Pearson New International Edition

Statistics for Business and Economics
James T. McClave   P. George Benson
Terry Sincich
Twelfth Edition

PEARSON®

Pearson Education Limited
Edinburgh Gate
Harlow
Essex CM20 2JE
England and Associated Companies throughout the world

Visit us on the World Wide Web at: www.pearsoned.co.uk

© Pearson Education Limited 2014

 ISBN 10: 1-292-02329-5
ISBN 13: 978-1-292-02329-8

British Library Cataloguing-in-Publication Data
A catalogue record for this book is available from the British Library

Printed by CPI UK

Table of Contents

CONTENTS

Where We're Going

- Introduce the field of statistics (1)
- Demonstrate how statistics applies to business (2)
- Introduce the language of statistics and the key elements of any statistical problem (3)
- Differentiate between population and sample data (3)
- Differentiate between descriptive and inferential statistics (3)
- Introduce the key elements of a process (4)
- Identify the different types of data and data-collection methods (5–6)
- Discover how critical thinking through statistics can help improve our quantitative literacy (7)

☐ Statistics, Data, and Statistical Thinking

STATISTICS in ACTION   **A *20/20* View of Surveys: Fact or Fiction?**

"Did you ever notice that, no matter where you stand on popular issues of the day, you can always find statistics or surveys to back up your point of view–whether to take vitamins, whether daycare harms kids, or what foods can hurt you or save you? There is an endless flow of information to help you make decisions, but is this information accurate, unbiased? John Stossel decided to check that out, and you may be surprised to learn if the picture you're getting doesn't seem quite right, maybe it isn't."

Barbara Walters gave this introduction to a segment of the popular prime-time ABC television program *20/20*. The story was titled "Fact or Fiction?—Exposés of So-Called Surveys." One of the surveys investigated by ABC correspondent John Stossel compared the discipline problems experienced by teachers in the 1940s and those experienced today. The results: In the 1940s, teachers worried most about students talking in class, chewing gum, and running in the halls. Today, they worry most about being assaulted! This information was highly publicized in the print media—in daily newspapers, weekly magazines, gossip columns, the *Congressional Quarterly,* and the *Wall Street Journal,* among others—and referenced in speeches by a variety of public figures, including former first lady Barbara Bush and former Education Secretary William Bennett.

"Hearing this made me yearn for the old days when life was so much simpler and gentler, but was life that simple then?" asks Stossel. "Wasn't there juvenile delinquency [in the 1940s]? Is the survey true?" With the help of a Yale School of Management professor, Stossel found the original source of the teacher survey—Texas oilman T. Colin Davis—and discovered it wasn't a survey at all! Davis had simply identified certain disciplinary problems encountered by teachers in a conservative newsletter—a list he admitted was not obtained from a statistical survey, but

From Chapter 1 of *Statistics for Business and Economics*, Twelfth Edition. James T. McClave, P. George Benson, Terry Sincich. Copyright © 2014 by Pearson Education, Inc. All rights reserved.
Content marked with a CD icon requires datasets or applets that can be found at http://www.pearsonhighered.com/mathstatsresources.

from Davis's personal knowledge of the problems in the 1940s. ("I was in school then") and his understanding of the problems today ("I read the papers").

Stossel's critical thinking about the teacher "survey" led to the discovery of research that is misleading at best and unethical at worst. Several more misleading (and possibly unethical) surveys, conducted by businesses or special interest groups with specific objectives in mind, were presented on the ABC program. These are listed below. Two other studies are also discussed.

The *20/20* segment ended with an interview of Cynthia Crossen, author of *Tainted Truth: The Manipulation of Fact in America,* an exposé of misleading and biased surveys. Crossen warns, "If everybody is misusing numbers and scaring us with numbers to get us to do something, however good [that something] is, we've lost the power of numbers. Now, we know certain things from research. For example, we know that smoking cigarettes is hard on your lungs and heart, and because we know that, many people's lives have been extended or saved. We don't want to lose the power of information to help us make decisions, and that's what I worry about."

Reported Information (Source)	Actual Study Information
1. Eating oat bran is a cheap and easy way to reduce your cholesterol. (Quaker Oats)	Diet must consist of nothing but oat bran to reduce your cholesterol count.
2. 150,000 women a year die from anorexia. (Feminist group)	Approximately 1,000 women a year die from problems that were likely caused by anorexia.
3. Domestic violence causes more birth defects than all medical issues combined. (March of Dimes)	No study–false report.
4. Only 29% of high school girls are happy with themselves, compared to 66% of elementary school girls. (American Association of University Women)	Of 3,000 high school girls, 29% responded, "Always true" to the statement "I am happy the way I am." Most answered, "Sort of true" and "Sometimes true."
5. One in four American children under age 12 is hungry or at risk of hunger. (Food Research and Action Center)	Based on responses to questions: "Do you ever cut the size of meals?" "Do you ever eat less than you feel you should?" "Did you ever rely on limited numbers of foods to feed your children because you were running out of money to buy food for a meal?"
6. There is a strong correlation between a CEO's golf handicap and the company's stock performance: The lower the CEO's handicap (i.e., the better the golfer), the better the stock performs. (*New York Times,* May 31, 1998)	Survey sent to CEOs of 300 largest U.S. companies; only 51 revealed their golf handicaps. Data for several top-ranking CEOs were excluded from the analysis.
7. If the federal government's health reform act is passed, 30% of employers are predicted to "definitely" or "probably" stop offering health coverage. (McKinsey & Company Survey, Feb. 2011)	Online survey of 1,329 private-sector employers in the United States. Respondents were asked leading questions that made it logical to stop offering health insurance.

In the following *Statistics in Action Revisited* sections, we discuss several key statistical concepts covered in this chapter that are relevant to misleading surveys like those exposed in the *20/20* program.

STATISTICS in ACTION REVISITED

- Identifying the population, sample, and inference
- Identifying the data-collection method and data type
- Critically assessing the ethics of a statistical study

1 The Science of Statistics

What does *statistics* mean to you? Does it bring to mind batting averages? Gallup polls, unemployment figures, or numerical distortions of facts (lying with statistics!)? Or is it simply a college requirement you have to complete? We hope to persuade you that statistics is a meaningful, useful science whose broad scope of applications to business, government, and the physical and social sciences is almost limitless. We also want to show that statistics can lie only when they are misapplied. Finally, we wish to demonstrate the key role statistics play in critical thinking—whether in the classroom, on the job, or in everyday life. Our objective is to leave you with the impression that the time you spend studying this subject will repay you in many ways.

Although the term can be defined in many ways, a broad definition of *statistics* is the science of collecting, classifying, analyzing, and interpreting information. Thus, a statistician isn't just someone who calculates batting averages at baseball games or tabulates the results of a Gallup poll. Professional statisticians are trained in *statistical science*—that is, they are trained in collecting information in the form of **data,** evaluating it, and drawing conclusions from it. Furthermore, statisticians determine what information is relevant in a given problem and whether the conclusions drawn from a study are to be trusted.

> **Statistics** is the science of data. It involves collecting, classifying, summarizing, organizing, analyzing, and interpreting numerical and categorical information.

In the next section, you'll see several real-life examples of statistical applications in business and government that involve making decisions and drawing conclusions.

2 Types of Statistical Applications in Business

BIOGRAPHY

FLORENCE NIGHTINGALE (1820–1910)
The Passionate Statistician

In Victorian England, the "Lady of the Lamp" had a mission to improve the squalid field hospital conditions of the British army during the Crimean War. Today, most historians consider Florence Nightingale to be the founder of the nursing profession. To convince members of the British Parliament of the need for supplying nursing and medical care to soldiers in the field, Nightingale compiled massive amounts of data from the army files. Through a remarkable series of graphs (which included the first "pie chart"), she demonstrated that most of the deaths in the war were due to illnesses contracted outside the battlefield or long after battle action from wounds that went untreated. Florence Nightingale's compassion and self-sacrificing nature, coupled with her ability to collect, arrange, and present large amounts of data, led some to call her the "Passionate Statistician."

Statistics means "numerical descriptions" to most people. Monthly unemployment figures, the failure rate of startup companies, and the proportion of female executives in a particular industry all represent statistical descriptions of large sets of data collected on some phenomenon. Often the data are selected from some larger set of data whose characteristics we wish to estimate. We call this selection process *sampling*. For example, you might collect the ages of a sample of customers of an online DVD movie rental company to estimate the average age of *all* customers of the company. Then you could use your estimate to target the firm's advertisements to the appropriate age group. Notice that statistics involves two different processes: (1) describing sets of data and (2) drawing conclusions (making estimates, decisions, predictions, etc.) about the sets of data based on sampling. So, the applications of statistics can be divided into two broad areas: *descriptive statistics* and *inferential statistics*.

> **Descriptive statistics** utilizes numerical and graphical methods to explore data, i.e., to look for patterns in a data set, to summarize the information revealed in a data set, and to present the information in a convenient form.

> **Inferential statistics** utilizes sample data to make estimates, decisions, predictions, or other generalizations about a larger set of data.

Although we'll discuss both descriptive and inferential statistics the primary theme of the text is **inference**.

Let's begin by examining some business studies that illustrate applications of statistics.

Study 1 "Best-Selling Girl Scout Cookies" (www.girlscouts.org): Since 1917, the Girl Scouts of America have been selling boxes of cookies. Currently, there are eight varieties for sale: Thin Mints, Samoas, Caramel deLites, Tagalongs, Peanut Butter Patties, Do-si-dos, Peanut Butter Sandwiches, and Trefoils. Each of the approximately 150 million boxes of Girl Scout cookies sold in 2006 was classified by variety. The results are summarized in Figure 1. From the graph, you can clearly see that the best-selling variety is Thin Mints (25%), followed by Samoas (19%) and Tagalongs (13%). Since Figure 1 *describes* the variety of categories of the boxes of Girl Scout cookies sold, the graphic is an example of *descriptive statistics*.

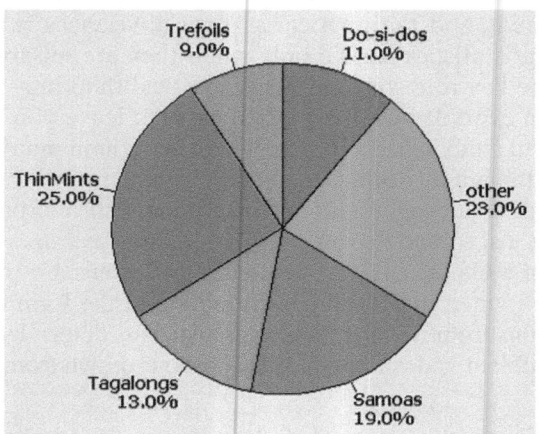

Figure 1

Best-selling Girl Scout cookies
Source: "Best-Selling Girl Scout Cookies" www.girlscouts.org.

Study 2 "The Executive Compensation Scoreboard" (*Forbes*, April 13, 2011): How much are the top corporate executives in the United States being paid, and are they worth it? To answer these questions, *Forbes* magazine compiles the "Executive Compensation Scoreboard" each year based on a survey of executives at the 500 largest U.S. companies. To determine which executives are worth their pay, *Forbes* also records the performance of shareholders' stock for the CEO's company over the previous 6 years. Based on a comparison of the stock's performance and the CEO's annual salary, each CEO is given an "efficiency" rating—the lower the rating, the more the CEO is worth his/her pay. An analysis of the scoreboard data for the highest-paid CEOs in 2011 is summarized in Table 1. The table reveals that CEOs in the business services industry have the lowest average efficiency rating (4.5), thus, they are the best performers. The CEOs in the telecommunications industry are the worst performers, with the highest efficiency rating (163). Armed with this sample information, *Forbes* might *infer* that, from the shareholders' perspective, typical chief executives in telecommunications are overpaid relative to CEOs in business services. Thus, this study is an example of *inferential statistics*.

Table 1	Average Pay-for-Performance Efficiency Ratings of CEOs, by Industry		
Industry	Average Efficiency Rating	Industry	Average Efficiency Rating
Aerospace and Defense	85	Hotels, Restaurants	31
Banking	59	Household Products	110
Business Services	4.5	Insurance	106
Capital Goods	85	Materials	54
Chemicals	131	Media	134
Conglomerates	126	Oil and Gas Operations	91
Construction	144	Retailing	107
Consumer Durables	11	Semiconductors	82
Diversified Financial	106	Software and Services	110
Drugs and Biotechnology	121	Technology Hardware	132
Food, Drink, and Tobacco	140	Telecommunications	163
		Transportation	51
Health Care Equipment	96	Utilities	127

Source: Data from "Executive Compensation Scoreboard," FORBES April 13, 2011.

Study 3 "Does rudeness really matter in the workplace?" (*Academy of Management Journal*, Oct. 2007): Previous studies have established that rudeness in the workplace can lead to retaliatory and counterproductive behavior. However, there has been little research on how rude behaviors influence a victim's task performance. In a recent study, college students enrolled in a management course were randomly assigned to one of two experimental conditions: rudeness condition (45 students) and control group (53 students). Each student was asked to write down as many uses for a brick as possible in 5 minutes; this value (total number of uses) was used as a performance measure for each student. For those students in the rudeness condition, the facilitator displayed rudeness by berating the students in general for being irresponsible and unprofessional (due to a late-arriving confederate). No comments were made about the late-arriving confederate to students in the control group. As you might expect, the researchers discovered that the performance levels for students in the rudeness condition were generally lower than the performance levels for students in the control group; thus, they concluded that rudeness in the workplace negatively effects job performance. As in Study 2, this study is an example of the use of inferential statistics. The researchers used data collected on 98 college students in a simulated work environment to make an inference about the performance levels of all workers exposed to rudeness on the job.

These studies provide three real-life examples of the uses of statistics in business, economics, and management. Notice that each involves an analysis of data, either for the purpose of describing the data set (Study 1) or for making inferences about a data set (Studies 2 and 3).

3 Fundamental Elements of Statistics

Statistical methods are particularly useful for studying, analyzing, and learning about *populations* of *experimental units*.

> An **experimental (or observational) unit** is an object (e.g., person, thing, transaction, or event) upon which we collect data.

> A **population** is a set of units (usually people, objects, transactions, or events) that we are interested in studying.

For example, populations may include (1) *all* employed workers in the United States, (2) *all* registered voters in California, (3) *everyone* who has purchased a particular brand of cellular telephone, (4) *all* the cars produced last year by a particular assembly line, (5) the *entire* stock of spare parts at United Airlines' maintenance facility, (6) *all* sales made at the drive-through window of a McDonald's restaurant during a given year, and (7) the set of *all* accidents occurring on a particular stretch of interstate during a holiday period. Notice that the first three population examples (1–3) are sets (groups) of people, the next two (4–5) are sets of objects, the next (6) is a set of transactions, and the last (7) is a set of events. Also notice that *each set includes all the experimental units in the population* of interest.

In studying a population, we focus on one or more characteristics or properties of the experimental units in the population. We call such characteristics *variables*. For example, we may be interested in the variables age, gender, income, and/or the number of years of education of the people currently unemployed in the United States.

> A **variable** is a characteristic or property of an individual experimental (or observational) unit.

The name *variable* is derived from the fact that any particular characteristic may vary among the experimental units in a population.

In studying a particular variable, it is helpful to be able to obtain a numerical representation for it. Often, however, numerical representations are not readily available, so the process of measurement plays an important supporting role in statistical studies. **Measurement** is the process we use to assign numbers to variables of individual population units. We might, for instance, measure the preference for a food product by asking a consumer to rate the product's taste on a scale from 1 to 10. Or we might measure workforce age by simply asking each worker, "How old are you?" In other cases, measurement involves the use of instruments such as stopwatches, scales, and calipers.

If the population we wish to study is small, it is possible to measure a variable for every unit in the population. For example, if you are measuring the starting salary for all University of Michigan MBA graduates last year, it is at least feasible to obtain every salary. When we measure a variable for every experimental unit of a population, the result is called a **census** of the population. Typically, however, the populations of interest in most applications are much larger, involving perhaps many thousands or even an infinite number of units. Examples of large populations include the seven listed above, as well as all invoices produced in the last year by a *Fortune* 500 company, all potential buyers of a new iPad, and all stockholders of a firm listed on the New York Stock Exchange. For such populations, conducting a census would be prohibitively time-consuming and/or costly. A reasonable alternative would be to select and study a *subset* (or portion) of the units in the population.

A **sample** is a subset of the units of a population.

For example, suppose a company is being audited for invoice errors. Instead of examining all 15,472 invoices produced by the company during a given year, an auditor may select and examine a sample of just 100 invoices (see Figure 2). If he is interested in the variable "invoice error status," he would record (measure) the status (error or no error) of each sampled invoice.

After the variable(s) of interest for every experimental unit in the sample (or population) is measured, the data are analyzed, either by descriptive or inferential statistical methods. The auditor, for example, may be interested only in *describing* the error rate in

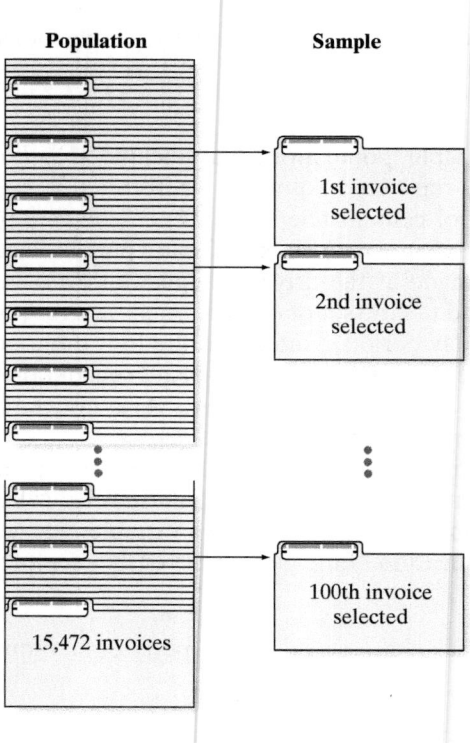

Figure 2

A sample of all company invoices

the sample of 100 invoices. More likely, however, he will want to use the information in the sample to make *inferences* about the population of all 15,472 invoices.

> A **statistical inference** is an estimate or prediction or some other generalization about a population based on information contained in a sample.

That is, we use the information contained in the sample to learn about the larger population.* Thus, from the sample of 100 invoices, the auditor may estimate the total number of invoices containing errors in the population of 15,472 invoices. The auditor's inference about the quality of the firm's invoices can be used in deciding whether to modify the firm's billing operations.

Example 1 **Key Elements of a Statistical Problem—Ages of TV Viewers**	**Problem** According to *Variety* (Aug. 10, 2010), the average age of viewers of television programs broadcast on CBS, NBC, and ABC is 51 years. Suppose a rival network (e.g., FOX) executive hypothesizes that the average age of FOX viewers is less than 51. To test her hypothesis, she samples 200 FOX viewers and determines the age of each. **a.** Describe the population. **b.** Describe the variable of interest. **c.** Describe the sample. **d.** Describe the inference. **Solution** **a.** The population is the set of units of interest to the TV executive, which is the set of all FOX viewers. **b.** The age (in years) of each viewer is the variable of interest. **c.** The sample must be a subset of the population. In this case, it is the 200 FOX viewers selected by the executive. **d.** The inference of interest involves the *generalization* of the information contained in the sample of 200 viewers to the population of all FOX viewers. In particular, the executive wants to *estimate* the average age of the viewers in order to determine whether it is less than 51 years. She might accomplish this by calculating the average age in the sample and using the sample average to estimate the population average. **Look Back** A key to diagnosing a statistical problem is to identify the data set collected (in this example, the ages of the 200 FOX TV viewers) as a population or sample.

Example 2 **Key Elements of a Statistical Problem— Pepsi vs. Coca-Cola**	**Problem** *Cola wars* is the popular term for the intense competition between Coca-Cola and Pepsi displayed in their marketing campaigns. Their campaigns have featured movie and television stars, rock videos, athletic endorsements, and claims of consumer preference based on taste tests. Suppose, as part of a Pepsi marketing campaign, 1,000 cola consumers are given a blind taste test (i.e., a taste test in which the two brand names are disguised). Each consumer is asked to state a preference for brand A or brand B.

---

*The terms *population* and *sample* are often used to refer to the sets of measurements themselves, as well as to the units on which the measurements are made. When a single variable of interest is being measured, this usage causes little confusion. But when the terminology is ambiguous, we'll refer to the measurements as *population data sets* and *sample data sets,* respectively.

a. Describe the population.

b. Describe the variable of interest.

c. Describe the sample.

d. Describe the inference.

Solution

a. Because we are interested in the responses of cola consumers in a taste test, a cola consumer is the experimental unit. Thus, the population of interest is the collection or set of all cola consumers.

b. The characteristic that Pepsi wants to measure is the consumer's cola preference as revealed under the conditions of a blind taste test, so cola preference is the variable of interest.

c. The sample is the 1,000 cola consumers selected from the population of all cola consumers.

d. The inference of interest is the *generalization* of the cola preferences of the 1,000 sampled consumers to the population of all cola consumers. In particular, the preferences of the consumers in the sample can be used to *estimate* the percentage of all cola consumers who prefer each brand.

Look Back In determining whether the statistical application is inferential or descriptive, we assess whether Pepsi is interested in the responses of only the 1,000 sampled customers (descriptive statistics) or in the responses for the entire population of consumers (inferential statistics).

Now Work Exercise 15b

The preceding definitions and examples identify four of the five elements of an inferential statistical problem: a population, one or more variables of interest in a sample, and an inference. But making the inference is only part of the story. We also need to know its **reliability**–that is, how good the inference is. The only way we can be certain that an inference about a population is correct is to include the entire population in our sample. However, because of *resource constraints* (e.g., insufficient time and/or money), we usually can't work with whole populations, so we base our inferences on just a portion of the population (a sample). Consequently, whenever possible, it is important to determine and report the reliability of each inference made. Reliability, then, is the fifth element of inferential statistical problems.

The measure of reliability that accompanies an inference separates the science of statistics from the art of fortune-telling. A palm reader, like a statistician, may examine a sample (your hand) and make inferences about the population (your life). However, unlike statistical inferences, the palm reader's inferences include no measure of reliability.

Suppose, like the TV executive in Example 1, we are interested in the *error of estimation* (i.e., the difference between the average age of the population of TV viewers and the average age of a sample of TV viewers). Using statistical methods, we can determine a *bound on the estimation error*. This bound is simply a number that our estimation error (the difference between the average age of the sample and the average age of the population) is not likely to exceed. This bound is a measure of the uncertainty of our inference. The reliability of statistical inferences is discussed throughout this text. For now, we simply want you to realize that an inference is incomplete without a measure of its reliability.

> A **measure of reliability** is a statement (usually quantified) about the degree of uncertainty associated with a statistical inference.

Let's conclude this section with a summary of the elements of both descriptive and inferential statistical problems and an example to illustrate a measure of reliability.

Four Elements of Descriptive Statistical Problems

1. The population or sample of interest
2. One or more variables (characteristics of the population or experimental units) that are to be investigated
3. Tables, graphs, or numerical summary tools
4. Identification of patterns in the data

Five Elements of Inferential Statistical Problems

1. The population of interest
2. One or more variables (characteristics of the population or experimental units) that are to be investigated
3. The sample of population units
4. The inference about the population based on information contained in the sample
5. A measure of reliability for the inference

Example 3

Reliability of an Inference—Pepsi vs. Coca-Cola

Problem Refer to Example 2, in which the cola preferences of 1,000 consumers were indicated in a taste test. Describe how the reliability of an inference concerning the preferences of all cola consumers in the Pepsi bottler's marketing region could be measured.

Solution When the preferences of 1,000 consumers are used to estimate the preferences of all consumers in the region, the estimate will not exactly mirror the preferences of the population. For example, if the taste test shows that 56% of the 1,000 consumers chose Pepsi, it does not follow (nor is it likely) that exactly 56% of all cola drinkers in the region prefer Pepsi. Nevertheless, we can use sound statistical reasoning (which is presented later in the text) to ensure that our sampling procedure will generate estimates that are almost certainly within a specified limit of the true percentage of all consumers who prefer Pepsi. For example, such reasoning might assure us that the estimate of the preference for Pepsi from the sample is almost certainly within 5% of the actual population preference. The implication is that the actual preference for Pepsi is between 51% [i.e., $(56 - 5)\%$] and 61% [i.e., $(56 + 5)\%$]—that is, $(56 \pm 5)\%$. This interval represents a measure of reliability for the inference.

Look Back The interval 56 ± 5 is called a *confidence interval*, because we are "confident" that the true percentage of customers who prefer Pepsi in a taste test falls into the range $(51, 61)$.

STATISTICS in ACTION REVISITED

Identifying the Population, Sample, and Inference

Consider the study on the link between a CEO's golf handicap and the company's stock performance, reported in the *New York Times* (May 31, 1998). The newspaper gathered information on golf handicaps of corporate executives obtained from a *Golf Digest* survey sent to CEOs of the 300 largest U.S. companies. (A golf handicap is a numerical "index" that allows golfers to compare skills; the lower the handicap, the better the golfer.) For the 51 CEOs who reported their handicaps, the *New York Times*

STATISTICS
in ACTION
REVISITED
CONTINUED

then determined each CEO's company stock market performance over a 3-year period (measured as a rate-of-return index, from a low value of 0 to a high value of 100). Thus, the experimental unit for the study is a corporate executive, and the two variables measured are golf handicap and stock performance index. Also, the data for the 51 CEOs represent a sample selected from the much larger population of all corporate executives in the United States. (These data are available in the **GLFCEO** file.)

The *New York Times* discovered a "statistical correlation" between golf handicap and stock performance. Thus, the newspaper inferred that the better the CEO is at golf, the better the company's stock performance.

Data Set: GLFCEO

4 Processes*

Sections 2 and 3 focused on the use of statistical methods to analyze and learn about populations, which are sets of *existing* units. Statistical methods are equally useful for analyzing and making inferences about *processes*.

> A **process** is a series of actions or operations that transforms inputs to outputs. A process produces or generates output over time.

The most obvious processes of interest to businesses are those of production or manufacturing. A manufacturing process uses a series of operations performed by people and machines to convert inputs, such as raw materials and parts, to finished products (the outputs). Examples include the process used to produce the paper on which these words are printed, automobile assembly lines, and oil refineries.

Figure 3 presents a general description of a process and its inputs and outputs. In the context of manufacturing, the process in the figure (i.e., the transformation process) could be a depiction of the overall production process or it could be a depiction of one of the many processes (sometimes called *subprocesses*) that exist within an overall production process. Thus, the output shown could be finished goods that will be shipped to an external customer or merely the output of one of the steps or subprocesses of the overall process. In the latter case, the output becomes input for the next subprocess. For example, Figure 3 could represent the overall automobile assembly process, with its output being fully assembled cars ready for shipment to dealers. Or, it could depict the windshield assembly subprocess, with its output of partially assembled cars with windshields ready for "shipment" to the next subprocess in the assembly line.

Besides physical products and services, businesses and other organizations generate streams of numerical data over time that are used to evaluate the performance of the organization. Examples include weekly sales figures, quarterly earnings, and yearly profits. The U.S. economy (a complex organization) can be thought of as generating streams of data that include the gross domestic product (GDP), stock prices, and the Consumer Price Index. Statisticians and other analysts conceptualize these data streams

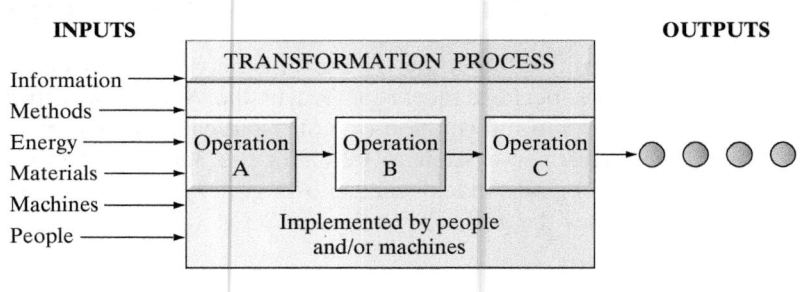

Figure 3

Graphical depiction of
a manufacturing process

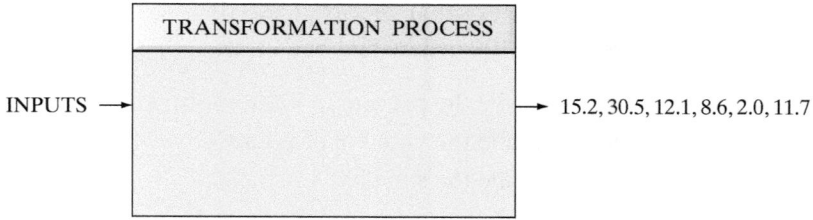

Figure 4

A black box process with numerical output

as being generated by processes. Typically, however, the series of operations or actions that cause particular data to be realized are either unknown or so complex (or both) that the processes are treated as *black boxes*.

> A process whose operations or actions are unknown or unspecified is called a **black box**.

Frequently, when a process is treated as a black box, its inputs are not specified either. The entire focus is on the output of the process. A black box process is illustrated in Figure 4.

In studying a process, we generally focus on one or more characteristics, or properties, of the output. For example, we may be interested in the weight or the length of the units produced or even the time it takes to produce each unit. As with characteristics of population units, we call these characteristics *variables*. In studying processes whose output is already in numerical form (i.e., a stream of numbers), the characteristic, or property, represented by the numbers (e.g., sales, GDP, or stock prices) is typically the variable of interest. If the output is not numeric, we use *measurement processes* to assign numerical values to variables.* For example, if in the automobile assembly process the weight of the fully assembled automobile is the variable of interest, a measurement process involving a large scale will be used to assign a numerical value to each automobile.

As with populations, we use sample data to analyze and make inferences (estimates, predictions, or other generalizations) about processes. But the concept of a sample is defined differently when dealing with processes. Recall that a population is a set of existing units and that a sample is a subset of those units. In the case of processes, however, the concept of a set of existing units is not relevant or appropriate. Processes generate or create their output *over time*—one unit after another. For example, a particular automobile assembly line produces a completed vehicle every 4 minutes. We define a sample from a process in the box.

> Any set of output (object or numbers) produced by a process is also called a **sample**.

Thus, the next 10 cars turned out by the assembly line constitute a sample from the process, as do the next 100 cars or every fifth car produced today.

Example 4

Key Elements of a Process—Waiting Time at a Fast-Food Window

Problem A particular fast-food restaurant chain has 6,289 outlets with drive-through windows. To attract more customers to its drive-through services, the company is considering offering a 50% discount to customers who wait more than a specified number of minutes to receive their order. To help determine what the time limit should be, the company decided to estimate the average waiting time at a particular drive-through window in Dallas, Texas. For 7 consecutive days, the worker taking customers' orders recorded the time that every order was placed. The worker who handed the order to the customer recorded the time of delivery. In both cases, workers used synchronized

---

*A process whose output is already in numerical form necessarily includes a measurement process as one of its subprocesses.

digital clocks that reported the time to the nearest second. At the end of the 7-day period, 2,109 orders had been timed.

a. Describe the process of interest at the Dallas restaurant.

b. Describe the variable of interest.

c. Describe the sample.

d. Describe the inference of interest.

e. Describe how the reliability of the inference could be measured.

Solution

a. The process of interest is the drive-through window at a particular fast-food restaurant in Dallas, Texas. It is a process because it "produces," or "generates," meals over time—that is, it services customers over time.

b. The variable the company monitored is customer waiting time, the length of time a customer waits to receive a meal after placing an order. Because the study is focusing only on the output of the process (the time to produce the output) and not the internal operations of the process (the tasks required to produce a meal for a customer), the process is being treated as a black box.

c. The sampling plan was to monitor every order over a particular 7-day period. The sample is the 2,109 orders that were processed during the 7-day period.

d. The company's immediate interest is in learning about the drive-through window in Dallas. They plan to do this by using the waiting times from the sample to make a statistical inference about the drive-through process. In particular, they might use the average waiting time for the sample to estimate the average waiting time at the Dallas facility.

e. As for inferences about populations, measures of reliability can be developed for inferences about processes. The reliability of the estimate of the average waiting time for the Dallas restaurant could be measured by a bound on the error of estimation—that is, we might find that the average waiting time is 4.2 minutes, with a bound on the error of estimation of 0.5 minutes. The implication would be that we could be reasonably certain that the true average waiting time for the Dallas process is between 3.7 and 4.7 minutes.

Look Back Notice that there is also a population described in this example: the company's 6,289 existing outlets with drive-through facilities. In the final analysis, the company will use what it learns about the process in Dallas and, perhaps, similar studies at other locations to make an inference about the waiting times in its population of outlets.

■ **Now Work Exercise 36**

Note that output already generated by a process can be viewed as a population. Suppose a soft-drink canning process produced 2,000 twelve-packs yesterday, all of which were stored in a warehouse. If we were interested in learning something about those 2,000 twelve-packs—such as the percentage with defective cardboard packaging—we could treat the 2,000 twelve-packs as a population. We might draw a sample from the population in the warehouse, measure the variable of interest, and use the sample data to make a statistical inference about the 2,000 twelve-packs, as described in Sections 2 and 3.

In this optional section, we have presented a brief introduction to processes and the use of statistical methods to analyze and learn about processes.

5   Types of Data

You have learned that statistics is the science of data and that data are obtained by measuring the values of one or more variables on the units in the sample (or population). All data (and hence the variables we measure) can be classified as one of two general types: *quantitative* and *qualitative*.

Quantitative data are data that are measured on a naturally occurring numerical scale.* The following are examples of quantitative data:

1. The temperature (in degrees Celsius) at which each unit in a sample of 20 pieces of heat-resistant plastic begins to melt
2. The current unemployment rate (measured as a percentage) for each of the 50 states
3. The scores of a sample of 150 MBA applicants on the GMAT, a standardized business graduate school entrance exam administered nationwide
4. The number of female executives employed in each of a sample of 75 manufacturing companies

> **Quantitative data** are measurements that are recorded on a naturally occurring numerical scale.

In contrast, qualitative data cannot be measured on a natural numerical scale; they can only be classified into categories.[†] Examples of qualitative data are as follows:

1. The political party affiliation (Democrat, Republican, or Independent) in a sample of 50 CEOs
2. The defective status (defective or not) of each of 100 computer chips manufactured by Intel
3. The size of a car (subcompact, compact, midsize, or full-size) rented by each of a sample of 30 business travelers
4. A taste tester's ranking (best, worst, etc.) of four brands of barbecue sauce for a panel of 10 testers

Often, we assign arbitrary numerical values to qualitative data for ease of computer entry and analysis. But these assigned numerical values are simply codes: They cannot be meaningfully added, subtracted, multiplied, or divided. For example, we might code Democrat = 1, Republican = 2, and Independent = 3. Similarly, a taste tester might rank the barbecue sauces from 1 (best) to 4 (worst). These are simply arbitrarily selected numerical codes for the categories and have no utility beyond that.

> **Qualitative data** are measurements that cannot be measured on a natural numerical scale; they can only be classified into one of a group of categories.

Example 5

Types of Data—Study of a River Contaminated by a Chemical Plant

Problem Chemical and manufacturing plants sometimes discharge toxic-waste materials such as DDT into nearby rivers and streams. These toxins can adversely affect the plants and animals inhabiting the river and the riverbank. The U.S. Army Corps of Engineers conducted a study of fish in the Tennessee River (in Alabama) and its three tributary creeks: Flint Creek, Limestone Creek, and Spring Creek. A total of 144 fish were captured, and the following variables were measured for each:

1. River/creek where each fish was captured
2. Species (channel catfish, largemouth bass, or smallmouth buffalo fish)
3. Length (centimeters)
4. Weight (grams)
5. DDT concentration (parts per million)

*Quantitative data can be subclassified as either *interval* or *ratio*. For ratio data, the origin (i.e., the value 0) is a meaningful number. But the origin has no meaning with interval data. Consequently, we can add and subtract interval data, but we can't multiply and divide them. Of the four quantitative data sets listed, (1) and (3) are interval data, while (2) and (4) are ratio data.

[†]Qualitative data can be subclassified as either *nominal* or *ordinal*. The categories of an ordinal data set can be ranked or meaningfully ordered, but the categories of a nominal data set can't be ordered. Of the four qualitative data sets listed, (1) and (2) are nominal and (3) and (4) are ordinal.

These data are saved in the **DDT** file. Classify each of the five variables measured as quantitative or qualitative.

Solution The variables length, weight, and DDT are quantitative because each is measured on a numerical scale: length in centimeters, weight in grams, and DDT in parts per million. In contrast, river/creek and species cannot be measured quantitatively: They can only be classified into categories (e.g., channel catfish, largemouth bass, and smallmouth buffalo fish for species). Consequently, data on river/creek and species are qualitative.

Look Back It is essential that you understand whether data are quantitative or qualitative in nature because the statistical method appropriate for describing, reporting, and analyzing the data depends on the data type (quantitative or qualitative).

■ **Now Work Exercise 18**

6 Collecting Data: Sampling and Related Issues

Once you decide on the type of data—quantitative or qualitative—appropriate for the problem at hand, you'll need to collect the data. Generally, you can obtain the data in three different ways:

1. Data from a *published source*
2. Data from a *designed experiment*
3. Data from an *observational study* (e.g., a *survey*)

Sometimes, the data set of interest has already been collected for you and is available in a **published source,** such as a book, journal, newspaper, or Web site. For example, you may want to examine and summarize the unemployment rates (i.e., percentages of eligible workers who are unemployed) in the 50 states of the United States. You can find this data set (as well as numerous other data sets) at your library in the *Statistical Abstract of the United States,* published annually by the U.S. government. Similarly, someone who is interested in monthly mortgage applications for new home construction would find this data set in the *Survey of Current Business,* another government publication. Other examples of published data sources include the *Wall Street Journal* (financial data) and the *The Sporting News* (sports information).* The Internet (World Wide Web) now provides a medium by which data from published sources are readily available.

A second method of collecting data involves conducting a **designed experiment,** in which the researcher exerts strict control over the units (people, objects, or events) in the study. For example, an often-cited medical study investigated the potential of aspirin in preventing heart attacks. Volunteer physicians were divided into two groups—the *treatment* group and the *control* group. In the treatment group, each physician took one aspirin tablet a day for 1 year, while each physician in the control group took an aspirin-free placebo (no drug) made to look like an aspirin tablet. The researchers, not the physicians under study, controlled who received the aspirin (the treatment) and who received the placebo. A properly designed experiment allows you to extract more information from the data than is possible with an uncontrolled study.

Finally, observational studies can be employed to collect data. In an **observational study,** the researcher observes the experimental units in their natural setting and records the variable(s) of interest. For example, a company psychologist might observe and record the level of "Type A" behavior of a sample of assembly line workers. Similarly, a

---

*With published data, we often make a distinction between the *primary source* and *secondary source*. If the publisher is the original collector of the data, the source is primary. Otherwise, the data are secondary source.

finance researcher may observe and record the closing stock prices of companies that are acquired by other firms on the day prior to the buyout and compare them to the closing prices on the day the acquisition is announced. Unlike a designed experiment, an observational study is one in which the researcher makes no attempt to control any aspect of the experimental units.

The most common type of observational study is a **survey,** where the researcher samples a group of people, asks one or more questions, and records the responses. Probably the most familiar type of survey is the political poll, conducted by any one of a number of organizations (e.g., Harris, Gallup, Roper, and CNN) and designed to predict the outcome of a political election. Another familiar survey is the Nielsen survey, which provides the major television networks with information on the most watched TV programs. Surveys can be conducted through the mail, with telephone interviews, or with in-person interviews. Although in-person interviews are more expensive than mail or telephone surveys, they may be necessary when complex information must be collected.

Regardless of the data-collection method employed, it is likely that the data will be a sample from some population. And if we wish to apply inferential statistics, we must obtain a *representative sample*.

> A **representative sample** exhibits characteristics typical of those possessed by the population of interest.

For example, consider a political poll conducted during a presidential election year. Assume the pollster wants to estimate the percentage of all 145 million registered voters in the United States who favor the incumbent president. The pollster would be unwise to base the estimate on survey data collected for a sample of voters from the incumbent's own state. Such an estimate would almost certainly be *biased* high; consequently, it would not be very reliable.

The most common way to satisfy the representative sample requirement is to select a simple random sample. A **simple random sample** ensures that every subset of fixed size in the population has the same chance of being included in the sample. If the pollster samples 1,500 of the 145 million voters in the population so that every subset of 1,500 voters has an equal chance of being selected, she has devised a simple random sample.

> A **simple random sample** of n experimental units is a sample selected from the population in such a way that every different sample of size n has an equal chance of selection.

The procedure for selecting a simple random sample typically relies on a **random number generator.** Random number generators are available in table form, online,* and in most statistical software packages. The Excel/XLSTAT, Minitab, and SPSS statistical software packages all have easy-to-use random number generators for creating a random sample. The next two examples illustrate the procedure.

Example 6

Generating a Simple Random Sample— Selecting Households for a Feasibility Study

Problem Suppose you wish to assess the feasibility of building a new high school. As part of your study, you would like to gauge the opinions of people living close to the proposed building site. The neighborhood adjacent to the site has 711 homes. Use a random number generator to select a simple random sample of 20 households from the neighborhood to participate in the study.

Solution In this study, your population of interest consists of the 711 households in the adjacent neighborhood. To ensure that every possible sample of 20 households selected from the 711 has an equal chance of selection (i.e., to ensure a simple random sample), first assign a number from 1 to 711 to each of the households in the population. These numbers were entered into an Excel worksheet. Now, apply the random number

*One of many free online random number generators is available at www.randomizer.org.

generator of Excel/ XLSTAT, requesting that 20 households be selected without replacement. Figure 5 shows the output from XLSTAT. You can see that households numbered $40, 63, 108, \ldots, 636$ are the households to be included in your sample.

	A	B	C	D	E	F	G	H	I	J	K
1		XLSTAT 2011.4.02 - Data sampling - on 11/4/2011 at 10:17:05 AM									
2		Data: Workbook = HOUSEHOLDS.xlsx / Sheet = Sheet1 / Range = Sheet1!$A:$A / 711 rows and 1 column									
3		Sampling method: Random without replacement									
4		Number of samples: 1									
5		Sample size: 20									
6		Seed (random numbers): 4186805									
7											
8											
9		Sampled data:									
10											
11		HOUSEHOLD									
12		40									
13		63									
14		108									
15		153									
16		190									
17		227									
18		283									
19		302									
20		309									
21		371									
22		379									
23		419									
24		434									
25		457									
26		463									
27		489									
28		536									
29		537									
30		560									
31		636									
32											

Figure 5

Random selection of
20 households using XLSTAT

Look Back It can be shown (proof omitted) that there are over 3×10^{38} possible samples of size 20 that can be selected from the 711 households. Random number generators guarantee (to a certain degree of approximation) that each possible sample has an equal chance of being selected.

■ **Now Work Exercise 14**

The notion of random selection and randomization is also key to conducting good research with a designed experiment. The next example illustrates a basic application.

Example   7

Randomization in a Designed Experiment— A Clinical Trial

Problem A designed experiment in the medical field involving human subjects is referred to as a *clinical trial*. One recent clinical trial was designed to determine the potential of using aspirin in preventing heart attacks. Volunteer physicians were randomly divided into two groups—the *treatment* group and the *control* group. Each physician in the treatment group took one aspirin tablet a day for one year, while the physicians in the control group took an aspirin-free placebo made to look identical to an aspirin tablet. Because the physicians did not know which group, treatment or control, they were assigned to, the clinical trial is called a *blind study*. Assume 20 physicians volunteered for the study. Use a random number generator to randomly assign half of the physicians to the treatment group and half to the control group.

Solution Essentially, we want to select a random sample of 10 physicians from the 20. The first 10 selected will be assigned to the treatment group; the remaining 10 will be assigned to the control group. (Alternatively, we could randomly assign each physician,

↓	C1	C2	C3
	Physician	Treatment	
1	1	3	
2	2	11	
3	3	10	
4	4	14	
5	5	2	
6	6	7	
7	7	6	
8	8	16	
9	9	17	
10	10	9	
11	11		
12	12		
13	13		
14	14		
15	15		
16	16		
17	17		
18	18		
19	19		
20	20		
21			

ASPIRIN-STUDY.MTW ***

Figure 6

Minitab worksheet with random assignment of physicians

one by one, to either the treatment or control group. However, this would not guarantee exactly 10 physicians in each group.)

The Minitab random sample procedure was employed, producing the printout shown in Figure 6. Numbering the physicians from 1 to 20, we see that physicians 3, 11, 10, 14, 2, 7, 6, 16, 17, and 9 are assigned to receive the aspirin (treatment). The remaining physicians are assigned the placebo (control).

Now Work Exercise 33e

In addition to simple random samples, there are more complex random sampling designs that can be employed. These include (but are not limited to) **stratified random sampling, cluster sampling, systematic sampling,** and **randomized response sampling**. Brief descriptions of each follow. (For more details on the use of these sampling methods, consult the References at the end of this chapter.)

Stratified random sampling is typically used when the experimental units associated with the population can be separated into two or more groups of units, called *strata*, where the characteristics of the experimental units are more similar within strata than across strata. Random samples of experimental units are obtained for each strata; then the units are combined to form the complete sample. For example, if you are gauging opinions of voters on a polarizing issue, like government-sponsored health care, you may want to stratify on political affiliation (Republicans and Democrats), making sure that representative samples of both Republicans and Democrats (in proportion to the number of Republicans and Democrats in the voting population) are included in your survey.

Sometimes it is more convenient and logical to sample natural groupings (*clusters*) of experimental units first, and then collect data from all experimental units within each cluster. This involves the use of *cluster sampling*. For example, suppose a marketer for a large upscale restaurant chain wants to find out whether customers like the new menu. Rather than collect a simple random sample of all customers (which would be very difficult and costly to do), the marketer will randomly sample 10 of the 150 restaurant locations (clusters), and then interview all customers eating at each of the 10 locations on a certain night.

Another popular sampling method is *systematic sampling*. This method involves systematically selecting every kth experimental unit from a list of all experimental units. For example, every fifth person who walks into a shopping mall could be asked his or her opinion on a business topic of interest. Or, a quality control engineer at a manufacturing plant may select every 10th item produced on an assembly line for inspection.

A fourth alternative to simple random sampling is *randomized response sampling*. This design is particularly useful when the questions of the pollsters are likely to elicit false answers. For example, suppose each person in a sample of wage earners is asked whether he or she ever cheated on an income tax return. A cheater might lie, thus biasing an estimate of the true likelihood of someone cheating on his or her tax return. To circumvent this problem, each person is presented with two questions, one being the object of the survey and the other an innocuous question, such as:

1. Did you ever cheat on your federal income tax return?
2. Did you drink coffee this morning?

One of the questions is chosen at random to be answered by the wage earner by flipping a coin; however, which particular question is answered is unknown to the interviewer. In this way, the random response method attempts to elicit an honest response to a sensitive question. Sophisticated statistical methods are then employed to derive an estimate of the percentage of "yes" responses to the sensitive question.

No matter what type of sampling design you employ to collect the data for your study, be careful to avoid *selection bias*. Selection bias occurs when some experimental units in the population have less chance of being included in the sample than others. This results in samples that are not representative of the population. Consider an opinion poll that employs either a telephone survey or mail survey.

After collecting a random sample of phone numbers or mailing addresses, each person in the sample is contacted via telephone or the mail and a survey conducted. Unfortunately, these types of surveys often suffer from selection bias due to *non-response*. Some individuals may not be home when the phone rings, or others may refuse to answer the questions or mail back the questionnaire. As a consequence, no data are obtained for the nonrespondents in the sample. If the nonrespondents and respondents differ greatly on an issue, then *nonresponse bias* exits. For example, those who choose to answer a question on a school board issue may have a vested interest in the outcome of the survey—say, parents with children of school age, schoolteachers whose jobs may be in jeopardy, or citizens whose taxes might be substantially affected. Others with no vested interest may have an opinion on the issue but might not take the time to respond.

> **Selection bias** results when a subset of experimental units in the population has little or no chance of being selected for the sample.

> **Nonresponse bias** is a type of selection bias that results when data on all experimental units in a sample are not obtained.

Finally, even if your sample is representative of the population, the data collected may suffer from *measurement error*. That is, the values of the data (quantitative or qualitative) may be inaccurate. In sample surveys, opinion polls, etc., measurement error often results from *ambiguous* or *leading questions*. Consider the survey question: "How often did you change the oil in your car last year?" It is not clear whether the researcher wants to know how often you personally changed the oil in your car or how often you took your car into a service station to get an oil change. The ambiguous question may lead to inaccurate responses. On the other hand, consider the question: "Does the new health plan offer more comprehensive medical services at less cost than the old one?" The way the question is phrased *leads* the reader to believe that the new plan is better and to a "yes" response—a response that is more desirable to the researcher. A better, more neutral way to phrase the question is: "Which health plan offers more comprehensive medical services at less cost, the old one or the new one?"

> **Measurement error** refers to inaccuracies in the values of the data collected. In surveys, the error may be due to ambiguous or leading questions and the interviewer's effect on the respondent.

We conclude this section with two examples involving actual sampling studies.

Example   8

Method of Data Collection—Survey of Online Shoppers

Problem How do consumers feel about using the Internet for online shopping? To find out, a customer-experience software company recently commissioned a nationwide survey of 1,859 U.S. adults who had conducted at least one online transaction at a banking, shopping, travel, or insurance Web site in the past year. The findings, reported on *BusinessWeek.com,* revealed that 1,655 respondents, or 89%, experienced technical problems with an online transaction. Also, more than one-third of the consumers go to a competitor's Web site when a glitch in the online transaction occurs.

a. Identify the data-collection method.

b. Identify the target population.

c. Are the sample data representative of the population?

Solution

a. The data-collection method is a survey: 1,859 adults completed the questionnaire.

b. Presumably, the software company who commissioned the survey is interested in all consumers who have made at least one online transaction in the past year. Consequently, the target population is *all* consumers who use the Internet for online transactions.

c. Because the 1,859 respondents clearly make up a subset of the target population, they do form a sample. Whether or not the sample is representative is unclear because *BusinessWeek.com* provided no detailed information on how the 1,859 respondents were selected. If the respondents were obtained using, say, random-digit telephone dialing, then the sample is likely to be representative because it is a random sample. However, if the questionnaire was made available to anyone surfing the Internet, then the respondents are *self-selected* (i.e., each Internet user who saw the survey chose whether or not to respond to it). Such a survey often suffers from *nonresponse* bias. It is possible that many Internet users who chose not to respond (or who never saw the questionnaire) would have answered the questions differently, leading to a lower (or higher) sample percentage.

Look Back Any inferences based on survey samples that employ self-selection are suspect due to potential nonresponse bias.

➤ Now Work Exercise 25

Example   9

Representative Data— Price Promotion Study

Problem Marketers use wording such as "was $100, now $80" to indicate a price promotion. The promotion is typically compared to the retailer's previous price or to a competitor's price. A study in the *Journal of Consumer Research* investigated whether between-store comparisons result in greater perceptions of value by consumers than within-store comparisons. Suppose 50 consumers were randomly selected from all consumers in a designated market area to participate in the study. The researchers randomly assigned 25 consumers to read a within-store price promotion advertisement ("was $100, now $80") and 25 consumers to read a between-store price promotion ("$100 there, $80 here"). The consumers then gave their opinion on the value of the discount offer on a 10-point scale (where 1 = lowest value and 10 = highest value). The value opinions of the two groups of consumers were compared.

a. Identify the data-collection method.

b. Are the sample data representative of the target population?

Solution

a. Here, the experimental units are the consumers. Because the researchers controlled which price promotion ad—"within-store" or "between-store"—the experimental units (consumers) were assigned to, a designed experiment was used to collect the data.

b. The sample of 50 consumers was randomly selected from all consumers in the designated market area. If the target population is all consumers in this market, it is likely that the sample is representative. However, the researchers warn that the sample data should not be used to make inferences about consumer behavior in other, dissimilar markets.

Look Back By using randomization in a designed experiment, the researcher is attempting to eliminate different types of bias, including self-selection bias.

➤ Now Work Exercise 17

STATISTICS
in ACTION
REVISITED

Identifying the Data-Collection Method and Data Type

Refer to the *New York Times* study on the link between a CEO's golf handicap and the company's stock performance. Recall that the newspaper gathered information on golf handicaps of corporate executives obtained from a *Golf Digest* survey that was sent to 300 corporate executives. Thus, the data-collection method is a survey. In addition to golf handicap (a numerical "index" that allows golfers to compare skills), the *Times* measured the CEO's company stock market performance over a 3-year period on a scale of 0 to 100. Because both variables, golf handicap and stock performance, are numerical in nature, they are quantitative data.

Data Set: GLFCEO

7   Critical Thinking with Statistics

According to H. G. Wells, author of such science-fiction classics as *The War of the Worlds* and *The Time Machine*, "*Statistical thinking* will one day be as necessary for efficient citizenship as the ability to read and write." Written more than a hundred years ago, Wells's prediction is proving true today.

BIOGRAPHY

H. G. WELLS (1866–1946)
Writer and Novelist

English-born Herbert George Wells published his first novel, *The Time Machine,* in 1895 as a parody of the English class division and as a satirical warning that human progress is inevitable. Although most famous as a science-fiction novelist, Wells was a prolific writer as a journalist, sociologist, historian, and philosopher. Wells's prediction about statistical thinking (see above) is just one of a plethora of observations he made about life on this world. Here are a few more of H. G. Wells's more famous quotes:

"Advertising is legalized lying."

"Crude classification and false generalizations are the curse of organized life."

"The crisis of today is the joke of tomorrow."

"Fools make researchers and wise men exploit them."

"The only true measure of success is the ratio between what we might have done and what we might have been on the one hand, and the thing we have made and the things we have made of ourselves on the other."

The growth in data collection associated with scientific phenomena, business operations, and government activities (quality control, statistical auditing, forecasting, etc.) has been remarkable in the past several decades. Every day the media present us with the published results of political, economic, and social surveys. In increasing government emphasis on drug and product testing, for example, we see vivid evidence of the need for **quantitative literacy,** i.e., the ability to evaluate data intelligently. Consequently, each of us has to develop a discerning sense—an ability to use rational thought to interpret and understand the meaning of data. Quantitative literacy can help you make intelligent decisions, inferences, and generalizations; that is, it helps you *think critically* using statistics.

> **Statistical thinking** involves applying rational thought and the science of statistics to critically assess data and inferences. Fundamental to the thought process is that variation exists in populations and process data.

To gain some insight into the role statistics plays in critical thinking, we present two examples of some misleading or faulty surveys.

Example 10

Biased Sample— Motorcycle Helmet Law

Problem An article in the *New York Times* considered the question of whether motorcyclists should be required by law to wear helmets. In supporting his argument for no helmets, the editor of a magazine for Harley-Davidson bikers presented the results of one study that claimed "nine states without helmet laws had a lower fatality rate (3.05 deaths per 10,000 motorcycles) than those that mandated helmets (3.38)" and a survey that found "of 2,500 bikers at a rally, 98% of the respondents opposed such laws." Based on this information, do you think it is safer to ride a motorcycle without a helmet? What further statistical information would you like?

Solution You can use statistical thinking to help you critically evaluate the study. For example, before you can evaluate the validity of the 98% estimate, you would want to know how the data were collected. If a survey was, in fact, conducted, it's possible that the 2,500 bikers in the sample were not selected at random from the target population of all bikers, but rather were "self-selected." (Remember, they were all attending a rally—a rally likely for bikers who oppose the law.) If the respondents were likely to have strong opinions regarding the helmet law (e.g., strongly oppose the law), the resulting estimate is probably biased high. Also, if the selection bias in the sample was intentional, with the sole purpose to mislead the public, the researchers would be guilty of **unethical statistical practice**.

ETHICS in STATISTICS

Intentionally selecting a biased sample in order to produce misleading statistics is considered unethical statistical practice.

You would also want more information about the study comparing the motorcycle fatality rate of the nine states without a helmet law to those states that mandate helmets. Were the data obtained from a published source? Were all 50 states included in the study, or were only certain states selected? That is, are you seeing sample data or population data? Furthermore, do the helmet laws vary among states? If so, can you really compare the fatality rates?

Look Back Questions such as these led a group of mathematics and statistics teachers attending an American Statistical Association course to discover a scientific and statistically sound study on helmets. The study reported a dramatic *decline* in motorcycle crash deaths after California passed its helmet law.

Example 11

Manipulative or Ambiguous Survey Questions—Satellite Radio Survey

Problem Talk-show host Howard Stern moved his controversial radio program from free, over-the-air (AM/FM) radio to Sirius XM satellite radio. The move was perceived in the industry to boost satellite radio subscriptions. This led American Media Services, a developer of AM/FM radio properties, to solicit a nationwide random-digit dialing phone survey of 1,008 people. The purpose of the survey was to determine how much interest Americans really have in buying satellite radio service. After providing some background on Howard Stern's controversial radio program, one of the questions asked, "How likely are you to purchase a subscription to satellite radio after Howard Stern's move to Sirius?" The result: 86% of the respondents stated that they aren't likely to buy satellite radio because of Stern's move. Consequently, American Media Services concluded that "the Howard Stern Factor is overrated" and that "few Americans expect to purchase satellite radio"—claims that made the headlines of news reports and Web blogs. Do you agree?

Solution First, we need to recognize that American Media Services had a vested interest in the outcome of the survey—the company makes its money from over-the-air broadcast radio stations. Second, although the phone survey was conducted using random-digit dialing, there is no information provided on the response rate. It's possible that nonrespondents (people who were not home or refused to answer the survey questions) tend to be people who use cell phones more than their landline phone, and, consequently, are more likely to use the latest in electronic technology, including satellite radio. Finally, the survey question itself is ambiguous. Do the respondents have negative feelings about satellite radio, Howard Stern, or both? If not for Howard Stern's program, would the respondents be more likely to buy satellite radio? To the critical thinker, it's unclear what the results of the survey imply.

Look Back Examining the survey results from the perspective of satellite radio providers, 14% of the respondents indicated that they would be likely to purchase satellite radio. Projecting the 14% back to the population of all American adults, this figure represents about 50 million people; what is interpreted as "few Americans" by American Media Services could be music to the ears of satellite radio providers.

ETHICS in STATISTICS

Intentionally selecting a nonrandom sample in an effort to support a particular viewpoint is considered *unethical statistical practice.*

As with many statistical studies, both the motorcycle helmet study and satellite radio study are based on survey data. Most of the problems with these surveys result from the use of *nonrandom* samples. These samples are subject to potential errors, such as *selection bias, nonresponse bias,* and *measurement error.* Researchers who are aware of these problems and continue to use the sample data to make inferences are practicing *unethical statistics.*

Successful managers rely heavily on statistical thinking to help them make decisions. The role statistics can play in managerial decision making is displayed in the flow diagram in Figure 7. Every managerial decision-making problem begins with a real-world problem. This problem is then formulated in managerial terms and framed as a managerial question. The next sequence of steps (proceeding counterclockwise around the flow diagram) identifies the role that statistics can play in this process. The managerial question is translated into a statistical question, the sample data are collected and analyzed, and the statistical question is answered. The next step in the process is using the answer to the statistical question to reach an answer to the managerial question. The answer to the managerial question may suggest a reformulation of the original managerial problem, suggest a new managerial question, or lead to the solution of the managerial problem.

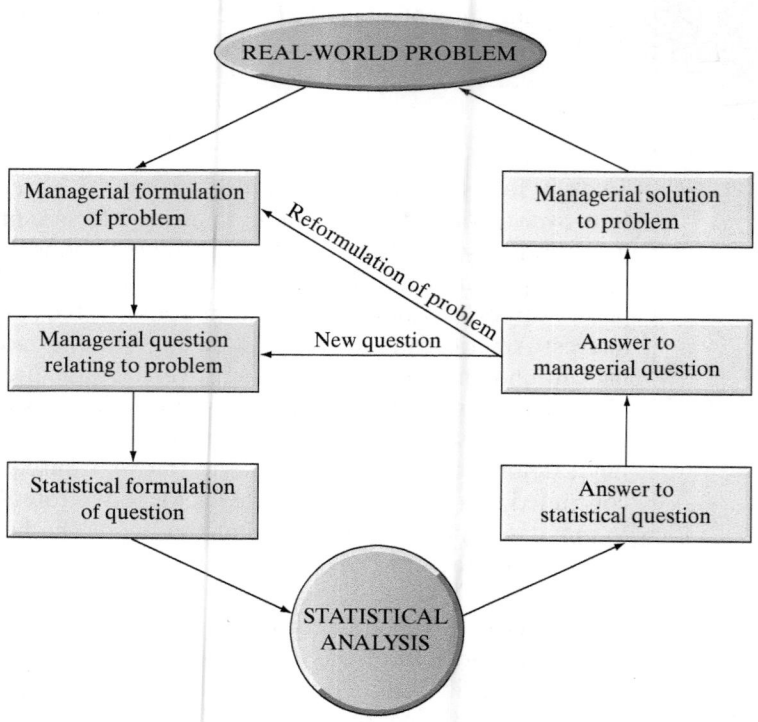

Figure 7

Flow diagram showing the role of statistics in managerial decision making

One of the most difficult steps in the decision-making process—one that requires a cooperative effort among managers and statisticians—is the translation of the managerial question into statistical terms (for example, into a question about a population). This statistical question must be formulated so that, when answered, it will provide the key to the answer to the managerial question. Thus, as in the game of chess, you must formulate the statistical question with the end result, the solution to the managerial question, in mind.

STATISTICS in ACTION REVISITED

Critically Assessing the Ethics of a Statistical Study

The *New York Times* reported a strong link between a corporate executive's golf handicap and his/her company's stock performance. Thus, the newspaper inferred that the better the CEO is at golf, the better the company's stock performance will be. To critically assess this study, consider the following facts:

1. *Golf Digest* sent surveys to the CEOs at the 300 largest U.S. firms. Only 74 executives agreed to reveal their golf handicaps. Of these 74 CEOs, the *Times* collected data on stock performance for only 51 of the companies. (The other 23 CEOs were not in the stock performance database used by the newspaper.)

2. The *New York Times* researcher who performed the analysis of the data stated that "for all the different factors I've tested as possible links to predicting which CEOs are going to perform well or poorly, [golf handicap] is certainly one of the ... strongest."

3. According to the *Times,* the researcher "scientifically sifted out a handful of CEOs because of their statistical extremes," in effect "removing seven CEOs from the final analysis because [their data] destroyed the trend lines."

These observations lead a critical thinker to doubt the validity of the inference made by the *New York Times* researcher. Consider first that the sample of CEOs analyzed was not randomly selected from all CEOs in the United States. In fact, it was self-selected—only those CEOs who chose to report their golf handicap were included in the study. (Not even all these "self-reporters" were included; some were eliminated because the newspaper did not have information on their company's stock performance in the database.) Thus, the potential for selection and/or nonresponse bias is extremely high.

Second, based on fact #2, it is likely that the researcher tested a multitude of factors and found only one (golf handicap) that had a link to stock performance. When a plethora of irrelevant variables are tested statistically, by chance one or more of the variables will be found "statistically significant."

Finally, the researcher removed the data for seven CEOs based on their "statistical extremes." It can be shown (using the methods outlined in the text) that these seven data points are not outliers. If the data points are included in the analysis, the link between golf handicap and stock performance is found to be weak, at best.

Data Set: GLFCEO

☐ Chapter Notes

Key Terms

Note: Starred (*) terms are from the optional section in this chapter.

*Black box
Census
Cluster sampling
Data
Descriptive statistics
Designed experiment
Experimental (or
  observational) unit
Inference
Inferential statistics
Measurement
Measurement error
Measure of reliability
Nonresponse bias
Observational study
Population
*Process
Published source
Qualitative data

Quantitative data
Quantitative literacy
Randomized response
  sampling
Random number generator
Reliability
Representative sample
Sample
Selection bias
Simple random sample
Statistical inference
Statistical thinking
Statistics
Stratified random sampling
Survey
Systematic sampling
Unethical statistical
  practice
Variable

Key Ideas

Types of Statistical Applications

Descriptive

1. Identify **population** or **sample** (collection of **experimental units**)
2. Identify **variable(s)**

3. Collect **data**
4. **Describe** data

Inferential

1. Identify **population** (collection of *all* **experimental units**)
2. Identify **variable(s)**
3. Collect **sample** data (*subset* of population)
4. **Inference** about population based on sample
5. **Measure of reliability** for inference

Types of Data

1. **Quantitative** (numerical in nature)
2. **Qualitative** (categorical in nature)

Data-Collection Methods

1. **Observational** (e.g., survey)
2. **Published source**
3. **Designed experiment**

Types of Random Samples

1. **Simple random sample**
2. **Stratified random sample**
3. **Cluster sample**
4. **Systematic sample**
5. **Random response sample**

Problems with Nonrandom Samples

1. **Selection bias**
2. **Nonresponse bias**
3. **Measurement error**

Exercises 1–39

Note: Starred (*) exercises are from the optional section in this chapter.

Learning the Mechanics

1 What is statistics?

2 Explain the difference between descriptive and inferential statistics.

3 List and define the four elements of a descriptive statistics problem.

4 List and define the five elements of an inferential statistical analysis.

5 List the three major methods of collecting data and explain their differences.

6 Explain the difference between quantitative and qualitative data.

7 Explain how populations and variables differ.

8 Explain how populations and samples differ.

9 What is a representative sample? What is its value?

10 Why would a statistician consider an inference incomplete without an accompanying measure of its reliability?

*11 Explain the difference between a population and a process.

12 Define *statistical thinking*.

13 Suppose you're given a data set that classifies each sample unit into one of four categories: A, B, C, or D. You plan to create a computer database consisting of these data, and you decide to code the data as A = 1, B = 2, C = 3, and D = 4. Are the data consisting of the classifications A, B, C, and D qualitative or quantitative? After the data are input as 1, 2, 3, or 4, are they qualitative or quantitative? Explain your answers.

14 Suppose that a population contains 200,000 experimental units. Use a random number generator to select a simple random sample of $n = 10$ units from the population.

☺ Applet Exercise 1

The *Random Numbers* applet generates a list of *n* random numbers from 1 to *N*, where *n* is the size of the sample and *N* is the size of the population. The list generated often contains repetitions of one or more numbers.

    a. Using the applet *Random Numbers*, enter 1 for the minimum value, 10 for the maximum value, and 10 for the sample size. Then click on *Sample*. Look at the results and list any numbers that are repeated and the number of times each of these numbers occurs.

b. Repeat part **a,** changing the maximum value to 20 and keeping the size of the sample fixed at 10. If you still have repetitions, repeat the process, increasing the maximum value by 10 each time but keeping the size of the sample fixed. What is the smallest maximum value for which you had no repetitions?

c. Describe the relationship between the population size (maximum value) and the number of repetitions in the list of random numbers as the population size increases and the sample size remains the same. What can you conclude about using a random number generator to choose a relatively small sample from a large population?

⚙ Applet Exercise 2

The *Random Numbers* applet can be used to select a random sample from a population, but can it be used to simulate data? In parts **a** and **b,** you will use the applet to create data sets. Then you will explore whether those data sets are realistic.

a. In the activity *Keep the Change* a data set called *Amounts Transferred* is described. Use the *Random Numbers* applet to simulate this data set by setting the minimum value equal to 0, the maximum value equal to 99, and the sample size equal to 30. Explain what the numbers in the list produced by the applet represent in the context of the activity. (You may need to read the activity.) Do the numbers produced by the applet seem reasonable? Explain.

b. Use the *Random Numbers* applet to simulate grades on a statistics test by setting the minimum value equal to 0, the maximum value equal to 100, and the sample size equal to 30. Explain what the numbers in the list produced by the applet represent in this context. Do the numbers produced by the applet seem reasonable? Explain.

c. Referring to parts **a** and **b,** why do the randomly generated data seem more reasonable in one situation than in the other? Comment on the usefulness of using a random number generator to produce data.

Applying the Concepts—Basic

15 **Zillow.com estimates of home values.** Zillow.com is a real estate Web site that provides free estimates of the market value of homes. A trio of University of Texas at San Antonio professors compared *Zillow* estimates to actual sale prices of homes and published their results in *The Appraisal Journal* (Winter 2010). The analysis was based on data collected for 2,045 single-family residential properties in Arlington, Texas, that sold during the last 6 months of 2006. Sale price and *Zillow* estimated value (in dollars) were measured for each property. *Zillow* claims that this market has one of its highest-accuracy ratings. However, the research revealed that *Zillow* overestimated the market value by more than 10% for nearly half of the properties.

a. What is the experimental unit for this study?

b. Describe the variables measured in the study. Do these variables produce quantitative or qualitative data?

c. Give a scenario where the 2,045 properties represent a population.

d. If the 2,045 properties represent a representative sample from a population, describe the population.

e. Suppose the relevant population is all single-family residential properties in the United States. Do you believe the 2,045 properties are representative of this population? Explain.

16 **Drafting NFL quarterbacks.** The National Football League (NFL) is a lucrative business, generating an annual revenue of about $8 million. One key to becoming a financially successful NFL team is drafting a good quarterback (QB) out of college. The NFL draft allows the worst-performing teams in the previous year the opportunity of selecting the best quarterbacks coming out of college. The *Journal of Productivity Analysis* (Vol. 35, 2011) published a study of how successful NFL teams are in drafting productive quarterbacks. Data were collected for all 331 quarterbacks drafted between 1970 and 2007. Several variables were measured for each QB, including draft position (one of the top 10 players picked, selection between picks 11–50, or selected after pick 50), NFL winning ratio (percentage of games won), and QB production score (higher scores indicate more productive QBs). The researchers discovered that draft position is only weakly related to a quarterback's performance in the NFL. They concluded that "quarterbacks taken higher [in the draft] do not appear to perform any better."

a. What is the experimental unit for this study?

b. Identify the type (quantitative or qualitative) of each variable measured.

c. Suppose you want to use this study to project the performance of future NFL QBs. Is this an application of descriptive or inferential statistics? Explain.

17 **Opinion polls.** Pollsters regularly conduct opinion polls to determine the popularity rating of the current president. Suppose a poll is to be conducted tomorrow in which 2,000 individuals will be asked whether the president is doing a good or bad job. The 2,000 individuals will be selected by random-digit telephone dialing and asked the question over the phone.

a. What is the relevant population?

b. What is the variable of interest? Is it quantitative or qualitative?

c. What is the sample?

d. What is the inference of interest to the pollster?

e. What method of data collection is employed?

f. How likely is the sample to be representative?

18 **College application data.** Colleges and universities are requiring an increasing amount of information about applicants before making acceptance and financial aid decisions. Classify each of the following types of data required on a college application as quantitative or qualitative.

a. High school GPA

b. Honors, awards

c. Applicant's score on the SAT or ACT

d. Gender of applicant

e. Parents' income

f. Age of applicant

19 **Microsoft survey of Windows.** Windows is a computer software product made by Microsoft Corporation. In designing a new version of Windows, Microsoft telephoned thousands of users of an earlier version of Windows and asked them how the product could be improved. Assume customers were asked the following questions:

a. Are you the most frequent user of Windows in your household?

b. What is your age?

c. Are the tutorial instructions that accompany Windows helpful?

d. When using a printer with Windows, do you most frequently use a laser printer or another type of printer?

e. If the speed of Windows could be changed, which one of the following would you prefer: slower, unchanged, or faster?

f. How many people in your household have used Windows at least once?

Each of these questions defines a variable of interest to the company. Classify the data generated for each variable as quantitative or qualitative. Justify your classification.

20 **Going online for health information.** A *cyberchondriac* is defined as a person who regularly searches the Web for health care information. Each year a Harris Poll is conducted to determine the number of cyberchondriacs in the United States. In 2011, the Harris Poll surveyed 1,019 U.S. adults by telephone and asked the following questions:

1. Have you ever gone online to look for health care information?

2. How many times per month do you look for health care information online?

3. In the past year, have you ever discussed with your doctor the information you found online?

a. For each question, determine whether the type of data collected is quantitative or qualitative.

b. Do the data collected for the 1,019 adults represent a sample or a population? Explain.

21 **The executive compensation scoreboard.** Each year, *Forbes* publishes its Executive Compensation Scoreboard. (See Study 2.) For the 2011 scoreboard, data were collected for chief executive officers at the 500 largest U.S. companies and the following variables were measured for each CEO: (1) the industry type of the CEO's company (e.g., banking, retailing, etc.), (2) the CEO's total compensation ($ millions) for the year, (3) the CEO's total compensation ($ millions) over the previous 5 years, (4) the number of company stock shares (millions) held, (5) the CEO's age (years), and (6) the CEO's efficiency rating.

a. Are the data for the 500 CEOs in the 2011 Executive Compensation Scoreboard a population or sample? Explain.

b. Identify the type (quantitative or qualitative) of each variable measured.

22 **Annual survey of computer crimes.** The Computer Security Institute (CSI) conducts an annual survey of computer crime at U.S. businesses. CSI sends survey questionnaries to computer security personnel at all U.S. corporations and government agencies. The 2010 CSI survey was sent by post or e-mail to 5,412 firms, and 351 organizations responded. Forty-one percent of the respondents admitted unauthorized use of computer systems at their firms

during the year. (*CSI Computer Crime and Security Survey, 2010/2011*)

a. Identify the population of interest to CSI.

b. Identify the data-collection method used by CSI. Are there any potential biases in the method used?

c. Describe the variable measured in the CSI survey. Is it quantitative or qualitative?

d. What inference can be made from the study result?

23 **Treasury deficit prior to the Civil War.** In *Civil War History* (June 2009), historian Jane Flaherty researched the condition of the U.S. Treasury on the eve of the Civil War in 1861. Between 1854 and 1857 (under President Franklin Pierce), the annual surplus/deficit was +18.8, +6.7, +5.3, and +1.3 million dollars, respectively. In contrast, between 1858 and 1861 (under President James Buchanan), the annual surplus/deficit was −27.3, −16.2, −7.2, and −25.2 million dollars, respectively. Flaherty used these data to aid in portraying the exhausted condition of the U.S. Treasury when Abraham Lincoln took office in 1861. Does this study represent a descriptive or inferential statistical study? Explain.

24 **The "lucky store effect" in lottery ticket sales.** In the *American Economic Review* (Vol. 98, 2008), University of Chicago researchers investigated the *lucky store effect* theory in lottery ticket sales, i.e., the theory that a lottery retail store that sold a large-prize-winning ticket will experience greater ticket sales the following week. The researchers examined the weekly ticket sales between January 2000 and June 2002 of all 24,400 active lottery retailers in Texas. Specifically, they focused on sales of the Lotto Texas ticket, with jackpots ranging from $1 to $50 million. The analysis showed that "the week following the sale of [a winning Lotto Texas ticket], the winning store experiences a 12 to 38 percent relative sales increase. . . ." Consequently, the researchers project that future winning lottery retail stores will experience the *lucky store effect*. Is this study an example of descriptive statistics or inferential statistics? Explain.

Applying the Concepts—Intermediate

25 **The economic return to earning an MBA.** What are the economic rewards (e.g., higher salary) to obtaining an MBA degree? This was the question of interest in an article published in the *International Economic Review* (August 2008). The researchers made inferences based on wage data collected for a sample of 3,244 individuals who sat for the Graduate Management Admissions Test (GMAT). (The GMAT exam is required for entrance into most MBA programs.) The following sampling scheme was employed. All those who took the GMAT exam in any of four selected time periods (Jan. 1990, Sep. 1991, Jan. 1993, and Jan. 1997) were mailed a questionnaire. Those who responded to the questionnaire were then sent three follow-up surveys (one survey every 3 months). The final sample of 3,244 represents only those individuals who responded to all four surveys. (For example, about 5,600 took the GMAT in Jan. 1990; of these, only about 800 responded to all four surveys.)

a. For this study, describe the population of interest.

b. What method was used to collect the sample data?

c. Do you think the final sample is representative of the population? Who or why not? Comment on potential biases in the sample.

26 Corporate sustainability and firm characteristics. *Corporate sustainability* refers to business practices designed around social and environmental considerations (e.g., "going green"). *Business and Society* (March 2011) published a paper on how firm size and firm type impact sustainability behaviors. The researchers added questions on sustainability to a quarterly survey of Certified Public Accountants (CPAs). The survey was sent to approximately 23,500 senior managers at CPA firms, of which 1,293 senior managers responded. (*Note:* It is not clear how the 23,500 senior managers were selected.) Due to missing data (incomplete survey answers), only 992 surveys were analyzed. These data were used to infer whether larger firms are more likely to report sustainability policies than smaller firms and whether public firms are more likely to report sustainability policies than private firms.

a. Identify the population of interest to the researchers.
b. What method was used to collect the sample data?
c. Comment on the representativeness of the sample.
d. How will your answer to part **c** impact the validity of the inferences drawn from the study?

27 Inspection of highway bridges. All highway bridges in the United States are inspected periodically for structural deficiency by the Federal Highway Administration (FHWA). Data from the FHWA inspections are compiled into the National Bridge Inventory (NBI). Several of the nearly 100 variables maintained by the NBI are listed below. Classify each variable as quantitative or qualitative.

a. Length of maximum span (feet)
b. Number of vehicle lanes
c. Toll bridge (yes or no)
d. Average daily traffic
e. Condition of deck (good, fair, or poor)
f. Bypass or detour length (miles)
g. Route type (interstate, U.S., state, county, or city)

28 Structurally deficient highway bridges. Refer to Exercise 27. The 2009 NBI data were analyzed and the results made available at the FHWA Web site (www.fhwa.dot.gov). Using the FHWA inspection ratings, each of the 608,272 highway bridges in the United States was categorized as structurally deficient, functionally obsolete, or safe. About 13.5% of the bridges were found to be structurally deficient, while 3.5% were functionally obsolete.

a. What is the variable of interest to the researchers?
b. Is the variable of part a quantitative or qualitative?
c. Is the data set analyzed a population or a sample? Explain.
d. How did the NBI obtain the data for the study?

*29 Monitoring product quality. The Wallace Company of Houston is a distributor of pipes, valves, and fittings to the refining, chemical, and petrochemical industries. The company was a recent winner of the Malcolm Baldrige National Quality Award. One of the steps the company takes to monitor the quality of its distribution process is to send out a survey twice a year to a subset of its current customers, asking the customers to rate the speed of deliveries, the accuracy of invoices, and the quality of the packaging of the products they have received from Wallace.

a. Describe the process studied.
b. Describe the variables of interest.
c. Describe the sample.
d. Describe the inferences of interest.
e. What are some of the factors that are likely to affect the reliability of the inferences?

30 Guilt in decision making. The effect of guilt emotion on how a decision maker focuses on the problem was investigated in the *Journal of Behavioral Decision Making* (January 2007). A total of 171 volunteer students participated in the experiment, where each was randomly assigned to one of three emotional states (guilt, anger, or neutral) through a reading/writing task. Immediately after the task, the students were presented with a decision problem (e.g., whether or not to spend money on repairing a very old car). The researchers found that a higher proportion of students in the guilty-state group chose to repair the car than those in the neutral-state and anger-state groups.

a. Identify the population, sample, and variables measured for this study.
b. Identify the data-collection method used.
c. What inference was made by the researcher?
d. The reliability of an inference is related to the size of the sample used. In addition to sample size, what factors might affect the reliability of the inference drawn in this study?

31 Accounting and Machiavellianism. *Behavioral Research in Accounting* (January 2008) published a study of Machiavellian traits in accountants. *Machiavellian* describes negative character traits that include manipulation, cunning, duplicity, deception, and bad faith. A questionnaire was administered to a random sample of 700 accounting alumni of a large southwestern university; however, due to nonresponse and incomplete answers, only 198 questionnaires could be analyzed. Several variables were measured, including age, gender, level of education, income, job satisfaction score, and Machiavellian ("Mach") rating score. The research findings suggest that Machiavellian behavior is not required to achieve success in the accounting profession.

a. What is the population of interest to the researcher?
b. What type of data (quantitative or qualitative) is produced by each of the variables measured?
c. Identify the sample.
d. Identify the data-collection method used.
e. What inference was made by the researcher?
f. How might the nonresponses impact the inference?

32 Sampling stocks on the NYSE. The results of the previous business day's transactions for stocks traded on the New York Stock Exchange (NYSE) and five regional exchanges—the Chicago, Pacific, Philadelphia, Boston, and Cincinnati stock exchanges—are summarized each business day in the NYSE—Composite Transactions table in the *Wall Street Journal*.

a. Examine the NYSE—Composite Transactions table in a recent issue of the *Wall Street Journal* and explain how to draw a simple random sample of stocks from the table.

b. Use the procedure you described in part **a** to draw a simple random sample of 20 stocks from a recent NYSE—Composite Transactions table. For each stock in the sample, list its name (i.e., the abbreviation given in the table), its sales volume, and its closing price.

33 Can money spent on gifts buy love? Is the gift you purchased for that special someone really appreciated? This was the question of interest to business professors at Stanford University. Their research was published in the *Journal of Experimental Social Psychology* (Vol. 45, 2009). In one study, the researchers investigated the link between engagement ring price (dollars) and level of appreciation of the recipient (measured on a 7-point scale where 1 = "not at all" and 7 = "to a great extent"). Participants for the study were those who used a popular Web site for engaged couples. The Web site's directory was searched for those with "average" American names (e.g., "John Smith," "Sara Jones"). These individuals were then invited to participate in an online survey in exchange for a $10 gift certificate. Of the respondents, those who paid really high or really low prices for the ring were excluded, leaving a sample size of 33 respondents.

a. Identify the experimental units for this study.

b. What are the variables of interest? Are they quantitative or qualitative in nature?

c. Describe the population of interest.

d. Do you believe the sample of 33 respondents is representative of the population? Explain.

e. In a second designed study, the researchers investigated whether the link between gift price and level of appreciation is stronger for birthday gift-givers than for birthday gift-receivers. The participants were randomly assigned to play the role of gift-giver or gift-receiver. Assume that the sample consists of 50 individuals. Use a random number generator to randomly assign 25 individuals to play the gift-receiver role and 25 to play the gift-giver role.

Applying the Concepts—Advanced

34 Random-digit dialing. To ascertain the effectiveness of their advertising compaigns, firms frequently conduct telephone interviews with consumers using *random-digit dialing*. With this approach, a random number generator mechanically creates the sample of phone numbers to be called. Each digit in the phone number is randomly selected from the possible digits 0, 1, 2, ..., 9. Use the procedure to generate five seven-digit telephone numbers whose first three digits (area code) are 373.

35 Bank corporate mergers. *Corporate merger* is a means through which one firm (the bidder) acquires control of the assets of another firm (the target). Recently, there was a frenzy of bank mergers in the United States, as the banking industry consolidated into more efficient and more competitive units.

a. Construct a brief questionnaire (two or three questions) that could be used to query a sample of bank presidents concerning their opinions of why the industry is consolidating and whether it will consolidate further.

b. Describe the population about which inferences could be made from the results of the survey.

c. Discuss the pros and cons of sending the questionnaire to all bank presidents versus a sample of 200.

*36 Monitoring the production of soft-drink cans. The Wakefield plant of Coca-Cola and Schweppes Beverages Limited (CCSB) can produce 4,000 cans of soft drink per minute. The automated process consists of measuring and dispensing the raw ingredients into storage vessels to create the syrup, and then injecting the syrup, along with carbon dioxide, into the beverage cans. In order to monitor the subprocess that adds carbon dioxide to the cans, five filled cans are pulled off the line every 15 minutes, and the amount of carbon dioxide in each of these five cans is measured to determine whether the amounts are within prescribed limits.

a. Describe the process studied.

b. Describe the variable of interest.

c. Describe the sample.

d. Describe the inference of interest.

e. *Brix* is a unit for measuring sugar concentration. If a technician is assigned the task of estimating the average brix level of all 240,000 cans of beverage stored in a warehouse near Wakefield, will the technician be examining a process or a population? Explain.

37 Current population survey. The employment status (employed or unemployed) of each individual in the U.S. workforce is a set of data that is of interest to economists, businesspeople, and sociologists. To obtain information about the employment status of the workforce, the U.S. Bureau of the Census conducts what is known as the *Current Population Survey*. Each month interviewers visit about 50,000 of the 117 million households in the United States and question the occupants over 14 years of age about their employment status. Their responses enable the Bureau of the Census to *estimate* the percentage of people in the labor force who are unemployed (the *unemployment rate*).

a. Define the population of interest to the Census Bureau.

b. What variable is being measured? Is it quantitative or qualitative?

c. Is the problem of interest to the Census Bureau descriptive or inferential?

d. In order to monitor the rate of unemployment, it is essential to have a definition of *unemployed*. Different economists and even different countries define it in various ways. Develop your own definition of an "unemployed person." Your definition should answer such questions as: Are students on summer vacation unemployed? Are college professors who do not teach summer school unemployed? At what age are people considered to be eligible for the workforce? Are people who are out of work but not actively seeking a job unemployed?

38 Sampling TV markets for a court case. A recent court case involved a claim of satellite television subscribers obtaining illegal access to local TV stations. The defendant (the satellite TV company) wanted to sample TV markets nationwide and determine the percentage of its subscribers in each sampled market who have illegal access to local TV stations. To do this, the defendant's expert witness drew a rectangular grid over the continental United States, with horizontal and vertical grid lines every .02 degrees of latitude and longitude, respectively. This created a total of

500 rows and 1,000 columns, or $(500)(1,000) = 500,000$ intersections. The plan was to randomly sample 900 intersection points and include the TV market at each intersection in the sample. Explain how you could use a random number generator to obtain a random sample of 900 intersections. Develop at least two plans: one that numbers the intersections from 1 to 500,000 prior to selection and another that selects the row and column of each sampled intersection (from the total of 500 rows and 1,000 columns).

Critical Thinking Challenge

39 *20/20* **survey exposé.** Refer to the "Statistics in Action" box of this chapter. Recall that the popular prime-time ABC television program *20/20* presented several misleading (and possibly unethical) surveys in a segment titled "Fact or Fiction?—Exposés of So-Called Surveys." The information reported from four of these surveys and a more recent survey are reproduced here (actual survey facts are provided in parentheses).

- *Quaker Oats study:* Eating oat bran is a cheap and easy way to reduce your cholesterol count. (Fact: Diet must consist of nothing but oat bran to achieve a slightly lower cholesterol count.)
- *March of Dimes report:* Domestic violence causes more birth defects than all medical issues combined. (Fact: No study—false report.)
- *American Association of University Women (AAUW) study:* Only 29% of high school girls are happy with themselves, compared to 66% of elementary school girls. (Fact: Of 3,000 high school girls, 29% responded, "Always true" to the statement "I am happy the way I am." Most answered, "Sort of true" and "Sometimes true.")
- *Food Research and Action Center study:* One in four American children under age 12 is hungry or at risk of hunger. (Fact: Based on responses to questions: "Do

you ever cut the size of meals?" and "Do you ever eat less than you feel you should?" and "Did you ever rely on limited numbers of foods to feed your children because you were running out of money to buy food for a meal?")

- *McKinsey survey on the health reform act:* Thirty percent of employers would "definitely" or "probably" stop offering health coverage to their employees if the government-sponsored act is passed. (Fact: Employers were asked leading questions that made it seem logical for them to stop offering insurance. For example, respondents were told that the new health insurance exchanges would become "an easy, affordable way for individuals to obtain health insurance" outside the company. Then they were given examples of how little their workers would pay for this insurance. Only then were they asked how likely they would be to stop offering health insurance.)

a. Refer to the Quaker Oats study relating oat bran to cholesterol levels. Discuss why it is unethical to report the results as stated.

b. Consider the false March of Dimes report on domestic violence and birth defects. Discuss the type of data required to investigate the impact of domestic violence on birth defects. What data-collection method would you recommend?

c. Refer to the AAUW study of self-esteem of high school girls. Explain why the results of the study are likely to be misleading. What data might be appropriate for assessing the self-esteem of high school girls?

d. Refer to the Food Research and Action Center study of hunger in America. Explain why the results of the study are likely to be misleading. What data would provide insight into the proportion of hungry American children?

e. Refer to the McKinsey survey on the health reform act. Explain what a "leading question" is and why it might produce responses that bias the results.

Activity   1   *Keep the Change:* Collecting Data

Bank of America has a savings program called *Keep the Change.* Each time a customer enrolled in the program uses his or her debit card to make a purchase, the difference between the purchase total and the next higher dollar amount is transferred from the customer's checking account to a savings account. For example, if you were enrolled in the program and used your debit card to purchase a latte for $3.75, then $0.25 would be transferred from your checking to your savings account. For the first 90 days that a customer is enrolled in the program, Bank of America matches the amounts transferred up to $250. In this and subsequent activities, we will investigate the potential benefit to the customer and cost to the bank.

1. Simulate the program by keeping track of all purchases that you make during one week that could be made with a debit card, even if you use a different form of payment. For each purchase, record both the purchase

total and the amount that would be transferred from checking to savings with the *Keep the Change* program.

2. You now have two sets of data: *Purchase Totals* and *Amounts Transferred.* Both sets contain quantitative data. For each data set, identify the corresponding naturally occurring numerical scale. Explain why each set has an obvious lower bound but only one set has a definite upper bound.

3. Find the total of the amounts transferred for the one-week period. Because 90 days is approximately 13 weeks, multiply the total by 13 to estimate how much the bank would have to match during the first 90 days. Form a third data set, *Bank Matching,* by collecting the 90-day estimates of all the students in your class. Identify the naturally occurring scale, including bounds, for this set of data.

We suggest you save the data using statistical software (e.g., Minitab) or a graphing calculator.

Activity 2 — Identifying Misleading Statistics

In the *Statistics in Action* feature at the beginning of this chapter, several examples of false or misleading statistics were discussed. Claims such as *One in four American children under age 12 is hungry or at risk of hunger* are often used to persuade the public or the government to donate or allocate more money to charitable groups that feed the poor. Researchers sometimes claim a relationship exists between two seemingly unrelated quantities such as a CEO's golf handicap and the company's stock performance; such relationships are often weak at best and of little practical importance. Read the *Statistics in Action* and *Statistics in Action Revisited* features in this chapter before completing this activity.

1. Look for an article in a newspaper or on the Internet in which a large proportion or percentage of a population is purported to be "at risk" of some calamity, as in the childhood hunger example. Does the article cite a source or provide any information to support the proportion or percentage reported? Is the goal of the article to persuade some individual or group to take some action? If so, what action is being requested? Do you believe that the writer of the article may have some motive for exaggerating the problem? If so, give some possible motives.

2. Look for another article in which a relationship between two seemingly unrelated quantities is purported to exist, as in the CEO golf handicap and stock performance study. Select an article that contains some information on how the data were collected. Identify the target population and the data-collection method. Based on what is presented in the article, do you believe that the data are representative of the population? Explain. Is the purported relationship of any practical interest? Explain.

References

Careers in Statistics, American Statistical Association, 2011 (www.amstat.org)

Cochran, W. G. *Sampling Techniques,* 3rd ed. New York: Wiley, 1977.

Deming, W. E. *Sample Design in Business Research.* New York: Wiley, 1963.

Dillman, D. A., Smyth, J. D., and Christian, L. M. *Internet, Mail, and Mixed-Mode Surveys: The Tailored Design Method.* New York: Wiley, 2008.

Ethical Guidelines for Statistical Practice, American Statistical Association, 1999 (www.amstat.org).

Hahn, G. J. and Doganaksoy, N. *The Role of Statistics in Business and Industry.* New York: Wiley, 2008.

Huff, D. *How to Lie with Statistics.* New York: Norton, 1982 (paperback 1993).

Hoerl, R. and Snee, R. *Statistical Thinking: Improving Business Performance.* Boston: Duxbury, 2002.

Kish, L. *Survey Sampling.* New York: Wiley, 1965 (paperback, 1995).

Peck, R., Casella, G., Cobb, G., Hoerl, R., Nolan, D., Starbuck, R., and Stern, H. *Statistics: A Guide to the Unknown,* 4th ed. Cengage Learning, 2005.

Scheaffer, R., Mendenhall, W., and Ott, R. L. *Elementary Survey Sampling,* 6th ed. Boston: Duxbury, 2005.

What Is a Survey? American Statistical Association (F. Scheuren, editor), 2nd ed., 2005 (www.amstat.org).

USING TECHNOLOGY   Technology images shown here are taken from SPSS Statistics Professional 20.0, Minitab 16, XLSTAT for Pearson, and Excel 2010.

SPSS: Accessing and Listing Data

When you start an SPSS session, you will see a screen similar to Figure S.1. The main portion of the screen is an empty spreadsheet, with columns representing variables and rows representing observations (or cases). The very top of the screen is the SPSS main menu bar, with buttons for the different functions and procedures available in SPSS. Once you have entered data into the spreadsheet, you can analyze the data by clicking the appropriate menu buttons.

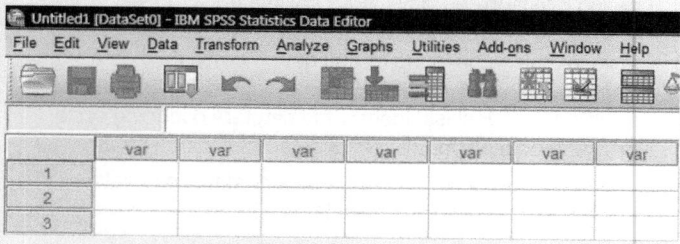

Figure S.1 Initial screen viewed by the SPSS user

Entering Data

Step 1 To create an SPSS data file, enter data directly into the spreadsheet. See Figure S.2 which shows data entered on a variable called "GPA."

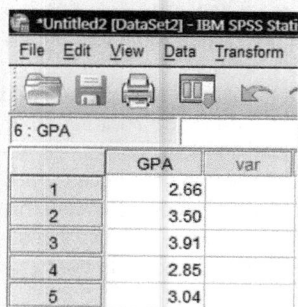

Figure S.2 Data entered into the SPSS spreadsheet

Step 2 Name the variables (columns) by selecting the "Variable View" button at the bottom of the screen and typing in the name of each variable.

Opening an SPSS Data File

If the data have been previously saved as an SPSS (.sav) file, access the data as follows.

Step 1 Click the "File" button on the menu bar, and then click "Open" and "Data," as shown in Figure S.3. A dialog box similar to Figure S.4 will appear.

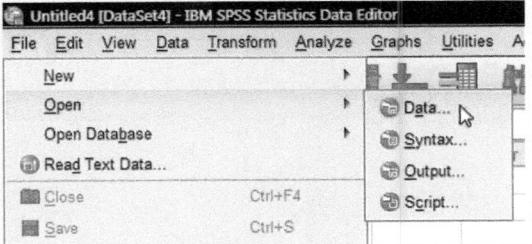

Figure S.3 Options for opening an SPSS data file

Step 2 Specify the location (folder) that contains the data, click on the SPSS data file, and then click "Open" (see Figure S.4). The data will appear in the SPSS spreadsheet, as shown in Figure S.5.

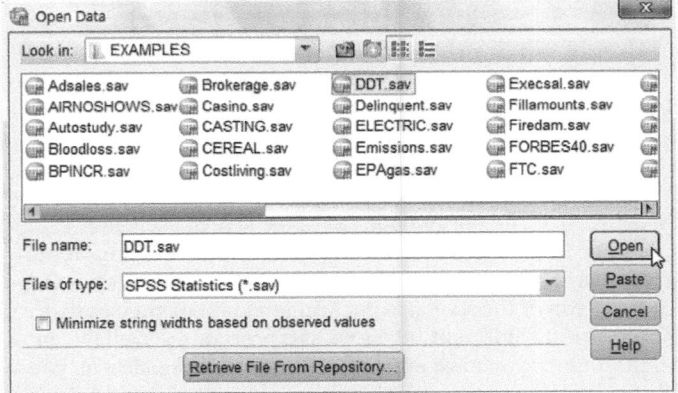

Figure S.4 Selecting the SPSS data file to open

	RIVER	MILE	SPECIES	LENGTH	WEIGHT	DDT
1	FCM	5	CHANNE...	42.5	732	10.00
2	FCM	5	CHANNE...	44.0	795	16.00
3	FCM	5	CHANNE...	41.5	547	23.00
4	FCM	5	CHANNE...	39.0	465	21.00
5	FCM	5	CHANNE...	50.5	1252	50.00
6	FCM	5	CHANNE...	52.0	1255	150.00

Figure S.5 The SPSS spreadsheet showing the opened SPSS data file

Accessing External Data from a File

If the data are saved in an external data file, you can access the data using the options available in SPSS.

Step 1 Click the "File" button on the menu bar, and then click "Read Text Data," as shown in Figure S.6. A dialog box similar to Figure S.7 will appear.

Figure S.6 SPSS options for reading data from an external file

Step 2 Specify the location (folder) that contains the data file, click on the data file, and then click "Open," as shown in Figure S.7. The SPSS Text Import Wizard Opens.

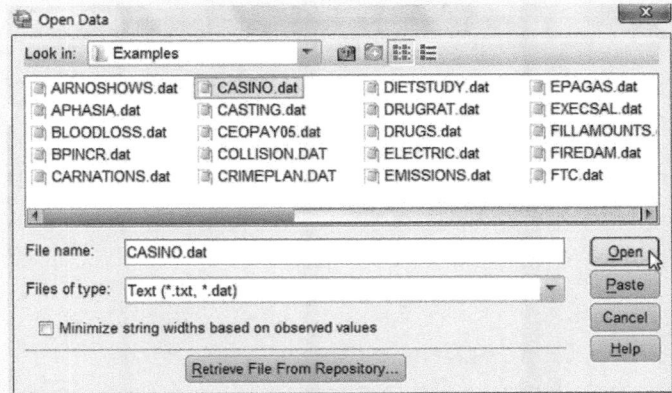

Figure S.7 Selecting the external data file in SPSS

Step 3 The Text Import Wizard is a series of six screen menus. Make the appropriate selections on the screen, and click "Next" to go to the next screen.

Step 4 When finished, click "Finish." The SPSS spreadsheet will reappear with the data from the external data file.

Reminder: The variable (columns) can be named by selecting the "Variable View" button at the bottom of the spreadsheet screen and typing in the name of each variable.

Listing (Printing) Data

Step 1 Click on the "Analyze" button on the SPSS main menu bar, then click on "Reports," and then on "Report Summaries in Rows" (see Figure S.8). The resulting menu, or dialog box, appears as in Figure S.9.

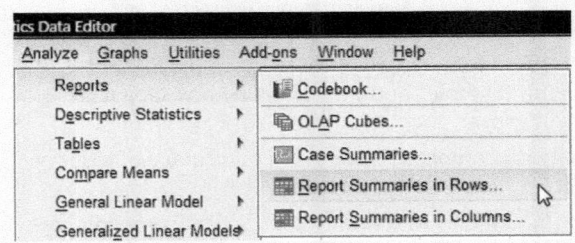

Figure S.8 SPSS menu options for obtaining a data listing

Step 2 Enter the names of the variables you want to print in the "Data Columns" box (you can do this by simply clicking on the variables), check the "Display cases" box at the bottom left, and then click "OK." The printout will show up on your screen.

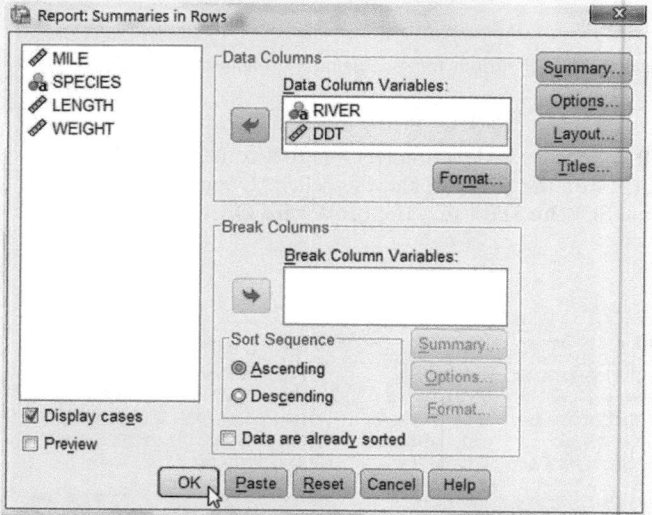

Figure S.9 SPSS data report dialog box

SPSS: Generating a Random Sample

Step 1 Click on are "Data" button on the SPSS menu bar and then click on "Select Cases" as shown in Figure S.10. The resulting menu list appears as shown in Figure S.11.

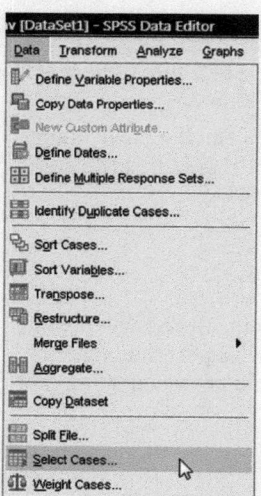

Figure S.10 SPSS menu options for sampling from a data set

Step 2 Select "Random sample of cases" from the list and then click on the "Sample" button. The dialog box shown in Figure S.12 will appear.

Step 3 Specify the sample size there as a percentage of cases or a raw number.

Step 4 Click "Continue" to return to the "Select Cases" dialog box (Figure S.11) and then click "OK." The SPSS spreadsheet will reappear with the selected (sampled) cases.

32

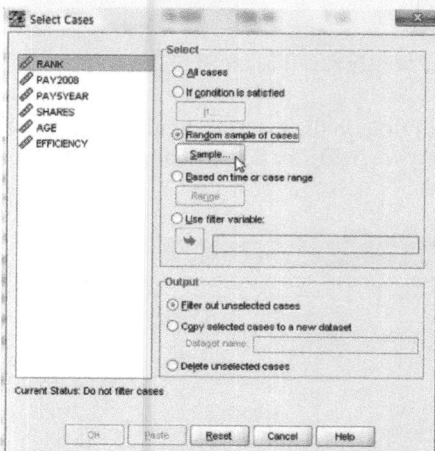

Figure S.11 SPSS options for selecting a random sample

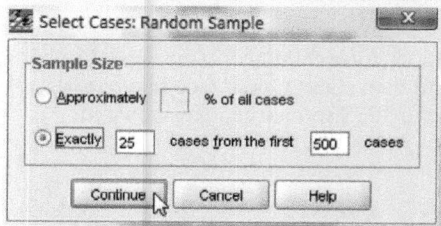

Figure S.12 SPSS random sample dialog box

Minitab: Accessing and Listing Data

When you start a Minitab session, you will see a screen similar to Figure M.1. The bottom portion of the screen is an empty spreadsheet—called a Minitab worksheet—with columns representing variables and rows representing observations (or cases). The very top of the screen is the Minitab main menu bar, with buttons for the different functions and procedures available in Minitab. Once you have entered data into the spreadsheet, you can analyze the data by clicking the appropriate menu buttons. The results will appear in the Session window.

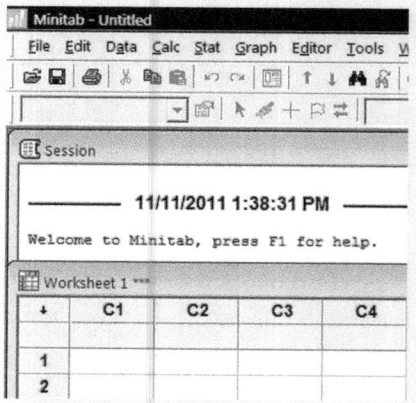

Figure M.1 Initial screen viewed by the Minitab user

Entering Data

Create a Minitab data file by entering data directly into the worksheet. Figure M.2 shows data entered for a variable called "GPA." Name the variables (columns) by typing in the name of each variable in the box below the column number.

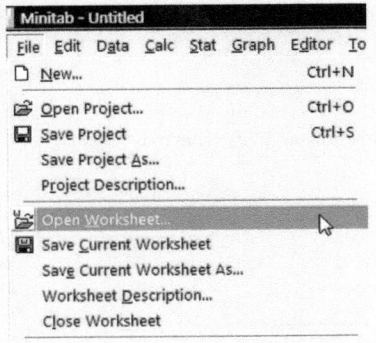

Figure M.2 Data entered into the Minitab worksheet

Opening a Minitab Data File

If the data have been previously saved as a Minitab (.mtw) file, access the data as follows.

Step 1 Click the "File" button on the menu bar, and then click "Open Worksheet," as shown in Figure M.3. A dialog box similar to Figure M.4 will appear.

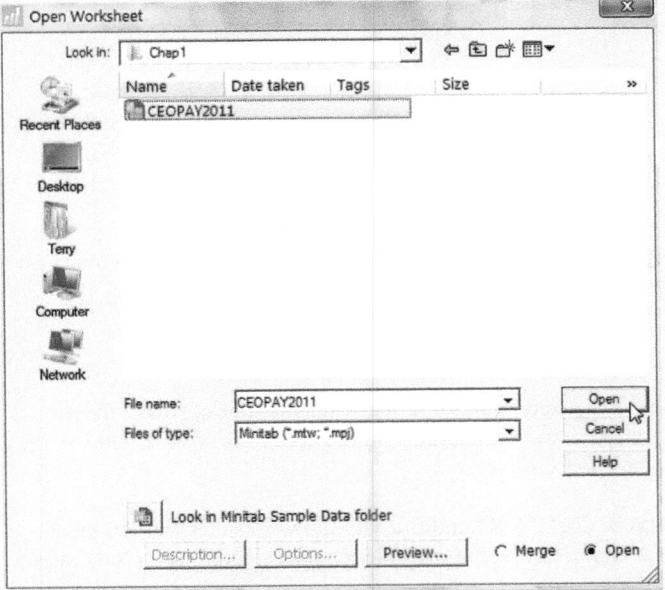

Figure M.3 Options for opening a Minitab data file

Figure M.4 Selecting the Minitab data file to open

Step 2 Specify the location (folder) that contains the data, click on the Minitab data file, and then click "Open" (see Figure M.4). The data will appear in the Minitab worksheet, as shown in Figure M.5 at bottom of the page.

Accessing External Data from a File

Step 1 Click the "File" button on the menu bar, and then click "Open Worksheet" as shown in Figure M.3. A dialog box similar to Figure M.6 will appear.

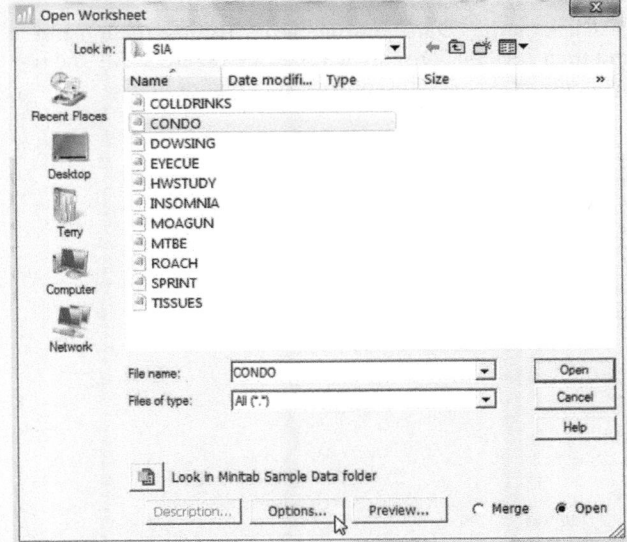

Figure M.6 Selecting the external data file in Minitab

Step 2 Specify the location (folder) that contains the external data file and the file type, and then click on the file name, as shown in Figure M.6.

Step 3 If the data set contains qualitative data or data with special characters, click on the "Options" button as shown in Figure M.6. The Options dialog box, shown in Figure M.7, will appear.

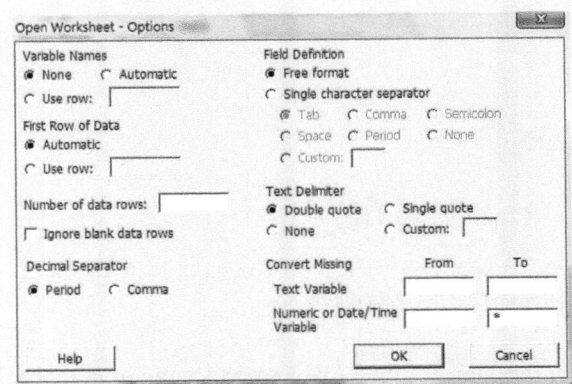

Figure M.7 Selecting the Minitab data input options

↓	C1	C2-T	C3-T	C4	C5
	Rank	Name	Company	Pay ($mil)	5-Yr Pay ($mil)
1	1	Hemsley, Stephen JStephen J Hemsley	UnitedHealth Group	101.965	120.472
2	2	Mueller, Edward AEdward A Mueller	Qwest Communications	65.800	75.003
3	3	Iger, Robert ARobert A Iger	Walt Disney	53.320	147.080
4	4	Paz, GeorgeGeorge Paz	Express Scripts	51.520	100.210
5	5	Frankfort, LewLew Frankfort	Coach	49.450	137.870
6	6	Lauren, RalphRalph Lauren	Polo Ralph Lauren	43.000	155.250

Figure M.5 The Minitab worksheet showing the opened Minitab data file

Step 4 Specify the appropriate options for the data set, and then click "OK" to return to the "Open Worksheet" dialog box (Figure M.6).

Step 5 Click "Open" and the Minitab worksheet will appear with the data from the external data file.

Reminder: The variables (columns) can be named by typing in the name of each variable in the box under the column number.

Listing (Printing) Data

Step 1 Click on the "Data" button on the Minitab main menu bar, and then click on "Display Data." (See Figure M.8.) The resulting menu, or dialog box, appears as in Figure M.9.

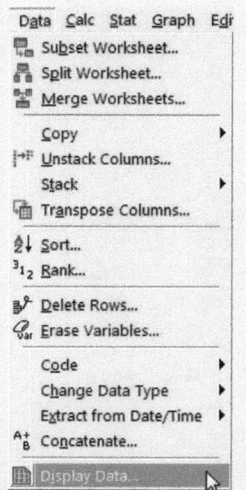

Figure M.8 Minitab options for displaying data

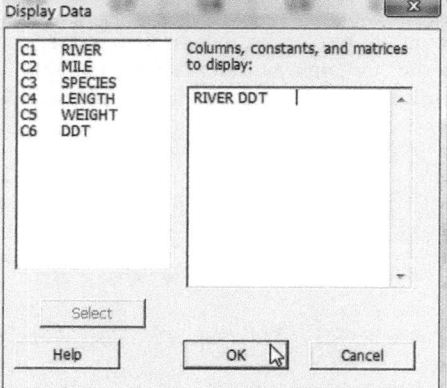

Figure M.9 Minitab Display Data dialog box

Step 2 Enter the names of the variables you want to print in the "Columns, constants, and matrices to display" box (you can do this by simply double clicking on the variables), and then click "OK." The printout will show up on your Minitab session screen.

Minitab: Generating a Random Sample

Step 1 Click on the "Calc" button on the Minitab menu bar and then click on "Random Data," and finally, click on "Sample From Columns," as shown in Figure M.10. The resulting dialog box appears as shown in Figure M.11.

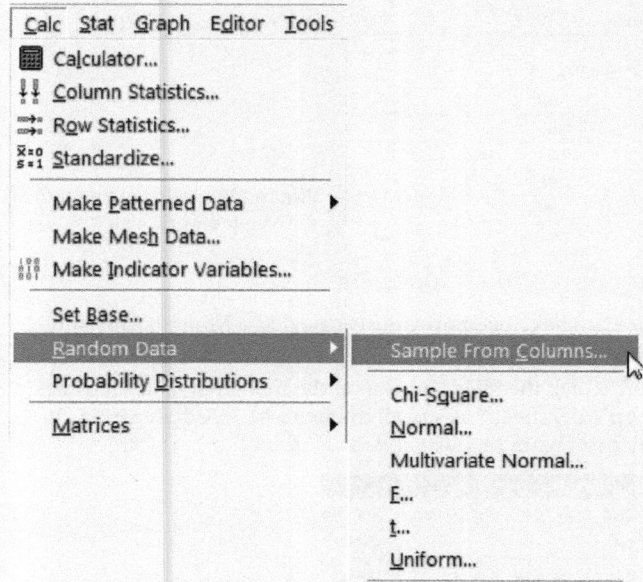

Figure M.10 Minitab menu options for sampling from a data set

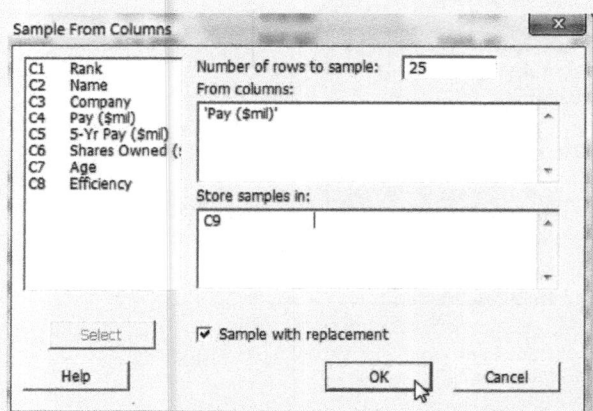

Figure M.11 Minitab options for selecting a random sample from worksheet columns

Step 2 Specify the sample size (i.e., number of rows), the variable(s) to be sampled, and the column(s) where you want to save the sample.

Step 3 Click "OK" and the Minitab worksheet will reappear with the values of the variable for the selected (sampled) cases in the column specified.

In Minitab, you can also generate a sample of case numbers.

Step 1 From the Minitab menu, click on the "Calc" button and then click on "Random Data," and finally, click on the "Uniform" option (see Figure M.10).

Step 2 In the resulting dialog box (shown in Figure M.12), specify the number of cases (rows, i.e., the sample size), and the column where the case numbers selected will be stored.

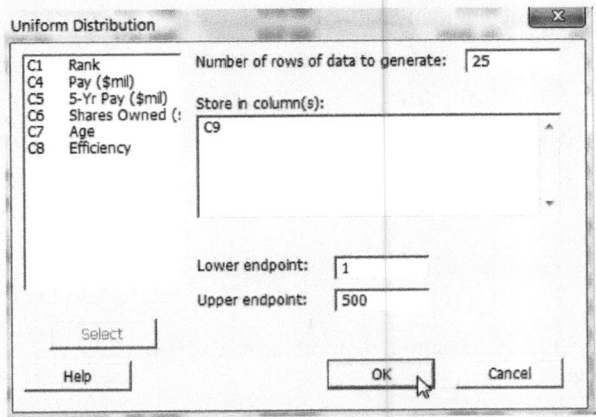

Figure M.12 Minitab options for selecting a random sample of cases

Step 3 Click "OK" and the Minitab worksheet will reappear with the case numbers for the selected (sampled) cases in the column specified.

[*Note:* If you want the option of generating the same (identical) sample multiple times from the data set, then first click on the "Set Base" option shown in Figure M.10. Specify an integer in the resulting dialog box. If you always select the same integer. Minitab will select the same sample when you choose the random sampling options.]

Excel: Accessing and Listing Data

When you open Excel, you will see a screen similar to Figure E.1. The majority of the screen window is a spreadsheet—called an Excel workbook—with columns (labeled A, B, C, etc.) representing variables, and rows representing observations (or cases). The very top of the screen is the Excel main menu bar, with buttons for the different functions and procedures available in Excel. Once you have entered data into the spreadsheet, you can analyze the data by clicking the appropriate menu buttons. The results will appear in a new workbook.

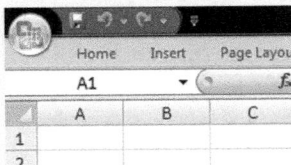

Figure E.1 Initial screen viewed by Excel user

Entering Data

Enter data directly into the appropriate row and column of the spreadsheet. Figure E.2 shows data entered in the first (A) column. Optionally, you can add names for the variables (columns) in the first row of the workbook.

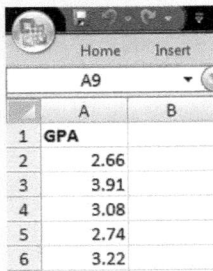

Figure E.2 Data entered into the Excel workbook

Opening an Excel File

If the data have been previously saved as an Excel (.xls) file, access the data as follows.

Step 1 Click the round Office button at the far left of the menu bar, and then click "Open," as shown in Figure E.3. A dialog box similar to Figure E.4 will appear.

Figure E.3 Options for opening an Excel file

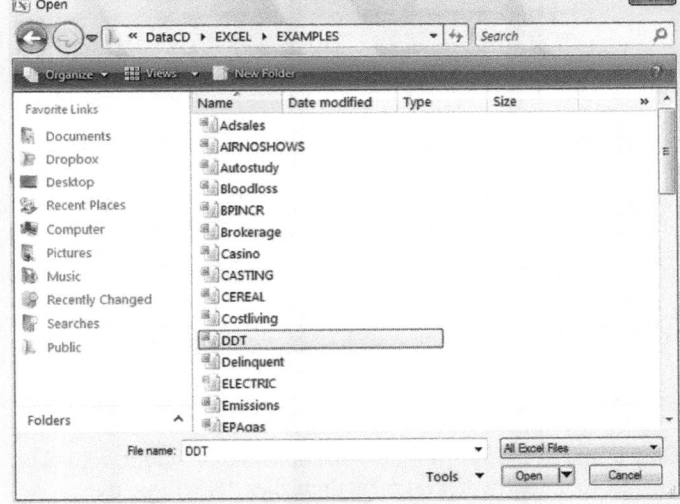

Figure E.4 Selecting the Excel file to open

Step 2 Specify the location (folder) that contains the data, click on the Excel file, and then click "Open" (see Figure E.4). The data will appear in the Excel spreadsheet as shown in Figure E.5.

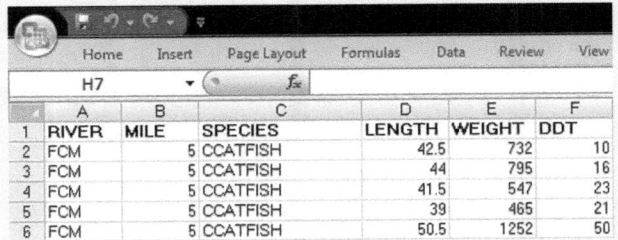

Figure E.5 The Excel spreadsheet showing the opened Excel file

Accessing External Data from a File

Step 1 Click the "Office" button on the menu bar, and then click "Open," as shown in Figure E.3. A dialog box similar to Figure E.6 will appear.

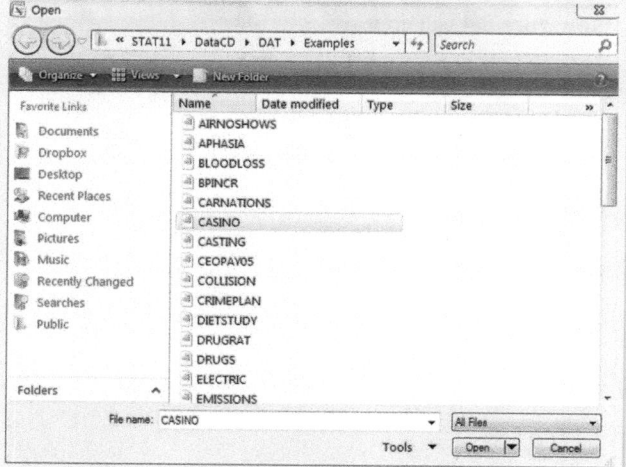

Figure E.6 Selecting the external data file in Excel

Step 2 Specify the location (folder) that contains the external data file and the file type, and then click on the file name and click on "Open," as shown in Figure E.6. The Excel Text Import Wizard opens (Figure E.7).

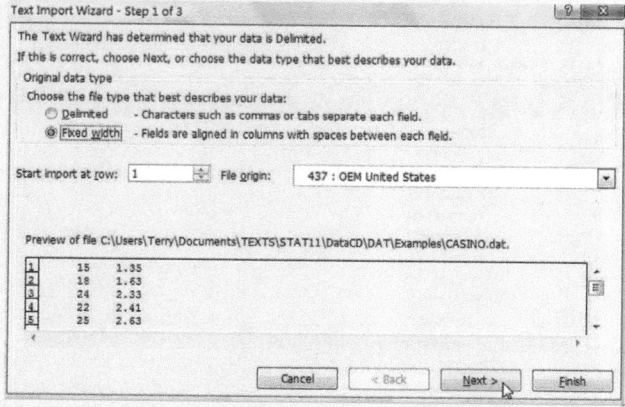

Figure E.7 Excel Text Import Wizard, Screen 1

Step 3 Make the appropriate selections on the screen, and click "Next" to go to the next screen; then click "Next" again.

Step 4 When finished, click "Finish." The Excel workbook will reappear with the data from the external data file.

Naming Variables

Step 1 Select "Insert" from the Excel main menu, and then select "Rows." A blank (empty) row will be added in the first row of the spreadsheet.

Step 2 Type the name of each variable in the first row under the appropriate column.

Listing (Printing) Data

Step 1 Click on the "Office" button on the Excel main menu bar.

Step 2 Click on "Print."

Excel: Generating a Random Sample

To obtain a random sample of numbers in Excel, perform the following:

Step 1 Select "Data," and then "Data Analysis" from the Excel main menu bar, as shown in Figure E.8 at bottom of the page.

Step 2 Select "Random Number Generation" from the Data Analysis dialog box and then click "OK," as shown in Figure E.9.

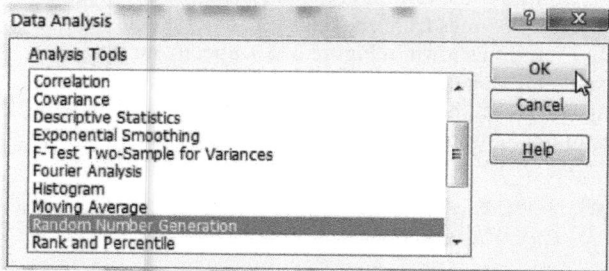

Figure E.9 Excel data analysis tools options: Random number generation

Step 3 In the resulting menu (shown in Figure E.10), specify the number of variables and number of random numbers you want to generate and select "Uniform" for the distribution. Click "OK" to generate the random numbers.

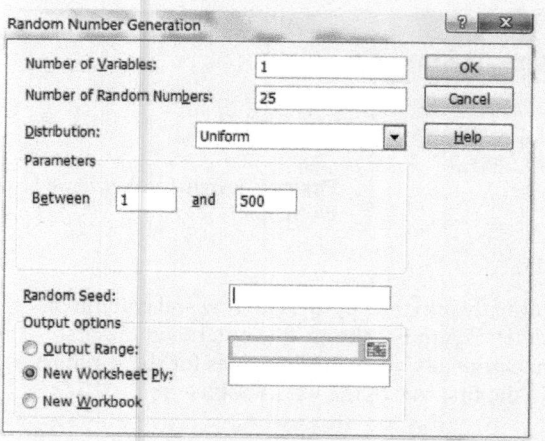

Figure E.10 Excel random number generation dialog box

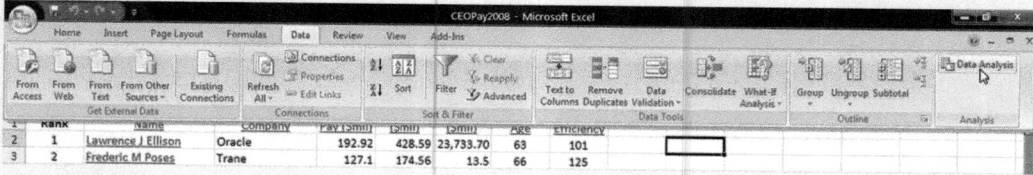

Figure E.8 Excel menu options for generating a random sample of numbers

❏ Answers to Selected Exercises

3 Population/sample; variable(s); collect data; describe **5** Published source; designed experiment; observationally **13** Qualitative; qualitative **15 a.** Single-family residential property **b.** Sale price and the Zillow estimated value; quantitative **c.** If the 2,045 properties were all the properties sold in Arlington, Texas, in the past 6 months **d.** All the singe-family residential properties sold in the last 6 months in Arlington, Texas **e.** No **17 a.** All U.S. citizens **b.** President's job performance; qualitative **c.** 2000 polled individuals **d.** Estimate the proportion of all citizens who believe the president is doing a good job. **e.** Survey **f.** Not very likely **19 a.** Qualitative **b.** Quantitative **c.** Qualitative **d.** Qualitative **e.** Qualitative **f.** Quantitative **21 a.** Sample, if interested in CEOs of all U.S. companies; population, if interested in only the 500 CEOs in the 2011 Scoreboard **b.** (1) qualitative; (2) quantitative; (3) quantitative; (4) quantitative; (5) quantitative; (6) quantitative **23** Descriptive **25 a.** All who took the GMAT between 1990 and 1997 **b.** Survey **c.** No; self-selection **27 a.** Quantitative **b.** Quantitative **c.** Qualitative **d.** Quantitative **e.** Qualitative **f.** Quantitative **g.** Qualitative **29 a.** Speed of the deliveries; accuracy of the invoices; quality of the packaging **b.** Total numbers of questionnaires received **31 a.** All accounting alumni of the large university **b.** Quantitative: age, income, job satisfaction score, Machiavellian rating; qualitative: gender, education level **c.** 198 alumni who returned the questionnaire **d.** Survey **e.** Machiavellian behavior is not required to achieve success in business. **f.** Nonrespondents may be more Machiavellian in nature, biasing the results. **33 a.** Engaged couples who used a particular Web site **b.** Price of the engagement ring (quantitative) and the level of appreciation (qualitative) **c.** All engaged couples **d.** No **35 a.** All bank presidents in the United States **37 a.** All persons over 14 in United States **b.** Unemployment status; qualitative **c.** Inferential

❏ Credits

❏ Technology Images

Where We're Going

- Describe qualitative data using graphs (1)
- Describe quantitative data using graphs (2)
- Describe quantitative data using numerical measures (3–7)
- Describe the relationship between two quantitative variables using graphs (8–9)
- Detecting descriptive methods that distort the truth (10)

☐ Methods for Describing Sets of Data

STATISTICS in ACTION   **Can Money Buy Love?**

*Every day, millions of shoppers hit the stores in full force—both online and on foot—searching frantically for the perfect gift.... Americans [spend] over $30 billion at retail stores in the month of December alone. [Yet] many dread the thought of buying gifts; they worry that their purchases will disappoint rather than delight the intended recipients.**

With this paragraph, Stanford University Graduate School of Business researchers Francis J. Flynn and Gabrielle S. Adams introduce their study "Money Can't Buy Love: Asymmetric Beliefs about Gift Price and Feelings of Appreciation," published in the *Journal of Experimental Social Psychology* (Vol. 45, 2009). The researchers investigated the relationship between the price paid for a gift and the level of appreciation felt by the recipient. Gift-givers who spend more money on a gift often do so in order to send a strong signal of their love to the recipient. The researchers theorized that these gift-givers would expect the recipient to express a high level of appreciation for the gift. However, the researchers did not expect gift-recipients to associate a greater level of appreciation with a higher gift price. That is, "The link between gift price and feelings of appreciation will be stronger for gift-givers than for gift-recipients."

In order to test this theory, the researchers conducted an experimental study involving a representative sample of 237 adults from across the nation. Each subject completed an online survey in exchange for a $5 gift certificate to a major online retailer. The survey asked questions about a birthday gift that the subject either received or gave. The participants were randomly assigned to the role of

*Source: "Money Can't Buy Love: Asymmetric Beliefs About Gift Price and Feelings of Appreciation" by Francis J. Flynn and Gabrielle S. Adams, from JOURNAL OF EXPERIMENTAL SOCIAL PSYCHOLOGY, February 2009, Volume 45(2).

either gift-giver or gift-receiver. (In other words, gift-givers were asked about a birthday gift they recently gave, while gift-recipients were asked about a birthday gift they recently received.) Gifts of cash, gift cards, or gift certificates were excluded from the study. Data were collected on the following variables measured for each participant:

1. *Role* (gift-giver or gift-recipient)

2. *Gender* (male or female)

3. *Gift price* (measured in dollars)

4. *Feeling of appreciation* (measured on a 7-point scale in response to the question: "To what extent do you or does the recipient appreciate this gift?," where 1 = "Not at all," 2 = "A little," 3 = "More than a little," 4 = "Somewhat," 5 = "Moderately so," 6 = "Very much," and 7 = "To a great extent")

5. *Feeling of gratefulness* (measured on a 7-point scale in response to the question: "To what extent do you or does the recipient feel grateful for this gift?," where 1 = "Not at all," 2 = "A little," 3 = "More than a little," 4 = "Somewhat," 5 = "Moderately so," 6 = "Very much," and 7 = "To a great extent")

6. *Overall level of appreciation* (measured as the sum of the two 7-point scales—possible values are 2, 3, 4,..., 13, and 14)

These data are saved in the **BUYLOV** file.

The Stanford University researchers' analysis of the data led them to conclude that "gift-givers and gift-receivers disagree about the link between gift price and gift-recipients' feelings of appreciation. Givers anticipated that recipients would appreciate more expensive gifts, but gift-recipients did not base their feelings of appreciation on how much the gift cost."

In the following *Statistics in Action Revisited* sections, we apply the graphical and numerical descriptive techniques of this chapter to the **BUYLOV** data to demonstrate the conclusions reached by the Stanford University researchers.

STATISTICS in ACTION REVISITED

▫ Interpreting pie charts and bar graphs

▫ Interpreting histograms

▫ Interpreting numerical descriptive measures

▫ Detecting outliers

▫ Interpreting scatterplots

Data Set: BUYLOVE

Suppose you wish to evaluate the managerial capabilities of a class of 400 MBA students based on their Graduate Management Aptitude Test (GMAT) scores. How would you describe these 400 measurements? Characteristics of the data set include the typical or most frequent GMAT score, the variability in the scores, the highest and lowest scores, the "shape" of the data, and whether or not the data set contains any unusual scores. Extracting this information by "eye-balling" the data isn't easy. The 400 scores may provide too many bits of information for our minds to comprehend. Clearly, we need some formal methods for summarizing and characterizing the information in such a data set. Methods for describing data sets are also essential for statistical inference. Most populations make for large data sets. Consequently, we need methods for describing a sample data set that let us make statements (inferences) about the population from which the sample was drawn.

Two methods for describing data are presented in this chapter, one *graphical* and the other *numerical*. Both play an important role in statistics. Section 1 presents both graphical and numerical methods for describing qualitative data. Graphical methods for describing quantitative data are presented in Sections 2, 7, 9, and optional Section 8; numerical descriptive methods for quantitative data are presented in Sections 3–6. We end this chapter with a section on the *misuse* of descriptive techniques.

1 Describing Qualitative Data

In addition to salary information, *Forbes* collects and reports personal data on CEOs, including level of education. Do most CEOs have advanced degrees, such as master's degrees or doctorates? To answer this question, Table 1 gives the highest college degree obtained (bachelor's, MBA, master's, law, PhD, or none) for each of the 40 best-paid CEOs in 2011.

For this study, the variable of interest, highest college degree obtained, is qualitative in nature. Qualitative data are nonnumerical; thus, the value of a qualitative variable can be classified only into categories called *classes*. The possible degree types—bachelor's, MBA, master's, law, PhD, or none—represent the classes for this qualitative variable. We can summarize such data numerically in two ways: (1) by computing the *class frequency*—the number of observations in the data set that fall into each class; or (2) by computing the *class relative frequency*—the proportion of the total number of observations falling into each class.

Table 1	Data on 40 Best-Paid Executives				
	CEO	Company	Salary ($ millions)	Age	Degree
1	Hemsley, Stephen	UnitedHealth Group	101.96	58	Bachelor's
2	Mueller, Edward	Qwest Communications	65.80	64	MBA
3	Iger, Robert	Walt Disney	53.32	60	Bachelor's
4	Paz, George	Express Scripts	51.52	56	Bachelor's
5	Frankfort, Lew	Coach	49.45	65	MBA
6	Lauren, Ralph	Polo Ralph Lauren	43.00	71	None
7	Martin, John	Gilead Sciences	42.72	59	PhD
8	Hackett, James	Anadarko Petroleum	38.94	57	MBA
9	Chambers, John	Cisco Systems	37.90	61	MBA
10	Seidenberg, Ivan	Verizon Commun	36.75	64	MBA
11	Pyott, David	Allergan	33.76	58	Master's
12	Lucier, Gregory	Life Technologies	33.75	46	MBA
13	Davidson, Charles	Noble Energy	33.44	61	Master's
14	Hammergren, John	McKesson	32.46	52	MBA
15	Tucci, Joseph	EMC	31.63	63	MBA
16	Huang, Jen-Hsun	Nvidia	31.41	48	Master's
17	Boyce, Gregory	Peabody Energy	30.66	56	Bachelor's
18	Merelli, F H	Cimarex Energy	30.53	75	None
19	Palmisano, Samuel	IBM	30.32	59	Bachelor's
20	Camilleri, Louis	Philip Morris Intl	30.09	56	Bachelor's
21	Watford, Michael	Ultra Petroleum	30.04	57	MBA
22	Schultz, Howard	Starbucks	29.73	57	Bachelor's
23	Novak, David	Yum Brands	29.67	58	Bachelor's
24	Thiry, Kent	DaVita	29.52	55	MBA
25	Farr, David	Emerson Electric	28.93	56	MBA
26	Cutler, Alexander	Eaton	28.47	59	MBA
27	Solomon, Howard	Forest Labs	27.10	83	Law
28	Moonves, Leslie	CBS	26.42	62	Bachelor's
29	Adkerson, Richard	Freeport Copper	25.30	64	MBA
30	Swanson, William	Raytheon	24.89	62	Bachelor's
31	Boyd, Jeffery	Priceline.com	24.39	54	None
32	Chenevert, Louis	United Technologies	23.97	53	Bachelor's
33	Washkewicz, Donald	Parker-Hannifin	23.88	60	MBA
34	Rose, Peter	Expeditors Intl	23.63	68	None
35	Buckley, George	3M	23.22	64	PhD
36	Daane, John	Altera	23.19	47	Bachelor's
37	Young, James	Union Pacific	23.06	59	Bachelor's
38	Larsen, Marshall	Goodrich	22.43	62	Master's
39	Hugin, Robert	Celgene	22.40	56	MBA
40	Snow, David	Medco Health	22.19	56	Master's

Source: Data from "America's Highest Paid Chief Executives," FORBES, April 13, 2011.　　*Data Set:* FRBS40

> A **class** is one of the categories into which qualitative data can be classified.

> The **class frequency** is the number of observations in the data set falling into a particular class.

> The **class relative frequency** is the class frequency divided by the total number of observations in the data set; that is,
>
> $$\text{class relative frequency} = \frac{\text{class frequency}}{n}$$

Examining Table 1, we observe that 4 of the 40 best-paid CEOs did not obtain a college degree, 13 obtained bachelor's degrees, 15 MBAs, 5 master's degrees, 2 PhDs, and 1 law degree. These numbers—4, 13, 15, 5, 2, and 1—represent the class frequencies for the six classes and are shown in the summary table, Figure 1, produced using SPSS.

> The **class percentage** is the class relative frequency multiplied by 100; that is,
>
> $$\text{class percentage} = (\text{class relative frequency}) \times 100$$

Figure 1 also gives the relative frequency of each of the five degree classes. We know that we calculate the relative frequency by dividing the class frequency by the total number of observations in the data set. Thus, the relative frequencies for the five degree types are

$$\text{Bachelor's: } \frac{13}{40} = .325$$

$$\text{Law: } \frac{1}{40} = .025$$

$$\text{Master's: } \frac{5}{40} = .125$$

$$\text{MBA: } \frac{15}{40} = .375$$

$$\text{None: } \frac{4}{40} = .10$$

$$\text{PhD: } \frac{2}{40} = .05$$

These values, expressed as a percentage, are shown in the "Percent" column in the SPSS summary table, Figure 1. If we sum the relative frequencies for MBA, master's, law,

DEGREE

		Frequency	Percent	Valid Percent	Cumulative Percent
Valid	Bachelors	13	32.5	32.5	32.5
	Law	1	2.5	2.5	35.0
	Masters	5	12.5	12.5	47.5
	MBA	15	37.5	37.5	85.0
	None	4	10.0	10.0	95.0
	PhD	2	5.0	5.0	100.0
	Total	40	100.0	100.0	

Figure 1

SPSS summary table for degrees of 40 CEOs

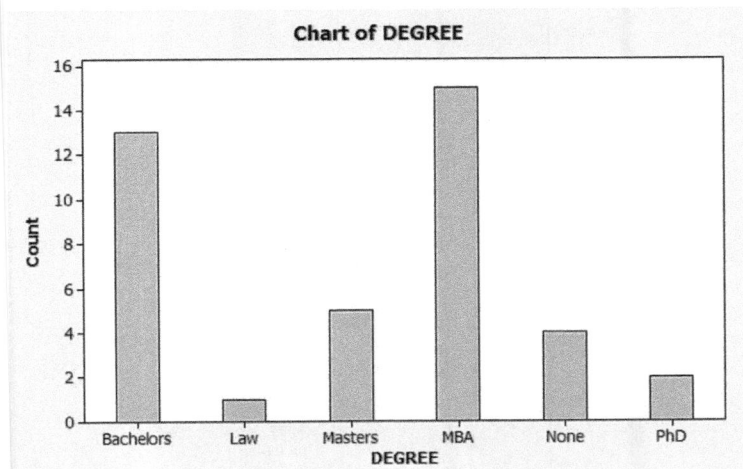

Figure 2

Minitab bar graph for degrees of 40 CEOs

**VILFREDO PARETO
(1843–1923)**

The Pareto Principle

Born in Paris to an Italian aristocratic family, Vilfredo Pareto was educated at the University of Turin, where he studied engineering and mathematics. After the death of his parents, Pareto quit his job as an engineer and began writing and lecturing on the evils of the economic policies of the Italian government. While at the University of Lausanne in Switzerland in 1896, he published his first paper, "Cours d'economie politique." In the paper, Pareto derived a complicated mathematical formula to prove that the distribution of income and wealth in society is not random but that a consistent pattern appears throughout history in all societies. Essentially, Pareto showed that approximately 80% of the total wealth in a society lies with only 20% of the families. This famous law about the "vital few and the trivial many" is widely known as the Pareto principle in economics.

and PhD, we obtain .375 + .125 + .025 + .05 = .575. Therefore, 57.5% of the 40 best-paid CEOs obtained at least a master's degree (MBA, master's, law, or PhD).

Although the summary table in Figure 1 adequately describes the data in Table 1, we often want a graphical presentation as well. Figures 2 and 3 show two of the most widely used graphical methods for describing qualitative data—**bar graphs** and **pie charts.** Figure 2 is a bar graph for "highest degree obtained" produced with Minitab. Note that the height of the rectangle, or "bar," over each class is equal to the class frequency. (Optionally, the bar heights can be proportional to class relative frequencies.) In contrast, Figure 3 (also created using Minitab) shows the relative frequencies (expressed as a percentage) of the six degree types in a *pie chart*. Note that the pie is a circle (spanning 360°), and the size (angle) of the "pie slice" assigned to each class is proportional to the class relative frequency. For example, the slice assigned to the MBA degree is 37.5% of 360°, or (.375)(360°) = 135°.

Before leaving the data set in Table 1, consider the bar graph shown in Figure 4, produced using SPSS with annotations. Note that the bars for the CEO degree categories are arranged in descending order of height from left to right across the horizontal axis—that is, the tallest bar (MBA) is positioned at the far left and the shortest bar is at the far right. This rearrangement of the bars in a bar graph is called a Pareto diagram. One goal of a Pareto diagram (named for the Italian economist Vilfredo Pareto) is to make it easy to locate the "most important" categories—those with the largest frequencies. For the 40 best-paid CEOs in 2011, an MBA degree was the highest degree obtained by the most CEOs (37.5%).

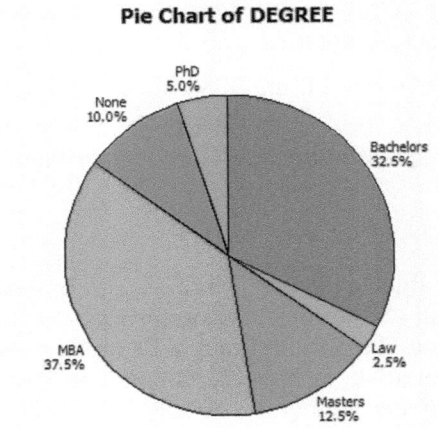

Figure 3

Minitab pie chart for degrees of 40 CEOs

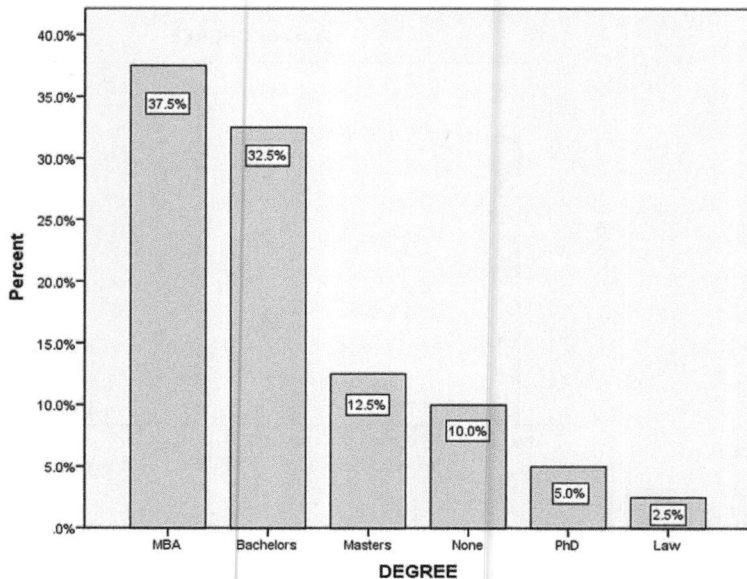

Figure 4
SPSS Pareto diagram for degrees
of 40 CEOs

Summary of Graphical Descriptive Methods for Qualitative Data

Bar graph: The categories (classes) of the qualitative variable are represented by bars, where the height of each bar is either the class frequency, class relative frequency, or class percentage.

Pie chart: The categories (classes) of the qualitative variable are represented by slices of a pie (circle). The size of each slice is proportional to the class relative frequency.

Pareto diagram: A bar graph with the categories (classes) of the qualitative variable (i.e., the bars) arranged by height in descending order from left to right.

Let's look at a practical example that requires interpretation of the graphical results.

Example 1

Graphing and Summarizing Qualitative Data—Blood Loss Study

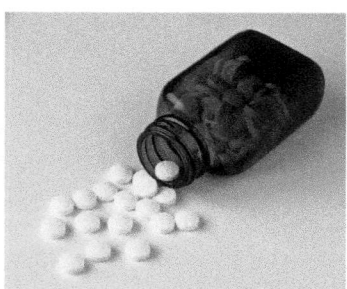

Problem A group of cardiac physicians in southwest Florida have been studying a new drug designed to reduce blood loss in coronary artery bypass operations. Blood loss data for 114 coronary artery bypass patients (some who received a dosage of the drug and others who did not) are saved in the **BLOOD** file. Although the drug shows promise in reducing blood loss, the physicians are concerned about possible side effects and complications. So their data set includes not only the qualitative variable, DRUG, which indicates whether or not the patient received the drug, but also the qualitative variable, COMP, which specifies the type (if any) of complication experienced by the patient. The four values of COMP recorded by the physicians are (1) redo surgery, (2) post-op infection, (3) both, or (4) none.

a. Figure 5, generated using SPSS, shows summary tables for the two qualitative variables, DRUG and COMP. Interpret the results.

b. Interpret the Minitab output shown in Figure 6 and the SPSS output shown in Figure 7.

Solution

a. The top table in Figure 5 is a summary frequency table for DRUG. Note that exactly half (57) of the 114 coronary artery bypass patients received the drug and half did not. The bottom table in Figure 5 is a summary frequency table for COMP. We see that about 69% of the 114 patients had no complications, leaving about 31% who experienced either a redo surgery, a post-op infection, or both.

DRUG

		Frequency	Percent	Valid Percent	Cumulative Percent
Valid	NO	57	50.0	50.0	50.0
	YES	57	50.0	50.0	100.0
	Total	114	100.0	100.0	

COMP

		Frequency	Percent	Valid Percent	Cumulative Percent
Valid	BOTH	6	5.3	5.3	5.3
	INFECT	15	13.2	13.2	18.4
	NONE	79	69.3	69.3	87.7
	REDO	14	12.3	12.3	100.0
	Total	114	100.0	100.0	

Figure 5

SPSS summary tables for DRUG and COMP

b. Figure 6 is a Minitab side-by-side bar graph for the data. The four bars on the left represent the frequencies of COMP for the 57 patients who did not receive the drug; the four bars on the right represent the frequencies of COMP for the 57 patients who did receive a dosage of the drug. The graph clearly shows that patients who did not get the drug suffered fewer complications. The exact percentages are displayed in the SPSS summary tables of Figure 7. About 56% of the patients who got the drug had no complications, compared to about 83% for the patients who did not get the drug.

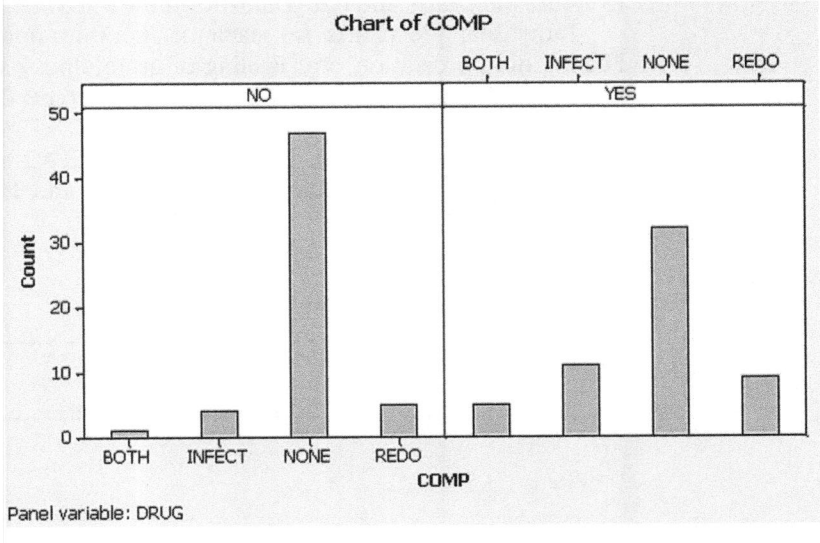

Figure 6

Minitab side-by-side bar graphs for COMP, by value of DRUG

COMP

DRUG				Frequency	Percent	Valid Percent	Cumulative Percent
NO	Valid	BOTH		1	1.8	1.8	1.8
		INFECT		4	7.0	7.0	8.8
		NONE		47	82.5	82.5	91.2
		REDO		5	8.8	8.8	100.0
		Total		57	100.0	100.0	
YES	Valid	BOTH		5	8.8	8.8	8.8
		INFECT		11	19.3	19.3	28.1
		NONE		32	56.1	56.1	84.2
		REDO		9	15.8	15.8	100.0
		Total		57	100.0	100.0	

Figure 7

SPSS summary tables for COMP by value of DRUG

Look Back Although these results show that the drug may be effective in reducing blood loss, Figures 6 and 7 imply that patients on the drug may have a higher risk of complications. But before using this information to make a decision about the drug, the physicians will need to provide a measure of reliability for the inference—that is, the physicians will want to know whether the difference between the percentages of patients with complications observed in this sample of 114 patients is generalizable to the population of all coronary artery bypass patients.

■ **Now Work Exercise 12**

STATISTICS in ACTION REVISITED

Interpreting Pie Charts and Bar Graphs

In the *Journal of Experimental Social Psychology* (Vol. 45, 2009) study on whether money can buy love, Stanford University researchers measured several qualitative (categorical) variables for each of 237 adults: *Gender* (male or female), *Role* (gift-giver or gift-recipient), *Feeling of appreciation for the gift* (measured on an ordinal 7-point scale), and *Feeling of gratefulness for the gift* (measured on an ordinal 7-point scale). We classify the last two variables listed as qualitative since the numerical values represent distinct response categories (e.g., 1 = "Not at all," 2 = "A little," 3 = "More than a little," 4 = "Somewhat," 5 = "Moderately so," 6 = "Very much," and 7 = "To a great extent") that portray an opinion on how one feels about giving or receiving a gift. Pie charts and bar graphs can be used to summarize and describe the responses for these variables. Recall that the data are saved in the **BUYLOV** file. We used Excel/XLSTAT and SPSS to create pie charts and bar graphs for these variables.

Individual pie charts for each of the four qualitative variables, Role, Gender, Feeling of appreciation, and Feeling of gratefulness, are shown in Figures SIA1–SIA4, respectively. First, notice in Figure SIA1 that of the 237 adults, 56.5% were gift-givers and 43.5% were gift-recipients. Figure SIA2 gives the gender breakdown: 62% were females and 38% were males. Figures SIA3 and SIA4 show the summary of the responses for the Feeling of gratefulness and Feeling of appreciation questions,

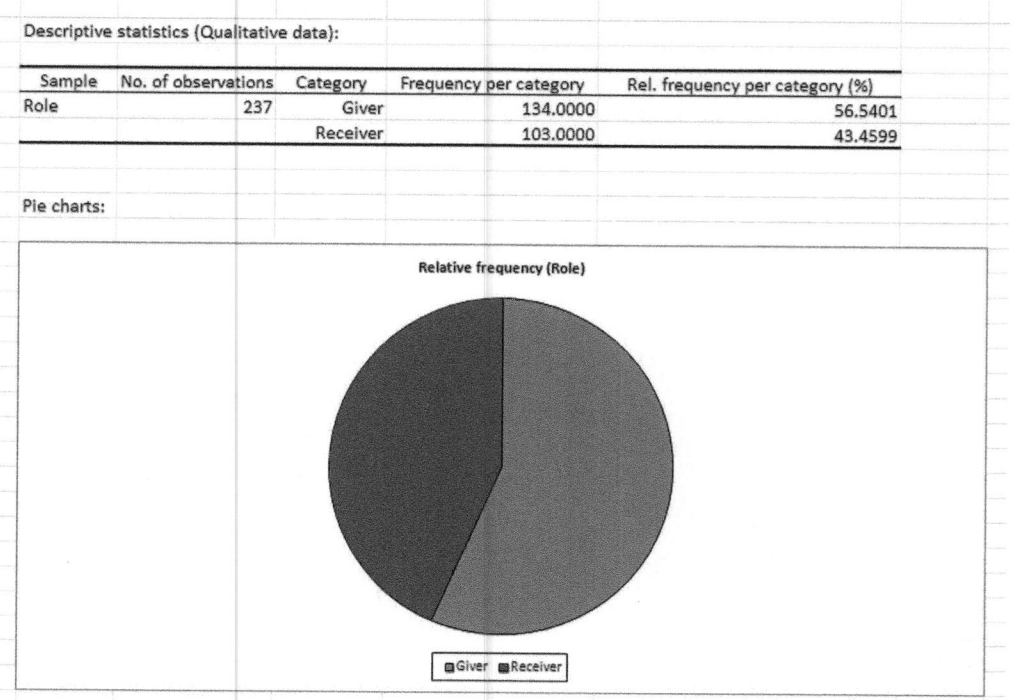

Descriptive statistics (Qualitative data):

Sample	No. of observations	Category	Frequency per category	Rel. frequency per category (%)
Role	237	Giver	134.0000	56.5401
		Receiver	103.0000	43.4599

Pie charts:

Relative frequency (Role)

□ Giver ■ Receiver

Figure SIA1

XLSTAT pie chart for role

Descriptive statistics (Qualitative data):

Sample	No. of observations	Category	Frequency per category	Rel. frequency per category (%)
Gender	237	Female	147.0000	62.0253
		Male	90.0000	37.9747

Pie charts:

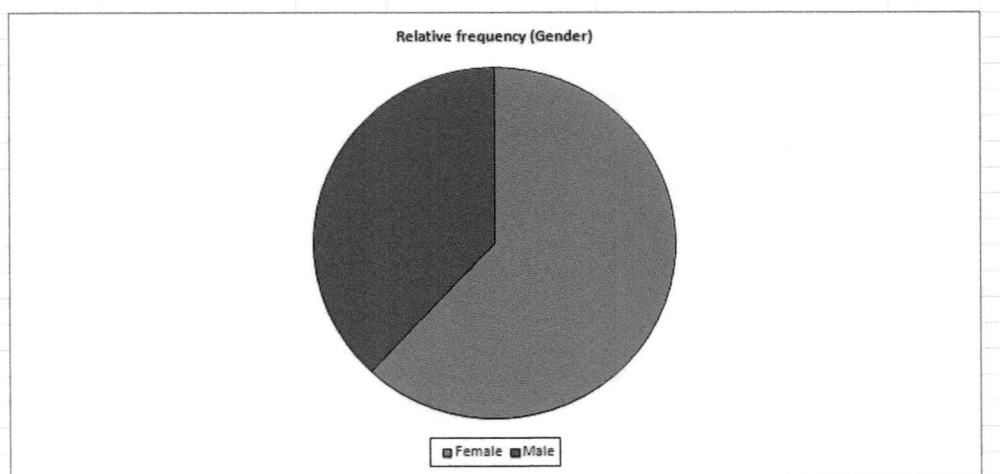

Figure SIA2

XLSTAT pie chart for gender

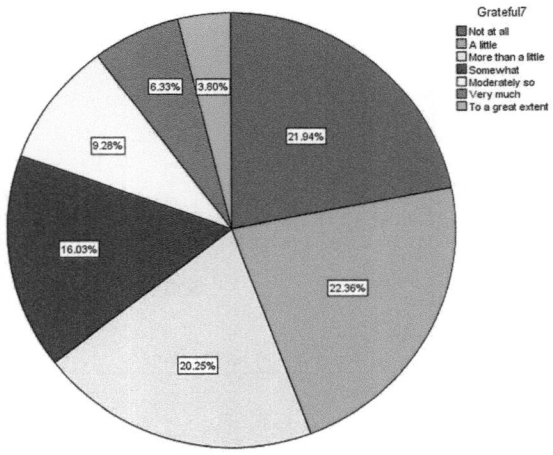

Figure SIA3

SPSS pie chart for feeling
of gratefulness

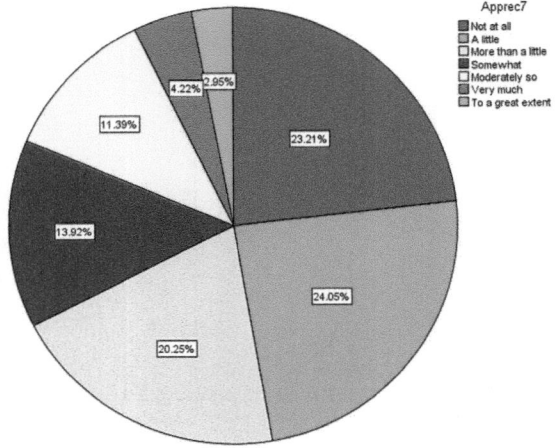

Figure SIA4

SPSS pie chart for feeling
of appreciation

respectively. The response percentages are very similar. For example, 23.2% of adults responded, "Not at all" to the Feeling of appreciation question compared to 21.9% for the Feeling of gratefulness question. Similarly, 24.0% of adults responded, "To a great extent" to the Feeling of appreciation question compared to 22.4% for the Feeling of gratefulness question.

Of interest in the study is whether gift-givers and gift-recipients would respond differently to the Feeling of gratefulness question. We can gain insight into this question by forming bar graphs of the Feeling of gratefulness responses, one graph for gift-givers and one for gift-recipients. These bar graphs are shown in Figure SIA5. You can see that about 32% of the gift-givers responded, "Not at all" (top graph) as compared to about 9% of the gift-recipients (bottom graph). Similarly, 10% of the gift-givers responded, "Somewhat" as compared to about 23% of the gift-recipients, and 2.2% of the gift-givers responded, "To a great extent" as compared to 5.8% of the gift-recipients Thus, it does

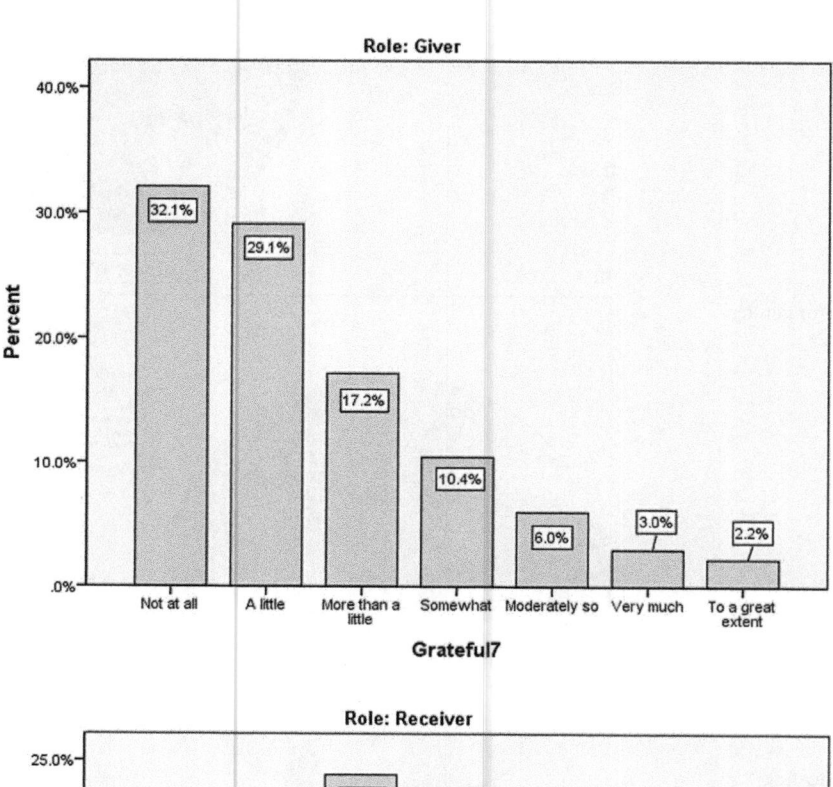

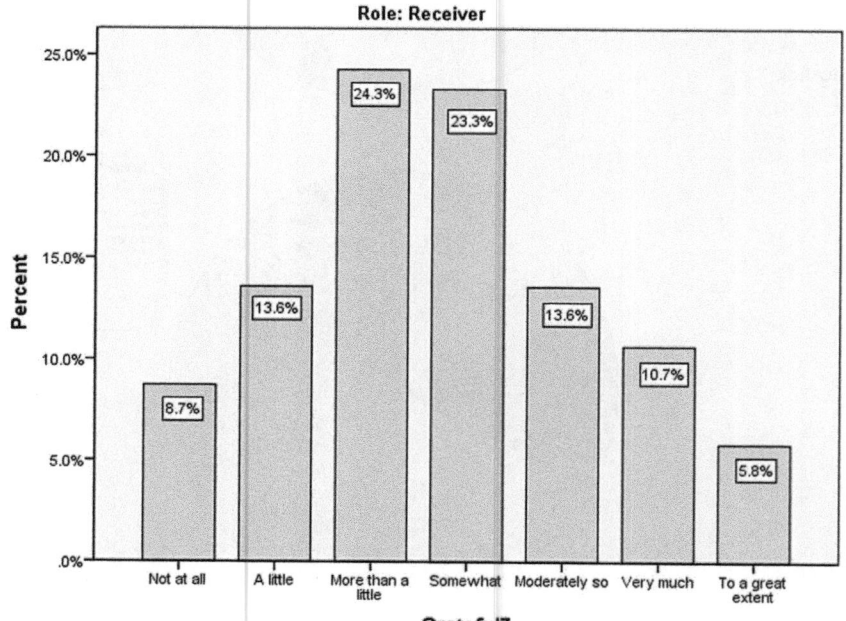

Figure SIA5

SPSS bar graphs for feeling
of gratefulness by role

appear that gift-givers and gift-recipients respond differently, with gift-recipients more likely to express a greater level of gratefulness for the gift than what gift-givers perceive.

Also of interest is whether males and females would respond differently to the Feeling of gratefulness question. Figure SIA6 is a set of bar graphs of the Feeling of gratefulness responses, one graph for each gender. The bar heights in these graphs look very similar, indicating that males and females responded about the same to the question.

Caution: The information produced in these graphs should be limited to describing the sample of 237 adults who participated in the study. If one is interested in making inferences about the population of all gift-givers and gift-recipients (as were the Stanford University researchers), inferential statistical methods need to be applied to the data.

Data Set: BUYLOVE

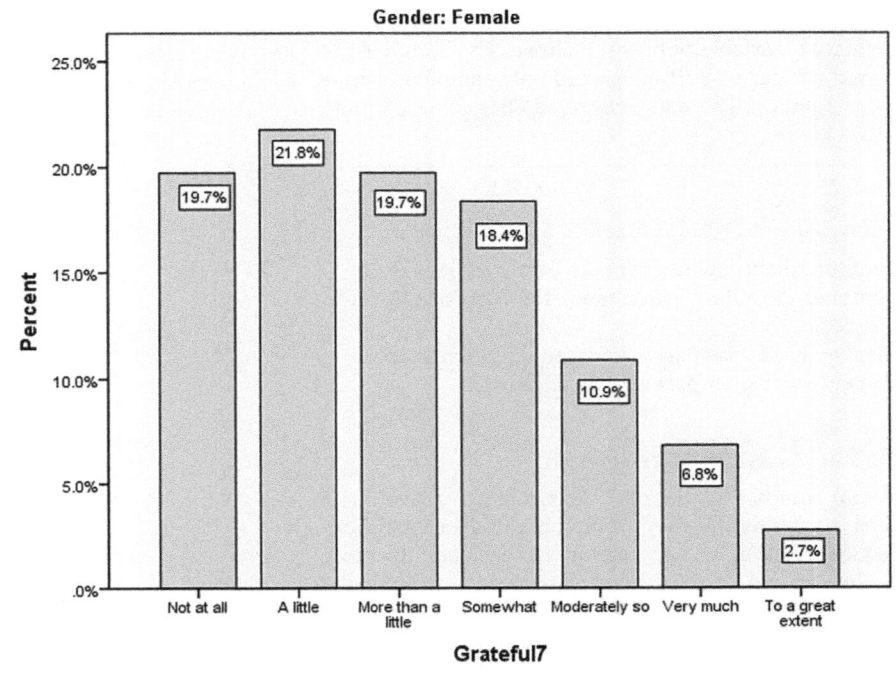

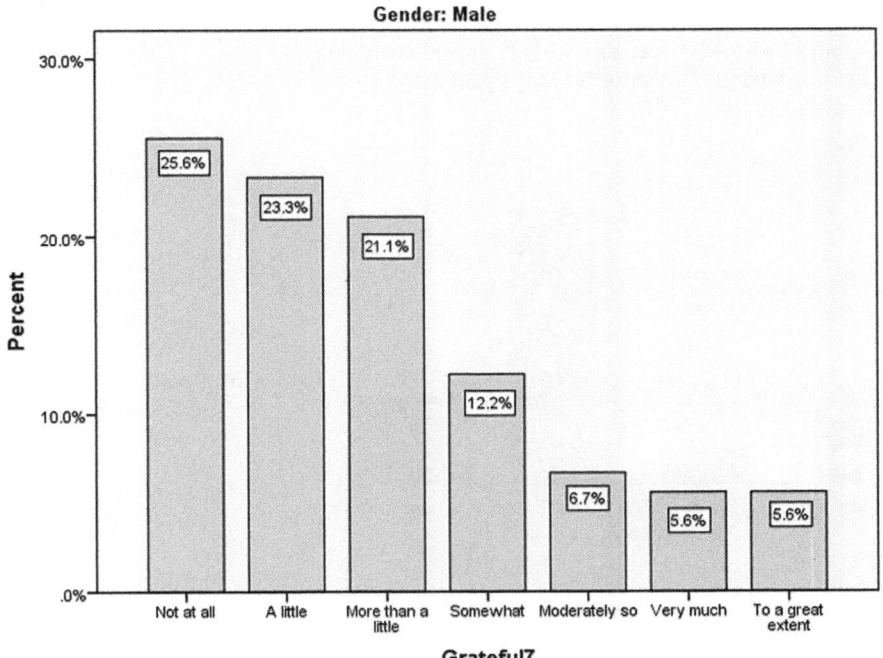

Figure SIA6

SPSS bar graphs for feeling of gratefulness by gender

Exercises 1–17

Please be aware that some of the following problems may require knowledge of concepts that are not presented in this chapter.

Learning the Mechanics

1 Complete the following table.

Grade on Business Statistics Exam	Frequency	Relative Frequency
A: 90–100	—	.08
B: 80–89	36	—
C: 65–79	90	—
D: 50–64	30	—
F: Below 50	28	—
Total	200	1.00

2 A qualitative variable with three classes (X, Y, and Z) is measured for each of 20 units randomly sampled from a target population. The data (observed class for each unit) are listed below.

```
Y  X  X  Z  X  Y  Y  Y  X  X  Z  X
Y  Y  X  Z  Y  Y  Y  X
```

a. Compute the frequency for each of the three classes.
b. Compute the relative frequency for each of the three classes.
c. Display the results, part **a,** in a frequency bar graph.
d. Display the results, part **b,** in a pie chart.

Applying the Concepts—Basic

3 **Do social robots walk or roll?** According to the United Nations, social robots now outnumber industrial robots worldwide. A social (or service) robot is designed to entertain, educate, and care for human users. In a paper published by the *International Conference on Social Robotics* (Vol. 6414, 2010), design engineers investigated the trend in the design of social robots. Using a random sample of 106 social robots obtained through a Web search, the engineers found that 63 were built with legs only, 20 with wheels only, 8 with both legs and wheels, and 15 with neither legs nor wheels. This information is portrayed in the accompanying graph.

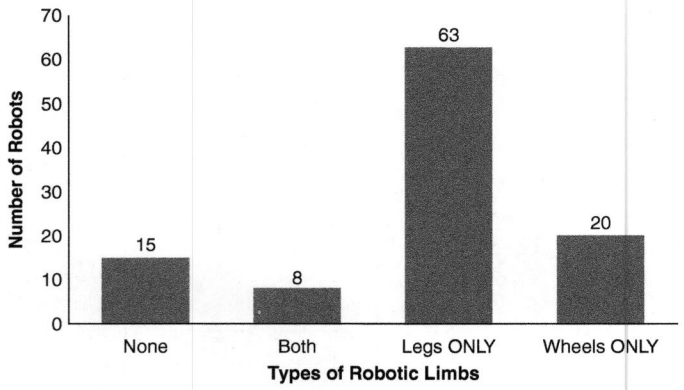

a. What type of graph is used to describe the data?
b. Indentify the variable measured for each of the 106 robot designs.

c. Use the graph to identify the social robot design that is currently used the most.
d. Compute class relative frequencies for the different categories shown in the graph.
e. Use the results from, part **d** to construct a Pareto diagram for the data.

4 **Paying for music downloads.** If you use the Internet, have you ever paid to access or download music? This was one **MUSIC** of the questions of interest in a recent *Pew Internet & American Life Project Survey* (October 2010). Telephone interviews were conducted on a representative sample of 1,003 adults living in the United States. For this sample, 248 adults stated that they do not use the Internet, 249 revealed that they use the Internet but have never paid to download music, and the remainder (506 adults) admitted that they use the Internet and have paid to download music. The results are summarized in the Minitab pie chart shown.

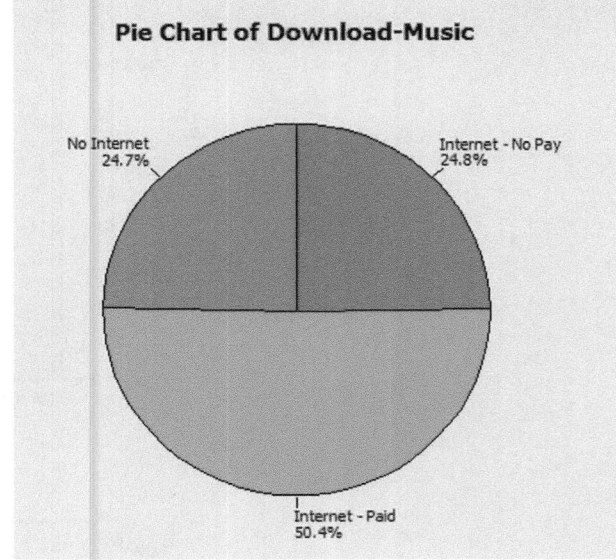

a. According to the pie chart, what proportion of the sample use the Internet and pay to download music? Verify the accuracy of this proportion using the survey results.
b. Now consider only the 755 adults in the sample that use the Internet. Create a graph that compares the proportions of these adults that pay to download music with the proportion that do not pay to download music.

5 **Profiling UK rental malls.** An analysis of the retail rental levels of tenants of United Kingdom regional shopping malls was published in *Urban Studies* (June 2011). One aspect of the study involved describing the type of tenant typically found at a UK shopping mall. Data were collected for 148 Shopping malls, which housed 1,821 stores. Tenants were categorized into five different-size groups based on amount of floor space: *anchor tenants* (more than 30,000 square feet), *major space users* (between 10,000 and 30,000 sq. ft.), *large standard tenants* (between 4,000 and 10,000 sq. ft.), *small standard* *tenants* (between 1,500 and 4,000 sq. ft.), and *small tenants* (less than 1,500 sq. ft.). The number of stores in each tenant category was reported as 14, 61, 216, 711, and 819, respectively. Use this information to construct a Pareto diagram for the distribution of tenant groups at UK shopping malls. Interpret the graph.

6 Who is to blame for rising health care costs? Rising health care costs are of major concern to Americans. A nationwide survey of 2,119 U.S. adults was conducted to elicit opinions on who is to blame for the rising costs (*The Harris Poll,* Oct. 28, 2008). The next table summarizes the responses to the question "When you think of the rising costs of health care, who do you think is most responsible?"

Most Responsible for Rising Health Care Costs	Number Responding
Insurance companies	869
Pharmaceutical companies	339
Government	338
Hospitals	127
Physicians	85
Other	128
Not at all sure	233
Total	2,119

a. Compute the relative frequencies in each response category.
b. Construct a relative frequency bar graph for the data.
c. Convert the relative frequency bar graph into a Pareto diagram. Interpret the graph.

7 PIN pad shipments. Personal identification number (PIN) pads are devices that connect to point-of-sale electronic cash registers for debit and credit card purchases. The PIN pad allows the customer's card to be accessed and the PIN encrypted before it is sent to the transaction manager. *The Nilson Report* (Oct. 2008) listed the volume of PIN pad shipments by manufacturers worldwide in 2007. For the 12 manufacturers listed in the table, a total of 334,039 PIN pads were shipped in 2007.

Manufacturer	Number Shipped (units)
Bitel	13,500
CyberNet	16,200
Fujian Landi	119,000
Glintt (ParaRede)	5,990
Intelligent	4,562
KwangWoo	42,000
Omron	20,000
Pax Tech.	10,072
ProvencoCadmus	20,000
SZZT Electronics	67,300
Toshiba TEC	12,415
Urmet	3,000

Source: Data from THE NILSON REPORT, No. 912, October 2008, p. 9.

a. One of the 334,039 PIN pads is selected and the manufacturer of the pad is determined. What type of data (quantitative or qualitative) is measured?
b. Construct a frequency bar chart for the data summarized in the table.
c. Convert the frequency bar chart, part **b**, into a Pareto diagram. Interpret the results.

Applying the Concepts—Intermediate

8 The economic return to earning an MBA. The *International Economic Review* (August 2008) did a study on the economic rewards to obtaining an MBA degree. Job status information was collected for a sample of 3,244 individuals who sat for the GMAT in each of four time periods (waves). Summary information (number of individuals) for Wave 1 (at the time of taking the GMAT) and Wave 4 (7 years later) is provided in the accompanying table. Use a graph to compare and contrast the job status distributions of GMAT takers in Wave 1 and Wave 4.

Job Status	Wave 1	Wave 4
Working, No MBA	2,657	1,787
Working, Have MBA	0	1,372
Not Working, Business School	0	7
Not Working, Other Graduate School	36	78
Not Working, 4-Year Institution	551	0
Total	3,244	3,244

Source: Data from P. Arcidiancono, P. Cooley, and A. Hussey, "The economic returns to an MBA," INTERNATIONAL ECONOMIC REVIEW, Vol. 49, No. 3, August 2008, Table 1.

9 Blogs for *Fortune* 500 firms. Web site communication through blogs and forums is becoming a key marketing tool for companies. The *Journal of Relationship Marketing* (Vol. 7, 2008) investigated the prevalence of blogs and forums at *Fortune* 500 firms with both English and Chinese web sites. Of the firms that provided blogs/forums as a marketing tool, the accompanying table gives a breakdown on the entity responsible for creating the blogs/forums. Use a graphical method to describe the data summarized in the table. Interpret the graph.

Blog/Forum	Percentage of Firms
Created by company	38.5
Created by employees	34.6
Created by third party	11.5
Creator not identified	15.4

Source: Data from K. Mishra and C. Li, "Relationship marketing in FORTUNE 500 U.S. and Chinese web sites," JOURNAL OF RELATIONSHIP MARKETING, Vol. 7, No. 1, 2008.

10 The Executive Compensation Scoreboard. *Forbes* published "Executive Compensation Scoreboard" for 2011. The industry type of the CEO's company (e.g., banking, retailing, etc.) was recorded for each of the 175 CEOs with the highest efficiency (pay-for-performance) ratings. Access the data file and use a graphical method to describe the frequency of occurrence of the industry types.

11 Doctors and ethics. For physicians confronted with ethical dilemmas (e.g., end-of-life issues or treatment of patients without insurance), many hospitals provide ethics consultation services. However, not all physicians take advantage of these services and some refuse to use ethics consultation. The extent to which doctors refuse ethics consults was studied in the *Journal of Medical*

Ethics (Vol. 32, 2006). Survey questionnaires were administered to all physicians on staff at a large community hospital in Tampa, Florida, and 118 physicians responded. Several qualitative variables were measured, including *previous use of ethics consultation* ("never used" or "used at least once"), *practitioner specialty* ("medical" or "surgical"), and *future use of ethics consultation* ("yes" or "no").

a. Access the file and generate a graph that describes the level to which the physicians on staff have previously used the ethics consultation services. What proportion of the sampled physicians have never used ethics consultation?

b. Repeat part **a** for *future use of ethics consultation*. What proportion of the sampled physicians state that they will not use the services in the future?

c. Generate side-by-side graphs that illustrate differences in previous use of ethics consultation by medical and surgical specialists. What inference can you make from the graphs?

d. Repeat part **c** for *future use of ethics consultation*.

12 **History of corporate acquisitions.** A corporate acquisition occurs when one corporation purchases all the stock shares of another, essentially taking over the other. The *Academy of Management Journal* (Aug. 2008) investigated the performance and timing of corporate acquisitions for a large sample of firms over the years 1980 to 2000. The accompanying data table gives the number of firms sampled and number that announced one or more acquisitions during the years 1980, 1990, and 2000. Construct side-by-side bar charts to describe the firms with and without acquisitions in the 3 years. Compare and contrast the bar charts.

Year	Number of Firms Sampled	Number with Acquisitions
1980	1,963	18
1990	2,197	350
2000	2,778	748

Source: Data from D. N. Iyer and K. D. Miller, "Performance feedback, slack, and the timing of acquisitions," ACADEMY OF MANAGEMENT JOURNAL, Vol. 51, No. 4, August 2008, pp. 808–822, Table 1.

13 **Motivation and right-oriented bias.** Evolutionary theory suggests that motivated decision makers tend to exhibit a right-oriented bias. (For example, if presented with two equally valued brands of detergent on a supermarket shelf, consumers are more likely to choose the brand on the right.) In *Psychological Science* (November 2011), researchers tested this theory using data on all penalty shots attempted in World Cup soccer matches (a total of 204 penalty shots). The researchers believed that goalkeepers, motivated to make a penalty-shot save but with little time to make a decision, would tend to dive to the right. The results of the study (percentages of dives to the left, middle, or right) are provided in the table. Note that the percentages in each row, corresponding to a certain match situation, add to 100%. Construct side-by-side bar graphs showing the distribution of dives for the three match situations. What inferences can you draw from the graphs?

Match Situation	Dive Left	Stay Middle	Dive Right
Team behind	29%	0%	71%
Tied	48%	3%	49%
Team ahead	51%	1%	48%

Source: Based on M. Roskes, et al., "The right side? Under time pressure, approach motivation leads to right-oriented bias," PSYCHOLOGICAL SCIENCE, Vol. 22, No. 11, November 2011 (adapted from Figure 2).

Applying the Concepts—Advanced

14 **Museum management.** What criteria do museums use to evaluate their performance? In a worldwide survey reported in *Museum Management and Curatorship* (June 2010), managers of 30 leading museums of contemporary art were asked to provide the performance measure used most often. A summary of the results is provided in the table. The researcher concluded that "there is a large amount of variation within the museum community with regard to . . . performance measurement and evaluation," Do you agree? Use a graph to support your conclusion.

Performance Measure	Number of Museums
Total visitors	8
Paying visitors	5
Big shows	6
Funds raised	7
Members	4

15 **Advertising with reader-response cards.** "Reader-response cards" are used by marketers to advertise their product and obtain sales leads. These cards are placed in magazines and trade publications. Readers detach and mail in the cards to indicate their interest in the product, expecting literature or a phone call in return. How effective are these cards (called "bingo cards" in the industry) as a marketing tool? Performark, a Minneapolis business that helps companies close on sales leads, attempted to answer this question by responding to 17,000 card-advertisements placed by industrial marketers in a wide variety of trade publications over a 6-year period. Performark kept track of how long it took for each advertiser to respond. A summary of the response times is given in the following table.

Advertiser's Response Time	Percentage
Never responded	21
13–59 days	33
60–120 days	34
More than 120 days	12
Total	100

a. Describe the variable measured by Performark.

b. These results were displayed in the form of a pie chart. Reconstruct the pie chart from the information given in the table.

c. How many of the 17,000 advertisers never responded to the sales lead?

d. Advertisers typically spend at least a million dollars on a reader-response card marketing campaign. Many industrial marketers feel these "bingo cards" are not worth their expense. Does the information in the pie chart, part **b,** support this contention? Explain why or why not. If not, what information can be gleaned from the pie chart to help potential "bingo card" campaigns?

16 **Stewardship at MBA programs.** *Business Ethics* (Fall 2005) reported on a survey designed to rank master in business administration (MBA) programs worldwide on how well they prepare students for social and environmental stewardship. Each business school was ranked according to four criteria: *student exposure* (class time dedicated to social and environmental issues), *student opportunity* (courses with social and environmental content), *course content* (courses emphasize business as a force for positive social and environmental change), and *faculty research* (published articles that examine business in a social/environmental context). Each area was rated from 1 star (lowest rating) to 5 stars (highest rating). Overall, Stanford University received the top ranking, followed by ESADE (Spain), York University (Canada), Monterrey Technical Institute (Mexico), and the University of Notre Dame. A summary of the rankings (star ratings) for the top 30 MBA programs is shown in the table.

Criteria	5 Stars	4 Stars	3 Stars	2 Stars	1 Star	Total
Student Exposure	2	9	14	5	0	30
Student Opportunity	3	10	14	3	0	30
Course Content	3	9	17	1	0	30
Faculty Research	3	10	11	4	0	28

Source: Data from Stewardship at MBA programs, D. Biello, "MBA Programs for Social and Environmental Stewardship," BUSINESS ETHICS, Fall 2005, p. 25.

a. Illustrate the differences and similarities of the star-ranking distributions for the four different criteria.

b. Give a plausible reason why there were no 1-star ratings for the 30 MBA programs.

17 **Groundwater contamination in wells.** In New Hampshire, about half the counties mandate the use of reformulated gasoline. This has led to an increase in the contamination of groundwater with methyl *tert*-butyl ether (MTBE).

Environmental Science & Technology (Jan. 2005) reported on the factors related to MTBE contamination in public and private New Hampshire wells. Data were collected for a sample of 223 wells. Three of the variables are qualitative in nature: well class (public or private), aquifer (bedrock or unconsolidated), and detectible level of MTBE (below limit or detect). [*Note:* A detectible level of MTBE occurs if the MTBE value exceeds .2 micrograms per liter.] The data for 11 selected wells are shown in the accompanying table.

Well Class	Aquifer	Detect MTBE
Private	Bedrock	Below Limit
Private	Bedrock	Below Limit
Public	Unconsolidated	Detect
Public	Unconsolidated	Below Limit
Public	Unconsolidated	Below Limit
Public	Unconsolidated	Below Limit
Public	Unconsolidated	Detect
Public	Unconsolidated	Below Limit
Public	Unconsolidated	Below Limit
Public	Bedrock	Detect
Public	Bedrock	Detect

Source: Based on Ayotte, J. D., Argue, D. M., and McGarry, F. J. "Methyl tert-Butyl Ether Occurrence and Related Factors in Public and Private Wells in Southeast New Hampshire." ENVIRONMENTAL SCIENCE & TECHNOLOGY, Vol. 39, No. 1, Jan. 2005, pp. 9–16.

a. Use graphical methods to describe each of the three qualitative variables for all 223 wells.

b. Use side-by-side bar charts to compare the proportions of contaminated wells for private and public well classes.

c. Use side-by-side bar charts to compare the proportions of contaminated wells for bedrock and unconsolidated aquifers.

d. What inferences can be made from the bar charts, parts **a–c**?

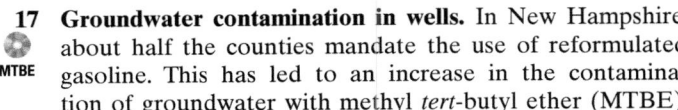

2 Graphical Methods for Describing Quantitative Data

Quantitative data sets consist of data that are recorded on a meaningful numerical scale. For describing, summarizing, and detecting patterns in such data, we can use three graphical methods: **dot plots, stem-and-leaf displays,** and **histograms.** Because almost all statistical software packages can produce these graphs, we'll focus here on their interpretations rather than their construction.

For example, suppose a financial analyst is interested in the amount of resources spent by computer hardware and software companies on research and development (R&D). She samples 50 of these high-technology firms and calculates the amount each spent last year on R&D as a percentage of their total revenue. The results are given in Table 2. As numerical measurements made on the sample of 50 units (the firms), these percentages represent quantitative data. The analyst's initial objective is to summarize and describe these data in order to extract relevant information.

A visual inspection of the data indicates some obvious facts. For example, the smallest R&D percentage is 5.2% (company 45) and the largest is 13.5% (companies 1 and 16). But it is difficult to provide much additional information on the 50 R&D percentages without resorting to some method of summarizing the data. One such method is a dot plot.

Table 2	Percentage of Revenues Spent on Research and Development						
Company	Percentage	Company	Percentage	Company	Percentage	Company	Percentage
1	13.5	14	9.5	27	8.2	39	6.5
2	8.4	15	8.1	28	6.9	40	7.5
3	10.5	16	13.5	29	7.2	41	7.1
4	9.0	17	9.9	30	8.2	42	13.2
5	9.2	18	6.9	31	9.6	43	7.7
6	9.7	19	7.5	32	7.2	44	5.9
7	6.6	20	11.1	33	8.8	45	5.2
8	10.6	21	8.2	34	11.3	46	5.6
9	10.1	22	8.0	35	8.5	47	11.7
10	7.1	23	7.7	36	9.4	48	6.0
11	8.0	24	7.4	37	10.5	49	7.8
12	7.9	25	6.5	38	6.9	50	6.5
13	6.8	26	9.5				

Data Set: R&D

Dot Plots

A **dot plot** for the 50 R&D percentages, produced using Minitab, is shown in Figure 8. The horizontal axis of Figure 8 is a scale for the quantitative variable, percent. The numerical value of each measurement in the data set is located on the horizontal scale by a dot. When data values repeat, the dots are placed above one another, forming a pile at that particular numerical location. As you can see, this dot plot shows that almost all of the R&D percentages are between 6% and 12%, with most falling between 7% and 9%.

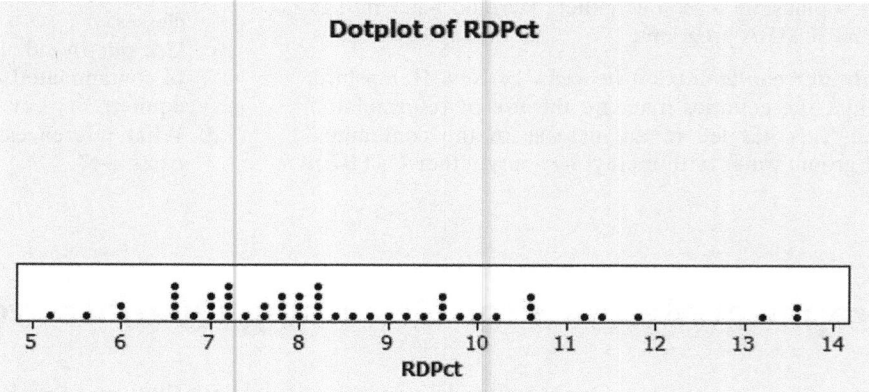

Figure 8

Minitab dot plot for 50 R&D percentages

Stem-and-Leaf Display

We used XLSTAT to generate another graphical representation of these same data, a **stem-and-leaf display,** in Figure 9. In this display the *stem* is the portion of the measurement (percentage) to the left of the decimal point, while the remaining portion to the right of the decimal point is the *leaf.*

The stems for the data set are listed in the first column of Figure 9 from the smallest (5) to the largest (13). Then the leaf for each observation is recorded in the row of the display corresponding to the observation's stem. For example, the leaf 5 of the first observation (13.5) in Table 2 is placed in the row corresponding to the stem 13. Similarly, the leaf 4 for the second observation (8.4) in Table 2 is recorded in the row corresponding to the stem 8, while the leaf 5 for the third observation (10.5) is recorded in the row corresponding to the stem 10. (The leaves for these first three observations are shaded in Figure 9.) Typically, the leaves in each row are ordered as shown in Figure 9.

Stem-and-leaf plot (RDPct):

Unit: 1

```
         5 2 6 9
         6 0 5 5 5 6 8 9 9 9
         7 1 1 2 2 4 5 5 7 7 8 9
         8 0 0 1 2 2 2 4 5 8
         9 0 2 4 5 5 6 7 9
        10 1 5 5 6
        11 1 3 7
        12
        13 2 5 5
```

Figure 9

XLSTAT stem-and-leaf display for 50 R&D percentages

The stem-and-leaf display presents another compact picture of the data set. You can see at a glance that most of the sampled computer companies (37 of 50) spent between 6.0% and 9.9% of their revenues on R&D, and 11 of them spent between 7.0% and 7.9%. Relative to the rest of the sampled companies, three spent a high percentage of revenues on R&D—in excess of 13%.

The definitions of the stem and leaf can be modified to alter the graphical display. For example, suppose we had defined the stem as the tens digit for the R&D percentage data, rather than the ones and tens digits. With this definition, the stems and leaves corresponding to the measurements 13.5 and 8.4 would be as follows:

Stem	Leaf		Stem	Leaf
1	3		0	8

Note that the decimal portion of the numbers has been dropped. Generally, only one digit is displayed in the leaf.

If you look at the data, you'll see why we didn't define the stem this way. All the R&D measurements fall below 13.5, so all the leaves would fall into just two stem rows—1 and 0—in this display. The picture resulting from using only a few stems would not be nearly as informative as Figure 9.

Histograms

A **Minitab histogram** for these 50 R&D measurements is displayed in Figure 10. The horizontal axis for Figure 10, which gives the percentage amounts spent on R&D for each company, is divided into **class intervals** commencing with the interval (5.0−6.0) and proceeding in intervals of equal size to (13.0−14.0). The vertical axis gives the number (or *frequency*) of the 50 measurements that fall in each class interval. You can see that the class interval (7.0−8.0) (i.e., the class with the highest bar) contains the largest frequency of 11 R&D percentage measurements; the remaining class intervals tend to contain a smaller number of measurements as R&D percentage gets smaller or larger.

Histograms can be used to display either the *frequency* or *relative frequency* of the measurements falling into the class intervals. The class intervals, frequencies, and relative frequencies for the 50 R&D measurements are shown in Table 3.* By summing the

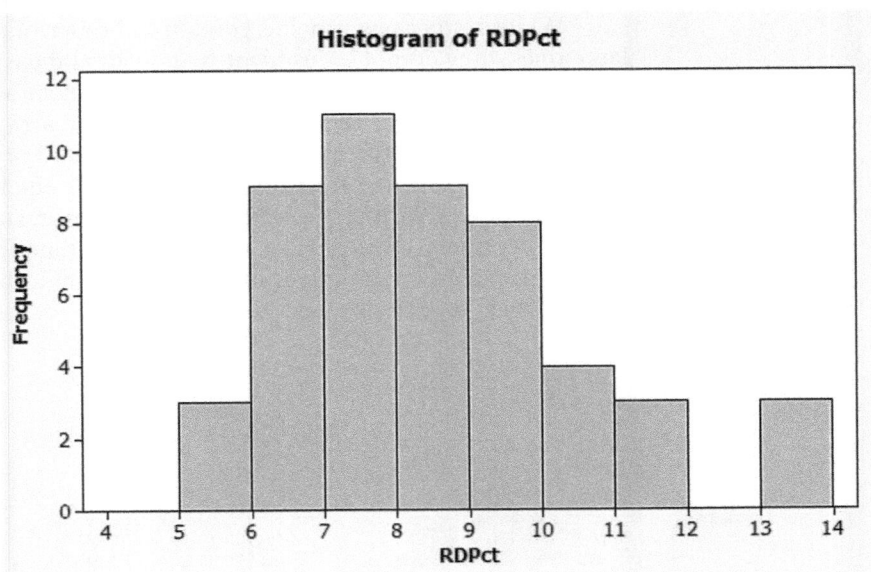

Figure 10

Minitab histogram for 50 R&D percentages

*Minitab, like many statistical software packages, will classify an observation that falls on the borderline of a class interval into the next highest class interval. For example, the R&D measurement of 8.0, which falls on the border between the intervals (7.0−8.0) and (8.0−9.0), is classified into the (8.0−9.0) interval. The frequencies in Table 3 reflect this convention.

Table 3	Class Intervals, Frequencies, and Relative Frequencies for the 50 R&D Measurements		
Class	Class Interval	Class Frequency	Class Relative Frequency
1	5.0–6.0	3	3/50 = .06
2	6.0–7.0	9	9/50 = .18
3	7.0–8.0	11	11/50 = .22
4	8.0–9.0	9	9/50 = .18
5	9.0–10.0	8	8/50 = .16
6	10.0–11.0	4	4/50 = .08
7	11.0–12.0	3	3/50 = .06
8	12.0–13.0	0	0/50 = .00
9	13.0–14.0	3	3/50 = .06
Totals		50	1.00

relative frequencies in the intervals (6.0–7.0), (7.0–8.0), (8.0–9.0), (9.0–10.0), and (10.0–11.0), we find that .18 + .22 + .18 + .16 + .08 = .82, or 82%, of the R&D measurements are between 6.0 and 11.0. Similarly, summing the relative frequencies in the last two intervals, (12.0–13.0) and (13.0–14.0), we find that 6% of the companies spent over 12.0% of their revenues on R&D. Many other summary statements can be made by further study of the histogram. Note that the sum of all class frequencies will always equal the sample size n.

When interpreting a histogram, consider two important facts. First, the proportion of the total area under the histogram that falls above a particular interval of the horizontal axis is equal to the relative frequency of measurements falling in the interval. For example, the relative frequency for the class interval 7.0–8.0 in Figure 10 is .22. Consequently, the rectangle above the interval contains 22% of the total area under the histogram.

Second, imagine the appearance of the relative frequency histogram for a very large set of data (say, a population). As the number of measurements in a data set is increased, you can obtain a better description of the data by decreasing the width of the class intervals. When the class intervals become small enough, a relative frequency histogram will (for all practical purposes) appear as a smooth curve (see Figure 11). Some recommendations for selecting the number of intervals in a histogram for smaller data sets are given in the box below Figure 11.

While histograms provide good visual descriptions of data sets–particularly very large ones–they do not let us identify individual measurements. In contrast, each of the original measurements is visible to some extent in a dot plot and clearly visible in a stem-and-leaf display. The stem-and-leaf display arranges the data in ascending order, so it's easy to locate the individual measurements. For example, in Figure 9, we can easily see that three of the R&D measurements are equal to 8.2, but we can't see that fact by inspecting the histogram in Figure 10. However, stem-and-leaf displays can become unwieldy for very large data sets. A very large number of stems and leaves causes the vertical and horizontal dimensions of the display to become cumbersome, diminishing the usefulness of the visual display.

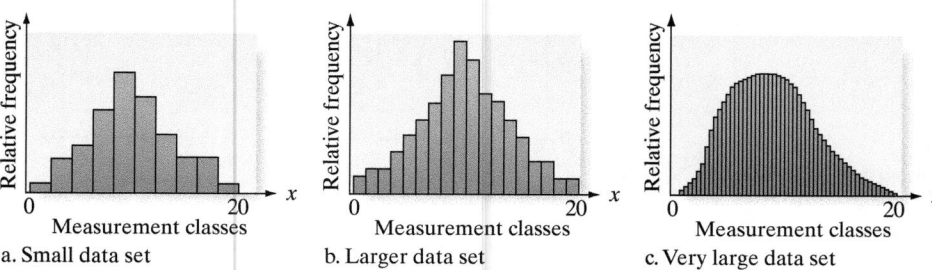

Figure 11

Effect of the size of a data set on the outline of a histogram

a. Small data set   b. Larger data set   c. Very large data set

Determining the Number of Classes in a Histogram

Number of Observations in Data Set	Number of Classes
Less than 25	5–6
25–50	7–14
More than 50	15–20

Example 2

Graphs for a Quantitative Variable— Lost Price Quotes

Problem A manufacturer of industrial wheels suspects that profitable orders are being lost because of the long time the firm takes to develop price quotes for potential customers. To investigate this possibility, 50 requests for price quotes were randomly selected from the set of all quotes made last year, and the processing time was determined for each quote. The processing times are displayed in Table 4, and each quote was classified according to whether the order was "lost" or not (i.e., whether or not the customer placed an order after receiving a price quote).

a. Use a statistical software package to create a frequency histogram for these data. Then shade the area under the histogram that corresponds to lost orders. Interpret the result.

b. Use a statistical software package to create a stem-and-leaf display for these data. Then shade each leaf of the display that corresponds to a lost order. Interpret the result.

Solution

a. We used SPSS to generate the frequency histogram in Figure 12. Note that 20 classes were formed by the SPSS program. The class intervals are (1.0–2.0), (2.0–3.0),..., (20.0–21.0). This histogram clearly shows the clustering of the measurements in the

Table 4	Price Quote Processing Time (Days)					
Request Number	Processing Time	Lost?	Request Number	Processing Time	Lost?
1	2.36	No	26	3.34	No
2	5.73	No	27	6.00	No
3	6.60	No	28	5.92	No
4	10.05	Yes	29	7.28	Yes
5	5.13	No	30	1.25	No
6	1.88	No	31	4.01	No
7	2.52	No	32	7.59	No
8	2.00	No	33	13.42	Yes
9	4.69	No	34	3.24	No
10	1.91	No	35	3.37	No
11	6.75	Yes	36	14.06	Yes
12	3.92	No	37	5.10	No
13	3.46	No	38	6.44	No
14	2.64	No	39	7.76	No
15	3.63	No	40	4.40	No
16	3.44	No	41	5.48	No
17	9.49	Yes	42	7.51	No
18	4.90	No	43	6.18	No
19	7.45	No	44	8.22	Yes
20	20.23	Yes	45	4.37	No
21	3.91	No	46	2.93	No
22	1.70	No	47	9.95	Yes
23	16.29	Yes	48	4.46	No
24	5.52	No	49	14.32	Yes
25	1.44	No	50	9.01	No

Data Set: QUOTES

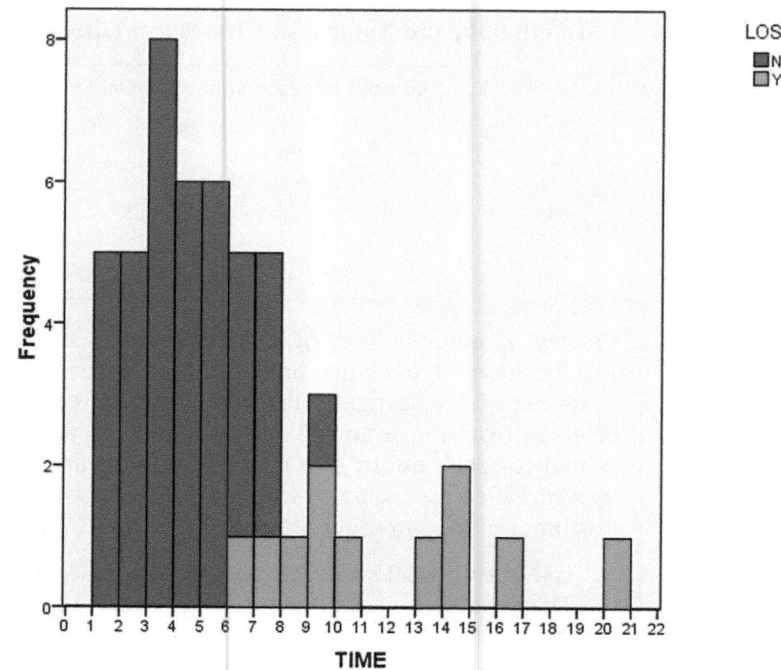

Figure 12

SPSS frequency histogram for price quote data

lower end of the distribution (between approximately 1 and 8 days), and the relatively few measurements in the upper end of the distribution (greater than 12 days). The shading of the area of the frequency histogram corresponding to lost orders (green bars) clearly indicates that they lie in the upper tail of the distribution.

b. We used Minitab to generate the stem-and-leaf display in Figure 13. Note that the stem (the second column of the printout) consists of the number of whole days (digits to the left of the decimal). The leaf (the third column of the printout) is the tenths digit (first digit after the decimal) of each measurement. Thus, the leaf 2 in the stem 20 (the last row of the printout) represents the time of 20.23 days. Like the histogram, the stem-and-leaf display shows the shaded "lost" orders in the upper tail of the distribution.

Look Back As is usually the case for data sets that are not too large (say, fewer than 100 measurements), the stem-and-leaf display provides more detail than the histogram without being unwieldy. For instance, the stem-and-leaf display in Figure 13 clearly indicates that the lost orders are associated with high processing times (as does the histogram in Figure 12), and exactly which of the times correspond to lost orders. Histograms are most useful for displaying very large data sets, when the overall shape of the distribution of measurements is more important than the identification of individual measurements. Nevertheless, the message of both graphical displays is clear: Establishing processing time limits may well result in fewer lost orders.

Now Work Exercise 22

```
Stem-and-leaf of TIME  N = 50
Leaf Unit = 0.10

   5   1   24789
  10   2   03569
  18   3   23344699
  24   4   034469
  (6)  5   114579
  20   6   01467
  15   7   24557
  10   8   2
   9   9   049
   6  10   0
   5  11
   5  12
   5  13   4
   4  14   03
   2  15
   2  16   2
   1  17
   1  18
   1  19
   1  20   2
```

Figure 13

Minitab stem-and-leaf display for price quote data

Most statistical software packages can be used to generate histograms, stem-and-leaf displays, and dot plots. All three are useful tools for graphically describing data sets. We recommend that you generate and compare the displays whenever you can. You'll find that histograms are generally more useful for very large data sets, while stem-and-leaf displays and dot plots provide useful detail for smaller data sets.

Summary of Graphical Descriptive Methods for Quantitative Data

Dot plot: The numerical value of each quantitative measurement in the data set is represented by a dot on a horizontal scale. When data values repeat, the dots are placed above one another vertically.

Stem-and-leaf display: The numerical value of the quantitative variable is partitioned into a "stem" and a "leaf." The possible stems are listed in order in a column. The leaf for each quantitative measurement in the data set is placed in the corresponding stem row. Leaves for observations with the same stem value are listed in increasing order horizontally.

Histogram: The possible numerical values of the quantitative variable are partitioned into class intervals, where each interval has the same width. These intervals form the scale of the horizontal axis. The frequency or relative frequency of observations in each class interval is determined. A horizontal bar is placed over each class interval, with height equal to either the class frequency or class relative frequency.

STATISTICS
in ACTION
REVISITED

Interpreting Histograms

In the *Journal of Experimental Social Psychology* (Vol. 45, 2009) study on whether money can buy love, the researchers randomly assigned participants to the role of either gift-giver or gift-receiver. (Gift-givers, recall, were asked about a birthday gift they recently gave, while gift-recipients were asked about a birthday gift they recently received.) Two quantitative variables were measured for each of the 237 participants: *gift price* (measured in dollars) and *overall level of appreciation for the gift* (measured as the sum of the two 7-point appreciation scales, with higher values indicating a higher level of appreciation). One of the objectives of the research was to investigate whether givers and receivers differ on the price of the gift reported and on the level of appreciation reported. We can explore this phenomenon graphically by forming side-by-side histograms for the quantitative variables, one histogram for gift-givers and one for gift-recipients. These histograms, produced from a Minitab analysis of the data in the **BUYLOV** file, are shown in Figures SIA7a and SIA7b.

First, examine the histograms for birthday gift price (Figure SIA7a). The prices reported by gift-recipients tended to be higher than the prices reported by gift-givers. For example, receivers reported more birthday gift prices of at least $300 than givers, while givers reported more prices of $100 or less than receivers.

Next, examine the histograms for overall level of appreciation (Figure SIA7b). For gift-givers, the histogram of appreciation scores is centered around 5 points, while

Figure SIA7a
Side-by-side histograms for birthday gift price

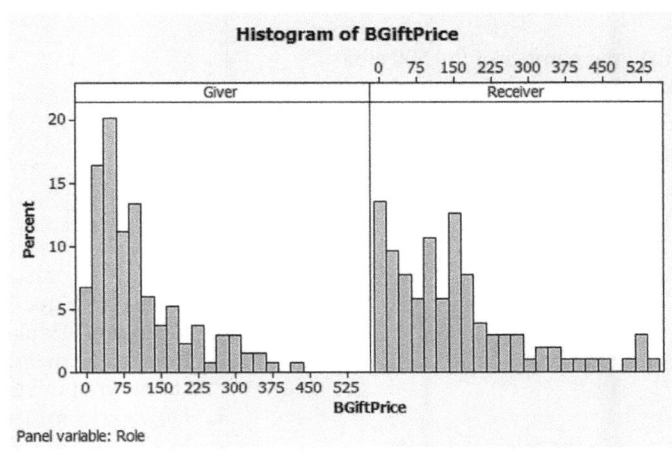

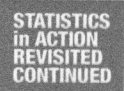

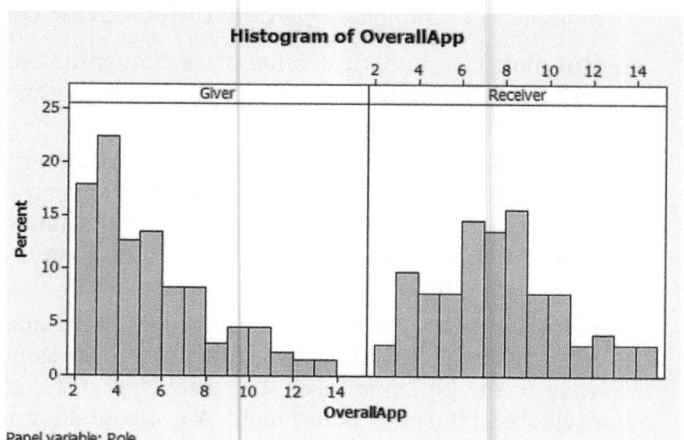

Figure SIA7b

Side-by-side histograms for overall
level of appreciation

for gift-recipients the histogram is centered higher, at about 8 points. Also from the
histograms you can see that about 65% of the givers reported an appreciation level
of less than 6 compared to about 28% for gift-recipients. As with the bar graphs in the
previous Statistics in Action Revisited, it appears that gift-givers and gift-recipients respond differently, with gift-recipients more likely to express a greater level of appreciation for the gift than what gift-givers perceive.

Data Set: BUYLOV

Exercises 18–34

Please be aware that some of the following problems may require knowledge of concepts that are not
presented in this chapter.

Learning the Mechanics

18 Graph the relative frequency histogram for the 500 measurements summarized in the accompanying relative frequency table.

Measurement Class	Relative Frequency
.5–2.5	.10
2.5–4.5	.15
4.5–6.5	.25
6.5–8.5	.20
8.5–10.5	.05
10.5–12.5	.10
12.5–14.5	.10
14.5–16.5	.05

19 Refer to Exercise 18. Calculate the number of the 500 measurements falling into each of the measurement classes.
Then graph a frequency histogram for these data.

20 Consider the stem-and-leaf display shown here.

Stem	Leaf
5	1
4	457
3	00036
2	1134599
1	2248
0	012

a. How many observations were in the original data set?

b. In the bottom row of the stem-and-leaf display, identify
the stem, the leaves, and the numbers in the original
data set represented by this stem and its leaves.

c. Re-create all the numbers in the data set and construct
a dot plot.

21 Minitab was used to generate the following histogram:

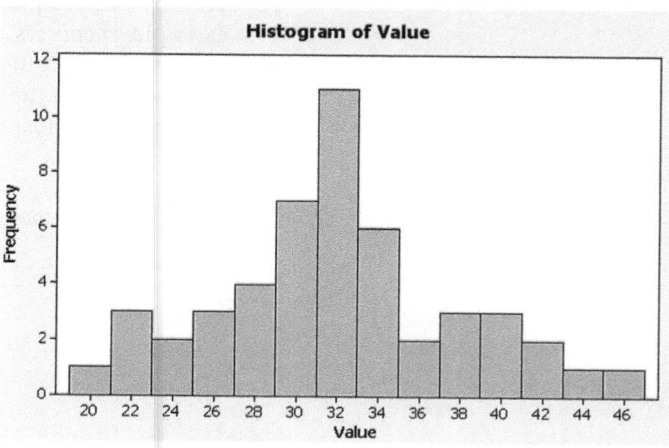

a. Is this a frequency histogram or a relative frequency
histogram? Explain.

b. How many measurement classes were used in the construction of this histogram?

c. How many measurements are in the data set described
by this histogram?

Applying the Concepts—Basic

22 Annual survey of computer crimes. This exercise references the 2010 *CSI Computer Crime and Security Survey.* 351 organizations responded on unauthorized use of computer systems. One of the survey questions asked respondents to indicate the percentage of monetary losses attributable to malicious actions by individuals within the organization (i.e., malicious insider actions). The following XLSTAT histogram summarizes the data for the 144 firms who experienced some monetary loss due to malicious insider actions.

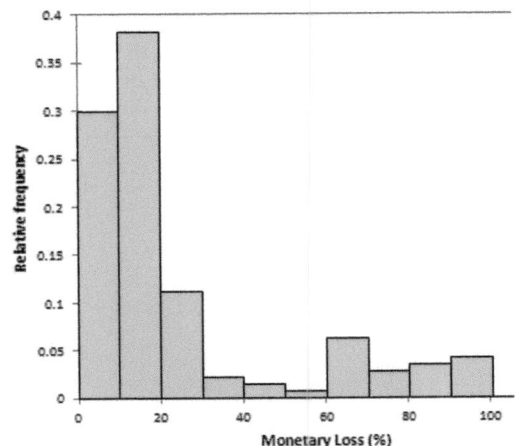

a. Which measurement class contains the highest proportion of respondents?

b. What is the approximate proportion of the 144 organizations that reported a percentage monetary loss from malicious insider actions less than 20%?

c. What is the approximate proportion of the 144 organizations that reported a percentage monetary loss from malicious insider actions greater than 60%?

d. About how many of the 144 organizations reported a percentage monetary loss from malicious insider actions between 20% and 30%?

23 Corporate sustainability of CPA firms. The *Business and Society* (March 2011) did a study on the sustainability behaviors of CPA corporations. *Corporate sustainability*, recall, refers to business practices designed around social and environmental considerations. Data on the level of support for corporate sustainability were obtained for 992 senior managers. Level of support was measured quantitatively. Simulation was used to convert the data from the study to a scale ranging from 0 to 160 points, where higher point values indicate a higher level of support for sustainability.

a. A histogram for level of support for sustainability is shown next. What type of histogram is produced, frequency or relative frequency?

b. Use the graph to estimate the percentage of the 992 senior managers who reported a high (100 points or greater) level of support for corporate sustainability.

Minitab histogram for Exercise 23

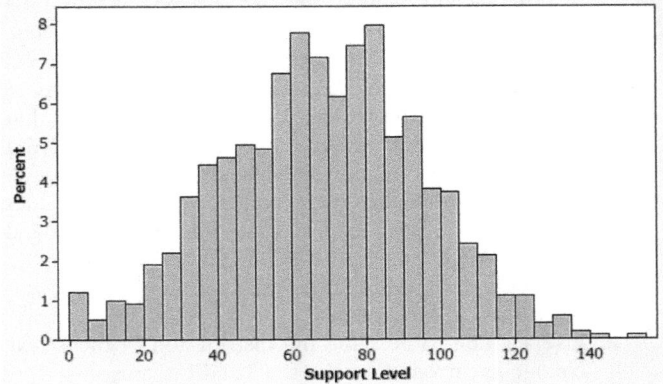

24 Sanitation inspection of cruise ships. To minimize the potential for gastrointestinal disease outbreaks, all passenger cruise ships arriving at U.S. ports are subject to unannounced sanitation inspections. Ships are rated on a 100-point scale by the Centers for Disease Control and Prevention. A score of 86 or higher indicates that the ship is providing an accepted standard of sanitation. The latest (as of Jan. 2010) sanitation scores for 186 cruise ships are saved in the accompanying file. The first five and last five observations in the data set are listed in the accompanying table.

Ship Name	Sanitation Score
Adventure of the Seas	98
AIDAaura	100
Albatross	69
Amadea	84
Amsterdam	99
⋮	⋮
Westerdam	99
Wind Spirit	97
Wind Surf	95
Zaandam	99
Zuiderdam	95

Source: Data from U.S. Department of Health and Human Services, Centers for Disease Control and Prevention/National Center for Environmental Health and Agency for Toxic Substances and Disease Registry, January 6, 2010.

a. Generate both a stem-and-leaf display and histogram of the data.

b. Use the graphs to estimate the proportion of ships that have an accepted sanitation standard. Which graph did you use?

c. Locate the inspection score of 69 (*Albatross*) on the graph. Which graph did you use?

25 History of corporate acquisitions. Refer to the *Academy of Management Journal* (Aug. 2008) study of corporate acquisitions from 1980 to 2000, Exercise 12. The data file includes the number of firms with at least one acquisition each year.

a. Construct either a dot plot or a stem-and-leaf display for the annual number of firms with at least one acquisition.

b. On the graph, part **a**, highlight (or circle) the values for the years 1996–2000. Do you detect a pattern? If so, what conclusion can you draw from the data?

Applying the Concepts—Intermediate

26 Most valuable NFL teams. Each year *Forbes* reports on the value of all teams in the National Football League. Although England's soccer team, Manchester United, is the most valuable team in the world ($1.8 billion), the NFL now has 15 teams worth at least $1 billion. For 2011, *Forbes* reports that the Dallas Cowboys are the most valuable team in the NFL, worth $1.85 billion. The current values (in $ millions) of all 32 NFL teams, as well as the percentage changes in values from 2010 to 2011, debt-to-value ratios, annual revenues, and operating incomes are listed in the first table below.

a. Use a graph to describe the distribution of current values for the 32 NFL teams.

b. Use a graph to describe the distribution of the 1-year change in current value for the 32 NFL teams.

c. Use a graph to describe the distribution of debt-to-value ratios for the 32 NFL teams.

d. Use a graph to describe the distribution of the annual revenues for the 32 NFL teams.

e. Use a graph to describe the distribution of operating incomes for the 32 NFL teams.

f. Compare and contrast the graphs, parts **a–e**.

27 State SAT scores. Educators are constantly evaluating the efficacy of public schools in the education and training of American students. One quantitative assessment of change over time is the difference in scores on the SAT, which has been used for decades by colleges and universities as one criterion for admission. Originally, the SAT provided scores in reading and mathematics. Now, three scores are provided: reading, mathematics, and critical writing. SAT scores for each of the 50 states and District of Columbia for the years 2011, 2010, and 2001 are saved in the accompanying file. Data for the first five and last two states are shown in the second table below.

Rank	Team	Current Value ($ mil)	1-Yr Value Change (%)	Debt/Value (%)	Revenue ($ mil)	Operating Income ($ mil)
1	Dallas Cowboys	1,850	2	18	406	119
2	Washington Redskins	1,555	0	26	352	65.6
3	New England Patriots	1,400	2	19	333	42.9
4	New York Giants	1,300	10	50	293	40.6
5	New York Jets	1,223	7	61	285	25.1
6	Houston Texans	1,202	3	17	283	41
7	Philadelphia Eagles	1,164	4	9	274	28.9
8	Chicago Bears	1,093	2	11	266	43.4
9	Green Bay Packers	1,089	7	2	259	12
10	Baltimore Ravens	1,088	1	25	262	24.9
11	Indianapolis Colts	1,057	2	4	252	32.8
12	Denver Broncos	1,046	0	14	255	28.5
13	Pittsburgh Steelers	1,018	2	25	255	28.3
14	Miami Dolphins	1,012	0	40	253	12.9
15	Carolina Panthers	1,002	−3	19	257	31.2
16	Seattle Seahawks	997	1	12	249	7.8
17	San Francisco 49ers	990	7	14	234	1.5
18	Kansas City Chiefs	986	2	14	252	14.5
19	Tampa Bay Buccaneers	981	−5	18	245	50.8
20	Cleveland Browns	977	−4	15	247	−2.9
21	New Orleans Saints	965	1	13	261	28.9
22	Tennessee Titans	964	−3	13	250	21.8
23	San Diego Chargers	920	1	14	241	34.2
24	Arizona Cardinals	901	−2	17	240	56.4
25	Cincinnati Bengals	875	−3	11	236	44.7
26	Detroit Lions	844	3	33	228	−7.7
27	Atlanta Falcons	814	−2	34	233	27.2
28	Minnesota Vikings	796	3	41	227	3.7
29	Buffalo Bills	792	−1	16	236	40.9
30	St. Louis Rams	775	−1	15	228	24.6
31	Oakland Raiders	761	0	16	217	23
32	Jacksonville Jaguars	725	0	17	236	32.8

Source: Based on Kurt Badenhausen, "The NFL's Most Valuable Teams," FORBES, September 7, 2011.

Data for Exercise 27

State	2011 Read	2011 Math	2011 Write	2010 Read	2010 Math	2010 Write	2001 Read	2001 Math
Alabama	546	541	536	556	550	543	559	554
Alaska	515	511	487	516	513	489	514	510
Arizona	517	523	499	518	524	498	523	525
Arkansas	568	570	554	564	564	550	562	550
California	499	515	499	501	516	500	498	517
Wisconsin	590	602	575	593	603	578	584	596
Wyoming	572	569	551	568	565	543	547	545

Source: Data from "SAT Trends: Background on the SAT Takers in the Class of 2011," The College Board, 2011.

a. Use graphs to display the SAT mathematics score distributions in 2011 and 2010. How did the distributions of state scores change over the year?

b. Repeat part **a,** but compare the distribution in 2011 with the one in 2001. How did the distributions of state scores change over the past 10 years?

c. As another method of comparing the 2011 and 2001 SAT mathematics scores, compute the *paired difference* by subtracting the 2001 score from the 2011 score for each state. Summarize these differences with a graph. Compare the results to those of part **b.**

d. Based on the graph, part **c,** what is the largest improvement in SAT mathematics score? Identify the state associated with this improvement.

28 Items arriving and departing a work center. In a manufacturing plant, a *work center* is a specific production facility that consists of one or more people and/or machines and is treated as one unit for the purposes of capacity requirements for planning and job scheduling. If jobs arrive at a particular work center at a faster rate than they depart, the work center impedes the overall production process and is referred to as a *bottleneck*. The data in the table at the bottom of the page were collected by an operations manager for use in investigating a potential bottleneck work center. Construct dot plots for the two sets of data. Do the dot plots suggest that the work center may be a bottleneck? Explain.

WRKCTR

29 Crude oil biodegradation. In order to protect their valuable resources, oil companies spend millions of dollars researching ways to prevent biodegradation of crude

BIODEG

oil. The *Journal of Petroleum Geology* (April 2010) published a study of the environmental factors associated with biodegradation in crude oil reservoirs. Sixteen water specimens were randomly selected from various locations in a reservoir on the floor of a mine. Two of the variables measured were (1) the amount of dioxide (milligrams/liter) present in the water specimen and (2) whether or not oil was present in the water specimen. These data are listed in the accompanying table in the left column. Construct a stem-and-leaf display for the dioxide data. Locate the dioxide levels associated with water specimens that contain oil. Highlight these data points on the stem-and-leaf display. Is there a tendency for crude oil to be present in water with lower levels of dioxide?

30 Is honey a cough remedy? Coughing at night is a common symptom of an upper respiratory tract infection, yet there is no accepted therapeutic cure. Does a teaspoon of honey before bed really calm a child's cough? To test the folk remedy, pediatric researchers at Pennsylvania State University carried out a designed study conducted over two nights (*Archives of Pediatrics and Adolescent Medicine*, Dec. 2007). A sample of 105 children who were ill with an upper respiratory tract infection and their parents participated in the study. On the first night, the parents rated their children's cough symptoms on a scale from 0 (no problems at all) to 6 (extremely severe) in five different areas. The total symptoms score (ranging from 0 to 30 points) was the variable of interest for the 105 patients. On the second night, the parents were instructed to give their sick child a dosage of liquid "medicine" prior to bedtime. Unknown to the parents, some were given a dosage of dextromethorphan (DM)—an over-the-counter cough medicine—while others were given a similar dose of honey. Also, a third group of parents (the control group) gave their sick children no dosage at all. Again, the parents rated their children's cough symptoms, and the improvement in total cough symptoms score was determined for each child. The data (improvement scores) for the study are shown in the table on the next page, followed by a Minitab dot plot of the data. Notice that the green dots represent the children who received a dose of honey, the red dots represent those who got the DM dosage, and the black dots represent the children in the control group. What conclusions can pediatric researchers draw from the graph? Do you agree with the statement (extracted from the article), "Honey may be a preferable treatment for the cough and sleep difficulty associated with childhood upper respiratory tract infection"?

HCOUGH

Dioxide Amount	Crude Oil Present
3.3	No
0.5	Yes
1.3	Yes
0.4	Yes
0.1	No
4.0	No
0.3	No
0.2	Yes
2.4	No
2.4	No
1.4	No
0.5	Yes
0.2	Yes
4.0	No
4.0	No
4.0	No

Source: Based on A. Permanyer, J. L. R. Gallego, M. A. Caja, and D. Dessort, "Crude Oil Biodegradation and Environmental Factors at the Riutort Oil Shale Mine, SE Pyrenees." JOURNAL OF PETROLEUM GEOLOGY, Vol. 33, No. 2, April 2010, Table 1.

Data for Exercise 28

Number of Items Arriving at Work Center per Hour											
155	115	156	150	159	163	172	143	159	166	148	175
151	161	138	148	129	135	140	152	139			

Number of Items Departing Work Center per Hour											
156	109	127	148	135	119	140	127	115	122	99	106
171	123	135	125	107	152	111	137	161			

Data for Exercise 30

Honey Dosage:	12	11	15	11	10	13	10	4	15	16	9	14
	10	6	10	8	11	12	12	8	9	5	12	
	12	9	11	15	10	15	9	13	8	12	10	8
DM Dosage:	4	6	9	4	7	7	7	9	12	10	11	6	3
	4	9	12	7	6	8	12	12	4	12	10	15	9
	13	7	10	13	9	4	4						
No Dosage (Control):	5	8	6	1	0	8	12	8	7	7	1	6	7
	7	12	7	9	7	9	5	11	9	5	1	4	3
	6	8	8	6	7	10	9	4	8	7	3		

Source: Based on Paul, I. M., et al. "Effect of honey, dextromethorphan, and no treatment on nocturnal cough and sleep quality for coughing children and their parents," *Archives of Pediatrices and Adolescent Medicine,* Vol. 161, No. 12, Dec. 2007 (data simulated).

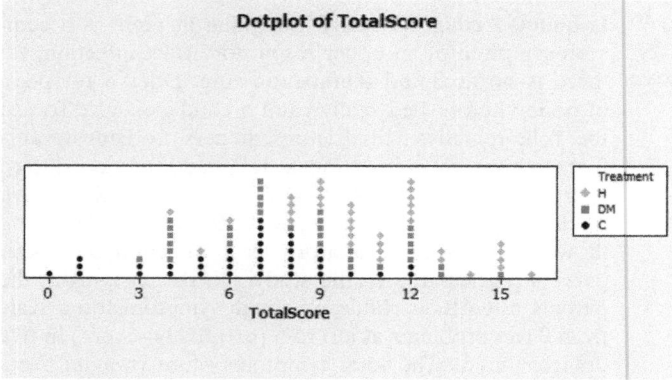

Applying the Concepts—Advanced

31 Doctors and ethics. Refer to the *Journal of Medical Ethics* (Vol. 32, 2006) study of physicians' use of ethics consultation, Exercise 11. In addition to the qualitative variable, *use of ethics consultation in the future* ("yes" or "no"), one of the quantitative variables measured in the survey of physicians was *length of time in practice* (i.e., years of experience). The medical researchers hypothesized that older, more experienced physicians would be less likely to use ethics consultation in the future. Access the file and generate two graphs to describe the distribution of years of experience—one for physicians who indicated they would use ethics consultation in the future and one for physicians who refused to use ethics consultation. Place the graphs side by side. Is there support for the researchers' assertion? Explain.

 ETHICS

32 Time in bankruptcy. Financially distressed firms can gain protection from their creditors while they restructure by filing for protection under U.S. Bankruptcy Codes. In a *prepackaged bankruptcy,* a firm negotiates a reorganization plan with its creditors prior to filing for bankruptcy. This can result in a much quicker exit from bankruptcy than tradional bankruptcy filings. A study of 49 prepackaged bankrupcies was published in *Financial Management* (Spring, 1995). For each firm, information was collected on the time (in months) in bankruptcy as well as the results of the board of directors' vote on the type of reorganization plan. Three types of plans were studied: "Joint"—a joint exachange offer with prepackaged bankruptcy solicitation; "Prepack"—prepackaged bankruptcy solicitation only; and "None"—no pre-filing vote held. The data for the 49 firms is provided in the accompanying table.

BNKRPT

Reorganization Plan	Time in Bankruptcy (months)						
None	3.9	10.1	4.1	3.0	3.2	4.2	
	2.9	2.4	7.8*	2.6*	2.4		
Prepack	1.5	1.0*	1.9	1.3*	4.1	1.1	1.0*
	3.8	1.0*	1.5	1.0	1.4*	1.2*	3.0*
	1.6*	1.4*	1.1*	1.2	1.5*	2.1*	1.4
	1.7	1.4	2.7	1.2	4.1	2.9*	
Joint	1.4	1.2*	1.2	1.5*	1.4	5.2	4.5*
	2.1	3.9*	1.4*	5.4			

Source: Data from B. L. Betker, "An empirical examination of prepackaged bankruptcy," FINANCIAL MANAGEMENT, Vol. 24, No. 1, Spring 1995, p. 6 (Table 2).

a. Construct a stem-and-leaf display for the length of time in bankruptcy for all 49 companies.

b. Summarize the information reflected in the stem-and-leaf display from part **a.** Make a general statement about the length of time in bankruptcy for firms using "prepacks."

c. Select a graphical method that will permit a comparison of the time-in-bankruptcy distributions for the three types or reorganization plans.

d. Firms that were reorganized through a leveraged buyout are identified by an asterisk in the table. Mark these firms on the stem-and-leaf display, part **a,** by circling their bankruptcy times. Do you observe any pattern in the graph? Explain.

33 Phishing attacks to e-mail accounts. *Phishing* is the term used to describe an attempt to extract personal/financial information (e.g., PIN numbers, credit card information, bank account numbers) from unsuspecting people through fraudulent e-mail. An article in *Chance* (Summer 2007) demonstrates how statistics can help identify phishing attempts and make e-commerce safer. Data from an actual phishing attack against an organization were used to determine whether the attack may have been an "inside job" that originated within the company. The company set up a publicized e-mail account—called a "fraud box"—that enabled employees to notify them if they suspected an e-mail phishing attack. The interarrival times, i.e., the time differences (in seconds), for 267 fraud box e-mail notifications were recorded and saved in the file. *Chance* showed that if there is minimal or no collaboration or collusion from within the company, the interarrival times would have a frequency distribution similar to the one shown in the accompanying figure. Construct a frequency histogram for the interarrival times. Give your opinion on whether the phishing attack against the organization was an "inside job."

 PHISH

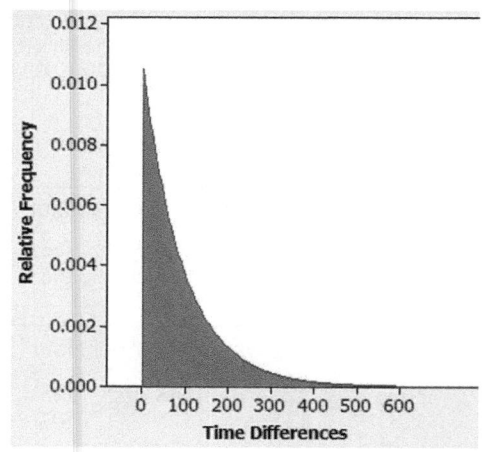

34 Made-to-order delivery times. Production processes may be classified as *make-to-stock processes* or *make-to-order processes*. Make-to-stock processes are designed to produce a standardized product that can be sold to customers from the firm's inventory. Make-to-order processes are designed to produce products according to customer specifications (Schroeder, *Operations Management,* 2008). In general, performance of make-to-order processes is measured by delivery time—the time from receipt of an order until the product is delivered to the customer. The accompanying data set is a sample of delivery times (in days) for a particular make-to-order firm last year. The delivery times marked by an asterisk are associated with customers who subsequently placed additional orders with the firm.

50*	64*	56*	43*	64*	82*	65*	49*	32*	63*	44*	71
54*	51*	102	49*	73*	50*	39*	86	33*	95	59*	51*
68											

Concerned that they are losing potential repeat customers because of long delivery times, the management would like to establish a guideline for the maximum tolerable delivery time. Use a graphical method to help suggest a guideline. Explain your reasoning.

3 Numerical Measures of Central Tendency

When we speak of a data set, we refer to either a sample or a population. If statistical inference is our goal, we'll wish ultimately to use sample **numerical descriptive measures** to make inferences about the corresponding measures for the population.

As you'll see, a large number of numerical methods are available to describe quantitative data sets. Most of these methods measure one of two data characteristics:

1. The **central tendency** of the set of measurements—that is, the tendency of the data to cluster, or center, about certain numerical values (see Figure 14a).

2. The **variability** of the set of measurements—that is, the spread of the data (see Figure 14b).

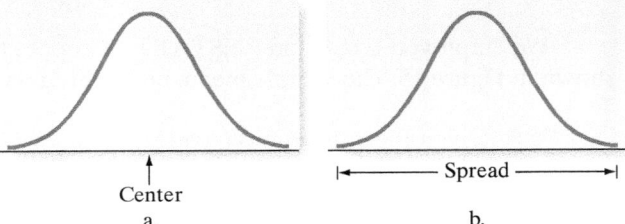

Figure 14
Numerical descriptive measures

In this section we concentrate on **measures of central tendency.** In the next section, we discuss measures of variability. The most popular and best-understood measure of central tendency for quantitative data is the arithmetic mean (or simply the mean) of a data set.

The **mean** of a set of quantitative data is the sum of the measurements divided by the number of measurements contained in the data set.

In everyday terms, the mean is the average value of the data set and is often used to represent a "typical" value. We denote the **mean of a sample** of measurements by $\bar{x}$ (read "x-bar") and represent the formula for its calculation as shown in the box below.

Formula for a Sample Mean

$$\bar{x} = \frac{\sum_{i=1}^{n} x_i}{n}$$

[*Note:* $\sum_{i=1}^{n} x_i = (x_1 + x_2 + \cdots + x_n)$). For more details on this summation notation, see Appendix: Summation Notation.]

Example	3

Calculating the Sample Mean

Problem Calculate the mean of the following five sample measurements: 5, 3, 8, 5, 6.

Solution Using the definition of sample mean and the summation notation, we find

$$\bar{x} = \frac{\sum_{i=1}^{5} x_i}{5} = \frac{5 + 3 + 8 + 5 + 6}{5} = \frac{27}{5} = 5.4$$

Thus, the mean of this sample is 5.4.

Look Back There is no specific rule for rounding when calculating $\bar{x}$ because $\bar{x}$ is specifically defined to be the sum of all measurements divided by n—that is, it is a specific fraction. When $\bar{x}$ is used for descriptive purposes, it is often convenient to round the calculated value of $\bar{x}$ to the number of significant figures used for the original measurements. When $\bar{x}$ is to be used in other calculations, however, it may be necessary to retain more significant figures.

■ Now Work Exercise 36

Example	4

Finding the Mean on a Printout—R&D Expenditures

Problem Calculate the sample mean for the R&D expenditure percentages of the 50 companies given in Table 2.

Solution The mean R&D percentage for the 50 companies is denoted

$$\bar{x} = \frac{\sum_{i=1}^{50} x_i}{50}$$

We employed Excel and XLSTAT to compute the mean. The XLSTAT printout is shown in Figure 15. The sample mean, highlighted on the printout, is $\bar{x} = 8.492$.

Look Back Given this information, you can visualize a distribution of R&D percentages centered in the vicinity $\bar{x} = 8.492$. An examination of the relative frequency histogram (Figure 10) confirms that $\bar{x}$ does, in fact, fall near the center of the distribution.

Descriptive statistics (Quantitative data):

Statistic	RDPct
No. of observations	50
Minimum	5.2000
Maximum	13.5000
Range	8.3000
1st Quartile	7.1000
Median	8.0500
3rd Quartile	9.5750
Mean	8.4920
Variance (n-1)	3.9228
Standard deviation (n-1)	1.9806

Figure 15

XLSTAT numerical descriptive measures for 50 R&D percentages

The sample mean $\bar{x}$ will play an important role in accomplishing our objective of making inferences about populations based on sample information. For this reason, we need to use a different symbol for the *mean of a population*–the mean of the set of measurements on every unit in the population. We use the Greek letter μ (mu) for the population mean.

Symbols for the Sample and Population Mean

In this text, we adopt a general policy of using Greek letters to represent population numerical descriptive measures and Roman letters to represent corresponding descriptive measures for the sample. The symbols for the mean are

$$\bar{x} = \text{Sample mean}$$
$$\mu = \text{Population mean*}$$

We'll often use the sample mean $\bar{x}$ to estimate (make an inference about) the population mean, μ. For example, the percentages of revenues spent on R&D by the population consisting of *all* U.S. companies has a mean equal to some value, μ. Our sample of 50 companies yielded percentages with a mean of $\bar{x} = 8.492$. If, as is usually the case, we don't have access to the measurements for the entire population, we could use $\bar{x}$ as an estimator or approximator for μ. Then we'd need to know something about the reliability of our inference—that is, we'd need to know how accurately we might expect $\bar{x}$ to estimate μ. This accuracy depends on two factors:

1. The *size of the sample*. The larger the sample, the more accurate the estimate will tend to be.
2. The *variability,* or *spread, of the data*. All other factors remaining constant, the more variable the data, the less accurate the estimate.

Another important measure of central tendency is the *median*.

The **median** of a quantitative data set is the middle number when the measurements are arranged in ascending (or descending) order.

The median is of most value in describing large data sets. If the data set is characterized by a relative frequency histogram (Figure 16), the median is the point on the *x*-axis such that half the area under the histogram lies above the median and half lies below. [*Note:* In Section 2, we observed that the relative frequency associated with a particular interval on the horizontal axis is proportional to the amount of area under the histogram that lies above the interval.] We denote the *median of a sample* by *m*. Like with the population mean, we use a Greek letter (η) to represent the population median.

Calculating a Sample Median, *m*

Arrange the *n* measurements from smallest to largest.

1. If *n* is odd, *m* is the middle number.
2. If *n* is even, *m* is the mean of the middle two numbers.

Figure 16

Location of the median

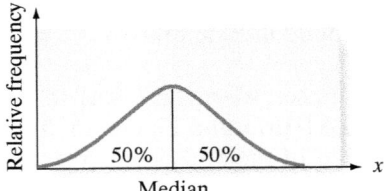

50%   50%

Median

*The population mean μ is calculated as $\mu = \dfrac{\sum\limits_{i=1}^{N} x_i}{N}$, where N is the population size.

> **Symbols for the Sample and Population Median**
>
> m = sample median
>
> η = population median*

Example **5**	**Problem** Consider the following sample of $n = 7$ measurements: 5, 7, 4, 5, 20, 6, 2.
Computing the Median	**a.** Calculate the median m of this sample.

b. Eliminate the last measurement (the 2) and calculate the median of the remaining $n = 6$ measurements.

Solution

a. The seven measurements in the sample are ranked in ascending order: 2, 4, 5, 5, 6, 7, 20. Because the number of measurements is odd, the median is the middle measurement. Thus, the median of this sample is $m = 5$ (the second 5 listed in the sequence).

b. After removing the 2 from the set of measurements, we rank the sample measurements in ascending order as follows: 4, 5, 5, 6, 7, 20. Now the number of measurements is even, so we average the middle two measurements. The median is $m = (5 + 6)/2 = 5.5$.

Look Back When the sample size n is even and the two middle numbers are different (as in part **b**), exactly half of the measurements will fall below the calculated median m. However, when n is odd (as in part **a**), the percentage of measurements that fall below m is approximately 50%. This approximation improves as n increases.

■ **Now Work Exercise 35**

In certain situations, the median may be a better measure of central tendency than the mean. In particular, the median is less sensitive than the mean to extremely large or small measurements. Note, for instance, that all but one of the measurements in part **a** of Example 5 center about $x = 5$. The single relatively large measurement, $x = 20$, does not affect the value of the median, 5, but it causes the mean, $\bar{x} = 7$, to lie to the right of most of the measurements.

As another example of data for which the central tendency is better described by the median than the mean, consider the salaries of professional athletes (e.g., National Basketball Association players). The presence of just a few athletes (e.g., LeBron James) with extremely high salaries will affect the mean more than the median. Thus, the median will provide a more accurate picture of the typical salary for the professional league. The mean could exceed the vast majority of the sample measurements (salaries), making it a misleading measure of central tendency.

Example **6**	**Problem** Calculate the median for the 50 R&D percentages given in Table 2. Compare the median to the mean found in Example 4.
Finding the Median on a Printout—R&D Expenditures	

Solution For this large data set, we again resort to a computer analysis. The median is highlighted on the XLSTAT printout, Figure 15. You can see that the median is 8.05. This value implies that half of the 50 R&D percentages in the data set fall below 8.05 and half lie above 8.05.

Note that the mean (8.492) for these data is larger than the median. This fact indicates that the data are **skewed** to the right–that is, there are more extreme

*The population median η is calculated like the sample median, but with all N observations in the population arranged from smallest to largest.

measurements in the right tail of the distribution than in the left tail (recall the histogram in Figure 10).

Look Back In general, extreme values (large or small) affect the mean more than the median because these values are used explicitly in the calculation of the mean. On the other hand, the median is not affected directly by extreme measurements because only the middle measurement (or two middle measurements) is explicitly used to calculate the median. Consequently, if measurements are pulled toward one end of the distribution (as with the R&D percentages), the mean will shift toward that tail more than the median.

A data set is said to be **skewed** if one tail of the distribution has more extreme observations than the other tail.

A comparison of the mean and the median gives us a general method for detecting skewness in data sets, as shown in the next box. With *rightward skewed* data, the right tail (high end) of the distribution has more extreme observations. These few, but large, measurements tend to pull the mean away from the median toward the right; that is, rightward skewness typically indicates that the mean is greater than the median. Conversely, with *leftward skewed* data, the left tail (low end) of the distribution has more extreme observations. These few, but small, measurements also tend to pull the mean away from the median but toward the left; consequently, leftward skewness typically implies that the mean is smaller than the median.

Detecting Skewness by Comparing the Mean and the Median

If the data set is skewed to the right, then typically the median is less than the mean.

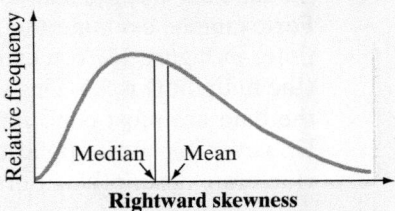

Rightward skewness

If the data set is symmetric, the mean equals the median.

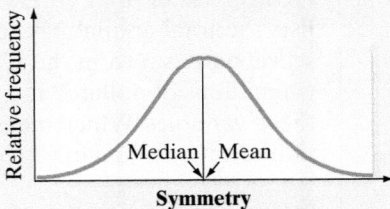

Symmetry

If the data set is skewed to the left, then typically the mean is less than (to the left of) the median.

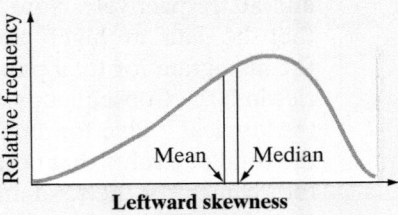

Leftward skewness

A third measure of central tendency is the *mode* of a set of measurements.

> The **mode** is the measurement that occurs most frequently in the data set.

<table>
<tr><td>

Example 7

Finding the Mode

</td><td>

Problem Each of 10 taste testers rated a new brand of barbecue sauce on a 10-point scale, where 1 = awful and 10 = excellent. Find the mode for the 10 ratings shown below.

8 7 9 6 8 10 9 9 5 7

Solution Because 9 occurs most often, the mode of the 10 taste-ratings is 9.

Look Back Note that the data are actually qualitative in nature (e.g., "awful," "excellent"). The mode is particularly useful for describing qualitative data. The modal category is simply the category (or class) that occurs most often.

■ **Now Work Exercise 39**

</td></tr>
</table>

Because it emphasizes data concentration, the mode is used with quantitative data sets to locate the region in which much of the data are concentrated. A retailer of men's clothing would be interested in the modal neck size and sleeve length of potential customers. The modal income class of the laborers in the United States is of interest to the Labor Department.

For some quantitative data sets, the mode may not be very meaningful. For example, consider the percentages of revenues spent on R&D by 50 companies, Table 2. A reexamination of the data reveals that three of the measurements are repeated three times: 6.5%, 6.9%, and 8.2%. Thus, there are three modes in the sample, and none is particularly useful as a measure of central tendency.

A more meaningful measure can be obtained from a relative frequency histogram for quantitative data. The class interval containing the largest relative frequency is called the **modal class.** Several definitions exist for locating the position of the mode within a modal class, but the simplest is to define the mode as the midpoint of the modal class. For example, examine the relative frequency histogram for the price quote processing times in Figure 12. You can see that the modal class is the interval (3.0–4.0). The mode (the midpoint) is 3.5. This modal class (and the mode itself) identifies the area in which the data are most concentrated, and in that sense it is a measure of central tendency. However, for most applications involving quantitative data, the mean and median provide more descriptive information than the mode.

<table>
<tr><td>

Example 8

Comparing the Mean, Median, and Mode— CEO Salaries

</td><td>

Problem Refer to *Forbes* magazine's "Executive Compensation Scoreboard," which lists the total annual pay for CEOs at the 500 largest U.S. firms. The data for the 2011 scoreboard, saved in the **CEO** file, includes the quantitative variables total annual pay (in millions of dollars) and age (in years). Find the mean, median, and mode for both of these variables. Which measure of central tendency is better for describing the distribution of total annual pay? Age?

Solution Measures of central tendency for the two variables were obtained using SPSS. The means, medians, and modes are displayed at the top of the SPSS printout, Figure 17.

For total annual pay, the mean, median, and mode are $9.25 million, $6.10 million, and $0, respectively. Note that the mean is much greater than the median, indicating that the data are highly skewed right. This rightward skewness (graphically shown on the histogram for total pay in Figure 17) is due to several exceptionally high CEO salaries in 2011. Consequently, we would probably want to use the median, $6.10 million, as the "typical" value for annual pay for CEOs at the 500 largest firms. The mode of $0 is the total pay value that occurs most often in the data set, but it is not very descriptive of the "center" of the total annual pay distribution. The mode reflects the fact that there were four CEOs who deferred their 2011 pay until the next year.

</td></tr>
</table>

Statistics

		CEO Pay ($mil)	Age (years)
N	Valid	478	500
	Missing	22	0
Mean		9.24692	56.62
Median		6.10000	56.00
Mode		.000	56

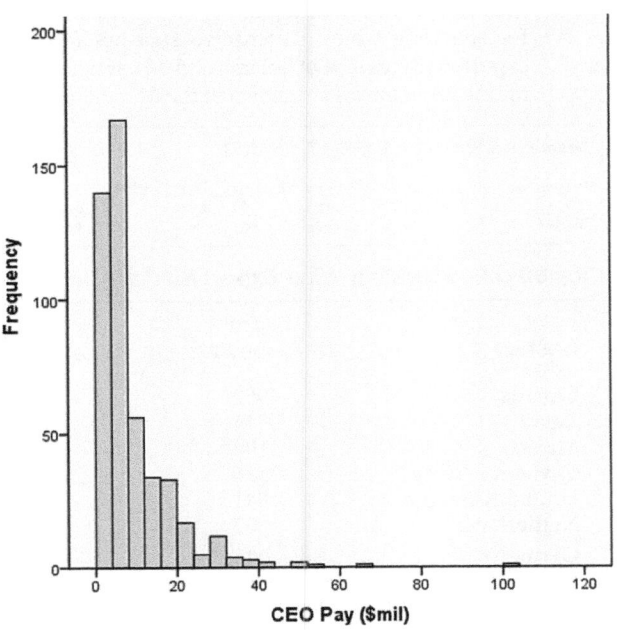

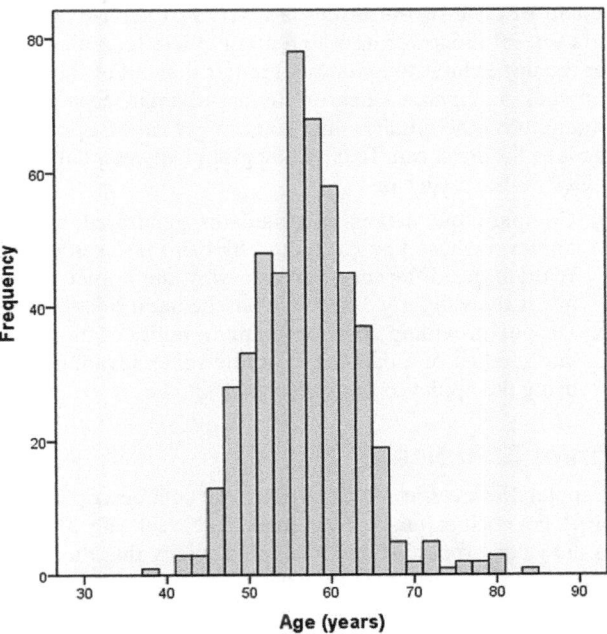

Figure 17
SPSS analysis of total 2011 pay and age for 500 CEOs

For age, the mean, median, and mode are 56.6, 56, and 56 years, respectively. All three values are nearly the same, which is typical of symmetric distributions. From the age histogram on the right in Figure 17, you can see that the age distribution is nearly symmetric. Consequently, any of the three measures of central tendency could be used to describe the "middle" of the age distribution.

Look Back The choice of which measure of central tendency to use will depend on the properties of the data set analyzed and on the application. Consequently, it is vital that you understand how the mean, median, and mode are computed.

■ **Now Work Exercise 44a, b**

Exercises 35–55

Learning the Mechanics

35 Calculate the mean and median of the following grade point averages:

NW

$$3.2 \quad 2.5 \quad 2.1 \quad 3.7 \quad 2.8 \quad 2.0$$

36 Calculate the mean for samples where

NW
a. $n = 10$, $\sum x = 85$
b. $n = 16$, $\sum x = 400$
c. $n = 45$, $\sum x = 35$
d. $n = 18$, $\sum x = 242$

37 Explain how the relationship between the mean and median provides information about the symmetry or skewness of the data's distribution.

38 Explain the difference between the calculation of the median for an odd and an even number of measurements. Construct one data set consisting of five measurements and another consisting of six measurements for which the medians are equal.

39 Calculate the mode, mean, and median of the following data:

NW

$$18 \quad 10 \quad 15 \quad 13 \quad 17 \quad 15 \quad 12 \quad 15 \quad 18 \quad 16 \quad 11$$

40 Calculate the mean, median, and mode for each of the following samples:

a. $7, -2, 3, 3, 0, 4$
b. $2, 3, 5, 3, 2, 3, 4, 3, 5, 1, 2, 3, 4$
c. $51, 50, 47, 50, 48, 41, 59, 68, 45, 37$

41 Describe how the mean compares to the median for a distribution as follows:
   a. Skewed to the left
   b. Skewed to the right
   c. Symmetric

⚙ Applet Exercise 1

Use the applet entitled *Mean versus Median* to find the mean and median of each of the three data sets in Exercise 40. For each data set, set the lower limit to a number less than all of the data, set the upper limit to a number greater than all of the data, and then click on *Update*. Click on the approximate location of each data item on the number line. You can get rid of a point by dragging it to the trash can. To clear the graph between data sets, simply click on the trash can.

   a. Compare the means and medians generated by the applet to those you calculated by hand in Exercise 40. If there are differences, explain why the applet might give values slightly different from the hand calculations.
   b. Despite providing only approximate values of the mean and median of a data set, describe some advantages of using the applet to find these values.

⚙ Applet Exercise 2

Use the applet *Mean versus Median* to illustrate your descriptions in Exercise 41. For each part **a, b,** and **c,** create a data set with 10 items that has the given property. Using the applet, verify that the mean and median have the relationship you described in Exercise 41.

⚙ Applet Exercise 3

Use the applet *Mean versus Median* to study the effect that an extreme value has on the difference between the mean and median. Begin by setting appropriate limits and plotting the given data on the number line provided in the applet.

0 6 7 7 8 8 8 9 9 10

   a. Describe the shape of the distribution and record the value of the mean and median. Based on the shape of the distribution, do the mean and median have the relationship that you would expect?
   b. Replace the extreme value of 0 with 2, then 4, and then 6. Record the mean and median each time. Describe what is happening to the mean as 0 is replaced by higher numbers. What is happening to the median? How is the difference between the mean and the median changing?
   c. Now replace 0 with 8. What values does the applet give you for the mean and the median? Explain why the mean and the median should be the same.

Applying the Concepts—Basic

42 Performance of stock screeners. Investment companies provide their clients with automated tools—called *stock screeners*—to help them select a portfolio of stocks to invest in. The American Association of Individual Investors (AAII) provides statistics on stock screeners at its Web site, www.aaii.com. The next table lists the annualized percentage return on investment (as compared to the Standard & Poor's 500 Index) for 13 randomly selected stock screeners. (*Note:* A negative annualized return reflects a stock portfolio that performed worse than the S&P 500.)

9.0 −.1 −1.6 14.6 16.0 7.7 19.9 9.8 3.2 24.8 17.6 10.7 9.1

   a. Compute the mean for the data set. Interpret its value.
   b. Compute the median for the data set. Interpret its value.

43 U.S. wine export markets. The data in the next table, compiled by the Center for International Trade Development (CITD), provide a listing of the top 30 U.S. export markets for sparkling wines. Descriptive statistics for the amount exported (thousands of dollars) and 3-year percentage change for the 30 countries are shown in the Minitab printout below.

Descriptive Statistics: EXPORT, CHANGE

Variable	N	N*	Mean	StDev	Minimum	Q1	Median	Q3	Maximum	IQR
EXPORT	30	0	653	1113	70	105	231	523	4952	418
CHANGE	28	2	481	1098	−49	21	156	499	5750	478

Top 30 U.S. Sparkling Wine Export Markets

Country	Export ($ Thousands)	3-Year Change (%)
Canada	4952	71.9
Japan	3714	−16.9
Mexico	2104	143.2
Cayman Islands	1576	280.7
United Kingdom	1041	465.8
Netherlands	807	550.8
Germany	645	658.8
Korea	482	20.5
France	449	−48.7
Russia	351	5750
Jamaica	350	21.5
China	339	539.6
Taiwan	309	505.9
Colombia	272	159
Hong Kong	232	114.8
Aruba	229	−31.6
Australia	225	1223.5
Haiti	191	478.8
Switzerland	181	70.8
Trinidad & Tobago	175	1490.9
Costa Rica	170	NA
Panama	126	447.8
Slovenia	106	NA
Neth. Antilles	103	−41.8
Bahamas	92	−20.7
New Zealand	91	193.5
Honduras	74	51
Philippines	72	242.9
Greece	71	153.6
Belgium	70	−16.7

Source: "Best Export Markets for U.S. Wines, 2008," *Center for International Trade Development* (Table 11.A-3). Copyright © 2008 by Center for International Trade Development. Reprinted with permission.

   a. Locate the mean amount exported on the printout and practically interpret its value.
   b. Locate the median amount exported on the printout and practically interpret its value.
   c. Locate the mean 3-year percentage change on the printout and practically interpret its value.
   d. Locate the median 3-year percentage change on the printout and practically interpret its value.

44 Surface roughness of oil field pipe. Oil field pipes are internally coated in order to prevent corrosion. Researchers at the University of Louisiana, Lafayette, investigated the influence that coating may have on the surface roughness of oil field pipes (*Anti-corrosion Methods and Materials*, Vol. 50, 2003). A scanning probe instrument was used to measure the surface roughness of each in a sample of 20 sections of coated interior pipe. The data (in micrometers) are provided in the table.

1.72	2.50	2.16	2.13	1.06	2.24	2.31	2.03	1.09	1.40
2.57	2.64	1.26	2.05	1.19	2.13	1.27	1.51	2.41	1.95

Source: Farshed, F., & Pesacreta, T. "Coated pipe interior surface roughness as measured by three scanning probe instruments." *Anti-corrosion Methods and Materials.* Vol. 50, No. 1, 2003 (Table III).

NW **a.** Find and interpret the mean of the sample.

NW **b.** Find and interpret the median of the sample.

c. Which measure of central tendency—the mean or the median—best describes the surface roughness of the sampled pipe sections? Explain.

45 **Top research universities.** Each year, the Center for Measuring University Performance produces a report on America's top research universities. The total expenditures (in thousands of dollars) for research for the top 20 ranked universities from the *2010 Annual Report* are listed in the table.

RESRCH

Rank	Institution	Expenditures ($ thousands)	Type
1	Johns Hopkins University	1,680,927	Private
2	University of California–San Francisco	885,182	Public
3	University of Wisconsin	881,777	Public
4	University of Michigan	876,390	Public
5	University of California–Los Angeles	871,478	Public
6	University of California–San Diego	842,027	Public
7	Duke University	766,906	Private
8	University of Washington	765,135	Public
9	University of Pennsylvania	708,244	Private
10	Ohio State University	702,592	Public
11	Stanford University	688,225	Private
12	University of Minnesota	682,662	Public
13	Massachusetts Institute of Technology	659,626	Private
14	University of California–Davis	642,519	Public
15	Pennsylvania State University	620,432	Public
16	University of Pittsburgh	595,627	Public
17	University of California–Berkeley	591,770	Public
18	University of Florida	584,170	Public
19	Texas A&M University	582,365	Public
20	Washington University–St. Louis	563,967	Private

Source: Based on Elizabeth D. Capaldi, John V. Lombardi, Craig W. Abbey, and Diane D. Craig, THE TOP AMERICAN RESEARCH UNIVERSITIES: 2010 Annual Report. © The Center for Measuring University Performance.

a. Find the mean of the research expenditures for the top 20 ranked universities. Interpret this value.

b. Find the median of the research expenditures for the top 20 ranked universities. Interpret this value.

c. Consider a university president who is interested in the distribution of research expenditures of all American universities. Would the mean, part **a,** be a good measure of the center of this distribution? Explain.

46 **Corporate sustainability of CPA firms.** Refer to the *Business and Society* (March 2011) study on the sustainability behaviors of CPA corporations, Exercise 23. Recall that the level of support for corporate sustainability (measured on a quantitative scale ranging from 0 to 160 points) was obtained for each 992 senior managers at CPA firms. Numerical measures of central tendency for level of support are shown in the accompanying Minitab printout.

CORSUS

Descriptive Statistics: Support

Variable	N	Mean	Minimum	Median	Maximum	Mode	N for Mode
Support	992	67.755	0.000	68.000	155.000	64	20

a. Locate the mean on the printout. Comment on the accuracy of the statement: "On average, the level of support for corporate sustainability for the 992 senior managers was 67.76 points."

b. Locate the median on the printout. Comment on the accuracy of the statement: "Half of the 992 senior managers reported a level of support for corporate sustainability below 68 points."

c. Locate the mode on the printout. Comment on the accuracy of the statement: "Most of the 992 senior managers reported a level of support for corporate sustainability below 64 points."

d. Based on the values of the measures of central tendency, make a statement about the type of skewness (if any) that exists in the distribution of 992 support levels. Check your answer by examining the histogram shown in Exercise 23.

Applying the Concepts—Intermediate

47 **Is honey a cough remedy?** Refer to the *Archives of Pediatrics and Adolescent Medicine* (Dec. 2007) study of honey as a remedy for coughing, Exercise 30. Recall that the 105 ill children in the sample were randomly divided into three groups: those who received a dosage of an over-the-counter cough medicine (DM), those who received a dosage of honey (H), and those who received no dosage (control group). The coughing improvement scores (as determined by the children's parents) for the patients are reproduced in the accompanying table.

HCOUGH

a. Find the median improvement score for the honey dosage group.

Honey Dosage:	12	11	15	11	10	13	10	4	15	16	9	14
	10	6	10	8	11	12	12	8	12	9	11	15
	10	15	9	13	8	12	10	8	9	5	12	

DM Dosage:	4	6	9	4	7	7	7	9	12	10	11	6	3	4
	9	12	7	6	8	12	12	4	12	13	7	10		
	13	9	4	4	10	15	9							

No Dosage (Control):	5	8	6	1	0	8	12	8	7	7	1	6	7	7	12
	7	9	7	9	5	11	9	5	6	8					
	8	6	7	10	9	4	8	7	3	1	4	3			

Source: Based on Paul, I. M., et al. "Effect of honey, dextromethorphan, and no treatment on nocturnal cough and sleep quality for coughing children and their parents." *Archives of Pediatrics and Adolescent Medicine,* Vol. 161, No. 12. Dec. 2007 (data simulated).

b. Find the median improvement score for the DM dosage group.

c. Find the median improvement score for the control group.

d. Based on the results, parts **a–c,** what conclusions can pediatric researchers draw?

48 Crude oil biodegradation. Refer to the *Journal of Petroleum Geology* (April 2010) study of the environmental factors associated with biodegradation in crude oil reservoirs, Exercise 29. Recall that amount of dioxide (milligrams/liter) and presence/absence of crude oil was determined for each of 16 water specimens collected from a mine reservoir. The data are repeated in the accompanying table.

BIODEG

Dioxide Amount	Crude Oil Present
3.3	No
0.5	Yes
1.3	Yes
0.4	Yes
0.1	No
4.0	No
0.3	No
0.2	Yes
2.4	No
2.4	No
1.4	No
0.5	Yes
0.2	Yes
4.0	No
4.0	No
4.0	No

Source: Based on A. Permanyer, J. L. R. Gallego, M. A. Caja, and D. Dessort, "Crude Oil Biodegradation and Environmental Factors at the Riutort Oil Shale Mine, SE Pyrenees." JOURNAL OF PETROLEUM GEOLOGY, Vol. 33, No. 2, April 2010, Table 1.

a. Find the mean dioxide level of the 16 water specimens. Interpret this value.

b. Find the median dioxide level of the 16 water specimens. Interpret this value.

c. Find the mode of the 16 dioxide levels. Interpret this value.

d. Find the median dioxide level of the 10 water specimens with no crude oil present.

e. Find the median dioxide level of the 6 water specimens with crude oil present.

f. Compare the results, parts **d** and **e.** Make a statement about the association between dioxide level and presence/absence of crude oil.

49 Symmetric or skewed? Would you expect the data sets described below to possess relative frequency distributions that are symmetric, skewed to the right, or skewed to the left? Explain.

a. The salaries of all persons employed by a large university

b. The grades on an easy test

c. The grades on a difficult test

d. The amounts of time students in your class studied last week

e. The ages of automobiles on a used-car lot

f. The amounts of time spent by students on a difficult examination (maximum time is 50 minutes)

50 Ranking driving performance of professional golfers. A group of Northeastern University researchers developed a new method for ranking the total driving performance of golfers on the Professional Golf Association (PGA) tour (*The Sport Journal,* Winter 2007). The method requires knowing a golfer's average driving distance (yards) and driving accuracy (percent of drives that land in the fairway). The values of these two variables are used to compute a driving performance index. Data for the top 40 PGA golfers (as ranked by the new method) are saved in the accompanying file. The first five and last five observations are listed in the table below.

PGA

Rank	Player	Driving Distance (yards)	Driving Accuracy (%)	Driving Performance Index
1	Woods	316.1	54.6	3.58
2	Perry	304.7	63.4	3.48
3	Gutschewski	310.5	57.9	3.27
4	Wetterich	311.7	56.6	3.18
5	Hearn	295.2	68.5	2.82
⋮	⋮	⋮	⋮	⋮
36	Senden	291	66	1.31
37	Mickelson	300	58.7	1.30
38	Watney	298.9	59.4	1.26
39	Trahan	295.8	61.8	1.23
40	Pappas	309.4	50.6	1.17

Source: Based on Frederick Wiseman, Ph.D., Mohamed Habibullah, Ph.D., and Mustafa Yilmaz, Ph.D, "Ranking Driving Performance on the PGA Tour." SPORTS JOURNAL, Vol. 10, No. 1, Winter 2007 (Table 2).

a. Find the mean, median, and mode for the 40 driving performance index values.

b. Interpret each of the measures of central tendency, part **a.**

c. Use the results, part **a,** to make a statement about the type of skewness in the distribution of driving performance indexes. Support your statement with a graph.

51 Semester hours taken by CPA candidates. In order to become a certified public accountant (CPA), you must pass the Uniform CPA Exam. Many states require a minimum of 150 semester hours of college education before a candidate can sit for the CPA exam. However, traditionally, colleges only require 128 semester hours for an undergraduate degree. A study of whether the "extra" 22 hours of college credit is warranted for CPA candidates was published in the *Journal of Accounting and Public Policy* (Spring 2002). For one aspect of the study, researchers sampled over 100,000 first-time candidates for the CPA exam and recorded the total semester hours of college credit for each candidate. The mean and median for the data set were 141.31 and 140 hours, respectively. Interpret these values. Make a statement about the type of skewness, if any, that exists in the distribution of total semester hours.

52 Doctors and ethics. Refer to the *Journal of Medical Ethics* (Vol. 32, 2006) study of physicians' use of ethics consultation, Exercise 31. In addition to the qualitative variable, *use of ethics consultation in the future* ("yes" or "no"), one of the quantitative variables measured in the survey of physicians was *length of time in practice* (i.e., years of experience). Recall that the medical researchers hypothesized that physicians who refused to use ethics consultation in the future would tend to be older, more experienced physicians.

ETHICS

a. Access the data file and find the mean, median, and mode for the *length of time in practice* (i.e., years of experience) variable. Give a practical interpretation of each of these measures of central tendency.

b. Consider only the physicians who would refuse to use ethics consultation in the future. Find the mean, median, and mode for the *length of time in practice* for these physicians. Practically interpret the results.

c. Repeat part **b** for physicians who would use ethics consultation in the future.

d. Use the results, parts **b** and **c,** to comment on the medical researchers' theory.

Applying the Concepts—Advanced

53 **Time in bankruptcy.** Refer to the *Financial Management* (Spring 1995) study of prepackaged bankruptcy filings, Exercise 32. Recall that each of 49 firms that negotiated a reorganization plan with its creditors prior to filing for bankruptcy was classified in one of three categories: joint exchange offer with prepack, prepack solicitation only, and no prefiling vote held. Consider the quantitative variable length of time in bankruptcy (months) saved in the accompanying file. Is it reasonable to use a single number (e.g., mean or median) to describe the center of the time-in-bankruptcy distributions? Or should three "centers" be calculated, one for each of the three categories of prepack firms? Explain.

BNKRPT

54 **Active nuclear power plants.** The U.S. Energy Information Administration monitors all nuclear power plants operating in the United States. The next table lists the number of active nuclear power plants operating in each of a sample of 20 states.

NUKES

a. Find the mean, median, and mode of this data set.

b. Eliminate the largest value from the data set and repeat part **a.** What effect does dropping this measurement have on the measures of central tendency found in part **a**?

c. Arrange the 20 values in the table from lowest to highest. Next, eliminate the lowest two values and the highest two values from the data set and find the mean of the remaining data values. The result is called a *10% trimmed mean,* because it is calculated after removing the highest 10% and the lowest 10% of the data values. What advantages does a trimmed mean have over the regular arithmetic mean?

State	Number of Power Plants	State	Number of Power Plants
Alabama	5	New Hampshire	1
Arizona	2	New York	6
California	4	North Carolina	5
Florida	5	Ohio	3
Georgia	4	Pennsylvania	9
Illinois	11	South Carolina	7
Kansas	1	Tennessee	3
Louisiana	2	Texas	4
Massachusetts	1	Vermont	1
Mississippi	1	Wisconsin	3

Source: Data from STATISTICAL ABSTRACT OF THE UNITED STATES, 2010 (Table 907). U.S. Energy Information Administration, Electric Power Annual.

55 **Professional athletes' salaries.** The salaries of superstar professional athletes receive much attention in the media. The multimillion-dollar long-term contract is now commonplace among this elite group. Nevertheless, rarely does a season pass without negotiations between one or more of the players' associations and team owners for additional salary and fringe benefits for *all* players in their particular sports.

a. If a players' association wanted to support its argument for higher "average" salaries, which measure of central tendency do you think it should use? Why?

b. To refute the argument, which measure of central tendency should the owners apply to the players' salaries? Why?

4 Numerical Measures of Variability

Measures of central tendency provide only a partial description of a quantitative data set. The description is incomplete without a **measure of the variability,** or **spread,** of the data set. Knowledge of the data's variability along with its center can help us visualize the shape of a data set as well as its extreme values.

For example, suppose we are comparing the profit margin per construction job (as a percentage of the total bid price) for 100 construction jobs for each of two cost estimators working for a large construction company. The histograms for the two sets of 100 profit margin measurements are shown in Figure 18. If you examine the two histograms, you will notice that both data sets are symmetric with equal modes, medians, and means. However, cost estimator A (Figure 18a) has profit margins spread with almost equal relative frequency over the measurement classes, while cost estimator B (Figure 18b) has profit margins clustered about the center of the distribution. Thus, estimator B's profit margins are *less variable* than estimator A's. Consequently, you can see that we need a measure of variability as well as a measure of central tendency to describe a data set.

Perhaps the simplest measure of the variability of a quantitative data set is its *range.*

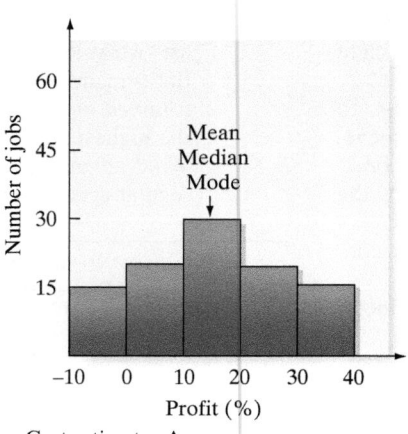

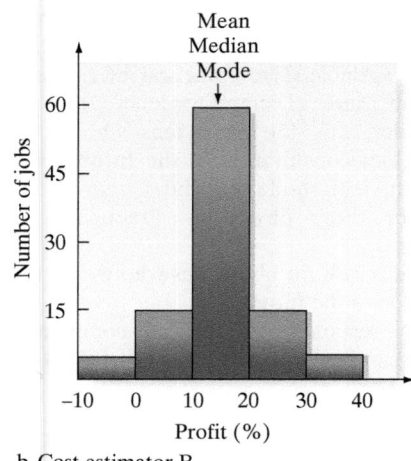

Figure 18

Profit margin histograms for two cost estimators

a. Cost estimator A

b. Cost estimator B

> The **range** of a quantitative data set is equal to the largest measurement minus the smallest measurement.

The range is easy to compute and easy to understand, but it is a rather insensitive measure of data variation when the data sets are large. This is because two data sets can have the same range and be vastly different with respect to data variation. This phenomenon is demonstrated in Figure 18. Although the ranges are equal and all central tendency measures are the same for these two symmetric data sets, there is an obvious difference between the two sets of measurements. The difference is that estimator B's profit margins tend to be more stable—that is, to pile up or to cluster about the center of the data set. In contrast, estimator A's profit margins are more spread out over the range, indicating a higher incidence of some high profit margins but also a greater risk of losses. Thus, even though the ranges are equal, the profit margin record of estimator A is more variable than that of estimator B, indicating a distinct difference in their cost-estimating characteristics.

Let's see if we can find a measure of data variation that is more sensitive than the range. Consider the two samples in Table 5: Each has five measurements. (We have ordered the numbers for convenience.)

Note that both samples have a mean of 3 and that we have also calculated the distance and direction, or *deviation*, between each measurement and the mean. What information do these deviations contain? If they tend to be large in magnitude, as in sample 1, the data are spread out, or highly variable, as shown in Figure 19a. If the deviations are mostly small, as in sample 2, the data are clustered around the mean, $\bar{x}$, and therefore do not exhibit much variability, as shown in Figure 19b. You can see that these deviations provide information about the variability of the sample measurements.

The next step is to condense the information in these deviations into a single numerical measure of variability. Averaging the deviations from $\bar{x}$ won't help because the negative and positive deviations cancel; that is, the sum of the deviations (and thus the average deviation) is always equal to zero.

Table 5	Two Hypothetical Data Sets	
	Sample 1	Sample 2
Measurements	$1, 2, 3, 4, 5$	$2, 3, 3, 3, 4$
Mean	$\bar{x} = \dfrac{1 + 2 + 3 + 4 + 5}{5} = \dfrac{15}{5} = 3$	$\bar{x} = \dfrac{2 + 3 + 3 + 3 + 4}{5} = \dfrac{15}{5} = 3$
Deviations of measurement values from $\bar{x}$	$(1 - 3), (2 - 3), (3 - 3), (4 - 3),$ $(5 - 3),$ or $-2, -1, 0, 1, 2$	$(2 - 3), (3 - 3), (3 - 3), (3 - 3),$ $(4 - 3),$ or $-1, 0, 0, 0, 1$

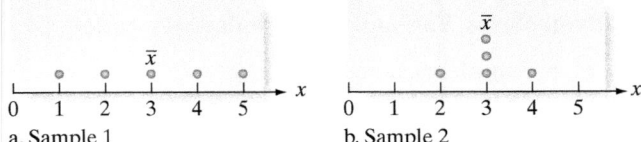

Figure 19
Dot plots for two data sets

a. Sample 1

b. Sample 2

Two methods come to mind for dealing with the fact that positive and negative deviations from the mean cancel. The first is to treat all the deviations as though they were positive, ignoring the sign of the negative deviations. We won't pursue this line of thought because the resulting measure of variability (the mean of the absolute values of the deviations) presents analytical difficulties beyond the scope of this text. A second method of eliminating the minus signs associated with the deviations is to square them. The quantity we can calculate from the squared deviations will provide a meaningful description of the variability of a data set and present fewer analytical difficulties in inference making.

To use the squared deviations calculated from a data set, we first calculate the *sample variance*.

> The **sample variance** for a sample of n measurements is equal to the sum of the squared deviations from the mean divided by $(n - 1)$. The symbol s^2 is used to represent the sample variance.

> **Formula for the Sample Variance**
>
> $$s^2 = \frac{\sum_{i=1}^{n}(x_i - \bar{x})^2}{n - 1}$$
>
> *Note:* A shortcut formula for calculating s^2 is
>
> $$s^2 = \frac{\sum_{i=1}^{n}x_i^2 - \frac{\left(\sum_{i=1}^{n}x_i\right)^2}{n}}{n - 1}$$

Referring to the two samples in Table 5, you can calculate the variance for sample 1 as follows:

$$s^2 = \frac{(1 - 3)^2 + (2 - 3)^2 + (3 - 3)^2 + (4 - 3)^2 + (5 - 3)^2}{5 - 1}$$

$$= \frac{4 + 1 + 0 + 1 + 4}{4} = 2.5$$

The second step in finding a meaningful measure of data variability is to calculate the *standard deviation* of the data set.

> The **sample standard deviation,** s, is defined as the positive square root of the sample variance, s^2. Thus, $s = \sqrt{s^2}$.

The population variance, denoted by the symbol σ^2 (sigma squared), is the average of the squared distances of the measurements on *all* units in the population from the mean, μ, and σ (sigma) is the square root of this quantity. Because we rarely, if ever, have access to the population data, we do not compute σ^2 or σ. We simply denote these two quantities by their respective symbols.*

*The population variance, σ^2, is calculated as $\sigma^2 = \dfrac{\sum_{i=1}^{N}(x_i - \mu)^2}{N}$, where N is the size of the population.

> **Symbols for Variance and Standard Deviation**
>
> s^2 = Sample variance
>
> s = Sample standard deviation
>
> σ^2 = Population variance
>
> σ = Population standard deviation

Notice that, unlike the variance, the standard deviation is expressed in the original units of measurement. For example, if the original measurements are in dollars, the variance is expressed in the peculiar units "dollars squared," but the standard deviation is expressed in dollars. Consequently, you can think of s as a "typical" distance of an observation x from its mean, $\bar{x}$.

You may wonder why we use the divisor $(n - 1)$ instead of n when calculating the sample variance. Wouldn't using n be more logical so that the sample variance would be the average squared deviation from the mean? The trouble is that using n tends to produce an underestimate of the population variance, σ^2, so we use $(n - 1)$ in the denominator to provide the appropriate correction for this tendency.* Because sample statistics such as s^2 are primarily used to estimate population parameters such as σ^2, $(n - 1)$ is preferred to n when defining the sample variance.

Example	9

Computing Measures of Variation

Problem Calculate the variance and standard deviation of the following sample: 2, 3, 3, 3, 4.

Solution If you calculate the values of s and s^2 using the formula in the box on the previous page, you first need to compute $\bar{x}$. From the table below, we see that $\Sigma x = 15$. Thus, $\bar{x} = \dfrac{\Sigma x}{n} = \dfrac{15}{5} = 3$. Now, for each measurement, find $(x - \bar{x})$ and $(x - \bar{x})^2$, as shown.

x	$(x - \bar{x})$	$(x - \bar{x})^2$
2	-1	1
3	0	0
3	0	0
3	0	0
4	1	1
$\Sigma x = 15$		$\Sigma(x - \bar{x})^2 = 2$

Then we use[†]

$$s^2 = \frac{\sum_{i=1}^{n}(x - \bar{x})^2}{n - 1} = \frac{2}{5 - 1} = \frac{2}{4} = .5$$

$$s = \sqrt{.5} = .71$$

Look Ahead As the sample size n increases, these calculations can become very tedious. As the next example shows, we can use the computer to find s^2 and s.

Now Work Exercise 57

*_Appropriate_ here means that s^2 with the divisor $(n - 1)$ is an _unbiased estimator_ of σ^2.
[†]When calculating s^2, how many decimal places should you carry? Although there are no rules for the rounding procedure, it's reasonable to retain twice as many decimal places in s^2 as you ultimately wish to have in s. If you wish to calculate s to the nearest hundredth (two decimal places), for example, you should calculate s^2 to the nearest ten-thousandth (four decimal places).

Example 10

Finding Measures of Variation on a Printout— R&D Expenditures

Descriptive statistics (Quantitative data):

Statistic	RDPct
No. of observations	50
Minimum	5.2000
Maximum	13.5000
Range	8.3000
1st Quartile	7.1000
Median	8.0500
3rd Quartile	9.5750
Mean	8.4920
Variance (n-1)	3.9228
Standard deviation (n-1)	1.9806

Figure 20

XLSTAT numerical descriptive measures for 50 R&D percentages

Problem Use the computer to find the sample variance s^2 and the sample standard deviation s for the 50 companies' percentages of revenues spent on R&D, given in Table 2.

Solution The XLSTAT printout describing the R&D percentage data is reproduced in Figure 20. The variance and standard deviation, highlighted on the printout, are $s^2 = 3.9228$ and $s = 1.9806$. The value $s = 1.98$ represents a typical deviation of an R&D percentage from the sample mean, $\bar{x} = 8.49\%$. We have more to say about the interpretation of s in the next section.

Now Work Exercise 67

You now know that the standard deviation measures the variability of a set of data. The larger the standard deviation, the more variable the data. The smaller the standard deviation, the less variable the data. But how can we practically interpret the standard deviation and use it to make inferences? This is the topic of Section 5.

Exercises 56–70

Learning the Mechanics

56 Answer the following questions about variability of data sets:
  a. What is the primary disadvantage of using the range to compare the variability of data sets?
  b. Describe the sample variance using words rather than a formula. Do the same with the population variance.
  c. Can the variance of a data set ever be negative? Explain. Can the variance ever be smaller than the standard deviation? Explain.

57 Calculate the range, variance, and standard deviation for the following samples:
  a. $4, 2, 1, 0, 1$
  b. $1, 6, 2, 2, 3, 0, 3$
  c. $8, -2, 1, 3, 5, 4, 4, 1, 3, 3$
  d. $0, 2, 0, 0, -1, 1, -2, 1, 0, -1, 1, -1, 0, -3, -2, -1, 0, 1$

58 Calculate the variance and standard deviation for samples where
  a. $n = 10, \Sigma x^2 = 84, \Sigma x = 20$
  b. $n = 40, \Sigma x^2 = 380, \Sigma x = 100$
  c. $n = 20, \Sigma x^2 = 18, \Sigma x = 17$

59 Compute $\bar{x}$, s^2, and s for each of the following data sets. If appropriate, specify the units in which your answer is expressed.
  a. $3, 1, 10, 10, 4$
  b. 8 feet, 10 feet, 32 feet, 5 feet
  c. $-1, -4, -3, 1, -4, -4$
  d. $\frac{1}{5}$ ounce, $\frac{1}{5}$ ounce, $\frac{1}{5}$ ounce, $\frac{2}{5}$ ounce, $\frac{1}{5}$ ounce, $\frac{4}{5}$ ounce

60 Calculate the range, variance, and standard deviation for the following samples:
  a. $39, 42, 40, 37, 41$
  b. $100, 4, 7, 96, 80, 3, 1, 10, 2$
  c. $100, 4, 7, 30, 80, 30, 42, 2$

61 Using only integers between 0 and 10, construct two data sets with at least 10 observations each that have the same range but different means. Construct a dot plot for each of your data sets, and mark the mean of each data set on its dot diagram.

62 Using only integers between 0 and 10, construct two data sets with at least 10 observations each so that the two sets have the same mean but different variances. Construct dot plots for each of your data sets and mark the mean of each data set on its dot diagram.

63 Consider the following sample of five measurements: 2, 1, 1, 0, 3.
  a. Calculate the range, s^2, and s.
  b. Add 3 to each measurement and repeat part **a.**
  c. Subtract 4 from each measurement and repeat part **a.**
  d. Considering your answers to parts **a, b,** and **c,** what seems to be the effect on the variability of a data set by adding the same number to or subtracting the same number from each measurement?

Applet Exercise 4

Use the applet entitled *Standard Deviation* to find the standard deviation of each of the four data sets in Exercise 57. For each data set, set the lower limit to a number less than all of the data, set the upper limit to a number greater than all of the data, and then click on *Update*. Click on the approximate location of each data item on the number line. You can get rid of a point by dragging it to the trash can. To clear the graph between data sets, simply click on the trash can.
  a. Compare the standard deviations generated by the applet to those you calculated by hand in Exercise 57. If there are differences, explain why the applet might give values slightly different from the hand calculations.
  b. Despite providing a slightly different value of the standard deviation of a data set, describe some advantages of using the applet.

Applet Exercise 5

Use the applet *Standard Deviation* to study the effect that multiplying or dividing each number in a data set by the same number has on the standard deviation. Begin by setting appropriate limits and plotting the given data on the number line provided in the applet.

0 1 1 1 2 2 3 4

a. Record the standard deviation. Then multiply each data item by 2, plot the new data items, and record the standard deviation. Repeat the process, first multiplying each of the original data items by 3 and then by 4. Describe what is happening to the standard deviation as the data items are multiplied by higher numbers. Divide each standard deviation by the standard deviation of the original data set. Do you see a pattern? Explain.

b. Divide each of the original data items by 2, plot the new data, and record the standard deviation. Repeat the process, first dividing each of the original data items by 3 and then by 4. Describe what is happening to the standard deviation as the data items are divided by higher numbers. Divide each standard deviation by the standard deviation of the original data set. Do you see a pattern? Explain.

c. Using your results from parts **a** and **b,** describe what happens to the standard deviation of a data set when each of the data items in the set is multiplied or divided by a fixed number *n*. Experiment by repeating parts **a** and **b** for other data sets if you need to.

Applet Exercise 6

Use the applet *Standard Deviation* to study the effect that an extreme value has on the standard deviation. Begin by setting appropriate limits and plotting the given data on the number line provided in the applet.

0 6 7 7 8 8 8 9 9 10

a. Record the standard deviation. Replace the extreme value of 0 with 2, then 4, and then 6. Record the standard deviation each time. Describe what is happening to the standard deviation as 0 is replaced by higher numbers.

b. How would the standard deviation of the data set compare to the original standard deviation if the 0 were replaced by 16? Explain.

Applying the Concepts—Basic

64 Performance of stock screeners. Refer to the American Association of Individual Investors (AAII) statistics on SCREEN stock screeners, Exercise 42. Annualized percentage return on investment (as compared to the Standard & Poor's 500 Index) for 13 randomly selected stock screeners are reproduced in the table.

| 9.0 | −.1 | −1.6 | 14.6 | 16.0 | 7.7 | 19.9 | 9.8 | 3.2 | 24.8 | 17.6 | 10.7 | 9.1 |

a. Find the range of the data for the 13 stock screeners. Give the units of measurement for the range.

b. Find the variance of the data for the 13 stock screeners. If possible, give the units of measurement for the variance.

c. Find the standard deviation of the data for the 13 stock screeners. Give the units of measurement for the standard deviation.

65 U.S. wine export markets. Refer to the data on the top 30 U.S. export markets for sparkling wines, compiled by WINEX the Center for International Trade Development (CITD), given in Exercise 43. The Minitab descriptive statistics printout for the amount exported (thousands of dollars) and 3-year percentage change for the 30 countries is reproduced below.

Descriptive Statistics: EXPORT, CHANGE

Variable	N	N*	Mean	StDev	Minimum	Q1	Median	Q3	Maximum	IQR
EXPORT	30	0	653	1113	70	105	231	523	4952	418
CHANGE	28	2	481	1098	-49	21	156	499	5750	478

a. Use the information on the printout to find the range of the amount exported.

b. Locate the standard deviation of the amount exported on the printout.

c. Use the result, part **b**, to find the variance of the amount exported.

66 Is honey a cough remedy? Refer to the *Archives of Pediatrics and Adolescent Medicine* (Dec. 2007) study of HCOUGH honey as a remedy for coughing, Exercise 30 and 47. The coughing improvement scores (as determined by the children's parents) for the patients in the over-the-counter cough medicine dosage (DM) group, honey dosage group, and control group are reproduced in the accompanying table.

Honey Dosage:	12	11	15	11	10	13	10	4	15	16	9
	14	10	6	10	8	11	12	12	8		
	12	9	11	15	10	15	9	13	8	12	10
	8	9	5	12							
DM Dosage:	4	6	9	4	7	7	7	9	12	10	11	6
	3	4	9	12	7	6	8	12	12	4	12	
	13	7	10	13	9	4	4	10	15	9		
No Dosage (Control):	5	8	6	1	0	8	12	8	7	7	1	6
	7	7	12	7	9	7	9	5	11	9	5	
	6	8	8	6	7	10	9	4	8	7	3	1	4	3

Source: Based on Paul, I. M., et al. "Effect of honey, dextromethorphan, and no treatment on nocturnal cough and sleep quality for coughing children and their parents," *Archives of Pediatrics and Adolescent Medicine*, Vol. 161, No. 12, Dec. 2007 (data simulated).

a. Find the standard deviation of the improvement scores for the honey dosage group.

b. Find the standard deviation of the improvement scores for the DM dosage group.

c. Find the standard deviation of the improvement scores for the control group.

d. Based on the results, parts **a–c,** which group appears to have the most variability in coughing improvement scores? The least variability?

Applying the Concepts—Intermediate

67 Corporate sustainability of CPA firms. Refer to the *Business and Society* (March 2011) study on the CORSUS sustainability behaviors of CPA corporations, Exercise 46. Numerical measures of variation for level of support for the 992 senior managers are shown in the accompanying Minitab printout.

Descriptive Statistics: Support

Variable	N	Mean	StDev	Variance	Minimum	Maximum	Range
Support	992	67.755	26.871	722.036	0.000	155.000	155.000

a. Locate the range on the printout. Comment on the accuracy of the statement: "The difference between the largest and smallest values of level of support for the 992 senior managers is 155 points."

b. Locate the variance on the printout. Comment on the accuracy of the statement: "On average, the level of support for corporate sustainability for the 992 senior managers is 722 points."

c. Locate the standard deviation on the printout. Does the distribution of support levels for the 992 senior managers have more or less variation than another distribution with a standard deviation of 50? Explain.

d. Which measure of variation best describes the distribution of 992 support levels? Explain.

68 **Doctors and ethics.** Refer to the *Journal of Medical Ethics* (Vol. 32, 2006) study of physicians' use of ethics consultation, Exercise 52. Again, consider an analysis of the quantitative variable, *length of time in practice* (i.e., years of experience).

ETHICS

a. Access the data file and find the range, variance, and standard deviation for the *length of time in practice* (i.e., years of experience) variable. If possible, give a practical interpretation of each of these measures of variation.

b. Consider only the physicians who would refuse to use ethics consultation in the future. Find the standard deviation for the *length of time in practice* for these physicians.

c. Repeat part **b** for physicians who would use ethics consultation in the future.

d. Use the results, parts **b** and **c**, to compare the variation in the length of time in practice distributions for physicians who would use and who would refuse ethics consultation in the future.

69 **Active nuclear power plants.** Refer to Exercise 54 and the U.S. Energy Information Administration's data on the number of nuclear power plants operating in each of 20 states.

NUKES

a. Find the range, variance, and standard deviation of this data set.

b. Eliminate the largest value from the data set and repeat part **a.** What effect does dropping this measurement have on the measures of variation found in part **a?**

c. Eliminate the smallest and largest value from the data set and repeat part **a.** What effect does dropping both of these measurements have on the measures of variation found in part **a?**

Applying the Concepts—Advanced

70 **Estimating production time.** A widely used technique for estimating the length of time it takes workers to produce a product is the **time study.** In a time study, the task to be studied is divided into measurable parts, and each is timed with a stopwatch or filmed for later analysis. For each worker, this process is repeated many times for each subtask. Then the average and standard deviation of the time required to complete each subtask are computed for each worker. A worker's overall time to complete the task under study is then determined by adding his or her subtask-time averages (Gaither and Frazier, *Operations Management*, 2001). The data (in minutes) given in the table are the result of a time study of a production operation involving two subtasks.

TIMES

	Worker A		Worker B	
Repetition	Subtask 1	Subtask 2	Subtask 1	Subtask 2
1	30	2	31	7
2	28	4	30	2
3	31	3	32	6
4	38	3	30	5
5	25	2	29	4
6	29	4	30	1
7	30	3	31	4

a. Find the overall time it took each worker to complete the manufacturing operation under study.

b. For each worker, find the standard deviation of the seven times for subtask 1.

c. In the context of this problem, what are the standard deviations you computed in part **b** measuring?

d. Repeat part **b** for subtask 2.

e. If you could choose workers similar to A or workers similar to B to perform subtasks 1 and 2, which type would you assign to each subtask? Explain your decisions on the basis of your answers to parts **a–d.**

5 Using the Mean and Standard Deviation to Describe Data

We've seen that if we are comparing the variability of two samples selected from a population, the sample with the larger standard deviation is the more variable of the two. Thus, we know how to interpret the standard deviation on a relative or comparative basis, but we haven't explained how it provides a measure of variability for a single sample.

To understand how the standard deviation provides a measure of variability of a data set, consider a specific data set and answer the following questions: How many measurements are within 1 standard deviation of the mean? How many measurements are within 2 standard deviations? For a specific data set, we can answer these questions by counting the number of measurements in each of the intervals. However, if we are interested in obtaining a general answer to these questions, the problem is more difficult.

Tables 6 and 7 give two sets of answers to the questions of how many measurements fall within 1, 2, and 3 standard deviations of the mean. The first, which applies to *any* set of data, is derived from a theorem proved by the Russian mathematician P. L. Chebyshev. The second, which applies to **mound-shaped, symmetric distributions** of data (where the mean, median, and mode are all about the same), is based upon empirical evidence that has accumulated over the years. However, the percentages given for the intervals in Table 7 provide remarkably good approximations even when the distribution of the data is slightly skewed or asymmetric. Note that both rules apply to either population data sets or sample data sets.

Table 6	Using the Mean and Standard Deviation to Describe Data: Chebyshev's Rule

Chebyshev's Rule applies to any data set, regardless of the shape of the frequency distribution of the data.

   a. No useful information is provided on the fraction of measurements that fall within 1 standard deviation of the mean [i.e., within the interval $(\bar{x} - s, \bar{x} + s)$ for samples and $(\mu - \sigma, \mu + \sigma)$ for populations].

   b. At least $\frac{3}{4}$ will fall within 2 standard deviations of the mean [i.e., within the interval $(\bar{x} - 2s, \bar{x} + 2s)$ for samples and $(\mu - 2\sigma, \mu + 2\sigma)$ for populations].

   c. At least $\frac{8}{9}$ of the measurements will fall within 3 standard deviations of the mean [i.e., within the interval $(\bar{x} - 3s, \bar{x} + 3s)$ for samples and $(\mu - 3\sigma, \mu + 3\sigma)$ for populations].

   d. Generally, for any number k greater than 1, at least $(1 - 1/k^2)$ of the measurements will fall within k standard deviations of the mean [i.e., within the interval $(\bar{x} - ks, \bar{x} + ks)$ for samples and $(\mu - k\sigma, \mu + k\sigma)$ for populations].

Table 7	Using the Mean and Standard Deviation to Describe Data: The Empirical Rule

The **Empirical Rule** is a rule of thumb that applies to data sets with frequency distributions that are mound-shaped and symmetric, as shown below.

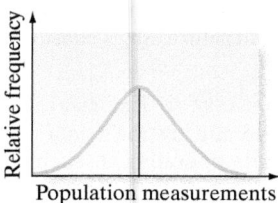

   a. Approximately 68% of the measurements will fall within 1 standard deviation of the mean [i.e., within the interval $(\bar{x} - s, \bar{x} + s)$ for samples and $(\mu - \sigma, \mu + \sigma)$ for populations].

   b. Approximately 95% of the measurements will fall within 2 standard deviations of the mean [i.e., within the interval $(\bar{x} - 2s, \bar{x} + 2s)$ for samples and $(\mu - 2\sigma, \mu + 2\sigma)$ for populations].

   c. Approximately 99.7% (essentially all) of the measurements will fall within 3 standard deviations of the mean [i.e., within the interval $(\bar{x} - 3s, \bar{x} + 3s)$ for samples and $(\mu - 3\sigma, \mu + 3\sigma)$ for populations].

Example   **11**

Interpreting the Standard Deviation—R&D Expenditures

Problem The 50 companies' percentages of revenues spent on R&D are repeated in Table 8. We have previously shown (see Figure 20) that the mean and standard deviation of these data (rounded) are 8.49 and 1.98, respectively. Calculate the fraction of these measurements that lie within the intervals $\bar{x} \pm s$, $\bar{x} \pm 2s$, and $\bar{x} \pm 3s$ and compare the results with those predicted in Tables 6 and 7.

Table 8	R&D Percentages for 50 Companies								
13.5	9.5	8.2	6.5	8.4	8.1	6.9	7.5	10.5	13.5
7.2	7.1	9.0	9.9	8.2	13.2	9.2	6.9	9.6	7.7
9.7	7.5	7.2	5.9	6.6	11.1	8.8	5.2	10.6	8.2
11.3	5.6	10.1	8.0	8.5	11.7	7.1	7.7	9.4	6.0
8.0	7.4	10.5	7.8	7.9	6.5	6.9	6.5	6.8	9.5

Data Set: R&D

**PAFNUTY L. CHEBYSHEV
(1821–1894)**

*The Splendid Russian
Mathematician*

P. L. Chebyshev was educated in
mathematical science at Moscow
University, eventually earning his
master's degree. Following his
graduation, Chebyshev joined
St. Petersburg (Russia) University
as a professor, becoming part of
the well-known "Petersburg mathematical school." It was here that
Chebyshev proved his famous
theorem about the probability of
a measurement being within k
standard deviations of the mean
(Table 6). His fluency in French
allowed him to gain international
recognition in probability theory.
In fact, Chebyshev once objected
to being described as a "splendid
Russian mathematician," saying
he surely was a "worldwide mathematician." One student remembered Chebyshev as "a wonderful
lecturer" who "was always prompt
for class," and "as soon as the bell
sounded, he immediately dropped
the chalk, and, limping, left the
auditorium."

Solution We first form the interval

$$(\bar{x} - s, \bar{x} + s) = (8.49 - 1.98, 8.49 + 1.98) = (6.51, 10.47)$$

A check of the measurements reveals that 34 of the 50 measurements, or 68%, are within
1 standard deviation of the mean.

The next interval of interest,

$$(\bar{x} - 2s, \bar{x} + 2s) = (8.49 - 3.96, 8.49 + 3.96) = (4.53, 12.45),$$

contains 47 of the 50 measurements, or 94%.

Finally, the 3-standard-deviation interval around $\bar{x}$,

$$(\bar{x} - 3s, \bar{x} + 3s) = (8.49 - 5.94, 8.49 + 5.94) = (2.55, 14.43),$$

contains all, or 100%, of the measurements.

In spite of the fact that the distribution of these data is skewed to the right (see
Figure 10), the percentages within 1, 2, and 3 standard deviations (68%, 94%, and 100%)
agree very well with the approximations of 68%, 95%, and 99.7% given by the Empirical
Rule (Table 7).

Look Back You will find that unless the distribution is extremely skewed, the mound-
shaped approximations will be reasonably accurate. Of course, no matter what the
shape of the distribution, Chebyshev's Rule (Table 6) ensures that at least 75% and at
least 89% of the measurements will lie within 2 and 3 standard deviations of the mean,
respectively.

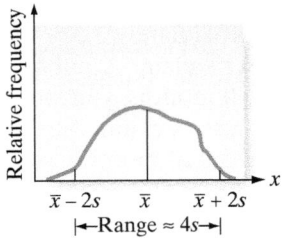 **Now Work Exercise 74**

Example **12**

**Check on the Calculation
of s—R&D Expenditures**

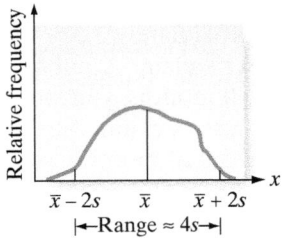

Figure 21

The relation between the range
and the standard deviation

Problem Chebyshev's Rule and the Empirical Rule are useful as a check on the calculation of the standard deviation. For example, suppose we calculated the standard deviation for the R&D percentages (Table 8) to be 3.92. Are there any "clues" in the data that
enable us to judge whether this number is reasonable?

Solution The range of the R&D percentages in Table 8 is $13.5 - 5.2 = 8.3$. From
Chebyshev's Rule and the Empirical Rule we know that most of the measurements
(approximately 95% if the distribution is mound-shaped) will be within 2 standard deviations of the mean. And, regardless of the shape of the distribution and the number
of measurements, almost all of them will fall within 3 standard deviations of the mean.
Consequently, we would expect the range of the measurements to be between 4 (i.e., $\pm 2s$)
and 6 (i.e., $\pm 3s$) standard deviations in length (see Figure 21).

For the R&D data, this means that s should fall between

$$\frac{\text{Range}}{6} = \frac{8.3}{6} = 1.38 \quad \text{and} \quad \frac{\text{Range}}{4} = \frac{8.3}{4} = 2.08$$

In particular, the standard deviation should not be much larger than $\frac{1}{4}$ of the range,
particularly for the data set with 50 measurements. Thus, we have reason to believe that
the calculation of 3.92 is too large. A check of our work reveals that 3.92 is the variance
s^2, not the standard deviation s (see Example 10). We "forgot" to take the square root (a
common error); the correct value is $s = 1.98$. Note that this value is between $\frac{1}{6}$ and $\frac{1}{4}$ of
the range.

Look Ahead In examples and exercises we'll sometimes use $s \approx \text{range}/4$ to obtain a
crude, and usually conservatively large, approximation for s. However, we stress that this
is no substitute for calculating the exact value of s when possible.

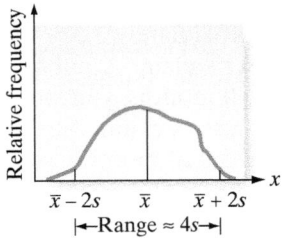 **Now Work Exercise 75**

In the next example, we use the concepts in Chebyshev's Rule and the Empirical Rule to build the foundation for statistical inference making.

Example 13

Making a Statistical Inference—Car Battery Guarantee

Problem A manufacturer of automobile batteries claims that the average length of life for its grade A battery is 60 months. However, the guarantee on this brand is for just 36 months. Suppose the standard deviation of the life length is known to be 10 months, and the frequency distribution of the life-length data is known to be mound-shaped.

a. Approximately what percentage of the manufacturer's grade A batteries will last more than 50 months, assuming the manufacturer's claim is true?

b. Approximately what percentage of the manufacturer's batteries will last less than 40 months, assuming the manufacturer's claim is true?

c. Suppose your battery lasts 37 months. What could you infer about the manufacturer's claim?

Solution If the distribution of life length is assumed to be mound-shaped with a mean of 60 months and a standard deviation of 10 months, it would appear as shown in Figure 22. Note that we can take advantage of the fact that mound-shaped distributions are (approximately) symmetric about the mean, so that the percentages given by the Empirical Rule can be split equally between the halves of the distribution on each side of the mean.

For example, because approximately 68% of the measurements will fall within 1 standard deviation of the mean, the distribution's symmetry implies that approximately $\frac{1}{2}(68\%) = 34\%$ of the measurements will fall between the mean and 1 standard deviation on each side. This concept is illustrated in Figure 22. The figure also shows that 2.5% of the measurements lie beyond 2 standard deviations in each direction from the mean. This result follows from the fact that if approximately 95% of the measurements fall within 2 standard deviations of the mean, then about 5% fall outside 2 standard deviations; if the distribution is approximately symmetric, then about 2.5% of the measurements fall beyond 2 standard deviations on each side of the mean.

a. It is easy to see in Figure 22 that the percentage of batteries lasting more than 50 months is approximately 34% (between 50 and 60 months) plus 50% (greater than 60 months). Thus, approximately 84% of the batteries should have life length exceeding 50 months.

b. The percentage of batteries that last less than 40 months can also be easily determined from Figure 22. Approximately 2.5% of the batteries should fail prior to 40 months, assuming the manufacturer's claim is true.

c. If you are so unfortunate that your grade A battery fails at 37 months, you can make one of two inferences: either your battery was one of the approximately 2.5% that fail prior to 40 months, or something about the manufacturer's claim is not true. Because the chances are so small that a battery fails before 40 months, you would have good reason to have serious doubts about the manufacturer's claim. A mean smaller than 60 months and/or a standard deviation longer than 10 months would both increase the likelihood of failure prior to 40 months.*

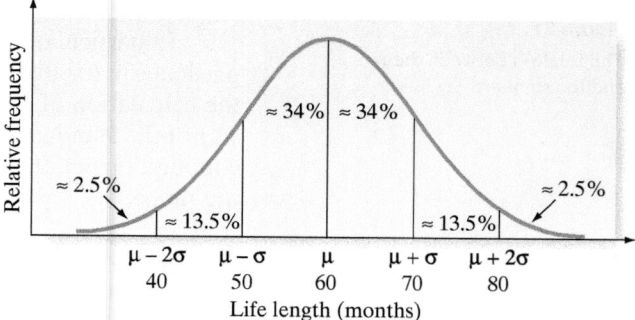

Figure 22
Battery life-length distribution:
Manufacturer's claim assumed true

*The assumption that the distribution is mound-shaped and symmetric may also be incorrect. However, if the distribution were skewed to the right, as life-length distributions often tend to be, the percentage of measurements more than 2 standard deviations *below* the mean would be even less than 2.5%.

Look Back The approximations given in Figure 22 are more dependent on the assumption of a mound-shaped distribution than those given by the Empirical Rule (Table 7) because the approximations in Figure 22 depend on the (approximate) symmetry of the mound-shaped distribution. We saw in Example 11 that the Empirical Rule can yield good approximations even for skewed distributions. This will *not* be true of the approximations in Figure 22; the distribution *must* be mound-shaped and approximately symmetric.

Example 13 is our initial demonstration of the statistical inference-making process. At this point you should realize that we'll use sample information (in Example 13, your battery's failure at 37 months) to make inferences about the population (in Example 13, the manufacturer's claim about the life length for the population of all batteries). We'll build on this foundation as we proceed.

STATISTICS
in ACTION
REVISITED

Interpreting Numerical Descriptive Measures

We return to the *Journal of Experimental Social Psychology* (Vol. 45, 2009) study on whether money can buy love for two groups of participants—those assigned the role of gift-giver and those assigned the role of gift-recipient. Recall that the researchers investigated whether givers and receivers differ on the price of the birthday gift reported and on the overall level of appreciation reported. The Minitab descriptive statistics printout for the **BUYLOV** data is displayed in Figure SIA8, with means and standard deviations highlighted.

First, we focus on the quantitative variable, *birthday gift price*. The sample mean gift price for givers is $105.84 compared to $149.00 for receivers. Our interpretation is that receivers report a higher average gift price than givers—a difference of about $43.

To interpret the gift price standard deviations (93.47 for givers and 134.5 for receivers), we substitute into the formula, $\bar{x} \pm 2s$, to obtain the following intervals:

Gift-Giver: $\quad \bar{x} \pm 2s = 105.84 \pm 2(93.47) = 105.84 \pm 186.94 = (-81.1, 292.78)$
Gift-Receiver: $\quad \bar{x} + 2s = 149.00 \pm 2(134.50) = 149 \pm 269 = (-120, 418)$

Because gift price cannot have a negative value, the two intervals for givers and receivers are more practically given as $(0, 293)$ and $(0, 418)$, respectively. Since the distributions of gift price are not mound-shaped and symmetric (see Figure SIA7a), we apply Chebyshev's Rule (Table 6). Thus, we know that at least 75% of the gift-givers in the study reported a gift price between $0 and $293, and at least 75% of the gift-recipients reported a gift price between $0 and $418. You can see that the upper endpoint of the interval for givers lies below that for receivers. Consequently, we can infer that prices reported by gift-recipients tend to be higher than the prices reported by gift-givers. Also, if a gift price of $400 is observed, it is much more likely to be reported by a gift-receiver than a gift-giver.

A similar analysis performed for the variable *overall level of appreciation* yielded the following intervals:

Gift-Giver: $\quad \bar{x} \pm 2s = 4.985 \pm 2(2.775) = 4.985 \pm 5.55 = (-.565, 10.535)$
Gift-Receiver: $\quad \bar{x} \pm 2s = 7.165 \pm 2(2.928) = 7.165 \pm 5.856 = (1.309, 13.021)$

Since overall level of appreciation cannot have a value less than 2 and is a whole number, the two intervals for givers and receivers are more practically given as $(2, 10)$ and $(2, 13)$,

Descriptive Statistics: BGiftPrice, OverallApp

Variable	Role	N	Mean	StDev	Variance	Minimum	Median	Maximum
BGiftPrice	Giver	134	105.84	93.47	8736.78	2.00	75.50	431.00
	Receiver	103	149.0	134.5	18083.8	1.0	133.0	548.0
OverallApp	Giver	134	4.985	2.775	7.699	2.000	4.000	13.000
	Receiver	103	7.165	2.928	8.571	2.000	7.000	14.000

Figure SIA8

Minitab descriptive statistics for gift price and appreciation level, by role

respectively. Applying Chebyshev's Rule, we know that at least 75% of the gift-givers in the study reported an appreciation level between 2 and 10 points, and at least 75% of the gift-recipients reported an appreciation level between 2 and 13 points. Again, the upper endpoint of the interval for givers lies below that for receivers; thus, we infer that overall levels of appreciation reported by gift-recipients tend to be higher than those reported by gift-givers.

Now, how does this information help the researchers determine whether there are "significant" differences in the means for gift-givers and gift-recipients?

Data Set: BUYLOVE

Exercises 71–89

Learning the Mechanics

71 The output from a statistical software package indicates that the mean and standard deviation of a data set consisting of 200 measurements are $1,500 and $300, respectively.
  a. What are the units of measurement of the variable of interest? Based on the units, what type of data is this: quantitative or qualitative?
  b. What can be said about the number of measurements between $900 and $2,100? Between $600 and $2,400? Between $1,200 and $1,800? Between $1,500 and $2,100?

72 For any set of data, what can be said about the percentage of the measurements contained in each of the following intervals?
  a. $\bar{x} - s$ to $\bar{x} + s$
  b. $\bar{x} - 2s$ to $\bar{x} + 2s$
  c. $\bar{x} - 3s$ to $\bar{x} + 3s$

73 For a set of data with a mound-shaped relative frequency distribution, what can be said about the percentage of the measurements contained in each of the intervals specified in Exercise 72?

74 The following is a sample of 25 measurements:

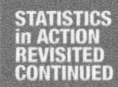
L02074

7	6	6	11	8	9	11	9	10	8	7	7
5	9	10	7	7	7	7	9	12	10	10	8	6

  a. Compute $\bar{x}$, s^2, and s for this sample.
  b. Count the number of measurements in the intervals $\bar{x} \pm s$, $\bar{x} \pm 2s$, $\bar{x} \pm 3s$. Express each count as a percentage of the total number of measurements.
  c. Compare the percentages found in part **b** to the percentages given by the Empirical Rule and Chebyshev's Rule.
  d. Calculate the range and use it to obtain a rough approximation for s. Does the result compare favorably with the actual value for s found in part **a?**

75 Given a data set with a largest value of 760 and a smallest value of 135, what would you estimate the standard deviation to be? Explain the logic behind the procedure you used to estimate the standard deviation. Suppose the standard deviation is reported to be 25. Is this feasible? Explain.

Applying the Concepts—Basic

76 Do social robots walk or roll? Refer to the *International Conference on Social Robotics* (Vol. 6414, 2010) study
ROBOTS on the current trend in the design of social robots,

Exercise 3. Recall that in a random sample of social robots obtained through a Web search, 28 were built with wheels. The number of wheels on each of the 28 robots is listed in the accompanying table.

4	4	3	3	3	6	4	2	2	2	1	3	3	3
3	4	4	3	2	8	2	2	3	4	3	3	4	2

Source: Based on Chew, S., et al. "Do social robots walk or roll?," *International Conference on Social Robotics,* Vol. 6414, 2010 (adapted from Figure 2).

  a. Generate a histogram for the sample data set. Is the distribution of number of wheels mound-shaped and symmetric?
  b. Find the mean and standard deviation for the sample data set.
  c. Form the interval, $\bar{x} \pm 2s$.
  d. According to Chebychev's rule, what proportion of sample observations will fall within the interval, part **c?**
  e. According to the Empirical Rule, what proportion of sample observations will fall within the interval, part **c?**
  f. Determine the actual proportion of sample observations that fall within the interval, part **c.** Even though the histogram, part **a,** is not perfectly symmetric, does the Empirical Rule provide a good estimate of the proportion?

77 College dropout study. The *American Economic Review* (Dec. 2008) published a study on whether the removal of credit constraints would impact the likelihood of a student dropping out of college. As part of the investigation, the researchers looked for factors other than credit constraints that would influence the college dropout decision. One factor of interest was expected GPA for a college student who studied 3 hours per day. In a representative sample of 307 college students, the researchers reported the following summary statistics for the expected GPA of those who studied 3 hours per day: $\bar{x} = 3.11, s = .66$.
  a. Give an interval that will contain most (at least 75% to approximately 95%) of the 307 GPAs.
  b. If you observe a GPA of 1.25, is it likely that this college student studied 3 hours per day? Explain.

78 Blogs for *Fortune* 500 firms. Refer to the *Journal of Relationship Marketing* (Vol. 7, 2008) study of the prevalence of blogs and forums at *Fortune* 500 firms with both English and Chinese Web sites, Exercise 9. In a sample of firms that provide blogs and forums as marketing tools, the mean number of blogs/forums per site was 4.25, with a standard deviation of 12.02.

a. Provide an interval that is likely to contain the number of blogs/forums per site for at least 75% of the *Fortune* 500 firms in the sample.

b. Do you expect the distribution of the number of blogs/forums to be symmetric, skewed right, or skewed left? Explain.

79 Semester hours taken by CPA candidates. Refer to the *Journal of Accounting and Public Policy* (Spring 2002) study of 100,000 first-time candidates for the CPA exam, Exercise 51. Recall that the mean number of semester hours of college credit taken by the candidates was 141.31 hours. The standard-deviation was reported to be 17.77 hours.

a. Compute the 2-standard-deviation interval around the mean.

b. Make a statement about the proportion of first-time candidates for the CPA exam who have total college credit hours within the interval, part **a.**

c. For the statement, part **b,** to be true, what must be known about the shape of the distribution of total semester hours?

80 Motivation of drug dealers. Researchers at Georgia State University investigated the personality characteristics of drug dealers in order to shed light on their motivation for participating in the illegal drug market (*Applied Psychology in Criminal Justice*, Sep. 2009). The sample consisted of 100 convicted drug dealers who attended a court-mandated counseling program. Each dealer was scored on the Wanting Recognition (WR) Scale, which provides a quantitative measure of a person's level of need for approval and sensitivity to social situations. (Higher scores indicate a greater need for approval.) The sample of drug dealers had a mean WR score of 39, with a standard deviation of 6. Assume the distribution of WR scores for drug dealers is mound-shaped and symmetric.

a. Give a range of WR scores that will contain about 95% of the scores in the drug dealer sample.

b. What proportion of the drug dealers had WR scores above 51?

c. Give a range of WR sores that contain nearly all the scores in the drug dealer sample.

Applying the Concepts—Intermediate

81 Sanitation inspection of cruise ships. Refer to the Centers for Disease Control and Prevention listing of the Jan. 2010 sanitation scores for 186 cruise ships, Exercise 24.

a. Find the mean and standard deviation of the sanitation scores.

b. Calculate the intervals $\bar{x} \pm s, \bar{x} \pm 2s, \bar{x} \pm 3s$.

c. Find the percentage of measurements in the data set that fall within each of the intervals, part **b.** Do these percentages agree with Chebyshev's Rule? The Empirical Rule?

82 Laptop use in middle school. Many middle schools have initiated a program that provides every student with a free laptop (notebook) computer. Student usage of laptops at a middle school that participates in the initiative was investigated in *American Secondary Education* (Fall 2009). In a sample of 106 students, the researchers reported the following statistics on how many minutes per day each student used his or her laptop for taking notes: $\bar{x} = 13.2, s = 19.5$.

a. Compute the interval, $\bar{x} \pm 2s$.

b. Explain why the distribution of laptop usage for taking notes for these 106 students cannot be symmetric.

c. Given your answer to part **b,** what percentage of the 106 students have laptop usages that fall within the $\bar{x} \pm 2s$ interval?

83 Bearing strength of concrete FRP strips. Fiber reinforced polymer (FRP) composite materials are the standard for strengthening, retrofitting, and repairing concrete structures. Typically, FRP strips are fastened to the concrete with epoxy adhesive. Engineers at the University of Wisconsin-Madison have developed a new method of fastening the FRP strips using mechanical anchors (*Composites Fabrication Magazine*, Sep. 2004). To evaluate the new fastening method, 10 specimens of pultruded FRP strips mechanically fastened to highway bridges were tested for bearing strength. The strength measurements (recorded in mega pascal units, Mpa) are shown in the table. Use the sample data to find an interval that is likely to contain the bearing strength of a pultruded FRP strip.

240.9	248.8	215.7	233.6	231.4	230.9	225.3	247.3	235.5	238.0

Source: Based on summary information provided in COMPOSITES FABRICATION MAGAZINE, September 2004, p. 32, Table 1.

84 Time in bankruptcy. Refer to the *Financial Management* (Spring 1995) study of 49 firms filing for prepackaged bankruptcy, Exercise 32. Data on the variable of interest, length of time (months) in bankruptcy for each firm, are saved in the accompanying file.

a. Construct a histogram for the 49 bankruptcy times. Comment on whether the Empirical Rule is applicable for describing the bankruptcy time distribution for firms filing for prepackaged bankruptcy.

b. Find numerical descriptive statistics for the data set. Use this information to construct an interval that captures at least 75% of the bankruptcy times.

c. Count the number of the 49 bankruptcy times that fall within the interval, part **b,** and convert the result to a percentage. Does the result agree with Chebyshev's Rule? The Empirical Rule?

d. A firm is considering filing a prepackaged bankruptcy plan. Estimate the length of time the firm will be in bankruptcy.

85 Shopping vehicle and judgment. While shopping at the grocery store, are you more likely to buy a vice product (e.g., a candy bar) when pushing a shopping cart or when carrying a shopping basket? This was the question of interest in a study published in the *Journal of Marketing Research* (Dec. 2011). The researchers believe that when your arm is flexed (as when carrying a basket), you are more likely to choose a vice product than when your arm is extended (as when pushing a cart). To test this theory in a laboratory setting, the researchers recruited 22 consumers and asked each to push his or her hand against a table while being asked a serious of shopping questions. Half of the consumers were told to put their arms in a flex position (similar to a shopping basket) and the other half were told to put their arms in an extended position (similar to a shopping cart). Participants were offered several choices between a vice and a virtue (e.g., a movie ticket vs. a shopping coupon, paying later with a larger amount vs. paying now), and a choice score (on a scale of 0 to 100) was determined for each. (Higher scores indicate a greater preference for vice options.) The average choice score for consumers with a flexed arm was 59, while the average for consumers with an extended arm was 43.

a. Suppose the standard deviations of the choice scores for the flexed arm and extended arm conditions are 4 and 2, respectively. Does this information support the researchers' theory? Explain.

b. Suppose the standard deviations of the choice scores for the flexed arm and extended arm conditions are 10 and 15, respectively. Does this information support the researchers' theory? Explain.

86 Buy-side vs. sell-side analysts' earnings forecasts. Financial analysts are hired by investment companies to make forecasts of stock prices and recommendations about whether to buy, sell, or hold specific securities. These analysts can be categorized as either "buy-side" analysts or "sell-side" analysts based on a variety of factors, including scope of industry coverage, sources of information used, and target audience. A group of Harvard Business School professors compared earnings forecasts of buy-side and sell-side analysts (*Financial Analysts Journal*, Jul/Aug 2008). Data were collected on 3,526 forecasts made by buy-side analysts and 58,562 forecasts made by sell-side analysts, and the relative absolute forecast error was determined for each.

a. Frequency distributions for buy-side and sell-side analysts forecast errors (with the sell-side distribution superimposed over the buy-side distribution) are shown in the accompanying figure. Based on the figure, the researchers concluded "that absolute forecast errors for buy-side analysts have a higher mean and variance than those for the sell-side analysts." Do you agree? Explain.

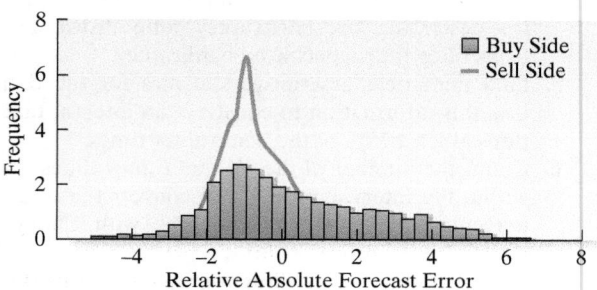

b. The mean and standard deviation of forecast errors for both buy-side and sell-side analysts are given in the following table. For each type of analyst, provide an interval that will contain approximately 95% of the forecast errors. Compare these intervals. Which type of analyst is likely to have a relative forecast error of +2.00 or higher?

	Buy-Side Analysts	Sell-Side Analysts
Mean	0.85	−0.05
Standard deviation	1.93	0.85

Source: Based on Groysberg, B., Healy, P., & Chapman, C. *Financial Analysis Journal*, Vol. 64, No. 4. Jul/Aug. 2008 (Table 2).

Applying the Concepts—Advanced

87 Land purchase decision. A buyer for a lumber company must decide whether to buy a piece of land containing 5,000 pine trees. If 1,000 of the trees are at least 40 feet tall,

the buyer will purchase the land; otherwise, he won't. The owner of the land reports that the height of the trees has a mean of 30 feet and a standard deviation of 3 feet. Based on this information, what is the buyer's decision?

88 Improving SAT scores. The National Education Longitudinal Survey (NELS) tracks a nationally representative sample of U.S. students from eighth grade through high school and college. Research published in *Chance* (Winter 2001) examined the Standardized Assessment Test (SAT) scores of 265 NELS students who paid a private tutor to help them improve their scores. The table summarizes the changes in both the SAT–Mathematics and SAT–Verbal scores for these students.

	SAT–Math	SAT–Verbal
Mean change in score	19	7
Standard deviation of score changes	65	49

a. Suppose one of the 265 students who paid a private tutor is selected at random. Give an interval that is likely to contain this student's change in the SAT–Math score.

b. Repeat part **a** for the SAT–Verbal score.

c. Suppose the selected student increased his score on one of the SAT tests by 140 points. Which test, the SAT–Math or SAT–Verbal, is the one most likely to have the 140-point increase? Explain.

89 Monitoring weights of flour bags. When it is working properly, a machine that fills 25-pound bags of flour dispenses an average of 25 pounds per fill; the standard deviation of the amount of fill is .1 pound. To monitor the performance of the machine, an inspector weighs the contents of a bag coming off the machine's conveyor belt every half hour during the day. If the contents of two consecutive bags fall more than 2 standard deviations from the mean (using the mean and standard deviation given above), the filling process is said to be out of control, and the machine is shut down briefly for adjustments. The data given in the following table are the weights measured by the inspector yesterday. Assume the machine is never shut down for more than 15 minutes at a time. At what times yesterday was the process shut down for adjustment? Justify your answer.

Time	Weight (pounds)
8:00 A.M.	25.10
8:30	25.15
9:00	24.81
9:30	24.75
10:00	25.00
10:30	25.05
11:00	25.23
11:30	25.25
12:00	25.01
12:30 P.M.	25.06
1:00	24.95
1:30	24.80
2:00	24.95
2:30	25.21
3:00	24.90
3:30	24.71
4:00	25.31
4:30	25.15
5:00	25.20

6   Numerical Measures of Relative Standing

We've seen that numerical measures of central tendency and variability describe the general nature of a quantitative data set (either a sample or a population). In addition, we may be interested in describing the *relative* quantitative location of a particular measurement within a data set. Descriptive measures of the relationship of a measurement to the rest of the data are called **measures of relative standing.**

One measure of the relative standing of a measurement is its **percentile ranking,** or **percentile score.** For example, if oil company A reports that its yearly sales are in the 90th percentile of all companies in the industry, the implication is that 90% of all oil companies have yearly sales less than company A's, and only 10% have yearly sales exceeding company A's. This is demonstrated in Figure 23. Similarly, if the oil company's yearly sales are in the 50th percentile (the median of the data set), 50% of all oil companies would have lower yearly sales and 50% would have higher yearly sales.

Percentile rankings are of practical value only for large data sets. Finding them involves a process similar to the one used in finding a median. The measurements are ranked in order, and a rule is selected to define the location of each percentile. Because we are primarily interested in interpreting the percentile rankings of measurements (rather than finding particular percentiles for a data set), we define the *pth percentile* of a data set.

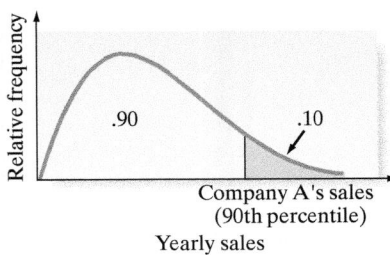

Figure 23

Location of 90th percentile for yearly sales of oil companies

> For any set of *n* measurements (arranged in ascending or descending order), the *pth* **percentile** is a number such that $p\%$ of the measurements fall below the *pth* percentile and $(100 - p)\%$ fall above it.

Example   14

Finding and Interpreting Percentiles — R&D Expenditures

Problem Refer to the percentages spent on R&D by the 50 high-technology firms listed in Table 8. A portion of the SPSS descriptive statistics printout is shown in Figure 24. Locate the 25th percentile and 95th percentile on the printout and interpret these values.

Solution Both the 25th percentile and 95th percentile are highlighted on the SPSS printout, Figure 24. These values are 7.05 and 13.335, respectively. Our interpretations are as follows: 25% of the 50 R&D percentages fall below 7.05 and 95% of the R&D percentages fall below 13.335.

Look Back The method for computing percentiles with small data sets varies according to the software used. As the sample size increases, these percentile values from the different software packages will converge to a single number.

Statistics

RDPCT

N	Valid	50
	Missing	0
Percentiles	5	5.765
	10	6.500
	25	7.050
	50	8.050
	75	9.625
	90	11.280
	95	13.335

Figure 24

SPSS percentiles for 50 R&D percentages

Now Work Exercise 91

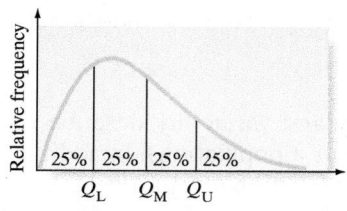

Figure 25

The quartiles for a data set

Percentiles that partition a data set into four categories, each category containing exactly 25% of the measurements, are called **quartiles.** The *lower quartile* (Q_L) is the 25th percentile, the *middle quartile* (Q_M) is the median or 50th percentile, and the *upper quartile* (Q_U) is the 75th percentile, as shown in Figure 25. Therefore, in Example 14, we have (from the SPSS printout, Figure 24), $Q_L = 7.05$, $Q_M = 8.05$, and $Q_U = 9.625$. Quartiles will prove useful in finding unusual observations in a data set (Section 7).

> The **lower quartile (Q_L)** is the 25th percentile of a data set. The **middle quartile (Q_M)** is the median or 50th percentile. The **upper quartile (Q_U)** is the 75th percentile.

Another measure of relative standing in popular use is the *z-score*. As you can see in the definition of *z*-score below, the *z*-score makes use of the mean and standard deviation of the data set in order to specify the relative location of a measurement. Note that the *z*-score is calculated by subtracting $\bar{x}$ (or μ) from the measurement x and then dividing the result by s (or σ). The final result, the *z*-score, represents the distance between a given measurement x and the mean, expressed in standard deviations.

> The **sample *z*-score** for a measurement x is
> $$z = \frac{x - \bar{x}}{s}$$
> The **population *z*-score** for a measurement x is
> $$z = \frac{x - \mu}{\sigma}$$

Example 15

Finding a z-Score—GMAT Results

Problem A random sample of 2,000 students who sat for the Graduate Management Admission Test (GMAT) is selected. For this sample, the mean GMAT score is $\bar{x} = 540$ points and the standard deviation is $s = 100$ points. One student from the sample, Kara Smith, had a GMAT score of $x = 440$ points. What is Kara's sample *z*-score?

Solution First, note that Kara's GMAT score lies below the mean score for the 2,000 students (see Figure 26). Now we compute

$$z = (x - \bar{x})/s = (440 - 540)/100 = -100/100 = -1.0$$

This *z*-score implies that Kara Smith's GMAT score is 1.0 standard deviations below the sample mean GMAT score, or, in short, her sample *z*-score is -1.0.

Look Back The numerical value of the *z*-score reflects the relative standing of the measurement. A large positive *z*-score implies that the measurement is larger than almost all other measurements, whereas a large (in magnitude) negative *z*-score indicates that the measurement is smaller than almost every other measurement. If a *z*-score is 0 or near 0, the measurement is located at or near the mean of the sample or population.

Figure 26

GMAT scores of a sample of test takers

					GMAT Score
240		440	540		840
$\bar{x} - 3s$		Kara Smith's GMAT	$\bar{x}$		$\bar{x} + 3s$

Now Work Exercise 90

If we know that the frequency distribution of the measurements is mound-shaped, the following interpretation of the z-score can be given.

Interpretation of z-Scores for Mound-Shaped Distributions of Data

1. Approximately 68% of the measurements will have a z-score between −1 and 1.
2. Approximately 95% of the measurements will have a z-score between −2 and 2.
3. Approximately 99.7% (almost all) of the measurements will have a z-score between −3 and 3.

Note that this interpretation of z-scores is identical to that given by the Empirical Rule for mound-shaped distributions (Table 7). The statement that a measurement falls in the interval $(\mu - \sigma)$ to $(\mu + \sigma)$ is equivalent to the statement that a measurement has a population z-score between −1 and 1 because all measurements between $(\mu - \sigma)$ and $(\mu + \sigma)$ are within 1 standard deviation of μ. These z-scores are displayed in Figure 27.

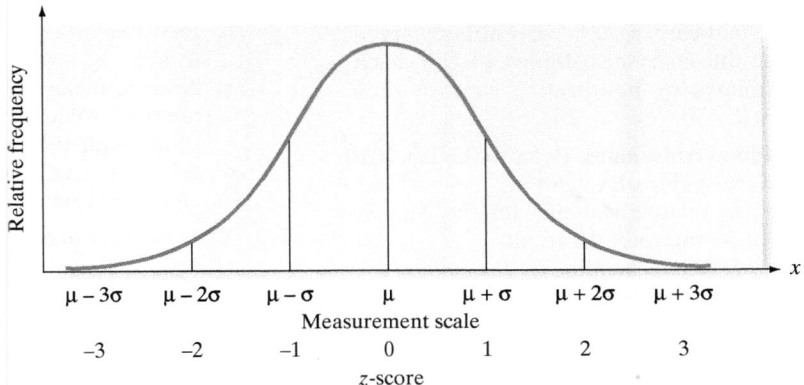

Figure 27

Population z-scores for a mound-shaped distribution

Exercises 90–105

Learning the Mechanics

90 Compute the z-score corresponding to each of the following
NW values of x:
   a. $x = 40, s = 5, \bar{x} = 30$
   b. $x = 90, \mu = 89, \sigma = 2$
   c. $\mu = 50, \sigma = 5, x = 50$
   d. $s = 4, x = 20, \bar{x} = 30$
   e. In parts **a–d**, state whether the z-score locates x within a sample or a population.
   f. In parts **a–d**, state whether each value of x lies above or below the mean and by how many standard deviations.

91 Give the percentage of measurements in a data set that are
NW above and below each of the following percentiles:
   a. 75th percentile
   b. 50th percentile
   c. 20th percentile
   d. 84th percentile

92 In terms of percentiles, define Q_L, Q_M, and Q_U.

93 Compare the z-scores to decide which of the following x values lie the greatest distance above the mean and the greatest distance below the mean.

   a. $x = 100, \mu = 50, \sigma = 25$
   b. $x = 1, \mu = 4, \sigma = 1$
   c. $x = 0, \mu = 200, \sigma = 100$
   d. $x = 10, \mu = 5, \sigma = 3$

94 Suppose that 40 and 90 are two elements of a population data set and that their z-scores are −2 and 3, respectively. Using only this information, is it possible to determine the population's mean and standard deviation? If so, find them. If not, explain why it's not possible.

Applying the Concepts—Basic

95 Mathematics assessment test scores. According to the National Center for Education Statistics (2009), scores on a mathematics assessment test for U.S. eighth graders have a mean of 283, a 25th percentile of 259, a 75th percentile of 308, and a 90th percentile of 329. Interpret each of these numerical descriptive measures.

96 Motivation of drug dealers. Refer to the *Applied Psychology in Criminal Justice* (Sep. 2009) study of convicted drug dealers' motivations, Exercise 80. Recall that the sample of drug dealers had a mean Wanting Recognition (WR) score of 39 points, with a standard deviation of 6 points.

a. Find and interpret the z-score for a drug dealer with a WR score of 30 points.

b. What proportion of the sampled drug dealers had WR scores below 39 points? (Assume the distribution of WR scores is mound-shaped and symmetric.)

c. If 5% of convicted drug dealers have WR scores above 49 points, give a percentile ranking for the WR score of 49.

97 Starting and mid-career salaries of bachelor's degree graduates. PayScale, Inc., an online provider of global compensation data, recently conducted a survey of 1.2 million bachelor's degree graduates with a minimum of 10 years of work experience. Three of the many variables measured by PayScale were the graduate's starting salary, mid-career salary, and the college or university where they obtained their degree. A summary of the starting and mid-career salary data was reported in *the Wall Street Journal* (July 31, 2008). Descriptive statistics were provided for each of the over 300 colleges and universities that graduates attended. For example, graduates of the University of South Florida (USF) had a median starting salary of $41,100, a median mid-career salary of $71,100, and a mid-career 90th percentile salary of $131,000. Describe the salary distribution of USF bachelor's degree graduates by interpreting each of these summary statistics.

98 Sanitation inspection of cruise ships. Refer to the Jan. 2010 sanitation levels of cruise ships, Exercise 81.

SANIT

a. Give a measure of relative standing for the *Nautilus Explorer* score of 74. Interpret the result.

b. Give a measure of relative standing for the *Rotterdam's* score of 92. Interpret the result.

Applying the Concepts—Intermediate

99 Lead in drinking water. The U.S. Environmental Protection Agency (EPA) sets a limit on the amount of lead permitted in drinking water. The EPA *Action Level* for lead is .015 milligrams per liter (mg/L) of water. Under EPA guidelines, if 90% of a water system's study samples have a lead concentration less than .015 mg/L, the water is considered safe for drinking. I (coauthor Sincich) received a recent report on a study of lead levels in the drinking water of homes in my subdivision. The 90th percentile of the study sample had a lead concentration of .00372 mg/L. Are water customers in my subdivision at risk of drinking water with unhealthy lead levels? Explain.

100 Corporate sustainability of CPA firms. Refer to the *Business and Society* (March 2011) study on the sustainability behaviors of CPA corporations, Exercise 67. Numerical descriptive measures for level of support for corporate sustainability for the 992 senior managers are repeated in the accompanying Minitab printout. One of the managers reported a support level of 155 points. Would you consider this support level to be typical of the study sample? Explain.

CORSUS

Descriptive Statistics: Support

Variable	N	Mean	StDev	Variance	Minimum	Median	Maximum
Support	992	67.755	26.871	722.036	0.000	68.000	155.000

101 Hazardous waste cleanup in Arkansas. The Superfund Act was passed by Congress to encourage state participation in the implementation of a law relating to the release and cleanup of hazardous substances. Hazardous waste sites financed by the Superfund Act are called *Superfund sites*. A total of 393 Superfund sites are operated by waste management companies in Arkansas (Tabor and Stanwick, *Arkansas Business and Economic Review,* Summer 1995). The numbers of these Superfund sites in each of Arkansas's 75 counties are shown in the next table.

SPRFND

3	3	2	1	2	0	5	3	5	2	1	8	2
12	3	5	3	1	3	0	8	0	9	6	8	6
2	16	0	6	0	5	5	0	1	25	0	0	0
6	2	10	12	3	10	3	17	2	4	2	1	21
4	2	1	11	5	2	2	7	2	3	1	8	2
0	0	0	2	3	10	2	3	48	21			

Source: Based on Tabor. R. H., & Stanwick, S. D. "Arkansas: An environmental perspective." *Arkansas Business and Economic Review.* Vol. 28, No. 2. Summer 1995, pp. 22–32 (Table 4).

a. Find the 10th percentile of the data set. Interpret the result.

b. Find the 95th percentile of the data set. Interpret the result.

c. Find the mean and standard deviation of the data; then use these values to calculate the z-score for an Arkansas county with 48 Superfund sites.

d. Based on your answer to part **c**, would you classify 48 as an extreme number of Superfund sites?

102 Blue- vs. red-colored exam study. In a study of how external clues influence performance, professors at the University of Alberta and Pennsylvania State University gave two different forms of a midterm examination to a large group of introductory students. The questions on the exam were identical and in the same order, but one exam was printed on blue paper and the other on red paper (*Teaching Psychology,* May 1998). Grading only the difficult questions on the exam, the researchers found that scores on the blue exam had a distribution with a mean of 53% and a standard deviation of 15%, while scores on the red exam had a distribution with a mean of 39% and a standard deviation of 12%. (Assume that both distributions are approximately mound-shaped and symmetric.)

a. Give an interpretation of the standard deviation for the students who took the blue exam.

b. Give an interpretation of the standard deviation for the students who took the red exam.

c. Suppose a student is selected at random from the group of students who participated in the study and the student's score on the difficult questions is 20%. Which exam form is the student more likely to have taken, the blue or the red exam? Explain.

103 Ranking PhD programs in economics. Thousands of students apply for admission to graduate schools in economics each year with the intention of obtaining a PhD. The *Southern Economic Journal* (Apr. 2008) published a guide to graduate study in economics by ranking the PhD programs at 129 colleges and universities. Each program was evaluated according to the number of publications published by faculty teaching in the PhD program and by the quality of the publications. Data obtained from the Social Science Citation Index (SSCI) were used to

ECOPHD

calculate an overall productivity score for each PhD program. The mean and standard deviation of these 129 productivity scores were then used to compute a z-score for each economics program. Harvard University had the highest z-score ($z = 5.08$) and, hence, was the top-ranked school; Howard University was ranked last because it had the lowest z-score ($z = -0.81$). The data (z-scores) for all 129 economic programs are saved in the data file.

a. Interpret the z-score for Harvard University.

b. Interpret the z-score for Howard University.

c. The authors of the *Southern Economic Journal* article note that "only 44 of the 129 schools have positive z-scores, indicating that the distribution of overall productivity is skewed to the right." Do you agree? (Check your answer by constructing a histogram for the z-scores in the file.)

Applying the Concepts—Advanced

104 Using z-scores for grades. At one university, the students are given z-scores at the end of each semester rather than the traditional GPAs. The mean and standard deviation of all students' cumulative GPAs, on which the z-scores are based, are 2.7 and .5, respectively.

a. Translate each of the following z-scores to the corresponding GPA: $z = 2.0$, $z = -1.0$, $z = .5$, $z = -2.5$.

b. Students with z-scores below -1.6 are put on probation. What is the corresponding probationary GPA?

c. The president of the university wishes to graduate the top 16% of the students with *cum laude* honors and the top 2.5% with *summa cum laude* honors. Where (approximately) should the limits be set in terms of z-scores? In terms of GPAs? What assumption, if any, did you make about the distribution of the GPAs at the university?

105 Ranking PhD programs in economics (cont'd). Refer to the *Southern Economic Journal* (Apr. 2008) study of PhD programs in economics, Exercise 103. The authors also made the following observation: "A noticeable feature of this skewness is that distinction between schools diminishes as the rank declines. For example, the top-ranked school, Harvard, has a z-score of 5.08, and the fifth-ranked school, Yale, has a z-score of 2.18, a substantial difference. However,…,the 70th-ranked school, the University of Massachusetts, has a z-score of -0.43, and the 80th-ranked school, the University of Delaware, has a z-score of -0.50, a very small difference. [Consequently] the ordinal rankings presented in much of the literature that ranks economics departments miss the fact that below a relatively small group of top programs, the differences in [overall] productivity become fairly small." Do you agree?

---

7 Methods for Detecting Outliers: Box Plots and z-Scores

Sometimes it is important to identify inconsistent or unusual measurements in a data set. An observation that is unusually large or small relative to the data values we want to describe is called an *outlier*.

Outliers are often attributable to one of several causes. First, the measurement associated with the outlier may be invalid. For example, the experimental procedure used to generate the measurement may have malfunctioned, the experimenter may have misrecorded the measurement, or the data might have been coded incorrectly in the computer. Second, the outlier may be the result of a misclassified measurement—that is, the measurement belongs to a population different from which the rest of the sample was drawn. Finally, the measurement associated with the outlier may be recorded correctly and be from the same population as the rest of the sample but represent a rare (chance) event. Such outliers occur most often when the relative frequency distribution of the sample data is extremely skewed because such a distribution has a tendency to include extremely large or small observations relative to the others in the data set.

An observation (or measurement) that is unusually large or small relative to the other values in a data set is called an **outlier**. Outliers typically are attributable to one of the following causes:

1. The measurement is observed, recorded, or entered into the computer incorrectly.

2. The measurement comes from a different population.

3. The measurement is correct but represents a rare (chance) event.

Two useful methods for detecting outliers, one graphical and one numerical, are **box plots** and z-scores. The box plot is based on the *quartiles* (defined in Section 6) of a data set. Specifically, a box plot is based on the *interquartile range* (IQR), the distance between the lower and upper quartiles:

$$IQR = Q_U - Q_L$$

> The **interquartile range (IQR)** is the distance between the lower and upper quartiles:
> $$IQR = Q_U - Q_L$$

An annotated Minitab box plot for the 50 companies' percentages of revenues spent on R&D (Table 2) is shown in Figure 28.* Note that a rectangle (the box) is drawn, with the top and bottom sides of the rectangle (the **hinges**) drawn at the quartiles Q_L and Q_U, respectively. Recall that Q_L represents the 25th percentile and Q_U represents the 75th percentile. By definition, then, the "middle" 50% of the observations—those between Q_L and Q_U—fall inside the box. For the R&D data, these quartiles are at 7.05 and 9.625 (see Figure 24). Thus,

$$IQR = 9.625 - 7.05 = 2.575$$

The median is shown at 8.05 by a horizontal line within the box.

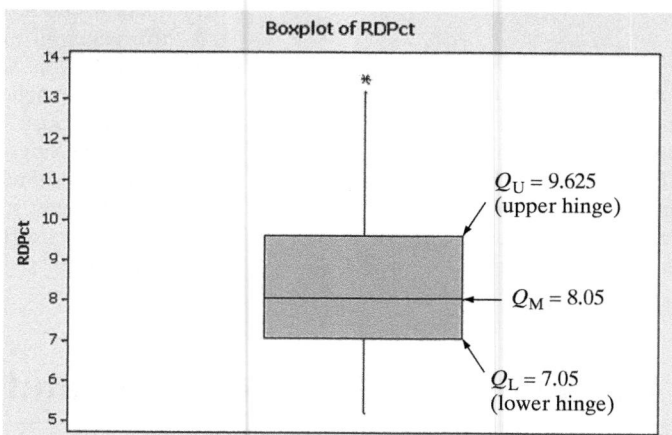

Figure 28

Annotated Minitab box plot for 50 R&D percentages

To guide the construction of the "tails" of the box plot, two sets of limits, called **inner fences** and **outer fences,** are used. Neither set of fences actually appears on the box plot. Inner fences are located at a distance of 1.5(IQR) from the hinges. Emanating from the hinges of the box are vertical lines called the **whiskers.** The two whiskers extend to the most extreme observation inside the inner fences. For example, the inner fence on the lower side (bottom) of the R&D percentage box plot is

$$\begin{aligned}
\text{Lower inner fence} &= \text{Lower hinge} - 1.5(IQR) \\
&= 7.05 - 1.5(2.575) \\
&= 7.05 - 3.863 = 3.187
\end{aligned}$$

The smallest measurement in the data set is 5.2, which is well inside this inner fence. Thus, the lower whisker extends to 5.2. Similarly, the upper whisker extends to the most extreme observation inside the upper inner fence, where

$$\begin{aligned}
\text{Upper inner fence} &= \text{Upper hinge} + 1.5(IQR) \\
&= 9.625 + 1.5(2.575) \\
&= 9.625 + 3.863 = 13.488
\end{aligned}$$

The largest measurement inside this fence is the third largest measurement, 13.2. Note that the longer upper whisker reveals the rightward skewness of the R&D distribution.

Values that are beyond the inner fences are deemed *potential outliers* because they are extreme values that represent relatively rare occurrences. In fact, for mound-shaped distributions, fewer than 1% of the observations are expected to fall outside the inner fences. Two of the 50 R&D measurements, both at 13.5, fall outside the upper inner fence. Each of these potential outliers is represented by the asterisk (*) at 13.5.

---

*Although box plots can be generated by hand, the amount of detail required makes them particularly well suited for computer generation. We use computer software to generate the box plots in this section.

The other two imaginary fences, the outer fences, are defined at a distance 3(IQR) from each end of the box. Measurements that fall beyond the outer fence are represented by 0s (zeros) and are very extreme measurements that require special analysis. Because less than one-hundredth of 1% (.01% or .0001) of the measurements from mound-shaped distributions are expected to fall beyond the outer fence, these measurements are considered to be *outliers*. No measurement in the R&D percentage box plot (Figure 28) is represented by a 0; thus there are no outliers.

Recall that outliers are extreme measurements that stand out from the rest of the sample and may be faulty: They may be incorrectly recorded observations, members of a population different from the rest of the sample, or, at the least, very unusual measurements from the same population. For example, the two R&D measurements at 13.5 (identified by an asterisk) may be considered outliers. When we analyze these measurements, we find that they are correctly recorded. However, it turns out that both represent R&D expenditures of relatively young and fast-growing companies. Thus, the outlier analysis may have revealed important factors that relate to the R&D expenditures of high-tech companies: their age and rate of growth. Outlier analysis often reveals useful information of this kind and therefore plays an important role in the statistical inference-making process.

In addition to detecting outliers, box plots provide useful information on the variation in a data set. The elements (and nomenclature) of box plots are summarized in the next box. Some aids to the interpretation of box plots are also given.

Elements of a Box Plot

1. A rectangle (the **box**) is drawn with the ends (the **hinges**) drawn at the lower and upper quartiles (Q_L and Q_U). The median (Q_M) of the data is shown in the box, usually by a line or a symbol (such as "+").

2. The points at distances 1.5(IQR) from each hinge define the **inner fences** of the data set. Lines (the **whiskers**) are drawn from each hinge to the most extreme measurement inside the inner fence. Thus,

$$\text{Lower inner fence} = Q_L - 1.5(\text{IQR})$$
$$\text{Upper inner fence} = Q_U + 1.5(\text{IQR})$$

3. A second pair of fences, the **outer fences,** are defined at a distance of 3 interquartile ranges, 3(IQR) from the hinges. One symbol (usually "*") is used to represent measurements falling between the inner and outer fences, and another (usually "0") is used to represent measurements beyond the outer fences. Outer fences are not shown unless one or more measurements lie beyond them:

$$\text{Lower outer fence} = Q_L - 3(\text{IQR})$$
$$\text{Upper outer fence} = Q_U + 3(\text{IQR})$$

4. The symbols used to represent the median and the extreme data points (those beyond the fences) will vary depending on the software you use to construct the box plot. (You may use your own symbols if you are constructing a box plot by hand.) You should consult the program's documentation to determine exactly which symbols are used.

Aids to the Interpretation of Box Plots

1. The line (median) inside the box represents the "center" of the distribution of data.

2. Examine the length of the box. The IQR is a measure of the sample's variability and is especially useful for the comparison of two samples (see Example 17).

3. Visually compare the lengths of the whiskers. If one is clearly longer, the distribution of the data is probably skewed in the direction of the longer whisker.

4. Analyze any measurements that lie beyond the fences. Fewer than 5% should fall beyond the inner fences, even for very skewed distributions. Measurements beyond the outer fences are probably outliers, with one of the following explanations:

a. The measurement is incorrect. It may have been observed, recorded, or entered into the computer incorrectly.

b. The measurement belongs to a population different from the population that the rest of the sample was drawn from (see Example 17).

c. The measurement is correct *and* from the same population as the rest. Generally, we accept this explanation only after carefully ruling out all others.

Example 16

Interpreting a Box Plot—Lost Price Quotes

Problem In Example 2 we analyzed 50 processing times (listed in Table 4) for the development of price quotes by the manufacturer of industrial wheels. The intent was to determine whether the success or failure in obtaining the order was related to the amount of time to process the price quotes. Each quote that corresponds to "lost" business was so classified. Use a statistical software package to draw a box plot for all 50 processing times. What does the box plot reveal about the data? Identify any outliers in the data set.

Solution The Minitab box plot printout for these data is shown in Figure 29. Note that the upper whisker is much longer than the lower whisker, indicating rightward skewness of the data. However, the most important feature of the data is made very obvious by the box plot: There are four measurements (indicated by asterisks) that are beyond the upper inner fence. Thus, the distribution is extremely skewed to the right, and several measurements—or outliers—need special attention in our analysis. Examination of the data reveals that these four outliers correspond to processing times 14.06, 14.32, 16.29, and 20.23 days.

Look Back Before removing outliers from the data set, a good analyst will make a concerted effort to find the cause of the outliers. We offer an explanation for these processing time outliers in the next example.

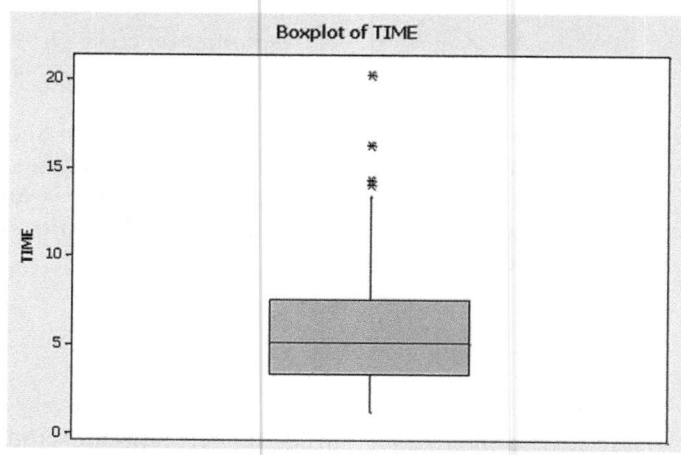

Figure 29

Minitab box plot for processing time data

Now Work Exercise 108

Example 17

Comparing Box Plots—Lost Price Quotes

Problem Refer to Example 16. The box plot for the 50 processing times (Figure 29) does not explicitly reveal the differences, if any, between the set of times corresponding to the success and the set of times corresponding to the failure to obtain the business. Box plots corresponding to the 39 "won" and 11 "lost" bids were generated using SPSS and are shown in Figure 30. Interpret them.

Solution The division of the data set into two parts, corresponding to won and lost bids, eliminates any observations that are beyond the inner fences. Furthermore, the skewness in the distributions has been reduced, as evidenced by the fact that the upper whiskers are only slightly longer than the lower. The box plots also reveal that the processing times corresponding to the lost bids tend to exceed those of the won bids. A plausible explanation for the outliers in the combined box plot (Figure 29) is that they are from a different population than the bulk of the times. In other words, there are two populations represented by the sample of processing times—one corresponding to lost bids and the other to won bids.

Look Back The box plots lend support to the conclusion that the price quote processing time and the success of acquiring the business are related. However, whether the visual differences between the box plots generalize to inferences about the populations corresponding to these two samples is a matter for inferential statistics, not graphical descriptions.

TIME

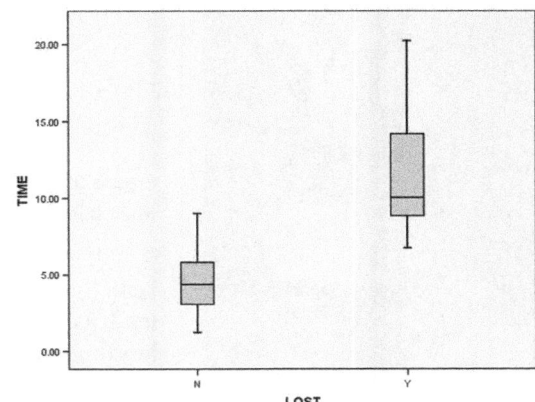

Figure 30
SPSS box plots of processing times for won and lost bids

■ **Now Work Exercise 110**

The following example illustrates how z-scores can be used to detect outliers and make inferences.

Example 18

Inference Using z-Scores—Salary Discrimination

Problem Suppose a female bank employee believes that her salary is low as a result of sex discrimination. To substantiate her belief, she collects information on the salaries of her male counterparts in the banking business. She finds that their salaries have a mean of $64,000 and a standard deviation of $2,000. Her salary is $57,000. Does this information support her claim of sex discrimination?

Solution The analysis might proceed as follows: First, we calculate the z-score for the woman's salary with respect to those of her male counterparts. Thus,

$$z = \frac{\$57,000 - \$64,000}{\$2,000} = -3.5$$

The implication is that the woman's salary is 3.5 standard deviations *below* the mean of the male salary distribution. Furthermore, if a check of the male salary data shows that the frequency distribution is mound-shaped, we can infer that very few salaries in this distribution should have a z-score less than -3, as shown in Figure 31. Clearly, a z-score of -3.5 represents an outlier. Either this female's salary is from a distribution different from the male salary distribution, or it is a very unusual (highly improbable) measurement from a distribution that is no different from the male salary distribution.

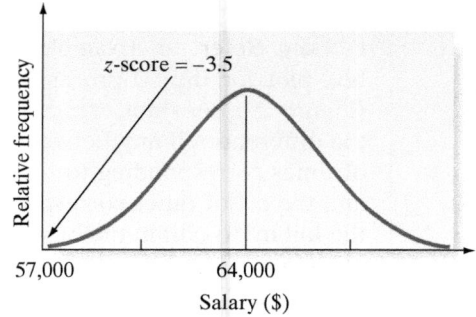

Figure 31

Male salary distribution

Look Back Which of the two situations do you think prevails? Statistical thinking would lead us to conclude that her salary does not come from the male salary distribution, lending support to the female bank employee's claim of sex discrimination. A careful investigator should aquire more information before inferring sex discrimination as the cause. We would want to know more about the data-collection technique the woman used and more about her competence at her job. Also, perhaps other factors such as length of employment should be considered in the analysis.

■ **Now Work Exercise 106**

Examples 17 and 18 exemplify an approach to statistical inference that might be called the **rare-event approach.** An experimenter hypothesizes a specific frequency distribution to describe a population of measurements. Then a sample of measurements is drawn from the population. If the experimenter finds it unlikely that the sample came from the hypothesized distribution, the hypothesis is concluded to be false. Thus, in Example 18 the woman believes her salary reflects discrimination. She hypothesizes that her salary should be just another measurement in the distribution of her male counterparts' salaries if no discrimination exists. However, it is so unlikely that the sample (in this case, her salary) came from the male frequency distribution that she rejects that hypothesis, concluding that the distribution from which her salary was drawn is different from the distribution for the men.

We conclude this section with some rules of thumb for detecting outliers.

Rules of Thumb for Detecting Outliers*

Box Plots: Observations falling between the inner and outer fences are deemed *suspect outliers*. Observations falling beyond the outer fence are deemed *highly suspect outliers*.

Suspect Outliers	Highly Suspect Outliers
Between $Q_L - 1.5(IQR)$ and $Q_L - 3(IQR)$ or Between $Q_U + 1.5(IQR)$ and $Q_U + 3(IQR)$	Below $Q_L - 3(IQR)$ or Above $Q_U + 3(IQR)$

z-scores: Observations with z-scores greater than 3 in absolute value are considered outliers. For some highly skewed data sets, observations with z-scores greater than 2 in absolute value may be outliers.

Possible Outliers	Outliers
$|z| > 2$	$|z| > 3$

*The z-score and box plot methods both establish rule-of-thumb limits outside of which a measurement is deemed to be an outlier. Usually, the two methods produce similar results. However, the presence of one or more outliers in a data set can inflate the computed value of s. Consequently, it will be less likely that an errant observation would have a z-score larger than 3 in absolute value. In contrast, the values of the quartiles used to calculate the intervals for a box plot are not affected by the presence of outliers.

STATISTICS
in ACTION
REVISITED

Detecting Outliers

In the *Journal of Experimental Social Psychology* (Vol. 45, 2009) study on whether money can buy love, recall that the researchers measured the quantitative variable *birthday gift price* (dollars) for each of the 237 participants. Are there any unusual reported prices in the **BUYLOV** data set? We will apply both the box plot and z-score methods to aid in identifying any outliers in the data. Since from previous analyses, there appears to be a difference in the distribution of reported prices for gift-givers and gift-recipients, we will analyze the data by role.

z-Score Method: To employ the z-score method, we require the mean and standard deviation of the data for each role type. These values were already computed in the previous Statistics in Action Revisited section. For gift-givers, $\bar{x} = \$105.84$ and $s = \$93.47$; for gift-recipients, $\bar{x} = \$149.00$ and $s = \$134.50$ (see Figure SIA8). Then, the 3-standard-deviation interval for each role is calculated as follows:

$$\text{Givers:} \quad \bar{x} \pm 3s = 105.84 \pm 3(93.47) = 105.84 \pm 280.41 = (0, 386.25)$$
$$\text{Receivers:} \quad \bar{x} \pm 3s = 149.00 \pm 3(134.50) = 149.00 \pm 403.50 = (0, 552.50)$$

(*Note:* Since price cannot be negative, we replaced negative lower endpoints with 0.) If you examine the gift prices for givers reported in the data set, you will find that only one ($431) falls beyond the 3-standard-deviation interval. None of the prices for receivers fall outside the 3-standard-deviation interval. Consequently, if we use the z-score approach, there is only one highly suspect outlier in the gift price data.

Box Plot Method: Box plots for the data are shown in Figure SIA9. Although several suspect outliers (asterisks) are shown on the box plot for each role type, there are no highly suspect outliers (zeros) shown. That is, no gift prices fall beyond the outer fences of the box plots.

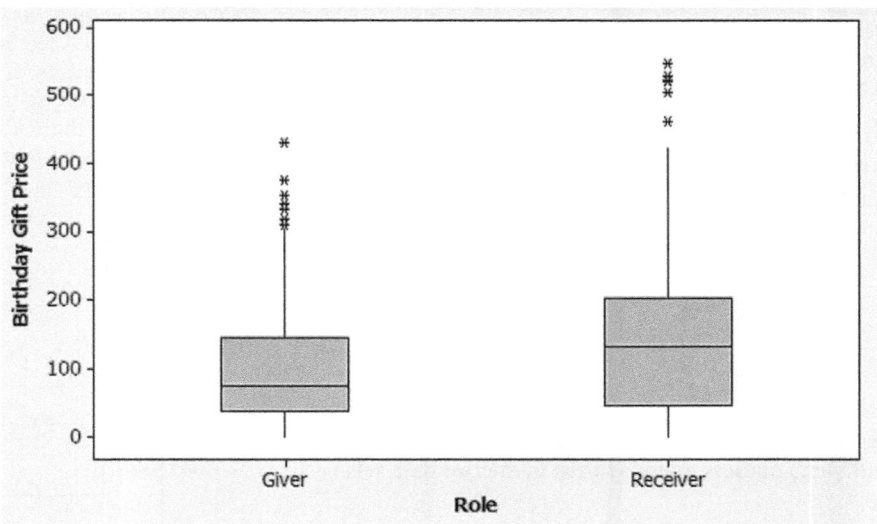

Figure SIA9

Minitab box plots for birthday gift price by role

Although not detected by the box plot method, the z-score method did detect one highly suspect outlier—the gift price of $431 reported by a birthday gift-giver. The researchers should investigate whether or not to include this observation in any analysis that leads to an inference about the population of gift-givers. Is the outlier a legitimate value (in which case it will remain in the data set for analysis), or is the outlier associated with a gift-giver who is not a member of the population of interest—say, a person who mistakenly reported on the price of a wedding gift rather than a birthday gift (in which case it will be removed from the data set prior to analysis)?

Data Set: BUYLOVE

Exercises 106–120

Learning the Mechanics

106 A sample data set has a mean of 57 and a standard deviation of 11. Determine whether each of the following sample measurements are outliers.

   a. 65
   b. 21
   c. 72
   d. 98

107 Suppose a data set consisting of exam scores has a lower quartile $Q_L = 60$, a median $Q_M = 75$, and an upper quartile $Q_U = 85$. The scores on the exam range from 18 to 100. Without having the actual scores available to you, construct as much of the box plot as possible.

108 Consider the horizontal box plot shown below.

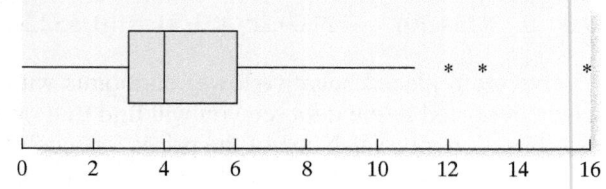

   a. What is the median of the data set (approximately)?
   b. What are the upper and lower quartiles of the data set (approximately)?
   c. What is the interquartile range of the data set (approximately)?
   d. Is the data set skewed to the left, skewed to the right, or symmetric?
   e. What percentage of the measurements in the data set lie to the right of the median? To the left of the upper quartile?
   f. Identify any outliers in the data.

109 Consider the following two sample data sets.

Sample A			Sample B		
121	171	158	171	152	170
173	184	163	168	169	171
157	85	145	190	183	185
165	172	196	140	173	206
170	159	172	172	174	169
161	187	100	199	151	180
142	166	171	167	170	188

   a. Construct a box plot for each data set.
   b. Identify any outliers that may exist in the two data sets.

Applet Exercise 7

Use the applet *Standard Deviation* to determine whether an item in a data set may be an outlier. Begin by setting appropriate limits and plotting the data below on the number line provided in the applet.

10 80 80 85 85 85 85 90 90 90 90 90 95 95 95 95 100 100

   a. The green arrow shows the approximate location of the mean. Multiply the standard deviation given by the applet by 3. Is the data item 10 more than 3 standard deviations away from the green arrow (the mean)? Can you conclude that the 10 is an outlier?

   b. Using the mean and standard deviation from part **a,** move the point at 10 on your plot to a point that appears to be about 3 standard deviations from the mean. Repeat the process in part **a** for the new plot and the new suspected outlier.

   c. When you replaced the extreme value in part **a** with a number that appeared to be within 3 standard deviations of the mean, the standard deviation got smaller and the mean moved to the right, yielding a new data set where the extreme value was not within 3 standard deviations of the mean. Continue to replace the extreme value with higher numbers until the new value is within 3 standard deviations of the mean in the new data set. Use trial and error to estimate the smallest number that can replace the 10 in the original data set so that the replacement is not considered to be an outlier.

Applying the Concepts—Basic

110 Treating psoriasis with the "Doctorfish of Kangal." Psoriasis is a skin disorder with no known cure and no proven effective pharmacological treatment. An alternative treatment for psoriasis is ichthyotherapy, also known as therapy with the "Doctorfish of Kangal." Fish from the hot pools of Kangal, Turkey, feed on the skin scales of bathers, reportedly reducing the symptoms of psoriasis. In one study, 67 patients diagnosed with psoriasis underwent 3 weeks of ichthyotherapy (*Evidence-Based Research in Complementary and Alternative Medicine,* Dec. 2006). The Psoriasis Area Severity Index (PASI) of each patient was measured both before and after treatment. (The lower the PASI score, the better is the skin condition.) Box plots of the PASI scores, both before (baseline) and after 3 weeks of ichthyotherapy treatment, are shown in the accompanying diagram.

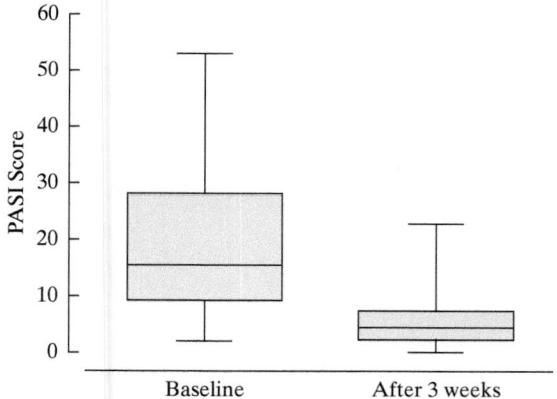

Source: Based on "Ichthyotherapy as alternative treatment for patients with psoriasis: A pilot study" by M. Grassberger and W. Hoch, from EVIDENCE-BASED RESEARCH IN COMPLEMENTARY AND ALTERNATIVE MEDICINE, December 2006, Volume 3(4).

   a. Find the approximate 25th percentile, the median, and the 75th percentile for the PASI scores before treatment.

b. Find the approximate 25th percentile, the median, and the 75th percentile for the PASI scores after treatment.

c. Comment on the effectiveness of ichthyotherapy in treating psoriasis.

111 Budget lapsing at army hospitals. Accountants use the term *budget lapsing* to describe the situation that occurs when unspent funds do not carry over from one budgeting period to the next. Due to budget lapsing, U.S. army hospitals tend to stockpile pharmaceuticals and other supplies toward the end of the fiscal year, leading to a spike in expenditures. This phenomenon was investigated in the *Journal of Management Accounting Research* (Vol. 19, 2007). Data on expenses per full-time equivalent employees for a sample of 1,751 army hospitals yielded the following summary statistics: $\bar{x} = \$6,563$, $m = \$6,232$, $s = \$2,484$, $Q_L = \$5,309$, and $Q_U = \$7,216$.

a. Interpret, practically, the measures of relative standing.

b. Compute the interquartile range, IQR, for the data.

c. What proportion of the 1,751 army hospitals have expenses between \$5,309 and \$7,216?

112 Salary offers to MBAs. Consider the top salary offer (in thousands of dollars) received by each member of a sample of 50 MBA students who graduated from the Graduate School of Management at Rutgers, the state university of New Jersey. Descriptive statistics and a box plot for the data are shown on the XLSTAT printouts below.

MBASAL

Statistic	SALARY
No. of observations	50
Minimum	35.0000
Maximum	75.0000
Range	40.0000
1st Quartile	45.7250
Median	51.0000
3rd Quartile	58.9000
Mean	52.3340
Variance (n-1)	85.0851
Standard deviation (n-1)	9.2242

Box plots:

Box plot (SALARY)

a. Find and interpret the z-score associated with the highest salary offer, the lowest salary offer, and the mean salary offer. Would you consider the highest offer to be unusually high? Why or why not?

b. Based on the box plot for this data set, which salary offers (if any) are suspect or highly suspect outliers?

113 Semester hours taken by CPA candidates. Refer to the *Journal of Accounting and Public Policy* (Spring 2002) study of 100,000 first-time candidates for the CPA exam, Exercise 51. The number of semester hours of college credit earned by the candidates had a mean of 141.31 hours and a standard deviation of 17.77 hours.

a. Find the z-score for a first-time candidate for the CPA exam who earned 160 semester hours of college credit. Is this observation considered an outlier?

b. Give a value of the number of semester hours that would, in fact, be considered an outlier in this data set.

Applying the Concepts—Intermediate

114 Corporate sustainability of CPA firms. Refer to the *Business and Society* (March 2011) study on the sustainability behaviors of CPA corporations, Exercise 100. Recall that data on the level of support for corporate sustainability were recorded for each of 992 senior managers. One of the managers reported a support level of 155 points. Use both a graph and a numerical technique to determine if this observation is an outlier.

CORSUS

115 Time in bankruptcy. Refer to the *Financial Management* (Spring 1995) study of 49 firms filing for prepackaged bankruptcies, Exercise 32. Recall that three types of "prepack" firms exist: (1) those who hold no prefiling vote, (2) those who vote their preference for a joint solution; and (3) those who vote their preference for a prepack.

BNKRPT

a. Construct a box plot for the time in bankruptcy (months) for each type of firm.

b. Find the median bankruptcy times for the three types.

c. How do the variabilities of the bankruptcy times compare for the three types?

d. The standard deviations of the bankruptcy times are 2.47 for "none," 1.72 for "joint," and 0.96 for "prepack." Do the standard deviations agree with the interquartile ranges with regard to the comparison of the variabilities of the bankruptcy times?

e. Is there evidence of outliers in any of the three distributions?

116 Hazardous waste cleanup in Arkansas. Refer to Exercise 101 and the data on the number of Superfund sites in each of 75 Arkansas counties.

SPRFND

a. There is at least one outlier in the data. Use the methods of this chapter to detect the outliers.

b. Delete the outlier(s) found in part **a** from the data set and recalculate measures of central tendency and variation. Which measures are most affected by the removal of the outlier(s)?

117 Sanitation inspection of cruise ships. Refer to Exercise 81 and the data on the sanitation levels of passenger cruise ships.

SANIT

a. Use the box plot method to detect any outliers in the data set.

b. Use the z-score method to detect any outliers in the data set.

c. Do the two methods agree? If not, explain why.

118 Network server downtime. A manufacturer of network computer server systems is interested in improving its customer support services. As a first step, its marketing department has been charged with the responsibility of summarizing the extent of customer problems in terms of system downtime. The 40 most recent customers were surveyed to determine the amount of downtime (in hours) they had experienced during the previous month. These data are listed in the table.

Customer Number	Downtime	Customer Number	Downtime
230	12	250	4
231	16	251	10
232	5	252	15
233	16	253	7
234	21	254	20
235	29	255	9
236	38	256	22
237	14	257	18
238	47	258	28
239	0	259	19
240	24	260	34
241	15	261	26
242	13	262	17
243	8	263	11
244	2	264	64
245	11	265	19
246	22	266	18
247	17	267	24
248	31	268	49
249	10	269	50

a. Construct a box plot for these data. Use the information reflected in the box plot to describe the frequency distribution of the data set. Your description should address central tendency, variation, and skewness.

b. Use your box plot to determine which customers are having unusually lengthy downtimes.

c. Find and interpret the z-scores associated with the customers you identified in part **b**.

Applying the Concepts—Advanced

119 Made-to-order delivery times. Refer to the data on delivery times for a made-to-order product, Exercise 34. The delivery times (in days) for a sample of 25 orders are repeated in the accompanying table. (Times marked by an asterisk are associated with customers who subsequently placed additional orders with the company.) Identify any unusual observations (outliers) in the data set, and then use the results to comment on the claim that repeat customers tend to have shorter delivery times than one-time customers.

50*	64*	56*	43*	64*	82*	65*	49*	32*	63*	44*	71	54*
51*	102	49*	73*	50*	39*	86	33*	95	59*	51*	68	

120 Sensor motion of a robot. Researchers at Carnegie Mellon University developed an algorithm for estimating the sensor motion of a robotic arm by mounting a camera with inertia sensors on the arm (*International Journal of Robotics Research*, Dec. 2004). One variable of interest is the error of estimating arm translation (measured in centimeters). Data for 10 experiments are listed in the following table. In each experiment, the perturbation of camera intrinsics and projections were varied. Suppose a trial resulted in a translation error of 4.5 cm. Is this value an outlier for trials with perturbed intrinsics but no perturbed projections? For trials with perturbed projections but no perturbed intrinsics? What type of camera perturbation most likely occurred for this trial?

Trial	Perturbed Intrinsics	Perturbed Projections	Translation Error (cm)
1	Yes	No	1.0
2	Yes	No	1.3
3	Yes	No	3.0
4	Yes	No	1.5
5	Yes	No	1.3
6	No	Yes	22.9
7	No	Yes	21.0
8	No	Yes	34.4
9	No	Yes	29.8
10	No	Yes	17.7

Source: Strelow. D., & Singh, S. "Motion estimation form image and intertial measurements," *International Journal of Robotics Research*, Vol. 23, No. 12, Dec. 2004 (Table 4). Dennis Strelow, © November 2004. Reprinted by permission of the author.

8 | Graphing Bivariate Relationships*

The claim is often made that the crime rate and the unemployment rate are "highly correlated." Another popular belief is that the gross domestic product (GDP) and the rate of inflation are "related." Some people even believe that the Dow Jones Industrial Average and the lengths of fashionable skirts are "associated." The words *correlated*, *related*, and *associated* imply a relationship between two variables—in the examples above, two *quantitative* variables.

One way to describe the relationship between two quantitative variables–called a **bivariate relationship**—is to plot the data in a **scatterplot**. A scatterplot is a two-dimensional graph, with one variable's values plotted along the vertical axis and the other variable's values plotted along the horizontal axis. For example, Figure 32 is a

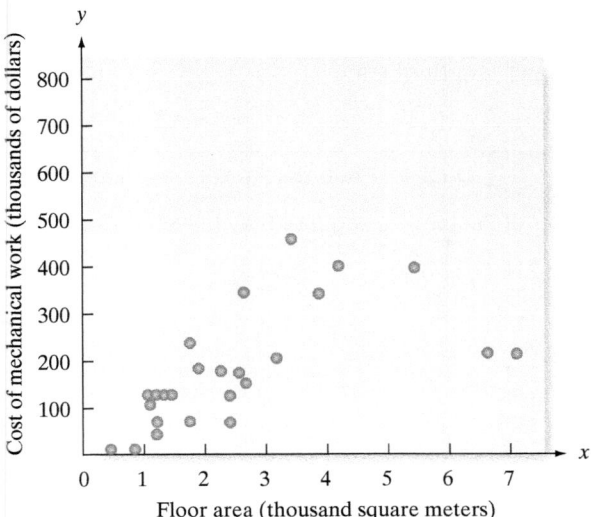

Figure 32

Scatterplot of cost vs. floor area

scatterplot relating (1) the cost of mechanical work (heating, ventilating, and plumbing) to (2) the floor area of the building for a sample of 26 factory and warehouse buildings. Note that the scatterplot suggests a general tendency for mechanical cost to increase as building floor area increases.

When an increase in one variable is generally associated with an increase in the second variable, we say that the two variables are "positively related" or "positively correlated." Figure 32 implies that mechanical cost and floor area are positively correlated. Alternatively, if one variable has a tendency to decrease as the other increases, we say the variables are "negatively correlated." Figure 33 shows hypothetical scatterplots that portray a positive bivariate relationship (Figure 33a), a negative bivariate relationship (Figure 33b), and a situation where the two variables are unrelated (Figure 33c).

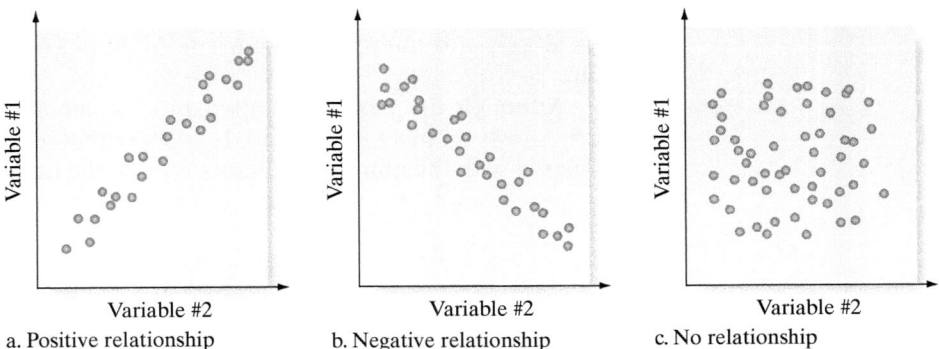

Figure 33

Hypothetical bivariate relationship

a. Positive relationship   b. Negative relationship   c. No relationship

Example   19

Graphing Bivariate Data—Hospital Length of Stay

Problem A medical item used to treat a hospital patient is called a *factor*. For example, factors can be intravenous (IV) tubing, IV fluid, needles, shave kits, bedpans, diapers, dressings, medications, and even code carts. The coronary care unit at Bayonet Point Hospital (St. Petersburg, Florida) recently investigated the relationship between the number of factors used per patient and the patient's length of stay (in days). Data on these two variables for a sample of 50 coronary care patients are given in Table 9. Use a scatterplot to describe the relationship between the two variables of interest: number of factors and length of stay.

Table 9	Data on Patient's Factors and Length of Stay		
Number of Factors	Length of Stay (days)	Number of Factors	Length of Stay (days)
231	9	354	11
323	7	142	7
113	8	286	9
208	5	341	10
162	4	201	5
117	4	158	11
159	6	243	6
169	9	156	6
55	6	184	7
77	3	115	4
103	4	202	6
147	6	206	5
230	6	360	6
78	3	84	3
525	9	331	9
121	7	302	7
248	5	60	2
233	8	110	2
260	4	131	5
224	7	364	4
472	12	180	7
220	8	134	6
383	6	401	15
301	9	155	4
262	7	338	8

Source: Based on Bayonet Point Hospital, Coronary Care Unit. *Data Set:* MEDFAC

Solution Rather than construct the plot by hand, we resort to a statistical software package. The XLSTAT plot of the data in Table 9, with length of stay (LOS) on the vertical axis and number of factors (FACTORS) on the horizontal axis, is shown in Figure 34.

Although the plotted points exhibit a fair amount of variation, the scatterplot clearly shows an increasing trend. It appears that a patient's length of stay is positively correlated with the number of factors used in the patient's care.

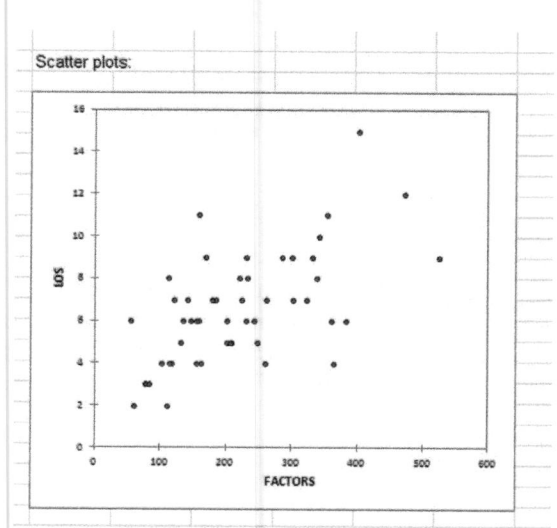

Figure 34

XLSTAT scatterplot of data in Table 9

Look Back If hospital administrators can be confident that the sample trend shown in Figure 34 accurately describes the trend in the population, then they may use this information to improve their forecasts of lengths of stay for future patients.

Now Work Exercise 123

The scatterplot is a simple but powerful tool for describing a bivariate relationship. However, keep in mind that it is only a graph. No measure of reliability can be attached to inferences made about bivariate populations based on scatterplots of sample data.

Interpreting Scatterplots

Refer, again, to the *Journal of Experimental Social Psychology* (Vol. 45, 2009) study on whether money can buy love. Two quantitative variables of interest to the Stanford University researchers were *birthday gift price* (dollars) and *overall level of appreciation for the gift* (measured on a scale from 2 to 14). To investigate a possible relationship between these two variables, we created a scatterplot for the data collected for each of the 237 participants. The Minitab scatterplot is displayed in Figure SIA10a.

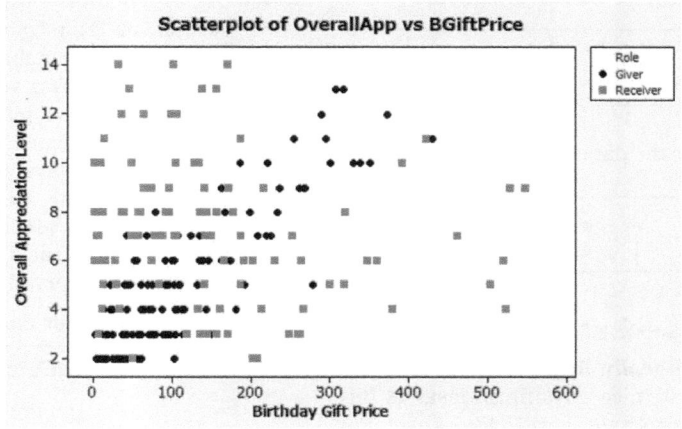

Figure SIA10a

Minitab scatterplot of appreciation level vs. gift price

At first glance, the graph appears to show little or no association between appreciation level and gift price. However, if you look closely you will see that the data points associated with gift-givers are plotted with a different symbol (black circle) than the data points associated with gift-recipients (red square). Focusing on just the black circles, a fairly strong positive trend is apparent. To see this trend more clearly, we generated side-by-side scatterplots for the data, one plot for givers and one for receivers. This graph is shown in Figure SIA10b.

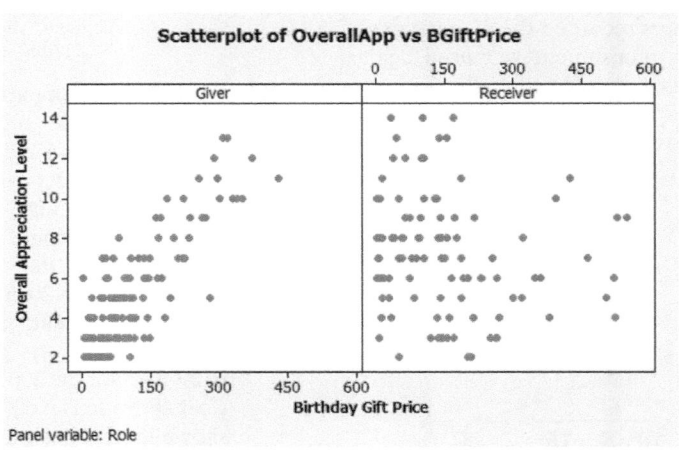

Figure SIA10b

Minitab side-by-side scatterplots for the study

The left panel of Figure SIA10b shows a fairly strong positive association between appreciation level and gift price for gift-givers. As gift price increases, the gift-giver anticipates that the level of appreciation for the gift will increase. Conversely, the right panel of Figure SIA10b shows little or no association between appreciation level and gift price for gift-recipients. This type of analysis led the Stanford University researchers to conclude that "gift-givers and gift-receivers disagree about the link between gift price and gift-recipients' feelings of appreciation. Givers anticipated that recipients would appreciate more expensive gifts, but gift-recipients did not base their feelings of appreciation on how much the gift cost."

Exercises 121–132

Learning the Mechanics

121 Construct a scatterplot for the data in the following table.

Variable 1:	5	1	1.5	2	2.5	3	3.5	4	4.5	5
Variable 2:	2	1	3	4	6	10	9	12	17	17

122 Construct a scatterplot for the data in the following table.

Variable 1:	5	3	−1	2	7	6	4	0	8
Variable 2:	14	3	10	1	8	5	3	2	12

Applying the Concepts—Basic

123 **In business, do nice guys really finish last?** In baseball, there is an old saying that "nice guys finish last." Is this true in the competitive corporate world? Researchers at Harvard University attempted to answer this question and reported their results in *Nature* (March 20, 2008). In the study, Boston-area college students repeatedly played a version of the game "prisoner's dilemma," where competitors choose cooperation, defection, or costly punishment. (Cooperation meant paying 1 unit for the opponent to receive 2 units; defection meant gaining 1 unit at a cost of 1 unit for the opponent; and punishment meant paying 1 unit for the opponent to lose 4 units.) At the conclusion of the games, the researchers recorded the average payoff and the number of times punishment was used against each player. A graph of the data is shown in the accompanying scatterplot. Does it appear that average payoff is associated with punishment use? The researchers concluded that "winners don't punish." Do you agree? Explain.

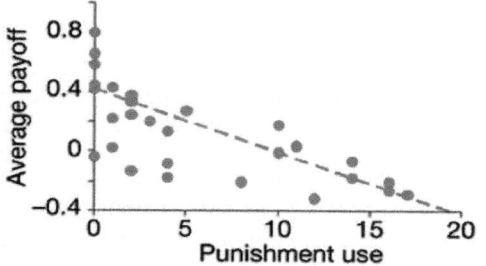

124 **Lobster trap placement.** Strategic placement of lobster traps is one of the keys for a successful lobster fisherman. An observational study of teams fishing for the red spiny lobster in Baja California Sur, Mexico, was conducted and the results published in *Bulletin of Marine Science* (April 2010). Two variables measured for each of eight teams from the Punta Abreojos (PA) fishing cooperative were y = total catch of lobsters (in kilograms) during the season and x = average percentage of traps allocated per day to exploring areas of unknown catch (called *search frequency*). These data are listed in the accompanying table. Graph the data in a scatterplot. What type of trend, if any, do you observe?

Lobster Fishing Study Data

Total Catch	Search Frequency
2,785	35
6,535	21
6,695	26
4,891	29
4,937	23
5,727	17
7,019	21
5,735	20

Source: Based on Shester, G. G. "Explaining catch variation among Baja California lobster fishers through spatial analysis of trap-placement decisions," *Bulletin of Marine Science*, Vol. 86, No. 2, April 2010 (Table 1), pp. 479–498.

125 **Does elevation impact hitting performance in baseball?** The Colorado Rockies play their Major League home baseball games at Coors Field, Denver. Each year, the Rockies are among the leaders in team batting statistics (e.g., home runs, batting average, and slugging percentage). Many baseball experts attribute this phenomenon to the "thin air" of Denver—called the "mile-high" city due to its elevation. *Chance* (Winter 2006) investigated the effects of elevation on slugging percentage in Major League Baseball. Data were compiled on players' composite slugging percentage at each of 29 cities for the 2003 season, as well as each city's elevation (feet above sea level). The data for selected observations are shown in the table on the next page. Construct a scatterplot of the data for all 29 cities. Do you detect a trend?

Data for Exercise 125

City	Slug Pct.	Elevation
Anaheim	.480	160
Arlington	.605	616
Atlanta	.530	1,050
Baltimore	.505	130
Boston	.505	20
⋮	⋮	⋮
Denver	.625	5,277
⋮	⋮	⋮
Seattle	.550	350
San Francisco	.510	63
St. Louis	.570	465
Tampa	.500	10
Toronto	.535	566

Source: Schaffer, J., & Heiny. E. L. "The effects of elevation on slugging percentage in Major League Baseball." *Chance*, Vol. 19, No. 1. Winter 2006 (adapted from Figure 2, p. 30).

126 State SAT scores. Refer to Exercise 27 and the data on state SAT scores. Construct a scatterplot for the data, with SATMAT 2001 Math SAT score on the horizontal axis and 2011 Math SAT score on the vertical axis. What type of trend do you detect?

127 Are geography journals worth their cost? In *Geoforum* (Vol. 37, 2006), Simon Fraser University professor Nicholas GEOJRN Blomley assessed whether the price of a geography journal is correlated with quality. He collected pricing data (cost for a 1-year subscription in U.S. dollars) for a sample of 28 geography journals. In addition to cost, three other variables were measured: Journal Impact Factor (JIF), defined as

Journal	Cost ($)	JIF	Cites	RPI
J. Econ. Geogr.	468	3.139	207	1.16
Prog. Hum. Geog.	624	2.943	544	0.77
T. I. Brit. Geogr.	499	2.388	249	1.11
Econ. Geogr.	90	2.325	173	0.30
A. A. A. Geogr.	698	2.115	377	0.93
Antipode	717	1.922	333	0.96
Reg. Stud.	1,312	1.652	445	1.49
Environ. Plan A	1,297	1.622	773	0.91
Environ. Plan D	479	1.591	297	0.99
Geoforum	1,118	1.560	298	1.58
Area	242	1.475	215	0.53
Polit. Geogr.	1,099	1.316	282	1.92
Int. J. Geogr. IS	1,733	1.234	240	3.42
Landscape. Ur. Plan	1,619	1.204	446	1.56
Sing. J. Trop. Geo.	197	1.029	62	1.13
Aust. Geogr.	345	0.947	72	1.83
Eur. Geogr. Eco.	499	0.780	62	1.99
Urban. Geogr.	530	0.667	135	1.81
J. Hist. Geogr.	388	0.661	96	1.44
Tij. Eco. Soc. Geo	343	0.518	99	1.00
Cult. Geogr.	538	0.500	24	NA
Pap. Reg. Sci.	397	0.481	89	1.36
Can. Geo. Can.	253	0.429	74	1.05
J. Geo. High. Ed.	1,115	0.413	79	4.33
Cartogr. J.	266	0.295	18	3.11
Geogr. Anal.	213	0.902	106	0.88
Geogr. J.	223	0.857	81	0.94
Appl. Geogr.	646	0.853	74	3.38

Source: Data from Blomley, N. "Is this journal worth US$1118?. "*Geoforum*, Vol. 37, 2006.

the average number of times articles from the journal have been cited; number of citations for a journal over the past 5 years; Relative Price Index (RPI), a measure developed by economists. [*Note:* A journal with an RPI less than 1.25 is considered a "good value."] The data for the 28 geography journals are listed in the accompanying table.

a. Construct a scatterplot for the variables JIF and cost. Do you detect a trend?

b. Construct a scatterplot for the variables number of cites and cost. Do you detect a trend?

c. Construct a scatterplot for the variables RPI and cost. Do you detect a trend?

Applying the Concepts—Intermediate

128 Spreading rate of spilled liquid. A contract engineer at DuPont Corp. studied the rate at which a spilled volatile LSPILL liquid will spread across a surface (*Chemical Engineering Progress,* Jan. 2005). Assume 50 gallons of methanol spills onto a level surface outdoors. The engineer used derived empirical formulas (assuming a state of turbulent-free convection) to calculate the mass (in pounds) of the spill after a period of time ranging from 0 to 60 minutes. The calculated mass values are given in the table. Is there evidence to indicate that the mass of the spill tends to diminish as time increases? Support your answer with a scatterplot.

Time (minutes)	Mass (pounds)
0	6.64
1	6.34
2	6.04
4	5.47
6	4.94
8	4.44
10	3.98
12	3.55
14	3.15
16	2.79
18	2.45
20	2.14
22	1.86
24	1.60
26	1.37
28	1.17
30	0.98
35	0.60
40	0.34
45	0.17
50	0.06
55	0.02
60	0.00

Source: Based on Barry. J. "Estimating rates of spreading and evaporation of volatile liquids." *Chemical Engineering Progress,*. Vol. 101, No. 1. Jan. 2005, p. 38.

129 Performance ratings of government agencies. The U.S. Office of Management and Budget (OMB) requires government agencies to produce annual performance and PARS accounting reports (PARS) each year. A research team at George Mason University evaluated the quality of the PARS for 24 government agencies (*The Public Manager,* Summer 2008). Evaluation scores ranged from 12 (lowest) to 60 (highest). The PARS evaluation scores for two consecutive years are shown in the next table.

Data for Exercise 129

Agency	Year 1	Year 2
Transportation	55	53
Labor	53	51
Veterans	51	51
NRC	39	34
Commerce	37	36
HHS	37	35
DHS	37	30
Justice	35	37
Treasury	35	35
GSA	34	40
Agriculture	33	35
EPA	33	36
Social Security	33	33
USAID	32	42
Education	32	36
Interior	32	31
NASA	32	32
Energy	31	34
HUD	31	30
NSF	31	31
State	31	50
OPM	27	28
SBA	22	31
Defense	17	32

Source: "Performance ratings of government agencies," by J. Ellig and H. Wray, from Measuring Performance Reporting Quality. THE PUBLIC MANAGER, Vol. 37.2, Summer 2008, p. 68. Copyright © 2008 by Jerry Ellig. Reprinted with permission.

a. Construct a scatterplot for the data. Do you detect a trend in the data?

b. Based on the graph, identify one or two agencies that had greater than expected PARS evaluation scores for year 2.

130 **Most valuable NFL teams.** Refer to the *Forbes* listing of the 2011 values of the 32 teams in the National Football League (NFL), Exercise 26. Construct a scatterplot to investigate the relationship between 2011 value ($ millions) and operating income ($ millions). Would you recommend that an NFL executive use operating income to predict a team's current value? Explain.

131 **Doctors and ethics.** Refer to the *Journal of Medical Ethics* (Vol. 32, 2006) study of physicians' use of ethics consultation, Exercise 68. In addition to *length of time in practice* (i.e., years of experience), the researchers also measured the *amount of exposure to ethics in medical school* (number of hours) for the sample of 118 physicians.

a. Use data from the accompanying file to create a scatterplot for these two variables. Plot years of experience on the vertical axis and amount of exposure to ethics in medical school on the horizontal axis. Comment on the strength of the association between these two variables.

b. Conduct an outlier analysis of the data for the variable *amount of exposure to ethics in medical school.* Identify the highly suspect outlier in the data set.

c. Remove the outlier, part **b**, from the data set and re-create the scatterplot of part **a**. What do you observe?

Applying the Concepts—Advanced

132 **Ranking driving performance of professional golfers.** Refer to *The Sport Journal* (Winter 2007) analysis of a new method for ranking the total driving performance of golfers on the PGA tour, Exercise 50. Recall that the method uses both the average driving distance (yards) and driving accuracy (percent of drives that land in the fairway). Data on these two variables for the top 40 PGA golfers are saved in the accompanying file. A professional golfer is practicing a new swing to increase his average driving distance. However, he is concerned that his driving accuracy will be lower. Is his concern a valid one? Explain.

9 The Time Series Plot*

Each of the previous sections has been concerned with describing the information contained in a sample or population of data. Often these data are viewed as having been produced at essentially the same point in time. Thus, time has not been a factor in any of the graphical methods described so far.

Data of interest to managers are often produced and monitored over time. Examples include the daily closing price of their company's common stock, the company's weekly sales volume and quarterly profits, and characteristics—such as weight and length—of products produced by the company.

> Data that are produced and monitored over time are called **time series data.**

A process is a series of actions or operations that generates output over time. Accordingly, measurements taken of a sequence of units produced by a process–such as a production process—are time series data. In general, any sequence of numbers produced over time can be thought of as being generated by a process.

When measurements are made over time, it is important to record both the numerical value and the time or the time period associated with each measurement. With this information, a **time series plot**—sometimes called a **run chart**—can be constructed to describe the time series data and to learn about the process that generated the data.

A time series plot is simply a scatterplot with the measurements on the vertical axis and time or the order in which the measurements were made on the horizontal axis. The plotted points are usually connected by straight lines to make it easier to see the changes and movement in the measurements over time. For example, Figure 35 is a time series plot of a particular company's monthly sales (number of units sold per month). And Figure 36 is a time series plot of the weights of 30 one-gallon paint cans that were consecutively filled by the same filling head. Notice that the weights are plotted against the order in which the cans were filled rather than some unit of time. When monitoring production processes, it is often more convenient to record the order rather than the exact time at which each measurement was made.

Time series plots reveal the movement (trend) and changes (variation) in the variable being monitored. Notice how sales trend upward in the summer and how the variation in the weights of the paint cans increases over time. This kind of information would not be revealed by stem-and-leaf displays or histograms, as the following example illustrates.

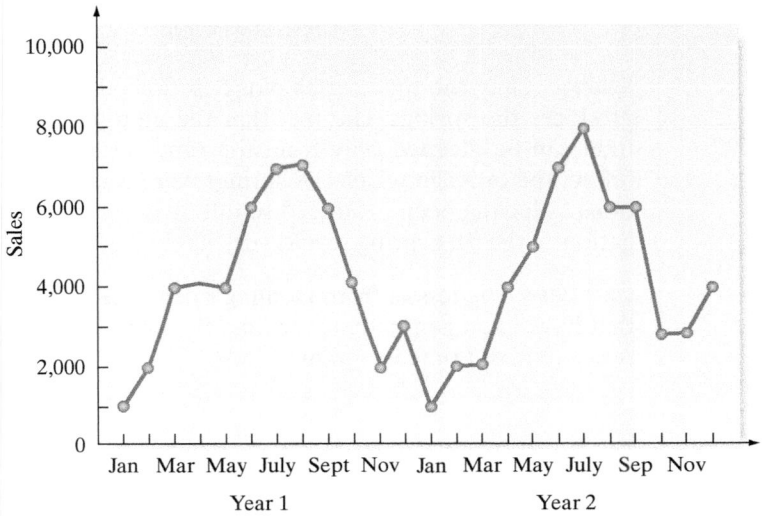

Figure 35

Time series plot of company sales

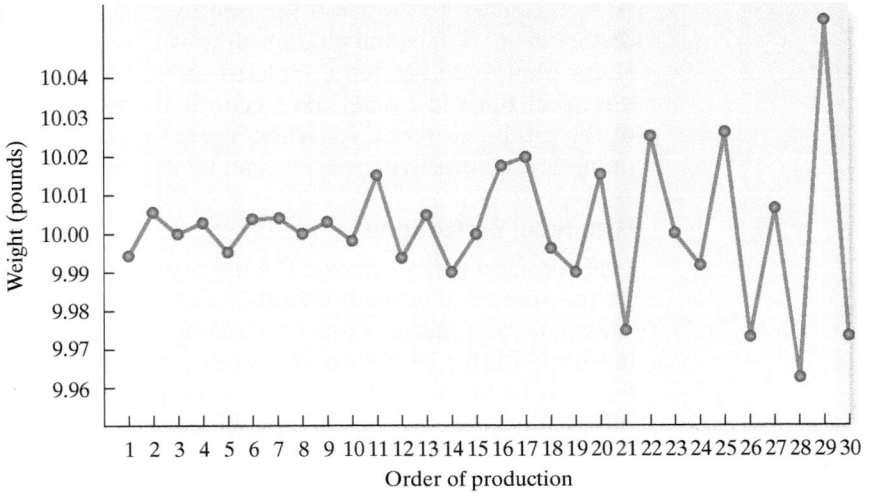

Figure 36

Time series plot of paint can weights

Example	20

Time Series Plot vs. a Histogram—Deming's Example

Problem W. Edwards Deming was one of America's most famous statisticians. He was best known for the role he played after World War II in teaching the Japanese how to improve the quality of their products by monitoring and continually improving their production processes. In his book *Out of the Crisis* (1986), Deming warned against the knee-jerk (i.e., automatic) use of histograms to display and extract information from data. As evidence, he offered the following example.

Fifty camera springs were tested in the order in which they were produced. The elongation of each spring was measured under the pull of 20 grams. Both a time series plot and a histogram were constructed from the measurements. They are shown in Figure 37, which has been reproduced from Deming's book. If you had to predict the elongation measurement of the next spring to be produced (i.e., spring 51) and could use only one of the two plots to guide your prediction, which would you use? Why?

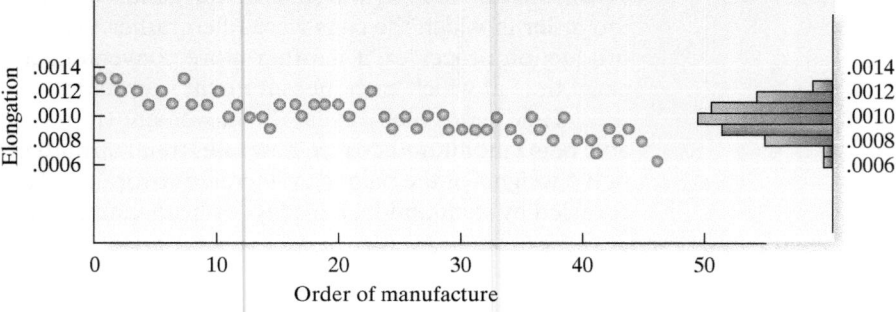

Figure 37

Deming's time series plot and histogram

Solution Only the time series plot describes the behavior *over time* of the process that produces the springs. The fact that the elongation measurements are decreasing over time can be gleaned only from the time series plot. Because the histogram does not reflect the order in which the springs were produced, it in effect represents all observations as having been produced simultaneously. Using the histogram to predict the elongation of the 51st spring would very likely lead to an overestimate.

Look Back The lesson from Deming's example is this: For displaying and analyzing data that have been generated over time by a process, the primary graphical tool is the time series plot, not the histogram.

10 Distorting the Truth with Descriptive Techniques

A picture may be "worth a thousand words," but pictures can also color messages or distort them. In fact, the pictures displayed in statistics (e.g., histograms, bar charts, time series plots, etc.) are susceptible to distortion, whether unintentional or as a result of unethical statistical practices. Accordingly, we begin this section by mentioning a few of the pitfalls to watch for when interpreting a chart or a graph. Then we discuss how numerical descriptive measures can be used to distort the truth.

Graphical Distortions

One common way to change the impression conveyed by a graph is to change the scale on the vertical axis, the horizontal axis, or both. For example, consider the data on collisions of large marine vessels operating in European waters over a 5-year period summarized in Table 10. Figure 38 is a Minitab bar graph showing the frequency of collisions for each of the three locations. The graph shows that "in port" collisions occur more often than collisions "at sea" or collisions in "restricted waters."

Table 10	Collisions of Marine Vessels by Location
Location	Number of Ships
At sea	376
Restricted waters	273
In port	478
TOTAL	1,127

Data Set: MARINE

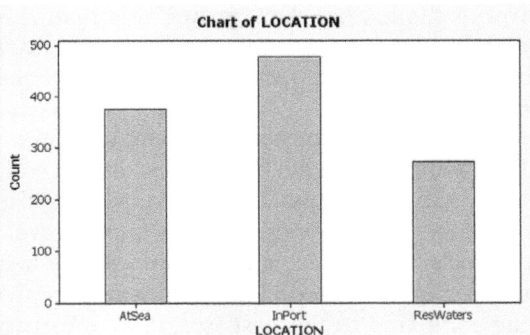

Figure 38

Minitab bar graph of vessel collisions by location

Suppose you want to use the same data to exaggerate the difference between the number of "in port" collisions and the number of collisions in "restricted waters." One way to do this is to increase the distance between successive units on the vertical axis—that is, to *stretch* the vertical axis by graphing only a few units per inch. A telltale sign of stretching is a long vertical axis, but this is often hidden by starting the vertical axis at some point above the origin, 0. Such a graph is shown in the SPSS printout, Figure 39. By starting the bar chart at 250 collisions (instead of at 0), it appears that the frequency of "in port" collisions is many times larger than the frequency of collisions in "restricted waters."

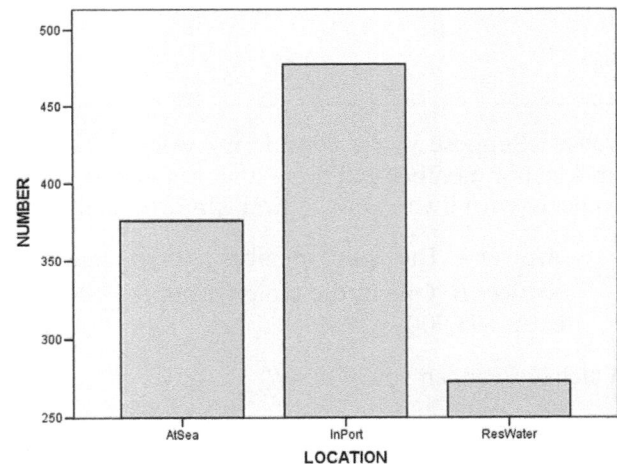

Figure 39

SPSS bar graph of vessel collisions by location—adjusted vertical axis

ETHICS in STATISTICS

Intentionally distorting a graph to portray a particular viewpoint is considered *unethical statistical practice*.

Another method of achieving visual distortion with bar graphs is by making the width of the bars proportional to the height. For example, look at the bar chart in Figure 40a, which depicts the percentage of a year's total automobile sales attributable to each of four major manufacturers. Now suppose we make both the width and the

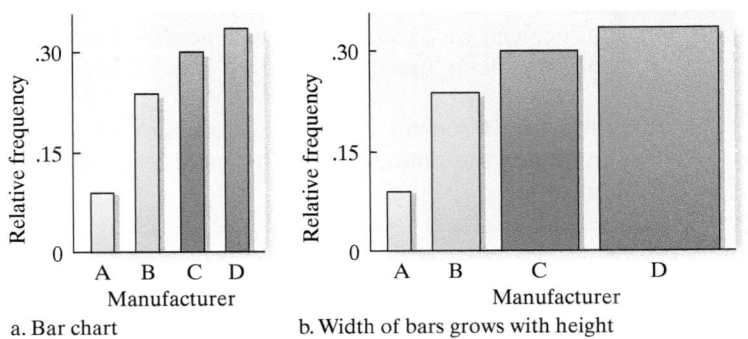

Figure 40

Relative share of the automobile market for each of four major manufacturers

Production declines again

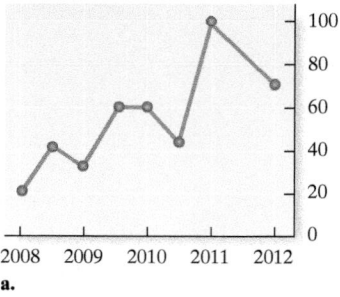

a.

2012: 2nd best year for production

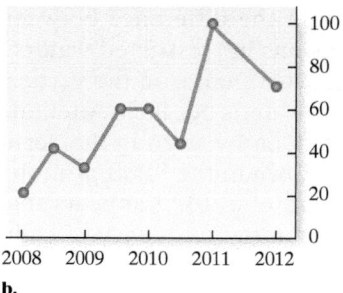

b.

Figure 41

Changing the verbal description to change a viewer's interpretation

height grow as the market share grows. This change is shown in Figure 40b. The distortion may lead the reader to equate the *area* of the bars with the relative market share of each manufacturer. But the fact is the true relative market share is proportional only to the *height* of the bars.

Sometimes, we do not need to manipulate the graph to distort the impression it creates. Modifying the verbal description that accompanies the graph can change the interpretation that will be made by the viewer. Figure 41 provides a good illustration of this ploy. The time series plots show the annual level of production of a firm. The only difference in the two graphs is the headings. The heading "Production declines again" in Figure 41a might be used if the firm wants to give the impression that it is underperforming compared to the past (say, in an effort to convince the government that it should not be prosecuted for monopolistic practices). In contrast, the heading "2012: 2nd best year for production" in Figure 41b might be intended for stockholders (to give the impression that the firm's stock is a wise investment).

Although we've discussed only a few of the ways that graphs can be used to convey misleading pictures of phenomena, the lesson is clear. Look at all graphical descriptions of data with a critical eye. Particularly, check the axes and the size of the units on each axis. Ignore the visual changes and concentrate on the actual numerical changes indicated by the graph or chart.

Misleading Numerical Descriptive Statistics

The information in a data set can also be distorted by using numerical descriptive measures, as Example 21 indicates.

Example 21

Misleading Descriptive Statistics—Your Average Salary

Problem Suppose you're considering working for a small law firm—one that currently has a senior member and three junior members. You inquire about the salary you could expect to earn if you join the firm. Unfortunately, you receive two answers:

Answer A: The senior member tells you that an "average employee" earns $107,500.
Answer B: One of the junior members later tells you that an "average employee" earns $95,000.

Which answer can you believe?

Solution The confusion exists because the phrase "average employee" has not been clearly defined. Suppose the four salaries paid are $95,000 for each of the three junior members and $145,000 for the senior member. Thus,

$$\text{Mean} = \frac{3(\$95,000) + \$145,000}{4} = \frac{\$430,000}{4} = \$107,500$$

$$\text{Median} = \$95,000$$

You can now see how the two answers were obtained. The senior member reported the mean of the four salaries, and the junior member reported the median. The information you received was distorted because neither person stated which measure of central tendency was being used.

Look Back Based on our earlier discussion of the mean and median, we would probably prefer the median as the measure that best describes the salary of the "average" employee.

Another distortion of information in a sample occurs when *only* a measure of central tendency is reported. Both a measure of central tendency and a measure of variability are needed to obtain an accurate mental image of a data set.

Suppose you want to buy a new car and are trying to decide which of two models to purchase. Because energy and economy are both important issues, you decide to purchase model A because its EPA mileage rating is 32 miles per gallon in the city, whereas the mileage rating for model B is only 30 miles per gallon in the city.

However, you may have acted too quickly. How much variability is associated with the ratings? As an extreme example, suppose that further investigation reveals that the standard deviation for model A mileages is 5 miles per gallon, whereas that for model B is only 1 mile per gallon. If the mileages form a mound-shaped distribution, they might appear as shown in Figure 42. Note that the larger amount of variability associated with model A implies that more risk is involved in purchasing model A—that is, the particular car you purchase is more likely to have a mileage rating that will greatly differ from the EPA rating of 32 miles per gallon if you purchase model A, while a model B car is not likely to vary from the 30-miles-per-gallon rating by more than 2 miles per gallon.

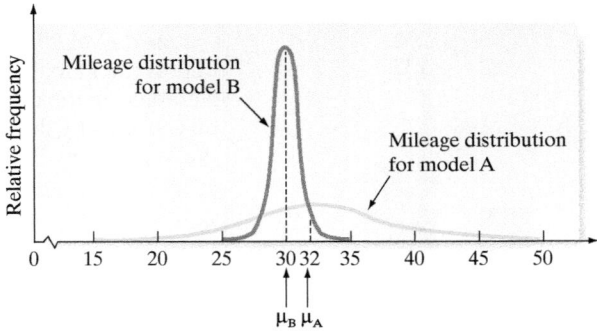

Figure 42

Mileage distributions for two car models

We conclude this section with another example on distorting the truth with numerical descriptive measures.

Example 22

More Misleading Descriptive Statistics— Delinquent Children

Problem *Children out of School in America* is a report on delinquency of school-age children prepared by the Children's Defense Fund (CDF), a government-sponsored organization. Consider the following three reported results of the CDF survey.

- Reported result 1: 25% of the 16- and 17-year-olds in the Portland, Maine, Bayside East Housing Project were out of school. Fact: *Only eight children were surveyed; two were found to be out of school.*

- Reported result 2: Of all the secondary-school students who had been suspended more than once in census tract 22 in Columbia, South Carolina, 33% had been suspended two times and 67% had been suspended three or more times. Fact: *CDF found only three children in that entire census tract who had been suspended; one child was suspended twice and the other two children, three or more times.*

- Reported result 3: In the Portland Bayside East Housing Project, 50% of all the secondary-school children who had been suspended more than once had been suspended three or more times. Fact: *The survey found two secondary-school children had been suspended in that area; one of them had been suspended three or more times.*

Identify the potential distortions in the results reported by the CDF.

Solution In each of these examples, the reporting of percentages (i.e., relative frequencies) instead of the numbers themselves is misleading. No inference we might draw from the cited examples would be reliable. In short, either the report should state the numbers alone instead of percentages, or, better yet, it should state that the numbers were too small to report by region.

Look Back If several regions were combined, the numbers (and percentages) would be more meaningful.

Exercises 133–136

Applying the Concepts—Intermediate

133 Museum management. Refer to the *Museum Management and Curatorship* (June 2010) study of how museums evaluate their performance, Exercise 14. Recall that managers of 30 museums of contemporary art identified the performance measure used most often. A summary of the results is reproduced in the table. Consider the bar graph shown. Identify two ways in which the bar graph might mislead the viewer by overemphasizing the importance of one of the performance measures.

Performance Measure	Number of Museums	Proportion of Museums
Total visitors	8	.267
Paying visitors	5	.167
Big shows	6	.200
Funds raised	7	.233
Members	4	.133

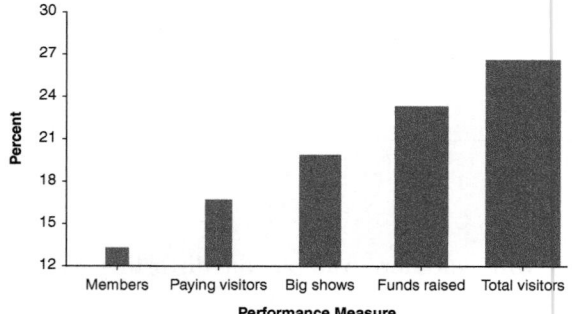

134 Trend in Iraq War casualties. While the United States was still actively fighting in the Iraq War, a news media outlet produced a graphic showing a dramatic decline in the annual number of American casualties. The number of deaths for the years 2003, 2004, 2005, and 2006 were (approximately) 475, 850, 820, and 130, respectively.

a. Create a time series plot showing the dramatic decline in the number of American deaths per year.

b. The graphic was based on data collected through February of 2006. Knowing this fact, why is the time series plot misleading?

c. What information would you like to have in order to construct a graph that accurately reflects the trend in American casualties from the Iraq War?

135 Misleading graph. Consider the following graphic, produced by the *Silicon Alley Insider*, an online publication

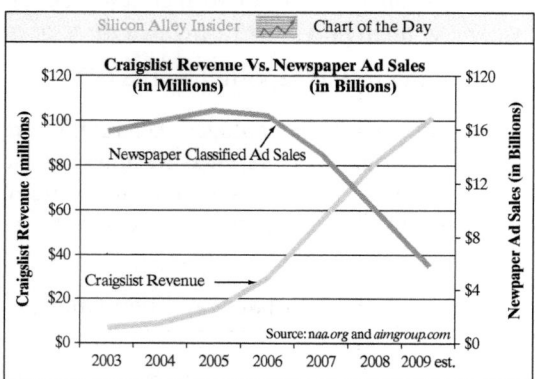

for business news. The graph is attempting to show the increasing trend in annual revenue produced by Craigslist as compared to the decrease in newspaper classified ad sales.

a. Why might the graph be misleading? [*Hint:* Focus on the units of measure on the two vertical axes.]

b. Redraw the graph, but use the same units of measure for both Craigslist revenue and newspaper ad sales. What conclusions can you draw from the redrawn graph?

136 BP oil leak. In the summer of 2010, an explosion on the Deepwater Horizon oil drilling rig caused a leak in one of British Petroleum (BP) Oil Company's wells in the Gulf of Mexico. Crude oil rushed unabated for 3 straight months into the Gulf until BP could fix the leak. During the disaster, BP used suction tubes to capture some of the gushing oil. In May of 2011, in an effort to demonstrate the daily improvement in the process, a BP representative presented a graphic on the daily number of 42-gallon barrels (bbl) of oil collected by the suctioning process. A graphic similar to the one used by BP is shown below.

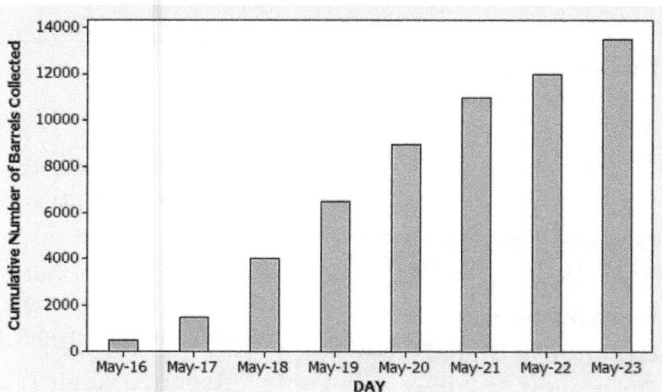

a. Note that the vertical axis represents the "cumulative" number of barrels collected per day. This is calculated by adding the amounts of the previous days' oil collection to the current day's oil collection. Explain why this graph is misleading.

b. Estimates of the actual number of barrels of oil collected per day for each of the 8 days are listed in the accompanying table. Construct a graph for this data that accurately depicts BP's progress in its daily collection of oil. What conclusions can you draw from the graph?

Estimates of Daily Collection of Oil

Day	Number of Barrels (bbl)
May 16	500
May 17	1,000
May 18	3,000
May 19	2,500
May 20	2,500
May 21	2,000
May 22	1,000
May 23	1,500

◼ Chapter Notes

Key Terms

Note: Starred (*) items are from the optional sections in this chapter.

Bar graph
*Bivariate relationship
Box plots
Central tendency
Chebyshev's Rule
Class
Class frequency
Class interval
Class percentage
Class relative frequency
Dot plot
Empirical Rule
Hinges
Histogram
Inner fences
Interquartile range (IQR)
Lower quartile
Mean
Mean of a sample
Measures of central
  tendency
Measures of relative
  standing
Measures of variability
Median
Middle quartile
Minitab histogram
Modal class
Mode
Mound-shaped distribution

Numerical descriptive
  measures
Outer fences
Outliers
Pareto diagram
Percentile ranking/score
Pie chart
Population z-score
pth percentile
Quartiles
Range
Rare-event approach
*Run chart
Sample standard deviation
Sample variance
Sample z-score
*Scatterplot
Skewness
Spread
Standard deviation
Stem-and-leaf display
Symmetric distribution
*Time series data
*Time series plot
Time study
Upper quartile
Variability
Variance
Whiskers
z-score

Key Symbols

	Sample	Population
Mean:	$\bar{x}$	μ
Variance:	s^2	σ^2
Std. Dev.:	s	σ
Median:	m or Q_M	η
Lower Quartile:	Q_L	
Upper Quartile:	Q_U	
Interquartile Range:	IQR	

Key Ideas

Describing Qualitative Data

1. Identify **category classes**
2. Determine **class frequencies**
3. **Class relative frequency** = (class frequency)$/n$
4. **Graph** relative frequencies

Pie Chart:

Bar Graph:

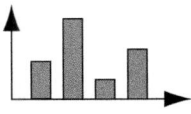

Pareto Diagram:

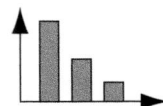

Graphing Quantitative Data

One Variable
1. Identify class intervals
2. Determine **class interval frequencies**
3. **Class interval relative frequency** =
   (class interval frequency)$/n$
4. **Graph** class interval relative frequencies

Dot Plot:

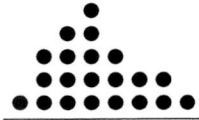

Stem-and-Leaf Display:

```
1 | 3
2 | 2489
3 | 126678
4 | 37
5 | 2
```

Histogram:

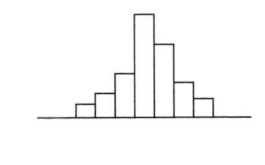

Box Plot:

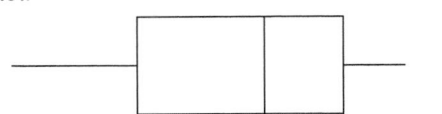

Two Variables

Scatterplot:

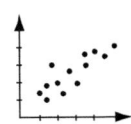

Time series plot:

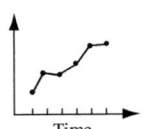

Time

Numerical Description of Quantitative Data

Central Tendency
Mean: $\bar{x} = (\Sigma x_i)/n$
Median: Middle value when data ranked in order
Mode: Value that occurs most often

Variation
Range: Difference between largest and smallest value
Variance:

$$s^2 = \frac{\Sigma(x_i - \bar{x})^2}{n-1} = \frac{\Sigma x_i^2 - \dfrac{(\Sigma x_i)^2}{n}}{n-1}$$

Std. Dev.: $s = \sqrt{s^2}$
Interquartile Range: $\text{IQR} = Q_U - Q_L$

Relative Standing
Percentile Score: Percentage of values that fall below x-score
z-score:

$$z = (x - \bar{x})/s$$
$$= (x - \mu)/\sigma$$

Rules for Detecting Quantitative Outliers

Interval	Chebyshev's Rule	Empirical Rule
$\bar{x} \pm s$	At least 0%	$\approx 68\%$
$\bar{x} \pm 2s$	At least 75%	$\approx 95\%$
$\bar{x} \pm 3s$	At least 89%	$\approx$ All

Rules for Detecting Quantitative Outliers

Method	Suspect	Highly Suspect
Box plot:	Values between inner & outer fences	Values beyond outer fences
z-score:	$2 < |z| < 3$	$|z| > 3$

Guide to Selecting the Data Description Method

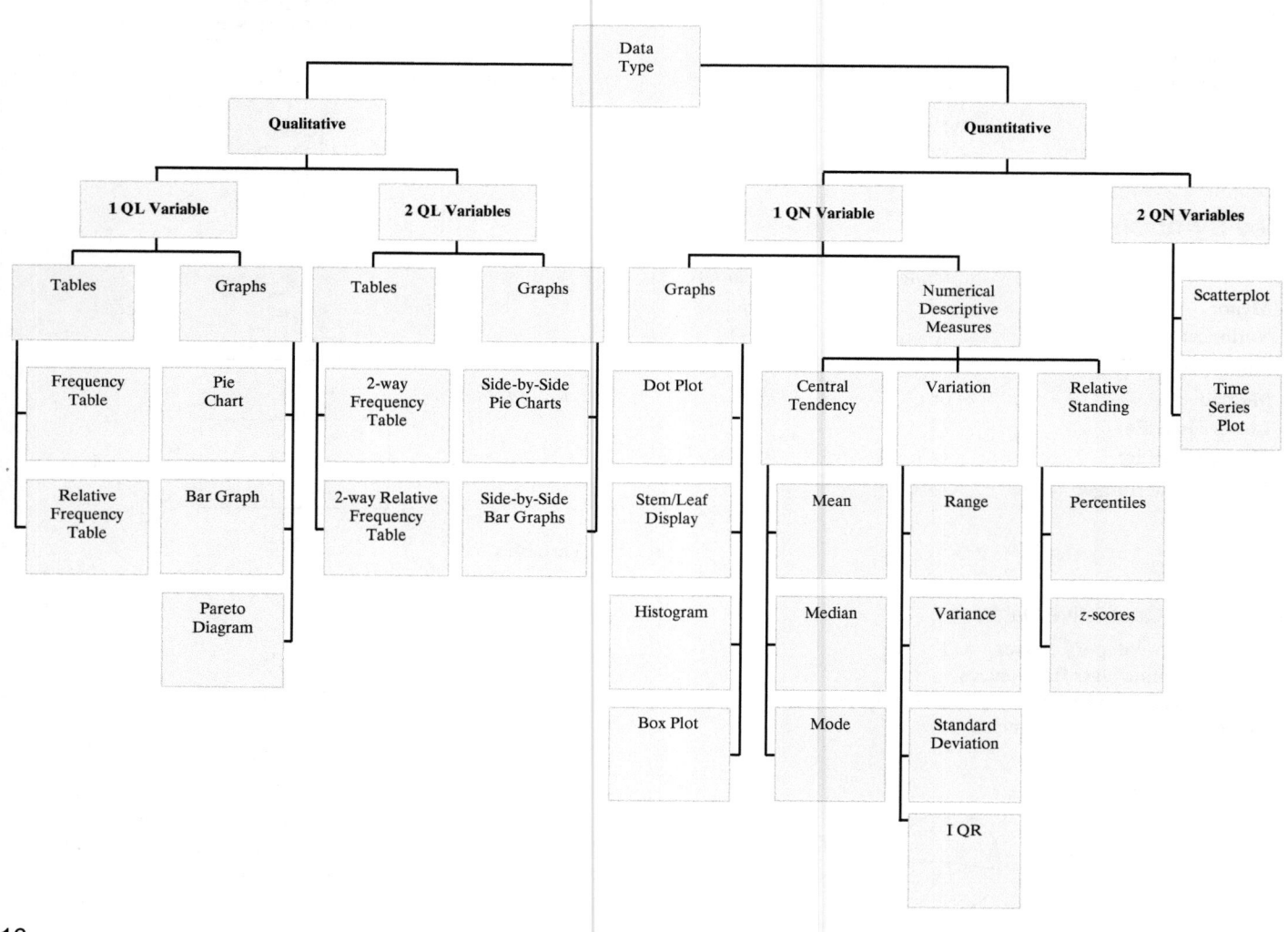

Supplementary Exercises 137–171

Note: Starred (*) exercises refer to the optional sections in this chapter.

Learning the Mechanics

137 Construct a relative frequency histogram for the data summarized in the accompanying table.

Measurement Class	Relative Frequency
.00–.75	.02
.75–1.50	.01
1.50–2.25	.03
2.25–3.00	.05
3.00–3.75	.10
3.75–4.50	.14
4.50–5.25	.19
5.25–6.00	.15
6.00–6.75	.12
6.75–7.50	.09
7.50–8.25	.05
8.25–9.00	.04
9.00–9.75	.01

138 Discuss the conditions under which the median is preferred to the mean as a measure of central tendency.

139 Consider the following three measurements: 50, 70, 80. Find the z-score for each measurement if they are from a population with a mean and standard deviation equal to
  a. $\mu = 60, \sigma = 10$
  b. $\mu = 50, \sigma = 5$
  c. $\mu = 40, \sigma = 10$
  d. $\mu = 40, \sigma = 100$

140 Refer to Exercise 139. For parts **a–d**, determine whether the values 50, 70, and 80 are outliers.

141 For each of the following data sets, compute $\bar{x}$, s^2, and s:
  a. 13, 1, 10, 3, 3
  b. 13, 6, 6, 0
  c. 1, 0, 1, 10, 11, 11, 15
  d. 3, 3, 3, 3

142 For each of the following data sets, compute $\bar{x}$, s^2, and s. If appropriate, specify the units in which your answers are expressed.
  a. 4, 6, 6, 5, 6, 7
  b. $-\$1, \$4, -\$3, \$0, -\$3, -\$6$
  c. $\frac{3}{5}\%, \frac{4}{5}\%, \frac{2}{5}\%, \frac{1}{5}\%, \frac{1}{16}\%$
  d. Calculate the range of each data set in parts **a–c.**

143 Explain why we generally prefer the standard deviation to the range as a measure of variability for quantitative data.

144 If the range of a set of data is 20, find a rough approximation to the standard deviation of the data set.

*145 Construct a scattergram for the data in the following table.

L02145
Variable 1:	174	268	345	119	400	520	190	448	307	252
Variable 2:	8	10	15	7	22	31	15	20	11	9

Applying the Concepts—Basic

146 **Management system failures.** The U.S. Chemical Safety and Hazard Investigation Board (CSB) is responsible for determining the root cause of industrial accidents (*Process*

Safety Progress, Dec. 2004). The accompanying table gives a breakdown of the root causes of 83 incidents caused by management system failures.

Management System Cause Category	Number of Incidents
Engineering & Design	27
Procedures & Practices	24
Management & Oversight	22
Training & Communication	10
Total	83

Source: Based on A. S. Blair, "Management system failures identified in incidents investigated by the U.S. Chemical Safety and Hazard Investigation Board," PROCESS SAFETY PROGRESS, Vol. 23, No. 4, December 2004, pp. 232–236 (Table 1).

  a. Find the relative frequency of the number of incidents for each cause category.
  b. Construct a Pareto diagram for the data.
  c. From the Pareto diagram, identify the cause categories with the highest (and lowest) relative frequency of incidents.

147 **Business marketing publications.** Business-to-business marketing describes the field of marketing between multiple business entities. The *Journal of Business-to-Business Marketing* (Vol. 15, 2008) produced a pie chart describing the number of business-to-business marketing articles published in all journals, by topical area, between 1971 and 2006. The data used to produce the pie chart are shown in the table.

MARPUB

Area	Number
Global Marketing	235
Sales Management	494
Buyer Behavior	478
Relationships	498
Innovation	398
Marketing Strategy	280
Channels/Distribution	213
Marketing Research	131
Services	136
Total	2,863

Source: Based on Peter J. LaPlaca, "Commentary on 'The Essence of Business Marketing…' by Lichtenthal, Mummalaneni, and Wilson: The JBBM Comes of Age," JOURNAL OF BUSINESS-TO-BUSINESS MARKETING, Vol. 15, No. 2, 2008 (Figure 4), p. 187.

  a. Compute the relative frequencies for the nine topical areas shown in the table. Interpret the relative frequency for Buyer Behavior.
  b. Use the relative frequencies, part **a,** to construct a pie chart for the data. Why is the slice for Marketing Research smaller than the slice for Sales Management?

*148 **A boom in U.S. bankruptcies.** The American Bankruptcy Institute and the National Bankruptcy Research Center monitor the number of consumer bankruptcy filings each month. The table on the next page lists the number of bankruptcy filings for each of the first 10 months of a recent year.
FILING
  a. Explain why the data in the table represent time series data.

b. Construct a time series plot for the monthly number of bankruptcy filings.

c. Do you detect a trend in the time series plot? Explain.

Month	Number of bankruptcy filings
January	66,050
February	76,120
March	86,165
April	92,291
May	91,214
June	82,770
July	94,124
August	96,413
September	88,663
October	106,266

149 Crash tests on new cars. The National Highway Traffic Safety Administration (NHTSA) crash-tests new car models to determine how well they protect the driver and front-seat passenger in a head-on collision. The NHTSA has developed a "star" scoring system for the frontal crash test, with results ranging from one star (*) to five stars (*****). The more stars in the rating, the better the level of crash protection in a head-on collision. The NHTSA crash test results for 98 cars (in a recent model year) are stored in the accompanying data file. The driver-side star ratings for the 98 cars are summarized in the Minitab printout shown below. Use the information in the printout to form a pie chart. Interpret the graph.

Tally for Discrete Variables: DRIVSTAR

```
DRIVSTAR   Count   Percent
       2       4      4.08
       3      17     17.35
       4      59     60.20
       5      18     18.37
      N=      98
```

150 Crash tests on new cars (cont'd). Refer to Exercise 149. One quantitative variable recorded by the NHTSA is driver's severity of head injury (measured on a scale from 0 to 1,500). The mean and standard deviation for the 98 driver head-injury ratings are displayed in the Minitab printout below.

Descriptive Statistics: DRIVHEAD

```
Variable    N    Mean   StDev   Minimum     Q1   Median     Q3   Maximum
DRIVHEAD    98   603.7   185.4     216.0  475.0    605.0  724.3    1240.0
```

a. Give a practical interpretation of the mean.

b. Use the mean and standard deviation to make a statement about where most of the head-injury ratings fall.

c. Find the z-score for a driver head-injury rating of 408. Interpret the result.

151 Defects in new automobiles. Consider the following data from the automobile industry (adapted from Kane 1989). All cars produced on a particular day were inspected for defects. The 145 defects found were categorized by type as shown in the accompanying table.

Defect Type	Number
Accessories	50
Body	70
Electrical	10
Engine	5
Transmission	10

a. Construct a Pareto diagram for the data. Use the graph to identify the most frequently observed type of defect.

b. All 70 car body defects were further classified as to type. The frequencies are provided in the following table. Form a Pareto diagram for type of body defect. (Adding this graph to the original Pareto diagram of part **a** is called *exploding the Pareto diagram*.) Interpret the result. What type of body defect should be targeted for special attention?

Body Defect	Number
Chrome	2
Dents	25
Paint	30
Upholstery	10
Windshield	3

152 Products "Made in the USA." "Made in the USA" is a claim stated in many product advertisements or on product labels. Advertisers want consumers to believe that the product is manufactured with 100% U.S. labor and materials—which is often not the case. What does "Made in the USA" mean to the typical consumer? To answer this question, a group of marketing professors conducted an experiment at a shopping mall in Muncie, Indiana (*Journal of Global Business*, Spring 2002). They asked every fourth adult entrant to the mall to participate in the study. A total of 106 shoppers agreed to answer the question, "'Made in the USA' means what percentage of U.S. labor and materials?" The responses of the 106 shoppers are summarized as follows: "100%" (64 shoppers), "75 to 99%" (20 shoppers), "50 to 74%" (18 shoppers), and "less than 50%" (4 shoppers).

a. What type of data-collection method was used?

b. What type of variable, quantitative or qualitative, is measured?

c. Present the data in graphical form. Use the graph to make a statement about the percentage of consumers who believe "Made in the USA" means 100% U.S. labor and materials.

153 Vehicle use of an intersection. For each day of last year, the number of vehicles passing through a certain intersection was recorded by a city engineer. One objective of this study was to determine the percentage of days that more than 425 vehicles used the intersection. Suppose the mean for the data was 375 vehicles per day and the standard deviation was 25 vehicles.

a. What can you say about the percentage of days that more than 425 vehicles used the intersection? Assume you know nothing about the shape of the relative frequency distribution for the data.

b. What is your answer to part **a** if you know that the relative frequency distribution for the data is mound-shaped?

154 Drivers stopped by police. According to the Bureau of Justice Statistics (June 2006), 75% of all licensed drivers stopped by police are 25 years or older. Give a percentile ranking for the age of 25 years in the distribution of all ages of licensed drivers stopped by police.

Applying the Concepts—Intermediate

155 Environmental failures of Arkansas companies. Failure of a corporation to obey both federal and state environmental regulations may result in irreparable damage to the environment and costly financial penalties to the firm. The accompanying table lists the financial penalties (thousands of dollars) assessed in 38 civil actions filed against Arkansas companies by the U.S. Department of Justice and the Environmnetal Protection Agency. The penalties were assessed for violations of at least one of several different environmental laws, including the Clean Air Act (CAA). (Penalties assessed due to CAA violations are marked with an asterisk in the table.)

91*	25*	25*	19*	35*	4*	30*	15*	105*	930
10	124	38	138	1000	25	30	100	43	190
15	20	40	20	40	850	35	25	40	15
20	400	85	30	300	25	90	3		

Source: Data from R. H. Tabor and S. D. Stanwick, "Arkansas: An environmental perspective," ARKANSAS BUSINESS AND ECONOMIC REVIEW, Vol. 28, No. 2, Summer 1995 (Table 4).

a. Construct a stem-and-leaf display for all 38 penalties.
b. Circle the individual leaves that are associated with penalties imposed for CAA violations.
c. What does the pattern of circles in part b suggest about the severity of the penalties imposed for CAA violations relative to the other types of violations reported in the table? Explain.

156 Color and clarity of diamonds. Diamonds are categorized according to the "four C's": carats, clarity, color, and cut. Each diamond stone that is sold on the open market is provided a certificate by an independent diamond assessor that lists these characteristics. Data for 308 diamonds were extracted from Singapore's *Business Times* (*Journal of Statistics Education*, Vol. 9, No. 1, 2001). Color is classified as D, E, F, G, H, or I, while clarity is classified as IF, VVS1, VVS2, VS1, or VS2. Use a graphical technique to summarize the color and clarity of the 308 diamond stones. What is the color and clarity that occurs most often? Least often?

157 Color and clarity of diamonds (cont'd). Refer to Exercise 156. In addition to color and clarity, the independent certification group (GIA, HRD, or IGI) and the number of carats were recorded for each of 308 diamonds for sale on the open market.
a. Use a graphical method to describe the carat distribution of all 308 diamonds.
b. Use a graphical method to describe the carat distribution of diamonds certified by the GIA group.
c. Repeat part b for the HRD and IGI certification groups.
d. Compare the three carat distributions, parts b and c. Is there one particular certification group that appears to be assessing diamonds with higher carats than the others?
e. Find and interpret the mean of the data set.
f. Find and interpret the median of the data set.
g. Find and interpret the mode of the data set.
h. Which measure of central tendency best describes the 308 carat values? Explain.
i. Use the mean and standard deviation to form an interval that will contain at least 75% of the carat values in the data set.

* 158 Characteristics of diamonds sold at retail. Refer to Exercise 157. In addition to the number of carats, the asking price for each of the 308 diamonds for sale on the open market was recorded. Construct a scatterplot for the data, with number of carats on the horizontal axis and price on the vertical axis. What type of trend do you detect?

159 Hull failures of oil tankers. Owing to several major ocean oil spills by tank vessels, Congress passed the 1990 Oil Pollution Act, which requires all tankers to be designed with thicker hulls. Further improvements in the structural design of a tank vessel have been proposed since then, each with the objective of reducing the likelihood of an oil spill and decreasing the amount of outflow in the event of a hull puncture. To aid in this development, *Marine Technology* (Jan. 1995) reported on the spillage amount (in thousands of metric tons) and cause of puncture for 42 major oil spills from tankers and carriers. [*Note:* Cause of puncture is classified as either collision (C), fire/explosion (FE), hull failure (HF), or grounding (G).] The data are saved in the accompanying file.
a. Use a graphical method to describe the cause of oil spillage for the 42 tankers. Does the graph suggest that any one cause is more likely to occur than any other? How is this information of value to the design engineers?
b. Find and interpret descriptive statistics for the 42 spillage amounts. Use this information to form an interval that can be used to predict the spillage amount of the next major oil spill.

160 Software defects. The Promise Software Engineering Repository is a collection of data sets available to serve businesses in building predictive software models. One such data set, saved in the accompanying file, contains information on 498 modules of software code. Each module was analyzed for defects and classified as "true" if it contained defective code and "false" if not. Access the data file and produce a bar graph or a pie chart for the defect variable. Use the graph to make a statement about the likelihood of defective software code.

161 Velocity of Winchester bullets. The *American Rifleman* (June 1993) reported on the velocity of ammunition fired from the FEG P9R pistol, a 9 mm gun manufactured in Hungary. Field tests revealed that Winchester bullets fired from the pistol had a mean velocity (at 15 feet) of 936 feet per second and a standard deviation of 10 feet per second. Tests were also conducted with Uzi and Black Hills ammunition.
a. Describe the velocity distribution of Winchester bullets fired from the FEG P9R pistol.
b. A bullet, brand unknown, is fired from the FEG P9R pistol. Suppose the velocity (at 15 feet) of the bullet is 1,000 feet per second. Is the bullet likely to be manufactured by Winchester? Explain.

162 Time to develop price quotes. A manufacturer of industrial wheels is losing many profitable orders because of the long time it takes the firm's marketing, engineering, and accounting departments to develop price quotes for potential customers. To remedy this problem, the firm's management would like to set guidelines for the length of time each department should spend developing price quotes. To help develop these guidelines, 50 requests for price quotes were randomly selected from the set of price quotes made last year: the processing time (in days) was determined for each price quote for each department. Several observations are displayed in the table below. The price quotes are also classified by whether or not they were "lost" (i.e., whether or not the customer placed an order after receiving the price quote).

Request Number	Marketing	Engineering	Accounting	Lost?
1	7.0	6.2	.1	No
2	.4	5.2	.1	No
3	2.4	4.6	.6	No
4	6.2	13.0	.8	Yes
5	4.7	.9	.5	No
⋮	⋮	⋮	⋮	⋮
46	6.4	1.3	6.2	No
47	4.0	2.4	13.5	Yes
48	10.0	5.3	.1	No
49	8.0	14.4	1.9	Yes
50	7.0	10.0	2.0	No

a. Construct a stem-and-leaf display for the total processing time for each department. Shade the leaves that correspond to "lost" orders in each of the displays, and interpret each of the displays.

b. Using your results from part a, develop "maximum processing time" guidelines for each department that, if followed, will help the firm reduce the number of lost orders.

c. Generate summary statistics for the processing times. Interpret the results.

d. Calculate the z-score corresponding to the maximum processing time guideline you developed in part b for each department, and for the total processing time.

e. Calculate the maximum processing time corresponding to a z-score of 3 for each of the departments. What percentage of the orders exceed these guidelines? How does this agree with Chebyshev's Rule and the Empirical Rule?

f. Repeat part e using a z-score of 2.

g. Compare the percentage of "lost" quotes with corresponding times that exceed at least one of the guidelines in part e to the same percentage using the guidelines in part f. Which set of guidelines would you recommend be adopted? Why?

163 **Misleading advertisement.** A time series plot similar to the one shown next appeared in a recent advertisement for a well-known golf magazine. One person might interpret the plot's message as the longer you subscribe to the magazine, the better golfer you should become. Another person might interpret it as indicating that if you subscribe for 3 years, your game should improve dramatically.

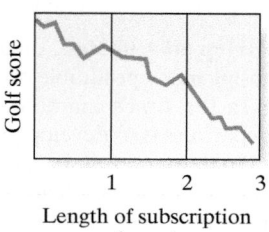

Length of subscription (years)

a. Explain why the plot can be interpreted in more than one way.

b. How could the plot be altered to rectify the current distortion?

*164 **History of corporate acquisitions.** Refer to the *Academy of Management Journal* (Aug. 2008) study of corporate acquisitions from 1980 to 2000, Exercise 12.

a. Construct a time series plot of the number of firms with at least one acquisition.

b. For each year, compute the percentage of sampled firms with at least one acquisition. Then construct a time series plot of these percentages.

c. Which time series plot, part a or part b, is more informative about the history of corporate acquisitions over time? Explain.

165 **Radiation levels in homes.** In some locations, radiation levels in homes are measured at well above normal background levels in the environment. As a result, many architects and builders are making design changes to ensure adequate air exchange so that radiation will not be "trapped" in homes. In one such location, 50 homes' levels were measured, and the mean level was 10 parts per billion (ppb), the median was 8 ppb, and the standard deviation was 3 ppb. Background levels in this location are at about 4 ppb.

a. Based on these results, is the distribution of the 50 homes' radiation levels symmetric, skewed to the left, or skewed to the right? Why?

b. Use both Chebyshev's Rule and the Empirical Rule to describe the distribution of radiation levels. Which do you think is most appropriate in this case? Why?

c. Use the results from part b to approximate the number of homes in this sample that have radiation levels above the background level.

d. Suppose another home is measured at a location 10 miles from the one sampled and has a level of 20 ppb. What is the z-score for this measurement relative to the 50 homes sampled in the other location? Is it likely that this new measurement comes from the same distribution of radiation levels as the other 50? Why? How would you go about confirming your conclusion?

166 **Amount of zinc phosphide in commercial rat poison.** A chemical company produces a substance composed of 98% cracked corn particles and 2% zinc phosphide for use in controlling rat populations in sugarcane fields. Production must be carefully controlled to maintain the 2% zinc phosphide because too much zinc phosphide will cause damage to the sugarcane and too little will be ineffective in controlling the rat population. Records from past production indicate that the distribution of the actual percentage of zinc phosphide present in the substance is approximately mound-shaped, with a mean of 2.0% and a standard deviation of .08%.

a. If the production line is operating correctly, approximately what proportion of batches from a day's production will contain less than 1.84% of zinc phosphide?

b. Suppose one batch chosen randomly actually contains 1.80% zinc phosphide. Does this indicate that there is too little zinc phosphide in today's production? Explain your reasoning.

167 U.S. peanut production. If not examined carefully, the graphical description of U.S. peanut production shown at the bottom of the page can be misleading.

a. Explain why the graph may mislead some readers.

b. Construct an undistorted graph of U.S. peanut production for the given years.

Applying the Concepts—Advanced

168 Investigating the claims of weight-loss clinics. The U.S. Federal Trade Commission assesses fines and other penalties against weight-loss clinics that make unsupported or misleading claims about the effectiveness of their programs. Brochures from two weight-loss clinics both advertise "statistical evidence" about the effectiveness of their programs. Clinic A claims that the *mean* weight loss during the first month is 15 pounds; Clinic B claims a *median* weight loss of 10 pounds.

a. Assuming the statistics are accurately calculated, which clinic would you recommend if you had no other information? Why?

b. Upon further research, the median and standard deviation for Clinic A are found to be 10 pounds and 20 pounds, respectively, while the mean and standard deviation for Clinic B are found to be 10 and 5 pounds, respectively. Both are based on samples of more than 100 clients. Describe the two clinics' weight-loss distributions as completely as possible given this additional information. What would you recommend to a prospective client now? Why?

c. Note that nothing has been said about how the sample of clients upon which the statistics are based was selected. What additional information would be important regarding the sampling techniques employed by the clinics?

169 Age discrimination study. The Age Discrimination in Employment Act mandates that workers 40 years of age or older be treated without regard to age in all phases of employment (hiring, promotions, firing, etc.). Age discrimination cases are of two types: *disparate treatment* and *disparate impact*. In the former, the issue is whether workers have been intentionally discriminated against. In the latter, the issue is whether employment practices adversely affect the protected class (i.e., workers 40 and over) even though

no such effect was intended by the employer. A small computer manufacturer laid off 10 of its 20 software engineers. The ages of all engineers at the time of the layoff are shown below. Analyze the data to determine whether the company may be vulnerable to a disparate impact claim.

Not laid off:	34	55	42	38	42	32	40	40	46	29
Laid off:	52	35	40	41	40	39	40	64	47	44

Critical Thinking Challenges

170 No Child Left Behind Act. According to the government, federal spending on K-12 education has increased dramatically over the past 20 years, but student performance has essentially stayed the same. Hence, in 2002, President George Bush signed into law the No Child Left Behind Act, a bill that promised improved student achievement for all U.S. children. *Chance* (Fall 2003) reported on a graphic

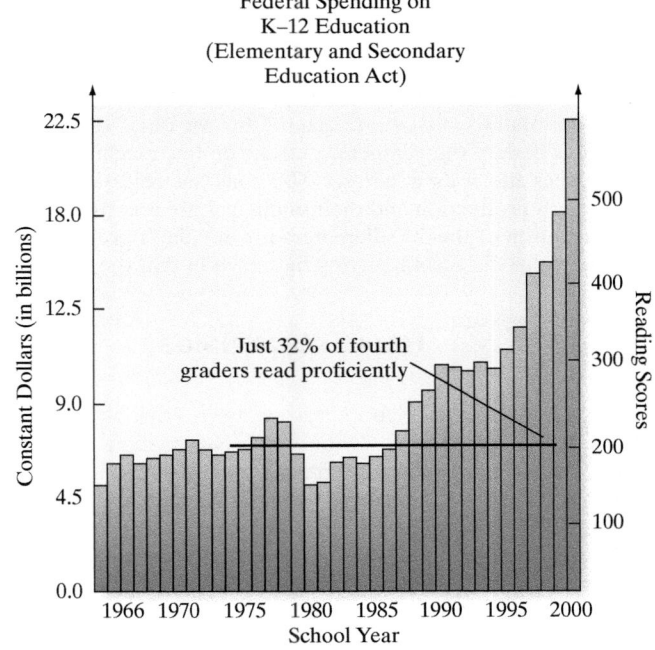

Source: Based on U.S. Department of Education.

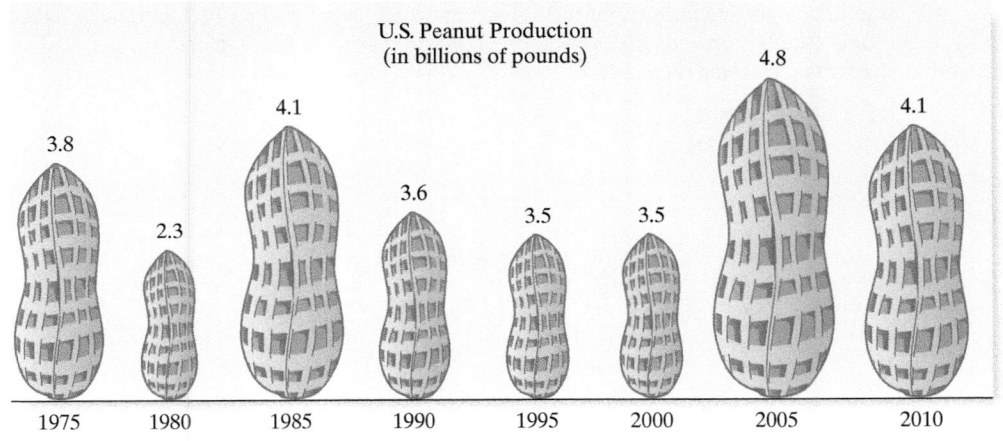

Graph for Exercise 167

obtained from the U.S. Department of Education Web site (www.ed.gov) that was designed to support the new legislation. The graphic is reproduced on the previous page. The bars in the graph represent annual federal spending on education, in billions of dollars (left-side vertical axis). The horizontal line represents the annual average fourth-grade children's reading ability score (right-side vertical axis). Critically assess the information portrayed in the graph. Does it, in fact, support the government's position that our children are not making classroom improvements despite federal spending on education? Use the following facts (divulged in the *Chance* article) to help you frame your answer: (1) The U.S. student population has also increased dramatically over the past 20 years, (2) fourth-grade reading test scores are designed to have an average of 250 with a standard deviation of 50, and (3) the reading test scores of seventh and twelfth graders and the mathematics scores of fourth graders did improve substantially over the past 20 years.

171 **Steel rod quality.** In his essay "Making Things Right," W. Edwards Deming considered the role of statistics in the quality control of industrial products.* In one example, Deming examined the quality-control process for a manufacturer of steel rods. Rods produced with diameters smaller than 1 centimeter fit too loosely in their bearings and ultimately must be rejected (thrown out). To determine whether the diameter setting of the machine that produces the rods is correct, 500 rods are selected from the day's production and their diameters are recorded. The distribution of the 500 diameters for one day's production is shown in the accompanying figure. Note that the symbol

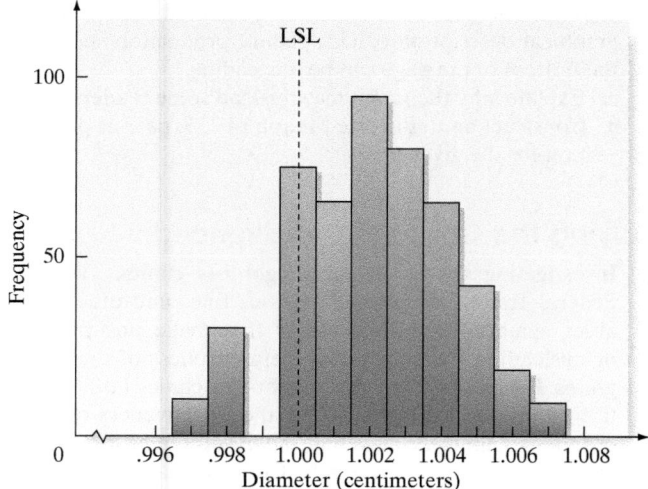

*From Tanur, J., et al., eds. *Statistics: A Guide to the Unknown*. San Francisco: Holden-Day, 1978, pp. 279–81.

LSL in the figure represents the 1-centimeter lower specification limit of the steel rod diameters. There has been speculation that some of the inspectors are unaware of the trouble that an undersized rod diameter would cause later in the manufacturing process. Consequently, these inspectors may be passing rods with diameters that are barely below the lower specification limit and recording them in the interval centered at 1.000 centimeter. According to the figure, is there any evidence to support this claim? Explain.

Activity 1   Real Estate Sales

In recent years, the price of real estate in America's major metropolitan areas has skyrocketed. Newspapers usually report recent real estate sales data in their Saturday editions, both hard copies and online. These data usually include the actual prices paid for homes by geographical location during a certain time period, usually a 1-week period 6 to 8 weeks earlier, and some summary statistics, which might include comparisons to real estate sales data in other geographical locations or during other time periods.

1. Locate the real estate sales data in a newspaper for a major metropolitan area. From the information given, identify the time period during which the homes listed were sold. Then describe the way the sales prices are organized. Are they categorized by type of home (single family or condominium), by neighborhood or address, by sales price, etc.?

2. What summary statistics and comparisons are provided with the sales data? Describe several groups of people who might be interested in this data and how each of the summary statistics and comparisons would be helpful to them. Why are the measures of central tendency listed more useful in the real estate market than other measures of central tendency?

3. Based on the lowest and highest sales prices represented in the data, create 10 intervals of equal size and use these intervals to create a relative frequency histogram for the sales data. Describe the shape of the histogram and explain how the summary statistics provided with the data are illustrated in the histogram. Based on the histogram, describe the "typical" home price.

References

Deming, W. E. *Out of the Crisis*. Cambridge, Mass.: M.I.T. Center for Advanced Engineering Study, 1986.

Gitlow, H., Oppenheim, A., Oppenheim, R., and Levine, D. *Quality Management*, 3rd ed. Homewood, Ill.: Irwin, 2004.

Huff, D. *How to Lie with Statistics*. New York: Norton, 1954.

Ishikawa, K. *Guide to Quality Control,* 2nd ed. Asian Productivity Organization, 1986.

Juran, J. M. *Juran on Quality by Design: The New Steps for Planning Quality into Goods and Services*. New York: The Free Press, 1992.

Tufte, E. R. *Beautiful Evidence*. Cheshire, Conn.: Graphics Press, 2006.

Tufte, E. R. *Envisioning Information*. Cheshire, Conn.: Graphics Press, 1990.

Tufte, E. R. *Visual Display of Quantiative Information*. Cheshire, Conn.: Graphics Press, 1983.

Tufte, E. R. *Visual Explanations*. Cheshire, Conn.: Graphics Press, 1997.

Tukey, J. *Exploratory Data Analysis*. Reading, Mass.: Addison-Wesley, 1977.

Zabel, S. L. "Statistical Proof of Employment Discrimination." *Statistics: A Guide to the Unknown*, 3rd ed. Pacific Grove, Calif.: Wadsworth, 1989.

USING TECHNOLOGY Technology images shown here are taken from SPSS Statistics Professional 20.0, Minitab 16, XLSTAT for Pearson, and Excel 2010.

SPSS: Describing Data

Graphing Data

Step 1 Click on the "Graphs" button on the SPSS menu bar and then select "Legacy Dialogs."

Step 2 Click on the graph of your choice (bar, pie, box plot, scatter/dot plot, or histogram) to view the appropriate dialog box. The dialog box for a histogram is shown in Figure S.1.

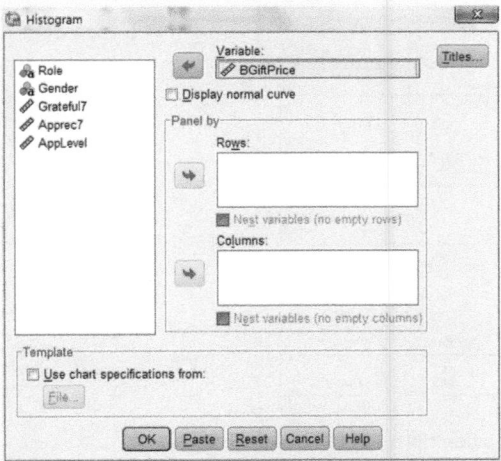

Figure S.1 SPSS histogram dialog box

Step 3 Make the appropriate variable selections and click "OK" to view the graph.

Stem-and-Leaf Plots

Step 1 Select "Analyze" from the main SPSS menu, then "Descriptive Statistics," and then "Explore."

Step 2 In the "Explore" dialog box, select the variable to be analyzed in the "Dependent List" box, as shown in Figure S.2.

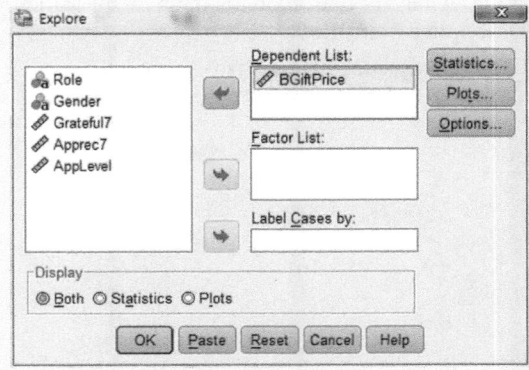

Figure S.2 SPSS explore dialog box

Step 3 Click on either "Both" or "Plots" in the "Display" options and then click "OK" to display the stem-and-leaf graph.

Pareto Diagrams

Step 1 Select "Analyze" from the main SPSS menu, then "Quality Control," and then "Pareto Charts."

Step 2 Click "Define" on the resulting menu and then select the variable to be analyzed and move it to the "Category Axis" box, as shown in Figure S.3.

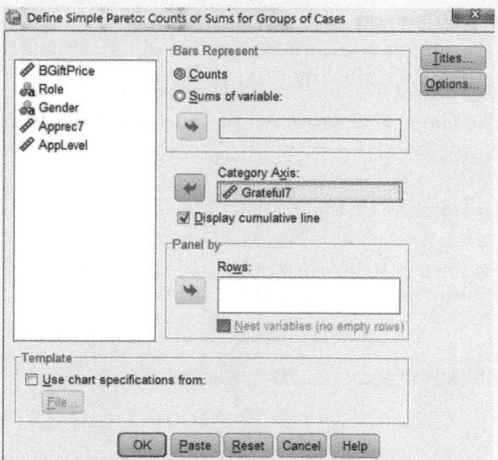

Figure S.3 SPSS Pareto chart dialog box

Step 3 Click "OK" to display the Pareto diagram.

Numerical Descriptive Statistics

Step 1 Click on the "Analyze" button on the main menu bar and then click on "Descriptive Statistics."

Step 2 Select "Descriptives;" the dialog box is shown in Figure S.4.

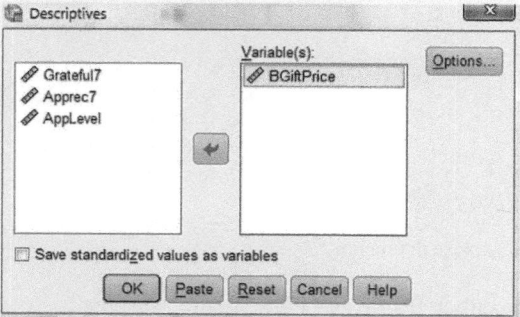

Figure S.4 SPSS descriptive statistics dialog box

Step 3 Select the quantitative variables you want to analyze and place them in the "Variable(s)" box. You can control which descriptive statistics appear by clicking the "Options" button on the dialog box and making your selections.

Step 4 Click "OK" to view the descriptive statistics printout.

Percentiles

Step 1 Select "Analyze" on the main menu bar, and then click on "Descriptive Statistics."

Step 2 Select "Explore" from the resulting menu.

Step 3 In the resulting dialog box (see Figure S.2), select the "Statistics" button and check the "Percentiles" box.

Step 4 Return to the "Explore" dialog box and click "OK" to generate the descriptive statistics.

Minitab: Describing Data

Graphing Data

Step 1 Click on the "Graph" button on the Minitab menu bar.

Step 2 Click on the graph of your choice (bar, pie, scatterplot, histogram, dot plot, or stem-and-leaf) to view the appropriate dialog box. The dialog box for a histogram is shown in Figure M.1.

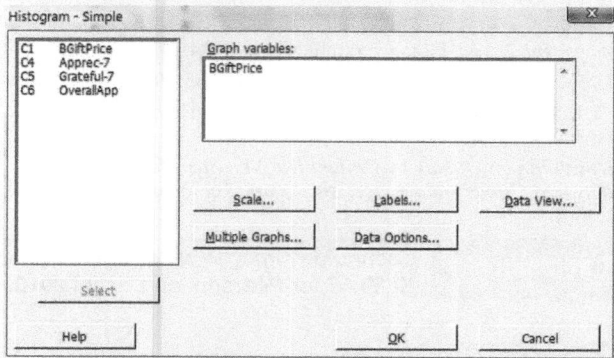

Figure M.1 Minitab histogram dialog box

Step 3 Make the appropriate variable selections and then click "OK" to view the graph.

Numerical Descriptive Statistics

Step 1 Click on the "Stat" button on the main menu bar, click on "Basic Statistics," and then click on "Display Descriptive Statistics." The resulting dialog box appears in Figure M.2.

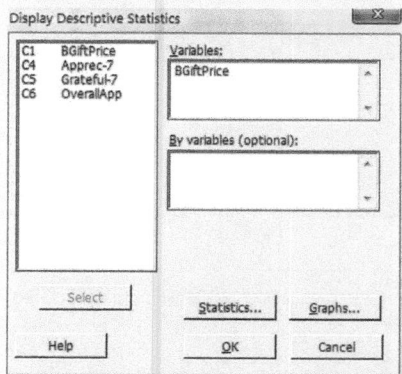

Figure M.2 Minitab descriptive statistics dialog box

Step 2 Select the quantitative variables you want to analyze and place them in the "Variables" box. You can control which descriptive statistics appear by clicking the "Statistics" button on the dialog box and making your selections. (As an option, you can create histograms and dot plots for the data by clicking the "Graphs" button and making the appropriate selections.)

Step 3 Click "OK" to view the descriptive statistics printout.

Excel/XLSTAT: Describing Data

Graphing Data

Step 1 Click the "XLSTAT" button on the Excel main menu bar and then click "Visualizing Data."

Step 2 From the resulting menu (see Figure E.1), select the graph of your choice. For bar graphs, pie charts, stem-and-leaf displays, or box plots, select "Univariate plots"; for histograms, select "Histogram"; and for scatterplots, select "Scatter plots."

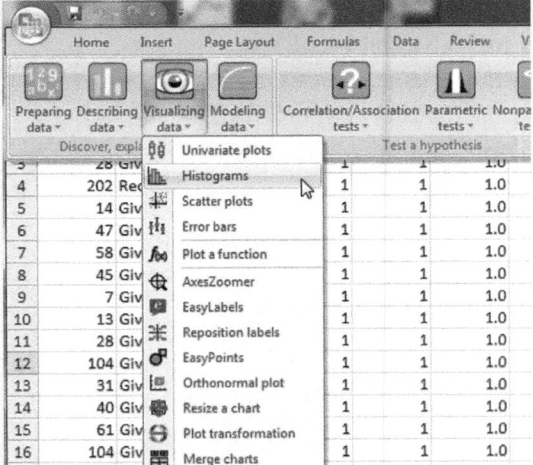

Figure E.1 XLSTAT menu for graphing data

Step 3 When the resulting dialog box appears, highlight the data column(s) you want to graph so that the column information appears in the appropriate entry (see, for example, Figure E.2).

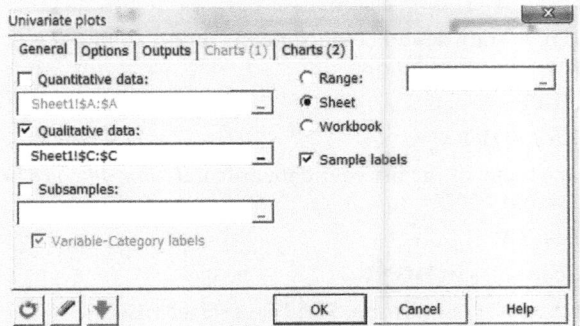

Figure E.2 XLSTAT graphing univariate plots dialog box

Step 4 For univariate plots only, click the "Charts (1)" option for quantitative data or the "Charts (2)" option for qualitative data, and then select the type of graph (e.g., pie chart, bar graph, stem-and-leaf display, or box plot) you want to display. (See Figure E.3.)

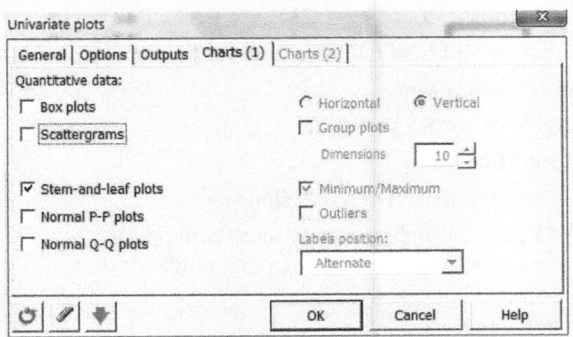

Figure E.3 XLSTAT univariate plots charts options

Step 5 Click "OK," and then "Continue" to display the graph.

Numerical Descriptive Statistics

Step 1 Click the "XLSTAT" button on the Excel main menu bar, click "Describing Data," and then click "Descriptive Statistics."

Step 2 When the resulting dialog box appears, highlight the data column(s) you want to graph so that the column information appears in the quantitative data entry.

Step 3 Click the "Outputs" option, and then select the descriptive statistics you want to produce. (See Figure E.4.)

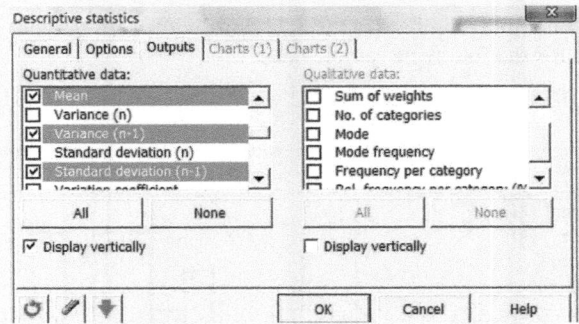

Figure E.4 XLSTAT descriptive statistics outputs options

Step 5 Click "OK," and then "Continue" to display the summary statistics.

TI-84 Graphing Calculator: Describing Data

Histogram from Raw Data

Step 1 *Enter the data*

- Press **STAT** and select **1:Edit**

Note: If the list already contains data, clear the old data. Use the up arrow to highlight "**L1**." Press **CLEAR ENTER.** Use the arrow and **ENTER** keys to enter the data set into **L1.**

Step 2 *Set up the histogram plot*

- Press **2nd** and press **Y =** for **STAT PLOT**
- Press **1** for **Plot1**
- Set the cursor so that **ON** is flashing
- For **Type,** use the arrow and **ENTER** keys to highlight and select the histogram
- For **Xlist,** choose the column containing the data (in most cases, L1)

Note: Press **2nd 1** for **L1.** **Freq** should be set to 1.

Step 3 *Select your window settings*

- Press **WINDOW** and adjust the settings as follows:

$$\textbf{X min} = \text{lowest class boundary}$$
$$\textbf{X max} = \text{highest class boundary}$$
$$\textbf{X scl} = \text{class width}$$
$$\textbf{Y min} = 0$$
$$\textbf{Y max} \geq \text{greatest class frequency}$$
$$\textbf{Y scl} = 1$$
$$\textbf{X res} = 1$$

Step 4 *View the graph*

- Press **GRAPH**

Optional *Read class frequencies and class boundaries*

Step You can press **TRACE** to read the class frequencies and class boundaries. Use the arrow keys to move between bars.

Example The following figures show TI-84 window settings and histogram for the following sample data:

86, 70, 62, 98, 73, 56, 53, 92, 86, 37, 62, 83, 78, 49, 78, 37, 67, 79, 57

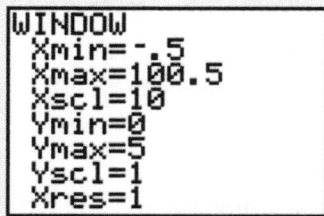 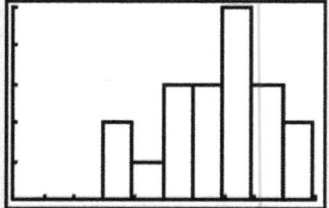

Histogram from a Frequency Table

Step 1 *Enter the data*

- Press **STAT** and select **1:Edit**

Note: If a list already contains data, clear the old data. Use the up arrow to highlight the list name, "L1" or "L2."

- Press **CLEAR ENTER**
- Enter the midpoint of each class into **L1**
- Enter the class frequencies or relative frequencies into **L2**

Step 2 *Set up the histogram plot*

- Press **2nd** and **Y =** for **STAT PLOT**
- Press **1** for **Plot1**
- Set the cursor so that **ON** is flashing
- For **Type,** use the arrow and **ENTER** keys to highlight and select the histogram
- For **Xlist,** choose the column containing the midpoints
- For **Freq,** choose the column containing the frequencies or relative frequencies

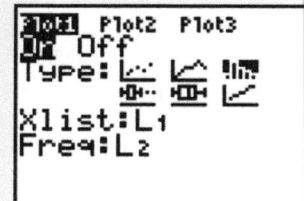

Step 3–4 *Follow steps 3–4 given above.*

Note: To set up the Window for relative frequencies, be sure to set **Ymax** to a value that is greater than or equal to the largest relative frequency.

One-Variable Descriptive Statistics

Step 1 *Enter the data*

- Press STAT and select **1:Edit**

Note: If the list already contains data, clear the old data. Use the up arrow to highlight "L1." Press **CLEAR ENTER.**

- Use the arrow and **ENTER** keys to enter the data set into L1

Step 2 *Calculate descriptive statistics*

- Press **STAT**
- Press the right arrow key to highlight **CALC**
- Press **ENTER** for **1-Var Stats**

- Enter the name of the list containing your data
- Press **2nd 1** for **L1** (or **2nd 2** for **L2**, etc.)
- Press **ENTER**

You should see the statistics on your screen. Some of the statistics are off the bottom of the screen. Use the down arrow to scroll through to see the remaining statistics. Use the up arrow to scroll back up.

Example The descriptive statistics for the sample data set

86, 70, 62, 98, 73, 56, 53, 92, 86, 37, 62, 83, 78, 49, 78, 37, 67, 79, 57

The output screens for this example are shown below.

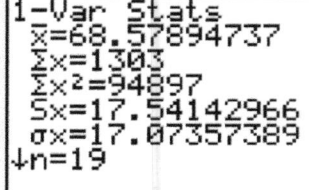 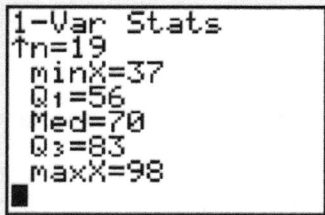

Sorting Data (to Find the Mode)

The descriptive statistics do not include the mode. To find the mode, sort your data as follows:

- Press **STAT**
- Press **2** for **SORTA(**
- Enter the name of the list your data are in. If your data are in **L1**, press **2nd 1**
- Press **ENTER**
- The screen will say: **DONE**
- To see the sorted data, press **STAT** and select **1:Edit**
- Scroll down through the list and locate the data value that occurs most frequently

Box Plot

Step 1 *Enter the data*

- Press **STAT** and select **1:Edit**

Note: If the list already contains data, clear the old data. Use the up arrow to highlight "**L1.**" Press **CLEAR ENTER.**

- Use the arrow and **ENTER** keys to enter the data set into **L1**

Step 2 *Set up the box plot*

- Press **2nd Y =** for **STAT PLOT**
- Press **1** for **Plot1**
- Set the cursor so that **"ON"** is flashing
- For **TYPE,** use the right arrow to scroll through the plot icons and select the box plot in the middle of the second row
- For **XLIST,** choose **L1**
- Set **FREQ** to 1

Step 3 *View the graph*

- Press **ZOOM** and select **9:ZoomStat**

Optional *Read the five-number summary*

- Press **TRACE**
- Use the left and right arrow keys to move between **minX, Q1, Med, Q3,** and **maxX**

Example Make a box plot for the given data:

86, 70, 62, 98, 73, 56, 53, 92, 86, 37, 62, 83, 78, 49, 78, 37, 67, 79, 57

The output screen for this example is shown below.

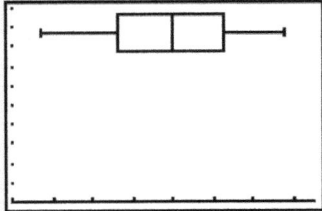

Scatterplots

Step 1 *Enter the data*

- Press **STAT** and select **1:Edit**

Note: If a list already contains data, clear the old data. Use the up arrow to highlight the list name, **"L1"** or **"L2."**

- Press **CLEAR ENTER**
- Enter your *x*-data in **L1** and your *y*-data in **L2**

Step 2 *Set up the scatterplot*

- Press **2nd Y =** for **STAT PLOT**
- Press **1** for **Plot1**

- Set the cursor so that **ON** is flashing
- For **Type,** use the arrow and **ENTER** keys to highlight and select the scatterplot (first icon in the first row)

- For **Xlist,** choose the column containing the *x*-data
- For **Ylist,** choose the column containing the *y*-data

Step 3 *View the scatterplot*

- Press **ZOOM 9** for **ZoomStat**

Example The figures below show a table of data entered on the T1-84 and the scatterplot of the data obtained using the steps given above.

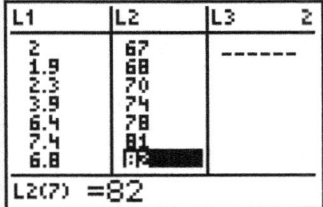 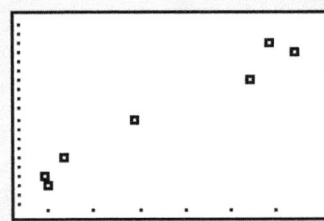

127

[ ] The Kentucky Milk Case

Many products and services are purchased by governments, cities, states, and businesses on the basis of scaled bids, and contracts are awarded to the lowest bidders. This process works extremely well in competitive markets, but it has the potential to increase the cost of purchasing if the markets are noncompetitive or if collusive practices are present.

An investigation that began with a statistical analysis of bids in the Florida school milk market led to the recovery of more than $33,000,000 from dairies that had conspired to rig the bids there. The investigation spread quickly to other states, and to date, settlements and fines from dairies exceed $100.000,000 for school milk bidrigging in 20 other states. This case concerns a school milk bidrigging investigation in Kentucky.

Each year, the Commonwealth of Kentucky invites bids from dairies to supply half-pint containers of fluid milk products for its school districts. The products include whole white milk, low-fat white milk, and low-fat chocolate milk. In 13 school districts in northern Kentucky, the suppliers (dairies) were accused of "price-fixing"—that is, conspiring to allocate the districts so that the "winner" was predetermined. Because these districts are located in Boone, Campbell, and Kenton counties, the geographic market they represent is designated as the "tri-county" market. Over a 9-year period, two dairies—Meyer Dairy and Trauth Dairy— were the only bidders on the milk contracts in the school districts in the tri-county market. Consequently, these two companies were awarded all the milk contracts in the market. (In contrast, a large number of different dairies won the milk contracts for the school districts in the remainder of the northern Kentucky market—called the "surrounding" market.) The

Commonwealth of Kentucky alleged that Meyer and Trauth conspired to allocate the districts in the tri-county market. To date, one of the dairies (Meyer) has admitted guilt, while the other (Trauth) steadfastly maintains its innocence.

The Commonwealth of Kentucky maintains a database on all bids received from the dairies competing for the milk contracts. Some of these data have been made available to you to analyze to determine whether there is empirical evidence of bid collusion in the tri-county market. The data, saved in the **MILK** file, are described in detail below. Some background information on the data and important economic theory regarding bid collusion is also provided. Use this information to guide your analysis. Prepare a professional document that presents the results of your analysis and gives your opinion regarding collusion.

Background Information

Collusive Market Environment

Certain economic features of a market create an environment in which collusion may be found. These basic features include the following:

1. *Few sellers and high concentration.* Only a few dairies control all or nearly all of the milk business in the market.

2. *Homogeneous products.* The products sold are essentially the same from the standpoint of the buyer (i.e., the school district).

3. *Inelastic demand.* Demand is relatively insensitive to price. (*Note:* The quantity of milk required by a school district is primarily determined by school enrollment, not price.)

4. *Similar costs.* The dairies bidding for the milk contracts face similar cost conditions. (*Note:* Approximately 60% of a dairy's production cost is raw milk, which is federally regulated. Meyer and Trauth are dairies of similar size, and both bought their raw milk from the same supplier.)

Although these market structure characteristics create an environment that makes collusive behavior easier, they do not necessarily indicate the existence of collusion. An analysis of the actual bid prices may provide additional information about the degree of competition in the market.

Variable	Type	Description
YEAR	QN	Year in which milk contract awarded
MARKET	QL	Northern Kentucky Market (TRI-COUNTY or SURROUND)
WINNER	QL	Name of winning dairy
WWBID	QN	Winning bid price of whole white milk (dollars per half-pint)
WWQTY	QN	Quantity of whole white milk purchased (number of half-pints)
LFWBID	QN	Winning bid price of low-fat white milk (dollars per half-pints)
LFWQTY	QN	Quantity of low-fat white milk purchased (number of half-pints)
LFCBID	QN	Winning bid price of low-fat chocolate milk (dollars per half-pint)
LFCQTY	QN	Quantity of low-fat chocolate milk purchased (number of half-pints)
DISTRICT	QL	School district number
KYFMO	QN	FMO minimum raw cost of milk (dollars per half-pint)
MILESM	QN	Distance (miles) from Meyer processing plant to school district
MILEST	QN	Distance (miles) from Trauth processing plant to school district
LETDATE	QL	Date on which bidding on milk contract began (month/day/year)

(Number of observations: 392) *Data Set:* MILK

Collusive Bidding Patterns

The analyses of patterns in sealed bids reveal much about the level of competition, or lack thereof, among the vendors serving the market. Consider the following bid analyses:

1. *Market shares.* A market share for a dairy is the number of milk half-pints supplied by the dairy over a given school year, divided by the total number of half-pints supplied to the entire market. One sign of potential collusive behavior is stable, nearly equal market shares over time for the dairies under investigation.

2. *Incumbency rates.* Market allocation is a common form of collusive behavior in bidrigging conspiracies. Typically, the same dairy controls the same school districts year after year. The incumbency rate for a market in a given school year is defined as the percentage of school districts that are won by the same vendor who won the previous year. An incumbency rate that exceeds 70% has been considered a sign of collusive behavior.

3. *Bid levels and dispersion.* In competitive sealed-bid markets, vendors do not share information about their bids. Consequently, more dispersion or variability among the bids is observed than in collusive markets, where vendors communicate about their bids and have a tendency to submit bids in close proximity to one another in an attempt to make the bidding appear competitive. Furthermore, in competitive markets the bid dispersion tends to be directly proportional to the level of the bid: When bids are submitted at relatively high levels, there is more variability among the bids than when they are submitted at or near marginal cost, which will be approximately the same among dairies in the same geographic market.

4. *Price versus cost/distance.* In competitive markets, bid prices are expected to track costs over time. Thus, if the market is competitive, the bid price of milk should be highly correlated with the raw milk cost. Lack of such a relationship is another sign of collusion. Similarly, bid price should be correlated to the distance the product must travel from the processing plant to the school (due to delivery costs) in a competitive market.

5. *Bid sequence.* School milk bids are submitted over the spring and summer months, generally at the end of one school year and before the beginning of the next. When the bids are examined in sequence in competitive markets, the level of bidding is expected to fall as the bidding season progresses. (This phenomenon is attributable to the learning process that occurs during the season, with bids adjusted accordingly. Dairies may submit relatively high bids early in the season to "test the market," confident that volume can be picked up later if the early high bids lose. But, dairies who do not win much business early in the season are likely to become more aggressive in their bidding as the season progresses, driving price levels down.) Constant or slightly increasing price patterns of sequential bids in a market where a single dairy wins year after year is considered another indication of collusive behavior.

6. *Comparison of average winning bid prices.* Consider two similar markets, one in which bids are possibly rigged and the other in which bids are competitively determined. In theory, the mean winning price in the "rigged" market will be significantly higher than the mean price in the competitive market for each year in which collusion occurs.

■ Answers to Selected Exercises

1 16; .18, .45, .15, .14   **3 a.** Bar graph **b.** Type of robotic limb **c.** Legs only **d.** None: .142; both: .075; legs only: .594; wheels only: .189
5 Most (84%) malls have small or small standard tenants   **7 a.** Qualitative   **9** Companies and employees created 73% of blogs/forums   **11 a.** .712 **b.** .195 **c.** Medical: .707; surgical: .721 **d.** Medical: .173; surgical: .233   **13** If team behind, goalie is likely to dive right   **15 a.** Response time **c.** 3,570   **17 d.** Most aquifers are bedrock; most MTBE levels are below the limit; 79% of private wells and 60% of public wells are not contaminated   **19** 50, 75, 125, 100, 25, 50, 50, 25   **21 a.** Frequency histogram **b.** 14 **c.** 49
23 a. Relative frequency **b.** 12%   **25 b.** Years 1996–2000 had the highest number of firms with at least one acquisition
27 a. Very little change **b.** Higher scores in 2011 **d.** 32; Michigan   **29** Yes   **31** More than 20 years of experience: "no" — 38%, "yes" — 19%   **33** "Inside job" not likely since histogram appears similar to frequency distribution   **35** $\bar{x} = 2.72, m = 2.65$ **37** mean > median: skewed right; mean < median: skewed left; mean = median: symmetric   **39** mode = 15; $\bar{x} = 14.55; m = 15$ **41 a.** mean < median **b.** mean > median **c.** Equal   **43 a.** mean = 653; average amount of sparkling wine exported by the 30 countries is $653,000 **b.** median = 231; half the 30 export values are above $231,000 **c.** mean = 481; average change in amount exported by the 30 countries is 481% **d.** median = 156; half the 30 percentage changes are above 156%   **45 a.** 759,601; average research expenditures of top 20 ranked universities is $759,601 thousand **b.** 695,408.5; half of top 20 ranked universities have research expenditures less than $695,405.8 thousand **c.** No; sample not representative of all American universities   **47 a.** 11 **b.** 9 **c.** 7 **d.** Honey dosage leads to greatest improvement
49 a. Skewed right **b.** Skewed left **c.** Skewed right **d.** Skewed right **e.** Symmetric **f.** Skewed left   **51** Average semester hours taken by sample of candidates is 141.31 hours; half of the sampled candidates take less than 140 semester hours; data likely to be symmetric   **53** Joint: $\bar{x} = 2.65, m = 1.5$; no prefiling: $\bar{x} = 4.24, m = 3.2$; prepack: $\bar{x} = 1.82, m = 1.4$; 3 centers   **55 a.** Median **b.** Mean
57 a. $R = 4, s^2 = 2.3, s = 1.52$ **b.** $R = 6, s^2 = 3.619, s = 1.90$ **c.** $R = 10, s^2 = 7.111, s = 2.67$ **d.** $R = 5, s^2 = 1.624, s = 1.274$
59 a. $\bar{x} = 5.6, s^2 = 17.3, s = 4.16$ **b.** $\bar{x} = 13.75$ feet, $s^2 = 152.25$ square feet, $s = 12.34$ feet **c.** $\bar{x} = -2.5, s^2 = 4.3, s = 2.07$ **d.** $\bar{x} = .33$ ounce, $s^2 = .0587$ square ounce, $s = .24$ ounce   **61** Data set 1: 0, 1, 2, 3, 4, 5, 6, 7, 8, 9; data set 2: 0, 0, 1, 1, 2, 2, 3, 3, 9, 9
63 a. $R = 3, s^2 = 1.3, s = 1.14$ **b.** $R = 3, s^2 = 1.3, s = 1.14$ **c.** $R = 3, s^2 = 1.3, s = 1.14$ **d.** No effect   **65 a.** $R = \$4,882$ thousand **b.** $s = \$1,113$ thousand **c.** $s^2 = 1,238,769$ **67 a.** 155; accurate **b.** 722.036; inaccurate **c.** 26.871; less **d.** standard deviation
69 a. $R = 10, s^2 = 7.67, s = 2.77$ **b.** $R = 8, s^2 = 5.15, s = 2.27$ **c.** $R = 8, s^2 = 5.06, s = 2.25$ **71 a.** Dollars; quantitative **b.** At least $\frac{3}{4}$; at least $\frac{8}{9}$; nothing; nothing   **73** Approx. 68%; approx. 95%; essentially all   **75** Between R/6 = 104.17 and R/4 = 156.25; no
77 a. (1.79, 4.43) **b.** No   **79 a.** (105.77, 176.85) **b.** At least $\frac{3}{4}$ **c.** Nothing   **81 a.** $\bar{x} = 95.7, s = 4.96$ **b.** (90.74, 100.66), (85.78, 105.62), (80.82, 110.58) **c.** 89.2%, 96.2%, 97.8%; Chebyshev's Rule   **83** $\bar{x} = 234.74, s = 9.91$; (205.0, 264.5)   **85 a.** Flexed: $\bar{x} \pm 2s = (51, 67)$; extended: $\bar{x} \pm 2s = (39, 47)$; yes **b.** Flexed: $\bar{x} \pm 2s = (39, 79)$; extended: $\bar{x} \pm 2s = (13, 73)$; no   **87** Do not buy   **89** 11:30 and 4:00   **91 a.** 25%, 75% **b.** 50%, 50% **c.** 80%, 20% **d.** 16%, 84%   **93 a.** $z = 2$ **b.** $z = -3$ **c.** $z = -2$ **d.** $z = 1.67$ **95** Average score is 283; 25% score below 259; 75% score below 308; 90% score below 329   **97** Half the graduates had starting salaries less than $41,100; half the graduates had mid-career salaries less than $71,100; 90% of the graduates had mid-career salaries less than $131,000   **99** No   **101 a.** 0 **b.** 21 **c.** $\bar{x} = 5.24, s = 7.24; z = 5.90$ **d.** Yes   **103 a.** Harvard's productivity score falls 5.08 standard deviations above the mean **b.** Howard's productivity score falls .81 standard deviation below the mean **c.** Yes   **105** Not necessarily, since the standard deviation will be large for right-skewed data   **107** IQR = 25   **109 a.** Sample A: IQR = 22; sample B: IQR = 15 **b.** Sample A: 84; sample B: 140 and 206   **111 a.** 50% of expenditures are less than $6,232; 25% are less than $5,309; 75% are less than $7,216 **b.** $1,907 **c.** $.75 - .25 = .50$ **113 a.** $z = 1.05$, no **b.** greater than 194.6 or less than 88   **115 b.** Joint: 1.5; none firms: 3.2; prepack: 1.4 **d.** No **e.** Yes   **117 a.** 10 outliers: 69, 73, 74, 78, 83, 84, 84, 86, 86, and 86 **b.** 7 outliers: 69, 73, 74, 78, 83, 84, and 84 **c.** No
119 No outliers; agree with claim   **123** Yes; yes, negative association between punishment use and average payoff   **125** No
127 a. No **b.** Positive trend **c.** Positive trend   **129 a.** Yes **b.** USAID and State   **131 a.** Weak association **b.** 1,000 **c.** Negative association   **133** Vertical axis is cut off; width of bars increases   **135 a.** Scales on two vertical axes differ **b.** Craigslist revenue much lower than newspaper ad sales   **139 a.** −1, 1, 2 **b.** 0, 4, 6 **c.** 1, 3, 4 **d.** .1, .3, .4   **141 a.** 6, 27, 5.20 **b.** 6.25, 28.25, 5.32 **c.** 7, 37.67, 6.14 **d.** 3, 0, 0
147 a. .082, .173, .167, .174, .139, .098, .074, .046, .048; 16.7% of articles published were in the Buyer Behavior area **b.** Lower percentage for Marketing Research   **149** 60% of cars with 4-star rating   **151 a.** Body defect **b.** Paint or dents   **153 a.** At most 25% **b.** ≈2.5%   **155 c.** Penalties for CAA tend to be smaller   **157 d.** HRD group **e.** $\bar{x} = .63$; average number of carats of 308 diamonds is .63 **f.** $m = .62$; 50% of the diamonds weigh less than .62 carat **g.** Mode = 1.0; carat value of 1.0 occurred the most often **h.** Mean or median **i.** (.077, 1.185)   **159 a.** Grounding and fire **b.** $\bar{x} = 66.19, s = 56.05$; (0, 234.34)   **161 a.** At least $\frac{8}{9}$ of the velocities fall within (906, 966) **b.** No   **163 a.** No scale on vertical axis **b.** Add vertical axis scale   **165 a.** Skewed right **c.** ≈38 **d.** No, z = 3.333   **167 a.** both height and width of bars change   **169** Laid off: $m = 40.5$; not laid off: $m = 40$; company probably not vulnerable   **171** Yes; no observations were recorded in the interval just below the interval centered at 1.000 cm

■ Credits

☐ Technology Images

Probability

CONTENTS

Where We're Going

- Develop probability as a measure of uncertainty (1)

- Introduce basic rules for finding probabilities (2–6)

- Use probability as a measure of reliability for an inference (2–6)

- Provide an advanced rule for finding probabilities (7)

☐ Probability

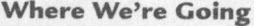 **STATISTICS in ACTION** **Lotto Buster!**

"Welcome to the Wonderful World of Lottery Bu$ters." So began the premier issue of Lottery Buster, *a monthly publication for players of the state lottery games.* Lottery Buster *provides interesting facts and figures on the 42 state lotteries and 2 multistate lotteries currently operating in the United States and, more importantly, tips on how to increase a player's odds of winning the lottery.*

New Hampshire, in 1963, was the first state in modern times to authorize a state lottery as an alternative to increasing taxes. (Prior to this time, beginning in 1895, lotteries were banned in America because of corruption.) Since then, lotteries have become immensely popular for two reasons: (1) They lure you with the opportunity to win millions of dollars with a $1 investment, and (2) when you lose, at least you believe your money is going to a good cause. Many state lotteries, such as Florida's, designate a high percentage of lottery revenues to fund state education.

The popularity of the state lottery has brought with it an avalanche of "experts" and "mathematical wizards" (such as the editors of *Lottery Buster*) who provide advice on how to win the lottery—for a fee, of course! Many offer guaranteed "systems" of winning through computer software products with catchy names such as Lotto Wizard, Lottorobics, Win4d, and Lotto-luck.

For example, most knowledgeable lottery players would agree that the "golden rule" or "first rule" in winning lotteries is *game selection*. State lotteries generally offer three types of games: an Instant (scratch-off tickets or online) game, Daily Numbers (Pick-3 or Pick-4), and a weekly Pick-6 Lotto game.

One version of the Instant game involves scratching off the thin opaque covering on a ticket with the edge of a coin to determine whether you have won or lost. The cost of a ticket ranges from 50¢ to $5, and the amount won ranges from $1 to $100,000 in most states, and to as much as $1 million in others. *Lottery Buster* advises against playing the Instant game because it is "a pure chance play, and you can win only by dumb luck. No skill can be applied to this game."

The Daily Numbers game permits you to choose either a three-digit (Pick-3) or four-digit (Pick-4) number at a cost of $1 per ticket. Each night, the winning number is drawn. If your number matches the winning number, you win a large sum of money, usually $100,000. You do have some control over the Daily Numbers game (because you pick the numbers that you play), and, consequently, there are strategies available to increase your chances of winning. However, the Daily Numbers game, like the Instant game, is not available for out-of-state play.

To play Pick-6 Lotto, you select six numbers of your choice from a field of numbers ranging from 1 to N, where N depends on which state's game you are playing. For example, Florida's current Lotto game involves picking six numbers ranging from 1 to 53. (See Figure SIA1.) The cost of a ticket is $1, and the payoff, if your six numbers match the winning numbers drawn, is $7 million or more, depending on the number of tickets purchased. (To date, Florida has had the largest individual state weekly payoff of over $200 million.) In addition to the grand prize, you can win second-, third-, and fourth-prize payoffs by matching five, four, and three of the six numbers drawn, respectively. And you don't have to be a resident of the state to play the state's Lotto game.

In this chapter, several Statistics in Action Revisited examples demonstrate how to use the basic concepts of probability to compute the odds of winning a state lottery game and to assess the validity of the strategies suggested by lottery "experts."

STATISTICS in ACTION REVISITED

- The Probability of Winning Lotto
- The Probability of Winning a Wheel System
- The Probability of Winning Cash 3 or Play 4

Recall that one branch of statistics is concerned with decisions about a population based on sample information. You can see how this is accomplished more easily if you understand the relationship between population and sample—a relationship that becomes clearer if we reverse the statistical procedure of making inferences from sample to population. In this chapter, then, we assume that the population is known and calculate the chances of obtaining various samples from the population. Thus, we show that probability is the reverse of statistics: **In probability, we use the population information to infer the probable nature of the sample.**

Probability plays an important role in inference making. Suppose, for example, you have an opportunity to invest in an oil exploration company. Past records show that out of 10 previous oil drillings (a sample of the company's experiences), all 10 came up dry. What do you conclude? Do you think the chances are better than 50:50 that the company will hit a gusher? Should you invest in this company? Chances are, your answer to these questions will be an emphatic "no." If the company's exploratory prowess is sufficient to hit a producing well 50% of the time, a record of 10 dry wells out of 10 drilled is an event that is just too improbable.

Or suppose you're playing poker with what your opponents assure you is a well-shuffled deck of cards. In three consecutive five-card hands, the person on your right is dealt four aces. Based on this sample of three deals, do you think the cards are being adequately shuffled? Again, your answer is likely to be "no" because dealing three hands of four aces is just too improbable if the cards were properly shuffled.

Note that the decisions concerning the potential success of the oil drilling company and the adequacy of card shuffling both involve knowing the chance–or probability–of a certain sample result. Both situations were contrived so that you could easily conclude that the probabilities of the sample results were small. Unfortunately, the probabilities of many observed sample results are not so easy to evaluate intuitively. For these cases we will need the assistance of a theory of probability.

1 Events, Sample Spaces, and Probability

Let's begin our treatment of probability with simple examples that are easily described. With the aid of simple examples, we can introduce important definitions that will help us develop the notion of probability more easily.

Suppose a coin is tossed once and the up face is recorded. The result we see and record is called an *observation*, or *measurement*, and the process of making an observation is called an *experiment*. Notice that our definition of *experiment* is broader than the one used in the physical sciences, where you would picture test tubes, microscopes, and other laboratory equipment. Among other things, statistical experiments may include recording an Internet user's preference for a Web browser, recording a change in the Dow Jones Industrial Average from one day to the next, recording the weekly sales of a business firm, and counting the number of errors on a page of an accountant's ledger. The point is that a statistical experiment can be almost any act of observation as long as the outcome is uncertain.

> An **experiment** is an act or process of observation that leads to a single outcome that cannot be predicted with certainty.

Consider another simple experiment consisting of tossing a die and observing the number on the up face. The six basic possible outcomes to this experiment are as follows:

1. Observe a 1
2. Observe a 2
3. Observe a 3
4. Observe a 4
5. Observe a 5
6. Observe a 6

Note that if this experiment is conducted once, *you can observe one and only one of these six basic outcomes, and the outcome cannot be predicted with certainty.* Also, these possibilities cannot be decomposed into more basic outcomes. Because observing the outcome of an experiment is similar to selecting a sample from a population, the basic possible outcomes to an experiment are called *sample points.**

> A **sample point** is the most basic outcome of an experiment.

Example 1

Listing the Sample Points for a Coin–Tossing Experiment

Problem Two coins are tossed, and their up faces are recorded. List all the sample points for this experiment.

Solution Even for a seemingly trivial experiment, we must be careful when listing the sample points. At first glance, we might expect three basic outcomes: Observe two heads, Observe two tails, or Observe one head and one tail. However, further reflection reveals that the last of these, Observe one head and one tail, can be decomposed into two outcomes: Head on coin 1, Tail on coin 2; and Tail on coin 1, Head on coin 2.

A useful tool for illustrating this notion is a **tree diagram.** Figure 1 shows a tree diagram for this experiment. At the top of the "tree," there are two branches, representing the two outcomes (H or T) for the first tossed coin. Each of these outcomes results in two more branches, representing the two outcomes (H or T) for the second tossed coin. Consequently, after tossing both coins, you can see that we have four sample points.

1. Observe HH **3.** Observe TH
2. Observe HT **4.** Observe TT

*Alternatively, the term *simple event* can be used.

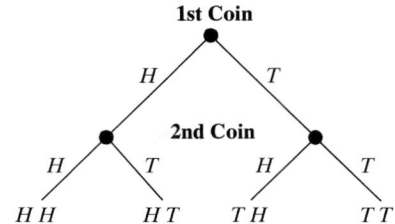

Figure 1
Tree diagram for the coin-tossing experiment

where H in the first position means "Head on coin 1," H in the second position means "Head on coin 2," and so on.

Look Back Even if the coins are identical in appearance, there are, in fact, two distinct coins. Thus, the sample points must account for this distinction.

■ **Now Work Exercise 7a**

We often wish to refer to the collection of all the sample points of an experiment. This collection is called the *sample space* of the experiment. For example, there are six sample points in the sample space associated with the die-toss experiment. The sample spaces for the experiments discussed thus far are shown in Table 1.

The **sample space** of an experiment is the collection of all its sample points.

Just as graphs are useful in describing sets of data, a pictorial method for presenting the sample space will often be useful. Figure 2 shows such a representation for each of the experiments in Table 1. In each case, the sample space is shown as a closed figure, labeled S, containing all possible sample points. Each sample point is represented by a solid dot (i.e., a "point") and labeled accordingly. Such graphical representations are called **Venn diagrams.**

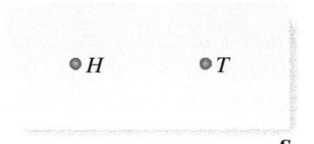

a. Experiment: Observe the up face on a coin

b. Experiment: Observe the up face on a die

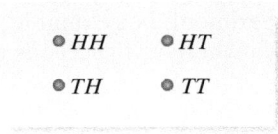

c. Experiment: Observe the up faces on two coins

Figure 2

Venn diagrams for the three experiments from Table 1

Table 1	Experiments and Their Sample Spaces

Experiment: Observe the up face on a coin.
Sample space: **1.** Observe a head
                 2. Observe a tail
This sample space can be represented in set notation as a set containing two sample points:

$$S: \{H, T\}$$

where H represents the sample point Observe a head and T represents the sample point Observe a tail.

Experiment: Observe the up face on a die.
Sample space: **1.** Observe a 1
                 2. Observe a 2
                 3. Observe a 3
                 4. Observe a 4
                 5. Observe a 5
                 6. Observe a 6
This sample space can be represented in set notation as a set of six sample points:

$$S: \{1, 2, 3, 4, 5, 6\}$$

Experiment: Observe the up faces on two coins.
Sample space: **1.** Observe HH
                 2. Observe HT
                 3. Observe TH
                 4. Observe TT
This sample space can be represented in set notation as a set of four sample points:

$$S: \{HH, HT, TH, TT\}$$

Now that we know that an experiment will result in *only one* basic outcome—called a *sample point*—and that the sample space is the collection of all possible sample points, we're ready to discuss the probabilities of the sample points. You've undoubtedly used the term *probability* and have some intuitive idea about its meaning. Probability is generally used synonymously with "chance," "odds," and similar concepts. For example, if a fair coin is tossed, we might reason that both the sample points, Observe a head and Observe a tail, have the same *chance* of occurring. Thus, we might state that "the probability of observing a head is 50%" or "the *odds* of seeing a head are 50:50." Both of these statements are based on an informal knowledge of probability. We'll begin our treatment of probability by using such informal concepts and then later solidify what we mean.

The probability of a sample point is a number between 0 and 1 inclusive that measures the likelihood that the outcome will occur when the experiment is performed. This number is usually taken to be the relative frequency of the occurrence of a sample point in a very long series of repetitions of an experiment.* For example, if we are assigning probabilities to the two sample points (Observe a head and Observe a tail) in the coin-toss experiment, we might reason that if we toss a balanced coin a very large number of times, the sample points Observe a head and Observe a tail will occur with the same relative frequency of .5.

Our reasoning is supported by Figure 3. The figure plots the relative frequency of the number of times that a head occurs when simulating (by computer) the toss of a coin N times, where N ranges from as few as 25 tosses to as many as 1,500 tosses of the coin. You can see that when N is large (i.e., $N = 1,500$), the relative frequency is converging to .5. Thus, the probability of each sample point in the coin-tossing experiment is .5.

For some experiments, we may have little or no information on the relative frequency of occurrence of the sample points; consequently, we must assign probabilities to the sample points based on general information about the experiment. For example, if the experiment is to invest in a business venture and to observe whether it succeeds or fails, the sample space would appear as in Figure 4.

We are unlikely to be able to assign probabilities to the sample points of this experiment based on a long series of repetitions because unique factors govern each performance of this kind of experiment. Instead, we may consider factors such as the personnel managing the venture, the general state of the economy at the time, the

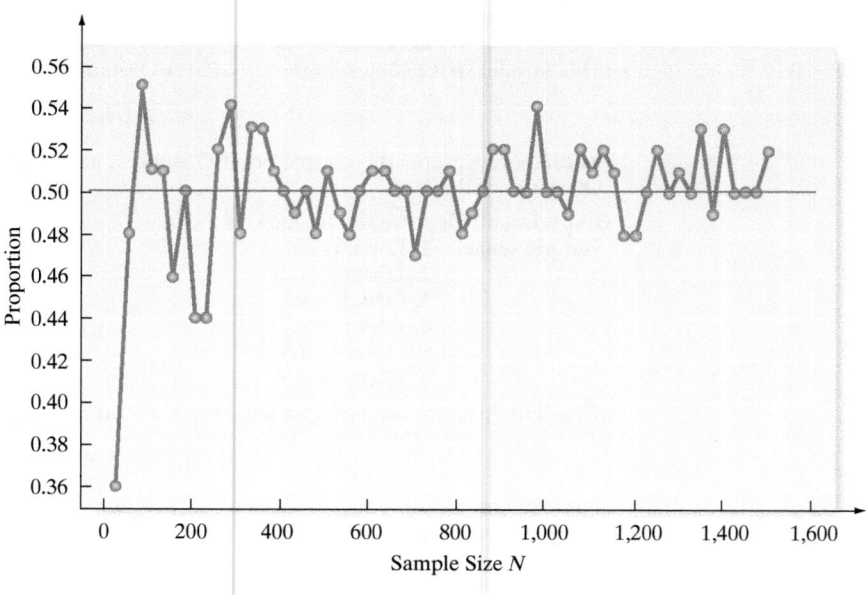

Figure 3

Proportion of heads in N coin tosses

*The result derives from an axiom in probability theory called the **Law of Large Numbers**. Phrased informally, this law states that the relative frequency of the number of times that an outcome occurs when an experiment is replicated over and over again (i.e., a large number of times) approaches the theoretical probability of the outcome.

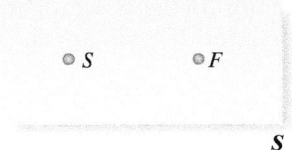

Figure 4
Experiment: Invest in a business venture and observe whether it succeeds (*S*) or fails (*F*)

rate of success of similar ventures, and any other pertinent information. If we finally decide that the venture has an 80% chance of succeeding, we assign a probability of .8 to the sample point Success. This probability can be interpreted as a measure of our degree of belief in the outcome of the business venture; that is, it is a subjective probability. Notice, however, that such probabilities should be based on expert information that is carefully assessed. If not, we may be misled on any decisions based on these probabilities or based on any calculations in which they appear. [*Note:* For a text that deals in detail with the subjective evaluation of probabilities, see Winkler (1972) or Lindley (1985).]

No matter how you assign the probabilities to sample points, the probabilities assigned must obey two rules:

> **Probability Rules for Sample Points**
>
> Let p_i represent the probability of sample point i.
>
> 1. All sample point probabilities *must* lie between 0 and 1 (i.e., $0 \leq p_i \leq 1$).
> 2. The probabilities of all the sample points within a sample space *must* sum to 1 (i.e., $\sum p_i = 1$).

Assigning probabilities to sample points is easy for some experiments. For example, if the experiment is to toss a fair coin and observe the face, we would probably all agree to assign a probability of $\frac{1}{2}$ to the two sample points, Observe a head and Observe a tail. However, many experiments have sample points whose probabilities are more difficult to assign.

Example	2

Sample Point Probabilities—Hotel Water Conservation

Problem *Going Green* is the term used to describe water conservation programs at hotels and motels. Many hotels now offer their guests the option of participating in these Going Green programs by reusing towels and bed linens. Suppose you randomly select one hotel from a registry of all hotels in Orange County, California, and check whether or not the hotel participates in a water conservation program. Show how this problem might be formulated in the framework of an experiment with sample points and a sample space. Indicate how probabilities might be assigned to the sample points.

Solution The experiment can be defined as the selection of an Orange County hotel and the observation of whether or not a water conservation program is offered to guests at the hotel. There are two sample points in the sample space for this experiment:

C: {The hotel offers a water conservation program.}

N: {The hotel does not offer a water conservation program.}

The difference between this and the coin-toss experiment becomes apparent when we attempt to assign probabilities to the two sample points. What probability should we assign to sample point *C*? If you answer .5, you are assuming that the events *C* and *N* occur with equal likelihood, just like the sample points Heads and Tails in the coin-toss experiment. But assigning sample point probabilities for the hotel water conservation experiment is not so easy. In fact, a recent report by the Orange County Water District stated that 70% of the hotels in the county now participate in a water conservation program of some type. In that case, it might be reasonable to approximate the probability of the sample point *C* as .7 and that of the sample point *N* as .3.

Look Back Here we see that sample points are not always equally likely, so assigning probabilities to them can be complicated—particularly for experiments that represent real applications (as opposed to coin- and die-toss experiments).

Now Work Exercise 9

Although the probabilities of sample points are often of interest in their own right, it is usually probabilities of collections of sample points that are important. Example 3 demonstrates this point.

Example 3

Probability of a Collection of Sample Points— Die-Tossing Experiment

Problem A fair die is tossed, and the up face is observed. If the face is even, you win $1. Otherwise, you lose $1. What is the probability that you win?

Solution Recall that the sample space for this experiment contains six sample points:

$$S: \{1, 2, 3, 4, 5, 6\}$$

Because the die is balanced, we assign a probability of $\frac{1}{6}$ to each of the sample points in this sample space. An even number will occur if one of the sample points, Observe a 2, Observe a 4, or Observe a 6, occurs. A collection of sample points such as this is called an *event*, which we denote by the letter A. Because the event A contains three sample points—each with probability $\frac{1}{6}$—and because no sample points can occur simultaneously, we reason that the probability of A is the sum of the probabilities of the sample points in A. Thus, the probability of A (i.e., the probability that you will win) is $\frac{1}{6} + \frac{1}{6} + \frac{1}{6} = \frac{1}{2}$.

Look Back Based on our notion of probability, $P(A) = \frac{1}{2}$ implies that, *in the long run*, you will win $1 half the time and lose $1 half the time.

Now Work Exercise 6

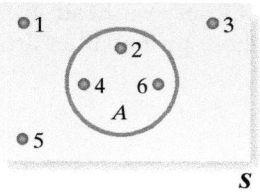

Figure 5
Die-toss experiment with event
A: Observe an even number

Figure 5 is a Venn diagram depicting the sample space associated with a die-toss experiment and the event A, Observe an even number. The event A is represented by the closed figure inside the sample space S. This closed figure A contains all the sample points that comprise it.

To decide which sample points belong to the set associated with an event A, test each sample point in the sample space S. If event A occurs, then that sample point is in the event A. For example, the event A, Observe an even number, in the die-toss experiment will occur if the sample point Observe a 2 occurs. By the same reasoning, the sample points Observe a 4 and Observe a 6 are also in event A.

To summarize, we have demonstrated that an event can be defined in words or it can be defined as a specific set of sample points. This leads us to the following general definition of an event:

> An **event** is a specific collection of sample points. Further, a **simple event** contains only a single sample point, while a **compound event** contains two or more sample points.

Example 4

The Probability of a Compound Event— Coin-Tossing Experiment

Problem Consider the experiment of tossing two *unbalanced* coins. Because the coins are *not* balanced, their outcomes (H or T) are not equiprobable. Suppose the correct probabilities associated with the sample points are given in the table. [*Note:* The necessary properties for assigning probabilities to sample points are satisfied.]
Consider the events

$$A: \{\text{Observe exactly one head}\}$$
$$B: \{\text{Observe at least one head}\}$$

Calculate the probability of A and the probability of B.

Sample Point	Probability
HH	$\frac{4}{9}$
HT	$\frac{2}{9}$
TH	$\frac{2}{9}$
TT	$\frac{1}{9}$

Solution Event A contains the sample points HT and TH; thus, A is a compound event. Because two or more sample points cannot occur at the same time, we can easily calculate the probability of event A by summing the probabilities of the two sample points. Thus, the probability of observing exactly one head (event A), denoted by the symbol $P(A)$, is

$$P(A) = P(\text{Observe } HT) + P(\text{Observe } TH) = \tfrac{2}{9} + \tfrac{2}{9} = \tfrac{4}{9}$$

Similarly, because B contains the sample points HH, HT, and TH,

$$P(B) = \tfrac{4}{9} + \tfrac{2}{9} + \tfrac{2}{9} = \tfrac{8}{9}$$

Look Back Again, these probabilities should be interpreted *in the long run*. For example, $P(B) = \tfrac{8}{9} \approx .89$ implies that if we were to toss two coins an infinite number of times, we would observe at least 2 heads on about 89% of the tosses.

Now Work Exercise 3

The preceding example leads us to a general procedure for finding the probability of an event A:

Probability of an Event

The probability of an event A is calculated by summing the probabilities of the sample points in the sample space for A.

Thus, we can summarize the steps for calculating the probability of any event, as indicated in the next box.

Steps for Calculating Probabilities of Events

Step 1 Define the experiment; that is, describe the process used to make an observation and the type of observation that will be recorded.

Step 2 List the sample points.

Step 3 Assign probabilities to the sample points.

Step 4 Determine the collection of sample points contained in the event of interest.

Step 5 Sum the sample point probabilities to get the event probability.

Example 5

Applying the Five Steps to Find a Probability— Diversity Training

Problem Diversity training of employees is the latest trend in U.S. business. *USA Today* reported on the primary reasons businesses give for making diversity training part of their strategic planning process. The reasons are summarized in Table 2. Assume that one business is selected at random from all U.S. businesses that use diversity training, and the primary reason is determined.

Table 2	Primary Reasons for Diversity Training
Reason	Percentage
Comply with personnel policies (CPP)	7
Increase productivity (IP)	47
Stay competitive (SC)	38
Social responsibility (SR)	4
Other (O)	4
Total	100

a. Define the experiment that generated the data in Table 2 and list the sample points.

b. Assign probabilities to the sample points.

c. What is the probability that the primary reason for diversity training is business related, that is, related to competition or productivity?

d. What is the probability that social responsibility is not a primary reason for diversity training?

Solution

a. The experiment is the act of determining the primary reason for diversity training of employees at a U.S. business. The sample points, the simplest outcomes of the experiment, are the five response categories listed in Table 2. These sample points are shown in the Venn diagram in Figure 6.

b. If, as in Example 1, we were to assign equal probabilities in this case, each of the response categories would have a probability of one-fifth, $\frac{1}{5}$, or .20. But, by examining Table 2 you can see that equal probabilities are not reasonable here because the response percentages are not even approximately the same in the five classifications. It is more reasonable to assign a probability equal to the response percentage in each class, as shown in Table 3.*

c. Let the symbol B represent the event that the primary reason for diversity training is business related. B is not a sample point because it consists of more than one of the response classifications (the sample points). In fact, as shown in Figure 6, B consists of two sample points, IP and SC. The probability of B is defined to be the sum of the probabilities of the sample points in B.

$$P(B) = P(IP) + P(SC) = .47 + .38 = .85$$

d. Let NSR represent the event that social responsibility is not a primary reason for diversity training. Then NSR consists of all sample points except SR, and the probability is the sum of the corresponding sample point probabilities:

$$P(NSR) = P(CPP) + P(IP) + P(SC) + P(O)$$
$$= .07 + .47 + .38 + .04 = .96$$

Look Back The key to solving this problem is to follow the steps outlined in the box. We defined the experiment (Step 1) and listed the sample points (Step 2) in part **a.** The assignment of probabilities to the sample points (Step 3) was done in part **b.** For each probability in parts **c** and **d,** we identified the collection of points in the event (Step 4) and summed their probabilities (Step 5).

Now Work Exercise 15

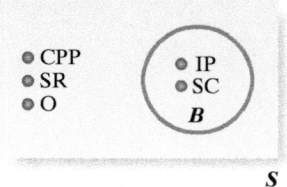

Figure 6

Venn diagram for diversity training survey

Table 3

Sample Point Probabilities for Diversity Training Survey

Sample Point	Probability
CPP	.07
IP	.47
SC	.38
SR	.04
O	.04

Example 6

Another Compound Event Probability—Investing in a Successful Venture

Problem You have the capital to invest in two of four ventures, each of which requires approximately the same amount of investment capital. Unknown to you, two of the investments will eventually fail and two will be successful. You research the four ventures because you think that your research will increase your probability of a successful choice over a purely random selection, and you eventually decide on two. If you used none of the information generated by your research and selected two ventures at random, what is the probability that you would select at least one successful venture?

Solution

Step 1: Denote the two successful enterprises as S_1 and S_2 and the two failing enterprises as F_1 and F_2. The experiment involves a random selection of two out of the four ventures, and each possible pair of ventures represents a sample point.

*The response percentages were based on a sample of U.S. businesses; consequently, these assigned probabilities are estimates of the true population-response percentages.

Step 2: The six sample points that make up the sample space are

    1. (S_1, S_2)

    2. (S_1, F_1)

    3. (S_1, F_2)

    4. (S_2, F_1)

    5. (S_2, F_2)

    6. (F_1, F_2)

Step 3: Next, we assign probabilities to the sample points. If we assume that the choice of any one pair is as likely as any other, then the probability of each sample point is $\frac{1}{6}$,

Step 4: The event of selecting at least one of the two successful ventures includes all the sample points except (F_1, F_2).

Step 5: Now, we find

$$P(\text{Select at least one success}) = P(S_1, S_2) + P(S_1, F_1) + P(S_1, F_2) +$$
$$P(S_2, F_1) + P(S_2, F_2)$$
$$= \tfrac{1}{6} + \tfrac{1}{6} + \tfrac{1}{6} + \tfrac{1}{6} + \tfrac{1}{6} = \tfrac{5}{6}$$

Therefore, with a random selection, the probability of selecting at least one successful venture out of two is $\frac{5}{6}$.

The preceding examples have one thing in common: The number of sample points in each of the sample spaces was small; hence, the sample points were easy to identify and list. How can we manage this when the sample points run into the thousands or millions? For example, suppose you wish to select five business ventures from a group of 1,000. Then each different group of five ventures would represent a sample point. How can you determine the number of sample points associated with this experiment?

One method of determining the number of sample points for a complex experiment is to develop a counting system. Start by examining a simple version of the experiment. For example, see if you can develop a system for counting the number of ways to select two ventures from a total of four (this is exactly what was done in Example 6). If the ventures are represented by the symbols V_1, V_2, V_3, and V_4, the sample points could be listed in the following pattern:

$$(V_1, V_2) \quad (V_2, V_3) \quad (V_3, V_4)$$
$$(V_1, V_3) \quad (V_2, V_4)$$
$$(V_1, V_4)$$

Note the pattern and now try a more complex situation—say, sampling three ventures out of five. List the sample points and observe the pattern. Finally, see if you can deduce the pattern for the general case. Perhaps you can program a computer to produce the matching and counting for the number of samples of five selected from a total of 1,000.

A second method of determining the number of sample points for an experiment is to use **combinatorial mathematics.** This branch of mathematics is concerned with developing counting rules for given situations. For example, there is a simple rule for finding the number of different samples of 5 ventures selected from 1,000. This rule, called the **Combinations Rule,** is given in the box.

Combinations Rule

A sample of n elements is to be drawn from a set of N elements. Then, the number of different samples possible is denoted by $\binom{N}{n}$ and is equal to

$$\binom{N}{n} = \frac{N!}{n!(N-n)!}$$

where the factorial symbol (!) means that

$$n! = n(n-1)(n-2)\cdots(3)(2)(1)$$

For example, $5! = 5 \cdot 4 \cdot 3 \cdot 2 \cdot 1$. [*Note:* The quantity 0! is defined to be equal to 1.]

Example 7
Using the Combinations Rule—Selecting 2 Investments from 4

Problem Refer to Example 6, where we selected two ventures from four in which to invest. Use the combinations rule to determine how many different selections can be made.

Solution For this example, $N = 4, n = 2$, and

$$\binom{4}{2} = \frac{4!}{2!2!} = \frac{4\cdot3\cdot2\cdot1}{(2\cdot1)(2\cdot1)} = \frac{4\cdot3}{2\cdot1} = \frac{12}{2} = 6$$

Look Back You can see that this agrees with the number of sample points obtained in Example 6.

Now Work Exercise 5

Example 8
Using the Combinations Rule—Selecting 5 Investments from 20

Problem Suppose you plan to invest equal amounts of money in each of five business ventures. If you have 20 ventures from which to make the selection, how many different samples of five ventures can be selected from the 20?

Solution For this example, $N = 20$ and $n = 5$. Then the number of different samples of 5 that can be selected from the 20 ventures is

$$\binom{20}{5} = \frac{20!}{5!(20-5)!} = \frac{20!}{5!15!}$$

$$= \frac{20\cdot19\cdot18\cdot\cdots\cdot3\cdot2\cdot1}{(5\cdot4\cdot3\cdot2\cdot1)(15\cdot14\cdot13\cdot\cdots\cdot3\cdot2\cdot1)} = \frac{20\cdot19\cdot18\cdot17\cdot16}{5\cdot4\cdot3\cdot2\cdot1} = 15{,}504$$

Look Back You can see that attempting to list all the sample points for this experiment would be an extremely tedious and time-consuming, if not practically impossible, task.

Now Work Exercise 20

The Combinations Rule is just one of a large number of counting rules that have been developed by combinatorial mathematicians. This counting rule applies to situations in which the experiment calls for selecting n elements from a total of N elements, without replacing each element before the next is selected. If you are interested in learning other methods for counting sample points for various types of experiments, you will find a few of the basic counting rules in Appendix: Basic Counting Rules. Others can be found in the chapter references.

The Probability of Winning Lotto

In Florida's state lottery game, called Pick-6 Lotto, you select six numbers of your choice from a set of numbers ranging from 1 to 53. We can apply the Combinations Rule to determine the total number of combinations of 6 numbers selected from 53 (i.e., the total number of sample points [or possible winning tickets]). Here, $N = 53$ and $n = 6$; therefore, we have

$$\binom{N}{n} = \frac{N!}{n!(N-n)!} = \frac{53!}{6!47!}$$

$$= \frac{(53)(52)(51)(50)(49)(48)(47!)}{(6)(5)(4)(3)(2)(1)(47!)}$$

$$= 22{,}957{,}480$$

Now, since the Lotto balls are selected at random, each of these 22,957,480 combinations is equally likely to occur. Therefore, the probability of winning Lotto is

$$P(\text{Win}\,6/53\,\text{Lotto}) = 1/(22,957,480) = .00000004356$$

This probability is often stated as follows: The odds of winning the game with a single ticket are 1 in 22,957,480, or 1 in approximately 23 million. For all practical purposes, this probability is 0, implying that you have almost no chance of winning the lottery with a single ticket. Yet each week there is almost always a winner in the Florida Lotto. This apparent contradiction can be explained with the following analogy.

Suppose there is a line of Smart cars, front to back, from New York City to Los Angeles, California. Based on the distance between the two cities and the length of a standard minivan, there would be approximately 23 million Smart cars in line. Lottery officials will select, at random, one of the Smart cars and put a check for $10 million dollars in the glove compartment. For a cost of $1, you may roam the country and select one (and only one) Smart car and check the glove compartment. Do you think you will find $10 million in the Smart car you choose? You can be almost certain that you won't. But now permit anyone to enter the lottery for $1 and suppose that 50 million people do so. With such a large number of participants, it is very likely that someone will find the Smart car with the $10 million—but it almost certainly won't be you! (This example illustrates an axiom in statistics called the Law of Large Numbers.)

Exercises 1–27

Please be aware that some of the following problems may require knowledge of concepts that are not presented in this chapter.

Learning the Mechanics

1 An experiment results in one of the following sample points: E_1, E_2, E_3, E_4, or E_5.
   a. Find $P(E_3)$ if $P(E_1) = .1, P(E_2) = .2, P(E_4) = .1$, and $P(E_5) = .1$.
   b. Find $P(E_3)$ if $P(E_1) = P(E_3), P(E_2) = .1, P(E_4) = .2$, and $P(E_5) = .1$.
   c. Find $P(E_3)$ if $P(E_1) = P(E_2) = P(E_4) = P(E_5) = .1$.

2 The diagram below describes the sample space of a particular experiment and events A and B.

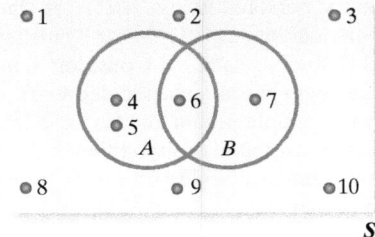

   a. What is this type of diagram called?
   b. Suppose the sample points are equally likely. Find $P(A)$ and $P(B)$.
   c. Suppose $P(1) = P(2) = P(3) = P(4) = P(5) = \frac{1}{20}$ and $P(6) = P(7) = P(8) = P(9) = P(10) = \frac{3}{20}$. Find $P(A)$ and $P(B)$.

3 The sample space for an experiment contains five sample points with probabilities as shown in the table. Find the probability of each of the following events:

Sample Points	Probabilities
1	.05
2	.20
3	.30
4	.30
5	.15

A: {Either 1, 2, or 3 occurs}

B: {Either 1, 3, or 5 occurs}

C: {4 does not occur}

4 Compute each of the following:
   a. $\binom{9}{4}$ b. $\binom{7}{2}$ c. $\binom{4}{4}$
   d. $\binom{5}{0}$ e. $\binom{6}{5}$

5 Compute the number of ways you can select n elements from N elements for each of the following:
   a. $n = 2, N = 5$
   b. $n = 3, N = 6$
   c. $n = 5, N = 20$

6 Two fair dice are tossed, and the face on each die is observed.

    a. Use a tree diagram to find the 36 sample points contained in the sample space.

    b. Assign probabilities to the sample points in part **a.**

    c. Find the probability of each of the following events:

        A = {3 showing on each die}

        B = {sum of two numbers showing is 7}

        C = {sum of two numbers showing is even}

7 Two marbles are drawn at random and without replacement from a box containing two blue marbles and three red marbles.

    a. List the sample points for this experiment.

    b. Assign probabilities to the sample points.

    c. Determine the probability of observing each of the following events:

        A: {Two blue marbles are drawn.}

        B: {A red and a blue marble are drawn.}

        C: {Two red marbles are drawn.}

8 Simulate the experiment described in Exercise 7 using any five identically shaped objects, two of which are one color and three another color. Mix the objects, draw two, record the results, and then replace the objects. Repeat the experiment a large number of times (at least 100). Calculate the proportion of time events *A*, *B*, and *C* occur. How do these proportions compare with the probabilities you calculated in Exercise 7? Should these proportions equal the probabilities? Explain.

◉ Applet Exercise 1

Use the applet *Simulating the Probability of Rolling a 6* to explore the relationship between the proportion of 6s rolled on several rolls of a die and the theoretical probability of rolling a 6 on a fair die.

    a. To simulate rolling a die one time, click on the *Roll* button on the screen while $n = 1$. The outcome of the roll appears in the list at the right, and the cumulative proportion of 6s for one roll is shown above the graph and as a point on the graph corresponding to 1. Click *Reset* and repeat the process with $n = 1$ several times. What are the possible values of the cumulative proportion of 6s for one roll of a die? Can the cumulative proportion of 6s for one roll of a die equal the theoretical probability of rolling a 6 on a fair die? Explain.

    b. Set $n = 10$ and click the *Roll* button. Repeat this several times, resetting after each time. Record the cumulative proportion of 6s for each roll. Compare the cumulative proportions for $n = 10$ to those for $n = 1$ in part **a.** Which tend to be closer to the theoretical probability of rolling a 6 on a fair die?

    c. Repeat part **b** for $n = 1,000$, comparing the cumulative proportions for $n = 1,000$ to those for $n = 1$ in part **a** and for $n = 10$ in part **b.**

    d. Based on your results for parts **a, b,** and **c,** do you believe that we could justifiably conclude that a die is unfair because we rolled it 10 times and didn't roll any 6s? Explain.

◉ Applet Exercise 2

Use the applet *Simulating the Probability of a Head with a Fair Coin* to explore the relationship between the proportion of heads on several flips of a coin and the theoretical probability of getting heads on one flip of a fair coin.

    a. Repeat parts **a–c** of Applet Exercise 1 for the experiment of flipping a coin and the event of getting heads.

    b. Based on your results for part **a,** do you believe that we could justifiably conclude that a coin is unfair because we flipped it 10 times and didn't get any heads? Explain.

Applying the Concepts–Basic

9 Colors of M&M's candies. In 1940, Forrest E. Mars Sr. formed the Mars Corporation to produce chocolate candies with a sugar shell that could be sold throughout the year and wouldn't melt during the summer. Originally, M&M's Plain Chocolate Candies came in only a brown color. Today, M&M's in standard bags come in six colors: brown, yellow, red, blue, orange, and green. According to Mars Corporation, today 24% of all M&M's produced are blue, 20% are orange, 16% are green, 14% are yellow, 13% are brown, and 13% are red. Suppose you purchase a randomly selected bag of M&M's Plain Chocolate Candies and randomly select one of the M&M's from the bag. The color of the selected M&M is of interest.

    a. Identify the outcomes (sample points) of this experiment.

    b. Assign reasonable probabilities to the outcomes, part **a.**

    c. What is the probability that the selected M&M is brown (the original color)?

    d. In 1960, the colors red, green, and yellow were added to brown M&Ms. What is the probability that the selected M&M is either red, green, or yellow?

    e. In 1995, based on voting by American consumers, the color blue was added to the M&M mix. What is the probability that the selected M&M is not blue?

10 Workers' unscheduled absence survey. Each year CCH, Inc., a firm that provides human resources and employment law information, conducts a survey on absenteeism in the workplace. The latest *CCH Unscheduled Absence Survey* found that of all unscheduled work absences, 34% are due to "personal illness," 22% for "family issues," 18% for "personal needs," 13% for "entitlement mentality," and 13% due to "stress." Consider a randomly selected employee who has an unscheduled work absence.

    a. List the sample points for this experiment.

    b. Assign reasonable probabilities to the sample points.

    c. What is the probability that the absence is due to something other than "personal illness"?

11 Male nannies. In a survey conducted by the International Nanny Association (INA) and reported at the INA Web site (*www.nanny.org*), 4,176 nannies were placed in a job in a given year. Only 24 of the nannies placed were men. Find the probability that a randomly selected nanny who was placed during the last year is a male nanny (a "mannie").

12 Predicting when a Florida hurricane occurs. Since the early 1900s, the state of Florida has exceeded $450 million in damages due to destructive hurricanes. Consequently, the value of property insured against windstorm damage in Florida is the highest in the nation. Researchers at Florida State University conducted a comprehensive analysis of damages caused by Florida hurricanes and published the results in *Southeastern Geographer* (Summer 2009). Part of their analysis included estimating the likelihood that a hurricane develops from a tropical storm based on the sequence number of the tropical storm within a season. The researchers discovered that of the 67 Florida hurricanes since 1900, 11 developed from the fifth tropical storm of the season (the sequence with the highest frequency). Also, only 5 hurricanes developed from a tropical storm with a sequence number of 12 or greater.

a. Estimate the probability that a Florida hurricane develops from the fifth tropical storm of the season.

b. Estimate the probability that a Florida hurricane develops before the 12th tropical storm of the season.

13 **Going online for health information.** A *cyberchondriac* is defined as a person who regularly searches the Web for health care information. A 2011 Harris Poll surveyed 1,019 U.S. adults by telephone and asked each respondent how often (in the past month) he/she looked for health care information online. The results are summarized in the following table. Consider the response category of a randomly selected person who participated in the Harris Poll.

Response (# per Month)	Percentage of Respondents
None	19
1 or 2	31
3–5	26
6–9	5
10 or more	19
Total	100

Source: Data from *The Harris Poll*, Sept. 15, 2011 (Table 4).

a. List the sample points for the experiment.

b. Assign reasonable probabilities to the sample points.

c. Find the probability that the respondent looks for health care information online more than two times per month.

14 **Working on summer vacation.** Is summer vacation a break from work? Not according to an *Adweek/Harris* (July 2011) poll of 3,304 U.S. adults. The poll found that 46% of the respondents work during their summer vacation, 35% do not work at all while on vacation, and 19% were unemployed. Consider the work status during summer vacation of a randomly selected poll respondent.

a. List the sample points for this experiment.

b. Assign reasonable probabilities to the sample points.

c. What is the probability that a randomly selected poll respondent will not work while on summer vacation or is unemployed?

Applying the Concepts—Intermediate

15 **Is a product "green"?** A "green" product (e.g., a product built from recycled materials) is one that has minimal impact on the environment and human health. How do consumers determine if a product is "green"? The *2011*

ImagePower Green Brands Survey asked this question of more than 9,000 international consumers. The results are shown in the following table.

Reason for Saying a Product Is Green	Percentage of Consumers
Certification mark on label	45
Packaging	15
Reading information about the product	12
Advertisement	6
Brand Web site	4
Other	18
Total	100

Source: Based on *2011 ImagePower Green Brands Survey*.

a. What method is an international consumer most likely to use to identify a green product?

b. Find the probability that an international consumer identifies a green product by a certification mark on the product label or by the product packaging.

c. Find the probability that an international consumer identifies a green product by reading about the product or from information at the brand's Web site.

d. Find the probability that an international consumer does not use advertisements to identify a green product.

16 **Museum management.** The *Museum Management and Curatorship* (June 2010) did a study of the criteria used to evaluate museum performance. The managers of 30 leading museums of contemporary art were asked to provide the performance measure used most often. A summary of the results is reproduced in the table.

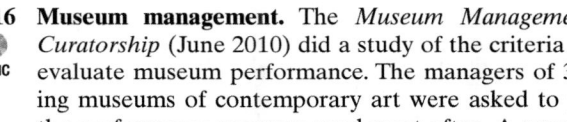

Performance Measure	Number of Museums
Total visitors	8
Paying visitors	5
Big shows	6
Funds raised	7
Members	4

a. If one of the 30 museums is selected at random, what is the probability that the museum uses total visitors or funds raised most often as a performance measure?

b. Consider two museums of contemporary art randomly selected from all such museums. Of interest is whether or not the museums use total visitors or funds raised most often as a performance measure. Use a tree diagram to aid in listing the sample points for this problem.

c. Assign reasonable probabilities to the sample points of part **b.** [*Hint*: Use the probability, part **a,** to estimate these probabilities.]

d. Refer to parts **b** and **c.** Find the probability that both museums use total visitors or funds raised most often as a performance measure.

17 **USDA chicken inspection.** The U.S. Department of Agriculture (USDA) reports that, under its standard inspection system, one in every 100 slaughtered chickens passes inspection with fecal contamination.

a. If a slaughtered chicken is selected at random, what is the probability that it passes inspection with fecal contamination?

b. The probability of part **a** was based on a USDA study that found that 306 of 32,075 chicken carcasses passed inspection with fecal contamination. Do you agree with the USDA's statement about the likelihood of a slaughtered chicken passing inspection with fecal contamination?

18 **PIN pad shipments.** Personal identification number (PIN) pads are devices that connect to point-of-sale electronic cash registers for debit and credit card purchases. *The Nilson Report* (Oct. 2008) published a listing of the volume of PIN pad shipments by manufacturers worldwide. For the 12 manufacturers listed in the table, a total of 334,039 PIN pads were shipped. Suppose you randomly select one of these PIN pads and identify the manufacturer.

Manufacturer	Number Shipped (units)
Bitel	13,500
CyberNet	16,200
Fujian Landi	119,000
Glintt (ParaRede)	5,990
Intelligent	4,562
KwangWoo	42,000
Omron	20,000
Pax Tech.	10,072
ProvencoCadmus	20,000
SZZT Electronics	67,300
Toshiba TEC	12,415
Urmet	3,000

Source: Data from *The Nilson Report*, No. 912, October 2008 (p. 9).

a. Find the probability that the PIN pad is shipped by either Fujian Landi or SZZT Electronics.

b. Suppose that 1,000 of the PIN pads shipped were found to be defective. Find the probability that the PIN pad selected is one of the defectives.

19 **Randomization in a study of TV commercials.** Gonzaga University professors conducted a study of more than 1,500 television commercials and published their results in the *Journal of Sociology, Social Work and Social Welfare* (Vol. 2, 2008). Commercials from eight networks—ABC, FAM, FOX, MTV, ESPN, CBS, CNN, and NBC—were sampled during an 8-day period, with one network randomly selected each day. The table below shows the actual order determined by random draw:

ABC—July 6 (Wed)
FAM—July 7 (Thr)
FOX—July 9 (Sat)
MTV—July 10 (Sun)
ESPN—July 11 (Mon)
CBS—July 12 (Tue)
CNN—July 16 (Sat)
NBC—July 17 (Sun)

a. What is the probability that ESPN was selected on Monday, July 11?

b. Consider the four networks chosen for the weekends (Saturday and Sunday). How many ways could the researchers select four networks from the eight for the weekend analysis of commercials? (Assume that the order of assignment for the four weekend days was immaterial to the analysis.)

c. Knowing that the networks were selected at random, what is the probability that ESPN was one of the four networks selected for the weekend analysis of commercials?

20 **Jai-alai bets.** The Quinella bet at the paramutual game of jai-alai consists of picking the jai-alai players that will place first and second in a game *irrespective* of order. In jai-alai, eight players (numbered 1, 2, 3,...,8) compete in every game.

a. How many different Quinella bets are possible?

b. Suppose you bet the Quinella combination of 2–7. If the players are of equal ability, what is the probability that you win the bet?

21 **Investing in stocks.** From a list of 15 preferred stocks recommended by your broker, you will select three to invest in. How many different ways can you select the three stocks from the 15 recommended stocks?

22 **Groundwater contamination in wells.** The *Environmental Science & Technology* (Jan. 2005) did a study of methyl *tert*-butyl ether (MTBE) contamination in New Hampshire wells. Data collected for a sample of 223 wells are saved in the accompanying file. Each well was classified according to well class (public or private), aquifer (bedrock or unconsolidated), and detectable level of MTBE (below limit or detect).

a. Consider an experiment in which the well class, aquifer, and detectable MTBE level of a well are observed. List the sample points for this experiment. [*Hint:* One sample point is private/bedrock/below limit.]

b. Use statistical software to find the number of the 223 wells in each sample point outcome. Then use this information to compute probabilities for the sample points.

c. Find and interpret the probability that a well has a detectable level of MTBE.

23 **Choosing portable grill displays.** University of Maryland marketing professor R. W. Hamilton studied how people attempt to influence the choices of others by offering undesirable alternatives (*Journal of Consumer Research*, Mar. 2003). Such a phenomenon typically occurs when family members propose a vacation spot, friends recommend a restaurant for dinner, and realtors show the buyer potential homes. In one phase of the study, the researcher had each of 124 college students select showroom displays for portable grills. Five different displays (representing five different-sized grills) were available, but only three displays would be selected. The students were instructed to select the displays to maximize purchases of Grill #2 (a smaller-sized grill).

a. In how many possible ways can the three grill displays be selected from the five displays? List the possibilities.

b. The table shows the grill display combinations and the number of each selected by the 124 students. Use this information to assign reasonable probabilities to the different display combinations.

c. Find the probability that a student who participated in the study selected a display combination involving Grill #1.

Grill Display Combination	Number of Students
1-2-3	35
1-2-4	8
1-2-5	42
2-3-4	4
2-3-5	1
2-4-5	34

Source: Based on Hamilton, R. W. "Why do people suggest what they do not want? Using context effects to influence others' choices," *Journal of Consumer Research*, Vol. 29, No. 4. Mar. 2003 (Table 1).

24 Highest-rated new cars. *Consumer Reports* magazine annually asks readers to evaluate their experiences in buying a new car during the previous year. Analysis of the questionnaires for a recent year revealed that readers were very satisfied with the following three new cars (in no particular order): Hyundai Elantra, Toyota Prius, and Subaru Forrester (*Consumer Reports,* Apr. 2011).

    a. List all possible sets of rankings for these top three cars.

    b. Assuming that each set of rankings in part **a** is equally likely, what is the probability that readers ranked Toyota Prius first? That readers ranked Hyundai Elantra third? That readers ranked Toyota Prius first and Subaru Forrester second?

Applying the Concepts—Advanced

25 Odds of winning a race. Handicappers for greyhound races express their belief about the probabilities that each greyhound will win a race in terms of **odds.** If the probability of event E is $P(E)$, then the *odds in favor of* E are $P(E)$ to $1 - P(E)$. Thus, if a handicapper assesses a probability of .25 that Oxford Shoes will win its next race, the odds in favor of Oxford Shoes are $\frac{25}{100}$ to $\frac{75}{100}$, or 1 to 3. It follows that the *odds against* E are $1 - P(E)$ to $P(E)$, or 3 to 1 against a win by Oxford Shoes. In general, if the odds in favor of event E are a to b, then $P(E) = a/(a + b)$.

    a. A second handicapper assesses the probability of a win by Oxford Shoes to be $\frac{1}{3}$. According to the second handicapper, what are the odds in favor of Oxford Shoes winning?

    b. A third handicapper assesses the odds in favor of Oxford Shoes to be 1 to 1. According to the third handicapper, what is the probability of Oxford Shoes winning?

    c. A fourth handicapper assesses the odds against Oxford Shoes winning to be 3 to 2. Find this handicapper's assessment of the probability that Oxford Shoes will win.

26 Lead bullets as forensic evidence. *Chance* (Summer 2004) published an article on the use of lead bullets as forensic evidence in a federal criminal case. Typically, the Federal Bureau of Investigation (FBI) will use a laboratory method to match the lead in a bullet found at the crime scene with unexpended lead cartridges found in possession of the suspect. The value of this evidence depends on the chance of a *false positive* (i.e., the probability that the FBI finds a match given that the lead at the crime scene and the lead in possession of the suspect are actually from two different "melts," or sources). To estimate the false-positive rate, the FBI collected 1,837 bullets that they were confident all came from different melts. The FBI then examined every possible pair of bullets and counted the number of matches using its established criteria. According to *Chance*, the FBI found 693 matches. Use this information to compute the chance of a false positive. Is this probability small enough for you to have confidence in the FBI's forensic evidence?

27 Making your vote count. The recent Democratic and Republican presidential state primary elections were highlighted by the difference in the way winning candidates were awarded delegates. In Republican states, the winner is awarded all the state's delegates; conversely, the Democratic state winner is awarded delegates in proportion to the percentage of votes. This led to a *Chance* (Fall 2007) article on making your vote count. Consider the following scenario where you are one of five voters (for example, on a county commission where you are one of the five commissioners voting on an issue).

    a. Determine the number of ways the five commissioners can vote, where each commissioner votes either for or against. (These outcomes represent the sample points for the experiment.)

    b. Assume each commissioner is equally likely to vote for or against. Assign reasonable probabilities to the sample points, part **a**.

    c. Your vote counts (i.e., is the decisive vote) only if the other four voters split, two in favor and two against. Assuming you are commissioner number 5, how many of the sample points in part **a** result in a 2-2 split for the other four commissioners?

    d. Use your answers to parts **a–c** to find the probability that your vote counts.

    e. Now suppose you convince two other commissioners to "vote in bloc," i.e., you all agree to vote among yourselves first, and whatever the majority decides is the way all three will vote. With only five total voters, this guarantees that the bloc vote will determine the outcome. In this scenario, your vote counts only if the other two commissioners in the bloc split votes, one in favor and one against. Find the probability that your vote counts.

2   Unions and Intersections

An event can often be viewed as a composition of two or more other events. Such events, which are called **compound events,** can be formed (composed) in two ways, as defined and illustrated here.

> The **union** of two events A and B is the event that occurs if either *A or B or* both occur on a single performance of the experiment. We denote the union of events A and B by the symbol $A \cup B$. $A \cup B$ consists of all the sample points that belong to *A or B or both*. (See Figure 7a.)

The **intersection** of two events *A and B* is the event that occurs if both *A and B* occur on a single performance of the experiment. We write $A \cap B$ for the intersection of *A* and *B*. $A \cap B$ consists of all the sample points belonging to *both A and B*. (See Figure 7b.)

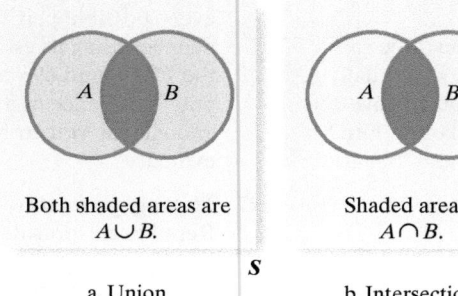

Both shaded areas are
$A \cup B$.

Shaded area is
$A \cap B$.

Figure 7

Venn diagrams for union
and intersection

a. Union   b. Intersection

| **Example** | **9** |

Probabilities of Unions and Intersections— Die-Toss Experiment

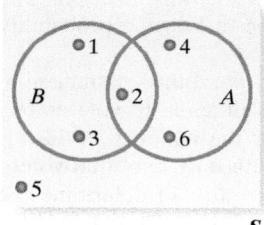

Figure 8

Venn diagram for die toss

Problem Consider the die-toss experiment. Define the following events:

> *A:* {Toss an even number}
> *B:* {Toss a number less than or equal to 3}

a. Describe $A \cup B$ for this experiment.
b. Describe $A \cap B$ for this experiment.
c. Calculate $P(A \cup B)$ and $P(A \cap B)$ assuming the die is fair.

Solution Draw the Venn diagram as shown in Figure 8.

a. The union of *A* and *B* is the event that occurs if we observe either an even number, a number less than or equal to 3, or both on a single throw of the die. Consequently, the sample points in the event $A \cup B$ are those for which *A* occurs, *B* occurs, or both *A* and *B* occur. Checking the sample points in the entire sample space, we find that the collection of sample points in the union of *A* and *B* is

$$A \cup B = \{1, 2, 3, 4, 6\}$$

b. The intersection of *A* and *B* is the event that occurs if we observe *both* an even number and a number less than or equal to 3 on a single throw of the die. Checking the sample points to see which imply the occurrence of *both* events *A* and *B*, we see that the intersection contains only one sample point:

$$A \cap B = \{2\}$$

In other words, the intersection of *A* and *B* is the sample point Observe a 2.

c. Recalling that the probability of an event is the sum of the probabilities of the sample points of which the event is composed, we have

$$P(A \cup B) = P(1) + P(2) + P(3) + P(4) + P(6)$$

$$= \tfrac{1}{6} + \tfrac{1}{6} + \tfrac{1}{6} + \tfrac{1}{6} + \tfrac{1}{6} = \tfrac{5}{6}$$

and

$$P(A \cap B) = P(2) = \tfrac{1}{6}$$

Look Back Since the six sample points are equally likely, the probabilities in part **c** are simply the number of sample points in the event of interest, divided by 6.

■ **Now Work Exercise 31a–d**

Unions and intersections can be defined for more than two events. For example, the event $A \cup B \cup C$ represents the union of three events: *A*, *B*, and *C*. This event, which includes the set of sample points in *A*, *B*, or *C*, will occur if any one (or more) of the events A, B, and C occurs. Similarly, the intersection $A \cap B \cap C$ is the event that all three of the events A, B, and C occur. Therefore, $A \cap B \cap C$ is the set of sample points that are in all three of the events.

Example 10	
Finding Probabilities in a Two-Way Table—Income vs. age	

Problem Many firms undertake direct marketing campaigns to promote their products. The campaigns typically involve mailing information to millions of households. The response rates are carefully monitored to determine the demographic characteristics of respondents. By studying tendencies to respond, the firms can better target future mailings to those segments of the population most likely to purchase their products.

Suppose a distributor of mail-order tools is analyzing the results of a recent mailing. The probability of response is believed to be related to income and age. The percentages of the total number of respondents to the mailing are given by income and age classification in Table 4. This table is called a **two-way table** because responses are classified according to two variables, income (columns) and age (rows).

Define the following events:

$$A: \{\text{A respondent's income is more than } \$50,000.\}$$

$$B: \{\text{A respondents age is 30 or more.}\}$$

a. Find $P(A)$ and $P(B)$.

b. Find $P(A \cup B)$.

c. Find $P(A \cap B)$.

Table 4	Two-Way Table with Percentage of Respondents in Age-Income Classes		
		Income	
Age	< $25,000	$25,000–$50,000	> $50,000
< 30 yrs	5%	12%	10%
30–50 yrs	14%	22%	16%
> 50 yrs	(B) 8%	10%	3%
			(A)

Solution Following the steps for calculating probabilities of events, we first note that the objective is to characterize the income and age distribution of respondents to the mailing. To accomplish this, we define the experiment to consist of selecting a respondent from the collection of all respondents and observing which income and age class he or she occupies. The sample points are the nine different age-income classifications:

$E_1: \{< 30 \text{ yrs}, < \$25,000\}$ $E_4: \{< 30 \text{ yrs}, \$25,000 - \$50,000\}$ $E_7: \{< 30 \text{ yrs}, > \$50,000\}$

$E_2: \{30 - 50 \text{ yrs}, < \$25,000\}$ $E_5: \{30 - 50 \text{ yrs}, \$25,000 - \$50,000\}$ $E_8: \{30 - 50 \text{ yrs}, > \$50,000\}$

$E_3: \{> 50 \text{ yrs}, < \$25,000\}$ $E_6: \{> 50 \text{ yrs}, \$25,000 - \$50,000\}$ $E_9: \{> 50 \text{ yrs}, > \$50,000\}$

Next, we assign probabilities to the sample points. If we blindly select one of the respondents, the probability that he or she will occupy a particular age-income classification is the proportion, or relative frequency, of respondents in the classification. These proportions are given (as percentages) in Table 4. Thus,

$$P(E_1) = \text{Relative frequency of respondents in age-income class}$$
$$\{< 30 \text{ yrs}, < \$25,000\} = .05$$
$$P(E_2) = .14$$
$$P(E_3) = .08$$
$$P(E_4) = .12$$
$$P(E_5) = .22$$
$$P(E_6) = .10$$

$$P(E_7) = .10$$
$$P(E_8) = .16$$
$$P(E_9) = .03$$

You may verify that the sample points probabilities add to 1.

a. To find $P(A)$, we first determine the collection of sample points contained in event A. Because A is defined as $\{> \$50,000\}$, we see from Table 4 that A contains the three sample points represented by the last column of the table (see shaded area). In other words, the event A consists of the income classification $\{> \$50,000\}$ in all three age classifications. The probability of A is the sum of the probabilities of the sample points in A:

$$P(A) = P(E_7) + P(E_8) + P(E_9) = .10 + .16 + .03 = .29$$

Similarly, $B = \{\geq 30 \text{ yrs}\}$ consists of the six sample points in the second and third rows of Table 4 (see shaded area):

$$P(B) = P(E_2) + P(E_3) + P(E_5) + P(E_6) + P(E_8) + P(E_9)$$
$$= .14 + .08 + .22 + .10 + .16 + .03 = .73$$

b. The union of events A and B, $A \cup B$, consists of all the sample points in *either A or B or both*—that is, the union of A and B consists of all respondents whose income exceeds \$50,000 *or* whose age is 30 or more. In Table 4 this is any sample point found in the third column *or* the last two rows. Thus,

$$P(A \cup B) = .10 + .14 + .22 + .16 + .08 + .10 + .03 = .83$$

c. The intersection of events A and B, $A \cap B$, consists of all sample points in *both A and B*—that is, the intersection of A and B consists of all respondents whose income exceeds \$50,000 *and* whose age is 30 or more. In Table 4 this is any sample point found in the third column *and* the last two rows. Thus,

$$P(A \cap B) = .16 + .03 = .19$$

Look Back As with previous problems, the key to finding the probabilities of parts **b** and **c** is to identify the sample points that comprise the event of interest. In a two-way table like Table 4, the number of sample points will be equal to the number of rows times the number of columns.

■ Now Work Exercise 33f–g

3 Complementary Events

A very useful concept in the calculation of event probabilities is the notion of **complementary events:**

> The **complement** of an event A is the event that A does *not* occur—that is, the event consisting of all sample points that are not in event A. We denote the complement of A by A^c.

An event A is a collection of sample points, and the sample points included in A^c are those not in A. Figure 9 demonstrates this idea. Note from the figure that all sample points in S are included in *either A or A^c* and that *no* sample point is in both A and A^c. This leads us to conclude that the probabilities of an event and its complement *must sum to 1:*

> **Rule of Complements**
>
> The sum of the probabilities of complementary events equals 1:
> $$P(A) + P(A^c) = 1.$$

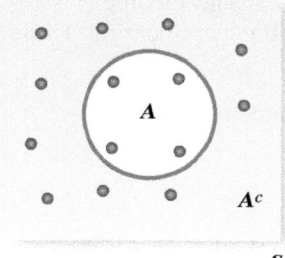

Figure 9

Venn diagram of complementary events

In many probability problems, calculating the probability of the complement of the event of interest is easier than calculating the event itself. Then, because

$$P(A) + P(A^c) = 1$$

we can calculate $P(A)$ by using the relationship

$$P(A) = 1 - P(A^c)$$

Example 11

Probability of a Complementary Event—Coin-Toss Experiment

Problem Consider the experiment of tossing fair coins. Define the following event: A: {Observing at least one head}.

a. Find $P(A)$ if 2 coins are tossed.

b. Find $P(A)$ if 10 coins are tossed.

Solution

a. When 2 coins are tossed, we know that the event A: {Observe at least one head.} consists of the sample points

$$A: \{HH, HT, TH\}$$

The complement of A is defined as the event that occurs when A does not occur. Therefore,

$$A^c: \{\text{Observe no heads.}\} = \{TT\}$$

This complementary relationship is shown in Figure 10. Since the coins are balanced, we have

$$P(A^c) = P(TT) = \tfrac{1}{4}$$

and

$$P(A) = 1 - P(A^c) = 1 - \tfrac{1}{4} = \tfrac{3}{4}$$

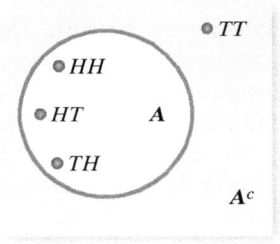

Figure 10

Complementary events in the toss of two coins

b. We solve this problem by following the five steps for calculating probabilities of events. (See Section 1.)

Step 1: Define the experiment. The experiment is to record the results of the 10 tosses of the coin.

Step 2: List the sample points. A sample point consists of a particular sequence of 10 heads and tails. Thus, one sample point is *HHTTTHTHTT,* which denotes head on first toss, head on second toss, tail on third toss, etc. Others are *HTHHHTTTTT* and *THHTHTHTT.* Obviously, the number of sample points is very large—too many to list. It can be shown that there are $2^{10} = 1,024$ sample points for this experiment.

Step 3: Assign probabilities. Since the coin is fair, each sequence of heads and tails has the same chance of occurring; therefore, all the sample points are equally likely. Then

$$P(\text{Each sample point}) = \frac{1}{1,024}$$

Step 4: Determine the sample points in event A. A sample point is in A if at least one H appears in the sequence of 10 tosses. However, if we consider the complement of A, we find that

$$A^c = \{\text{No heads are observed in 10 tosses.}\}$$

Thus, A^c contains only one sample point:

$$A^c: \{TTTTTTTTTT\}$$

and $P(A^c) = \dfrac{1}{1{,}024}$

Step 5: Now we use the relationship of complementary events to find $P(A)$:

$$P(A) = 1 - P(A^c) = 1 - \frac{1}{1{,}024} = \frac{1{,}023}{1{,}024} = .999$$

Look Back In part **a,** we can find $P(A)$ by summing the probabilities of the sample points *HH, HT,* and *TH* in A. Many times, however, it is easier to find $P(A^c)$ by using the rule of complements.

Look Forward Since $P(A) = .999$ in part **b,** we are virtually certain of observing at least one head in 10 tosses of the coin.

■ **Now Work Exercise 31e–f**

4   The Additive Rule and Mutually Exclusive Events

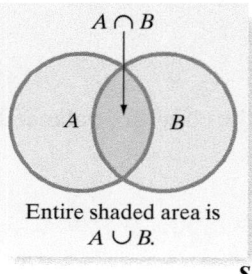

$A \cap B$

A B

Entire shaded area is
$A \cup B$.

S

Figure 11
Venn diagram of union

In Section 2 we saw how to determine which sample points are contained in a union and how to calculate the probability of the union by adding the probabilities of the sample points in the union. It is also possible to obtain the probability of the union of two events by using the **additive rule of probability.**

The union of two events will often contain many sample points because the union occurs if either one or both of the events occur. By studying the Venn diagram in Figure 11, you can see that the probability of the union of two events, A and B, can be obtained by summing $P(A)$ and $P(B)$ and subtracting the probability corresponding to $A \cap B$. We must subtract $P(A \cap B)$ because the sample point probabilities in $A \cap B$ have been included twice—once in $P(A)$ and once in $P(B)$. The formula for calculating the probability of the union of two events is given in the next box.

Additive Rule of Probability

The probability of the union of events A and B is the sum of the probabilities of events A and B minus the probability of the intersection of events A and B—that is,

$$P(A \cup B) = P(A) + P(B) - P(A \cap B)$$

Example   12

Applying the Additive Rule—Hospital Admission Study

Problem Hospital records show that 12% of all patients are admitted for surgical treatment, 16% are admitted for obstetrics, and 2% receive both obstetrics and surgical treatment. If a new patient is admitted to the hospital, what is the probability that the patient will be admitted either for surgery, obstetrics, or both?

Solution Consider the following events:

$A:$ {A patient admitted to the hospital receives surgical treatment.}

$B:$ {A patient admitted to the hospital receives obstetrics treatment.}

Then, from the given information,

$$P(A) = .12$$
$$P(B) = .16$$

and the probability of the event that a patient receives both obstetrics and surgical treatment is

$$P(A \cap B) = .02$$

The event that a patient admitted to the hospital receives either surgical treatment, obstetrics treatment, or both is the union $A \cup B$. The probability of $A \cup B$ is given by the additive rule of probability:

$$P(A \cup B) = P(A) + P(B) - P(A \cap B) = .12 + .16 - .02 = .26$$

Thus, 26% of all patients admitted to the hospital receive either surgical treatment, obstetrics treatment, or both.

Look Back From the information given, it is not possible to list and assign probabilities to all the sample points. Consequently, we cannot proceed through the five-step process for finding the probability of an event and must use the additive rule.

Now Work Exercise 28c

A very special relationship exists between events A and B when $A \cap B$ contains no sample points. In this case we call the events A and B *mutually exclusive events*.

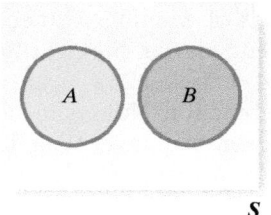

Figure 12
Venn diagram of mutually exclusive events

> Events A and B are **mutually exclusive** if $A \cap B$ contains no sample points—that is, if A and B have no sample points in common.

Figure 12 shows a Venn diagram of two mutually exclusive events. The events A and B have no sample points in common—that is, A and B cannot occur simultaneously, and $P(A \cap B) = 0$. Thus, we have the important relationship given in the box.

> **Probability of Union of Two Mutually Exclusive Events**
>
> If two events A and B are *mutually exclusive*, the probability of the union of A and B equals the sum of the probabilities of A and B; that is, $P(A \cup B) = P(A) + P(B)$.

> ⚠ **CAUTION** The formula just shown is *false* if the events are *not* mutually exclusive. For two nonmutually exclusive events, you must apply the general additive rule of probability.

Example 13

The Union of Two Mutually Exclusive Events—Coin-Tossing Experiment

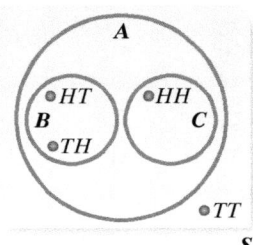

Figure 13
Venn diagram for coin-toss experiment

Problem Consider the experiment of tossing two balanced coins. Find the probability of observing *at least* one head.

Solution Define the events

$$A: \{\text{Observe at least one head}\}$$
$$B: \{\text{Observe exactly one head}\}$$
$$C: \{\text{Observe exactly two heads}\}$$

Note that

$$A = B \cup C$$

and that $B \cap C$ contains no sample points (see Figure 13). Thus, B and C are mutually exclusive, so that

$$P(A) = P(B \cup C) = P(B) + P(C) = \tfrac{1}{2} + \tfrac{1}{4} = \tfrac{3}{4}$$

Look Back Although this example is very simple, it shows us that writing events with verbal descriptions that include the phrases *at least* or *at most* as unions of mutually exclusive events is very useful. This practice enables us to find the probability of the event by adding the probabilities of the mutually exclusive events.

Now Work Exercise 37

The Probability of Winning a Wheeling System

Refer to Florida's Pick-6 Lotto game in which you select six numbers of your choice from a field of numbers ranging from 1 to 53. In Section 1, we learned that the probability of winning Lotto on a single ticket is only 1 in approximately 23 million. The "experts" at *Lottery Buster* recommend many strategies for increasing the odds of winning the lottery. One strategy is to employ a wheeling system. In a complete wheeling system, you select more than six numbers, say, seven, and play every combination of six of those seven numbers.

Suppose you choose to "wheel" the following seven numbers: 2, 7, 18, 23, 30, 32, and 51. Every combination of six of these seven numbers is listed in Table SIA1 You can see that there are seven different possibilities. (Use the Combinations Rule with $N = 7$ and $n = 6$ to verify this.) Thus, we would purchase seven tickets (at a cost of $7) corresponding to these different combinations in a complete wheeling system.

To determine if this strategy does, in fact, increase our odds of winning, we need to find the probability that one of these seven combinations occurs during the $\frac{6}{53}$ Lotto draw—that is, we need to find the probability that either Ticket 1 or Ticket 2 or Ticket 3 or Ticket 4 or Ticket 5 or Ticket 6 or Ticket 7 is the winning combination. Note that this probability is stated using the word *or*, implying a union of seven events. Letting T1 represent the event that Ticket 1 wins, and defining T2, T3,..., T7 in a similar fashion, we want to find

$$P(\text{T1 or T2 or T3 or T4 or T5 or T6 or T7})$$

Recall (Section 1) that the 22,957,480 possible combinations in Pick-6 Lotto are mutually exclusive and equally likely to occur. Consequently, the probability of the union of the seven events is simply the sum of the probabilities of the individual events, where each event has probability of 1/(22,957,480):

$$P(\text{win Lotto with 7 wheeled numbers})$$
$$= P(\text{T1 or T2 or T3 or T4 or T5 or T6 or T7})$$
$$= 7/(22,957,480) = .0000003$$

In terms of odds, we now have 3 chances in 10 million of winning the Lotto with the complete wheeling system. The "experts" are correct—our odds of winning Lotto have increased (from 1 in 23 million). However, the probability of winning is so close to 0 we question whether the $7 spent on lottery tickets is worth the negligible increase in odds. In fact, it can be shown that to increase your chance of winning the $\frac{6}{53}$ Lotto to 1 chance in 100 (i.e., .01) using a complete wheeling system, you would have to wheel 26 of your favorite numbers—a total of 230,230 combinations at a cost of $230,230!

Table SIA1	Wheeling the Seven Numbers 2, 7, 18, 23, 30, 32, and 51					
Ticket 1:	2	7	18	23	30	32
Ticket 2:	2	7	18	23	30	51
Ticket 3:	2	7	18	23	32	51
Ticket 4:	2	7	18	30	32	51
Ticket 5:	2	7	23	30	32	51
Ticket 6:	2	18	23	30	32	51
Ticket 7:	7	18	23	30	32	51

Exercises 28–48

Please be aware that some of the following problems may require knowledge of concepts that are not presented in this chapter.

Learning the Mechanics

28 Suppose $P(A) = .4$, $P(B) = .7$, and $P(A \cap B) = .3$. Find the following probabilities:
  a. $P(B^c)$
  b. $P(A^c)$
  c. $P(A \cup B)$

29 A fair coin is tossed three times, and the events A and B are defined as follows:

  A: {At least one head is observed.}
  B: {The number of heads observed is odd.}

  a. Identify the sample points in the events A, B, $A \cup B$, A^c, and $A \cap B$.
  b. Find $P(A)$, $P(B)$, $P(A \cup B)$, $P(A^c)$, and $P(A \cap B)$ by summing the probabilities of the appropriate sample points.
  c. Find $P(A \cup B)$ using the additive rule. Compare your answer to the one you obtained in part **b.**
  d. Are the events A and B mutually exclusive? Why?

30 A pair of fair dice is tossed. Define the following events:

  A: {You will roll a 7.} (i.e., The sum of the dots on the up faces of the two dice is equal to 7.)
  B: {At least one of the two dice shows a 4.}

  a. Identify the sample points in the events A, B, $A \cap B$, $A \cup B$ and A^c.
  b. Find $P(A)$, $P(B)$, $P(A \cap B)$, $P(A \cup B)$, and $P(A^c)$ by summing the probabilities of the appropriate sample points.
  c. Find $P(A \cup B)$ using the additive rule. Compare your answer to that for the same event in part **b.**
  d. Are A and B mutually exclusive? Why?

31 Consider the Venn diagram below, where

$$P(E_1) = P(E_2) = P(E_3) = \tfrac{1}{5}, P(E_4) = P(E_5) = \tfrac{1}{20},$$
$$P(E_6) = \tfrac{1}{10}, \text{ and } P(E_7) = \tfrac{1}{5}.$$

Find each of the following probabilities:

  a. $P(A)$ **e.** $P(A^c)$
  b. $P(B)$ **f.** $P(B^c)$
  c. $P(A \cup B)$ **g.** $P(A \cup A^c)$
  d. $P(A \cap B)$ **h.** $P(A^c \cap B)$

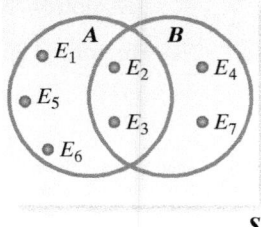

32 Consider the Venn diagram in the next column, where

$$P(E_1) = .10, P(E_2) = .05, P(E_3) = P(E_4) = .2,$$
$$P(E_5) = .06, P(E_6) = .3, P(E_7) = .06, \text{ and}$$
$$P(E_8) = .03.$$

Find the following probabilities:
  a. $P(A^c)$
  b. $P(B^c)$
  c. $P(A^c \cap B)$
  d. $P(A \cup B)$
  e. $P(A \cap B)$
  f. $P(A^c \cap B^c)$
  g. Are events A and B mutually exclusive? Why?

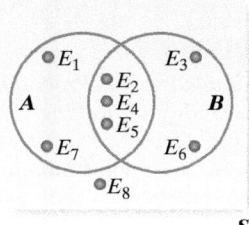

33 The outcomes of two variables are (Low, Medium, High) and (On, Off), respectively. An experiment is conducted in which the outcomes of each of the two variables are observed. The probabilities associated with each of the six possible outcome pairs are given in the accompanying two-way table.

	Low	Medium	High
On	.50	.10	.05
Off	.25	.07	.03

Consider the following events:

  A: {On}
  B: {Medium or On}
  C: {Off and Low}
  D: {High}

  a. Find $P(A)$.
  b. Find $P(B)$.
  c. Find $P(C)$.
  d. Find $P(D)$.
  e. Find $P(A^c)$.
  f. Find $P(A \cup B)$.
  g. Find $P(A \cap C)$.
  h. Consider each pair of events (A and B, A and C, A and D, B and C, B and D, C and D). List the pairs of events that are mutually exclusive. Justify your choices.

34 Refer to Exercise 33. Use the same event definitions to do the following exercises.
  a. Write the event that the outcome is "On" and "High" as an intersection of two events.
  b. Write the event that the outcome is "Low" or "Medium" as the complement of an event.

Applet Exercise 3

Use the applets *Simulating the Probability of Rolling a 6* and *Simulating the Probability of Rolling a 3 or 4* to explore the additive rule for probability.
  a. Explain why the applet *Simulating the Probability of Rolling a 6* can also be used to simulate the probability

of rolling a 3. Then use the applet with $n = 1,000$ to simulate the probability of rolling a 3. Record the cumulative proportion. Repeat the process to simulate the probability of rolling a 4.

b. Use the applet *Simulating the Probability of Rolling a 3 or 4* with $n = 1,000$ to simulate the probability of rolling a 3 or 4. Record the cumulative proportion.

c. Add the two cumulative proportions from part **a.** How does this sum compare to the cumulative proportion in part **b?** How does this illustrate the additive rule for probability?

⚙ Applet Exercise 4

Use the applets *Simulating the Probability of Rolling a 6* and *Simulating the Probability of Rolling a 3 or 4* to simulate the probability of the complement of an event.

a. Explain how the applet *Simulating the Probability of Rolling a 6* can also be used to simulate the probability of the event *rolling a 1, 2, 3, 4, or 5*. Then use the applet with $n = 1,000$ to simulate this probability.

b. Explain how the applet *Simulating the Probability of Rolling a 3 or 4* can also be used to simulate the probability of the event *rolling a 1, 2, 5, or 6*. Then use the applet with $n = 1,000$ to simulate this probability.

c. Which applet could be used to simulate the probability of the event *rolling a 1, 2, 3, or 4*? Explain.

Applying the Concepts—Basic

35 Study of analysts' forecasts. The *Journal of Accounting Research* (March 2008) published a study on relationship incentives and degree of optimism among analysts' forecasts. Participants were analysts at either a large or small brokerage firm who made their forecasts either early or late in the quarter. Also, some analysts were only concerned with making an accurate forecast, while others were also interested in their relationship with management. Suppose one of these analysts is randomly selected. Consider the following events:

A = {The analyst is concerned only with making an accurate forecast.}

B = {The analyst makes the forecast early in the quarter.}

C = {The analyst is from a small brokerage firm.}

Describe each of the following events in terms of unions, intersections, and complements (e.g., $A \cup B$, $A \cap B$, A^c, etc.).

a. The analyst makes an early forecast and is concerned only with accuracy.

b. The analyst is not concerned only with accuracy.

c. The analyst is from a small brokerage firm or makes an early forecast.

d. The analyst makes a late forecast and is not concerned only with accuracy.

36 Problems at major companies. The *Organization Development Journal* (Summer 2006) reported on the results of a survey of human resource officers (HROs) at major employers located in a southeastern city. The focus of the study was employee behavior, namely absenteeism, promptness to work, and turnover. The study found that 55% of the HROs had problems with employee absenteeism; also, 41% had problems with turnover. Suppose that 22% of the HROs had problems with both

absenteeism and turnover. Use this information to find the probability that an HRO selected from the group surveyed had problems with either employee absenteeism or employee turnover.

37 Do social robots walk or roll? The *International Conference on Social Robotics* (Vol. 6414, 2010) did a study of the trend in the design of social robots. In a random sample of 106 social (or service) robots designed to entertain, educate, and care for human users, 63 were built with legs only, 20 with wheels only, 8 with both legs and wheels, and 15 with neither legs nor wheels. One of the 106 social robots is randomly selected and the design (e.g., wheels only) is noted.

a. List the sample points for this study.

b. Assign reasonable probabilities to the sample points.

c. What is the probability that the selected robot is designed with wheels?

d. What is the probability that the selected robot is designed with legs?

e. Use the rule of complements to find the probability that the selected robot is designed with either legs or wheels.

38 Scanning errors at Wal-Mart. The National Institute for Standards and Technology (NIST) mandates that for every 100 items scanned through the electronic checkout scanner at a retail store, no more than 2 should have an inaccurate price. A study of the accuracy of checkout scanners at Wal-Mart stores in California was conducted (*Tampa Tribune*, Nov. 22, 2005). Of the 60 Wal-Mart stores investigated, 52 violated the NIST scanner accuracy standard. If one of the 60 Wal-Mart stores is randomly selected, what is the probability that the store does not violate the NIST scanner accuracy standard?

39 Inactive oil and gas structures. U.S. federal regulations require that operating companies clear all inactive offshore oil and gas structures within 1 year after production ceases. Researchers at the Louisiana State University Center for Energy Studies gathered data on both active and inactive oil and gas structures in the Gulf of Mexico (*Oil & Gas Journal*, Jan. 3, 2005). They discovered that the Gulf of Mexico has 2,175 active and 1,225 idle (inactive) structures. The following table breaks down these structures by type (caisson, well protector, or fixed platform). Consider the structure type and active status of one of these oil/gas structures.

	Structure Type			
	Caisson	Well Protector	Fixed Platform	Totals
Active	503	225	1,447	2,175
Inactive	598	177	450	1,225

Source: Data from Kaiser, M., and Mesyanzhinov, D. "Study tabulates idle Gulf of Mexico structures," *Oil & Gas Journal*, Vol. 103, No. 1, Jan. 3, 2005 (Table 2).

a. List the simple events for this experiment.

b. Assign reasonable probabilities to the simple events.

c. Find the probability that the structure is active.

d. Find the probability that the structure is a well protector.

e. Find the probability that the structure is an inactive caisson.

f. Find the probability that the structure is either inactive or a fixed platform.

g. Find the probability that the structure is not a caisson.

40 **Social networking Web sites in the United Kingdom.** In the United States, MySpace and Facebook are considered the two most popular social networking Web sites. In the United Kingdom (UK), the competition for social networking is between MySpace and Bebo. According to Nielsen/NetRatings (April 2006), 4% of UK citizens visit MySpace, 3% visit Bebo, and 1% visit both MySpace and Bebo.

a. Draw a Venn diagram to illustrate the use of social networking sites in the United Kingdom.

b. Find the probability that a UK citizen visits either the MySpace or Bebo social networking site.

c. Use your answer to part **b** to find the probability that a UK citizen does not visit either social networking site.

Applying the Concepts—Intermediate

41 **Study of why EMS workers leave the job.** An investigation into why emergency medical service (EMS) workers leave the profession was published in the *Journal of Allied Health* (Fall 2011). The researchers surveyed a sample of 244 former EMS workers, of which 127 were fully compensated while on the job, 45 were partially compensated, and 72 had noncompensated volunteer positions. The numbers of EMS workers who left because of retirement were 7 for fully compensated workers, 11 for partially compensated workers, and 10 for noncompensated volunteers. One of the 244 former EMS workers is selected at random.

a. Find the probability that the former EMS worker was fully compensated while on the job.

b. Find the probability that the former EMS worker was fully compensated while on the job and left due to retirement.

c. Find the probability that the former EMS worker was not fully compensated while on the job.

d. Find the probability that the former EMS worker was either fully compensated while on the job or left due to retirement.

42 **Stock market participation and IQ.** *The Journal of Finance* (December 2011) published a study of whether the decision to invest in the stock market is dependent on IQ. Information on a sample of 158,044 adults living in Finland formed the database for the study. An IQ score (from a low score of 1 to a high score of 9) was determined for each Finnish citizen as well as whether or not the citizen invested in the stock market. The next table gives the number of Finnish citizens in each IQ score/investment category. Suppose one of the 158,044 citizens is selected at random.

a. What is the probability that the Finnish citizen invests in the stock market?

b. What is the probability that the Finnish citizen has an IQ score of 6 or higher?

c. What is the probability that the Finnish citizen invests in the stock market and has an IQ score of 6 or higher?

d. What is the probability that the Finnish citizen invests in the stock market or has an IQ score of 6 or higher?

IQ Score	Invest in Market	No Investment	Totals
1	893	4,659	5,552
2	1,340	9,409	10,749
3	2,009	9,993	12,002
4	5,358	19,682	25,040
5	8,484	24,640	33,124
6	10,270	21,673	31,943
7	6,698	11,260	17,958
8	5,135	7,010	12,145
9	4,464	5,067	9,531
Totals	44,651	113,393	158,044

Source: Based on Grinblatt, M., Keloharju, M., & Linnainaa, J. "IQ and Stock Market Participation," *The Journal of Finance,* Vol. 66, No. 6, December 2011 (adapted from Table 1 and Figure 1).

e. What is the probability that the Finnish citizen does not invest in the stock market?

f. Are the events {Invest in the stock market} and {IQ score of 1} mutually exclusive?

43 **Characteristics of a new product.** The long-run success of a business depends on its ability to market products with superior characteristics that maximize consumer satisfaction and that give the firm a competitive advantage (Kotler & Keller, *Marketing Management*, 2006). Ten new products have been developed by a food-products firm. Market research has indicated that the 10 products have the characteristics described by the following Venn diagram:

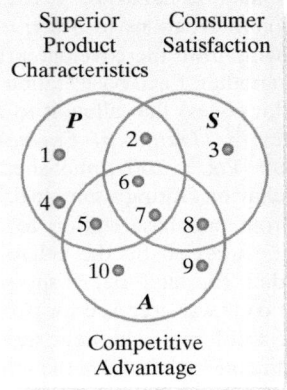

a. Write the event that a product possesses all the desired characteristics as an intersection of the events defined in the Venn diagram. Which products are contained in this intersection?

b. If one of the 10 products were selected at random to be marketed, what is the probability that it would possess all the desired characteristics?

c. Write the event that the randomly selected product would give the firm a competitive advantage or would satisfy consumers as a union of the events defined in the Venn diagram. Find the probability of this union.

d. Write the event that the randomly selected product would possess superior product characteristics and satisfy consumers. Find the probability of this intersection.

44 **Guilt in decision making.** The effect of guilt emotion on how a decision maker focuses on a problem was investigated in the Jan. 2007 issue of the *Journal of Behavioral*

Decision Making. A total of 171 volunteer students participated in the experiment, where each was randomly assigned to one of three emotional states (guilt, anger, or neutral) through a reading/writing task. Immediately after the task, students were presented with a decision problem where the stated option had predominantly negative features (e.g., spending money on repairing a very old car). The results (number responding in each category) are summarized in the accompanying table. Suppose one of the 171 participants is selected at random.

Emotional State	Choose Stated Option	Do Not Choose Stated Option	Totals
Guilt	45	12	57
Anger	8	50	58
Neutral	7	49	56
Totals	60	111	171

Source: Based on Gangemi, A., & Mancini, F. "Guilt and focusing in decision-making," *Journal of Behavioral Decision Making,* Vol. 20, Jan. 2007 (Table 2).

a. Find the probability that the respondent is assigned to the guilty state.
b. Find the probability that the respondent chooses the stated option (repair the car).
c. Find the probability that the respondent is assigned to the guilty state and chooses the stated option.
d. Find the probability that the respondent is assigned to the guilty state or chooses the stated option.

45 **Cell phone handoff behavior.** A "handoff" is a term used in wireless communications to describe the process of a cell phone moving from the coverage area of one base station to that of another. Each base station has multiple channels (called color codes) that allow it to communicate with the cell phone. The *Journal of Engineering, Computing and Architecture* (Vol. 3., 2009) published a study of cell phone handoff behavior. During a sample driving trip that involved crossing from one base station to another, the different color codes accessed by the cell phone were monitored and recorded. The table below shows the number of times each color code was accessed for two identical driving trips, each using a different cell phone model. (*Note:* The table is similar to the one published in the article.) Suppose you randomly select one point during the combined driving trips.

	Color Code				
	0	5	b	c	Total
Model 1	20	35	40	0	85
Model 2	15	50	6	4	75
Total	35	85	46	4	160

a. What is the probability that the cell phone was using color code 5?
b. What is the probability that the cell phone was using color code 5 or color code 0?
c. What is the probability that the cell phone used was Model 2 and the color code was 0?

46 **Likelihood of a tax return audit.** At the beginning of each year, the Internal Revenue Service (IRS) releases information on the likelihood of a tax return being audited.

In 2010, the IRS audited 1,581,394 individual tax returns from the total of 142,823,105 filed returns; also, the IRS audited 29,803 returns from the total of 2,143,808 corporation returns filed (*IRS 2010 Data Book*).

a. Suppose an individual tax return from 2010 is randomly selected. What is the probability that the return was audited by the IRS?
b. Refer to part **a.** Determine the probability that an individual return was not audited by the IRS.
c. Suppose a corporation tax return from 2010 is randomly selected. What is the probability that the return was audited by the IRS?
d. Refer to part **c.** Determine the probability that a corporation return was not audited by the IRS.

47 **Reliability of gas station air guages.** Tire and automobile manufacturers and consumer safety experts all recommend that drivers maintain proper tire pressure in their cars. Consequently, many gas stations now provide air pumps and air gauges for their customers. In a *Research Note* (Nov. 2001), the National Highway Traffic Safety Administration studied the reliability of gas station air guages. The next table gives the percentage of gas stations that provide air gauges that overreport the pressure level in the tire.

Station Gauge Pressure	Overreport by 4 psi or More (%)	Overreport by 6 psi or More (%)	Overreport by 8 psi or More (%)
25 psi	16	2	0
35 psi	19	9	0
45 psi	19	14	5
55 psi	20	15	9

a. If the gas station air pressure gauge reads 35 psi, what is the probability that the pressure is overreported by 6 psi or more?
b. If the gas station air pressure gauge reads 55 psi, what is the probability that the pressure is overreported by 8 psi or more?
c. If the gas station air pressure gauge reads 25 psi, what is the probability that the pressure is not overreported by 4 psi or more?
d. Are the events $A = $ {overreport by 4 psi or more} and $B = $ {overreport by 6 psi or more} mutually exclusive? Explain.
e. Based on your answer to part **d,** why do the probabilities in the table not sum to 1?

Applying the Concepts—Advanced

48 **Galileo's Passedix game.** Passedix is a game of chance played with three fair dice. Players bet whether the sum of the faces shown on the dice will be above or below 10. During the late sixteenth century, the astronomer and mathematician Galileo Galilei was asked by the Grand Duke of Tuscany to explain why "the chance of throwing a total of 9 with three fair dice was less than that of throwing a total of 10" (*Interstat*, Jan. 2004). The grand duke believed that the chance should be the same because "there are an equal number of partitions of the numbers 9 and 10." Find the flaw in the grand duke's reasoning and answer the question posed to Galileo.

5 Conditional Probability

The event probabilities we've been discussing give the relative frequencies of the occurrences of the events when the experiment is repeated a very large number of times. Such probabilities are often called **unconditional probabilities** because no special conditions are assumed, other than those that define the experiment.

Often, however, we have additional knowledge that might affect the likelihood of the outcome of an experiment, so we need to alter the probability of an event of interest. A probability that reflects such additional knowledge is called the **conditional probability** of the event. For example, we've seen that the probability of observing an even number (event A) on a toss of a fair die is $\frac{1}{2}$. But suppose we're given the information that on a particular throw of the die, the result was a number less than or equal to 3 (event B). Would the probability of observing an even number on that throw of the die still be equal to $\frac{1}{2}$? It can't be because making the assumption that B has occurred reduces the sample space from six sample points to three sample points (namely, those contained in event B). This reduced sample space is as shown in Figure 14.

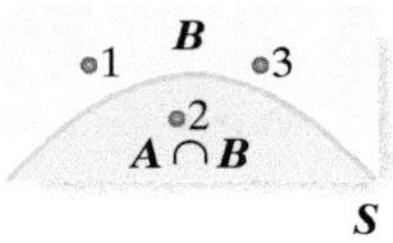

Because the sample points for the die-toss experiment are equally likely, each of the three sample points in the reduced sample space is assigned an equal *conditional probability* of $\frac{1}{3}$. Because the only even number of the three in the reduced sample space B is the number 2 and the die is fair, we conclude that the probability that A occurs *given that B occurs* is $\frac{1}{3}$. We use the symbol $P(A|B)$ to represent the probability of event A given that event B occurs. For the die-toss example, $P(A|B) = \frac{1}{3}$.

To get the probability of event A given that event B occurs, we proceed as follows: We divide the probability of the part of A that falls within the reduced sample space B, namely $P(A \cap B)$, by the total probability of the reduced sample space, namely $P(B)$. Thus, for the die-toss example with event A: {Observe an even number} and event B: {Observe a number less than or equal to 3}, we find

$$P(A|B) = \frac{P(A \cap B)}{P(B)} = \frac{P(2)}{P(1) + P(2) + P(3)} = \frac{\frac{1}{6}}{\frac{3}{6}} = \frac{1}{3}$$

The formula for $P(A|B)$ is true in general:

Figure 14

Reduced sample space for the die-toss experiment given that event B has occurred

---

Conditional Probability Formula

To find the *conditional probability that event A occurs given that event B occurs*, divide the probability that *both A* and *B* occur by the probability that *B* occurs—that is,

$$P(A|B) = \frac{P(A \cap B)}{P(B)} \quad \text{[We assume that } P(B) \neq 0.]$$

This formula adjusts the probability of $A \cap B$ from its original value in the complete sample space S to a conditional probability in the reduced sample space B. If the sample points in the complete sample space are equally likely, then the formula will assign equal probabilities to the sample points in the reduced sample space, as in the die-toss experiment. If, on the other hand, the sample points have unequal probabilities, the formula will assign conditional probabilities proportional to the probabilities in the complete sample space. This is illustrated by the following practical examples.

Example 14	Problem To develop programs for business travelers staying at convention hotels, a major hotel chain commissioned a study of executives who play golf. The study revealed that 55% of the executives admitted they had cheated at golf. Also, 20% of the executives admitted they had cheated at golf and had lied in business. Given an executive who had cheated at golf, what is the probability that the executive also had lied in business?
The Conditional Probability Formula— Executives Who Cheat at Golf	

Solution Let's define events A and B as follows:

$$A = \{\text{Executive who had cheated at golf}\}$$

$$B = \{\text{Executive who had lied in business}\}$$

From the study, we know that 55% of executives had cheated at golf, so $P(A) = .55$. Now, executives who both cheat at golf (event A) *and* lie in business (event B) represent the compound event $A \cap B$. From the study, $P(A \cap B) = .20$. We want to know the probability that an executive lied in business (event B), given that he or she cheated at golf (event A)—that is, we want to know the conditional probability $P(A|B)$. Applying the preceding conditional probability formula, we have

$$P(B|A) = \frac{P(A \cap B)}{P(A)} = \frac{.20}{.55} = .364$$

Thus, given an executive who had cheated at golf, the probability that the executive also had lied in business is .364.

Look Back One of the keys to correctly applying the formula is to write the information in the study in the form of probability statements involving the events of interest. The word *and* in the statement "cheat at golf *and* lie in business" implies an intersection of the two events, A and B. The word *given* in the phrase "*given* an executive who cheats at golf" implies that event A is the given event.

■ **Now Work Exercise 58b**

Example	**15**

Applying the Conditional Probability Formula to a Two-Way Table— Customer Desire to Buy

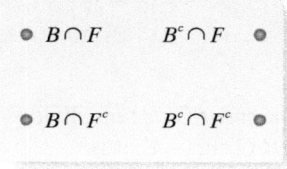

Figure 15

Sample space for contacting a sales prospect

Problem Suppose you are interested in the probability of the sale of a large piece of earthmoving equipment. A single prospect is contacted. Let F be the event that the buyer has sufficient money (or credit) to buy the product and let F^c denote the complement of F (the event that the prospect does not have the financial capability to buy the product). Similarly, let B be the event that the buyer wishes to buy the product and let B^c be the complement of that event. Then the four sample points associated with the experiment are shown in Figure 15, and their probabilities are given in Table 5. Use the sample point probabilities to find the probability that a single prospect will buy, given that the prospect is able to finance the purchase.

Table 5	**Probabilities of Customer Desire to Buy and Ability to Finance**		
			Desire
		To Buy, B	Not to Buy, B^c
Able to Finance	Yes, F	.2	.1
	No, F^c	.4	.3

Solution Suppose you consider the large collection of prospects for the sale of your product and randomly select one person from this collection. What is the probability that the person selected will buy the product? In order to buy the product, the customer must be financially able *and* have the desire to buy, so this probability would correspond to the entry in Table 5 {To buy, B} and next to {Yes, F}, or $P(B \cap F) = .2$. This is the unconditional probability of the event $B \cap F$.

In contrast, suppose you know that the prospect selected has the financial capability for purchasing the product. Now you are seeking the probability that the customer will buy given (the condition) that the customer has the financial ability to pay. This probability, the conditional probability of B given that F has occurred and denoted by the symbol $P(B|F)$, would be determined by considering only the sample points in the reduced sample space containing the sample points $B \cap F$ and $B^c \cap F$—that is, sample points that imply the prospect is financially able to buy. (This reduced sample space is shaded in Figure 16.) From our definition of conditional probability,

$$P(B|F) = \frac{P(B \cap F)}{P(F)}$$

where $P(F)$ is the sum of the probabilities of the two sample points corresponding to $B \cap F$ and $B^c \cap F$ (given in Table 5). Then

$$P(F) = P(B \cap F) + P(B^c \cap F) = .2 + .1 = .3$$

and the conditional probability that a prospect buys, given that the prospect is financially able, is

$$P(B|F) = \frac{P(B \cap F)}{P(F)} = \frac{.2}{.3} = .667$$

As we would expect, the probability that the prospect will buy, given that he or she is financially able, is higher than the unconditional probability of selecting a prospect who will buy.

Look Back Note that the conditional probability formula assigns a probability to the event $(B \cap F)$ in the reduced sample space that is proportional to the probability of the event in the complete sample space. To see this, note that the two sample points in the reduced sample space, $(B \cap F)$ and $(B^c \cap F)$, have probabilities of .2 and .1, respectively, in the complete sample space S. The formula assigns conditional probabilities $\frac{2}{3}$ and $\frac{1}{3}$ (use the formula to check the second one) to these sample points in the reduced sample space F so that the conditional probabilities retain the 2-to-1 proportionality of the original sample point probabilities.

■ Now Work Exercise 49a–b

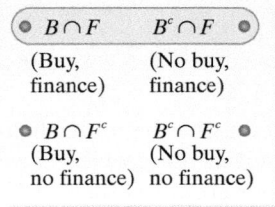

Figure 16

Reduced sample space (shaded) containing sample points implying a financially able prospect

---

Example 16

Applying the Conditional Probability Formula to a Two-Way Table— Customer Complaints

Problem The investigation of consumer product complaints by the Federal Trade Commission (FTC) has generated much interest by manufacturers in the quality of their products. A manufacturer of an electromechanical kitchen utensil conducted an analysis of a large number of consumer complaints and found that they fell into the six categories shown in Table 6. If a consumer complaint is received, what is the probability that the cause of the complaint was product appearance given that the complaint originated during the guarantee period?

Table 6	Distribution of Product Complaints			
	Reason for Complaint			
Complaint Origin	Electrical	Mechanical	Appearance	Totals
During Guarantee Period	18%	13%	32%	63%
After Guarantee Period	12%	22%	3%	37%
Totals	30%	35%	35%	100%

Solution Let A represent the event that the cause of a particular complaint is product appearance and let B represent the event that the complaint occurred during the guarantee period. Checking Table 6, you can see that $(18 + 13 + 32)\% = 63\%$ of the complaints occur during the guarantee period. Hence, $P(B) = .63$. The percentage of complaints that were caused by appearance and occurred during the guarantee period (the event $A \cap B$) is 32%. Therefore, $P(A \cap B) = .32$

Using these probability values, we can calculate the conditional probability $P(A|B)$ that the cause of a complaint is appearance, given that the complaint occurred during the guarantee time:

$$P(A|B) = \frac{P(A \cap B)}{P(B)} = \frac{.32}{.63} = .51$$

Consequently, we can see that slightly more than half the complaints that occurred during the guarantee period were due to scratches, dents, or other imperfections in the surface of the kitchen devices.

Look Back Note that the answer, $\frac{.32}{.63}$, is the proportion for the event of interest A (.32) divided by the row total proportion for the given event B (.63) — that is, it is the proportion of the time A occurs within the given event B.

Now Work Exercise 60

6 The Multiplicative Rule and Independent Events

The probability of an intersection of two events can be calculated using the multiplicative rule, which employs the conditional probabilities we defined in the previous section. Actually, we have already developed the formula in another context (Section 5). You will recall that the formula for calculating the conditional probability of A given B is

$$P(A|B) = \frac{P(A \cap B)}{P(B)}$$

Multiplying both sides of this equation by $P(B)$, we obtain a formula for the probability of the intersection of events A and B. This is often called the **multiplicative rule of probability.**

> **Multiplicative Rule of Probability**
> $P(A \cap B) = P(A)P(B|A)$ or, equivalently, $P(A \cap B) = P(B)P(A|B)$

Example 17 **Applying the Multiplicative Rule — Wheat Futures**	**Problem** An investor in wheat futures is concerned with the following events: $\quad$ B: {U.S. production of wheat will be profitable next year.} $\quad$ A: {A serious drought will occure next year.} Based on available information, the investor believes that the probability is .01 that production of wheat will be profitable *assuming* a serious drought will occur in the same year and that the probability is .05 that a serious drought will occur — that is, $\quad P(B|A) = .01$ and $P(A) = .05$ Based on the information provided, what is the probability that a serious drought will occur and that a profit will be made? That is, find $P(A \cap B)$, the probability of the intersection of events A and B. **Solution** We want to calculate $P(A \cap B)$. Using the formula for the multiplicative rule, we obtain $\quad P(A \cap B) = P(A)P(B|A) = (.05)(.01) = .0005$ The probability that a serious drought occurs and the production of wheat is profitable is only .0005. As we might expect, this intersection is a very rare event. **Look Back** The multiplicative rule can be expressed in two ways: $P(A \cap B) = P(A) \cdot P(B|A)$ or $P(A \cap B) = P(B) \cdot P(A|B)$. Select the formula that involves a given event for which you know the probability (e.g., event B in the example).

Now Work Exercise 61

Intersections often contain only a few sample points. In this case, the probability of an intersection is easy to calculate by summing the appropriate sample point probabilities. However, the formula for calculating intersection probabilities is invaluable when the intersection contains numerous sample points, as the next example illustrates.

Example 18	**Problem** A county welfare agency employs 10 welfare workers who interview prospective food stamp recipients. Periodically the supervisor selects, at random, the forms completed by 2 workers to audit for illegal deductions. Unknown to the supervisor, 3 of the workers have regularly been giving illegal deductions to applicants. What is the probability that both of the 2 workers chosen have been giving illegal deductions?

Applying the Multiplicative Rule—Study of Welfare Workers

Solution Define the following two events:

$$A: \{\text{First worker selected gives illegal deductions}\}$$
$$B: \{\text{Second worker selected gives illegal deductions}\}$$

We want to find the probability of the event that both selected workers have been giving illegal deductions. This event can be restated as {First worker gives illegal deductions *and* second worker gives illegal deductions}. Thus, we want to find the probability of the intersection, $A \cap B$. Applying the multiplicative rule, we have

$$P(A \cap B) = P(A)P(B|A)$$

To find $P(A)$, it is helpful to consider the experiment as selecting 1 worker from the 10. Then the sample space for the experiment contains 10 sample points (representing the 10 welfare workers), where the 3 workers giving illegal deductions are denoted by the symbol I (I_1, I_2, I_3), and the 7 workers not giving illegal deductions are denoted by the symbol N ($N_1, \ldots, N_7$). The resulting Venn diagram is illustrated in Figure 17.

Because the first worker is selected at random from the 10, it is reasonable to assign equal probabilities to the 10 sample points. Thus, each sample point has a probability of $\frac{1}{10}$. The sample points in event A are $\{I_1, I_2, I_3,\}$—the 3 workers who are giving illegal deductions. Thus,

$$P(A) = P(I_1) + P(I_2) + P(I_3) = \tfrac{1}{10} + \tfrac{1}{10} + \tfrac{1}{10} = \tfrac{3}{10}$$

To find the conditional probability, $P(B|A)$, we need to alter the sample space S. Because we know A has occurred [the first worker selected is giving illegal deductions (say I_3)], only 2 of the 9 remaining workers in the sample space are giving illegal deductions. The Venn diagram for this new sample space (S') is shown in Figure 18. Each of these nine sample points are equally likely, so each is assigned a probability of $\frac{1}{9}$. Because the event $(B|A)$ contains the sample points $\{I_1, I_2\}$, we have

$$P(B|A) = P(I_1) + P(I_2) = \tfrac{1}{9} + \tfrac{1}{9} = \tfrac{2}{9}$$

Substituting $P(A) = \frac{3}{10}$ and $P(B|A) = \frac{2}{9}$ into the formula for the multiplicative rule, we find

$$P(A \cap B) = P(A)P(B|A) = \left(\tfrac{3}{10}\right)\left(\tfrac{2}{90}\right) = \tfrac{6}{90} = \tfrac{1}{15}$$

Thus, there is a 1 in 15 chance that both workers chosen by the supervisor have been giving illegal deductions to food stamp recipients.

Look Back The key words *both* and *and* in the statement "both A and B occur" imply an intersection of two events, which in turn implies that we should *multiply* probabilities to obtain the probability of interest.

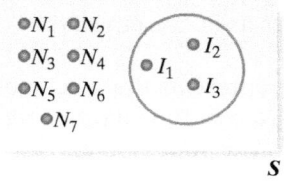

Figure 17
Venn diagram for finding $P(A)$

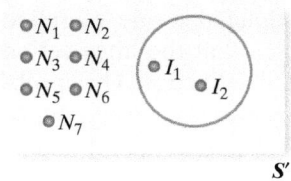

Figure 18
Venn diagram for finding $P(B|A)$

■ **Now Work Exercise 53c**

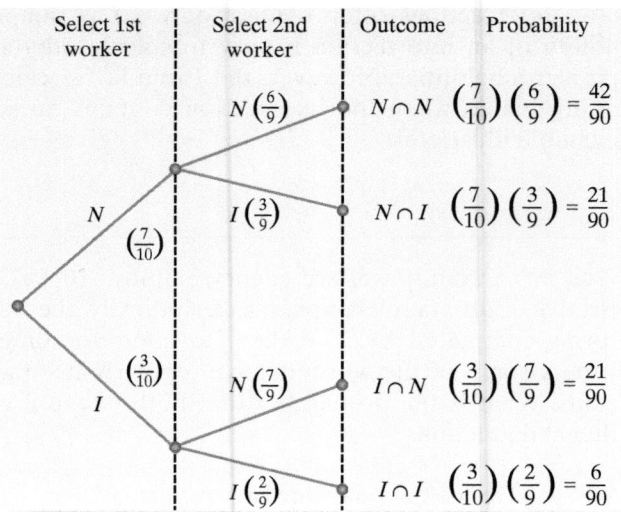

Figure 19
Tree diagram for Example 18

The sample space approach is only one way to solve the problem posed in Example 18. An alternative method employs the tree diagram (introduced in Example 1). Tree diagrams are helpful for calculating the probability of an intersection.

To illustrate, a tree diagram for Example 18 is displayed in Figure 19. The tree begins at the far left with two branches. These branches represent the two possible outcomes N (no illegal deductions) and I (illegal deductions) for the first worker selected. The unconditional probability of each outcome is given (in parentheses) on the appropriate branch—that is, for the first worker selected, $P(N) = \frac{7}{10}$ and $P(I) = \frac{3}{10}$. (These can be obtained by summing sample point probabilities as in Example 18.)

The next level of the tree diagram (moving to the right) represents the outcomes for the second worker selected. The probabilities shown here are conditional probabilities because the outcome for the first worker is assumed to be known. For example, if the first worker is giving illegal deductions *(I)*, the probability that the second worker is also giving illegal deductions *(I)* is $\frac{2}{10}$ because of the 9 workers left to be selected, only 2 remain who are giving illegal deductions. This conditional probability, $\frac{2}{9}$, is shown in parentheses on the bottom branch of Figure 19.

Finally, the four possible outcomes of the experiment are shown at the end of each of the four tree branches. These events are intersections of two events (outcome of first worker and outcome of second worker). Consequently, the multiplicative rule is applied to calculate each probability, as shown in Figure 19. You can see that the intersection $\{I \cap I\}$ (i.e., the event that both workers selected are giving illegal deductions) has probability $\frac{6}{90} = \frac{1}{15}$—the same value obtained in Example 18.

In Section 5 we showed that the probability of an event A may be substantially altered by the knowledge that an event B has occurred. However, this will not always be the case. In some instances, the assumption that event B has occurred will *not* alter the probability of event A at all. When this is true, we say that the two events A and B are *independent events*.

Events A and B are **independent events** if the occurrence of B does not alter the probability that A has occurred; that is, events A and B are independent if

$$P(A|B) = P(A)$$

When events A and B are independent, it is also true that

$$P(B|A) = P(B)$$

Events that are not independent are said to be **dependent.**

Example 19

Checking for Independence— Die-Tossing Experiment

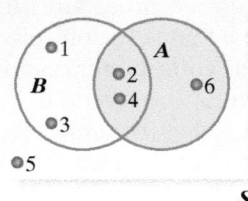

Figure 20
Venn diagram for die-toss experiment

Problem Consider the experiment of tossing a fair die and let

$$A: \{\text{Observe an even number.}\}$$
$$B: \{\text{Observe a number less than or equal to 4.}\}$$

Are events A and B independent?

Solution The Venn diagram for this experiment is shown in Figure 20. We first calculate

$$P(A) = P(2) + P(4) + P(6) = \tfrac{1}{2}$$
$$P(B) = P(1) + P(2) + P(3) + P(4) = \tfrac{2}{3}$$
$$P(A \cap B) = P(2) + P(4) = \tfrac{1}{3}$$

Now assuming B has occurred, the conditional probability of A given B is

$$P(A|B) = \frac{P(A \cap B)}{P(B)} = \frac{\tfrac{1}{3}}{\tfrac{2}{3}} = \frac{1}{2} = P(A)$$

Thus, assuming that event B occurring does not alter the probability of observing an even number, $P(A)$ remains $\tfrac{1}{2}$. Therefore, the events A and B are independent.

Look Back Note that if we calculate the conditional probability of B given A, our conclusion is the same:

$$P(B|A) = \frac{P(A \cap B)}{P(A)} = \frac{\tfrac{1}{3}}{\tfrac{1}{2}} = \frac{2}{3} = P(B)$$

■ **Now Work Exercise 58c**

BIOGRAPHY

BLAISE PASCAL (1623–1662)
Solver of Chevalier's Dilemma

As a precocious child growing up in France, Blaise Pascal showed an early inclination toward mathematics. Although his father would not permit Pascal to study mathematics before the age of 15 (removing all math texts from his house), at age 12 Pascal discovered on his own that the sum of the angles of a triangle are two right triangles.

Pascal went on to become a distinguished mathematician, as well as a physicist, theologian, and the inventor of the first digital calculator. Most historians attribute the beginning of the study of probability to the correspondence between Pascal and Pierre de Fermat in 1654. The two solved the Chevalier's dilemma—a gambling problem related to Pascal by his friend and Paris gambler the Chevalier de Mere. The problem involved determining the expected number of times one could roll two dice without throwing a double 6. (Pascal proved that the breakeven point is 25 rolls.)

Example 20

Checking for Independence— Consumer Product Complaint Study

Problem Refer to the consumer product complaint study in Example 16. The percentages of complaints of various types during and after the guarantee period are shown in Table 6. Define the following events:

$$A: \{\text{Cause of complaint is product appearance.}\}$$
$$B: \{\text{Complaint occurred during the guarantee term.}\}$$

Are A and B independent events?

Solution Events A and B are independent if $P(A|B) = P(A)$. We calculated $P(A|B)$ in Example 16 to be .51, and from Table 6 we see that

$$P(A) = .32 + .03 = .35$$

Therefore, $P(A|B)$ is not equal to $P(A)$, and A and B are dependent events.

■ **Now Work Exercise 49c**

To gain an intuitive understanding of independence, think of situations in which the occurrence of one event does not alter the probability that a second event will occur. For example, suppose two small companies are being monitored by a financier for possible investment. If the businesses are in different industries and they are otherwise unrelated, then the success or failure of one company may be *independent* of the success or failure of the other—that is, the event that company A fails may not alter the probability that company B will fail.

As a second example, consider an election poll in which 1,000 registered voters are asked their preference between two candidates. Pollsters try to use procedures for selecting a sample of voters so that the responses are independent—that is, the objective of the pollster is to select the sample so the event that one polled voter prefers candidate A does not alter the probability that a second polled voter prefers candidate A.

We will make three final points about independence. The first is that the property of independence, unlike the mutually exclusive property, cannot be shown on or gleaned from a Venn diagram. This means *you can't trust your intuition*. In general, the only way to check for independence is by performing the calculations of the probabilities in the definition.

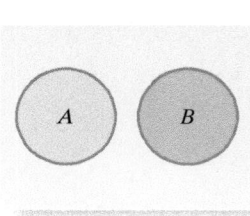

Figure 21

Mutually exclusive events are dependent events

The second point concerns the relationship between the mutually exclusive and independence properties. Suppose that events A and B are mutually exclusive, as shown in Figure 21, and both events have nonzero probabilities. Are these events independent or dependent? That is, does the assumption that B occurs alter the probability of the occurrence of A? It certainly does, because if we assume that B has occurred, it is impossible for A to have occurred simultaneously—that is, $P(A|B) = 0$. Thus, *mutually exclusive events are dependent events* because $P(A) \neq P(A|B)$.

The third point is that the probability of the intersection of independent events is very easy to calculate. Referring to the formula for calculating the probability of an intersection, we find

$$P(A \cap B) = P(A)P(B|A)$$

Thus, because $P(B|A) = P(B)$ when A and B are independent, we have the following useful rule:

Probability of Intersection of Two Independent Events

If events A and B are independent, the probability of the intersection of A and B equals the product of the probabilities of A and B; that is,

$$P(A \cap B) = P(A)P(B)$$

The converse is also true: If $P(A \cap B) = P(A)P(B)$, then events A and B are independent.

In the die-toss experiment, we showed in Example 19 that the events *A:* {Observe an even number} and *B:* {Observe a number less than or equal to 4} are independent if the die is fair. Thus,

$$P(A \cap B) = P(A)P(B) = \left(\tfrac{1}{2}\right)\left(\tfrac{2}{3}\right) = \tfrac{1}{3}$$

This agrees with the result that we obtained in the example:

$$P(A \cap B) = P(2) + P(4) = \tfrac{2}{6} = \tfrac{1}{3}$$

Example 21

Probability of Independent Events Occurring Simultaneously—Diversity Training Study

Problem Refer to Example 5. Recall that *USA Today* found that of all U.S. firms that use diversity training, 38% state that their primary reason for using it is to stay competitive.

a. What is the probability that in a sample of two firms that use diversity training, both primarily use it to stay competitive?

b. What is the probability that in a sample of 10 firms that use diversity training, all 10 primarily use it to stay competitive?

Solution

a. Let C_1 represent the event that firm 1 gives "stay competitive" as the primary reason for using diversity training. Define C_2 similarly for firm 2. The event that *both* firms give "stay competitive" as their primary reason is the intersection of the two events, $C_1 \cap C_2$. Based on the survey that found that 38% of U.S. firms use diversity training to stay competitive, we could reasonably conclude that $P(C_1) = .38$ and $P(C_2) = .38$. However, in order to compute the probability of $C_1 \cap C_2$ from the multiplicative rule, we must make the assumption that the two events are independent. Because the classification of any firm using diversity training is not likely to affect the classification of another firm, this assumption is reasonable. Assuming independence, we have

$$P(C_1 \cap C_2) = P(C_1)P(C_2) = (.38)(.38) = .1444$$

b. To see how to compute the probability that 10 of 10 firms will give "stay competitive" as their primary reason, first consider the event that 3 of 3 firms give "stay competitive" as the primary reason. Using the notation defined earlier, we want to compute the probability of the intersection $C_1 \cap C_2 \cap C_3$. Again assuming independence of the classifications, we have

$$P(C_1 \cap C_2 \cap C_3) = P(C_1)P(C_2)P(C_3) = (.38)(.38)(.38) = .054872$$

Similar reasoning leads us to the conclusion that the intersection of 10 such events can be calculated as follows:

$$P(C_1 \cap C_2 \cap C_3 \cap \ldots \cap C_{10}) = P(C_1)P(C_2) \ldots P(C_{10}) = (.38)^{10} = .0000628$$

Thus, the probability that 10 of 10 firms all give "stay competitive" as their primary reason for using diversity training is about 63 in 1 million, assuming the events (stated reasons for using diversity training) are independent.

Look Back The very small probability in part **b** makes it extremely unlikely that 10 of 10 firms would give "stay competitive" as their primary reason for diversity training. If this event should actually occur, we would need to reassess our estimate of the probability of .38 used in the calculation. If all 10 firms' reason is staying competitive, then the probability that any one firm gives staying competitive as their reason is much higher than .38. (This conclusion is another application of the rare event approach to statistical inference.)

■ **Now Work Exercise 72a**

STATISTICS
in ACTION
REVISITED

The Probability of Winning Cash 3 or Play 4

In addition to biweekly Lotto 6/53, the Florida Lottery runs several other games. Two popular daily games are "Cash 3" and "Play 4." In Cash 3, players pay $1 to select three numbers in sequential order, where each number ranges from 0 to 9. If the three numbers selected (e.g., 2-8-4) match exactly the order of the three numbers drawn, the player wins $500. Play 4 is similar to Cash 3, but players must match four numbers (each number ranging from 0 to 9). For a $1 Play 4 ticket (e.g., 3-8-3-0), the player will win $5,000 if the numbers match the order of the four numbers drawn.

During the official drawing for Cash 3, 10 Ping-Pong balls numbered 0, 1, 2, 3, 4, 5, 6, 7, 8, and 9 are placed into each of three chambers. The balls in the first chamber are colored pink, the balls in the second chamber are blue, and the balls in the third chamber are yellow. One ball of each color is randomly drawn, with the official order as pink-blue-yellow. In Play 4, a fourth chamber with orange balls is added, and the official order is pink-blue-yellow-orange. Because the draws of the colored balls are random and independent, we can apply an extension of the Probability Rule for the Intersection

of Two Independent Events to find the odds of winning Cash 3 and Play 4. The probability of matching a numbered ball being drawn from a chamber is $\frac{1}{10}$; therefore,

$$P(\text{Win Cash 3}) = P(\text{match pink}) \text{ AND (match blue) AND (match yellow)}$$
$$= P(\text{match pink}) \times P(\text{match blue}) \times P(\text{match yellow})$$
$$= \left(\tfrac{1}{10}\right)\left(\tfrac{1}{10}\right)\left(\tfrac{1}{10}\right) = \tfrac{1}{1000} = .001$$

$$P(\text{Win Play 4}) = P(\text{match pink AND match blue}$$
$$\text{AND match yellow AND match orange})$$
$$= P(\text{match pink}) \times P(\text{match blue}) \times$$
$$P(\text{match yellow}) \times P(\text{match orange})$$
$$= \left(\tfrac{1}{10}\right)\left(\tfrac{1}{10}\right)\left(\tfrac{1}{10}\right)\left(\tfrac{1}{10}\right)$$
$$= \tfrac{1}{10,000} = .0001$$

Although the odds of winning one of these daily games is much better than the odds of winning Lotto $\frac{6}{53}$, there is still only a 1 in 1,000 chance (for Cash 3) or a 1 in 10,000 chance (for Play 4) of winning the daily game. And the payoffs ($500 or $5,000) are much smaller. In fact, it can be shown that you will lose an average of 50¢ every time you play either Cash 3 or Play 4!

Exercises 49–76

Please be aware that some of the following problems may require knowledge of concepts that are not presented in this chapter.

Learning the Mechanics

49 For two events, A and B, $P(A) = .4$, $P(B) = .2$, and $P(A \cap B) = .1$:
a. Find $P(A|B)$.
b. Find $P(B|A)$.
c. Are A and B independent events?

50 For two events, A and B, $P(A) = .4$, $P(B) = .2$, and $P(A|B) = .6$:
a. Find $P(A \cap B)$.
b. Find $P(B|A)$.

51 For two independent events, A and B, $P(A) = .4$ and $P(B) = .2$:
a. Find $P(A \cap B)$
b. Find $P(A|B)$.
c. Find $P(A \cup B)$

52 An experiment results in one of three mutually exclusive events, A, B, or C. It is known that $P(A) = .30$, $P(B) = .55$, and $P(C) = .15$. Find each of the following probabilities:
a. $P(A \cup B)$
b. $P(A \cap C)$
c. $P(A|B)$
d. $P(B \cup C)$
e. Are B and C independent events? Explain.

53 Consider the experiment depicted by the Venn diagram, with the sample space S containing five sample points. The sample points are assigned the following probabilities: $P(E_1) = .20$, $P(E_2) = .30, P(E_3) = .30, P(E_4) = .10, P(E_5) = .10$.

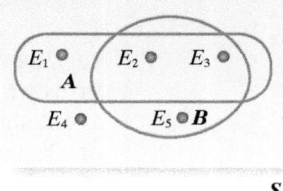

a. Calculate $P(A), P(B)$, and $P(A \cap B)$
b. Suppose we know that event A has occurred, so that the reduced sample space consists of the three sample points in A—namely, E_1, E_2, and E_3. Use the formula for conditional probability to adjust the probabilities of these three sample points for the knowledge that A has occurred [i.e., $P(E_i|A)$]. Verify that the conditional probabilities are in the same proportion to one another as the original sample point probabilities.
c. Calculate the conditional probability $P(B|A)$ in two ways: (1) Add the adjusted (conditional) probabilities of the sample points in the intersection $A \cap B$, as these represent the event that B occurs given that A has occurred; (2) use the formula for conditional probability:

$$P(B|A) = \frac{P(A \cap B)}{P(A)}$$

Verify that the two methods yield the same result.
d. Are events A and B independent? Why or why not?

54 Two fair coins are tossed, and the following events are defined:

> A: {Observe at least one head}
> B: {Observe exactly one head}

a. Draw a Venn diagram for the experiment, showing events A and B. Assign probabilities to the sample points.
b. Find $P(A), P(B),$ and $P(A \cap B)$
c. Use the formula for conditional probability to find $P(A|B)$ and $P(B|A)$. Verify your answer by inspecting the Venn diagram and using the concept of reduced sample spaces.

55 An experiment results in one of five sample points with the following probabilities: $P(E_1) = .22,$ $P(E_2) = .31,$ $P(E_3) = .15,$ $P(E_4) = .22,$ and $P(E_5) = .1.$ The following events have been defined:

> A: {E_1, E_3}
> B: {E_2, E_3, E_4}
> C: {E_1, E_5}

Find each of the following probabilities:
a. $P(A)$
b. $P(B)$
c. $P(A \cap B)$
d. $P(A|B)$
e. $P(B \cap C)$
f. $P(C|B)$
g. Consider each pair of events: A and B, A and C, and B and C. Are any of the pairs of events independent? Why?

56 Two fair dice are tossed, and the following events are defined:

> A: {Sum of the numbers showing is odd}
> B: {Sum of the numbers showing is 9, 11, or 12}

Are events A and B independent? Why?

57 A sample space contains six sample points and events A, B, and C as shown in the Venn diagram. The probabilities of the sample points are

> $P(1) = .20, P(2) = .05, P(3) = .30, P(4) = .10,$
> $P(5) = .10, P(6) = .25.$

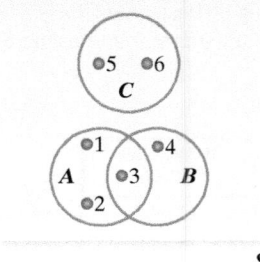

a. Which pairs of events, if any, are mutually exclusive? Why?
b. Which pairs of events, if any, are independent? Why?
c. Find $P(A \cup B)$ by adding the probabilities of the sample points and then by using the additive rule. Verify that the answers agree. Repeat for $P(A \cup C)$

Applet Exercise 5

Use the applet *Simulating the Probability of Rolling a 6* to simulate conditional probabilities. Begin by running the applet twice with $n = 10$ without resetting between runs. The data on your screen represent 20 rolls of a die. The diagram above the *Roll* button shows the frequency of each of the six possible outcomes. Use this information to find each of the probabilities.

a. The probability of 6 given the outcome is 5 or 6
b. The probability of 6 given the outcome is even
c. The probability of 4 or 6 given the outcome is even
d. The probability of 4 or 6 given the outcome is odd

Applying the Concepts—Basic

58 **On-the-job arrogance and task performance.** *Human Performance* (Vol. 23, 2010) published the results of a study that found that arrogant workers are more likely to have poor performance ratings. Suppose that 15% of all full-time workers exhibit arrogant behaviors on the job and that 10% of all full-time workers will receive a poor performance rating. Also, assume that 5% of all full-time workers exhibit arrogant behaviors and receive a poor performance rating. Let A be the event that a full-time worker exhibits arrogant behavior on the job. Let B be the event that a full-time worker will receive a poor performance rating.
a. Are the events A and B mutually exclusive? Explain.
b. Find $P(B|A)$.
c. Are the events A and B independent? Explain.

59 **World's largest public companies.** *Forbes* (Apr. 20 , 2011) conducted a survey of the 20 largest public companies in the world. Of these 20 companies, 4 were banking or investment companies based in the United States. A total of 9 U.S. companies were on the top 20 list. Suppose we select one of these 20 companies at random. Given that the company is based in the United States, what is the probability that it is a banking or investment company?

60 **Guilt in decision making.** Refer to the *Journal of Behavioral Decision Making* (Jan. 2007) study of the effect of guilt emotion on how a decision maker focuses on a problem, Exercise 44. The results (number responding in each category) for the 171 study participants are reproduced in the table below. Suppose one of the 171 participants is selected at random.

Emotional State	Choose Stated Option	Do Not Choose Stated Option	Totals
Guilt	45	12	57
Anger	8	50	58
Neutral	7	49	56
Totals	60	111	171

Source: Based on Gangemi, A., & Mancini, F. "Guilt and focusing in decision-making," *Journal of Behavioral Decision Making*, Vol. 20, Jan. 2007 (Table 2).

a. Given that the respondent is assigned to the guilty state, what is the probability that the respondent chooses the stated option?
b. If the respondent does not choose to repair the car, what is the probability that the respondent is in the anger state?
c. Are the events {repair the car} and {guilty state} independent?

61 Twitter and wireless Internet. According to the *Pew Internet & American Life Project* (Oct. 2009), 54% of Internet users have a wireless connection to the Internet via a laptop, cell phone, game console, or other mobile device. Of these wireless users, 25% use Twitter to share updates about themselves. What is the probability that an Internet user has a wireless connection and uses Twitter?

62 Identity theft victims. According to *The National Crime Victimization Survey* (December 2010), published by the U.S. Department of Justice, about 11.7 million people were victims of identity theft over the past 2 years. This number represents 5% of all persons age 16 or older in the United States. Of these victims, 53% reported that the identity theft occurred from the unauthorized use of a credit card. Consider a randomly selected person of age 16 or older in the United States.
  a. What is the probability that this person was a victim of identity theft?
  b. What is the probability that this person was a victim of identity theft that occurred from the unauthorized use of a credit card?

63 Study of why EMS workers leave the job. Refer to the *Journal of Allied Health* (Fall 2011) study of why emergency medical service (EMS) workers leave the profession, Exercise 41. Recall that in a sample of 244 former EMS workers, 127 were fully compensated while on the job, 45 were partially compensated, and 72 had noncompensated volunteer positions. Also, the numbers of EMS workers who left because of retirement were 7 for fully compensated workers, 11 for partially compensated workers, and 10 for noncompensated volunteers.
  a. Given that the former EMS worker was fully compensated while on the job, estimate the probability that the worker left the EMS profession due to retirement.
  b. Given that the former EMS worker had a noncompensated volunteer position, estimate the probability that the worker left the EMS profession due to retirement.
  c. Are the events {a former EMS worker was fully compensated on the job} and {a former EMS worker left the job due to retirement} independent? Explain.

Applying the Concepts–Intermediate

64 Working on summer vacation. Refer to the *Adweek/Harris* (July 2011) poll of whether U.S. adults work during their summer vacation, Exercise 14. Recall that the poll found that 46% of the respondents work during their summer

vacation, 35% do not work at all while on vacation, and 19% were unemployed. Also, 35% of those who work while on vacation do so by monitoring their business e-mails.
  a. Given that a randomly selected poll respondent will work while on summer vacation, what is the probability that the respondent will monitor business e-mails?
  b. What is the probability that a randomly selected poll respondent will work while on summer vacation and will monitor business e-mails?
  c. What is the probability that a randomly selected poll respondent will not work while on summer vacation and will monitor business e-mails?

65 Stock market participation and IQ. Refer to *The Journal of Finance* (December 2011) study of whether the decision to invest in the stock market is dependent on IQ, Exercise 42. The summary table giving the number of the 158,044 Finnish citizens in each IQ score/investment category is reproduced below. Again, suppose one of the citizens is selected at random.

IQ Score	Invest in Market	No Investment	Totals
1	893	4,659	5,552
2	1,340	9,409	10,749
3	2,009	9,993	12,002
4	5,358	19,682	25,040
5	8,484	24,640	33,124
6	10,270	21,673	31,943
7	6,698	11,260	17,958
8	5,135	7,010	12,145
9	4,464	5,067	9,531
Totals	44,651	113,393	158,044

Source: Based on Grinblatt, M., Keloharju, M., & Linnainaa, J. "IQ and Stock Market Participation," *The Journal of Finance*, Vol. 66, No. 6, December 2011 (data from Table 1 and Figure 1).

  a. Given that the Finnish citizen has an IQ score of 6 or higher, what is the probability that he/she invests in the stock market?
  b. Given that the Finnish citizen has an IQ score of 5 or lower, what is the probability that he/she invests in the stock market?
  c. Based on the results, parts **a** and **b,** does it appear that investing in the stock market is dependent on IQ? Explain.

66 Degrees of best-paid CEOs. *Forbes* (April 13, 2011) did a survey of the top 40 best-paid CEOs. The data on highest degree obtained are summarized in the SPSS printout below.

DEGREE

		Frequency	Percent	Valid Percent	Cumulative Percent
Valid	Bachelors	13	32.5	32.5	32.5
	Law	1	2.5	2.5	35.0
	Masters	5	12.5	12.5	47.5
	MBA	15	37.5	37.5	85.0
	None	4	10.0	10.0	95.0
	PhD	2	5.0	5.0	100.0
	Total	40	100.0	100.0	

SPSS output for Exercise 66

Suppose you randomly select five of the CEOs (without replacement) and record the highest degree obtained by each.

a. What is the probability that the highest degree obtained by the first CEO you select is a bachelor's degree?

b. Suppose the highest degree obtained by each of the first four CEOs you select is a bachelor's degree. What is the probability that the highest degree obtained by the fifth CEO you select is a bachelor's degree?

67 Ambulance response time. *Geographical Analysis* (Jan. 2010) presented a study of emergency medical service (EMS) ability to meet the demand for an ambulance. In one example, the researchers presented the following scenario. An ambulance station has one vehicle and two demand locations, A and B. The probability that the ambulance can travel to a location in under 8 minutes is .58 for location A and .42 for location B. The probability that the ambulance is busy at any point in time is .3.

a. Find the probability that EMS can meet the demand for an ambulance at location A.

b. Find the probability that EMS can meet the demand for an ambulance at location B.

68 Working mothers with children. The U.S. Census Bureau reports a decline in the percentage of mothers in the workforce who have infant children. The following table gives a breakdown of the marital status and working status of the 1.8 million mothers with infant children in the year 2010. (The numbers in the table are reported in thousands.) Consider the following events: $A = \{$Mom with infant works$\}$, $B = \{$Mom with infant is married and living with husband$\}$. Are A and B independent events?

	Working	Not Working
Married/living with husband	1,174	89
All other arrangements	416	121

Source: Data from U.S. Census Bureau, Bureau of Labor Statistics, 2010.

69 Intrusion detection systems. A computer intrusion detection system (IDS) is designed to provide an alarm whenever an intrusion (e.g., unauthorized access) is being attempted into a computer system. A probabilistic evaluation of a system with two independently operating intrusion detection systems (a double IDS) was published in the *Journal of Research of the National Institute of Standards and Technology* (November/December 2003). Consider a double IDS with system A and system B. If there is an intruder, system A sounds an alarm with probability .9, and system B sounds an alarm with probability .95. If there is no intruder, the probability that system A sounds an alarm (i.e., a false alarm) is .2, and the probability that system B sounds an alarm is .1. Assume that under a given condition (intruder or not), systems A and B operate independently.

a. Using symbols, express the four probabilities given in the example.

b. If there is an intruder, what is the probability that both systems sound an alarm?

c. If there is no intruder, what is the probability that both systems sound an alarm?

d. Given an intruder, what is the probability that at least one of the systems sounds an alarm?

70 Wine quality and soil. The *Journal of Wine Research* (Vol. 21, 2010) published a study of the effects of soil and climate on the quality of wine produced in Spain. The soil at two vineyards—Llarga and Solar—was the focus of the analysis. Wine produced from grapes grown in each of the two vineyards was evaluated for each of three different years (growing seasons) by a wine-tasting panel. Based on the taste tests, the panel (as a group) selected the wine with the highest quality.

a. How many different wines were evaluated by the panel, where one wine was produced for each vineyard/growing season combination?

b. If the wines were all of equal quality, what is the probability that the panel selected a Llarga wine as the wine with the highest quality?

c. If the wines were all of equal quality, what is the probability that the panel selected a wine produced in year 3 as the wine with the highest quality?

d. The panel consisted of four different wine tasters who performed the evaluations independently of each other. If the wines were all of equal quality, what is the probability that all four tasters selected a Llarga wine as the wine with the highest quality?

71 Are you really being served red snapper? Red snapper is a rare and expensive reef fish served at upscale restaurants. Federal law prohibits restaurants from serving a cheaper, look-alike variety of fish (e.g., vermillion snapper or lane snapper) to customers who order red snapper. Researchers at the University of North Carolina used DNA analysis to examine fish specimens labeled "red snapper" that were purchased from vendors across the country (*Nature*, July 15, 2004). The DNA tests revealed that 77% of the specimens were not red snapper but the cheaper, look-alike variety of fish.

a. Assuming the results of the DNA analysis are valid, what is the probability that you are actually served red snapper the next time you order it at a restaurant?

b. If there are five customers at a restaurant, all who have ordered red snapper, what is the probability that at least one customer is actually served red snapper?

72 Lie detector test. The software for a lie detector based on voice stress levels—called the computerized voice stress analyzer (CVSA)—is available for about $10,000. The manufacturer claims that the CVSA is 98% accurate, and, unlike a polygraph machine, will not be thrown off by drugs and medical factors. However, laboratory studies by the U.S. Defense Department found that the CVSA had an accuracy rate of 49.8%—slightly less than pure chance. Suppose the CVSA is used to test the veracity of four suspects. Assume the suspects' responses are independent.

a. If the manufacturer's claim is true, what is the probability that the CVSA will correctly determine the veracity of all four suspects?

b. If the manufacturer's claim is true, what is the probability that the CVSA will yield an incorrect result for at least one of the four suspects?

c. Suppose that in a laboratory experiment conducted by the U.S. Defense Department on four suspects, the CVSA yielded incorrect results for two of the suspects. Use this result to make an inference about the true accuracy rate of the lie detector.

Applying the Concepts—Advanced

73 Patient medical instruction sheets. Physicians and pharmacists sometimes fail to inform patients adequately about the proper application of prescription drugs and about the precautions to take in order to avoid potential side effects. One method of increasing patients' awareness of the problem is for physicians to provide patient medication instruction (PMI) sheets. The American Medical Association, however, has found that only 20% of the doctors who prescribe drugs frequently distribute PMI sheets to their patients. Assume that 20% of all patients receive the PMI sheet with their prescriptions and that 12% receive the PMI sheet and are hospitalized because of a drug-related problem. What is the probability that a person will be hospitalized for a drug-related problem given that the person received the PMI sheet?

74 Risk of a natural gas pipeline accident. *Process Safety Progress* (Dec. 2004) published a risk analysis for a natural gas pipeline between Bolivia and Brazil. The most likely scenario for an accident would be natural gas leakage from a hole in the pipeline. The probability that the leak ignites immediately (causing a jet fire) is .01. If the leak does not immediately ignite, it may result in a delayed ignition of a gas cloud. Given no immediate ignition, the probability of delayed ignition (causing a flash fire) is .01. If there is no delayed ignition, the gas cloud will harmlessly disperse. Suppose a leak occurs in the natural gas pipeline. Find the probability that either a jet fire or a flash fire will occur. Illustrate with a tree diagram.

75 Most likely coin-tossing sequence. In *Parade Magazine*'s (Nov. 26, 2000) column "Ask Marilyn," the following question was posed: "I have just tossed a [balanced] coin 10 times, and I ask you to guess which of the following three sequences was the result. One (and only one) of the sequences is genuine."

$$(1)\ \text{H H H H H H H H H H}$$
$$(2)\ \text{H H T T H T T H H H}$$
$$(3)\ \text{T T T T T T T T T T}$$

a. Demonstrate that prior to actually tossing the coins, the three sequences are equally likely to occur.

b. Find the probability that the 10 coin tosses result in all heads or all tails.

c. Find the probability that the 10 coin tosses result in a mix of heads and tails.

d. Marilyn's answer to the question posed was "Though the chances of the three specific sequences occurring randomly are equal . . . it's reasonable for us to choose

sequence (2) as the most likely genuine result." If you know that only one of the three sequences actually occurred, explain why Marilyn's answer is correct. [*Hint:* Compare the probabilities in parts **b** and **c**.]

76 Software defects in NASA spacecraft instrument code.
SWDEF Portions of computer software code that may contain undetected defects are called *blind spots*. The issue of blind spots in software code evaluation was addressed at the *8th IEEE International Symposium on High Assurance Software Engineering* (March 2004). The researchers developed guidelines for assessing methods of predicting software defects using data on 498 modules of software code written in "C" language for a NASA spacecraft instrument. One simple prediction algorithm is to count the lines of code in the module; any module with more than 50 lines of code is predicted to have a defect. The accompanying file contains the predicted and actual defect status of all 498 modules. A standard approach to evaluating a software defect prediction algorithm is to form a two-way summary table similar to the one shown here. In the table, *a, b, c,* and *d* represent the number of modules in each cell. Software engineers use these table entries to compute several probability measures, called *accuracy, detection rate, false alarm rate,* and *precision.*

		Module Has Defects	
		False	True
Algorithm	No	*a*	*b*
Predicts Defects	Yes	*c*	*d*

a. *Accuracy* is defined as the probability that the prediction algorithm is correct. Write a formula for *accuracy* as a function of the table values *a, b, c,* and *d.*

b. The *detection rate* is defined as the probability that the algorithm predicts a defect, given that the module actually is a defect. Write a formula for *detection rate* as a function of the table values *a, b, c,* and *d.*

c. The *false alarm rate* is defined as the probability that the algorithm predicts a defect, given that the module actually has no defect. Write a formula for *false alarm rate* as a function of the table values *a, b, c,* and *d.*

d. *Precision* is defined as the probability that the module has a defect, given that the algorithm predicts a defect. Write a formula for *precision* as a function of the table values *a, b, c,* and *d.*

e. Access the accompanying file and compute the values of accuracy, detection rate, false alarm rate, and precision. Interpret the results.

7 Bayes's Rule

An early attempt to employ probability in making inferences is the basis for a branch of statistical methodology known as **Bayesian statistical methods.** The logic employed by the English philosopher Thomas Bayes in the mid-1700s involves converting an unknown conditional probability, say $P(B|A)$, to one involving a known conditional probability, say $P(A|B)$. The method is illustrated in the next example.

Example 22

Applying Bayes's Logic— Intruder Detection System

Problem An unmanned monitoring system uses high-tech video equipment and microprocessors to detect intruders. A prototype system has been developed and is in use outdoors at a weapons munitions plant. The system is designed to detect intruders with a probability of .90. However, the design engineers expect this probability to vary with weather conditions. The system automatically records the weather condition each time an intruder is detected. Based on a series of controlled tests, in which an intruder was released at the plant under various weather conditions, the following information is available: Given the intruder was, in fact, detected by the system, the weather was clear 75% of the time, cloudy 20% of the time, and raining 5% of the time. When the system failed to detect the intruder, 60% of the days were clear, 30% cloudy, and 10% rainy. Use this information to find the probability of detecting an intruder, given rainy weather conditions. (Assume that an intruder has been released at the plant.)

Solution Define D to be the event that the intruder is detected by the system. Then D^c is the event that the system fails to detect the intruder. Our goal is to calculate the conditional probability, $P(D|\text{Rainy})$. From the statement of the problem, the following information is available:

$$P(D) = .90 \qquad P(D^c) = .10$$
$$P(\text{Clear}|D) = .75 \qquad P(\text{Clear}|D^c) = .60$$
$$P(\text{Cloudy}|D) = .20 \qquad P(\text{Cloudy}|D^c) = .30$$
$$P(\text{Rainy}|D) = .05 \qquad P(\text{Rainy}|D^c) = .10$$

Note that $P(D|\text{Rainy})$ is not one of the conditional probabilities that is known. However, we can find

$$P(\text{Rainy} \cap D) = P(D)P(\text{Rainly}|D) = (.90)(.05) = .045$$

and

$$P(\text{Rainy} \cap D^c) = P(D^c)P(\text{Rainy}|D^c) = (.10)(.10) = .01$$

using the multiplicative rule of probability. These two probabilities are highlighted on the tree diagram for the problem in Figure 22.

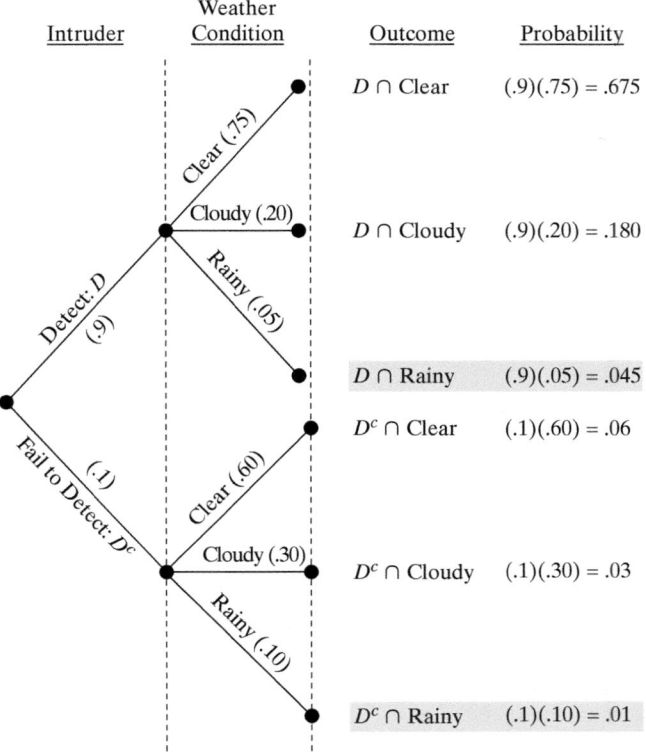

Figure 22

Tree diagram for Example 22

Now the event Rainy is the union of two mutually exclusive events, (Rainy $\cap D$) and (Rainy $\cap D^c$). Thus, applying the additive rule of probability, we have

$$P(\text{Rainy}) = P(\text{Rainy} \cap D) + P(\text{Rainy} \cap D^c) = .045 + .01 = .055$$

We now apply the formula for conditional probability to obtain

$$P(D|\text{Rainy}) = \frac{P(\text{Rainy} \cap D)}{P(\text{Rainy})} = \frac{P(\text{Rainy} \cap D)}{P(\text{Rainy} \cap D) + P(\text{Rainy} \cap D^c)}$$
$$= \frac{.045}{.055} = .818$$

Therefore, under rainy weather conditions, the prototype system can detect the intruder with a probability of .818—a value lower than the designed probability of .90.

Look Back One key to solving a problem of this type is recognizing that the conditional probability of interest, $P(D|\text{Rainy})$, is not the same as the conditional probability given, $P(\text{Rainy}|D)$.

■ **Now Work Exercise 77**

The technique utilized in Example 22, called **Bayes's Rule,** can be applied when an observed event A occurs with any one of several mutually exclusive and exhaustive events, $B_1, B_2, \ldots, B_k$. The formula for finding the appropriate conditional probabilities is given in the box.

Bayes's Rule

Given k mutually exclusive and exhaustive events, $B_1, B_2, \ldots, B_k$, such that $P(B_1) + P(B_2) + \cdots + P(B_k) = 1$, and an observed event A, then

$$P(B_i|A) = \frac{P(B_i \cap A)}{P(A)}$$
$$= \frac{P(B_i)P(A|B_i)}{P(B_1)P(A|B_1) + P(B_2)P(A|B_2) + \cdots + P(B_k)P(A|B_k)}$$

In applying Bayes's Rule to Example 22, the observed event $A = \{\text{Rainy}\}$ and the $k = 2$ mutually exclusive and exhaustive events are the complementary events $D = \{\text{intruder detected}\}$ and $D^c = \{\text{intruder not detected}\}$. Hence, the formula

$$P(D|\text{Rainy}) = \frac{P(D)P(\text{Rainy}|D)}{P(D)P(\text{Rainy}|D) + P(D^c)P(\text{Rainy}|D^c)}$$
$$= \frac{(.90)(.05)}{(.90)(.05) + (.10)(.10)} = .818$$

Example 23

Bayes's Rule Application— Wheelchair Control

Problem Electric wheelchairs are difficult to maneuver for many disabled people. In a paper presented at the *1st International Workshop on Advances in Service Robotics* (March 2003), researchers applied Bayes's Rule to evaluate an "intelligent" robotic controller that aims to capture the intent of the wheelchair user and aid in navigation. Consider the following scenario. From a certain location in a room, a wheelchair user will either (1) turn sharply to the left and navigate through a door, (2) proceed straight to the other side of the room, or (3) turn slightly right and stop at a table. Denote these three events as D (for door), S (for straight), and T (for table). Based on previous trips, $P(D) = .5$, $P(S) = .2$, and $P(T) = .3$. The wheelchair is installed with a robot-controlled joystick. When the user intends to go through the door, he points the joystick straight 30% of the time; when the user intends to go straight, he points the joystick straight 40% of the time; and when the user intends to go to the table, he points the joystick straight 5% of the time. If the wheelchair user points the joystick straight, where is his most likely destination?

Solution Let $J = \{$joystick is pointed straight$\}$. The user intention percentages can be restated as the following conditional probabilities: $P(J|D) = .3$, $P(J|S) = .4$, and $P(J|T) = .05$. Since the user has pointed the joystick straight, we want to find the following probabilities: $P(D|J)$, $P(S|J)$, and $P(T|J)$. Now, the three events, D, S, and T, represent mutually exclusive and exhaustive events, where $P(D) = .5$, $P(S) = .2$, and $P(T) = .3$. Consequently, we can apply Bayes's Rule as follows:

$$P(D|J) = P(J|D) \cdot P(D)/[P(J|D) \cdot P(D) + P(J|S) \cdot P(S) + P(J|T) \cdot P(T)]$$
$$= (.3)(.5)/[(.3)(.5) + (.4)(.2) + (.05)(.3)] = .15/.245 = .612$$
$$P(S|J) = P(J|S) \cdot P(S)/[P(J|D) \cdot P(D) + P(J|S) \cdot P(S) + P(J|T) \cdot P(T)]$$
$$= (.4)(.2)/[(.3)(.5) + (.4)(.2) + (.05)(.3)] = .08/.245 = .327$$
$$P(T|J) = P(J|T) \cdot P(T)/[P(J|D) \cdot P(D) + P(J|S) \cdot P(S) + P(J|T) \cdot P(T)]$$
$$= (.05)(.3)/[(.3)(.5) + (.4)(.2) + (.05)(.3)] = .015/.245 = .061$$

Note that the largest conditional probability is $P(D|J) = 612$. Thus, if the joystick is pointed straight, the wheelchair user is most likely headed through the door.

■ **Now Work Exercise 82**

Exercises 77–89

Please be aware that some of the following problems may require knowledge of concepts that are not presented in this chapter.

Learning the Mechanics

77 Suppose the events B_1 and B_2 are mutually exclusive and complementary events, such that $P(B_1) = .75$ and $P(B_2) = .25$. Consider another event A such that $P(A|B_1) = .3$ and $P(A|B_2) = .5$.
   a. Find $P(B_1 \cap A)$.
   b. Find $P(B_2 \cap A)$.
   c. Find $P(A)$ using the results in parts **a** and **b**.
   d. Find $P(B_1|A)$.
   e. Find $P(B_2|A)$.

78 Suppose the events B_1, B_2, and B_3 are mutually exclusive and complementary events, such that $P(B_1) = .2$, $P(B_2) = .15$, and $P(B_3) = .65$. Consider another event A such that $P(A|B_1) = .4$, $P(A|B_2) = .25$, and $P(A|B_3) = .6$. Use Bayes's Rule to find
   a. $P(B_1|A)$
   b. $P(B_2|A)$
   c. $P(B_3|A)$

79 Suppose the events B_1, B_2, and B_3 are mutually exclusive and complementary events, such that $P(B_1) = .2$, $P(B_2) = .15$, and $P(B_3) = .65$. Consider another event A such that $P(A) = .4$. If A is independent of B_1, B_2, and B_3, use Bayes's Rule to show that $P(B_1|A) = P(B_1) = .2$.

Applying the Concepts—Basic

80 **Tests for Down syndrome.** Currently, there are three diagnostic tests available for chromosome abnormalities in a developing fetus: triple serum marker screening, ultrasound, and amniocentesis. The safest (to both the mother and fetus) and least expensive of the three is the ultrasound test. Two San Diego State University statisticians investigated the accuracy of using ultrasound to test for Down syndrome (*Chance*, Summer 2007). Let D denote that the fetus has a genetic marker for Down syndrome and N denote that the ultrasound test is normal (i.e., no indication of chromosome abnormalities). Then,

the statisticians desired the probability $P(D/N)$. Use Bayes's Rule and the following probabilities (provided in the article) to find the desired probability: $P(D) = \frac{1}{180}$, $P(D^c) = \frac{79}{80}$, $P(N|D) = \frac{1}{2}$, $P(N^c|D) = \frac{1}{2}$, $P(N|D^c) = 1$, and $P(N^c|D^c) = 0$.

81 **Fingerprint expertise.** Contrary to what is presented on TV shows like *CSI*, fingerprint identification is not fully automated. Expert examiners are required to identify the person who left the fingerprint. A study published in *Psychological Science* (August 2011) tested the accuracy of experts and novices in identifying fingerprints. Participants were presented pairs of fingerprints and asked to judge whether the prints in each pair matched. The pairs were presented under three different conditions: prints from the same individual (*match condition*), nonmatching but similar prints (*similar distracter condition*), and nonmatching and very dissimilar prints (*nonsimilar distracter condition*). The percentages of correct decisions made by the two groups under each of the three conditions are listed in the table.

Condition	Fingerprint Experts	Novices
Match	92.12%	74.55%
Similar Distracter	99.32%	44.82%
Nonsimilar Distracter	100%	77.03%

Source: Based on Tangen, J. M., Thompson, M. B., & McCarthy, D. J. "Identifying fingerprint expertise," *Psychological Science*, Vol. 22, No. 8, August 2011 (Figure 1).

   a. Given a pair of matched prints, what is the probability that an expert failed to identify the match?
   b. Given a pair of matched prints, what is the probability that a novice failed to identify the match?
   c. Assume the study included 10 participants, 5 experts and 5 novices. Suppose that a pair of matched prints was presented to a randomly selected study participant and the participant failed to identify the match. Is the participant more likely to be an expert or a novice?

82 Errors in estimating job costs. A construction company employs three sales engineers. Engineers 1, 2, and 3 estimate the costs of 30%, 20%, and 50%, respectively, of all jobs bid by the company. For $i = 1, 2, 3$, define E_i to be the event that a job is estimated by engineer i. The following probabilities describe the rates at which the engineers make serious errors in estimating costs:

$$P(\text{error}|E_1) = .01, P(\text{error}|E_2) = .03, \text{ and}$$
$$P(\text{error}|E_3) = .02$$

a. If a particular bid results in a serious error in estimating job cost, what is the probability that the error was made by engineer 1?

b. If a particular bid results in a serious error in estimating job cost, what is the probability that the error was made by engineer 2?

c. If a particular bid results in a serious error in estimating job cost, what is the probability that the error was made by engineer 3?

d. Based on the probabilities, parts **a–c**, which engineer is most likely responsible for making the serious error?

83 Fish contaminated by a plant's toxic discharge. The U.S. Army Corps of Engineers' did a study on the DDT contamination of fish in the Tennessee River (Alabama). Part of the investigation focused on how far upstream the contaminated fish have migrated. (A fish is considered to be contaminated if its measured DDT concentration is greater than 5.0 parts per million.)

a. Considering only the contaminated fish captured from the Tennessee River, the data reveal that 52% of the fish are found between 275 and 300 miles upstream, 39% are found 305 to 325 miles upstream, and 9% are found 330 to 350 miles upstream. Use these percentages to determine the probabilities, $P(275-300)$, $P(305-325)$, and $P(330-350)$.

b. Given that a contaminated fish is found a certain distance upstream, the probability that it is a channel catfish (CC) is determined from the data as $P(CC|275-300) = .775$, $P(CC|305-325) = .77$, and $P(CC|330-350) = .86$. If a contaminated channel catfish is captured from the Tennessee River, what is the probability that it was captured 275–300 miles upstream?

84 Drug testing in athletes. Due to inaccuracies in drug-testing procedures (e.g., false positives and false negatives) in the medical field, the results of a drug test represent only one factor in a physician's diagnosis. Yet, when Olympic athletes are tested for illegal drug use (i.e., doping), the results of a single positive test are used to ban the athlete from competition. In *Chance* (Spring 2004), University of Texas biostatisticians D. A. Berry and L. Chastain demonstrated the application of Bayes's Rule for making inferences about testosterone abuse among Olympic athletes. They used the following example: In a population of 1,000 athletes, suppose 100 are illegally using testosterone. Of the users, suppose 50 would test positive for testosterone. Of the nonusers, suppose 9 would test positive.

a. Given that the athlete is a user, find the probability that a drug test for testosterone will yield a positive result. (This probability represents the *sensitivity* of the drug test.)

b. Given the athlete is a nonuser, find the probability that a drug test for testosterone will yield a negative result. (This probability represents the *specificity* of the drug test.)

c. If an athlete tests positive for testosterone, use Bayes's Rule to find the probability that the athlete is really doping. (This probability represents the *positive predictive value* of the drug test.)

Applying the Concepts—Intermediate

85 Mining for dolomite. Dolomite is a valuable mineral that is found in sedimentary rock. During mining operations, dolomite is often confused with shale. The radioactivity features of rock can aid miners in distinguishing between dolomite and shale rock zones. For example, if the Gamma ray reading of a rock zone exceeds 60 API units, the area is considered to be mostly shale (and is not mined); if the Gamma ray reading of a rock zone is less than 60 API units, the area is considered to be abundant in dolomite (and is mined). Data on 771 core samples in a rock quarry collected by the Kansas Geological Survey revealed the following: 476 of the samples are dolomite and 295 of the samples are shale. Of the 476 dolomite core samples, 34 had a Gamma ray reading greater than 60. Of the 295 shale core samples, 280 had a Gamma ray reading greater than 60. Suppose you obtain a Gamma ray reading greater than 60 at a certain depth of the rock quarry. Should this area be mined?

86 Nondestructive evaluation. Nondestructive evaluation (NDE) describes methods that quantitatively characterize materials, tissues, and structures by noninvasive means, such as X-ray computed tomography, ultrasonics, and acoustic emission. Recently, NDE was used to detect defects in steel castings (*JOM*, May 2005). Assume that the probability that NDE detects a "hit" (i.e., predicts a defect in a steel casting) when, in fact, a defect exists is .97. (This is often called the *probability of detection.*) Also assume that the probability that NDE detects a hit when, in fact, no defect exists is .005. (This is called the *probability of a false call.*) Past experience has shown a defect occurs once in every 100 steel castings. If NDE detects a hit for a particular steel casting, what is the probability that an actual defect exists?

87 Purchasing microchips. An important component of your desktop or laptop personal computer (PC) is a microchip. The table gives the proportions of microchips that a certain PC manufacturer purchases from seven suppliers.

Supplier	Proportion
S_1	.15
S_2	.05
S_3	.10
S_4	.20
S_5	.12
S_6	.20
S_7	.18

a. It is known that the proportions of defective microchips produced by the seven suppliers are .001, .0003, .0007, .006, .0002, .0002, and .001, respectively. If a single PC microchip failure is observed, which supplier is most likely responsible?

b. Suppose the seven suppliers produce defective microchips at the same rate, .0005. If a single PC microchip failure is observed, which supplier is most likely responsible?

88 Intrusion detection systems. Refer to the *Journal of Research of the National Institute of Standards and Technology* (Nov.–Dec. 2003) study of a double intrusion detection system with independent systems, Exercise 69. Recall that if there is an intruder, system A sounds an alarm with probability .9, and system B sounds an alarm with probability .95. If there is no intruder, system A sounds an alarm with probability .2, and system B sounds an alarm with probability .1. Now assume that the probability of an intruder is .4. Also assume that under a given condition (intruder or not), systems A and B operate independently. If both systems sound an alarm, what is the probability that an intruder is detected?

Applying the Concepts—Advanced

89 Forensic analysis of JFK assassination bullets. Following the assassination of President John F. Kennedy (JFK) in 1963, the House Select Committee on Assassinations (HSCA) conducted an official government investigation. The HSCA concluded that although there was a probable conspiracy involving at least one shooter in addition to Lee Harvey Oswald, the additional shooter missed all limousine occupants. A recent analysis of assassination bullet fragments, reported in the *Annals of Applied Statistics* (Vol. 1, 2007), contradicted these findings, concluding that the evidence used by the HSCA to rule out a second assassin is fundamentally flawed. It is well documented that at least two different bullets were the source of bullet fragments found after the assassination. Let E = {bullet evidence used by the HSCA}, T = {two bullets used in the aassassination}, and T^c = {more than two bullets used in the assassination}. Given the evidence (E), which is more likely to have occurred—two bullets used (T) or more than two bullets used (T^c)?

a. The researchers demonstrated that the ratio, $P(T|E)/P(T^c|E)$, is less than 1. Explain why this result supports the theory of more than two bullets used in the assassination of JFK.

b. To obtain the result, part **a,** the researchers first showed that

$$P(T|E)/P(T^c|E) = [P(E|T) \cdot P(T)]/[P(E|T^c) \cdot P(T^c)]$$

Demonstrate this equality using Bayes's Rule.

◻ Chapter Notes

Key Terms

Additive rule of probability	Multiplicative rule of probability
Bayesian statistical methods	Mutually exclusive events
Bayes's Rule	Odds
Combinations Rule	Probability of an event
Combinatorial mathematics	Probability rules (sample points)
Complementary events	Rule of complements
Compound event	Sample point
Conditional probability	Sample space
Dependent events	Simple event
Event	Tree diagram
Experiment	Two-way table
Independent events	Unconditional probabilities
Intersection	Union
Law of Large Numbers	Venn diagram

Key Symbols

S	**sample space** (collection of all sample points)
$A: \{1,2\}$	set of **sample points in event A**
$P(A)$	**probability** of event A
$A \cup B$	**union** of events A and B (either A or B can occur)
$A \cap B$	**intersection** of events A and B (both A and B occur)
A^c	**complement** of A (event A does not occur)
$A\|B$	event A occurs, **given** event B occurs
$\binom{N}{n}$	number of **combinations** of N elements taken n at a time
$N!$	**N factorial** $= N(N-1)(N-2)\cdots(2)(1)$

Key Ideas

Probability Rules for k Sample Points, $S_1, S_2, S_3, \ldots, S_k$

1. $0 \le P(S_i) \le 1$

2. $\sum P(S_i) = 1$

Combinations Rule

Counting number of samples of n elements selected from N elements

$$\binom{N}{n} = \frac{N!}{n!(N-n)!} = \frac{N(N-1)(N-2)\cdots(N-n+1)}{n(n-1)(n-2)\cdots(2)(1)}$$

Bayes's Rule

For mutually exclusive events $B_1, B_2, \ldots, B_k$, such that $P(B_1) + P(B_2) + \cdots + P(B_k) = 1$,

$$P(B_i|A) = \frac{P(B_i)P(A|B_i)}{P(B_1)P(A|B_1) + P(B_2)P(A|B_2) + \cdots + P(B_k)P(A|B_k)}$$

Guide to Selecting Probability Rules

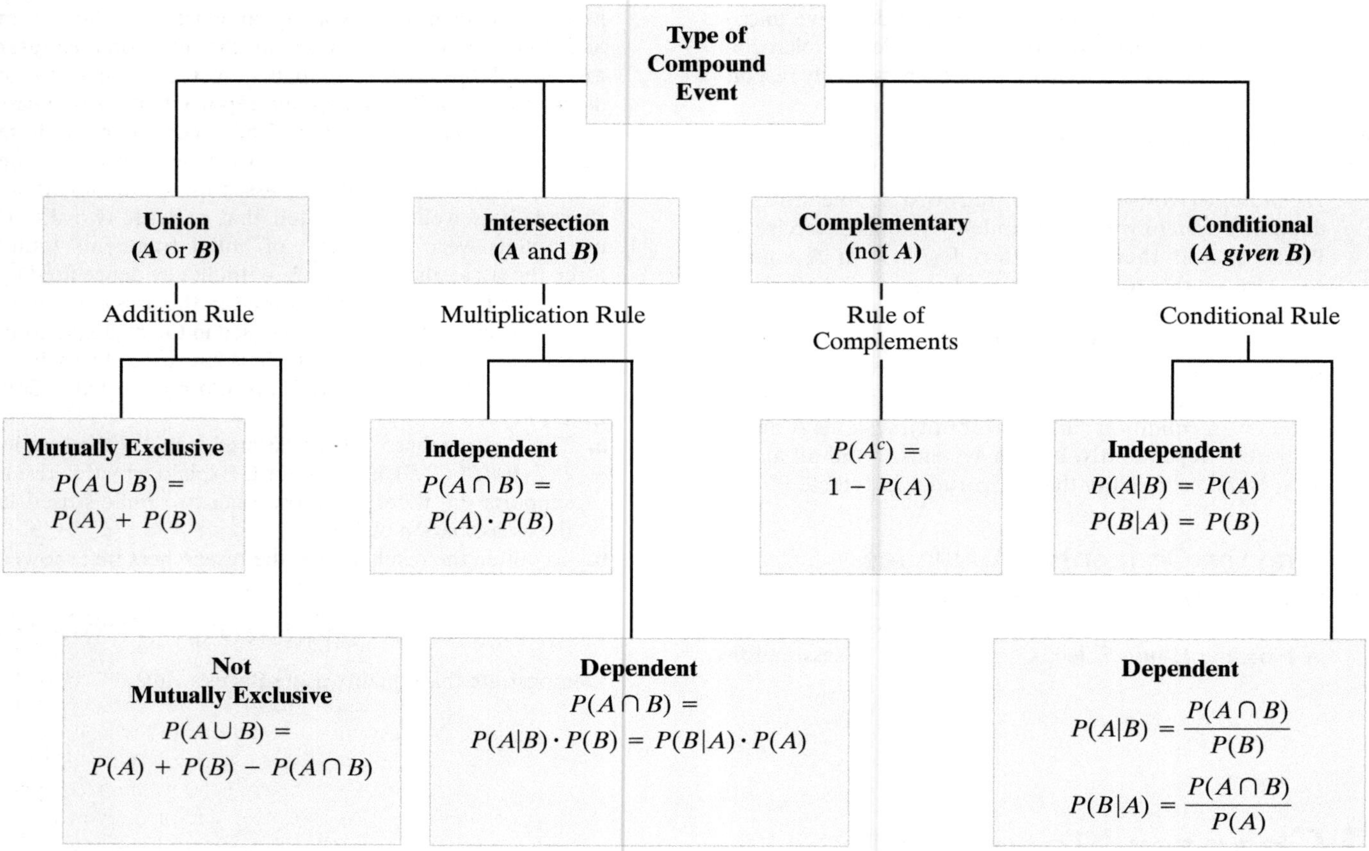

Type of Compound Event

Union (*A* or *B*)	Intersection (*A* and *B*)	Complementary (not *A*)	Conditional (*A* given *B*)
Addition Rule	Multiplication Rule	Rule of Complements	Conditional Rule

Mutually Exclusive
$$P(A \cup B) =$$
$$P(A) + P(B)$$

Independent
$$P(A \cap B) =$$
$$P(A) \cdot P(B)$$

$$P(A^c) =$$
$$1 - P(A)$$

Independent
$$P(A|B) = P(A)$$
$$P(B|A) = P(B)$$

Not Mutually Exclusive
$$P(A \cup B) =$$
$$P(A) + P(B) - P(A \cap B)$$

Dependent
$$P(A \cap B) =$$
$$P(A|B) \cdot P(B) = P(B|A) \cdot P(A)$$

Dependent
$$P(A|B) = \frac{P(A \cap B)}{P(B)}$$
$$P(B|A) = \frac{P(A \cap B)}{P(A)}$$

Supplementary Exercises 90–130

Please be aware that some of the following problems may require knowledge of concepts that are not presented in this chapter.

Learning the Mechanics

90 Which of the following pairs of events are mutually exclusive? Justify your response.
  a. {The Dow Jones Industrial Average increases on Monday.}, {A large New York bank decreases its prime interest rate on Monday.}
  b. {The next sale by a PC retailer is a notebook computer.}, {The next sale by a PC retailer is a desktop computer.}
  c. {You reinvest all your dividend income in a limited partnership.}, {You reinvest all your dividend income in a money market fund.}

91 A sample space consists of four sample points, where $P(S_1) = .2$, $P(S_2) = .1$, $P(S_3) = .3$, and $P(S_4) = .4$.
  a. Show that the sample points obey the two probability rules for a sample space.
  b. If an event $A = \{S_1, S_4\}$, find $P(A)$.

92 For two events A and B, suppose $P(A) = .7$, $P(B) = .5$, and $P(A \cap B) = .4$. Find $P(A \cup B)$.

93 A and B are mutually exclusive events, with $P(A) = .2$ and $P(B) = .3$.
  a. Find $P(A|B)$.
  b. Are A and B independent events?

94 Two events, A and B, are independent, with $P(A) = .3$ and $P(B) = .1$.
  a. Are A and B mutually exclusive? Why?
  b. Find $P(A|B)$ and $P(B|A)$.
  c. Find $P(A \cup B)$.

95 Given that $P(A \cap B) = .4$ and $P(A|B) = .8$, find $P(B)$.

96 A random sample of $n = 5$ is to be selected from $N = 50$. In how many different ways can the sample be drawn?

97 The Venn diagram below illustrates a sample space containing six sample points and three events, A, B, and C. The probabilities of the sample points are $P(1) = .3$, $P(2) = .2$, $P(3) = .1$, $P(4) = .1$, $P(5) = .1$, and $P(6) = .2$.

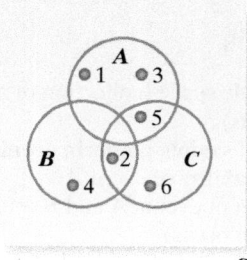

a. Find $P(A \cap B)$, $P(B \cap C)$, $P(A \cup C)$, $P(A \cup B \cup C)$, $P(B^c)$, $P(A^c \cap B)$, $P(B|C)$, and $P(B|A)$.

b. Are A and B independent? Mutually exclusive? Why?

c. Are B and C independent? Mutually exclusive? Why?

98 Find the numerical value of

a. $6!$ **b.** $\binom{10}{9}$ **c.** $\binom{10}{1}$ **d.** $\binom{6}{3}$ **e.** $0!$

🔘 Applet Exercise 6

Use the applet entitled *Random Numbers* to generate a list of 50 numbers between 1 and 100, inclusive. Use this list to find each of the probabilities.

a. The probability that a number chosen from the list is less than or equal to 50

b. The probability that a number chosen from the list is even

c. The probability that a number chosen from the list is less than or equal to 50 and even

d. The probability that a number chosen from the list is less than or equal to 50 given that the number is even

e. Do your results from parts **a–d** support the conclusion that the events *less than or equal to 50* and *even* are independent? Explain.

Applying the Concepts—Basic

99 **Management system failures.** The *Process Safety Progress* (Dec. 2004) did a study of 83 industrial accidents caused by management system failures. A summary of the root causes of these 83 incidents is reproduced in the following table. One of the 83 incidents is randomly selected and the root cause is determined.

Management System Cause Category	Number of Incidents
Engineering and Design	27
Procedures and Practices	24
Management and Oversight	22
Training and Communication	10
Total	83

Source: Based on *Blair*, A. S. "Management system failures identified in incidents investigated by the U.S. Chemical Safety and Hazard Investigation Board," *Process Safety Progress*, Vol. 23, No. 4, Dec. 2004, pp. 232–236 (Table 1).

a. List the sample points for this problem and assign reasonable probabilities to them.

b. Find and interpret the probability that an industrial accident is caused by faulty engineering and design.

c. Find and interpret the probability that an industrial accident is caused by something other than faulty procedures and practices.

100 **Annual compensation and benefits report.** Each year, Hudson Institute conducts a survey of 10,000 U.S. workers about their total compensation packages. One question in Hudson's *Compensation and Benefits Report* focused on employees who received raises in the past year. Of these employees, 35% reported that their raise was based on job performance, 50% reported that it was based on a standard cost of living, and the remainder (15%) were unsure how their raises were determined. Suppose we select (at random) one of the U.S. workers surveyed who received a raise last year and inquire about how that worker's raise was determined.

a. List the sample points for this experiment.

b. Assign reasonable probabilities to the sample points.

c. Find the probability that the raise was based either on job performance or a standard cost of living.

101 **Ownership of small businesses.** According to the *Journal of Business Venturing* (Vol. 17, 2002), 27% of all small businesses owned by non-Hispanic whites nationwide are women-owned firms. If we select, at random, a small business owned by a non-Hispanic white, what is the probability that it is a male-owned firm?

102 **Condition of public school facilities.** The National Center for Education Statistics (NCES) conducted a survey on the condition of America's public school facilities. The survey revealed the following information. The probability that a public school building has inadequate plumbing is .25. Of the buildings with inadequate plumbing, the probability that the school has plans for repairing the building is .38. Find the probability that a public school building has inadequate plumbing and will be repaired.

103 **New car crash tests.** The National Highway Traffic Safety Administration (NHTSA) did crash tests of new car models. The NHTSA has developed a "star" scoring system, with results ranging from one star (*) to five stars (*****). The more stars in the rating, the better the level of crash protection in a head-on collision. A summary of the driver-side star ratings for 98 cars is reproduced in the accompanying Minitab printout. Assume that one of the 98 cars is selected at random. State whether each of the following is true or false.

a. The probability that the car has a rating of two stars is 4.

b. The probability that the car has a rating of four or five stars is .7857.

c. The probability that the car has a rating of one star is 0.

d. The car has a better chance of having a two-star rating than of having a five-star rating.

Tally for Discrete Variables: DRIVSTAR

DRIVSTAR	Count	Percent
2	4	4.08
3	17	17.35
4	59	60.20
5	18	18.37
N=	98	

104 **Speeding linked to fatal car crashes.** According to the National Highway Traffic and Safety Administration's National Center for Statistics and Analysis (NCSA), "Speeding is one of the most prevalent factors contributing to fatal traffic crashes" (*NHTSA Technical Report*, Aug. 2005). The probability that speeding is a cause of a fatal crash is .3. Furthermore, the probability that speeding and missing a curve are causes of a fatal crash is .12. Given speeding is a cause of a fatal crash, what is the probability that the crash occurred on a curve?

105 Survey on energy conservation. A state energy agency mailed questionnaires on energy conservation to 1,000 homeowners in the state capital. Five hundred questionnaires were returned. Suppose an experiment consists of randomly selecting and reviewing one of the returned questionnaires. Consider the events:

> A: {The home is constructed of brick.}
> B: {The home is more than 30 years old.}
> C: {The home is heated with oil.}

Describe each of the following events in terms of unions, intersections, and complements (i.e., $A \cup B$, $A \cap B$, A^c, etc.):
a. The home is more than 30 years old and is heated with oil.
b. The home is not constructed of brick.
c. The home is heated with oil or is more than 30 years old.
d. The home is constructed of brick and is not heated with oil.

106 Identifying urban counties. *Urban* and *rural* describe geographic areas for which land zoning regulations, school district policy, and public service policy are often set. However, the characteristics of urban/rural areas are not clearly defined. Researchers at the University of Nevada (Reno) asked a sample of county commissioners to give their perception of the single most important factor in identifying urban counties (*Professional Geographer*, Feb. 2000). In all, five factors were mentioned by the commissioners: total population, agricultural change, presence of industry, growth, and population concentration. The survey results are displayed in the pie chart below. Suppose one of the commissioners is selected at random and the most important factor specified by the commissioner is recorded.
a. List the sample points for this experiment.
b. Assign reasonable probabilities to the sample points.
c. Find the probability that the most important factor specified by the commissioner is population related.

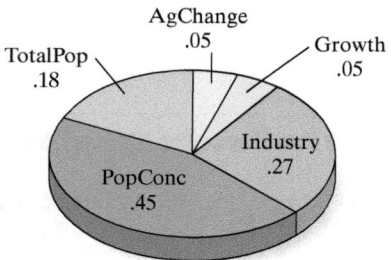

107 Use of country club facilities. A local country club has a membership of 600 and operates facilities that include an 18-hole championship golf course and 12 tennis courts. Before deciding whether to accept new members, the club president would like to know how many members regularly use each facility. A survey of the membership indicates that 70% regularly use the golf course, 50% regularly use the tennis courts, and 5% use neither of these facilities regularly.
a. Construct a Venn diagram to describe the results of the survey.
b. If one club member is chosen at random, what is the probability that the member uses either the golf course or the tennis courts or both?

c. If one member is chosen at random, what is the probability that the member uses both the golf and the tennis facilities?
d. A member is chosen at random from among those known to use the tennis courts regularly. What is the probability that the member also uses the golf course regularly?

108 Monitoring quality of power equipment. *Mechanical Engineering* (Feb. 2005) reported on the need for wireless networks to monitor the quality of industrial equipment. For example, consider Eaton Corp., a company that develops distribution products. Eaton estimates that 90% of the electrical switching devices it sells can monitor the quality of the power running through the device. Eaton further estimates that of the buyers of electrical switching devices capable of monitoring quality, 90% do not wire the equipment up for that purpose. Use this information to estimate the probability that an Eaton electrical switching device is capable of monitoring power quality and is wired up for that purpose.

Applying the Concepts—Intermediate

109 Appeals of federal civil trials. The *Journal of the American Law and Economics Association* (Vol. 3, 2001) published the results of a study of appeals of federal civil trials. The following table, extracted from the article, gives a breakdown of 2,143 civil cases that were appealed by either the plaintiff or the defendant. The outcome of the appeal, as well as the type of trial (judge or jury), was determined for each civil case. Suppose one of the 2,143 cases is selected at random and both the outcome of the appeal and type of trial are observed.

	Jury	Judge	Totals
Plaintiff trial win—reversed	194	71	265
Plaintiff trial win—affirmed/dismissed	429	240	669
Defendant trial win—reversed	111	68	179
Defendant trial win—affirmed/dismissed	731	299	1,030
Totals	1,465	678	2,143

a. Find $P(A)$, where $A = \{$jury trial$\}$.
b. Find $P(B)$, where $B = \{$plaintiff trial win is reversed$\}$.
c. Are A and B mutually exclusive events?
d. Find $P(A^c)$.
e. Find $P(A \cup B)$.
f. Find $P(A \cap B)$.

110 Assembling a panel of energy experts. The state legislature has appropriated $1 million to be distributed in the form of grants to individuals and organizations engaged in the research and development of alternative energy sources. You have been hired by the state's energy agency to assemble a panel of five energy experts whose task it will be to determine which individuals and organizations should receive the grant money. You have identified 11 equally qualified individuals who are willing to serve on the panel. How many different panels of five experts could be formed from these 11 individuals?

111 Testing a watch manufacturer's claim. A manufacturer of electronic digital watches claims that the probability of its watch running more than 1 minute slow or 1 minute fast after 1 year of use is .05. A consumer protection agency has purchased four of the manufacturer's watches with the intention of testing the claim.

   a. Assuming that the manufacturer's claim is correct, what is the probability that none of the watches are as accurate as claimed?

   b. Assuming that the manufacturer's claim is correct, what is the probability that exactly two of the four watches are as accurate as claimed?

   c. Suppose that only one of the four tested watches is as accurate as claimed. What inference can be made about the manufacturer's claim? Explain.

   d. Suppose that none of the watches tested are as accurate as claimed. Is it necessarily true that the manufacturer's claim is false? Explain.

112 Ranking razor blades. The corporations in the highly competitive razor blade industry do a tremendous amount of advertising each year. Corporation G gave a supply of three top-name brands, G, S, and W, to a consumer and asked her to use them and rank them in order of preference. The corporation was, of course, hoping the consumer would prefer its brand and rank it first, thereby giving them some material for a consumer interview advertising campaign. If the consumer did not prefer one blade over any other but was still required to rank the blades, what is the probability that

   a. The consumer ranked brand G first?

   b. The consumer ranked brand G last?

   c. The consumer ranked brand G last and brand W second?

   d. The consumer ranked brand W first, brand G second, and brand S third?

113 Link between cigar smoking and cancer. The *Journal of the National Cancer Institute* (Feb. 16, 2000) published the results of a study that investigated the association between cigar smoking and death from tobacco-related cancers. Data were obtained for a national sample of 137,243 American men. The results are summarized in the table. Each male in the study was classified according to his cigar-smoking status and whether or not he died from a tobacco-related cancer.

	Died from Cancer	Did Not Die from Cancer	Totals
Never Smoked Cigars	782	120,747	121,529
Former Cigar Smoker	91	7,757	7,848
Current Cigar Smoker	141	7,725	7,866
Totals	1,014	136,229	137,243

Source: Based on Shapiro, J. A., Jacobs, E. J., & Thun, M. J. "Cigar smoking in men and risk of death from tobacco-related cancers," *Journal of the National Cancer Institute*, Vol. 92, No. 4, Feb. 16, 2000. pp. 333–337 (Table 2).

   a. Find the probability that a man who never smoked cigars died from cancer.

   b. Find the probability that a former cigar smoker died from cancer.

   c. Find the probability that a current cigar smoker died from cancer.

114 Which events are independent? Use your intuitive understanding of independence to form an opinion about whether each of the following scenarios represents independent events.

   a. The results of consecutive tosses of a coin

   b. The opinions of randomly selected individuals in a preelection poll

   c. A Major League Baseball player's results in two consecutive at-bats

   d. The amount of gain or loss associated with investments in different stocks if these stocks are bought on the same day and sold on the same day 1 month later

   e. The amount of gain or loss associated with investments in different stocks that are bought and sold in different time periods, 5 years apart

   f. The prices bid by two different development firms in response to a building construction proposal

115 Home modifications for wheelchair users. The *American Journal of Public Health* (Jan. 2002) reported on a study of elderly wheelchair users who live at home. A sample of 306 wheelchair users, age 65 or older, were surveyed about whether they had an injurious fall during the year and whether their home features any one of five structural modifications: bathroom modifications, widened doorways/hallways, kitchen modifications, installed railings, and easy-open doors. The responses are summarized in the accompanying table. Suppose we select, at random, one of the 306 surveyed wheelchair users.

Home Features	Injurious Fall(s)	No Falls	Totals
All 5	2	7	9
At least 1 but not all	26	162	188
None	20	89	109
Totals	48	258	306

Source: Based on Berg, K., Hines, M., & Allen, S. "Wheelchair users at home: Few home modifications and many injurious falls," *American Journal of Public Health*, Vol. 92, No. 1, Jan. 2002 (Table 1).

   a. Find the probability that the wheelchair user had an injurious fall.

   b. Find the probability that the wheelchair user had all five features installed in the home.

   c. Find the probability that the wheelchair user had no falls and none of the features installed in the home.

   d. Given the wheelchair user had all five features installed, what is the probability that the user had an injurious fall?

   e. Given the wheelchair user had none of the features installed, what is the probability that the user had an injurious fall?

116 World Cup soccer match draws. Every 4 years the world's 32 best national soccer teams compete for the World Cup. Run by FIFA (Fédération Internationale de Football Association), national teams are placed into eight groups of four teams, with the group winners advancing to play for the World Cup. *Chance* (Spring 2007) investigated the fairness of the 2006 World Cup draw. Each of the top 8 seeded teams (teams ranked 1–8, called pot 1) were placed into one of the eight groups (named Group A, B, C, D, E, F, G, and H). The remaining 24 teams were assigned to 3 pots of 8 teams each to achieve the best possible geographical distribution between the groups. The teams in pot 2 were assigned to groups as follows: the first team drawn was placed into Group A, the second team drawn was placed in to Group B, etc. Teams in pots 3 and 4 were assigned to the groups in similar fashion. Because teams in pots 2–4 are not necessarily placed there based on their world ranking, this typically leads to a "group of death," i.e., a group involving at least two highly seeded teams where only one can advance.

a. In 2006, Germany (as the host country) was assigned as the top seed in Group A. What is the probability that Paraguay (with the highest ranking in pot 2) was assigned to Group A?

b. Many soccer experts viewed the South American teams (Ecuador and Paraguay) as the most dangerous teams in pot 2. What is the probability one of the South American teams was assigned to Group A?

c. In 2006, Group B was considered the "group of death," with England (world rank 2), Paraguay (highest rank in pot 2), Sweden (2nd highest rank in pot 3), and Trinidad and Tobago. What is the probability that Group B included the team with the highest rank in pot 2 and the team with one of the top two ranks in pot 3?

d. In drawing teams from pot 2, there was a notable exception in 2006. If a South American team (either Ecuador or Paraguay) was drawn into a group with another South American team, it was automatically moved to the next group. This rule impacted Group C (Argentina as the top seed) and Group F (Brazil as the top seed), because they already had South American teams, and groups that followed these groups in the draw. Now Group D included the eventual champion Italy as its top seed. What is the probability that Group D was not assigned one of the dangerous South American teams in pot 2?

117 Chance of an Avon sale. The probability that an Avon salesperson sells beauty products to a prospective customer on the first visit to the customer is .4. If the salesperson fails to make the sale on the first visit, the probability that the sale will be made on the second visit is .65. The salesperson never visits a prospective customer more than twice. What is the probability that the salesperson will make a sale to a particular customer?

118 Repairing a computer network. The local area network (LAN) for the College of Business computing system at a large university is temporarily shut down for repairs. Previous shutdowns have been due to hardware failure, software failure, or power failure. Maintenance engineers have determined that the probabilities of hardware, software, and power problems are .01, .05, and .02, respectively. They have also determined that if the system experiences hardware problems, it shuts down 73% of the time. Similarly, if software problems occur, the system shuts down 12% of the time; and if power failure occurs, the system shuts down 88% of the time. What is the probability that the current shutdown of the LAN is due to hardware failure? Software failure? Power failure?

119 Profile of a sustainable farmer. *Sustainable development or sustainable farming* means finding ways to live and work the Earth without jeopardizing the future. Studies were conducted in five Midwestern states to develop a profile of a sustainable farmer. The results revealed that farmers can be classified along a sustainability scale, depending on whether they are likely (L) or unlikely (U) to engage in the following practices: (1) Raise a broad mix of crops; (2) raise livestock; (3) use chemicals sparingly; and (4) use techniques for regenerating the soil, such as crop rotation.

a. List the different sets of classifications that are possible for the four practices (e.g., LUUL).

b. Suppose you are planning to interview farmers across the country to determine the frequency with which they fall into the classification sets you listed for part **a.** Because no information is yet available, assume initially that there is an equal chance of a farmer falling into any single classification set. Using that assumption, what is the probability that a farmer will be classified as unlikely on all four criteria (i.e., classified as a nonsustainable farmer)?

c. Using the same assumption as in part b, what is the probability that a farmer will be classified as likely on at least three of the criteria (i.e., classified as a near-sustainable farmer)?

120 Evaluating the performance of quality inspectors. The performance of quality inspectors affects both the quality of outgoing products and the cost of the products. A product that passes inspection is assumed to meet quality standards; a product that fails inspection may be reworked, scrapped, or reinspected. Quality engineers at an electric company evaluated performances of inspectors in judging the quality of solder joints by comparing each inspector's classifications of a set of 153 joints with the consensus evaluation of a panel of experts. The results for a particular inspector are shown in the table. One of the 153 solder joints was selected at random.

| | Inspector's Judgment | |
Committee's Judgment	Joint Acceptable	Joint Rejectable
Joint acceptable	101	10
Joint rejectable	23	19

a. What is the probability that the inspector judged the joint to be acceptable? That the committee judged the joint to be acceptable?

b. What is the probability that both the inspector and the committee judged the joint to be acceptable? That neither judged the joint to be acceptable?

c. What is the probability that the inspector and the committee disagreed? Agreed?

121 System components operating in series and parallel. Consider the two systems shown in the schematic at the top of the next page. System A operates properly only if all three components operate properly. (The three components are said to operate *in series*.) The probability of failure for system A components 1, 2, and 3 are .12, .09, and .11, respectively. Assume the components operate independently of each other. System B comprises two subsystems said to operate *in parallel*. Each subsystem has two components that operate in series. System B will operate properly as long as at least one of the subsystems functions properly. The probability of failure for each component in the system is .1. Assume the components operate independently of each other.

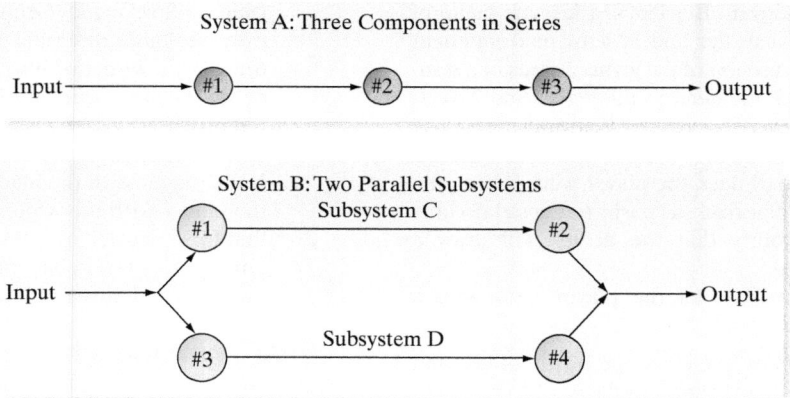

Figures for Exercise 121

a. Find the probability that system A operates properly.

b. What is the probability that at least one of the components in system A will fail and therefore that the system will fail?

c. Find the probability that system B operates properly.

d. Find the probability that exactly one subsystem in system B fails.

e. Find the probability that system B fails to operate properly.

f. How many parallel subsystems like the two shown here would be required to guarantee that the system operates properly at least 99% of the time?

122 Probability of winning a war. Before a country enters into a war, a prudent government will assess the cost, utility, and probability of a victory. University of Georgia professor P. L. Sullivan has developed a statistical model for determining the probability of winning a war based on a government's capabilities and resources (*Journal of Conflict Resolution,* Vol. 51, 2007). Now consider the recently ended U.S.-Iraq conflict. One researcher used the model to estimate that the probability of a successful regime change in Iraq was .70 prior to the start of the war. Of course, we now know that the successful regime change was achieved. However, the model also estimates that given the mission was extended to support a weak Iraqi government, the probability of ultimate success was only .26. Assume these probabilities are accurate.

a. Prior to the start of the U.S.-Iraq war, what was the probability that a successful regime change would not be achieved?

b. Given that the mission was extended to support a weak Iraqi government, what was the probability that a successful regime change would ultimately be achieved?

c. Suppose the probability of the United States extending the mission to support a weak Iraqi government had been .55. Find the probability that the mission would be extended and would result in a successful regime change.

123 Detecting traces of TNT. University of Florida researchers in the Department of Materials Science and Engineering have invented a technique to rapidly detect traces of TNT (*Today,* Spring 2005). The method, which involves shining a laser light on a potentially contaminated object, provides instantaneous results and gives no false positives. In this application, a false positive would occur if the laser light detects traces of TNT when, in fact, no TNT is actually present on the object. Let A be the event that the laser light detects traces of TNT. Let B be the event that the object contains no traces of TNT. The probability of a false positive is 0. Write this probability in terms of A and B using symbols such as $\cup$, $\cap$, and |.

Applying the Concepts—Advanced

124 Malfunctioning production lines. A manufacturing operation utilizes two production lines to assemble electronic fuses. Both lines produce fuses at the same rate and generally produce 2.5% defective fuses. However, production line 1 recently suffered mechanical difficulty and produced 6.0% defectives during a 3-week period. This situation was not known until several lots of electronic fuses produced in this period were shipped to customers. If one of the two fuses tested by a customer was found to be defective, what is the probability that the lot from which it came was produced on malfunctioning line 1? (Assume all the fuses in the lot were produced on the same line.)

125 Scrap rate of machine parts. A press produces parts used in the manufacture of large-screen plasma televisions. If the press is correctly adjusted, it produces parts with a scrap rate of 5%. If it is not adjusted correctly, it produces scrap at a 50% rate. From past company records, the machine is known to be correctly adjusted 90% of the time. A quality-control inspector randomly selects one part from those recently produced by the press and discovers it is defective. What is the probability that the machine is incorrectly adjusted?

126 Chance of winning at "craps." A version of the dice game "craps" is played in the following manner. A player starts by rolling two balanced dice. If the roll (the sum of the two numbers showing on the dice) results in a 7 or 11, the player wins. If the roll results in a 2 or 3 (called *craps*), the player loses. For any other roll outcome, the player continues to throw the dice until the original roll outcome recurs (in which case the player wins) or until a 7 occurs (in which case the player loses).

a. What is the probability that a player wins the game on the first roll of the dice?

b. What is the probability that a player loses the game on the first roll of the dice?

c. If the player throws a total of 4 on the first roll, what is the probability that the game ends (win or lose) on the next roll?

127 Chance of winning blackjack. Blackjack, a favorite game of gamblers, is played by a dealer and at least one opponent (called a *player*). In one version of the game, 2 cards of a standard 52-card bridge deck are dealt to the player and 2 cards to the dealer. For this exercise, assume that drawing an ace and a face card is called *blackjack*. If the dealer does not draw a blackjack and the player does, the player wins. If both the dealer and player draw blackjack, a "push" (i.e., a tie) occurs.

a. What is the probability that the dealer will draw a blackjack?

b. What is the probability that the player wins with a blackjack?

128 Strategy in the game "Go." "Go" is one of the oldest and most popular strategic board games in the world, especially in Japan and Korea. The University of Virginia requires MBA students to learn Go to understand how the Japanese conduct business. This two-player game is played on a flat surface marked with 19 vertical and 19 horizontal lines. The objective is to control territory by placing pieces, called *stones,* on vacant points on the board. Players alternate placing their stones. The player using black stones goes first, followed by the player using white stones. *Chance* (Summer 1995) published an article that investigated the advantage of playing first (i.e., using the black stones) in Go. The results of 577 games recently played by professional Go players were analyzed.

a. In the 577 games, the player with the black stones won 319 times, and the player with the white stones won 258 times. Use this information to assess the probability of winning when you play first in Go.

b. Professional Go players are classified by level. Group C includes the top-level players, followed by Group B (middle-level) and Group A (low-level) players. The previous table describes the number of games won by the player with the black stones, categorized by level of the black player and level of the opponent. Assess the probability of winning when you play first in Go for each combination of player and opponent level.

c. If the player with the black stones is ranked higher than the player with the white stones, what is the probability that black wins?

d. Given the players are of the same level, what is the probability that the player with the black stones wins?

Critical Thinking Challenges

129 "Let's Make a Deal." Marilyn vos Savant, who is listed in *Guinness Book of World Records Hall of Fame* for "Highest IQ," writes a weekly column in the Sunday newspaper supplement *Parade Magazine.* Her column, "Ask Marilyn," is devoted to games of skill, puzzles, and mind-bending riddles. In one issue (*Parade Magazine*, Feb. 24, 1991), vos Savant posed the following question:

Suppose you're on a game show, and you're given a choice of three doors. Behind one door is a car; behind the others, goats. You pick a door—say, #1—and the host, who knows what's behind the doors, opens another door—say #3—which has a goat. He then says to you, "Do you want to pick door #2?" Is it to your advantage to switch your choice?

Marilyn's answer: "Yes, you should switch. The first door has a $\frac{1}{3}$ chance of winning [the car], but the second has a $\frac{2}{3}$ chance [of winning the car]." Predictably, vos Savant's surprising answer elicited thousands of critical letters, many of them from PhD mathematicians, who disagreed with her. Who is correct, the PhDs or Marilyn?

130 Flawed Pentium computer chip. In October 1994, a flaw was discovered in the Pentium microchip installed in personal computers. The chip produced an incorrect result when dividing two numbers. Intel, the manufacturer of the Pentium chip, initially announced that such an error would occur once in 9 billion divisions, or "once in every 27,000 years" for a typical user; consequently, it did not immediately offer to replace the chip.

Depending on the procedure, statistical software packages (e.g., Minitab) may perform an extremely large number of divisions to produce the required output. For heavy users of the software, 1 billion divisions over a short time frame is not unusual. Will the flawed chip be a problem for a heavy Minitab user? [*Note:* Two months after the flaw was discovered, Intel agreed to replace all Pentium chips free of charge.]

Black Player Level	Opponent Level	Number of Wins	Number of Games
C	A	34	34
C	B	69	79
C	C	66	118
B	A	40	54
B	B	52	95
B	C	27	79
A	A	15	28
A	B	11	51
A	C	5	39
Totals		319	577

Source: Kim, J., & Kim, H. J. "The advantage of playing first in Go," *Chance,* Vol. 8, No. 3, Summer 1995, p. 26 (Table 3). Copyright © 1995 by the American Statistical Association. Reprinted with permission.

Activity 1 *Exit Polls:* **Conditional Probability**

Exit polls are conducted in selected locations as voters leave their polling places after voting. In addition to being used to predict the outcome of elections before the votes are counted, these polls are used to gauge tendencies among voters. The results are usually stated in terms of conditional probabilities.

The table on the next page shows the results of exit polling that suggest men were almost evenly spit on voting for John McCain or Barack Obama, while women were more likely to vote for Obama in the 2008 presidential election. In addition, the table also suggests that more women than men voted in the election. The six percentages in the last three columns represent conditional probabilities where the given event is gender.

2008 Presidential Election, Vote by Gender

	Obama	McCain	Other
Male (47%)	49%	48%	3%
Female (53%)	56%	43%	1%

Source: Data from CNN (www.cnn.com).

1. Find similar exit poll results where the voters are categorized by race, income, education, or some other criterion for a recent national, state, or local election. Choose two different examples and interpret the percentages given as probabilities, or conditional probabilities where appropriate.

2. Use the multiplicative rule of probability to find the probabilities related to the percentages given. [For example, in the table on the left find *P* (Obama and Male) using the multiplicative rule.] Then interpret each of these probabilities and use them to determine the total percentage of the electorate who voted for each candidate.

3. Describe a situation where a business might use a form of exit polling to gauge customer reaction to a new product or service. Identify the type of business, the product or service, the criterion used to categorize customers, and how the customers' reactions will be determined. Then describe how the results will be summarized as conditional probabilities. How might the results of the poll benefit the business?

References

Bennett, D. J. *Randomness.* Cambridge, Mass.: Harvard University Press, 1998.

Epstein, R. A. *The Theory of Gambling and Statistical Logic*, rev. ed. New York: Academic Press, 1977.

Feller, W. *An Introduction to Probability Theory and Its Applications*, 3rd ed., Vol. 1. New York: Wiley, 1968.

Lindley, D. V. *Making Decisions*, 2nd ed. London: Wiley, 1985.

Parzen, E. *Modern Probability Theory and Its Applications.* New York: Wiley, 1960.

Wackerly, D., Mendenhall, W., and Scheaffer, R. L. *Mathematical Statistics with Applications,* 7th ed. Boston: Duxbury, 2008.

Williams, B. *A Sampler on Sampling.* New York: Wiley, 1978.

Winkler, R. L. *An Introduction to Bayesian Inference and Decision.* New York: Holt, Rinehart and Winston, 1972.

Wright, G., & Ayton, P., eds. *Subjective Probability.* New York: Wiley, 1994.

Note: Automated commands for generating combinations and permutations are not available in SPSS.

Minitab: Combinations and Permutations

Combinations—Choosing *n* Elements from *N* Elements

Step 1 Click "Calc" from the main menu bar, and then select "Calculator."

Step 2 On the resulting dialog box, specify the column you want to store the result in, and then enter "COMBINATIONS(N,n)" in the "Expression" box. (See Figure M.1.)

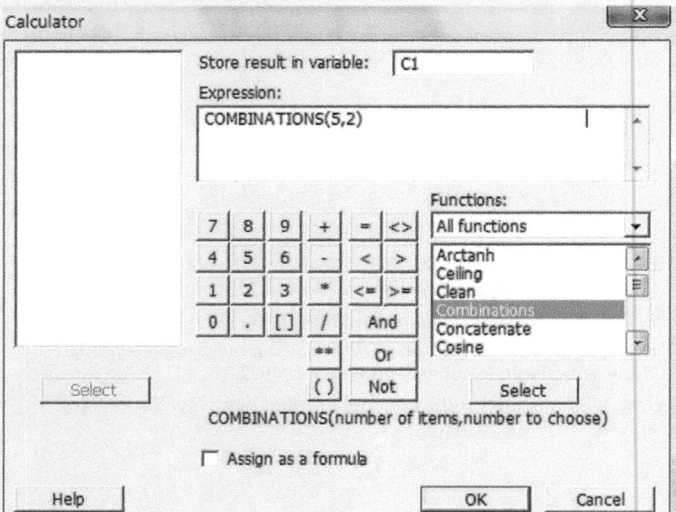

Figure M.1 Minitab calculator dialog box entries for combinations

Step 3 Specify the values of *N* and *n,* as shown in Figure M.1.

Step 4 Click "OK" and the result will appear in the specified column in the Minitab worksheet.

Permutations—Choosing *n* Elements from *N* Elements (See Appendix: Summation Notation for an application.)

Step 1 Click "Calc" from the main menu bar, and then select "Calculator."

Step 2 On the resulting dialog box, specify the column you want to store the result in, and then enter "PERMUTATIONS(N, n)" in the "Expression" box. (See Figure M.2.)

Step 3 Specify the values of *N* and *n,* as shown in Figure M.2.

Step 4 Click "OK" and the result will appear in the specified column in the Minitab worksheet.

Excel: Combinations and Permutations

Combinations—Choosing *n* Elements from *N* Elements

Step 1 Click on the cell in the Excel worksheet where you want the result to appear.

Step 2 In the formula bar, enter "=" followed by "COMBIN(N,n)."

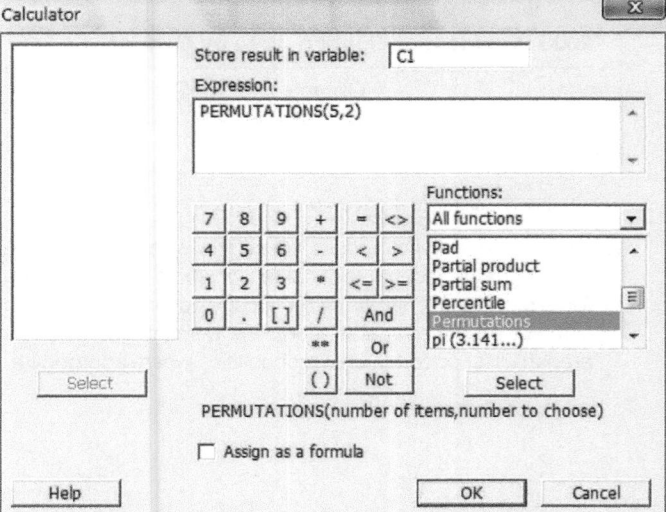

Figure M.2 Minitab calculator dialog box entries for permutations

Step 3 Specify the values of *N* and *n,* as shown in Figure E.1.

Step 4 Click "Enter" and the result will appear in the selected cell (see Figure E.1).

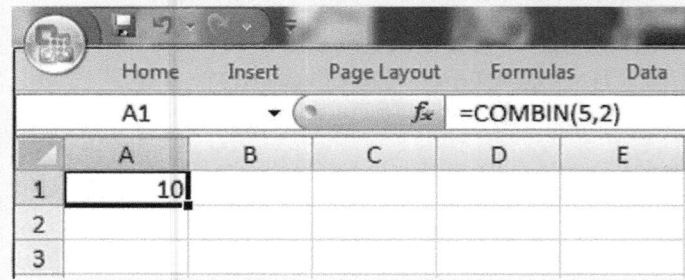

Figure E.1 Excel formula for combinations

Permutations—Choosing *n* Elements from *N* Elements (See Appendix: Summation Notation for an application.)

Step 1 Click on the cell in the Excel worksheet where you want the result to appear.

Step 2 In the formula bar, enter "=" followed by "PERMUT(N,n)."

Step 3 Specify the values of *N* and *n,* as shown in Figure E.2.

Step 4 Click "Enter" and the result will appear in the selected cell (see Figure E.2).

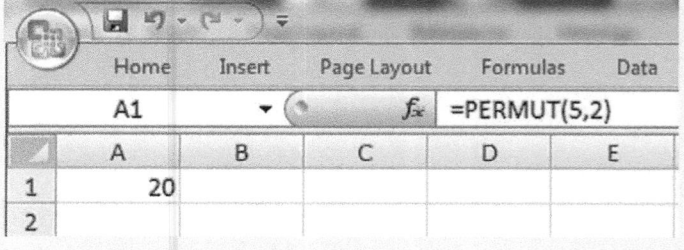

Figure E.2 Excel formula for permutations

TI-84 Graphing Calculator: Combinations and Permutations

Combinations — Choosing *n* Elements from *N* Elements

Step 1 Enter the value of *N*.

Step 2 Press **MATH**, and then select **PRB**.

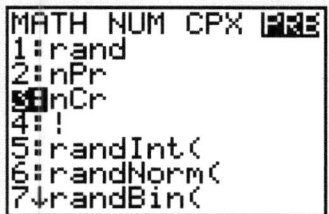

Step 3 Press **nCr** for combinations.

Step 4 Enter the value of *n;* press **ENTER.**

Permutations — Choosing *n* Elements from *N* Elements (See Appendix: Summation Notation for an application.)

Step 1 Enter the value of *N*.

Step 2 Press **MATH,** and then select **PRB**.

Step 3 Press **nPr** for permutations.

Step 4 Enter the value of *n;* press **ENTER.**

❑ Answers to Selected Exercises

1 a. .5 **b.** .3 **c.** .6 **3** $P(A) = .55$, $P(B) = .50$, $P(C) = .70$ **5 a.** 10 **b.** 20 **c.** 15,504 **7 a.** (B_1, B_2), (B_1, R_1), (B_1, R_2), (B_1, R_3), (B_2, R_1), (B_2, R_2), (B_2, R_3), (R_1, R_2), (R_1, R_3), (R_2, R_3) **b.** $P(E_i) = \frac{1}{10}$ **c.** $P(A) = \frac{1}{10}$, $P(B) = \frac{3}{5}$, $P(C) = \frac{3}{10}$ **9 a.** Brown, yellow, red, blue, orange, and green **b.** $P(\text{Br}) = 0.13$, $P(\text{Y}) = 0.14$, $P(\text{R}) = 0.13$, $P(\text{Bl}) = 0.24$, $P(\text{O}) = 0.2$, $P(\text{G}) = 0.16$ **c.** .13 **d.** .43 **e.** .76 **11** .0057 **13 a.** None, 1 or 2, 3–5, 6–9, 10 or more **b.** $P(\text{none}) = 0.19$, $P(1 \text{ or } 2) = 0.31$, $P(3{-}5) = 0.26$, $P(6{-}9) = 0.05$, $P(10 \text{ or more}) = 0.19$ **c.** .50 **15 a.** Certification mark on label **b.** .60 **c.** .16 **d.** .94 **17 a.** $\frac{1}{100} = .01$ **b.** .0095; yes **19 a.** $\frac{1}{8}$ **b.** 70 **c.** .5 **21** 455 **23 a.** 6; $(G_1 G_2 G_3)$, $(G_1 G_2 G_4)$, $(G_1 G_2 G_5)$, $(G_2 G_3 G_4)$, $(G_2 G_3 G_5)$, $(G_2 G_4 G_5)$ **b.** .282, .065, .339, .032, .008, .274 **c.** .686 **25 a.** 1 to 2 **b.** $\frac{1}{2}$ **c.** $\frac{2}{5}$ **27 a.** 32 **b.** $\frac{1}{32}$ **c.** 12 **d.** $\frac{12}{32} = .375$ **e.** .5 **29 b.** $P(A) = \frac{7}{8}$, $P(B) = \frac{1}{2}$, $P(A \cup B) = \frac{7}{8}$, $P(A^c) = \frac{1}{8}$, $P(A \cap B) = \frac{1}{2}$ **31 a.** $\frac{3}{4}$ **b.** $\frac{13}{20}$ **c.** 1 **d.** $\frac{2}{5}$ **e.** $\frac{1}{4}$ **f.** $\frac{7}{20}$ **g.** 1 **h.** $\frac{1}{4}$ **33 a.** .65 **b.** .72 **c.** .25 **d.** .08 **e.** .35 **f.** .72 **g.** 0 **h.** A and C, B and C, C and D **35 a.** $A \cap B$ **b.** A^c **c.** $C \cup B$ **d.** $B^c \cap A^c$ **37 a.** {L, W, B, N} **b.** .594, .189, .075, .142 **c.** .264 **d.** .669 **e.** .858 **39 a.** AC, AW, AF, IC, IW, and IF **b.** .148, .066, .426, .176, .052, .132 **c.** .640 **d.** .118 **e.** .176 **f.** .786 **g.** .676 **41 a.** $\frac{127}{244}$ **b.** $\frac{7}{244}$ **c.** $\frac{117}{244}$ **d.** $\frac{148}{244}$ **43 a.** $P \cap S \cap A$ **b.** $\frac{1}{5}$ **c.** $A \cup S$; $\frac{4}{5}$ **d.** $P \cap S$; $\frac{3}{10}$ **45 a.** .531 **b.** .75 **c.** .094 **47 a.** .09 **b.** .09 **c.** .84 **d.** No **e.** Column events not mutually exclusive **49 a.** .5 **b.** .25 **c.** No **51 a.** .08 **b.** .4 **c.** .52 **53 a.** .8, .7, .6 **b.** .25, .375, .375 **d.** No **55 a.** .37 **b.** .68 **c.** .15 **d.** .2206 **e.** 0 **f.** 0 **g.** No **57 a.** A and C, B and C **b.** None **c.** .65, .90 **59** .444 **61** .135 **63 a.** .055 **b.** .139 **c.** No **65 a.** .371 **b.** .209 **c.** Yes **67 a.** .406 **b.** .294 **69 a.** $P(A|I) = .9$, $P(B|I) = .95$, $P(A|I^c) = .2$, $P(B|I^c) = .1$ **b.** .855 **c.** .02 **d.** .995 **71 a.** .23 **b.** .729 **73** .60 **75 a.** $(.5)^{10} = .000977$ **b.** .00195 **c.** .99805 **77 a.** .225 **b.** .125 **c.** .35 **d.** .643 **e.** .357 **81 a.** .0788 **b.** .2545 **c.** Novice **83 a.** .52, .39, .09 **b.** .516 **85** No; $P(D|G > 60) = .1075$ **87 a.** Supplier 4; $P(S_4|D) = .7147$ **b.** Suppliers 4 or 6 **91 b.** .6 **93 a.** 0 **b.** No **95** .5 **97 a.** 0, .2, .9, 1, .7, .3, .4, 0 **b.** No; yes **c.** No; no **99 a.** E and D, P and P, M and O, T and C **b.** .325 **c.** .711 **101** .73 **103 a.** False **b.** True **c.** True **d.** False **105 a.** $B \cap C$ **b.** A^c **c.** $C \cup B$ **d.** $A \cap C^c$ **107 b.** .95 **c.** .25 **d.** .5 **109 a.** .684 **b.** .124 **c.** No **d.** .316 **e.** .717 **f.** .091 **111 a.** .00000625 **b.** .0135 **c.** Doubt validity of the manufacturer's claim **d.** No **113 a.** .006 **b.** .012 **c.** .018 **115 a.** .157 **b.** .029 **c.** .291 **d.** .222 **e.** .183 **117** .79 **119 a.** LLLL, LLLU, LLUL, LULL, ULLL, LLUU, LULU, LUUL, ULLU, ULUL, UULL, LUUU, ULUU, UULU, UUUL, UUUU **b.** $\frac{1}{16}$ **c.** $\frac{5}{16}$ **121 a.** .7127 **b.** .2873 **c.** .9639 **d.** .3078 **e.** .0361 **f.** 3 **123** $P(A|B) = 0$ **125** .526 **127 a.** .0362 **b.** .0352 **129** Marilyn

❑ Credits

❑ Technology Images

Random Variables and
Probability Distributions

From Chapter 4 of *Statistics for Business and Economics*, Twelfth Edition. James T. McClave, P. George Benson, Terry Sincich. Copyright © 2014 by Pearson Education, Inc. All rights reserved.

CONTENTS

Where We're Going

- Develop the notion of a random variable (1)
- Learn that numerical data are observed values of either discrete or continuous random variables (2, 5)
- Study two important types of random variables and their probability models: the binomial and normal models (3, 6, 7)
- Present some additional discrete and continuous random variables (4, 8)

■ Random Variables and Probability Distributions

STATISTICS in ACTION **Probability in a Reverse Cocaine Sting: Was Cocaine Really Sold?**

The American Statistician *described an interesting application of a discrete probability distribution in a case involving illegal drugs. It all started with a "bust" in a midsized Florida city. During the bust, police seized approximately 500 foil packets of a white, powdery substance, presumably cocaine. Since it is not a crime to buy or sell nonnarcotic cocaine look-alikes (e.g., inert powders), detectives had to prove that the packets actually contained cocaine in order to convict their suspects of drug trafficking. When the police laboratory randomly selected and chemically tested 4 of the packets, all 4 tested positive for cocaine. This finding led to the conviction of the traffickers.*

After the conviction, the police decided to use the remaining foil packets (i.e., those not tested) in reverse sting operations. Two of these packets were randomly selected and sold by undercover officers to a buyer. Between the sale and the arrest, however, the buyer disposed of the evidence. The key question is, Beyond a reasonable doubt, did the defendant really purchase cocaine?

In court, the defendant's attorney argued that his client should not be convicted, because the police could not prove that the missing foil packets contained cocaine. The police contended, however, that since 4 of the original packets tested positive for cocaine, the 2 packets sold in the reverse sting were also highly likely to contain cocaine. In this chapter, two Statistics in Action Revisited examples demonstrate how to use probability models to solve the dilemma posed by the police's reverse sting. (The case represented Florida's first cocaine-possession conviction without the actual physical evidence.) (*The American Statistician*, May 1991.)

STATISTICS in ACTION REVISITED

▫ Using the Binomial Model to Solve the Cocaine Sting Case
▫ Using the Hypergeometric Model to Solve the Cocaine Sting Case

The Consumer Price Index, the unemployment rate, the number of sales made in a week, and the yearly profit of a company are all examples of numerical measurements of some phenomenon. Thus, most experiments have sample points that correspond to values of some numerical variable.

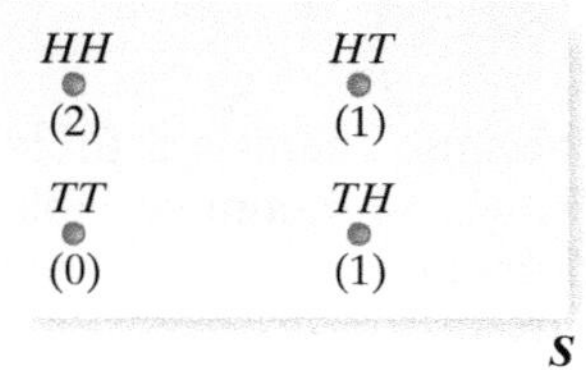

    To illustrate, consider a coin-tossing experiment. Figure 1 is a Venn diagram showing the sample points when two coins are tossed and the up faces (heads or tails) of the coins are observed. One possible numerical outcome is the total number of heads observed. These values (0, 1, or 2) are shown in parentheses on the Venn diagram, one numerical value associated with each sample point. In the jargon of probability, the variable "total number of heads observed when two coins are tossed" is called a *random variable.*

HH (2)	*HT* (1)
TT (0)	*TH* (1)

S

Figure 1

Venn diagram for coin-tossing experiment

> A **random variable** is a variable that assumes numerical values associated with the random outcomes of an experiment, where one (and only one) numerical value is assigned to each sample point.

    The term *random variable* is more meaningful than the term *variable* because the adjective *random* indicates that the coin-tossing experiment may result in one of the several possible values of the variable—0, 1, or 2—according to the *random* outcome of the experiment, *HH, HT, TH,* and *TT.* Similarly, if the experiment is to count the number of customers who use the drive-up window of a bank each day, the random variable (the number of customers) will vary from day to day, partly because of random phenomena that influence whether customers use the drive-up window. Thus, the possible values of this random variable range from 0 to the maximum number of customers the window could possibly serve in a day.

    We define two different types of random variables, *discrete* and *continuous,* in Section 1. Then we spend the remainder of this chapter discussing specific types of both discrete and continuous random variables and the aspects that make them important in business applications.

1   Two Types of Random Variables

Recall that the sample point probabilities corresponding to an experiment must sum to 1. Dividing one unit of probability among the sample points in a sample space and consequently assigning probabilities to the values of a random variable is not always easy. If the number of sample points can be completely listed, the job is straightforward. But if the experiment results in an infinite number of numerical sample points that are impossible to list, the task of assigning probabilities to the sample points is impossible without the aid of a probability model. The next three examples demonstrate the need for different probability models depending on the number of values that a random variable can assume.

Example   1

Values of a Discrete Random Variable—Wine Ratings

Problem A panel of 10 experts for the *Wine Spectator* (a national publication) is asked to taste a new white wine and assign a rating of 0, 1, 2, or 3. A score is then obtained by adding together the ratings of the 10 experts. How many values can this random variable assume?

Solution A sample point is a sequence of 10 numbers associated with the rating of each expert. For example, one sample point is

$$\{1, 0, 0, 1, 2, 0, 0, 3, 1, 0\}$$

The random variable assigns a score to each one of these sample points by adding the 10 numbers together. Thus, the smallest score is 0 (if all 10 ratings are 0), and the largest score is 30 (if all 10 ratings are 3). Because every integer between 0 and 30 is a possible score, the random variable denoted by the symbol x can assume 31 values. Note that the value of the random variable for the sample point above is $x = 8$.*

Look Back This is an example of a *discrete random variable* because there is a finite number of distinct possible values. Whenever all the possible values a random variable can assume can be listed (or counted), the random variable is discrete.

Example 2

Values of a Discrete Random Variable—EPA Application

Problem Suppose the Environmental Protection Agency (EPA) takes readings once a month on the amount of pesticide in the discharge water of a chemical company. If the amount of pesticide exceeds the maximum level set by the EPA, the company is forced to take corrective action and may be subject to penalty. Consider the random variable, x, the number of months before the company's discharge exceeds the EPA's maximum level. What values can x assume?

Solution The company's discharge of pesticide may exceed the maximum allowable level on the first month of testing, the second month of testing, and so on. It is possible that the company's discharge will *never* exceed the maximum level. Thus, the set of possible values for the number of months until the level is first exceeded is the set of all positive integers

$$1, 2, 3, 4, \ldots$$

Look Back If we can list the values of a random variable x, even though the list is never ending, we call the list **countable** and the corresponding random variable *discrete*. Thus, the number of months until the company's discharge first exceeds the limit is a *discrete random variable*.

Now Work Exercise 4

Example 3

Values of a Continuous Random Variable— Another EPA Application

Problem Refer to Example 2. A second random variable of interest is the amount x of pesticide (in milligrams per liter) found in the monthly sample of discharge waters from the chemical company. What values can this random variable assume?

Solution Unlike the *number* of months before the company's discharge exceeds the EPA's maximum level, the set of all possible values for the *amount* of discharge *cannot* be listed—that is, it is not countable. The possible values for the amounts of pesticide would correspond to the points on the interval between 0 and the largest possible value the amount of the discharge could attain, the maximum number of milligrams that could occupy 1 liter of volume. (Practically, the interval would be much smaller, say, between 0 and 500 milligrams per liter.)

Look Ahead When the values of a random variable are not countable but instead correspond to the points on some interval, we call it a *continuous random variable*. Thus, the *amount* of pesticide in the chemical plant's discharge waters is a *continuous random variable*.

Now Work Exercise 5

---

*The standard mathematical convention is to use a capital letter (e.g., X) to denote the theoretical random variable. The possible values (or realizations) of the random variable are typically denoted with a lowercase letter (e.g., x). Thus, in Example 1, the random variable X can take on the values $x = 0, 1, 2, \ldots, 30$. Because this notation can be confusing for introductory statistics students, we simplify the notation by using the lowercase x to represent the random variable throughout.

> Random variables that can assume a *countable* number (finite or infinite) of values are called **discrete.**

> Random variables that can assume values corresponding to any of the points contained in one or more intervals (i.e., values that are infinite and *uncountable*) are called **continuous.**

Several more examples of discrete random variables follow:

1. The number of sales made by a salesperson in a given week: $x = 0, 1, 2, \ldots$
2. The number of consumers in a sample of 500 who favor a particular product over all competitors: $x = 0, 1, 2, \ldots, 500$
3. The number of bids received in a bond offering: $x = 0, 1, 2, \ldots$
4. The number of errors on a page of an accountant's ledger: $x = 0, 1, 2, \ldots$
5. The number of customers waiting to be served in a restaurant at a particular time: $x = 0, 1, 2, \ldots$

Note that each of the examples of discrete random variables begins with the words "The number of...." This wording is very common because the discrete random variables most frequently observed are counts.

We conclude this section with some more examples of continuous random variables:

1. The length of time between arrivals at a hospital clinic: $0 \le x < \infty$ (infinity)
2. For a new apartment complex, the length of time from completion until a specified number of apartments are rented: $0 \le x < \infty$
3. The amount of carbonated beverage loaded into a 12-ounce can in a can-filling operation: $0 \le x \le 12$
4. The depth at which a successful oil-drilling venture first strikes oil: $0 \le x \le c$, where c is the maximum depth obtainable
5. The weight of a food item bought in a supermarket: $0 \le x \le 500$ [*Note*: Theoretically, there is no upper limit on x, but it is unlikely that it would exceed 500 pounds.]

Discrete random variables and their probability distributions are discussed in Part I—Sections 2–4. Continuous random variables and their probability distributions are the topic of Part II—Sections 5–8.

Exercises 1–10

Please be aware that some of the following problems may require knowledge of concepts that are not presented in this chapter.

Applying the Concepts—Basic

1 Types of random variables. Which of the following describe continuous random variables? Which describe discrete random variables?

a. The number of newspapers sold by the *New York Times* each month

b. The amount of ink used in printing a Sunday edition of the *New York Times*

c. The actual number of ounces in a 1-gallon bottle of laundry detergent

d. The number of defective parts in a shipment of nuts and bolts

e. The number of people collecting unemployment insurance each month

2 Types of finance random variables. Security analysts are professionals who devote full-time efforts to evaluating the investment worth of a narrow list of stocks. The following variables are of interest to security analysts. Which are discrete and which are continuous random variables?

a. The closing price of a particular stock on the New York Stock Exchange

b. The number of shares of a particular stock that are traded each business day

c. The quarterly earnings of a particular firm

d. The percentage change in yearly earnings between 2011 and 2012 for a particular firm

e. The number of new products introduced per year by a firm

f. The time until a pharmaceutical company gains approval from the U.S. Food and Drug Administration to market a new drug

3 NHTSA crash tests. The National Highway Traffic Safety Administration (NHTSA) does crash tests of new car models. The NHTSA developed a driver-side "star" scoring system, with results ranging from one star (*) to five stars (*****). The more stars in the rating, the better the level of crash protection in a head-on collision. Suppose that a car is selected from the data and its driver-side star rating is determined. Let x equal the number of stars in the rating. Is x a discrete or continuous random variable?

4 Customers in line at a Subway shop. The number of customers, x, waiting in line to order sandwiches at a Subway shop at noon is of interest to the store manager. What values can x assume? Is x a discrete or continuous random variable?

5 Executive Compensation Scoreboard. *Forbes'* publishes a 2011 "Executive Compensation Scoreboard." One variable saved in the file is the CEO's compensation (in $ millions) in 2011. Is x a discrete or continuous random variable?

Applying the Concepts—Intermediate

6 Banking. Give an example of a discrete random variable that would be of interest to a banker.

7 Economics. Give an example of a continuous random variable that would be of interest to an economist.

8 Hotel management. Give an example of a discrete random variable that would be of interest to the manager of a hotel.

9 Retailing. Give two examples of discrete random variables that would be of interest to the manager of a clothing store.

10 Stock market. Give an example of a continuous random variable that would be of interest to a stockbroker.

PART I: DISCRETE RANDOM VARIABLES

2 Probability Distributions for Discrete Random Variables

A complete description of a discrete random variable requires that we *specify the possible values the random variable can assume and the probability associated with each value.* To illustrate, consider Example 4.

Example	4

Finding a Probability Distribution—Coin-Tossing Experiment

HH	HT
$x = 2$	$x = 1$
TH	TT
$x = 1$	$x = 0$

S

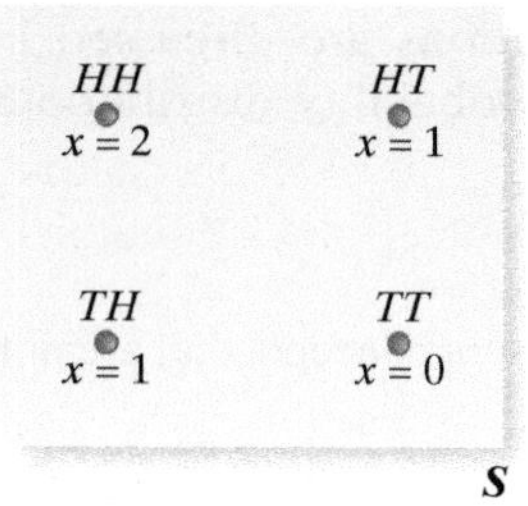

Figure 2

Venn diagram for the two-coin-toss experiment

Table 1

Probability Distribution for Coin-Toss Experiment: Tabular Form

x	$p(x)$
0	$\frac{1}{4}$
1	$\frac{1}{2}$
2	$\frac{1}{4}$

Problem Recall the experiment of tossing two coins (Section 1) and let x be the number of heads observed. Find the probability associated with each value of the random variable x, assuming the two coins are fair. Display these values in a table or graph.

Solution The sample space and sample points for this experiment are reproduced in Figure 2. Note that the random variable x can assume values 0, 1, and 2. The probability associated with each of the four sample points is $\frac{1}{4}$. Then, identifying the probabilities of the sample points associated with each of these values of x, we have

$$P(x = 0) = P(TT) = \tfrac{1}{4}$$
$$P(x = 1) = P(TH) + P(HT) = \tfrac{1}{4} + \tfrac{1}{4} = \tfrac{1}{2}$$
$$P(x = 2) = P(HH) = \tfrac{1}{4}$$

Thus, we now know the values the random variable can assume (0, 1, 2) and how the probability is *distributed over* these values $\left(\tfrac{1}{4}, \tfrac{1}{2}, \tfrac{1}{4}\right)$. This completely describes the random variable and is referred to as the *probability distribution,* denoted by the symbol $p(x)$.* The probability distribution for the coin-toss example is shown in tabular form in Table 1 and in graphical form in Figure 3. Because the probability distribution for a discrete random variable is concentrated at specific points (values of x), the graph in Figure 3a represents the probabilities as the heights of vertical lines over the corresponding values of x. Although the representation of the probability distribution as a histogram, as in Figure 3b, is less precise (because the probability is spread over a unit interval), the histogram representation will prove useful when we approximate probabilities of certain discrete random variables in Section 4.

*In standard mathematical notation, the probability that a random variable X takes on a value x is denoted $P(X = x) = p(x)$. Thus, $P(X = 0) = p(0), P(X = 1) = p(1)$, etc. In this introductory text, we adopt the simpler $p(x)$ notation.

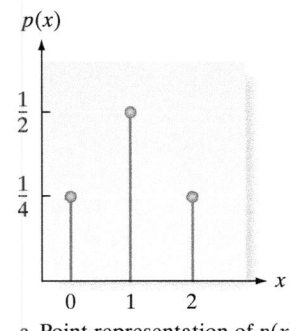
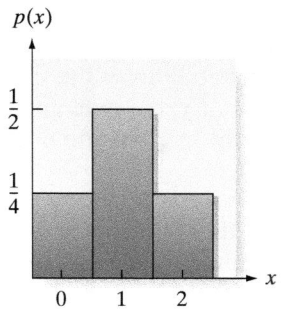

Figure 3
Probability distribution for coin-toss experiment: graphical form

a. Point representation of $p(x)$ b. Histogram representation of $p(x)$

Look Ahead We could also present the probability distribution for x as a formula, but this would unnecessarily complicate a very simple example. We give the formulas for the probability distributions of some common discrete random variables later in this chapter.

■ **Now Work Exercise 16**

> The **probability distribution** of a **discrete random variable** is a graph, table, or formula that specifies the probability associated with each possible value the random variable can assume.

Two requirements must be satisfied by all probability distributions for discrete random variables.

> **Requirements for the Probability Distribution of a Discrete Random Variable, x**
>
> 1. $p(x) \geq 0$ for all values of x
> 2. $\Sigma p(x) = 1$
>
> where the summation of $p(x)$ is over all possible values of x.*

Example 5

Probability Distribution from a Graph—Playing Craps

Problem Craps is a popular casino game in which a player throws two dice and bets on the outcome (the sum total of the dots showing on the upper faces of the two dice). Consider a $5 wager. On the first toss (called the *come-out* roll), if the total is 7 or 11 the roller wins $5. If the outcome is a 2, 3, or 12, the roller loses $5 (i.e., the roller wins −$5). For any other outcome (4, 5, 6, 8, 9, or 10), a *point* is established and no money is lost or won on that roll (i.e., the roller wins $0). In a computer simulation of repeated tosses of two dice, the outcome x of the come-out roll wager (−$5, $0, or +$5) was recorded. A relative frequency histogram summarizing the results is shown in Figure 4. Use the histogram to find the approximate probability distribution of x.

Solution The histogram shows that the relative frequencies of the outcomes $x = -\$5$, $x = \$0$, and $x = \$5$ are .1, .65, and .25, respectively. For example, in repeated tosses of

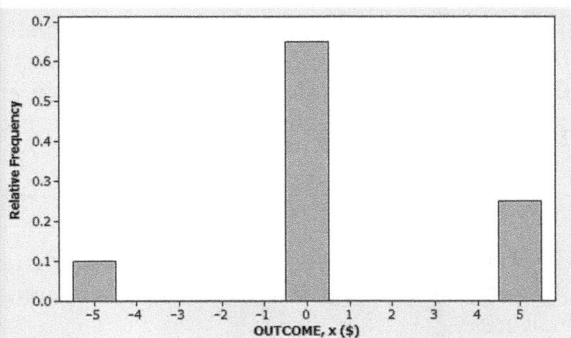

Figure 4
Histogram for $5 wager on come-out roll in craps

*Unless otherwise indicated, summations will always be over all possible values of x.

two dice, 25% of the outcomes resulted in a sum of 7 or 11 (a $5 win for the roller). Based on a long-run definition of probability, these relative frequencies estimate the probabilities of the three outcomes. Consequently, the approximate probability distribution of x, the outcome of the come-out wager in craps, is $p(-\$5) = .1$, $p(\$0) = .65$, and $p(\$5) = .25$. Note that these probabilities sum to 1.

Look Back When two dice are tossed, there are a total of 36 possible outcomes. (Can you list these outcomes, or sample points?) Of these, 4 result in a sum of 2, 3, or 12; 24 result in a sum of 4, 5, 6, 8, 9, or 10; and 8 result in a sum of 7 or 11. Using the rules of probability, you can show that the actual probability distribution for x is $p(-\$5) = 4/36 = .1111$, $p(\$0) = 24/36 = .6667$, and $p(\$5) = 8/36 = .2222$.

■ **Now Work Exercise 11**

Examples 4 and 5 illustrate how the probability distribution for a discrete random variable can be derived, but for many practical situations, the task is much more difficult. Fortunately, many experiments and associated discrete random variables observed in business possess identical characteristics. Thus, you might observe a random variable in a marketing experiment that possesses the same characteristics as a random variable observed in accounting, economics, or management. We classify random variables according to type of experiment, derive the probability distribution for each of the different types, and then use the appropriate probability distribution when a particular type of random variable is observed in a practical situation. The probability distributions for most commonly occurring discrete random variables have already been derived. This fact simplifies the problem of finding the appropriate probability distributions for the business analyst, as the next example illustrates.

Example 6
Probability Distribution Using a Formula—Texas Droughts

Problem A drought is a period of abnormal dry weather that causes serious problems in the farming industry of the region. University of Arizona researchers used historical annual data to study the severity of droughts in Texas. The researchers showed that the distribution of x, the number of consecutive years that must be sampled until a dry (drought) year is observed, can be modeled using the formula

$$p(x) = (.3)(.7)^{x-1}, x = 1, 2, 3, \ldots$$

Find the probability that exactly 3 years must be sampled before a drought year occurs.

Solution We want to find the probability that $x = 3$. Using the formula, we have

$$p(3) = (.3)(.7)^{3-1} = (.3)(.7)^2 = (.3)(.49) = .147$$

Thus, there is about a 15% chance that exactly 3 years must be sampled before a drought year occurs in Texas.

Look Back The probability of interest can also be derived using the principles of probability. The event of interest is $N_1N_2D_3$, where N_1 represents no drought occurs in the first sampled year, N_2 represents no drought occurs in the second sampled year, and D_3 represents a drought occurs in the third sampled year. The researchers discovered that the probability of a drought occurring in any sampled year is .3 (and, consequently, the probability of no drought occurring in any sampled year is .7). Using the multiplicative rule of probability for independent events, the probability of interest is $(.7)(.7)(.3) = .147$.

■ **Now Work Exercise 29**

Because probability distributions are analogous to relative frequency distributions, it should be no surprise that the mean and standard deviation are useful descriptive measures.

If a discrete random variable x were observed a very large number of times, and the data generated were arranged in a relative frequency distribution, the relative

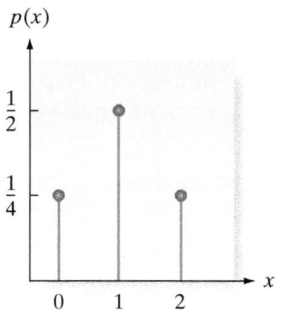

$p(x)$

Figure 5
Probability distribution
for a two-coin toss

frequency distribution would be indistinguishable from the probability distribution for the random variable. Thus, the probability distribution for a random variable is a theoretical model for the relative frequency distribution of a population. To the extent that the two distributions are equivalent (and we will assume they are), the probability distribution for x possesses a mean μ and a variance σ^2 that are identical to the corresponding descriptive measures for the population. How can you find the mean value for a random variable? We illustrate the procedure with an example.

Examine the probability distribution for x (the number of heads observed in the toss of two fair coins) in Figure 5. Try to locate the mean of the distribution intuitively. We may reason that the mean μ of this distribution is equal to 1 as follows: In a large number of experiments—say, $100,000-\frac{1}{4}$ (or 25,000) should result in $x = 0, \frac{1}{2}$ (or 50,000) in $x = 1$, and $\frac{1}{4}$ (or 25,000) in $x = 2$ heads. Therefore, the average number of heads is

$$\mu = \frac{0(25,000) + 1(50,000) + 2(25,000)}{100,000} = 0\left(\tfrac{1}{4}\right) + 1\left(\tfrac{1}{2}\right) + 2\left(\tfrac{1}{4}\right) = 0 + \tfrac{1}{2} + \tfrac{1}{2} = 1$$

Note that to get the population mean of the random variable x, we multiply each possible value of x by its probability $p(x)$ and then sum this product over all possible values of x. The *mean of x* is also referred to as the *expected value of x*, denoted $E(x)$.

> The **mean**, or **expected value**, of a discrete random variable x is
> $$\mu = E(x) = \sum xp(x)$$

Expected is a mathematical term and should not be interpreted as it is typically used. Specifically, a random variable might never be equal to its "expected value." Rather, the expected value is the mean of the probability distribution or a measure of its central tendency. You can think of μ as the mean value of x in a *very large* (actually, *infinite*) number of repetitions of the experiment, where the values of x occur in proportions equivalent to the probabilities of x.

Example	7

Finding an Expected Value—An Insurance Application

Problem Suppose you work for an insurance company, and you sell a $10,000 one-year term insurance policy at an annual premium of $290. Actuarial tables show that the probability of death during the next year for a person of your customer's age, sex, health, etc., is .001. What is the expected gain (amount of money made by the company) for a policy of this type?

Solution The experiment is to observe whether the customer survives the upcoming year. The probabilities associated with the two sample points, Live and Die, are .999 and .001, respectively. The random variable you are interested in is the gain x, which can assume the values shown in the following table.

Gain, x	Sample Point	Probability
$290	Customer lives	.999
−$9,710	Customer dies	.001

If the customer lives, the company gains the $290 premium as profit. If the customer dies, the gain is negative because the company must pay $10,000, for a net "gain" of $(290 - 10,000) = -\$9,710$. The expected gain is therefore

$$\mu = E(x) = \sum xp(x)$$
$$= (290)(.999) + (-9,710)(.001) = \$280$$

In other words, if the company were to sell a very large number of one-year $10,000 policies to customers possessing the characteristics previously described, it would (on the average) net $280 per sale in the next year.

Look Back Note that $E(x)$ need not equal a possible value of x—that is, the expected value is \$280, but x will equal either \$290 or $-\$9,710$ each time the experiment is performed (a policy is sold and a year elapses). The expected value is a measure of central tendency—and in this case represents the average over a very large number of one-year policies—but is not a possible value of x.

■ **Now Work Exercise 32a**

The mean and other measures of central tendency tell only part of the story about a set of data. The same is true about probability distributions. We need to measure variability as well. Because a probability distribution can be viewed as a representation of a population, we will use the population variance to measure its variability.

The *population variance* σ^2 is defined as the average of the squared distance of x from the population mean μ. Because x is a random variable, the squared distance, $(x - \mu)^2$, is also a random variable. Using the same logic used to find the mean value of x, we find the mean value of $(x - \mu)^2$ by multiplying all possible values of $(x - \mu)^2$ by $p(x)$ and then summing over all possible x values.* This quantity,

$$E[(x - \mu)^2] = \sum (x - \mu)^2 p(x)$$

is also called the *expected value of the squared distance from the mean;* that is, $\sigma^2 = E[(x - \mu)^2]$. The standard deviation of x is defined as the square root of the variance σ^2.

The **variance** of a **discrete random variable** x is

$$\sigma^2 = E[(x - \mu)^2] = \sum(x - \mu)^2 p(x)$$

The **standard deviation** of a **discrete random variable** is equal to the square root of the variance, i.e., $\sigma = \sqrt{\sigma^2} = \sqrt{\sum(x - \mu)^2 \, p(x)}$.

Knowing the mean μ and standard deviation σ of the probability distribution of x, in conjunction with Chebyshev's Rule and the Empirical Rule, we can make statements about the likelihood that values of x will fall within the intervals $\mu \pm \sigma$, $\mu \pm 2\sigma$, and $\mu \pm 3\sigma$. These probabilities are given in the box.

Probability Rules for a Discrete Random Variable

Let x be a discrete random variable with probability distribution $p(x)$, mean μ, and standard deviation σ. Then, depending on the shape of $p(x)$, the following probability statements can be made:

	Chebyshev's Rule	Empirical Rule
	Applies to any probability distribution (see Figure 6a)	Applies to probability distributions that are mound-shaped and symmetric (see Figure 6b)
$P(\mu - \sigma < x < \mu + \sigma)$	≥ 0	$\approx .68$
$P(\mu - 2\sigma < x < \mu + 2\sigma)$	$\geq \frac{3}{4}$	$\approx .95$
$P(\mu - 3\sigma < x < \mu + 3\sigma)$	$\geq \frac{8}{9}$	≈ 1.00

---

*It can be shown that $E[(x - \mu^2)] = E(x^2) - \mu^2$, where $E(x^2) = \sum x^2 p(x)$. Note the similarity between this expression and the shortcut formula $\sum(x - \bar{x})^2 = \sum x^2 - \frac{(\sum x)^2}{n}$.

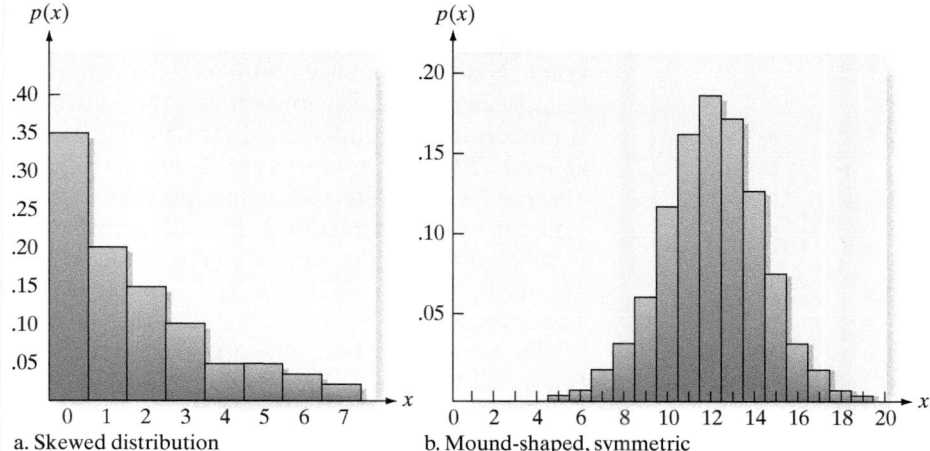

Figure 6

Shapes of two probability distributions for a discrete random variable x

a. Skewed distribution

b. Mound-shaped, symmetric

Example 8

Finding μ and σ—Internet Business Venture

Problem Suppose you invest a fixed sum of money in each of five Internet business ventures. Assume you know that 70% of such ventures are successful, the outcomes of the ventures are independent of one another, and the probability distribution for the number, x, of successful ventures out of five is

x	0	1	2	3	4	5
$p(x)$	.002	.029	.132	.309	.360	.168

a. Find $\mu = E(x)$. Interpret the result.

b. Find $\sigma = \sqrt{E[(x - \mu)^2]}$. Interpret the result.

c. Graph $p(x)$. Locate μ and the interval $\mu \pm 2\sigma$ on the graph. Use either Chebyshev's Rule or the Empirical Rule to approximate the probability that x falls in this interval. Compare this result with the actual probability.

d. Would you expect to observe fewer than two successful ventures out of five?

Solution

a. Applying the formula,

$$\mu = E(x) = \sum xp(x) = 0(.002) + 1(.029) + 2(.132) + 3(.309)$$
$$+ 4(.360) + 5(.168) = 3.50$$

On average, the number of successful ventures out of five will equal 3.5. Remember that this expected value has meaning only when the experiment—investing in five Internet business ventures—is repeated a large number of times.

b. Now we calculate the variance of x:

$$\sigma^2 = E[(x - \mu)^2] = \sum (x - \mu)^2 p(x)$$
$$= (0 - 3.5)^2(.002) + (1 - 3.5)^2(.029) + (2 - 3.5)^2(.132)$$
$$+ (3 - 3.5)^2(.309) + (4 - 3.5)^2(.360) + (5 - 3.5)^2(.168)$$
$$= 1.05$$

Thus, the standard deviation is

$$\sigma = \sqrt{\sigma^2} = \sqrt{1.05} = 1.02$$

This value measures the spread of the probability distribution of x, the number of successful ventures out of five. A more useful interpretation is obtained by answering parts **c** and **d**.

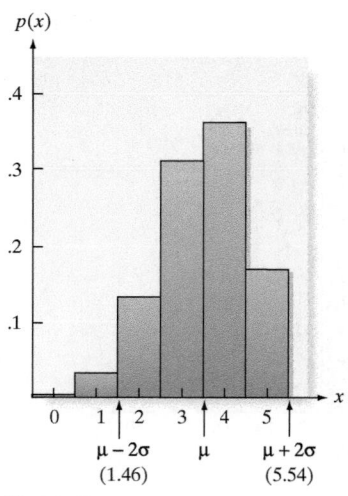

$p(x)$

Figure 7
Graph of $p(x)$ for Example 8

c. The graph of $p(x)$ in histogram form is shown in Figure 7 with the mean μ and the interval $\mu \pm 2\sigma = 3.50 \pm 2(1.02) = 3.50 \pm 2.04 = (1.46, 5.54)$ shown on the graph. Note particularly that $\mu = 3.5$ locates the center of the probability distribution. Because this distribution is a theoretical relative frequency distribution that is moderately mound-shaped (see Figure 7), we expect (from Chebyshev's Rule) at least 75% and, more likely (from the Empirical Rule), approximately 95% of observed x values to fall in the interval $\mu \pm 2\sigma$—that is, between 1.46 and 5.54. You can see from Figure 7 that the actual probability that x falls in the interval $\mu \pm 2\sigma$ includes the sum of $p(x)$ for the values $x = 2$, $x = 3$, $x = 4$, and $x = 5$. This probability is $p(2) + p(3) + p(4) + p(5) = .132 + .309 + .360 + .168 = .969$. Therefore, 96.9% of the probability distribution lies within 2 standard deviations of the mean. This percentage is consistent with both Chebyshev's Rule and the Empirical Rule.

d. Fewer than two successful ventures out of five implies that $x = 0$ or $x = 1$. Because both these values of x lie outside the interval $\mu \pm 2\sigma$, we know from the Empirical Rule that such a result is unlikely (approximate probability of .05). The exact probability, $P(x \le 1)$, is $p(0) + p(1) = .002 + .029 = .031$. Consequently, in a single experiment where we invest in five Internet business ventures, we would not expect to observe fewer than two successful ones.

■ **Now Work Exercise 17**

Exercises 11–39

Please be aware that some of the following problems may require knowledge of concepts that are not presented in this chapter.

Learning the Mechanics

11 A discrete random variable x can assume five possible values: 20, 21, 22, 23, and 24. The following Minitab histogram shows the likelihood of each value.
  a. What is $p(22)$?
  b. What is the probability that x equals 20 or 24?
  c. What is $P(x \le 23)$?

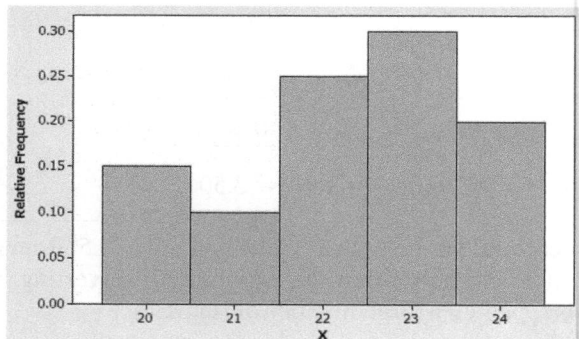

12 The random variable x has the following discrete probability distribution:

x	1	3	5	7	9
$p(x)$	.1	.2	.4	.2	.1

  a. List the values x may assume.
  b. What value of x is most probable?
  c. Display the probability distribution as a graph.
  d. Find $P(x = 7)$.
  e. Find $P(x \ge 5)$.
  f. Find $P(x > 2)$.
  g. Find $E(x)$.

13 A discrete random variable x can assume five possible values: 2, 3, 5, 8, and 10. Its probability distribution is shown here:

x	2	3	5	8	10
$p(x)$	.15	.10	–	.25	.25

  a. What is $p(5)$?
  b. What is the probability that x equals 2 or 10?
  c. What is $P(x \le 8)$?

14 Explain why each of the following is or is not a valid probability distribution for a discrete random variable x:

a.

x	0	1	2	3
$p(x)$	.1	.3	.3	.2

b.

x	−2	−1	0
$p(x)$	.25	.50	.25

c.

x	4	9	20
$p(x)$	−.3	.4	.3

d.

x	2	3	5	6
$p(x)$	.15	.15	.45	.35

15 A die is tossed. Let x be the number of spots observed on the upturned face of the die.
  a. Find the probability distribution of x and display it in tabular form.
  b. Display the probability distribution of x in graphical form.

16 Toss three fair coins and let x equal the number of heads observed.
  a. Identify the sample points associated with this experiment and assign a value of x to each sample point.

b. Calculate $p(x)$ for each value of x.
c. Construct a graph for $p(x)$.
d. What is $P(x = 2 \text{ or } x = 3)$?

🔘 Applet Exercise 1

Use the applet *Random Numbers* to generate a list of 25 numbers between 1 and 3, inclusive. Let x represent a number chosen from this list.

a. What are the possible values of x?
b. Write a probability distribution for x in table form.
c. Use the probability distribution in part **b** to find the expected value of x.
d. Let y be a number randomly chosen from the set $\{1, 2, 3\}$. Write a probability distribution for y in table form and use it to find the expected value of y.
e. Compare the expected values of x and y in parts **c** and **d**. Why should these two numbers be approximately the same?

🔘 Applet Exercise 2

Run the applet *Simulating the Probability of a Head with a Fair Coin* 10 times with $n = 2$, resetting between runs, to simulate flipping two coins 10 times. Count and record the number of heads each time. Let x represent the number of heads on a single flip of the two coins.

a. What are the possible values of x?
b. Use the results of the simulation to write a probability distribution for x in table form and then use it to find the expected value of x.
c. Explain why the expected value in part **b** should be close to 1.

17 Consider the probability distribution shown here:

x	-4	-3	-2	-1	0	1	2	3	4
$p(x)$	.02	.07	.10	.15	.30	.18	.10	.06	.02

a. Calculate μ, σ^2, and σ.
b. Graph $p(x)$. Locate μ, $\mu - 2\sigma$, and $\mu + 2\sigma$ on the graph.
c. What is the probability that x is in the interval $\mu \pm 2\sigma$?

18 Consider the probability distribution for the random variable x shown here:

x	10	20	30	40	50	60
$p(x)$	.05	.20	.30	.25	.10	.10

a. Find μ, σ^2, and σ.
b. Graph $p(x)$.
c. Locate μ and the interval $\mu \pm 2\sigma$ on your graph. What is the probability that x will fall within the interval $\mu \pm 2\sigma$?

19 Consider the probability distributions shown here:

x	0	1	2	y	0	1	2
$p(x)$	.3	.4	.3	$p(y)$	.1	.8	.1

a. Use your intuition to find the mean for each distribution. How did you arrive at your choice?

b. Which distribution appears to be more variable? Why?
c. Calculate μ and σ^2 for each distribution. Compare these answers to your answers in parts **a** and **b**.

Applying the Concepts—Basic

20 Size of TV households. According to Nielsen's *Television Audience Report, 2010 & 2011*, 26% of all U.S. TV households have a size of 1 person, 32% have a household size of 2, 17% have a household size of 3, and 25% have a household size of 4 or more. Let x represent the size (number of people) in a randomly selected TV household.

a. List the possible values of the discrete random variable x.
b. What is the probability that $x = 1$?
c. What is the probability that $x \geq 4$?
d. Explain why you cannot compute $E(x)$.

21 NHTSA crash tests. Refer to the NHTSA crash tests of new car models, Exercise 3. A summary of the driver-side star ratings for the 98 cars in the file is reproduced in the accompanying Minitab printout. Assume that one of the 98 cars is selected at random and let x equal the number of stars in the car's driver-side star rating.

Tally for Discrete Variables: DRIVSTAR

DRIVSTAR	Count	Percent
2	4	4.08
3	17	17.35
4	59	60.20
5	18	18.37
N=	98	

a. Use the information in the printout to find the probability distribution for x.
b. Find $P(x = 5)$.
c. Find $P(x \leq 2)$.
d. Find $\mu = E(x)$ and practically interpret the result.

22 Ages of "dot-com" employees. The age distribution for the employees of a highly successful "dot-com" company headquartered in Atlanta is shown in the next table. An employee is to be randomly selected from this population.

Age	20 21 22 23 24 25 26 27 28 29 30 31 32 33
Proportion	.02 .04 .05 .07 .04 .02 .07 .02 .11 .07 .09 .13 .15 .12

Source: Data provided by P. George Benson, University of Charleston.

a. Can the relative frequency distribution in the table be interpreted as a probability distribution? Explain.
b. Graph the probability distribution.
c. What is the probability that the randomly selected employee is over 30 years of age? Over 40 years of age? Under 30 years of age?
d. What is the probability that the randomly selected employee will be 25 or 26 years old?

23 Downloading "apps" to your cell phone. According to an August 2011 survey by the Pew Internet & American Life Project, nearly 40% of adult cell phone owners have downloaded an application ("app") to their cell phone. The next table gives the probability distribution for x, the number of "apps" used at least once a week by cell phone owners who have downloaded an "app" to their phone. (The probabilities in the table are based on information from the Pew Internet & American Life Project survey.)

Number of "Apps" Used, x	p(x)
0	.17
1	.10
2	.11
3	.11
4	.10
5	.10
6	.07
7	.05
8	.03
9	.02
10	.02
11	.02
12	.02
13	.02
14	.01
15	.01
16	.01
17	.01
18	.01
19	.005
20	.005

a. Show that the properties of a probability distribution for a discrete random variable are satisfied.
b. Find $P(x \geq 10)$.
c. Find the mean and variance of x.
d. Give an interval that will contain the value of x with a probability of at least .75.

24 **Choosing portable grill displays.** The *Journal of Consumer Research* (Mar. 2003) did a marketing study of influencing consumer choices by offering undesirable alternatives. Each of 124 college students selected showroom displays for portable grills. Five different displays (representing five different-sized grills) were available, but the students were instructed to select only three displays in order to maximize purchases of Grill #2 (a smaller-sized grill). The table shows the grill display combinations and the number of times each was selected by the 124 students. Suppose one of the 124 students is selected at random. Let x represent the sum of the grill numbers selected by this student. (This value is an indicator of the size of the grills selected.)
a. Find the probability distribution for x.
b. What is the probability that x exceeds 10?

Grill Display Combination	Number of Students
1-2-3	35
1-2-4	8
1-2-5	42
2-3-4	4
2-3-5	1
2-4-5	34

Source: Based on Hamilton, R. W. "Why do people suggest what they do not want? Using context effects to influence others' choices," *Journal of Consumer Research*, Vol. 29, Mar. 2003 (Table 1).

25 **Do social robots walk or roll?** The *International Conference on Social Robotics* (Vol. 6414, 2010) did a study of the trend in the design of social robots. In a random sample

of 106 social (or service) robots designed to entertain, educate, and care for human users, 63 were built with legs only, 20 with wheels only, 8 with both legs and wheels, and 15 with neither legs nor wheels. Assume the following: Of the 63 robots with legs only, 50 have two legs, 5 have three legs, and 8 have four legs; of the 8 robots with both legs and wheels, all 8 have two legs. Suppose one of the 106 social robots is randomly selected. Let x equal the number of legs on the robot.
a. List the possible values of x.
b. Find the probability distribution of x.
c. Find $E(x)$ and give a practical interpretation of its value.

26 **Predicting when a Florida hurricane occurs.** The *Southeastern Geographer* (Summer 2009) did a comprehensive analysis of damages caused by Florida hurricanes. In an effort to minimize the monetary losses that result from a devastating Florida hurricane, part of the researchers' analysis included a graphic showing the sequence number of tropical storms within a season that are most likely to develop into a hurricane. Data for 67 hurricanes are summarized in the table. Let x represent the sequence number of a Florida tropical storm within a season that develops into a hurricane.

HCANE

Sequence of Storm	Number That Develop into Hurricanes
1	4
2	10
3	5
4	6
5	11
6	5
7	5
8	5
9	4
10	2
11	5
12	1
13	1
14	1
15	1
22	1

Source: Based on Malmstadt, J., Scheitlin, K., & Elsner, J. "Florida Hurricanes and Damage Costs," *Southeastern Geographer*, Vol. 49, No. 2, Summer 2009 (adapted from Figure 3).

a. Explain why x represents a discrete random variable.
b. Specify the probability distribution for x.
c. Find $P(x = 5)$.
d. Find $P(x < 5)$.
e. Find $E(x)$ and interpret the result.
f. Is it likely to observe a hurricane after the 15th tropical storm of the season? Explain.

Applying the Concepts—Intermediate

27 **Solar energy cells.** According to *Wired* (June 2008), 35% of the world's solar energy cells are manufactured in China. Consider a random sample of five solar energy cells and let x represent the number in the sample that are manufactured in China. In the next section, we show that the probability distribution for x is given by the formula,

$$p(x) = \frac{(5!)(.35)^x(.65)^{5-x}}{(x!)(5-x)!}, \text{ where}$$

$$n! = (n)(n-1)(n-2)\cdots(2)(1)$$

a. Explain why x is a discrete random variable.
b. Find $p(x)$ for $x = 0, 1, 2, 3, 4,$ and 5.
c. Show that the properties for a discrete probability distribution are satisfied.
d. Find the probability that at least four of the five solar energy cells in the sample are manufactured in China.

28 USDA chicken inspection. One in every 100 slaughtered chickens passes USDA inspection with fecal contamination. Consider a random sample of three slaughtered chickens that all pass USDA inspection. Let x equal the number of chickens in the sample that have fecal contamination.
a. Find $p(x)$ for $x = 0, 1, 2, 3$.
b. Graph $p(x)$.
c. Find $P(x \le 1)$.

29 Contaminated gun cartridges. A weapons manufacturer
[NW] uses a liquid propellant to produce gun cartridges. During the manufacturing process, the propellant can get mixed with another liquid to produce a contaminated cartridge. A University of South Florida statistician, hired by the company to investigate the level of contamination in the stored cartridges, found that 23% of the cartridges in a particular lot were contaminated. Suppose you randomly sample (without replacement) gun cartridges from this lot until you find a contaminated one. Let x be the number of cartridges sampled until a contaminated one is found. It is known that the probability distribution for x is given by the formula

$$p(x) = (.23)(.77)^{x-1}, x = 1, 2, 3, \ldots$$

a. Find $p(1)$. Interpret this result.
b. Find $p(5)$. Interpret this result.
c. Find $P(x \ge 2)$. Interpret this result.

30 The "last name" effect in purchasing. The *Journal of Consumer Research* (August 2011) published a study demonstrating the "last name" effect—i.e., the tendency for consumers with last names that begin with a later letter of the alphabet to purchase an item before consumers with last names that begin with earlier letters. To facilitate the analysis, the researchers assigned a number, x, to each consumer based on the first letter of the consumer's last name. For example, last names beginning with "A" were assigned $x = 1$; last names beginning with "B" were assigned $x = 2$; and last names beginning with "Z" were assigned $x = 26$.
a. If the first letters of consumers' last names are equally likely, find the probability distribution for x.
b. Find $E(x)$ using the probability distribution, part **a**. If possible, give a practical interpretation of this value.
c. Do you believe the probability distribution, part **a**, is realistic? Explain. How might you go about estimating the true probability distribution for x?

31 Mailrooms contaminated with anthrax. During autumn 2001, there was a highly publicized outbreak of anthrax cases among U.S. Postal Service workers. In *Chance* (Spring 2002), research statisticians discussed the problem of sampling mailrooms for the presence of anthrax spores. Let x equal the number of mailrooms contaminated with anthrax spores in a random sample of n mailrooms selected from a population of N mailrooms. The researchers showed that the probability distribution for x is given by the formula

$$p(x) = \frac{\binom{k}{x}\binom{N-k}{n-x}}{\binom{N}{n}}$$

where k is the number of contaminated mailrooms in the population. (In Section 4 we identify this probability distribution as the *hypergeometric distribution*.) Suppose $N = 100$, $n = 3$, and $k = 20$.
a. Find $p(0)$.   **b.** Find $p(1)$.
c. Find $p(2)$.   **d.** Find $p(3)$.

32 Investment risk analysis. The risk of a portfolio of financial assets is sometimes called *investment risk*. In general, investment risk is typically measured by computing the variance or standard deviation of the probability distribution that describes the decision maker's potential outcomes (gains or losses). The greater the variation in potential outcomes, the greater the uncertainty faced by the decision maker; the smaller the variation in potential outcomes, the more predictable the decision maker's gains or losses. The two discrete probability distributions given in the next table were developed from historical data. They describe the potential total physical damage losses next year to the fleets of delivery trucks of two different firms.

Firm A		Firm B	
Loss Next Year	Probability	Loss Next Year	Probability
$ 0	.01	$ 0	.00
500	.01	200	.01
1,000	.01	700	.02
1,500	.02	1,200	.02
2,000	.35	1,700	.15
2,500	.30	2,200	.30
3,000	.25	2,700	.30
3,500	.02	3,200	.15
4,000	.01	3,700	.02
4,500	.01	4,200	.02
5,000	.01	4,700	.01

[NW] **a.** Verify that both firms have the same expected total physical damage loss.
b. Compute the standard deviation of each probability distribution and determine which firm faces the greater risk of physical damage to its fleet next year.

33 Ryder Cup miracle in golf. The Ryder Cup is a 3-day golf tournament played between a team of golf professionals from the United States and a team from Europe. A total of 28 matches are played between the teams; one point is awarded to the team winning a match and half a point is awarded to each team if the match ends in a tie (draw). The team with the most points wins the tournament. In 1999, the United States was losing 10 points to 6 when it miraculously won 8.5 of a possible 12 points on the last day of the tournament to seal the win. On the last day, 12 single matches are played. A total of 8.5 points can be won in a variety of ways, as shown in the next table. Given one team scores at least 8.5 points on the last day of the tournament, *Chance* (Fall 2009) determined the probabilities of each of these outcomes assuming each team is equally likely to win a match. Let x be the points scored by the winning team on the last day of the tournament when the team scores at least 8.5 points. Find the probability distribution of x.

Wins	Ties	Points	Probability
5	7	8.5	.000123
6	5	8.5	.008823
6	6	9.0	.000456
7	3	8.5	.128030
7	4	9.0	.020086
7	5	9.5	.001257
8	1	8.5	.325213
8	2	9.0	.153044
8	3	9.5	.032014
8	4	10.0	.002514
9	0	9.0	.115178
9	1	9.5	.108400
9	2	10.0	.032901
9	3	10.5	.003561
10	0	10.0	.034552
10	1	10.5	.021675
10	2	11.0	.003401
11	0	11.0	.006284
11	1	11.0	.001972
12	0	12.0	.000518

34 **Stock market participation and IQ.** *The Journal of Finance* (December 2011) did a study of whether the decision to invest in the stock market is dependent on IQ. An IQ score (from a low score of 1 to a high score of 9) was determined for each in a sample of 158,044 Finnish citizens. Also recorded was whether or not the citizen invested in the stock market. The accompanying table gives the number of Finnish citizens in each IQ score/investment category. Which group of Finnish citizens (market investors or noninvestors) has the highest average IQ score?

IQ Score	Invest in Market	No Investment	Totals
1	893	4,659	5,552
2	1,340	9,409	10,749
3	2,009	9,993	12,002
4	5,358	19,682	25,040
5	8,484	24,640	33,124
6	10,270	21,673	31,943
7	6,698	11,260	17,958
8	5,135	7,010	12,145
9	4,464	5,067	9,531
Totals	44,651	113,393	158,044

Source: Based on Grinblatt, M., Keloharju, M., & Linnainaa, J. "IQ and Stock Market Participation," *The Journal of Finance*, Vol. 66, No. 6, December 2011 (data from Table 1 and Figure 1).

35 **Expected loss due to flood damage.** The National Weather Service issues precipitation forecasts that indicate the likelihood of measurable precipitation ($\geq$ .01 inch) at a specific point (the official rain gauge) during a given time period. Suppose that if a measurable amount of rain falls during the next 24 hours, a river will reach flood stage and a business will incur damages of $300,000.

The National Weather Service has indicated that there is a 30% chance of a measurable amount of rain during the next 24 hours.
  a. Construct the probability distribution that describes the potential flood damages.
  b. Find the firm's expected loss due to flood damage.

36 **Expected Lotto winnings.** Most states offer weekly lotteries to generate revenue for the state. Despite the long odds of winning, residents continue to gamble on the lottery each week. The chance of winning Florida's Pick-6 Lotto game is 1 in approximately 23 million. Suppose you buy a $1 Lotto ticket in anticipation of winning the $7 million grand prize. Calculate your expected net winnings. Interpret the result.

37 **The showcase showdown.** On the popular television game show *The Price Is Right*, contestants can play "The Showcase Showdown." The game involves a large wheel with 20 nickel values, 5, 10, 15, 20,…,95, 100, marked on it. Contestants spin the wheel once or twice, with the objective of obtaining the highest total score *without going over a dollar* (*100*). [According to the *American Statistician* (Aug. 1995), the optimal strategy for the first spinner in a three-player game is to spin a second time only if the value of the initial spin is 65 or less.] Let x represent the total score for a single contestant playing "The Showcase Showdown." Assume a "fair" wheel (i.e., a wheel with equally likely outcomes). If the total of the player's spins exceeds 100, the total score is set to 0.
  a. If the player is permitted only one spin of the wheel, find the probability distribution for x.
  b. Refer to part **a.** Find $E(x)$ and interpret this value.
  c. Refer to part **a.** Give a range of values within which x is likely to fall.
  d. Suppose the player will spin the wheel twice, no matter what the outcome of the first spin. Find the probability distribution for x.
  e. What assumption did you make to obtain the probability distribution, part **d**? Is it a reasonable assumption?
  f. Find μ and σ for the probability distribution, part **d**, and interpret the results.
  g. Refer to part **d.** What is the probability that in two spins the player's total score exceeds a dollar (i.e., is set to 0)?
  h. Suppose the player obtains a 20 on the first spin and decides to spin again. Find the probability distribution for x.
  i. Refer to part **h.** What is the probability that the player's total score exceeds a dollar?
  j. Given the player obtains a 65 on the first spin and decides to spin again, find the probability that the player's total score exceeds a dollar.
  k. Repeat part **j** for different first-spin outcomes. Use this information to suggest a strategy for the one-player game.

Applying the Concepts—Advanced

38 **Robot-sensor system configuration.** Engineers at Broadcom Corp. and Simon Fraser University collaborated on research involving a robot-sensor system in an unknown environment (*International Journal of Robotics Research*, Dec. 2004). As an example, the engineers presented the three-point, single-link robotic system shown in the accompanying figure. Each point (A, B, or C) in the physical space of the system has either an "obstacle" status or a "free" status. There are two single links in the system: $A \leftrightarrow B$ and $B \leftrightarrow C$. A link has a "free" status if and only if both points in the link are "free." Otherwise, the link has an "obstacle" status. Of interest is the random variable Y, the total number of links in the system that are "free."

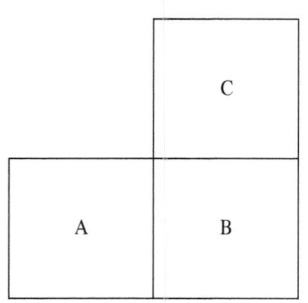

a. List the possible values of Y for the system.

b. The researchers stated that the probability of any point in the system having a "free" status is .5. Assuming the three points in the system operate independently, find the probability distribution for Y.

39 Parlay card betting. Odds makers try to predict which professional and college football teams will win and by how much (the *spread*). If the odds makers do this accurately, adding the spread to the underdog's score should make the final score a tie. Suppose a bookie will give you $6 for every $1 you risk if you pick the winners in three games (adjusted by the spread) on a "parlay" card. Thus, for every $1 bet, you will either lose $1 or gain $5. What is the bookie's expected earnings per dollar wagered?

---

3   The Binomial Distribution

Many experiments result in *dichotomous* responses—that is, responses for which there exist two possible alternatives, such as Yes-No, Pass-Fail, Defective-Nondefective, or Male-Female. A simple example of such an experiment is the coin-toss experiment. A coin is tossed a number of times, say 10. Each toss results in one of two outcomes, Head or Tail. Ultimately, we are interested in the probability distribution of x, the number of heads observed. Many other experiments are equivalent to tossing a coin (either balanced or unbalanced) a fixed number n of times and observing the number x of times that one of the two possible outcomes occurs. Random variables that possess these characteristics are called **binomial random variables.**

Public opinion and consumer preference polls (e.g., the CNN, Gallup, and Harris polls) frequently yield observations on binomial random variables. For example, suppose a sample of 100 current customers is selected from a firm's database and each person is asked whether he or she prefers the firm's product (a Head) or prefers a competitor's product (a Tail). Suppose we are interested in x, the number of customers in the sample who prefer the firm's product. Sampling 100 customers is analogous to tossing the coin 100 times. Thus, you can see that consumer preference polls like the one described here are real-life equivalents of coin-toss experiments. We have been describing a **binomial experiment;** it is identified by the following characteristics.

Characteristics of a Binomial Experiment

1. The experiment consists of n identical trials.

2. There are only two possible outcomes on each trial. We will denote one outcome by S (for success) and the other by F (for failure).

3. The probability of S remains the same from trial to trial. This probability is denoted by p, and the probability of F is denoted by q. Note that $q = 1 - p$.

4. The trials are independent.

5. The binomial random variable x is the number of S's in n trials.

Example 9

Assessing Whether x Is Binomial—Business Problems

BIOGRAPHY

JACOB BERNOULLI
(1654–1705)
The Bernoulli Distribution

Son of a magistrate and spice maker in Basel, Switzerland, Jacob Bernoulli completed a degree in theology at the University of Basel. While at the university, however, he studied mathematics secretly and against the will of his father. Jacob taught mathematics to his younger brother Johan, and they both went on to become distinguished European mathematicians. At first the brothers collaborated on the problems of the time (e.g., calculus); unfortunately, they later became bitter mathematical rivals. Jacob applied his philosophical training and mathematical intuition to probability and the theory of games of chance, where he developed the Law of Large Numbers. In his book *Ars Conjectandi,* published in 1713 (eight years after his death), the binomial distribution was first proposed. Jacob showed that the binomial distribution is a sum of independent 0–1 variables, now known as "Bernoulli" random variables.

Problem For the following examples, decide whether x is a binomial random variable.

a. You randomly select 3 bonds out of a possible 10 for an investment portfolio. Unknown to you, 8 of the 10 will maintain their present value, and the other 2 will lose value due to a change in their ratings. Let x be the number of the 3 bonds you select that lose value.

b. Before marketing a new product on a large scale, many companies will conduct a consumer preference survey to determine whether the product is likely to be successful. Suppose a company develops a new diet soda and then conducts a taste preference survey in which 100 randomly chosen consumers state their preferences among the new soda and the two leading sellers. Let x be the number of the 100 who choose the new brand over the two others.

c. Some surveys are conducted by using a method of sampling other than simple random sampling. For example, suppose a television cable company plans to conduct a survey to determine the fraction of households in the city that would use the cable television service. The sampling method is to choose a city block at random and then survey every household on that block. This sampling technique is called *cluster sampling.* Suppose 10 blocks are so sampled, producing a total of 124 household responses. Let x be the number of the 124 households that would use the television cable service.

Solution

a. In checking the binomial characteristics in the box, a problem arises with both characteristic 3 (probabilities remaining the same from trial to trial) and characteristic 4 (independence). The probability that the first bond you pick loses value is clearly $\frac{2}{10}$. Now suppose the first bond you picked was 1 of the 2 that will lose value. This reduces the chance that the second bond you pick will lose value to $\frac{1}{9}$ because now only 1 of the 9 remaining bonds are in that category. Thus, the choices you make are dependent, and therefore $x,$ the number of 3 bonds you select that lose value, is *not* a binomial random variable.

b. Surveys that produce dichotomous responses and use random sampling techniques are classic examples of binomial experiments. In our example, each randomly selected consumer either states a preference for the new diet soda or does not. The sample of 100 consumers is a very small proportion of the totality of potential consumers, so the response of one would be, for all practical purposes, independent of another.* Thus, x is a binomial random variable.

c. This example is a survey with dichotomous responses (Yes or No to the cable service), but the sampling method is not simple random sampling. Again, the binomial characteristic of independent trials would probably not be satisfied. The responses of households within a particular block would be dependent because the households within a block tend to be similar with respect to income, level of education, and general interests. Thus, the binomial model would not be satisfactory for x if the cluster sampling technique were employed.

Look Back Nonbinomial random variables with two outcomes on every trial typically occur because they do not satisfy characteristics 3 or 4 of a binomial distribution.

■ **Now Work Exercise 49a**

---

*In most real-life applications of the binomial distribution, the population of interest has a finite number of elements (trials), denoted N. When N is large and the sample size n is small relative to N, say $n/N \leq .05$, the sampling procedure, for all practical purposes, satisfies the conditions of a binomial experiment.

Example   10

Deriving the Binomial Probability Distribution in a PC Purchase Application

Problem A computer retailer sells both desktop and laptop personal computers (PCs) online. Assume that 80% of the PCs that the retailer sells online are desktops and 20% are laptops.

a. Find the probability that all of the next four online PC purchases are laptops.

b. Find the probability that three of the next four online PC purchases are laptops.

c. Let x represent the number of the next four online PC purchases that are laptops. Explain why x is a binomial random variable.

d. Use the answers to parts **a** and **b** to derive a formula for $p(x)$, the probability distribution of the binomial random variable x.

Solution

a. **1.** The first step is to define the experiment. Here we are interested in observing the type of PC purchased online by each of the next four (buying) customers: desktop (D) or laptop (L).

2. Next, we list the sample points associated with the experiment. Each sample point consists of the purchase decisions made by the four online customers. For example, $DDDD$ represents the sample point that all four purchase desktop PCs, while $LDDD$ represents the sample point that customer 1 purchases a laptop, while customers 2, 3, and 4 purchase desktops. The tree diagram, Figure 8, shows that there are 16 sample points. These 16 sample points are also listed in Table 2.

3. We now assign probabilities to the sample points. Note that each sample point can be viewed as the intersection of four customers' decisions and, assuming the

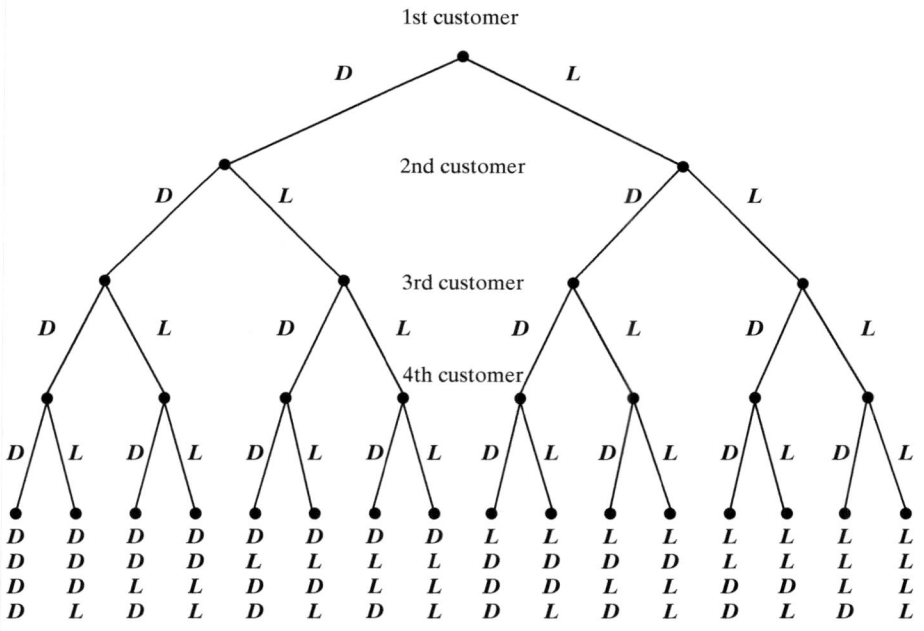

Figure 8

Tree diagram showing outcomes for PC purchases

Table 2	Sample Points for PC Experiment of Example 9			
$DDDD$	$LDDD$	$LLDD$	$DLLL$	LLLL
	$DLDD$	$LDLD$	$LDLL$	
	$DDLD$	$LDDL$	$LLDL$	
	$DDDL$	$DLLD$	$LLLD$	
		$DLDL$		
		$DDLL$		

decisions are made independently, the probability of each sample point can be obtained using the multiplicative rule, as follows:

$$P(DDDD) = P[(\text{customer 1 chooses desktop}) \cap (\text{customer 2 chooses desktop})$$
$$\cap (\text{customer 3 chooses desktop}) \cap (\text{customer 4 chooses desktop})]$$

$$= P(\text{customer 1 chooses desktop}) \times P(\text{customer 2 chooses desktop}) \times P(\text{customer 3 chooses desktop})$$
$$\times P(\text{customer 4 chooses desktop})$$

$$= (.8)(.8)(.8)(.8) = (.8)^4 = .4096$$

All other sample point probabilities are calculated using similar reasoning. For example,

$$P(LDDD) = (.2)(.8)(.8)(.8) = (.2)(.8)^3 = .1024$$

You can check that this reasoning results in sample point probabilities that add to 1 over the 16 points in the sample space.

4. Finally, we add the appropriate sample point probabilities to obtain the desired event probability. The event of interest is that all four online customers purchase laptops. In Table 2 we find only one sample point, *LLLL*, contained in this event. All other sample points imply that at least one desktop is purchased. Thus,

$$P(\text{All four purchase laptops}) = P(LLLL) = (.2)^4 = .0016$$

That is, the probability is only 16 in 10,000 that all four customers purchase laptop PCs.

b. The event that three of the next four online buyers purchase laptops consists of the four sample points in the fourth column of Table 2: *DLLL, LDLL, LLDL,* and *LLLD.* To obtain the event probability, we add the sample point probabilities:

$$P(3 \text{ of next 4 customers purchase laptops})$$
$$= P(DLLL) + P(LDLL) + P(LLDL) + P(LLLD)$$
$$= (.2)^3(.8) + (.2)^3(.8) + (.2)^3(.8) + (.2)^3(.8)$$
$$= 4(.2)^3(.8) = .0256$$

Note that each of the four sample point probabilities is the same because each sample point consists of three *L*'s and one *D;* the order does not affect the probability because the customers' decisions are (assumed) independent.

c. We can characterize the experiment as consisting of four identical trials—the four customers' purchase decisions. There are two possible outcomes to each trial, *D* or *L,* and the probability of *L, p* = .2, is the same for each trial. Finally, we are assuming that each customer's purchase decision is independent of all others, so that the four trials are independent. Then it follows that *x,* the number of the next four purchases that are laptops, is a binomial random variable.

d. The event probabilities in parts **a** and **b** provide insight into the formula for the probability distribution $p(x)$. First, consider the event that three purchases are laptops (part **b**). We found that

$$P(x = 3) = (\text{Number of sample points for which } x = 3)$$
$$\times (.2)^{\text{Number of laptops purchased}} \times (.8)^{\text{Number of desktops purchased}}$$
$$= 4(.2)^3(.8)^1$$

In general, we can use combinatorial mathematics to count the number of sample points. For example,

Number of sample points for which $x = 3$

= Number of different ways of selecting 3 of the 4 trials for L purchases

$$= \binom{4}{3} = \frac{4!}{3!(4-3)!} = \frac{4 \cdot 3 \cdot 2 \cdot 1}{(3 \cdot 2 \cdot 1) \cdot 1} = 4$$

The formula that works for any value of x can be deduced as follows. Because

$$P(x = 3) = \binom{4}{3}(.2)^3(.8)^1,$$

then $p(x) = \binom{4}{x}(.2)^x(.8)^{4-x}$

The component $\binom{4}{x}$ counts the number of sample points with x laptops and the component $(.2)^x(.8)^{4-x}$ is the probability associated with each sample point having x laptops. For the general binomial experiment, with n trials and probability of success p on each trial, the probability of x successes is

$$p(x) = \binom{n}{x} \cdot \underbrace{p^x(1-p)^{n-x}}$$

Number of sample points with x S's	Probability of x S's and $(n - x)$ F's in any sample point

Look Ahead In theory, you could always resort to the principles developed in this example to calculate binomial probabilities; list the sample points and sum their probabilities. However, as the number of trials (n) increases, the number of sample points grows very rapidly (the number of sample points is 2^n). Thus, we prefer the formula for calculating binomial probabilities because its use avoids listing sample points.

The binomial distribution* is summarized in the box.

The Binomial Probability Distribution

$$p(x) = \binom{n}{x}p^x q^{n-x} \quad (x = 0, 1, 2, \ldots, n)$$

where

p = Probability of a success on a single trial

$q = 1 - p$

n = Number of trials

x = Number of successes in n trials

$n - x$ = Number of failures in n trials

$$\binom{n}{x} = \frac{n!}{x!(n-x)!}$$

The symbol 5! means $5 \cdot 4 \cdot 3 \cdot 2 \cdot 1 = 120$. Similarly, $n! = n(n-1)(n-2) \ldots 3 \cdot 2 \cdot 1$; remember, $0! = 1$.

---

*The binomial distribution is so named because the probabilities, $p(x), x = 0, 1, \ldots, n$, are terms of the binomial expansion $(q + p)^n$.

Example 11

Applying the Binomial Distribution—Manufacture of Automobiles

Problem A machine that produces stampings for automobile engines is malfunctioning and producing 10% defectives. The defective and nondefective stampings proceed from the machine in a random manner. If the next five stampings are tested, find the probability that three of them are defective.

Solution Let x equal the number of defectives in $n = 5$ trials. Then x is a binomial random variable with p, the probability that a single stamping will be defective, equal to .1, and $q = 1 - p = 1 - .1 = .9$. The probability distribution for x is given by the expression

$$p(x) = \binom{n}{x} p^x q^{n-x} = \binom{5}{x} (.1)^x (.9)^{5-x}$$

$$= \frac{5!}{x!(5-x)!} (.1)^x (.9)^{5-x} \qquad (x = 0, 1, 2, 3, 4, 5)$$

To find the probability of observing $x = 3$ defectives in a sample of $n = 5$, substitute $x = 3$ into the formula for $p(x)$ to obtain

$$p(3) = \frac{5!}{3!(5-3)!} (.1)^3 (.9)^{5-3} = \frac{5!}{3!2!} (.1)^3 (.9)^2$$

$$= \frac{5 \cdot 4 \cdot 3 \cdot 2 \cdot 1}{(3 \cdot 2 \cdot 1)(2 \cdot 1)} (.1)^3 (.9)^2 = 10(.1)^3 (.9)^2$$

$$= .0081$$

Look Back Note that the binomial formula tells us that there are 10 sample points having 3 defectives (check this by listing them), each with probability $(.1)^3 (.9)^2$.

Now Work Exercise 47c

The mean, variance, and standard deviation for the binomial random variable x are shown in the box.

Mean, Variance, and Standard Deviation for a Binomial Random Variable

$$\text{Mean: } \mu = np$$
$$\text{Variance: } \sigma^2 = npq$$
$$\text{Standard deviation: } \sigma = \sqrt{npq}$$

The mean and standard deviation provide measures of the central tendency and variability, respectively, of a distribution. Thus, we can use μ and σ to obtain a rough visualization of the probability distribution for x when the calculation of the probabilities is too tedious. The next example illustrates this idea.

Example 12

Finding μ and σ—Automobile Manufacturing Application

Problem Refer to Example 11 and find the values of $p(0), p(1), p(2), p(4)$ and $p(5)$. Graph $p(x)$. Calculate the mean μ and standard deviation σ. Locate μ and the interval $\mu - 2\sigma$ to $\mu + 2\sigma$ on the graph. If the experiment were to be repeated many times, what proportion of the x observations would fall within the interval $\mu - 2\sigma$ to $\mu + 2\sigma$?

Solution Again, $n = 5$, $p = .1$, and $q = .9$. Then, substituting into the formula for $p(x)$:

$$p(0) = \frac{5!}{0!(5-0)!} (.1)^0 (.9)^{5-0} = \frac{5 \cdot 4 \cdot 3 \cdot 2 \cdot 1}{(1)(5 \cdot 4 \cdot 3 \cdot 2 \cdot 1)} (1)(.9)^5 = .59049$$

$$p(1) = \frac{5!}{1!(5-1)!} (.1)^1 (.9)^{5-1} = 5(.1)(.9)^4 = .32805$$

$$p(2) = \frac{5!}{2!(5-2)!} (.1)^2 (.9)^{5-2} = (10)(.1)^2(.9)^3 = .07290$$

$$p(3) = .0081 \text{ (from Example 11)}$$

$$p(4) = \frac{5!}{4!(5-4)!} (.1)^4 (.9)^{5-4} = (5)(.1)^4(.9) = .00045$$

$$p(5) = \frac{5!}{5!(5-5)!} (.1)^5 (.9)^{5-5} = (.1)^5 = .00001$$

The graph of $p(x)$ is shown as a probability histogram in Figure 9.

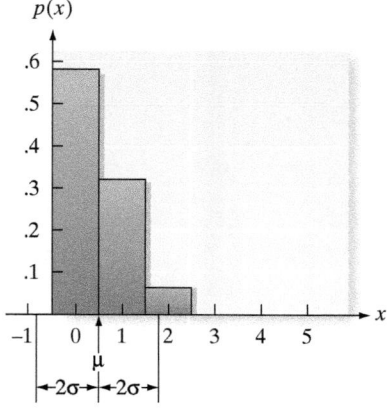

To calculate the values of μ and σ, substitute $n = 5$ and $p = .1$ into the following formulas:

$$\mu = np = (5)(.1) = .5$$

$$\sigma = \sqrt{npq} = \sqrt{(5)(.1)(.9)} = \sqrt{.45} = .67$$

To find the interval $\mu - 2\sigma$ to $\mu + 2\sigma$, we calculate

$$\mu - 2\sigma = .5 - 2(.67) = -.84$$

$$\mu + 2\sigma = .5 + 2(.67) = 1.84$$

If the experiment was repeated a large number of times, what proportion of the x observations would fall within the interval $\mu - 2\sigma$ to $\mu + 2\sigma$? You can see from Figure 9 that all observations equal to 0 or 1 will fall within the interval. The probabilities corresponding to these values are .5905 and .3280, respectively. Consequently, you would expect .5905 + .3280 = .9185, or approximately 91.9%, of the observations to fall within the interval $\mu - 2\sigma$ to $\mu + 2\sigma$.

Figure 9
The binomial distribution: $n = 5, p = .1$

Look Back This result again emphasizes that for most probability distributions, observations rarely fall more than 2 standard deviations from μ.

Now Work Exercise 57

Using Tables and Software to Find Binomial Probabilities

Calculating binomial probabilities becomes tedious when n is large. For some values of n and p, the binomial probabilities have been tabulated in Table I in Appendix: Tables. Part of Table I is shown in Table 3; a graph of the binomial probability distribution for $n = 10$ and $p = .10$ is shown in Figure 10. Table I actually contains a total of nine tables, labeled (a) through (i), each one corresponding to $n = 5, 6, 7, 8, 9, 10, 15, 20,$ and 25. In each of these tables, the columns correspond to values of p, and the rows correspond to values (k) of the random variable x. The entries in the table represent

Table 3	Reproduction of Part of Table I in Appendix: Tables: Binomial Probabilities for $n = 10$												
	p												
k	.01	.05	.10	.20	.30	.40	.50	.60	.70	.80	.90	.95	.99
0	.904	.599	.349	.107	.028	.006	.001	.000	.000	.000	.000	.000	.000
1	.996	.914	.736	.376	.149	.046	.011	.002	.000	.000	.000	.000	.000
2	1.000	.988	.930	.678	.383	.167	.055	.012	.002	.000	.000	.000	.000
3	1.000	.999	.987	.879	.650	.382	.172	.055	.011	.001	.000	.000	.000
4	1.000	1.000	.998	.967	.850	.633	.377	.166	.047	.006	.000	.000	.000
5	1.000	1.000	1.000	.994	.953	.834	.623	.367	.150	.033	.002	.000	.000
6	1.000	1.000	1.000	.999	.989	.945	.828	.618	.350	.121	.013	.001	.000
7	1.000	1.000	1.000	1.000	.998	.988	.945	.833	.617	.322	.070	.012	.000
8	1.000	1.000	1.000	1.000	1.000	.998	.989	.954	.851	.624	.264	.086	.004
9	1.000	1.000	1.000	1.000	1.000	1.000	.999	.994	.972	.893	.651	.401	.096

cumulative binomial probabilities, $p(x \le k)$. Thus, for example, the entry in the column corresponding to $p = .10$ and the row corresponding to $k = 2$ is .930 (shaded), and its interpretation is

$$P(x \le 2) = P(x = 0) + P(x = 1) + P(x = 2) = .930$$

This probability is also shaded in the graphical representation of the binomial distribution with $n = 10$ and $p = .10$ in Figure 10.

You can also use Table I to find the probability that x equals a specific value. For example, suppose you want to find the probability that $x = 2$ in the binomial distribution with $n = 10$ and $p = .10$. This is found by subtraction as follows:

$$P(x = 2) = [P(x = 0) + P(x = 1) + P(x = 2)] - [P(x = 0) + P(x = 1)]$$
$$= P(x \le 2) - P(x \le 1) = .930 - .736 = .194$$

The probability that a binomial random variable exceeds a specified value can be found using Table I and the notion of complementary events. For example, to find the probability that x exceeds 2 when $n = 10$ and $p = .10$, we use

$$P(x > 2) = 1 - P(x \le 2) = 1 - .930 = .070$$

Note that this probability is represented by the unshaded portion of the graph in Figure 10.

All probabilities in Table I are rounded to three decimal places. Thus, although none of the binomial probabilities in the table is exactly zero, some are small enough (less than .0005) to round to .000. For example, using the formula to find $P(x = 0)$ when $n = 10$ and $p = .6$, we obtain

$$P(x = 0) = \binom{10}{0}(.6)^0(.4)^{10-0} = .4^{10} = .00010486$$

but this is rounded to .000 in Table I in Appendix: Tables (see Table 3).

Similarly, none of the table entries is exactly 1.0, but when the cumulative probabilities exceed .9995, they are rounded to 1.000. The row corresponding to the largest possible value for x, $x = n$, is omitted because all the cumulative probabilities in that row are equal to 1.0 (exactly). For example, in Table 3, with $n = 10$, $P(x \le 10) = 1.0$, no matter what the value of p.

Of course, you can also use a statisitical software package to find binomial probabilities. The following example further illustrates the use of Table I and statistical software.

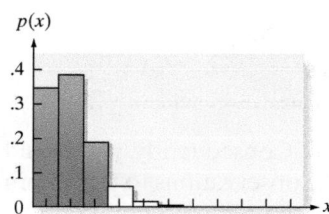

Figure 10

Binomial probability distribution for $n = 10$ and $p = .10$; $P(x \le 2)$ shaded

---

| **Example** | **13** |

Using the Binomial Table and Computer Software— Worker Unionization Problem

Problem Suppose a poll of 20 employees is taken in a large company. The purpose is to determine x, the number who favor unionization. Suppose that 60% of all the company's employees favor unionization.

a. Find the mean and standard deviation of x.

b. Use Table I in Appendix: Tables to find the probability that $x \le 10$. Verify this probability using Minitab.

c. Use Table I to find the probability that $x > 12$.

d. Use Table I to find the probability that $x = 11$. Verify this probability using Minitab.

e. Graph the probability distribution of x and locate the interval $\mu \pm 2\sigma$ on the graph.

Solution

a. The number of employees polled is presumably small compared with the total number of employees in this company. Thus, we may treat x, the number of the 20 who favor unionization, as a binomial random variable. The value of p is the fraction of the total employees who favor unionization; that is, $p = .6$. Therefore, we calculate the mean and variance:

$$\mu = np = 20(.6) = 12$$
$$\sigma^2 = npq = 20(.6)(.4) = 4.8$$
$$\sigma = \sqrt{4.8} = 2.19$$

b. Looking in the $k = 10$ row and the $p = .6$ column of Table I (Appendix: Tables) for $n = 20$, we find the value of .245. Thus,

$$P(x \leq 10) = .245$$

This value agrees (to three decimal places) with the cumulative probability shaded at the top of the Minitab printont shown in Figure 11.

Cumulative Distribution Function

```
Binomial with n = 20 and p = 0.6

   x   P( X <= x )
  10      0.244663
```

Probability Density Function

```
Binomial with n = 20 and p = 0.6

   x   P( X = x )
  11      0.159738
```

---

c. To find the probability

$$P(x > 12) = \sum_{x=13}^{20} p(x)$$

we use the fact that for all probability distributions, $\sum_{\text{All } x} p(x) = 1$. Therefore,

$$P(x > 12) = 1 - P(x \leq 12) = 1 - \sum_{x=0}^{12} p(x)$$

Consulting Table I, we find the entry in row $k = 12$, column $p = .6$ to be .584. Thus,

$$P(x > 12) = 1 - .584 = .416$$

d. To find the probability that exactly 11 employees favor unionization, recall that the entries in Table I are cumulative probabilities and use the relationship

$$P(x = 11) = [p(0) + p(1) + \cdots + p(11)] - [p(0) + p(1) + \cdots + p(10)]$$
$$= P(x \leq 11) - P(x \leq 10)$$

Then

$$P(x = 11) = .404 - .245 = .159$$

Again, this value agrees (to three decimal places) with the probability shaded at the bottom of the Minitab printont, Figure 11.

e. The probability distribution for x in this example is shown in Figure 12. Note that

$$\mu - 2\sigma = 12 - 2(2.2) = 7.6$$
$$\mu + 2\sigma = 12 + 2(2.2) = 16.4$$

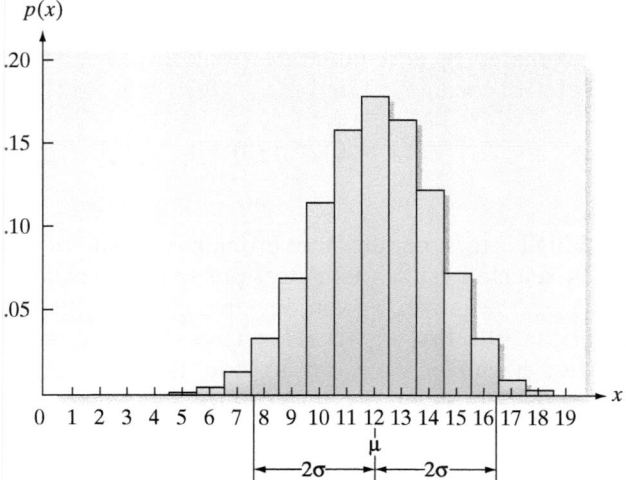

Figure 11
Minitab output for Example 13

Figure 12
The binomial probability distribution for x in Example 13: $n = 20, p = .6$

The interval (7.6, 16.4) is also shown in Figure 12. The probability that x falls in this interval is $P(x = 8, 9, 10, \ldots, 16) = P(x \le 16) - P(x \le 7) = .984 - .021 = .963$. This probability is very close to the .95 given by the Empirical Rule. Thus, we expect the number of employees in the sample of 20 who favor unionization to be between 8 and 16.

■ Now Work Exercise 51

STATISTICS
in ACTION
REVISITED

Using the Binomial Model to Solve the Cocaine Sting Case

Refer to the reverse cocaine sting case described at the beginning of the chapter. During a drug bust, police seized 496 foil packets of a white, powdery substance that appeared to be cocaine. The police laboratory randomly selected 4 packets and found that all 4 tested positive for cocaine. This finding led to the conviction of the drug traffickers. Following the conviction, the police used 2 of the remaining 492 foil packets (i.e., those not tested) in a reverse sting operation. The 2 randomly selected packets were sold by undercover officers to a buyer, who disposed of the evidence before being arrested. Is there evidence beyond a reasonable doubt that the 2 packets contained cocaine?

To solve the dilemma, we will assume that, of the 496 original packets confiscated, 331 contained cocaine and 165 contained an inert (legal) powder. (A statistician hired as an expert witness on the case showed that the chance of the defendant being found not guilty is maximized when 331 packets contain cocaine and 165 do not.) First, we'll find the probability that 4 packets randomly selected from the original 496 will test positive for cocaine. Then we'll find the probability that the 2 packets sold in the reverse sting did not contain cocaine. Finally, we'll find the probability that both events occur (i.e., that the first 4 packets selected test positive for cocaine, but that the next 2 packets selected do not). In each of these probability calculations, we will apply the binomial probability distribution to approximate the probabilities.

Let x be the number of packets that contain cocaine in a sample of n selected from the 496 packets. Here, we are defining a success as a packet that contains cocaine. If n is small, say, $n = 2$ or $n = 4$, then x has an approximate binomial distribution with probability of success $p = 331/496 \approx .67$.

The probability that the first 4 packets selected contain cocaine [i.e., $P(x = 4)$] is obtained from the binomial formula with $n = 4$ and $p = .67$:

$$P(x = 4) = p(4) = \binom{4}{4}p^4(1 - p)^0 = \frac{4!(.67)^4(.33)^0}{4!0!}$$
$$= (.67)^4 = .202$$

Thus, there is about a 20% chance that all 4 of the randomly selected packets contain cocaine.

Given that 4 of the original packets tested positive for cocaine, the probability that the 2 packets randomly selected and sold in the reverse sting *do not* contain cocaine is approximated by a binomial distribution with $n = 2$ and $p = .67$. Since a success is a packet with cocaine, we find $P(x = 0)$:

$$P(x = 0) = p(0) = \binom{2}{0}p^0(1 - p)^2 = \frac{2!(.67)^0(.33)^2}{0!2!}$$
$$= (.33)^2 = .109$$

Finally, to compute the probability that, of the original 496 foil packets, the first 4 selected (at random) test positive for cocaine and the next 2 selected (at random) test negative, we employ the multiplicative law of probability. Let A be the event that the first 4 packets test positive. Let B be the event that the next 2 packets test negative. We want to find the probability of both events occurring [i.e., $P(A \text{ and } B) = P(A \cap B) = P(B|A)P(A)$]. Note that this probability is the product of the two previously calculated probabilities:

$$P(A \text{ and } B) = (.109)(.201) = .022$$

Consequently, there is only a .022 probability (i.e., about 2 chances in a hundred) that the first 4 packets will test positive for cocaine and the next 2 packets will test negative for cocaine. A reasonable jury would likely believe that an event with such a small probability is unlikely to occur and conclude that the 2 "lost" packets contained cocaine. In other words, most of us would infer that the defendant in the reverse cocaine sting was guilty of drug trafficking.

[*Epilogue:* Several of the defendant's lawyers believed that the .022 probability was too high for jurors to conclude guilt "beyond a reasonable doubt." The argument was made moot, however, when, to the surprise of the defense, the prosecution revealed that the remaining 490 packets had not been used in any other reverse sting operations and offered to test a sample of them. On the advice of the statistician, the defense requested that an additional 20 packets be tested. All 20 tested positive for cocaine! As a consequence of this new evidence, the defendant was convicted by the jury.]

Exercises 40–60

Please be aware that some of the following problems may require knowledge of concepts that are not presented in this chapter.

Learning the Mechanics

40 Compute the following:

a. $\dfrac{6!}{2!(6-2)!}$ **b.** $\dbinom{5}{2}$ **c.** $\dbinom{7}{0}$ **d.** $\dbinom{6}{6}$ **e.** $\dbinom{4}{3}$

41 Consider the following probability distribution:

$$p(x) = \binom{5}{x}(.7)^x (.3)^{5-x} \quad (x = 0, 1, 2, \ldots, 5)$$

a. Is x a discrete or a continuous random variable?
b. What is the name of this probability distribution?
c. Graph the probability distribution.
d. Find the mean and standard deviation of x.
e. Show the mean and the 2-standard-deviation interval on each side of the mean on the graph you drew in part **c.**

42 Suppose x is a binomial random variable with $n = 3$ and $p = .3$.
a. Calculate the value of $p(x)$, $x = 0, 1, 2, 3$, using the formula for a binomial probability distribution.
b. Using your answers to part **a,** give the probability distribution for x in tabular form.

43 If x is a binomial random variable, compute $p(x)$ for each of the following cases:
a. $n = 5, x = 1, p = .2$
b. $n = 4, x = 2, q = .4$
c. $n = 3, x = 0, p = .7$
d. $n = 5, x = 3, p = .1$
e. $n = 4, x = 2, q = .6$
f. $n = 3, x = 1, p = .9$

44 If x is a binomial random variable, use Table I in Appendix: Tables to find the following probabilities:
a. $P(x = 2)$ for $n = 10, p = .4$
b. $P(x \le 5)$ for $n = 15, p = .6$
c. $P(x > 1)$ for $n = 5, p = .1$
d. $P(x < 10)$ for $n = 25, p = .7$
e. $P(x \ge 10)$ for $n = 15, p = .9$
f. $P(x = 2)$ for $n = 20, p = .2$

45 If x is a binomial random variable, calculate μ, σ^2, and σ for each of the following:
a. $n = 25, p = .5$
b. $n = 80, p = .2$

c. $n = 100, p = .6$
d. $n = 70, p = .9$
e. $n = 60, p = .8$
f. $n = 1,000, p = .04$

46 The binomial probability distribution is a family of probability distributions with each single distribution depending on the values of n and p. Assume that x is a binomial random variable with $n = 4$.
a. Determine a value of p such that the probability distribution of x is symmetric.
b. Determine a value of p such that the probability distribution of x is skewed to the right.
c. Determine a value of p such that the probability distribution of x is skewed to the left.
d. Graph each of the binomial distributions you obtained in parts **a, b,** and **c.** Locate the mean for each distribution on its graph.
e. In general, for what values of p will a binomial distribution be symmetric? Skewed to the right? Skewed to the left?

⚙ Applet Exercise 3

Use the applets *Simulating the Probability of a Head with an Unfair Coin (P(H) = .2),* and *Simulating the Probability of a Head with an Unfair Coin (P(H) = .8)* to study the mean μ of a binomial distribution.
a. Run each applet mentioned above once with $n = 1,000$ and record the cumulative proportions. How does the cumulative proportion for each applet compare to the value of $P(H)$ given for the applet?
b. Using the cumulative proportion from each applet as p, compute $\mu = np$ for each applet where $n = 1,000$. What does the value of μ represent in terms of the results from running each applet in part **a?**
c. In your own words, describe what the mean μ of a binomial distribution represents.

⚙ Applet Exercise 4

Open the applet *Sample from a Population.* On the pull-down menu to the right of the top graph, select *Binary.* Set $n = 10$ as the sample size and repeatedly choose samples from the population. For each sample, record the number of 1s in the sample. Let x be the number of 1s in a sample of size 10. Explain why x is a binomial random variable.

⊙ Applet Exercise 5

Use the applet *Simulating the Stock Market* to estimate the probability that the stock market will go up each of the next two days. Repeatedly run the applet for $n = 2$, recording the number of up's each time. Use the proportion of 2s among your results as the estimate of the probability. Compare to the binomial probability where $x = 2, n = 2$, and $p = 0.5$.

Applying the Concepts — Basic

47 Working on summer vacation. An *Adweek/Harris* (July 2011) poll found that 35% of U.S. adults do not work at all while on summer vacation. In a random sample of 10 U.S. adults, let x represent the number who do not work during summer vacation.
   a. For this experiment, define the event that represents a "success."
   b. Explain why x is (approximately) a binomial random variable.
   c. Give the value of p for this binomial experiment.
   NW **d.** Find $P(x = 3)$.
   e. Find the probability that 2 or fewer of the 10 U.S. adults do not work during summer vacation.

48 Hotel guest satisfaction. Each year, J.D. Power and Associates publishes the results of its North American Hotel Guest Satisfaction Index Study. For 2009, the study revealed that 66% of hotel guests were aware of the hotel's "green" conservation program. Among these guests, 72% actually participated in the program by reusing towels and bed linens. In a random sample of 15 hotel guests, consider the number (x) of guests who were aware of and participated in the hotel's conservation efforts.
   a. Explain why x is (approximately) a binomial random variable.
   b. Use the rules of probability to determine the value of p for this binomial experiment.
   c. Assume $p = .45$. Find the probability that at least 10 of the 15 hotel guests were aware of and participated in the hotel's conservation efforts.

49 Paying for music downloads. A *Pew Internet & American Life Project Survey* (October 2010) revealed that half of all U.S. adults use the Internet and have paid to download music. In a random sample of 250 U.S. adults, let x be the number who use the Internet and pay to download music.
   NW **a.** Explain why x is a binomial random variable (to a reasonable degree of approximation).
   b. What is the value of p? Interpret this value.
   c. What is the expected value of x? Interpret this value.

50 Physicians' opinions on a career in medicine. Many primary care doctors feel overworked and burdened by potential lawsuits. In fact, the Physicians' Foundation reported that 60% of all general practice physicians in the United States do not recommend medicine as a career (*Reuters*, Nov. 18, 2008). Let x represent the number of sampled general practice physicians who do not recommend medicine as a career.
   a. Explain why x is approximately a binomial random variable.
   b. Use the Physicians' Foundation report to estimate p for the binomial random variable.

   c. Consider a random sample of 25 general practice physicians. Use p from part **b** to find the mean and standard deviation of x, the number who do not recommend medicine as a career.
   d. For the sample of part **c**, find the probability that at least one general practice physician does not recommend medicine as a career.

51 Job satisfaction of law librarians. According to the *Canadian Journal of Information and Library Science* (Vol. 33, 2009), nearly 90% of workers in law libraries are satisfied with their job. Assume the true proportion of law librarians in Canada who are satisfied with their job is .9. In a random sample of 20 law librarians in Canada, what is the probability that at most 2 are unsatisfied with their job?

Applying the Concepts — Intermediate

52 Immediate feedback to incorrect exam answers. Researchers from the Educational Testing Service (ETS) found that providing immediate feedback to students answering open-ended questions can dramatically improve students' future performance on exams (*Educational and Psychological Measurement,* Feb. 2010). The ETS researchers used questions from the Graduate Record Examination (GRE) in the experiment. After obtaining feedback, students could revise their answers. Consider one of these questions. Initially, 50% of the students answered the question correctly. After providing immediate feedback to students who had answered incorrectly, 70% answered correctly. Consider a bank of 100 open-ended questions similar to those on the GRE.
   a. In a random sample of 20 students, what is the probability that more than half initially answered the question correctly?
   b. Refer to part **a**. After receiving immediate feedback, what is the probability that more than half of the students answered the question correctly?

53 Fingerprint expertise. The *Psychological Science* (August 2011) did a study of fingerprint identification. The study found that when presented with prints from the same individual, a fingerprint expert will correctly identify the match 92% of the time. In contrast, a novice will correctly identify the match 75% of the time. Consider a sample of five different pairs of fingerprints, where each pair is a match.
   a. What is the probability that an expert will correctly identify the match in all five pairs of fingerprints?
   b. What is the probability that a novice will correctly identify the match in all five pairs of fingerprints?

54 Making your vote count. *Chance* (Fall 2007) did a study on making your vote count. Imagine a scenario where you are one of five county commissioners voting on an issue, and each commissioner is equally likely to vote for or against.
   a. Your vote counts (i.e., is the decisive vote) only if the other four voters split, two in favor and two against. Use the binomial distribution to find the probability that your vote counts.
   b. If you convince two other commissioners to "vote in bloc" (i.e., you all agree to vote among yourselves first, and whatever the majority decides is the way all three will vote, guaranteeing that the issue is decided

by the bloc), your vote counts only if these two commissioners split their bloc votes, one in favor and one against. Again, use the binomial distribution to find the probability that your vote counts.

55 Bridge inspection ratings. According to the National Bridge Inspection Standard (NBIS), public bridges over 20 feet in length must be inspected and rated every 2 years. The NBIS rating scale ranges from 0 (poorest rating) to 9 (highest rating). University of Colorado engineers used a probabilistic model to forecast the inspection ratings of all major bridges in Denver (*Journal of Performance of Constructed Facilities*, Feb. 2005). For the year 2020, the engineers forecast that 9% of all major Denver bridges will have ratings of 4 or below.

   a. Use the forecast to find the probability that in a random sample of 10 major Denver bridges, at least 3 will have an inspection rating of 4 or below in 2020.

   b. Suppose that you actually observe 3 or more of the sample of 10 bridges with inspection ratings of 4 or below in 2020. What inference can you make? Why?

56 Tax returns audited by the IRS. According to the Internal Revenue Service (IRS), the chances of your tax return being audited are about 1 in 100 if your income is less than $1 million and 9 in 100 if your income is $1 million or more (*IRS Enforcement and Services Statistics*).

   a. What is the probability that a taxpayer with income less than $1 million will be audited by the IRS? With income $1 million or more?

   b. If five taxpayers with incomes under $1 million are randomly selected, what is the probability that exactly one will be audited? That more than one will be audited?

   c. Repeat part **b** assuming that five taxpayers with incomes of $1 million or more are randomly selected.

   d. If two taxpayers with incomes under $1 million are randomly selected and two with incomes more than $1 million are randomly selected, what is the probability that none of these taxpayers will be audited by the IRS?

   e. What assumptions did you have to make in order to answer these questions using the methodology presented in this section?

57 FDA report on pesticides in food. Every quarter, the Food and Drug Administration (FDA) produces a report called the *Total Diet Study*. The FDA's report covers a variety of food items, each of which is analyzed for potentially harmful chemical compounds. A *Total Diet Study* reported that no pesticides at all were found in 65% of the domestically produced food samples (*FDA Pesticide Program: Residue Monitoring*, 2008). Consider a random sample of 800 food items analyzed for the presence of pesticides.

   a. Compute μ and σ for the random variable x, the number of food items found that showed no trace of pesticide.

   b. Based on a sample of 800 food items, is it likely you would observe less than half without any traces of pesticide? Explain.

Applying the Concepts—Advanced

58 Purchasing decision. Suppose you are a purchasing officer for a large company. You have purchased 5 million electrical switches, and your supplier has guaranteed that the shipment will contain no more than .1% defectives. To check the shipment, you randomly sample 500 switches, test them, and find that four are defective. Based on this evidence, do you think the supplier has complied with the guarantee? Explain.

59 USGA golf ball specifications. According to the U.S. Golf Association (USGA), "The weight of the [golf] ball shall not be greater than 1.620 ounces avoirdupois (45.93 grams). ... The diameter of the ball shall not be less than 1.680 inches. ... The velocity of the ball shall not be greater than 250 feet per second" (USGA, 2002). The USGA periodically checks the specifications of golf balls sold in the United States by randomly sampling balls from pro shops around the country. Two dozen of each kind are sampled, and if more than three do not meet size and/or velocity requirements, that kind of ball is removed from the USGA's approved-ball list.

   a. What assumptions must be made and what information must be known in order to use the binomial probability distribution to calculate the probability that the USGA will remove a particular kind of golf ball from its approved-ball list?

   b. Suppose 10% of all balls produced by a particular manufacturer are less than 1.680 inches in diameter, and assume that the number of such balls, x, in a sample of two dozen balls can be adequately characterized by a binomial probability distribution. Find the mean and standard deviation of the binomial distribution.

   c. Refer to part **b.** If x has a binomial distribution, then so does the number, y, of balls in the sample that meet the USGA's minimum diameter. [*Note*: $x + y = 24$.] Describe the distribution of y. In particular, what are p, q, and n? Also, find $E(y)$ and the standard deviation of y.

60 Reliability of a "one-shot" device. A "one-shot" device can be used only once; after use, the device (e.g., a nuclear weapon, space shuttle, automobile air bag) is either destroyed or must be rebuilt. The destructive nature of a one-shot device makes repeated testing either impractical or too costly. Hence, the reliability of such a device must be determined with minimal testing. Consider a one-shot device that has some probability, p, of failure. Of course, the true value of p is unknown, so designers will specify a value of p that is the largest defective rate they are willing to accept. Designers will conduct n tests of the device and determine the success or failure of each test. If the number of observed failures, x, is less than or equal to some specified value, K, then the device is considered to have the desired failure rate. Consequently, the designers want to know the minimum sample size n needed so that observing K or fewer defectives in the sample will demonstrate that the true probability of failure for the one-shot device is no greater than p.

   a. Suppose the desired failure rate for a one-shot device is $p = .10$. Also, suppose designers will conduct $n = 20$ tests of the device and conclude that the device is performing to specifications if $K = 1$ (i.e., if 1 or no failures are observed in the sample). Find $P(x \leq 1)$.

   b. In reliability analysis, $1 - P(x \leq K)$ is often called the *level of confidence* for concluding that the true failure rate is less than or equal to p. Find the level of confidence for the one-shot device described in part **a.** In your opinion, is this an acceptable level? Explain.

c. Demonstrate that the confidence level can be increased by either (1) increasing the sample size n or (2) decreasing the number K of failures allowed in the sample.

d. Typically, designers want a confidence level of .90, .95, or .99. Find the values of n and K to use so that the designers can conclude (with at least 95% confidence)

that the failure rate for the one-shot device of part **a** is no greater than $p = .10$.

[*Note:* The U.S. Department of Defense Reliability Analysis Center (DoD RAC) provides designers with free access to tables and toolboxes that give the minimum sample size n required to obtain a desired confidence level for a specified number of observed failures in the sample.]

4   Other Discrete Distributions: Poisson and Hypergeometric

Poisson Random Variable

A type of discrete probability distribution that is often useful in describing the number of rare events that will occur in a specific period of time or in a specific area or volume is the **Poisson distribution** (named after the eighteenth-century physicist and mathematician Siméon Poisson). Typical examples of random variables for which the Poisson probability distribution provides a good model are as follows:

1. The number of industrial accidents per month at a manufacturing plant
2. The number of noticeable surface defects (scratches, dents, etc.) found by quality inspectors on a new automobile
3. The parts per million of some toxin found in the water or air emission from a manufacturing plant
4. The number of customer arrivals per unit of time at a supermarket checkout counter
5. The number of death claims received per day by an insurance company
6. The number of errors per 100 invoices in the accounting records of a company

---

Characteristics of a Poisson Random Variable

1. The experiment consists of counting the number of times a certain event occurs during a given unit of time or in a given area or volume (or weight, distance, or any other unit of measurement).

2. The probability that an event occurs in a given unit of time, area, or volume is the same for all the units.

3. The number of events that occur in one unit of time, area, or volume is independent of the number that occur in any other mutually exclusive unit.

4. The mean (or expected) number of events in each unit is denoted by the Greek letter lambda, λ.

The characteristics of the Poisson random variable are usually difficult to verify for practical examples. The examples given satisfy them well enough that the Poisson distribution provides a good model in many instances. As with all probability models, the real test of the adequacy of the Poisson model is in whether it provides a reasonable approximation to reality–that is, whether empirical data support it.

The probability distribution, mean, and variance for a Poisson random variable are shown in the next box.

Probability Distribution, Mean, and Variance for a Poisson Random Variable*

$$p(x) = \frac{\lambda^x e^{-\lambda}}{x!} \quad (x = 0, 1, 2, \ldots)$$

$$\mu = \lambda$$

$$\sigma^2 = \lambda$$

*The Poisson probability distribution also provides a good approximation to a binomial distribution with mean $\lambda = np$ when n is large and p is small (say, $np \leq 7$).

where

λ = Mean number of events during given unit of time, area, volume, etc.
e = 2.71828 $\cdots$

The calculation of Poisson probabilities is made easier by the use of statistical software, as illustrated in Example 14.

Example 14

Finding Poisson Probabilities—Worker Absenteeism

Problem Suppose the number, x, of a company's employees who are absent on Mondays has (approximately) a Poisson probability distribution. Furthermore, assume that the average number of Monday absentees is 2.6.

a. Find the mean and standard deviation of x, the number of employees absent on Monday.

b. Use Minitab to find the probability that exactly five employees are absent on a given Monday.

c. Use Minitab to find the probability that fewer than two employees are absent on a given Monday.

d. Use Minitab to find the probability that more than five employees are absent on a given Monday.

Solution

a. The mean and variance of a Poisson random variable are both equal to λ. Thus, for this example,

$$\mu = \lambda = 2.6$$

$$\sigma^2 = \lambda = 2.6$$

Then the standard deviation of x is

$$\sigma = \sqrt{2.6} = 1.61$$

Remember that the mean measures the central tendency of the distribution and does not necessarily equal a possible value of x. In this example, the mean is 2.6 absences, and although there cannot be 2.6 absences on a given Monday, the average number of Monday absences is 2.6. Similarly, the standard deviation of 1.61 measures the variability of the number of absences per week. Perhaps a more helpful measure is the interval $\mu \pm 2\sigma$, which in this case stretches from $-.62$ to 5.82. We expect the number of absences to fall in this interval most of the time–with at least 75% relative frequency (according to Chebyshev's Rule) and probably with approximately 95% relative frequency (the Empirical Rule). The mean and the 2-standard-deviation interval around it are shown in Figure 13.

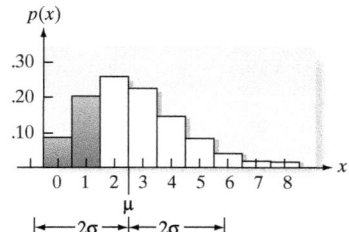

Figure 13

Probability distribution for number of Monday absences

Probability Density Function

```
Poisson with mean = 2.6

x   P( X = x )
5   0.0735394
```

Cumulative Distribution Function

```
Poisson with mean = 2.6

x   P( X <= x )
1   0.267385
```

Cumulative Distribution Function

```
Poisson with mean = 2.6

x   P( X <= x )
5   0.950963
```

Figure 14

Minitab output for Example 14

b. Since x represents the number of employees absent on a given Monday, we want to find $P(x = 5)$. Like for binomial probabilities, tables and computer software give Poisson probabilities of the form $P(x = k)$ or cumulative probabilities of the form $P(x \leq k)$. Setting $\lambda = 2.6$ as an option in Minitab and specifying the value "5" for a Poisson probability, we obtain the value (shaded) shown at the top of the Minitab printout, Figure 14:

$$P(x = 5) = .0735$$

c. Here, we want to find $P(x < 2)$. Since x is a discrete whole number, we know that

$$P(x < 2) = P(x \leq 1)$$

This probability is now in the form of a cumulative probability and can be found using statistical software. Setting $\lambda = 2.6$ as an option in Minitab and specifying the value "1" for a cumulative Poisson probability, we obtain the value (shaded) shown in the middle of the Minitab printout, Figure 14:

$$P(x < 2) = P(x \leq 1) = .2674$$

d. To find the probability that more than five employees are absent on a given Monday, we consider the complementary event

$$P(x > 5) = 1 - P(x \leq 5)$$

Again, we select $\lambda = 2.6$ as an option in Minitab and now specify the value "5" for a cumulative Poisson probability. This yields the probability, .951, shaded at the bottom of the Minitab printout, Figure 14. Now, we compute:

$$P(x > 5) = 1 - P(x \leq 5) = 1 - .951 = .049$$

Look Back Note from Figure 13 that the probability of part **d** is in the area in the interval $\mu \pm 2\sigma$, or $2.6 \pm 2(1.61) = (-.62, 5.82)$. Then, the number of absences should exceed 5—or, equivalently, should be more than 2 standard deviations from the mean—during only about 4.9% of all Mondays. This percentage agrees remarkably well with that given by the Empirical Rule for mound-shaped distributions, which informs us to expect about 5% of the measurements (values of the random variable x) to lie farther than 2 standard deviations from the mean.

■ **Now Work Exercise 71**

Hypergeometric Random Variable

The **hypergeometric probability distribution** provides a realistic model for some types of enumerative (countable) data. The characteristics of the hypergeometric distribution are listed in the following box:

Characteristics of a Hypergeometric Random Variable

1. The experiment consists of randomly drawing n elements without replacement from a set of N elements, r of which are S's (for success) and $(N - r)$ of which are F's (for failure).
2. The hypergeometric random variable x is the number of S's in the draw of n elements.

Note that both the hypergeometric and binomial characteristics stipulate that each draw, or trial, results in one of two outcomes. The basic difference between these random variables is that the hypergeometric trials are dependent, while the binomial trials are independent. The draws are dependent because the probability of drawing an S (or an F) is dependent on what occurred on preceding draws.

To illustrate the dependence between trials, we note that the probability of drawing an S on the first draw is r/N. Then the probability of drawing an S on the second draw depends on the outcome of the first. It will be either $(r - 1)/(N - 1)$ or $r/(N - 1)$, depending on whether the first draw was an S or an F. Consequently, the results of the draws represent dependent events.

For example, suppose we define x as the number of women hired in a random selection of three applicants from a total of six men and four women. This random variable satisfies the characteristics of a **hypergeometric random variable** with $N = 10$ and $n = 3$. The possible outcomes on each trial are either the selection of a female (S) or the selection of a male (F). Another example of a hypergeometric random variable is the number x of defective large-screen plasma televisions in a random selection of $n = 4$ from a shipment of $N = 8$. Finally, as a third example, suppose $n = 5$ stocks are randomly selected from a list of $N = 15$ stocks. Then the number x of the five companies selected that pay regular dividends to stockholders is a hypergeometric random variable.

The hypergeometric probability distribution is summarized in the following box:

Probability Distribution, Mean, and Variance of the Hypergeometric Random Variable

$$p(x) = \frac{\binom{r}{x}\binom{N-r}{n-x}}{\binom{N}{n}} \quad [x = \text{Maximum}\,[0, n - (N - r)], \ldots, \text{Minimum}(r, n)]$$

$$\mu = \frac{nr}{N} \qquad \sigma^2 = \frac{r(N-r)n(N-n)}{N^2(N-1)}$$

where

N = Total number of elements

r = Number of S's in the N elements

n = Number of elements drawn

x = Number of S's drawn in the n elements

Example 15

Applying the Hypergeometric Distribution—Selecting Teaching Assistants

Problem Suppose a marketing professor randomly selects three new teaching assistants from a total of ten applicants—six male and four female students. Let x be the number of females who are hired.

a. Find the mean and standard deviation of x.

b. Find the probability that no females are hired.

Solution

a. Because x is a hypergeometric random variable with $N = 10, n = 3$, and $r = 4$, the mean and variance are

$$\mu = \frac{nr}{N} = \frac{(3)(4)}{10} = 1.2$$

$$\sigma^2 = \frac{r(N-r)n(N-n)}{N^2(N-1)} = \frac{4(10-4)3(10-3)}{(10)^2(10-1)}$$

$$= \frac{(4)(6)(3)(7)}{(100)(9)} = .56$$

The standard deviation is

$$\sigma = \sqrt{.56} = .75$$

b. The probability that no female students are hired by the professor, assuming that the selection is truly random, is

$$P(x = 0) = p(0) = \frac{\binom{4}{0}\binom{10-4}{3-0}}{\binom{10}{3}}$$

$$= \frac{\dfrac{4!}{0!(4-0)!}\dfrac{6!}{3!(6-3)!}}{\dfrac{10!}{3!(10-3)!}} = \frac{(1)(20)}{120} = \frac{1}{6} = .1667$$

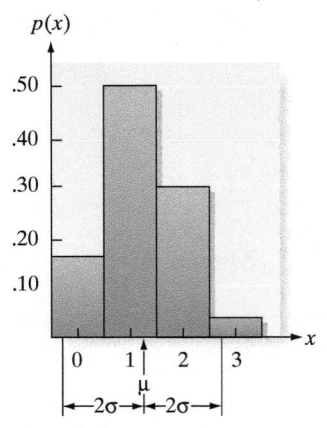

$p(x)$

.50
.40
.30
.20
.10

x

0   1   2   3
μ

←2σ→←2σ→

Figure 16
Probability distribution for x in
Example 15

We verified this calculation using statistical software. The probability, .166667, shaded on the Minitab printont, Figure 15, agrees with our answer.

Probability Density Function

Hypergeometric with N = 10, M = 4, and n = 3

```
x    P( X = x )
0      0.166667
```

Figure 15
Minitab output for Example 15

Look Back The entire probability distribution for x is shown in Figure 16. The mean $\mu = 1.2$ and the interval $\mu \pm 2\sigma = (-.3, 2.7)$ are indicated. You can see that if this random variable were to be observed over and over again a large number of times, most of the values of x would fall within the interval $\mu \pm 2\sigma$.

Now Work Exercise 75

STATISTICS
in ACTION
REVISITED

Using the Hypergeometric Model to Solve the Cocaine Sting Case

The reverse cocaine sting case solved in Section 3 can also be solved by applying the hypergeometric distribution. In fact, the probabilities obtained with the hypergeometric distribution are *exact* probabilities, compared with the approximate probabilities obtained with the binomial distribution.

Our objective, you will recall, is to find the probability that 4 packets (randomly selected from 496 packets confiscated in a drug bust) will contain cocaine and 2 packets (randomly selected from the remaining 492) will not contain cocaine. We assumed that, of the 496 original packets, 331 contained cocaine and 165 contained an inert (legal) powder. Since we are sampling *without replacement* from the 496 packets, the probability of a success (i.e., the probability of a packet containing cocaine) does not remain *exactly* the same from trial to trial. For example, for the first randomly selected packet, the probability of a success is $\frac{331}{496} = .66734$. If we find that the first 3 packets selected contain cocaine, the probability of success for the fourth packet selected is now $\frac{328}{493} = .66531$. You can see that these probabilities are not exactly the same. Hence, the binomial distribution will only approximate the distribution of x, the number of packets that contain cocaine in a sample of size n.

To find the probability that 4 packets randomly selected from the original 496 will test positive for cocaine under the hypergeometric distribution, we first identify the parameters of the distribution:

$N = 496$ is the total number of packets in the population

$S = 331$ is the number of successes (cocaine packets) in the population

$n = 4$ is the sample size

$x = 4$ is the number of successes (cocaine packets) in the sample

Substituting into the formula for $p(x)$ (above), we obtain

$$P(x = 4) = p(4) = \frac{\binom{331}{4}\binom{165}{0}}{\binom{496}{4}} = \frac{\left(\frac{331!}{4!327!}\right)\left(\frac{165!}{0!165!}\right)}{\left(\frac{496!}{4!492!}\right)}$$

$$= .197$$

To find the probability that 2 packets randomly selected from the remaining 492 will test negative for cocaine, *assuming that the first 4 packets tested positive*, we identify the parameters of the relevant hypergeometric distribution:

$N = 492$ is the total number of packets in the population

$S = 327$ is the number of successes (cocaine packets) in the population

$n = 2$ is the sample size

$x = 0$ is the number of successes (cocaine packets) in the sample

Again, we substitute into the formula for $p(x)$ to obtain

$$P(x = 0) = p(0) = \frac{\binom{327}{0}\binom{165}{2}}{\binom{492}{2}} = \frac{\left(\frac{327!}{0!327!}\right)\left(\frac{165!}{2!163!}\right)}{\left(\frac{492!}{2!490!}\right)}$$

$$= .112$$

By the multiplicative law of probability, the probability that the first 4 packets test positive for cocaine and the next 2 packets test negative is the product of the two probabilities just given:

$$P \text{ (first 4 positive and next 2 negative)} = (.197)(.112)$$

$$= .0221$$

Note that this exact probability is almost identical to the approximate probability computed with the binomial distribution in Section 3.

Exercises 61–83

Please be aware that some of the following problems may require knowledge of concepts that are not presented in this chapter.

Learning the Mechanics

61 Consider the probability distribution shown here:

$$p(x) = \frac{3^x e^{-3}}{x!} \quad (x = 0, 1, 2, \ldots)$$

a. Is x a discrete or continuous random variable? Explain.

b. What is the name of this probability distribution?

c. Graph the probability distribution.

d. Find the mean and standard deviation of x.

62 Assume that x is a random variable having a Poisson probability distribution with a mean of 1.5. Use statistical software to find the following probabilities:

a. $P(x \leq 3)$ **b.** $P(x \geq 3)$

c. $P(x = 3)$ **d.** $P(x = 0)$

e. $P(x > 0)$ **f.** $P(x > 6)$

63 Given that x is a hypergeometric random variable, compute $p(x)$ for each of the following cases:

a. $N = 5, n = 3, r = 3, x = 1$

b. $N = 9, n = 5, r = 3, x = 3$

c. $N = 4, n = 2, r = 2, x = 2$

d. $N = 4, n = 2, r = 2, x = 0$

64 Given that x is a hypergeometric random variable with $N = 8, n = 3$, and $r = 5$, compute the following:

a. $P(x = 1)$ **b.** $P(x = 0)$

c. $P(x = 3)$ **d.** $P(x \geq 4)$

65 Given that x is a random variable for which a Poisson probability distribution provides a good approximation, use statistical software to find the following:

a. $P(x \leq 2)$ when $\lambda = 1$

b. $P(x \leq 2)$ when $\lambda = 2$

c. $P(x \leq 2)$ when $\lambda = 3$

d. What happens to the probability of the event $\{x \leq 2\}$ as λ increases from 1 to 3? Is this intuitively reasonable?

66 Suppose x is a random variable for which a Poisson probability distribution with $\lambda = 5$ provides a good characterization.

a. Graph $p(x)$ for $x = 0, 1, 2, \ldots, 15$.

b. Find μ and σ for x and locate μ and the interval $\mu \pm 2\sigma$ on the graph.

c. What is the probability that x will fall within the interval $\mu \pm 2\sigma$?

67 Suppose you plan to sample 10 items from a population of 100 items and would like to determine the probability of observing 4 defective items in the sample. Which probability distribution should you use to compute this probability under the conditions listed here? Justify your answers.

a. The sample is drawn without replacement.

b. The sample is drawn with replacement.

68 Given that x is a hypergeometric random variable with $N = 10, n = 5$, and $r = 7$:

a. Display the probability distribution for x in tabular form.

b. Compute the mean and variance of x.

c. Graph $p(x)$ and locate μ and the interval $\mu \pm 2\sigma$ on the graph.

d. What is the probability that x will fall within the interval $\mu \pm 2\sigma$?

Applying the Concepts—Basic

69 Do social robots walk or roll? Refer to the *International Conference on Social Robotics* (Vol. 6414, 2010) study of the trend in the design of social robots, Exercise 25. The study found that of 106 social robots, 63 were built with legs only, 20 with wheels only, 8 with both legs and wheels, and 15 with neither legs nor wheels. Suppose you randomly select 10 of the 106 social robots and count the number, *x*, with neither legs nor wheels.

  a. Demonstrate why the probability distribution for *x* should not be approximated by the binomial distribution.

  b. Show that the properties of the hypergeometric probability distribution are satisfied for this experiment.

  c. Find μ and σ for the probability distribution for *x*.

  d. Calculate the probability that $x = 2$.

70 FDIC bank failures. The Federal Deposit Insurance Corporation (FDIC) normally insures deposits of up to $100,000 in banks that are members of the Federal Reserve System against losses due to bank failure or theft. Over the last 10 years, the average number of bank failures per year among insured banks was 45 (*FDIC Failed Bank List,* Dec. 2011). Assume that *x,* the number of bank failures per year among insured banks, can be adequately characterized by a Poisson probability distribution with mean 45.

  a. Find the expected value and standard deviation of *x*.

  b. In 2011, 360 banks failed. How far (in standard deviations) does $x = 360$ lie above the mean of the Poisson distribution? That is, find the *z*-score for $x = 360$.

  c. In 2010, 65 banks failed. Find $P(x \leq 65)$

71 Airline fatalities. U.S. airlines average about 4.5 fatalities per month (*Statistical Abstract of the United States: 2012*). Assume the probability distribution for *x,* the number of fatalities per month, can be approximated by a Poisson probability distribution.

  a. What is the probability that no fatalities will occur during any given month?

  b. What is the probability that one fatality will occur during a month?

  c. Find $E(x)$ and the standard deviation of *x*.

72 Male nannies. According to the International Nanny Association (INA), 4,176 nannies were placed in a job during a recent year (www.nanny.org). Of these, only 24 were men. Use the hypergeometric distribution to find the probability that in a random sample of 10 nannies who were placed during a recent year, at least 1 is a man.

73 Contaminated gun cartridges. Refer to the investigation of contaminated gun cartridges at a weapons manufacturer, presented in Exercise 29. In a sample of 158 cartridges from a certain lot, 36 were found to be contaminated and 122 were "clean." If you randomly select 5 of these 158 cartridges, what is the probability that all 5 will be "clean"?

74 NASA and rare planet transits. A "planet transit" is a rare celestial event in which a planet appears to cross in front of its star as seen from Earth. The planet transit causes a noticeable dip in the star's brightness, allowing scientists to detect a new planet even though it is not directly visible.

The National Aeronautics and Space Administration (NASA) recently launched its Kepler mission, designed to discover new planets in the Milky Way by detecting extrasolar planet transits. After 1 year of the mission in which 3,000 stars were monitored, NASA announced that five planet transits had been detected (NASA, American Astronomical Society, Jan. 4, 2010). Assume that the number of planet transits discovered for every 3,000 stars follows a Poisson distribution with $\lambda = 5$. What is the probability that, in the next 3,000 stars monitored by the Kepler mission, more than 10 planet transits will be seen?

Applying the Concepts—Intermediate

75 Museum management. The *Museum Management and Curatorship* (June 2010) did a study of the criteria used to evaluate museum performance. The managers of 30 leading museums of contemporary art were asked to provide the performance measure used most often. Of these 30 museums, 8 specified "total visitors" as the performance measure. Consider a random sample of 5 museums selected from the 30. How likely is it that none of the museums in the sample specified "total visitors" as the performance measure?

76 Traffic fatalities and sporting events. The relationship between close sporting events and game-day traffic fatalities was investigated in the *Journal of Consumer Research* (December 2011). The researchers found that closer football and basketball games are associated with more traffic fatalities. The methodology used by the researchers involved modeling the traffic fatality count for a particular game as a Poisson random variable. For games played at the winner's location (home court or home field), the mean number of traffic fatalities was .5. Use this information to find the probability that at least three game-day traffic fatalities will occur at the winning team's location.

77 Cell phone handoff behavior. The *Journal of Engineering, Computing and Architecture* (Vol. 3., 2009) did a study of cell phone handoff behavior. A "handoff" describes the process of a cell phone moving from one base channel (identified by a color code) to another. During a particular driving trip, a cell phone changed channels (color codes) 85 times. Color code "b" was accessed 40 times on the trip. You randomly select 7 of the 85 handoffs. How likely is it that the cell phone accessed color code "b" only twice for these 7 handoffs?

78 Guilt in decision making. The *Journal of Behavioral Decision Making* (Jan. 2007) published a study of how guilty feelings impact on-the-job decisions. In one experiment, 57 participants were assigned to a guilty state through a reading/writing task. Immediately after the task, the participants were presented with a decision problem where the stated option had predominantly negative features (e.g., spending money on repairing a very old car). Of these 57 participants, 45 chose the stated option. Suppose 10 of the 57 guilty-state participants are selected at random. Define *x* as the number in the sample of 10 who chose the stated option.

  a. Find $P(x = 5)$.

  b. Find $P(x = 8)$.

  c. What is the expected value (mean) of *x*?

79 Flaws in plastic-coated wire. The British Columbia Institute of Technology provides on its Web site (www.math.bcit.ca) practical applications of statistics at mechanical engineering firms. The following is a Poisson application. A roll of plastic-coated wire has an average of .8 flaws per 4-meter length of wire. Suppose a quality-control engineer will sample a 4-meter length of wire from a roll of wire 220 meters in length. If no flaws are found in the sample, the engineer will accept the entire roll of wire. What is the probability that the roll will be rejected? What assumption did you make to find this probability?

80 Noise in laser imaging. Penumbrol imaging is a technique used by scanning companies for imaging objects (e.g., X-rays and lasers) that emit high-energy photons. In *IEICE Transactions on Information & Systems* (Apr. 2005), researchers demonstrated that penumbrol images are always degraded by noise, where the number x of noise events occurring in a unit of time follows a Poisson process with mean λ. Suppose that $\lambda = 9$ for a particular image.
a. Find and interpret the mean of x.
b. Find the standard deviation of x.
c. The signal-to-noise ratio (SNR) for a penumbrol image is defined as SNR $= \mu/\sigma$, where μ and σ are the mean and standard deviation, respectively, of the noise process. Find the SNR for x.

81 Making high-stakes insurance decisions. The *Journal of Economic Psychology* (Sep. 2008) published the results of a high-stakes experiment where subjects were asked how much they would pay for insuring a valuable painting. The painting was threatened by fire and theft, hence, the need for insurance. To make the risk realistic, the subjects were informed that if it rained on exactly 24 days in July,

the painting was considered to be stolen; if it rained on exactly 23 days in August, the painting was considered to be destroyed by fire. Although the probability of these two events, "fire" and "theft," was ambiguous for the subjects, the researchers estimated their probabilities of occurrence at .0001. Rain frequencies for the months of July and August were shown to follow a Poisson distribution with a mean of 10 days per month.
a. Find the probability that it will rain on exactly 24 days in July.
b. Find the probability that it will rain on exactly 23 days in August.
c. Are the probabilities, parts **a** and **b**, good approximations to the probabilities of "fire" and "theft"?

Applying the Concepts—Advanced

82 Waiting for a car wash. An automatic car wash takes exactly 5 minutes to wash a car. On average, 10 cars per hour arrive at the car wash. Suppose that 30 minutes before closing time, 5 cars are in line. If the car wash is in continuous use until closing time, is it likely anyone will be in line at closing time?

83 Gender discrimination suit. The *Journal of Business & Economic Statistics* (July 2000) presented a case in which a charge of gender discrimination was filed against the U.S. Postal Service. At the time, there were 302 U.S. Postal Service employees (229 men and 73 women) who applied for promotion. Of the 72 employees who were awarded promotion, 5 were female. Make an inference about whether or not females at the U.S. Postal Service were promoted fairly.

PART II: CONTINUOUS RANDOM VARIABLES

5 Probability Distributions for Continuous Random Variables

The graphical form of the probability distribution for a **continuous random variable** x is a smooth curve that might appear as shown in Figure 17. This curve, a function of x, is denoted by the symbol $f(x)$ and is variously called a **probability density function (pdf)**, a **frequency function,** or a **probability distribution.**

The areas under a probability distribution correspond to probabilities for x. For example, the area A beneath the curve between the two points a and b, as shown in Figure 17, is the probability that x assumes a value between a and b ($a < x < b$). Because there is no area over a point, say $x = a$, it follows that (according to our model) the probability associated with a particular value of x is equal to 0; that is, $P(x = a) = 0$ and hence $P(a < x < b) = P(a \le x \le b)$. In other words, the probability is the same whether or not you include the endpoints of the interval. Also, because areas over intervals represent probabilities, it follows that the total area under a probability distribution, the probability assigned to all values of x, should equal 1. Note that probability distributions for continuous random variables possess different shapes depending on the relative frequency distributions of real data that the probability distributions are supposed to model.

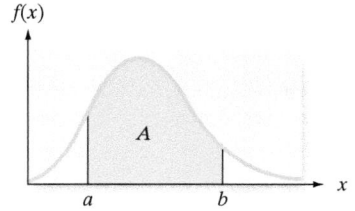

$f(x)$

Figure 17

A probability distribution $f(x)$ for a continuous random variable x

The **probability distribution for a continuous random variable, x,** can be represented by a smooth curve—a function of x, denoted $f(x)$. The curve is called a **density function** or **frequency function.** The probability that x falls between two values, a and b, i.e., $P(a < x < b)$, is the area under the curve between a and b.

The areas under most probability distributions are obtained by using calculus or numerical methods.* Because these methods often involve difficult procedures, we will give the areas for one of the most common probability distributions in tabular form in Appendix: Tables. Then, to find the area between two values of x, say $x = a$ and $x = b$, you simply have to consult the appropriate table. Of course, you can always use statistical software to find this area.

For each of the continuous random variables presented in this chapter, we will give the formula for the probability distribution along with its mean μ and standard deviation σ. These two numbers will enable you to make some approximate probability statements about a random variable even when you do not have access to a table of areas under the probability distribution.

6   The Normal Distribution

One of the most commonly observed continuous random variables has a **bell-shaped** probability distribution (or **bell curve**), as shown in Figure 18. It is known as a **normal random variable,** and its probability distribution is called a **normal distribution.**

The normal distribution plays a very important role in the science of statistical inference. Moreover, many business phenomena generate random variables with probability distributions that are very well approximated by a normal distribution. For example, the monthly rate of return for a particular stock is approximately a normal random variable, and the probability distribution for the weekly sales of a corporation might be approximated by a normal probability distribution. The normal distribution might also provide an accurate model for the distribution of scores on an employment aptitude test. You can determine the adequacy of the normal approximation to an existing population by comparing the relative frequency distribution of a large sample of the data to the normal probability distribution. Methods to detect disagreement between a set of data and the assumption of normality are presented in Section 7.

The normal distribution is perfectly symmetric about its mean μ, as can be seen in the examples in Figure 19. Its spread is determined by the value of its standard deviation σ. The formula for the normal probability distribution is shown in the next box. When plotted, this formula yields a curve like that shown in Figure 18.

Note that the mean μ and standard deviation σ appear in this formula, so no separate formulas for μ and σ are necessary. To graph the normal curve, we have to know the numerical values of μ and σ. Computing the area over intervals under the normal

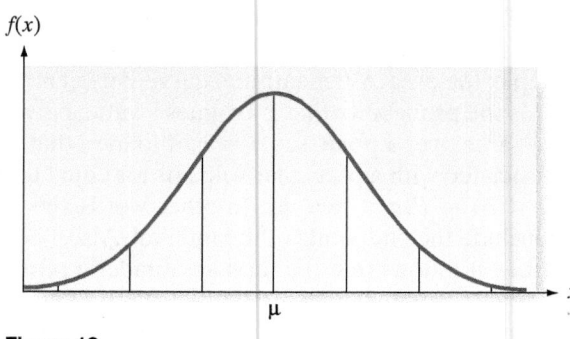

Figure 18

A normal probability distribution

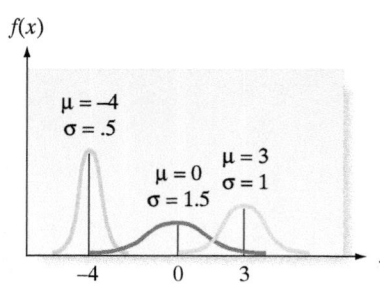

Figure 19

Several normal distributions with different means and standard deviations

*Students with knowledge of calculus should note that the probability that x assumes a value in the interval $a < x < b$ is $P(a < x < b) = \int_a^b f(x)dx$, assuming the integral exists. Similar to the requirement for a discrete probability distribution, we require $f(x) \geq 0$ and $\int_{-\infty}^{\infty} f(x)dx = 1$.

THE GAUSSIAN DISTRIBUTION (1777–1855)
Carl F. Gauss

The normal distribution began in the eighteenth century as a theoretical distribution for errors in disciplines where fluctuations in nature were believed to behave randomly. Although he may not have been the first to discover the formula, the normal distribution was named the Gaussian distribution after Carl Friedrich Gauss. A well-known and respected German mathematician, physicist, and astronomer, Gauss applied the normal distribution while studying the motion of planets and stars. Gauss's prowess as a mathematician was exemplified by one of his most important discoveries. At the young age of 22, Gauss constructed a regular 17-gon by ruler and compasses—a feat that was the most major advance in mathematics since the time of the ancient Greeks. In addition to publishing close to 200 scientific papers, Gauss invented the heliograph as well as a primitive telegraph device.

Probability Distribution for a Normal Random Variable x

Probability density function: $f(x) = \dfrac{1}{\sigma\sqrt{2\pi}}\, e^{-(\frac{1}{2})[(x-\mu)/\sigma]^2}$

where

μ = Mean of the normal random variable x

σ = Standard deviation

π = 3.1415 ...

e = 2.71828 ...

$P(x < a)$ is obtained from a table of normal probabilities or using statistical software.

---

probability distribution is a difficult task.* Consequently, we will use the computed areas listed in Table II in Appendix: Tables. Although there are an infinitely large number of normal curves–one for each pair of values for μ and σ—we have formed a single table that will apply to any normal curve.

Table II is based on a normal distribution with mean $\mu = 0$ and standard deviation $\sigma = 1$, called a *standard normal distribution*. A random variable with a standard normal distribution is typically denoted by the symbol z. The formula for the probability distribution of z is given by

$$f(z) = \frac{1}{\sqrt{2\pi}}\, e^{-(\frac{1}{2})z^2}$$

Figure 20 shows the graph of a standard normal distribution.

The **standard normal distribution** is a normal distribution with $\mu = 0$ and $\sigma = 1$. A random variable with a standard normal distribution, denoted by the symbol z, is called a *standard normal random variable*.

Because we will ultimately convert all normal random variables to standard normal in order to use Table II to find probabilities, it is important that you learn to use Table II well. A partial reproduction of Table II is shown in Table 4. Note that the values of the standard normal random variable z are listed in the left-hand column. The entries in the body of the table give the area (probability) between 0 and z. Examples 16–19 illustrate the use of the table.

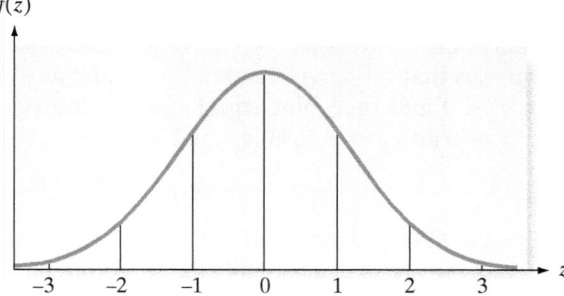

Figure 20

Standard normal distribution:
$\mu = 0, \sigma = 1$

---

*The student with knowledge of calculus should note that there is not a closed-form expression for $P(a < x < b) = \displaystyle\int_a^b f(x)\, dx$ for the normal probability distribution. The value of this definite integral can be obtained to any desired degree of accuracy by numerical approximation procedures. For this reason, it is tabulated for the user.

Table 4		Reproduction of Part of Table II in Appendix: Tables							

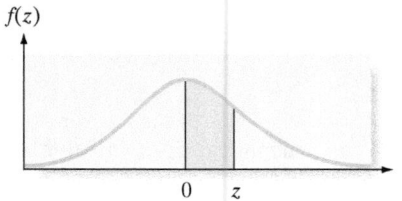

f(z)

z	.00	.01	.02	.03	.04	.05	.06	.07	.08	.09
.0	.0000	.0040	.0080	.0120	.0160	.0199	.0239	.0279	.0319	.0359
.1	.0398	.0438	.0478	.0517	.0557	.0596	.0636	.0675	.0714	.0753
.2	.0793	.0832	.0871	.0910	.0948	.0987	.1026	.1064	.1103	.1141
.3	.1179	.1217	.1255	.1293	.1331	.1368	.1406	.1443	.1480	.1517
.4	.1554	.1591	.1628	.1664	.1700	.1736	.1772	.1808	.1844	.1879
.5	.1915	.1950	.1985	.2019	.2054	.2088	.2123	.2157	.2190	.2224
.6	.2257	.2291	.2324	.2357	.2389	.2422	.2454	.2486	.2517	.2549
.7	.2580	.2611	.2642	.2673	.2704	.2734	.2764	.2794	.2823	.2852
.8	.2881	.2910	.2939	.2967	.2995	.3023	.3051	.3078	.3106	.3133
.9	.3159	.3186	.3212	.3238	.3264	.3289	.3315	.3340	.3365	.3389
1.0	.3413	.3438	.3461	.3485	.3508	.3531	.3554	.3577	.3599	.3621
1.1	.3643	.3665	.3686	.3708	.3729	.3749	.3770	.3790	.3810	.3830
1.2	.3849	.3869	.3888	.3907	.3925	.3944	.3962	.3980	.3997	.4015
1.3	.4032	.4049	.4066	.4082	.4099	.4115	.4131	.4147	.4162	.4177
1.4	.4192	.4207	.4222	.4236	.4251	.4265	.4279	.4292	.4306	.4319
1.5	.4332	.4345	.4357	.4370	.4382	.4394	.4406	.4418	.4429	.4441

Example 16

Using the Standard Normal Table to Find $P(-z_0 < z < z_0)$

Problem Find the probability that the standard normal random variable z falls between -1.33 and 1.33.

Solution The standard normal distribution is shown again in Figure 21. Because all probabilities associated with standard normal random variables can be depicted as areas under the standard normal curve, you should always draw the curve and then equate the desired probability to an area.

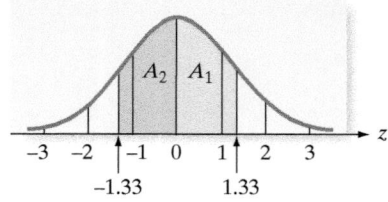

Figure 21
Areas under the standard normal curve for Example 16

In this example, we want to find the probability that z falls between -1.33 and 1.33, which is equivalent to the area between -1.33 and 1.33, shown shaded in Figure 21. Table II provides the area between $z = 0$ and any positive value of z, so that if we look up $z = 1.33$ (the value in the 1.3 row and .03 column, as shown in Table 4), we find that the area between $z = 0$ and $z = 1.33$ is .4082. This is the area labeled A_1 in Figure 21. To find the area A_2 located between $z = 0$ and $z = -1.33$, we note that the symmetry of the normal distribution implies that the area between $z = 0$ and any point to the left is equal to the area between $z = 0$ and the point equidistant to the right. Thus, in this example, the area between $z = 0$ and $z = -1.33$ is equal to the area between $z = 0$ and $z = 1.33$. That is,

$$A_1 = A_2 = .4082$$

The probability that z falls between -1.33 and 1.33 is the sum of the areas of A_1 and A_2. We summarize in probabilistic notation:

$$P(-1.33 < z < 1.33) = P(-1.33 < z < 0) + P(0 < z < 1.33)$$

$$= A_1 + A_2 = .4082 + .4082 = .8164$$

Look Back Remember that "<" and "≤" are equivalent in events involving z because the inclusion (or exclusion) of a single point does not alter the probability of an event involving a continuous random variable.

■ Now Work Exercise 87

Example 17

Using the Standard Normal Table to Find $P(z > z_0)$

Problem Find the probability that a standard normal random variable exceeds 1.64; that is, find $P(z > 1.64)$.

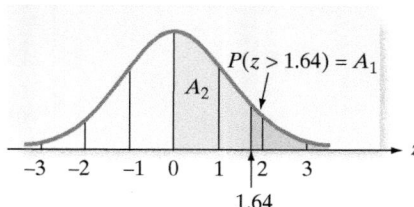

Solution The area under the standard normal distribution to the right of 1.64 is the shaded area labeled A_1 in Figure 22. This area represents the desired probability that z exceeds 1.64. However, when we look up $z = 1.64$ in Table II, we must remember that the probability given in the table corresponds to the area between $z = 0$ and $z = 1.64$ (the area labeled A_2 in Figure 22). From Table II, we find that $A_2 = .4495$. To find the area A_1 to the right of 1.64, we make use of two facts:

Figure 22

Areas under the standard normal curve for Example 17

1. The standard normal distribution is symmetric about its mean, $z = 0$.
2. The total area under the standard normal probability distribution equals 1.

Taken together, these two facts imply that the areas on either side of the mean $z = 0$ equal .5; thus, the area to the right of $z = 0$ in Figure 22 is $A_1 + A_2 = .5$. Then

$$P(z > 1.64) = A_1 = .5 - A_2 = .5 - .4495 = .0505$$

Look Back To attach some practical significance to this probability, note that the implication is that the chance of a standard normal random variable exceeding 1.64 is approximately .05.

■ Now Work Exercise 85a

Example 18

Using the Standard Normal Table to Find $P(z < z_0)$

Problem Find the probability that a standard normal random variable lies to the left of .67.

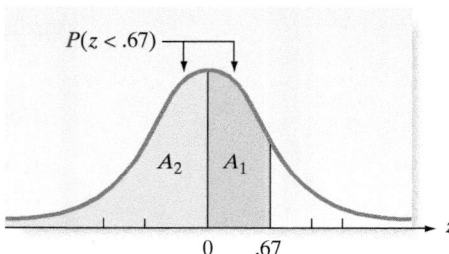

Solution The event is shown as the highlighted area in Figure 23. We want to find $P(z < .67)$. We divide the highlighted area into two parts: the area A_1 between $z = 0$ and $z = .67$ and the area A_2 to the left of $z = 0$. We must always make such a division when the desired area lies on both sides of the mean ($z = 0$) because Table II contains areas between $z = 0$ and the point you look up. We look up $z = .67$

Figure 23

Areas under the standard normal curve for Example 18

in Table II to find that $A_1 = .2486$. The symmetry of the standard normal distribution also implies that half the distribution lies on each side of the mean, so the area A_2 to the left of $z = 0$ is .5. Then

$$P(z < .67) = A_1 + A_2 = .2486 + .5 = .7486$$

Look Back Note that this probability is approximately .75. Thus, about 75% of the time the standard normal random variable z will fall below .67. This implies that $z = .67$ represents the approximate 75th percentile for the distribution.

■ Now Work Exercise 86f

Example   19

Using the Standard Normal Table to Find $P(|z| > z_0)$

Problem Find the probability that a standard normal random variable exceeds 1.96 in absolute value.

Solution We want to find

$$P(|z| > 1.96) = P(z < -1.96 \text{ or } z > 1.96)$$

This probability is the shaded area in Figure 24. Note that the total shaded area is the sum of two areas, A_1 and A_2—areas that are equal because of the symmetry of the normal distribution.

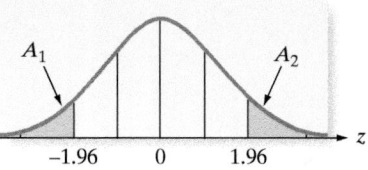

Figure 24

Areas under the standard normal curve for Example 19

We look up $z = 1.96$ and find the area between $z = 0$ and $z = 1.96$ to be .4750. Then the area to the right of 1.96, A_2, is $.5 - .4750 = .0250$, so that

$$P(|z| > 1.96) = A_1 + A_2 = .0250 + .0250 = .05$$

Look Back We emphasize, again, the importance of drawing the standard normal curve when finding normal probabilities.

To apply Table II to a normal random variable x with any mean μ and any standard deviation σ, we must first convert the value of x to a z-score. The population z-score for a measurement was defined as the *distance* between the measurement and the population mean, divided by the population standard deviation. Thus, the z-score gives the distance between a measurement and the mean in units equal to the standard deviation. In symbolic form, the z-score for the measurement x is

$$z = \frac{x - \mu}{\sigma}$$

Note that when $x = \mu$, we obtain $z = 0$.

An important property of the normal distribution is that if x is normally distributed with any mean and any standard deviation, z is always normally distributed with mean 0 and standard deviation 1. That is, z is a standard normal random variable.

Converting a Normal Distribution to a Standard Normal Distribution

If x is a normal random variable with mean μ and standard deviation σ, then the random variable z, defined by the formula

$$z = \frac{x - \mu}{\sigma}$$

has a standard normal distribution. The value z describes the number of standard deviations between x and μ.

Recall from Example 19 that $P(|z| > 1.96) = .05$. This probability coupled with our interpretation of z implies that any normal random variable lies more than 1.96 standard deviations from its mean only 5% of the time. Compare this to the Empirical Rule, which tells us that about 5% of the measurements in mound-shaped distributions will lie beyond 2 standard deviations from the mean. The normal distribution actually provides the model on which the Empirical Rule is based, along with much "empirical" experience with real data that often approximately obey the rule, whether drawn from a normal distribution or not.

Example	20

Finding the Probability of a Normal Random Variable—Cell Phone Application

Problem Assume that the length of time, x, between charges of a cellular phone is normally distributed with a mean of 10 hours and a standard deviation of 1.5 hours. Find the probability that the cell phone will last between 8 and 12 hours between charges.

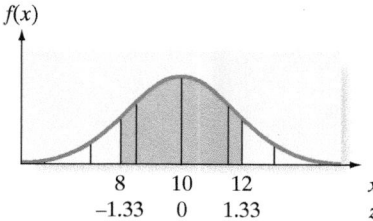

Figure 25

Areas under the normal curve for Example 20

Solution The normal distribution with mean $\mu = 10$ and $\sigma = 1.5$ is shown in Figure 25. The desired probability that the charge lasts between 8 and 12 hours is shaded. In order to find the probability, we must first convert the distribution to standard normal, which we do by calculating the z-score:

$$z = \frac{x - \mu}{\sigma}$$

The z-scores corresponding to the important values of x are shown beneath the x values on the horizontal axis in Figure 25. Note that $z = 0$ corresponds to the mean of $\mu = 10$ hours, whereas the x values 8 and 12 yield z-scores of -1.33 and 1.33, respectively. Thus, the event that the cell phone charge lasts between 8 and 12 hours is equivalent to the event that a standard normal random variable lies between -1.33 and 1.33. We found this probability in Example 16 (see Figure 21) by doubling the area corresponding to $z = 1.33$ in Table II. That is,

$$P(8 \leq x \leq 12) = P(-1.33 \leq z \leq 1.33) = 2(.4082) = .8164$$

■ **Now Work Exercise 100a–c**

Table II in Appendix: Tables provides good approximations to probabilities under the normal curve. However, if you do not have access to a normal table, you can always rely on statistical software to compute the desired probability. With most statistical software, you will need to specify the mean and standard deviation of the normal distribution, as well as the key values of the variable for which you desire probabilities. In Example 20, we desire $P(8 \leq x \leq 12)$, where $\mu = 10$ and $\sigma = 1.5$. To find this probability using Minitab's normal probability function, we enter 10 for the mean and 1.5 for the standard deviation, and then find two cumulative probabilities: $P(x \leq 12)$ and $P(x < 8)$. These two probabilities are shown (shaded) on the Minitab printout, Figure 26. The difference between the two probabilities yields the desired result:

$$P(8 \leq x \leq 12) = P(x \leq 12) - P(x < 8) = .908789 - .0912112 = .8175778$$

Note that this probability agrees with the value computed using Table II to two decimal places. The difference is due to rounding of the probabilities given in Table II.

The steps to follow when calculating a probability corresponding to a normal random variable are shown in the box on the next page.

Cumulative Distribution Function

```
Normal with mean = 10 and standard deviation = 1.5

 x   P( X <= x )
12      0.908789
```

Cumulative Distribution Function

```
Normal with mean = 10 and standard deviation = 1.5

 x   P( X <= x )
 8      0.0912112
```

Figure 26

Minitab output with cumulative normal probabilities

Steps for Finding a Probability Corresponding to a Normal Random Variable

1. Sketch the normal distribution and indicate the mean of the random variable x. Then shade the area corresponding to the probability you want to find.

2. Convert the boundaries of the shaded area from x values to standard normal random variable z values using the formula

$$z = \frac{x - \mu}{\sigma}$$

   Show the z values under the corresponding x values on your sketch.

3. Use Table II in Appendix: Tables or statistical software to find the areas corresponding to the z values. If necessary, use the symmetry of the normal distribution to find areas corresponding to negative z values and the fact that the total area on each side of the mean equals .5 to convert the areas to the probabilities of the event you have shaded.

Example 21

Using Normal Probabilities to Make an Inference—Advertised Gas Mileage

Problem Suppose an automobile manufacturer introduces a new model that has an advertised mean in-city mileage of 27 miles per gallon. Although such advertisements seldom report any measure of variability, suppose you write the manufacturer for the details of the tests, and you find that the standard deviation is 3 miles per gallon. This information leads you to formulate a probability model for the random variable x, the in-city mileage for this car model. You believe that the probability distribution of x can be approximated by a normal distribution with a mean of 27 and a standard deviation of 3.

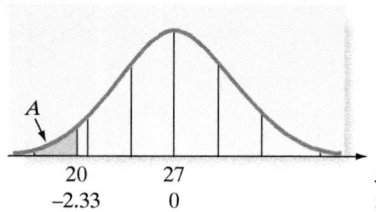

Figure 27

Areas under the normal curve for Example 21

a. If you were to buy this model of automobile, what is the probability that you would purchase one that averages less than 20 miles per gallon for in-city driving? In other words, find $P(x < 20)$.

b. Suppose you purchase one of these new models and it does get less than 20 miles per gallon for in-city driving. Should you conclude that your probability model is incorrect?

Solution

a. The probability model proposed for x, the in-city mileage, is shown in Figure 27. We are interested in finding the area A to the left of 20 because this area corresponds to the probability that a measurement chosen from this distribution falls below 20. In other words, if this model is correct, the area A represents the fraction of cars that can be expected to get less than 20 miles per gallon for in-city driving. To find A, we first calculate the z-value corresponding to $x = 20$. That is,

$$z = \frac{x - \mu}{\sigma} = \frac{20 - 27}{3} = -\frac{7}{3} = -2.33$$

Then

$$P(x < 20) = P(z < -2.33)$$

as indicated by the shaded area in Figure 27. Because Table II gives areas only to the right of the mean (and because the normal distribution is symmetric about its mean), we look up 2.33 in Table II and find that the corresponding area is .4901. This is equal to the area between $z = 0$ and $z = -2.33$, so we find

$$P(x < 20) = A = .5 - .4901 = .0099 \approx .01$$

According to this probability model, you should have only about a 1% chance of purchasing a car of this make with an in-city mileage under 20 miles per gallon.

b. Now you are asked to make an inference based on a sample—the car you purchased. You are getting less than 20 miles per gallon for in-city driving. What do you infer? We think you will agree that one of two possibilities is true:

1. The probability model is correct. You simply were unfortunate to have purchased one of the cars in the 1% that get less than 20 miles per gallon in the city.

2. The probability model is incorrect. Perhaps the assumption of a normal distribution is unwarranted or the mean of 27 is an overestimate, or the standard deviation of 3 is an underestimate, or some combination of these errors was made. At any rate, the form of the actual probability model certainly merits further investigation.

You have no way of knowing with certainty which possibility is correct, but the evidence points to the second one. We are again relying on the rare-event approach to statistical inference that we introduced earlier. The sample (one measurement in this case) was so unlikely to have been drawn from the proposed probability model that it casts serious doubt on the model. We would be inclined to believe that the model is somehow in error.

Look Back When applying the rare-event approach, the calculated probability must be small (say, less than or equal to .05) in order to infer that the observed event is, indeed, unlikely.

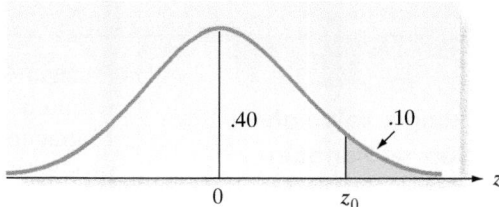

Now Work Exercise 100d

Occasionally you will be given a probability and will want to find the values of the normal random variable that correspond to the probability. For example, suppose the scores on a college entrance examination are known to be normally distributed, and a certain prestigious university will consider for admission only those applicants whose scores exceed the 90th percentile of the test score distribution. To determine the minimum score for admission consideration, you will need to be able to use Table II or statistical software in reverse, as demonstrated in the following example.

Example 22

Finding a z-value Associated with a Normal Probability

Problem Find the value of z, call it z_0, in the standard normal distribution that will be exceeded only 10% of the time—that is, find z_0 such that $P(z \geq z_0) = .10$.

Solution In this case we are given a probability, or an area, and asked to find the value of the standard normal random variable that corresponds to the area. Specifically, we want to find the value z_0 such that only 10% of the standard normal distribution exceeds z_0 (see Figure 28).

.40   .10

0   z_0 z

Figure 28

Area under the standard normal curve for Example 22

We know that the total area to the right of the mean $z = 0$ is .5, which implies that z_0 must lie to the right of (above) 0. To pinpoint the value, we use the fact that the area to the right of z_0 is .10, which implies that the area between $z = 0$ and z_0 is $.5 - .1 = .4$. But areas between $z = 0$ and some other z-value are exactly the types given in Table II. Therefore, we look up the area .4000 in the body of Table II and find that the corresponding z-value is (to the closest approximation) $z_0 = 1.28$. The implication is that the point 1.28 standard deviations above the mean is the 90th percentile of a normal distribution.

We can also arrive at this answer using statistical software. In Minitab, we use the inverse cumulative distribution function for a normal random variable and specify the cumulative probability,

$$P(z \leq z_0) = .9$$

237

Figure 29
Minitab output for Example 22

Inverse Cumulative Distribution Function

Normal with mean = 0 and standard deviation = 1

P(X <= x)   x
       0.9   1.28155

The value of z_0 is shown (shaded) on the Minitab printout, Figure 29. You can see that this value agrees with our solution using the normal table.

Look Back As with earlier problems, it is critical to draw correctly the normal probability of interest on the normal curve. Placement of z_0 to the left or right of 0 is the key. Be sure to shade the probability (area) involving z_0. If it does not agree with the probability of interest (i.e., the shaded area is greater than .5 and the probability of interest is smaller than .5), then you need to place z_0 on the opposite side of 0.

■ **Now Work Exercise 89**

Example	**23**

Finding a z-Value Associated with a Normal Probability

Problem Find the value of z_0 such that 95% of the standard normal z values lie between $-z_0$ and z_0; that is, $P(-z_0 \le z \le z_0) = .95$.

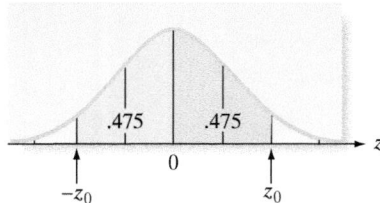

Solution Here we wish to move an equal distance z_0 in the positive and negative directions from the mean $z = 0$ until 95% of the standard normal distribution is enclosed. This means that the area on each side of the mean will be equal to $\frac{1}{2}(.95) = .475$, as shown in Figure 30. Because the area between $z = 0$ and z_0 is .475, we look up .475 in the body of Table II to find the value $z_0 = 1.96$. Thus, as we found in the reverse order in Example 22, 95% of a normal distribution lies between -1.96 and 1.96 standard deviations of the mean.

Figure 30
Areas under the standard normal curve for Example 23

■ **Now Work Exercise 92**

Now that you have learned how to find a standard normal z-value that corresponds to a specified probability, we demonstrate a practical application in Example 24.

Example	**24**

Finding a Value of a Normal Random Variable—Paint Manufacturing Application

Problem Suppose a paint manufacturer has a daily production, x, that is normally distributed with a mean of 100,000 gallons and a standard deviation of 10,000 gallons. Management wants to create an incentive bonus for the production crew when the daily production exceeds the 90th percentile of the distribution, in hopes that the crew will, in turn, become more productive. At what level of production should management pay the incentive bonus?

Solution In this example, we want to find a production level, x_0, such that 90% of the daily levels (x values) in the distribution fall below x_0 and only 10% fall above x_0—that is,

$$P(x \le x_0) = .90$$

Converting x to a standard normal random variable, where $\mu = 100,000$ and $\sigma = 10,000$, we have

$$P(x \le x_0) = P\left(z \le \frac{x_0 - \mu}{\sigma}\right)$$

$$= P\left(z \le \frac{x_0 - 100,000}{10,000}\right) = .90$$

In Example 22 (see Figure 28) we found the 90th percentile of the standard normal distribution to be $z_0 = 1.28$—that is, we found $P(z \le 1.28) = .90$. Consequently, we know the production level x_0 at which the incentive bonus is paid corresponds to a z-score of 1.28; that is,

$$\frac{x_0 - 100{,}000}{10{,}000} = 1.28$$

If we solve this equation for x_0, we find

$$x_0 = 100{,}000 + 1.28(10{,}000) = 100{,}000 + 12{,}800 = 112{,}800$$

This x value is shown in Figure 31. Thus, the 90th percentile of the production distribution is 112,800 gallons. Management should pay an incentive bonus when a day's production exceeds this level if its objective is to pay only when production is in the top 10% of the current daily production distribution.

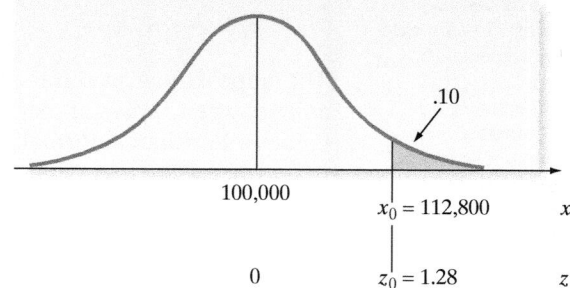

Figure 31

Area under the normal curve
for Example 24

Look Back As this example shows, in practical applications of the normal table in reverse, first find the value of z_0, then convert the value to the units of x using the z-score formula in reverse.

Now Work Exercise 97a

We close this section with one final application of the normal distribution. When n is large, a normal probability distribution may be used to provide a good approximation to the probability distribution of the discrete binomial random variable (Section 3). To show how this approximation works, we refer to Example 13, in which we used the binomial distribution to model the number x of 20 employees who favor unionization. We assumed that 60% of the company's employees favored unionization. The mean and standard deviation of x were found to be $\mu = 12$ and $\sigma = 2.2$. The binomial distribution for $n = 20$ and $p = .6$ is shown in Figure 32 and the approximating normal distribution with mean $\mu = 12$ and standard deviation $\sigma = 2.2$ is superimposed.

As part of Example 13, we used Table I to find the probability that $x \leq 10$. This probability, which is equal to the sum of the areas contained in the rectangles (shown in Figure 32) that correspond to $p(0), p(1), p(2), \ldots, p(10)$, was found to equal .245. The portion of the approximating normal curve that would be used to approximate the

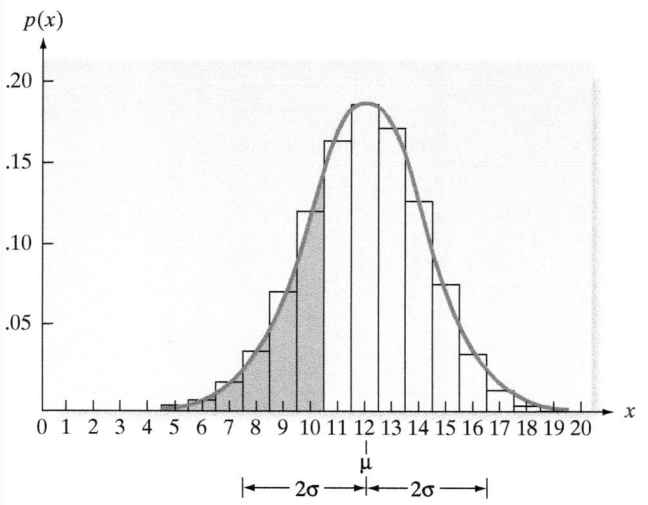

Figure 32

Binomial distribution for $n = 20$,
$p = .6$, and normal distribution
with $\mu = 12$, $\sigma = 2.2$

239

area $p(0) + p(1) + p(2) + \cdots + p(10)$ is shaded in Figure 32. Note that this shaded area lies to the left of 10.5 (not 10), so we may include all of the probability in the rectangle corresponding to $p(10)$. Because we are approximating a discrete distribution (the binomial) with a continuous distribution (the normal), we call the use of 10.5 (instead of 10 or 11) a **correction for continuity**, that is, we are correcting the discrete distribution so that it can be approximated by the continuous one. The use of the correction for continuity leads to the calculation of the following standard normal z-value:

$$z = \frac{x - \mu}{\sigma} = \frac{10.5 - 12}{2.2} = -.68$$

Using Table II, we find the area between $z = 0$ and $z = .68$ to be .2517. Then the probability that x is less than or equal to 10 is approximated by the area under the normal distribution to the left of 10.5, shown shaded in Figure 32—that is,

$$P(x \le 10) \approx P(z \le -.68) = .5 - P(-.68 < z \le 0) = .5 - .2517 = .2483$$

The approximation differs only slightly from the exact binomial probability, .245. Of course, when tables of exact binomial probabilities are available, we will use the exact value rather than a normal approximation.

Use of the normal distribution will not always provide a good approximation for binomial probabilities. The following is a useful rule of thumb to determine when n is large enough for the approximation to be effective: *The interval $\mu \pm 3\sigma$ should lie within the range of the binomial random variable x (i.e., 0 to n) in order for the normal approximation to be adequate.* The rule works well because almost all of the normal distribution falls within 3 standard deviations of the mean, so if this interval is contained within the range of x values, there is "room" for the normal approximation to work.

As shown in Figure 33a for the preceding example with $n = 20$ and $p = .6$, the interval $\mu \pm 3\sigma = 12 \pm 3(2.2) = (5.4, 18.6)$ lies within the range 0 to 20. However, if we were to try to use the normal approximation with $n = 10$ and $p = .1$, the interval $\mu \pm 3\sigma$ is $1 \pm 3(.95)$, or $(-1.85, 3.85)$. As shown in Figure 33b, this interval is

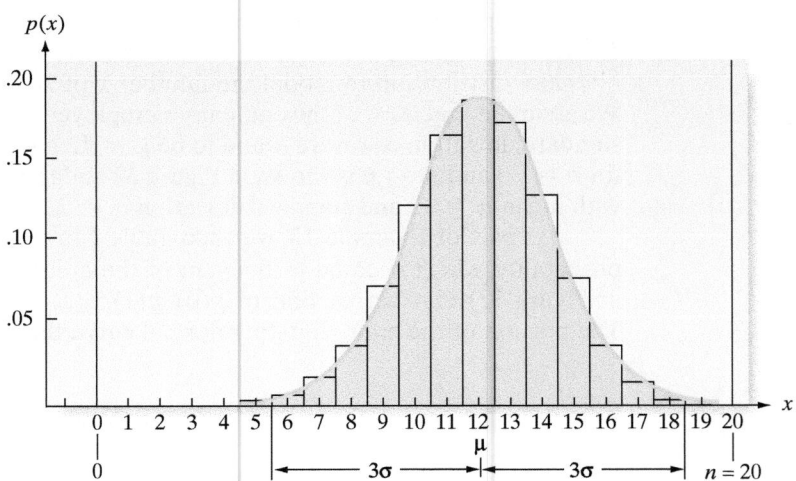

a. $n = 20, p = .6$: Normal approximation is good

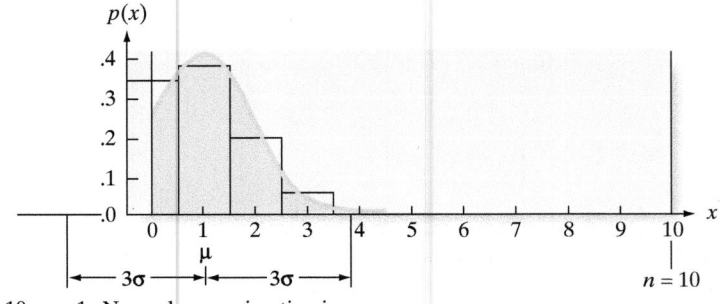

Figure 33

Rule of thumb for normal approximation to binomial probabilities

b. $n = 10, p = .1$: Normal approximation is poor

not contained within the range of x because $x = 0$ is the lower bound for a binomial random variable. Note in Figure 33b that the normal distribution will not "fit" in the range of x, and therefore it will not provide a good approximation to the binomial probabilities.

Example   25

Applying the Normal Approximation to a Binomial Probability—Lot Acceptance Sampling

Problem One problem with any product (e.g., a graphing calculator) that is mass produced is quality control. The process must somehow be monitored or audited to be sure the output of the process conforms to requirements. One method of dealing with this problem is *lot acceptance sampling,* in which items being produced are sampled at various stages of the production process and are carefully inspected. The lot of items from which the sample is drawn is then accepted or rejected, based on the number of defectives in the sample. Lots that are accepted may be sent forward for further processing or may be shipped to customers; lots that are rejected may be reworked or scrapped. For example, suppose a manufacturer of calculators chooses 200 stamped circuits from the day's production and determines x, the number of defective circuits in the sample. Suppose that up to a 6% rate of defectives is considered acceptable for the process.

a. Find the mean and standard deviation of x, assuming the defective rate is 6%.

b. Use the normal approximation to determine the probability that 20 or more defectives are observed in the sample of 200 circuits (i.e., find the approximate probability that $x \geq 20$).

Solution

a. The random variable x is binomial with $n = 200$ and the fraction defective $p = .06$. Thus,

$$\mu = np = 200(.06) = 12$$
$$\sigma = \sqrt{npq} = \sqrt{200(.06)(.94)} = \sqrt{11.28} = 3.36$$

We first note that

$$\mu \pm 3\sigma = 12 \pm 3(3.36) = 12 \pm 10.08 = (1.92, 22.08)$$

lies completely within the range from 0 to 200. Therefore, a normal probability distribution should provide an adequate approximation to this binomial distribution.

b. Using the rule of complements, $P(x \geq 20) = 1 - P(x \leq 19)$. To find the approximating area corresponding to $x \leq 19$, refer to Figure 34. Note that we want to include all the binomial probability histogram from 0 to 19, inclusive. Because the event is of the form $x \leq a$, the proper correction for continuity is $a + .5 = 19 + .5 = 19.5$. Thus, the z-value of interest is

$$z = \frac{(a + .5) - \mu}{\sigma} = \frac{19.5 - 12}{3.36} = \frac{7.5}{3.36} = 2.23$$

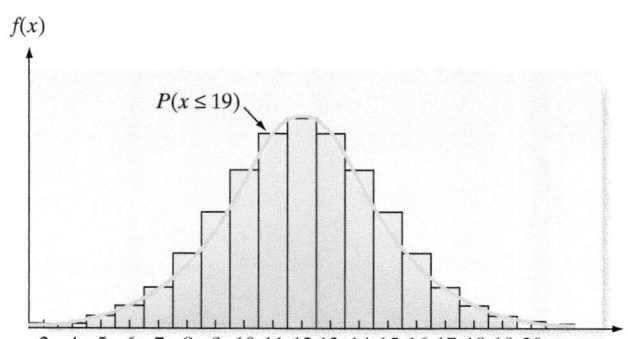

Figure 34

Normal approximation to the binomial distribution with $n = 200, p = .06$

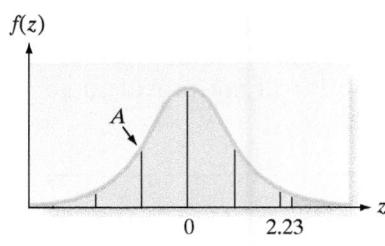

Figure 35
Standard normal distribution

Referring to Table II in Appendix: Tables, we find that the area to the right of the mean 0 corresponding to $z = 2.23$ (see Figure 35) is .4871. So the area $A = P(z \le 2.23)$ is

$$A = .5 + .4871 = .9871$$

Thus, the normal approximation to the binomial probability we seek is

$$P(x \ge 20) = 1 - P(x \le 19) \approx 1 - .9871 = .0129$$

In other words, the probability is extremely small that 20 or more defectives will be observed in a sample of 200 circuits—*if in fact the true fraction of defectives is .06.*

Look Back If the manufacturer observes $x \ge 20$, the likely reason is that the process is producing more than the acceptable 6% defectives. The lot acceptance sampling procedure is another example of using the rare-event approach to make inferences.

■ **Now Work Exercise 95**

The steps for approximating a binomial probability by a normal probability are given in the next box.

Using a Normal Distribution to Approximate Binomial Probabilities

1. After you have determined n and p for the binomial distribution, calculate the interval

$$\mu \pm 3\sigma = np \pm 3\sqrt{npq}$$

If the interval lies in the range 0 to n, the normal distribution will provide a reasonable approximation to the probabilities of most binomial events.

2. Express the binomial probability to be approximated in the form $P(x \le a)$ or $P(x \le b) - P(x \le a)$. For example,

$$P(x < 3) = P(x \le 2)$$
$$P(x \ge 5) = 1 - P(x \le 4)$$
$$P(7 \le x \le 10) = P(x \le 10) - P(x \le 6)$$

3. For each value of interest a, the correction for continuity is $(a + .5)$, and the corresponding standard normal z-value is

$$z = \frac{(a + .5) - \mu}{\sigma} \quad \text{(see Figure 36)}$$

4. Sketch the approximating normal distribution and shade the area corresponding to the probability of the event of interest, as in Figure 36. Verify that the rectangles you have included in the shaded area correspond to the event probability you wish to approximate. Using Table II and the z-value(s) you calculated in step 3, find the shaded area. This is the approximate probability of the binomial event.

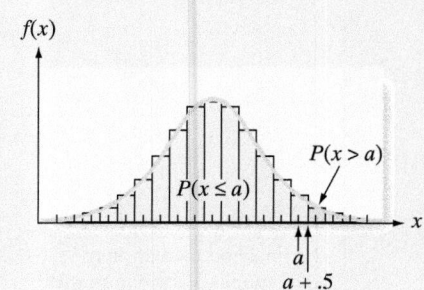

Figure 36
Approximating binomial probabilities by normal probabilities

Exercises 84–116

Please be aware that some of the following problems may require knowledge of concepts that are not presented in this chapter.

Learning the Mechanics

84 Find the area under the standard normal probability distribution between the following pairs of z-scores:
  a. $z = 0$ and $z = 2.00$ **b.** $z = 0$ and $z = 3$
  c. $z = 0$ and $z = 1.5$ **d.** $z = 0$ and $z = .80$

85 Find the following probabilities for the standard normal
NW random variable z:
  a. $P(z > 1.46)$ **b.** $P(z < -1.56)$
  c. $P(.67 \leq z < 2.41)$ **d.** $P(-1.96 \leq z < -.33)$
  e. $P(z \geq 0)$ **f.** $P(-2.33 < z < 1.50)$

86 Find the following probabilities for the standard normal random variable z:
  a. $P(-1 < z < 1)$ **b.** $P(-2 < z < 2)$
  c. $P(-2.16 \leq z \leq .55)$ **d.** $P(-.42 < z < 1.96)$
  e. $P(z \geq -2.33)$ **NW f.** $P(z < 2.33)$

87 Find each of the following probabilities for the standard
NW normal random variable z:
  a. $P(-1 \leq z \leq 1)$ **b.** $P(-1.96 \leq z \leq 1.96)$
  c. $P(-1.645 \leq z \leq 1.645)$ **d.** $P(-2 \leq z \leq 2)$

88 Find a value of the standard normal random variable z, call it z_0, such that
  a. $P(z \geq z_0) = .05$ **b.** $P(z \geq z_0) = .025$
  c. $P(z \leq z_0) = .025$ **d.** $P(z \geq z_0) = .10$
  e. $P(z > z_0) = .10$

89 Find a value of the standard normal random variable z, call
NW it z_0, such that
  a. $P(z \leq z_0) = .2090$
  b. $P(z \leq z_0) = .7090$
  c. $P(-z_0 \leq z < z_0) = .8472$
  d. $P(-z_0 \leq z < z_0) = .1664$
  e. $P(z_0 \leq z \leq 0) = .4798$
  f. $P(-1 < z < z_0)$

90 Give the z-score for a measurement from a normal distribution for the following:
  a. 1 standard deviation above the mean
  b. 1 standard deviation below the mean
  c. Equal to the mean
  d. 2.5 standard deviations below the mean
  e. 3 standard deviations above the mean

91 Suppose the random variable x is best described by a normal distribution with $\mu = 30$ and $\sigma = 4$. Find the z-score that corresponds to each of the following x values:
  a. $x = 20$ **b.** $x = 30$
  c. $x = 2.75$ **d.** $x = 15$
  e. $x = 35$ **f.** $x = 25$

92 The random variable x has a normal distribution with
NW $\mu = 1,000$ and $\sigma = 10$.
  a. Find the probability that x assumes a value more than 2 standard deviations from its mean. More than 3 standard deviations from μ.
  b. Find the probability that x assumes a value within 1 standard deviation of its mean. Within 2 standard deviations of μ.
  c. Find the value of x that represents the 80th percentile of this distribution. The 10th percentile.

93 Suppose x is a normally distributed random variable with $\mu = 11$ and $\sigma = 2$. Find each of the following:
  a. $P(10 \leq x \leq 12)$ **b.** $P(6 \leq x \leq 10)$
  c. $P(13 \leq x \leq 16)$ **d.** $P(7.8 \leq x \leq 12.6)$
  e. $P(x \geq 13.24)$ **f.** $P(x \geq 7.62)$

94 Suppose x is a normally distributed random variable with $\mu = 50$ and $\sigma = 3$. Find a value of the random variable, call it x_0, such that
  a. $P(x \leq x_0) = .8413$
  b. $P(x > x_0) = .025$
  c. $P(x > x_0) = .95$
  d. $P(41 \leq x < x_0) = .8630$
  e. 10% of the values of x are less than x_0.
  f. 1% of the values of x are greater than x_0.

95 Suppose x is a binomial random variable with $p = .4$ and
NW $n = 25$.
  a. Would it be appropriate to approximate the probability distribution of x with a normal distribution? Explain.
  b. Assuming that a normal distribution provides an adequate approximation to the distribution of x, what are the mean and variance of the approximating normal distribution?
  c. Use Table I in Appendix: Tables to find the exact value of $P(x \geq 9)$.
  d. Use the normal approximation to find $P(x \geq 9)$.

96 Assume that x is a binomial random variable with $n = 1,000$ and $p = .50$. Use a normal approximation to find each of the following probabilities:
  a. $P(x > 500)$
  b. $P(490 \leq x < 500)$
  c. $P(x > 550)$

⚽ Applet Exercise 6

Open the applet *Sample from a Population*. On the pull-down menu to the right of the top graph, select *Bell shaped*. The box to the left of the top graph displays the population mean, median, and standard deviation.
  a. Run the applet for each available value of n on the pull-down menu for the sample size. Go from the smallest to the largest value of n. For each value of n, observe the shape of the graph of the sample data and record the mean, median, and standard deviation of the sample.
  b. Describe what happens to the shape of the graph and the mean, median, and standard deviation of the sample as the sample size increases.

Applying the Concepts—Basic

97 **Tomato as a taste modifier.** Miraculin—a protein naturally produced in a rare tropical fruit—can convert a sour taste into a sweet taste. Consequently, miraculin has the potential to be an alternative low-calorie sweetener. In *Plant Science* (May 2010), a group of Japanese environmental scientists investigated the ability of a hybrid tomato plant to produce miraculin. For a particular generation of the tomato plant, the amount x of miraculin produced (measured in micrograms per gram of fresh weight) had a mean of 105.3 and a standard deviation of 8.0. Assume that x is normally distributed.

a. Find $P(x > 120)$.

b. Find $P(100 < x < 110)$.

NW **c.** Find the value a for which $P(x < a) = .25$.

98 **Corporate sustainability of CPA firms.** *Business and Society* (March 2011) did a study on the sustainability behaviors of CPA corporations. The level of support for corporate sustainability (measured on a quantitative scale ranging from 0 to 160 points) was obtained for each of 992 senior managers at CPA firms. The accompanying Minitab printout gives the mean and standard deviation for the level of support variable. It can be shown that level of support is approximately normally distributed.

a. Find the probability that the level of support for corporate sustainability of a randomly selected senior manager is less than 40 points.

b. Find the probability that the level of support for corporate sustainability of a randomly selected senior manager is between 40 and 120 points.

c. Find the probability that the level of support for corporate sustainability of a randomly selected senior manager is greater than 120 points.

d. One-fourth of the 992 senior managers indicated a level of support for corporate sustainability below what value?

Descriptive Statistics: Support

Variable	N	Mean	StDev	Variance	Minimum	Maximum	Range
Support	992	67.755	26.871	722.036	0.000	155.000	155.000

99 **Shopping vehicle and judgment.** The *Journal of Marketing Research* (Dec. 2011) did a study of whether you are more likely to choose a vice product (e.g., a candy bar) when your arm is flexed (as when carrying a shopping basket) than when your arm is extended (as when pushing a shopping cart). The study measured choice scores (on a scale of 0 to 100, where higher scores indicate a greater preference for vice options) for consumers shopping under each of the two conditions. The average choice score for consumers with a flexed arm was 59, while the average for consumers with an extended arm was 43. For both conditions, assume that the standard deviation of the choice scores is 5. Also assume that both distributions are approximately normally distributed.

a. In the flexed arm condition, what is the probability that a consumer has a choice score of 60 or greater?

b. In the extended arm condition, what is the probability that a consumer has a choice score of 60 or greater?

100 **The business of casino gaming.** Casino gaming yields over $35 billion in revenue each year in the United States. In *Chance* (Spring 2005), University of Denver statistician R. C. Hannum discussed the business of casino gaming and its reliance on the laws of probability. Casino games of pure chance (e.g., craps, roulette, baccarat, and keno) always yield a "house advantage." For example, in the game of double-zero roulette, the expected casino win percentage is 5.26% on bets made on whether the outcome will be either black or red. (This implies that for every $5 bet on black or red, the casino will earn a net of about 25¢.)

It can be shown that in 100 roulette plays on black/red, the average casino win percentage is normally distributed with mean 5.26% and standard deviation 10%. Let x represent the average casino win percentage after 100 bets on black/red in double-zero roulette.

a. Find $P(x > 0)$. (This is the probability that the casino wins money.)

b. Find $P(5 < x < 15)$.

c. Find $P(x < 1)$.

d. If you observed an average casino win percentage of -25% after 100 roulette bets on black/red, what would you conclude?

101 **Buy-side vs. sell-side analysts' earnings forecasts.** Financial analysts who make forecasts of stock prices are categorized as either "buy-side" analysts or "sell-side" analysts. *Financial Analysts Journal* (Jul./Aug. 2008) did a comparison of earnings forecasts of buy-side and sell-side analysts. The mean and standard deviation of forecast errors for both types of analysts are reproduced in the table. Assume that the distribution of forecast errors are approximately normally distributed.

a. Find the probability that a buy-side analyst has a forecast error of +2.00 or higher.

b. Find the probability that a sell-side analyst has a forecast error of +2.00 or higher.

	Buy-Side Analysts	Sell-Side Analysts
Mean	0.85	-0.05
Standard Deviation	1.93	0.85

Source: Based on Groysberg, B., Healy, P., & Chapman, C. *Financial Analysis Journal*, Vol. 64, No. 4, Jul./Aug. 2008.

102 **NHTSA crash safety tests.** Refer to Exercise 21 and the NHTSA crash test data for new cars. One of the variables saved in the accompanying file is the severity of a driver's head injury when the car is in a head-on collision with a fixed barrier while traveling at 35 miles per hour. The more points assigned to the head-injury rating, the more severe the injury. The head-injury ratings can be shown to be approximately normally distributed with a mean of 605 points and a standard deviation of 185 points. One of the crash-tested cars is randomly selected from the data, and the driver's head-injury rating is observed.

a. Find the probability that the rating will fall between 500 and 700 points.

b. Find the probability that the rating will fall between 400 and 500 points.

c. Find the probability that the rating will be less than 850 points.

d. Find the probability that the rating will exceed 1,000 points.

103 **Paying for music downloads.** In Exercise 49 you learned that half of all U.S. adults use the Internet and have paid to download music (*Pew Internet & American Life Project Survey*, October 2010). In a random sample of 250 U.S. adults, let x be the number who use the Internet and pay to download music.

a. Find the mean of x. (This value should agree with your answer to Exercise 49c.)

b. Find the standard deviation of x.

c. Find the z-score for the value $x = 200$.

d. Find the approximate probability that the number of the 250 adults who use the Internet and pay to download music is less than or equal to 200.

104 **LASIK surgery complications.** According to studies, 1% of all patients who undergo laser surgery (i.e., LASIK) to correct their vision have serious postlaser vision problems (*All About Vision*, 2012). In a sample of 100,000 patients, what is the approximate probability that fewer than 950 will experience serious postlaser vision problems?

Applying the Concepts—Intermediate

105 **Optimal goal target in soccer.** When attempting to score a goal in soccer, where should you aim your shot? Should you aim for a goalpost (as some soccer coaches teach), the middle of the goal, or some other target? To answer these questions, *Chance* (Fall 2009) utilized the normal probability distribution. Suppose the accuracy x of a professional soccer player's shots follows a normal distribution with a mean of 0 feet and a standard deviation of 3 feet. (For example, if the player hits his target, $x = 0$; if he misses his target 2 feet to the right, $x = 2$; and if he misses 1 foot to the left, $x = -1$.) Now, a regulation soccer goal is 24 feet wide. Assume that a goalkeeper will stop (save) all shots within 9 feet of where he is standing; all other shots on goal will score. Consider a goalkeeper who stands in the middle of the goal.

a. If the player aims for the right goalpost, what is the probability that he will score?

b. If the player aims for the center of the goal, what is the probability that he will score?

c. If the player aims for halfway between the right goalpost and the outer limit of the goalkeeper's reach, what is the probability that he will score?

106 **Mean shifts on a production line.** *Six Sigma* is a comprehensive approach to quality goal setting that involves statistics. An article in *Aircraft Engineering and Aerospace Technology* (Vol. 76, No. 6, 2004) demonstrated the use of the normal distribution in Six Sigma goal setting at Motorola Corporation. Motorola discovered that the average defect rate for parts produced on an assembly line varies from run to run and is approximately normally distributed with a mean equal to 3 defects per million. Assume that the goal at Motorola is for the average defect rate to vary no more than 1.5 standard deviations above or below the mean of 3. How likely is it that the goal will be met?

107 **Rating employee performance.** Almost all companies utilize some type of year-end performance review for their employees. Human Resources (HR) at the University of Texas Health Science Center provides guidelines for supervisors rating their subordinates. For example, raters are advised to examine their ratings for a tendency to be either too lenient or too harsh. According to HR, "If you have this tendency, consider using a normal distribution—10% of employees (rated) exemplary, 20% distinguished, 40% competent, 20% marginal, and 10% unacceptable." Suppose you are rating an employee's performance on a scale of 1 (lowest) to 100 (highest). Also, assume the ratings follow a normal distribution with a mean of 50 and a standard deviation of 15.

a. What is the lowest rating you should give to an "exemplary" employee if you follow the University of Texas HR guidelines?

b. What is the lowest rating you should give to a "competent" employee if you follow the University of Texas HR guidelines?

108 **Ambulance response time.** Ambulance response time is measured as the time (in minutes) between the initial call to emergency medical services (EMS) and when the patient is reached by ambulance. *Geographical Analysis* (Vol. 41, 2009) investigated the characteristics of ambulance response time for EMS calls in Edmonton, Alberta. For a particular EMS station (call it Station A), ambulance response time is known to be normally distributed with $\mu = 7.5$ minutes and $\sigma = 2.5$ minutes.

a. Regulations require that 90% of all emergency calls be reached in 9 minutes or less. Are the regulations met at EMS Station A? Explain.

b. A randomly selected EMS call in Edmonton has an ambulance response time of 2 minutes. Is it likely that this call was serviced by Station A? Explain.

109 **Personnel dexterity tests.** Personnel tests are designed to test a job applicant's cognitive and/or physical abilities. The Wonderlic IQ test is an example of the former; the Purdue Pegboard speed test involving the arrangement of pegs on a peg board is an example of the latter. A particular dexterity test is administered nationwide by a private testing service. It is known that for all tests administered last year, the distribution of scores was approximately normal with mean 75 and standard deviation 7.5.

a. A particular employer requires job candidates to score at least 80 on the dexterity test. Approximately what percentage of the test scores during the past year exceeded 80?

b. The testing service reported to a particular employer that one of its job candidate's scores fell at the 98th percentile of the distribution (i.e., approximately 98% of the scores were lower than the candidate's, and only 2% were higher). What was the candidate's score?

110 **Manufacturing hourly pay rate.** Government data indicate that the mean hourly wage for manufacturing workers in the United States is $18.50 (*Statistical Abstract of the United States: 2012*). Suppose the distribution of manufacturing wage rates nationwide can be approximated by a normal distribution with standard deviation $1.25 per hour. The first manufacturing firm contacted by a particular worker seeking a new job pays $19.80 per hour.

a. If the worker were to undertake a nationwide job search, approximately what proportion of the wage rates would be greater than $19.80 per hour?

b. If the worker were to randomly select a U.S. manufacturing firm, what is the probability the firm would pay more than $19.80 per hour?

c. The population median, call it η, of a continuous random variable x is the value such that $P(x \geq \eta) = P(x \leq \eta) = .5$—that is, the median is the value η such that half the area under the probability distribution lies above η and half lies below it. Find the median of the random variable corresponding to the wage rate and compare it to the mean wage rate.

111 California's electoral college votes. During a presidential election, each state is allotted a different number of votes in the Electoral College depending on population. For example, California is allotted 55 votes (the most) while several states (including the District of Columbia) are allotted 3 votes each (the least). When a presidential candidate wins the popular vote in a state, the candidate wins all the Electoral College votes in that state. To become president, a candidate must win 270 of the total of 538 votes in the Electoral College. *Chance* (Winter 2010) demonstrated the impact on the presidential election of winning California. Assuming a candidate wins California's 55 votes, the number of additional Electoral College votes the candidate will win can be approximated by a normal distribution with $\mu = 241.5$ votes and $\sigma = 49.8$ votes. If a presidential candidate wins the popular vote in California, what are the chances that he or she becomes the next U.S. president?

112 Hotel guest satisfaction. Refer to the North American Hotel Guest Satisfaction Index Study, Exercise 48. You determined that the probability of a hotel guest participating in the hotel's "green" conservation program by reusing towels and bed linens is .45. Suppose a large hotel chain randomly samples 200 of its guests. The chain's national director claims that more than 110 of these guests participated in the conservation program. Do you believe this claim? Explain.

113 Credit card market shares. The following table reports the U.S. credit card industry's market share data for 2011. A random sample of 100 credit card users is to be questioned regarding their satisfaction with their credit card company. For simplification, assume that each credit card user carries just one credit card and that the market share percentages are the percentages of all credit card customers that carry each brand.

Credit Card	Market Share %
Visa	50
MasterCard	33
Discover	9
American Express	8

Source: Based on *Nilson Report* data, May 2008.

a. Propose a procedure for randomly selecting the 100 credit card users.
b. For random samples of 100 credit card users, what is the expected number of customers who carry Visa? Discover?
c. What is the probability that half or more of the sample of credit card users carry Visa? American Express?
d. Justify the use of the normal approximation to the binomial in answering the question in part **c**.

Applying the Concepts—Advanced

114 Industrial filling process. The characteristics of an industrial filling process in which an expensive liquid is injected into a container were investigated in the *Journal of Quality Technology* (July 1999). The quantity injected per container is approximately normally distributed with mean 10 units and standard deviation .2 units. Each unit of fill costs $20 per unit. If a container contains less than 10 units (i.e., is underfilled), it must be reprocessed at a cost of $10. A properly filled container sells for $230.

a. Find the probability that a container is underfilled. Not underfilled.
b. A container is initially underfilled and must be reprocessed. Upon refilling, it contains 10.60 units. How much profit will the company make on this container?
c. The operations manager adjusts the mean of the filling process upward to 10.10 units in order to make the probability of underfilling approximately zero. Under these conditions, what is the expected profit per container?

115 Executive coaching and meeting effectiveness. Poor executive leadership during business meetings can result in counterproductive outcomes (e.g., negative employee attitudes, ambiguous objectives). Can executive coaching help improve business meeting effectiveness? This was the question of interest in an article published in *Consulting Psychology Journal: Practice and Research* (Vol. 61, 2009). Certain behaviors by leaders during meetings were categorized as content behaviors (e.g., seeking information, disagreeing/attacking) or process behaviors (e.g., asking clarifying questions, summarizing). The goal of executive coaching is to reduce content behaviors in favor of process behaviors. The study reported that prior to receiving executive coaching, the percentage of observed process behaviors of leaders had a mean of 75% with a standard deviation of 8.5%. In contrast, after receiving executive coaching, the percentage of observed process behaviors of leaders had a mean of 52% with a standard deviation of 7.5%. Assume that the percentage of observed process behaviors is approximately normally distributed for both leaders with and without executive coaching. Suppose you observe 70% process behaviors by the leader of a business meeting. Give your opinion on whether or not the leader has received executive coaching.

116 Box plots and the standard normal distribution. What relationship exists between the standard normal distribution and the box-plot methodology for describing distributions of data using quartiles? The answer depends on the true underlying probability distribution of the data. Assume for the remainder of this exercise that the distribution is normal.

a. Calculate the values of the standard normal random variable z, call them z_L and z_U, that correspond to the hinges of the box plot—that is, the lower and upper quartiles, Q_L and Q_U—of the probability distribution.
b. Calculate the z values that correspond to the inner fences of the box plot for a normal probability distribution.
c. Calculate the z values that correspond to the outer fences of the box plot for a normal probability distribution.
d. What is the probability that an observation lies beyond the inner fences of a normal probability distribution? The outer fences?
e. Can you better understand why the inner and outer fences of a box plot are used to detect outliers in a distribution? Explain.

7   Descriptive Methods for Assessing Normality

Several techniques for making inferences about the population based on information in the sample are based on the assumption that the population is approximately normally distributed. Consequently, it will be important to determine whether the sample data come from a normal population before we can properly apply these techniques.

Several descriptive methods can be used to check for normality. In this section, we consider the four methods summarized in the box.

Determining Whether the Data Are from an Approximately Normal Distribution

1. Construct either a histogram or stem-and-leaf display for the data and note the shape of the graph. If the data are approximately normal, the shape of the histogram or stem-and-leaf display will be similar to the normal curve, Figure 18 (i.e., mound-shaped and symmetric about the mean).

2. Compute the intervals $\bar{x} \pm s$, $\bar{x} \pm 2s$, and $\bar{x} \pm 3s$, and determine the percentage of measurements falling in each. If the data are approximately normal, the percentages will be approximately equal to 68%, 95%, and 100%, respectively.

3. Find the interquartile range, IQR, and standard deviation, s, for the sample, then calculate the ratio IQR/s. If the data are approximately normal, then IQR/$s \approx 1.3$.

4. Examine a *normal probability plot* for the data. If the data are approximately normal, the points will fall (approximately) on a straight line.

The first two methods come directly from the properties of a normal distribution established in Section 6. Method 3 is based on the fact that for normal distributions, the z values corresponding to the 25th and 75th percentiles are $-.67$ and $.67$, respectively (see Example 18). Because $\sigma = 1$ for a standard normal distribution,

$$\frac{\text{IQR}}{\sigma} = \frac{Q_U - Q_L}{\sigma} = \frac{.67 - (-.67)}{1} = 1.34$$

The final descriptive method for checking normality is based on a *normal probability plot*. In such a plot, the observations in a data set are ordered from smallest to largest and then plotted against the expected z-scores of observations calculated under the assumption that the data come from a normal distribution. When the data are, in fact, normally distributed, a linear (straight-line) trend will result. A nonlinear trend in the plot suggests that the data are nonnormal.

A **normal probability plot** for a data set is a scatterplot with the ranked data values on one axis and their corresponding expected z-scores from a standard normal distribution on the other axis. [*Note:* Computation of the expected standard normal z-scores is beyond the scope of this text. Therefore, we will rely on available statistical software packages to generate a normal probability plot.]

Example   26

Checking for Normal Data—EPA Estimated Gas Mileages

Problem The Environmental Protection Agency (EPA) performs extensive tests on all new car models to determine their mileage ratings. The results of 100 EPA tests on a certain new car model are displayed in Table 5. Numerical and graphical descriptive measures for the data are shown on the Minitab and SPSS printouts, Figures 37a–c. Determine whether the EPA mileage ratings are from an approximate normal distribution.

Table 5	EPA Gas Mileage Ratings for 100 Cars (miles per gallon)								
36.3	41.0	36.9	37.1	44.9	36.8	30.0	37.2	42.1	36.7
32.7	37.3	41.2	36.6	32.9	36.5	33.2	37.4	37.5	33.6
40.5	36.5	37.6	33.9	40.2	36.4	37.7	37.7	40.0	34.2
36.2	37.9	36.0	37.9	35.9	38.2	38.3	35.7	35.6	35.1
38.5	39.0	35.5	34.8	38.6	39.4	35.3	34.4	38.8	39.7
36.3	36.8	32.5	36.4	40.5	36.6	36.1	38.2	38.4	39.3
41.0	31.8	37.3	33.1	37.0	37.6	37.0	38.7	39.0	35.8
37.0	37.2	40.7	37.4	37.1	37.8	35.9	35.6	36.7	34.5
37.1	40.3	36.7	37.0	33.9	40.1	38.0	35.2	34.8	39.5
39.9	36.9	32.9	33.8	39.8	34.0	36.8	35.0	38.1	36.9

Data Set: EPAGAS

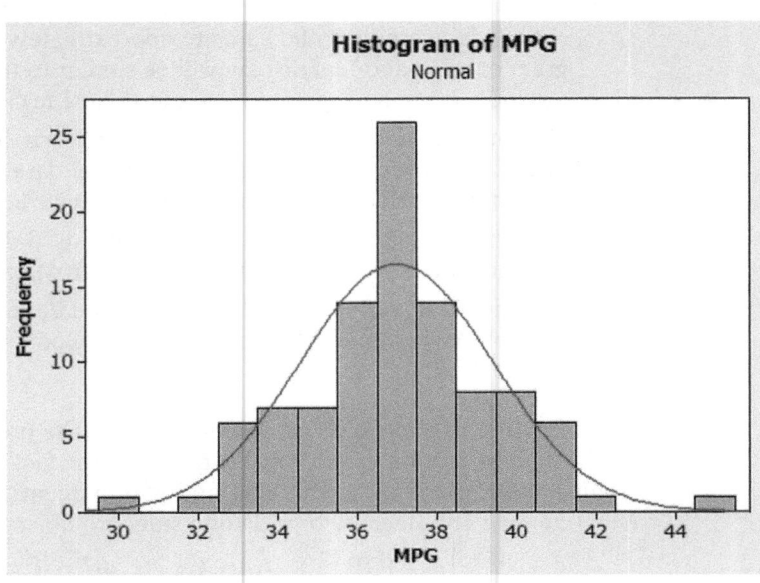

Figure 37a

Minitab histogram for gas mileage data

Figure 37b

Minitab descriptive statistics for gas mileage data

Descriptive Statistics: MPG

Variable	N	Mean	StDev	Minimum	Q1	Median	Q3	Maximum
MPG	100	36.994	2.418	30.000	35.625	37.000	38.375	44.900

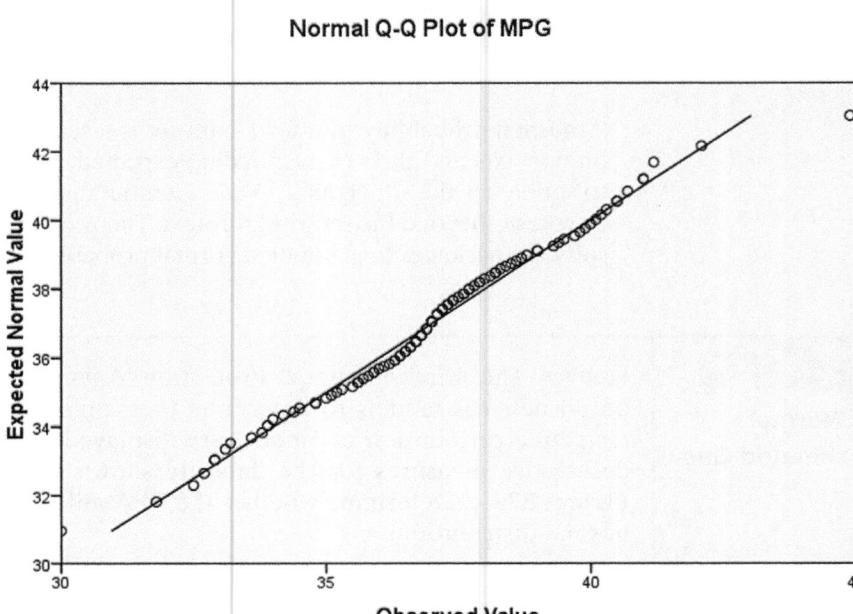

Figure 37c

SPSS normal probability plot for gas mileage data

Table 6

Describing the 100 EPA Mileage Ratings

Interval	Percentage in Interval
$\bar{x} \pm s = (34.6, 39.4)$	68
$\bar{x} \pm 2s = (32.2, 41.8)$	96
$\bar{x} \pm 3s = (29.8, 44.2)$	99

Solution As a first check, we examine the Minitab histogram of the data shown in Figure 37a. Clearly, the mileages fall in an approximately mound-shaped, symmetric distribution centered around the mean of approximately 37 mpg. Note that a normal curve is superimposed on the figure. Therefore, using check #1 in the box, the data appear to be approximately normal.

To apply check #2, we obtain $\bar{x} = 37$ and $s = 2.4$ from the Minitab printout, Figure 37b. The intervals $\bar{x} \pm s, \bar{x} \pm 2s$ and $\bar{x} \pm 3s$ are shown in Table 6, as well as the percentage of mileage ratings that fall in each interval. These percentages agree almost exactly with those from a normal distribution.

Check #3 in the box requires that we find the ratio IQR/s. From Figure 37b, the 25th percentile (called Q_1 by Minitab) is $Q_L = 35.625$, and the 75th percentile (labeled Q_3 by Minitab) is $Q_U = 38.375$. Then, IQR $= Q_U - Q_L = 2.75$, and the ratio is

$$\frac{IQR}{s} = \frac{2.75}{2.4} = 1.15$$

Because this value is approximately equal to 1.3, we have further confirmation that the data are approximately normal.

A fourth descriptive method is to interpret a normal probability plot. An SPSS normal probability plot for the mileage data is shown in Figure 37c. Notice that the ordered mileage values (shown on the horizontal axis) fall reasonably close to a straight line when plotted against the expected z-scores from a normal distribution. Thus, check #4 also suggests that the EPA mileage data are likely to be approximately normally distributed.

Look Back The checks for normality given in the box are simple, yet powerful, techniques to apply, but they are only descriptive in nature. It is possible (although unlikely) that the data are nonnormal even when the checks are reasonably satisfied. Thus, we should be careful not to claim that the 100 EPA mileage ratings of Example 26 are, in fact, normally distributed. We can only state that it is reasonable to believe that the data are from a normal distribution.*

Now Work Exercise 120

Several inferential methods of analysis require the data to be approximately normal. If the data are clearly nonnormal, inferences derived from the method may be invalid. Therefore, it is advisable to check the normality of the data prior to conducting the analysis.

Exercises 117–131

Please be aware that some of the following problems may require knowledge of concepts that are not presented in this chapter.

Learning the Mechanics

117 If a population data set is normally distributed, what is the proportion of measurements you would expect to fall within the following intervals?
a. $\mu \pm \sigma$
b. $\mu \pm 2\sigma$
c. $\mu \pm 3\sigma$

118 Consider a sample data set with the following summary statistics: $s = 95, Q_L = 72, Q_U = 195$.
a. Calculate IQR.
b. Calculate IQR/s.
c. Is the value of IQR/s approximately equal to 1.3? What does this imply?

119 Normal probability plots for three data sets are shown on the next page. Which plot indicates that the data are approximately normally distributed?

120 Examine the sample data in the accompanying table.

5.9	5.3	1.6	7.4	8.6	1.2	2.1
4.0	7.3	8.4	8.9	6.7	4.5	6.3
7.6	9.7	3.5	1.1	4.3	3.3	8.4
1.6	8.2	6.5	1.1	5.0	9.4	6.4

a. Construct a stem-and-leaf plot to assess whether the data are from an approximately normal distribution.
b. Compute s for the sample data.

*Statistical tests of normality that provide a measure of reliability for the inference are available. However, these tests tend to be very sensitive to slight departures from normality (i.e., they tend to reject the hypothesis of normality for any distribution that is not perfectly symmetrical and mound-shaped). Consult the references (see Ramsey & Ramsey, 1990) if you want to learn more about these tests.

Normal probability plots for Exercise 119

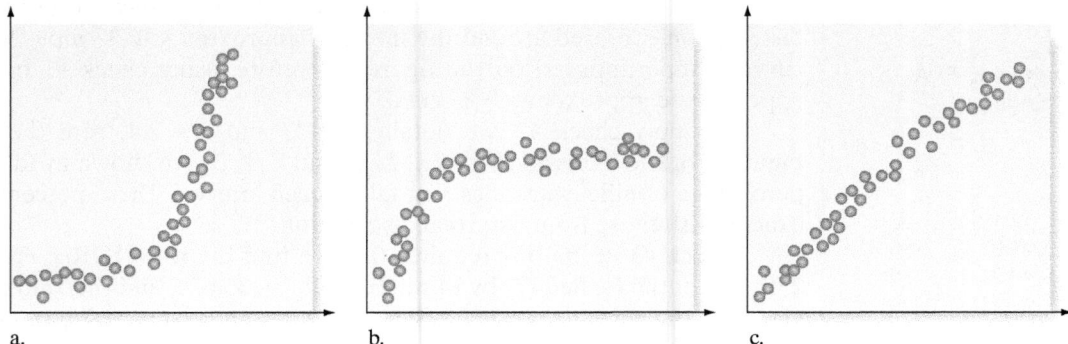

a. b. c.

c. Find the values of Q_L and Q_U and the value of s from part **b** to assess whether the data come from an approximately normal distribution.

d. Generate a normal probability plot for the data and use it to assess whether the data are approximately normal.

Applying the Concepts—Basic

121 **Corporate sustainability of CPA firms.** Refer to the *Business and Society* (March 2011) study on the sustainability behaviors of CPA corporations, Exercise 98. Data on the level of support for corporate sustainability (measured on a quantitative scale ranging from 0 to 160 points) for each of 992 senior managers at CPA firms are saved in the accompanying file. In Exercise 98 you assumed that the level of support variable was approximately normally distributed.

a. Construct a histogram for the data and use it to evaluate the validity of the normality assumption.

b. Obtain the mean and standard deviation for the data and use these statistics to evaluate the validity of the normality assumption.

c. Obtain the interquartile range (IQR) for the data and use it to evaluate the validity of the normality assumption.

d. Construct a normal probability plot for the data and use it to evaluate the validity of the normality assumption.

122 **Shear strength of rock fractures.** Understanding the characteristics of rock masses, especially the nature of the fractures, is essential when building dams and power plants. The shear strength of rock fractures was investigated in *Engineering Geology* (May 12, 2010). The Joint Roughness Coefficient (JRC) was used to measure shear strength. Civil engineers collected JRC data for over 750 rock fractures. The results (simulated from information provided in the article) are summarized in the accompanying SPSS histogram. Should the engineers use the normal probability distribution to model the behavior of shear strength for rock fractures? Explain.

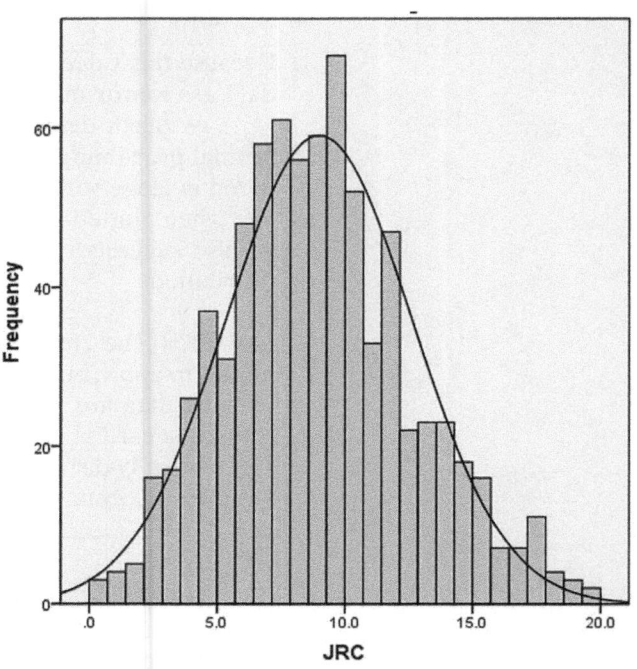

123 **Drug content assessment.** Scientists at GlaxoSmithKline Medicines Research Center used high-performance liquid chromatography (HPLC) to determine the amount of drug in a tablet produced by the company (*Analytical Chemistry,* Dec. 15, 2009). Drug concentrations (measured as a percentage) for 50 randomly selected tablets are listed in the table below and saved in the accompanying file.

a. Descriptive statistics for the drug concentrations are shown at the top of the XLSTAT printout on the next page. Use this information to assess whether the data are approximately normal.

b. An XLSTAT normal probability plot follows. Use this information to assess whether the data are approximately normal.

91.28	92.83	89.35	91.90	82.85	94.83	89.83	89.00	84.62
86.96	88.32	91.17	83.86	89.74	92.24	92.59	84.21	89.36
90.96	92.85	89.39	89.82	89.91	92.16	88.67	89.35	86.51
89.04	91.82	93.02	88.32	88.76	89.26	90.36	87.16	91.74
86.12	92.10	83.33	87.61	88.20	92.78	86.35	93.84	91.20
93.44	86.77	83.77	93.19	81.79				

Source: Based on Borman, P. J., Marion, J. C., Damjanov, I., & Jackson, P. "Design and analysis of method equivalence studies," *Analytical Chemistry,* Vol. 81, No. 24, December 15, 2009 (Table 3).

Descriptive statistics (Quantitative data):	
Statistic	**Content**
No. of observations	50
Minimum	81.7900
Maximum	94.8300
Range	13.0400
1st Quartile	87.2725
Median	89.3750
3rd Quartile	91.8800
Mean	89.2906
Variance (n-1)	10.1343
Standard deviation (n-1)	3.1834

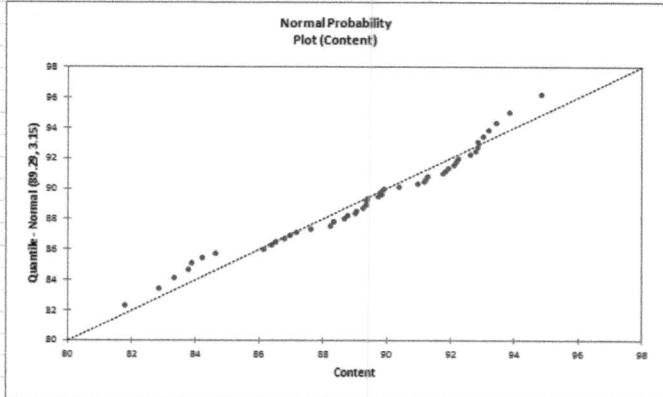

XLSTAT output for Exercise 123

124 Ranking PhD programs in economics. The *Southern Economic Journal* (Apr. 2008) published rankings of PhD ECOPHO programs in economics at 129 colleges and universities. The number of publications published by faculty teaching in the PhD program and the quality of the publications were used to calculate an overall productivity score for each program. The mean and standard deviation of these 129 productivity scores were then used to compute a z-score for each economics program. The data (z-scores) for all 129 economic programs are saved in the accompanying file. A Minitab normal probability plot for the z-scores is shown below. Use the graph to assess whether the data are approximately normal.

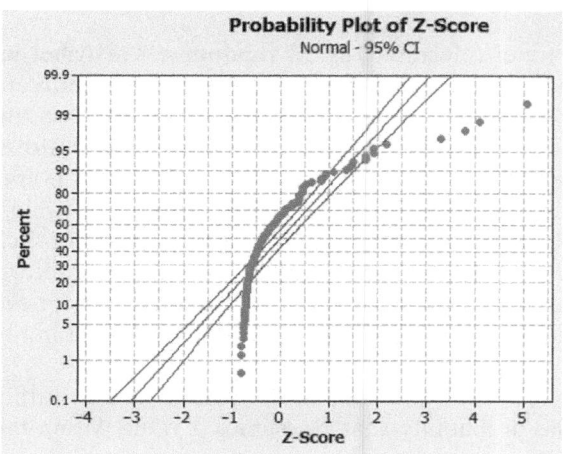

125 Software file updates. Software configuration management was used to monitor a software engineering team's performance at Motorola, Inc. (*Software Quality Professional*, Nov. 2004). One of the variables of interest was the number of updates to a file that was changed because of a problem report. Summary statistics for $n = 421$ files yielded the following results: $\bar{x} = 4.71$, $s = 6.09$, $Q_L = 1$, and $Q_U = 6$. Are these data approximately normally distributed? Explain.

Applying the Concepts—Intermediate

126 Wear-out of used display panels. Wear-out failure time of electronic components is often assumed to have a normal distribution. Can the normal distribution be applied PANEL to the wear-out of used manufactured products, such as colored display panels? A lot of 50 used display panels was purchased by an outlet store. Each panel displays 12 to 18 color characters. Prior to acquisition, the panels had been used for about one-third of their expected lifetimes. The data in the accompanying table (saved in the file) give the failure times (in years) of the 50 used panels. Use the techniques of this section to determine whether the used panel wear-out times are approximately normally distributed.

0.01	1.21	1.71	2.30	2.96	0.19	1.22	1.75	2.30	2.98	0.51
1.24	1.77	2.41	3.19	0.57	1.48	1.79	2.44	3.25	0.70	1.54
1.88	2.57	3.31	0.73	1.59	1.90	2.61	1.19	0.75	1.61	1.93
2.62	3.50	0.75	1.61	2.01	2.72	3.50	1.11	1.62	2.16	2.76
3.50	1.16	1.62	2.18	2.84	3.50					

Source: Based on Irony, T. Z., Lauretto, M., Pereira, C., & Stern, J. M. "A Weibull wearout test: Full Bayesian approach," paper presented at *Mathematical Sciences Colloquium*, Binghamton University, Bringhamton, UK, December 2001.

127 NHTSA crash tests. Refer to the NHTSA crash test data for new cars. Assume that the driver's head-injury rating is CRASH approximately normally distributed. Apply the methods of this chapter to the data saved in the accompanying file to support this assumption.

128 Sanitation inspection of cruise ships. Refer to the data on the Dec. 2008 sanitation scores for 186 cruise ships. The data SANIT are saved in the accompanying file. Assess whether the sanitation scores are approximately normally distributed.

129 Ranking driving performance of professional golfers. *The Sport Journal* (Winter 2007) published an article on a new PGA method for ranking the driving performance of PGA golfers. The method incorporates a golfer's average driving distance (yards) and driving accuracy (percent of drives that land in the fairway) into a driving performance index. Data on these three variables for the top 40 PGA golfers are saved in the accompanying file. Determine which of these variables—driving distance, driving accuracy, and driving performance index—are approximately normally distributed.

130 Department of Defense START sheets. The DoD RAC publishes START sheets for government and industry. TENSIL These START sheets are designed to improve the reliability, maintainability, supportability, and quality of manufactured components and systems. In Volume 11 (2004), the DoD analyzed the following data set on tensile strength measurements taken at two different temperatures. (The data are saved in the accompanying file.) In the START

Temperature	Strength
75	328.2
75	334.7
75	347.8
75	346.3
75	338.7
75	340.8
−67	343.6
−67	334.2
−67	348.7
−67	356.3
−67	344.1

sheet, the DoD demonstrated that the data for the 11 tensile strength measurements were sampled from an approximately normal distribution. Do you agree?

Applying the Concepts—Advanced

131 **Semester hours taken by CPA candidates.** The *Journal of Accounting and Public Policy* (Spring 2002) did a study of first-time candidates for the CPA exam. The variable of interest is the total semester hours of college credit for each candidate. The mean and median for the data set were 141.31 and 140 hours, respectively, and the standard deviation was 17.77 hours. Demonstrate why the probability distribution for the variable, total semester hours, is unlikely to be normally distributed.

8 Other Continuous Distributions: Uniform and Exponential

Uniform Random Variable

Continuous random variables that appear to have equally likely outcomes over their range of possible values possess a **uniform probability distribution.** For example, if a short exists in a 5-meter stretch of electrical wire, it may have an equal probability of being in any particular 1-centimeter segment along the line. Or if a safety inspector plans to choose a time at random during the four afternoon work hours to pay a surprise visit to a certain area of a plant, then each 1-minute time interval in this 4-work-hour period will have an equally likely chance of being selected for the visit.

Suppose the random variable x can assume values only in an interval $c \leq x \leq d$. Then the **uniform frequency function** has a rectangular shape, as shown in Figure 38. Note that the possible values of x consist of all points in the interval between point c and point d. The height of $f(x)$ is constant in that interval and equals $1/(d - c)$. Therefore, the total area under $f(x)$ is given by

$$\text{Total area of rectangle} = (\text{Base})(\text{Height}) = (d - c)\left(\frac{1}{d - c}\right) = 1$$

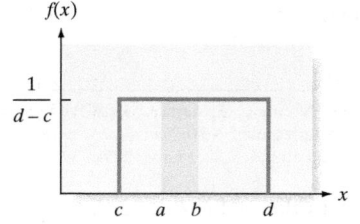

Figure 38

The uniform probability distribution

The uniform probability distribution provides a model for continuous random variables that are *evenly distributed* over a certain interval—that is, a uniform random variable is one that is just as likely to assume a value in one interval as it is to assume a value in any other interval of equal size. There is no clustering of values around any value; instead, there is an even spread over the entire region of possible values.

The uniform distribution is sometimes referred to as the **randomness distribution** because one way of generating a uniform random variable is to perform an experiment in which a point is *randomly selected* on the horizontal axis between the points c and d. If we were to repeat this experiment infinitely often, we would create a uniform probability distribution like that shown in Figure 38. The random selection of points in an interval can also be used to generate random numbers such as those in Table I in Appendix: Basic Counting Rules. Recall that random numbers are selected in such a way that every number would have an equal probability of selection. Therefore, random numbers are realizations of a uniform random variable. The formulas for the uniform probability distribution, its mean, and its standard deviation are shown in the next box.

Suppose the interval $a < x < b$ lies within the domain of x; that is, it falls within the larger interval $c \leq x \leq d$. Then the probability that x assumes a value within the

Probability Distribution for a Uniform Random Variable x

Probability density function: $f(x) = \dfrac{1}{d - c} \quad c \leq x \leq d$

Mean: $\mu = \dfrac{c + d}{2}$ Standard deviation: $\sigma = \dfrac{d - c}{\sqrt{12}}$

$P(a < x < b) = (b - a)/(d - c), c \leq a < b \leq d$

interval $a < x < b$ is equal to the area of the rectangle over the interval, namely, $(b - a)/(d - c).$* (See the shaded area in Figure 38.)

Example 27

Applying the Uniform Distribution—Steel Manufacturing

Problem Suppose the research department of a steel manufacturer believes that one of the company's rolling machines is producing sheets of steel of varying thickness. The thickness is a uniform random variable with values between 150 and 200 millimeters. Any sheets less than 160 millimeters must be scrapped because they are unacceptable to buyers.

a. Calculate and interpret the mean and standard deviation of x, the thickness of the sheets produced by this machine.

b. Graph the probability distribution of x, and show the mean on the horizontal axis. Also show 1- and 2-standard-deviation intervals around the mean.

c. Calculate the fraction of steel sheets produced by this machine that have to be scrapped.

Solution

a. To calculate the mean and standard deviation for x, we substitute 150 and 200 millimeters for c and d, respectively, in the formulas for uniform random variables. Thus,

$$\mu = \frac{c + d}{2} = \frac{150 + 200}{2} = 175 \text{ millimeters}$$

and

$$\sigma = \frac{d - c}{\sqrt{12}} = \frac{200 - 150}{\sqrt{12}} = \frac{50}{3.464} = 14.43 \text{ millimeters}$$

Our interpretations follow:

The average thickness of all manufactured steel sheets is $\mu = 175$ millimeters. From Chebyshev's Rule, we know that at least 75% of the thickness values, x, in the distribution will fall in the interval

$$\mu \pm 2\sigma = 175 \pm 2(14.43)$$
$$= 175 \pm 28.86$$

or between 146.14 and 203.86 millimeters. (This demonstrates, once again, the conservativeness of Chebyshev's Rule because we know that all values of x fall between 150 and 200 millimeters.)

b. The uniform probability distribution is

$$f(x) = \frac{1}{d - c} = \frac{1}{200 - 150} = \frac{1}{50} (150 \leq x \leq 200)$$

The graph of this function is shown in Figure 39. The mean and 1- and 2-standard-deviation intervals around the mean are shown on the horizontal axis.

*The student with knowledge of calculus should note that

$$P(a < x < b) = \int_a^b f(x)d(x) = \int_a^b 1/(d - c)dx = (b - a)/(d - c)$$

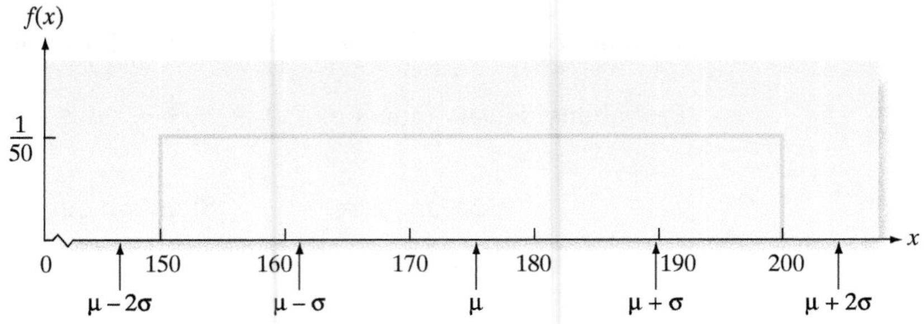

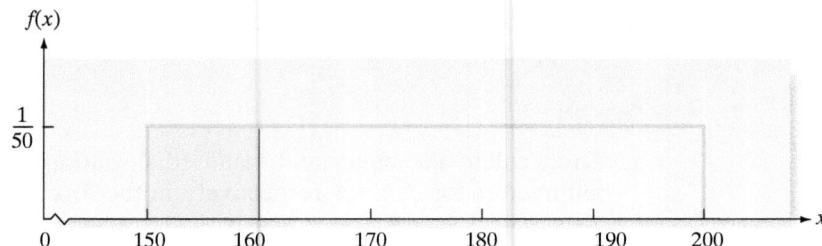

Figure 39

Distribution for x in Example 27

c. To find the fraction of steel sheets produced by the machine that have to be scrapped, we must find the probability that x, the thickness, is less than 160 millimeters. As indicated in Figure 40, we need to calculate the area under the frequency function $f(x)$ between the points $x = 150$ and $x = 160$. Therefore, in this case, $a = 150$ and $b = 160$. Applying the formula in the box, we have

$$P(x < 160) = P(150 < x < 160)$$
$$= \frac{b - a}{d - c} = \frac{160 - 150}{200 - 150} = \frac{10}{50} = \frac{1}{5} = .2$$

That is, 20% of all the sheets made by this machine must be scrapped.

Figure 40

Probability that sheet thickness, x, is between 150 and 160 millimeters

Look Back The calculated probability in part **c** is the area of a rectangle with base $160 - 150 = 10$ and height $\frac{1}{50}$. Alternatively, we can find the fraction that has to be scrapped as

$$P(x < 160) = (\text{Base})(\text{Height}) = (10)\left(\frac{1}{50}\right) = \frac{1}{5} = .2$$

Or, we can use statistical software to find the probability, as shown on the Minitab printout, Figure 41.

Cumulative Distribution Function

```
Continuous uniform on 150 to 200

  x    P( X <= x )
160         0.2
```

Figure 41

Minitab output for Example 27

■ **Now Work Exercise 142**

Exponential Random Variable

The length of time between emergency arrivals at a hospital, the length of time between breakdowns of manufacturing equipment, and the length of time between catastrophic events (e.g., a stock market crash), are all continuous random phenomena that we might want to describe probabilistically. The length of time or the distance between occurrences of random events like these can often be described by the **exponential probability distribution.** For this reason, the exponential distribution is sometimes called the **waiting-time distribution.** The formula for the exponential probability distribution is shown in the following box, along with its mean and standard deviation.

Unlike the normal distribution, which has a shape and location determined by the values of the two quantities μ and σ, the shape of the exponential distribution is governed by a single quantity: θ. Further, it is a probability distribution with the property that its mean equals its standard deviation. Exponential distributions corresponding to $\theta = .5, 1$, and 2 are shown in Figure 42.

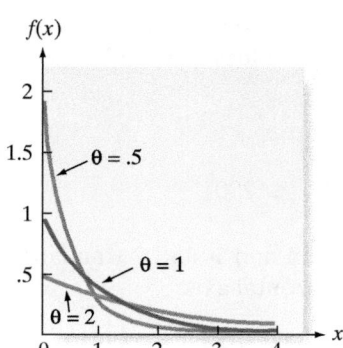

Figure 42

Exponential distributions

254

Probability Distribution for an Exponential Random Variable x

Probability density function: $f(x) = \dfrac{1}{\theta} e^{-x/\theta} \ (x > 0)$

Mean: $\mu = \theta$

Standard deviation: $\sigma = \theta$

To calculate probabilities of **exponential random variables,** we need to be able to find areas under the exponential probability distribution. Suppose we want to find the area A to the right of some number a, as shown in Figure 43. This area can be calculated by means of the formula shown in the box that follows or by using statistical software.

Finding the Area A to the Right of a Number a for an Exponential Distribution*

$$A = P(x \geq a) = e^{-a/\theta}$$

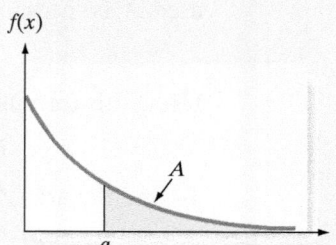

Figure 43

The area A to the right of a number a for an exponential distribution

---

Example 28

Finding an Exponential Probability—Hospital Emergency Arrivals

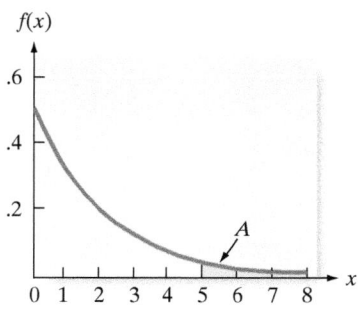

Figure 44

Area to the right of $a = 5$ for Example 28

Problem Suppose the length of time (in hours) between emergency arrivals at a certain hospital is modeled as an exponential distribution with $\theta = 2$. What is the probability that more than 5 hours pass without an emergency arrival?

Solution The probability we want is the area A to the right of $a = 5$ in Figure 44. To find this probability, we use the area formula:

$$A = e^{-a/\theta} = e^{-(5/2)} = e^{-2.5}$$

Using a calculator with an exponential function, we find that

$$A = e^{-2.5} = .082085$$

Our exponential model indicates that the probability that more than 5 hours pass between emergency arrivals is about .08 for this hospital.

Look Back The desired probability can also be found with a statistical software package. We accessed the exponential probability function of Minitab, specified a mean of 2, and requested the cumulative probability, $P(x \leq 5)$. This probability is shaded in Figure 45. Using the rule of complements, the desired probability is

Cumulative Distribution Function

Exponential with mean = 2

x   P(X <= x)
5   0.917915

Figure 45

Minitab output for Example 28

$$P(x > 5) = 1 - P(x \leq 5) = 1 - .917915 = .082085$$

■ **Now Work Exercise 135**

*For students with a knowledge of calculus, the shaded area in Figure 43 corresponds to the integral

$$\int_a^b \frac{1}{\theta} e^{-x/\theta} dx = -e^{-x/\theta} \Big|_a^\infty = e^{-a/\theta}.$$

Example 29

The Mean and Variance of an Exponential Random Variable—Length of Life of a Microwave Oven

Problem A manufacturer of microwave ovens is trying to determine the length of warranty period it should attach to its magnetron tube, the most critical component in the oven. Preliminary testing has shown that the length of life (in years), x, of a magnetron tube has an exponential probability distribution with $\theta = 6.25$.

a. Find the mean and standard deviation of x.

b. Suppose a warranty period of 5 years is attached to the magnetron tube. What fraction of tubes must the manufacturer plan to replace, assuming that the exponential model with $\theta = 6.25$ is correct?

c. Find the probability that the length of life of a magnetron tube will fall within the interval $\mu - 2\sigma$ to $\mu + 2\sigma$.

Solution

a. Because $\theta = \mu = \sigma$, both μ and σ equal 6.25.

b. To find the fraction of tubes that will have to be replaced before the 5-year warranty period expires, we need to find the area between 0 and 5 under the distribution. This area, A, is shown in Figure 46. To find the required probability, we recall the formula

$$P(x > a) = e^{-a/\theta}$$

Using this formula, we find that

$$P(x > 5) = e^{-a/\theta} = e^{-5/6.25} = e^{-.80} = .449329$$

To find the area A, we use the complementary relationship:

$$P(x \le 5) = 1 - P(x > 5) = 1 - .449329 = .550671$$

So approximately 55% of the magnetron tubes will have to be replaced during the 5-year warranty period.

c. We would expect the probability that the life of a magnetron tube, x, falls within the interval $\mu - 2\sigma$ to $\mu + 2\sigma$ to be quite large. A graph of the exponential distribution showing the interval from $\mu - 2\sigma$ to $\mu + 2\sigma$ is given in Figure 47. Because the point $\mu - 2\sigma$ lies below $x = 0$, we need to find only the area between $x = 0$ and $x = \mu + 2\sigma = 6.25 + 2(6.25) = 18.75$.

This area, P, which is shaded in Figure 47, is

$$P = 1 - P(x > 18.75) = 1 - e^{-18.75/\theta} = 1 - e^{-18.75/6.25} = 1 - e^{-3}$$

Using a calculator, we find that $e^{-3} = .049787$. Therefore, the probability that the life x of a magnetron tube will fall within the interval $\mu - 2\sigma$ to $\mu + 2\sigma$ is

$$P = 1 - e^{-3} = 1 - .049787 = .950213$$

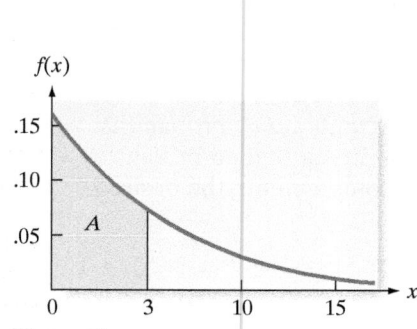

Figure 46
Area to the left of $a = 5$ for Example 29

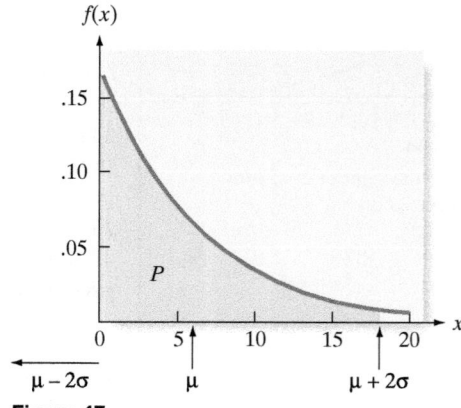

Figure 47
Area in the interval $\mu \pm 2\sigma$ for Example 29

> **Look Back** You can see that this probability agrees well with the interpretation of a standard deviation given by the Empirical Rule, even though the probability distribution that we were given is not mound-shaped. (It is strongly skewed to the right.)

Exercises 132–155

Please be aware that some of the following problems may require knowledge of concepts that are not presented in this chapter.

Learning the Mechanics

132 Suppose x is a random variable best described by a uniform probability distribution with $c = 3$ and $d = 7$.
a. Find $f(x)$.
b. Find the mean and standard deviation of x.
c. Find $P(\mu - \sigma \leq x \leq \mu + \sigma)$.

133 Suppose x is a random variable best described by a uniform probability distribution with $c = 20$ and $d = 45$.
a. Find $f(x)$.
b. Find the mean and standard deviation of x.
c. Graph $f(x)$ and locate μ and the interval $\mu \pm 2\sigma$ on the graph. Note that the probability that x assumes a value within the interval $\mu \pm 2\sigma$ is equal to 1.

134 Refer to Exercise 133. Find the following probabilities:
a. $P(20 \leq x \leq 30)$ b. $P(20 < x \leq 30)$
c. $P(x \geq 30)$ d. $P(x \geq 45)$
e. $P(x \leq 40)$ f. $P(x < 40)$
g. $P(15 \leq x \leq 35)$ h. $P(21.5 \leq x \leq 31.5)$

135 Suppose x has an exponential distribution with $\theta = 1$. Find the following probabilities:
a. $P(x > 1)$ b. $P(x \leq 3)$
c. $P(x > 1.5)$ d. $P(x \leq 5)$

136 Suppose x has an exponential distribution with $\theta = 2.5$. Find the following probabilities:
a. $P(x \leq 4)$ b. $P(x > 5)$
c. $P(x \leq 2)$ d. $P(x > 3)$

137 The random variable x is best described by a uniform probability distribution with $c = 100$ and $d = 200$. Find the probability that x assumes a value
a. More than 2 standard deviations from μ.
b. Less than 3 standard deviations from μ.
c. Within 2 standard deviations of μ.

138 The random variable x can be adequately approximated by an exponential probability distribution with $\theta = 2$. Find the probability that x assumes a value
a. More than 3 standard deviations from μ.
b. Less than 2 standard deviations from μ.
c. Within half a standard deviation of μ.

⚙ Applet Exercise 7

Open the applet *Sample from a Population*. On the pull-down menu to the right of the top graph, select *Uniform*. The box to the left of the top graph displays the population mean, median, and standard deviation.
a. Run the applet for each available value of n on the pull-down menu for the sample size. Go from the smallest to the largest value of n. For each value of n,

observe the shape of the graph of the sample data and record the mean, median, and standard deviation of the sample.
b. Describe what happens to the shape of the graph and the mean, median, and standard deviation of the sample as the sample size increases.

⚙ Applet Exercise 8

Suppose we set the *Random Numbers* applet to generate one number between 1 and 100, inclusive. We let the value of the random variable x be the number generated when the *Sample* button is clicked. Explain why the distribution of x is approximately uniform even though x is a discrete rather than continuous random variable.

Applying the Concepts—Basic

139 **Requests to a Web server.** According to Brighton Webs LTD, a British company that specializes in data analysis, the arrival time of requests to a Web server within each hour can be modeled by a uniform distribution (www. brighton-webs.co.uk). Specifically, the number of seconds x from the start of the hour that the request is made is uniformly distributed between 0 and 3,600 seconds. Find the probability that a request is made to a Web server sometime during the last 15 minutes of the hour.

140 **Preventative maintenance tests.** The optimal scheduling of preventative maintenance tests of some (but not all) of n independently operating components was developed in *Reliability Engineering and System Safety* (Jan. 2006). The time (in hours) between failures of a component was approximated by an exponential distribution with mean θ.
a. Suppose $\theta = 1,000$ hours. Find the probability that the time between component failures ranges between 1,200 and 1,500 hours.
b. Again, assume $\theta = 1,000$ hours. Find the probability that the time between component failures is at least 1,200 hours.
c. Given that the time between failures is at least 1,200 hours, what is the probability that the time between failures is less than 1,500 hours?

141 **Maintaining pipe wall temperature.** Maintaining a constant pipe wall temperature in some hot-process applications is critical. A technique that utilizes bolt-on trace elements to maintain temperature was presented in the *Journal of Heat Transfer* (Nov. 2000). Without bolt-on trace elements, the pipe wall temperature of a switch condenser used to produce plastic has a uniform distribution ranging from 260° to 290°F. When several bolt-on trace elements are attached to the piping, the wall temperature is uniform from 278° to 285°F.

a. Ideally, the pipe wall temperature should range between 280° and 284°F. What is the probability that the temperature will fall in this ideal range when no bolt-on trace elements are used? When bolt-on trace elements are attached to the pipe?

b. When the temperature is 268°F or lower, the hot liquid plastic hardens (or plates), causing a buildup in the piping. What is the probability of plastic plating when no bolt-on trace elements are used? When bolt-on trace elements are attached to the pipe?

142 New method for detecting anthrax. Researchers at the University of South Florida Center for Biological Defense have developed a safe method for rapidly detecting anthrax spores in powders and on surfaces (*USF Magazine*, Summer 2002). The method has been found to work well even when there are very few anthrax spores in a powder specimen. Consider a powder specimen that has exactly 10 anthrax spores. Suppose that the number of anthrax spores in the sample detected by the new method follows an approximate uniform distribution between 0 and 10.

a. Find the probability that 8 or fewer anthrax spores are detected in the powder specimen.

b. Find the probability that between 2 and 5 anthrax spores are detected in the powder specimen.

143 Lead in metal shredder residue. On the basis of data collected from metal shredders across the nation, the amount x of extractable lead in metal shredder residue has an approximate exponential distribution with mean $\theta = 2.5$ milligrams per liter (Florida Shredder's Association).

a. Find the probability that x is greater than 2 milligrams per liter.

b. Find the probability that x is less than 5 milligrams per liter.

144 Critical-part failures in NASCAR vehicles. In NASCAR races such as the Daytona 500, 43 drivers start the race; however, about 10% of the cars do not finish due to the failure of critical parts. University of Portland professors conducted a study of critical-part failures from 36 NASCAR races (*The Sport Journal*, Winter 2007). The researchers discovered that the time (in hours) until the first critical-part failure is exponentially distributed with a mean of .10 hour.

a. Find the probability that the time until the first critical-part failure is 1 hour or more.

b. Find the probability that the time until the first critical-part failure is less than 30 minutes.

Applying the Concepts—Intermediate

145 Social network densities. Social networking sites for business professionals are used to promote one's business. Each social network involves interactions (connections) between members of the network. Researchers define network density as the ratio of actual network connections to the number of possible one-to-one connections. For example, a network with 10 members has $\binom{10}{2} = 45$ total possible connections. If that network has only 5 connections, the network density is $\frac{5}{45} = .111$. Sociologists at the

University of Michigan assumed that the density x of a social network would follow a uniform distribution between 0 and 1 (*Social Networks*, 2010).

a. On average, what is the density of a randomly selected social network?

b. What is the probability that the randomly selected network has a density higher than .7?

c. Consider a social network with only 2 members. Explain why the uniform model would not be a good approximation for the distribution of network density.

146 Marine losses for an oil company. The frequency distribution shown in the next table depicts the property and marine losses incurred by a large oil company over the last 2 years. This distribution can be used by the company to predict future losses and to help determine an appropriate level of insurance coverage. In analyzing the losses within an interval of the distribution, for simplification, analysts may treat the interval as a uniform probability distribution (*Research Review*, Summer 1998). In the insurance business, intervals like these are often called *layers*.

Layer	Property and Marine Losses (millions of $)	Frequency
1	0.00–0.01	668
2	0.01–0.05	38
3	0.05–0.10	7
4	0.10–0.25	4
5	0.25–0.50	2
6	0.50–1.00	1
7	1.00–2.50	0

Source: Based on Cozzolino, J. M., & Mikolaj, P. J. "Applications of the piecewise constant pareto distribution," *Research Review*, Summer 1998, pp. 39–59.

a. Use a uniform distribution to model the loss amount in layer 2. Graph the distribution. Calculate and interpret its mean and variance.

b. Repeat part **a** for layer 6.

c. If a loss occurs in layer 2, what is the probability that it exceeds $10,000? That it is under $25,000?

d. If a layer-6 loss occurs, what is the probability that it is between $750,000 and $1,000,000? That it exceeds $900,000? That it is exactly $900,000?

147 Soft-drink dispenser. The manager of a local soft-drink bottling company believes that when a new beverage-dispensing machine is set to dispense 7 ounces, it in fact dispenses an amount x at random anywhere between 6.5 and 7.5 ounces inclusive. Suppose x has a uniform probability distribution.

a. Is the amount dispensed by the beverage machine a discrete or a continuous random variable? Explain.

b. Graph the frequency function for x, the amount of beverage the manager believes is dispensed by the new machine when it is set to dispense 7 ounces.

c. Find the mean and standard deviation for the distribution graphed in part **b** and locate the mean and the interval $\mu \pm 2\sigma$ on the graph.

d. Find $P(x \geq 7)$.

e. Find $P(x < 6)$.

f. Find $P(6.5 \leq x \leq 7.25)$.

g. What is the probability that each of the next six bottles filled by the new machine will contain more than

7.25 ounces of beverage? Assume that the amount of beverage dispensed in one bottle is independent of the amount dispensed in another bottle.

148 Phishing attacks to e-mail accounts. *Chance* (Summer 2007) published an article on phishing attacks at a company. *Phishing* describes an attempt to extract personal/financial information through fraudulent e-mail. The company set up a publicized e-mail account—called a "fraud box"—that enabled employees to notify them if they suspected an e-mail phishing attack. If there is minimal or no collaboration or collusion from within the company, the interarrival times (i.e., the time between successive e-mail notifications, in seconds) have an approximate exponential distribution with a mean of 95 seconds.

a. What is the probability of observing an interarrival time of at least 2 minutes?

b. Data for a sample of 267 interarrival times are saved in the accompanying file. Do the data appear to follow an exponential distribution with $\theta = 95$?

149 Product failure behavior. An article in *Hotwire* (Dec. 2002) discussed the length of time till failure of a product produced at Hewlett-Packard. At the end of the product's lifetime, the time till failure is modeled using an exponential distribution with mean 500 thousand hours. In reliability jargon this is known as the "wear-out" distribution for the product. During its normal (useful) life, assume the product's time till failure is uniformly distributed over the range 100 thousand to 1 million hours.

a. At the end of the product's lifetime, find the probability that the product fails before 700 thousand hours.

b. During its normal (useful) life, find the probability that the product fails before 700 thousand hours.

c. Show that the probability of the product failing before 830 thousand hours is approximately the same for both the normal (useful) life distribution and the wear-out distribution.

150 Cycle availability of a system. In the jargon of system maintenance, *cycle availability* is defined as the probability that the system is functioning at any point in time. The DoD developed a series of performance measures for assessing system cycle availability (START, Vol. 11, 2004). Under certain assumptions about the failure time and maintenance time of a system, cycle availability is shown to be uniformly distributed between 0 and 1. Find the following parameters for cycle availability: mean, standard deviation, 10th percentile, lower quartile, and upper quartile. Interpret the results.

151 Gouges on a spindle. A tool-and-die machine shop produces extremely high-tolerance spindles. The spindles are 18-inch slender rods used in a variety of military equipment. A piece of equipment used in the manufacture of the spindles malfunctions on occasion and places a single gouge somewhere on the spindle. However, if the spindle can be cut so that it has 14 consecutive inches without a gouge, then the spindle can be salvaged for other purposes. Assuming that the location of the gouge along the spindle is random, what is the probability that a defective spindle can be salvaged?

152 Reliability of CD-ROMs. In *Reliability Ques* (March 2004), the exponential distribution was used to model the lengths of life of CD-ROM drives in a two-drive system. The two CD-ROM drives operate independently, and at least one drive must be operating for the system to operate successfully. Both drives have a mean length of life of 25,000 hours.

a. The reliability $R(t)$ of a single CD-ROM drive is the probability that the life of the drive exceeds t hours. Give a formula for $R(t)$.

b. Use the result from part **a** to find the probability that the life of the single CD-ROM drive exceeds 8,760 hours (the number of hours of operation in a year).

c. The reliability $S(t)$ of the two-drive/CD-ROM system is the probability that the life of at least one drive exceeds t hours. Give a formula for $S(t)$. [*Hint*: Use the rule of complements and the fact that the two drives operate independently.]

d. Use the result from part **c** to find the probability that the two-drive CD-ROM system has a life whose length exceeds 8,760 hours.

e. Compare the probabilities you found in parts **b** and **d**.

Applying the Concepts—Advanced

153 Acceptance sampling of a product. An essential tool in the monitoring of the quality of a manufactured product is *acceptance sampling*. An acceptance sampling plan involves knowing the distribution of the life length of the item produced and determining how many items to inspect from the manufacturing process. The *Journal of Applied Statistics* (Apr. 2010) demonstrated the use of the exponential distribution as a model for the life length x of an item (e.g., a bullet). The article also discussed the importance of using the median of the lifetime distribution as a measure of product quality, since half of the items in a manufactured lot will have life lengths exceeding the median. For an exponential distribution with mean θ, give an expression for the median of the distribution. (*Hint:* Your answer will be a function of θ.)

154 Reliability of a robotic device. The *reliability* of a piece of equipment is frequently defined to be the probability, p, that the equipment performs its intended function successfully for a given period of time under specific conditions (Render and Heizer, *Principles of Operations Management*, 1995). Because p varies from one point in time to another, some reliability analysts treat p as if it were a random variable. Suppose an analyst characterizes the uncertainty about the reliability of a particular robotic device used in an automobile assembly line using the following distribution:

$$f(p) = \begin{cases} 1 & 0 \le p \le 1 \\ 0 & \text{otherwise} \end{cases}$$

a. Graph the analyst's probability distribution for p.

b. Find the mean and variance of p.

c. According to the analyst's probability distribution for p, what is the probability that p is greater than .95? Less than .95?

d. Suppose the analyst receives the additional information that p is definitely between .90 and .95, but that there is complete uncertainty about where it lies between these values. Describe the probability distribution the analyst should now use to describe p.

155 Length of life of a halogen bulb. For a certain type of halogen light bulb, an old bulb that has been in use for a while tends to have a longer life than a new bulb. Let x represent the life (in hours) of a new halogen light bulb and assume that x has an exponential distribution with mean $\theta = 250$ hours. According to *Microelectronics and Reliability* (Jan. 1986), the "life" distribution of x is considered *new better than used* (NBU) if

$$P(x > a + b) \leq P(x > a)P(x > b)$$

Alternatively, a "life" distribution is considered *new worse than used* (NWU) if

$$P(x > a + b) \geq P(x > a)P(x > b)$$

a. Show that when $a = 300$ and $b = 200$, the exponential distribution is both NBU and NWU.

b. Choose any two positive numbers a and b and repeat part **a**.

c. Show that, in general, for any positive a and b, the exponential distribution with mean θ is both NBU and NWU. Such a "life" distribution is said to be *new same as used*, or *memoryless*. Explain why.

◻ Chapter Notes

Key Terms

Bell curve
Bell-shaped distribution
Binomial experiment
Binomial probability distribution
Binomial random variable
Continuous random variable
Correction for continuity
Countable
Cumulative binomial probabilities
Discrete random variable
Expected value
Exponential probability distribution
Exponential random variable
Frequency function
Hypergeometric probability distribution
Hypergeometric random variable
Mean of a binomial random variable
Mean of a discrete random variable
Mean of a hypergeometric random variable
Mean of a Poisson random variable
Normal distribution
Normal probability plot
Normal random variable
Poisson distribution
Poisson random variable
Probability density function

Probability distribution
Probability distribution of a discrete random variable
Probability distribution of an exponential random variable
Probability distribution of a hypergeometric random variable
Probability distribution of a normal random variable
Probability distribution of a Poisson random variable
Probability distribution for a uniform random variable
Random variable
Randomness distribution
Standard deviation of a binomial random variable
Standard deviation of a discrete random variable
Standard normal distribution
Uniform frequency function
Uniform probability distribution
Uniform random variable
Variance of a binomial random variable
Variance of a discrete random variable
Variance of a hypergeometric random variable
Variance of a Poisson random variable
Waiting-time distribution

Key Symbols

$p(x)$ Probability distribution for discrete random variable, x

$f(x)$ Probability distribution for continuous random variable, x

S Outcome of binomial trial denoted "success"

F Outcome of binomial trial denoted "failure"

p $P(S)$ in binomial trial

q $P(F)$ in binomial trial $= 1 - p$

e Constant used in normal and Poisson probability distributions, $e = 2.71828\ldots$

π Constant used in normal probability distributions, $\pi = 3.1415\ldots$

Key Ideas

Properties of Probability Distributions

Discrete Distributions

1. $p(x) \geq 0$

2. $\displaystyle\sum_{\text{all } x} p(x) = 1$

Continuous Distributions

1. $P(x = a) = 0$

2. $P(a < x < b)$ is area under curve between a and b

Normal Approximation to Binomial

x is binomial (n, p)
$P(x \leq a) \approx P\{z < (a + .5) - \mu\}$

Methods for Assessing Normality

1. *Histogram*

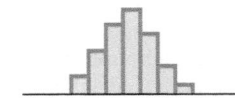

2. *Stem-and-leaf display*

```
1 | 7
2 | 3389
3 | 245677
4 | 19
5 | 2
```

3. $(IQR)/S \approx 1.3$

4. *Normal probability plot*

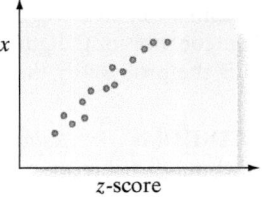

z-score

Key Formulas

Random Variable	Probability Distribution	Mean	Variance
General Discrete:	Table, formula, or graph for $p(x)$	$\displaystyle\sum_{\text{all } x} x \cdot p(x)$	$\displaystyle\sum_{\text{all } x}(x - \mu)^2 \cdot p(x)$
Binomial:	$p(x) = \binom{n}{x}p^x q^{n-x}$ $x = 0, 1, 2, \cdots, n$	np	npq
Poisson:	$p(x) = \dfrac{\lambda^x e^{-\lambda}}{x!}$ $x = 0, 1, 2, \cdots$	λ	λ
Hypergeometric	$p(x) = \dfrac{\binom{r}{x}\binom{N-r}{n-x}}{\binom{N}{n}}$	$\dfrac{nr}{N}$	$\dfrac{r(N-r)n(N-n)}{N^2(N-1)}$
Uniform:	$f(x) = 1/(d - c)$ $(c \le x \le d)$	$(c + d)/2$	$(d - c)^2/12$
Normal:	$f(x) = \dfrac{1}{\sigma\sqrt{2\pi}} e^{-\frac{1}{2}[(x-\mu)/\sigma]^2}$	μ	σ^2
Exponential	$f(x) = \dfrac{1}{\theta} e^{-x/\theta}$	θ	θ
Standard Normal:	$f(z) = \dfrac{1}{\sqrt{2\pi}} e^{-\frac{1}{2}(z)^2}$ $z = (x - \mu)/\sigma$	$\mu = 0$	$\sigma^2 = 1$

Guide to Selecting a Probability Distribution

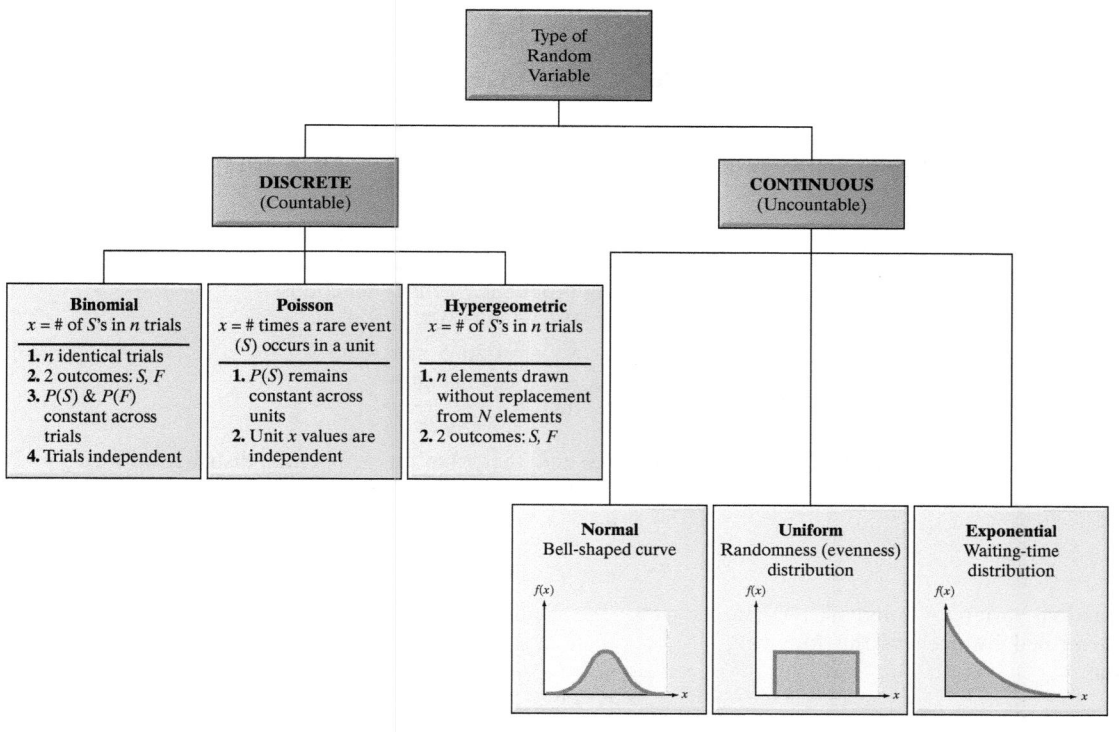

Supplementary Exercises 156–206

Please be aware that some of the following problems may require knowledge of concepts that are not presented in this chapter.

Learning the Mechanics

156 For each of the following examples, decide whether x is a binomial random variable and explain your decision:
  a. A manufacturer of computer chips randomly selects 100 chips from each hour's production in order to estimate the proportion defective. Let x represent the number of defectives in the 100 sampled chips.
  b. Of five applicants for a job, two will be selected. Although all applicants appear to be equally qualified, only three have the ability to fulfill the expectations of the company. Suppose that the two selections are made at random from the five applicants and let x be the number of qualified applicants selected.
  c. A software developer establishes a support hotline for customers to call in with questions regarding use of the software. Let x represent the number of calls received on the support hotline during a specified workday.
  d. Florida is one of a minority of states with no state income tax. A poll of 1,000 registered voters is conducted to determine how many would favor a state income tax in light of the state's current fiscal condition. Let x be the number in the sample who would favor the tax.

157 Given that x is a binomial random variable, compute $p(x)$ for each of the following cases:
  a. $n = 7, x = 3, p = .5$
  b. $n = 4, x = 3, p = .8$
  c. $n = 15, x = 1, p = .1$

158 Consider the discrete probability distribution shown here.

x	10	12	18	20
$p(x)$	.2	.3	.1	.4

  a. Calculate μ, σ^2, and σ.
  b. What is $P(x < 15)$?
  c. Calculate $\mu \pm 2\sigma$.
  d. What is the probability that x is in the interval $\mu \pm 2\sigma$?

159 Suppose x is a binomial random variable with $n = 20$ and $p = .7$.
  a. Find $P(x = 14)$.
  b. Find $P(x \le 12)$.
  c. Find $P(x > 12)$.
  d. Find $P(9 \le x \le 18)$.
  e. Find $P(8 < x < 18)$.
  f. Find μ, σ^2, and σ.
  g. What is the probability that x is in the interval $\mu \pm 2\sigma$?

160 Suppose x is a Poisson random variable. Compute $p(x)$ for each of the following cases:
  a. $\lambda = 2, x = 3$
  b. $\lambda = 1, x = 4$
  c. $\lambda = .5, x = 2$

161 Identify the type of random variable—binomial, Poisson, or hypergeometric—described by each of the following probability distributions:
  a. $p(x) = \dfrac{.5^x e^{-5}}{x!}$ $(x = 0, 1, 2, \dots)$

  b. $p(x) = \dbinom{6}{x}(.2)^x(.8)^{6-x}$ $(x = 0, 1, 2, \dots, 6)$

  c. $p(x) = \dfrac{10!}{x!(10 - x)!}(.9)^x(.1)^{10-x}$

  d. $(x = 0, 1, 2, \dots, 10)$

162 Given that x is a hypergeometric random variable, compute $p(x)$ for each of the following cases:
  a. $N = 8, n = 5, r = 3, x = 2$
  b. $N = 6, n = 2, r = 2, x = 2$
  c. $N = 5, n = 4, r = 4, x = 3$

163 Which of the following describe discrete random variables, and which describe continuous random variables?
  a. The number of damaged inventory items
  b. The average monthly sales revenue generated by a salesperson over the past year
  c. Square feet of warehouse space a company rents
  d. The length of time a firm must wait before its copying machine is fixed

164 Assume that x is a random variable best described by a uniform distribution with $c = 10$ and $d = 90$.
  a. Find $f(x)$.
  b. Find the mean and standard deviation of x.
  c. Graph the probability distribution for x and locate its mean and the interval $\mu \pm 2\sigma$ on the graph.
  d. Find $P(x \le 60)$.
  e. Find $P(x \ge 90)$.
  f. Find $P(x \le 80)$.
  g. Find $P(\mu - \sigma \le x \le \mu + \sigma)$.
  h. Find $P(x > 75)$.

165 Find the following probabilities for the standard normal random variable z:
  a. $P(z \le 2.1)$ **b.** $P(z \ge 2.1)$
  c. $P(z \ge -1.65)$ **d.** $P(-2.13 \le z \le -.41)$
  e. $P(-1.45 \le z \le 2.15)$ **f.** $P(z \le -1.43)$

166 Find a z-score, call it z_0, such that
  a. $P(z \le z_0) = .5080$
  b. $P(z \ge z_0) = .5517$
  c. $P(z \ge z_0) = .1492$
  d. $P(z_0 \le z \le .59) = .4773$

167 Identify the type of continuous random variable—uniform, normal, or exponential—described by each of the following probability density functions:
  a. $f(x) = (e^{-x/7})/7, x > 0$
  b. $f(x) = 1/20, 5 < x < 25$
  c. $f(x) = \dfrac{e^{-.5[(x-10)/5]^2}}{5\sqrt{2\pi}}$

168 Assume that x has an exponential distribution with $\theta = 3$. Find
  a. $P(x \le 1)$ **b.** $P(x > 1)$
  c. $P(x = 1)$ **d.** $P(x \le 6)$
  e. $P(2 \le x \le 10)$

169 The random variable x has a normal distribution with $\mu = 75$ and $\sigma = 10$. Find the following probabilities:
  a. $P(x \le 80)$ **b.** $P(x \ge 85)$
  c. $P(70 \le x \le 75)$ **d.** $P(x > 80)$
  e. $P(x = 78)$ **f.** $P(x \le 110)$

170 Assume that x is a binomial random variable with $n = 100$ and $p = .5$. Use the normal probability distribution to approximate the following probabilities:

a. $P(x \leq 48)$ **b.** $P(50 \leq x \leq 65)$

c. $P(x \geq 70)$ **d.** $P(55 \leq x \leq 58)$

e. $P(x = 62)$ **f.** $P(x \leq 49 \text{ or } x \geq 72)$

171 The random variable x has a normal distribution with $\mu = 40$ and $\sigma^2 = 36$. Find a value of x, call it x_0, such that

a. $P(x \geq x_0) = .10$ **b.** $P(\mu \leq x < x_0) = .40$

c. $P(x < x_0) = .05$ **d.** $P(x \geq x_0) = .40$

e. $P(x_0 \leq x < \mu) = .45$

Applying the Concepts—Basic

172 Analysis of bottled water. Is the bottled water you're drinking really purified water? A 4-year study of bottled water brands conducted by the Natural Resources Defense Council found that 25% of bottled water is just tap water packaged in a bottle (*Scientific American*, July 2003). Consider a sample of five bottled water brands and let x equal the number of these brands that use tap water.

a. Explain why x is (approximately) a binomial random variable.

b. Give the probability distribution for x as a formula.

c. Find $P(x = 2)$.

d. Find $P(x \leq 1)$.

e. In a random sample of 65 bottled water brands, is it likely that 20 or more brands will contain tap water? Explain.

173 Dentists' use of laughing gas. According to the American Dental Association, 60% of all dentists use nitrous oxide in their practice. If x equals the number of dentists in a random sample of five dentists who use laughing gas in practice, then the probability distribution of x is

x	0	1	2	3	4	5
$p(x)$	.0102	.0768	.2304	.3456	.2592	.0778

a. Verify that the probabilities for x sum to 1.

b. Find $P(x = 4)$.

c. Find $P(x < 2)$.

d. Find $P(x \geq 3)$.

e. Find $\mu = E(x)$ and practically interpret this value.

174 Transmission delays in wireless technology. Resource reservation protocol (RSVP) was originally designed to establish signaling links for stationary networks. In *Mobile Networks and Applications* (Dec. 2003), RSVP was applied to mobile wireless technology (e.g., a PC notebook with wireless LAN card for Internet access). A simulation study revealed that the transmission delay (measured in milliseconds) of an RSVP linked wireless device has an approximate normal distribution with mean $\mu = 48.5$ milliseconds and $\sigma = 8.5$ milliseconds.

a. What is the probability that the transmission delay is less than 57 milliseconds?

b. What is the probability that the transmission delay is between 40 and 60 milliseconds?

175 Trajectory of an electrical circuit. Researchers at the University of California–Berkeley have designed, built, and tested a switched-capacitor circuit for generating random signals (*International Journal of Circuit Theory and Applications,* May–June 1990). The circuit's

trajectory was shown to be uniformly distributed on the interval $(0, 1)$.

a. Give the mean and variance of the circuit's trajectory.

b. Compute the probability that the trajectory falls between .2 and .4.

c. Would you expect to observe a trajectory that exceeds .995? Explain.

176 Spare line replacement units. The DoD RAC publishes Selected Topics in Assurance Related Technologies (START) sheets to help improve the quality of manufactured components and systems. One START sheet, titled "Application of the Poisson Distribution" (Vol. 9, No. 1, 2002), focuses on a spare line replacement unit (LRU). Failures of LRUs are assumed to follow a Poisson distribution with a mean failure rate of 1.2 failures per 10,000 hours.

a. Find the probability that there are no LRU failures during the next 10,000 hours of operation.

b. Find the probability that there are at least two LRU failures during the next 10,000 hours of operation.

177 Hospital patient interarrival times. The length of time between arrivals at a hospital clinic has an approximately exponential probability distribution. Suppose the mean time between arrivals for patients at a clinic is 4 minutes.

a. What is the probability that a particular interarrival time (the time between the arrival of two patients) is less than 1 minute?

b. What is the probability that the next four interarrival times are all less than 1 minute?

c. What is the probability that an interarrival time will exceed 10 minutes?

178 Dutch elm disease. A nursery advertises that it has 10 elm trees for sale. Unknown to the nursery, 3 of the trees have already been infected with Dutch elm disease and will die within a year.

a. If a buyer purchases 2 trees, what is the probability that both trees will be healthy?

b. Refer to part **a.** What is the probability that at least 1 of the trees is infected?

179 Tracking missiles with satellite imagery. The U.S. government has devoted considerable funding to missile defense research over the past 20 years. The latest development is the Space-Based Infrared System (SBIRS), which uses satellite imagery to detect and track missiles (*Chance,* Summer 2005). The probability that an intruding object (e.g., a missile) will be detected on a flight track by SBIRS is .8. Consider a sample of 20 simulated tracks, each with an intruding object. Let x equal the number of these tracks where SBIRS detects the object.

a. Demonstrate that x is (approximately) a binomial random variable.

b. Give the values of p and n for the binomial distribution.

c. Find $P(x = 15)$, the probability that SBIRS will detect the object on exactly 15 tracks.

d. Find $P(x \geq 15)$, the probability that SBIRS will detect the object on at least 15 tracks.

e. Find $E(x)$ and interpret the result.

180 Estimating demand for white bread. A bakery has determined that the number of loaves of its white bread demanded daily has a normal distribution with mean 7,200 loaves and standard deviation 300 loaves. Based on cost considerations, the company has decided that its best strategy is to produce a sufficient number of loaves so that it will fully supply demand on 94% of all days.

a. How many loaves of bread should the company produce?

b. Based on the production in part **a,** on what percentage of days will the company be left with more than 500 loaves of unsold bread?

181 **Machine repair times.** An article in *IEEE Transactions* (Mar. 1990) gave an example of a flexible manufacturing system with four machines operating independently. The repair rates for the machines (i.e., the time, in hours, it takes to repair a failed machine) are exponentially distributed with means $\mu_1 = 1$, $\mu_2 = 2$, $\mu_3 = .5$, and $\mu_4 = .5$, respectively.

a. Find the probability that the repair time for machine 1 exceeds 1 hour.

b. Repeat part **a** for machine 2.

c. Repeat part **a** for machines 3 and 4.

d. If all four machines fail simultaneously, find the probability that the repair time for the entire system exceeds 1 hour.

182 **Public transit deaths.** Millions of suburban commuters use the public transit system (e.g., subway trains) as an alternative to the automobile. While generally perceived as a safe mode of transportation, the average number of deaths per week due to public transit accidents is a surprisingly high 16 (Bureau of Transportation Statistics, 2010).

a. Construct arguments both for and against the use of the Poisson distribution to characterize the number of deaths per week due to public transit accidents.

b. For the remainder of this exercise, assume the Poisson distribution is an adequate approximation for x, the number of deaths per week due to public transit accidents. Find $E(x)$ and the standard deviation of x.

c. Based strictly on your answers to part **b,** is it likely that only four or fewer deaths occur next week? Explain.

d. Find $P(x \le 4)$. Is this probability consistent with your answer to part **c**? Explain.

183 **On-site treatment of hazardous waste.** The Resource Conservation and Recovery Act mandates the tracking and disposal of hazardous waste produced at U.S. facilities. *Professional Geographer* (Feb. 2000) reported the hazardous-waste generation and disposal characteristics of 209 facilities. Only 8 of these facilities treated hazardous waste on-site. Use the hypergeometric distribution to answer the following:

a. In a random sample of 10 of the 209 facilities, what is the expected number in the sample that treat hazardous waste on-site? Interpret this result.

b. Find the probability that 4 of the 10 selected facilities treat hazardous waste on-site.

184 **Random numbers.** The data set listed in the table (next column) was created using the Minitab random number RANUNI generator. Construct a relative frequency histogram for the data. Except for the expected variation in relative frequencies among the class intervals, does your histogram suggest that the data are observations on a uniform random variable with $c = 0$ and $d = 100$? Explain.

38.8759	98.0716	64.5788	60.8422	.8413
88.3734	31.8792	32.9847	.7434	93.3017
12.4337	11.7828	87.4506	94.1727	23.0892
47.0121	43.3629	50.7119	88.2612	69.2875
62.6626	55.6267	78.3936	28.6777	71.6829
44.0466	57.8870	71.8318	28.9622	23.0278
35.6438	38.6584	46.7404	11.2159	96.1009
95.3660	21.5478	87.7819	12.0605	75.1015

185 **Time in bankruptcy.** The *Financial Management* (Spring 1995) did a study of 49 companies that filed for a prepack-BNKRPT aged bankruptcy. The time in bankruptcy (measured in months) for each company is saved in the accompanying file. Determine whether the bankruptcy times are approximately normally distributed.

186 **Environmental failures of Arkansas companies.** Refer to the study of 38 Arkansas corporations that were penalized ARKAIR for violating one or more environmental laws. The financial penalties assessed to the companies are saved in the accompanying file. Determine whether the financial penalties are approximately normally distributed.

Applying the Concepts—Intermediate

187 **Errors in measuring truck weights.** To help highway planners anticipate the need for road repairs and design future construction projects, data are collected on the estimated volume and weight of truck traffic on specific roadways (*Transportation Planning Handbook,* 2008) using specialized "weigh-in-motion" equipment. In an experiment performed by the Minnesota Department of Transportation involving repeated weighing of a 27,907-pound truck, it was found that the weights recorded by the weigh-in-motion equipment were approximately normally distributed with a mean of 27,315 and a standard deviation of 628 pounds (Minnesota Department of Transportation). It follows that the difference between the actual weight and recorded weight, the error of measurement, is normally distributed with a mean of 592 pounds and a standard deviation of 628 pounds.

a. What is the probability that the weigh-in-motion equipment understates the actual weight of the truck?

b. If a 27,907-pound truck was driven over the weigh-in-motion equipment 100 times, approximately how many times would the equipment overstate the truck's weight?

c. What is the probability that the error in the weight recorded by the weigh-in-motion equipment for a 27,907-pound truck exceeds 400 pounds?

d. It is possible to adjust (or *calibrate*) the weigh-in-motion equipment to control the mean error of measurement. At what level should the mean error be set so the equipment will understate the weight of a 27,907-pound truck 50% of the time? Only 40% of the time?

188 **Detecting a computer virus attack.** *Chance* (Winter 2004) presented basic methods for detecting virus attacks (e.g., Trojan programs or worms) on a network computer that are sent from a remote host. These viruses reach the network through requests for communication (e.g., e-mail, Web chat, or remote log-in) that are identified as "packets." For example, the "SYN flood" virus ties up the network computer by "flooding" the network with multiple packets. Cybersecurity experts can detect this type of virus attack if at least one packet is observed by a network sensor. Assume that the probability of observing a single packet sent from a new virus is only .001. If the virus actually sends 150 packets to a network computer, what is the probability that the virus is detected by the sensor?

189 Whistle-blowing among federal employees. *Whistle-blowing* refers to an employee's reporting of wrongdoing by coworkers. A survey found that about 5% of employees contacted had reported wrongdoing during the past 12 months. Assume that a sample of 25 employees in one agency are contacted and let x be the number who have observed and reported wrongdoing in the last 12 months. Assume that the probability of whistle-blowing is .05 for any federal employee over the past 12 months.
a. Find the mean and standard deviation of x. Can x be equal to its expected value? Explain.
b. Write the event that at least 5 of the employees are whistle-blowers in terms of x. Find the probability of the event.
c. If 5 of the 25 contacted have been whistle-blowers over the past 12 months, what would you conclude about the applicability of the 5% assumption to this agency? Use your answer to part b to justify your conclusion.

190 Cotton crop yield study. The crop yield for a particular farm in a particular year is typically measured as the amount of the crop produced per acre. For example, cotton is measured in pounds per acre. It has been demonstrated that the normal distribution can be used to characterize crop yields over time (*American Journal of Agricultural Economics*, May 1999). Historical data indicate that next summer's cotton yield for a particular Georgia farmer can be characterized by a normal distribution with mean 1,500 pounds per acre and standard deviation 250. The farm in question will be profitable if it produces at least 1,600 pounds per acre.
a. What is the probability that the farm will lose money next summer?
b. Assume the same normal distribution is appropriate for describing cotton yield in each of the next two summers. Also assume that the two yields are statistically independent. What is the probability that the farm will lose money for two straight years?
c. What is the probability that the cotton yield falls within 2 standard deviations of 1,500 pounds per acre next summer?

191 Awarding of home improvement grants. A curious event was described in the *Minneapolis Star and Tribune*. The Minneapolis Community Development Agency (MCDA) makes home improvement grants each year to homeowners in depressed city neighborhoods. Of the $708,000 granted one year, $233,000 was awarded by the city council via a "random selection" of 140 homeowners' applications from among a total of 743 applications: 601 from the north side, and 142 from the south side, of Minneapolis. Oddly, all 140 grants awarded were from the north side—clearly a highly improbable outcome if, in fact, the 140 winners were randomly selected from among the 743 applicants.
a. Suppose the 140 winning applications were randomly selected from among the total of 743 and let x equal the number in the sample from the north side. Find the mean and standard deviation of x.

b. Use the results of part **a** to support a contention that the grant winners were not randomly selected.

192 Time delays at a bus stop. A bus is scheduled to stop at a certain bus stop every half hour on the hour and the half hour. At the end of the day, buses still stop after every 30 minutes, but because delays often occur earlier in the day, the bus is never early and is likely to be late. The director of the bus line claims that the length of time a bus is late is uniformly distributed, and the maximum time that a bus is late is 20 minutes.
a. If the director's claim is true, what is the expected number of minutes a bus will be late?
b. If the director's claim is true, what is the probability that the last bus on a given day will be more than 19 minutes late?
c. If you arrive at the bus stop at the end of a day at exactly half past the hour and must wait more than 19 minutes for the bus, what would you conclude about the director's claim? Why?

193 Reliability of a flow network. The journal *Networks* periodically publishes studies on the reliability of flow networks. For example, *Networks* (Sep. 2007) provided applications in mobile ad hoc and sensor networks. Consider a similar network with four activities, called *arcs*. The probability distribution of the capacity x for each of the four arcs is provided in the following table.

Arc 1	x	0	1	2	3
	$p(x)$	.05	.10	.25	.60

Arc 2	x	0	1	2	3
	$p(x)$	.10	.30	.60	0

Arc 3	x	0	1	2	3
	$p(x)$	.05	.25	.70	0

Arc 4	x	0	1	2	3
	$p(x)$	.90	.10	0	0

Source: Adapted from Lin, J. "On Reliability Evaluation of Capacitated-Flow Network in Terms of Minimal Pathsets." *Networks,* Vol. 25, No. 3, May 1995 (Table 1).

a. Verify that the properties of discrete probability distributions are satisfied for each arc capacity distribution.
b. Find the probability that the capacity for Arc 1 will exceed 1.
c. Repeat part **b** for each of the remaining three arcs.
d. Compute μ for each arc and interpret the results.
e. Compute σ for each arc and interpret the results.

194 Doctors and ethics. The *Journal of Medical Ethics* (Vol. 32, 2006) did a study of the extent to which doctors refuse ethics consultation. Consider a random sample of 10 doctors, each of whom is confronted with an ethical dilemma (e.g., an end-of-life issue or treatment of a patient without insurance). What is the probability that at least two of the doctors refuse ethics consultation? Estimate p, the probability that a doctor will refuse to use ethics consultation.

195 LAN video conferencing. A network administrator is installing a video conferencing module to a local area network (LAN) computer system. Of interest is the capacity of the

LAN to handle users who attempt to call in for video conferencing during peak hours. Calls are blocked if the user finds all LAN lines are "busy." The capacity is directly related to the rate at which calls are blocked ("Traffic Engineering Model for LAN Video Conferencing," Intel, 2005). Let x equal the number of calls blocked during the peak hour (busy) video conferencing call time. The network administrator believes that x has a Poisson distribution with mean $\lambda = 5$.

a. Find the probability that fewer than three calls are blocked during the peak hour.

b. Find $E(x)$ and interpret its value.

196 Testing for spoiled wine. Suppose that you are purchasing cases of wine (12 bottles per case) and that, periodically, you select a test case to determine the adequacy of the bottles' seals. To do this, you randomly select and test 3 bottles in the case. If a case contains 1 spoiled bottle of wine, what is the probability that this bottle will turn up in your sample?

197 Testing a manufacturer's claim. A manufacturer of CD-ROMs claims that 99.4% of its CDs are defect-free. A large software company that buys and uses a large number of the CDs wants to verify this claim, so it selects 1,600 CDs to be tested. The tests reveal 12 CDs to be defective. Assuming that the manufacturer's claim is correct, what is the probability of finding 12 or more defective CDs in a sample of 1,600? Does your answer cast doubt on the manufacturer's claim? Explain.

198 Checkout lanes at a supermarket. A team of consultants working for a large national supermarket chain based in the New York metropolitan area developed a statistical model for predicting the annual sales of potential new store locations. Part of their analysis involved identifying variables that influence store sales, such as the size of the store (in square feet), the size of the surrounding population, and the number of checkout lanes. They surveyed 52 supermarkets in a particular region of the country and constructed the relative frequency distribution shown below to describe the number of checkout lanes per store, x.

x	1	2	3	4	5	6	7	8	9	10
Relative Frequency	.01	.04	.04	.08	.10	.15	.25	.20	.08	.05

Source: Based on Chow, W., et.al. "A model for predicting a supermarket's annual sales per square foot." Graduate School of Management, Rutgers University, 1994.

a. Why do the relative frequencies in the table represent the approximate probabilities of a randomly selected supermarket having x number of checkout lanes?

b. Find $E(x)$ and interpret its value in the context of the problem.

c. Find the standard deviation of x.

d. According to Chebyshev's Rule, what percentage of supermarkets would be expected to fall within $\mu \pm \sigma$? Within $\mu \pm 2\sigma$?

e. What is the actual number of supermarkets that fall within $\mu \pm \sigma$? $\mu \pm 2\sigma$? Compare your answers to those of part **d**. Are the answers consistent?

199 Model for long-term construction cost. Before negotiating a long-term construction contract, building contractors must carefully estimate the total cost of completing the project. Benzion Barlev of New York University proposed a model for total cost of a long-term contract based on the normal distribution (*Journal of Business Finance and Accounting*, July 1995). For one particular construction contract, Barlev assumed total cost, x, to be normally distributed with mean $850,000 and standard deviation $170,000. The revenue, R, promised to the contractor is $1,000,000.

a. The contract will be profitable if revenue exceeds total cost. What is the probability that the contract will be profitable for the contractor?

b. What is the probability that the project will result in a loss for the contractor?

c. Suppose the contractor has the opportunity to renegotiate the contract. What value of R should the contractor strive for in order to have a .99 probability of making a profit?

200 Ship-to-shore transfer times. Lack of port facilities or shallow water may require cargo on a large ship to be transferred to a pier in smaller craft. The smaller craft may have to cycle back and forth from ship to shore many times. Researchers G. Horne (Center for Naval Analysis) and T. Irony (George Washington University) developed models of this transfer process that provide estimates of ship-to-shore transfer times (*Naval Research Logistics*, Vol. 41, 1994). They used an exponential distribution to model the time between arrivals of the smaller craft at the pier.

a. Assume that the mean time between arrivals at the pier is 17 minutes. Give the value of θ for this exponential distribution. Graph the distribution.

b. Suppose there is only one unloading zone at the pier available for the small craft to use. If the first craft docks at 10:00 A.M. and doesn't finish unloading until 10:15 A.M., what is the probability that the second craft will arrive at the unloading zone and have to wait before docking?

Applying the Concepts—Advanced

201 How many questionnaires to mail? The probability that a consumer responds to a marketing department's mailed questionnaire is .4. How many questionnaires should be mailed if you want to be reasonably certain that at least 100 will be returned?

202 Establishing tolerance limits. The *tolerance limits* for a particular quality characteristic (e.g., length, weight, or strength) of a product are the minimum and/or maximum values at which the product will operate properly. Tolerance limits are set by the engineering design function of the manufacturing operation (*Total Quality Management*, Vol. 11, 2000). The tensile strength of a particular metal part can be characterized as being normally distributed with a mean of 25 pounds and a standard deviation of 2 pounds. The upper and lower tolerance limits for the part are 30 pounds and 21 pounds, respectively. A part that falls within the tolerance limits results in a profit of $10. A part that falls below the lower tolerance limit costs the company $2; a part that falls above the upper tolerance limit costs the company $1. Find the company's expected profit per metal part produced.

203 Load on frame structures. In the *Journal of the International Association for Shell and Spatial Structures* (Apr. 2004), Japanese environmental researchers studied the performance of truss and frame structures subjected to uncertain loads. The load was assumed to have a normal distributions with a mean of 20,000 pounds. Also, the probability that the load is between 10,000 and 30,000 pounds is .95. Based on this information, find the standard deviation of the load distribution.

204 **Luggage inspection at Newark airport.** *New Jersey Business* reports that Newark Liberty International Airport's new terminal handles an average of 3,000 international passengers an hour but is capable of handling twice that number. Also, after scanning all luggage, 20% of arriving international passengers are detained for intrusive luggage inspection. The inspection facility can handle 600 passengers an hour without unreasonable delays for the travelers.
   a. When international passengers arrive at the rate of 1,500 per hour, what is the expected number of passengers who will be detained for luggage inspection?
   b. In the future, it is expected that as many as 4,000 international passengers will arrive per hour. When that occurs, what is the expected number of passengers who will be detained for luggage inspection?
   c. Refer to part **b.** Find the approximate probability that more than 600 international passengers will be detained for luggage inspection. (This is also the probability that travelers will experience unreasonable luggage inspection delays.)

Critical Thinking Challenges

205 **Super weapons development.** The U.S. Army is working with a major defense contractor (not named here for both confidentiality and security reasons) to develop a "super" weapon. The weapon is designed to fire a large number of sharp tungsten bullets—called flechettes—with a single shot that will destroy a large number of enemy soldiers. (Flechettes are about the size of an average nail, with small fins at one end to stabilize them in flight.) The defense contractor has developed a prototype gun that fires 1,100 flechettes with a single round. In range tests, three 2-feet-wide targets were set up at a distance of 500 meters (approximately 1500 feet) from the weapon. Using a number line as a reference, the centers of the three targets were at 0, 5, and 10 feet, respectively, as shown in the accompanying figure. The prototype gun was aimed at the middle target (center at 5 feet) and fired once. The point x where each of the 1,100 flechettes landed at the 500-meter distance was measured using a horizontal grid. For example, a flechette with a horizontal value of $x = 5.5$ (shown in the figure) hit the middle target, but a flechette with a horizontal value of $x = 2.0$ (also shown in the figure) did not hit any of the three targets. The 1,100 measurements on the random variable x are saved in the accompanying file. (The data are simulated for confidentiality reasons.)

   The defense contractor is interested in the likelihood of any one of the targets being hit by a flechette, and in

particular, wants to set the gun specifications to maximize the number of target hits. The weapon is designed to have a mean horizontal value, $E(x)$, equal to the aim point (e.g., $\mu = 5$ feet when aimed at the center target). By changing specifications, the contractor can vary the standard deviation, σ. The data file contains flechette measurements for three different range tests—one with a standard deviation of $\sigma = 1$ foot, one with $\sigma = 2$ feet, and one with $\sigma = 4$ feet. Let x_1, x_2, and x_4 represent the random variables for horizontal measurements with $\sigma = 1$, $\sigma = 2$, and $\sigma = 4$, respectively. From past experience, the defense contractor has found that the distribution of the horizontal flechette measurements is closely approximated by a normal distribution.
   a. For each of the three values of σ, use the normal distribution to find the approximate probability that a single flechette shot from the weapon will hit any one of the three targets. [*Hint:* Note that the three targets range from −1 to 1, 4 to 6, and 9 to 11 feet on the horizontal grid.]
   b. The actual results of the three range tests are saved in the data file. Use this information to calculate the proportion of the 1,100 flechettes that actually hit each target— called the hit ratio—for each value of σ. How do these actual hit ratios compare to the estimated probabilities of a hit using the normal distribution?
   c. If the U.S. Army wants to maximize the chance of hitting the target that the prototype gun is aimed at, what setting should be used for σ? If the Army wants to hit multiple targets with a single shot of the weapon, what setting should be used for σ?

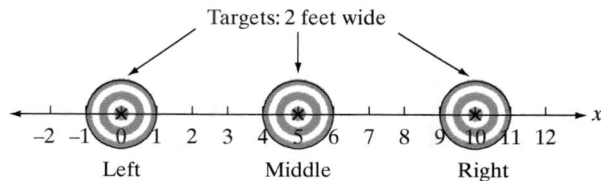

Targets: 2 feet wide

Left   Middle   Right

206 **Space shuttle disaster.** On January 28, 1986, the space shuttle *Challenger* exploded, killing all seven astronauts aboard. An investigation concluded that the explosion was caused by the failure of the O ring seal in the joint between the two lower segments of the right solid rocket booster. In a report made 1 year prior to the catastrophe, the National Aeronautics and Space Administration (NASA) claimed that the probability of such a failure was about $\frac{1}{60,000}$, or about once in every 60,000 flights. But a risk-assessment study conducted for the Air Force at about the same time assessed the probability to be $\frac{1}{35}$, or about once in every 35 missions. (*Note:* The shuttle had flown 24 successful missions prior to the disaster.) Given the events of January 28, 1986, which risk assessment—NASA's or the Air Force's— appears to be more appropriate?

Activity 1 **Warehouse Club Memberships: Exploring a Binomial Random Variable**

Warehouse clubs are retailers that offer lower prices than traditional retailers, but they sell only to customers who have purchased memberships and often merchandise must be purchased in large quantities. A warehouse club may offer more than one type of membership, such as a regular

membership *R* for a low annual fee and an upgraded membership *U* for a higher annual fee. The upgraded membership has additional benefits that might include extended shopping hours, additional discounts on certain products, or cash back on purchases.

(Continued)

A local warehouse club has determined that 20% of its customer base has the upgraded membership.

1. What is the probability $P(U)$ that a randomly chosen customer entering the store has an upgraded membership? What is the probability $P(R)$ that a randomly chosen customer entering the store has a regular (not upgraded) membership?

   In an effort to sell more upgraded memberships, sales associates are placed at the entrance to the store to explain the benefits of the upgraded membership to customers as they enter. Suppose that in a given time period five customers enter the store.

2. Given that 20% of the store's customers have an upgraded membership, how many of the five customers would you expect to have an upgraded membership?

3. Because there are five customers and each customer either has an upgraded membership (U) or does not (R), there are $2^5 = 32$ different possible combinations of membership types among the five customers. List these 32 possibilities.

4. Find the probability of each of the 32 outcomes. Assume that each of the five customers' membership type is independent of each of the other customers' membership type

and use your probabilities $P(U)$ and $P(R)$ with the multiplicative rule. For example, $P(RRUUR) = P(R)P(R)P(U)P(U)P(R)$.

5. Notice that $P(URRRR) = P(RURRR) = P(RRURR) = P(RRRUR) = P(RRRRU) = P(U)^1 P(R)^4$ so that $P(\text{exactly one } U) = P(URRRR) + P(RURRR) + P(RRURR) + P(RRRUR) + P(RRRRU) = 5P(U)^1 P(R)^4$ where 5 is the number of ways that exactly one U can occur. Find $P(\text{exactly one } U)$. Use similar reasoning to establish that $P(\text{no } U\text{'s}) = 1P(U)^0 P(R)^5$, $P(\text{exactly two } U\text{'s}) = 10P(U)^2 (R)^3$, $P(\text{exactly three } U\text{'s}) = 10P(U)^3 P(R)^2$, $P(\text{exactly four } U\text{'s}) = 5P(U)^4 P(R)^1$, and $P(\text{five } U\text{'s}) = 1P(U)^5 P(R)^0$.

6. Let x be the number of upgraded memberships U in a sample of five customers. Use the results of Part 5 to write a probability distribution for the random variable x in table form. Find the mean and standard deviation of the distribution using the formulas in Section 2.

7. Calculate np and $\sqrt{npq}$ where $n = 5$, $p = P(U)$, and $q = P(R)$. How do these numbers compare to the mean and standard deviation of the random variable x in Part **6** and to the expected number of customers with upgraded memberships in Part **1**?

8. Explain how the characteristics of a binomial random variable are illustrated in this activity.

Activity **2**   ## Identifying the Type of Probability Distribution

Collect data for at least 50 observations on a variable of interest to you (e.g., scores on a statistics exam, monthly sales of a pre-owned auto dealership, time spent preparing for the GMAT, number of bank failures per year). Be sure to identify the experimental unit prior to beginning your data search.

1. Before you actually collect the data, identify the probability distribution that you believe will be the best model

for the variable you selected. (Be sure to check the properties of the different random variables presented in this chapter.)

2. Enter the data into a statistical software package and graph the distribution. Does the graph match the probability distribution you identified?

References

Deming, W. E. *Out of the Crisis.* Cambridge, Mass.: MIT Center for Advanced Engineering Study, 1986.

Hogg, R. V., McKean, J. W., and Craig, A. T. *Introduction to Mathematical Statistics,* 6th ed. Upper Saddle River, N.J.: Prentice Hall, 2005.

Larsen, R. J., & Marx, M. L. *An Introduction to Mathematical Statistics and Its Applications,* 4th ed. Upper Saddle River, N.J.: Prentice Hall, 2005.

Lindgren, B. W. *Statistical Theory,* 4th ed. New York: Chapman & Hall, 1993.

Ramsey, P. P., & Ramsey, P. H. "Simple tests of normality in small samples," *Journal of Quality Technology,* Vol. 22, 1990.

Wackerly, D., Mendenhall, W., and Scheaffer, R. *Mathematical Statistics with Applications,* 7th ed. North Scituate, Mass.: Duxbury, 2008.

USING TECHNOLOGY   **Technology images shown here are taken from SPSS Statistics Professional 20.0, Minitab 16, XLSTAT for Pearson, and Excel 2010.**

SPSS: Discrete Probabilities, Continuous Probabilities, and Normal Probability Plots

Discrete and Continuous Probabilities

Step 1 Select "Transform" on the SPSS menu bar and then click on "Compute Variable," as shown in Figure S.1. The resulting dialog box appears as shown in Figure S.2.

Figure S.1 SPSS menu options for obtaining discrete and continuous probabilities

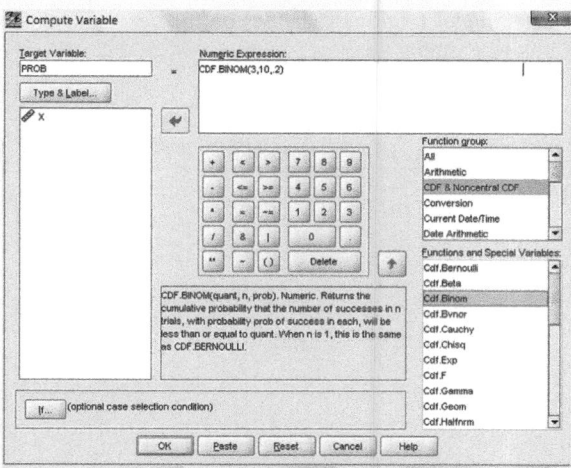

Figure S.2 SPSS compute cumulative binomial probabilities dialog box

Step 2 Specify a name for the "Target Variable."

Step 3 Select either "CDF" (for cumulative probabilities) or "PDF" (for exact probabilities) in the "Function group" box.

Step 4 Select the appropriate probability distribution in the "Functions and Special Variables" box. (For example, for cumulative probabilities of the binomial, use the function CDF.BINOM. For exact binomial probabilities, use the PDF.BINOM function.)

Step 5 Enter the parameters of the distribution in the "Numeric Expression" box. For example, Figure S.2 shows the cumulative binomial function with parameters of $x = 3$ (the first number in the function), $n = 10$ (the second number), and $p = .2$ (the third number).

Step 6 Click "OK"; SPSS will compute the requested probability (in this example, the cumulative binomial probability that x is less than or equal to 3) and display it on the SPSS spreadsheet. Similarly, for example, Figure S.3 shows the cumulative normal function with parameters of $x = 3.7$ (the first number in the function), $\mu = 5$ (the second number), and $\sigma = 2$ (the third number). When you click "OK," SPSS will compute the requested probability (in this example, the cumulative normal probability that x is less than 3.7) and display it on the SPSS spreadsheet.

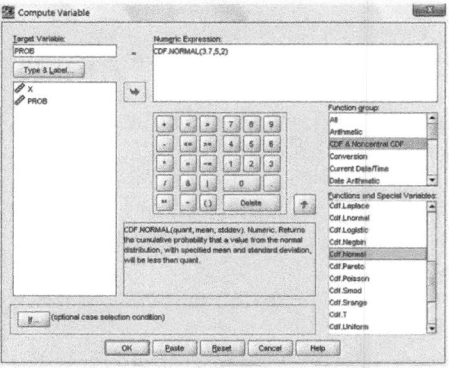

Figure S.3 SPSS compute cumulative normal probabilities dialog box

Normal Probability Plot

Step 1 Select "Analyze" on the SPSS menu bar, and then select "Descriptive Statistics" and "Q-Q Plots," as shown in Figure S.4. The resulting dialog box appears as shown in Figure S.5.

Step 2 Specify the variable of interest in the "Variables" box and select "Normal" in the "Test Distribution" box.

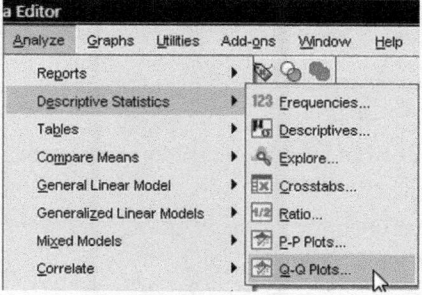

Figure S.4 SPSS options for a normal probability plot

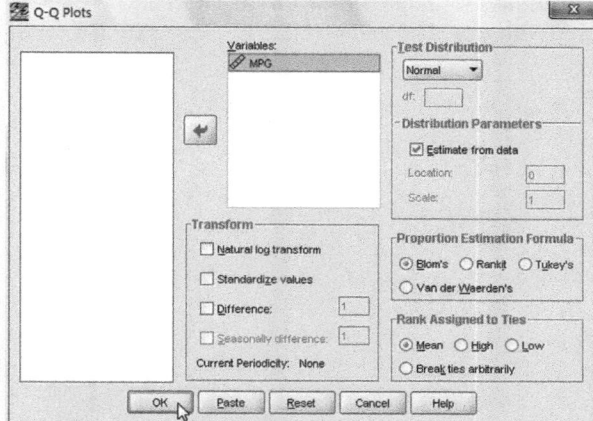

Figure S.5 SPSS normal probability plot dialog box

Step 3 Click "OK" to generate the normal probability plot.

Minitab: Discrete Probabilities, Continuous Probabilities, and Normal Probability Plots

Discrete and Continuous Probabilities

Step 1 Select the "Calc" button on the Minitab menu bar, click on "Probability Distributions," and then finally select the distribution of your choice (e.g., "Binomial"), as shown in Figure M.1.

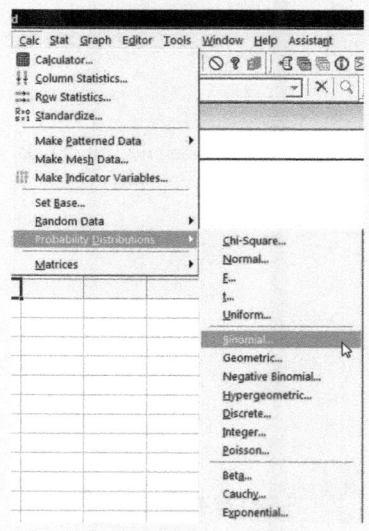

Figure M.1 Minitab menu options for obtaining discrete and continuous probabilities

Step 2 Select either "Probability" or "Cumulative probability" on the resulting dialog box.

Step 3 Specify the parameters of the distribution (e.g., sample size n, probability of success p, μ or σ.)

Step 4 Specify the value of x of interest in the "Input constant" box.

Step 5 Click "OK." The probability for the value of x will appear on the Minitab session window.

[*Note:* Figure M.2 gives the specifications for finding $P(x = 1)$ in a binomial distribution with $n = 5$ and $p = .2$. Figure M.3 gives the specifications for finding $P(x \leq 20)$ in a normal distribution with $\mu = 24.5$ and $\sigma = 3.1$.]

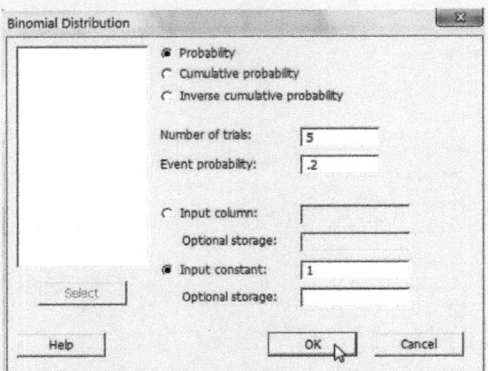

Figure M.2 Minitab binomial distribution dialog box

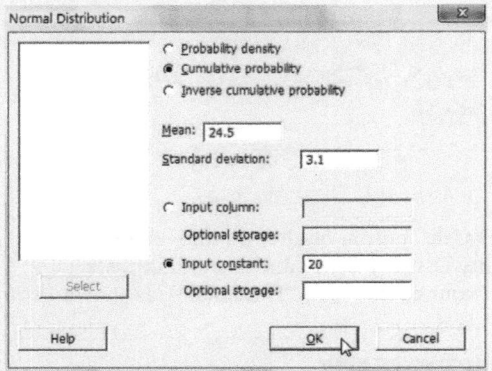

Figure M.3 Minitab normal distribution dialog box

Normal Probability Plot

Step 1 Select "Graph" on the Minitab menu bar and then click on "Probability Plot," as shown in Figure M.4.

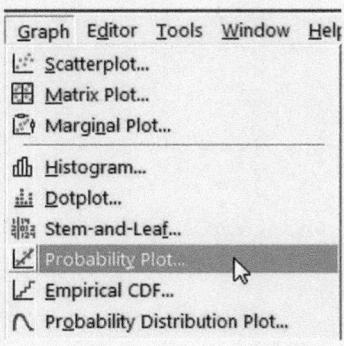

Figure M.4 Minitab options for a normal probability plot

Step 2 Select "Single" (for one variable) on the next box, and the dialog box will appear as shown in Figure M.5.

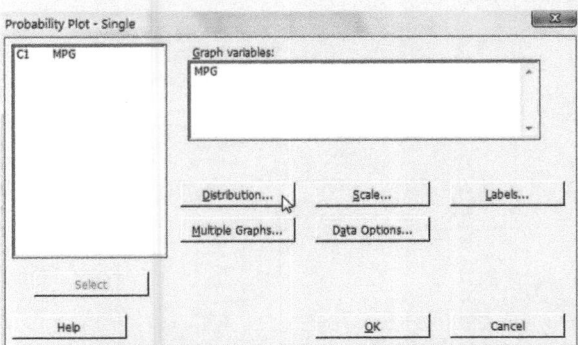

Figure M.5 Minitab normal probability plot dialog box

Step 3 Specify the variable of interest in the "Graph variables" box and then click the "Distribution" button and select the "Normal" option. Click "OK" to return to the Probability Plot dialog box.

Step 4 Click "OK" to generate the normal probability plot.

Excel/XLSTAT: Discrete Probabilities, Continuous Probabilities, and Normal Probability Plots

Discrete and Continuous Probabilities

Step 1 Click on the cell in the Excel worksheet where you want the probability to appear.

Step 2 In the formula bar, enter "=" followed by the appropriate probability function. A list of different probability functions is shown in Figure E.1.

Type of Probability	Excel Function
Binomial Probability, $P(x = a)$	$= \text{BINOMDIST}\,(a, n, p, \text{FALSE})$
Cumulative Binomial Probability, $P(X \leq a)$	$= \text{BINOMDIST}\,(a, n, p, \text{TRUE})$
Poisson Probability, $P(X = a)$	$= \text{POISSON}\,(a, \lambda, \text{FALSE})$
Cumulative Poisson Probability, $P(x \leq a)$	$= \text{POISSON}\,(a, \lambda, \text{TRUE})$
Hypergeometric Probability, $P(x = a)$	$= \text{HYPERGEOMDIST}\,(a, n, r, N)$
Cumulative Normal Probability, $P(X \leq a)$	$= \text{NORMDIST}\,(a, \mu, \sigma, \text{TRUE})$
Value of Normal Variable, given Probability p	$= \text{NORMINV}(p, \mu, \sigma)$
Cumulative Exponential Probability, $P(X \leq a)$	$= \text{EXPONDIST}(a, \sigma, \text{TRUE})$

Note: Probabilities from the uniform distribution function are not available in Excel.

Figure E.1 List of probability functions in Excel

Step 3 Specify the parameters (e.g., n, p, μ, and σ) of the probability distribution as well as a specific value of the random variable (denoted "a") in the probability function on the formula bar, as shown in Figure E.2.

Step 4 Click "Enter" and the probability will appear in the selected cell (see Figure E.2).

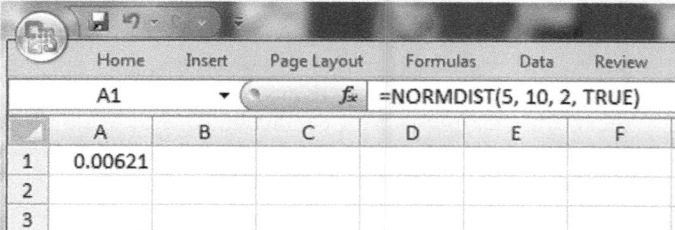

Figure E.2 Normal probability function in Excel

Normal Probability Plot

Step 1 Click the "XLSTAT" button on the Excel main menu bar and then click "Describing Data."

Step 2 From the resulting menu, select "Normality tests" (see Figure E.3).

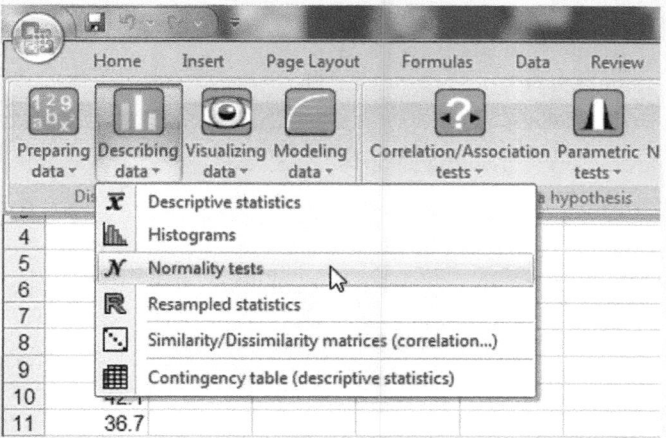

Figure E.3 XLSTAT menu options for describing data

Step 3 When the resulting dialog box appears, highlight the data column(s) you want to graph so that the column information appears in the "Data" entry (see Figure E.4).

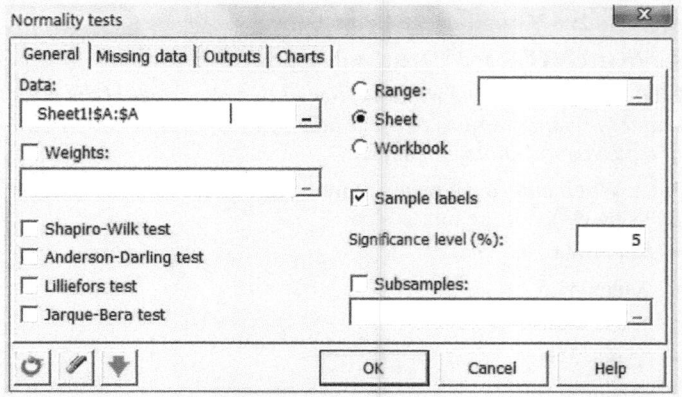

Figure E.4 XLSTAT normality tests dialog box

Step 4 Click the "Charts" tab, and then select "Normal Q-Q plots" on the resulting menu.

Step 5 Click "OK" and then "Continue" to display the normal probability plot.

TI-84 Graphing Calculator: Discrete and Continuous Random Variables Normal Probability Plots

Calculating the Mean and Standard Deviation of a Discrete Random Variable

Step 1 *Enter the data*

- Press **STAT** and select **1:Edit**

Note: If the lists already contain data, clear the old data. Use the up **ARROW** to highlight **L1**

- Press **CLEAR ENTER**
- Use the up **ARROW** to highlight **L2**
- Press **CLEAR ENTER**
- Use the **ARROW** and **ENTER** keys to enter the x-values of the variable into **L1**
- Use the **ARROW** and **ENTER** keys to enter the probabilities, $P(x)$, into **L2**

Step 2 *Access the Calc Menu*

- Press **STAT**
- Arrow right to **CALC**
- Select **1-Var Stats**
- Press **ENTER**
- Press **2nd 1** for **L1**
- Press **COMMA**
- Select **2nd 2** for **L2**
- Press **ENTER**

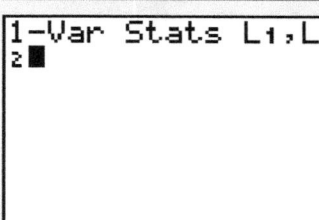

The mean and standard deviation will be displayed on the screen, as well as the quartiles, min, and max.

Calculating Binomial Probabilities
I. $P(x = k)$

To compute the probability of k successes in n trials, where p is the probability of success for each trial, use the **binompdf(** command. *Binompdf* stands for "binomial probability density function." This command is under the **DISTR**ibution menu and has the format **binompdf(n, p, k)**.

Example Compute the probability of 5 successes in 8 trials, where the probability of success for a single trial is 40%. In this example, $n = 8$, $p = .4$, and $k = 5$.

Step 1 *Enter the binomial parameters*

- Press **2nd VARS** for **DISTR**
- Press the down **ARROW** key until **binompdf** is highlighted
- Press **ENTER**

- After **binompdf(**, type
  8, .4, 5) (*Note:* Be sure to use
  the **COMMA** key between
  each parameter)
- Press **ENTER**
- You should see

```
binompdf(8,.4,5)
           .12386304
```

Thus, $P(x = 5)$ is about 12.4%.

II. $P(x \le k)$

To compute the probability of k or fewer successes in n trials, where p is the probability of success for each trial, use the **binomcdf(** command. *Binomcdf* stands for "binomial *cumulative* probability density function." This command is under the **DISTR**ibution menu and has the format **binomcdf(n, p, k)**.

Example Compute the probability of 5 or fewer successes in 8 trials, where the probability of success for a single trial is 40%. In this example, $n = 8$, $p = .4$, and $k = 5$.

Step 2 *Enter the binomial parameters*

- Press **2nd VARS** for **DISTR**
- Press down the **ARROW** key until **binomcdf** is highlighted
- Press **ENTER**
- After **binomcdf(**, type
  8, .4, 5)
- Press **ENTER**
- You should see

```
binomcdf(8,.4,5)
           .95019264
```

Thus, $P(x \le k)$ is about 95%.

III. $P(x < k)$, $(x > k)$, $(x \ge k)$

To find the probability of fewer than k successes $P(x < k)$, more than k successes $P(x > k)$, or at least k successes $P(x \ge k)$, variations of the **binomcdf(** command must be used as shown below.

- $P(x < k)$ use **binomcdf(n, p, k − 1)**
- $P(x > k)$ use **1 − binomcdf(n, p, k)**
- $P(x \ge k)$ use **1 − binomcdf(n, p, k − 1)**

Calculating Poisson Probabilities
I. $P(x = k)$

To compute $P(x = k)$, the probability of exactly k successes in a specified interval where λ is the mean number of successes in the interval, use the **poissonpdf(** command. *Poissonpdf* stands for "Poisson probability density function." This command is under the **DISTR**ibution menu and has the format **poissonpdf( )**.

Example Suppose that the number, x, of reported sightings per week of blue whales is recorded. Assume that x has approximately a Poisson probability distribution and that the average number of weekly sightings is 2.6. Compute the probability that exactly five sightings are made during a given week. In this example, $\lambda = 2.6$ and $k = 5$.

Step 1 *Enter the Poisson parameters*

- Press **2nd VARS** for **DISTR**
- Press the down **ARROW** key until **poissonpdf** is highlighted
- Press **ENTER**

- After **poissonpdf(**, type **2.6, 5)** (*Note:* Be sure to use the **COMMA** key between each parameter)
- Press **ENTER**
- You should see

```
poissonpdf(2.6,5
)
         .0735393591
```

Thus, the $P(x = 5)$ is about 7.4%.

II. $P(x \le k)$

To compute the probability of k or fewer successes in a specified interval, where λ is the mean number of successes in the interval, use the **poissoncdf(** command. *Poissoncdf* stands for "Poisson *cumulative* probability density function." This command is under the **DISTR**ibution menu and has the format **poissoncdf(**.

Example In the preceding example, compute the probability that five or fewer sightings are made during a given week. In this example, $\lambda = 2.6$ and $k = 5$.

Step 2 *Enter the Poisson parameters*

- Press **2nd VARS** for **DISTR**
- Press the down **ARROW** key until **poissoncdf** is highlighted
- Press **ENTER**
- After **poissoncdf(**, type **2.6, 5)**
- Press **ENTER**
- You should see

```
poissoncdf(2.6,5
)
         .9509628481
```

Thus, the $P(x = 5)$ is about 95.1%.

III. $P(x < k)$, $(x > k)$, $(x \ge k)$

To find the probability of fewer than k successes, more than k successes, or at least k successes, variations of the **poissoncdf(** command must be used as shown below.

- $P(x < k)$ use **poissoncdf(λ, k − 1)**
- $P(x > k)$ use **1 − poissoncdf(λ, k)**
- $P(x \ge k)$ use **1 − poissoncd(λ, k − 1)**

Graphing the Area under the Standard Normal Curve

Step 1 *Turn off all plots*

- Press **2nd PRGM** and select **1:ClrDraw**
- Press **ENTER** and "Done" will appear on the screen
- Press **2nd Y=** and select **4:PlotsOff**
- Press **ENTER** and "Done" will appear on the screen

Step 2 *Set the viewing window (Recall that almost all of the area under the standard normal curve falls between −5 and 5. A height of 0.5 is a good choice for Ymax.)*

Note: When entering a negative number, be sure to use the negative sign (−), not the minus sign.

- Set **Xmin** = −5
- **Xmax** = 5
- **Xscl** = 1
- **Ymin** = 0
- **Ymax** = .5
- **Yscl** = 0
- **Xres** = 1

Step 3 *View graph*

- Press **2nd VARS**
- Arrow right to **DRAW**
- Press **ENTER** to select **1:ShadeNorm(**
- Enter your lower limit (e.g., −5)
- Press **COMMA**
- Enter your upper limit (e.g., 1.5)
- Press **)**
- Press **ENTER**

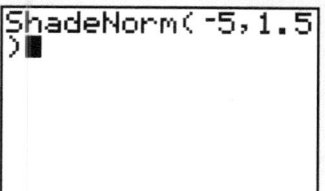

The graph will be displayed along with the area, lower limit, and upper limit.

Thus, $P(z < 1.5) = .9332$.

Nonstandard Normal Probabilities

I. Finding Normal Probabilities without a Graph

To compute probabilities for a normal distribution, use the **normalcdf(** command. *Normalcdf* stands for "normal cumulative density function." This command is under the **DISTR**ibution menu and has the format **normalcdf(*lower limit, upper limit, mean, standard deviation*).**

Step 1 *Find probability*

- Press **2nd VARS** for **DISTR** and select **Normalcdf(**
- After **Normalcdf(,** type in the lower limit
- Press **COMMA**
- Enter the upper limit
- Press **COMMA**
- Enter the mean
- Press **COMMA**
- Enter the standard deviation
- Press **)**
- Press **ENTER**

The probability will be displayed on the screen.

Example What is $P(x < 115)$ for a normal distribution with $\mu = 100$ and $\sigma = 10$?

In this example, the lower limit is $-\infty$, the upper limit is 115, the mean is 100, and the standard deviation is 10. To represent $-\infty$ on the calculator, enter **(−) 1**, press **2nd** and press the **COMMA** key for **EE**, and then press **99**. The screen appears as follows:

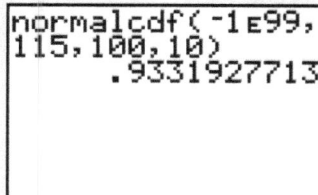

Thus, $P(x < 115)$ is .9332.

II. Finding Normal Probabilities with a Graph

Step 1 *Turn off all plots*

- Press **Y=** and **CLEAR** all functions from the Y registers
- Press **2nd Y =** and select **4:PlotsOff**
- Press **ENTER ENTER**, and 'Done' will appear on the screen

Step 2 *Set the viewing window (These values depend on the mean and standard deviation of the data.) Note:* When entering a negative number, be sure to use the negative sign (−), not the minus sign.

- Press **WINDOW**
- Set **Xmin** $= \mu - 5\sigma$
- **Xmax** $= \mu + 5\sigma$
- **Xscl** $= \sigma$
- **Ymin** $= -.125/gs$
- **Ymax** $= .5/\sigma$
- **Yscl** $= 1$
- **Xres** $= 1$

Step 3 *View graph*

- Press **2nd VARS**
- **ARROW** right to **DRAW**
- Press **ENTER** to select **1:ShadeNorm(**
- Enter the lower limit
- Press **COMMA**
- Enter the upper limit
- Press **COMMA**
- Enter the mean
- Press **COMMA**
- Enter the standard deviation
- Press **)**
- Press **ENTER**

The graph will be displayed along with the area, lower limit, and upper limit.

Example What is $P(x < 115)$ for a normal distribution with $\mu = 100$ and $\sigma = 10$? In this example, the lower limit is $-\infty$, the upper limit is 115, the mean is 100, and the standard deviation is 10. To represent $-\infty$ on the calculator, enter (−)**1**, press **2nd** and press the **COMMA** key for **EE**, and then press **99**. The screens appear as follows:

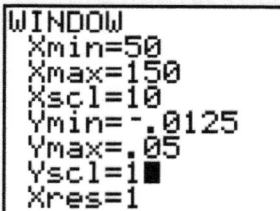
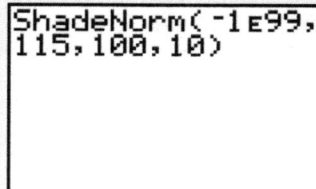

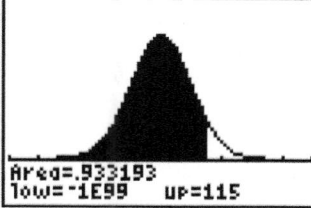

Graphing a Normal Probability Plot

Step 1 *Enter the data*

- Press **STAT** and select **1:Edit**

Note: If the list already contains data, clear the old data. Use the up **ARROW** to highlight **L1**.

- Press **CLEAR ENTER**
- Use the **ARROW** and **ENTER** keys to enter the data set into **L1**

Step 2 *Set up the normal probability plot*

- Press **Y=** and **CLEAR** all functions from the Y registers
- Press **2nd** and press **Y=** for **STAT PLOT**
- Press **1** for **Plot 1**
- Set the cursor so that **ON** is flashing
- For **Type**, use the **ARROW** and **ENTER** keys to highlight and select the last graph in the bottom row
- For **Data List**, choose the column containing the data (in most cases, L1) (*Note:* Press **2nd 1** for **L1**)
- For **Data Axis**, choose **X** and press **ENTER**

Step 3 *View plot*

- Press **ZOOM 9**

Your data will be displayed against the expected *z*-scores from a normal distribution. If you see a "generally" linear relationship, your data set is approximately normal.

◼ Answers to Selected Exercises

1 a. Discrete **b.** Continuous **c.** Continuous **d.** Discrete **e.** Discrete **3** Discrete **5** Discrete **7** Inflation rate **9** Number of returns per day; number of new salespeople hired **11 a.** .25 **b.** .35 **d.** .80 **13 a.** .25 **b.** .40 **c.** .75 **15 a.** $p(x) = \frac{1}{6}$ for all *x* values **17 a.** $\mu = 0, \sigma^2 = 2.94, \sigma = 1.72$ **c.** .96 **19 a.** 1; 1 **b.** *x* **c.** $\mu = 1, \sigma^2 = .6; \mu = 1, \sigma^2 = .2$ **21 a.** $p(1) = 0, p(2) = .0408, p(3) = .1735,$ $p(4) = .6020, p(5) = .1837$ **b.** .1837 **c.** .0408 **d.** 3.93 **23 b.** .14 **c.** $\mu = 4.655, \sigma^2 = 19.856$ **d.** $(-4.26, 13.57)$ **25 a.** 0, 2, 3, 4 **b.** $p(0) = .3302, p(2) = .5472, p(3) = .0472, p(4) = .0755$ **c.** 1.538 **27 b.** $p(0) = .1160, p(1) = .3124, p(2) = .3364, p(3) = .1811,$ $p(4) = .0488, p(5) = .0053$ **d.** .0541 **29 a.** .23 **b.** .0809 **c.** .77 **31 a.** .508 **b.** .391 **c.** .094 **d.** .007 **33** $p(8.5) = .4622, p(9) = .2888,$ $p(9.5) = .1417, p(10) = .0700, p(10.5) = .0252, p(11) = .0117, p(12) = .00052$ **35 a.** $p(\$300{,}000) = .3, p(\$0) = .7$ **b.** $\$90{,}000$ **37 a.** $p(x) = .05$ for all *x*-values **b.** 52.5 **c.** $(-5.16, 110.16)$ **f.** 33.25, 38.3577 **g.** .525 **i.** .20 **j.** .65 **39** $\$.25$ **41 a.** Discrete **b.** Binomial **d.** 3.5; 1.02 **43 a.** .4096 **b.** .3456 **c.** .027 **d.** .0081 **e.** .3456 **f.** .027 **45 a.** 12.5, 6.25, 2.5 **b.** 16, 12.8, 3.578 **c.** 60, 24, 4.899 **d.** 63, 6.3, 2.510 **e.** 48, 9.6, 3.098 **f.** 40, 38.4, 6.197 **47 a.** Adult who does not work in the summer **c.** .35 **d.** .2522 **e.** .2616 **49 b.** .5 **c.** 125 **51** .677 **53 a.** .6591 **b.** .2373 **55 a.** .055 **b.** In 2020, more than 9% of Denver bridges will have a rating of 4 or below **57 a.** $\mu = 520, \sigma = 13.49$ **b.** No, $z = -8.90$ **59 b.** $\mu = 2.4, \sigma = 1.47$ **c.** $p = .90, q = .10, n = 24, \mu = 21.60, \sigma = 1.47$ **61 a.** Discrete **b.** Poisson **d.** $\mu = 3,$ $\sigma = 1.73$ **63 a.** .3 **b.** .119 **c.** .167 **d.** .167 **65 a.** .9197 **b.** .6767 **c.** .4232 **d.** Decreases **67 a.** Hypergeometric **b.** Binomial **69 c.** $\mu = 1.415, \sigma = 1.054$ **d.** .280 **71 a.** .0111 **b.** .05 **c.** $\mu = 4.5, \sigma = 2.12$ **73** .2693 **75** .1848 **77** .1931 **79** .5507 **81 a.** ≈ 0 **b.** ≈ 0 **c.** Yes **83** No; probability of only 5 females selected is ≈ 0 **85 a.** .0721 **b.** .0594 **c.** .2434 **d.** .3457 **e.** .5 **f.** .9233 **87 a.** .6826 **b.** .9500 **c.** .90 **d.** .9544 **89 a.** $-.81$ **b.** .55 **c.** 1.43 **d.** .21 **e.** -2.05 **f.** .50 **91 a.** -2.5 **b.** 0 **c.** -6.81 **d.** -3.75 **e.** 1.25 **f.** -1.25 **93 a.** .3830 **b.** .3023 **c.** .1525 **d.** .7333 **e.** .1314 **f.** .9545 **95 a.** Yes **b.** 10, 6 **c.** .726 **d.** .7291 **97 a.** .0331 **b.** .4677 **c.** 99.9 **99 a.** .4207 **b.** .000337 **101 a.** .2743 **b.** .008 **103 a.** 125 **b.** 7.91 **c.** 9.49 **d.** 1 **105 a.** .3413 **b.** .0026 **c.** .3830 **107 a.** 69.2 **b.** 42.2 **109 a.** 25.14% **b.** 90.375 **111** .703 **113 b.** 50; 9 **c.** .5398; 0 **115** $z = -.588$ if no coaching, $z = 2.4$ if coaching; more likely that leader did not receive coaching **117 a.** .68 **b.** .95 **c.** 1.00 **119** Plot c **121 b.** $\bar{x} = 67.76, s = 26.87; 94.5\%$ of observations within $\bar{x} \pm 2s$ **c.** IQR = 37, IQR/*s* = 1.38 **123 a.** Approx. normal **b.** Approx. normal **125** No **127** IQR/*s* = 1.3 **129** None **131** $z = -.75$ for minimum value of 128 **133 a.** $f(x) = .04$ $(20 \le x \le 45), 0$ otherwise **b.** 32.5, 7.22 **135 a.** .367879 **b.** .950213 **c.** .223130 **d.** .993262 **137 a.** 0 **b.** 1 **c.** 1 **139** .25 **141 a.** .133; .571 **b.** .267; 0 **143 a.** .449329 **b.** .864665 **145 a.** .5 **b.** .3 **c.** Only 1 possible connection **147 a.** Continuous **c.** 7, .2887, (6.422, 7.577) **d.** .5 **e.** 0 **f.** .75 **g.** .0002 **149 a.** .753403 **b.** .667 **c.** .811 **151** .4444 **153** $-\theta \ln(.5) = .6931470$ **157 a.** .2734 **b.** .4096 **c.** .3432 **159 a.** .192 **b.** .228 **c.** .772 **d.** .987 **e.** .960 **f.** 14, 4.2, 2.049 **g.** .975 **161 a.** Poisson **b.** Binomial **c.** Binomial **163 a.** Discrete **b.** Continuous **c.** Continuous **d.** Continuous **165 a.** .9821 **b.** .0179 **c.** .9505 **d.** .3243 **e.** .9107 **f.** .0764 **167 a.** Exponential **b.** Uniform **c.** Normal **169 a.** .6915 **b.** .1587 **c.** .1915 **d.** .3085 **e.** 0 **f.** 1 **171 a.** 47.68 **b.** 47.68 **c.** 30.13 **d.** 41.5 **e.** 30.13 **173 b.** .2592 **c.** .0870 **d.** .6826 **e.** 3.00 **175 a.** .5, .289 **b.** .2 **c.** No, $p = .005$ **177 a.** .221199 **b.** .002394 **c.** .082085 **179 b.** $n = 20, p = .8$ **c.** .175 **d.** .804 **e.** 16 **181 a.** .367869 **b.** .606531 **c.** .135335; .135335 **d.** .814046 **183 a.** .383 **b.** .0002 **185** No **187 a.** .8264 **b.** 17 times **c.** .6217 **d.** 0, -157 **189 a.** 1.25, 1.09; no **b.** .007 **c.** Not applicable **191 a.** $\mu = 113.24, \sigma = 4.19$ **b.** $z = 6.38$ **193 b.** .85 **c.** .6, .7, 0 **d.** A_1: 2.4; A_2: 1.5; A_3: 1.65; A_4: .10 **e.** A_1: .86; A_2: .67; A_3: .57; A_4: .3 **195 a.** .125 **b.** 5 **197** .2676; no **199 a.** .8106 **b.** .1894 **c.** $\$1{,}246{,}100$ **201** 292 **203** 5,102 **205 a.** $\sigma = 1$: .6826; $\sigma = 2$: .4260; $\sigma = 4$: .3734 **b.** $\sigma = 1$: .6945; $\sigma = 2$: .42; $\sigma = 4$: .3709 **c.** $\sigma = 1$; $\sigma = 2$

◼ Credits

The photo credits below are listed in order of appearance.

Mario Beauregard/Fotolia
Soupstock/Fotolia
Shock/Fotolia
Michaeljung/Shutterstock
Andrea Lehmkuhl/Fotolia
Sebastian Duda/iStockphoto

◻ Technology Images

CONTENTS

Where We're Going

- Establish that a sample statistic is a random variable with a probability distribution (1)

- Define a *sampling distribution* as the probability distribution of a sample statistic (1)

- Give two important properties of sampling distributions (2)

- Learn that the sampling distribution of both the sample mean and sample proportion tends to be approximately normal (3, 4)

☐ Sampling Distributions

STATISTICS in ACTION **The Insomnia Pill: Is It Effective?**

More than 15 years ago, neuroscientists at the Massachusetts Institute of Technology (MIT) began experimenting with melatonin—a hormone secreted by the pineal gland in the brain—as a sleep-inducing hormone. Their original study, published in the Proceedings of the National Academy of Sciences *(March 1994), brought encouraging news to insomniacs and travelers who suffer from jet lag: Melatonin was discovered to be effective in reducing sleep onset latency (the amount of time between a person lying down to sleep and the actual onset of stage one sleep). Furthermore, since the hormone is naturally produced, it is nonaddictive.*

Since then, pharmaceutical companies that produce melatonin pills for treating insomnia have received negative reports on the efficacy of the drug. Many people don't think the melatonin pills work. Consequently, the MIT researchers undertook a follow-up study and published their results in *Sleep Medicine Reviews* (Feb. 2005). They reported that commercially available melatonin pills contain too high a dosage of the drug. When the melatonin receptors in the brain are exposed to too much of the hormone, they become unresponsive. The researchers' analysis of all previous studies on melatonin as a sleep inducer confirmed that, taken in small doses, melatonin is effective in reducing sleep onset latency.

In this Statistics in Action, our focus is on the original MIT study. Young male volunteers were given various doses of melatonin or a placebo (a dummy medication containing no melatonin). Then they were placed in a dark room at midday and told to close their eyes for 30 minutes. The variable of interest was sleep onset latency (in minutes).

According to the lead investigator, Professor Richard Wurtman, "Our volunteers fall asleep in 5 or 6 minutes on melatonin, while those on placebo take

STATISTICS
in ACTION
CONTINUED

about 15 minutes." Wurtman warned, however, that uncontrolled doses of melatonin could cause mood-altering side effects.

Now, consider a random sample of 40 young males, each of whom is given a dosage of the sleep-inducing hormone melatonin. The times taken (in minutes) to fall asleep for these 40 males are listed in Table SIA1 and saved in the **SLEEP** file. The researchers know that with the placebo (i.e., no hormone), the mean sleep onset latency is $\mu = 15$ minutes and the standard deviation is $\sigma = 10$ minutes. They want to use the data to make an inference about the true value of μ for those taking the melatonin. Specifically, the researchers want to know whether melatonin is an effective drug against insomnia.

In this chapter, a Statistics in Action Revisited example demonstrates how we can use one of the topics discussed in the chapter—the Central Limit Theorem—to make an inference about the effectiveness of melatonin as a sleep-inducing hormone.

STATISTICS in ACTION REVISITED

▫ Making an Inference about the Mean Sleep Onset Latency for Insomnia Pill Takers

Table SIA1	Times Taken (in Minutes) for 40 Male Volunteers to Fall Asleep								
7.6	2.1	1.4	1.5	3.6	17.0	14.9	4.4	4.7	20.1
7.7	2.4	8.1	1.5	10.3	1.3	3.7	2.5	3.4	10.7
2.9	1.5	15.9	3.0	1.9	8.5	6.1	4.5	2.2	2.6
7.0	6.4	2.8	2.8	22.8	1.5	4.6	2.0	6.3	3.2

[Note: These data are simulated sleep times based on summary information provided in the MIT study.]

🌀 *Data Set:* SLEEP

A **parameter** is a numerical descriptive measure of a population. Because it is based on the observations in the population, its value is almost always unknown.

The sample mean $\bar{x}$ sample variance s^2, sample standard deviation s, and the like, are numerical descriptive measures calculated from the sample. (See Table 1 for a list of the statistics.) We will often use the information contained in these *sample statistics* to make inferences about the parameters of a population.

A **sample statistic** is a numerical descriptive measure of a sample. It is calculated from the observations in the sample.

Table 1	List of Population Parameters and Corresponding Sample Statistics	
	Population Parameter	Sample Statistic
Mean:	μ	$\bar{x}$
Median:	η	m
Variance:	σ^2	s^2
Standard deviation:	σ	s
Binomial proportion:	p	$\hat{p}$

Note that the term *statistic* refers to a *sample* quantity and the term *parameter* refers to a *population* quantity.

Before we can show you how to use sample statistics to make inferences about population parameters, we need to be able to evaluate their properties. Does one sample statistic contain more information than another about a population parameter? On what basis should we choose the "best" statistic for making inferences about a parameter? The purpose of this chapter is to answer these questions.

1 The Concept of a Sampling Distribution

If we want to estimate a parameter of a population—say, the population mean μ—we can use a number of sample statistics for our estimate. Two possibilities are the sample mean $\bar{x}$ and the sample median m. Which of these do you think will provide a better estimate of μ?

Before answering this question, consider the following example: Toss a fair die, and let x equal the number of dots showing on the up face. Suppose the die is tossed three times, producing the sample measurements 2, 2, 6. The sample mean is then $\bar{x} = 3.33$, and the sample median is $m = 2$. Since the population mean of x is $\mu = 3.5$, you can see that, for this sample of three measurements, the sample mean $\bar{x}$ provides an estimate that falls closer to μ than does the sample median (see Figure 1a). Now suppose we toss the die three more times and obtain the sample measurements 3, 4, 6. Then the mean and median of this sample are $\bar{x} = 4.33$ and $m = 4$, respectively. This time m is closer to μ. (See Figure 1b.)

This simple example illustrates an important point: Neither the sample mean nor the sample median will *always* fall closer to the population mean. Consequently, we cannot compare these two sample statistics, or, in general, any two sample statistics, on the basis of their performance for a single sample. Instead, we need to recognize that sample statistics are themselves random variables because different samples can lead to different values for the sample statistics. As random variables, sample statistics must be judged and compared on the basis of their probability distributions (i.e., the *collection* of values and associated probabilities of each statistic that would be obtained if the sampling experiment was repeated a *very large number of times*). We will illustrate this concept with another example.

Suppose it is known that the connector module manufactured for a certain brand of pacemaker has a mean length of $\mu = .3$ inch and a standard deviation of .005 inch. Consider an experiment consisting of randomly selecting 25 recently manufactured connector modules, measuring the length of each, and calculating the sample mean length $\bar{x}$. If this experiment was repeated a very large number of times, the value of $\bar{x}$ would vary from sample to sample. For example, the first sample of 25 length measurements might have a mean $\bar{x} = .301$, the second sample a mean $\bar{x} = .298$, the third sample a mean

Figure 1

Comparing the sample mean ($\bar{x}$) and sample median (m) as estimators of the population mean (μ)

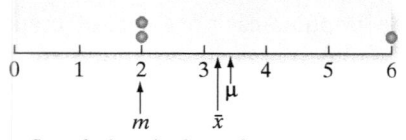

a. Sample 1: $\bar{x}$ is closer than m to μ

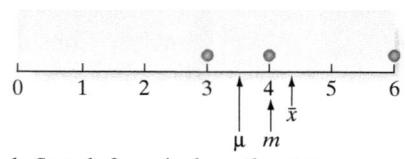

b. Sample 2: m is closer than $\bar{x}$ to μ

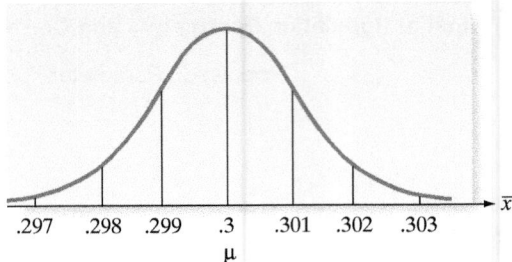

Figure 2

Sampling distribution for $\bar{x}$ based on a sample of $n = 25$ length measurements

$\bar{x} = .303$, etc. If the sampling experiment were repeated a very large number of times, the resulting histogram of sample means would be approximately the probability distribution of $\bar{x}$. If $\bar{x}$ is a good estimator of μ, we would expect the values of $\bar{x}$ to cluster around μ, as shown in Figure 2. This probability distribution is called a *sampling distribution* because it is generated by repeating a sampling experiment a very large number of times.

> The **sampling distribution** of a sample statistic calculated from a sample of n measurements is the probability distribution of the statistic.

In actual practice, the sampling distribution of a statistic is obtained mathematically or (at least approximately) by simulating the sample on a computer using a procedure similar to that just described.

If $\bar{x}$ has been calculated from a sample of $n = 25$ measurements selected from a population with mean $\mu = .3$ and standard deviation $\sigma = .005$, the sampling distribution (Figure 2) provides information about the behavior of $\bar{x}$ in repeated sampling. For example, the probability that you will draw a sample of 25 length measurements and obtain a value of $\bar{x}$ in the interval $.299 \leq \bar{x} \leq .3$ will be the area under the sampling distribution over that interval.

Because the properties of a statistic are typified by its sampling distribution, it follows that to compare two sample statistics, you compare their sampling distributions. For example, if you have two statistics, A and B, for estimating the same parameter (for purposes of illustration, suppose the parameter is the population variance σ^2) and if their sampling distributions are as shown in Figure 3, you would choose statistic A in preference to statistic B. You would make this choice because the sampling distribution for statistic A centers over σ^2 and has less spread (variation) than the sampling distribution for statistic B. When you draw a single sample in a practical sampling situation, the probability is higher that statistic A will fall nearer σ^2.

Remember that in practice we will not know the numerical value of the unknown parameter σ^2, so we will not know whether statistic A or statistic B is closer to σ^2 for a sample. We have to rely on our knowledge of the theoretical sampling distributions to choose the best sample statistic and then use it sample after sample. The procedure for finding the sampling distribution for a statistic is demonstrated in Example 1.

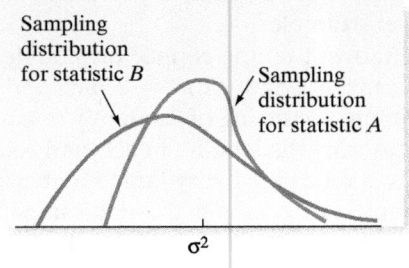

Figure 3

Two sampling distributions for estimating the population variance, σ^2

Example	1

Finding a Sampling Distribution—Come-Out Roll in Craps

Problem Consider the popular casino game of craps, in which a player throws two dice and bets on the outcome (the sum total of the dots showing on the upper faces of the two dice). Let's look at the possible outcomes of a $5 wager on the first toss (called the *come-out* roll). If the sum total of the dice is 7 or 11, the roller wins $5; if the total is a 2, 3, or 12, the roller loses $5 (i.e., the roller "wins" $-\$5$); and,

for any other total (4, 5, 6, 8, 9, or 10) no money is lost or won on that roll (i.e., the roller wins $0). Let x represent the result of the come-out roll wager ($-$5$, 0, or $+$5$). We showed in Example 5 that the actual probability distribution of x is:

Outcome of wager, x	-5	0	5
$p(x)$	1/9	6/9	2/9

Now, consider a random sample of $n = 3$ come-out rolls.

a. Find the sampling distribution of the sample mean, $\bar{x}$.

b. Find the sampling distribution of the sample median, m.

Solution The outcomes for every possible sample of $n = 3$ come-out rolls are listed in Table 2, along with the sample mean and median. The probability of each sample is obtained using the multiplicative rule. For example, the probability of the sample $(0, 0, 5)$ is $p(0) \cdot p(0) \cdot p(5) = \left(\frac{6}{9}\right)\left(\frac{6}{9}\right)\left(\frac{2}{9}\right) = \frac{72}{729} = .099$. The probability for each sample is also listed in Table 2. Note that the sum of these probabilities is equal to 1.

a. From Table 2, you can see that $\bar{x}$ can assume the values -5, -3.33, -1.67, 0, 1.67, 3.33, and 5. Because $\bar{x} = -5$ occurs only in one sample, $P(\bar{x} = -5) = \frac{1}{729}$. Similarly, $\bar{x} = -3.33$ occurs in three samples, $(-5, -5, 0)$, $(-5, 0, -5)$, and $(0, -5, -5)$. Therefore, $P(\bar{x} = -3.33) = \frac{6}{729} + \frac{6}{729} + \frac{6}{729} = \frac{18}{729}$. Calculating the probabilities of the remaining values of $\bar{x}$ and arranging them in a table, we obtain the following probability distribution:

$\bar{x}$	-5	-3.33	-1.67	0	1.67	3.33	5
$p(\bar{x})$	1/729 = .0014	18/729 = .0247	114/729 = .1564	288/729 = .3951	288/729 = .3127	72/729 = .0988	8/729 = .0110

Table 2	All Possible Samples of $n = 3$ Come-Out Rolls in Craps		
Possible Samples	$\bar{x}$	m	Probability
$-5, -5, -5$	-5	-5	$(1/9)(1/9)(1/9) = 1/729$
$-5, -5, 0$	-3.33	-5	$(1/9)(1/9)(6/9) = 6/729$
$-5, -5, 5$	-1.67	-5	$(1/9)(1/9)(2/9) = 2/729$
$-5, \;\;\, 0, -5$	-3.33	-5	$(1/9)(6/9)(1/9) = 6/729$
$-5, \;\;\, 0, 0$	-1.67	0	$(1/9)(6/9)(6/9) = 36/729$
$-5, \;\;\, 0, 5$	0	0	$(1/9)(6/9)(2/9) = 12/729$
$-5, \;\;\, 5, -5$	-1.67	-5	$(1/9)(2/9)(1/9) = 2/729$
$-5, \;\;\, 5, 0$	0	0	$(1/9)(2/9)(6/9) = 12/729$
$-5, \;\;\, 5, 5$	1.67	5	$(1/9)(2/9)(2/9) = 4/729$
$0, -5, -5$	-3.33	-5	$(6/9)(1/9)(1/9) = 6/729$
$0, -5, 0$	-1.67	0	$(6/9)(1/9)(6/9) = 36/729$
$0, -5, 5$	0	0	$(6/9)(1/9)(2/9) = 12/729$
$0, \;\;\, 0, -5$	-1.67	0	$(6/9)(6/9)(1/9) = 36/729$
$0, \;\;\, 0, 0$	0	0	$(6/9)(6/9)(6/9) = 216/729$
$0, \;\;\, 0, 5$	1.67	0	$(6/9)(6/9)(2/9) = 72/729$
$0, \;\;\, 5, -5$	0	0	$(6/9)(2/9)(1/9) = 12/729$
$0, \;\;\, 5, 0$	1.67	0	$(6/9)(2/9)(6/9) = 72/729$
$0, \;\;\, 5, 5$	3.33	5	$(6/9)(2/9)(2/9) = 24/729$
$5, -5, -5$	-1.67	-5	$(2/9)(1/9)(1/9) = 2/729$
$5, -5, 0$	0	0	$(2/9)(1/9)(6/9) = 12/729$
$5, -5, 5$	1.67	5	$(2/9)(1/9)(2/9) = 4/729$
$5, \;\;\, 0, -5$	0	0	$(2/9)(6/9)(1/9) = 12/729$
$5, \;\;\, 0, 0$	1.67	0	$(2/9)(6/9)(6/9) = 72/729$
$5, \;\;\, 0, 5$	3.33	5	$(2/9)(6/9)(2/9) = 24/729$
$5, \;\;\, 5, -5$	1.67	5	$(2/9)(2/9)(1/9) = 4/729$
$5, \;\;\, 5, 0$	3.33	5	$(2/9)(2/9)(6/9) = 24/729$
$5, \;\;\, 5, 5$	5	5	$(2/9)(2/9)(2/9) = 8/729$

$$Sum = 729/729 = 1$$

This is the sampling distribution for $\bar{x}$ because it specifies the probability associated with each possible value of $\bar{x}$. You can see that the most likely mean outcome after 3 randomly selected come-out rolls is $\bar{x} = \$0$; this result occurs with probability $\frac{288}{729} = .3951$.

b. In Table 2, you can see that the median m can assume one of three values: $-5, 0$, or 5. The value $m = -5$ occurs in 7 different samples. Therefore, $P(m = -5)$ is the sum of the probabilities associated with these 7 samples; that is, $P(m = -5) = \frac{1}{729} + \frac{6}{729} + \frac{2}{729} + \frac{6}{729} + \frac{2}{729} + \frac{6}{729} + \frac{2}{729} = \frac{25}{729}$. Similarly, $m = 0$ occurs in 13 samples and $m = 5$ occurs in 7 samples. These probabilities are obtained by summing the probabilities of their respective sample points. After performing these calculations, we obtain the following probability distribution for the median m:

m	-5	0	5
$p(m)$	25/729 = .0343	612/729 = .8395	92/729 = .1262

Once again, the most likely median outcome after 3 randomly selected come-out rolls is $\bar{x} = \$0$—a result that occurs with probability $\frac{612}{729} = .8395$.

Look Back The sampling distributions of parts **a** and **b** are found by first listing all possible distinct values of the statistic and then calculating the probability of each value. Note that if the values of x were equally likely, the 27 sample points in Table 2 would all have the same probability of occurring, namely, $\frac{1}{27}$.

▬ **Now Work Exercise 1**

Example 1 demonstrates the procedure for finding the exact sampling distribution of a statistic when the number of different samples that could be selected from the population is relatively small. In the real world, populations often consist of a large number of different values, making samples difficult (or impossible) to enumerate. When this situation occurs, we may choose to obtain the approximate sampling distribution for a statistic by simulating the sampling over and over again and recording the proportion of times different values of the statistic occur. Example 2 illustrates this procedure.

Example 2

Simulating a Sampling Distribution—Thickness of Steel Sheets

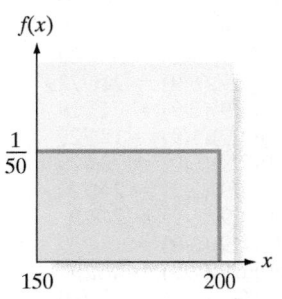

Figure 4
Uniform distribution for thickness of steel sheets

Problem The thickness of a steel sheet follows a uniform distribution with values between 150 and 200 millimeters. Suppose we perform the following experiment over and over again: Randomly sample 11 steel sheets from the production line and record the thickness, x, of each. Calculate the two sample statistics

$$\bar{x} = \text{Sample mean} = \frac{\Sigma x}{11}$$

$$m = \text{Median} = \text{Sixth sample measurement when the 11 thicknesses are arranged in ascending order}$$

Obtain approximations to the sampling distributions of $\bar{x}$ and m.

Solution The population of thicknesses follows the uniform distribution shown in Figure 4. We used Minitab to generate 1,000 samples from this population, each with $n = 11$ observations. Then we compute $\bar{x}$ and m for each sample. Our goal is to obtain approximations to the sampling distributions of $\bar{x}$ and m to find out which sample statistic ($\bar{x}$ or m) contains more information about μ. [*Note:* In this particular example, we *know* the population mean is $\mu = 175$ mm.]

Table 3	First 10 Samples of $n = 11$ Thickness Measurements from Uniform Distribution												
Sample	Thickness Measurements											Mean	Median
1	173	171	187	151	188	181	182	157	162	169	193	174.00	173
2	181	190	182	171	187	177	162	172	188	200	193	182.09	182
3	192	195	187	187	172	164	164	189	179	182	173	180.36	182
4	173	157	150	154	168	174	171	182	200	181	187	172.45	173
5	169	160	167	170	197	159	174	174	161	173	160	169.46	169
6	179	170	167	174	173	178	173	170	173	198	187	176.55	173
7	166	177	162	171	154	177	154	179	175	185	193	172.09	175
8	164	199	152	153	163	156	184	151	198	167	180	169.73	164
9	181	193	151	166	180	199	180	184	182	181	175	179.27	181
10	155	199	199	171	172	157	173	187	190	185	150	176.18	173

Data Set: SIMUNI

The first 10 of the 1,000 samples generated are presented in Table 3. For instance, the first computer-generated sample from the uniform distribution (arranged in ascending order) contain the following thickness measurements: 151, 157, 162, 169, 171, 173, 181, 182, 187, 188, and 193 millimeters. The sample mean $\bar{x}$ and median m computed for this sample are

$$\bar{x} = \frac{151 + 157 + \cdots + 193}{11} = 174.0$$

$$m = \text{Sixth ordered measurement} = 173$$

The Minitab relative frequency histograms for $\bar{x}$ and m for the 1,000 samples of size $n = 11$ are shown in Figure 5. These histograms represent approximations to the true sampling distributions of $\bar{x}$ and m.

Look Back You can see that the values of $\bar{x}$ tend to cluster around μ to a greater extent than do the values of m. Thus, on the basis of the observed sampling distributions, we conclude that $\bar{x}$ contains more information about μ than m does—at least for samples of $n = 11$ measurements from the uniform distribution.

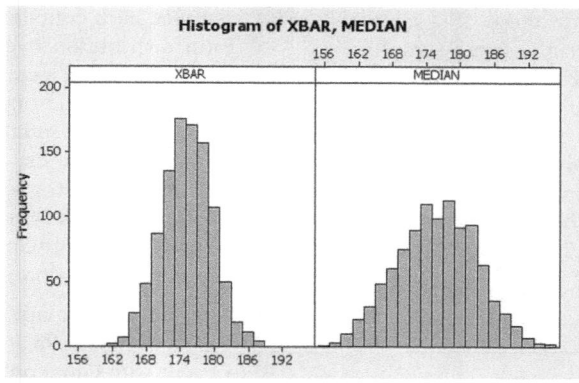

Figure 5

Minitab histograms for sample mean and sample median, Example 2

Now Work Exercise 6

As noted earlier, many sampling distributions can be derived mathematically, but the theory necessary to do this is beyond the scope of this text. Consequently, when we need to know the properties of a statistic, we will present its sampling distribution and simply describe its properties. Several of the important properties we look for in sampling distributions are discussed in the next section.

Exercises 1–7

Learning the Mechanics

1 The probability distribution shown here describes a population of measurements that can assume values of 0, 2, 4, and 6, each of which occurs with the same relative frequency:

x	0	2	4	6
$p(x)$	$\frac{1}{4}$	$\frac{1}{4}$	$\frac{1}{4}$	$\frac{1}{4}$

   a. List all the different samples of $n = 2$ measurements that can be selected from this population.

   b. Calculate the mean of each different sample listed in part **a**.

   c. If a sample of $n = 2$ measurements is randomly selected from the population, what is the probability that a specific sample will be selected?

   d. Assume that a random sample of $n = 2$ measurements is selected from the population. List the different values of $\bar{x}$ found in part **b** and find the probability of each. Then give the sampling distribution of the sample mean $\bar{x}$ in tabular form.

   e. Construct a probability histogram for the sampling distribution of $\bar{x}$.

2 Simulate sampling from the population described in Exercise 1 by marking the values of x, one on each of four identical coins (or poker chips, etc.). Place the coins (marked 0, 2, 4, and 6) into a bag, randomly select one, and observe its value. Replace this coin, draw a second coin, and observe its value. Finally, calculate the mean $\bar{x}$ for this sample of $n = 2$ observations randomly selected from the population (Exercise 1, part **b**). Replace the coins, mix, and using the same procedure, select a sample of $n = 2$ observations from the population. Record the numbers and calculate $\bar{x}$ for this sample. Repeat this sampling process until you acquire 100 values of $\bar{x}$. Construct a relative frequency distribution for these 100 sample means. Compare this distribution to the exact sampling distribution of $\bar{x}$ found in part **e** of Exercise 1. [*Note:* The distribution obtained in this exercise is an approximation to the exact sampling distribution. But, if you were to repeat the sampling procedure, drawing two coins not 100 times but 10,000 times, the relative frequency distribution for the 10,000 sample means would be almost identical to the sampling distribution of $\bar{x}$ found in Exercise 1, part **e**.]

3 Consider the population described by the probability distribution shown below.

x	1	2	3	4	5
$p(x)$	.2	.3	.2	.2	.1

The random variable x is observed twice. If these observations are independent, verify that the different samples of size 2 and their probabilities are as shown in the next column.

Sample	Probability	Sample	Probability
1, 1	.04	3, 4	.04
1, 2	.06	3, 5	.02
1, 3	.04	4, 1	.04
1, 4	.04	4, 2	.06
1, 5	.02	4, 3	.04
2, 1	.06	4, 4	.04
2, 2	.09	4, 5	.02
2, 3	.06	5, 1	.02
2, 4	.06	5, 2	.03
2, 5	.03	5, 3	.02
3, 1	.04	5, 4	.02
3, 2	.06	5, 5	.01
3, 3	.04		

   a. Find the sampling distribution of the sample mean $\bar{x}$.

   b. Construct a probability histogram for the sampling distribution of $\bar{x}$.

   c. What is the probability that $\bar{x}$ is 4.5 or larger?

   d. Would you expect to observe a value of $\bar{x}$ equal to 4.5 or larger? Explain.

4 Refer to Exercise 3 and find $E(x) = \mu$. Then use the sampling distribution of $\bar{x}$ found in Exercise 3 to find the expected value of $\bar{x}$. Note that $E(\bar{x}) = \mu$.

5 Refer to Exercise 3. Assume that a random sample of $n = 2$ measurements is randomly selected from the population.

   a. List the different values that the sample median m may assume and find the probability of each. Then give the sampling distribution of the sample median.

   b. Construct a probability histogram for the sampling distribution of the sample median and compare it with the probability histogram for the sample mean (Exercise 3, part **b**).

6 In Example 2 we used a computer to generate 1,000 samples, each containing $n = 11$ observations, from a uniform distribution over the interval from 150 to 200. For this exercise, use a computer to generate 500 samples, each containing $n = 15$ observations, from this population.

   a. Calculate the sample mean for each sample. To approximate the sampling distribution of $\bar{x}$, construct a relative frequency histogram for the 500 values of $\bar{x}$.

   b. Repeat part **a** for the sample median. Compare this approximate sampling distribution with the approximate sampling distribution of $\bar{x}$ found in part **a**.

7 Consider a population that contains values of x equal to 00, 01, 02, 03,..., 96, 97, 98, 99. Assume that these values of x occur with equal probability. Use a computer to generate 500 samples, each containing $n = 25$ measurements, from this population. Calculate the sample mean $\bar{x}$ and sample variance s^2 for each of the 500 samples.

   a. To approximate the sampling distribution of $\bar{x}$, construct a relative frequency histogram for the 500 values of $\bar{x}$.

   b. Repeat part **a** for the 500 values of s^2.

2 Properties of Sampling Distributions: Unbiasedness and Minimum Variance

The simplest type of statistic used to make inferences about a population parameter is a *point estimator*—a rule or formula that tells us how to use the sample data to calculate a single number that is intended to estimate the value of some population parameter. For example, the sample mean $\bar{x}$ is a point estimator of the population mean μ. Similarly, the sample variance s^2 is a point estimator of the population variance σ^2.

> A **point estimator** of a population parameter is a rule or formula that tells us how to use the sample data to calculate a single number that can be used as an *estimate* of the population parameter.

Often, many different point estimators can be found to estimate the same parameter. Each will have a sampling distribution that provides information about the point estimator. By examining the sampling distribution, we can determine how large the difference between an estimate and the true value of the parameter (called the **error of estimation**) is likely to be. We can also tell whether an estimator is more likely to overestimate or to underestimate a parameter.

Example 3 **Comparing Two Statistics**	**Problem** Suppose two statistics, A and B, exist to estimate the same population parameter θ (theta). (Note that θ could be any parameter: μ, σ^2, σ, etc.) Suppose the two statistics have sampling distributions as shown in Figure 6. On the basis of these sampling distributions, which statistic is more attractive as an estimator of θ?

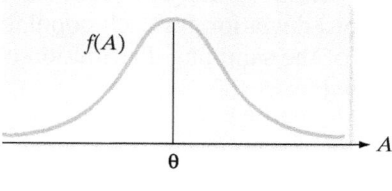

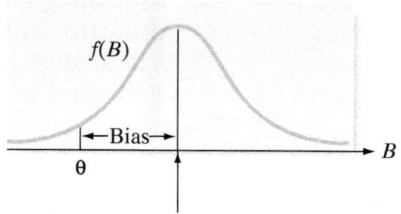

Mean of sampling distribution

Figure 6

Sampling distributions of unbiased and biased estimators

a. Unbiased sample statistic for the parameter θ

b. Biased sample statistic for the parameter θ

Solution As a first consideration, we would like the sampling distribution to center over the value of the parameter we wish to estimate. One way to characterize this property is in terms of the mean of the sampling distribution. Consequently, we say that a statistic is *unbiased* if the mean of the sampling distribution is equal to the parameter it is intended to estimate. This situation is shown in Figure 6a, where the mean μ_A of statistic A is equal to θ. If the mean of a sampling distribution is *not* equal to the parameter it is intended to estimate, the statistic is said to be *biased*. The sampling distribution for a biased statistic is shown in Figure 6b. The mean μ_B of the sampling distribution for statistic B is not equal to θ; in fact, it is shifted to the right of θ.

Look Back You can see that biased statistics tend either to overestimate or to underestimate a parameter. Consequently, when other properties of statistics tend to be equivalent, we will choose an unbiased statistic to estimate a parameter of interest.*

Now Work Exercise 8

*Unbiased statistics do not exist for all parameters of interest, but they do exist for all the parameters considered in this text.

If the sampling distribution of a sample statistic has a mean equal to the population parameter the statistic is intended to estimate, the statistic is said to be an **unbiased estimate** of the parameter.

If the mean of the sampling distribution is not equal to the parameter, the statistic is said to be a **biased estimate** of the parameter.

The standard deviation of a sampling distribution measures another important property of statistics: the spread of these estimates generated by repeated sampling. Suppose two statistics, *A* and *B,* are both unbiased estimators of the population parameter. Since the means of the two sampling distributions are the same, we turn to their standard deviations in order to decide which will provide estimates that fall closer to the unknown population parameter we are estimating. Naturally, we will choose the sample statistic that has the smaller standard deviation. Figure 7 depicts sampling distributions for *A* and *B*. Note that the standard deviation of the distribution for *A* is smaller than the standard deviation of the distribution for *B*, indicating that, over a large number of samples, the values of *A* cluster more closely around the unknown population parameter than do the values of *B*. Stated differently, the probability that *A* is close to the parameter value is higher than the probability that *B* is close to the parameter value.

In sum, to make an inference about a population parameter, we use the sample statistic with a sampling distribution that is unbiased and has a small standard deviation (usually smaller than the standard deviation of other unbiased sample statistics). The derivation of this sample statistic will not concern us, because the "best" statistic for estimating specific parameters is a matter of record. We will simply present an unbiased estimator with its standard deviation for each population parameter we consider. [*Note:* The standard deviation of the sampling distribution of a statistic is also called the **standard error of the statistic**.]

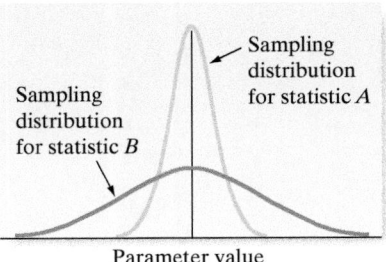

Figure 7

Sampling distributions for two unbiased estimators

Example	4

Biased and Unbiased Estimators—Craps Application

Problem Refer to Example 1 and the outcome *x* of a $5 wager in craps. We found the sampling distributions of the sample mean $\bar{x}$ and the sample median *m* for random samples of *n* = 3 dice rolls from a population defined by the following probability distribution:

x	−5	0	5
p(x)	$\frac{1}{9}$	$\frac{6}{9}$	$\frac{2}{9}$

The sampling distributions of $\bar{x}$ and *m* were found to be as follows:

x	−5	−3.33	−1.67	0	1.67	3.33	5
$p(\bar{x})$	$\frac{1}{729}$	$\frac{18}{729}$	$\frac{114}{729}$	$\frac{288}{729}$	$\frac{228}{729}$	$\frac{72}{729}$	$\frac{8}{729}$

m	−5	0	5
p(m)	$\frac{25}{729}$	$\frac{612}{729}$	$\frac{92}{729}$

a. Show that $\bar{x}$ is an unbiased estimator of μ in this situation.

b. Show that *m* is a biased estimator of μ in this situation.

Solution

a. The expected value of a discrete random variable x is defined as $E(x) = \Sigma x p(x)$, where the summation is over all values of x. Then

$$E(x) = \mu = \Sigma x p(x) = (-5)\left(\tfrac{1}{9}\right) + (0)\left(\tfrac{6}{9}\right) + (5)\left(\tfrac{2}{9}\right) = \frac{5}{9} = .556$$

The expected value of the discrete random variable $\bar{x}$ is

$$E(\bar{x}) = \Sigma(\bar{x})p(\bar{x})$$

summed over all values of $\bar{x}$, or

$$E(\bar{x}) = (-5)\left(\tfrac{1}{729}\right) + (-3.33)\left(\tfrac{18}{729}\right) + (-1.67)\left(\tfrac{114}{729}\right) + \cdots + (5)\left(\tfrac{8}{729}\right) = .556$$

Since $E(\bar{x}) = \mu, \bar{x}$ is an unbiased estimator of μ.

b. The expected value of the sample median m is

$$E(m) = \Sigma m p(m) = (-5)\left(\tfrac{25}{729}\right) + (0)\left(\tfrac{612}{729}\right) + (5)\left(\tfrac{92}{729}\right) = \frac{335}{729} = .460$$

Since the expected value of m is not equal to $\mu(\mu = .556)$, the sample median m is a biased estimator of μ.

■ **Now Work Exercise 10 a, b, c, d**

Example   5

Variance of Estimators—Craps Application

Problem Refer to Example 4 and find the standard deviations of the sampling distributions of $\bar{x}$ and m. Which statistic would appear to be a better estimator of μ?

Solution The variance of the sampling distribution of $\bar{x}$ (we denote it by the symbol $\sigma_{\bar{x}}^2$) is found to be

$$\sigma_{\bar{x}}^2 = E\{[\bar{x} - E(\bar{x})]^2\} = \Sigma(\bar{x} - \mu)^2 p(\bar{x})$$

where, from Example 4,

$$E(\bar{x}) = \mu = .556$$

Then

$$\sigma_{\bar{x}}^2 = (-5 - .556)^2\left(\tfrac{1}{729}\right) + (-3.33 - .556)^2\left(\tfrac{18}{729}\right) + \cdots (5 - .556)^2\left(\tfrac{8}{729}\right)$$

$$= 2.675$$

and

$$\sigma_{\bar{x}} = \sqrt{2.675} = 1.64$$

Similarly, the variance of the sampling distribution of m (we denote it by σ_m^2) is

$$\sigma_m^2 = E\{[m - E(m)]^2\}$$

where, from Example 4, the expected value of m is $E(m) = .460$. Then

$$\sigma_m^2 = E\{[m - E(m)]^2\} = \Sigma[m - E(m)]^2 p(m)$$

$$= (-5 - .460)\left(\tfrac{25}{729}\right) + (0 - .460)\left(\tfrac{612}{729}\right) + (5 - .460)\left(\tfrac{92}{729}\right) = 3.801$$

and

$$\sigma_m = \sqrt{3.801} = 1.95$$

Which statistic appears to be the better estimator for the population mean μ, the sample mean $\bar{x}$ or the median m? To answer this question, we compare the sampling distributions of the two statistics. The sampling distribution of the sample median m is biased (i.e., it is located to the left of the mean μ), and its standard deviation $\sigma_m = 1.95$ is larger than the standard deviation of the sampling distribution of $\bar{x}$, $\sigma_{\bar{x}} = 1.64$. Consequently, for the population in question, the sample mean $\bar{x}$ would be a better estimator of the population mean μ than the sample median m would be.

Look Back Ideally, we desire an estimator that is unbiased *and* has the smallest variance among all unbiased estimators. We call this statistic the **minimum-variance unbiased estimator (MVUE)**.

> **Now Work Exercise 10 e, f**

Exercises 8–14

Learning the Mechanics

8 Consider the following probability distribution:

x	0	1	4
$p(x)$	$\frac{1}{3}$	$\frac{1}{3}$	$\frac{1}{3}$

  a. Find μ and σ^2.
  b. Find the sampling distribution of the sample mean $\bar{x}$ for a random sample of $n = 2$ measurements from this distribution.
  c. Show that $\bar{x}$ is an unbiased estimator of μ. [*Hint:* Show that $E(\bar{x}) = \Sigma \bar{x} p(\bar{x}) = \mu$.]
  d. Find the sampling distribution of the sample variance s^2 for a random sample of $n = 2$ measurements from this distribution.
  e. Show that s^2 is an unbiased estimator for σ^2.

9 Consider the following probability distribution:

x	2	4	9
$p(x)$	$\frac{1}{3}$	$\frac{1}{3}$	$\frac{1}{3}$

  a. Calculate μ for this distribution.
  b. Find the sampling distribution of the sample mean $\bar{x}$ for a random sample of $n = 3$ measurements from this distribution, and show that $\bar{x}$ is an unbiased estimator of μ.
  c. Find the sampling distribution of the sample median m for a random sample of $n = 3$ measurements from this distribution, and show that the median is a biased estimator of μ.
  d. If you wanted to use a sample of three measurements from this population to estimate μ, which estimator would you use? Why?

10 Consider the following probability distribution:

x	0	1	2
$p(x)$	$\frac{1}{3}$	$\frac{1}{3}$	$\frac{1}{3}$

  a. Find μ.
  b. For a random sample of $n = 3$ observations from this distribution, find the sampling distribution of the sample mean.
  c. Find the sampling distribution of the median of a sample of $n = 3$ observations from this population.
  d. Refer to parts **b** and **c**, and show that both the mean and median are unbiased estimators of μ for this population.
  e. Find the variances of the sampling distributions of the sample mean and the sample median.
  f. Which estimator would you use to estimate μ? Why?

11 Use the computer to generate 500 samples, each containing $n = 25$ measurements, from a population that contains values of x equal to 1, 2, ..., 48, 49, 50. Assume that these values of x are equally likely. Calculate the sample mean $\bar{x}$ and median m for each sample. Construct relative frequency histograms for the 500 values of $\bar{x}$ and the 500 values of m. Use these approximations to the sampling distributions of $\bar{x}$ and m to answer the following questions:
  a. Does it appear that $\bar{x}$ and m are unbiased estimators of the population mean? [*Note:* $\mu = 25.5$.]
  b. Which sampling distribution displays greater variation?

12 Refer to Exercise 3.
  a. Show that $\bar{x}$ is an unbiased estimator of μ.
  b. Find $\sigma_{\bar{x}}^2$.
  c. Find the probability that $\bar{x}$ will fall within $2\sigma_{\bar{x}}$ of μ.

13 Refer to Exercise 3.
  a. Find the sampling distribution of s^2.
  b. Find the population variance σ^2.
  c. Show that s^2 is an unbiased estimator of σ^2.
  d. Find the sampling distribution of the sample standard deviation s.
  e. Show that s is a biased estimator of σ.

14 Refer to Exercise 5, in which we found the sampling distribution of the sample median. Is the median an unbiased estimator of the population mean μ?

3 The Sampling Distribution of the Sample Mean and the Central Limit Theorem

Estimating the mean useful life of automobiles, the mean monthly sales for all iPhone dealers in a large city, and the mean breaking strength of new plastic are practical problems with something in common. In each case, we are interested in making an inference about the mean μ of some population. The sample mean $\bar{x}$ is, in general, a good estimator of μ. We now develop pertinent information about the sampling distribution for this useful statistic. We will show that $\bar{x}$ is the minimum-variance unbiased estimator (MVUE) of μ.

Example 6

Describing the Sampling Distribution of $\bar{x}$

Problem Suppose a population has the uniform probability distribution given in Figure 8. The mean and standard deviation of this probability distribution are $\mu = 175$ and $\sigma = 14.43$. Now suppose a sample of 11 measurements is selected from this population. Describe the sampling distribution of the sample mean $\bar{x}$ based on the 1,000 sampling experiments discussed in Example 2.

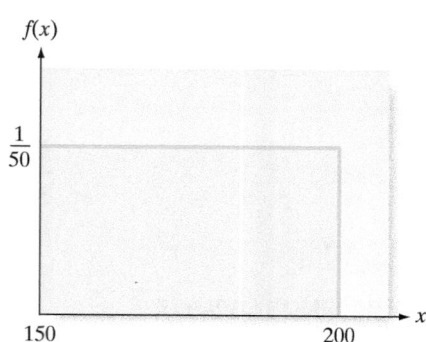

Figure 8
Sampled uniform population

Solution You will recall that in Example 2 we generated 1,000 samples of $n = 11$ measurements each. The Minitab histogram for the 1,000 sample means is shown in Figure 9 with a normal probability distribution superimposed. You can see that this normal probability distribution approximates the computer-generated sampling distribution very well.

To fully describe a normal probability distribution, it is necessary to know its mean and standard deviation. Minitab gives these statistics for the 1,000 $\bar{x}$'s in the upper right corner of the histogram, Figure 9. You can see that the mean is 175.2, and the standard deviation is 4.383.

To summarize our findings based on 1,000 samples, each consisting of 11 measurements from a uniform population, the sampling distribution of $\bar{x}$ appears to be approximately normal with a mean of about 175 and a standard deviation of about 4.38.

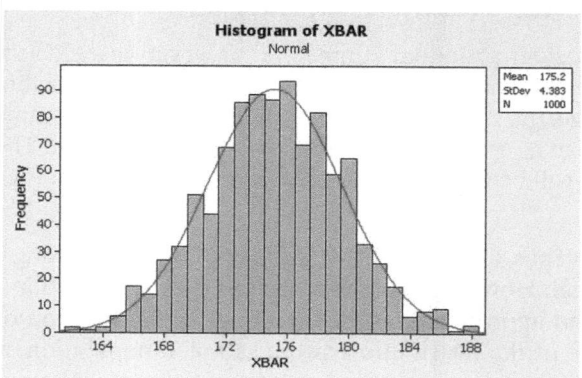

Figure 9

Minitab histogram for sample mean in 1,000 samples

Look Back Note that the simulated value $\mu_{\bar{x}} = 175.2$ is very close to $\mu = 175$ for the uniform distribution—that is, the simulated sampling distribution of $\bar{x}$ appears to provide an accurate estimate of μ.

The true sampling distribution of $\bar{x}$ has the properties given in the next box, assuming only that a random sample of n observations has been selected from *any* population.

Properties of the Sampling Distribution of $\bar{x}$

1. Mean of sampling distribution equals mean of sampled population, that is, $\mu_{\bar{x}} = E(\bar{x}) = \mu$.

2. Standard deviation of sampling distribution equals

$$\frac{\text{Standard deviation of sampled population}}{\text{Square root of sample size}}$$

That is, $\sigma_{\bar{x}} = \sigma/\sqrt{n}$.*

The standard deviation $\sigma_{\bar{x}}$ is often referred to as the **standard error of the mean.**

You can see that our approximation to $\mu_{\bar{x}}$ in Example 6 was precise because property 1 assures us that the mean is the same as that of the sampled population: 175. Property 2 tells us how to calculate the standard deviation of the sampling distribution of $\bar{x}$. Substituting $\sigma = 14.43$, the standard deviation of the sampled uniform distribution, and the sample size $n = 11$ into the formula for $\sigma_{\bar{x}}$, we find

$$\sigma_{\bar{x}} = \frac{\sigma}{\sqrt{n}} = \frac{14.43}{\sqrt{11}} = 4.35$$

Thus, the approximation we obtained in Example 6, $\sigma_{\bar{x}} = 4.38$, is very close to the exact value, $\sigma_{\bar{x}} = 4.35$. It can be shown (proof omitted) that the value of $\sigma_{\bar{x}}^2$ is the smallest variance among all unbiased estimators of μ; thus, $\bar{x}$ is the MVUE for μ.

What about the shape of the sampling distribution of $\bar{x}$? Two important theorems provide this information. One is applicable whenever the original population data are normally distributed. The other, applicable when the sample size n is large, represents one of the most important theoretical results in statistics: the **Central Limit Theorem.**

Theorem 1

If a random sample of n observations is selected from a population with a normal distribution, the sampling distribution of $\bar{x}$ will be a normal distribution.

Theorem 2 (Central Limit Theorem)

Consider a random sample of n observations selected from a population (*any* probability distribution) with mean μ and standard deviation σ. Then, when n is sufficiently large, the sampling distribution of $\bar{x}$ will be approximately a normal distribution with mean $\mu_{\bar{x}} = \mu$ and standard deviation $\sigma_{\bar{x}} = \sigma/\sqrt{n}$. The larger the sample size, the better will be the normal approximation to the sampling distribution of $\bar{x}$.†

Thus, for sufficiently large samples, the sampling distribution of $\bar{x}$ is approximately normal. How large must the sample size n be so that the normal distribution provides a good approximation for the sampling distribution of $\bar{x}$? The answer depends on the shape of the distribution of the sampled population, as shown by Figure 10. Generally speaking, the greater the skewness of the sampled population distribution, the larger the

*If the sample size, n, is large relative to the number, N, of elements in the population (e.g., 5% or more), $\sigma/\sqrt{n}$ must be multiplied by a finite population correction factor, $\sqrt{(N-n)/(N-1)}$. For most sampling situations, this correction factor will be close to 1 and can be ignored.

†Moreover, because of the Central Limit Theorem, the sum of a random sample on n observations, Σx, will possess a sampling distribution that is approximately normal for large samples. This distribution will have a mean equal to $n\mu$ and a variance equal to $n\sigma^2$. Proof of the Central Limit Theorem is beyond the scope of this text, but it can be found in many mathematical statistics texts.

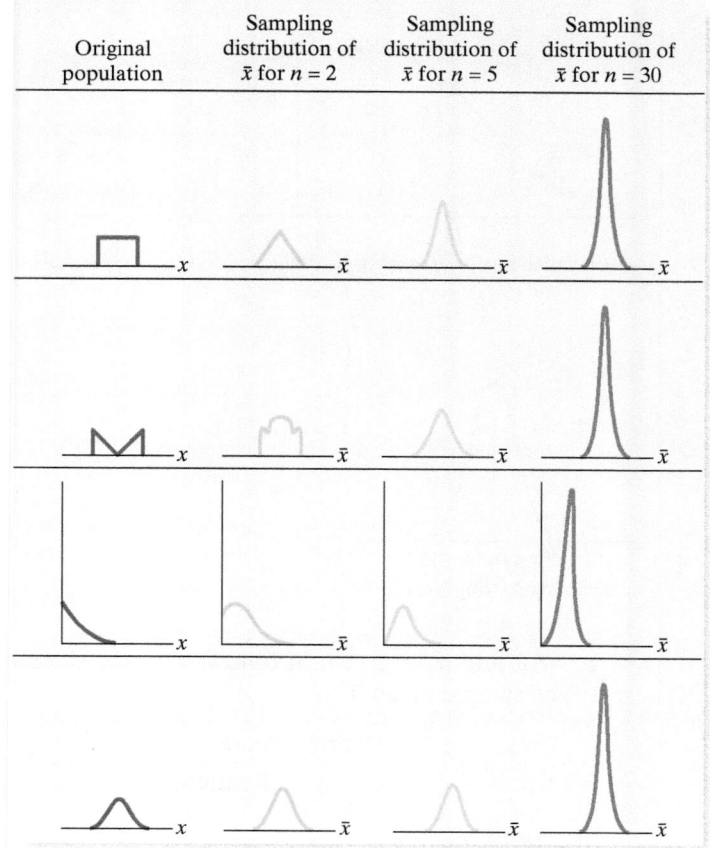

	Original population	Sampling distribution of $\bar{x}$ for $n = 2$	Sampling distribution of $\bar{x}$ for $n = 5$	Sampling distribution of $\bar{x}$ for $n = 30$

Figure 10

Sampling distributions of $\bar{x}$ for different populations and different sample sizes (*Note*: Distributions not drawn to scale. All areas under the curves are equal to 1.)

sample size must be before the normal distribution is an adequate approximation for the sampling distribution of $\bar{x}$. For most sampled populations, sample sizes of $n \geq 30$ will suffice for the normal approximation to be reasonable.

Example 7

Using the Central Limit Theorem to Find a Probability

Problem Suppose we have selected a random sample of $n = 36$ observations from a population with mean equal to 80 and standard deviation equal to 6. It is known that the population is not extremely skewed.

a. Sketch the relative frequency distributions for the population and for the sampling distribution of the sample mean, $\bar{x}$.

b. Find the probability that $\bar{x}$ will be larger than 82.

Solution

a. We do not know the exact shape of the population relative frequency distribution, but we do know that it should be centered about $\mu = 80$, its spread should be measured by $\sigma = 6$, and it is not highly skewed. One possibility is shown in Figure 11a. From the Central Limit Theorem, we know that the sampling distribution of $\bar{x}$ will be approximately normal because the sampled population distribution is not extremely skewed. We also know that the sampling distribution will have mean and standard deviation

$$\mu_{\bar{x}} = \mu = 80 \quad \text{and} \quad \sigma_{\bar{x}} = \frac{\sigma}{\sqrt{n}} = \frac{6}{\sqrt{36}} = 1$$

The sampling distribution of $\bar{x}$ is shown in Figure 11b.

b. The probability that $\bar{x}$ will exceed 82 is equal to the darker shaded area in Figure 12. To find this area, we need to find the z-value corresponding to $\bar{x} = 82$. Recall that the standard normal random variable z is the difference between any normally distributed random variable and its mean, expressed in units of its standard deviation. Because $\bar{x}$ is approximately a normally distributed random variable with mean

291

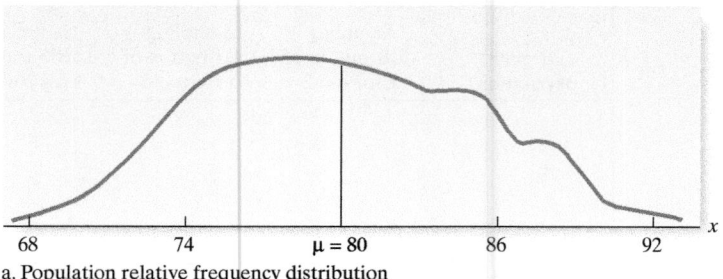

Figure 11

A population relative frequency distribution and the sampling distribution for $\bar{x}$

a. Population relative frequency distribution

b. Sampling distribution of $\bar{x}$

$\mu_{\bar{x}} = \mu$ and $\sigma_{\bar{x}} = \sigma/\sqrt{n}$, it follows that the standard normal z-value corresponding to the sample mean, $\bar{x}$, is

$$z = \frac{(\text{Normal random variable}) - (\text{Mean})}{\text{Standard deviation}} = \frac{\bar{x} - \mu_{\bar{x}}}{\sigma_{\bar{x}}}$$

Therefore, for $\bar{x} = 82$, we have

$$z = \frac{\bar{x} - \mu_{\bar{x}}}{\sigma_{\bar{x}}} = \frac{82 - 80}{1} = 2$$

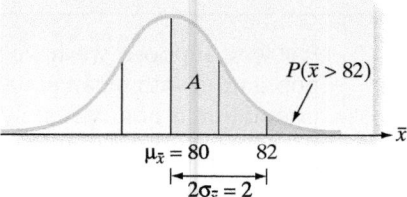

Figure 12

The sampling distribution of $\bar{x}$

The area A in Figure 12 corresponding to $z = 2$ is given in the table of areas under the normal curve (see Table II in Appendix: Tables) as .4772. Therefore, the tail area corresponding to the probability that $\bar{x}$ exceeds 82 is

$$P(\bar{x} > 82) = P(z > 2) = .5 - .4772 = .0228$$

Look Back The key to finding the probability, part **b,** is to recognize that the distribution of $\bar{x}$ is normal with mean $\mu_{\bar{x}} = \mu$ and $\sigma_{\bar{x}} = \sigma/\sqrt{n}$.

Now Work Exercises 18–19

Example	8

Application of the Central Limit Theorem—Testing a Manufacturer's Claim

Problem A manufacturer of automobile batteries claims that the distribution of the lengths of life of its best battery has a mean of 54 months and a standard deviation of 6 months. Recently, the manufacturer has received a rash of complaints from unsatisfied customers whose batteries have died earlier than expected. Suppose a consumer group decides to check the manufacturer's claim by purchasing a sample of 50 of these batteries and subjecting them to tests that determine battery life.

a. Assuming that the manufacturer's claim is true, describe the sampling distribution of the mean lifetime of a sample of 50 batteries.

b. Assuming that the manufacturer's claim is true, what is the probability that the consumer group's sample has a mean life of 52 or fewer months?

Solution

a. Even though we have no information about the shape of the probability distribution of the lives of the batteries, we can use the Central Limit Theorem to deduce that the sampling distribution for a sample mean lifetime of 50 batteries is approximately normally distributed. Furthermore, the mean of this sampling distribution is the same as the mean of the sampled population, which is $\mu = 54$ months according to the manufacturer's claim. Finally, the standard deviation of the sampling distribution is given by

$$\sigma_{\bar{x}} = \frac{\sigma}{\sqrt{n}} = \frac{6}{\sqrt{50}} = .85 \text{ month}$$

Note that we used the claimed standard deviation of the sampled population, $\sigma = 6$ months. Thus, if we assume that the claim is true, the sampling distribution for the mean life of the 50 batteries sampled is as shown in Figure 13.

b. If the manufacturer's claim is true, the probability that the consumer group observes a mean battery life of 52 or fewer months for their sample of 50 batteries, $P(\bar{x} \leq 52)$, is equivalent to the darker shaded area in Figure 13. Because the sampling distribution is approximately normal, we can find this area by computing the standard normal z-value:

$$z = \frac{\bar{x} - \mu_{\bar{x}}}{\sigma_{\bar{x}}} = \frac{52 - 54}{.85} = -2.35$$

where $\mu_{\bar{x}}$, the mean of the sampling distribution of $\bar{x}$, is equal to μ, the mean of the lives of the sampled population, and $\sigma_{\bar{x}}$ is the standard deviation of the sampling distribution of $\bar{x}$. Note that z is the familiar standardized distance (z-score) of Section 7 and because $\bar{x}$ is approximately normally distributed, it will possess (approximately) the standard normal distribution of Section 6.

Figure 13

Sampling distribution of $\bar{x}$ in Example 8 for $n = 50$

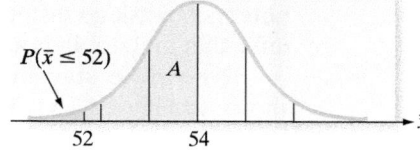

The area A shown in Figure 13 between $\bar{x} = 52$ and $\bar{x} = 54$ (corresponding to $z = -2.35$) is found in Table II in Appendix: Tables to be .4906. Therefore, the area to the left of $\bar{x} = 52$ is

$$P(\bar{x} \leq 52) = .5 - A = .5 - .4906 = .0094$$

Thus, the probability that the consumer group will observe a sample mean of 52 or less is only .0094 if the manufacturer's claim is true.

Look Back If the 50 tested batteries do exhibit a mean of 52 or fewer months, the consumer group will have strong evidence that the manufacturer's claim is untrue because such an event is very unlikely to occur if the claim is true. (This is still another application of the *rare-event approach to statistical inference.*)

■ **Now Work Exercise 24**

We conclude this section with two final comments on the sampling distribution of $\bar{x}$. First, from the formula $\sigma_{\bar{x}} = \sigma/\sqrt{n}$, we see that the standard deviation of the sampling distribution of $\bar{x}$ gets smaller as the sample size n gets larger. For example, we computed $\sigma_{\bar{x}} = .85$ when $n = 50$ in Example 8. However, for $n = 100$, we obtain $\sigma_{\bar{x}} = \sigma/\sqrt{n} = 6/\sqrt{100} = .60$. This relationship will hold true for most of the sample statistics encountered in this text–that is, *the standard deviation of the sampling distribution decreases as the sample size increases.* Consequently, the larger the sample size, the more accurate the sample statistic (e.g., $\bar{x}$) is in estimating a population parameter (e.g., μ).

Our second comment concerns the Central Limit Theorem. In addition to providing a very useful approximation for the sampling distribution of a sample mean, the Central Limit Theorem offers an explanation for the fact that many relative frequency distributions of data possess mound-shaped distributions. Many of the measurements we take in business are really means or sums of a large number of small phenomena. For example, a company's sales for 1 year are the total of the many individual sales the company made during the year. Similarly, we can view the length of time a construction company takes to build a house as the total of the times taken to complete a multitude of distinct jobs, and we can regard the monthly demand for blood at a hospital as the total of the many individual patients' needs. Whether or not the observations entering into these sums satisfy the assumptions basic to the Central Limit Theorem is open to question. However, it is a fact that many distributions of data in nature are mound-shaped and possess the appearance of normal distributions.

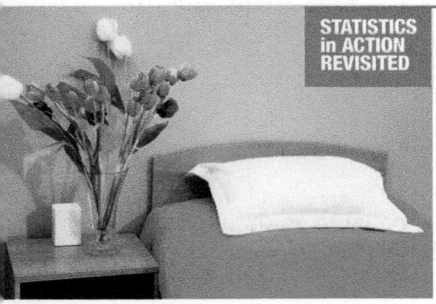

STATISTICS
in ACTION
REVISITED

Making an Inference about the Mean Sleep Onset Latency for Insomnia Pill Takers

In a Massachusetts Institute of Technology (MIT) study, each member of a sample of 40 young male volunteers was given a dosage of the sleep-inducing hormone melatonin or a placebo, was placed in a dark room at midday, and was told to close his eyes for 30 minutes. The researchers measured the time (in minutes) elapsed before each volunteer fell asleep—called sleep onset latency. Recall that the data (shown in Table SIA1) are saved in the **SLEEP** file.

Previous research established that with the placebo (i.e., no hormone), the mean sleep onset latency is $\mu = 15$ minutes and the standard deviation is $\sigma = 10$ minutes. If the true value of μ for those taking the melatonin is $\mu < 15$ (i.e., if, on average, the volunteers fall asleep faster with the drug than with the placebo), then the researchers can infer that melatonin is an effective drug against insomnia.

Descriptive statistics for the 40 sleep times are displayed in the SPSS printout shown in Figure SIA1. You can see that the mean for the sample is $\bar{x} = 5.935$ minutes. If the drug is not effective in reducing sleep times, then the distribution of sleep times will be no different from the distribution with the placebo. That is, if the drug is not effective, the mean and standard deviation of the population of sleep times are $\mu = 15$ and $\sigma = 10$. If this is true, how likely is it to observe a sample mean that is below 6 minutes?

To answer this question, we desire the probability $P(\bar{x} < 6)$. To find this probability, we invoke the Central Limit Theorem. According to the theorem, the sampling distribution of $\bar{x}$ has the following mean and standard deviation:

$$\mu_{\bar{x}} = \mu = 15$$
$$\sigma_{\bar{x}} = \sigma/\sqrt{n} = 10/\sqrt{40} = 1.58$$

Descriptive Statistics

	N	Minimum	Maximum	Mean	Std. Deviation
SLEEPTIME	40	1.3	22.8	5.935	5.3917
Valid N (listwise)	40				

Figure SIA1

SPSS descriptive statistics for sleep time data

The theorem also states that $\bar{x}$ is approximately normally distributed. Therefore, we find the desired probability (using the standard normal table) as follows:

$$P(\bar{x} < 6) = P\left(z < \frac{6 - \mu_{\bar{x}}}{\sigma_{\bar{x}}}\right)$$

$$= P\left(z < \frac{6 - 15}{1.58}\right) = P(z < -5.70) \approx 0$$

In other words, the probability that we observe a sample mean below $\bar{x} = 6$ minutes *if the mean and standard deviation of the sleep times are,* respectively, $\mu = 15$ and $\sigma = 10$ *(i.e., if the drug is not effective),* is almost 0. Therefore, either the drug is not effective and the researchers have observed an extremely rare event (one with almost no chance of happening), or the true value of μ for those taking the melatonin pill is much less than 15 minutes. The rare-event approach to making statistical inferences, of course, would favor the second conclusion. Melatonin appears to be an effective insomnia pill, one that lowers the average time it takes the volunteers to fall asleep.

Data Set: SLEEP

Exercises 15–35

Please be aware that some of the following problems may require knowledge of concepts that are not presented in this chapter.

Learning the Mechanics

15 Will the sampling distribution of $\bar{x}$ always be approximately normally distributed? Explain.

16 Suppose a random sample of $n = 25$ measurements is selected from a population with mean μ and standard deviation σ. For each of the following values of μ and σ, give the values of $\mu_{\bar{x}}$ and $\sigma_{\bar{x}}$.
   a. $\mu = 10, \sigma = 3$
   b. $\mu = 100, \sigma = 25$
   c. $\mu = 20, \sigma = 40$
   d. $\mu = 10, \sigma = 100$

17 Suppose a random sample of n measurements is selected from a population with mean $\mu = 100$ and variance $\sigma^2 = 100$. For each of the following values of n, give the mean and standard deviation of the sampling distribution of the sample mean $\bar{x}$.
   a. $n = 4$ **b.** $n = 25$
   c. $n = 100$ **d.** $n = 50$
   e. $n = 500$ **f.** $n = 1,000$

18 A random sample of $n = 64$ observations is drawn from a population with a mean equal to 20 and a standard deviation equal to 16.
   a. Give the mean and standard deviation of the (repeated) sampling distribution of $\bar{x}$.
   b. Describe the shape of the sampling distribution of $\bar{x}$. Does your answer depend on the sample size?
   c. Calculate the standard normal z-score corresponding to a value of $\bar{x} = 15.5$.
   d. Calculate the standard normal z-score corresponding to $\bar{x} = 23$.

19 Refer to Exercise 18. Find the probability that
   a. $\bar{x}$ is less than 16.
   b. $\bar{x}$ is greater than 23.

   c. $\bar{x}$ is greater than 25.
   d. $\bar{x}$ falls between 16 and 22.
   e. $\bar{x}$ is less than 14.

20 A random sample of $n = 900$ observations is selected from a population with $\mu = 100$ and $\sigma = 10$.
   a. What are the largest and smallest values of $\bar{x}$ that you would expect to see?
   b. How far, at the most, would you expect $\bar{x}$ to deviate from μ?
   c. Did you have to know μ to answer part **b**? Explain.

21 A random sample of $n = 100$ observations is selected from a population with $\mu = 30$ and $\sigma = 16$. Approximate the following probabilities:
   a. $P(\bar{x} \geq 28)$
   b. $P(22.1 \leq \bar{x} \leq 26.8)$
   c. $P(\bar{x} \leq 28.2)$
   d. $P(\bar{x} \geq 27.0)$

22 Consider a population that contains values of x equal to 0, 1, 2, ..., 97, 98, 99. Assume that the values of x are equally likely. For each of the following values of n, use a computer to generate 500 random samples and calculate $\bar{x}$ for each sample. For each sample size, construct a relative frequency histogram of the 500 values of $\bar{x}$. What changes occur in the histograms as the value of n increases? What similarities exist? Use $n = 2, n = 5, n = 10, n = 30$, and $n = 50$.

Applet Exercise 1

Open the applet *Sampling Distributions.* On the pull-down menu to the right of the top graph, select *Binary.*
   a. Run the applet for the sample size $n = 10$ and the number of samples $N = 1,000$. Observe the shape of the graph of the sample proportions and record the mean, median, and standard deviation of the sample proportions.

b. How does the mean of the sample proportions compare to the mean $\mu = 0.5$ of the original distribution?

c. Compute the standard deviation of the original distribution using the formula $\sigma = \sqrt{np(1-p)}$ where $n = 1$ and $p = 0.5$. Divide the result by $\sqrt{10}$, the square root of the sample size used in the sampling distribution. How does this result compare to the standard deviation of the sample proportions?

d. Explain how the graph of the distribution of sample proportions suggests that the distribution may be approximately normal.

e. Explain how the results of parts **b–d** illustrate the Central Limit Theorem.

● Applet Exercise 2

Open the applet *Sampling Distributions*. On the pull-down menu to the right of the top graph, select *Uniform*. The box to the left of the top graph displays the population mean, median, and standard deviation of the original distribution.

a. Run the applet for the sample size $n = 30$ and the number of samples $N = 1,000$. Observe the shape of the graph of the sample means and record the mean, median, and standard deviation of the sample means.

b. How does the mean of the sample means compare to the mean of the original distribution?

c. Divide the standard deviation of the original distribution by $\sqrt{30}$, the square root of the sample size used in the sampling distribution. How does this result compare to the standard deviation of the sample proportions?

d. Explain how the graph of the distribution of sample means suggests that the distribution may be approximately normal.

e. Explain how the results of parts **b–d** illustrate the Central Limit Theorem.

Applying the Concepts—Basic

23 Phishing attacks to e-mail accounts. *Phishing* describes an attempt to extract personal/financial information from unsuspecting people through fraudulent e-mail. Data from an actual phishing attack against an organization were presented in *Chance* (Summer 2007). The interarrival times, i.e., the time differences (in seconds), for 267 fraud box e-mail notifications, were recorded and are saved in the accompanying file. For this exercise, consider these interarrival times to represent the population of interest.

a. Construct a histogram for the interarrival times. Describe the shape of the population of interarrival times.

b. Find the mean and standard deviation of the population of interarrival times.

c. Now consider a random sample of $n = 40$ interarrival times selected from the population. Describe the shape of the sampling distribution of $\bar{x}$, the sample mean. Theoretically, what are $\mu_{\bar{x}}$ and $\sigma_{\bar{x}}$?

d. Find $P(\bar{x} < 90)$.

e. Use a random number generator to select a random sample of $n = 40$ interarrival times from the population, and calculate the value of $\bar{x}$. (Every student in the class should do this.)

f. Refer to part **e.** Obtain the values of $\bar{x}$ computed by the students and combine them into a single data set. Form a histogram for these values of $\bar{x}$. Is the shape approximately normal?

g. Refer to part **f.** Find the mean and standard deviation of the $\bar{x}$-values. Do these values approximate $\mu_{\bar{x}}$ and $\sigma_{\bar{x}}$, respectively?

24 Salary of a travel management professional. According to a National Business Travel Association (NBTA) 2010 survey, the average salary of a travel management professional is \$96,850. Assume that the standard deviation of such salaries is \$30,000. Consider a random sample of 50 travel management professionals and let $\bar{x}$ represent the mean salary for the sample.

a. What is $\mu_{\bar{x}}$?

b. What is $\sigma_{\bar{x}}$?

c. Describe the shape of the sampling distribution of $\bar{x}$.

d. Find the z-score for the value $\bar{x} = 89,500$.

e. Find $P(\bar{x} > 89,500)$.

25 Corporate sustainability of CPA firms. The journal *Business and Society* (March 2011) did a study on the sustainability behaviors of CPA corporations. *Corporate sustainability,* refers to business practices designed around social and environmental considerations. The level of support senior managers have for corporate sustainability was measured quantitatively on a scale ranging from 0 to 160 points, where higher point values indicate a higher level of support for sustainability. The study provided the following information on the distribution of levels of support for sustainability: $\mu = 68$, $\sigma = 27$. Now consider a random sample of 45 senior managers and let $\bar{x}$ represent the sample mean level of support.

a. Give the value of $\mu_{\bar{x}}$, the mean of the sampling distribution of $\bar{x}$, and interpret the result.

b. Give the value of $\sigma_{\bar{x}}$, the standard deviation of the sampling distribution of $\bar{x}$, and interpret the result.

c. What does the Central Limit Theorem say about the shape of the sampling distribution of $\bar{x}$?

d. Find $P(\bar{x} > 65)$.

26 Critical-part failures in NASCAR vehicles. *The Sport Journal* (Winter 2007) did an analysis of critical-part failures at NASCAR races. Researchers found that the time x (in hours) until the first critical-part failure is exponentially distributed with $\mu = .10$ and $\sigma = .10$. Now consider a random sample of $n = 50$ NASCAR races and let $\bar{x}$ represent the sample mean time until the first critical-part failure.

a. Find $E(\bar{x})$ and $\text{Var}(\bar{x})$.

b. Although x has an exponential distribution, the sampling distribution of $\bar{x}$ is approximately normal. Why?

c. Find the probability that the sample mean time until the first critical-part failure exceeds .13 hour.

27 Tomato as a taste modifier. Miraculin is a protein naturally produced in a rare tropical fruit that can convert a sour taste into a sweet taste. The journal *Plant Science* (May 2010) did an investigation of the ability of a hybrid tomato plant to produce miraculin. The amount x of miraculin produced in the plant had a mean of 105.3 micrograms per gram of fresh weight with a standard deviation of 8.0. Consider a random sample of $n = 64$

hybrid tomato plants and let $\bar{x}$ represent the sample mean amount of miraculin produced. Would you expect to observe a value of $\bar{x}$ less than 103 micrograms per gram of fresh weight? Explain.

Applying the Concepts—Intermediate

28 Requests to a Web server. Brighton Webs LTD modeled the arrival time of requests to a Web server within each hour using a uniform distribution. Specifically, the number of seconds x from the start of the hour that the request is made is uniformly distributed between 0 and 3,600 seconds. In a random sample of $n = 60$ Web server requests, let $\bar{x}$ represent the sample mean number of seconds from the start of the hour that the request is made.
  a. Find $E(\bar{x})$ and interpret its value.
  b. Find $Var(\bar{x})$.
  c. Describe the shape of the sampling distribution of $\bar{x}$.
  d. Find the probability that $\bar{x}$ is between 1,700 and 1,900 seconds.
  e. Find the probability that $\bar{x}$ exceeds 2,000 seconds.

29 Levelness of concrete slabs. Geotechnical engineers use water-level "manometer" surveys to assess the levelness of newly constructed concrete slabs. Elevations are typically measured at eight points on the slab; of interest is the maximum differential between elevations. The *Journal of Performance of Constructed Facilities* (Feb. 2005) published an article on the levelness of slabs in California residential developments. Elevation data collected for over 1,300 concrete slabs *before tensioning* revealed that maximum differential, x, has a mean of $\mu = .53$ inch and a standard deviation of $\sigma = .193$ inch. Consider a sample of $n = 50$ slabs selected from those surveyed and let $\bar{x}$ represent the mean of the sample.
  a. Fully describe the sampling distribution of $\bar{x}$.
  b. Find $P(\bar{x} > .58)$.
  c. The study also revealed that the mean maximum differential of concrete slabs measured *after tensioning and loading* is $\mu = .58$ inch. Suppose the sample data yield $\bar{x} = .59$ inch. Comment on whether the sample measurements were obtained before tensioning or after tensioning and loading.

30 Surface roughness of pipe. *Anti-Corrosion Methods and Materials* (Vol. 50, 2003) did a study of the surface roughness of oil field pipes. A scanning probe instrument was used to measure the surface roughness x (in micrometers) of 20 sampled sections of coated interior pipe. Consider the sample mean, $\bar{x}$.
  a. Assume that the surface roughness distribution has a mean of $\mu = 1.8$ micrometers and a standard deviation of $\sigma = .5$ micrometer. Use this information to find the probability that $\bar{x}$ exceeds 1.85 micrometers.
  b. The sample data are reproduced in the following table. Compute $\bar{x}$.
  c. Based on the result, part **b**, comment on the validity of the assumptions made in part **a**.

| 1.72 | 2.50 | 2.16 | 2.13 | 1.06 | 2.24 | 2.31 | 2.03 | 1.09 | 1.40 |
| 2.57 | 2.64 | 1.26 | 2.05 | 1.19 | 2.13 | 1.27 | 1.51 | 2.41 | 1.95 |

Source: Based on Farshad, F., & Pesacreta, T. "Coated pipe interior surface roughness as measured by three scanning probe instruments," *Anti-Corrosion Methods and Materials,* Vol. 50, No. 1, 2003 (Table III).

31 Is exposure to a chemical in Teflon-coated cookware hazardous? Perfluorooctanoic acid (PFOA) is a chemical used in Teflon-coated cookware to prevent food from sticking. The EPA is investigating the potential risk of PFOA as a cancer-causing agent (*Science News Online*, August 27, 2005). It is known that the blood concentration of PFOA in people in the general population has a mean of $\mu = 6$ parts per billion (ppb) and a standard deviation of $\sigma = 10$ ppb. *Science News Online* reported on tests for PFOA exposure conducted on a sample of 326 people who live near DuPont's Teflon-making Washington (West Virginia) Works facility.
  a. What is the probability that the average blood concentration of PFOA in the sample is greater than 7.5 ppb?
  b. The actual study resulted in $\bar{x} = 300$ ppb. Use this information to make an inference about the true mean μ PFOA concentration for the population of people who live near DuPont's Teflon facility.

32 Rental car fleet evaluation. National Car Rental Systems, Inc., commissioned the U.S. Automobile Club (USAC) to conduct a survey of the general condition of the cars rented to the public by Hertz, Avis, National, and Budget Rent-a-Car.* USAC officials evaluate each company's cars using a demerit point system. Each car starts with a perfect score of 0 points and incurs demerit points for each discrepancy noted by the inspectors. One measure of the overall condition of a company's cars is the mean of all scores received by the company (i.e., the company's *fleet mean score*). To estimate the fleet mean score of each rental car company, 10 major airports were randomly selected, and 10 cars from each company were randomly rented for inspection from each airport by USAC officials (i.e., a sample of size $n = 100$ cars from each company's fleet was drawn and inspected).
  a. Describe the sampling distribution of $\bar{x}$, the mean score of a sample of $n = 100$ rental cars.
  b. Interpret the mean of $\bar{x}$ in the context of this problem.
  c. Assume $\mu = 30$ and $\sigma = 60$ for one rental car company. For this company, find $P(\bar{x} \geq 45)$.
  d. Refer to part **c**. The company claims that their true fleet mean score "couldn't possibly be as high as 30." The sample mean score tabulated by USAC for this company was 45. Does this result tend to support or refute the claim? Explain.

33 Motivation of drug dealers. *Applied Psychology in Criminal Justice* (Sep. 2009) did an investigation of the personality characteristics of drug dealers. Convicted drug dealers were scored on the Wanting Recognition (WR) Scale—a scale that provides a quantitative measure of a person's level of need for approval and sensitivity to social situations. (Higher scores indicate a greater need for approval.) Based on the study results, we can assume that the WR scores for the population of convicted drug dealers has a mean of 40 and a standard deviation of 5. Suppose that in a sample of 100 people, the mean WR scale score is $\bar{x} = 42$. Is this sample likely to have been selected from the population of convicted drug dealers? Explain.

*Information by personal communication with Rajiv Tandon, corporate vice president and general manager of the Car Rental Division, National Car Rental Systems, Inc., Minneapolis, Minnesota.

Applying the Concepts—Advanced

34 **Plastic fill process.** University of Louisville researchers J. Usher, S. Alexander, and D. Duggins examined the process of filling plastic pouches of dry blended biscuit mix (*Quality Engineering,* Vol. 91, 1996). The current fill mean of the process is set at $\mu = 406$ grams, and the process fill standard deviation is $\sigma = 10.1$ grams. (According to the researchers, "The high level of variation is due to the fact that the product has poor flow properties and is, therefore, difficult to fill consistently from pouch to pouch.") Operators monitor the process by randomly sampling 36 pouches each day and measuring the amount of biscuit mix in each. Consider $\bar{x}$, the mean fill amount of the sample of 36 products. Suppose that on one particular day, the operators observe $\bar{x} = 400.8$. One of the operators believes that this indicates that the true process fill mean μ for that day is less than 406 grams. Another operator argues that $\mu = 406$, and the small value of $\bar{x}$ observed is due to random variation in the fill process. Which operator do you agree with? Why?

35 **Handwashing vs. handrubbing.** The *British Medical Journal* (Aug. 17, 2002) published the results of a study to compare the effectiveness of handwashing with soap and handrubbing with alcohol. Health care workers who used handrubbing had a mean bacterial count of 35 per hand with a standard deviation of 59. Health care workers who used handwashing had a mean bacterial count of 69 per hand with a standard deviation of 106. In a random sample of 50 health care workers, all using the same method of cleaning their hands, the mean bacterial count per hand, $\bar{x}$, is less than 30. Give your opinion on whether this sample of workers used handrubbing with alcohol or handwashing with soap.

4   The Sampling Distribution of the Sample Proportion

Suppose you want to estimate the proportion of voters in favor of a bill to legalize gambling in your state, or the percentage of store customers who use a store credit card to make a purchase, or the fraction of company CEOs who defer their annual pay. In each case, the data of interest are categorical in nature with two outcomes (e.g., favor or do not favor); consequently, we want to make an inference about a binomial proportion, p.

Just as the sample mean is a good estimator of the population mean, the sample proportion—denoted $\hat{p}$—is a good estimator of the population proportion p. How good the estimator $\hat{p}$ is will depend on the sampling distribution of the statistic. This sampling distribution has properties similar to those of the sampling distribution of $\bar{x}$, as shown in the following example.

Example 9

Simulating the Sampling Distribution of $\hat{p}$—Worker Unionization

Problem Refer to the problem of sampling workers to determine whether they are in favor of unionization. We assumed that 60% of all workers at a large plant were, in fact, in favor of unionization. Suppose we will randomly sample 100 plant workers and ask each if he or she is or is not in favor of unionization. Use a computer and statistical software to simulate the sampling distribution of $\hat{p}$, the sample proportion of workers in favor of unionization. What properties do you observe?

Solution Consider a single random sample of 100 workers. If we define a "success" as a worker in favor of unionization, and if 58 of the 100 are in favor of unionization, then our estimate of the binomial proportion p is $\hat{p} = 58/100 = .58$. By repeatedly taking samples in this manner and calculating $\hat{p}$ each time, we can simulate the sampling distribution.

We used SPSS to generate 1,000 samples of size $n = 100$ from a binomial population with probability of success $p = .6$. For each sample, we calculated $\hat{p} = x/n$, where x is the number of successes in the sample. The estimated proportions for the first 20 samples are shown in Table 4. An SPSS histogram for all 1,000 estimated proportions is shown in Figure 14. This histogram approximates the sampling distribution of $\hat{p}$.

First, note that the sampling distribution appears to be normally distributed. Thus, the sampling distribution of $\hat{p}$ has the same property as the sampling distribution of $\bar{x}$—normally distributed for large n. Second, you can see that the sampling distribution is centered around the value $p = .6$. That is, it appears that the mean of the sampling distribution is equal to p, the proportion being estimated.

Look Back The normal distribution property identified with computer simulation becomes obvious once you recognize that the sample proportion $\hat{p}$ can be written as an average of 0s and 1s, where 1 represents a "success" (a worker in favor of unionization)

Table 4	Results for First 20 Samples of $n = 100$ Workers	
Sample	Number of Success, x	Sample Proportion, $\hat{p}$
1	60	.60
2	58	.58
3	56	.56
4	61	.61
5	54	.54
6	67	.67
7	54	.54
8	55	.55
9	56	.56
10	69	.69
11	59	.59
12	64	.64
13	53	.53
14	65	.65
15	66	.66
16	61	.61
17	60	.60
18	55	.55
19	57	.57
20	61	.61

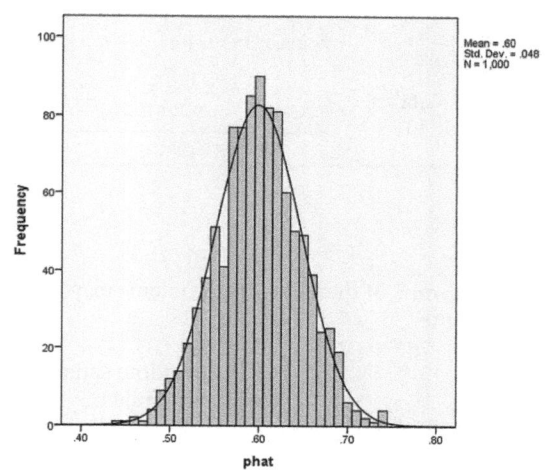

Mean = .60
Std. Dev. = .048
N = 1,000

Descriptive Statistics

	N	Minimum	Maximum	Mean	Std. Deviation
phat	1000	.44	.74	.5988	.04823
Valid N (listwise)	1000				

Figure 14

SPSS histogram of 1,000 values of $\hat{p}$, Example 9

and 0 represents a "failure" (a worker not in favor of unionization). In the first sample shown in Table 4, there were 60 successes and 40 failures; thus

$$\hat{p} = \frac{(60)(1) + (40)(0)}{100} = 60/100 = .60$$

Since $\hat{p}$ is a mean, the Central Limit Theorem can be applied when the sample size n is large.

The true sampling distribution of $\hat{p}$ has the properties listed in the next box.

Sampling Distribution of $\hat{p}$

1. Mean of the sampling distribution is equal to the true binomial proportion, p; that is, $E(\hat{p}) = p$. Consequently, $\hat{p}$ is an unbiased estimator of p.
2. Standard deviation of the sampling distribution is equal to $\sqrt{p(1-p)/n}$; that is, $\sigma_{\hat{p}} = \sqrt{p(1-p)/n}$.
3. For large samples, the sampling distribution is approximately normal. (A sample is considered large if $n\hat{p} \geq 15$ and $n(1-\hat{p}) \geq 15$.)

In Example 9, $p = .6$. Thus, the true mean of the sampling distribution of $\hat{p}$ is equal to .6. Also, the true standard deviation of the sampling distribution of $\hat{p}$ is

$$\sigma_{\hat{p}} = \sqrt{p(1-p)/n} = \sqrt{(.6)(.4)/100} = .049$$

Note that our estimates of the mean and standard deviation using simulation—.599 and .048, respectively—closely approximate the true values.

Example 10

Finding a Probability Involving $\hat{p}$—Workers in Favor of Unionization

Problem Refer to Example 9. Again, assume that 60% of all workers at a large plant are in favor of unionization. In a random sample of 100 plant workers, what is the probability that fewer than half are in favor of unionization?

Solution We want to find the probability that the sample proportion is less than .5, i.e., $P(\hat{p} < .5)$. From previous work, we know that the sampling distribution of $\hat{p}$ is normally distributed (since n is large), with mean $p = .6$ and standard deviation $\sigma_{\hat{p}} = .049$. Consequently,

$$P(\hat{p} < .5) = P\{(\hat{p} - p)/\sigma_{\hat{p}} < (.5 - p)/\sigma_{\hat{p}}\} = P\{z < (.5 - .6)/.049\} = P(z < -2.04)$$

Using Minitab software (see Figure 15), we find $P(\hat{p} < .5) = P(z < -2.04) = .021$.

Cumulative Distribution Function

```
Normal with mean = 0 and standard deviation = 1

     x    P( X <= x )
 -2.04      0.0206752
```

Figure 15

Minitab output for a normal probability, Example 10

▪ **Now Work Exercise 39**

Exercises 36–49

Please be aware that some of the following problems may require knowledge of concepts that are not presented in this chapter.

Learning the Mechanics

36 Suppose a random sample of n measurements is selected from a binomial population with probability of success $p = .2$. For each of the following values of n, give the mean and standard deviation of the sampling distribution of the sample proportion, $\hat{p}$.
 a. $n = 50$
 b. $n = 1,000$
 c. $n = 400$

37 Suppose a random sample of $n = 500$ measurements is selected from a binomial population with probability of success p. For each of the following values of p, give the mean and standard deviation of the sampling distribution of the sample proportion, $\hat{p}$.
 a. $p = .1$
 b. $p = .5$
 c. $p = .7$

38 A random sample of $n = 80$ measurements is drawn from a binomial population with probability of success .3.
 a. Give the mean and standard deviation of the sampling distribution of the sample proportion, $\hat{p}$.
 b. Describe the shape of the sampling distribution of $\hat{p}$.
 c. Calculate the standard normal z-score corresponding to a value of $\hat{p} = .35$.
 d. Find $P(\hat{p} > .35)$.

39 A random sample of $n = 250$ measurements is drawn from a binomial population with probability of success .85.
 a. Find $E(\hat{p})$ and $\sigma_{\hat{p}}$.
 b. Describe the shape of the sampling distribution of $\hat{p}$.
 c. Find $P(\hat{p} < .9)$.

40 A random sample of $n = 1,500$ measurements is drawn from a binomial population with probability of success .4. What are the smallest and largest values of $\hat{p}$ you would expect to see?

41 Consider a population with values of x equal to 0 or 1. Assume that the values of x are equally likely. For each of the following values of n, use a computer to generate 500 random samples and calculate the sample proportion of 1s observed for each sample. Then construct a histogram of the 500 sample proportions for each sample.
 a. $n = 10$
 b. $n = 25$
 c. $n = 100$
 d. Refer to the histograms, parts **a–c**. What changes occur as the value of n increases? What similarities exist?

Applying the Concepts—Basic

42 Do social robots walk or roll? *International Conference on Social Robotics* (Vol. 6414, 2010) did a study of the trend in the design of social robots.

The researchers obtained a random sample of 106 social robots through a Web search and determined the number that were designed with legs, but no wheels. Let $\hat{p}$ represent the sample proportion of social robots designed with legs, but no wheels. Assume that in the population of all social robots, 40% are designed with legs, but no wheels.

a. Give the mean and standard deviation of the sampling distribution of $\hat{p}$.

b. Describe the shape of the sampling distribution of $\hat{p}$.

c. Find $P(\hat{p} > .59)$.

d. The researchers found that 63 of the 106 robots were built with legs only. Does this result cast doubt on the assumption that 40% of all social robots are designed with legs, but no wheels? Explain.

43 **Paying for music downloads.** According to a recent *Pew Internet & American Life Project Survey* (October 2010), 67% of adults who use the Internet have paid to download music. In a random sample of $n = 1,000$ adults who use the Internet, let $\hat{p}$ represent the proportion who have paid to download music.

a. Find the mean of the sampling distribution of $\hat{p}$.

b. Find the standard deviation of the sampling distribution of $\hat{p}$.

c. What does the Central Limit Theorem say about the shape of the sampling distribution of $\hat{p}$?

d. Compute the probability that $\hat{p}$ is less than .75.

e. Compute the probability that $\hat{p}$ is greater than .50.

44 **Working on summer vacation.** According to an *Adweek/Harris* (July 2011) poll of U.S. adults, about 45% work during their summer vacation. Assume that the true proportion of all U.S. adults that work during summer vacation is $p = .45$. Now consider a random sample of 500 U.S. adults.

a. What is the probability that between 40% and 50% of the sampled adults work during summer vacation?

b. What is the probability that over 60% of the sampled adults work during summer vacation?

45 **Study of why EMS workers leave the job.** A study of full-time emergency medical service (EMS) workers published in the *Journal of Allied Health* (Fall 2011) found that only about 3% leave their job in order to retire. Assume that the true proportion of all full-time EMS workers who leave their job in order to retire is $p = .03$. In a random sample of 1,000 full-time EMS workers, let $\hat{p}$ represent the proportion who leave their job in order to retire.

a. Describe the properties of the sampling distribution of $\hat{p}$.

b. Compute $P(\hat{p} < .05)$. Interpret this result.

c. Compute $P(\hat{p} > .025)$. Interpret this result.

Applying the Concepts—Intermediate

46 **Stock market participation and IQ.** *The Journal of Finance* (December 2011) did a study of whether the decision to invest in the stock market is dependent on IQ. The researchers found that the probability of a Finnish citizen investing in the stock market differed depending on IQ score. For those with a high IQ score, the probability is .44; for those with an average IQ score, the probability is .26; and for those with a low IQ score, the probability is .14.

a. In a random sample of 500 Finnish citizens with high IQ scores, what is the probability that more than 150 invest in the stock market?

b. In a random sample of 500 Finnish citizens with average IQ scores, what is the probability that more than 150 invest in the stock market?

c. In a random sample of 500 Finnish citizens with low IQ scores, what is the probability that more than 150 invest in the stock market?

47 **Downloading "apps" to your cell phone.** An August 2011 survey by the Pew Internet & American Life Project found that 40% of adult cell phone owners have downloaded an application ("app") to their cell phone. Assume this percentage applies to the population of all adult cell phone owners.

a. In a random sample of 50 adult cell phone owners, how likely is it to find that more than 60% have downloaded an "app" to their cell phone?

b. Refer to part **a.** Suppose you observe a sample proportion of .62. What inference can you make about the true proportion of adult cell phone owners who have downloaded an "app"?

c. Suppose the sample of 50 cell phone owners is obtained at a convention for the International Association for the Wireless Telecommunications Industry. How will your answer to part **b** change, if at all?

48 **Hotel guest satisfaction.** The results of the 2009 North American Hotel Guest Satisfaction Index Study showed that 66% of hotel guests were aware of the hotel's "green" conservation program; of these guests, 72% actually participated in the program by reusing towels and bed linens. In a random sample of 100 hotel guests, find the probability that fewer than 42 were aware of and participated in the hotel's conservation efforts.

49 **Fingerprint expertise.** *Psychological Science* (August 2011) did a study of fingerprint identification. When presented with prints from the same individual, a fingerprint expert will correctly identify the match 92% of the time. Consider a forensic database of 1,000 different pairs of fingerprints, where each pair is a match.

a. What proportion of the 1,000 pairs would you expect an expert to correctly identify as a match?

b. What is the probability that an expert will correctly identify fewer than 900 of the fingerprint matches?

◻ Chapter Notes

Key Terms

Biased estimate
Central Limit Theorem
Error of estimation
Minimum-variance unbiased
   estimator (MVUE)
Parameter

Point estimator
Sample statistic
Sampling distribution
Standard error of the mean
Standard error of the statistic
Unbiased estimate

Key Formulas

	Mean	Standard Deviation	z-score
Sampling distribution of $\bar{x}$:	$\mu_{\bar{x}} = \mu$	$\sigma_{\bar{x}} = \dfrac{\sigma}{\sqrt{n}}$	$z = \dfrac{\bar{x} - \mu_{\bar{x}}}{\sigma_{\bar{x}}}$ $= \dfrac{\bar{x} - \mu}{\sigma/\sqrt{n}}$
Sampling distribution of $\hat{p}$:	p	$\sigma_{\hat{p}} = \sqrt{p(1-p)/n}$	$z = \dfrac{\hat{p} - p}{\sqrt{p(1-p)/n}}$

Key Ideas

Sampling distribution of a statistic—the theoretical probability distribution of the statistic in repeated sampling

Unbiased estimator—a statistic with a sampling distribution mean equal to the population parameter being estimated

Central Limit Theorem—the sampling distribution of the sample mean, $\bar{x}$, or the sample proportion, $\hat{p}$, is approximately normal for large n

$\bar{x}$ is the **minimum-variance unbiased estimator (MVUE)** of μ

$\hat{p}$ is the MVUE of p

Key Symbols

θ	Population parameter (general)
$\mu_{\bar{x}}$	True mean of sampling distribution of $\bar{x}$
$\sigma_{\bar{x}}$	True standard deviation of sampling distribution of $\bar{x}$
p	True mean of sampling distribution of $\hat{p}$
$\sigma_{\hat{p}}$	True standard deviation of sampling distribution of $\hat{p}$

Generating the Sampling Distribution of $\bar{x}$

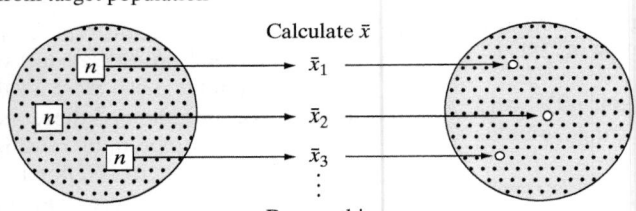

Select sample size n (large) from target population

Calculate $\bar{x}$

$\bar{x}_1$
$\bar{x}_2$
$\bar{x}_3$

Population:
   Mean = μ
   Std. Dev. = σ
   Unknown shape

Repeat this process an infinite number of times

Sampling distribution of $\bar{x}$
(i.e., theoretical population of x's)
   Mean = $\mu_{\bar{x}} = \mu$
   Std. Dev. = $\sigma_{\bar{x}} = \sigma/\sqrt{n}$
   Normal distribution (Central Limit Theorem)

Supplementary Exercises 50–75

Please be aware that some of the following problems may require knowledge of concepts that are not presented in this chapter.

Learning the Mechanics

50 The standard deviation (or, as it is usually called, the *standard error*) of the sampling distribution for the sample mean, $\bar{x}$, is equal to the standard deviation of the population from which the sample was selected, divided by the square root of the sample size. That is,

$$\sigma_{\bar{x}} = \frac{\sigma}{\sqrt{n}}$$

a. As the sample size is increased, what happens to the standard error of $\bar{x}$? Why is this property considered important?

b. Suppose a sample statistic has a standard error that is not a function of the sample size. In other words, the standard error remains constant as n changes. What would this imply about the statistic as an estimator of a population parameter?

c. Suppose another unbiased estimator (call it A) of the population mean is a sample statistic with a standard error equal to

$$\sigma_A = \frac{\sigma}{\sqrt[3]{n}}$$

Which of the sample statistics, $\bar{x}$ or A, is preferable as an estimator of the population mean? Why?

d. Suppose that the population standard deviation σ is equal to 10 and that the sample size is 64. Calculate the standard errors of $\bar{x}$ and A. Assuming that the sampling distribution of A is approximately normal, interpret the standard errors. Why is the assumption of (approximate) normality unnecessary for the sampling distribution of $\bar{x}$?

51 Consider a sample statistic A. As with all sample statistics, A is computed by utilizing a specified function (formula) of the sample measurements. (For example, if A were the sample mean, the specified formula would sum the measurements and divide by the number of measurements.)

a. Describe what we mean by the phrase "the sampling distribution of the sample statistic A."

b. Suppose A is to be used to estimate a population parameter θ. What is meant by the assertion that A is an unbiased estimator of θ?

c. Consider another sample statistic, B. Assume that B is also an unbiased estimator of the population parameter α. How can we use the sampling distributions of A and B to decide which is the better estimator of θ?

d. If the sample sizes on which A and B are based are large, can we apply the Central Limit Theorem and assert that the sampling distributions of A and B are approximately normal? Why or why not?

52 A random sample of 40 observations is to be drawn from a large population of measurements. It is known that 30% of the measurements in the population are 1s, 20% are 2s, 20% are 3s, and 30% are 4s.

a. Give the mean and standard deviation of the (repeated) sampling distribution of $\bar{x}$, the sample mean of the 40 observations.

b. Describe the shape of the sampling distribution of $\bar{x}$. Does your answer depend on the sample size?

53 A random sample of $n = 68$ observations is selected from a population with $\mu = 19.6$ and $\sigma = 3.2$. Approximate each of the following probabilities:

a. $P(\bar{x} \le 19.6)$
b. $P(\bar{x} \le 19)$
c. $P(\bar{x} \ge 20.1)$
d. $P(19.2 \le \bar{x} \le 20.6)$

54 A random sample of $n = 500$ observations is selected from a binomial population with $p = .35$.

a. Give the mean and standard deviation of the (repeated) sampling distribution of $\hat{p}$, the sample proportion of successes for the 500 observations.

b. Describe the shape of the sampling distribution of $\hat{p}$. Does your answer depend on the sample size?

55 A random sample of $n = 300$ observations is selected from a binomial population with $p = .8$. Approximate each of the following probabilities:

a. $P(\hat{p} < .83)$
b. $P(\hat{p} > .75)$
c. $P(.79 < \hat{p} < .81)$

56 Use a statistical software package to generate 100 random samples of size $n = 2$ from a population characterized by a normal probability distribution with a mean of 100 and a standard deviation of 10. Compute $\bar{x}$ for each sample, and plot a frequency distribution for the 100 values of $\bar{x}$. Repeat this process for $n = 5, 10, 30,$ and 50. How does the fact that the sampled population is normal affect the sampling distribution of $\bar{x}$?

57 Use a statistical software package to generate 100 random samples of size $n = 2$ from a population characterized by a uniform probability distribution with $c = 0$ and $d = 10$. Compute $\bar{x}$ for each sample, and plot a frequency distribution for the 100 $\bar{x}$ values. Repeat this process for $n = 5, 10, 30,$ and 50. Explain how your plots illustrate the Central Limit Theorem.

58 Suppose x equals the number of heads observed when a single coin is tossed; that is, $x = 0$ or $x = 1$ The population corresponding to x is the set of 0s and 1s generated when the coin is tossed repeatedly a large number of times. Suppose we select $n = 2$ observations from this population. (That is, we toss the coin twice and observe two values of x.)

a. List the three different samples (combinations of 0s and 1s) that could be obtained.

b. Calculate the value of $\bar{x}$ for each of the samples.

c. Show that the sample proportion of 1s, $\hat{p}$, is equal to $\bar{x}$.

d. List the values that $\hat{p}$ can assume, and find the probabilities of observing these values.

e. Construct a graph of the sampling distribution of $\hat{p}$.

59 A random sample of size n is to be drawn from a large population with mean 100 and standard deviation 10, and the sample mean $\bar{x}$ is to be calculated. To see the effect of different sample sizes on the standard deviation of the sampling distribution of $\bar{x}$, plot $\sigma/\sqrt{n}$ against n for $n = 1, 5, 10, 20, 30, 40,$ and 50.

Applying the Concepts—Basic

60 **Semester hours taken by CPA candidates.** The *Journal of Accounting and Public Policy* (Spring 2002) did a study of first-time candidates for the CPA exam. The number of semester hours of college credit taken by candidates has a distribution with a mean of 141 hours and a standard deviation of 18 hours. Consider a random sample of 100 first-time candidates for the CPA exam and let $\bar{x}$ represent the mean number of hours of college credit taken for the sample.

a. What is $\mu_{\bar{x}}$?
b. What is $\sigma_{\bar{x}}$?
c. Describe the shape of the sampling distribution of $\bar{x}$.
d. Find the z-score for the value $\bar{x} = 142$ hours.
e. Find $P(\bar{x} > 142)$.

61 **Improving SAT scores.** *Chance* (Winter 2001) examined the Scholastic Assessment Test (SAT) scores of students who pay a private tutor to help them improve their results. On the SAT—Mathematics test, these students had a mean score change of $+19$ points, with a standard deviation of 65 points. In a random sample of 100 students who pay a private tutor to help them improve their results, what is the likelihood that the sample mean score change is less than 10 points?

62 **Back injuries at work.** A poll by the Gallup Organization sponsored by Philadelphia-based CIGNA Integrated Care found that about 40% of employees have missed work due to a musculoskeletal (back) injury of some kind (*National Underwriter,* Apr. 5, 1999). Let x be the number of sampled workers who have missed work due to a back injury.

a. Explain why x is approximately a binomial random variable.

b. Use the Gallup poll data to estimate p for the binomial random variable of part **a.**

c. A random sample of 100 workers is to be drawn from a particular manufacturing plant. Use the p from part **b** to find the mean and standard deviation of $\hat{p}$ the proportion of workers who missed work due to back injuries in the sample.

d. Refer to part **c.** Find the probability that the sample proportion is less than .38.

63 **Dentists' use of laughing gas.** According to the American Dental Association, 60% of all dentists use nitrous oxide in their practice. In a random sample of 75 dentists, let $\hat{p}$ represent the proportion who use laughing gas in practice.

a. Find $E(\hat{p})$.

b. Find $\sigma_{\hat{p}}$.

c. Describe the shape of the sampling distribution of $\hat{p}$.

d. Find $P(\hat{p} > .70)$.

64 **Ocean quahog harvesting.** The ocean quahog is a type of clam found in the coastal waters of New England and the mid-Atlantic states. A federal survey of offshore ocean quahog harvesting in New Jersey, conducted from 1980 to 1992, revealed an average catch per unit effort (CPUE) of 89.34 clams. The CPUE standard deviation was 7.74 (*Journal of Shellfish Research,* June 1995). Let $\bar{x}$ represent the mean CPUE for a sample of 35 attempts to catch ocean quahogs off the New Jersey shore.

a. Compute $\mu_{\bar{x}}$ and $\sigma_{\bar{x}}$. Interpret their values.

b. Sketch the sampling distribution of $\bar{x}$.

c. Find $P(\bar{x} > 88)$.

d. Find $P(\bar{x} < 87)$.

Applying the Concepts—Intermediate

65 **Analysis of supplier lead time.** In determining when to place orders to replenish depleted product inventories, a retailer should take into consideration the lead times for the products. *Lead time* is the time between placing the order and having the product available to satisfy customer demand. It includes time for placing the order, receiving the shipment from the supplier, inspecting the units received, and placing them in inventory (Clauss, *Applied Management Science and Spreadsheet Modeling,* 1996). Interested in average lead time, μ, for a particular supplier of men's apparel, the purchasing department of a national department store chain randomly sampled 50 of the supplier's lead times and found $\bar{x} = 44$ days.

a. Describe the shape of the sampling distribution of $\bar{x}$.

b. If μ and σ are really 40 and 12, respectively, what is the probability that a second random sample of size 50 would yield $\bar{x}$ greater than or equal to 44?

c. Using the values for μ and σ in part **b,** what is the probability that a sample of size 50 would yield a sample mean within the interval $\mu \pm 2\sigma/\sqrt{n}$?

66 **Producing machine bearings.** To determine whether a metal lathe that produces machine bearings is properly adjusted, a random sample of 25 bearings is collected and the diameter of each is measured.

a. If the standard deviation of the diameters of the bearings measured over a long period of time is .001 inch, what is the approximate probability that the mean diameter $\bar{x}$ of the sample of 25 bearings will lie within .0001 inch of the population mean diameter of the bearings?

b. If the population of diameters has an extremely skewed distribution, how will your approximation in part **a** be affected?

67 **Quality control.** Refer to Exercise 66. The mean diameter of the bearings produced by the machine is supposed to be .5 inch. The company decides to use the sample mean from Exercise 66 to decide whether the process is in control (i.e., whether it is producing bearings with a mean diameter of .5 inch). The machine will be considered out of control if the mean of the sample of $n = 25$ diameters is less than .4994 inch or larger than .5006 inch. If the true mean diameter of the bearings produced by the machine is .501 inch, what is the approximate probability that the test will imply that the process is out of control?

68 **Length of job tenure.** Researchers at the Terry College of Business at the University of Georgia sampled 344 business students and asked them this question: "Over the course of your lifetime, what is the maximum number of years you expect to work for any one employer?" The sample resulted in $\bar{x} = 19.1$ years. Assume that the sample of students was randomly selected from the 6,000 undergraduate students at the Terry College and that $\sigma = 6$ years.

a. Describe the sampling distribution of $\bar{x}$

b. If the mean for the 6,000 undergraduate students is $\mu = 18.5$ years, find $P(\bar{x} > 19.1)$

c. If the mean for the 6,000 undergraduate students is $\mu = 19.5$ years, find $P(\bar{x} > 19.1)$

d. If $P(\bar{x} > 19.1) = .5$, what is μ?

e. If $P(\bar{x} > 19.1) = .2$, is μ greater than or less than 19.1 years? Explain.

69 **Switching banks after a merger.** Banks that merge with others to form "mega-banks" sometimes leave customers dissatisfied with the impersonal service. A poll by the Gallup Organization found 20% of retail customers switched banks after their banks merged with another. One year after the acquisition of First Fidelity by First Union, a random sample of 250 retail customers who had banked with First Fidelity were questioned. Let $\hat{p}$ be the proportion of those customers who switched their business from First Union to a different bank.

a. Find the mean and the standard deviation of $\hat{p}$.

b. Calculate the interval $E(\hat{p}) \pm 2\sigma_{\hat{p}}$.

c. If samples of size 250 were drawn repeatedly a large number of times and $\hat{p}$ determined for each sample, what proportion of the $\hat{p}$ values would fall within the interval you calculated in part **c**?

70 **Piercing rating of fencing safety jackets.** A manufacturer produces safety jackets for competitive fencers. These jackets are rated by the minimum force, in newtons, that will

allow a weapon to pierce the jacket. When this process is operating correctly, it produces jackets that have ratings with an average of 840 newtons and a standard deviation of 15 newtons. FIE, the international governing body for fencing, requires jackets to be rated at a minimum of 800 newtons. To check whether the process is operating correctly, a manager takes a sample of 50 jackets from the process, rates them, and calculates $\bar{x}$, the mean rating for jackets in the sample. She assumes that the standard deviation of the process is fixed but is worried that the mean rating of the process may have changed.

a. What is the sampling distribution of $\bar{x}$ if the process is still operating correctly?

b. Suppose the manager's sample has a mean rating of 830 newtons. What is the probability of getting an $\bar{x}$ of 830 newtons or lower if the process is operating correctly?

c. Given the manager's assumption that the standard deviation of the process is fixed, what does your answer to part **b** suggest about the current state of the process (i.e., does it appear that the mean jacket rating is still 840 newtons)?

d. Now suppose that the mean of the process has not changed, but the standard deviation of the process has increased from 15 newtons to 45 newtons. What is the sampling distribution of $\bar{x}$ in this case? What is the probability of getting an $\bar{x}$ of 830 newtons or lower when $\bar{x}$ has this distribution?

71 **Errors in filling prescriptions** A large number of preventable errors (e.g., overdoses, botched operations, misdiagnoses) are being made by doctors and nurses in U.S. hospitals. A study of a major metropolitan hospital revealed that of every 100 medications prescribed or dispensed, 1 was in error, but only 1 in 500 resulted in an error that caused significant problems for the patient. It is known that the hospital prescribes and dispenses 60,000 medications per year.

a. What is the expected proportion of errors per year at this hospital? The expected proportion of significant errors per year?

b. Within what limits would you expect the proportion significant errors per year to fall?

72 **Purchasing decision.** A building contractor has decided to purchase a load of factory-reject aluminum siding as long as the average number of flaws per piece of siding in a sample of size 35 from the factory's reject pile is 2.1 or less. If it is known that the number of flaws per piece of siding in the factory's reject pile has a Poisson probability distribution with a mean of 2.5, find the approximate probability that the contractor will not purchase a load of siding.

Applying the Concepts—Advanced

73 **Machine repair time.** An article in *Industrial Engineering* (August 1990) discussed the importance of modeling machine downtime correctly in simulation studies. As an illustration, the researcher considered a single-machine-tool system with repair times (in minutes) that can be modeled by an exponential distribution with $\theta = 60$. Of interest is the mean repair time $\bar{x}$ of a sample of 100 machine breakdowns.

a. Find $E(\bar{x})$ and the variance of $\bar{x}$.

b. What probability distribution provides the best model of the sampling distribution of $\bar{x}$? Why?

c. Calculate the probability that the mean repair time $\bar{x}$ is no longer than 30 minutes.

Critical Thinking Challenges

74 **Soft-drink bottles.** A soft-drink bottler purchases glass bottles from a vendor. The bottles are required to have an internal pressure of at least 150 pounds per square inch (psi). A prospective bottle vendor claims that its production process yields bottles with a mean internal pressure of 157 psi and a standard deviation of 3 psi. The bottler strikes an agreement with the vendor that permits the bottler to sample from the vendor's production process to verify the vendor's claim. The bottler randomly selects 40 bottles from the last 10,000 produced, measures the internal pressure of each, and finds the mean pressure for the sample to be 1.3 psi below the process mean cited by the vendor.

a. Assuming the vendor's claim to be true, what is the probability of obtaining a sample mean this far or farther below the process mean? What does your answer suggest about the validity of the vendor's claim?

b. If the process standard deviation were 3 psi as claimed by the vendor, but the mean were 156 psi, would the observed sample result be more or less likely than in part **a**? What if the mean were 158 psi?

c. If the process mean were 157 psi as claimed, but the process standard deviation were 2 psi, would the sample result be more or less likely than in part **a**? What if instead the standard deviation were 6 psi?

75 **Fecal pollution at Huntington Beach.** The state of California mandates fecal indicator bacteria monitoring at all public beaches. When the concentration of fecal bacteria in the water exceeds a certain limit (400 colony-forming units of fecal coliform per 100 milliliters), local health officials must post a sign (called surf zone posting) warning beachgoers of potential health risks upon entering the water. For fecal bacteria, the state uses a single-sample standard; that is, if the fecal limit is exceeded in a single sample of water, surf zone posting is mandatory. This single-sample standard policy has led to a recent rash of beach closures in California.

Joon Ha Kim and Stanley B. Grant, engineers at the University of California at Irvine, conducted a study of the surf water quality at Huntington Beach in California and reported the results in *Environmental Science & Technology* (September 2004). The researchers found that beach closings were occurring despite low pollution levels in some instances, while in others, signs were not posted when the fecal limit was exceeded. They attributed these "surf zone posting errors" to the variable nature of water quality in the surf zone (for example, fecal bacteria concentration tends to be higher during ebb tide and at night) and the inherent time delay between when a water sample is collected and when a sign is posted or removed. In order to prevent posting errors, the researchers recommend using an averaging method, rather than a single sample, to determine unsafe water quality. (For example, one simple averaging method is to take a random sample of multiple water specimens and compare the average fecal bacteria level of the sample with the limit of 400 cfu/100 mL in order to determine whether the water is safe.)

Discuss the pros and cons of using the single-sample standard versus the averaging method. Part of your discussion should address the probability of posting a sign when in fact the water is safe and the probability of posting a sign when in fact the water is unsafe. (Assume that the fecal bacteria concentrations of water specimens at Huntington Beach follow an approximately normal distribution.)

Simulating a Sampling Distribution—Cell Phone Usage

[*Note:* This activity is designed for small groups or the entire class.] Consider the length of time a student spends making a cell phone call, sending/retrieving a text message, or accessing e-mail on his/her cell phone. Let x represent the length of time, in seconds, for a single cell phone activity (call, text, or e-mail). Here, we are interested in the sampling distribution of $\bar{x}$, the mean length of time for a sample of size n cell phone activities.

1. Keep track of the time lengths for all cell phone activities you engage in over the next week.

2. Pool your time length data with data from other class members or the entire class so that the pooled data set has at least 100 observations. Designate someone in the group to calculate the mean and standard deviation of the pooled data set.

3. Devise a convenient way to choose random samples from the pooled data set. (For example, you could assign each observation a number beginning with "1" and use a random number generator to select a sample.)

4. Choose a random sample of size $n = 30$ from the pooled data, and find the mean of the sample. Group members should repeat the process of choosing a sample of size $n = 30$ from the pooled data and finding the sample mean until the group has accumulated at least 25 sample means. (Call this data set *Sample Means.*)

5. Find the mean and standard deviation of the *Sample Means* data set. Also, form a histogram for the *Sample Means* data set. Explain how the Central Limit Theorem is illustrated in this activity.

References

Hogg, R. V., McKean, J. W., and Craig, A. T. *Introduction to Mathematical Statistics,* 6th ed. Upper Saddle River, N.J.: Prentice Hall, 2005.

Larsen, R. J., & Marx, M. L. *An Introduction to Mathematical Statistics and Its Applications,* 4th ed. Upper Saddle River, N.J.: Prentice Hall, 2005.

Lindgren, B. W. *Statistical Theory,* 3rd ed. New York: Macmillan, 1976.

Wackerly, D., Mendenhall, W., & Scheaffer, R. L. *Mathematical Statistics with Applications,* 7th ed. North Scituate, Mass.: Duxbury, 2008.

USING TECHNOLOGY Technology images shown here are taken from SPSS Statistics Professional 20.0, Minitab 16, XLSTAT for Pearson, and Excel 2010.

SPSS: Simulating a Sampling Distribution

Generating a sampling distribution with SPSS is not a simple process. Consult the SPSS user's guide for help with this feature.

Minitab: Simulating a Sampling Distribution

Step 1 Select "Calc" on the Minitab menu bar, and then click on "Random Data" (see Figure M.1).

Step 2 On the resulting menu list, click on the distribution of your choice (e.g., "Uniform"). A dialog box similar to the one (the Uniform Distribution) shown in Figure M.2 will appear.

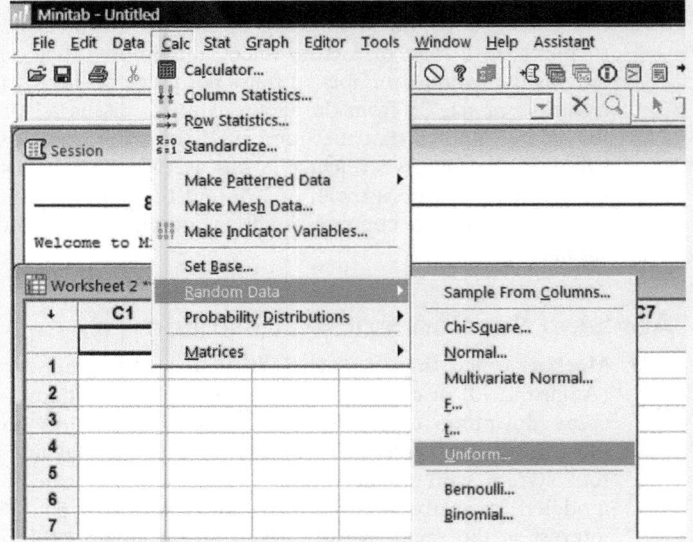

Figure M.1 Minitab options for generating random data

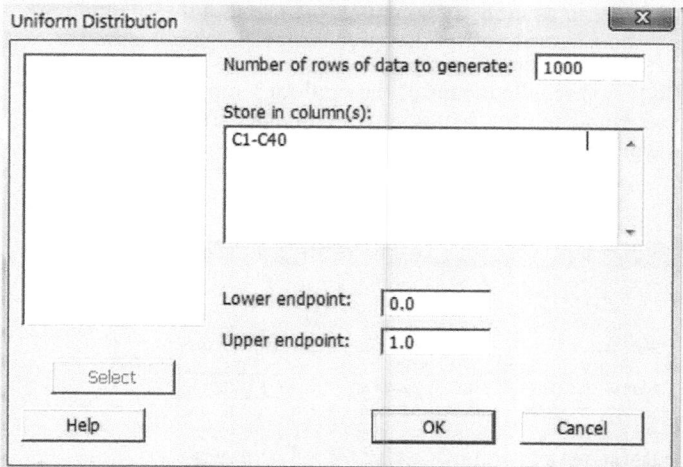

Figure M.2 Minitab dialog box for simulating the uniform distribution

Step 3 Specify the number of samples (e.g., 1,000) to generate in the "Number of rows of data to generate" box and the columns where the data will be stored in the "Store in columns" box. (The number of columns will be equal to the sample size, e.g., 40.) Finally, specify the parameters of the distribution (e.g., the lower and upper range of the uniform distribution). When you click "OK," the simulated data will appear on the Minitab worksheet.

Step 4 Calculate the value of the sample statistic of interest for each sample. To do this, click on the "Calc" button on the Minitab menu bar, and then click on "Row Statistics," as shown in Figure M.3. The resulting dialog box appears in Figure M.4.

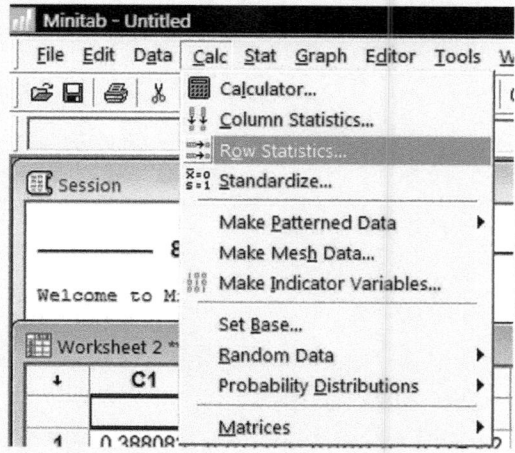

Figure M.3 Minitab selections for generating sample statistics for the simulated data

Step 5 Check the sample statistic (e.g., the mean) you want to calculate, specify the "Input variables" (or columns), and the column where you want the value of the sample statistic to be saved. Click "OK" and the value of the statistic for each sample will appear on the Minitab worksheet.

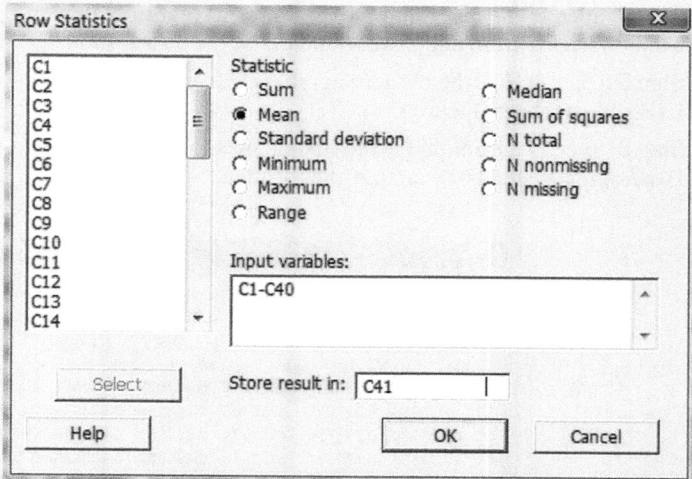

Figure M.4 Minitab row statistics dialog box

Excel: Simulating a Sampling Distribution

Step 1 Select "Data" on the main menu bar and then click on "Data Analysis." The resulting menu is shown in Figure E.1.

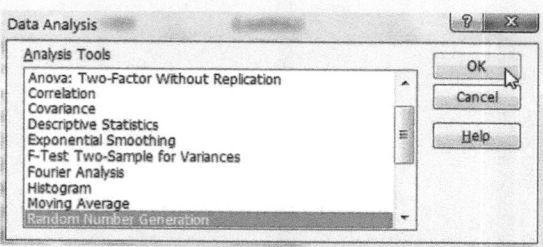

Figure E.1 Excel data analysis menu options

Step 2 Select "Random Number Generation" from the Data Analysis menu and then click "OK." The dialog box in Figure E.2 will appear.

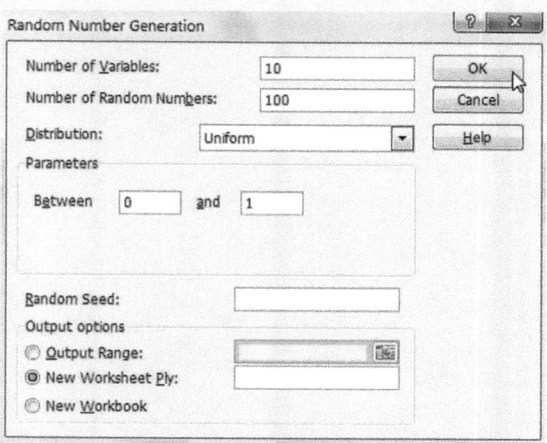

Figure E.2 Excel dialog box for generating uniform random numbers

Step 3 Specify the number of samples (e.g., 10) to generate in the "Number of Variables" box and the sample size of each (e.g., 100) in the "Number of Random Numbers" box.

Step 4 Specify the distribution (e.g., uniform) that the samples will be selected from and the parameters of the distribution.

Step 5 Click "OK"; the random numbers will appear on a new Excel spreadsheet (Figure E.3).

Step 6 Specify a formula for the sample mean on the resulting Excel spreadsheet. For example, the formula "=AVERAGE (A2:J2)" in column "L" computes the mean of the 10 random numbers in each row of the spreadsheet shown in Figure E.3.

Step 7 Once the means of the random samples are computed, you can generate a histogram or summary statistics for the mean.

	A	B	C	D	E	F	G	H	I	J	K	L
1	x1	x2	x3	x4	x4	x6	x7	x8	x9	x10		xbar
2	0.969176	0.277139	0.916257	0.403027	0.950652	0.123386	0.140416	0.037599	0.338603	0.445662		0.460192
3	0.63094	0.445875	0.718406	0.760155	0.523515	0.668569	0.124577	0.992676	0.451064	0.074862		0.539064
4	0.145299	0.791559	0.730979	0.426191	0.856349	0.349895	0.022736	0.527482	0.991668	0.518906		0.536106
5	0.11301	0.497971	0.2566	0.493667	0.983428	0.192145	0.189734	0.852351	0.817957	0.802454		0.519932
6	0.479904	0.230049	0.106357	0.174749	0.144536	0.408826	0.499008	0.868191	0.475753	0.104892		0.349226
7	0.570299	0.490005	0.159734	0.234474	0.146428	0.337565	0.477035	0.939207	0.353862	0.877773		0.458638

Figure E.3 Excel formula for computing sample means from random numbers

MAKING BUSINESS DECISIONS

The Furniture Fire Case

A wholesale furniture retailer stores in-stock items at a large warehouse located in Tampa, Florida. Early in the year, a fire destroyed the warehouse and all the furniture in it. After determining the fire was an accident, the retailer sought to recover costs by submitting a claim to its insurance company.

As is typical in a fire insurance policy of this type, the furniture retailer must provide the insurance company with an estimate of "lost" profit for the destroyed items. Retailers calculate profit margin in percentage form using the Gross Profit Factor (GPF). By definition, the GPF for a single sold item is the ratio of the profit to the item's selling price measured as a percentage, that is,

Item GPF = (Profit/Sales price) $\times$ 100%

Of interest to both the retailer and the insurance company is the average GPF for all of the items in the warehouse. Because these furniture pieces were all destroyed, their eventual selling prices and profit values are obviously unknown. Consequently, the average GPF for all the warehouse items is unknown.

One way to estimate the mean GPF of the destroyed items is to use the mean GPF of similar, recently sold items. The retailer sold 3,005 furniture items in the year prior to the fire and kept paper invoices on all sales. Rather than calculate the mean GPF for all 3,005 items (the data were not computerized), the retailer sampled a total of 253 of the invoices and computed the mean GPF for these items. The 253 items were obtained by first selecting a sample of 134 items and then augmenting this sample with a second sample of 119 items. The mean GPFs for the two subsamples were calculated to be 50.6% and 51.0%, respectively, yielding an overall average GPF of 50.8%. This average GPF can be applied to the costs of the furniture items destroyed in the fire to obtain an estimate of the "lost" profit.

According to experienced claims adjusters at the insurance company, the GPF for sale items of the type destroyed in the fire rarely exceeds 48%. Consequently, the estimate of 50.8% appeared to be unusually high. (A 1% increase in GPF for items of this type equates to, approximately, an additional $16,000 in profit.) When the insurance company questioned the retailer on this issue, the retailer responded, "Our estimate was based on selecting two independent, random samples from the population of 3,005 invoices. Because the samples were selected randomly and the total sample size is large, the mean GPF estimate of 50.8% is valid."

A dispute arose between the furniture retailer and the insurance company, and a lawsuit was filed. In one portion of the suit, the insurance company accused the retailer of fraudulently representing their sampling methodology. Rather than selecting the samples randomly, the retailer was accused of selecting an unusual number of "high-profit" items from the population in order to increase the average GPF of the overall sample.

To support their claim of fraud, the insurance company hired a CPA firm to independently assess the retailer's Gross Profit Factor. Through the discovery process, the CPA firm legally obtained the paper invoices for the entire population of 3,005 items sold and input the information into a computer. The selling price, profit, profit margin, and month sold for these 3,005 furniture items are stored in the **FIRE** file, described below.

Your objective in this case is to use these data to determine the likelihood of fraud. Is it

(Making Business
Decisions Continued)

likely that a random sample of 253 items selected from the population of 3,005 items would yield a mean GPF of at least 50.8%? Or, is it likely that two independent, random samples of sizes 134 and 119 would yield mean GPFs of at least 50.6% and 51.0%, respectively? (These were the questions posed to a statistician retained by the CPA firm.) Use the ideas of probability and sampling distributions to guide your analysis.

Prepare a professional document that presents the results of your analysis and gives your opinion regarding fraud. Be sure to describe the assumptions and methodology used to arrive at your findings.

Variable	Type	Description
MONTH	QL	Month in which item was sold in 1991
INVOICE	QN	Invoice number
SALES	QN	Sales price of item in dollars
PROFIT	QN	Profit amount of item in dollars
MARGIN	QN	Profit margin of item = (Profit/Sales) × 100%

Data Set: FIRE

■ Answers to Selected Exercises

1 a. $(0, 0), (0, 2), (0, 4), (0, 6), (2, 0), (2, 2), (2, 4), (2, 6), (4, 0), (4, 2), (4, 4), (4, 6), (6, 0), (6, 2), (6, 4), (6, 6)$ **b.** $0, 1, 2, 3, 1, 2, 3, 4, 2, 3, 4, 5, 3, 4, 5, 6$ **c.** $\frac{1}{16}$ **d.** $p(0) = \frac{1}{16}, p(1) = \frac{2}{16}, p(2) = \frac{3}{16}, p(3) = \frac{4}{16}, p(4) = \frac{3}{16}, p(5) = \frac{2}{16}, p(6) = \frac{1}{16}$ **3 a.** $p(1) = .04, p(1.5) = .12,$ $p(2) = .17, p(2.5) = .20, p(3) = .20, p(3.5) = .14, p(4) = .08, p(4.5) = .04, p(5) = .01$ **c.** $.05$ **d.** No **5 a.** Same as Exercise 3a **9 a.** 5 **b.** $E(\bar{x}) = 5$ **c.** $E(m) = 4.778$ **d.** $\bar{x}$ **11 a.** yes **b.** median **13 b.** 1.61 **c.** $E(s^2) = 1.61$ **e.** $E(s) = 1.004$ **15** No **17 a.** 100, 5 **b.** 100, 2 **c.** 100, 1 **d.** 100, 1.414 **e.** 100, .447 **f.** 100, .316 **19 a.** .0228 **b.** .0668 **c.** .0062 **d.** .8185 **e.** .0013 **21 a.** .8944 **b.** .0228 **c.** .1292 **d.** .9699 **23 a.** Skewed right **b.** $\mu = 95.52, \sigma = 91.45$ **c.** Normal; $\mu_{\bar{x}} = 95.52$ and $\sigma_{\bar{x}} = 14.47$ **d.** .3520 **25 a.** 68 **b.** 4.02 **c.** Approx. normal **d.** .7734 **27** No; $P(\bar{x} < 103) = .0107$ **29 a.** $\approx$ normal with $\mu_{\bar{x}} = .53$ and $\sigma_{\bar{x}} = .0273$ **b.** .0336 **c.** Before: $p = .0139$; after: $p = .3557$; after **31 a.** .0034 **b.** ≈ 0; true mean is larger than 6 ppb **33** Not likely; $P(\bar{x} > 42) \approx 0$ **35** Handrubbing: $p = .2743$; handwashing: $p = .0047$; handrubbing **37 a.** $\mu_{\hat{p}} = .1, \sigma_{\hat{p}} = .0134$ **b.** $\mu_{\hat{p}} = .5, \sigma_{\hat{p}} = .0224$ **c.** $\mu_{\hat{p}} = .7,$ $\sigma_{\hat{p}} = .0205$ **39 a.** $E(\hat{p}) = .85, \sigma_{\hat{p}} = .0226$ **b.** Approx. normal **c.** .9864 **41 d.** As n increases, $\sigma_{\hat{p}}$ decreases; distributions all approx. normal **43 a.** .67 **b.** .0149 **c.** Approx. normal **d.** 1 **e.** 1 **45 a.** Approx. normal with $\mu_{\hat{p}} = .03$ and $\sigma_{\hat{p}} = .0054$ **b.** .9999 **c.** .8238 **47 a.** .0019 **b.** True $p > .4$ **c.** Sample not representative of target population **49 a.** .92 **b.** .0099 **51 b.** $E(A) = \theta$ **c.** Choose estimator with smaller variance **53 a.** .5 **b.** .0606 **c.** .0985 **d.** .8436 **55 a.** .9032 **b.** .9850 **c.** .3328 **61** .0838 **63 a.** .6 **b.** .0566 **c.** Approx. normal **d.** .0384 **65 a.** $\approx$ normal **b.** .0091 **c.** .9544 **67** .9772 **69 a.** $\mu_{\hat{p}} = .2, \sigma_{\hat{p}} = .0253$ **b.** $(.1494, .2596)$ **c.** .9544 **71 a.** .01; .002 **b.** $(.00164, .00236)$ **73 a.** 60; 6 **b.** Normal **c.** 0

■ Credits

☐ Technology Images

Where We're Going

◻ Estimate a population parameter
  (means, proportion, or variance)
  based on a large sample selected
  from the population (1)

◻ Use the sampling distribution of
  a statistic to form a confidence
  interval for the population
  parameter (2–4, 6, 7)

◻ Show how to select the proper
  sample size for estimating a
  population parameter (5)

◻ Inferences Based on a Single
Sample *Estimation with Confidence Intervals*

STATISTICS in ACTION **Medicare Fraud Investigations**

United States Department of Justice (USDOJ) press release (Feb. 17, 2011): *The Medicare Fraud Strike Force today charged 111 defendants in nine cities, including doctors, nurses, health care company owners and executives, and others, for their alleged participation in Medicare fraud schemes involving more than $225 million in false billing.*

The joint Department of Justice (DOJ) and Health and Human Services (HHS) Medicare Fraud Strike Force is a multi-agency team of federal, state, and local investigators designed to combat Medicare fraud through the use of Medicare data analysis techniques and an increased focus on community policing. More than 700 law enforcement agents from the FBI, HHS-Office of Inspector General (HHS-OIG), multiple Medicaid Fraud Control Units, and other state and local law enforcement agencies participated in today's operation. In addition to making arrests, agents also executed 16 search warrants across the country in connection with ongoing strike force investigations.

In Miami, 32 defendants . . . were charged for their participation in various fraud schemes involving a total of $55 million in false billings for home health care, durable medical equipment and prescription drugs.

Twenty-one defendants . . . were charged in Detroit for schemes to defraud Medicare of more than $23 million. [These] cases involve false claims for home health care, nerve conduction tests, psychotherapy, physical therapy and podiatry.

In Brooklyn, N.Y., 10 individuals . . . were charged with fraud schemes involving $90 million in false billings for physical therapy, proctology services and nerve conduction tests.

STATISTICS
in ACTION
CONTINUED

Ten defendants were charged in Tampa for participating in schemes involving more than $5 million related to false claims for physical therapy, durable medical equipment and pharmaceuticals.

Nine individuals were charged in Houston for schemes involving $8 million in fraudulent Medicare claims for physical therapy, durable medical equipment, home health care and chiropractor services.

In Dallas, seven defendants were indicted for conspiring to submit $2.8 million in false billing to Medicare related to durable medical equipment and home health care.

Five defendants were charged in Los Angeles for their roles in schemes to defraud Medicare of more than $28 million. [These] cases involve false claims for durable medical equipment and home health care.

In Baton Rouge, La., six individuals were charged for a durable medical equipment fraud scheme involving more than $9 million in false claims.

In Chicago, charges were filed against 11 individuals associated with businesses that have billed Medicare more than $6 million for home health [care], diagnostic testing and prescription drugs.

As the above press release implies, the U.S. Department of Justice (USDOJ) and its Medicare Fraud Strike Force conduct investigations into suspected fraud and abuse of the Medicare system by health care providers. According to published reports, the Strike Force is responsible for 25% of the Medicare fraud charges brought nationwide.

One way in which Medicare fraud occurs is through the use of "upcoding," which refers to the practice of providers coding Medicare claims at a higher level of care than was actually provided to the patient. For example, suppose a particular kind of claim can be coded at three levels, where Level 1 is a routine office visit, Level 2 is a thorough examination involving advanced diagnostic tests, and Level 3 involves performing minor surgery. The amount of Medicare payment is higher for each increased level of claim. Thus, upcoding would occur if Level 1 services were billed at Level 2 or Level 3 payments, or if Level 2 services were billed at Level 3 payment.

The USDOJ relies on sound statistical methods to help identify Medicare fraud. Once the USDOJ has determined that possible upcoding has occurred, it next seeks to further investigate whether it is the result of legitimate practice (perhaps the provider is a specialist giving higher levels of care) or the result of fraudulent action on the part of the provider. To further its investigation, the USDOJ will next ask a statistician to select a sample of the provider's claims. For example, the statistician might determine that a random sample of 52 claims from the 1,000 claims in question will provide a sufficient sample to estimate the overcharge reliably. The USDOJ then asks a health care expert to audit each of the medical files corresponding to the sampled claims and determine whether the level of care matches the level billed by the provider, and, if not, to determine what level should have been billed. Once the audit has been completed, the USDOJ will calculate the overcharge.

In this chapter, we present a recent Medicare fraud case investigated by the USDOJ. Results for the audit of 52 sampled claims, with the amount paid for each claim, the amount disallowed by the auditor, and the amount that should have been paid for each claim, are saved in the **MFRAUD** file.* Knowing that a total of $103,500 was paid for the 1,000 claims, the USDOJ wants to use the sample results to extrapolate the overpayment amount to the entire population of 1,000 claims.

STATISTICS in ACTION REVISITED

- Estimating the Mean Overpayment
- Estimating the Coding Error Rate
- Determining Sample Size

Data Set: MFRAUD

*Data provided (with permission) from Info Tech, Inc., Gainesville, Florida.

1 Identifying and Estimating the Target Parameter

In this chapter, our goal is to estimate the value of an unknown population parameter, such as a population mean or a proportion from a binomial population. For example, we might want to know the mean gas mileage for a new car model, the average expected life of a flat-screen computer monitor, or the proportion of dot-com companies that fail within a year of start-up.

You'll see that different techniques are used for estimating a mean or proportion, depending on whether a sample contains a large or small number of measurements. Nevertheless, our objectives remain the same. We want to use the sample information to estimate the population parameter of interest (called the **target parameter**) and assess the reliability of the estimate.

> The unknown population parameter (e.g., mean or proportion) that we are interested in estimating is called the **target parameter.**

Often, there are one or more key words in the statement of the problem that indicate the appropriate target parameter. Some key words associated with the two parameters covered in this section are listed in the following box.

Determining the Target Parameter

Parameter	Key Words or Phrases	Type of Data
μ	Mean; average	Quantitative
p	Proportion; percentage; fraction; rate	Qualitative
σ^2 (optional)	Variance; variability; spread	Quantitative

For the examples given above, the words *mean* in *mean gas mileage* and *average* in *average life expectancy* imply that the target parameter is the population mean, μ. The word *proportion* in *proportion of dot-com companies that fail within one year of start-up* indicates that the target parameter is the binomial proportion, p.

In addition to key words and phrases, the type of data (quantitative or qualitative) collected is indicative of the target parameter. With quantitative data, you are likely to be estimating the mean or variance of the data. With qualitative data with two outcomes (success or failure), the binomial proportion of successes is likely to be the parameter of interest.

A single number calculated from the sample that estimates a target population parameter is called a **point estimator.** For example, we'll use the sample mean, $\bar{x}$, to estimate the population mean μ. Consequently, $\bar{x}$ is a point estimator. Similarly, we'll learn that the sample proportion of successes, denoted $\hat{p}$, is a point estimator for the binomial proportion p and that the sample variance s^2 is a point estimator for the population variance σ^2. Also, we will attach a measure of reliability to our estimate by obtaining an **interval estimator**—a range of numbers that contain the target parameter with a high degree of confidence. For this reason the interval estimate is also called a **confidence interval.**

> A **point estimator** of a population parameter is a rule or formula that tells us how to use the sample data to calculate a *single* number that can be used as an *estimate* of the target parameter.

> An **interval estimator** (or **confidence interval**) is a formula that tells us how to use the sample data to calculate an *interval* that *estimates* the target parameter.

We consider confidence intervals for estimating a population mean in Sections 2 and Section 3. Confidence intervals for a population proportion are presented in Section 4. In Section 5, we show how to determine the sample sizes necessary for reliable estimates of the target parameters based on simple random sampling. Optional Section 6 presents a method to apply when the sample size is large relative to the population size. Finally, in Section 7 we discuss estimation of a population variance.

2   Confidence Interval for a Population Mean: Normal (z) Statistic

Suppose a large bank wants to estimate the average amount of money owed by its delinquent debtors (i.e., debtors who are more than 2 months behind in payment). To accomplish this objective, the bank plans to randomly sample 100 of its delinquent accounts and use the sample mean, $\bar{x}$, of the amounts overdue to estimate μ, the mean for *all* delinquent accounts. Because the sample mean $\bar{x}$ represents a single number estimator, it is the *point estimator* of the target parameter μ. How can we assess the accuracy of this point estimator?

According to the Central Limit Theorem, the sampling distribution of the sample mean is approximately normal for large samples, as shown in Figure 1. Let us calculate the interval estimator:

$$\bar{x} \pm 1.96\sigma_{\bar{x}} = \bar{x} \pm \frac{1.96\sigma}{\sqrt{n}}$$

That is, we form an interval from 1.96 standard deviations below the sample mean to 1.96 standard deviations above the mean. *Prior to drawing the sample,* what are the chances that this interval will enclose μ, the population mean?

To answer this question, refer to Figure 1. If the 100 measurements yield a value of $\bar{x}$ that falls between the two lines on either side of μ (i.e., within 1.96 standard deviations of μ), then the interval $\bar{x} \pm 1.96\sigma_{\bar{x}}$ will contain μ; if $\bar{x}$ falls outside these boundaries, the interval $\bar{x} \pm 1.96\sigma_{\bar{x}}$ will not contain μ. We know that the area under the normal curve (the sampling distribution of $\bar{x}$) between these boundaries is exactly .95. Thus, the probability that a randomly selected interval, $\bar{x} \pm 1.96\sigma_{\bar{x}}$, will contain μ is equal to .95.

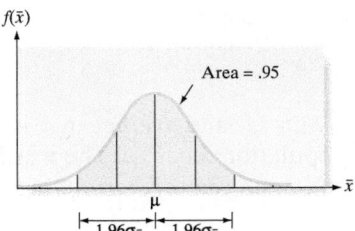

$f(\bar{x})$

Area = .95

$\bar{x}$

μ

$1.96\sigma_{\bar{x}}$ $1.96\sigma_{\bar{x}}$

Figure 1

Sampling distribution of $\bar{x}$

Example   1

Estimating the Mean, σ Known—Delinquent Debtors

Problem Consider the large bank that wants to estimate the average amount of money owed by its delinquent debtors, μ. The bank randomly samples $n = 100$ of its delinquent accounts and finds that the sample mean amount owed is $\bar{x} = \$230$. Also, suppose it is known that the standard deviation of the amount owed for all delinquent accounts is $\sigma = \$90$. Use the interval estimator $\bar{x} \pm 1.96\sigma_{\bar{x}}$ to calculate a confidence interval for the target parameter, μ.

Solution Substituting $\bar{x} = 230$ and $\sigma = 90$ into the interval estimator formula, we obtain:

$$\bar{x} \pm 1.96\sigma_{\bar{x}} = \bar{x} \pm (1.96)\sigma/\sqrt{n} = 230 \pm (1.96)(90/\sqrt{100}) = 230 \pm 17.64$$

Or, (212.36, 247.64). We can also obtain this confidence interval using statistical software, as shown (highlighted) on the Minitab printout, Figure 2.

One-Sample Z

The assumed standard deviation = 90

Figure 2

Minitab output showing 95%
confidence interval for μ, σ known

N	Mean	SE Mean	95% CI
100	230.00	9.00	(212.36, 247.64)

Look Back Because we know the probability that the interval $\bar{x} \pm 1.96\sigma_{\bar{x}}$ will contain μ is .95, we call the interval estimator a *95% confidence interval* for μ.

■ **Now Work Exercise 3a**

The interval $\bar{x} \pm 1.96\sigma_{\bar{x}}$ in Example 1 is called a *large-sample* 95% confidence interval for the population mean μ. The term *large-sample* refers to the sample being of sufficiently large size that we can apply the Central Limit Theorem and the normal (z) statistic to determine the form of the sampling distribution of $\bar{x}$. Empirical research suggests that a sample size n exceeding a value between 20 and 30 will usually yield a sampling distribution of $\bar{x}$ that is approximately normal. This result led many practitioners to adopt the rule of thumb that a sample size of $n \geq 30$ is required to use large-sample confidence interval procedures. Keep in mind, though, that 30 is not a magical number and, in fact, is quite arbitrary.

Also, *note that the large-sample interval estimator requires knowing the value of the population standard deviation, σ*. In most (if not nearly all) practical business applications, however, the value of σ will be unknown. For large samples, the fact that σ is unknown poses only a minor problem because the sample standard deviation s provides a very good approximation to σ*. The next example illustrates the more realistic large-sample confidence interval procedure.

Example 2

Estimating the Mean, σ Unknown—Delinquent Debtors

Problem Refer to Example 1 and the problem of estimating μ, the average amount of money owed by a bank's delinquent debtors. The overdue amounts for the $n = 100$ delinquent accounts are shown in Table 1. Use the data to find a 95% confidence interval for μ and interpret the result.

Table 1	Overdue Amounts (in Dollars) for 100 Delinquent Accounts								
195	243	132	133	209	400	142	312	221	289
221	162	134	275	355	293	242	458	378	148
278	222	236	178	202	222	334	208	194	135
363	221	449	265	146	215	113	229	221	243
512	193	134	138	209	207	206	310	293	310
237	135	252	365	371	238	232	271	121	134
203	178	180	148	162	160	86	234	244	266
119	259	108	289	328	331	330	227	162	354
304	141	158	240	82	17	357	187	364	268
368	274	278	190	344	157	219	77	171	280

 Data Set: OVRDUE

	A	B
1	AMOUNT	
2		
3	Mean	233.28
4	Standard Error	9.033988347
5	Median	222
6	Mode	221
7	Standard Deviation	90.33988347
8	Sample Variance	8161.294545
9	Kurtosis	0.254810234
10	Skewness	0.476799829
11	Range	495
12	Minimum	17
13	Maximum	512
14	Sum	23328
15	Count	100

Figure 3a

Excel summary statistics for overdue amounts

Solution The large bank almost surely does not know the true standard deviation, σ, of the population of overdue amounts. However, because the sample size is large, we will use the sample standard deviation, s, as an estimate for σ in the confidence interval formula. An Excel printout of summary statistics for the sample of 100 overdue amounts is shown in Figure 3a. From the shaded portion of the printout, we

*It can be shown that s is an *unbiased* estimator of σ.

find $\bar{x} = 233.28$ and $s = 90.34$. Substituting these values into the interval estimator formula, we obtain:

$$\bar{x} \pm (1.96)\sigma/\sqrt{n} \approx \bar{x} \pm (1.96)s/\sqrt{n} = 233.28 \pm (1.96)(90.34)/\sqrt{100} = 233.28 \pm 17.71$$

Or, $(215.57, 250.99)$. That is, we estimate the mean amount of delinquency for all accounts to fall within the interval $215.57 to $250.99.

Look Back The confidence interval is also shown (highlighted) at the bottom of the Excel/XLSTAT printout, Figure 3b. Note that the endpoints of the interval vary slightly from those computed in the example. This is due to the fact that when σ is unknown and n is large, the sampling distribution of $\bar{x}$ will deviate slightly from the normal (z) distribution. In practice, these differences can be ignored.

Statistic	AMOUNT
No. of observations	100
Minimum	17.0000
Maximum	512.0000
Mean	233.2800
Standard deviation (n-1)	90.3399
Lower bound on mean (95%)	215.3546
Upper bound on mean (95%)	251.2054

Figure 3b

XLSTAT output showing 95% confidence interval for μ, σ unknown

Now Work Exercise 14

Can we be sure that μ, the true mean, is in the interval $(215.57, 250.99)$ in Example 2? We cannot be certain, but we can be reasonably confident that it is. This confidence is derived from the knowledge that if we were to draw repeated random samples of 100 measurements from this population and form the interval $\bar{x} \pm 1.96\sigma_{\bar{x}}$ each time, 95% of the intervals would contain μ. We have no way of knowing (without looking at all the delinquent accounts) whether our sample interval is one of the 95% that contains μ or one of the 5% that does not, but the odds certainly favor its containing μ. The probability, .95, that measures the confidence we can place in the interval estimate is called a *confidence coefficient*. The percentage, 95%, is called the *confidence level* for the interval estimate.

> The **confidence coefficient** is the probability that a randomly selected confidence interval encloses the population parameter—that is, the relative frequency with which similarly constructed intervals enclose the population parameter when the estimator is used repeatedly a very large number of times. The **confidence level** is the confidence coefficient expressed as a percentage.

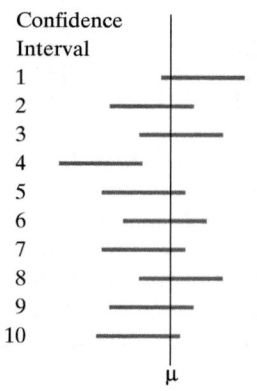

Confidence
Interval
1
2
3
4
5
6
7
8
9
10

μ

Figure 4

Confidence intervals for μ: 10 samples

Now we have seen how an interval can be used to estimate a population mean. When we use an interval estimator, we can usually calculate the probability that the estimation *process* will result in an interval that contains the true value of the population mean—that is, the probability that the interval contains the parameter in repeated usage is usually known. Figure 4 shows what happens when 10 different samples are drawn from a population, and a confidence interval for μ is calculated from each. The location of μ is indicated by the vertical line in the figure. Ten confidence intervals, each based on one of 10 samples, are shown as horizontal line segments. Note that the confidence intervals move from sample to sample—sometimes containing μ and other times missing μ. *If our confidence level is 95%, then in the long run, 95% of our confidence intervals will contain μ and 5% will not.*

Suppose you wish to choose a confidence coefficient other than .95. Notice in Figure 1 that the confidence coefficient .95 is equal to the total area under the sampling distribution, less .05 of the area, which is divided equally between the two tails. Using this idea, we can construct a confidence interval with any desired confidence coefficient by increasing or decreasing the area (call it α) assigned to the tails of the sampling distribution (see Figure 5). For example, if we place area $\frac{\alpha}{2}$ in each tail and if $z_{\alpha/2}$ is the z-value such that the area $\frac{\alpha}{2}$ lies to its right, then the confidence interval with confidence coefficient $(1 - \alpha)$ is

$$\bar{x} \pm (z_{\alpha/2})\sigma_{\bar{x}}$$

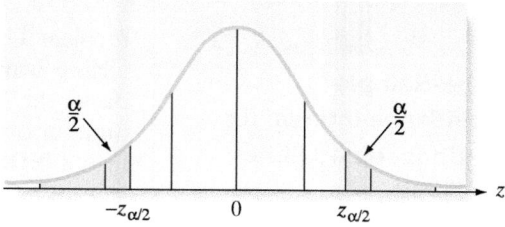

Figure 5

Locating $z_{\alpha/2}$ on the standard normal curve

The value z_α is defined as the value of the standard normal random variable z such that the area α will lie to its right. In other words, $P(z > z_\alpha) = \alpha$.

To illustrate, for a confidence coefficient of .90, we have $(1 - \alpha) = .90$, $\alpha = .10$, and $\frac{\alpha}{2} = .05$; $z_{.05}$ is the z-value that locates area .05 in the upper tail of the sampling distribution. Recall that Table II in Appendix: Tables gives the areas between the mean and a specified z-value. Because the total area to the right of the mean is .5, we find that $z_{.05}$ will be the z-value corresponding to an area of $.5 - .05 = .45$ to the right of the mean (see Figure 6). This z-value is $z_{.05} = 1.645$.

Confidence coefficients used in practice usually range from .90 to .99. The most commonly used confidence coefficients with corresponding values of α and $z_{\alpha/2}$ are shown in Table 2.

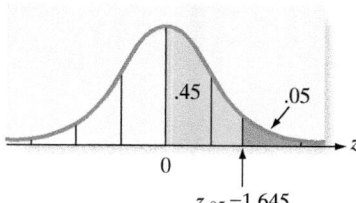

Figure 6

The z-value $(z_{.05})$ corresponding to an area equal to .05 in the upper tail of the z-distribution

---

Large-Sample $100(1 - \alpha)\%$ Confidence Interval for μ, Based on a Normal (z) Statistic

$$\sigma \text{ known: } \bar{x} \pm (z_{\alpha/2})\sigma_{\bar{x}} = \bar{x} \pm (z_{\alpha/2})(\sigma/\sqrt{n})$$
$$\sigma \text{ unknown: } \bar{x} \pm (z_{\alpha/2})\sigma_{\bar{x}} \approx \bar{x} \pm (z_{\alpha/2})(s/\sqrt{n})$$

where $z_{\alpha/2}$ is the z-value corresponding to an area $\frac{\alpha}{2}$ in the tail of a standard normal distribution (see Figure 5), $\sigma_{\bar{x}}$ is the standard deviation of the sampling distribution of $\bar{x}$, σ is the standard deviation of the population, and s is the standard deviation of the sample.

Conditions Required for a Valid Large-Sample Confidence Interval for μ

1. A random sample is selected from the target population.
2. The sample size n is large (i.e., $n \geq 30$). Due to the Central Limit Theorem, this condition guarantees that the sampling distribution of $\bar{x}$ is approximately normal. (Also, for large n, s will be a good estimator of σ.)

BIOGRAPHY

JERZEY NEYMAN (1894–1981)
Speaking Statistics with a Polish Accent

Polish-born Jerzey Neyman was educated at the University of Kharkov (Russia) in elementary mathematics but taught himself graduate mathematics by studying journal articles on the subject. After receiving his doctorate in 1924 from the University of Warsaw (Poland), Neyman accepted a position at University College (London). There, he developed a friendship with Egon Pearson; Neyman and Pearson together developed the theory of hypothesis testing. In 1934, in a talk to the Royal Statistical Society, Neyman first proposed the idea of interval estimation, which he called *confidence intervals*. (It is interesting that Neyman rarely receives credit in textbooks as the originator of the confidence interval procedure.) In 1938, he immigrated to the United States and the University of California at Berkeley. At Berkeley, he built one of the strongest statistics departments in the country. Jerzey Neyman is considered one of the great founders of modern statistics. He was a superb teacher and innovative researcher who loved his students, always sharing his ideas with them. Neyman's influence on those he met is best expressed by a quote from prominent statistician David Salsburg: "We have all learned to speak statistics with a Polish accent."

Table 2	Commonly Used Values of $z_{\alpha/2}$		
Confidence Level			
$100(1 - \alpha)$	α	$\alpha/2$	$z_{\alpha/2}$
90%	.10	.05	1.645
95%	.05	.025	1.960
98%	.02	.01	2.326
99%	.01	.005	2.576

Example 3

Large-Sample Confidence Interval for μ — Unoccupied Seats per Flight

Problem Unoccupied seats on flights cause airlines to lose revenue. Suppose a large airline wants to estimate its average number of unoccupied seats per flight over the past year. To accomplish this, the records of 225 flights are randomly selected, and the number of unoccupied seats is noted for each of the sampled flights. (The data are saved in the **NOSHOW** file.) Descriptive statistics for the data are displayed in the Minitab printout, Figure 7.

```
Variable    N    Mean   StDev  SE Mean      90% CI
NOSHOWS    225  11.596  4.103    0.274  (11.144, 12.047)
```

Figure 7
Minitab confidence interval for mean, Example 3

Estimate μ, the mean number of unoccupied seats per flight during the past year, using a 90% confidence interval.

Solution The general form of the 90% confidence interval for a population mean is

$$\bar{x} \pm z_{\alpha/2}\sigma_{\bar{x}} = \bar{x} \pm z_{.05}\sigma_{\bar{x}} = \bar{x} \pm 1.645\left(\frac{\sigma}{\sqrt{n}}\right)$$

From Figure 7, we find (after rounding) $\bar{x} = 11.6$. Because we do not know the value of σ (the standard deviation of the number of unoccupied seats per flight for all flights of the year), we use our best approximation—the sample standard deviation s. Then the 90% confidence interval is, approximately,

$$11.6 \pm 1.645\left(\frac{4.1}{\sqrt{225}}\right) = 11.6 \pm .45$$

or from 11.15 to 12.05—that is, at the 90% confidence level, we estimate the mean number of unoccupied seats per flight to be between 11.15 and 12.05 during the sampled year. This result is verified (except for rounding) on the right side of the Minitab printout in Figure 7.

Look Back We stress that the confidence level for this example, 90%, refers to the procedure used. If we were to apply this procedure repeatedly to different samples, approximately 90% of the intervals would contain μ. Although we do not know whether this particular interval (11.15, 12.05) is one of the 90% that contain μ or one of the 10% that do not, our knowledge of probability gives us "confidence" that the interval contains μ.

Now Work Exercise 12

The interpretation of confidence intervals for a population mean is summarized in the next box.

Interpretation of a Confidence Interval for a Population Mean

When we form a $100(1 - \alpha)\%$ confidence interval for μ, we usually express our confidence in the interval with a statement such as, "We can be $100(1 - \alpha)\%$ confident that μ lies between the lower and upper bounds of the confidence interval," where for a particular application, we substitute the appropriate numerical values for the confidence and for the lower and upper bounds. *The statement reflects our confidence in the estimation process rather than in the particular interval that is calculated from the sample data.* We know that repeated application of the same procedure will result in different lower and upper bounds on the interval. Furthermore, we know that $100(1 - \alpha)\%$ of the resulting intervals will contain μ. There is (usually) no way to determine whether any particular interval is one of those that contain μ, or one that does not. However, unlike point estimators, confidence intervals have some measure of reliability, the confidence coefficient, associated with them. For that reason they are generally preferred to point estimators.

Sometimes, the estimation procedure yields a confidence interval that is too wide for our purposes. In this case, we will want to reduce the width of the interval to obtain a more precise estimate of μ. One way to accomplish this is to decrease the confidence coefficient, $1 - \alpha$. For example, reconsider the problem of estimating the mean amount owed, μ, for all delinquent accounts. Recall that for a sample of 100 accounts, $\bar{x} = \$233.28$ and $s = \$90.34$. A 90% confidence interval for μ is

$$\bar{x} \pm 1.645\sigma/\sqrt{n} \approx 233.28 \pm (1.645)(90.34/\sqrt{100}) = 233.28 \pm 14.86$$

or ($218.42, $248.14). You can see that this interval is narrower than the previously calculated 95% confidence interval ($215.57, $250.99). Unfortunately, we also have "less confidence" in the 90% confidence interval. An alternative method used to decrease the width of an interval without sacrificing "confidence" is to increase the sample size n. We demonstrate this method in Section 5.

Exercises 1–22

Please be aware that some of the following problems may require knowledge of concepts that are not presented in this chapter.

Learning the Mechanics

1 Find $z_{\alpha/2}$ for each of the following:
a. $\alpha = .10$ **b.** $\alpha = .01$
c. $\alpha = .05$ **d.** $\alpha = .20$

2 What is the confidence level of each of the following confidence intervals for μ?

a. $\bar{x} \pm 1.96\left(\dfrac{\sigma}{\sqrt{n}}\right)$ **b.** $\bar{x} \pm 1.645\left(\dfrac{\sigma}{\sqrt{n}}\right)$

c. $\bar{x} \pm 2.575\left(\dfrac{\sigma}{\sqrt{n}}\right)$ **d.** $\bar{x} \pm 1.282\left(\dfrac{\sigma}{\sqrt{n}}\right)$

e. $\bar{x} \pm .99\left(\dfrac{\sigma}{\sqrt{n}}\right)$

3 A random sample of n measurements was selected from a population with unknown mean μ and known standard deviation σ. Calculate a 95% confidence interval for μ for each of the following situations:
a. $n = 75, \bar{x} = 28, \sigma^2 = 12$
b. $n = 200, \bar{x} = 102, \sigma^2 = 22$
c. $n = 100, \bar{x} = 15, \sigma = .3$
d. $n = 100, \bar{x} = 4.05, \sigma = .83$
e. Is the assumption that the underlying population of measurements is normally distributed necessary to ensure the validity of the confidence intervals in parts **a–d**? Explain.

4 A random sample of 90 observations produced a mean $\bar{x} = 25.9$ and a standard deviation $s = 2.7$.
a. Find an approximate 95% confidence interval for the population mean μ.
b. Find an approximate 90% confidence interval for μ.
c. Find an approximate 99% confidence interval for μ.

5 A random sample of 70 observations from a normally distributed population possesses a sample mean equal to 26.2 and a sample standard deviation equal to 4.1.
a. Find an approximate 95% confidence interval for μ.
b. What do you mean when you say that a confidence coefficient is .95?
c. Find an approximate 99% confidence interval for μ.

d. What happens to the width of a confidence interval as the value of the confidence coefficient is increased while the sample size is held fixed?
e. Would your confidence intervals of parts **a** and **c** be valid if the distribution of the original population was not normal? Explain.

Applet Exercise 1

Use the applet *Confidence Intervals for a Mean (the impact of confidence level)* to investigate the situation in Exercise 5 further. For this exercise, assume that $\mu = 2.62$ is the population mean and $\sigma = 4.1$ is the population standard deviation.
a. Using $n = 70$ and the normal distribution with the mean and standard deviation above, run the applet one time. How many of the 95% confidence intervals contain the mean? How many would you expect to contain the mean? How many of the 99% confidence intervals contain the mean? How many would you expect to contain the mean?
b. Which confidence level has a greater frequency of intervals that contain the mean? Is this result what you would expect? Explain.
c. Without clearing, run the applet several more times. What happens to the proportion of 95% confidence intervals that contain the mean as you run the applet more and more? What happens to the proportion of 99% confidence intervals that contain the mean as you run the applet more and more? Interpret these results in terms of the meanings of the 95% confidence interval and the 99% confidence interval.
d. Change the distribution to *right skewed*, clear, and run the applet several more times. Do you get the same results as in part **c?** Would you change your answer to part **e** of Exercise 5? Explain.

Applet Exercise 2

Use the applet *Confidence Intervals for a Mean (the impact of confidence level)* to investigate the effect of the sample size on the proportion of confidence intervals that contain the mean when the underlying distribution is skewed. Set the distribution to *right skewed*, the mean to 10, and the standard deviation to 1.

a. Using $n = 30$, run the applet several times without clearing. What happens to the proportion of 95% confidence intervals that contain the mean as you run the applet more and more? What happens to the proportion of 99% confidence intervals that contain the mean as you run the applet more and more? Do the proportions seem to be approaching the values that you would expect?

b. Clear and run the applet several times using $n = 100$. What happens to the proportions of 95% confidence intervals and 99% confidence intervals that contain the mean this time? How do these results compare to your results in part **a**?

c. Clear and run the applet several times using $n = 1,000$. How do the results compare to your results in parts **a** and **b**?

d. Describe the effect of sample size on the likelihood that a confidence interval contains the mean for a skewed distribution.

6 Explain what is meant by the statement, "We are 95% confident that an interval estimate contains μ."

7 Explain the difference between an interval estimator and a point estimator for μ.

8 The mean and standard deviation of a random sample of n measurements are equal to 33.9 and 3.3, respectively.
a. Find a 95% confidence interval for μ if $n = 100$.
b. Find a 95% confidence interval for μ if $n = 400$.
c. Find the widths of the confidence intervals found in parts **a** and **b**. What is the effect on the width of a confidence interval of quadrupling the sample size while holding the confidence coefficient fixed?

9 Will a large-sample confidence interval be valid if the population from which the sample is taken is not normally distributed? Explain.

Applying the Concepts—Basic

10 **Bankruptcy effect on U.S. airfares.** Recently, both Delta Airlines and USAir filed for bankruptcy. A study of the impact of bankruptcy on the fares charged by U.S. airlines was published in *Research in Applied Economics* (Vol. 2, 2010). The researchers collected data on Orlando-bound airfares for three airlines in 2005—Southwest (a stable airline), Delta (just entering bankruptcy at the time), and USAir (emerging from bankruptcy). A large sample of nonrefundable ticket prices was obtained for each airline following USAir's emergence from bankruptcy, and then a 95% confidence interval for the true mean airfare was obtained for each. The results for 7-day advanced bookings are shown in the accompanying table.

Airline	95% Confidence Interval
Southwest	($412, $496)
Delta	($468, $500)
USAir	($247, $372)

Source: Based on Sturm, R. R & Winters, D. B. "The Effect of Bankruptcy on U.S. Air Fares," *Research in Applied Economics* Vol. 2, No. 2, © 2010 Macrothink Institute.

a. What confidence coefficient was used to generate the confidence intervals?
b. Give a practical interpretation of each of the 95% confidence intervals. Use the phrase "95% confident" in your answer.

c. When you say you are "95% confident," what do you mean?
d. If you want to reduce the width of each confidence interval, should you use a smaller or larger confidence coefficient? Explain.

11 **College dropout study.** The *American Economic Review* (Dec. 2008) did a study of college dropouts. One factor thought to influence the college dropout decision was expected GPA for a student who studied 3 hours per day. In a representative sample of 307 college students who studied 3 hours per day, the mean GPA was $\bar{x} = 3.11$ and the standard deviation was $s = .66$. Of interest is μ, the true mean GPA of all college students who study 3 hours per day.
a. Give a point estimate for μ.
b. Give an interval estimate for μ. Use a confidence coefficient of .98.
c. Comment on the validity of the following statement: "98% of the time, the true mean GPA will fall in the interval computed in part **b**."
d. It is unlikely that the GPA values for college students who study 3 hours per day are normally distributed. In fact, it is likely that the GPA distribution is highly skewed. If so, what impact, if any, does this have on the validity of inferences derived from the confidence interval?

12 **Corporate sustainability of CPA firms.** *Corporate sustainability* refers to business practices designed around social and environmental considerations. *Business and Society* (March 2011) did a study on the sustainability behaviors of CPA corporations. The level of support for corporate sustainability (measured on a quantitative scale ranging from 0 to 160 points) was obtained for each in a sample of 992 senior managers at CPA firms. Higher point values indicate a higher level of support for sustainability. The accompanying Minitab printout gives a 90% confidence interval for the mean level of support for all senior managers at CPA firms.

CORSUS
NW

One-Sample T: Support

Variable	N	Mean	StDev	SE Mean	90% CI
Support	992	67.755	26.871	0.853	(66.350, 69.160)

a. Locate the 90% confidence interval on the printout.
b. Use the sample mean and standard deviation on the printout to calculate the 90% confidence interval. Does your result agree with the interval shown on the printout?
c. Give a practical interpretation of the 90% confidence interval.
d. Suppose the CEO of a CPA firm claims that the true mean level of support for sustainability is 75 points. Do you believe this claim Explain.

13 **Budget lapsing at army hospitals.** Budget lapsing occurs when unspent funds do not carry over from one budgeting period to the next. The *Journal of Management Accounting Research* (Vol. 19, 2007) did a study on budget lapsing at U.S. Army hospitals. Because budget lapsing often leads to a spike in expenditures at the end of the fiscal year, the researchers recorded expenses per full-time equivalent employee for each in a sample of 1,751 army hospitals. The sample yielded the following summary statistics: $\bar{x} = \$6,563$ and $s = \$2,484$. Estimate the mean expenses per full-time equivalent employee of all U.S. Army hospitals using a 90% confidence interval. Interpret the result.

14 Wear-out of used display panels. A study was done on the wear-out failure time of used colored display panels purchased by an outlet store. Prior to acquisition, the panels had been used for about one-third of their expected lifetimes. The failure times (in years) for a sample of 50 used panels are reproduced in the table. An SPSS printout of the analysis is shown below.

PANEL
NW

a. Locate a 95% confidence interval for the true mean failure time of used colored display panels on the printout.
b. Give a practical interpretation of the interval, part **a.**
c. In repeated sampling of the population of used colored display panels, where a 95% confidence interval for the mean failure time is computed for each sample, what proportion of all the confidence intervals generated will capture the true mean failure time?

0.01	1.21	1.71	2.30	2.96	0.19	1.22	1.75	2.30	2.98	0.51
1.24	1.77	2.41	3.19	0.57	1.48	1.79	2.44	3.25	0.70	1.54
1.88	2.57	3.31	0.73	1.59	1.90	2.61	1.19	0.75	1.61	1.93
2.62	3.50	0.75	1.61	2.01	2.72	3.50	1.11	1.62	2.16	2.76
3.50	1.16	1.62	2.18	2.84	3.50					

Source: Based on Irony, T. Z., Lauretto, M., Pereira, C., & Stern, J. M. "A Weibull wearout Test: Full Bayesian approach," paper presented at *Mathematical Sciences Colloquium*, Binghamton University, Binghamton, UK, December 2001.

Applying the Concepts—Intermediate

15 Do social robots walk or roll? The *International Conference on Social Robotics* (Vol. 6414, 2010) did a study on the current trend in the design of social robots. In a random sample of social robots obtained through a Web search, 28 were built with wheels. The number of wheels on each of the 28 robots are reproduced in the next table.

ROBOTS

a. Estimate μ, the average number of wheels used on all social robots built with wheels, with 99% confidence.
b. Practically interpret the interval, part **a.**

c. Refer to part **a.** In repeated sampling, what proportion of all similarly constructed confidence intervals will contain the true mean, μ?

4	4	3	3	3	6	4	2	2	2	1	3	3	3
3	4	4	3	2	8	2	2	3	4	3	3	4	2

Source: Based on Chew, S., et al. "Do social robots walk or roll?," *International Conference on Social Robotics,* Vol. 6414, 2010 (adapted from Figure 2).

16 Shopping on Black Friday. The day after Thanksgiving—called Black Friday—is one of the largest shopping days in the United States. Winthrop University researchers conducted interviews with a sample of 38 women shopping on Black Friday to gauge their shopping habits and reported the results in the *International Journal of Retail and Distribution Management* (Vol. 39, 2011). One question was "How many hours do you usually spend shopping on Black Friday?" Data for the 38 shoppers are listed in the accompanying table.

BLKFRI

a. Describe the population of interest to the researchers.
b. What is the quantitative variable of interest to the researchers?
c. Use the information in the table to estimate the population mean number of hours spent shopping on Black Friday with a 95% confidence interval.
d. Give a practical interpretation of the interval.
e. A retail store advertises that the true mean number of hours spent shopping on Black Friday is 5.5 hours. Can the store be sued for false advertising? Explain.

6	6	4	4	3	16	4	4	5	6	6	5	5	4
6	5	6	4	5	4	4	4	7	12	5	8	6	10
5	8	8	3	3	8	5	6	10	11				

Source: Based on Thomas, J. B., & Peters, C. "An exploratory investigation of Black Friday consumption rituals," *International Journal of Retail and Distribution Management,* Vol. 39, No. 7, 2011 (Table I).

17 Executive Compensation Scoreboard. Refer to *Forbes'* 2011 "Executive Compensation Scoreboard." Recall that the data file contains the 2011 salaries (in $ millions) of the 500 CEOs that participated in the *Forbes'* survey. Suppose you are interested in estimating the mean 2011 salary for these 500 CEOs.

CEOPAY

a. What is the target parameter?
b. Obtain a random sample of 50 salaries from the data set.

Descriptives

			Statistic	Std. Error
FAILTIME	Mean		1.9350	.13133
	95% Confidence Interval for Mean	Lower Bound	1.6711	
		Upper Bound	2.1989	
	5% Trimmed Mean		1.9454	
	Median		1.8350	
	Variance		.862	
	Std. Deviation		.92865	
	Minimum		.01	
	Maximum		3.50	
	Range		3.49	
	Interquartile Range		1.43	
	Skewness		-.008	.337
	Kurtosis		-.755	.662

SPSS output for Exercise 14

c. Find the mean of the 50 salaries, part **b.**

d. Verify that the standard deviation for the population of 500 salaries is $\sigma = \$9.84$ million.

e. Use the information, parts **c** and **d,** to form a 99% confidence interval for the true mean 2011 salary of the 500 CEOs in the *Forbes'* survey.

f. Give a practical interpretation of the interval, part **e.**

g. Find the true mean salary of the 500 CEOs and check to see if this value falls within the 99% confidence interval, part **e.**

18 **401(k) Participation rates.** Named for the section of the 1978 Internal Revenue Code that authorized them, 401(k) plans permit employees to shift part of their before-tax salaries into investments such as mutual funds. Employers typically match 50% of the employee's contribution up to about 6% of salary. One company, concerned with what it believed was a low employee participation rate in its 401(k) plan, sampled 30 other companies with similar plans and asked for their 401(k) participation rates. The following rates (in percentages) were obtained.

PR401K

80	76	81	77	82	80	85	60	80	79	82	70
88	85	80	79	83	75	87	78	80	84	72	75
90	84	82	77	75	86						

a. Construct a 90% confidence interval for the mean participation rate for all companies that have 401(k) plans.

b. Interpret the interval in the context of this problem.

c. What assumption is necessary to ensure the validity of this confidence interval?

d. If the company that conducted the sample has a 71% participation rate, can it safely conclude that its rate is below the population mean rate for all companies with 401(k) plans? Explain.

e. If in the data set the 60% had been 80%, how would the center and width of the confidence interval you constructed in part **a** be affected?

19 **Accounting and Machiavellianism.** *Behavioral Research in Accounting* (Jan. 2008) did a study of Machiavellian traits in accountants. *Machiavellian* describes negative character traits that include manipulation, cunning, duplicity, deception, and bad faith. A Machiavellian ("Mach") rating score was determined for each in a sample of accounting alumni of a large southwestern university. Scores range from a low of 40 to a high of 160, with the theoretical neutral Mach rating score of 100. The 122 purchasing managers in the sample had a mean Mach rating score of 99.6, with a standard deviation of 12.6.

a. From the sample, estimate the true mean Mach rating score of all purchasing managers.

b. Form a 95% confidence interval for the estimate, part **b.**

c. Give a practical interpretation of the interval, part **c.**

d. A director of purchasing at a major firm claims that the true mean Mach rating score of all purchasing managers is 85. Is there evidence to dispute this claim?

20 **Facial structure of CEOs.** In *Psychological Science* (Vol. 22, 2011), researchers reported that a chief executive officer's facial structure can be used to predict a firm's financial performance. The study involved measuring the facial width-to-height ratio (WHR) for each in a sample of 55 CEOs at publicly traded *Fortune* 500 firms. These WHR values (determined by a computer analyzing a photo of the CEO's face) had a mean of $\bar{x} = 1.96$ and a standard deviation of $s = .15$.

a. Find and interpret a 95% confidence interval for μ, the mean facial WHR for all CEOs at publicly traded *Fortune* 500 firms.

b. The researchers found that CEOs with wider faces (relative to height) tended to be associated with firms that had greater financial performance. They based their inference on an equation that uses facial WHR to predict financial performance. Suppose an analyst wants to predict the financial performance of a *Fortune* 500 firm based on the value of the true mean facial WHR of CEOs. The analyst wants to use the value of $\mu = 2.2$. Do you recommend he use this value?

Applying the Concepts—Advanced

21 **Improving SAT scores.** *Chance* (Winter 2001) and National Education Longitudinal Survey (NELS) did a study of 265 students who paid a private tutor to help them improve their SAT scores. The changes in both the SAT–Mathematics and SAT–Verbal scores for these students are reproduced in the table. Suppose the true population mean change in score on one of the SAT tests for all students who paid a private tutor is 15. Which of the two tests, SAT–Mathematics or SAT–Verbal, is most likely to have this mean change? Explain.

	SAT–Math	SAT–Verbal
Mean change in score	19	7
Standard deviation of score changes	65	49

22 **The "Raid" test kitchen.** According to scientists, the cockroach has had 300 million years to develop a resistance to destruction. In a study conducted by researchers for S. C. Johnson & Son, Inc. (manufacturers of Raid and Off!), 5,000 roaches (the expected number in a roach-infested house) were released in the Raid test kitchen. One week later, the kitchen was fumigated, and 16,298 dead roaches were counted, a gain of 11,298 roaches for the 1-week period. Assume that none of the original roaches died during the 1-week period and that the standard deviation of x, the number of roaches produced per roach in a 1-week period, is 1.5. Use the number of roaches produced by the sample of 5,000 roaches to find a 95% confidence interval for the mean number of roaches produced per week for each roach in a typical roach-infested house.

3 Confidence Interval for a Population Mean: Student's *t*-Statistic

Federal legislation requires pharmaceutical companies to perform extensive tests on new drugs before they can be marketed. Initially, a new drug is tested on animals. If the drug is deemed safe after this first phase of testing, the pharmaceutical company is then permitted to begin human testing on a limited basis. During this second phase, inferences must be made about the safety of the drug based on information in very small samples.

Suppose a pharmaceutical company must estimate the average increase in blood pressure of patients who take a certain new drug. Assume that only six patients (randomly selected from the population of all patients) can be used in the initial phase of human testing. The use of a *small sample* in making an inference about μ presents two immediate problems when we attempt to use the standard normal z as a test statistic.

Problem 1   The shape of the sampling distribution of the sample mean $\bar{x}$ (and the z-statistic) now depends on the shape of the population that is sampled. We can no longer assume that the sampling distribution of $\bar{x}$ is approximately normal because the Central Limit Theorem ensures normality only for samples that are sufficiently large.

Solution to Problem 1   The sampling distribution of $\bar{x}$ (and z) is exactly normal, even for small samples, if the sampled population is normal. It is approximately normal if the sampled population is approximately normal.

Problem 2   The population standard deviation σ is almost always unknown. Although it is still true that $\sigma_{\bar{x}} = \frac{\sigma}{\sqrt{n}}$, the sample standard deviation s may provide a poor approximation for σ when the sample size is small.

Solution to Problem 2   Instead of using the standard normal statistic

$$z = \frac{\bar{x} - \mu}{\sigma_{\bar{x}}} = \frac{\bar{x} - \mu}{\sigma/\sqrt{n}}$$

which requires knowledge of or a good approximation to σ, we define and use the statistic

$$t = \frac{\bar{x} - \mu}{s/\sqrt{n}}$$

in which the sample standard deviation, s, replaces the population standard deviation, σ.

If we are sampling from a normal distribution, the *t*-statistic has a sampling distribution very much like that of the *z*-statistic: mound-shaped, symmetric, with mean 0. The primary difference between the sampling distributions of *t* and *z* is that the *t*-statistic is more variable than the *z*, which follows intuitively when you realize that *t* contains two random quantities ($\bar{x}$ and *s*), whereas *z* contains only one ($\bar{x}$).

The actual amount of variability in the sampling distribution of *t* depends on the sample size *n*. A convenient way of expressing this dependence is to say that the *t*-statistic has $(n - 1)$ **degrees of freedom (df).** Recall that the quantity $(n - 1)$ is the divisor that appears in the formula for s^2. This number plays a key role in the sampling distribution of s^2. In particular, the smaller the number of degrees of freedom associated with the *t*-statistic, the more variable will be its sampling distribution.

In Figure 8 we show both the sampling distribution of *z* and the sampling distribution of a *t*-statistic with 4 and 20 df. Note that the *t*-distribution is more variable than the *z*-distribution, and this variability increases as the degrees of freedom decrease. Also, the increased variability of the *t*-statistic means that the *t*-value, t_α, that locates an area α in the upper tail of the *t*-distribution is larger than the corresponding value z_α. For any given value of α, the *t*-value t_α increases as the df decreases. Values of *t* that will be used in forming small-sample confidence intervals of μ are given in Table III in Appendix: Tables. A partial reproduction of this table is shown in Table 3

Figure 8

Standard normal (*z*) distribution and *t*-distributions

Table 3 Reproduction of Part of Table III in Appendix: Tables

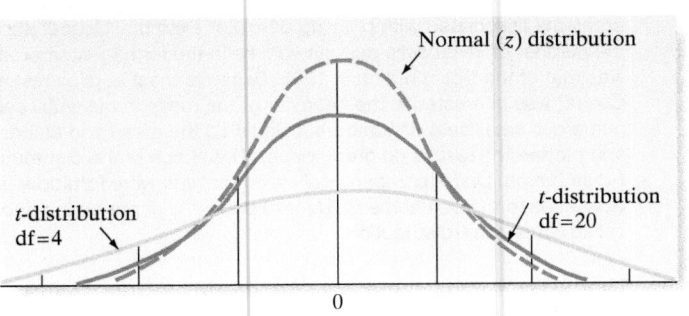

Degrees of Freedom	$t_{.100}$	$t_{.050}$	$t_{.025}$	$t_{.010}$	$t_{.005}$	$t_{.001}$	$t_{.0005}$
1	3.078	6.314	12.706	31.821	63.657	318.13	636.62
2	1.886	2.920	4.303	6.965	9.925	22.326	21.598
3	1.638	2.353	3.182	4.541	5.841	10.213	12.924
4	1.533	2.132	2.776	3.747	4.604	7.173	8.610
5	1.476	2.015	2.571	3.365	4.032	5.893	6.869
6	1.440	1.943	2.447	3.132	3.707	5.208	5.959
7	1.415	1.895	2.365	2.998	3.499	4.785	5.408
8	1.397	1.860	2.306	2.896	3.355	4.501	5.041
9	1.383	1.833	2.262	2.821	3.250	4.297	4.781
10	1.372	1.812	2.228	2.764	3.169	4.144	4.587
11	1.363	1.796	2.201	2.718	3.106	4.025	4.437
12	1.356	1.782	2.179	2.681	3.055	3.930	4.318
13	1.350	1.771	2.160	2.650	3.012	3.852	4.221
14	1.345	1.761	2.145	2.624	2.977	3.787	4.140
15	1.341	1.753	2.131	2.602	2.947	3.733	4.073
⋮	⋮	⋮	⋮	⋮	⋮	⋮	⋮
∞	1.282	1.645	1.960	2.326	2.576	3.090	3.291

Note that t_α values are listed for various degrees of freedom, where α refers to the tail area under the t-distribution to the right of t_α. For example, if we want the t-value with an area of .025 to its right and 4 df, we look in the table under the column $t_{.025}$ for the entry in the row corresponding to 4 df. This entry, $t_{.025} = 2.776$, is highlighted in Figure 8. Recall that the corresponding standard normal z-score is $z_{.025} = 1.96$.

The last row of Table III, where df $= \infty$ (infinity), contains the standard normal z-values. This follows from the fact that as the sample size n grows very large, s becomes closer to σ and thus t becomes closer in distribution to z. In fact, when df $= 29$, there is little difference between corresponding tabulated values of z and t. Thus, researchers often choose the arbitrary cutoff of $n = 30$ (df $= 29$) to distinguish between the large-sample and small-sample inferential techniques when σ is unknown.

Example 4

A Confidence Interval for μ Using the t-statistic — Blood Pressure Drug

Table 4

Blood Pressure Increases for $n = 6$ Patients

1.7	3.0	.8	3.4	2.7	2.1

 *Data Set:* BPINCR

Problem Consider the pharmaceutical company that desires an estimate of the mean increase in blood pressure of patients who take a new drug. The blood pressure increases (points) for the $n = 6$ patients in the human testing phase are shown in Table 4. Use this information to construct a 95% confidence interval for μ, the mean increase in blood pressure associated with the new drug for all patients in the population.

Solution First, note that we are dealing with a sample too small to assume that the sample mean $\bar{x}$ is approximately normally distributed by the Central Limit Theorem — that is, we do not get the normal distribution of $\bar{x}$ "automatically" from the Central Limit Theorem when the sample size is small. Instead, the measured variable, in this case the increase in blood pressure, must be normally distributed in order for the distribution of $\bar{x}$ to be normal.

Second, unless we are fortunate enough to know the population standard deviation σ, which in this case represents the standard deviation of *all* the patients' increases in blood pressure when they take the new drug, we cannot use the standard normal z-statistic to form our confidence interval for μ. Instead, we must use the t-distribution, with $(n - 1)$ degrees of freedom.

In this case, $n - 1 = 5$ df, and the t-value is found in Table 3 to be $t_{.025} = 2.571$ with 5 df. Recall that the large-sample confidence interval would have been of the form

$$\bar{x} \pm z_{\alpha/2}\sigma_{\bar{x}} = \bar{x} \pm z_{\alpha/2}\frac{\sigma}{\sqrt{n}} = \bar{x} \pm z_{.025}\frac{\sigma}{\sqrt{n}}$$

where 95% is the desired confidence level. To form the interval for a small sample from *a normal distribution, we simply substitute t for z and s for σ in the preceding formula:*

$$\bar{x} \pm t_{\alpha/2}\frac{s}{\sqrt{n}}$$

An SPSS printout showing descriptive statistics for the six blood pressure increases is displayed in Figure 9. Note that $\bar{x} = 2.283$ and $s = .950$. Substituting these numerical values into the confidence interval formula, we get

$$2.283 \pm (2.571)\left(\frac{.950}{\sqrt{6}}\right) = 2.283 \pm .997$$

or 1.286 to 3.280 points. Note that this interval agrees (except for rounding) with the confidence interval generated by SPSS in Figure 9.

We interpret the interval as follows: We can be 95% confident that the mean increase in blood pressure associated with taking this new drug is between 1.286 and 3.28 points. As with our large-sample interval estimates, our confidence is in the process, not in

Descriptives

			Statistic	Std. Error
BPINCR	Mean		2.283	.3877
	95% Confidence Interval for Mean	Lower Bound	1.287	
		Upper Bound	3.280	
	5% Trimmed Mean		2.304	
	Median		2.400	
	Variance		.902	
	Std. Deviation		.9496	
	Minimum		.8	
	Maximum		3.4	
	Range		2.6	
	Interquartile Range		1.625	
	Skewness		−.573	.845
	Kurtosis		−.389	1.741

Figure 9

SPSS confidence interval for mean blood pressure increase

this particular interval. We know that if we were to repeatedly use this estimation procedure, 95% of the confidence intervals produced would contain the true mean μ, *assuming that the probability distribution of changes in blood pressure from which our sample was selected is normal.* The latter assumption is necessary for the small-sample interval to be valid.

Look Back What price did we pay for having to use a small sample to make the inference? First, we had to assume the underlying population was normally distributed, and if the assumption was invalid, our interval might also have been invalid.* Second, we had to form the interval using a *t*-value of 2.571 rather than a *z*-value of 1.96, resulting in a wider interval to achieve the same 95% level of confidence. If the interval from 1.286 to 3.28 is too wide to be of use, then we know how to remedy the situation: increase the number of patients sampled to decrease the interval width (on average).

━ **Now Work Exercise 24**

The procedure for forming a small-sample confidence interval is summarized in the accompanying boxes.

Small-Sample Confidence Interval for μ, Student's t-statistic

$$\sigma \text{ unknown: } \bar{x} \pm t_{\alpha/2}\left(\frac{s}{\sqrt{n}}\right)$$

where $t_{\alpha/2}$ is the *t*-value corresponding to an area $\frac{\alpha}{2}$ in the upper tail of the student's *t*-distribution based on $(n - 1)$ degrees of freedom.

$$\sigma \text{ known: } \bar{x} \pm z_{\alpha/2}\left(\frac{\sigma}{\sqrt{n}}\right)$$

Conditions Required for a Valid Small-Sample Confidence Interval for μ

1. A random sample is selected from the target population.
2. The population has a relative frequency distribution that is approximately normal.

---

*By *invalid*, we mean that the probability that the procedure will yield an interval that contains μ is not equal to $(1 - \alpha)$. Generally, if the underlying population is approximately normal, then the confidence coefficient will approximate the probability that a randomly selected interval contains μ.

Example 5

A Small-Sample Confidence Interval for μ — Destructive Sampling

Table 5

Number of Characters (in Millions) for $n = 15$ Printhead Tests

1.13	1.55	1.43	.92	1.25
1.36	1.32	.85	1.07	1.48
1.20	1.33	1.18	1.22	1.29

Data Set: PRHEAD

Problem Some quality-control experiments require *destructive sampling* (i.e., the test to determine whether the item is defective destroys the item) in order to measure some particular characteristic of the product. The cost of destructive sampling often dictates small samples. For example, suppose a manufacturer of printers for personal computers wishes to estimate the mean number of characters printed before the printhead fails. Suppose the printer manufacturer tests $n = 15$ randomly selected printheads and records the number of characters printed until failure for each. These 15 measurements (in millions of characters) are listed in Table 5, followed by an XLSTAT summary statistics printout in Figure 10.

a. Form a 99% confidence interval for the mean number of characters printed before the printhead fails. Interpret the result.

b. What assumption is required for the interval, part **a**, to be valid? Is it reasonably satisfied?

Solution

a. For this small sample ($n = 15$), we use the t-statistic to form the confidence interval. We use a confidence coefficient of .99 and $n - 1 = 14$ degrees of freedom to find $t_{\alpha/2}$ in Table III:

$$t_{\alpha/2} = t_{.005} = 2.977$$

[*Note:* The small sample forces us to extend the interval almost 3 standard deviations (of $\bar{x}$) on each side of the sample mean in order to form the 99% confidence interval.] From the XLSTAT printout, Figure 10, we find $\bar{x} = 1.239$ and $s = .193$. Substituting these values into the confidence interval formula, we obtain

Statistic	NUMBER
No. of observations	15
Minimum	0.8500
Maximum	1.5500
Mean	1.2387
Standard deviation (n-1)	0.1932
Lower bound on mean (99%)	1.0902
Upper bound on mean (99%)	1.3871

Figure 10

XLSTAT output showing summary statistics and 95% confidence interval for μ, Example 5

$$\bar{x} \pm t_{.005}\left(\frac{s}{\sqrt{n}}\right) = 1.239 \pm 2.977\left(\frac{.193}{\sqrt{15}}\right)$$

$$= 1.239 \pm .148 \text{ or } (1.091, 1.387)$$

This interval is shown (shaded) at the bottom of the printout, Figure 10.

Our interpretation is as follows: The manufacturer can be 99% confident that the printhead has a mean life of between 1.091 and 1.387 million characters. If the manufacturer were to advertise that the mean life of its printheads is (at least) 1 million characters, the interval would support such a claim. Our confidence is derived from the fact that 99% of the intervals formed in repeated applications of this procedure would contain μ.

b. Because n is small, we must assume that the number of characters printed before printhead failure is a random variable from a normal distribution—that is, we assume that the population from which the sample of 15 measurements is selected is distributed normally. One way to check this assumption is to graph the distribution of data in Table 5. If the sample data are approximately normal, then the population from which the sample is selected is very likely to be normal. A Minitab stem-and-leaf plot for the sample data is displayed in Figure 11. The distribution is mound-shaped and nearly symmetric. Therefore, the assumption of normality appears to be reasonably satisfied.

Stem-and-Leaf Display: NUMBER

```
Stem-and-leaf of NUMBER  N  = 15
Leaf Unit = 0.010

  1     8   5
  2     9   2
  3    10   7
  5    11   38
 (4)   12   0259
  6    13   236
  3    14   38
  1    15   5
```

Figure 11

Minitab stem-and-leaf display of data in Table 5

Look Back Other checks for normality, such as a normal probability plot and the ratio IQR/S, may also be used to verify the normality condition.

■ **Now Work Exercise 35**

We have emphasized throughout this section that an assumption that the population is approximately normally distributed is necessary for making small-sample inferences about μ when σ is unknown and when using the t-statistic. Although many phenomena do have approximately normal distributions, it is also true that many random phenomena have distributions that are not normal or even mound-shaped. Empirical evidence acquired over the years has shown that confidence intervals based on the t-distribution are rather insensitive to moderate departures from normality—that is, use of the t-statistic when sampling from slightly or moderately skewed mound-shaped populations generally produces credible results; however, for cases in which the distribution is distinctly nonnormal, we must either take a large sample or use a *nonparametric method*.

STATISTICS
in ACTION
REVISITED

Estimating the Mean Overpayment

Refer to the Medicare fraud investigation described in the Statistics in Action. Recall that the United States Department of Justice (USDOJ) obtained a random sample of 52 claims from a population of 1,000 Medicare claims. For each claim, the amount paid, the amount disallowed (denied) by the auditor, and the amount that should have been paid (allowed) were recorded and saved in the **MFRAUD** file. The USDOJ wants to use these data to calculate an estimate of the overpayment for all 1,000 claims in the population.

One way to do this is to first use the sample data to estimate the mean overpayment per claim for the population, then use the estimated mean to extrapolate the overpayment amount to the population of all 1,000 claims. The difference between the amount paid and the amount allowed by the auditor represents the overpayment for each claim. This value is recorded as the amount denied in the **MFRAUD** file. These overpayment amounts in dollars are listed in the accompanying table.

Minitab software is used to find a 95% confidence interval for μ, the mean overpayment amount. The Minitab printout is displayed in Figure SIA1. The 95% confidence interval for μ (highlighted on the printout) is (16.51, 27.13). Thus, the USDOJ can be 95% confident that the mean overpayment amount for the population of 1,000 claims is between $16.51 and $27.13.

Table SIA1	Overpayment Amounts (Dollars) for Sample of 52 Claims						
0.00	31.00	0.00	37.20	37.20	0.00	43.40	0.00
37.20	43.40	0.00	37.20	0.00	24.80	0.00	0.00
37.20	0.00	37.20	0.00	37.20	37.20	37.20	0.00
37.20	37.20	0.00	0.00	37.20	0.00	43.40	37.20
0.00	37.20	0.00	37.20	37.20	0.00	37.20	37.20
0.00	37.20	43.40	0.00	37.20	37.20	37.20	0.00
43.40	0.00	43.40	0.00				

Data Set: MFRAUD

```
Variable        N   Mean  StDev  SE Mean      95% CI
Denied_Amount  52  21.82  19.08     2.65  (16.51, 27.13)
```

Figure SIA1

Minitab confidence interval for mean overpayment

Now, let x_i represent the overpayment amount for the ith claim. If the true mean μ were known, then the total overpayment amount for all 1,000 claims would be equal to

$$\sum_{i=1}^{1,000} x_i = (1,000)\left[\sum_{i=1}^{1,000} x_i\right]/(1,000) = (1,000)\mu$$

Consequently, to estimate the total overpayment amount for the 1,000 claims, the USDOJ will simply multiply the endpoints of the interval by 1,000. This yields the 95% confidence interval ($16,510, $27,130).* Typically, the USDOJ is willing to give the Medicare provider in question the benefit of the doubt by demanding a repayment equal to the lower 95% confidence bound—in this case, $16,510.

Exercises 23–39

Please be aware that some of the following problems may require knowledge of concepts that are not presented in this chapter.

Learning the Mechanics

23 Suppose you have selected a random sample of $n = 5$ measurements from a normal distribution. Compare the standard normal z-values with the corresponding t-values if you were forming the following confidence intervals.
   a. 80% confidence interval
   b. 90% confidence interval
   c. 95% confidence interval
   d. 98% confidence interval
   e. 99% confidence interval
   f. Use the table values you obtained in parts **a–e** to sketch the z-and t-distributions. What are the similarities and differences?

◉ Applet Exercise 3

Use the applet *Confidence Intervals for a Mean (the impact of not knowing the standard deviation)* to compare proportions of z-intervals and t-intervals that contain the mean for a population that is normally distributed.
   a. Using $n = 5$ and the normal distribution with mean 50 and standard deviation 10, run the applet several times. How do the proportions of z-intervals and t-intervals that contain the mean compare?
   b. Repeat part **a** first for $n = 10$ and then for $n = 20$. Compare your results to part **a**.
   c. Describe any patterns you observe between the proportion of z-intervals that contain the mean and the proportion of t-intervals that contain the mean as the sample size increases.

◉ Applet Exercise 4

Use the applet *Confidence Intervals for a Mean (the impact of not knowing the standard deviation)* to compare proportions of z-intervals and t-intervals that contain the mean for a population with a skewed distribution.
   a. Using $n = 5$ and the right skewed distribution with mean 50 and standard deviation 10, run the applet several times. How do the proportions of z-intervals and t-intervals that contain the mean compare?
   b. Repeat part **a** first for $n = 10$ and then for $n = 20$. Compare your results to part **a**.

   c. Describe any patterns you observe between the proportion of z-intervals that contain the mean and the proportion of t-intervals that contain the mean as the sample size increases.
   d. How does skewedness of the underlying distribution affect the proportions of z-intervals and t-intervals that contain the mean?

24 Explain the differences in the sampling distributions of $\bar{x}$ for large and small samples under the following assumptions.
   a. The variable of interest, x, is normally distributed.
   b. Nothing is known about the distribution of the variable x.

25 Let t_0 be a particular value of t. Use Table III in Appendix: Tables to find t_0 values such that the following statements are true.
   a. $P(-t_0 < t < t_0) = .95$ where df $= 10$
   b. $P(t \leq -t_0 \text{ or } t \geq t_0)$ where df $= 10$
   c. $P(t \leq t_0) = .05$ where df $= 10$
   d. $P(t \leq -t_0 \text{ or } t \geq t_0) = .10$ where df $= 20$
   e. $P(t \leq -t_0 \text{ or } t \geq t_0) = .01$ where df $= 5$

26 Let t_0 be a specific value of t. Use Table III in Appendix: Tables to find t_0 values such that the following statements are true.
   a. $P(t \geq t_0) = .025$ where df $= 11$
   b. $P(t \geq t_0) = .01$ where df $= 9$
   c. $P(t \leq t_0) = .005$ where df $= 6$
   d. $P(t \leq t_0) = .05$ where df $= 18$

27 The following random sample was selected from a normal distribution: 4, 6, 3, 5, 9, 3.
   a. Construct a 90% confidence interval for the population mean μ.
   b. Construct a 95% confidence interval for the population mean μ.
   c. Construct a 99% confidence interval for the population mean μ.
   d. Assume that the sample mean $\bar{x}$ and sample standard deviation s remain exactly the same as those you just calculated but are based on a sample of $n = 25$ observations rather than $n = 6$ observations. Repeat parts **a–c**. What is the effect of increasing the sample size on the width of the confidence intervals?

*This interval represents an approximation to the true 95% confidence interval for the total amount of overpayment. The precise interval involves use of a continuity correction for population size (see Section 6).

28 The following sample of 16 measurements was selected from a population that is approximately normally distributed:

L06028

91	80	99	110	95	106	78	121	106	100	97	82
100	83	115	104								

a. Construct an 80% confidence interval for the population mean.

b. Construct a 95% confidence interval for the population mean and compare the width of this interval with that of part **a.**

c. Carefully interpret each of the confidence intervals and explain why the 80% confidence interval is narrower.

Applying the Concepts—Basic

29 Lobster trap placement. Strategic placement of lobster traps is one of the keys for a successful lobster fisherman. An observational study of teams fishing for the red spiny lobster in Baja California Sur, Mexico, was conducted and the results published in *Bulletin of Marine Science* (April 2010). One of the variables of interest was the average distance separating traps—called *trap spacing*—deployed by the same team of fishermen. Trap-spacing measurements (in meters) for a sample of seven teams of red spiny lobster fishermen are shown in the accompanying table. Of interest is the mean trap spacing for the population of red spiny lobster fishermen fishing in Baja California Sur, Mexico.

TRAPS

93	99	105	94	82	70	86

Source: Based on Shester, G. G. "Explaining catch variation among Baja California lobster fishers through spatial analysis of trap-placement decisions," *Bulletin of Marine Science*, Vol. 86, No. 2, April 2010 (Table 1), pp. 479–498.

a. Identify the target parameter for this study.

b. Compute a point estimate of the target parameter.

c. What is the problem with using the normal (z) statistic to find a confidence interval for the target parameter?

d. Find a 95% confidence interval for the target parameter.

e. Give a practical interpretation of the interval, part **d.**

f. What conditions must be satisfied for the interval, part **d,** to be valid?

30 Radon exposure in Egyptian tombs. Many ancient Egyptian tombs were cut from limestone rock that contained uranium. Since most tombs are not well ventilated, guards, tour guides, and visitors may be exposed to deadly radon gas. In *Radiation Protection Dosimetry* (December 2010), a study of radon exposure in tombs in the Valley of Kings, Luxor, Egypt (recently opened for public tours), was conducted. The radon levels—measured in becquerels per cubic meter (Bq/m^3)—in the inner chambers of a sample of 12 tombs were determined. Summary statistics follow: $\bar{x} = 3,643 \ Bq/m^3$ and $s = 4,487 \ Bq/m^3$. Use this information to estimate, with 95% confidence, the true mean level of radon exposure in tombs in the Valley of Kings. Interpret the resulting interval.

TOMBS

31 Assessing the bending strength of a wooden roof. The white wood material used for the roof of an ancient Japanese temple is imported from Northern Europe. The wooden roof must withstand as much as 100 centimeters of snow in the winter. Architects at Tohoku University (Japan) conducted a study to estimate the mean bending strength of the white wood roof (*Journal of the*

International Association for Shell and Spatial Structures, Aug. 2004). A sample of 25 pieces of the imported wood was tested and yielded the following statistics on breaking strength (MPa): $\bar{x} = 75.4, s = 10.9$. Estimate the true mean breaking strength of the white wood with a 90% confidence interval. Interpret the result.

32 Hospital length of stay. Health insurers and the federal government are both putting pressure on hospitals to shorten the average length of stay (LOS) of their patients. The average LOS for men in the United States is 5.4 days, and the average for women is 4.6 days (*Statistical Abstract of the United States: 2012*). A random sample of 20 hospitals in one state had a mean LOS for women of 3.8 days and a standard deviation of 1.2 days.

a. Use a 90% confidence interval to estimate the population mean LOS for women for the state's hospitals.

b. Interpret the interval in terms of this application.

c. What is meant by the phrase "90% confidence interval"?

33 Surface roughness of pipe. *Anti-corrosion Methods and Materials* (Vol. 50, 2003) did a study of the surface roughness of coated interior pipe used in oil fields. The data (in micrometers) for 20 sampled pipe sections are reproduced in the accompanying table; a Minitab analysis of the data appears below.

RPIPE

1.72	2.50	2.16	2.13	1.06	2.24	2.31	2.03	1.09	1.40
2.57	2.64	1.26	2.05	1.19	2.13	1.27	1.51	2.41	1.95

Source: Data from Farshad, F., & Pesacreta, T. "Coated pipe interior surface roughness as measured by three scanning probe instruments," *Anti-corrosion Methods and Materials*, Vol. 50, No. 1, 2003 (Table III).

a. Locate a 95% confidence interval for the mean surface roughness of coated interior pipe on the accompanying Minitab printout.

b. Would you expect the average surface roughness to be as high as 2.5 micrometers? Explain.

One-Sample T: ROUGH

```
Variable   N     Mean     StDev    SE Mean       95% CI
ROUGH      20   1.88100  0.52391  0.11715  (1.63580, 2.12620)
```

Applying the Concepts—Intermediate

34 Performance of stock screeners. Stock screeners are automated tools used by investment companies to help clients select a portfolio of stocks to invest in. The table below lists the annualized percentage return on investment (as compared to the Standard & Poor's 500 Index) for 13 randomly selected stock screeners provided by the American Association of Individual Investors (AAII).

SCREEN

9.0	−.1	−1.6	14.6	16.0	7.7	19.9	9.8	3.2	24.8	17.6	10.7	9.1

a. Find a 90% confidence interval for the average annualized percentage return on investment of all stock screeners provided by AAII. Interpret the result.

b. A negative annualized return reflects a stock portfolio that performed worse than the S&P 500. On average, do the AAII stock screeners perform worse or better than the S&P 500? Explain.

c. What assumption about the distribution of the annualized percentage returns on investment is required for the inference, part **b**, to be valid? Is this assumption reasonably satisfied?

35 Minimizing tractor skidding distance. When planning for a new forest road to be used for tree harvesting, planners must select the location to minimize tractor skidding distance. In the *Journal of Forest Engineering* (July 1999), researchers wanted to estimate the true mean skidding distance along a new road in a European forest. The skidding distances (in meters) were measured at 20 randomly selected road sites. These values are given in the accompanying table.

a. Estimate the true mean skidding distance for the road with a 95% confidence interval.

b. Give a practical interpretation of the interval, part **a.**

c. What conditions are required for the inference, part **b**, to be valid? Are these conditions reasonably satisfied?

d. A logger working on the road claims the mean skidding distance is at least 425 meters. Do you agree?

488	350	457	199	285	409	435	574	439	546
385	295	184	261	273	400	311	312	141	425

Source: Based on Tujek, J., & Pacola, E. "Algorithms for skidding distance modeling on a raster digital terrain model" *Journal of Forest Engineering,* Vol. 10, No. 1, July 1999 (Table 1).

36 Contamination of New Jersey wells. Methyl *t*-butyl ether (MTBE) is an organic water contaminant that often results from gasoline spills. The level of MTBE (in parts per billion) was measured for a sample of 12 well sites located near a gasoline service station in New Jersey (*Environmental Science & Technology,* Jan. 2005). The data are listed in the accompanying table.

150	367	38	12	11	134
12	251	63	8	13	107

Source: Based on Kuder, T., et al. "Enrichment of stable carbon and hydrogen isotopes during anaerobic biodegradation of MTBE: Microcosm and field evidence," *Environmental Science & Technology,* Vol. 39, No. 1, Jan. 2005, pp. 213–220 (Table 1).

a. Give a point estimate for μ, the true mean MTBE level for all well sites located near the New Jersey gasoline service station.

b. Calculate and interpret a 99% confidence interval for μ.

c. What assumptions are required for the interval, part **b**, to be valid? Are these assumptions reasonably satisfied?

37 Crude oil biodegradation. The *Journal of Petroleum Geology* (April 2010) did a study of the environmental factors associated with biodegradation in crude oil reservoirs. One indicator of biodegradation is the level of dioxide in the water. 16 water specimens were randomly selected from various locations in a reservoir on the floor of a mine and the amount of dioxide (milligrams/liter) as well as presence of oil were determined for each specimen. These data are reproduced in the next table.

a. Estimate the true mean amount of dioxide present in water specimens that contain oil using a 95% confidence interval. Give a practical interpretation of the interval.

b. Repeat part **a** for water specimens that do not contain oil.

c. Based on the results, parts **a** and **b,** make an inference about biodegradation at the mine reservoir.

Dioxide Amount	Crude Oil Present
3.3	No
0.5	Yes
1.3	Yes
0.4	Yes
0.1	No
4.0	No
0.3	No
0.2	Yes
2.4	No
2.4	No
1.4	No
0.5	Yes
0.2	Yes
4.0	No
4.0	No
4.0	No

Source: Based on Permanyer, A., et al. "Crude oil biodegradation and environmental factors at the Riutort oil shale mine, SE Pyrenees," *Journal of Petroleum Geology,* Vol. 33, No. 2, April 2010 (Table 1).

38 Overbooking policies for major airlines. Airlines overbook flights in order to reduce the odds of flying with unused seats. An article in *Transportation Research* (Vol. 38, 2002) investigated the optimal overbooking policies for major airlines. One of the variables measured for each airline was the compensation (in dollars) per bumped passenger required to maximize future revenue. Consider the *threshold* levels of compensation for a random sample of 10 major airlines shown in the table. Estimate the true mean threshold compensation level for all major worldwide airlines using a 90% confidence interval. Interpret the result practically.

825	850	1,210	1,370	1,415
1,500	1,560	1,625	2,155	2,220

Source: Data from Suzuki, Y. "An empirical analysis of the optimal overbooking policies for US major airlines." *Transportation Research, Part E,* Vol. 38, 2002, pp. 135–149 (Table 4).

39 Largest private companies. IPOs—initial public offerings of stock—create billions of dollars of new wealth for owners, managers, and employees of companies that were previously privately owned. Nevertheless, hundreds of large and thousands of small companies remain privately owned. The revenues of a random sample of 15 firms from *Forbes* 212 Largest Private Companies list is given in the table below.

Company	Revenue (in billions)
Enterprise Rent-A-Car	$14.10
Pilot Flying J	17.77
Tenaska Energy	9.95
Wawa	6.99
Gulf States Toyota	5.10
Brookshire Grocery	2.30
BrightStar	4.61
Bose	2.28
Mary Kay	2.50
Drummoend	3.03
Petco	2.80
SAS	2.43
Forever 21	2.60
Burger King	2.33
Conair	2.01

Source: Data from "America's Largest Private Companies," *Forbes,* Nov. 16, 2011.

a. Describe the population from which the random sample was drawn.

b. Use a 98% confidence interval to estimate the mean revenue of the population of companies in question.

c. Interpret your confidence interval in the context of the problem.

d. What characteristic must the population possess to ensure the appropriateness of the estimation procedure used in part **b?**

e. Suppose *Forbes* reports that the true mean revenue of the 212 companies on the list is $5.0 billion. Is the claim believable?

4 Large-Sample Confidence Interval for a Population Proportion

The number of public opinion polls has grown at an astounding rate in recent years. Almost daily, the news media report the results of some poll. Pollsters regularly determine the percentage of people who approve of the president's on-the-job performance, the fraction of voters in favor of a certain candidate, the fraction of customers who prefer a particular product, and the proportion of households that watch a particular TV program. In each case, we are interested in estimating the percentage (or proportion) of some group with a certain characteristic. In this section, we consider methods for making inferences about population proportions when the sample is large.

Example	**6**

Estimating a Population Proportion—Preference for Breakfast Cereal

Problem A food-products company conducted a market study by randomly sampling and interviewing 1,000 consumers to determine which brand of breakfast cereal they prefer. Suppose 313 consumers were found to prefer the company's brand. How would you estimate the true fraction of *all* consumers who prefer the company's cereal brand?

Solution In this study, consumers are asked which brand of breakfast cereal they prefer. Note that "brand" is a qualitative variable and that what we are asking is how you would estimate the probability p of success in a binomial experiment, where p is the probability that a chosen consumer prefers the company's brand. One logical method of estimating p for the population is to use the proportion of successes in the sample—that is, we can estimate p by calculating

$$\hat{p} = \frac{\text{Number of consumers sampled who prefer the company's brand}}{\text{Number of consumers sampled}}$$

where $\hat{p}$ is read "p hat." Thus, in this case,

$$\hat{p} = \frac{313}{1,000} = .313$$

Look Back To determine the reliability of the estimator $\hat{p}$, we need to know its sampling distribution—that is, if we were to draw samples of 1,000 consumers over and over again, each time calculating a new estimate $\hat{p}$, what would be the frequency distribution of all the $\hat{p}$ values? The answer lies in viewing $\hat{p}$ as the average, or mean, number of successes per trial over the n trials. If each success is assigned a value equal to 1 and a failure is assigned a value of 0, then the sum of all n sample observations is x, the total number of successes, and $\hat{p} = x/n$ is the average, or mean, number of successes per trial in the n trials. The Central Limit Theorem tells us that the *relative frequency distribution of the sample mean for any population is approximately normal for sufficiently large samples.*

Now Work Exercise 49a

The repeated sampling distribution of $\hat{p}$ has the characteristics given in the next box and shown in Figure 12.

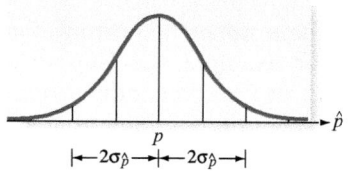

Figure 12
Sampling distribution of $\hat{p}$

Properties of the Sampling Distribution of $\hat{p}$

1. The mean of the sampling distribution of $\hat{p}$ is p; that is, $\hat{p}$ is an unbiased estimator of p.
2. The standard deviation of the sampling distribution of $\hat{p}$ is $\sqrt{pq/n}$; that is, $\sigma_{\hat{p}} = \sqrt{pq/n}$, where $q = 1 - p$.
3. For large samples, the sampling distribution of $\hat{p}$ is approximately normal. A sample size is considered large if both $n\hat{p} \geq 15$ and $n\hat{q} \geq 15$.

The fact that $\hat{p}$ is a "sample mean number of successes per trial" allows us to form confidence intervals about p in a manner that is completely analogous to that used for large-sample estimation of μ.

Large-Sample Confidence Interval for $\hat{p}$

$$\hat{p} \pm z_{\alpha/2}\sigma_{\hat{p}} = \hat{p} \pm z_{\alpha/2}\sqrt{\frac{pq}{n}} \approx \hat{p} \pm z_{\alpha/2}\sqrt{\frac{\hat{p}\hat{q}}{n}}$$

where $\hat{p} = \dfrac{x}{n}$ and $\hat{q} = 1 - \hat{p}$

Note: When n is large, $\hat{p}$ can approximate the value of p in the formula for $\sigma_{\hat{p}}$.

Conditions Required for a Valid Large-Sample Confidence Interval for p

1. A random sample is selected from the target population.
2. The sample size n is large. (This condition will be satisfied if both $n\hat{p} \geq 15$ and $n\hat{q} \geq 15$. Note that $n\hat{p}$ and $n\hat{q}$ are simply the number of successes and number of failures, respectively, in the sample.)

Thus, if 313 of 1,000 consumers prefer the company's cereal brand, a 95% confidence interval for the proportion of *all* consumers who prefer the company's brand is

$$\hat{p} \pm z_{\alpha/2}\sigma_{\hat{p}} = .313 \pm 1.96\sqrt{\frac{pq}{1,000}}$$

Table 6		
Values of *pq* for Several Different Values of *p*		
p	*pq*	$\sqrt{pq}$
.5	.25	.50
.6 or .4	.24	.49
.7 or .3	.21	.46
.8 or .2	.16	.40
.9 or .1	.09	.30

where $q = 1 - p$. Just as we needed an approximation for σ in calculating a large-sample confidence interval for μ, we now need an approximation for p. As Table 6 shows, the approximation for p does not have to be especially accurate because the value of $\sqrt{pq}$ needed for the confidence interval is relatively insensitive to changes in p. Therefore, we can use $\hat{p}$ to approximate p. Keeping in mind that $\hat{q} = 1 - \hat{p}$, we substitute these values into the formula for the confidence interval:

$$\hat{p} \pm 1.96\sqrt{\frac{pq}{1,000}} \approx \hat{p} \pm 1.96\sqrt{\frac{\hat{p}\hat{q}}{1,000}}$$

$$= .313 \pm 1.96\sqrt{\frac{(.313)(.687)}{1,000}}$$

$$= .313 \pm .029$$

$$= (.284, .342)$$

The company can be 95% confident that the interval from 28.4% to 34.2% contains the true percentage of *all* consumers who prefer its brand—that is, in repeated construction of confidence intervals, approximately 95% of all samples would produce confidence intervals that enclose p. Note that the guidelines for interpreting a confidence interval about μ also apply to interpreting a confidence interval for p because p is the "population fraction of successes" in a binomial experiment.

Example 7

Large-Sample Confidence Interval for *p*—Proportion Optimistic about the Economy

Problem Many public polling agencies conduct surveys to determine the current consumer sentiment concerning the state of the economy. For example, the Bureau of Economic and Business Research (BEBR) at the University of Florida conducts quarterly surveys to gauge consumer sentiment in the Sunshine State. Suppose that the BEBR randomly samples 484 consumers and finds that 157 are optimistic about the state of the economy. Use a 90% confidence interval to estimate the proportion of all consumers in Florida who are optimistic about the state of the economy. Based on the confidence interval, can BEBR infer that a minority of Florida consumers is optimistic about the economy?

Solution The number, *x*, of the 484 sampled consumers who are optimistic about the Florida economy is a binomial random variable if we can assume that the sample was randomly selected from the population of Florida consumers and that the poll was conducted identically for each sampled consumer.

The point estimate of the proportion of Florida consumers who are optimistic about the economy is

$$\hat{p} = \frac{x}{n} = \frac{157}{484} = .324$$

We first check to be sure that the sample size is sufficiently large that the normal distribution provides a reasonable approximation for the sampling distribution of $\hat{p}$. We require the number of successes in the sample, $n\hat{p}$, and the number of failures, $n\hat{q}$, to both be at least 15. Since the number of successes is $n\hat{p} = 157$ and the number of failures is $n\hat{q} = 327$, we may conclude that the normal approximation is reasonable.

We now proceed to form the 90% confidence interval for *p*, the true proportion of Florida consumers who are optimistic about the state of the economy:

$$\hat{p} \pm z_{\alpha/2}\sigma_{\hat{p}} = \hat{p} \pm z_{\alpha/2}\sqrt{\frac{pq}{n}} \approx \hat{p} \pm z_{\alpha/2}\sqrt{\frac{\hat{p}\hat{q}}{n}}$$

$$= .324 \pm 1.645\sqrt{\frac{(.324)(.676)}{484}} = .324 \pm .035 = (.289, .359)$$

(This interval is also shown on the Minitab printout, Figure 13.) Thus, we can be 90% confident that the proportion of all Florida consumers who are confident about the economy is between .289 and .359. As always, our confidence stems from the fact that 90% of all similarly formed intervals will contain the true proportion *p* and not from any knowledge about whether this particular interval does.

Test and CI for One Proportion

Sample	X	N	Sample p	90% CI
1	157	484	0.324380	(0.289379, 0.359381)

Using the normal approximation.

Figure 13

Minitab output showing 95% confidence interval for *p*, Example 7

Can we conclude that a minority of Florida consumers is optimistic about the economy based on this interval? If we wished to use this interval to infer that a minority is optimistic, the interval would have to support the inference that *p* is less than .5—that is, that less than 50% of the Florida consumers are optimistic about the economy. Note that the interval contains only values below .5. Therefore, we can conclude that the true value of *p* is less than .5 based on this 90% confidence interval.

Look Back If the confidence interval includes .5 (e.g., an interval from .42 to .54), then we could not conclude that the true proportion of consumers who are optimistic is less than .5. (This is because it is possible that *p* is as high as .54.)

Now Work Exercise 49

We conclude this section with a warning and an illustrative example.

> ⚠️ **CAUTION** Unless n is extremely large, the large-sample procedure presented in this section performs poorly when p is near 0 or near 1.

The problem stated in the above warning can be illustrated as follows. Suppose you want to estimate the proportion of executives who die from a work-related injury using a sample size of $n = 100$. This proportion is likely to be near 0, say $p \approx .001$. If so, then $np \approx 100(.001) = .1$ is less than the recommended value of 15. Consequently, a confidence interval for p based on a sample of $n = 100$ will probably be misleading.

To overcome this potential problem, an *extremely* large sample size is required. Because the value of n required to satisfy "extremely large" is difficult to determine, statisticians (see Agresti & Coull, 1998) have proposed an alternative method, based on the Wilson (1927) point estimator of p. The procedure is outlined in the box below. Researchers have shown that this confidence interval works well for any p, even when the sample size n is very small.

Adjusted $(1 - \alpha)100\%$ Confidence Interval for a Population Proportion, p

$$\widetilde{p} \pm z_{\alpha/2}\sqrt{\frac{\widetilde{p}(1 - \widetilde{p})}{n + 4}}$$

where $\widetilde{p} = \frac{x + 2}{n + 4}$ is the adjusted sample proportion of observations with the characteristic of interest, x is the number of successes in the sample, and n is the sample size.

<table>
<tr><td>

Example 8

Adjusted Confidence Interval Procedure for p—Injury Rate at a Jewelry Store

</td><td>

Problem According to the Bureau of Labor Statistics (2012), the probability of injury while working at a jewelry store is less than .01. Suppose that in a random sample of 200 jewelry store workers, 3 were injured on the job. Estimate the true proportion of jewelry store workers who are injured on the job using a 95% confidence interval.

Solution Let p represent the true proportion of all jewelry store workers who are injured on the job. Because p is near 0, an "extremely large" sample is required to estimate its value using the usual large-sample method. Note that the number of "successes," 3, is less than 15. Thus, we doubt whether the sample size of 200 is large enough to apply the large-sample method. Alternatively, we will apply the adjustment outlined in the box.

Because the number of "successes" (i.e., number of injured jewelry store workers) in the sample is $x = 3$, the adjusted sample proportion is

$$\widetilde{p} = \frac{x + 2}{n + 4} = \frac{3 + 2}{200 + 4} = \frac{5}{204} = .025$$

</td></tr>
</table>

Note that this adjusted sample proportion is obtained by adding a total of four observations—two "successes" and two "failures"—to the sample data. Substituting $\widetilde{p} = .025$ into the equation for a 95% confidence interval, we obtain

$$\widetilde{p} \pm 1.96\sqrt{\frac{\widetilde{p}(1 - \widetilde{p})}{n + 4}} = .025 \pm 1.96\sqrt{\frac{(.025)(.975)}{204}}$$

$$= .025 \pm .021$$

or (.004, .046). Consequently, we are 95% confident that the true proportion of jewelry store workers who are injured while on the job falls between .004 and .046.

Look Back If we apply the standard large-sample confidence interval formula, where $\hat{p} = \frac{3}{200} = .015$, we obtain

$$\hat{p} \pm 1.96\sqrt{\frac{\hat{p}\hat{q}}{200}} = .015 \pm 1.96\sqrt{\frac{(.015)(.985)}{200}}$$

$$= .015 \pm .017 \text{ or } (-.002, .032)$$

Note that the interval contains negative (nonsensical) values for the true proportion. Such a result is typical when the large-sample method is misapplied.

■ Now Work Exercise 50

STATISTICS
in ACTION
REVISITED

Estimating the Coding Error Rate

In the previous Statistics in Action Revisited, we showed how to estimate the mean overpayment amount for claims in a Medicare fraud study. In addition to estimating overcharges, the USDOJ also is interested in estimating the *coding error rate* of a Medicare provider. The coding error rate is defined as the proportion of Medicare claims that are coded incorrectly. Thus, for this inference, the USDOJ is interested in estimating a population proportion, p. Typically, the USDOJ finds that about 50% of the claims in a Medicare fraud case are incorrectly coded.

If you examine the sample data in Table SIA6.1, you can verify that of the 52 audited claims, 31 were determined to be coded incorrectly, resulting in an overcharge. These are the claims with a disallowed amount greater than $0. Therefore, an estimate of the coding error rate, p, for this Medicare provider is

$$\hat{p} = 31/52 = .596$$

A 95% confidence interval for p can be obtained with the use of a confidence interval formula or with statistical software.

The **MFRAUD** file includes a qualitative variable (called "Coding Error") at two levels, where "Yes" represents that the claim is coded incorrectly and "No" represents that the claim is coded correctly. Thus, the USDOJ desires an estimate of the proportion of "Yes" values for the "Coding Error" variable. A confidence interval for the proportion of incorrectly coded claims is highlighted on the accompanying Minitab printout, Figure SIA2. The interval, (.45, .73), implies that the true coding error rate for the 1,000 claims in the population falls between .45 and .73, with 95% confidence. Note that the value .5—the proportion of incorrectly coded claims expected by the USDOJ—falls within the 95% confidence interval.

Figure SIA2

Minitab confidence interval for coding error rate

```
Event = Yes

Variable       X   N   Sample p      95% CI
Coding_Error  31  52   0.596154   (0.451016, 0.729940)
```

Data Set: MFRAUD

Exercises 40–59

Please be aware that some of the following problems may require knowledge of concepts that are not presented in this chapter.

Learning the Mechanics

40 Describe the sampling distribution of $\hat{p}$ based on large samples of size n—that is, give the mean, the standard deviation, and the (approximate) shape of the distribution of $\hat{p}$ when large samples of size n are (repeatedly) selected from the binomial distribution with probability of success p.

⬤ Applet Exercise 5

Use the applet *Confidence Intervals for a Proportion* to investigate the effect of the value of p on the number of confidence intervals that contain the population proportion p for a fixed sample size. For this exercise, use sample size $n = 10$.

   a. Run the applet several times without clearing for $p = .1$. What proportion of the 95% confidence intervals contain p? What proportion of the 99% confidence intervals contain p? Do the results surprise you? Explain.

   b. Repeat part **a** for each value of p: $p = .2$, $p = .3$, $p = .4$, $p = .5$, $p = .6$, $p = .7$, $p = .8$, and $p = .9$.

   c. Which value of p yields the greatest proportion of each type of interval that contain p?

   d. Based on your results, what values of p will yield more reliable confidence intervals for a fixed sample size n? Explain.

⬤ Applet Exercise 6

Use the applet *Confidence Intervals for a Proportion* to investigate the effect of the sample size on the number of confidence intervals that contain the population proportion p for a value of p close to 0 or 1.

   a. Run the applet several times without clearing for $p = .5$ and $n = 50$. Record the proportion of the 99% confidence intervals containing p.

   b. Now set $p = .1$ and run the applet several times without clearing for $n = 50$. How does the proportion of the 99% confidence intervals containing p compare to that in part **a?**

c. Repeat part **b** keeping $p = .1$ and increasing the sample size by 50 until you find a sample size that yields a similar proportion of the 99% confidence intervals containing p as that in part **a**.

d. Based on your results, describe how the value of p affects the sample size needed to guarantee a certain level of confidence.

41 For the binomial sample information summarized in each part, indicate whether the sample size is large enough to use the methods of this chapter to construct a confidence interval for p.
a. $n = 400, \hat{p} = .10$ **b.** $n = 50, \hat{p} = .10$
c. $n = 20, \hat{p} = .5$ **d.** $n = 20, \hat{p} = .3$

42 A random sample of size $n = 121$ yielded $\hat{p} = .88$.
a. Is the sample size large enough to use the methods of this section to construct a confidence interval for p? Explain.
b. Construct a 90% confidence interval for p.
c. What assumption is necessary to ensure the validity of this confidence interval?

43 A random sample of size $n = 225$ yielded $\hat{p} = .46$.
a. Is the sample size large enough to use the methods of this section to construct a confidence interval for p? Explain.
b. Construct a 95% confidence interval for p.
c. Interpret the 95% confidence interval.
d. Explain what is meant by the phrase "95% confidence interval."

44 A random sample of 50 consumers taste-tested a new snack food. Their responses were coded (0: do not like; 1: like; 2: indifferent) and recorded as follows:

1	0	0	1	2	0	1	1	0	0
0	1	0	2	0	2	2	0	0	1
1	0	0	0	0	1	0	2	0	0
0	1	0	0	1	0	0	1	0	1
0	2	0	0	1	1	0	0	0	1

a. Use an 80% confidence interval to estimate the proportion of consumers who like the snack food.
b. Provide a statistical interpretation for the confidence interval you constructed in part **a**.

Applying the Concepts—Basic

45 **Zillow.com estimates of home values.** Zillow.com is a real estate Web site that provides free estimates of the market value of homes. *The Appraisal Journal* (Winter 2010) did a study of the accuracy of Zillow's estimates. Data were collected for a sample of 2,045 single-family residential properties in Arlington, Texas. The researchers determined that Zillow overestimated by more than 10% the market value of 818 of the 2,045 homes. Suppose you want to estimate p, the true proportion of Arlington, Texas, homes with market values that are overestimated by more than 10% by Zillow.
a. Find $\hat{p}$, the point estimate of p.
b. Describe the sampling distribution of $\hat{p}$.
c. Find a 95% confidence interval for p.
d. Give a practical interpretation of the confidence interval, part **c**.

e. Suppose a *Zillow* representative claims that $p = .3$. Is the claim believable? Explain.

46 **Paying for music downloads.** If you use the Internet, have you ever paid to access or download music? This was one of the questions of interest in a recent *Pew Internet & American Life Project Survey* (October 2010). Telephone interviews were conducted on a representative sample of 1,003 adults living in the United States. For this sample, 506 adults admitted that they have paid to download music.
a. Use the survey information to find a point estimate for the true proportion of U.S. adults who have paid to download music.
b. Find an interval estimate for the proportion, part **a**. Use a 90% confidence interval.
c. Give a practical interpretation of the interval, part **b**. Your answer should begin with "We are 90% confident…."
d. Explain the meaning of the phrase "90% confident."

47 **Is Starbucks coffee overpriced?** The *Minneapolis Star Tribune* (August 12, 2008) reported that 73% of Americans say that Starbucks coffee is overpriced. The source of this information was a national telephone survey of 1,000 American adults conducted by Rasmussen Reports.
a. Identify the population of interest in this study.
b. Identify the sample for the study.
c. Identify the parameter of interest in the study.
d. Find and interpret a 95% confidence interval for the parameter of interest.

48 **Do social robots walk or roll?** *International Conference on Social Robotics* (Vol. 6414, 2010) did a study of the trend in the design of social robots. The researchers obtained a random sample of 106 social robots through a Web search and determined that 63 were designed with legs, but no wheels.
a. Find a 99% confidence interval for the proportion of all social robots designed with legs, but no wheels. Interpret the result.
b. In Exercise 42, you assumed that 40% of all social robots are designed with legs, but no wheels. Comment on the validity of this assumption.

49 **Cell phone use by drivers.** Studies have shown that drivers who use cell phones while operating a motor passenger vehicle increase their risk of an accident. Nevertheless, drivers continue to make cell phone calls while driving. A June 2011 *Harris Poll* of 2,163 adults found that 60% (1,298 adults) use cell phones while driving.
a. Give a point estimate of p, the true driver cell phone use rate (i.e., the proportion of all drivers who are using a cell phone while operating a motor passenger vehicle).
b. Find a 95% confidence interval for p.
c. Give a practical interpretation of the interval, part **b**.

50 **Nannies who work for celebrities.** The International Nanny Association reports that in a sample of 528 in-home child care providers (nannies), 20 work for either a nationally known, locally known, or internationally known celebrity (*2011 International Nanny Association Salary and Benefits Survey*). Use Wilson's adjustment to find a 95% confidence interval for the true proportion of all nannies who work for a celebrity. Interpret the resulting interval.

Applying the Concepts—Intermediate

51 Annual survey of computer crimes. *CSI Computer Crime and Security Survey (2010/2011)* showed that of the 351 organizations that responded to the survey, 144 (or 41%) admitted unauthorized use of computer systems at their firms during the year. Estimate the probability of unauthorized use of computer systems at an organization with a 90% confidence interval. Explain how 90% is used as a measure of reliability for the confidence interval.

52 Minority ownership of franchises. According to *Franchised Business Ownership: By Minority and Gender Groups* (2011), a report for IFA Educational Foundation, 20.5% of all franchised businesses in the United States are minority owned. (This information is based on the U.S. Census Bureau's survey of 27 million business owners.) Suppose that you obtain a sample of 100 franchised businesses located in Mississippi and find that 15 are owned by minorities. Does this result lead you to conclude that the percentage of minority-owned franchises in Mississippi is less than the national value of 20.5%? Explain.

53 History of corporate acquisitions. *Academy of Management Journal* (Aug. 2008) did an investigation of the performance and timing of corporate acquisitions. A corporate acquisition occurs when one corporation purchases all the stock shares of another. The investigation discovered that in a sample of 2,778 firms, 748 announced one or more acquisitions during the year 2000. Estimate the true percentage of all firms that announced one or more acquisitions during the year 2000 using a 90% confidence interval. Interpret the result.

54 Interviewing candidates for a job. The costs associated with conducting interviews for a job opening have skyrocketed over the years. According to a Harris Interactive survey, 211 of 502 senior human resources executives at U.S. companies believe that their hiring managers are interviewing too many people to find qualified candidates for the job (*Business Wire*, June 8, 2006).
a. Describe the population of interest in this study.
b. Identify the population parameter of interest, p.
c. Is the sample size large enough to provide a reliable estimate of p?
d. Find and interpret an interval estimate for the true proportion of senior human resources executives who believe that their hiring managers interview too many candidates during a job search. Use a confidence level of 98%.
e. If you had constructed a 90% confidence interval, would it be wider or narrower?

55 Splinting in mountain climbing accidents. The most common injury that occurs among mountain climbers is trauma to the lower extremity (leg). Consequently, rescuers must be proficient in immobilizing and splinting fractures. In *High Altitude Medicine & Biology* (Vol. 10, 2009), researchers provided official recommendations for mountain emergency medicine. As part of the document, the researchers examined the likelihood of mountain climbers needing certain types of splints. A Scottish Mountain Rescue study reported that there was 1 femoral shaft splint needed among 333 live casualties. The researchers will use

this study to estimate the proportion of all mountain casualties that require a femoral shaft splint.
a. Is the sample large enough to apply the large-sample estimation method of this section? Show why or why not.
b. Use Wilson's adjustment to find a 95% confidence interval for the true proportion of all mountain casualties that require a femoral shaft splint. Interpret the result.

56 Diamonds sold on the open market. Refer to the sample of 308 diamond stones that were listed for sale on the open market in Singapore's *Business Times*. Recall that the color of each diamond is classified as D, E, F, G, H, or I, while the clarity of each is classified as VVS1, VVS2, VS1, or VS2.
a. Find a 99% confidence interval for the proportion of all diamonds for sale on the open market that are classified as "D" color. Interpret the result.
b. Find a 99% confidence interval for the proportion of all diamonds for sale on the open market that are classified as "VS1" clarity. Interpret the result.

57 Are you really being served red snapper? *Nature* (July 15, 2004) did a study of fish specimens labeled "red snapper." Federal law prohibits restaurants from serving a cheaper, look-alike variety of fish (e.g., vermillion snapper or lane snapper) to customers who order red snapper. A team of University of North Carolina (UNC) researchers analyzed the meat from each in a sample of 22 "red snapper" fish fillets purchased from vendors across the United States in an effort to estimate the true proportion of fillets that are really red snapper. DNA tests revealed that 17 of the 22 fillets (or 77%) were not red snapper but the cheaper, look-alike variety of fish.
a. Identify the parameter of interest to the UNC researchers.
b. Explain why a large-sample confidence interval is inappropriate to apply in this study.
c. Construct a 95% confidence interval for the parameter of interest using Wilson's adjustment.
d. Give a practical interpretation of the confidence interval.

Applying the Concepts—Advanced

58 Eye shadow, mascara, and nickel allergies. Pigmented makeup products like mascara and eye shadow may contain metal (e.g., nickel) allergens. Is a nickel allergy more likely to occur in women who report cosmetic dermatitis from using eye shadow or mascara? This was the question of interest in a paper published in the *Journal of the European Academy of Dermatology and Venereology* (June 2010). In a sample of 131 women with cosmetic dermatitis from using eye shadow, 12 were diagnosed with a nickel allergy. In a sample of 250 women with cosmetic dermatitis from using mascara, 25 were diagnosed with a nickel allergy.
a. Compute a 95% confidence interval for the proportion of women with cosmetic dermatitis from using eye shadow who have a nickel allergy. Interpret the result.

b. Compute a 95% confidence interval for the proportion of women with cosmetic dermatitis from using mascara who have a nickel allergy. Interpret the result.

c. Suppose you are informed that the true proportion with a nickel allergy for one of the two groups (eye shadow or mascara) is .12. Can you determine which group is referenced? Explain.

59 U.S. Postal Service's performance. The U.S. Postal Service (USPS) reports that 95% of first-class mail within the same city is delivered on time (i.e., within 2 days of the time of mailing). To gauge the USPS performance, Price Waterhouse monitored the delivery of first-class mail items between Dec. 10 and Mar. 3—the most difficult delivery season due to bad weather conditions and holidays. In a sample of 332,000 items, Price Waterhouse determined that 282,200 were delivered on time. Comment on the performance of USPS first-class mail service over this time period.

5   Determining the Sample Size

One way to collect the relevant data for a study used to make inferences about the population is to implement a designed (planned) experiment. Perhaps the most important design decision faced by the analyst is to determine the size of the sample. We show in this section that the appropriate sample size for making an inference about a population mean or proportion depends on the desired reliability.

Estimating a Population Mean

Consider Example 2, in which we estimated the mean overdue amount for all delinquent accounts in a large credit corporation. A sample of 100 delinquent accounts produced the 95% confidence interval $\bar{x} \pm 1.96\sigma_{\bar{x}} \approx 233.28 \pm 17.71$. Consequently, our estimate $\bar{x}$ was within $17.71 of the true mean amount due, μ, for all the delinquent accounts at the 95% confidence level—that is, the 95% confidence interval for μ was $2(17.71) = \$35.42$ wide when 100 accounts were sampled. This is illustrated in Figure 14a.

Now suppose we want to estimate μ to within $5 with 95% confidence—that is, we want to narrow the width of the confidence interval from $35.42 to $10, as shown in Figure 14b. How much will the sample size have to be increased to accomplish this? If we want the estimator $\bar{x}$ to be within $5 of μ, we must have

$$1.96\sigma_{\bar{x}} = 5 \quad \text{or, equivalently,} \quad 1.96\left(\frac{\sigma}{\sqrt{n}}\right) = 5$$

The necessary sample size is obtained by solving this equation for n. To do this, we need an approximation for σ. We have an approximation from the initial sample of

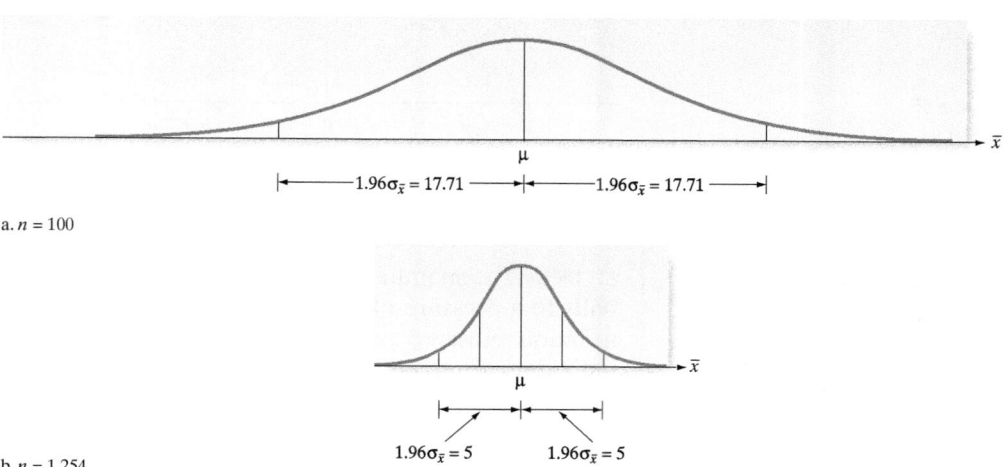

a. $n = 100$

Figure 14

Relationship between sample size and width of confidence interval: delinquent debtors example

b. $n = 1,254$

100 accounts—namely, the sample standard deviation, $s = 90.34$ (see the Solution to Example 2). Thus,

$$1.96\left(\frac{\sigma}{\sqrt{n}}\right) \approx 1.96\left(\frac{s}{\sqrt{n}}\right) = 1.96\left(\frac{90.34}{\sqrt{n}}\right) = 5$$

$$\sqrt{n} = \frac{1.96(90.34)}{5} = 35.413$$

$$n = (35.413)^2 = 1{,}254.1 \approx 1{,}254$$

Approximately 1,254 accounts will have to be randomly sampled to estimate the mean overdue amount μ to within \$5 with (approximately) 95% confidence. The confidence interval resulting from a sample of this size will be approximately \$10 wide (see Figure 14b).

In general, we express the reliability associated with a confidence interval for the population mean μ by specifying the **margin of sampling error,** within which we want to estimate μ with $100(1 - \alpha)\%$ confidence. The margin of error (denoted ME), then, is equal to the half-width of the confidence interval, as shown in Figure 15.

Sample Size Determination for $100(1 - \alpha)\%$ Confidence Interval for μ

In order to estimate μ with a margin of error ME and with $100(1 - \alpha)\%$ confidence, the required sample size is found as follows:

$$z_{\alpha/2}\left(\frac{\sigma}{\sqrt{n}}\right) = \text{ME}$$

The solution for n is given by the equation

$$n = \left[\frac{(z_{\alpha/2})\sigma}{\text{ME}}\right]^2$$

Note: The value of σ is usually unknown. It can be estimated by the standard deviation, s, from a prior sample. Alternatively, we may approximate the range R of observations in the population, and (conservatively) estimate $\sigma \approx \frac{R}{4}$. In any case, you should round the value of n obtained *upward* to ensure that the sample size will be sufficient to achieve the specified reliability.

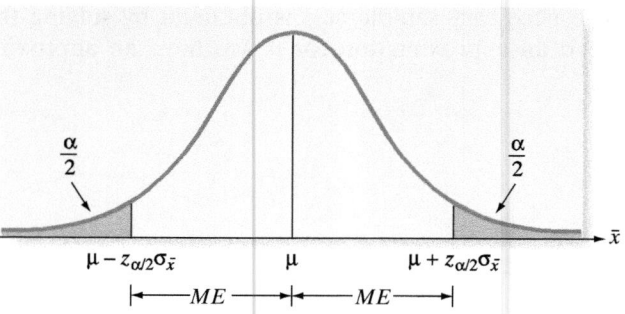

Figure 15

Specifying the sampling error as the half-width of a confidence interval

---

Example	9

Sample Size for Estimating μ—Mean Inflation Pressure of Footballs

Problem The manufacturer of official NFL footballs uses a machine to inflate its new balls to a pressure of 13.5 pounds. When the machine is properly calibrated, the mean inflation pressure is 13.5 pounds, but uncontrollable factors cause the pressures of individual footballs to vary randomly from about 13.3 to 13.7 pounds. For quality-control purposes, the manufacturer wishes to estimate the mean inflation pressure to within .025 pound of its true value with a 99% confidence interval. What sample size should be used?

Solution We desire a 99% confidence interval that estimates μ with a margin of error of ME = .025 pound. For a 99% confidence interval, we have $z_{\alpha/2} = z_{.005} = 2.576$. No previous estimate of s is available; however, we are given that the range of observations is $R = 13.7 - 13.3 = .4$. A conservative estimate (based on Chebychev's Rule) is $\sigma \approx R/4 = .1$. Now we use the formula derived in the box to find the sample size n:

$$n = \left[\frac{(z_{\alpha/2})\sigma}{\text{ME}} \right]^2 = \left[\frac{(2.576)(.1)}{.025} \right]^2 = 106.17$$

We round this up to $n = 107$. Realizing that σ was approximated by $R/4$, we might even advise that the sample size be specified as $n = 110$ to be more certain of attaining the objective of a 99% confidence interval with a sampling error of .025 pound or less.

Look Back To determine the value of the margin of error ME, look for the value that follows the key words "estimate μ to within. . . ."

Now Work Exercise 70

Sometimes the formula will yield a small sample size (say, $n < 30$). Unfortunately, this solution is invalid because the procedures and assumptions for small samples differ from those for large samples, as we discovered in Section 3. Therefore, if the formulas yield a small sample size, one simple strategy is to select a sample size $n = 30$.

Estimating a Population Proportion

The method outlined above is easily applied to a population proportion p. To illustrate, in Example 6 a company used a sample of 1,000 consumers to estimate the proportion of consumers who prefer its cereal brand. As a follow-up, we obtained the 95% confidence interval, $.313 \pm .029$. Suppose the company wishes to estimate its market share more precisely, say to within .015 with a 95% confidence interval.

The company wants a confidence interval with a margin of error for the estimate of p of ME = .015. The sample size required to generate such an interval is found by solving the following equation for n (see Figure 16):

$$z_{\alpha/2}\sigma_{\hat{p}} = \text{ME} \qquad \text{or} \qquad z_{\alpha/2}\sqrt{\frac{pq}{n}} = .015$$

Since a 95% confidence interval is desired, the appropriate z-value is $z_{\alpha/2} = z_{.025} = 1.96$. We must approximate the value of the product pq before we can solve the equation for n. As shown in Table 6, the closer the values of p and q to .5, the larger the product pq. Thus, to find a conservatively large sample size that will generate a confidence interval with the specified reliability, we generally choose an approximation of p close to .5. In the case of the food-products company, however, we have an initial sample estimate of $\hat{p} = .313$. A conservatively large estimate of pq can therefore be obtained by using, say, $p = .35$. We now substitute into the equation and solve for n:

$$1.96\sqrt{\frac{(.35)(.65)}{n}} = .015$$

$$n = \frac{(1.96)^2(.35)(.65)}{(.015)^2}$$

$$= 3,884.28 \approx 3,885$$

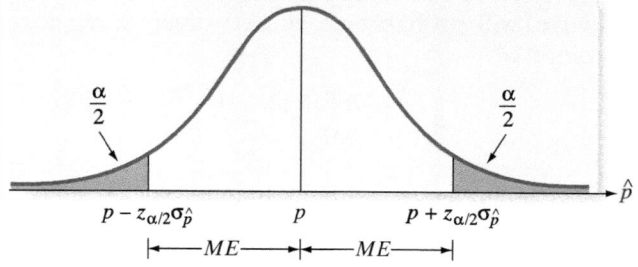

Figure 16

Specifying the sampling error of a confidence interval for a population proportion p

The company must sample about 3,885 consumers to estimate the percentage who prefer its brand to within .015 with a 95% confidence interval.

The procedure for finding the sample size necessary to estimate a population proportion p with a specified margin of error ME is given in the box.

Sample Size Determination for $100(1 - \alpha)\%$ Confidence Interval for p

In order to estimate a binomial probability p with margin of error ME and with $100(1 - \alpha)\%$ confidence, the required sample size is found by solving the following equation for n:

$$z_{\alpha/2} \sqrt{\frac{pq}{n}} = \text{ME}$$

The solution for n can be written as follows:

$$n = \frac{(z_{\alpha/2})^2 (pq)}{(\text{ME})^2}$$

Note: Because the value of the product pq is unknown, it can be estimated by using the sample fraction of successes, $\hat{p}$, from a prior sample. Remember (Table 6) that the value of pq is at its maximum when p equals .5, so you can obtain conservatively large values of n by approximating p by .5 or values close to .5. In any case, you should round the value of n obtained *upward* to ensure that the sample size will be sufficient to achieve the specified reliability.

Example	10

Sample Size for Estimating p—Fraction of Defective Cell Phones

Problem A cellular telephone manufacturer that entered the postregulation market too quickly has an initial problem with excessive customer complaints and consequent returns of the cell phones for repair or replacement. The manufacturer wants to determine the magnitude of the problem in order to estimate its warranty liability. How many cellular telephones should the company randomly sample from its warehouse and check in order to estimate the fraction defective, p, to within .01 with 90% confidence?

Solution In order to estimate p to within .01 of its true value, we set the half-width of the confidence interval equal to ME = .01, as shown in Figure 17.

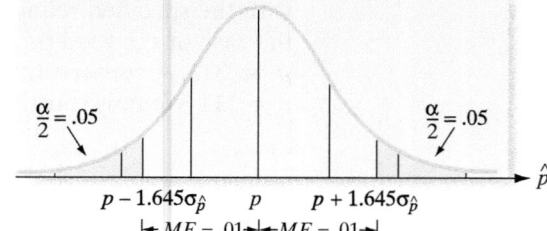

Figure 17

Specified reliability for estimate of fraction defective in Example 10

The equation for the sample size n requires an estimate of the product pq. We could most conservatively estimate $pq = .25$ (i.e., use $p = .5$), but this may be overly conservative when estimating a fraction defective. A value of .1, corresponding to 10% defective, will probably be conservatively large for this application. The solution is therefore

$$n = \frac{(z_{\alpha/2})^2 (pq)}{(\text{ME})^2} = \frac{(1.645)^2 (.1)(.9)}{(.01)^2} = 2,435.4 \approx 2,436$$

Thus, the manufacturer should sample 2,436 cellular telephones in order to estimate the fraction defective, p, to within .01 with 90% confidence.

> **Look Back** Remember that this answer depends on our approximation for pq, where we used .09. If the fraction defective is closer to .05 than to .10, we can use a sample of 1,286 cell phones (check this) to estimate p to within .01 with 90% confidence.

■ **Now Work Exercise 71**

The cost of sampling will also play an important role in the final determination of the sample size to be selected to estimate either μ or p. Although more complex formulas can be derived to balance the reliability and cost considerations, we will solve for the necessary sample size and note that the sampling budget may be a limiting factor. (Consult the references for a more complete treatment of this problem.) Once the sample size n is determined, be sure to devise a sampling plan that will ensure a representative sample is selected from the target population.

STATISTICS in ACTION REVISITED

Determining Sample Size

In the previous Statistics in Action applications in this chapter, we used confidence intervals (1) to estimate μ, the mean overpayment amount for claims in a Medicare fraud study, and (2) to estimate p, the coding error rate (i.e., proportion of claims that are incorrectly coded) of a Medicare provider. Both of these confidence intervals were based on selecting a random sample of 52 claims from the population of claims handled by the Medicare provider. How does the USDOJ determine how many claims to sample for auditing?

Consider the problem of estimating the coding error rate, p. As stated in a previous Statistics in Action Revisited, the USDOJ typically finds that about 50% of the claims in a Medicare fraud case are incorrectly coded. Suppose the USDOJ wants to estimate the true coding error rate of a Medicare provider to within .1 with 95% confidence. How many claims should be randomly sampled for audit in order to attain the desired estimate?

Here, the USDOJ desires a margin of error of ME = .1, a confidence level of $1 - \alpha = .95$ (for which $z_{\alpha/2} = 1.96$), and uses an estimate $p \approx .50$. Substituting these values into the sample size formula, we obtain:

$$n = (z_{\alpha/2})^2(pq)/(ME)^2$$
$$= (1.96)^2(.5)(.5)/(.1)^2$$
$$= 96.04$$

Consequently, the USDOJ should audit about 97 randomly selected claims to attain a 95% confidence interval for p with a sampling error of .10.

[*Note:* You may wonder why the sample actually used in the fraud analysis included only 52 claims. The sampling strategy employed involved more than selecting a simple random sample; rather, it used a more sophisticated sampling scheme, called stratified random sampling. The 52 claims represented the sample for just one of the strata.]

Exercises 60–78

Please be aware that some of the following problems may require knowledge of concepts that are not presented in this chapter.

Learning the Mechanics

60 If you wish to estimate a population mean with a margin of error of ME = .3 using a 95% confidence interval, and you know from prior sampling that σ^2 is approximately equal to 7.2, how many observations would have to be included in your sample?

61 Suppose you wish to estimate a population mean correct to within .20 with probability equal to .90. You do not know σ^2, but you know that the observations will range in value between 30 and 34.

a. Find the approximate sample size that will produce the desired accuracy of the estimate. You wish to be conservative to ensure that the sample size will be ample to achieve the desired accuracy of the estimate. [*Hint:* Using your knowledge of data variation and assume that the range of the observations will equal 4σ.]

b. Calculate the approximate sample size, making the less conservative assumption that the range of the observations is equal to 6σ.

62 In each case, find the approximate sample size required to construct a 95% confidence interval for p that has margin of error of ME = .08.

    a. Assume p is near .2.

    b. Assume you have no prior knowledge about p, but you wish to be certain that your sample is large enough to achieve the specified accuracy for the estimate.

63 The following is a 90% confidence interval for p: (.26, .54). How large was the sample used to construct this interval?

64 It costs you $10 to draw a sample of size $n = 1$ and measure the attribute of interest. You have a budget of $1,500.

    a. Do you have sufficient funds to estimate the population mean for the attribute of interest with a 95% confidence interval 5 units in width? Assume $\sigma = 14$.

    b. If you used a 90% confidence level, would your answer to part **a** change? Explain.

65 Suppose you wish to estimate the mean of a normal population using a 95% confidence interval, and you know from prior information that $\sigma^2 \approx 1$.

    a. To see the effect of the sample size on the width of the confidence interval, calculate the width of the confidence interval for $n = 16, 25, 49, 100,$ and 400.

    b. Plot the width as a function of sample size n on graph paper. Connect the points by a smooth curve and note how the width decreases as n increases.

66 If nothing is known about p, .5 can be substituted for p in the sample size formula for a population proportion. But when this is done, the resulting sample size may be larger than needed. Under what circumstances will using $p = .5$ in the sample size formula yield a sample size larger than needed to construct a confidence interval for p with a specified bound and a specified confidence level?

Applying the Concepts—Basic

67 **Lobster trap placement.** Refer to the *Bulletin of Marine Science* (April 2010) study of lobster trap placement, Exercise 29. Recall that you used a 95% confidence interval to estimate the mean trap spacing (in meters) for the population of red spiny lobster fishermen fishing in Baja California Sur, Mexico. How many teams of fishermen would need to be sampled in order to reduce the width of the confidence interval to 5 meters? Use the sample standard deviation from Exercise 29 in your calculation.

68 **Do social robots walk or roll?** Refer to the *International Conference on Social Robotics* (Vol. 6414, 2010) study of the trend in the design of social robots, Exercise 48. Recall that you used a 99% confidence interval to estimate the proportion of all social robots designed with legs, but no wheels. How many social robots would need to be sampled in order to estimate the proportion to within .075 of its true value?

69 **Assessing the bending strength of a wooden roof.** Refer to the *Journal of the International Association for Shell and Spatial Structures* (Aug. 2004) study to estimate the mean bending strength of imported white wood used on the roof of an ancient Japanese temple, Exercise 31. Suppose you want to estimate the true mean breaking strength of the white wood to within 4 MPa using a 90% confidence interval. How many pieces of the imported wood need to be tested? Recall that the sample standard deviation of the breaking strengths from the study was 10.9 MPa.

70 **Accounting and Machiavellianism.** Refer to the *Behavioral Research in Accounting* (Jan. 2008) study of Machiavellian traits in accountants, Exercise 19 where a Mach rating score was determined for each in a sample of accounting alumni who work as purchasing managers. Suppose you want to reduce the width of the 95% confidence interval for the true mean Mach rating score of all purchasing managers you obtained in Exercise 19b. How many purchasing managers should be included in the sample if you desire a sampling error of only 1.5 Mach rating points? Use $\sigma \approx 12$ in your calculations.

71 **Aluminum cans contaminated by fire.** A gigantic warehouse located in Tampa, Florida, stores approximately 60 million empty aluminum beer and soda cans. Recently, a fire occurred at the warehouse. The smoke from the fire contaminated many of the cans with blackspot, rendering them unusable. A University of South Florida statistician was hired by the insurance company to estimate p, the true proportion of cans in the warehouse that were contaminated by the fire. How many aluminum cans should be randomly sampled to estimate p to within .02 with 90% confidence?

Applying the Concepts—Intermediate

72 **Shopping on Black Friday.** Refer to the *International Journal of Retail and Distribution Management* (Vol. 39, 2011) survey of Black Friday shoppers, Exercise 16. One question was "How many hours do you usually spend shopping on Black Friday?"

    a. How many Black Friday shoppers should be included in a sample designed to estimate the average number of hours spent shopping on Black Friday if you want the estimate to deviate no more than .5 hour from the true mean?

    b. Devise a sampling plan for collecting the data that will likely result in a representative sample.

73 **Bacteria in bottled water.** Is the bottled water you drink safe? The Natural Resources Defense Council warns that the bottled water you are drinking may contain more bacteria and other potentially carcinogenic chemicals than allowed by state and federal regulations. Of the more than 1,000 bottles studied, nearly one-third exceeded government levels (www.nrdc.org). Suppose that the Natural Resources Defense Council wants an updated estimate of the population proportion of bottled water that violates at least one government standard. Determine the sample size (number of bottles) needed to estimate this proportion to within ± 0.01 with 99% confidence.

74 **Eye shadow, mascara and nickel allergies.** Refer to the *Journal of the European Academy of Dermatology and Venereology* (June 2010) study of the link between nickel allergies and use of mascara or eye shadow, Exercise 58. Recall that two groups of women were sampled—one group with cosmetic dermatitis from using eye shadow and another group with cosmetic dermatitis from using mascara. In either group, how many women would need to be sampled in order to yield an estimate of the population percentage with a nickel allergy that falls no more than 3% from the true value?

75 Monitoring phone calls to a toll-free number. A large food-products company receives about 100,000 phone calls a year from consumers on its toll-free number. A computer monitors and records how many rings it takes for an operator to answer, how much time each caller spends "on hold," and other data. However, the reliability of the monitoring system has been called into question by the operators and their labor union. As a check on the computer system, approximately how many calls should be manually monitored during the next year to estimate the true mean time that callers spend on hold to within 3 seconds with 95% confidence? Answer this question for the following values of the standard deviation of waiting times (in seconds): 10, 20, and 30.

76 USGA golf ball tests. The United States Golf Association (USGA) tests all new brands of golf balls to ensure that they meet USGA specifications. One test conducted is intended to measure the average distance traveled when the ball is hit by a machine called "Iron Byron," a name inspired by the swing of the famous golfer Byron Nelson. Suppose the USGA wishes to estimate the mean distance for a new brand to within 1 yard with 90% confidence. Assume that past tests have indicated that the standard deviation of the distances Iron Byron hits golf balls is approximately 10 yards. How many golf balls should be hit by Iron Byron to achieve the desired accuracy in estimating the mean?

Applying the Concepts—Advanced

77 Is caffeine addictive? Does the caffeine in coffee, tea, and cola induce an addiction similar to that induced by alcohol, tobacco, heroin, and cocaine? In an attempt to answer this question, researchers at Johns Hopkins University examined 27 caffeine drinkers and found 25 who displayed some type of withdrawal symptoms when abstaining from caffeine. [*Note:* The 27 caffeine drinkers volunteered for the study.] Furthermore, of 11 caffeine drinkers who were diagnosed as caffeine dependent, 8 displayed dramatic withdrawal symptoms (including impairment in normal functioning) when they consumed a caffeine-free diet in a controlled setting. The National Coffee Association claimed, however, that the study group was too small to draw conclusions. Is the sample large enough to estimate the true proportion of caffeine drinkers who are caffeine dependent to within .05 of the true value with 99% confidence? Explain.

78 Preventing production of defective items. It costs more to produce defective items—because they must be scrapped or reworked—than it does to produce nondefective items. This simple fact suggests that manufacturers should ensure the quality of their products by perfecting their production processes rather than through inspection of finished products (*Out of the Crisis,* Deming, 1986). In order to better understand a particular metal-stamping process, a manufacturer wishes to estimate the mean length of items produced by the process during the past 24 hours.
a. How many parts should be sampled in order to estimate the population mean to within .1 millimeter (mm) with 90% confidence? Previous studies of this machine have indicated that the standard deviation of lengths produced by the stamping operation is about 2 mm.
b. Time permits the use of a sample size no larger than 100. If a 90% confidence interval for μ is constructed using $n = 100$, will it be wider or narrower than would have been obtained using the sample size determined in part **a**? Explain.
c. If management requires that μ be estimated to within .1 mm and that a sample size of no more than 100 be used, what is (approximately) the maximum confidence level that could be attained for a confidence interval that meets management's specifications?

6 Finite Population Correction for Simple Random Sampling*

The large-sample confidence intervals for a population mean μ and a population proportion p presented in the previous sections are based on a simple random sample selected from the target population. Although we did not state it, the procedure also assumes that the number N of measurements (i.e., sampling units) in the population is large relative to the sample size n.

In some sampling situations, the sample size n may represent 5% or perhaps 10% of the total number N of sampling units in the population. When the sample size is large relative to the number of measurements in the population (see the next box), the standard errors of the estimators of μ and p given in Sections 2 and 4, respectively, should be multiplied by a **finite population correction factor.**

The form of the finite population correction factor depends on how the population variance σ^2 is defined. In order to simplify the formulas of the standard errors, it is common to define σ^2 as division of the sum of squares of deviations by $N - 1$ *rather than by* N (analogous to the way we defined the sample variance). If we adopt this convention, the finite population correction factor becomes $\sqrt{(N - n)/N}$. Then the estimated standard errors of $\bar{x}$ (the estimator of μ) and $\hat{p}$ (the estimator of p) are as shown in the box.*

*For most surveys and opinion polls, the finite population correction factor is approximately equal to 1 and, if desired, can be safely ignored. However, if $n/N > .05$, the finite population correction factor should be included in the calculation of the standard error.

Rule of Thumb for Finite Population Correction Factor

Use the finite population correction factor (shown in the next box) when $n/N > .05$.

Simple Random Sampling with Finite Population of Size N
Estimation of the Population Mean

Estimated standard error:

$$\hat{\sigma}_{\bar{x}} = \frac{s}{\sqrt{n}} \sqrt{\frac{N - n}{N}}$$

Approximate 95% confidence interval: $\bar{x} \pm 2\hat{\sigma}_{\bar{x}}$

Estimation of the Population Proportion

Estimated standard error:

$$\hat{\sigma}_{\hat{p}} = \sqrt{\frac{\hat{p}(1 - \hat{p})}{n}} \sqrt{\frac{N - n}{N}}$$

Approximate 95% confidence interval: $\hat{p} \pm 2\hat{\sigma}_{\hat{p}}$

Note: The confidence intervals are "approximate" because we are using 2 to approximate the value $z_{.025} = 1.96$.

Example	**11**

Applying the Finite Population Correction Factor—Manufacture of Sheet Aluminum Foil

Problem A specialty manufacturer wants to purchase remnants of sheet aluminum foil. The foil, all of which is the same thickness, is stored on 1,462 rolls, each containing a varying amount of foil. To obtain an estimate of the total number of square feet of foil on all the rolls, the manufacturer randomly sampled 100 rolls and measured the number of square feet on each roll. The sample mean was 47.4, and the sample standard deviation was 12.4.

a. Find an approximate 95% confidence interval for the mean amount of foil on the 1,462 rolls.

b. Estimate the total number of square feet of foil on all the rolls by multiplying the confidence interval, part **a,** by 1,462. Interpret the result.

Solution

a. Each roll of foil is a sampling unit, and there are $N = 1,462$ units in the population, and the sample size is $n = 100$. Because $\frac{n}{N} = \frac{100}{1,462} = .068$ exceeds .05, we need to apply the finite population correction factor. We have $n = 100$, $\bar{x} = 47.4$, and $s = 12.4$. Substituting these quantities, we obtain the approximate 95% confidence interval:

$$\bar{x} \pm 2\frac{s}{\sqrt{n}} \sqrt{\frac{(N - n)}{N}} = (47.4) \pm 2\frac{12.4}{\sqrt{100}} \sqrt{\frac{(1,462 - 100)}{1,462}}$$

$$= 47.4 \pm 2.39$$

or, $(45.01, 49.79)$.

b. For finite populations of size N, the sum of all measurements in the population—called a *population total*—is

$$\sum_{i=1}^{N} x_i = N\mu$$

Because the confidence interval, part **a,** estimates μ, an estimate of the population total is obtained by multiplying the endpoints of the interval by N. For we have

$$\text{Lower Limit} = N(45.01) = 1,462(45.01) = 65,804.6$$
$$\text{Upper Limit} = N(49.79) = 1,462(49.79) = 72,793.0$$

Consequently, the manufacturer estimates the total amount of foil to be in the interval of 65,805 square feet to 72,793 square feet with 95% confidence.

Look Back If the manufacturer wants to adopt a conservative approach, the bid for the foil will be based on the lower confidence limit, 65,805 square feet of foil.

■ **Now Work Exercise 86a**

Exercises 79–91

Learning the Mechanics

79 Calculate the percentage of the population sampled and the finite population correction factor for each of the following situations.
  a. $n = 1,000, N = 2,500$
  b. $n = 1,000, N = 5,000$
  c. $n = 1,000, N = 10,000$
  d. $n = 1,000, N = 100,000$

80 Suppose the standard deviation of the population is known to be $\sigma = 200$. Calculate the standard error of $\bar{x}$ for each of the situations described in Exercise 79.

81 Suppose $N = 10,000, n = 2,000$, and $s = 50$.
  a. Compute the standard error of $\bar{x}$ using the finite population correction factor.
  b. Repeat part **a** assuming $n = 4,000$.
  c. Repeat part **a** assuming $n = 10,000$.
  d. Compare parts **a, b,** and **c** and describe what happens to the standard error of $\bar{x}$ as n increases.
  e. The answer to part **c** is 0. This indicates that there is no sampling error in this case. Explain.

82 Suppose $N = 5,000, n = 64$, and $s = 24$.
  a. Compare the size of the standard error of $\bar{x}$ computed with and without the finite population correction factor.
  b. Repeat part **a,** but this time assume $n = 400$.
  c. Theoretically, when sampling from a finite population, the finite population correction factor should always be used in computing the standard error of $\bar{x}$. However, when n is small relative to N, the finite population correction factor is close to 1 and can safely be ignored. Explain how parts **a** and **b** illustrate this point.

83 Suppose you want to estimate a population proportion, p, and $\hat{p} = .42, N = 6,000$, and $n = 1,600$. Find an approximate 95% confidence interval for p.

84 Suppose you want to estimate a population mean, μ, and $\bar{x} = 422, s = 14, N = 375$, and $n = 40$. Find an approximate 95% confidence interval for μ.

85 A random sample of size $n = 30$ was drawn from a population of size $N = 300$. The following measurements were obtained:

L06085

21	33	19	29	22	38	58	29	52	36	37	30
53	37	29	18	35	42	36	41	35	36	33	38
29	38	39	54	42	42

  a. Estimate μ with an approximate 95% confidence interval.
  b. Estimate p, the proportion of measurements in the population that are greater than 30, with an approximate 95% confidence interval.

Applying the Concepts—Basic

86 **Magazine subscriber salaries.** Each year, the trade magazine *Quality Progress* publishes a study of subscribers' salaries. One year, the 223 vice presidents sampled had a mean salary of $116,754 and a standard deviation of $39,185. Suppose the goal of the study is to estimate the true mean salary of all vice presidents who subscribe to *Quality Progress*.
  a. If 2,193 vice presidents subscribe to *Quality Progress*, [NW] estimate the mean with an approximate 95% confidence interval.
  b. Interpret the result.

87 **NFL player survey.** Researchers at the University of Pennsylvania's Wharton Sports Business Initiative collaborated with the National Football League Players Association (NFLPA) to produce the first NFL Player Survey. Of the 1,696 active NFL players, 1,355 (almost 80%) responded to the survey. One of the survey questions asked, "Who is the coach—professional, college, or high school—that has been the most influential in your career?" Of the 1,355 respondents, 759 selected an NFL (professional) coach.
  a. Construct a 95% confidence interval for the true proportion of active NFL players who select a professional coach as the most influential in their careers.
  b. Why is it necessary to use the continuity correction factor in the construction of the interval, part **a?**
  c. Give a practical interpretation of the interval, part **a.**

Applying the Concepts—Intermediate

88 **Furniture brand familiarity.** A brand name that consumers recognize is a highly valued commodity in any industry. To assess brand familiarity in the furniture industry, NPD (a market research firm) surveyed 1,333 women who head U.S. households that have incomes of $25,000 or more. The sample was drawn from a database of 25,000 households that match the criteria listed above. Of the 10 furniture brands evaluated, La-Z-Boy was the most recognized brand; 70.8% of the respondents indicated they were "very familiar" with La-Z-Boy.
  a. Describe the population being investigated by NPD.
  b. In constructing a confidence interval to estimate the proportion of households that are very familiar with the La-Z-Boy brand, is it necessary to use the finite population correction factor? Explain.
  c. What estimate of the standard error of $\hat{p}$ should be used in constructing the confidence interval of part **b?**
  d. Construct a 90% confidence interval for the true proportion and interpret it in the context of the problem.

89 Auditing sampling methods. Traditionally, auditors have relied to a great extent on sampling techniques, rather than 100% audits, to help them test and evaluate the financial records of a client firm. When sampling is used to obtain an estimate of the total dollar value of an account—the account balance—the examination is known as *a substantive test* (*Audit Sampling—AICPA Audit Guide*, 2012). In order to evaluate the reasonableness of a firm's stated total value of its parts inventory, an auditor randomly samples 100 of the total of 500 parts in stock, prices each part, and reports the results shown in the next table.

Part Number	Part Price	Sample Size
002	$ 108	3
101	55	2
832	500	1
077	73	10
688	300	1
910	54	4
839	92	6
121	833	5
271	50	9
399	125	12
761	1,000	2
093	62	8
505	205	7
597	88	11
830	100	19

a. Give a point estimate of the mean value of the parts inventory.

b. Find the estimated standard error of the point estimate of part **a.**

c. Construct an approximate 95% confidence interval for the mean value of the parts inventory.

d. The firm reported a mean parts inventory value of $300. What does your confidence interval of part **c** suggest about the reasonableness of the firm's reported figure? Explain.

90 Invoice errors in a billing system. In a study of invoice errors in a company's new billing system, an auditor randomly sampled 35 invoices produced by the new system and recorded actual amount (*A*), invoice amount (*I*), and the difference (or error), $x = (A - I)$. The results were $\bar{x} = \$1$ and $s = \$124$. At the time that the sample was drawn, the new system had produced 1,500 invoices. Use this information to find an approximate 95% confidence interval for the true mean error per invoice of the new system. Interpret the result.

Applying the Concepts—Advanced

91 Pesticide residue in corn products. The U.S. Environmental Protection Agency (EPA) bans use of the cancer-causing pesticide ethylene dibromide (EDB) as a fumigant for grain- and flour-milling equipment. EDB was once used to protect against infestation by microscopic roundworms called *nematodes*. The EPA sets maximum safe levels for EDB presence in raw grain, flour, cake mixes, cereals, bread, and other grain products on supermarket shelves and in warehouses. Of the 3,000 corn-related products sold in one state, tests indicated that 15 of a random sample of 175 had EDB residues above the safe level. Will more than 7% of the corn-related products in this state have to be removed from shelves and warehouses? Explain.

7 Confidence Interval for a Population Variance*

In the previous sections, we considered interval estimation for population means or proportions. In this optional section, we discuss a confidence interval for a population variance, σ^2.

The U.S. Army Corps of Engineers studies contaminated fish in the Tennessee River, Alabama. It is important for the Corps of Engineers to know how stable the weights of the contaminated fish are. That is, how large is the variation in the fish weights? The key word "variation" indicates that the target population parameter is σ^2, the variance of the weights of all contaminated fish inhabiting the Tennessee River. Of course, the exact value of σ^2 will be unknown. Consequently, the Corps of Engineers wants to estimate its value with a high level of confidence.

Intuitively, it seems reasonable to use the sample variance, s^2, to estimate σ^2. However, unlike with sample means and proportions, the sampling distribution of s^2 does not follow a normal (z) distribution or a Student's t-distribution. Rather, when certain assumptions are satisfied (we discuss these later), the sampling distribution of s^2 possesses approximately a **chi-square (χ^2) distribution.** The chi-square probability distribution, like the t-distribution, is characterized by a quantity called the *degrees of freedom* (df) associated with the distribution. Several chi-square distributions with different df values are shown in Figure 18. You can see that unlike z- and t-distributions, the chi-square distribution is not symmetric about 0.

The upper-tail areas for this distribution have been tabulated and are given in Table IV in Appendix: Tables, a portion of which is reproduced in Table 7. The table gives the values of χ^2, denoted as χ^2_α, that locate an area of α in the upper tail of the chi-square distribution; that is, $P(\chi^2 > \chi^2_\alpha) = \alpha$. As with the t-statistic, the degrees

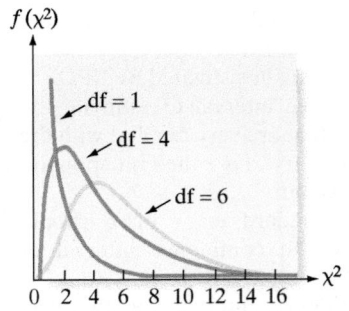

$f(\chi^2)$

df = 1
df = 4
df = 6

Figure 18
Several χ^2 probability distributions

Table 7	Reproduction of Part of Table IV in Appendix: Tables: Critical Values of Chi Square

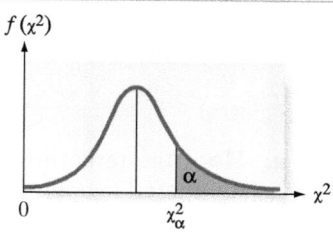

Degrees of Freedom	$\chi^2_{.100}$	$\chi^2_{.050}$	$\chi^2_{.025}$	$\chi^2_{.010}$	$\chi^2_{.005}$
1	2.70554	3.84146	5.02389	6.63490	7.87944
2	4.60517	5.99147	7.37776	9.21034	10.5966
3	6.25139	7.81473	9.34840	11.3449	12.8381
4	7.77944	9.48773	11.1433	13.2767	14.8602
5	9.23635	11.0705	12.8325	15.0863	16.7496
6	10.6446	12.5916	14.4494	16.8119	18.5476
7	12.0170	14.0671	16.0128	18.4753	20.2777
8	13.3616	15.5073	17.5346	20.0902	21.9550
9	14.6837	16.9190	19.0228	21.6660	23.5893
10	15.9871	18.3070	20.4831	23.2093	25.1882
11	17.2750	19.6751	21.9200	24.7250	25.7569
12	18.5494	21.0261	23.3367	26.2170	28.2995
13	19.8119	22.3621	24.7356	27.6883	29.8194
14	21.0642	23.6848	26.1190	29.1413	31.3193
15	22.3072	24.9958	27.4884	30.5779	32.8013
16	23.5418	26.2862	28.8454	31.9999	34.2672
17	24.7690	27.5871	30.1910	33.4087	35.7185
18	25.9894	28.8693	31.5264	34.8053	37.1564
19	27.2036	30.1435	32.8523	36.1908	38.5822

of freedom associated with s^2 are $(n - 1)$. Thus, for $n = 10$ and an upper-tail value $\alpha = .05$, you will have $n - 1 = 9$ df and $\chi^2_{.05} = 16.9190$ (highlighted in Table 7).

The chi-square distribution is used to find a confidence interval for σ^2, as shown in the box. An illustrative example follows.

A 100(1 − α) Confidence Interval for σ^2

$$\frac{(n - 1)s^2}{\chi^2_{\alpha/2}} \leq \sigma^2 \leq \frac{(n - 1)s^2}{\chi^2_{(1-\alpha/2)}}$$

where $\chi^2_{\alpha/2}$ and $\chi^2_{(1-\alpha/2)}$ are values corresponding to an area of $\alpha/2$ in the right (upper) and left (lower) tails, respectively, of the chi-square distribution based on $(n - 1)$ degrees of freedom.

Conditions Required for a Valid Confidence Interval for σ^2

1. A random sample is selected from the target population.
2. The population of interest has a relative frequency distribution that is approximately normal.

Example 12

Estimating σ^2—Weight Variance of Contaminated Fish

Problem Refer to the U.S. Army Corps of Engineers study of contaminated fish in the Tennessee River. The Corps of Engineers has collected data for a random sample of 144 fish contaminated with DDT. (The engineers made sure to capture contaminated fish in several different randomly selected streams and tributaries of the river.) The fish weights (in grams) are saved in the **DDT** file. The Army Corps of Engineers wants to

estimate the true variation in fish weights in order to determine whether the fish are stable enough to allow further testing for DDT contamination.

a. Use the sample data to find a 95% confidence interval for the parameter of interest.

b. Determine whether the confidence interval, part **a,** is valid.

Solution

a. Here, the target parameter is σ^2, the variance of the population of weights of contaminated fish. First we need to find the sample variance, s^2, to compute the interval estimate. The Minitab printout, Figure 19 gives descriptive statistics for the sample weights saved in the **DDT** file. You can see that $s = 376.5$ grams. Consequently, $s^2 = (376.5)^2 = 141{,}752.25$.

Descriptive Statistics: WEIGHT

Variable	N	Mean	StDev	Minimum	Median	Maximum
WEIGHT	144	1049.7	376.5	173.0	1000.0	2302.0

Next, we require the critical values $\chi^2_{\alpha/2}$ and $\chi^2_{(1-\alpha/2)}$ for a chi-square distribution. For a 95% confidence interval, $\alpha = .05$, $\alpha/2 = .025$, and $(1 - \alpha/2) = .975$. Therefore, we need $\chi^2_{.025}$ and $\chi^2_{.975}$. Now, for a sample size $n = 144$, the degrees of freedom associated with the distribution is df $= (n - 1) = 143$. Looking in the df $= 150$ row of Table IV, Appendix: Tables (the row with the df value closest to 143), we find $\chi^2_{.025} = 185.800$ and $\chi^2_{.975} = 117.985$.

Substituting the appropriate values into the formula given in the box, we obtain

$$\frac{(144 - 1)(376.5)^2}{185.500} \leq \sigma^2 \leq \frac{(144 - 1)(376.5)^2}{117.985}$$

Or,

$$109{,}275 \leq \sigma^2 \leq 171{,}806$$

Thus, the Army Corps of Engineers can be 95% confident that the variance in weights of the population of contaminated fish ranges between 109,275 and 171,806.

b. According to the box, two conditions are required for the confidence interval to be valid. First, the sample must be randomly selected from the population. The Army Corps of Engineers did, indeed, collect a random sample of contaminated fish, making sure to sample fish from different location in the Tennessee River. Second, the population data (the fish weights) must be approximately normally distributed. A Minitab histogram for the sampled fish weights (with a normal curve superimposed) is displayed in Figure 20. Clearly, the data appear to be approximately normally distributed. Thus, the confidence interval is valid.

Figure 19

Minitab descriptive statistics for fish weights, Example 12

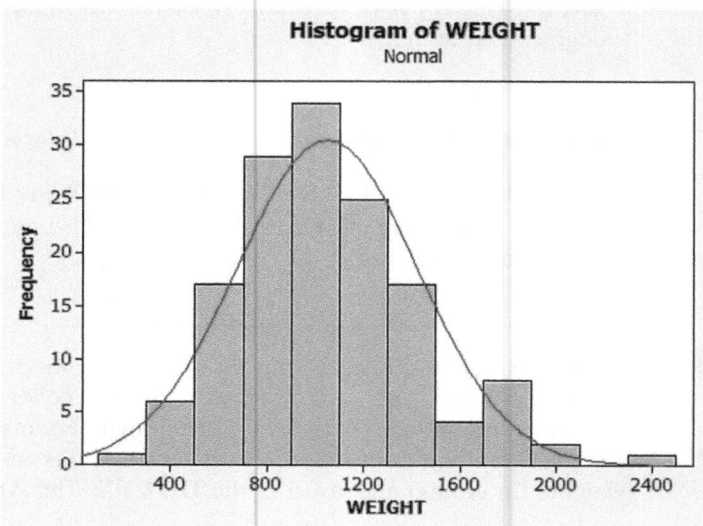

Figure 20

Minitab histogram of fish weights, Example 12

Look Ahead Will this confidence interval to practically useful in helping the Corps of Engineers decide whether the weights of the fish are stable? Only if it is clear what a weight variance of, say, 150,000 grams^2 implies. Most likely, the Corps of Engineers will want the interval in the same units as the weight measurement—grams. Consequently, a confidence interval for σ, the standard deviation of the population of fish weights, is desired. We demonstrate how to obtain this interval estimate in the next example.

■ **Now Work Exercise 98a, b**

Example   13

Estimating σ—Weight Standard Deviation of Contaminated Fish

Problem Refer to Example 12. Find a 95% confidence interval for σ, the true standard deviation of the contaminated fish weights.

Solution A confidence interval for σ is obtained by taking the square roots of the lower and upper endpoints of a confidence interval for σ^2. Consequently, the 95% confidence interval for σ is:

$$\sqrt{109{,}275} \le \sigma \le \sqrt{171{,}806}$$

Or,

$$330.5 \le \sigma \le 414.5$$

Thus, the engineers can be 95% confident that the true standard deviation of fish weights is between 330.5 grams and 414.5 grams.

Look Back Suppose the Corps of Engineers' threshold is $\sigma = 500$ grams. That is, if the standard deviation in fish weights is 500 grams or higher, further DDT contamination tests will be suspended due to the unstableness of the fish weights. Since the 95% confidence interval for σ lies below 500 grams, the engineers will continue the DDT contamination tests on the fish.

■ **Now Work Exercise 98c, d, e, f**

> ⚠ **CAUTION** The procedure for estimating either σ^2 or σ requires an assumption regardless of whether the sample size n is large or small (see the condition in the box). The sampled data must come from a population that has an approximate normal distribution. Unlike small-sample confidence intervals for μ based on the t-distribution, *slight to moderate departures from normality will render the chi-square confidence interval for σ^2 invalid.*

Exercises 92–104

Please be aware that some of the following problems may require knowledge of concepts that are not presented in this chapter.

Learning the Mechanics

92 For each of the following combinations of α and degrees of freedom (df), use Table IV in Appendix: Tables to find the values of $\chi^2_{\alpha/2}$ and $\chi^2_{(1-\alpha/2)}$ that would be used to form a confidence interval for σ^2.
   a. $\alpha = .05, df = 7$
   b. $\alpha = .10, df = 16$
   c. $\alpha = .01, df = 20$
   d. $\alpha = .05, df = 20$

93 Given the following values of $\bar{x}$, s, and n, form a 90% confidence interval for σ^2.
   a. $\bar{x} = 21, s = 2.5, n = 50$
   b. $\bar{x} = 1.3, s = .02, n = 15$
   c. $\bar{x} = 167, s = 31.6, n = 22$
   d. $\bar{x} = 9.4, s = 1.5, n = 5$

94 Refer to Exercise 93. For each part, **a–d,** form a 90% confidence interval for σ.

95 A random sample of $n = 6$ observations from a normal distribution resulted in the data shown in the table. Compute a 95% confidence interval for σ^2.

L06095

8	2	3	7	11	6

Applying the Concepts—Basics

96 **Motivation of drug dealers.** *Applied Psychology in Criminal Justice* (Sep. 2009) did a study of the personality characteristics of convicted drug dealers.

A random sample of 100 drug dealers had a mean Wanting Recognition (WR) score of 39 points, with a standard deviation of 6 points. The researchers are interested in σ^2, the variation in WR scores for all convicted drug dealers.

a. Identify the target parameter, in symbols and words.

b. Compute a 99% confidence interval for σ^2.

c. What does it mean to say that the target parameter lies within the interval with "99% confidence"?

d. What assumption about the data must be satisfied in order for the confidence interval to be valid?

e. To obtain a practical interpretation of the interval, part b, explain why a confidence interval for the standard deviation, σ, is desired.

f. Use the results, part b, to compute a 99% confidence interval for σ. Give a practical interpretation of the interval.

97 **Facial structure of CEOs.** Refer to the *Psychological Science* (Vol. 22, 2011) study of a chief executive officer's facial structure, Exercise 20. Recall that the facial width-to-height ratio (WHR) was determined by computer analysis for each in a sample of 55 CEOs at publicly traded *Fortune* 500 firms, with the following results: $\bar{x} = 1.96, s = .15$.

a. Find and interpret a 95% confidence interval for the standard deviation, σ, of the facial WHR values for all CEOs at publicly traded *Fortune* 500 firms. Interpret the result.

b. For the interval, part a, to be valid, the population of WHR values should be distributed how? Draw a sketch of the required distribution to support your answer.

98 **Corporate sustainability of CPA firms.** Refer to the *Business and Society* (March 2011) study on the sustainability behaviors of CPA corporations, Exercise 12. Recall that the level of support for corporate sustainability (measured on a quantitative scale ranging from 0 to 160 points) was obtained for each in a sample of 992 senior managers at CPA firms. The accompanying Minitab printout gives 90% confidence intervals for both the variance and standard deviation of level of support for all senior managers at CPA firms.

```
Statistics

Variable    N    StDev    Variance
Support    992    26.9       722


90% Confidence Intervals

                       CI for        CI for
Variable   Method      StDev         Variance
Support    Chi-Square  (25.9, 27.9)  (672, 779)
```

a. Locate the 90% confidence interval for σ^2 on the printout. Interpret the result.

b. Use the sample variance on the printout to calculate the 90% confidence interval for σ^2. Does your result agree with the interval shown on the printout?

c. Locate the 90% confidence interval for σ on the printout.

d. Use the result, part a, to calculate the 90% confidence interval for σ. Does your result agree with the interval shown on the printout?

e. Give a practical interpretation of the 90% confidence interval for σ.

f. What assumption about the distribution of level of support is required for the inference, part e, to be valid? Is this assumption reasonably satisfied?

99 **Radon exposure in Egyptian tombs.** Refer to the *Radiation Protection Dosimetry* (December 2010) study of radon exposure in tombs carved from limestone in the Egyptian Valley of Kings, Exercise 30. The radon levels in the inner chambers of a sample of 12 tombs were determined, yielding the following summary statistics: $\bar{x} = 3,643$ Bq/m³ and $s = 4,487$ Bq/m³. Use this information to estimate, with 95% confidence, the true standard deviation of radon levels in tombs in the Valley of Kings. Interpret the resulting interval.

Applying the Concepts—Intermediate

100 **Jitter in a water power system.** *Jitter* is a term used to describe the variation in conduction time of a water power system. Low throughput jitter is critical to successful waterline technology. An investigation of throughput jitter in the opening switch of a prototype system (*Journal of Applied Physics*) yielded the following descriptive statistics on conduction time for $n = 18$ trials: $\bar{x} = 334.8$ nanoseconds, $s = 6.3$ nanoseconds. (Conduction time is defined as the length of time required for the downstream current to equal 10% of the upstream current.)

a. Construct a 95% confidence interval for the true standard deviation of conduction times of the prototype system.

b. Practically interpret the confidence interval, part a.

c. A system is considered to have low throughput jitter if the true conduction time standard deviation is less than 7 nanoseconds. Does the prototype system satisfy this requirement? Explain.

101 **Drug content assessment.** *Analytical Chemistry* (Dec. 15, 2009) did a study of a new method used by GlaxoSmithKline Medicines Research Center to determine the amount of drug in a tablet. Drug concentrations (measured as a percentage) for 50 randomly selected tablets are repeated in the accompanying table. For comparisons against a standard method, the scientists at GlaxoSmithKline desire an estimate of the variability in drug concentrations for the new method. Obtain the estimate for the scientists using a 99% confidence interval. Interpret the interval.

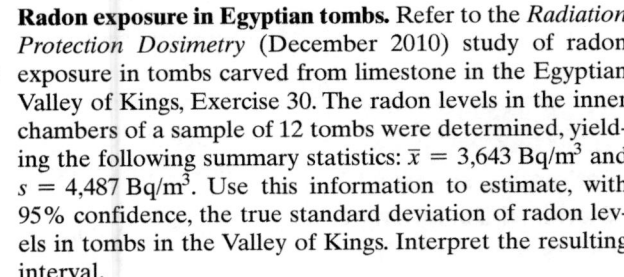

91.28	92.83	89.35	91.90	82.85	94.83	89.83	89.00	84.62
86.96	88.32	91.17	83.86	89.74	92.24	92.59	84.21	89.36
90.96	92.85	89.39	89.82	89.91	92.16	88.67	89.35	86.51
89.04	91.82	93.02	88.32	88.76	89.26	90.36	87.16	91.74
86.12	92.10	83.33	87.31	88.20	92.78	86.35	93.84	91.20
93.44	86.77	83.77	93.19	81.79				

Source: Based on Borman, P. J., Marion, J. C., Damjanov, I., & Jackson, P. "Design and analysis of method equivalence studies," *Analytical Chemistry,* Vol. 81, No. 24, December 15, 2009 (Table 3).

102 **Phishing attacks on e-mail accounts.** *Chance* (Summer 2007) did a study of an actual phishing attack against an organization. *Phishing* describes an attempt to extract personal/financial information from unsuspecting people through fraudulent e-mail. The interarrival times (in seconds) for 267 fraud box e-mail notifications are saved in the accompanying file. Consider these interarrival times to represent the population of interest.

a. Obtain a random sample of $n = 10$ interarrival times from the population.

b. Use the sample, part **b,** to obtain an interval estimate of the population variance of the interarrival times. What is the measure of reliability for your estimate?

c. Find the true population variance for the data. Does the interval, part **b,** contain the true variance? Give one reason why it may not.

103 **Lobster trap placement.** Refer to the *Bulletin of Marine Science* (April 2010) observational study of teams fishing for the red spiny lobster in Baja California Sur, Mexico, Exercise 29. Trap-spacing measurements (in meters) for a sample of seven teams of red spiny lobster fishermen are repeated in the table. The researchers want to know how variable the trap-spacing measurements are for the population of red spiny lobster fishermen fishing in Baja California Sur, Mexico. Provide the researchers with an estimate of the target parameter using a 99% confidence interval.

93	99	105	94	82	70	86

Source: Based on Shester, G. G. "Explaining catch variation among Baja California lobster fishers through spatial analysis of trap-placement decisions," *Bulletin of Marine Science,* Vol. 86, No. 2, April 2010 (Table 1) , pp. 479–498.

104 **Is honey a cough remedy?** *Archives of Pediatrics and Adolescent Medicine* (Dec. 2007) did a study of honey as a remedy for coughing. The 105 ill children in the sample were randomly divided into groups. One group received a dosage of an over-the-counter cough medicine (DM); another group received a dosage of honey (H). The coughing improvement scores (as determined by the children's parents) for the patients in the two groups are reproduced in the accompanying table. The pediatric researchers desire information on the variation in coughing improvement scores for each of the two groups.

a. Find a 90% confidence interval for the standard deviation in improvement scores for the honey dosage group.

b. Repeat part **a** for the DM dosage group.

c. Based on the results, parts **a** and **b,** what conclusions can the pediatric researchers draw about which group has the smaller variation in improvement scores?

Honey Dosage:	12 11 15 11 10 13 10 4 15 16 9 14 10 6 10 8 11 12 12 8 12 9 11 15 10 15 9 13 8 12 10 8 9 5 12
DM Dosage:	4 6 9 4 7 7 7 9 12 10 11 6 3 4 9 12 7 6 8 12 12 4 12 13 7 10 13 9 4 4 10 15 9

Source: Based on Paul, I. M., et al. "Effect of honey, dextromethorphan, and no treatment on nocturnal cough and sleep quality for coughing children and their parents," *Archives of Pediatrics and Adolescent Medicine,* Vol. 161, No. 12, Dec. 2007 (data simulated).

■ Chapter Notes

Key Terms

Note: Asterisks (*) denote items from the optional sections of this chapter.

Adjusted $(1 - \alpha)100\%$ confidence interval for a population parameter
*Chi-square distribution
Confidence coefficient
Confidence interval
Confidence level
Degrees of freedom
*Finite population correction factor

Interval estimator
Large-sample confidence interval for p
Margin of sampling error
Point estimator
Target parameter
t-statistic
z-statistic

Key Symbols

θ General population parameter (theta)
μ Population mean
σ^2 Population variance
σ Population standard deviation
p Population proportion; $P(\text{Success})$ in binomial trial

q $1 - p$
$\bar{x}$ Sample mean (estimator of μ)
$\hat{p}$ Sample proportion (estimator of p)
*s^2 Sample variance (estimator of σ^2)
$\mu_{\bar{x}}$ Mean of the population sampling distribution of $\bar{x}$
$\sigma_{\bar{x}}$ Standard deviation of the sampling distribution of $\bar{x}$
$\sigma_{\hat{p}}$ Standard deviation of the sampling distribution of $\hat{p}$
ME   Margin of sampling error in estimation
α $(1 - \alpha)$ represents the confidence coefficient
$z_{\alpha/2}$ z-value used in a $100(1 - \alpha)\%$ large-sample confidence interval for μ or p
$t_{\alpha/2}$ Student's t-value used in a $100(1 - \alpha)\%$ small-sample confidence interval for μ
*N Number of observations in the target population
*$\chi^2_{\alpha/2}$ Chi-square value used in a $100(1 - \alpha)\%$ confidence interval for σ^2

Key Ideas

Population Parameters, Estimators, and Standard Errors

Parameter (θ)	Estimator ($\hat{\theta}$)	Standard Error of Estimator ($\sigma_{\hat{\theta}}$)	Estimated Std. Error ($\hat{\sigma}_{\hat{\theta}}$)
Mean, μ	$\bar{x}$	$\sigma/\sqrt{n}$	$s/\sqrt{n}$
Proportion, p	$\hat{p}$	$\sqrt{pq/n}$	$\sqrt{\hat{p}\hat{q}/n}$
*Variance, σ^2	s^2	—	—

Confidence Interval: An interval that encloses an unknown population parameter with a certain level of confidence $(1 - \alpha)$

Confidence Coefficient: The probability $(1 - \alpha)$ that a randomly selected confidence interval encloses the true value of the population parameter.

Key Words for Identifying the Target Parameter

μ—Mean, Average
p—Proportion, Fraction, Percentage, Rate, Probability
*σ^2—Variance, Variation, Spread

Commonly Used z-Values for a Large-Sample Confidence Interval

90% CI:	$(1 - \alpha) = .10$	$z_{.05} = 1.645$
95% CI:	$(1 - \alpha) = .05$	$z_{.025} = 1.96$
98% CI:	$(1 - \alpha) = .02$	$z_{.01} = 2.326$
99% CI:	$(1 - \alpha) = .01$	$z_{.005} = 2.576$

Determining the Sample Size $\textbf{\textit{n}}$

Estimating μ: $n = (z_{\alpha/2})^2(\sigma^2)/(\text{ME})^2$
Estimating p: $n = (z_{\alpha/2})^2(pq)/(\text{ME})^2$

*Finite Population Correction Factor

Required when $n/N > .05$

Illustrating the Notion of "95% Confidence"

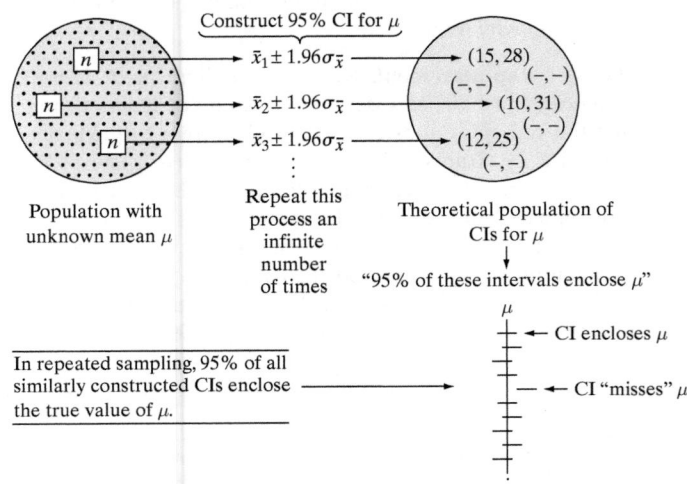

Guide to Forming a Confidence Interval

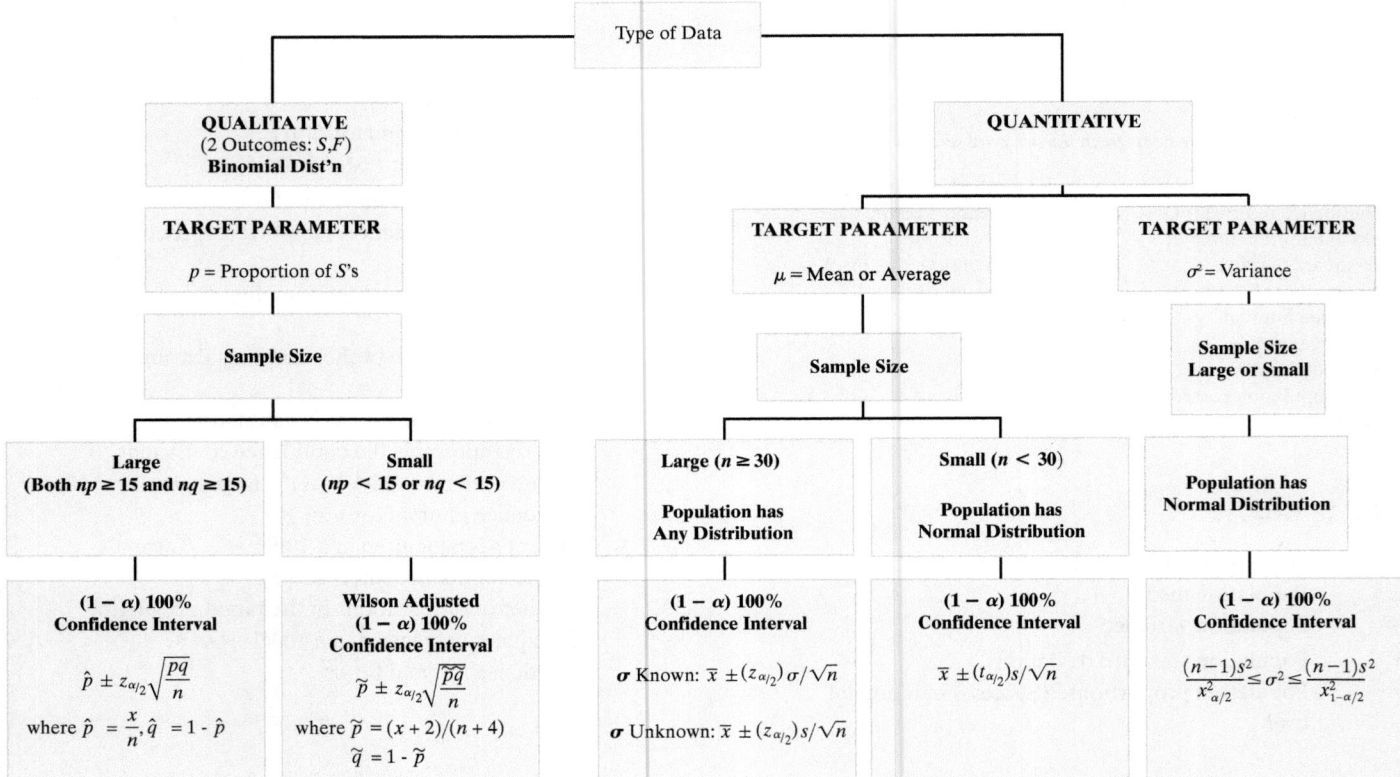

Supplementary Exercises 105–137

Please be aware that some of the following problems may require knowledge of concepts that are not presented in this chapter.

Note: List the assumptions necessary for the valid implementation of the statistical procedures you use in solving all these exercises. Exercises marked with an asterisk (*) are from the optional sections in this chapter.

Learning the Mechanics

105 Let t_0 represent a particular value of t from Table III in Appendix: Tables. Find the table values such that the following statements are true.
 a. $P(t \leq t_0) = .05$ where df $= 20$
 b. $P(t \geq t_0) = .005$ where df $= 9$
 c. $P(t \leq -t_0 \text{ or } t \leq t_0) = .10$ where df $= 8$
 d. $P(t \leq -t_0 \text{ or } t \geq t_0) = .01$ where df $= 17$

106 In each of the following instances, determine whether you would use a z- or t-statistic (or neither) to form a 95% confidence interval and then look up the appropriate z- or t-value.
 a. Random sample of size $n = 23$ from a normal distribution with unknown mean μ and standard deviation σ
 b. Random sample of size $n = 135$ from a normal distribution with unknown mean μ and standard deviation σ
 c. Random sample of size $n = 10$ from a normal distribution with unknown mean μ and standard deviation $s = 5$
 d. Random sample of size $n = 73$ from a distribution about which nothing is known
 e. Random sample of size $n = 12$ from a distribution about which nothing is known

107 A random sample of 225 measurements is selected from a population, and the sample mean and standard deviation are $\bar{x} = 32.5$ and $s = 30.0$, respectively.
 a. Use a 99% confidence interval to estimate the mean of the population, μ.
 b. How large a sample would be needed to estimate m to within .5 with 99% confidence?
 *c. Use a 99% confidence interval to estimate the population variance, σ^2.
 d. What is meant by the phrase *99% confidence* as it is used in this exercise?

108 In a random sample of 400 measurements, 227 of the measurements possess the characteristic of interest, A.
 a. Use a 95% confidence interval to estimate the true proportion p of measurements in the population with characteristic A.
 b. How large a sample would be needed to estimate p to within .02 with 95% confidence?

* 109 Find $\chi^2_{\alpha/2}$ and $\chi^2_{(1-\alpha/2)}$ from Table IV, Appendix: Tables, for each of the following:
 a. $n = 10, \alpha = .05$
 b. $n = 20, \alpha = .05$
 c. $n = 50, \alpha = .01$

* 110 Calculate the finite population correction factor for each of the following situations:
 a. $n = 50, N = 2,000$
 b. $n = 20, N = 100$
 c. $n = 300, N = 1,500$

Applying the Concepts—Basic

111 General health survey. The Centers for Disease Control and Prevention (CDCP) in Atlanta, Georgia, conducts an annual survey of the general health of the U.S. population as part of its Behavioral Risk Factor Surveillance System. Using random-digit dialing, the CDCP telephones U.S. citizens over 18 years of age and asks them the following four questions:
 1. Is your health generally excellent, very good, good, fair, or poor?
 2. How many days during the previous 30 days was your physical health not good because of injury or illness?
 3. How many days during the previous 30 days was your mental health not good because of stress, depression, or emotional problems?
 4. How many days during the previous 30 days did your physical or mental health prevent you from performing your usual activities?

 Identify the parameter of interest for each question.

112 Latex allergy in health care workers. Health care workers who use latex gloves with glove powder on a daily basis are particularly susceptible to developing a latex allergy. Symptoms of a latex allergy include conjunctivitis, hand eczema, nasal congestion, skin rash, and shortness of breath. Each in a sample of 46 hospital employees who were diagnosed with latex allergy based on a skin-prick test reported on their exposure to latex gloves (*Current Allergy & Clinical Immunology,* Mar. 2004). Summary statistics for the number of latex gloves used per week are $\bar{x} = 19.3, s = 11.9$.
 a. Give a point estimate for the average number of latex gloves used per week by all health care workers with a latex allergy.
 b. Form a 95% confidence interval for the average number of latex gloves used per week by all health care workers with a latex allergy.
 c. Give a practical interpretation of the interval, part **b.**
 d. Give the conditions required for the interval, part **b,** to be valid.

113 Material safety data sheets. For more than 20 years, the Occupational Safety & Health Administration has required companies that handle hazardous chemicals to complete material safety data sheets (MSDSs). These MSDSs have been criticized for being too hard to understand and complete by workers. Although improvements were implemented in 1990, a more recent study of 150 MSDSs revealed that only 11% were satisfactorily completed (*Chemical & Engineering News,* Feb. 7, 2005).
 a. Give a point estimate of p, the true proportion of MSDSs that are satisfactorily completed.
 b. Find a 95% confidence interval for p.
 c. Give a practical interpretation of the interval, part **b.**

114 Products "Made in the USA." *Journal of Global Business* (Spring 2002) did a survey to determine what "Made in the USA" means to consumers. 106 shoppers at a shopping mall in Muncie, Indiana, responded to the question, "'Made in the USA' means what percentage of U.S. labor and materials?" Sixty-four shoppers answered, "100%."

a. Define the population of interest in the survey.

b. What is the characteristic of interest in the population?

c. Estimate the true proportion of consumers who believe "Made in the USA" means 100% U.S. labor and materials using a 90% confidence interval.

d. Give a practical interpretation of the interval, part **c.**

e. Explain what the phrase "90% confidence" means for this interval.

f. Compute the sample size necessary to estimate the true proportion to within .05 using a 90% confidence interval.

115 Water pollution testing. The EPA wants to test a randomly selected sample of n water specimens and estimate the mean daily rate of pollution produced by a mining operation. If the EPA wants a 95% confidence interval estimate with a sampling error of 1 milligram per liter (mg/L), how many water specimens are required in the sample? Assume prior knowledge indicates that pollution readings in water samples taken during a day are approximately normally distributed with a standard deviation equal to 5 mg/L.

116 Lead and copper in drinking water. Periodically, the Hillsborough County (Florida) Water Department tests the drinking water of homeowners for contaminants such as lead and copper. The lead and copper levels in water specimens collected for a sample of 10 residents of the Crystal Lakes Manors subdivision are shown below, followed by a Minitab printout analyzing the data.

Lead (μg/L)	Copper (mg/L)
1.32	.508
0	.279
13.1	.320
.919	.904
.657	.221
3.0	.283
1.32	.475
4.09	.130
4.45	.220
0	.743

Source: Data from Hillsborough Country Water Department Environmental Laboratory, Tampa, Florida.

```
Variable   N    Mean    StDev   SE Mean      90% CI
LEAD      10    2.89     3.92     1.24    ( 0.61,    5.16)
COPPER    10   0.4083   0.2495   0.0789   (0.2637, 0.5529)
```

a. Locate a 90% confidence interval for the mean lead level in water specimens from Crystal Lakes Manors on the printout.

b. Locate a 90% confidence interval for the mean copper level in water specimens from Crystal Lakes Manors on the printout.

c. Interpret the intervals, parts **a** and **b,** in the words of the problem.

d. Discuss the meaning of the phrase "90% confident."

*117 Employees with substance abuse problems. According to the New Jersey *Governor's Council for a Drug-Free Workplace Report,* 50 of the 72 sampled businesses that are members of the council admitted that they had employees with substance abuse problems. At the time of the survey, 251 New Jersey businesses were members of the Governor's Council. Use the finite population correction factor to find a 95% confidence interval for the proportion of all New Jersey Governor's Council business members who have employees with substance abuse problems. Interpret the resulting interval.

118 Sick leave taken by employees. A company is interested in estimating μ, the mean number of days of sick leave taken by all its employees. The firm's statistician selects at random 100 personnel files and notes the number of sick days taken by each employee. The following sample statistics are computed: $\bar{x} = 12.2$ days, $s = 10$ days.

a. Estimate μ using a 90% confidence interval. Interpret the result.

b. How many personnel files would the statistician have to select in order to estimate μ to within 2 days with a 99% confidence interval?

*c. Estimate σ using a 90% confidence interval. Interpret the result.

119 Blogs for *Fortune* 500 firms. The *Journal of Relationship Marketing* (Vol. 7, 2008) did a study of the prevalence of blogs and forums at *Fortune* 500 firms with both English and Chinese Web sites. In a sample of 56 firms that provide blogs and forums as marketing tools, the mean number of blogs/forums per site was 4.25, with a standard deviation of 12.02.

a. Find a 99% confidence interval for the mean number of blogs/forums per site of all *Fortune* 500 firms that provide blogs and forums as marketing tools.

b. Give a practical interpretation of the interval, part **a.**

c. The number of blogs/forums per site is known to have a highly skewed distribution. Does this impact the validity of the inference, part **b?**

Applying the Concepts—Intermediate

120 Size of diamonds sold at retail. Refer to the *Journal of Statistics Education* data on diamonds saved in the accompanying file. Consider the quantitative variable, number of carats, recorded for each of the 308 diamonds for sale on the open market.

a. Select a random sample of 30 diamonds from the 308 diamonds.

b. Find the mean and standard deviation of the number of carats per diamond for the sample.

c. Use the sample information, part **b,** to construct a 95% confidence interval for the mean number of carats in the population of 308 diamonds.

d. Interpret the phrase *95% confidence* when applied to the interval, part **c.**

e. Find the mean of all 308 diamonds. Does the "population" mean fall within the confidence interval of part **c?**

121 Fish contaminated by a plant's discharge. The U.S. Army Corps of Engineers collected data on a sample of 144 contaminated fish collected from the river adjacent to a chemical plant. Estimate the proportion of contaminated fish that are of the channel catfish species. Use a 90% confidence interval and interpret the result.

122 Improving the productivity of chickens. Farmers have discovered that the more domestic chickens peck at objects placed in their environment, the healthier and more productive the chickens seem to be. White string has been found to be a particularly attractive pecking stimulus. In one experiment, 72 chickens were exposed to a string stimulus. Instead of white string, blue-colored string was used. The number of pecks each chicken took at the blue string over a specified time interval was recorded. Summary statistics for the 72 chickens were $\bar{x} = 1.13$ pecks, $s = 2.21$ pecks (*Applied Animal Behaviour Science*, Oct. 2000).

a. Estimate the population mean number of pecks made by chickens pecking at blue string using a 99% confidence interval. Interpret the result.

b. Previous research has shown that $\mu = 7.5$ pecks if chickens are exposed to white string. Based on the results, part **a**, is there evidence that chickens are more apt to peck at white string than blue string? Explain.

123 Petroleum waste contamination. Accidental spillage and misguided disposal of petroleum wastes have resulted in extensive contamination of soils across the country. A common hazardous compound found in the contaminated soil is benzo(a)pyrene [B(a)p]. An experiment was conducted to determine the effectiveness of a method designed to remove B(a)p from soil (*Journal of Hazardous Materials,* June 1995). Three soil specimens contaminated with a known amount of B(a)p were treated with a toxin that inhibits microbial growth. After 95 days of incubation, the percentage of B(a)p removed from each soil specimen was measured. The experiment produced the following summary statistics: $\bar{x} = 49.3$ and $s = 1.5$.

a. Use a 99% confidence interval to estimate the mean percentage of B(a)p removed from a soil specimen in which the toxin was used.

b. Interpret the interval in terms of this application.

c. What assumption is necessary to ensure the validity of this confidence interval?

d. Comment on whether the true mean percent removed could be as high as 50%.

*e. Find and interpret a 90% confidence interval for the true variance in the percentages of B(a)p removed.

124 IRS answers to gift tax questions. According to estimates made by the General Accounting Office, the Internal Revenue Service (IRS) answered 18.3 million telephone inquiries during a recent tax season, and 17% of the IRS offices provided wrong answers. These estimates were based on data collected from sample calls to numerous IRS offices. How many IRS offices should be randomly selected and contacted in order to estimate the proportion of IRS offices that fail to correctly answer questions about gift taxes with a 90% confidence interval of width .06?

125 IQ comparison of older vs. younger workers. The Age Discrimination in Employment Act (ADEA) made it illegal to discriminate against workers 40 years of age and older. Opponents of the law argue that there are sound economic reasons why employers would not want to hire and train workers who are very close to retirement. They also argue that people's abilities tend to deteriorate with age. Do 25-year-olds score significantly higher than 60-year-olds on the Wechsler Adult Intelligence Scale, the most popular IQ test? The data in the next table are raw test scores (i.e., not the familiar normalized IQ scores) for a sample of thirty-six 25-year-olds and thirty-six 60-year-olds.

25-Year-Olds					
54	61	80	92	41	63
59	68	66	76	82	80
82	47	81	77	88	94
49	86	55	82	45	51
70	72	63	50	52	67
75	60	58	49	63	68

60-Year-Olds					
42	54	38	22	58	37
60	49	51	60	45	42
73	28	65	65	60	34
34	33	40	28	36	60
45	61	47	30	45	45
45	37	27	40	37	58

a. Estimate the mean raw test score for all 25-year-olds using a 99% confidence interval. Give a practical interpretation of the confidence interval.

b. What assumption(s) must hold for the method of estimation used in part **a** to be appropriate?

c. Find a 95% confidence interval for the mean raw score of all 60-year-olds and interpret your result.

126 Air bags pose danger for children. By law, all new cars must be equipped with both driver-side and passenger-side safety air bags. There is concern, however, over whether air bags pose a danger to children sitting on the passenger side. In a National Highway Traffic Safety Administration (NHTSA) study of 55 people killed by the explosive force of air bags, 35 were children seated on the front-passenger side (*www.nhtsa.org*). This study led some car owners with children to disconnect the passenger-side air bag. Consider all fatal automobile accidents in which it is determined that air bags were the cause of death. Let p represent the true proportion of these accidents involving children seated on the front-passenger side.

a. Use the data from the NHTSA study to estimate p.

b. Construct a 99% confidence interval for p.

c. Interpret the interval, part **b**, in the words of the problem.

d. NHTSA investigators determined that 24 of the 35 children killed by the air bags were not wearing seat belts or were improperly restrained. How does this information impact your assessment of the risk of an air bag fatality?

e. How many fatal accidents should the NHTSA sample in order to estimate the proportion to within .1 of its true value using a 99% confidence interval?

127 Accuracy of price scanners at Wal-Mart. The National Institute for Standards and Technology (NIST) mandates that for every 100 items scanned through the electronic checkout scanner at a retail store, no more than 2 should have an inaccurate price. A study of the accuracy of checkout scanners at Wal-Mart stores in California was conducted. At each of 60 randomly selected Wal-Mart stores, 100 random items were scanned. The researchers found that 52 of the 60 stores had more than 2 items that were inaccurately priced.

a. Give an estimate of p, the proportion of Wal-Mart stores in California that have more than 2 inaccurately priced items per 100 items scanned.

b. Construct a 95% confidence interval for p.

c. Give a practical interpretation of the interval, part **b.**

d. Suppose a Wal-Mart spokesperson claims that 99% of California Wal-Mart stores are in compliance with the NIST mandate on accuracy of price scanners. Comment on the believability of this claim.

e. Are the conditions required for a valid large-sample confidence interval for p satisfied in this application? If not, comment on the validity of the inference in part **d.**

f. Determine the number of Wal-Mart stores that must be sampled in order to estimate the true proportion to within .05 with 90% confidence using the large-sample method.

128 **Performance appraisal process.** The relationship between an employee's participation in the performance appraisal process and subsequent subordinate reactions toward the appraisal was investigated in the *Journal of Applied Psychology* (Aug. 1998). A quantitative measure of the relationship between two variables is called the *coefficient of correlation r*. The researchers obtained r for a sample of 34 studies that examined the relationship between appraisal participation and a subordinate's satisfaction with the appraisal. These correlations are listed in the table. (Values of r near +1 reflect a strong positive relationship between the variables.) Find a 95% confidence interval for the mean of the data and interpret it in the words of the problem.

.50	.58	.71	.46	.63	.66	.31	.35	.51	.06	.35	.19
.40	.63	.43	.16	−.08	.51	.59	.43	.30	.69	.25	.20
.39	.20	.51	.68	.74	.65	.34	.45	.31	.27		

Source: Data from Cawley, B. D., Keeping, L. M., & Levy, P. E. "Participation in the performance appraisal process and employees reactions: A meta-analytic review of field investigations," *Journal of Applied Psychology,* Vol. 83, No. 4, Aug. 1998, pp. 632–633 (Appendix).

129 **Vacation times at major companies.** The primary determinant of the amount of vacation time U.S. employees receive is their length of service. According to data released by Hewitt Associates, more than 8 of 10 employers provide 2 weeks of vacation after the first year. After 5 years, 75% of employers provide 3 weeks, and after 15 years most provide 4-week vacations. To more accurately estimate p, the proportion of U.S. employers who provide only 2 weeks of vacation to new hires, a random sample of 24 major U.S. companies was contacted. The following vacation times were reported (in days).

10	12	10	10	10	10
15	10	10	10	10	10
10	10	10	10	10	15
10	10	15	10	10	10

a. Construct a 95% confidence interval for p.

b. Is the sample size large enough to ensure that the normal distribution provides a reasonable approximation to the sampling distribution of $\hat{p}$? Justify your answer.

c. How large a sample would be required to estimate p to within .02 with 95% confidence?

130 **Salmonella poisoning from eating an ice cream bar.** Recently, a case of salmonella (bacterial) poisoning was traced to a particular brand of ice cream bar, and the manufacturer removed the bars from the market. Despite this response, many consumers refused to purchase *any* brand of ice cream bars for some period of time after the event (McClave, personal consulting). One manufacturer conducted a survey of consumers 6 months after the outbreak. A sample of 244 ice cream bar consumers was contacted, and 23 respondents indicated that they would not purchase ice cream bars because of the potential for food poisoning.

a. What is the point estimate of the true fraction of the entire market who refuse to purchase bars 6 months after the outbreak?

b. Is the sample size large enough to use the normal approximation for the sampling distribution of the estimator of the binomial probability? Justify your response.

c. Construct a 95% confidence interval for the true proportion of the market who still refuses to purchase ice cream bars 6 months after the event.

d. Interpret both the point estimate and confidence interval in terms of this application.

131 **Salmonella poisoning from eating an ice cream bar (cont'd).** Refer to Exercise 130. Suppose it is now 1 year after the outbreak of food poisoning was traced to ice cream bars. The manufacturer wishes to estimate the proportion who still will not purchase bars to within .02 using a 95% confidence interval. How many consumers should be sampled?

132 **Latex allergy in health care workers.** Refer to the *Current Allergy & Clinical Immunology* (Mar. 2004) study of health care workers who use latex gloves, Exercise 112. In addition to the 46 hospital employees who were diagnosed with a latex allergy based on a skin-prick test, another 37 health care workers were diagnosed with the allergy using a latex-specific serum test. Of these 83 workers with confirmed latex allergy, only 36 suspected that they had the allergy when asked on a questionnaire. Make a statement about the likelihood that a health care worker with latex allergy suspects he or she actually has the allergy. Attach a measure of reliability to your inference.

133 **Interpreting margin of sampling error.** When a poll reports, for example, that 61% of the public supports a program of national health insurance, it usually also reports the sampling error. For example, a poll might report that the estimate is accurate to within plus or minus 3%. A classic essay in *Time* magazine ("How not to read polls," Apr. 28, 1980) points out the following:

> *Readers consistently misinterpret the meaning of this "warning label." …[The sampling error warning] says nothing about errors that might be caused by a sloppily worded question or a biased one or a single question that evokes complex feelings. Example: "Are you satisfied with your job?" Most important of all, warning labels about sampling error say nothing about whether or not the public is conflict-ridden or has given a subject much thought. This is the most serious source of opinion poll misinterpretation.*

Carefully explain the difference between sampling error and nonsampling error, both in general and in the context of the above quotation.

Applying the Concepts—Advanced

134 Accountants' salary survey. Each year, *Management Accounting* reports the results of a salary survey of the members of the Institute of Management Accountants (IMA). One year, the 2,112 members responding had a salary distribution with a 20th percentile of $35,100; a median of $50,000; and an 80th percentile of $73,000.

  a. Use this information to determine the minimum sample size that could be used in next year's survey to estimate the mean salary of IMA members to within $2,000 with 98% confidence. [*Hint*: To estimate *s*, first apply Chebyshev's Theorem to find *k* such that at least 60% of the data fall within *k* standard deviations of μ. Then find $s \approx$ (80th percentile – 20th percentile)/$2k$.]

  b. Explain how you estimated the standard deviation required for the sample size calculation.

  c. List any assumptions you make.

135 Internal auditing of invoices. A firm's president, vice presidents, department managers, and others use financial data generated by the firm's accounting system to help them make decisions regarding such things as pricing, budgeting, and plant expansion. To provide reasonable certainty that the system provides reliable data, internal auditors periodically perform various checks of the system (Horngren, Foster, and Datar, *Cost Accounting: A Managerial Emphasis*, 2005). Suppose an internal auditor is interested in determining the proportion of sales invoices in a population of 5,000 sales invoices for which the "total sales" figure is in error. She plans to estimate the true proportion of invoices in error based on a random sample of size 100.

  a. Assume that the population of invoices is numbered from 1 to 5,000 and that every invoice ending with a 0 is in error (i.e., 10% are in error). Use a random number generator to draw a random sample of 100 invoices from the population of 5,000 invoices. For example, random number 456 stands for invoice number 456. List the invoice numbers in your sample and indicate which of your sampled invoices are in error (i.e., those ending in a 0).

  b. Use the results of your sample of part **a** to construct a 90% confidence interval for the true proportion of invoices in error.

  c. Recall that the true population proportion of invoices in error is equal to .1. Compare the true proportion with the estimate of the true proportion you developed in part **b**. Does your confidence interval include the true proportion?

Critical Thinking Challenge

136 "Out of control" production process. When companies employ control charts to monitor the quality of their products, a series of small samples is typically used to determine if the process is "in control" during the period of time in which each sample is selected. Suppose a concrete-block manufacturer samples nine blocks per hour and tests the breaking strength of each. During 1 hour's test, the mean and standard deviation are 985.6 pounds per square inch (psi) and 22.9 psi, respectively. The process is to be considered "out of control"

if the true mean strength differs from 1,000 psi. The manufacturer wants to be reasonably certain that the process is really out of control before shutting down the process and trying to determine the problem. What is your recommendation?

137 Scallops, sampling, and the law. *Interfaces* (March–April 1995) presented the case of a ship that fishes for scallops off the coast of New England. In order to protect baby scallops from being harvested, the U.S. Fisheries and Wildlife Service requires that "the average meat per scallop weigh at least $\frac{1}{36}$ of a pound." The ship was accused of violating this weight standard. Author Arnold Barnett lays out the scenario:

SCALWT

> *The vessel arrived at a Massachusetts port with 11,000 bags of scallops, from which the harbormaster randomly selected 18 bags for weighing. From each such bag, his agents took a large scoopful of scallops; then, to estimate the bag's average meat per scallop, they divided the total weight of meat in the scoopful by the number of scallops it contained. Based on the 18 [numbers] thus generated, the harbormaster estimated that each of the ship's scallops possessed an average of $\frac{1}{39}$ of a pound of meat (that is, they were about seven percent lighter than the minimum requirement). Viewing this outcome as conclusive evidence that the weight standard had been violated, federal authorities at once confiscated 95 percent of the catch (which they then sold at auction). The fishing voyage was thus transformed into a financial catastrophe for its participants.*

The actual scallop weight measurements for each of the 18 sampled bags are listed in the table below. For ease of exposition, Barnett expressed each number as a multiple of $\frac{1}{36}$ of a pound, the minimum permissible average weight per scallop. Consequently, numbers below 1 indicate individual bags that do not meet the standard.

The ship's owner filed a lawsuit against the federal government, declaring that his vessel had fully complied with the weight standard. A Boston law firm was hired to represent the owner in legal proceedings, and Barnett was retained by the firm to provide statistical litigation support and, if necessary, expert witness testimony.

  a. Recall that the harbormaster sampled only 18 of the ship's 11,000 bags of scallops. One of the questions the lawyers asked Barnett was, "Can a reliable estimate of the mean weight of all the scallops be obtained from a sample of size 18?" Give your opinion on this issue.

  b. As stated in the article, the government's decision rule is to confiscate a catch if the sample mean weight of the scallops is less than $\frac{1}{36}$ of a pound. Do you see any flaws in this rule?

  c. Develop your own procedure for determining whether a ship is in violation of the minimum-weight restriction. Apply your rule to the data. Draw a conclusion about the ship in question.

.93	.88	.85	.91	.91	.84	.90	.98	.88
.89	.98	.87	.91	.92	.99	1.14	1.06	.93

Source: Based on Barnett, A. "Misapplications review: Jail terms," *Interfaces*, Vol. 25, No. 2, Mar.–Apr. 1995, p. 20.

Activity 1 Conducting a Pilot Study

Choose a population parameter pertinent to your major area of interest—a population that has an unknown mean, or if the population is binomial, an unknown probability of success. For example, a marketing major may be interested in the proportion of consumers who prefer a certain brand of diet cola. An economics or finance major might want to estimate the mean annual salary of Internet Web site designers. A management major may wish to estimate the proportion of companies that have mandatory sensitivity training for all employees. A pre-med student might desire an estimate of the average number of patients treated daily in the emergency room. An accounting major may want to find the percentage of audits that result in substantive changes to a company's accounting

system. We could continue with examples, but the point should be clear: Choose something of interest to you.

Define the parameter you want to estimate and conduct a *pilot study* to obtain an initial estimate of the parameter of interest and, more importantly, an estimate of the variability associated with the estimator. A pilot study is a small experiment (perhaps 15 to 20 observations) used to gain information about some phenomenon. The purpose of the study is to help plan more elaborate future experiments. Using the results of your pilot study, determine the sample size necessary to estimate the parameter to within a reasonable bound (of your choice) with a 95% confidence interval. Present the results to your class.

References

Agresti, A., & Coull, B. A. "Approximate is better than 'exact' for interval estimation of binomial proportions," *The American Statistician,* Vol. 52, No. 2, May 1998, pp. 119–126.

Arkin, H. *Sampling Methods for the Auditor.* New York: McGraw-Hill, 1982.

Cochran, W. G. *Sampling Techniques,* 3rd ed. New York: Wiley, 1977.

Freedman, D., Pisani, R., & Purves, R. *Statistics.* New York: Norton, 1978.

Kish, L. *Survey Sampling.* New York: Wiley, 1965.

Mendenhall, W., Beaver, R. J., & Beaver, B. *Introduction to Probability and Statistics,* 13th ed. Belmont, CA: Brooks/Cole, 2009.

Wilson, E. G. "Probable inference, the law of succession, and statistical inference," *Journal of the American Statistical Association,* Vol. 22, 1927, pp. 209–212.

USING TECHNOLOGY Technology images shown here are taken from SPSS Statistics Professional 20.0, Minitab 16, XLSTAT for Pearson, and Excel 2010.

SPSS: Confidence Intervals

SPSS can be used to obtain one-sample confidence intervals for a population mean and a population proportion, but cannot currently produce confidence intervals for a population variance.

Confidence Interval for a Mean

Step 1 Access the SPSS spreadsheet file that contains the sample data.

Step 2 Click on the "Analyze" button on the SPSS menu bar and then click on "Descriptive Statistics" and "Explore," as shown in Figure S.1.

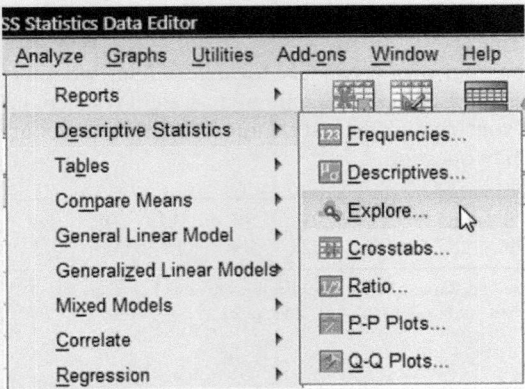

Figure S.1 SPSS menu options—confidence interval for the mean

Step 3 On the resulting dialog box (shown in Figure S.2), specify the quantitative variable of interest in the "Dependent List" and then click on the "Statistics" button.

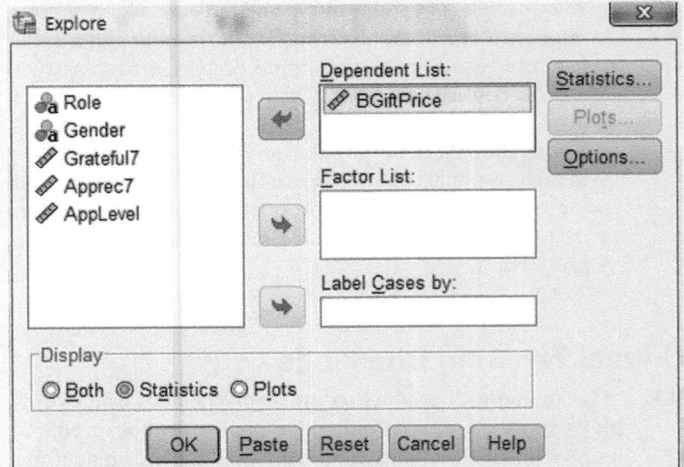

Figure S.2 SPSS explore dialog box

Step 4 Specify the confidence level in the resulting dialog box, as shown in Figure S.3.

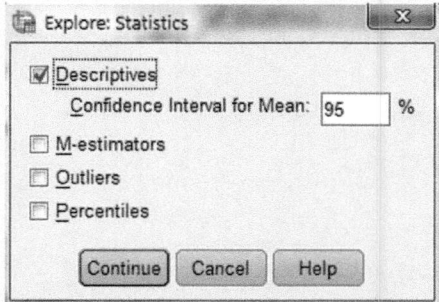

Figure S.3 SPSS explore statistics options

Step 5 Click "Continue" to return to the "Explore" dialog box and then click "OK" to produce the confidence interval.

Confidence Interval for a Proportion

Step 1 Access the SPSS spreadsheet that contains the qualitative variable of interest.

Step 2 Click on the "Analyze" button on the main menu bar, and then click on "Nonparametric Tests" and "1 Sample" (see Figure S.1).

Step 3 Click the "Fields" option, and then on the resulting dialog box (shown in Figure S.4), move the qualitative (categorical) variable to the "Test Fields" box.

Step 4 Click the "Settings" option, and then on the resulting dialog box (shown in Figure S.5), select "Customize Tests" and "Compare observed binary probability to hypothesized (Binomial test)." Then click "Options."

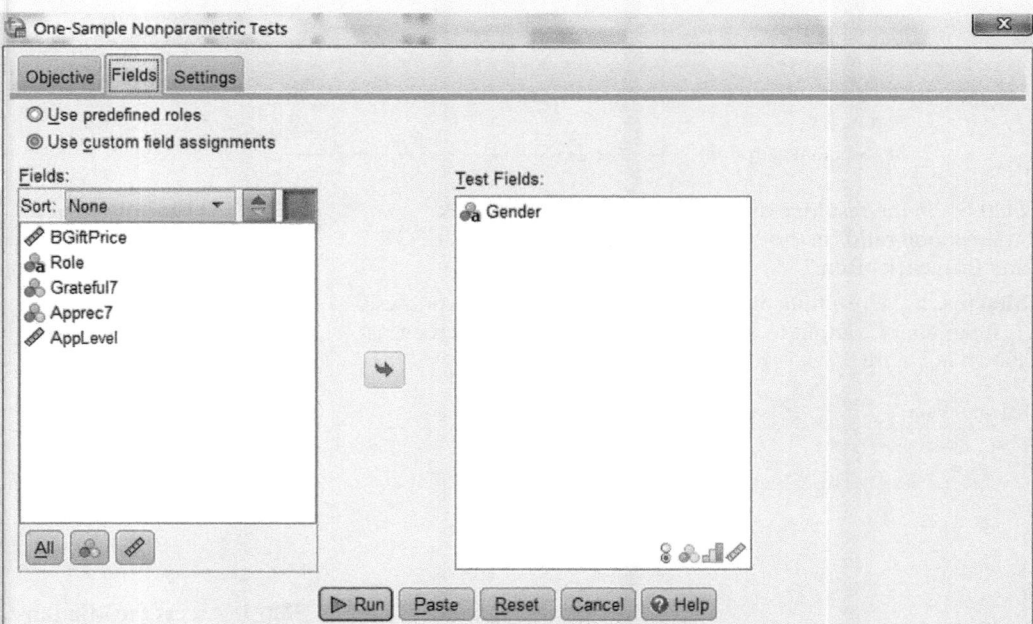

Figure S.4

SPSS field options for binomial confidence interval

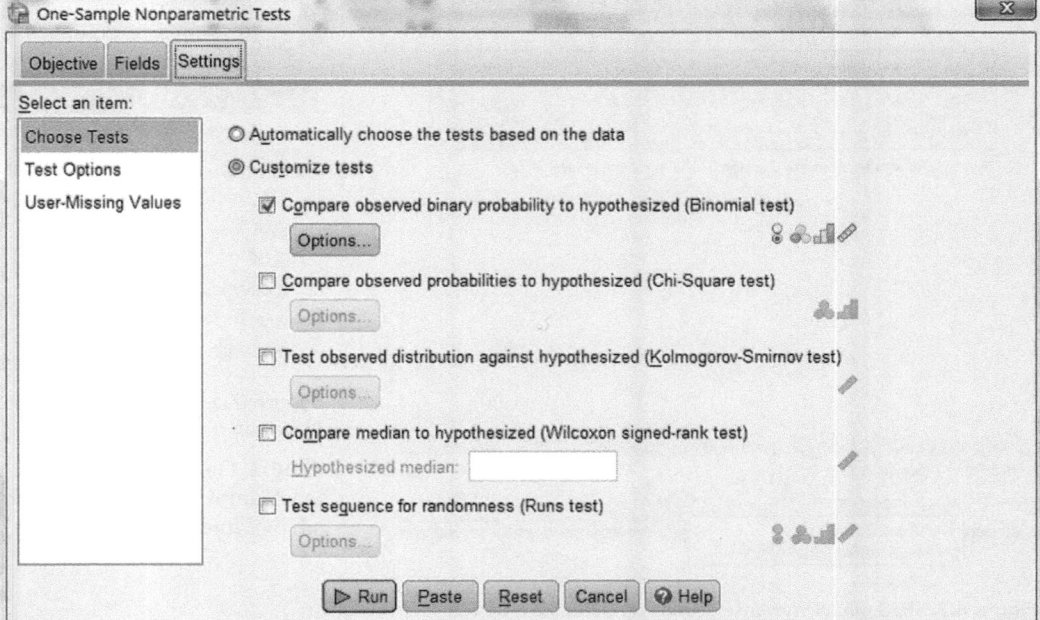

Figure S.5

SPSS settings options for binomial confidence interval

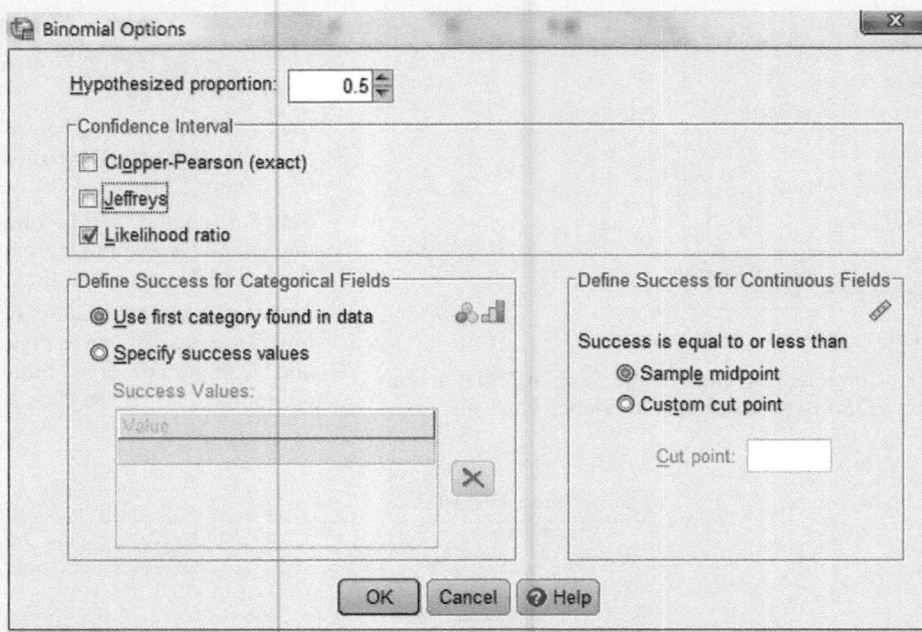

Figure S.6
SPSS binomial options

Step 5 On the resulting dialog box (see Figure S.6), click "Likelihood ratio" in the "Confidence Interval" box, click "OK," and then click "Run."

Step 6 On the resulting output, double click on the "Hypothesis Test Summary" output to display the "Model Viewer" screen, as shown in Figure S.7.

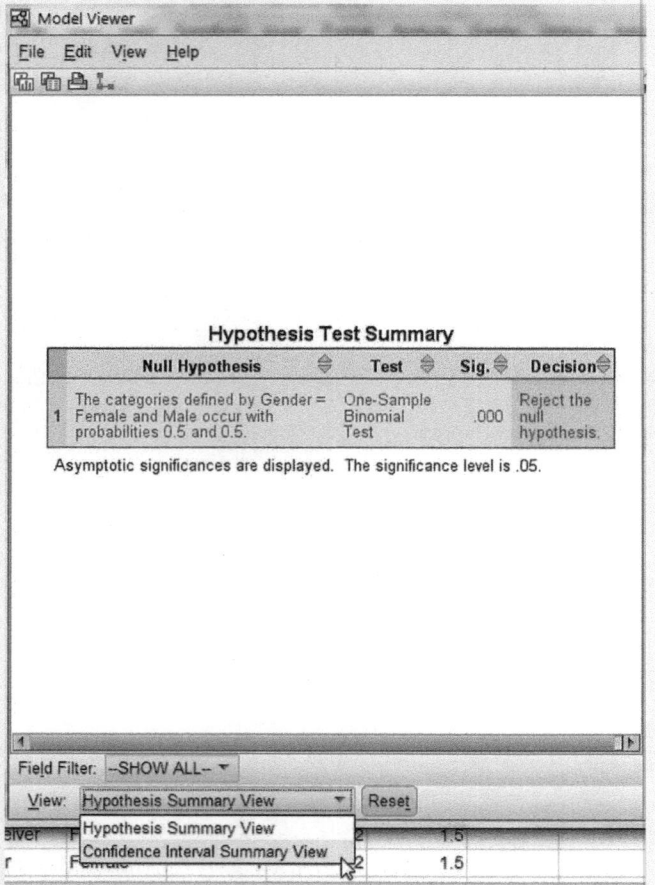

Figure S.7 SPSS model viewer selections for binomial confidence interval

Step 7 At the bottom of the "Model Viewer" screen, select "Confidence Interval Summary View" (as shown in Figure S.7) to view the resulting 95% confidence interval.

Minitab: Confidence Intervals

Minitab can be used to obtain one-sample confidence intervals for a population mean, a population proportion, and a population variance.

Confidence Interval for a Mean

Step 1 Access the Minitab data worksheet that contains the quantitative variable of interest.

Step 2 Click on the "Stat" button on the Minitab menu bar and then click on "Basic Statistics" and "1-Sample t," as shown in Figure M.1.

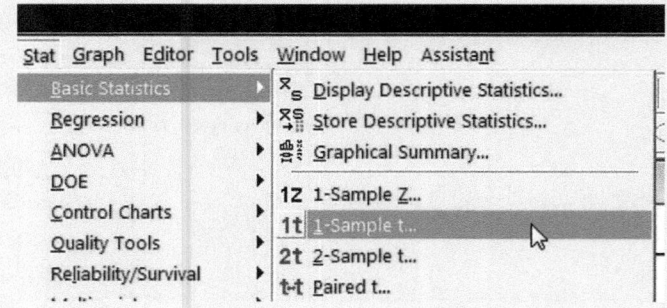

Figure M.1 Minitab menu options—confidence interval for the mean

Step 3 On the resulting dialog box (shown in Figure M.2.), click on "Samples in columns," and then specify the quantitative variable of interest in the open box.

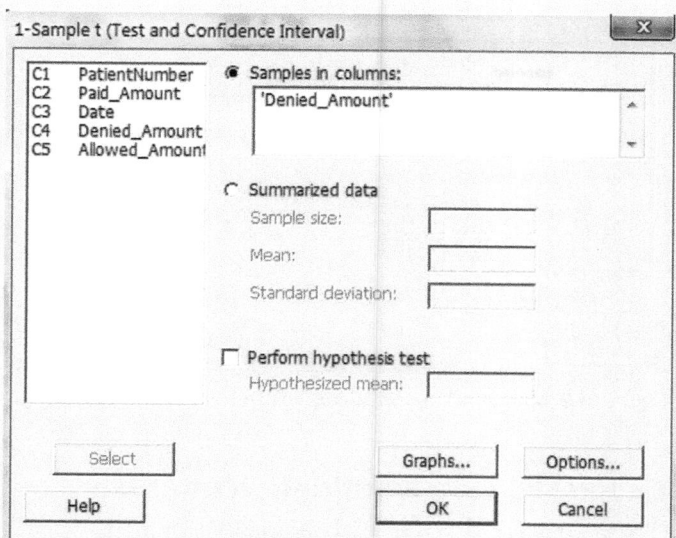

Figure M.2 Minitab 1-sample t dialog box

Step 4 Click on the "Options" button at the bottom of the dialog box and specify the confidence level in the resulting dialog box, as shown in Figure M.3.

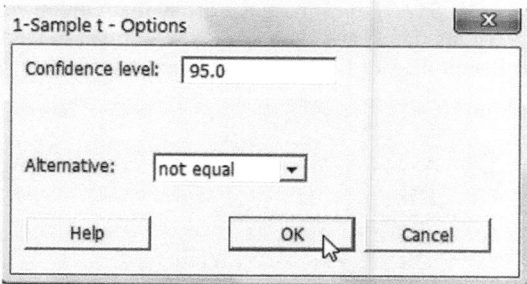

Figure M.3 Minitab 1-sample t options

Step 5 Click "OK" to return to the "1-Sample t" dialog box, and then click "OK" again to produce the confidence interval.

Note: If you want to produce a confidence interval for the mean from summary information (e.g., the sample mean, sample standard deviation, and sample size), click on "Summarized data" in the "1-Sample t" dialog box, as shown in Figure M.4. Enter the values of the summary statistics and then click "OK."

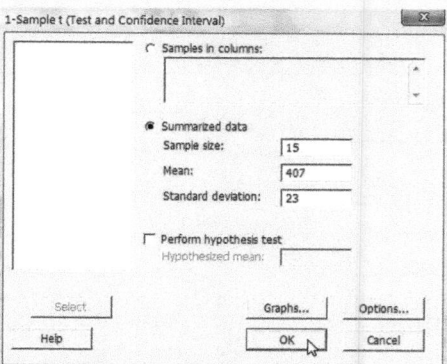

Figure M.4 Minitab 1-sample t dialog box with summary statistics options

Important: The Minitab 1-sample t procedure uses the *t*-statistic to generate the confidence interval. When the sample size *n* is small, this is the appropriate method. When the sample size *n* is large, the *t*-value will be approximately equal to the large-sample *z*-value and the resulting interval will still be valid. If you have a large sample and you know the value of the population standard deviation σ (which will rarely be the case), select "1-Sample z" from the "Basic Statistics" menu options (see Figure M.1) and make the appropriate selections.

Confidence Interval for a Proportion

Step 1 Access the Minitab data worksheet that contains the qualitative variable of interest.

Step 2 Click on the "Stat" button on the Minitab menu bar and then click on "Basic Statistics" and "1 Proportion" (see Figure M.1).

Step 3 On the resulting dialog box (shown in Figure M.5), click on "Samples in Columns" and then specify the qualitative variable of interest in the open box.

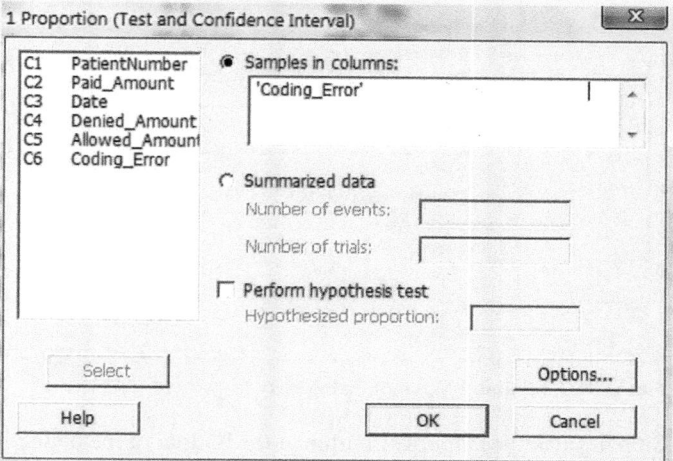

Figure M.5 Minitab 1-proportion dialog box

Step 4 Click on the "Options" button at the bottom of the dialog box and specify the confidence level in the resulting dialog box, as shown in Figure M.6. Also, check the "Use test and interval based on normal distribution" box at the bottom.

1 Proportion - Options

Confidence level: 95.0

Alternative: not equal

☑ Use test and interval based on normal distribution

Help   OK   Cancel

Figure M.6 Minitab 1-proportion dialog box options

Step 5 Click "OK" to return to the "1-Proportion" dialog box and then click "OK" again to produce the confidence interval.

Note: If you want to produce a confidence interval for a proportion from summary information (e.g., the number of successes and the sample size), click on "Summarized data" in the "1-Proportion" dialog box (see Figure M.5). Enter the value for the number of trials (i.e., the sample size) and the number of events (i.e., the number of successes) and then click "OK."

Confidence Interval for a Variance

Step 1 Access the Minitab data worksheet that contains the quantitative variable of interest.

Step 2 Click on the "Stat" button on the main Minitab menu bar, and then click on "Basic Statistics" and "1 Variance" (Figure M.1).

Step 3 On the resulting dialog box (shown in Figure M.7), select "Samples in columns" in the "Data" box, and then specify the quantitative variable of interest in the "Columns" box.

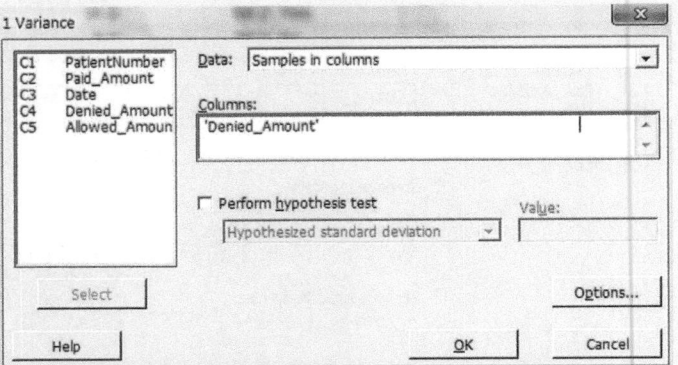

Figure M.7 Minitab 1 Variance dialog box

Step 4 Click the "Options" button at the bottom of the dialog box and specify the confidence level in the resulting menu, as shown in Figure M.8.

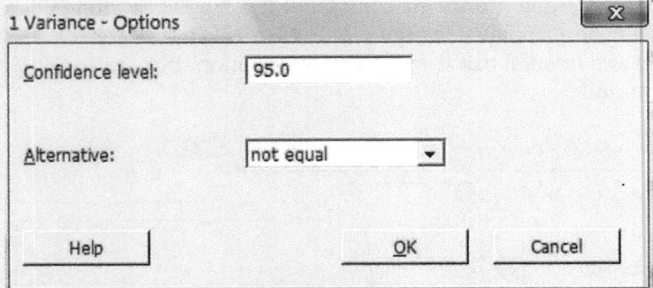

Figure M.8 Minitab 1 Variance options

Step 5 Click "OK" to return to the "1 Variance" dialog box and then click "OK" again to produce the confidence interval.

Note: If you want to produce a confidence interval for a variance from summary information (e.g., the sample variance), select "Sample variance" in the "Data" box of the "1 Variance" dialog box (see Figure M.9). Enter the values of the sample size and sample variance in the appropriate boxes, and then click "OK."

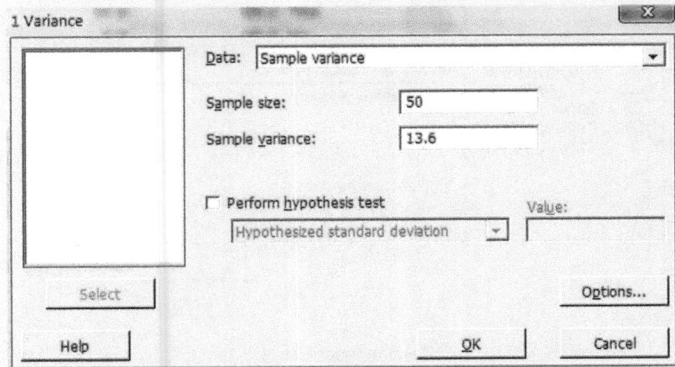

Figure M.9 Minitab 1 Variance dialog box with summary statistics option

Excel/XLSTAT: Confidence Intervals

XLSTAT can produce a confidence interval for a population mean or a population proportion. Currently, confidence intervals for a population variance are not available in XLSTAT.

Confidence Interval for a Mean

Step 1 Click the "XLSTAT" button on the Excel main menu bar, select "Describing data," and then click "Descriptive Statistics," as shown in Figure E.1.

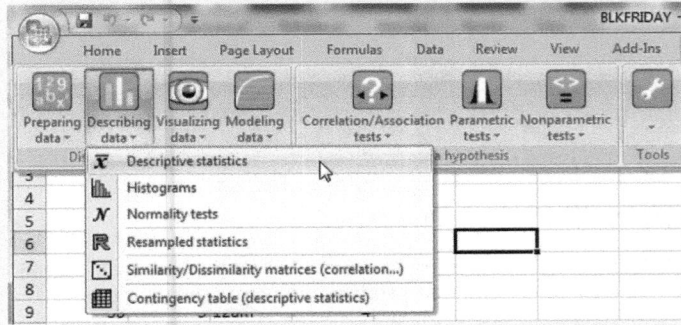

Figure E.1 XLSTAT menu options for descriptive statistics

Step 2 When the resulting dialog box appears, check "Quantitative data" and then highlight the column that contains the values of the quantitative variable you want to analyze so that the column appears in the appropriate entry (see, for example, Figure E.2).

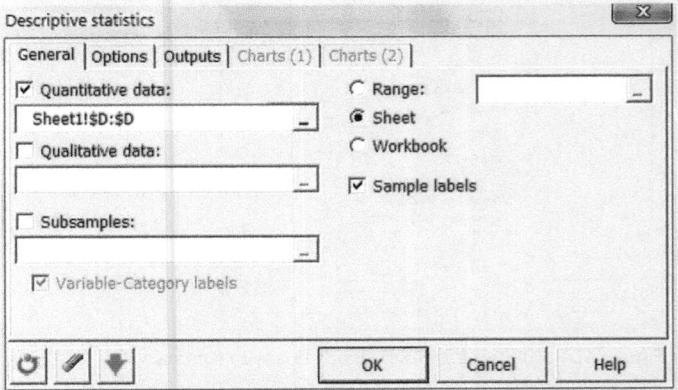

Figure E.2 XLSTAT descriptive statistics dialog box

Step 3 Click the "Options" tab, and then select "Descriptive statistics" and specify the confidence level in the open box, as shown in Figure E.3.

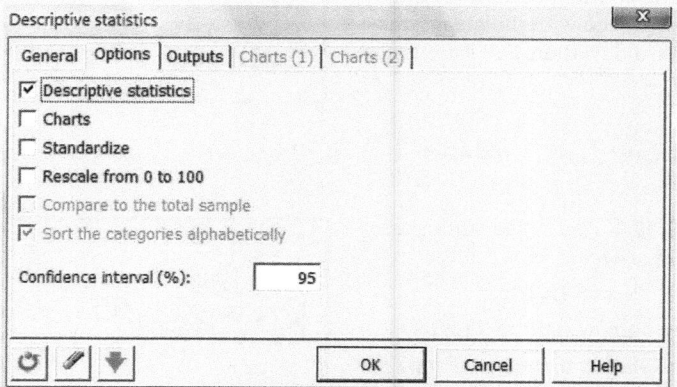

Figure E.3 XLSTAT options for a confidence interval for the mean

Step 4 Click "OK" and then "Continue" to display the confidence interval.

Confidence Interval for a Proportion

[*Note:* To form a confidence interval for a binomial proportion using XLSTAT, you will need summary information on your qualitative data, e.g., the sample size and either the number of successes or the proportion of successes in the sample.]

Step 1 Click the "XLSTAT" button on the Excel main menu bar, select "Parametric tests," and then click "Tests for one proportion," as shown in Figure E.4.

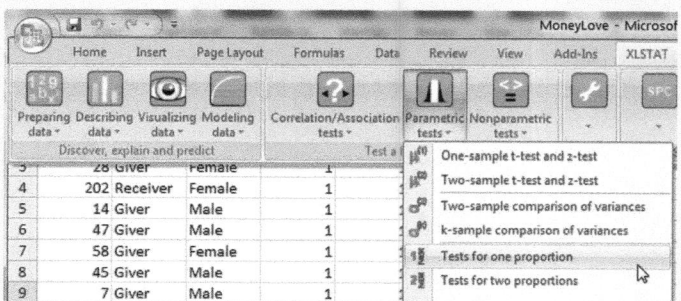

Figure E.4 XLSTAT menu options for a binomial proportion

Step 2 When the resulting dialog box appears, check "Frequency" in the "Data format" area, and then enter the number of successes and the sample size in the "Frequency" and "Sample size" boxes, respectively, as shown in Figure E.5. (Alternatively, you can check "Proportion" in the "Data format" area and enter the sample proportion in the "Test proportion" box.)

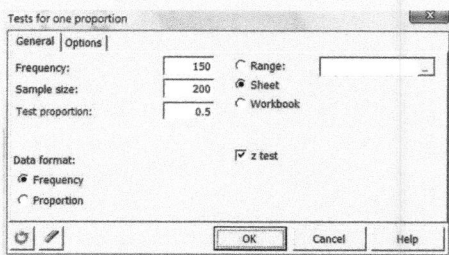

Figure E.5 XLSTAT test for one proportion dialog box

Step 3 Click "OK" to display the confidence interval.

TI-84 Graphing Calculator: Confidence Intervals

Confidence Interval for a Population Mean (Known σ or $n \geq 30$)

Step 1 *Enter the data (skip to Step 2 if you have summary statistics, not raw data)*

- Press **STAT** and select **1:Edit**

Note: If the list already contains data, clear the old data. Use the up **ARROW** to highlight "**L1**."

- Press **CLEAR ENTER**

- Use the **ARROW** and **ENTER** keys to enter the data set into **L1**

Step 2 *Access the Statistical Tests Menu*

- Press **STAT**
- Arrow right to **TESTS**
- Arrow down to **ZInterval**
- Press **ENTER**

Step 3 *Choose "Data" or "Stats." ("Data" is selected when you have entered the raw data into a List. "Stats" is selected when you are given only the mean, standard deviation, and sample size.)*

- Press **ENTER**

If you selected "Data," enter a value for σ (the best approximation is s, the sample standard deviation)

- Set **List** to **L1**
- Set **Freq** to **1**
- Set **C-Level** to the confidence level
- Arrow down to "**Calculate**"
- Press **ENTER**

If you selected "Stats," enter a value for σ (the best approximation is s, the sample standard deviation)

- Enter the sample mean and sample size
- Set **C-Level** to the confidence level
- Arrow down to "**Calculate**"
- Press **ENTER**

(The bottom screen at right is set up for an example with a standard deviation of 20, a mean of 200, and a sample size of 40.) The confidence interval will be displayed along with the sample mean and the sample size.

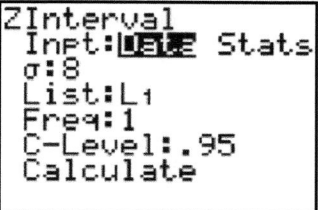

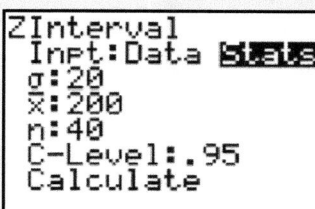

Confidence Interval for a Population Mean ($n < 30$)

Step 1 *Enter the data (skip to Step 2 if you have summary statistics, not raw data)*

- Press **STAT** and select **1:Edit**

Note: If the list already contains data, clear the old data. Use the up **ARROW** to highlight "**L1.**"

- Press **CLEAR ENTER**
- Use the **ARROW** and **ENTER** keys to enter the data set into **L1**

Step 2 *Access the Statistical Tests Menu*

- Press **STAT**
- Arrow right to **TESTS**
- Arrow down to **TInterval**
- Press **ENTER**

Step 3 *Choose "**Data**" or "**Stats.**" ("Data" is selected when you have entered the raw data into a List. "Stats" is selected when you are given only the mean, standard deviation, and sample size.)*

- Press **ENTER**
- If you selected "Data," set **List** to **L1**
- Set **Freq** to **1**
- Set **C-Level** to the confidence level

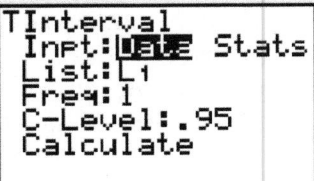

- Arrow down to "**Calculate**"
- Press **ENTER**

If you selected "Stats," enter the mean, standard deviation, and sample size.

- Set **C-Level** to the confidence level
- Arrow down to "**Calculate**"
- Press **ENTER**

(The screen here is set up for an example with a mean of 100 and a standard deviation of 10.)

The confidence interval will be displayed with the mean, standard deviation, and sample size.

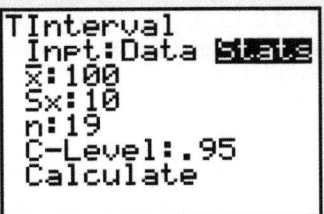

Confidence Interval for a Population Proportion (Large Samples)

Step 1 *Access the Statistical Tests Menu*

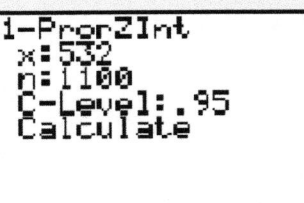

- Press **STAT**
- Arrow right to **TESTS**
- Arrow down to **1-PropZInt**
- Press **ENTER**

Step 2 *Enter the values for x, n, and C-Level*

- where x = number of successes

- n = sample size
- **C-Level** = level of Confidence
- Arrow down to "**Calculate**"
- Press **ENTER**

(The screens at the right are set up for an example with $x = 532$, $n = 1,100$, and confidence level of .95.)

Answers to Selected Exercises

1 a. 1.645 **b.** 2.576 **c.** 1.96 **d.** 1.282 **3 a.** $28 \pm .784$ **b.** $102 \pm .65$ **c.** $15 \pm .0588$ **d.** $4.05 \pm .163$ **e.** No **5 a.** $26.2 \pm .96$ **b.** In repeated sampling, 95% of all confidence intervals constructed will include μ. **c.** 26.2 ± 1.26 **d.** Increases **e.** Yes **7** Point estimator is a single number **9** Yes **11 a.** 3.11 **b.** (3.02, 3.30) **c.** Incorrect **d.** No impact—CLT applies **13** $6,563 \pm 97.65$ **15 a.** (2.55, 3.98) **b.** 99% confident that true mean number of wheels on all social robots is between 2.55 and 3.98 **c.** .99 **17 a.** μ = mean salary of all 500 CEOs **19 a.** 99.6 **b.** 99.6 ± 2.24 **c.** 95% confident that true Mach rating score of all purchasing managers is between 97.36 and 101.84. **d.** Yes **21** SAT–Math **23 a.** $z_{.10} = 1.282, t_{.10} = 1.533$ **b.** $z_{.05} = 1.645, t_{.05} = 2.132$ **c.** $z_{.025} = 1.96, t_{.025} = 2.776$ **d.** $z_{.01} = 2.326, t_{.01} = 3.747$ **e.** $z_{.005} = 2.576, t_{.005} = 4.604$ **25 a.** 2.228 **b.** 2.228 **c.** -1.812 **d.** 1.725 **e.** 4.032 **27 a.** 5 ± 1.88 **b.** 5 ± 2.39 **c.** 5 ± 3.75 **d.** $5 \pm .78, 5 \pm .94, 5 \pm 1.28$; decreased width **29 a.** μ = mean trap spacing for the population of red spiny lobster fishermen **b.** 89.86 **c.** Sampling distribution of $\bar{x}$ is unknown **d.** (79.10, 100.62) **e.** 95% confident that true mean trap spacing is between 79.10 and 100.62 meters **f.** Population of trap spacings is normally distributed **31** (71.67, 79.13) **33 a.** (1.64, 2.13) **b.** No **35 a.** (303.4, 413.6) **b.** 95% confident that true mean skidding distance falls between 303.4 and 413.6 meters **c.** $\approx$ normal **d.** No **37 a.** (.09, .94) **b.** (1.49, 3.69) **c.** Mean is lower in water containing oil **39 a.** All 212 firms in *Forbes* Largest Private Companies list **b.** (2.10, 8.68) **c.** 98% confident that true mean revenue is between \$2.10 and \$8.68 billion. **d.** $\approx$ normal **e.** Yes **41 a.** Yes **b.** No **c.** No **d.** No **43 a.** Yes **b.** $.46 \pm .065$ **c.** 95% confident p is between .395 and .525 **d.** 95% of all similarly constructed intervals contain the true value of p **45 a.** .4 **b.** Approx. normal **c.** (.38, .42) **d.** 95% confident that true proportion of Arlington homes with market values that are overestimated by more than 10% falls between .38 and .42 **e.** No **47 a.** All American adults **b.** 1,000 adults surveyed **c.** Proportion of all American adults who think Starbucks coffee is overpriced **d.** $.73 \pm .028$ **49 a.** .60 **b.** (.58, .62) **c.** 95% confident that true proportion of all adults who use cell phones while driving falls between .58 and .62 **51** (.367, .453) **53** $.269 \pm .014$; 90% confident that true percentage of all firms with acquisitions is between 25.5% and 28.3% **55 a.** No **b.** (0, .019) **57 a.** True proportion of all fillets that are red snapper **c.** $.27 \pm .17$ **d.** 95% confident that true proportion of all fillets that are red snapper is between .10 and .44 **59** 95% CI for p: (.849, .851); actual performance is below claim of $p = .95$ **61 a.** 68 **b.** 31 **63** 34 **65 a.** 0.98, 0.784, 0.56, 0.392, 0.196 **67** 84 **69** 21 **71** 1,692 **73** 14,735 **75** 43; 171; 385 **77** No **79 a.** .7746 **b.** .8944 **c.** .9487 **d.** .995 **81 a.** 1.00 **b.** .6124 **c.** 0 **d.** As n increases, standard error decreases. **83** $.42 \pm .021$ **85 a.** 36.03 ± 3.40 **b.** $.7 \pm .16$ **87 a.** $.56 \pm .012$ **c.** 95% confident that true proportion of active NFL players who select a professional coach as most influential is between .548 and .572 **89 a.** 156.46 **b.** 18.70 **c.** 156.46 ± 37.405 **d.** Not reasonable **91** No; $.086 \pm .041$ **93 a.** (4.54, 8.81) **b.** (.00024, .00085) **c.** (641.86, 1809.09) **d.** (.95, 12.66) **95** (4.27, 65.90) **97 a.** (.13, .19); 95% confident that true standard deviation of facial WHR for CEOs is between .13 and .19 **b.** Approx. normal **99** (3178.6, 7618.4); 95% confident that true standard deviation of radon levels in tombs is between 3,178.6 and 7,618.4 Bq/m^3 **101** (6.25, 17.74); 99% confident that true variance in drug concentrations is between 6.67 and 17.74 **103** (43.72, 1199.95) **105 a.** -1.725 **b.** 3.250 **c.** 1.860 **d.** 2.898 **107 a.** 32.5 ± 5.15 **b.** 23,871 **c.** (714.2, 1163.7) **109 a.** 19.0228; 2.70039 **b.** 32.8523; 8.90655 **c.** 79.49; 27.9907 **111 (1)** p = proportion with excellent health; **(2), (3),** and **(4)** μ = mean number of days health not good **113 a.** .11 **b.** $.11 \pm .050$ **115** 97 **117** $.694 \pm .092$ **119 a.** 4.25 ± 4.14 **b.** 99% confident that true mean number of blogs/forums falls between .11 and 8.39 **c.** No; apply the Central Limit Theorem **121** $.667 \pm .065$ **123 a.** 49.3 ± 8.6 **b.** 99% confident that mean amount removed from all soil specimens is between 40.70% and 57.90% **c.** Normal distribution **d.** Possible **e.** (.75, 45) **125 a.** 66.83 ± 6.17 **c.** 45.31 ± 4.15 **127 a.** .867 **b.** (.781, .953) **c.** 95% confident that true proportion of Wal-Mart stores with more than 2 inaccurately scanned items is between .781 and .953 **d.** Not believable **e.** No **f.** 126 **129 a.** $.833 \pm .149$ **b.** No **c.** 1,337 **131** 818 **137 a.** Yes **b.** Missing measure of reliability **c.** 95% CI for μ: $.932 \pm .037$

Credits

The photo credits below are listed in order of appearance.

Jacquelyn Martin/AP Images
Pressmaster/Fotolia
Svetlana Lukienko/Shutterstock
Iofoto/Fotolia
DIGIcal/iStockphoto

☐ Technology Images

CONTENTS

Where We're Going

- Introduce the concept of a *test of hypothesis* (1–2)
- Provide a measure of reliability for the hypothesis test, called the *significance level* of the test (2, 3)
- Test a specific value of a population parameter (mean, proportion or variance) called a *test of hypothesis* (4–7)
- Show how to estimate the reliability of a test (8)

Inferences Based on a Single Sample *Tests of Hypotheses*

STATISTICS in ACTION

Diary of a Kleenex® User—How Many Tissues in a Box?

In 1924, Kimberly-Clark Corporation invented a facial tissue for removing cold cream and began marketing it as Kleenex® brand tissues. Today, Kleenex® is recognized as the top-selling brand of tissue in the world. A wide variety of Kleenex® products are available, ranging from extra-large tissues to tissues with lotion. Over the past 80 years, Kimberly-Clark Corporation has packaged the tissues in boxes of different sizes and shapes and varied the number of tissues packaged in each box. For example, currently a family-size box contains 144 two-ply tissues, a cold-care box contains 70 tissues (coated with lotion), and a convenience pocket pack contains 15 miniature tissues.

How does Kimberly-Clark Corp. decide how many tissues to put in each box? According to the *Wall Street Journal*, marketing experts at the company use the results of a survey of Kleenex® customers to help determine how many tissues should be packed in a box. In the mid-1980s, when Kimberly-Clark Corp. developed the cold-care box designed especially for people who have a cold, the company conducted their initial survey of customers for this purpose. Hundreds of customers were asked to keep count of their Kleenex® use in diaries. According to the *Wall Street Journal* report, the survey results left "little doubt that the company should put 60 tissues in each box." The number 60 was "the average number of times people blow their nose during a cold." In 2000, the company increased the number of tissues packaged in a cold-care box to 70 based on the results of a more recent survey.

From summary information provided in the *Wall Street Journal* article, we constructed a data set that represents the results of a survey similar to the one described above. In the data file named **TISSUE,** we recorded the number of

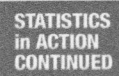

tissues used by each of 250 consumers during a period when they had a cold. We apply the hypothesis-testing methodology presented in this chapter to this data set in several Statistics in Action Revisited examples.

STATISTICS in ACTION REVISITED

▫ Key Elements of a Hypothesis Test

▫ Testing a Population Mean

▫ Testing a Population Proportion

Data Set: TISSUE

Suppose you wanted to determine whether the mean waiting time in the drive-through line of a fast-food restaurant is less than 5 minutes, or whether the majority of consumers are optimistic about the economy. In both cases you are interested in making an inference about how the value of a parameter relates to a specific numerical value. Is it less than, equal to, or greater than the specified number? This type of inference, called a **test of hypothesis,** is the subject of this chapter.

We introduce the elements of a test of hypothesis in Sections 1–3. We then show how to conduct a large-sample test of hypothesis about a population mean in Section 4. In Section 5 we use small samples to conduct tests about means. Large-sample tests about binomial probabilities are the subject of Section 6, and a test about a population variance is covered in Section 7. Finally, some advanced methods for determining the reliability of a test are covered in Section 8.

1   The Elements of a Test of Hypothesis

Suppose building specifications in a certain city require that the average breaking strength of residential sewer pipe be more than 2,400 pounds per foot of length (i.e., per linear foot). Each manufacturer who wants to sell pipe in this city must demonstrate that its product meets the specification. Note that we are interested in making an inference about the mean μ of a population. However, in this example we are less interested in estimating the value of μ than we are in testing a **hypothesis** about its value—that is, *we want to decide whether the mean breaking strength of the pipe exceeds 2,400 pounds per linear foot.*

> A statistical **hypothesis** is a statement about the numerical value of a population parameter.

The method used to reach a decision is based on the rare-event concept. We define two hypotheses: (1) The **null hypothesis** is that which represents the status quo to the party performing the sampling experiment—the hypothesis that will be accepted unless the data provide convincing evidence that it is false. (2) The **alternative,** or **research, hypothesis** is that which will be accepted only if the data provide convincing evidence of its truth. From the point of view of the city conducting the tests, the null hypothesis is that the manufacturer's pipe does *not* meet specifications unless the tests provide convincing evidence otherwise. The null and alternative hypotheses are therefore

Null hypothesis (H_0): $\mu \leq 2{,}400$

(i.e., the manufacturer's pipe does not meet specifications)

Alternative (research) hypothesis (H_a): $\mu > 2{,}400$

(i.e., the manufacturer's pipe meets specifications)

> The **null hypothesis,** denoted H_0, represents the hypothesis that will be accepted unless the data provide convincing evidence that it is false. This usually represents the "status quo" or some claim about the population parameter that the researcher wants to test.

> The **alternative (research) hypothesis,** denoted H_a, represents the hypothesis that will be accepted only if the data provide convincing evidence of its truth. This usually represents the values of a population parameter for which the researcher wants to gather evidence to support.

How can the city decide when enough evidence exists to conclude that the manufacturer's pipe meets specifications? Because the hypotheses concern the value of the population mean μ, it is reasonable to use the sample mean $\bar{x}$ to make the inference. The city will conclude that the pipe meets specifications only when the sample mean $\bar{x}$ convincingly indicates that the population mean exceeds 2,400 pounds per linear foot.

"Convincing" evidence in favor of the alternative hypothesis will exist when the value of $\bar{x}$ exceeds 2,400 by an amount that cannot be readily attributed to sampling variability. To decide, we compute a **test statistic,** i.e., a numerical value computed from the sample. Here, the test statistic is the z-value that measures the distance (in units of the standard deviation) between the value of $\bar{x}$ and the value of μ specified in the null hypothesis. When the null hypothesis contains more than one value of μ, as in this case (H_0: $\mu \le 2,400$), we use the value of μ closest to the values specified in the alternative hypothesis. The idea is that if the hypothesis that μ *equals* 2,400 can be rejected in favor of $\mu > 2,400$, then μ *less than or equal to* 2,400 can certainly be rejected. Thus, the test statistic is

$$z = \frac{\bar{x} - 2,400}{\sigma_{\bar{x}}} = \frac{\bar{x} - 2,400}{\sigma/\sqrt{n}}$$

Note that a value of $z = 1$ means that $\bar{x}$ is 1 standard deviation above $\mu = 2,400$; a value of $z = 1.5$ means that $\bar{x}$ is 1.5 standard deviations above $\mu = 2,400$; and so on. How large must z be before the city can be convinced that the null hypothesis can be rejected in favor of the alternative and conclude that the pipe meets specifications?

> The **test statistic** is a sample statistic, computed from information provided in the sample, that the researcher uses to decide between the null and alternative hypotheses.

If you examine Figure 1, you will note that the chance of observing $\bar{x}$ more than 1.645 standard deviations above 2,400 is only .05 — *if in fact the true mean μ is 2,400.* Thus, if the sample mean is more than 1.645 standard deviations above 2,400, either H_0 is true and a relatively rare event has occurred (.05 probability), or H_a is true and the

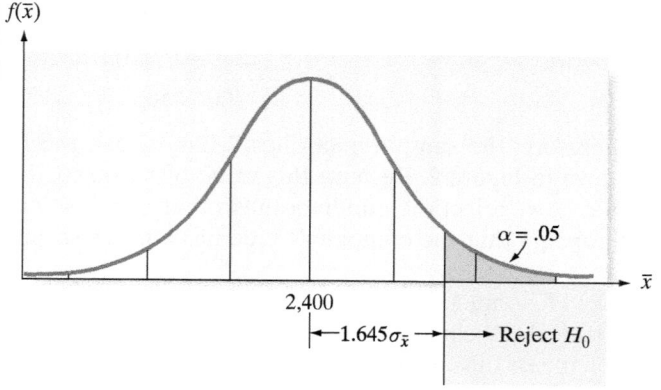

Figure 1

The sampling distribution of $\bar{x}$, assuming $\mu = 2,400$

population mean exceeds 2,400. Because we would most likely reject the notion that a rare event has occurred, we would reject the null hypothesis ($\mu \le 2,400$) and conclude that the alternative hypothesis ($\mu > 2,400$) is true. What is the probability that this procedure will lead us to an incorrect decision?

Such an incorrect decision—deciding that the null hypothesis is false when in fact it is true—is called a **Type I error.** As indicated in Figure 1, the risk of making a Type I error is denoted by the symbol α—that is,

$$\alpha = P(\text{Type I error})$$
$$= P(\text{Rejecting the null hypothesis when in fact the null hypothesis is true})$$

> A **Type I error** occurs if the researcher rejects the null hypothesis in favor of the alternative hypothesis when, in fact, H_0 is true. The probability of committing a Type I error is denoted by α.

In our example,

$$\alpha = P(z > 1.645 \text{ when in fact } \mu = 2,400) = .05$$

We now summarize the elements of the test:

H_0: $\mu \le 2,400$ (Pipe does not meet specifications)

H_a: $\mu > 2,400$ (Pipe meets specifications)

Test statistic: $z = \dfrac{\bar{x} - 2,400}{\sigma_{\bar{x}}}$

Rejection region: $z > 1.645$, which corresponds to $\alpha = .05$

Note that the **rejection region** refers to the values of the test statistic for which we will *reject the null hypothesis.*

> The **rejection region** of a statistical test is the set of possible values of the test statistic for which the researcher will reject H_0 in favor of H_a.

To illustrate the use of the test, suppose we test 50 sections of sewer pipe and find the mean and standard deviation for these 50 measurements to be

$$\bar{x} = 2,460 \text{ pounds per linear foot}$$
$$s = 200 \text{ pounds per linear foot}$$

As in the case of estimation, we can use s to approximate σ when s is calculated from a large set of sample measurements.

The test statistic is

$$z = \frac{\bar{x} - 2,400}{\sigma_{\bar{x}}} = \frac{\bar{x} - 2,400}{\sigma/\sqrt{n}} \approx \frac{\bar{x} - 2,400}{s/\sqrt{n}}$$

Substituting $\bar{x} = 2,460$, $n = 50$, and $s = 200$, we have

$$z \approx \frac{2,460 - 2,400}{200/\sqrt{50}} = \frac{60}{28.28} = 2.12$$

Therefore, the sample mean lies $2.12\sigma_{\bar{x}}$ above the hypothesized value of μ, 2,400, as shown in Figure 2. Because this value of z exceeds 1.645, it falls in the rejection region. That is, we reject the null hypothesis that $\mu = 2,400$ and conclude that $\mu > 2,400$. Thus, it appears that the company's pipe has a mean strength that exceeds 2,400 pounds per linear foot.

How much faith can be placed in this conclusion? What is the probability that our statistical test could lead us to reject the null hypothesis (and conclude that the company's pipe meets the city's specifications) when in fact the null hypothesis is true? The answer

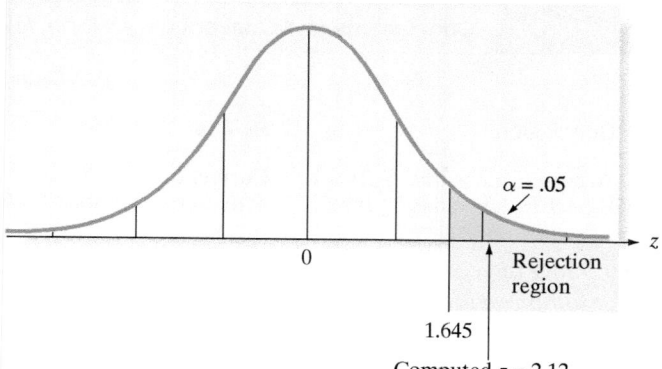

Figure 2

Location of the test statistic
for a test of the hypothesis
$H_0: \mu = 2,400$

**EGON S. PEARSON
(1895–1980)**
The Neyman-Pearson Lemma

Egon Pearson was the only son
of noteworthy British statistician
Karl Pearson (see Biography). As
you might expect, Egon developed
an interest in the statistical methods developed by his father and,
upon completing graduate school,
accepted a position to work for
Karl in the Department of Applied
Statistics at University College,
London. Egon is best known
for his collaboration with Jerzey
Neyman on the development of
the theory of hypothesis testing.
One of the basic concepts in the
Neyman-Pearson approach was
that of the "null" and "alternative" hypotheses. Their famous
Neyman-Pearson lemma was
published in *Biometrika* in 1928.
Egon Pearson had numerous other
contributions to statistics and was
known as an excellent teacher and
lecturer. In his last
major work, Egon fulfilled a
promise made to his father by
publishing an annotated version
of Karl Pearson's lectures on the
early history of statistics.

is $\alpha = .05$ — that is, we selected the level of risk, α, of making a Type I error when we constructed the test. Thus, the chance is only 1 in 20 that our test would lead us to con- clude the manufacturer's pipe satisfies the city's specifications when in fact the pipe does *not* meet specifications.

Now, suppose the sample mean breaking strength for the 50 sections of sewer pipe turned out to be $\bar{x} = 2,430$ pounds per linear foot. Assuming that the sample standard deviation is still $s = 200$, the test statistic is

$$z = \frac{2,430 - 2,400}{200/\sqrt{50}} = \frac{30}{28.28} = 1.06$$

Therefore, the sample mean $\bar{x} = 2,430$ is only 1.06 standard deviations above the null hypothesized value of $\mu = 2,400$. As shown in Figure 3, this value does not fall into the rejection region ($z > 1.645$). Therefore, we know that we cannot reject H_0 using $\alpha = .05$. Even though the sample mean exceeds the city's specification of 2,400 by 30 pounds per linear foot, it does not exceed the specification by enough to provide *convincing* evidence that the *population mean* exceeds 2,400.

Should we accept the null hypothesis $H_0: \mu \le 2,400$ and conclude that the manufacturer's pipe does not meet specifications? To do so would be to risk a **Type II error** — that of concluding that the null hypothesis is true (the pipe does not meet specifications) when in fact it is false (the pipe does meet specifications). We denote the probability of committing a Type II error by β, and we show in Section 8 that β is often difficult to determine precisely. Rather than make a decision (accept H_0) for which the probability of error (β) is unknown, we avoid the potential Type II error by

> A **Type II error** occurs if the researcher accepts the null hypothesis when, in fact, H_0 is false. The probability of committing a Type II error is denoted by β.

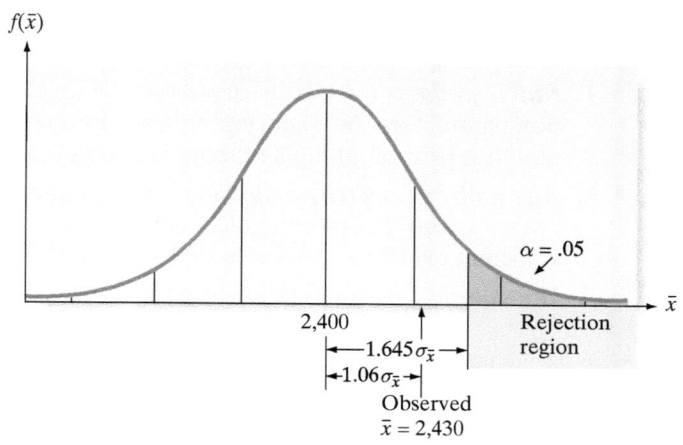

Figure 3

Location of test statistic
when $\bar{x} = 2,430$

Table 1	Conclusions and Consequences for a Test of Hypothesis	
	True State of Nature	
Conclusion	H_0 True	H_a True
Accept H_0 (Assume H_0 True)	Correct decision	Type II error (probability β)
Reject H_0 (Assume H_a True)	Type I error (probability α)	Correct decision

avoiding the conclusion that the null hypothesis is true. Instead, we will simply state that *the sample evidence is insufficient to reject H_0 at $\alpha = .05$.* Because the null hypothesis is the "status-quo" hypothesis, the effect of not rejecting H_0 is to maintain the status quo. In our pipe-testing example, the effect of having insufficient evidence to reject the null hypothesis that the pipe does not meet specifications is probably to prohibit the use of the manufacturer's pipe unless and until there is sufficient evidence that the pipe does meet specifications—that is, until the data indicate convincingly that the null hypothesis is false, we usually maintain the status quo implied by its truth.

Table 1 summarizes the four possible outcomes (i.e., **conclusions**) of a test of hypothesis. The "true state of nature" columns in Table 1 refer to the fact that either the null hypothesis H_0 is true or the alternative hypothesis H_a is true. Note that the true state of nature is unknown to the researcher conducting the test. The "decision" rows in Table 1 refer to the action of the researcher, assuming that he or she will either conclude that H_0 is true or that H_a is true, based on the results of the sampling experiment. Note that a Type I error can be made *only* when the null hypothesis is rejected in favor of the alternative hypothesis, and a Type II error can be made *only* when the null hypothesis is accepted. Our policy will be to make a decision only when we know the probability of making the error that corresponds to that decision. Because α is usually specified by the analyst, we will generally be able to reject H_0 (accept H_a) when the sample evidence supports that decision. However, because β is usually not specified, *we will generally avoid the decision to accept H_0, preferring instead to state that the sample evidence is insufficient to reject H_0 when the test statistic is not in the rejection region.*

 CAUTION Be careful not to "accept H_0" when conducting a test of hypothesis because the measure of reliability, $\beta = P$(Type II error), is almost always unknown. If the test statistic does not fall into the rejection region, it is better to state the conclusion as "insufficient evidence to reject H_0."*

The elements of a test of hypothesis are summarized in the following box. Note that the first four elements are all specified *before* the sampling experiment is performed. In no case will the results of the sample be used to determine the hypotheses; the data are collected to test the predetermined hypotheses, not to formulate them.

Elements of a Test of Hypothesis

1. *Null hypothesis* (H_0): A theory about the specific values of one or more population parameters. The theory generally represents the status quo, which we adopt until it is proven false. The theory is always stated as H_0: parameter = value.

2. *Alternative (research) hypothesis* (H_a): A theory that contradicts the null hypothesis. The theory generally represents that which we will adopt only when sufficient evidence exists to establish its truth.

3. *Test statistic:* A sample statistic used to decide whether to reject the null hypothesis.

*In many practical business applications of hypothesis testing, nonrejection leads management to behave as if the null hypothesis were accepted. Accordingly, the distinction between acceptance and nonrejection is frequently blurred in practice. We discuss the issues connected with the acceptance of the null hypothesis and the calculation of β in more detail in Section 8.

4. *Rejection region:* The numerical values of the test statistic for which the null hypothesis will be rejected. The rejection region is chosen so that the probability is α that it will contain the test statistic when the null hypothesis is true, thereby leading to a Type I error. The value of α is usually chosen to be small (e.g., .01, .05, or .10) and is referred to as the **level of significance** of the test.

5. *Assumptions:* Clear statement(s) of any assumptions made about the population(s) being sampled.

6. *Experiment and calculation of test statistic:* Performance of the sampling experiment and determination of the numerical value of the test statistic.

7. *Conclusion:*

   a. If the numerical value of the test statistic falls in the rejection region, we reject the null hypothesis and conclude that the alternative hypothesis is true. We know that the hypothesis-testing process will lead to this conclusion incorrectly (Type I error) only $100\alpha\%$ of the time when H_0 is true.

   b. If the test statistic does not fall in the rejection region, we do not reject H_0. Thus, we reserve judgment about which hypothesis is true. We do not conclude that the null hypothesis is true because we do not (in general) know the probability β that our test procedure will lead to an incorrect acceptance of H_0 (Type II error).

As with confidence intervals, the methodology for testing hypotheses varies depending on the target population parameter. In this chapter, we develop methods for testing a population mean, a population proportion, and a population variance. Some key words and the type of data associated with these target parameters are listed in the accompanying box.

Determining the Target Parameter

Parameter	Key Words or Phrases	Type of Data
μ	Mean; average	Quantitative
p	Proportion; percentage; fraction; rate	Qualitative
σ^2	Variance; variability; spread	Quantitative

2 Formulating Hypotheses and Setting Up the Rejection Region

In Section 1 we learned that the null and alternative hypotheses form the basis for inference using a test of hypothesis. The null and alternative hypotheses may take one of several forms. In the sewer pipe example, we tested the null hypothesis that the population mean strength of the pipe is less than or equal to 2,400 pounds per linear foot against the alternative hypothesis that the mean strength exceeds 2,400—that is, we tested

$$H_0: \mu \leq 2,400 \quad \text{(Pipe does not meet specifications)}$$
$$H_a: \mu > 2,400 \quad \text{(Pipe meets specifications)}$$

This is a **one-tailed** (or **one-sided**) **statistical test** because the alternative hypothesis specifies that the population parameter (the population mean μ in this example) is strictly greater than a specified value (2,400 in this example). If the null hypothesis had been $H_0: \mu \geq 2,400$ and the alternative hypothesis had been $H_a: \mu < 2,400$, the test would still be one-sided because the parameter is still specified to be on "one side" of the null hypothesis value. Some statistical investigations seek to show that the population parameter is *either larger or smaller* than some specified value. Such an alternative hypothesis is called a **two-tailed** (or **two-sided**) **hypothesis.**

While alternative hypotheses are always specified as strict inequalities, such as $\mu < 2{,}400$, $\mu > 2{,}400$, or $\mu \neq 2{,}400$, null hypotheses are usually specified as equalities, such as $\mu = 2{,}400$. Even when the null hypothesis is an inequality, such as $\mu \leq 2{,}400$, we specify $H_0: \mu = 2{,}400$, reasoning that if sufficient evidence exists to show that $H_a: \mu > 2{,}400$ is true when tested against $H_0: \mu = 2{,}400$, then surely sufficient evidence exists to reject $\mu < 2{,}400$ as well. Therefore, the null hypothesis is specified as the value of μ closest to a one-sided alternative hypothesis and as the only value *not* specified in a two-tailed alternative hypothesis. The steps for selecting the null and alternative hypotheses are summarized in the following box.

Steps for Selecting the Null and Alternative Hypotheses

1. Select the *alternative hypothesis* as that which the sampling experiment is intended to establish. The alternative hypothesis will assume one of three forms:
   a. One-tailed, **upper-tailed** (e.g., $H_a: \mu > 2{,}400$)
   b. One-tailed, **lower-tailed** (e.g., $H_a: \mu < 2{,}400$)
   c. Two-tailed (e.g., $H_a: \mu \neq 2{,}400$)

2. Select the *null hypothesis* as the status quo, that which will be presumed true unless the sampling experiment conclusively establishes the alternative hypothesis. The null hypothesis will be specified as that parameter value closest to the alternative in one-tailed tests and as the complementary (or only unspecified) value in two-tailed tests.

$$\text{(e.g., } H_0: \mu = 2{,}400)$$

A **one-tailed test** of hypothesis is one in which the alternative hypothesis is directional and includes the symbol "<" or ">."

A **two-tailed test** of hypothesis is one in which the alternative hypothesis does not specify departure from H_0 in a particular direction and is written with the symbol "$\neq$."

Example 1

Formulating H_0 and H_a for a Test of a Population Mean—Quality Control

Problem A metal lathe is checked periodically by quality-control inspectors to determine whether it is producing machine bearings with a mean diameter of .5 inch. If the mean diameter of the bearings is larger or smaller than .5 inch, then the process is out of control and must be adjusted. Formulate the null and alternative hypotheses for a test to determine whether the bearing production process is out of control.

Solution The hypotheses must be stated in terms of a population parameter. Here, we define μ as the true mean diameter (in inches) of all bearings produced by the metal lathe. If either $\mu > .5$ or $\mu < .5$, then the lathe's production process is out of control. Because the inspectors want to be able to detect either possibility (indicating that the process is in need of adjustment), these values of μ represent the alternative (or research) hypothesis. Alternatively, because $\mu = .5$ represents an in-control process (the status quo), this represents the null hypothesis. Therefore, we want to conduct the two-tailed test:

$$H_0: \mu = .5 \text{ (i.e., the process is in control)}$$
$$H_a: \mu \neq .5 \text{ (i.e., the process is out of control)}$$

Look Back Here, the alternative hypothesis is not necessarily the hypothesis that the quality-control inspectors desire to support. However, they will make adjustments to the metal lathe settings only if there is strong evidence to indicate that the process is out of control. Consequently, $\mu \neq .5$ must be stated as the alternative hypothesis.

■ **Now Work Exercise 10a**

Example 2

Formulating H_0 and H_a for a Test of a Population Proportion—Cigarette Advertisements

Problem Cigarette advertisements are required by federal law to carry the following statement: "Warning: The surgeon general has determined that cigarette smoking is dangerous to your health." However, this warning is often located in inconspicuous corners of the advertisements and printed in small type. Suppose the Federal Trade Commission (FTC) claims that 80% of cigarette consumers fail to see the warning. A marketer for a large tobacco firm wants to gather evidence to show that the FTC's claim is too high, i.e., that fewer than 80% of cigarette consumers fail to see the warning. Specify the null and alternative hypotheses for a test of the FTC's claim.

Solution The marketer wants to make an inference about p, the true proportion of all cigarette consumers who fail to see the surgeon general's warning. In particular, the marketer wants to collect data to show that fewer than 80% of cigarette consumers fail to see the warning, i.e., $p < .80$. Consequently, $p < .80$. represents the alternative hypothesis and $p = .80$ (the claim made by the FTC) represents the null hypothesis. That is, the marketer desires the one-tailed (lower-tailed) test:

$$H_0: p = .80 \text{ (i.e., the FTC's claim is true)}$$
$$H_a: p < .80 \text{ (i.e., the FTC's claim is false)}$$

Look Back Whenever a claim is made about the value of a particular population parameter and the researcher wants to test the claim, believing that it is false, the claimed value will represent the null hypothesis.

■ **Now Work Exercise 11**

The rejection region for a two-tailed test differs from that for a one-tailed test. When we are trying to detect departure from the null hypothesis in *either* direction, we must establish a rejection region in both tails of the sampling distribution of the test statistic. Figures 4a and 4b show the one-tailed rejection regions for lower- and upper-tailed tests, respectively. The two-tailed rejection region is illustrated in Figure 4c. Note that a rejection region is established in each tail of the sampling distribution for a two-tailed test.

The rejection regions corresponding to typical values selected for α are shown in Table 2 for one- and two-tailed tests. Note that the smaller the α you select, the more evidence (the larger the z) you will need before you can reject H_0.

Figure 4
Rejection regions corresponding to one- and two-tailed tests

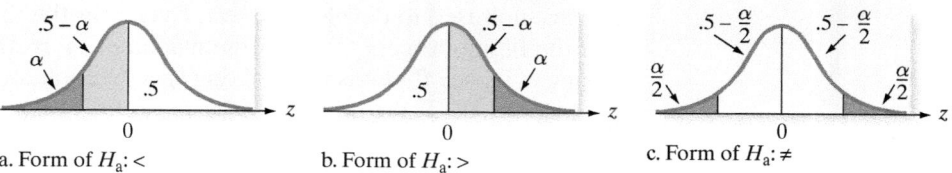

a. Form of $H_a: <$ b. Form of $H_a: >$ c. Form of $H_a: \neq$

Table 2	Rejection Regions for Common Values of α		
	Alternative Hypotheses		
	Lower-Tailed	Upper-Tailed	Two-Tailed
$\alpha = .10$	$z < -1.282$	$z > 1.282$	$z < -1.645$ or $z > 1.645$
$\alpha = .05$	$z < -1.645$	$z > 1.645$	$z < -1.96$ or $z > 1.96$
$\alpha = .01$	$z < -2.326$	$z > 2.326$	$z < -2.576$ or $z > 2.576$

Example 3

Setting Up a Hypothesis Test for μ—Mean Amount of Cereal in a Box

Problem A manufacturer of cereal wants to test the performance of one of its filling machines. The machine is designed to discharge a mean amount of 12 ounces per box, and the manufacturer wants to detect any departure from this setting. This quality study calls for randomly sampling 100 boxes from today's production run and determining whether the mean fill for the run is 12 ounces per box. Set up a test of hypothesis for this study, using $\alpha = .01$.

Solution The key word *mean* in the statement of the problem implies that the target parameter is μ, the mean amount of cereal discharged into each box. Because the manufacturer wishes to detect a departure from the setting of $\mu = 12$ in either direction, $\mu < 12$ or $\mu > 12$, we conduct a two-tailed statistical test. Following the procedure for selecting the null and alternative hypotheses, we specify as the alternative hypothesis that the mean differs from 12 ounces because detecting the machine's departure from specifications is the purpose of the quality-control study. The null hypothesis is the presumption that the filling machine is operating properly unless the sample data indicate otherwise. Thus,

$H_0: \mu = 12$ (Population mean fill amount is 12 ounces)

$H_a: \mu \neq 12$ (i.e., $\mu < 12$ or $\mu > 12$; machine is under- or overfilling each box)

The test statistic measures the number of standard deviations between the observed value of $\bar{x}$ and the null hypothesized value $\mu = 12$:

$$\textit{Test statistic: } z = \frac{\bar{x} - 12}{\sigma_{\bar{x}}}$$

The rejection region must be designated to detect a departure from $\mu = 12$ in *either* direction, so we will reject H_0 for values of z that are either too small (negative) or too large (positive). To determine the precise values of z that comprise the rejection region, we first select α, the probability that the test will lead to incorrect rejection of the null hypothesis. Then we divide α equally between the lower and upper tails of the distribution of z, as shown in Figure 5. In this example, $\alpha = .01$, so $\frac{\alpha}{2} = .005$ is placed in each tail. The areas in the tails correspond to $z = -2.576$ and $z = 2.576$, respectively (from Table 2):

Rejection region: $z < -2.576$ or $z > 2.576$ (see Figure 5)

Assumptions: Because the sample size of the experiment is large enough $(n > 30)$, the Central Limit Theorem will apply, and no assumptions need be made about the population of fill measurements. The sampling distribution of the sample mean fill of 100 boxes will be approximately normal regardless of the distribution of the individual boxes' fills.

Look Back Note that the test is set up *before* the sampling experiment is conducted. The data are not used to develop the test. Evidently, the manufacturer does not want to disrupt the filling process to adjust the machine, unless the sample data provide very convincing evidence that it is not meeting specifications, because the value of α has been set quite low at .01. If the sample evidence results in the rejection of H_0, the manufacturer will confidently conclude that the machine needs adjustment because there is only a .01 probability of a Type I error.

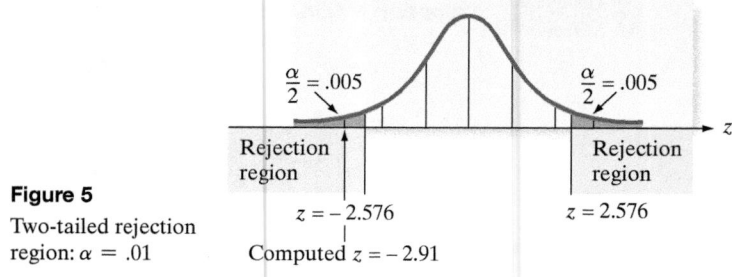

Figure 5
Two-tailed rejection
region: $\alpha = .01$

■ **Now Work Exercise 10b, c**

Once the test is set up, the manufacturer is ready to perform the sampling experiment and conduct the test. The test is performed in the next section.

STATISTICS
in ACTION
REVISITED

Key Elements of a Hypothesis Test

In Kimberly-Clark Corp.'s survey of people with colds, each of 250 customers was asked to keep count of his or her use of Kleenex® tissues in diaries. One goal of the company was to determine how many tissues to package in a cold-care box of Kleenex®; consequently, the total number of tissues used was recorded for each person surveyed. Since the number of tissues is a quantitative variable, the parameter of interest is either μ, the mean number of tissues used by all customers with colds, or σ^2, the variance of the number of tissues used.

Recall that in 2000, the company increased from 60 to 70 the number of tissues it packages in a cold-care box of Kleenex® tissues. The decision was based on a claim made by marketing experts that the average number of times a person will blow his or her nose during a cold exceeds the previous mean of 60. The key word *average* implies that the parameter of interest is μ, and the marketers are claiming that $\mu > 60$. In order to test the claim, we set up the following null and alternative hypotheses:

$$H_0: \mu = 60 \qquad H_a: \mu > 60$$

We'll conduct this test in the next Statistics in Action Revisited.

Exercises 1–18

Please be aware that some of the following problems may require knowledge of concepts that are not presented in this chapter.

Learning the Mechanics

1 Which hypothesis, the null or the alternative, is the status-quo hypothesis? Which is the research hypothesis?

2 Which element of a test of hypothesis is used to decide whether to reject the null hypothesis in favor of the alternative hypothesis?

3 What is the level of significance of a test of hypothesis?

4 What is the difference between Type I and Type II errors in hypothesis testing? How do α and β relate to Type I and Type II errors?

5 List the four possible results of the combinations of decisions and true states of nature for a test of hypothesis.

6 We reject the null hypothesis when the test statistic falls in the rejection region, but we do not accept the null hypothesis when the test statistic does not fall in the rejection region. Why?

7 If you test a hypothesis and reject the null hypothesis in favor of the alternative hypothesis, does your test prove that the alternative hypothesis is correct? Explain.

8 For each of the following rejection regions, sketch the sampling distribution for z and indicate the location of the rejection region.
  a. $z > 1.96$
  b. $z > 1.645$
  c. $z > 2.576$
  d. $z < -1.282$
  e. $z < -1.645$ or $z > 1.645$
  f. $z < -2.576$ or $z > 2.576$
  g. For each of the rejection regions specified in parts **a–f,** what is the probability that a Type I error will be made?

⚙ Applet Exercise 1

Use the applet *Hypothesis Test for a Mean* to investigate the frequency of Type I and Type II errors. For this exercise, use $n = 100$ and the normal distribution with mean 50 and standard deviation 10.
  a. Set the null mean equal to 50 and the alternative to *not equal.* Run the applet one time. How many times was the null hypothesis rejected at level .05? In this case, the null hypothesis is true. Which type of error occurred each time the true null hypothesis was rejected? What is the probability of rejecting a true null hypothesis at level .05? How does the proportion of times the null hypothesis was rejected compare to this probability?
  b. Clear the applet, then set the null mean equal to 47 and keep the alternative at *not equal.* Run the applet one time. How many times was the null hypothesis *not* rejected at level .05? In this case, the null hypothesis is false. Which type of error occurred each time the null hypothesis was *not* rejected? Run the applet several more times without clearing. Based on your results, what can you conclude about the probability of failing to reject the null hypothesis for the given conditions?

Applying the Concepts—Basic

9 **Effectiveness of online courses.** The Sloan Survey of Online Learning, "Going the Distance: Online Education in the United States, 2011," reported that 68% of college presidents believe that their online education courses are as good as or superior to courses that use traditional, face-to-face instruction.
  a. Give the null hypothesis for testing the claim made by the Sloan Survey.
  b. Give the rejection region for a two-tailed test conducted at $\alpha = .01$.

10 Play Golf America program. The Professional Golf Association (PGA) and *Golf Digest* have developed the Play Golf America program, in which teaching professionals at participating golf clubs provide a free 10-minute lesson to new customers. According to *Golf Digest* (July 2008), golf facilities that participate in the program gain, on average, $2,400 in greens, fees, lessons, or equipment expenditures. A teaching professional at a golf club believes that the average gain in greens fees, lessons, or equipment expenditures for participating golf facilities exceeds $2,400.

a. In order to support the claim made by the teaching professional, what null and alternative hypotheses should you test?

b. Suppose you select $\alpha = .05$. Interpret this value in the words of the problem.

c. For $\alpha = .05$, specify the rejection region of a large-sample test.

11 Student loan default rate. The national student loan default rate has fluctuated over the last several years. A few years ago, the Department of Education reported the default rate (i.e., the proportion of college students who default on their loans) at .07. Set up the null and alternative hypotheses if you want to determine if the student loan default rate this year is less than .07.

12 Work travel policy. American Express Consulting reported in *USA Today* (June 15, 2001) that 80% of U.S. companies have formal, written travel and entertainment policies for their employees. Give the null hypothesis for testing the claim made by American Express Consulting.

13 Calories in school lunches. A University of Florida economist conducted a study of Virginia elementary school lunch menus. During the state-mandated testing period, school lunches averaged 863 calories (National Bureau of Economic Research, Nov. 2002). The economist claims that after the testing period ends, the average caloric content of Virginia school lunches drops significantly. Set up the null and alternative hypotheses to test the economist's claim.

14 Libor interest rate. The interest rate at which London banks lend money to one another is called the *London interbank offered rate,* or *Libor.* The British Bankers Association regularly surveys international banks for the Libor rate. One recent report (*Bankrate.com*, Jan. 25, 2012) had the average Libor rate at 1.10% for 1-year loans—a value considered high by many Western banks. Set up the null and alternative hypotheses for testing the reported value.

Applying the Concepts—Intermediate

15 FDA certification of new drugs. According to *Chemical Marketing Reporter,* pharmaceutical companies spend $15 billion per year on research and development of new drugs. The pharmaceutical company must subject each new drug to lengthy and involved testing before receiving the necessary permission from the Food and Drug Administration (FDA) to market the drug. The FDA's policy is that the pharmaceutical company must provide substantial evidence that a new drug is safe prior to receiving FDA approval, so that the FDA can confidently certify the safety of the drug to potential consumers.

a. If the new drug testing were to be placed in a test of hypothesis framework, would the null hypothesis be that the drug is safe or unsafe? The alternative hypothesis?

b. Given the choice of null and alternative hypotheses in part **a**, describe Type I and Type II errors in terms of this application. Define α and β in terms of this application.

c. If the FDA wants to be very confident that the drug is safe before permitting it to be marketed, is it more important that α or β be small? Explain.

16 Authorizing computer users. At high-technology industries, computer security is achieved by using a *password*—a collection of symbols (usually letters and numbers) that must be supplied by the user before the computer permits access to the account. The problem is that persistent hackers can create programs that enter millions of combinations of symbols into a target system until the correct password is found. The newest systems solve this problem by requiring authorized users to identify themselves by unique body characteristics. For example, a system developed by Palmguard, Inc. tests the hypothesis

H_0: The proposed user is authorized
H_a: The proposed user is unauthorized

by checking characteristics of the proposed user's palm against those stored in the authorized users' data bank.

a. Define a Type I error and Type II error for this test. Which is the more serious error? Why?

b. Palmguard reports that the Type I error rate for its system is less than 1%, whereas the Type II error rate is .00025%. Interpret these error rates.

c. Another successful security system, the EyeDentifyer, "spots authorized computer users by reading the one-of-a-kind patterns formed by the network of minute blood vessels across the retina at the back of the eye." The EyeDentifyer reports Type I and II error rates of .01% (1 in 10,000) and .005% (5 in 100,000), respectively. Interpret these rates.

Applying the Concepts—Advanced

17 Jury trial outcomes. Sometimes, the outcome of a jury trial defies the "common sense" expectations of the general public (e.g., the O. J. Simpson verdict and the 2011 Casey Anthony verdict). Such a verdict is more acceptable if we understand that the jury trial of an accused murderer is analogous to the statistical hypothesis-testing process. The null hypothesis in a jury trial is that the accused is innocent. (The status-quo hypothesis in the U.S. system of justice is innocence, which is assumed to be true until proven *beyond a reasonable doubt.*) The alternative hypothesis is guilt, which is accepted only when sufficient evidence exists to establish its truth. If the vote of the jury is unanimous in favor of guilt, the null hypothesis of innocence is rejected, and the court concludes that the accused murderer is guilty. Any vote other than a unanimous one for guilt results in a "not guilty" verdict. The court never accepts the null hypothesis; that is, the court never declares the accused "innocent." A "not guilty" verdict (as in the Casey Anthony) implies that the court could not find the defendant guilty *beyond a reasonable doubt.*

a. Define Type I and Type II errors in a murder trial.

b. Which of the two errors is the more serious? Explain.

c. The court does not, in general, know the values of α and β; but ideally, both should be small. One of these probabilities is assumed to be smaller than the other in a jury trial. Which one, and why?

d. The court system relies on the belief that the value of α is made very small by requiring a unanimous vote before guilt is concluded. Explain why this is so.

e. For a jury prejudiced against a guilty verdict as the trial begins, will the value of α increase or decrease? Explain.

f. For a jury prejudiced against a guilty verdict as the trial begins, will the value of β increase or decrease? Explain.

18 Intrusion detection systems. The *Journal of Research of the National Institute of Standards and Technology* (Nov.–Dec. 2003) did a study of a computer intrusion detection system (IDS). An IDS is designed to provide an alarm whenever unauthorized access e.g., an intrusion) to a computer system occurs. The probability of the system giving a false alarm (i.e., providing a warning when no intrusion occurs) is defined by the symbol α, while the probability of a missed detection (i.e., no warning given when an intrusion occurs) is defined by the symbol β. These symbols are used to represent Type I and Type II error rates, respectively, in a hypothesis-testing scenario.

a. What is the null hypothesis, H_0?

b. What is the alternative hypothesis, H_a?

c. According to actual data on the EMERALD system collected by the Massachusetts Institute of Technology Lincoln Laboratory, only 1 in 1,000 computer sessions with no intrusions resulted in a false alarm. For the same system, the laboratory found that only 500 of 1,000 intrusions were actually detected. Use this information to estimate the values of α and β.

3   Observed Significance Levels: *p*-Values

According to the statistical test procedure described in Section 2, the rejection region and, correspondingly, the value of α are selected prior to conducting the test, and the conclusions are stated in terms of rejecting or not rejecting the null hypothesis. A second method of presenting the results of a statistical test is one that reports the extent to which the test statistic disagrees with the null hypothesis and leaves to the reader the task of deciding whether to reject the null hypothesis. This measure of disagreement is called the *observed significance level* (or *p-value*) for the test.

> The **observed significance level,** or *p*-value, for a specific statistical test is the probability (assuming H_0 is true) of observing a value of the test statistic that is at least as contradictory to the null hypothesis, and supportive of the alternative hypothesis, as the actual one computed from the sample data.

Recall testing H_0: $\mu = 2{,}400$ versus H_a: $\mu = 2{,}400$, where μ is the mean breaking strength of sewer pipe (Section 1). The value of the test statistic computed for the sample of $n = 50$ sections of sewer pipe was $z = 2.12$. Because the test is one-tailed—that is, the alternative (research) hypothesis of interest is H_a: $\mu > 2{,}400$—values of the test statistic even more contradictory to H_0 than the one observed would be values larger than $z = 2.12$. Therefore, the observed significance level (*p*-value) for this test is

$$p\text{-value} = P(z > 2.12)$$

or, equivalently, the area under the standard normal curve to the right of $z = 2.12$ (see Figure 6).

The area A in Figure 6 is given in Table II in Appendix: Tables as .4830. Therefore, the upper-tail area corresponding to $z = 2.12$ is

$$p\text{-value} = .5 - .4830 = .0170$$

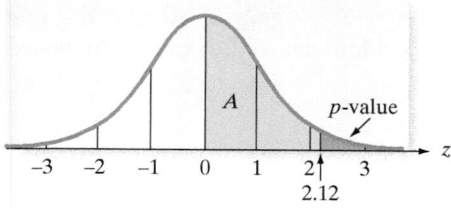

Figure 6

Finding the *p*-value for an upper-tailed test when $z = 2.12$

Consequently, we say that these test results are "very significant" (i.e., they disagree rather strongly with the null hypothesis, H_0: $\mu = 2,400$, and favor H_a: $\mu > 2,400$). The probability of observing a z-value as large as 2.12 is only .0170, if in fact the true value of μ is 2,400.

If you are inclined to select $\alpha = .05$ for this test, then you would reject the null hypothesis because the p-value for the test, .0170, is less than .05. In contrast, if you choose $\alpha = .01$, you would not reject the null hypothesis because the p-value for the test is larger than .01. Thus, the use of the observed significance level is identical to the test procedure described in the preceding sections except that the choice of α is left to you.

The steps for calculating the p-value corresponding to a test statistic for a population mean are given in the next box.

Steps for Calculating the p-Value for a Test of Hypothesis

1. Determine the value of the test statistic z corresponding to the result of the sampling experiment.

2. **a.** If the test is one-tailed, the p-value is equal to the tail area beyond z in the same direction as the alternative hypothesis. Thus, if the alternative hypothesis is of the form $>$, the p-value is the area to the right of, or above, the observed z-value. Conversely, if the alternative is of the form $<$, the p-value is the area to the left of, or below, the observed z-value. (See Figure 7.)

   b. If the test is two-tailed, the p-value is equal to twice the tail area beyond the observed z-value in the direction of the sign of z—that is, if z is positive, the p-value is twice the area to the right of, or above, the observed z-value. Conversely, if z is negative, the p-value is twice the area to the left of, or below, the observed z-value. (See Figure 8.)

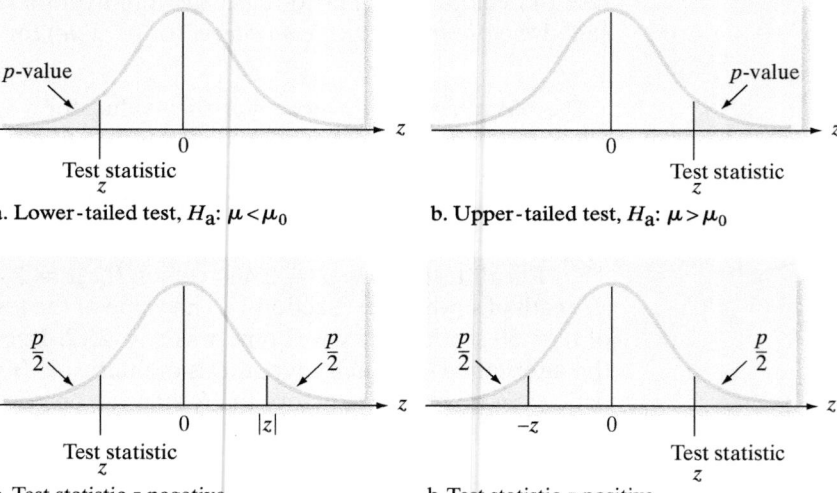

Figure 7
Finding the p-value for a one-tailed test

a. Lower-tailed test, H_a: $\mu < \mu_0$ b. Upper-tailed test, H_a: $\mu > \mu_0$

Figure 8
Finding the p-value for a two-tailed test: p-value $= 2\left(\frac{p}{2}\right)$

a. Test statistic z negative b. Test statistic z positive

Example 4

Comparing Rejection Regions to p-Values

Problem Consider the one-tailed test of hypothesis, H_0: $\mu = 100$ versus H_a: $\mu > 100$.

a. Suppose the test statistic is $z = 1.44$. Find the p-value of the test and the rejection region for the test when $\alpha = .05$. Then show that the conclusion using the rejection region approach will be identical to the conclusion based on the p-value.

b. Now suppose the test statistic is $z = 3.01$; find the p-value and rejection region for the test when $\alpha = .05$. Again, show that the conclusion using the rejection region approach will be identical to the conclusion based on the p-value.

Solution

a. The p-value for the test is the probability of observing a test statistic more contradictory to the null hypothesis (i.e., more supportive of the alternative hypothesis) than the value $z = 1.44$. Since we are conducting an upper-tailed test ($H_a: \mu > 100$), the probability we seek is:

$$p\text{-value} = P(z > 1.44) = 1 - P(z < 1.44)$$

The latter probability in the expression is a cumulative probability that can be obtained from the standard normal table (Table II, Appendix: Tables) or using statistical software. The Minitab printout giving this probability is shown in Figure 9.

Cumulative Distribution Function

Normal with mean = 0 and standard deviation = 1

Figure 9

Minitab normal probability for Example 4a

```
    x   P( X <= x )
 1.44      0.925066
```

Therefore, we compute

$$p\text{-value} = P(z > 1.44) = 1 - P(z < 1.44) = 1 - .925 = .075$$

This p-value is shown on Figure 10.

Since $\alpha = .05$ and the test is upper-tailed, the rejection region for the test is $z > 1.645$ (see Table 2). This rejection region is also shown in Figure 10. Observe that the test statistic ($z = 1.44$) falls outside the rejection region, implying that we fail to reject H_0. Also, $\alpha = .05$ is less than p-value $= .075$. This result also implies that we should fail to reject H_0. Consequently, both decision rules agree—there is insufficient evidence to reject H_0.

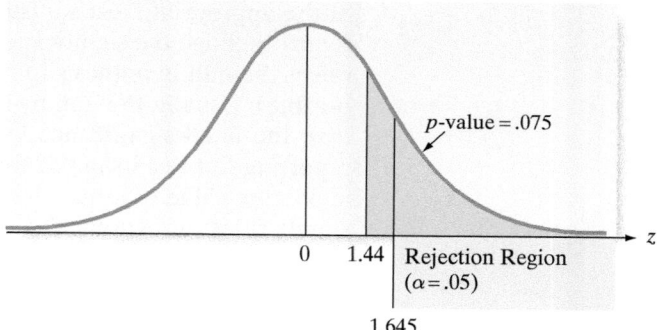

Figure 10

Test for Example 4a—Fail to reject H_0

b. For $z = 3.01$, the observed significance level of the test is:

$$p\text{-value} = P(z > 3.01) = 1 - P(z < 3.01)$$

A Minitab printout giving the cumulative probability, $P(z < 3.01)$, is shown in Figure 11.

Cumulative Distribution Function

Normal with mean = 0 and standard deviation = 1

Figure 11

Minitab normal probability for Example 4b

```
    x   P( X <= x )
 3.01      0.998694
```

Thus, we have

$$p\text{-value} = P(z > 3.01) = 1 - P(z < 3.01) = 1 - .9987 = .0013.$$

This p-value is shown on Figure 12.

Again, for $\alpha = .05$ and an upper-tailed test, the rejection region is $z > 1.645$. This rejection region is also shown in Figure 12. Now the test statistic ($z = 3.01$) falls within the rejection region, leading us to reject H_0. And, $\alpha = .05$ now exceeds the p-value

(.0013), which also implies that we should reject H_0. Once again, both decision rules agree—and they always will if the same value of α is used to make the decision.

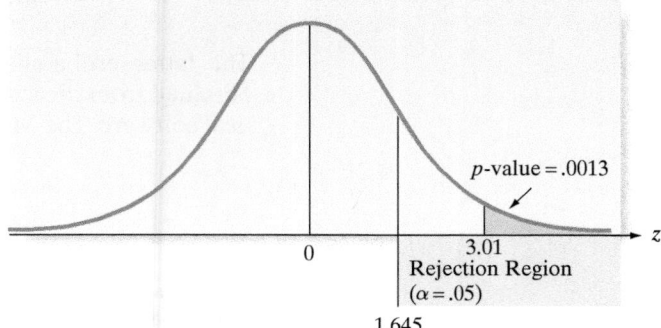

Figure 12

Test for Example 4b—Reject H_0

Look Ahead Since *p*-values are easily computed using statistical software, most analysts and researchers utilize the *p*-value approach to hypothesis testing. In future examples, we will adopt this approach generally, although we'll continue to show the appropriate rejection regions where necessary for illustrative purposes.

Now Work: Exercise 19

When publishing the results of a statistical test of hypothesis in journals, case studies, reports, and so on, many researchers make use of *p*-values. Instead of selecting α beforehand and then conducting a test, as outlined in this chapter, the researcher computes (usually with the aid of a statistical software package) and reports the value of the appropriate test statistic and its associated *p*-value. It is left to the reader of the report to judge the significance of the result (i.e., the reader must determine whether to reject the null hypothesis in favor of the alternative hypothesis, based on the reported *p*-value). Usually, the null hypothesis is rejected if the observed significance level is *less than* the fixed significance level, α, chosen by the reader. The inherent advantage of reporting test results in this manner are twofold: (1) Readers are permitted to select the maximum value of α that they would be willing to tolerate if they actually carried out a standard test of hypothesis in the manner outlined in this chapter, and (2) a measure of the degree of significance of the result (i.e., the *p*-value) is provided.

ETHICS in STATISTICS

Selecting the value of α *after* computing the observed significance level (*p*-value) in order to guarantee a preferred conclusion is considered *unethical statistical practice.*

Reporting Test Results as *p*-Values: How to Decide Whether to Reject H_0

1. Choose the maximum value of α that you are willing to tolerate.
2. If the observed significance level (p-value) of the test is less than the chosen value of α, reject the null hypothesis. Otherwise, do not reject the null hypothesis.

Note: Some statistical software packages (e.g., SPSS) will conduct only two-tailed tests of hypothesis. For these packages, you obtain the *p*-value for a one-tailed test as shown in the box:

Converting a Two-Tailed *p*-Value from a Printout to a One-Tailed *p*-Value

$$p = \frac{\text{Reported } p\text{-value}}{2} \quad \text{if} \begin{cases} H_a \text{ is of form} > \text{ and } z \text{ is positive} \\ H_a \text{ is of form} < \text{ and } z \text{ is negative} \end{cases}$$

$$p = 1 - \left(\frac{\text{Reported } p\text{-value}}{2} \right) \quad \text{if} \begin{cases} H_a \text{ is of form} > \text{ and } z \text{ is negative} \\ H_a \text{ is of form} < \text{ and } z \text{ is positive} \end{cases}$$

Exercises 19–27

Learning the Mechanics

19 Consider the test of $H_0: \mu = 7$. For each of the following, find the p-value of the test:
   a. $H_a: \mu > 7, z = 1.20$
   b. $H_a: \mu < 7, z = -1.20$
   c. $H_a: \mu \neq 7, z = 1.20$

20 If a hypothesis test were conducted using $\alpha = .05$, for which of the following p-values would the null hypothesis be rejected?
   a. .06   **b.** .10
   c. .01   **d.** .001
   e. .251   **f.** .042

21 For each α and observed significance level (p-value) pair, indicate whether the null hypothesis would be rejected.
   a. $\alpha = .05, p\text{-value} = .10$
   b. $\alpha = .10, p\text{-value} = .05$
   c. $\alpha = .01, p\text{-value} = .001$
   d. $\alpha = .025, p\text{-value} = .05$
   e. $\alpha = .10, p\text{-value} = .45$

22 In a test of the hypothesis $H_0: \mu = 50$ versus $H_a: \mu > 50$, a sample of $n = 100$ observations possessed mean $\bar{x} = 49.4$ and standard deviation $s = 4.1$. Find and interpret the p-value for this test.

23 In a test of $H_0: \mu = 100$ against $H_a: \mu > 100$, the sample data yielded the test statistic $z = 2.17$. Find and interpret the p-value for the test.

24 In a test of the hypothesis $H_0: \mu = 10$ versus $H_a: \mu \neq 10$, a sample of $n = 50$ observations possessed mean $\bar{x} = 10.7$ and standard deviation $s = 3.1$. Find and interpret the p-value for this test.

25 In a test of $H_0: \mu = 100$ against $H_a: \mu \neq 100$, the sample data yielded the test statistic $z = 2.17$. Find the p-value for the test.

26 In a test of $H_0: \mu = 75$ performed using the computer, SPSS reports a two-tailed p-value of .1032. Make the appropriate conclusion for each of the following situations:
   a. $H_a: \mu < 75, z = -1.63, \alpha = .05$
   b. $H_a: \mu < 75, z = 1.63, \alpha = .10$
   c. $H_a: \mu > 75, z = 1.63, \alpha = .10$
   d. $H_a: \mu \neq 75, z = -1.63, \alpha = .01$

27 An analyst tested the null hypothesis $\mu \geq 20$ against the alternative hypothesis that $\mu < 20$. The analyst reported a p-value of .06. What is the smallest value of α for which the null hypothesis would be rejected?

4 Test of Hypothesis about a Population Mean: Normal (z) Statistic

When testing a hypothesis about a population mean μ, the test statistic we use will depend on whether the sample size n is large (say, $n \geq 30$) or small, and whether or not we know the value of the population standard deviation, σ. In this section, we consider the large-sample case.

Because the sample size is large, the Central Limit Theorem guarantees that the sampling distribution of $\bar{x}$ is approximately normal. Consequently, the test statistic for a test based on large samples will be based on the normal z-statistic. Although the z-statistic requires that we know the true population standard deviation σ, we rarely if ever know σ. However when n is large, the sample standard deviation s provides a good approximation to σ, and the z-statistic can be approximated as follows:

$$z = \frac{\bar{x} - \mu_0}{\sigma_{\bar{x}}} = \frac{\bar{x} - \mu_0}{\sigma/\sqrt{n}} \approx \frac{\bar{x} - \mu_0}{s/\sqrt{n}}$$

where μ_0 represents the value of μ specified in the null hypothesis.

The setup of a large-sample test of hypothesis about a population mean is summarized in the following boxes. Both the one- and two-tailed tests are shown.

> **Conditions Required for a Valid Large-Sample Hypothesis Test for μ**
>
> **1.** A random sample is selected from the target population.
>
> **2.** The sample size n is large (i.e., $n \geq 30$). (Due to the Central Limit Theorem, this condition guarantees that the test statistic will be approximately normal regardless of the shape of the underlying probability distribution of the population.)

Large-Sample Test of Hypothesis about μ Based on a Normal (z) Statistic

One-Tailed Test	Two-Tailed Test
$H_0: \mu = \mu_0$ $H_a: \mu < \mu_0$ (or $H_a: \mu > \mu_0$)	$H_0: \mu = \mu_0$ $H_a: \mu \neq \mu_0$
Test statistic (σ known): $z = \dfrac{\bar{x} - \mu_0}{\sigma/\sqrt{n}}$	Test statistic (σ known): $z = \dfrac{\bar{x} - \mu_0}{\sigma/\sqrt{n}}$
Test statistic (σ unknown): $z \approx \dfrac{\bar{x} - \mu_0}{\sigma/\sqrt{n}}$	Test statistic (σ unknown): $z \approx \dfrac{\bar{x} - \mu_0}{s\sqrt{n}}$
Rejection region: $z < -z_\alpha$ (or $z > z_\alpha$ when $H_a: \mu > \mu_0$) where z_α is chosen so that $P(z > z_\alpha) = \alpha$	Rejection region: $\lvert z \rvert > z_{\alpha/2}$ where $z_{\alpha/2}$ is chosen so that $P(\lvert z \rvert > z_{\alpha 2}) = \alpha/2$

Note: μ_0 is the symbol for the numerical value assigned to μ under the null hypothesis.

Once the test has been set up, the sampling experiment is performed and the test statistic and corresponding p-value are calculated. The next box reviews possible conclusions for a test of hypothesis, depending on the result of the sampling experiment.

Possible Conclusions for a Test of Hypothesis

1. If the calculated test statistic falls in the rejection region (or, $\alpha > p$-value), reject H_0 and conclude that the alternative hypothesis H_a is true. State that you are rejecting H_0 at the α level of significance. Remember that the confidence is in the testing *process,* not in the particular result of a single test.

2. If the test statistic does not fall in the rejection region (or, $\alpha < p$-value), conclude that the sampling experiment does not provide sufficient evidence to reject H_0 at the α level of significance. [Generally, we will not "accept" the null hypothesis unless the probability β of a Type II error has been calculated (see Section 8).]

Example 5

Carrying Out a Hypothesis Test for μ—Mean Amount of Cereal in a Box

Problem Refer to the quality-control test set up in Example 3. Recall that a machine is designed to discharge a mean of 12 ounces of cereal per box. A sample of 100 boxes yielded the fill amounts (in ounces) shown in Table 3. Use these data to conduct the following test:

$$H_0: \mu = 12 \quad \text{(Population mean fill amount is 12 ounces)}$$
$$H_a: \mu \neq 12 \quad \text{(Machine is under- or overfilling the box)}$$

Table 3	Fill Amounts from Quality-Control Tests								
12.3	12.2	12.9	11.8	12.1	11.7	11.8	11.3	12.0	11.7
11.0	12.7	11.2	11.8	11.4	11.3	11.5	12.1	12.5	11.7
12.3	11.7	11.6	11.6	11.1	12.1	12.4	11.4	11.6	11.4
10.9	11.0	11.5	11.6	11.6	11.4	11.9	11.1	11.7	12.1
12.2	11.7	11.6	11.4	12.4	11.0	11.8	12.9	13.2	11.5
11.5	12.0	11.9	11.8	12.5	11.8	12.4	12.0	12.2	12.4
11.8	12.6	11.8	11.8	11.5	12.0	12.7	11.5	11.0	11.8
11.2	12.6	12.0	12.6	12.0	12.0	12.5	12.0	12.8	11.8
12.6	12.4	10.9	12.0	11.9	11.6	11.3	12.1	11.8	12.2
12.2	11.5	12.7	11.5	11.0	11.7	12.5	11.6	11.3	11.1

 Data Set: CEREAL

Descriptive Statistics: FILL

Variable	N	Mean	StDev	Minimum	Q1	Median	Q3	Maximum
FILL	100	11.851	0.512	10.900	11.500	11.800	12.200	13.200

Figure 13

Minitab descriptive statistics for fill amounts, Example 5

Solution To carry out the test, we need to find the values of $\bar{x}$ and s. These values, $\bar{x} = 11.851$ and $s = .512$, are shown (highlighted) on the Minitab printout, Figure 13. Now, we substitute these sample statistics into the test statistic and obtain:

$$z = \frac{\bar{x} - 12}{\sigma_{\bar{x}}} = \frac{\bar{x} - 12}{\sigma/\sqrt{n}} = \frac{11.851 - 12}{\sigma/\sqrt{100}}$$

$$\approx \frac{11.851 - 12}{s/10} = \frac{-.149}{.512/10} = -2.91$$

The implication is that the sample mean, 11.851, is (approximately) 3 standard deviations below the null hypothesized value of 12.0 in the sampling distribution of $\bar{x}$. You can see in Figure 5 that this value of z is in the lower-tail rejection region, which consists of all values of $z < -2.576$. These sample data provide sufficient evidence to reject H_0 and conclude, at the $\alpha = .01$ level of significance, that the mean fill differs from the specification of $\mu = 12$ ounces. It appears that the machine is, on average, underfilling the boxes.

Look Back Three points about the test of hypothesis in this example apply to all statistical tests:

1. Because z is less than -2.576, it is tempting to state our conclusion at a significance level lower than $\alpha = .01$. We resist the temptation because the level of α is determined before the sampling experiment is performed. If we decide that we are willing to tolerate a 1% Type I error rate, the result of the sampling experiment should have no effect on that decision. In general, *the same data should not be used both to set up and to conduct the test.*

2. When we state our conclusion at the .01 level of significance, we are referring to the failure rate of the procedure, not the result of this particular test. We know that the test procedure will lead to the rejection of the null hypothesis only 1% of the time when in fact $\mu = 12$. Therefore, *when the test statistic falls in the rejection region, we infer that the alternative $\mu \neq 12$ is true and express our confidence in the procedure by quoting the α level of significance, or the $100(1 - \alpha)\%$ confidence level.*

3. Although a test may lead to a "statistically significant" result (i.e., rejecting H_0 at significance level α, as in the test above), it may not be "practically significant." For example, suppose the quality-control study tested $n = 100{,}000$ cereal boxes, resulting in $\bar{x} = 11.995$ and $s = .5$. Now, a two-tailed hypothesis test of H_0: $\mu = 12$ results in a test statistic of $z = \dfrac{(11.995 - 12)}{.5/\sqrt{100{,}000}} = -3.16$.

   This result at $\alpha = .01$ leads us to "reject H_0" and conclude that the mean, μ, is "statistically different" from 12. However, for all practical purposes, the sample mean, $\bar{x} = 11.995$, and hypothesized mean, $\mu = 12$, are the same. Because the result is not "practically significant," the company is not likely to spend money fixing a machine that, for all practical purposes, is dispensing an average of 12 ounces of cereal into the boxes. Consequently, *not all "statistically significant" results are "practically significant."*

◀ **Now Work Exercise 34**

Example 6

Using p-Values—Test of Mean Filling Weight

Problem Find the observed significance level (p-value) for the test of the mean filling weight in Examples 3 and 5. Interpret the result.

Solution Again, we are testing H_0: $\mu = 12$ ounces versus H_a: $\mu \neq 12$ ounces. The observed value of the test statistic in Example 5 was $z = -2.91$, and any value of z less than -2.91 or greater than 2.91 (because this is a two-tailed test) would be even more contradictory to H_0. Therefore, the observed significance level for the test is

$$p\text{-value} = P(z < -2.91 \text{ or } z > 2.91) = P(|z| > 2.91)$$

Thus, we calculate the area below the observed z-value, $z = -2.91$, and double it. Consulting Table II in Appendix: Tables, we find that $P(z < -2.91) = .5 - .4982 = .0018$. Therefore, the p-value for this two-tailed test is

$$2P(z < -2.91) = 2(.0018) = .0036$$

This p-value can also be obtained using statistical software. The rounded p-value is shown (highlighted) on the Minitab printout, Figure 14. Since $\alpha = .01$ is greater than p-value $= .0036$, our conclusion is identical to that in Example 5—reject H_0.

Figure 14

Minitab test of mean fill amount, Example 6

```
Test of mu = 12 vs not = 12

Variable    N     Mean    StDev   SE Mean      95% CI          T      P
FILL       100  11.8510  0.5118   0.0512  (11.7495, 11.9525)  -2.91  0.004
```

Look Back We can interpret this p-value as a strong indication that the machine is not filling the boxes according to specifications because we would observe a test statistic this extreme or more extreme only 36 in 10,000 times if the machine were meeting specifications ($\mu = 12$). The extent to which the mean differs from 12 could be better determined by calculating a confidence interval for μ.

■ Now Work Exercise 25

Example 7

Using p-Values—Test of Mean Hospital Length of Stay

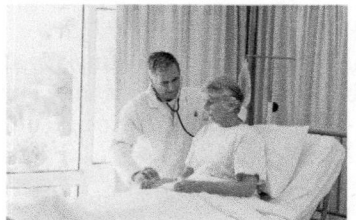

Problem Knowledge of the amount of time a patient occupies a hospital bed—called *length of stay* (LOS)—is important for allocating resources. At one hospital, the mean LOS was determined to be 5 days. A hospital administrator believes the mean LOS may now be less than 5 days due to a newly adopted managed health care system. To check this, the LOSs (in days) for 100 randomly selected hospital patients were recorded; these data are listed in Table 4. Suppose we want to test the hypothesis that the true mean length of stay at the hospital is less than 5 days; that is,

$$H_0: \mu = 5 \text{(Mean LOS after adoption is 5 days)}$$

$$H_a: \mu < 5 \text{(Mean LOS after adoption is less than 5 days)}$$

Assuming that $\sigma = 3.68$, use the data in the table to conduct the test at $\alpha = .05$.

Table 4	Lengths of Stay for 100 Hospital Patients								
2	3	8	6	4	4	6	4	2	5
8	10	4	4	4	2	1	3	2	10
1	3	2	3	4	3	5	2	4	1
2	9	1	7	17	9	9	9	4	4
1	1	1	3	1	6	3	3	2	5
1	3	3	14	2	3	9	6	6	3
5	1	4	6	11	22	1	9	6	5
2	2	5	4	3	6	1	5	1	6
17	1	2	4	5	4	4	3	2	3
3	5	2	3	3	2	10	2	4	2

Data Set: LOS

Solution The data were entered into a computer and Minitab was used to conduct the analysis. The Minitab printout for the lower-tailed test is displayed in Figure 15. Both the test statistic, $z = -1.28$, and the p-value of the test, $p = .101$, are highlighted on the Minitab printout. Since the p-value exceeds our selected α value, $\alpha = .05$, we cannot reject the null hypothesis. Hence, there is insufficient evidence (at $\alpha = .05$) to conclude that the true mean LOS at the hospital is less than 5 days.

One-Sample Z: LOS

```
Test of mu = 5 vs < 5
The assumed standard deviation = 3.68
```

Variable	N	Mean	StDev	SE Mean	95% Upper Bound	Z	P
LOS	100	4.530	3.678	0.368	5.135	-1.28	0.101

Figure 15

Minitab lower-tailed test of mean LOS, Example 7

Look Back A hospital administrator, desirous of a mean length of stay less than 5 days, may be tempted to select an α level that leads to a rejection of the null hypothesis *after* determining p-value $= .101$. There are two reasons one should resist this temptation. First, the administrator would need to select $\alpha > .101$ (say, $\alpha = .15$) in order to conclude that $H_a: \mu < 5$ is true. A Type I error rate of 15% is considered too large by most researchers. Second, and more importantly, such a strategy is considered unethical statistical practice.

Now Work Exercise 32

In the next section, we demonstrate how to conduct a test for μ when the sample size is small.

STATISTICS in ACTION REVISITED

Testing a Population Mean

Refer to Kimberly-Clark Corporation's survey of 250 people who kept a count of their use of Kleenex® tissues in diaries. We want to test the claim made by marketing experts that μ, the average number of tissues used by people with colds, is greater than 60 tissues. That is, we want to test

$$H_0: \mu = 60 \quad H_a: > 60$$

We will select $\alpha = .05$ as the level of significance for the test.

The survey results for the 250 sampled Kleenex® users are stored in the **TISSUE** data file. A Minitab analysis of the data yielded the printout displayed in Figure SIA1.

The observed significance level of the test, highlighted on the printout, is p-value $= 000$. Since this p-value is less than $\alpha = .05$, we have sufficient evidence to reject H_0; therefore, we conclude that the mean number of tissues used by a person with a cold is greater than 60 tissues. This result supports the company's decision to put 70 tissues in a cold-care box of Kleenex.

```
Test of mu = 60 vs > 60
```

Variable	N	Mean	StDev	SE Mean	95% Lower Bound	T	P
NUMUSED	250	68.68	25.03	1.58	66.06	5.48	0.000

Figure SIA1

Minitab test of $\mu = 60$ for Kleenex survey

Data Set: TISSUE

391

Exercises 28–46

Please be aware that some of the following problems may require knowledge of concepts that are not presented in this chapter.

Learning the Mechanics

28 Consider the test $H_0: \mu = 70$ versus $H_a: \mu > 70$ using a large sample of size $n = 400$. Assume $\sigma = 20$.
  a. Describe the sampling distribution of $\bar{x}$.
  b. Find the value of the test statistic if $\bar{x} = 72.5$.
  c. Refer to part **b.** Find the p-value of the test.
  d. Find the rejection region of the test for $\alpha = .01$.
  e. Refer to parts **c** and **d.** Use the p-value approach to make the appropriate conclusion.
  f. Repeat part **e,** but use the rejection region approach.
  g. Do the conclusions, parts **e** and **f,** agree?

29 Suppose you are interested in conducting the statistical test of $H_0: \mu = 255$ against $H_a: \mu > 255$, and you have decided to use the following decision rule: Reject H_0 if the sample mean of a random sample of 81 items is more than 270. Assume that the standard deviation of the population is 63.
  a. Express the decision rule in terms of z.
  b. Find α, the probability of making a Type I error, by using this decision rule.

30 A random sample of 100 observations from a population with standard deviation 60 yielded a sample mean of 110.
  a. Test the null hypothesis that $\mu = 100$ against the alternative hypothesis that $\mu > 100$ using $\alpha = .05$. Interpret the results of the test.
  b. Test the null hypothesis that $\mu = 100$ against the alternative hypothesis that $\mu \neq 100$ using $\alpha = .05$. Interpret the results of the test.
  c. Compare the results of the two tests you conducted. Explain why the results differ.

31 A random sample of 64 observations produced the following summary statistics: $\bar{x} = .323$ and $s^2 = .034$.
  a. Test the null hypothesis that $\mu = .36$ against the alternative hypothesis that $\mu < .36$ using $\alpha = .10$.
  b. Test the null hypothesis that $\mu = .36$ against the alternative hypothesis that $\mu \neq .36$ using $\alpha = .10$. Interpret the result.

🔵 Applet Exercise 2

Use the applet *Hypotheses Test for a Mean* to investigate the effect of the underlying distribution on the proportion of Type I errors. For this exercise use $n = 100$, mean = 50, standard deviation = 10, null mean = 50, and alternative <.
  a. Select the normal distribution and run the applet several times without clearing. What happens to the proportion of times the null hypothesis is rejected at the .05 level as the applet is run more and more times?
  b. Clear the applet and then repeat part **a** using the right skewed distribution. Do you get similar results? Explain.
  c. Describe the effect that the underlying distribution has on the probability of making a Type I error.

🔵 Applet Exercise 3

Use the applet *Hypotheses Test for a Mean* to investigate the effect of the underlying distribution on the proportion of

Type II errors. For this exercise use $n = 100$, mean = 50, standard deviation = 10, null mean = 52, and alternative <.
  a. Select the normal distribution and run the applet several times without clearing. What happens to the proportion of times the null hypothesis is rejected at the .01 level as the applet is run more and more times? Is this what you would expect? Explain.
  b. Clear the applet and then repeat part **a** using the right skewed distribution. Do you get similar results? Explain.
  c. Describe the effect that the underlying distribution has on the probability of making a Type II error.

🔵 Applet Exercise 4

Use the applet *Hypotheses Test for a Mean* to investigate the effect of the null mean on the probability of making a Type II error. For this exercise use $n = 100$, mean = 50, standard deviation = 10, and alternative < with the normal distribution. Set the null mean to 55 and run the applet several times without clearing. Record the proportion of Type II errors that occurred at the .01 level. Clear the applet and repeat for null means of 54, 53, 52, and 51. What can you conclude about the probability of a Type II error as the null mean gets closer to the actual mean? Can you offer a reasonable explanation for this?

Applying the Concepts—Basic

32 Corporate sustainability of CPA firms. *Business and Society* (March 2011) did a study on the sustainability behaviors of CPA corporations. The level of support for corporate sustainability (measured on a quantitative scale ranging from 0 to 160 points) was obtained for each in a sample of 992 senior managers at CPA firms. The data (where higher point values indicate a higher level of support for sustainability) are saved in the accompanying file. The CEO of a CPA firm claims that the true mean level of support for sustainability is 75 points.
  a. Specify the null and alternative hypotheses for testing this claim.
  b. For this problem, what is a Type I error? A Type II error?
  c. The XLSTAT printout on the following page gives the results of the test. Locate the test statistic and p-value on the printout.
  d. At $\alpha = .05$, give the appropriate conclusion.
  e. What assumptions, if any, about the distribution of support levels must hold true in order for the inference derived from the test to be valid? Explain.

33 Packaging of a children's health food. Junk foods (e.g., potato chips) are typically packaged to appeal to children. Can similar packaging of a healthy food product influence children's desire to consume the product? This was the question of interest in an article published in the *Journal of Consumer Behaviour* (Vol. 10, 2011). A fictitious brand of a healthy food product—sliced apples—was packaged to appeal to children (a smiling cartoon apple was on the front of the package). The researchers showed the packaging to a sample of 408 school children and asked each whether he or she was willing to eat the product. Willingness to eat

	B	C	D	E	F	G
	XLSTAT 2011.4.02 - One-sample t-test and z-test					
	Theoretical mean: 75					
	Significance level (%): 5					
	Summary statistics		▼			

Summary statistics:

Variable	Observations	Minimum	Maximum	Mean	Std. deviation
Support	992	0.0000	155.0000	67.7550	26.8707

One-sample z-test / Two-tailed test:

95% confidence interval on the mean:
(66.0829, 69.4271)

Difference	-7.2450
z (Observed value)	-8.4923
|z| (Critical value)	1.9600
p-value (Two-tailed)	< 0.0001
alpha	0.05

XLSTAT output for Exercise 32

was measured on a 5-point scale, with 1 = "not willing at all" and 5 = "very willing." The data are summarized as follows: $\bar{x} = 3.69$, $s = 2.44$. Suppose the researchers knew that the mean willingness to eat an actual brand of sliced apples (which is not packaged for children) is $\mu = 3$.

a. Conduct a test to determine whether the true mean willingness to eat the brand of sliced apples packaged for children exceeded 3. Use $\alpha = .05$ to make your conclusion.

b. The data (willingness to eat values) are not normally distributed. How does this impact (if at all) the validity of your conclusion in part a? Explain.

34 Accounting and Machiavellianism. *Behavioral Research in Accounting* (Jan. 2008) did a study of Machiavellian traits in accountants. A Mach rating score was determined for each in a random sample of 122 purchasing managers, with the following results: $\bar{x} = 99.6$, $s = 12.6$. A director of purchasing at a major firm claims that the true mean Mach rating score of all purchasing managers is 85.

a. Suppose you want to test the director's claim. Specify the null and alternative hypotheses for the test.

b. Give the rejection region for the test using $\alpha = .10$.

c. Find the value of the test statistic.

d. Use the result, part **c**, to make the appropriate conclusion.

35 Facial structure of CEOs. *Psychological Science* (Vol. 22, 2011) did a study on using a chief executive officer's facial structure to predict a firm's financial performance. The facial width-to-height ratio (WHR) for each in a sample of 55 CEOs at publicly traded *Fortune* 500 firms was determined. The sample resulted in $\bar{x} = 1.96$ and $s = .15$. An analyst wants to predict the financial performance of a *Fortune* 500 firm based on the value of the true mean

facial WHR of CEOs. The analyst wants to use the value of $\mu = 2.2$. Do you recommend he use this value? Conduct a test of hypothesis for μ to help you answer the question. Specify all the elements of the test: H_0, H_a, test statistic, p-value, α, and your conclusion.

36 Trading skills of institutional investors. Managers of stock portfolios make decisions as to what stocks to buy and sell in a given quarter. The trading skills of these institutional investors were quantified and analyzed in *The Journal of Finance* (April 2011). The study focused on "round-trip" trades, i.e., trades in which the same stock was both bought and sold in the same quarter. Consider a random sample of 200 round-trip trades made by institutional investors. Suppose the sample mean rate of return is 2.95% and the sample standard deviation is 8.82%. If the true mean rate of return of round-trip trades is positive, then the population of institutional investors is considered to have performed successfully.

a. Specify the null and alternative hypotheses for determining whether the population of institutional investors performed successfully.

b. Find the rejection region for the test using $\alpha = .05$.

c. Interpret the value of α in the words of the problem.

d. A Minitab printout of the analysis is shown below. Locate the test statistic and p-value on the printout. [*Note:* For large samples, $z \approx t$.]

e. Give the appropriate conclusion in the words of the problem.

```
Test of mu = 0 vs > 0


                                   95% Lower
  N    Mean   StDev   SE Mean      Bound      T      P
 200   2.950  8.820    0.624       1.919    4.73   0.000
```

37 Producer's and consumer's risk. In quality-control applications of hypothesis testing, the null and alternative hypotheses are frequently specified as

TEES

H_0: The production process is performing satisfactorily.

H_a: The process is performing in an unsatisfactory manner.

Accordingly, α is sometimes referred to as the *producer's risk*, while β is called the *consumer's risk* (Stevenson, *Operations Management*, 2008). An injection molder produces plastic golf tees. The process is designed to produce tees with a mean weight of .250 ounce. To investigate whether the injection molder is operating satisfactorily, 40 tees were randomly sampled from the last hour's production. Their weights (in ounces) are listed in the following table.

.247	.251	.254	.253	.253	.248	.253	.255	.256	.252
.253	.252	.253	.256	.254	.256	.252	.251	.253	.251
.253	.253	.248	.251	.253	.256	.254	.250	.254	.255
.249	.250	.254	.251	.251	.255	.251	.253	.252	.253

a. Write H_0 and H_a in terms of the true mean weight of the golf tees, μ.
b. Access the data and find $\bar{x}$ and s.
c. Calculate the test statistic.
d. Find the p-value for the test.
e. Locate the rejection region for the test using $\alpha = .01$.
f. Do the data provide sufficient evidence to conclude that the process is not operating satisfactorily?
g. In the context of this problem, explain why it makes sense to call α the producer's risk and β the consumer's risk.

Applying the Concepts—Intermediate

38 Birth order, IQ, and earnings. Recent research suggests that your annual pay is linked to your birth order—firstborn individuals tend to earn higher salaries than non-firstborn individuals. The evidence on whether IQ is associated with birth order is not as conclusive. An international team of economists investigated the possible link between IQ and birth order in *CESifo Economic Studies* (Vol. 57, 2011). The data source for the research was the Medical Birth Registry of Norway. It is known that the mean IQ (measured in stanines) for all Norway residents is 5.2 points. In the study, a sample of 581 Norway residents who were the sixth-born or later in their families had a mean IQ score of 4.7 points with a standard deviation of 1.8 points. Is this sufficient evidence to conclude that the mean IQ score of all Norway residents who were the sixth-born or later in their families is lower than the country mean of 5.2 points? Use $\alpha = .01$ as a measure of reliability for your inference.

39 Time required to complete a task. When a person is asked, "How much time will you require to complete this task?"

cognitive theory posits that people (e.g., a business consultant) will typically underestimate the time required. Would the opposite theory hold if the question was phrased in terms of how much work could be completed in a given amount of time? This was the question of interest to researchers writing in *Applied Cognitive Psychology* (Vol. 25, 2011). For one study conducted by the researchers, each in a sample of 40 University of Oslo students was asked how many minutes it would take to read a 32-page report. In a second study, 42 students were asked how many pages of a lengthy report they could read in 48 minutes. (The students in either study did not actually read the report.) Numerical descriptive statistics (based on summary information published in the article) for both studies are provided in the accompanying table.

	Estimated Time (minutes)	Estimated Number of Pages
Sample size, n	40	42
Sample mean, $\bar{x}$	60	28
Sample standard deviation, s	41	14

a. The researchers determined that the actual mean time it takes to read the report is $\mu = 48$ minutes. Is there evidence to support the theory that the students, on average, overestimated the time it would take to read the report? Test using $\alpha = .10$.
b. The researchers also determined that the actual mean number of pages of the report that is read within the allotted time is $\mu = 32$ pages. Is there evidence to support the theory that the students, on average, underestimated the number of report pages that could be read? Test using $\alpha = .10$.
c. The researchers noted that the distribution of both estimated time and estimated number of pages is highly skewed (i.e., not normally distributed). Does this fact impact the inferences derived in parts **a** and **b**? Explain.

40 Cooling method for gas turbines. During periods of high electricity demand, especially during the hot summer months, the power output from a gas turbine engine can drop dramatically. One way to counter this drop in power is by cooling the inlet air to the gas turbine. An increasingly popular cooling method uses high-pressure inlet fogging. The performance of a sample of 67 gas turbines augmented with high-pressure inlet fogging was investigated in the *Journal of Engineering for Gas Turbines and Power* (Jan. 2005). One measure of performance is heat rate (kilojoules per kilowatt per hour). Heat rates for the 67 gas turbines are listed in the table below. Suppose that a standard gas turbine has, on average, a heat rate of 10,000 kJ/kWh. Conduct a test to determine if the mean heat rate of gas turbines augmented with high-pressure inlet fogging exceeds 10,000 kJ/kWh. Use $\alpha = .05$.

14622	13196	11948	11289	11964	10526	10387	10592	10460	10086
14628	13396	11726	11252	12449	11030	10787	10603	10144	11674
11510	10946	10508	10604	10270	10529	10360	14796	12913	12270
11842	10656	11360	11136	10814	13523	11289	11183	10951	9722
10481	9812	9669	9643	9115	9115	11588	10888	9738	9295
9421	9105	10233	10186	9918	9209	9532	9933	9152	9295
16243	14628	12766	8714	9469	11948	12414			

Data for Exercise 40

41 Point spreads of NFL games. During the National Football League (NFL) season, Las Vegas odds makers establish a point spread on each game for betting purposes. For example, the New England Patriots were established as 3.5-point favorites over the eventual champion New York Giants in the 2012 Super Bowl. The final scores of NFL games were compared against the final point spreads established by the odds makers in *Chance* (Fall 1998). The difference between the game outcome and point spread (called a *point-spread error*) was calculated for 240 NFL games. The mean and standard deviation of the point-spread errors are $\bar{x} = -1.6$ and $s = 13.3$. Use this information to test the hypothesis that the true mean point-spread error for all NFL games differs from 0. Conduct the test at $\alpha = .01$ and interpret the result.

42 Revenue for a full-service funeral. According to the National Funeral Directors Association (NFDA), the nation's 22,000 funeral homes collected an average of $6,500 per full-service funeral in 2009 (www.nfda.org). A random sample of 36 funeral homes reported revenue data for the current year. Among other measures, each reported its average fee for a full-service funeral. These data (in thousands of dollars) are shown in the following table.

7.4	9.4	5.3	8.4	7.5	6.5	6.2	8.3	6.7
11.6	6.3	5.9	6.7	5.8	5.2	6.4	6.0	7.4
7.2	6.6	6.3	5.3	6.6	5.6	8.4	7.2	7.4
5.8	6.3	6.1	7.0	7.2	6.1	5.4	7.4	6.6

a. What are the appropriate null and alternative hypotheses to test whether the average full-service fee of U. S. funeral homes this year exceeds $6,500?

b. Conduct the test at $\alpha = .05$. Do the sample data provide sufficient evidence to conclude that the average fee this year is higher than in 2009?

c. In conducting the test, was it necessary to assume that the population of average full-service fees was normally distributed? Justify your answer.

43 Buy-side vs. sell-side analysts' earnings forecasts. The *Financial Analysts Journal* (Jul./Aug. 2008) did a study of earnings forecasts of buy-side and sell-side analysts. Buy-side analysts differ from sell-side analysts on a variety of factors, including scope of industry coverage, sources of information used, and target audience. Data were collected on 3,526 forecasts made by buy-side analysts and 58,562 forecasts made by sell-side analysts, and the relative absolute forecast error was determined for each. A positive forecast error indicates that the analyst is overestimating earnings, while a negative forecast error implies that the analyst is underestimating earnings. Summary statistics for the forecast errors in the two samples are reproduced in the table below.

	Buy-Side Analysts	Sell-Side Analysts
Mean	0.85	−0.05
Standard Deviation	1.93	0.85

Source: Based on Groysberg, B., Healy, P., & Chapman, C. "Buy-side vs. sell-side analysts' earnings forecast," *Financial Analysts Journal,* Vol. 64, No. 4, Jul./Aug. 2008.

a. Conduct a test (at $\alpha = .01$) to determine if the true mean forecast error for buy-side analysts is positive.

Use the observed significance level (*p*-value) of the test to make your decision and state your conclusion in the words of the problem.

b. Conduct a test (at $\alpha = .01$) to determine if the true mean forecast error for sell-side analysts is negative. Use the observed significance level (*p*-value) of the test to make your decision and state your conclusion in the words of the problem.

44 Solder-joint inspections. Current technology uses high-resolution X-rays and lasers for inspection of solder-joint defects on printed circuit boards (PCBs) (*Global SMT & Packaging,* April 2008). A particular manufacturer of laser-based inspection equipment claims that its product can inspect on average at least 10 solder joints per second when the joints are spaced .1 inch apart. The equipment was tested by a potential buyer on 48 different PCBs. In each case, the equipment was operated for exactly 1 second. The number of solder joints inspected on each run follows:

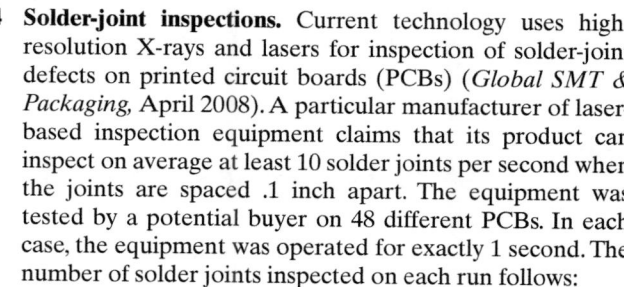

10	9	10	10	11	9	12	8	8	9	6	10
7	10	11	9	9	13	9	10	11	10	12	8
9	9	9	7	12	6	9	10	10	8	7	9
11	12	10	0	10	11	12	9	7	9	9	10

a. The potential buyer wants to know whether the sample data refute the manufacturer's claim. Specify the null and alternative hypotheses that the buyer should test.

b. In the context of this exercise, what is a Type I error? A Type II error?

c. Conduct the hypothesis test you described in part **a** and interpret the test's results in the context of this exercise. Use $\alpha = .05$.

Applying the Concepts—Advanced

45 Why do small firms export? What motivates small firms to export their products? To answer this question, California State University Professor Ralph Pope conducted a survey of 137 exporting firms listed in the *California International Trade Register* (*Journal of Small Business Management,* Vol. 40, 2002). Firm CEOs were asked to respond to the statement "Management believes that the firm can achieve economies of scale by exporting" on a scale of 1 (strongly disagree) to 5 (strongly agree). Summary statistics for the $n = 137$ scale scores were reported as $\bar{x} = 3.85$ and $s = 1.5$. In the journal article, the researcher hypothesized that if the true mean scale score exceeds 3.5, then CEOs at all California small firms generally agree with the statement.

a. Conduct the appropriate test using $\alpha = .05$. State your conclusion in the words of the problem.

b. Explain why the results of the study, although "statistically significant," may not be practically significant.

c. The scale scores for the sample of 137 small firms are unlikely to be normally distributed. Does this invalidate the inference you made in part **a**? Explain.

46 Salaries of postgraduates. The *Economics of Education Review* (Vol. 21, 2002) published a paper on the relationship between education level and earnings. The data for the research were obtained from the National Adult Literacy Survey of more than 25,000 respondents. The survey revealed that males with a postgraduate degree have a mean salary of $61,340 (with standard error $s_{\bar{x}} = \$2,185$), while females with a postgraduate degree have a mean of $32,227 (with standard error $s_{\bar{x}} = \$932$).

a. The article reports that a 95% confidence interval for μ_M, the population mean salary of all males with postgraduate degrees, is ($57,050, $65,631). Based on this interval, is there evidence to say that μ_M differs from $60,000? Explain.

b. Use the summary information to test the hypothesis that the true mean salary of males with postgraduate degrees differs from $60,000. Use $\alpha = .05$.

c. Explain why the inferences in parts **a** and **b** agree.

d. The article reports that a 95% confidence interval for μ_F, the population mean salary of all females with postgraduate degrees, is ($30,396, $34,058). Based on this interval, is there evidence to say that μ_F differs from $33,000? Explain.

e. Use the summary information to test the hypothesis that the true mean salary of females with postgraduate degrees differs from $33,000. Use $\alpha = .05$.

f. Explain why the inferences in parts **d** and **e** agree.

5   Test of Hypothesis about a Population Mean: Student's *t*-Statistic

A manufacturing operation consists of a single-machine-tool system that produces an average of 15.5 transformer parts every hour. After undergoing a complete overhaul, the system was monitored by observing the number of parts produced in each of 17 randomly selected 1-hour periods. The mean and standard deviation for the 17 production runs are

$$\bar{x} = 15.42 \qquad s = .16$$

Does this sample provide sufficient evidence to conclude that the true mean number of parts produced every hour by the overhauled system differs from 15.5?

This inference can be placed in a test of hypothesis framework. We establish the preoverhaul mean as the null hypothesized value and use a two-tailed alternative that the true mean of the overhauled system differs from the preoverhaul mean:

$H_0: \mu = 15.5$ (Mean of overhauled system equals 15.5 parts per hour.)

$H_a: \mu \neq 15.5$ (Mean of overhauled system differs from 15.5 parts per hour.)

When we are faced with making inferences about a population mean using the information in a small sample, two problems emerge:

1. The normality of the sampling distribution for $\bar{x}$ does not follow from the Central Limit Theorem when the sample size is small. We must assume that the distribution of measurements from which the sample was selected is approximately normally distributed in order to ensure the approximate normality of the sampling distribution of $\bar{x}$.

2. If the population standard deviation σ is unknown, as is usually the case, then we cannot assume that s will provide a good approximation for σ when the sample size is small. Instead, we must use the *t*-distribution rather than the standard normal *z*-distribution to make inferences about the population mean μ.

Therefore, as the test statistic of a small-sample test of a population mean, we use the *t*-statistic:

$$\text{Test statistic: } t = \frac{\bar{x} - \mu_0}{s/\sqrt{n}} = \frac{\bar{x} - 15.5}{s/\sqrt{n}}$$

where μ_0 is the null hypothesized value of the population mean μ. In our example, $\mu_0 = 15.5$.

To find the rejection region, we must specify the value of α, the probability that the test will lead to rejection of the null hypothesis when it is true, and then consult either the *t*-table (Table III in Appendix : Tables) or use computer software. Using $\alpha = .05$, the two-tailed rejection region is

$$\text{Rejection region: } t_{\alpha/2} = t_{.025} = 2.120 \text{ with } n - 1 = 16 \text{ df}$$
$$\text{Reject } H_0 \text{ if } t < -2.120 \text{ or } t > 2.120$$

The rejection region is shown in Figure 16.

We are now prepared to calculate the test statistic and reach a conclusion:

$$t = \frac{\bar{x} - \mu_0}{s/\sqrt{n}} = \frac{15.42 - 15.50}{.16/\sqrt{n}} = \frac{-.08}{.0388} = -2.06$$

Because the calculated value of t does not fall in the rejection region (Figure 16), we cannot reject H_0 at the $\alpha = .05$ level of significance. Based on the sample evidence, we should not conclude that the mean number of parts produced per hour by the over-hauled system differs from 15.5.

It is interesting to note that the calculated t-value, -2.06, is *less than* $-z_{.05} = -1.96$. The implication is that if we had *incorrectly* used a z-statistic for this test, we would have rejected the null hypothesis at $\alpha = .05$, concluding that the mean production per hour of the over-hauled system differs from 15.5 parts. The important point is that the statistical procedure to be used must always be closely scrutinized, with all the assumptions understood. Many statistical distortions are the result of misapplications of otherwise valid procedures.

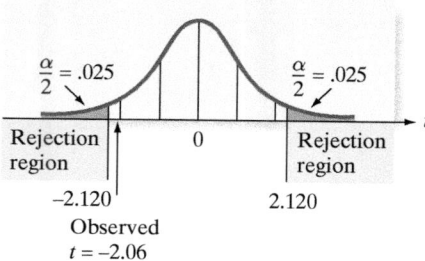

Figure 16

Two-tailed rejection region for small-sample t-test

The technique for conducting a small-sample test of hypothesis about a population mean is summarized in the following box.

Small-Sample Test of Hypothesis about μ Based on Student's t-Statistic

One-Tailed Test	Two-Tailed Test
$H_0: \mu = \mu_0$	$H_0: \mu = \mu_0$
$H_a: \mu < \mu_0$ (or $H_a: \mu > \mu_0$)	$H_a: \mu \neq \mu_0$
Test statistic: $t = \dfrac{\bar{x} - \mu_0}{s/\sqrt{n}}$	Test statistic: $t = \dfrac{\bar{x} - \mu_0}{s/\sqrt{n}}$
Rejection region: $t < -t_\alpha$ (or $t > t_\alpha$ when $H_a: \mu > \mu_0$)	Rejection region: $|t| > t_{\alpha/2}$

where t_α and $t_{\alpha/2}$ are based on $(n - 1)$ degrees of freedom

---

Conditions Required for a Valid Small-Sample Hypothesis Test for μ

1. A random sample is selected from the target population.
2. The population from which the sample is selected has a distribution that is approximately normal.

Example 8

Small-Sample Test for μ — Does a New Engine Meet Air Pollution Standards?

Problem A major car manufacturer wants to test a new engine to determine whether it meets new air pollution standards. The mean emission μ of all engines of this type must be less than 20 parts per million of carbon. Ten engines are manufactured for testing purposes, and the emission level of each is determined. The data (in parts per million) are listed in Table 5.

Do the data supply sufficient evidence to allow the manufacturer to conclude that this type of engine meets the pollution standard? Assume that the production process is stable and the manufacturer is willing to risk a Type I error with probability $\alpha = .01$.

Table 5	Emission Levels for Ten Engines								
15.6	16.2	22.5	20.5	16.4	19.4	19.6	17.9	12.7	14.9

Data Set: CARBON

Solution The manufacturer wants to support the research hypothesis that the mean emission level μ for all engines of this type is less than 20 parts per million. The elements of this small-sample one-tailed test are

$$H_0: \mu = 20 \qquad \text{(Mean emission level equals 20 ppm.)}$$

$$H_a: \mu < 20 \qquad \text{(Mean emission level is less than 20 ppm— i.e., engine meets pollution standard.)}$$

Test statistic: $t = \dfrac{\bar{x} - 20}{s/\sqrt{n}}$

Rejection region: For $\alpha = .01$ and df $= n - 1 = 9$, the one-tailed rejection region (see Figure 17) is $t < -t_{.01} = -2.821$.

Assumption: The relative frequency distribution of the population of emission levels for all engines of this type is approximately normal. Based on the shape of the Minitab stem-and-leaf display of the data shown in Figure 18, this assumption appears to be reasonably satisfied.

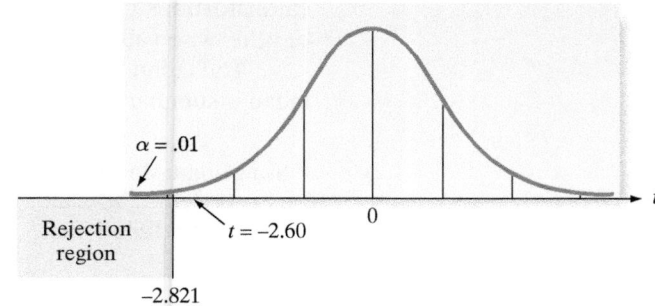

Figure 17

A *t*-distribution with 9 df and the rejection region for Example 8

To calculate the test statistic, we entered the data into a computer and analyzed it using Minitab. The Minitab printout is shown in Figure 18. From the printout, we obtain $\bar{x} = 17.57$, $s = 2.95$. Substituting these values into the test statistic formula, we get

$$t = \frac{\bar{x} - 20}{s/\sqrt{n}} = \frac{17.57 - 20}{2.95/\sqrt{10}} = -2.60$$

Stem-and-Leaf Display: E-LEVEL

```
Stem-and-leaf of E-LEVEL   N  = 10
Leaf Unit = 1.0


    1    1  2
    3    1  45
   (3)   1  667
    4    1  99
    2    2  0
    1    2  2
```

One-Sample T: E-LEVEL

```
Test of mu = 20 vs < 20
```

Figure 18

Minitab analysis of 10 emission levels, Example 8

Variable	N	Mean	StDev	SE Mean	95% Upper Bound	T	P
E-LEVEL	10	17.5700	2.9522	0.9336	19.2814	-2.60	0.014

Because the calculated t falls outside the rejection region (see Figure 17), the manufacturer cannot reject H_0. There is insufficient evidence to conclude that $\mu < 20$ parts per million. Consequently, we cannot conclude that the new engine type meets the pollution standard.

Look Back Are you satisfied with the reliability associated with this inference? The probability is only $\alpha = .01$ that the test would support the research hypothesis if, in fact, it were false.

Now Work Exercise 50a, b

Example	9

The *p*-Value for a Small-Sample Test of μ

Problem Find the observed significance level for the test described in Example 8. Interpret the result.

Solution The test of Example 8 was a lower-tailed test: $H_0: \mu = 20$ versus $H_a: \mu < 20$. Because the value of t computed from the sample data was $t = -2.60$, the observed significance level (or p-value) for the test is equal to the probability that t would assume a value less than or equal to -2.60 if, in fact, H_0 were true. This is equal to the area in the lower tail of the t-distribution (shaded in Figure 19).

One way to find this area (i.e., the p-value for the test) is to consult the t-table (Table III in Appendix : Tables). Unlike the table of areas under the normal curve, Table III gives only the t-values corresponding to the areas .100, .050, .025, .010, .005, .001, and .0005. Therefore, we can only approximate the p-value for the test. Because the observed t-value was based on 9 degrees of freedom, we use the df $= 9$ row in Table III and move across the row until we reach the t-values that are closest to the observed $t = -2.60$. [*Note:* We ignore the minus sign.]

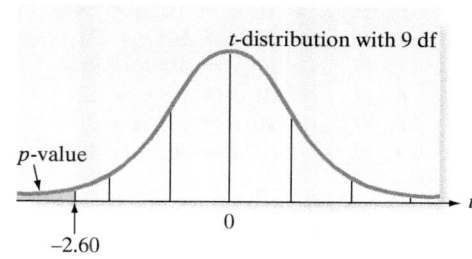

Figure 19

The observed significance level for the test of Example 8

The t-values corresponding to p-values of .010 and .025 are 2.821 and 2.262, respectively. Because the observed t-value falls between $t_{.010}$ and $t_{.025}$, the p-value for the test lies between .010 and .025. In other words, $.010 < p\text{-value} < .025$. Thus, we would reject the null hypothesis, $H_0: \mu = 20$ parts per million, for any value of α larger than .025 (the upper bound of the p-value).

A second, more accurate, way to obtain the p-value is to use a statistical software package to conduct the test of hypothesis. The Minitab printout shown in Figure 18 gives both the test statistic (-2.60) and p-value $(.014)$.

You can see that the actual p-value of the test falls within the bounds obtained from Table III. Based on the actual p-value, we will reject $H_0: \mu = 20$ in favor of $H_a: \mu < 20$ for any α level larger than .014.

Now Work Exercise 50c

Small-sample inferences typically require more assumptions and provide less information about the population parameter than do large-sample inferences. Nevertheless, the t-test is a method of testing a hypothesis about a population mean of a normal distribution when only a small number of observations are available. What can be done if you know that the population relative frequency distribution is decidedly nonnormal, say highly skewed?

Exercises 47–63

Please be aware that some of the following problems may require knowledge of concepts that are not presented in this chapter.

Learning the Mechanics

47 a. Consider testing $H_0: \mu = 80$. Under what conditions should you use the *t*-distribution to conduct the test?

b. In what ways are the distributions of the *z*-statistic and *t*-test statistic alike? How do they differ?

48 For each of the following rejection regions, sketch the sampling distribution of *t* and indicate the location of the rejection region on your sketch:

a. $t > 1.440$ where df $= 6$

b. $t < -1.782$ where df $= 12$

c. $t < -2.060$ or $t > 2.060$ where df $= 25$

d. For each of parts **a–c,** what is the probability that a Type I error will be made?

49 A random sample of *n* observations is selected from a normal population to test the null hypothesis that $\mu = 10$. Specify the rejection region for each of the following combinations of H_a, α, and *n*:

a. $H_a: \mu \neq 10; \alpha = .05; n = 14$

b. $H_a: \mu > 10; \alpha = .01; n = 24$

c. $H_a: \mu > 10; \alpha = .10; n = 9$

d. $H_a: \mu < 10; \alpha = .01; n = 12$

e. $H_a: \mu \neq 10; \alpha = .10; n = 20$

f. $H_a: \mu < 10; \alpha = .05; n = 4$

50 A sample of five measurements, randomly selected from a normally distributed population, resulted in the following summary statistics: $\bar{x} = 4.8, s = 1.3$.

a. Test the null hypothesis that the mean of the population is 6 against the alternative hypothesis, $\mu < 6$. Use $\alpha = .05$.

b. Test the null hypothesis that the mean of the population is 6 against the alternative hypothesis, $\mu \neq 6$. Use $\alpha = .05$.

c. Find the observed significance level for each test.

51 Suppose you conduct a *t*-test for the null hypothesis $H_0: \mu = 1,000$ versus the alternative hypothesis $H_a: \mu > 1,000$ based on a sample of 17 observations. The test results are $t = 1.89$ and *p*-value $= .038$.

a. What assumptions are necessary for the validity of this procedure?

b. Interpret the results of the test.

c. Suppose the alternative hypothesis had been the two-tailed $H_a: \mu \neq 1,000$. If the *t*-statistic were unchanged, then what would the *p*-value be for this test? Interpret the *p*-value for the two-tailed test.

Applying the Concepts—Basic

52 **Lobster trap placement.** The *Bulletin of Marine Science* (April 2010) did an observational study of lobster trap placement by **TRAPS** teams fishing for the red spiny lobster in Baja California Sur, Mexico. Trap-spacing measurements (in meters) for a sample of seven teams of red spiny lobster fishermen are reproduced in the accompanying table. Let μ represent the average of the trap-spacing measurements for the population of red spiny lobster fishermen fishing in Baja California Sur, Mexico. Assume the mean and standard deviation of the sample measurements to be $\bar{x} = 89.9$ meters and $s = 11.6$ meters, respectively. Suppose you want to determine if the true value of μ differs from 95 meters.

93	99	105	94	82	70	86

Source: Based on Shester, G. G. "Explaining catch variation among Baja California lobster fishers through spatial analysis of trap-placement decisions," *Bulletin of Marine Science,* Vol. 86, No. 2, April 2010 (Table 1), pp. 479–498.

a. Specify the null and alternative hypotheses for this test.

b. Since $\bar{x} = 89.9$ is less than 95, a fisherman wants to reject the null hypothesis. What are the problems with using such a decision rule?

c. Compute the value of the test statistic.

d. Find the approximate *p*-value of the test.

e. Select a value of α, the probability of a Type I error. Interpret this value in the words of the problem.

f. Give the appropriate conclusion, based on the results of parts **d** and **e.**

g. What conditions must be satisfied for the test results to be valid?

h. Assume a 95% confidence interval for μ. Does this interval support your conclusion in part **f?**

53 **Radon exposure in Egyptian tombs.** The *Radiation Protection Dosimetry* (December 2010) did a study of radon **TOMBS** exposure in Egyptian tombs. The radon levels—measured in becquerels per cubic meter (Bq/m^3)—in the inner chambers of a sample of 12 tombs are listed in the table (next page). For the safety of the guards and visitors, the Egypt Tourism Authority (ETA) will temporarily close the tombs if the true mean level of radon exposure in the tombs rises to

One-Sample Statistics

	N	Mean	Std. Deviation	Std. Error Mean
RADON	12	3642.50	4486.929	1295.265

One-Sample Test

					95% Confidence Interval of the Difference	
					Test Value = 6000	
	t	df	Sig. (2-tailed)	Mean Difference	Lower	Upper
RADON	-1.820	11	.096	-2357.500	-5208.36	493.36

SPSS output for Exercise 53

One-Sample T: ROUGH

Test of mu = 2 vs not = 2

Variable	N	Mean	StDev	SE Mean	95% CI	T	P
ROUGH	20	1.88100	0.52391	0.11715	(1.63580, 2.12620)	-1.02	0.322

Minitab output for Exercise 55

6,000 Bq/m^3. Consequently, the ETA wants to conduct a test to determine if the true mean level of radon exposure in the tombs is less than 6,000 Bq/m^3, using a Type I error probability of .10. An SPSS analysis of the data is shown (bottom). Specify all the elements of the test: H_0, H_a, test statistic, p-value, α, and your conclusion.

50	910	180	580	7800	4000
390	12100	3400	1300	11900	1100

54 **A new dental bonding agent.** When bonding teeth, orthodontists must maintain a dry field. A new bonding adhesive (called *Smartbond*) has been developed to eliminate the necessity of a dry field. However, there is concern that the new bonding adhesive is not as strong as the current standard, a composite adhesive (*Trends in Biomaterials & Artificial Organs,* Jan. 2003). Tests on a sample of 10 extracted teeth bonded with the new adhesive resulted in a mean breaking strength (after 24 hours) of $\bar{x} = 5.07$ Mpa and a standard deviation of $s = .46$ Mpa. Orthodontists want to know if the true mean breaking strength of the new bonding adhesive is less than 5.70 Mpa, the mean breaking strength of the composite adhesive.

a. Set up the null and alternative hypotheses for the test.
b. Find the rejection region for the test using $\alpha = .01$.
c. Compute the test statistic.
d. Give the appropriate conclusion for the test.
e. What conditions are required for the test results to be valid?

55 **Surface roughness of pipe.** *Anti-corrosion Methods and Materials* (Vol. 50, 2003) did a study of the surface roughness of coated interior pipe used in oil fields. The data (in micrometers) for 20 sampled pipe sections are reproduced in the next table.

a. Give the null and alternative hypotheses for testing whether the mean surface roughness of coated interior pipe, μ, differs from 2 micrometers.
b. Find the test statistic for the hypothesis test.
c. Give the rejection region for the hypothesis test, using $\alpha = .05$.

d. State the appropriate conclusion for the hypothesis test.
e. A Minitab printout giving the test results is shown at the top of the page. Find and interpret the p-value of the test.
f. Assume a 95% confidence interval for μ. Explain why the confidence interval and test lead to the same conclusion about μ.

1.72	2.50	2.16	2.13	1.06	2.24	2.31	2.03	1.09	1.40
2.57	2.64	1.26	2.05	1.19	2.13	1.27	1.51	2.41	1.95

Source: Data from Farshad, F., & Pesacreta, T. "Coated pipe interior surface roughness as measured by three scanning probe instruments," *Anti-corrosion Methods and Materials,* Vol. 50, No. 1, 2003 (Table III).

56 **Performance of stock screeners.** Stock screeners are automated tools used by investment companies to help clients select a portfolio of stocks to invest in. The data on the annualized percentage return on investment (as compared to the Standard & Poor's 500 Index) for 13 randomly selected stock screeners provided by the American Association of Individual Investors (AAII)

	B	C	D	E	F	G
XLSTAT 2011.4.02 - One-sample t-test and z-test						
Theoretical mean: 0						
Significance level (%): 5						
Summary statistics	▼					
Summary statistics:						
Variable	Observations	Minimum	Maximum	Mean	Std. deviation	
ROI	13	-1.6000	24.8000	10.8231	7.7115	
One-sample t-test / Upper-tailed test:						
95% confidence interval on the mean:						
(7.0112, +Inf)						
Difference	10.8231					
t (Observed value)	5.0604					
t (Critical value)	1.7823					
DF	12					
p-value (one-tailed)	0.0001					
alpha	0.05					

XLSTAT output for Exercise 56

are repeated in the accompanying table. You want to determine whether μ, the average annualized return for all AAII stock screeners, is positive (which implies that the stock screeners perform better, on average, than the S&P 500). An XLSTAT printout of the analysis is shown on previous page.

9.0	−.1	−1.6	14.6	16.0	7.7	19.9	9.8	3.2	24.8	17.6	10.7	9.1

a. State H_0 and H_a for this test.
b. Locate the values of $\bar{x}$ and s on the printout, and then use these values to compute the test statistic. Verify that your calculation is correct by comparing it to the test statistic value shown on the printout.
c. Locate the observed significance level (p-value) on the printout.
d. Give the appropriate conclusion if you test using $\alpha = .05$.
e. What assumption about the data must hold in order for the inference derived from the test to be valid?

Applying the Concepts—Intermediate

57 **Water distillation with solar energy.** In countries with a water shortage, converting salt water to potable water is big business. The standard method of water distillation is with a single-slope solar still. Several enhanced solar energy water distillation systems were investigated in *Applied Solar Energy* (Vol. 46, 2010). One new system employs a sun-tracking meter and a step-wise basin. The new system was tested over 3 randomly selected days at a location in Amman, Jordan. The daily amounts of distilled water collected by the new system over the 3 days were 5.07, 5.45, and 5.21 liters per square meter (l/m^2). Suppose it is known that the mean daily amount of distilled water collected by the standard method at the same location in Jordan is $\mu = 1.4 \ l/m^2$.
  a. Set up the null and alternative hypotheses for determining whether the mean daily amount of distilled water collected by the new system is greater than 1.4.
  b. For this test, give a practical interpretation of the value $\alpha = .10$.
  c. Find the mean and standard deviation of the distilled water amounts for the sample of 3 days.
  d. Use the information from part c to calculate the test statistic.
  e. Find the observed significance level (p-value) of the test.
  f. State, practically, the appropriate conclusion.

58 **Shopping vehicle and judgment.** The *Journal of Marketing Research* (Dec. 2011) did a study of when grocery store shoppers' judgments. For one part of the study, 11 consumers were told to put their arm in a flex position (similar to a shopping basket) and then each consumer was offered several choices between a vice product and a virtue product (e.g., a movie ticket vs. a shopping coupon, pay later with a larger amount vs. pay now). Based on these choices, a vice choice score was determined on a scale of 0 to 100 (where higher scores indicate a greater preference for vice options). The data in the next table are (simulated) choice scores for

the 11 consumers. Suppose that the average choice score for consumers with an extended arm position (similar to pushing a shopping cart) is known to be $\mu = 50$. The researchers theorize that the mean choice score for consumers shopping with a flexed arm will be higher than 43 (reflecting their higher propensity to select a vice product. Test the theory at $\alpha = .05$.

56	76	62	57	55	61	62	43	57	61	58

59 **Minimizing tractor skidding distance.** The *Journal of Forest Engineering* (July 1999) did a study of minimizing tractor skidding distances along a new road in a European forest. The skidding distances (in meters) were measured at 20 randomly selected road sites. The data are repeated below. A logger working on the road claims the mean skidding distance is at least 425 meters. Is there sufficient evidence to refute this claim? Use $\alpha = .10$.

488	350	457	199	285	409	435	574	439	546
385	295	184	261	273	400	311	312	141	425

Source: Based on Tujek, J., & Pacola, E. "Algorithms for skidding distance modeling on a raster digital terrain model," *Journal of Forest Engineering,* Vol. 10, No. 1, July 1999 (Table 1).

60 **Crude oil biodegradation.** The *Journal of Petroleum Geology* (April 2010) did a study of the environmental factors associated with biodegradation in crude oil reservoirs. 16 water specimens were randomly selected from various locations in a reservoir on the floor of a mine and that the amount of dioxide (milligrams/liter)—a measure of biodegradation—as well as presence of oil were determined for each specimen. These data are reproduced in the accompanying table.
  a. Conduct a test to determine if the true mean amount of dioxide present in water specimens that contained oil was less than 3 milligrams/liter. Use $\alpha = .10$.

  b. Repeat part a for water specimens that did not contain oil.

Dioxide Amount	Crude Oil Present
3.3	No
0.5	Yes
1.3	Yes
0.4	Yes
0.1	No
4.0	No
0.3	No
0.2	Yes
2.4	No
2.4	No
1.4	No
0.5	Yes
0.2	Yes
4.0	No
4.0	No
4.0	No

Source: Based on Permanyer, A., et al. "Crude oil biodegradation and environmental factors at the Riutort oil shale mine, SE Pyrenees," *Journal of Petroleum Geology,* Vol. 33, No. 2, April 2010 (Table 1).

61 **Crack intensity of paved highways.** The Mississippi Department of Transportation collected data on the number of cracks (called *crack intensity*) in an undivided two-lane highway using van-mounted, state-of-the-art video technology (*Journal of Infrastructure Systems*, Mar. 1995). The mean number of cracks found in a sample of eight 50-meter sections of the highway was $\bar{x} = .210$, with a variance of $s^2 = .011$. Suppose the American Association of State Highway and Transportation Officials (AASHTO) recommends a maximum mean crack intensity of .100 for safety purposes. Is there evidence to say that the true mean crack intensity of the Mississippi highway exceeds the AASHTO recommended maximum? Use $\alpha = .01$ in the test.

62 **Active nuclear power plants.** The U.S. Energy Information Administration's compiled a list of active nuclear power plants operating in each of a sample of 20 states. The data are reproduced in the next table.

NUKES

a. Is there sufficient evidence to claim that the mean number of active nuclear power plants operating in all states exceeds 3? Test using $\alpha = .10$.

b. Are the conditions required for a valid small-sample test reasonably satisfied? Explain.

c. Eliminate the lowest two values and the highest two values from the data set, then conduct the test of part **a** on the smaller data set. What impact does this have on the test results?

d. Why is it dangerous to eliminate data points in order to satisfy an assumption for a test of hypothesis?

State	Number of Power Plants	State	Number of Power Plants
Alabama	5	New Hampshire	1
Arizona	2	New York	6
California	4	North Carolina	5
Florida	5	Ohio	3
Georgia	4	Pennsylvania	9
Illinois	11	South Carolina	7
Kansas	1	Tennessee	3
Louisiana	2	Texas	4
Massachusetts	1	Vermont	1
Mississippi	1	Wisconsin	3

Source: Data from *Statistical Abstract of the United States*, 2010 (Table 906). U.S. Energy Information Administration. Electric Power Annual.

Applying the Concepts—Advanced

63 **Arsenic in smelters.** The Occupational Safety and Health Act (OSHA) allows issuance of engineering standards to ensure safe workplaces for all Americans. The maximum allowable mean level of arsenic in smelters, herbicide production facilities, and other places where arsenic is used is .004 milligrams per cubic meter of air. Suppose smelters at two plants are being investigated to determine whether they are meeting OSHA standards. Two analyses of the air are made at each plant, and the results (in milligrams per cubic meter of air) are shown in the table. A claim is made that the OSHA standard is violated at Plant 2 but not at Plant 1. Do you agree?

OSHA

Plant 1		Plant 2	
Observation	Arsenic Level	Observation	Arsenic Level
1	.01	1	.05
2	.005	2	.09

6 Large-Sample Test of Hypothesis about a Population Proportion

Inferences about population proportions (or percentages) are often made in the context of the probability, *p*, of "success" for a binomial distribution. We consider tests of hypotheses about *p*.

For example, consider the problem of *insider trading* in the stock market. Insider trading is the buying and selling of stock by an individual privy to inside information in a company, usually a high-level executive in the firm. The Securities and Exchange Commission (SEC) imposes strict guidelines about insider trading so that all investors can have equal access to information that may affect the stock's price. An investor wishing to test the effectiveness of the SEC guidelines monitors the market for a period of a year and records the number of times a stock price increases the day following a significant purchase of stock by an insider. For a total of 576 such transactions, the stock increased the following day 327 times. Does this sample provide evidence that the stock price may be affected by insider trading?

We first view this as a binomial experiment, with the 576 transactions as the trials, and with success representing an increase in the stock's price the following day. Let *p* represent the probability that the stock price will increase following a large insider purchase. If the insider purchase has no effect on the stock price (that is, if the information available to the insider is identical to that available to the general market), then the investor expects the probability of a stock increase to be the same as that of a decrease, or $p = .5$. On the other hand, if insider trading affects the stock price (indicating that the market has not fully accounted for the information known to the insiders), then the investor expects the stock either to decrease or to increase more than half the time following significant insider transactions; that is, $p \neq .5$.

We can now place the problem in the context of a test of hypothesis:

$$H_0: p = .5 \text{ (Probability of stock increase equals .5—}$$
$$\text{i.e., insider purchase has no effect on stock price.)}$$

$$H_a: p \neq .5 \text{ (Probability of stock increase differs from .5—}$$
$$\text{i.e., insider trading effects stock price.)}$$

The sample proportion, $\hat{p}$, is really just the sample mean of the outcomes of the individual binomial trials and, as such, is approximately normally distributed (for large samples) according to the Central Limit Theorem. Thus, for large samples, we can use the standard normal z as the test statistic:

$$\textit{Test statistic: } z = \frac{\text{Sample proportion } - \text{ Null hypothesized proportion}}{\text{Standard deviation of sample proportion}}$$

$$= \frac{\hat{p} - p_0}{\sigma_{\hat{p}}}$$

where we use the symbol p_0 to represent the null hypothesized value of p.

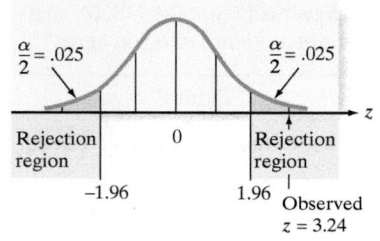

$\frac{\alpha}{2} = .025$　　$\frac{\alpha}{2} = .025$

Rejection region　　0　　Rejection region

-1.96　　　1.96　　Observed
　　　　　　　　　$z = 3.24$

Figure 20

Rejection region for insider trading example

Rejection region: We use the standard normal distribution to find the appropriate rejection region for the specified value of α. Using $\alpha = .05$, the two-tailed rejection region is

$$z < -z_{\alpha/2} = -z_{.025} = -1.96 \text{ or } z > z_{\alpha/2} = z_{.025} = 1.96$$

See Figure 20.

We are now prepared to calculate the value of the test statistic. Before doing so, we want to be sure that the sample size is large enough to ensure that the normal approximation for the sampling distribution of $\hat{p}$ is reasonable. We require both np and nq to be at least 15. Because the null hypothesized value, p_0, is assumed to be the true value of p until our test procedure indicates otherwise, we check to see if $np_0 \geq 15$ and $nq_0 \geq 15$ (where $q_0 = 1 - p_0$). Now, $np_0 = (576)(.5) = 288$ and $nq_0 = (576)(.5) = 288$; therefore, the normal distribution will provide a reasonable approximation for the sampling distribution of $\hat{p}$.

Returning to the hypothesis test at hand, the proportion of the sampled transactions that resulted in a stock increase is

$$\hat{p} = \frac{327}{576} = .568$$

Finally, we calculate the number of standard deviations (the z-value) between the sampled and hypothesized values of the binomial proportion:

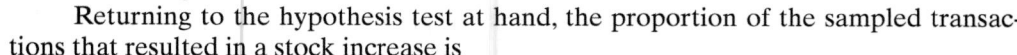

$$z = \frac{\hat{p} - p_0}{\sigma_{\hat{p}}} = \frac{\hat{p} - p_0}{\sqrt{p_0 q_0/n}} = \frac{.568 - .5}{.021} = \frac{.068}{.021} = 3.24$$

The implication is that the observed sample proportion is (approximately) 3.24 standard deviations above the null hypothesized proportion .5 (Figure 20). Therefore, we reject the null hypothesis, concluding at the .05 level of significance that the true probability of an increase or decrease in a stock's price differs from .5 the day following insider purchase of the stock. It appears that an insider purchase significantly increases the probability that the stock price will increase the following day. (To estimate the magnitude of the probability of an increase, a confidence interval can be constructed.)

The test of hypothesis about a population proportion p is summarized in the next box. Note that the procedure is entirely analogous to that used for conducting large-sample tests about a population mean.

Large-Sample Test of Hypothesis about p: Normal (z) Statistic

One-Tailed Test	Two-Tailed Test
$H_0: p = p_0$	$H_0: p = p_0$
$H_a: p < p_0 \ (\text{or } H_a: p > p_0)$	$H_a: p \neq p_0$
Test statistic: $z = \dfrac{\hat{p} - p_0}{\sigma_{\hat{p}}}$	Test statistic: $z = \dfrac{\hat{p} - p_0}{\sigma_{\hat{p}}}$

where, according to H_0, $\sigma_{\hat{p}} = \sqrt{p_0 q_0/n}$ and $q_0 = 1 - p_0$

Rejection region: $z < -z_\alpha$ (or $z > z_\alpha$ when $H_a: p > p_0$)

Rejection region: $|z| > z_{\alpha/2}$

Note: p_0 is the symbol for the numerical value of p assigned in the null hypothesis.

Conditions Required for a Valid Large-Sample Hypothesis Test for p

1. A random sample is selected from a binomial population.
2. The sample size n is large. (This condition will be satisfied if both $np_0 \geq 15$ and $nq_0 \geq 15$.)

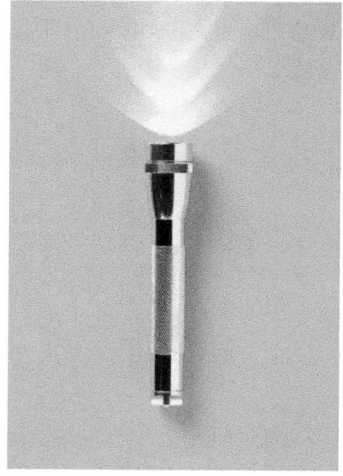

Example 10

Hypothesis Test for p—Proportion of Defective Batteries

Problem The reputations (and hence sales) of many businesses can be severely damaged by shipments of manufactured items that contain a large percentage of defectives. For example, a manufacturer of alkaline batteries may want to be reasonably certain that fewer than 5% of its batteries are defective. Suppose 300 batteries are randomly selected from a very large shipment; each is tested, and 10 defective batteries are found. Does this provide sufficient evidence for the manufacturer to conclude that the fraction defective in the entire shipment is less than .05? Use $\alpha = .01$.

Solution The objective of the sampling is to determine whether there is sufficient evidence to indicate that the fraction defective, p, is less than .05. Consequently, we will test the null hypothesis that $p = .05$ against the alternative hypothesis that $p < .05$. The elements of the test are

$H_0: p = .05$ (Fraction of defective batteries equals .05.)

$H_a: p < .05$ (Fraction of defective batteries is less than .05.)

Test statistic: $z = \dfrac{\hat{p} - p_0}{\sigma_{\hat{p}}}$

Rejection region: $z < -z_{.01} = -2.326$ (see Figure 21)

Before conducting the test, we check to determine whether the sample size is large enough to use the normal approximation to the sampling distribution of $\hat{p}$. Because $np_0 = (300)(.05) = 15$ and $nq_0 = (300)(.95) = 285$ are both at least 15, the normal approximation will be adequate.

We now calculate the test statistic:

$$z = \frac{\hat{p} - .05}{\sigma_{\hat{p}}} = \frac{(10/300) - .05}{\sqrt{p_0 q_0/n}} = \frac{.03333 - .05}{\sqrt{p_0 q_0/300}}$$

Notice that we use p_0 to calculate $\sigma_{\hat{p}}$ because, in contrast to calculating $\sigma_{\hat{p}}$ for a confidence interval, the test statistic is computed on the assumption that the null hypothesis

405

is true—that is, $p = p_0$. Therefore, substituting the values for $\hat{p}$ and p_0 into the z-statistic, we obtain

$$z \approx \frac{-.01667}{\sqrt{(.05)(.95)/300}} = \frac{-.01667}{.0126} = -1.32$$

As shown in Figure 21, the calculated z-value does not fall in the rejection region. Therefore, there is insufficient evidence at the .01 level of significance to indicate that the shipment contains fewer than 5% defective batteries.

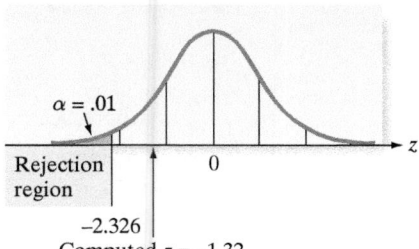

Figure 21

Rejection region for Example 10

$\alpha = .01$

Rejection region

-2.326

Computed $z = -1.32$

■ **Now Work Exercise 64a, b**

Example 11

The p-Value for a Test about a Population Proportion p

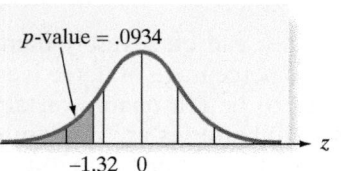

p-value $= .0934$

$-1.32 \quad 0$

Figure 22

The observed significance level for Example 11

Problem In Example 10 we found that we did not have sufficient evidence, at the $\alpha = .01$ level of significance, to indicate that the fraction defective p of alkaline batteries was less than $p = .05$. How strong was the weight of evidence favoring the alternative hypothesis ($H_a: p < .05$)? Find the observed significance level for the test.

Solution The computed value of the test statistic z was $z = -1.32$. Therefore, for this lower-tailed test, the observed significance level is

$$\text{Observed significance level} = P(z \le -1.32)$$

This lower-tail area is shown in Figure 22. The area between $z = 0$ and $z = 1.32$ is given in Table II in Appendix: Tables as .4066. Therefore, the observed significance level is $.5 - .4066 = .0934$.

Note: The observed significance level can also be obtained with statistical software. The Minitab printout shown in Figure 23 gives the p-value (highlighted).

Test and CI for One Proportion

```
Test of p = 0.05 vs p < 0.05


                              95% Upper
Sample   X    N   Sample p      Bound   Z-Value   P-Value
1       10  300  0.033333     0.050380    -1.32     0.093

Using the normal approximation.
```

Figure 23

Minitab lower-tailed test of p, Example 11

Look Back Although we did not reject $H_0: p = .05$ at $\alpha = .01$, the probability of observing a z-value as small as or smaller than -1.32 is only .0934 if, in fact, H_0 is true. Therefore, we would reject H_0 if we choose $\alpha = .10$ (because the observed significance level is less than .10), and we would not reject H_0 (the conclusion of Example 10) if we choose $\alpha = .05$ or $\alpha = .01$.

■ **Now Work Exercise 64c**

Small-sample test procedures are also available for p, although most surveys use samples that are large enough to employ the large-sample tests presented in this section.

Testing a Population Proportion

In the previous Statistics in Action Revisited we investigated Kimberly-Clark Corporation's assertion that the company should put more than 60 tissues in a cold-care box of Kleenex® tissues. We did this by testing the claim that the mean number of tissues used by a person with a cold is $\mu = 60$, using data collected from a survey of 250 Kleenex® users. Another approach to the problem is to consider the proportion of Kleenex® users who use more than 60 tissues when they have a cold. Now the population parameter of interest is p, the proportion of all Kleenex® users who use more than 60 tissues when they have a cold.

Kimberly-Clark Corporation's belief that the company should put more than 60 tissues in a cold-care box will be supported if over half of the Kleenex® users surveyed used more than 60 tissues (i.e., if $p > .5$). Is there evidence to indicate that the population proportion exceeds .5? To answer this question, we set up the following null and alternative hypotheses:

$$H_0: p = .5 \quad H_a: p > .5$$

Recall that the survey results for the 250 sampled Kleenex® users are stored in the **TISSUE** data file. In addition to the number of tissues used by each person, the file contains a qualitative variable—called USED60—representing whether the person used fewer or more than 60 tissues. (The values of USED60 in the data set are "LESS" or "MORE.") A Minitab analysis of this variable yielded the printout displayed in Figure SIA2.

On the Minitab printout, x represents the number of the 250 people with colds who used more than 60 tissues. Note that $x = 154$. This value is used to compute the test statistic $z = 3.67$, highlighted on the printout. The p-value of the test, also highlighted on the printout, is p-value $= .000$. Since this value is less than $\alpha = .05$, there is sufficient evidence (at $\alpha = .05$) to reject H_0; we conclude that the proportion of all Kleenex® users who use more than 60 tissues when they have a cold exceeds 5. This conclusion supports again the company's decision to put more than 60 tissues in a cold-care box of Kleenex.

Test and CI for One Proportion: USED60

```
Test of p = 0.5 vs p > 0.5

Event = MORE

                                    95% Lower
Variable   X    N   Sample p         Bound   Z-Value   P-Value
USED60    154  250  0.616000       0.565404     3.67     0.000

Using the normal approximation.
```

Figure SIA2

Minitab test of $p = .5$ for Kleenex survey

Data Set: TISSUE

Exercises 64–81

Please be aware that some of the following problems may require knowledge of concepts that are not presented in this chapter.

Learning the Mechanics

64 Suppose a random sample of 100 observations from a binomial population gives a value of $\hat{p} = .63$ and you wish to test the null hypothesis that the population parameter p is equal to .70 against the alternative hypothesis that p is less than .70.

a. Noting that $\hat{p} = .63$, what does your intuition tell you? Does the value of $\hat{p}$ appear to contradict the null hypothesis?

b. Use the large-sample z-test to test $H_0: p = .70$ against the alternative hypothesis, $H_a: p < .70$. Use $\alpha = .05$. How do the test results compare with your intuitive decision from part **a**?

c. Find and interpret the observed significance level of the test you conducted in part **b**.

65 Suppose the sample in Exercise 64 has produced $\hat{p} = .83$ and we wish to test $H_0: p = .9$ against the alternative $H_a: p < .9$.

a. Calculate the value of the z-statistic for this test.

b. Note that the numerator of the z-statistic ($\hat{p} - p_0 = .83 - .90 = -.07$) is the same as for Exercise 64. Considering this, why is the absolute value of z for this exercise larger than that calculated in Exercise 64?

c. Complete the test using $\alpha = .05$ and interpret the result.

d. Find the observed significance level for the test and interpret its value.

66 A statistics student used a computer program to test the null hypothesis $H_0: p = .5$ against the one-tailed alternative,

$H_a: p > .5$. A sample of 500 observations are input into SPSS, which returns the following results: $z = .44$, two-tailed p-value $= .33$.

a. The student concludes, based on the p-value, that there is a 33% chance that the alternative hypothesis is true. Do you agree? If not, correct the interpretation.

b. How would the p-value change if the alternative hypothesis was two-tailed, $H_a: p \neq .5$? Interpret this p-value.

67 In this study, 50 consumers taste-tested a new snack food. Their responses (where $0 =$ do not like; $1 =$ like; $2 =$ indifferent) are reproduced below.

SNACK

a. Test $H_0: p = .5$ against $H_a: p > .5$, where p is the proportion of customers who do not like the snack food.

b. Find the observed significance level of your test.

1	0	0	1	2	0	1	1	0	0	0	1
0	2	0	2	2	0	0	1	1	0	0	0
0	1	0	2	0	0	0	1	0	0	1	0
0	1	0	1	0	2	0	0	1	1	0	0
0	1										

68 For the binomial sample sizes and null hypothesized values of p in each part, determine whether the sample size is large enough to use the normal approximation methodology presented in this section to conduct a test of the null hypothesis $H_0: p = p_0$.

a. $n = 900, p_0 = .975$
b. $n = 125, p_0 = .01$
c. $n = 40, p_0 = .75$
d. $n = 15, p_0 = .75$
e. $n = 12, p_0 = .62$

Applet Exercise 5

Use the applet *Hypotheses Test for a Proportion* to investigate the relationships between the probabilities of Type I and Type II errors occurring at levels .05 and .01. For this exercise, use $n = 100$, true $p = 0.5$, and alternative *not equal*.

a. Set null $p = .5$. What happens to the proportion of times the null hypothesis is rejected at the .05 level and at the .01 level as the applet is run more and more times? What type of error has occurred when the null hypothesis is rejected in this situation? Based on your results, is this type of error more likely to occur at level .05 or at level .01? Explain.

b. Set null $p = .6$. What happens to the proportion of times the null hypothesis is *not* rejected at the .05 level and at the .01 level as the applet is run more and more times? What type of error has occurred when the null hypothesis is *not* rejected in this situation? Based on your results, is this type of error more likely to occur at level .05 or at level .01? Explain.

c. Use your results from parts a and b to make a general statement about the probabilities of Type I and Type II errors at levels .05 and .01.

Applet Exercise 6

Use the applet *Hypotheses Test for a Proportion* to investigate the effect of the true population proportion p on the probability of a Type I error occurring. For this exercise, use $n = 100$, and alternative *not equal*.

a. Set true $p = .5$ and null $p = .5$. Run the applet several times and record the proportion of times the null hypothesis is rejected at the .01 level.

b. Clear the applet and repeat part a for true $p = .1$ and null $p = .1$. Then repeat one more time for true $p = .01$ and null $p = .01$.

c. Based on your results from parts a and b, what can you conclude about the probability of a Type I error occurring as the true population proportion gets closer to 0?

Applying the Concepts—Basic

69 **Paying for music downloads.** If you use the Internet, have you ever paid to access or download music? This was one of the questions of interest in a *Pew Internet & American Life Project Survey* (October 2010). In a representative sample of 755 adults who use the Internet, 506 admitted that they have paid to download music. Let p represent the true proportion of all Internet-using adults who have paid to download music.

a. Compute a point estimate of p.

b. Set up the null and alternative hypotheses for testing whether the true proportion of all Internet-using adults who have paid to download music exceeds .7.

c. Compute the test statistic for part b.

d. Find the rejection region for the test if $\alpha = .01$.

e. Find the p-value for the test.

f. Make the appropriate conclusion using the rejection region.

g. Make the appropriate conclusion using the p-value.

70 **Satellite radio in cars.** A spokesperson for the National Association of Broadcasters (NAB) claims that 80% of all satellite radio subscribers have a satellite radio receiver in their car. In a recent survey of 501 satellite radio subscribers, 396 have a satellite receiver in their car. Consider a test of the NAB spokesperson's claim.

a. Define the parameter of interest to the NAB spokesperson.

b. Set up the null hypothesis for testing the claim.

c. Specify the alternative hypothesis if you believe that the spokesperson's claim is too high.

d. Compute the value of the test statistic.

e. Determine the rejection region for the test using $\alpha = .10$.

f. Compute the p-value of the test.

g. Make the appropriate conclusion. Show that the decision based on the rejection region agrees with the decision based on the p-value.

71 **History of corporate acquisitions.** The *Academy of Management Journal* (Aug. 2008) did an investigation of the performance and timing of corporate acquisitions. The investigation discovered that in a random sample of 2,778 firms, 748 announced one or more acquisitions during the year 2000. Does the sample provide sufficient evidence to indicate that the true percentage of all firms that announced one or more acquisitions during the year 2000 is less than 30%? Use $\alpha = .05$ to make your decision.

72 **Gummi Bears: Red or yellow?** Companies that produce candies typically offer different colors of their candies to provide consumers a choice. Presumably, the consumer will choose one color over another because of taste. *Chance* (Winter 2010) presented an experiment designed to test this taste theory. Students were blindfolded and then given a red-colored or yellow-colored Gummi Bear to chew. (Half the students were randomly assigned to receive the red Gummi Bear and half to receive the yellow Bear. The students could not see what color Gummi Bear they were given.) After chewing, the students were asked to guess the color of the candy based on the flavor. Of the 121 students who participated in the study, 97 correctly identified the color of the Gummi Bear.

a. If there is no relationship between color and Gummi Bear flavor, what proportion of the population of students would correctly identify the color?

b. Specify the null and alternative hypotheses for testing whether color and flavor are related.

c. Carry out the test and give the appropriate conclusion at $\alpha = .01$. Use the *p*-value of the test, shown on the accompanying SPSS printout, to make your decision.

Binomial Test

		Category	N	Observed Prop.	Test Prop.	Exact Sig. (2-tailed)
ID_Color	Group 1	Yes	97	.80	.50	.000
	Group 2	No	24	.20		
	Total		121	1.00		

73 Toothpaste brands with the ADA seal. *Consumer Reports* evaluated and rated 46 brands of toothpaste. One attribute examined in the study was whether or not a toothpaste brand carries an American Dental Association (ADA) seal verifying effective decay prevention. The data for the 46 brands (coded 1 = ADA seal, 0 = no ADA seal) are listed here.

0	0	0	0	0	0	1	1	1	0	0	1
0	1	0	0	0	0	1	1	1	0	1	1
1	1	0	0	0	0	0	1	0	0	1	1
1	0	1	0	1	1	1	0	0	0		

a. Give the null and alternative hypotheses for testing whether the true proportion of toothpaste brands with the ADA seal verifying effective decay prevention is less than .5.

b. Locate the *p*-value on the Minitab printout below.

c. Make the appropriate conclusion using $\alpha = .10$.

```
Test of p = 0.5 vs p < 0.5

Event = 1

                                  95%
                               Upper     Exact
Variable    X    N  Sample p   Bound   P-Value
ADASEAL    20   46  0.434783  0.566289  0.231
```

74 Vacation-home owners. The National Association of Realtors (NAR) reported the results of a March 2010 survey of home buyers. In a random sample of 1,982 residential properties purchased during the year, 198 were purchased as a vacation home. Five years ago, 14% of residential properties were vacation homes.

a. Do the survey results allow the NAR to conclude (at $\alpha = .01$) that the percentage of all residential properties purchased for vacation homes is less that 14%.

b. The NAR sent the survey questionnaire to a nationwide sample of 45,000 new home owners, of which 1,982 responded to the survey. How might this bias the results?

Applying the Concepts—Intermediate

75 Organic-certified coffee. Coffee markets that conform to organic standards focus on the environmental aspects of coffee growing, such as the use of shade trees and a reduced reliance on chemical pesticides. A study of organic coffee growers was published in *Food Policy* (Vol. 36, 2010). In a representative sample of 845 coffee growers from southern Mexico, 417 growers were certified to sell to organic coffee markets while 77 growers were transitioning to become organic certified. In the United States, 60% of coffee growers are organic certified. Is there evidence to indicate that fewer than 60% of the coffee growers in southern Mexico are either organic certified or transitioning to become organic certified? State your conclusion so that there is only a 5% chance of making a Type I error.

76 Unemployment and a reduced workweek. In an effort to increase employment, France mandated in February 2000 that all companies with 20 or more employees reduce the workweek to 35 hours. The economic impact of the shortened workweek was analyzed in *Economic Policy* (July 2008). The researchers focused on several key variables such as hourly wages, dual-job holdings, and level of employment. Assume that in the year prior to the 35-hour-workweek law, unemployment in France was at 12%. Suppose that in a random sample of 500 French citizens (eligible workers) taken several years after the law was enacted, 53 were unemployed. Conduct a test of hypothesis to determine if the French unemployment rate dropped after the enactment of the 35-hour-workweek law. Test using $\alpha = .05$.

77 Effectiveness of skin cream. Pond's Age-Defying Complex, a cream with alpha hydroxy acid, advertised that it could reduce wrinkles and improve the skin. In a study published in *Archives of Dermatology* (June 1996), 33 middle-aged women used a cream with alpha hydroxy acid for 22 weeks. At the end of the study period, a dermatologist judged whether each woman exhibited skin improvement. The results for the 33 women (where I = improved skin and N = no improvement) are listed in the next table. [*Note:* Pond's recently discontinued the production of this cream product, replacing it with Age-Defying Towlettes.]

a. Do the data provide sufficient evidence to conclude that the cream improved the skin of more than 60% of middle-aged women? Test using $\alpha = .05$.

b. Find and interpret the *p*-value of the test.

I	I	N	I	N	N	I	I	I	I	I	I
N	I	I	I	N	I	I	N	I	N	I	N	I
I	I	I	I	N	I	I	I	N			

78 Detection of motorcycles while driving. Motorcycle fatalities have increased dramatically over the past decade. As a result, manufacturers of powered two-wheelers (PTWs) are tweaking with their design in order to improve visibility by automobile drivers. The factors that impact the visibility of PTWs on the road were investigated in *Accident Analysis and Prevention* (Vol. 44, 2012). A visual search study was conducted in which viewers were presented with pictures of driving scenarios and asked to identify the presence or absence of a PTW. Of interest to the researchers is the detection rate, i.e., the proportion of pictures showing a PTW in which the viewer actually detected the presence of the PTW. Suppose that, in theory, the true detection rate for pictures of PTWs is .70. The study revealed that in a sample of 2,376 pictures that included a PTW, only 1,554 were detected by the viewers. Use this results to test the theory at $\alpha = .10$.

79 TVs with DVRs. According to Nielsen's *Television Audience Report* (2011), 41% of all households with televisions in the United States have a digital video recorder (DVR). Develop a sampling plan that will allow you to test this claim. Identify the target population, experimental units, variable to be measured, parameter of interest, null and alternative hypotheses, and the form of the test statistic.

Applying the Concepts—Advanced

80 Choosing portable grill displays. The *Journal of Consumer Research* (Mar. 2003) did an experiment on influencing the choices of others by offering undesirable alternatives. Each of 124 college students selected three portable grills

from five to display on the showroom floor. The students were instructed to include Grill #2 (a smaller-sized grill) and select the remaining two grills in the display to maximize purchases of Grill #2. If the six possible grill display combinations (1-2-3, 1-2-4, 1-2-5, 2-3-4, 2-3-5, and 2-4-5) were selected at random, then the proportion of students selecting any display was $\frac{1}{6} = .167$. One theory tested by the researcher was that the students would tend to choose the three-grill display so that Grill #2 was a compromise between a more desirable and a less desirable grill (i.e., display 1-2-3, 1-2-4, or 1-2-5). Of the 124 students, 85 selected a three-grill display that was consistent with this theory. Use this information to test the theory proposed by the researcher at $\alpha = .05$.

81 The Pepsi Challenge. "Take the Pepsi Challenge" was a famous marketing campaign used by the Pepsi-Cola Company. Coca-Cola drinkers participated in a blind taste test where they were asked to taste unmarked cups of Pepsi and Coke and were asked to select their favorite. In one Pepsi television commercial, an announcer stated that "in recent blind taste tests, more than half the Diet Coke drinkers surveyed said they preferred the taste of Diet Pepsi." Suppose 100 Diet Coke drinkers took the Pepsi Challenge and 56 preferred the taste of Diet Pepsi. Determine if more than half of all Diet Coke drinkers selected Diet Pepsi in the blind taste test. Select α to minimize the probability of a Type I error. What were the consequences of the test results from Coca-Cola's perspective?

7 Test of Hypothesis about a Population Variance

Although many practical problems involve inferences about a population mean (or proportion), it is sometimes of interest to make an inference about a population variance, σ^2. To illustrate, a quality-control supervisor in a cannery knows that the exact amount each can contains will vary because there are certain uncontrollable factors that affect the amount of fill. The mean fill per can is important, but equally important is the variation of fill. If σ^2, the variance of the fill, is large, some cans will contain too little and others too much. Suppose regulatory agencies specify that the standard deviation of the amount of fill should be less than .1 ounce. To determine whether the process is meeting this specification, the supervisor randomly selects 10 cans and weighs the contents of each. The results are given in Table 6.

Table 6	Fill Weights (in Ounces) of 10 Cans								
16.00	16.06	15.95	16.04	16.10	16.05	16.02	16.03	15.99	16.02

Data Set: FILLWT

Do these data provide sufficient evidence to indicate that the variability is as small as desired? To answer this question, we need a procedure for testing a hypothesis about σ^2.

Intuitively, it seems that we should compare the sample variance σ^2 to the hypothesized value of σ^2 (or s to σ) in order to make a decision about the population's variability. The quantity

$$\frac{(n-1)s^2}{\sigma^2}$$

is known to have a **chi-square** (χ^2) **sampling distribution** when the population from which the sample is taken is *normally distributed*.

Since the distribution of $\frac{(n-1)s^2}{\sigma^2}$ is known, we can use this quantity as a test statistic in a test of hypothesis for a population variance, as illustrated in the next example.

FRIEDRICH R. HELMERT (1843–1917)
Helmert Transformations

German Friedrich Helmert studied engineering sciences and mathematics at Dresden University, where he earned his PhD, then accepted a position as a professor of geodesy—the scientific study of the earth's size and shape—at the technical school in Aachen. Helmert's mathematical solutions to geodesy problems led him to several statistics-related discoveries. His greatest statistical contribution occurred in 1876, when he was the first to prove that the sampling distribution of the sample variance, s^2, is a chi-square distribution. Helmert used a series of mathematical transformations to obtain the distribution of s^2—transformations that have since been named "Helmert transformations" in his honor. Later in life, Helmert was appointed professor of advanced geodesy at the prestigious University of Berlin and director of the Prussian Geodesic Institute.

Example 12

Test for σ^2—Fill Weight Variance

Problem Refer to the fill weights for the sample of ten 16-ounce cans in Table 6. Do the data provide sufficient evidence to indicate that the true standard deviation σ of the fill measurements of all 16-ounce cans is less than .1 ounce?

Solution Here, we want to test whether $\sigma < .1$. Because the null and alternative hypotheses must be stated in terms of σ^2 rather than σ, we want to test the null hypothesis that $\sigma^2 = (.1)^2 = .01$ against the alternative that $\sigma^2 < .01$. Therefore, the elements of the test are

H_0: $\sigma^2 = .01$ (Fill variance equals .01—i.e., process specifications are not met.)
H_a: $\sigma^2 < .01$ (Fill variance is less than .01—i.e., process specifications are met.)

Test statistic: $\chi^2 = \dfrac{(n-1)s^2}{\sigma^2}$

Assumption: The distribution of the amounts of fill is approximately normal.

Rejection region: The smaller the value of s^2 we observe, the stronger the evidence in favor of H_a. Thus, we reject H_0 for "small values" of the test statistic. The chi-square distribution depends on $(n-1)$ degrees of freedom. With $\alpha = .05$ and $(n-1) = 9$ df, the χ^2 value for rejection is found in Table IV and pictured in Figure 24. We will reject H_0 if $\chi^2 < 3.32511$.

[*Note:* The area given in Table IV is the area to the *right* of the numerical value in the table. Thus, to determine the lower-tail value, which has $\alpha = .05$ to its *left*, we used the $\chi^2_{.95}$ column in Table IV.]

A Minitab analysis of the data in Table 6 is displayed in Figure 25. The value of s (highlighted) on the printout is $s = .0412$. Substituting into the formula for the test statistic, we have

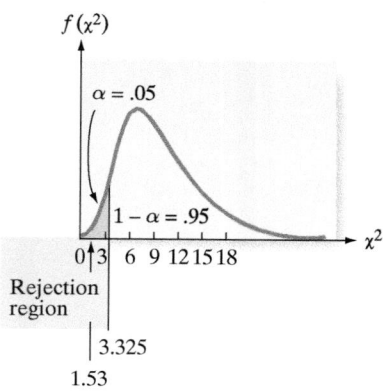

$f(\chi^2)$

$\alpha = .05$

$1 - \alpha = .95$

Rejection region

3.325

1.53

Figure 24
Rejection region for Example 12

$$\chi^2 = \frac{(n-1)s^2}{\sigma^2} = \frac{9(.0412)^2}{.01} = 1.53$$

Test and CI for One Variance: WEIGHT

```
Method

Null hypothesis          Sigma = 0.1
Alternative hypothesis   Sigma < 0.1

The chi-square method is only for the normal distribution.
The Bonett method is for any continuous distribution.


Statistics

Variable   N    StDev  Variance
WEIGHT     10   0.0412  0.00169


95% One-Sided Confidence Intervals

                         Upper Bound   Upper Bound
Variable   Method         for StDev   for Variance
WEIGHT     Chi-Square       0.0677       0.00458
           Bonett           0.0732       0.00536


Tests

                          Test
Variable   Method       Statistic  DF  P-Value
WEIGHT     Chi-Square      1.52      9   0.003
           Bonett          -        -    0.010
```

Figure 25

Minitab analysis of fill weight variance, Example 12

Because the test statistic falls into the rejection region, we reject H_0 in favor of H_a—that is, the supervisor can conclude that the variance σ^2 of the population of all amounts of fill is less than .01 ($\sigma < .1$) with probability of a Type I error equal to $\alpha = .05$. If this procedure is repeatedly used, it will incorrectly reject H_0 only 5% of the time. Thus, the quality-control supervisor is confident in the decision that the cannery is operating within the desired limits of variability.

Look Back Note that both the test statistic (rounded) and the lower-tailed p-value of the test (.003) are highlighted at the bottom of the printout, Figure 25. Because $\alpha = .05$ exceeds the p-value, our decision to reject H_0 is confirmed.

Now Work Exercise 87

One-tailed and two-tailed tests of hypothesis for σ^2 are given in the following box.

Test of a Hypothesis about σ^2

One-Tailed Test	Two-Tailed Test
$H_0: \sigma^2 = \sigma_0^2$	$H_0: \sigma^2 = \sigma_0^2$
$H_a: \sigma^2 < \sigma_0^2$ (or $H_a: \sigma^2 > \sigma_0^2$)	$H_a: \sigma^2 \neq \sigma_0^2$
Test statistic: $\chi^2 = \dfrac{(n-1)s^2}{\sigma_0^2}$	Test statistic: $\chi^2 = \dfrac{(n-1)s^2}{\sigma_0^2}$
Rejection region: $\chi^2 < \chi^2_{(1-\alpha)}$	Rejection region: $\chi^2 < \chi^2_{(1-\alpha/2)}$ or
(or $\chi^2 > \chi^2_\alpha$ when $H_a: \sigma^2 > \sigma_0^2$)	$\chi^2 > \chi^2_{(\alpha/2)}$

where σ_0^2 is the hypothesized variance and the distribution of χ^2 is based on $(n-1)$ degrees of freedom.

> **Conditions Required for a Valid Hypothesis Test for s^2**
>
> 1. A random sample is selected from the target population.
> 2. The population from which the sample is selected has a distribution that is approximately normal.

> ⚠ **CAUTION** The procedure for conducting a hypothesis test for σ^2 in the above examples requires an assumption regardless of whether the sample size n is large or small. We must assume that the population from which the sample is selected has an approximate normal distribution. Unlike small-sample tests for μ based on the t-statistic, *slight to moderate departures from normality will render the chi-square test invalid.*

Exercises 82–95

Please be aware that some of the following problems may require knowledge of concepts that are not presented in this chapter.

Learning the Mechanics

82 Let χ_0^2 be a particular value of χ^2. Find the value of χ_0^2 such that
   a. $P(\chi^2 > \chi_0^2) = .10$ for $n = 12$
   b. $P(\chi^2 > \chi_0^2) = .05$ for $n = 9$
   c. $P(\chi^2 > \chi_0^2) = .025$ for $n = 5$

83 A random sample of n observations is selected from a normal population to test the null hypothesis that $\sigma^2 = 25$. Specify the rejection region for each of the following combinations of H_a, α, and n:
   a. H_a: $\sigma^2 \neq 25$; $\alpha = .05$; $n = 16$
   b. H_a: $\sigma^2 > 25$; $\alpha = .01$; $n = 23$
   c. H_a: $\sigma^2 > 25$; $\alpha = .10$; $n = 15$
   d. H_a: $\sigma^2 < 25$; $\alpha = .01$; $n = 13$
   e. H_a: $\sigma^2 \neq 25$; $\alpha = .10$; $n = 7$
   f. H_a: $\sigma^2 < 25$; $\alpha = .05$; $n = 25$

84 A random sample of seven measurements gave $\bar{x} = 9.4$ and $s^2 = 4.84$.
   a. What assumptions must you make concerning the population in order to test a hypothesis about σ^2?
   b. Suppose the assumptions in part **a** are satisfied. Test the null hypothesis, $\sigma^2 = 1$, against the alternative hypothesis, $\sigma^2 > 1$. Use $\alpha = .05$.
   c. Test the null hypothesis that $\sigma^2 = 1$ against the alternative hypothesis that $\sigma^2 \neq 1$. Use $\alpha = .05$.

85 Refer to Exercise 84. Suppose we had $n = 100$, $\bar{x} = 9.4$, and $s^2 = 4.84$.
   a. Test the null hypothesis, H_0: $\sigma^2 = 1$, against the alternative hypothesis, H_a: $\sigma^2 > 1$.
   b. Compare your test result with that of Exercise 84.

86 A random sample of $n = 7$ observations from a normal population produced the following measurements: 4, 0, 6, 3, 3, 5, 9. Do the data provide sufficient evidence to indicate that $\sigma^2 < 1$? Test using $\alpha = .05$.

Applying the Concepts—Basic

87 **Trading skills of institutional investors.** Refer to *The Journal of Finance* (April 2011) analysis of trading skills of institutional investors, Exercise 36. Recall that the study focused on "round-trip" trades, i.e., trades in which the same stock was both bought and sold in the same quarter. In a random sample of 200 round-trip trades made by institutional investors, the sample standard deviation of the rates of return was 8.82%. One property of a consistent performance of institutional investors is a small variance in the rates of return of round-trip trades, say, a standard deviation of less than 10%.
   a. Specify the null and alternative hypotheses for determining whether the population of institutional investors performs consistently.
   b. Find the rejection region for the test using $\alpha = .05$.
   c. Interpret the value of α in the words of the problem.
   d. A Minitab printout of the analysis is shown below. Locate the test statistic and p-value on the printout.
   e. Give the appropriate conclusion in the words of the problem.
   f. What assumptions about the data are required for the inference to be valid?

Test and CI for One Variance

```
Method

Null hypothesis          Sigma = 10
Alternative hypothesis   Sigma < 10

The chi-square method is only for the normal distribution.
The Bonett method cannot be calculated with summarized data.

Statistics

  N   StDev   Variance
 200   8.82     77.8

Tests
                    Test
Method          Statistic   DF   P-Value
Chi-Square        154.81    199    0.009
```

---

88 Lobster trap placement. Refer to the *Bulletin of Marine Science* (April 2010) observational study of lobster trap placement by teams fishing for the red spiny lobster in Baja California Sur, Mexico, Exercise 52. Trap-spacing measurements (in meters) for a sample of seven teams of red spiny lobster fishermen are repeated in the table. (These measurements are for the BT cooperative in the accompanying data file.) The researchers want to know whether σ^2, the variation in the population of trap-spacing measurements, is larger than 10 m². They will conduct a test of hypothesis using $\alpha = .05$.

TRAPS

93	99	105	94	82	70	86

Source: Based on Shester, G. G. "Explaining catch variation among Baja California lobster fishers through spatial analysis of trap-placement decisions," *Bulletin of Marine Science,* Vol. 86, No. 2, April 2010 (Table 1), pp. 479–498.

a. Specify the null and alternative hypotheses for this test.

b. Find the variance of the sample data, s^2.

c. Note that $s^2 > 10$. Consequently, a fisherman wants to reject the null hypothesis. What are the problems with using such a decision rule?

d. Compute the value of the test statistic.

e. Use statistical software to find the *p*-value of the test.

f. Give the appropriate conclusion.

g. What conditions must be satisfied for the test results to be valid?

89 Golf tees produced from an injection mold. Refer to Exercise 37 and the weights of tees produced by an injection mold process. If operating correctly, the process will produce tees with a weight variance of .000004 (ounces)². If the weight variance differs from .000004, the injection molder is out of control.

TEES

a. Set up the null and alternative hypotheses for testing whether the injection mold process is out of control.

b. Use the data saved in the accompanying file to conduct the test, part **a.** Use $\alpha = .01$.

c. What conditions are required for inferences derived from the test to be valid? Are they reasonably satisfied?

90 A new dental bonding agent. Refer to the *Trends in Biomaterials & Artificial Organs* (Jan. 2003) study of a new dental bonding adhesive (called *Smartbond*), Exercise 54. Recall that tests on a sample of 10 extracted teeth bonded with the new adhesive resulted in a mean breaking strength (after 24 hours) of $\bar{x} = 5.07$ Mpa and a standard deviation of $s = .46$ Mpa. The manufacturer must demonstrate that the breaking strength variance of the new adhesive is less than the variance of the standard composite adhesive, $\sigma^2 = .25$.

a. Set up the null and alternative hypotheses for the test.

b. Find the rejection region for the test using $\alpha = .01$.

c. Compute the test statistic.

d. Give the appropriate conclusion for the test.

e. What conditions are required for the test results to be valid?

Applying the Concepts—Intermediate

91 Jitter in a water power system. The *Journal of Applied Physics* investigation of throughput jitter in the opening switch of a prototype water power system. Low throughput jitter is critical to successful waterline technology. An analysis of conduction time for a sample of 18 trials of the prototype system yielded $\bar{x} = 334.8$ nanoseconds and $s = 6.3$ nanoseconds. (Conduction time is defined as the length of time required for the downstream current to equal 10% of the upstream current.) A system is considered to have low throughput jitter if the true conduction time standard deviation is less than 7 nanoseconds. Does the prototype system satisfy this requirement? Test using $\alpha = .01$.

92 Drug content assessment. *Analytical Chemistry* (Dec. 15, 2009) did a study of a new method used by GlaxoSmithKline Medicines Research Center to determine the amount of drug in a tablet. Drug concentrations (measured as a percentage) for 50 randomly selected tablets are repeated in the accompanying table. The standard method of assessing drug content yields a concentration variance of 9. Can the scientists at GlaxoSmithKline conclude that the new method of determining drug concentration is less variable than the standard method? Test using $\alpha = .01$.

HPLC

91.28	92.83	89.35	91.90	82.85	94.83	89.83	89.00	84.62
86.96	88.32	91.17	83.86	89.74	92.24	92.59	84.21	89.36
90.96	92.85	89.39	89.82	89.91	92.16	88.67	89.35	86.51
89.04	91.82	93.02	88.32	88.76	89.26	90.36	87.16	91.74
86.12	92.10	83.33	87.61	88.20	92.78	86.35	93.84	91.20
93.44	86.77	83.77	93.19	81.79				

Source: Based on Borman, P. J., Marion, J. C., Damjanov, I., & Jackson, P. "Design and analysis of method equivalence studies," *Analytical Chemistry,* Vol. 81, No. 24, December 15, 2009 (Table 3).

93 Do ball bearings conform to specifications? It is essential in the manufacture of machinery to use parts that conform to specifications. In the past, diameters of the ball bearings produced by a certain manufacturer had a variance of .00156. To cut costs, the manufacturer instituted a less expensive production method. The variance of the diameters of 100 randomly sampled bearings produced by the new process was .00211. Do the data provide sufficient evidence to indicate that diameters of ball bearings produced by the new process are more variable than those produced by the old process?

94 Cooling method for gas turbines. Refer to the *Journal of Engineering for Gas Turbines and Power* (Jan. 2005) study of the performance of augmented gas turbine engines, Exercise 40. Recall that performance for each in a sample of 67 gas turbines was measured by heat rate (kilojoules per kilowatt per hour). The data are saved in the accompanying file. Suppose that standard gas turbines have heat rates with a standard deviation of 1,500 kJ/kWh. Is there sufficient evidence to indicate that the heat rates of the augmented gas turbine engine are more variable than the heat rates of the standard gas turbine engine? Test using $\alpha = .05$.

GASTRB

Applying the Concepts—Advanced

95 Why do small firms export? Refer to the *Journal of Small Business Management* (Vol. 40, 2002) study of what motivates small firms to export, Exercise 45. Recall that in a survey of 137 exporting firms, each CEO was asked to respond to the statement "Management believes that the firm can achieve economies of scale by exporting" on a scale of 1 (strongly disagree) to 5 (strongly agree). Summary statistics for the $n = 137$ scale scores were reported as $\bar{x} = 3.85$ and $s = 1.5$.

a. Explain why the researcher will be unable to conclude that the true mean scale score exceeds 3.5 (as in Exercise 45) if the standard deviation of the scale scores is too large.

b. Give the largest value of the true standard deviation, σ, for which you will reject the null hypothesis $H_0: \mu = 3.5$ in favor of the alternative hypothesis $H_a: \mu > 3.5$ using $\alpha = .01$.

c. Based on the study results, is there evidence (at $\alpha = .01$) to indicate that σ is smaller than the value you determined in part **b**?

8   Calculating Type II Error Probabilities: More about β*

In our introduction to hypothesis testing in Section 1, we showed that the probability of committing a Type I error, α, can be controlled by the selection of the rejection region for the test. Thus, when the test statistic falls in the rejection region and we make the decision to reject the null hypothesis, we do so knowing the error rate for incorrect rejections of H_0. The situation corresponding to accepting the null hypothesis, and thereby risking a Type II error, is not generally as controllable. For that reason, we adopted a policy of nonrejection of H_0 when the test statistic does not fall in the rejection region, rather than risking an error of unknown magnitude.

To see how β, the probability of a Type II error, can be calculated for a test of hypothesis, recall the example in Section 1 in which a city tests a manufacturer's sewer pipe to see whether it meets the requirement that the mean strength exceeds 2,400 pounds per linear foot. The setup for the test is as follows:

$$H_0: \mu = 2,400$$

$$H_a: \mu > 2,400$$

Test statistic: $z = \dfrac{\bar{x} - 2,400}{\sigma/\sqrt{n}}$

Rejection region: $z > 1.645$ for $\alpha = .05$

Figure 26a shows the rejection region for the **null distribution**—that is, the distribution of the test statistic assuming the null hypothesis is true. The area in the rejection region is .05, and this area represents α, the probability that the test statistic leads to rejection of H_0 when in fact H_0 is true.

The Type II error probability β is calculated assuming that the null hypothesis is false because it is defined as the *probability of accepting H_0 when it is false.* Because H_0 is false for any value of μ exceeding 2,400, one value of β exists for each possible value of μ greater than 2,400 (an infinite number of possibilities). Figures 26b–d show three of the possibilities, corresponding to alternative hypothesis values of μ equal to 2,425, 2,450, and 2,475, respectively. Note that β is the area in the *nonrejection* (or *acceptance*) *region* in each of these distributions and that β decreases as the true value of μ moves farther from the null hypothesized value of $\mu = 2,400$. This is sensible because the probability of incorrectly accepting the null hypothesis should decrease as the distance between the null and alternative values of μ increases.

In order to calculate the value of β for a specific value of μ in H_a, we proceed as follows:

1. Calculate the value of $\bar{x}$ that corresponds to the border between the acceptance and rejection regions. For the sewer pipe example, this is the value of $\bar{x}$ that lies 1.645 standard deviations above $\mu = 2,400$ in the sampling distribution of $\bar{x}$.

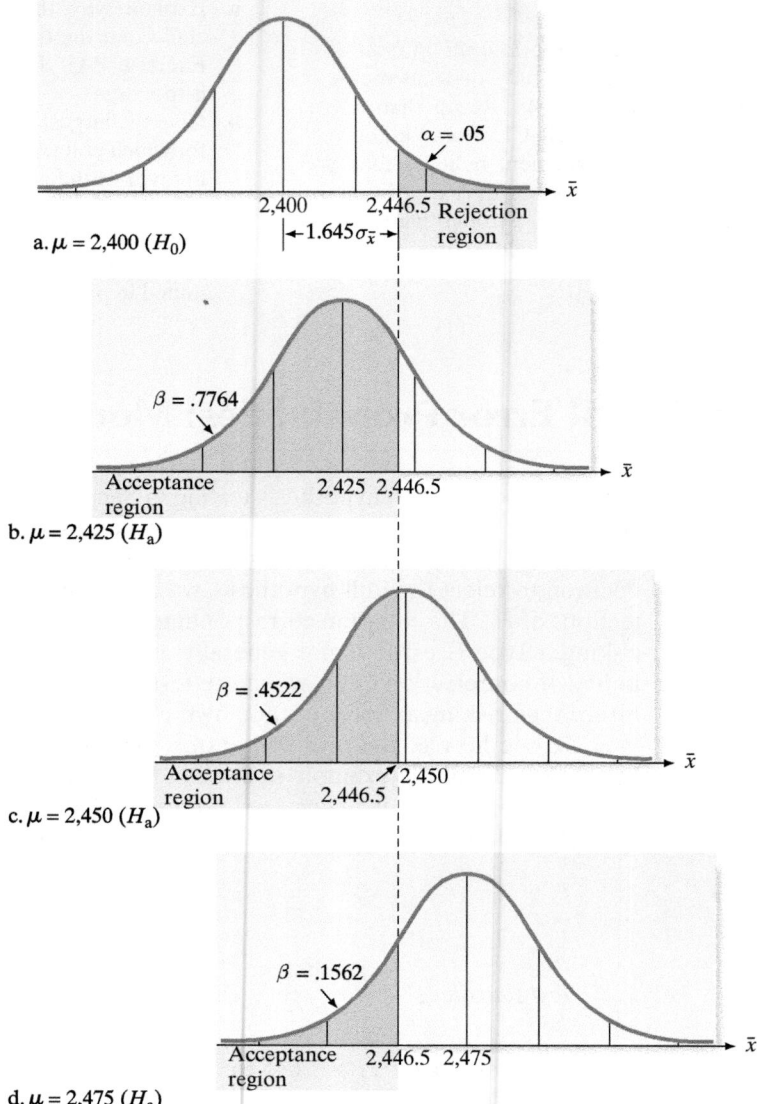

Figure 26

Values of α and β for various values of μ

a. $\mu = 2{,}400$ (H_0)

b. $\mu = 2{,}425$ (H_a)

c. $\mu = 2{,}450$ (H_a)

d. $\mu = 2{,}475$ (H_a)

Denoting this value by $\bar{x}_0$, corresponding to the largest value of $\bar{x}$ that supports the null hypothesis, we find (recalling that $s = 200$ and $n = 50$)

$$\bar{x}_0 = \mu_0 + 1.645\sigma_{\bar{x}} = 2{,}400 + 1.645\left(\frac{\sigma}{\sqrt{n}}\right)$$

$$\approx 2{,}400 + 1.645\left(\frac{s}{\sqrt{n}}\right) = 2{,}400 + 1.645\left(\frac{200}{\sqrt{50}}\right)$$

$$= 2{,}400 + 1.645(28.28) = 2{,}446.5$$

2. For a particular alternative distribution corresponding to a value of μ, denoted by μ_a, we calculate the z-value corresponding to $\bar{x}_0$, the border between the rejection and acceptance regions. We then use this z-value and Table II in Appendix: Tables to determine the area in the *acceptance region* under the alternative distribution. This area is the value of β corresponding to the particular alternative μ_a. For example, for the alternative $\mu_a = 2{,}425$, we calculate

$$z = \frac{\bar{x}_0 - 2{,}425}{\sigma_{\bar{x}}} = \frac{\bar{x}_0 - 2{,}425}{\sigma/\sqrt{n}}$$

$$\approx \frac{\bar{x}_0 - 2{,}425}{\sigma_{\bar{x}}} = \frac{2{,}446.5 - 2{,}425}{28.28} = .76$$

Note in Figure 26b that the area in the acceptance region is the area to the left of $z = .76$. This area is

$$\beta = .5 + .2764 = .7764$$

Thus, the probability that the test procedure will lead to an incorrect acceptance of the null hypothesis $\mu = 2{,}400$ when in fact $\mu = 2{,}425$ is about .78. As the average strength of the pipe increases to 2,450, the value of β decreases to .4522 (Figure 26c). If the mean strength is further increased to 2,475, the value of β is further decreased to .1562 (Figure 26d). Thus, even if the true mean strength of the pipe exceeds the minimum specification by 75 pounds per linear foot, the test procedure will lead to an incorrect acceptance of the null hypothesis (rejection of the pipe) approximately 16% of the time. The upshot is that the pipe must be manufactured so that the mean strength well exceeds the minimum requirement if the manufacturer wants the probability of its acceptance by the city to be large (i.e., β to be small).

The steps for calculating β for a large-sample test about a population mean and a population proportion are summarized in the following boxes.

Steps for Calculating β for a Large-Sample Test about μ

1. Calculate the value(s) of $\bar{x}$ corresponding to the border(s) of the rejection region. There will be one border value for a one-tailed test and two for a two-tailed test. The formula is one of the following, corresponding to a test with level of significance α:

$$\textit{Upper-tailed test: } \bar{x}_0 = \mu_0 + z_\alpha \sigma_{\bar{x}} \approx \mu_0 + z_\alpha \left(\frac{s}{\sqrt{n}} \right)$$
$$(H_a: \mu > \mu_0)$$

$$\textit{Lower-tailed test: } \bar{x}_0 = \mu_0 - z_\alpha \sigma_{\bar{x}} \approx \mu_0 - z_\alpha \left(\frac{s}{\sqrt{n}} \right)$$
$$(H_a: \mu < \mu_0)$$

$$\textit{Two-tailed test: } \bar{x}_{0,L} = \mu_0 - z_{\alpha/2} \sigma_{\bar{x}} \approx \mu_0 - z_{\alpha/2} \left(\frac{s}{\sqrt{n}} \right)$$
$$(H_a: \mu \neq \mu_0)$$

$$\bar{x}_{0,U} = \mu_0 + z_{\alpha/2} \sigma_{\bar{x}} \approx \mu_0 + z_{\alpha/2} \left(\frac{s}{\sqrt{n}} \right)$$

2. Specify the value of μ_a in the alternative hypothesis for which the value of β is to be calculated. Then convert the border value(s) of $\bar{x}_0$ to z-value(s) using the alternative distribution with mean μ_a. The general formula for the z-value is

$$z = \frac{\bar{x}_0 - \mu_a}{\sigma_{\bar{x}}}$$

3. Sketch the alternative distribution (centered at μ_a), and shade the area in the acceptance (nonrejection) region. Use the z-statistic(s) and Table II of Appendix: Tables to find the shaded area, which is β.

$$\textit{Lower-tailed test: } \beta = P\left(z > \frac{\bar{x}_0 - \mu_a}{\sigma_{\bar{x}}} \right)$$
$$(H_a: \mu < \mu_0)$$

$$\textit{Upper-tailed test: } \beta = P\left(z < \frac{\bar{x}_0 - \mu_a}{\sigma_{\bar{x}}} \right)$$
$$(H_a: \mu > \mu_0)$$

$$\textit{Two-tailed test: } \beta = P\left(\frac{\bar{x}_{0,L} - \mu_a}{\sigma_{\bar{x}}} < z < \frac{\bar{x}_{0,U} - \mu_a}{\sigma_{\bar{x}}} \right)$$
$$(H_a: \mu \neq \mu_0)$$

Steps for Calculating β for a Large-Sample Test about p

1. Calculate the value(s) of $\hat{p}$ corresponding to the border(s) of the rejection region. There will be one border for a one-tailed test and two for a two-tailed test. The formula is one of the following, corresponding to a test with level of significance α.

$$\text{Upper-tailed test: } \hat{p}_0 = p_0 + z_\alpha\sigma_p = p_0 + z_\alpha\sqrt{\frac{p_0q_0}{n}}$$
$$(H_a: p > p_0)$$

$$\text{Lower-tailed test: } \hat{p}_0 = p_0 - z_\alpha\sigma_p = p_0 + z_\alpha\sqrt{\frac{p_0q_0}{n}}$$
$$(H_a: p < p_0)$$

$$\text{Two-tailed test: } \hat{p}_{0,L} = p_0 - z_{\alpha/2}\sigma_p = p_0 - z_{\alpha/2}\sqrt{\frac{p_0q_0}{n}}$$
$$(H_a: p \neq p_0)$$

$$\hat{p}_{0,U} = p_0 + z_{\alpha/2}\sigma_p = p_0 + z_{\alpha/2}\sqrt{\frac{p_0q_0}{n}}$$

2. Specify the value of p_a in the alternative hypothesis for which the value of β is to be calculated. Then covert the border values of $\hat{p}_0$ to z-value(s), using the alternative distribution with mean p_a. The general formula for the z-value is:

$$z = (\hat{p}_0 - p_a)/\sigma_p = \frac{\hat{p}_0 - p_a}{\sqrt{\frac{p_0q_0}{n}}}$$

3. Sketch the alternative distribution (centered at p_a), and shade the area in the acceptance (nonrejection) region. Use the z-statistic(s) and Table II of Appendix: Tables to find the shaded area, which is β.

$$\text{Upper-tailed test: } \beta = P\left(z < \frac{\hat{p}_0 - p_a}{\sqrt{\frac{p_0q_0}{n}}}\right)$$

$$(H_a: p > p_0)$$

$$\text{Lower-tailed test: } \beta = P\left(z > \frac{\hat{p}_0 - p_a}{\sqrt{\frac{p_0q_0}{n}}}\right)$$

$$(H_a: p < p_0)$$

$$\text{Two-tailed test: } \beta = P\left(\frac{\hat{p}_{0,L} - p_a}{\sqrt{\frac{p_0q_0}{n}}} < z < \frac{\hat{p}_{0,U} - p_a}{\sqrt{\frac{p_0q_0}{n}}}\right)$$

$$(H_a: p \neq p_0)$$

Following the calculation of β for a particular value of the parameter in H_a you should interpret the value in the context of the hypothesis-testing application. It is often useful to interpret the value of $1 - \beta$, which is known as the **power of the test** corresponding to a particular alternative, say, μ_a for a population mean. Since β is the probability of accepting the null hypothesis when the alternative hypothesis is true with $\mu = \mu_a$, $1 - \beta$ is the probability of the complementary event, or the probability of rejecting the null hypothesis when the alternative $H_a: \mu = \mu_a$ is true. That is, the power $(1 - \beta)$ measures the likelihood that the test procedure will lead to the correct decision (reject H_0) for a particular value of the mean (or proportion) in the alternative hypothesis.

The **power of a test** is the probability that the test will correctly lead to the rejection of the null hypothesis for a particular value of μ or p in the alternative hypothesis. The power is equal to $(1 - \beta)$ for the particular alternative considered.

For example, in the sewer pipe example we found that $\beta = .7764$ when $\mu = 2,425$. This is the probability that the test leads to the (incorrect) acceptance of the null hypothesis when $\mu = 2,425$. Or, equivalently, the power of the test is $1 - .7764 = .2236$, which means that the test will lead to the (correct) rejection of the null hypothesis only 22% of the time when the pipe exceeds specifications by 25 pounds per linear foot. When the manufacturer's pipe has a mean strength of 2,475 (that is, 75 pounds per linear foot in excess of specifications), the power of the test increases to $1 - .1562 = .8438$— that is, the test will lead to the acceptance of the manufacturer's pipe 84% of the time if $\mu = 2,475$.

Example **13**	**Problem** Recall the quality-control study in Example 5, in which we tested to determine whether a cereal box filling machine was deviating from the specified mean fill of $\mu = 12$ ounces. The test setup is repeated here:
The Power of a Test— Quality-Control Study	

$$H_0: \mu = 12$$
$$H_a: \mu \neq 12 \ (\text{i.e., } \mu < 12 \text{ or } \mu > 12)$$

Test statistic: $z = \dfrac{\bar{x} - 12}{\sigma_{\bar{x}}}$

Rejection region: $z < -1.96$ or $z > 1.96$ for $\alpha = .05$
$$z < -2.575 \text{ or } z > 2.575 \text{ for } \alpha = .01$$

Note that two rejection regions have been specified corresponding to values of $\alpha = .05$ and $\alpha = .01$, respectively. Assume that $n = 100$ and $s = .5$.

a. Suppose the machine is underfilling the boxes by an average of .1 ounce (i.e., $\mu = 11.9$). Calculate the values of β corresponding to the two rejection regions. Discuss the relationship between the values of α and β.

b. Calculate the power of the test for each of the rejection regions when $\mu = 11.9$.

Solution

a. We first consider the rejection region corresponding to $\alpha = .05$. The first step is to calculate the border values of $\bar{x}$ corresponding to the two-tailed rejection region, $z < -1.96$ or $z > 1.96$:

$$\bar{x}_{0,L} = \mu_0 - 1.96\sigma_{\bar{x}} \approx \mu_0 - 1.96\left(\frac{s}{\sqrt{n}}\right) = 12 - 1.96\left(\frac{.5}{10}\right) = 11.902$$

$$\bar{x}_{0,U} = \mu_0 + 1.96\sigma_{\bar{x}} \approx \mu_0 + 1.96\left(\frac{s}{\sqrt{n}}\right) = 12 + 1.96\left(\frac{.5}{10}\right) = 12.098$$

These border values are shown in Figure 27a.

Next, we convert these values to z-values in the alternative distribution with $\mu_a = 11.9$:

$$z_L = \frac{\bar{x}_{0,L} - \mu_a}{\sigma_{\bar{x}}} \approx \frac{11.902 - 11.9}{.05} = .04$$

$$z_U = \frac{\bar{x}_{0,U} - \mu_a}{\sigma_{\bar{x}}} \approx \frac{12.098 - 11.9}{.05} = 3.96$$

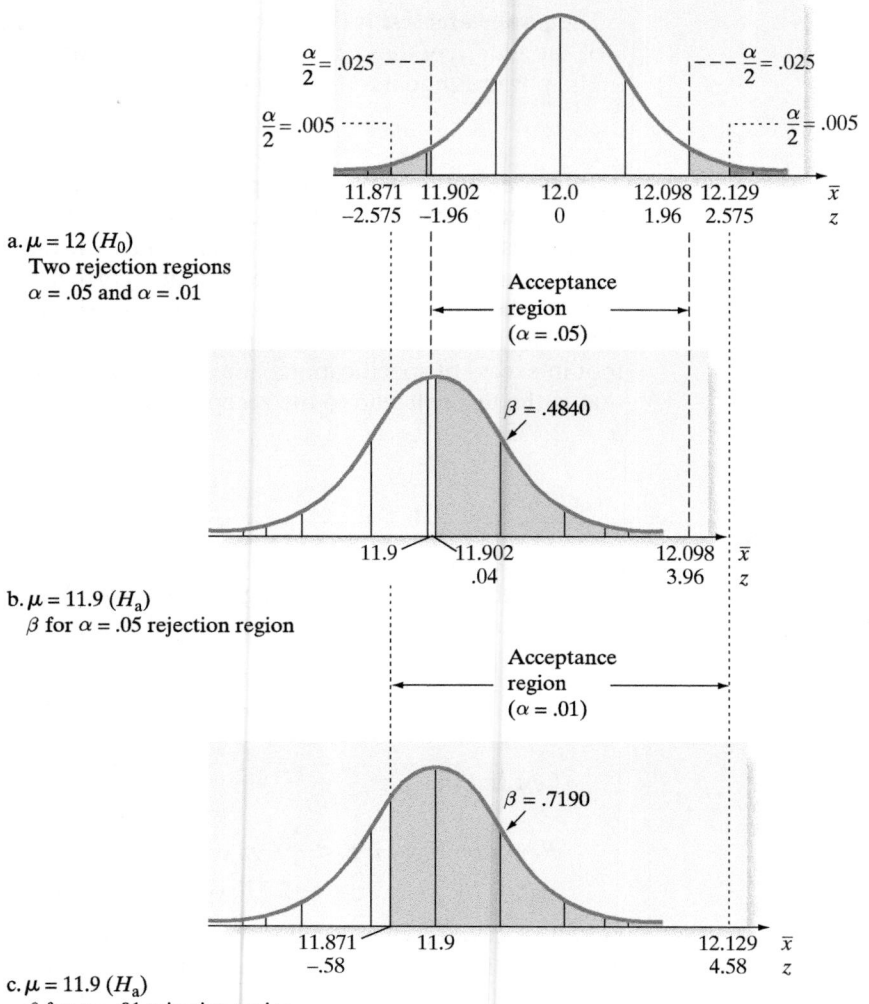

a. $\mu = 12$ (H_0)
Two rejection regions
$\alpha = .05$ and $\alpha = .01$

b. $\mu = 11.9$ (H_a)
β for $\alpha = .05$ rejection region

c. $\mu = 11.9$ (H_a)
β for $\alpha = .01$ rejection region

Figure 27

Calculation of β for filling machine process, Example 13

These z-values are shown in Figure 27b: You can see that the acceptance (or nonrejection) region is the area between them. Using Table II in Appendix: Tables, we find that the area between $z = 0$ and $z = .04$ is .0160, and the area between $z = 0$ and $z = 3.96$ is (approximately) .5 (because $z = 3.96$ is off the scale of Table II). Then the area between $z = .04$ and $z = 3.96$ is, approximately,

$$\beta = .5 - .0160 = .4840$$

Thus, the test with $\alpha = .05$ will lead to a Type II error about 48% of the time when the machine is underfilling, on average, by .1 ounce.

For the rejection region corresponding to $\alpha = .01$, $z < -2.575$, or $z > 2.575$, we find

$$\bar{x}_{0,L} = 12 - 2.575\left(\frac{.5}{10}\right) = 11.871$$

$$\bar{x}_{0,U} = 12 + 2.575\left(\frac{.5}{10}\right) = 12.129$$

These border values of the rejection region are shown in Figure 27c.

Converting these two border values to z-values in the alternative distribution with $\mu_a = 11.9$, we find $z_L = -.58$ and $z_U = 4.58$. The area between these values is, approximately,

$$\beta = P(-.58 < z < 4.58) = .2190 + .5 = .7190$$

Thus, the chance that the test procedure with $\alpha = .01$ will lead to an incorrect acceptance of H_0 is about 72%.

Note that the value of β increases from .4840 to .7190 when we decrease the value of α from .05 to .01. This is a general property of the relationship between α and β: *as α is decreased (increased), β is increased (decreased).*

b. The power is defined to be the probability of (correctly) rejecting the null hypothesis when the alternative is true. When $\mu = 11.9$ and $\alpha = .05$, we find

$$\text{Power} = 1 - \beta = 1 - .4840 = .5160$$

When $\mu = 11.9$ and $\alpha = .01$, we find

$$\text{Power} = 1 - \beta = 1 - .7190 = .2810$$

You can see that the power of the test is decreased as the level of α is decreased. This means that as the probability of incorrectly rejecting the null hypothesis is decreased, the probability of correctly accepting the null hypothesis for a given alternative is also decreased.

Look Back A key point of this example is that the value of α must be selected carefully, with the realization that a test is made less capable of detecting departures from the null hypothesis when the value of α is decreased.

Now Work Exercise 102

Note: Most statistical software packages now have options for computing the power of standard tests of hypothesis. Usually you will need to specify the type of test (z-test or t-test), form of H_a ($<$, $>$, or $\neq$), standard deviation, sample size, and the value of the parameter in H_a (or the difference between the value in H_0 and the value in H_a). The Minitab power analysis for Example 13 when $\alpha = .05$ is displayed in Figure 28. The power of the test (.516) is highlighted on the printout.

Power and Sample Size

```
1-Sample Z Test

Testing mean = null (versus not = null)
Calculating power for mean = null + difference
Alpha = 0.05   Assumed standard deviation = 0.5
```

Figure 28

Minitab power analysis for Example 13

```
               Sample
Difference      Size      Power
      0.1        100   0.516005
```

We have shown that the probability of committing a Type II error, β, is inversely related to α (Example 13) and that the value of β decreases as the value of μ_a moves farther from the null hypothesis value (sewer pipe example). The sample size n also affects β. Remember that the standard deviation of the sampling distribution of $\bar{x}$ is inversely proportional to the square root of the sample size ($\sigma_{\bar{x}} = \sigma/\sqrt{n}$). Thus, as illustrated in Figure 29, the variability of both the null and alternative sampling distributions is decreased as n is increased. If the value of α is specified and remains fixed, the value of β decreases as n increases, as illustrated in Figure 29. Conversely, the power of the test for a given alternative hypothesis is increased as the sample size is increased. The properties of β and power are summarized in the box.

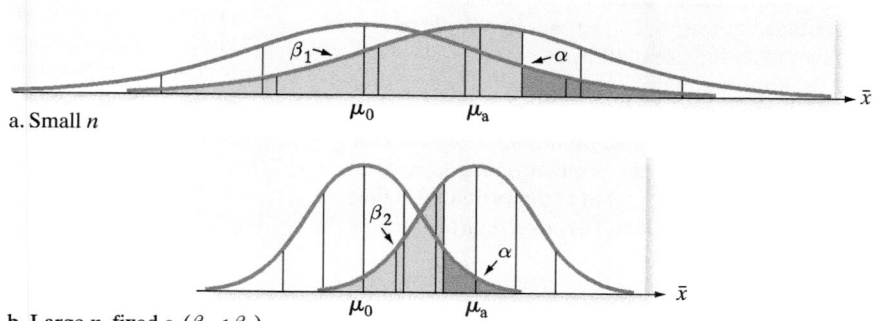

a. Small n

Figure 29

Relationship between α, β, and n

b. Large n, fixed α ($\beta_2 < \beta_1$)

> ### Properties of β and Power
>
> 1. For fixed n and α, the value of β decreases, and the power increases as the distance between the specified null value μ_0 (or, p_0) and the specified alternative value μ_a (or, p_a) increases (see Figure 26).
> 2. For fixed n and values of μ_0 and μ_a (or, p_0 and p_a), the value of β increases, and the power decreases as the value of α is decreased (see Figure 27).
> 3. For fixed α and values of μ_0 and μ_a (or, p_0 and p_a), the value of β decreases, and the power increases as the sample size n is increased (see Figure 29).

Exercises 96–107

Learning the Mechanics

96 a. List three factors that will increase the power of a test.
b. What is the relationship between β, the probability of committing a Type II error, and the power of a test?

97 Suppose you want to test H_0: $\mu = 500$ against H_a: $\mu > 500$ using $\alpha = .05$. The population in question is normally distributed with standard deviation 100. A random sample of size $n = 25$ will be used.
a. Sketch the sampling distribution of $\bar{x}$ assuming that H_0 is true.
b. Find the value of $\bar{x}_0$, that value of $\bar{x}$ above which the null hypothesis will be rejected. Indicate the rejection region on your graph of part **a**. Shade the area above the rejection region and label it α.
c. On your graph of part **a**, sketch the sampling distribution of $\bar{x}$ if $\mu = 550$. Shade the area under this distribution that corresponds to the probability that $\bar{x}$ falls in the nonrejection region when $\mu = 550$. Label this area β.
d. Find β.
e. Compute the power of this test for detecting the alternative H_a: $\mu = 550$.

98 Refer to Exercise 97.
a. If $\mu = 575$ instead of 550, what is the probability that the hypothesis test will incorrectly fail to reject H_0? That is, what is β?
b. If $\mu = 575$, what is the probability that the test will correctly reject the null hypothesis? That is, what is the power of the test?
c. Compare β and the power of the test when $\mu = 575$ to the values you obtained in Exercise 97 for $\mu = 550$. Explain the differences.

99 It is desired to test H_0: $\mu = 75$ against H_a: $\mu < 75$ using $\alpha = .10$. The population in question is uniformly distributed with standard deviation 15. A random sample of size 49 will be drawn from the population.
a. Describe the (approximate) sampling distribution of $\bar{x}$ under the assumption that H_0 is true.
b. Describe the (approximate) sampling distribution of $\bar{x}$ under the assumption that the population mean is 70.
c. If μ were really equal to 70, what is the probability that the hypothesis test would lead the investigator to commit a Type II error?
d. What is the power of this test for detecting the alternative H_a: $\mu = 70$?

100 Refer to Exercise 99.
a. Find β for each of the following values of the population mean: 74, 72, 70, 68, and 66.
b. Plot each value of β you obtained in part **a** against its associated population mean. Show β on the vertical axis and μ on the horizontal axis. Draw a curve through the five points on your graph.
c. Use your graph of part **b** to find the approximate probability that the hypothesis test will lead to a Type II error when $\mu = 73$.
d. Convert each of the β values you calculated in part **a** to the power of the test at the specified value of μ. Plot the power on the vertical axis against μ on the horizontal axis. Compare the graph of part **b** to the *power curve* of this part.
e. Examine the graphs of parts **b** and **d**. Explain what they reveal about the relationships among the distance between the true mean μ and the null hypothesized mean μ_0, the value of β, and the power.

101 Suppose you want to conduct the two-tailed test of H_0: $p = .7$ against H_a: $p \neq .7$ using $\alpha = .05$. A random sample of size 100 will be drawn from the population in question.
a. Describe the sampling distribution of $\hat{p}$ under the assumption that H_0 is true.
b. Describe the sampling distribution of $\hat{p}$ under the assumption that $p = .65$.
c. If p were really equal to .65, find the value of β associated with the test.
d. Find the value of β for the alternative H_a: $p = .71$.

Applying the Concepts—Intermediate

102 Square footage of new California homes. The average size of single-family homes built in the United States is 2,390 square feet (*Statistical Abstract of the United States*, 2011). A random sample of 100 new homes sold in California yielded the following size information: $\bar{x} = 2,507$ square feet and $s = 257$ square feet.
a. Assume the average size of U.S. homes is known with certainty. Do the sample data provide sufficient evidence to conclude that the mean size of California homes built exceeds the national average? Test using $\alpha = .01$.
b. Suppose the actual mean size of new California homes was 2,490 square feet. What is the power of the test in part **a** to detect this 100-square-foot difference?

c. If the California mean were actually 2,440 square feet, what is the power of the test in part **a** to detect this 50-square-foot difference?

103 Manufacturers that practice sole sourcing. If a manufacturer (the vendee) buys all items of a particular type from a particular vendor, the manufacturer is practicing *sole sourcing* (Schonberger and Knod, *Operations Management*, 2001). As part of a sole-sourcing arrangement, a vendor agrees to periodically supply its vendee with sample data from its production process. The vendee uses the data to investigate whether the mean length of rods produced by the vendor's production process is truly 5.0 millimeters (mm) or more, as claimed by the vendor and desired by the vendee.

a. If the production process has a standard deviation of .01 mm, the vendor supplies $n = 100$ items to the vendee, and the vendee uses $\alpha = .05$ in testing $H_0: \mu = 5.0$ mm against $H_a: \mu < 5.0$ mm, what is the probability that the vendee's test will fail to reject the null hypothesis when in fact $\mu = 4.9975$ mm? What is the name given to this type of error?

b. Refer to part **a.** What is the probability that the vendee's test will reject the null hypothesis when in fact $\mu = 5.0$? What is the name given to this type of error?

c. What is the power of the test to detect a departure of .0025 mm below the specified mean rod length of 5.0 mm?

104 Satellite radio in cars. Refer to the National Association of Broadcasters (NAB) survey of 501 satellite radio subscribers, Exercise 70. Recall that an NAB spokesperson claims that 80% of all satellite radio subscribers have a satellite radio receiver in their car. You conducted a test to determine if the claimed value is too high using $\alpha = .10$. What is the probability that the test will conclude that the claim is too high, if in fact the true percentage of all satellite radio subscribers who have a satellite radio receiver in their car is 82%?

105 Gummi Bears: Red or yellow? Refer to the *Chance* (Winter 2010) experiment to determine if color of a Gummi Bear is related to its flavor, Exercise 72. You tested the null hypothesis of $p = .5$ against the two-tailed alternative hypothesis of $p \neq .5$ using $\alpha = .01$, where p represents the true proportion of blind folded students who correctly identified the color of the Gummi Bear. Recall that of the 121 students who participated in the study, 97 correctly identified the color. Find the power of the test if the true proportion is $p = .65$.

106 Fuel economy of the Honda Civic. According to the Environmental Protection Agency (EPA) *Fuel Economy Guide,* the 2011 Honda Civic automobile obtains a mean of 36 miles per gallon (mpg) on the highway. Suppose Honda claims that the EPA has underestimated the Civic's mileage. To support its assertion, the company selects $n = 50$ model 2011 Civic cars and records the mileage obtained for each car over a driving course similar to the one used by the EPA. The following data resulted: $\bar{x} = 38.3$ mpg, $s = 6.4$ mpg.

a. If Honda wishes to show that the mean mpg for 2011 Civic autos is greater than 36 mpg, what should the alternative hypothesis be? The null hypothesis?

b. Do the data provide sufficient evidence to support the auto manufacturer's claim? Test using $\alpha = .05$. List any assumptions you make in conducting the test.

c. Calculate the power of the test for the mean values of 36.5, 37.0, 37.5, 38.0, and 38.5, assuming $s = 6.4$ is a good estimate of σ.

d. Plot the power of the test on the vertical axis against the mean on the horizontal axis. Draw a curve through the points.

e. Use the power curve of part **d** to estimate the power for the mean value $\mu = 37.75$. Calculate the power for this value of μ and compare it to your approximation.

f. Use the power curve to approximate the power of the test when $\mu = 41$. If the true value of the mean mpg for this model is really 41, what (approximately) are the chances that the test will fail to reject the null hypothesis that the mean is 36?

107 Solder-joint inspections. Refer to Exercise 44 in which the performance of a particular type of laser-based inspection equipment was investigated. Assume that the standard deviation of the number of solder joints inspected on each run is 1.2. If $\alpha = .05$ is used in conducting the hypothesis test of interest using a sample of 48 circuit boards, and if the true mean number of solder joints that can be inspected is really equal to 9.5, what is the probability that the test will result in a Type II error?

☐ Chapter Notes

Key Terms

Note: Asterisks (*) denote items from the optional sections of this chapter.

Alternative (research) hypothesis
Chi-square sampling distribution
Conclusions
Hypothesis
Level of significance
Lower-tailed test
Null distribution
Null hypothesis
Observed significance level (*p*-value)

One-tailed (one-sided) statistical test
*Power of the test
Rejection region
Test of hypothesis
Test statistic
Two-tailed (two-sided) hypothesis
Type I error
Type II error
Upper-tailed test

Key Symbols

μ	Population mean
p	Population proportion, $P(\text{Success})$, in binomial trial
σ^2	Population variance
$\bar{x}$	Sample mean (estimator of μ)
$\hat{p}$	Sample proportion (estimator of p)
s^2	Sample variance (estimator of σ^2)
H_0	Null hypothesis
H_a	Alternative hypothesis
α	Probability of a Type I error
β	Probability of a Type II error
χ^2	Chi-square (sampling distribution of s^2 for normal data)

Key Ideas

Key Words for Identifying the Target Parameter

μ—Mean, Average
p—Proportion, Fraction, Percentage, Rate, Probability
σ^2—Variance, Variability, Spread

Elements of a Hypothesis Test

1. *Null hypothesis* (H_0)
2. *Alternative hypothesis* (H_a)
3. *Test statistic* $(z, t, or \chi^2)$
4. *Significance level* (α)
5. *p-value*
6. *Conclusion*

Probabilities in Hypothesis Testing

$\alpha = P(\textbf{Type I Error}) = P(\text{Reject } H_0 \text{ when } H_0 \text{ is true})$
$\beta = P(\textbf{Type II Error}) = P(\text{Accept } H_0 \text{ when } H_0 \text{ is false})$
$1 - \beta = \textbf{Power of a Test} = P(\text{Reject } H_0 \text{ when } H_0 \text{ is false})$

Forms of Alternative Hypothesis

Lower-tailed: $H_a\text{: } \mu < 50$
Upper-tailed: $H_a\text{: } \mu > 50$
Two-tailed: $H_a\text{: } \mu \neq 50$

Using p-Values to Decide

1. Choose significance level (α)
2. Obtain *p*-value of the test
3. If $\alpha > p$-value, reject H_0

Guide to Selecting a One-Sample Hypothesis Test

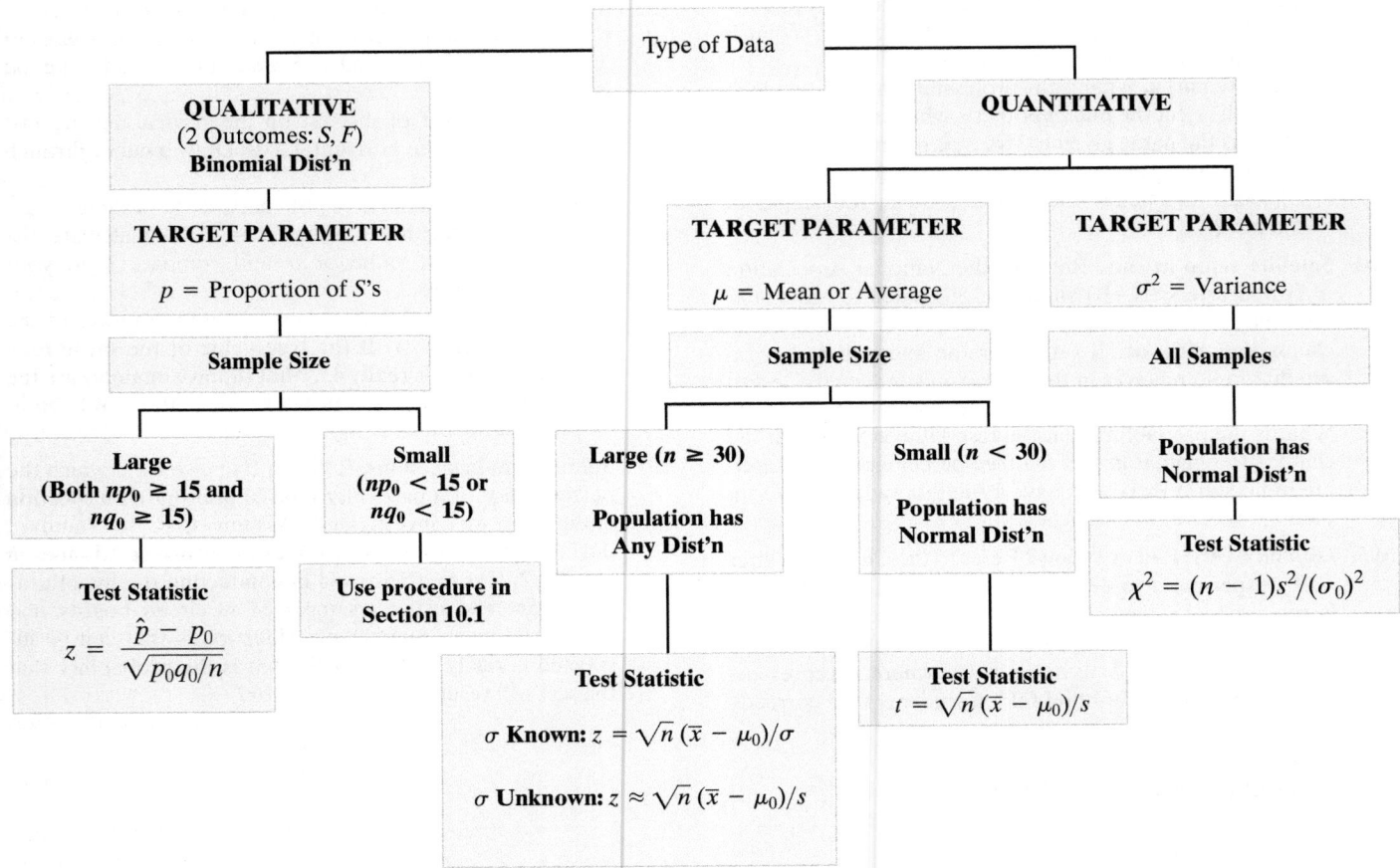

Supplementary Exercises 108–145

Please be aware that some of the following problems may require knowledge of concepts that are not presented in this chapter.

Note: List the assumptions necessary for the valid implementation of the statistical procedures you use in solving all these exercises. Exercises marked with an asterisk (*) are from the optional section in this chapter.

Learning the Mechanics

108 Specify the differences between a large-sample and small-sample test of hypothesis about a population mean μ. Focus on the assumptions and test statistics.

109 *Complete the following statement:* The smaller the *p*-value associated with a test of hypothesis, the stronger the support for the ____ hypothesis. Explain your answer.

110 Which of the elements of a test of hypothesis can and should be specified *prior* to analyzing the data that are to be used to conduct the test?

111 If you select a very small value for α when conducting a hypothesis test, will β tend to be big or small? Explain.

112 If the rejection of the null hypothesis of a particular test would cause your firm to go out of business, would you want α to be small or large? Explain.

113 A random sample of 20 observations selected from a normal population produced $\bar{x} = 72.6$ and $s^2 = 19.4$.
  a. Test $H_0: \mu = 80$ against $H_a: \mu < 80$. Use $\alpha = .05$.
  b. Test $H_0: \mu = 80$ against $H_a: \mu \neq 80$. Use $\alpha = .01$.

114 A random sample of 175 measurements possessed a mean $\bar{x} = 8.2$ and a standard deviation $s = .79$.
  a. Test $H_0: \mu = 8.3$ against $H_a: \mu \neq 8.3$. Use $\alpha = .05$.
  b. Test $H_0: \mu = 8.4$ against $H_a: \mu \neq 8.4$. Use $\alpha = .05$.
  c. Test $H_0: \sigma = 1$ against $H_a: \sigma \neq 1$. Use $\alpha = .05$.
  *d. Find the power of the test, part **a**, if $\mu_a = 8.5$.

115 A random sample of $n = 200$ observations from a binomial population yields $\hat{p} = .29$.
  a. Test $H_0: p = .35$ against $H_a: p < .35$. Use $\alpha = .05$.
  b. Test $H_0: p = .35$ against $H_a: p \neq .35$. Use $\alpha = .05$.

116 A t-test is conducted for the null hypothesis $H_0: \mu = 10$ versus the alternative $H_a: \mu > 10$ for a random sample of $n = 17$ observations. The test results are $t = 1.174$, p-value $= .1288$.
  a. Interpret the p-value.
  b. What assumptions are necessary for the validity of this test?
  c. Calculate and interpret the p-value assuming the alternative hypothesis was instead $H_a: \mu \neq 10$.

117 A random sample of 41 observations from a normal population possessed a mean $\bar{x} = 88$ and a standard deviation $s = 6.9$.
  a. Test $H_0: \sigma^2 = 30$ against $H_a: \sigma^2 > 30$. Use $\alpha = .05$.
  b. Test $H_0: \sigma^2 = 30$ against $H_a: \sigma^2 \neq 30$. Use $\alpha = .05$.

Applying the Concepts—Basic

118 **Latex allergy in health care workers.** *Current Allergy & Clinical Immunology* (Mar. 2004) did a study of $n = 46$ hospital employees who were diagnosed with a latex allergy from exposure to the powder on latex gloves. The number of latex gloves used per week by the sampled workers is summarized as follows: $\bar{x} = 19.3$ and $s = 11.9$. Let μ represent the mean number of latex gloves used per week by all hospital employees. Consider testing $H_0: \mu = 20$ against $H_a: \mu < 20$.
  a. Give the rejection region for the test at a significance level of $\alpha = .01$.
  b. Calculate the value of the test statistic.
  c. Use the results, parts **a** and **b**, to make the appropriate conclusion.

119 **Latex allergy in health care workers (cont'd).** Refer to Exercise 118. Let σ^2 represent the variance in the number of latex gloves used per week by all hospital employees. Consider testing $H_0: \sigma^2 = 100$ against $H_a: \sigma^2 \neq 100$.
  a. Give the rejection region for the test at a significance level of $\alpha = .01$.
  b. Calculate the value of the test statistic.
  c. Use the results, parts **a** and **b**, to make the appropriate conclusion.

120 **"Made in the USA" survey.** Refer to the *Journal of Global Business* (Spring 2002) study of what "Made in the USA" means to consumers. Recall that 64 of 106 randomly selected shoppers believed "Made in the USA" means 100% of labor and materials are from the United States. Let p represent the true proportion of consumers who believe "Made in the USA" means 100% of labor and materials are from the United States.
  a. Calculate a point estimate for p.
  b. A claim is made that $p = .70$. Set up the null and alternative hypotheses to test this claim.
  c. Calculate the test statistic for the test, part **b**.
  d. Find the rejection region for the test if $\alpha = .01$.
  e. Use the results, parts **c** and **d**, to make the appropriate conclusion.

121 **Beta value of a stock.** The "beta coefficient" of a stock is a measure of the stock's volatility (or risk) relative to the market as a whole. Stocks with beta coefficients greater than 1 generally bear greater risk (more volatility) than the market, whereas stocks with beta coefficients less than 1 are less risky (less volatile) than the overall market (Alexander, Sharpe, and Bailey, *Fundamentals of Investments*, 2000). A random sample of 15 high-technology stocks was selected at the end of 2009, and the mean and standard deviation of the beta coefficients were calculated: $\bar{x} = 1.23$, $s = .37$.
  a. Set up the appropriate null and alternative hypotheses to test whether the average high-technology stock is riskier than the market as a whole.
  b. Establish the appropriate test statistic and rejection region for the test. Use $\alpha = .10$.
  c. What assumptions are necessary to ensure the validity of the test?
  d. Calculate the test statistic and state your conclusion.
  e. What is the approximate p-value associated with this test? Interpret it.
  f. Conduct a test to determine if the variance of the stock beta values differs from .15. Use $\alpha = .05$.

122 **Accuracy of price scanners at Wal-Mart.** A study was done of the accuracy of checkout scanners at Wal-Mart stores in California. The National Institute for Standards and Technology (NIST) mandates that for every 100 items scanned through the electronic checkout scanner at a retail store, no more than two should have an inaccurate price. A study of random items purchased at California Wal-Mart stores found that 8.3% had the wrong price (*Tampa Tribune*, Nov. 22, 2005). Assume that the study included 1,000 randomly selected items.
  a. Identify the population parameter of interest in the study.
  b. Set up H_0 and H_a for a test to determine if the true proportion of items scanned at California Wal-Mart stores exceeds the 2% NIST standard.
  c. Find the test statistic and rejection region (at $\alpha = .05$) for the test.
  d. Give a practical interpretation of the test.
  e. What conditions are required for the inference, part **d**, to be valid? Are these conditions met?

123 **A camera that detects liars.** According to *New Scientist* (Jan. 2, 2002), a new thermal imaging camera that detects small temperature changes is now being used as a polygraph device. The U.S. Department of Defense Polygraph Institute (DDPI) claims the camera can correctly detect liars 75% of the time by monitoring the temperatures of their faces.

a. Give the null hypothesis for testing the claim made by the DDPI.

b. What is a Type I error for this problem? A Type II error?

124 Size of diamonds sold at retail. Refer to the *Journal of Statistics Education* data on diamonds saved in the file. Let μ represent the mean number of carats in the population of 308 diamonds. Suppose you want to test H_0: $\mu = .6$ against H_a: $\mu \neq .6$.

a. In the words of the problem, define a Type I error and a Type II error.

b. Use the sample information to conduct the test at a significance level of $\alpha = .05$.

c. Conduct the test, part **b**, using $\alpha = .10$.

d. What do the results suggest about the choice of α in a test of hypothesis?

125 Cost-of-living index. Each year, Kiplinger's complies its list of *Best Value Cities*. One of the statistics used in the rankings is the cost-of-living index, complied by the U.S. Bureau of Labor Statistics. The index measures the cost of living in a city relative to the national average of 100. In 2011, the New York metropolitan area had a cost-of-living index of 218, the highest in the nation. This means that the cost of living in New York City is 118% higher than the average cost of living for the nation. In contrast, Pueblo, Colorado, had the lowest cost-of-living index (84). The table lists the cost-of-living index for each in a sample of seven Southeastern cities.

City	Cost-of-living Index (U.S. mean = 100)
Charlotte, NC	93.0
Birmingham, AL	89.6
Florence, SC	100.0
Tampa, FL	92.1
Atlanta, GA	95.2
Knoxville, TN	89.7
Miami, FL	107.7

Source: Data from U.S. Bureau of Labor Statistics, 2011.

a. Specify the null and alternative hypotheses for testing whether the true mean cost-of-living index for Southeastern cities differs from the national cost-of-living index of 100.

b. What assumptions about the sample and population must hold in order for the test, part **a**, to yield valid results?

c. Conduct the hypothesis test using $\alpha = .05$.

d. Is the observed significance level of the test greater or less than .05? Justify your answer.

Applying the Concepts—Intermediate

126 Consumers' use of discount coupons. In 1894, druggist Asa Candler began distributing handwritten tickets to his customers for free glasses of Coca-Cola at his soda fountain. That was the genesis of the discount coupon. In 1975, it was estimated that 65% of U.S. consumers regularly used discount coupons when shopping. In a more recent consumer survey, 72% said they regularly redeem coupons (Prospectiv 2008 Consumer Coupon Poll). Assume the recent survey consisted of a random sample of 1,000 shoppers.

a. Does the survey provide sufficient evidence that the percentage of shoppers using cents-off coupons exceeds 65%? Test using $\alpha = .05$.

b. Is the sample size large enough to use the inferential procedures presented in this section? Explain.

c. Find the observed significance level for the test you conducted in part **a** and interpret its value.

127 Errors in medical tests. Medical tests have been developed to detect many serious diseases. A medical test is designed to minimize the probability that it will produce a "false positive" or a "false negative." A *false positive* refers to a positive test result for an individual who does not have the disease, whereas a false negative is a negative test result for an individual who does have the disease.

a. If we treat a medical test for a disease as a statistical test of hypothesis, what are the null and alternative hypotheses for the medical test?

b. What are the Type I and Type II errors for the test? Relate each to false positives and false negatives.

c. Which of the errors has graver consequences? Considering this error, is it more important to minimize α or β? Explain.

128 Drivers' use of the Lincoln Tunnel. The Lincoln Tunnel (under the Hudson River) connects suburban New Jersey to midtown Manhattan. On Mondays at 8:30 A.M., the mean number of cars waiting in line to pay the Lincoln Tunnel toll is 1,220. Because of the substantial wait during rush hour, the Port Authority of New York and New Jersey is considering raising the amount of the toll between 7:30 and 8:30 A.M. to encourage more drivers to use the tunnel at an earlier or later time. Suppose the Port Authority experiments with peak-hour pricing for 6 months, increasing the toll from $4 to $7 during the rush hour peak. On 10 different workdays at 8:30 A.M. aerial photographs of the tunnel queues are taken and the number of vehicles counted. The results follow:

1,260 1,052 1,201 942 1,062 999 931 849 867 735

Analyze the data for the purpose of determining whether peak-hour pricing succeeded in reducing the average number of vehicles attempting to use the Lincoln Tunnel during the peak rush hour.

129 Point spreads of NFL games. Refer to the *Chance* (Fall 1998) study of point-spread errors in NFL games, Exercise 41. Recall that the difference between the actual game outcome and the point spread established by odds makers—the point-spread error—was calculated for 240 NFL games. The results are summarized as follows: $\bar{x} = -1.6$, $s = 13.3$. Suppose the researcher wants to know whether the true standard deviation of the point-spread errors exceeds 15. Conduct the analysis using $\alpha = .10$.

130 Improving the productivity of chickens. *Applied Animal Behaviour Science* (Oct. 2000) did a study of the color of string preferred by pecking domestic chickens. $n = 72$ chickens were exposed to blue string and the number of pecks each chicken took at the string over a specified time interval had a mean of $\bar{x} = 1.13$ pecks and a standard deviation of $s = 2.21$ pecks. Previous research had shown that $\mu = 7.5$ pecks if chickens are exposed to white string.

a. Conduct a test (at $\alpha = .01$) to determine if the true mean number of pecks at blue string is less than $\mu = 7.5$ pecks.

b. Use a 99% confidence interval as evidence that chickens are more apt to peck at white string than blue string. Do the test results, part **a**, support this conclusion? Explain.

131 **Are manufacturers satisfied with trade promotions?** Sales promotions that are used by manufacturers to entice retailers to carry, feature, or push the manufacturer's products are called *trade promotions*. A survey of 132 manufacturers conducted by Nielsen found that 36% of the manufacturers were satisfied with their spending for trade promotions (*Survey of Trade Promotion Practices,* 2004). Is this sufficient evidence to reject a previous claim by the American Marketing Association that no more than half of all manufacturers are dissatisfied with their trade promotion spending?

a. Conduct the appropriate hypothesis test at $\alpha = .02$. Begin your analysis by determining whether the sample size is large enough to apply the testing methodology presented in this chapter.

b. Report the observed significance level of the test and interpret its meaning in the context of the problem.

c. Calculate β, the probability of a Type II error, if in fact 55% of all manufacturers are dissatisfied with their trade promotion spending.

132 **Arresting shoplifters.** Shoplifting in the United States costs retailers about $35 million a day. Despite the seriousness of the problem, the National Association of shoplifting Prevention (NASP) claims that only 50% of all shoplifters are turned over to police (www.shopliftingprevention.org). A random sample of 40 U.S. retailers were questioned concerning the disposition of the most recent shoplifter they apprehended. A total of 24 were turned over to police. Do these data provide sufficient evidence to contradict the NASP?

a. Conduct a hypothesis test to answer the question of interest. Use $\alpha = .05$.

b. Is the sample size large enough to use the inferential procedure of part **a**?

c. Find the observed significance level of the hypothesis test in part **a**. Interpret the value.

d. For what values of α would the observed significance level be sufficient to reject the null hypothesis of the test you conducted in part **b**?

* 133 **Arresting shoplifters (cont'd).** Refer to Exercise 132.

a. Describe a Type II error in terms of this application.

b. Calculate the probability β of a Type II error for this test assuming that the true fraction of shoplifters turned over to the police is $p = .55$.

c. Suppose the number of retailers sampled is increased from 40 to 100. How does this affect the probability of a Type II error for $p = .55$?

134 **Frequency marketing programs by restaurants.** To instill customer loyalty, airlines, hotels, rental car companies, **PROFIT** and credit card companies (among others) have initiated *frequency marketing programs* that reward their regular

customers. More than 80 million people are members of the frequent flier programs of the airline industry (www.frequentflier.com). A large fast-food restaurant chain wished to explore the profitability of such a program. They randomly selected 12 of their 1,200 restaurants nationwide and instituted a frequency program that rewarded customers with a $5.00 gift certificate after every 10 meals purchased at full price. They ran the trial program for 3 months. The restaurants not in the sample had an average increase in profits of $1,050 over the previous 3 months, whereas the restaurants in the sample had the following changes in profit.

$2,232.90	$ 545.47	$3,440.70	$1,809.10
$6,552.70	$4,798.70	$2,965.00	$2,610.70
$3,381.30	$1,591.40	$2,376.20	−$2,191.00

Note that the last number is negative, representing a decrease in profits.

a. Specify the appropriate null and alternative hypotheses for determining whether the mean profit change for restaurants with frequency programs was significantly greater (in a statistical sense) than $1,050.

b. Conduct the test of part **b** using $\alpha = .05$. Does it appear that the frequency program would be profitable for the company if adopted nationwide?

135 **EPA limits on vinyl chloride.** The EPA sets an airborne limit of 5 parts per million (ppm) on vinyl chloride, a colorless gas used to make plastics, adhesives, and other chemicals. It is both a carcinogen and a mutagen (New Jersey Department of Health, *Hazardous Substance Fact Sheet,* 2010). A major plastics manufacturer, attempting to control the amount of vinyl chloride its workers are exposed to, has given instructions to halt production if the mean amount of vinyl chloride in the air exceeds 3.0 ppm. A random sample of 50 air specimens produced the following statistics: $\bar{x} = 3.1$ ppm, $s = .5$ ppm.

a. Do these statistics provide sufficient evidence to halt the production process? Use $\alpha = .01$.

b. If you were the plant manager, would you want to use a large or a small value for α for the test in part **a**? Explain.

c. Find the p-value for the test and interpret its value.

* 136 **EPA limits vinyl chloride (cont'd).** Refer to Exercise 135.

a. In the context of the problem, define a Type II error.

b. Calculate β for the test described in part **a** of Exercise 135, assuming that the true mean is $\mu = 3.1$ ppm.

c. What is the power of the test to detect a departure from the manufacturer's 3.0 ppm limit when the mean is 3.1 ppm?

d. Repeat parts **b** and **c** assuming that the true mean is 3.2 ppm. What happens to the power of the test as the plant's mean vinyl chloride level departs further from the limit?

* 137 **EPA limits on vinyl chloride (cont'd).** Refer to Exercises 135 and 136.

a. Suppose an α value of .05 is used to conduct the test. Does this change favor halting production? Explain.

b. Determine the value of β and the power for the test when $\alpha = .05$ and $\mu = 3.1$.

c. What happens to the power of the test when α is increased?

138 Evaluating a measuring instrument. One way of evaluating a measuring instrument is to repeatedly measure the same item and compare the average of these measurements to the item's known measured value. The difference is used to assess the instrument's accuracy (American Society for Quality). To evaluate a particular Metlar scale, an item whose weight is known to be 16.01 ounces is weighed five times by the same operator. The measurements (in ounces) follow:

15.99	16.00	15.97	16.01	15.96

a. In a statistical sense, does the average measurement differ from 16.01? Conduct the appropriate hypothesis test at $\alpha = .05$. What does your analysis suggest about the accuracy of the instrument?

b. List any assumptions you make in conducting the hypothesis test, part **a.**

c. Evaluate the instrument's precision by testing whether the standard deviation of the weight measurements is greater than .01. Use $\alpha = .05$.

139 Graduation rates of student-athletes. Are student-athletes at Division I universities poorer students than non-athletes? The National Collegiate Athletic Association (NCAA) measures the academic outcomes of student-athletes with the Graduation Success Rate (GSR). The GSR is measured as the percentage of eligible athletes who graduate within 6 years of entering college. It is well known that the GSR for all students at Division I colleges is 60%.

a. Suppose the NCAA reports that in a sample of 500 student-athletes, 315 graduated within 6 years. Is this sufficient information to conclude that the GSR for all student athletes at Division I institutions differs from 60%? Test using $\alpha = .01$.

b. The GSR statistics are also broken down by gender and sport. It is known that the GSR for all male college students is 58%. In a sample of 200 male basketball players at Division I institutions, 84 graduated within 6 years. Is this sufficient information to conclude that the GSR for all male basketball players at Division I institutions differs from 58%? Test using $\alpha = .01$.

140 Feminized faces in TV commercials. Television commercials most often employ females or "feminized" males to pitch a company's product. Research published in *Nature* (Aug. 27, 1998) revealed that people are, in fact, more attracted to "feminized" faces, regardless of gender. In one experiment, 50 human subjects viewed both a Japanese female face and a Caucasian male face on a computer. Using special computer graphics, each subject could morph the faces (by making them more feminine or more masculine) until they attained the "most attractive" face. The level of feminization x (measured as a percentage) was measured.

a. For the Japanese female face, $\bar{x} = 10.2\%$ and $s = 31.3\%$. The researchers used this sample information to test the null hypothesis of a mean level of feminization equal to 0%. Verify that the test statistic is equal to 2.3.

b. Refer to part **a.** The researchers reported the *p*-value of the test as $p = .021$. Verify and interpret this result.

c. For the Caucasian male face, $\bar{x} = 15.0\%$ and $s = 25.1\%$. The researchers reported the test statistic (for the test of the null hypothesis stated in part **a**) as

4.23 with an associated *p*-value of approximately 0. Verify and interpret these results.

141 Identifying type of urban land cover. For planning purposes, urban land cover must be identified as either grassland, commercial, or residential. This is typically done using remote sensing data from satellite pictures. In *Geographical Analysis* (Oct. 2006), researchers from Arizona State, Florida State, and Louisiana State universities collaborated on a new method for analyzing remote sensing data. A satellite photograph of an urban area was divided into 4×4 meter areas (called pixels). Of interest is a numerical measure of the distribution of gaps or hole sizes in the pixel, called *lacunarity*. The mean and standard deviation of the lacunarity measurements for a sample of 100 pixels randomly selected from a specific urban area are 225 and 20, respectively. It is known that the mean lacunarity measurement for all grassland pixels is 220. Do the data suggest that the area sampled is grassland? Test at $\alpha = .01$.

Applying the Concepts—Advanced

142 Ages of cable TV shoppers. In a paper presented at the 2000 Conference of the International Association for Time Use Research, professor Margaret Sanik of Ohio State University reported the results of her study on American cable TV viewers who purchase items from one of the home shopping channels. She found that the average age of these cable TV shoppers was 51 years. Suppose you want to test the null hypothesis, H_0: $\mu = 51$, using a sample of $n = 50$ cable TV shoppers.

a. Find the *p*-value of a two-tailed test if $\bar{x} = 52.3$ and $s = 7.1$.

b. Find the *p*-value of an upper-tailed test if $\bar{x} = 52.3$ and $s = 7.1$.

c. Find the *p*-value of a two-tailed test if $\bar{x} = 52.3$ and $s = 10.4$.

d. For each of the tests, parts **a–c,** give a value of α that will lead to a rejection of the null hypothesis.

e. If $\bar{x} = 52.3$, give a value of s that will yield a two-tailed *p*-value of .01 or less.

143 Factors that inhibit learning in marketing. What factors inhibit the learning process in the classroom? To answer this question, researchers at Murray State University surveyed 40 students from a senior-level marketing class (*Marketing Education Review*). Each student was given a list of factors and asked to rate the extent to which each factor inhibited the learning process in courses offered in their department. A 7-point rating scale was used, where 1 = "not at all" and 7 = "to a great extent." The factor with the highest rating was instructor related: "Professors who place too much emphasis on a single right answer rather than overall thinking and creative ideas." Summary statistics for the student ratings of this factor are $\bar{x} = 4.70$, $s = 1.62$.

a. Conduct a test to determine if the true mean rating for this instructor-related factor exceeds 4. Use $\alpha = .05$. Interpret the test results.

b. Examine the results of the study from a practical view, then discuss why "statistically significant" does not always imply "practically significant."

c. Because the variable of interest, rating, is measured on a 7-point scale, it is unlikely that the population of ratings will be normally distributed. Consequently, some analysts may perceive the test, part **a**, to be invalid and search for alternative methods of analysis. Defend or refute this argument.

144 **Testing the placebo effect.** The *placebo effect* describes the phenomenon of improvement in the condition of a patient taking a placebo—a pill that looks and tastes real but contains no medically active chemicals. Physicians at a clinic in La Jolla, California, gave what they thought were drugs to 7,000 asthma, ulcer, and herpes patients. Although the doctors later learned that the drugs were really placebos, 70% of the patients reported an improved condition. Use this information to test (at $\alpha = .05$) the placebo effect at the clinic. Assume that if the placebo is ineffective, the probability of a patient's condition improving is .5.

Critical Thinking Challenge

145 **The hot tamale caper.** "Hot tamales" are chewy, cinnamon-flavored candies. A bulk vending machine is known to **TAMALE** dispense, on average, 15 hot tamales per bag with a standard deviation of 3 per bag. *Chance* (Fall 2000) published an article on a classroom project in which students were required to purchase bags of hot tamales from the machine and count the number of candies per bag. One student group claimed they purchased five bags that had the following candy counts: 25, 23, 21, 21, and 20. These data are saved in the file. There was some question as to whether the students had fabricated the data. Use a hypothesis test to gain insight into whether or not the data collected by the students were fabricated. Use a level of significance that gives the benefit of the doubt to the students.

Activity 1   *Challenging a Company's Claim:* Tests of Hypotheses

Use the Internet or a newspaper or magazine to find an example of a claim made by a company about the reliability or efficiency of one of its products. In this activity, you represent a consumer group that believes the claim may be false.

1. In your example, what kinds of evidence might exist that would cause one to suspect that the claim might be false and therefore worthy of a statistical study? Be specific. If the claim were false, how would consumers be hurt?

2. Describe what data are relevant and how those data may be collected.

3. Explain the steps necessary to reject the company's claim at level α. State the null and alternative hypotheses. If you reject the claim, does it mean that the claim is false?

4. If you reject the claim when the claim is actually true, what type of error has occurred? What is the probability of this error occurring?

5. If you were to file a lawsuit against the company based on your rejection of its claim, how might the company use your results to defend itself?

References

Snedecor, G. W., & Cochran, W. G. *Statistical Methods,* 7th ed. Ames: Iowa State University Press, 1980.

Wackerly, D., Mendenhall, W., & Scheaffer, R. *Mathematical Statistics with Applications,* 7th ed. Belmont, CA: Thomson, Brooks/Cole, 2008.

USING TECHNOLOGY Technology images shown here are taken from SPSS Statistics Professional 20.0, Minitab 16, XLSTAT for Pearson, and Excel 2010.

SPSS: Tests of Hypotheses

Note: SPSS cannot currently conduct a test for a population variance.

Testing μ

Step 1 Access the SPSS spreadsheet file that contains the sample data.

Step 2 Click on the "Analyze" button on the SPSS menu bar and then click on "Compare Means" and "One-Sample T Test," as shown in Figure S.1.

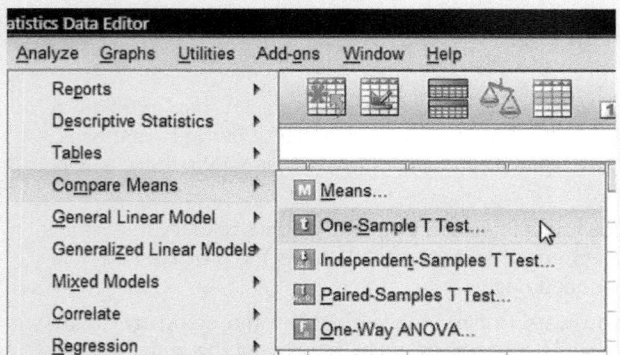

Figure S.1 SPSS menu options for a test on a mean

Step 3 On the resulting dialog box (shown in Figure S.2), specify the quantitative variable of interest in the "Test Variable(s)" box and the value of μ_0 for the null hypothesis in the "Test Value" box.

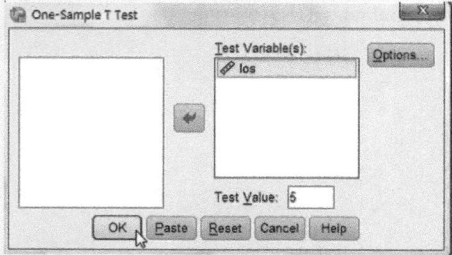

Figure S.2 SPSS 1-sample t-test for mean dialog box

Step 4 Click "OK." SPSS will automatically conduct a two-tailed test of hypothesis.

Important Note: The SPSS one-sample t-procedure uses the t-statistic to conduct the test of hypothesis. When the sample size n is small, this is the appropriate method. When the sample size n is large, the t-value will be approximately equal to the large-sample z-value and the resulting test will still be valid.

Testing p

Step 1 Access the SPSS spreadsheet file that contains the sample data.

Step 2 Click on the "Analyze" button on the SPSS menu bar, then click on "Nonparametric Tests," "Legacy Dialogs," and "Binomial" (see Figure S.3).

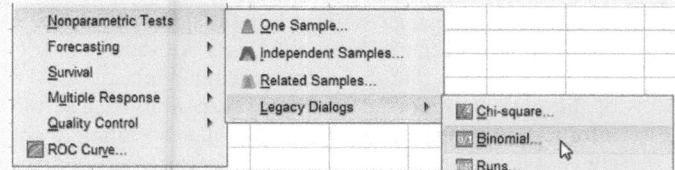

Figure S.3 SPSS menu options for test on a proportion

Step 3 On the resulting dialog box (shown in Figure S.4), specify the binomial variable of interest in the "Test Variable List" box and the value of p_0 for the null hypothesis in the "Test Proportion" box.

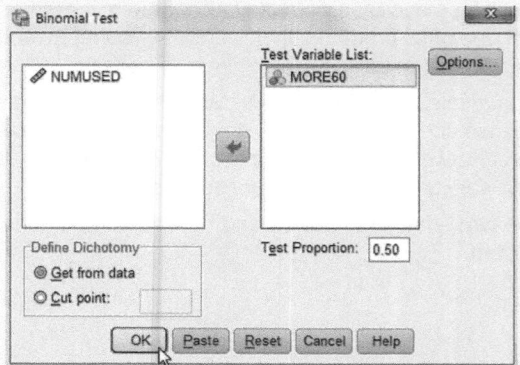

Figure S.4 SPSS binomial test for proportion dialog box

Step 4 Click "OK" to generate the two-tailed test of hypothesis.

Important: SPSS requires the binomial variable to be entered as a quantitative variable. Typically, this is accomplished by entering two numerical values (e.g., 0 and 1) for the two outcomes of the variable. If the data have been entered in this fashion, select the "Get from data" option in the "Define Dichotomy" area of the dialog box.

You can also create the two outcome values for a quantitative variable by selecting the "Cut point" option in the "Define Dichotomy" area and specifying a numerical value. All values of the variables less than or equal to the cut point value are assigned to one group (success), and all other values are assigned to the other group (failure).

Minitab: Tests of Hypotheses

Testing μ

Step 1 Access the Minitab data worksheet that contains the sample data.

Step 2 Click on the "Stat" button on the Minitab menu bar and then click on "Basic Statistics" and "1-Sample t," as shown in Figure M.1.

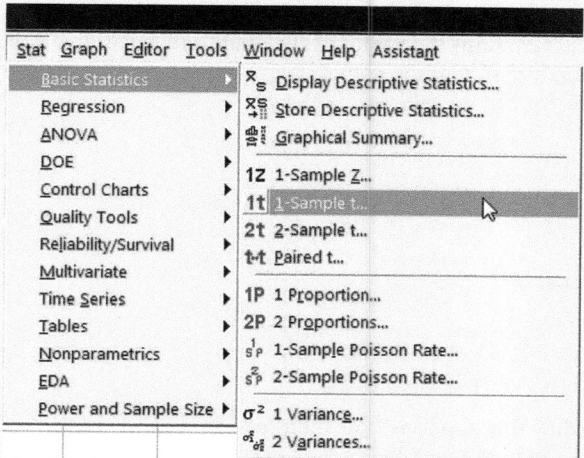

Figure M.1 Minitab menu options for a test on a mean

Step 3 On the resulting dialog box (shown in Figure M.2), click on "Samples in columns" and then specify the quantitative variable of interest in the open box.

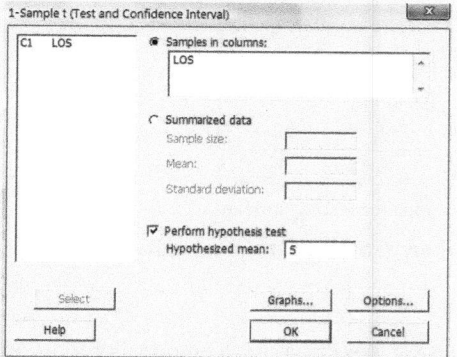

Figure M.2 Minitab 1-sample *t*-test for mean dialog box

Step 4 Check "Perform hypothesis test" and then specify the value of μ_0 for the null hypothesis in the "Hypothesized mean" box.

Step 5 Click on the "Options" button at the bottom of the dialog box and specify the form of the alternative hypothesis, as shown in Figure M.3.

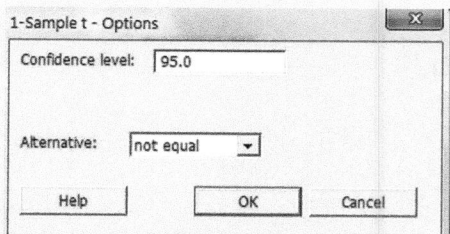

Figure M.3 Minitab 1-sample *t*-test options

Step 6 Click "OK" to return to the "1-Sample t" dialog box and then click "OK" again to produce the hypothesis test.

Note: If you want to produce a test for the mean from summary information (e.g., the sample mean, sample standard deviation, and sample size), click on "Summarized data" in the "1-Sample t" dialog box, enter the values of the summary statistics and μ_0, and then click "OK."

Important: The Minitab one-sample *t*-procedure uses the *t*-statistic to generate the hypothesis test. When the sample size *n*

is small, this is the appropriate method. When the sample size *n* is large, the *t*-value will be approximately equal to the large-sample *z*-value, and the resulting test will still be valid. If you have a large sample and you know the value of the population standard deviation σ (which is rarely the case), select "1-Sample Z" from the "Basic Statistics" menu options (see Figure M.1) and make the appropriate selections.

Testing p

Step 1 Access the Minitab data worksheet that contains the sample data.

Step 2 Click on the "Stat" button on the Minitab menu bar and then click on "Basic Statistics" and "1 Proportion" (see Figure M.1).

Step 3 On the resulting dialog box (shown in Figure M.4), click on "Samples in columns," and then specify the qualitative variable of interest in the open box.

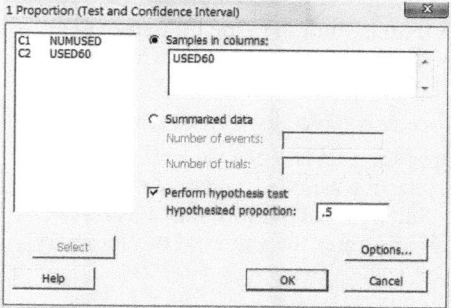

Figure M.4 Minitab 1 proportion test dialog box

Step 4 Check "Perform hypothesis test" and then specify the null hypothesis value p_0 in the "Hypothesized proportion" box.

Step 5 Click "Options," then specify the form of the alternative hypothesis in the resulting dialog box, as shown in Figure M.5. Also, check the "Use test and interval based on normal distribution" box at the bottom.

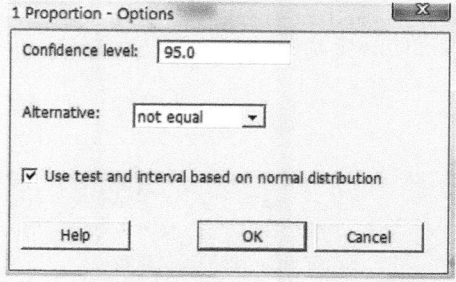

Figure M.5 Minitab 1 proportion test options

Step 6 Click "OK" to return to the "1 Proportion" dialog box and then click "OK" again to produce the test results.

Note: If you want to produce a confidence interval for a proportion from summary information (e.g., the number of successes and the sample size), click on "Summarized data" in the "1 Proportion" dialog box (see Figure M.4). Enter the value for the number of trials (i.e., the sample size) and the number of events (i.e., the number of successes), and then click "OK."

Testing σ^2

Step 1 Access the Minitab data worksheet that contains the sample data set.

Step 2 Click on the "Stat" button on the Minitab menu bar and and then click on "Basic Statistics" and "1 Variance" (see Figure M.1).

Step 3 Once the resulting dialog box appears (see Figure M.6), click on "Samples in columns" and then specify the quantitative variable of interest in the open box.

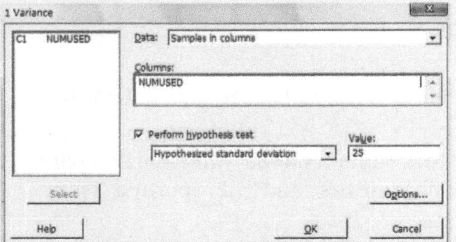

Figure M.6 Minitab 1 variance test dialog box

Step 4 Check "Perform hypothesis test" and specify the null hypothesis value of the standard deviation σ_0 in the open box.

Step 5 Click on the "Options" button at the bottom of the dialog box and specify the form of the alternative hypothesis (similar to Figure M.3).

Step 6 Click "OK" twice to produce the hypothesis test.

Note: If you want to produce a test for the variance from summary information (e.g., the sample standard deviation and sample size), click on "Summarized data" in the "1 Variance" dialog box (Figure M.6) and enter the values of the summary statistics.

Excel/XLSTAT: Tests of Hypotheses

Currently, tests of hypothesis for a population variance are not available in XLSTAT.

Testing μ

Step 1 Click the "XLSTAT" button on the Excel main menu bar, select "Parametric tests," and then click "One-sample t-test and z-test," as shown in Figure E.1.

Step 2 When the resulting dialog box appears, highlight the column that contains the values of the quantitative variable you want to analyze so that the column appears in the appropriate entry (see, for example, Figure E.2).

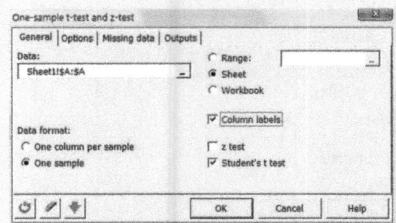

Figure E.2 XLSTAT test mean dialog box

Step 3 Click the "Options" tab, then specify the form of the alternative hypothesis, value of the hypothesized (theoretical) mean, and the value of α (significance level) in the appropriate boxes, as shown in Figure E.3.

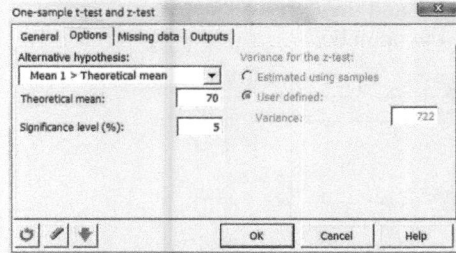

Figure E.3 XLSTAT options for testing a mean

Step 4 Click "OK," then "Continue" to display the test results.

Testing p

[*Note:* To conduct a test of hypothesis for a binomial proportion using XLSTAT, you will need summary information on your qualitative data, e.g., the sample size and either the number of successes or proportion of successes in the sample.]

Step 1 Click the "XLSTAT" button on the Excel main menu bar, select "Parametric tests," and then click "Tests for one proportion," as shown in Figure E.4.

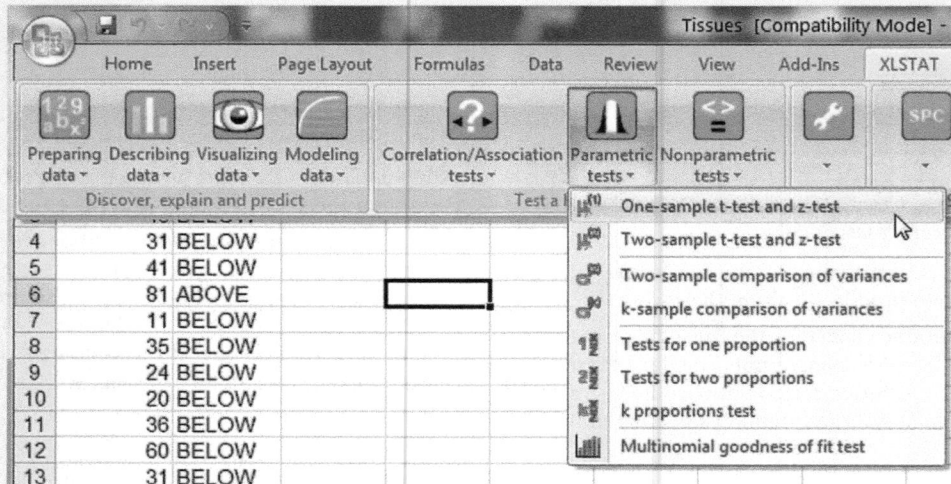

Figure E.1 XLSTAT menu options for testing a mean

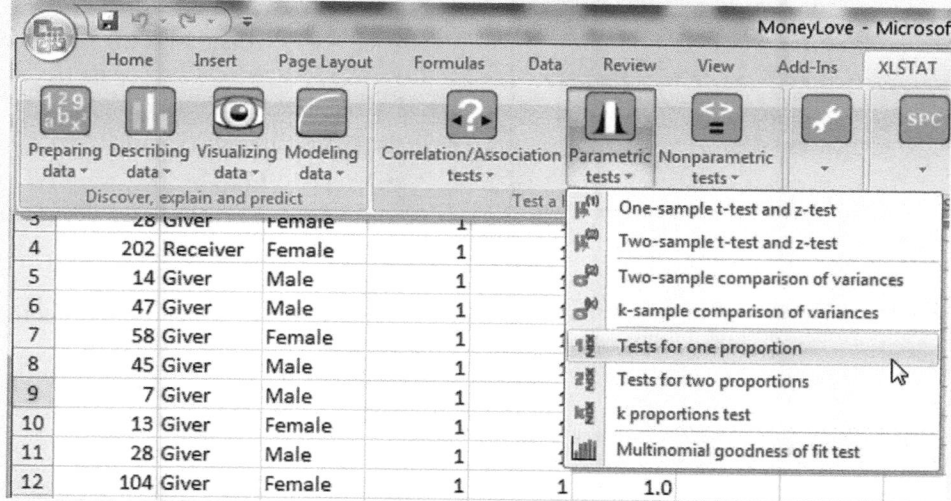

Figure E.4 XLSTAT menu options for a binomial proportion

Step 2 When the resulting dialog box appears, check "Frequency" in the "Data format" area, enter the number of successes and the sample size in the "Frequency" and "Sample size" boxes, respectively, and then specify the value of the hypothesized (test) proportion, as shown in Figure E.5. (Alternatively, you can check "Proportion" in the "Data format" area and enter the sample proportion in the Test "proportion" box.)

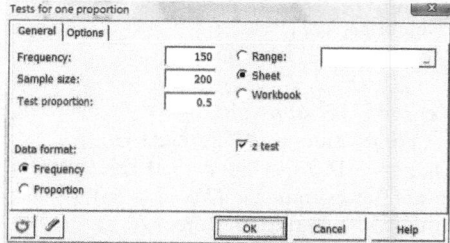

Figure E.5 XLSTAT test for proportion dialog box

Step 3 Click the "Options" tab, specify the form of the alternative hypothesis, and then enter "0" for the hypothesized difference and the value of α (significance level) in the appropriate boxes, as shown in Figure E.6.

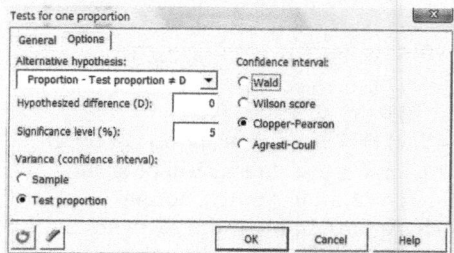

Figure E.6 XLSTAT options for testing a proportion

Step 4 Click "OK" to display the test results.

TI-84 Graphing Calculator: Tests of Hypotheses

Note: The TI-84 graphing calculator cannot currently conduct a test for a population variance.

Hypothesis Test for a Population Mean (Large-Sample Case)

Step 1 *Enter the Data (Skip to Step 2 if you have summary statistics, not raw data)*

- Press **STAT** and select **1:Edit**

Note: If the list already contains data, clear the old data. Use the up **ARROW** to highlight "**L1**."

- Press **CLEAR ENTER**

- Use the **ARROW** and **ENTER** keys to enter the data set into **L1**

Step 2 *Access the Statistical Tests Menu*

- Press **STAT**

- Arrow right to **TESTS**

- Press **ENTER** to select either **Z-Test** (if large sample and known) or **T-Test** (if unknown)

Step 3 *Choose "Data" or "Stats." ("Data" is selected when you have entered the raw data into a List. "Stats" is selected when you are given only the mean, standard deviation, and sample size.)*

- Press **ENTER**

If you selected "Data," enter the values for the hypothesis test where μ_0 = the value for μ in the null hypothesis, σ = assumed value of the population standard deviation.

- Set **List** to **L1**

- Set **Freq** to **1**

- Use the **ARROW** to highlight the appropriate alternative hypothesis

- Press **ENTER**

- Arrow down to "**Calculate**"

- Press **ENTER**

If you selected "Stats," enter the values for the hypothesis test where μ_0 = the value for μ in the null hypothesis, σ = assumed value of the population standard deviation.

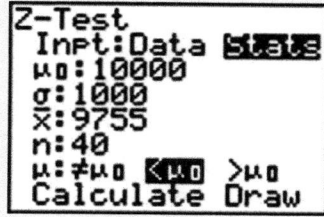

- Enter the sample mean, sample standard deviation, and sample size
- Use the **ARROW** to highlight the appropriate alternative hypothesis
- Press **ENTER**
- Arrow down to "**Calculate**"
- Press **ENTER**

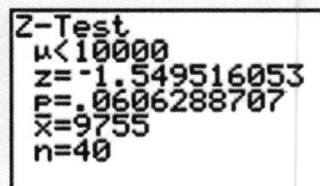

```
Z-Test
 μ<10000
 z=-1.549516053
 P=.0606288707
 x̄=9755
 n=40
```

The chosen test will be displayed as well as the z (or t) test statistic, the p-value, the sample mean, and the sample size.

Testing p

Step 1 *Enter the Data (Skip to Step 2 if you have summary statistics, not raw data)*

- Press **STAT** and select **1:Edit**

Note: If the list already contains data, clear the old data. Use the up **ARROW** to highlight "**L1**."

- Press **CLEAR ENTER**
- Use the **ARROW** and **ENTER** keys to enter the data set into **L1**

Step 2 *Access the Statistical Tests Menu*

- Press **STAT**
- Arrow right to **TESTS**
- Press **ENTER** after selecting **1-Prop Z Test**

Step 3 *Enter the hypothesized proportion p_0, the number of success x, and the sample size n*

- Use the **ARROW** to highlight the appropriate alternative hypothesis
- Press **ENTER**
- Arrow down to "**Calculate**"
- Press **ENTER**

The chosen test will be displayed as well as the z-test statistic and the p-value.

◻ Answers to Selected Exercises

1 Null; alternative   **3** α **5** Reject H_0 when H_0 is true; accept H_0 when H_0 is true; Reject H_0 when H_0 is false; accept H_0 when H_0 is false   **7** No   **9 a.** H_0: $p = .68$ **b.** $|z| > 2.576$ **11** H_0: $p = .07$, H_a: $p < .07$ **13** H_0: $\mu = 863$, H_a: $\mu < 863$ **15 a.** Unsafe; safe   **c.** α **17 c.** α **e.** Decrease   **f.** Increase   **19 a.** .1151   **b.** .1151   **c.** .2302   **21 a.** Do not reject H_0 **b.** Reject H_0 **c.** Reject H_0 **d.** Do not reject H_0 **e.** Do not reject H_0 **23** .0150   **25** .03   **27** .06   **29 a.** $z > 2.14$ **b.** .0162   **31 a.** $z = -1.61$, reject H_0 **b.** $z = -1.61$, do not reject H_0 **33 a.** $z = 5.71$, reject H_0 **b.** Test valid due to CLT   **35** H_0: $\mu = 2.2$, H_a: $\mu \neq 2.2$, p-value ≈ 0, reject H_0 for any reasonable α **37 a.** H_0: $\mu = .250$, H_a: $\mu \neq .250$ **b.** $\bar{x} = .25248$, $s = .00223$ **c.** $z = 7.03$ **d.** p-value ≈ 0 **e.** $|z| > 2.576$ **f.** Yes, reject H_0 **39 a.** Yes; $z = 1.85$, p-value $= .0322$, reject H_0 **b.** Yes; $z = -1.85$, p-value $= .0322$, reject H_0 **c.** No; apply CLT   **41** $z = -1.86$, do not reject H_0 **43 a.** $z = 26.15$, p-value ≈ 0, reject H_0 **b.** $z = -14.24$, p-value ≈ 0, reject H_0 **45 a.** $z = 2.73$, reject H_0 **c.** No   **47 a.** Small n, data normal   **b.** Mound-shaped and symmetric; t is flatter than z **49 a.** $|t| > 2.160$ **b.** $t > 2.500$ **c.** $t > 1.397$ **d.** $t < -2.718$ **e.** $|t| > 1.729$ **f.** $t < -2.353$ **51 a.** Population is normally distributed   **b.** Reject H_0 at $\alpha = .05$ **c.** .076   **53** H_0: $\mu = 6,000$, H_a: $\mu < 6,000$, p-value $= .096/2 = .048$, $\alpha = .10$, reject H_0 **55 a.** H_0: $\mu = 2$, H_a: $\mu \neq 2$ **b.** $t = -1.02$ **c.** $|t| > 2.093$ **d.** Do not reject H_0 **e.** .322   **57 a.** H_0: $\mu = 1.4$, H_a: $\mu > 1.4$ **b.** Chance of concluding $\mu > 1.4$ when $\mu = 1.4$ is .10   **c.** $\bar{x} = 5.243$, $s = .192$ **d.** $t = 34.67$ **e.** p-value $= 0$ **f.** Reject H_0 **59** Yes, $t = -2.53$ **61** No, $t = 2.97$ **63** Yes, using $\alpha = .05$; Plant 1: p-value $= .197$; Plant 2: p-value $= .094$ **65 a.** -2.33 **c.** Reject H_0 **d.** .0099   **67 a.** $z = 1.13$, do not reject H_0 **b.** .1292   **69 a.** $\hat{p} = .67$ **b.** H_0: $p = .7$, H_a: $p > .7$ **c.** $z = -1.80$ **d.** $z > 2.326$ **e.** p-value $= .9641$ **f.** Do not reject H_0 **g.** Do not reject H_0 **71** Yes, $z = -3.54$ **73 a.** H_0: $p = .5$, H_a: $p < .5$ **b.** .231   **c.** Do not reject H_0 **75** No; $z = -.89$ **77 a.** No, $z = 1.49$ **b.** .0681   **79** Population: all U.S. households with TVs; experimental unit: individual household with a TV; variable: whether or not the household has a DVR; parameter: $p = $ proportion all households with DVRs; H_0: $p = .41$, H_a: $p \neq .41$; test statistic: $z = (\hat{p} - .41)/\sqrt{(.41)(.59)/n}$ **81** $z = 1.20$, do not reject H_0 **83 a.** $\chi^2 < 6.26214$ or $\chi^2 > 27.4884$ **b.** $\chi^2 > 40.2894$ **c.** $\chi^2 > 21.0642$ **d.** $\chi^2 < 3.57056$ **e.** $\chi^2 < 1.63539$ or $\chi^2 > 12.5916$ **f.** $\chi^2 < 13.8484$ **85 a.** $\chi^2 = 479.16$, reject H_0 **87 a.** H_0: $\sigma^2 = 100$, H_a: $\sigma^2 < 100$ **b.** $\chi^2 < 167.361$ **c.** Chance of concluding $\sigma < 10$ when $\sigma = 10$ is .05   **d.** $\chi^2 = 154.81$, p-value $= .009$ **e.** Reject H_0 **f.** Rates of return $\approx$ normal   **89 a.** H_0: $\sigma^2 = .000004$, H_a: $\sigma^2 \neq .000004$ **b.** $\chi^2 = 48.49$, do not reject H_0 **c.** Tee weights $\approx$ normal   **91** No, $\chi^2 = 13.77$ **93** At $\alpha = .05$, yes; $\chi^2 = 133.90$ **95 a.** With large s, test statistic will be small   **b.** 1.76   **c.** Yes; $\chi^2 = 99$ **97 b.** 532.9   **d.** .1949   **e.** .8051   **99 a.** Approx. normal with $\mu_{\bar{x}} = 75$ and $\sigma_{\bar{x}} = 2.14$ **b.** Approx. normal with $\mu_{\bar{x}} = 70$ and $\sigma_{\bar{x}} = 2.14$ **c.** .1469   **d.** .8531   **101 a.** Approx. normal with $\mu_{\hat{p}} = .7$ and $\sigma_{\hat{p}} = .046$ **b.** Approx. normal with $\mu_{\hat{p}} = .65$ and $\sigma_{\hat{p}} = .048$ **c.** .7979   **d.** .9469   **103 a.** .1949, Type II error   **b.** .05, Type I error   **c.** .8051   **105** .7764   **107** .1075   **109** Alternative   **111** Large   **113 a.** $t = -7.51$, reject H_0 **b.** $t = -7.51$, reject H_0 **115 a.** $z = -1.78$, reject H_0 **b.** $z = -1.78$, do not reject H_0 **117 a.** $\chi^2 = 63.48$, reject H_0 **b.** $\chi^2 = 63.48$, reject H_0 **119 a.** $\chi^2 < 24.3$ or $\chi^2 > 73.1$ **b.** $\chi^2 = 63.72$ **c.** Do not reject H_0 **121 a.** H_0: $\mu = 1$, H_a: $\mu > 1$ **b.** Reject H_0 if $t > 1.345$ **d.** $t = 2.41$ **e.** $.01 < p$-value $< .025$, reject H_0 **f.** $\chi^2 = 12.78$, do not reject H_0 **123 a.** H_0: $p = .75$ **b.** Type I error: conclude p differs from .75 when $p = .75$; Type II error: conclude $p = .75$ when p differs from .75   **125 a.** H_0: $\mu = 100$, H_a: $\mu \neq 100$ **b.** Random sample; population of cost-of-living indexes $\approx$ normal   **c.** $t = -1.89$, do not reject H_0 **d.** p-value $= .108$ **127 a.** H_0: No disease, H_a: Disease   **b.** Type I error $=$ false positive; Type II error $=$ false negative   **c.** Type II error; β **129** $\chi^2 = 187.9$, do not reject H_0 **131 a.** $z = -3.22$, do not reject H_0 **b.** p-value ≈ 1 **c.** .8159

133 a. Concluding that percentage of shoplifters turned over to police is 50% when, in fact, the percentage is higher than 50% **b.** .8461 **c.** Decreases to .7389   **135 a.** No, $z = 1.41$ **b.** Small **c.** .0793   **137 a.** No **b.** $\beta = .5910$, power $= .4090$ **c.** Increases   **139 a.** No, $z = 1.37$ **b.** Yes, $z = -4.58$ **141** Yes; $z = 2.50$, do not reject H_0: $\mu = 220$ **143 a.** $z = 2.73$, reject H_0 **c.** Sampling distribution of $\bar{x}$ is approx. normal by CLT   **145** $z = 7.83$, reject H_0

☐ Credits

The photo credits below are listed in order of appearance.

Jeff Chiu/AP Images
Ellen Creager/KRT/Newscom
Wavebreakmedia Ltd./Shutterstock
Michael Shake/Fotolia; Dorling Kindersley, Ltd.

☐ Technology Images

CONTENTS

Where We're Going

- Learn how to identify the target parameter for comparing two populations (1)
- Learn how to compare two population means using confidence intervals and tests of hypotheses (2–3)
- Apply these inferential methods to problems where we want to compare two population proportions or two population variances (4, 6)
- Determine the sizes of the samples necessary to estimate the difference between two population parameters with a specified margin of error (5)

☐ Inferences Based on Two Samples *Confidence Intervals*

and Tests of Hypotheses

STATISTICS in ACTION *ZixIt Corp. v. Visa USA Inc.*—A Libel Case

The *National Law Journal (Aug. 26–Sep. 2, 2002) reported on an interesting court case involving ZixIt Corp., a start-up Internet credit card clearing center. ZixIt claimed that its new online credit card processing system would allow Internet shoppers to make purchases without revealing their credit card numbers. This claim violated the established protocols of most major credit card companies, including Visa. Without the company's knowledge, a Visa vice president for technology research and development began writing e-mails and Web site postings on a Yahoo! message board for ZixIt investors, challenging ZixIt's claim and urging investors to sell their ZixIt stock. The Visa executive posted more than 400 e-mails and notes before he was caught. Once it was discovered that a Visa executive was responsible for the postings, ZixIt filed a lawsuit against Visa Corp., alleging that Visa—using the executive as its agent—had engaged in a "malicious two-part scheme to disparage and interfere with ZixIt" and its efforts to market the new online credit card processing system. In the libel case ZixIt asked for $699 million in damages.*

Dallas lawyers Jeff Tillotson and Mike Lynn, of the law firm Lynn Tillotson & Pinker, were hired to defend Visa in the lawsuit. The lawyers, in turn, hired Dr. James McClave (coauthor of this text) as their expert statistician. McClave testified in court on an "event study" he did matching the Visa executive's e-mail postings with movement of ZixIt's stock price the next business day. McClave's testimony,

STATISTICS in ACTION CONTINUED

showing that there was an equal number of days when the stock went up as went down after a posting, helped the lawyers representing Visa to prevail in the case. *The National Law Journal* reported that, after two-and-a-half days of deliberation, "the jurors found [the Visa executive] was not acting in the scope of his employment and that Visa had not defamed ZixIt or interfered with its business."

In this chapter, we demonstrate several of the statistical analyses McClave used to infer that the Visa executive's postings had no effect on ZixIt's stock price. The daily ZixIt stock prices as well as the timing of the Visa executive's postings are saved in the **ZIXITVISA** file.* We apply the statistical methodology presented in this chapter to this data set in two Statistics in Action Revisited examples.

STATISTICS in ACTION REVISITED

□ Comparing Mean Price Changes

□ Comparing Proportions

 *Data Set:* ZIXVSA

1   Identifying the Target Parameter

Many experiments involve a comparison of two populations. For instance, a realtor may want to estimate the difference in mean sales price between city and suburban homes. A consumer group might test whether two major brands of food freezers differ in the average amount of electricity they use. A television market researcher wants to estimate the difference in the proportions of younger and older viewers who regularly watch a popular TV program. A golf ball supplier may be interested in comparing the variability in the distance that two competing brands of golf balls travel when struck with the same club. In this chapter, we consider techniques for using two samples to compare the populations from which they were selected.

The same procedures that are used to estimate and test hypotheses about a single population can be modified to make inferences about two populations. The methodology used will depend on the sizes of the samples and the parameter of interest (i.e., the *target parameter*). Some key words and the type of data associated with the parameters covered in this chapter are listed in the box.

Determining the Target Parameter

Parameter	Key Words or Phrases	Type of Data
$\mu_1 - \mu_2$	Mean difference; difference in averages	Quantitative
$p_1 - p_2$	Difference between proportions, percentages, fractions, or rates; compare proportions	Qualitative
$(\sigma_1)^2/(\sigma_2)^2$	Ratio of variances; difference in variability or spread; compare variation	Quantitative

You can see that the key words *difference* and *compare* help identify the fact that two populations are to be compared. For the examples given above, the words *mean* in *mean sales price* and *average* in *average amount of electricity* imply that the target parameter is the difference in population means, $\mu_1 - \mu_2$. The word *proportions* in *proportions of younger and older viewers* indicates that the target parameter is the difference in proportions, $p_1 - p_2$. Finally, the key word *variability* in *variability in the distance* identifies the ratio of population variances, $(\sigma_1)^2/(\sigma_2)^2$, as the target parameter.

As with inferences about a single population, the type of data (quantitative or qualitative) collected on the two samples is also indicative of the target parameter. With

*Data provided (with permission) from Info Tech, Inc., Gainesville, Florida.

quantitative data, you are likely to be interested in comparing the means or variances of the data. With qualitative data with two outcomes (success or failure), a comparison of the proportions of successes is likely to be of interest.

We consider methods for comparing two population means in Sections 2 and 3. A comparison of population proportions is presented in Section 4 and population variances in Section 6. We show how to determine the sample sizes necessary for reliable estimates of the target parameters in Section 5.

2   Comparing Two Population Means: Independent Sampling

In this section we develop both large-sample and small-sample methodologies for comparing two population means. In the large-sample case, we use the z-statistic (where $z \approx t$ when the population variances are unknown), while in the small-sample case we use the t-statistic.

Large Samples

Example   1

Large-Sample Confidence Interval for $(\mu_1 - \mu_2)$— Comparing Mean Car Prices

Problem In recent years, the United States and Japan have engaged in intense negotiations regarding restrictions on trade between the two countries. One of the claims made repeatedly by U.S. officials is that many Japanese manufacturers price their goods higher in Japan than in the United States, in effect subsidizing low prices in the United States by extremely high prices in Japan. According to the U.S. argument, Japan accomplishes this by keeping competitive U.S. goods from reaching the Japanese marketplace.

An economist decided to test the hypothesis that higher retail prices are being charged for Japanese automobiles in Japan than in the United States. She obtained independent random samples of 50 retail sales in the United States and 50 retail sales in Japan over the same time period and for the same model of automobile and converted the Japanese sales prices from yen to dollars using current conversion rates. The data, saved in the **AUTOS** file, are listed in Table 1. Form a 95% confidence interval for the difference between the population mean retail prices of this automobile model for the two countries. Interpret the result.

Solution Recall that the general form of a large-sample confidence interval for a single mean μ is $\bar{x} \pm z_{\alpha/2}\sigma_{\bar{x}}$—that is, we add and subtract $z_{\alpha/2}$ standard deviations of the sample estimate, $\bar{x}$, to the value of the estimate. We employ a similar procedure to form the confidence interval for the difference between two population means.

Let μ_1 represent the mean of the population of retail sales prices for this car model sold in the United States. Let μ_2 be similarly defined for retail sales in Japan. We wish to form a confidence interval for $(\mu_1 - \mu_2)$. An intuitively appealing estimator for

Table 1	Automobile Retail Prices (Thousands of Dollars)								
USA Sales:	18.2	16.2	17.2	18.7	18.4	16.6	14.9	16.8	12.1	10.8
	18.5	15.5	16.2	16.3	18.2	19.5	13.2	16.8	12.9	17.2
	18.2	16.3	16.8	16.4	18.6	15.6	17.1	18.1	18.9	19.0
	17.3	18.8	14.9	16.7	20.3	17.1	14.6	17.2	13.0	18.4
	16.9	13.3	16.3	15.9	16.6	17.6	16.0	17.1	14.6	18.0
Japan Sales:	18.5	14.0	18.2	21.1	13.9	18.7	14.9	16.4	16.3	18.0
	16.8	19.8	17.3	16.6	14.9	16.3	16.5	15.4	17.6	20.1
	16.4	18.0	17.5	18.4	19.8	14.8	18.2	16.7	20.2	16.2
	20.4	17.9	15.5	15.4	17.7	17.1	17.9	17.4	18.2	16.2
	18.5	16.9	17.6	14.4	21.6	18.6	16.2	14.3	12.5	20.0

Data Set: AUTOS

Group Statistics

	COUNTRY	N	Mean	Std. Deviation	Std. Error Mean
PRICE	USA	50	16596.00	1981.440	280.218
	JAPAN	50	17236.00	1974.093	279.179

Independent Samples Test

		Levene's Test for Equality of Variances		t-test for Equality of Means					95% Confidence Interval of the Difference	
		F	Sig.	t	df	Sig. (2-tailed)	Mean Difference	Std. Error Difference	Lower	Upper
PRICE	Equal variances assumed	.118	.732	-1.618	98	.109	-640.000	395.554	-1424.964	144.964
	Equal variances not assumed			-1.618	97.999	.109	-640.000	395.554	-1424.964	144.964

Figure 1

SPSS summary statistics and confidence interval for automobile price study

$(\mu_1 - \mu_2)$ is the difference between the sample means, $(\bar{x}_1 - \bar{x}_2)$. Thus, we will form the confidence interval of interest by

$$(\bar{x}_1 - \bar{x}_2) \pm z_{\sigma/2}\sigma_{(\bar{x}_1-\bar{x}_2)}$$

Assuming the two samples are independent, the standard deviation of the difference between the sample means is

$$\sigma_{(\bar{x}_1 - \bar{x}_2)} = \sqrt{\frac{\sigma_1^2}{n_1} + \frac{\sigma_2^2}{n_2}} \approx \sqrt{\frac{s_1^2}{n_1} + \frac{s_2^2}{n_2}}$$

Note that we have substituted s_1^2 and s_2^2 for the usually unknown values of σ_1^2 and σ_2^2, respectively. With large samples, this will be a good approximation.

Summary statistics for the car sales data are displayed in the SPSS printout, Figure 1. Note that $\bar{x}_1 = \$16,596$, $\bar{x}_2 = \$17,236$, $s_1 = \$1,981$, and $s_2 = \$1,974$. Using these values and noting that $\alpha = .05$ and $z_{.025} = 1.96$, we find that the 95% confidence interval is, approximately,

$$(16,596 - 17,236) \pm 1.96\sqrt{\frac{(1,981)^2}{50} + \frac{(1,974)^2}{50}} = -640 \pm (1.96)(396)$$

$$= -640 \pm 776$$

or $(-1416, 136)$. This interval is also given at the bottom of Figure 1. (Differences in the results are due to rounding and normal approximation.)

Using this estimation procedure over and over again for different samples, we know that approximately 95% of the confidence intervals formed in this manner will enclose the difference in population means $(\mu_1 - \mu_2)$. Therefore, we are highly confident that the difference in mean retail prices in the United States and Japan is between $-\$1,416$ and $\$136$. Because 0 falls in this interval, it is possible for the difference to be 0 (i.e., for $\mu_1 = \mu_2$); thus, the economist cannot conclude that a significant difference exists between the mean retail prices in the two countries.

Look Back If the confidence interval for $(\mu_1 - \mu_2)$ contains all positive numbers [e.g., $(527, 991)$], then we would conclude that the difference between the means is positive and that $\mu_1 > \mu_2$. Alternatively, if the interval contains all negative numbers [e.g., $(-722, -145)$], then we would conclude that the difference between the means is negative and that $\mu_1 < \mu_2$.

Now Work Exercise 3a

The justification for the procedure used in Example 1 to estimate $(\mu_1 - \mu_2)$ relies on the properties of the sampling distribution of $(\bar{x}_1 - \bar{x}_2)$. The performance of the estimator in repeated sampling is pictured in Figure 2, and its properties are summarized in the box on the next page.

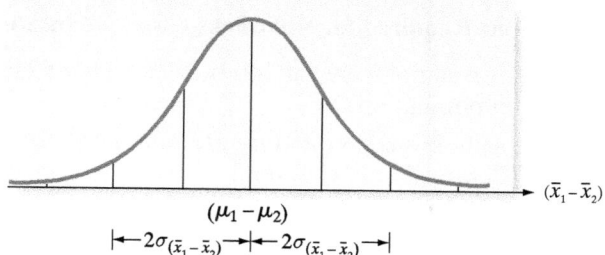

Figure 2
Sampling distribution of $(\bar{x}_1 - \bar{x}_2)$

Properties of the Sampling Distribution of $(\bar{x}_1 - \bar{x}_2)$

1. The mean of the sampling distribution $(\bar{x}_1 - \bar{x}_2)$ is $(\mu_1 - \mu_2)$.
2. If the two samples are independent, the standard deviation of the sampling distribution is

$$\sigma_{(\bar{x}_1 - \bar{x}_2)} = \sqrt{\frac{\sigma_1^2}{n_1} + \frac{\sigma_2^2}{n_2}}$$

where σ_1^2 and σ_2^2 are the variances of the two populations being sampled, and n_1 and n_2 are the respective sample sizes. We also refer to $\sigma_{(\bar{x}_1 - \bar{x}_2)}$ as the **standard error** of the statistic $(\bar{x}_1 - \bar{x}_2)$.

3. The sampling distribution of $(\bar{x}_1 - \bar{x}_2)$ is approximately normal for *large samples* by the Central Limit Theorem.

In Example 1, we noted the similarity in the procedures for forming a large-sample confidence interval for one population mean and a large-sample confidence interval for the difference between two population means. When we are testing hypotheses, the procedures are again very similar. The general large-sample procedures for forming confidence intervals and testing hypotheses about $(\mu_1 - \mu_2)$ are summarized in the following boxes.

Large, Independent Samples Confidence Interval for $(\mu_1 - \mu_2)$: Normal (z) Statistic

σ_1^2 and σ_2^2 known: $(\bar{x}_1 - \bar{x}_2) \pm z_{\alpha/2}\sigma_{(\bar{x}_1 - \bar{x}_2)} = (\bar{x}_1 - \bar{x}_2) \pm z_{\alpha/2}\sqrt{\frac{\sigma_1^2}{n_1} + \frac{\sigma_2^2}{n_2}}$

σ_1^2 and σ_2^2 unknown: $(\bar{x}_1 - \bar{x}_2) \pm z_{\alpha/2}\sigma_{(\bar{x}_1 - \bar{x}_2)} \approx (\bar{x}_1 - \bar{x}_2) \pm z_{\alpha/2}\sqrt{\frac{s_1^2}{n_1} + \frac{s_2^2}{n_2}}$

Large, Independent Samples Test of Hypothesis for $(\mu_1 - \mu_2)$: Normal (z) Statistic

One-Tailed Test	Two-Tailed Test
$H_0: (\mu_1 - \mu_2) = D_0$	$H_0: (\mu_1 - \mu_2) = D_0$
$H_a: (\mu_1 - \mu_2) < D_0$	$H_a: (\mu_1 - \mu_2) \neq D_0$
[or $H_a: (\mu_1 - \mu_2) > D_0$]	

where D_0 = Hypothesized difference between the means (this difference is often hypothesized to be equal to 0)

Test statistic:

$$z = \frac{(\bar{x}_1 - \bar{x}_2) - D_0}{\sigma_{(\bar{x}_1 - \bar{x}_2)}} \quad \text{where} \quad \sigma_{(\bar{x}_1 - \bar{x}_2)} = \sqrt{\frac{\sigma_1^2}{n_1} + \frac{\sigma_2^2}{n_2}} \text{ if } \sigma_1^2 \text{ and } \sigma_2^2 \text{ are known}$$

$$\approx \sqrt{\frac{s_1^2}{n_1} + \frac{s_2^2}{n_2}} \text{ if } \sigma_1^2 \text{ and } \sigma_2^2 \text{ are unknown}$$

Rejection region: $z < -z_\alpha$ *Rejection region:* $|z| > z_{\alpha/2}$
[or $z > z_\alpha$ when
$H_a: (\mu_1 - \mu_2) > D_0$]

> **Conditions Required for Valid Large-Sample Inferences about $(\mu_1 - \mu_2)$**
>
> 1. The two samples are randomly selected in an independent manner from the two target populations.
> 2. The sample sizes, n_1 and n_2, are both large (i.e., $n_1 \geq 30$ and $n_2 \geq 30$). [Due to the Central Limit Theorem, this condition guarantees that the sampling distribution of $(\bar{x}_1 - \bar{x}_2)$ will be approximately normal regardless of the shapes of the underlying probability distributions of the populations. Also, s_1^2 and s_2^2 will provide good approximations to σ_1^2 and σ_2^2 when the samples are both large.]

Example 2

Large-Sample Test for $(\mu_1 - \mu_2)$—Comparing Mean Car Prices

Problem Refer to the study of retail prices of an automobile sold in the United States and Japan, Example 1. Another way to compare the mean retail prices for the two countries is to conduct a test of hypothesis. Use the information on the SPSS printout, Figure 1, to conduct the test. Use $\alpha = .05$.

Solution Again, we let μ_1 and μ_2 represent the population mean retail sales prices in the United States and Japan, respectively. If the claim made by the U.S. government is true, then the mean retail price in Japan will exceed the mean in the United States [i.e., $\mu_1 < \mu_2$ or $(\mu_1 - \mu_2) < 0$]. Thus, the elements of the test are as follows:

$H_0: (\mu_1 - \mu_2) = 0$ (i.e., $\mu_1 = \mu_2$; note that $D_0 = 0$ for this hypothesis test)

$H_a: (\mu_1 - \mu_2) < 0$ (i.e., $\mu_1 < \mu_2$)

$$\text{Test statistic: } z = \frac{(\bar{x}_1 - \bar{x}_2) - D_0}{\sigma_{(\bar{x}_1 - \bar{x}_2)}} = \frac{(\bar{x}_1 - \bar{x}_2) - 0}{\sigma_{(\bar{x}_1 - \bar{x}_2)}}$$

Rejection region: $z < -z_{.05} = -1.645$ (see Figure 3)

Substituting the summary statistics given in Figure 1 into the test statistic, we obtain

$$z = \frac{(\bar{x}_1 - \bar{x}_2) - 0}{\sigma_{(\bar{x}_1 - \bar{x}_2)}} = \frac{(16,596 - 17,236)}{\sqrt{\dfrac{\sigma_1^2}{n_1} + \dfrac{\sigma_2^2}{n_2}}}$$

$$\approx \frac{-640}{\sqrt{\dfrac{s_1^2}{n_1} + \dfrac{s_2^2}{n_2}}} = \frac{-640}{\sqrt{\dfrac{(1,981)^2}{50} + \dfrac{(1,974)^2}{50}}} = \frac{-640}{396} = -1.62$$

[*Note:* This value of the test statistic is shown (highlighted) at the bottom of the SPSS printout, Figure 1.]

As you can see in Figure 3, the calculated z-value does not fall in the rejection region. Therefore, the samples do not provide sufficient evidence, at $\alpha = .05$, for the economist to conclude that the mean retail price in Japan exceeds that in the United States.

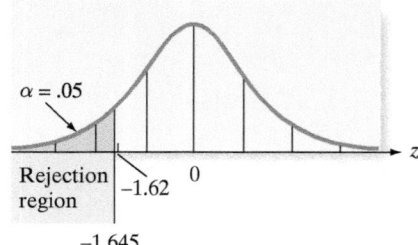

Figure 3

Rejection region for Example 2

Look Back First, note that this conclusion agrees with the inference drawn from the 95% confidence interval in Example 1. Generally, however, a confidence interval will provide more information on the difference in means than a test. A test can detect only whether or not a difference between the means exists, while the confidence interval provides information on the magnitude of the difference. Second, a one-tailed hypothesis test and a confidence interval (which is two-tailed) may not always agree. However, a two-tailed test of hypothesis and a confidence interval will *always* give the same inference about the target parameter, as long as the value of α is the same for both.

<table>
<tr><td>Example</td><td>3</td></tr>
</table>

The *p*-Value of a Test for
$(\mu_1 - \mu_2)$

Problem Find the observed significance level for the test in Example 2. Interpret the result.

Solution The alternative hypothesis in Example 2, H_a: $(\mu_1 - \mu_2) < 0$, required a lower one-tailed test using

$$z = \frac{\bar{x}_1 - \bar{x}_2}{\sigma_{(\bar{x}_1 - \bar{x}_2)}}$$

as a test statistic. Because the approximate *z*-value calculated from the sample data was -1.62, the observed significance level (*p*-value) for the lower-tailed test is the probability of observing a value of *z* more contradictory to the null hypothesis as $z = -1.62$; that is,

$$p\text{-value} = P(z < -1.62)$$

This probability is computed assuming H_0 is true and is equal to the shaded area shown in Figure 4.

The tabulated area corresponding to $z = 1.62$ in Table II in Appendix: Tables is .4474. Therefore, the observed significance level of the test is

$$p\text{-value} \approx .5 - .4474 = .0526$$

Because our selected α value, .05, is less than this *p*-value, we have insufficient evidence to reject H_0: $(\mu_1 - \mu_2) = 0$ in favor of H_a: $(\mu_1 - \mu_2) < 0$.

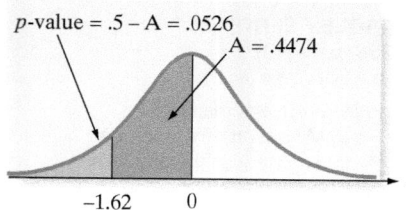

Figure 4

The observed significance level for Example 2

Look Back The *p*-value of the test is more easily obtained from a statistical software package. A Minitab printout for the hypothesis test is displayed in Figure 5. The one-tailed *p*-value, highlighted on the printout, is .054, which agrees (except for rounding) with our approximated *p*-value.

Two-Sample T-Test and CI: USA, JAPAN

```
Two-sample T for USA vs JAPAN

         N    Mean   StDev   SE Mean
USA     50   16596    1981      280
JAPAN   50   17236    1974      279


Difference = mu (USA) - mu (JAPAN)
Estimate for difference:  -640.000
95% upper bound for difference:  16.838
T-Test of difference = 0 (vs <): T-Value = -1.62   P-Value = 0.054   DF = 98
Both use Pooled StDev = 1977.7703
```

Figure 5

Minitab analysis for comparing U.S. and Japan mean auto prices

■ **Now Work Exercise 3b**

Small Samples

When comparing two population means with small samples (say, $n_1 < 30$ or $n_2 < 30$), the methodology of the previous three examples is invalid. The reason? When the sample sizes are small, estimates of σ_1^2 and σ_2^2 are unreliable, and the Central Limit Theorem (which guarantees that the *z*-statistic is normal) can no longer be applied. But as in the case of a single mean, we use the familiar Student's *t*-distribution.

To use the t-*distribution, both sampled populations must be approximately normally distributed with equal population variances, and the random samples must be*

selected independently of each other. The normality and equal variances assumptions imply relative frequency distributions for the populations that would appear as shown in Figure 6.

Because we assume the two populations have equal variances ($\sigma_1^2 = \sigma_2^2 = \sigma^2$), it is reasonable to use the information contained in *both* samples to construct a **pooled sample estimator of σ^2** for use in confidence intervals and test statistics.* Thus, if s_1^2 and s_2^2 are the two sample variances (both estimating the variance σ^2 common to both populations), the pooled estimator of σ^2, denoted as s_p^2, is

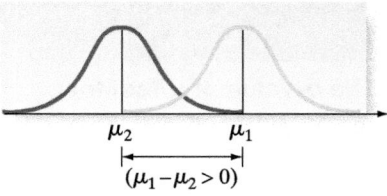

Figure 6

Assumptions for the two-sample t: (1) normal populations, (2) equal variances

$$s_p^2 = \frac{(n_1 - 1)s_1^2 + (n_2 - 1)s_2^2}{(n_1 - 1) + (n_2 - 1)} = \frac{(n_1 - 1)s_1^2 + (n_2 - 1)s_2^2}{n_1 + n_2 - 2}$$

or

$$s_p^2 = \frac{\overbrace{\sum(x_1 - \bar{x}_1)^2}^{\text{From sample 1}} + \overbrace{\sum(x_2 - \bar{x}_2)^2}^{\text{From sample 2}}}{n_1 + n_2 - 2}$$

where x_1 represents a measurement from sample 1 and x_2 represents a measurement from sample 2. The term *degrees of freedom* means 1 less than the sample size. Thus, in this case, we have $(n_1 - 1)$ degrees of freedom for sample 1 and $(n_2 - 1)$ degrees of freedom for sample 2. Because we are pooling the information on σ^2 obtained from both samples, the degrees of freedom associated with the pooled variance s_p^2 is equal to the sum of the degrees of freedom for the two samples, namely, the denominator of s_p^2; that is, $(n_1 - 1) + (n_2 - 1) = n_1 + n_2 - 2$.

Note that the second formula given for s_p^2 shows that the pooled variance is simply a *weighted average* of the two sample variances, s_1^2 and s_2^2. The weight given each variance is proportional to its degrees of freedom. If the two variances have the same number of degrees of freedom (i.e., if the sample sizes are equal), then the pooled variance is a simple average of the two sample variances. The result is an average or "pooled" variance that is a better estimate of σ^2 than either s_1^2 or s_2^2 alone.

Both the confidence interval and the test of hypothesis procedures for comparing two population means with small samples are summarized in the following boxes.

Small, Independent Samples Confidence Interval for $(\mu_1 - \mu_2)$: Student's t-Statistic

$$(\bar{x}_1 - \bar{x}_2) \pm t_{\alpha/2}\sqrt{s_p^2\left(\frac{1}{n_1} + \frac{1}{n_2}\right)}$$

where $s_p^2 = \dfrac{(n_1 - 1)s_1^2 + (n_2 - 1)s_2^2}{n_1 + n_2 - 2}$

and $t_{\alpha/2}$ is based on $(n_1 + n_2 - 2)$ degrees of freedom.

---

*s_p^2 can be shown to be the minimum-variance unbiased estimator (MVUE) of σ^2 when $\sigma^2 = \sigma_1^2 = \sigma_2^2$.

Small, Independent Samples Test of Hypothesis for $(\mu_1 - \mu_2)$: Student's t-Statistic

One-Tailed Test	Two-Tailed Test
$H_0: (\mu_1 - \mu_2) = D_0$	$H_0: (\mu_1 - \mu_2) = D_0$
$H_a: (\mu_1 - \mu_2) < D_0$	$H_a: (\mu_1 - \mu_2) \neq D_0$
$[\text{or } H_a: (\mu_1 - \mu_2) > D_0]$	

$$\text{Test statistic: } t = \frac{(\bar{x}_1 - \bar{x}_2) - D_0}{\sqrt{s_p^2\left(\frac{1}{n_1} + \frac{1}{n_2}\right)}}$$

Rejection region: $t < -t_\alpha$ Rejection region: $|t| > t_{\alpha/2}$
$[\text{or } t > t_\alpha \text{ when } H_a: (\mu_1 - \mu_2) > D_0]$
where t_α and $t_{\alpha/2}$ are based on $(n_1 + n_2 - 2)$ degrees of freedom.

Conditions Required for Valid Small-Sample Inferences about $(\mu_1 - \mu_2)$

1. The two samples are randomly selected in an independent manner from the two target populations.
2. Both sampled populations have distributions that are approximately normal.
3. The population variances are equal (i.e., $\sigma_1^2 = \sigma_2^2$).

Example 4

Small-Sample Confidence Interval for $(\mu_1 - \mu_2)$— Managerial Success

Problem Behavioral researchers have developed an index designed to measure managerial success. The index (measured on a 100-point scale) is based on the manager's length of time in the organization and his or her level within the firm; the higher the index, the more successful the manager. Suppose a researcher wants to compare the average success index for two groups of managers at a large manufacturing plant. Managers in group 1 engage in a high volume of interactions with people outside the manager's work unit. (Such interactions include phone and face-to-face meetings with customers and suppliers, outside meetings, and public relations work.) Managers in group 2 rarely interact with people outside their work unit. Independent random samples of 12 and 15 managers are selected from groups 1 and 2, respectively, and the success index of each is recorded. The results of the study are given in Table 2.

a. Use the data in the table to estimate the true mean difference between the success indexes of managers in the two groups. Use a 95% confidence interval.
b. Interpret the interval, part **a**.
c. What assumptions must be made so that the estimate is valid? Are they reasonably satisfied?

Table 2	Managerial Success Indexes for Two Groups of Managers										
	Group 1						Group 2				
	Interaction with Outsiders						Few Interactions				
65	58	78	60	68	69	62	53	36	34	56	50
66	70	53	71	63	63	42	57	46	68	48	42
						52	53	43			

Data Set: SUCCES

```
Two-sample T for SUCCESS

GROUP   N    Mean   StDev  SE Mean
1       12   65.33   6.61     1.9
2       15   49.47   9.33     2.4


Difference = mu (1) - mu (2)
Estimate for difference:  15.87
95% CI for difference:  (9.29, 22.45)
T-Test of difference = 0 (vs not =): T-Value = 4.97  P-Value = 0.000  DF = 25
Both use Pooled StDev = 8.2472
```

Figure 7

Minitab printout for Example 4

Solution

a. For this experiment, let μ_1 and μ_2 represent the mean success index of group 1 and group 2 managers, respectively. Then, the objective is to obtain a 95% confidence interval for $(\mu_1 - \mu_2)$.

The first step in constructing the confidence interval is to obtain summary statistics (e.g., $\bar{x}$ and s) on the success index for each group of managers. The data of Table 2 were entered into a computer, and Minitab was used to obtain these descriptive statistics. The Minitab printout appears in Figure 7. Note that $\bar{x}_1 = 65.33$, $s_1 = 6.61$, $\bar{x}_2 = 49.47$, and $s_2 = 9.33$.

Next, we calculate the pooled estimate of variance:

$$s_p^2 = \frac{(n_1 - 1)s_1^2 + (n_2 - 1)s_2^2}{n_1 + n_2 - 2}$$

$$= \frac{(12 - 1)(6.61)^2 + (15 - 1)(9.33)^2}{12 + 15 - 2} = 67.97$$

where s_p^2 is based on $(n_1 + n_2 - 2) = (12 + 15 - 2) = 25$ degrees of freedom. Also, we find $t_{\alpha/2} = t_{.025} = 2.06$ (based on 25 degrees of freedom) from Table III in Appendix: Tables.

Finally, the 95% confidence interval for $(\mu_1 - \mu_2)$, the difference between mean managerial success indexes for the two groups, is

$$(\bar{x}_1 - \bar{x}_2) \pm t_{\alpha/2}\sqrt{s_p^2\left(\frac{1}{n_1} + \frac{1}{n_2}\right)} = 65.33 - 49.47 \pm t_{.025}\sqrt{67.97\left(\frac{1}{12} + \frac{1}{15}\right)}$$

$$= 15.86 \pm (2.06)(3.19)$$

$$= 15.86 \pm 6.58$$

or $(9.28, 22.44)$. This interval agrees (except for rounding) with the one shown at the bottom of the Minitab printout, Figure 7.

b. Notice that the confidence interval includes positive differences only. Consequently, we are 95% confident that $(\mu_1 - \mu_2)$ exceeds 0. In fact, we estimate the mean success index, μ_1, for managers with a high volume of outsider interaction (group 1) to be anywhere between 9.28 and 22.44 points higher than the mean success index, μ_2, of managers with few interactions (group 2).

c. To properly use the small-sample confidence interval, the following assumptions must be satisfied:

1. The samples of managers are randomly and independently selected from the populations of group 1 and group 2 managers.
2. The success indexes are normally distributed for both groups of managers.
3. The variance of the success indexes is the same for the two populations (i.e., $\sigma_1^2 = \sigma_2^2$).

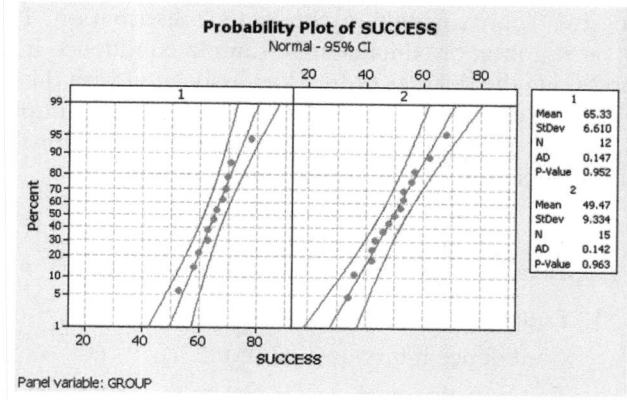

Figure 8

Minitab normal probability plots for manager success index

The first assumption is satisfied, based on the information provided about the sampling procedure in the problem description. To check the plausibility of the remaining two assumptions, we resort to graphical methods. Figure 8 is a Minitab printout that displays normal probability plots for the success indexes of the two samples of managers. The near straight-line trends on both plots indicate that the success index distributions are approximately mound-shaped and symmetric. Consequently, each sample data set appears to come from a population that is approximately normal.

One way to check assumption #3 is to test the null hypothesis $H_0: \sigma_1^2 = \sigma_2^2$. This test is covered in Section 6. Another approach is to examine box plots for the sample data. Figure 9 is a Minitab printout that shows side-by-side vertical box plots for the success indexes in the two samples. The box plot represents the "spread" of a data set. The two box plots appear to have about the same spread; thus, the samples appear to come from populations with approximately the same variance.

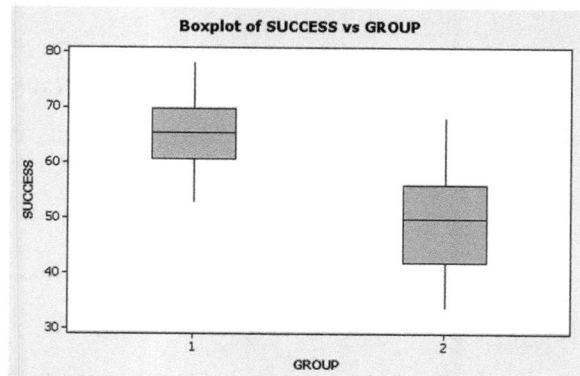

Figure 9

Minitab box plots for manager success index

Look Back All three assumptions appear to be reasonably satisfied for this application of the small-sample confidence interval.

Now Work Exercise 7

The two-sample t-statistic is a powerful tool for comparing population means when the assumptions are satisfied. It has also been shown to retain its usefulness when the sampled populations are only approximately normally distributed. And when the sample sizes are equal, the assumption of equal population variances can be relaxed—that is, if $n_1 = n_2$, then σ_1^2 and σ_2^2 can be quite different, and the test statistic will still possess, approximately, a Student's t-distribution. In the case where $\sigma_1^2 \neq \sigma_2^2$ and $n_1 \neq n_2$, an approximate small-sample confidence interval or test can be obtained by modifying the degrees of freedom associated with the t-distribution.

The next box gives the approximate small-sample procedures to use when the assumption of equal variances is violated. The test for the "unequal sample sizes" case is based on Satterthwaite's (1946) approximation.

Approximate Small-Sample Procedures when $\sigma_1^2 \neq \sigma_2^2$

1. **Equal sample sizes ($n_1 = n_2 = n$)**

   Confidence interval: $(\bar{x}_1 - \bar{x}_2) \pm t_{\alpha/2}\sqrt{(s_1^2 + s_1^2)/n}$

   Test statistic for $H_0: (\mu_1 - \mu_2) = 0$: $\quad t = (\bar{x}_2 - \bar{x}_2)/\sqrt{(s_1^2 + s_2^2)/n}$

   where t is based on $\nu = n_1 + n_2 - 2 = 2(n - 1)$ degrees of freedom.

2. **Unequal sample sizes ($n_1 \neq n_2$)**

   Confidence interval: $(\bar{x}_1 - \bar{x}_2) \pm t_{\alpha/2}\sqrt{(s_1^2/n_1) + (s_2^2/n_2)}$

   Test statistic for $H_0: (\mu_1 - \mu_2) = 0$: $t = (\bar{x}_1 - \bar{x}_2)/\sqrt{(s_1^2/n_1) + (s_2^2/n_2)}$ where t is based on degrees of freedom equal to

   $$\nu = \frac{(s_1^2/n_1 + s_2^2/n_2)^2}{\dfrac{(s_1^2/n_1)^2}{n_1 - 1} + \dfrac{(s_1^2/n_2)^2}{n_2 - 1}}$$

Note: The value of ν will generally not be an integer. Round ν down to the nearest integer to use the t-table.

When the assumptions are clearly not satisfied, you can select larger samples from the populations or you can use other available statistical tests (nonparametric statistical tests).

What Should You Do if the Assumptions Are Not Satisfied?

Answer: If you are concerned that the assumptions are not satisfied, use the Wilcoxon rank sum test for independent samples to test for a shift in population distributions.

STATISTICS in ACTION REVISITED

Comparing Mean Price Changes

Refer to the *ZixIt v. Visa* court case described in the Statistics in Action. Recall that a Visa executive wrote e-mails and made Web site postings in an effort to undermine a new online credit card processing system developed by ZixIt. ZixIt sued Visa for libel, asking for $699 million in damages. An expert statistician, hired by the defendants (Visa), performed an "event study" in which he matched the Visa executive's e-mail postings with movement of ZixIt's stock price the next business day. The data were collected daily from September 1 to December 30, 1999 (an 83-day period) and are available in the **ZIXVSA** file. In addition to daily closing price (dollars) of ZixIt stock, the file contains a variable for whether or not the Visa executive posted an e-mail and the change in price of the stock the following business day. During the 83-day period, the executive posted e-mails on 43 days and had no postings on 40 days.

If the daily postings by the Visa executive had a negative impact on ZixIt stock, then the average price change following nonposting days should exceed the average

---

Two-Sample T-Test and CI: PriceChange, Posting

```
Two-sample T for PriceChange

Posting  N   Mean   StDev  SE Mean
NO       40  -0.13  3.46   0.55
POST     43  0.06   2.20   0.34


Difference = mu (NO) - mu (POST)
Estimate for difference:  -0.188
95% CI for difference:  (-1.470, 1.093)
T-Test of difference = 0 (vs not =): T-Value = -0.29  P-Value = 0.770  DF = 65
```

Figure SIA1

Minitab comparison of two price change means

price change following posting days. Consequently, one way to analyze the data is to conduct a comparison of two population means through either a confidence interval or a test of hypothesis. Here, we let μ_1 represent the mean price change of ZixIt stock following all nonposting days and μ_2 represent the mean price change of ZixIt stock following posting days. If, in fact, the charges made by ZixIt are true, then μ_1 will exceed μ_2. However, if the data do not support ZixIt's claim, then we will not be able to reject the null hypothesis H_0: $(\mu_1 - \mu_2) = 0$ in favor of H_a: $(\mu_1 - \mu_2) > 0$. Similarly, if a confidence interval for $(\mu_1 - \mu_2)$ contains the value 0, then there will be no evidence to support ZixIt's claim.

Because both sample sizes ($n_1 = 40$ and $n_2 = 43$) are large, we can apply the large-sample z-test or large-sample confidence interval procedure for independent samples. A Minitab printout for this analysis is shown in Figure SIA1. Both the 95% confidence interval and p-value for a two-tailed test of hypothesis are highlighted on the printout. Note that the 95% confidence interval, ($-\$1.47$, $\$1.09$), includes the value $\$0$, and the p-value for the two-tailed hypothesis test (.770) implies that the two population means are not significantly different. Also, interestingly, the sample mean price change after posting days ($\bar{x}_1 = \$.06$) is small and positive, while the sample mean price change after nonposting days ($\bar{x}_2 = -\$.13$) is small and negative, totally contradicting ZixIt's claim.

The statistical expert for the defense presented these results to the jury, arguing that the "average price change following posting days is small and similar to the average price change following nonposting days" and "the difference in the means is not statistically significant."

Note: The statistician also compared the mean ZixIt trading volume (number of ZixIt stock shares traded) after posting days to the mean trading volume after nonposting days. These results are shown in Figure SIA2. You can see that the 95% confidence interval for the difference in mean trading volume (highlighted) includes 0, and the p-value for a two-tailed test of hypothesis for a difference in means (also highlighted) is not statistically significant. These results were also presented to the jury in defense of Visa.

```
Two-sample T for VolumeAfter

Posting  N    Mean    StDev   SE Mean
NO       40   719645  430837  68121
POST     43   578665  333921  50922


Difference = mu (NO) - mu (POST)
Estimate for difference:  140980
95% CI for difference:  (-28526, 310485)
T-Test of difference = 0 (vs not =): T-Value = 1.66  P-Value = 0.102  DF = 73
```

Figure SIA2

Minitab comparison of two trading volume means analysis

Data Set: ZIXVSA

Exercises 1–25

Please be aware that some of the following problems may require knowledge of concepts that are not presented in this chapter.

Learning the Mechanics

1 The purpose of this exercise is to compare the variability of $\bar{x}_1$ and $\bar{x}_2$ with the variability of $(\bar{x}_1 - \bar{x}_2)$.

   a. Suppose the first sample is selected from a population with mean $\mu_1 = 150$ and variance $\sigma_1^2 = 900$. Within what range should the sample mean vary about 95% of the time in repeated samples of 100 measurements from this distribution? That is, construct an interval extending 2 standard deviations of $\bar{x}_1$ on each side of μ_1.

   b. Suppose the second sample is selected independently of the first from a second population with mean $\mu_2 = 150$ and variance $\sigma_2^2 = 1,600$. Within what range should the sample mean vary about 95% of the time in repeated samples of 100 measurements from this distribution? That is, construct an interval extending 2 standard deviations of $\bar{x}_2$ on each side of μ_2.

   c. Now consider the difference between the two sample means $(\bar{x}_1 - \bar{x}_2)$. What are the mean and standard deviation of the sampling distribution of $(\bar{x}_1 - \bar{x}_2)$?

   d. Within what range should the difference in sample means vary about 95% of the time in repeated independent samples of 100 measurements each from the two populations?

   e. What, in general, can be said about the variability of the difference between independent sample means relative to the variability of the individual sample means?

2 Independent random samples of 64 observations each are chosen from two normal populations with the following means and standard deviations:

Population 1	Population 2
$\mu_1 = 12$	$\mu_2 = 10$
$\sigma_1 = 4$	$\sigma_2 = 3$

Let $\bar{x}_1$ and $\bar{x}_2$ denote the two sample means.

   a. Give the mean and standard deviation of the sampling distribution of $\bar{x}_1$.

   b. Give the mean and standard deviation of the sampling distribution of $\bar{x}_2$.

   c. Suppose you were to calculate the difference between the sample means $(\bar{x}_1 - \bar{x}_2)$. Find the mean and standard deviation of the sampling distribution of $(\bar{x}_1 - \bar{x}_2)$.

   d. Will the statistic $(\bar{x}_1 - \bar{x}_2)$ be normally distributed? Explain.

3 In order to compare the means of two populations, independent random samples of 400 observations are selected from each population, with the following results:

Sample 1	Sample 2
$\bar{x}_1 = 5{,}275$	$\bar{x}_2 = 5{,}240$
$s_1 = 150$	$s_2 = 200$

   a. Use a 95% confidence interval to estimate the difference between the population means $(\mu_1 - \mu_2)$. Interpret the confidence interval.

   b. Test the null hypothesis $H_0: (\mu_1 - \mu_2) = 0$ versus the alternative hypothesis $H_a: (\mu_1 - \mu_2) \neq 0$. Give the significance level of the test and interpret the result.

   c. Suppose the test in part b was conducted with the alternative hypothesis $H_a: (\mu_1 - \mu_2) > 0$. How would your answer to part b change?

   d. Test the null hypothesis $H_0: (\mu_1 - \mu_2) = 25$ versus $H_a: (\mu_1 - \mu_2) \neq 25$. Give the significance level and interpret the result. Compare your answer to the test conducted in part b.

   e. What assumptions are necessary to ensure the validity of the inferential procedures applied in parts a–d?

4 To use the t-statistic to test for a difference between the means of two populations, what assumptions must be made about the two populations? About the two samples?

5 Two populations are described in each of the following cases. In which cases would it be appropriate to apply the small-sample t-test to investigate the difference between the population means?

   a. Population 1: Normal distribution with variance σ_1^2. Population 2: Skewed to the right with variance $\sigma_2^2 = \sigma_1^2$.

   b. Population 1: Normal distribution with variance σ_1^2. Population 2: Normal distribution with variance $\sigma_2^2 \neq \sigma_1^2$.

   c. Population 1: Skewed to the left with variance σ_1^2. Population 2: Skewed to the left with variance $\sigma_2^2 = \sigma_1^2$.

   d. Population 1: Normal distribution with variance σ_1^2. Population 2: Normal distribution with variance $\sigma_2^2 = \sigma_1^2$.

   e. Population 1: Uniform distribution with variance σ_1^2. Population 2: Uniform distribution with variance $\sigma_2^2 = \sigma_1^2$.

6 Assume that $\sigma_1^2 = \sigma_2^2 = \sigma^2$. Calculate the pooled estimator of σ^2 for each of the following cases:

   a. $s_1^2 = 120$, $s_2^2 = 100$, $n_1 = n_2 = 25$
   b. $s_1^2 = 12$, $s_2^2 = 20$, $n_1 = 20$, $n_2 = 10$
   c. $s_1^2 = .15$, $s_2^2 = .20$, $n_1 = 6$, $n_2 = 10$
   d. $s_1^2 = 3{,}000$, $s_2^2 = 2{,}500$, $n_1 = 16$, $n_2 = 17$

Note that the pooled estimate is a weighted average of the sample variances. To which of the variances does the pooled estimate fall nearer in each of the above cases?

7 Independent random samples from normal populations produced the results shown in the next table.

Sample 1	Sample 2
1.2	4.2
3.1	2.7
1.7	3.6
2.8	3.9
3.0	

   a. Calculate the pooled estimate of σ^2.

   b. Do the data provide sufficient evidence to indicate that $\mu_2 > \mu_1$? Test using $\alpha = .10$.

   c. Find a 90% confidence interval for $(\mu_1 - \mu_2)$.

L08007

d. Which of the two inferential procedures, the test of hypothesis in part **b** or the confidence interval in part **c**, provides more information about $(\mu_1 - \mu_2)$?

8 Two independent random samples have been selected— 100 observations from population 1 and 100 from population 2. Sample means $\bar{x}_1 = 26.6$ and $\bar{x}_2 = 15.5$ were obtained. From previous experience with these populations, it is known that the variances are $\sigma_1^2 = 9$ and $\sigma_2^2 = 16$.

a. Find $\sigma_{(\bar{x}_1 - \bar{x}_2)}$.

b. Sketch the approximate sampling distribution for $(\bar{x}_1 - \bar{x}_2)$ assuming $(\mu_1 - \mu_2) = 10$.

c. Locate the observed value of $(\bar{x}_1 - \bar{x}_2)$ on the graph you drew in part **b**. Does it appear that this value contradicts the null hypothesis $H_0: (\mu_1 - \mu_2) = 10$?

d. Use the z-table to determine the rejection region for the test of $H_0: (\mu_1 - \mu_2) = 10$ against $H_0: (\mu_1 - \mu_2) \neq 10$. Use $\alpha = .05$.

e. Conduct the hypothesis test of part **d** and interpret your result.

f. Construct a 95% confidence interval for $(\mu_1 - \mu_2)$. Interpret the interval.

g. Which inference provides more information about the value of $(\mu_1 - \mu_2)$—the test of hypothesis in part **e** or the confidence interval in part **f**?

9 Independent random samples of $n_1 = 233$ and $n_2 = 312$ are selected from two populations and used to test the hypothesis $H_0: (\mu_1 - \mu_2) = 0$ against the alternative $H_a: (\mu_1 - \mu_2) \neq 0$.

a. The two-tailed p-value of the test is .1150. Interpret this result.

b. If the alternative hypothesis had been $H_a: (\mu_1 - \mu_2) < 0$, how would the p-value change? Interpret the p-value for this one-tailed test.

10 Independent random samples from approximately normal populations produced the results shown below.

L08010

Sample 1				Sample 2			
52	33	42	44	52	43	47	56
41	50	44	51	62	53	61	50
45	38	37	40	56	52	53	60
44	50	43		50	48	60	55

a. Do the data provide sufficient evidence to conclude that $(\mu_2 - \mu_1) > 10$? Test using $\alpha = .01$.

b. Construct a 98% confidence interval for $(\mu_2 - \mu_1)$. Interpret your result.

11 Independent random samples selected from two normal populations produced the sample means and standard deviations shown below.

Sample 1	Sample 2
$n_1 = 17$	$n_2 = 12$
$\bar{x}_1 = 5.4$	$\bar{x}_2 = 7.9$
$s_1 = 3.4$	$s_2 = 4.8$

a. Conduct the test $H_0: (\mu_1 - \mu_2) = 0$ against $H_a: (\mu_1 - \mu_2) \neq 0$. Interpret the results.

b. Estimate $(\mu_1 - \mu_2)$ using a 95% confidence interval.

Applying the Concepts—Basic

12 Lobster trap placement. The *Bulletin of Marine Science* (April 2010) did a study of lobster trap placement. The variable of interest was the average distance separating traps—called *trap spacing*—deployed by teams of fishermen fishing for the red spiny lobster in Baja California Sur, Mexico. The trap-spacing measurements (in meters) for a sample of seven teams from the Bahia Tortugas (BT) fishing cooperative are repeated in the table. In addition, trap-spacing measurements for eight teams from the Punta Abreojos (PA) fishing cooperative are listed. For this problem, we are interested in comparing the mean trap-spacing measurements of the two fishing cooperatives.

TRAPS

BT Cooperative:	93	99	105	94	82	70	86	
PA Cooperative:	118	94	106	72	90	66	153	98

Source: Based on Shester, G. G. "Explaining catch variation among Baja California lobster fishers through spatial analysis of trap-placement decisions," *Bulletin of Marine Science*, Vol. 86, No. 2, April 2010 (Table 1).

a. Identify the target parameter for this study.

b. Compute a point estimate of the target parameter.

c. What is the problem with using the normal (z) statistic to find a confidence interval for the target parameter?

d. Find a 90% confidence interval for the target parameter.

e. Use the interval, part **d**, to make a statement about the difference in mean trap-spacing measurements of the two fishing cooperatives.

f. What conditions must be satisfied for the inference, part **e**, to be valid?

13 Last name and acquisition timing. The speed with which consumers decide to purchase a product was investigated in the *Journal of Consumer Research* (August 2011). The researchers theorized that consumers with last names that begin with letters later in the alphabet will tend to acquire items faster than those whose last names begin with letters earlier in the alphabet—called the *last name effect*. MBA students were offered up to four free tickets to attend a top-ranked women's college basketball game for which there was a limited supply of tickets. The first letter of the last name of those who responded to an e-mail offer in time to receive the tickets was noted as well as the response time (measured in minutes). The researchers compared the response times for two groups of MBA students: (1) those with last names beginning with one of the first nine letters of the alphabet and (2) those with last names beginning with one of the last nine letters of the alphabet. Summary statistics for the two groups are provided in the table.

	First 9 Letters: A–I	Last 9 Letters: R–Z
Sample size:	25	25
Mean response time (minutes):	25.08	19.38
Standard deviation (minutes):	10.41	7.12

Source: Based on Carlson, K. A., & Conrad, J. M. "The last name effect: How last name influences acquisition timing," *Journal of Consumer Research*, Vol. 38, No. 2, August 2011.

a. Construct a 95% confidence interval for the difference between the true mean response times for MBA students in the two groups.

b. Based on the interval, part **a,** which group has the shorter mean response time? Does this result support the researchers' *last name effect* theory? Explain.

14 **Effectiveness of teaching software.** Educational software—ranging from video-game-like programs played on Sony PlayStations to rigorous drilling exercises used on computers—has become very popular in school districts across the country. The U.S. Department of Education (DOE) recently conducted a national study of the effectiveness of educational software. In one phase of the study, a sample of 1,516 first-grade students in classrooms that used educational software was compared to a sample of 1,103 first-grade students in classrooms that did not use the technology. In its *Report to Congress* (March 2007), the DOE concluded that "[mean] test scores [of students on the SAT reading test] were not significantly higher in classrooms using reading... software products" than in classrooms that did not use educational software.

a. Identify the parameter of interest to the DOE.

b. Specify the null and alternative hypotheses for the test conducted by the DOE.

c. The *p*-value for the test was reported as .62. Based on this value, do you agree with the conclusion of the DOE? Explain.

15 **Children's recall of TV ads.** Marketing professors at Robert Morris and Kent State Universities examined children's recall and recognition of television advertisements (*Journal of Advertising,* Spring 2006). Two groups of children were shown a 60-second commercial for Sunkist FunFruit Rock-n-Roll Shapes. One group (the A/V group) was shown the ad with both audio and video; the second group (the video only group) was shown only the video portion of the commercial. Following the viewing, the children were asked to recall 10 specific items from the ad. The number of the 10 items recalled correctly by each child is summarized in the table. The researchers theorized that "children who receive an audiovisual presentation will have the same level of mean recall of ad information as those who receive only the visual aspects of the ad."

Video Only Group	A/V Group
$n_1 = 20$	$n_2 = 20$
$\bar{x}_1 = 3.70$	$\bar{x}_2 = 3.30$
$s_1 = 1.98$	$s_2 = 2.13$

Source: Based on Maher, J. K., Hu, M. Y., & Kolbe, R. H. "Children's recall of television ad elements," *Journal of Advertising,* Spring 2006, Volume 35(1).

a. Set up the appropriate null and alternative hypotheses to test the researchers' theory.

b. Find the value of the test statistic.

c. Give the rejection region for $\alpha = .10$.

d. Make the appropriate inference. What can you say about the researchers' theory?

e. The researchers reported the *p*-value of the test as *p*-value = .542. Interpret this result.

f. What conditions are required for the inference to be valid?

16 **Drug content assessment.** *Analytical Chemistry* (Dec. 15, 2009) did a study in which scientists used high-performance liquid chromatography to determine the amount of drug in a tablet. Twenty-five tablets were produced at each of two different, independent sites. Drug concentrations (measured as a percentage) for the tablets produced at the two sites are listed in the table below. The scientists want to know whether there is any difference between the mean drug concentration in tablets produced at Site 1 and the corresponding mean at Site 2. Use the accompanying Minitab printout to help the scientists draw a conclusion.

Site 1

91.28	92.83	89.35	91.90	82.85	94.83	89.83	89.00	84.62
86.96	88.32	91.17	83.86	89.74	92.24	92.59	84.21	89.36
90.96	92.85	89.39	89.82	89.91	92.16	88.67		

Site 2

89.35	86.51	89.04	91.82	93.02	88.32	88.76	89.26	90.36
87.16	91.74	86.12	92.10	83.33	87.61	88.20	92.78	86.35
93.84	91.20	93.44	86.77	83.77	93.19	81.79		

Source: Borman, P. J., Marion, J. C., Damjanov, I., & Jackson, P. "Design and analysis of method equivalence studies," *Analytical Chemistry,* Vol. 81, No. 24, December 15, 2009 (Table 3).

Two-Sample T-Test and CI: Content, Site

```
Two-sample T for Content

Site   N    Mean   StDev   SE Mean
1      25   89.55  3.07    0.61
2      25   89.03  3.34    0.67


Difference = mu (1) - mu (2)
Estimate for difference:  0.515
95% CI for difference:  (-1.308, 2.338)
T-Test of difference = 0 (vs not =): T-Value = 0.57  P-Value = 0.573  DF = 48
Both use Pooled StDev = 3.2057
```

Minitab output for Exercise 16

17 Buy-side vs. sell-side analysts' earnings forecasts. The *Financial Analysts Journal* (Jul./Aug. 2008) did a study of financial analysts' forecast earnings. Data were collected on 3,526 forecasts made by buy-side analysts and 58,562 forecasts made by sell-side analysts, and the relative absolute forecast error was determined for each. The mean and standard deviation of forecast errors for both types of analysts are given in the table.

	Buy-Side Analysts	Sell-Side Analysts
Sample Size	3,526	58,562
Mean	0.85	−0.05
Standard Deviation	1.93	0.85

Source: Groysberg, B., Healy, P., & Chapman, C. "Buy-side vs. sell-side analysts' earnings forecasts," *Financial Analysts Journal,* Vol. 64, No. 4, Jul./Aug. 2008.

a. Construct a 95% confidence interval for the difference between the mean forecast error of buy-side analysts and the mean forecast error of sell-side analysts.

b. Based on the interval, part **a,** which type of analysis has the greater mean forecast error? Explain.

c. What assumptions about the underlying populations of forecast errors (if any) are necessary for the validity of the inference, part **b**?

Applying the Concepts—Intermediate

18 Homework assistance for accounting students. How much assistance should accounting professors provide students for completing homework? Is too much assistance counterproductive? These were some of the questions of interest in a *Journal of Accounting Education* (Vol. 25, 2007) article. A total of 75 junior-level accounting majors who were enrolled in Intermediate Financial Accounting participated in an experiment. All students took a pretest on a topic not covered in class; then each was given a homework problem to solve on the same topic. However, the students were randomly assigned different levels of assistance on the homework. Some (20 students) were given the completed solution, some (25 students) were given check figures at various steps of the solution, and the rest (30 students) were given no help. After finishing the homework, each student was given a posttest on the subject. One of the variables of interest to the researchers was the knowledge gain (or, test score improvement), measured as the difference between the posttest and pretest scores. The sample mean knowledge gains for the three groups of students are provided in the table.

	No Solutions	Check Figures	Completed Solutions
Sample Size	30	25	20
Sample Mean	2.43	2.72	1.95

Source: Based on Lindquist, T. M., & Olsen, L. M. "How much help, is too much help? An experimental investigation of the use of check figures and completed solutions in teaching intermediate accounting," *Journal of Accounting Education,* Vol. 25, No. 3, 2007, pp. 103–117 (Table 1, Panel B).

a. The researchers theorized that as the level of homework assistance increased, the test score improvement

from pretest to posttest would decrease. Do the sample means reported in the table support this theory?

b. What is the problem with using only the sample means to make inferences about the population mean knowledge gains for the three groups of students?

c. The researchers conducted a statistical test of hypothesis to compare the mean knowledge gain of students in the "no solutions" group to the mean knowledge gain of students in the "check figures" group. Based on the theory, part **a,** set up the null and alternative hypotheses for the test.

d. The observed significance level of the t-test of part *c* was reported as .8248. Using $\alpha = .05$, interpret this result.

e. The researchers conducted a statistical test of hypothesis to compare the mean knowledge gain of students in the "completed solutions" group to the mean knowledge gain of students in the "check figures" group. Based on the theory, part **a,** set up the null and alternative hypotheses for the test.

f. The observed significance level of the *t*-test of part **e** was reported as .1849. Using $\alpha = .05$, interpret this result.

g. The researchers conducted a statistical test of hypothesis to compare the mean knowledge gain of students in the "no solutions" group to the mean knowledge gain of students in the "completed solutions" group. Based on the theory, part **a,** set up the null and alternative hypotheses for the test.

h. The observed significance level of the *t*-test of part **g** was reported as .2726. Using $\alpha = .05$, interpret this result.

19 Patent infringement case. *Chance* (Fall 2002) described a lawsuit where Intel Corp. was charged with infringing on a patent for an invention used in the automatic manufacture of computer chips. In response, Intel accused the inventor of adding material to his patent notebook after the patent was witnessed and granted. The case rested on whether a patent witness' signature was written on top of key text in the notebook or under the key text. Intel hired a physicist who used an X-ray beam to measure the relative concentration of certain elements (e.g., nickel, zinc, potassium) at several spots on the notebook page. The zinc measurements for three notebook locations—on a text line, on a witness line, and on the intersection of the witness and text lines—are provided in the table.

PATENT

Text Line	.335	.374	.440			
Witness Line	.210	.262	.188	.329	.439	.397
Intersection	.393	.353	.285	.295	.319	

a. Use a test or a confidence interval (at $\alpha = .05$) to compare the mean zinc measurement for the text line with the mean for the intersection.

b. Use a test or a confidence interval (at $\alpha = .05$) to compare the mean zinc measurement for the witness line with the mean for the intersection.

c. From the results, parts **a** and **b,** what can you infer about the mean zinc measurements at the three notebook locations?

d. What assumptions are required for the inferences to be valid? Are they reasonably satisfied?

Data for Exercise 21

Control Group:

1	24	5	16	21	7	20	1	9	20	19	10	23	16	0	4	9	13	17	13	0	2	12	11	7	3	11
1	19	9	12	18	5	21	30	15	4	2	12	11	10	13	11	3	6	10	13	16	12	28	19	12	20	

Rudeness Condition:

4	11	18	11	9	6	5	11	9	12	7	5	7	3	11	1	9	11	10	7	8	9	10	7
11	4	13	5	4	7	8	3	8	15	9	16	10	0	7	15	13	9	2	13	10			

20 Producer willingness to supply biomass. The conversion of biomass to energy is critical for producing transportation fuels. How willing are producers to supply biomass products such as cereal straw, corn stover, and surplus hay? To answer this question, economists conducted a survey of producers in both mid-Missouri and southern Illinois (*Biomass and Energy,* Vol. 36, 2012). Independent samples of 431 Missouri producers and 508 Illinois producers participated in the survey. Each producer was asked to give the maximum proportion of hay produced that he or she would be willing to sell to the biomass market. Summary statistics for the two groups of producers are listed in the table. Does the mean amount of surplus that hay producers are willing to sell to the biomass market differ for the two areas, Missouri and Illinois? Use $\alpha = .05$ to make the comparison.

	Missouri Producers	Illinois Producers
Sample Size	431	508
Mean Amount of Hay (%)	21.5	22.2
Standard Deviation (%)	33.4	34.9

Source: Based on Altman, I., & Sanders, D. "Producer willingness and ability to supply biomass: Evidence from the U.S. Midwest," *Biomass and Energy,* Vol. 36, No. 8, 2012 (Tables 3 and 7).

21 Does rudeness really matter in the workplace? Studies have established that rudeness in the workplace can lead to retaliatory and counterproductive behavior. However, there has been little research on how rude behaviors influence a victim's task performance. Such a study was conducted, with the results published in the *Academy of Management Journal* (Oct. 2007). College students enrolled in a management course were randomly assigned to one of two experimental conditions: rudeness condition (45 students) and control group (53 students). Each student was asked to write down as many uses for a brick as possible in 5 minutes. For those students in the rudeness condition, the facilitator displayed rudeness by generally berating students for being irresponsible and

unprofessional (due to a late-arriving confederate). No comments were made about the late-arriving confederate to students in the control group. The number of different uses for a brick was recorded for each of the 98 students and is shown at the top of the page. Conduct a statistical analysis (at $\alpha = .01$) to determine if the true mean performance level for students in the rudeness condition is lower than the true mean performance level for students in the control group.

22 Service without a smile. "Service with a smile" is a slogan that many businesses adhere to. However, there are some jobs (e.g., those of judges, law enforcement officers, pollsters) that require neutrality when dealing with the public. An organization will typically provide "display rules" to guide employees on what emotions they should use when interacting with the public. A *Journal of Applied Psychology* (Vol. 96, 2011) study compared the results of surveys conducted using two different types of display rules: positive (requiring a strong display of positive emotions) and neutral (maintaining neutral emotions at all times). In this designed experiment, 145 undergraduate students were randomly assigned to either a positive display rule condition ($n_1 = 78$) or a neutral display rule condition ($n_2 = 67$). Each participant was trained on how to conduct the survey using the display rules. As a manipulation check, the researchers asked each participant to rate, on a scale of 1 = "strongly agree" to 5 = "strongly disagree," the statement, "This task requires me to be neutral in my expressions."

a. If the manipulation of the participants was successful, which group should have the larger mean response? Explain.

b. The data for the study (simulated based on information provided in the journal article) are listed in the table below. Access the data and run an analysis to determine if the manipulation was successful. Conduct a test of hypothesis using $\alpha = .05$.

c. What assumptions, if any, are required for the inference from the test to be valid?

Data for Exercise 22

Positive Display Rule:

2	4	3	3	3	3	4	4	4	4	4	4	4	4	4	4	4	4	4	5
4	4	4	4	4	4	4	4	4	4	4	4	4	4	4	5	5	5	5	5
5	5	5	5	5	5	5	5	5	5	5	5	5	5	5	5	5	5	5	5
5	5	5	5	5	5	5	5	5	5	5	5	5	5	5	5	5	5		

Neutral Display Rule:

3	3	2	1	2	1	1	1	2	2	1	2	2	2	3	2	2	1	2
2	2	2	2	1	2	2	2	2	2	2	1	2	2	2	2	2	2	2
3	2	1	2	2	2	1	2	1	2	2	3	2	2	2	2	2	2	2
2	2	2	2	1	2	2	2	2	2									

23 Is honey a cough remedy? *Archives of Pediatrics and Adolescent Medicine* (Dec. 2007) did a study of honey as a children's cough remedy. Children who were ill with an upper respiratory tract infection and their parents participated in the study. Parents were instructed to give their sick child a dosage of liquid "medicine" prior to bedtime. Unknown to the parents, some were given a dosage of dextromethorphan (DM)—an over-the-counter cough medicine—while others were given a similar dose of honey. (*Note*: A third group gave their children no medicine.) Parents then rated their children's cough symptoms, and the improvement in total cough symptoms score was determined for each child. The data (improvement scores) for the 35 children in the DM dosage group and the 35 children in the honey dosage group are reproduced in the table below. Do you agree with the statement (extracted from the article), "Honey may be a preferable treatment for the cough and sleep difficulty associated with childhood upper respiratory tract infection"? Use the comparison of two means methodology presented in this section to answer the question.

Honey Dosage:

12 11 15 11 10 13 10 4 15 16 9 14 10 6 10 8 11
12 12 8 12 9 11 15 10 15 9 13 8 12 10 8 9 5 12

DM Dosage:

4 6 9 4 7 7 7 9 12 10 11 6 3 4 9 7 8
12 12 4 12 13 7 10 13 9 4 4 10 15 9 12 6

Source: Paul, I. M., et al. "Effect of honey, dextromethorphan, and no treatment on nocturnal cough and sleep quality for coughing children and their parents," *Archives of Pediatrics and Adolescent Medicine*, Vol. 161, No. 12, Dec. 2007 (data simulated).

24 Cooling method for gas turbines. The *Journal of Engineering for Gas Turbines and Power* (Jan. 2005) did a study of gas turbines augmented with high-pressure inlet fogging. The researchers classified gas turbines into three categories: traditional, advanced, and aeroderivative. Summary statistics on heat rate (kilojoules per kilowatt per hour) for each of the three types of gas turbines are shown in the Minitab printout (at the top of the next column).
a. Is there sufficient evidence of a difference between the mean heat rates of traditional augmented gas turbines and aeroderivative augmented gas turbines? Test using $\alpha = .05$.
b. Is there sufficient evidence of a difference between the mean heat rates of advanced augmented gas turbines and aeroderivative augmented gas turbines? Test using $\alpha = .05$.

Minitab Output for Exercise 24

Descriptive Statistics: HEATRATE

Variable	ENGINE	N	Mean	StDev	Minimum	Maximum
HEATRATE	Advanced	21	9764	639	9105	11588
	Aeroderiv	7	12312	2652	8714	16243
	Traditional	39	11544	1279	10086	14796

Applying the Concepts—Advanced

25 Ages of self-employed immigrants. Is self-employment for immigrant workers a faster route to economic advancement in the country? This was one of the questions studied in research published in the *International Journal of Manpower* (Vol. 32, 2011). One aspect of the study involved comparing the ages of self-employed and wage-earning immigrants. The researcher found that in Sweden, native wage earners tend to be younger than self-employed natives. However, immigrant wage earners tend to be older than self-employed immigrants. This inference was based on summary statistics for male Swedish immigrants shown in the table.

	Self-Employed Immigrants	Wage-Earning Immigrants
Sample Size	870	84,875
Mean Age (years)	44.88	46.79

Source: Based on Andersson, L. "Occupational choice and returns to self-employment among immigrants," *International Journal of Manpower*, Vol. 32, No. 8, 2011 (Table I).

a. Based on the information given, why is it impossible to provide a measure of reliability for the inference "Self-employed immigrants are younger, on average, than wage-earning immigrants in Sweden"?
b. What information do you need to obtain a measure of reliability for the inference, part **a**?
c. Give a value of the test statistic that would lead you to conclude that the true mean age of self-employed immigrants is less than the true mean age of wage-earning immigrants if you are willing to risk a Type I error rate of .01.
d. Assume that σ, the standard deviation of the ages, is the same for both self-employed and wage-earning immigrants. Give an estimate of σ that would lead you to conclude that the true mean age of self-employed immigrants is less than the true mean age of wage-earning immigrants using $\alpha = .01$.
e. Is the true value of σ likely to be larger or smaller than the one you calculated in part **d**?

3 Comparing Two Population Means: Paired Difference Experiments

Suppose you want to compare the mean daily sales of two restaurants located in the same city. If you were to record the restaurants' total sales for each of 12 randomly selected days during a 6-month period, the results might appear as shown in Table 3. Do these data provide evidence of a difference between the mean daily sales of the two restaurants?

Table 3	Daily Sales for Two Restaurants	
Day	Restaurant 1 (x_1)	Restaurant 2 (x_2)
1 (Wednesday)	$1,005	$ 918
2 (Saturday)	2,073	1,971
3 (Tuesday)	873	825
4 (Wednesday)	1,074	999
5 (Friday)	1,932	1,827
6 (Thursday)	1,338	1,281
7 (Thursday)	1,449	1,302
8 (Monday)	759	678
9 (Friday)	1,905	1,782
10 (Monday)	693	639
11 (Saturday)	2,106	2,049
12 (Tuesday)	981	933

Data Set: SALES2

We want to test the null hypothesis that the mean daily sales, μ_1 and μ_2, for the two restaurants are equal against the alternative hypothesis that they differ; that is,

$$H_0: (\mu_1 - \mu_2) = 0$$

$$H_a: (\mu_1 - \mu_2) \neq 0$$

Many researchers mistakenly use the t-statistic for two independent samples (Section 2) to conduct this test. The analysis is shown on the Excel/XLSTAT printout, Figure 10. The test statistic, $t = .38$, is highlighted on the printout, as well as the p-value of the test, p-value $= .7047$. At $\alpha = .10$, the p-value exceeds α. Thus, from *this* analysis we might conclude that insufficient evidence exists to infer that there is a difference in mean daily sales for the two restaurants.

Summary statistics:

Variable	Observations	Minimum	Maximum	Mean	Std. deviation
SALES1	12	693.0000	2106.0000	1349.0000	530.0744
SALES2	12	639.0000	2049.0000	1267.0000	516.0370

t-test for two independent samples / Two-tailed test:

95% confidence interval on the difference between the means:
(−360.8877 , 524.8877)

Difference	82.0000
t (Observed value)	0.3840
|t| (Critical value)	2.0739
DF	22
p-value (Two-tailed	0.7047
alpha	0.05

Figure 10

Excel/XLSTAT printout of an invalid analysis of the data in Table 3

If you carefully examine the data in Table 3, however, you will find this conclusion difficult to accept. The sales of restaurant 1 exceed those of restaurant 2 *for every one of the randomly selected 12 days.* This, in itself, is strong evidence to indicate that μ_1 differs from μ_2, and we will subsequently confirm this fact. Why, then, was the t-test unable to detect this difference? The answer is, *the independent samples* t-*test is not a valid procedure to use with this set of data.*

The t-test is inappropriate because the assumption of independent samples is invalid. We have randomly chosen *days;* thus, once we have chosen the sample of days for restaurant 1, we have *not* independently chosen the sample of days for restaurant

2. The dependence between observations within days can be seen by examining the pairs of daily sales, which tend to rise and fall together as we go from day to day. This pattern provides strong visual evidence of a violation of the assumption of independence required for the two-sample t-test of Section 2. Also, substituting $s_1^2 = 530.07$ and $s_2^2 = 516.04$ (obtained from the printout, Figure 10) into the formula for s_p^2, we obtain

$$s_p^2 = \frac{(n_1 - 1)s_1^2 + (n_2 - 1)s_2^2}{n_1 + n_2 - 2}$$

$$= \frac{(12 - 1)(530.07)^2 + (12 - 1)(516.04)^2}{12 + 12 - 2} = 273{,}635.7$$

Thus, there is a *large variation within samples* (reflected by the large value of s_p^2) in comparison to the relatively *small difference between the sample means*. Because s_p^2 is so large, the t-test of Section 2 is unable to detect a possible difference between μ_1 and μ_2.

Table 4	Daily Sales and Differences for Two Restaurants		
Day	Restaurant 1 (x_1)	Restaurant 2 (x_2)	Difference $d = x_1 - x_2$
1 (Wednesday)	$1,005	$ 918	$ 87
2 (Saturday)	2,073	1,971	102
3 (Tuesday)	873	825	48
4 (Wednesday)	1,074	999	75
5 (Friday)	1,932	1,827	105
6 (Thursday)	1,338	1,281	57
7 (Thursday)	1,449	1,302	147
8 (Monday)	759	678	81
9 (Friday)	1,905	1,782	123
10 (Monday)	693	639	54
11 (Saturday)	2,106	2,049	57
12 (Tuesday)	981	933	48

We now consider a valid method of analyzing the data of Table 3. In Table 4, we add the column of differences between the daily sales of the two restaurants, $d = x_1 - x_2$. We can regard these daily differences in sales as a random sample of all daily differences, past and present. Then we can use this sample to make inferences about the mean of the population of differences, μ_d, which is equal to the difference $(\mu_1 - \mu_2)$—that is, the mean of the population (and sample) of differences equals the difference between the population (and sample) means. Thus, our test becomes

$$H_0: \mu_d = 0 \ [\text{i.e.,} \ (\mu_1 - \mu_2) = 0]$$
$$H_a: \mu_d \neq 0 \ [\text{i.e.,} \ (\mu_1 - \mu_2) \neq 0]$$

The test statistic is a one-sample t because we are now analyzing a single sample of differences for small n:

$$\textit{Test statistic: } t = \frac{\overline{d} - 0}{s_d/\sqrt{n_d}}$$

where $\overline{d}$ = Sample mean difference
  s_d = Sample standard deviation of differences
  n_d = Number of differences = number of pairs

Assumptions: The population of differences in daily sales is approximately normally distributed. The sample differences are randomly selected from the population differences. [*Note:* We do not need to make the assumption that $\sigma_1^2 = \sigma_2^2$.]

Rejection region: At significance level $\alpha = .05$, we will reject H_0 if $|t| > t_{.05}$, where $t_{.05}$ is based on $(n_d - 1)$ degrees of freedom.

Referring to Table III in Appendix: Tables, we find the t-value corresponding to $\alpha = .025$ and $n_d - 1 = 12 - 1 = 11$ df to be $t_{.025} = 2.201$. Then we will reject the null hypothesis if $|t| > 2.201$ (see Figure 11). Note that the number of degrees of freedom has decreased from $n_1 + n_2 - 2 = 22$ to 11 when we use the paired difference experiment rather than the two independent random samples design.

Summary statistics for the $n = 12$ differences are shown on the Minitab printout, Figure 12. Note that $\bar{d} = 82.0$ and $s_d = 32.0$ (rounded). Substituting these values into the formula for the test statistic, we have

$$t = \frac{\bar{d} - 0}{s_d/\sqrt{n_d}} = \frac{82}{32/\sqrt{12}} = 8.88$$

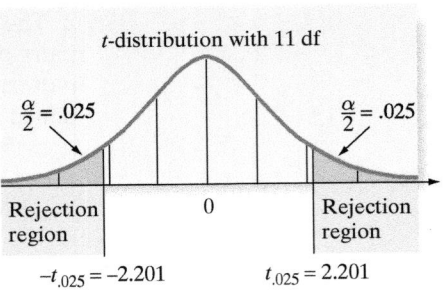

Figure 11

Rejection region for restaurant sales example

Because this value of t falls in the rejection region, we conclude (at $\alpha = .05$) that the difference in population mean daily sales for the two restaurants differs from 0. We can reach the same conclusion by noting that the p-value of the test, highlighted in Figure 12, is approximately 0. The fact that $(\bar{x}_1 - \bar{x}_2) = \bar{d} = \$82.00$ strongly suggests that the mean daily sales for restaurant 1 exceed the mean daily sales for restaurant 2.

```
Paired T for SALES1 - SALES2

             N    Mean   StDev   SE Mean
SALES1       12   1349    530       153
SALES2       12   1267    516       149
Difference   12   82.00   31.99     9.23


95% CI for mean difference: (61.68, 102.32)
T-Test of mean difference = 0 (vs not = 0): T-Value = 8.88  P-Value = 0.000
```

Figure 12

Minitab analysis of differences in daily restaurant sales

This kind of experiment, in which observations are paired and the differences are analyzed, is called a **paired difference experiment.** In many cases, a paired difference experiment can provide more information about the difference between population means than an independent samples experiment. The idea is to compare population means by comparing the differences between pairs of experimental units (objects, people, etc.) that were very similar prior to the experiment. The differencing removes sources of variation that tend to inflate σ^2. For instance, in the restaurant example, the day-to-day variability in daily sales is removed by analyzing the differences between the restaurants' daily sales. Making comparisons within groups of similar experimental units is called **blocking,** and the paired difference experiment is an example of a **randomized block experiment.** In our example, the days represent the blocks.

Some other examples for which the paired difference experiment might be appropriate are the following:

1. Suppose you want to estimate the difference $(\mu_1 - \mu_2)$ in mean price per gallon between two major brands of premium gasoline. If you choose two independent random samples of stations for each brand, the variability in price due to geographic location may be large. To eliminate this source of variability, you could choose pairs of stations of similar size, one station for each brand, in close geographic proximity and use the sample of differences between the prices of the brands to make an inference about $(\mu_1 - \mu_2)$.

2. A college placement center wants to estimate the difference $(\mu_1 - \mu_2)$ in mean starting salaries for men and women graduates who seek jobs through the center. If it independently samples men and women, the starting salaries may vary because of their different college majors and differences in grade point averages. To eliminate these sources of variability, the placement center could match male and female job seekers according to their majors and grade point

averages. Then the differences between the starting salaries of each pair in the sample could be used to make an inference about $(\mu_1 - \mu_2)$.

3. To compare the performance of two automobile salespeople, we might test a hypothesis about the difference $(\mu_1 - \mu_2)$ in their respective mean monthly sales. If we randomly choose n_1 months of salesperson 1's sales and independently choose n_2 months of salesperson 2's sales, the month-to-month variability caused by the seasonal nature of new car sales might inflate s_p^2 and prevent the two-sample t-statistic from detecting a difference between μ_1 and μ_2, if such a difference actually exists. However, by taking the difference in monthly sales for the two salespeople for each of n months, we eliminate the month-to-month variability (seasonal variation) in sales, and the probability of detecting a difference between μ_1 and μ_2, if a difference exists, is increased.

The hypothesis-testing procedures and the method of forming confidence intervals for the difference between two means using a paired difference experiment are summarized in the following boxes for both large and small n.

Paired Difference Confidence Interval for $\mu_d = (\mu_1 - \mu_2)$

Large Sample, Normal (z) Statistic:

$$\bar{d} \pm z_{\alpha/2} \frac{\sigma_d}{\sqrt{n_d}} \approx \bar{d} \pm z_{\alpha/2} \frac{s_d}{\sqrt{n_d}}$$

Small Sample, Student's t-Statistic:

$$\bar{d} \pm t_{\alpha/2} \frac{s_d}{\sqrt{n_d}}$$

where $t_{\alpha/2}$ is based on $(n_d - 1)$ degrees of freedom.

Paired Difference Test of Hypothesis for $\mu_d = (\mu_1 - \mu_2)$

One-Tailed Test	Two-Tailed Test
H_0: $\mu_d = D_0$	H_0: $\mu_d = D_0$
H_a: $\mu_d < D_0$	H_a: $\mu_d \neq D_0$
[or H_a: $\mu_d > D_0$]	

Large Sample, Normal (z) Statistic

Test statistic: $z = \dfrac{\bar{d} - D_0}{\sigma_d/\sqrt{n_d}} \approx \dfrac{\bar{d} - D_0}{s_d/\sqrt{n_d}}$

Rejection region: $z < -z_\alpha$ Rejection region: $|z| > z_{\alpha/2}$
[or $z > z_\alpha$ when H_a: $\mu_d > D_0$]

Small Sample, Student's t-Statistic

Test statistic: $t = \dfrac{\bar{d} - D_0}{s_d/\sqrt{n_d}}$

Rejection region: $t < -t_\alpha$ Rejection region: $|t| > t_{\alpha/2}$
[or $t > t_\alpha$ when H_a: $\mu_d > D_0$]
where t_α and $t_{\alpha/2}$ are based on $(n_d - 1)$ degrees of freedom

---

Conditions Required for Valid Large-Sample Inferences about μ_d

1. A random sample of differences is selected from the target population of differences.

2. The sample size n_d is large (i.e., $n_d \geq 30$). (By the Central Limit Theorem, this condition guarantees that the test statistic will be approximately normal regardless of the shape of the underlying probability distribution of the population.)

> ### Conditions Required for Valid Small-Sample Inferences about μ_d
>
> 1. A random sample of differences is selected from the target population of differences.
> 2. The population of differences has a distribution that is approximately normal.

Example 5

Confidence Interval for μ_d—Comparing Mean Salaries of Males and Females

Problem An experiment is conducted to compare the starting salaries of male and female college graduates who find jobs. Pairs are formed by choosing a male and a female with the same major and similar grade point averages (GPAs). Suppose a random sample of 10 pairs is formed in this manner and the starting annual salary of each person is recorded. The results are shown in Table 5. Compare the mean starting salary, μ_1, for males to the mean starting salary, μ_2, for females using a 95% confidence interval. Interpret the results.

Table 5	Data on Annual Salaries for Matched Pairs of College Graduates		
Pair	Male x_1	Female x_2	Difference $d = x_1 - x_2$
1	$29,300	$28,800	$500
2	41,500	41,600	−100
3	40,400	39,800	600
4	38,500	38,500	0
5	43,500	42,600	900
6	37,800	38,000	−200
7	69,500	69,200	300
8	41,200	40,100	1,100
9	38,400	38,200	200
10	59,200	58,500	700

Data Set: PAIRS

Solution Because the data on annual salary are collected in pairs of males and females matched on GPA and major, a paired difference experiment is performed. To conduct the analysis, we first compute the differences between the salaries, as shown in Table 5. Summary statistics for these $n = 10$ differences are displayed in the Minitab printout, Figure 13.

```
Paired T for MALE - FEMALE

              N    Mean   StDev  SE Mean
MALE         10   43930   11665     3689
FEMALE       10   43530   11617     3674
Difference   10     400     435      137


95% CI for mean difference: (89, 711)
T-Test of mean difference = 0 (vs not = 0): T-Value = 2.91   P-Value = 0.017
```

Figure 13

Minitab analysis of salary differences

The 95% confidence interval for $\mu_d = (\mu_1 - \mu_2)$ for this small sample is

$$\bar{d} \pm t_{\alpha/2} \frac{s_d}{\sqrt{n_d}}$$

where $t_{\alpha/2} = t_{.025} = 2.262$ (obtained from Table III Appendix: Tables) is based on $n_d - 1 = 9$ degrees of freedom. Substituting the values of $\bar{d} = 400$ and $s_d = 435$ shown on the printout, we obtain

$$\bar{d} \pm t_{.025} \frac{s_d}{\sqrt{n_d}} = 400 \pm 2.262 \left(\frac{435}{\sqrt{10}}\right)$$

$$= 400 \pm 311 = (\$89, \$711)$$

[*Note:* This interval is also shown on the Minitab printout, Figure 13.] Our interpretation is that the true mean difference between the starting salaries of males and females falls between $89 and $711, with 95% confidence. Because the interval falls above 0, we infer that $\mu_1 - \mu_2 > 0$; that is, that the mean salary for males exceeds the mean salary for females.

Look Back Remember that $\mu_d = \mu_1 - \mu_2$. So, if $\mu_d > 0$, then $\mu_1 > \mu_2$. Alternatively, if $\mu_d < 0$, then $\mu_1 < \mu_2$.

■ **Now Work Exercise 39**

To measure the amount of information about $(\mu_1 - \mu_2)$ gained by using a paired difference experiment in Example 5 rather than an independent samples experiment, we can compare the relative widths of the confidence intervals obtained by the two methods. A 95% confidence interval for $(\mu_1 - \mu_2)$ using the paired difference experiment is, from Example 5, ($89, $711). If we mistakenly analyzed the same data as though this were an independent samples experiment,* we would first obtain the descriptive statistics shown in the SPSS printout, Figure 14.

Then we would substitute the sample means and standard deviations shown on the printout into the formula for a 95% confidence interval for $(\mu_1 - \mu_2)$ using independent samples:

$$(\bar{x}_1 - \bar{x}_2) \pm t_{.025}\sqrt{s_p^2\left(\frac{1}{n_1} + \frac{1}{n_2}\right)}$$

where

$$s_p^2 = \frac{(n_1 - 1)s_1^2 + (n_2 - 1)s_2^2}{n_1 + n_2 - 2}$$

SPSS performed these calculations and obtained the interval $(-\$10{,}537.50, \$11{,}337.50)$. This interval is highlighted in Figure 14.

Notice that the independent samples interval includes 0. Consequently, if we were to use this interval to make an inference about $(\mu_1 - \mu_2)$, we would incorrectly conclude that the mean starting salaries of males and females do not differ! You can see that the confidence interval for the independent sampling experiment is about five times wider than for the corresponding paired difference confidence interval. Blocking out the variability due to differences in majors and grade point averages significantly increases the information about the difference in male and female mean starting salaries by providing a much more accurate (smaller confidence interval for the same confidence coefficient) estimate of $(\mu_1 - \mu_2)$.

Group Statistics

	GENDER	N	Mean	Std. Deviation	Std. Error Mean
SALARY	M	10	43930.00	11665.148	3688.844
	F	10	43530.00	11616.946	3673.601

Independent Samples Test

		Levene's Test for Equality of Variances		t-test for Equality of Means						
									95% Confidence Interval of the Difference	
		F	Sig.	t	df	Sig. (2-tailed)	Mean Difference	Std. Error Difference	Lower	Upper
SALARY	Equal variances assumed	.000	.991	.077	18	.940	400.00	5206.046	-10537.5	11337.50
	Equal variances not assumed			.077	18.000	.940	400.00	5206.046	-10537.5	11337.51

Figure 14

SPSS analysis of salaries, assuming independent samples

*This is done only to provide a measure of the increase in the amount of information obtained by a paired design in comparison to an unpaired design. Actually, if an experiment is designed using pairing, an unpaired analysis would be invalid because the assumption of independent samples would not be satisfied.

You may wonder whether conducting a paired difference experiment is always superior to an independent samples experiment. The answer is—most of the time but not always. We sacrifice half the degrees of freedom in the t-statistic when a paired difference design is used instead of an independent samples design. This is a loss of information, and unless this loss is more than compensated for by the reduction in variability obtained by blocking (pairing), the paired difference experiment will result in a net loss of information about $(\mu_1 - \mu_2)$. Thus, we should be convinced that the pairing will significantly reduce variability before performing the paired difference experiment. Most of the time this will happen.

One final note: The pairing of the observations is determined before the experiment is performed (that is, by the *design* of the experiment). A paired difference experiment is *never* obtained by pairing the sample observations after the measurements have been acquired.

ETHICS in STATISTICS

In a two-group analysis, intentionally pairing observations after the data have been collected in order to produce a desired result is considered *unethical statistical practice*.

What Do You Do When the Assumption of a Normal Distribution for the Population of Differences Is Not Satisfied?

Answer: Use the Wilcoxon signed rank test for the paired difference design.

Exercises 26–42

Please be aware that some of the following problems may require knowledge of concepts that are not presented in this chapter.

Learning the Mechanics

26 A paired difference experiment produced the following results:

$$n_d = 38 \quad \bar{x}_1 = 92 \quad \bar{x}_2 = 95.5 \quad \bar{d} = -3.5 \quad s_d^2 = 21$$

a. Determine the values of z for which the null hypothesis, $\mu_1 - \mu_2 = 0$, would be rejected in favor of the alternative hypothesis, $\mu_1 - \mu_2 < 0$. Use $\alpha = .10$.

b. Conduct the paired difference test described in part **a.** Draw the appropriate conclusions.

c. What assumptions are necessary so that the paired difference test will be valid?

d. Find a 90% confidence interval for the mean difference μ_d.

e. Which of the two inferential procedures, the confidence interval of part **d** or the test of hypothesis of part **b**, provides more information about the differences between the population means?

27 A paired difference experiment yielded n_d pairs of observations. In each case, what is the rejection region for testing $H_0: \mu_d > 2$?

a. $n_d = 12, \alpha = .05$

b. $n_d = 24, \alpha = .10$

c. $n_d = 4, \alpha = .025$

d. $n_d = 80, \alpha = .01$

28 The data for a random sample of six paired observations are shown in the next table.

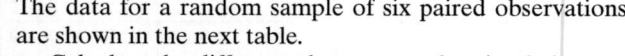

a. Calculate the difference between each pair of observations by subtracting observation 2 from observation 1. Use the differences to calculate $\bar{d}$ and s_d^2.

b. If μ_1 and μ_2 are the means of populations 1 and 2, respectively, express μ_d in terms of μ_1 and μ_2.

Pair	Sample from Population 1 (Observation 1)	Sample from Population 2 (Observation 2)
1	7	4
2	3	1
3	9	7
4	6	2
5	4	4
6	8	7

c. Form a 95% confidence interval for μ_d.

d. Test the null hypothesis $H_0: \mu_d = 0$ against the alternative hypothesis $H_a: \mu_d \neq 0$. Use $\alpha = .05$.

29 The data for a random sample of 10 paired observations are shown in the table below.

Pair	Sample from Population 1	Sample from Population 2
1	19	24
2	25	27
3	31	36
4	52	53
5	49	55
6	34	34
7	59	66
8	47	51
9	17	20
10	51	55

a. If you wish to test whether these data are sufficient to indicate that the mean for population 2 is larger than that for population 1, what are the appropriate null and alternative hypotheses? Define any symbols you use.

b. Conduct the test, part **a,** using $\alpha = .10$.

c. Find a 90% confidence interval for μ_d. Interpret this result.

d. What assumptions are necessary to ensure the validity of this analysis?

30 A paired difference experiment yielded the following results:

$$n_d = 40 \quad \Sigma d = 468 \quad \Sigma d^2 = 6,880$$

a. Test $H_0: \mu_d = 10$ against $H_a: \mu_d \neq 10$, where $\mu_d = (\mu_1 - \mu_2)$. Use $\alpha = .05$.

b. Report the p-value for the test you conducted in part **a.** Interpret the p-value.

c. Do you need to assume that the population of differences is normally distributed? Explain.

Applying the Concepts—Basic

31 Summer weight-loss camp. Camp Jump Start is an 8-week summer camp for overweight and obese adolescents. Counselors develop a weight-management program for each camper that centers on nutrition education and physical activity. To justify the cost of the camp, counselors must provide empirical evidence that the weight-management program is effective. In a study published in *Pediatrics* (April 2010), the body mass index (BMI) was measured for each of 76 campers both at the start and end of camp. Summary statistics on BMI measurements are shown in the table.

	Mean	Standard Deviation
Starting BMI	34.9	6.9
Ending BMI	31.6	6.2
Paired Differences	3.3	1.5

Source: Based on Huelsing, J., Kanafani, N., Mao, J., & White, N. H. "Camp Jump Start: Effects of a residential summer weight-loss camp for older children and adolescents," *Pediatrics,* Vol. 125, No. 4, April 2010 (Table 3).

a. Give the null and alternative hypotheses for determining whether the mean BMI at the end of camp is less than the mean BMI at the start of camp.

b. How should the data be analyzed, as an independent samples test or as a paired difference test? Explain.

c. Calculate the test statistic using the formula for an independent samples test. (*Note:* This is *not* how the test should be conducted.)

d. Calculate the test statistic using the formula for a paired difference test.

e. Compare the test statistics, parts **c** and **d.** Which test statistic provides more evidence in support of the alternative hypothesis?

f. The p-value of the test, part **d,** was reported as $p < .0001$. Interpret this result assuming $\alpha = .01$.

g. Do the differences in BMI values need to be normally distributed in order for the inference, part **f,** to be valid? Explain.

h. Find a 99% confidence interval for the true mean change in BMI for Camp Jump Start campers. Interpret the result.

32 Performance ratings of government agencies. The U.S. Office of Management and Budget (OMB) requires government agencies to produce annual performance and accounting reports (PARS) each year. A research team at George Mason University evaluated the quality of the PARS for 24 government agencies (*The Public Manager,* Summer 2008), where evaluation scores ranged from 12 (lowest) to 60 (highest). The accompanying file contains evaluation scores for all 24 agencies for two consecutive years. Data for a random sample of five of these agencies are shown in the accompanying table. Suppose you want to conduct a paired difference test to determine whether the true mean evaluation score of government agencies in year 2 exceeds the true mean evaluation score in year 1.

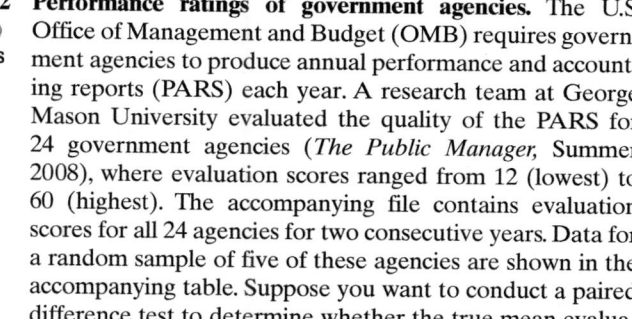

Agency	Year 1 Score	Year 2 Score
GSA	34	40
Agriculture	33	35
Social Security	33	33
USAID	32	42
Defense	17	32

Source: Ellig, J., & Wray, H. "Measuring performance reporting quality," *The Public Manager,* Vol. 37, No. 2, Summer 2008 (p. 66). Copyright © 2008 by Jerry Ellig. Reprinted with permission.

a. Explain why the data should be analyzed using a paired difference test.

b. Compute the difference between the year 2 score and the year 1 score for each sampled agency.

c. Find the mean and standard deviation of the differences, part **b.**

d. Use the summary statistics, part **c,** to find the test statistic.

e. Give the rejection region for the test using $\alpha = .10$.

f. Make the appropriate conclusion in the words of the problem.

33 Twinned drill holes. A traditional method of verifying mineralization grades in mining is to drill twinned holes, i.e., the drilling of a new hole, or "twin," next to an earlier drill hole. The use of twinned drill holes was investigated in *Exploration and Mining Geology* (Vol. 18, 2009). Geologists use data collected at both holes to estimate the total amount of heavy minerals (THM) present at the drilling site. The data in the table on the next page (based on information provided in the journal article) represent THM percentages for a sample of 15 twinned holes drilled at a diamond mine in Africa. The geologists want to know if there is any evidence of a difference in the true THM means of all original holes and their twin holes drilled at the mine.

a. Explain why the data should be analyzed as paired differences.

b. Compute the difference between the "1st Hole" and "2nd Hole" measurements for each drilling location.

c. Find the mean and standard deviation of the differences, part **b.**

d. Use the summary statistics, part **c,** to find a 90% confidence interval for the true mean difference ("1st Hole" minus "2nd Hole") in THM measurements.

e. Interpret the interval, part **d.** Can the geologists conclude that there is no evidence of a difference in the true THM means of all original holes and their twin holes drilled at the mine?

Location	1st Hole	2nd Hole
1	5.5	5.7
2	11.0	11.2
3	5.9	6.0
4	8.2	5.6
5	10.0	9.3
6	7.9	7.0
7	10.1	8.4
8	7.4	9.0
9	7.0	6.0
10	9.2	8.1
11	8.3	10.0
12	8.6	8.1
13	10.5	10.4
14	5.5	7.0
15	10.0	11.2

34 Packaging of a children's health food. The *Journal of Consumer Behaviour* (Vol. 10, 2011) did a study of packaging of a children's health food product. A fictitious brand of a healthy food product—sliced apples—was packaged to appeal to children (a smiling cartoon apple was on the front of the package). The researchers compared the appeal of this fictitious brand to the appeal of a commercially available brand of sliced apples, which was not packaged for children. Each of 408 schoolchildren rated both brands on a 5-point "willingness to eat" scale, with 1 = "not willing at all" and 5 = "very willing." The fictitious brand had a sample mean score of 3.69, while the commercially available brand had a sample mean score of 3.00. The researchers wanted to compare the population mean score for the fictitious brand, μ_F, to the population mean score for the commercially available brand, μ_C. They theorized that μ_F would be greater than μ_C.

a. Specify the null and alternative hypotheses for the test.

b. Explain how the researchers should analyze the data and why.

c. The researchers reported a test statistic value of 5.71. Interpret this result. Use $\alpha = .05$ to make your conclusion.

d. Find the approximate p-value of the test.

e. Could the researchers have tested at $\alpha = .01$ and arrived at the same conclusion?

35 "I am not selling anything" surveys. To improve response rates in telephone surveys, interviewers are often instructed by the polling company to state, "I am not selling anything" at the outset of the call. The effectiveness of the "I am not selling anything" strategy was investigated in the *International Journal of Public Opinion Research* (Winter 2004). The sample consisted of 29 different telephone surveys. However, in each survey about half the people were contacted by interviewers using the "I am not selling anything" introduction and the other half were contacted by interviewers using the standard (no mention of "not selling") introduction. Thus, for each of the 29 surveys, both the "not selling" and standard interviewing techniques were employed. Summary statistics on response

rates (proportion of people called who actually responded to the survey questions) are given in the accompanying table. The goal of the researchers was to compare the mean response rates of the two interviewing methods with the specific purpose to determine if the mean response rate for "not selling" was higher than that for the standard.

	"Not selling" Introduction	Standard Introduction
Number of Surveys	29	29
Mean Response Rate	.262	.246
Standard Deviation	.12	.11

Source: De Leeuw, E. D., & Hox, J. J. "I am not selling anything: 29 experiments in telephone introductions," *International Journal of Public Opinion Research*, Vol. 16, No. 4, Winter 2004, pp. 464–473 (Table 1). Copyright © 2004 by Oxford University Press. Reprinted with permission.

a. Explain why the data should be analyzed as a paired difference experiment.

b. Analyze the data in the table using the independent samples t-test. Do you detect a significant difference between the mean response rates of the two methods using $\alpha = .05$?

c. The researchers applied the paired difference t procedure and obtained an observed significance level of p-value = .001. Interpret this result if $\alpha = 0.5$.

d. Compare the inferences you made in parts **b** and **c.**

36 NHTSA new car crash tests. Refer to the National Highway Traffic Safety Administration (NHTSA) crash-test data for new cars saved in the file. Crash-test dummies were placed in the driver's seat and front passenger's seat of a new car model, and the car was steered by remote control into a head-on collision with a fixed barrier while traveling at 35 miles per hour. Two of the variables measured for each of the 98 new cars in the data set are (1) the severity of the driver's chest injury and (2) the severity of the passenger's chest injury. (The more points assigned to the chest injury rating, the more severe the injury.) Suppose the NHTSA wants to determine whether the true mean driver chest injury rating exceeds the true mean passenger chest injury rating and, if so, by how much.

 CRASH

a. State the parameter of interest to the NHTSA.

b. Explain why the data should be analyzed as matched pairs.

c. Find a 99% confidence interval for the true difference between the mean chest injury ratings of drivers and front-seat passengers.

d. Interpret the interval, part **c.** Does the true mean driver chest injury rating exceed the true mean passenger chest injury rating? If so, by how much?

e. What conditions are required for the analysis to be valid? Do these conditions hold for these data?

Applying the Concepts—Intermediate

37 Taking "power naps" during work breaks. Lack of sleep costs companies about $18 billion a year in lost productivity, according to the National Sleep Foundation. Companies are waking up to the problem, however. Some even have quiet rooms available for study or sleep. "Power naps" are in vogue (*Athens Daily News,* Jan. 9, 2000). A major airline recently began encouraging reservation agents to nap during their breaks. The accompanying table lists the number of complaints received about each of a sample of 10 reservation agents during the 6 months before naps were encouraged and during the 6 months after the policy change.

a. Do the data present sufficient evidence to conclude that the new napping policy reduced the mean number of customer complaints about reservation agents? Test using $\alpha = .05$.

b. What assumptions must hold to ensure the validity of the test?

c. What variables, not controlled in the study, could lead to an invalid conclusion?

Operator	Before Policy	After Policy
1	10	5
2	3	0
3	16	7
4	11	4
5	8	6
6	2	4
7	1	2
8	14	3
9	5	5
10	6	1

38 Acidity of mouthwash. Acid has been found to be a primary cause of dental caries (cavities). It is theorized that oral mouthwashes contribute to the development of caries due to the antiseptic agent oxidizing into acid over time. This theory was tested in the *Journal of Dentistry, Oral Medicine and Dental Education* (Vol. 3, 2009). Three bottles of mouthwash, each of a different brand, were randomly selected from a drugstore. The pH level (where lower pH levels indicate higher acidity) of each bottle was measured on the date of purchase and after 30 days. The data are shown in the table. Conduct an analysis to determine if the mean initial pH level of mouthwash differs significantly from the mean pH level after 30 days. Use $\alpha = .05$ as your level of significance.

MOWASH

Mouthwash Brand	Initial pH	Final pH
LMW	4.56	4.27
SMW	6.71	6.51
RMW	5.65	5.58

Source: Based on Chunhye, K. L., & Schmitz, B. C. "Determination of pH, total acid, and total ethanol in oral health products: Oxidation of ethanol and recommendations to mitigate its association with dental caries," *Journal of Dentistry, Oral Medicine and Dental Education,* Vol. 3, No. 1, 2009 (Table 1).

39 Testing electronic circuits. Japanese researchers have developed a compression/depression method of testing electronic circuits based on Huffman coding (*IEICE Transactions on Information & Systems,* Jan. 2005). The new method is designed to reduce the time required for input decompression and output compression—called the *compression ratio.* Experimental results were obtained by testing a sample of 11 benchmark circuits (all of different sizes) from a SUN Blade 1000 workstation. Each circuit was tested using the standard compression/depression

CIRCUT
NW

method and the new Huffman-based coding method, and the compression ratio was recorded. The data are given in the accompanying table. Compare the two methods with a 95% confidence interval. Which method has the smaller mean compression ratio?

Circuit	Standard Method	Huffman-coding Method
1	.80	.78
2	.80	.80
3	.83	.86
4	.53	.53
5	.50	.51
6	.96	.68
7	.99	.82
8	.98	.72
9	.81	.45
10	.95	.79
11	.99	.77

Source: Based on Ichihara, H., Shintani, M., & Inoue, T. "Huffman-based test response coding," *IEICE Transactions on Information & Systems,* Vol. E88-D, No. 1, Jan. 2005 (Table 3).

40 Impact of red light cameras on car crashes. To combat red-light-running crashes—the phenomenon of a motorist entering an intersection after the traffic signal turns red and causing a crash—many states are adopting photo-red enforcement programs. In these programs, red light cameras installed at dangerous intersections photograph the license plates of vehicles that run the red light. How effective are photo-red enforcement programs in reducing red-light-running crash incidents at intersections? The Virginia Department of Transportation (VDOT) conducted a comprehensive study of its newly adopted photo-red enforcement program and published the results in a June 2007 report. In one portion of the study, the VDOT provided crash data both before and after installation of red light cameras at several intersections. The data (measured as the number of crashes caused by red light running per intersection per year) for 13 intersections in Fairfax County, Virginia, are given in the table. Analyze the data for the VDOT. What do you conclude?

REDLIT

Intersection	Before Camera	After Camera
1	3.60	1.36
2	0.27	0
3	0.29	0
4	4.55	1.79
5	2.60	2.04
6	2.29	3.14
7	2.40	2.72
8	0.73	0.24
9	3.15	1.57
10	3.21	0.43
11	0.88	0.28
12	1.35	1.09
13	7.35	4.92

Source: Based on "Research report: The impact of red light cameras (photo-red enforcement) on crashes in Virginia" from Virginia Transportation Research Council.

41 Evaluating a new drug. Merck Research Labs conducted an experiment to evaluate the effect of a new drug using the single-T swim maze. Nineteen impregnated dam rats were captured and allocated a dosage of 12.5 milligrams of

RATPUP

the drug. One male and one female rat pup were randomly selected from each resulting litter to perform in the swim maze. Each pup was placed in the water at one end of the maze and allowed to swim until it escaped at the opposite end. If the pup failed to escape after a certain period of time, it was placed at the beginning of the maze and given another chance. The experiment was repeated until each pup accomplished three successful escapes. The table below reports the number of swims required by each pup to perform three successful escapes. Is there sufficient evidence of a difference between the mean number of swims required by male and female pups? Conduct the test (at $\alpha = .10$). Comment on the assumptions required for the test to be valid.

Litter	Male	Female	Litter	Male	Female
1	8	5	11	6	5
2	8	4	12	6	3
3	6	7	13	12	5
4	6	3	14	3	8
5	6	5	15	3	4
6	6	3	16	8	12
7	3	8	17	3	6
8	5	10	18	6	4
9	4	4	19	9	5
10	4	4			

Source: Copyright © 2012 by Merck Research Laboratories. Reprinted with permission.

Applying the Concepts—Advanced

42 Alcoholic fermentation in wines. Determining alcoholic fermentation in wine is critical to the wine-making process.
WINE40 Must/wine density is a good indicator of the fermentation point because the density value decreases as sugars are converted into alcohol. For decades, winemakers have measured must/wine density with a hydrometer. Although accurate, the hydrometer employs a manual process that is very time-consuming. Consequently, large wineries are searching for more rapid measures of density measurement. An alternative method uses the hydrostatic balance instrument (similar to the hydrometer but digital). A winery in Portugal collected the must/wine density measurements for white wine samples randomly selected from the fermentation process for a recent harvest. For each sample, the density of the wine at 20°C was measured with both the hydrometer and the hydrostat balance. The densities for 40 wine samples are saved in the file. The first five and last five observations are shown in the table. The winery will use the alternative method of measuring wine density only if it can be demonstrated that the mean difference between the density measurements of the two methods does not exceed .002. Perform the analysis for the winery. Provide the winery with a written report of your conclusions.

Sample	Hydrometer	Hydrostatic
1	1.08655	1.09103
2	1.00270	1.00272
3	1.01393	1.01274
4	1.09467	1.09634
5	1.10263	1.10518
⋮	⋮	⋮
36	1.08084	1.08097
37	1.09452	1.09431
38	0.99479	0.99498
39	1.00968	1.01063
40	1.00684	1.00526

Source: Cooperative Cellar of Borba (*Adega Cooperative de Borba*), Portugal.

4 Comparing Two Population Proportions: Independent Sampling

Suppose a personal water craft (PWC) manufacturer wants to compare the potential market for its products in the northeastern United States to the market in the southeastern United States. Such a comparison would help the manufacturer decide where to concentrate sales efforts. Using telephone directories, the company randomly chooses 1,000 households in the southeast (SE) and 1,000 households in the northeast (NE) and determines whether each household plans to buy a PWC within the next 5 years. The objective is to use this sample information to make an inference about the difference $(p_1 - p_2)$ between the proportion p_1 of *all* households in the SE and the proportion p_2 of *all* households in the NE that plan to purchase a PWC within 5 years.

The two samples represent independent binomial experiments. The binomial random variables are the numbers x_1 and x_2 of the 1,000 sampled households in each area that indicate they will purchase a PWC within 5 years. The results are summarized in Table 6.

We can now calculate the sample proportions $\hat{p}_1$ and $\hat{p}_2$ of the households in the SE and NE, respectively, that are prospective buyers:

Table 6	Results of Telephone Survey
SE	**NE**
$n_1 = 1,000$	$n_2 = 1,000$
$x_1 = 42$	$x_2 = 24$

$$\hat{p}_1 = \frac{x_1}{n_1} = \frac{42}{1,000} = .042$$

$$\hat{p}_2 = \frac{x_2}{n_2} = \frac{24}{1,000} = .024$$

The difference between the sample proportions $(\hat{p}_1 - \hat{p}_2)$ makes an intuitively appealing point estimator of the difference between the population parameters $(p_1 - p_2)$. For our example, the estimate is

$$(\hat{p}_1 - \hat{p}_2) = .042 - .024 = .018$$

To judge the reliability of the estimator $(\hat{p}_1 - \hat{p}_2)$, we must observe its performance in repeated sampling from the two populations—that is, we need to know the sampling distribution of $(\hat{p}_1 - \hat{p}_2)$. The properties of the sampling distribution are given in the next box. Remember that $\hat{p}_1$ and $\hat{p}_2$ can be viewed as means of the number of successes per trial in the respective samples, so the Central Limit Theorem applies when the sample sizes are large.

Properties of the Sampling Distribution of $(p_1 - p_2)$

1. The mean of the sampling distribution of $(\hat{p}_1 - \hat{p}_2)$ is $(p_1 - p_2)$; that is,

$$E(\hat{p}_1 - \hat{p}_2) = p_1 - p_2$$

Thus, $(\hat{p}_1 - \hat{p}_2)$ is an unbiased estimator of $(p_1 - p_2)$.

2. The standard deviation of the sampling distribution of $(\hat{p}_1 - \hat{p}_2)$ is

$$\sigma_{(\hat{p}_1 - \hat{p}_2)} = \sqrt{\frac{p_1 q_1}{n_1} + \frac{p_2 q_2}{n_2}}$$

3. If the sample sizes n_1 and n_2 are large, the sampling distribution of $(\hat{p}_1 - \hat{p}_2)$ is approximately normal.

Because the distribution of $(\hat{p}_1 - \hat{p}_2)$ in repeated sampling is approximately normal, we can use the z-statistic to derive confidence intervals for $(p_1 - p_2)$ or test a hypothesis about $(p_1 - p_2)$.

For the PWC example, a 95% confidence interval for the difference $(p_1 - p_2)$ is

$$(\hat{p}_1 - \hat{p}_2) \pm 1.96\sigma_{(\hat{p}_1 - \hat{p}_2)} \quad \text{or} \quad (\hat{p}_1 - \hat{p}_2) \pm 1.96\sqrt{\frac{p_1 q_1}{n_1} + \frac{p_2 q_2}{n_2}}$$

The quantities $p_1 q_1$ and $p_2 q_2$ must be estimated to complete the calculation of the standard deviation $\sigma_{(\hat{p}_1 - \hat{p}_2)}$ and hence the calculation of the confidence interval. The value of pq is relatively insensitive to the value chosen to approximate p. Therefore, $\hat{p}_1 \hat{q}_1$ and $\hat{p}_2 \hat{q}_2$ will provide satisfactory estimates to approximate $p_1 q_1$ and $p_2 q_2$, respectively. Then

$$\sqrt{\frac{p_1 q_1}{n_1} + \frac{p_2 q_2}{n_2}} \approx \sqrt{\frac{\hat{p}_1 \hat{q}_1}{n_1} + \frac{\hat{p}_2 \hat{q}_2}{n_2}}$$

and we will approximate the 95% confidence interval by

$$(\hat{p}_1 - \hat{p}_2) \pm 1.96\sqrt{\frac{\hat{p}_1 \hat{q}_1}{n_1} + \frac{\hat{p}_2 \hat{q}_2}{n_2}}$$

Substituting the sample quantities yields

$$(.042 - .024) \pm 1.96\sqrt{\frac{(.042)(.958)}{1,000} + \frac{(.024)(.976)}{1,000}}$$

or, $.018 \pm .016$. Thus, we are 95% confident that the interval from .002 to .034 contains $(p_1 - p_2)$. We infer that there are between .2% and 3.4% more households in the southeast than in the northeast that plan to purchase PWCs in the next 5 years.

The general form of a confidence interval for the difference $(p_1 - p_2)$ between population proportions is given in the following box.

Large-Sample $(1 - \alpha)\%$ Confidence Interval for $(p_1 - p_2)$: Normal (z) Statistic

$$(\hat{p}_1 - \hat{p}_2) \pm z_{\alpha/2}\sigma_{(\hat{p}_1 - \hat{p}_2)} = (\hat{p}_1 - \hat{p}_2) \pm z_{\alpha/2}\sqrt{\frac{p_1 q_1}{n_1} + \frac{p_2 q_2}{n_2}}$$

$$\approx (\hat{p}_1 - \hat{p}_2) \pm z_{\alpha/2}\sqrt{\frac{\hat{p}_1 \hat{q}_1}{n_1} + \frac{\hat{p}_2 \hat{q}_2}{n_2}}$$

Conditions Required for Valid Large-Sample Inferences about $(p_1 - p_2)$

1. The two samples are randomly selected in an independent manner from the two target populations.
2. The sample sizes, n_1 and n_2, are both large so that the sampling distribution of $(\hat{p}_1 - \hat{p}_2)$ will be approximately normal. (This condition will be satisfied if both $n_1\hat{p}_1 \geq 15, n_1\hat{q}_1 \geq 15$, and $n_2\hat{p}_2 \geq 15, n_2\hat{q}_2 \geq 15$.)

The z-statistic,

$$z = \frac{(\hat{p}_1 - \hat{p}_2) - (p_1 - p_2)}{\sigma_{(\hat{p}_1 - \hat{p}_2)}}$$

is used to test the null hypothesis that $(p_1 - p_2)$ equals some specified difference, say D_0. For the special case where $D_0 = 0$—that is, where we want to test the null hypothesis $H_0: (p_1 - p_2) = 0$ (or, equivalently, $H_0: p_1 = p_2$)—the best estimate of $p_1 = p_2 = p$ is obtained by dividing the total number of successes $(x_1 + x_2)$ for the two samples by the total number of observations $(n_1 + n_2)$; that is,

$$\hat{p} = \frac{x_1 + x_2}{n_1 + n_2} \quad \text{or} \quad \hat{p} = \frac{n_1\hat{p}_1 + n_2\hat{p}_2}{n_1 + n_2}$$

The second equation shows that $\hat{p}$ is a weighted average of $\hat{p}_1$ and $\hat{p}_2$, with the larger sample receiving more weight. If the sample sizes are equal, then $\hat{p}$ is a simple average of the two sample proportions of successes.

We now substitute the weighted average $\hat{p}$ for both p_1 and p_2 in the formula for the standard deviation of $(\hat{p}_1 - \hat{p}_2)$:

$$\sigma_{(\hat{p}_1 - \hat{p}_2)} = \sqrt{\frac{p_1 q_1}{n_1} + \frac{p_2 q_2}{n_2}} \approx \sqrt{\frac{\hat{p}\hat{q}}{n_1} + \frac{\hat{p}\hat{q}}{n_2}} = \sqrt{\hat{p}\hat{q}\left(\frac{1}{n_1} + \frac{1}{n_2}\right)}$$

The test is summarized in the next box.

Large-Sample Test of Hypothesis about $(p_1 - p_2)$: Normal (z) Statistic

One-Tailed Test	Two-Tailed Test
$H_0: (p_1 - p_2) = 0^*$	$H_0: (p_1 - p_2) = 0$
$H_a: (p_1 - p_2) < 0$	$H_a: (p_1 - p_2) \neq 0$
[or $H_a: (p_1 - p_2) > 0$]	

$$\text{Test statistic: } z = \frac{(\hat{p}_1 - \hat{p}_2)}{\sigma_{(\hat{p}_1 - \hat{p}_2)}}$$

Rejection region: $z < -z_\alpha$	Rejection region: $|z| > z_{\alpha/2}$
[or $z > z_\alpha$ when $H_a: (p_1 - p_2) > 0$]	

$$\text{Note: } \sigma_{(\hat{p}_1 - \hat{p}_2)} = \sqrt{\frac{p_1 q_1}{n_1} + \frac{p_2 q_2}{n_2}} \approx \sqrt{\hat{p}\hat{q}\left(\frac{1}{n_1} + \frac{1}{n_2}\right)}, \text{ where } \hat{p} = \frac{x_1 + x_2}{n_1 + n_2}.$$

*The test can be adapted to test for a difference $D_0 \neq 0$. Because most applications call for a comparison of p_1 and p_2, implying $D_0 = 0$, we will confine our attention to this case.

Example 6

Large-Sample Test about $(p_1 - p_2)$—Comparing Car Repair Rates

Problem A consumer advocacy group wants to determine whether there is a difference between the proportions of the two leading automobile models that need major repairs (more than \$500) within 2 years of their purchase. A sample of 400 two-year owners of model 1 is contacted, and a sample of 500 two-year owners of model 2 is contacted. The numbers x_1 and x_2 of owners who report that their cars needed major repairs within the first 2 years are 53 and 78, respectively. Test the null hypothesis that no difference exists between the proportions in populations 1 and 2 needing major repairs against the alternative that a difference does exist. Use $\alpha = .10$.

Solution If we define p_1 and p_2 as the true proportions of model 1 and model 2 owners, respectively, whose cars needed major repairs within 2 years, the elements of the test are

$$H_0: (p_1 - p_2) = 0$$
$$H_a: (p_1 - p_2) \neq 0$$

$$\text{Test statistic: } z = \frac{(\hat{p}_1 - \hat{p}_2) - 0}{\sigma_{(\hat{p}_1 - \hat{p}_2)}}$$

Rejection region ($\alpha = .10$): $|z| > z_{\alpha/2} = z_{.05} = 1.645$ (see Figure 15)

We now calculate the sample proportions of owners who needed major car repairs,

$$\hat{p}_1 = \frac{x_1}{n_1} = \frac{53}{400} = .1325$$

$$\hat{p}_2 = \frac{x_2}{n_2} = \frac{78}{500} = .1560$$

Then

$$z = \frac{(\hat{p}_1 - \hat{p}_2) - 0}{\sigma_{(\hat{p}_1 - \hat{p}_2)}} \approx \frac{(\hat{p}_1 - \hat{p}_2)}{\sqrt{\hat{p}\hat{q}\left(\dfrac{1}{n_1} + \dfrac{1}{n_2}\right)}}$$

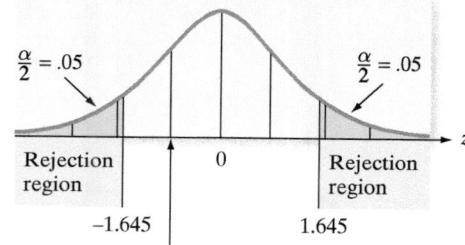

$\dfrac{\alpha}{2} = .05$ $\dfrac{\alpha}{2} = .05$

Rejection region   0   Rejection region

−1.645   1.645

Observed $z = -.99$

Figure 15
Rejection region for Example 6

where

$$\hat{p} = \frac{x_1 + x_2}{n_1 + n_2} = \frac{53 + 78}{400 + 500} = .1456$$

Note that $\hat{p}$ is a weighted average of $\hat{p}_1$ and $\hat{p}_2$, with more weight given to the larger sample of model 2 owners.

Thus, the computed value of the test statistic is

$$z = \frac{.1325 - .1560}{\sqrt{(.1456)(.8544)\left(\dfrac{1}{400} + \dfrac{1}{500}\right)}} = \frac{-.0235}{.0237} = -.99$$

The samples provide insufficient evidence at $\alpha = .10$ to detect a difference between the proportions of the two models that needed repairs within 2 years.

Look Back Even though 2.35% more sampled owners of model 2 found they needed major repairs, this difference is less than 1 standard deviation ($z = -.99$) from the hypothesized zero difference between the true proportions. Thus, a 95% confidence interval for $(p_1 - p_2)$ would include 0—also implying no evidence of a difference.

Now Work Exercise 49

<table>
<tr><td>

Example 7

Finding the Observed Significance Level of a Test for $p_1 - p_2$

</td><td>

Problem Use a statistical software package to conduct the test in Example 6. Find and interpret the p-value of the test.

Solution We entered the sample sizes (n_1 and n_2) and number of successes (x_1 and x_2) into Excel/XLSTAT and obtained the printout shown in Figure 16. The test statistic for this two-tailed test is shaded on the printout, as well as the observed significance level (p-value). Note that p-value $= .3205$ exceeds $\alpha = .10$. Consequently, there is no evidence of a difference between the true population proportions.

</td></tr>
</table>

z-test for two proportions / Two-tailed test:

95% confidence interval on the difference between the proportions:
(−0.0699 , 0.0229)

Difference	−0.0235
z (Observed value)	−0.9934
z (Critical value)	1.9600
p-value (Two-tailed)	0.3205
alpha	0.05

Figure 16
Excel/XLSTAT printout for test of two proportions

STATISTICS
in ACTION
REVISITED

Comparing Proportions

In the first Statistics in Action Revisited in this chapter, we demonstrated how the expert statistician used a comparison of two means to defend Visa in a libel case. Recall that ZixIt claimed that a Visa executive's e-mail postings had a negative impact on ZixIt's attempt to develop a new online credit card processing system. Here, we demonstrate another way to analyze the data, one successfully presented in court by the statistician.

In addition to daily closing price and trading volume of ZixIt stock, the **ZIXVSA** file also contains a qualitative variable that indicates whether the stock price increased or not (decreased or stayed the same) on the following day. This variable was created by the statistician to compare the proportion of days on which ZixIt stock went up for posting and nonposting days. Let p_1 represent the proportion of days where the ZixIt stock price increased following all nonposting days and p_2 represent the proportion of days where the ZixIt stock price increased following posting days. Then, if the charges made by ZixIt were true (i.e., that postings had a negative impact on ZixIt stock), p_1 will exceed p_2. Thus, a comparison of two population proportions is appropriate. Recall that during the 83-day period of interest, the executive posted e-mails on 43 days and had no postings on 40 days. Again, both sample sizes ($n_1 = 40$ and $n_2 = 43$) are large, so we can apply the large-sample z-test or large-sample confidence interval procedure for independent samples. (Can you demonstrate this?) A Minitab printout for this analysis is shown in Figure SIA3.

From the printout you can see that following the 40 nonposting days, the price increased on 20 days; following the 43 posting days, the stock price increased on 18 days. Thus, the sample proportions are $p_1 = 20/40 = .5$ and $p_2 = 18/43 = .42$. Are these sample proportions different enough for us to conclude that the population proportions are different and that ZixIt's claim was true? Not according to the statistical analysis. Note that the 95% confidence interval for $(p_1 - p_2)$, $(-.133, .295)$, includes the value 0, and the p-value for the two-tailed test of H_0: $(p_1 - p_2) = 0$, p-value $= .456$, exceeds, say $\alpha = .05$. Both imply that the two population proportions are not significantly different.

Test and CI for Two Proportions: Up/Down, Posting

```
Event = UP

Posting   X    N    Sample p
NO        20   40   0.500000
POST      18   43   0.418605


Difference = p (NO) - p (POST)
Estimate for difference:  0.0813953
95% CI for difference:  (-0.132500, 0.295291)
Test for difference = 0 (vs not = 0):  Z = 0.75  P-Value = 0.456

Fisher's exact test: P-Value = 0.513
```

Figure SIA3

Minitab comparison of two proportions analysis

Also, neither sample proportion is significantly different from .5. (Can you demonstrate this?) Consequently, in courtroom testimony, the statistical expert used these results to conclude that "the direction of ZixIt's stock price movement following days with postings is random, just like days with no postings."

Data Set: ZIXVSA

Exercises 43–60

Please be aware that some of the following problems may require knowledge of concepts that are not presented in this chapter.

Learning the Mechanics

43 Consider making an inference about $p_1 - p_2$, where there are x_1 successes in n_1 binomial trials and x_2 successes in n_2 binomial trials.
  a. Describe the distributions of x_1 and x_2.
  b. Explain why the Central Limit Theorem is important in finding an approximate distribution for $(\hat{p}_1 - \hat{p}_2)$.

44 For each of the following values of α, find the values of z for which $H_0: (p_1 - p_2) = 0$ would be rejected in favor of $H_a: (p_1 - p_2) < 0$.
  a. $\alpha = .01$ **b.** $\alpha = .025$
  c. $\alpha = .05$ **d.** $\alpha = .10$

45 In each case, determine whether the sample sizes are large enough to conclude that the sampling distribution of $(\hat{p}_1 - \hat{p}_2)$ is approximately normal.
  a. $n_1 = 12, n_2 = 14, \hat{p}_1 = .42, \hat{p}_2 = .57$
  b. $n_1 = 12, n_2 = 14, \hat{p}_1 = .92, \hat{p}_2 = .86$
  c. $n_1 = n_2 = 30, \hat{p}_1 = .70, \hat{p}_2 = .73$
  d. $n_1 = 100, n_2 = 250, \hat{p}_1 = .93, \hat{p}_2 = .97$
  e. $n_1 = 125, n_2 = 200, \hat{p}_1 = .08, \hat{p}_2 = .12$

46 Construct a 95% confidence interval for $(p_1 - p_2)$ in each of the following situations:
  a. $n_1 = 400, \hat{p}_1 = .65; n_2 = 400, \hat{p}_2 = .58$
  b. $n_1 = 180, \hat{p}_1 = .31; n_2 = 250, \hat{p}_2 = .25$
  c. $n_1 = 100, \hat{p}_1 = .46; n_2 = 120, \hat{p}_2 = .61$

47 Independent random samples, each containing 800 observations, were selected from two binomial populations. The samples from populations 1 and 2 produced 320 and 400 successes, respectively.
  a. Test $H_0: (p_1 - p_2) = 0$ against $H_a: (p_1 - p_2) > 0$. Use $\alpha = .05$.
  b. Test $H_0: (p_1 - p_2) = 0$ against $H_a: (p_1 - p_2) \neq 0$. Use $\alpha = .01$.
  c. Test $H_0: (p_1 - p_2) = 0$ against $H_a: (p_1 - p_2) < 0$. Use $\alpha = .01$.
  d. Form a 90% confidence interval for $(p_1 - p_2)$.

48 Random samples of size $n_1 = 55$ and $n_2 = 65$ were drawn from populations 1 and 2, respectively. The samples yielded $\hat{p}_1 = .7$ and $\hat{p}_2 = .6$. Test $H_0: (p_1 - p_2) = 0$ against $H_a: (p_1 - p_2) > 0$ using $\alpha = .05$.

Applying the Concepts—Basic

49 **The "winner's curse" in auction bidding.** In auction bidding, the "winner's curse" is the phenomenon of the winning (or highest) bid price being above the expected value of the item being auctioned. *The Review of Economics and Statistics* (Aug. 2001) published a study on whether bid experience impacts the likelihood of the winner's curse occurring. Two groups of bidders in a sealed-bid auction were compared: (1) super-experienced bidders and (2) less-experienced bidders. In the super-experienced group, 29 of 189 winning bids were above the item's expected value; in the less-experienced group, 32 of 149 winning bids were above the item's expected value.
  a. Find an estimate of p_1, the true proportion of super-experienced bidders who fell prey to the winner's curse.
  b. Find an estimate of p_2, the true proportion of less-experienced bidders who fell prey to the winner's curse.
  c. Construct a 90% confidence interval for $p_1 - p_2$.
  d. Give a practical interpretation of the confidence interval, part **c.** Make a statement about whether bid experience impacts the likelihood of the winner's curse occurring.

50 **Is steak your favorite barbeque food?** July is National Grilling Month in the United States. On July 1, 2008, *The Harris Poll #70* reported on a survey of Americans' grilling preferences. When asked about their favorite food prepared on a barbeque, 662 of 1,250 randomly sampled Democrats preferred steak, as compared to 586 of 930 randomly sampled Republicans.
  a. Give a point estimate for the proportion of all Democrats who prefer steak as their favorite barbeque food.

b. Give a point estimate for the proportion of all Republicans who prefer steak as their favorite barbeque food.

c. Give a point estimate for the difference between the proportions of all Democrats and all Republicans who prefer steak as their favorite barbeque food.

d. Construct a 95% confidence interval for the difference between the proportions of all Democrats and all Republicans who prefer steak as their favorite barbeque food.

e. Give a practical interpretation of the interval, part **d.**

f. Explain the meaning of the phrase 95% confident in your answer to part **e.**

51 **Producer willingness to supply biomass.** Refer to the *Biomass and Energy* (Vol. 36, 2012) study of the willingness of producers to supply biomass products such as surplus hay, Exercise 20. Recall that independent samples of Missouri producers and Illinois producers were surveyed. Another aspect of the study focused on the services producers were willing to supply. One key service involves windrowing (mowing and piling) of hay. Of the 558 Missouri producers surveyed, 187 were willing to offer windrowing services; of the 940 Illinois producers surveyed, 380 were willing to offer windrowing services. The researchers want to know if the proportion of producers who were willing to offer windrowing services to the biomass market differs for the two areas, Missouri and Illinois.

a. Specify the parameter of interest to the researchers.

b. Set up the null and alternative hypotheses for testing whether the proportion of producers who were willing to offer windrowing services differs in Missouri and Illinois.

c. A Minitab analysis of the data is shown below. Locate the test statistic on the printout.

d. Give the rejection region for the test using $\alpha = .01$.

e. Locate the *p*-value of the test on the printout.

f. Make the appropriate conclusion using both the *p*-value and rejection region approach. Your conclusions should agree.

Test and CI for Two Proportions

```
Sample   X    N    Sample p
1       187  558   0.335125
2       380  940   0.404255


Difference = p (1) - p (2)
Estimate for difference:  -0.0691299
99% CI for difference:  (-0.135079, -0.00318070)
Test for difference = 0 (vs not = 0):  Z = -2.67  P-Value = 0.008

Fisher's exact test: P-Value = 0.008
```

---

52 **Planning habits survey.** *American Demographics* (Jan. 2002) reported the results of a survey on the planning habits of men and women. In response to the question, "What is your preferred method of planning and keeping track of meetings, appointments, and deadlines?," 56% of the men and 46% of the women answered, "Keep them in my head." A nationally representative sample of 1,000 adults participated in the survey; therefore, assume that 500 were men and 500 were women.

a. Set up the null and alternative hypotheses for testing whether the percentage of men who prefer keeping track of appointments in their head is larger than the corresponding percentage of women.

b. Compute the test statistic for the test.

c. Give the rejection region for the test using $\alpha = .01$.

d. Find the *p*-value for the test.

e. Make the appropriate conclusion.

53 **Hospital administration of malaria patients.** One of the most serious health problems in India is malaria. Consequently, Indian hospital administrators must have the resources to treat the high volume of malaria patients that are admitted. Research published in the *National Journal of Community Medicine* (Vol. 1, 2010) investigated whether the malaria admission rate is higher in some months than in others. In a sample of 192 hospital patients admitted in January, 32 were treated for malaria. In an independent sample of 403 patients admitted in May (4 months later), 34 were treated for malaria.

a. Describe the two populations of interest in this study.

b. Give a point estimate of the difference in the malaria admission rates in January and May.

c. Find a 90% confidence interval for the difference in the malaria admission rates in January and May.

d. Based on the interval, part **c,** can you conclude that a difference exists in the true malaria admission rates in January and May? Explain.

Applying the Concepts—Intermediate

54 **Electronic vs. printed surveys.** The rapid evolution of computer hardware and software has made it easy for businesses to conduct computer-based and Web-based (i.e., electronic) surveys. Professors at Michigan State and DePaul Universities collaborated on a study designed to compare the response rates of electronic surveys and traditional print surveys (Decision Sciences Institute, *Decision Line,* July 2001). The two surveys were developed for customers who had purchased products over the Internet from a leading retailer of office supplies. Of the 631 customers mailed the printed survey, 261 returned usable responses. Of the 414 customers who were sent a computer disk with the electronic survey, 155 returned usable responses.

a. Estimate the difference between the response rates of the two survey types using a 90% confidence interval. Interpret the result.

b. If the difference in response rates is 5% or less, the researchers will infer that there is no "practical" difference in response rates for the two surveys. Are the researchers able to make this inference? Explain.

55 **Salmonella in produce.** Salmonella is the most common type of bacterial food-borne illness in the United States. How prevalent is salmonella in produce grown in the major agricultural region of Monterey, California? Researchers from the U.S. Department of Agriculture (USDA) conducted tests for salmonella in produce grown in the region and published their results in *Applied and Environmental Microbiology* (April 2011). In a sample of 252 cultures obtained from water used to irrigate the region, 18 tested positive for salmonella. In an independent sample of 476 cultures obtained from the region's wildlife (e.g., birds), 20 tested positive for salmonella. Is this sufficient evidence for the USDA to state that the prevalence of salmonella in the region's water differs from the prevalence of salmonella in the region's wildlife? Use $\alpha = .01$ to make your decision.

56 Angioplasty's benefits challenged. More than 1 million heart patients each year undergo an angioplasty. The benefits of an angioplasty were challenged in a recent study of 2,287 patients (2007 Annual Conference of the American College of Cardiology, New Orleans). All the patients had substantial blockage of the arteries but were medically stable. All were treated with medication such as aspirin and beta-blockers. However, half the patients were randomly assigned to get an angioplasty and half were not. After 5 years, the researchers found that 211 of the 1,145 patients in the angioplasty group had subsequent heart attacks compared to 202 of 1,142 patients in the medication-only group. Do you agree with the study's conclusion, "There was no significant difference in the rate of heart attacks for the two groups"? Support your answer with a 95% confidence interval.

57 Entrepreneurial careers of MBA alumni. Are African American MBA students more likely to begin their careers as entrepreneurs than white MBA students? This was a question of interest to the Graduate Management Admission Council (GMAC). *GMAC Research Reports* (Oct. 3, 2005) published the results of a survey of MBA alumni. Of the 1,304 African Americans who responded to the survey, 209 reported their employment status after graduation as self-employed or a small business owner. Of the 7,120 whites who responded to the survey, 356 reported their employment status after graduation as self-employed or a small business owner. Use this information to answer the research question.

58 Predicting software defects. Refer to the PROMISE Software Engineering Repository data on 498 modules of software code written in "C" language for a NASA spacecraft instrument, saved in the file. The software code in each module was evaluated for defects; 49 were classified as "true" (i.e., module has defective code), and 449 were classified as "false" (i.e., module has correct code). Consider these to be independent random samples of software code modules. Researchers predicted the defect status of each module using the simple algorithm, "If number of lines of code in the module exceeds 50, predict the module to have a defect." The accompanying SPSS printout shows the number of modules in each of the two samples that were predicted to have defects (PRED_LOC = "yes") and predicted to have no defects (PRED_LOC = "no"). Now, define the *accuracy rate* of the algorithm as the proportion of modules that were correctly predicted. Compare the accuracy rate of the algorithm when applied to modules with defective code to the accuracy rate of the algorithm when applied to modules with correct code. Use a 99% confidence interval.

DEFECT * PRED_LOC Crosstabulation

Count

		PRED_LOC		Total
		no	yes	
DEFECT	false	400	49	449
	true	29	20	49
Total		429	69	498

Applying the Concepts—Advanced

59 Food craving study. Do you have an insatiable craving for chocolate or some other food? Because many North Americans apparently do, psychologists are designing scientific studies to examine the phenomenon. According to the *New York Times* (Feb. 22, 1995), one of the largest studies of food cravings involved a survey of 1,000 McMaster University (Canada) students. The survey revealed that 97% of the women in the study acknowledged specific food cravings while only 67% of the men did.

a. How large do n_1 and n_2 need to be to conclude that the true proportion of women who acknowledged having food cravings exceeds the corresponding proportion of men? Assume $\alpha = .01$.

b. Why is it dangerous to conclude from the study that women have a higher incidence of food cravings than men?

60 Religious symbolism in TV commercials. Gonzaga University professors conducted a study of television commercials and published their results in the *Journal of Sociology, Social Work and Social Welfare* (Vol. 2, 2008). The key research question was: "Do television advertisers use religious symbolism to sell goods and services?" In a sample of 797 TV commercials collected in 1998, only 16 commercials used religious symbolism. Of the sample of 1,499 TV commercials examined in the more recent study, 51 commercials used religious symbolism. Conduct an analysis to determine if the percentage of TV commercials that use religious symbolism has changed since the 1998 study. If you detect a change, estimate the magnitude of the difference and attach a measure of reliability to the estimate.

5 Determining the Required Sample Size

You can find the appropriate sample size to estimate the difference between a pair of parameters with a specified margin of error (ME) and degree of reliability by estimating the difference between a pair of parameters correct to within ME units with confidence level $(1 - \alpha)$, let $z_{\alpha/2}$ standard deviations of the sampling distribution of the estimator equal ME. Then solve for the sample size. To do this, you have to solve the problem for a specific ratio between n_1 and n_2. Most often, you will want to have equal sample sizes — that is, $n_1 = n_2 = n$. We will illustrate the procedure with two examples.

| Example | 8 |

Finding the Sample Sizes for Estimating $(\mu_1 - \mu_2)$ — Comparing Mean Crop Yields

Problem New fertilizer compounds are often advertised with the promise of increased crop yields. Suppose we want to compare the mean yield μ_1 of wheat when a new fertilizer is used to the mean yield μ_2 with a fertilizer in common use. The estimate of the difference in mean yield per acre is to be correct to within .25 bushel with a confidence coefficient of .95. If the sample sizes are to be equal, find $n_1 = n_2 = n$, the number of 1-acre plots of wheat assigned to each fertilizer.

Solution To solve the problem, you need to know something about the variation in the bushels of yield per acre. Suppose from past records you know the yields of wheat possess a range of approximately 10 bushels per acre. You could then approximate $\sigma_1 = \sigma_2 = \sigma$ by letting the range equal 4σ. Thus,

$$4\sigma \approx 10 \text{ bushels}$$
$$\sigma \approx 2.5 \text{ bushels}$$

The next step is to solve the equation

$$z_{\alpha/2}\sigma_{(\bar{x}_1 - \bar{x}_2)} = \text{ME} \qquad \text{or} \qquad z_{\alpha/2}\sqrt{\frac{\sigma_1^2}{n_1} + \frac{\sigma_2^2}{n_2}} = \text{ME}$$

for n, where $n = n_1 = n_2$. Because we want the estimate to lie within ME $= .25$ of $(\mu_1 - \mu_2)$ with confidence coefficient equal to .95, we have $z_{\alpha/2} = z_{.025} = 1.96$. Then, letting $\sigma_1 = \sigma_2 = 2.5$ and solving for n, we have

$$1.96\sqrt{\frac{(2.5)^2}{n} + \frac{(2.5)^2}{n}} = .25$$

$$1.96\sqrt{\frac{2(2.5)^2}{n}} = .25$$

$$n = 768.32 \approx 769 \text{ (rounding up)}$$

Consequently, you will have to sample 769 acres of wheat for each fertilizer to estimate the difference in mean yield per acre to within .25 bushel.

Look Back Because $n = 769$ would necessitate extensive and costly experimentation, you might decide to allow a larger margin of error (say, ME $= .50$ or ME $= 1$) to reduce the sample size, or you might decrease the confidence coefficient. The point is that we can obtain an idea of the experimental effort necessary to achieve a specified precision in our final estimate by determining the approximate sample size *before* the experiment is started.

Now Work Exercise 62a

| Example | 9 |

Finding the Sample Sizes for Estimating $(p_1 - p_2)$ — Comparing Defect Rates of Two Machines

Problem A production supervisor suspects a difference exists between the proportions p_1 and p_2 of defective items produced by two different machines. Experience has shown that the proportion defective for each of the two machines is in the neighborhood of .03. If the supervisor wants to estimate the difference in the proportions to within .005 using a 95% confidence interval, how many items must be randomly sampled from the production of each machine? (Assume that the supervisor wants $n_1 = n_2 = n$.)

Solution In this sampling problem, the margin of error is ME $= .005$, and for the specified level of reliability, $(1 - \alpha) = .95$, $z_{\alpha/2} = z_{.025} = 1.96$. Then, letting $p_1 = p_2 = .03$ and $n_1 = n_2 = n$, we find the required sample size per machine by solving the following equation for n:

$$z_{\alpha/2}\sigma_{(\hat{p}_1 - \hat{p}_2)} = \text{ME}$$

or

$$z_{\alpha/2} \sqrt{\frac{p_1 q_1}{n_1} + \frac{p_2 q_2}{n_2}} = \text{ME}$$

$$1.96 \sqrt{\frac{(.03)(.97)}{n} + \frac{(.03)(.97)}{n}} = .005$$

$$1.96 \sqrt{\frac{2(.03)(.97)}{n}} = .005$$

$$n = 8{,}943.2$$

Look Back This large n will likely result in a tedious sampling procedure. If the supervisor insists on estimating $(p_1 - p_2)$ correct to within .005 with 95% confidence, approximately 9,000 items will have to be inspected for each machine.

■ **Now Work Exercise 61a**

You can see from the calculations in Example 9 that $\sigma_{(\hat{p}_1 - \hat{p}_2)}$ (and hence the solution, $n_1 = n_2 = n$) depends on the actual (but unknown) values of p_1 and p_2. In fact, the required sample size $n_1 = n_2 = n$ is largest when $p_1 = p_2 = .5$. Therefore, if you have no prior information on the approximate values of p_1 and p_2, use $p_1 = p_2 = .5$ in the formula for $\sigma_{(\hat{p}_1 - \hat{p}_2)}$. If p_1 and p_2 are in fact close to .5, then the values of n_1 and n_2 that you have calculated will be correct. If p_1 and p_2 differ substantially from .5, then your solutions for n_1 and n_2 will be larger than needed. Consequently, using $p_1 = p_2 = .5$ when solving for n_1 and n_2 is a conservative procedure because the sample sizes n_1 and n_2 will be at least as large as (and probably larger than) needed.

The procedures for determining the sample sizes necessary for estimating $(\mu_1 - \mu_2)$ or $(p_1 - p_2)$ for the case $n_1 = n_2$ are given in the boxes that follow.

Determination of Sample Size for Estimating $(\mu_1 - \mu_2)$

To estimate $(\mu_1 - \mu_2)$ with a given margin of error ME and with confidence level $(1 - \alpha)$, use the following formula to solve for equal sample sizes that will achieve the desired reliability:

$$n_1 = n_2 = \frac{(z_{\alpha/2})^2 (\sigma_1^2 + \sigma_2^2)}{(\text{ME})^2}$$

You will need to substitute estimates for the values of σ_1^2 and σ_2^2 before solving for the sample size. These estimates might be sample variances s_1^2 and s_2^2 from prior sampling (e.g., a pilot sample) or from an educated (and conservatively large) guess based on the range—that is, $s \approx R/4$.

Determination of Sample Size for Estimating $(p_1 - p_2)$

To estimate $(p_1 - p_2)$ with a given margin of error ME and with confidence level $(1 - \alpha)$, use the following formula to solve for equal sample sizes that will achieve the desired reliability:

$$n_1 = n_2 = \frac{(z_{\alpha/2})^2 (p_1 q_1 + p_2 q_2)}{(\text{ME})^2}$$

You will need to substitute estimates for the values of p_1 and p_2 before solving for the sample size. These estimates might be based on prior samples, obtained from educated guesses, or, most conservatively, specified as $p_1 = p_2 = .5$.

Exercises 61–72

Learning the Mechanics

61 Assuming that $n_1 = n_2$, find the sample sizes needed to estimate $(p_1 - p_2)$ for each of the following situations:

NW **a.** Margin of error = .01 with 99% confidence. Assume that $p_1 \approx .4$ and $p_2 \approx .7$.

b. A 90% confidence interval of width .05. Assume that there is no prior information available to obtain approximate values of p_1 and p_2.

c. Margin of error = .03 with 90% confidence. Assume that $p_1 \approx .2$ and $p_2 \approx .3$.

62 Find the appropriate values of n_1 and n_2 (assume $n_1 = n_2$) needed to estimate $(\mu_1 - \mu_2)$ for each of the following situations:

NW **a.** A margin of error equal to 3.2 with 95% confidence. From prior experience it is known that $\sigma_1 \approx 15$ and $\sigma_2 \approx 17$.

b. A margin of error equal to 8 with 99% confidence. The range of each population is 60.

c. A 90% confidence interval of width 1.0. Assume that $\sigma_1^2 \approx 5.8$ and $\sigma_2^2 \approx 7.5$.

63 Suppose you want to estimate the difference between two population means correct to within 1.8 with a 95% confidence interval. If prior information suggests that the population variances are approximately equal to $\sigma_1^2 = \sigma_2^2 = 14$ and you want to select independent random samples of equal size from the populations, how large should the sample sizes, n_1 and n_2, be?

64 Enough money has been budgeted to collect independent random samples of size $n_1 = n_2 = 100$ from populations 1 and 2 to estimate $(\mu_1 - \mu_2)$. Prior information indicates that $\sigma_1 = \sigma_2 = 10$. Have sufficient funds been allocated to construct a 90% confidence interval for $(\mu_1 - \mu_2)$ of width 5 or less? Justify your answer.

Applying the Concepts—Basic

65 **Last name and acquisition timing.** Refer to the *Journal of Consumer Research* (August 2011) study of the *last name effect* in acquisition timing, Exercise 13. Recall that the mean response times (in minutes) to acquire basketball tickets were compared for two groups of MBA students— those students with last names beginning with one of the first nine letters of the alphabet and those with last names beginning with one of the last nine letters of the alphabet. How many MBA students from each group would need to be selected to estimate the difference in mean times to within 2 minutes of its true value with 95% confidence? (Assume equal sample sizes were selected for each group and that the response time standard deviation for both groups is $\sigma \approx 9$ minutes.)

66 **Homework assistance for accounting students.** Refer to the *Journal of Accounting Education* (Vol. 25, 2007) study of providing homework assistance to accounting students, Exercise 18. Recall that one group of students was given a completed homework solution and another group was given only check figures at various steps of the solution. The researchers wanted to compare the average test score improvement of the two groups. How many students should be sampled in each group to estimate the difference in the averages to within .5 point with 99% confidence? Assume that the standard deviations of the test score improvements for the two groups are approximately equal to 1.

67 **Electronic vs. printed surveys.** Refer to the *Decision Line* (July 2001) study designed to compare the response rates of electronic surveys and traditional print surveys, Exercise 54. Recall that the two surveys were developed for customers who had purchased products over the Internet from a leading retailer of office supplies. How many customers should be sampled to estimate the difference between the response rates of the two survey types to within .01 using a 90% confidence interval? Assume the same number of customers should be sampled for each survey.

68 **Conducting a political poll.** A pollster wants to estimate the difference between the proportions of men and women who favor a particular national candidate using a 90% confidence interval of width .04. Suppose the pollster has no prior information about the proportions. If equal numbers of men and women are to be polled, how large should the sample sizes be?

Applying the Concepts—Intermediate

69 **Life expectancies of working women and housewives.** Is housework hazardous to your health? A study in *Public Health Reports* compared the life expectancies of 25-year-old white women in the labor force to those who are housewives. How large a sample would have to be taken from each group in order to be 95% confident that the estimate of difference in average life expectancies for the two groups is within 1 year of the true difference in average life expectancies? Assume that equal sample sizes will be selected from the two groups and that the standard deviation for both groups is approximately 15 years.

70 **Users of home shopping services.** All cable companies carry at least one home shopping channel. Who uses these home shopping services? Are the shoppers primarily men or women? Suppose you want to estimate the difference in the proportions of men and women who say they have used or expect to use televised home shopping using an 80% confidence interval of width .06 or less.

a. Approximately how many people should be included in your samples?

b. Suppose you want to obtain individual estimates for the two proportions of interest. Will the sample size found in part **a** be large enough to provide estimates of each proportion correct to within .02 with probability equal to .90? Justify your response.

71 **Angioplasty's benefits challenged.** Refer to the study of patients with substantial blockage of the arteries presented at the 2007 Annual Conference of the American College of Cardiology, Exercise 56. Recall that half the patients were randomly assigned to get an angioplasty and half were not. The researchers compared the proportion of patients with subsequent heart attacks for the two groups and reported no significant difference between the two proportions. Although the study involved over

2,000 patients, the sample size may have been too small to detect a difference in heart attack rates.

a. How many patients must be sampled in each group to estimate the difference in heart attack rates to within .015 with 95% confidence? (Use summary data from Exercise 56 in your calculation.)

b. Comment on the practicality of carrying out the study with the sample sizes determined in part **a.**

c. Comment on the practical significance of the difference detected in the confidence interval for the study, part **a.**

72 **Average housing space per person.** Even though Japan is an economic superpower, Japanese workers are in many ways worse off than their U.S. and European counterparts. For example, the estimated average housing space per person (in square feet) is 645 in the United States but only 344 in Japan (Diawa House Industry, Co., Japan). Suppose a team of economists and sociologists from the United Nations plans to reestimate the difference in the mean housing space per person for U.S. and Japanese workers. Assume that equal sample sizes will be used for each country and that the standard deviation is 35 square feet for Japan and 80 for the United States. How many people should be sampled in each country to estimate the difference to within 10 square feet with 95% confidence?

6   Comparing Two Population Variances: Independent Sampling

Many times, it is of practical interest to use the techniques developed in this chapter to compare the means or proportions of two populations. However, there are also important instances when we wish to compare two population variances. For example, when two devices are available for producing precision measurements (scales, calipers, thermometers, etc.), we might want to compare the variability of the measurements of the devices before deciding which one to purchase. Or when two standardized tests can be used to rate job applicants, the variability of the scores for both tests should be taken into consideration before deciding which test to use.

For problems like these, we need to develop a statistical procedure to compare population variances. The common statistical procedure for comparing population variances, σ_1^2 and σ_2^2, makes an inference about the ratio $\frac{\sigma_1^2}{\sigma_2^2}$. In this section, we will show how to test the null hypothesis that the ratio $\frac{\sigma_1^2}{\sigma_2^2}$ equals 1 (the variances are equal) against the alternative hypothesis that the ratio differs from 1 (the variances differ):

$$H_0: \frac{\sigma_1^2}{\sigma_2^2} = 1 \qquad (\sigma_1^2 = \sigma_2^2)$$

$$H_a: \frac{\sigma_1^2}{\sigma_2^2} \neq 1 \qquad (\sigma_1^2 \neq \sigma_2^2)$$

To make an inference about the ratio $\frac{\sigma_1^2}{\sigma_2^2}$, it seems reasonable to collect sample data and use the ratio of the sample variances, $\frac{s_1^2}{s_2^2}$. We will use the test statistic

$$F = \frac{s_1^2}{s_2^2}$$

To establish a rejection region for the test statistic, we need to know the sampling distribution of $\frac{s_1^2}{s_2^2}$. As you will subsequently see, the sampling distribution of $\frac{s_1^2}{s_2^2}$ is based on two of the assumptions already required for the *t*-test:

1. The two sampled populations are normally distributed.

2. The samples are randomly and independently selected from their respective populations.

When these assumptions are satisfied and when the null hypothesis is true (that is, $\sigma_1^2 = \sigma_2^2$), the sampling distribution of $F = \frac{s_1^2}{s_2^2}$ is the **F-distribution** with $(n_1 - 1)$ numerator degrees of freedom and $(n_2 - 1)$ denominator degrees of freedom, respectively. The shape of the F-distribution depends on the degrees of freedom associated with s_1^2 and s_2^2—that is, on $(n_1 - 1)$ and $(n_2 - 1)$. An F-distribution with 7 and 9 df is shown in Figure 17. As you can see, the distribution is skewed to the right because $\frac{s_1^2}{s_2^2}$ cannot be less than 0 but can increase without bound.

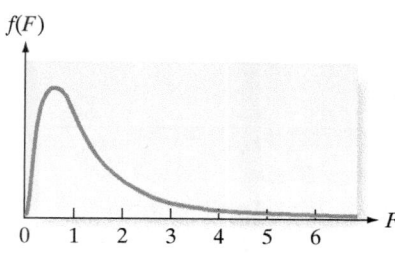

Figure 17

An F-distribution with 7 numerator and 9 denominator degrees of freedom

We need to be able to find F values corresponding to the tail areas of this distribution to establish the rejection region for our test of hypothesis because we expect the ratio F of the sample variances to be either very large or very small when the population variances are unequal. The upper-tail F values for $\alpha = .10, .05, .025$, and $.01$ can be found in Tables V, VI, VII, and VIII in Appendix: Tables. Table VI is partially reproduced in Table 7. It gives F values that correspond to $\alpha = .05$ upper-tail areas for different degrees of freedom ν_1 for the numerator sample variance, s_1^2, whereas the rows correspond to the degrees of freedom ν_2 for the denominator sample variance, s_2^2. Thus, if the numerator degrees of freedom is $\nu_1 = 7$ and the denominator degrees of freedom is $\nu_2 = 9$, we look in the seventh column and ninth row to find $F_{.05} = 3.29$. As shown in Figure 18, $\alpha = .05$ is the tail area to the right of 3.29 in the F-distribution with 7 and 9 df—that is, if $\sigma_1^2 = \sigma_2^2$, then the probability that the F-statistic will exceed 3.29 is $\alpha = .05$.

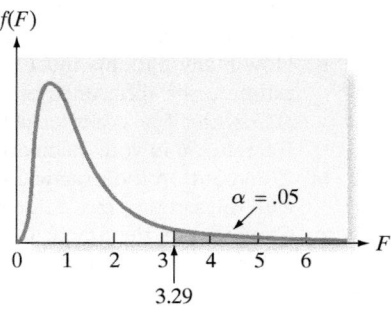

Figure 18

An F-distribution for $\nu_1 = 7$ df and $\nu_2 = 9$ df; $\alpha = .05$

Table 7	Reproduction of Part of Table VI in Appendix: Tables: Percentage Points of the F-Distribution, $\alpha = .05$

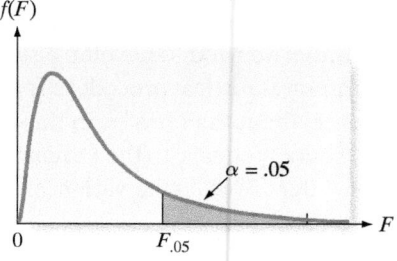

Numerator Degrees of Freedom

ν_2 \ ν_1	1	2	3	4	5	6	7	8	9
1	161.4	199.5	215.7	224.6	230.2	234.0	236.8	238.9	240.5
2	18.51	19.00	19.16	19.25	19.30	19.33	19.35	19.37	19.38
3	10.13	9.55	9.28	9.12	9.01	8.94	8.89	8.85	8.81
4	7.71	6.94	6.59	6.39	6.26	6.16	6.09	6.04	6.00
5	6.61	5.79	5.41	5.19	5.05	4.95	4.88	4.82	4.77
6	5.99	5.14	4.76	4.53	4.39	4.28	4.21	4.15	4.10
7	5.59	4.74	4.35	4.12	3.97	3.87	3.79	3.73	3.68
8	5.32	4.46	4.07	3.84	3.69	3.58	3.50	3.44	3.39
9	5.12	4.26	3.86	3.63	3.48	3.37	3.29	3.23	3.18
10	4.96	4.10	3.71	3.48	3.33	3.22	3.14	3.07	3.02
11	4.84	3.98	3.59	3.36	3.20	3.09	3.01	2.95	2.90
12	4.75	3.89	3.49	3.25	3.11	3.00	2.91	2.85	2.80
13	4.67	3.81	3.41	3.18	3.03	2.92	2.83	2.77	2.71
14	4.60	3.74	3.34	3.11	2.96	2.85	2.76	2.70	2.65

Denominator Degrees of Freedom

Example	10

An *F*-Test Application— Comparing Paper Mill Production Variation

Problem A manufacturer of paper products wants to compare the variation in daily production levels at two paper mills. Independent random samples of days are selected from each mill, and the production levels (in units) are recorded. The data are shown in Table 8. Do these data provide sufficient evidence to indicate a difference in the variability of production levels at the two paper mills? (Use $\alpha = .10$.)

Table 8	Production Levels at Two Paper Mills								
Mill 1:	34	18	28	21	40	23	29		
	25	10	38	32	22	22			
Mill 2:	31	13	27	19	22	18	23	22	21
	18	15	24	13	19	18	19	23	13

Data Set:

Solution Let

$$\sigma_1^2 = \text{Population variance of production levels at mill 1}$$
$$\sigma_2^2 = \text{Population variance of production levels at mill 2}$$

The hypotheses of interest, then, are

$$H_0: \frac{\sigma_1^2}{\sigma_2^2} = 1 \qquad (\sigma_1^2 = \sigma_2^2)$$

$$H_a: \frac{\sigma_1^2}{\sigma_2^2} \neq 1 \qquad (\sigma_1^2 \neq \sigma_2^2)$$

The nature of the F-tables given in Appendix: Tables affects the form of the test statistic. To form the rejection region for a two-tailed F-test, we want to make certain that the upper tail is used because only the upper-tail values of F are shown in the tables in Appendix: Tables. To accomplish this, *we will always place the larger sample variance in the numerator of the* F-*test statistic.* This doubles the tabulated value for α because we double the probability that the F-ratio will fall in the upper tail by always placing the larger sample variance in the numerator—that is, we establish a one-tailed rejection region by putting the larger variance in the numerator rather than establishing rejection regions in both tails.

Thus, for our example, we have a numerator s_1^2 with df $= \nu_1 = n_1 - 1 = 12$ and a denominator s_2^2 with df $= \nu_2 = n_2 - 1 = 17$. Therefore, the test statistic will be

$$F = \frac{\text{Larger sample variance}}{\text{Smaller sample variance}} = \frac{s_1^2}{s_2^2}$$

and we will reject $H_0: \sigma_1^2 = \sigma_2^2$ for $\alpha = .10$ when the calculated value of F exceeds the tabulated value:

$$F_{\alpha/2} = F_{.05} = 2.38 \qquad \text{(see Figure 19)}$$

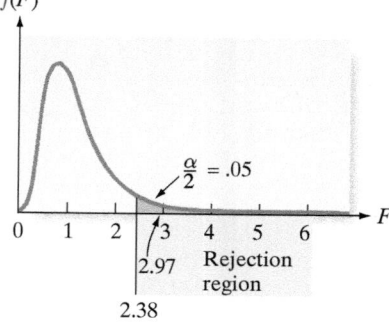

Figure 19

Rejection region for Example 10

To calculate the value of the test statistic, we require the sample variances. Summary statistics for the data in Table 8 are shown on the Minitab printout, Figure 20. The sample standard deviations (shaded) are $s_1 = 8.36$ and $s_2 = 4.85$. Therefore,

$$F = \frac{s_1^2}{s_2^2} = \frac{(8.36)^2}{(4.85)^2} = 2.97$$

When we compare this result to the rejection region shown in Figure 19, we see that $F = 2.97$ falls in the rejection region. Therefore, the data provide sufficient evidence to indicate that the population variances differ. It appears that the variation in production levels at mill 1 tends to be higher than the variation at mill 2.

Descriptive Statistics: LEVEL

```
Variable  MILL   N    Mean   StDev  Minimum  Median  Maximum
LEVEL      1    13   26.31   8.36    10.00   25.00    40.00
           2    18   19.89   4.85    13.00   19.00    31.00
```

Figure 20

Minitab summary statistics for data in Table 8

Look Back What would you have concluded if the value of F calculated from the samples had not fallen in the rejection region? Would you have concluded that the null hypothesis of equal variances is true? No, because then you risk the possibility of a Type II error (accepting H_0 if H_a is true) without knowing the value of β, the probability of accepting $H_0: \sigma_1^2 = \sigma_2^2$ if, in fact, it is false. Because we will not consider the calculation of β for specific alternatives in this text, when the F-statistic does not fall in the rejection region, we simply conclude that insufficient sample evidence exists to refute the null hypothesis that $\sigma_1^2 = \sigma_2^2$.

■ **Now Work Exercise 78a**

The F-test for equal population variances is summarized in the following boxes.*

F-Test for Equal Population Variances

One-Tailed Test	Two-Tailed Test>
$H_0: \sigma_1^2 = \sigma_2^2$	$H_0: \sigma_1^2 = \sigma_2^2$
$H_a: \sigma_1^2 < \sigma_2^2$ (or $H_a: \sigma_1^2 > \sigma_2^2$)	$H_a: \sigma_1^2 \neq \sigma_2^2$
Test statistic:	*Test statistic:*
$F = \dfrac{s_2^2}{s_1^2}$	$F = \dfrac{\text{Larger sample variance}}{\text{Smaller sample variance}}$
$\left(\text{or } F = \dfrac{s_1^2}{s_2^2} \text{ when } H_a: \sigma_1^2 > \sigma_2^2\right)$	$= \dfrac{s_1^2}{s_2^2} \text{ when } s_1^2 > s_2^2$
	$\left(\text{or } \dfrac{s_2^2}{s_1^2} \text{ when } s_2^2 > s_1^2\right)$
Rejection region:	*Rejection region:*
$F > F_\alpha$	$F > F_{\alpha/2}$

where F_α and $F_{\alpha/2}$ are based on $\nu_1 =$ numerator degrees of freedom and $\nu_2 =$ denominator degrees of freedom; ν_1 and ν_2 are the degrees of freedom for the numerator and denominator sample variances, respectively.

Conditions Required for a Valid F-Test for Equal Variances

1. Both sampled populations are normally distributed.
2. The samples are random and independent.

Example 11

The Observed Significance Level of an F-Test

Problem Find the p-value for the test in Example 10 using the F-tables in Appendix: Tables. Compare this to the exact p-value obtained from a computer printout.

Solution Because the observed value of the F-statistic in Example 10 was 2.97, the observed significance level of the test would equal the probability of observing a value of F at least as contradictory to $H_0: \sigma_1^2 = \sigma_2^2$ as $F = 2.97$, if, in fact, H_0 is true. Because we give the F-tables in Appendix: Tables only for values of α equal to .10, .05, .025, and .01, we can only approximate the observed significance level. Checking Tables VII and VIII, we find $F_{.025} = 2.82$ and $F_{.01} = 3.46$. Because the observed value of F exceeds $F_{.025}$ but

---

*Although a test of a hypothesis of equality of variances is the most common application of the F-test, it can also be used to test a hypothesis that the ratio between the population variances is equal to some specified value: $H_0: \sigma_1^2/\sigma_2^2 = k$. The test is conducted in exactly the same way as specified in the box, except that we use the test statistic

$$F = \frac{s_1^2}{s_2^2}\left(\frac{1}{k}\right)$$

is less than $F_{.01}$, the observed significance level for the test is less than $2(.025) = .05$ but greater than $2(.01) = .02$—that is,

$$.02 < p\text{-value} < .05$$

The exact p-value of the test is shown on the Minitab printout, Figure 21. This value (highlighted) is .04.

Test for Equal Variances: LEVEL versus MILL

95% Bonferroni confidence intervals for standard deviations

```
MILL  N    Lower    StDev    Upper
  1   13  5.73182  8.36047  14.9507
  2   18  3.49950  4.84936   7.7455
```

F-Test (normal distribution)
Test statistic = 2.97, p-value = 0.040

Levene's Test (any continuous distribution)
Test statistic = 3.78, p-value = 0.062

Figure 21

Minitab F-test for equal variances

Look Back We double the α value shown in Tables VII and VIII because this is a two-tailed test.

◼ **Now Work Exercise 78b**

As a final example of an application, consider the comparison of population variances as a check of the assumption $\sigma_1^2 = \sigma_2^2$ needed for the two-sample t-test. Rejection of the null hypothesis $\sigma_1^2 = \sigma_2^2$ would indicate that the assumption is invalid. [*Note:* Nonrejection of the null hypothesis does *not* imply that the assumption is valid.] We illustrate with an example.

Example **12**

Checking the Assumption of Equal Variances

Problem In Example 4 (Section 2) we used the two-sample t-statistic to compare the success indexes of two groups of managers. The data are repeated in Table 9 for convenience. The use of the t-statistic was based on the assumption that the population variances of the managerial success indexes were equal for the two groups. Conduct a test of hypothesis to check this assumption at $\alpha = .10$.

Table 9	Managerial Success Indexes for Two Groups of Managers										
	Group 1						Group 2				
	Interaction with Outsiders						Few Interactions				
65	58	78	60	68	69	62	53	36	34	56	50
66	70	53	71	63	63	42	57	46	68	48	42
						52	53	43			

Data Set: SUCCES

Solution We want to test

$$H_0: \sigma_1^2 = \sigma_2^2$$
$$H_a: \sigma_1^2 \neq \sigma_2^2$$

This F-test is shown on the Excel/XLSTAT printout, Figure 22. Both the test statistic, $F = .5$, and two-tailed p-value, $p\text{-value} = .2554$, are highlighted on the printout. Because $\alpha = .10$ is less than the p-value, we do not reject the null hypothesis that the population variances of the success indexes are equal. It is here that the temptation to misuse the F-test is strongest. *We cannot conclude that the data justify the use of the t-statistic.* This is equivalent to accepting H_0, and we have repeatedly warned against this conclusion because the probability of a Type II error, β, is unknown. The α level of .10 protects us only against rejecting H_0 if it is true. This use of the F-test may prevent us from abusing the t-procedure when we obtain a value of F that leads to a rejection of the assumption that $\sigma_1^2 = \sigma_2^2$. But when the F-statistic does not fall in the rejection region, we know little more about the validity of the assumption than before we conducted the test.

Summary statistics:

Variable	Observations	Minimum	Maximum	Mean	Std. deviation
SUCCESS | 1	12	53.0000	78.0000	65.3333	6.6104
SUCCESS | 2	15	34.0000	68.0000	49.4667	9.3340

Fisher's F-test / Two-tailed test:

90% confidence interval on the ratio of variances:
(0.1955, 1.3736)

Ratio	0.5016
F (Observed value)	0.5016
F (Critical value)	2.5655
DF1	11
DF2	14
p-value (Two-tailed)	0.2554
alpha	0.1

Figure 22

Excel/XLSTAT analysis for testing assumption of equal variances

Look Back A 90% confidence interval for the ratio σ_1^2/σ_2^2 is shown in the middle of the Excel/XLSTAT printont of Figure 22. Note that the interval (.196, 1.374) includes 1; hence, we cannot conclude that the ratio differs from 1. Thus, the confidence interval leads to the same conclusion as the two-tailed test does: There is insufficient evidence of a difference between the population variances.

■ **Now Work Exercise 84**

What Do You Do If the Assumption of Normal Population Distributions Is Not Satisfied?

Answer: The F-test is much less robust (i.e., much more sensitive) to departures from normality than the t-test for comparing the population means (Section 2). If you have doubts about the normality of the population frequency distributions, use a **nonparametric method** (e.g., *Levene's test*) for comparing the two population variances.

Exercises 73–88

Learning the Mechanics

73 Use Tables V, VI, VII, and VIII in Appendix: Tables to find
NW each of the following F-values:
  a. $F_{.05}$ where $\nu_1 = 9$ and $\nu_2 = 6$
  b. $F_{.01}$ where $\nu_1 = 18$ and $\nu_2 = 14$
  c. $F_{.025}$ where $\nu_1 = 11$ and $\nu_2 = 4$
  d. $F_{.10}$ where $\nu_1 = 20$ and $\nu_2 = 5$

74 Given ν_1 and ν_2, find the following probabilities:
  a. $\nu_1 = 2, \nu_2 = 30, P(F \geq 5.39)$
  b. $\nu_1 = 24, \nu_2 = 10, P(F < 2.74)$
  c. $\nu_1 = 7, \nu_2 = 1, P(F \leq 236.8)$
  d. $\nu_1 = 40, \nu_2 = 40, P(F > 2.11)$

75 For each of the following cases, identify the rejection region that should be used to test $H_0: \sigma_1^2 = \sigma_2^2$ against $H_a: \sigma_1^2 > \sigma_2^2$. Assume $\nu_1 = 30$ and $\nu_2 = 20$.
- **a.** $\alpha = .10$
- **b.** $\alpha = .05$
- **c.** $\alpha = .025$
- **d.** $\alpha = .01$

76 For each of the following cases, identify the rejection region that should be used to test $H_0: \sigma_1^2 = \sigma_2^2$ against $H_a: \sigma_1^2 \neq \sigma_2^2$. Assume $\nu_1 = 10$ and $\nu_2 = 12$.
- **a.** $\alpha = .20$
- **b.** $\alpha = .10$
- **c.** $\alpha = .05$
- **d.** $\alpha = .02$

77 Specify the appropriate rejection region for testing $H_0: \sigma_1^2 = \sigma_2^2$ in each of the following situations:
- **a.** $H_a: \sigma_1^2 > \sigma_2^2; \alpha = .05, n_1 = 25, n_2 = 20$
- **b.** $H_a: \sigma_1^2 < \sigma_2^2; \alpha = .05, n_1 = 10, n_2 = 15$
- **c.** $H_a: \sigma_1^2 \neq \sigma_2^2; \alpha = .10, n_1 = 21, n_2 = 31$
- **d.** $H_a: \sigma_1^2 < \sigma_2^2; \alpha = .01, n_1 = 31, n_2 = 41$
- **e.** $H_a: \sigma_1^2 \neq \sigma_2^2; \alpha = .05, n_1 = 7, n_2 = 16$

78 Independent random samples were selected from each of two normally distributed populations, $n_1 = 12$ from population 1 and $n_2 = 27$ from population 2. The means and variances for the two samples are shown in the table.

Sample 1	Sample 2
$n_1 = 12$	$n_2 = 27$
$\bar{x}_1 = 31.7$	$\bar{x}_2 = 37.4$
$s_1^2 = 3.87$	$s_2^2 = 8.75$

- **a.** Test the null hypothesis $H_0: \sigma_1^2 = \sigma_2^2$ against the alternative hypothesis $H_a: \sigma_1^2 \neq \sigma_2^2$. Use $\alpha = .10$.
- **b.** Find and interpret the approximate p-value of the test.

79 Independent random samples were selected from each of two normally distributed populations, $n_1 = 6$ from population 1 and $n_2 = 5$ from population 2. The data are shown in the table.

Sample 1	Sample 2
3.1	2.3
4.4	1.4
1.2	3.7
1.7	8.9
.7	5.5
3.4	

- **a.** Test $H_0: \sigma_1^2 = \sigma_2^2$ against $H_a: \sigma_1^2 < \sigma_2^2$. Use $\alpha = .01$.
- **b.** Find and interpret the approximate p-value of the test.

Applying the Concepts—Basic

80 **Lobster trap placement.** Refer to the *Bulletin of Marine Science* (April 2010) study of lobster trap placement, Exercise 12. The data are repeated here (next column). You used the small-sample t-statistic to form a confidence interval for the difference between the mean trap-spacing measurements of the two fishing cooperatives. This method requires the variance of the population of trap spacings for the BT cooperative, $(\sigma_{BT})^2$, to be the same as the population variance for the PA cooperative, $(\sigma_{PA})^2$.

BT Cooperative:	93	99	105	94	82	70	86	
PA Cooperative:	118	94	106	72	90	66	153	98

Source: Shester, G. G. "Explaining catch variation among Baja California lobster fishers through spatial analysis of trap-placement decisions," *Bulletin of Marine Science*, Vol. 86, No. 2, April 2010 (Table 1).

- **a.** Set up the null and alternative hypotheses for testing the equality of variances.
- **b.** Find the sample variances for the two cooperatives.
- **c.** Compute the test statistic.
- **d.** Find the approximate p-value of the test.
- **e.** Make the appropriate conclusion using $\alpha = .01$.

81 **Children's recall of TV ads.** Refer to the *Journal of Advertising* (Spring 2006) study of children's recall of television commercials, Exercise 15. You used a small-sample t-test to test the null hypothesis $H_0: (\mu_1 - \mu_2) = 0$, where μ_1 = mean number of ads recalled by children in the video only group and μ_2 = mean number of ads recalled by children in the A/V group. Summary statistics for the study are reproduced in the table below. The validity of the inference derived from the test is based on the assumption of equal group variances, i.e., $\sigma_1^2 = \sigma_2^2$.

- **a.** Set up the null and alternative hypotheses for testing this assumption.
- **b.** Compute the test statistic.
- **c.** Find the rejection region for the test using $\alpha = .10$.
- **d.** Make the appropriate conclusion in the words of the problem.
- **e.** Comment on the validity of the inference derived about the difference in population means in Exercise 15.

Video Only Group	A/V Group
$n_1 = 20$	$n_2 = 20$
$\bar{x}_1 = 3.70$	$\bar{x}_2 = 3.30$
$s_1 = 1.98$	$s_2 = 2.13$

82 **Mental health of workers and the unemployed.** A study in the *Journal of Occupational and Organizational Psychology* investigated the relationship of employment status and mental health. A sample of working and unemployed people was selected, and each person was given a mental health examination using the General Health Questionnaire (GHQ), a widely recognized measure of mental health. Although the article focused on comparing the mean GHQ levels, a comparison of the variability of GHQ scores for employed and unemployed men and women is of interest as well.

- **a.** In general terms, what does the amount of variability in GHQ scores tell us about the group?
- **b.** What are the appropriate null and alternative hypotheses to compare the variability of the mental health scores of the employed and unemployed groups? Define any symbols you use.
- **c.** The standard deviation for a sample of 142 employed men was 3.26, while the standard deviation for 49 unemployed men was 5.10. Conduct the test you set up in part **b** using $\alpha = .05$. Interpret the results.
- **d.** What assumptions are necessary to ensure the validity of the test?

83 Drug content assessment. Refer to Exercise 16 and the *Analytical Chemistry* (Dec. 15, 2009) study in which scientists used high-performance liquid chromatography to determine the amount of drug in a tablet. Recall that 25 tablets were produced at each of two different, independent sites. The researchers want to determine if the two sites produced drug concentrations with different variances. A Minitab printout of the analysis follows. Locate the test statistic and *p*-value on the printout. Use these values and $\alpha = .05$ to conduct the appropriate test for the researchers.

Test and CI for Two Variances: Content vs Site

```
Method

Null hypothesis          Variance(1) / Variance(2) = 1
Alternative hypothesis   Variance(1) / Variance(2) not = 1
Significance level       Alpha = 0.05


Statistics

Site   N   StDev   Variance
1      25  3.067    9.406
2      25  3.339   11.147


Ratio of standard deviations = 0.919
Ratio of variances = 0.844


95% Confidence Intervals

                              CI for
Distribution   CI for StDev   Variance
of Data        Ratio          Ratio
Normal         (0.610, 1.384) (0.372, 1.915)
Continuous     (0.497, 1.315) (0.247, 1.729)


Tests

                                        Test
Method                      DF1  DF2  Statistic  P-Value
F Test (normal)             24   24   0.84       0.681
Levene's Test (any continuous) 1  48  0.64       0.427
```

Applying the Concepts—Intermediate

84 Patent infringement case. Refer to the *Chance* (Fall 2002) description of a patent infringement case against Intel Corp., Exercise 19. The zinc measurements for three locations on the original inventor's notebook—on a text line, on a witness line, and on the intersection of the witness and text line—are reproduced in the table.

Text Line	.335	.374	.440			
Witness Line	.210	.262	.188	.329	.439	.397
Intersection	.393	.353	.285	.295	.319	

a. Use a test (at $\alpha = .05$) to compare the variation in zinc measurements for the text line with the corresponding variation for the intersection.

b. Use a test (at $\alpha = .05$) to compare the variation in zinc measurements for the witness line with the corresponding variation for the intersection.

c. From the results, parts **a** and **b**, what can you infer about the variation in zinc measurements at the three notebook locations?

d. What assumptions are required for the inferences to be valid? Are they reasonably satisfied? (You checked these assumptions when answering Exercise 19d.)

85 Analyzing human inspection errors. Tests of product quality using human inspectors can lead to serious inspection error problems (*Journal of Quality Technology*). To evaluate the performance of inspectors in a new company, a quality manager had a sample of 12 novice inspectors evaluate 200 finished products. The same 200 items were evaluated by 12 experienced inspectors. The quality of each item—whether defective or nondefective—was known to the manager. The table lists the number of inspection errors (classifying a defective item as nondefective or vice versa) made by each inspector.

Novice Inspectors				Experienced Inspectors			
30	35	26	40	31	15	25	19
36	20	45	31	28	17	19	18
33	29	21	48	24	10	20	21

a. Prior to conducting this experiment, the manager believed the variance in inspection errors was lower for experienced inspectors than for novice inspectors. Do the sample data support her belief? Test using $\alpha = .05$.

b. What is the appropriate *p*-value of the test you conducted in part **a?**

86 Cooling method for gas turbines. Refer to the *Journal of Engineering for Gas Turbines and Power* (Jan. 2005) study of gas turbines augmented with high-pressure inlet fogging, Exercise 24. Heat rate data (kilojoules per kilowatt per hour) for each of three types of gas turbines (advanced, aeroderivative, traditional) are saved in the accompanying file. In order to compare the mean heat rates of two types of gas turbines, you assumed that the heat rate variances were equal.

a. Conduct a test (at $\alpha = .05$) for equality of heat rate variances for traditional and aeroderivative augmented gas turbines. Use the result to make a statement about the validity of the inference derived in Exercise 24a.

b. Conduct a test (at $\alpha = .05$) for equality of heat rate variances for advanced and aeroderivative augmented gas turbines. Use the result to make a statement about the validity of the inference derived in Exercise 24b.

87 "Just-in-time" deliveries from factories to foxholes. Following the initial Persian Gulf War, the Pentagon changed its logistics processes to be more corporate-like. The extravagant "just-in-case" mentality was replaced with "just-in-time" systems. Emulating FedEx and United Parcel Service, deliveries from factories to foxholes are now expedited using bar codes, laser cards, radio tags, and databases to track supplies. The table below contains order-to-delivery times (in days) for a sample of shipments from the United States to the Persian Gulf and a sample of shipments to Bosnia.

Persian Gulf	Bosnia
28.0	15.1
20.0	6.4
26.5	5.0
10.6	11.4
9.1	6.5
35.2	6.5
29.1	3.0
41.2	7.0
27.5	5.5

Source: Based on Crock, S. "The Pentagon goes to B-school," *Business Week,* December 11, 1995, p. 98.

a. Is there sufficient evidence to indicate that the variances in order-to-delivery times for Persian Gulf and Bosnia shipments differ? Use $\alpha = .05$.

b. Given your answer to part **a**, is it appropriate to construct a confidence interval for the difference between the mean order-to-delivery times? Explain.

88 Is honey a cough remedy? Refer to the *Archives of Pediatrics and Adolescent Medicine* (Dec. 2007) study HCOUGH of honey as a children's cough remedy, Exercise 23.

The data (cough improvement scores) for the 33 children in the DM dosage group and the 35 children in the honey dosage group are reproduced in the table below. In Exercise 23, you used a comparison of two means to determine whether "honey may be a preferable treatment for the cough and sleep difficulty associated with childhood upper respiratory tract infection." The researchers also want to know if the variability in coughing improvement scores differs for the two groups. Conduct the appropriate analysis, using $\alpha = .10$.

Honey Dosage:	12	11	15	11	10	13	10	4	15	16	9	14	10	6	10	11	12	15
	12	9	11	15	10	9	13	8	12	10	8	9	5	12	8	12	8	
DM Dosage:	4	6	9	4	7	7	7	9	12	10	11	3	9	7	8	12	12	
	13	7	10	13	9	4	4	10	15	9	6	4	12	6	12	4		

Source: Paul, I. M., et al. "Effect of honey, dextromethorphan, and no treatment on nocturnal cough and sleep quality for coughing children and their parents," *Archives of Pediatrics and Adolescent Medicine*, Vol. 161, No. 12, Dec. 2007 (data simulated).

◻ Chapter Notes

Key Terms

Blocking
F-distribution
Nonparametric method
Paired difference experiment

Pooled sample estimator of σ^2
Randomized block experiment
Standard error

Key Symbols

$\mu_1 - \mu_2$	Difference between population means
μ_d	Paired difference in population means
$p_1 - p_2$	Difference between population proportions
$\frac{\sigma_1^2}{\sigma_2^2}$	Ratio of population variances
D_0	Hypothesized value of difference
$\bar{x}_1 - \bar{x}_2$	Difference between sample means
$\bar{d}$	Mean of sample differences
$\hat{p}_1 - \hat{p}_2$	Difference between sample proportions
$\frac{s_1^2}{s_2^2}$	Ratio of sample variances
$\sigma_{(\bar{x}_1 - \bar{x}_2)}$	Standard error for $\bar{x}_1 - \bar{x}_2$
$\sigma_{\bar{d}}$	Standard error for $\bar{d}$
$\sigma_{(\hat{p}_1 - \hat{p}_2)}$	Standard error for $\hat{p}_1 - \hat{p}_2$
F_α	Critical value for *F*-distribution
ν_1	Numerator degrees of freedom for *F*-distribution
ν_2	Denominator degrees of freedom for *F*-distribution
ME	Margin of error in estimation

Key Ideas

Key Words for Identifying the Target Parameter

$\mu_1 - \mu_2$	Difference in means or averages
μ_d	Paired difference in means or averages
$p_1 - p_2$	Difference in proportions, fractions, percentages, rates
$\frac{\sigma_1^2}{\sigma_2^2}$	Ratio (or difference) in variances, spreads

Determining the Sample Size

Estimating $\mu_1 - \mu_2$: $n_1 = n_2 = (z_{\alpha/2})^2(\sigma_1^2 + \sigma_2^2)/(\text{ME})^2$

Estimating $p_1 - p_2$: $n_1 = n_2 = (z_{\alpha/2})^2(p_1q_1 + p_2q_2)/(\text{ME})^2$

Conditions Required for Inferences about $\mu_1 - \mu_2$

Large samples:
1. Independent random samples
2. $n_1 \geq 30$, $n_2 \geq 30$

Small samples:
1. Independent random samples
2. Both populations normal
3. $\sigma_1^2 = \sigma_2^2$

Conditions Required for Inferences about $\frac{\sigma_1^2}{\sigma_2^2}$

Large or small samples:
1. Independent random samples
2. Both populations normal

Conditions Required for Inferences about μ_d

Large samples:
1. Random sample of paired differences
2. $n_d \geq 30$

Small samples:
1. Random sample of paired differences
2. Population of differences is normal

Conditions Required for Inferences about $p_1 - p_2$

Large samples:
1. Independent random samples
2. $n_1p_1 \geq 15$, $n_1q_1 \geq 15$
3. $n_2p_2 \geq 15$, $n_2q_2 \geq 15$

Using a Confidence Interval for $(\mu_1 - \mu_2)$ or $(p_1 - p_2)$ to Determine whether a Difference Exists

1. If the confidence interval includes all *positive* numbers $(+, +)$: $\rightarrow$ Infer $\mu_1 > \mu_2$ or $p_1 > p_2$
2. If the confidence interval includes all *negative* numbers $(-, -)$: $\rightarrow$ Infer $\mu_1 < \mu_2$ or $p_1 < p_2$
3. If the confidence interval includes 0 $(-, +)$: $\rightarrow$ Infer no evidence of a difference

Guide to Selecting a Two-Sample Hypothesis Test and Confidence Interval

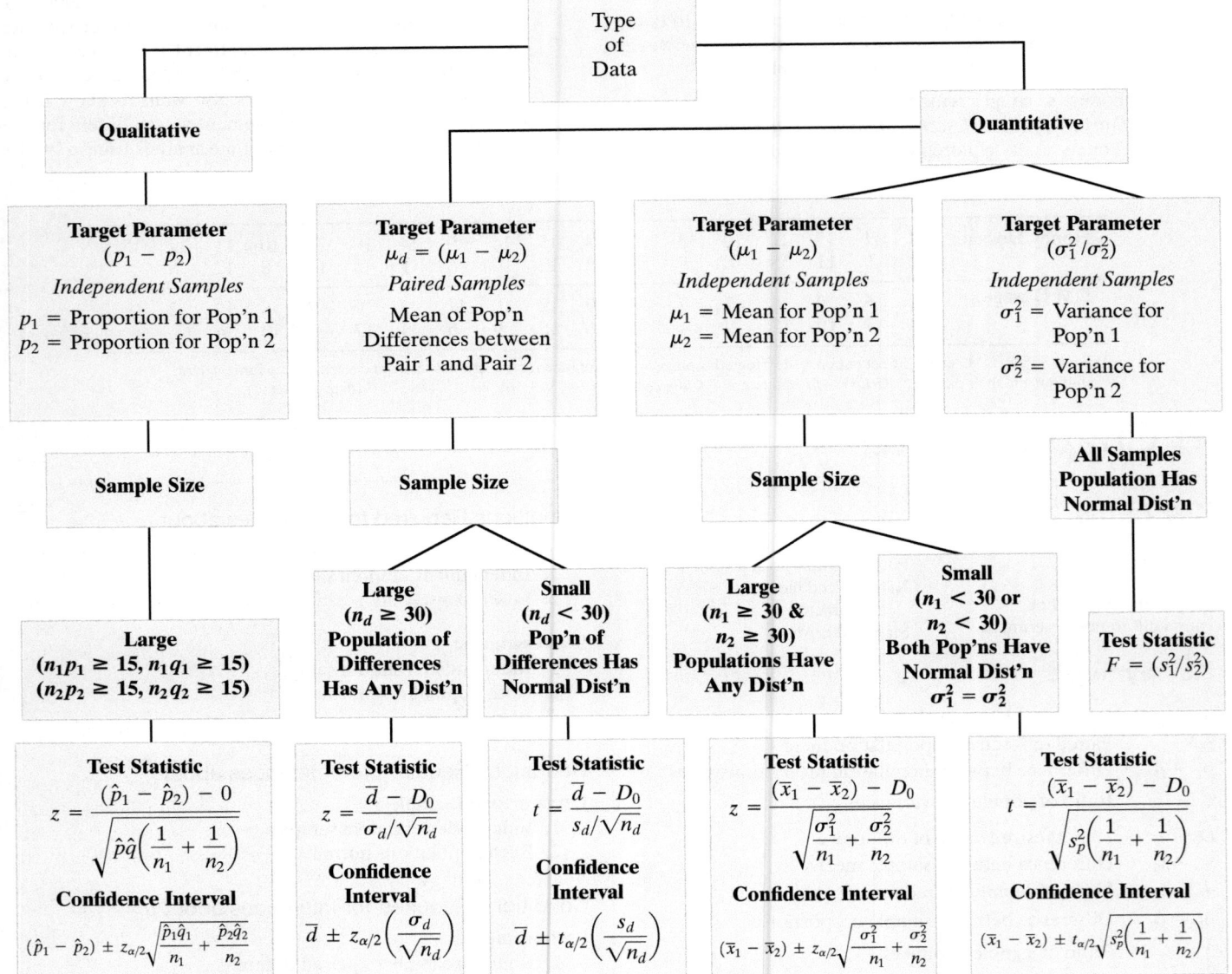

Supplementary Exercises 89–123

Please be aware that some of the following problems may require knowledge of concepts that are not presented in this chapter.

Learning the Mechanics

89 List the assumptions necessary for each of the following inferential techniques:

a. Large-sample inferences about the difference $(\mu_1 - \mu_2)$ between population means using a two-sample z-statistic

b. Small-sample inferences about $(\mu_1 - \mu_2)$ using an independent samples design and a two-sample t-statistic

c. Small-sample inferences about $(\mu_1 - \mu_2)$ using a paired difference design and a single-sample t-statistic to analyze the differences

d. Large-sample inferences about the differences $(p_1 - p_2)$ between binomial proportions using a two-sample z-statistic

e. Inferences about the ratio $\frac{\sigma_1^2}{\sigma_2^2}$ of two population variances using an F-test.

90 Two independent random samples were selected from normally distributed populations with means and variances (μ_1, σ_1^2) and (μ_2, σ_2^2), respectively. The sample sizes, means, and variances are shown in the following table.

Sample 1	Sample 2
$n_1 = 20$	$n_2 = 15$
$\bar{x}_1 = 123$	$\bar{x}_2 = 116$
$s_1^2 = 31.3$	$s_2^2 = 120.1$

a. Test $H_0: \sigma_1^2 = \sigma_2^2$ against $H_a: \sigma_1^2 \neq \sigma_2^2$. Use $\alpha = .05$.

b. Would you be willing to use a small sample t-test to test the null hypothesis $H_0: (\mu_1 - \mu_2) = 0$ against the alternative hypothesis $H_a: (\mu_1 - \mu_2) \neq 0$? Why?

91 Independent random samples were selected from two normally distributed populations with means μ_1 and μ_2, respectively. The sample sizes, means, and variances are shown in the following table.

Sample 1	Sample 2
$n_1 = 12$	$n_2 = 14$
$\bar{x}_1 = 17.8$	$\bar{x}_2 = 15.3$
$s_1^2 = 74.2$	$s_2^2 = 60.5$

a. Test $H_0: (\mu_1 - \mu_2) = 0$ against $H_a: (\mu_1 - \mu_2) > 0$. Use $\alpha = .05$.

b. Form a 99% confidence interval for $(\mu_1 - \mu_2)$.

c. How large must n_1 and n_2 be if you wish to estimate $(\mu_1 - \mu_2)$ to within 2 units with 99% confidence? Assume that $n_1 = n_2$.

92 Independent random samples were selected from two binomial populations. The sizes and number of observed successes for each sample are shown in the following table.

Sample 1	Sample 2
$n_1 = 200$	$n_2 = 200$
$x_1 = 110$	$x_2 = 130$

a. Test $H_0: (p_1 - p_2) = 0$ against $H_a: (p_1 - p_2) < 0$. Use $\alpha = .10$.

b. Form a 95% confidence interval for $(p_1 - p_2)$.

c. What sample sizes would be required if we wish to use a 95% confidence interval of width .01 to estimate $(p_1 - p_2)$?

93 Two independent random samples are taken from two populations. The results of these samples are summarized in the next table.

Sample 1	Sample 2
$n_1 = 135$	$n_2 = 148$
$\bar{x}_1 = 12.2$	$\bar{x}_2 = 8.3$
$s_1^2 = 2.1$	$s_2^2 = 3.0$

a. Form a 90% confidence interval for $(\mu_1 - \mu_2)$.

b. Test $H_0: (\mu_1 - \mu_2) = 0$ against $H_a: (\mu_1 - \mu_2) \neq 0$. Use $\alpha = .01$.

c. What sample sizes would be required if you wish to estimate $(\mu_1 - \mu_2)$ to within .2 with 90% confidence? Assume that $n_1 = n_2$.

94 A random sample of five pairs of observations were selected, one of each pair from a population with mean μ_1, the other from a population with mean μ_2. The data are shown in the accompanying table.

L08094

Pair	Value from Population 1	Value from Population 2
1	28	22
2	31	27
3	24	20
4	30	27
5	22	20

a. Test the null hypothesis $H_0: \mu_d = 0$ against $H_a: \mu_d \neq 0$, where $\mu_d = \mu_1 - \mu_2$. Use $\alpha = .05$.

b. Form a 95% confidence interval for μ_d.

c. When are the procedures you used in parts **a** and **b** valid?

Applying the Concepts—Basic

95 Determining the target parameter. For each of the following studies, give the parameter of interest and state any assumptions that are necessary for the inferences to be valid.

a. To investigate a possible link between jet lag and memory impairment, a University of Bristol (England) neurologist recruited 20 female flight attendants who worked flights across several time zones. Half of the attendants had only a short recovery time between flights and half had a long recovery time between flights. The average size of the right temporal lobe of the brain for the short-recovery group was significantly smaller than the average size of the right temporal lobe of the brain for the long-recovery group (*Tampa Tribune*, May 23, 2001).

b. In a study presented at the March 2001 meeting of the Association for the Advancement of Applied Sport Psychology, researchers revealed that the proportion of athletes who have a good self-image of their body is 20% higher than the corresponding proportion of nonathletes.

c. A University of Florida animal sciences professor has discovered that feeding chickens corn oil causes them to produce larger eggs (*UF News*, April 11, 2001). The weight of eggs produced by each of a sample of chickens on a regular feed diet was recorded. Then, the same chickens were fed a diet supplemented by corn oil, and the weight of eggs produced by each was recorded. The mean weight of the eggs produced with corn oil was 3 grams heavier than the mean weight produced with the regular diet.

96 Financial incentives for college students. A study reported in *Inside Higher Education News* (May 22, 2006) found that financial incentives can improve low-income college students' grades and retention. As part of their "Opening Doors" program, a Louisiana community college offered to pay students $1,000 per semester on condition that they maintain at least half-time enrollment and at least a 2.0 grade point average (GPA).

a. About 61% of Opening Doors students enrolled full time as opposed to about 52% of traditional students. Identify the target parameter for this comparison.

b. The mean GPA of Opening Doors students was 2.3 as compared to the mean GPA of 2.1 for traditional students. Identify the target parameter for this comparison.

97 Rating service at five-star hotels. A study published in *The Journal of American Academy of Business, Cambridge* (March 2002) examined whether the perception of service quality at five-star hotels in Jamaica differed by gender. Hotel guests were randomly selected from the lobby and restaurant areas and asked to rate 10 service-related items (e.g., "The personal attention you received from our employees"). Each item was rated on a 5-point scale (1 = "much worse than I expected," 5 = "much better than I expected"), and the sum of the items for each guest was determined. A summary of the guest scores is provided in the table.

Gender	Sample Size	Mean Score	Standard Deviation
Males	127	39.08	6.73
Females	114	38.79	6.94

487

a. Construct a 90% confidence interval for the difference between the population mean service-rating scores given by male and female guests at Jamaican five-star hotels.

b. Conduct a test to determine if the service-rating score variances differ by gender. Use $\alpha = .10$

c. Use the results, parts a and b, to make an inference about whether the perception of service quality at five-star hotels in Jamaica differs by gender.

98 Hull failures of oil tankers. *Marine Technology* (Jan. 1995) did a study of major oil spills from tankers and carriers. **HULL** The data for the 42 recent spills are saved in the accompanying file.

a. Construct a 90% confidence interval for the difference between the mean spillage amount of accidents caused by collision and the mean spillage amount of accidents caused by fire/explosion. Interpret the result.

b. Conduct a test of hypothesis to compare the mean spillage amount of accidents caused by grounding to the corresponding mean of accidents caused by hull failure. Use $\alpha = .05$.

c. Refer to parts a and b. State any assumptions required for the inferences derived from the analyses to be valid. Are these assumptions reasonably satisfied?

d. Conduct a test of hypothesis to compare the variation in spillage amounts for accidents caused by collision and accidents caused by grounding. Use $\alpha = .02$.

99 Financial incentives for college students. Do students who play virtual-reality educational software games perform better in school? If so, software designers will use this information to create more attractive and motivating educational software. In a study published in *Educational Technology & Society* (April 2005), a class of 90 elementary schoolchildren were randomly divided into two groups of 45. One group used a virtual-reality game called VR-ENGAGE to learn about geography. The other group learned geography on the computer with a simple user interface. All students were given an exam at the beginning and the end of the learning period. The difference in test scores was used to find the percentage improvement in scores for each student. The following table summarizes the results for the two groups.

	VR-ENGAGE	Simple User Interface
n:	45	45
$\bar{x}$:	43.15	32.48
s:	12.57	9.26

Source: Based on Virvou, M., Katsionis, G., & Manos, K. "Combining software games with education: Evaluation of its educational effectiveness," *Educational Technology & Society*, Vol. 8, No. 2, April 2005 (Table 2).

a. Visually inspect the summary results. Does it appear that the mean improvement in scores for the virtual-reality group is greater than the mean for the simple user interface group?

b. Conduct an analysis (either a confidence interval or a test of hypothesis) at $\alpha = .05$ to support your observation in part a.

100 Durability of shock absorbers. A manufacturer of automobile shock absorbers was interested in comparing the **SHOCK** durability of its shocks with that of the shocks produced by

its biggest competitor. To make the comparison, one of the manufacturer's and one of the competitor's shocks were randomly selected and installed on the rear wheels of each of six cars. After the cars had been driven 20,000 miles, the strength of each test shock was measured, coded, and recorded. Results of the examination are shown in the table.

Car Number	Manufacturer's Shock	Competitor's Shock
1	8.8	8.4
2	10.5	10.1
3	12.5	12.0
4	9.7	9.3
5	9.6	9.0
6	13.2	13.0

a. Explain why the data are collected as matched pairs.

b. Do the data present sufficient evidence to conclude that there is a difference in the mean strength of the two types of shocks after 20,000 miles of use? Use $\alpha = .05$.

c. Find the approximate observed significance level for the test and interpret its value.

d. What assumptions are necessary to apply a paired difference analysis to the data?

e. Construct a 95% confidence interval for μ_d. Interpret the confidence interval.

f. Suppose the data are based on independent random samples. Construct a 95% confidence interval for $(\mu_1 - \mu_2)$. Interpret your result.

g. Compare the confidence intervals you obtained in parts e and f. Which is wider? To what do you attribute the difference in width? Assuming in each case that the appropriate assumptions are satisfied, which interval provides you with more information about $(\mu_1 - \mu_2)$? Explain.

h. Are the results of an unpaired analysis valid if the data come from a paired experiment?

101 Life expectancy of Oscar winners. Movie actors who win an Oscar usually can command a greater fee for their next motion picture. Does winning an Academy of Motion Picture Arts and Sciences award (aka, an Oscar) lead to long-term mortality for movie actors? In an article in the *Annals of Internal Medicine* (May 15, 2001), researchers sampled 762 Academy Award winners and matched each one with another actor of the same sex who was in the same winning film and was born in the same era. The life expectancy (age) of each pair of actors was compared.

a. Explain why the data should be analyzed as a paired difference experiment.

b. Set up the null hypothesis for a test to compare the mean life expectancies of Academy Award winners and nonwinners.

c. The sample mean life expectancies of Academy Award winners and nonwinners were reported as 79.7 years and 75.8 years, respectively. The *p*-value for comparing the two population means was reported as $p = .003$. Interpret this value in the context of the problem.

102 Diamonds sold at retail. Refer to the data for 308 diamonds saved in the file. Two quantitative variables in the **DIAMND** data set are number of carats and selling price. One of the qualitative variables is the independent certification body that assessed each of the stones. Three certification bodies were used: GIA, IGI, and HRD. The Minitab printout shown below gives the means and standard deviations of the quantitative variables for each certification body.

Descriptive Statistics: CARAT, PRICE

Variable	CERT	N	Mean	StDev
CARAT	GIA	151	0.6723	0.2456
	HRD	79	0.8129	0.1831
	IGI	78	0.3665	0.2163
PRICE	GIA	151	5310	3247
	HRD	79	7181	2898
	IGI	78	2267	2121

a. Construct a 95% confidence interval for the difference between the mean carat size of diamonds certified by GIA and the mean carat size of diamonds certified by HRD.

b. Interpret the result, part **a.** Specifically, which (if either) of the two population means compared is larger and by how much?

c. Construct a 95% confidence interval for the difference between the mean carat size of diamonds certified by GIA and the mean carat size of diamonds certified by IGI.

d. Interpret the result, part **c.** Specifically, which (if either) of the two population means is larger and by how much?

e. Construct a 95% confidence interval for the difference between the mean selling price of diamonds certified by HRD and the mean selling price of diamonds certified by IGI.

f. Interpret the result, part **e.** Specifically, which (if either) of the two population means is larger and by how much?

g. Conduct a test to determine whether the variation in carat size differs for diamonds certified by GIA and diamonds certified by HRD. Use $\alpha = .05$.

h. Conduct a test to determine whether the variation in carat size differs for diamonds certified by GIA and diamonds certified by IGI. Use $\alpha = .05$.

i. Conduct a test to determine whether the variation in selling price differs for diamonds certified by HRD and diamonds certified by IGI. Use $\alpha = .05$.

j. Use a statistical software package (and the data in the accompanying file) to determine whether the assumption of normally distributed data for each certification group is reasonably satisfied.

103 **Ages of cable TV shoppers.** The International Association for Time Use Research did a study on cable TV viewers who purchase items from one of the home shopping channels. The 1,600 sampled viewers described their motivation for watching cable TV shopping networks by giving their level of agreement (on a 5-point scale, where 1 = strongly disagree and 5 = strongly agree) with the statement, "I have nothing else to do." The researcher wanted to compare the mean responses of viewers who watch the shopping network at noon with those viewers who do not watch at noon.

a. Give the null and alternative hypotheses for determining whether the mean response of noontime watchers differs from the mean response of non-noontime watchers.

b. The researcher found the p-value for the test, part **a,** to be .02. Interpret this result, assuming $\alpha = .05$.

c. Interpret the result, part **b,** assuming $\alpha = .01$.

d. The sample means for noontime watchers and non-watchers were found to be 3.3 and 3.4, respectively. Comment on the practical significance of this result.

104 **Career success expectations.** In evaluating the usefulness and validity of a questionnaire, researchers often pretest the questionnaire on different independently selected samples of respondents. Knowledge of the differences and similarities of the samples and their respective populations is important for interpreting the questionnaire's validity. *Educational and Psychological Measurement* (Feb. 1998) reported on a questionnaire developed for measuring the career success expectations of employees. The instrument was tested on the two independent samples described in the following table.

	Managers and Professionals	Part-Time MBA Students
Sample size	162	109
Gender (% males)	95.0	68.9
Marital status (% married)	91.2	53.4

Source: Based on Stephens, G. K., Szajna, B., & Broome, K. M., "The career success expectation scale: An exploratory and confirmatory factor analysis," *Educational and Psychological Measurement,* Vol. 58, No. 1, Feb. 1998, pp.129–141.

a. Does the population of managers and professionals from which the sample was drawn consist of more males than the part-time MBA population does? Conduct the appropriate test using $\alpha = .05$.

b. Describe any assumptions you made in conducting the test of part **a** and why you made them.

c. Does the population of managers and professionals consist of more married individuals than the part-time MBA population does? Conduct the appropriate hypothesis test using $\alpha = .01$.

d. What assumptions must hold for the test of part **c** to be valid?

105 **Likelihood of getting a routine medical checkup.** Who is more likely to get a routine medical checkup—employed or unemployed people? To answer this question, a team of physicians and public health professors collected data on a sample of over 2,200 individuals (*American Journal of Public Health,* Jan. 2002). Of the 1,140 individuals who were employed, 642 visited a physician for a routine checkup within the past year. In contrast, 740 of the 1,106 unemployed individuals had a routine medical checkup within the past year.

a. Specify the parameter of interest to the research team.

b. Set up the null and alternative hypotheses for testing whether there is a difference between the percentages of employed and unemployed people who had a recent routine medical checkup.

c. Compute the test statistic for the test.

d. Give the rejection region for the test using $\alpha = .01$.

e. The research team reported the p-value for the test as p-value ≈ 0. Do you agree?

f. Make the appropriate conclusion.

106 **Turnover rates in the United States and Japan.** High job
turnover rates are often associated with high product
defect rates because high turnover rates mean more
inexperienced workers who are unfamiliar with the company's product lines (Stevenson, *Production/Operations
Management*, 2000). In a study, five Japanese and five U.S.
plants that manufacture air conditioners were randomly
sampled; their turnover rates are listed in the table.

U.S. Plants	Japanese Plants
7.11%	3.52%
6.06	2.02
8.00	4.91
6.87	3.22
4.77	1.92

a. Do the data provide sufficient evidence to indicate
that the mean annual percentage turnover for U.S.
plants exceeds the corresponding mean percentage for
Japanese plants? Test using $\alpha = .05$.
b. Find and interpret the observed significance level of
the test you conducted in part **a.**
c. List any assumptions you made in conducting the hypothesis test of part **a.** Comment on their validity for
this application.

107 **Cell phone usage differs by gender.** The role of the cell
phone in modern life was investigated by a Pew Internet
& American Life Project (April 2006) survey. A total of
1,286 cell phone users were interviewed in the sample.
One of the objectives was to compare male and female
cell phone users. For example, 32% of men admitted they
sometimes don't drive safely while talking or texting on a
cell phone compared to 25% of women. Also, 71% of men
used their cell phone in an emergency compared to 77%
of women. Assume that half (643) of the cell phone users
in the sample were men and half (643) were women.
a. Describe the two populations of interest in the survey.
b. Give an estimate of the proportion of men and the
proportion of women who sometimes do not drive
safely while talking or texting on a cell phone.
c. Find a 90% confidence interval for the difference between the proportions of men and women who sometimes do not drive safely while talking or texting on a
cell phone.
d. From your answer to part **c,** can you conclude that
men are more likely than women to sometimes not
drive safely while talking or texting on a cell phone?
Explain.
e. Give an estimate of the proportion of men and the
proportion of women who used their cell phone in an
emergency.
f. Conduct a test to determine whether the proportions
of men and women who used their cell phone in an
emergency differ. Use $\alpha = .10$.

Applying the Concepts—Intermediate

108 **Sampling plan for a movie promotion.** Advertising companies often try to characterize the average user of a client's product so ads can be targeted at particular segments
of the buying community. A new movie is about to be
released, and the advertising company wants to determine
whether to aim the ad campaign at people under or over

25 years of age. It plans to arrange an advance showing of
the movie to an audience from each group and then obtain
an opinion about the movie from each individual. How
many individuals should be included in each sample if the
advertising company wants to estimate the difference in
the proportions of viewers in each age group who will like
the movie to within .05 with 90% confidence? Assume the
sample size for each group will be the same and about half
of each group will like the movie.

109 **Comparing purchasers and nonpurchasers of toothpaste.**
Marketing strategists would like to predict consumer
response to new products and their accompanying promotional schemes. Consequently, studies that examine the
differences between buyers and nonbuyers of a product
are of interest. One classic study conducted by Shuchman
and Riesz (*Journal of Marketing Research*) was aimed
at characterizing the purchasers and nonpurchasers of
Crest toothpaste. The researchers demonstrated that both
the mean household size (number of persons) and mean
household income were significantly larger for purchasers
than for nonpurchasers. A similar study used independent
random samples of size 20 and yielded the data shown in
the following table on the age of the householder primarily responsible for buying toothpaste.
a. Do the data present sufficient evidence to conclude
there is a difference in the mean age of purchasers and
nonpurchasers? Use $\alpha = .10$.
b. What assumptions are necessary in order to answer
part **a**?
c. Find the observed significance level for the test and
interpret its value.
d. Calculate and interpret a 90% confidence interval for
the difference between the mean ages of purchasers
and nonpurchasers.

Purchasers						Nonpurchasers					
34	35	23	44	52	46	28	22	44	33	55	63
28	48	28	34	33	52	45	31	60	54	53	58
41	32	34	49	50	45	52	52	66	35	25	48
29	59					59	61				

110 **Killing moths with carbon dioxide.** A University of South
Florida biologist conducted an experiment to determine
whether increased levels of carbon dioxide kill leaf-eating
moths (*USF Magazine*, Winter 1999). Moth larvae were
placed in open containers filled with oak leaves. Half the
containers had normal carbon dioxide levels, while the
other half had double the normal level of carbon dioxide.
Ten percent of the larvae in the containers with high carbon dioxide levels died, compared to 5% in the containers with normal levels. Assume that 80 moth larvae were
placed, at random, in each of the two types of containers.
Do the experimental results demonstrate that an increased
level of carbon dioxide is effective in killing a higher percentage of leaf-eating moth larvae? Test using $\alpha = .01$.

111 **Racial profiling by the LAPD.** *Racial profiling* is a term
used to describe any police action that relies on ethnicity
rather than behavior to target suspects engaged in criminal activities. Does the Los Angeles Police Department
(LAPD) invoke racial profiling in stops and searches
of LA drivers? This question was addressed in *Chance*
(Spring 2006).

a. Data on stops and searches of both African Americans and white drivers are summarized in the accompanying table. Conduct a test (at $\alpha = .05$) to determine if there is a disparity in the proportions of African American and white drivers who are searched by the LA police after being stopped.

b. The LAPD defines a *hit rate* as the proportion of searches that result in a discovery of criminal activity. Use the data in the table to estimate the disparity in the hit rates for African American and white drivers using a 95% confidence interval. Interpret the results.

Race	Number Stopped	Number Searched	Number of "Hits"
African American	61,688	12,016	5,134
White	106,892	5,312	3,006

Source: Based on Khadjavi, L. S. "Driving while black in the City of Angels," *Chance*, Vol. 19, No. 2.

112 **State SAT scores.** Refer to the data on average math SAT
scores for each of the 50 states and District of Columbia for
SATMAT the years 2001 and 2011. The data are saved in the file. (The first five observations and last two observations in the data set are shown in the table below.)

State	2001	2011
Alabama	554	541
Alaska	510	511
Arizona	525	523
Arkansas	550	570
California	517	515
⋮	⋮	⋮
Wisconsin	596	602
Wyoming	545	569

Source: Based on "SAT trends: Background on the SAT takers in the class of 2011," from The CollegeBoard.

a. You can compute the *paired differences* of SAT scores by subtracting the 2001 score from the 2011 score for each state. Find the mean of these 51 paired differences. This value is μ_d, the mean difference in SAT scores for the population of 50 states and the District of Columbia.

b. Explain why there is no need to employ the confidence interval or test procedures of this section to make an inference about μ_d.

c. Now, suppose the 50 paired differences of part **a** represent a sample of SAT score differences for 50 randomly selected high school students. Use the data in the file to make an inference about whether the true mean SAT score of high school students in 2011 differs from the true mean in 2001. Use a confidence level of .90.

113 **Rat damage to sugarcane fields.** Poisons are used to prevent rat damage in sugarcane fields. The U.S. Department of Agriculture is investigating whether the rat poison should be located in the middle of the field or on the outer perimeter. One way to answer this question is to determine where the greater amount of damage occurs. If damage is measured by the proportion of cane stalks that have been damaged by rats, how many stalks from each section of the field should be sampled to estimate the true difference between proportions of stalks damaged in the two sections to within .02 with 95% confidence?

114 **Environmental impact study.** Some power plants are located near rivers or oceans so that the available water can be used for cooling the condensers. Suppose that, as part of an environmental impact study, a power company wants to estimate the difference in mean water temperature between the discharge of its plant and the offshore waters. How many sample measurements must be taken at each site to estimate the true difference between means to within $.2°C$ with 95% confidence? Assume that the range in readings will be about $4°C$ at each site and the same number of readings will be taken at each site.

115 **Instrument precision.** When new instruments are developed to perform chemical analyses of products (food, INSTAB medicine, etc.), they are usually evaluated with respect to two criteria: accuracy and precision. *Accuracy* refers to the ability of the instrument to identify correctly the nature and amounts of a product's components. *Precision* refers to the consistency with which the instrument will identify the components of the same material. Thus, a large variability in the identification of a single batch of a product indicates a lack of precision. Suppose a pharmaceutical firm is considering two brands of an instrument designed to identify the components of certain drugs. As part of a comparison of precision, 10 test-tube samples of a well-mixed batch of a drug are selected and then 5 are analyzed by instrument A and 5 by instrument B. The data shown below are the percentages of the primary component of the drug given by the instruments. Do these data provide evidence of a difference in the precision of the two machines? Use $\alpha = .10$.

Instrument A	Instrument B
43	46
48	49
37	43
52	41
45	48

116 **Computer-mediated communication study.** Computer-
mediated communication (CMC) is a form of interaction
CMC that heavily involves technology (e.g., instant messaging, e-mail). A study was conducted to compare relational intimacy in people interacting via CMC to people meeting face-to-face (FTF) *(Journal of Computer-Mediated Communication,* April 2004). Participants were 48 undergraduate students, of which half were randomly assigned to the CMC group and half assigned to the FTF group. Each group was given a task that required communication with the group members. Those in the CMC group used the "chat" mode of instant-messaging software; those in the FTF group met in a conference room. The variable of interest, relational intimacy score, was measured (on a 7-point scale) for each participant after each of three different meeting sessions and is saved in the accompanying file. Scores for the first meeting session are given in the table on the next page. The researchers hypothesized that, after the first meeting, the mean relational intimacy score for participants in the CMC group would be lower than the mean relational intimacy score for participants in the FTF group. Test the researchers' hypothesis using $\alpha = .10$.

Data for Exercise 116

CMC	4	3	3	4	3	3	3	3	4	4	3	4
	3	3	2	4	2	4	5	4	4	4	5	3
FTF	5	4	4	4	3	3	3	4	3	3	3	3
	4	4	4	4	4	3	3	3	4	4	2	4

Note: Data simulated from descriptive statistics provided in article.

117 **Computer-mediated communication study (cont'd).** Refer to Exercise 116. The researchers also hypothesized that the mean relational intimacy score for participants in the CMC group would significantly increase between the first and third meetings, but the difference between the first and third meetings would not significantly change for participants in the FTF group.

   a. For the CMC group comparison, give the null and alternative hypotheses of interest.

   b. The researchers made the comparison, part **a,** using a paired *t*-test. Explain why the data should be analyzed as matched pairs.

   c. For the CMC group comparison, the reported test statistic was $t = 3.04$ with *p*-value = .003. Interpret these results. Is the researchers' hypothesis supported?

   d. For the FTF group comparison, give the null and alternative hypotheses of interest.

   e. For the FTF group comparison, the reported test statistic was $t = .39$ with *p*-value = .70. Interpret these results. Is the researchers' hypothesis supported?

118 **Positive spillover effects from self-managed work teams.** To improve quality, productivity, and timeliness, many American industries employ self-managed work teams (SMWTs). A team typically consists of 5 to 15 workers who are collectively responsible for making decisions and performing all tasks related to a particular project. Because SMWTs require that employees be trained in interpersonal skills, they can have potential positive spillover effects on a worker's family life. The link between SMWT work characteristics and workers' perceptions of positive spillover into family life was investigated in the *Quality Management Journal* (Summer 1995). Survey data were collected from 114 AT&T employees who work in 1 of 15 SMWTs at an AT&T technical division. The workers were divided into two groups: (1) those who reported positive spillover of work skills to family life and (2) those who did not report positive work spillover. The two groups were compared on a variety of job and demographic characteristics, one of which was the use of creative ideas (measured on a 7-point scale, where the larger the number, the more of the characteristic indicated). The data (simulated from summary information provided in the *Quality Management Journal* article) are saved in the file.

   a. One comparison of interest to the researchers is whether the mean creative use of ideas scale score for employees who report positive spillover of work skills to family life differs from the mean scale score for employees who did not report positive work spillover. Give the null and alternative hypotheses that will allow the researchers to make the comparison.

   b. Discuss whether it is appropriate to apply the large-sample z-test to test the hypotheses, part **a.**

   c. The results of the test are shown in the SPSS printout below. Interpret these results. Make the appropriate conclusion using $\alpha = .05$.

   d. A 95% confidence interval for the difference between the mean use of creative ideas scale scores is shown in the last column of the SPSS printout. Interpret this interval. Does the inference derived from the confidence interval agree with that from the hypothesis test?

   e. The data also include the qualitative variable, Gender, for each worker. The researchers want to know whether the proportion of male workers in the two groups are significantly different. A Minitab printout of the analysis is shown below. Fully interpret the results in the words of the problem.

Applying the Concepts—Advanced

119 **Impact of gender on advertising.** How does gender affect the type of advertising that proves to be most effective? An article in the *Journal of Advertising Research* (May/June 1990)

SPSS output for Exercise 118

Independent Samples Test

		Levene's Test for Equality of Variances		t-test for Equality of Means						95% Confidence Interval of the Difference	
		F	Sig.	t	df	Sig. (2-tailed)	Mean Difference	Std. Error Difference	Lower	Upper
CREATIVE	Equal variances assumed	16.479	.000	8.565	112	.000	.808	.094	.621	.994
	Equal variances not assumed			8.847	108.727	.000	.808	.091	.627	.988

Minitab output for Exercise 118

Test and CI for Two Proportions: GENDER, GROUP

```
Event = MALE


GROUP      X   N   Sample p
NOSPILL   59  67   0.880597
SPILLOV   39  47   0.829787


Difference = p (NOSPILL) - p (SPILLOV)
Estimate for difference:  0.0508098
95% CI for difference:  (-0.0817519, 0.183371)
Test for difference = 0 (vs not = 0):  Z = 0.75   P-Value = 0.453
```

makes reference to numerous studies that conclude males tend to be more competitive with others than with themselves. To apply this conclusion to advertising, the author created two ads promoting a new brand of soft drink:

Ad 1: Four men are shown competing in racquetball
Ad 2: One man is shown competing against himself in racquetball

The author hypothesized that the first ad would be more effective when shown to males. To test this hypothesis, 43 males were shown both ads and asked to measure their attitude toward the advertisement (Aad), their attitude toward the brand of soft drink (Ab), and their intention to purchase the soft drink (Intention). Each variable was measured using a 7-point scale, with higher scores indicating a more favorable attitude. The results are shown in the table below. Do you agree with the author's hypothesis?

	Sample Means		
	Aad	Ab	Intention
Ad 1	4.465	3.311	4.366
Ad 2	4.150	2.902	3.813
Level of Significance	$p = .091$	$p = .032$	$p = .050$

120 Salaries of postgraduates. *Economics of Education Review* (Vol. 21, 2002) did a study of the relationship between education level and earnings. A National Adult Literacy Survey revealed that males with a postgraduate degree had a sample mean salary of \$61,340 (with standard error $s_{\bar{x}_M} = \$2,185$), while females with a postgraduate degree had a sample mean salary of \$32,227 (with standard error $s_{\bar{x}_F} = \$932$). Let μ_M represent the population mean salary of all males with postgraduate degrees and μ_F represent the population mean salary of all females with postgraduate degrees.
   a. Set up the null and alternative hypotheses for determining whether μ_M exceeds μ_F.
   b. Calculate the test statistic for the test, part **a.** [*Note:* $s_{\bar{x}_M - \bar{x}_F} = \sqrt{(s_{\bar{x}_M}^2 + s_{\bar{x}_F}^2)}.$]
   c. Find the rejection region for the test using $\alpha = .01$.
   d. Use the results, parts **b** and **c,** to make the appropriate conclusion.

121 Gambling in public high schools. With the rapid growth in legalized gambling in the United States, there is concern that the involvement of youth in gambling activities is also increasing. University of Minnesota Professor Randy Stinchfield compared the rates of gambling among Minnesota public school students between 1992 and 1998 (*Journal of Gambling Studies,* Winter 2001). Based on survey data, the table (next column) shows the percentages of ninth-grade boys who gambled weekly or daily on any game (e.g., cards, sports betting, lotteries) for the 2 years.
   a. Are the percentages of ninth-grade boys who gambled weekly or daily on any game in 1992 and 1998 significantly different? (Use $\alpha = .01$.)
   b. Professor Stinchfield states that "because of the large sample sizes, even small differences may achieve statistical significance, so interpretations of the differences should include a judgment regarding the magnitude of the difference and its public health significance." Do

you agree with this statement? If not, why not? If so, obtain a measure of the magnitude of the difference between 1992 and 1998 and attach a measure of reliability to the difference.

	1992	1998
Number of Ninth-Grade Boys in Survey	21,484	23,199
Number Who Gambled Weekly/Daily	4,684	5,313

122 CareerBank.com annual salary survey. CareerBank.com conducts an annual salary survey of accounting, finance, and banking professionals. For one survey, data were collected for 2,800 responses submitted online by professionals across the country who voluntarily responded to CareerBank.com's Web-based survey. Salary comparisons were made by gender, education, and marital status. Some of the results are shown in the accompanying table.

	Males	Females
Mean Salary	\$69,848	\$52,012
Number of Respondents	1,400	1,400

   a. Suppose you want to make an inference about the difference between the mean salaries of male and female accounting/finance/banking professionals at a 95% level of confidence. Why is this impossible to do using the information in the table?
   b. Give values of the missing standard deviations that would lead you to conclude that the mean salary for males is significantly higher than the mean salary for females at a 95% level of confidence.
   c. In your opinion, are the sample standard deviations, part **b,** reasonable values for the salary data? Explain.
   d. How does the data-collection method impact any inferences derived from the data?

Critical Thinking Challenge

123 Facility layout study. Facility layout and material flowpath design are major factors in the productivity analysis of automated manufacturing systems. Facility layout is concerned with the location arrangement of machines and buffers for work-in-process. Flowpath design is concerned with the direction of manufacturing material flows (e.g., unidirectional or bidirectional; Lee, Lei, and Pinedo, *Annals of Operations Research,* 1997). A manufacturer of printed circuit boards is interested in evaluating two alternative existing layout and flowpath designs. The output of each design was monitored for 8 consecutive working days. The data (shown below) are saved in the file. Design 2 appears to be superior to Design 1. Do you agree? Explain fully.

Working Days	Design 1 (units)	Design 2 (units)
8/16	1,220	1,273
8/17	1,092	1,363
8/18	1,136	1,342
8/19	1,205	1,471
8/20	1,086	1,299
8/23	1,274	1,457
8/24	1,145	1,263
8/25	1,281	1,368

Activity   1   *Box Office Receipts:* Comparing Population Means

Use the Internet to find the daily box office receipts for two different hit movies during the first 8 weeks after their releases. In this activity, you will compare the mean daily box office receipts of these movies in two different ways.

1. Independently select random samples of size $n = 30$ from the data sets for each of the movies' daily box office receipts. Find the mean and standard deviation of each sample. Then find a confidence interval for the difference of the means.

2. Now pair the data for the two movies by day, that is, the box office receipts for the day of release for each movie are paired, the box office receipts for each movie's second day are paired, and so forth. Calculate the difference in box office receipts for each day and select a random sample of size $n = 30$ from the daily differences. Then find a confidence interval for the sample mean.

3. Compare the confidence intervals from Exercises 1 and 2. Explain how the sampling for the paired difference experiment is different from the independent sampling. How might this sampling technique yield a better comparison of the two means in the box office example?

4. Compute the actual means for the daily box office receipts for each of the movies and then find the difference of the means. Does the difference of the means lie in both confidence intervals you found? Is the exact difference remarkably closer to one of the estimates? Explain.

References

Freedman, D., Pisani, R., & Purves, R. *Statistics.* New York: W. W. Norton and Co., 1978.

Gibbons, J. D. *Nonparametric Statistical Inference,* 2nd ed. New York: McGraw-Hill, 1985.

Hollander, M., & Wolfe, D. A. *Nonparametric Statistical Methods.* New York: Wiley, 1973.

Koehler, K. *Snedecor and Cochran's Statistical Methods,* 9th ed. New York: Blackwell Publishing, 2012.

Mendenhall, W., Beaver, R. J., & Beaver, B. M. *Introduction to Probability and Statistics,* 13th ed. Belmont, CA: Brooks/Cole, 2009.

Satterthwaite, F. W. "An approximate distribution of estimates of variance components," *Biometrics Bulletin,* Vol. 2, 1946, pp. 110–114.

Steel, R. G. D., & Torrie, J. H. *Principles and Procedures of Statistics,* 2nd ed. New York: McGraw-Hill, 1980.

USING TECHNOLOGY

SPSS: Two-Sample Inferences

SPSS can be used to make two-sample inferences about $\mu_1 - \mu_2$ for independent samples, μ_d for paired samples, $p_1 - p_2$, and $\frac{\sigma_1^2}{\sigma_2^2}$.

Comparing Means with Independent Samples

Step 1 Access the SPSS spreadsheet file that contains the sample data. The data file should contain one quantitative variable (which the means will be calculated on) and one qualitative variable with either two numerical coded values (e.g., 1 and 2) or two short categorical levels (e.g., "yes" and "no"). These two values represent the two groups or populations to be compared.

Step 2 Click on the "Analyze" button on the SPSS menu bar and then click on "Compare Means" and "Independent-Samples T Test," as shown in Figure S.1.

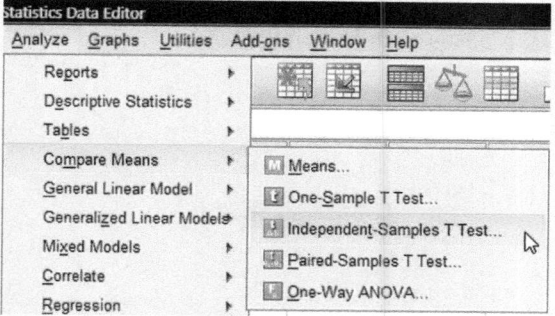

Figure S.1 SPSS menu options for comparing two means

Step 3 On the resulting dialog box (shown in Figure S.2), specify the quantitative variable of interest in the "Test Variable(s)" box and the qualitative variable in the "Grouping Variable" box.

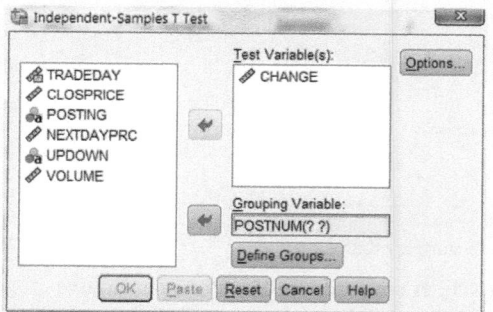

Figure S.2 SPSS independent-samples T test dialog box

Step 4 Click the "Define Groups" button and specify the values of the two groups in the resulting dialog box (see Figure S.3).

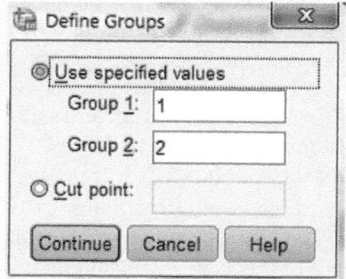

Figure S.3 SPSS define groups dialog box

Step 5 Click "Continue" to return to the "Independent-Samples T Test" dialog screen. Without any further menu selections, SPSS will automatically conduct a two-tailed test of the null hypothesis, $H_0: \mu_1 - \mu_2 = 0$.

Step 6 If you want to generate a confidence interval for $\mu_1 - \mu_2$, click the "Options" button and specify the confidence level on the resulting menu screen, as shown in Figure S.4. Click "Continue" to return to the "T Test" dialog box.

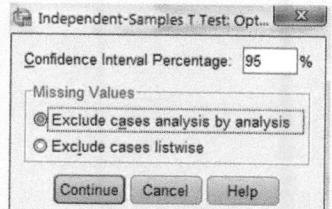

Figure S.4 SPSS options dialog box

Step 7 Click "OK" to generate the SPSS printout.

Important Note: The SPSS two-sample *t*-procedure uses the *t*-statistic to conduct the test of hypothesis. When the sample sizes are small, this is the appropriate method. When the sample sizes are large, the *t*-value will be approximately equal to the large-sample *z*-value, and the resulting test will still be valid.

Comparing Means with Paired Samples

Step 1 Access the SPSS spreadsheet file that contains the sample data. The data file should contain two quantitative variables—one with the data values for the first group (or population) and one with the data values for the second group. (*Note:* The sample size should be the same for each group.)

Step 2 Click on the "Analyze" button on the SPSS menu bar and then click on "Compare Means" and "Paired-Samples T Test" (see Figure S.1).

Step 3 On the resulting dialog box (shown in Figure S.5), specify the two quantitative variables of interest in the "Paired Variables" box. Without any further menu selections, SPSS will automatically conduct a two-tailed test of the null hypothesis, $H_0: \mu_d = 0$.

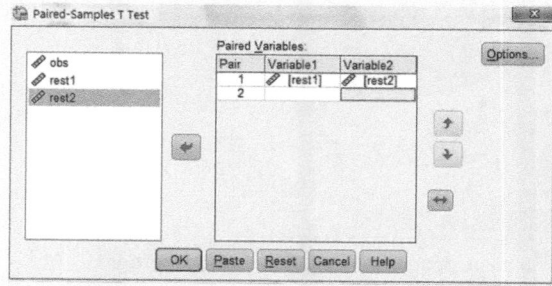

Figure S.5 SPSS paired-samples dialog box

Step 4 If you want to generate a confidence interval for μ_d, click the "Options" button and specify the confidence level on the resulting menu screen (as shown in Figure S.4). Click "Continue" to return to the "Paired-Samples" dialog box.

Step 5 Click "OK" to generate the SPSS printout.

Comparing Proportions with Independent Samples

Step 1 SPSS requires summary data to compare population proportions. Create a data file with three variables (columns)—(1) SAMPLE, (2) OUTCOME, and (3) NUMBER—and four rows. Each row will give the sample number, outcome (success or failure), and number of observations. For example, Figure S.6 shows the data file for a problem with 60 out of 100 successes for sample 1 and 50 out of 100 successes for sample 2.

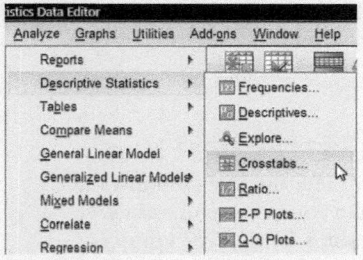

SAMPLE	OUTCOME	NUMBER
1	S	60
1	F	40
2	S	50
2	F	50

Figure S.6 SPSS data file for comparing two proportions

Step 2 Click on the "Data" button on the SPSS menu bar and then click on "Weight Cases". Enter the "Number" variable into the "Frequency Variable" box, then click "OK."

Step 3 Click on the "Analyze" button on the SPSS menu bar and then click on "Descriptive Statistics" and "Crosstabs." (See Figure S.7.)

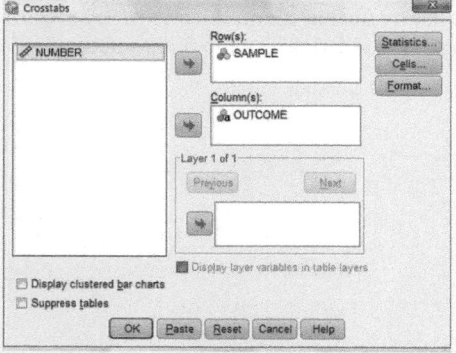

Figure S.7 SPSS menu options for comparing two proportions

Step 4 On the resulting menu, specify "SAMPLE" in the "Row" box and "OUTCOME" in the "Column(s)" box as shown in Figure S.8. Also, click the "Statistics" option button and select "Chi-square," then click the "Cells" option button and select "Observed Counts" and "Row Percentages."

Figure S.8 SPSS menu options for comparing two proportions

Step 5 Click "Continue," then click "OK." On the resulting SPSS printout, look for the p-value associated with the "Likelihood Ratio" test (this is equivalent to the large-sample z-test).

Comparing Variances with Independent Samples

Follow the steps outlined for "Comparing Means with Independent Samples" above. On the resulting SPSS printout, there will be an F-test for comparing population variances. (This test, called Levene's Test, is a nonparametric test that is similar to the F-test presented in the text.)

Minitab: Two-Sample Inferences

Minitab can be used to make two-sample inferences about $\mu_1 - \mu_2$ or independent samples, μ_d for paired samples, $p_1 - p_2$ and $\frac{\sigma_1^2}{\sigma_2^2}$.

Comparing Means with Independent Samples

Step 1 Access the Minitab worksheet that contains the sample data.

Step 2 Click on the "Stat" button on the Minitab menu bar and then click on "Basic Statistics" and "2-Sample t," as shown in Figure M.1. The resulting dialog box appears as shown in Figure M.2.

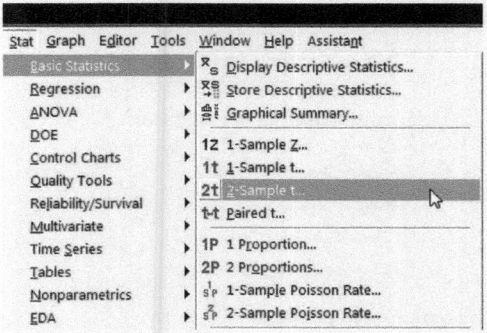

Figure M.1 Minitab menu options for comparing two means

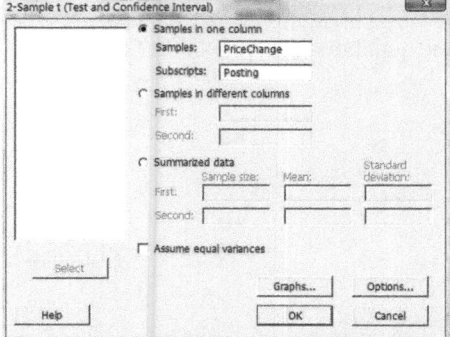

Figure M.2 Minitab 2-sample t dialog box

Step 3a If the worksheet contains data for one quantitative variable (which the means will be computed on) and one qualitative variable (which represents the two groups or populations), select "Samples in one column" and then specify the quantitative variable in the "Samples" area and the qualitative variable in the "Subscripts" area. (See Figure M.2.)

Step 3b If the worksheet contains the data for the first sample in one column and the data for the second sample in another column, select "Samples in different columns" and then specify the "First" and "Second" variables. Alternatively, if you have only summarized data (i.e., sample sizes, sample means, and sample standard deviations), select "Summarized data" and enter these summarized values in the appropriate boxes.

Step 4 Click the "Options" button on the Minitab "2-Sample t" dialog box. Specify the confidence level for a confidence interval, the null hypothesized value of the difference, $\mu_1 - \mu_2$, and the form of the alternative hypothesis (lower-tailed, two-tailed, or upper-tailed) in the resulting dialog box, as shown in Figure M.3.

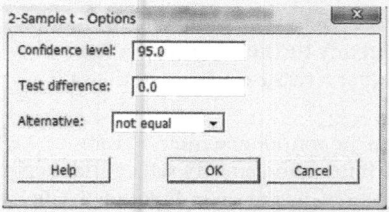

Figure M.3 Minitab options dialog box

Step 5 Click "OK" to return to the "2-Sample t" dialog box and then click "OK" again to generate the Minitab printout.

Important Note: The Minitab two-sample *t*-procedure uses the *t*-statistic to conduct the test of hypothesis. When the sample sizes are small, this is the appropriate method. When the sample sizes are large, the *t*-value will be approximately equal to the large-sample *z*-value, and the resulting test will still be valid.

Comparing Means with Paired Samples

Step 1 Access the Minitab worksheet that contains the sample data. The data file should contain two quantitative variables—one with the data values for the first group (or population) and one with the data values for the second group. (*Note:* The sample size should be the same for each group.)

Step 2 Click on the "Stat" button on the Minitab menu bar and then click on "Basic Statistics" and "Paired t" (see Figure M.1).

Step 3 On the resulting dialog box, select the "Samples in columns" option and specify the two quantitative variables of interest in the "First sample" and "Second sample" boxes, as shown in Figure M.4. [Alternatively, if you have only summarized data of the paired differences, select the "Summarized data (differences)" option and enter the sample size, sample mean, and sample standard deviation in the appropriate boxes.]

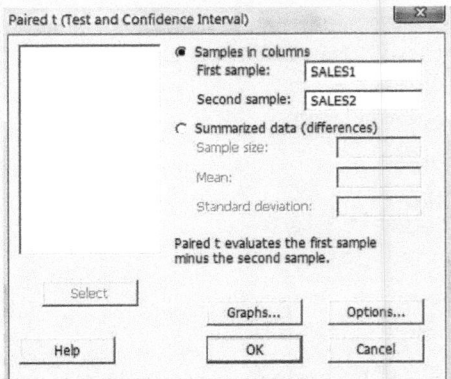

Figure M.4 Minitab paired-samples *t* dialog box

Step 4 Click the "Options" button and specify the confidence level for a confidence interval, the null hypothesized value of the difference, μ_d, and the form of the alternative hypothesis (lower-tailed, two-tailed, or upper-tailed) in the resulting dialog box. (See Figure M.3.)

Step 5 Click "OK" to return to the "Paired t" dialog box and then click "OK" again to generate the Minitab printout.

Comparing Proportions with Large Independent Samples

Step 1 Access the Minitab worksheet that contains the sample data.

Step 2 Click on the "Stat" button on the Minitab menu bar and then click on "Basic Statistics" and "2 Proportions," as shown in Figure M.1.

Step 3 On the resulting dialog box (shown in Figure M.5), select the data option ("Samples in one column" or "Samples in different columns" or "Summarized data") and make the appropriate menu choices. (Figure M.5 shows the menu options when you select "Summarized data.")

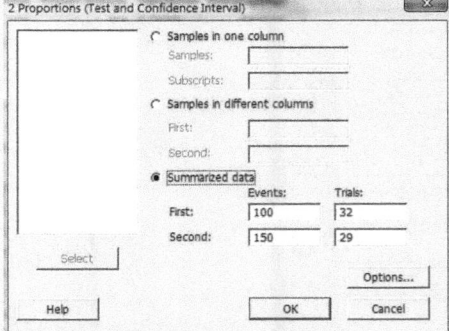

Figure M.5 Minitab 2 proportions dialog box

Step 4 Click the "Options" button and specify the confidence level for a confidence interval, the null hypothesized value of the difference, and the form of the alternative hypothesis (lower-tailed, two-tailed, or upper-tailed) in the resulting dialog box, as shown in Figure M.6. (If you desire a pooled estimate of *p* for the test, be sure to check the appropriate box.)

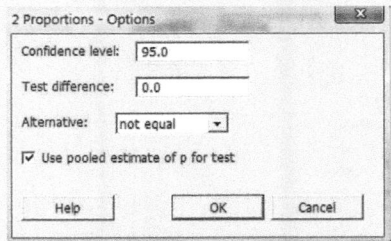

Figure M.6 Minitab 2 proportions options

Step 5 Click "OK" to return to the "2 Proportions" dialog box and then click "OK" again to generate the Minitab printout.

Comparing Variances with Independent Samples

Step 1 Access the Minitab worksheet that contains the sample data.

Step 2 Click on the "Stat" button on the Minitab menu bar and then click on "Basic Statistics" and "2 Variances" (Figure M.1.)

Step 3 On the resulting dialog box (shown in Figure M.7), the menu selections and options are similar to those for the two-sample *t*-test.

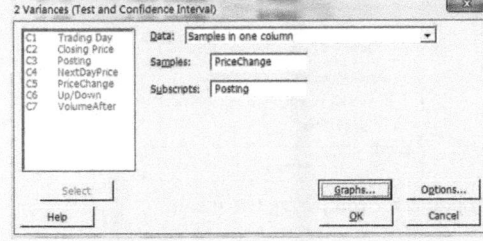

Figure M.7 Minitab 2 variances dialog box

Step 4 Click "OK" to produce the Minitab *F*-test printout.

Excel/XLSTAT: Two-Sample Inferences

Comparing Means with Independent Samples

Step 1 Click the "XLSTAT" button on the Excel main menu bar, select "Parametric tests," and then click "Two-sample t-test and z-test," as shown in Figure E.1.

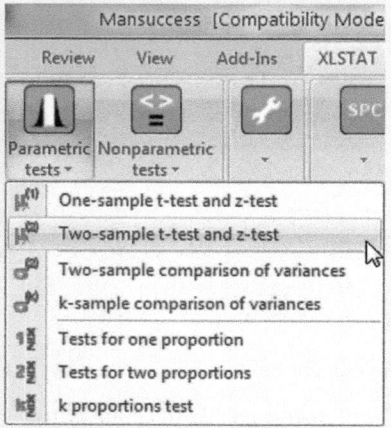

Figure E.1 XLSTAT menu options for testing a mean

Step 2 When the resulting dialog box appears, select the proper "Data format" (e.g., "One column per variable"), and then select the appropriate columns (e.g., one column for the variable being analyzed and one for the variable that represents the two different samples). Also, check the "z test" box (if large samples) or the "Student's t test" box (if small samples). See, for example, Figure E.2.

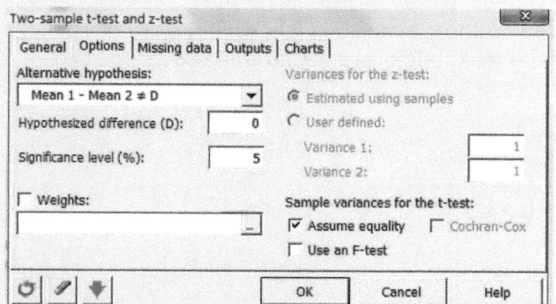

Figure E.2 XLSTAT two-sample test dialog box

Step 3 Click the "Options" tab, then specify the form of the alternative hypothesis, the value of the hypothesized (theoretical) difference in means, and the value of α (significance level) in the appropriate boxes, as shown in Figure E.3.

Figure E.3 XLSTAT options for comparing two means

Step 4 Click "OK," then "Continue" to display the test results.

Comparing Means with Paired Samples

Step 1 Click the "XLSTAT" button on the Excel main menu bar, select "Parametric tests," then click "Two-sample t-test and z-test," as shown in Figure E.1.

Step 2 When the resulting dialog box appears, select "Paired samples" as the "Data format," and then select the appropriate columns containing the data for the two samples, as shown in Figure E.4. Also, check the "z test" box (if large samples) or the "Student's t test" box (if small samples).

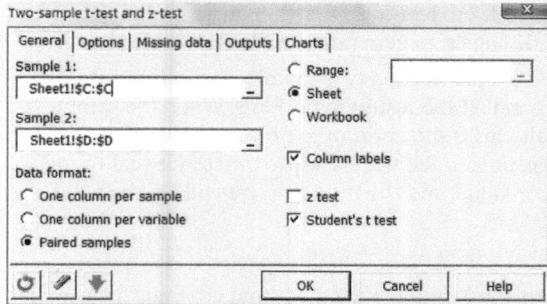

Figure E.4 XLSTAT options for paired samples

Step 3 Click the "Options" tab, and then specify the form of the alternative hypothesis, the value of the hypothesized (theoretical) difference in means, and the value of α (significance level) in the appropriate boxes, similar to Figure E.3.

Step 4 Click "OK," then "Continue" to display the test results.

Comparing Proportions with Independent Samples

[*Note:* To compare two binomial proportions using XLSTAT, you will need summary information on your qualitative data, e.g., the sample sizes and either the number of successes or proportion of successes for both samples.]

Step 1 Click the "XLSTAT" button on the Excel main menu bar, select "Parametric tests," then click "Tests for two proportions," as shown in Figure E.5.

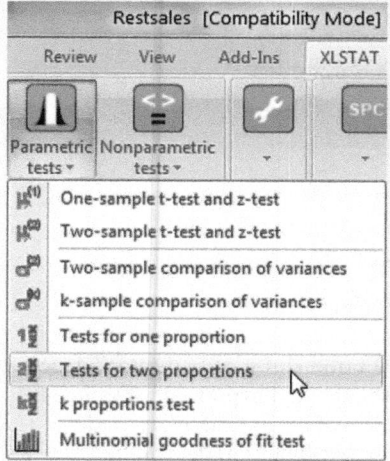

Figure E.5 XLSTAT menu options for comparing proportions

Step 2 When the resulting dialog box appears, check "Frequencies" in the "Data format" area, then enter the number of successes and the sample size for each sample in the appropriate boxes, as shown in Figure E.6. (Alternatively, you can check "Proportions" in the "Data format" area and enter the sample proportions.)

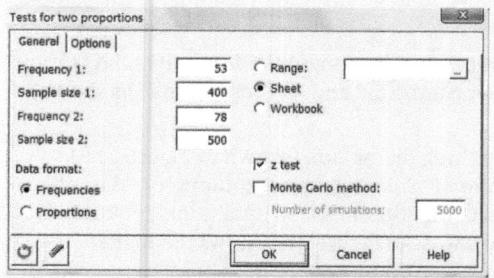

Figure E.6 XLSTAT test for two proportions dialog box

Step 3 Click the "Options" tab, specify the form of the alternative hypothesis, and then enter "0" for the hypothesized difference and the value of α (significance level) in the appropriate boxes, as shown in Figure E.7.

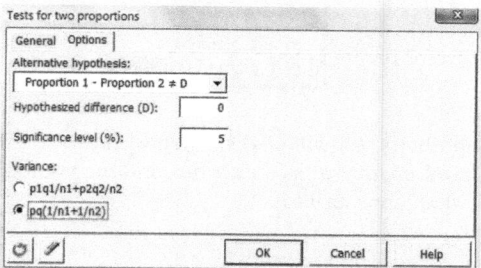

Figure E.7 XLSTAT options for testing proportions

Step 4 Click "OK" to display the test results.

Comparing Variances with Independent Samples

Step 1 Click the "XLSTAT" button on the Excel main menu bar, select "Parametric tests," then click "Two-sample comparison of variances" (see Figure E.1).

Step 2 When the resulting dialog box appears, select the proper "Data format" (e.g., "One column per variable"), and then select the appropriate columns (e.g., one column for the variable being analyzed and one for the variable that represents the two different samples). Also, check the "Fisher's F-test" box, as shown in Figure E.8.

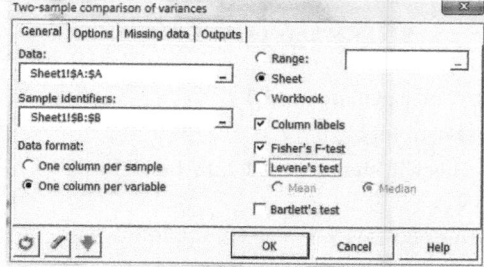

Figure E.8 XLSTAT two-sample variance test dialog box

Step 3 Click the "Options" tab, and then specify the form of the alternative hypothesis, the value of the hypothesized (theoretical) ratio of variances, and the value of α (significance level) in the appropriate boxes, as shown in Figure E.9.

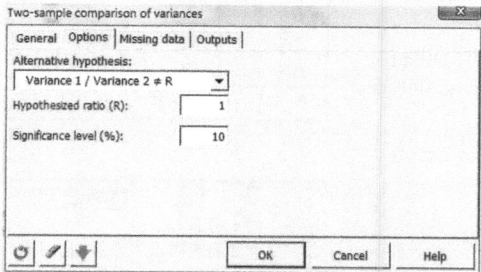

Figure E.9 XLSTAT options for comparing two variances

Step 4 Click "OK," then "Continue" to display the test results.

TI-83/TI-84 Graphing Calculator: Two-Sample Inferences

The TI-84 graphing calculator can be used to conduct tests and form confidence intervals for the difference between two means

with independent samples, the difference between two means with matched pairs, the difference between two proportions for large independent samples, and the ratio of two variances.

Confidence Interval for $\mu_1 - \mu_2$

Step 1 *Enter the data (Skip to Step 2 if you have summary statistics, not raw data)*

- Press **STAT** and select **1:Edit**

Note: If the lists already contain data, clear the old data. Use the up **ARROW** to highlight "**L1**."

- Press **CLEAR ENTER**
- Use the up **ARROW** to highlight "**L2**"
- Press **CLEAR ENTER**
- Use the **ARROW** and **ENTER** keys to enter the first data set into **L1**
- Use the **ARROW** and **ENTER** keys to enter the second data set into **L2**

Step 2 *Access the Statistical Tests Menu*

- Press **STAT**
- Arrow right to **TESTS**
- Arrow down to **2-SampTInt**
- Press **ENTER**

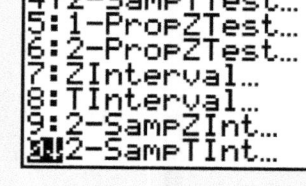

Step 3 *Choose "Data" or "Stats" ("Data" is selected when you have entered the raw data into the Lists. "Stats" is selected when you are given only the means, standard deviations, and sample sizes.)*

- Press **ENTER**
- If you selected "Data," set **List1** to **L1** and **List2** to **L2**
- Set **Freq1** to **1** and set **Freq2** to **1**
- Set **C-Level** to the confidence level
- If you are assuming that the two populations have equal variances, select **Yes** for **Pooled**
- If you are not assuming equal variances, select **No**
- Press **ENTER**
- Arrow down to "**Calculate**"
- Press **ENTER**
- If you selected "Stats," enter the means, standard deviations, and sample sizes
- Set **C-Level** to the confidence level

- If you are assuming that the two populations have equal variances, select **Yes** for **Pooled**
- If you are not assuming equal variances, select **No**
- Press **ENTER**
- Arrow down to "**Calculate**"
- Press **ENTER**

(The accompanying screen is set up for an example with a mean of 100, a standard deviation of 10, and a sample size of 15 for the first data set and a mean of 105, a standard

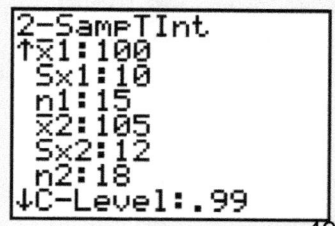

deviation of 12, and a sample size of 18 for the second data set.)

The confidence interval will be displayed with the degrees of freedom, the sample statistics, and the pooled standard deviation (when appropriate).

Hypothesis Test for $\mu_1 - \mu_2$

Step 1 *Enter the data (Skip to Step 2 if you have summary statistics, not raw data)*

- Press **STAT** and select **1:Edit**

Note: If the lists already contain data, clear the old data. Use the up **ARROW** to highlight "**L1**."

- Press **CLEAR ENTER**
- Use the up **ARROW** to highlight "**L2**"
- Press **CLEAR ENTER**
- Use the **ARROW** and **ENTER** keys to enter the first data set into **L1**
- Use the **ARROW** and **ENTER** keys to enter the second data set into **L2**

Step 2 *Access the Statistical Tests Menu*

- Press **STAT**
- Arrow right to **TESTS**
- Arrow down to **2-SampTTest**
- Press **ENTER**

Step 3 *Choose "Data" or "Stats" ("Data" is selected when you have entered the raw data into the Lists. "Stats" is selected when you are given only the means, standard deviations, and sample sizes.)*

- Press **ENTER**
- If you selected "Data," set **List1** to **L1** and **List2** to **L2**
- Set **Freq1** to **1** and set **Freq2** to **1**
- Use the **ARROW** to highlight the appropriate alternative hypothesis
- Press **ENTER**
- If you are assuming that the two populations have equal variances, select **Yes** for **Pooled**
- If you are not assuming equal variances, select **No**
- Press **ENTER**
- Arrow down to "**Calculate**"
- Press **ENTER**
- If you selected "**Stats,**" enter the means, standard deviations, and sample sizes
- Use the **ARROW** to highlight the appropriate alternative hypothesis
- Press **ENTER**
- If you are assuming that the two populations have equal variances, select **Yes** for **Pooled**
- If you are not assuming equal variances, select **No**
- Press **ENTER**
- Arrow down to "**Calculate**"
- Press **ENTER**

(The screen at the right is set up for an example with a mean of 100, a standard deviation of 10, and a sample size of 15 for the first data set and a mean of 120, a standard deviation of 12, and a sample size of 18 for the second data set.)

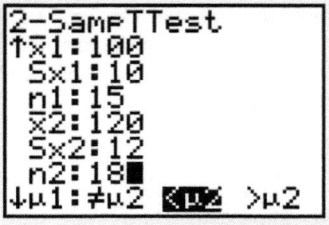

The results of the hypothesis test will be displayed with the *p*-value, degrees of freedom, the sample statistics, and the pooled standard deviation (when appropriate).

Confidence Interval for a Paired Difference Mean

Note: There is no paired difference option on the calculator. These instructions demonstrate how to calculate the differences and then use the 1-sample *t*-interval.

Step 1 *Enter the data and calculate the differences.*

- Press **STAT** and select **1:Edit**

Note: If the lists already contain data, clear the old data. Use the up **ARROW** to highlight "**L1**."

- Press **CLEAR ENTER**
- Use the up **ARROW** to highlight "**L2**"
- Press **CLEAR ENTER**
- Use the **ARROW** and **ENTER** keys to enter the first data set into **L1**
- Use the **ARROW** and **ENTER** keys to enter the second data set into **L2**
- The differences will be calculated in **L3**
- Use the up **ARROW** to highlight "**L3**"
- Press **CLEAR—** This will clear any old data, but **L3** will remain highlighted
- To enter the equation L3 = L1 − L2, use the following keystrokes:
  - Press **2ND** "**1**" (this will enter L1)
  - Press the **MINUS** button
  - Press **2ND** "**2**" (this will enter L2)

(Notice the equation at the bottom of the screen.)

- Press **ENTER** (the differences should be calculated in L3)

Step 2 *Access the Statistical Tests Menu*

- Press **STAT**
- Arrow right to **TESTS**
- Arrow down to **TInterval** (**even for large-sample case**)
- Press **ENTER**

Step 3 *Choose "Data"*

- Press **ENTER**
- Set **List** to **L3**

500

- Set **Freq** to **1**
- Set **C-Level** to the confidence level
- Arrow down to "**Calculate**"
- Press **ENTER**

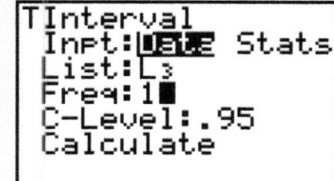

The confidence interval will be displayed with the mean, standard deviation, and sample size of the differences.

Hypothesis Test for a Paired Difference Mean

Note: There is no paired difference option on the calculator. These instructions demonstrate how to calculate the differences and then use the 1-sample *t*-test.

Step 1 *Enter the data and calculate the differences.*

- Press **STAT** and select **1:Edit**

Note: If the lists already contain data, clear the old data. Use the up **ARROW** to highlight "**L1.**"

- Press **CLEAR ENTER**
- Use the up **ARROW** to highlight "**L2**"
- Press **CLEAR ENTER**
- Use the **ARROW** and **ENTER** keys to enter the first data set into **L1**
- Use the **ARROW** and **ENTER** keys to enter the second data set into **L2**
- The differences will be calculated in **L3**
- Use the up **ARROW** to highlight "**L3**"
- Press **CLEAR**—this will clear any old data, but **L3** will remain highlighted
- To enter the equation L3 = L1 − L2, use the following keystrokes:
  - Press **2ND** "**1**" (this will enter L1)
  - Press the **MINUS** button
  - Press **2ND** "**2**" (this will enter L2)

(Notice the equation at the bottom of the screen.)

- Press **ENTER** (the differences should be calculated in L3)

Step 2 *Access the Statistical Tests Menu*

- Press **STAT**
- Arrow right to **TESTS**
- Arrow down to **T-Test** (even for large-sample case)
- Press **ENTER**

Step 3 *Choose "Data"*

- Press **ENTER**
- Enter the values for the hypothesis test, where μ_0 = the value for μ_d in the null hypothesis
- Set **List** to **L3**

- Set **Freq** to **1**
- Use the **ARROW** to highlight the appropriate alternative hypothesis
- Press **ENTER**
- Arrow down to "**Calculate**"
- Press **ENTER**

The test statistic and the *p*-value will be displayed, as well as the sample mean, standard deviation, and sample size of the differences.

Confidence Interval for ($p_1 - p_2$)

Step 1 *Access the Statistical Tests Menu*

- Press **STAT**
- Arrow right to **TESTS**
- Arrow down to **2-PropZInt**
- Press **ENTER**

Step 2 *Enter the values from the sample information and the confidence level*

where x_1 = number of successes in the first sample (e.g., 53)

n_1 = sample size for the first sample (e.g., 400)

x_2 = number of successes in the second sample (e.g., 78)

n_2 = sample size for the second sample (e.g., 500)

- Set **C-Level** to the confidence level
- Arrow down to "**Calculate**"
- Press **ENTER**

Hypothesis Test for ($p_1 - p_2$)

Step 1 *Access the Statistical Tests Menu*

- Press **STAT**
- Arrow right to **TESTS**
- Arrow down to **2-PropZ-Test**
- Press **ENTER**

Step 2 *Enter the values from the sample information and select the alternative hypothesis*

where x_1 = number of successes in the first sample (e.g., 53)

n_1 = sample size for the first sample (e.g., 400)

x_2 = number of successes in the second sample (e.g., 78)

n_2 = sample size for the second sample (e.g., 500)

- Use the **ARROW** to highlight the appropriate alternative hypothesis
- Press **ENTER**
- Arrow down to "**Calculate**"
- Press **ENTER**

Hypothesis Test for $\left(\dfrac{\sigma_1^2}{\sigma_2^2}\right)$

Step 1 *Enter the data (Skip to Step 2 if you have summary statistics, not raw data)*

• Press **STAT** and select **1:Edit**

Note: If the lists already contain data, clear the old data. Use the up **ARROW** to highlight "**L1**."

• Press **CLEAR ENTER**

• Use the up **ARROW** to highlight "**L2**"

• Press **CLEAR ENTER**

• Use the **ARROW** and **ENTER** keys to enter the first data set into **L1**

• Use the **ARROW** and **ENTER** keys to enter the second data set into **L2**

Step 2 *Access the Statistical Tests Menu*

• Press **STAT**

• Arrow right to **TESTS**

• Arrow down to **2-SampFTest**

• Press **ENTER**

Step 3 *Choose "Data" or "Stats" ("Data" is selected when you have entered the raw data into the Lists. "Stats" is selected when you are given only the means, standard deviations, and sample sizes.)*

• Press **ENTER**

• If you selected "Data"

  • Set **List1** to **L1** and **List2** to **L2**

  • Set **Freq1** to **1** and set **Freq2** to **1**

  • Use the **ARROW** to highlight the appropriate alternative hypothesis

  • Press **ENTER**

  • Arrow down to "**Calculate**"

  • Press **ENTER**

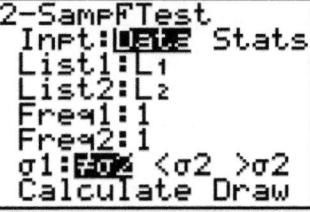

• If you selected "Stats," enter the standard deviations and sample sizes

  • Use the **ARROW** to highlight the appropriate alternative hypothesis

  • Press **ENTER**

  • Arrow down to "**Calculate**"

  • Press **ENTER**

The results of the hypothesis test will be displayed with the *p*-value and the input data used.

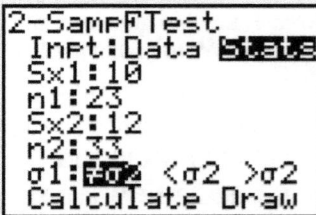

■ MAKING BUSINESS DECISIONS

The Kentucky Milk Case

You should prepare a professional document that presents the results of the analyses and any implications regarding collusionary practices in the tri-county Kentucky milk market.

1. *Incumbency rates.* Recall that market allocation (where the same dairy controls the same school districts year after year) is a common form of collusive behavior in bid-rigging conspiracies. Market allocation is typically gauged by the incumbency rate for a market in a given school year—defined as the percentage of school districts that are won by the same milk vendor who won the previous year. Past experience with milk bids in a competitive market reveals that a "normal" incumbency rate is about .7—that is, 70% of the school districts are expected to purchase their milk from the same vendor who supplied the milk the previous year. In the 13-district tri-county Kentucky market, 13 vendor transitions potentially exist each year. Over the 1985–1988 period (when bid collusion was alleged to have occurred), there were 52 potential vendor transitions. Based on the actual number of vendor transitions that occurred each year and over the 1985–1988 period, make an inference regarding bid collusion.

2. *Bid price dispersion.* Recall that in competitive, sealed-bid markets, more dispersion or variability among the bids is observed than in collusive markets. (This is due to conspiring vendors sharing information about their bids.) Consequently, if collusion exists, the variation in bid prices in the tri-county market should be significantly smaller than the corresponding variation in the surrounding market. For each milk product, conduct an analysis to compare the bid price variances of the two markets each year. Make the appropriate inferences.

3. *Average winning bid price.* According to collusion theorists, the mean winning bid price in the "rigged" market will exceed the mean winning bid price in the competitive market for each year in which collusion occurs. In addition, the difference between the competitive average and the "rigged" average tends to grow over time when collusionary tactics are employed over several consecutive years. For each milk product, conduct an analysis to compare the winning bid price means of the tri-county and surrounding markets each year. Make the appropriate inferences.

🔵 *Data Set:* MILK

Answers to Selected Exercises

1 a. 150 ± 6 **b.** 150 ± 8 **c.** $0;5$ **d.** 0 ± 10 **e.** Variability of the difference is greater **3 a.** 35 ± 24.5 **b.** $z = 2.8$, p-value $= .0052$, reject H_0 **c.** p-value $= .0026$ **d.** $z = .8$, p-value $= .4238$, do not reject H_0 **e.** Independent random samples **5 a.** No **b.** No **c.** No **d.** Yes **e.** No **7 a.** $.5989$ **b.** Yes, $t = -2.39$ **c.** $-1.24 \pm .98$ **d.** Confidence interval **9 a.** Do not reject H_0 **b.** $.0575$ **11 a.** $t = -1.646$, do not reject H_0 **b.** -2.50 ± 3.12 **13 a.** 5.70 ± 5.07 **b.** R–Z group; yes **15 a.** $H_0: \mu_1 - \mu_2 = 0$, $H_a: \mu_1 - \mu_2 \neq 0$ **b.** $t = .62$ **c.** $|t| > 1.684$ **d.** Do not reject H_0 **e.** Do not reject H_0 **f.** Independent random samples, both populations normal, $\sigma_1^2 = \sigma_2^2$ **17 a.** $.90 \pm .064$ **b.** Buy-side **c.** Large, independent random samples **19 a.** $t = 1.56$, do not reject $H_0: \mu_T = \mu_I$ **b.** $t = -.50$, do not reject $H_0: \mu_W = \mu_I$ **c.** No differences **21** $z = -2.81$, reject $H_0: \mu_C = \mu_R$ **23** Yes, $z = 3.20$, sufficient evidence to conclude $\mu_{\text{Honey}} > \mu_{\text{DM}}$ **25 a.** No sample variances **b.** s_1^2 and s_2^2 **c.** $z < -2.326$ **d.** $.24$ **e.** Smaller **27 a.** $t > 1.796$ **b.** $t > 1.319$ **c.** $t > 3.182$ **d.** $t > 2.374$ **29 a.** $H_0: \mu_d = 0$, $H_a: \mu_d < 0$ **b.** $t = -5.29$, p-value $= .0003$, reject H_0 **c.** $(-4.98, -2.42)$ **d.** Population of differences is normal **31 a.** $H_0: \mu_d = 0$, $H_a: \mu_d > 0$ **b.** Paired test **c.** $z = 3.10$ **d.** $z = 19.18$ **e.** Paired test **f.** Reject H_0 **g.** No **h.** $(2.86, 3.74)$ **33 a.** Two hole measurements at each location **c.** $\bar{d} = .14$, $s_d = 1.26$ **d.** $(-.435, .715)$ **e.** Yes **35 a.** Response rates observed twice for each survey **b.** No, $t = .53$ **c.** Reject H_0 **37 a.** Yes, $t = 2.864$ **39** $(.036, .224)$; Huffman-coding **41** $t = .46$, p-value $= 0.65$, do not reject H_0 **43 a.** Binomial distributions **b.** Distribution is approx. normal for large n's **45 a.** No **b.** No **c.** No **d.** No **e.** No **47 a.** $z = -4.02$, reject H_0 **b.** $z = -4.02$, reject H_0 **c.** $z = -4.02$, reject H_0 **d.** $-.1 \pm .041$ **49 a.** $.153$ **b.** $.215$ **c.** $(-.132, .008)$ **d.** No evidence of a difference **51 a.** $p_1 - p_2$ **b.** $H_0: p_1 - p_2 = 0$, $H_a: p_1 - p_2 \neq 0$ **c.** $z = -2.67$ **d.** $|z| > 2.576$ **e.** $.008$ **f.** Reject H_0 **53 a.** All January patients; all May patients **b.** $.083$ **c.** $(.033, .133)$ **d.** Yes **55** No, $z = 1.68$ **57** Yes; 95% CI for $(p_{\text{AA}} - p_{\text{White}}) = (.089, .131)$, $z = 14.64$ **59 a.** $500, 46$ **b.** Sample may not be representative **61 a.** $29,954$ **b.** $2,165$ **c.** $1,113$ **63** 34 **65** 156 **67** $13,531$ for each survey **69** $1,729$ **71 a.** $5,051$ **73 a.** 4.10 **b.** 3.57 **c.** 8.81 **d.** 3.21 **75 a.** $F > 1.74$ **b.** $F > 2.04$ **c.** $F > 2.35$ **d.** $F > 2.78$ **77 a.** $F > 2.11$ **b.** $F > 3.01$ **c.** $F > 2.04$ **d.** $F > 2.30$ **e.** $F > 5.27$ **79 a.** $F = 4.29$, do not reject H_0 **b.** $.05 < p$-value $< .10$ **81 a.** $H_0: \sigma_1^2 = \sigma_2^2$, $H_a: \sigma_1^2 \neq \sigma_2^2$ **b.** $F = 1.16$ **c.** $F > 2.16$ **d.** Fail to reject H_0 **e.** Valid **83** $F = .844$, p-value $= .681$, fail to reject H_0 **85 a.** No, $F = 2.27$ **b.** $.05 < p$-value $< .10$ **87 a.** Yes, $F = 8.29$ **b.** No **91 a.** $t = .78$, do not reject H_0 **b.** 2.50 ± 8.99 **c.** 225 **93 a.** $3.90 \pm .31$ **b.** $z = 20.60$, reject H_0 **c.** 346 **95 a.** $\mu_1 - \mu_2$ **b.** $p_1 - p_2$ **c.** μ_d **97 a.** $.29 \pm 1.45$ **b.** $F = 1.06$, do not reject H_0 **c.** No significant difference **99 a.** Yes **b.** $z = 4.58$, reject H_0 **101 b.** $H_0: \mu_d = 0$, $H_a: \mu_d \neq 0$ **c.** Reject H_0 **103 a.** $H_0: \mu_1 = \mu_2$, $H_a: \mu_1 \neq \mu_2$ **b.** Reject H_0 **c.** Do not reject H_0 **d.** No practical difference **105 a.** $p_1 - p_2$ **b.** $H_0: p_1 - p_2 = 0$, $H_a: p_1 - p_2 \neq 0$ **c.** $z = -5.16$ **d.** $|z| > 2.58$ **e.** Yes **f.** Reject H_0 **107 a.** All male and all female cell phone users **b.** $.32; .25$ **c.** $.07 \pm .04$ **d.** Yes **e.** $.71; .77$ **f.** $z = -2.45$, reject H_0 **109 a.** Yes, $t = -1.96$ **c.** $.058$ **d.** -7.4 ± 6.38 **111 a.** $z = 94.35$, reject H_0 **b.** $(-.155, -.123)$ **113** $4,802$ **115** No, $F = 2.79$ **117 a.** $H_0: \mu_1 = \mu_2$, $H_a: \mu_1 > \mu_2$ **c.** Reject H_0; yes **d.** $H_0: \mu_1 = \mu_2$, $H_a: \mu_1 \neq \mu_2$ **e.** Do not reject H_0; yes **119** Aad: no, at $\alpha = .05$; Ab: yes, at $\alpha = .05$; Intention: no, at $\alpha = .05$ **121 a.** yes, $z = -2.79$ **b.** 95% CI: $-.011 \pm .0077$ **123** Yes; 95% confidence interval for μ_d: $(-242.29, -106.96)$

Credits

Technology Images

Design of Experiments and Analysis of Variance

From Chapter 9 of *Statistics for Business and Economics*, Twelfth Edition. James T. McClave, P. George Benson, Terry Sincich. Copyright © 2014 by Pearson Education, Inc. All rights reserved.

CONTENTS

Where We're Going

- Discuss the critical elements in the design of a sampling experiment (1)

- Learn how to set up three of the more popular experimental designs for comparing more than two population means: *completely randomized, randomized block,* and *factorial designs* (2, 4, 5)

- Show how to analyze data collected from a designed experiment using a technique called an *analysis of variance* (2, 4, 5)

- Present a follow-up analysis to an ANOVA: Ranking means (3)

☐ Design of Experiments and Analysis of Variance

STATISTICS in ACTION

Pollutants at a Housing Development—A Case of Mishandling Small Samples

According to the Environmental Protection Agency (EPA), "Polycyclic aromatic hydrocarbons (PAHs) are a group of over 100 different chemicals that are formed during the incomplete burning of oil, gas, coal, garbage, or other organic substances like tobacco or charbroiled meat and from motor vehicle exhaust" (www.epa.gov). The EPA considers PAHs to be potentially dangerous pollutants; consequently, industries are monitored regularly for the production of PAHs.

In this Statistics in Action, we consider a legal case involving a developer who purchased a large parcel of Florida land that he planned to turn into a residential community. Unfortunately, the parcel turned out to have significant deposits of PAHs. Environmental regulatory agencies required the developer to remove the PAHs from the site prior to commencing development. The cleanup was finally completed, but the housing bubble burst and the development was a bust. The developer blamed the failure of his plan on the discovery of the pollutants, and filed suit against two industries that were within 25 miles of the site, both of which produced some PAH waste materials as part of their industrial processes. Not only did the developer want the industries to pay the costs of the cleanup, but he also wanted recompense for the more than $100 million in lost profits he claimed would have been earned had the development been built out on schedule.

Both industries denied responsibility, and each hired experts to investigate the degree of similarity between pollutants at their industrial sites and those at the development site. Unfortunately, only limited PAH data had been collected at the proximate time that the pollution was discovered at the development site. Nonetheless, one biochemical expert undertook a statistical analysis comparing two different types of PAH measurements for the three sites. The biochemical expert concluded that the data showed that Industry B was more likely to be responsible for the pollution at the development site than was his client, Industry A. Subsequently, an expert statistician hired by Industry B analyzed the same data and testified that "the data and statistical tests shed essentially no light on the matter."

Given the two contradictory expert opinions, how should the trial judge rule? To answer this question, we will analyze the data (saved in the **PAH** file) using the methods developed in this chapter and present the results in two Statistics in Action Revisited examples. Specifically, we want (1) to compare the mean PAH measurements at the different sites and (2) if the means differ, to determine which industry is more likely to be responsible for the pollution at the housing development site.

STATISTICS in ACTION REVISITED

▫ Testing for Differences in Mean PAH Measurements

▫ Ranking Mean PAH Measurements

In *observational studies,* the analyst has little or no control over the variables under study and merely observes their values. In contrast, *designed experiments* are those in which the analyst attempts to control the levels of one or more variables to determine their effect on a variable of interest. When properly designed, such experiments allow the analyst to determine whether a change in the controlled variable *causes* a change in the response variable, that is, it allows one to infer *cause and effect*. Although many practical business situations do not present the opportunity for such control, it is instructive, even for observational experiments, to have a working knowledge of the analysis and interpretation of data that result from designed experiments and to know the basics of how to design experiments when the opportunity arises.

We first present the basic elements of an experimental design in Section 1. We then discuss three of the simpler, and more popular, experimental designs in Sections 2, 4, and 5. In Section 3 we show how to rank the population means, from smallest to largest.

1   Elements of a Designed Experiment

Certain elements are common to almost all designed experiments, regardless of the specific area of application. For example, the *response* is the variable of interest in the experiment. The response might be the SAT scores of a high school senior, the total sales of a firm last year, or the total income of a particular household this year. The response is also called the *dependent variable*. Typically, the response variable is quantitative in nature since one of the objectives of a designed experiment is to compare response variable means.

> The **response variable** is the variable of interest to be measured in the experiment. We also refer to the response as the **dependent variable**. Typically, the response/dependent variable is quantitative in nature.

The intent of most statistical experiments is to determine the effect of one or more variables on the response. These variables are usually referred to as the *factors* in a designed experiment. Factors are either *quantitative* or *qualitative,* depending on whether the variable is measured on a numerical scale or not. For example, we might want to explore the effect of the qualitative factor Gender on the response SAT score.

In other words, we want to compare the SAT scores of male and female high school seniors. Or, we might wish to determine the effect of the quantitative factor Number of salespeople on the response Total sales for retail firms. Often two or more factors are of interest. For example, we might want to determine the effect of the quantitative factor Number of wage earners and the qualitative factor Location on the response Household income.

Factors are those variables whose effect on the response is of interest to the experimenter. **Quantitative factors** are measured on a numerical scale, whereas **qualitative factors** are those that are not (naturally) measured on a numerical scale. Factors are also referred to as **independent variables.**

Levels are the values of the factors that are used in the experiment. The levels of qualitative factors are categorical in nature. For example, the levels of Gender are Male and Female, and the levels of Location might be North, East, South, and West.* The levels of quantitative factors are numerical values. For example, the Number of salespeople may have levels 1, 3, 5, 7, and 9. The factor Years of education may have levels 8, 12, 16, and 20.

Factor levels are the values of the factor used in the experiment.

When a *single factor* is employed in an experiment, the *treatments* of the experiment are the levels of the factor. For example, if the effect of the factor Gender on the response SAT score is being investigated, the treatments of the experiment are the two levels of Gender—Female and Male. Or, if the effect of the Number of wage earners on Household income is the subject of the experiment, the numerical values assumed by the quantitative factor Number of wage earners are the treatments. If *two or more factors* are used in an experiment, the treatments are the factor-level combinations used. For example, if the effects of the factors Gender and Socioeconomic Status (SES) on the response SAT score are being investigated, the treatments are the combinations of the levels of Gender and SES used; thus (Female, high SES), (Male, high SES), and (Female, low SES) would all be treatments.

The **treatments** of an experiment are the factor-level combinations used.

The objects on which the response variable and factors are observed are the *experimental units.* For example, SAT score, High school GPA, and Gender are all variables that can be observed on the same experimental unit—a high school senior. Or, the Total sales, the Earnings per share, and the Number of salespeople can be measured on a particular firm in a particular year, and the firm-year combination is the experimental unit. The Total income, the Number of female wage earners, and the Location can be observed for a household at a particular point in time, and the household-time combination is the experimental unit. Every experiment, whether observational or designed, has experimental units on which the variables are observed. However, the identification of the experimental units is more important in designed experiments, when the experimenter must actually sample the experimental units and measure the variables.

*The levels of a qualitative variable may bear numerical labels. For example, the Locations could be numbered 1, 2, 3, and 4. However, in such cases, the numerical labels for a qualitative variable will usually be codes representing categorical levels.

SIR RONALD A. FISHER
(1890–1962)
The Founder of Modern
Statistics

At a young age, Ronald Fisher demonstrated special abilities in mathematics, astronomy, and biology. (Fisher's biology teacher once divided all his students for "sheer brilliance" into two groups—Fisher and the rest.) Fisher graduated from prestigious Cambridge University in London in 1912 with a BA in astronomy, and, after several years teaching mathematics, he found work at the Rothamsted Agricultural Experiment station. There, Fisher began his extraordinary career as a statistician. Many consider Fisher to be the leading founder of modern statistics. His contributions to the field include the notion of unbiased statistics, the development of *p*-values for hypothesis tests, the invention of analysis of variance for designed experiments, maximum likelihood estimation theory, and the mathematical distributions of several well-known statistics. Fisher's book *Statistical Methods for Research Workers* (written in 1925) revolutionized applied statistics, demonstrating how to analyze data and interpret the results with very readable and practical examples. In 1935, Fisher wrote *The Design of Experiments,* where he first described his famous experiment on the "lady tasting tea." (Fisher showed, through a designed experiment, that the lady really could determine whether tea poured into milk tastes better than milk poured into tea.) Before his death, Fisher was elected a Fellow of the Royal Statistical Society, was awarded numerous medals, and was knighted by the Queen of England.

> An **experimental unit** is the object on which the response and factors are observed or measured.*

When the specification of the treatments and the method of assigning the experimental units to each of the treatments are controlled by the analyst, the study is said to be *designed.* In contrast, if the analyst is just an observer of the treatments on a sample of experimental units, the study is *observational.* For example, if you give one randomly selected group of employees a training program and withhold it from another randomly selected group to evaluate the effect of the training on worker productivity, then you are designing a study. If, on the other hand, you compare the productivity of employees with college degrees with the productivity of employees without college degrees, the study is observational.

> A **designed study** is one for which the analyst controls the specification of the treatments and the method of assigning the experimental units to each treatment. An **observational study** is one for which the analyst simply observes the treatments and the response on a sample of experimental units.

The diagram in Figure 1 provides an overview of the experimental process and a summary of the terminology introduced in this section. Note that the experimental unit

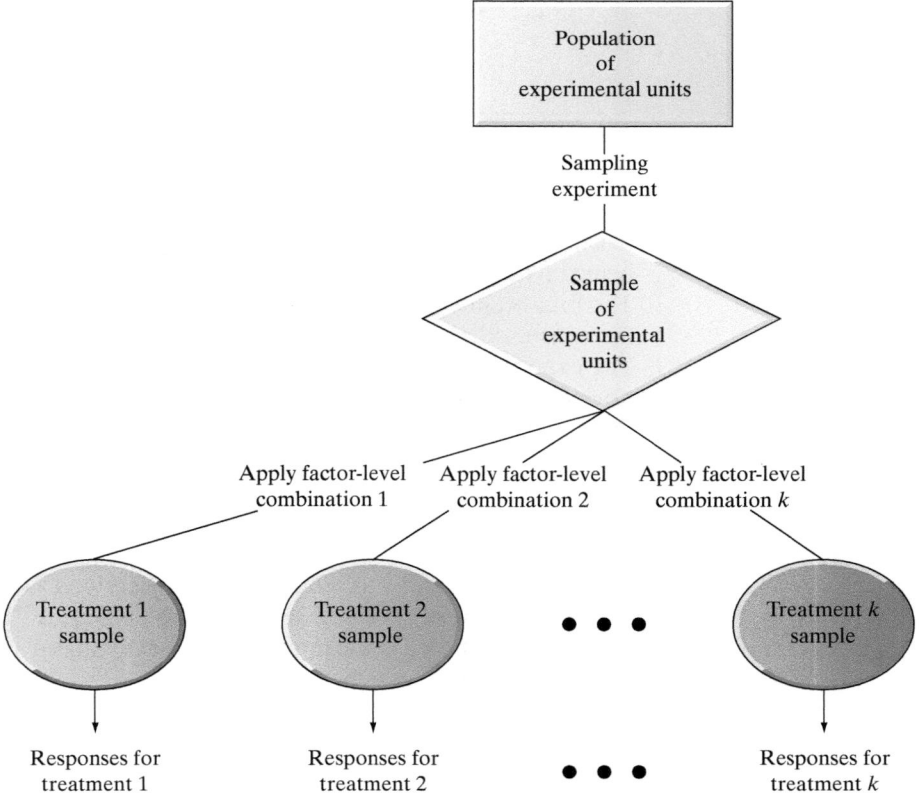

Figure 1
Sampling experiment: Process and terminology

*The set of all experimental units is the population.

is at the core of the process. The method by which the sample of experimental units is selected from the population determines the type of experiment. The level of every factor (the treatment) and the response are all variables that are observed or measured on each experimental unit.

Example 1

Key Elements of a Designed Experiment— Testing Golf Ball Brands

Problem The USGA (United States Golf Association) regularly tests golf equipment to ensure that it conforms to USGA standards. Suppose it wishes to compare the mean distance traveled by four different brands of golf balls when struck by a driver (the club used to maximize distance). The following experiment is conducted: 10 balls of each brand are randomly selected. Each is struck by "Iron Byron" (the USGA's golf robot named for the famous golfer Byron Nelson) using a driver, and the distance traveled is recorded. A layout of the experimental design is portrayed in Figure 2. Identify each of the following elements in this experiment: response, factors, factor types, levels, treatments, and experimental units.

Brand A	Brand B	Brand C	Brand D
—	—	—	—
—	—	—	—
—	—	—	—
⋮	⋮	⋮	⋮
—	—	—	—

Distances for 10 randomly selected balls from Brand B lot

Figure 2
Layout of designed study for Example 1

Solution The response is the variable of interest, Distance traveled. The only factor being investigated is the Brand of golf ball, and it is nonnumerical and therefore qualitative. The four brands (say A, B, C, and D) represent the levels of this factor. Because only one factor is used, the treatments are the four levels of this factor—that is, the four brands. The experimental unit is a golf ball; more specifically, it is a golf ball at a particular position in the striking sequence, because the distance traveled can be recorded only when the ball is struck, and we would expect the distance to be different (due to random factors such as wind resistance, landing place, and so forth) if the same ball is struck a second time. Note that 10 experimental units are sampled for each treatment, generating a total of 40 observations.

Look Back This study, like many real applications, is a blend of designed and observational: The analyst cannot control the assignment of the brand to each golf ball (observational), but he or she can control the assignment of each ball to the position in the striking sequence (designed).

■ **Now Work Exercise 5**

Example 2

A Two-Factor Experiment— Testing Golf Ball Brands

Problem Suppose the USGA is interested in comparing the mean distances the four brands of golf balls travel when struck by a five-iron and by a driver. Ten balls of each brand are randomly selected, five to be struck by the driver and five by the five-iron. Identify the elements of the experiment and construct a schematic diagram similar to Figure 1 to provide an overview of this experiment.

Solution The response is the same as in Example 1—Distance traveled. The experiment now has two factors: Brand of golf ball and Club used. There are four levels of Brand (A, B, C, and D) and two of Club (driver and five-iron, or 1 and 5). Treatments are factor-level combinations, so there are $4 \times 2 = 8$ treatments in this experiment: (A, 1), (A, 5), (B, 1), (B, 5), (C, 1), (C, 5), (D, 1), and (D, 5). The experimental units are still the golf balls. Note that five experimental units are sampled per treatment, generating 40 observations. The experiment is summarized in Figure 3.

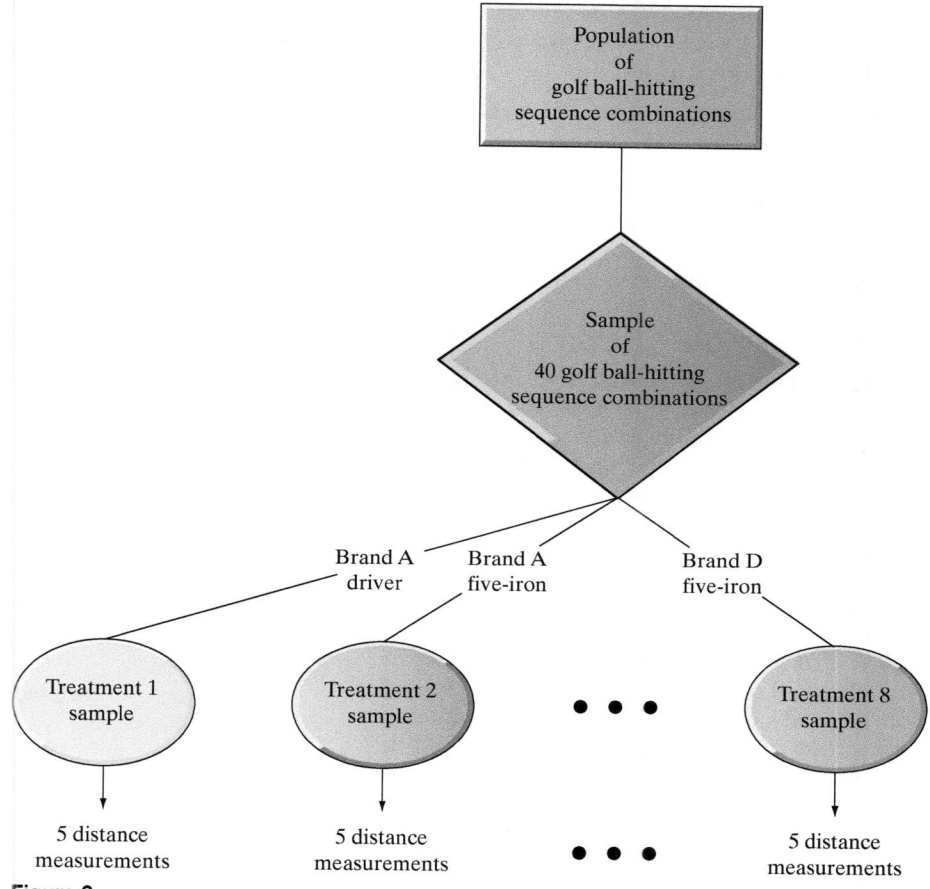

Figure 3

Two-factor golf experiment summary: Example 2

Look Back Whenever there are two or more factors in an experiment, remember to combine the levels of the factors—one level from each factor—to obtain the treatments.

Now Work Exercise 10

Our objective in designing a study is usually to maximize the amount of information obtained about the relationship between the treatments and the response. Of course, we are almost always subject to constraints on budget, time, and even the availability of experimental units. Nevertheless, designed studies are generally preferred to observational studies. Not only do we have better control of the amount and quality of the information collected, but we also avoid the biases inherent in observational studies in the selection of the experimental units representing each treatment. Inferences based on observational studies always carry the implicit assumption that the sample has no hidden bias that was not considered in the statistical analysis. Better understanding of the potential problems with observational studies is a by-product of our study of experimental design in the remainder of this chapter.

Exercises 1–14

Please be aware that some of the following problems may require knowledge of concepts that are not presented in this chapter.

Learning the Mechanics

1 What are the treatments for a designed experiment that uses one qualitative factor with four levels—A, B, C, and D?

2 What are the treatments for a designed experiment with two factors, one qualitative with two levels (A and B) and one quantitative with five levels (50, 60, 70, 80, and 90)?

3 What is the difference between an observational experiment and a designed experiment?

4 What are the experimental units on which each of the following responses are observed?
  a. College GPA
  b. Household income
  c. Gasoline mileage rating for an automobile model
  d. Number of defective sectors on a computer disk
  e. December unemployment rate for a state

Applying the Concepts—Basic

5 **Identifying the type of experiment.** Brief descriptions of a number of experiments are given next. Determine whether each is observational or designed and explain your reasoning.
  a. An economist obtains the unemployment rate and gross state product for a sample of states over the past 10 years, with the objective of examining the relationship between the unemployment rate and the gross state product by census region.
  b. A manager in a paper production facility installs one of three incentive programs in each of nine plants to determine the effect of each program on productivity.
  c. A marketer of personal computers runs ads in each of four national publications for one quarter and keeps track of the number of sales that are attributable to each publication's ad.
  d. An electric utility engages a consultant to monitor the discharge from its smokestack on a monthly basis over a 1-year period to relate the level of sulfur dioxide in the discharge to the load on the facility's generators.
  e. Intrastate trucking rates are compared before and after governmental deregulation of prices changed, with the comparison also taking into account distance of haul, goods hauled, and the price of diesel fuel.

6 **Drafting NFL quarterbacks.** The *Journal of Productivity Analysis* (Vol. 35, 2011) did a study of how successful NFL teams are in drafting productive quarterbacks. The researchers measured two variables for each of the 331 quarterbacks drafted between 1970 and 2007: (1) Draft position (Top 10, between picks 11–50, or after pick 50) and (2) QB production score (where higher scores indicate more productive QBs). Suppose we want to compare the mean production score of quarterbacks in the three draft position groups. Identify each of the following elements for this study:
  a. Response variable
  b. Factor(s)
  c. Treatments
  d. Experimental units

7 **Corporate sustainability and firm characteristics.** *Business and Society* (March 2011) did a study on how firm size and firm type impact corporate sustainability behaviors. Certified Public Accountants (CPAs) were surveyed on their firms' likelihood of reporting sustainability policies (measured as a probability between 0 and 1). The CPAs were divided into four groups depending on firm size (large or small) and firm type (public or private): large/public, large/private, small/public, and small/private. One goal of the analysis was to determine whether the mean likelihood of reporting sustainability policies differs depending on firm size and firm type. Identify each of the following elements for this study:
  a. Experimental units
  b. Response variable
  c. Factor(s)
  d. Factor levels
  e. Treatments

8 **Accounting and Machiavellianism.** A study of Machiavellian traits in accountants was published in *Behavioral Research in Accounting* (January 2008). *Machiavellian* describes negative character traits such as manipulation, cunning, duplicity, deception, and bad faith. A Mach rating score was determined for each in a sample of accounting alumni of a large southwestern university. The accountants were then classified as having high, moderate, or low Mach rating scores. For one portion of the study, the researcher investigated the impact of both Mach score classification and gender on the average income of an accountant. For this experiment, identify each of the following:
  a. Experimental unit
  b. Response variable
  c. Factors
  d. Levels of each factor
  e. Treatments

9 **Can money spent on gifts buy love?** The *Journal of Experimental Social Psychology* (Vol. 45, 2009) did a study of whether buying gifts truly buys love. Study participants were randomly assigned to play the role of gift-giver or gift-receiver. Gift-receivers were asked to provide the level of appreciation (measured on a 7-point scale where 1 = "not at all" and 7 = "to a great extent") they had for the last birthday gift they received from a loved one. Gift-givers were asked to recall the last birthday gift they gave to a loved one and to provide the level of appreciation the loved one had for the gift. The researchers wanted to know if the average level of appreciation is higher for birthday gift-givers than for birthday gift-receivers.
  a. Why is this study designed?
  b. Specify the key elements of the study: experimental unit, response variable, factor, and treatments.

Applying the Concepts—Intermediate

10 **Value perceptions of consumers.** The *Journal of Consumer Research* did a study of whether between-store comparisons result in greater perceptions of value by consumers than within-store comparisons. 50 consumers were randomly selected from all consumers in a designated market area to participate in the study. The researchers randomly assigned 25 consumers to read a within-store price promotion advertisement ("was $100,

now $80") and 25 consumers to read a between-store price promotion ("$100 there, $80 here"). The consumers then gave their opinion on the value of the discount offer on a 10-point scale (where 1 = lowest value and 10 = highest value). The goal was to compare the average discount values of the two groups of consumers.
a. What is the response variable for this study?
b. What are the treatments for this study?
c. What is the experimental unit for this study?

11 Value perceptions of consumers (cont'd). Refer to Exercise 10. In addition to the factor, Type of advertisement (within-store price promotion and between-store price promotion), the researchers also investigated the impact of a second factor—Location where ad is read (at home or in the store). About half of the consumers who were assigned to the within-store price promotion read the ad at home, and the other half read the ad in the store. Similarly, about half of the consumers who were assigned to the between-store price promotion read the ad at home, and the other half read the ad in the store. In this second experiment, the goal was to compare the average discount values of the groups of consumers created by combining Type of advertisement with Location.
a. How many treatments are involved in this experiment?
b. Identify the treatments.

12 Baker's vs. brewer's yeast. The *Electronic Journal of Biotechnology* (Dec. 15, 2003) published an article on a comparison of two yeast extracts—baker's yeast and brewer's yeast. Brewer's yeast is a surplus by-product obtained from a brewery; hence it is less expensive than primary-grown baker's yeast. Samples of both yeast extracts were prepared at four different temperatures (45, 48, 51, and 54°C), and the autolysis yield (recorded as a percentage) was measured for each of the yeast-temperature combinations. The goal of the analysis was to investigate the impact of yeast extract and temperature on mean autolysis yield.
a. Identify the factors (and factor levels) in the experiment.
b. Identify the response variable.
c. How many treatments are included in the experiment?
d. What type of experimental design is employed?

13 Exam performance study. In *Teaching of Psychology* (August 1998), a study investigated whether final exam performance is affected by whether students take a practice test. Students in an introductory psychology class at Pennsylvania State University were initially divided into three groups based on their class standing: Low, Medium, or High. Within each group, students were randomly assigned to either attend a review session or take a practice test prior to the final exam. Thus, six groups were formed: (Low, Review), (Low, Practice exam), (Medium, Review), (Medium, Practice exam), (High, Review), and (High, Practice exam). One goal of the study was to compare the mean final exam scores of the six groups of students.
a. What is the experimental unit for this study?
b. Is the study a designed experiment? Why?
c. What are the factors in the study?
d. Give the levels of each factor.
e. How many treatments are in the study? Identify them.
f. What is the response variable?

Applying the Concepts—Advanced

14 Testing a new pain-reliever tablet. Paracetamol is the active ingredient in drugs designed to relieve mild to moderate pain and fever. To save costs, pharmaceutical companies are looking to produce paracetamol tablets from locally available materials. The properties of paracetamol tablets derived from khaya gum were studied in the *Tropical Journal of Pharmaceutical Research* (June 2003). Three factors believed to affect the properties of paracetamol tablets are (1) the nature of the binding agent, (2) the concentration of the binding agent, and (3) the relative density of the tablet. In the experiment, binding agent was set at two levels (khaya gum and PVP), binding concentration at two levels (.5% and 4.0%), and relative density at two levels (low and high). One of the dependent variables investigated in the study was tablet dissolution time (i.e., the amount of time [in minutes] for 50% of the tablet to dissolve). The goal of the study was to determine the effect of binding agent, binding concentration, and relative density on mean dissolution time.
a. Identify the dependent (response) variable in the study.
b. What are the factors investigated in the study? Give the levels of each.
c. How many treatments are possible in the study? List them.

2 The Completely Randomized Design: Single Factor

The simplest experimental design, a *completely randomized design,* consists of the *independent random selection* of experimental units representing each treatment. For example, we could independently select random samples of 20 female and 15 male high school seniors to compare their mean SAT scores. Or, we could independently select random samples of 30 households from each of four census districts to compare the mean income per household among the districts. In both examples, our objective is to compare treatment means by selecting random, independent samples for each treatment.

> Consider an experiment that involves a single factor with k treatments. A **completely randomized design** is a design in which the experimental units are randomly assigned to the k treatments or in which independent random samples of experimental units are selected for each treatment.*

*We use *completely randomized* design to refer to both designed and observational studies. Thus, the only requirement is that the experimental units to which treatments are applied (designed) or on which treatments are observed (observational) are independently selected for each treatment.

Example	3

Assigning Treatments in a Completely Randomized Design—Bottled Water Brands Study

Problem Suppose we want to compare the taste preferences of consumers for three different brands of bottled water (say, Brands A, B, and C) using a random sample of 15 bottled water consumers. Set up a completely randomized design for this purpose—that is, assign the experimental units to the treatments for this design.

Solution In this study, the experimental units are the 15 consumers, and the treatments are the three brands of bottled water. One way to set up the completely randomized design is to randomly assign one of the three brands to each consumer to taste. Then we could measure (say, on a 1-to-10-point scale) the taste preference of each consumer. A good practice is to assign the same number of consumers to each brand—in this case, five consumers to each of the three brands. (When an equal number of experimental units are assigned to each treatment, we call the design a **balanced design.**)

A random number generator or statistical software can be used to make the random assignments. Figure 4 is a Minitab worksheet showing the random assignments made with the Minitab "Random Data" function. You can see that Minitab randomly assigned consumers numbered 2, 11, 1, 13, and 3 to taste Brand A, consumers numbered 15, 14, 7, 10, and 8 to taste Brand B, and consumers numbered 6, 5, 12, 9, and 4 to taste Brand C.

Look Back In some experiments, it will not be possible to randomly assign treatments to the experimental units or vice versa—the units will already be associated with one of the treatments. (For example, if the treatments are Male and Female, you cannot change a person's gender.) In this case, a completely randomized design is one where you select independent random samples of experimental units from each treatment.

CRD3brands.MTW ***

↓	C1	C2	C3	C4	C5
	Consumer	BrandA	BrandB	BrandC	
1	1	2	15	6	
2	2	11	14	5	
3	3	1	7	12	
4	4	13	10	9	
5	5	3	8	4	
6	6				
7	7				
8	8				
9	9				
10	10				
11	11				
12	12				
13	13				
14	14				
15	15				
16					

Figure 4

Minitab random assignments of consumers to brands

■ **Now Work Exercise 24d**

The objective of a completely randomized design is usually to compare the treatment means. If we denote the true, or population, means of the k treatments as $\mu_1, \mu_2, \ldots, \mu_k$, then we will test the null hypothesis that the treatment means are all equal against the alternative that at least two of the treatment means differ:

$$H_0: \mu_1 = \mu_2 = \cdots = \mu_k$$
$$H_a: \text{At least two of the } k \text{ treatment means differ}$$

The μ's might represent the means of *all* female and male high school seniors' SAT scores or the means of *all* households' income in each of four census regions.

To conduct a statistical test of these hypotheses, we will use the means of the independent random samples selected from the treatment populations using the completely randomized design—that is, we compare the k sample means, $\bar{x}_1, \bar{x}_2, \ldots, \bar{x}_k$.

Design of Experiments and Analysis of Variance

Table 1	SAT Scores for High School Students
Females	Males
530	490
560	520
590	550
620	580
650	610

Data Set: HSSAT1

For example, suppose you select independent random samples of five female and five male high school seniors and record their SAT scores. The data are shown in Table 1. A Minitab analysis of the data, shown in Figure 5, reveals that the sample mean SAT scores (shaded) are 590 for females and 550 for males. Can we conclude that the population of female high school students scores higher, on average, than the population of male students?

Descriptive Statistics: Females, Males

```
Variable  N   Mean  StDev  Variance  Minimum  Maximum
Females   5  590.0   47.4    2250.0    530.0    650.0
Males     5  550.0   47.4    2250.0    490.0    610.0
```

Figure 5

Minitab descriptive statistics for data in Table 1

To answer this question, we must consider the amount of sampling variability among the experimental units (students). The SAT scores in Table 1 are depicted in the dot plot shown in Figure 6. Note that the difference between the sample means is small relative to the sampling variability of the scores within the treatments, namely, Female and Male. We would be inclined not to reject the null hypothesis of equal population means in this case.

In contrast, if the data are as depicted in the dot plot of Figure 7, then the sampling variability is small relative to the difference between the two means. We would be inclined to favor the alternative hypothesis that the population means differ in this case.

You can see that the key is to compare the difference between the treatment means to the amount of sampling variability. To conduct a formal statistical test of the hypotheses requires numerical measures of the difference between the treatment means and the sampling variability within each treatment. The variation between the treatment means is measured by the **Sum of Squares for Treatments (SST),** which is calculated by squaring the distance between each treatment mean and the overall mean of *all* sample measurements, then multiplying each squared distance by the number of sample

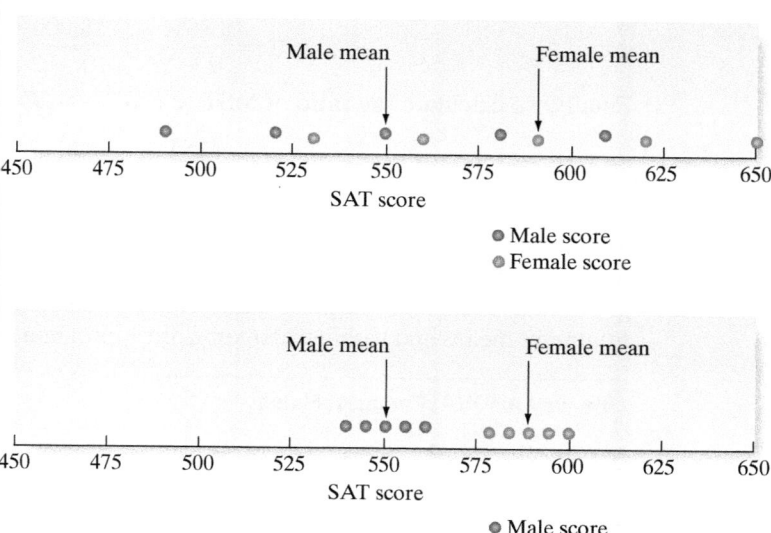

Figure 6

Dot plot of SAT scores: Difference between means dominated by sampling variability

Figure 7

Dot plot of SAT scores: Difference between means large relative to sampling variability

Now Work Exercise 17a

517

measurements for the treatment, and finally, adding the results over all treatments. For the data in Table 1, the overall mean is 570. Thus, we have:

$$\text{SST} = \sum_{i=1}^{k} n_i(\bar{x}_i - \bar{x})^2 = 5(550 - 570)^2 + 5(590 - 570)^2 = 4,000$$

In this equation we use $\bar{x}$ to represent the overall mean response of all sample measurements—that is, the mean of the combined samples. The symbol n_i is used to denote the sample size for the ith treatment. You can see that the value of SST is 4,000 for the two samples of five female and five male SAT scores depicted in Figures 6 and 7.

Next, we must measure the sampling variability within the treatments. We call this the **Sum of Squares for Error (SSE)** because it measures the variability around the treatment means that is attributed to sampling error. The value of SSE is computed by summing the squared distance between each response measurement and the corresponding treatment mean and then adding the squared differences over all measurements in the entire sample:

$$\text{SSE} = \sum_{j=1}^{n_1} (x_{1j} - \bar{x}_1)^2 + \sum_{j=1}^{n_2} (x_{2j} - \bar{x}_2)^2 + \cdots + \sum_{j=1}^{n_k} (x_{kj} - \bar{x}_k)^2$$

Here, the symbol x_{1j} is the jth measurement in sample 1, x_{2j} is the jth measurement in sample 2, and so on. This rather complex-looking formula can be simplified by recalling the formula for the sample variance, s^2:

$$s^2 = \sum_{i=1}^{n} \frac{(x_i - \bar{x})^2}{n - 1}$$

Note that each sum in SSE is simply the numerator of s^2 for that particular treatment. Consequently, we can rewrite SSE as

$$\text{SSE} = (n_1 - 1)s_1^2 + (n_2 - 1)s_2^2 + \cdots + (n_k - 1)s_k^2$$

where $s_1^2, s_2^2, \ldots, s_k^2$ are the sample variances for the k treatments. For the SAT scores in Table 1, the Minitab printout (Figure 5) shows that $s_1^2 = 2,250$ (for females) and $s_2^2 = 2,250$ (for males); then we have

$$\text{SSE} = (5 - 1)(2,250) + (5 - 1)(2,250) = 18,000$$

To make the two measurements of variability comparable, we divide each by the degrees of freedom to convert the sums of squares to mean squares. First, the **Mean Square for Treatments (MST),** which measures the variability among the treatment means, is equal to

$$\text{MST} = \frac{\text{SST}}{k - 1} = \frac{4,000}{2 - 1} = 4,000$$

where the number of degrees of freedom for the k treatments is $(k - 1)$. Next, the **Mean Square for Error (MSE),** which measures the sampling variability within the treatments, is

$$\text{MSE} = \frac{\text{SSE}}{n - k} = \frac{18,000}{10 - 2} = 2,250$$

Finally, we calculate the ratio of MST to MSE—an **F-statistic:**

$$F = \frac{\text{MST}}{\text{MSE}} = \frac{4,000}{2,250} = 1.78$$

These quantities—MST, MSE, and F—are shown (highlighted) on the Minitab printout displayed in Figure 8.

Values of the F-statistic near 1 indicate that the two sources of variation, between treatment means and within treatments, are approximately equal. In this case, the difference

One-way ANOVA: Females, Males

Source	DF	SS	MS	F	P
Factor	1	4000	4000	1.78	0.219
Error	8	18000	2250		
Total	9	22000			

S = 47.43   R-Sq = 18.18%   R-Sq(adj) = 7.95%

Figure 8

Minitab printout with ANOVA results for data in Table 1

between the treatment means may well be attributable to sampling error, which provides little support for the alternative hypothesis that the population treatment means differ. Values of F well in excess of 1 indicate that the variation among treatment means well exceeds that within treatments and therefore support the alternative hypothesis that the population treatment means differ.

When does F exceed 1 by enough to reject the null hypothesis that the means are equal? This depends on the degrees of freedom for treatments and for error and on the value of α selected for the test. We compare the calculated F-value to a table of F-values (Tables V–VIII in Appendix: Tables) with $v_1 = (k - 1)$ degrees of freedom in the numerator and $v_2 = (n - k)$ degrees of freedom in the denominator and corresponding to a Type I error probability of α. For the SAT score example, the F-statistic has $v_1 = (2 - 1) = 1$ numerator degree of freedom and $v_2 = (10 - 2) = 8$ denominator degrees of freedom. Thus, for $\alpha = .05$, we find (Table VI in Appendix: Tables)

$$F_{.05} = 5.32$$

The implication is that MST would have to be 5.32 times greater than MSE before we could conclude at the .05 level of significance that the two population treatment means differ. Because the data yielded $F = 1.78$, our initial impressions from the dot plot in Figure 6 are confirmed—there is insufficient information to conclude that the mean SAT scores differ for the populations of female and male high school seniors. The rejection region and the calculated F value are shown in Figure 9.

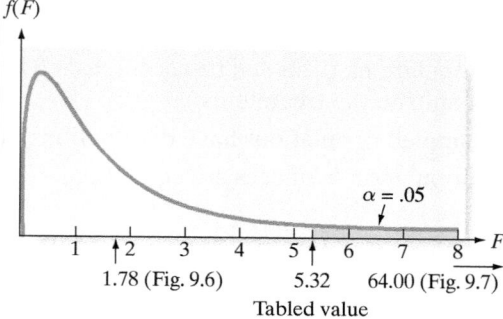

Figure 9

Rejection region and calculated F values for SAT score samples

In contrast, consider the dot plot in Figure 7. The SAT scores depicted in this dot plot are listed in Table 2, followed by Minitab descriptive statistics in Figure 10. Note that the sample means for females and males, 590 and 550, respectively, are the same as in the previous example. Consequently, the variation between the means is the same, namely, MST = 4,000. However, the variation within the two treatments appears to be considerably smaller. In fact, Figure 10 shows that $s_1^2 = 62.5$ and $s_2^2 = 62.5$. Thus, the variation within the treatments is measured by

$$\text{SSE} = (5 - 1)(62.5) + (5 - 1)(62.5) = 500$$

$$\text{MSE} = \frac{\text{SSE}}{n - k} = \frac{500}{8} = 62.5 \text{ (shaded on Figure 10)}$$

Then the F-ratio is

$$F = \frac{\text{MST}}{\text{MSE}} = \frac{4,000}{62.5} = 64.0 \text{ (shaded on Figure 10)}$$

Table 2

SAT Scores for High School Students Shown in Figure 7

Females	Males
580	540
585	545
590	550
595	555
600	560

Data Set: HSSAT2

Descriptive Statistics: Females, Males

Variable	N	Mean	StDev	Variance	Minimum	Maximum
Females	5	590.00	7.91	62.50	580.00	600.00
Males	5	550.00	7.91	62.50	540.00	560.00

One-way ANOVA: Females, Males

Source	DF	SS	MS	F	P
Factor	1	4000.0	4000.0	64.00	0.000
Error	8	500.0	62.5		
Total	9	4500.0			

Figure 10

Minitab descriptive statistics and ANOVA results for data in Table 2

Again, our visual analysis of the dot plot is confirmed statistically: $F = 64.0$ well exceeds the tabled F-value, 5.32, corresponding to the .05 level of significance. We would therefore reject the null hypothesis at that level and conclude that the SAT mean score of males differs from that of females.

Now Work Exercise 17b–h

The **analysis of variance F-test** for comparing treatment means is summarized in the accompanying box.

ANOVA F-Test to Compare k Treatment Means: Completely Randomized Design

$H_0: \mu_1 = \mu_2 = \cdots = \mu_k$

H_a: At least two treatment means differ

Test statistic: $F = \dfrac{\text{MST}}{\text{MSE}}$

Rejection region: $F > F_\alpha$ where F_α is based on $(k - 1)$ numerator degrees of freedom (associated with MST) and $(n - k)$ denominator degrees of freedom (associated with MSE), or $\alpha > p$-value.

Conditions Required for a Valid ANOVA F-Test: Completely Randomized Design

1. The samples are randomly selected in an independent manner from the k treatment populations. (This can be accomplished by randomly assigning the experimental units to the treatments.)
2. All k sampled populations have distributions that are approximately normal.
3. The k population variances are equal (i.e., $\sigma_1^2 = \sigma_2^2 = \sigma_3^2 = \cdots = \sigma_k^2$).

Computational formulas for MST and MSE are given in Appendix: Calculation Formulas for Analysis of Variance. We will rely on some of the many statistical software packages available to compute the F statistic, concentrating on the interpretation of the results rather than their calculations.

Example 4

Conducting an ANOVA F-Test—Comparing Golf Ball Brands

Problem Suppose the USGA wants to compare the mean distances associated with four different brands of golf balls when struck with a driver. A completely randomized design is employed, with Iron Byron, the USGA's robotic golfer, using a driver to hit a random sample of 10 balls of each brand in a random sequence. The distance is recorded for each hit, and the results are shown in Table 3, organized by brand.

a. Set up the test to compare the mean distances for the four brands. Use $\alpha = .10$.

b. Use statistical software to obtain the test statistic and p-value. Interpret the results.

Table 3	Results of Completely Randomized Design: Iron Byron Driver			
	Brand A	Brand B	Brand C	Brand D
	251.2	263.2	269.7	251.6
	245.1	262.9	263.2	248.6
	248.0	265.0	277.5	249.4
	251.1	254.5	267.4	242.0
	260.5	264.3	270.5	246.5
	250.0	257.0	265.5	251.3
	253.9	262.8	270.7	261.8
	244.6	264.4	272.9	249.0
	254.6	260.6	275.6	247.1
	248.8	255.9	266.5	245.9
Sample Means	250.8	261.1	270.0	249.3

Data Set: GLFCRD

Solution

a. To compare the mean distances of the four brands, we first specify the hypotheses to be tested. Denoting the population mean of the ith brand by μ_i, we test

$$H_0: \mu_1 = \mu_2 = \mu_3 = \mu_4$$

H_a: The mean distances differ for at least two of the brands

The test statistic compares the variation among the four treatment (Brand) means to the sampling variability within each of the treatments.

$$\text{Test statistic: } F = \frac{\text{MST}}{\text{MSE}}$$

$$\text{Rejection region: } F > F_\alpha = F_{.10}$$

$$\text{with } v_1 = (k - 1) = 3 \text{ df and } v_2 = (n - k) = 36 \text{ df}$$

From Table V in Appendix: Tables, we find $F_{.10} \approx 2.25$ for 3 and 36 df. Thus, we will reject H_0 if $F > 2.25$. (See Figure 11.)

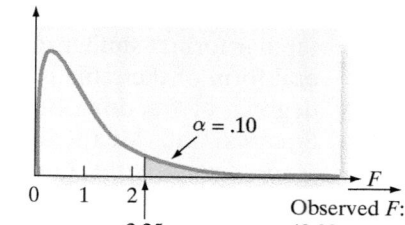

Figure 11

F-test for completely randomized design: Golf ball experiment

The assumptions necessary to ensure the validity of the test are as follows:

1. The samples of 10 golf balls for each brand are selected randomly and independently.
2. The probability distributions of the distances for each brand are normal.
3. The variances of the distance probability distributions for each brand are equal.

b. The Excel printout for the data in Table 3 resulting from this completely randomized design is given in Figure 12. The values of the mean squares, MST = 931.46 and MSE = 21.175, are highlighted on the printout. The F-ratio, 43.99, also highlighted on the printout, exceeds the tabled value of 2.25. We therefore reject the null hypothesis at the .10 level of significance, concluding that at least two of the brands differ with respect to mean distance traveled when struck by the driver.

We can also arrive at the appropriate conclusion by noting that the observed significance level of the F-test (highlighted on the printout) is approximately 0. This implies that we would reject the null hypothesis that the means are equal at any reasonably selected α level.

Figure 12

Excel printout for ANOVA of golf ball distance data

	A	B	C	D	E	F	G
1	Anova: Single Factor						
2							
3	SUMMARY						
4	Groups	Count	Sum	Average	Variance		
5	BrandA	10	2507.8	250.78	22.42178		
6	BrandB	10	2610.6	261.06	14.94711		
7	BrandC	10	2699.5	269.95	20.25833		
8	BrandD	10	2493.2	249.32	27.07289		
9							
10							
11	ANOVA						
12	Source of Variation	SS	df	MS	F	P-value	F crit
13	Between Groups	2794.389	3	931.4629	43.98875	3.97E-12	2.866266
14	Within Groups	762.301	36	21.17503			
15							
16	Total	3556.69	39				

[*Note:* Excel uses exponential notation to display the *p*-value. The value 3.97E-12 is equal to .00000000000397.]

Look Ahead Now that we know the mean driving distances differ, a logical follow-up question is: "Which ball brand travels farthest, on average, when hit with a driver?" In Section 3 we present a method for ranking treatment means in an ANOVA.

Now Work Exercise 21

Table 4	General ANOVA Summary Table for a Completely Randomized Design			
Source	df	SS	MS	F
Treatments	$k-1$	SST	$MST = \dfrac{SST}{k-1}$	$\dfrac{MST}{MSE}$
Error	$n-k$	SSE	$MSE = \dfrac{SSE}{n-k}$	
Total	$n-1$	SS(Total)		

The results of an **analysis of variance (ANOVA)** can be summarized in a simple tabular format similar to that obtained from the Excel printout in Example 4. The general form of the table is shown in Table 4, where the symbols df, SS, and MS stand for degrees of freedom, Sum of Squares, and Mean Square, respectively. Note that the two sources of variation, Treatments and Error, add to the Total Sum of Squares, SS(Total). The ANOVA summary table for Example 4 is given in Table 5, and the partitioning of the Total Sum of Squares into its two components is illustrated in Figure 13.

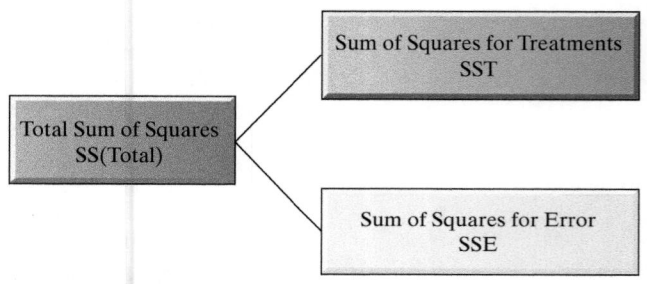

Figure 13

Partitioning of the Total Sum of Squares for the completely randomized design

Table 5	ANOVA Summary Table for Example 4				
Source	df	SS	MS	F	*p*-value
Brands	3	2,794.39	931.46	43.99	.0000
Error	36	762.30	21.18		
Total	39	3,556.69			

Example 5

Checking the ANOVA Assumptions

Problem Refer to the completely randomized design ANOVA conducted in Example 4. Are the assumptions required for the test approximately satisfied?

Solution The assumptions for the test are repeated below.

1. The samples of golf balls for each brand are selected randomly and independently.
2. The probability distributions of the distances for each brand are normal.
3. The variances of the distance probability distributions for each brand are equal.

Since the sample consisted of 10 randomly selected balls of each brand and the robotic golfer Iron Byron was used to drive all the balls, the first assumption of independent random samples is satisfied. To check the next two assumptions, we will employ two graphical methods:

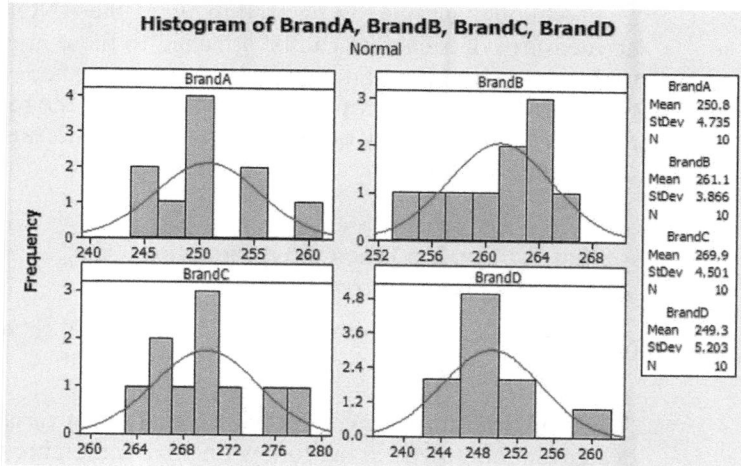

Figure 14

Minitab histograms for golf ball distances

histograms and box plots. A Minitab histogram of driving distances for each brand of golf ball is shown in Figure 14, followed by SPSS box plots in Figure 15.

The normality assumption can be checked by examining the histograms in Figure 14. With only 10 sample measurements for each brand, however, the displays are not very informative. More data would need to be collected for each brand before we could assess whether the distances come from normal distributions. Fortunately, analysis of variance has been shown to be a very **robust method** when the assumption of normality is not satisfied exactly—that is, *moderate departures from normality do not have much effect on the significance level of the ANOVA F-test or on confidence coefficients.* Rather than spend the time, energy, or money to collect additional data for this experiment to verify the normality assumption, we will rely on the robustness of the ANOVA methodology.

Box plots are a convenient way to obtain a rough check on the assumption of equal variances. With the exception of a possible outlier for Brand D (indicated by a circle in Figure 15) the box plots in Figure 15 show that the spread of the distance measurements is about the same for each brand. Because the sample variances appear to be the same, the assumption of equal population variances for the brands is probably satisfied. Although robust with respect to the normality assumption, ANOVA is *not robust* with respect to the equal variances assumption. Departures from the assumption of equal population variances can affect the associated measures of reliability (e.g., p-values and confidence levels). Fortunately, the effect is slight when the sample sizes are equal, as in this experiment.

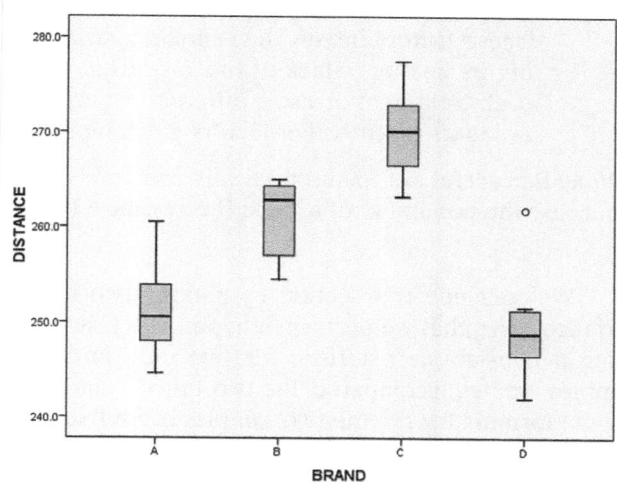

Figure 15

SPSS box plots for golf ball distances

Now Work Exercise 28

Although graphs can be used to check the ANOVA assumptions, as in Example 5, no measures of reliability can be attached to these graphs. When you have a plot that is unclear as to whether or not an assumption is satisfied, you can use formal statistical tests, which are beyond the scope of this text. (Consult the references for information on these tests.) When the validity of the ANOVA assumptions is in doubt, nonparametric statistical methods are useful.

What Do You Do When the Assumptions Are Not Satisfied for an ANOVA for a Completely Randomized Design?

Answer: Use a nonparametric statistical method such as the Kruskal-Wallis *H*-test.

The procedure for conducting an analysis of variance for a completely randomized design is summarized in the following box. Remember that the hallmark of this design is independent random samples of experimental units associated with each treatment. We discuss a design with dependent samples in Section 4.

Steps for Conducting an ANOVA for a Completely Randomized Design

1. Be sure the design is truly completely randomized, with independent random samples for each treatment.
2. Check the assumptions of normality and equal variances.
3. Create an ANOVA summary table that specifies the variability attributable to treatments and error, making sure that it leads to the calculation of the *F*-statistic for testing the null hypothesis that the treatment means are equal in the population. Use a statistical software program to obtain the numerical results. (If no such package is available, use the calculation formulas in Appendix: Calculation Formulas for Analysis of Variance.)
4. If the *F*-test leads to the conclusion that the means differ,
   a. Conduct a multiple comparisons procedure for as many of the pairs of means as you wish to compare (see Section 3). Use the results to summarize the statistically significant differences among the treatment means.
   b. If desired, form confidence intervals for one or more individual treatment means.
5. If the *F*-test leads to the nonrejection of the null hypothesis that the treatment means are equal, consider the following possibilities:
   a. The treatment means are equal—that is, the null hypothesis is true.
   b. The treatment means really differ, but other important factors affecting the response are not accounted for by the completely randomized design. These factors inflate the sampling variability, as measured by MSE, resulting in smaller values of the *F*-statistic. Either increase the sample size for each treatment or use a different experimental design (as in Section 4) that accounts for the other factors affecting the response.

Note: Be careful not to automatically conclude that the treatment means are equal because the possibility of a Type II error must be considered if you accept H_0.

We conclude this section by making two important points about an analysis of variance. First, that we perform a hypothesis test for the difference between two means, using a two-sample *t*-statistic for two independent samples. When two independent samples are being compared, the two-tailed *t*- and *F*-tests are equivalent. To see this, apply the formula for *t* to the two samples of SAT scores in Table 2:

$$t = \frac{\bar{x}_1 - \bar{x}_2}{\sqrt{s_p^2\left(\frac{1}{n_1} + \frac{1}{n_2}\right)}} = \frac{590 - 550}{\sqrt{(62.5)\left(\frac{1}{5} + \frac{1}{5}\right)}} = \frac{40}{5} = 8$$

Here, we used the fact that $s_p^2 = $ MSE, which you can verify by comparing the formulas. Note that the calculated F for these samples ($F = 64$) equals the square of the calculated t for the same samples ($t = 8$). Likewise, the critical F-value (5.32) equals the square of the critical t-value at the two-sided .05 level of significance ($t_{.025} = 2.306$ with 8 df). Because both the rejection region and the calculated values are related in the same way, the tests are equivalent. Moreover, the assumptions that must be met to ensure the validity of the t- and F-tests are the same:

1. The probability distributions of the populations of responses associated with each treatment must all be approximately normal.
2. The probability distributions of the populations of responses associated with each treatment must have equal variances.
3. The samples of experimental units selected for the treatments must be random and independent.

In fact, the only real difference between the tests is that the F-test can be used to compare *more than two* treatment means, whereas the t-test is applicable to two samples only.

For our second point, refer to Example 4. Our conclusion that at least two of the brands of golf balls have different mean distances traveled when struck with a driver leads naturally to the following questions: Which of the brands differ? How are the brands ranked with respect to mean distance?

One way to obtain this information is to construct a confidence interval for the difference between the means of any pair of treatments using the method as described previously. For example, if a 95% confidence interval for ($\mu_A - \mu_C$) in Example 4 is found to be ($-24, -13$), we are confident that the mean distance for Brand C exceeds the mean for Brand A (because all differences in the interval are negative). Constructing these confidence intervals for all possible brand pairs will allow you to rank the brand means. A method for conducting these *multiple comparisons*—one that controls for Type I errors—is presented in Section 3.

STATISTICS
in ACTION
REVISITED

Testing for Differences in Mean PAH Measurements

We now return to the case of the Florida land developer who blamed the failure of his housing plan on the discovery of pollutants (PAHs) at the site and who filed suit against two industries that produced PAH waste materials as part of their industrial processes. Soil specimens were collected at each of four locations: 7 at the housing development site, 8 at Industry A, 5 at Industry B, and 2 at Industry C. Two different molecular diagnostic ratios for measuring level of PAH in soil were determined for each soil specimen. These data are displayed in Table SIA1. Recall that the objective is to compare the mean PAH ratios at the four different locations.

Since the soil samples were obtained independently from the four different sites, we can treat the data as coming from a completely randomized design. There are two different response (dependent) variables: PAH Ratio 1 and PAH Ratio 2. The design employs a single factor (independent variable): Site (or location). The four levels of Site (Industry A, Industry B, Industry C, and Development) represent the treatments in the experiment. Then, the appropriate null and alternative hypotheses are:

$H_0: \mu_A = \mu_B = \mu_C = \mu_D$,

H_a: At least two of the means, $\mu_A, \mu_B, \mu_C, \mu_D$, are different

A Flawed Analysis of the Data

The biochemical expert hired by Industry A chose to analyze the data using a series of t-tests for comparing two means. That is, he conducted a two-sample t-test for each possible pair of sites—Industry A vs. Industry B, Industry A vs. Industry C, Industry A vs. Development, Industry B vs. Industry C, Industry B vs. Development, and Industry C vs. Development. The results of these six t-tests for the second PAH ratio variable are shown in the Minitab printouts, Figure SIA1a–f.

STATISTICS in ACTION REVISITED CONTINUED

Table SIA1	Data on PAH Ratios at Four Sites		
		Ratio	
Soil Specimen	Site	PAH1	PAH2
1	Development	0.620	1.040
2	Development	0.630	1.020
3	Development	0.660	1.070
4	Development	0.670	1.180
5	Development	0.610	1.020
6	Development	0.670	1.090
7	Development	0.660	1.100
8	Industry A	0.620	0.950
9	Industry A	0.660	1.090
10	Industry A	0.700	0.960
11	Industry A	0.560	0.970
12	Industry A	0.560	1.000
13	Industry A	0.570	1.030
14	Industry A	0.600	0.970
15	Industry A	0.580	1.015
16	Industry B	0.770	1.130
17	Industry B	0.720	1.110
18	Industry B	0.560	0.980
19	Industry B	0.705	1.130
20	Industry B	0.670	1.140
21	Industry C	0.675	1.115
22	Industry C	0.650	1.060

Source: Info Tech, Inc. (For confidentiality purposes, data values have been altered.)

🔵 *Data Set:* PAH

a. Development Site vs. Industry A

```
Two-sample T for PAH2

SITE          N    Mean    StDev   SE Mean
Development   7   1.0743   0.0565   0.021
IndustryA     8   0.9981   0.0464   0.016


Difference = mu (Development) - mu (IndustryA)
Estimate for difference:  0.0762
95% CI for difference:  (0.0188, 0.1336)
T-Test of difference = 0 (vs not =): T-Value = 2.87  P-Value = 0.013  DF = 13
Both use Pooled StDev = 0.0513
```

b. Development Site vs. Industry B

```
Two-sample T for PAH2

SITE          N    Mean    StDev   SE Mean
Development   7   1.0743   0.0565   0.021
IndustryB     5   1.0980   0.0669   0.030


Difference = mu (Development) - mu (IndustryB)
Estimate for difference:  -0.0237
95% CI for difference:  (-0.1031, 0.0557)
T-Test of difference = 0 (vs not =): T-Value = -0.67  P-Value = 0.521  DF = 10
Both use Pooled StDev = 0.0609
```

c. Development Site vs. Industry C

```
Two-sample T for PAH2

SITE          N    Mean    StDev   SE Mean
Development   7   1.0743   0.0565   0.021
IndustryC     2   1.0875   0.0389   0.027


Difference = mu (Development) - mu (IndustryC)
Estimate for difference:  -0.0132
95% CI for difference:  (-0.1163, 0.0898)
T-Test of difference = 0 (vs not =): T-Value = -0.30  P-Value = 0.771  DF = 7
Both use Pooled StDev = 0.0544
```

Figure SIA1

Minitab output for two-sample *t*-tests to compare PAH2 ratio means

d. Industry A vs. Industry B

```
Two-sample T for PAH2

SITE       N    Mean    StDev   SE Mean
IndustryA  8  0.9981  0.0464    0.016
IndustryB  5  1.0980  0.0669    0.030


Difference = mu (IndustryA) - mu (IndustryB)
Estimate for difference:  -0.0999
95% CI for difference:  (-0.1686, -0.0312)
T-Test of difference = 0 (vs not =): T-Value = -3.20  P-Value = 0.008  DF = 11
Both use Pooled StDev = 0.0548
```

e. Industry A vs. Industry C

```
Two-sample T for PAH2

SITE       N    Mean    StDev   SE Mean
IndustryA  8  0.9981  0.0464    0.016
IndustryC  2  1.0875  0.0389    0.027


Difference = mu (IndustryA) - mu (IndustryC)
Estimate for difference:  -0.0894
95% CI for difference:  (-0.1724, -0.0063)
T-Test of difference = 0 (vs not =): T-Value = -2.48  P-Value = 0.038  DF = 8
Both use Pooled StDev = 0.0456
```

f. Industry B vs. Industry C

```
Two-sample T for PAH2

SITE       N    Mean    StDev   SE Mean
IndustryB  5  1.0980  0.0669    0.030
IndustryC  2  1.0875  0.0389    0.027


Difference = mu (IndustryB) - mu (IndustryC)
Estimate for difference:  0.0105
95% CI for difference:  (-0.1234, 0.1444)
T-Test of difference = 0 (vs not =): T-Value = 0.20  P-Value = 0.848  DF = 5
Both use Pooled StDev = 0.0623
```

Figure SIA1

(Continued)

Each of the t-tests is a test of the null hypothesis, H_0: $\mu_i = \mu_j$, where μ_i and μ_j represent the two population means being compared. The biochemical expert conducted each test using a significance level of $\alpha = .05$. Comparing α to the p-value of each test (highlighted on Figure SIA1), the expert concluded the following:

1. The mean PAH2 ratio at **Industry A** is *statistically different* from the corresponding mean at **Industry B** since p-value $= .008$ (see Figure SIA1d).

2. The mean PAH2 ratio at the **development** site is *statistically different* from the corresponding mean at **Industry A** since p-value $= .013$ (see Figure SIA1a).

3. The mean PAH2 ratio at the **development** site is *not statistically different* from the corresponding mean at **Industry B** since p-value $= .521$ (see Figure SIA1b).

The last two inferences led the expert to argue that the source of the PAH contamination at the housing development site was more likely to have been derived from Industry A than from Industry B.

The statistician hired to rebut this testimony argued that the analysis was flawed. To see why, consider the fact that the biochemical expert conducted six independent t-tests on the data, each using $\alpha = P(\text{Type I error}) = .05$. Now, the probability of the expert concluding that a difference in means exists when, in fact, there is no difference (i.e., the probability of committing a Type I error) is .05 for any individual test. However, the expert drew his final conclusion based on the results of all six tests. It can be shown (proof omitted) that the probability of committing at least one Type I error—called the *overall Type I error rate*—when six tests are conducted at $\alpha = .05$ is approximately .265. In other words, there is more than a one in four chance that the expert erroneously concluded that a difference in means exists when there is actually no difference. This error rate is unacceptably high.

A second problem with the testimony of the biochemical expert is that of "accepting the null hypothesis." When the expert's test failed to show a significant difference in means, he declared the mean PAH ratio at the two sites being compared to be "statistically indistinguishable," implying that the population means are equal. By accepting the null hypothesis of equal means, the expert failed to account for the possibility of a Type II error (i.e., the error of accepting H_0 when H_0 is false). The probability of a Type II error, β, is typically unknown and is not controlled for in the series of two-sample t-tests and is likely to be large with the very small samples collected at the sites.

A Statistically Valid Analysis of the Data

Based on our discussion in this section, the appropriate way to analyze the data is with an analysis of variance (ANOVA). Since there is a single null hypothesis tested in an ANOVA, the probability of making a Type I error (i.e., the probability of concluding that the means differ when, in fact, they are the same) is simply $\alpha = .05$. A Minitab printout of the ANOVA results for both dependent variables, PAH Ratio 1 and PAH Ratio 2, is shown in Figure SIA2a–b.

The F-value and p-value of each test are highlighted on the printouts. For the first PAH ratio, p-value $= .083$. Consequently, at $\alpha = .05$ there is *insufficient evidence*

---

a. Dependent Variable = PAH1

One-way ANOVA: PAH1 versus SITE

```
Source  DF      SS       MS      F      P
SITE     3   0.02041  0.00680  2.61  0.083
Error   18   0.04697  0.00261
Total   21   0.06738

S = 0.05108    R-Sq = 30.29%    R-Sq(adj) = 18.67%


                                 Individual 95% CIs For Mean Based on
                                 Pooled StDev
Level          N    Mean    StDev   ------+---------+---------+---------+---
Development    7  0.64571  0.02507              (-------*-------)
IndustryA      8  0.60625  0.05097   (------*-------)
IndustryB      5  0.68500  0.07858             (---------*---------)
IndustryC      2  0.66250  0.01768   (--------------*---------------)
                                   ------+---------+---------+---------+---
                                      0.600     0.650     0.700     0.750

Pooled StDev = 0.05108
```

b. Dependent Variable = PAH2

One-way ANOVA: PAH2 versus SITE

```
Source  DF      SS       MS      F      P
SITE     3   0.03977  0.01326  4.45  0.017
Error   18   0.05366  0.00298
Total   21   0.09343

S = 0.05460    R-Sq = 42.56%    R-Sq(adj) = 32.99%



Level          N   Mean    StDev
Development    7  1.0743  0.0565
IndustryA      8  0.9981  0.0464
IndustryB      5  1.0980  0.0669
IndustryC      2  1.0875  0.0389

              Individual 95% CIs For Mean Based on Pooled StDev
Level          +---------+---------+---------+---------
Development              (------*------)
IndustryA      (-----*------)
IndustryB                  (--------*--------)
IndustryC               (-------------*-------------)
               +---------+---------+---------+---------
              0.960     1.020     1.080     1.140

Pooled StDev = 0.0546
```

Figure SIA2

Minitab output for ANOVA to compare PAH ratio means

of differences in the mean PAH ratios in the population of soil samples collected at the four sites. This result contradicts the conclusions drawn by conducting a series of independent samples t-tests on the data. Now, the p-value for the second PAH ratio ($p = .017$) indicates that there are some differences in the four PAH ratio means. To determine which sites have significantly different means, a follow-up analysis is required. This will involve ranking the means while controlling the overall Type I error rate. We pursue this analysis in the next Statistics in Action Revisited.

Exercises 15–34

Please be aware that some of the following problems may require knowledge of concepts that are not presented in this chapter.

Learning the Mechanics

15 Use Tables V, VI, VII, and VIII in Appendix: Tables to find each of the following F values:
  a. $F_{.05}, v_1 = 4, v_2 = 4$
  b. $F_{.01}, v_1 = 4, v_2 = 4$
  c. $F_{.10}, v_1 = 30, v_2 = 40$
  d. $F_{.025}, v_1 = 15, v_2 = 12$

16 Find the following probabilities:
  a. $P(F \leq 3.48)$ for $v_1 = 5, v_2 = 9$
  b. $P(F > 3.09)$ for $v_1 = 15, v_2 = 20$
  c. $P(F > 2.40)$ for $v_1 = 15, v_2 = 15$
  d. $P(F \leq 1.83)$ for $v_1 = 8, v_2 = 40$

17 Consider dot plots 1 and 2 shown below. Assume that the two samples represent independent, random samples corresponding to two treatments in a completely randomized design.
  a. In which plot is the difference between the sample means small relative to the variability within the sample observations? Justify your answer.
  b. Calculate the treatment means (i.e., the means of samples 1 and 2) for both dot plots.
  c. Use the means to calculate the Sum of Squares for Treatments (SST) for each dot plot.
  d. Calculate the sample variance for each sample and use these values to obtain the Sum of Squares for Error (SSE) for each dot plot.
  e. Calculate the Total Sum of Squares [SS(Total)] for the two dot plots by adding the Sums of Squares for Treatments and Error. What percentage of SS(Total) is accounted for by the treatments—that is, what percentage of the Total Sum of Squares is the Sum of Squares for Treatments—in each case?
  f. Convert the Sums of Squares for Treatments and Error to mean squares by dividing each by the appropriate number of degrees of freedom. Calculate the F-ratio of the Mean Square for Treatments (MST) to the Mean Square for Error (MSE) for each dot plot.

  g. Use the F-ratios to test the null hypothesis that the two samples are drawn from populations with equal means. Use $\alpha = .05$.
  h. What assumptions must be made about the probability distributions corresponding to the responses for each treatment to ensure the validity of the F-tests conducted in part **g**?

18 Refer to Exercise 17. Conduct a two-sample t-test of the null hypothesis that the two treatment means are equal for each dot plot. Use $\alpha = .05$ and two-tailed tests. In the course of the test, compare each of the following with the F-tests in Exercise 17:
  a. The pooled variances and the MSEs
  b. The t- and F-test statistics
  c. The tabled values of t and F that determine the rejection regions
  d. The conclusions of the t- and F-tests
  e. The assumptions that must be made to ensure the validity of the t- and F-tests

19 Refer to Exercises 17 and 18. Complete the following ANOVA table for each of the two dot plots:

Source	df	SS	MS	F
Treatments				
Error				
Total				

20 A partially completed ANOVA table for a completely randomized design is shown here:

Source	df	SS	MS	F
Treatments	6	17.5	—	—
Error	—	—	—	
Total	41	46.5		

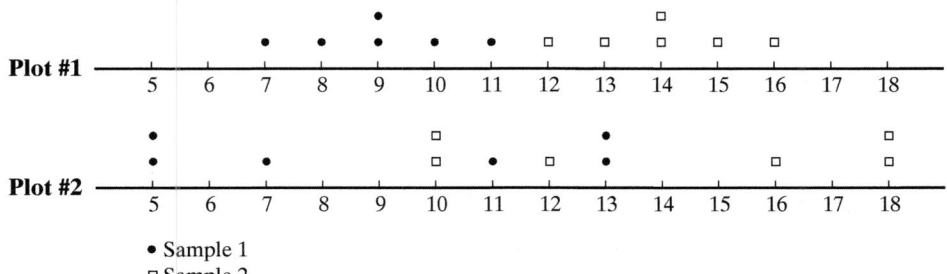

Plot #1

Plot #2

• Sample 1
□ Sample 2

Dot plots for Exercise 17

a. Complete the ANOVA table.

b. How many treatments are involved in the experiment?

c. What is the total sample size, n, for the experiment?

d. Use a random number generator to randomly assign each experimental unit to one of the treatments. Assume the sample size will be the same for each treatment.

e. Do the data provide sufficient evidence to indicate a difference among the population means? Test using $\alpha = .10$.

f. Find the approximate observed significance level for the test in part **c** and interpret it.

g. Suppose that $\bar{x}_1 = 3.7$ and $\bar{x}_2 = 4.1$. Do the data provide sufficient evidence to indicate a difference between μ_1 and μ_2? Assume that there are six observations for each treatment. Test using $\alpha = .10$.

h. Refer to part **g.** Find a 90% confidence interval for $(\mu_1 - \mu_2)$. [*Hint:* Use $s = \sqrt{MSE}$ as an estimate of both σ_1 and σ_2.]

i. Refer to part **g.** Find a 90% confidence interval for μ_1. [*Hint:* Use $s = \sqrt{MSE}$ as an estimate of σ_1.]

21 The data in the next table resulted from an experiment that used a completely randomized design.

Treatment 1	Treatment 2	Treatment 3
3.8	5.4	1.3
1.2	2.0	0.7
4.1	4.8	2.2
5.5	3.8	
2.3		

a. Use statistical software (or the appropriate calculation formulas in Appendix: Calculation Formulas for Analysis of Variance to complete the following ANOVA table:

Source	df	SS	MS	F
Treatments				
Error				
Total				

b. Test the null hypothesis that $\mu_1 = \mu_2 = \mu_3$, where μ_i represents the true mean for treatment i, against the alternative that at least two of the means differ. Use $\alpha = .01$.

Applying the Concepts—Basic

22 **How workers respond to wage cuts.** A randomized field experiment was carried out to determine how workers respond to wage cuts and the results published in *Institute for the Study of Labor: Discussion Paper Series* (March 2011). A company formed teams of two employees for a temporary promotion campaign. Both team members had identical individual tasks (sell promotional cards for entrance to a nightclub) and were initially paid the same hourly wage. After a short period of time on the job, teams were unknowingly randomly assigned to one of three treatments. In the "unilateral wage cut" treatment, one worker's pay was cut by 25%; in the "general wage cut" treatment, both workers' pay was cut by 25%; and in the "baseline" treatment, neither worker received a pay cut. The variable of interest was the decrease in the number of promotional cards sold after implementation of the pay cuts. The researchers wanted to know if the average decrease in cards sold differed depending on whether one or more of the workers received a pay cut.

a. Identify the type of experimental design used in the study.

b. Identify the dependent variable of interest.

c. What is the factor in this experiment? The factor levels?

d. Specify the null hypothesis of interest to the researchers.

e. The ANOVA F-test was carried out and resulted in a p-value less than .001. Interpret these results using $\alpha = .01$.

23 **Performance of a bus depot.** The performances of public bus depots in India were evaluated and ranked in the *International Journal of Engineering Science and Technology* (February 2011). A survey was administered to 150 customers selected randomly and independently at each of three different bus depots (Depot 1, Depot 2, and Depot 3); thus, the total sample consisted of 450 bus customers. Based on responses to 16 different items (e.g., bus punctuality, seat comfort, luggage service, etc.), a performance score (out of 100 total points) was calculated for each customer. The average performance scores were compared across the three bus depots using an analysis of variance. The ANOVA F-test resulted in a p-value of .0001.

a. Give details (experimental units, dependent variable, factor, treatments) on the experimental design utilized in this study.

b. The researchers concluded that the "mean customer performance scores differed across the three bus depots at a 95% confidence level." Do you agree?

24 **Making high-stakes insurance decisions.** The *Journal of Economic Psychology* (Sep. 2008) published the results of a high-stakes experiment where subjects (university students) were asked how much they would pay for insuring a valuable painting. The painting was threatened by both fire and theft, hence, the need for insurance. Of interest was the amount the subject was willing to pay (WTP) for insurance (thousands of dollars). For one part of the experiment, a total of 252 subjects were randomly assigned to one of three groups. Group 1 subjects ($n_1 = 84$) were informed of the hazards (both fire and theft) but were not told the exact probabilities of the hazards occurring. These subjects provided a separate WTP value for fire and theft. Group 2 subjects ($n_2 = 84$) were also informed of the hazards (fire/theft) and were not told the exact probabilities of the hazards occurring. However, these subjects provided a single WTP value covering both fire and theft. Group 3 subjects ($n_3 = 84$) were told of the hazards in sequential order (fire first, then theft). After being given the exact probability of fire occurring, the subjects provided a WTP value for fire. Then they were given the exact probability of theft occurring and were asked to provide a WTP value for theft. The researchers investigated whether the mean total WTP value differed for the three groups.

a. Explain why the experimental design employed is a completely randomized design.

b. Identify the dependent (response) variable and treatments for the design.

c. Give the null and alternative hypotheses of interest to the researchers.

NW **d.** Use a random number generator to randomly assign each of the 252 subjects to one of the three groups. Be sure to assign 84 subjects to each group.

25 **Contingent valuation of homes in contaminated areas.** Contingent valuation (CV) is a method of estimating property values that uses survey responses from potential homeowners. CV surveys were employed to determine the impact of contamination on property values in the *Journal of Real Estate Research* (Vol. 27, 2005). Homeowners were randomly selected from each of seven states—Kentucky, Pennsylvania, Ohio, Alabama, Illinois, South Carolina, and Texas. Each homeowner was asked to estimate the property value of a home located in an area contaminated by petroleum leaking from underground storage tanks (LUST). The dependent variable of interest was the LUST discount percentage (i.e., the difference between the current home value and estimated LUST value, as a percentage). The researchers were interested in comparing the mean LUST discount percentages across the seven states.

a. Give the null and alternative hypotheses of interest to the researchers.

b. An ANOVA summary table is shown below. Use the information provided to conduct the hypothesis test, part **a.** Use $\alpha = .10$.

Source	df	SS	MS	F-Value	p-Value
States	6	.1324	.0221	1.60	0.174
Error	59	.8145	.0138		
Total	65	.9469			

26 **Study of mutual fund performance.** Mutual funds are classified as large-cap funds, medium-cap funds, or small-cap funds, depending on the capitalization of the companies in the fund. Hawaii Pacific University researchers S. Shi and M. Seiler investigated whether the average performance of a mutual fund is related to capitalization size (*American Business Review,* Jan. 2002). Independent random samples of 30 mutual funds were selected from each of the three fund groups, and the 90-day rate of return was determined for each fund. The data for the 90 funds were subjected to an analysis of variance, with the results shown in the ANOVA summary table below.

Source	df	SS	MS	F	p-Value
Fund group	2	409.566	204.783	6.965	.002
Error	87	2,557.860	29.401		
Total	89	2,967.426			

Source: Shi, S. W. W., & Seiler, M. J. "Growth and value style comparison of U.S. stock mutual funds," *American Business Review,* January 2002 (Table 3). Copyright © by Taylor & Francis, Inc. Reprinted with permission.

a. State the null and alternative hypotheses for the ANOVA.

b. Give the rejection region for the test using $\alpha = .01$.

c. Make the appropriate conclusion using either the test statistic or the *p*-value.

27 **Income and road rage.** Is a driver's propensity to engage in road rage related to his or her income? Researchers at Mississippi State University attempted to answer this

question by conducting a survey of a representative sample of over 1,000 U.S. adult drivers (*Accident Analysis and Prevention,* Vol. 34, 2002). Based on how often each driver engaged in certain road rage behaviors (e.g., making obscene gestures at, tailgating, and thinking about physically hurting another driver), a road rage score was assigned. (Higher scores indicate a greater pattern of road rage behavior.) The drivers were also grouped by annual income: under $30,000, between $30,000 and $60,000, and over $60,000. The data were subjected to an analysis of variance, with the results summarized in the table. Is there evidence to indicate that the mean road rage score differs for the three income groups? Test using $\alpha = .05$.

Income Group	Sample Size	Mean Road Rage Score
Under $30,000	379	4.60
$30,000 to $60,000	392	5.08
Over $60,000	267	5.15
ANOVA Results:	*F*-value = 3.90	*p*-value < .01

Source: Wells-Parker, E., et al. "An exploratory study of the relationship between road rage and crash experience in a representative sample of US Drivers," *Accident Analysis and Prevention,* Vol. 34, 2002 (Table 2). Copyright © by Elsevier, Ltd. Reprinted with permission.

Applying the Concepts—Intermediate

28 **Study of recall of TV commercials.** Do TV shows with violence and sex impair memory for commercials? To answer this question, Iowa State researchers conducted a designed experiment in which 324 adults were randomly assigned to one of three viewer groups of 108 participants each (*Journal of Applied Psychology,* June 2002). One group watched a TV program with a violent content code (V) rating, the second group viewed a show with a sex content code (S) rating, and the last group watched a neutral TV program with neither a V nor an S rating. Nine commercials were embedded into each TV show. After viewing the program, each participant was scored on his or her recall of the brand names in the commercial messages, with scores ranging from 0 (no brands recalled) to 9 (all brands recalled). The data (simulated from information provided in the article) are saved in the accompanying file. The researchers compared the mean recall scores of the three viewing groups with an analysis of variance for a completely randomized design.

a. Identify the experimental units in the study.

b. Identify the dependent (response) variable in the study.

c. Identify the factor and treatments in the study.

d. The sample mean recall scores for the three groups were $\bar{x}_V = 2.08$, $\bar{x}_S = 1.71$, and $\bar{x}_{Neutral} = 3.17$. Explain why one should not draw an inference about differences in the population mean recall scores on the basis of only these summary statistics.

e. An ANOVA on the data yielded the results shown in the Minitab printout on the next page. Locate the test statistic and *p*-value on the printout.

f. Interpret the results from part **e,** using $\alpha = 0.01$. What can the researchers conclude about the three groups of TV ad viewers?

g. Check that the ANOVA assumptions are reasonably satisfied.

Minitab Output for Exercise 28

One-way ANOVA: VIOLENT, SEX, NEUTRAL

```
Source    DF      SS      MS      F      P
Factor     2   123.27   61.63   20.45  0.000
Error    321   967.35    3.01
Total    323  1090.62

S = 1.736    R-Sq = 11.30%    R-Sq(adj) = 10.75%
```

29 Does the media influence your attitude toward tanning?
Dermatologists' primary recommendation to prevent skin cancer is minimal exposure to the sun. Yet, models used in product advertisements are typically well tanned. Do such advertisements influence a consumer's attitude toward tanning? University of California and California State University researchers designed an experiment to investigate this phenomenon and published their results in *Basic and Applied Social Psychology* (May 2010). College student participants were randomly assigned to one of three conditions: (1) view product advertisements featuring models with a tan, (2) view product advertisements featuring models without a tan, or (3) view products advertised with no models (control group). The objective was to determine whether the mean attitude toward tanning differs across the three conditions. A tanning attitude index (measured on a scale of 0 to 5 points) was recorded for each participant. The results are summarized in the accompanying table.

	Tanned Models	Models with No Tan	No Models
Sample Size	56	56	56
Mean	2.40	2.11	2.50
Standard Deviation	.85	.73	.82

Source: Based on Mahler, H., et al. "Effects of media images on attitudes toward tanning," *Basic and Applied Social Psychology*, Vol. 32, No. 2, May 2010 (adapted from Table 1).

a. Identify the type of experimental design utilized by the researchers.

b. Identify the experimental units, dependent variable, and treatments for the design.

c. Set up the null hypothesis for a test to compare the treatment means.

d. The sample means shown in the table are obviously different. Explain why the researchers should not use these means alone to test the hypothesis, part **c**.

e. The researchers conducted an ANOVA on the data and reported the following results: $F = 3.60$, p-value $= .03$. Carry out the test, part **c**. Use $\alpha = .05$ to draw your conclusion.

f. What assumptions are required for the inferences derived from the test to be valid?

30 Homework assistance for accounting students. The *Journal of Accounting Education* (Vol. 25, 2007) did a study of assisting accounting students with their homework. A total of 75 junior-level accounting majors who were enrolled in Intermediate Financial Accounting participated in the experiment. Students took a pretest on a topic not covered in class and then each was given a homework problem to solve on the same topic. A completely randomized design was employed, with students randomly assigned to receive one of three different levels of assistance on the homework: (1) the completed solution, (2) check figures at various steps of the solution, and (3) no help at all. After finishing the homework, each student was given a posttest on the subject. The response variable of interest to the researchers was the knowledge gain (or, test score improvement), measured as the difference between the posttest and pretest scores. The data (simulated from descriptive statistics published in the article) are saved in the accompanying file.

a. Give the null and alternative hypotheses tested in an analysis of variance of the data.

b. Summarize the results of the analysis in an ANOVA table.

c. Interpret the results, practically.

31 Effectiveness of sales closing techniques. Industrial sales professionals have long debated the effectiveness of various sales closing techniques. For example, a University of Akron study investigated the impact of five different closing techniques and a no-close condition on the level of a sales prospect's trust in the salesperson (*Industrial Marketing Management,* Sept. 1996). More recently, a *B2B Marketing Insider* blog (Oct. 7, 2010) examined five currently-used sales closing techniques. Consider the following study. Sales scenarios are presented to a sample of 230 purchasing executives. Each subject received one of the five closing techniques or a scenario in which no close was achieved. After reading the sales scenario, each executive was asked to rate his/her level of trust in the salesperson on a 7-point scale. The table reports the six treatments employed in the study and the number of subjects receiving each treatment.

Treatments: Closing Techniques	Sample Size
1. No close	35
2. Financial close	35
3. Time Line close	30
4. Sympathy close	40
5. The Visual close	35
6. Thermometer close	55

Source: Based on Hawes, J. M. "Do Closing Techniques Diminish Prospect Trust?" from *Industrial Marketing Management*, September 1996, Volume 25(5).

a. Consider the following hypotheses:

H_0: The salesperson's level of prospect trust is not influenced by the choice of closing method.

H_a: The salesperson's level of prospect trust is influenced by the choice of closing method.

Rewrite these hypotheses in the form required for an analysis of variance.

b. Assume the ANOVA F-statistic is $F = 2.21$. Is there sufficient evidence to reject H_0 at $\alpha = .05$?

c. What assumptions must be met for the test of part **a** to be valid?

d. Would you classify this experiment as observational or designed? Explain.

32 Is honey a cough remedy? Pediatric researchers at Pennsylvania State University carried out a designed study to test whether a teaspoon of honey before bed calms a child's cough and published their results in *Archives of Pediatrics and Adolescent Medicine* (Dec. 2007). A sample of 105 children who were ill with an upper respiratory tract infection and their parents participated in the study. On the first night, the parents rated their children's cough symptoms on a scale from 0 (no problems at all) to 6 (extremely severe) in five different areas. The total symptoms score (ranging from 0 to 30 points) was the variable of interest for the 105 patients. On the second night, the parents were instructed to give their sick children a dosage of liquid "medicine" prior to bedtime. Unknown to the parents, some were given a dosage of dextromethorphan (DM)—an over-the-counter cough medicine—while others were given a similar dose of honey. Also, a third group of parents (the control group) gave their sick children no dosage at all. Again, the parents rated their children's cough symptoms, and the improvement in total cough symptoms score was determined for each child. The data (improvement scores) for the study are shown in the accompanying table. The goal of the researchers was to compare the mean improvement scores for the three treatment groups.

a. Identify the type of experimental design employed. What are the treatments?

b. Conduct an analysis of variance on the data and interpret the results.

c. Check the validity of the ANOVA assumptions.

Honey Dosage:	12	11	15	11	10	13	10	4	15	16	9	14
	10	6	10	8	11	12	12	8	12	9	11	15
	10	15	9	13	8	12	10	8	9	5	12	
DM Dosage:	4	6	9	4	7	7	7	9	12	10	11	
	6	3	4	9	12	7	6	8	12	12	4	
	12	13	7	10	13	9	4	4	10	15	9	
No Dosage (Control):	5	8	6	1	0	8	12	8	7	7	1	6
	7	7	12	7	9	5	11	9	5	6	8	8
	6	7	10	9	4	8	7	3	1	4	3	

Source: Paul, I. M., et al. "Effect of honey, dextromethorphan, and no treatment on nocturnal cough and sleep quality for coughing children and their parents," *Archives of Pediatrics and Adolescent Medicine,* Vol. 161, No. 12, Dec. 2007 (data simulated).

33 Commercial eggs produced from different housing systems. In the production of commercial eggs in Europe, four different types of housing systems for the chickens are used: cage, barn, free range, and organic. The characteristics of eggs produced from the four housing systems were investigated in *Food Chemistry* (Vol. 106, 2008). Twenty-eight commercial grade A eggs were randomly selected from supermarkets—10 of which were produced in cages, 6 in barns, 6 with free range, and 6 organic. A number of quantitative characteristics were measured for each egg, including shell thickness (millimeters), whipping capacity (percent overrun), and penetration strength (newtons). The data (simulated from summary statistics provided in the journal article) are saved in the accompanying file. For each characteristic, the researchers compared the means of the four housing systems. Minitab descriptive statistics and ANOVA printouts for each characteristic are shown (next column). Fully interpret the results. Identify the characteristics for which the housing systems differ.

Minitab output for Exercise 33

Descriptive Statistics: THICKNESS, OVERRUN, STRENGTH

Variable	HOUSING	N	Mean	StDev	Minimum	Maximum
THICKNESS	BARN	6	0.50000	0.01414	0.48000	0.52000
	CAGE	10	0.4230	0.0350	0.3700	0.4700
	FREE	6	0.5017	0.0279	0.4700	0.5500
	ORGANIC	6	0.4817	0.0387	0.4300	0.5200
OVERRUN	BARN	6	513.33	8.38	501.00	526.00
	CAGE	10	480.60	12.91	462.00	502.00
	FREE	6	517.50	8.17	510.00	531.00
	ORGANIC	6	529.17	10.65	511.00	544.00
STRENGTH	BARN	6	39.333	1.120	37.600	40.300
	CAGE	10	37.320	2.127	33.000	40.200
	FREE	6	37.17	3.79	31.50	40.60
	ORGANIC	6	35.97	3.04	32.60	40.20

One-way ANOVA: THICKNESS versus HOUSING

Source	DF	SS	MS	F	P
HOUSING	3	0.034291	0.011430	11.74	0.000
Error	24	0.023377	0.000974		
Total	27	0.057668			

One-way ANOVA: OVERRUN versus HOUSING

Source	DF	SS	MS	F	P
HOUSING	3	10788	3596	31.36	0.000
Error	24	2752	115		
Total	27	13540			

One-way ANOVA: STRENGTH versus HOUSING

Source	DF	SS	MS	F	P
HOUSING	3	35.12	11.71	1.70	0.193
Error	24	164.82	6.87		
Total	27	199.94			

Applying the Concepts—Advanced

34 Animal-assisted therapy for heart patients. Chief executive officers of hospitals are adopting unconventional therapeutic methods to shorten the length of stay of patients. At an *American Heart Association Conference* (Nov. 2005), a study to gauge whether animal-assisted therapy can improve the physiological responses of heart failure patients was presented. In the study, 76 heart patients were randomly assigned to one of three groups. Each patient in group T was visited by a human volunteer accompanied by a trained dog; each patient in group V was visited by a volunteer only; and the patients in group C were not visited at all. The anxiety level of each patient was measured (in points) both before and after the visits. The table below gives summary statistics for the drop in anxiety level for patients in the three groups. The mean drops in anxiety levels of the three groups of patients were compared using an analysis of variance. Although the ANOVA table was not provided in the article, sufficient information is provided to reconstruct it.

	Sample Size	Mean Drop	Std. Dev.
Group T: Volunteer + Trained Dog	26	10.5	7.6
Group V: Volunteer only	25	3.9	7.5
Group C: Control group (no visit)	25	1.4	7.5

Source: Cole, K., et al. "Animal assisted therapy decreases hemodynamics, plasma epinephrine and state anxiety in hospitalized heart failure patients," *American Heart Association Conference,* Dallas, Texas, Nov. 2005. Copyright © 2005 by American Heart Association. Reprinted with permission.

a. Compute SST for the ANOVA, using the formula

$$\text{SST} = \sum_{i=1}^{3} n_i (\bar{x}_i - \bar{x})^2$$

where $\bar{x}$ is the overall mean drop in anxiety level of all 76 subjects. [*Hint:* $\bar{x} = (\sum_{i=1}^{3} n_i(\bar{x}_i))/76.$]

b. Recall that SSE for the ANOVA can be written as

$$SSE = (n_1 - 1)s_1^2 + (n_2 - 1)s_2^2 + (n_3 - 1)s_3^2$$

where s_1^2, s_2^2, and s_3^2 are the sample variances associated with the three treatments. Compute SSE for the ANOVA.

c. Use the results from parts **a** and **b** to construct the ANOVA table.

d. Is there sufficient evidence (at $\alpha = .01$) of differences among the mean drops in anxiety levels by the patients in the three groups?

e. Comment on the validity of the ANOVA assumptions. How might this affect the results of the study?

3 Multiple Comparisons of Means

Consider a completely randomized design with three treatments, A, B, and C. Suppose we determine that the treatment means are statistically different via the ANOVA F-test of Section 2. To complete the analysis, we want to rank the three treatment means. As mentioned in Section 2, we start by placing confidence intervals on the difference between various pairs of treatment means in the experiment. In the three-treatment experiment, for example, we would construct confidence intervals for the following differences: $\mu_A - \mu_B$, $\mu_A - \mu_C$, and $\mu_B - \mu_C$.

Determining the Number of Pairwise Comparisons of Treatment Means

In general, if there are k treatment means, there are

$$c = \frac{k(k-1)}{2}$$

pairs of means that can be compared.

CARLO E. BONFERRONI
(1892–1960)
Bonferroni Inequalities

During his childhood years in Turin, Italy, Carlo Bonferroni developed an aptitude for mathematics while studying music. He went on to obtain a degree in mathematics at the University of Turin. Bonferroni's first appointment as a professor of mathematics was at the University of Bari in 1923. Ten years later, he became chair of financial mathematics at the University of Florence, where he remained until his death. Bonferroni was a prolific writer, authoring over 65 research papers and books. His interest in statistics included various methods of calculating a mean and a correlation coefficient. Among statisticians, however, Bonferroni is most well known for developing his Bonferroni inequalities in probability theory in 1935. Later, other statisticians proposed using these inequalities for finding simultaneous confidence intervals, which led to the development of the Bonferroni multiple comparisons method in ANOVA. Bonferroni balanced these scientific accomplishments with his music, becoming an excellent pianist and composer.

If we want to have $100(1 - \alpha)\%$ confidence that each of the c confidence intervals contains the true difference it is intended to estimate, we must use a smaller value of α for each individual confidence interval than we would use for a single interval. For example, suppose we want to rank the means of the three treatments, A, B, and C, with 95% confidence that all three confidence intervals comparing the means contain the true differences between the treatment means. Then each individual confidence interval will need to be constructed using a level of significance smaller than $\alpha = .05$ in order to have 95% confidence that the three intervals collectively include the true differences.*

Now Work Exercise 35

To make **multiple comparisons of a set of treatment means,** we can use a number of procedures that, under various assumptions, ensure that the overall confidence level associated with all the comparisons remains at or above the specified $100(1 - \alpha)\%$ level. Three widely used techniques are the Bonferroni, Scheffé, and Tukey methods. For each of these procedures, the risk of making a Type I error applies to the comparisons of the treatment means in the experiment; thus, the value of α selected is called an **experimentwise error rate** (in contrast to a **comparisonwise error rate**).

For a single comparison of two means in a designed experiment, the probability of making a Type I error (i.e., the probability of concluding that a difference in the means exists, given that the means are the same) is called a **comparisonwise error rate (CER).**

---

*The reason each interval must be formed at a higher confidence level than that specified for the collection of intervals can be demonstrated as follows:

$P\{$At least one of c intervals fails to contain the true difference$\}$
$= 1 - P\{$All c intervals contain the true differences$\}$
$= 1 - (1 - \alpha)^c \geq \alpha$

Thus, to make this probability of at least one failure equal to α, we must specify the individual levels of significance to be less than α.

For multiple comparisons of means in a designed experiment, the probability of making at least one Type I error (i.e., the probability of concluding that at least one difference in means exists, given that the means are all the same) is called an **experimentwise error rate (EER)**.

The choice of a multiple comparisons method in ANOVA will depend on the type of experimental design used and the comparisons of interest to the analyst. For example, **Tukey** (1949) developed his procedure specifically for pairwise comparisons when the sample sizes of the treatments are equal. The **Bonferroni method** (see Miller, 1981), like the Tukey procedure, can be applied when pairwise comparisons are of interest; however, Bonferroni's method does not require equal sample sizes. **Scheffé** (1953) developed a more general procedure for comparing all possible linear combinations of treatment means (called *contrasts*). Consequently, when making pairwise comparisons, the confidence intervals produced by Scheffé's method will generally be wider than the Tukey or Bonferroni confidence intervals.

The formulas for constructing confidence intervals for differences between treatment means using the Tukey, Bonferroni, or Scheffé method are provided in Appendix: Calculation Formulas for Analysis of Variance. However, because these procedures (and many others) are available in the ANOVA programs of most statistical software packages, we use the computer to conduct the analysis. The programs generate a confidence interval for the difference between two treatment means for all possible pairs of treatments based on the experimentwise error rate (α) selected by the analyst.

| **Example** | **6** |

Ranking Treatment Means—Golf Ball Experiment

Problem Refer to the completely randomized design of Example 4, in which we concluded that at least two of the four brands of golf balls are associated with different mean distances traveled when struck with a driver.

a. Use Tukey's multiple comparisons procedure to rank the treatment means with an overall confidence level of 95%.

b. Estimate the mean distance traveled for balls manufactured by the brand with the highest rank.

Solution

a. To rank the treatment means with an overall confidence level of .95, we require the experimentwise error rate of $\alpha = .05$. The confidence intervals generated by Tukey's method appear at the top of the SPSS printout, Figure 16. [*Note*: SPSS uses the number 1 for Brand A, 2 for Brand B, etc.] For any pair of means, μ_i and μ_j, SPSS computes two confidence intervals—one for $(\mu_i - \mu_j)$ and one for $(\mu_j - \mu_i)$. Only one of these intervals is necessary to decide whether the means differ significantly.

In this example, we have $k = 4$ brand means to compare. Consequently, the number of relevant pairwise comparisons—that is, the number of nonredundant confidence intervals—is $c = 4(3)/2 = 6$. These six intervals, highlighted in Figure 16, are given in Table 6.

We are 95% confident that the intervals *collectively* contain all the differences between the true brand mean distances. Note that intervals that contain 0, such as the Brand A–Brand D interval from −4.08 to 7.00, do not support a conclusion that the true brand mean distances differ. If both endpoints of the interval are positive, as with the Brand B–Brand D interval from 6.20 to 17.28, the implication is that the first Brand (B) mean distance exceeds the second (D). Conversely, if both endpoints of the interval are negative, as with the Brand A–Brand C interval from −24.71 to −13.63, the implication is that the second Brand (C) mean distance exceeds the first Brand (A) mean distance.

A convenient summary of the results of the Tukey multiple comparisons is a listing of the brand means from highest to lowest, with a solid line connecting those

Multiple Comparisons

Dependent Variable: DISTANCE
Tukey HSD

(I) BRANDNUM	(J) BRANDNUM	Mean Difference (I-J)	Std. Error	Sig.	95% Confidence Interval Lower Bound	95% Confidence Interval Upper Bound
1	2	-10.2800*	2.0579	.000	-15.822	-4.738
	3	-19.1700*	2.0579	.000	-24.712	-13.628
	4	1.4600	2.0579	.893	-4.082	7.002
2	1	10.2800*	2.0579	.000	4.738	15.822
	3	-8.8900*	2.0579	.001	-14.432	-3.348
	4	11.7400*	2.0579	.000	6.198	17.282
3	1	19.1700*	2.0579	.000	13.628	24.712
	2	8.8900*	2.0579	.001	3.348	14.432
	4	20.6300*	2.0579	.000	15.088	26.172
4	1	-1.4600	2.0579	.893	-7.002	4.082
	2	-11.7400*	2.0579	.000	-17.282	-6.198
	3	-20.6300*	2.0579	.000	-26.172	-15.088

*. The mean difference is significant at the .05 level.

DISTANCE

Tukey HSD[a]

BRANDNUM	N	Subset for alpha = .05 1	Subset for alpha = .05 2	Subset for alpha = .05 3
4	10	249.320		
1	10	250.780		
2	10		261.060	
3	10			269.950
Sig.		.893	1.000	1.000

Means for groups in homogeneous subsets are displayed.
 a. Uses Harmonic Mean Sample Size = 10.000.

Figure 16

SPSS printout of Tukey's multiple comparisons for the golf ball data

Table 6	Pairwise Comparisons for Example 6
Brand Comparison	**Confidence Interval**
$(\mu_A - \mu_B)$	$(-15.82, -4.74)$
$(\mu_A - \mu_C)$	$(-24.71, -13.63)$
$(\mu_A - \mu_D)$	$(-4.08, 7.00)$
$(\mu_B - \mu_C)$	$(-14.43, -3.35)$
$(\mu_B - \mu_D)$	$(6.20, 17.28)$
$(\mu_C - \mu_D)$	$(15.09, 26.17)$

that are *not* significantly different. This summary is shown in Figure 17. A similar summary is shown at the bottom of the SPSS printout, Figure 16. The interpretation is that Brand C's mean distance exceeds all others; Brand B's mean exceeds that of Brands A and D; and the means of Brands A and D do not differ significantly. All these inferences are made simultaneously with 95% confidence, the overall confidence level of the Tukey multiple comparisons.

Figure 17

Summary of Tukey multiple comparisons

Mean: 249.3 250.8 261.1 270.0
Brand: D   A   B   C

b. Brand C is ranked highest; thus, we want a confidence interval for μ_C. Because the samples were selected independently in a completely randomized design, a confidence interval for an individual treatment mean is obtained with the one-sample t confidence interval, using the mean square for error, MSE, as the measure of sampling variability for the experiment. A 95% confidence interval on the mean distance traveled by Brand C (apparently the "longest ball" of those tested), is

$$\bar{x}_C \pm t_{.025} \sqrt{\frac{\text{MSE}}{n}}$$

where $n = 10$, $t_{.025} \approx 2$ (based on 36 degrees of freedom), and MSE = 21.175 (obtained from the Excel printout, Figure 12). Substituting, we obtain

$$270.0 \pm (2)\sqrt{\frac{21.175}{10}} = 270.0 \pm 2.9 \text{ or } (267.1, 272.9)$$

Thus, we are 95% confident that the true mean distance traveled for Brand C is between 267.1 and 272.9 yards, when hit with a driver by Iron Byron.

Look Back The easiest way to create a summary table like the one in Figure 17 is to first list the treatment means in rank order. Begin with the largest mean and compare it to (in order) the second largest mean, the third largest mean, and so on, by examining the appropriate confidence intervals shown on the computer printout. If a confidence interval contains 0, then connect the two means with a line. (These two means are not significantly different.) Continue in this manner by comparing the second largest mean with the third largest, fourth largest, and so on, until all possible $c = \frac{(k)(k + 1)}{2}$ comparisons are made.

Now Work Exercise 39

Remember that the Tukey method—designed for comparing pairs of treatment means with equal sample sizes—is just one of numerous multiple comparisons procedures available. Another technique may be more appropriate for the experimental design you employ. Consult the references for details on these other methods and when they should be applied. Guidelines for using the Tukey, Bonferroni, and Scheffé methods are given in the box.

Guidelines for Selecting a Multiple Comparisons Method in ANOVA

Method	Treatment Sample Sizes	Types of Comparisons
Tukey	Equal	Pairwise
Bonferroni	Equal or unequal	Pairwise or general contrasts (number of contrasts known)
Scheffé	Equal or unequal	General contrasts

Note: For equal sample sizes and pairwise comparisons, Tukey's method will yield simultaneous confidence intervals with the smallest width, and the Bonferroni intervals will have smaller widths than the Scheffé intervals.

STATISTICS in ACTION REVISITED

Ranking Mean PAH Measurements

We return to the problem posed in the previous Statistics in Action Revisited that is, determining the industry that is most likely to have been responsible for PAH contamination at a housing development site. Recall that we used an ANOVA for a completely randomized design to compare the mean PAH ratios for soil samples at four different locations (Development, Industry A, Industry B, and Industry C). The ANOVA F-test for the first PAH ratio revealed no significant differences among the means at the four sites. However, the ANOVA F-test for the second PAH ratio led us to conclude that the mean PAH ratios at the four sites differed in some fashion.

Now, we follow up these ANOVAs with multiple comparisons of the site (treatment) means. Since the sample sizes associated with the four sites are not equal, and because we desire pairwise comparisons of the means, the method with the highest power (i.e., the one with the greatest chance of detecting a difference when differences actually exist) is the Bonferroni multiple comparisons method. Also, this method explicitly controls the comparisonwise error rate (i.e., the overall Type I error rate).

For this problem there are four treatments (sites). Consequently, there are $c = \frac{k(k - 1)}{2} = \frac{4(3)}{2} = 6$ comparisons of interest. Using the symbol μ, to represent the

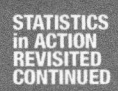

population mean PAH ratio at site j, the six comparisons we desire are: $(\mu_A - \mu_B)$, $(\mu_A - \mu_C)$, $(\mu_A - \mu_D)$, $(\mu_B - \mu_C)$, $(\mu_B - \mu_C)$, and $(\mu_C - \mu_D)$. We used Excel/XLSTAT to perform the multiple comparisons for the data saved in the **PAH** file. The results for the two dependent variables, both using an experimentwise error rate of .05, are shown in Figure SIA3a–b. Based on the confidence intervals for the differences in means, XLSTAT determines which means are significantly different. Treatments with the same letter in the "Groups" column are not significantly different.

For the first PAH ratio, all four sites have the same letter (see Figure SIA3a). Consequently, none of the four PAH ratio means differ significantly. Of course, this result is consistent with the ANOVA F-test we conducted in the previous Statistics in Action Revisited section.

The results for the second PAH ratio are shown in Figure SIA3b. You can see that the development site, Industry B, and Industry C do not have significantly different means. Similarly, the development site, Industry C, and Industry A do not have significantly different means. The only two sites found to have significantly different mean PAH2 ratios are Industry A and Industry B (since they do not have the same "Group" letter). These inferences can be made with an overall 5% chance of a Type I error.

The expert statistician used these results to conclude that although the two industries in question, Industry A and Industry B, have PAH2 ratio means that are significantly different, neither mean is significantly different from either the housing development site mean or the Industry C mean. Consequently, based on the available data, it is impossible to determine which industry (A or B) was most likely to have contaminated the development site. In fact, according to the statistician's court testimony, "The results provide clear evidence that these samples are simply too small to make a reliable determination about the sites' similarity or dissimilarity with respect to [PAH] diagnostic ratios." The statistician went on to conclude that "the small samples relied upon by [the biochemical expert] shed no light on the issue of whether [Industry A and Industry B] are similar or dissimilar to the [development] site…."

a. Development Variable = PAH1

Category	LS means	Groups
IndustryB	0.6850	A
IndustryC	0.6625	A
Development	0.6457	A
IndustryA	0.6063	A

b. Development Variable = PAH2

Category	LS means	Groups	
IndustryB	1.0980	A	
IndustryC	1.0875	A	B
Development	1.0743	A	B
IndustryA	0.9981		B

Figure SIA3
XLSTAT output for multiple comparisons of PAH ratio means

Concluding Note: The trial judge ultimately decided that the biochemist's statistical analyses and his opinions based on them would be excluded from the evidence used to decide the case. As of this date, the issue of responsibility for the pollution has still not been decided.

Exercises 35–49

Please be aware that some of the following problems may require knowledge of concepts that are not presented in this chapter.

Learning the Mechanics

35 Consider a completely randomized design with k treatments. Assume all pairwise comparisons of treatment means are to be made using a multiple comparisons procedure. Determine the total number of pairwise comparisons for the following values of k.

a. $k = 3$　　**b.** $k = 5$
c. $k = 4$　　**d.** $k = 10$

36 Define an experimentwise error rate.

37 Define a comparisonwise error rate.

38 Consider a completely randomized design with five treatments, A, B, C, D, and E. The ANOVA F-test revealed significant differences among the means. A multiple comparisons procedure was used to compare all possible pairs of treatment means at $\alpha = .05$. The ranking of the five treatment means is summarized in each part below. Identify which pairs of means are significantly different.

a. $\overline{A\ C\ E}\ \overline{B\ D}$ **b.** $\overline{A\ C\ E}\ \ B\ D$

c. $\overline{A\ C\ E\ B\ D}$ **d.** $A\ \overline{C\ E\ B}\ D$

39 A multiple comparison procedure for comparing four treatment means produced the confidence intervals shown here. Rank the means from smallest to largest. Which means are significantly different?

NW

$(\mu_1 - \mu_2)$: $(2, 15)$
$(\mu_1 - \mu_3)$: $(4, 7)$
$(\mu_1 - \mu_4)$: $(-10, 3)$
$(\mu_2 - \mu_3)$: $(-5, 11)$
$(\mu_2 - \mu_4)$: $(-12, -6)$
$(\mu_3 - \mu_4)$: $(-8, -5)$

Applying the Concepts—Basic

40 **How workers respond to wage cuts.** Refer to the *Institute for the Study of Labor: Discussion Paper Series* (March 2011) study of how workers respond to wage cuts, Exercise 22. Recall that teams of workers were divided into three wage cut groups: "unilateral wage cut," "general wage cut," and "baseline" (no wage cut). The researchers determined that the average decrease in promotional cards sold differed depending on the wage cut treatment group. Now the researchers want to rank the treatment means by making all possible pairwise comparisons.

a. How many pairwise comparisons make up this phase of the study? List them.

b. Why is a multiple comparisons procedure like Tukey's recommended for the analysis?

c. The confidence interval for the difference between the means for "baseline" and "general wage cut," i.e., for $(\mu_{baseline} - \mu_{general})$, includes only positive values. Interpret this result.

41 **Performance of a bus depot.** Refer to the *International Journal of Engineering Science and Technology* (February 2011) study of public bus depot performance, Exercise 23. Recall that 150 customers provided overall performance ratings at each of three different bus depots (Depot 1, Depot 2, and Depot 3). The average performance scores were determined to be significantly different at $\alpha = .05$ using an ANOVA F-test. The sample mean performance scores were reported as $\bar{x}_1 = 67.17$, $\bar{x}_2 = 58.95$, and $\bar{x}_3 = 44.49$. The researchers employed the Bonferroni method to rank the three performance means using an experimentwise error rate of .05. Adjusted 95% confidence intervals for the differences between each pair of treatment means are shown in the table. Use this information to rank the mean performance scores at the three bus depots.

Comparison	Adjusted 95% CI
$(\mu_1 - \mu_2)$	$(1.50, 14.94)$
$(\mu_1 - \mu_3)$	$(15.96, 29.40)$
$(\mu_2 - \mu_3)$	$(7.74, 21.18)$

42 **Guilt in decision making.** The effect of guilt emotion on how a decision maker focuses on a problem was investigated in the Jan. 2007 issue of the *Journal of Behavioral Decision Making*. A sample of 77 volunteer students participated in one portion of the experiment, where each was randomly assigned to one of three emotional states (guilt, anger, or neutral) through a reading/writing task. Immediately after the task, students were presented with a decision problem where the stated option had predominantly negative features (e.g., spending money on repairing a very old car). Prior to making the decision, the researchers asked each subject to list possible, more attractive alternatives. The researchers then compared the mean number of alternatives listed across the three emotional states with an analysis of variance for a completely randomized design. A partial ANOVA summary table is shown below.

Source	df	F-Value	p-Value
Emotional State	2	22.68	0.001
Error	74		
Total	76		

a. What conclusion can you draw from the ANOVA results?

b. A multiple comparisons of means procedure was applied to the data using an experimentwise error rate of .05. Explain what the .05 represents.

c. The multiple comparisons yielded the following results. What conclusion can you draw?

Sample mean:	1.90	2.17	4.75
Emotional state:	Angry	Neutral	Guilt

43 **Study of mutual fund performance.** Refer to the *American Business Review* (Jan. 2002) comparison of large-cap, medium-cap, and small-cap mutual funds, Exercise 26. Using an experimentwise error rate of .05, Tukey confidence intervals for the difference between mean rates of return for all possible pairs of fund types are given below.

Comparison	Tukey Confidence Interval
$\mu_{Large} - \mu_{Medium}$	$(-.1847, 5.3807)$
$\mu_{Large} - \mu_{Small}$	$(2.4426, 8.0080)$
$\mu_{Medium} - \mu_{Small}$	$(-.1554, 5.4100)$

a. Why is the Tukey multiple comparisons method preferred over another method?

b. Is there a significant difference between the treatment means for large-cap and medium-cap mutual funds? Explain.

c. Is there a significant difference between the treatment means for large-cap and small-cap mutual funds? Explain.

d. Is there a significant difference between the treatment means for medium-cap and small-cap mutual funds? Explain.

e. Use your answers to parts **b–d** to rank the treatment means.

f. Give a measure of reliability for the inference in part **e**.

44 Does the media influence your attitude toward tanning? Refer to the *Basic and Applied Social Psychology* (May 2010) study of whether product advertisements influence consumers' attitudes toward tanning, Exercise 29. Recall that college students were randomly assigned to one of three conditions—view product advertisements featuring models with a tan, view product advertisements featuring models without a tan, or view products advertised with no models. An ANOVA *F*-test revealed that the mean attitude toward tanning differed across the conditions. The researchers followed up this analysis with a multiple comparisons of means using an experimentwise error rate of .05. These results are summarized below. Fully interpret the results. Does it appear that the type of product advertisement can influence a consumer's attitude toward tanning?

Mean:	2.11	2.40	2.50
Condition:	Models/No Tan	Tanned Models	No Models

Applying the Concepts—Intermediate

45 Income and road rage. Refer to the *Accident Analysis and Prevention* (Vol. 34, 2002) study of road rage, Exercise 27. Recall that the mean road rage scores of drivers in the three income groups, under $30,000, between $30,000 and $60,000, and over $60,000, were 4.60, 5.08, and 5.15, respectively.

a. An experimentwise error rate of .01 was used to rank the three means. Give a practical interpretation of this error rate.

b. How many pairwise comparisons are necessary to compare the three means? List them.

c. A multiple comparisons procedure revealed that the means for the income groups $30,000–$60,000 and over $60,000 were not significantly different. All other pairs of means were found to be significantly different. Summarize these results in table form.

d. Which of the comparisons of part **b** will yield a confidence interval that does not contain 0?

46 Study of recall of TV commercials. Refer to the *Journal of Applied Psychology* (June 2002) completely randomized design study to compare the mean commercial recall scores of viewers of three TV programs, presented in Exercise 28. Recall that one program had a violent content code (V) rating, one had a sex content code (S) rating, and one was a neutral TV program. Using Tukey's method, the researchers conducted multiple comparisons of the three mean recall scores.

 ADREC

a. How many pairwise comparisons were made in this study?

b. The multiple comparison procedure was applied to the data and the results are shown in the Minitab printout at the bottom of the page. An experimentwise error rate of .05 was used. Locate the confidence interval for the comparison of the V and S groups. Interpret this result practically.

c. Repeat part **b** for the remaining comparisons. Which of the groups has the largest mean recall score?

d. In the journal article, the researchers concluded that "memory for [television] commercials is impaired after watching violent or sexual programming." Do you agree?

47 Effectiveness of sales closing techniques. Refer to the *B2B Marketing Insider* (Oct. 7, 2010) comparison of six sales closing techniques, Exercise 31. Assume the "level of trust" means for prospects of salespeople using each of the six closing techniques are listed in the table.

Minitab output for Exercise 46

```
Grouping Information Using Tukey Method

            N   Mean  Grouping
NEUTRAL   108   3.167  A
VIOLENT   108   2.083      B
SEX       108   1.713      B

Means that do not share a letter are significantly different.


Tukey 95% Simultaneous Confidence Intervals
All Pairwise Comparisons

Individual confidence level = 98.01%


VIOLENT subtracted from:

          Lower   Center  Upper   -------+---------+---------+---------+--
SEX      -0.923  -0.370  0.183            (----*----)
NEUTRAL   0.530   1.083  1.636                      (----*----)
                                  -------+---------+---------+---------+--
                                     -1.2      0.0       1.2       2.4


SEX subtracted from:

          Lower   Center  Upper   -------+---------+---------+---------+--
NEUTRAL   0.901   1.454  2.007                     (---*----)
                                  -------+---------+---------+---------+--
                                     -1.2      0.0       1.2       2.4
```

A multiple comparisons of means analysis was conducted (at $\alpha = .05$), with the results shown in the third column of the table. Fully interpret the results.

Treatments: Closing Technique	Mean Level of Trust	Differing Treatments
1. No close	4.70	1 from 5 and 6
2. Financial close	4.50	2 from 6
3. Time Line close	4.40	No differences
4. Sympathy close	4.35	No differences
5. The Visual close	4.00	5 from 1
6. Thermometer close	3.95	6 from 1 and 2

48 Is honey a cough remedy? Refer to the *Archives of Pediatrics and Adolescent Medicine* (Dec. 2007) study of treatments for children's cough symptoms, Exercise 32. Do you agree with the statement (extracted from the article), "Honey may be a preferable treatment for the cough and sleep difficulty associated with childhood upper respiratory tract infection"? Perform a multiple comparisons of means to answer the question.

HCOUGH

49 Commercial eggs produced from different housing systems. Refer to the *Food Chemistry* (Vol. 106, 2008)

EGGS

study of four different types of egg housing systems, Exercise 33. Recall that you analyzed the data file and discovered that the mean shell thickness (millimeters) differed for cage, barn, free range, and organic egg housing systems. A multiple comparisons of means was conducted using the Bonferroni method with an experimentwise error rate of .05. The results are displayed in the SPSS printout below.

a. Locate the confidence interval for $(\mu_{CAGE} - \mu_{BARN})$ on the printout and interpret the result.

b. Locate the confidence interval for $(\mu_{CAGE} - \mu_{FREE})$ on the printout and interpret the result.

c. Locate the confidence interval for $(\mu_{CAGE} - \mu_{ORGANIC})$ on the printout and interpret the result.

d. Locate the confidence interval for $(\mu_{BARN} - \mu_{FREE})$ on the printout and interpret the result.

e. Locate the confidence interval for $(\mu_{BARN} - \mu_{ORGANIC})$ on the printout and interpret the result.

f. Locate the confidence interval for $(\mu_{FREE} - \mu_{ORGANIC})$ on the printout and interpret the result.

g. Based on the results, parts **a–f**, provide a ranking of the housing system means. Include the experimentwise error rate as a statement of reliability.

SPSS output for Exercise 49

Multiple Comparisons

THICKNESS
Bonferroni

(I) HOUSE	(J) HOUSE	Mean Difference (I-J)	Std. Error	Sig.	95% Confidence Interval	
					Lower Bound	Upper Bound
CAGE	BARN	-.07867*	.01612	.000	-.1250	-.0323
	FREE	-.07700*	.01612	.000	-.1233	-.0307
	ORGANIC	-.05867*	.01612	.008	-.1050	-.0123
BARN	CAGE	.07867*	.01612	.000	.0323	.1250
	FREE	.00167	.01802	1.000	-.0501	.0535
	ORGANIC	.02000	.01802	1.000	-.0318	.0718
FREE	CAGE	.07700*	.01612	.000	.0307	.1233
	BARN	-.00167	.01802	1.000	-.0535	.0501
	ORGANIC	.01833	.01802	1.000	-.0335	.0701
ORGANIC	CAGE	.05867*	.01612	.008	.0123	.1050
	BARN	-.02000	.01802	1.000	-.0718	.0318
	FREE	-.01833	.01802	1.000	-.0701	.0335

*. The mean difference is significant at the 0.05 level.

4 The Randomized Block Design

If the completely randomized design results in nonrejection of the null hypothesis that the treatment means differ because the sampling variability (as measured by MSE) is large, we may want to consider an experimental design that better controls the variability. In contrast to the selection of independent samples of experimental units specified by the completely randomized design, the *randomized block design* uses experimental units that are *matched sets,* assigning one from each set to each treatment. The matched sets of experimental units are called *blocks.* The theory behind the randomized block design is that the sampling variability of the experimental units in each block will be reduced, in turn reducing the measure of error, MSE.

The **randomized block design** consists of a two-step procedure:

1. Matched sets of experimental units, called **blocks,** are formed, each block consisting of k experimental units (where k is the number of treatments). The b blocks should consist of experimental units that are as similar as possible.
2. One experimental unit from each block is randomly assigned to each treatment, resulting in a total of $n = bk$ responses.

For example, if we wish to compare the SAT scores of female and male high school seniors, we could select independent random samples of five females and five males, and analyze the results of the completely randomized design as outlined in Section 2. Or, we could select matched pairs of females and males according to their scholastic records and analyze the SAT scores of the pairs. For instance, we could select pairs of students with approximately the same GPAs from the same high school. Five such pairs (blocks) are depicted in Table 7. Note that this is just a *paired difference experiment.*

As before, the variation between the treatment means is measured by squaring the distance between each treatment mean and the overall mean, multiplying each squared distance by the number of measurements for the treatment, and summing over treatments:

$$\text{SST} = \sum_{i=1}^{k} b(\bar{x}_{T_i} - \bar{x})^2$$
$$= 5(606 - 600)^2 + 5(594 - 600)^2 = 360$$

where $\bar{x}_{T_i}$ represents the sample mean for the ith treatment, b (the number of blocks) is the number of measurements for each treatment, and k is the number of treatments.

The blocks also account for some of the variation among the different responses — that is, just as SST measures the variation between the female and male means, we can calculate a measure of variation among the five block means representing different schools and scholastic abilities. Analogous to the computation of SST, we sum the squares of the differences between each block mean and the overall mean, multiplying each squared difference by the number of measurements for each block, and sum over blocks to calculate the **Sum of Squares for Blocks (SSB):**

$$\text{SSB} = \sum_{i=1}^{b} k(\bar{x}_{B_i} - \bar{x})^2$$
$$= 2(535 - 600)^2 + 2(560 - 600)^2 + 2(585 - 600)^2$$
$$+ 2(630 - 600)^2 + 2(690 - 600)^2$$
$$= 30{,}100$$

where $\bar{x}_{B_i}$ represents the sample mean for the ith block and k (the number of treatments) is the number of measurements in each block. As we expect, the variation in SAT scores attributable to schools and levels of scholastic achievement is apparently large.

Now, we want to compare the variability attributed to treatments with that which is attributed to sampling variability. In a randomized block design, the sampling variability is measured by subtracting that portion attributed to treatments and blocks from the

Table 7	Randomized Block Design: SAT Score Comparison		
Block	Female SAT Score	Male SAT Score	Block Mean
1 (school A, 2.75 GPA)	540	530	535
2 (school B, 3.00 GPA)	570	550	560
3 (school C, 3.25 GPA)	590	580	585
4 (school D, 3.50 GPA)	640	620	630
5 (school E, 3.75 GPA)	690	690	690
Treatment Mean	606	594	

Data Set: HSSAT3

Total Sum of Squares, SS(Total). The total variation is the sum of squared differences of each measurement from the overall mean:

$$SS(Total) = \sum_{i=1}^{n}(x_i - \bar{x})^2$$

$$= (540 - 600)^2 + (530 - 600)^2 + (570 - 600)^2 + (550 - 600)^2$$

$$+ \cdots + (690 - 600)^2$$

$$= 30,600$$

Then the variation attributable to sampling error is found by subtraction:

$$SSE = SS(Total) - SST - SSB = 30,600 - 360 - 30,100 = 140$$

In summary, the Total Sum of Squares—30,600—is divided into three components: 360 attributed to treatments (Gender), 30,100 attributed to blocks (Scholastic ability and School), and 140 attributed to sampling error.

The mean squares associated with each source of variability are obtained by dividing the sum of squares by the appropriate number of degrees of freedom. The partitioning of the Total Sum of Squares and the total degrees of freedom for a randomized block experiment is summarized in Figure 18.

To determine whether we can reject the null hypothesis that the treatment means are equal in favor of the alternative that at least two of them differ, we calculate

$$MST = \frac{SST}{k-1} = \frac{360}{2-1} = 360$$

$$MSE = \frac{SSE}{n-b-k+1} = \frac{140}{10-5-2+1} = 35$$

The F-ratio that is used to test the hypothesis is

$$F = \frac{360}{35} = 10.29$$

Comparing this ratio to the tabled F value corresponding to $\alpha = .05$, $v_1 = (k-1) = 1$ degree of freedom in the numerator, and $v_2 = (n-b-k+1) = 4$ degrees of freedom in the denominator, we find that

$$F = 10.29 > F_{.05} = 7.71$$

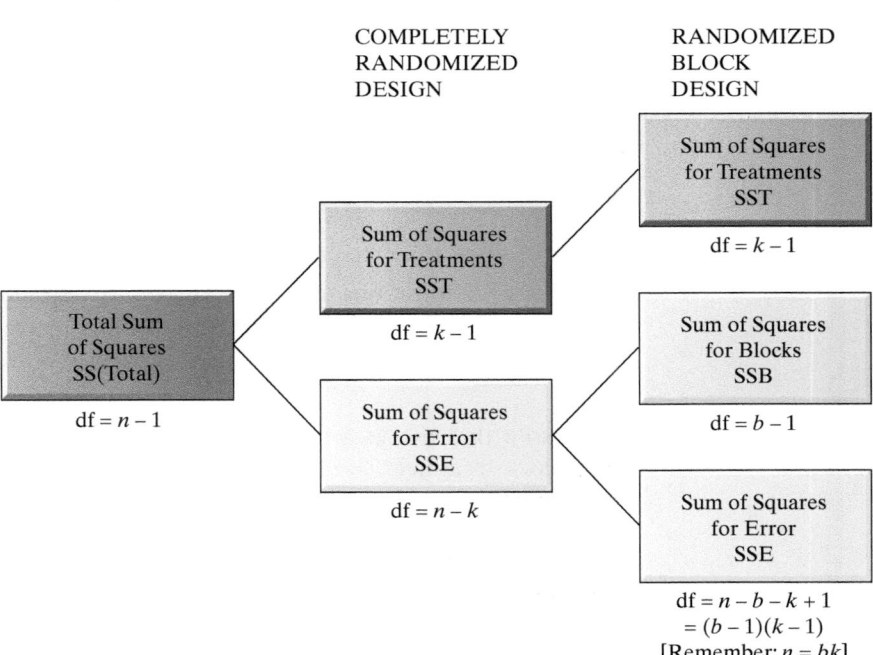

Figure 18

Partitioning of the total sum of squares for the randomized block design

Two-way ANOVA: SAT versus GENDER, BLOCK

Source	DF	SS	MS	F	P
GENDER	1	360	360	10.29	0.033
BLOCK	4	30100	7525	215.00	0.000
Error	4	140	35		
Total	9	30600			

Figure 19

Minitab printout with ANOVA results for the data in Table 7

which indicates that we should reject the null hypothesis and conclude that the mean SAT scores differ for females and males. All of these calculations, of course, can be obtained using statistical software. The output for the Minitab analysis of the data in Table 7 is shown in Figure 19. The values of SST, SSE, MST, MSE, and F are highlighted on the printout.

Comment: The analysis of a paired difference experiment results in a one-sample t-test on the differences between the treatment responses within each block. Applying the procedure to the differences between female and male scores in Table 7, we find

$$t = \frac{\bar{x}_d}{s_d/\sqrt{n_d}} = \frac{12}{\sqrt{70}/\sqrt{5}} = 3.207$$

At the .05 level of significance with $(n_d - 1) = 4$ degrees of freedom,

$$t = 3.21 > t_{.025} = 2.776$$

Since $t^2 = (3.207)^2 = 10.29$ and $t_{.025}^2 = (2.776)^2 = 7.71$, we find that the paired difference t-test and the ANOVA F-test are equivalent, with both the calculated test statistics and the rejection region related by the formula $F = t^2$. The difference between the tests is that the paired difference t-test can be used to compare only two treatments in a randomized block design, whereas the F-test can be applied to *two or more* treatments in a randomized block design.

The F-test is summarized in the following box.

ANOVA F-Test to Compare k Treatment Means: Randomized Block Design

$H_0: \mu_1 = \mu_2 = \cdots = \mu_k$

$H_a:$ At least two treatment means differ

Test statistic: $F = \dfrac{MST}{MSE}$

Rejection region: $F > F_\alpha$, where F_α is based on $(k - 1)$ numerator degrees of freedom and $(n - b - k + 1)$ denominator degrees of freedom.

Conditions Required for a Valid ANOVA F-Test: Randomized Block Design

1. The b blocks are randomly selected, and all k treatments are applied (in random order) to each block.

2. The distributions of observations corresponding to all bk block-treatment combinations are approximately normal.

3. The bk block-treatment distributions have equal variances.

Note that the assumptions concern the probability distributions associated with each block-treatment combination. The experimental unit selected for each combination is assumed to have been randomly selected from all possible experimental units for that combination, and the response is assumed to be normally distributed with the same variance for each of the block-treatment combinations. For example, the F-test comparing female and male SAT score means requires the scores for each combination of gender and scholastic ability (e.g., females with 3.25 GPA from School C) to be normally distributed with the same variance as the other combinations employed in the experiment.

For those who are interested, the calculation formulas for randomized block designs are given in Appendix: Calculation Formulas for Analysis of Variance. Throughout this section, we will rely on statistical software packages to analyze randomized block designs and to obtain the necessary ingredients for testing the null hypothesis that the treatment means are equal.

Example **7**	**Problem** Refer to Examples 4–6. Suppose the USGA wants to compare the mean distances associated with the four brands of golf balls when struck by a driver but wishes to employ human golfers rather than the robot Iron Byron. Assume that 10 balls of each brand are to be used in the experiment.

Experimental Design Principles

a. Explain how a completely randomized design could be employed.

b. Explain how a randomized block design could be employed.

c. Which design is likely to provide more information about the differences among the brand mean distances?

Solution

a. Because the completely randomized design calls for independent samples, we can employ such a design by randomly selecting 40 golfers and then randomly assigning 10 golfers to each of the four brands. Finally, each golfer will strike the ball of the assigned brand, and the distance will be recorded. The design is illustrated in Figure 20a.

b. The randomized block design employs blocks of relatively homogeneous experimental units. For example, we could randomly select 10 golfers and permit each golfer to hit four balls, one of each brand, in a random sequence. Then each golfer is a block, with each treatment (brand) assigned to each block (golfer). The design is summarized in Figure 20b.

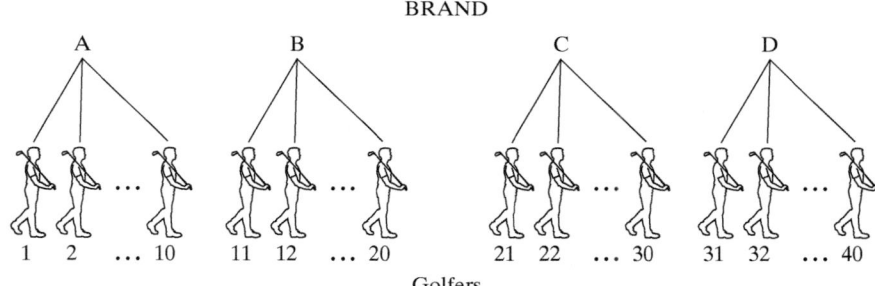

BRAND

a. Completely randomized design

BRAND

		A	B	C	D
Golfers	1	Hit 3	Hit 1	Hit 4	Hit 2
	2	Hit 2	Hit 4	Hit 3	Hit 1
	⋮	⋮	⋮	⋮	⋮
	10	Hit 4	Hit 3	Hit 1	Hit 2

b. Randomized block design

Figure 20

Illustration of completely randomized design and randomized block design: comparison of four golf ball brands

c. Because we expect much more variability among distances generated by "real" golfers than by Iron Byron, we would expect the randomized block design to control the variability better than the completely randomized design—that is, with 40 different golfers, we would expect the sampling variability among the measured distances within each brand to be greater than that among the four distances generated by each of 10 golfers hitting one ball of each brand.

◾ **Now Work Exercise 54**

Example 8

Randomized Block Design—Comparing Golf Ball Brands

Problem Refer to Example 7. Suppose the randomized block design of part **b** is employed, employing a random sample of 10 golfers, with each golfer using a driver to hit four balls, one of each brand, in a random sequence.

a. Set up a test of the research hypothesis that the brand mean distances differ. Use $\alpha = .05$.

b. The data for the experiment are given in Table 8. Use statistical software to analyze the data and conduct the test set up in part **a**.

Solution

a. We want to test whether the data in Table 8 provide sufficient evidence to conclude that the brand mean distances differ. Denoting the population mean of the ith brand by μ_i, we test

$$H_0: \mu_1 = \mu_2 = \mu_3 = \mu_4$$

H_a: The mean distances differ for at least two of the brands.

The test statistic compares the variation among the four treatment (brand) means to the sampling variability within each of the treatments.

$$\text{Test statistic: } F = \frac{\text{MST}}{\text{MSE}}$$

Rejection region: $F > F_\alpha = F_{.05}$, with $v_1 = (k - 1) = 3$ numerator degrees of freedom and $v_2 = (n - k - b + 1) = 27$ denominator degrees of freedom. From Table VI in Appendix: Tables we find $F_{.05} = 2.96$. Thus, we will reject H_0 if $F > 2.96$.

The assumptions necessary to ensure the validity of the test are as follows: (1) The probability distributions of the distances for each brand–golfer combination are normal. (2) The variances of the distance probability distributions for each brand–golfer combination are equal.

b. Minitab was used to analyze the data in Table 8, and the result is shown in Figure 21. The values of MST and MSE (highlighted on the printout) are 1,099.6 and 20.2, respectively. The F-ratio for Brand (also highlighted on the printout) is

Table 8	Distance Data for Randomized Block Design			
Golfer (Block)	Brand A	Brand B	Brand C	Brand D
1	202.4	203.2	223.7	203.6
2	242.0	248.7	259.8	240.7
3	220.4	227.3	240.0	207.4
4	230.0	243.1	247.7	226.9
5	191.6	211.4	218.7	200.1
6	247.7	253.0	268.1	244.0
7	214.8	214.8	233.9	195.8
8	245.4	243.6	257.8	227.9
9	224.0	231.5	238.2	215.7
10	252.2	255.2	265.4	245.2
Sample Means	227.0	233.2	245.3	220.7

💿 *Data Set:* GLFRBD

Figure 21

Minitab randomized block design ANOVA: golf ball brand comparison

```
Two-way ANOVA: DISTANCE versus BRAND, GOLFER

Source   DF      SS      MS       F      P
BRAND     3   3298.7  1099.55  54.31  0.000
GOLFER    9  12073.9  1341.54  66.26  0.000
Error    27    546.6    20.25
Total    39  15919.2

S = 4.499   R-Sq = 96.57%   R-Sq(adj) = 95.04%
```

$F = 54.31$, which exceeds the tabled value of 2.96. We therefore reject the null hypothesis at the $\alpha = .05$ level of significance, concluding that at least two of the brands differ with respect to mean distance traveled when struck by the driver.

Look Back The result of part **b** can also be obtained by noting that the observed significance level of the test, highlighted on the printout, is $p \approx 0$.

■ **Now Work Exercise 56**

The results of an ANOVA can be summarized in a simple tabular format, similar to that used for the completely randomized design in Section 2. The general form of the table is shown in Table 9, and that for Example 8 is given in Table 10. Note that the randomized block design is characterized by three sources of variation—Treatments, Blocks, and Error—which sum to the Total Sum of Squares. We hope that employing blocks of experimental units will reduce the error of variability, thereby making the test for comparing treatment means more powerful.

When the F-test results in the rejection of the null hypothesis that the treatment means are equal, we will usually want to compare the various pairs of treatment means to determine which specific pairs differ. We can employ a multiple comparisons procedure as in Section 3. The number of pairs of means to be compared will again be $c = \frac{k(k-1)}{2}$, where k is the number of treatment means. In Example 8, $c = \frac{4(3)}{2} = 6$; that is, there are six pairs of golf ball brand means to be compared.

Table 9	General ANOVA Summary Table for a Randomized Block Design			
Source	df	SS	MS	F
Treatments	$k-1$	SST	MST	MST/MSE
Blocks	$b-1$	SSB	MSB	
Error	$n-k-b+1$	SSE	MSE	
Total	$n-1$	SS(Total)		

Table 10	ANOVA Table for Example 8				
Source	df	SS	MS	F	p
Treatments (brand)	3	3,298.7	1,099.6	54.31	.000
Blocks (golfer)	9	12,073.9	1,341.5		
Error	27	546.6	20.2		
Total	39	15,919.2			

Example   9

Ranking Treatment Means in a Randomized Block Design—Golf Ball Study

Problem Apply Bonferroni's procedure to the data in Example 8. Use an experiment-wise error rate (EER) of .05 to rank the mean distances of the four golf ball brands. Interpret the results.

Solution We used Excel/XLSTAT to obtain the rankings of the means with Bonferroni's method. The XLSTAT printout is shown in Figure 22. Since there are $k = 4$ treatments (brands) in this design, there are $c = \frac{4(3)}{2} = 6$ pairwise

comparisons of brand means to be analyzed. These comparisons (contrasts) are shown at the top of Figure 22. Rather than give a confidence interval for each comparison, XLSTAT provides information to determine whether the two means being compared are significantly different. You can see that when EER = .05, all six comparisons yield significant differences. (This is equivalent to stating that none of the six confidence intervals contain 0.) Consequently, with overall 95% confidence we can conclude that the true mean driving distances for all four golf ball brands differ from each other.

BRAND / Bonferroni / Analysis of the differences between the categories with a confidence interval of 95%:

Contrast	Difference	Standardized difference	Critical value	Pr > Diff	Significant
BrandC vs BrandD	24.6000	12.2253	2.8469	< 0.0001	Yes
BrandC vs BrandA	18.2800	9.0845	2.8469	< 0.0001	Yes
BrandC vs BrandB	12.1500	6.0381	2.8469	< 0.0001	Yes
BrandB vs BrandD	12.4500	6.1872	2.8469	< 0.0001	Yes
BrandB vs BrandA	6.1300	3.0464	2.8469	0.0051	Yes
BrandA vs BrandD	6.3200	3.1408	2.8469	0.0041	Yes
Modified significance level:			0.0083		

Category	Mean		Groups		
BrandC	245.3300	A			
BrandB	233.1800		B		
BrandA	227.0500			C	
BrandD	220.7300				D

Figure 22

XLSTAT output of Bonferroni rankings of golf ball brand means

The bottom of Figure 22 gives the rankings of the four brands as well as the sample mean driving distances. (Note that each brand is associated with a different group letter.) So, with overall 95% confidence, we have $\mu_C > \mu_B > \mu_A > \mu_D$.

■ Now Work Exercise 57d

Unlike the completely randomized design, the randomized block design cannot, in general, be used to estimate individual treatment means. Whereas the completely randomized design employs a random sample for each treatment, the randomized block design does not necessarily employ a random sample of experimental units for each treatment. The experimental units within the blocks are assumed to be randomly selected, but the blocks themselves may not be randomly selected.

We can, however, test the hypothesis that the block means are significantly different. We simply compare the variability attributable to differences among the block means to that associated with sampling variability. The ratio of MSB to MSE is an F-ratio similar to that formed in testing treatment means. The F-statistic is compared to a tabled value for a specific value of α, with numerator degrees of freedom $(b - 1)$ and denominator degrees of freedom $(n - k - b + 1)$. The test is usually given on the same printout as the test for treatment means. Refer to the Minitab printout in Figure 21 and note that the test statistic for comparing the block means is

$$F = \frac{MSB}{MSE} = \frac{MS(\text{Golfers})}{MS(\text{Error})} = \frac{1,341.5}{20.2} = 66.26$$

with a p-value of .000. Because $\alpha = .05$ exceeds this p-value, we conclude that the block means are different. The results of the test are summarized in Table 11.

In the golf example, the test for block means confirms our suspicion that the golfers vary significantly; therefore, use of the block design was a good decision. However,

Table 11	ANOVA Table for Randomized Block Design: Test for Blocks Included				
Source	df	SS	MS	F	p
Treatments (brands)	3	3,298.7	1,099.6	54.31	.000
Blocks (golfers)	9	12,073.9	1,341.5	66.26	.000
Error	27	546.6	20.2		
Total	39	15,919.2			

be careful not to conclude that the block design was a mistake if the F-test for blocks does not result in rejection of the null hypothesis that the block means are the same. Remember that the possibility of a Type II error exists, and we are not controlling its probability as we are the probability α of a Type I error. If the experimenter believes that the experimental units are more homogeneous within blocks than between blocks, then he or she should use the randomized block design regardless of the results of a single test comparing the block means.

The procedure for conducting an analysis of variance for a randomized block design is summarized in the next box. Remember that the hallmark of this design is using blocks of homogeneous experimental units in which each treatment is represented.

Steps for Conducting an ANOVA for a Randomized Block Design

1. Be sure the design consists of blocks (preferably, blocks of homogeneous experimental units) and that each treatment is randomly assigned to one experimental unit in each block.

2. If possible, check the assumptions of normality and equal variances for all block-treatment combinations. [*Note:* This may be difficult to do because the design will likely have only one observation for each block-treatment combination.]

3. Create an ANOVA summary table that specifies the variability attributable to Treatments, Blocks, and Error, which leads to the calculation of the F-statistic to test the null hypothesis that the treatment means are equal in the population. Use a statistical software package or the calculation formulas in Appendix: Calculation Formulas for Analysis of Variance to obtain the necessary numerical ingredients.

4. If the F-test leads to the conclusion that the means differ, use the Bonferroni, Tukey, or similar procedure to conduct multiple comparisons of as many of the pairs of means as you wish. Use the results to summarize the statistically significant differences among the treatment means. Remember that, in general, the randomized block design cannot be used to form confidence intervals for individual treatment means.

5. If the F-test leads to the nonrejection of the null hypothesis that the treatment means are equal, several possibilities exist:
   a. The treatment means are equal—that is, the null hypothesis is true.
   b. The treatment means really differ, but other important factors affecting the response are not accounted for by the randomized block design. These factors inflate the sampling variability, as measured by MSE, resulting in smaller values of the F-statistic. Either increase the sample size for each treatment or conduct an experiment that accounts for the other factors affecting the response (as in Section 5). Do not automatically reach the former conclusion because the possibility of a Type II error must be considered if you accept H_0.

6. If desired, conduct the F-test of the null hypothesis that the block means are equal. Rejection of this hypothesis lends statistical support to using the randomized block design.

Note: It is often difficult to check whether the assumptions for a randomized block design are satisfied. There is usually only one observation for each block-treatment combination. When you feel these assumptions are likely to be violated, a nonparametric procedure is advisable.

What Do You Do When Assumptions Are Not Satisfied for the Analysis of Variance for a Randomized Block Design?

Answer: Use a nonparametric statistical method such as the Friedman F_r test.

Exercises 50–63

Learning the Mechanics

50 A randomized block design yielded the following ANOVA table.

Source	df	SS	MS	F
Treatments	4	501	125.25	9.109
Blocks	2	225	112.50	8.182
Error	8	110	13.75	
Total	14	836		

a. How many blocks and treatments were used in the experiment?

b. How many observations were collected in the experiment?

c. Specify the null and alternative hypotheses you would use to compare the treatment means.

d. What test statistic should be used to conduct the hypothesis test of part **c**?

e. Specify the rejection region for the test of parts **c** and **d**. Use $\alpha = .01$.

f. Conduct the test of parts **c–e** and state the proper conclusion.

g. What assumptions are necessary to ensure the validity of the test you conducted in part **f**?

51 An experiment was conducted using a randomized block design. The data from the experiment are displayed in the following table.

L09051

	Block		
Treatment	1	2	3
1	2	3	5
2	8	6	7
3	7	6	5

a. Fill in the missing entries in the ANOVA table.

Source	df	SS	MS	F
Treatments	2	21.5555		
Blocks	2			
Error	4			
Total	8	30.2222		

b. Specify the null and alternative hypotheses you would use to investigate whether a difference exists among the treatment means.

c. What test statistic should be used in conducting the test of part **b**?

d. Describe the Type I and Type II errors associated with the hypothesis test of part **b**.

e. Conduct the hypothesis test of part **b** using $\alpha = .05$.

52 A randomized block design was used to compare the mean responses for three treatments. Four blocks of three homogeneous experimental units were selected, and each treatment was randomly assigned to one experimental unit within each block. The data are shown in the next table, and the SPSS ANOVA printout for this experiment is shown below.

L09052

	Block			
Treatment	1	2	3	4
A	3.4	5.5	7.9	1.3
B	4.4	5.8	9.6	2.8
C	2.2	3.4	6.9	.3

Tests of Between-Subjects Effects

Dependent Variable: RESPONSE

Source	Type III Sum of Squares	df	Mean Square	F	Sig.
Corrected Model	83.781ᵃ	5	16.756	141.935	.000
Intercept	238.521	1	238.521	2020.412	.000
TRTMENT	12.032	2	6.016	50.958	.000
BLOCK	71.749	3	23.916	202.586	.000
Error	.708	6	.118		
Total	323.010	12			
Corrected Total	84.489	11			

a. R Squared = .992 (Adjusted R Squared = .985)

Multiple Comparisons

Dependent Variable: RESPONSE
Tukey HSD

(I) TRTMENT	(J) TRTMENT	Mean Difference (I-J)	Std. Error	Sig.	95% Confidence Interval	
					Lower Bound	Upper Bound
A	B	−1.125*	.2430	.009	−1.870	−.380
	C	1.325*	.2430	.004	.580	2.070
B	A	1.125*	.2430	.009	.380	1.870
	C	2.450*	.2430	.000	1.705	3.195
C	A	−1.325*	.2430	.004	−2.070	−.580
	B	−2.450*	.2430	.000	−3.195	−1.705

Based on observed means.

*. The mean difference is significant at the .05 level.

a. Use the printout to fill in the entries in the following ANOVA table.

Source	df	SS	MS	F
Treatments				
Blocks				
Error				
Total				

b. Do the data provide sufficient evidence to indicate that the treatment means differ? Use $\alpha = .05$.

c. Do the data provide sufficient evidence to indicate that blocking was effective in reducing the experimental error? Use $\alpha = .05$.

d. Use the printout to rank the treatment means at $\alpha = .05$.

e. What assumptions are necessary to ensure the validity of the inferences made in parts **b, c,** and **d**?

53 Suppose an experiment employing a randomized block design has four treatments and nine blocks, for a total of $4 \times 9 = 36$ observations. Assume that the Total Sum of Squares for the response is SS(Total) = 500. For each of the following partitions of SS(Total), test the null hypothesis that the treatment means are equal and test the null hypothesis that the block means are equal. Use $\alpha = .05$ for each test.

a. The Sum of Squares for Treatments (SST) is 20% of SS(Total), and the Sum of Squares for Blocks (SSB) is 30% of SS(Total).

b. SST is 50% of SS(Total), and SSB is 20% of SS(Total).

c. SST is 20% of SS(Total), and SSB is 50% of SS(Total).

d. SST is 40% of SS(Total), and SSB is 40% of SS(Total).

e. SST is 20% of SS(Total), and SSB is 20% of SS(Total).

Applying the Concepts—Basic

54 **Making high-stakes insurance decisions.** Refer to the *Journal of Economic Psychology* (Sep. 2008) study on high-stakes insurance decisions, Exercise 24. A second experiment involved only the group 2 subjects. In part A of the experiment, these 84 subjects were informed of the hazards (both fire and theft) of owning a valuable painting but were not told the exact probabilities of the hazards occurring. The subjects then provided an amount they were willing to pay (WTP) for insuring the painting. In part B of the experiment, these same subjects were informed of the exact probabilities of the hazards (fire and theft) of owning a valuable sculpture. The subjects then provided a WTP amount for insuring the sculpture. The researchers were interested in comparing the mean WTP amounts for the painting and the sculpture.

a. Explain why the experimental design employed is a randomized block design.

b. Identify the dependent (response) variable, treatments, and blocks for the design.

c. Give the null and alternative hypotheses of interest to the researchers.

55 **Peer mentor training at a firm.** Peer mentoring occurs when a more experienced employee provides one-on-one support and knowledge sharing with a less experienced employee. The *Journal of Managerial Issues* (Spring 2008) published a study of the impact of peer mentor training at a large software company. Participants were 222 employees who volunteered to attend a 1-day peer mentor training session. One variable of interest was the employee's level of competence in peer mentoring (measured on a 7-point scale). The competence level of each trainee was measured at three different times in the study: 1 week before training, 2 days after training, and 2 months after training. One goal of the experiment was to compare the mean competence levels of the three time periods.

a. Explain why these data should be analyzed using a randomized block design. As part of your answer, identify the blocks and the treatments.

b. A partial ANOVA table for the experiment is shown below. Explain why there is enough information in the table to make conclusions.

Source	df	SS	MS	F-Value	p-Value
Time Period	2	—	—	—	0.001
Blocks	221	—	—	—	0.001
Error	442	—	—		
Total	665	—			

c. State the null hypothesis of interest to the researcher.

d. Make the appropriate conclusion.

e. A multiple comparisons of means for the three time periods (using an experimentwise error rate of .10) is summarized below. Fully interpret the results.

Sample mean:	3.65	4.14	4.17
Time period:	*before*	*2 months after*	*2 days after*

56 **Forecasting electrical consumption.** Two different methods of forecasting monthly electrical consumption were compared and the results published in *Applied Mathematics and Computation* (Vol. 186, 2007). The two methods were Artificial Neural Networks (ANN) and Time Series Regression (TSR). Forecasts were made using each method for each of 4 months. These forecasts were also compared to the actual monthly consumption values. A layout of the design is shown in the accompanying table. The researchers want to compare the mean electrical consumption values of the ANN forecast, TSR forecast, and Actual consumption.

Month	ANN Forecast	TSR Forecast	Actual Consumption
1	—	—	—
2	—	—	—
3	—	—	—
4	—	—	—
Sample Mean	13.480	13.260	13.475

a. Indentify the experimental design employed in the study.

b. A partial ANOVA table for the study is provided on next page. Fill in the missing entries.

Source	df	SS	MS	F-Value	p-Value
Forecast Method	—	—	.195	2.83	.08
Month	3	—	10.780	—	<.01
Error	—	.414	.069		
Total	11	33.144			

c. Use the information in the table to conduct the appropriate ANOVA F-test using $\alpha = .05$. State your conclusion in the words of the problem.

57 Interactive video games and physical fitness. Wii Fit is an interactive video game marketed to consumers who want to increase their physical fitness level. The effectiveness of Wii Fit activities relative to other physical activities was investigated in the *Journal of Physical Activity and Health* (Vol. 7, 2010). A sample of 15 young adults (ages 21–38 years) participated in the study. Each adult completed a total of eight activities—rest, handheld gaming, Wii yoga, Wii muscle conditioning, Wii balance, Wii aerobics, brisk treadmill walking, and treadmill jogging. At the end of each session, the heart rate (beats per minute) of the participant was recorded. Since the goal was to compare mean heart rates across the eight activities, and since each adult completed all activities, a randomized block design ANOVA was conducted.

a. Identify the treatments for this experiment.
b. Identify the blocks for this experiment.
c. The ANOVA F-test for treatments resulted in a p-value of .001. Interpret this result using $\alpha = .01$.
d. Multiple comparisons (with an experimentwise error rate of .05) of the mean heart rates for the eight activities revealed the following. (*Note:* Means with the same letter are not significantly different.) Provide a ranking of the treatment means.

	Mean Heart Rate
Rest	58.3 a
Handheld gaming	65.6 a
Wii balance	76.7 b
Wii yoga	77.6 b
Wii muscle conditioning	82.4 b
Wii aerobics	94.5 b
Brisk treadmill walking	108.3 c
Treadmill jogging	153.7 d

58 Rotary oil rigs. An economist wants to compare the average monthly number of rotary oil rigs running in three states—California, Utah, and Alaska. In order to account for month-to-month variation, 3 months were randomly selected over a 2-year period, and the number of oil rigs running in each state in each month was obtained from data provided from *World Oil* (Jan. 2002) magazine. The data, reproduced in the accompanying table, were analyzed using a randomized block design.

Month	California	Utah	Alaska
1	27	17	11
2	34	20	14
3	36	15	14

a. Why is a randomized block design preferred over a completely randomized design for comparing the mean number of oil rigs running monthly in California, Utah, and Alaska?
b. Identify the treatments for the experiment.
c. Identify the blocks for the experiment.
d. State the null hypothesis for the ANOVA F-test.
e. Locate the test statistic and p-value on the XLSTAT printout shown below. Interpret the results.

Analysis of variance:

Source	DF	Sum of squares	Mean squares	F	Pr > F
Model	4	648.4444	162.1111	19.9863	0.0066
Error	4	32.4444	8.1111		
Corrected	8	680.8889			

Computed against model Y=Mean(Y)

Type III Sum of Squares analysis:

Source	DF	Sum of squares	Mean squares	F	Pr > F
State	2	617.5556	308.7778	38.0685	0.0025
Month	2	30.8889	15.4444	1.9041	0.2624

f. A Tukey multiple comparisons of means (at $\alpha = .05$) is summarized in the XLSTAT printout below. Which state(s) have the significantly largest mean number of oil rigs running monthly?

XLSTAT output for Exercise 58f

State / Tukey (HSD) / Analysis of the differences between the categories with a confidence interval of 95%:

Contrast	Difference	Standardized difference	Critical value	Pr > Diff	Significant
CAL vs AL	19.3333	8.3140	3.5641	0.0025	Yes
CAL vs UT	15.0000	6.4505	3.5641	0.0066	Yes
UT vs AL	4.3333	1.8635	3.5641	0.2624	No
Tukey's d critical value:			5.0404		

Category	Mean		Groups	
CAL	32.3333	A		
UT	17.3333		B	
AL	13.0000		B	

Applying the Concepts—Intermediate

59 **A new method of evaluating health care research reports.** When evaluating research reports in health care, a popular tool is the Assessment of Multiple Systematic Reviews (AMSTAR). AMSTAR, which incorporates 11 items (questions), has been widely accepted by professional health associations. A group of dental researchers has revised the assessment tool and named it R-AMSTAR (*The Open Dentistry Journal,* Vol. 4, 2010). The revised assessment tool was validated on five systematic reviews (named R1, R2, R3, R4, and R5) on rheumatoid arthritis. For each review, scores on the 11 R-AMSTAR items (all measured on a 4-point scale) were obtained. The data are shown in the table at the bottom of the page.

a. One goal of the study was to compare the mean item scores of the five reviews. Set up the null and alternative hypotheses for this test.

b. Examine the data in the table and explain why a randomized block ANOVA is appropriate to apply.

c. The Minitab output for a randomized block ANOVA of the data (with Review as treatments and Item as blocks) appears below. Interpret the *p*-values of the tests shown.

d. The Minitab printout also reports the results of a Tukey multiple comparison analysis of the five Review means. Which pairs of means are significantly different? Do these results agree with your conclusion in part **c**?

e. The experimentwise error rate used in the analysis of part **d** is .05. Interpret this value.

```
Analysis of Variance for SCORE, using Adjusted SS for Tests

Source  DF  Seq SS   Adj SS   Adj MS    F     P
REVIEW   4   2.5182   2.5182  0.6295   1.22  0.319
ITEM    10  43.5000  43.5000  4.3500   8.41  0.000
Error   40  20.6818  20.6818  0.5170
Total   54  66.7000

S = 0.719059   R-Sq = 68.99%   R-Sq(adj) = 58.14%

Grouping Information Using Tukey Method and 95.0% Confidence

REVIEW   N   Mean   Grouping
R5      11   3.182    A
R2      11   3.045    A
R4      11   2.864    A
R3      11   2.864    A
R1      11   2.545    A

Means that do not share a letter are significantly different.
```

60 **Reducing on-the-job stress.** Plant therapists believe that plants can reduce on-the-job stress. A Kansas State University study was conducted to investigate this phenomenon. Two weeks prior to final exams, 10 undergraduate students took part in an experiment to determine what effect the presence of a live plant, a photo of a plant, or absence of a plant has on a student's ability to relax while isolated in a dimly lit room. Each student participated in three sessions—one with a live plant, one with a plant photo, and one with no plant (control).* During each session, finger temperature was measured at 1-minute intervals for 20 minutes. Because increasing finger temperature indicates an increased level of relaxation, the maximum temperature (in degrees) was used as the response variable. For example, one student's finger measured 95.6° in the "Live Plant" condition, 92.6° in the "Plant Photo" condition, and 96.6° in the "No Plant" condition. The temperatures under the three conditions for the other nine students follow: Student 2 (95.6°, 94.8°, 96.0°), Student 3 (96.0°, 97.2°, 96.2°), Student 4 (95.2°, 94.6°, 95.7°), Student 5 (96.7°, 95.5°, 94.8°), Student 6 (96.0°, 96.6°, 93.5°), Student 7 (93.7°, 96.2°, 96.7°), Student 8 (97.0°, 95.8°, 95.4°), Student 9 (94.9°, 96.6°, 90.5°), Student 10 (91.4°, 93.5°, 96.6°). These data (based on data from Elizabeth Schreiber. Department of Statistics, Kansas State University, Manhattan, Kansas) are saved in the accompanying file. Conduct an ANOVA and make the proper inferences at $\alpha = .10$.

61 **Absentee rates at a jeans plant.** A plant that manufactures denim jeans in the United Kingdom introduced a computerized automated handling system. The new system delivers garments to the assembly line operators by means of an overhead conveyor. Although the automated system minimizes operator handling time, it inhibits operators from working ahead and taking breaks from their machine. A study in *New Technology, Work, and Employment* (July 2001) investigated the impact of the new handling system on worker absentee rates at the jeans plant. One theory is that the mean absentee rate will vary by day of the week, as operators decide to indulge in 1-day absences to relieve work pressure. Nine weeks were randomly selected, and the absentee rate (percentage of workers absent) determined for each day (Monday through Friday) of the workweek. The data are listed in the table on the next page. Conduct a complete analysis of the data to determine whether the mean absentee rate differs across the 5 days of the workweek.

Data for Exercise 59

Review	Item 1	Item 2	Item 3	Item 4	Item 5	Item 6	Item 7	Item 8	Item 9	Item 10	Item 11
R1	4.0	1.0	4.0	2.0	3.5	3.5	3.5	3.5	1.0	1.0	1.0
R2	3.5	2.5	4.0	4.0	3.5	4.0	3.5	2.5	3.5	1.5	1.0
R3	4.0	4.0	3.5	4.0	1.5	2.5	3.5	3.5	2.5	1.5	1.0
R4	3.5	2.0	4.0	4.0	2.0	4.0	3.5	3.0	3.5	1.0	1.0
R5	3.5	4.0	4.0	3.0	2.5	4.0	4.0	4.0	2.5	1.0	2.5

Source: Kung, J., et al. "From systematic reviews to clinical recommendations to clinical-based health care: Validation of revised assessment of multiple systematic reviews (R-AMSTAR) for grading of clinical relevance," *The Open Dentistry Journal,* Vol. 4, 2010 (Table 2).

*The experiment is simplified for this exercise. The actual experiment involved 30 students who participated in 12 sessions.

Data for Exercise 61

Week	Mon	Tues	Wed	Thur	Fri
1	5.3	0.6	1.9	1.3	1.6
2	12.9	9.4	2.6	0.4	0.5
3	0.8	0.8	5.7	0.4	1.4
4	2.6	0.0	4.5	10.2	4.5
5	23.5	9.6	11.3	13.6	14.1
6	9.1	4.5	7.5	2.1	9.3
7	11.1	4.2	4.1	4.2	4.1
8	9.5	7.1	4.5	9.1	12.9
9	4.8	5.2	10.0	6.9	9.0

Source: Based on Boggis, J. J. "The eradication of leisure," *New Technology, Work, and Employment,* Vol. 16, No. 2, July 2001, pp. 118–129 (Table 3).

62 **Stress in cows prior to slaughter.** What is the level of stress (if any) that cows undergo prior to being slaughtered? To answer this question, researchers designed an experiment involving cows bred in Normandy, France (*Applied Animal Behaviour Science,* June 2010). The heart rate (beats per minute) of a cow was measured at four different pre-slaughter phases—(1) first phase of visual contact with pen mates, (2) initial isolation from pen mates for prepping, (3) restoration of visual contact with pen mates, and (4) first contact with human prior to slaughter. Data for eight cows (simulated from information provided in the article) are shown in the accompanying table. The researchers analyzed the data using an analysis of variance for a randomized block design. Their objective was to determine whether the mean heart rate of cows differed in the four pre-slaughter phases.

COW	PHASE			
	1	2	3	4
1	124	124	109	107
2	100	98	98	99
3	103	98	100	106
4	94	91	98	95
5	122	109	114	115
6	103	92	100	106
7	98	80	99	103
8	120	84	107	110

Source: Based on *Applied Animal Behaviour Science.*

a. Identify the treatments and blocks for this experimental design.
b. Conduct the appropriate analysis using a statistical software package. Summarize the results in an ANOVA table.
c. Is there evidence of differences among the mean heart rates of cows in the four pre-slaughter phases? Test using $\alpha = .05$.
d. If warranted, conduct a multiple comparisons procedure to rank the four treatment means. Use an experimentwise error rate of $\alpha = .05$.

Applying the Concepts—Advanced

63 **Anticorrosive behavior of steel coated with epoxy.** Organic coatings that use epoxy resins are widely used for protecting steel and metal against weathering and corrosion. Researchers at National Technical University (Athens, Greece) examined the steel anticorrosive behavior of different epoxy coatings formulated with zinc pigments in an attempt to find the epoxy coating with the best corrosion inhibition (*Pigment & Resin Technology,* Vol. 32, 2003). The experimental units were flat, rectangular panels cut from steel sheets. Each panel was coated with one of four different coating systems, S1, S2, S3, and S4. Three panels were prepared for each coating system. (These panels are labeled S1-A, S1-B, S1-C, S2-A, S2-B, …, S4-C.) The characteristics of the four coating systems are listed at the bottom of the page.

EPOXY

Each coated panel was immersed in deionized and deaerated water and then tested for corrosion. Because exposure time is likely to have a strong influence on anticorrosive behavior, the researchers attempted to remove this extraneous source of variation through the experimental design. Exposure times were fixed at 24 hours, 60 days, and 120 days. For each of the coating systems, one panel was exposed to water for 24 hours, one exposed to water for 60 days, and one exposed to water for 120 days in random order. The design is illustrated in the accompanying table.

Exposure Time	Coating System/Panel Exposed
24 hours	S1-A, S2-C, S3-C, S4-B
60 days	S1-C, S2-A, S3-B, S4-A
120 days	S1-B, S2-B, S3-A, S4-C

Following exposure, the corrosion rate (nanoamperes per square centimeter) was determined for each panel. The lower the corrosion rate, the greater the anticorrosion performance of the coating system. The data are shown in the next table. Are there differences among the epoxy treatment means? If so, which of the epoxy coating systems yields the lowest corrosion rate?

Exposure Time	System S1	System S2	System S3	System S4
24 hours	6.7	7.5	8.2	6.1
60 days	8.7	9.1	10.5	8.3
120 days	11.8	12.6	14.5	11.8

Source: Kouloumbi, N., Pantazopoulou, P., & Moundoulas, P. "Anticorrosion performance of epoxy coatings on steel surface exposed to deionized water," *Pigment & Resin Technology,* Vol. 32, No. 2, 2003, pp. 89–99 (Table II). © Emerald Group Publishing Limited. All rights reserved.

Coating systems characteristics for Exercise 63

Coating System	1st Layer	2nd Layer
S1	Zinc dust	Epoxy paint, 100 micrometers thick
S2	Zinc phosphate	Epoxy paint, 100 micrometers thick
S3	Zinc phosphate with mica	Finish layer, 100 micrometers thick
S4	Zinc phosphate with mica	Finish layer, 200 micrometers thick

5 Factorial Experiments: Two Factors

All of the experiments discussed in Sections 2–4 were **single-factor experiments.** The treatments were levels of a single factor, with the sampling of experimental units performed using either a completely randomized or a randomized block design. However, most responses are affected by more than one factor, and we will therefore often wish to design experiments involving more than one factor.

Consider an experiment in which the effects of two factors on the response are being investigated. Assume that factor A is to be investigated at a levels and factor B at b levels. Recalling that treatments are factor-level combinations, you can see that the experiment has, potentially, ab treatments that could be included in the experiment. A *complete factorial experiment* is one in which all possible ab treatments are employed.

> A **complete factorial experiment** is one in which every factor-level combination is employed—that is, the number of treatments in the experiment equals the total number of factor-level combinations.

For example, suppose the USGA wants to determine not only the relationship between distance and brand of golf ball but also between distance and the club used to hit the ball. If they decide to use four brands and two clubs (say, driver and five-iron) in the experiment, then a complete factorial would call for employing all $4 \times 2 = 8$ Brand-Club combinations. This experiment is referred to more specifically as a *complete 4×2 factorial.* A layout for a two-factor factorial experiment (we are henceforth referring to a *complete factorial* when we use the term *factorial*) is given in Table 12. The factorial experiment is also referred to as a **two-way classification** because it can be arranged in the row-column format exhibited in Table 12.

Table 12	Schematic Layout of Two-Factor Factorial Experiment				
		Factor B at b Levels			
	Level	1	2	3	...	b
	1	Trt. 1	Trt. 2	Trt. 3	...	Trt. b
Factor A	2	Trt. $b + 1$	Trt. $b + 2$	Trt. $b + 3$	...	Trt. $2b$
at a Levels	3	Trt. $2b + 1$	Trt. $2b + 2$	Trt. $2b + 3$	...	Trt. $3b$
	⋮	⋮	⋮	⋮	...	⋮
	a	Trt. $(a-1)b + 1$	Trt. $(a-1)b + 2$	Trt. $(a-1)b + 3$	...	Trt. ab

In order to complete the specification of the experimental design, the treatments must be assigned to the experimental units. If the assignment of the ab treatments in the factorial experiment is random and independent, the design is completely randomized. For example, if the machine Iron Byron is used to hit 80 golf balls, 10 for each of the eight Brand-Club combinations, in a random sequence, the design would be completely randomized. In the remainder of this section, we confine our attention to factorial experiments employing completely randomized designs.

If we employ a completely randomized design to conduct a factorial experiment with ab treatments, we can proceed with the analysis in exactly the same way as we did in Section 2—that is, we calculate (or let the computer calculate) the measure of treatment mean variability (MST) and the measure of sampling variability (MSE) and use the F-ratio of these two quantities to test the null hypothesis that the treatment means are equal. However, if this hypothesis is rejected, so that we conclude some differences exist among the treatment means, important questions remain. Are both factors affecting the response or only one? If both, do they affect the response independently, or do they interact to affect the response?

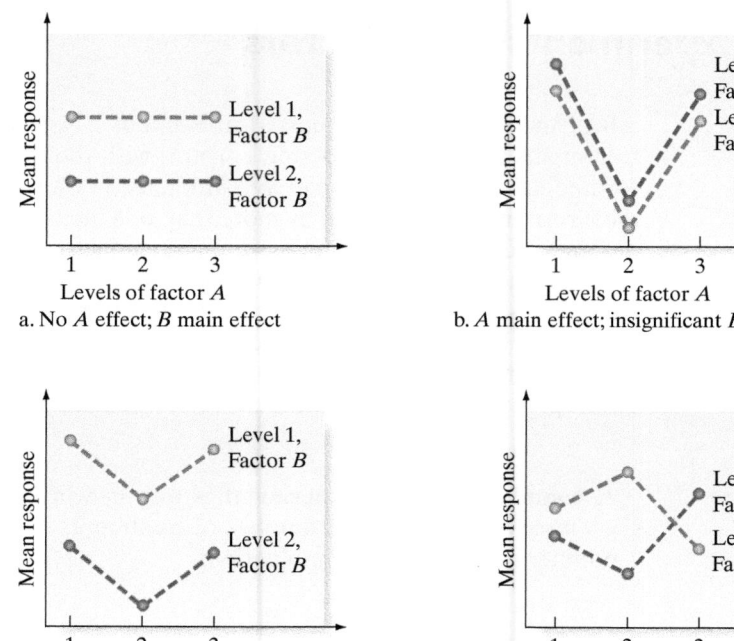

Figure 23

Illustration of possible treatment effects: factorial experiment

For example, suppose the distance data indicate that at least two of the eight treatment (Brand-Club combinations) means differ in the golf experiment. Does the brand of ball (factor A) or the club used (factor B) affect mean distance, or do both affect it? Several possibilities are shown in Figure 23. In Figure 23a, the brand means are equal (only three are shown for the purpose of illustration), but the distances differ for the two levels of factor B (Club). Thus, there is no effect of Brand on distance, but a Club main effect is present. In Figure 23b, the Brand means differ, but the Club means are equal for each Brand. Here a Brand main effect is present, but no effect of Club is present.

Figures 23c and 23d illustrate cases in which both factors affect the response. In Figure 23c, the mean distances between Clubs does not change for the three Brands, so that the effect of Brand on distance is independent of Club—that is, the two factors Brand and Club *do not interact*. In contrast, Figure 23d shows that the difference between mean distances between Clubs varies with Brand. Thus, the effect of Brand on distance depends on Club, and therefore the two factors *do interact*.

To determine the nature of the treatment effect, if any, on the response in a factorial experiment, we need to break the treatment variability into three components: Interaction between Factors A and B, Main Effect of Factor A, and Main Effect of Factor B. The **Factor Interaction** component is used to test whether the factors combine to affect the response, while the **Factor Main Effect** components are used to determine whether the factors separately affect the response.

Now Work Exercise 71c

The partitioning of the Total Sum of Squares into its various components is illustrated in Figure 24. Notice that at stage 1, the components are identical to those in the one-factor, completely randomized designs of Section 2; the Sums of Squares for Treatments and Error sum to the Total Sum of Squares. The degrees of freedom for treatments is equal to $(ab - 1)$, one less than the number of treatments. The degrees of freedom for error is equal to $(n - ab)$, the total sample size minus the number of treatments. Only at stage 2 of the partitioning does the factorial experiment differ from those previously discussed. Here we divide the Treatments Sum of Squares into its three

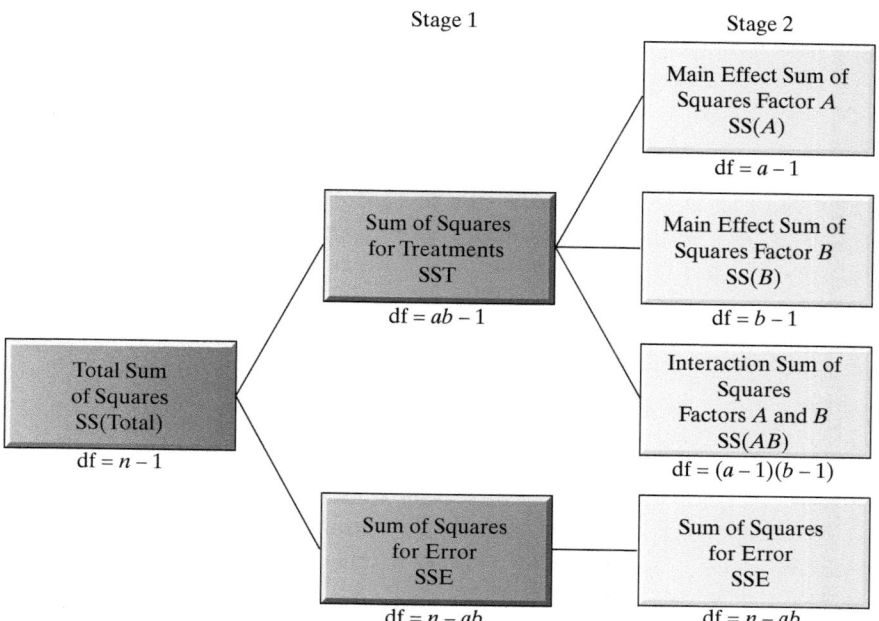

Figure 24

Partitioning the Total Sum of
Squares for a two-factor factorial

components: Interaction and the two Main Effects. These components can then be used
to test the nature of the differences, if any, among the treatment means.

There are a number of ways to proceed in the testing and estimation of factors in a
factorial experiment. We present one approach in the next box.

Procedure for Analysis of Two-Factor Factorial Experiment

1. Partition the Total Sum of Squares into the Treatments and Error components
   (stage 1 of Figure 24). Use either a statistical software package or the calculation formulas in Appendix: Calculation Formulas for Analysis of Variance to
   accomplish the partitioning.

2. Use the F-ratio of Mean Square for Treatments to Mean Square for Error to
   test the null hypothesis that the treatment means are equal.*
   a. If the test results in nonrejection of the null hypothesis, consider refining the experiment by increasing the number of replications or introducing other factors.
   Also consider the possibility that the response is unrelated to the two factors.
   b. If the test results in rejection of the null hypothesis, then proceed to step 3.

3. Partition the Treatments Sum of Squares into the Main Effect and Interaction
   Sum of Squares (stage 2 of Figure 24). Use either a statistical software package
   or the calculation formulas in Appendix: Calculation Formulas for Analysis of
   Variance to accomplish the partitioning.

4. Test the null hypothesis that factors A and B do not interact to affect the response
   by computing the F-ratio of the Mean Square for Interaction to the Mean
   Square for Error.
   a. If the test results in nonrejection of the null hypothesis, proceed to step 5.
   b. If the test results in rejection of the null hypothesis, conclude that the two
   factors interact to affect the mean response. Then proceed to step 6a.

5. Conduct tests of two null hypotheses that the mean response is the same at
   each level of factor A and factor B. Compute two F-ratios by comparing the
   Mean Square for each Factor Main Effect to the Mean Square for Error.
   a. If one or both tests result in rejection of the null hypothesis, conclude that
   the factor affects the mean response. Proceed to step 6b.

(Continued)

---

*Some analysts prefer to proceed directly to test the interaction and main effect components, skipping the test
of treatment means. We begin with this test to be consistent with our approach in the one-factor completely
randomized design.

b. If both tests result in nonrejection, an apparent contradiction has occurred. Although the treatment means apparently differ (step 2 test), the interaction (step 4) and main effect (step 5) tests have not supported that result. Further experimentation is advised.

6. Compare the means:
   a. If the test for interaction (step 4) is significant, use a multiple comparisons procedure to compare any or all pairs of the treatment means.
   b. If the test for one or both main effects (step 5) is significant, use a multiple comparisons procedure to compare the pairs of means corresponding to the levels of the significant factor(s).

We assume the completely randomized design is a balanced design, meaning that the same number of observations are made for each treatment—that is, we assume that r experimental units are randomly and independently selected for each treatment. The numerical value of r must exceed 1 in order to have any degrees of freedom with which to measure the sampling variability. [Note that if $r = 1$, then $n = ab$, and the degrees of freedom associated with Error (Figure 24) is df $= n - ab = 0$.] The value of r is often referred to as the number of **replicates** of the factorial experiment because we assume that all ab treatments are repeated, or replicated, r times. Whatever approach is adopted in the analysis of a factorial experiment, several tests of hypotheses are usually conducted. The tests are summarized in the next box.

ANOVA Tests Conducted for Factorial Experiments: Completely Randomized Design, r Replicates per Treatment

Test for Treatment Means

H_0: No difference among the ab treatment means

H_a: At least two treatment means differ

Test statistic: $F = \dfrac{\text{MST}}{\text{MSE}}$

Rejection region: $F \geq F_{\alpha}$, based on $(ab - 1)$ numerator and $(n - ab)$ denominator degrees of freedom [Note: $n = abr$.]

Test for Factor Interaction

H_0: Factors A and B do not interact to affect the response mean.

H_a: Factors A and B do interact to affect the response mean.

Test statistic: $F = \dfrac{\text{MS}(AB)}{\text{MSE}}$

Rejection region: $F \geq F_{\alpha}$, based on $(a - 1)(b - 1)$ numerator and $(n - ab)$ denominator degrees of freedom

Test for Main Effect of Factor A

H_0: No difference among the a mean levels of factor A

H_a: At least two factor A mean levels differ

Test statistic: $F = \dfrac{\text{MS}(A)}{\text{MSE}}$

Rejection region: $F \geq F_{\alpha}$, based on $(a - 1)$ numerator and $(n - ab)$ denominator degrees of freedom

Test for Main Effect of Factor B

H_0: No difference among the b mean levels of factor B

H_a: At least two factor B mean levels differ

Test statistic: $F = \dfrac{MS(B)}{MSE}$

Rejection region: $F \geq F_\alpha$, based on $(b - 1)$ numerator and $(n - ab)$ denominator degrees of freedom

---

Conditions Required for Valid *F*-Tests in Factorial Experiments

1. The response distribution for each factor-level combination (treatment) is normal.

2. The response variance is constant for all treatments.

3. Random and independent samples of experimental units are associated with each treatment.

Example   10

Conducting a Factorial ANOVA—Golf Ball Study

Problem The USGA is interested in knowing whether the difference in distance traveled by any two golf ball brands depends on the club used. Consequently, the USGA tests four different brands (A, B, C, D) of golf balls and two different clubs (driver, five-iron) in a completely randomized design. Each of the eight Brand-Club combinations (treatments) is randomly and independently assigned to four experimental units, each experimental unit consisting of a specific position in the sequence of hits by Iron Byron. The distance response is recorded for each of the 32 hits, and the results are shown in Table 13.

Table 13	Distance Data for 4 × 2 Factorial Golf Experiment			
		Brand		
		A	B	C	D
Club	**Driver**	226.4 232.6 234.0 220.7	238.3 231.7 227.7 237.2	240.5 246.9 240.3 244.7	219.8 228.7 232.9 237.6
	Five-Iron	163.8 179.4 168.6 173.4	184.4 180.6 179.5 186.2	179.0 168.0 165.2 156.5	157.8 161.8 162.1 160.3

Data Set: GLFAC1

a. Use a statistical software package to partition the Total Sum of Squares into the components necessary to analyze this 4 × 2 factorial experiment.

b. Conduct the appropriate ANOVA tests and interpret the results of your analysis. Use $\alpha = .10$ for each test you conduct.

c. If appropriate, conduct multiple comparisons of the treatment means. Use an experimentwise error rate of .10. Illustrate the comparisons with a graph.

Solution

a. The SPSS printout that partitions the Total Sum of Squares [i.e., SS(Total)] for this factorial experiment is given in Figure 25. The value SS(Total) = 34,482.049, shown as "Corrected Total SS" at the bottom of the printout, is partitioned into

Tests of Between-Subjects Effects

Dependent Variable: DISTANCE

Source	Type III Sum of Squares	df	Mean Square	F	Sig.
Corrected Model	33659.809ᵃ	7	4808.544	140.354	.000
Intercept	1306778.61	1	1306778.611	38142.98	.000
BRAND	800.736	3	266.912	7.791	.001
CLUB	32093.111	1	32093.111	936.752	.000
BRAND * CLUB	765.961	3	255.320	7.452	.001
Error	822.240	24	34.260		
Total	1341260.66	32			
Corrected Total	34482.049	31			

a. R Squared = .976 (Adjusted R Squared = .969)

Figure 25

SPSS ANOVA for factorial experiment on golf ball data

the "Corrected Model" (i.e., Treatment) and Error Sums of Squares. Note that SST = 33,659.09 (with 7 df) and SSE = 822.24 (with 24 df) add to SS(Total) (with 31 df). The Treatment Sum of Squares, SST, is further divided into Main Effect (Brand and Club) and Interaction Sum of Squares. These values, highlighted on Figure 25, are SS(Brand) = 800.7 (with 3 df), SS(Club) = 32,093.1 (with 1 df), and SS(Brand × Club) = 766.0 (with 3 df).

b. Once partitioning is accomplished, our first test is

H_0: The eight treatment means are equal.

H_a: At least two of the eight means differ.

$$\text{Test statistic: } F = \frac{MST}{MSE} = 140.354 \quad \text{(top line of printout)}$$

$$\text{Observed significance level: } p = .000 \quad \text{(top line of printout)}$$

Because $\alpha = .10$ exceeds p, we reject this null hypothesis and conclude that at least two of the Brand-Club combinations differ in mean distance.

After accepting the hypothesis that the treatment means differ, and therefore that the factors Brand and/or Club somehow affect the mean distance, we want to determine how the factors affect the mean response. We begin with a test of interaction between Brand and Club:

H_0: The factors Brand and Club do not interact to affect the mean response.

H_a: Brand and Club interact to affect mean response.

$$\text{Test statistic: } F = \frac{MS(AB)}{MSE} = \frac{MS(\text{Brand} \times \text{Club})}{MSE}$$

$$= \frac{255.32}{34.26} = 7.452 \quad \text{(bottom of printout)}$$

$$\text{Observed significance level: } p = .001 \quad \text{(bottom of printout)}$$

Because $\alpha = .10$ exceeds the p-value, we conclude that the factors Brand and Club interact to affect mean distance.

Because the factors interact, we do not test the main effects for Brand and Club. Instead, we compare the treatment means in an attempt to learn the nature of the interaction in part **c.**

c. Rather than compare all $8(7)/2 = 28$ pairs of treatment means, we test for differences only between pairs of brands within each club. That differences exist *between* clubs can be assumed. Therefore, only $4(3)/2 = 6$ pairs of means need to be compared for each club, or a total of 12 comparisons for the two clubs. The results of these comparisons using Tukey's method with an experimentwise error rate of $\alpha = .10$ for each club are displayed in the SPSS printout, Figure 26. For each club, the brand means are listed in descending order in Figure 26, and those not significantly different are listed in the same "Homogeneous Subset" column.

CLUB=5IRON

Tukey HSD[a,b]

BRAND	N	Subset	
		1	2
D	4	160.500	
C	4	167.175	
A	4	171.300	
B	4		182.675
Sig.		.103	1.000

Means for groups in homogeneous subsets are displayed.
Based on Type III Sum of Squares
The error term is Mean Square(Error) = 36.108.
  a. Uses Harmonic Mean Sample Size = 4.000.
   b. Alpha = .10.

CLUB=DRIVER

Tukey HSD[a,b]

BRAND	N	Subset	
		1	2
A	4	228.425	
D	4	229.750	
B	4	233.725	233.725
C	4		243.100
Sig.		.570	.146

Means for groups in homogeneous subsets are displayed.
Based on Type III Sum of Squares
The error term is Mean Square(Error) = 32.412.
  a. Uses Harmonic Mean Sample Size = 4.000.
   b. Alpha = .10.

Figure 26

SPSS ranking of brand means
for each level of club

As shown in Figure 26, the picture is unclear with respect to Brand means. For the five-iron (top of Figure 26), the Brand B mean significantly exceeds all other brands. However, when hit with a driver (bottom of Figure 26), Brand B's mean is not significantly different from any of the other brands. The Club × Brand interaction can be seen in the SPSS plot of means in Figure 27. Note that the difference between the mean distances of the two clubs (driver and five-iron) varies depending on brand. The biggest difference appears for Brand C, while the smallest difference is for Brand B.

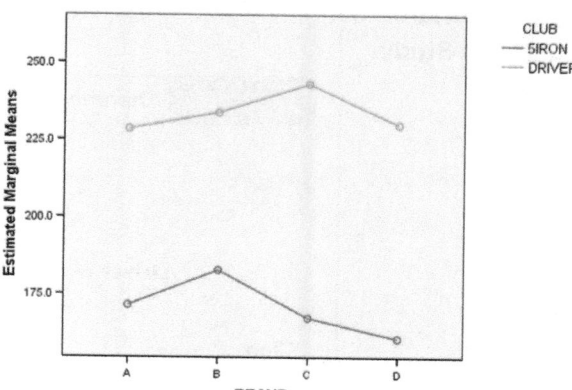

Estimated Marginal Means of DISTANCE

Figure 27

SPSS means plot for factorial
golf ball experiment

Look Back Note the nontransitive nature of the multiple comparisons. For example, for the driver, the Brand C mean can be "the same" as the Brand B mean, and the Brand B mean can be "the same" as the Brand D mean, and yet the Brand C mean can significantly exceed the Brand D mean. The reason lies in the definition of "the same"—we must be careful not to conclude two means are equal simply because they are placed in the same subgroup or connected by a vertical line. The line indicates only that *the connected means are not significantly different.* You should conclude (at the overall α level of significance) only that means not connected are different, while withholding judgment on those that are connected. The picture of which means differ and by how much will become clearer as we increase the number of replicates of the factorial experiment.

Now Work Exercise 72

As with completely randomized and randomized block designs, the results of a factorial ANOVA are typically presented in an ANOVA summary table. Table 14 gives the general form of the ANOVA table, while Table 15 gives the ANOVA table for the golf ball data analyzed in Example 10. A two-factor factorial is characterized by four sources of variation—Factor A, Factor B, $A \times B$ interaction, and Error—which sum to the total Sum of Squares.

Table 14	General ANOVA Summary Table for a Two-Factor Factorial Experiment with r Replicates, where Factor A Has a Levels and Factor B Has b Levels			
Source	df	SS	MS	F
A	$a-1$	SSA	MSA	MSA/MSE
B	$b-1$	SSB	MSB	MSB/MSE
AB	$(a-1)(b-1)$	SSAB	MSAB	MSAB/MSE
Error	$ab(r-1)$	SSE	MSE	
Total	$n-1$	SS(Total)		

Table 15	ANOVA Summary Table for Example 10			
Source	df	SS	MS	F
Brand	1	32,093.11	32,093.11	936.75
Club	3	800.74	266.91	7.79
Interaction	3	765.96	255.32	7.45
Error	24	822.24	34.26	
Total	31	34,482.05		

Example 11

More Practice on Conducting a Factorial Analysis—Golf Ball Study

Problem Refer to Example 10. Suppose the same factorial experiment is performed on four other brands (E, F, G, and H), and the results are as shown in Table 16. Repeat the factorial analysis and interpret the results.

Table 16	Distance Data for Second Factorial Golf Experiment			
		Brand		
		E	F	G	H
Club	Driver	238.6	261.4	264.7	235.4
		241.9	261.3	262.9	239.8
		236.6	254.0	253.5	236.2
		244.9	259.9	255.6	237.5
	Five-Iron	165.2	179.2	189.0	171.4
		156.9	171.0	191.2	159.3
		172.2	178.0	191.3	156.6
		163.2	182.7	180.5	157.4

Data Set: GLFAC2

Solution The Minitab printout for the second factorial experiment is shown in Figure 28. We conduct several tests, as outlined in the box.

Two-way ANOVA: DISTANCE versus BRAND, CLUB

Source	DF	SS	MS	F	P
BRAND	3	3410.3	1136.8	46.21	0.000
CLUB	1	46443.9	46443.9	1887.94	0.000
Interaction	3	105.2	35.1	1.42	0.260
Error	24	590.4	24.6		
Total	31	50549.8			

$S = 4.960$ R-Sq = 98.83%   R-Sq(adj) = 98.49%

Figure 28

Minitab analysis for second factorial golf experiment

Test for Equality of Treatment Means

Note that Minitab (unlike SPSS) does not automatically conduct the F-test for treatment differences. Consequently, to conduct this test, we must first calculate the Sum of Squares for Treatments. Using the Sums of Squares for Brands, Clubs, and Interaction shown on the printout, we obtain

$$SS(\text{Treatments}) = SS(\text{Clubs}) + SS(\text{Brands}) + SS(\text{Interaction})$$
$$= 46{,}443.9 + 3{,}410.3 + 105.2 = 49{,}959.4$$

For this 4×2 factorial experiment, there are eight treatments. Then

$$MS(\text{Treatments}) = SS(\text{Treatments})/(8 - 1) = 49{,}959.4/7 = 7{,}137.1$$

The test statistic is

$$F = MS(\text{Treatments})/MSE = 7{,}137.1/24.6 = 290.1$$

Because this F-value exceeds the critical value of $F_{.10} = 1.98$ (obtained from Table V in Appendix: Tables, we reject the null hypothesis of no treatment differences and conclude that at least two of the Brand-Club combinations have significantly different mean distances.

Test for Interaction

Next, we test for interaction between Brand and Club:

$$F = \frac{MS(\text{Brand} \times \text{Club})}{MSE} = 1.42 \text{ (highlighted on the printout)}$$

Because this F-ratio does not exceed the tabled value of $F_{.10} = 2.33$ with 3 and 24 df (obtained from Table V in Appendix: Tables, we cannot conclude at the .10 level of significance that the factors interact. In fact, note that the observed significance level (on the Minitab printout) for the test of interaction is .26. Thus, at any level of significance lower than $\alpha = .26$, we could not conclude that the factors interact. We therefore test the main effects for Brand and Club.

Test for Brand Main Effect

We first test the Brand main effect:

H_0: No difference exists among the true Brand mean distances.

H_a: At least two Brand mean distances differ.

Test statistic: $F = \dfrac{MS(\text{Brand})}{MSE} = \dfrac{1{,}136.77}{24.60} = 46.21$ (highlighted on the printout)

Observed significance level: $p = .000$ (highlighted on the printout)

Since $\alpha = .10$ exceeds the p-value, we conclude that at least two of the brand means differ. We will subsequently determine which brand means differ using Tukey's multiple comparisons procedure. But first, we want to test the Club main effect.

Test for Club Main Effect

H_0: No differences exist between the Club mean distances.

H_a: The Club mean distances differ.

Test statistic: $F = \dfrac{MS(\text{Club})}{MSE} = \dfrac{46{,}443.9}{24.60} = 1{,}887.94$

Observed significance level: $p = .000$

Since $\alpha = .10$ exceeds the *p*-value, we conclude that the two clubs are associated with different mean distances. Because only two levels of Club were used in the experiment, this *F*-test leads to the inference that the mean distance differs for two clubs. It is no surprise (to golfers) that the mean distance for balls hit with the driver is significantly greater than the mean distance for those hit with the five-iron.

Ranking of Means

To determine which of the Brands' mean distances differ, we want to compare the $k = 4$ Brand means using Tukey's method at $\alpha = .10$. The results of these multiple comparisons are displayed in the Minitab printout, Figure 29. Minitab computes simultaneous 90% confidence intervals for the $c = 4(3)/2 = 6$ possible comparisons of the form $\mu_i - \mu_j$. These intervals are highlighted on the printout. Any interval that does not include 0 implies a significant difference between the two treatment means.

A summary of these pairwise comparisons is shown at the top of the Minitab printout. You can see that Brands G and F are associated with significantly greater mean distances than Brands E and H, but we cannot distinguish between Brands G and F or between Brands E and H.

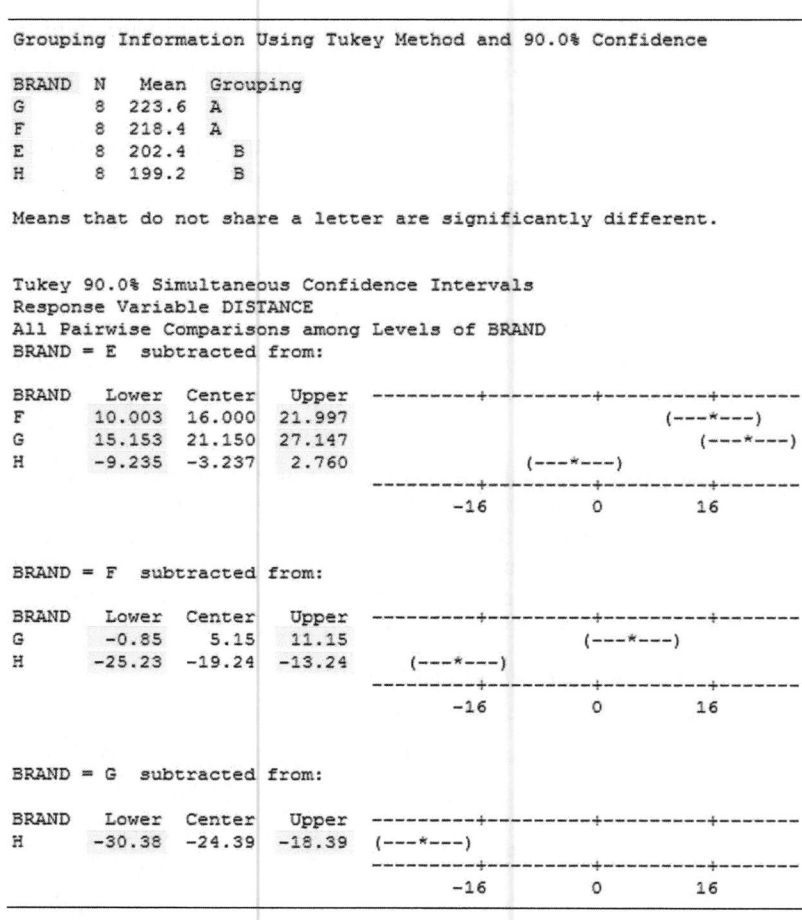

Figure 29

Minitab printout with Tukey multiple comparisons for brand

Look Back Because the interaction between Brand and Club was not significant, we conclude that this difference among brands applies to both clubs. The sample means for all Club-Brand combinations are shown in Figure 30 and appear to support the conclusions of the tests and comparisons. Note that the Brand means maintain their relative positions for each Club—brands F and G dominate brands E and H for both the driver and the five-iron.

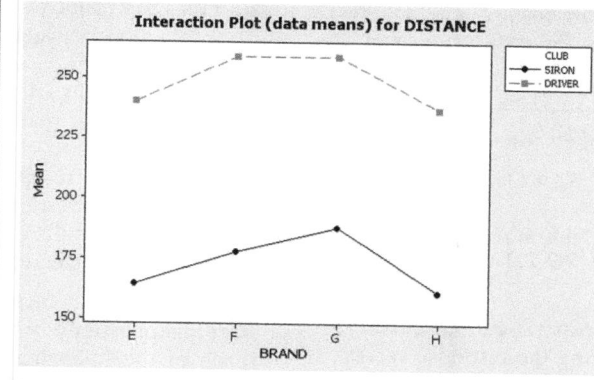

Figure 30

Minitab means plot for second factorial golf ball experiment

■ Now Work Exercise 74

The analysis of factorial experiments can become complex if the number of factors is increased. Even the two-factor experiment becomes more difficult to analyze if some factor combinations have different numbers of observations than others. We have provided an introduction to these important experiments using two-factor factorials with equal numbers of observations for each treatment. Although similar principles apply to most factorial experiments, you should consult the references at the end of this chapter if you need to design and analyze more complex factorials.

Exercises 64–81

Learning the Mechanics

64 Suppose you conduct a 4×3 factorial experiment.
  a. How many factors are used in the experiment?
  b. Can you determine the factor type(s)—qualitative or quantitative—from the information given? Explain.
  c. Can you determine the number of levels used for each factor? Explain.
  d. Describe a treatment for this experiment and determine the number of treatments used.
  e. What problem is caused by using a single replicate of this experiment? How is the problem solved?

65 The partially completed ANOVA for a 3×4 factorial experiment with two replications is shown below.

Source	df	SS	MS	F
A	–	.8	–	–
B	–	5.3	–	–
AB	–	9.6	–	–
Error	–	–	–	
Total	–	17.0		

  a. Complete the ANOVA table.
  b. Which sums of squares are combined to find the Sum of Squares for Treatments? Do the data provide sufficient evidence to indicate that the treatment means differ? Use $\alpha = .05$.
  c. Does the result of the test in part **b** warrant further testing? Explain.

d. What is meant by *factor interaction*, and what is the practical implication if it exists?
  e. Test to determine whether these factors interact to affect the response mean. Use $\alpha = .05$ and interpret the result.
  f. Does the result of the interaction test warrant further testing? Explain.

66 The partially complete ANOVA table given here is for a two-factor factorial experiment.

Source	df	SS	MS	F
Treatments	7	4.1	–	–
A	3	–	.75	–
B	1	.95	–	–
AB	–	–	.30	–
Error	–	–	–	
Total	23	6.5		

  a. Give the number of levels for each factor.
  b. How many observations were collected for each factor-level combination?
  c. Complete the ANOVA table.
  d. Test to determine whether the treatment means differ. Use $\alpha = .10$.
  e. Conduct the tests of factor interaction and main effects, each at the $\alpha = .10$ level of significance. Which of the tests are warranted as part of the factorial analysis? Explain.

67 The following two-way table gives data for a 2×3 factorial experiment with two observations for each factor-level combination.

L09067

		Factor B		
	Level	1	2	3
Factor A	1	3.1, 4.0	4.6, 4.2	6.4, 7.1
	2	5.9, 5.3	2.9, 2.2	3.3, 2.5

a. Identify the treatments for this experiment. Calculate and plot the treatment means, using the response variable as the y-axis and the levels of factor B as the x-axis. Use the levels of factor A as plotting symbols. Do the treatment means appear to differ? Do the factors appear to interact?

b. The Minitab ANOVA printout for this experiment is shown below. Sum the appropriate sums of squares and test to determine whether the treatment means differ at the $\alpha = .05$ level of significance. Does the test support your visual interpretation from part **a**?

c. Does the result of the test in part **b** warrant a test for interaction between the two factors? If so, perform it using $\alpha = .05$.

d. Do the results of the previous tests warrant tests of the two factor main effects? If so, perform them using $\alpha = .05$.

e. Interpret the results of the tests. Do they support your visual interpretation from part **a**?

Two-way ANOVA: Response versus A, B

```
Source        DF     SS       MS       F       P
A              1   4.4408   4.44083   18.06   0.005
B              2   4.1267   2.06333    8.39   0.018
Interaction    2  18.0067   9.00333   36.62   0.000
Error          6   1.4750   0.24583
Total         11  28.0492

S = 0.4958   R-Sq = 94.74%   R-Sq(adj) = 90.36%
```

68 The next table gives data for a 2×2 factorial experiment with two observations per factor-level combination.

L09068

		Factor B	
	Level	1	2
Factor A	1	29.6, 35.2	47.3, 42.1
	2	12.9, 17.6	28.4, 22.7

a. Identify the treatments for this experiment. Calculate and plot the treatment means, using the response variable as the y-axis and the levels of factor B as the x-axis. Use the levels of factor A as plotting symbols. Do the treatment means appear to differ? Do the factors appear to interact?

b. Use the computational formulas in Appendix: Calculation Formulas for Analysis of Variance to create an ANOVA table for this experiment.

c. Test to determine whether the treatment means differ at the $\alpha = .05$ level of significance. Does the test support your visual interpretation from part **a**?

d. Does the result of the test in part **b** warrant a test for interaction between the two factors? If so, perform it using $\alpha = .05$.

e. Do the results of the previous tests warrant tests of the two factor main effects? If so, perform them using $\alpha = .05$. Yes.

f. Interpret the results of the tests. Do they support your visual interpretation from part **a**?

g. Given the results of your tests, which pairs of means, if any, should be compared?

69 Suppose a 3×3 factorial experiment is conducted with three replications. Assume that SS(Total) = 1,000. For each of the following scenarios, form an ANOVA table, conduct the appropriate tests, and interpret the results.

a. The Sum of Squares of factor A main effect [SS(A)] is 20% of SS(Total), the Sum of Squares for factor B main effect [SS(B)] is 10% of SS(Total), and the Sum of Squares for interaction [SS(AB)] is 10% of SS(Total).

b. SS(A) is 10%, SS(B) is 10%, and SS(AB) is 50% of SS(Total).

c. SS(A) is 40%, SS(B) is 10%, and SS(AB) is 20% of SS(Total).

d. SS(A) is 40%, SS(B) is 40%, and SS(AB) is 10% of SS(Total).

Applying the Concepts—Basic

70 Eggshell quality in laying hens. Introducing calcium into a hen's diet can improve the shell quality of the eggs laid. One way to do this is with a limestone diet. In *Animal Feed Science and Technology* (June 2010), researchers investigated the effect of hen's age and limestone diet on eggshell quality. Two different diets were studied—fine limestone (FL) and coarse limestone (CL). Hens were classified as either younger hens (24–36 weeks old) or older hens (56–68 weeks old). The study used 120 younger hens and 120 older hens. Within each age group, half the hens were fed a fine limestone diet and the other half a coarse limestone diet. Thus, there were 60 hens in each of the four combinations of age and diet. The characteristics of the eggs produced from the laying hens were recorded, including shell thickness.

a. Identify the type of experimental design employed by the researchers.

b. Identify the factors and the factor levels (treatments) for this design.

c. Identify the experimental unit.

d. Identify the dependent variable.

e. The researchers found no evidence of factor interaction. Interpret this result, practically.

f. The researchers found no evidence of a main effect for hen's age. Interpret this result, practically.

g. The researchers found statistical evidence of a main effect for limestone diet. Interpret this result, practically. (*Note:* The mean shell thickness for eggs produced by hens on a CL diet was larger than the corresponding mean for hens on an FL diet.)

71 Corporate social responsibility study. The importance that consumers place on the social responsibility of firms has grown over the past decade. As a consequence, corporations are developing more socially responsible strategies and procedures (e.g., corporate sustainability, fair-trade policies). The perceptions consumers have of these strategies were investigated in the *Journal of Marketing* (November 2009). Undergraduate marketing students were provided information on a firm's irresponsible behaviors as well as public statements made by the firm to promote its corporate social responsibility policy. Each student then rated the level of hypocrisy in the statements on a 7-point scale. Students were divided into groups depending on the type of *statement* they were given (concrete or abstract) and on the *order of information* provided (statement first or corporate behavior first). The researchers analyzed the data using a 2×2 factorial design.

a. Identify the factors and treatments in this experiment.
b. An ANOVA *F*-test for the interaction between statement type and order of information was found to be significant (*p*-value $< .01$). Practically interpret this result.
c. The means for the four treatments are shown in the table. Graph these means to demonstrate the nature of the interaction.
d. Based on the result, part **b**, advise the researchers on whether or not they should perform main effect tests.

Statement Type	Order of Information	Treatment Mean
Concrete	Statement first	5.90
Concrete	Behavior first	4.60
Abstract	Statement first	5.33
Abstract	Behavior first	5.26

72 Baker's vs. brewer's yeast. The *Electronic Journal of Biotechnology* (Dec. 15, 2003) published an article on a comparison of two yeast extracts, baker's yeast and brewer's yeast. Brewer's yeast is a surplus by-product obtained from a brewery, hence it is less expensive than primary-grown baker's yeast. Samples of both yeast extracts were prepared at four different temperatures (45, 48, 51, and 54°C); thus, a 2×4 factorial design with yeast extract at two levels and temperature at four levels was employed. The response variable was the autolysis yield (recorded as a percentage).
a. How many treatments are included in the experiment?
b. An ANOVA found sufficient evidence of factor interaction at $\alpha = .05$. Interpret this result practically.
c. Give the null and alternative hypotheses for testing the main effects of yeast extract and temperature.
d. Explain why the tests, part **c**, should not be conducted.
e. Multiple comparisons of the four temperature means were conducted for each of the two yeast extracts. Interpret the results shown below.

Baker's yeast:	Mean yield (%):	41.1	47.5	48.6	50.3
	Temperature (°C):	54	45	48	51
Brewer's yeast:	Mean yield (%):	39.4	47.3	49.2	49.6
	Temperature (°C):	54	51	48	45

73 Purchase of fair-trade products. "Just-world" theory proposes that people receive the rewards and/or punishments that they deserve. Marketing researchers examined just-world theory in the context of fair trade (*Journal of Marketing*, January 2012). In particular, the researchers wanted to know if manipulating market conditions has an impact on whether consumers purchase fair-trade products. A designed experiment with two manipulated

market factors was employed. One factor was *justice reparation potential* (low or high); a second factor was *producer need* (moderate or high). A sample of business students was divided into four groups—34 students were randomly assigned to each of the $2 \times 2 = 4$ market condition treatments. After reading a news article and press release that manipulated their condition, each student reported on their intention to purchase a fair-trade product. Intention was measured on a scale ranging from 0 to 6 points. The data for all 136 students (simulated based on information provided in the journal article) are saved in the accompanying file. An ANOVA for the data is shown in the accompanying Minitab printout.

```
Analysis of Variance for INT

Source      DF       SS       MS       F       P
JRP          1    1.360    1.360    1.25   0.266
NEED         1    0.622    0.622    0.57   0.451
JRP*NEED     1   22.405   22.405   20.55   0.000
Error      132  143.948    1.091
Total      135  168.335


S = 1.04428    R-Sq = 14.49%    R-Sq(adj) = 12.54%
```

a. For this designed experiment, explain (practically) what it means to have factor interaction.
b. Conduct the *F*-test for factor interaction using $\alpha = .01$. What do you conclude?
c. In the journal article, the researchers reported on the ANOVA *F*-tests for main effects. Is this necessary? Explain.
d. A plot of the sample means for the four treatments is shown below in the Minitab graph. Explain why this graph supports your answer to part **b**.
e. The researchers hypothesized that when justice restoration potential is low, fair-trade purchase intentions will be lower when Need is high rather than moderate. Conversely, when justice restoration potential is high, purchase intentions will be greater when Need is high rather than moderate. Is there evidence to support this theory?

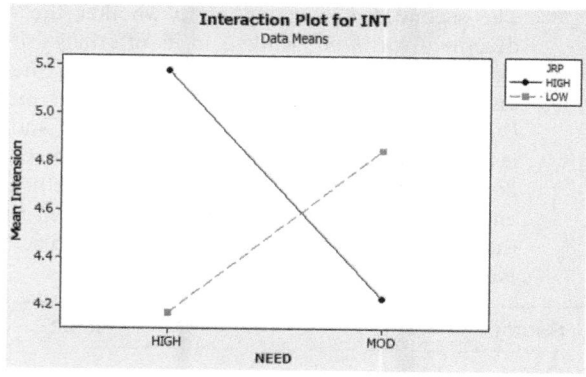

74 Insomnia and education. Many workers suffer from stress and chronic insomnia. Is insomnia related to education status? Researchers at the Universities of Memphis, Alabama at Birmingham, and Tennessee investigated this question in the *Journal of Abnormal Psychology* (Feb. 2005). Adults living in Tennessee were selected to participate in the study using a random-digit telephone dialing procedure. In addition to insomnia status (normal sleeper or chronic insomnia), the researchers classified each participant into one of four education categories (college graduate, some college, high school graduate, and high school dropout). One dependent variable of interest to the researchers was a quantitative measure of daytime functioning called the Fatigue Severity Scale (FSS). The data were analyzed as a 2×4 factorial experiment, with Insomnia status and Education level as the two factors.

a. Determine the number of treatments for this study. List them.

b. The researchers reported that "the Insomnia $\times$ Education interaction was not statistically significant." Practically interpret this result. (Illustrate with a graph.)

c. The researchers discovered that the sample mean FSS for people with insomnia was greater than the sample mean FSS for normal sleepers, and this difference was statistically significant. Practically interpret this result.

d. The researchers reported that the main effect of Education was statistically significant. Practically interpret this result.

e. Refer to part **d.** In a follow-up analysis, the sample mean FSS values for the four Education levels were compared using Tukey's method ($\alpha = .05$), with the results shown below. What do you conclude?

Mean:	3.3	3.6	3.7	4.2
Education:	College graduate	Some college	HS graduate	HS dropout

Applying the Concepts—Intermediate

75 **Temptation in consumer choice.** Are you willing to pay more for a tempting vice option (e.g., eating a hamburger, surfing the Internet) than a virtuous option (e.g., eating broccoli, reading the newspaper)? The costs and benefits of consumer temptation choice were investigated in the *Journal of Marketing Research* (February 2012). In one experiment, the researchers used a 2×2 factorial design involving a sample of 180 consumers. The first factor varied as to whether consumers were asked to imagine ordering a steak (*vice*) or organic pasta (*virtue*) at a restaurant. The second factor varied as to whether the restaurant described was *homogeneous* in its offerings (either "only tasty, less healthy dishes like steak" or "only healthy, less tasty dishes like organic pasta") or offered a *mixed menu* (both "tasty, less healthy dishes like steak" and "healthy, less tasty dishes like organic pasta"). Consumers were randomly assigned to one of the four order/menu conditions and then asked to give the maximum amount (in dollars) they would be willing to pay for their choice. A partial ANOVA table for the data is shown below.

Source	df	F-Value	p-Value
Order (vice/virtue)	–	–	–
Menu (homogeneous/mixed)	–	–	–
Order × Menu	–	11.25	<.001
Error	–		
Total	179		

a. Fill in the missing degrees of freedom values in the ANOVA table.

b. Give a practical interpretation of the test for interaction using $\alpha = .05$.

c. The F-values (and corresponding p-values) missing in the table were not provided in the journal article. Are these results required to complete the analysis of the data? Explain.

d. In a follow-up to the ANOVA, the researchers compared the mean willing to pay values for the homogeneous and mixed-menu conditions at each level of the order condition. In the virtue condition, the mean for the homogeneous menu ($11.08) was significantly lower than the mean for the mixed menu ($13.26). In the vice condition, the mean for the homogeneous menu ($17.11) was significantly higher than the mean for the mixed menu ($15.00). Demonstrate why these results support your answer to part **b.** Illustrate with a graph.

76 **Commercial eggs produced from different housing systems.** Refer to the *Food Chemistry* (Vol. 106, 2008) study of four different types of egg housing systems, Exercise 33. Recall that the four housing systems were cage, barn, free range, and organic. In addition to housing system, the researchers also determined the weight class (medium or large) for each sampled egg. The data on whipping capacity (percent overrun) for the 28 sampled eggs are shown in the accompanying table. The researchers want to investigate the effect of both housing system and weight class on the mean whipping capacity of the eggs. In particular, they want to know whether the difference between the mean whipping capacity of medium and large eggs depends on the housing system.

EGGS

Housing	Wtclass	Overrun (%)
Cage	M	495, 462, 488, 471, 471
	L	502, 472, 474, 492, 479
Free	M	513, 510, 510
	L	520, 531, 521
Barn	M	515, 516, 514
	L	526, 501, 508
Organic	M	532, 511, 527
	L	530, 544, 531

a. Identify the factors and treatments for this experiment.

b. Use statistical software to conduct an ANOVA on the data. Report the results in an ANOVA table.

c. Is there evidence of interaction between housing system and weight class? Test using $\alpha = .05$. [*Hint:* Due to an unbalanced design, you will need to analyze the data using the general linear model procedure of your statistical software.] What does this imply, practically?

d. Interpret the main effect test for housing system (using $\alpha = .05$). What does this imply, practically?

e. Interpret the main effect test for weight class (using $\alpha = .05$). What does this imply, practically?

77 **Testing a new pain-reliever tablet.** Refer to the *Tropical Journal of Pharmaceutical Research* (June 2003) study of the impact of binding agent, binding concentration, and relative density on the mean dissolution time of pain-relief tablets, Exercise 14. Recall that the binding agent was set at two levels (khaya gum and PVP), binding concentration at two levels (.5% and 4.0%), and relative density at two levels (low and high); thus, a $2 \times 2 \times 2$ factorial design was employed. The sample mean dissolution times for the treatments associated with the factors binding agent and relative density when the other factor (binding concentration) is held fixed at .5% are $\bar{x}_{Gum/Low} = 4.70$, $\bar{x}_{Gum/High} = 7.95$, $\bar{x}_{PVP/Low} = 3.00$, and $\bar{x}_{PVP/High} = 4.10$. Do the results suggest there is an interaction between binding agent and relative density? Explain.

78 **Eyewitnesses and mugshots.** When an eyewitness to a crime examines a set of mugshots at a police station, the photos are usually presented in groups (e.g., six mugshots at a time). Criminologists at Niagara University investigated whether mugshot group size has an effect on the selections made by eyewitnesses (*Applied Psychology in Criminal Justice*, April 2010). A sample of 90 college students was shown a video of a simulated theft. Shortly thereafter, each student was shown 180 mugshots and asked to select a photo that most closely resembled the thief. (Multiple photos could be selected.) The students were randomly assigned to view either 3, 6, or 12 mugshots at a time. Within each mugshot group size, the students were further randomly divided into three sets. In the first set, the researchers focused on the selections made in the first 60 photos shown; in the second set, the focus was on selections made in the middle 60 photos shown; and in the third set, selections made in the last 60 photos were recorded. The dependent variable of interest was the number of mugshot selections. Simulated data for this 3 × 3 factorial ANOVA, with mugshot group size at three levels (3, 6, or 12 photos) and photo set at three levels (first 60, middle 60, and last 60) are saved in the accompanying file. Fully analyze the data for the researchers. In particular, the researchers want to know if mugshot group size has an effect on the mean number of selections, and, if so, which group size leads to the most selections. Also, are there a higher number of selections made in the first 60, middle 60, or last 60 photos viewed?

79 **TV ad recall study.** Refer to the *Journal of Applied Psychology* (June 2002) study of the effect of violence and sex on a television viewer's ability to recall a TV commercial, Exercise 28. Recall that 324 adults were randomly assigned to one of three TV content groups, with 108 subjects in each group. One group watched a TV program with a violent content code (V) rating; the second group viewed a show with a sex content code (S) rating; and the last group watched a neutral TV program. Commercials were imbedded into each TV show, and after the participants viewed the show, the advertisement recall score was measured for each participant. In addition, the researchers recorded whether or not the subject had previously seen the commercial. The layout for the full experimental design is shown in the accompanying schematic. Note that there are two factors in this experiment—TV content group at three levels and watched commercial before status at two levels—and the design is a 3 × 2 factorial. The researchers want to know whether the two factors, TV content group and watched commercial before status, impact mean recall score. Conduct a two-way factorial analysis of variance on the data saved in the accompanying file. The researchers concluded that (1) the Neutral TV content group has the highest mean recall score, but that there is no significant difference between the mean recall scores of the Violent and Sex content groups and (2) there is no significant difference between the mean recall

scores of those who had previously watched the commercial and those who had not. Do you agree?

Layout of Experimental Design for TV Ad Recall Study

	TV Content Group		
	Violent (V)	Sex (S)	Neutral (N)
Watched commercial before: *Yes*	$n = 48$	$n = 60$	$n = 54$
No	$n = 60$	$n = 48$	$n = 54$

Applying the Concepts—Advanced

80 **On the trail of the cockroach.** Knowledge of how cockroaches forage for food is valuable for companies that develop and manufacture roach bait and traps. Many entomologists believe, however, that the navigational behavior of cockroaches scavenging for food is random. D. Miller of Virginia Tech University challenged the "random-walk" theory by designing an experiment to test a cockroach's ability to follow a trail of their fecal material (*Explore, Research at the University of Florida*, Fall 1998).

A methanol extract from roach feces—called a *pheromone*—was used to create a chemical trail. German cockroaches were released at the beginning of the trail, one at a time, and a video surveillance camera was used to monitor the roach's movements. In addition to the trail containing the fecal extract (the treatment), a trail using methanol only (the control) was created. To determine if trail-following ability differed among cockroaches of different age, sex, and reproductive status, four roach groups were used in the experiment: adult males, adult females, gravid (pregnant) females, and nymphs (immatures). Twenty roaches of each type were randomly assigned to the treatment trail, and 10 of each type were randomly assigned to the control trail. Thus, a total of 120 roaches were used in the experiment. The movement pattern of each cockroach was measured (in "pixels") as the average trail deviation. The data for the 120 cockroaches in the study are stored in the accompanying file. (The first 5 and last 5 observations in the data set are listed here.) Conduct a complete analysis of the data. Determine whether roaches can distinguish between the fecal extract and control trail and whether trail-following ability differs according to age, sex, and reproductive status.

Trail Deviation	Roach Group	Trail
3.1	Adult Male	Extract
42.0	Adult Male	Control
6.2	Adult Male	Extract
22.7	Adult Male	Control
34.0	Adult Male	Extract
⋮	⋮	⋮
23.8	Nymph	Extract
5.1	Nymph	Extract
3.8	Nymph	Extract
3.1	Nymph	Extract
2.8	Nymph	Extract

81 **Impact of flavor name on consumer choice.** Do consumers react favorably to products with ambiguous colors or names? Marketing Professors E. G. Miller and B. E. Kahn investigated this phenomenon in the *Journal of Consumer Research* (June 2005). As a "reward" for participating in an unrelated experiment, 100 consumers were told they could have some jelly beans available in several cups on a table. Half the consumers were assigned to take jelly beans with common descriptive flavor names (e.g., watermelon green), while the other half were assigned to take jelly beans with ambiguous flavor names (e.g., monster green). Within each group, half of the consumers took the jelly beans and left (low cognitive load condition), while the other half were distracted with additional questions designed to distract them while they were taking their jelly beans (high cognitive load condition). Consequently, a 2×2 factorial experiment was employed— with Flavor Name (common or ambiguous) and Cognitive Load (low or high) as the two factors—with 25 consumers assigned to each of four treatments. The dependent variable of interest was the number of jelly beans taken by each consumer. The means and standard deviations of the four treatments are shown in the accompanying table.

	Ambiguous		Common	
	Mean	Std. Dev.	Mean	Std. Dev.
Low load	18.0	15.0	7.8	9.5
High load	6.1	9.5	6.3	10.0

Source: Based on Miller, E. G., & Kahn, B. E. "Shades of meaning: The effect of color and flavor names on consumer choice," *Journal of Consumer Research,* Vol. 32, No. 1, June 2005 (Table 1).

a. Calculate the total of the $n = 25$ measurements for each of the four categories in the 2×2 factorial experiment.

b. Calculate the correction for mean, CM. (See Appendix: Calculation Formulas for Analysis of Variance for computational formulas.)

c. Use the results of parts **a** and **b** to calculate the sums of squares for Load, Name, and Load $\times$ Name interaction.

d. Calculate the sample variance for each treatment. Then calculate the sum of squares of deviations within each sample for the four treatments.

e. Calculate SSE. (*Hint:* SSE is the pooled sum of squares for the deviations calculated in part **d.**)

f. Now that you know SS(Load), SS(Name), SS(Load $\times$ Name), and SSE, find SS(Total).

g. Summarize the calculations in an ANOVA table.

h. The researchers reported the F-value for Load $\times$ Name interaction as $F = 5.34$. Do you agree?

i. Conduct a complete analysis of these data. Use $\alpha = .05$ for any inferential techniques you employ. Illustrate your conclusions graphically.

j. What assumptions are necessary to ensure the validity of the inferential techniques you used? State them in terms of this experiment.

◻ Chapter Notes

Key Terms

Analysis of variance (ANOVA)
Balanced design
Blocks
Bonferroni multiple comparisons procedure
Comparisonwise error rate (CER)
Complete factorial experiment
Completely randomized design
Dependent variable
Designed study
Experimental unit
Experimentwise error rate (EER)
Factor interaction
Factor levels
Factor main effect
Factors
F-statistic
F-test
Independent variables
Mean Square for Error (MSE)

Mean Square for Treatments (MST)
Multiple comparisons of a set of treatment means
Observational study
Qualitative factors
Quantitative factors
Randomized block design
Replicates
Response variable
Robust method
Scheffé multiple comparisons procedure
Single-factor experiment
Sum of Squares for Blocks (SSB)
Sum of Squares for Error (SSE)
Sum of Squares for Treatments (SST)
Treatments
Tukey multiple comparisons procedure
Two-way classification

MST	Mean Square for Treatments
SSB	Sum of Squares for Blocks
MSB	Mean Square for Blocks
SSE	Sum of Squares for Error
MSE	Mean Square for Error
$a \times b$ factorial	Factorial design with one factor at a levels and the other factor at b levels
SS(A)	Sum of Squares for main effect factor A
MS(A)	Mean Square for main effect factor A
SS(B)	Sum of Squares for main effect factor B
MS(B)	Mean Square for main effect factor B
SS(AB)	Sum of Squares for factor $A \times B$ interaction
MS(AB)	Mean Square for factor $A \times B$ interaction

Key Ideas

Key Elements of a Designed Experiment

1. *Response (dependent) variable*—quantitative
2. *Factors*—quantitative or qualitative
3. *Factor levels (values of factors)*—selected by the experimenter
4. *Treatments*—combinations of factor levels
5. *Experimental units*—assign treatments to experimental units and measure response for each

Key Symbols/Notation

ANOVA	Analysis of variance
SST	Sum of Squares for Treatments

Balanced design
Sample sizes for each treatment are equal.

Tests for main effects in a factorial design
Only appropriate if the test for factor interaction is nonsignificant.

Robust method
Slight to moderate departures from normality do not have impact on validity of the ANOVA results.

Conditions Required for Valid F-Test in a Completely Randomized Design

1. All k treatment populations are approximately normal.
2. $\sigma_1^2 = \sigma_2^2 = \cdots = \sigma_k^2$

Conditions Required for Valid F-Test in a Randomized Block Design

1. All treatment-block populations are approximately normal.
2. All treatment-block populations have the same variance.

Conditions Required for Valid F-Tests in a Complete Factorial Design

1. All treatment populations are approximately normal.
2. All treatment populations have the same variance.

Mulitiple Comparisons of Means Methods

Number of pairwise comparisons with k treatment means
$$c = k(k-1)/2$$

Tukey method:
1. Balanced design
2. Pairwise comparisons of means

Bonferroni method:
1. Either balanced or unbalanced design
2. Pairwise comparisons of means

Scheffé method:
1. Either balanced or unbalanced design
2. General contrasts of means

Experimentwise error rate (EER)
Risk of making at least one Type I error when making multiple comparisons of means in ANOVA

Guide to Selecting the Experimental Design

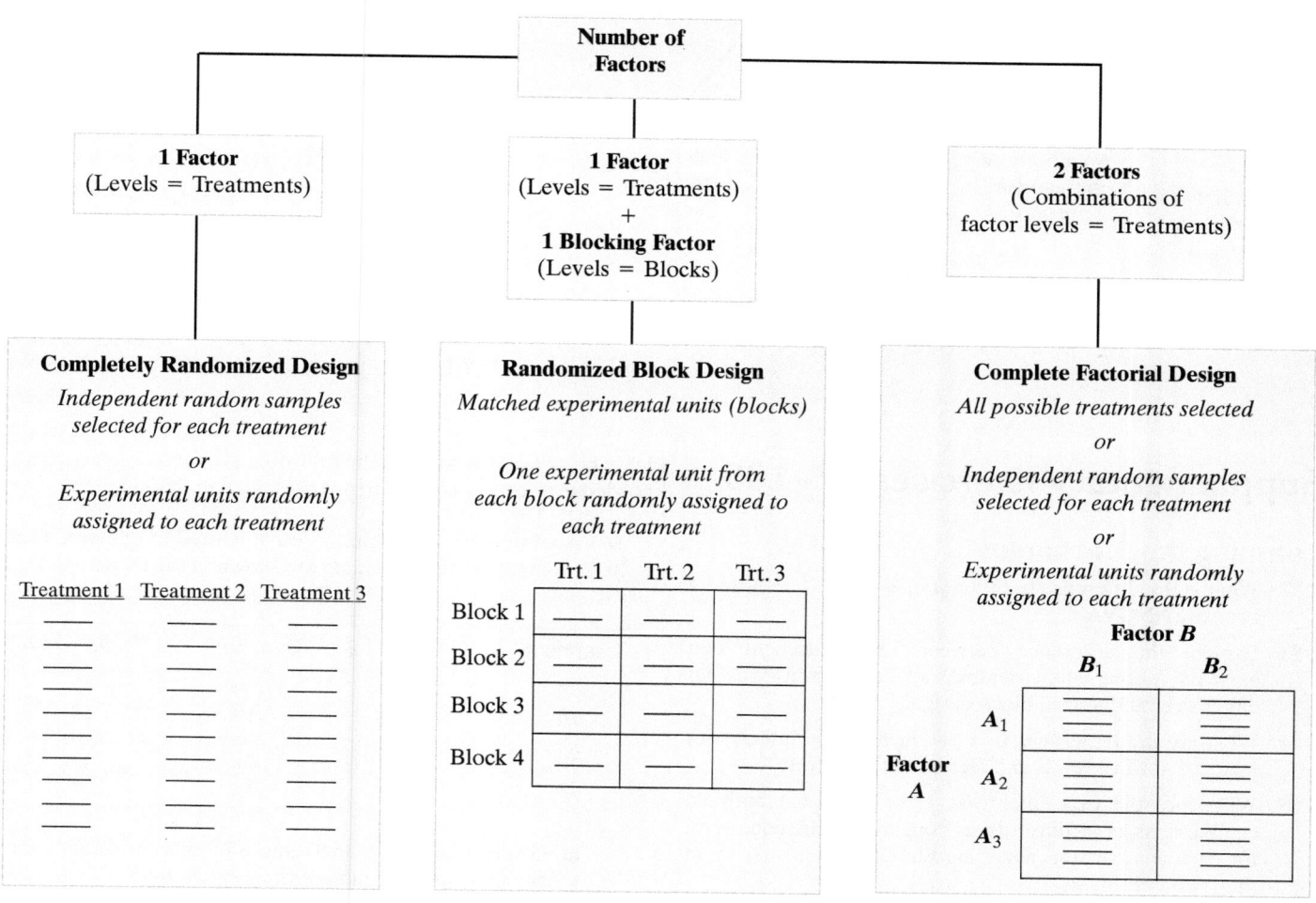

571

Guide to Conducting ANOVA *F*-Tests

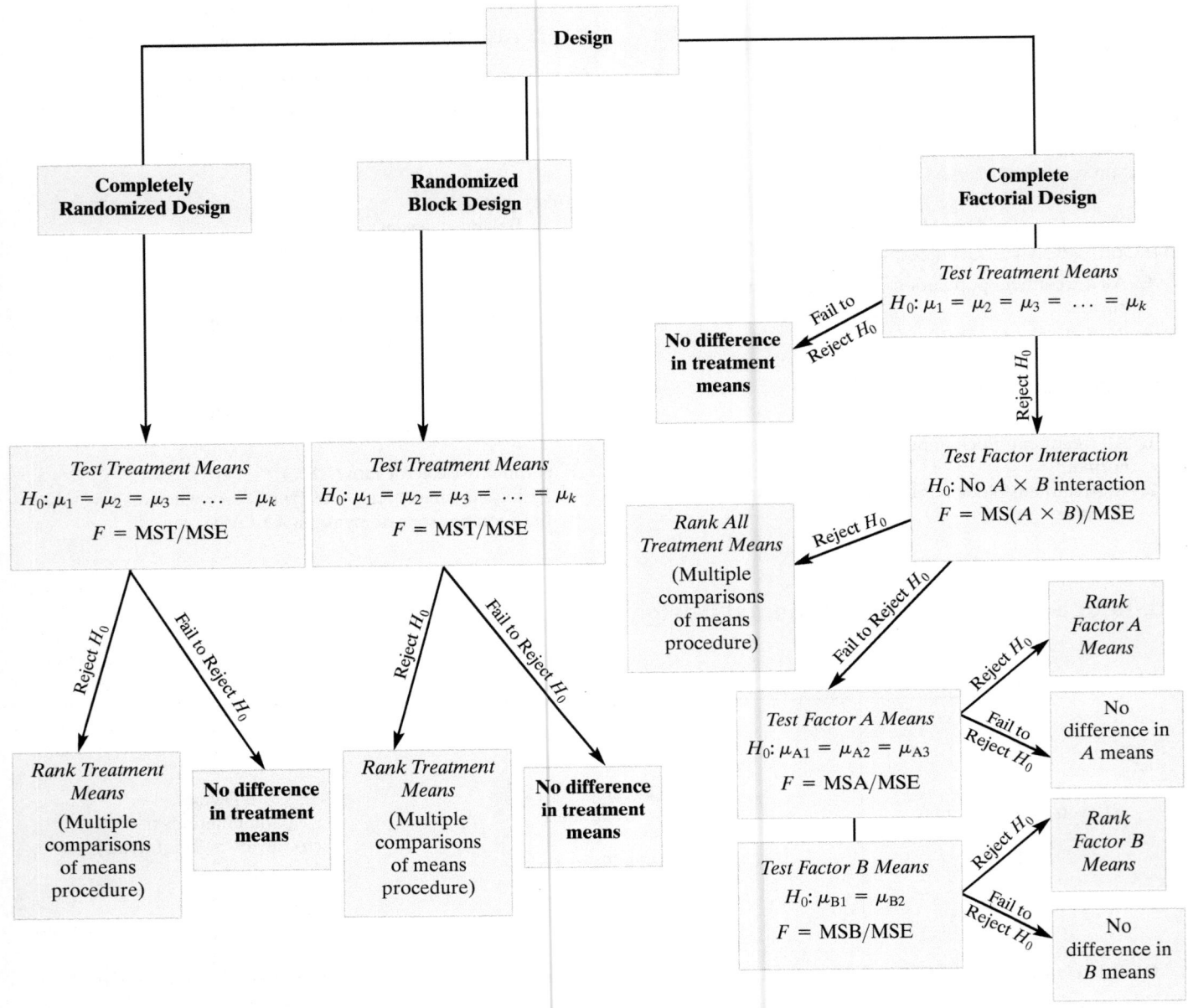

Supplementary Exercises 82–109

Please be aware that some of the following problems may require knowledge of concepts that are not presented in this chapter.

Learning the Mechanics

82 What is the difference between a one-way ANOVA and a two-way ANOVA?

83 Explain the difference between an experiment that employs a completely randomized design and one that employs a randomized block design.

84 What are the treatments in a two-factor experiment, with factor A at three levels and factor B at two levels?

85 Why does the experimentwise error rate of a multiple comparisons procedure differ from the significance level for each comparison (assuming the experiment has more than two treatments)?

86 A completely randomized design is used to compare four treatment means. The data are shown in the table.

L09086

Treatment 1	Treatment 2	Treatment 3	Treatment 4
8	6	9	12
10	9	10	13
9	8	8	10
10	8	11	11
11	7	12	11

a. Given that SST = 36.95 and SS(Total) = 62.55, complete an ANOVA table for this experiment.

b. Is there evidence that the treatment means differ? Use $\alpha = .10$.

c. Place a 90% confidence interval on the mean response for treatment 4.

87 An experiment employing a randomized block design was conducted to compare the mean responses for four treatments—A, B, C, and D. The treatments were randomly assigned to the four experimental units in each of five blocks. The data are shown in the following table.

L09087

Treatment	Block				
	1	2	3	4	5
A	8.6	7.5	8.7	9.8	7.4
B	7.3	6.3	7.3	8.4	6.3
C	9.1	8.3	9.0	9.9	8.2
D	9.3	8.2	9.2	10.0	8.4

a. Given that SS(Total) = 22.31 and SS(Block) = 10.688 and SSE = .288, complete an ANOVA table for the experiment.

b. Do the data provide sufficient evidence to indicate a difference among treatment means? Test using $\alpha = .05$.

c. Does the result of the test in part **b** warrant further comparison of the treatment means? If so, how many pairwise comparisons need to be made?

d. Is there evidence that the block means differ? Use $\alpha = .05$.

88 The following table shows a partially completed ANOVA table for a two-factor factorial experiment.

Source	df	SS	MS	F
A	3	2.6	–	–
B	5	9.2	–	–
A × B	–	–	3.1	–
Error	–	18.7		
Total	47			

a. Complete the ANOVA table.

b. How many levels were used for each factor? How many treatments were used? How many replications were performed?

c. Find the value of the Sum of Squares for Treatments. Test to determine whether the data provide evidence that the treatment means differ. Use $\alpha = .05$.

d. Is further testing of the nature of factor effects warranted? If so, test to determine whether the factors interact. Use $\alpha = .05$. Interpret the result.

Applying the Concepts—Basic

89 **Robots trained to behave like ants.** Robotic researchers investigated whether robots could be trained to behave like ants in an ant colony (*Nature*, Aug. 2000). Robots were trained and randomly assigned to "colonies" (i.e., groups) consisting of 3, 6, 9, or 12 robots. The robots were assigned the task of foraging for "food" and to recruit another robot when they identified a resource-rich area. One goal of the experiment was to compare the mean energy expended (per robot) of the four different colony sizes.

a. What type of experimental design was employed?

b. Identify the treatments and the dependent variable.

c. Set up the null and alternative hypotheses of the test.

d. The following ANOVA results were reported: $F = 7.70$, numerator df = 3, denominator df = 56, p-value < .001. Conduct the test at a significance level of $\alpha = .05$ and interpret the result.

e. Multiple comparisons of mean energy expended for the four colony sizes were conducted using an experiment-wise error rate of .05. The results are summarized below.

Sample mean:	.97	.95	.93	.80
Group size:	3	6	9	12

How many pairwise comparisons are conducted in this analysis?

f. Refer to part **e.** Interpret the results shown in the table.

90 **Ethics of salespeople.** Within marketing, the area of personal sales has long suffered from a poor ethical image, particularly in the eyes of college students. An article in *Journal of Business Ethics* (Vol. 15, 1996) investigated whether such opinions by college students are a function of the type of sales job (high tech vs. low tech) and/or the sales task (new account development vs. account maintenance). Four different samples of college students were confronted with the four different situations (new account development in a high-tech sales task, new account development in a low-tech sales task, account maintenance in a high-tech sales task, and account maintenance in a low-tech sales task) and were asked to evaluate the ethical behavior of the salesperson on a 7-point scale ranging from 1 (not a serious ethical violation) to 7 (a very serious ethical violation). Identify each of the following elements of the experiment:

a. Response   **b.** Factor(s) and factor level(s)

c. Treatments   **d.** Experimental units

91 **Impact of paper color on exam scores.** A study published in *Teaching Psychology* (May 1998) examined how external clues influence student performance. Undergraduate students were randomly assigned to one of four different midterm examinations. Form 1 was printed on blue paper and contained difficult questions, while form 2 was also printed on blue paper but contained simple questions. Form 3 was printed on red paper, with difficult questions; form 4 was printed on red paper with simple questions. The researchers were interested in the impact that Color (red or blue) and Question (simple or difficult) had on mean exam score.

Form	Color	Question	Mean Score
1	Blue	Difficult	53.3
2	Blue	Simple	80.0
3	Red	Difficult	39.3
4	Red	Simple	73.6

a. What experimental design was employed in this study? Identify the factors and treatments.

b. The researchers conducted an ANOVA and found a significant interaction between Color and Question (p-value < .03). Interpret this result.

c. The sample mean scores (percentage correct) for the four exam forms are listed in the table above. Plot the four means on a graph to illustrate the Color × Question interaction.

92 Flower production of dwarf shrubs. Dwarf shrubs are popular with model home landscapers. Stetson University researchers conducted an experiment to determine the effects of fire on the shrub's growth (*Florida Scientist,* Spring 1997). Twelve experimental plots of land were selected in a pasture where the shrub is abundant. Within each plot, three dwarf shrubs were randomly selected and treated as follows: one shrub was subjected to fire, another to clipping, and the third was left unmanipulated (a control). After 5 months, the number of flowers produced by each of the 36 shrubs was determined. The objective of the study was to compare the mean number of flowers produced by dwarf shrubs for the three treatments (fire, clipping, and control).

   a. Identify the type of experimental design employed, including the treatments, response variable, and experimental units.

   b. Illustrate the layout of the design using a graphic similar to Figure 20.

   c. The ANOVA of the data resulted in a test statistic of $F = 5.42$ for treatments, with an associated p-value of $p = .009$. Interpret this result.

   d. The three treatment means were compared using Tukey's method at $\alpha = .05$. Interpret the results shown below.

Mean number of flowers:	1.17	10.58	17.08
Treatment:	*Control*	*Clipping*	*Burning*

93 *Fortune's* E-50 list. The *Fortune* E-50 is a listing of the top 50 electronic commerce and Internet-based companies, as determined by *Fortune* magazine each year. *Fortune* groups the companies into four categories: (1) e-companies, (2) Internet software and service, (3) Internet hardware, and (4) Internet communication. Consider a study to compare the mean rates of return for the stock of companies in the four *Fortune* categories. Because the age of an electronic commerce or Internet-based company may have an impact on rate of return, the study is designed to remove any age variation. Four 1-year-old companies, four 3-year-old companies, and four 5-year-old companies were selected; within each age group, one company was randomly selected from category 1, one from category 2, one from category 3, and one from category 4.

   a. What type of experimental design is employed?

   b. Identify the key elements of the experiment (i.e., treatments, blocks, response variable, and experimental unit).

94 College tennis recruiting with a team Web site. Most university athletic programs now have a Web site with information on individual sports and a Prospective Student Athlete Form that allows high school athletes to submit their academic and sports achievements directly to the college coach. *The Sport Journal* (Winter 2004) published a study of how important team Web sites are to the recruitment of college tennis players. A survey was conducted of NCAA tennis coaches, of which 53 were from Division I schools, 20 were from Division II schools, and 53 were from Division III schools. Coaches were asked to respond to a series of statements, including "The Prospective Student Athlete Form on the Web site contributes very little to the recruiting process." Responses were measured on a 7-point scale (where $1 =$ strongly disagree and $7 =$ strongly agree). In order to compare the mean responses of tennis coaches from the three NCAA divisions, the data were analyzed with a completely randomized design ANOVA.

   a. Identify the experimental unit, dependent (response) variable, factor, and treatments for this study.

   b. Give the null and alternative hypotheses for the ANOVA F-test.

   c. The observed significance level of the test was found to be p-value $< .003$. What conclusion can you draw if you want to test at $\alpha = .05$?

   d. The mean responses are listed and ranked in the next table. The results were obtained using a multiple comparisons procedure with an experimentwise error rate of .05. Interpret the results practically.

Mean:	4.51	3.60	3.21
Division:	I	II	III

95 Leadership style and subordinate behavior. Leadership acts occur when one person tries to influence the behavior of others toward the attainment of some goal. The effects of leadership style on the behavior of subordinates were investigated in *Accounting, Organizations and Society* (Vol. 20, 1995). Four types of leadership style were defined based on two variables: the degree of control applied (high or low) and the level of consideration shown for subordinates (high or low). A sample of 257 senior auditors in Big-Six accounting firms yielded the following distribution of leadership styles for the auditors' leaders:

Leadership Style	*n*
A. High control, low consideration	51
B. Low control, low consideration	63
C. High control, high consideration	79
D. Low control, high consideration	64
Total	257

All subjects were asked to indicate (confidentially) how frequently their auditing fieldwork had been intentionally substandard in a particular way. They were asked to respond using a scale that ranged from 1 (never) to 5 (always). These data are summarized in the following table. An ANOVA conducted to test for differences in the four treatment means yielded $F = 30.4$.

Leadership Style	Mean	Standard Deviation	Bonferroni Analysis: Significantly Smaller Means
A	4.27	1.13	B, C, D
B	2.83	1.18	D
C	2.54	1.24	None
D	2.87	1.31	None
Overall	3.04	1.42	

Source: Otley, D. T., & Pierce, B. J. "The control problem in public accounting firms: An empirical study of the impact of leadership style," *Accounting Organizations and Society,* Vol. 20, No. 5, 1995, pp. 405–420. Copyright © 1995 by Elsevier, Ltd. Reprinted with permission.

   a. Do the data indicate that leadership style affects the behavior of subordinates? Test using $\alpha = .05$.

   b. The Bonferroni multiple comparisons procedure was used to rank the four treatment means at an experimentwise error rate of $\alpha = .05$. Carefully interpret the results shown in the table.

   c. What assumptions must hold to ensure the validity of the Bonferroni procedure?

96 Effectiveness of geese decoys. What type of decoy should you purchase for hunting waterfowl? A study in the *Journal of Wildlife Management* (July 1995) compared the effectiveness of three different decoy types—taxidermy-mounted decoys, plastic shell decoys, and full-bodied plastic decoys—in attracting Canada geese to sunken pit blinds. In order to account for an extraneous source of variation, three pit blinds were used as blocks in the experiment. Thus, a randomized block design with three treatments (decoy types) and three blocks (pit blinds) was employed. The response variable was the percentage of a goose flock to approach within 46 meters of the pit blind on a given day. The data are given in the table.* A Minitab printout of the analysis follows. Locate the *p*-value for treatments on the printout and interpret the result.

Blind	Shell	Full-Bodied	Taxidermy-Mounted
1	7.3	13.6	17.8
2	12.6	10.4	17.0
3	16.4	23.4	13.6

Source: Harrey, W. F., Hindman, L. J., & Rhodes. W. E. "Vulnerability of Canada geese to taxidermy-mounted decoys," *Journal of Wildlife Management,* Vol. 59, No. 3, July 1995, p. 475 (Table 1). Copyright © 1995 by John Wiley & Sons. Reproduced with permission.

Two-way ANOVA: PERCENT versus DECOY, BLIND

```
Source   DF      SS      MS      F      P
DECOY    2    30.069  15.0344  0.61  0.589
BLIND    2    44.149  22.0744  0.89  0.479
Error    4    99.338  24.8344
Total    8   173.556

S = 4.983    R-Sq = 42.76%    R-Sq(adj) = 0.00%
```

97 Removing bacteria from water. A coagulation-microfiltration process for removing bacteria from water was investigated in *Environmental Science & Engineering* (Sept. 1, 2000). Chemical engineers at Seoul National University performed a designed experiment to estimate the effect of both the level of the coagulant and acidity (pH) level on the coagulation efficiency of the process. Six levels of coagulant (5, 10, 20, 50, 100, and 200 milligrams per liter) and six pH levels (4.0, 5.0, 6.0, 7.0, 8.0, and 9.0) were employed. Water specimens collected from the Han River in Seoul, Korea, were placed in jars, and each jar was randomly assigned to receive one of the $6 \times 6 = 36$ combinations of coagulant level and pH level.

a. What type of experimental design was applied in this study?

b. Give the factors, factor levels, and treatments for the study.

Applying the Concepts—Intermediate

98 A managerial decision problem. A direct-mail company assembles and stores paper products (envelopes, letters, brochures, order cards, etc.) for its customers. The company estimates the total number of pieces received in a shipment by estimating the weight per piece and then weighing the entire shipment. The company is unsure whether the

*The actual design employed in the study was more complex than the randomized block design shown here. In the actual study, each number in the table represented the mean daily percentage of goose flocks attracted to the blind, averaged over 13–17 days.

sample of pieces used to estimate the mean weight per piece should be drawn from a single carton, or whether it is worth the extra time required to pull a few pieces from several cartons. To aid management in making a decision, eight brochures were pulled from each of five cartons of a typical shipment and weighed. The weights (in pounds) are shown in the table.

Carton 1	Carton 2	Carton 3	Carton 4	Carton 5
.01851	.01872	.01869	.01899	.01882
.01829	.01861	.01853	.01917	.01895
.01844	.01876	.01876	.01852	.01884
.01859	.01886	.01880	.01904	.01835
.01854	.01896	.01880	.01923	.01889
.01853	.01879	.01882	.01905	.01876
.01844	.01879	.01862	.01924	.01891
.01833	.01879	.01860	.01893	.01879

a. Identify the response, factor(s), treatments, and experimental units.

b. Do these data provide sufficient evidence to indicate differences in the mean weight per brochure among the five cartons?

c. What assumptions must be satisfied in order for the test of part **b** to be valid?

d. Use Tukey's method to compare all pairs of means, with $\alpha = .05$ as the overall level of significance.

e. Given the results, make a recommendation to management about whether to sample from one carton or from many cartons.

99 Ethics of downsizing. A major strategic alternative for many U.S. firms is to reduce the size of their workforce, i.e., to "downsize." The ethics of downsizing decisions from the employees' perspective was investigated in the *Journal of Business Ethics* (Vol. 18,1999). The researchers surveyed a sample of 209 employees who were enrolled in an Executive MBA Program or weekend program at one of three Colorado universities. These individuals were divided into five distinct groups, depending on their job situation at a previous or current firm. The groups were named (1) Casualties, (2) Survivors, (3) Implementors/casualties, (4) Implementors/survivors, and (5) Formulators. The sampled employees completed a questionnaire on their ethical perceptions of downsizing. One item asked employees to respond to the statement: "It is unethical for a downsizing decision to be announced or implemented on or prior to a major holiday." Responses were measured using a 5-point Likert scale, where 1 = strongly agree, 2 = agree, 3 = neutral, 4 = disagree, and 5 = strongly disagree. Data on both the qualitative variable "Group" and the quantitative variable "Ethics response" are saved in the accompanying file. The researchers' goal was to determine if any differences exist among the mean ethics scores for the five groups.

a. The data were analyzed using an ANOVA for a completely randomized design. Identify the factor, treatments, response variable, and experimental units for this design.

b. Specify the null and alternative hypotheses tested.

c. A Minitab printout of the ANOVA is displayed on the next page. Can you conclude that the mean ethics scores of the five groups of employees are significantly different? Explain.

Minitab output for Exercise 99

One-way ANOVA: CASUAL, SURVIVE, IMPCAS, IMPSUR, FORMUL

```
Source    DF      SS     MS     F      P
Factor     4   40.84  10.21  9.85  0.000
Error    204  211.35   1.04
Total    208  252.19

S = 1.018    R-Sq = 16.19%    R-Sq(adj) = 14.55%


                            Individual 95% CIs For Mean Based on Pooled StDev
Level     N    Mean   StDev   +---------+---------+---------+---------
CASUAL   47   1.787   0.832         (----*----)
SURVIVE  71   1.845   1.023         (---*---)
IMPCAS   27   1.593   0.636   (------*-----)
IMPSUR   33   2.545   1.301                  (----*-----)
FORMUL   31   2.871   1.176                     (-----*-----)
                                +---------+---------+---------+---------
                             1.20      1.80      2.40      3.00


Pooled StDev = 1.018
```

---

d. Access the data and check that the assumptions required for the ANOVA *F*-test are reasonably satisfied.

e. Multiple comparisons of the treatment (group) means were conducted using the Bonferroni method with an experimentwise error rate of .05. Explain why the Bonferroni method is preferred over another multiple comparisons method (e.g., Tukey or Scheffé).

f. Refer to part **e**. Determine the number of pairwise comparisons for this analysis.

g. The sample mean ethics scores for the five groups and Bonferroni rankings are summarized below. Identify the groups with the significantly largest mean ethics scores.

1.59	1.79	1.84	2.45	2.87
Implementors/ casualties	Casualties	Survivors	Implementors/ survivors	Formulators
Group 3	Group 1	Group 2	Group 4	Group 5

100 Study of anticoagulant drugs. Three anticoagulant drugs are studied to compare their effectiveness in dissolving blood clots. Each of five subjects receives the drugs at equally spaced time intervals and in random order. Time periods between drug applications permit a drug to be passed out of a subject's body before the subject receives the next drug. After each drug is in the bloodstream, the length of time (in seconds) required for a cut of specified size to stop bleeding is recorded. The results are shown in the following table.

		Drug	
Person	A	B	C
1	127.5	129.0	135.5
2	130.6	129.1	138.0
3	118.3	111.7	110.1
4	155.5	144.3	162.3
5	180.7	174.4	181.8

a. What type of experimental design was used in this study? Identify the response, factor(s), factor type(s), treatments, and experimental units.

b. Is there evidence of a difference in mean clotting time among the three drugs? Test using $\alpha = .10$.

c. What is the observed significance level of the test you conducted in part **a**? Interpret it.

d. Was blocking effective in reducing the variation among the data? That is, do the data support the contention that the mean clotting time varies from person to person?

e. If warranted, use a multiple comparisons technique to determine whether one of the drugs is most effective. Use an overall significance level of $\alpha = .10$.

101 Steel ingot quality study. A quality-control supervisor measures the quality of a steel ingot on a scale of 0 to 10. He designs an experiment in which three different temperatures (ranging from 1,100 to 1,200 °F) and five different pressures (ranging from 500 to 600 psi) are used, with 20 ingots produced at each Temperature-Pressure combination. Identify the following elements of the experiment:

a. Response   b. Factor(s) and factor type(s)
c. Treatments   d. Experimental units

102 Factors that impact a customer's willingness to buy. Advancements in information technology have yielded services that compete against products, with each providing roughly the same benefits to the consumer (e.g., home answering machines and voice-mail services). With the advent of such services, consumers also face different types of pricing schemes. Using a 2×2 factorial design, D. Fortin and T. Greenlee of the University of Rhode Island investigated the effects of the type of message retrieval system (answering machine vs. voice-mail service) and the type of pricing (lump sum amount for 5 years of use vs. monthly cost for 5 years of use) on consumers' willingness to buy (*Journal of Business Research,* Vol. 41, 1998). The first pricing option requires the consumer to do mental arithmetic to determine the total cost of the system; the second provides the true full cost. Thirty subjects were randomly assigned to each of the four treatments. Each was exposed to a purchase situation involving the relevant product or service and payment description and was asked to indicate his or her willingness to buy the item on a 5-point scale (1 = definitely would not buy;

5 = definitely would buy). The results are presented in the incomplete ANOVA table below.

a. Fill in the degrees of freedom (df) column in the ANOVA table.

b. Specify the null and alternative hypotheses that should be used in testing for interaction effects between type of message retrieval system and pricing option.

c. Conduct the test of part **b** using $\alpha = .05$. Interpret the results in the context of the problem.

d. Given the results of part **c**, is it advisable to conduct main effects tests? Why or why not? If so, perform the appropriate main effects tests using $\alpha = .05$.

Source	df	SS	MS	F
Type of message retrieval system	–	–	–	2.001
Pricing option	–	–	–	5.019
Type of system × pricing option	–	–	–	4.986
Error	–	–	–	
Total	119	–		

Source: Based on Fortin, D., & Greenlee, T. "Using a product/service evaluation frame: An experiment on the economic equivalence of product versus service alternatives for message retrieval systems," *Journal of Business Research*, Vol. 41, 1998, pp. 205–214.

103 Diamonds sold at retail. The *Journal of Statistics Education*
⊙ study of 308 diamonds for sale on the open market. The
DIAMND file contains information on the quantitative variables, size (number of carats) and price (in dollars), and on the qualitative variables, color (D, E, F, G, H, and I), clarity (IF, VS1, VS2, VVS1, and VVS2), and independent certification group (GIA, HRD, or IGI). Select one of the quantitative variables and one of the qualitative variables.

a. Set up the null and alternative hypotheses for determining whether the means of the quantitative variable differ for the levels of the qualitative variable.

b. Use the data to conduct the test, part **a**, at $\alpha = 10$. State the conclusion in the words of the problem.

c. Check any assumptions required for the methodology used in part **b** to be valid.

d. Follow up the analysis with multiple comparisons of the treatment means. Use an experimentwise error rate of .05. Interpret the results practically.

104 Participation in a company's walking program. A study was
⊙ conducted to investigate the effect of prompting in a walking
WALKS program instituted at a large corporation (*Health Psychology,*

Mar. 1995). Five groups of walkers—27 in each group—agreed to participate by walking for 20 minutes at least one day per week over a 24-week period. The participants were prompted to walk each week via telephone calls, but different prompting schemes were used for each group. Walkers in the control group received no prompting phone calls; walkers in the "frequent/low" group received a call once a week with low structure (i.e., "just touching base"); walkers in the "frequent/high" group received a call once a week with high structure (i.e., goals are set); walkers in the "infrequent/low" group received a call once every 3 weeks with low structure; and walkers in the "infrequent/high" group received a call once every 3 weeks with high structure. The table at the bottom of the page lists the number of participants in each group who actually walked the minimum requirement each week for weeks 1, 4, 8, 12, 16, and 24. The data were subjected to an analysis of variance for a randomized block design, with the five walker groups representing the treatments and the six time periods (weeks) representing the blocks.

Source	df	SS	MS	F	p-Value
Prompt	4	1185.000	–	–	0.0000
Week	–	386.400	77.28000	10.40	0.0001
Error	20	148.600	7.43000		
Total	29	1720.00			

a. What is the purpose of blocking on weeks in this study?

b. Fill in the missing entries on the ANOVA summary table shown above.

c. Is there sufficient evidence of a difference in the mean number of walkers per week among the five walker groups? Use $\alpha = .05$.

d. Tukey's technique was used to compare all pairs of treatment means with an experimentwise error rate of $\alpha = .05$. The rankings are shown at the bottom of the page. Interpret these results.

e. What assumptions must hold to ensure the validity of the inferences in parts **c** and **d**?

105 Manager's trust and job-related tension. Research published in *Accounting, Organizations and Society* (Vol. 19, 1994) investigated whether the effects of different performance evaluation styles (PES) on the level of job-related tension is affected by trust. Three performance evaluation styles were considered. Each is related to the way in which accounting information is used for the purpose of

Table for Exercise 104

Week	Control	Frequent/Low	Frequent/High	Infrequent/Low	Infrequent/High
1	7	23	25	21	19
4	2	19	25	10	12
8	2	18	19	9	9
12	2	7	20	8	2
16	2	18	18	8	7
24	1	17	17	7	6

Source: Lombard, D. N., Lombard, T. N., & Winett, R. A. "Walking to meet health guidelines: The effect of prompting frequency and prompt structure," *Health Psychology*, Vol. 14, No. 2, Mar. 1995, p. 167 (Table 2).

Tukey Rankings for Exercise 104

Mean:	2.67	9.17	10.50	17.00	20.67
Prompt:	*Control*	*Infr./High*	*Infr./Low*	*Frequent/Low*	*Frequent/High*

evaluation. The three styles are budget-constrained (BC), profit-conscious (PC), and the nonaccounting style (NA), which focuses on factors such as quality of output and attitude toward the job. Consider a questionnaire (similar to the one used in the study) administered to 200 managers. It measures the performance evaluation style of each manager's superior (on a 10-point scale), the manager's job-related tension, and the manager's level of trust (low, medium, and high) in his or her superior. These data were used to produce the partial ANOVA table and table of treatment means shown next.

Source	df	SS	MS	F
PES	2	4.35	–	–
Trust	–	15.20	–	–
PES × trust	4	3.50	–	–
Error	191	–		
Total	199	301.55		

		Performance Evaluation Style		
		BC	PC	NA
	Low	6.5	6.2	6.3
		($n = 30$)	($n = 20$)	($n = 20$)
Trust	Medium	5.5	5.6	5.3
		($n = 25$)	($n = 30$)	($n = 15$)
	High	4.6	4.8	4.7
		($n = 20$)	($n = 25$)	($n = 15$)

Source: Based on Ross, A. "Trust as a moderator of the effect of performance evaluation style on job-related tension: A research note," from *Accounting, Organizations, and Society,* October 1994, Volume 19(7).

a. Describe the treatments of this study.
b. Complete the ANOVA table.
c. Investigate the presence of an interaction effect by conducting the appropriate hypothesis test using $\alpha = .05$.
d. Use a plot of treatment means to investigate the interaction effect. Interpret your results. Are your results of parts **c** and **d** consistent?
e. Given your answers to parts **c** and **d**, should the F-tests for the two main effects be conducted?

106 Testing the effectiveness of supermarket sales strategies.
Factorial designs are commonly employed in marketing research to evaluate the effectiveness of sales strategies. At
SUPMKT one supermarket, two of the factors were price level (regular, reduced price, cost to supermarket) and Display level (normal display space, normal display space plus end-of-aisle display, twice the normal display space). A 3 × 3 complete factorial design was employed, where each treatment was applied three times to a particular product at a particular supermarket. The dependent variable of interest was unit sales for the week. (To minimize treatment carryover effects, each treatment was preceded and followed by a week in which the product was priced at its regular price and was displayed in its normal manner.) The next table reports the data collected.
a. How many treatments are considered in this study?
b. Do the data indicate that the mean sales differ among the treatments? Test using $\alpha = .10$.
c. Is the test of interaction between the factors price and Display warranted as a result of the test in part **b**? If so, conduct the test using $\alpha = .10$.

d. Are the tests of the main effects for Price and Display warranted as a result of the previous tests? If so, conduct them using $\alpha = .10$.
e. Which pairs of treatment means should be compared as a result of the tests in parts **b–d**?

		Price		
		Regular	Reduced	Cost to Supermarket
		989	1,211	1,577
	Normal	1,025	1,215	1,559
		1,030	1,182	1,598
		1,191	1,860	2,492
Display	Normal Plus	1,233	1,910	2,527
		1,221	1,926	2,511
		1,226	1,516	1,801
	Twice Normal	1,202	1,501	1,833
		1,180	1,498	1,852

Applying the Concepts—Advanced

107 Testing a new insect repellent. Traditionally, people protect themselves from mosquito bites by applying insect repellent to their skin and clothing. Research suggests that permethrin, an insecticide with low toxicity to humans, can provide protection from mosquitoes. A study in the *Journal of the American Mosquito Control Association* (Mar. 1995) investigated whether a tent sprayed with a commercially available 1% permethrin formulation would protect people, both inside and outside the tent, against biting mosquitoes. Two canvas tents—one treated with permethrin, the other untreated—were positioned 25 meters apart on flat, dry ground in an area infested with mosquitoes. Eight people participated in the experiment, with four randomly assigned to each tent. Of the four stationed at each tent, two were randomly assigned to stay inside the tent (at opposite corners) and two to stay outside the tent (at opposite corners). During a specified 20-minute period during the night, each person kept count of the number of mosquito bites received. The goal of the study was to determine the effect of both Tent type (treated or untreated) and Location (inside or outside the tent) on the mean mosquito bite count.
a. What type of design was employed in the study?
b. Identify the factors and treatments.
c. Identify the response variable.
d. The study found statistical evidence of interaction between Tent type and Location. Give a practical interpretation of this result.

108 Improving the output of an industrial lathe. *Quality Engineering* (Vol. 6, 1994) reported the results of an experiment that was designed to find ways to improve the
LATHE output of an industrial lathe. The lathe is controlled by a computer that automatically feeds bar stock, cuts the stock, machines the surface finish, and releases the part. As it is machined, the bar stock spins and is held in place by a collet. The lathe operator sets the feed (the rate at which bars are machined) and the speed (spin rate). The product characteristic of interest is surface finish. It is measured on a gauge that records the vertical distance a probe travels as it moves along a given horizontal distance on the bar. The

rougher the surface, the higher the gauge measurement. The factors that were manipulated in the experiment were speed, feed, collet tightness, and tool wear. The table below reports the factor-level settings and the resulting surface-finish measurements (H = High; L = Low).

a. What type of experimental design was used?

b. How many different treatments were applied?

c. Perform an ANOVA for these data.

d. Do significant interaction effects exist? Test using $\alpha = .05$. Interpret your results.

e. Is it necessary to perform main effect tests? Why or why not? If so, perform the tests using $\alpha = .05$.

f. What assumptions must hold to ensure the validity of your results in parts **c, d,** and **e**?

Speed	Feed	Collet Tightness	Surface Tool Wear	Finish
H	H	H	H	216
L	H	H	H	212
H	L	H	H	48
L	L	H	H	40
H	H	L	H	232
L	H	L	H	248
H	L	L	H	514
L	L	L	H	298
H	H	H	L	238
L	H	H	L	219
H	L	H	L	40
L	L	H	L	33
H	H	L	L	230
L	H	L	L	253
H	L	L	L	273
L	L	L	L	101
H	H	H	H	217
L	H	H	H	221
H	L	H	H	39
L	L	H	H	31
H	H	L	H	235
L	H	L	H	238
H	L	L	H	437
L	L	L	H	87
H	H	H	L	245
L	H	H	L	226
H	L	H	L	51
L	L	H	L	33
H	H	L	L	226
L	H	L	L	214
H	L	L	L	691
L	L	L	L	130

Source: Collins, W. H., & Colins, C. B. "Including residual analysis in designed experiments: Case studies," *Quality Engineering,* Vol. 6, No. 4, 1994, pp. 547–565. Copyright © 1994 by Taylor & Francis. Reprinted with permission.

Critical Thinking Challenge

109 **Exam performance study.** Refer to the *Teaching of Psychology* (August 1998) study of whether a practice test helps students prepare for a final exam, Exercise 13. Recall that undergraduate students were grouped according to their class standing and whether they attended a review session or took a practice test prior to the final exam. The experimental design was a 3×2 factorial design, with Class Standing at three levels (low, medium, or high) and Exam Preparation at two levels (practice exam or review session). There were 22 students in each of the $3 \times 2 = 6$ treatment groups. After completing the final exam, each student rated his/her exam preparation on an 11-point scale ranging from 0 (not helpful at all) to 10 (extremely helpful). The data for this experiment (simulated from summary statistics provided in the article) are saved in the accompanying file. The first 5 and last 5 observations in the data set are listed below. Conduct a complete analysis of variance of the helpfulness ratings data, including (if warranted) multiple comparisons of means. Do your findings support the research conclusion that "students at all levels of academic ability benefit from a…practice exam"?

Exam Preparation	Class Standing	Helpfulness Rating
Practice	Low	6
Practice	Low	7
Practice	Low	7
Practice	Low	5
Practice	Low	3
⋮	⋮	⋮
Review	High	5
Review	High	2
Review	High	5
Review	High	4
Review	High	3

Source: Balch, W. R. "Practice versus review exams and final exam performance," *Teaching of Psychology,* Vol. 25, No. 3. Copyright © 1998 by Sage Publications. Reprinted with permission.

References

Cochran, W. G., & Cox, G. M. *Experimental Designs,* 2nd ed. New York: Wiley, 1957.

Hsu, J. C. *Multiple Comparisons: Theory and Methods.* London: Chapman & Hall, 1996.

Koehler, K. *Snedecor and Cochran's Statistical Methods*, 9th ed. New York: Blackwell Publishing, 2012.

Kramer, C. Y. "Extension of multiple range tests to group means with unequal number of replications," *Biometrics,* Vol. 12, 1956, pp. 307–310.

Kutner, M., Nachtsheim, C., Neter, J., & Li, W. *Applied Linear Statistical Models,* 5th ed. New York: McGraw-Hill/Irwin, 2005.

Mason, R. L., Gunst, R. F., & Hess, J. L. *Statistical Design and Analysis of Experiments.* New York: Wiley, 1989.

Mendenhall, W. *Introduction to Linear Models and the Design and Analysis of Experiments.* Belmont, Calif.: Wadsworth, 1968.

Miller, R. G., Jr. *Simultaneous Statistical Inference.* New York: Springer-Verlag, 1981.

Scheffé, H. "A method for judging all contrasts in the analysis of variance," *Biometrica,* Vol. 40, 1953, pp. 87–104.

Scheffé, H. *The Analysis of Variance.* New York: Wiley, 1959.

Steele, R. G. D., & Torrie, J. H. *Principles and Procedures of Statistics: A Biometrical Approach,* 2nd ed. New York: McGraw-Hill, 1980.

Tukey, J. "Comparing individual means in the analysis of variance," *Biometrics,* Vol. 5, 1949, pp. 99–114.

Winer, B. J. *Statistical Principles in Experimental Design,* 2nd ed. New York: McGraw-Hill, 1971.

USING TECHNOLOGY   Technology images shown here are taken from SPSS Statistics Professional 20.0, Minitab 16, XLSTAT for Pearson, and Excel 2010.

SPSS: Analysis of Variance

SPSS can conduct ANOVAs for all three types of experimental designs discussed in this chapter: completely randomized, randomized block, and factorial designs.

Completely Randomized Design

Step 1   Access the SPSS spreadsheet file that contains the sample data. The data file should contain one quantitative variable (the response, or dependent, variable) and one factor variable with at least two levels. (These values must be numbers, e.g., 1, 2, 3, …)

Step 2   Click on the "Analyze" button on the SPSS menu bar, then click on "Compare Means" and "One-Way ANOVA," as shown in Figure S.1.

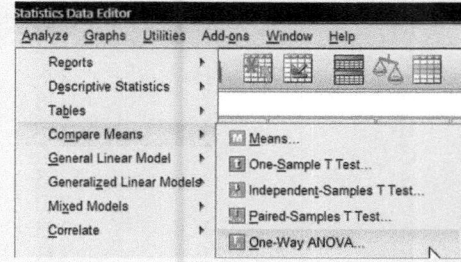

Figure S.1

SPSS menu options for one-way ANOVA

Step 3   In the resulting dialog box (shown in Figure S.2), specify the response variable under "Dependent List" and the factor variable under "Factor."

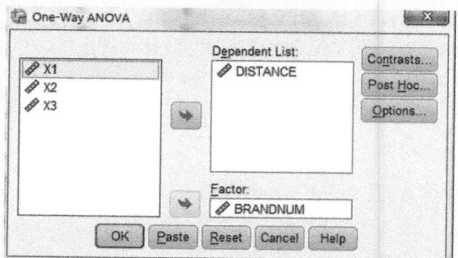

Figure S.2 SPSS one-way ANOVA dialog box

Step 4 Click the "Post Hoc" button and select a multiple comparisons method and experimentwise error rate in the resulting dialog box (see Figure S.3).

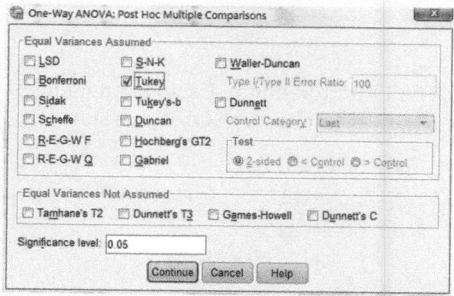

Figure S.3 SPSS multiple comparisons dialog box

Step 5 Click "Continue" to return to the "One-Way ANOVA" dialog screen and then click "OK" to generate the SPSS printout.

Randomized Block and Factorial Designs

Step 1 Access the SPSS spreadsheet file that contains the sample data. The data file should contain one quantitative variable (the response, or dependent, variable) and at least two other variables that represent the factors and/or blocks.

Step 2 Click on the "Analyze" button on the SPSS menu bar and then click on "General Linear Model" and "Univariate," as shown in Figure S.4

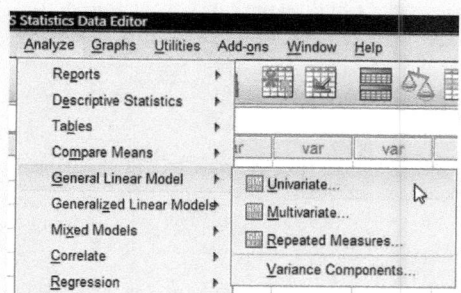

Figure S.4 SPSS menu options for two-way ANOVA

Step 3 On the resulting dialog box (Figure S.5.), specify the response variable under "Dependent Variable" and the factor variable(s) and block variable under "Fixed Factor(s)."

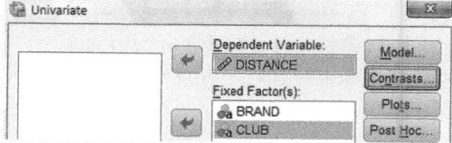

Figure S.5 SPSS two-way ANOVA dialog box

Step 4 Click the "Post Hoc" button and select the factor variable of interest, a multiple comparisons method, and experimentwise error rate in the resulting dialog box (similar to Figure S.3).

Step 5 Click "Continue" to return to the "Two-Way ANOVA" dialog screen and then click the "Model" button to specify the type of experimental design (randomized block or factorial) on the resulting dialog screen (as shown in Figure S.6). For factorial designs, select the "Full factorial" option; for randomized block designs, select the "Custom" option and specify the treatment and blocking factors under "Model."

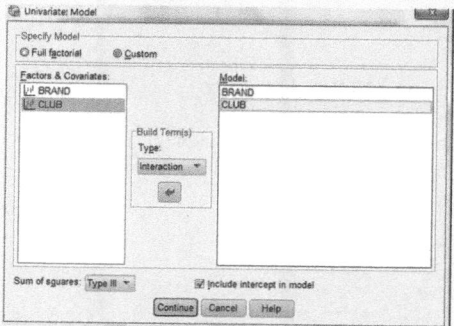

Figure S.6 SPSS design (model) specification box

Step 6 Click "Continue" to return to the "Two-Way ANOVA" dialog screen and then click "OK" to generate the SPSS printout.

Minitab: Analysis of Variance

Minitab can conduct ANOVAs for all three types of experimental designs discussed in this chapter: completely randomized, randomized block, and factorial designs.

Completely Randomized Design

Step 1 Access the Minitab worksheet file that contains the sample data. The data file should contain one quantitative variable (the response, or dependent, variable) and one factor variable with at least two levels.

Step 2 Click on the "Stat" button on the Minitab menu bar and then click on "ANOVA" and "One-Way," as shown in Figure M.1.

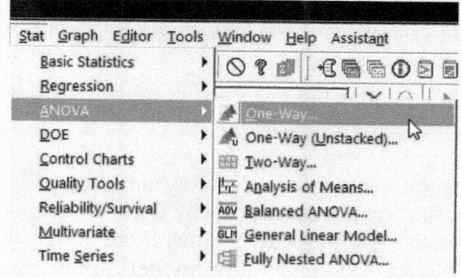

Figure M.1 Minitab menu options for one-way ANOVA

Step 3 On the resulting dialog screen (Figure M.2), specify the response variable in the "Response" box and the factor variable in the "Factor" box.

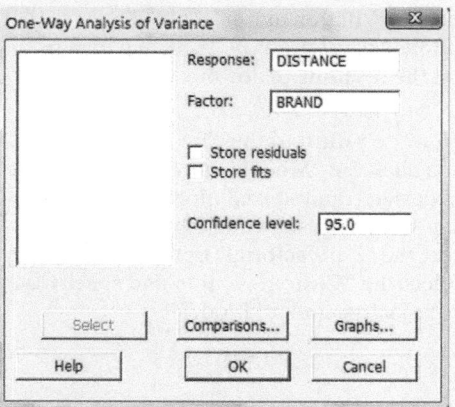

Figure M.2 Minitab one-way ANOVA dialog box

Step 4 Click the "Comparisons" button and select a multiple comparisons method and experimentwise error rate in the resulting dialog box (see Figure M.3).

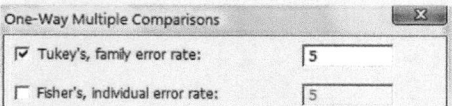

Figure M.3 Minitab multiple comparisons dialog box

Step 5 Click "OK" to return to the "One-Way ANOVA" dialog screen and then click "OK" to generate the Minitab printout.

Randomized Block and Factorial Designs

Step 1 Access the Minitab worksheet file that contains the sample data. The data file should contain one quantitative variable (the response, or dependent, variable) and two other variables that represent the factors and/or blocks.

Step 2 Click on the "Stat" button on the Minitab menu bar and then click on "ANOVA" and "Two-Way" (see Figure M.1). The resulting dialog screen appears as shown in Figure M.4.

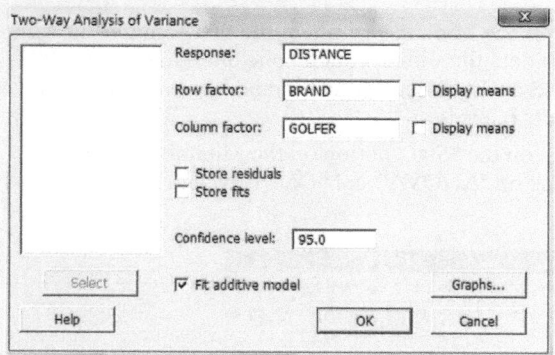

Figure M.4 Minitab two-way ANOVA dialog box

Step 3 Specify the response variable in the "Response" box, the first factor variable in the "Row factor" box, and the second factor or block variable in the "Column factor" box. If the design is a randomized block, select the "Fit additive model" option, as shown in Figure M.4. If the design is factorial, leave the "Fit additive model" option unselected.

Step 4 Click "OK" to generate the Minitab printout.

Note: Multiple comparisons of treatment means are obtained by selecting "Stat," then "ANOVA," and then "General Linear Model." Specify the factors in the "Model" box and then select "Comparisons" and put the factor of interest in the "Terms" box. Press "OK" twice.

Excel/XLSTAT: Analysis of Variance

XLSTAT can conduct ANOVAs for all three types of experimental designs discussed in this chapter: completely randomized design, randomized block design, and two-factor factorial designs. The Excel workbook file should include a column for the quantitative dependent (response) variable, and columns for the qualitative factors.

Completely Randomized Design

Step 1 Click the "XLSTAT" button on the Excel main menu bar, select "Modeling Data," then click "ANOVA," as shown in Figure E.1.

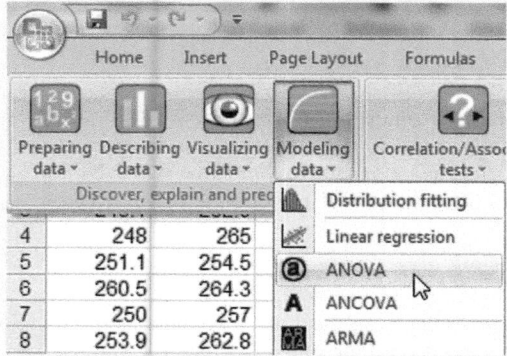

Figure E.1 XLSTAT menu options for analysis of variance

Step 2 When the resulting dialog box appears, enter the appropriate column for the quantitative dependent variable in the "Y / Dependent variables" box and the appropriate column for the qualitative factor variable in the "X / Explanatory variables" box. (*Note:* Be sure to check "Qualitative" and enter the factor column in this box.) See, for example, Figure E.2.

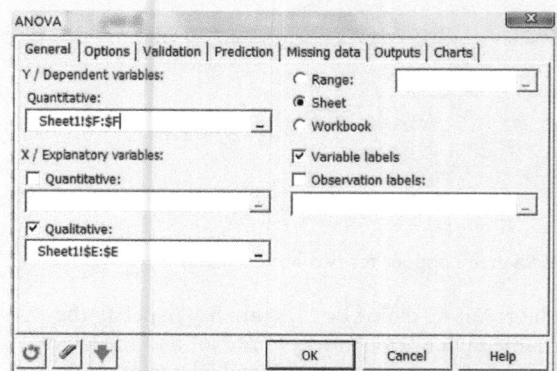

Figure E.2 XLSTAT ANOVA dialog box

Step 3 Click the "Outputs" tab to run a multiple comparisons of means. On the resulting dialog box, check "Pairwise comparisons," then select the method (e.g., Tukey), as shown in Figure E.3. [*Note:* The default EER is .05. If you want to change the EER value, click the "Options" tab on the ANOVA dialog box and specify a different confidence interval percentage (e.g., 90%).]

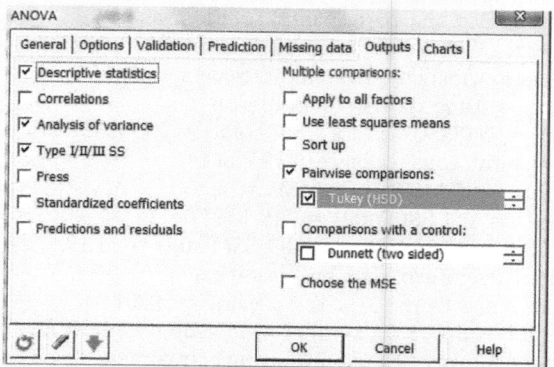

Figure E.3 XLSTAT output options for analysis of variance

Step 4 Click "OK," then "Continue" to display the test results.

Randomized Block and Factorial Designs

Step 1 Click the "XLSTAT" button on the Excel main menu bar, select "Modeling Data," then click "ANOVA," as shown in Figure E.1.

Step 2 When the resulting dialog box appears, enter the appropriate column for the quantitative dependent variable in the "Y / Dependent variables" box and the appropriate columns for the qualitative factor variables in the "X / Explanatory variables" box. (*Note:* Be sure to check "Qualitative" and enter the factor columns in this box.) See, for example, Figure E.2.

Step 3 To run a factorial ANOVA, click the "Options" tab and check "Interactions" on the resulting screen, as shown in Figure E.4. [*Note:* Do not check "Interactions" when running a randomized block ANOVA.]

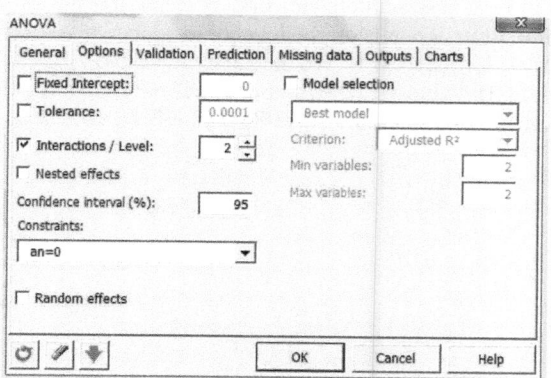

Figure E.4 XLSTAT ANOVA options

Step 4 Click the "Outputs" tab to run a multiple comparisons of means. On the resulting dialog box, check "Pairwise comparisons," then select the method (e.g., Tukey), as shown in Figure E.3. [*Note:* The default EER is .05. If you want to change the EER value, click the "Options" tab on the ANOVA dialog box and specify a different confidence interval percentage (e.g., 90%).]

Step 5 Click "OK," then "Continue" to display the test results. [*Note:* For two-factor designs, XLSTAT will prompt you to select the effects you want to estimate in the ANOVA and the factors

you want to rank means on. (See Figure E.5.) Make the appropriate selections and click "OK."]

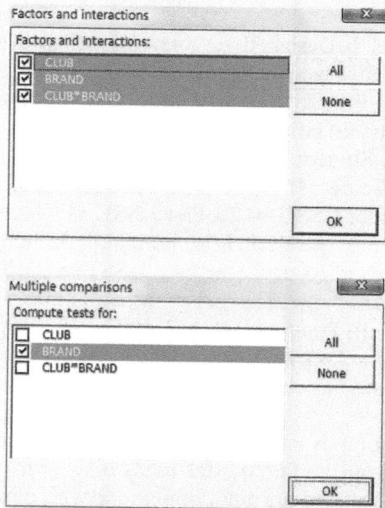

Figure E.5 XLSTAT ANOVA model selections

TI-84 Graphing Calculator: Analysis of Variance

The TI-84 graphing calculator can be used to compute a one-way ANOVA for a completely randomized design but not a two-way ANOVA for either a randomized block or factorial design.

Completely Randomized Design

Step 1 *Enter each data set into its own list (i.e., sample 1 into L1, sample 2 into L2, sample 3 into L3, etc.).*

Step 2 *Access the Statistical Test Menu*

- Press **STAT**
- Arrow right to **TESTS**
- Arrow down to **ANOVA(**
- Press **ENTER**
- Type in each List name separated by commas (*e.g., L1, L2, L3, L4*)
- Press **ENTER**

Step 3 *View Display*

The calculator will display the *F*-test statistic, as well as the *p*-value, the factor degrees of freedom, sum of squares, mean square, and by arrowing down, the Error degrees of freedom, sum of squares, mean square, and the pooled standard deviation.

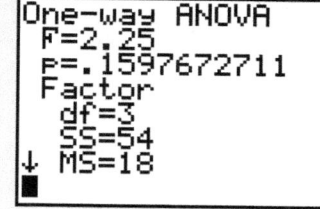
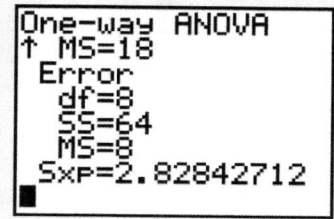

◻ Answers to Selected Exercises

1 A, B, C, D **5 a.** Observational **b.** Designed **c.** Observational **d.** Observational **e.** Observational **7 a.** CPAs **b.** Likelihood of reporting sustainability policies **c.** Firm size; firm type **d.** Size: large or small; type: public or private **e.** large/public, large/private, small/public, and small/private **9 a.** Experimental units randomly assigned to treatments **b.** Exp. unit: participant; response: level of appreciation; factor: role; treatments: gift giver, gift receiver **11 a.** 4 **b.** (Within-store/home), (Within-store/in store), (Between-store/home), (Between-store/in store) **13 a.** Student **b.** Yes **c.** Class standing and study group **d.** Class: low, medium, high; study: review session, practice test **e.** 6 **f.** Final exam score **15 a.** 6.39 **b.** 15.98 **c.** 1.54 **d.** 3.18 **17 a.** Plot 2 **b.** $\bar{x}_1 = 9$ and $\bar{x}_2 = 14$ for both plots **c.** SST = 75 for both plots **d.** Plot 1: SSE = 20; Plot 2: SSE = 144 **e.** Plot 1: SS(Total) = 95 (78.95%); Plot 2: SS(Total) = 219 (34.25%) **f.** Plot 1: $F = 37.5$; Plot 2: $F = 5.21$ **g.** reject H_0 for both plots **h.** Both populations normal with equal variances **19** Plot 1: df(Treatments) = 1, df(Error) = 10, df(Total) = 11, SST = 75, SSE = 20, SS(Total) = 95, MST = 75, MSE = 2, $F = 37.5$; Plot 2: df(Treatments) = 1, df(Error) = 10, df(Total) = 11, SST = 75, SSE = 144, SS(Total) = 219, MST = 75, MSE = 14.4, $F = 5.21$ **21 a.** df(Treatments) = 2, df(Error) = 9, df(Total) = 11, SST = 12.30, SSE = 18.89, SS(Total) = 31.19, MST = 6.15, MSE = 2.10, $F = 2.93$ **b.** Do not reject H_0 **23 a.** Completely randomized design; exp. units: bus customers; dependent variable: performance score; factor: bus depot; treatments: Depot 1, Depot 2, and Depot 3 **b.** Yes; p-value = .0001 **25 a.** $H_0: \mu_1 = \mu_2 = \mu_3 = \mu_4 = \mu_5 = \mu_6 = \mu_7$, H_a: At least two treatment means differ **b.** $F = 1.60$, p-value = .174, do not reject H_0 **27** Yes, $F = 3.90$ **29 a.** Completely randomized design **b.** Exp. units: students; dependent variable: tanning attitude; treatments: models with a tan, models with no tan, and no model **c.** $H_0: \mu_{Tan} = \mu_{NoTan} = \mu_{NoModel}$ **d.** No measure of variance **e.** Reject H_0 **f.** Independent random samples from normal populations with equal variances **31** $H_0: \mu_1 = \mu_2 = \mu_3 = \mu_4 = \mu_5 = \mu_6$ **b.** No **d.** Designed **33** Reject $H_0: \mu_1 = \mu_2 = \mu_3 = \mu_4$ for shell thickness and whipping capacity **35 a.** 3 **b.** 10 **c.** 6 **d.** 45 **37** P(Type I error) for a single comparison **39** $(\mu_1, \mu_4) > (\mu_2, \mu_3)$ **41** $\mu_1 > \mu_2 > \mu_3$ **43 b.** No **c.** Yes **d.** No **e.** $\mu_{Large} > \mu_{Small}$; no other significant differences **f.** 95% confidence **45 a.** Probability of claiming at least 2 means are different when they are not is .01 **b.** 3 **b.** $(\mu_{Under30} - \mu_{30to60})$; $(\mu_{Under30} - \mu_{Over60})$ **47** $\mu_{NC} > (\mu_{AC}, \mu_{EO})$; $\mu_{IE} > \mu_{EO}$ **49 a.** $(-.125, -.032)$; $\mu_{Barn} > \mu_{Cage}$ **b.** $(-.1233, -.0307)$; $\mu_{Free} > \mu_{Cage}$ **c.** $(-.105, -.0123)$; $\mu_{Organic} > \mu_{Cage}$ **d.** $(-.0501, .0535)$; no difference **e.** $(-.0318, .0718)$; no difference **f.** $(-.0335, .0701)$; no difference **g.** $(\mu_{Barn}, \mu_{Free}, \mu_{Organic}) > \mu_{Cage}$; .05 **51 a.** SSB = .8889, SSE = 7.7778, MST = 10.7778, MSB = .4445, MSE = 1.9445, F(Treatments) = 5.54, F(Blocks) = .23 **b.** $H_0: \mu_1 = \mu_2 = \mu_3$ **c.** $F = 5.54$ **e.** Do not reject H_0 **53 a.** $F = 3.20$; $F = 1.80$ **b.** $F = 13.33$; $F = 2.00$ **c.** $F = 5.33$; $F = 5.00$ **d.** $F = 16.00$; $F = 6.00$ **e.** $F = 2.67$; $F = 1.00$ **55 a.** Blocks: employees; treatments: time periods **b.** p-values given **c.** $H_0: \mu_{Before} = \mu_{2months} = \mu_{2days}$ **d.** Mean competence levels differ for three time periods **e.** $\mu_{Before} < (\mu_{2months}, \mu_{2days})$ **57 a.** 8 activities **b.** 15 adults **c.** Reject H_0: all treatment means are equal **d.** $(\mu_{rest}, \mu_{gaming}) > (\mu_{balance}, \mu_{muscle}, \mu_{aerobics}) > (\mu_{walking}, \mu_{jogging})$ **59** $H_0: \mu_1 = \mu_2 = \mu_3 = \mu_4 = \mu_5$ **c.** p-value = .319, do not reject H_0 **d.** No differences; yes **e.** P(at least one Type I error) = .05 **61** $F = 2.00$, fail to reject $H_0: \mu_M = \mu_T = \mu_W = \mu_R = \mu_F$ **63** Yes, $F = 34.12$; S4 and S1 **65** df(A) = 2, df(B) = 3, df(AB) = 6, df(Error) = 12, df(Total) = 23, SSE = 1.3, MS(A) = .4, MS(B) = 1.7667, MS(AB) = 1.6, MSE = .1083, $F(A) = 3.69$, $F(B) = 16.31$, $F(AB) = 14.77$ **b.** SSA + SSB + SSAB; yes, $F = 13.18$ **c.** Yes **e.** $F = 14.77$, reject H_0 **f.** No **67 a.** (1, 1), (1, 2), (1, 3), (2, 1), (2, 2), (2, 3) **b.** Yes, $F = 21.62$ **c.** Yes; $F = 36.62$, reject H_0 **d.** No **69 a.** $F(AB) = .75$, $F(A) = 3.00$, $F(B) = 1.50$ **b.** $F(AB) = 7.50$, $F(A) = 3.00$, $F(B) = 3.00$ **c.** $F(AB) = 3.00$, $F(A) = 12.00$, $F(B) = 3.00$ **d.** $F(AB) = 4.50$, $F(A) = 36.00$, $F(B) = 36.00$ **71 a.** Factors: statement type and information order; treatments: concrete/statement first, concrete/behavior first, abstract/statement first, abstract/behavior first **b.** Reject H_0: no interaction **d.** No main effect tests **73 a.** Effect of justice reparation potential on intention depends on the level of producer **b.** Reject H_0 **c.** No **e.** Yes **75 a.** df(Order) = 1, df(Menu) = 1, df(Order × Menu) = 1, df(Error) = 176 **b.** Reject H_0 **c.** No **77** Yes **79** Do not reject H_0: no interaction (p-value = .289); reject $H_0: \mu_V = \mu_S = \mu_N$ (p-value = .000); do not reject $H_0: \mu_{1yes} = \mu_{no}$ (p-value = .145) **81 a.** 450; 152.5; 195; 157.5 **b.** 9,120.25 **c.** 1,222.25; 625; 676 **d.** 225; 90.25; 90.25; 100 **e.** 12,132 **f.** 14,555.25 **g.**

Source	df	SS	MS	F
Load	1	1,122.25	1,122.25	8.88
Name	1	625.00	625.00	4.95
Load × Name	1	676.00	676.00	5.35
Error	96	12,132.00	126.375	
Total	99	14,555.25		

h. Yes **i.** evidence of interaction **j.** Normal distributions for each treatment, with equal variances
87 a.

Source	df	SS	MS	F
Treatment	3	11.332	3.777	157.39
Block	4	10.688	2.672	111.33
Error	12	0.288	0.024	
Total	19	22.308		

b. Yes, $F = 157.39$ **c.** Yes, 6 **d.** Yes, $F = 111.33$ **89 a.** Completely randomized design **b.** Treatments: 3, 6, 9, and 12 robots; dependent variable: energy expended **c.** $H_0: \mu_3 = \mu_6 = \mu_9 = \mu_{12}$ **d.** reject H_0 **e.** 6 **f.** $(\mu_3, \mu_6, \mu_9) > \mu_{12}$ **91 a.** 2 × 2 factorial; factors: color and question; treatments: (red/simple), (red/difficult), (blue/simple), (blue/difficult) **b.** Difference between red and blue exam means depends on question difficulty **93 a.** Randomized block **b.** Experimental units: electronic commerce/internet-based companies; response: rate of return; treatments: e-companies, Internet software/service, Internet hardware, and Internet communication; blocks: 1 year, 3 year, and 5 year **95 a.** Yes, $F = 30.4$ **b.** $\mu_A > (\mu_B, \mu_C, \mu_D); \mu_B > \mu_D$ **97 a.** Complete 6×6 factorial design **b.** Factors: coagulant (5, 10, 20, 50, 100, and 200), pH level (4.0, 5.0, 6.0, 7.0, 8.0, and 9.0); $6 \times 6 = 36$ treatments **99 a.** Factor = Group; treatments = 5 levels of Group; response variable = ethics score; experimental units = employees **b.** $H_0: \mu_1 = \mu_2 = \mu_3 = \mu_4 = \mu_5$, H_a: At least two treatment means differ **c.** yes; $F = 9.85$, p-value = 0 **d.** Assumption of constant variance is violated **e.** Unequal sample sizes **f.** 10 **g.** Implementors/survivors and formulators **101 a.** Quality **b.** Temperature and pressure **c.** $3 \times 5 = 15$ combinations of temperature and pressure **d.** Steel ingots **103 a.** $H_0: \mu_D = \mu_E = \mu_F = \mu_G = \mu_H$ **b.** $F = 2.11$, p-value = .064, reject H_0 **c.** No differences at $\alpha = .05$ **105 a.** low/BC, low/PC, low/NA, medium/BC, medium/PC, medium/NA, high/BC, high/PC, high/NA **b.** df(Trust) = 2, SSE = 149.5641, MS(PES) = 1.0887, MS(Trust) = 3.81835, MS(PES $\times$ Trust) = .4345, F(PES) = 1.4995, F(Trust) = 5.2592, F(PES $\times$ Trust) = .5984 **c.** Do not reject H_0 **d.** Yes **e.** Yes **107 a.** 2×2 factorial experiment **b.** Factors: tent type and location; 4 treatments: (treated/inside), (treated/outside), (untreated/inside), and (untreated/outside) **c.** Number of mosquito bites received in a 20-minute interval **d.** Effect of tent type on mean number of bites depends on location **109** $F = 1.77$, no evidence of interaction; $F = 2.17$, no evidence of Class main effect; $F = 14.40$, evidence of Preparation main effect

◻ Credits

The photo credits below are listed in order of appearance.

Jesse Kunerth/Shutterstock
Isogood/iStockphoto
Sian Irvine/Dorling Kindersley, Ltd.
Ben Blankenburg/iStockphoto
Akreinick/Dreamstime

◻ Technology Images

Categorical Data Analysis

CONTENTS

Where We're Going

- Discuss qualitative (i.e., categorical) data with more than two outcomes (1)
- Present a *chi-square* hypothesis test for comparing the category proportions associated with a single qualitative variable—called a *one-way analysis* (2)
- Present a *chi-square* hypothesis test for relating two qualitative variables—called a *two-way analysis* (3)
- Caution about the misuse of chi-square tests (4)

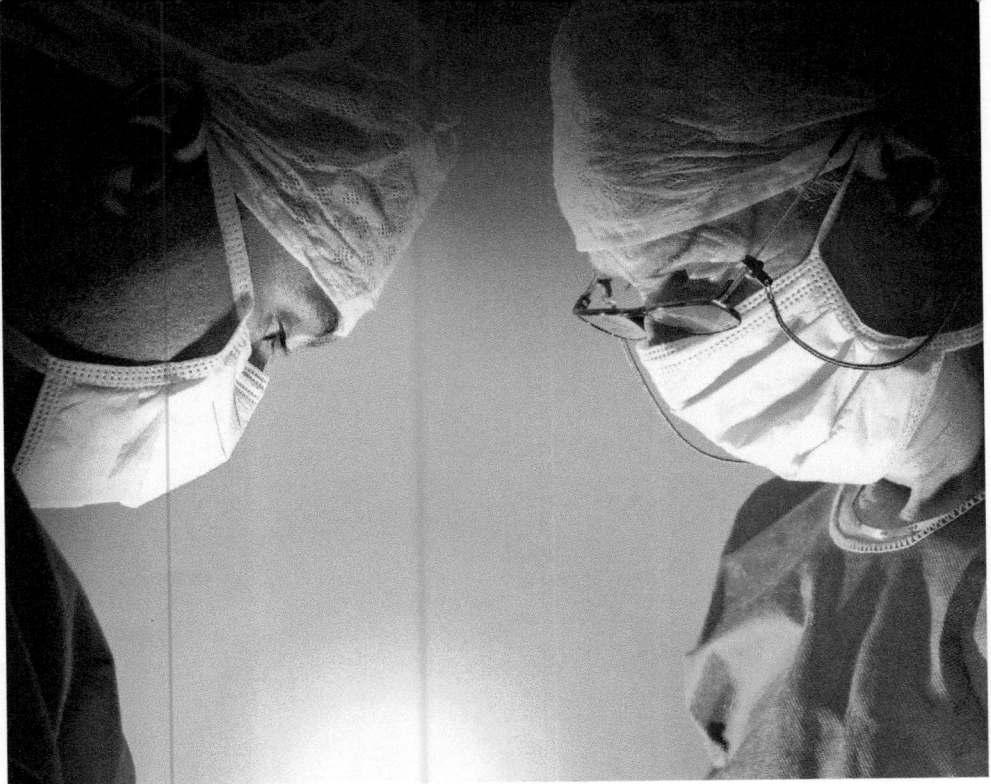

☐ Categorical Data Analysis

STATISTICS in ACTION

The Case of the Ghoulish Transplant Tissue—Who Is Responsible for Paying Damages?

According to Organ and Tissue Transplantation and Alternatives *(January 1, 2011), published by BCC Research, "The global market for transplantation products, devices, and pharmaceuticals was valued at nearly $54 billion in 2010 and is projected to grow at an 8.3% compound annual growth rate to reach $80 billion in 2015." In other words, the worldwide tissue transplant market is big business. Here in the United States, tissue implants are routinely performed to aid patients in various types of surgery, including joint replacements, spinal surgery, sports-related surgeries (tendons and ligaments), and others.**

The process of obtaining a tissue transplant involves several parties. First, of course, is the donor, who has agreed to have tissue removed upon death and whose family has approved the donation. The tissue is then "harvested" by an approved tissue bank. Next, the harvested tissue is sent to a processor, who sterilizes the tissue. Finally, the processor either sends it directly to the hospital/surgeon doing the implant or sends it to a distributor, who inventories the tissue and ultimately sends it on to the hospital/surgeon. The entire process is highly regulated by the Federal Trade Commission (FTC), particularly the harvesting and processing aspects.

Given this background, we consider an actual case that began in the early 2000s when the owner of a tissue bank—Biomedical Tissue Services (BTS)—became a ringleader of a group of funeral home directors that harvested tissue illegally and without the permission of donors or their families. In some cases the cadavers were cancerous or infected with HIV or hepatitis, all of which would, of course, disqualify them as donors. BTS then sent the tissue to processors without divulging that it had obtained the tissue illegally. (*Note:* The owner is currently serving a sentence

*Source: "Organ and Tissue Transplantations," BBC Research Report.

of 18–24 years in a New York prison.) The unsuspecting processors sterilized the tissue and sent it on for use as surgical implants. When the news story broke about how the tissue had been obtained, the processors and their distributors were required to send FTC-mandated recall notices to the hospitals/surgeons who had received the tissue. Some of the BTS tissue was recovered; however, much of the tissue had already been implanted, and hospitals and surgeons were required to inform patients who had received implants of the potentially infectious tissue. Although few patients subsequently became infected, a number filed suit against the distributors and processors (and BTS) asking for monetary damages.

After the bulk of the lawsuits had been either tried or settled, a dispute arose between a processor and one of its distributors regarding ultimate responsibility for the payment of damages to litigating patients. In particular, the processor claimed that the distributor should be held more responsible for the damages since in its recall package, the distributor had of its own volition included some salacious, inflammatory newspaper articles describing in graphic detail the "ghoulish" acts that had been committed. None of the patients who received implants that had been sterilized by this processor ever became infected, but many still filed suit.

To establish its case against the distributor, the processor collected data on the patients who had received implants of BTS tissue that it had processed and on the number of those patients who subsequently filed suit: The data revealed that of a total of 8,914 patients, 708 filed suit. A consulting statistician subdivided this information according to whether the recall notice had been sent to the patient's surgeon by the processor or one of its distributors that had sent only the notice, or by the distributor that had included the newspaper articles. The breakdown was as shown in Table SIA1:

Table SIA1	Data for the Tainted Tissue Case*	
Recall Notice Sender	Number of Patients	Number of Lawsuits
Processor/Other distributor	1,751	51
Distributor in question	6,163	657
Totals	8,914	708

Source: Info Tech, Inc.

Do these data provide evidence of a difference in the probability that a patient would file a lawsuit depending on which party sent the recall notice? If so, and if the probability is significantly higher for the distributor in question, then the processor can argue in court that the distributor who sent the inflammatory newspaper articles is more responsible for the damages.

We apply the statistical methodology presented in this chapter to solve the case of the ghoulish transplant tissue in the following Statistics in Action Revisited example.

STATISTICS in ACTION REVISITED

▫ Testing Whether Likelihood of a Lawsuit Is Related to Recall Notice Sender

1 Categorical Data and the Multinomial Experiment

Observations on a qualitative variable can be categorized only. For example, consider the highest level of education attained by each in a group of salespersons. Level of education is a qualitative variable, and each salesperson would fall in one and only one of the following five categories: some high school, high school diploma, some college, college degree, and graduate degree. The result of the categorization would be a count of the numbers of salespersons falling into the respective categories.

*For confidentiality purposes, the parties in the case cannot be identified. Permission to use the data in this Statistics in Action has been granted by the consulting statistician.

When the qualitative variable results in one of two responses (yes or no, success or failure, favor or do not favor, etc.), the data—called *counts*—can be analyzed using the binomial probability distribution. However, qualitative variables, such as level of education, that allow for more than two categories for a response are much more common, and these must be analyzed using a different method.

Qualitative data that fall in more than two categories often result from a **multinomial experiment**. The characteristics for a multinomial experiment with k outcomes are described in the box. The binomial experiment is a multinomial experiment with $k = 2$.

Properties of the Multinomial Experiment

1. The experiment consists of n identical trials.
2. There are k possible outcomes to each trial. These outcomes are called **classes, categories**, or **cells.**
3. The probabilities of the k outcomes, denoted by $p_1, p_2, \ldots, p_k$, remain the same from trial to trial, where $p_1 + p_2 + \cdots + p_k = 1$.
4. The trials are independent.
5. The random variables of interest are the **cell counts,** $n_1, n_2, \ldots, n_k$, of the number of observations that fall in each of the k classes.

Example 1

Identifying a Multinomial Experiment

Problem Consider the problem of determining the highest level of education attained by each of $n = 100$ salespersons at a large company. Suppose we categorize level of education into one of five categories—some high school, high school diploma, some college, college degree, and graduate degree—and count the number of the 100 salespeople that fall into each category. Is this a multinomial experiment to a reasonable degree of approximation?

Solution Checking the five properties of a multinomial experiment shown in the box, we have the following:

1. The experiment consists of $n = 100$ identical trials, where each trial is to determine the highest level of education of a salesperson.
2. There are $k = 5$ possible outcomes to each trial corresponding to the five education-level categories.
3. The probabilities of the $k = 5$ outcomes, p_1, p_2, p_3, p_4, and p_5, remain (to a reasonable degree of approximation) the same from trial to trial, where p_i represents the true probability that a salesperson attains level of education i.
4. The trials are independent (i.e., the education level attained by one salesperson does not affect the level attained by any other salesperson).
5. We are interested in the count of the number of salespeople who fall into each of the five categories. These five *cell counts* are denoted n_1, n_2, n_3, n_4, and n_5.

Thus, the properties of a multinomial experiment are satisfied.

In this chapter, we are concerned with the analysis of categorical data—specifically, the data that represent the counts for each category of a multinomial experiment. In Section 2, we learn how to make inferences about category probabilities for data classified according to a single qualitative (or categorical) variable. Then, in Section 3, we consider inferences about category probabilities for data classified according to two qualitative variables. The statistic used for these inferences is one that possesses, approximately, the familiar chi-square distribution.

2 Testing Category Probabilities: One-Way Table

In this section, we consider a multinomial experiment with k outcomes that correspond to categories of a *single* qualitative variable. The results of such an experiment are summarized in a **one-way table**. The term *one-way* is used because only one variable is classified. Typically, we want to make inferences about the true proportions that occur in the k categories based on the sample information in the one-way table.

To illustrate, suppose a large supermarket chain conducts a consumer-preference survey by recording the brand of bread purchased by customers in its stores. Assume the chain carries three brands of bread—two major brands (A and B) and its own store brand. The brand preferences of a random sample of 150 consumers are observed, and the number preferring each brand is tabulated; the resulting count data appear in Table 1.

Note that our consumer-preference survey satisfies the properties of a multinomial experiment for the qualitative variable brand of bread. The experiment consists of randomly sampling $n = 150$ buyers from a large population of consumers containing an unknown proportion p_1 who prefer brand A, a proportion p_2 who prefer brand B, and a proportion p_3 who prefer the store brand. Each buyer represents a single trial that can result in one of three outcomes: The consumer prefers brand A, B, or the store brand with probabilities $p_1, p_2,$ and p_3, respectively. (Assume that all consumers will have a preference.) The buyer preference of any single consumer in the sample does not affect the preference of another; consequently, the trials are independent. And, finally, you can see that the recorded data are the number of buyers in each of three consumer-preference categories. Thus, the consumer-preference survey satisfies the five properties of a multinomial experiment.

In the consumer-preference survey, and in most practical applications of the multinomial experiment, the k outcome probabilities $p_1, p_2, \ldots, p_k$ are unknown, and we typically want to use the survey data to make inferences about their values. The unknown probabilities in the consumer-preference survey are

$$p_1 = \text{Proportion of all buyers who prefer brand A}$$
$$p_2 = \text{Proportion of all buyers who prefer brand B}$$
$$p_3 = \text{Proportion of all buyers who prefer the store brand}$$

For example, to decide whether the consumers have a preference for any of the brands, we will want to test the null hypothesis that the brands of bread are equally preferred (that is, $p_1 = p_2 = p_3 = \frac{1}{3}$) against the alternative hypothesis that one brand is preferred (that is, at least one of the probabilities $p_1, p_2,$ and p_3 exceeds $\frac{1}{3}$). Thus, we want to test

$$H_0: p_1 = p_2 = p_3 = \tfrac{1}{3} \text{ (no preference)}$$
$$H_a: \text{At least one of the proportions exceeds } \tfrac{1}{3} \text{ (a preference exists)}$$

If the null hypothesis is true and $p_1 = p_2 = p_3 = \frac{1}{3}$, the expected value (mean value) of the number of customers who prefer brand A is given by

$$E_1 = np_1 = (n)\tfrac{1}{3} = (150)\tfrac{1}{3} = 50$$

Similarly, $E_2 = E_3 = 50$ if the null hypothesis is true and no preference exists.

The following test statistic—the **chi-square test**—measures the degree of disagreement between the data and the null hypothesis:

$$\chi^2 = \frac{[n_1 - E_1]^2}{E_1} + \frac{[n_2 - E_2]^2}{E_2} + \frac{[n_3 - E_3]^2}{E_3}$$
$$= \frac{(n_1 - 50)^2}{50} + \frac{(n_2 - 50)^2}{50} + \frac{(n_3 - 50)^2}{50}$$

Note that the farther the observed numbers $n_1, n_2,$ and n_3 are from their expected value (50), the larger χ^2 will become—that is, large values of χ^2 imply that the null hypothesis is false.

Table 1		
Results of Consumer Preference Survey		
A	B	Store Brand
61	53	36

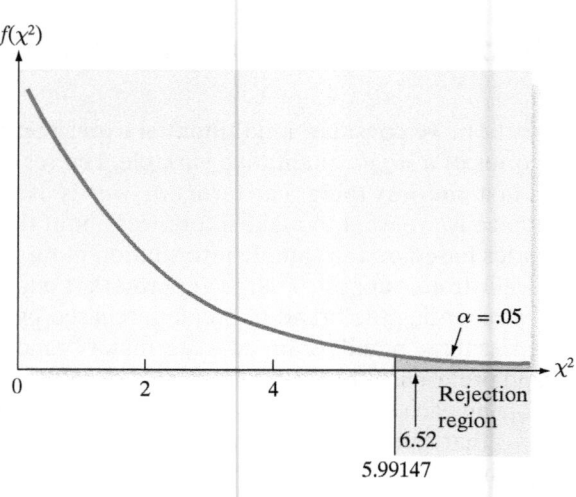

Figure 1

Rejection region for consumer-preference survey

KARL PEARSON (1857–1936)
The Father of Statistics

While attending college, London-born Karl Pearson exhibited a wide range of interests, including mathematics, physics, religion, history, socialism, and Darwinism. After earning a law degree at Cambridge University and a PhD in political science at the University of Heidelberg (Germany), Pearson became a professor of applied mathematics at University College in London. His 1892 book, *The Grammar of Science,* illustrated his conviction that statistical data analysis lies at the foundation of all knowledge; consequently, many consider Pearson to be the "father of statistics." A few of Pearson's many contributions to the field include introducing the term *standard deviation* and its associated symbol (σ), developing the distribution of the correlation coefficient, cofounding and editing the prestigious statistics journal *Biometrika,* and (what many consider his greatest achievement) creating the first chi-square "goodness-of-fit" test. Pearson inspired his students (including his son, Egon, and William Gossett) with his wonderful lectures and enthusiasm for statistics.

We have to know the distribution of χ^2 in repeated sampling before we can decide whether the data indicate that a preference exists. For this one-way classification, the χ^2 distribution has $(k - 1)$ degrees of freedom.* The rejection region for the consumer-preference survey for $\alpha = .05$ and $k - 1 = 3 - 1 = 2$ df is

$$\text{Rejection region: } \chi^2 > \chi^2_{.05}$$

The value of $\chi^2_{.05}$ (found in Table IV in Appendix: Tables) is 5.99147. (See Figure 1.) The computed value of the test statistic is

$$\chi^2 = \frac{(n_1 - 50)^2}{50} + \frac{(n_2 - 50)^2}{50} + \frac{(n_3 - 50)^2}{50}$$

$$= \frac{(61 - 50)^2}{50} + \frac{(53 - 50)^2}{50} + \frac{(36 - 50)^2}{50} = 6.52$$

Since the computed $\chi^2 = 6.52$ exceeds the critical value of 5.99147, we conclude at the $\alpha = .05$ level of significance that a consumer preference exists for one or more of the brands of bread.

The general form for a test of a hypothesis concerning multinomial probabilities is shown in the next box.

A Test of a Hypothesis about Multinomial Probabilities: One-Way Table

$$H_0: p_1 = p_{1,0}, p_2 = p_{2,0}, \ldots, p_k = p_{k,0}$$

where $p_{1,0}, p_{2,0}, \ldots, p_{k,0}$ represent the hypothesized values of the multinomial probabilities.

H_a: At least one of the multinomial probabilities does not equal its hypothesized value.

$$\text{Test statistic: } \chi^2 = \sum \frac{[n_i - E_i]^2}{E_i}$$

where $E_i = np_{i,0}$ is the **expected cell count**—that is, the expected number of outcomes of type i assuming that H_0 is true. The total sample size is n.

$$\text{Rejection region: } \chi^2 > \chi^2_\alpha \quad (\text{or, } \alpha > p\text{-value})$$

where χ^2_α has $(k - 1)$ df.

---

*The derivation of the degrees of freedom for χ^2 involves the number of linear restrictions imposed on the count data. In the present case, the only constraint is that $\Sigma n_i = n$, where n (the sample size) is fixed in advance. Therefore, df $= k - 1$. For other cases, we will give the degrees of freedom for each usage of χ^2 and refer the interested reader to the references for more detail.

Conditions Required for a Valid χ^2 Test: One-Way Table

1. A multinomial experiment has been conducted. This is generally satisfied by taking a random sample from the population of interest.

2. The sample size n is large. This is satisfied if for every cell, the expected cell count E_i will be equal to 5 or more.*

Example 2

A One-Way χ^2 Test— Evaluating a Firm's Merit-Increase Plan

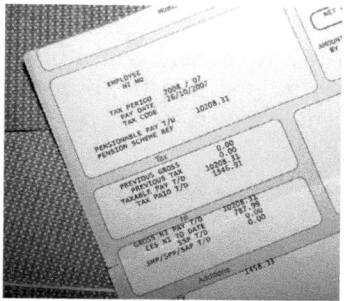

Table 2

Distribution of Pay Increases

None	Standard	Merit
42	365	193

Data Set: PAYINC

Problem A large firm has established what it hopes is an objective system of deciding on annual pay increases for its employees. The system is based on a series of evaluation scores determined by the supervisors of each employee. Employees with scores above 80 receive a merit pay increase, those with scores between 50 and 80 receive the standard increase, and those below 50 receive no increase. The firm designed the plan with the objective that, on the average, 25% of its employees would receive merit increases, 65% would receive standard increases, and 10% would receive no increase. After 1 year of operation using the new plan, the distribution of pay increases for a random sample of 600 company employees was as shown in Table 2. Test at the $\alpha = .01$ level to determine whether these data indicate that the distribution of pay increases differs significantly from the proportions established by the firm.

Solution Define the population proportions for the three pay increase categories to be

p_1 = Proportion of employees who receive no pay increase

p_2 = Proportion of employees who receive a standard increase

p_3 = Proportion of employees who receive a merit increase

Then the null hypothesis representing the distribution of percentages in the firm's proposed plan is

$$H_0: p_1 = .10, p_2 = .65, p_3 = .25$$

and the alternative is

H_a: At least two of the proportions differ from the firm's proposed plan.

Now, we have

$$\text{Test statistic: } \chi^2 = \sum \frac{[n_i - E_i]^2}{E_i}$$

where

$$E_1 = np_{1,0} = 600(.10) = 60$$
$$E_2 = np_{2,0} = 600(.65) = 390$$
$$E_3 = np_{3,0} = 600(.25) = 150$$

Since all these values are larger than 5, the χ^2 approximation is appropriate. Also, since the employees were randomly selected, the properties of the multinomial distribution are satisfied.

Rejection region: For $\alpha = .01$ and df $= k - 1 = 2$, reject H_0 if $\chi^2 > \chi^2_{.01}$, where (from Table IV in Appendix: Tables) $\chi^2_{.01} = 9.21034$.

We now calculate the test statistic:

$$\chi^2 = \frac{(42 - 60)^2}{60} + \frac{(365 - 390)^2}{390} + \frac{(193 - 150)^2}{150} = 19.33$$

*The assumption that all expected cell counts are at least 5 is necessary to ensure that the χ^2 approximation is appropriate. Exact methods for conducting the test of a hypothesis exist and may be used for small expected cell counts, but these methods are beyond the scope of this text. Also, some researchers relax this assumption somewhat, requiring expected cell counts to be at least 1 and no more than 20% to be less than 5.

This value exceeds the table value of χ^2 (9.21034); therefore, the data provide strong evidence ($\alpha = .01$) that the company's actual pay plan distribution differs from its proposed plan.

The χ^2 test can also be conducted using statistical software. Figure 2 is an Excel/XLSTAT printout of the analysis of the data in Table 2; note that the p-value of the test is reported as less than .0001. Because $\alpha = .01$ exceeds this p-value, there is sufficient evidence to reject H_0.

Figure 2

Excel/XLSTAT multinomial chi-square test for data in Table 2

Chi-square test:	
Chi-square (Observed value)	19.3292
Chi-square (Critical value)	5.9915
DF	2
p-value	< 0.0001
alpha	0.05

Look Back If the conclusion for the χ^2 test is "fail to reject H_0," then there is insufficient evidence to conclude that the actual pay plan distribution differs from the proposed plan as stated in H_0. Be careful not to "accept H_0" and conclude that $p_1 = .10, p_2 = .65$, and $p_3 = .25$. The probability (β) of a Type II error is unknown.

Now Work Exercise 7a

If we want a 95% confidence interval for the proportion of the company's employees who will receive merit increases under the new system, we calculate

$$\hat{p}_3 \pm 1.96\sigma_{\hat{p}_3} \approx \hat{p}_3 \pm 1.96\sqrt{\frac{\hat{p}_3(1 - \hat{p}_3)}{n}} \quad \text{where } \hat{p}_3 = \frac{n_3}{n} = \frac{193}{600} = .32$$

$$= .32 \pm 1.96\sqrt{\frac{(.32)(1 - .32)}{600}} = .32 \pm .04$$

Thus, we estimate that between 28% and 36% of the firm's employees will qualify for merit increases under the new plan. It appears that the firm will have to raise the requirements for merit increases in order to achieve the stated goal of a 25% employee qualification rate.

Exercises 1–18

Please be aware that some of the following problems may require knowledge of concepts that are not presented in this chapter.

Learning the Mechanics

1 Find the rejection region for a one-dimensional χ^2 test of a null hypothesis concerning $p_1, p_2, \ldots, p_k$ if
- **a.** $k = 3; \alpha = .05$
- **b.** $k = 5; \alpha = .10$
- **c.** $k = 4; \alpha = .01$

2 What are the characteristics of a multinomial experiment? Compare the characteristics to those of a binomial experiment.

3 What conditions must n satisfy to make the χ^2 test valid?

4 A multinomial experiment with $k = 3$ cells and $n = 320$ produced the data shown in the following one-way table. Do these data provide sufficient evidence to contradict the null hypothesis that $p_1 = .25, p_2 = .25$, and $p_3 = .50$? Test using $\alpha = .05$.

	Cell		
	1	2	3
n_i	78	60	182

5 A multinomial experiment with $k = 4$ cells and $n = 205$ produced the data shown in the one-way table below.

L10005

	Cell			
	1	2	3	4
n_i	43	56	59	47

a. Do these data provide sufficient evidence to conclude that the multinomial probabilities differ? Test using $\alpha = .05$.

b. What are the Type I and Type II errors associated with the test of part **a?**

c. Construct a 95% confidence interval for the multinomial probability associated with cell 3.

Applying the Concepts—Basic

6 **Do social robots walk or roll?** *International Conference on Social Robotics* (Vol. 6414, 2010) did a study of how engineers design social robots. A social (or service) robot is designed to entertain, educate, and care for human users. In a random sample of 106 social robots obtained through a Web search, the researchers found that 63 were built with legs only, 20 with wheels only, 8 with both legs and wheels, and 15 with neither legs nor wheels. Prior to obtaining these sample results, a robot design engineer stated that 50% of all social robots produced have legs only, 30% have wheels only, 10% have both legs and wheels, and 10% have neither legs nor wheels.

NW

SOCROB

a. Explain why the data collected for each sampled social robot are categorical in nature.

b. Specify the null and alternative hypotheses for testing the design engineer's claim.

c. Assuming the claim is true, determine the number of social robots in the sample that you expect to fall into each design category.

d. Use the results to compute the chi-square test statistic.

e. Make the appropriate conclusion using $\alpha = .05$.

7 **Museum management.** *Museum Management and Curatorship* (June 2010) did a worldwide survey of 30 leading museums of contemporary art. Each museum manager was asked to provide the performance measure used most often for internal evaluation. A summary of the results is provided in the table (next column). The data were analyzed using a chi-square test for a multinomial experiment. The results are shown in the Minitab printout below.

MMC

Performance Measure	Number of Museums
Total visitors	8
Paying visitors	5
Big shows	6
Funds raised	7
Members	4

a. Is there evidence to indicate that one performance measure is used more often than any of the others? Test using $\alpha = .10$.

NW

b. Find a 90% confidence interval for the proportion of museums worldwide that use total visitors as their performance measure. Interpret the result.

8 **Rankings of MBA programs.** *Business Ethics* (Fall 2005) compiled rankings of master in business administration (MBA) programs worldwide. Each of 30 business schools was rated according to student exposure to social and environmental issues in the classroom. Ratings ranged from 1 star (lowest-rated group) to 5 stars (highest-rated group). A summary of the star ratings assigned to the 30 MBA programs is reproduced in the table.

MBASTR

Criteria	5 stars	4 stars	3 stars	2 stars	1 star	Total
Student Exposure	2	9	14	5	0	30

Source: Biello, D. "MBA programs for social and environmental stewardship," *Business Ethics,* Fall 2005, p. 25. Copyright © 2005 by Springer. Reprinted with permission.

a. Identify the categorical variable (and its levels) measured in this study.

b. How many of the sampled MBA programs would you expect to observe in each star rating category if there are no differences in the category proportions in the population of all MBA programs?

c. Specify the null and alternative hypotheses for testing whether there are differences in the star rating category proportions in the population of all MBA programs.

d. Calculate the χ^2 test statistic for testing the hypotheses in part **c.**

e. Give the rejection region for the test using $\alpha = .05$.

f. Use the results, parts **d** and **e,** to make the appropriate conclusion.

Chi-Square Goodness-of-Fit Test for Observed Counts in Variable: NUMBER

```
Using category names in PERFORM


                               Test              Contribution
Category          Observed  Proportion  Expected    to Chi-Sq
Total visitors           8         0.2         6     0.666667
Paying visitors          5         0.2         6     0.166667
Big shows                6         0.2         6     0.000000
Funds raised             7         0.2         6     0.166667
Members                  4         0.2         6     0.666667


 N  DF   Chi-Sq  P-Value
30   4  1.66667    0.797
```

Minitab output for Exercise 7

g. Find and interpret a 95% confidence interval for the proportion of all MBA programs that are ranked in the three-star category.

9 **Survey on giving and volunteering.** The *National Tax Journal* (Dec. 2001) published a study of charitable givers based on data collected from the Independent Sector Survey on Giving and Volunteering. A total of 1,072 charitable givers reported that their charitable contributions were motivated by tax considerations. The number of these 1,072 givers in each of 10 household income categories (saved in the accompanying file) is shown in the table below.

Household Income Group	Number of Charitable Givers
Under $10,000	42
$10,000–$20,000	93
$20,000–$30,000	99
$30,000–$40,000	153
$40,000–$50,000	91
$50,000–$60,000	114
$60,000–$70,000	157
$70,000–$80,000	101
$80,000–$100,000	95
Over $100,000	127

Source: Tiehen, L. "Tax policy and charitable contributions of money." *National Tax Journal,* Vol. 54, No. 4, Dec. 2001, p. 717 (adapted from Table 5). Copyright © 2001 by the National Tax Association. Reprinted with permission.

a. If the true proportions of charitable givers in each household income group are the same, how many of the 1,072 sampled givers would you expect to find in each income category?

b. Give the null hypothesis for testing whether the true proportions of charitable givers in each household income group are the same.

c. Compute the chi-square test statistic for testing the null hypothesis, part **b**.

d. Find the rejection region for the test if $\alpha = .10$.

e. Give the appropriate conclusion for the test in the words of the problem.

10 **Offshoring companies.** "Offshoring" is a term that describes a company's practice of relocating jobs and/or production to another country to reduce labor costs. *The Journal of Applied Business Research* (Jan/Feb 2011) published a study on the phenomenon of offshoring and how prevalent it is worldwide. The article included the results from a recent survey of CEOs at U.S. firms, where each CEO was asked about his or her firm's position on offshoring. A summary of the results (similar to the actual study) is shown in the accompanying table.

Firm's Position	Number of Firms
Currently offshoring	126
Not currently offshoring, but plan to do so in the future	72
Offshored in the past, but no more	30
Offshoring not applicable	372
Total	600

a. Identify the qualitative variable of interest (and its levels) for this study.

b. Are the proportions of U.S. firms in the four offshoring position categories significantly different? Conduct the appropriate chi-square test using $\alpha = .05$.

c. Construct a 95% confidence interval for the proportion of U.S. firms who are currently offshoring. Interpret the result.

Applying the Concepts—Intermediate

11 **Mobile device typing strategies.** Researchers estimate that in a typical month, about 75 billion text messages are sent in the United States. Text messaging on mobile devices (e.g., cell phones, smartphones) often requires typing in awkward positions that may lead to health issues. A group of Temple University public health professors investigated this phenomenon and published their results in *Applied Ergonomics* (March, 2012). One portion of the study focused on the typing styles of mobile device users. Typing style was categorized as (1) device held with both hands/both thumbs typing, (2) device held with right hand/right thumb typing, (3) device held with left hand/left thumb typing, (4) device held with both hands/right thumb typing, (5) device held with left hand/right index finger typing, or (6) other. In a sample of 859 college students observed typing on their mobile devices, the professors observed 396, 311, 70, 39, 18, and 25, respectively, in the six categories. Is this sufficient evidence to conclude that the proportions of mobile device users in the six texting style categories differ? Use $\alpha = .10$ to answer the question.

12 **Profiling UK rental malls.** *Urban Studies* (June 2011) did an analysis of tenants renting space in United Kingdom regional shopping malls. Tenants were categorized into five different-size groups based on amount of floor space: *anchor tenants* (more than 30,000 sq. ft.), *major space users* (between 10,000 and 30,000 sq. ft.), *large standard tenants* (between 4,000 and 10,000 sq. ft.), *small standard tenants* (between 1,500 and 4,000 sq. ft.), and *small tenants* (less than 1,500 sq. ft.). Suppose that a UK mall developer believes that the proportions of tenants in each category are .01, .05, .10, .40, and .44, respectively. In the actual study, 1,821 stores were sampled and the number of stores in each tenant category was reported as 14, 61, 216, 711, and 819, respectively. Use this information to test the mall developer's belief (at $\alpha = .01$). What do you conclude?

13 **Who is to blame for rising health care costs?** This exercise refers to *The Harris Poll* (Oct. 28, 2008) on who is to blame for the rising costs of health care. A nationwide survey of 2,119 U.S. adults answered the question "When you think of the rising costs of health care, who do you think is most responsible?" The responses are summarized in the table on the next page. One theory is that 50% of adults blame insurance companies, 10% blame pharmaceutical companies, 10% blame government, 10% blame hospitals, 10% blame physicians, 5% blame some other entity, and 5% are unsure.

a. Explain why the data come from a multinomial experiment.

b. Specify the null hypothesis for a test of the theory.

c. Use statistical software to conduct the test using $\alpha = .01$. What do you conclude?

Most Responsible for Rising Health Care Costs	Number Responding
Insurance companies	869
Pharmaceutical companies	339
Government	338
Hospitals	127
Physicians	85
Other	128
Not sure	233
Total	2,119

14 Attitudes toward top corporate managers. Scandals involving large U.S. corporations (e.g., Enron, WorldCom, and Adelphia) have had a major impact on the public's attitude toward business managers. In a Harris Poll administered immediately after the Enron scandal, a national sample of 2,023 adults were asked to agree or disagree with the following statement: "Top company managers have become rich at the expense of ordinary workers" (*The Harris Poll*, #55, Oct. 18, 2002). The response categories (and number of respondents in each) were strongly agree (1,173), somewhat agree (587), somewhat disagree (182), and strongly disagree (81). Suppose that prior to the Enron scandal, the percentages of all U.S. adults falling into the four response categories were 45%, 35%, 15%, and 5%, respectively. Is there evidence to infer that the percentages of all U.S. adults falling into the four response categories changed after the Enron scandal? Test using $\alpha = .01$.

15 Coupon user study. A hot topic in marketing research is the exploration of a technology-based self-service (TBSS) encounter, e.g., ATMs, automated hotel checkout, online banking, and express package tracking. Marketing Professor Dan Ladik (University of Suffolk) investigated a customer's motivation to use a TBSS developed for a firm's discount coupons. The coupon users received the coupons in one of three ways—mail only (nontechnology user), Internet only (TBSS user), and both mail and Internet. One of the variables of interest in the study was *Type of coupon user*. In particular, the professor wants to know if the true proportions of mail only, Internet only, and both mail and Internet users differ. In a sample of 440 coupon users, the professor discovered that 262 received coupons via only mail, 43 via only the Internet, and 135 via both mail and Internet. Conduct the appropriate analysis for the professor. Use $\alpha = .01$.

16 Cell phone user survey. If you subscribe to a cell phone plan, how many different cell phone numbers do you own? This was one question of interest in *Public Opinion Quarterly* (Vol. 70, No. 5, 2006). According to the Current Population Survey (CPS) Cell Phone Supplement, 51% of cell phone plans have only one cell number, 37% have two numbers, 9% have three numbers, and 3% have four or more numbers. An independent survey of 943 randomly selected cell phone users found that 473 pay for only one number, 334 pay for two numbers, 106 pay for three numbers, and 30 pay for four or more numbers. Conduct a test to determine if the data from the independent survey contradict the percentages reported by the CPS Cell Phone Supplement. Use $\alpha = .01$.

Applying the Concepts—Advanced

17 Overloading in the trucking industry. Although illegal, overloading is common in the trucking industry. A state highway planning agency (Minnesota Department of Transportation) monitored the movements of overweight trucks on an interstate highway using an unmanned, computerized scale that is built into the highway. Unknown to the truckers, the scale weighed their vehicles as they passed over it. Each day's proportion of 1 week's total truck traffic (five-axle tractor truck semitrailers) is shown in the first column of the table below. During the same week, the number of overweight trucks per day is given in the second column. This information is saved in the accompanying file. The planning agency would like to know whether the number of overweight trucks per week is distributed over the 7 days of the week in direct proportion to the volume of truck traffic. Test using $\alpha = .05$.

Day	Proportion	Number
Monday	.191	90
Tuesday	.198	82
Wednesday	.187	72
Thursday	.180	70
Friday	.155	51
Saturday	.043	18
Sunday	.046	31

18 Political representation of religious groups. Do those elected to the U.S. House of Representatives really "represent" their constituents demographically? This was a question of interest in *Chance* (Summer 2002). One of several demographics studied was religious affiliation. The accompanying table gives the proportion of the U.S. population for several religions, as well as the number of the 435 seats in the House of Representatives that are affiliated with that religion. Give your opinion on whether or not the House of Representatives is statistically representative of the religious affiliations of their constituents in the United States.

Religion	Proportion of U.S. Population	Number of Seats in House
Catholic	.28	117
Methodist	.04	61
Jewish	.02	30
Other	.66	227
Totals	1.00	435

3 Testing Category Probabilities: Two-Way (Contingency) Table

In Section 1, we introduced the multinomial probability distribution and considered data classified according to a single qualitative criterion. We now consider multinomial experiments in which the data are classified according to two criteria—that is, *classification with respect to two qualitative factors.*

For example, consider a study published in the *Journal of Marketing* on the impact of using celebrities in television advertisements. The researchers investigated the relationship between gender of a viewer and the viewer's brand awareness. Three hundred TV viewers were asked to identify products advertised by male celebrity spokespersons. The data are summarized in the **two-way table** shown in Table 3. This table is called a **contingency table;** it presents multinomial count data classified on two scales, or **dimensions, of classification**—namely, gender of viewer and brand awareness.

The symbols representing the cell counts for the multinomial experiment in Table 3 are shown in Table 4a; and the corresponding cell, row, and column probabilities are shown in Table 4b. Thus, n_{11} represents the number of viewers who are male and could identify the brand, and p_{11} represents the corresponding cell probability. Note the symbols for the row and column totals and also the symbols for the probability totals. The latter are called **marginal probabilities** for each row and column. The marginal probability p_{r1} is the probability that a TV viewer identifies the product; the marginal probability p_{c1} is the probability that the TV viewer is male. Thus,

$$p_{r1} = p_{11} + p_{12} \quad \text{and} \quad p_{c1} = p_{11} + p_{21}$$

Table 3	Contingency Table for Marketing Example			
		Gender		
		Male	Female	Totals
Brand Awareness	Could Identify Product	95	41	136
	Could Not Identify Product	50	114	164
	Totals	145	155	300

 *Data Set:* CELEB

Table 4a	Observed Counts for Contingency Table 3			
		Gender		
		Male	Female	Totals
Brand Awareness	Could Identify Product	n_{11}	n_{12}	R_1
	Could Not Identify Product	n_{21}	n_{22}	R_2
	Totals	C_1	C_2	n

Table 4b	Probabilities for Contingency Table 3			
		Gender		
		Male	Female	Totals
Brand Awareness	Could Identify Product	p_{11}	p_{12}	p_{r1}
	Could Not Identify Product	p_{21}	p_{22}	p_{r2}
	Totals	p_{c1}	p_{c2}	1

We can see, then, that this really is a multinomial experiment with a total of 300 trials, $(2)(2) = 4$ cells or possible outcomes, and probabilities for each cell as shown in Table 4b. If the 300 TV viewers are randomly chosen, the trials are considered independent, and the probabilities are viewed as remaining constant from trial to trial.

Suppose we want to know whether the two classifications, gender and brand awareness, are dependent—that is, if we know the gender of the TV viewer, does that information give us a clue about the viewer's brand awareness? In a probabilistic sense, we know that independence of events A and B implies $P(AB) = P(A)P(B)$. Similarly, in the contingency table analysis, if the **two classifications are independent**, the probability that an item is classified in any particular cell of the table is the product of the corresponding marginal probabilities. Thus, under the hypothesis of independence, in Table 4b, we must have

$$p_{11} = p_{r1}p_{c1}, \quad p_{21} = p_{r2}p_{c1}$$
$$p_{12} = p_{r1}p_{c_2}, \quad p_{22} = p_{r2}p_{c2}$$

To test the hypothesis of independence, we use the same reasoning employed in the one-dimensional tests of Section 2. First, we calculate the *expected, or mean, count in each cell*, assuming that the null hypothesis of independence is true. We do this by noting that the expected count in a cell of the table is just the total number of multinomial trials, n, times the cell probability. Recall that n_{ij} represents the **observed count** in the cell located in the ith row and jth column. Then the expected cell count for the upper left-hand cell (first row, first column) is

$$E_{11} = np_{11}$$

or, when the null hypothesis (the classifications are independent) is true,

$$E_{11} = np_{r1}p_{c1}$$

Since these true probabilities are not known, we estimate p_{r1} and p_{c1} by the proportions $\hat{p}_{r1} = R_1/n$ and $\hat{p}_{c1} = C_1/n$, where R_1 and C_1 represent the totals for row 1 and column 1, respectively. Thus, the estimate of the expected value E_{11} is

$$\hat{E}_{11} = n\left(\frac{R_1}{n}\right)\left(\frac{C_1}{n}\right) = \frac{R_1C_1}{n}$$

Similarly, for each i, j,

$$\hat{E}_{ij} = \frac{(\text{Row total})(\text{Column total})}{\text{Total sample size}}$$

Thus,

$$\hat{E}_{12} = \frac{R_1C_2}{n}$$

$$\hat{E}_{21} = \frac{R_2C_1}{n}$$

$$\hat{E}_{22} = \frac{R_2C_2}{n}$$

Finding Expected Cell Counts for a Two-Way Contingency Table

The estimate of the expected number of observations falling into the cell in row i and column j is given by

$$\hat{E}_{ij} = \frac{R_iC_j}{n}$$

where R_i = total for row i, C_j = total for column j, and n = sample size.

Using the data in Table 3, we find

$$\hat{E}_{11} = \frac{R_1 C_1}{n} = \frac{(136)(145)}{300} = 65.73$$

$$\hat{E}_{12} = \frac{R_1 C_2}{n} = \frac{(136)(155)}{300} = 70.27$$

$$\hat{E}_{21} = \frac{R_1 C_2}{n} = \frac{(164)(145)}{300} = 79.27$$

$$\hat{E}_{22} = \frac{R_1 C_2}{n} = \frac{(164)(155)}{300} = 84.73$$

These estimated expected values are more easily obtained using computer software. Figure 3 is a Minitab printout of the analysis, with expected values highlighted.

Tabulated statistics: AWARE, GENDER

```
Using frequencies in NUMBER


Rows: AWARE    Columns: GENDER

               Male   Female    All

ID-Product       95       41    136
               65.7     70.3  136.0

No-ID            50      114    164
               79.3     84.7  164.0

All             145      155    300
              145.0    155.0  300.0

Cell Contents:       Count
                     Expected count
```

Figure 3

Minitab contingency table analysis of data in Table 3

```
Pearson Chi-Square = 46.135, DF = 1, P-Value = 0.000
Likelihood Ratio Chi-Square = 47.362, DF = 1, P-Value = 0.000
```

We now use the χ^2 statistic to compare the observed and expected (estimated) counts in each cell of the contingency table:

$$\chi^2 = \frac{[n_{11} - \hat{E}_{11}]^2}{\hat{E}_{11}} + \frac{[n_{12} - \hat{E}_{12}]^2}{\hat{E}_{12}} + \frac{[n_{21} - \hat{E}_{21}]^2}{\hat{E}_{21}} + \frac{[n_{22} - \hat{E}_{22}]^2}{\hat{E}_{22}}$$

$$= \sum \frac{[n_{ij} - \hat{E}_{ij}]^2}{\hat{E}_{ij}}$$

(*Note:* The use of Σ in the context of a contingency table analysis refers to a sum over all cells in the table.)

Substituting the data of Table 3 into this expression, we get

$$\chi^2 = \frac{(95 - 65.73)^2}{65.73} + \frac{(41 - 70.27)^2}{70.27} + \frac{(50 - 79.27)^2}{79.27} + \frac{(114 - 84.73)^2}{84.73} = 46.14$$

Note that this value is also shown (highlighted) in Figure 3.

Large values of χ^2 imply that the observed counts do not closely agree, and hence, the hypothesis of independence is false. To determine how large χ^2 must be before it is too large to be attributed to chance, we make use of the fact that the sampling distribution of χ^2 is approximately a χ^2 probability distribution when the classifications are independent.

When testing the null hypothesis of independence in a two-way contingency table, the appropriate degrees of freedom will be $(r - 1)(c - 1)$, where r is the number of rows and c is the number of columns in the table. For the brand awareness example, the degrees of freedom for χ^2 are $(r - 1)(c - 1) = (2 - 1)(2 - 1) = 1$. Then, for $\alpha = .05$, we reject the hypothesis of independence when

$$\chi^2 > \chi^2_{.05} = 3.8146$$

Because the computed $\chi^2 = 46.14$ exceeds the value 3.84146, we conclude that viewer gender and brand awareness are dependent events. This result may also be obtained by noting that the p-value of the test (highlighted in Figure 3) is approximately 0.

The pattern of **dependence** can be seen more clearly by expressing the data as percentages. We first select one of the two classifications to be used as the base variable. In the preceding example, suppose we select gender of the TV viewer as the classificatory variable to be the base. Next, we represent the responses for each level of the second categorical variable (brand awareness in our example) as a percentage of the subtotal for the base variable. For example, from Table 3, we convert the response for males who identify the brand (95) to a percentage of the total number of male viewers (145)—that is,

$$\left(\tfrac{95}{145}\right)100\% = 65.5\%$$

The conversions of all Table 3 entries are similarly computed, and the values are shown in Table 5. The value shown at the right of each row is the row's total expressed as a percentage of the total number of responses in the entire table. Thus, the percentage of TV viewers who identify the product is $\left(\tfrac{136}{300}\right)100\% = 45.3\%$ (rounded to the nearest 10th of a percent).

Table 5	Percentage of TV Viewers Who Identify Brand, by Gender			
		Gender		
		Male	Female	Totals
Brand Awareness	Could Identify Product	65.5	26.5	45.3
	Could Not Identify Product	34.5	73.5	54.7
	Totals	100	100	100

If the gender and brand awareness variables are independent, then the percentages in the cells of the table are expected to be approximately equal to the corresponding row percentages. Thus, we would expect the percentages who identify the brand for each gender to be approximately 45% if the two variables are independent. The extent to which each gender's percentage departs from this value determines the dependence of the two classifications, with greater variability of the row percentages meaning a greater degree of dependence. A plot of the percentages helps summarize the observed pattern. In the SPSS bar graph in Figure 4, we show the gender of the viewer (the base variable) on the horizontal axis, and the percentages of TV viewers who identify the brand (green bars) on the vertical axis. The "expected" percentage under the assumption of independence is shown as a horizontal line.

Figure 4 clearly indicates the reason that the test resulted in the conclusion that the two classifications in the contingency table are dependent. The percentage of male TV viewers who identify the brand promoted by a male celebrity is more than twice as high as the percentage of female

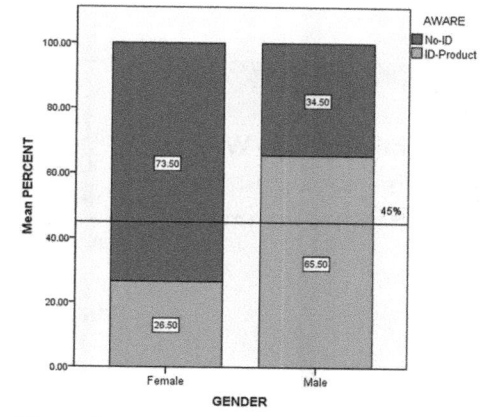

Figure 4

SPSS bar graph showing percent of viewers who identify TV product

TV viewers who identify the brand.* Statistical measures of the degree of dependence and procedures for making comparisons of pairs of levels for classifications are available. They are beyond the scope of this text but can be found in the references. We will, however, use descriptive summaries such as Figure 4 to examine the degree of dependence exhibited by the sample data.

The general form of a two-way contingency table containing r rows and c columns (called an $r \times c$ contingency table) is shown in Table 6. Note that the observed count in the (ij) cell is denoted by n_{ij}, the ith row total is R_i, the jth column total is C_j, and the total sample size is n. Using this notation, we give the general form of the contingency table test for independent classifications in the next box.

Table 6	General $r \times c$ Contingency Table				
Column	1	2	$\cdots$	c	Row Totals
Row 1	n_{11}	n_{12}	$\cdots$	n_{1c}	R_1
2	n_{21}	n_{22}	$\cdots$	n_{2c}	R_2
$\vdots$	$\vdots$	$\vdots$		$\vdots$	$\vdots$
r	n_{r1}	n_{r2}	$\cdots$	n_{rc}	R_r
Column Totals	C_1	C_2	$\cdots$	C_c	n

General Form of a Two-Way (Contingency) Table Analysis: χ^2-Test for Independence

H_0: The two classifications are independent.

H_a: The two classifications are dependent.

Test statistic: $\chi^2 = \Sigma \dfrac{[n_{ij} - \hat{E}_{ij}]^2}{\hat{E}_{ij}}$

where $\hat{E}_{ij} = \dfrac{R_i C_j}{n}$

Rejection region: $\chi^2 > \chi_\alpha^2$, where χ_α^2 has $(r - 1)(c - 1)$ df.
(or, $\alpha < p$-value)

Conditions Required for a Valid χ^2-Test: Contingency Table

1. The n observed counts are a random sample from the population of interest. We may then consider this to be a multinomial experiment with $r \times c$ possible outcomes.

2. The sample size, n, will be large enough so that, for every cell, the estimated expected count, $\hat{E}_{ij}$, will be equal to 5 or more.

| Example | 3 | |

Conducting a Two-Way Analysis—Broker Rating and Customer Income

Problem A large brokerage firm wants to determine whether the service it provides to affluent clients differs from the service it provides to lower-income clients. A sample of 500 clients is selected, and each client is asked to rate his or her broker. The results are shown in Table 7.

a. Test to determine whether there is evidence that broker rating and customer income are dependent. Use $\alpha = .05$.

b. Graph the data and describe the patterns revealed. Is the result of the test supported by the plot?

---

*Another way to make this comparison is to make an inference about the difference ($p_1 - p_2$), where p_1 is the proportion of males who identify the brand and p_2 is the corresponding proportion for females. In fact, a χ^2-analysis for a 2×2 contingency table is equivalent to a test of the null hypothesis, H_0: $p_1 - p_2 = 0$.

Solution

a. The first step is to obtain estimated expected cell frequencies under the assumption that the classifications are independent. Rather than compute these values by hand, we resort to statistical software. The Excel/XLSTAT printout of the analysis of Table 7 is displayed in Figure 5. Each cell in the "Theoretical frequencies" table of Figure 5 contains the expected frequency in that cell. Note that $\hat{E}_{11}$ the estimated expected count for the Outstanding, Under \$30,000 cell is 53.86. Similarly, the estimated expected count for the Outstanding, \$30,000–\$60,000 cell is $\hat{E}_{12} = 66.40$. Because all the estimated expected cell frequencies are greater than 5, the χ^2 approximation for the test statistic is appropriate. Assuming the clients chosen were randomly selected from all clients of the brokerage firm, the characteristics of the multinomial probability distribution are satisfied.

Table 7	Survey Results (Observed Clients), Example 3			

		Client's Income			
		Under \$30,000	\$30,000–\$60,000	Over \$60,000	Totals
Broker Rating	Outstanding	48	64	41	153
	Average	98	120	50	268
	Poor	30	33	16	79
	Totals	176	217	107	500

Data Set: BROKER

Test of independence between the rows and the columns (RATING / INCOME):

Chi-square (Observed value)	4.2777
Chi-square (Critical value)	9.4877
DF	4
p-value	0.3697
alpha	0.05

Observed frequencies (RATING / INCOME):

	1:UND30K	2:30K-60K	3:OVR60K	Total
1:OUTSTANDING	48	64	41	153
2:AVERAGE	98	120	50	268
3:POOR	30	33	16	79
Total	176	217	107	500

Theoretical frequencies (RATING / INCOME):

	1:UND30K	2:30K-60K	3:OVR60K	Total
1:OUTSTANDING	53.8560	66.4020	32.7420	153
2:AVERAGE	94.3360	116.3120	57.3520	268
3:POOR	27.8080	34.2860	16.9060	79
Total	176	217	107	500

Percentages / Column (RATING / INCOME):

	1:UND30K	2:30K-60K	3:OVR60K	Total
1:OUTSTANDING	27.2727	29.4931	38.3178	30.6000
2:AVERAGE	55.6818	55.2995	46.7290	53.6000
3:POOR	17.0455	15.2074	14.9533	15.8000
Total	100	100	100	100

Figure 5

XLSTAT contingency table analysis for brokerage data

The null and alternative hypotheses we want to test are

H_0: The rating a client gives his or her broker is independent of client's income.

H_a: Broker rating and client income are dependent.

The test statistic, $\chi^2 = 4.28$, is highlighted at the top of the printout, as is the observed significance level (p-value) of the test. Because $\alpha = .05$ is less than $p = .370$, we fail to reject H_0. This survey does not support the firm's alternative hypothesis that affluent clients receive different broker service than lower-income clients. (Note that we could not reject H_0 even with $\alpha = .10$.)

b. The broker rating frequencies are expressed as percentages of income category frequencies in the bottom table of the XLSTAT printout, Figure 5. The expected percentages under the assumption of independence are shown in the "Total" column of the printout. A Minitab side-by-side bar graph of the data is shown in Figure 6. Note that the response percentages deviate only slightly from those expected under the assumption of independence, supporting the result of the test in part **a**—that is, neither the descriptive plot nor the statistical test provides evidence that the rating given for broker services depends on (varies with) the customer's income.

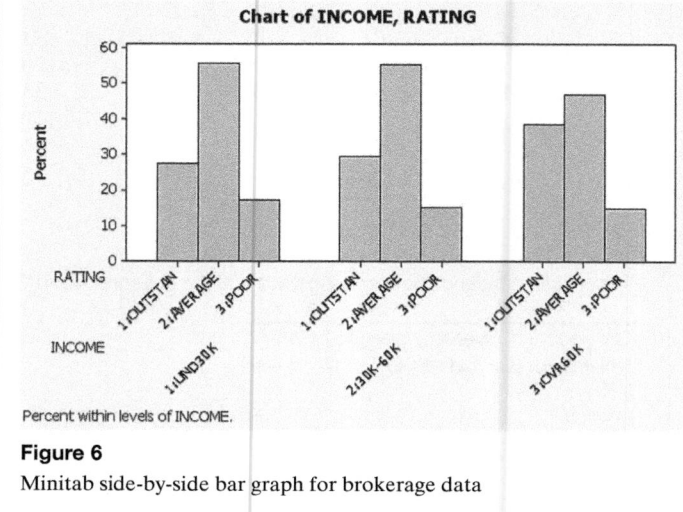

Figure 6

Minitab side-by-side bar graph for brokerage data

Now Work Exercise 26

Contingency Tables with Fixed Marginals

In the *Journal of Marketing* study on celebrities in TV ads, a single random sample was selected from the target population of all TV viewers and the outcomes—values of gender and brand awareness—were recorded for each viewer. For this type of study, the researchers had no *apriori* knowledge of how many observations would fall into the categories of the qualititative variables. In other words, prior to obtaining the sample, the researchers did not know how many males or how many brand identifiers would make up the sample. Oftentimes, it is advantageous to select a random sample from each of the levels of one of the qualitative variables.

For example, in the *Journal of Marketing* study, the researchers may want to be sure of an equivalent number of males and females in their sample. Consequently, they will select independent random samples of 150 males and 150 females. (In fact, this was the sampling plan for the actual study.) Summary data for this type of study yield a **contingency table with fixed marginals** since the column totals for one qualitative variable (e.g., gender) are known in advance.* The goal of the analysis does not change—determine whether the two qualitative variables (e.g., gender and brand awareness) are dependent.

The procedure for conducting a chi-square analysis for a contingency table with fixed marginals is identical to the one outlined above, since it can be shown (proof omitted) that the χ^2 test statistic for this type of sampling also has an approximate chi-square distribution with $(r - 1)(c - 1)$ degrees of freedom. One reason why you might choose this

*Data from this type of study are also known as *product binomial data*.

alternative sampling plan is to obtain sufficient observations in each cell of the contingency table to ensure that the chi-square approximation is valid. Remember, this will usually occur when the expected cell counts are all greater than or equal to 5. By selecting a large sample (150 observations) for each gender in the *Journal of Marketing* study, the researchers improved the odds of obtaining large expected cell counts in the contingency table.

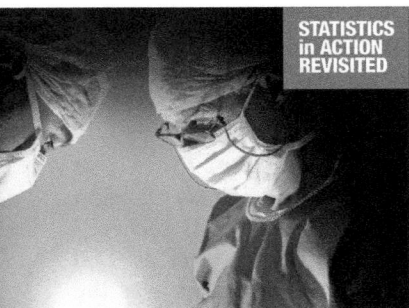

STATISTICS in ACTION REVISITED

Testing Whether Likelihood of a Lawsuit Is Related to Recall Notice Sender

We return to the case involving tainted transplant tissue. Recall that a processor of the tainted tissue filed a lawsuit against a tissue distributor, claiming that the distributor was more responsible than the processor for paying damages to litigating transplant patients. Why? Because the distributor in question had sent recall notices (as required by the FTC) to hospitals and surgeons with unsolicited newspaper articles describing in graphic detail the "ghoulish" acts that had been committed. According to the processor, by including the articles in the recall package, this distributor inflamed the tissue recipients, increasing the likelihood that the patients would file a lawsuit.

To prove its case in court, the processor needed to establish a statistical link between the likelihood of a lawsuit and the sender of the recall notice. More specifically, can the processor show that the probability of a lawsuit is higher for the patients of surgeons who received the recall notice with the inflammatory articles than for the patients of surgeons who only received the recall notice?

A statistician serving as an expert consultant for the processor reviewed data for the 7,914 patients who received recall notices (of which 708 filed suit). These data are saved in the **GHOUL1** file. For each patient, the file contains information on the SENDER of the recall notice (Processor or Distributor) and whether or not a LAWSUIT was filed (Yes or No). Since both of these variables are qualitative, and we want to know whether the probability of a LAWSUIT depended on the SENDER of the recall notice, a contingency table analysis is appropriate.

Figure SIA1 shows the Minitab contingency table analysis. The null and alternative hypotheses for the test are

H_0: Lawsuit and Sender are independent
H_a: Lawsuit and Sender are dependent

Tabulated statistics: SENDER, LAWSUIT

```
Rows: SENDER    Columns: LAWSUIT

                   No      Yes      All

Distributor       5506      657     6163
                 89.34    10.66   100.00
                  5612      551     6163
                 1.989   20.244        *

Processor         1700       51     1751
                 97.09     2.91   100.00
                  1594      157     1751
                 7.001   71.252        *

All               7206      708     7914
                 91.05     8.95   100.00
                  7206      708     7914
                     *        *        *

Cell Contents:        Count
                      % of Row
                      Expected count
                      Contribution to Chi-square


Pearson Chi-Square = 100.485, DF = 1, P-Value = 0.000
Likelihood Ratio Chi-Square = 124.748, DF = 1, P-Value = 0.000
```

Figure SIA1

Minitab contingency table analysis—likelihood of lawsuit vs. recall notice sender

Both the chi-square test statistic (100.5) and *p*-value of the test (.000) are highlighted on the printout. If we conduct the test at $\alpha = .01$, there is sufficient evidence to reject H_0. That is, the data provide evidence to indicate that the likelihood of a tainted transplant patient filing a lawsuit is associated with the sender of the recall notice.

To determine which sender had the higher percentage of patients to file a lawsuit, examine the row percentages (highlighted) in the contingency table of Figure SIA1 You can see that of the 1,751 patients sent recall notices by the processor, 51 (or 2.91%) filed lawsuits. In contrast, of the 6,163 patients sent recall notices by the distributor in question, 657 (or 66%) filed lawsuits. Thus, the probability of a patient filing a lawsuit was almost five times higher for the distributor's patients than for the processor's patients.

Before testifying on these results in court, the statistician decided to do one additional analysis: He eliminated from the sample data any patients whose surgeon had been sent notices by both parties. Why? Since these patients' surgeons received both recall notices, the underlying reason for filing a lawsuit would be unclear. Did the patient file simply because he or she received tainted transplant tissue, or was the filing motivated by the inflammatory articles that accompanied the recall notice? After eliminating these patients, the data looked like that shown in Table SIA2. A Minitab contingency table analysis on this reduced data set (saved in the **GHOUL2** file) is shown in Figure SIA2.

Table SIA2	Data for the Tainted Tissue Case, Dual Recall Notices Eliminated		
Recall Notice Sender		Number of Patients	Number of Lawsuits
Processor/other distributor		1,522	31
Distributor in question		5,705	606
Totals		7,227	637

Source: Info Tech, Inc.

```
Tabulated statistics: SENDER, LAWSUIT

Rows: SENDER    Columns: LAWSUIT

                  No      Yes      All

Distributor      5099      606     5705
                89.38    10.62   100.00
                 5202      503     5705
                2.045   21.160        *

Processor        1491       31     1522
                97.96     2.04   100.00
                 1388      134     1522
                7.667   79.315        *

All              6590      637     7227
                91.19     8.81   100.00
                 6590      637     7227
                    *        *        *


Cell Contents:      Count
                    % of Row
                    Expected count
                    Contribution to Chi-square
```

Figure SIA2

Minitab contingency table analysis, with dual recall notices eliminated

```
Pearson Chi-Square = 110.187, DF = 1, P-Value = 0.000
Likelihood Ratio Chi-Square = 144.862, DF = 1, P-Value = 0.000
```

As in the previous analysis, the chi-square test statistic (12) and *p*-value of the test (.000)—both highlighted on the printout—imply that the likelihood of a tainted transplant patient filing a lawsuit is associated with the sender of the recall notice, at $\alpha = .01$. Also, the percentage of patients filing lawsuits when sent a recall notice by the distributor (62%) is again five times higher than the percentage of patients filing lawsuits when sent a recall notice by the processor (2.04%).

The results of both analyses were used to successfully support the processor's claim in court. Nonetheless, we need to point out one caveat to the contingency table analyses. Be careful not to conclude that the data are proof that the inclusion of the inflammatory articles *caused* the probability of litigation to increase. Without controlling all possible variables that may relate to filing a lawsuit (e.g., a patient's socioeconomic status, whether or not a patient has filed a lawsuit in the past), we can only say that the two qualitative variables, lawsuit status and recall notice sender, are statistically associated. However, the fact that the likelihood of a lawsuit was almost five times higher when the notice was sent by the distributor shifts the burden of proof to the distributor to explain why this occurred and to convince the court that it should not be held accountable for paying the majority of the damages.

Alternative Analysis: As mentioned in a footnote in this Section 3, a 2×2 contingency table analysis is equivalent to a comparison of two population proportions. In the tainted tissue case, we want to compare p_1, the proportion of lawsuits filed by patients who were sent recall notices by the processor, to p_2, the proportion of lawsuits filed by patients who were sent recall notices by the distributor who included the inflammatory articles. Both a test of the null hypothesis, H_0: $(p_1 - p_2) = 0$, and a 95% confidence interval for the difference, $(p_1 - p_2)$ using the reduced sample data, are shown (highlighted) on the Minitab printout, Figure SIA3.

Test and CI for Two Proportions

```
Sample     X     N   Sample p
1         31  1522   0.020368
2        606  5705   0.106223


Difference = p (1) - p (2)
Estimate for difference:   -0.0858547
95% CI for difference:  (-0.0965452, -0.0751641)
Test for difference = 0 (vs not = 0):  Z = -10.50  P-Value = 0.000

Fisher's exact test: P-Value = 0.000
```

Figure SIA3

Minitab output with 95% confidence interval and test for difference in proportions of lawsuits filed

The p-value for the test (.000) indicates that the two proportions are significantly different at $\alpha = 05$. The 95% confidence interval, $(-.097, -.075)$, shows that the proportion of lawsuits associated with patients who were sent recall notices from the distributor ranges between .075 and .097 higher than the corresponding proportion for the processor. Both results support the processor's case, namely, that the patients who were sent recall notices with the inflammatory news articles were more likely to file a lawsuit than those who were sent only recall notices.

Exercises 19–37

Please be aware that some of the following problems may require knowledge of concepts that are not presented in this chapter.

Learning the Mechanics

19 Find the rejection region for a test of independence of two classifications where the contingency table contains r rows and c columns.
  a. $r = 5, c = 5, \alpha = .05$
  b. $r = 3, c = 6, \alpha = .10$
  c. $r = 2, c = 3, \alpha = .01$

20 Consider the 2×3 (i.e., $r = 2$ and $c = 3$) contingency table shown below.

L10020

		Column		
		1	2	3
Row	1	9	34	53
	2	16	30	25

a. Specify the null and alternative hypotheses that should be used in testing the independence of the row and column classifications.

b. Specify the test statistic and the rejection region that should be used in conducting the hypothesis test of part **a.** Use $\alpha = .01$.

c. Assuming the row classification and the column classification are independent, find estimates for the expected cell counts.

d. Conduct the hypothesis test of part **a.** Interpret your result.

21 Refer to Exercise 20.
  a. Convert the frequency responses to percentages by calculating the percentage of each column total falling in each row. Also convert the row totals to percentages of the total number of responses. Display the percentages in a table.

b. Create a bar graph with row 1 percentage on the vertical axis and column number on the horizontal axis. Show the row 1 total percentage as a horizontal line on the graph.

c. What pattern do you expect to see if the rows and columns are independent? Does the plot support the result of the test of independence in Exercise 20?

22 Test the null hypothesis of independence of the two classifications, A and B, in the 3×3 contingency table shown below. Test using $\alpha = .05$.

L10022

		B		
		B_1	B_2	B_3
	A_1	40	72	42
A	A_2	63	53	70
	A_3	31	38	30

23 Refer to Exercise 22.

a. Convert the responses to percentages by calculating the percentage of each B class total falling into each A classification.

b. Calculate the percentage of the total number of responses that constitute each of the A classification totals.

c. Create a bar graph with row A_1 percentage on the vertical axis and B classification on the horizontal axis. Does the graph support the result of the test of hypothesis in Exercise 22? Explain.

d. Repeat part **c** for the row A_2 percentages.

e. Repeat part **c** for the row A_3 percentages.

Applying the Concepts—Basic

24 **Safety of hybrid cars.** According to the Highway Loss Data Institute (HLDI), "Hybrid [automobiles] have a safety edge over their conventional twins when it comes to shielding their occupants from injuries in crashes" (*HLDI Bulletin*, Sept. 2011). Consider data collected by the HLDI on Honda Accords in 2002–2010. In a sample of 50,132 collision claims for conventional Accords, 5,364 involved injuries; in a sample of 1,505 collision claims for hybrid Accords, 137 involved injuries. You want to use this information to determine whether the injury rate for hybrid Accords is less than the injury rate for conventional Accords.

a. Identify the two qualitative variables measured for each Honda Accord collision claim.

b. Form a contingency table for this data, giving the number of claims in each combination of the qualitative variable categories.

c. Give H_0 and H_a for testing whether injury rate for collision claims depends on Accord model (hybrid or conventional).

d. Find the expected number of claims in each cell of the contingency table, assuming that H_0 is true.

e. Compute the χ^2 test statistic and compare your answer to the test statistic shown on the accompanying XLSTAT printout (next column).

f. Find the rejection region for the test using $\alpha = .05$ and compare your answer to the critical value shown on the accompanying XLSTAT printout.

XLSTAT Output for Exercise 24

Results for the variables Model and Claim:

Contingency table (Model / Claim):

	Injury	No Injury
Conventional	5364	44768
Hybrid	137	1368

Test of independence between the rows and the columns (Model / Claim):

Chi-square (Observed value)	3.9139
Chi-square (Critical value)	3.8415
DF	1
p-value	0.0479
alpha	0.05

g. Make the appropriate conclusion using both the rejection region method and the *p*-value (shown on the XLSTAT printout).

h. Find a 95% confidence interval for the difference between the injury rates of conventional and hybrid Honda Accords. (See Section 3.) Use the interval to determine whether the injury rate for hybrid Accords is less than the injury rate for conventional Accords.

25 **Purchasing souvenirs.** A major tourist activity is shopping. Travel researchers estimate that nearly one-third of total travel expenditures are used on shopping for souvenirs (*Journal of Travel Research*, May 2011). To investigate the impact of gender on souvenir shopping, a survey of 3,200 tourists was conducted. One question asked how often the tourist purchases photographs, postcards, or paintings of the region visited. Responses were recorded as "Always," "Often," "Occasionally," or "Rarely or Never." The table shows the percentages of tourists responding in each category, by gender.

Photos, Postcards, Paintings	Male Tourist	Female Tourist
Always	16%	28%
Often	27	31
Occasionally	35	29
Rarely or never	22	12
Totals	100%	100%

Source: Wilkins, H. "Souvenirs: What and why we buy," *Journal of Travel Research*, Vol. 50, No. 3, May 2011 (adapted from Table 2).

a. Based on the percentages shown in the table, do you think male and female tourists differ in their responses to purchasing photographs, postcards, or paintings? Why are these percentages alone insufficient to draw a conclusion about the true response category proportions?

b. Assume that 1,500 males and 1,700 females participated in the survey. Use these sample sizes and the percentages in the table to compute the counts of tourists in each of the Response/Gender categories. This represents the contingency table for the study.

c. Specify the null and alternative hypotheses for testing whether male and female tourists differ in their responses to purchasing photographs, postcards, or paintings.

d. An SPSS printout of the contingency table analysis is shown below. Locate the test statistic and *p*-value on the printout.

e. Make the appropriate conclusion using $\alpha = .01$.

RESPONSE * GENDER Crosstabulation

			GENDER Female	GENDER Male	Total
RESPONSE	1:Always	Count	476	240	716
		Expected Count	380.4	335.6	716.0
	2:Often	Count	527	405	932
		Expected Count	495.1	436.9	932.0
	3:Occasionally	Count	493	525	1018
		Expected Count	540.8	477.2	1018.0
	4:Rarely/Never	Count	204	330	534
		Expected Count	283.7	250.3	534.0
Total		Count	1700	1500	3200
		Expected Count	1700.0	1500.0	3200.0

Chi-Square Tests

	Value	df	Asymp. Sig. (2-sided)
Pearson Chi-Square	112.433[a]	3	.000
Likelihood Ratio	113.788	3	.000
N of Valid Cases	3200		

a. 0 cells (0.0%) have expected count less than 5. The minimum expected count is 250.31.

26 Stereotyping in deceptive and authentic news stories. Major newspapers lose their credibility (and subscribers) when they are found to have published deceptive or misleading news stories. In *Journalism and Mass Communication Quarterly* (Summer 2007), University of Texas researchers investigated whether certain stereotypes (e.g., negative references to certain nationalities) occur more often in deceptive news stories than in authentic news stories. The researchers analyzed 183 news stories that were proven to be deceptive in nature and 128 news stories that were considered authentic. Specifically, the researchers determined whether each story was negative, neutral, or positive in tone. The accompanying table gives the number of news stories found in each tone category.

	Authentic News Stories	Deceptive News Stories
Negative tone	59	111
Neutral tone	49	61
Positive tone	20	11
Totals	128	183

Source: Based on Lasorsa, D., & Dai, J. "When news reporters deceive: The production of stereotypes," *Journalism and Mass Communication Quarterly,* Vol. 84, No. 2, Summer 2007 (Table 2).

a. Find the sample proportion of negative tone news stories that are deceptive.

b. Find the sample proportion of neutral news stories that are deceptive.

c. Find the sample proportion of positive news stories that are deceptive.

d. Compare the sample proportions, parts **a–c**. Does it appear that the proportion of news stories that are deceptive depends on story tone?

Minitab output for Exercise 26

Tabulated statistics: TONE, STORY

```
Using frequencies in NUMBER

Rows: TONE    Columns: STORY

            Authentic  Deceptive    All

Negative          59        111      170
               69.97     100.03   170.00

Neutral           49         61      110
               45.27      64.73   110.00

Positive          20         11       31
               12.76      18.24    31.00

All              128        183      311
              128.00     183.00   311.00

Cell Contents:      Count
                    Expected count
```

Pearson Chi-Square = 10.427, DF = 2, P-Value = 0.005
Likelihood Ratio Chi-Square = 10.348, DF = 2, P-Value = 0.006

e. Give the null hypothesis for testing whether the authenticity of a news story depends on tone.

f. Use the Minitab printout above to conduct the test, part **e.** Test at $\alpha = .05$.

27 Are travel professionals equitably paid? *Business Travel News* (July 17, 2006) reported the results of its annual Travel Manager Salary & Attitude survey. A total of 277 travel professionals, 103 males and 174 females, participated in the 2005 survey. One question asked for the travel professional's opinion on the fairness of his/her salary. Responses were classified as "salary too low," "equitable/fair," or "paid well." The table below gives a breakdown of the responses in each category by gender.

	Males	Females
Salary too low	29	89
Equitable/fair	58	64
Paid well	16	21
Totals	103	174

a. Find the proportion of male travel professionals who believe their salary is too low and compare it to the proportion of female travel professionals who believe their salary is too low.

b. Repeat part **a** but compare the proportions who believe their salary is equitable/fair.

c. Repeat part **a** but compare the proportions who believe they are paid well.

d. Based on the comparisons, parts **a–c**, do you think opinion on the fairness of a travel professional's salary differs for males and females?

e. Refer to part **d**. Conduct the appropriate statistical test using $\alpha = .10$.

f. Construct and interpret a 90% confidence interval for the difference between the proportions of part **a**.

28 Eyewitnesses and mugshots. *Applied Psychology in Criminal Justice* (April 2010) did a study of mugshot choices by eyewitnesses to a crime.

A sample of 96 college students was shown a video of a simulated theft, then asked to select a mugshot that most closely resembled the thief. The students were randomly assigned to view either 3, 6, or 12 mugshots at a time, with 32 students in each group. The number of students in the 3-, 6-, and 12-photos-per-page groups who selected the target mugshot were 19, 19, and 15, respectively.

a. For each photo group, compute the proportion of students who selected the target mugshot. Which group yielded the lowest proportion?

b. Create a contingency table for these data, with photo group in the rows and whether or not the target mugshot was selected in the columns.

c. Analyze the contingency table, part **b.** Are there differences in the proportions who selected the target mugshot among the three photo groups? Test using $\alpha = .10$.

Applying the Concepts—Intermediate

29 Offshoring companies. Refer to *The Journal of Applied Business Research* (Jan/Feb 2011) study of offshoring companies, Exercise 10. In addition to U.S. firms, CEOs from international companies were also surveyed on their offshoring positions. The number of firms in each position category (adapted from the results of the actual study) is shown in the accompanying table. Does a firm's position on offshoring depend on the firm's nationality? Test using $\alpha = .05$.

OFSHR2

Firm's Position	United States	Europe	South America	Asia-Pacific
Currently offshoring	126	75	35	93
Not currently offshoring, but plan to do so in the future	72	36	10	27
Offshored in the past, but no more	30	9	4	6
Offshoring not applicable	372	180	51	174
Totals	600	300	100	300

30 Guilt in decision making. The effect of guilt emotion on how a decision maker focuses on a problem was investigated in the Jan. 2007 issue of the *Journal of Behavioral Decision Making*. A total of 171 volunteer students participated in the experiment, where each was randomly assigned to one of three emotional states (guilt, anger, or neutral) through a reading/writing task. Immediately after the task, students were presented with a decision problem where the stated option had predominantly negative features (e.g., spending

GUILT

Emotional State	Choose Stated Option	Do Not Choose Stated Option	Totals
Guilt	45	12	57
Anger	8	50	58
Neutral	7	49	56
Totals	60	111	171

Source: Gangemi, A., and Mancini, F. "Guilt and focusing in decision-making," *Journal of Behavioral Decision Making,* Vol. 20, Jan. 2007 (Table 2).

money on repairing a very old car). The results (number responding in each category) are summarized in the accompanying table. Is there sufficient evidence (at $\alpha = .10$) to claim that the option choice depended on emotional state? Use the data saved to answer the question.

31 Mobile device typing strategies. Refer to the *Applied Ergonomics* (March 2012) study of mobile device typing strategies, Exercise 11. Recall that typing style of mobile device users was categorized as (1) device held with both hands/both thumbs typing, (2) device held with right hand/right thumb typing, (3) device held with left hand/left thumb typing, (4) device held with both hands/right thumb typing, (5) device held with left hand/right index finger typing, or (6) other. The researchers' main objective was to determine if there are gender differences in typing strategies. Typing strategy and gender were observed for each in a sample of 859 college students observed typing on their mobile devices. The data are summarized in the accompanying table. Is this sufficient evidence to conclude that the proportions of mobile device users in the six texting style categories depend on whether a male or a female is texting? Use $\alpha = .10$ to answer the question.

TXTMS2

Typing Strategy	Number of Males	Number of Females
Both hands hold/both thumbs type	161	235
Right hand hold/right thumb type	118	193
Left hand hold/left thumb type	29	41
Both hands hold/right thumb type	10	29
Left hand hold/right index type	6	12
Other	11	14

Source: Gold, J. E., et al. "Postures, typing strategies, and gender differences in mobile device usage: An observational study," *Applied Ergonomics,* Vol. 43, No. 2, March 2012 (Table 2).

32 "Cry Wolf" effect in air traffic controlling. Researchers at Alion Science Corporation and New Mexico State University collaborated on a study of how air traffic controllers respond to false alarms (*Human Factors,* Aug. 2009). The researchers theorize that the high rate of false alarms regarding mid-air collisions leads to the "cry wolf" effect, i.e., the tendency for air traffic controllers to ignore true alerts in the future. The investigation examined data on a random sample of 437 conflict alerts. Each alert was first classified as a "true" or "false" alert. Then, each was classified according to whether or not there was a human controller response to the alert. A summary of the responses is provided in the accompanying table. Do the data indicate that the response rate of air traffic controllers to mid-air collision alarms differs for true and false alerts? Test using $\alpha = .05$. What inference can you make concerning the "cry wolf" effect?

ATC

	No Response	Response	Totals
True alert	3	231	234
False alert	37	166	203
Totals	40	397	437

Source: Based on Wickens, C. D., et al. "False alerts in air traffic control conflict alerting system: Is there a 'cry wolf' effect?" *Human Factors,* Vol. 51, No. 4, August 2009 (Table 2).

33 **Creating menus to influence others.** The *Journal of Consumer Research* (Mar. 2003) did a study on influencing the choices of others by offering undesirable alternatives. In another experiment conducted by the researcher, 96 subjects were asked to imagine that they had just moved to an apartment with two others and that they were shopping for a new appliance (e.g., television, microwave oven). Each subject was asked to create a menu of three brand choices for their roommates; then subjects were randomly assigned (in equal numbers) to one of three different "goal" conditions—(1) create the menu in order to influence roommates to buy a preselected brand, (2) create the menu in order to influence roommates to buy a brand of your choice, and (3) create the menu with no intent to influence roommates. The researcher theorized that the menus created to influence others would likely include undesirable alternative brands. Consequently, the number of menus in each goal condition that was consistent with the theory was determined. The data are summarized in the table below. Analyze the data for the purpose of determining whether the proportion of subjects who selected menus consistent with the theory depends on goal condition. Use $\alpha = .01$.

Goal Condition	Number Consistent with Theory	Number Not Consistent with Theory	Totals
Influence/preselected brand	15	17	32
Influence/own brand	14	18	32
No influence	3	29	32

Source: Based on Hamilton, R. W. "Why do people suggest what they do not want? Using context effects to influence others' choices," *Journal of Consumer Research*, Vol. 29, No. 4, March 2003 (Table 2).

34 **Coupon user study.** Refer to the study of a customer's motivation to use a technology-based self-service (TBSS) encounter developed for a firm's discount coupons, Exercise 15. Recall that the coupon users received the coupons in one of three ways—mail only (nontechnology user), Internet only (TBSS user), and both mail and Internet. The researcher wants to know if there are differences in customer characteristics—specifically gender (male or female) and coupon usage satisfaction (satisfied, unsatisfied, or indifferent)—among the three types of coupon users. That is, does type of coupon user depend on gender? Does type depend on coupon usage satisfaction level? Data on these categorical variables were collected for a sample of 440 coupon users and are saved in the file. Conduct the appropriate analyses for the researcher. Use $\alpha = .01$ for each analysis. Present your conclusions in a professional report.

35 **Classifying air threats with heuristics.** The *Journal of Behavioral Decision Making* (Jan. 2007) published a study on the use of heuristics to classify the threat level of approaching aircraft. Of special interest was the use of a fast and frugal heuristic—a computationally simple procedure for making judgments with limited information—named "Take-the-Best-for-Classification" (TTBC). Subjects were 48 men and women; some were from a Canadian Forces reserve unit, and others were university students. Each subject was presented with a radar screen on which simulated approaching aircraft were identified with asterisks. By using the computer mouse to click on the asterisk, further information about the aircraft was provided. The goal was to identify the aircraft as "friend" or "foe" as fast as possible. Half the subjects were given cue-based instructions for determining the type of aircraft, while the other half were given pattern-based instructions. The researcher also classified the heuristic strategy used by the subject as TTBC, Guess, or Other. Data on the two variables, instruction type and strategy, measured for each of the 48 subjects are saved in the file. (Data for the first five and last five subjects are shown in the table below.) Do the data provide sufficient evidence (at $\alpha = .05$) to indicate that choice of heuristic strategy depends on type of instruction provided? At $\alpha = .01$?

Instruction	Strategy
Pattern	Other
Pattern	Other
Pattern	Other
Cue	TTBC
Cue	TTBC
⋮	⋮
Pattern	TTBC
Cue	Guess
Cue	TTBC
Cue	Guess
Pattern	Guess

Source: Bryant, D. J. "Classifying simulated air threats with fast and frugal heuristics," *Journal of Behavioral Decision Making*, Vol. 20, January 2007 (Appendix C).

Applying the Concepts—Advanced

36 **Examining the "Monty Hall Dilemma."** There is a classic game show problem in which you decide whether or not to switch your choice of three doors—one of which hides a prize—after the host reveals what is behind a door not chosen. (Despite the natural inclination of many to keep one's first choice, the correct answer is that you should switch your choice of doors.) This problem is sometimes called the "Monty Hall Dilemma," named for Monty Hall, the host of the popular TV game show *Let's Make a Deal*. In *Thinking & Reasoning* (Aug. 2007), Wichita State University professors set up an experiment designed to influence subjects to switch their original choice of doors. Each subject participated in 23 trials. In trial #1, three doors (boxes) were presented on a computer screen, only one of which hid a prize. In each subsequent trial, an additional box was presented, so that in trial #23, 25 boxes were presented. After selecting a box in each trial, all the remaining boxes except for one were either (1) shown to be empty (*Empty* condition), (2) disappeared (*Vanish* condition),

Condition	First Trial (#1)		Last Trial (#23)	
	Switch Boxes	No Switch	Switch Boxes	No Switch
Empty	10	17	23	4
Vanish	3	24	12	15
Steroids	5	22	21	6
Steroids2	8	19	19	8

Source: Based on Howard, J. N., Lambdin, C. G., & Datteri, D. L. "Let's make a deal: Quality and availability of second-stage information as a catalyst for change," *Thinking & Reasoning*, Vol. 13, No. 3, August 2007, pp. 248–272 (Table 2).

(3) disappeared and the chosen box enlarged (*Steroids* condition), or (4) disappeared and the remaining box not chosen enlarged (*Steroids2* condition). A total of 27 subjects were assigned to each condition. The number of subjects who ultimately switched boxes is tallied, by condition, in the table on the previous page for both the first trials and the last trial.

a. For a selected trial, does the likelihood of switching boxes depend on condition?

b. For a given condition, does the likelihood of switching boxes depend on trial number?

c. Based on the results, parts **a** and **b**, what factors influence a subject to switch choices?

37 Efficacy of an HIV vaccine. New, effective AIDS vaccines are now being developed using the process of "sieving" (i.e., sifting out infections with some strains of HIV). Harvard School of Public Health Statistician Peter Gilbert demonstrated how to test the efficacy of an HIV vaccine in *Chance* (Fall 2000). As an example, Gilbert reported the results of VaxGen's preliminary HIV vaccine trial using the 2×2 table below. The vaccine was designed to eliminate a particular strain of the virus, called the "MN strain." The trial consisted of 7 AIDS patients vaccinated with the new drug and 31 AIDS patients who were treated with a placebo (no vaccination). The table (saved in the **HIV1** file) shows the number of patients who tested positive and negative for the MN strain in the trial follow-up period.

	MN Strain		
Patient Group	Positive	Negative	Totals
Unvaccinated	22	9	31
Vaccinated	2	5	7
Totals	24	14	38

Source: Gilbert, P. "Developing an AIDS vaccine by sieving," *Chance*, Vol. 13, No. 4, Fall 2000, pp. 16–21 (adapted Table 1, p. 19). Copyright © 2000 by the American Statistical Association. All rights reserved.

a. Conduct a test to determine whether the vaccine is effective in treating the MN strain of HIV. Use $\alpha = .05$.

b. Are the assumptions for the test, part **a,** satisfied? What are the consequences if the assumptions are violated?

c. In the case of a 2×2 contingency table, R. A. Fisher (1935) developed a procedure for computing the exact *p*-value for the test (called *Fisher's exact test*). The method uses the *hypergeometric probability distribution.* Consider the hypergeometric probability

$$\frac{\binom{7}{2}\binom{31}{22}}{\binom{38}{24}}$$

This represents the probability that 2 out of 7 vaccinated AIDS patients test positive and 22 out of 31 unvaccinated patients test positive (i.e., the probability of the table result given the null hypothesis of independence is true). Compute this probability (called the *probability of the contingency table*).

d. Refer to part **c.** Two contingency tables (with the same marginal totals as the original table) that are more contradictory to the null hypothesis of independence than the observed table follow and are saved in the **HIV2** and **HIV3** files. First, explain why these tables provide more evidence to reject H_0 than the original table; then compute the probability of each table using the hypergeometric formula.

	MN Strain		
Patient Group	Positive	Negative	Totals
Unvaccinated	23	8	31
Vaccinated	1	6	7
Totals	24	14	38

SPSS output for Exercise 37

GROUP * MNSTRAIN Crosstabulation

			MNSTRAIN		
			NEG	POS	Total
GROUP	UNVAC	Count	9	22	31
		Expected Count	11.4	19.6	31.0
	VACC	Count	5	2	7
		Expected Count	2.6	4.4	7.0
Total		Count	14	24	38
		Expected Count	14.0	24.0	38.0

Chi-Square Tests

	Value	df	Asymp. Sig. (2-sided)	Exact Sig. (2-sided)	Exact Sig. (1-sided)
Pearson Chi-Square	4.411[b]	1	.036		
Continuity Correction[a]	2.777	1	.096		
Likelihood Ratio	4.289	1	.038		
Fisher's Exact Test				.077	.050
N of Valid Cases	38				

a. Computed only for a 2x2 table

b. 2 cells (50.0%) have expected count less than 5. The minimum expected count is 2.58.

Patient Group	MN Strain		
	Positive	Negative	Totals
Unvaccinated	24	7	31
Vaccinated	0	7	7
Totals	24	14	38

e. The *p*-value of Fisher's exact test is the probability of observing a result at least as contradictory to the null hypothesis as the observed contingency table, given the same marginal totals. Sum the probabilities of parts **c** and **d** to obtain the *p*-value of Fisher's exact test. (To verify your calculations, check the *p*-value at the bottom of the SPSS printout on the previous page.) Interpret this value in the context of the vaccine trial.

4 A Word of Caution about Chi-Square Tests

Because the χ^2 statistic for testing hypotheses about multinomial probabilities is one of the most widely applied statistical tools, it is also one of the most abused statistical procedures. Consequently, the user should always be certain that the experiment satisfies the assumptions given with each procedure. Furthermore, the user should be certain that the sample is drawn from the correct population—that is, from the population about which the inference is to be made.

The use of the χ^2 probability distribution as an approximation to the sampling distribution for χ^2 should be avoided when the expected counts are very small. The approximation can become very poor when these expected counts are small, and thus the true α level may be quite different from the tabled value. As a rule of thumb, an expected cell count of at least 5 means that the χ^2 probability distribution can be used to determine an approximate critical value.

If the χ^2 value does not exceed the established critical value of χ^2, *do not accept the hypothesis of independence.* You would be risking a Type II error (accepting H_0 if it is false), and the probability β of committing such an error is unknown. The usual alternative hypothesis is that the classifications are dependent. Because the number of ways in which two classifications can be dependent is virtually infinite, it is difficult to calculate one or even several values of β to represent such a broad alternative hypothesis. Therefore, we avoid concluding that two classifications are independent, even when χ^2 is small.

Finally, if a contingency table χ^2 value does exceed the critical value, we must be careful to avoid inferring that a *causal* relationship exists between the classifications. Our alternative hypothesis states that the two classifications are statistically dependent—and a statistical dependence does not imply causality. Therefore, *the existence of a causal relationship cannot be established by a contingency table analysis.*

ETHICS in STATISTICS

Using the results of a chi-square analysis to make a desired influence when you are fully aware that the sample is too small or that the assumptions are violated is considered *unethical statistical practice.*

◻ Chapter Notes

Key Terms

Categories
Cell counts
Cells
Chi-square test
Classes
Contingency table
Contingency table with fixed marginals
Dependence

Dimensions of classification
Expected cell count
Independence of two classifications
Marginal probabilities
Multinomial experiment
Observed cell count
One-way table
Two-way table

n_i	Number of observed outcomes in cell i of a one-way table
E_i	Expected number of outcomes in cell i of a one-way table
p_{ij}	Probability of an outcome in row i and column j of a two-way table
n_{ij}	Number of observed outcomes in row i and column j of a two-way table
$\hat{E}_{ij}$	Estimated expected number of outcomes in row i and column j of a two-way table
R_i	Total number of outcomes in row i of a two-way table
C_j	Total number of outcomes in column j of a two-way table

Key Symbols/Notation

$p_{i,0}$ Value of multinomial probability p_i hypothesized in H_0
χ^2 Chi-square test statistic used in analysis of categorical data

Key Ideas

Multinomial data
Qualitative data that fall into more than two categories (or classes)

Properties of a Multinomial Experiment
1. n identical trials
2. k possible outcomes to each trial
3. probabilities of the k outcomes $(p_1, p_2, \ldots, p_k)$ remain the same from trial to trial, where $p_1 + p_2 + \cdots + p_k = 1$
4. trials are independent
5. variables of interest: *cell counts* (i.e., number of observations falling into each outcome category), denoted $n_1, n_2, \ldots, n_k$

One-way table
Summary table for a *single* qualitative variable

Two-way (contingency) table
Summary table for *two* qualitative variables

Chi-square (χ^2) statistic
used to test category probabilities in one-way and two-way tables

Chi-square tests for independence
should **not** be used to *infer a causal relationship between 2 QLs*

Conditions Required for Valid χ^2-Tests
1. multinomial experiment
2. sample size n is large (expected cell counts are all greater than or equal to 5)

Categorical Data Analysis Guide

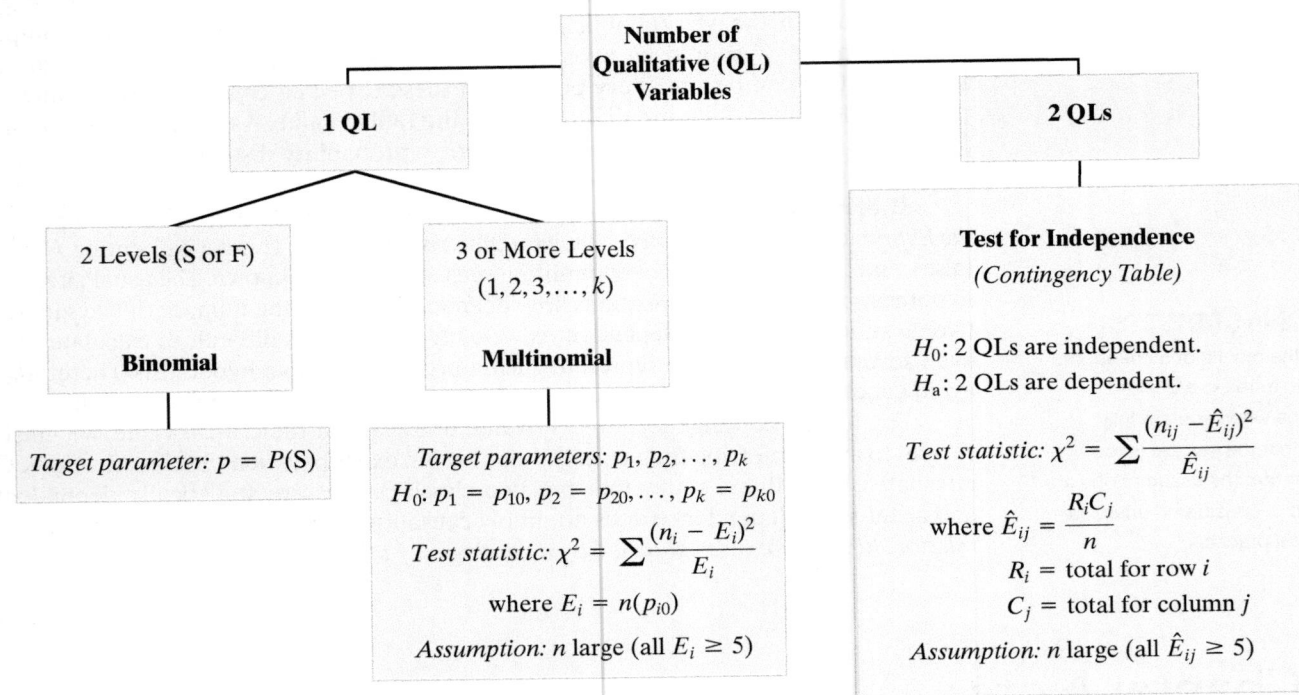

Supplementary Exercises 38–57

Please be aware that some of the following problems may require knowledge of concepts that are not presented in this chapter.

Learning the Mechanics

38 A random sample of 250 observations was classified according to the row and column categories shown in the table below.

L10038

		Column		
		1	2	3
	1	20	20	10
Row	2	10	20	70
	3	20	50	30

a. Do the data provide sufficient evidence to conclude that the rows and columns are dependent? Test using $\alpha = .05$.
b. Would the analysis change if the row totals were fixed before the data were collected?
c. Do the assumptions required for the analysis to be valid differ according to whether the row (or column) totals are fixed? Explain.
d. Convert the table entries to percentages by using each column total as a base and calculating each row response as a percentage of the corresponding column total. In addition, calculate the row totals and convert them to percentages of all 250 observations.

e. Create a bar graph with row 1 percentage on the vertical axis against the column number on the horizontal axis. Draw horizontal lines corresponding to the row 1 percentages. Does the graph support the result of the test conducted in part **a**?

39 A random sample of 150 observations was classified into the categories shown in the table below.

L10039

	Category				
	1	2	3	4	5
n_i	28	35	33	25	29

a. Do the data provide sufficient evidence that the categories are not equally likely? Use $\alpha = .10$.

b. Form a 90% confidence interval for p_2, the probability that an observation will fall in category 2.

Applying the Concepts—Basic

40 **Location of major sports venues.** There has been a trend for professional sports franchises to build new stadiums and ballparks in urban, downtown venues. An article in *Professional Geographer* (Feb. 2000) investigated whether there has been a significant suburban-to-urban shift in the location of major sports facilities. In 1985, 40% of all major sports facilities were located downtown, 30% in a central city, and 30% in suburban areas. In contrast, of the 113 major sports franchises that existed in 1997, 58 were built downtown, 26 in a central city, and 29 in a suburban area.

a. Describe the qualitative variable of interest in the study. Give the levels (categories) associated with the variable.

b. Give the null hypothesis for a test to determine whether the proportions of major sports facilities in downtown, central city, and suburban areas in 1997 were the same as in 1985.

c. If the null hypothesis, part **b**, is true, how many of the 113 sports facilities in 1997 would you expect to be located in downtown, central city, and suburban areas, respectively?

d. Find the value of the chi-square statistic for testing the null hypothesis, part **b**.

e. Find the *p*-value of the test and give the appropriate conclusion in the words of the problem. Assume $\alpha = .05$.

41 **"Made in the USA" survey.** The *Journal of Global Business* (Spring 2002) did a study of what "Made in the USA" on product labels means to the typical consumer. 106 shoppers participated in the survey. Their responses, given as a percentage of U.S. labor and materials in four categories, are summarized in the table. Suppose a consumer advocate group claims that half of all consumers believe that "Made in the USA" means "100%" of labor and materials are produced in

Response to "Made in the USA"	Number of Shoppers
100%	64
75% to 99%	20
50% to 74%	18
Less than 50%	4

Source: "'Made in the USA': Consumer perceptions, deception and policy alternatives," *Journal of Global Business*, Vol. 13, No. 24, Spring 2002 (Table 3).

the United States, one-fourth believe that "75% to 99%" are produced in the United States, one-fifth believe that "50% to 74%" are produced in the United States, and 5% believe that "less than 50%" are produced in the United States.

a. Describe the qualitative variable of interest in the study. Give the levels (categories) associated with the variable.

b. What are the values of p_1, p_2, p_3, and p_4, the probabilities associated with the four response categories hypothesized by the consumer advocate group?

c. Give the null and alternative hypotheses for testing the consumer advocate group's claim.

d. Compute the test statistic for testing the hypotheses, part **c**.

e. Find the rejection region of the test at $\alpha = .10$.

f. State the conclusion in the words of the problem.

g. Find and interpret a 90% confidence interval for the true proportion of consumers who believe "Made in the USA" means "100%" of labor and materials are produced in the United States.

42 **Survey on giving and volunteering.** Refer to the study of charitable givers published in the *National Tax Journal* (Dec. 2001), Exercise 9. In addition to the 1,072 charitable givers who reported that their charitable contributions were motivated by tax considerations, another 1,693 givers reported no tax motivation, giving a total sample of 2,765 charitable givers. Of the 1,072 who were motivated by tax considerations, 691 itemized deductions on their income tax returns. Of the 1,693 who were not motivated by tax considerations, 794 itemized deductions.

a. Consider the two categorical variables, tax motivation (yes or no) and itemize deductions (yes or no). Form a 2×2 contingency table for these variables.

b. Compute the expected cell counts for the contingency table, part **a**.

c. Compute the value of χ^2 for a test of independence.

d. At $\alpha = .05$, what inference can you make about whether the two variables, tax motivation and itemize deductions, are related for charitable givers?

e. Create a bar graph that will visually support your conclusion in part **d**.

43 **Dust plumes from farm equipment.** Fugitive dust plumes generated by farm equipment can be hazardous to human health. In the *Journal of Agricultural, Biological, and Environmental Sciences* (Mar. 2001), environmental engineers developed a model for dust particle concentrations in plumes produced by a tractor operating in a wheat field. The tractor traveled along six parallel, equi-length paths in the field. A remote sensing instrument with a laser beam, placed at the edge of the field, measured the particulate matter in the dust every .5 seconds. Unfortunately, a few of the measurements were censored (i.e., higher than the signal level of the instrument). This usually occurred when the tractor was a short distance from the instrument's laser beam. The table on the next page shows the number of censored measurements for each of the six tractor lines.

a. Calculate and compare the sample proportion of censored measurements for the six tractor lines.

b. Do the data provide sufficient evidence to indicate that the proportion of censored measurements differs for the six tractor lines? Test using $\alpha = .01$.

c. Comment on the practical versus statistical significance of the test.

Data for Exercise 43

Tractor Line	Uncensored Measurements	Censored Measurements	Totals
1	6,047	175	6,222
2	4,456	236	4,692
3	6,821	319	7,140
4	5,889	231	6,120
5	9,873	480	10,353
6	4,607	187	4,794
Totals	37,693	1,628	39,321

Source: Based on Johns, C., Holmen, B., Niemeier, A., & Shumway, R. "Nonlinear regression for modeling censored one-dimensional concentration profiles of fugitive dust plumes," *Journal of Agricultural, Biological, and Environmental Sciences,* Vol. 6, No. 1, March 2001.

44 **JAMA study of heart patients.** The *Journal of the American Medical Association* (Apr. 18, 2001) published the results of a study of alcohol consumption in patients suffering from acute myocardial infarction (AMI). The patients were classified according to average number of alcoholic drinks per week and whether or not they had congestive heart failure. A summary of the results for 1,913 AMI patients is shown in the table.

Congestive Heart Failure	Alcohol Consumption		
	Abstainers	Less than 7 Drinks/Week	7 or More Drinks/Week
Yes	146	106	29
No	750	590	292
Totals	896	696	321

Source: Mukamal, K. J., et al. "Prior alcohol consumption and mortality following acute myocardial infarction," *Journal of the American Medical Association,* Vol. 285, No. 15, April 18, 2001 (Table 1).

a. Find the sample proportion of abstainers with congestive heart failure.

b. Find the sample proportion of moderate drinkers (patients who have less than 7 drinks per week) with congestive heart failure.

c. Find the sample proportion of heavy drinkers (patients who have 7 or more drinks per week) with congestive heart failure.

d. Compare the sample proportions, parts **a–c**. Does it appear that the proportion of AMI patients with congestive heart failure depends on alcohol consumption?

e. Give the null hypothesis for testing whether the proportion of AMI patients with congestive heart failure depends on alcohol consumption.

f. Conduct the test, part **e**, using $\alpha = .05$. What do you conclude?

45 **Colors of M&M's candies.** M&M's plain chocolate candies come in six different colors: dark brown, yellow, red, orange, green, and blue. According to the manufacturer (Mars, Inc.), the color ratio in each large production batch is 30% brown, 20% yellow, 20% red, 10% orange, 10% green, and 10% blue. To test this claim, a professor at Carleton College (Minnesota) had students count the colors of M&M's found in "fun size" bags of the candy. The results for 400 M&M's sampled in a similar study are displayed in the next table.

Brown	Yellow	Red	Orange	Green	Blue	Total
100	75	85	50	40	50	400

a. Assuming the manufacturer's stated percentages are accurate, calculate the expected numbers falling into the six categories.

b. Calculate the value of χ^2 for testing the manufacturer's claim.

c. Conduct a test to determine whether the true percentages of the colors produced differ from the manufacturer's stated percentages. Use $\alpha = .05$.

Applying the Concepts—Intermediate

46 **Top Internet search engines.** Nielsen/NetRatings is a global leader in Internet media and market research. In a recent year, the firm reported on the "search" shares (i.e., percentage of all Internet searches) for the most popular search engines available on the Web. Google accounted for 50% of all searches, Yahoo! for 22%, MSN for 11%, and all other search engines for 17%. Suppose that in a random sample of 1,000 recent Internet searches, 487 used Google, 245 used Yahoo!, 121 used MSN, and 147 used another search engine.

a. Do the sample data disagree with the percentages reported by Nielsen/NetRatings? Test using $\alpha = .05$.

b. Find and interpret a 95% confidence interval for the percentage of all Internet searches that use the Google search engine.

47 **Ethical behavior of accountants.** University of Louisville Professor Julia Karcher conducted an experiment to investigate the ethical behavior of accountants (*Journal of Business Ethics,* Vol. 15, 1996). She focused on auditor abilities to detect ethical problems that may not be obvious. Seventy auditors from Big-Six accounting firms were given a detailed case study that contained several problems, including tax evasion by the client. In 35 of the cases, the tax evasion issue was severe; in the other 35 cases, it was moderate. The auditors were asked to identify any problems they detected in the case. The following table summarizes the results for the ethical issue.

	Severity of Ethical Issue	
	Moderate	Severe
Ethical Issue Identified	27	26
Ethical Issue Not Identified	8	9

Source: Karcher, J. "Auditors' ability to discern the presence of ethical problems," *Journal of Business Ethics,* Vol. 15(10), 1996, p. 1041 (Table V). Copyright © 1996 Springer. Reprinted with kind permission from Springer Science+Business Media B.V.

a. Did the severity of the ethical issue influence whether the issue was identified or not by the auditors? Test using $\alpha = .05$.

b. Suppose the left-hand column of the table contained the counts 35 and 0 instead of 27 and 8. Should the test of part **a** still be conducted? Explain.

c. Keeping the sample size the same, change the numbers in the contingency table so that the answer you would get for the question posed in part **a** changes.

48 Pig farm study. An article in *Sociological Methods & Research* (May 2001) analyzed the data presented in the table. A sample of 262 Kansas pig farmers was classified according to their education level (college or not) and size of their pig farm (number of pigs). Conduct a test to determine whether a pig farmer's education level has an impact on the size of the pig farm. Use $\alpha = .05$ and support your answer with a graph.

Farm Size	Education Level		
	No College	College	Totals
<1,000 pigs	42	53	95
1,000–2,000 pigs	27	42	69
2,000–5,000 pigs	22	20	42
>5,000 pigs	27	29	56
Totals	118	144	262

Source: Based on Agresti, A., & Liu, I. "Strategies for modeling a categorical variable allowing multiple category choices," *Sociological Methods & Research,* Vol. 29, No. 4, May 2001 (Table 1).

49 Management system failures. *Process Safety Progress* (Dec. 2004) and U.S. Chemical Safety and Hazard Investigation Board did a study of industrial accidents caused by management system failures. The table below gives a breakdown of the root causes of a sample of 83 incidents. Are there significant differences in the percentage of incidents in the four cause categories? Test using $\alpha = .05$.

Management System Cause	Number of Incidents
Engineering & Design	27
Procedures & Practices	24
Management & Oversight	22
Training & Communication	10
Total	83

Source: Blair, A. S. "Management system failures identified in incidents investigated by the U.S. Chemical Safety and Hazard Investigation Board," *Process Safety Progress,* Vol. 23, No. 4, Dec. 2004, pp. 232–236 (Table 1). Copyright © 2004 by John Wiley & Sons. Reprinted with permission.

50 History of corporate acquisitions. The *Academy of Management Journal* (Aug. 2008) did an investigation of the performance and timing of corporate acquisitions. Data on the number of firms sampled and number that announced one or more acquisitions during the year from 1980 to 2000 are saved in the accompanying file. Suppose you want to determine if the proportion of firms with acquisitions differed annually from 1990 to 2000, that is, you want to determine if year and acquisition status were dependent from 1990 to 2000.
a. Identify the two qualitative variables (and their respective categories) to be analyzed.
b. Set up the null and alternative hypotheses for the test.
c. Use the Minitab printout at the bottom of the page to conduct the test at $\alpha = .5$.

51 Performance of solder-joint inspectors. Westinghouse Electric Company has experimented with different means of evaluating the performance of solder-joint inspectors. One approach involves comparing an individual inspector's classifications with those of the group of experts that comprise Westinghouse's Work Standards Committee. In one experiment conducted by Westinghouse, 153 solder connections were evaluated by the committee, and 111 were classified as acceptable. An inspector evaluated the same 153 connections and classified 124 as acceptable. Of the items rejected by the inspector, the committee agreed with 19.
a. Construct a contingency table that summarizes the classifications of the committee and the inspector.
b. Based on a visual examination of the table you constructed in part **a**, does it appear that there is a relationship between the inspector's classifications and the committee's? Explain. (A graph of the percentage rejected by committee and inspector will aid your examination.)
c. Conduct a chi-square test of independence for these data. Use $\alpha = .05$. Carefully interpret the results of your test in the context of the problem.

Minitab output for Exercise 50

Tabulated statistics: ACQUISITION, YEAR

```
Using frequencies in NUMBER


Rows: ACQUISITION    Columns: YEAR

        1990   1991   1992   1993   1994   1995   1996   1997   1998   1999   2000    All

No      1847   1891   1936   2050   2149   2238   2319   2300   2047   2049   2030   22856
        1689   1738   1817   1985   2134   2222   2360   2383   2240   2152   2136   22856

Yes      350    370    427    532    626    652    751    799    866    750    748    6871
         508    523    546    597    641    668    710    716    673    647    642    6871

All     2197   2261   2363   2582   2775   2890   3070   3099   2913   2799   2778   29727
        2197   2261   2363   2582   2775   2890   3070   3099   2913   2799   2778   29727

Cell Contents:      Count
                    Expected count


Pearson Chi-Square = 297.048, DF = 10, P-Value = 0.000
Likelihood Ratio Chi-Square = 303.612, DF = 10, P-Value = 0.000
```

---

52 Multiple sclerosis drug. Interferons are proteins produced naturally by the human body that help fight infections and regulate the immune system. A drug developed from interferons, called Avonex, is now available for treating patients with multiple sclerosis (MS). In a clinical study, 85 MS patients received weekly injections of Avonex over a 2-year period. The number of exacerbations (i.e., flare-ups of symptoms) was recorded for each patient and is summarized in the accompanying table. For MS patients who take a placebo (no drug) over a similar two-week period, it is known from previous studies that 26% will experience no exacerbations, 30% one exacerbation, 11% two exacerbations, 14% three exacerbations, and 19% four or more exacerbations.

Number of Exacerbations	Number of Patients
0	32
1	26
2	15
3	6
4 or more	6

Source: Biogen, Inc.

a. Conduct a test to determine whether the exacerbation distribution of MS patients who take Avonex differs from the percentages reported for placebo patients. Test using $\alpha = .05$.

b. Find a 95% confidence interval for the true proportion of Avonex MS patients who are exacerbation free during a 2-year period.

c. Refer to part **b**. Is there evidence that Avonex patients are more likely to have no exacerbations than placebo patients? Explain.

53 Flight response of geese to helicopter traffic. Offshore oil drilling near an Alaskan estuary has led to increased air traffic—mostly large helicopters—in the area. The U.S. Fish and Wildlife Service commissioned a study to investigate the impact these helicopters have on the flocks of Pacific brant geese that inhabit the estuary in fall before migrating (*Statistical Case Studies: A Collaboration between Academe and Industry,* 1998). Two large helicopters were flown repeatedly over the estuary at different altitudes and lateral distances from the flock. The flight responses of the geese (recorded as "low" or "high"), altitude (hundreds of meters), and lateral distance (hundreds of meters) for each of

Overflight	Altitude	Lateral Distance	Flight Response
1	0.91	4.99	High
2	0.91	8.21	High
3	0.91	3.38	High
4	9.14	21.08	Low
5	1.52	6.60	High
6	0.91	3.38	High
7	3.05	0.16	High
8	6.10	3.38	High
9	3.05	6.60	High
10	12.19	6.60	High

Source: Erickson, W., Nick, T., & Ward, D. "Investigating flight response of Pacific brant to helicopters at Izembek Lagoon, Alaska, by using logistic regression," *Statistical Case Studies: A Collaboration between Academe and Industry,* Copyright © 1998 Society for Industrial and Applied Mathematics. Reprinted with permission. All rights reserved.

the 464 helicopter overflights were recorded and are saved in the file. (The data for the first 10 overflights are shown in the preceding table.)

a. The researchers categorized altitude as follows: less than 300 meters, 300–600 meters, and 600 or more meters. Summarize the data in the file by creating a contingency table for altitude category and flight response.

b. Conduct a test to determine if flight response of the geese depends on altitude of the helicopter. Test using $\alpha = .01$.

c. The researchers categorized lateral distance as follows: less than 1,000 meters, 1,000–2,000 meters, 2,000–3,000 meters, and 3,000 or more meters. Summarize the data in the file by creating a contingency table for lateral distance category and flight response.

d. Conduct a test to determine if flight response of the geese depends on lateral distance of the helicopter from the flock. Test using $\alpha = .01$.

e. The current Federal Aviation Authority (FAA) minimum altitude standard for flying over the estuary is 2,000 feet (approximately 610 meters). Based on the results, parts **a–d**, what changes to the FAA regulations do you recommend to minimize the effects to Pacific brant geese?

54 "Fitness for use" of gasoline filters. Product or service quality is often defined as *fitness for use.* This means the product or service meets the customer's needs. Generally speaking, fitness for use is based on five quality characteristics: technological (e.g., strength, hardness), psychological (taste, beauty), time-oriented (reliability), contractual (guarantee provisions), and ethical (courtesy, honesty). The quality of a service may involve all these characteristics, while the quality of a manufactured product generally depends on technological and time-oriented characteristics (Schroeder, *Operations Management,* 2008). After a barrage of customer complaints about poor quality, a manufacturer of gasoline filters for cars had its quality inspectors sample 600 filters—200 per work shift—and check for defects. The data in the table resulted.

Shift	Defectives Produced
First	25
Second	35
Third	80

a. Do the data indicate that the quality of the filters being produced may be related to the shift producing the filter? Test using $\alpha = .05$.

b. Estimate the proportion of defective filters produced by the first shift. Use a 95% confidence interval.

Applying the Concepts—Advanced

55 Goodness-of-fit test. A statistical analysis is to be done on a set of data consisting of 1,000 monthly salaries. The analysis requires the assumption that the sample was drawn from a normal distribution. A preliminary test, called the χ^2 *goodness-of-fit test,* can be used to help determine whether it is reasonable to assume that the sample is from a normal distribution. Suppose the mean and standard deviation of

Table for Exercise 55

Interval	Probability	Expected Frequency	Observed Frequency
Less than $800	.023	23	26
Between $800 and $1,000	.136	136	146
Between $1,000 and $1,200	.341	341	361
Between $1,200 and $1,400	.341	341	311
Between $1,400 and $1,600	.136	136	143
Above $1,600	.023	23	13

the 1,000 salaries are hypothesized to be $1,200 and $200, respectively. Using the standard normal table, we can approximate the probability of a salary being in the intervals listed in the table above. The third column represents the expected number of the 1,000 salaries to be found in each interval if the sample was drawn from a normal distribution with $\mu = \$1,200$ and $\Sigma = \$200$. Suppose the last column contains the actual observed frequencies in the sample. Large differences between the observed and expected frequencies cast doubt on the normality assumption.

a. Compute the χ^2 statistic based on the observed and expected frequencies—just as you did in Section 2.

b. Find the tabulated χ^2 value when $\alpha = .05$ and there are 5 degrees of freedom. (There are $k - 1 = 5$ df associated with this χ^2 statistic.)

c. Based on the χ^2 statistic and the tabulated χ^2 value, is there evidence that the salary distribution is nonnormal?

d. Find an approximate observed significance level for the test in part **c.**

56 **Software defects.** The PROMISE Software Engineering Repository at the University of Ottawa provides researchers SWDEF with data sets for building predictive software models. Data on 498 modules of software code written in "C" language for a NASA spacecraft instrument are saved in the file. Each module was analyzed for defects and classified as "true" if it contained defective code and "false" if not. One algorithm for predicting whether or not a module has defects is "essential complexity" (denoted EVG), where a module with at least 15 subflow graphs with D-structured primes is predicted to have a defect. When the method predicts a defect, the predicted EVG value is "yes"; otherwise, it is "no." Would you recommend the essential complexity algorithm as a predictor of defective software modules? Explain.

Critical Thinking Challenge

57 **A "rigged" election?** *Chance* (Spring 2004) presented data from a recent election held to determine the board of directors of a local community. There were 27 candidates for RIGGED the board, and each of 5,553 voters was allowed to choose 6 candidates. The claim was that "a fixed vote with fixed percentages (was) assigned to each and every candidate making it impossible to participate in an honest election." Votes were tallied in six time periods: after 600 total votes were in, after 1,200, after 2,444, after 3,444, after 4,444, and after 5,553 votes. The data for three of the candidates (Smith, Coppin, and Montes) are shown in the following table. A residential organization believes that "there was nothing random about the count and tallies each time period and specific unnatural or rigged percentages were being assigned to each and every candidate." Give your opinion. Is the probability of a candidate receiving votes independent of the time period? If so, does this imply a rigged election?

	Time Period					
	1	2	3	4	5	6
Votes for Smith	208	208	451	392	351	410
Votes for Coppin	55	51	109	98	88	104
Votes for Montes	133	117	255	211	186	227
Total Votes	600	600	1,244	1,000	1,000	1,109

Source: Based on Gelman, A. "55,000 residents desperately need your help!" *Chance*, Vol. 17, No. 2, Spring 2004, p. 32 (Figures 1 and 5, p. 34).

Activity 1   Binomial vs. Multinomial Experiments

In this activity, you will study the difference between binomial and multinomial experiments.

1. A television station has hired an independent research group to determine whether television viewers in the area prefer its local news program to the news programs of two other stations in the same city. Explain why a multinomial experiment would be appropriate and design a poll that satisfies the five properties of a multinomial experiment. State the null and alternative hypotheses for the corresponding χ^2-test.

2. Suppose the television station believes that a majority of local viewers prefer its news program to those of its two competitors. Explain why a binomial experiment would be appropriate to support this claim and design a poll that satisfies the five properties of a binomial experiment. State the null and alternative hypotheses for the corresponding test.

3. Generalize the situations in Exercises 1 and 2 to describe conditions under which a multinomial experiment can be rephrased as a binomial experiment. Is there any advantage in doing so? Explain.

References

Agresti, A. *Categorical Data Analysis*. New York: Wiley, 1990.

Cochran, W. G. "The χ^2 test of goodness of fit," *Annals of Mathematical Statistics*, 1952, 23.

Conover, W. J. *Practical Nonparametric Statistics*, 2nd ed. New York: Wiley, 1980.

DeGroot, M. H., Fienberg, S. E., & Kadane, J. B., eds. *Statistics and the Law*. New York: Wiley, 1986.

Fisher, R. A. "The logic of inductive inference (with discussion)," *Journal of the Royal Statistical Society*, Vol. 98, 1935, pp. 39–82.

Hollander, M., & Wolfe, D. A. *Nonparametric Statistical Methods*. New York: Wiley, 1973.

Savage, I. R. "Bibliography of nonparametric statistics and related topics," *Journal of the American Statistical Association*, 1953, 48.

USING TECHNOLOGY | Technology images shown here are taken from SPSS Statistics Professional 20.0, Minitab 16, XLSTAT for Pearson, and Excel 20

SPSS: Chi-Square Analyses

SPSS can conduct chi-square tests for both one-way and two-way (contingency) tables.

One-Way Table

Step 1 Access the SPSS spreadsheet file that contains the variable with category values for each of the *n* observations in the data set. (*Note:* SPSS requires that these categories be specified numerically, e.g., 1, 2, 3.)

Step 2 Click on the "Analyze" button on the SPSS menu bar and then click on "Nonparametric Tests," "Legacy Dialogs," and "Chi-square," as shown in Figure S.1. The resulting dialog box appears as shown in Figure S.2.

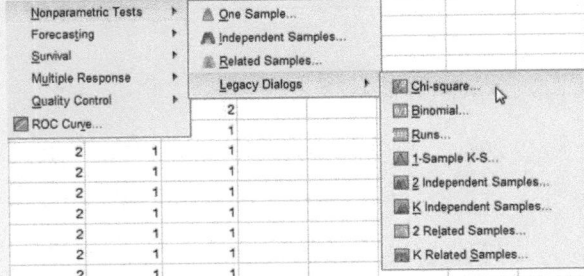

Figure S.1 SPSS menu options for a one-way chi-square analysis

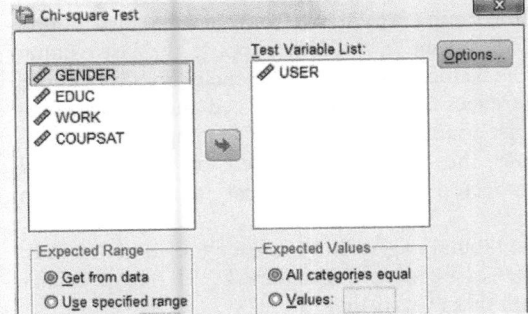

Figure S.2 SPSS one-way chi-square dialog box

Step 3 Specify the qualitative variable of interest in the "Test Variable List" box.

Step 4 If you want to test for equal cell probabilities in the null hypothesis, then select the "All categories equal" option under the "Expected Values" box (as shown in Figure S.2). If the null hypothesis specifies unequal cell probabilities, then select the "Values" option under the "Expected Values" box. Enter the hypothesized cell probabilities in the adjacent box, one at a time, clicking "Add" after each specification.

Step 5 Click "OK" to generate the SPSS printout.

Two-Way Table

Step 1 Access the SPSS spreadsheet file that contains the sample data. The data file should contain two qualitative variables, with category values for each of the *n* observations in the data set.

Step 2 Click on the "Analyze" button on the SPSS menu bar and then click on "Descriptive Statistics" and "Crosstabs," as shown in Figure S.3. The resulting dialog box appears as shown in Figure S.4.

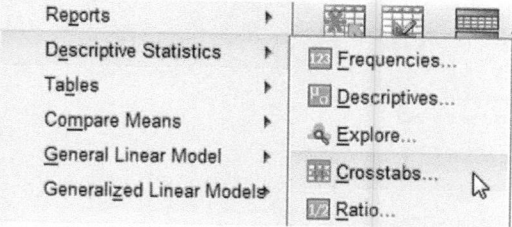

Figure S.3 SPSS menu options for two-way chi-square analysis

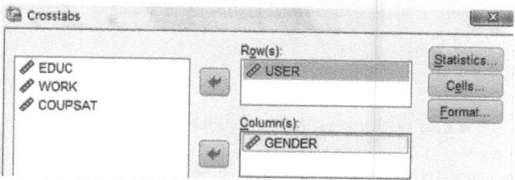

Figure S.4 SPSS crosstabs dialog box

Step 3 Specify one qualitative variable in the "Row(s)" box and the other qualitative variable in the "Column(s)" box.

Step 4 Click the "Statistics" button and select the "Chi-square" option, as shown in Figure S.5.

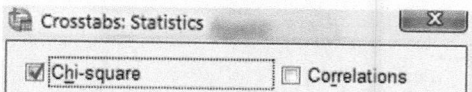

Figure S.5 SPSS statistics menu selections for the two-way analysis

Step 5 Click "Continue" to return to the "Crosstabs" dialog box. If you want the contingency table to include expected values, row percentages, and/or column percentages, click the "Cells" button and make the appropriate menu selections.

Step 6 When you return to the "Crosstabs" menu screen, click "OK" to generate the SPSS printout.

Note: If your SPSS spreadsheet contains summary information (i.e., the cell counts for the contingency table) rather than the actual categorical data values for each observation, you must weight each observation in your data file by the cell count for that observation prior to running the chi-square analysis. Do this by selecting the "Data" button on the SPSS menu bar and then click on "Weight Cases" and specify the variable that contains the cell counts.

Minitab: Chi-Square Analyses

Minitab can conduct chi-square tests for both one-way and two-way (contingency) tables.

One-Way Table

Step 1 Access the Minitab worksheet file that contains the sample data for the qualitative variable of interest.

[*Note:* The data file can have actual values (levels) of the variable for each observation, or, alternatively, two columns—one column listing the levels of the qualitative variable and the other column with the observed counts for each level.]

Step 2 Click on the "Stat" button on the Minitab menu bar and then click on "Tables" and "Chi-Square Goodness-of-Fit Test (One Variable)," as shown in Figure M.1. The resulting dialog box appears as shown in Figure M.2.

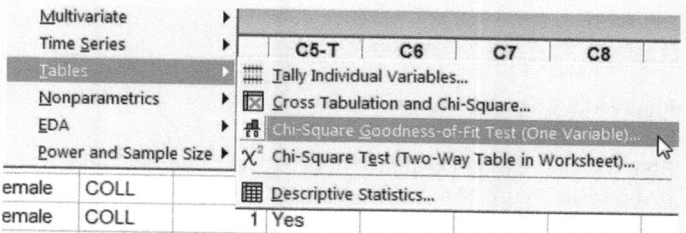

Figure M.1 Minitab menu options for a one-way chi-square analysis

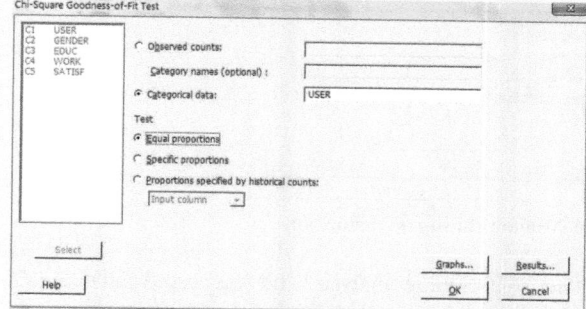

Figure M.2 Minitab one-way chi-square dialog box

Step 3 If your data have one column of values for your qualitative variable, select "Categorical data" and specify the variable name (or column) in the box. If your data have summary information in two columns (see above), select "Observed counts" and specify the column with the counts and the column with the variable names in the respective boxes.

Step 4 Select "Equal proportions" for a test of equal proportions or select "Specific proportions" and enter the hypothesized proportion next to each level in the resulting box.

Step 5 Click "OK" to generate the Minitab printout.

Two-Way Table

Step 1 Access the Minitab worksheet file that contains the sample data. The data file should contain two qualitative variables, with category values for each of the *n* observations in the data set. Alternatively, the worksheet can contain the cell counts for each of the categories of the two qualitative variables.

Step 2 Click on the "Stat" button on the Minitab menu bar and then click on "Tables" and "Cross Tabulation and Chi-Square," (see Figure M.1). The resulting dialog box appears as shown in Figure M.3.

Step 3 Specify one qualitative variable in the "For rows" box and the other qualitative variable in the "For columns" box. [*Note:* If your worksheet contains cell counts for the categories, enter the variable with the cell counts in the "Frequencies are in" box.]

Step 4 Select the summary statistics (e.g., counts, percentages) you want to display in the contingency table.

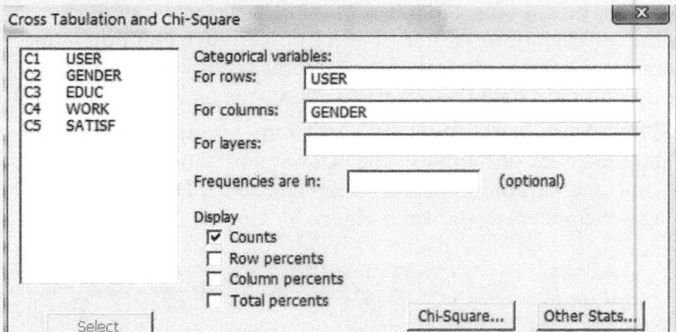

Figure M.3 Minitab cross tabulation dialog box

Step 5 Click the "Chi-Square" button. The resulting dialog box is shown in Figure M.4.

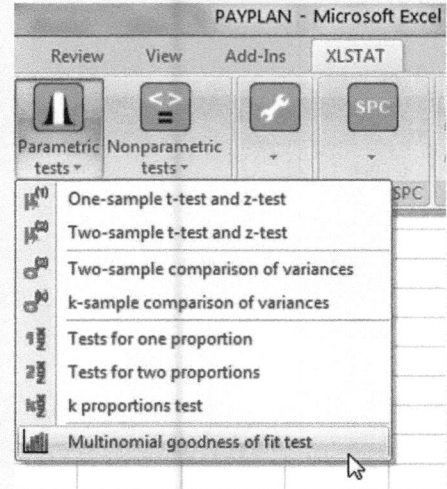

Figure M.4 Minitab chi-square dialog box

Step 6 Select "Chi-Square analysis" and "Expected cell counts" and click "OK."

Step 7 When you return to the "Cross Tabulation" menu screen, click "OK" to generate the Minitab printout.

Note: If your Minitab worksheet contains only the cell counts for the contingency table in columns, click the "Chi-Square Test (Two-Way Table in Worksheet)" menu option (see Figure M.1) and specify the columns in the "Columns containing the table" box. Click "OK" to produce the Minitab printout.

Excel/XLSTAT: Chi-Square Analyses

XLSTAT can conduct a chi-square analysis for both one-way and two-way (contingency) tables. The Excel workbook file should include a column for the quantitative dependent (response) variable, and columns for the qualitative factors.

One-Way Table

Step 1 First, create a workbook with columns representing the levels (categories) of the qualitative variable, the cell (category) counts, and the hypothesized proportions for the levels, as shown in Figure E.1.

	A	B	C
1	**Category**	**Number**	**Proportion**
2	NONE	42	0.1
3	STANDARD	365	0.65
4	MERIT	193	0.25

Figure E.1 Excel workbook format for one-way chi-square analysis

Step 2 Click the "XLSTAT" button on the Excel main menu bar, select "Parametric tests," then click "Multinomial goodness of fit test," as shown in Figure E.2.

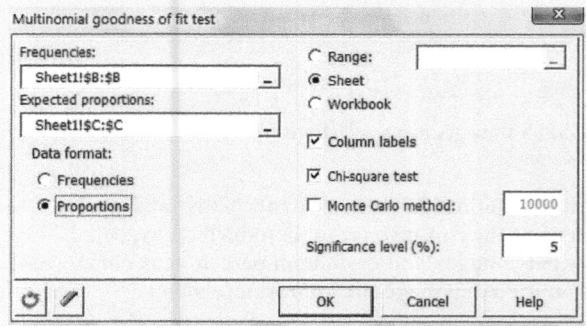

Figure E.2 XLSTAT menu options for one-way chi-square test

Step 3 When the resulting dialog box appears (Figure E.3), enter the column containing the cell counts in the "Frequencies" box. Check the "Proportions" option in the "Data format" area, then enter the column containing the hypothesized proportions in the "Expected proportions" box. Also, select the "Chi-square test" option.

Figure E.3 XLSTAT dialog box for one-way chi-square test

Step 4 Click "OK," then "Continue" to display the test results.

Two-Way Table

Step 1 Create a workbook with one column representing the levels (categories) of the first qualitative variable, a second column representing the levels (categories) of the second qualitative variable, and a third column containing the cell counts, as shown in Figure E.4.

	A	B	C
1	**Model**	**Claim**	**Number**
2	Conventional	Injury	5364
3	Hybrid	Injury	1505
4	Conventional	No Injury	44768
5	Hybrid	No Injury	3859

Figure E.4 Excel workbook format for two-way chi-square analysis

Step 2 Click the "XLSTAT" button on the Excel main menu bar, select "Correlation/Association tests," then click "Tests on contingency tables (Chi-square)," as shown in Figure E.5.

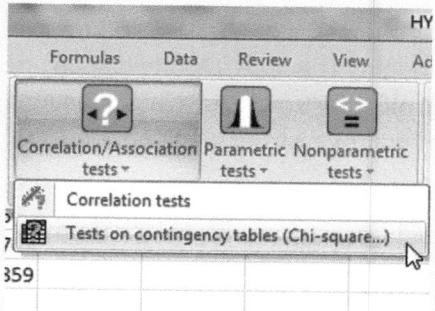

Figure E.5 XLSTAT menu options for two-way chi-square test

Step 3 When the resulting dialog box appears (Figure E.6), enter the column for one qualitative variable in the "Row variables" box and the column for the other qualitative variable in the "Column variables" box. Check the "Weights" option, then enter the column containing the cell counts in the appropriate box.

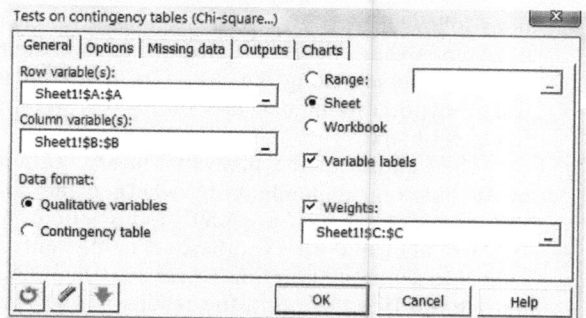

Figure E.6 XLSTAT dialog box for two-way chi-square test

Step 4 Click the "Options" tab, then check "Chi-square test" in the resulting dialog box, as shown in Figure E.7. Click "OK."

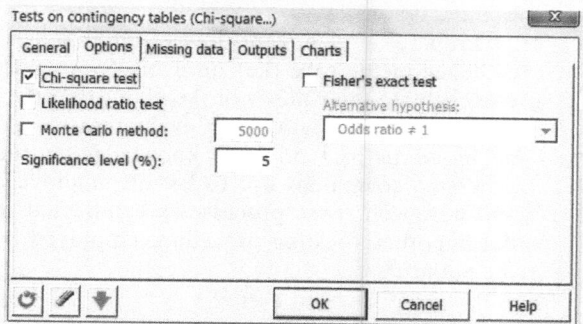

Figure E.7 XLSTAT options for two-way chi-square test

Step 5 (Optional) Click the "Outputs" tab, then select the statistics you want to display in the contingency table (e.g., observed frequencies, expected frequencies). Click "OK."

Step 6 Click "OK," then "Continue" to display the test results.

TI-84 Graphing Calculator: Chi-Square Analyses

One-Way Table

Step 1 *Enter the data for the observed and expected values*

- Press **STAT**, then select **1:Edit**
- Enter the observed category values in **L1** and the expected category values in **L2**

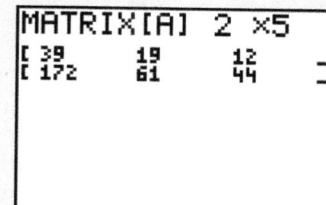

Step 2 *Access the statistical tests menu and perform the chi-square test*

- Press **STAT**
- Arrow right to **TESTS**
- Arrow down to χ^2: **GOF-Test**
- Press **ENTER**
- Arrow down to **Calculate**
- Press **ENTER**

Two-Way (Contingency) Table

Step 1 *Access the Matrix menu to enter the observed values*

- Press **2nd x^{-1}** for **MATRX**
- Arrow right to **EDIT**
- Press **ENTER**
- Use the **ARROW** key to enter the row and column dimensions of your observed Matrix
- Use the **ARROW** key to enter your observed values into Matrix [A]

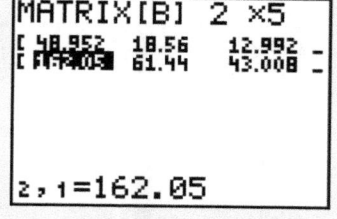

Step 2 *Access the Matrix menu to enter the expected values*

- Press **2nd x^{-1}** for **MATRX**
- Arrow right to **EDIT**
- Arrow down to **2:[B]**
- Press **ENTER**
- Use the **ARROW** key to enter the row and column dimensions of your expected matrix (The dimensions will be the same as in Matrix A)
- Use the **ARROW** key to enter your expected values into Matrix [B]

Step 3 *Access the Statistical Tests menu and perform the chi-square test*

- Press **STAT**
- Arrow right to **TESTS**
- Arrow down to χ^2 **Test**
- Press **ENTER**
- Arrow down to **Calculate**
- Press **ENTER**

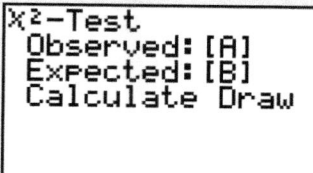

Discrimination in the Workplace

Title VII of the Civil Rights Act of 1964 prohibits discrimination in the workplace on the basis of race, color, religion, gender, or national origin. The Age Discrimination in Employment Act of 1967 (ADEA) protects workers age 40 to 70 against discrimination based on age. The potential for discrimination exists in such processes as hiring, promotion, compensation, and termination.

In 1971 the U.S. Supreme Court established that employment discrimination cases fall into two categories: **disparate treatment** and **disparate impact.** In the former, the issue is whether the employer intentionally discriminated against a worker. For example, if the employer considered an individual's race in deciding whether to terminate him, the case is one of disparate treatment. In a disparate impact case, the issue is whether employment practices have an adverse impact on a protected group or class of people, even when the employer does not intend to discriminate.

Part I: Downsizing at a Computer Firm

Disparate impact cases almost always involve the use of statistical evidence and expert testimony by professional statisticians. Attorneys for the plaintiffs frequently use hypothesis test results in the form of *p*-values in arguing the case for their clients.

Table C.1 was recently introduced as evidence in a race case that resulted from a round of layoffs during the downsizing of a division of a computer manufacturer. The company had selected 51 of the division's 1,215 employees to lay off. The plaintiffs—in this case 15 of the 20 African Americans who were laid off—were suing the company for $20 million in damages.

Table C1		Summary of Downsizing Data for Race Case	
		Decision	
		Retained	Laid off
Race	White	1,051	31
	Black	113	20

Source: P. George Benson.　　　🖸 *Data Set:* LAYOFF

The company's lawyers argued that the selections followed from a performance-based ranking of all employees. The plaintiffs' legal team and their expert witnesses, citing the results of a statistical test of hypothesis, argued that the layoffs were a function of race.

The validity of the plaintiffs' interpretation of the data is dependent on whether the assumptions of the test are met in this situation. In particular, like all hypothesis tests presented in this text, the assumption of random sampling must hold. If it does not, the results of the test may be due to the violation of this assumption rather than to discrimination. In general, the appropriateness of the testing procedure is dependent on the test's ability to capture the relevant aspects of the employment process in question (DeGroot, Fienberg, and Kadane, *Statistics and the Law,* 1986).

Prepare a document to be submitted as evidence in the case (i.e., an exhibit) in which you evaluate the validity of the plaintiffs' interpretation of the data. Your evaluation should be based in part on your knowledge of the processes companies use to lay off employees and how well those processes are reflected in the hypothesis-testing procedure employed by the plaintiffs.

Part II: Age Discrimination—You Be the Judge

As part of a significant restructuring of product lines, AJAX Pharmaceuticals (a fictitious name for a real company) laid off 24 of 55 assembly line workers in its Pittsburgh manufacturing plant. Citing the ADEA, 11 of the laid-off workers claimed they were discriminated against on

Table C2	**Data for Age Discrimination Case**		
Employee	Yearly Wages	Age	Employment Status
*Adler, C. J.	$41,200	45	Terminated
Alario, B. N.	39,565	43	Active
Anders, J. M.	30,980	41	Active
Bajwa, K. K.	23,225	27	Active
Barny, M. L.	21,250	26	Active
*Berger, R. W.	41,875	45	Terminated
Brenn, L. O.	31,225	41	Active
Cain, E. J.	30,135	36	Terminated
Carle, W. J.	29,850	32	Active
Castle, A. L.	21,850	22	Active
Chan, S. D.	43,005	48	Terminated
Cho, J. Y.	34,785	41	Active
Cohen, S. D.	25,350	27	Active
Darel, F. E.	36,300	42	Active
*Davis, D. E.	40,425	46	Terminated
*Dawson, P. K.	39,150	42	Terminated
Denker, U. H.	19,435	19	Active
Dorando, T. R.	24,125	28	Active
Dubois, A. G.	30,450	40	Active
England, N.	24,750	25	Active
Estis, K. B.	22,755	23	Active
Fenton, C. K.	23,000	24	Active
Finer, H. R.	42,000	46	Terminated
*Frees, O. C.	44,100	52	Terminated
Gary, J. G.	44,975	55	Terminated
Gillen, D. J.	25,900	27	Active
Harvey, D. A.	40,875	46	Terminated
Higgins, N. M.	38,595	41	Active
*Huang, T. J.	42,995	48	Terminated
Jatho, J. A.	31,755	40	Active
Johnson, C. H.	29,540	32	Active
Jurasik, T. B.	34,300	41	Active
Klein, K. L.	43,700	51	Terminated
Lang, T. F.	19,435	22	Active
Liao, P. C.	28,750	32	Active
*Lostan, W. J.	44,675	52	Terminated
Mak, G. L.	35,505	38	Terminated
Maloff, V. R.	33,425	38	Terminated
McCall, R. M.	31,300	36	Terminated
*Nadeau, S. R.	42,300	46	Terminated
*Nguyen, O. L.	43,625	50	Terminated
Oas, R. C.	37,650	42	Active
*Patel, M. J.	38,400	43	Terminated
Porter, K. D.	32,195	35	Terminated
Rosa, L. M.	19,435	21	Active
Roth, J. H.	32,785	39	Terminated
Sayino, G. L.	37,900	42	Active
Scott, I. W.	29,150	30	Terminated
Smith, E. E.	35,125	41	Active
Teel, Q. V.	27,655	33	Active
*Walker, F. O.	42,545	47	Terminated
Wang, T. G.	22,200	32	Active
Yen, D. O.	40,350	44	Terminated
Young, N. L.	28,305	34	Active
Zeitels, P. W.	36,500	42	Active

Denotes plaintiffs

the basis of age and sued AJAX for $5,000,000. Management disputed the claim, saying that because the workers were essentially interchangeable, they had used random sampling to choose the 24 workers to be terminated.

Table C.2 lists the 55 assembly line workers and identifies which were terminated and which remained active. Plaintiffs are denoted by an asterisk. These data were used by both the plaintiffs and the defendants to determine whether the layoffs had an adverse impact on workers age 40 and over and to establish the credibility of management's random sampling claim.

Using whatever statistical methods you think are appropriate, build a case that supports the plaintiffs' position. (Call documents related to this issue Exhibit A.) Similarly, build a case that supports the defendants' position. (Call these documents Exhibit B.) Then discuss which of the two cases is more convincing and why. [*Note:* The data for this case are available in the file, described in the table.]

Variable	Type
LASTNAME	QL
WAGES	QN
AGE	QN
STATUS	QL

(Number of observations: 55)　　　*Data Set:* DISCRM

Answers to Selected Exercises

1 a. $\chi^2 > 5.99147$ **b.** $\chi^2 > 7.77944$ **c.** $\chi^2 > 11.3449$ **3** $E(n_i) \geq 5$ **5 a.** $\chi^2 = 3.29$ **c.** $(.226, .350)$ **7 a.** No; $\chi^2 = 1.67$, *p*-value $= .797$ **b.** $(.134, .400)$ **9 a.** 107.2 **b.** $H_0: p_1 = p_2 = \ldots = p_{10} = .10$ **c.** 93.15 **d.** $\chi^2 > 14.6837$ **e.** Reject H_0 **11** Yes, $\chi^2 = 963.4$ **13 b.** $H_0: p_1 = .5, p_2 = .1, p_3 = .1, p_4 = .1, p_5 = .1, p_6 = .05, p_7 = .05$ **c.** $\chi^2 = 452.48$, reject H_0 **15** $\chi^2 = 164.9$, reject H_0 **17** $\chi^2 = 12.37$, do not reject H_0 **19 a.** $\chi^2 > 26.2962$ **b.** $\chi^2 > 15.9871$ **c.** $\chi^2 > 9.21034$ **21 a.** column 1: 36%, 64%; column 2: 53%, 47%; column 3: 68%, 32%; row 1: 9.4%, 35.4%, 55.2%; row 2: 22.5%, 42.3%, 35.2% **c.** yes **23 a.** B_1: 30%, 47%, 23%; B_2: 44%, 33%, 23%; B_3: 30%, 49%, 21% **b.** A_1: 35%; A_2: 42%; A_3: 23% **c.** Yes **25 a.** Yes **b.** Always/Male: 240; Always/Female: 476; Often/Male: 405; Often/Female: 527; Occasional/Male: 525; Occasional/Female: 493; Never/Male: 330; Never/Female: 204 **c.** H_0: Gender and Purchasing are independent **d.** ≈ 0 **e.** Reject H_0 **27 a.** .282; .511 **b.** .563; .368 **c.** .155; .121 **d.** Yes **e.** $\chi^2 = 14.21$, reject H_0 **f.** $(-.15, -.133)$ **29** Yes, $\chi^2 = 21.24$, *p*-value $= .012$ **31** No; $\chi^2 = 4.21$ **33** $\chi^2 = 12.47$, reject H_0 **35** Yes, $\chi^2 = 7.38$, *p*-value $= .025$; no **37 a.** $\chi^2 = 4.41$, reject H_0 **b.** No **c.** .04378 **d.** .00571, .00027 **e.** .04976 **39 a.** No, $\chi^2 = 2.133$ **b.** $.233 \pm .057$ **41 a.** Levels: 100%, 75–99%, 50–74%, less than 50% **b.** .50, .25, .20, .05 **c.** $H_0: p_1 = .5, p_2 = .25, p_3 = .20, p_4 = .05$ **d.** 4.68 **e.** $\chi^2 > 6.25139$ **f.** Do not reject H_0 **g.** $(.526, .682)$ **43 a.** .028, .050, .045, .038, .046, .039 **b.** Yes, $\chi^2 = 48.09$ **45 a.** 120, 80, 80, 40, 40, 40 **b.** 8.96 **c.** Do not reject H_0 **47 a.** No, $\chi^2 = .078$ **b.** No **49** Yes, $\chi^2 = 8.04$ **51 a.** Inspector Accept/Committee Accept: 101; Accept/Reject: 23; Reject/Accept: 10; Reject/Reject: 19 **b.** Yes **c.** $\chi^2 = 26.034$, reject H_0 **53 a.** Low/<300: 85; Low/300–600: 77; Low/>600: 17; High/<300: 105; High/300–600: 121; High/>600: 59 **b.** $\chi^2 = 11.48$, reject H_0 **c.** Low/<1,000: 37; Low/1,000–2,000: 68; Low/2,000–3,000: 44; Low/>3,000: 30; High/<1,000: 243; High/1,000–2,000: 37; High/2,000–3,000: 4; High/>3,000: 1 **d.** $\chi^2 = 207.81$, reject H_0 **e.** Maximum height: 300 m; minimum distance: 3,000 m **55 a.** 9.65 **b.** 11.0705 **c.** No **d.** $.05 < p\text{-value} < .10$ **57** Yes, $\chi^2 = 2.28$, do not reject H_0; yes, implies rigged election

Credits

The photo credits below are listed in order of appearance.

◻ Technology Images

Where We're Going

◻ Introduce the straight-line (*simple linear regression*) model as a means of relating one quantitative variable to another quantitative variable (1)

◻ Assess how well the simple linear regression model fits the sample data (2–4)

◻ Introduce the *correlation coefficient* as a means of relating one quantitative variable to another quantitative variable (5)

◻ Employ the simple linear regression model for predicting the value of one variable from a specified value of another variable (6–7)

◻ Simple Linear Regression

STATISTICS in ACTION   **Legal Advertising—Does It Pay?**

According to the American Bar Association, there are over 1 million lawyers competing for your business. To gain a competitive edge, these lawyers aggressively advertise their services. The advertising of legal services has long been a controversial subject, with many believing that it constitutes an unethical (and in some cases even illegal) practice. Nonetheless, legal advertisements appear in nearly all media, ranging from the covers of telephone directories to infomercials on television, as well as a significant presence on the Internet. In fact, Erickson Marketing, Inc., reports that "attorneys are the #1 category of advertising in the Yellow Pages."

For this *Statistics in Action,* we present an actual recent case involving two former law partners. One partner (A) sued the other (B) over who should pay what share of the expenses of their former partnership. Partner A handled personal injury (PI) cases, while partner B handled only worker's compensation (WC) cases. The firm's advertising was focused on personal injury only, but partner A claimed that the ads resulted in the firm getting more WC cases for partner B, and therefore partner B should share the advertising expenses.

Table SIA1 shows the firm's new PI and WC cases each month over a 48-month period for this partnership. Also shown is the total expenditure on advertising each month and over the previous 6 months. Do these data provide support for the hypothesis that increased advertising expenditures are associated with more PI cases? With more WC cases? If advertising expenditures have a statistically significant association with the number of cases, does this necessarily mean that there is a causal relationship, that is, that spending more on advertising causes an increase in the number of cases? Based on these data, should partner A or partner B bear the brunt of the advertising expenditures?

Table SIA1	Legal Advertising Data			
Month	Advertising Expenditure ($)	New PI Cases	New WC Cases	6 Months Cumulative Adv. Exp. ($)
1	9,221.55	7	26	n/a
2	6,684.00	9	33	n/a
3	200.00	12	18	n/a
4	14,546.75	27	15	n/a
5	5,170.14	9	19	n/a
6	5,810.30	13	26	n/a
7	5,816.20	11	24	41,632.74
8	8,236.38	7	22	38,227.39
9	−2,089.55	13	12	39,779.77
10	29,282.24	7	15	37,490.22
11	9,193.58	9	21	52,225.71
12	9,499.18	8	24	56,249.15
13	11,128.76	18	25	59,938.03
14	9,057.64	9	19	65,250.59
15	13,604.54	25	12	66,071.85
16	14,411.76	26	33	81,765.94
17	13,724.28	27	32	66,895.46
18	13,419.42	12	21	71,426.16
19	17,372.33	14	18	75,346.40
20	6,296.35	5	25	81,589.97
21	13,191.59	22	12	78,828.68
22	26,798.80	15	7	78,415.73
23	18,610.95	12	22	90,802.77
24	829.53	18	27	95,689.44
25	16,976.53	20	25	83,099.55
26	14,076.98	38	26	82,703.75
27	24,791.75	13	28	90,484.38
28	9,691.25	18	31	102,084.54
29	28,948.25	21	40	84,976.99
30	21,373.52	7	39	95,314.29
31	9,675.25	16	41	115,858.28
32	33,213.55	12	48	108,557.00
33	19,859.85	15	28	127,693.57
34	10,475.25	18	29	122,761.67
35	24,790.84	30	20	123,545.67
36	36,660.94	12	27	119,388.26
37	8,812.50	30	26	134,675.68
38	41,817.75	20	45	133,812.93
39	27,399.33	19	30	142,417.13
40	25,723.10	29	33	149,956.61
41	16,312.10	58	24	165,204.46
42	26,332.78	42	40	156,725.72
43	60,207.58	24	36	146,397.56
44	42,485.39	47	29	197,792.64
45	35,601.92	24	17	198,460.28
46	72,071.50	14	13	206,662.87
47	12,797.11	31	15	253,011.27
48	12,310.50	26	16	249,496.28

Source: Info Tech, Inc.

Data Set: LEGADV

The data for the case are saved in the **LEGADV** file. In the *Statistics in Action Revisited* sections of this chapter, we examine the relationship between monthly advertising expenditure and the number of new legal cases in an attempt to answer these questions.

STATISTICS in ACTION REVISITED

- Estimating a Straight-Line Regression Model
- Assessing How Well a Straight-Line Regression Model Fits Data
- Using the Coefficient of Correlation and the Coefficient of Determination
- Prediction Using the Straight-Line Model

There are methods for making inferences about population means. The mean of a population can be treated as a *constant*, using sample data to estimate or to test hypotheses about this constant mean. In many applications, the mean of a population is not viewed as a constant but rather as a variable. For example, the mean sale price of residences sold this year in a large city might be treated as a variable that depends on the square feet of living space in the residence. For example, the relationship might be

$$\text{Mean sale price} = \$30{,}000 + \$60 \text{ (square feet)}$$

This formula implies that the mean sale price of 1,000-square-foot homes is $90,000, the mean sale price of 2,000-square-foot homes is $150,000, and the mean sale price of 3,000-square-foot homes is $210,000.

In this chapter, we discuss situations in which the mean of the population is treated as a variable, dependent on the value of another variable. The dependence of residential sale price on the square feet of living space is one illustration. Other examples include the dependence of mean sales revenue of a firm on advertising expenditure, the dependence of mean starting salary of a college graduate on the student's GPA, and the dependence of mean monthly production of automobiles on the total number of sales in the previous month.

We begin our discussion with the simplest of all models relating a population mean to another variable—*the straight-line model*. We show how to use the sample data to estimate the straight-line relationship between the mean value of one variable, *y*, as it relates to a second variable, *x*. The methodology of estimating and using a straight-line relationship is referred to as *simple linear regression analysis*.

1   Probabilistic Models

An important consideration in merchandising a product is the amount of money spent on advertising. Suppose you want to model the monthly sales revenue of an appliance store as a function of the monthly advertising expenditure. The first question to be answered is this: "Do you think an exact relationship exists between these two variables?" That is, do you think it is possible to state the exact monthly sales revenue if the amount spent on advertising is known? We think you will agree with us that this is *not* possible for several reasons. Sales depend on many variables other than advertising expenditure—for example, time of year, the state of the general economy, inventory, and price structure. Even if many variables are included in a model, it is still unlikely that we would be able to predict the monthly sales *exactly*. There will almost certainly be some variation in monthly sales due strictly to *random phenomena* that cannot be modeled or explained.

If we were to construct a model that hypothesized an exact relationship between variables, it would be called a **deterministic model.** For example, if we believe that *y*, the monthly sales revenue, will be exactly 15 times *x*, the monthly advertising expenditure, we write

$$y = 15x$$

This represents a *deterministic relationship* between the variables *y* and *x*. It implies that *y* can always be determined exactly when the value of *x* is known. *There is no allowance for error in this prediction.*

If, on the other hand, we believe there will be unexplained variation in monthly sales—perhaps caused by important but unincluded variables or by random phenomena— we discard the deterministic model and use a model that accounts for this **random error.** This **probabilistic model** includes both a deterministic component and a random error component. For example, if we hypothesize that the sales *y* are related to advertising expenditure *x* by

$$y = 15x + \text{Random error}$$

General Form of Probabilistic Models

$$y = \text{Deterministic component} + \text{Random error}$$

where y is the variable of interest. We always assume that the mean value of the random error equals 0. This is equivalent to assuming that the mean value of y, $E(y)$, equals the deterministic component of the model; that is,

$$E(y) = \text{Deterministic component}$$

we are hypothesizing a *probabilistic relationship* between y and x. Note that the deterministic component of this probabilistic model is $15x$.

Figure 1a shows the possible values of y and x for five different months, when the model is deterministic. All the pairs of (x, y) data points must fall exactly on the line because a deterministic model leaves no room for error.

Figure 1b shows a possible set of points for the same values of x when we are using a probabilistic model. Note that the deterministic part of the model (the straight line itself) is the same. Now, however, the inclusion of a random error component allows the monthly sales to vary from this line. Because we know that the sales revenue does vary randomly for a given value of x, the probabilistic model provides a more realistic model for y than does the deterministic model.

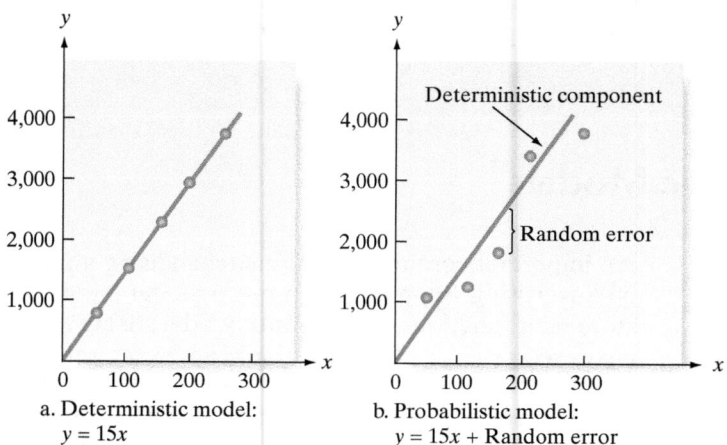

Figure 1

Possible sales revenues, y, for five different months, x

a. Deterministic model: $y = 15x$

b. Probabilistic model: $y = 15x + \text{Random error}$

In this chapter, we present the simplest of probabilistic models—the **straight-line model**—which derives its name from the fact that the deterministic portion of the model graphs as a straight line. Fitting this model to a set of data is an example of **regression analysis,** or **regression modeling.** The elements of the straight-line model are summarized in the next box.

A First-Order (Straight-Line) Probabilistic Model

$$y = \beta_0 + \beta_1 x + \varepsilon$$

where

$y = $ **Dependent** *or* **response variable** (variable to be modeled)

$x = $ **Independent** *or* **predictor variable** (variable used as a predictor of y)*

$E(y) = \beta_0 + \beta_1 x = $ Deterministic component

ε (epsilon) $= $ Random error component

β_0 (beta zero) $= $ **y-intercept of the line,** that is, the point at which the line *intercepts or cuts through the y-axis* (see Figure 2)

*The word *independent* should not be interpreted in a probabilistic sense. The phrase *independent variable* is used in regression analysis to refer to a predictor variable for the response y.

BIOGRAPHY

FRANCIS GALTON (1822–1911)
The Law of Universal Regression

Francis Galton was the youngest of seven children born to a middle-class English family of Quaker faith. A cousin of Charles Darwin, Galton attended Trinity College (Cambridge, England) to study medicine. Due to the death of his father, Galton was unable to obtain his degree. His competence in both medicine and mathematics, however, led Galton to pursue a career as a scientist. Galton made major contributions to the fields of genetics, psychology, meteorology, and anthropology. Some consider Galton to be the first social scientist for his applications of the novel statistical concepts of the time—in particular, regression and correlation. While studying natural inheritance in 1886, Galton collected data on the heights of parents and adult children. He noticed the tendency for tall (or short) parents to have tall (or short) children, but the children were not as tall (or short), on average, as their parents. Galton called this phenomenon the "law of universal regression," for the average heights of adult children tend to "regress" to the mean of the population. Galton, with the help of his friend and disciple, Karl Pearson, applied the straight-line model to the height data, and the term *regression* model was coined.

β_1 (beta one) = **Slope of the line,** that is, the change (amount of increase or decrease) in the deterministic component of y for every 1-unit increase in x

[*Note:* A *positive* slope implies that $E(y)$ *increases* by the amount β_1 for each unit increase in x (see Figure 2). A *negative* slope implies that $E(y)$ *decreases* by the amount β_1.]

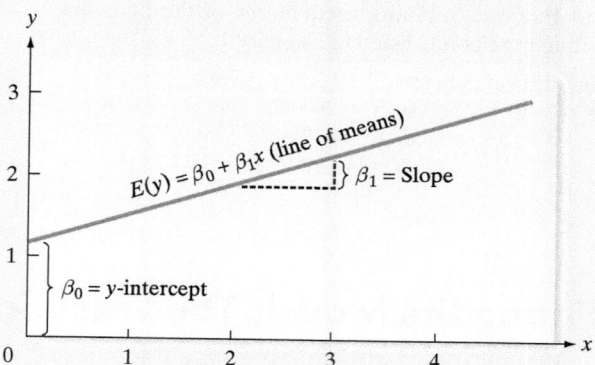

Figure 2
The straight-line model

In the probabilistic model, the deterministic component is referred to as the **line of means** because the mean of y, $E(y)$, is equal to the straight-line component of the model—that is,

$$E(y) = \beta_0 + \beta_1 x$$

Note that the Greek symbols β_0 and β_1, respectively, represent the y-intercept and slope of the model. They are population parameters that will be known only if we have access to the entire population of (x, y) measurements. Together with a specific value of the independent variable x, they determine the mean value of y, which is a specific point on the line of means (Figure 2).

The values of β_0 and β_1 will be unknown in almost all practical applications of regression analysis. The process of developing a model, estimating the unknown parameters, and using the model can be viewed as the five-step procedure shown in the next box.

Step 1: Hypothesize the deterministic component of the model that relates the mean, $E(y)$, to the independent variable x (Section 1).

Step 2: Use the sample data to estimate unknown parameters in the model (Section 2).

Step 3: Specify the probability distribution of the random error term and estimate the standard deviation of this distribution (Section 3).

Step 4: Statistically evaluate the usefulness of the model (Sections 4 and 5).

Step 5: When satisfied that the model is useful, use it for prediction, estimation, and other purposes (Section 6).

Exercises 1–9

Learning the Mechanics

1 In each case, graph the line that passes through the given points.
  a. $(1, 1)$ and $(5, 5)$
  b. $(0, 3)$ and $(3, 0)$
  c. $(-1, 1)$ and $(4, 2)$
  d. $(-6, -3)$ and $(2, 6)$

2 Give the slope and y-intercept for each of the lines graphed in Exercise 1.

3 The equation for a straight line (deterministic model) is

$$y = \beta_0 + \beta_1 x$$

If the line passes through the point $(-2, 4)$, then $x = -2$, $y = 4$ must satisfy the equation; that is,

$$4 = \beta_0 + \beta_1(-2)$$

Similarly, if the line passes through the point $(4, 6)$, then $x = 4$, $y = 6$ must satisfy the equation; that is,

$$6 = \beta_0 + \beta_1(4)$$

Use these two equations to solve for β_0 and β_1; then find the equation of the line that passes through the points $(-2, 4)$ and $(4, 6)$.

4 Refer to Exercise 3. Find the equations of the lines that pass through the points listed in Exercise 1.

5 Plot the following lines:
a. $y = 4 + x$ **b.** $y = 5 - 2x$
c. $y = -4 + 3x$ **d.** $y = -2x$
e. $y = x$ **f.** $y = .50 + 1.5x$

6 Give the slope and y-intercept for each of the lines graphed in Exercise 5.

7 Why do we generally prefer a probabilistic model to a deterministic model? Give examples for when the two types of models might be appropriate.

8 What is the line of means?

9 If a straight-line probabilistic relationship relates the mean $E(y)$ to an independent variable x, does it imply that every value of the variable y will always fall exactly on the line of means? Why or why not?

2 Fitting the Model: The Least Squares Approach

After the straight-line model has been hypothesized to relate the mean $E(y)$ to the independent variable x, the next step is to collect data and to estimate the (unknown) population parameters, the y-intercept β_0 and the slope β_1.

To begin with a simple example, suppose an appliance store conducts a 5-month experiment to determine the effect of advertising on sales revenue. The results are shown in Table 1. (The number of measurements and the measurements themselves are unrealistically simple to avoid arithmetic confusion in this introductory example.) This set of data will be used to demonstrate the five-step procedure of regression modeling given in Section 1. In this section, we hypothesize the deterministic component of the model and estimate its unknown parameters (steps 1 and 2). The model assumptions and the random error component (step 3) are the subjects of Section 3, whereas Sections 4 and 5 assess the utility of the model (step 4). Finally, we use the model for prediction and estimation (step 5) in Section 6.

Step 1: *Hypothesize the deterministic component of the probabilistic model.* As stated before, we will consider only straight-line models in this chapter. Thus, the complete model to relate mean sales revenue $E(y)$ to advertising expenditure x is given by

$$E(y) = \beta_0 + \beta_1 x$$

Step 2: *Use sample data to estimate unknown parameters in the model.* This step is the subject of this section—namely, how can we best use the information in the sample of five observations in Table 1 to estimate the unknown y-intercept β_0 and slope β_1?

To determine whether a linear relationship between y and x is plausible, it is helpful to plot the sample data in a **scatterplot** (or **scattergram**). A scatterplot locates each of the five data points on a graph, as shown in Figure 3. Note that the scatterplot suggests a general tendency for y to increase as x increases. If you

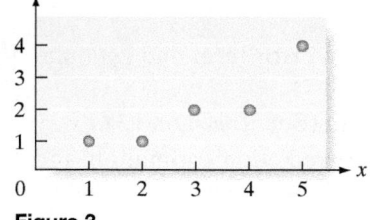

Figure 3

Scatterplot for data in Table 1

Table 1	Advertising-Sales Data	
Month	Advertising Expenditure, x ($100s)	Sales Revenue, y ($1,000s)
1	1	1
2	2	1
3	3	2
4	4	2
5	5	4

Data Set: ADSALE

place a ruler on the scatterplot, you will see that a line may be drawn through three of the five points, as shown in Figure 4. To obtain the equation of this visually fitted line, note that the line intersects the y-axis at $y = -1$, so the y-intercept is -1. Also, y increases exactly 1 unit for every 1-unit increase in x, indicating that the slope is $+1$. Therefore, the equation is

$$\tilde{y} = -1 + 1(x) = -1 + x$$

where $\tilde{y}$ is used to denote the predicted y from the visual model.

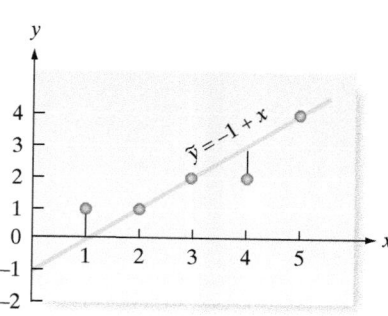

One way to decide quantitatively how well a straight line fits a set of data is to note the extent to which the data points deviate from the line. For example, to evaluate the model in Figure 4, we calculate the magnitude of the *deviations* (i.e., the differences between the observed and the predicted values of y). These deviations, or **errors of prediction,** are the vertical distances between observed and predicted values (see Figure 4).* The observed and predicted values of y, their differences, and their squared differences are shown in

Figure 4

Visual straight line fitted to the data in Figure 3

Table 2. Note that the *sum of errors* equals 0 and the *sum of squares of the errors* (SSE), which gives greater emphasis to large deviations of the points from the line, is equal to 2.

Table 2		Comparing Observed and Predicted Values for the Visual Model		
x	y	$\tilde{y} = -1 + x$	$(y - \tilde{y})$	$(y - \tilde{y})^2$
1	1	0	$(1 - 0) = 1$	1
2	1	1	$(1 - 1) = 0$	0
3	2	2	$(2 - 2) = 0$	0
4	2	3	$(2 - 3) = -1$	1
5	4	4	$(4 - 4) = 0$	0
			Sum of errors $= 0$	Sum of squared errors (SSE) $= 2$

You can see by shifting the ruler around the graph that it is possible to find many lines for which the sum of errors is equal to 0, but it can be shown that there is one (and only one) line for which the SSE is a *minimum*. This line is called the **least squares line,** the **regression line,** or the **least squares prediction equation.** The methodology used to obtain this line is called the **method of least squares.**

Now Work Exercise 12a, b, c, d

To find the least squares prediction equation for a set of data, assume that we have a sample of n data points consisting of pairs of values of x and y, say (x_1, y_1), $(x_2, y_2), \ldots, (x_n, y_n)$. For example, the $n = 5$ data points shown in Table 2 are $(1,1), (2,1)$, $(3,2), (4,2)$, and $(5,4)$. The fitted line, which we will calculate based on the five data points, is written as

$$\hat{y} = \hat{\beta}_0 + \hat{\beta}_1 x$$

The "hats" indicate that the symbols below them are estimates: $\hat{y}$ (y-hat) is an estimator of the mean value of y, $E(y)$, and a predictor of some future value of y; and $\hat{\beta}_0$ and $\hat{\beta}_1$ are estimators of β_0 and β_1, respectively.

For a given data point, say the point (x_i, y_i), the observed value of y is y_i, and the predicted value of y would be obtained by substituting x_i into the prediction equation:

$$\hat{y}_i = \hat{\beta}_0 + \hat{\beta}_1 x_i$$

---

*These errors of prediction can be referred to as **regression residuals.** An Analysis of residuals is essential in establishing a useful regression model.

And the deviation of the ith value of y from its predicted value is

$$(y_i - \hat{y}_i) = [y_i - (\hat{\beta}_0 + \hat{\beta}_1 x_i)]$$

Then the sum of squares of the deviations of the y-values about their predicted values for all the n points is

$$\text{SSE} = \sum [y_i - (\hat{\beta}_0 + \hat{\beta}_1 x_i)]^2$$

The quantities $\hat{\beta}_0$ and $\hat{\beta}_1$ that make the SSE a minimum are called the **least squares estimates** of the population parameters β_0 and β_1, and the prediction equation $\hat{y} = \hat{\beta}_0 + \hat{\beta}_1 x$ is called the *least squares line*.

The **least squares line** $\hat{y} = \hat{\beta}_0 + \hat{\beta}_1 x$ is one that has the following two properties:

1. The sum of the errors equals 0, i.e., mean error $= 0$.
2. The sum of squared errors (SSE) is smaller than for any other straight-line model, i.e., the error variance is minimum.

The values of $\hat{\beta}_0$ and $\hat{\beta}_1$ that minimize the SSE are (proof omitted) given by the formulas in the box.*

Formulas for the Least Squares Estimates

$$\text{Slope: } \hat{\beta}_1 = \frac{\text{SS}_{xy}}{\text{SS}_{xx}}$$

$$\text{y-intercept: } \hat{\beta}_0 = \bar{y} - \hat{\beta}_1 \bar{x}$$

$$\text{where}^\dagger \quad \text{SS}_{xy} = \sum (x_i - \bar{x})(y_i - \bar{y})$$

$$\text{SS}_{xx} = \sum (x_i - \bar{x})^2$$

$$n = \text{Sample size}$$

| Example | 1 |

Applying the Method of Least Squares— Advertising–Sales Data

Problem Refer to the advertising–monthly–sales data presented in Table 1. Consider the straight-line model, $E(y) = \beta_0 + \beta_1 x$, where $y = $ sales revenue (thousands of dollars) and $x = $ advertising expenditure (hundreds of dollars).

a. Use the method of least squares to estimate the values of β_0 and β_1.
b. Predict the sales revenue when advertising expenditure is $200 (i.e., when $x = 2$).
c. Find SSE for the analysis.
d. Give practical interpretations to β_0 and β_1.

Solution

a. We used Excel to make the preliminary computations for finding the least squares line. The Excel spreadsheet is shown in Figure 5. Using the values on the spreadsheet, we find

---

*Students who are familiar with calculus should note that the values of β_0 and β_1 that minimize $\text{SSE} = \sum (y_i - \hat{y}_i)^2$ are obtained by setting the two partial derivatives $\partial \text{SSE}/\partial \beta_0$ and $\partial \text{SSE}/\partial \beta_1$ equal to 0. The solutions to these two equations yield the formulas shown in the box. Furthermore, we denote the *sample* solutions to the equations by $\hat{\beta}_0$ and $\hat{\beta}_1$, where the "hat" denotes that these are sample estimates of the true population intercept β_0 and true population slope β_1.

†Alternatively, you can use the following "shortcut" formulas:

$$\text{SS}_{xy} = \sum x_i y_i - \frac{(\sum x_i)(\sum y_i)}{n}; \quad \text{SS}_{xx} = \sum x_i^2 - \frac{(\sum x_i)^2}{n}$$

Figure 5

Excel spreadsheet showing calculations for advertising-sales example

	A	B	C	D	E	F	G	H
		AdvExp (X)	SalesRev (Y)	(X - 3)	(Y - 2)	(X-3)(Y-2)	(X-3)(X-3)	(Y-2)(Y-2)
1								
2		1	1	-2	-1	2	4	1
3		2	1	-1	-1	1	1	1
4		3	2	0	0	0	0	0
5		4	2	1	0	0	1	0
6		5	4	2	2	4	4	4
7								
8	Totals	15	10	0	0	7	10	6
9	Mean	3	2					

$$\bar{x} = \frac{\Sigma x}{5} = \frac{15}{5} = 3$$

$$\bar{y} = \frac{\Sigma y}{5} = \frac{10}{5} = 2$$

$$SS_{xy} = \Sigma(x - \bar{x})(y - \bar{y}) = \Sigma(x - 3)(y - 2) = 7$$

$$SS_{xx} = \Sigma(x - \bar{x})^2 = \Sigma(x - 3)^2 = 10$$

Then the slope of the least squares line is

$$\hat{\beta}_1 = \frac{SS_{xy}}{SS_{xx}} = \frac{7}{10} = .7$$

and the y-intercept is

$$\hat{\beta}_0 = \bar{y} - \hat{\beta}_1\bar{x} = 2 - (.7)(3) = 2 - 2.1 = -.1$$

The least squares line is thus

$$\hat{y} = \hat{\beta}_0 + \hat{\beta}_1 x = -.1 + .7x$$

The graph of this line is shown in Figure 6.

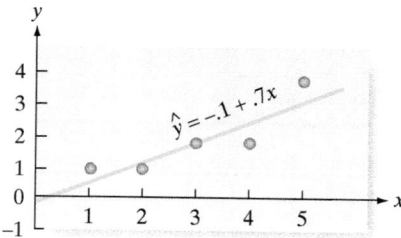

Figure 6

The line $\hat{y} = -.1 + .7x$ fitted to the data

b. The predicted value of y for a given value of x can be obtained by substituting into the formula for the least squares line. Substituting $x = 2$ into the least squares equation yields

$$\hat{y} = -.1 + .7x = -.1 + .7(2) = 1.3$$

Thus, when advertising expenditure is $200, we predict monthly sales revenue to be $1,300. We show how to find a prediction interval for y in Section 6.

c. The observed and predicted values of y, the deviations of the y values about their predicted values, and the squares of these deviations are shown in the Excel spreadsheet, Figure 7. Note that SSE = 1.10, and (as we would expect) this is less than the SSE = 2.0 obtained in Table 2 for the visually fitted line.

d. The estimated y-intercept, $\hat{\beta}_0 = -.1$, appears to imply that the estimated mean sales revenue is equal to $-.1$, or $-$100, when the advertising expenditure, x, is equal to $0. Because negative sales revenues are not possible, this seems to make the model nonsensical. However, *the model parameters should be interpreted only within the*

	A	B	C	D	E	F
1	AdvExp (X)	SalesRev (Y)	Predicted Y=-.1+.7X (Y-hat)	(Y-Yhat)	(Y-Yhat)(Y-Yhat)	
2	1	1	0.6	0.4	0.16	
3	2	1	1.3	-0.3	0.09	
4	3	2	2	0	0	
5	4	2	2.7	-0.7	0.49	
6	5	4	3.4	0.6	0.36	
7						
8			Sum	0	1.1	
9						
10						

Figure 7

Excel spreadsheet comparing observed and predicted values for advertising-sales example

sampled range of the independent variable—in this case, for advertising expenditures between $100 and $500. Thus, the y-intercept—which is, by definition, at $x = 0$ ($0 advertising expenditure)—is not within the range of the sampled values of x and is not subject to meaningful interpretation.

The slope of the least squares line, $\hat{\beta}_1 = .7$, implies that for every unit increase of x, the mean value of y is estimated to increase by .7 unit. In terms of this example, for every $100 increase in advertising, the mean sales revenue is estimated to increase by $700 *over the sampled range of advertising expenditures from $100 to $500.* Thus, the model does not imply that increasing the advertising expenditures from $500 to $1,000 will result in an increase in mean sales of $3,500, because the range of x in the sample does not extend to $1,000 ($x = 10$). Be careful to interpret the estimated parameters only within the sampled range of x.

Look Back The calculations required to obtain $\hat{\beta}_0, \hat{\beta}_1$, and SSE in simple linear regression, although straightforward, can become rather tedious. Even with the use of an Excel spreadsheet, the process is laborious, especially when the sample size is large. Fortunately, a statistical software package can significantly reduce the labor involved in regression calculations. The SPSS, Minitab, and Excel/XLSTAT outputs for the simple linear regression of the data in Table 1 are displayed in Figures 8a–c. The values of $\hat{\beta}_0$ and $\hat{\beta}_1$ are highlighted on the printouts. These values, $\hat{\beta}_0 = -.1$ and $\hat{\beta}_1 = .7$, agree exactly with our calculated values. The value of SSE = 1.10 is also highlighted on the printouts.

Model Summary

Model	R	R Square	Adjusted R Square	Std. Error of the Estimate
1	.904[a]	.817	.756	.606

a. Predictors: (Constant), ADVEXP_X

ANOVA[b]

Model		Sum of Squares	df	Mean Square	F	Sig.
1	Regression	4.900	1	4.900	13.364	.035[a]
	Residual	1.100	3	.367		
	Total	6.000	4			

a. Predictors: (Constant), ADVEXP_X
b. Dependent Variable: SALES_Y

Coefficients[a]

Model		Unstandardized Coefficients		Standardized Coefficients	t	Sig.
		B	Std. Error	Beta		
1	(Constant)	-.100	.635		-.157	.885
	ADVEXP_X	.700	.191	.904	3.656	.035

a. Dependent Variable: SALES_Y

Figure 8a

SPSS printout for the advertising-sales regression

Regression Analysis: SALES_Y versus ADVEXP_X

```
The regression equation is
SALES_Y = - 0.100 + 0.700 ADVEXP_X


Predictor     Coef   SE Coef      T      P
Constant    -0.1000   0.6351   -0.16  0.885
ADVEXP_X     0.7000   0.1915    3.66  0.035


S = 0.605530   R-Sq = 81.7%   R-Sq(adj) = 75.6%


Analysis of Variance

Source          DF     SS      MS      F      P
Regression       1  4.9000  4.9000  13.36  0.035
Residual Error   3  1.1000  0.3667
Total            4  6.0000
```

Figure 8b

Minitab printout for the advertising-sales regression

Regression of variable SALES_Y:

Goodness of fit statistics:

Observations	5.0000
Sum of weights	5.0000
DF	3.0000
R²	0.8167
Adjusted R²	0.7556
MSE	0.3667
RMSE	0.6055
DW	2.5091

Analysis of variance:

Source	DF	Sum of squares	Mean squares	F	Pr > F
Model	1	4.9000	4.9000	13.3636	0.0354
Error	3	1.1000	0.3667		
Corrected Total	4	6.0000			

Computed against model Y=Mean(Y)

Model parameters:

Source	Value	Standard error	t	Pr > |t|	Lower bound (95%)	Upper bound (95%)
Intercept	-0.1000	0.6351	-0.1575	0.8849	-2.1211	1.9211
ADVEXP_X	0.7000	0.1915	3.6556	0.0354	0.0906	1.3094

Equation of the model:

SALES_Y =-0.10000+0.70000*ADVEXP_X

Figure 8c

XLSTAT printout of sales-advertising regression model

Now Work Exercise 15

Interpreting the Estimates of β_0 and β_1 in Simple Linear Regression

y-intercept: $\hat{\beta}_0$ represents the predicted value of y when x = 0 (*Caution:* This value will not be meaningful if the value x = 0 is nonsensical or outside the range of the sample data.)

slope: $\hat{\beta}_1$ represents the increase (or decrease) in y for every 1-unit increase in x (*Caution:* This interpretation is valid only for x-values within the range of the sample data.)

Even when the interpretations of the estimated parameters in a simple linear regression are meaningful, we need to remember that they are only estimates based on the sample. As such, their values will typically change in repeated sampling. How much confidence do we have that the estimated slope, $\hat{\beta}_1$, accurately approximates the true slope, β_1? This requires statistical inference, in the form of confidence intervals and tests of hypotheses, which we address in Section 4.

To summarize, we defined the best-fitting straight line to be the one that minimizes the sum of squared errors around the line, and we called it the *least squares line*. We should interpret the least squares line only within the sampled range of the independent variable. In subsequent sections, we show how to make statistical inferences about the model.

Estimating a Straight-Line Regression Model

We return to the legal advertising case involving two former law partners. Recall that partner A (who handled PI cases) sued partner B (who handled WC cases) over who should pay what share of the advertising expenses of their former partnership. Monthly data were collected on the number of new PI cases, number of new WC cases, and the total amount spent (in thousands of dollars) on advertising over the previous 6 months. These data (shown in Table SIA1) are saved in the **LEGADV** file. Do these data provide support for the hypothesis that increased advertising expenditures are associated with more PI cases? Define y as the number of new PI cases per month and x as the cumulative 6-month advertising expenditures (in thousands of dollars). One way to investigate the link between these two variables is to fit the straight-line model, $E(y) = \beta_0 + \beta_1 x$, to the data in Table SIA1.

A Minitab scatterplot of the data and a simple linear regression printout are shown in Figure SIA1. Note that the least squares line is also displayed on the scatterplot. You can see that the line has a positive slope and, although there is some variation of the data points around the line, it appears that advertising expenditure (x) is fairly strongly related to the number of new PI cases (y). The estimated slope of the line (highlighted on Figure SIA1) is $\hat{\beta}_1 = .113$. Thus, we estimate a .113 increase in the number of new PI cases for every \$1,000 increase in cumulative advertising expenditures.

Does such a relationship also exist between number of new WC cases and advertising expenditure? Now let y = number of new WC cases per month and x = cumulative

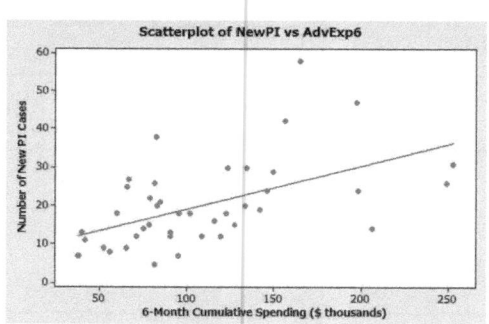

Regression Analysis: NewPI versus AdvExp6

The regression equation is
NewPI = 7.77 + 0.113 AdvExp6

Predictor	Coef	SE Coef	T	P
Constant	7.767	3.385	2.29	0.027
AdvExp6	0.11289	0.02793	4.04	0.000

S = 9.67521 R-Sq = 29.0% R-Sq(adj) = 27.2%

Analysis of Variance

Source	DF	SS	MS	F	P
Regression	1	1529.5	1529.5	16.34	0.000
Residual Error	40	3744.4	93.6		
Total	41	5273.9			

Figure SIA1

Minitab analysis of new PI cases vs. 6-month cumulative advertising expenditure

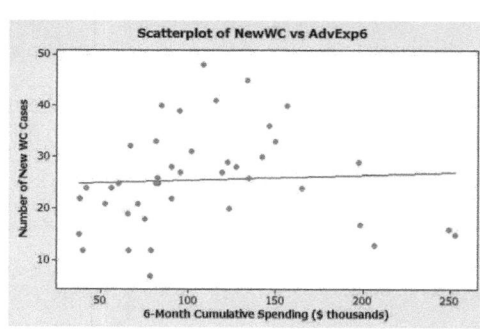

Regression Analysis: NewWC versus AdvExp6

The regression equation is
NewWC = 24.6 + 0.0098 AdvExp6

Predictor	Coef	SE Coef	T	P
Constant	24.574	3.367	7.30	0.000
AdvExp6	0.00982	0.02778	0.35	0.725

S = 9.62296 R-Sq = 0.3% R-Sq(adj) = 0.0%

Analysis of Variance

Source	DF	SS	MS	F	P
Regression	1	11.58	11.58	0.13	0.725
Residual Error	40	3704.06	92.60		
Total	41	3715.64			

Figure SIA2

Minitab analysis of new WC cases vs. 6-month cumulative advertising expenditure

6-month advertising expenditures. A Minitab scatterplot and simple linear regression analysis for these two variables are shown in Figure SIA2. Compared to the previous scatterplot, the slope of the least squares line shown in Figure SIA2 is much flatter, and the variation of the data points around the line is much larger. Consequently, it does not appear that number of new WC cases is very strongly related to advertising expenditure. In fact, the estimated slope (highlighted in Figure SIA2) implies that a $1,000 increase in cumulative advertising expenditures will lead to only a $\hat{\beta}_1 = .0098$ increase in the number of new WC cases per month.

Based on these descriptive statistics (scatterplots and least squares lines), it appears that partner A's argument that partner B should share the advertising expenses is weak, at best. In the *Statistics in Action Revisited* sections that follow, we will provide a measure of reliability to this inference and investigate the legal advertising data further.

Exercises 10–26

Please be aware that some of the following problems may require knowledge of concepts that are not presented in this chapter.

Learning the Mechanics

10 The following table is similar to Table 2. It is used for making the preliminary computations for finding the least squares line for the given pairs of x and y values.

x_i	y_i	x_i^2	$x_i y_i$
7	2		
4	4		
6	2		
2	5		
1	7		
1	6		
3	5		
Totals $\Sigma x_i =$	$\Sigma y_i =$	$\Sigma x_i^2 =$	$\Sigma x_i y_i =$

a. Complete the table. **b.** Find SS_{xy}.
c. Find SS_{xx}. **d.** Find $\hat{\beta}_1$.
e. Find $\bar{x}$ and $\bar{y}$. **f.** Find $\hat{\beta}_0$.
g. Find the least squares line.

11 Refer to Exercise 10. After the least squares line has been obtained, the table below (which is similar to Table 2) can be used for (1) comparing the observed and the predicted values of y and (2) computing SSE.

x	y	$\hat{y}$	$(y - \hat{y})$	$(y - \hat{y})^2$
7	2			
4	4			
6	2			
2	5			
1	7			
1	6			
3	5			
			$\Sigma(y - \hat{y}) =$	SSE $= \Sigma(y - \hat{y})^2 =$

a. Complete the table.
b. Plot the least squares line on a scatterplot of the data. Plot the following line on the same graph: $\hat{y} = 14 - 2.5x$.
c. Show that SSE is larger for the line in part **b** than it is for the least squares line.

12 Construct a scatterplot for the data in the following table.

x	.5	1	1.5
y	2	1	3

a. Plot the following two lines on your scatterplot:
$$y = 3 - x \quad \text{and} \quad y = 1 + x$$
b. Which of these lines would you choose to characterize the relationship between x and y? Explain.
c. Show that the sum of the errors of prediction for both of these lines equals 0.
d. Which of these lines has the smaller SSE?
e. Find the least squares line for the data and compare it to the two lines described in part **a**.

13 Consider the following pairs of measurements:

x	8	5	4	6	2	5	3
y	1	3	6	3	7	2	5

a. Construct a scatterplot for these data.
b. What does the scatterplot suggest about the relationship between x and y?
c. Find the least squares estimates of β_0 and β_1.
d. Plot the least squares line on your scatterplot. Does the line appear to fit the data well? Explain.

⚙ Applet Exercise 1

Use the applet *Regression by Eye* to explore the relationship between the pattern of data in a scatterplot and the corresponding least squares model.

a. Run the applet several times. For each time, attempt to move the green line into a position that appears to minimize the vertical distances of the points from the line. Then click *Show regression line* to see the actual regression line. How close is your line to the actual line? Click *New data* to reset the applet.
b. Click the trash can to clear the graph. Use the mouse to place five points on the scatterplot that are approximately in a straight line. Then move the green line to approximate the regression line. Click *Show regression line* to see the actual regression line. How close were you this time?

c. Continue to clear the graph and plot sets of five points with different patterns among the points. Use the green line to approximate the regression line. How close do you come to the actual regression line each time?

d. Based on your experiences with the applet, explain why we need to use more reliable methods of finding the regression line than just "eyeing" it.

Applying the Concepts—Basic

14 In business, do nice guys finish first or last? *Nature* (March 20, 2008) did a study of whether "nice guys finish last" in the business world. College students repeatedly played a version of the game "prisoner's dilemma," where competitors choose cooperation, defection, or costly punishment. (Cooperation meant paying 1 unit for the opponent to receive 2 units, defection meant gaining 1 unit at a cost of 1 unit for the opponent, and punishment meant paying 1 unit for the opponent to lose 4 units.) At the conclusion of the games, the researchers recorded the average payoff and the number of times cooperation, defection, and punishment were used for each player. The scatterplots below plot average payoff (*y*) against level of cooperation use, defection use, and punishment use, respectively.

a. Consider cooperation use (*x*) as a predictor of average payoff (*y*). Based on the scatterplot, is there evidence of a linear trend?

b. Consider defection use (*x*) as a predictor of average payoff (*y*). Based on the scatterplot, is there evidence of a linear trend?

c. Consider punishment use (*x*) as a predictor of average payoff (*y*). Based on the scatterplot (reproduced from Exercise 2.123), is there evidence of a linear trend?

d. Refer to part **c.** Is the slope of the line relating punishment use (*x*) to average payoff (*y*) positive or negative?

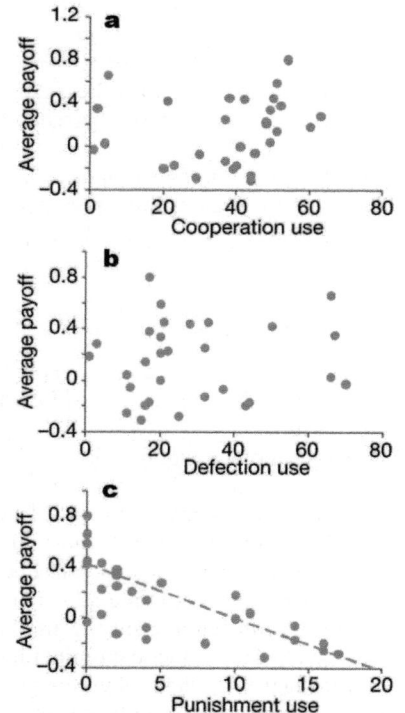

15 State Math SAT scores. Refer to the data file on average state Math SAT scores for 2001 and 2011. The first five observations and last two observations in the file are reproduced in the next table. Examine the relationship between the 2001 Math SAT scores and the 2011 Math SAT scores with a scatterplot.

State	2001	2011
Alabama	554	541
Alaska	510	511
Arizona	525	523
Arkansas	550	570
California	517	515
⋮	⋮	⋮
Wisconsin	596	602
Wyoming	545	569

Source: Based on "SAT Trends: Background on the SAT Takers in the Class of 2011." The College Board.

a. Write the equation of a straight-line model relating 2011 Math SAT score (*y*) to 2001 Math SAT score (*x*).

b. An SPSS simple linear regression printout for the data is shown on the next page. Find the least squares prediction equation.

c. Give a practical interpretation of the *y*-intercept of the least squares line. If a practical interpretation is not possible, explain why.

d. Give a practical interpretation of the slope of the least squares line. Over what range of *x* is the interpretation meaningful?

16 Lobster fishing study. The *Bulletin of Marine Science* (April 2010) did a study of teams of fishermen fishing for the red spiny lobster in Baja California Sur, Mexico. Two variables measured for each of 15 teams from two fishing cooperatives were *y* = total catch of lobsters (in kilograms) during the season and *x* = average percentage of traps allocated per day to exploring areas of unknown catch (called *search frequency*). These data are listed in the table.

Total Catch	Search Frequency	Total Catch	Search Frequency
9,998	18	6,535	21
7,767	14	6,695	26
8,764	4	4,891	29
9,077	18	4,937	23
8,343	9	5,727	17
9,222	5	7,019	21
6,827	8	5,735	20
2,785	35		

Source: Based on Shester, G. G. "Explaining catch variation among Baja California lobster fishers through spatial analysis of trap-placement decisions," *Bulletin of Marine Science,* Vol. 86, No. 2, April 2010 (Table 1).

a. Graph the data in a scatterplot. What type of trend, if any, do you observe?

b. A simple linear regression analysis was conducted using XLSTAT. A portion of the regression printout is shown on the next page. Find the estimates of β_0 and β_1 on the printout.

SPSS Output for Exercise 15

Coefficients[a]

Model		Unstandardized Coefficients		Standardized Coefficients	t	Sig.
		B	Std. Error	Beta		
1	(Constant)	-97.414	26.668		-3.653	.001
	MATH2001	1.188	.050	.959	23.830	.000

a. Dependent Variable: MATH2011

XLSTAT output for Exercise 16

Model parameters:

Source	Value	Standard error	t	Pr > |t|	Lower bound (95%)	Upper bound (95%)
Intercept	9877.8300	829.0411	11.9148	< 0.0001	8086.7957	11668.8643
SEARCHFR	-163.6024	41.9014	-3.9045	0.0018	-254.1249	-73.0799

Equation of the model:

CATCH = 9877.82997-163.60242*SEARCHFREQ

c. If possible, give a practical interpretation of the estimate of β_0. If no practical interpretation is possible, explain why.

d. If possible, give a practical interpretation of the estimate of β_1. If no practical interpretation is possible, explain why.

17 Drug controlled-release rate study. Researchers at Dow Chemical Co. investigated the effect of tablet surface area and volume on the rate at which a drug is released in a controlled-release dosage (*Drug Development and Industrial Pharmacy*, Vol. 28, 2002). Six similarly shaped tablets were prepared with different weights and thicknesses, and the ratio of surface area to volume was measured for each. Using a dissolution apparatus, each tablet was placed in 900 milliliters of deionized water, and the diffusional drug release rate (percentage of drug released divided by the square root of time) was determined. The experimental data are listed in the table below.

Drug Release Rate (% released/√time)	Surface Area to Volume (mm²/mm³)
60	1.50
48	1.05
39	.90
33	.75
30	.60
29	.65

Source: Reynolds, T., Mitchell, S., & Balwinski, K.M. "Investigation of the effect of table surface area/volume on drug release from hydroxypropyl-methylcellulose controlled-release matrix tablets," *Drug Development and Industrial Pharmacy,* Vol. 28, No. 4, 2002, pp. 457–466 (Figure 3). Reprinted by permission of the publisher (Taylor & Francis Group, www.informaworld.com).

a. Fit the simple linear model, $E(y) = \beta_0 + \beta_1 x$, where y = release rate and x = surface-area-to-volume ratio.

b. Interpret the estimates of β_0 and β_1.

c. Predict the drug release rate for a tablet that has a surface area/volume ratio of .50.

d. Comment on the reliability of the prediction in part **c.**

18 Extending the life of an aluminum smelter pot. An investigation of the properties of bricks used to line aluminum smelter pots was published in *The American Ceramic Society Bulletin* (Feb. 2005). Six different commercial bricks were evaluated. The life length of a smelter pot depends on the porosity of the brick lining (the less porosity, the longer the life); consequently, the researchers measured the apparent porosity of each brick specimen, as well as the mean pore diameter of each brick. The data are given in the accompanying table.

Brick	Apparent Porosity (%)	Mean Pore Diameter (micrometers)
A	18.8	12.0
B	18.3	9.7
C	16.3	7.3
D	6.9	5.3
E	17.1	10.9
F	20.4	16.8

Source: Based on Bonadia, P., et al. "Aluminosilicate refractories for aluminum cell linings," *The American Ceramic Society Bulletin,* Vol. 84, No. 2, Feb. 2005, pp. 26–31 (Table II).

a. Find the least squares line relating porosity (y) to mean pore diameter (x).

b. Interpret the y-intercept of the line.

c. Interpret the slope of the line.

d. Predict the apparent porosity percentage for a brick with a mean pore diameter of 10 micrometers.

19 Software millionaires and birthdays. In *Outliers: The Story of Success* (Little, Brown, 2008), the author notes that a disproportionate number of software millionaires were born around the year 1955. Is this a coincidence, or does birth year matter when gauging whether a software founder will be successful? On his Web blog (www.measuringusability.com), statistical consultant Jeff Sauro investigated this question by analyzing the data shown in the table on the next page.

Data for Exercise 19

Decade	Total U.S. Births (millions)	Number of Software Millionaire Birthdays	Number of CEO Birthdays (in a random sample of 70 companies from the *Fortune* 500 list)
1920	28.582	3	2
1930	24.374	1	2
1940	31.666	10	23
1950	40.530	14	38
1960	38.808	7	9
1970	33.309	4	0

Source: Sauro, J. "Were most software millionaires born around 1955?" *Measuring Usability,* November 17, 2010. Copyright © 2010 by Measuring Usability LLC. Reprinted with permission.

a. Fit a simple linear regression model relating number (y) of software millionaire birthdays in a decade to total number (x) of U.S. births. Give the least squares prediction equation.

b. Practically interpret the estimated y-intercept and slope of the model, part **a.**

c. Predict the number of software millionaire birthdays that will occur in a decade where the total number of U.S. births is 35 million.

d. Fit a simple linear regression model relating number (y) of software millionaire birthdays in a decade to number (x) of CEO birthdays. Give the least squares prediction equation.

e. Practically interpret the estimated y-intercept and slope of the model, part **d.**

f. Predict the number of software millionaire birthdays that will occur in a decade where the number of CEO birthdays (from a random sample of 70 companies) is 10.

Applying the Concepts—Intermediate

20 Public corruption and bad weather. The Federal Emergency Management Agency (FEMA) provides disaster relief for states impacted by natural disasters (e.g., hurricanes, tornados, floods). Do these bad weather windfalls lead to public corruption? This was the research question of interest in an article published in the *Journal of Law and Economics* (Nov. 2008). Data on y = average annual number of public corruption convictions (per 100,000 residents) and x = average annual FEMA relief (in dollars) per capita for each of the 50 states were used in the investigation.

a. Access the data, saved in the file, and construct a scatterplot. Do you observe a trend?

b. Fit the simple linear regression model, $E(y) = \beta_0 + \beta_1 x$, to the data and obtain estimates of the y-intercept and slope.

c. Practically interpret the estimated y-intercept and estimated slope.

21 Ranking driving performance of professional golfers. *The Sport Journal* (Winter 2007) did a study of a new method for ranking the total driving performance of golfers on the Professional Golf Association (PGA) tour. The method computes a driving performance index based on a golfer's average driving distance (yards) and driving accuracy (percent of drives that land in the fairway). Data for the top 40 PGA golfers

(as ranked by the new method) are saved in the file. (The first five and last five observations are listed in the table.)

Rank	Player	Driving Distance (yards)	Driving Accuracy (%)	Driving Performance Index
1	Woods	316.1	54.6	3.58
2	Perry	304.7	63.4	3.48
3	Gutschewski	310.5	57.9	3.27
4	Wetterich	311.7	56.6	3.18
5	Hearn	295.2	68.5	2.82
⋮	⋮	⋮	⋮	⋮
36	Senden	291	66	1.31
37	Mickelson	300	58.7	1.30
38	Watney	298.9	59.4	1.26
39	Trahan	295.8	61.8	1.23
40	Pappas	309.4	50.6	1.17

Source: Wiseman, F., et al. "A new method for ranking total driving performance on the PGA Tour," *The Sport Journal,* Vol. 10, No. 1, Winter 2007 (Table 2).

a. Write the equation of a straight-line model relating driving accuracy (y) to driving distance (x).

b. Fit the model, part **a,** to the data using simple linear regression. Give the least squares prediction equation.

c. Interpret the estimated y-intercept of the line.

d. Interpret the estimated slope of the line.

e. A professional golfer, practicing a new swing to increase his average driving distance, is concerned that his driving accuracy will be lower. Which of the two estimates, y-intercept or slope, will help you determine if the golfer's concern is a valid one? Explain.

22 Sweetness of orange juice. The quality of the orange juice produced by a manufacturer (e.g., Minute Maid, Tropicana) is constantly monitored. There are numerous sensory and chemical components that combine to make the best-tasting orange juice. For example, one manufacturer has developed a quantitative index of the "sweetness" of orange juice. (The higher the index, the sweeter the juice.) Is there a relationship between the sweetness index and a chemical measure such as the amount of water-soluble pectin (parts per million) in the orange juice? Data collected on these two variables for 24 production runs at a juice manufacturing plant are shown in the table on the next page. Suppose a manufacturer wants to use simple linear regression to predict the sweetness (y) from the amount of pectin (x).

Data for Exercise 22

Run	Sweetness Index	Pectin (ppm)
1	5.2	220
2	5.5	227
3	6.0	259
4	5.9	210
5	5.8	224
6	6.0	215
7	5.8	231
8	5.6	268
9	5.6	239
10	5.9	212
11	5.4	410
12	5.6	256
13	5.8	306
14	5.5	259
15	5.3	284
16	5.3	383
17	5.7	271
18	5.5	264
19	5.7	227
20	5.3	263
21	5.9	232
22	5.8	220
23	5.8	246
24	5.9	241

Note: The data in the table are authentic. For confidentiality reasons, the manufacturer cannot be disclosed.

a. Find the least squares line for the data.

b. Interpret $\hat{\beta}_0$ and $\hat{\beta}_1$ in the words of the problem.

c. Predict the sweetness index if amount of pectin in the orange juice is 300 ppm. [*Note:* A measure of reliability of such a prediction is discussed in Section 6]

23 **Forecasting movie revenues with Twitter.** Marketers are keenly interested in how social media (e.g., Facebook, Twitter) may influence consumers who buy their products. Researchers at HP Labs (Palo Alto, CA) investigated whether the volume of chatter on Twitter.com could be used to forecast the box office revenues of movies (*IEEE International Conference on Web Intelligence and Intelligent Agent Technology,* 2010). Opening weekend box office revenue data (in $millions of dollars) were collected for a sample of 23 recent movies. In addition, the researchers computed each movie's *tweet rate,* i.e., the average number of tweets (at Twitter.com) referring to the movie per hour 1 week prior to the movie's release. The data (simulated based on information provided in the study) are listed in the accompanying table. Assuming that movie revenue and tweet rate are linearly related, how much do you estimate a movie's opening weekend revenue to change as the tweet rate for the movie increases by an average of 100 tweets per hour?

24 **FCAT scores and poverty.** In the state of Florida, elementary school performance is based on the average score obtained by students on a standardized exam, called the Florida Comprehensive Assessment Test (FCAT). An analysis of the link between FCAT scores and sociodemographic factors was published in the *Journal of Educational and Behavioral Statistics* (Spring 2004). Data on average math and reading FCAT scores of third graders, as well as the percentage of students below the poverty level, for a sample of 22 Florida elementary schools are listed in the table below.

a. Propose a straight-line model relating math score (y) to percentage (x) of students below the poverty level.

b. Fit the model to the data using the method of least squares.

c. Graph the least squares line on a scatterplot of the data. Is there visual evidence of a relationship between the two variables? Is the relationship positive or negative?

d. Interpret the estimates of the y-intercept and slope in the words of the problem.

e. Now consider a model relating reading score (y) to percentage (x) of students below the poverty level. Repeat parts **a–d** for this model.

Tweet Rate	Revenue (millions)
1365.8	142
1212.8	77
581.5	61
310.1	32
455	31
290	30
250	21
680.5	18
150	18
164.5	17
113.9	16
144.5	15
418	14
98	14
100.8	12
115.4	11
74.4	10
87.5	9
127.6	9
52.2	9
144.1	8
41.3	2
2.75	0.3

Elementary School	FCAT-Math	FCAT-Reading	% Below Poverty
1	166.4	165.0	91.7
2	159.6	157.2	90.2
3	159.1	164.4	86.0
4	155.5	162.4	83.9
5	164.3	162.5	80.4
6	169.8	164.9	76.5
7	155.7	162.0	76.0
8	165.2	165.0	75.8
9	175.4	173.7	75.6
10	178.1	171.0	75.0
11	167.1	169.4	74.7
12	177.0	172.9	63.2
13	174.2	172.7	52.9
14	175.6	174.9	48.5
15	170.8	174.8	39.1
16	175.1	170.1	38.4
17	182.8	181.4	34.3
18	180.3	180.6	30.3
19	178.8	178.0	30.3
20	181.4	175.9	29.6
21	182.8	181.6	26.5
22	186.1	183.8	13.8

Source: Based on Tekwe, C. D., et al. "An empirical comparison of statistical models for value-added assessment of school performance," *Journal of Educational and Behavioral Statistics,* Vol. 29, No. 1, Spring 2004, pp. 11–36 (Table 2).

Data for Exercise 25

School	Enrollment (# full-time students)	Annual Tuition ($)	Mean GMAT	% with Job Offer	Avg. Salary ($)
Dartmouth	503	38,400	704	—	119,800
Michigan	1,873	33,076	690	91	105,986
Carnegie Mellon	661	38,800	691	93	95,531
Northwestern	2,650	38,844	700	94	117,060
Yale	468	36,800	696	86	104,018
Pennsylvania	1,840	40,458	716	92	117,471
Cal., Berkeley	1,281	21,512	701	92	112,699
Columbia	1,796	38,290	709	95	126,319
North Carolina	855	16,375	652	86	92,565
Southern Cal.	1,588	37,558	685	82	88,839

Source: "Wall Street Journal's annual rankings of business schools," *The Wall Street Journal,* Sep. 25, 2005. Copyright 2005 by Dow Jones & Company, Inc. Reproduced with permission.

25 Survey of the top business schools. Each year, the *Wall Street Journal* and *Harris Interactive* track the opinions and experiences of college recruiters for large corporations and summarize the results in the Business School Survey. One of these surveys included rankings of 76 business schools. Survey data for the top 10 business schools are given in the table above. All the data are saved in the file.

TOPBUS

a. Select one of the variables as the dependent variable, *y*, and another as the independent variable, *x*. Use your knowledge of the subject area and common sense to help you select the variables.

b. Fit the simple linear model, $E(y) = \beta_0 + \beta_1 x$, to the data for all 76 business schools. Interpret the estimates of the slope and *y*-intercept.

Applying the Concepts—Advanced

26 Spreading rate of spilled liquid. *Chemical Engineering Progress* (Jan. 2005) did a study of the rate at which a spilled volatile liquid will spread across a surface. A DuPont Corp. engineer calculated the mass (in pounds) of a 50-gallon methanol spill after a period of time ranging

LSPILL

from 0 to 60 minutes. Do the data in the table below indicate that the mass of the spill tends to diminish as time increases? If so, how much will the mass diminish each minute?

Time (minutes)	Mass (pounds)	Time (minutes)	Mass (pounds)
0	6.64	22	1.86
1	6.34	24	1.60
2	6.04	26	1.37
4	5.47	28	1.17
6	4.94	30	0.98
8	4.44	35	0.60
10	3.98	40	0.34
12	3.55	45	0.17
14	3.15	50	0.06
16	2.79	55	0.02
18	2.45	60	0.00
20	2.14		

Source: Barry, J. "Estimating rates of spreading and evaporation of volatile liquids," *Chemical Engineering Progress,* Vol. 101, No. 1, Jan. 2005. Reproduced with permission. Copyright © 2005 AICHE.

3 Model Assumptions

In Section 2, we assumed that the probabilistic model relating the firm's sales revenue *y* to the advertising dollars is

$$y = \beta_0 + \beta_1 x + \varepsilon$$

We also recall that the least squares estimate of the deterministic component of the model, $\beta_0 + \beta_1 x$, is

$$\hat{y} = \hat{\beta}_0 + \hat{\beta}_1 x = -.1 + .7x$$

Now we turn our attention to the random component ε of the probabilistic model and its relation to the errors in estimating β_0 and β_1. We will use a probability distribution to characterize the behavior of ε. We will see how the probability distribution of ε determines how well the model describes the relationship between the dependent variable *y* and the independent variable *x*.

Step 3 in a regression analysis requires us to specify the probability distribution of the random error ε. We will make four basic assumptions about the general form of this probability distribution:

Assumption 1: The mean of the probability distribution of ε is 0—that is, the average of the values of ε over an infinitely long series of experiments is 0 for each setting of the independent variable x. This assumption implies that the mean value of y, $E(y)$, for a given value of x is $E(y) = \beta_0 + \beta_1 x$.

Assumption 2: The variance of the probability distribution of ε is constant for all settings of the independent variable x. For our straight-line model, this assumption means that the variance of ε is equal to a constant, say σ^2, for all values of x.

Assumption 3: The probability distribution of ε is normal.

Assumption 4: The values of ε associated with any two observed values of y are independent—that is, the value of ε associated with one value of y has no effect on the values of ε associated with other y values.

The implications of the first three assumptions can be seen in Figure 9, which shows distributions of errors for three values of x, namely, x_1, x_2, and x_3. Note that the relative frequency distributions of the errors are normal with a mean of 0 and a constant variance σ^2. (All the distributions shown have the same amount of spread or variability.) The straight line shown in Figure 9 is the line of means. It indicates the mean value of y for a given value of x. We denote this mean value as $E(y)$. Then, the line of means is given by the equation

$$E(y) = \beta_0 + \beta_1 x$$

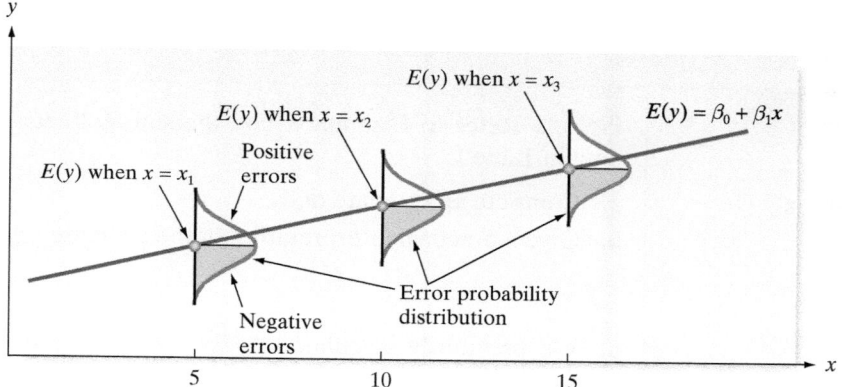

Figure 9

The probability distribution of ε

These assumptions make it possible for us to develop measures of reliability for the least squares estimators and to develop hypothesis tests for examining the usefulness of the least squares line. We have various techniques for checking the validity of these assumptions, and we have remedies to apply when they appear to be invalid. Fortunately, the assumptions need not hold exactly in order for least squares estimators to be useful. The assumptions will be satisfied adequately for many applications encountered in practice.

It seems reasonable to assume that the greater the variability of the random error ε (which is measured by its variance σ^2), the greater will be the errors in the estimation of the model parameters β_0 and β_1 and in the error of prediction when $\hat{y}$ is used to predict y for some value of x. Consequently, you should not be surprised, as we proceed through this chapter, to find that σ^2 appears in the formulas for all confidence intervals and test statistics that we will be using.

In most practical situations, σ^2 is unknown, and we must use our data to estimate its value. The best estimate of σ^2, denoted by s^2, is obtained by dividing the sum of squares of the deviations of the y values from the prediction line,

$$\text{SSE} = \sum (y_i - \hat{y}_i)^2$$

by the number of degrees of freedom associated with this quantity. We use 2 df to estimate the two parameters β_0 and β_1 in the straight-line model, leaving $(n - 2)$ df for the error variance estimation.

> **Estimation of σ^2 for a (First-Order) Straight-Line Model**
>
> $$s^2 = \frac{SSE}{\text{Degrees of freedom for error}} = \frac{SSE}{n-2}$$
>
> where $SSE = \Sigma(y_i - \hat{y}_i)^2 = SS_{yy} - \hat{\beta}_1 SS_{xy}$
>
> $$SS_{yy} = \Sigma(y_i - \bar{y})^2 *$$
>
> To estimate the standard deviation σ of ε, we calculate
>
> $$s = \sqrt{s^2} = \sqrt{\frac{SSE}{n-2}}$$
>
> We will refer to s as the **estimated standard error of the regression model.**

> ⚠️ **CAUTION** When performing these calculations, you may be tempted to round the calculated values of SS_{yy}, $\hat{\beta}_1$, and SS_{xy}. Be certain to carry at least six significant figures for each of these quantities to avoid substantial errors in calculation of the SSE.

Example	2

Estimating σ — Advertising-Sales Regression

Problem Refer to Example 1 and the simple linear regression of the advertising-sales data in Table 1.

a. Compute an estimate of σ.

b. Give a practical interpretation of the estimate.

Solution

a. We previously calculated $SSE = 1.10$ for the least squares line $\hat{y} = -.1 + .7x$. Recalling that there were $n = 5$ data points, we have $n - 2 = 5 - 2 = 3$ df for estimating σ^2. Thus,

$$s^2 = \frac{SSE}{n-2} = \frac{1.10}{3} = .367$$

is the estimated variance, and

$$s = \sqrt{.367} = .61$$

is the standard error of the regression model.

b. You may be able to grasp s intuitively by recalling the interpretation of a standard deviation and remembering that the least squares line estimates the mean value of y for a given value of x. Because s measures the spread of the distribution of y values about the least squares line, we should not be surprised to find that most of the observations lie within $2s$, or $2(.61) = 1.22$, of the least squares line. For this simple example (only five data points), all five sales revenue values fall within $2s$ (or \$1,220) of the least squares line. In Section 6, we use s to evaluate the error of prediction when the least squares line is used to predict a value of y to be observed for a given value of x.

Look Back The values of s^2 and s can also be obtained from a simple linear regression printout. The Minitab printout for the advertising-sales example is reproduced in Figure 10. The value of s^2 is highlighted at the bottom of the printout in the

*Alternatively, you can use the following "shortcut" formula:

$$SS_{yy} = \Sigma y^2 - \frac{(\Sigma y)^2}{n}$$

Regression Analysis: SALES_Y versus ADVEXP_X

```
The regression equation is
SALES_Y = - 0.100 + 0.700 ADVEXP_X


Predictor      Coef  SE Coef       T      P
Constant    -0.1000   0.6351   -0.16  0.885
ADVEXP_X     0.7000   0.1915    3.66  0.035


S = 0.605530    R-Sq = 81.7%    R-Sq(adj) = 75.6%


Analysis of Variance

Source          DF      SS      MS      F      P
Regression       1  4.9000  4.9000  13.36  0.035
Residual Error   3  1.1000  0.3667
Total            4  6.0000
```

Figure 10

Minitab printout for the advertising-sales regression

MS (Mean Square) column in the row labeled **Residual Error.** (In regression, the estimate of σ^2 is called Mean Square for Error, or MSE.) The value, $s^2 = .3667$, agrees with the one calculated by hand. The value of s is also highlighted in Figure 10. This value, $s = .60553$, agrees (except for rounding) with our hand-calculated value.

Now Work Exercise 32

Interpretation of s, the Estimated Standard Deviation of ε

We expect most ($\approx 95\%$) of the observed y values to lie within $2s$ of their respective least squares predicted values, $\hat{y}$.

Exercises 27–40

Please be aware that some of the following problems may require knowledge of concepts that are not presented in this chapter.

Learning the Mechanics

27 Visually compare the scatterplots shown below. If a least squares line were determined for each data set, which do you think would have the smallest variance, s^2? Explain.

28 Calculate SSE and s^2 for each of the following cases:
a. $n = 20$, $SS_{yy} = 95$, $SS_{xy} = 50$, $\hat{\beta}_1 = .75$
b. $n = 40$, $\Sigma y^2 = 860$, $\Sigma y = 50$, $SS_{xy} = 2,700$, $\hat{\beta}_1 = .2$
c. $n = 10$, $\Sigma(y_i - \bar{y})^2 = 58$, $SS_{xy} = 91$, $SS_{xx} = 170$

29 Suppose you fit a least squares line to 26 data points and the calculated value of SSE is 8.34.
a. Find s^2, the estimator of σ^2 (the variance of the random error term ε).
b. What is the largest deviation that you might expect between any one of the 26 points and the least squares line?

30 Refer to Exercise 10. Calculate SSE, s^2, and s for the least squares line. Use the value of s to determine where most of the errors of prediction lie.

a.
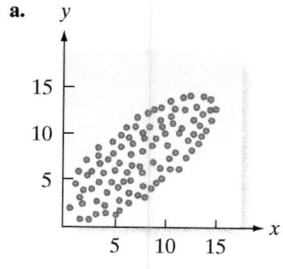

b.
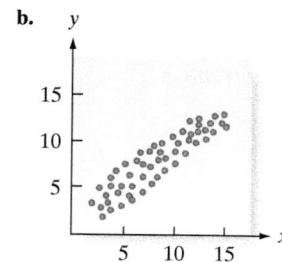

c.
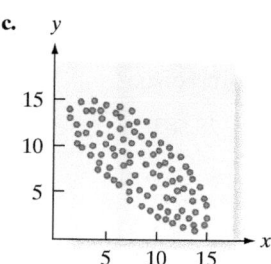

Scatterplots for Exercise 27

Applying the Concepts—Basic

31 Do nice guys really finish last in business? Refer to the *Nature* (March 20, 2008) study of whether "nice guys finish last" in business, Exercise 14. Recall that college students repeatedly played a version of the game "prisoner's dilemma," where competitors choose cooperation, defection, or costly punishment. At the conclusion of the games, the researchers recorded the average payoff and the number of times punishment was used for each player. Based on a scatterplot of the data, the simple linear regression relating average payoff (y) to punishment use (x) resulted in SSE = 1.04.

   a. Assuming a sample size of $n = 28$, compute the estimated standard deviation of the error distribution, s.

   b. Give a practical interpretation of s.

32 State Math SAT scores. Refer to the simple linear regression relating $y = 2011$ Math SAT scores to $x = 2001$ Math SAT scores, Exercise 15. A portion of the SPSS printout of the analysis is shown below.

   a. Locate the values of SSE, s^2, and s on the SPSS printout.

Model Summary

Model	R	R Square	Adjusted R Square	Std. Error of the Estimate
1	.959[a]	.921	.919	11.912

a. Predictors: (Constant), MATH2001

ANOVA[a]

Model		Sum of Squares	df	Mean Square	F	Sig.
1	Regression	80575.988	1	80575.988	567.864	.000[b]
	Residual	6952.757	49	141.893		
	Total	87528.745	50			

a. Dependent Variable: MATH2011
b. Predictors: (Constant), MATH2001

   b. Give a practical interpretation of the value of s.

33 Drug controlled-release rate study. Refer to the simple linear regression relating the drug release rate (y) to surface area-to-volume ratio (x), Exercise 17.

   a. Find the value of s for the straight-line model fit in Exercise 17a.

   b. Give a practical interpretation of the value of s.

34 Structurally deficient highway bridges. Data was compiled on structurally deficient highway bridges by the Federal Highway Administration (FHWA) into the National Bridge Inventory (NBI). For each state, the NBI lists the number of structurally deficient bridges and the total area (thousands of square feet) of the deficient bridges. The data for the 50 states (plus the District of Columbia and Puerto Rico) are saved in the file. (The first five and last five observations are listed in the table in the next column.) For

State	Number	Area (thousands of sq. ft.)
Alabama	1,899	432.7
Alaska	155	60.9
Arizona	181	110.5
Arkansas	997	347.3
California	3,140	5,177.9
⋮	⋮	⋮
Washington	400	502.0
West Virginia	1,058	331.5
Wisconsin	1,302	399.8
Wyoming	389	143.4
Puerto Rico	241	195.4

future planning and budgeting, the FHWA wants to estimate the total area of structurally deficient bridges in a state based on the number of deficient bridges.

   a. Write the equation of a straight-line model relating total area (y) to number of structurally deficient bridges (x).

   b. The model, part **a,** was fit to the data using Minitab, as shown below. Find the least squares prediction equation on the printout.

   c. List the assumptions required for the regression analysis.

   d. Locate the estimated standard error of the regression model, s, on the printout.

   e. Use the value of s to find a range where most (about 95%) of the errors of prediction will fall.

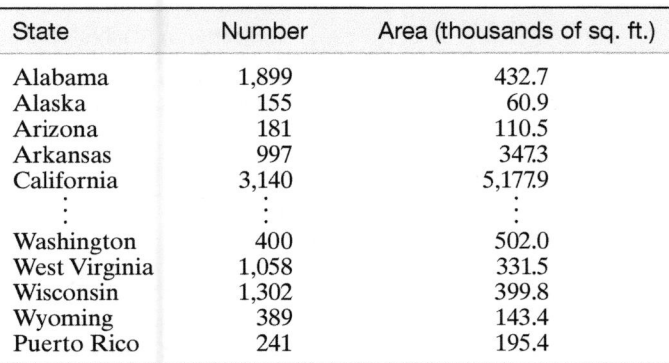

```
Regression Analysis: SDArea versus NumberSD

The regression equation is
SDArea = 120 + 0.346 NumberSD


Predictor    Coef    SE Coef     T      P
Constant     119.9    123.0    0.97   0.335
NumberSD    0.34560  0.06158   5.61   0.000


S = 635.187    R-Sq = 38.7%    R-Sq(adj) = 37.4%


Analysis of Variance

Source          DF       SS         MS       F       P
Regression       1    12710141   12710141   31.50   0.000
Residual Error  50    20173111    403462
Total           51    32883252
```

35 Software millionaires and birthdays. Refer to Exercise 19 and the study of software millionaires and their birthdays. The data are reproduced below.

   a. Find SSE, s^2, and s for the simple linear regression model relating number (y) of software millionaire birthdays in a decade to total number (x) of U.S. births.

Data for Exercise 35

Decade	Total U.S. Births (millions)	Number of Software Millionaire Birthdays	Number of CEO Birthdays (in a random sample of 70 companies from the *Fortune* 500 list)
1920	28.582	3	2
1930	24.374	1	2
1940	31.666	10	23
1950	40.530	14	38
1960	38.808	7	9
1970	33.309	4	0

Source: Sauro, J. "Were most software millionaires born around 1955?" *Measuring Usability,* November 17, 2010. Copyright © 2010 by Measuring Usability LLC. Reprinted with permission.

b. Find SSE, s^2, and s for the simple linear regression model relating number (y) of software millionaire birthdays in a decade to number (x) of CEO birthdays.

c. Which of the two models' fit will have smaller errors of prediction? Why?

Applying the Concepts—Intermediate

36 Public corruption and bad weather. Refer to the *Journal of Law and Economics* (Nov. 2008) study of the link between Federal Emergency Management Agency (FEMA) disaster relief and public corruption, Exercise 20. You used the data in the file to fit a straight-line model relating a state's average annual number of public corruption convictions (y) to the state's average annual FEMA relief (x).

a. Estimate σ^2, the variance of the random error term in the model.

b. Estimate σ, the standard deviation of the random error term in the model.

c. Which of the estimates, part **a** or **b**, can be interpreted practically? Why?

d. Make a statement about how accurate the model is in predicting a state's average annual number of public corruption convictions.

37 Sweetness of orange juice. Refer to the study of the quality of orange juice produced at a juice manufacturing plant, Exercise 22. Recall that simple linear regression was used to predict the sweetness index (y) from the amount of pectin (x) in the orange juice.

a. Find the values of SSE, s^2, and s for this regression.

b. Explain why it is difficult to give a practical interpretation to s^2.

c. Give a practical interpretation of the value of s.

38 Are geography journals worth their cost? *Geoforum* (Vol. 37, 2006) did a study of whether the price of a geography journal is correlated with quality. Several quantitative variables were recorded for each in a sample of 28 geography journals: cost of a 1-year subscription (dollars); Journal Impact Factor (JIF)—the average number of times articles from the journal have been cited; number of citations for the journal over the past 5 years; and Relative Price Index (RPI). The data for the 28 journals are saved in the file. (Selected observations are listed below.)

Journal	Cost ($)	JIF	Cites	RPI
J. Econ. Geogr.	468	3.139	207	1.16
Prog. Hum. Geog.	624	2.943	544	0.77
T. I. Brit. Geogr.	499	2.388	249	1.11
Econ. Geogr.	90	2.325	173	0.30
A. A. A. Geogr.	698	2.115	377	0.93
Geogr. Anal.	213	0.902	106	0.88
Geogr. J.	223	0.857	81	0.94
Appl. Geogr.	646	0.853	74	3.38

Source: Based on Blomley, N. "Is this journal worth US$1118?" *Geoforum,* Vol. 37, 2006.

a. Fit a straight-line model relating cost (y) to JIF (x). Find an estimate of σ, the standard deviation of the error term, and interpret its value.

b. Fit a straight-line model relating cost (y) to number of citations (x). Find an estimate of σ, the standard deviation of the error term, and interpret its value.

c. Fit a straight-line model relating cost (y) to RPI (x). Find an estimate of σ, the standard deviation of the error term, and interpret its value.

d. Which predictor of cost—JIF, number of citations, or RPI—leads to a regression line with the smallest errors of prediction?

39 FCAT scores and poverty. Refer to the *Journal of Educational and Behavioral Statistics* (Spring 2004) study of scores on the Florida Comprehensive Assessment Test (FCAT), Exercise 24.

a. Consider the simple linear regression relating math score (y) to percentage (x) of students below the poverty level. Find and interpret the value of s for this regression.

b. Consider the simple linear regression relating reading score (y) to percentage (x) of students below the poverty level. Find and interpret the value of s for this regression.

c. Which dependent variable, math score or reading score, can be more accurately predicted by percentage (x) of students below the poverty level? Explain.

Applying the Concepts—Advanced

40 Life tests of cutting tools. To improve the quality of the output of any production process, it is necessary first to understand the capabilities of the process (Gitlow, et al., *Quality Management: Tools and Methods for Improvement,* 1995). In a particular manufacturing process, the useful life of a cutting tool is related to the speed at which the tool is operated. The data in the table below were derived from life tests for the two different brands of cutting tools currently used in the production process. For which brand would you feel more confident in using the least squares line to predict useful life for a given cutting speed? Explain.

Cutting Speed (meters per minute)	Useful Life (Hours) Brand A	Brand B
30	4.5	6.0
30	3.5	6.5
30	5.2	5.0
40	5.2	6.0
40	4.0	4.5
40	2.5	5.0
50	4.4	4.5
50	2.8	4.0
50	1.0	3.7
60	4.0	3.8
60	2.0	3.0
60	1.1	2.4
70	1.1	1.5
70	.5	2.0
70	3.0	1.0

4 Assessing the Utility of the Model: Making Inferences about the Slope β_1

Now that we have specified the probability distribution of ε and found an estimate of the variance σ^2, we are ready to make statistical inferences about the model's usefulness for predicting the response y. This is step 4 in our regression modeling procedure.

Refer again to the data of Table 1 and suppose the appliance store's sales revenue is *completely unrelated* to the advertising expenditure. What could be said about the values of β_0 and β_1 in the hypothesized probabilistic model

$$y = \beta_0 + \beta_1 x + \varepsilon$$

if x contributes no information for the prediction of y? The implication is that the mean of y—that is, the deterministic part of the model $E(y) = \beta_0 + \beta_1 x$—does not change as x changes. In the straight-line model, this means that the true slope, β_1, is equal to 0 (see Figure 11). Therefore, to test the null hypothesis that the linear model contributes no information for the prediction of y against the alternative hypothesis that the linear model is useful in predicting y, we test

$$H_0: \beta_1 = 0 \text{ against } H_a: \beta_1 \neq 0$$

Figure 11

Graph of the straight-line model when slope is zero, i.e., $y = \beta_0 + \varepsilon$

If the data support the alternative hypothesis, we will conclude that x does contribute information for the prediction of y using the straight-line model (although the true relationship between $E[y]$ and x could be more complex than a straight line). Thus, in effect, this is a test of the usefulness of the hypothesized model.

The appropriate test statistic is found by considering the sampling distribution of $\hat{\beta}_1$, the least squares estimator of the slope β_1, as shown in the following box.

Sampling Distribution of $\hat{\beta}_1$

If we make the four assumptions about ε (see Section 3), the sampling distribution of the least squares estimator $\hat{\beta}_1$ of the slope will be normal with mean β_1 (the true slope) and standard deviation

$$\sigma_{\hat{\beta}_1} = \frac{\sigma}{\sqrt{SS_{xx}}} \quad \text{(see Figure 12)}$$

We estimate $\sigma_{\hat{\beta}_1}$ by $s_{\hat{\beta}_1} = \frac{s}{\sqrt{SS_{xx}}}$ and refer to this quantity as the **estimated standard error of the least squares slope $\hat{\beta}_1$.**

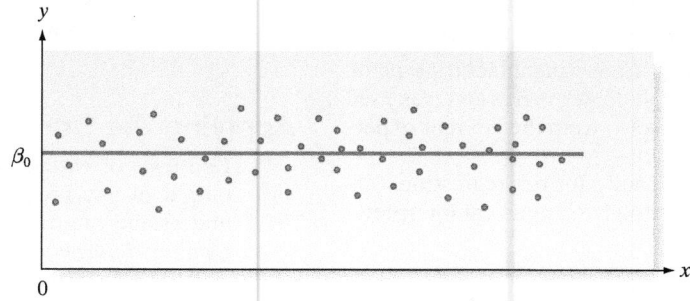

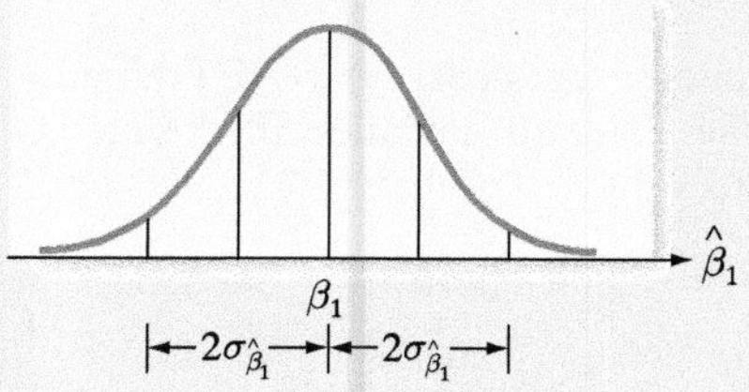

Figure 12

Sampling distribution of $\hat{\beta}_1$

Because σ is usually unknown, the appropriate test statistic is a t-statistic, formed as follows:

$$t = \frac{\hat{\beta}_1 - \text{Hypothesized value of } \beta_1}{s_{\hat{\beta}_1}} \qquad \text{where } s_{\hat{\beta}} = \frac{s}{\sqrt{\text{SS}_{xx}}}$$

Thus,

$$t = \frac{\hat{\beta}_1 - 0}{s/\sqrt{\text{SS}_{xx}}}$$

Note that we have substituted the estimator s for σ and then formed the estimated standard error $s_{\hat{\beta}_1}$ by dividing s by $\sqrt{\text{SS}_{xx}}$. The number of degrees of freedom associated with this t-statistic is the same as the number of degrees of freedom associated with s. Recall that this number is $(n - 2)$ df when the hypothesized model is a straight line (see Section 3). The setup of our test of the usefulness of the straight-line model is summarized in the following boxes.

A Test of Model Utility: Simple Linear Regression

One-Tailed Test	Two-Tailed Test
$H_0: \beta_1 = 0$	$H_0: \beta_1 = 0$
$H_a: \beta_1 < 0 \text{ (or } H_a: \beta_1 > 0)$	$H_a: \beta_1 \neq 0$

$$\text{Test statistic: } t = \frac{\hat{\beta}_1}{s_{\hat{\beta}_1}} = \frac{\hat{\beta}_1}{s/\sqrt{\text{SS}_{xx}}}$$

Rejection region: $t < -t_\alpha$ Rejection region: $|t| > t_{\alpha/2}$
(or $t > t_\alpha$ when $H_a: \beta_1 > 0$)

where t_α and $t_{\alpha/2}$ are based on $(n - 2)$ degrees of freedom

---

Conditions Required for a Valid Test: Simple Linear Regression

Refer to the four assumptions about ε listed in Section 3.

Example	3

Testing the Regression Slope, β_1—Sales Revenue Model

Problem Refer to the simple linear regression analysis of the advertising-sales data, Examples 1 and 2. Conduct a test (at $\alpha = .05$) to determine if sales revenue (y) is linearly related to advertising expenditure (x).

Solution As stated previously, we want to test $H_0: \beta_1 = 0$ against $H_a: \beta_1 \neq 0$. For this example, $n = 5$. Thus t will be based on $n - 2 = 3$ df, and the rejection region (at $\alpha = .05$) will be

$$|t| > t_{.025} = 3.182$$

We previously calculated $\hat{\beta}_1 = .7$, $s = .61$, and $\text{SS}_{xx} = 10$. Thus, the test statistic is

$$t = \frac{\hat{\beta}_1}{s/\sqrt{\text{SS}_{xx}}} = \frac{.7}{.61/\sqrt{10}} = \frac{.7}{.19} = 3.7$$

Because this calculated t-value falls into the upper-tail rejection region (see Figure 13), we reject the null hypothesis and conclude that the slope β_1 is not 0. The sample evidence indicates that advertising expenditure x contributes information for the production of sales revenue y when a linear model is used.

[*Note:* We can reach the same conclusion by using the observed significance level (p-value) of the test from a computer printout. The Minitab printout for the advertising-sales example is reproduced in Figure 14. The test statistic and *two-tailed p*-value are highlighted on the printout. Because the *p*-value is smaller than $\alpha = .05$, we will reject H_0.]

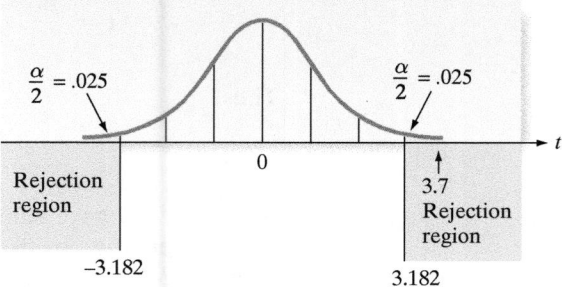

Figure 13

Rejection region and calculated *t*-value for testing $H_0: \beta_1 = 0$ versus $H_a: \beta_1 \neq 0$

Regression Analysis: SALES_Y versus ADVEXP_X

```
The regression equation is
SALES_Y = - 0.100 + 0.700 ADVEXP_X


Predictor      Coef   SE Coef       T      P
Constant    -0.1000    0.6351   -0.16  0.885
ADVEXP_X     0.7000    0.1915    3.66  0.035


S = 0.605530   R-Sq = 81.7%   R-Sq(adj) = 75.6%


Analysis of Variance

Source          DF       SS      MS      F      P
Regression       1   4.9000  4.9000  13.36  0.035
Residual Error   3   1.1000  0.3667
Total            4   6.0000
```

Figure 14

Minitab printout for the advertising-sales regression

Look Back What conclusion can be drawn if the calculated *t*-value does not fall in the rejection region or if the observed significance level of the test exceeds α? We know from previous discussions of the philosophy of hypothesis testing that such a *t*-value does *not* lead us to accept the null hypothesis—that is, we do not conclude that $\beta_1 = 0$. Additional data might indicate that β_1 differs from 0, or a more complex relationship may exist between x and y, requiring the fitting of a model other than the straight-line model.

Now Work Exercise 46

Interpreting *p*-Values for β Coefficients in Regression

Almost all statistical computer software packages report a *two-tailed p*-value for each of the β parameters in the regression model. For example, in simple linear regression, the *p*-value for the two-tailed test $H_0: \beta_1 = 0$ versus $H_a: \beta_1 \neq 0$ is given on the printout. If you want to conduct a *one-tailed* test of hypothesis, you will need to adjust the *p*-value reported on the printout as follows:

$$\text{Upper-tailed test } (H_a: \beta_1 > 0): \quad p\text{-value} = \begin{cases} p/2 & \text{if } t > 0 \\ 1 - p/2 & \text{if } t < 0 \end{cases}$$

$$\text{Lower-tailed test } (H_a: \beta_1 < 0): \quad p\text{-value} = \begin{cases} p/2 & \text{if } t < 0 \\ 1 - p/2 & \text{if } t > 0 \end{cases}$$

where p is the *p*-value reported on the printout and t is the value of the test statistic.

Another way to make inferences about the slope β_1 is to estimate it using a confidence interval. This interval is formed as shown in the next box.

A 100(1 − α)% Confidence Interval for the Simple Linear Regression Slope β_1

$$\hat{\beta}_1 \pm t_{\alpha/2}s_{\hat{\beta}_1}$$

where the estimated standard error $\hat{\beta}_1$ is calculated by

$$s_{\hat{\beta}_1} = \frac{s}{\sqrt{SS_{xx}}}$$

and $t_{\alpha/2}$ is based on $(n − 2)$ degrees of freedom.

Conditions Required for a Valid Confidence Interval: Simple Linear Regression

Refer to the four assumptions about ϵ listed in Section 3.

For the simple linear regression of sales revenue (Examples 1–3), $t_{\alpha/2}$ is based on $(n − 2) = 3$ degrees of freedom, and, for $\alpha = .05$, $t_{.025} = 3.182$. Therefore, a 95% confidence interval for the slope β_1, the expected change in sales revenue for a $100 increase in advertising expenditure, is

$$\hat{\beta}_1 \pm (t_{.025})s_{\hat{\beta}_1} = .7 \pm 3.182\left(\frac{s}{\sqrt{SS_{xx}}}\right) = .7 \pm 3.182\left(\frac{.61}{\sqrt{10}}\right) = .7 \pm .61$$

Thus, the interval estimate of the slope parameter β_1 is .09 to 1.31. [*Note:* This interval can also be obtained using statistical software and is highlighted on the SPSS printout, Figure 15.] In terms of this example, the implication is that we can be 95% confident that the *true* mean increase in monthly sales revenue per additional $100 of advertising expenditure is between $90 and $1,310. This inference is meaningful only over the sampled range of x—that is, from $100 to $500 of advertising expenditures.

Figure 15

SPSS printout with 95% confidence intervals for the advertising-sales regression β's

Coefficients[a]

Model		Unstandardized Coefficients B	Unstandardized Coefficients Std. Error	Standardized Coefficients Beta	t	Sig.	95% Confidence Interval for B Lower Bound	95% Confidence Interval for B Upper Bound
1	(Constant)	−.100	.635		−.157	.885	−2.121	1.921
	ADVEXP_X	.700	.191	.904	3.656	.035	.091	1.309

a. Dependent Variable: SALES_Y

Because all the values in this interval are positive, it appears that β_1 is positive and that the mean of y, $E(y)$, increases as x increases. However, the rather large width of the confidence interval reflects the small number of data points (and, consequently, a lack of information) in the experiment. Particularly bothersome is the fact that the lower end of the confidence interval implies that we are not even recovering our additional expenditure because a $100 increase in advertising may produce as little as a $90 increase in mean sales. If we wish to tighten this interval, we need to increase the sample size.

STATISTICS in ACTION REVISITED

Assessing How Well a Straight-Line Regression Model Fits Data

In the previous *Statistics in Action Revisited*, we fit the straight-line model, $E(y) = \beta_0 + \beta_1 x$, where x = cumulative 6-month advertising expenditures and y represents either the number of new PI cases or the number of new WC cases per month. The SPSS regression printouts for the two analyses are shown in Figure SIA3. (The regression for y = number of new PI cases is shown at the top, and the regression for y = number of new WC cases is shown at the bottom of the printout.) The objective is to determine whether one or both of the dependent variables are statistically linearly related to cumulative 6-month advertising expenditures.

The two-tailed p-values for testing the null hypothesis, H_0: $\beta_1 = 0$ (highlighted on the printouts), are p-value ≈ 0 for number of new PI cases and p-value $= .725$ for number

Coefficients[a]

Model		Unstandardized Coefficients		Standardized Coefficients	t	Sig.	95% Confidence Interval for B	
		B	Std. Error	Beta			Lower Bound	Upper Bound
1	(Constant)	7.767	3.385		2.295	.027	.926	14.609
	CUM. ADV (thous)	.113	.028	.539	4.042	.000	.056	.169

a. Dependent Variable: New PI Cases

Coefficients[a]

Model		Unstandardized Coefficients		Standardized Coefficients	t	Sig.	95% Confidence Interval for B	
		B	Std. Error	Beta			Lower Bound	Upper Bound
1	(Constant)	24.574	3.367		7.299	.000	17.770	31.379
	CUM. ADV (thous)	.010	.028	.056	.354	.725	−.046	.066

a. Dependent Variable: New WC Cases

Figure SIA3

SPSS simple linear regressions for legal advertising data

of new WC cases. For y = number of new PI cases, there is sufficient evidence to reject H_0 (at $\alpha = .01$) and conclude that number of new PI cases is linearly related to cumulative 6-month advertising expenditures. In contrast, for y = number of WC cases, there is insufficient evidence to reject H_0 (at $\alpha = .01$); thus, there is no evidence of a linear relationship between the number of new WC cases and cumulative 6-month advertising expenditures.

We can gain further insight into this phenomenon by examining a 95% confidence interval for the slope, β_1. For y = number of new PI cases, the interval (highlighted on the SPSS printout) is (.056, .169). With 95% confidence, we can state that for every $1,000 increase in monthly advertising expenditures, the number of new PI cases each month will increase between .056 and .169. Now, a more realistic increase in cumulative 6-month advertising expenditures is, say, $20,000. Multiplying the endpoints of the interval by 20, we see that this increase in advertising spending leads to an increase of anywhere between 1 and 3 new PI cases.

Now, for y = number of new WC cases, the 95% confidence interval for the slope (also highlighted on the SPSS printout) is (−.046, .066). Because the interval spans the value 0, we draw the same conclusion as we did with the hypothesis test—there is no statistical evidence of a linear relationship between the number of new WC cases and cumulative 6-month advertising expenditures.

Recall that partner A (who handled the PI cases) sued partner B (who handled the WC cases) for not paying a fair share of the advertising expenses. These results do not support partner A's argument because there is no evidence that partner B benefitted from advertising.

Exercises 41–58

Please be aware that some of the following problems may require knowledge of concepts that are not presented in this chapter.

Learning the Mechanics

41 Construct both a 95% and a 90% confidence interval for β_1 for each of the following cases:
a. $\hat{\beta}_1 = 31, s = 3, SS_{xx} = 35, n = 10$
b. $\hat{\beta}_1 = 64, SSE = 1,960, SS_{xx} = 30, n = 14$
c. $\hat{\beta}_1 = -8.4, SSE = 146, SS_{xx} = 64, n = 20$

42 Consider the following pairs of observations:

L11042

x	1	4	3	2	5	6	0
y	1	3	3	1	4	7	2

a. Construct a scatterplot for the data.
b. Use the method of least squares to fit a straight line to the seven data points in the table.
c. Plot the least squares line on your scatterplot of part **a.**
d. Specify the null and alternative hypotheses you would use to test whether the data provide sufficient evidence

to indicate that x contributes information for the (linear) prediction of y.
e. What is the test statistic that should be used in conducting the hypothesis test of part **d?** Specify the degrees of freedom associated with the test statistic.
f. Conduct the hypothesis test of part **d** using $\alpha = .05$.

43 Refer to Exercise 42. Construct an 80% and a 98% confidence interval for β_1.

44 Do the accompanying data provide sufficient evidence to conclude that a straight line is useful for characterizing the relationship between x and y?

L11044

x	4	2	4	3	2	4
y	1	6	5	3	2	4

Applying the Concepts—Basic

45 State Math SAT Scores. Refer to the SPSS simple linear regression relating y = average state SAT Math score in 2011 with x = average state SAT Math score in 2001, Exercise 15.

SATMAT

a. Give the null and alternative hypotheses for determining whether a positive linear relationship exists between y and x.

b. Locate the p-value of the test on the SPSS printout. Interpret the result if $\alpha = .05$.

c. Find a 95% confidence interval for the slope, β_1. Interpret the result.

46 Lobster fishing study. Refer to the *Bulletin of Marine Science* (April 2010) study of teams of fishermen fishing for the red spiny lobster in Baja California Sur, Mexico, Exercise 16. A simple linear regression model relating y = total catch of lobsters (in kilograms) and x = average percentage of traps allocated per day to exploring areas of unknown catch (called *search frequency*) was fit to the data in the file. A portion of the XLSTAT printout is reproduced at the bottom of the page.

TRAPS

a. Give the null and alternative hypotheses for testing whether total catch (y) is negatively linearly related to search frequency (x).

b. Find the p-value of the test on the XLSTAT printout.

c. Give the appropriate conclusion of the test, part **c**, using $\alpha = .05$.

47 Congress voting on women's issues. The *American Economic Review* (March 2008) published research on how the gender mix of a U.S. legislator's children can influence the legislator's votes in Congress. Specifically, the researcher investigated how having daughters influences voting on women's issues. The American Association of University Women (AAUW) uses voting records of each member of Congress to compute an AAUW score, where higher scores indicate more favorable voting for women's rights. The researcher modeled AAUW score (y) as a function of the number of daughters (x) a legislator has. Data collected for the 434 members of the 107th Congress were used to fit the straight-line model, $E(y) = \beta_0 + \beta_1 x$.

a. If it is true that having daughters influences voting on women's issues, will the sign of β_1 be positive or negative? Explain.

b. The following statistics were reported in the article: $\hat{\beta}_1 = .27$ and $s_{\hat{\beta}_1} = .74$. Find a 95% confidence interval for β_1.

c. Use the result, part **b,** to make an inference about the model.

48 Generation Y's entitlement mentality. The current workforce is dominated by "Generation Y"—people born between 1982 and 1999. These workers have a reputation as having an entitlement mentality (e.g., they believe they have a right to a high-paying job, without the work ethic). The reasons behind this phenomenon were investigated in *Proceedings of the Academy of Educational Leadership* (Vol. 16, 2011). A sample of 272 undergraduate business students was administered a questionnaire designed to capture the behaviors that lead to an entitlement mentality. The responses were used to measure the following two quantitative variables for each student: entitlement score (y)—where higher scores indicate a greater level of entitlement, and "helicopter parents" score (x)—where higher scores indicate that the student's parents had a higher level of involvement in his or her everyday experiences and problems.

a. Give the equation of a simple linear regression model relating y to x.

b. The researchers theorize that helicopter parents lead to an entitlement mentality. Based on this theory, would you expect β_0 to be positive or negative (or are you unsure)? Would you expect β_1 to be positive or negative (or are you unsure)? Explain.

c. The p-value for testing $H_0: \beta_1 = 0$ versus $H_a: \beta_1 > 0$ was reported as .002. Use this result to test the researchers' entitlement theory at $\alpha = .01$.

49 Drug controlled-release rate study. Refer to the simple linear regression analysis relating y = drug release rate to x = surface-area-to-volume ratio, Exercise 17. Use the results of the regression to form a 90% confidence interval for the slope, β_1. Interpret the result.

DOW

50 Sweetness of orange juice. Refer to the simple linear regression relating y = sweetness index of an orange juice sample with x = amount of water-soluble pectin, Exercise 22. Use the results of the regression to form a 95% confidence interval for the slope, β_1. Interpret the result.

OJUICE

Applying the Concepts—Intermediate

51 Software millionaires and birthdays. Refer to Exercise 19 and the study of whether birth decade can predict the number of software millionaires born in the decade. The data are reproduced in the next table.

BDAYS

Model parameters:

Source	Value	Standard error	t	Pr > |t|	Lower bound (95%)	Upper bound (95%)
Intercept	9877.8300	829.0411	11.9148	< 0.0001	8086.7957	11668.8643
SEARCHFR	–163.6024	41.9014	–3.9045	0.0018	–254.1249	–73.0799

Equation of the model:

CATCH = 9877.82997–163.60242*SEARCHFREQ

XLSTAT output for Exercise 46

Data for Exercise 51

Decade	Total U.S. Births (millions)	Number of Software Millionaire Birthdays	Number of CEO Birthdays (in a random sample of 70 companies from the *Fortune* 500 list)
1920	28.582	3	2
1930	24.374	1	2
1940	31.666	10	23
1950	40.530	14	38
1960	38.808	7	9
1970	33.309	4	0

Source: Sauro, J. "Were most software millionaires born around 1955?" *Measuring Usability,* November 17, 2010. Copyright © 2010 by Measuring Usability LLC. Reprinted with permission.

a. Construct a 95% confidence interval for the slope of the model, $E(y) = \beta_0 + \beta_1 x$, where x = total number of U.S. births and y = number of software millionaire birthdays. Give a practical interpretation of the interval.

b. Construct a 95% confidence interval for the slope of the model, $E(y) = \beta_0 + \beta_1 x$, where x = number of CEO birthdays (in a sample of 70 companies) and y = number of software millionaire birthdays. Give a practical interpretation of the interval.

c. Can you conclude that number of software millionaires born in a decade is linearly related to total number of people born in the United States? Number of CEOs born in the decade?

52 Beauty and electoral success. Are good looks an advantage when running for political office? This was the question of interest in an article published in the *Journal of Public Economics* (Feb. 2010). The researchers focused on a sample of 641 nonincumbent candidates for political office in Finland. Photos of each candidate were evaluated by non-Finnish subjects; each evaluator assigned a beauty rating—measured on a scale of 1 (lowest rating) to 5 (highest rating)—to each candidate. The beauty ratings for each candidate were averaged, then the average was divided by the standard deviation for all candidates to yield a beauty index for each candidate. (*Note:* A 1-unit increase in the index represents a 1-standard-deviation increase in the beauty rating.) The relative success (measured as a percentage of votes obtained) of each candidate was used as the dependent variable (y) in a regression analysis. One of the independent variables in the model was beauty index (x).

a. Write the equation of a simple linear regression relating y to x.

b. Does the y-intercept of the equation, part **a**, have a practical interpretation? Explain.

c. The article reported the estimated slope of the equation, part **a**, as 22.91. Give a practical interpretation of this value.

d. The standard error of the slope estimate was reported as 3.73. Use this information and the estimate from part **c** to conduct a test for a positive slope at $\alpha = .01$. Give the appropriate conclusion in the words of the problem.

53 Ranking driving performance of professional golfers. Refer to *The Sport Journal* (Winter 2007) study of a new method for ranking the total driving performance of golfers on the PGA tour, Exercise 21. You fit a straight-line model relating driving accuracy (y) to driving distance (x) to the data saved in the file.

a. Give the null and alternative hypotheses for testing whether driving accuracy (y) decreases linearly as driving distance (x) increases.

b. Find the test statistic and p-value of the test, part **a**.

c. Make the appropriate conclusion at $\alpha = .01$.

54 Are geography journals worth their cost? Refer to the *Geoforum* (Vol. 37, 2006) study of whether the price of a geography journal is correlated with quality, Exercise 38.

a. In Exercise 38a, you fit a straight-line model relating cost (y) to JIF (x). Find and interpret a 95% confidence interval for the slope of the line.

b. In Exercise 38b, you fit a straight-line model relating cost (y) to number of citations (x). Find and interpret a 95% confidence interval for the slope of the line.

c. In Exercise 38c, you fit a straight-line model relating cost (y) to RPI (x). Find and interpret a 95% confidence interval for the slope of the line.

55 Survey of the top business schools. Refer to the *Wall Street Journal* (Sep. 25, 2005) Business School Survey, Exercise 25. If you pay more in tuition to go to a top business school, will it necessarily result in a higher probability of a job offer at graduation? Let y = percentage of graduates with job offers and x = tuition cost; then fit the simple linear model, $E(y) = \beta_0 + \beta_1 x$, to the data in the file. Is there sufficient evidence (at $\alpha = .10$) of a positive linear relationship between y and x?

56 Public corruption and bad weather. Refer to the *Journal of Law and Economics* (Nov. 2008) study of the link between Federal Emergency Management Agency (FEMA) disaster relief and public corruption, Exercise 20 and 36. Evaluate the overall adequacy of the straight-line model relating a state's average annual number of public corruption convictions (y) to the state's average annual FEMA relief (x). Use $\alpha = .01$.

Applying the Concepts—Advanced

57 Does elevation impact hitting performance in baseball? *Chance* (Winter 2006) did an investigation of the effects of elevation on slugging percentage in Major League Baseball. Data were compiled on players' composite slugging percentage at each of 29 cities for a recent season, as well as each city's elevation (feet above sea level). The data are saved in the file. (Selected observations are shown in the table on the following page.) Consider a straight-line model relating slugging percentage (y) to elevation (x).

a. Is there sufficient evidence (at $\alpha = .01$) of a positive linear relationship between elevation (x) and slugging percentage (y)?

Selected data for Exercise 57

City	Slug Pct.	Elevation
Anaheim	.480	160
Arlington	.605	616
Atlanta	.530	1,050
Baltimore	.505	130
Boston	.505	20
$\vdots$	$\vdots$	$\vdots$
Denver	.625	5,277
$\vdots$	$\vdots$	$\vdots$
Seattle	.550	350
San Francisco	.510	63
St. Louis	.570	465
Tampa	.500	10
Toronto	.535	566

Source: Based on Schaffer, J., & Heiny, E.L. "The effects of elevation on slugging percentage in Major League Baseball," *Chance,* Vol. 19, No. 1, Winter 2006 (adapted from Figure 2, p. 30).

b. Construct a scatterplot for the data and draw the least squares line on the graph. Locate the data point for Denver on the graph. What do you observe?

c. The Colorado Rockies, who play their home games in Coors Field, Denver, typically lead the league in team slugging percentage. Many baseball experts attribute this to the "thin air" of Denver—called the "mile-high" city due to its elevation. Remove the data point for Denver from the data set and refit the straight-line model to the remaining data. What conclusions can you draw about the "thin air" theory from this analysis?

58 Spreading rate of spilled liquid. Refer to the *Chemical Engineering Progress* (Jan. 2005) study of the rate at which a spilled volatile liquid will spread across a surface, Exercise 26. Recall that the data on mass of the spill and elapsed time of the spill are saved in the file. Is there sufficient evidence (at $\alpha = .05$) to indicate that the mass of the spill tends to diminish linearly as time increases? If so, give an interval estimate (with 95% confidence) of the decrease in spill mass for each minute of elapsed time.

LSPILL

---

5   The Coefficients of Correlation and Determination

In this section, we present two statistics that describe the adequacy of a model: the *coefficient of correlation* and the *coefficient of determination.*

Coefficient of Correlation

A **bivariate relationship** describes a relationship—or correlation—between two variables, x and y. Scatterplots are used to graphically describe a bivariate relationship. In this section, we will discuss the concept of **correlation** and show how it can be used to measure the linear relationship between two variables x and y. A numerical descriptive measure of the linear association between x and y is provided by the *coefficient of correlation, r.*

The **coefficient of correlation,*** r, is a measure of the strength of the *linear* relationship between two variables x and y. It is computed (for a sample of n measurements on x and y) as follows:

$$r = \frac{SS_{xy}}{\sqrt{SS_{xx}SS_{yy}}}$$

where

$$SS_{xy} = \Sigma(x - \bar{x})(y - \bar{y})$$
$$SS_{xx} = \Sigma(x - \bar{x})^2$$
$$SS_{yy} = \Sigma(y - \bar{y})^2$$

Note that the computational formula for the correlation coefficient r given in the definition involves the same quantities that were used in computing the least squares prediction equation. In fact, because the numerators of the expressions for $\hat{\beta}_1$ and r are

*The value of r is often called the *Pearson correlation coefficient* to honor its developer, Karl Pearson.

identical, you can see that $r = 0$ when $\hat{\beta}_1 = 0$ (the case where x contributes no information for the prediction of y), and r is positive when the slope is positive and negative when the slope is negative. Unlike $\hat{\beta}_1$, the correlation coefficient r is *scaleless* and assumes a value between -1 and $+1$, regardless of the units of x and y.

A value of r near or equal to 0 implies little or no linear relationship between y and x. In contrast, the closer r comes to 1 or -1, the stronger the linear relationship between y and x. And if $r = 1$ or $r = -1$, all the sample points fall exactly on the least squares line. Positive values of r imply a positive linear relationship between y and x; that is, y increases as x increases. Negative values of r imply a negative linear relationship between y and x; that is, y decreases as x increases. Each of these situations is portrayed in Figure 16.

Now Work Exercise 60

We demonstrate how to calculate the coefficient of correlation r using the data in Table 1 for the advertising-sales example. The quantities needed to calculate r are SS_{xy}, SS_{xx}, and SS_{yy}. The first two quantities have been calculated previously as $SS_{xy} = 7$ and $SS_{xx} = 10$. The calculation for $SS_{yy} = \Sigma(y - \bar{y})^2$ is shown on the last column of the Excel spreadsheet, Figure 5. The result is $SS_{yy} = 6$.

We now find the coefficient of correlation:

$$r = \frac{SS_{xy}}{\sqrt{SS_{xx}SS_{yy}}} = \frac{7}{\sqrt{(10)(6)}} = \frac{7}{\sqrt{60}} = .904$$

The fact that r is positive and near 1 in value indicates that the sales revenue y tends to increase as advertising expenditure x increases—*for this sample of 5 months*. This is the same conclusion we reached when we found the calculated value of the least squares slope to be positive.

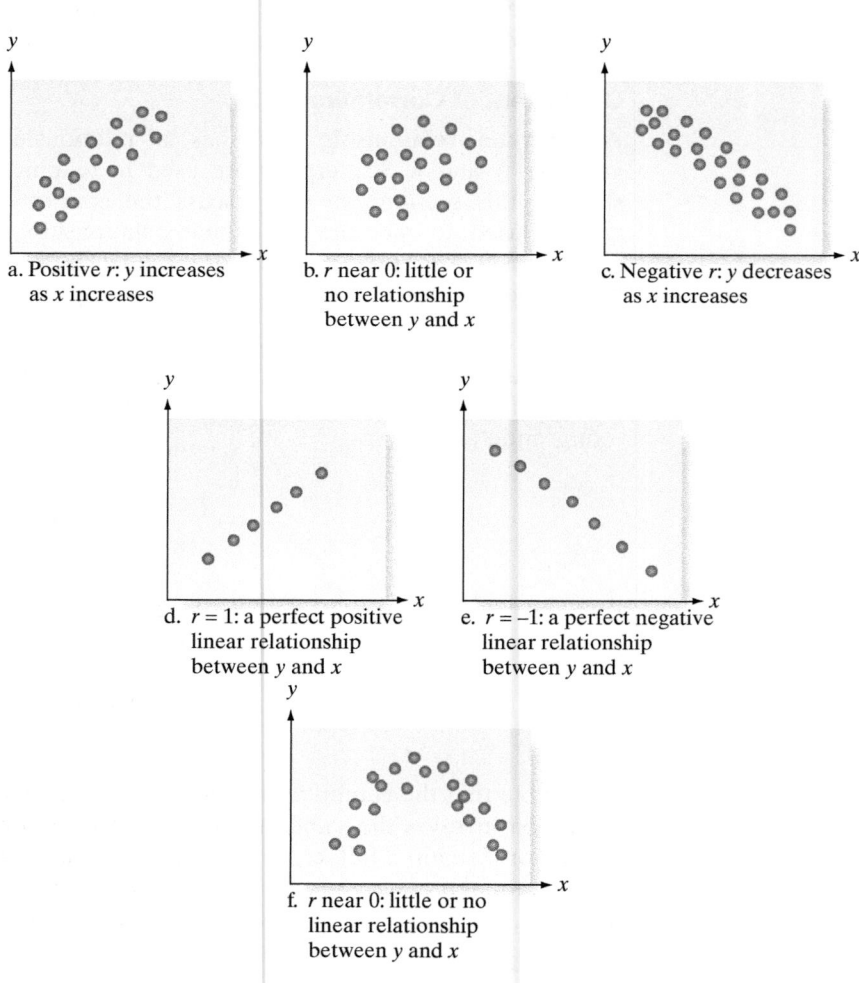

a. Positive r: y increases as x increases

b. r near 0: little or no relationship between y and x

c. Negative r: y decreases as x increases

d. $r = 1$: a perfect positive linear relationship between y and x

e. $r = -1$: a perfect negative linear relationship between y and x

f. r near 0: little or no linear relationship between y and x

Figure 16

Values of r and their implications

Example   4

Using the Correlation Coefficient—Relating Crime Rate and Casino Employment

Problem Legalized gambling is available on several riverboat casinos operated by a city in Mississippi. The mayor of the city wants to know the correlation between the number of casino employees and the yearly crime rate. The records for the past 10 years are examined, and the results listed in Table 3 are obtained. Calculate the coefficient of correlation r for the data. Interpret the result.

Table 3	Data on Casino Employees and Crime Rate, Example 4	
Year	Number of Casino Employees, x (thousands)	Crime Rate, y (number of crimes per 1,000 population)
2003	15	1.35
2004	18	1.63
2005	24	2.33
2006	22	2.41
2007	25	2.63
2008	29	2.93
2009	30	3.41
2010	32	3.26
2011	35	3.63
2012	38	4.15

Data Set: CASINO

Solution Rather than use the computing formula given in the definition, we resort to using a statistical software package. The data of Table 3 were entered into a computer, and Minitab was used to compute r. The Minitab printout is shown in Figure 17.

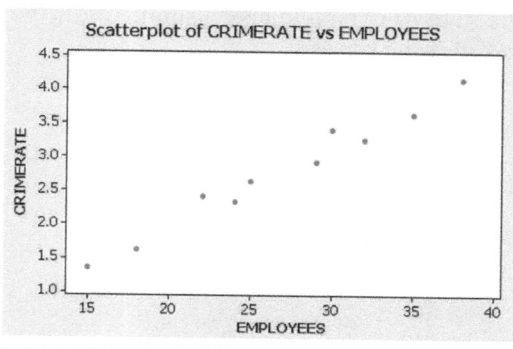

Correlations: EMPLOYEES, CRIMERAT

```
Pearson correlation of EMPLOYEES and CRIMERAT = 0.987
P-Value = 0.000
```

Figure 17

Minitab correlation printout for Example 4

The coefficient of correlation, highlighted at the top on the printout, is $r = .987$. Thus, the size of the casino workforce and crime rate in this city are very highly correlated—at least over the past 10 years. The implication is that a strong positive linear relationship exists between these variables (see the scatterplot at the bottom of Figure 17). We must be careful, however, not to jump to any unwarranted conclusions. For instance, the mayor may be tempted to conclude that hiring more casino workers next year will increase the crime rate—that is, that there is a *causal relationship* between the two variables. However, high correlation does not imply causality. The fact is, many things have probably contributed both to the increase in the casino workforce and to the increase in crime rate. The city's tourist trade has undoubtedly grown since riverboat casinos were legalized, and it is likely that the casinos have expanded both in services offered and in number. *We cannot infer a causal relationship on the basis of high sample correlation. When a high correlation is observed in the sample data, the only safe conclusion is that a linear trend may exist between* x *and* y.

ETHICS in STATISTICS

Intentionally using the correlation coefficient only to make an inference about the relationship between two variables in situations where a nonlinear relationship may exist is considered *unethical statistical practice*.

Look Back Another variable, such as the increase in tourism, may be the underlying cause of the high correlation between x and y.

Now Work Exercise 75

> **CAUTION** When using the sample correlation coefficient, r, to infer the nature of the relationship between x and y, two caveats exist: (1) A *high correlation* does not necessarily imply that a causal relationship exists between x and y—only that a linear trend may exist; (2) a *low correlation* does not necessarily imply that x and y are unrelated—only that x and y are not strongly *linearly* related.

Keep in mind that the correlation coefficient r measures the linear association between x values and y values in the sample, and a similar linear coefficient of correlation exists for the population from which the data points were selected. The **population correlation coefficient** is denoted by the symbol ρ (rho). As you might expect, ρ is estimated by the corresponding sample statistic, r. Or, instead of estimating ρ, we might want to test the null hypothesis $H_0: \rho = 0$ against $H_a: \rho \neq 0$—that is, we can test the hypothesis that x contributes no information for the prediction of y by using the straight-line model against the alternative that the two variables are at least linearly related.

However, we already performed this *identical* test in Section 4 when we tested $H_0: \beta_1 = 0$ against $H_a: \beta_1 \neq 0$—that is, the null hypothesis $H_0: \rho = 0$ is equivalent to the hypothesis $H_0: \beta_1 = 0$.* When we tested the null hypothesis $H_0: \beta_1 = 0$ in connection with the advertising-sales example, the data led to a rejection of the null hypothesis at the $\alpha = .05$ level. This rejection implies that the null hypothesis of a 0 correlation between the two variables (sales revenue and advertising expenditure) can also be rejected at the $\alpha = .05$ level. The only real difference between the least squares slope $\hat{\beta}_1$ and the coefficient of correlation r is the measurement scale. Therefore, the information they provide about the usefulness of the least squares model is to some extent redundant. Consequently, we will use the slope to make inferences about the existence of a positive or negative linear relationship between two variables.

For the sake of completeness, a summary of the test for linear correlation is provided in the following boxes.

A Test for Linear Correlation

One-Tailed Test	Two-Tailed Test
$H_0: \rho = 0$	$H_0: \rho = 0$
$H_a: \rho > 0$ (or $H_a: \rho < 0$)	$H_a: \rho \neq 0$

$$\text{Test statistic: } t = \frac{r\sqrt{n-2}}{\sqrt{1-r^2}} = \frac{\hat{\beta}_1}{s_{\hat{\beta}_1}}$$

Rejection region: $t > t_\alpha$ (or $t < -t_\alpha$)   *Rejection region:* $|t| > t_{\alpha/2}$

where the distribution of t depends on $(n-2)$ df.

Condition Required for a Valid Test of Correlation

The sample of (x, y) values is randomly selected from a normal population.

Coefficient of Determination

Another way to measure the usefulness of the model is to measure the contribution of x in predicting y. To accomplish this, we calculate how much the errors of prediction of y were reduced by using the information provided by x. To illustrate, consider the sample

*The two tests are equivalent in simple linear regression only.

shown in the scatterplot of Figure 18a. If we assume that x contributes no information for the prediction of y, the best prediction for a value of y is the sample mean $\bar{y}$, which is shown as the horizontal line in Figure 18b. The vertical line segments in Figure 18b are the deviations of the points about the mean $\bar{y}$. Note that the sum of squares of deviations for the prediction equation $\hat{y} = \bar{y}$ is

$$SS_{yy} = \sum (y_i - \bar{y})^2$$

Now suppose you fit a least squares line to the same set of data and locate the deviations of the points about the line as shown in Figure 18c. Compare the deviations about the prediction lines in Figures 18b and 18c. You can see that

1. If x contributes little or no information for the prediction of y, the sums of squares of deviations for the two lines,

$$SS_{yy} = \sum (y_i - \bar{y})^2 \quad \text{and} \quad SSE = \sum (y_i - \hat{y}_i)^2$$

will be nearly equal.

2. If x does contribute information for the prediction of y, the SSE will be smaller than SS_{yy}. In fact, if all the points fall on the least squares line, then SSE = 0.

Then the reduction in the sum of squares of deviations that can be attributed to x, expressed as a proportion of SS_{yy}, is

$$\frac{SS_{yy} - SSE}{SS_{yy}}$$

Note that SS_{yy} is the "total sample variation" of the observations around the mean $\bar{y}$ and that SSE is the remaining "unexplained sample variability" after fitting the line $\bar{y}$. Thus,

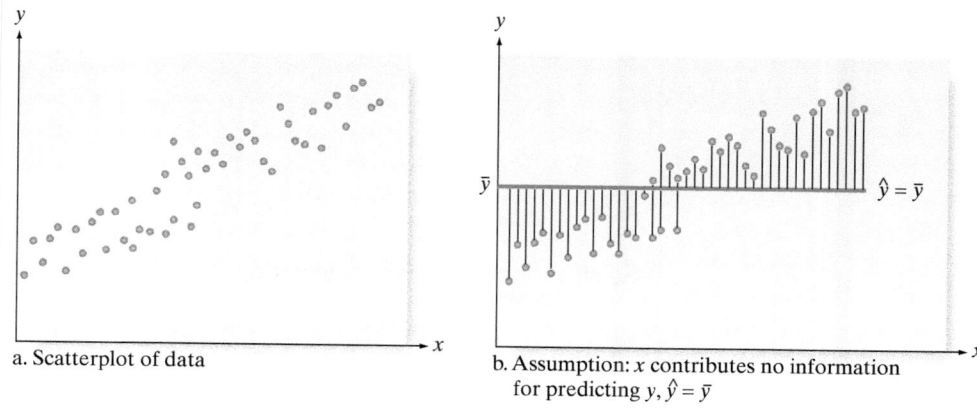

a. Scatterplot of data

b. Assumption: x contributes no information for predicting y, $\hat{y} = \bar{y}$

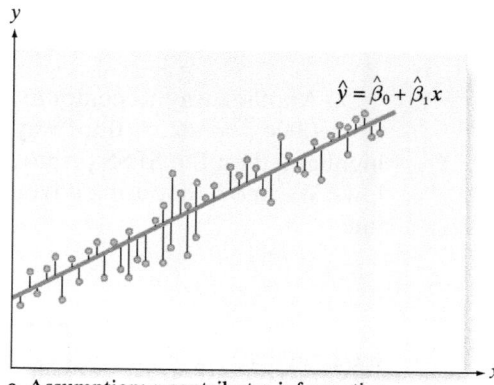

c. Assumption: x contributes information for predicting y, $\hat{y} = \hat{\beta}_0 + \hat{\beta}_1 x$

Figure 18

A comparison of the sum of squares of deviations for two models

the difference (SS_{yy} − SSE) is the "explained sample variability" attributable to the linear relationship with x. Then a verbal description of the proportion is

$$\frac{SS_{yy} - SSE}{SS_{yy}} = \frac{\text{Explained sample variability}}{\text{Total sample variablity}}$$

$$= \text{Proportion of total sample variability explained by the linear relationship}$$

In simple linear regression, it can be shown that this proportion—called the *coefficient of determination*—is equal to the square of the simple linear coefficient of correlation r.

Coefficient of Determination

$$r^2 = \frac{SS_{yy} - SSE}{SS_{yy}} = 1 - \frac{SSE}{SS_{yy}}$$

It represents the proportion of the total sample variability around $\bar{y}$ that is explained by the linear relationship between y and x. (In simple linear regression, it may also be computed as the square of the coefficient of correlation r.)

Note that r^2 is always between 0 and 1 because r is between −1 and +1. Thus, an r^2 of .60 means that the sum of squares of deviations of the y values about their predicted values has been reduced 60% by the use of the least squares equation $\hat{y}$, instead of $\bar{y}$, to predict y.

Example 5

Obtaining the Value of r^2—Sales Revenue Model

Problem Calculate the coefficient of determination for the advertising-sales example. The data are repeated in Table 4 for convenience. Interpret the result.

Table 4	Advertising-Sales Data
Advertising Expenditure, x ($100s)	Sales Revenue, y ($1,000s)
1	1
2	1
3	2
4	2
5	4

Data Set: ADSALE

Solution From previous calculations,

$$SS_{yy} = 6 \quad \text{and} \quad SSE = \sum (y - \hat{y})^2 = 1.10$$

Then, from the definition, the coefficient of determination is given by

$$r^2 = \frac{SS_{yy} - SSE}{SS_{yy}} = \frac{6.0 - 1.1}{6.0} = \frac{4.9}{6.0} = .82$$

Another way to compute r^2 is to recall (Section 2) that $r = .904$. Then we have $r^2 = (.904)^2 = .82$. A third way to obtain r^2 is from a computer printout. This value is highlighted on the SPSS printout reproduced in Figure 19. Our interpretation is as follows: We know that using advertising expenditure, x, to predict y with the least squares line

$$\hat{y} = -.1 + .7x$$

Model Summary

Figure 19

Portion of SPSS printout for advertising-sales regression

Model	R	R Square	Adjusted R Square	Std. Error of the Estimate
1	.904[a]	.817	.756	.606

a. Predictors: (Constant), ADVEXP_X

accounts for 82% of the total sum of squares of deviations of the five sample y values about their mean. Or, stated another way, 82% of the sample variation in sales revenue (y) can be "explained" by using advertising expenditure (x) in a straight-line model.

■ Now Work Exercise 64a

Practical Interpretation of the Coefficient of Determination, r^2

About $100(r^2)$% of the sample variation in y (measured by the total sum of squares of deviations of the sample y values about their mean $\bar{y}$) can be explained by (or attributed to) using x to predict y in the straight-line model.

STATISTICS in ACTION REVISITED

Using the Coefficient of Correlation and the Coefficient of Determination

In the previous *Statistics in Action Revisited*, we discovered that cumulative 6-month advertising expenditures was a statistically useful linear predictor of number of new PI cases but not a useful linear predictor of number of new WC cases. Both the coefficients of correlation and determination (highlighted on the Minitab printouts in Figures SIA4 and SIA5) also support this conclusion.

Regression Analysis: NewPI versus AdvExp6

```
The regression equation is
NewPI = 7.77 + 0.113 AdvExp6

Predictor      Coef  SE Coef      T      P
Constant      7.767    3.385   2.29  0.027
AdvExp6     0.11289  0.02793   4.04  0.000

S = 9.67521   R-Sq = 29.0%   R-Sq(adj) = 27.2%

Analysis of Variance

Source           DF      SS      MS      F      P
Regression        1  1529.5  1529.5  16.34  0.000
Residual Error   40  3744.4    93.6
Total            41  5273.9
```

Correlations: NewPI, AdvExp6

```
Pearson correlation of NewPI and AdvExp6 = 0.539
P-Value = 0.000
```

Figure SIA4

Minitab printout with coefficients of correlation and determination for y = number of new PI cases

---

Regression Analysis: NewWC versus AdvExp6

```
The regression equation is
NewWC = 24.6 + 0.0098 AdvExp6

Predictor      Coef  SE Coef      T      P
Constant     24.574    3.367   7.30  0.000
AdvExp6     0.00982  0.02778   0.35  0.725

S = 9.62296   R-Sq = 0.3%   R-Sq(adj) = 0.0%

Analysis of Variance

Source           DF       SS      MS     F      P
Regression        1    11.58   11.58  0.13  0.725
Residual Error   40  3704.06   92.60
Total            41  3715.64
```

Correlations: NewWC, AdvExp6

```
Pearson correlation of NewWC and AdvExp6 = 0.056
P-Value = 0.725
```

Figure SIA5

Minitab printout with coefficients of correlation and determination for y = number of new WC cases

For y = number of new PI cases, the correlation coefficient value of $r = .539$ is statistically significantly different from 0 and indicates a moderate positive linear relationship between the variables. The coefficient of determination, $r^2 = .29$, implies that almost 30% of the sample variation in number of new PI cases can be explained by using advertising expenditure (x) in the straight-line model. In contrast, for y = number of new WC cases, $r = .056$ is not statistically different from 0 and $r^2 = .003$ implies that only 0.3% of the sample variation in number of new WC cases can be explained by using advertising expenditure (x) in the straight-line model.

Exercises 59–75

Please be aware that some of the following problems may require knowledge of concepts that are not presented in this chapter.

Learning the Mechanics

59 Describe the slope of the least squares line if
   a. $r = .7$ **b.** $r = -.7$
   c. $r = 0$ **d.** $r^2 = .64$

60 Explain what each of the following sample correlation coefficients tells you about the relationship between the x and y values in the sample:
   a. $r = 1$ **b.** $r = -1$
   c. $r = 0$ **d.** $r = -.90$
   e. $r = .10$ **f.** $r = -.88$

61 Calculate r^2 for the least squares line in each of the following exercises. Interpret their values.
   a. Exercise 10   **b.** Exercise 13

62 Construct a scatterplot for each data set. Then calculate r and r^2 for each data set. Interpret their values.

a.

x	-2	-1	0	1	2
y	-2	1	2	5	6

b.

x	-2	-1	0	1	2
y	6	5	3	2	0

c.

x	1	2	2	3	3	3	4
y	2	1	3	1	2	3	2

d.

x	0	1	3	5	6
y	0	1	2	1	0

🌐 Applet Exercise 2

Use the applet *Correlation by Eye* to explore the relationship between the pattern of data in a scatterplot and the corresponding correlation coefficient.

   a. Run the applet several times. Each time, guess the value of the correlation coefficient. Then click *Show r* to see the actual correlation coefficient. How close is your value to the actual value of r? Click *New data* to reset the applet.

   b. Click the trash can to clear the graph. Use the mouse to place five points on the scatterplot that are approximately in a straight line. Then guess the value of the correlation coefficient. Click *Show r* to see the actual correlation coefficient. How close were you this time?

   c. Continue to clear the graph and plot sets of five points with different patterns among the points. Guess the value of r. How close do you come to the actual value of r each time?

   d. Based on your experiences with the applet, explain why we need to use more reliable methods of finding the correlation coefficient than just "eyeing" it.

Applying the Concepts—Basic

63 **Going for it on fourth-down in the NFL.** Each week coaches in the National Football League (NFL) face a decision during the game. On fourth-down, should the team punt the ball or go for a first-down? To aid in the decision-making process, statisticians at California State University, Northridge, developed a regression model for predicting the number of points scored (y) by a team that has a first-down with a given number of yards (x) from the opposing goal line (*Chance,* Winter 2009). One of the models fit to data collected on five NFL teams from a recent season was the simple linear regression model, $E(y) = \beta_0 + \beta_1 x$. The regression yielded the following results: $\hat{y} = 4.42 - 048x, r^2 = .18$.
   a. Give a practical interpretation of the coefficient of determination, r^2.
   b. Compute the value of the coefficient of correlation, r, from the value of r^2. Is the value of r positive or negative? Why?

64 **Lobster fishing study.** Refer to the *Bulletin of Marine Science* (April 2010) study of teams of fishermen fishing for the red spiny lobster in Baja California Sur, Mexico, Exercise 46. Recall that simple linear regression was used to model y = total catch of lobsters (in kilograms) during the season as a function of x = average percentage of traps allocated per day to exploring areas of unknown catch (called *search frequency*). Another portion of the XLSTAT printout of the analysis is shown on the next page.
   a. Locate and interpret the coefficient of determination, r^2, on the printout.
   b. Locate and interpret the coefficient of correlation, r, on the printout.
   c. In Exercise 46, you conducted a test to determine that total catch (y) is negatively linearly related to search frequency (x). Which of the two statistics, r or r^2, can be used to partially support this inference? Explain.

XLSTAT output for Exercise 64

Correlation matrix:

Variables	SEARCHFREQ	CATCH
SEARCHFREQ	**1.0000**	−0.7347
CATCH	−0.7347	**1.0000**

Regression of variable CATCH:

Goodness of fit statistics:

Observations	15.0000
Sum of weights	15.0000
DF	13.0000
R²	0.5397
Adjusted R²	0.5043
MSE	1902741.2024
RMSE	1379.3989
DW	1.4475

65 RateMyProfessors.com. A popular Web site among college students is RateMyProfessors.com (RMP). Established over 10 years ago, RMP allows students to post quantitative ratings of their instructors. In *Practical Assessment, Research & Evaluation* (May 2007), University of Maine researchers investigated whether instructor ratings posted on RMP are correlated with the formal in-class student evaluations of teaching (SET) that all universities are required to administer at the end of the semester. Data collected for $n = 426$ University of Maine instructors yielded a correlation between RMP and SET ratings of .68.

a. Give the equation of a linear model relating SET rating (y) to RMP rating (x).

b. Give a practical interpretation of the value $r = .68$.

c. Is the estimated slope of the line, part **a,** positive or negative? Explain.

d. A test of the null hypothesis H_0: $\rho = 0$ yielded a p-value of .001. Interpret this result.

e. Compute the coefficient of determination, r^2, for the regression analysis. Interpret the result.

66 In business, do nice guys finish first or last? Refer to the *Nature* (March 20, 2008) study of the use of punishment in cooperation games, Exercise 14. Recall that college students repeatedly played a version of the game "prisoner's dilemma," and the researchers recorded the average payoff and the number of times cooperation, defection, and punishment were used for each player.

a. A test of no correlation between cooperation use (x) and average payoff (y) yielded a p-value of .33. Interpret this result.

b. A test of no correlation between defection use (x) and average payoff (y) yielded a p-value of .66. Interpret this result.

c. A test of no correlation between punishment use (x) and average payoff (y) yielded a p-value of .001. Interpret this result.

67 Women in top management. An empirical analysis of women in upper management positions at U.S. firms was published in the *Journal of Organizational Culture, Communications and Conflict* (July 2007). Monthly data ($n = 252$ months) were collected for several variables, including the number of females in managerial positions, the number of females with a college degree, and the number of female high school graduates with no college degree. Similar data were collected for males.

a. The correlation coefficient relating number of females in managerial positions and number of females with a college degree was reported as $r = .983$. Interpret this result.

b. The correlation coefficient relating number of females in managerial positions and number of female high school graduates with no college degree was reported as $r = .074$. Interpret this result.

c. The correlation coefficient relating number of males in managerial positions and number of males with a college degree was reported as $r = .722$. Interpret this result.

d. The correlation coefficient relating number of males in managerial positions and number of male high school graduates with no college degree was reported as $r = .528$. Interpret this result.

68 Last name and acquisition timing. The *Journal of Consumer Research* (August 2011) did a study of the speed with which consumers decide to purchase a product. The researchers theorized that consumers with last names that begin with letters later in the alphabet would tend to acquire items faster than those whose last names begin with letters earlier in the alphabet (i.e., the *last name effect*). Each in a sample of 50 MBA students was offered free tickets to attend a college basketball game for which there was a limited supply of tickets. The first letter of the last name of those who responded to an e-mail offer in time to receive the tickets was noted and given a numerical value (e.g., "A" = 1, "B" = 2, etc.). Each student's response time (measured in minutes) was also recorded.

a. The researchers computed the correlation between the two variables as $r = -.271$. Interpret this result.

b. The observed significance level for testing for a negative correlation in the population was reported as p-value = .018. Interpret this result for $\alpha = .05$.

c. Does this analysis support the researchers' *last name effect* theory? Explain.

Applying the Concepts—Intermediate

69 Software millionaires and birthdays. Refer to Exercise 19 and the study of the seemingly disproportionate number of software millionaires born around the year 1955. The data are reproduced in the table on the following page.

a. Find the coefficient of determination for the simple linear regression model relating number (y) of software millionaire birthdays in a decade to total number (x) of U.S. births. Interpret the result.

b. Find the coefficient of determination for the simple linear regression model relating number (y) of software millionaire birthdays in a decade to number (x) of CEO birthdays. Interpret the result.

c. The consulting statistician argued that the software industry appears to be no different from any other industry with respect to producing millionaires in a decade. Do you agree? Explain.

Data for Exercise 69

Decade	Total U.S. Births (millions)	Number of Software Millionaire Birthdays	Number of CEO Birthdays (in a random sample of 70 companies from the *Fortune* 500 list)
1920	28.582	3	2
1930	24.374	1	2
1940	31.666	10	23
1950	40.530	14	38
1960	38.808	7	9
1970	33.309	4	0

Source: Sauro, J. "Were most software millionaires born around 1955?" *Measuring Usability,* November 17, 2010. Copyright © 2010 by Measuring Usability LLC. Reprinted with permission.

70 Child labor in diamond mines. The role of child laborers on Africa's colonial-era diamond mines was the subject of research published in the *Journal of Family History* (Vol. 35, 2010). One particular mining company lured children to the mines by offering incentives for adult male laborers to relocate their families close to the diamond mine. The success of the incentive program was examined by determining the annual *accompaniment rate,* i.e., the percentage of wives (or sons, or daughters) who accompanied their husbands (or fathers) in relocating to the mine. Information from the journal article was used to simulate accompaniment rates for nine consecutive years. Those rates are shown in the table below.

a. Find the correlation coefficient relating the accompaniment rates for wives and sons. Interpret this value.

b. Find the correlation coefficient relating the accompaniment rates for wives and daughters. Interpret this value.

c. Find the correlation coefficient relating the accompaniment rates for sons and daughters. Interpret this value.

Year	Wives	Sons	Daughters
1	28.7	2.4	14.3
2	41.6	1.7	13.1
3	37.2	0.5	10
4	39.3	3.7	19.6
5	39.5	5.6	19.4
6	39.9	11.2	21.7
7	40.2	12.1	15.3
8	31.3	8.8	15.1
9	25.3	7.6	19.6

Source: Based on Cleveland, T., "Minors in name only: Child laborers on the diamond mines of the *Companhia de Diamantes de Angola* (Diamang), 1917–1975." *Journal of Family History,* Vol. 35, No. 1, 2010 (Table 1).

71 Sweetness of orange juice. Refer to the simple linear regression relating y = sweetness index of an orange juice sample with x = amount of water-soluble pectin, Exercise 22 and the data saved in the file. Find and interpret the coefficient of determination, r^2, and the coefficient of correlation, r.

72 Performance ratings of government agencies. The U.S. Office of Management and Budget (OMB) requires government agencies to produce annual performance and accounting reports (PARS) each year. *The Public Manager* (Summer 2008) compiled a listing of PARS evaluation scores for 24 government agencies. Evaluation scores ranged from 12 (lowest) to 60 (highest). The PARS evaluation scores for two consecutive years are reproduced in the following table.

a. Calculate and interpret the coefficient of correlation between the PARS scores in year 1 and year 2.

b. Is there sufficient evidence of a positive linear relationship between year 2 PARS score (y) and year 1 PARS score (x)? Test using $\alpha = .05$.

Agency	Year 1	Year 2
Transportation	55	53
Labor	53	51
Veterans	51	51
NRC	39	34
Commerce	37	36
HHS	37	35
DHS	37	30
Justice	35	37
Treasury	35	35
GSA	34	40
Agriculture	33	35
EPA	33	36
Social Security	33	33
USAID	32	42
Education	32	36
Interior	32	31
NASA	32	32
Energy	31	34
HUD	31	30
NSF	31	31
State	31	50
OPM	27	28
SBA	22	31
Defense	17	32

Source: Ellig, J., & Wray, H. "Measuring performance reporting quality," *The Public Manager,* Vol. 37, No. 2, Summer 2008 (p. 66). Copyright © 2008 by Jerry Ellig. Reprinted with permission.

73 Survey of the top business schools. Refer to the *Wall Street Journal* (Sep. 25, 2005) Business School Survey, Exercise 25 and the data saved in the file. Find and interpret r and r^2 for the simple linear regression relating y = percentage of graduates with job offers and x = tuition cost and then fit the simple linear model.

74 Spreading rate of spilled liquid. Refer to the *Chemical Engineering Progress* (Jan. 2005) study of the rate at which a spilled volatile liquid will spread across a surface, Exercise 26 and the data saved in the file. Find and interpret r and r^2 for the simple linear regression y = mass of the spill and x = elapsed time of the spill.

Applying the Concepts—Advanced

75 Salary linked to height. Are short people short-changed when it comes to salary? According to Business Professors T. A. Judge (University of Florida) and D. M. Cable (University of North Carolina), tall people tend to earn more money over their careers than short people (*Journal of Applied Psychology*, June 2004). Using data collected from participants in the National Longitudinal Surveys begun in 1979, the researchers computed the correlation between average earnings from 1985 to 2000 (in dollars) and height (in inches) for several occupations. The results are given in the table. Are average earnings positively related to height? For all occupations? If so, can you conclude that a person taller than you will earn a higher salary? Explain.

Occupation	Correlation, r	Sample Size, n
Sales	.41	117
Managers	.35	455
Blue Collar	.32	349
Service Workers	.31	265
Professional/ Technical	.30	453
Clerical	.25	358
Crafts/ Forepersons	.24	250

Source: Judge, T. A., & Cable, D. M. "The effect of physical height on workplace success and income: Preliminary test of a theoretical model," *Journal of Applied Psychology*, Vol. 89, No. 3, June 2004 (Table 5).

6 Using the Model for Estimation and Prediction

If we are satisfied that a useful model has been found to describe the relationship between x and y, we are ready for step 5 in our regression modeling procedure: using the model for estimation and prediction.

The most common uses of a probabilistic model for making inferences can be divided into two categories. The first is using the model to estimate the mean value of y, $E(y)$, *for a specific value of* x. For our advertising-sales example, we may want to estimate the mean sales revenue for *all* months during which \$400 ($x = 4$) is expended on advertising.

The second use of the model entails predicting a new individual y *value for a given* x. That is, if we decide to expend \$400 in advertising next month, we may want to predict the firm's sales revenue for that month.

In the first case, we are attempting to *estimate the mean value of* y *for a very large number of experimental units at the given* x *value.* In the second case, we are trying to *predict the outcome for a single experimental unit at the given* x *value.* Which of these model uses—estimating the mean value of y or predicting an individual new value of y (for the same value of x)—can be accomplished with the greater accuracy?

Before answering this question, we first consider the problem of choosing an estimator (or predictor) of the mean (or a new individual) y value. We will use the least squares prediction equation

$$\hat{y} = \hat{\beta}_0 + \hat{\beta}_1 x$$

both to estimate the mean value of y and to predict a specific new value of y for a given value of x. For our example, we found

$$\hat{y} = -.1 + .7x$$

so that the estimated mean sales revenue for all months when $x = 4$ (advertising is \$400) is

$$\hat{y} = -.1 + .7(4) = 2.7$$

or \$2,700. (Recall that the units of y are thousands of dollars.) The same value is used to predict a new y value when $x = 4$—that is, both the estimated mean and the predicted value of y are $\hat{y} = 2.7$ when $x = 4$, as shown in Figure 20.

The difference between these two model uses lies in the relative accuracy of the estimate and the prediction. These accuracies are best measured by using the sampling errors of the least squares line when it is used as an estimator and as a predictor, respectively. These errors are reflected in the standard deviations given in the next box.

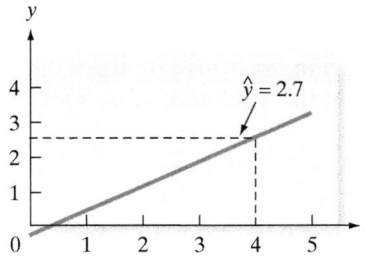

Figure 20

Estimated mean value and predicted individual value of sales revenue y for $x = 4$

Sampling Errors for the Estimator of the Mean of y and the Predictor of an Individual New Value of y

1. The *standard deviation* of the sampling distribution of the estimator $\hat{y}$ of the *mean value of* x, say x_p, is

$$\sigma_{\hat{y}} = \sigma\sqrt{\frac{1}{n} + \frac{(x_p - \bar{x})^2}{SS_{xx}}}$$

where σ is the standard deviation of the random error ε. We refer to $\sigma_{\hat{y}}$ as the **standard error of $\hat{y}$.**

2. The *standard deviation* of the prediction error for the predictor $\hat{y}$ of an individual *new y value* at a specific value of x is

$$\sigma_{(y-\hat{y})} = \sigma\sqrt{1 + \frac{1}{n} + \frac{(x_p - \bar{x})^2}{SS_{xx}}}$$

where σ is the standard deviation of the random error ε. We refer to $\sigma_{(y-\hat{y})}$ as the **standard error of the prediction.**

The true value of σ is rarely known, so we estimate σ by s and calculate the estimation and prediction intervals as shown in the next two boxes.

A $100(1 - \alpha)\%$ Confidence Interval for the Mean Value of y at $x = x_p$

$$\hat{y} \pm t_{\alpha/2}(\text{Estimated standard error of } \hat{y})$$

or

$$\hat{y} \pm t_{\alpha/2}s\sqrt{\frac{1}{n} + \frac{(x_p - \bar{x})^2}{SS_{xx}}}$$

where $t_{\alpha/2}$ is based on $(n - 2)$ degrees of freedom.

A $100(1 - \alpha)\%$ Prediction Interval* for an Individual New Value of y at $x = x_p$

$$\hat{y} \pm t_{\alpha/2}(\text{Estimated standard error of prediction})$$

or

$$\hat{y} \pm t_{\alpha/2}s\sqrt{1 + \frac{1}{n} + \frac{(x_p - \bar{x})^2}{SS_{xx}}}$$

where $t_{\alpha/2}$ is based on $(n - 2)$ degrees of freedom.

Example 6

Estimating the Mean of y—Sales Revenue Model

Problem Refer to the sales-appraisal simple linear regression in previous examples. Find a 95% confidence interval for the mean monthly sales when the appliance store spends $400 on advertising.

Solution Here, we desire a confidence interval for the mean, $E(y)$, for *all* months when the store spends $400 on advertising. For a $400 advertising expenditure, $x = 4$, and the confidence interval for the mean value of y is

$$\hat{y} \pm t_{\alpha/2}s\sqrt{\frac{1}{n} + \frac{(x_p - \bar{x})^2}{SS_{xx}}} = \hat{y} \pm t_{.025}s\sqrt{\frac{1}{5} + \frac{(4 - \bar{x})^2}{SS_{xx}}}$$

*The term *prediction interval* is used when the interval formed is intended to enclose the value of a random variable. The term *confidence interval* is reserved for the estimation of population parameters (such as the mean).

where $t_{.025}$ is based on $n - 2 = 5 - 2 = 3$ degrees of freedom. Recall that $\hat{y} = 2.7$, $s = .61, \bar{x} = 3$, and $SS_{xx} = 10$. From Table III in Appendix: Tables, $t_{.025} = 3.182$. Thus, we have

$$2.7 \pm (3.182)(.61)\sqrt{\frac{1}{5} + \frac{(4 - 3)^2}{10}} = 2.7 \pm (3.182)(.61)(.55)$$

$$= 2.7 \pm (3.182)(.34)$$

$$= 2.7 \pm 1.1 = (1.6, 3.8)$$

Therefore, when the store spends $400 a month on advertising, we are 95% confident that the mean sales revenue for these months is between $1,600 and $3,800.

Look Back Note that we used a small amount of data (small in size) for purposes of illustration in fitting the least squares line. The interval would probably be narrower if more information had been obtained from a larger sample.

Now Work Exercise 76a–d

Example 7

Predicting an Individual value of y—Sales Revenue Model

Problem Refer, again, to the sales-appraisal regression. Predict the monthly sales for next month if $400 is spent on advertising. Use a 95% prediction interval.

Solution Here, our focus is on a *single* month when the store spends $400 on advertising. To predict the sales for a particular month for which $x_p = 4$, we calculate the 95% prediction interval as

$$\hat{y} \pm t_{\alpha/2}s\sqrt{1 + \frac{1}{n} + \frac{(x_p - \bar{x})^2}{SS_{xx}}} = 2.7 \pm (3.182)(.61)\sqrt{1 + \frac{1}{5} + \frac{(4 - 3)^2}{10}}$$

$$= 2.7 \pm (3.182)(.61)(1.14)$$

$$= 2.7 \pm (3.182)(.70)$$

$$= 2.7 \pm 2.2 = (.5, 4.9)$$

Therefore, we predict with 95% confidence that the sales revenue next month (a month in which we spend $400 in advertising) will fall in the interval from $500 to $4,900.

Look Back Like the confidence interval for the mean value of y, the prediction interval for y is quite large. This is because we have chosen a simple example (only five data points) to fit the least squares line. The width of the prediction interval could be reduced by using a larger number of data points.

Now Work Exercise 76e

Both the confidence interval for $E(y)$ and prediction interval for y can be obtained using a statistical software package. Figure 21 is a Minitab printout showing the confidence interval and prediction interval for the data in the advertising-sales example. The 95% confidence interval for $E(y)$ when $x = 4$, highlighted under "95% CI" in Figure 21, is (1.645, 3.755). The 95% prediction interval for y when $x = 4$, highlighted in Figure 21 under "95% PI," is (.503, 4.897). Both intervals agree with the ones computed in Examples 6–7.

```
Predicted Values for New Observations

New
Obs    Fit   SE Fit      95% CI           95% PI
 1   2.700   0.332   (1.645, 3.755)   (0.503, 4.897)


Values of Predictors for New Observations

New
Obs   ADVEXP_X
 1       4.00
```

Figure 21

Minitab printout giving 95% confidence interval for $E(y)$ and 95% prediction interval for y

Note that the prediction interval for an individual new value of y is *always* wider than the corresponding confidence interval for the mean value of y. To see this, consider the following. The error in estimating the mean value of y, $E(y)$, for a given value of x, say x_p, is the distance between the least squares line and the true line of means, $E(y) = \beta_0 + \beta_1 x$. This error, $[\hat{y} - E(y)]$, is shown in Figure 22. In contrast, *the error* $(y_p - \hat{y})$ *in predicting some future value of* y *is the sum of two errors*—the error of estimating the mean of y, $E(y)$, plus the random error that is a component of the value of y to be predicted (see Figure 23). Consequently, the error of predicting a particular value of y will be larger than the error of estimating the mean value of y for a particular value of x. Note from their formulas that both the error of estimation and the error of prediction take their smallest values when $x_p = \bar{x}$. The farther x_p lies from $\bar{x}$, the larger will be the errors of estimation and prediction. You can see why this is true by noting the deviations for different values of x_p between the line of means $E(y) = \beta_0 + \beta_1 x$ and the predicted line of means $\hat{y} = \hat{\beta}_0 + \hat{\beta}_1 x$ shown in Figure 23. The deviation is larger at the extremes of the interval where the largest and smallest values of x in the data set occur.

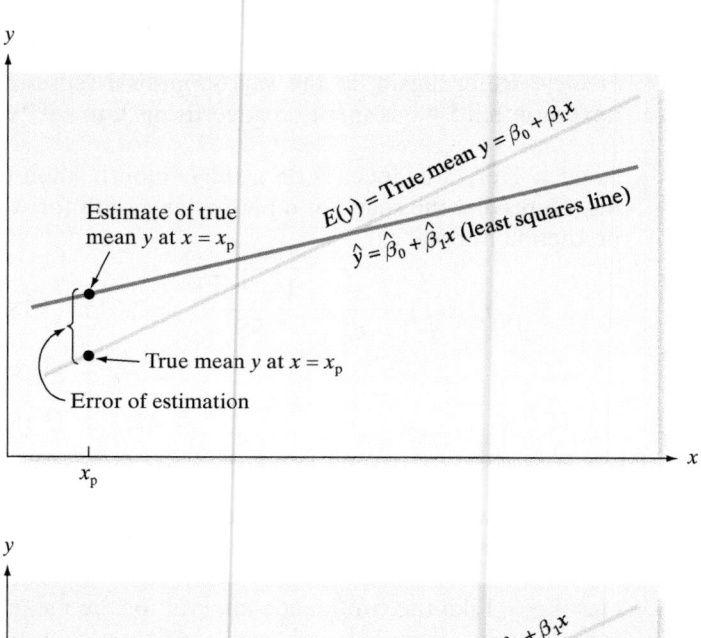

Figure 22

Error of estimating the mean value of y for a given value of x

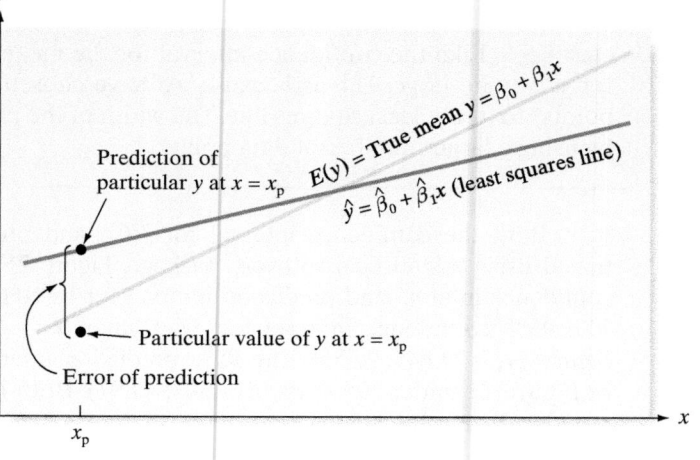

Figure 23

Error of predicting a future value of y for a given value of x

Both the confidence intervals for mean values and the prediction intervals for new values are depicted over the entire range of the regression line in Figure 24. You can see that the confidence interval is always narrower than the prediction interval, and they are both narrowest at the mean $\bar{x}$, increasing steadily as the distance $|x - \bar{x}|$ increases. In fact, when x is selected far enough away from $\bar{x}$ so that it falls outside the range of the sample data, it is dangerous to make any inferences about $E(y)$ or y.

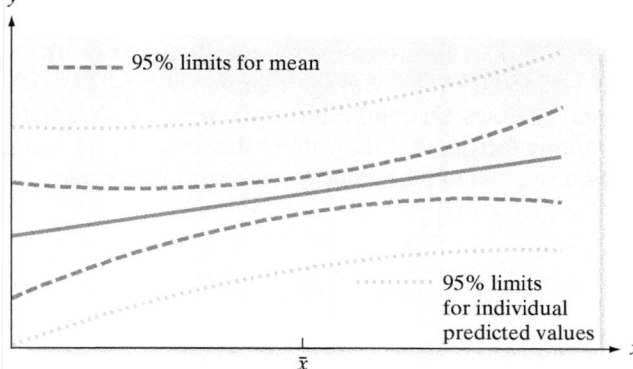

Figure 24

Confidence intervals for mean values and prediction intervals for new values

> ⚠️ **CAUTION** Using the least squares prediction equation to estimate the mean value of y or to predict a particular value of y for values of x that fall *outside the range* of the values of x contained in your sample data may lead to errors of estimation or prediction that are much larger than expected. Although the least squares model may provide a very good fit to the data over the range of x values contained in the sample, it could give a poor representation of the true model for values of x outside this region.

The confidence interval width grows smaller as n is increased; thus, in theory, you can obtain as precise an estimate of the mean value of y as desired (at any given x) by selecting a large enough sample. The prediction interval for a new value of y also grows smaller as n increases, but there is a lower limit on its width. If you examine the formula for the prediction interval, you will see that the interval can get no smaller than $\hat{y} \pm z_{\alpha/2}\sigma.$* Thus, the only way to obtain more accurate predictions for new values of y is to reduce the standard deviation of the regression model, σ. This can be accomplished only by improving the model, either by using a curvilinear (rather than linear) relationship with x or by adding new independent variables to the model, or both.

STATISTICS in ACTION REVISITED

Prediction Using the Straight-Line Model

In the two previous *Statistics in Action Revisited* sections, we demonstrated that $x =$ cumulative 6-month advertising expenditures is a useful linear predictor of $y =$ the number of new PI cases. The Minitab printout shown in Figure SIA6 gives a 95% prediction interval for the number of new PI cases in a month where cumulative spending on advertising over the past 6 months is $x = \$150,000$. The highlighted interval is $(4.78, 44.62)$. Thus, we can be 95% confident that for a given month with a 6-month cumulative advertising expenditure of \$150,000, the law firm will add between 5 and 44 new PI cases that month.

```
Predicted Values for New Observations

New
Obs    Fit   SE Fit     95% CI          95% PI
  1   24.70    1.89   (20.89, 28.51)   (4.78, 44.62)


Values of Predictors for New Observations

New
Obs   AdvExp6
  1      150
```

Figure SIA6

Minitab prediction interval for legal advertising straight-line model

*The result follows from the facts that, for large n, $t_{\alpha/2} \approx z_{\alpha/2}$, $s \approx \sigma$, and the last two terms under the radical in the standard error of the predictor are approximately 0.

The 95% *confidence interval for the mean of y* (also highlighted on the printout) is (20.89, 28.51). This indicates that for all months with cumulative spending on advertising of $x = \$150,000$, the average number of new PI cases each month will range between 21 and 28 cases. Of course, if these projections are to be useful for future planning, other economic factors that may affect the firm's business must be similar to those during the period over which the sample data were generated.

Exercises 76–90

Learning the Mechanics

76 Consider the following pairs of measurements:

x	-2	0	2	4	6	8	10
y	0	3	2	3	8	10	11

L11076

a. Construct a scatterplot for these data.
b. Find the least squares line and plot it on your scatterplot.
c. Find s^2 and s.
d. Find a 90% confidence interval for the mean value of y when $x = 3$. Plot the upper and lower bounds of the confidence interval on your scatterplot.
e. Find a 90% prediction interval for a new value of y when $x = 3$. Plot the upper and lower bounds of the prediction interval on your scatterplot.
f. Compare the widths of the intervals you constructed in parts **d** and **e**. Which is wider and why?

77 Consider the pairs of measurements shown in the table. For these data, $SS_{xx} = 38.9$, $SS_{yy} = 33.6$, $SS_{xy} = 32.8$, and $\hat{y} = -.414 + .843x$.

L11077

x	4	6	0	5	2	3	2	6	2	1
y	3	5	-1	4	3	2	0	4	1	1

a. Construct a scatterplot for these data.
b. Plot the least squares line on your scatterplot.
c. Use a 95% confidence interval to estimate the mean value of y when $x_p = 6$. Plot the upper and lower bounds of the interval on your scatterplot.
d. Repeat part **c** for $x_p = 3.2$ and $x_p = 0$.
e. Compare the widths of the three confidence intervals you constructed in parts **c** and **d** and explain why they differ.

78 Refer to Exercise 77.
a. Using no information about x, estimate and calculate a 95% confidence interval for the mean value of y.
b. Plot the estimated mean value and the confidence interval as horizontal lines on your scatterplot.
c. Compare the confidence intervals you calculated in parts **c** and **d** of Exercise 77 with the one you calculated in part **a** of this exercise. Does x appear to contribute information about the mean value of y?
d. Check the answer you gave in part **c** with a statistical test of the null hypothesis H_0: $\beta_1 = 0$ against H_a: $\beta_1 \neq 0$. Use $\alpha = .05$.

79 In fitting a least squares line to $n = 10$ data points, the following quantities were computed:

$SS_{xx} = 32$ $\bar{x} = 3$ $SS_{yy} = 26$ $\bar{y} = 4$ $SS_{xy} = 28$

a. Find the least squares line.
b. Graph the least squares line.
c. Calculate SSE.
d. Calculate s^2.
e. Find a 95% confidence interval for the mean value of y when $x_p = 2.5$.
f. Find a 95% prediction interval for y when $x_p = 4$.

Applying the Concepts—Basic

80 In business, do nice guys finish first or last? Refer to the *Nature* (March 20, 2008) study of the use of punishment in cooperation games, Exercise 14. Recall that simple linear regression was used to model a player's average payoff (y) as a straight-line function of the number of times punishment was used (x) by the player.
a. If the researchers want to predict average payoff for a single player who used punishment 10 times, how should they proceed?
b. If the researchers want to predict the mean of the average payoffs for all players who used punishment 10 times, how should they proceed?

81 Lobster fishing study. Refer to the *Bulletin of Marine Science* (April 2010) study of teams of fishermen fishing for the red spiny lobster in Baja California Sur, Mexico, Exercise 16. Recall that simple linear regression was used to model y = total catch of lobsters (in kilograms) during the season as a function of x = average percentage of traps allocated per day to exploring areas of unknown catch (called *search frequency*). A portion of the Minitab printout giving a 95% confidence interval for $E(y)$ and a 95% prediction interval for y when $x = 25$ is shown below.

```
Predicted Values for New Observations

New Obs    Fit   SE Fit      95% CI         95% PI
     1    5788      465  (4783, 6792)  (2643, 8933)


Values of Predictors for New Observations

New Obs   SEARCHFREQ
     1         25.0
```

a. Locate and interpret the 95% confidence interval for $E(y)$.
b. Locate and interpret the 95% prediction interval for y.

XLSTAT output for Exercise 82

Observation	Pred(RelRate)	Lower bound 90% (Mean)	Upper bound 90% (Mean)	Lower bound 90% (Observation)	Upper bound 90% (Observation)
1.5	61.08	57.26	64.91	55.33	66.83
1.05	44.92	42.99	46.85	40.21	49.63
0.9	39.53	37.78	41.29	34.90	44.17
0.75	34.15	32.17	36.12	29.42	38.87
0.6	28.76	26.27	31.25	23.80	33.72
0.65	30.55	28.26	32.85	25.69	35.42

Predictions for the new observations:

82 Drug controlled-release rate study. Refer to the *Drug Development and Industrial Pharmacy* (Vol. 28, 2002) drug controlled-release rate study, Exercise 17. Recall that data for six drug tablets were used to fit the simple linear model, $E(y) = \beta_0 + \beta_1 x$, where y = drug release rate and x = surface-area-to-volume ratio. An Excel/XLSTAT printout giving a 90% prediction interval for each of the $n = 6$ observations in the sample is shown above. Select an observation and give a practical interpretation for this prediction interval.

83 Sweetness of orange juice. Refer to the simple linear regression of sweetness index y and amount of pectin x for $n = 24$ orange juice samples, Exercise 22. A 90% confidence interval for the mean sweetness index, $E(y)$, for each of the first 12 runs is shown on the SPSS spreadsheet below. Select an observation and interpret this interval.

84 Public corruption and bad weather. Refer to the *Journal of Law and Economics* (Nov. 2008) study of the link between Federal Emergency Management Agency (FEMA) disaster relief and public corruption, Exercise 56. You determined that the p-value for testing the adequacy of the straight-line model relating a state's average annual number of public corruption convictions (y) to the state's average annual FEMA relief (x) was $p = .102$. Based on

this result, would you recommend using the model to predict the number of public corruption convictions in a state with an annual FEMA relief of $x = 5$ thousand dollars? Explain.

Applying the Concepts—Intermediate

85 Software millionaires and birthdays. Refer to Exercise 35 and the study of software millionaires and their birthdays. The data are reproduced on the next page. Recall that simple linear regression was used to model number (y) of software millionaire birthdays in a decade as a straight-line function of number (x) of CEO birthdays.

a. Consider a future decade where the number of CEO birthdays (in a random sample of 70 companies) is 25. Find a 95% prediction interval for the number of software millionaire birthdays in this decade. Interpret the result.

b. Consider another future decade where the number of CEO birthdays (in a random sample of 70 companies) is 10. Will the 95% prediction interval for the number of software millionaire birthdays in this decade be narrower or wider than the interval, part **b**? Explain.

	run	sweet	pectin	lower90m	upper90m
1	1	5.2	220	5.64898	5.83848
2	2	5.5	227	5.63898	5.81613
3	3	6.0	259	5.57819	5.72904
4	4	5.9	210	5.66194	5.87173
5	5	5.8	224	5.64337	5.82560
6	6	6.0	215	5.65564	5.85493
7	7	5.8	231	5.63284	5.80379
8	8	5.6	268	5.55553	5.71011
9	9	5.6	239	5.61947	5.78019
10	10	5.9	212	5.65946	5.86497
11	11	5.4	410	5.05526	5.55416
12	12	5.6	256	5.58517	5.73592
13	13	5.8	306	5.43785	5.65219
14	14	5.5	259	5.57819	5.72904
15	15	5.3	284	5.50957	5.68213
16	16	5.3	383	5.15725	5.57694
17	17	5.7	271	5.54743	5.70434
18	18	5.5	264	5.56591	5.71821
19	19	5.7	227	5.63898	5.81613
20	20	5.3	263	5.56843	5.72031
21	21	5.9	232	5.63125	5.80075
22	22	5.8	220	5.64898	5.83848
23	23	5.8	246	5.60640	5.76091
24	24	5.9	241	5.61587	5.77454

SPSS output for Exercise 83

Data for Exercise 85

Decade	Total U.S. Births (millions)	Number of Software Millionaire Birthdays	Number of CEO Birthdays (in a random sample of 70 companies from the *Fortune* 500 list)
1920	28.582	3	2
1930	24.374	1	2
1940	31.666	10	23
1950	40.530	14	38
1960	38.808	7	9
1970	33.309	4	0

Source: Sauro, J. "Were most software millionaires born around 1955?" *Measuring Usability,* November 17, 2010. Copyright © 2010 by Measuring Usability LLC. Reprinted with permission.

86 Ranking driving performance of professional golfers. Refer to *The Sport Journal* (Winter 2007) study of a new method for ranking the total driving performance of golfers on the PGA tour, Exercise 21. You fit a straight-line model relating driving accuracy (y) to driving distance (x) to the data saved in the file. Of interest is predicting y and estimating $E(y)$ when $x = 300$ yards.

a. Find and interpret a 95% prediction interval for y.

b. Find and interpret a 95% confidence interval for $E(y)$.

c. If you are interested in knowing the average driving accuracy of all PGA golfers who have a driving distance of 300 yards, which of the intervals is relevant? Explain.

87 Spreading rate of spilled liquid. Refer to the *Chemical Engineering Progress* (Jan. 2005) study of the rate at which a spilled volatile liquid will spread across a surface, Exercise 26. Recall that simple linear regression was used to model y = mass of the spill as a function of x = elapsed time of the spill.

a. Find a 99% confidence interval for the mean mass of all spills with an elapsed time of 15 minutes. Interpret the result.

b. Find a 99% prediction interval for the mass of a single spill with an elapsed time of 15 minutes. Interpret the result.

c. Compare the intervals, parts **a** and **b**. Which interval is wider? Will this always be the case? Explain.

88 Forecasting managerial needs. Managers are an important part of any organization's resource base. Accordingly, the organization should be just as concerned about forecasting its future managerial needs as it is with forecasting its needs for, say, the natural resources used in its production process (Northcraft and Neale, *Organizational Behavior: A Management Challenge,* 2001). A common forecasting procedure is to model the relationship between sales and the number of managers needed because the demand for managers is the result of the increases and decreases in the demand for products and services that a firm offers its customers. To develop this relationship, the data shown in the following table are collected from a firm's records.

a. Test the usefulness of the model. Use $\alpha = .05$. State your conclusion in the context of the problem.

b. The company projects that it will sell 39 units next month. Use the least squares model to construct a 90% prediction interval for the number of managers needed next month.

c. Interpret the interval in part **b.** Use the interval to determine the reliability of the firm's projection.

Units Sold, x	Managers, y	Units Sold, x	Managers, y
5	10	30	22
4	11	31	25
8	10	36	30
7	10	38	30
9	9	40	31
15	10	41	31
20	11	51	32
21	17	40	30
25	19	48	32
24	21	47	32

89 Predicting quit rates in manufacturing. The reasons given by workers for quitting their jobs generally fall into one of two categories: (1) worker quits to seek or take a different job, or (2) worker quits to withdraw from the labor force. Economic theory suggests that wages and quit rates are related. The table below lists quit rates (quits per 100 employees) and the average hourly wage in a sample of 15 manufacturing industries. Consider the simple linear regression of quit rate y on average wage x.

Industry	Quit Rate, y	Average Wage, x
1	1.4	$ 8.20
2	.7	10.35
3	2.6	6.18
4	3.4	5.37
5	1.7	9.94
6	1.7	9.11
7	1.0	10.59
8	.5	13.29
9	2.0	7.99
10	3.8	5.54
11	2.3	7.50
12	1.9	6.43
13	1.4	8.83
14	1.8	10.93
15	2.0	8.80

a. Do the data present sufficient evidence to conclude that average hourly wage rate contributes useful information for the prediction of quit rates? What does your model suggest about the relationship between quit rates and wages?

b. Find a 95% prediction interval for the quit rate in an industry with an average hourly wage of $9.00. Interpret the result.

c. Find a 95% confidence interval for the mean quit rate for industries with an average hourly wage of $9.00. Interpret this result.

Applying the Concepts—Advanced

90 Life tests of cutting tools. Refer to the data saved in the file, Exercise 40.

TOOLS **a.** Use a 90% confidence interval to estimate the mean useful life of a brand A cutting tool when the cutting speed is 45 meters per minute. Repeat for brand B. Compare the widths of the two intervals and comment on the reasons for any difference.

b. Use a 90% prediction interval to predict the useful life of a brand A cutting tool when the cutting speed is 45 meters per minute. Repeat for brand B. Compare the widths of the two intervals to each other and to the two intervals you calculated in part **a.** Comment on the reasons for any differences.

c. Note that the estimation and prediction you performed in parts **a** and **b** were for a value of x that was not included in the original sample—that is, the value $x = 45$ was not part of the sample. However, the value is within the range of x values in the sample, so the regression model spans the x value for which the estimation and prediction were made. In such situations, estimation and prediction represent *interpolations.* Suppose you were asked to predict the useful life of a brand A cutting tool for a cutting speed of $x = 100$ meters per minute. Because the given value of x is outside the range of the sample x values, the prediction is an example of **extrapolation.** Predict the useful life of a brand A cutting tool that is operated at 100 meters per minute and construct a 95% prediction interval for the actual useful life of the tool. What additional assumption do you have to make in order to ensure the validity of an extrapolation?

7   A Complete Example

In the preceding sections, we have presented the basic elements necessary to fit and use a straight-line regression model. In this section, we will assemble these elements by applying them in an example with the aid of a computer.

Suppose a fire insurance company wants to relate the amount of fire damage in major residential fires to the distance between the burning house and the nearest fire station. The study is to be conducted in a large suburb of a major city; a sample of 15 recent fires in this suburb is selected. The amount of damage, y, and the distance between the fire and the nearest fire station, x, are recorded for each fire. The results are shown in Table 5 and saved in the **RFIRES** file.

Step 1: First, we hypothesize a model to relate fire damage, y, to the distance from the nearest fire station, x. We hypothesize a straight-line probabilistic model:

$$y = \beta_0 + \beta_1 x + \varepsilon$$

Step 2: Next, we open the **RFIRES** file and use a statistical software package to estimate the unknown parameters in the deterministic component of the hypothesized model. The Excel printout for the simple linear regression analysis is

Table 5	Fire Damage Data
Distance from Fire Station, x (miles)	Fire Damage, y (thousands of dollars)
3.4	26.2
1.8	17.8
4.6	31.3
2.3	23.1
3.1	27.5
5.5	36.0
.7	14.1
3.0	22.3
2.6	19.6
4.3	31.3
2.1	24.0
1.1	17.3
6.1	43.2
4.8	36.4
3.8	26.1

Data Set: RFIRES

Simple Linear Regression

Regression Analysis					
Regression Statistics					
Multiple R	0.960977715				
R Square	0.923478169				
Adjusted R Square	0.917591874				
Standard Error	2.316346184				
Observations	15				
ANOVA					
	df	SS	MS	F	Significance F
Regression	1	841.766358	841.766358	156.8861596	1.2478E-08
Residual	13	69.75097535	5.365459643		
Total	14	911.5173333			
	Coefficients	Standard Error	t Stat	P-value	Lower 95%	Upper 95%
Intercept	10.27792855	1.420277811	7.236562082	8.58556E-06	7.209605476	13.34625162
DISTANCE	4.919330727	0.392747749	12.52542054	1.2478E-08	4.070850963	5.767810491

Figure 25

Excel printout for fire damage regression analysis

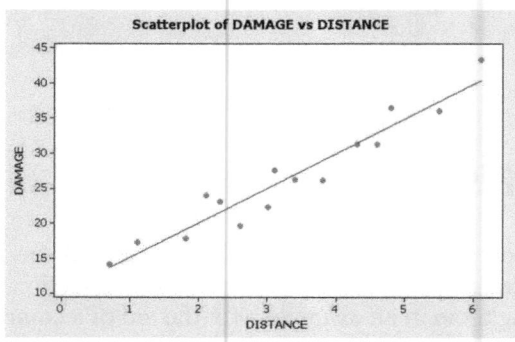

Figure 26

Minitab scatterplot with least squares line for fire damage regression analysis

shown in Figure 25. The least squares estimates of the slope β_1 and intercept β_0, highlighted on the printout, are

$$\hat{\beta}_1 = 4.919331$$
$$\hat{\beta}_0 = 10.277929$$

and the least squares equation is (rounded)

$$\hat{y} = 10.278 + 4.919x$$

This prediction equation is graphed in the Minitab scatterplot, Figure 26.

The least squares estimate of the slope, $\hat{\beta}_1 = 4.919$, implies that the estimated mean damage increases by \$4,919 for each additional mile from the fire station. This interpretation is valid over the range of x, or from .7 to 6.1 miles from the station. The estimated y-intercept, $\hat{\beta}_0 = 10.278$, has the interpretation that a fire 0 miles from the fire station has an estimated mean damage of \$10,278. Although this would seem to apply to the fire station itself, remember that the y-intercept is meaningfully interpretable only if $x = 0$ is within the sampled range of the independent variable. Because $x = 0$ is outside the range in this case, $\hat{\beta}_0$ has no practical interpretation.

Step 3: Now we specify the probability distribution of the random error component ε. The assumptions about the distribution are identical to those listed in Section 3. Although we know that these assumptions are not completely satisfied (they rarely are for practical problems), we are willing to assume they are approximately satisfied for this example. The estimate of the standard deviation σ of ε, highlighted on the Excel printout (Figure 25) is

$$s = 2.31635$$

This implies that most of the observed fire damage (y) values will fall within approximately $2s = 4.64$ thousand dollars of their respective predicted values when using the least squares line. [*Note:* A more precise prediction interval for y is given in step 5.]

Step 4: We can now check the usefulness of the hypothesized model—that is, whether x really contributes information for the prediction of y using the straight-line model. First, test the null hypothesis that the slope β_1 is 0—that is, that there is no linear relationship between fire damage and the distance from the nearest fire station, against the alternative hypothesis that fire damage increases as the distance increases. We test

$$H_0: \beta_1 = 0$$

$$H_a: \beta_1 > 0$$

The test statistic value (highlighted on the printout) is $t = 12.53$. Also, the two-tailed observed significance level for testing $H_a: \beta_1 \neq 0$, (highlighted on the printout) is approximately 0. When we divide this value in half, the p-value for our one-tailed test is also approximately 0. This small p-value leaves little doubt that mean fire damage and distance between the fire and station are at least linearly related, with mean fire damage increasing as the distance increases.

We gain additional information about the relationship by forming a 95% confidence interval for the slope β_1. The lower and upper endpoints of this interval are highlighted on the Excel printout shown in Figure 25.

This yields the interval (4.070, 5.768). We estimate (with 95% confidence) that the interval from \$4,070 to \$5,768 encloses the mean increase (β_1) in fire damage per additional mile distance from the fire station.

Another measure of the utility of the model is the coefficient of determination, r^2. The value (highlighted on Figure 25) is $r^2 = .9235$, which implies that about 92% of the sample variation in fire damage (y) is explained by the distance (x) between the fire and the fire station.

The coefficient of correlation, r, that measures the strength of the linear relationship between y and x is not shown on the Excel printout and must be calculated. Using the facts that $r = \sqrt{r^2}$ in simple linear regression and that r and $\hat{\beta}_1$ have the same sign, we find

$$r = +\sqrt{r^2} = \sqrt{.9235} = .96$$

The high correlation confirms our conclusion that β_1 is greater than 0; it appears that fire damage and distance from the fire station are positively correlated. All signs point to a strong linear relationship between y and x.

Step 5: We are now prepared to use the least squares model. Suppose the insurance company wants to predict the fire damage if a major residential fire were to occur 3.5 miles from the nearest fire station. A 95% confidence interval for $E(y)$ and prediction interval for y when $x = 3.5$ are shown on the Minitab printout, Figure 27. The predicted value (highlighted on the printout) is $\hat{y} = 27.496$, while the 95% prediction interval (also highlighted) is (22.3239, 32.6672). Therefore, with 95% confidence we predict fire damage in a major residential fire 3.5 miles from the nearest station to be between \$22,324 and \$32,667.

```
Predicted Values for New Observations

New
Obs    Fit   SE Fit       95% CI            95% PI
  1  27.496  0.604   (26.190, 28.801)   (22.324, 32.667)


Values of Predictors for New Observations

New
Obs   DISTANCE
  1     3.50
```

Figure 27

Minitab confidence and prediction intervals for fire damage regression

> ⚠ **CAUTION** We would not use this prediction model to make predictions outside the scope of the model, i.e., for homes less than .7 mile or more than 6.1 miles from the nearest fire station. A look at the data in Table 7 reveals that all the x values fall between .7 and 6.1. It is dangerous to use the model to make predictions outside the region in which the sample data fall. A straight line might not provide a good model for the relationship between the mean value of y and the value of x when stretched over a wider range of x values.

Exercises 91–93

Applying the Concepts—Intermediate

91 Prices of recycled materials. Prices of recycled materials (e.g., plastics, paper, and glass) are highly volatile due to the fact that supply is constant, rather than tied to demand. An exploratory study of the prices of recycled products in the United Kingdom was published in *Resources, Conservation, and Recycling* (Vol. 60, 2012). The researchers employed simple linear regression to model y = the monthly price of recycled colored plastic bottles as a function of x = the monthly price of naphtha (a primary material in plastics). The following results were obtained for monthly data collected over a recent 10-year period (n = 120 months):

$\hat{y} = -32.35 + 4.82x$, $t = 16.60$ (for testing H_0: $\beta_1 = 0$)
$r = .83$, $r^2 = .69$

Use this information to conduct the first four steps of a complete simple linear regression analysis. Give your conclusions in the words of the problem.

92 Forecasting movie revenues with Twitter. Refer to the *IEEE International Conference on Web Intelligence and Intelligent Agent Technology* (2010) study of how social media (e.g., Twitter.com) may influence the products consumers buy, Exercise 23. Recall that opening weekend box office revenue (in millions of dollars) and *tweet rate* (average number of tweets referring to the movie per hour)

Tweet Rate	Revenue (millions)
1365.8	142
1212.8	77
581.5	61
310.1	32
455	31
290	30
250	21
680.5	18
150	18
164.5	17
113.9	16
144.5	15
418	14
98	14
100.8	12
115.4	11
74.4	10
87.5	9
127.6	9
52.2	9
144.1	8
41.3	2
2.75	0.3

were collected for a sample of 23 recent movies. The data are reproduced in the table. Conduct a complete simple linear regression analysis of the relationship between revenue (y) and tweet rate (x). Write all your conclusions in the words of the problem.

93 An MBA's work-life balance. The importance of having employees with a healthy work-life balance has been recognized by U.S. companies for decades. Many business schools offer courses that assist MBA students with developing good work-life balance habits, and most large companies have developed work-life balance programs for their employees. In April 2005, the Graduate Management Admission Council (GMAC) conducted a survey of over 2,000 MBA alumni to explore the work-life balance issue. (For example, one question asked alumni to state their level of agreement with the statement "My personal and work demands are overwhelming.") Based on these responses, the GMAC determined a work-life balance scale score for each MBA alumnus. Scores ranged from 0 to 100, with lower scores indicating a higher imbalance between work and life. Many other variables, including average number of hours worked per week, were also measured. The data for the work-life balance study are saved in the file. (The first 15 observations are listed in the accompanying table.) Let x = average number of hours worked per week and y = work-life balance scale score for each MBA alumnus. Investigate the link between these two variables by conducting a complete simple linear regression analysis of the data. Summarize your findings in a professional report.

WLB Score	Hours
75.22	50
64.98	45
49.62	50
44.51	55
70.10	50
54.74	60
55.98	55
21.24	60
59.86	50
70.10	50
29.00	70
64.98	45
36.75	40
35.45	40
45.75	50

Source: Schoenfeld, G. "Work-life balance: An MBA alumni report," *Graduate Management Admission Council (GMAC) Research Report* (Oct. 13, 2005). Copyright © 2005 by the Graduate Management Admissions Council (GMAC). Reprinted with permission.

◻ Chapter Notes

Key Terms

Bivariate relationship
Coefficient of correlation
Coefficient of
  determination
Confidence interval
  for mean of y
Correlation
Dependent variable
Deterministic model
Errors of prediction
Estimated standard error
  of the least squares
  slope
Estimated standard error
  of regression model
Extrapolation
Independent variable
Least squares estimates
Least squares line
Least squares prediction
  equation

Line of means
Method of least squares
Population correlation
  coefficient
Prediction interval for y
Predictor variable
Probabilistic model
Random error
Regression analysis
Regression line
Regression modeling
Regression residuals
Response variable
Scatterplot
Slope
Standard error of the
  prediction
Standard error of $\hat{y}$
Straight-line (first-order)
  model
y-intercept

Key Symbols/Notation

y	Dependent variable (variable to be predicted)
x	Independent variable (variable used to predict y)
$E(y)$	Expected value (mean) of y
β_0	y-intercept of true line
β_1	Slope of true line
$\hat{\beta}_0$	Least squares estimate of y-intercept
$\hat{\beta}_1$	Least squares estimate of slope
ε	Random error
$\hat{y}$	Predicted value of y for a given x-value
$(y - \hat{y})$	Estimated error of prediction
SSE	Sum of squared errors of prediction
r	Coefficient of correlation
r^2	Coefficient of determination
x_p	Value of x used to predict y
$r^2 = \dfrac{SS_{yy} - SSE}{SS_{yy}}$	Coefficient of determination
$\hat{y} \pm t_{\alpha/2}s\sqrt{\dfrac{1}{n} + \dfrac{(x_p - \bar{x})^2}{SS_{xx}}}$	$100\%(1 - \alpha)$ confidence interval for $E(y)$ when $x = x_p$

$$\hat{y} \pm t_{\alpha/2}s\sqrt{1 + \frac{1}{n} + \frac{(x_p - \bar{x})^2}{SS_{xx}}}$$ $100\%(1 - \alpha)$ prediction interval for y when $x = x_p$

Key Ideas

Simple Linear Regression variables

y = **Dependent** variable (quantitative)
x = **Independent** variable (quantitative)

Method of Least Squares Properties

  1. average error of prediction $= 0$
  2. sum of squared errors is minimum

Practical Interpretation of y-Intercept

Predicted y-value when $x = 0$

(no practical interpretation if $x = 0$ is either nonsensical or outside range of sample data)

Practical Interpretation of Slope

Increase (or decrease) in mean y for every 1-unit increase in x

First-Order (Straight-Line) Model

$$E(y) = \beta_0 + \beta_1 x$$

where $E(y)$ = mean of y

  β_0 = **y-intercept** of line (point where line intecepts y-axis)
  β_1 = **slope** of line (change in mean of y for every 1-unit change in x)

Coefficient of Correlation, r

  1. ranges between -1 and $+1$
  2. measures strength of *linear relationship* between y and x

Coefficient of Determination, r^2

  1. ranges between 0 and 1
  2. measures proportion of sample variation in y "explained" by the model

Practical Interpretation of Model Standard Deviation, s

Ninety-five percent of y-values fall within $2s$ of their respected predicted values

Width of *confidence interval for $E(y)$* will always be **narrower** than width of prediction interval for y

Guide to Simple Linear Regression

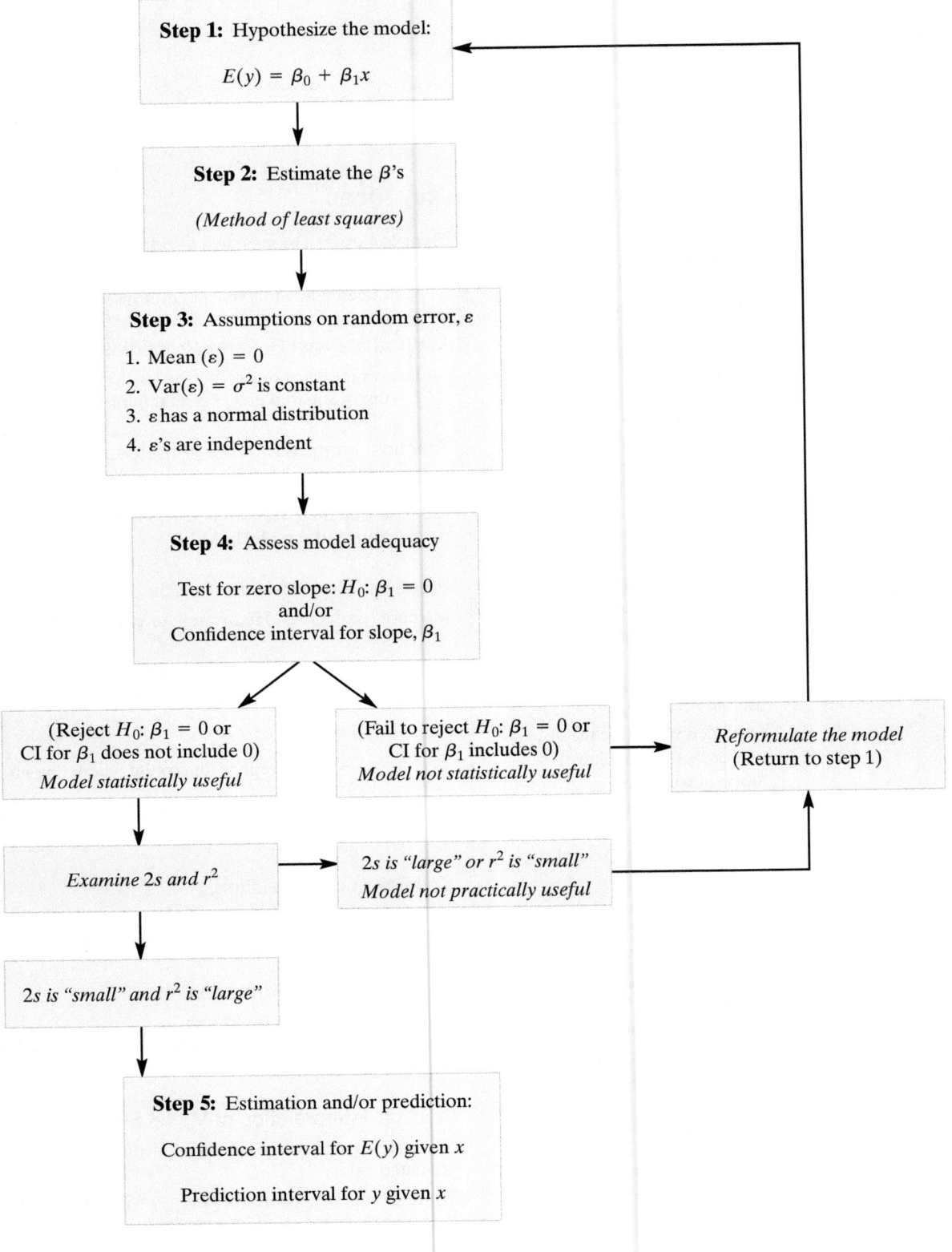

Supplementary Exercises 94–112

Please be aware that some of the following problems may require knowledge of concepts that are not presented in this chapter.

Learning the Mechanics

94 Consider the following sample data:

y	5	1	3
x	5	1	3

a. Construct a scatterplot for the data.

b. It is possible to find many lines for which $\sum(y - \hat{y}) = 0$. For this reason, the criterion $\sum(y - \hat{y}) = 0$ is not used for identifying the "best-fitting" straight line. Find two lines that have $\sum(y - \hat{y}) = 0$.

c. Find the least squares line.

d. Compare the value of SSE for the least squares line to that of the two lines you found in part **b.** What principle of least squares is demonstrated by this comparison?

95 In fitting a least squares line to $n = 15$ data points, the following quantities were computed: $SS_{xx} = 55$, $SS_{yy} = 198$, $SS_{xy} = -88$, $\bar{x} = 1.3$, and $\bar{y} = 35$.

a. Find the least squares line.

b. Graph the least squares line.

c. Calculate SSE.

d. Calculate s^2.

e. Find a 90% confidence interval for β_1. Interpret this estimate.

f. Find a 90% confidence interval for the mean value of y when $x = 15$.

g. Find a 90% prediction interval for y when $x = 15$.

96 Consider the following 10 data points:

L11096

x	3	5	6	4	3	7	6	5	4	7
y	4	3	2	1	2	3	3	5	4	2

a. Plot the data on a scatterplot.

b. Calculate the values of r and r^2.

c. Is there sufficient evidence to indicate that x and y are linearly correlated? Test at the $\alpha = .10$ level of significance.

Applying the Concepts—Basic

97 "Metaskills" and career management. Effective management of one's own career requires a skill set that includes adaptability, tolerance for ambiguity, self-awareness, and ability to identify change. Management professors at Pace University (New York) used correlation coefficients to investigate the relationship between these "metaskills" and effective career management (*International Journal of Manpower*, Aug. 2000). Data were collected for 446 business graduates who had all completed a management metaskills course. Two of the many variables measured were self-knowledge skill level (x) and goal-setting ability (y). The correlation coefficient for these two variables was $r = .70$.

a. Give a practical interpretation of the value of r.

b. The p-value for a test of no correlation between the two variables was reported as p-value $= .001$. Interpret this result.

c. Find the coefficient of determination, r^2, and interpret the result.

98 **Burnout of human services professionals.** Emotional exhaustion, or *burnout*, is a significant problem for people with careers in the field of human services. Regression analysis was used to investigate the relationship between burnout and aspects of the human services professional's job and job-related behavior (*Journal of Applied Behavioral Science*, Vol. 22, 1986). Emotional exhaustion was measured with the Maslach Burnout Inventory, a questionnaire. One of the independent variables considered, called *concentration*, was the proportion of social contacts with individuals who belong to a person's work group. The next table lists the values of the emotional exhaustion index (higher values indicate greater exhaustion) and concentration for a sample of 25 human services professionals who work in a large public hospital. A Minitab printout of the simple linear regression is provided below.

Exhaustion Index, y	Concentration, x	Exhaustion Index, y	Concentration, x
100	20%	493	86%
525	60	892	83
300	38	527	79
980	88	600	75
310	79	855	81
900	87	709	75
410	68	791	77
296	12	718	77
120	35	684	77
501	70	141	17
920	80	400	85
810	92	970	96
506	77		

```
The regression equation is
EXHAUST = - 29 + 8.87 CONCEN


Predictor    Coef   SE Coef       T       P
Constant    -29.5     106.7   -0.28   0.785
CONCEN      8.865     1.471    6.03   0.000


S = 174.207    R-Sq = 61.2%    R-Sq(adj) = 59.5%


Analysis of Variance

Source          DF        SS        MS       F       P
Regression       1   1102408   1102408   36.33   0.000
Residual Error  23    698009     30348
Total           24   1800417


Predicted Values for New Observations

New
Obs    Fit   SE Fit       95% CI            95% PI
  1  679.7     38.7   (599.7, 759.8)   (310.6, 1048.9)


Values of Predictors for New Observations

New
Obs   CONCEN
  1     80.0
```

a. Construct a scatterplot for the data. Do the variables x and y appear to be related?

b. Find the correlation coefficient for the data and interpret its value. Does your conclusion mean that concentration causes emotional exhaustion? Explain.

c. Test the usefulness of the straight-line relationship with concentration for predicting burnout. Use $\alpha = .05$.

d. Find the coefficient of determination for the model and interpret it.

e. Find a 95% confidence interval for the slope β_1. Interpret the result.

f. Use a 95% confidence interval to estimate the mean exhaustion level for all professionals who have 80% of their social contacts within their work groups. Interpret the interval.

99 Retaliation against company "whistle-blowers." Individuals who report perceived wrongdoing of a corporation or public agency are known as *whistle-blowers*. Two researchers developed an index to measure the extent of retaliation against a whistle-blower (*Journal of Applied Psychology*, 1986). The index was based on the number of forms of reprisal actually experienced, the number of forms of reprisal threatened, and the number of people within the organization (e.g., coworkers or immediate supervisor) who retaliated against them. The table below lists the retaliation index (higher numbers indicate more extensive retaliation) and salary for a sample of 15 whistle-blowers from federal agencies.

RETAL

Retaliation Index	Salary	Retaliation Index	Salary
301	$62,000	535	$19,800
550	36,500	455	44,000
755	21,600	615	46,600
327	24,000	700	15,100
500	30,100	650	70,000
377	35,000	630	21,000
290	47,500	360	16,900
452	54,000		

Source: Based on Near, J. P., & Miceli, M. P. "Retaliation against whistle blowers: Predictors and effects," *Journal of Applied Psychology*, Vol. 71, No. 1, 1986, pp. 137–145.

a. Construct a scatterplot for the data. Does it appear that the extent of retaliation increases, decreases, or stays the same with an increase in salary? Explain.

b. Use the method of least squares to fit a straight line to the data.

c. Graph the least squares line on your scatterplot. Does the least squares line support your answer to the question in part **a**? Explain.

d. Interpret the y-intercept, $\hat{\beta}_0$ of the least squares line in terms of this application. Is the interpretation meaningful?

e. Interpret the slope, $\hat{\beta}_1$, of the least squares line in terms of this application. Over what range of x is this interpretation meaningful?

f. Test the adequacy of the model using $\alpha = .05$.

100 Buying income of households. *Sales and Marketing Management* determined the "effective buying income" (EBI) of the average household in a state. Can the EBI be used to predict retail sales per household in the store-group category "eating and drinking places"?

EBI

a. Use the data for 13 states given in the table below to find the least squares line relating retail sales per household (y) to average household EBI (x).

b. Plot the least squares line, as well as the actual data points, on a scatterplot.

c. Based on the graph, part **b**, give your opinion regarding the predictive ability of the least squares line.

d. Find a 95% confidence interval for the slope of the line.

e. Use the results, part **d**, to assess the adequacy of the straight-line model.

State	Average Household Buying Income ($)	Retail Sales: Eating and Drinking Places ($ per household)
Connecticut	60,998	2,553.8
New Jersey	63,853	2,154.8
Michigan	46,915	2,523.3
Minnesota	44,717	2,278.6
Florida	42,442	2,475.8
South Carolina	37,848	2,358.4
Mississippi	34,490	1,538.4
Oklahoma	34,830	2,063.1
Texas	44,729	2,363.5
Colorado	44,571	3,214.9
Utah	43,421	2,653.8
California	50,713	2,215.0
Oregon	40,597	2,144.0

Source: "The survey of buying power," *Sales and Marketing Management*, 1995. Copyright © 1995 by Sales and Marketing Management. Reprinted with permission.

101 Diamonds sold at retail. The *Journal of Statistics Education* did a study of 308 diamonds sold on the open market. For this exercise, relate the size of the diamond (number of carats) to the asking price (dollars) using a scatterplot.

DIAMND

a. Write the equation of a straight-line model relating asking price (y) to number of carats (x).

b. An XLSTAT simple linear regression printout for the analysis is shown on the following page. Find the equation of the least squares line.

c. Give a practical interpretation of the y-intercept of the least squares line. If a practical interpretation is not possible, explain why.

d. Locate a 95% confidence interval for the slope of the least squares line on the printout and practically interpret the result. Over what range is the interpretation meaningful?

e. Locate the estimated standard deviation of the random error on the printout and practically interpret this value.

f. Specify the null and alternative hypotheses for determining whether a positive linear relationship exists between asking price and size.

g. Locate the p-value of the test, part **f**, on the printout. Interpret the result if $\alpha = .05$.

h. Locate the coefficient of determination, r^2, on the printout and interpret the result.

i. Locate the coefficient of correlation, r, on the printout and interpret the result.

j. Locate a 95% prediction interval for the asking price when carat size is .5 on the printout and practically interpret the result.

XLSTAT output for Exercise 101

Variables	CARAT	PRICE
CARAT	**1.0000**	0.9447
PRICE	0.9447	**1.0000**

Regression of variable PRICE:

Goodness of fit statistics:

Observatic	308.0000
Sum of we	308.0000
DF	306.0000
R²	0.8925
Adjusted R	0.8922
MSE	1248949.7531
RMSE	1117.5642
DW	1.2156

Analysis of variance:

Source	DF	Sum of squares	Mean squares	F	Pr > F
Model	1	3173248722.4667	3173248722.4667	2540.7337	< 0.0001
Error	306	382178624.4521	1248949.7531		
Corrected	307	3555427346.9188			

Computed against model Y=Mean(Y)

Model parameters:

Source	Value	Standard error	t	Pr > |t|	Lower bound (95%)	Upper bound (95%)
Intercept	-2298.3576	158.5306	-14.4979	< 0.0001	-2610.3056	-1986.4096
CARAT	11598.8840	230.1106	50.4057	< 0.0001	11146.0846	12051.6834

Equation of the model:

PRICE = -2298.35760+11598.88401*CARAT

Predictions for the new observations:

Observation	Pred(PRICE)	Lower bound 95% (Mean)	Upper bound 95% (Mean)	Lower bound 95% (Observation)	Upper bound 95% (Observation)
0.5	3501.0844	3362.4670	3639.7018	1297.6366	5704.5322

k. Locate a 95% confidence interval for the mean asking price when carat size is .5 on the printout and practically interpret the result.

102 Sports news on local TV broadcasts. *The Sports Journal* (Winter 2004) published the results of a study conducted to assess the factors that impact the time allotted to sports news on local television news broadcasts. Information on total time (in minutes) allotted to sports and audience ratings of the TV news broadcast (measured on a 100-point scale) was obtained from a national sample of 163 news directors. A correlation analysis on the data yielded $r = .43$.
a. Interpret the value of the correlation coefficient, r.
b. Find and interpret the value of the coefficient of determination, r^2.

Applying the Concepts—Intermediate

103 Evaluating managerial success. H. Mintzberg's classic book *The Nature of Managerial Work* (1973) identified the roles found in all managerial jobs. An observational study of

MINDEX

19 managers from a medium-sized manufacturing plant extended Mintzberg's work by investigating which activities *successful* managers actually perform (*Journal of Applied Behavioral Science,* Aug. 1985). To measure success, the researchers devised an index based on the manager's length of time in the organization and his or her level within the firm; the higher the index, the more successful the manager. The table on the following page presents data that can be used to determine whether managerial success is related to the extensiveness of a manager's network-building interactions with people outside the manager's work unit. Such interactions include phone and face-to-face meetings with customers and suppliers, attending outside meetings, and doing public relations work.
a. Construct a scatterplot for the data.
b. Find the prediction equation for managerial success.
c. Find s for your prediction equation. Interpret the standard deviation s in the context of this problem.
d. Plot the least squares line on your scatterplot of part **a.** Does it appear that the number of interactions

Data for Exercise 103

Manager	Manager Success Index, y	Number of Interactions with Outsiders, x
1	40	12
2	73	71
3	95	70
4	60	81
5	81	43
6	27	50
7	53	42
8	66	18
9	25	35
10	63	82
11	70	20
12	47	81
13	80	40
14	51	33
15	32	45
16	50	10
17	52	65
18	30	20
19	42	21

with outsiders contributes information for the prediction of managerial success? Explain.

e. Conduct a formal statistical hypothesis test to answer the question posed in part **d**. Use $\alpha = .05$.

f. Construct a 95% confidence interval for β_1. Interpret the interval in the context of the problem.

g. A particular manager was observed for 2 weeks, as in the *Journal of Applied Behavioral Science* study. She made 55 contacts with people outside her work unit. Predict the value of the manager's success index. Use a 90% prediction interval.

h. A second manager was observed for 2 weeks. This manager made 110 contacts with people outside his work unit. Why should caution be exercised in using the least squares model developed from the given data set to construct a prediction interval for this manager's success index?

i. In the context of this problem, determine the value of x for which the associated prediction interval for y is the narrowest.

104 Doctors and ethics. The *Journal of Medical Ethics* (Vol. 32, 2006) did a study of physicians' use of ethics consultation. The medical researchers measured the *length of time in practice* (i.e., years of experience) and the *amount of exposure to ethics in medical school* (number of hours) for a sample of 118 physicians. Consider a straight-line regression model relating hours of exposure (y) to time in practice (x).

a. Fit the model to the data saved in the file and conduct a test (at $\alpha = .05$) for a linear relationship between the two variables.

b. First, identify a highly suspect outlier for hours of exposure. Then remove this outlier from the data set and rerun the analysis, part **a**. What do you observe?

105 Do New Jersey banks serve minority communities? Financial institutions have a legal and social responsibility to serve all communities, both inner-city and suburban neighborhoods, both poor

and wealthy communities? In New Jersey, banks have been charged with withdrawing from urban areas with a high percentage of minorities. To examine this charge, a regional New Jersey newspaper, the *Asbury Park Press*, compiled county-by-county data on the number (y) of people in each county per branch bank in the county and the percentage (x) of the population in each county that is minority. These data for each of New Jersey's 21 counties are provided in the table below.

County	Number of People per Bank Branch	Percentage of Minority Population
Atlantic	3,073	23.3
Bergen	2,095	13.0
Burlington	2,905	17.8
Camden	3,330	23.4
Cape May	1,321	7.3
Cumberland	2,557	26.5
Essex	3,474	48.8
Gloucester	3,068	10.7
Hudson	3,683	33.2
Hunterdon	1,998	3.7
Mercer	2,607	24.9
Middlesex	3,154	18.1
Monmouth	2,609	12.6
Morris	2,253	8.2
Ocean	2,317	4.7
Passaic	3,307	28.1
Salem	2,511	16.7
Somerset	2,333	12.0
Sussex	2,568	2.4
Union	3,048	25.6
Warren	2,349	2.8

Source: D'Ambrosio, P., & Chambers, S. "No checks and balances," *Asbury Park Press,* September 10, 1995. Copyright © 1995 by Asbury Park Press. Reprinted with permission.

a. Plot the data in a scatterplot. What pattern, if any, does the plot reveal?

b. Consider the linear model $E(y) = \beta_0 + \beta_1 x$. If, in fact, the charge against the New Jersey banks is true, then an increase in the percentage of minorities (x) will lead to a decrease in the number of bank branches in a county and therefore will result in an increase in the number of people (y) per branch. Will the value of β_1 be positive or negative in this situation?

c. Do these data support or refute the charge made against the New Jersey banking community? Test using $\alpha = .01$.

106 Monetary values of NFL teams. *Forbes* magazine did a 2011 report on the financial standings of each team in the National Football League (NFL). The table listing the current value (without deduction for debt, except stadium debt) and operating income for each team is reproduced on the next page.

a. Propose a straight-line model relating an NFL team's current value (y) to its operating income (x).

b. Fit the model to the data using the method of least squares.

c. Interpret the least squares estimates of the slope and y-intercept in the words of the problem.

d. Statistically assess the adequacy of the model. Do you recommend using it to predict an NFL team's value?

Data for Exercise 106

Rank	Team	Current Value ($mil)	1-Yr Value Change (%)	Debt/Value (%)	Revenue ($mil)	Operating Income ($mil)
1	Dallas Cowboys	1,850	2	18	406	119
2	Washington Redskins	1,555	0	26	352	65.6
3	New England Patriots	1,400	2	19	333	42.9
4	New York Giants	1,300	10	50	293	40.6
5	New York Jets	1,223	7	61	285	25.1
6	Houston Texans	1,202	3	17	283	41
7	Philadelphia Eagles	1,164	4	9	274	28.9
8	Chicago Bears	1,093	2	11	266	43.4
9	Green Bay Packers	1,089	7	2	259	12
10	Baltimore Ravens	1,088	1	25	262	24.9
11	Indianapolis Colts	1,057	2	4	252	32.8
12	Denver Broncos	1,046	0	14	255	28.5
13	Pittsburgh Steelers	1,018	2	25	255	28.3
14	Miami Dolphins	1,012	0	40	253	12.9
15	Carolina Panthers	1,002	−3	19	257	31.2
16	Seattle Seahawks	997	1	12	249	7.8
17	San Francisco 49ers	990	7	14	234	1.5
18	Kansas City Chiefs	986	2	14	252	14.5
19	Tampa Bay Buccaneers	981	−5	18	245	50.8
20	Cleveland Browns	977	−4	15	247	−2.9
21	New Orleans Saints	965	1	13	261	28.9
22	Tennessee Titans	964	−3	13	250	21.8
23	San Diego Chargers	920	1	14	241	34.2
24	Arizona Cardinals	901	−2	17	240	56.4
25	Cincinnati Bengals	875	−3	11	236	44.7
26	Detroit Lions	844	3	33	228	−7.7
27	Atlanta Falcons	814	−2	34	233	27.2
28	Minnesota Vikings	796	3	41	227	3.7
29	Buffalo Bills	792	−1	16	236	40.9
30	St. Louis Rams	775	−1	15	228	24.6
31	Oakland Raiders	761	0	16	217	23
32	Jacksonville Jaguars	725	0	17	236	32.8

Source: Based on "Football's Most Valuable Teams," *Forbes,* September 7, 2011.

107 Evaluating a truck weigh-in-motion program. The Minnesota Department of Transportation installed a state-of-the-art weigh-in-motion scale in the concrete surface of the eastbound lanes of Interstate 494 in Bloomington, Minnesota. After installation, a study was undertaken to determine whether the scale's readings

Trial Number	Static Weight of Truck, x (thousand pounds)	Weigh-in-Motion Reading Prior to Calibration Adjustment, y_1 (thousand pounds)	Weigh-in-Motion Reading After Calibration Adjustment, y_2 (thousand pounds)
1	27.9	26.0	27.8
2	29.1	29.9	29.1
3	38.0	39.5	37.8
4	27.0	25.1	27.1
5	30.3	31.6	30.6
6	34.5	36.2	34.3
7	27.8	25.1	26.9
8	29.6	31.0	29.6
9	33.1	35.6	33.0
10	35.5	40.2	35.0

Source: Based on Wright, J. L., Owen, F., and Pena, D. "Status of MN/DOT's weigh-in-motion program," St. Paul: Minnesota Department of Transportation, January 1983.

correspond with the static weights of the vehicles being monitored. (Studies of this type are known as *calibration studies.*) After some preliminary comparisons using a two-axle, six-tire truck carrying different loads (see the accompanying table), calibration adjustments were made in the software of the weigh-in-motion system, and the scales were reevaluated.

a. Construct two scatterplots, one of y_1 versus x and the other of y_2 versus x.

b. Use the scatterplots of part **a** to evaluate the performance of the weigh-in-motion scale both before and after the calibration adjustment.

c. Calculate the correlation coefficient for both sets of data and interpret their values. Explain how these correlation coefficients can be used to evaluate the weigh-in-motion scale.

d. Suppose the sample correlation coefficient for y_2 and x was 1. Could this happen if the static weights and the weigh-in-motion readings disagreed? Explain.

108 Energy efficiency of buildings. Firms planning to build new plants or make additions to existing facilities have become very conscious of the energy efficiency of proposed new structures and are interested in the relation between yearly energy consumption and the number of square feet of building shell. The table on the next page lists the energy consumption in British thermal units (a BTU is the amount of heat required to raise 1 pound of water 1°F) for 22 buildings that were all subjected to the same climatic conditions. Consider a straight-line model relating BTU consumption, y, to building shell area, x.

a. Find the least squares estimates of the intercept β_0 and the slope β_1.

b. Investigate the usefulness of the model you developed in part **a.** Is yearly energy consumption positively linearly related to the shell area of the building? Test using $\alpha = .10$.

c. Find the observed significance level of the test of part **b.** Interpret its value.

d. Find the coefficient of determination r^2 and interpret its value.

e. A company wishes to build a new warehouse that will contain 8,000 square feet of shell area. Find the predicted value of energy consumption and associated 95% prediction interval. Comment on the usefulness of this interval.

f. The application of the model you developed in part **a** to the warehouse problem of part **e** is appropriate only if certain assumptions can be made about the new warehouse. What are these assumptions?

BTU/Year (thousands)	Shell Area (square feet)
3,870,000	30,001
1,371,000	13,530
2,422,000	26,060
672,200	6,355
233,100	4,576
218,900	24,680
354,000	2,621
3,135,000	23,350
1,470,000	18,770
1,408,000	12,220
2,201,000	25,490
2,680,000	23,680
337,500	5,650
567,500	8,001
555,300	6,147
239,400	2,660
2,629,000	19,240
1,102,000	10,700
423,500	9,125
423,500	6,510
1,691,000	13,530
1,870,000	18,860

109 Foreign investment risk. One of the most difficult tasks of developing and managing a global portfolio is assessing the risks of potential foreign investments. Duke University researcher C. R. Henry collaborated with two First Chicago Investment Management Company directors to examine the use of country credit ratings as a means of evaluating foreign investments (*Journal of Portfolio Management*, Winter 1995). To be effective, such a measure should help explain and predict the volatility of the foreign market in question. Data on annualized risk (y) and average credit rating (x) for 40 fictitious countries (based on the study results) are saved in the file. (The first and last five countries are shown in the table.)

a. Do the data provide sufficient evidence to conclude that country credit risk (x) contributes information for the prediction of market volatility (y)?

Country	Annualized Risk (%)	Average Credit Rating
1	85.9	30.7
2	25.8	77.1
3	25.2	82.7
4	20.9	77.3
5	63.7	35.1
⋮	⋮	⋮
36	73.0	31.5
37	20.7	86.5
38	14.3	95.3
39	44.9	43.9
40	34.5	23.4

b. Use a graph to visually locate any unusual data points (outliers).

c. Eliminate the outlier(s), part **b**, from the data set and rerun the simple linear regression analysis. Note any dramatic changes in the results.

Applying the Concepts—Advanced

110 Regression through the origin. Sometimes it is known from theoretical considerations that the straight-line relationship between two variables, x and y, passes through the origin of the xy-plane. Consider the relationship between the total weight of a shipment of 50-pound bags of flour, y, and the number of bags in the shipment, x. Because a shipment containing $x = 0$ bags (i.e., no shipment at all) has a total weight of $y = 0$, a straight-line model of the relationship between x and y should pass through the point $x = 0$, $y = 0$. In such a case, you could assume $\beta_0 = 0$ and characterize the relationship between x and y with the following model:

$$y = \beta_1 x + \varepsilon$$

The least squares estimate of β_1 for this model is

$$\hat{\beta}_1 = \frac{\sum x_i y_i}{\sum x_i^2}$$

From the records of past flour shipments, 15 shipments were randomly chosen, and the data shown in the table below were recorded.

Weight of Shipment	Number of 50-Pound Bags in Shipment
5,050	100
10,249	205
20,000	450
7,420	150
24,685	500
10,206	200
7,325	150
4,958	100
7,162	150
24,000	500
4,900	100
14,501	300
28,000	600
17,002	400
16,100	400

a. Find the least squares line for the given data under the assumption that $\beta_0 = 0$. Plot the least squares line on a scatterplot of the data.

b. Find the least squares line for the given data using the model

$$y = \beta_0 + \beta_1 x + \varepsilon$$

(i.e., do not restrict β_0 to equal 0). Plot this line on the same scatterplot you constructed in part **a**.

c. Refer to part **b**. Why might $\hat{\beta}_0$ be different from 0 even though the true value of β_0 is known to be 0?

d. The estimated standard error of $\hat{\beta}_0$ is equal to

$$s\sqrt{\frac{1}{n} + \frac{\bar{x}^2}{SS_{xx}}}$$

Use the t-statistic

$$t = \frac{\hat{\beta}_0 - 0}{s\sqrt{(1/n) + (\bar{x}^2/SS_{xx})}}$$

to test the null hypothesis $H_0: \beta_0 = 0$ against the alternative $H_a: \beta_0 \neq 0$. Use $\alpha = .10$. Should you include β_0 in your model?

Critical Thinking Challenges

111 Comparing cost functions. Managers are interested in modeling past cost behavior in order to make more accurate predictions of future costs. Models of past cost behavior are called *cost functions*. Factors that influence costs are called *cost drivers* (Horngren, Datar, and Rajan, *Cost Accounting*, 2011). The cost data shown below are from a rug manufacturer. Indirect manufacturing labor costs consist of machine maintenance costs and setup labor costs. Machine-hours and direct manufacturing labor-hours are cost drivers. Your task is to estimate and compare two alternative cost functions for indirect manufacturing labor costs. In the first, machine-hours is the independent variable; in the second, direct manufacturing labor-hours is the independent variable. Prepare a report that compares the two cost functions and recommends which should be used to explain and predict indirect manufacturing labor costs. Be sure to justify your choice.

Week	Indirect Manufacturing Labor Costs	Machine-Hours	Direct Manufacturing Labor-Hours
1	$1,190	68	30
2	1,211	88	35
3	1,004	62	36
4	917	72	20
5	770	60	47
6	1,456	96	45
7	1,180	78	44
8	710	46	38
9	1,316	82	70
10	1,032	94	30
11	752	68	29
12	963	48	38

Source: Based on Horngren, C. T., Datar, S. M., & Rajan, M. *Cost Accounting: A Managerial Emphasis,* 14th ed. Upper Saddle River, N.J.: Prentice Hall, 2011.

112 Spall damage in bricks. A civil suit revolved around a five-building brick apartment complex located in the Bronx, New York, which began to suffer *spalling* damage (i.e., a separation of some portion of the face of a brick from its body). The owner of the complex alleged that the bricks were defectively manufactured. The brick manufacturer countered that poor design and shoddy management led to the damage. To settle the suit, an estimate of the rate of damage per 1,000 bricks, called the *spall rate,* was required (*Chance,* Summer 1994). The owner estimated the spall rate using several *scaffold-drop* surveys. (With this method, an engineer lowers a scaffold down at selected places on building walls and counts the number of visible spalls for every 1,000 bricks in the observation area.) The brick manufacturer conducted its own survey by dividing the walls of the complex into 83 wall segments and taking a photograph of each wall segment. (The number of spalled bricks that could be made out from each photo was recorded, and the sum over all 83 wall segments was used as an estimate of total spall damage.) In this court case, the jury was faced with the following dilemma: The scaffold-drop survey provided the most accurate estimate of spall rates in a given wall segment. Unfortunately, the drop areas were not selected at random from the entire complex; rather, drops were made at areas with high spall concentrations, leading to an overestimate of the total damage. On the other hand, the photo survey was complete in that all 83 wall segments in the complex were checked for spall damage. But the spall rate estimated by the photos, at least in areas of high spall concentration, was biased low (spalling damage cannot always be seen from a photo), leading to an underestimate of the total damage.

Drop Location	Drop Spall Rate (per 1,000 bricks)	Photo Spall Rate (per 1,000 bricks)
1	0	0
2	5.1	0
3	6.6	0
4	1.1	.8
5	1.8	1.0
6	3.9	1.0
7	11.5	1.9
8	22.1	7.7
9	39.3	14.9
10	39.9	13.9
11	43.0	11.8

Source: Fairley, W. B., et al. "Bricks, buildings, and the Bronx: Estimating masonry deterioration," *Chance,* Vol. 7. No. 3, Summer 1994, p. 36 (Figure 3). Reprinted with permission from *Chance.* © 1994 by the American Statistical Association. All rights reserved. [*Note:* The data points are estimated from the points shown on a scatterplot.]

The data in the table are the spall rates obtained using the two methods at 11 drop locations. Use the data, as did expert statisticians who testified in the case, to help the jury estimate the true spall rate at a given wall segment. Then explain how this information, coupled with the data (not given here) on all 83 wall segments, can provide a reasonable estimate of the total spall damage (i.e., total number of damaged bricks).

Activity 1 — Applying Simple Linear Regression to Your Favorite Data

Many dependent variables in business serve as the subjects of regression modeling efforts. We list five such variables here:

1. Rate of return of a stock
2. Annual unemployment rate
3. Grade point average of an accounting student
4. Gross domestic product of the United States
5. Salary cap space available for your favorite NFL team

Choose one of these dependent variables, or choose some other dependent variable, for which you want to construct a prediction model. There may be a large number of independent variables that should be included in a prediction equation for the dependent variable you choose. List three potentially important independent variables, x_1, x_2, and x_3,

that you think might be (individually) strongly related to your dependent variable. Next, obtain 25 data values, each of which consists of a measure of your dependent variable y and the corresponding values of x_1, x_2, and x_3.

a. Use the least squares formulas given in this chapter to fit three straight-line models–one for each independent variable–for predicting y.

b. Interpret the sign of the estimated slope coefficient $\hat{\beta}_1$ in each case, and test the utility of each model by testing H_0: $\beta_1 = 0$ against H_a: $\beta_1 \neq 0$. What assumptions must be satisfied to ensure the validity of these tests?

c. Calculate the coefficient of determination, r^2, for each model. Which of the independent variables predicts y best for the 25 sampled sets of data? Is this variable necessarily best in general (i.e., for the entire population)? Explain.

References

Chatterjee, S., & Price, B. *Regression Analysis by Example,* 2nd ed. New York: Wiley, 1991.

Draper, N., & Smith, H. *Applied Regression Analysis,* 3rd ed. New York: Wiley, 1987.

Gitlow, H., Oppenheim, A., & Oppenheim, R. *Quality Management: Tools and Methods for Improvement,* 2nd ed. Burr Ridge, Ill.: Irwin, 1995.

Graybill, F. *Theory and Application of the Linear Model.* North Scituate, Mass.: Duxbury, 1976.

Kleinbaum, D., & Kupper, L. *Applied Regression Analysis and Other Multivariable Methods,* 2nd ed. North Scituate, Mass.: Duxbury, 1997.

Kutner, M., Nachtsheim, C., Neter, J., & Li, W. *Applied Linear Statistical Models,* 5th ed. New York: McGraw-Hill, 2006.

Mendenhall, W. *Introduction to Linear Models and the Design and Analysis of Experiments.* Belmont, CA.: Wadsworth, 1968.

Mendenhall, W., & Sincich, T. A. *Second Course in Statistics: Regression Analysis,* 7th ed. Upper Saddle River, N.J.: Prentice Hall, 2011.

Montgomery, D., Peck, E., & Vining, G. *Introduction to Linear Regression Analysis,* 3rd ed. New York: Wiley, 2001.

Mosteller, F., & Tukey, J. W. *Data Analysis and Regression: A Second Course in Statistics.* Reading, Mass.: Addison-Wesley, 1977.

Rousseeuw, P. J., & Leroy, A. M. *Robust Regression and Outlier Detection.* New York: Wiley, 1987.

Weisburg, S. *Applied Linear Regression,* 2nd ed. New York: Wiley, 1985.

USING TECHNOLOGY Technology images shown here are taken from SPSS Statistics Professional 20.0, Minitab 16, XLSTAT for Pearson, and Excel 2010.

SPSS: Simple Linear Regression

Regression Analysis

Step 1 Access the SPSS spreadsheet file that contains the two quantitative variables (dependent and independent variables).

Step 2 Click on the "Analyze" button on the SPSS menu bar and then click on "Regression" and "Linear," as shown in Figure S.1.

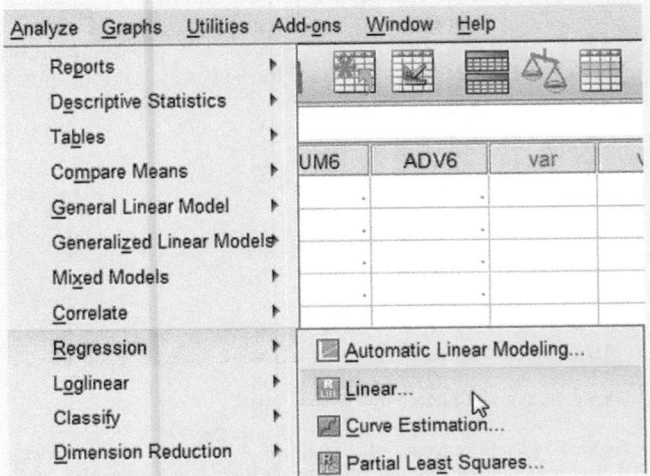

Figure S.1 SPSS menu options for regression

Step 3 On the resulting dialog box (see Figure S.2), specify the dependent variable in the "Dependent" box and the independent variable in the "Independent(s)" box. Be sure to select "Enter" in the "Method" box.

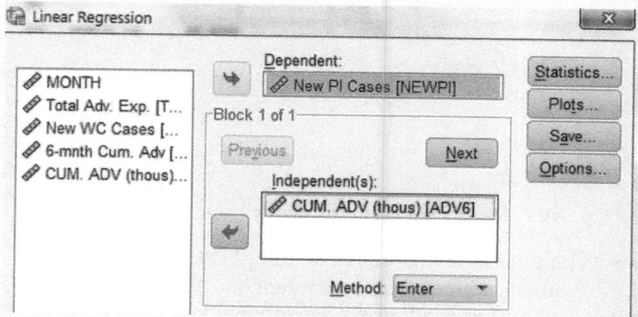

Figure S.2 SPSS linear regression dialog box

Step 4 To produce confidence intervals for the model parameters, click the "Statistics" button and check the appropriate menu items in the resulting menu list.

Step 5 To obtain prediction intervals for y and confidence intervals for $E(y)$, click the "Save" button and check the appropriate items in the resulting menu list, as shown in Figure S.3. (The prediction intervals will be added as new columns to the SPSS data spreadsheet.)

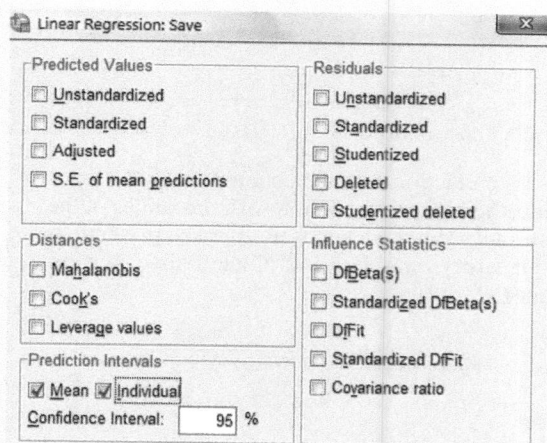

Figure S.3 SPSS linear regression save dialog box

Step 6 To return to the main Regression dialog box from any of these optional screens, click "Continue." Click "OK" on the Regression dialog box to view the linear regression results.

Correlation Analysis

Step 1 Click on the "Analyze" button on the main menu bar and then click on "Correlate" (see Figure S.1).

Step 2 Click on "Bivariate." The resulting dialog box appears in Figure S.4.

Step 3 Enter the variables of interest in the "Variables" box and check the "Pearson" option.

Step 4 Click "OK" to obtain a printout of the correlation.

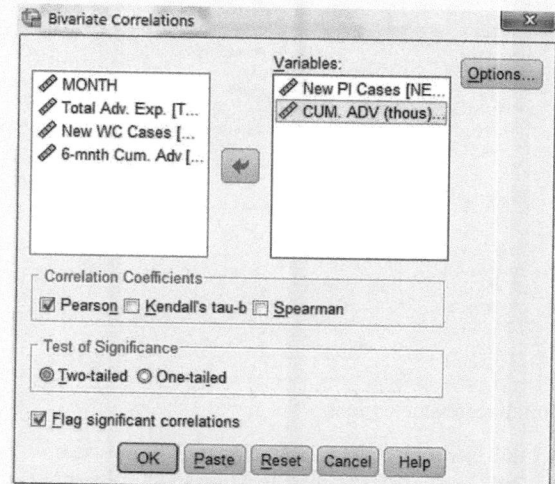

Figure S.4 SPSS correlation dialog box

Minitab: Simple Linear Regression

Regression Analysis

Step 1 Access the Minitab worksheet file that contains the two quantitative variables (dependent and independent variables).

Step 2 Click on the "Stat" button on the Minitab menu bar and then click on "Regression" and "Regression" again, as shown in Figure M.1.

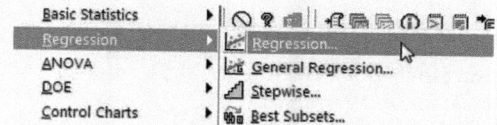

Figure M.1 Minitab menu options for regression

Step 3 On the resulting dialog box (see Figure M.2), specify the dependent variable in the "Response" box and the independent variable in the "Predictors" box.

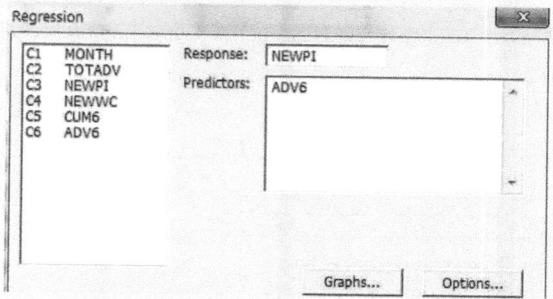

Figure M.2 Minitab regression dialog box

Step 4 To produce prediction intervals for y and confidence intervals for $E(y)$, click the "Options" button. The resulting dialog box is shown in Figure M.3.

Step 5 Check "Confidence limits" and/or "Prediction limits," specify the "Confidence level," and enter the value of x in the "Prediction intervals for new observations" box.

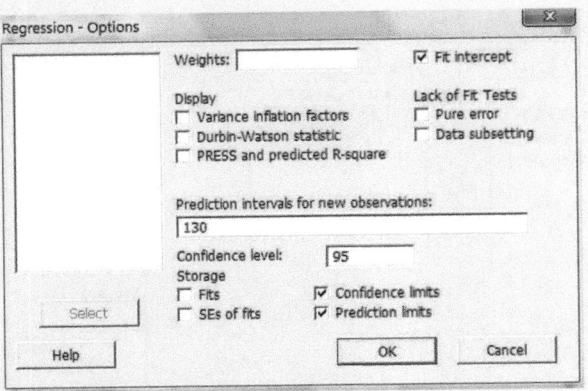

Figure M.3 Minitab regression options

Step 6 Click "OK" to return to the main Regression dialog box and then click "OK" again to produce the Minitab simple linear regression printout.

Correlation Analysis

Step 1 Click on the "Stat" button on the Minitab main menu bar, then click on "Basic Statistics," and then click on "Correlation," as shown in Figure M.4.

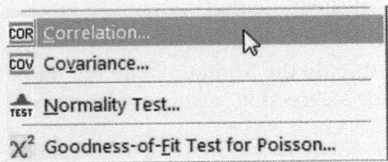

Figure M.4 Minitab menu options for correlation

Step 2 On the resulting dialog box (see Figure M.5), enter the two variables of interest in the "Variables" box.

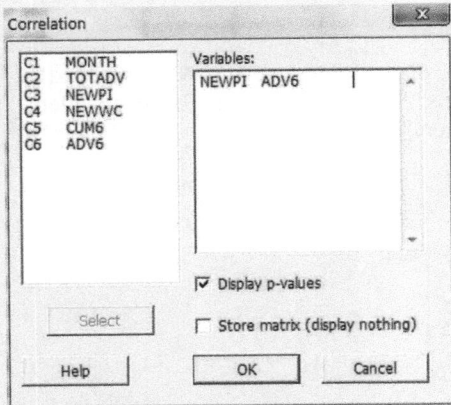

Figure M.5 Minitab correlation dialog box

Step 3 Click "OK" to obtain a printout of the correlation.

Excel/XLSTAT: Simple Linear Regression

Regression/Correlation Analysis

Step 1 First, create a workbook with two columns, one representing the quantitative dependent variable and the other the quantitative independent variable.

Step 2 Click the "XLSTAT" button on the Excel main menu bar, select "Modeling data," then click "Linear regression," as shown in Figure E.1.

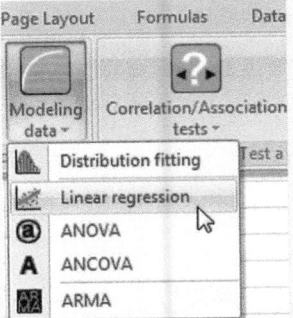

Figure E.1 XLSTAT menu options for simple linear regression

Step 3 When the resulting dialog box appears (Figure E.2), enter the column containing the dependent variable in the "Y / Dependent variables" box. Check the "Quantitative" option and then enter the column containing the independent variable in the "X / Explanatory variables" box.

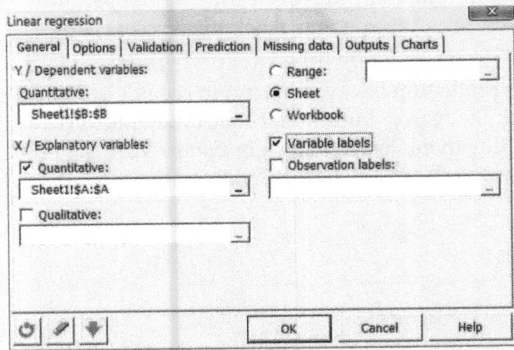

Figure E.2 XLSTAT dialog box for linear regression

Step 4 To obtain prediction/confidence intervals, select the "Prediction" tab, then enter the column with the values of the independent variable for which you want to make predictions in the "X / Explanatory variables" and "Quantitative" box, as shown in Figure E.3.

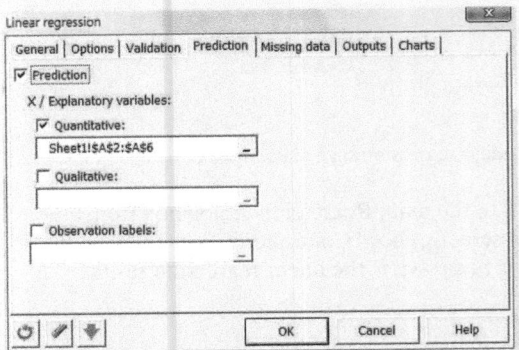

Figure E.3 XLSTAT dialog box for predictions

Step 5 Click "OK," then "Continue" to display the test results.

TI-84 Graphing Calculator: Simple Linear Regression

Finding the Least Squares Regression Equation

Step 1 *Enter the data*

• Press **STAT** and select **1:Edit**

Note: If a list already contains data, clear the old data.

- Use the up arrow to highlight the list name, "**L1**" or "**L2**"
- Press **CLEAR ENTER**
- Enter your *x*-data in **L1** and your *y*-data in **L2**

Step 2 *Find the equation*

- Press **STAT** and highlight **CALC**
- Press **4** for **LinReg(ax + b)**
- Press **ENTER**
- The screen will show the values for *a* and *b* in the equation $y = ax + b$.

Finding *r* and r^2

Use this procedure if *r* and r^2 do not already appear on the LinReg screen from part I:

Step 1 *Turn the diagnostics feature on*

- Press **2nd 0** for **CATALOG**
- Press the **ALPHA** key and x^{-1} for **D**
- Press the down **ARROW** until **DiagnosticsOn** is highlighted
- Press **ENTER** twice

Step 2 *Find the regression equation as shown in part I above*

The values for r and r^2 will appear on the screen as well.

Graphing the Least Squares Line with the Scatterplot

Step 1 *Enter the data as shown in part I above*

Step 2 *Set up the data plot*

- Press **Y=** and **CLEAR** all functions from the Y registers
- Press **2nd Y=** for **STAT PLOT**
- Press **1** for **Plot1**
- Set the cursor so that **ON** is flashing and press **ENTER**
- For **Type,** use the **ARROW** and **ENTER** keys to highlight and select the scatterplot (first icon in the first row)
- For **Xlist,** choose the column containing the *x*-data
- For **Ylist,** choose the column containing the *y*-data

Step 3 *Find the regression equation and store the equation in Y1*

- Press **STAT** and highlight **CALC**
- Press **4** for **LinReg(ax + b)** (Note: Don't press ENTER here because you want to store the regression equation in Y1.)
- Press **VARS**
- Use the right arrow to highlight **Y-VARS**
- Press **ENTER** to select **1:Function**
- Press **ENTER** to select **1:Y1**
- Press **ENTER**

Step 4 *View the scatterplot and regression line*

- Press **ZOOM** and then press **9** to select **9:ZoomStat**

You should see the data graphed along with the regression line.

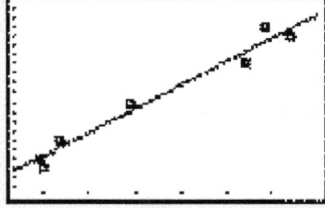

◻ Answers to Selected Exercises

3 $\beta_1 = \frac{1}{3}, \beta_0 = \frac{14}{3}, y = \frac{14}{3} + (1/3)x$ **9** No **11 a.** $\Sigma(y - \hat{y}) = 0.02$, SSE $= 1.2204$ **c.** SSE $= 108.00$ **13 b.** Negative linear relationship **c.** $8.54, -.994$ **15 a.** $y = \beta_0 + \beta_1 x + \varepsilon$ **b.** $\hat{y} = -97.41 + 1.19x$ **c.** No practical interpretation **d.** For every 1-point increase in 2001 Math SAT score, estimate 2011 Math SAT score to increase 1.19 points **17 a.** $\hat{y} = 7.21 + 35.92x$ **b.** y-intercept: no practical interpretation; slope: for each unit change in surface area to volume, estimate drug release rate to increase by 35.92 **c.** 25.17 **d.** Not reliable; $x = .50$ is outside range **19 a.** $\hat{y} = -14.14 + .63x$ **b.** For each additional 1 million births, estimate number of software millionaire birthdays to increase by .63 **c.** 7.83 **d.** $\hat{y} = 2.72 + .31x$ **e.** For each additional CEO birthday, estimate number of software millionaire birthdays to increase by .63 **f.** 5.79 **21 a.** $E(y) = \beta_0 + \beta_1 x$ **b.** $\hat{y} = 250.14 - .629x$ **c.** No practical interpretation **d.** For every 1-yard increase in driving distance, driving accuracy to decrease .629% **e.** Slope **23** \$7.88 million **27** Plot b **29 a.** .3475 **b.** 1.179 **31 a.** .2 **b.** About 95% of the observed payoffs fall within .4 unit of their predicted values **33 a.** 2.01 **b.** About 95% of the observed release rates fall within 4% of their predicted values **35 a.** SSE $= 44.16, s^2 = 11.04, s = 3.32$ **b.** SSE $= 9.69, s^2 = 2.42, s = 1.56$ **c.** $x = $ CEO birthdays **37 a.** SSE $= 1.017, s^2 = .0462, s = .215$ **c.** About 95% of the observed sweetness index values fall within .43 units of their predicted values **39 a.** $s = 5.37$; about 95% of the observed FCAT-Math scores fall within 10.74 points of their predicted values **b.** $s = 3.42$; about 95% of the observed FCAT-Reading scores fall within 6.84 points of their predicted values **c.** Reading score **41 a.** 95% CI:31 ± 1.13; 90% CI:$31 \pm .92$ **b.** 95% CI:64 ± 4.28; 90% CI:64 ± 3.53 **c.** 95% CI: $-8.4 \pm .67$; 90% CI:$-8.4 \pm .55$ **43** 80% CI:$.82 \pm .33$; 98% CI: $.82 \pm .76$ **45 a.** $H_0: \beta_1 = 0, H_a: \beta_1 > 0$ **b.** Reject H_0, p-value ≈ 0 **c.** $(1.09, 1.29)$ **47 a.** Positive **b.** $(-1.18, 1.72)$ **c.** Insufficient evidence of a linear relationship **49** $(30.17, 41.67)$; 90% confident that for each additional unit increase in surface area to volume, the increase in the drug release rate is between 30.17 and 41.67 **51 a.** $(-.048, 1.304)$ **b.** $(.179, .434)$ **c.** No; yes **53 a.** $H_0: \beta_1 = 0, H_a: \beta_1 < 0$ **b.** $t = -13.23$, p-value ≈ 0 **c.** Reject H_0 **55** No, $t = .66$ **57 a.** Yes, p-value $= \frac{.008}{2} = .004$ **b.** Possible outlier **c.** p-value $= \frac{.332}{2} = .166$, do not reject H_0 **59 a.** Positive **b.** Negative **c.** 0 slope **d.** Positive or negative **61 a.** .944 **b.** .802 **63 a.** 18% of sample variation in points scored is explained by the linear relationship with yards from goal line **b.** $-.424$; negative **65 a.** $E(y) = \beta_0 + \beta_1 x$ **b.** Moderately strong positive linear relationship between RMP and SET ratings **c.** Positive **d.** Reject $H_0: \rho = 0$ **e.** .4624 **67 a.** Strong positive linear relationship between number of females in managerial positions and number of females with college degree **b.** Very weak positive linear relationship between number of females in managerial positions and number of female HS graduates with no college **c.** Moderately strong positive linear relationship between number of males in managerial positions and number of males with college degree **d.** Moderate positive linear relationship between number of males in managerial positions and number of male HS graduates with no college **69 a.** .624; 62.4% of sample variation in software millionaire birthdays is explained by the linear relationship with number of U.S. births **b.** .917; 91.7% of sample variation in software millionaire birthdays is explained by the linear relationship with number of CEO births **c.** Yes **71** $r^2 = .2286, r = -.478$ **73** $r = .243, r^2 = .059$ **75** Yes, reject $H_0: \rho = 0$ for all occupations; no **77 c.** 4.64 ± 1.12 **d.** $2.28 \pm .63$; $-.41 \pm 1.17$ **79 a.** $\hat{y} = 1.375 + .875x$ **c.** 1.5 **d.** .1875 **e.** $(3.23, 3.89)$ **f.** $(3.81, 5.94)$ **81 a.** $(4783, 6792)$ **b.** $(2643, 8933)$ **83** For run $= 1$:90% confident that mean sweetness index of all runs with pectin value of 220 falls between 5.65 and 5.84 **85 a.** $(5.44, 15.32)$ **b.** Narrower **87 a.** $(2.955, 4.066)$; 99% confident that the mean mass of all spills with elapsed time of 15 minutes is between 2.995 and 4.066 **b.** $(1.02, 6.00)$; 99% confident that the actual mass of a single spill with elapsed time of 15 minutes is between 1.02 and 6.0 **c.** Prediction interval for y; yes **89 a.** Yes, $t = -5.91$; negative **b.** $(.656, 2.829)$ **c.** $(1.467, 2.018)$ **91** $\hat{y} = -32.35 + 4.82x$; $t = 16.60$, p-value $= 0$, reject H_0; $r^2 = .69$ **93** $\hat{y} = 62.449 - .34673x$; $t = -12.56$, p-value $= 0$, reject H_0; $r^2 = .07$ **95 a.** $\hat{y} = 37.08 - 1.6x$ **c.** 57.2 **d.** 4.4 **e.** $-1.6 \pm .5$ **f.** 13.08 ± 6.93 **g.** 13.08 ± 7.86 **97 a.** Moderately strong positive linear relationship between skill level and goal-setting ability **b.** Reject H_0 at $\alpha = .01$ **c.** .49 **99 b.** $\hat{y} = 569.58 - .0019x$ **e.** Range of x: \$15,100 to \$70,000 **f.** $t = -.82$, do not reject H_0 **101 a.** $E(y) = \beta_0 + \beta_1 x$ **b.** $\hat{y} = -2,298.4 + 11,598.9x$ **c.** No practical interpretation **d.** $(11,146.1, 12,051.7)$ **e.** 1,117.6 **f.** $H_0: \beta_1 = 0, H_a: \beta_1 > 0$ **g.** p-value $< .0001$ **h.** .8925 **i.** .9447 **j.** $(1,297.6, 5,704.6)$ **k.** $(3,362.5, 3,639.7)$ **103 b.** $\hat{y} = 44.13 + .237x$ **c.** 19.40 **d.** Possibly **e.** $t = 1.27$, do not reject H_0 **f.** $(-.16, .63)$ **g.** 57.143 ± 34.818 **h.** $x = 110$ outside range **i.** $\bar{x} = 44.1579$ **105 a.** Increasing trend **b.** Positive **c.** Support; $t = 4.60$, reject H_0 **107 c.** $r_1 = .965, r_2 = .996$ **d.** Yes **109 a.** Yes, $t = -4.37$ **111** Machine-hours: $t = 3.30$, $p = .008$, reject $H_0, r^2 = .521$; labor-hours: $t = 1.43, p = .183$, do not reject $H_0, r^2 = .170$

◻ Credits

The photo credits below are listed in order of appearance.

◨ Technology Images

Multiple Regression
and Model Building

From Chapter 12 of *Statistics for Business and Economics*, Twelfth Edition. James T. McClave, P. George Benson, Terry Sincich. Copyright © 2014 by Pearson Education, Inc. All rights reserved.
Content marked with a CD icon requires datasets or applets that can be found at http://www.pearsonhighered.com/mathstatsresources.

CONTENTS

☐ Multiple Regression and Model Building

STATISTICS in ACTION **Bid Rigging in the Highway Construction Industry**

In the United States, commercial contractors bid for the right to construct state highways and roads. A state government agency, usually the Department of Transportation (DOT), notifies various contractors of the state's intent to build a highway. Sealed bids are submitted by the contractors, and the contractor with the lowest bid (building cost) is awarded the road construction contract. The bidding process works extremely well in competitive markets but has the potential to increase construction costs if the markets are noncompetitive or if collusive practices are present. The latter occurred in the 1980s in Florida. Numerous road contractors either admitted or were found guilty of price fixing (i.e., setting the cost of construction above the fair, or competitive, cost through bid rigging or other means).

This Statistics in Action involves data collected by the Florida attorney general shortly following the price-fixing crisis. The attorney general's objective is to build a model for the cost (*y*) of a road construction contract awarded using the sealed-bid system. The **FLAG** file contains data for a sample of 235 road contracts. The variables measured for each contract are listed in Table SIA1. Ultimately, the attorney general wants to use the model to predict the costs of future road contracts in the state.

In several Statistics in Action Revisited sections in this chapter, we show how to analyze the data using a multiple regression analysis.

Where We're Going

- Introduce a *multiple regression* model as a means of relating a dependent variable *y* to two or more independent variables (1)

- Present several different multiple regression models involving both quantitative and qualitative independent variables (2, 5–8)

- Assess how well the multiple regression model fits the sample data (3)

- Demonstrate how to use the model for prediction (4)

- Present some model-building techniques (9–10)

- Show how an analysis of the model's *residuals* can aid in detecting violations of model assumptions and in identifying model modifications (11)

- Alert the analyst to some regression pitfalls (12)

Table SIA1	Variables in the FLAG Data File	
Variable Name	Type	Description
CONTRACT	Quantitative	Road contract number
COST	Quantitative	Low bid contract cost (thousands of dollars)
DOTEST	Quantitative	DOT engineer's cost estimate (thousands of dollars)
STATUS	Qualitative	Bid status (1 = fixed, 0 = competitive)
B2B1RAT	Quantitative	Ratio of second lowest bid to low bid
B3B1RAT	Quantitative	Ratio of third lowest bid to low bid
BHB1RAT	Quantitative	Ratio of highest bid to low bid
DISTRICT	Qualitative	Location of road (1 = south Florida, 0 = north Florida)
BTPRATIO	Quantitative	Ratio of number of bidders to number of plan holders
DAYSEST	Quantitative	DOT engineer's estimate of number of workdays required

Data Set: FLAG

STATISTICS in ACTION REVISITED

- Evaluating a First-Order Model
- Variable Screening and Model Building
- A Residual Analysis

1 Multiple Regression Models

Most practical applications of regression analysis employ models that are more complex than the simple straight-line model. For example, a realistic probabilistic model for monthly sales revenue would include more than just the amount of advertising expenditure. Factors such as last month's sales, number of sales competitors, and advertising medium are some of the many variables that might be related to sales revenue. Thus, we would want to incorporate these and other potentially important independent variables into the model in order to make accurate predictions.

Probabilistic models that include more than one independent variable are called **multiple regression models.** The general form of these models is

$$y = \beta_0 + \beta_1 x_1 + \beta_2 x_2 + \cdots + \beta_k x_k + \varepsilon$$

The dependent variable y is now written as a function of k independent variables, $x_1, x_2, \ldots, x_k$. The random error term is added to make the model probabilistic rather than deterministic. The value of the coefficient β_i determines the contribution of the independent variable x_i, and β_0 is the y-intercept. The coefficients $\beta_0, \beta_1, \ldots, \beta_k$ are usually unknown because they represent population parameters.

At first glance it might appear that the regression model shown above would not allow for anything other than straight-line relationships between y and the independent variables, but this is not true. Actually, $x_1, x_2, \ldots, x_k$ can be functions of variables as long as the functions do not contain unknown parameters. For example, the monthly sales revenue, y, could be a function of the independent variables

$$x_1 = \text{Advertising expenditure}$$
$$x_2 = \text{Number of sales competitors}$$
$$x_3 = (x_1)^2$$
$$x_4 = 1 \text{ if TV advertising, 0 if not}$$

The x_3 term is called a **higher-order term** because it is the value of a quantitative variable (x_1) squared (i.e., raised to the second power). The x_4 term is a **coded variable** representing a qualitative variable (advertising medium). The multiple regression model is quite versatile and can be made to model many different types of response variables.

The General Multiple Regression Model*

$$y = \beta_0 + \beta_1 x_1 + \beta_2 x_2 + \cdots + \beta_k x_k + \varepsilon$$

where

y is the dependent variable.

$x_1, x_2, \ldots, x_k$ are the independent variables.

$E(y) = \beta_0 + \beta_1 x_1 + \beta_2 x_2 + \cdots + \beta_k x_k$ is the deterministic portion of the model.

β_i determines the contribution of the independent variable x_i.

Note: The symbols $x_1, x_2, \ldots, x_k$ may represent higher-order terms for quantitative predictors or terms that represent qualitative predictors.

As shown in the box, the steps used to develop the multiple regression model are similar to those used for the simple linear regression model.**Analyzing a Multiple**

Regression Model

Step 1 Hypothesize the deterministic component of the model. This component relates the mean, $E(y)$, to the independent variables $x_1, x_2, \ldots, x_k$. This involves the choice of the independent variables to be included in the model (Sections 2, 5–10).

Step 2 Use the sample data to estimate the unknown model parameters $\beta_0, \beta_1, \beta_2, \ldots, \beta_k$ in the model (Section 2).

Step 3 Specify the probability distribution of the random error term, ε, and estimate the standard deviation of this distribution, σ (Section 3).

Step 4 Check that the assumptions on ε are satisfied and make model modifications if necessary (Section 11).

Step 5 Statistically evaluate the usefulness of the model (Sections 3).

Step 6 When satisfied that the model is useful, use it for prediction, estimation, and other purposes (Section 4).

The assumptions we make about the random error ε of the multiple regression model are also similar to those in a simple linear regression. These are summarized below.

Assumptions for Random Error ε

For any given set of values of $x_1, x_2, \ldots, x_k$, the random error ε has a probability distribution with the following properties:

1. Mean equal to 0

2. Variance equal to σ^2

3. Normal distribution

4. Random errors are independent (in a probabilistic sense).

Throughout this chapter, we introduce several different types of models that form the foundation of **model building** (or useful model construction). In the next several sections, we consider the most basic multiple regression model, called the *first-order model.*

*Technically, this model is referred to as a general multiple *linear* regression model since the equation is a linear function of the β's.

PART I: FIRST-ORDER MODELS WITH QUANTITATIVE INDEPENDENT VARIABLES

2 Estimating and Making Inferences about the β Parameters

BIOGRAPHY

GEORGE U. YULE (1871–1951)
Yule Processes

Born on a small farm in Scotland, George Yule received an extensive childhood education. After graduating from University College (London), where he studied civil engineering, Yule spent a year employed in engineering work-shops. However, he made a career change in 1893, accepting a teaching position back at University College under the guid-ance of statistician Karl Pearson. Inspired by Pearson's work, Yule produced a series of important ar-ticles on the statistics of regression and correlation. Yule is considered the first to apply the method of least squares in regression analy-sis, and he developed the theory of multiple regression. He eventu-ally was appointed a lecturer in statistics at Cambridge University and later became the president of the prestigious Royal Statistical Society. Yule made many other contributions to the field, includ-ing the invention of time series analysis and the development of Yule processes and the Yule distribution.

A model that includes terms only for *quantitative* independent variables, called a **first-order model,** is described in the box. Note that the first-order model does not include any higher-order terms (such as x_1^2).

A First-Order Model in Five Quantitative Independent (Predictor) Variables*

$$E(y) = \beta_0 + \beta_1 x_1 + \beta_2 x_2 + \beta_3 x_3 + \beta_4 x_4 + \beta_5 x_5$$

where $x_1, x_2, \ldots, x_5$ are all quantitative variables that *are not* functions of other independent variables.

Note: β_i represents the slope of the line relating y to x_i when all the other x's are held fixed.

The method of fitting first-order models—and multiple regression models in general—is identical to that of fitting the simple straight-line model: the **method of least squares**—that is, we choose the estimated model

$$\hat{y} = \hat{\beta}_0 + \hat{\beta}_1 x_1 + \cdots + \hat{\beta}_k x_k$$

that (1) has an average error of prediction of 0, i.e., $\Sigma(y - \hat{y}) = 0$
and (2) minimizes SSE $= (y - \hat{y})^2$

As in the case of the simple linear model, the sample estimates $\hat{\beta}_0, \hat{\beta}_1, \ldots, \hat{\beta}_k$ are obtained as a solution to a set of simultaneous linear equations.[†]

The primary difference between fitting the simple and multiple regression models is computational difficulty. The $(k + 1)$ simultaneous linear equations that must be solved to find the $(k + 1)$ estimated coefficients $\hat{\beta}_0, \hat{\beta}_1, \ldots, \hat{\beta}_k$ cannot be written in simple equation form; rather, the estimates are obtained using matrices and matrix algebra. Instead of presenting the complex matrix algebra required to fit the models, we resort to statistical software and present output from SPSS, Minitab, and Excel.

Example 1

Fitting a First-Order Model: Price of an Antique Clock

Problem A collector of antique grandfather clocks sold at auction believes that the price received for the clocks depends on both the age of the clocks and the number of bidders at the auction. Thus, he hypothesizes the first-order model

$$y = \beta_0 + \beta_1 x_1 + \beta_2 x_2 + \varepsilon$$

where

$$y = \text{Auction price (dollars)}$$
$$x_1 = \text{Age of clock (years)}$$
$$x_2 = \text{Number of bidders}$$

A sample of 32 auction prices of grandfather clocks, along with their age and the num-ber of bidders, is given in Table 1.

a. Use scatterplots to plot the sample data. Interpret the plots.

b. Use the method of least squares to estimate the unknown parameters β_0, β_1, and β_2 of the model.

---

*The terminology *first order* is derived from the fact that each x in the model is raised to the first power.

[†]Students who are familiar with calculus should note that $\hat{\beta}_0, \hat{\beta}_1, \ldots, \hat{\beta}_k$ are the solutions to the set of equations $\partial SSE/\partial\hat{\beta}_0 = 0, \partial SSE/\partial\hat{\beta}_1 = 0, \ldots, \partial SSE/\partial\hat{\beta}_k = 0$. The solution is usually given in matrix form, but we do not present the details here. See the references for details.

Table 1		Auction Price Data			
Age, x_1	Number of Bidders, x_2	Auction Price, y	Age, x_1	Number of Bidders, x_2	Auction Price, y
127	13	$1,235	170	14	$2,131
115	12	1,080	182	8	1,550
127	7	845	162	11	1,884
150	9	1,522	184	10	2,041
156	6	1,047	143	6	845
182	11	1,979	159	9	1,483
156	12	1,822	108	14	1,055
132	10	1,253	175	8	1,545
137	9	1,297	108	6	729
113	9	946	179	9	1,792
137	15	1,713	111	15	1,175
117	11	1,024	187	8	1,593
137	8	1,147	111	7	785
153	6	1,092	115	7	744
117	13	1,152	194	5	1,356
126	10	1,336	168	7	1,262

Data Set: CLOCKS

c. Find the value of SSE that is minimized by the least squares method.

d. Estimate σ, the standard deviation of the model, and interpret the result.

Solution

a. Minitab side-by-side scatterplots for examining the bivariate relationships between y and x_1, and between y and x_2, are shown in Figure 1. Of the two variables, age (x_1) appears to have the stronger linear relationship with auction price (y).

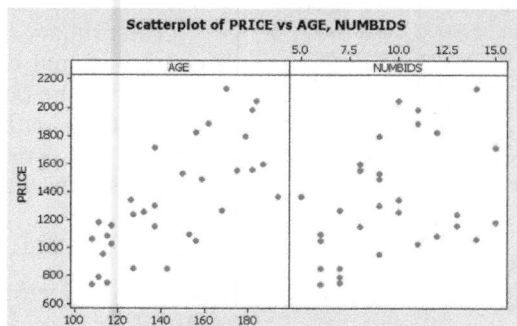

Figure 1

Minitab side-by-side scatterplots for the data of Table 1

b. The model hypothesized is fit to the data of Table 1 with Minitab. A portion of the printout is reproduced in Figure 2. The least squares estimates of the β parameters (highlighted) are $\hat{\beta}_0 = -1,339$, $\hat{\beta}_1 = 12.74$, and $\hat{\beta}_2 = 85.95$. Therefore, the equation that minimizes SSE for this data set (i.e., the **least squares prediction equation**) is

$$\hat{y} = -1,339 + 12.74x_1 + 85.95x_2$$

c. The minimum value of the sum of the squared errors, also highlighted in Figure 2, is SSE $= 516,727$.

d. Recall that the estimator of σ^2 for the straight-line model is $s^2 = \text{SSE}/(n-2)$, and note that the denominator is ($n -$ number of estimated β parameters), which is ($n - 2$) in the straight-line model. Because we must estimate the three parameters β_0, β_1, and β_2 for the first-order model, the estimator of σ^2 is

$$s^2 = \frac{\text{SSE}}{n-3} = \frac{\text{SSE}}{32-3} = \frac{516,727}{29} = 17,818$$

This value, often called the **mean square for error (MSE),** is also highlighted at the bottom of the Minitab printout in Figure 2. The estimate of σ, then, is

$$s = \sqrt{17,818} = 133.5$$

Regression Analysis: PRICE versus AGE, NUMBIDS

```
The regression equation is
PRICE = - 1339 + 12.7 AGE + 86.0 NUMBIDS


Predictor       Coef  SE Coef       T      P
Constant     -1339.0    173.8   -7.70  0.000
AGE          12.7406   0.9047   14.08  0.000
NUMBIDS       85.953    8.729    9.85  0.000


S = 133.485    R-Sq = 89.2%    R-Sq(adj) = 88.5%


Analysis of Variance

Source           DF       SS       MS       F      P
Regression        2  4283063  2141531  120.19  0.000
Residual Error   29   516727    17818
Total            31  4799790
```

Figure 2

Minitab analysis of the auction price model

which is highlighted in the middle of the Minitab printout in Figure 2. One useful interpretation of the estimated standard deviation s is that the interval $\pm 2s$ will provide a rough approximation to the accuracy with which the model will predict future values of y for given values of x. Thus, we expect the model to provide predictions of auction price to within about $\pm 2s = \pm 2(133.5) = \pm 267$ dollars.*

Look Back As with simple linear regression, we will use the estimator of σ^2 both to check the utility of the model (Section 3) and to provide a measure of reliability of predictions and estimates when the model is used for those purposes (Section 4). Thus, you can see that the estimation of σ^2 plays an important part in the development of a regression model.

Now Work Exercise 2a–c

Estimator of σ^2 for a Multiple Regression Model with k Independent Variables

$$s^2 = \frac{\text{SSE}}{n - \text{number of estimated } \beta \text{ parameters}} = \frac{\text{SSE}}{n - (k + 1)}$$

After obtaining the least squares prediction equation, the analyst will usually want to make meaningful interpretations of the β estimates. In the straight-line model

$$y = \beta_0 + \beta_1 x + \varepsilon$$

β_0 represents the y-intercept of the line, and β_1 represents the slope of the line. β_1 has a practical interpretation—it represents the mean change in y for every 1-unit increase in x. When the independent variables are quantitative, the β parameters in the first-order model specified in Example 1 have similar interpretations. The difference is that when we interpret the β that multiplies one of the variables (e.g., x_1), we must be certain to hold the values of the remaining independent variables (e.g., x_2, x_3) fixed.

To see this, suppose that the mean $E(y)$ of a response y is related to two quantitative independent variables, x_1 and x_2, by the first-order model

$$E(y) = 1 + 2x_1 + x_2$$

In other words, $\beta_0 = 1, \beta_1 = 2$, and $\beta_2 = 1$.

Now, when $x_2 = 0$, the relationship between $E(y)$ and x_1 is given by

$$E(y) = 1 + 2x_1 + (0) = 1 + 2x_1$$

---

*The $\pm 2s$ approximation will improve as the sample size is increased. We will provide more precise methodology for the construction of prediction intervals in Section 4.

A Minitab graph of this relationship (a straight line) is shown in Figure 3. Similar graphs of the relationship between $E(y)$ and x_1 for $x_2 = 1$,

$$E(y) = 1 + 2x_1 + (1) = 2 + 2x_1$$

and for $x_2 = 2$,

$$E(y) = 1 + 2x_1 + (2) = 3 + 2x_1$$

also are shown in Figure 3. Note that the slopes of the three lines are all equal to $\beta_1 = 2$, the coefficient that multiplies x_1.

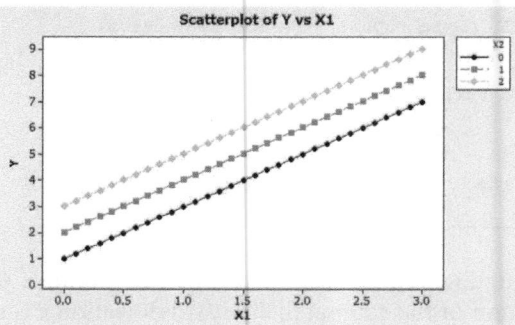

Figure 3

Minitab graph of
$E(y) = 1 + 2x_1 + x_2$ for
$x_2 = 0, 1, 2$

Figure 3 exhibits a characteristic of all first-order models: If you graph $E(y)$ versus any one variable—say, x_1—for fixed values of the other variables, the result will always be a *straight line* with slope equal to β_1. If you repeat the process for other values of the fixed independent variables, you will obtain a set of *parallel* straight lines. This indicates that the effect of the independent variable x_i on $E(y)$ is independent of all the other independent variables in the model, and this effect is measured by the slope β_i.

A Minitab three-dimensional graph of the model $E(y) = 1 + 2x_1 + x_2$ is shown in Figure 4. Note that the model graphs as a plane. If you slice the plane at a particular value of x_2 (say, $x_2 = 0$), you obtain a straight line relating $E(y)$ to x_1 (e.g., $E[y] = 1 + 2x_1$). Similarly, if you slice the plane at a particular value of x_1, you obtain a straight line relating $E(y)$ to x_2. Because it is more difficult to visualize three-dimensional and, in general, k-dimensional surfaces, we will graph all the models presented in this chapter in two dimensions. *The key to obtaining these graphs is to hold fixed all but one of the independent variables in the model.*

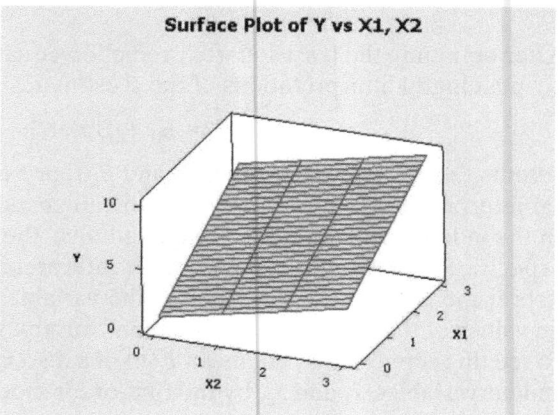

Figure 4

Minitab 3-dimensional graph of
$E(y) = 1 + 2x_1 + x_2$

Example	2

**Interpreting the
β Estimates: Clock
Auction Price Model**

Problem Refer to the first-order model for auction price (y) considered in Example 1. Interpret the estimates of the β parameters in the model.

Solution The least squares prediction equation, as given in Example 1, is $\hat{y} = -1,339 + 12.74x_1 + 85.95x_2$. We know that with first-order models, β_1 represents the slope of the line relating y to x_1 for fixed x_2. That is, β_1 measures the change in $E(y)$ for every 1-unit increase in x_1 when the other independent variable in the model is held fixed. A similar statement can be made about β_2: β_2 measures the change in $E(y)$ for every 1-unit increase in x_2 when the other x in the model is held fixed. Consequently, we obtain the following interpretations:

$\hat{\beta}_1 = 12.74$: We estimate the mean auction price $E(y)$ of an antique clock to increase \$12.74 for every 1-year increase in age (x_1) when the number of bidders (x_2) is held fixed.

$\hat{\beta}_2 = 85.95$: We estimate the mean auction price $E(y)$ of an antique clock to increase \$85.95 for every 1-bidder increase in the number of bidders (x_2) when age (x_1) is held fixed.

The value $\hat{\beta}_0 = -1,339$ does not have a meaningful interpretation in this example. To see this, note that $\hat{y} = \hat{\beta}_0$ when $x_1 = x_2 = 0$. Thus, $\hat{\beta}_0 = -1,339$ represents the estimated mean auction price when the values of all the independent variables are set equal to 0. Because an antique clock with these characteristics—an age of 0 years and 0 bidders on the clock—is not practical, the value of $\hat{\beta}_0$ has no meaningful interpretation.

Look Back In general, $\hat{\beta}_0$ will not have a practical interpretation unless it makes sense to set the values of the x's simultaneously equal to 0.

Now Work Exercise 14a, b

> ⚠ **CAUTION** The interpretation of the β parameters in a multiple regression model will depend on the terms specified in the model. The interpretations above are for a first-order linear model only. In practice, you should be sure that a first-order model is the correct model for $E(y)$ before making these β interpretations. (We discuss alternative models for $E(y)$ in Sections 5–8.)

Inferences about the individual β parameters in a model are obtained using either a confidence interval or a test of hypothesis, as outlined in the following two boxes.*

A $100(1 - \alpha)\%$ Confidence Interval for a β Parameter

$$\hat{\beta}_i \pm t_{\alpha/2}s_{\hat{\beta}_i}$$

where $t_{\alpha/2}$ is based on $n - (k + 1)$ degrees of freedom and

n = Number of observations

$k + 1$ = Number of β parameters in the model

Test of an Individual Parameter Coefficient in the Multiple Regression Model

One-Tailed Test	Two-Tailed Test
$H_0: \beta_i = 0$	$H_0: \beta_i = 0$
$H_a: \beta_i < 0$ [or $H_a: \beta_i > 0$]	$H_a: \beta_i \neq 0$

$$\text{Test statistic: } t = \frac{\hat{\beta}_i}{s_{\hat{\beta}_i}}$$

Rejection region: $t < -t_\alpha$	Rejection region: $\|t\| > t_{\alpha/2}$
[or $t > t_\alpha$ when $H_a: \beta_i > 0$]	

where t_α and $t_{\alpha/2}$ are based on $n - (k + 1)$ degrees of freedom and

n = Number of observations

$k + 1$ = Number of β parameters in the model

---

*The formulas for computing $\hat{\beta}_i$ and its standard error are so complex that the only reasonable way to present them is by using matrix algebra. We do not assume a prerequisite of matrix algebra for this text, and, in any case, we think the formulas can be omitted in an introductory course without serious loss. They are programmed into almost all statistical software packages with multiple regression routines and are presented in some of the texts listed in the references.

> **Conditions Required for Valid Inferences about the β Parameters**
>
> Refer to the four assumptions about the probability distribution for the random error ε.

We illustrate these methods with another example.

Example   3

Inferences about the β Parameters—Auction Price Model

Problem Refer to Examples 1 and 2. The collector of antique grandfather clocks knows that the price (y) received for the clocks increases linearly with the age (x_1) of the clocks. Moreover, the collector hypothesizes that the auction price (y) will increase linearly as the number of bidders (x_2) increases. Use the information on the Minitab printout shown in Figure 2 to

a. Test the hypothesis that the mean auction price of a clock increases as the number of bidders increases when age is held constant, that is, test $\beta_2 > 0$. Use $\alpha = .05$.

b. Form a 90% confidence interval for β_1 and interpret the result.

Solution

a. The hypotheses of interest concern the parameter β_2. Specifically,

$$H_0: \beta_2 = 0$$
$$H_a: \beta_2 > 0$$

The test statistic is a t-statistic formed by dividing the sample estimate $\hat{\beta}_2$ of the parameter β_2 by the estimated standard error of $\hat{\beta}_2$ (denoted $s_{\hat{\beta}_2}$). These estimates, $\hat{\beta}_2 = 85.953$ and $s_{\hat{\beta}_2} = 8.729$, as well as the calculated t-value,

$$\text{Test statistic: } t = \frac{\hat{\beta}_2}{s_{\hat{\beta}_2}} = \frac{85.953}{8.729} = 9.85$$

are highlighted on the Minitab printout in Figure 2.

The rejection region for the test is found in exactly the same way as the rejection regions for t-tests—that is, we consult Table III in Appendix: Tables to obtain an upper-tail value of t. This is a value t_α such that $P(t > t_\alpha) = \alpha$. We can then use this value to construct rejection regions for either one-tailed or two-tailed tests.

For $\alpha = .05$ and $n - (k + 1) = 32 - (2 + 1) = 29$ df, the critical t-value obtained from Table III is $t_{.05} = 1.699$. Therefore,

$$\text{Rejection region: } t > 1.699 \text{ (see Figure 5)}$$

Because the test statistic value, $t = 9.85$, falls in the rejection region, we have sufficient evidence to reject H_0. Thus, the collector can conclude that the mean auction price of a clock increases as the number of bidders increases, when age is held constant. Note that the two-tailed observed significance level of the test is also highlighted on the printout. Because the one-tailed p-value (half this value) is p-value ≈ 0, any nonzero α (e.g., $\alpha = .01$) will lead us to reject H_0.

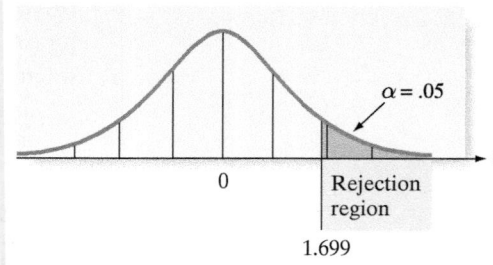

Figure 5

Rejection region for $H_0: \beta_2 = 0$ vs. $H_a: \beta_2 > 0$

b. A 90% confidence interval for β_1 is:

$$\hat{\beta}_1 \pm t_{\alpha/2}s_{\hat{\beta}_1} = \hat{\beta}_1 \pm t_{.05}s_{\hat{\beta}_1}$$

Substituting $\hat{\beta}_1 = 12.74$, $s_{\hat{\beta}_1} = .905$ (both obtained from the Minitab printout, Figure 2), and $t_{.05} = 1.699$ (from part **a**) into the equation, we obtain

$$12.74 \pm 1.699(.905) = 12.74 \pm 1.54$$

or (11.20, 14.28). Thus, we are 90% confident that β_1 falls between 11.20 and 14.28. Because β_1 is the slope of the line relating auction price (y) to age of the clock (x_1), we conclude that the price increases between \$11.20 and \$14.28 for every 1-year increase in age, holding number of bidders (x_2) constant.

Look Back When interpreting the β multiplied by one x, be sure to hold fixed the values of the other x's in the model.

Now Work Exercise 14c, d

3 Evaluating Overall Model Utility

In Section 2, we demonstrated the use of t-tests in making inferences about β parameters in the multiple regression model. There are caveats, however, with conducting these t-tests for the purposes of determining which x's are useful for predicting y. Several of these are listed next.

Use Caution when Conducting t-Tests on the β Parameters

It is dangerous to conduct t-tests on the individual β parameters in a *first-order linear model* for the purpose of determining which independent variables are useful for predicting y and which are not. If you fail to reject H_0: $\beta_i = 0$, several conclusions are possible:

1. There is no relationship between y and x_i.
2. A straight-line relationship between y and x exists (holding the other x's in the model fixed), but a Type II error occurred.
3. A relationship between y and x_i (holding the other x's in the model fixed) exists but is more complex than a straight-line relationship (e.g., a curvilinear relationship may be appropriate). The most you can say about a β parameter test is that there is either sufficient (if you reject H_0: $\beta_i = 0$) or insufficient (if you do not reject H_0: $\beta_i = 0$) evidence of a *linear* (straight-line) relationship between y and x_i.

In addition, conducting t-tests on each β parameter in a model is *not* the best way to determine whether the overall model is contributing information for the prediction of y. If we were to conduct a series of t-tests to determine whether the independent variables are contributing to the predictive relationship, we would be very likely to make one or more errors in deciding which terms to retain in the model and which to exclude.

For example, suppose you fit a first-order model in 10 quantitative x variables and decide to conduct t-tests on all 10 of the individual β's in the model, each at $\alpha = .05$. Even if all the β parameters (except β_0) are equal to 0, approximately 40% of the time you will incorrectly reject the null hypothesis at least once and conclude that some β parameter differs from 0.* Thus, in multiple regression models for which a large number

---

*The proof of this result (assuming independence of tests) proceeds as follows:

$P(\text{Reject } H_0 \text{ at least once} \mid \beta_1 = \beta_2 = \cdots = \beta_{10} = 0)$
$= 1 - P(\text{Reject } H_0 \text{ no times} \mid \beta_1 = \beta_2 = \cdots = \beta_{10} = 0)$
$\leq 1 - [P(\text{Accept } H_0: \beta_1 = 0 \mid \beta_1 = 0) \cdot P(\text{Accept } H_0: \beta_2 = 0 \mid \beta_2 = 0) \cdot \cdots \cdot P(\text{Accept } H_0: \beta_{10} = 0 \mid \beta_{10} = 0)]$
$= 1 - [(1 - \alpha)^{10}] = 1 - (.95)^{10} = .401$

For dependent tests, the Bonferroni inequality states that
$P(\text{Reject } H_0 \text{ at least once} \mid \beta_1 = \beta_2 = \cdots = \beta_{10} = 0) \leq 10(\alpha) = 10(.05) = .50.$

of independent variables are being considered, conducting a series of t-tests may include a large number of insignificant variables and exclude some useful ones. To test the utility of a multiple regression model, we need a *global test* (one that encompasses all the β parameters). We would also like to find some statistical quantity that measures how well the model fits the data.

We commence with the easier problem—finding a measure of how well a linear model fits a set of data. For this we use the multiple regression equivalent of r^2, the coefficient of determination for the straight-line model, as shown in the box.

The **multiple coefficient of determination, R^2,** is defined as

$$R^2 = 1 - \frac{\text{SSE}}{\text{SS}_{yy}} = \frac{\text{SS}_{yy} - \text{SSE}}{\text{SS}_{yy}} = \frac{\text{Explained variablilty}}{\text{Total variability}}$$

Just like r^2 in the simple linear model, R^2 represents the fraction of the sample variation of the y values (measured by SS_{yy}) that is explained by the least squares prediction equation. Thus, $R^2 = 0$ implies a complete lack of fit of the model to the data, and $R^2 = 1$ implies a perfect fit, with the model passing through every data point. In general, the larger the value of R^2, the better the model fits the data.

To illustrate, the value $R^2 = .892$ for the auction price model of Examples 1–3 is highlighted on the SPSS printout for the analysis shown in Figure 6. This high value of R^2 implies that using the independent variables age and number of bidders in a first-order model explains 89.2% of the total *sample variation* (measured by SS_{yy}) in auction price (y). Thus, R^2 is a sample statistic that tells how well the model fits the data and thereby represents a measure of the usefulness of the entire model.

Model Summary

Mode l	R	R Square	Adjusted R Square	Std. Error of the Estimate
1	.945[a]	.892	.885	133.485

a. Predictors: (Constant), NUMBIDS, AGE

ANOVA[b]

Model		Sum of Squares	df	Mean Square	F	Sig.
1	Regression	4283062.960	2	2141531.480	120.188	.000[a]
	Residual	516726.540	29	17818.157		
	Total	4799789.500	31			

a. Predictors: (Constant), NUMBIDS, AGE
b. Dependent Variable: PRICE

Coefficients[a]

Model		Unstandardized Coefficients		Standardized Coefficients	t	Sig.	95% Confidence Interval for B	
		B	Std. Error	Beta			Lower Bound	Upper Bound
1	(Constant)	−1338.951	173.809		−7.704	.000	−1694.432	−983.471
	AGE	12.741	.905	.887	14.082	.000	10.890	14.591
	NUMBIDS	85.953	8.729	.620	9.847	.000	68.101	103.805

a. Dependent Variable: PRICE

Figure 6

SPSS analysis of the auction price model

A large value of R^2 computed from the *sample* data does not necessarily mean that the model provides a good fit to all of the data points in the *population*. For example, a first-order linear model that contains three parameters will provide a perfect fit to a sample of three data points, and R^2 will equal 1. Likewise, you will always obtain a perfect fit ($R^2 = 1$) to a set of n data points if the model contains exactly n parameters. Consequently, if you want to use the value of R^2 as a measure of how useful the model will be for predicting y, it should be based on a sample that contains substantially more data points than the number of parameters in the model.

> ⚠️ **CAUTION** In a multiple regression analysis, use the value of R^2 as a measure of how useful a linear model will be for predicting y only if the sample contains substantially more data points than the number of β parameters in the model.

As an alternative to using R^2 as a measure of model adequacy, the *adjusted multiple coefficient of determination*, denoted R_a^2, is often reported. The formula for R_a^2 is shown in the box.

The **adjusted multiple coefficient of determination** is given by

$$R_a^2 = 1 - \left[\frac{(n-1)}{n-(k+1)} \right] \left(\frac{\text{SSE}}{\text{SS}_{yy}} \right)$$

$$= 1 - \left[\frac{(n-1)}{n-(k+1)} \right](1 - R^2)$$

Note: $R_a^2 \leq R^2$

R^2 and R_a^2 have similar interpretations. However, unlike R^2, R_a^2 takes into account ("adjusts" for) both the sample size n and the number of β parameters in the model. R_a^2 will always be smaller than R^2 and, more importantly, cannot be "forced" to 1 by simply adding more and more independent variables to the model. Consequently, analysts prefer the more conservative R_a^2 when choosing a measure of model adequacy. The value of R_a^2 is also highlighted in Figure 6. Note that $R_a^2 = .885$, a value only slightly smaller than R^2.

Despite their utility, R^2 and R_a^2 are only sample statistics. Therefore, it is dangerous to judge the global usefulness of a model based solely on these values. A better method is to conduct a test of hypothesis involving *all* the β parameters (except β_0) in a model. In particular, for the general multiple regression model $E(y) = \beta_0 + \beta_1 x_1 + \beta_2 x_2 + \cdots + \beta_k x_k$, we would test

$$H_0: \beta_1 = \beta_2 = \cdots = \beta_k = 0$$

H_a: At least one of the coefficients is nonzero.

The test statistic used to test this hypothesis is an F-statistic, and several equivalent versions of the formula can be used (although we will usually rely on the computer to calculate the F-statistic):

$$\textit{Test statistic: } F = \frac{(\text{SS}_{yy} - \text{SSE})/k}{\text{SSE}/[n-(k+1)]}$$

$$= \frac{\text{Mean Square (Model)}}{\text{Mean Square (Error)}} = \frac{R^2/k}{(1-R^2)/[n-(k+1)]}$$

These formulas indicate that the F-statistic is the ratio of the *explained* variability divided by the model degrees of freedom to the *unexplained* variability divided by the error degrees of freedom. Thus, the larger the proportion of the total variability accounted for by the model, the larger the F-statistic.

To determine when the ratio becomes large enough that we can confidently reject the null hypothesis and conclude that the model is more useful than no model at all for predicting y, we compare the calculated F-statistic to a tabulated F value with k df in the numerator and $[n - (k + 1)]$ df in the denominator. Recall that tabulations of the F-distribution for various values of α are given in Tables V, VI, VII, and VIII in Appendix: Tables.

> *Rejection region:* $F > F_\alpha$, where F is based on k numerator and
> $n - (k + 1)$ denominator degrees of freedom.

The analysis of variance F-test for testing the usefulness of the model is summarized in the next box.

Testing Global Usefulness of the Model: The Analysis of Variance F-Test

H_0: $\beta_1 = \beta_2 = \cdots = \beta_k = 0$ (All model terms are unimportant for predicting y.)

H_a: At least one $\beta_i \neq 0$ (At least one model term is useful for predicting y.)

$$\text{Test statistic: } F = \frac{(SS_{yy} - SSE)/k}{SSE/[n - (k + 1)]} = \frac{R^2/k}{(1 - R^2)/[n - (k + 1)]}$$

$$= \frac{\text{Mean Square (Model)}}{\text{Mean Square (Error)}}$$

where n is the sample size and k is the number of terms in the model.

Rejection region: $F > F_\alpha$, with k numerator degrees of freedom and $[n - (k + 1)]$ denominator degrees of freedom.

Conditions Required for the Global F-Test in Regression to Be Valid

refer to the standard regression assumptions about the random error component (Section 1).

⚠ **CAUTION** A rejection of the null hypothesis H_0: $\beta_1 = \beta_2 = \cdots = \beta_k$ in the *global F-test* leads to the conclusion [with $100(1 - \alpha)\%$ confidence] that the model is statistically useful. However, statistically "useful" does not necessarily mean "best." Another model may prove even more useful in terms of providing more reliable estimates and predictions. This global F-test is usually regarded as a test that the model *must* pass to merit further consideration.

Example 4

Assessing Overall Adequacy—Clock Auction Price Model

Problem Refer to Examples 1–3, in which an antique collector modeled the auction price (y) of grandfather clocks as a function of the age of the clock (x_1) and the number of bidders (x_2). Recall that the hypothesized first-order model is

$$y = \beta_0 + \beta_1 x_1 + \beta_2 x_2 + \varepsilon$$

The SPSS printout for the analysis is shown in Figure 6.

a. Find and interpret the adjusted coefficient of determination R_a^2.

b. Conduct the global F-test of model usefulness at the $\alpha = .05$ level of significance.

Solution

a. The R_a^2 value (highlighted in Figure 6) is .885. This implies that the least squares model has explained about 88.5% of the total sample variation in y values (auction prices), after adjusting for sample size and number of independent variables in the model.

b. The elements of the global test of the model follow:

H_0: $\beta_1 = \beta_2 = 0$ (*Note*: $k = 2$)

H_a: At least one of the two model coefficients, β_1 and β_2, is nonzero.

$$\text{Test statistic: } F = \frac{\text{MS (Model)}}{\text{MSE}} = \frac{2{,}141{,}531}{17{,}818} = 120.19 \text{ (see Figure 6)}$$

p-value ≈ 0

Conclusion: Because $\alpha = .05$ exceeds the observed significance level, ($p \approx 0$), the data provide strong evidence that at least one of the model coefficients is nonzero. The overall model appears to be statistically useful for predicting auction prices.

Look Back Can we be sure that the best prediction model has been found if the global F-test indicates that a model is useful? Unfortunately, we cannot. The addition of other independent variables may improve the usefulness of the model. We consider more complex multiple regression models in Sections 5–8.

■ Now Work Exercise 15d–h

In this section, we discussed several different statistics for assessing the utility of a multiple regression model: t-tests on individual β parameters, R^2, R_a^2, and the global F-test. Both R^2 and R_a^2 are indicators of how well the prediction equation fits the data. Intuitive evaluations of the contribution of the model based on R^2 must be examined with care. Unlike R_a^2, the value of R^2 increases as more and more variables are added to the model. Consequently, you could force R^2 to take a value very close to 1 even though the model contributes no information for the prediction of y. In fact, R^2 equals 1 when the number of terms in the model (including β_0) equals the number of data points. Therefore, you should not rely solely on the value of R^2 (or even R_a^2) to tell you whether the model is useful for predicting y.

Conducting t-tests on all of the individual β parameters is also not the best method of testing the global utility of the model because these multiple tests result in a high probability of making at least one Type I error. Use the F-test for testing the global utility of the model.

After we have determined that the overall model is useful for predicting y using the F-test, we may elect to conduct one or more t-tests on the individual β parameters. However, the test (or tests) to be conducted should be decided a priori—that is, prior to fitting the model. Also, we should limit the number of t-tests conducted to avoid the potential problem of making too many Type I errors. Generally, the regression analyst will conduct t-tests only on the "most important" β's. We provide insight in identifying the most important β's in a linear model in Sections 5–8.

Recommendation for Checking the Utility of a Multiple Regression Model

1. First, conduct a test of overall model adequacy using the F-test—that is, test

$$H_0: \beta_1 = \beta_2 = \cdots = \beta_k = 0$$

If the model is deemed adequate (that is, if you reject H_0), then proceed to step 2. Otherwise, you should hypothesize and fit another model. The new model may include more independent variables or higher-order terms.

2. Conduct t-tests on those β parameters in which you are particularly interested (that is, the "most important" β's). As we will see in Sections 5 and 6, these usually involve only the β's associated with higher-order terms (x^2, $x_1 x_2$, etc.). However, it is a safe practice to limit the number of β's that are tested. Conducting a series of t-tests leads to a high overall Type I error rate α.

Exercises 1–24

Please be aware that some of the following problems may require knowledge of concepts that are not presented in this chapter.

Learning the Mechanics

1 Write a first-order model relating $E(y)$ to
   a. two quantitative independent variables.
   b. four quantitative independent variables.
   c. five quantitative independent variables.

2 Minitab was used to fit the model
   $E(y) = \beta_0 + \beta_1 x_1 + \beta_2 x_2$ to $n = 20$ data points, and the printout shown on the next page was obtained.

a. What are the sample estimates of β_0, β_1, and β_2?
b. What is the least squares prediction equation?
c. Find SSE, MSE, and s. Interpret the standard deviation in the context of the problem.
d. Test $H_0: \beta_1 = 0$ against $H_0: \beta_1 \neq 0$. Use $\alpha = .05$.
e. Use a 95% confidence interval to estimate β_2.
f. Find R^2 and R_a^2 and interpret these values.
g. Find the test statistic for testing $H_0: \beta_1 = \beta_2 = 0$.
h. Find the observed significance level of the test, part **g**. Interpret the result.

Minitab output for Evxercise 2

```
The regression equation is
Y = 506.35 - 941.9 X1 - 429.1 X2


Predictor    Coef   SE Coef      T      P
Constant   506.346    45.17   11.21  0.000
X1        -941.900   275.08   -3.42  0.003
X2        -429.060   379.83   -1.13  0.274


S = 94.251    R-Sq = 45.9%    R-Sq(adj) = 39.6%


Analysis of Variance

Source          DF      SS      MS     F      P
Regression       2  128329   64165  7.22  0.005
Residual Error  17  151016    8883
Total           19  279345
```

3 Suppose you fit the multiple regression model

$$y = \beta_0 + \beta_1 x_1 + \beta_2 x_2 + \beta_3 x_3 + \varepsilon$$

to $n = 30$ data points and obtain the following result:

$$\hat{y} = 3.4 - 4.6x_1 + 2.7x_2 + .93x_3$$

The estimated standard errors of $\hat{\beta}_2$ and $\hat{\beta}_3$ are 1.86 and .29, respectively.

a. Test the null hypothesis $H_0: \beta_2 = 0$ against the alternative hypothesis $H_a: \beta_2 \neq 0$. Use $\alpha = .05$.
b. Test the null hypothesis $H_0: \beta_3 = 0$ against the alternative hypothesis $H_a: \beta_3 \neq 0$. Use $\alpha = .05$.
c. The null hypothesis $H_0: \beta_2 = 0$ is not rejected. In contrast, the null hypothesis $H_0: \beta_3 = 0$ is rejected. Explain how this can happen even though $\hat{\beta}_2 > \hat{\beta}_3$.

4 Suppose you fit the first-order multiple regression model

$$y = \beta_0 + \beta_1 x_1 + \beta_2 x_2 + \varepsilon$$

to $n = 25$ data points and obtain the prediction equation

$$\hat{y} = 6.4 + 3.1x_1 + .92x_2$$

The estimated standard deviations of the sampling distributions of $\hat{\beta}_1$ and $\hat{\beta}_2$ are 2.3 and .27, respectively.
a. Test $H_0: \beta_1 = 0$ against $H_a: \beta_1 > 0$. Use $\alpha = .05$.
b. Test $H_0: \beta_2 = 0$ against $H_a: \beta_2 \neq 0$. Use $\alpha = .05$.
c. Find a 90% confidence interval for β_1. Interpret the interval.
d. Find a 99% confidence interval for β_2. Interpret the interval.

5 How is the number of degrees of freedom available for estimating σ^2 (the variance of ε) related to the number of independent variables in a regression model?

6 Consider the first-order model equation in three quantitative independent variables

$$E(y) = 1 + 2x_1 + x_2 - 3x_3$$

a. Graph the relationship between y and x_1 for $x_2 = 1$ and $x_3 = 3$.
b. Repeat part **a** for $x_2 = -1$ and $x_3 = 1$.
c. How do the graphed lines in parts **a** and **b** relate to each other? What is the slope of each line?
d. If a linear model is first-order in three independent variables, what type of geometric relationship will you obtain when $E(y)$ is graphed as a function of one of the independent variables for various combinations of values of the other independent variables?

7 Suppose you fit the first-order model

$$y = \beta_0 + \beta_1 x_1 + \beta_2 x_2 + \beta_3 x_3 + \beta_4 x_4 + \beta_5 x_5 + \varepsilon$$

to $n = 30$ data points and obtain

$$SSE = .33 \quad R^2 = .92$$

a. Do the values of SSE and R^2 suggest that the model provides a good fit to the data? Explain.
b. Is the model of any use in predicting y? Test the null hypothesis $H_0: \beta_1 = \beta_2 = \beta_3 = \beta_4 = \beta_5 = 0$ against the alternative hypothesis H_a: At least one of the parameters $\beta_1, \beta_2, \ldots, \beta_5$ is nonzero. Use $\alpha = .05$.

8 If the analysis of variance F-test leads to the conclusion that at least one of the model parameters is nonzero, can you conclude that the model is the best predictor for the dependent variable y? Can you conclude that all of the terms in the model are important for predicting y? What is the appropriate conclusion?

Applying the Concepts—Basic

9 **Usability professionals salary survey.** The Usability Professionals' Association (UPA) supports people who research, design, and evaluate the user experience of products and services. Recently, the UPA conducted a salary survey of its members (*UPA Salary Survey*, August 18, 2009). One of the report's authors, Jeff Sauro, investigated how much having a PhD affects salaries in this profession and discussed his analysis on the blog, www.measuringusability.com. Sauro fit a first-order multiple regression model for salary (y, in dollars) as a function of years of experience (x_1), PhD status ($x_2 = 1$ if PhD, 0 if not), and manager status ($x_3 = 1$ if manager, 0 if not). The following prediction equation was obtained:

$$\hat{y} = 52{,}484 + 2{,}941x_1 + 16{,}880x_2 + 11{,}108x_3$$

a. Predict the salary of a UPA member with 10 years of experience who does not have a PhD, but is a manager.
b. Predict the salary of a UPA member with 10 years of experience who does have a PhD, but is not a manager.
c. The following coefficient was reported: $R_a^2 = .32$. Give a practical interpretation of this value.
d. A 95% confidence interval for β_1 was reported as (2700, 3200). Give a practical interpretation of this result.
e. A 95% confidence interval for β_2 was reported as (11,500, 22,300). Give a practical interpretation of this result.
f. A 95% confidence interval for β_3 was reported as (7,600, 14,600). Give a practical interpretation of this result.

10 **Forecasting movie revenues with Twitter.** The *IEEE International Conference on Web Intelligence and Intelligent Agent Technology* (2010) did a study on using the volume of chatter on Twitter.com to forecast movie box office revenue. Opening weekend box office revenue data (in millions of dollars) were collected for a sample of 24 recent movies. In addition to each movie's *tweet rate*, i.e., the average number of tweets referring to the movie per hour 1 week prior to the movie's release, the researchers also computed the ratio of positive to negative tweets (called the *PN-ratio*).
a. Give the equation of a first-order model relating revenue (y) to both tweet rate (x_1) and PN-ratio (x_2).

b. Which β in the model, part **a,** represents the change in revenue (y) for every 1-tweet increase in the tweet rate (x_1), holding PN-ratio (x_2) constant?

c. Which β in the model, part **a,** represents the change in revenue (y) for every 1-unit increase in the PN-ratio (x_2), holding tweet rate (x_1) constant?

d. The following coefficients were reported: $R^2 = .945$ and $R_a^2 = .940$. Give a practical interpretation for both R^2 and R_a^2.

e. Conduct a test of the null hypothesis, $H_0: \beta_1 = \beta_2 = 0$. Use $\alpha = .05$.

f. The researchers reported the p-values for testing $H_0: \beta_1 = 0$ and $H_0: \beta_2 = 0$ as both less than .0001. Interpret these results (use $\alpha = .01$).

11 Accounting and Machiavellianism. *Behavioral Research in Accounting* (Jan. 2008) did a study of Machiavellian traits (e.g., manipulation, cunning, duplicity, deception, and bad faith) in accountants. A Mach rating score was determined for each in a sample of accounting alumni of a large southwestern university. For one portion of the study, the researcher modeled an accountant's Mach score (y) as a function of age, gender, education, and income. Data on $n = 198$ accountants yielded the results shown in the table.

Independent Variable	t-value for $H_0: \beta_i = 0$	p-value
Age (x_1)	0.10	$> .10$
Gender (x_2)	-0.55	$> .10$
Education (x_3)	1.95	$< .01$
Income (x_4)	0.52	$> .10$

Overall model: $R^2 = .13, F = 4.74$ (p-value $< .01$)

a. Conduct a test of overall model utility. Use $\alpha = .05$.

b. Interpret the coefficient of determination, R^2.

c. Is there sufficient evidence (at $\alpha = .05$) to say that income is a statistically useful predictor of Mach score?

12 Characteristics of lead users. During new product development, companies often involve "lead users," i.e., creative individuals who are on the leading edge of an important market trend. *Creativity and Innovation Management* (Feb. 2008) published an article on identifying the social network characteristics of lead users of children's computer games. Data were collected for $n = 326$ children, and the following variables were measured: lead-user rating (y, measured on a 5-point scale), gender ($x_1 = 1$ if female, 0 if male), age (x_2, years), degree of centrality (x_3, measured as the number of direct ties to other peers in the network), and betweenness centrality (x_4, measured as the number of shortest paths between peers). A first-order model for y was fit to the data, yielding the following least squares prediction equation:

$$\hat{y} = 3.58 + .01x_1 - .06x_2 - .01x_3 + .42x_4$$

a. Give two properties of the errors of prediction that result from using the method of least squares to obtain the parameter estimates.

b. Give a practical interpretation of the estimate of β_4 in the model.

c. A test of $H_0: \beta_4 = 0$ resulted in a p-value of .002. Make the appropriate conclusion at $\alpha = .05$.

13 Highway crash data analysis. Researchers at Montana State University have written a tutorial on an empirical method for analyzing before and after highway crash data (Montana Department of Transportation, Research Report, May 2004). The initial step in the methodology is to develop a Safety Performance Function (SPF)—a mathematical model that estimates crash occurrence for a given roadway segment. Using data collected for over 100 roadway segments, the researchers fit the model, $E(y) = \beta_0 + \beta_1 x_1 + \beta_2 x_2$, where $y =$ number of crashes per 3 years, $x_1 =$ roadway length (miles), and $x_2 = $ AADT $=$ average annual daily traffic (number of vehicles). The results are shown in the following tables.

Interstate Highways

Variable	Parameter Estimate	Standard Error	t-value
Intercept	1.81231	.50568	3.58
Length (x_1)	.10875	.03166	3.44
AADT (x_2)	.00017	.00003	5.19

Noninterstate Highways

Variable	Parameter Estimate	Standard Error	t-value
Intercept	1.20785	.28075	4.30
Length (x_1)	.06343	.01809	3.51
AADT (x_2)	.00056	.00012	4.86

a. Give the least squares prediction equation for the interstate highway model.

b. Give practical interpretations of the β estimates, part **a.**

c. Refer to part **a.** Find a 99% confidence interval for β_1 and interpret the result.

d. Refer to part **a.** Find a 99% confidence interval for β_2 and interpret the result.

e. Repeat parts **a–d** for the noninterstate highway model.

14 Predicting runs scored in baseball. In *Chance* (Fall 2000), statistician Scott Berry built a multiple regression model for predicting total number of runs scored by a Major League Baseball team during a season. Using data on all teams over a 9-year period (a sample of $n = 234$), the results in the following table were obtained.

Independent Variable	β Estimate	Standard Error
Intercept	3.70	15.00
Walks (x_1)	.34	.02
Singles (x_2)	.49	.03
Doubles (x_3)	.72	.05
Triples (x_4)	1.14	.19
Home runs (x_5)	1.51	.05
Stolen bases (x_6)	.26	.05
Caught stealing (x_7)	$-.14$	.14
Strikeouts (x_8)	$-.10$	.01
Outs (x_9)	$-.10$	.01

Source: Table from Berry, S. M. "A statistician reads the sports pages: Modeling offensive ability in baseball," *Chance*, Vol. 13, No. 4, Fall 2000, pp. 56–59 (Table 2). Reprinted with permission from *Chance*. © 2000 by the American Statistical Association. Reprinted with permission.

a. Write the least squares prediction equation for $y =$ total number of runs scored by a team in a season.

b. Interpret, practically, the β estimates in the model.

c. Conduct a test of $H_0: \beta_7 = 0$ against $H_a: \beta_7 < 0$ at $\alpha = .05$. Interpret the results.

d. Form a 95% confidence interval for β_5. Interpret the results.

Applying the Concepts—Intermediate

15 **Novelty of a vacation destination.** Many tourists choose a
NW vacation destination based on the newness or uniqueness (i.e., the novelty) of the itinerary. Texas A&M University professor J. Petrick investigated the relationship between novelty and vacationing golfers' demographics (*Annals of Tourism Research*, Vol. 29, 2002). Data were obtained from a mail survey of 393 golf vacationers to a large coastal resort in the southeastern United States. Several measures of novelty level (on a numerical scale) were obtained for each vacationer, including "change from routine," "thrill," "boredom-alleviation," and "surprise." The researcher employed four independent variables in a regression model to predict each of the novelty measures. The independent variables were $x_1 =$ number of rounds of golf per year, $x_2 =$ total number of golf vacations taken, $x_3 =$ number of years played golf, and $x_4 =$ average golf score.

a. Give the hypothesized equation of a first-order model for $y =$ change from routine.

b. A test of $H_0: \beta_3 = 0$ versus $H_a: \beta_3 < 0$ yielded a p-value of .005. Interpret this result if $\alpha = .01$.

c. The estimate of β_3 was found to be negative. Based on this result (and the result of part **b**), the researcher concluded that "those who have played golf for more years are less apt to seek change from their normal routine in their golf vacations." Do you agree with this statement? Explain.

d. The regression results for three dependent novelty measures, based on data collected for $n = 393$ golf vacationers, are summarized in the table below. Give the null hypothesis for testing the overall adequacy of the first-order regression model.

e. Give the rejection region for the test, part **d,** for $\alpha = .01$.

f. Use the test statistics reported in the table and the rejection region from part **e** to conduct the test for each of the dependent measures of novelty.

g. Verify that the p-values reported in the table support your conclusions in part **f.**

h. Interpret the values of R^2 reported in the table.

Dependent Variable	F-value	p-value	R^2
Thrill	5.56	< .001	.055
Change from routine	3.02	.018	.030
Surprise	3.33	.011	.023

Source: Based on Petrick, J. F. "An examination of golf vacationers' novelty," *Annals of Tourism Research*, Vol. 29, No. 2, 2002, pp. 384–400.

16 **Arsenic in groundwater.** *Environmental Science & Technology*
WELLS (Jan. 2005) reported on a study of the reliability of a commercial kit to test for arsenic in groundwater. The field kit was used to test a sample of 328 groundwater wells in

Bangladesh. In addition to the arsenic level (micrograms per liter), the latitude (degrees), longitude (degrees), and depth (feet) of each well were measured. The data are saved in the file. (The first and last 5 observations are listed in the table below.)

Well ID	Latitude	Longitude	Depth	Arsenic
10	23.7887	90.6522	60	331
14	23.7886	90.6523	45	302
30	23.7880	90.6517	45	193
59	23.7893	90.6525	125	232
85	23.7920	90.6140	150	19
⋮	⋮	⋮	⋮	⋮
7353	23.7949	90.6515	40	48
7357	23.7955	90.6515	30	172
7890	23.7658	90.6312	60	175
7893	23.7656	90.6315	45	624
7970	23.7644	90.6303	30	254

a. Write a first-order model for arsenic level (y) as a function of latitude, longitude, and depth.

b. Fit the model to the data using the method of least squares.

c. Give practical interpretations of the β estimates.

d. Find the model standard deviation, s, and interpret its value.

e. Find and interpret the values of R^2 and R_a^2.

f. Conduct a test of overall model utility at $\alpha = .05$.

g. Based on the results, parts **d–f,** would you recommend using the model to predict arsenic level (y)? Explain.

17 **Reality TV and cosmetic surgery.** How much influence does
BDYIMG the media, especially reality television programs, have on one's decision to undergo cosmetic surgery? This was the question of interest to psychologists who published an article in *Body Image: An International Journal of Research* (March 2010). In the study, 170 college students answered questions about their impressions of reality TV shows featuring cosmetic surgery, level of self-esteem, satisfaction with one's own body, and desire to have cosmetic surgery to alter one's body. The variables analyzed in the study were measured as follows: DESIRE—scale ranging from 5 to 25, where the higher the value, the greater the interest in having cosmetic surgery; GENDER—1 if male, 0 if female; SELFESTM—scale ranging from 4 to 40, where the higher the value, the greater the level of self-esteem; BODYSAT—scale ranging from 1 to 9, where the higher the value, the greater the satisfaction with one's own body; and IMPREAL—scale ranging from 1 to 7, where the higher the value, the more one believes reality television shows featuring cosmetic surgery are realistic. The data for the study (simulated based on statistics reported in the journal article) are saved in the file. Selected observations are listed in the next table. The psychologists used multiple regression to model desire to have cosmetic surgery (y) as a function of gender (x_1), self-esteem (x_2), body satisfaction (x_3), and impression of reality TV (x_4).

a. Fit the first-order model, $E(y) = \beta_0 + \beta_1 x_1 + \beta_2 x_2 + \beta_3 x_3 + \beta_4 x_4$, to the data in the file. Give the least squares prediction equation.

b. Interpret the β estimates in the words of the problem.

Data for Exercise 17 (first and last five observations)

STUDENT	DESIRE	GENDER	SELFESTM	BODYSAT	IMPREAL
1	11	0	24	3	4
2	13	0	20	3	4
3	11	0	25	4	5
4	11	1	22	9	4
5	18	0	8	1	6
⋮	⋮	⋮	⋮	⋮	⋮
166	18	0	25	3	5
167	13	0	26	4	5
168	9	1	13	5	6
169	14	0	20	3	2
170	6	1	27	8	3

River	Mile	Species	Length	Weight	DDT
FC	5	CHANNELCATFISH	42.5	732	10.00
FC	5	CHANNELCATFISH	44.0	795	16.00
FC	5	CHANNELCATFISH	41.5	547	23.00
FC	5	CHANNELCATFISH	39.0	465	21.00
FC	5	CHANNELCATFISH	50.5	1,252	50.00
⋮	⋮	⋮	⋮	⋮	⋮
TR	345	LARGEMOUTHBASS	23.5	358	2.00
TR	345	LARGEMOUTHBASS	30.0	856	2.20
TR	345	LARGEMOUTHBASS	29.0	793	7.40
TR	345	LARGEMOUTHBASS	17.5	173	0.35
TR	345	LARGEMOUTHBASS	36.0	1,433	1.90

c. Is the overall model statistically useful for predicting desire to have cosmetic surgery? Test using $\alpha = .01$.

d. Which statistic, R^2 or R_a^2, is the preferred measure of model fit? Practically interpret the value of this statistic.

e. Conduct a test to determine whether desire to have cosmetic surgery decreases linearly as level of body satisfaction increases. Use $\alpha = .05$.

f. Find a 95% confidence interval for β_4. Practically interpret the result.

18 Contamination from a plant's discharge. The U.S. Army Corps of Engineers compiled data on fish contaminated from the toxic discharges of a chemical plant located on the banks of the Tennessee River in Alabama. The engineers measured the length (in centimeters), weight (in grams), and DDT level (in parts per million) for 144 captured fish. In addition, the number of miles upstream from the river was recorded. The data are saved in the file. (The first and last five observations are shown in the table in the next column.)

a. Fit the first-order model, $E(y) = \beta_0 + \beta_1 x_1 + \beta_2 x_2 + \beta_3 x_3$, to the data, where $y = $ DDT level, $x_1 = $ mile, $x_2 = $ length, and $x_3 = $ weight. Report the least squares prediction equation.

b. Find the estimate of the standard deviation of ε for the model and give a practical interpretation of its value.

c. Conduct a test of the global utility of the model. Use $\alpha = .05$.

d. Do the data provide sufficient evidence to conclude that DDT level increases as length increases? Report the observed significance level of the test and reach a conclusion using $\alpha = .05$.

e. Find and interpret a 95% confidence interval for β_3.

19 Cooling method for gas turbines. The *Journal of Engineering for Gas Turbines and Power* (Jan. 2005) did a study of a high-pressure inlet fogging method for a gas turbine engine. The heat rate (kilojoules per kilowatt per hour) was measured for each in a sample of 67 gas turbines augmented with high-pressure inlet fogging. In addition, several other variables were measured, including cycle speed (revolutions per minute), inlet temperature (°C), exhaust gas temperature (°C), cycle pressure ratio, and air mass flow rate (kilograms per second). The data are saved in the file. (The first and last five observations are listed in the table at the bottom of the page.)

a. Write a first-order model for heat rate (y) as a function of speed, inlet temperature, exhaust temperature, cycle pressure ratio, and airflow rate.

b. Fit the model to the data using the method of least squares.

c. Give practical interpretations of the β estimates.

d. Find the model standard deviation, s, and interpret its value.

e. Conduct a test for overall model utility using $\alpha = .01$.

f. Find and interpret R_a^2.

g. Is there sufficient evidence (at $\alpha = .01$) to indicate that heat rate (y) is linearly related to inlet temperature?

Data for Exercise 19 (selected observations)

RPM	CP Ratio	Inlet Temp.	Exhaust Temp.	Airflow	Heat Rate
27,245	9.2	1,134	602	7	14,622
14,000	12.2	950	446	15	13,196
17,384	14.8	1,149	537	20	11,948
11,085	11.8	1,024	478	27	11,289
14,045	13.2	1,149	553	29	11,964
⋮	⋮	⋮	⋮	⋮	⋮
18,910	14.0	1,066	532	8	12,766
3,600	35.0	1,288	448	152	8,714
3,600	20.0	1,160	456	84	9,469
16,000	10.6	1,232	560	14	11,948
14,600	13.4	1,077	536	20	12,414

Source: Based on Bhargava, R., & Meher-Homji, C. B. "Parametric analysis of existing gas turbines with inlet evaporative and overspray fogging," *Journal of Engineering for Gas Turbines and Power*, Vol. 127, No. 1, Jan. 2005, pp. 145–158.

20 Extracting water from oil. In the oil industry, water that mixes with crude oil during production and transportation must be removed. Chemists have found that the oil can be extracted from the water/oil mix electrically. Researchers at the University of Bergen (Norway) conducted a series of experiments to study the factors that influence the voltage (y) required to separate the water from the oil (*Journal of Colloid and Interface Science*, Aug. 1995). The seven independent variables investigated in the study are listed in the table below. (Each variable was measured at two levels—a "low" level and a "high" level.) Sixteen water/oil mixtures were prepared using different combinations of the independent variables; then each emulsion was exposed to a high electric field. In addition, three mixtures were tested when all independent variables were set to 0. The data for all 19 experiments are saved in the file (selected observations are shown in the table at the bottom of the page).

a. Propose a first-order model for y as a function of all seven independent variables.

b. Use a statistical software package to fit the model to the data in the table.

c. Fully interpret the β estimates.

d. Evaluate the overall utility of the model at $\alpha = .10$.

21 Occupational safety study. An important goal in occupational safety is "active caring." Employees demonstrate active caring (AC) about the safety of their coworkers when they identify environmental hazards and unsafe work practices and then implement appropriate corrective actions for these unsafe conditions or behaviors. Three factors hypothesized to increase the propensity for an employee to actively care for safety are (1) high self-esteem, (2) optimism, and (3) group cohesiveness. *Applied & Preventive Psychology* (Winter 1995) attempted to establish empirical support for the AC hypothesis by fitting the model $E(y) = \beta_0 + \beta_1 x_1 + \beta_2 x_2 + \beta_3 x_3$, where

y = AC score (active caring score, 15-point scale)

x_1 = Self-esteem score

x_2 = Optimism score

x_3 = Group cohesion score

The regression analysis, based on data collected for $n = 31$ hourly workers at a large fiber-manufacturing plant, yielded a multiple coefficient of determination of $R^2 = .362$.

a. Interpret the value of R^2.

b. Use the R^2 value to test the global utility of the model. Use $\alpha = .05$.

22 R^2 and model fit. Because the coefficient of determination R^2 always increases when a new independent variable is added to the model, it is tempting to include many variables in a model to force R^2 to be near 1. However, doing so reduces the degrees of freedom available for estimating σ^2, which adversely affects our ability to make reliable inferences. Suppose you want to use 18 economic indicators to predict next year's gross domestic product (GDP). You fit the model

$$y = \beta_0 + \beta_1 x_1 + \beta_2 x_2 + \cdots + \beta_{17} x_{17} + \beta_{18} x_{18} + \varepsilon$$

where y = GDP and $x_1, x_2, \ldots, x_{18}$ are the economic indicators. Only 20 years of data ($n = 20$) are used to fit the model, and you obtain $R^2 = .95$. Test to see whether this impressive-looking R^2 is large enough for you to infer that the model is useful—that is, that at least one term in the model is important for predicting GDP. Use $\alpha = .05$.

Applying the Concepts—Advanced

23 Bordeaux wine sold at auction. The vineyards in the Bordeaux region of France are known for producing excellent red wines. However, the uncertainty of the weather during the growing season, the phenomenon that wine tastes better with age, and the fact that some Bordeaux vineyards produce better wines than others encourage speculation concerning the value of a case of wine produced by a certain vineyard during a certain year (or vintage). As a result, many wine experts attempt to predict the auction price of a case of Bordeaux wine. The publishers of a newsletter titled *Liquid Assets: The International Guide to Fine Wine* discussed a multiple regression approach to predicting the London auction price of red Bordeaux wine in *Chance* (Fall 1995). The natural logarithm of the price y (in dollars) of a case containing a dozen bottles of red wine was modeled as a function of weather during growing season and age of vintage using data collected for the vintages of 1952–1980. Three models were fit to the data. The results of the regressions are summarized in the table on the next page.

Data for Exercise 20 (selected observations)

Experiment Number	Voltage, y (kw/cm)	Disperse Phase Volume, x_1 (%)	Salinity, x_2 (%)	Temperature, x_3 (°C)	Time Delay, x_4 (hours)	Surfactant Concentration, x_5 (%)	Span: Triton, x_6	Solid Particles, x_7 (%)
1	.64	40	1	4	.25	2	.25	.5
2	.80	80	1	4	.25	4	.25	2
3	3.20	40	4	4	.25	4	.75	.5
4	.48	80	4	4	.25	2	.75	2
5	1.72	40	1	23	.25	4	.75	2
⋮	⋮	⋮	⋮	⋮	⋮	⋮	⋮	⋮
16	.72	80	4	23	24	4	.75	2
17	1.08	0	0	0	0	0	0	0
18	1.08	0	0	0	0	0	0	0
19	1.04	0	0	0	0	0	0	0

Source: Based on Førdedal, H., et al. "A multivariate analysis of W/O emulsions in high external electric fields as studied by means of dielectric time domain spectroscopy," *Journal of Colloid and Interface Science*, Vol. 173, No. 2, Aug. 1995, p. 398 (Table 2).

Results for Exercise 23

Independent Variables	Beta Estimates (Standard Errors)		
	Model 1	Model 2	Model 3
x_1 = Vintage year	.0354 (.0137)	.0238 (.00717)	.0240 (.00747)
x_2 = Average growing season temperature(°C)	(not included)	.616 (.0952)	.608 (.116)
x_3 = Sept./Aug. rainfall (cm)	(not included)	−.00386 (.00081)	−.00380 (.00095)
x_4 = Rainfall in months preceding vintage (cm)	(not included)	.0001173 (.000482)	.00115 (.000505)
x_5 = Average Sept. temperature(°C)	(not included)	(not included)	.00765 (.565)
	$R^2 = .212$	$R^2 = .828$	$R^2 = .828$
	$s = .575$	$s = .287$	$s = .293$

a. For each model, conduct a t-test (at $\alpha = .05$) for each of the β parameters in the model. Interpret the results.

b. When the natural log of y is used as a dependent variable, the antilogarithm of a β coefficient minus 1—that is $e^{\beta_i} - 1$—represents the percentage change in y for every 1-unit increase in the associated x value. Use this information to interpret the β estimates of each model.

c. Based on the values of R^2 and s, which of the three models would you recommend for predicting Bordeaux wine prices? Explain.

24 Cost analysis for a shipping department. Multiple regression is used by accountants in cost analysis to shed light on the factors that cause costs to be incurred and the magnitudes of their effects. Sometimes, it is desirable to use physical units instead of cost as the dependent variable in a cost analysis (e.g., if the cost associated with the activity of interest is a function of some physical unit, such as hours of labor). The advantage of this approach is that the regression model will provide estimates of the number of labor hours required under different circumstances, and these hours can then be costed at the current labor rate (Horngren, Foster, and Datar, *Cost Accounting*, 2006). The sample data shown in the table below have been collected from a firm's accounting and production records to provide cost

information about the firm's shipping department. These data are saved in the file. Consider the model

$$y = \beta_0 + \beta_1 x_1 + \beta_2 x_2 + \beta_3 x_3 + \varepsilon$$

a. Find the least squares prediction equation.

b. Use an F-test to investigate the usefulness of the model specified in part **a.** Use $\alpha = .01$ and state your conclusion in the context of the problem.

c. Test $H_0: \beta_2 = 0$ versus $H_a: \beta_2 \neq 0$ using $\alpha = .05$. What do the results of your test suggest about the magnitude of the effects of x_2 on labor costs?

d. Find R^2 and interpret its value in the context of the problem.

e. If shipping department employees are paid $7.50 per hour, how much less, on average, will it cost the company per week if the average number of pounds per shipment increases from a level of 20 to 21? Assume that x_1 and x_2 remain unchanged. Your answer is an estimate of what is known in economics as the *expected marginal cost* associated with a 1-pound increase in x_3.

f. With what approximate precision can this model be used to predict the hours of labor? [*Note:* The precision of multiple regression predictions is discussed in Section 4.]

g. Can regression analysis alone indicate what factors *cause* costs to increase? Explain.

Data for Exercise 24

Week	Labor, y (hr)	Pounds Shipped, x_1 (1,000s)	Percentage of Units Shipped by Truck, x_2	Average Shipment Weight, x_3 (lb)
1	100	5.1	90	20
2	85	3.8	99	22
3	108	5.3	58	19
4	116	7.5	16	15
5	92	4.5	54	20
6	63	3.3	42	26
7	79	5.3	12	25
8	101	5.9	32	21
9	88	4.0	56	24
10	71	4.2	64	29
11	122	6.8	78	10
12	85	3.9	90	30
13	50	3.8	74	28
14	114	7.5	89	14
15	104	4.5	90	21
16	111	6.0	40	20
17	110	8.1	55	16
18	100	2.9	64	19
19	82	4.0	35	23
20	85	4.8	58	25

4   Using the Model for Estimation and Prediction

The least squares line can be used for estimating the mean value of y, $E(y)$, for some particular value of x, say $x = x_p$. The same fitted model can also be used to predict, when $x = x_p$, some new value of y to be observed in the future. The least squares line yielded the same value for both the estimate of $E(y)$ and the prediction of some future value of y—that is, both are the result of substituting x_p into the prediction equation $\hat{y} = \hat{\beta}_0 + \hat{\beta}_1 x$ and calculating $\hat{y}_p$. There the equivalence ends. The confidence interval for the mean $E(y)$ is narrower than the prediction interval for y because of the additional uncertainty attributable to the random error ε when predicting some future value of y.

These same concepts carry over to the multiple regression model. Consider a first-order model relating sale price (y) of a residential property to land value (x_1), appraised improvements value (x_2), and home size (x_3). Suppose we want to estimate the mean sale price for a given property with $x_1 = \$15,000$, $x_2 = \$50,000$, and $x_3 = 1,800$ square feet. Assuming that the first-order model represents the true relationship between sale price and the three independent variables, we want to estimate

$$E(y) = \beta_0 + \beta_1 x_1 + \beta_2 x_2 + \beta_3 x_3 = \beta_0 + \beta_1(15,000) + \beta_2(50,000) + \beta_3(1,800)$$

After obtaining the least squares estimates $\hat{\beta}_0, \hat{\beta}_1, \hat{\beta}_2,$ and $\hat{\beta}_3$, the estimate of $E(y)$ will be

$$\hat{y} = \hat{\beta}_0 + \hat{\beta}_1(15,000) + \hat{\beta}_2(50,000) + \hat{\beta}_3(1,800)$$

To form a confidence interval for the mean, we need to know the standard deviation of the sampling distribution for the estimator $\hat{y}$. For multiple regression models, the form of this standard deviation is rather complex. However, the regression routines of statistical computer software packages allow us to obtain the confidence intervals for mean values of y for any given combination of values of the independent variables. We illustrate with an example.

Example 5

Estimating $E(y)$ and Predicting y—Auction Price Model

Problem Refer to Examples 1–4 and the first-order model, $E(y) = \beta_0 + \beta_1 x_1 + \beta_2 x_2$, where y = auction price of a grandfather clock, x_1 = age of the clock, and x_2 = number of bidders.

a. Estimate the average auction price for all 150-year-old clocks sold at auction with 10 bidders using a 95% confidence interval. Interpret the result.

b. Predict the auction price for a single 150-year-old clock sold at an auction with 10 bidders using a 95% prediction interval. Interpret the result.

c. Suppose you want to predict the auction price for one clock that is 50 years old and has 2 bidders. How should you proceed?

Solution

a. Here, the key words *average* and *for all* imply we want to estimate the mean of y, $E(y)$. We want a 95% confidence interval for $E(y)$ when $x_1 = 150$ years and $x_2 = 10$ bidders. A Minitab printout for this analysis is shown in Figure 7. The confidence interval (highlighted under **"95% CI"**) is (1,381.4, 1,481.9). Thus, we are 95% confident that the mean auction price for all 150-year-old clocks sold at an auction with 10 bidders lies between \$1,381.40 and \$1,481.90.

b. The key words *predict* and *for a single* imply that we want a 95% prediction interval for y when $x_1 = 150$ years and $x_2 = 10$ bidders. This interval (highlighted under "95% PI" on the Minitab printout, Figure 7) is (1,154.1, 1,709.3). We say, with 95% confidence, that the auction price for a single 150-year-old clock sold at an auction with 10 bidders falls between \$1,154.10 and \$1,709.30.

c. Now, we want to predict the auction price, y, for a single (*one*) grandfather clock when $x_1 = 50$ years and $x_2 = 2$ bidders. Consequently, we desire a 95% prediction interval for y. However, before we form this prediction interval, we should check

---

Regression Analysis: PRICE versus AGE, NUMBIDS

```
The regression equation is
PRICE = - 1339 + 12.7 AGE + 86.0 NUMBIDS

Predictor      Coef   SE Coef       T      P
Constant    -1339.0     173.8   -7.70  0.000
AGE         12.7406    0.9047   14.08  0.000
NUMBIDS      85.953     8.729    9.85  0.000

S = 133.485   R-Sq = 89.2%   R-Sq(adj) = 88.5%

Analysis of Variance

Source          DF        SS       MS       F      P
Regression       2   4283063  2141531  120.19  0.000
Residual Error  29    516727    17818
Total           31   4799790

Predicted Values for New Observations

New
Obs     Fit  SE Fit         95% CI             95% PI
  1  1431.7    24.6  (1381.4, 1481.9)  (1154.1, 1709.3)

Values of Predictors for New Observations

New
Obs  AGE  NUMBIDS
  1  150     10.0
```

Figure 7

Minitab printout with 95% confidence intervals for grandfather clock model

to make sure that the selected values of the independent variables, $x_1 = 50$ and $x_2 = 2$, are both reasonable and within their respective sample ranges. If you examine the sample data shown in Table 1, you will see that the range for age is $108 \le x_1 \le 194$, and the range for number of bidders is $5 \le x_2 \le 15$. Thus, both selected values fall well *outside* their respective ranges. Be aware of the dangers of using the model to predict y for a value of an independent variable that is not within the range of the sample data. Doing so may lead to an unreliable prediction.

Look Back If we want to make the prediction requested in part **c,** we would need to collect additional data on clocks with the requested characteristics (i.e., $x_1 = 50$ years and $x_2 = 2$ bidders) and then refit the model.

Now Work Exercise 29

STATISTICS in ACTION REVISITED

Evaluating a First-Order Model

The Florida attorney general wants to develop a model for the cost (y) of a road construction contract awarded using the sealed-bid system and to use the model to predict the costs of future road contracts in the state. In addition to contract cost, the **FLAG** file contains data on eight potential predictor variables for a sample of 235 road contracts. (See Table SIA1.) Minitab scatterplots (with the dependent variable, COST, plotted against each of the potential predictors) for the data are shown in Figure SIA1. From the scatterplots, it appears that the DOT engineer's cost estimate (DOTEST) and estimate of work days (DAYSEST) would be good predictors of contract cost. [In a future Statistics in Action Revisited section, we will learn that the two best predictors of contract cost are actually DOTEST and the fixed or competitive status (STATUS) of the contract.] However, in this section, we will fit the first-order regression model using all eight independent variables.

The Minitab printout for the regression analysis is shown in Figure SIA2. The global F-statistic ($F = 1,166.68$) and associated p-value (.000) shown on the printout indicate that the overall model is statistically useful for predicting construction cost. The value of R^2 indicates that the model can explain 97.6% of the sample variation in contract cost. Both of these results provide strong statistical support for using the model for estimation and prediction.

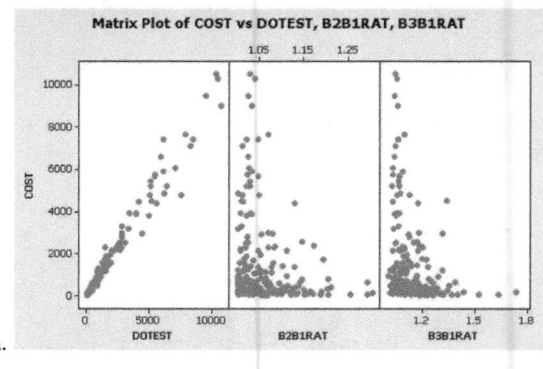

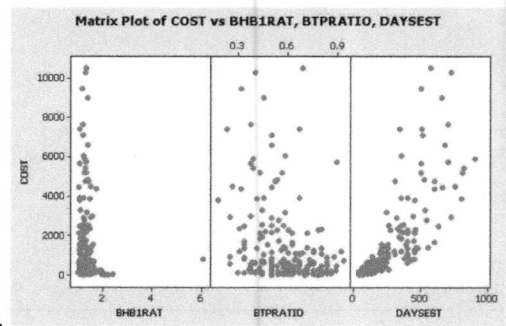

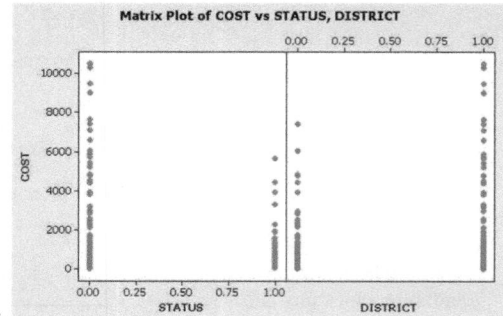

Figure SIA1
Minitab scatterplots for **FLAG** data

a.

b.

c.

```
The regression equation is
COST = 124 + 0.906 DOTEST - 147 B2B1RAT - 84 B3B1RAT - 59.1 BHB1RAT + 148 STA>>
       + 37.8 DISTRICT + 218 BTPRATIO + 0.344 DAYSEST


Predictor      Coef   SE Coef       T       P
Constant      123.9     426.8    0.29   0.772
DOTEST      0.90647   0.01659   54.64   0.000
B2B1RAT      -147.1     419.0   -0.35   0.726
B3B1RAT       -83.8     245.4   -0.34   0.733
BHB1RAT      -59.09     54.90   -1.08   0.283
STATUS       148.16     51.48    2.88   0.004
DISTRICT      37.75     43.07    0.88   0.382
BTPRATIO      217.6     139.6    1.56   0.120
DAYSEST      0.3439    0.1803    1.91   0.058


S = 304.589    R-Sq = 97.6%    R-Sq(adj) = 97.6%


Analysis of Variance

Source          DF         SS         MS       F       P
Regression       8  865907936  108238492  1166.68  0.000
Residual Error 226   20967037      92774
Total          234  886874973
```

Figure SIA2
Minitab regression output for first-order model of road construction cost

[*Note:* Not all of the independent variables have statistically significant t-values. However, we caution against dropping the insignificant variables from the model at this stage. One reason (discussed in Section 3) is that performing a large number of t-tests will yield an inflated probability of at least one Type I error. In later sections of this chapter, we develop other reasons for why the multiple t-test approach is not a good strategy for determining which independent variables to keep in the model.]

The Minitab printout shown in Figure SIA3 gives a 95% prediction interval for cost and a 95% confidence interval for the mean cost for the x-values associated with the last observation (contract) in the **FLAG** file. These x-values are engineer's cost estimate (DOTEST) = 497 thousand dollars, ratio of second lowest bid to lowest bid (B2B1RAT) = 1.07, ratio of third lowest bid to lowest bid (B3B1RAT) = 1.08, ratio of highest bid to lowest bid (BHB1RAT) = 1.19, competitive bid (STATUS = 0), south

Florida contract (DISTRICT = 1), bidders to planholders ratio (BTPRATIO) = 0.5, and estimated work days (DAYSEST) = 90. The 95% confidence interval of (339.2, 528.2) implies that for all road contracts with these x-values, the mean contract cost falls between 339.2 and 528.2 thousand dollars, with 95% confidence.

```
Predicted Values for New Observations

New
Obs    Fit  SE Fit       95% CI            95% PI
  1  433.7    48.0  (339.2, 528.2)  (-173.9, 1041.2)


Values of Predictors for New Observations

New
Obs  DOTEST  B2B1RAT  B3B1RAT  BHB1RAT    STATUS  DISTRICT  BTPRATIO  DAYSEST
  1     497     1.07     1.08     1.19  0.000000      1.00     0.500     90.0
```

Figure SIA3

Minitab printout with 95% confidence and prediction intervals

The 95% prediction interval of (−173.9, 1,041.2) implies that for an individual road contract with these x-values, the contract cost falls between 0 (because cost cannot be negative) and 1,041.2 thousand dollars, with 95% confidence. Note the wide range of the prediction interval. This is due to the large magnitude of the model standard deviation, $s = 305$ thousand dollars. Although the model is deemed statistically useful for predicting contract cost, it may not be "practically" useful. To reduce the magnitude of s, we will need to improve the model's predictive ability. (We consider such a model in the next Statistics in Action Revisited section.)

Data Set: FLAG

Exercises 25–33

Please be aware that some of the following problems may require knowledge of concepts that are not presented in this chapter.

Applying the Concepts—Basic

25 Characteristics of lead users. Refer to the *Creativity and Innovation Management* (Feb. 2008) study of lead users of children's computer games, Exercise 12. Recall that the researchers modeled lead-user rating (y, measured on a 5-point scale) as a function of gender ($x_1 = 1$ if female, 0 if male), age (x_2, years), degree of centrality (x_3, measured as the number of direct ties to other peers in the network), and betweenness centrality (x_4, measured as the number of shortest paths between peers). The least squares prediction equation was $\hat{y} = 3.58 + .01x_1 - .06x_2 - .01x_3 + .42x_4$.

  a. Compute the predicted lead-user rating of a 10-year-old female child with 5 direct ties to other peers in her social network and with 2 shortest paths between peers.

  b. Compute an estimate for the mean lead-user rating of all 8-year-old male children with 10 direct ties to other peers and with 4 shortest paths between peers.

26 Predicting runs scored in baseball. Refer to the *Chance* (Fall 2000) study of runs scored in Major League Baseball games, Exercise 14. Multiple regression was used to model total number of runs scored (y) of a team during the season as a function of number of walks (x_1), number of singles (x_2), number of doubles (x_3), number of triples (x_4), number of

home runs (x_5), number of stolen bases (x_6), number of times caught stealing (x_7), number of strikeouts (x_8), and total number of outs (x_9). Using the β estimates given in Exercise 14, predict the number of runs scored by your favorite Major League Baseball team last year. How close is the predicted value to the actual number of runs scored by your team? [*Note:* You can find data on your favorite team on the Internet at www.mlb.com.]

27 Reality TV and cosmetic surgery. Refer to the *Body Image: An International Journal of Research* (March 2010) study of the impact of reality TV shows on one's desire to undergo cosmetic surgery, Exercise 17. Recall that psychologists used multiple regression to model desire to have cosmetic surgery (y) as a function of gender (x_1), self-esteem (x_2), body satisfaction (x_3), and impression of reality TV (x_4). The SPSS printout below shows a confidence interval for $E(y)$ for each of the first five students in the study.

  a. Interpret the confidence interval for $E(y)$ for student 1.

  b. Interpret the confidence interval for $E(y)$ for student 4.

28 Chemical plant contamination. Refer to Exercise 18 and the U.S. Army Corps of Engineers study. You fit the first-order model, $E(y) = \beta_0 + \beta_1 x_1 + \beta_2 x_2 + \beta_3 x_3$,

STUDENT	DESIRE	GENDER	SELFESTM	BODYSAT	IMPREAL	Lower95CL_Mean	Upper95CL_Mean
1	1	11	0	24	3	4	13.42	14.31
2	2	13	0	20	3	4	13.56	14.55
3	3	11	0	25	4	5	13.42	14.56
4	4	11	1	22	9	4	8.79	10.89
5	5	18	0	8	1	6	15.18	17.34

SPSS output for Exercise 27

XLSTAT output for Exercise 28

Observation	Pred(DDT)	Lower bound 90% (Mean)	Upper bound 90% (Mean)	Lower bound 90% (Observation)	Upper bound 90% (Observation)
MILE=300, LNGTH=40, WT=1000	18.8803	3.8650	33.8956	-143.2178	180.9784

to the data, where y = DDT level (parts per million), x_1 = number of miles upstream, x_2 = length (centimeters), and x_3 = weight (grams). Use the Excel/XLSTAT printout above to predict, with 90% confidence, the DDT level of a fish caught 300 miles upstream with a length of 40 centimeters and a weight of 1,000 grams. Interpret the result.

29 Cooling method for gas turbines. Refer to the *Journal of Engineering for Gas Turbines and Power* (Jan. 2005) study of a high-pressure inlet fogging method for a gas turbine engine, Exercise 19. Recall that you fit a first-order model for heat rate (y) as a function of speed (x_1), inlet temperature (x_2), exhaust temperature (x_3), cycle pressure ratio (x_4), and airflow rate (x_5). A Minitab printout with both a 95% confidence interval for $E(y)$ and prediction interval for y for selected values of the x's is shown below.

GASTRB
NW

a. Interpret the 95% prediction interval for y in the words of the problem.
b. Interpret the 95% confidence interval for $E(y)$ in the words of the problem.
c. Will the confidence interval for $E(y)$ always be narrower than the prediction interval for y? Explain.

```
Predicted Values for New Observations

New
Obs     Fit   SE Fit      95% CI              95% PI
  1  12632.5  237.3  (12157.9, 13107.1)  (11599.6, 13665.5)


Values of Predictors for New Observations

New
Obs   RPM   INLET-TEMP  EXH-TEMP  CPRATIO  AIRFLOW
  1  7500      1000       525      13.5     10.0
```

Applying the Concepts—Intermediate

30 Arsenic in groundwater. Refer to the *Environmental Science & Technology* (Jan. 2005) study of the reliability of a commercial kit to test for arsenic in groundwater, Exercise 16. You fit a first-order model for arsenic level (y) as a function of latitude, longitude, and depth. Based on the model statistics, the researchers concluded that the arsenic level is highest at a low latitude, high longitude, and low depth. Do you agree? If so, find a 95% prediction interval for arsenic level for the lowest latitude, highest longitude, and lowest depth that are within the range of the sample data. Interpret the result.

WELLS

31 Pay-for-performance efficiency of CEOs. This exercise refers to *Forbes* magazine's "Executive Compensation Scoreboard." *Forbes* (April 13, 2011) determined which CEOs are worth their pay based on a comparison of the firm's stock performance and the CEO's annual salary. Data for 175 of the top performers are saved in the file. Some of the variables measured for each CEO include pay-for-performance efficiency rating (x_1), value of shares owned (x_2), age (x_3), and the CEO's average salary over the past 5 years (y).

TOP175

(The lower the efficiency rating, the more the CEO is worth his/her pay.) Consider the first-order model $E(y) = \beta_0 + \beta_1 x_1 + \beta_2 x_2 + \beta_3 x_3$.
a. Fit the model to the data and give the least squares prediction equation.
b. Conduct a test of overall model adequacy using $\alpha = .05$.
c. Predict, with 95% confidence, the 5-year pay of a CEO with $x_1 = 173$, $x_2 = \$102.9$ million, and $x_3 = 59$ years. (*Note:* These values represent the data for Sam Palmisano, CEO of IBM.) Interpret the result.

32 Extracting water from oil. Refer to Exercise 20 and the study on separating water from oil. The researchers concluded that "in order to break a water-oil mixture with the lowest possible voltage, the volume fraction of the disperse phase (x_1) should be high, while the salinity (x_2) and the amount of surfactant (x_5) should be low." Use this information and the first-order model of Exercise 20 to find a 95% prediction interval for this "low" voltage (y). Interpret the interval.

H2OOIL

33 Boiler drum production. In a production facility, an accurate estimate of man-hours needed to complete a task is crucial to management in making such decisions as the proper number of workers to hire, an accurate deadline to quote a client, or cost-analysis decisions regarding budgets. A manufacturer of boiler drums wants to use regression to predict the number of man-hours needed to erect the drums in future projects. To accomplish this, data for 35 boilers were collected. In addition to man-hours (y), the variables measured were boiler capacity (x_1 = lb/hr), boiler design pressure (x_2 = pounds per square inch or psi), boiler type (x_3 = 1 if industry field erected, 0 if utility field erected), and drum type (x_4 = 1 if steam, 0 if mud). The data are saved in the file. (The first five and last five observations are listed in the accompanying table.)

BOILER

a. Fit the model $E(y) = \beta_0 + \beta_1 x_1 + \beta_2 x_2 + \beta_3 x_3 + \beta_4 x_4$ to the data. Give the estimates of the β's.
b. Conduct a test for the global utility of the model. Use $\alpha = .01$.
c. Find a 95% confidence interval for $E(y)$ when $x_1 = 150,000$, $x_2 = 500$, $x_3 = 1$, and $x_4 = 0$. Interpret the result.

Man-Hours, y	Boiler Capacity, x_1	Design Pressure, x_2	Boiler Type, x_3	Drum Type, x_4
3,137	120,000	375	1	1
3,590	65,000	750	1	1
4,526	150,000	500	1	1
10,825	1,073,877	2,170	0	1
4,023	150,000	325	1	1
⋮	⋮	⋮	⋮	⋮
4,206	441,000	410	1	0
4,006	441,000	410	1	0
3,728	627,000	1,525	0	0
3,211	610,000	1,500	0	0
1,200	30,000	325	1	0

Source: Dr. Kelly Uscategui.

PART II: MODEL BUILDING IN MULTIPLE REGRESSION

5   Interaction Models

In Section 2, we demonstrated the relationship between $E(y)$ and the independent variables in a first-order model. When $E(y)$ is graphed against any one variable (say, x_1) for fixed values of the other variables, the result is a set of *parallel* straight lines (see Figure 3). When this situation occurs (as it always does for a first-order model), we say that the relationship between $E(y)$ and any one independent variable *does not depend* on the values of the other independent variables in the model.

However, if the relationship between $E(y)$ and x_1 does, in fact, depend on the values of the remaining x's held fixed, then the first-order model is not appropriate for predicting y. In this case, we need another model that will take into account this dependence. Such a model includes the *cross products* of two or more x's.

For example, suppose that the mean value $E(y)$ of a response y is related to two quantitative independent variables, x_1 and x_2, by the model

$$E(y) = 1 + 2x_1 - x_2 + 3x_1x_2$$

A graph of the relationship between $E(y)$ and x_1 for $x_2 = 0, 1$, and 2 is displayed in the Minitab graph, Figure 8.

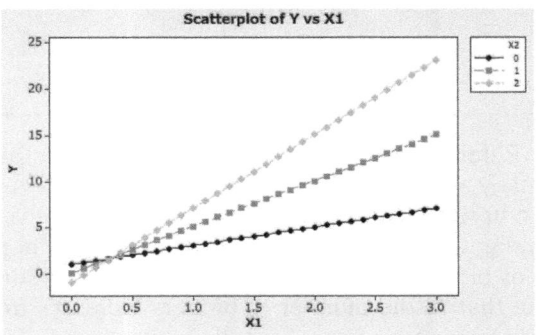

Figure 8

Minitab graphs of $1 + 2x_1 - x_2 + 3x_1x_2$ for $x_2 = 0, 1, 2$

Note that the graph shows three nonparallel straight lines. You can verify that the slopes of the lines differ by substituting each of the values $x_2 = 0, 1$, and 2 into the equation.

For $x_2 = 0$:

$$E(y) = 1 + 2x_1 - (0) + 3x_1(0) = 1 + 2x_1 \quad \text{(slope} = 2\text{)}$$

For $x_2 = 1$,

$$E(y) = 1 + 2x_1 - (1) + 3x_1(1) = 0 + 5x_1 \quad \text{(slope} = 5\text{)}$$

For $x_2 = 2$,

$$E(y) = 1 + 2x_1 - (2) + 3x_1(2) = -1 + 8x_1 \quad \text{(slope} = 8\text{)}$$

Note that the slope of each line is represented by $\beta_1 + \beta_3x_2 = 2 + 3x_2$. Thus, the effect on $E(y)$ of a change in x_1 (i.e., the slope) now *depends* on the value of x_2. When this situation occurs, we say that x_1 and x_2 **interact.** The cross-product term, x_1x_2, is called an **interaction term,** and the model $E(y) = \beta_0 + \beta_1x_1 + \beta_2x_2 + \beta_3x_1x_2$ is called an **interaction model** with two quantitative variables.

An Interaction Model Relating $E(y)$ to Two Quantitative Independent Variables

$$E(y) = \beta_0 + \beta_1x_1 + \beta_2x_2 + \beta_3x_1x_2$$

where

$(\beta_1 + \beta_3x_2)$ represents the change in $E(y)$ for every 1-unit increase in x_1, holding x_2 fixed

$(\beta_2 + \beta_3x_1)$ represents the change in $E(y)$ for every 1-unit increase in x_2, holding x_1 fixed

---

A three-dimensional graph (generated in Minitab) of the interaction model in two quantitative x's is shown in Figure 9. Unlike the flat planar surface displayed in Figure 4, the interaction model traces a ruled surface (twisted plane) in three-dimensional space. If we slice the twisted plane at a fixed value of x_2, we obtain a straight line relating $E(y)$ to x_1; however, the slope of the line will change as we change the value of x_2. Consequently, an interaction model is appropriate when the linear relationship between y and one independent variable depends on the value of another independent variable. The next example illustrates this idea.

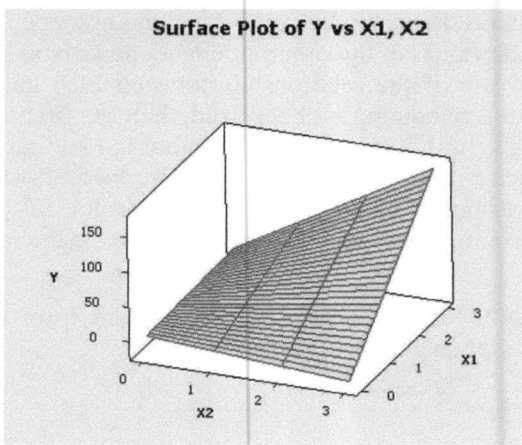

Figure 9

Minitab 3-dimensional graph of
$1 + 2x_1 - x_2 + 3x_1x_2$

Example 6

Evaluating an Interaction Model—Clock Auction Prices

Problem Refer to Examples 1–4. Suppose the collector of grandfather clocks, having observed many auctions, believes that the *rate of increase* of the auction price with age will be driven upward by a large number of bidders. Thus, instead of a relationship like that shown in Figure 10a, in which the rate of increase in price with age is the same for any number of bidders, the collector believes the relationship is like that shown in Figure 10b. Note that as the number of bidders increases from 5 to 15, the slope of the price versus age line increases.

Consequently, the interaction model is proposed:

$$y = \beta_0 = \beta_1x_1 + \beta_2x_2 + \beta_3x_1x_2 + \varepsilon$$

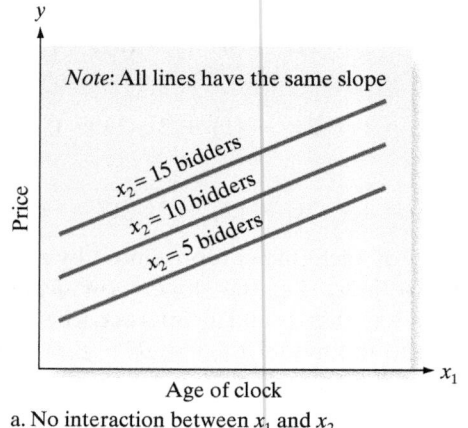
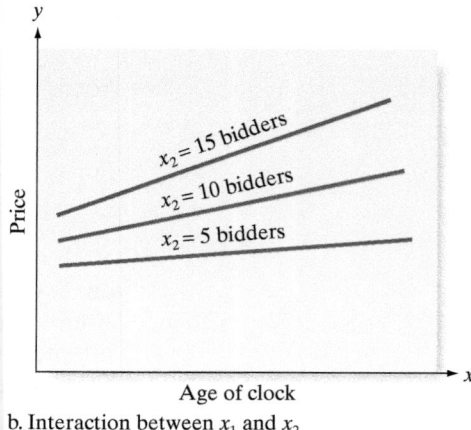

a. No interaction between x_1 and x_2 b. Interaction between x_1 and x_2

Figure 10

Examples of no-interaction and interaction models

The 32 data points listed in Table 1 were used to fit the model with interaction. A portion of the Minitab printout is shown in Figure 11.

a. Test the overall utility of the model using the global F-test at $\alpha = .05$.

b. Test the hypothesis (at $\alpha = .05$) that the price-age slope increases as the number of bidders increases—that is, that age and number of bidders, x_2, interact positively.

c. Estimate the change in auction price of a 150-year-old grandfather clock, y, for each additional bidder.

Regression Analysis: PRICE versus AGE, NUMBIDS, AGEBID

```
The regression equation is
PRICE = 320 + 0.88 AGE - 93.3 NUMBIDS + 1.30 AGEBID


Predictor     Coef   SE Coef      T      P
Constant     320.5    295.1    1.09  0.287
AGE          0.878    2.032    0.43  0.669
NUMBIDS     -93.26    29.89   -3.12  0.004
AGEBID      1.2978   0.2123    6.11  0.000


S = 88.9145   R-Sq = 95.4%   R-Sq(adj) = 94.9%


Analysis of Variance

Source           DF       SS       MS       F      P
Regression        3  4578427  1526142  193.04  0.000
Residual Error   28   221362     7906
Total            31  4799790
```

Figure 11

Minitab printout for interaction model of auction price

Solution

a. The global F-test is used to test the null hypothesis

$$H_0: \beta_1 = \beta_2 = \beta_3 = 0$$

The test statistic and p-value of the test (highlighted on the Minitab printout) are $F = 193.04$ and p-value $= 0$, respectively. Because $\alpha = .05$ exceeds the p-value, there is sufficient evidence to conclude that the model fit is a statistically useful predictor of auction price, y.

b. The hypotheses of interest to the collector concern the interaction parameter β_3. Specifically,

$$H_0: \beta_3 = 0$$
$$H_a: \beta_3 > 0$$

Because we are testing an individual β parameter, a t-test is required. The test statistic and two-tailed p-value (highlighted on the printout) are $t = 6.11$ and p-value $= 0$, respectively. The upper-tailed p-value, obtained by dividing the two-tailed p-value in half, is $0/2 = 0$. Because $\alpha = .05$ exceeds the p-value, the collector can reject H_0 and conclude that the rate of change of the mean price of the clocks with age increases as the number of bidders increases; that is, x_1 and x_2 interact positively. Thus, it appears that the interaction term should be included in the model.

c. To estimate the change in auction price, y, for every 1-unit increase in number of bidders, x_2, we need to estimate the slope of the line relating y to x_2 when the age of the clock, x_1, is 150 years old. An analyst who is not careful may estimate this slope as $\hat{\beta}_2 = -93.26$. Although the coefficient of x_2 is negative, this does *not* imply that auction price decreases as the number of bidders increases. Since interaction is present, the rate of change (slope) of mean auction price with the number of bidders *depends* on x_1, the age of the clock. For a fixed value of age (x_1), we can rewrite the interaction model as follows:

$$E(y) = \beta_0 + \beta_1 x_1 + \beta_2 x_2 + \beta_3 x_1 x_2 = \underbrace{(\beta_0 + \beta_1 x_1)}_{y\text{-intercept}} + \underbrace{(\beta_2 + \beta_3 x_1)}_{\text{slope}} x_2$$

Thus, the estimated rate of change of y for a 1-unit increase in x_2 (one new bidder) for a 150-year-old clock is

$$\text{Estimated slope of the } y \text{ versus } x_2 \text{ line} = \hat{\beta}_2 + \hat{\beta}_3 x_1$$

$$= -93.26 + 1.30(150) = 101.74$$

In other words, we estimate that the auction price of a 150-year-old clock will *increase* by about $101.74 for every additional bidder.

Look Back Although the rate of increase will vary as x_1 is changed, it will remain positive for the range of values of x_1 included in the sample. Extreme care is needed in interpreting the signs and sizes of coefficients in a multiple regression model.

Now Work Exercise 40

Example 6 illustrates an important point about conducting t-tests on the β parameters in the interaction model. The key β parameter in this model is the interaction β, β_3. [Note that this β is also the one associated with the highest-order term in the model, x_1x_2.]* Consequently, we will want to test $H_0: \beta_3 = 0$ after we have determined that the overall model is useful for predicting y. Once interaction is detected (as in Example 6), however, tests on the first-order terms x_1 and x_2 should *not* be conducted because they are meaningless tests; the presence of interaction implies that both x's are important.

> ⚠ **CAUTION** Once interaction has been deemed important in the model $E(y) = \beta_0 + \beta_1x_1 + \beta_2x_2 + \beta_3x_1x_2$, do not conduct t-tests on the β coefficients of the first-order terms x_1 and x_2. These terms should be kept in the model regardless of the magnitude of their associated p-values shown on the printout.

Exercises 34–48

Learning the Mechanics

34 Write an interaction model relating the mean value of y, $E(y)$ to
  a. two quantitative independent variables
  b. three quantitative independent variables [*Hint:* Include all possible two-way cross-product terms.]

35 Suppose the true relationship between $E(y)$ and the quantitative independent variables x_1 and x_2 is

$$E(y) = 3 + x_1 + 2x_2 - x_1x_2$$

  a. Describe the corresponding three-dimensional response surface.
  b. Plot the linear relationship between y and x_2 for $x_1 = 0, 1, 2$, where $0 \le x_2 \le 5$.
  c. Explain why the lines you plotted in part **b** are not parallel.
  d. Use the lines you plotted in part **b** to explain how changes in the settings of x_1 and x_2 affect $E(y)$.
  e. Use your graph from part **b** to determine how much $E(y)$ changes when x_1 is changed from 2 to 0 and x_2 is simultaneously changed from 4 to 5.

36 Suppose you fit the interaction model

$$y = \beta_0 + \beta_1x_1 + \beta_2x_2 + \beta_3x_1x_2 + \varepsilon$$

to $n = 32$ data points and obtain the following results:

$$\text{SS}_{yy} = 479 \quad \text{SSE} = 21 \quad \hat{\beta}_3 = 10 \quad s_{\hat{\beta}_3} = 4$$

  a. Find R^2 and interpret its value.
  b. Is the model adequate for predicting y? Test at $\alpha = .05$.

  c. Use a graph to explain the contribution of the x_1x_2 term to the model.
  d. Is there evidence that x_1 and x_2 interact? Test at $\alpha = .05$.

37 The Minitab printout below was obtained from fitting the model

$$y = \beta_0 + \beta_1x_1 + \beta_2x_2 + \beta_3x_1x_2 + \varepsilon$$

to $n = 15$ data points.
  a. What is the prediction equation for the response surface?
  b. Describe the geometric form of the response surface of part **a**.

```
The regression equation is
Y = -2.55 + 3.82 X1 + 2.63 X2 -1.29 X1X2


Predictor     Coef   SE Coef      T       P
Constant    -2.550     1.142   -2.23   0.043
X1           3.815     0.529    7.22   0.000
X2           2.630     0.344    7.64   0.000
X1X2        -1.285     0.159   -8.06   0.000


S = 0.713     R-Sq = 85.6%     R-Sq(adj) = 81.6%


Analysis of Variance

Source          DF        SS       MS       F       P
Regression       3    33.149   11.050   21.75   0.000
Residual Error  11     5.587    0.508
Total           14    38.736
```

*The order of a term is equal to the sum of the exponents of the quantitative variables included in the term. Thus, when x_1 and x_2 are both quantitative variables, the cross product, x_1x_2, is a second-order term.

c. Plot the prediction equation for the case when $x_2 = 1$. Do this twice more on the same graph for the cases when $x_2 = 3$ and $x_2 = 5$.

d. Explain what it means to say that x_1 and x_2 interact. Explain why your graph of part **c** suggests that x_1 and x_2 interact.

e. Specify the null and alternative hypotheses you would use to test whether x_1 and x_2 interact.

f. Conduct the hypothesis test of part **e** using $\alpha = .01$.

Applying the Concepts—Basic

38 Tipping behavior in restaurants. By law, food servers at restaurants are not entitled to minimum wages since they are tipped by customers. Can food servers increase their tips by complimenting the customers they are waiting on? To answer this question, researchers collected data on the customer tipping behavior for a sample of 348 dining parties and reported their findings in the *Journal of Applied Social Psychology* (Vol. 40, 2010). Tip size (y, measured as a percentage of the total food bill) was modeled as a function of size of the dining party (x_1) and whether or not the server complimented the customers' choice of menu items (x_2). One theory states that the effect of size of the dining party on tip size is independent of whether or not the server compliments the customers' menu choices. A second theory hypothesizes that the effect of size of the dining party on tip size is greater when the server compliments the customers' menu choices as opposed to when the server refrains from complimenting menu choices.

a. Write a model for $E(y)$ as a function of x_1 and x_2 that corresponds to Theory 1.

b. Write a model for $E(y)$ as a function of x_1 and x_2 that corresponds to Theory 2.

c. The researchers summarized the results of their analysis with the following graph. Based on the graph, which of the two models would you expect to fit the data better? Explain.

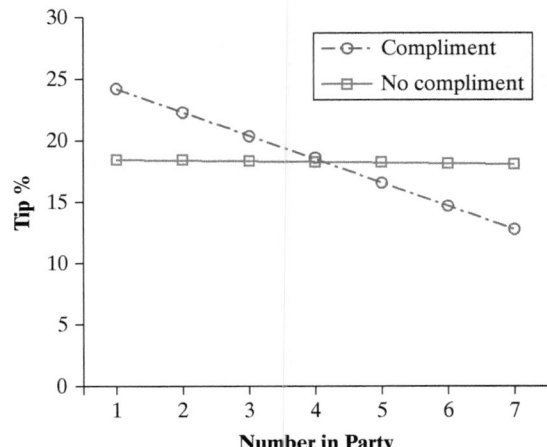

Number in Party

39 Forecasting movie revenues with Twitter. Refer to the *IEEE International Conference on Web Intelligence and Intelligent Agent Technology* (2010) study on using the volume of chatter on Twitter.com to forecast movie box office revenue, Exercise 10. The researchers modeled a movie's opening weekend box office revenue (y) as a function of tweet rate (x_1) and ratio of positive to negative tweets (x_2) using a first-order model.

a. Write the equation of an interaction model for $E(y)$ as a function of x_1 and x_2.

b. In terms of the β's in the model, part **a**, what is the change in revenue (y) for every 1-tweet increase in the tweet rate (x_1), holding PN-ratio (x_2) constant at a value of 2.5?

c. In terms of the β's in the model, part **a,** what is the change in revenue (y) for every 1-tweet increase in the tweet rate (x_1), holding PN-ratio (x_2) constant at a value of 5.0?

d. In terms of the β's in the model, part **a**, what is the change in revenue (y) for every 1-unit increase in the PN-ratio (x_2), holding tweet rate (x_1) constant at a value of 100?

e. Give the null hypothesis for testing whether tweet rate (x_1) and PN-ratio (x_2) interact to affect revenue (y).

40 Role of retailer interest on shopping behavior. Retail interest is defined by marketers as the level of interest a consumer has in a given retail store. Marketing professors at the University of Tennessee at Chattanooga and the University of Alabama investigated the role of retailer interest in consumers' shopping behavior (*Journal of Retailing*, Summer 2006). Using survey data collected for $n = 375$ consumers, the professors developed an interaction model for $y =$ willingness of the consumer to shop at a retailer's store in the future (called *repatronage intentions*) as a function of $x_1 =$ consumer satisfaction and $x_2 =$ retailer interest. The regression results are shown below.

Variable	$\hat{\beta}$	t-value	p-value
Satisfaction (x_1)	.426	7.33	$< .01$
Retailer interest (x_2)	.044	0.85	$> .10$
Interaction (x_1x_2)	−.157	−3.09	$< .01$

$R^2 = .65$, $F = 226.35$, p-value $< .001$

a. Is the overall model statistically useful for predicting y? Test using $\alpha = .05$.

b. Conduct a test for interaction at $\alpha = .05$.

c. Use the β estimates to sketch the estimated relationship between repatronage intentions (y) and satisfaction (x_1) when retailer interest is $x_2 = 1$ (a low value).

d. Repeat part **c** when retailer interest is $x_2 = 7$ (a high value).

e. Sketch the two lines, parts **c** and **d,** on the same graph to illustrate the nature of the interaction.

41 Defects in nuclear missile housing parts. The technique of multivariable testing (MVT) was discussed in the *Journal of the Reliability Analysis Center* (First Quarter, 2004). MVT was shown to improve the quality of carbon-foam rings used in nuclear missile housings. The rings are produced via a casting process that involves mixing ingredients, oven curing, and carving the finished part. One type of defect analyzed was the number y of black streaks in the manufactured ring. Two variables found to impact the number of defects were turntable speed (revolutions per minute), x_1, and cutting-blade position (inches from center), x_2.

a. The researchers discovered "an interaction between blade position and turntable speed." Hypothesize a regression model for $E(y)$ that incorporates this interaction.

b. The researchers reported a positive linear relationship between number of defects (y) and turntable speed (x_1)

but found that the slope of the relationship was much steeper for lower values of cutting-blade position (x_2). What does this imply about the interaction term in the model, part **a**? Explain.

42 Consumer behavior while waiting in line. While waiting in a long line for service (e.g., to use an ATM or at the post office), at some point you may decide to leave the queue. The *Journal of Consumer Research* (Nov. 2003) published a study of consumer behavior while waiting in a queue. A sample of $n = 148$ college students was asked to imagine that they were waiting in line at a post office to mail a package and that the estimated waiting time is 10 minutes or less. After a 10-minute wait, students were asked about their level of negative feelings (annoyed, anxious) on a scale of 1 (strongly disagree) to 9 (strongly agree). Before answering, however, the students were informed about how many people were ahead of them and behind them in the line. The researchers used regression to relate negative feelings score (y) to number ahead in line (x_1) and number behind in line (x_2).

a. The researchers fit an interaction model to the data. Write the hypothesized equation of this model.

b. In the words of the problem, explain what it means to say that "x_1 and x_2 interact to affect y."

c. A t-test for the interaction β in the model resulted in a p-value greater than .25. Interpret this result.

d. From their analysis, the researchers concluded that "the greater the number of people ahead, the higher the negative feeling score" and "the greater the number of people behind, the lower the negative feeling score." Use this information to determine the signs of β_1 and β_2 in the model.

Applying the Concepts—Intermediate

43 Reality TV and cosmetic surgery. Refer to the *Body Image: An International Journal of Research* (March 2010) study
BDYIMG of the impact of reality TV shows on a college student's decision to undergo cosmetic surgery, Exercise 17. Recall

that the data for the study (simulated based on statistics reported in the journal article) are saved in the file. Consider the interaction model, $E(y) = \beta_0 + \beta_1 x_1 + \beta_2 x_4 + \beta_3 x_1 x_4$, where y = desire to have cosmetic surgery (25-point scale), $x_1 = \{1$ if male, 0 if female$\}$, and x_4 = impression of reality TV (7-point scale). The model was fit to the data and the resulting SPSS printout appears at the bottom of the page.

a. Give the least squares prediction equation.

b. Find the predicted level of desire (y) for a male college student with an impression-of-reality-TV-scale score of 5.

c. Conduct a test of overall model adequacy. Use $\alpha = .10$.

d. Give a practical interpretation of R_a^2.

e. Give a practical interpretation of s.

f. Conduct a test (at $\alpha = .10$) to determine if gender (x_1) and impression of reality TV show (x_4) interact in the prediction of level of desire for cosmetic surgery (y).

44 Factors that impact an auditor's judgment. A study was conducted to determine the effects of linguistic delivery style and client credibility on auditors' judgments (*Advances in Accounting and Behavioral Research*, 2004). Two hundred auditors from Big 5 accounting firms were each asked to assume that he or she was an audit team supervisor of a new manufacturing client and was performing an analytical review of the client's financial statement. The researchers gave the auditors different information on the client's credibility and linguistic delivery style of the client's explanation. Each auditor then provided an assessment of the likelihood that the client-provided explanation accounted for the fluctuation in the financial statement. The three variables of interest—credibility (x_1), linguistic delivery style (x_2), and likelihood (y)—were all measured on a numerical scale. Regression analysis was used to fit the interaction model, $y = \beta_0 + \beta_1 x_1 + \beta_2 x_2 + \beta_3 x_1 x_2 + \varepsilon$. The results are summarized in the table on the next page.

Model Summary

Model	R	R Square	Adjusted R Square	Std. Error of the Estimate
1	.670[a]	.449	.439	2.350

a. Predictors: (Constant), GENDER_IMPREAL, IMPREAL, GENDER

ANOVA[a]

Model		Sum of Squares	df	Mean Square	F	Sig.
1	Regression	747.001	3	249.000	45.086	.000[b]
	Residual	916.787	166	5.523		
	Total	1663.788	169			

a. Dependent Variable: DESIRE

b. Predictors: (Constant), GENDER_IMPREAL, IMPREAL, GENDER

Coefficients[a]

Model		Unstandardized Coefficients		Standardized Coefficients	t	Sig.
		B	Std. Error	Beta		
1	(Constant)	11.779	.674		17.486	.000
	GENDER	−1.972	1.179	−.303	−1.672	.096
	IMPREAL	.585	.162	.258	3.617	.000
	GENDER_IMPREAL	−.553	.276	−.378	−2.004	.047

a. Dependent Variable: DESIRE

SPSS output for Exercise 43

Results for Exercise 44

	Beta Estimate	Std Error	*t*-statistic	*p*-value
Constant	15.865	10.980	1.445	0.150
Client credibility (x_1)	0.037	0.339	0.110	0.913
Linguistic delivery style (x_2)	−0.678	0.328	−2.064	0.040
Interaction (x_1x_2)	0.036	0.009	4.008	< 0.005

F-statistic = 55.35 ($p < 0.0005$): $R_a^2 = .450$

a. Interpret the phrase *client credibility and linguistic delivery style interact* in the words of the problem.

b. Give the null and alternative hypotheses for testing the overall adequacy of the model.

c. Conduct the test, part **b**, using the information in the table.

d. Give the null and alternative hypotheses for testing whether client credibility and linguistic delivery style interact.

e. Conduct the test, part **d**, using the information in the table.

f. The researchers estimated the slope of the likelihood–linguistic delivery style line at a low level of client credibility ($x_1 = 22$). Obtain this estimate and interpret it in the words of the problem.

g. The researchers also estimated the slope of the likelihood–linguistic delivery style line at a high level of client credibility ($x_1 = 46$). Obtain this estimate and interpret it in the words of the problem.

45 Arsenic in groundwater. Refer to the *Environmental Science & Technology* (Jan. 2005) study of the reliability of a commercial kit to test for arsenic in groundwater, Exercise 16. Recall that you fit a first-order model for arsenic level (*y*) as a function of latitude (x_1), longitude (x_2), and depth (x_3).

a. Write a model for arsenic level (*y*) that includes first-order terms for latitude, longitude, and depth, as well as terms for interaction between latitude and depth and interaction between longitude and depth.

b. Use statistical software to fit the interaction model, part **a**, to the data. Give the least squares prediction equation.

c. Conduct a test (at $\alpha = .05$) to determine whether latitude and depth interact to affect arsenic level.

d. Conduct a test (at $\alpha = .05$) to determine whether longitude and depth interact to affect arsenic level.

e. Practically interpret the results of the tests, parts **c** and **d**.

46 Cooling method for gas turbines. Refer to the *Journal of Engineering for Gas Turbines and Power* (Jan. 2005) study of a high-pressure inlet fogging method for a gas turbine engine, Exercise 19. Recall that you fit a first-order model for heat rate (*y*) as a function of speed (x_1), inlet temperature (x_2), exhaust temperature (x_3), cycle pressure ratio (x_4), and airflow rate (x_5).

a. Researchers hypothesize that the linear relationship between heat rate (*y*) and temperature (both inlet and exhaust) depends on airflow rate. Write a model for heat rate that incorporates the researchers' theories.

b. Use statistical software to fit the interaction model, part **a**, to the data. Give the least squares prediction equation.

c. Conduct a test (at $\alpha = .05$) to determine whether inlet temperature and airflow rate interact to affect heat rate.

d. Conduct a test (at $\alpha = .05$) to determine whether exhaust temperature and airflow rate interact to affect heat rate.

e. Practically interpret the results of the tests, parts **c** and **d**.

47 Extracting water from oil. Refer to the *Journal of Colloid and Interface Science* study of water/oil mixtures, Exercise 20. Recall that three of the seven variables used to predict voltage (*y*) were volume (x_1), salinity (x_2), and surfactant concentration (x_5). The model the researchers fit is

$$E(y) = \beta_0 + \beta_1 x_1 + \beta_2 x_2 + \beta_3 x_5 + \beta_4 x_1 x_2 + \beta_5 x_1 x_5$$

a. Note that the model includes interaction between disperse phase volume (x_1) and salinity (x_2) as well as interaction between disperse phase volume (x_1) and surfactant concentration (x_5). Discuss how these interaction terms affect the hypothetical relationship between *y* and x_1. Draw a sketch to support your answer.

b. Fit the interaction model to the data. Does this model appear to fit the data better than the first-order model in Exercise 20? Explain.

c. Interpret the β estimates of the interaction model.

48 Therapists' reactions to child-abuse reports. Licensed therapists are mandated by law to report child abuse by their clients. This requires the therapist to breach confidentiality and possibly lose the client's trust. A national survey of licensed psychotherapists was conducted to investigate clients' reactions to legally mandated child-abuse reports (*American Journal of Orthopsychiatry*, Jan. 1997). The sample consisted of 303 therapists who had filed a child-abuse report against one of their clients. The researchers were interested in finding the best predictors of a client's reaction (*y*) to the report, where *y* is measured on a 30-point scale. (The higher the value, the more favorable the client's response to the report.) The independent variables found to have the most predictive power are listed here.

x_1 = Therapist's age (years)

x_2 = Therapist's gender (1 if male, 0 if female)

x_3 = Degree of therapist's role strain (25-point scale)

x_4 = Strength of client-therapist relationship (40-point scale)

x_5 = Type of case (1 if family, 0 if not)

x_1x_2 = Age × gender interaction

a. Hypothesize a first-order model relating *y* to each of the five independent variables.

b. Give the null hypothesis for testing the contribution of x_4, strength of client-therapist relationship, to the model.

c. The test statistic for the test, part **b**, was $t = 4.408$ with an associated *p*-value of .001. Interpret this result.

d. The estimated β coefficient for the x_1x_2 interaction term was positive and highly significant ($p < .001$). According to the researchers, "This interaction suggests that ... as the age of the therapist increased, ... male therapists were less likely to get negative client reactions than were female therapists." Do you agree?

e. For this model, $R^2 = .2946$. Interpret this value.

6   Quadratic and Other Higher-Order Models

All of the models discussed in the previous sections proposed straight-line relationships between $E(y)$ and each of the independent variables in the model. In this section, we consider models that allow for curvature in the two-dimensional relationship between y and an independent variable. Each of these models is a **second-order model** because it will include an x^2 term.

First, we consider a model that includes only one independent variable x. The form of this model, called the **quadratic model,** is

$$y = \beta_0 + \beta_1 x + \beta_2 x^2 + \varepsilon$$

The term involving x^2, called a **quadratic term** (or **second-order term**), enables us to hypothesize curvature in the graph of the response model relating y to x. Graphs of the quadratic model for two different values of β_2 are shown in Figure 12. When the curve opens upward, the sign of β_2 is positive (see Figure 12a); when the curve opens downward, the sign of β_2 is negative (see Figure 12b).

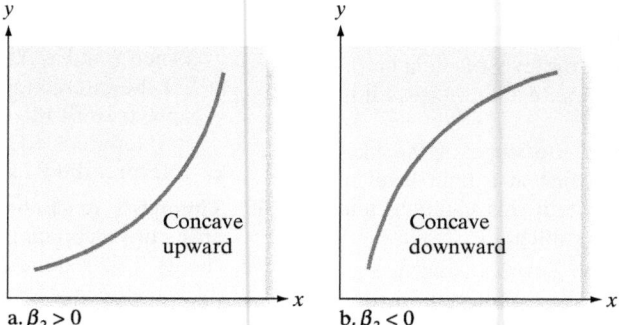

Figure 12

Graphs for two quadratic models

a. $\beta_2 > 0$ b. $\beta_2 < 0$

A Quadratic (Second-Order) Model in a Single Quantitative Independent Variable

$$E(y) = \beta_0 + \beta_1 x + \beta_2 x^2$$

where

β_0 is the y-intercept of the curve.

β_1 is a shift parameter.

β_2 is the rate of curvature.

Example 7

Analyzing a Quadratic Model—Predicting Electrical Usage

Problem In all-electric homes, the amount of electricity expended is of interest to consumers, builders, and groups involved with energy conservation. Suppose we wish to investigate the monthly electrical usage, y, in all-electric homes and its relationship to the size, x, of the home. Moreover, suppose we think that monthly electrical usage in all-electric homes is related to the size of the home by the quadratic model

$$y = \beta_0 + \beta_1 x + \beta_2 x^2 + \varepsilon$$

To fit the model, the values of y and x are collected for 15 homes during a particular month. The data are shown in Table 2.

a. Construct a scatterplot for the data. Is there evidence to support the use of a quadratic model?

b. Use the method of least squares to estimate the unknown parameters β_0, β_1, and β_2 in the quadratic model.

c. Graph the prediction equation and assess how well the model fits the data, both visually and numerically.

d. Interpret the β estimates.

Table 2	Home Size–Electrical Usage Data
Size of Home, x (sq. ft.)	Monthly Usage, y (kilowatt-hours)
1,290	1,182
1,350	1,172
1,470	1,264
1,600	1,493
1,710	1,571
1,840	1,711
1,980	1,804
2,230	1,840
2,400	1,986
2,710	2,007
2,930	1,984
3,000	1,960
3,210	2,001
3,240	1,928
3,520	1,945

Data Set: KWHRS

e. Is the overall model useful (at $\alpha = .01$) for predicting electrical usage y?

f. Is there sufficient evidence of downward curvature in the home size–electrical usage relationship? Test using $\alpha = .01$.

Solution

a. A Minitab scatterplot for the data in Table 2 is shown in Figure 13. The figure illustrates that electrical usage appears to increase in a curvilinear manner with the size of the home. This provides some support for the inclusion of the quadratic term x^2 in the model.

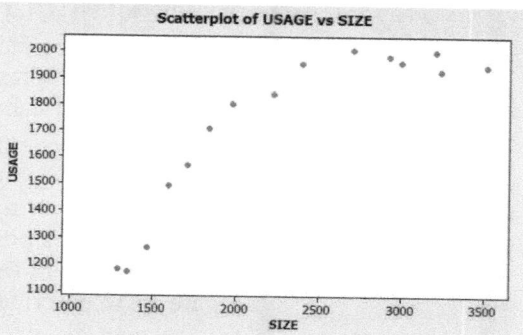

Figure 13

Minitab scatterplot for electrical usage data

b. We used Excel to fit the model to the data in Table 2. Part of the Excel regression output is displayed in Figure 14. The least squares estimates of the β parameters (highlighted) are $\hat{\beta}_0 = -806.7$, $\hat{\beta}_1 = 1.9616$, and $\hat{\beta}_2 = -.00034$. Therefore, the equation that minimizes the SSE for the data is

$$\hat{y} = -806.7 + 1.9616x - .00034x^2$$

SUMMARY OUTPUT

Regression Statistics	
Multiple R	0.988576
R Square	0.977283
Adjusted R Square	0.973496
Standard Error	50.19975
Observations	15

ANOVA

	df	SS	MS	F	Significance F
Regression	2	1300900.218	650450.1	258.1135719	0.0000000001
Residual	12	30240.18169	2520.015		
Total	14	1331140.4			

	Coefficients	Standard Error	t Stat	P-value	Lower 95%	Upper 95%
Intercept	-806.717	166.8720911	-4.83434	0.0004089596	-1170.299712	-443.134
SIZE	1.961617	0.152524384	12.861	0.0000000223	1.629294434	2.293939
SIZESQ	-0.00034	0.00003212	-10.599	0.0000001903	-0.000410426	-0.00027

Figure 14

Excel regression output for electrical usage model

c. Figure 15 is a Minitab graph of the least squares prediction equation. Note that the graph provides a good fit to the data of Table 2. A numerical measure of fit is obtained with the adjusted coefficient of determination, R_a^2. This value (highlighted on Figure 14) is $R_a^2 = .973$. This implies that about 97% of the sample variation in electrical usage (y) can be explained by the quadratic model (after adjusting for sample size and degrees of freedom).

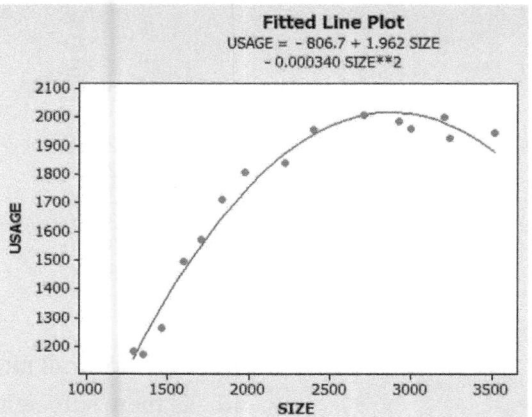

Figure 15

Minitab plot of least squares model for electrical usage

d. The interpretation of the estimated coefficients in a quadratic model must be undertaken cautiously. First, the estimated y-intercept, $\hat{\beta}_0$, can be meaningfully interpreted only if the range of the independent variable includes zero—that is, if $x = 0$ is included in the sampled range of x. Although $\hat{\beta}_0 = -806.7$ seems to imply that the estimated electrical usage is negative when $x = 0$, this zero point is not in the range of the sample (the lowest value of x is 1,290 square feet), and the value is nonsensical (a home with 0 square feet); thus the interpretation of $\hat{\beta}_0$ is not meaningful.

The estimated coefficient of x is $\hat{\beta}_1 = 1.9616$, but in the presence of the quadratic term x^2, it no longer represents a slope.* The estimated coefficient of the first-order term x will not, in general, have a meaningful interpretation in the quadratic model.

The sign of the coefficient, $\hat{\beta}_2 = -.00034$, of the quadratic term, x^2, is the indicator of whether the curve is concave downward (mound-shaped) or concave upward (bowl-shaped). A negative $\hat{\beta}_2$ implies downward concavity, as in this example (Figure 15), and a positive $\hat{\beta}_2$ implies upward concavity. Rather than interpreting the numerical value of $\hat{\beta}_2$ itself, we employ a graphical representation of the model, as in Figure 15, to describe the model.

Note that Figure 15 implies that the estimated electrical usage is leveling off as the home sizes increase beyond 2,500 square feet. In fact, the convexity of the model would lead to decreasing usage estimates if we were to display the model out to 4,000 square feet and beyond (see Figure 16). However, model interpretations are not meaningful outside the range of the independent variable, which has a maximum value of 3,520 square feet in this example. Thus, although the model appears to support the hypothesis that the *rate of increase* per square foot *decreases* for home sizes near the high end of the sampled values, the conclusion that usage will actually begin to decrease for very large homes would be a *misuse* of the model because no homes of 3,600 square feet or more were included in the sample.

e. To test whether the quadratic model is statistically useful, we conduct the global F-test:

$$H_0: \beta_1 = \beta_2 = 0$$

$$H_a: \text{At least one of the above coefficients is nonzero.}$$

---

*For students with knowledge of calculus, note that the slope of the quadratic model is the first derivative $\partial y/\partial x = \beta_1 + 2\beta_2 x$. Thus, the slope varies as a function of x, rather than the constant slope associated with the straight-line model.

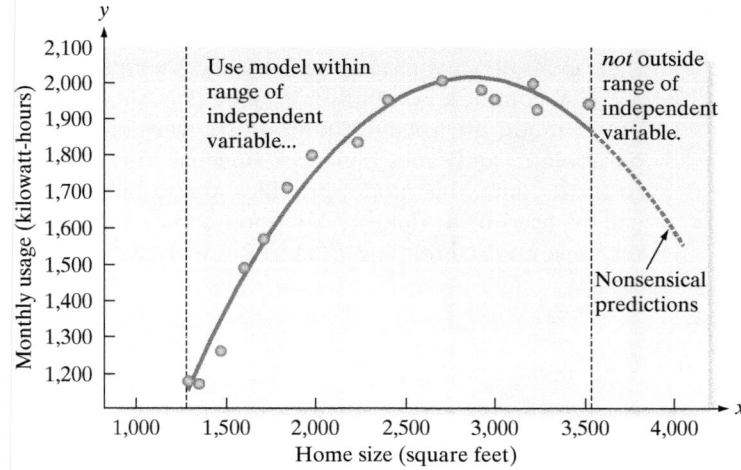

Figure 16

Potential misuse of quadratic model

From the Excel printout, Figure 14, the test statistic (highlighted) is $F = 258.11$ with an associated p-value of approximately 0. For any reasonable α, we reject H_0 and conclude that the overall model is a useful predictor of electrical usage, y.

f. Figure 15 shows concave downward curvature in the relationship between size of a home and electrical usage in the sample of 15 data points. To determine if this type of curvature exists in the population, we want to test

$$H_0: \beta_2 = 0 \text{ (no curvature in the response curve)}$$
$$H_a: \beta_2 < 0 \text{ (downward concavity exists in the response curve)}$$

The test statistic for testing β_2, highlighted on the printout, is $t = -10.599$, and the associated two-tailed p-value is .0000002. Because this is a one-tailed test, the appropriate p-value is $(.0000002)/2 = .0000001$. Now $\alpha = .01$ exceeds this p-value. Thus, there is very strong evidence of downward curvature in the population—that is, electrical usage increases more slowly per square foot for large homes than for small homes.

Look Back Note that the Excel printout in Figure 14 also provides the t-test statistic and corresponding two-tailed p-values for the tests of $H_0: \beta_0 = 0$ and $H_0: \beta_1 = 0$. Because the interpretation of these parameters is not meaningful for this model, the tests are not of interest.

Now Work Exercise 56

When two or more quantitative independent variables are included in a second-order model, we can incorporate squared terms for each x in the model, as well as the interaction between the two independent variables. A model that includes all possible second-order terms in two independent variables—called a **complete second-order model**—is given in the box below.

Complete Second-Order Model with Two Quantitative Independent Variables

$$E(y) = \beta_0 + \beta_1 x_1 + \beta_2 x_2 + \beta_3 x_2 x_2 + \beta_4 x_1^2 + \beta_5 x_2^2$$

Comments on the Parameters

β_0: y-intercept, the value of $E(y)$ when $x_1 = x_2 = 0$

β_1, β_2: Changing β_1 and β_2 causes the surface to shift along the x_1- and x_2-axes

β_3: Controls the rotation of the surface

β_4, β_5: Signs and values of these parameters control the type of surface and the rates of curvature.

Three types of three-dimensional graphs (called **response surfaces**) are produced by a second-order model:* a **paraboloid** that opens upward (Figure 17a), a paraboloid that opens downward (Figure 17b), and a **saddle-shaped surface** (Figure 17c).

A complete second-order model is the three-dimensional equivalent of a quadratic model in a single quantitative variable. Instead of tracing parabolas, it traces paraboloids and saddle surfaces. Because only a portion of the complete surface is used to fit the data, this model provides a very large variety of gently curving surfaces that can be used to fit data. It is a good choice for a model if you expect curvature in the response surface relating $E(y)$ to x_1 and x_2.

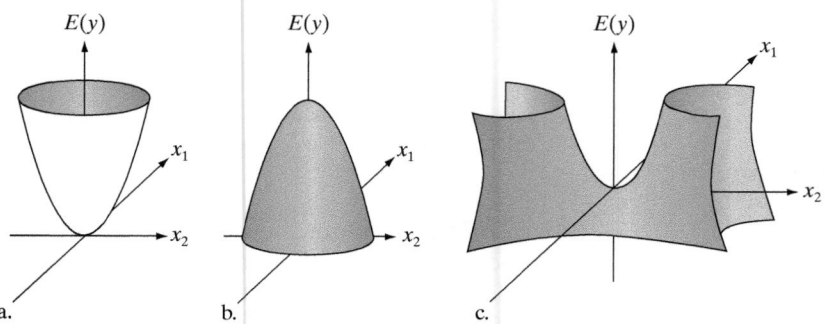

Figure 17

Graphs for three second-order surfaces

Example	8

A More Complex Second-Order Model—Predicting Hours Worked per Week

Problem A social scientist would like to relate the number of hours worked per week (outside the home) by a married woman to the number of years of formal education she has completed and the number of children in her family.

a. Identify the dependent variable and the independent variables.

b. Write the first-order model for this example.

c. Modify the model in part **b** to include an interaction term.

d. Write a complete second-order model for $E(y)$.

Solution

a. The dependent variable is

$$y = \text{Number of hours worked per week by a married woman}$$

The two independent variables, both quantitative in nature, are

$x_1 = $ Number of years of formal education completed by the woman

$x_2 = $ Number of children in the family

b. The first-order model is

$$E(y) = \beta_0 + \beta_1 x_1 + \beta_2 x_2$$

This model would probably not be appropriate in this situation because x_1 and x_2 may interact and/or curvature terms corresponding to x_1^2 and x_2^2 may be needed to obtain a good model for $E(y)$.

c. Adding the interaction term, we obtain

$$E(y) = \beta_0 + \beta_1 x_1 + \beta_2 x_2 + \beta_3 x_1 x_2$$

This model should be better than the model in part **b** because we have now allowed for interaction between x_1 and x_2.

---

*The saddle-shaped surface (Figure 17c) is produced when $\beta_3^2 > 4\beta_4\beta_5$; the paraboloid opens upward (Figure 17a) when $\beta_4 + \beta_5 > 0$ and opens downward (Figure 17b) when $\beta_4 + \beta_5 < 0$.

d. The complete second-order model is

$$E(y) = \beta_0 + \beta_1 x_1 + \beta_2 x_2 + \beta_3 x_1 x_2 + \beta_4 x_1^2 + \beta_5 x_2^2$$

Because it would not be surprising to find curvature in the response surface, the complete second-order model would be preferred to the models in parts **b** and **c.**

Look Back How can we tell whether the complete second-order model really does provide better predictions of hours worked than the models in parts **b** and **c**? The answers to these and similar questions are examined in Section 9.

■ **Now Work Exercise 59**

Most relationships between $E(y)$ and two or more quantitative independent variables are second order and require the use of either the interactive or the complete second-order model to obtain a good fit to a data set. As in the case of a single quantitative independent variable, however, the curvature in the response surface may be very slight over the range of values of the variables in the data set. When this happens, a first-order model may provide a good fit to the data.

Exercises 49–65

Please be aware that some of the following problems may require knowledge of concepts that are not presented in this chapter.

Learning the Mechanics

49 Write a second-order model relating the mean of y, $E(y)$, to
  a. one quantitative independent variable
  b. two quantitative independent variables
  c. three quantitative independent variables [*Hint:* Include all possible two-way cross-product terms and squared terms.]

50 Suppose you fit the second-order model

$$y = \beta_0 + \beta_1 x + \beta_2 x^2 + \varepsilon$$

to $n = 25$ data points. Your estimate of β_2 is $\hat{\beta}_2 = .47$, and the estimated standard error of the estimate is .15.

  a. Test $H_0: \beta_2 = 0$ against $H_a: \beta_2 \neq 0$. Use $\alpha = .05$.
  b. Suppose you want to determine only whether the quadratic curve opens upward; that is, as x increases, the slope of the curve increases. Give the test statistic and the rejection region for the test for $\alpha = .05$. Do the data support the theory that the slope of the curve increases as x increases? Explain.

51 Suppose you fit the quadratic model

$$E(y) = \beta_0 + \beta_1 x + \beta_2 x^2$$

to a set of $n = 20$ data points and found $R^2 = .91$, $SS_{yy} = 29.94$, and $SSE = 2.63$.

  a. Is there sufficient evidence to indicate that the model contributes information for predicting y? Test using $\alpha = .05$.
  b. What null and alternative hypotheses would you test to determine whether upward curvature exists?
  c. What null and alternative hypotheses would you test to determine whether downward curvature exists?

52 Consider the following quadratic models:
  (1) $y = 1 - 2x + x^2$
  (2) $y = 1 + 2x + x^2$
  (3) $y = 1 + x^2$
  (4) $y = 1 - x^2$
  (5) $y = 1 + 3x^2$

  a. Graph each of the quadratic models, side by side, on the same sheet of graph paper.
  b. What effect does the first-order term $(2x)$ have on the graph of the curve?
  c. What effect does the second-order term (x^2) have on the graph of the curve?

53 Minitab was used to fit the complete second-order model

$$E(y) = \beta_0 + \beta_1 x_1 + \beta_2 x_2 + \beta_3 x_1 x_2 + \beta_4 x_1^2 + \beta_5 x_2^2$$

to $n = 39$ data points. The printout is shown below.

```
The regression equation is
Y = -24.56 + 1.12 X1 + 27.99 X2 - 0.54 X1X2 - 0.004 X1SQ + 0.002 X2SQ


Predictor        Coef      SE Coef       T       P
Constant      -24.563        6.531   -3.76   0.001
X1            1.19848        0.1103   10.86   0.000
X2             27.988        79.489    0.35   0.727
X1X2          -0.5397        1.0338   -0.52   0.605
X1SQ          -0.0043        0.0004  -10.74   0.000
X2SQ           0.0020        0.0033    0.60   0.550


S = 2.762     R-Sq = 79.7%     R-Sq(adj) = 76.6%

Analysis of Variance

Source          DF      SS       MS       F       P
Regression       5  989.30   197.86   25.93   0.000
Residual Error  33  251.81     7.63
Total           38 1241.11
```

Minitab output for Exercise 53

a. Is there sufficient evidence to indicate that at least one of the parameters—$\beta_1, \beta_2, \beta_3, \beta_4$, and β_5—is nonzero? Test using $\alpha = .05$.

b. Test $H_0: \beta_4 = 0$ against $H_a: \beta_4 \neq 0$. Use $\alpha = .01$.

c. Test $H_0: \beta_5 = 0$ against $H_a: \beta_5 \neq 0$. Use $\alpha = .01$.

d. Use graphs to explain the consequences of the tests in parts **b** and **c**.

Applying the Concepts—Basic

54 **Personality traits and job performance.** When attempting to predict job performance using personality traits, researchers typically assume that the relationship is linear. A study published in the *Journal of Applied Psychology* (Jan. 2011) investigated a curvilinear relationship between job task performance and a specific personality trait—conscientiousness. Using data collected for 602 employees of a large public organization, task performance was measured on a 30-point scale (where higher scores indicate better performance) and conscientiousness was measured on a scale of -3 to $+3$ (where higher scores indicate a higher level of conscientiousness).

a. The coefficient of correlation relating task performance score to conscientiousness score was reported as $r = .18$. Explain why the researchers should not use this statistic to investigate the curvilinear relationship between task performance and conscientiousness.

b. Give the equation of a curvilinear (quadratic) model relating task performance score (y) to conscientiousness score (x).

c. The researchers theorized that task performance increases as level of conscientiousness increases, but at a decreasing rate. Draw a sketch of this relationship.

d. If the theory in part **c** is supported, what is the expected sign of β_2 in the model, part **b**?

e. The researchers reported $\hat{\beta}_2 = -.32$ with an associated p-value of less than .05. Use this information to test the researchers' theory at $\alpha = .05$.

55 **Going for it on fourth-down in the NFL.** *Chance* (Winter 2009) did a study of fourth-down decisions by coaches in the National Football League (NFL). Statisticians at California State University, Northridge, fit a straight-line model for predicting the number of points scored (y) by a team that has a first-down with a given number of yards (x) from the opposing goal line. A second model fit to data collected on five NFL teams from a recent season was the quadratic regression model, $E(y) = \beta_0 + \beta_1 x + \beta_2 x^2$. The regression yielded the following results: $\hat{y} = 6.13 + .141x - .0009x^2$, $R^2 = .226$.

a. If possible, give a practical interpretation of each of the β estimates in the model.

b. Give a practical interpretation of the coefficient of determination, R^2.

c. The coefficient of correlation for the straight-line model was reported as $R^2 = .18$. Does this statistic alone indicate that the quadratic model is a better fit than the straight-line model? Explain.

d. What test of hypothesis would you conduct to determine if the quadratic model is a better fit than the straight-line model?

56 **Catalytic converters in cars.** A quadratic model was applied to motor vehicle toxic emissions data collected in Mexico City (*Environmental Science & Engineering*, Sept. 1, 2000). The following equation was used to predict the percentage (y) of motor vehicles without catalytic converters in the Mexico City fleet for a given year (x):

$$\hat{y} = 325{,}790 - 321.67x + .0794x^2.$$

a. Explain why the value $\hat{\beta}_0 = 325{,}790$ has no practical interpretation.

b. Explain why the value $\hat{\beta}_1 = -321.67$ should not be interpreted as a slope.

c. Examine the value of $\hat{\beta}_2$ to determine the nature of the curvature (upward or downward) in the sample data.

d. The researchers used the model to estimate "that just after the year 2021 the fleet of cars with catalytic converters will completely disappear." Comment on the danger of using the model to predict y in the year 2021. (*Note:* The model was fit to data collected between 1984 and 1999.)

57 **Testing tires for wear.** Underinflated or overinflated tires can increase tire wear. A new tire was tested for wear at different pressures, with the results shown in the following table.

Pressure, x (pounds per square inch)	Mileage, y (thousands)
30	29
31	32
32	36
33	38
34	37
35	33
36	26

a. Plot the data on a scatterplot.

b. If you were given only the information for $x = 30, 31, 32, 33$, what kind of model would you suggest? For $x = 33, 34, 35, 36$? For all the data?

58 **Assertiveness and leadership.** Management professors at Columbia University examined the relationship between assertiveness and leadership (*Journal of Personality and Social Psychology,* Feb. 2007). The sample represented 388 people enrolled in a full-time MBA program. Based on answers to a questionnaire, the researchers measured two variables for each subject: assertiveness score (x) and leadership ability score (y). A quadratic regression model was fit to the data, with the following results:

Independent Variable	β Estimate	t-value	p-value
x	.57	2.55	.01
x^2	$-.088$	-3.97	$< .01$
Model $R^2 = .12$			

a. Conduct a test of overall model utility. Use $\alpha = .05$.

b. The researchers hypothesized that leadership ability increases at a decreasing rate with assertiveness. Set up the null and alternative hypotheses to test this theory.

c. Use the reported results to conduct the test, part **b**. Give your conclusion (at $\alpha = .05$) in the words of the problem.

59 **Goal congruence in top management teams.** Do chief executive officers (CEOs) and their top managers always agree on the goals of the company? Goal importance congruence between CEOs and vice presidents (VPs) was studied in the *Academy of Management Journal* (Feb. 2008). The researchers used regression to model a VP's attitude toward the goal of improving efficiency (y) as a function of the two quantitative independent variables level of CEO leadership (x_1) and level of congruence between the CEO and the VP (x_2). A complete second-order model in x_1 and x_2 was fit to data collected for $n = 517$ top management team members at U.S. credit unions.

a. Write the complete second-order model for $E(y)$.

b. The coefficient of determination for the model, part **a**, was reported as $R^2 = .14$. Interpret this value.

c. The estimate of the β-value for the $(x_2)^2$ term in the model was found to be negative. Interpret this result, practically.

d. A t-test on the β-value for the interaction term in the model, x_1x_2, resulted in a p-value of .02. Practically interpret this result, using $\alpha = .05$.

Applying the Concepts—Intermediate

60 Shopping on Black Friday. The *International Journal of Retail and Distribution Management* (Vol. 39, 2011) did a study of shopping on Black Friday (the day after Thanksgiving). Researchers conducted interviews with a sample of 38 women shopping on Black Friday to gauge their shopping habits. Two of the variables measured for each shopper were age (x) and number of years shopping on Black Friday (y). Data on these two variables for the 38 shoppers are listed in the accompanying table.

a. Fit the quadratic model, $E(y) = \beta_0 + \beta_1 x + \beta_2 x^2$, to the data using statistical software. Give the prediction equation.

b. Conduct a test of the overall adequacy of the model. Use $\alpha = .01$.

c. Conduct a test to determine if the relationship between age (x) and number of years shopping on Black Friday (y) is best represented by a linear or quadratic function. Use $\alpha = .01$.

Age	Years	Age	Years
32	5	21	5
27	3	52	10
40	12	40	18
62	35	38	5
47	20	56	8
53	30	60	5
24	8	35	15
27	2	50	25
47	24	56	10
40	25	20	2
45	11	20	4
22	11	21	4
25	5	22	5
60	35	50	10
22	3	30	6
50	15	28	16
70	22	25	7
50	10	30	6
21	6	49	30

Source: Thomas, J. B., & Peters, C. "An exploratory investigation of Black Friday consumption rituals," *International Journal of Retail and Distribution Management*, Vol. 39, No. 7, 2011 (Table I). Copyright © 2011 by Emerald Group Publishing Limited. Reprinted with permission.

61 Revenues of popular movies. The *Internet Movie Database* (www.imdb.com) monitors the gross revenues for all major motion pictures. The accompanying table gives both the domestic (United States and Canada) and international gross revenues for a sample of 19 popular movies.

Movie Title (year)	Domestic Gross ($ millions)	International Gross ($ millions)
Avatar (2009)	760.5	2,021.0
Titanic (1997)	600.8	1,234.6
The Dark Knight (2008)	533.3	464.0
E.T. (1982)	439.9	321.8
Pirates of the Caribbean: Dead Man's Chest (2006)	423.0	642.9
Jurassic Park (1993)	356.8	563.0
Lion King (1994)	328.4	455.0
Harry Potter and the Sorcerer's Stone (2001)	317.6	651.1
Inception (2010)	291.4	468.2
The Hangover (2009)	277.3	201.6
Sixth Sense (1999)	293.5	368.0
Jaws (1975)	260.0	210.6
Ghost (1990)	217.6	300.0
Saving Private Ryan (1998)	216.1	263.2
Gladiator (2000)	187.7	268.6
Dances with Wolves (1990)	184.2	240.0
The Exorcist (1973)	204.6	153.0
My Big Fat Greek Wedding (2002)	241.4	115.1
Rocky IV (1985)	127.9	172.6

Source: Based on information from *The Internet Movie Database* (http://www.imdb.com).

a. Write a first-order model for foreign gross revenues (y) as a function of domestic gross revenues (x).

b. Write a second-order model for international gross revenues y as a function of domestic gross revenues x.

c. Construct a scatterplot for these data. Which of the models from parts **a** and **b** appears to be the better choice for explaining the variation in foreign gross revenues?

d. Fit the model of part **b** to the data and investigate its usefulness. Is there evidence of a curvilinear relationship between international and domestic gross revenues? Try using $\alpha = .05$.

e. Based on your analysis in part **d**, which of the models from parts **a** and **b** better explains the variation in international gross revenues? Compare your answer to your preliminary conclusion from part **c**.

62 Estimating change-point dosage. A standard method for studying toxic substances and their effects on humans is to observe the responses of rodents exposed to various doses of the substance over time. In the *Journal of Agricultural, Biological, and Environmental Statistics* (June 2005), researchers used least squares regression to estimate the *change-point* dosage—defined as the largest dose level that has no adverse effects. Data were obtained from a dose-response study of rats exposed to the toxic substance aconiazide. A sample of 50 rats was evenly divided into five dosage groups: 0, 100, 200, 500, and 750 milligrams per kilogram of body weight. The dependent variable y measured was the weight change (in grams) after a

2-week exposure. The researchers fit the quadratic model $E(y) = \beta_0 + \beta_1 x + \beta_2 x^2$, where x = dosage level, with the following results: $\hat{y} = 10.25 + .0053x - .0000266x^2$.

a. Construct a rough sketch of the least squares prediction equation. Describe the nature of the curvature in the estimated model.

b. Estimate the weight change (y) for a rat given a dosage of 500 mg/kg of aconiazide.

c. Estimate the weight change (y) for a rat given a dosage of 0 mg/kg of aconiazide. (This dosage is called the *control* dosage level.)

d. Of the five dosage groups in the study, find the largest dosage level x that yields an estimated weight change that is closest to but below the estimated weight change for the control group. This value is the *change-point* dosage.

63 **Failure times of silicon wafer microchips.** Researchers at National Semiconductor experimented with tin-lead solder **WAFER** bumps used to manufacture silicon wafer integrated circuit chips (International Wafer Level Packaging Conference, Nov. 3–4, 2005). The failure times of the microchips (in hours) was determined at different solder temperatures (degrees Celsius). The data for one experiment are given in the table. The researchers want to predict failure time (y) based on solder temperature (x).

a. Construct a scatterplot for the data. What type of relationship, linear or curvilinear, appears to exist between failure time and solder temperature?

b. Fit the model, $E(y) = \beta_0 + \beta_1 x + \beta_2 x^2$, to the data. Give the least squares prediction equation.

c. Conduct a test to determine if there is upward curvature in the relationship between failure time and solder temperature. (Use $\alpha = .05$.)

Temperature (°C)	Time to Failure (hours)
165	200
162	200
164	1,200
158	500
158	600
159	750
156	1,200
157	1,500
152	500
147	500
149	1,100
149	1,150
142	3,500
142	3,600
143	3,650
133	4,200
132	4,800
132	5,000
134	5,200
134	5,400
125	8,300
123	9,700

Source: Gee, S., & Nguyen, L. "Mean time to failure in wafer level-CSP packages with SnPb and SnAgCu solder bmps," International Wafer Level Packaging Conference, San Jose, CA, Nov. 3–4, 2005 (adapted from Figure 7). Reprinted with permission.

64 **Public perceptions of health risks.** In the *Journal of Experimental Psychology: Learning, Memory, and Cognition* **INFECT** (July 2005), University of Basel (Switzerland) psychologists

tested the ability of people to judge risk of an infectious disease. The researchers asked German college students to estimate the number of people who are infected with a certain disease in a typical year. The median estimates as well as the actual incidence rate for each in a sample of 24 infections are provided in the table. Consider the quadratic model $E(y) = \beta_0 + \beta_1 x + \beta_2 x^2$, where y = actual incidence rate and x = estimated rate.

Infection	Incidence Rate	Estimate
Polio	0.25	300
Diphtheria	1	1,000
Trachoma	1.75	691
Rabbit fever	2	200
Cholera	3	17.5
Leprosy	5	0.8
Tetanus	9	1,000
Hemorrhagic fever	10	150
Trichinosis	22	326.5
Undulant fever	23	146.5
Well's disease	39	370
Gas gangrene	98	400
Parrot fever	119	225
Typhoid	152	200
Q fever	179	200
Malaria	936	400
Syphilis	1,514	1,500
Dysentery	1,627	1,000
Gonorrhea	2,926	6,000
Meningitis	4,019	5,000
Tuberculosis	12,619	1,500
Hepatitis	14,889	10,000
Gastroenteritis	203,864	37,000
Botulism	15	37,500

Source: Hertwig, R., Pachur, T., & Kurzenhauser, S. "Judgments of risk frequencies: Tests of possible cognitive mechanisms," *Journal of Experimental Psychology: Learning, Memory, and Cognition*, Vol. 31, No. 4, July 2005 (Table 1).

a. Fit the quadratic model to the data and then conduct a test to determine if incidence rate is curvilinearly related to estimated rate. (Use $\alpha = .05$.)

b. Construct a scatterplot for the data. Locate the data point for botulism on the graph. What do you observe?

c. Repeat part **a** but omit the data point for botulism from the analysis. Has the fit of the model improved? Explain.

65 **Orange juice demand study.** A chilled orange juice warehousing operation in New York City was experiencing too **NYOJ** many out-of-stock situations with its 96-ounce containers. To better understand current and future demand for this product, the company examined the last 40 days of sales, which are shown in the table on the next page. One of the company's objectives is to model demand, y, as a function of sale day, x (where $x = 1, 2, 3, \ldots, 40$).

a. Construct a scatterplot for these data.

b. Does it appear that a second-order model might better explain the variation in demand than a first-order model? Explain.

c. Fit a first-order model to these data.

d. Fit a second-order model to these data.

e. Compare the results in parts **c** and **d** and decide which model better explains variation in demand. Justify your choice.

Data for Exercise 65

Sale Day, x	Demand for 96 oz. Containers, y (in cases)	Sale Day, x	Demand for 96 oz. Containers, y (in cases)
1	4,581	21	5,902
2	4,239	22	2,295
3	2,754	23	2,682
4	4,501	24	5,787
5	4,016	25	3,339
6	4,680	26	3,798
7	4,950	27	2,007
8	3,303	28	6,282
9	2,367	29	3,267
10	3,055	30	4,779
11	4,248	31	9,000
12	5,067	32	9,531
13	5,201	33	3,915
14	5,133	34	8,964
15	4,211	35	6,984
16	3,195	36	6,660
17	5,760	37	6,921
18	5,661	38	10,005
19	6,102	39	10,153
20	6,099	40	11,520

Source: Tom Metzler and Rick Campbell.

7   Qualitative (Dummy) Variable Models

Multiple regression models can also be written to include **qualitative** (or **categorical**) independent variables. Qualitative variables, unlike quantitative variables, cannot be measured on a numerical scale. Therefore, we must code the values of the qualitative variables (called **levels**) as numbers before we can fit the model. These coded qualitative variables are called **dummy** (or **indicator**) **variables** because the numbers assigned to the various levels are arbitrarily selected.

To illustrate, suppose a female executive at a certain company claims that male executives earn higher salaries, on average, than female executives with the same education, experience, and responsibilities. To support her claim, she wants to model the salary y of an executive using a qualitative independent variable representing the gender of an executive (male or female).

A convenient method of coding the values of a qualitative variable at two levels involves assigning a value of 1 to one of the levels and a value of 0 to the other. For example, the dummy variable used to describe gender could be coded as follows:

$$x = \begin{cases} 1 & \text{if male} \\ 0 & \text{if female} \end{cases}$$

The choice of which level is assigned to 1 and which is assigned to 0 is arbitrary. The model then takes the following form:

$$E(y) = \beta_0 + \beta_1 x$$

The advantage of using a 0–1 coding scheme is that the β coefficients are easily interpreted. The model above allows us to compare the mean executive salary $E(y)$ for males with the corresponding mean for females.

$$\text{Males } (x = 1): E(y) = \beta_0 + \beta_1(1) = \beta_0 + \beta_1$$
$$\text{Females } (x = 0): E(y) = \beta_0 + \beta_1(0) = \beta_0$$

These two means are illustrated in the bar graph in Figure 18.

First note that β_0 represents the mean salary for females (say, μ_F). When a 0–1 coding convention is used, β_0 will always represent the mean response associated with the level of the qualitative variable assigned the value 0 (called the **base level**).

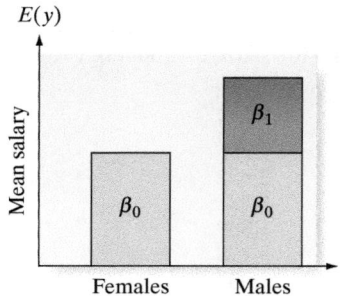

$E(y)$

Mean salary

β_1

β_0 β_0

Females   Males

Figure 18

Bar graph comparing $E(y)$ for males and females

The difference between the mean salary for males and the mean salary for females, $\mu_M - \mu_F$, is represented by β_1—that is,

$$\mu_M - \mu_F = (\beta_0 + \beta_1) - (\beta_0) = \beta_1$$

This difference is shown in Figure 18.* With a 0–1 coding convention, β_1 will always represent the difference between the mean response for the level assigned the value 1 and the mean for the base level. Thus, for the executive salary model, we have

$$\beta_0 = \mu_F$$
$$\beta_1 = \mu_M - \mu_F$$

The model relating a mean response $E(y)$ to a qualitative independent variable at two levels is summarized in the following box.

A Model Relating $E(y)$ to a Qualitative Independent Variable with Two Levels

$$E(y) = \beta_0 + \beta_1 x$$

where

$$x = \begin{cases} 1 & \text{if level A} \\ 0 & \text{if level B} \end{cases}$$

Interpretation of β's:

$$\beta_0 = \mu_B \text{ (mean for base level)}$$
$$\beta_1 = \mu_A - \mu_B$$

Note: μ_i represents the mean of y, $E(y)$, for level i of the dummy variable.

Now carefully examine the model with a single qualitative independent variable at two levels; we will use exactly the same pattern for any number of levels. Moreover, the interpretation of the parameters will always be the same. One level (say, level A) is selected as the base level. Then for the 0–1 coding† for the dummy variables,

$$\mu_A = \beta_0$$

The coding for all dummy variables is as follows: To represent the mean value of y for a particular level, let that dummy variable equal 1; otherwise, the dummy variable is set equal to 0. Using this system of coding,

$$\mu_B = \beta_0 + \beta_1$$
$$\mu_C = \beta_0 + \beta_2$$

and so on. Because $\mu_A = \beta_0$, any other model parameter will represent the difference between means for that level and the base level:

$$\beta_1 = \mu_B - \mu_A$$
$$\beta_2 = \mu_C - \mu_A$$

and so on. Consequently, each β multiplied by a dummy variable represents the difference between $E(y)$ at one level of the qualitative variable and $E(y)$ at the base level.

A Model Relating $E(y)$ to One Qualitative Independent Variable with k Levels

Always use a number of dummy variables that is one less than the number of levels of the qualitative variable. Thus, for a qualitative variable with k levels, use $k - 1$ dummy variables:

$$E(y) = \beta_0 + \beta_1 x_1 + \beta_2 x_2 + \cdots + \beta_{k-1} x_{k-1}$$

---

*Note that β_1 could be negative. If β_1 were negative, the height of the bar corresponding to males would be *reduced* (rather than increased) from the height of the bar for females by the amount β_1. Figure 18 is constructed assuming that β_1 is a positive quantity.

†You do not have to use a 0–1 system of coding for the dummy variables. Any two-value system will work, but the interpretation given to the model parameters will depend on the code. Using the 0–1 system makes the model parameters easy to interpret.

where x_i is the dummy variable for level $i + 1$ and

$$x_i = \begin{cases} 1 & \text{if } y \text{ is observed at level } i + 1 \\ 0 & \text{otherwise} \end{cases}$$

Then, for this system of coding

$$\begin{aligned} \mu_A &= \beta_0 & &\text{and} & \beta_1 &= \mu_B - \mu_A \\ \mu_B &= \beta_0 + \beta_1 & & & \beta_2 &= \mu_C - \mu_A \\ \mu_C &= \beta_0 + \beta_2 & & & \beta_3 &= \mu_D - \mu_A \\ \mu_D &= \beta_0 + \beta_3 & & & &\vdots \end{aligned}$$

Note: μ_i represents the mean of y, $E(y)$, for level i of the qualitative variable.

Example 9

A Model with One Qualitative Independent Variable—Credit Card Debt

Problem Suppose an economist wants to compare the mean dollar amounts owed by delinquent credit card customers in three different socioeconomic classes: (1) lower class, (2) middle class, and (3) upper class. A sample of 10 customers with delinquent accounts is selected from each group, and the amount owed by each is recorded, as shown in Table 3.

Table 3	Dollars Owed, Example 9	
Group 1 (lower class)	Group 2 (middle class)	Group 3 (upper class)
$148	$513	$335
76	264	643
393	433	216
520	94	536
236	535	128
134	327	723
55	214	258
166	135	380
415	280	594
153	304	465

Data Set: CCDEBT

a. Hypothesize a regression model for amount owed (y) using socioeconomic class as an independent variable.

b. Interpret the β's in the model.

c. Fit the model to the data and give the least squares prediction equation.

d. Use the model to determine if the mean dollar amounts owed by customers differ significantly for the three socioeconomic groups at $\alpha = .05$.

Solution

a. Note that socioeconomic status (low, middle, upper class) is a qualitative variable (measured on an ordinal scale). For a three-level qualitative variable, we need two dummy variables in the regression model. The model relating $E(y)$ to this single qualitative variable, socioeconomic group, is

$$E(y) = \beta_0 + \beta_1 x_1 + \beta_2 x_2$$

where (arbitrarily choosing group 1 as the base level)

$$x_1 = \begin{cases} 1 & \text{if group 2} \\ 0 & \text{if not} \end{cases} \qquad x_2 = \begin{cases} 1 & \text{if group 3} \\ 0 & \text{if not} \end{cases}$$

b. For this model

$$\begin{aligned} \beta_0 &= \mu_1 \\ \beta_1 &= \mu_2 - \mu_1 \\ \beta_2 &= \mu_3 - \mu_1 \end{aligned}$$

where μ_1, μ_2, and μ_3 are the mean responses for socioeconomic groups 1, 2, and 3, respectively—that is, β_0 represents the mean amount owed for group 1 (lower class), β_1 represents the mean difference in amounts owed for group 2 (middle) and group 1 (lower), and β_2 represents the mean difference in amounts owed for group 3 (upper) and group 1 (lower).

c. The Minitab printout of the regression analysis is shown in Figure 19. The least squares estimates of the β's are highlighted on the printout, yielding the following least squares prediction equation:

$$\hat{y} = 229.6 + 80.3x_1 + 198.2x_2$$

Regression Analysis: Amount versus X1, X2

```
The regression equation is
Amount = 230 + 80.3 X1 + 198 X2

Predictor    Coef   SE Coef    T      P
Constant   229.60    53.43   4.30  0.000
X1          80.30    75.56   1.06  0.297
X2         198.20    75.56   2.62  0.014

S = 168.948   R-Sq = 20.5%   R-Sq(adj) = 14.6%

Analysis of Variance

Source          DF      SS      MS     F      P
Regression       2  198772   99386  3.48  0.045
Residual Error  27  770671   28543
Total           29  969443
```

Descriptive Statistics: Amount

```
Variable  Class   N   Mean   StDev  Minimum  Maximum
Amount    L      10  229.6   158.2     55.0    520.0
          M      10  309.9   147.9     94.0    535.0
          U      10  427.8   196.8    128.0    723.0
```

Figure 19

Minitab output for model with dummy variables

The interpretations of the β's in part **b** allow us to obtain the β estimates from the sample means associated with the different levels of the qualitative variable.*

Because $\beta_0 = \mu_1$, then the estimate of β_0 is the estimated mean delinquent amount for the lower-class group. This sample mean, highlighted at the bottom of the Minitab printout, is 229.6; thus $\hat{\beta}_0 = 229.6$.

Now $\beta_1 = \mu_2 - \mu_1$; therefore, the estimate of β_1 is the difference between the sample mean delinquent amounts for the middle- and lower-class groups. Based on the sample means highlighted at the bottom of the Minitab printout, we have $\hat{\beta}_1 = 309.9 - 229.6 = 80.3$.

Similarly, the estimate of $\beta_2 = \mu_3 - \mu_1$ is the difference between the sample mean delinquent amounts for the upper- and lower-class groups. From the sample means highlighted at the bottom of the Minitab printout, we have $\hat{\beta}_2 = 427.8 - 229.6 = 198.2$.

d. Testing the null hypothesis that the means for the three groups are equal—that is, $\mu_1 = \mu_2 = \mu_3$—is equivalent to testing

$$H_0: \beta_1 = \beta_2 = 0$$

You can see this by observing that if $\beta_1 = \mu_2 - \mu_1 = 0$, then $\mu_1 = \mu_2$. Similarly, if $\beta_2 = \mu_3 - \mu_1 = 0$, then $\mu_3 = \mu_1$. Thus, if H_0 is true, then μ_1, μ_2, and μ_3 must be equal. The alternative hypothesis is

H_a: At least one of the parameters, β_1 and β_2, differs from 0, which implies that at least two of the three means (μ_1, μ_2, and μ_3) differ.

*The least squares method and the sample means method will yield equivalent β estimates when the sample sizes associated with the different levels of the qualitative variable are equal.

To test this hypothesis, we conduct the global F-test for the model. The value of the F-statistic for testing the adequacy of the model, $F = 3.48$, and the observed significance level of the test, p-value $= .045$, are both highlighted on Figure 19. Because $\alpha = .05$ exceeds the p-value, we reject H_0 and conclude that at least one of the parameters, β_1 and β_2, differs from 0. Or, equivalently, we conclude that the data provide sufficient evidence to indicate that the mean indebtedness does vary from one socioeconomic group to another.

Look Back This global F-test is equivalent to the analysis of variance F-test for a completely randomized design.

■ **Now Work Exercise 78**

⚠ **CAUTION** A common mistake of regression analysts is to use a single dummy variable x for a qualitative variable at k levels, where $x = 1, 2, 3, \ldots, k$. Such a regression model will have unestimable β's and β's that are difficult to interpret. Remember, when modeling $E(y)$ with a single qualitative independent variable, the number of 0–1 dummy variables to include in the model will always be one less than the number of levels of the qualitative variable.

Exercises 66–81

Please be aware that some of the following problems may require knowledge of concepts that are not presented in this chapter.

Learning the Mechanics

66 Write a regression model relating the mean value of y to a qualitative independent variable that can assume two levels. Interpret all the terms in the model.

67 Write a regression model relating $E(y)$ to a qualitative independent variable that can assume three levels. Interpret all the terms in the model.

68 The Minitab printout below resulted from fitting the following model to $n = 15$ data points:

$$y = \beta_0 + \beta_1 x_1 + \beta_2 x_2 + \varepsilon$$

where

$$x_1 = \begin{cases} 1 & \text{if level 2} \\ 0 & \text{if not} \end{cases} \qquad x_2 = \begin{cases} 1 & \text{if level 3} \\ 0 & \text{if not} \end{cases}$$

a. Report the least squares prediction equation.
b. Interpret the values of β_1 and β_2.
c. Interpret the following hypotheses in terms of μ_1, μ_2, and μ_3:

```
The regression equation is
Y = 80.0 + 16.8 X1 + 40.4 X2

Predictor    Coef   SE Coef      T       P
Constant   80.000    4.082   19.60   0.000
X1         16.800    5.774    2.91   0.013
X2         40.400    5.774    7.00   0.000

S = 9.129      R-Sq = 80.5%    R-Sq(adj) = 77.2%

Analysis of Variance

Source        DF      SS      MS      F       P
Regression     2   4118.9  2059.5  24.72   0.000
Residual Error 12  1000.0    83.3
Total          14  5118.9
```

$H_0: \beta_1 = \beta_2 = 0$
H_a: At least one of the parameters β_1 and β_2 differs from 0
d. Conduct the hypothesis test of part **c.**

69 The following model was used to relate $E(y)$ to a single qualitative variable with four levels:

$$E(y) = \beta_0 + \beta_1 x_1 + \beta_2 x_2 + \beta_3 x_3$$

where

$$x_1 = \begin{cases} 1 & \text{if level 2} \\ 0 & \text{if not} \end{cases} \quad x_2 = \begin{cases} 1 & \text{if level 3} \\ 0 & \text{if not} \end{cases} \quad x_3 = \begin{cases} 1 & \text{if level 4} \\ 0 & \text{if not} \end{cases}$$

This model was fit to $n = 30$ data points, and the following result was obtained:

$$\hat{y} = 10.2 - 4x_1 + 12x_2 + 2x_3$$

a. Use the least squares prediction equation to find the estimate of $E(y)$ for each level of the qualitative independent variable.
b. Specify the null and alternative hypotheses you would use to test whether $E(y)$ is the same for all four levels of the independent variable.

Applying the Concepts—Basic

70 **Can money spent on gifts buy love?** The *Journal of Experimental Social Psychology* (Vol. 45, 2009) did a study of whether buying gifts truly buys love. Study participants were randomly assigned to play the role of gift-giver or gift-receiver. Gift-receivers were asked to provide the level of appreciation (measured on a 7-point scale where 1 = "not at all" and 7 = "to a great extent") they had for the last birthday gift they received from a loved one. Gift-givers were asked to recall the last birthday gift they gave to a loved one and to provide the level of appreciation the loved one had for the gift.

a. Write a dummy variable regression model that will allow the researchers to compare the average level of appreciation for birthday gift-givers (μ_G) to the average for birthday gift-receivers (μ_R).

b. Express each of the model's β parameters in terms of μ_G and μ_R.

c. The researchers hypothesize that the average level of appreciation is higher for birthday gift-givers than for birthday gift-receivers. Explain how to test this hypothesis using the regression model.

71 Production technologies, terroir, and quality of Bordeaux wine. In addition to state-of-the-art technologies, the production of quality wine is strongly influenced by the natural endowments of the grape-growing region—called the "terroir." *The Economic Journal* (May 2008) published an empirical study of the factors that yield a quality Bordeaux wine. A quantitative measure of wine quality (y) was modeled as a function of several qualitative independent variables, including grape-picking method (manual or automated), soil type (clay, gravel, or sand), and slope orientation (east, south, west, southeast, or southwest).

a. Create the appropriate dummy variables for each of the qualitative independent variables.

b. Write a model for wine quality (y) as a function of grape-picking method. Interpret the β's in the model.

c. Write a model for wine quality (y) as a function of soil type. Interpret the β's in the model.

d. Write a model for wine quality (y) as a function of slope orientation. Interpret the β's in the model.

72 Impact of race on football card values. University of Colorado sociologists investigated the impact of race on the value of professional football players' "rookie" cards (*Electronic Journal of Sociology*, 2007). The sample consisted of 148 rookie cards of National Football League (NFL) players who were inducted into the Football Hall of Fame. The price of the card (in dollars) was modeled as a function of several qualitative independent variables: race of player (black or white), card availability (high or low), and player position (quarterback, running back, wide receiver, tight end, defensive lineman, linebacker, defensive back, or offensive lineman).

a. Create the appropriate dummy variables for each of the qualitative independent variables.

b. Write a model for price (y) as a function of race. Interpret the β's in the model.

c. Write a model for price (y) as a function of card availability. Interpret the β's in the model.

d. Write a model for price (y) as a function of position. Interpret the β's in the model.

73 Accuracy of software effort estimates. Periodically, software engineers must provide estimates of their effort in developing new software. In the *Journal of Empirical Software Engineering* (Vol. 9, 2004), multiple regression was used to predict the accuracy of these effort estimates. The dependent variable, defined as the relative error in estimating effort,

$$y = (\text{actual effort} - \text{estimated effort})/(\text{actual effort})$$

was determined for each in a sample of $n = 49$ software development tasks. Several qualitative independent variables were evaluated as potential predictors of relative error. Some of these variables are described in the table.

Estimator role (developer or project leader)
Task complexity (low, medium, or high)
Contract type (fixed price or hourly rate)
Customer priority (time of delivery, cost, or quality)

---

a. Write a model for $E(y)$ as a function of estimator role. Interpret the β's.

b. Write a model for $E(y)$ as a function of task complexity. Interpret the β's.

c. Write a model for $E(y)$ as a function of contract type. Interpret the β's.

d. Write a model for $E(y)$ as a function of customer priority. Interpret the β's.

74 Buy-side vs. sell-side analysts' earnings forecasts. The *Financial Analysts Journal* (Jul./Aug. 2008) did a comparison of earnings forecasts of buy-side and sell-side analysts. The Harvard Business School professors used regression to model the relative optimism (y) of the analysts' 3-month horizon forecasts. One of the independent variables used to model forecast optimism was the dummy variable $x = \{1$ if the analyst worked for a buy-side firm, 0 if the analyst worked for a sell-side firm$\}$.

a. Write the equation of the model for $E(y)$ as a function of type of firm.

b. Interpret the value of β_0 in the model, part **a**.

c. The professors write that the value of β_1 in the model, part **a**, "represents the mean difference in relative forecast optimism between buy-side and sell-side analysts." Do you agree?

d. The professors also argue that "if buy-side analysts make less optimistic forecasts than their sell-side counterparts, the [estimated value of β_1] will be negative." Do you agree?

75 Do blondes raise more funds? During fundraising, does the physical appearance of the solicitor impact the level of capital raised? An economist at the University of Nevada-Reno designed an experiment to answer this question and published the results in *Economic Letters* (Vol. 100, 2008). Each in a sample of 955 households was contacted by a female solicitor and asked to contribute to the Center for Natural Hazards Mitigation Research. The level of contribution (in dollars) was recorded as well as the hair color of the solicitor (blond Caucasian, brunette Caucasian, or minority female).

a. Consider a model for the mean level of contribution, $E(y)$, that allows for different means depending on the hair color of the solicitor. Create the appropriate number of dummy variables for hair color. (Use minority female as the base level.)

b. Write the equation of the model, part **a**, incorporating the dummy variables.

c. In terms of the β's in the model, what is the mean level of contribution for households contacted by a blond Caucasian solicitor?

d. In terms of the β's in the model, what is the difference between the mean level of contribution for households contacted by a blond solicitor and those contacted by a minority female?

e. One theory posits that blond solicitors will achieve the highest mean contribution level, but that there will be no difference between the mean contribution levels attained by brunette Caucasian and minority females. If this theory is true, give the expected signs of the β's in the model.

f. The researcher found the β-estimate for the dummy variable for blond Caucasian to be positive and significantly different from 0 (p-value $< .01$). The β-estimate for the dummy variable for brunette Caucasian was also positive, but not significantly different from 0 (p-value $> .10$). Do these results support the theory, part **e**?

Applying the Concepts—Intermediate

76 **Deferred tax allowance study.** A study was conducted to identify accounting choice variables that influence a manager's decision to change the level of the deferred tax asset allowance at the firm (*The Engineering Economist*, Jan./Feb. 2004). Data were collected for a sample of 329 firms that reported deferred tax assets in 2000. The dependent variable of interest (DTVA) is measured as the change in the deferred tax asset valuation allowance divided by the deferred tax asset. The independent variables used as predictors of DTVA are listed as follows:

LEVERAGE: $x_1 = $ ratio of debt book value to shareholder's equity

BONUS: $x_2 = 1$ if firm maintains a management bonus plan, 0 if not

MVALUE: $x_3 = $ market value of common stock

BBATH: $x_4 = 1$ if operating earnings negative and lower than last year, 0 if not

EARN: $x_5 = $ change in operating earnings divided by total assets

A first-order model was fit to the data with the following results (p-values in parentheses):

$$R_a^2 = .280$$

$$\hat{y} = .044 + .006x_1 - .035x_2 - .001x_3 + .296x_4 + .010x_5$$
$$(.070) \quad (.228) \quad (.157) \quad (.678) \quad (.001) \quad (.869)$$

a. Interpret the estimate of the β coefficient for x_4.

b. The "Big Bath" theory proposed by the researchers states that the mean DTVA for firms with negative earnings and earnings lower than last year will exceed the mean DTVA of other firms. Is there evidence to support this theory? Test using $\alpha = .05$.

c. Interpret the value of R_a^2.

77 **Corporate sustainability and firm characteristics.** *Business and Society* (March 2011) did a study on how firm size and firm type impact corporate sustainability behaviors. Certified Public Accountants (CPAs) were surveyed on their firms' likelihood of reporting sustainability policies (measured as a probability between 0 and 1). The CPAs were divided into four groups depending on firm size (large or small) and firm type (public or private): large/public, large/private, small/public, and small/private. One goal of the analysis is to determine whether the mean likelihood of reporting sustainability policies differs depending on firm size and firm type.

a. Consider a single qualitative variable representing the four size/type categories. Create the appropriate dummy variables for representing this qualitative variable as an independent variable in a regression model for predicting likelihood of reporting sustainability policies (y).

b. Give the equation of the model, part **a,** and interpret each of the model parameters.

c. The global F-test for the model resulted in p-value $< .001$. Give a practical interpretation of this result.

d. Now consider treating firm size and firm type as two different qualitative independent variables in a model for likelihood of reporting sustainability policies (y). Create the appropriate dummy variables for representing these qualitative variables in the model.

e. Refer to part **d.** Write a model for $E(y)$ as a function of firm size and firm type, but do not include interaction. (This model is called the *main effects* model.)

f. Refer to the model, part **e.** For each combination of firm size and firm type (e.g., large/public), write $E(y)$ as a function of the model parameters.

g. Use the results, part **f,** to show that for the main effects model, the difference between the mean likelihoods for large and small firms does not depend on firm type.

h. Write a model for $E(y)$ as a function of firm size, firm type, and size $\times$ type interaction.

i. Refer to the model, part **h.** For each combination of firm size and firm type (e.g., large/public), write $E(y)$ as a function of the model parameters.

j. Use the results, part **i,** to show that for the interaction model, the difference between the mean likelihoods for large and small firms does depend on firm type.

78 **Homework assistance for accounting students.** The *Journal of Accounting Education* (Vol. 25, 2007) did a study of assisting accounting students with their homework. 175 accounting students took a pretest on a topic not covered in class and then each was given a homework problem to solve on the same topic. The students were assigned to one of three homework assistance groups. Some students received the completed solution, some were given check figures at various steps of the solution, and some received no help at all. After finishing the homework, the students were all given a posttest on the subject. The dependent variable of interest was the knowledge gain (or test score improvement). These data are saved in the file.

a. Propose a model for the knowledge gain (y) as a function of the qualitative variable, homework assistance group.

b. In terms of the β's in the model, give an expression for the difference between the mean knowledge gains of students in the "completed solution" and "no help" groups.

c. Fit the model to the data and give the least squares prediction equation.

d. Conduct the global F-test for model utility using $\alpha = .05$. Interpret the results, practically.

79 **Comparing mosquito repellents.** Which insect repellents protect best against mosquitoes? *Consumer Reports* (June 2000) tested 14 products that all claim to be an effective mosquito repellent. Each product was classified as either lotion/cream or aerosol/spray. The cost of the product (in dollars) was divided by the amount of the repellent needed to cover exposed areas of the skin (about 1/3 ounce) to obtain a cost-per-use value. Effectiveness was measured as the maximum number of hours of protection (in half-hour increments) provided when human testers exposed their arms to 200 mosquitoes. The data from the report are listed in the table.

Insect Repellent	Type	Cost/ Use	Maximum Protection
Amway Hour Guard 12	Lotion/Cream	$2.08	13.5 hours
Avon Skin-So-Soft	Aerosol/Spray	0.67	0.5
Avon BugGuard Plus	Lotion/Cream	1.00	2.0
Ben's Backyard Formula	Lotion/Cream	0.75	7.0
Bite Blocker	Lotion/Cream	0.46	3.0
BugOut	Aerosol/Spray	0.11	6.0
Cutter Skinsations	Aerosol/Spray	0.22	3.0
Cutter Unscented	Aerosol/Spray	0.19	5.5
Muskoll Ultra6Hours	Aerosol/Spray	0.24	6.5
Natrapel	Aerosol/Spray	0.27	1.0
Off! Deep Woods	Aerosol/Spray	1.77	14.0
Off! Skintastic	Lotion/Cream	0.67	3.0
Sawyer Deet Formula	Lotion/Cream	0.36	7.0
Repel Permanone	Aerosol/Spray	2.75	24.0

Source: Based on "Buzz off and Insect repellants: Which keep bugs at bay?" *Consumer Reports,* June 2000.

a. Suppose you want to use repellent type to model the cost per use (y). Create the appropriate number of dummy variables for repellent type and write the model.

b. Fit the model, part **a,** to the data.

c. Give the null hypothesis for testing whether repellent type is a useful predictor of cost per use (y).

d. Conduct the test, part **c,** and give the appropriate conclusion. Use $\alpha = .10$.

e. Repeat parts **a–d** if the dependent variable is the maximum number of hours of protection (y).

Applying the Concepts—Advanced

80 Manipulating rates of return with stock splits. Some firms have been accused of using stock splits to manipulate their stock prices before being acquired by another firm. An article in *Financial Management* (Winter 2008) investigated the impact of stock splits on long-run stock performance for acquiring firms. A simplified version of the model fit by the researchers follows:

$$E(y) = \beta_0 + \beta_1 x_1 + \beta_2 x_2 + \beta_3 x_1 x_2,$$

where

$y = $ Firm's 3-year buy-and-hold return rate (%)

$x_1 = \{1$ if stock split prior to acquisition, 0 if not$\}$

$x_2 = \{1$ if firm's discretionary accrual is high, 0 if discreionary accrual is low$\}$

a. In terms of the β's in the model, what is the mean buy-and-hold return rate (BAR) for a firm with no stock split and a high discretionary accrual (DA)?

b. In terms of the β's in the model, what is the mean BAR for a firm with no stock split and a low DA?

c. For firms with no stock split, find the difference between the mean BAR for firms with high and low DA. (*Hint:* Use your answers to parts **a** and **b.**)

d. Repeat part **c** for firms with a stock split.

e. Note that the differences, parts **c** and **d,** are not the same. Explain why this illustrates the notion of interaction between x_1 and x_2.

f. A test for $H_0: \beta_3 = 0$ yielded a p-value of .027. Using $\alpha = .05$, interpret this result.

g. The researchers reported that the estimated values of both β_2 and β_3 are negative. Consequently, they conclude that "high-DA acquirers perform worse compared with low-DA acquirers. Moreover, the underperformance is even greater if high-DA acquirers have a stock split before acquistion." Do you agree?

81 Study of recall of TV commercials. The *Journal of Applied Psychology* (June 2002) did a study of recall of television commercials. Participants were assigned to watch one of three types of TV programs, with nine commercials embedded in each show. Group V watched a TV program with a violent content code rating (e.g., *Tour of Duty*); group S viewed a show with a sex content code rating (e.g., *Strip Mall*); and group N watched a neutral TV program with neither a V nor an S rating (e.g., *Candid Camera*). The dependent variable measured for each participant was a score (y) on his/her recall of the brand names in the commercial messages, with scores ranging from 0 (no brands recalled) to 9 (all brands recalled).

a. Write a model for $E(y)$ as a function of viewer group.

b. Fit the model, part **a,** to the data saved in the file. Give the least squares prediction equation.

c. Conduct a test of overall model utility at $\alpha = .01$. Interpret the results.

d. The sample mean recall scores for the three groups were $\bar{y}_V = 2.08$, $\bar{y}_S = 1.71$, and $\bar{y}_N = 3.17$. Show how to find these sample means using only the β estimates obtained in part **b.**

---

8 Models with Both Quantitative and Qualitative Variables

Suppose you want to relate the mean monthly sales $E(y)$ of a company to monthly advertising expenditure x for three different advertising media (say newspaper, radio, and television) and you wish to use first-order (straight-line) models to model the responses for all three media. Graphs of these three relationships might appear as shown in Figure 20.

Because the lines in Figure 20 are hypothetical, a number of practical questions arise. Is one advertising medium as effective as any other? That is, do the three mean sales lines differ for the three advertising media? Do the increases in mean sales per dollar input in advertising differ for the three advertising media? That is, do the slopes of the three lines differ? Note that the two practical questions have been rephrased into questions about the parameters that define the three lines in Figure 20. To answer them, we must write a single regression model that will characterize the three lines of Figure 20 and that, by testing hypotheses about the lines, will answer the questions.

The response described previously, monthly sales, is a function of *two* independent variables, one quantitative (advertising expenditure x_1)

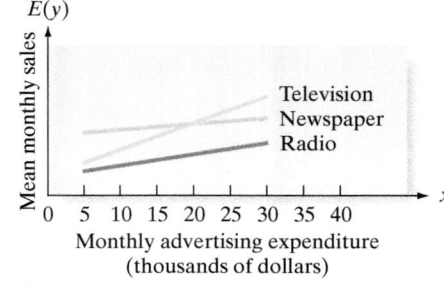

Figure 20

Graphs of the relationship between mean sales $E(y)$ and advertising expenditure x

and one qualitative (type of medium). We will proceed, in stages, to build a model relating $E(y)$ to these variables and will show graphically the interpretation we would give to the model at each stage. This will help you to see the contributions of the various terms in the model.

1. The straight-line relationship between mean sales $E(y)$ and advertising expenditure is the same for all three media—that is, a single line will describe the relationship between $E(y)$ and advertising expenditure x_1 for all the media (see Figure 21).

$$E(y) = \beta_0 + \beta_1 x \qquad \text{where } x_1 = \text{advertising expenditure}$$

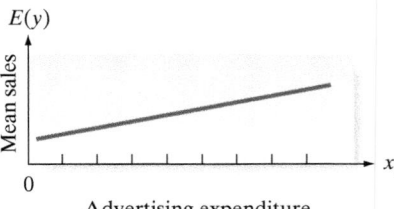

Figure 21

The relationship between $E(y)$ and x_1 is the same for all media

2. The straight lines relating mean sales $E(y)$ to advertising expenditure x_1 differ from one medium to another, but the rate of increase in mean sales per increase in dollar advertising expenditure x_1 is the same for all media—that is, the lines are parallel but possess different y-intercepts (see Figure 22).

$$E(y) = \beta_0 + \beta_1 x_1 + \beta_2 x_2 + \beta_3 x_3$$

where

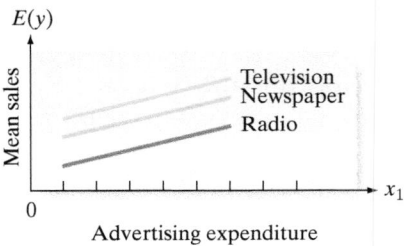

Figure 22

Parallel response lines for the three media

$$x_1 = \text{advertising expenditure}$$

$$x_2 = \begin{cases} 1 & \text{if radio medium} \\ 0 & \text{if not} \end{cases}$$

$$x_3 = \begin{cases} 1 & \text{if television medium} \\ 0 & \text{if not} \end{cases}$$

Notice that this model is essentially a combination of a first-order model with a single quantitative variable and the model with a single qualitative variable:

First-order model with a single
quantitative variable: $\qquad\qquad E(y) = \beta_0 + \beta_1 x_1$

Model with single qualitative
variable at three levels: $\qquad\qquad E(y) = \beta_0 + \beta_2 x_2 + \beta_3 x_3$

where x_1, x_2, and x_3 are as just defined. The model described here implies no interaction between the two independent variables, which are advertising expenditure x_1 and the qualitative variable (type of advertising medium). The change in $E(y)$ for a 1-unit increase in x_1 is identical (the slopes of the lines are equal) for all three advertising media. The terms corresponding to each of the independent variables are called **main effect terms** because they imply no interaction.

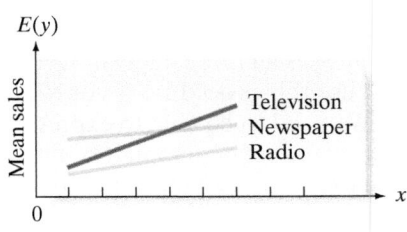

Figure 23

Different response lines for the three media

3. The straight lines relating mean sales $E(y)$ to advertising expenditure x_1 differ for the three advertising media—that is, both the line intercepts and the slopes differ (see Figure 23). As you will see, this interaction model is obtained by

adding terms involving the cross-product terms, one each from each of the two independent variables:

$$E(y) = \overbrace{\beta_0 + \beta_1 x_1}^{\substack{\text{Main effect,} \\ \text{advertising} \\ \text{expenditure}}} + \overbrace{\beta_2 x_2 + \beta_3 x_3}^{\substack{\text{Main effect,} \\ \text{type of} \\ \text{medium}}} + \overbrace{\beta_4 x_1 x_2 + \beta_5 x_1 x_3}^{\text{Interaction}}$$

Note that each of the preceding models is obtained by adding terms to model 1, the single first-order model used to model the responses for all three media. Model 2 is obtained by adding the main effect terms for type of medium, the qualitative variable. Model 3 is obtained by adding the interaction terms to model 2.

Example 10

Interpreting the β's in a Model with Mixed Independent Variables

Problem Substitute the appropriate values of the dummy variables in model 3 (above) to obtain the equations of the three response lines in Figure 23.

Solution The complete model that characterizes the three lines in Figure 23 is

$$E(y) = \beta_0 + \beta_1 x_1 + \beta_2 x_2 + \beta_3 x_3 + \beta_4 x_1 x_2 + \beta_5 x_1 x_3$$

where

$$x_1 = \text{advertising expenditure}$$

$$x_2 = \begin{cases} 1 & \text{if radio medium} \\ 0 & \text{if not} \end{cases}$$

$$x_3 = \begin{cases} 1 & \text{if television medium} \\ 0 & \text{if not} \end{cases}$$

Examining the coding, you can see that $x_2 = x_3 = 0$ when the advertising medium is newspaper. Substituting these values into the expression for $E(y)$, we obtain the newspaper medium line:

$$E(y) = \beta_0 + \beta_1 x_1 + \beta_2(0) + \beta_3(0) + \beta_4 x_1(0) + \beta_5 x_1(0) = \beta_0 + \beta_1 x_1$$

Similarly, we substitute the appropriate values of x_2 and x_3 into the expression for $E(y)$ to obtain the radio medium line ($x_2 = 1, x_3 = 0$):

$$E(y) = \beta_0 + \beta_1 x_1 + \beta_2(1) + \beta_3(0) + \beta_4 x_1(1) + \beta_5 x_1(0)$$

$$= \overbrace{(\beta_0 + \beta_2)}^{\text{y-intercept}} + \overbrace{(\beta_1 + \beta_4)}^{\text{Slope}} x_1$$

and the television medium line: ($x_2 = 0, x_3 = 1$):

$$E(y) = \beta_0 + \beta_1 x_1 + \beta_2(0) + \beta_3(1) + \beta_4 x_1(0) + \beta_5 x_1(1)$$

$$= \overbrace{(\beta_0 + \beta_3)}^{\text{y-intercept}} + \overbrace{(\beta_1 + \beta_5)}^{\text{Slope}} x_1$$

Look Back If you were to fit model 3, obtain estimates of $\beta_0, \beta_1, \beta_2, \ldots, \beta_5$, and substitute them into the equations for the three media lines, you would obtain exactly the same prediction equations as you would obtain if you were to fit three separate straight lines, one to each of the three sets of media data. You may ask why we would not fit the three lines separately. Why bother fitting a model that combines all three lines (model 3) into the same equation? The answer is that you need to use this procedure if you wish to use statistical tests to compare the three media lines. We need to be able to express a practical question about the lines in terms of a hypothesis that a set of parameters in the model equals 0. (We demonstrate this procedure in the next section.) You could not do this if you were to perform three separate regression analyses and fit a line to each set of media data.

Now Work Exercise 82

<table>
<tr><td>Example 11 </td></tr>
</table>

Example **11**

Testing for Two Different Slopes—Worker Productivity

Problem An industrial psychologist conducted an experiment to investigate the relationship between worker productivity and a measure of salary incentive for two manufacturing plants: One plant operates under "disciplined management practices," and the other plant uses a traditional management style. The productivity y per worker was measured by recording the number of machined castings that a worker could produce in a 4-week period of 40 hours per week. The incentive was the amount x_1 of bonus (in cents per casting) paid for all castings produced in excess of 1,000 per worker for the 4-week period. Nine workers were selected from each plant, and three from each group of nine were assigned to receive a 20¢ bonus per casting, three a 30¢ bonus, and three a 40¢ bonus. The productivity data for the 18 workers, three for each plant type and incentive combination, are shown in Table 4.

Table 4	Productivity Data for Example 11								
Management style	Incentive								
	20¢/casting			30¢/casting			40¢/casting		
Traditional	1,435	1,512	1,491	1,583	1,529	1,610	1,601	1,574	1,636
Disciplined	1,575	1,512	1,488	1,635	1,589	1,661	1,645	1,616	1,689

Data Set: CAST

a. Write a model for mean productivity, $E(y)$, assuming that the relationship between $E(y)$ and incentive x_1 is first-order.

b. Fit the model and graph the prediction equations for the disciplined and traditional management styles.

c. Do the data provide sufficient evidence to indicate that the rate of increase of worker productivity is different for disciplined and traditional plants? Test at $\alpha = .10$.

Solution

a. If we assume that a first-order model* is adequate to detect a change in mean productivity as a function of incentive x_1, then the model that produces two straight lines, one for each plant, is

$$E(y) = \beta_0 + \beta_1 x_1 + \beta_2 x_2 + \beta_3 x_1 x_2$$

where

$$x_1 = \text{incentive} \qquad x_2 = \begin{cases} 1 & \text{if disciplined management style} \\ 0 & \text{if traditional management style} \end{cases}$$

b. The SPSS printout for the regression analysis is shown in Figure 24. Reading the parameter estimates highlighted at the bottom of the printout, you can see that

$$\hat{y} = 1{,}365.833 + 6.217x_1 + 47.778x_2 + .033x_1 x_2$$

The prediction equation for the plant using a traditional management style can be obtained (see the coding) by substituting $x_2 = 0$ into the general prediction equation. Then

$$\hat{y} = \hat{\beta}_0 + \hat{\beta}_1 x_1 + \hat{\beta}_2(0) + \hat{\beta}_3 x_1(0) = \hat{\beta}_0 + \hat{\beta}_1 x_1$$
$$= 1{,}365.833 + 6.217x_1$$

*Although the model contains a term involving $x_1 x_2$, it is first-order (graphs as a straight line) in the quantitative variable x_1. The variable x_2 is a dummy variable that introduces or deletes terms in the model. The order of a model is determined only by the quantitative variables that appear in the model.

Model Summary

Model	R	R Square	Adjusted R Square	Std. Error of the Estimate
1	.843[a]	.711	.649	40.839

a. Predictors: (Constant), INC_PDUM, INCENTIV, PDUMMY

ANOVA[b]

Model		Sum of Squares	df	Mean Square	F	Sig.
1	Regression	57332.39	3	19110.796	11.459	.000[a]
	Residual	23349.22	14	1667.802		
	Total	80681.61	17			

a. Predictors: (Constant), INC_PDUM, INCENTIV, PDUMMY

b. Dependent Variable: CASTINGS

Coefficients[a]

Model		Unstandardized Coefficients		Standardized Coefficients	t	Sig.
		B	Std. Error	Beta		
1	(Constant)	1365.833	51.836		26.349	.000
	INCENTIV	6.217	1.667	.758	3.729	.002
	PDUMMY	47.778	73.308	.357	.652	.525
	INC_PDUM	.033	2.358	.008	.014	.989

a. Dependent Variable: CASTINGS

Figure 24

SPSS printout of the complete model for the casting data

Similarly, the prediction equation for the plant with a disciplined management style can be obtained by substituting $x_2 = 1$ into the general prediction equation. Then

$$\hat{y} = \hat{\beta}_0 + \hat{\beta}_1 x_1 + \hat{\beta}_2 x_2 + \hat{\beta}_3 x_1 x_2$$
$$= \hat{\beta}_0 + \hat{\beta}_1 x_1 + \hat{\beta}_2(1) + \hat{\beta}_3 x_1(1)$$
$$= \underbrace{(\beta_0 + \beta_2)}_{y\text{-intercept}} + \underbrace{(\beta_1 + \beta_3)}_{Slope} x_1$$
$$= (1{,}365.833 + 47.778) + (6.217 + .033)x_1$$
$$= 1{,}413.611 + 6.250 x_1$$

A Minitab graph of these prediction equations is shown in Figure 25. Note that the slopes of the two lines are nearly identical (6.217 for traditional and 6.250 for disciplined).

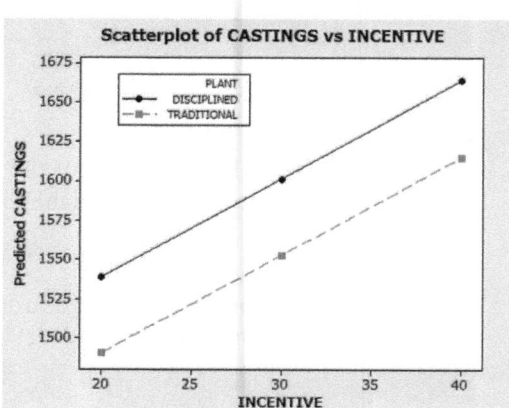

Figure 25

Minitab plot of prediction equations for two plants

c. If the rate of increase of productivity with incentive (i.e., the slope) for plants with the disciplined management style is different from the corresponding slope for traditional plants, then the interaction β (i.e., β_3) will differ from 0. Consequently, we want to test

$$H_0: \beta_3 = 0$$
$$H_a: \beta_3 \neq 0$$

This test is conducted using the t-test of Section 3. From the SPSS printout, the test statistic and corresponding p-value are

$$t = .014 \qquad p = .989$$

Because $\alpha = .10$ is less than the p-value, we fail to reject H_0. There is insufficient evidence to conclude that the traditional and disciplined shapes differ. Thus, the test supports our observation of two nearly identical slopes in part **b**.

Look Back Because interaction is not significant, we will drop the $x_1 x_2$ term from the model and use the simpler model, $E(y) = \beta_0 + \beta_1 x_1 + \beta_2 x_2$, to predict productivity.

■ **Now Work Exercise 88**

Models with both quantitative and qualitative x's may also include higher-order (e.g., second-order) terms. In the problem of relating mean monthly sales $E(y)$ of a company to monthly advertising expenditure x_1 and type of medium, suppose we think that the relationship between $E(y)$ and x_1 is curvilinear. We will construct the model, stage by stage, to enable you to compare the procedure with the stage-by-stage construction of the first-order model in the beginning of this section. The graphical interpretations will help you understand the contributions of the model terms.

1. The mean sales curves are identical for all three advertising media—that is, a single second-order curve will suffice to describe the relationship between $E(y)$ and x_1 for all the media (see Figure 26):

$$E(y) = \beta_0 + \beta_1 x_1 + \beta_2 x_1^2$$

where $x_1 =$ advertising expenditure

2. The response curves possess the same shapes but different y-intercepts (see Figure 27):

$$E(y) = \beta_0 + \beta_1 x_1 + \beta_2 x_1^2 + \beta_3 x_2 + \beta_4 x_3$$

where

$$x_1 = \text{advertising expenditure}$$

$$x_2 = \begin{cases} 1 & \text{if radio medium} \\ 0 & \text{if not} \end{cases}$$

$$x_3 = \begin{cases} 1 & \text{if television medium} \\ 0 & \text{if not} \end{cases}$$

Figure 26

The relationship between $E(y)$ and x_1 is the same for all media

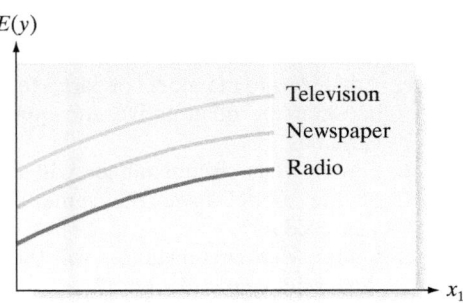

Figure 27

The response curves have the same shapes but different y-intercepts

3. The response curves for the three advertising media are different (i.e., advertising expenditure and type of medium interact), as shown in Figure 28:

$$E(y) = \beta_0 + \beta_1 x_1 + \beta_2 x_1^2 + \beta_3 x_2 + \beta_4 x_3 + \beta_5 x_1 x_2 + \beta_6 x_1 x_3 + \beta_7 x_1^2 x_2 + \beta_8 x_1^2 x_3$$

Now that you know how to write a model with two independent variables—one qualitative and one quantitative—we ask, Why do it? Why not write a separate second-order model for each type of medium where $E(y)$ is a function of only advertising expenditure? As stated earlier, one reason we wrote the single model representing all three response curves is so that we can test to determine whether the curves are different. We illustrate this procedure in Section 9. A second reason for writing a single model is that we obtain a pooled estimate of σ^2, the variance of the random error component ε. If the variance of ε is truly the same for each type of medium, the pooled estimate is superior to three separate estimates calculated by fitting a separate model for each type of medium.

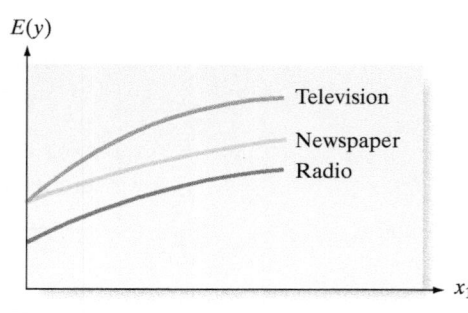

Figure 28
The response curves for the three media differ

Exercises 82–96

Learning the Mechanics

82 Consider a multiple regression model for a response y, with one quantitative independent variable x_1 and one qualitative variable at three levels.

a. Write a first-order model that relates the mean response $E(y)$ to the quantitative independent variable.

b. Add the main effect terms for the qualitative independent variable to the model of part **a.** Specify the coding scheme you use.

c. Add terms to the model of part **b** to allow for interaction between the quantitative and qualitative independent variables.

d. Under what circumstances will the response lines of the model in part **c** be parallel?

e. Under what circumstances will the model in part **c** have only one response line?

83 Refer to Exercise 82.

a. Write a complete second-order model that relates $E(y)$ to the quantitative variable.

b. Add the main effect terms for the qualitative variable (at three levels) to the model of part **a.**

c. Add terms to the model of part **b** to allow for interaction between the quantitative and qualitative independent variables.

d. Under what circumstances will the response curves of the model have the same shape but different y-intercepts?

e. Under what circumstances will the response curves of the model be parallel lines?

f. Under what circumstances will the response curves of the model be identical?

84 Consider the model:

$$y = \beta_0 + \beta_1 x_1 + \beta_2 x_2 + \beta_3 x_3 + \varepsilon$$

where x_1 is a quantitative variable and x_2 and x_3 are dummy variables describing a qualitative variable at three levels using the coding scheme

$$x_2 = \begin{cases} 1 & \text{if level 2} \\ 0 & \text{otherwise} \end{cases} \qquad x_3 = \begin{cases} 1 & \text{if level 3} \\ 0 & \text{otherwise} \end{cases}$$

The resulting least squares prediction equation is

$$\hat{y} = 44.8 + 2.2 x_1 + 9.4 x_2 + 15.6 x_3$$

a. What is the response line (equation) for $E(y)$ when $x_2 = x_3 = 0$? When $x_2 = 1$ and $x_3 = 0$? When $x_2 = 0$ and $x_3 = 1$?

b. What is the least squares prediction equation associated with level 1? Level 2? Level 3? Plot these on the same graph.

85 Consider the model:

$$y = \beta_0 + \beta_1 x_1 + \beta_2 x_1^2 + \beta_3 x_2 + \beta_4 x_3 + \\ \beta_5 x_1 x_2 + \beta_6 x_1 x_3 + \beta_7 x_1^2 x_2 + \beta_8 x_1^2 x_3 + \varepsilon$$

where x_1 is a quantitative variable and

$$x_2 = \begin{cases} 1 & \text{if level 2} \\ 0 & \text{otherwise} \end{cases} \qquad x_3 = \begin{cases} 1 & \text{if level 3} \\ 0 & \text{otherwise} \end{cases}$$

The resulting least squares prediction equation is

$$\hat{y} = 48.8 - 3.4 x_1 + .07 x_1^2 - 2.4 x_2 - 7.5 x_3 + \\ 3.7 x_1 x_2 + 2.7 x_1 x_3 - .02 x_1^2 x_2 - .04 x_1^2 x_3$$

a. What is the equation of the response curve for $E(y)$ when $x_2 = 0$ and $x_3 = 0$? When $x_2 = 1$ and $x_3 = 0$? When $x_2 = 0$ and $x_3 = 1$?

b. On the same graph, plot the least squares prediction equation associated with level 1, with level 2, and with level 3.

86 Write a model that relates $E(y)$ to two independent variables—one quantitative and one qualitative at four levels. Construct a model that allows the associated response curves to be second-order but does not allow for interaction between the two independent variables.

Applying the Concepts—Basic

87 Reality TV and cosmetic surgery. Refer to the *Body Image: An International Journal of Research* (March 2010) study of the impact of reality TV shows on a college student's decision to undergo cosmetic surgery, Exercise 43. The data saved in the file were used to fit the interaction model, $E(y) = \beta_0 + \beta_1 x_1 + \beta_2 x_4 + \beta_3 x_1 x_4$, where y = desire to have cosmetic surgery (25-point scale), $x_1 = \{1$ if male, 0 if female$\}$, and x_4 = impression of reality TV (7-point scale). From the SPSS printout, the estimated equation is:

$$\hat{y} = 11.78 - 1.97x_1 + .58x_4 - .55x_1 x_4$$

a. Give an estimate of the change in desire (y) for every 1-point increase in impression of reality TV show (x_4) for female students.

b. Repeat part **a** for male students.

88 Do blondes raise more funds? Refer to the *Economic Letters* (Vol. 100, 2008) study of whether the color of a female solicitor's hair impacts the level of capital raised, Exercise 75. Recall that 955 households were contacted by a female solicitor to raise funds for hazard mitigation research. In addition to the household's level of contribution (in dollars) and the hair color of the solicitor (blond Caucasian, brunette Caucasian, or minority female), the researcher also recorded the beauty rating of the solicitor (measured quantitatively, on a 10-point scale).

a. Write a first-order model (with no interaction) for mean contribution level, $E(y)$, as a function of a solicitor's hair color and her beauty rating.

b. Refer to the model, part **a**. For each hair color, express the change in contribution level for each 1-point increase in a solicitor's beauty rating in terms of the model parameters.

c. Write an interaction model for mean contribution level, $E(y)$, as a function of a solicitor's hair color and her beauty rating.

d. Refer to the model, part **c**. For each hair color, express the change in contribution level for each 1-point increase in a solicitor's beauty rating in terms of the model parameters.

e. Refer to the model, part **c**. Illustrate the interaction with a graph.

89 Impact of race on football card values. Refer to the *Electronic Journal of Sociology* (2007) study of the impact of race on the value of professional football players' "rookie" cards, Exercise 72. Recall that the sample consisted of 148 rookie cards of NFL players who were inducted into the Football Hall of Fame (HOF). The researchers modeled the natural logarithm of card price (y) as a function of the following independent variables:

Race:	$x_1 = 1$ if black, 0 if white
Card availability:	$x_2 = 1$ if high, 0 if low
Card vintage:	$x_3 =$ year card printed
Finalist:	$x_4 =$ natural logarithm of number of times player on final HOF ballot
Position-QB:	$x_5 = 1$ if quarterback, 0 if not
Position-RB:	$x_7 = 1$ if running back, 0 if not
Position-WR:	$x_8 = 1$ if wide receiver, 0 if not
Position-TE:	$x_9 = 1$ if tight end, 0 if not
Position-DL:	$x_{10} = 1$ if defensive lineman, 0 if not
Position-LB:	$x_{11} = 1$ if linebacker, 0 if not
Position-DB:	$x_{12} = 1$ if defensive back, 0 if not

[*Note:* For position, offensive lineman is the base level.]

a. The model $E(y) = \beta_0 + \beta_1 x_1 + \beta_2 x_2 + \beta_3 x_3 + \beta_4 x_4 + \beta_5 x_5 + \beta_6 x_6 + \beta_7 x_7 + \beta_8 x_8 + \beta_9 x_9 + \beta_{10} x_{10} + \beta_{11} x_{11} + \beta_{12} x_{12}$ was fit to the data with the following results: $R^2 = .705, R_a^2 = .681, F = 26.9$. Interpret the results, practically. Make an inference about the overall adequacy of the model.

b. Refer to part **a**. Statistics for the race variable were reported as follows: $\hat{\beta}_1 = -.147, s_{\hat{\beta}_1} = .145, t = -1.014$, p-value $= .312$. Use this information to make an inference about the impact of race on the value of professional football players' rookie cards.

c. Refer to part **a**. Statistics for the card vintage variable were reported as follows: $\hat{\beta}_3 = -.074, s_{\hat{\beta}_3} = .007$, $t = -10.92$, p-value $= .000$. Use this information to make an inference about the impact of card vintage on the value of professional football players' rookie cards.

d. Write a first-order model for $E(y)$ as a function of card vintage (x_3) and position (x_5–x_{12}) that allows for the relationship between price and vintage to vary depending on position.

90 Buy-side vs. sell-side analysts' earnings forecasts. Refer to the *Financial Analysts Journal* (Jul./Aug. 2008) comparison of earnings forecasts of buy-side and sell-side analysts, Exercise 74. Recall that the Harvard Business School professors used regression to model the relative optimism (y) of the analysts' 3-month horizon forecasts. The following model was fit to data collected on 11,121 forecasts: $E(y) = \beta_0 + \beta_1 x_1 + \beta_2 x_2 + \beta_3 x_3$, where

$x_1 = \{1$ if the analyst worked for a buy-side firm, 0 if the analyst worked for a sell-side firm$\}$

$x_2 =$ number of days between forecast and fiscal year-end (i.e., forecast horizon)

$x_3 =$ natural logarithm of the number of quarters the analyst had worked with the firm

a. The coefficient of determination for the model was reported as $R^2 = .069$. Interpret this value.

b. Use the value of R^2 in part **a** to conduct a test of the global utility of the model. Use $\alpha = .01$.

c. The value of β_1 was estimated as 1.07, with an associated t-value of 4.3. Use this information to test ($\alpha = .01$.) whether x_1 contributes significantly to the prediction of y.

d. The professors concluded that "after controlling for forecast horizon and analyst experience, earnings forecasts by the analysts at buy-side firms are more optimistic than forecasts made by analysts at sell-side firms." Do you agree?

91 Workplace bullying and intention to leave. Workplace bullying (e.g., work-related harassment, persistent criticism, withholding key information, spreading rumors, intimidation) has been shown to have a negative psychological effect on victims, often leading the victim to quit or resign. In *Human Resource Management Journal* (Oct. 2008), researchers employed multiple regression to examine whether perceived organizational support (POS) would moderate the relationship between workplace bullying and victims' intention to leave the firm. The dependent variable in the analysis, intention to leave (y), was measured on a quantitative scale. The two key independent variables in the study were bullying (x_1, measured on a quantitative scale) and perceived organizational support (measured qualitatively as "low," "neutral," or "high").

a. Set up the dummy variables required to represent POS in the regression model.

b. Write a model for $E(y)$ as a function of bullying and POS that hypothesizes three parallel straight lines, one for each level of POS.

c. Write a model for $E(y)$ as a function of bullying and POS that hypothesizes three nonparallel straight lines, one for each level of POS.

d. The researchers discovered that the effect of bullying on intention to leave was greater at the low level of POS than at the high level of POS. Which of the two models, parts **b** and **c**, support these findings?

Applying the Concepts—Intermediate

92 Agreeableness, gender, and wages. Do agreeable individuals get paid less, on average, than those who are less agreeable on the job? And is this gap greater for males than for females? These questions were addressed in the *Journal of Personality and Social Psychology* (Feb. 2012). Several variables were measured for each in a sample of individuals enrolled in the National Survey of Midlife Development in the U.S. Three of these variables are: (1) level of agreeableness score (where higher scores indicate a greater level of agreeableness), (2) gender (male or female), and (3) annual income (dollars). The researchers modeled mean income, $E(y)$, as a function of both agreeableness score (x_1) and a dummy variable for gender ($x_2 = 1$ if male, 0 if female). Data for a sample of 100 individuals (simulated, based on information provided in the study) are saved in the file. The first 10 observations are listed in the accompanying table.

Data for First 10 Individuals in Study

Income	Agree Score	Gender
44,770	3.0	1
51,480	2.9	1
39,600	3.3	1
24,370	3.3	0
15,460	3.6	0
43,730	3.8	1
48,330	3.2	1
25,970	2.5	0
17,120	3.5	0
20,140	3.2	0

a. Consider the model, $E(y) = \beta_0 + \beta_1 x_1 + \beta_2 x_2$. The researchers theorized that for either gender, income would decrease as agreeableness score increases. If this theory is true, what is the expected sign of β_1 in the model?

b. The researchers also theorized that the rate of decrease of income with agreeableness score would be steeper for males than for females (i.e., the income gap between males and females would be greater the less agreeable the individuals are). Can this theory be tested using the model, part **a**? Explain.

c. Consider the interaction model, $E(y) = \beta_0 + \beta_1 x_1 + \beta_2 x_2 + \beta_3 x_1 x_2$. If the theory, part **b**, is true, give the expected sign of β_1. The expected sign of β_3.

d. Fit the model, part **c**, to the sample data. Check the signs of the estimated β coefficients. How do they compare to the expected values, part **c**?

e. Refer to the interaction model, part **c**. Give the null and alternative hypotheses for testing whether the rate of decrease of income with agreeableness score is steeper for males than for females.

f. Conduct the test, part **e**. Use $\alpha = .05$. Is the researchers' theory supported?

93 Chemical plant contamination. Refer to Exercise 18 and the model relating the mean DDT level $E(y)$ of contaminated fish to $x_1 = $ miles captured upstream, $x_2 = $ length, and $x_3 = $ weight. Now consider a model for $E(y)$ as a function of both weight and species (channel catfish, largemouth bass, and smallmouth buffalo).

a. Set up the appropriate dummy variables for species.

b. Write the equation of a model that proposes parallel straight-line relationships between mean DDT level $E(y)$ and weight, one line for each species.

c. Write the equation of a model that proposes nonparallel straight-line relationships between mean DDT level $E(y)$ and weight, one line for each species.

d. Fit the model, part **b**, to the data saved in the file. Give the least squares prediction equation.

e. Refer to part **d**. Interpret the value of the least squares estimate of the beta coefficient multiplied by weight.

f. Fit the model, part **c**, to the data saved in the file. Give the least squares prediction equation.

g. Refer to part **f**. Find the estimated slope of the line relating DDT level (y) to weight for the channel catfish species.

94 Personality traits and job performance. Refer to the *Journal of Applied Psychology* (Jan. 2011) study of the relationship between task performance and conscientiousness, Exercise 54. Recall that the researchers used a quadratic model to relate $y = $ task performance score (measured on a 30-point scale) to $x_1 = $ conscientiousness score (measured on a scale of -3 to $+3$). In addition, the researchers included job complexity in the model, where $x_2 = \{1$ if highly complex job, 0 if not$\}$. The complete model took the form

$$E(y) = \beta_0 + \beta_1 x_1 + \beta_2 (x_1)^2 + \beta_3 x_2 + \beta_4 x_1 x_2 + \beta_5 (x_1)^2 x_2$$

a. For jobs that are not highly complex, write the equation of the model for $E(y)$ as a function of x_1. (Substitute $x_2 = 0$ into the equation.)

b. Refer to part **a.** What do each of the β's represent in the model?

c. For highly complex jobs, write the equation of the model for $E(y)$ as a function of x_1. (Substitute $x_2 = 1$ into the equation.)

d. Refer to part **c.** What do each of the β's represent in the model?

e. Does the model support the researchers' theory that the curvilinear relationship between task performance score (y) and conscientiousness score (x_1) depends on job complexity (x_2)? Explain.

95 Recently sold, single-family homes. The National Association of Realtors maintains a database consisting of sales information on homes sold in the United States. The next table lists the sale prices for a sample of 28 recently sold, single-family homes. The table also identifies the region of the country in which the home is located and the total number of homes sold in the region during the month the home sold.

Home Price	Region	Sales Volume
$218,200	NE	55,156
235,900	NE	61,025
192,888	NE	48,991
200,990	NE	55,156
345,300	NE	60,324
178,999	NE	51,446
240,855	NW	61,025
183,200	NW	94,166
165,225	NW	92,063
160,633	NW	89,485
173,900	NW	91,772
241,000	NW	99,025
188,950	NW	94,166
192,880	NW	95,688
193,000	S	155,666
211,980	S	160,000
179,500	S	153,540
185,650	S	148,668
250,900	S	163,210
190,990	S	141,822
242,790	S	163,611
258,900	W	109,083
202,420	W	101,111
365,900	W	116,983
219,900	W	108,773
228,250	W	105,106
235,300	W	107,839
269,800	W	109,026

Source: Based on information from National Association of Realtors, www.realtor.org.

a. Propose a complete second-order model for the sale price of a single-family home as a function of region and sales volume.

b. Give the equation of the curve relating sale price to sales volume for homes sold in the West.

c. Repeat part **b** for homes sold in the Northwest.

d. Which β's in the model, part **a,** allow for differences among the mean sale prices for homes in the four regions?

e. Fit the model, part **a,** to the data using an available statistical software package. Is the model statistically useful for predicting sale price? Test using $\alpha = .01$.

96 Volatility of foreign stocks. The relationship between country credit ratings and the volatility of the countries' stock markets was examined in the *Journal of Portfolio Management* (Spring 1996). The researchers point out that this volatility can be explained by two factors: the countries' credit ratings and whether the countries in question have developed or emerging markets. Data on the volatility (measured as the standard deviation of stock returns), credit rating (measured as a percentage), and market type (developed or emerging) for a sample of 30 fictitious countries are saved in the file. (Selected observations are shown in the table below.)

a. Write a model that describes the relationship between volatility (y) and credit rating (x_1) as two nonparallel lines, one for each type of market. Specify the dummy variable coding scheme you use.

b. Plot volatility y against credit rating x_1 for all the developed markets in the sample. On the same graph, plot y against x_1 for all emerging markets in the sample. Does it appear that the model specified in part **a** is appropriate? Explain.

c. Fit the model, part **a,** to the data using a statistical software package. Report the least squares prediction equation for each of the two types of markets.

d. Plot the two prediction equations of part **c** on a scatterplot of the data.

e. Is there evidence to conclude that the slope of the linear relationship between volatility y and credit rating x_1 depends on market type? Test using $\alpha = .01$.

Country	Volatility (standard deviation of return), y	Credit Rating, x_1	Developed (D) or Emerging (E), x_2
1	56.9	9.5	E
2	25.1	72.4	D
3	28.4	58.2	E
4	56.2	9.9	E
5	21.5	92.1	D
⋮	⋮	⋮	⋮
26	47.5	16.9	E
27	22.0	89.0	D
28	21.5	91.9	D
29	38.1	30.7	E
30	37.4	32.2	E

9 Comparing Nested Models

To be successful model builders, we require a statistical method that will allow us to determine (with a high degree of confidence) which one among a set of candidate models best fits the data. In this section, we present such a technique for *nested models*.

> Two models are **nested** if one model contains all the terms of the second model and at least one additional term. The more complex of the two models is called the **complete** (or **full**) model, and the simpler of the two is called the **reduced** model.

To illustrate the concept of nested models, consider the straight-line interaction model for the mean auction price $E(y)$ of a grandfather clock as a function of two quantitative variables: age of the clock (x_1) and number of bidders (x_2). The interaction model, fit in Example 6, is

$$E(y) = \beta_0 + \beta_1 x_1 + \beta_2 x_2 + \beta_3 x_1 x_2$$

If we assume that the relationship between auction price (y), age (x_1), and bidders (x_2) is curvilinear, then the complete second-order model is more appropriate:

$$E(y) = \underbrace{\beta_0 + \beta_1 x_1 + \beta_2 x_2 + \beta_3 x_1 x_2}_{\text{Terms in interaction model}} + \underbrace{\beta_4 x_1^2 + \beta_5 x_2^2}_{\text{Quadratic terms}}$$

Note that the curvilinear model contains quadratic terms for x_1 and x_2, as well as the terms in the interaction model. Therefore, the models are nested models. In this case, the interaction model is nested within the more complex curvilinear model. Thus, the curvilinear model is the *complete* model, and the interaction model is the *reduced* model.

Suppose we want to know whether the more complex curvilinear model contributes more information for the prediction of y than the straight-line interaction model. This is equivalent to determining whether the quadratic terms β_4 and β_5 should be retained in the model. To test whether these terms should be retained, we test the null hypothesis

H_0: $\beta_4 = \beta_5 = 0$ (i.e., quadratic terms are not important for predicting y)

against the alternative hypothesis

H_a: At least one of the parameters β_4 and β_5 is nonzero (i.e., at least one of the quadratic terms is useful for predicting y).

Note that the terms being tested are those additional terms in the complete (curvilinear) model that are not in the reduced (straight-line interaction) model.

In Section 3, we presented the t-test for a single β coefficient and the global F-test for *all* the β parameters (except β_0) in the model. We now need a test for a *subset* of the β parameters in the complete model. The test procedure is intuitive. First, we use the method of least squares to fit the reduced model and calculate the corresponding sum of squares for error, SSE_R (the sum of squares of the deviations between observed and predicted y-values). Next, we fit the complete model and calculate its sum of squares for error, SSE_C. Then we compare SSE_R to SSE_C by calculating the difference, $SSE_R - SSE_C$. If the additional terms in the complete model are significant, then SSE_C should be much smaller than SSE_R, and the difference $SSE_R - SSE_C$ will be large.

Because SSE will always decrease when new terms are added to the model, the question is whether the difference $SSE_R - SSE_C$ is large enough to conclude that it is due to more than just an increase in the number of model terms and to chance. The formal statistical test uses an F-statistic, as shown in the box.

When the assumptions listed in Section 1 about the random error term are satisfied, this F-statistic has an F-distribution with ν_1 and ν_2 df. Note that ν_1 is the number of

β parameters being tested, and ν_2 is the number of degrees of freedom associated with s^2 in the complete model.

F-Test for Comparing Nested Models

Reduced model: $E(y) = \beta_0 + \beta_1 x_1 + \cdots + \beta_g x_g$

Complete model: $E(y) = \beta_0 + \beta_1 x_1 + \cdots + \beta_g x_g + \beta_{g+1} x_{g+1} + \cdots + \beta_k x_k$

$H_0: \beta_{g+1} = \beta_{g+2} = \cdots = \beta_k = 0$

$H_a:$ At least one of the β parameters under test is nonzero.

$$\text{Test statistic: } F = \frac{(SSE_R - SSE_C)/(k - g)}{SSE_C/[n - (k + 1)]}$$

$$= \frac{(SSE_R - SSE_C)/\#\beta\text{'s tested in } H_0}{MSE_C}$$

where

SSE_R = Sum of squared errors for the reduced model

SSE_C = Sum of squared errors for the complete model

MSE_C = Mean square error (s^2) for the complete model

$k - g$ = Number of β parameters specified in H_0 (i.e., number of β parameters tested)

$k + 1$ = Number of β parameters in the complete model (including β_0)

n = Total sample size

Rejection region: $F > F_\alpha$

where F is based on $\nu_1 = k - g$ numerator degrees of freedom and $\nu_2 = n - (k + 1)$ denominator degrees of freedom.

Example	12

Analyzing a Complete Second-Order Model— Auction Price Data

Problem Refer to the problem of modeling the auction price (y) of an antique grandfather clock, Examples 1–6. In these examples, we discovered that price was related to both age (x_1) of the clock and number of bidders (x_2), and age and number of bidders had an interactive effect on price. Both the first-order model of Example 1 and the interaction model of Example 6, however, propose only straight-line (linear) relationships. We did not consider the possibility that the relationship between price (y) and age (x_1) is curvilinear, or that the relationship between price (y) and number of bidders (x_2) is curvilinear.

a. Propose a complete second-order model for price (y) as a function of age (x_1) and number of bidders (x_2).

b. Fit the model to the data for the 32 clocks in Table 1 and give the least squares prediction equation.

c. Do the data provide sufficient evidence to indicate that the quadratic terms in the model contribute information for the prediction of price (y)? That is, is there evidence of curvature in the price-age and price-bidders relationships?

Solution

a. Because both age (x_1) and number of bidders (x_2) are quantitative variables, we write the complete second-order model as follows:

$$E(y) = \beta_0 + \beta_1 x_1 + \beta_2 x_2 + \beta_3 x_1 x_2 + \beta_4 (x_1)^2 + \beta_5 (x_2)^2$$

Note that we have added two quadratic terms, $\beta_4 (x_1)^2$ and $\beta_5 (x_2)^2$, to the interaction model of Example 6.

Figure 29

Minitab analysis of complete second-order model for auction price

```
Regression Analysis: PRICE versus AGE, NUMBIDS, AGE-BID, AGESQ, NUMBIDSQ

The regression equation is
PRICE = - 332 + 3.21 AGE + 14.8 NUMBIDS + 1.12 AGE-BID - 0.0030 AGESQ
        - 4.18 NUMBIDSQ

Predictor       Coef  SE Coef       T      P
Constant      -331.9    764.9   -0.43  0.668
AGE            3.208    8.947    0.36  0.723
NUMBIDS        14.81    62.21    0.24  0.814
AGE-BID       1.1232   0.2316    4.85  0.000
AGESQ       -0.00300  0.02748   -0.11  0.914
NUMBIDSQ      -4.179    2.145   -1.95  0.062

S = 86.1019   R-Sq = 96.0%   R-Sq(adj) = 95.2%

Analysis of Variance

Source          DF       SS      MS       F      P
Regression       5  4607038  921408  124.29  0.000
Residual Error  26   192752    7414
Total           31  4799790
```

b. We used Minitab to fit the model to the data in Table 2. The Minitab output is shown in Figure 29. The least squares prediction equation, highlighted on the printout, is

$$\hat{y} = -332 + 3.21x_1 + 14.8x_2 + 1.12x_1x_2 - .003(x_1)^2 - 4.18(x_2)^2$$

Note that the estimates of the quadratic terms, β_4 and β_5, are both negative, implying downward curvature in both the price-age and price-bidders relationships.

c. To determine whether the quadratic terms are useful for predicting price (y), we want to test

$$H_0: \beta_4 = \beta_5 = 0$$

H_a: At least one of the parameters, β_4 and β_5, differs from 0.

Because the null hypothesis involves a subset of β's, we will need to perform a nested model F-test. The complete model is the complete second-order model of part **a.** The reduced model is obtained by dropping the quadratic terms out of the complete model. Doing so yields:

Reduced model: $E(y) = \beta_0 + \beta_1x_1 + \beta_2x_2 + \beta_3x_1x_2$

We fit this model in Example 6. The Minitab printout for this reduced model is reproduced in Figure 30.

To conduct this test, we first obtain the SSE values for the complete and reduced models. These values (highlighted, respectively, on Figures 29 and 30) are

$$\text{SSE}_C = 192,752 \text{ and } \text{SSE}_R = 221,362$$

Also, s^2 for the complete model (highlighted on Figure 29) is

$$s^2 = \text{MSE}_C = 7,414$$

Recall that $n = 32$ and that there are $k = 5$ terms in the complete model and $g = 3$ terms in the reduced model. Therefore, the calculated value of the test statistic is

$$\textit{Test statistic: } F = \frac{(\text{SSE}_R - \text{SSE}_C)/(k - g)}{\text{MSE}_C} = \frac{(221,362 - 192,752)/2}{7,414} = 1.93$$

The critical F-value for the rejection region is based on $\nu_1 = (k - g) = 2$ numerator df and $\nu_2 = [n - (k + 1)] = 26$ denominator df. If we choose $\alpha = .05$, this critical value is $F_{.05} = 3.37$ and the rejection region is

Rejection region: $F > 3.37$

Because the test statistic, $F = 1.93$, falls outside the rejection region, we fail to reject H_0. That is, there is insufficient evidence (at $\alpha = .05$) to conclude that at least one

Regression Analysis: PRICE versus AGE, NUMBIDS, AGEBID

```
The regression equation is
PRICE = 320 + 0.88 AGE - 93.3 NUMBIDS + 1.30 AGEBID


Predictor      Coef   SE Coef      T       P
Constant      320.5     295.1    1.09   0.287
AGE           0.878     2.032    0.43   0.669
NUMBIDS      -93.26     29.89   -3.12   0.004
AGEBID       1.2978    0.2123    6.11   0.000


S = 88.9145   R-Sq = 95.4%   R-Sq(adj) = 94.9%


Analysis of Variance

Source            DF       SS       MS       F       P
Regression         3  4578427  1526142  193.04   0.000
Residual Error    28   221362     7906
Total             31  4799790
```

Figure 30

Minitab analysis of reduced model for auction price

of the quadratic terms contributes information for the prediction of auction price (y). Consequently, there is no evidence of curvature in either the price-age or price-bidders relationship. It appears that the first-order, interaction (reduced) model is adequate for predicting auction price.

Look Back Some statistical software packages will perform the desired nested model F-test if requested. The test statistic and p-value for the test above are highlighted on the SPSS printout, Figure 31. Note that p-value $= .165$ exceeds $\alpha = .05$; thus, there is insufficient evidence to reject H_0.

Now Work Exercise 100

Model Summary

Mode l	R	R Square	Adjusted R Square	Std. Error of the Estimate	Change Statistics				
					R Square Change	F Change	df1	df2	Sig. F Change
1	.977[a]	.954	.949	88.915	.954	193.041	3	28	.000
2	.980[b]	.960	.952	86.102	.006	1.930	2	26	.165

a. Predictors: (Constant), AGE_BID, AGE, NUMBIDS

b. Predictors: (Constant), AGE_BID, AGE, NUMBIDS, NUMBIDSQ, AGESQ

Figure 31

SPSS printout of nested model F-test for auction price

The nested model F-test can be used to determine whether *any* subset of terms should be included in a complete model by testing the null hypothesis that a particular set of β parameters simultaneously equals 0. For example, we may want to test to determine whether a set of interaction terms for quantitative variables or a set of main effect terms for a qualitative variable should be included in a model. If we reject H_0, the complete model is the better of the two nested models. If we fail to reject H_0, as in Example 12, we favor the reduced model. Although we must be cautious about accepting H_0, most practitioners of regression analysis adopt the principle of *parsimony*—that is, in situations where two competing models are found to have essentially the same predictive power (as in Example 12), the model with the fewer number of β's (i.e., the more parsimonious model) is selected. Based on this principle, we would drop the two quadratic terms and select the first-order, interaction (reduced) model over the second-order (complete) model.

A **parsimonious model** is a general linear model with a small number of β parameters. In situations where two competing models have essentially the same predictive power (as determined by an F-test), choose the more parsimonious of the two.

Guidelines for Selecting Preferred Model in a Nested Model *F*-Test

Conclusion		Preferred Model
Reject H_0	$\rightarrow$	Complete Model
Fail to reject H_0	$\rightarrow$	Reduced Model

When the candidate models in model building are nested models, the *F*-test developed in this section is the appropriate procedure to apply to compare the models. However, if the models are not nested, this *F*-test is not applicable. In this situation, the analyst must base the choice of the best model on statistics such as R_a^2 and *s*. It is important to remember that decisions based on these and other numerical descriptive measures of model adequacy cannot be supported with a measure of reliability and are often very subjective in nature.

Exercises 97–110

Learning the Mechanics

97 Determine which pairs of the following models are "nested" models. For each pair of nested models, identify the complete and reduced model.
a. $E(y) = \beta_0 + \beta_1 x_1 + \beta_2 x_2$
b. $E(y) = \beta_0 + \beta_1 x_1$
c. $E(y) = \beta_0 + \beta_1 x_1 + \beta_2 x_1^2$
d. $E(y) = \beta_0 + \beta_1 x_1 + \beta_2 x_2 + \beta_3 x_1 x_2$
e. $E(y) = \beta_0 + \beta_1 x_1 + \beta_2 x_2 + \beta_3 x_1 x_2 + \beta_4 x_1^2 + \beta_5 x_2^2$

98 Suppose you fit the regression model

$$y = \beta_0 + \beta_1 x_1 + \beta_2 x_2 + \beta_3 x_1 x_2 + \beta_4 x_1^2 + \beta_5 x_2^2 + \varepsilon$$

to $n = 30$ data points and wish to test

$$H_0: \beta_3 = \beta_4 = \beta_5 = 0$$

a. State the alternative hypothesis H_a.
b. Give the reduced model appropriate for conducting the test.
c. What are the numerator and denominator degrees of freedom associated with the *F*-statistic?
d. Suppose the SSE's for the reduced and complete models are $SSE_R = 1,250.2$ and $SSE_C = 1,125.2$. Conduct the hypothesis test and interpret the results of your test. Test using $\alpha = .05$.

99 The complete model

$$y = \beta_0 + \beta_1 x_1 + \beta_2 x_2 + \beta_3 x_3 + \beta_4 x_4 + \varepsilon$$

was fit to $n = 20$ data points, with SSE = 152.66. The reduced model, $y = \beta_0 + \beta_1 x_1 + \beta_2 x_2 + \varepsilon$, was also fit, with SSE = 160.44.
a. How many β parameters are in the complete model? The reduced model?
b. Specify the null and alternative hypotheses you would use to investigate whether the complete model contributes more information for the prediction of *y* than the reduced model.
c. Conduct the hypothesis test of part **b.** Use $\alpha = .05$.

Applying the Concepts—Basic

100 Mental health of a community. An article in the *Community Mental Health Journal* (Aug. 2000) used multiple regression analysis to model the level of community adjustment of clients of the Department of Mental Health and Addiction Services in Connecticut. The dependent variable, community adjustment (*y*), was measured quantitatively based on staff ratings of the clients. (Lower scores indicate better adjustment.) The complete model was a first-order model with 21 independent variables. The independent variables were categorized as Demographic (4 variables), Diagnostic (7 variables), Treatment (4 variables), and Community (6 variables).
a. Write the equation of $E(y)$ for the complete model.
b. Give the null hypothesis for testing whether the 7 Diagnostic variables contribute information for the prediction of *y*.
c. Give the equation of the reduced model appropriate for the test, part **b.**
d. The test, part **b,** resulted in a test statistic of $F = 59.3$ and *p*-value < .0001. Interpret this result in the words of the problem.

101 Buy-side vs. sell-side analysts' earnings forecasts. Refer to the *Financial Analysts Journal* (Jul./Aug. 2008) comparison of earnings forecasts of buy-side and sell-side analysts, Exercise 90. Recall that the Harvard Business School professors used regression to model the relative optimism (*y*) of the analysts' 3-month horizon forecasts as a function of $x_1 = \{1$ if the analyst worked for a buy-side firm, 0 if the analyst worked for a sell-side firm} and $x_2 =$ number of days between forecast and fiscal year-end (i.e., forecast horizon). Consider the complete second-order model

$$E(y) = \beta_0 + \beta_1 x_1 + \beta_2 x_2 + \beta_3 x_1 x_2 + \beta_4 (x_2)^2 + \beta_5 x_1 (x_2)^2$$

a. What null hypothesis would you test to determine whether the quadratic terms in the model are statistically useful for predicting relative optimism (*y*)?

b. Give the complete and reduced models for conducting the test, part **a.**

c. What null hypothesis would you test to determine whether the interaction terms in the model are statistically useful for predicting relative optimism (*y*)?

d. Give the complete and reduced models for conducting the test, part **c.**

e. What null hypothesis would you test to determine whether the dummy variable terms in the model are statistically useful for predicting relative optimism (*y*)?

f. Give the complete and reduced models for conducting the test, part **e.**

102 Workplace bullying and intention to leave. Refer to the *Human Resource Management Journal* (Oct. 2008) study of workplace bullying, Exercise 91. Recall that multiple regression was used to model an employee's intention to leave (*y*) as a function of bullying (x_1, measured on a quantitative scale) and perceived organizational support (measured qualitatively as "low POS," "neutral POS," or "high POS"). In Exercise 91b, you wrote a model for $E(y)$ as a function of bullying and POS that hypothesizes three parallel straight lines, one for each level of POS. In Exercise 91c, you wrote a model for $E(y)$ as a function of bullying and POS that hypothesizes three nonparallel straight lines, one for each level of POS.

a. Explain why the two models are nested. Which is the complete model? Which is the reduced model?

b. Give the null hypothesis for comparing the two models.

c. If you reject H_0 in part **b,** which model do you prefer? Why?

d. If you fail to reject H_0 in part **b,** which model do you prefer? Why?

103 Cooling method for gas turbines. Refer to the *Journal of Engineering for Gas Turbines and Power* (Jan. 2005) study of a high-pressure inlet fogging method for a gas turbine engine, Exercise 19. Consider a model for heat rate (kilojoules per kilowatt per hour) of a gas turbine as a function of cycle speed (revolutions per minute) and cycle pressure ratio. The data are saved in the file.

a. Write a complete second-order model for heat rate (*y*).

b. Give the null and alternative hypotheses for determining whether the curvature terms in the complete second-order model are statistically useful for predicting heat rate (*y*).

c. For the test in part **b,** identify the complete and reduced model.

d. Portions of the Minitab printouts for the two models are shown below. Find the values of SSE_R, SSE_C, and MSE_C on the printouts.

e. Compute the value of the test statistics for the test of part **b.**

f. Find the rejection region for the test of part **b** using $\alpha = .10$.

g. State the conclusion of the test in the words of the problem.

104 Personality traits and job performance. Refer to the *Journal of Applied Psychology* (Jan. 2011) study of the relationship between task performance and conscientiousness, Exercise 94. Recall that *y* = task performance score (measured on a 30-point scale) was modeled as a function of x_1 = conscientiousness score (measured on a scale of −3 to +3) and x_2 = {1 if highly complex job, 0 if not} using the complete model

$$E(y) = \beta_0 + \beta_1 x_1 + \beta_2 (x_1)^2 + \beta_3 x_2 + \beta_4 x_1 x_2 + \beta_5 (x_1)^2 x_2$$

a. Specify the null hypothesis for testing the overall adequacy of the model.

Complete Model

```
The regression equation is
HEATRATE = 15583 + 0.078 RPM - 523 CPRATIO + 0.00445 RPM_CPR - 0.000000 RPMSQ
           + 8.84 CPRSQ


S = 563.513    R-Sq = 88.5%    R-Sq(adj) = 87.5%


Analysis of Variance


Source          DF         SS         MS      F      P
Regression       5  148526859   29705372  93.55  0.000
Residual Error  61   19370350     317547
Total           66  167897208
```

Reduced Model

```
The regression equation is
HEATRATE = 12065 + 0.170 RPM - 146 CPRATIO - 0.00242 RPM_CPR


S = 633.842    R-Sq = 84.9%    R-Sq(adj) = 84.2%


Analysis of Variance


Source          DF         SS         MS      F      P
Regression       3  142586570   47528857  118.30  0.000
Residual Error  63   25310639     401756
Total           66  167897208
```

Minitab output for Exercise 103

b. Specify the null hypothesis for testing whether task performance score (y) and conscientiousness score (x_1) are curvilinearly related.

c. Specify the null hypothesis for testing whether the curvilinear relationship between task performance score (y) and conscientiousness score (x_1) depends on job complexity (x_2).

d. Explain how each of the tests, parts **a–c,** should be conducted (i.e., give the forms of the test statistic and the reduced model).

Applying the Concepts—Intermediate

105 **Reality TV and cosmetic surgery.** Refer to the *Body Image: An International Journal of Research* (March 2010) study of the influence of reality TV shows on one's desire to undergo cosmetic surgery, Exercise 17. Recall that psychologists modeled desire to have cosmetic surgery (y) as a function of gender (x_1), self-esteem (x_2), body satisfaction (x_3), and impression of reality TV (x_4). The psychologists theorized that one's impression of reality TV will "moderate" the impact that each of the first three independent variables has on one's desire to have cosmetic surgery. If so, then x_4 will interact with each of the other independent variables.

a. Give the equation of the model for $E(y)$ that matches the theory.

b. Fit the model, part **a,** to the simulated data saved in the file. Evaluate the overall utility of the model.

c. Give the null hypothesis for testing the psychologists' theory.

d. Conduct a nested model F-test to test the theory. What do you conclude?

106 **Study of supervisor-targeted aggression.** "Moonlighters" are workers who hold two jobs at the same time. What are the factors that impact the likelihood of a moonlighting worker becoming aggressive toward his/her supervisor? This was the research question of interest in the *Journal of Applied Psychology* (July 2005). Completed questionnaires were obtained from $n = 105$ moonlighters, and the data were used to fit several multiple regression models for supervisor-directed aggression score (y). Two of the models (with R^2 values in parentheses) are given below:

Model 1: $E(y) = \beta_0 + \beta_1(\text{Age}) + \beta_2(\text{Gender}) + \beta_3(\text{Interatctional injustice at 2nd job}) + \beta_4(\text{Abusive supervisor at 2nd job})$

($R^2 = .101$)

Model 2: $E(y) = \beta_0 + \beta_1(\text{Age}) + \beta_2(\text{Gender}) + \beta_3(\text{Interactional injustice at 2nd job}) + \beta_4(\text{Abusive supervisor at 2nd job}) + \beta_5(\text{Self-esteem}) + \beta_6(\text{History of aggression}) + \beta_7(\text{Interactional injustice at primary job}) + \beta_8(\text{Abusive supervisor at primary job})$

($R^2 = .555$)

---

a. Interpret the R^2 values for the models.

b. Give the null and alternative hypotheses for comparing the fits of models 1 and 2.

c. Are the two models nested? Explain.

d. The nested F-test for comparing the two models resulted in $F = 42.13$ and p-value $< .001$. What can you conclude from these results?

e. A third model was fit, one that hypothesizes all possible pairs of interactions between self-esteem, history of aggression, interactional injustice at primary job, and abusive supervisor at primary job. Give the equation of this model (model 3).

f. A nested F-test to compare models 2 and 3 resulted in a p-value $> .10$. What can you conclude from this result?

107 **Agreeableness, gender, and wages.** Refer to the *Journal of Personality and Social Psychology* (Feb. 2012) study of on-the-job agreeableness and wages, Exercise 92. The researchers modeled mean income, $E(y)$, as a function of both agreeableness score (x_1) and a dummy variable for gender ($x_2 = 1$ if male, 0 if female). Suppose the researchers theorize that for either gender, income will decrease at a decreasing rate as agreeableness score increases. Consequently, they want to fit a second-order model.

a. Consider the model, $E(y) = \beta_0 + \beta_1 x_1 + \beta_2(x_1)^2 + \beta_3 x_2$. If the researchers' belief is true, what is the expected sign of β_2 in the model?

b. Draw a sketch of the model, part **a,** showing how gender impacts the income-agreeableness score relationship.

c. Write a complete second-order model for $E(y)$ as a function of x_1 and x_2.

d. Draw a sketch of the model, part **c,** showing how gender impacts the income-agreeableness score relationship.

e. What null hypothesis would you test in order to compare the two models, parts **a** and **c**?

f. Fit the models to the sample data saved in the file and carry out the test, part **e.** What do you conclude? (Test using $\alpha = .10$.)

108 **Recently sold, single-family homes.** Refer to the National Association of Realtors data on sales price (y), region (NE, NW, S, or W), and sales volume for 28 recently sold, single-family homes, Exercise 95. You fit a complete second-order model for $E(y)$ as a function of region and sales volume.

a. Conduct a nested-model F-test to determine whether the quadratic terms in the model are statistically useful for predicting sales price (y). Use $\alpha = .05$.

b. Based on the result, part **a,** which of the nested models (the complete or the reduced model) do you prefer to use in predicting sales price (y)? Explain.

c. Refer to part **b.** Treat the preferred model as the complete model and conduct a nested model F-test to determine whether region and sales volume interact to affect sales price (y). Use $\alpha = .05$.

d. Based on the result, part **c,** which of the nested models (the complete or the reduced model) do you prefer to use in predicting sales price (y)? Explain.

109 **Glass as a waste encapsulant.** Because glass is not subject to radiation damage, encapsulation of waste in glass is considered to be one of the most promising solutions to the problem of low-level nuclear waste in the environment. However, chemical reactions may weaken the glass.

This concern led to a study undertaken jointly by the Department of Materials Science and Engineering at the University of Florida and the U.S. Department of Energy to assess the utility of glass as a waste encapsulant.* Corrosive chemical solutions (called *corrosion baths*) were prepared and applied directly to glass samples containing one of three types of waste (TDS-3A, FE, and AL); the chemical reactions were observed over time. A few of the key variables measured were

y = Amount of silicon (in parts per million) found in solution at end of experiment. (This is both a measure of the degree of breakdown in the glass and a proxy for the amount of radioactive species released into the environment.)

x_1 = Temperature (°C) of the corrosion bath

x_2 = 1 if waste type TDS-3A, 0 if not

x_3 = 1 if waste type FE, 0 if not

(Waste type AL is the base level.) Suppose we want to model amount y of silicon as a function of temperature (x_1) and type of waste (x_2, x_3).

a. Write a model that proposes parallel straight-line relationships between amount of silicon and temperature, one line for each of the three waste types.

b. Add terms for the interaction between temperature and waste type to the model of part **a.**

c. Refer to the model of part **b.** For each waste type, give the slope of the line relating amount of silicon to temperature.

d. Explain how you could test for the presence of temperature–waste type interaction.

Applying the Concepts—Advanced

110 **Emotional distress in firefighters.** The *Journal of Human Stress* (Summer 1987) reported on a study of "psychological response of firefighters to chemical fire." It is thought that the following complete second-order model will be adequate to describe the relationship between emotional distress and years of experience for two groups of firefighters—those exposed to a chemical fire and those unexposed:

$$E(y) = \beta_0 + \beta_1 x_1 + \beta_2 x_1^2 + \beta_3 x_2 + \beta_4 x_1 x_2 + \beta_5 x_1^2 x_2$$

where

y = Emotional distress

x_1 = Experience (years)

x_2 = 1 if exposed to chemical fire, 0 if not

a. How would you determine whether the *rate* of increase of emotional distress with experience is different for the two groups of firefighters?

b. How would you determine whether there are differences in mean emotional distress levels that are attributable to exposure group?

10 Stepwise Regression

Consider the problem of predicting the salary y of an executive. Perhaps the biggest problem in building a model to describe executive salaries is choosing the important independent variables to be included in the model. The list of potentially important independent variables is extremely long (e.g., age, experience, tenure, education level, etc.), and we need some objective method of screening out those that are not important.

The problem of deciding which of a large set of independent variables to include in a model is a common one. Trying to determine which variables influence the profit of a firm, affect blood pressure of humans, or are related to a student's performance in college are only a few examples.

A systematic approach to building a model with a large number of independent variables is difficult because the interpretation of multivariable interactions and higher-order terms is tedious. We therefore turn to a screening procedure, available in most statistical software packages, known as **stepwise regression.**

The most commonly used stepwise regression procedure works as follows. The user first identifies the response, y, and the set of potentially important independent variables, $x_1, x_2, \ldots, x_k$, where k is generally large. [*Note:* This set of variables could include both first-order and higher-order terms. However, we may often include only the main effects of both quantitative variables (first-order terms) and qualitative variables (dummy variables) because the inclusion of second-order terms greatly increases the number of independent variables.] The response and independent variables are then entered into the computer software, and the stepwise procedure begins.

Step 1: The software program fits all possible one-variable models of the form

$$E(y) = \beta_0 + \beta_1 x_i$$

*The background information for this exercise was provided by Dr. David Clark, Department of Materials Science and Engineering, University of Florida.

to the data, where x_i is the ith independent variable, $i = 1, 2, \ldots, k$. For each model, the test of the null hypothesis

$$H_0: \beta_1 = 0$$

against the alternative hypothesis

$$H_a: \beta_1 \neq 0$$

is conducted using the t-test (or the equivalent F-test) for a single β parameter. The independent variable that produces the largest (absolute) t-value is declared the best one-variable predictor of y.* Call this independent variable x_1.

Step 2: The stepwise program now begins to search through the remaining $(k - 1)$ independent variables for the best two-variable model of the form

$$E(y) = \beta_0 + \beta_1 x_1 + \beta_2 x_i$$

This is done by fitting all two-variable models containing x_1 and each of the other $(k - 1)$ options for the second variable x_i. The t-values for the test $H_0: \beta_2 = 0$ are computed for each of the $(k - 1)$ models (corresponding to the remaining independent variables, $x_i, i = 2, 3, \ldots, k$), and the variable having the largest t is retained. Call this variable x_2.

At this point, some software packages diverge in methodology. The better packages now go back and check the t-value of $\hat{\beta}_1$ after $\hat{\beta}_2 x_2$ has been added to the model. If the t-value has become nonsignificant at some specified α level (say $\alpha = .10$), the variable x_1 is removed and a search is made for the independent variable with a β parameter that will yield the most significant t-value in the presence of $\hat{\beta}_2 x_2$. Other packages do not recheck the significance of $\hat{\beta}_1$ but proceed directly to step 3.†

The reason the t-value for x_1 may change from step 1 to step 2 is that the meaning of the coefficient $\hat{\beta}_1$ changes. In step 2, we are approximating a complex response surface in two variables with a plane. The best-fitting plane may yield a different value for $\hat{\beta}_1$ than that obtained in step 1. Thus, both the value of $\hat{\beta}_1$ and its significance usually change from step 1 to step 2. For this reason, the software packages that recheck the t-values at each step are preferred.

Step 3: The stepwise procedure now checks for a third independent variable to include in the model with x_1 and x_2—that is, we seek the best model of the form

$$E(y) = \beta_0 + \beta_1 x_1 + \beta_2 x_2 + \beta_3 x_i$$

To do this, we fit all the $(k - 2)$ models using x_1, x_2, and each of the $(k - 2)$ remaining variables, x_i, as a possible x_3. The criterion is again to include the independent variable with the largest t-value. Call this best third variable x_3.

The better programs now recheck the t-values corresponding to the x_1 and x_2 coefficients, removing the variables with t-values that have become nonsignificant. This procedure is continued until no further independent variables can be found that yield significant t-values (at the specified α level) in the presence of the variables already in the model.

The result of the stepwise procedure is a model containing only those terms with t-values that are significant at the specified α level. Thus, in most practical situations, only several of the large number of independent variables remain. However, it is very important *not* to jump to the conclusion that all the independent variables important for predicting y have been identified or that the unimportant independent variables have been eliminated. Remember, the stepwise procedure is using only *sample estimates* of the true model coefficients (β's) to select the important variables. An extremely large

*In step 1, note that the variable with the largest t-value is also the one with the largest (absolute) Pearson product moment correlation, r with y.

†*Forward selection* is the name given to stepwise routines that *do not* recheck the significance of each previously entered independent variable. This is in contrast to *stepwise selection* routines, which perform the rechecks. A third approach is to use *backward selection,* where initially, all terms are entered and then eliminated one by one.

number of single β parameter t-tests have been conducted, and the probability is very high that one or more errors have been made in including or excluding variables—that is, we have very probably included some unimportant independent variables in the model (Type I errors) and eliminated some important ones (Type II errors).

There is a second reason why we might not have arrived at a good model. When we choose the variables to be included in the stepwise regression, we may often omit higher-order terms (to keep the number of variables manageable). Consequently, we may have initially omitted several important terms from the model. Thus, we should recognize stepwise regression for what it is: an **objective variable screening procedure.**

Successful model builders will now consider second-order terms (for quantitative variables) and other interactions among variables screened by the stepwise procedure. It would be best to develop this response surface model with a second set of data independent of that used for the screening, so that the results of the stepwise procedure can be partially verified with new data. This is not always possible, however, because in many modeling situations only a small amount of data is available.

Do not be deceived by the impressive-looking t-values that result from the stepwise procedure—it has retained only the independent variables with the largest t-values. Also, be certain to consider second-order terms in systematically developing the prediction model. Finally, if you have used a first-order model for your stepwise procedure, remember that it may be greatly improved by the addition of higher-order terms.

⚠ **CAUTION** Be wary of using the results of stepwise regression to make inferences about the relationship between $E(y)$ and the independent variables in the resulting first-order model. First, an extremely large number of t-tests have been conducted, leading to a high probability of making one or more Type I or Type II errors. Second, the stepwise model does not include any higher-order or interaction terms. Stepwise regression should be used only when necessary—that is, when you want to determine which of a large number of potentially important independent variables should be used in the model-building process.

Example 13

Running a Stepwise Regression—Modeling Executive Salary

Problem An international management consulting company develops multiple regression models for executive salaries of its client firms. The consulting company has found that models that use the natural logarithm of salary as the dependent variable have better predictive power than those using salary as the dependent variable.* A preliminary step in the construction of these models is the determination of the most important independent variables. For one firm, 10 potential independent variables (7 quantitative and 3 qualitative) were measured in a sample of 100 executives. The data, described in Table 5, are

Table 5	Independent Variables in the Executive Salary Example	
Independent Variable	Description	Type
x_1	Experience (years)	Quantitative
x_2	Education (years)	Quantitative
x_3	Bonus eligibility (1 if yes, 0 if no)	Qualitative
x_4	Number of employees supervised	Quantitative
x_5	Corporate assets (millions of dollars)	Quantitative
x_6	Board member (1 if yes, 0 if no)	Qualitative
x_7	Age (years)	Quantitative
x_8	Company profits (past 12 months, millions of dollars)	Quantitative
x_9	Has international responsibility (1 if yes, 0 if no)	Qualitative
x_{10}	Company's total sales (past 12 months, millions of dollars)	Quantitative

  Data Set: EXSAL

---

*This is probably because salaries tend to be incremented in *percentages* rather than dollar values. When a response variable undergoes percentage changes as the independent variables are varied, the logarithm of the response variable will be more suitable as a dependent variable.

saved in the file. Because it would be very difficult to construct a complete second-order model with all of the 10 independent variables, use stepwise regression to decide which of the 10 variables should be included in the building of the final model for the natural log of executive salaries.

Solution We will use stepwise regression with the main effects of the 10 independent variables to identify the most important variables. The dependent variable y is the natural logarithm of the executive salaries. The Minitab stepwise regression printout is shown in Figure 32.

```
 Alpha-to-Enter: 0.15   Alpha-to-Remove: 0.15


Response is Y on 10 predictors, with N = 100


Step               1        2        3        4        5
Constant      11.091   10.968   10.783   10.278    9.962


X1            0.0278   0.0273   0.0273   0.0273   0.0273
T-Value        12.62    15.13    18.80    24.68    26.50
P-Value        0.000    0.000    0.000    0.000    0.000


X3                     0.197    0.233    0.232    0.225
T-Value                 7.10    10.17    13.30    13.74
P-Value                0.000    0.000    0.000    0.000


X4                            0.00048  0.00055  0.00052
T-Value                          7.32    10.92    11.06
P-Value                         0.000    0.000    0.000


X2                                     0.0300   0.0291
T-Value                                  8.38     8.72
P-Value                                 0.000    0.000


X5                                              0.00196
T-Value                                            3.95
P-Value                                           0.000


S              0.161    0.131    0.106   0.0807   0.0751
R-Sq           61.90    74.92    83.91    90.75    92.06
R-Sq(adj)      61.51    74.40    83.41    90.36    91.64
Mallows C-p    343.9    195.5     93.8     16.8      3.6
```

Figure 32

Minitab stepwise regression printout for executive salary data

Note that the first variable included in the model is x_1, years of experience. At the second step, x_3, a dummy variable for the qualitative variable, bonus eligibility or not, is brought into the model. In steps 3, 4, and 5, the variables x_4 (number of employees supervised), x_2 (years of education), and x_5 (corporate assets), respectively, are selected for model inclusion. Minitab stops after five steps because no other independent variables met the criterion for admission into the model. As a default, Minitab uses $\alpha = .15$ in the t-tests conducted. In other words, if the p-value associated with a β coefficient exceeds $\alpha = .15$, the variable is *not* included in the model.

The results of the stepwise regression suggest that we should concentrate on these five independent variables. Models with second-order terms and interactions should be proposed and evaluated to determine the best model for predicting executive salaries.

Now Work Exercise 113

⚠ **RECOMMENDATION** Do *not* use the stepwise regression model as the *final* model for predicting y. Recall that the stepwise procedure tends to perform a large number of t-tests, inflating the overall probability of a Type I error, and does not automatically include higher-order terms (e.g., interactions and squared terms) in the final model. Use stepwise regression as a variable screening tool when there exists a large number of potentially important independent variables. Then begin building models for y using the variables identified by stepwise.

Variable Screening and Model Building

In the previous Statistics in Action Revisited section, we used all eight of the independent variables in Table SIA1 to fit a first-order model for the cost (y) of a road construction contract awarded using the sealed-bid system. Although the model was deemed statistically useful for predicting y, the standard deviation of the model ($s = 305$ thousand dollars) was probably too large for the model to be practically useful. A more complex model—one involving higher-order terms (interactions and squared terms)—needs to be considered. A complete second-order model involving all eight of the independent variables, however, would require over 100 terms! Consequently, we'll use stepwise regression to select the best subset of independent variables and then form a complete second-order model with just these variables.

Figure SIA4 is a Minitab printout of the stepwise regression. You can see that the DOT engineer's cost estimate (DOTEST) is the first variable selected, followed by bid status (STATUS), estimated work days (DAYSEST), and bids to plan holders ratio (BTPRATIO). Recall that Minitab uses a default α level of .15. If we reduce the significance level for entry to $\alpha = .05$, only DOTEST and STATUS are selected because the p-values (highlighted on the printout) for DAYSEST and BTPRATIO are both greater than .05.

```
Alpha-to-Enter: 0.15   Alpha-to-Remove: 0.15


Response is COST on 8 predictors, with N = 235


Step              1        2        3        4
Constant       20.91   -20.54   -55.22  -212.85

DOTEST        0.9263   0.9308   0.9110   0.9132
T-Value        93.89    95.52    56.86    57.11
P-Value        0.000    0.000    0.000    0.000

STATUS                     166      167      171
T-Value                   3.38     3.40     3.50
P-Value                  0.001    0.001    0.001

DAYSEST                            0.27     0.33
T-Value                            1.55     1.85
P-Value                           0.122    0.065

BTPRATIO                                    241
T-Value                                    1.81
P-Value                                   0.072

S                313      306      305      304
R-Sq           97.42    97.55    97.57    97.60
R-Sq(adj)      97.41    97.52    97.54    97.56
Mallows C-p     15.2      5.7      5.2      4.0
```

Figure SIA4

Minitab stepwise regression for the road cost data

Because bid status is a qualitative variable ($x_2 = 1$ if fixed and 0 if competitive), a complete second-order model for contract cost (y) using DOTEST (x_1) and STATUS (x_2) is given by the equation

$$E(y) = \beta_0 + \beta_1 x_1 + \beta_2(x_1)^2 + \beta_3 x_2 + \beta_4 x_1 x_2 + \beta_5(x_1)^2 x_2$$

The Minitab printout for this model is shown in Figure SIA5. Note that the global F-test for the model is statistically significant (p-value $= .000$), and the model standard deviation, $s = 296.6$, is smaller than the standard deviation of the first-order model.

Are the second-order terms in the model, $\beta_2(x_1)^2$ and $\beta_5(x_1)^2 x_2$, necessary? If not, we can simplify the model by dropping these curvature terms. The hypothesis of interest is $H_0: \beta_2 = \beta_5 = 0$. To test this subset of β's, we compare the complete second-order model to a model without the curvilinear terms. The reduced model takes the form

$$E(y) = \beta_0 + \beta_1 x_1 + \beta_3 x_2 + \beta_4 x_1 x_2$$

```
The regression equation is
COST = - 3.0 + 0.916 DOTEST + 0.000001 DOTEST2 - 36.7 STATUS + 0.324 STA_DOT
       - 0.000036 STA_DOT2


Predictor          Coef       SE Coef       T      P
Constant          -2.98         30.89   -0.10  0.923
DOTEST          0.91553       0.02917   31.39  0.000
DOTEST2      0.00000072    0.00000340    0.21  0.833
STATUS           -36.72         74.77   -0.49  0.624
STA_DOT          0.3242        0.1192    2.72  0.007
STA_DOT2     -0.00003576    0.00002478   -1.44  0.150


S = 296.646   R-Sq = 97.7%   R-Sq(adj) = 97.7%


Analysis of Variance

Source            DF         SS          MS        F       P
Regression         5  866723202   173344640  1969.85   0.000
Residual Error   229   20151771       87999
Total            234  886874973
```

Figure SIA5

Minitab regression printout for the complete second-order model of contract cost

The results of this nested model (or partial) *F*-test are shown at the bottom of the SPSS printout, Figure SIA6. The *p*-value of the test (highlighted on the SPSS printout) is .355. Because this *p*-value is greater than $\alpha = .05$, there is insufficient evidence to reject H_0—that is, there is no evidence to indicate that the two curvature terms are useful predictors of road construction cost. Consequently, the reduced model is selected as the better predictor of cost.

Model Summary

Model	R	R Square	Adjusted R Square	Std. Error of the Estimate	R Square Change	F Change	df1	df2	Sig. F Change
					Change Statistics				
1	.988ᵃ	.977	.977	296.69515	.977	3281.312	3	231	.000
2	.989ᵇ	.977	.977	296.64238	.000	1.041	2	229	.355

a. Predictors: (Constant), STA_DOT, DOTEST, STATUS
b. Predictors: (Constant), STA_DOT, DOTEST, STATUS, DOTEST2, STA_DOT2

Figure SIA6

SPSS printout of test to compare the complete second-order model of contract cost to the reduced model

The Minitab printout for the reduced model is shown in Figure SIA7. The overall model is statistically useful (*p*-value = .000 for global *F*-test), explaining about 98% of the sample variation in contract costs. The model standard deviation, $s = 296.7$, implies that we can predict costs to within about 593 thousand dollars. Also, the *t*-test for the interaction term, $\beta_4 x_1 x_2$, is significant (*p*-value = .000), implying that the relationship between contract cost (*y*) and DOT cost estimate depends on bid status (fixed or competitive).

```
The regression equation is
COST = - 6.4 + 0.921 DOTEST + 28.7 STATUS + 0.163 STA_DOT


Predictor          Coef     SE Coef       T      P
Constant          -6.43       26.21   -0.25  0.806
DOTEST         0.921336    0.009723   94.75  0.000
STATUS           28.67       58.66    0.49  0.625
STA_DOT         0.16328     0.04043    4.04  0.000


S = 296.699   R-Sq = 97.7%   R-Sq(adj) = 97.7%


Analysis of Variance

Source            DF         SS          MS        F       P
Regression         3  866540004   288846668  3281.22   0.000
Residual Error   231   20334968       88030
Total            234  886874973
```

Figure SIA7

Minitab regression printout for the reduced model of contract cost

The nature of the interaction is illustrated in the Minitab graph of the least squares prediction equation for the reduced model, Figure SIA8. You can see that the rate of increase of contract cost (y) with the DOT engineer's estimate of cost (x_1) is steeper for fixed contracts than for competitive contracts.

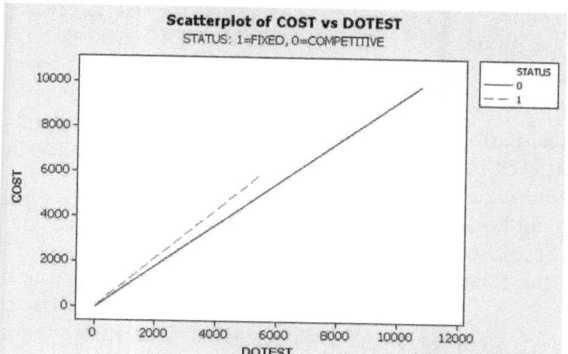

Figure SIA8

Minitab plot of least squares prediction equation for the reduced model of contract cost

Exercises 111–118

Learning the Mechanics

111 There are six independent variables, x_1, x_2, x_3, x_4, x_5, and x_6, that might be useful in predicting a response y. A total of $n = 50$ observations is available, and it is decided to employ stepwise regression to help in selecting the independent variables that appear to be useful. The software fits all possible one-variable models of the form

$$E(y) = \beta_0 + \beta_1 x_i$$

where x_i is the ith independent variable, $i = 1, 2, \ldots, 6$. The information in the table is provided from the computer printout.

Independent Variable	$\hat{\beta}_i$	$s_{\hat{\beta}_i}$
x_1	1.6	.42
x_2	−.9	.01
x_3	3.4	1.14
x_4	2.5	2.06
x_5	−4.4	.73
x_6	.3	.35

a. Which independent variable is declared the best one-variable predictor of y? Explain.

b. Would this variable be included in the model at this stage? Explain.

c. Describe the next phase that a stepwise procedure would execute.

Applying the Concepts—Basic

112 Teacher pay and pupil performance. In *Economic Policy* (January 2011), researchers from the London School of Economics conducted a cross-country analysis of the relationship between teacher's pay and pupils' performance. Data collected for 39 countries were used to model y = the country's average standardized score of its pupils. The independent variables under consideration were: x_1 = country's total teaching staff as a percentage of the country's labor force, x_2 = percentage of women on country's total teaching staff, x_3 = country's

pupil-teacher ratio, x_4 = average teacher's salary after 15 years on staff, x_5 = average teaching hours per year, x_6 = GDP growth of country (%), x_7 = country's educational spending per year, and x_8 = percentile position of country's teachers' salaries after 15 years on staff. Consider a stepwise regression run on the data.

a. What is the form of the model fit in step 1? How many models are fit? How is the "best" independent variable selected in this step?

b. What is the form of the model fit in step 2? How many models are fit? How is the "best" independent variable selected in this step?

c. What is the form of the model fit in step 3? How many models are fit? How is the "best" independent variable selected in this step?

d. The variables x_3, x_4, and x_6 were deemed the best variables for predicting y. How do you recommend the researchers proceed from here? Why?

113 Entry-level job preferences. *Benefits Quarterly* (First Quarter, 1995) published a study of entry-level job preferences. A number of independent variables were used to model the job preferences (measured on a 10-point scale) of 164 business school graduates. Suppose stepwise regression is used to build a model for job preference score (y) as a function of the following independent variables:

$$x_1 = \begin{cases} 1 & \text{if flextime position} \\ 0 & \text{if not} \end{cases}$$

$$x_2 = \begin{cases} 1 & \text{if day care support required} \\ 0 & \text{if not} \end{cases}$$

$$x_3 = \begin{cases} 1 & \text{if spousal transfer support required} \\ 0 & \text{if not} \end{cases}$$

x_4 = Number of sick days allowed

$$x_5 = \begin{cases} 1 & \text{if applicant married} \\ 0 & \text{if not} \end{cases}$$

x_6 = Number of children of applicant

$$x_7 = \begin{cases} 1 & \text{if male applicant} \\ 0 & \text{if female applicant} \end{cases}$$

a. How many models are fit to the data in step 1? Give the general form of these models.

b. How many models are fit to the data in step 2? Give the general form of these models.

c. How many models are fit to the data in step 3? Give the general form of these models.

d. Explain how the procedure determines when to stop adding independent variables to the model.

e. Describe two major drawbacks to using the final stepwise model as the best model for job preference score y.

114 Accuracy of software effort estimates. Periodically, software engineers must provide estimates of their effort in developing new software. In the *Journal of Empirical Software Engineering* (Vol. 9, 2004), multiple regression was used to predict the accuracy of these effort estimates. The dependent variable, defined as the relative error in estimating effort,

$$y = (\text{Actual effort} - \text{Estimated effort})/(\text{Actual effort})$$

was determined for each in a sample of $n = 49$ software development tasks. Eight independent variables were evaluated as potential predictors of relative error using stepwise regression. Each of these was formulated as a dummy variable, as shown in the table.

Company role of estimator:	$x_1 = 1$ if developer, 0 if project leader
Task complexity:	$x_2 = 1$ if low, 0 if medium/high
Contract type:	$x_3 = 1$ if fixed price, 0 if hourly rate
Customer importance:	$x_4 = 1$ if high, 0 if low/medium
Customer priority:	$x_5 = 1$ if time of delivery, 0 if cost or quality
Level of knowledge:	$x_6 = 1$ if high, 0 if low/medium
Participation:	$x_7 = 1$ if estimator participates in work, 0 if not
Previous accuracy:	$x_8 = 1$ if more than 20% accurate, 0 if less than 20% accurate

a. In step 1 of the stepwise regression, how many different one-variable models are fit to the data?

b. In step 1, the variable x_1 is selected as the best one-variable predictor. How is this determined?

c. In step 2 of the stepwise regression, how many different two-variable models (where x_1 is one of the variables) are fit to the data?

d. The only two variables selected for entry into the stepwise regression model were x_1 and x_8. The stepwise regression yielded the following prediction equation:

$$\hat{y} = .12 - .28x_1 + .27x_8$$

Give a practical interpretation of the β estimates multiplied by x_1 and x_8.

e. Why should a researcher be wary of using the model, part **d,** as the final model for predicting effort (y)?

Applying the Concepts — Intermediate

115 Diet of ducks bred for broiling. Corn is high in starch content; consequently, it is considered excellent feed for domestic chickens. Does corn possess the same potential in feeding ducks bred for broiling? This was the

subject of research published in *Animal Feed Science and Technology* (April 2010). The objective of the study was to establish a prediction model for the true metabolizable energy (TME) of corn regurgitated from ducks. The researchers considered 11 potential predictors of TME: dry matter (DM), crude protein (CP), ether extract (EE), ash (ASH), crude fiber (CF), neutral detergent fiber (NDF), acid detergent fiber (ADF), gross energy (GE), amylose (AM), amylopectin (AP), and amylopectin/amylose (AMAP). Stepwise regression was used to find the best subset of predictors. The final stepwise model yielded the following results:

$$\widehat{TME} = 7.70 + 2.14(\text{AMAP}) + .16(\text{NDF}), R^2 = .988,$$
$$s = .07, \text{Global } F \text{ } p\text{-value} = .001$$

a. Determine the number of t-tests performed in step 1 of the stepwise regression.

b. Determine the number of t-tests performed in step 2 of the stepwise regression.

c. Give a full interpretation of the final stepwise model regression results.

d. Explain why it is dangerous to use the final stepwise model as the "best" model for predicting TME.

e. Using the independent variables selected by the stepwise routine, write a complete second-order model for TME.

f. Refer to part **e.** How would you determine if the terms in the model that allow for curvature are statistically useful for predicting TME?

116 Reality TV and cosmetic surgery. Refer to the *Body Image: An International Journal of Research* (March 2010) study of the influence of reality TV shows on one's desire to undergo cosmetic surgery, Exercise 17. Recall that psychologists modeled desire to have cosmetic surgery (y) as a function of gender (x_1), self-esteem (x_2), body satisfaction (x_3), and impression of reality TV (x_4). Suppose you want to determine which subset of these four independent variables is best for predicting one's desire to have cosmetic surgery. Consequently, you will run a stepwise regression.

a. In step 1 of the stepwise regression, how many t-tests will be performed?

b. In step 2 of the stepwise regression, how many t-tests will be performed?

c. Access the data saved in the file and run the stepwise regression. Which independent variables comprise the best subset of variables for predicting one's desire to have cosmetic surgery?

d. Do you recommend using the resulting stepwise regression model for predicting one's desire to have cosmetic surgery or do you recommend further analysis? Explain your reasoning.

117 Bus Rapid Transit study. Bus Rapid Transit (BRT) is a rapidly growing trend in the provision of public transportation in America. The Center for Urban Transportation Research (CUTR) at the University of South Florida conducted a survey of BRT customers in Miami (*Transportation Research Board* Annual Meeting, Jan. 2003). Data on the following variables (all measured on a 5-point scale, where 1 = very unsatisfied and 5 = very satisfied) were collected for a sample of over 500 bus riders: overall satisfaction with BRT (y), safety on bus (x_1), seat availability (x_2), dependability (x_3), travel time (x_4), cost (x_5), information/maps (x_6), convenience of routes (x_7), traffic signals (x_8), safety at bus stops (x_9), hours of service (x_{10}), and frequency of service (x_{11}). CUTR analysts used stepwise regression to model overall satisfaction (y).

a. How many models are fit at step 1 of the stepwise regression?

b. How many models are fit at step 2 of the stepwise regression?

c. How many models are fit at step 11 of the stepwise regression?

d. The stepwise regression selected the following eight variables to include in the model (in order of selection): $x_{11}, x_4, x_2, x_7, x_{10}, x_1, x_9,$ and x_3. Write the equation for $E(y)$ that results from stepwise regression.

e. The model, part **d**, resulted in $R^2 = .677$. Interpret this value.

f. Explain why the CUTR analysts should be cautious in concluding that the best model for $E(y)$ has been found.

118 Adverse effects of hot-water runoff. A marine biologist was hired by the EPA to determine whether the hot-water runoff from a particular power plant located near a large gulf is having an adverse effect on the marine life in the area. The biologist's goal is to acquire a prediction equation for the number of marine animals located at certain designated areas, or stations, in the gulf. Based on past experience, the EPA considered the following environmental factors as predictors for the number of animals at a particular station:

x_1 = Temperature of water (TEMP)

x_2 = Salinity of water (SAL)

x_3 = Dissolved oxygen content of water (DO)

x_4 = Turbidity index, a measure of the turbidity of the water (TI)

x_5 = Depth of the water at the station (ST_DEPTH)

x_6 = Total weight of sea grasses in sampled area (TGRSWT)

As a preliminary step in the construction of this model, the biologist used a stepwise regression procedure to identify the most important of these six variables. A total of 716 samples were taken at different stations in the gulf, producing the SPSS printout shown below. (The response measured was y, the logarithm of the number of marine animals found in the sampled area.)

a. According to the SPSS printout, which of the six independent variables should be used in the model? (Use $\alpha = .10$.)

b. Are we able to assume that the marine biologist has identified all the important independent variables for the prediction of y? Why?

c. Using the variables identified in part **a**, write the first-order model with interaction that may be used to predict y.

d. How would the marine biologist determine whether the model specified in part **c** is better than the first-order model?

e. Note the small value of R^2. What action might the biologist take to improve the model?

Variables Entered/Removed[a]

Model	Variables Entered	Variables Removed	Method
1	ST_DEPTH	.	Stepwise (Criteria: Probability-of-F-to-enter <= .050, Probability-of-F-to-remove >= .100).
2	TGRSWT	.	Stepwise (Criteria: Probability-of-F-to-enter <= .050, Probability-of-F-to-remove >= .100).
3	TI	.	Stepwise (Criteria: Probability-of-F-to-enter <= .050, Probability-of-F-to-remove >= .100).

a. Dependent Variable: LOGNUM

Model Summary

Model	R	R Square	Adjusted R Square	Std. Error of the Estimate
1	.329[a]	.122	.121	.7615773
2	.427[b]	.182	.180	.7348470
3	.432[c]	.187	.184	.7348469

a. Predictors: (Constant), ST_DEPTH

b. Predictors: (Constant), ST_DEPTH, TGRSWT

c. Predictors: (Constant), ST_DEPTH, TGRSWT, TI

PART III: MULTIPLE REGRESSION DIAGNOSTICS

11 Residual Analysis: Checking the Regression Assumptions

When we apply regression analysis to a set of data, we never know for certain whether the assumptions of Section 1 are satisfied. How far can we deviate from the assumptions and still expect regression analysis to yield results that will have the reliability stated in this chapter? How can we detect departures (if they exist) from the assumptions, and what can we do about them? We provide some answers to these questions in this section.

Recall from Section 1 that for any given set of values of $x_1, x_2, \ldots, x_k$, we assume that the random error term ε has the following properties:

1. mean equal to 0
2. constant variance (σ^2)
3. normal probability distribution
4. probabilistically independent

It is unlikely that these assumptions are ever satisfied exactly in a practical application of regression analysis. Fortunately, experience has shown that least squares regression analysis produces reliable statistical tests, confidence intervals, and prediction intervals as long as the departures from the assumptions are not too great. In this section, we present some methods for determining whether the data indicate significant departures from the assumptions.

Because the assumptions all concern the random error component, ε, of the model, the first step is to estimate the random error. Because the actual random error associated with a particular value of y is the difference between the actual y value and its unknown mean, we estimate the error by the difference between the actual y-value and the *estimated* mean. This estimated error is called the *regression residual*, or simply the **residual,** and is denoted by $\hat{\varepsilon}$. The actual error ε and residual $\hat{\varepsilon}$ are shown in Figure 33.

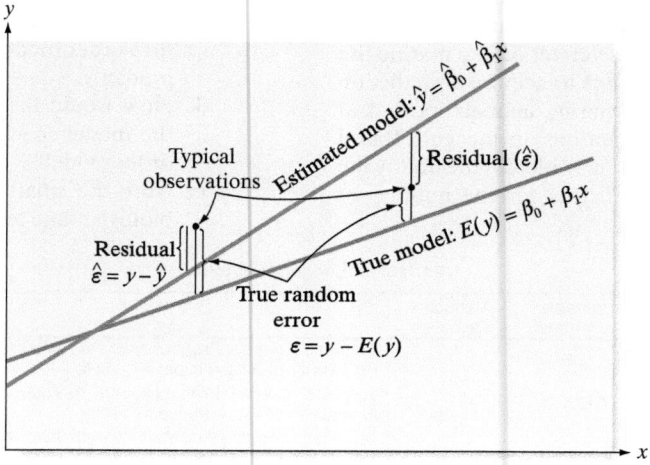

Figure 33

Actual random error ε and regression residual $\hat{\varepsilon}$

A **regression residual,** $\hat{\varepsilon}$, is defined as the difference between an observed y value and its corresponding predicted value:

$$\hat{\varepsilon} = (y - \hat{y}) = y - (\hat{\beta}_0 + \hat{\beta}_1 x_1 + \hat{\beta}_2 x_2 + \cdots + \hat{\beta}_k x_k)$$

Because the true mean of y (that is, the true regression model) is not known, the actual random error cannot be calculated. However, because the residual is based on the estimated mean (the least squares regression model), it can be calculated and used to estimate the random error and to check the regression assumptions. Such checks are generally referred to as **residual analyses.** Two useful properties of residuals are given in the next box.

Properties of Regression Residuals

1. The mean of the residuals is equal to 0. This property follows from the fact that the sum of the differences between the observed y values and their least squares predicted $\hat{y}$ values is equal to 0.

$$\sum (\text{Residuals}) = \sum (y - \hat{y}) = 0$$

2. The standard deviation of the residuals is equal to the standard deviation of the fitted regression model, s. This property follows from the fact that the sum of the squared residuals is equal to SSE, which when divided by the error degrees of freedom is equal to the variance of the fitted regression model, s^2. The square root of the variance is both the standard deviation of the residuals and the standard deviation of the regression model.

$$\sum (\text{Residuals})^2 = \sum (y - \hat{y})^2 = \text{SSE}$$

$$s = \sqrt{\frac{\sum (\text{Residuals})^2}{n - (k + 1)}} = \sqrt{\frac{\text{SSE}}{n - (k + 1)}}$$

BIOGRAPHY

FRANCIS J. ANSCOMBE (1918–2001)
Anscombe's Data

British citizen Frank Anscombe grew up in a small town near the English Channel. He attended Trinity College in Cambridge, England, on a merit scholarship, graduating with first class honors in mathematics in 1939. He later earned his master's degree in 1943. During World War II, Anscombe worked for the British Ministry of Supply, developing a mathematical solution for aiming antiaircraft rockets at German bombers and buzz bombs. Following the war, Anscombe worked at the Rothamsted Experimental Station, applying statistics to agriculture. There, he formed his appreciation for solving problems with social relevance. During his career as a professor of statistics, Anscombe served on the faculty of Cambridge, Princeton, and Yale universities. He was a pioneer in the application of computers to statistical analysis and was one of the original developers of residual analysis in regression. Anscombe is famous for a paper he wrote in 1973, in which he showed that one regression model could be fit by four very different data sets ("Anscombe's data"). While Anscombe published 50 research articles on statistics, he also had serious interests in classical music, poetry, and art.

The following examples show how a graphical analysis of regression residuals can be used to verify the assumptions associated with the model and to support improvements to the model when the assumptions do not appear to be satisfied. We rely on statistical software to generate the appropriate graphs in the examples and exercises.

Checking Assumption #1: Mean $\varepsilon = 0$

First, we demonstrate how a residual plot can detect a model in which the hypothesized relationship between $E(y)$ and an independent variable x is misspecified. The assumption of mean error of 0 is violated in these types of models.*

Example 14

Analyzing Residuals—Electrical Usage Model

Problem Refer to the problem of modeling the relationship between home size (x) and electrical usage (y) in Example 7. The data for $n = 15$ homes are repeated in Table 6. Minitab printouts for a straight-line model and a quadratic model fitted to the data are shown in Figures 34a and 34b, respectively. The residuals from these models are highlighted in the printouts. The residuals are then plotted on the vertical axis against the variable x, size of home, on the horizontal axis in Figures 35a and 35b, respectively.

a. Verify that each residual is equal to the difference between the observed y value and the estimated mean value, $\hat{y}$.

b. Analyze the residual plots.

---

*For a misspecified model, the hypothesized mean of y, denoted by $E_h(y)$, will not equal the true mean of y, $E(y)$. Because $y = E_h(y) + \varepsilon$, then $\varepsilon = y - E_h(y)$ and $E(\varepsilon) = E[y - E_h(y)] = E(y) - E_h(y) \neq 0$.

Table 6	Home Size–Electrical Usage Data
Size of Home, x (sq. ft.)	Monthly Usage, y (kilowatt-hours)
1,290	1,182
1,350	1,172
1,470	1,264
1,600	1,493
1,710	1,571
1,840	1,711
1,980	1,804
2,230	1,840
2,400	1,956
2,710	2,007
2,930	1,984
3,000	1,960
3,210	2,001
3,240	1,928
3,520	1,945

Solution

a. For the straight-line model, the residual is calculated for the first y value as follows:

$$\hat{\varepsilon} = (y - \hat{y}) = 1{,}182 - 1{,}362.2 = -180.2$$

where $\hat{y}$ is the first number in the column labeled **Fit** on the Minitab printout in Figure 34a. Similarly, the residual for the first y value using the quadratic model (Figure 34b) is

$$\hat{\varepsilon} = 1{,}182 - 1{,}157.2 = 24.8$$

Both residuals agree with the first values given in the column labeled **Residual** in Figures 34a and 34b, respectively. Although the residuals both correspond to the same observed y value, 1,182, they differ because the predicted mean value changes depending on whether the straight-line model or quadratic model is used. Similar calculations produce the remaining residuals.

Regression Analysis: USAGE versus SIZE

```
The regression equation is
USAGE = 903 + 0.356 SIZE

Predictor      Coef   SE Coef     T       P
Constant      903.0     132.1   6.83   0.000
SIZE        0.35594   0.05477   6.50   0.000

S = 155.251    R-Sq = 76.5%    R-Sq(adj) = 74.7%

Analysis of Variance

Source           DF        SS        MS       F       P
Regression        1   1017803   1017803   42.23   0.000
Residual Error   13    313338     24103
Total            14   1331140

Obs   SIZE   USAGE     Fit   SE Fit   Residual   St Resid
  1   1290  1182.0  1362.2    68.3     -180.2      -1.29
  2   1350  1172.0  1383.5    65.6     -211.5      -1.50
  3   1470  1264.0  1426.2    60.6     -162.2      -1.13
  4   1600  1493.0  1472.5    55.4       20.5       0.14
  5   1710  1571.0  1511.7    51.4       59.3       0.41
  6   1840  1711.0  1557.9    47.3      153.1       1.04
  7   1980  1804.0  1607.8    43.7      196.2       1.32
  8   2230  1840.0  1696.8    40.3      143.2       0.96
  9   2400  1956.0  1757.3    40.5      198.7       1.33
 10   2710  2007.0  1867.6    46.0      139.4       0.94
 11   2930  1984.0  1945.9    52.9       38.1       0.26
 12   3000  1960.0  1970.8    55.5      -10.8      -0.07
 13   3210  2001.0  2045.6    64.0      -44.6      -0.32
 14   3240  1928.0  2056.3    65.3     -128.3      -0.91
 15   3520  1945.0  2155.9    78.0     -210.9      -1.57
```

Figure 34a

Minitab printout for straight-line model of electrical usage

Regression Analysis: USAGE versus SIZE, SIZESQ

```
The regression equation is
USAGE = - 807 + 1.96 SIZE - 0.000340 SIZESQ

Predictor          Coef      SE Coef       T       P
Constant          -806.7       166.9    -4.83   0.000
SIZE             1.9616        0.1525   12.86   0.000
SIZESQ        -0.00034044  0.00003212  -10.60   0.000

S = 50.1998    R-Sq = 97.7%    R-Sq(adj) = 97.3%

Analysis of Variance

Source          DF       SS       MS       F       P
Regression       2  1300900   650450  258.11   0.000
Residual Error  12    30240     2520
Total           14  1331140

Obs  SIZE   USAGE     Fit  SE Fit  Residual  St Resid
  1  1290  1182.0  1157.2    29.3      24.8      0.61
  2  1350  1172.0  1221.0    26.2     -49.0     -1.14
  3  1470  1264.0  1341.2    21.2     -77.2     -1.70
  4  1600  1493.0  1460.3    18.0      32.7      0.70
  5  1710  1571.0  1552.2    17.1      18.8      0.40
  6  1840  1711.0  1650.1    17.6      60.9      1.30
  7  1980  1804.0  1742.6    19.0      61.4      1.32
  8  2230  1840.0  1874.7    21.2     -34.7     -0.76
  9  2400  1956.0  1940.2    21.7      15.8      0.35
 10  2710  2007.0  2009.0    20.0      -2.0     -0.04
 11  2930  1984.0  2018.2    18.4     -34.2     -0.73
 12  3000  1960.0  2014.1    18.4     -54.1     -1.16
 13  3210  2001.0  1982.1    21.5      18.9      0.42
 14  3240  1928.0  1975.1    22.5     -47.1     -1.05
 15  3520  1945.0  1880.0    36.2      65.0      1.87
```

Figure 34b

Minitab printout for quadratic model of electrical usage

b. The Minitab plot of the residuals for the straight-line model (Figure 35a) reveals a nonrandom pattern. The residuals exhibit a curved shape, with the residuals for the small values of x below the horizontal 0 (mean of the residuals) line, the residuals corresponding to the middle values of x above the 0 line, and the residuals for the largest values of x again below the 0 line. The indication is that the mean value of the random error ε *within* each of these ranges of x (small, medium, large) may not be equal to 0. Such a pattern usually indicates that curvature needs to be added to the model.

When the second-order term is added to the model, the nonrandom pattern disappears. In Figure 35b, the residuals appear to be randomly distributed around the 0 line, as expected. Note, too, that the residuals on the quadratic residual plot vary between -75 and 50, compared to between -200 and 200 on the straight-line plot. In fact, $s \approx 50$ for the quadratic model is much smaller than $s \approx 155$ for the straight-line model. The implication is that the quadratic model provides a considerably better model for predicting electrical usage.

Figure 35a

Minitab residual plot for straight-line model of electrical usage

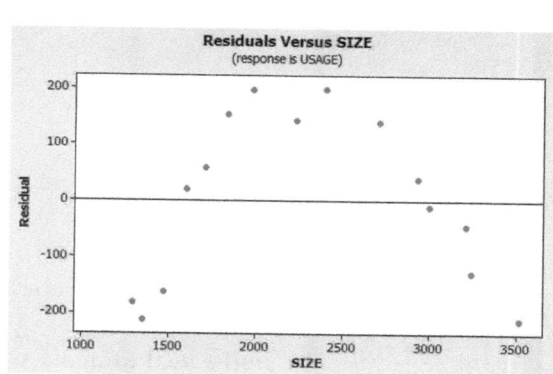

775

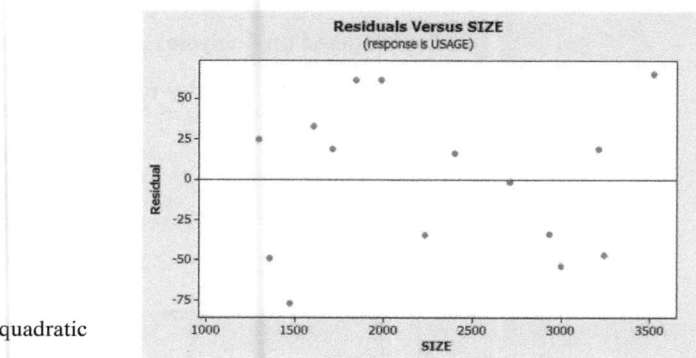

Figure 35b

Minitab residual plot for quadratic model of electrical usage

Look Back The residual analysis verifies our conclusions from Example 7, where we found the t-test for the quadratic term, $\beta_2 x^2$, to be statistically significant.

Now Work Exercise 120a

Checking Assumption #2: Constant Error Variance

Residual plots can also be used to detect violations of the assumption of constant error variance. For example, a plot of the residuals versus the predicted value $\hat{y}$ may display one of the patterns shown in Figure 36. In these figures, the range in values of the residuals increases (or decreases) as $\hat{y}$ increases, thus indicating that the variance of the random error, ε, becomes larger (or smaller) as the estimate of $E(y)$ increases in value. Because $E(y)$ depends on the x values in the model, this implies that the variance of ε is not constant for all settings of the x's.

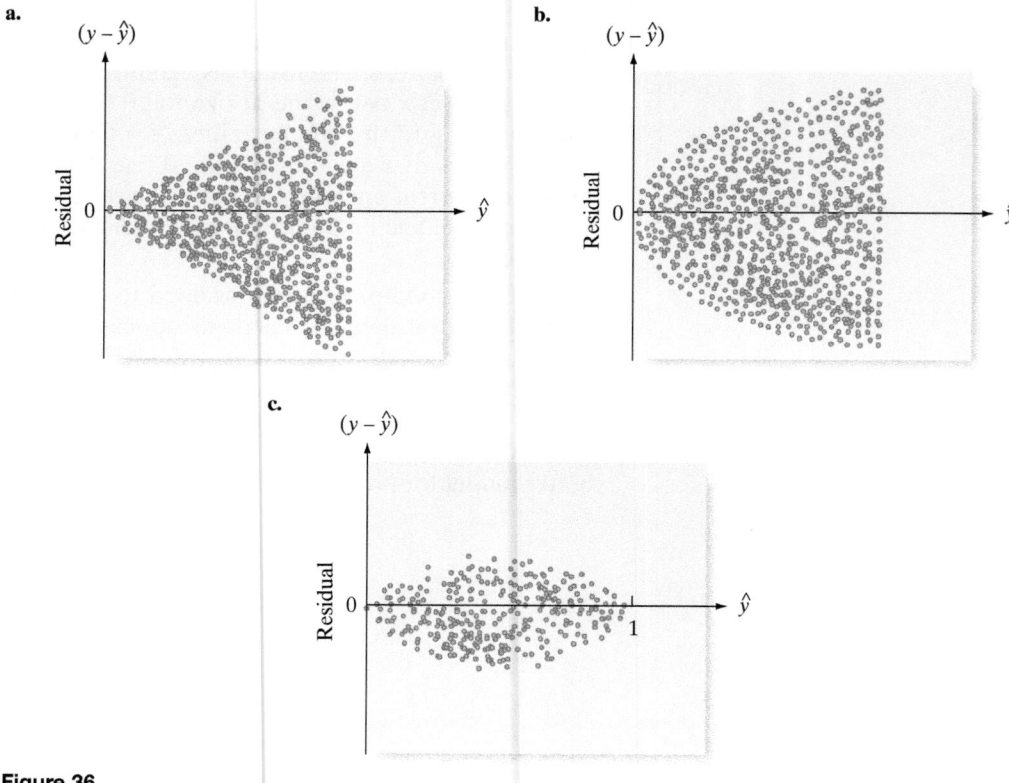

Figure 36

Residual plots showing changes in the variance of ε

In the next example, we demonstrate how to use this plot to detect a nonconstant variance and suggest a useful remedy.

Example 15

Using Residuals to Check Equal Variances—Social Workers' Salaries

Problem The data in Table 7 are the salaries, y, and years of experience, x, for a sample of 50 social workers. The first-order model $E(y) = \beta_0 + \beta_1 x$ was fitted to the data using SPSS. The SPSS printout is shown in Figure 37, followed by a plot of the residuals versus $\hat{y}$ in Figure 38. Interpret the results. Make model modifications, if necessary.

Solution The SPSS printout, Figure 37, suggests that the first-order model provides an adequate fit to the data. The R^2-value indicates that the model explains 78.7% of the sample variation in salaries. The t-value for testing β_1, 13.31, is highly significant (p-value ≈ 0) and indicates that the model contributes information for the prediction of y. However, an examination of the residuals plotted against $\hat{y}$ (Figure 38) reveals a

Table 7	Salary Data for Example 15				
Years of Experience, x	Salary, y	Years of Experience, x	Salary, y	Years of Experience, x	Salary, y
7	$26,075	21	$43,628	28	$99,139
28	79,370	4	16,105	23	52,624
23	65,726	24	65,644	17	50,594
18	41,983	20	63,022	25	53,272
19	62,308	20	47,780	26	65,343
15	41,154	15	38,853	19	46,216
24	53,610	25	66,537	16	54,288
13	33,697	25	67,447	3	20,844
2	22,444	28	64,785	12	32,586
8	32,562	26	61,581	23	71,235
20	43,076	27	70,678	20	36,530
21	56,000	20	51,301	19	52,745
18	58,667	18	39,346	27	67,282
7	22,210	1	24,833	25	80,931
2	20,521	26	65,929	12	32,303
18	49,727	20	41,721	11	38,371
11	33,233	26	82,641		

Data Set: SOCIAL

Model Summary[b]

Model	R	R Square	Adjusted R Square	Std. Error of the Estimate
1	.887[a]	.787	.782	8642.441

a. Predictors: (Constant), ESP
b. Dependent Variable: SALARY

ANOVA[b]

Model		Sum of Squares	df	Mean Square	F	Sig.
1	Regression	1.3E+10	1	1.324E+10	177.257	.000[a]
	Residual	3.6E+09	48	74691793.28		
	Total	1.7E+10	49			

a. Predictors: (Constant), ESP
b. Dependent Variable: SALARY

Coefficients[a]

Model		Unstandardized Coefficients		Standardized Coefficients	t	Sig.
		B	Std. Error	Beta		
1	(Constant)	11368.72	3160.317		3.597	.001
	ESP	2141.381	160.839	.887	13.314	.000

a. Dependent Variable: SALARY

Figure 37

SPSS regression printout for first-order model of salary

potential problem. Note the "cone" shape of the residual variability; the size of the residuals increases as the estimated mean salary increases, implying that the constant variance assumption is violated.

One way to stabilize the variance of ε is to refit the model using a transformation on the dependent variable y. With economic data (e.g., salaries), a useful **variance-stabilizing transformation** is the natural logarithm of y, denoted $\ln(y)$.* We fit the model

$$\ln(y) = \beta_0 + \beta_1 x + \varepsilon$$

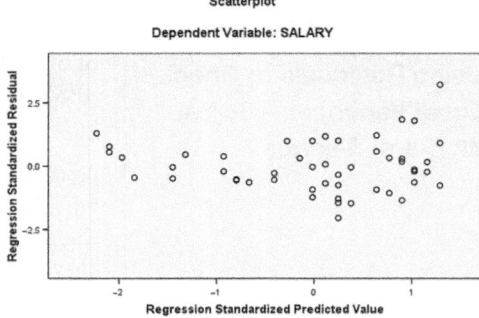

Figure 38

SPSS residual plot for first-order model of salary

to the data of Table 7. Figure 39 shows the SPSS regression analysis printout for the $n = 50$ measurements, while Figure 40 shows a plot of the residuals from the log model.

Model Summary[b]

Model	R	R Square	Adjusted R Square	Std. Error of the Estimate
1	.929[a]	.864	.861	.1541127

a. Predictors: (Constant), ESP

b. Dependent Variable: LNSALARY

ANOVA[b]

Model		Sum of Squares	df	Mean Square	F	Sig.
1	Regression	7.212	1	7.212	303.660	.000[a]
	Residual	1.140	48	.024		
	Total	8.352	49			

a. Predictors: (Constant), ESP

b. Dependent Variable: LNSALARY

Figure 39

SPSS regression printout for model of log salary

Coefficients[a]

Model		Unstandardized Coefficients		Standardized Coefficients		
		B	Std. Error	Beta	t	Sig.
1	(Constant)	9.841	.056		174.631	.000
	ESP	.050	.003	.929	17.426	.000

a. Dependent Variable: LNSALARY

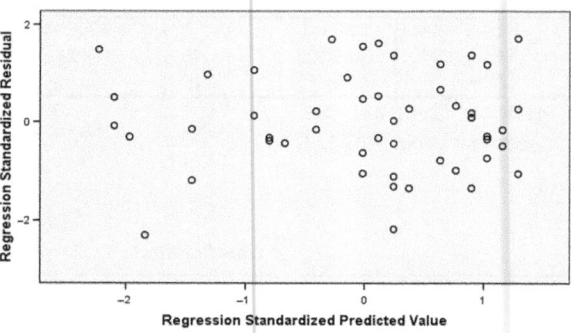

Figure 40

SPSS residual plot for model of ln(salary)

*Other variance-stabilizing transformations that are used successfully in practice are $\sqrt{y}$ and $\sin^{-1}\sqrt{y}$. Consult the references for more details on these transformations.

You can see that the logarithmic transformation has stabilized the error variances. Note that the cone shape is gone; there is no apparent tendency of the residual variance to increase as mean salary increases. We therefore are confident that inferences using the $\ln(y)$ model are more reliable than those using the untransformed model.

Look Back With transformed models, the analyst should be wary when interpreting model statistics such as $\hat{\beta}_1$ and s. These interpretations must take into account that the dependent variable is not some function of y. For example, the antilogarithm of $\hat{\beta}_1$ in the $\ln(y)$ model for salary (y) represents the percentage change in salary for every 1 year increase in experience (x).

■   **Now Work Exercise 120b**

Checking Assumption #3: Errors Normally Distributed

Several graphical methods are available for assessing whether the random error ε has an approximate normal distribution. Recall that stem-and-leaf displays, histograms, and normal probability plots are useful for checking whether the data are normally distributed. We illustrate these techniques in an example. But first, we discuss a related problem—using residuals to check for *outliers*.

If the assumption of normally distributed errors is satisfied, then we expect approximately 95% of the residuals to fall within 2 standard deviations of the mean of 0, and almost all of the residuals to lie within 3 standard deviations of the mean of 0. Residuals that are extremely far from 0 and disconnected from the bulk of the other residuals are called **regression outliers** and should receive special attention from the analyst.

> A **regression outlier** is a residual that is larger than $3s$ (in absolute value).

Example 16

Identifying Outliers— Grandfather Clock Price Model

Problem Refer to Example 6 in which we modeled the auction price (y) of a grandfather clock as a function of age (x_1) and number of bidders (x_2). The data for this example are repeated in Table 8, with one important difference: The auction price of the clock at the top of the sixth column has been changed from \$2,131 to \$1,131 (highlighted in Table 8). The interaction model

$$E(y) = \beta_0 + \beta_1 x_1 + \beta_2 x_2 + \beta_3 x_1 x_2$$

is again fit to these (modified) data, with the Minitab printout shown in Figure 41. The residuals are shown highlighted in the printout and then plotted against the number of bidders, x_2, in Figure 42. Analyze the residual plot.

Table 8	Altered Auction Price Data				
Age, x_1 (years)	Number of Bidders, x_2	Auction Price, y (\$)	Age, x_1 (years)	Number of Bidders, x_2	Auction Price, y (\$)
127	13	1,235	170	14	1,131
115	12	1,080	182	8	1,550
127	7	845	162	11	1,884
150	9	1,522	184	10	2,041
156	6	1,047	143	6	845
182	11	1,979	159	9	1,483
156	12	1,822	108	14	1,055
132	10	1,253	175	8	1,545
137	9	1,297	108	6	729
113	9	946	179	9	1,792
137	15	1,713	111	15	1,175
117	11	1,024	187	8	1,593
137	8	1,147	111	7	785
153	6	1,092	115	7	744
117	13	1,152	194	5	1,356
126	10	1,336	168	7	1,262

Data Set: CLOCK2

```
The regression equation is
PRICE = - 513 + 8.17 AGE + 19.9 NUMBIDS + 0.320 AGE_BIDS


Predictor      Coef   SE Coef       T      P
Constant     -512.8     665.9   -0.77  0.448
AGE           8.165     4.585    1.78  0.086
NUMBIDS       19.89     67.44    0.29  0.770
AGE_BIDS     0.3196    0.4790    0.67  0.510


S = 200.598   R-Sq = 72.9%   R-Sq(adj) = 70.0%


Analysis of Variance

Source           DF        SS       MS      F      P
Regression        3   3033587  1011196  25.13  0.000
Residual Error   28   1126703    40239
Total            31   4160290

Obs  AGE    PRICE      Fit   SE Fit   Residual   St Resid
  1  127   1235.0   1310.4     59.3      -75.4      -0.39
  2  115   1080.0   1105.9     62.1      -25.9      -0.14
  3  127    845.0    947.5     61.1     -102.5      -0.54
  4  150   1522.0   1322.5     37.1      199.5       1.01
  5  156   1047.0   1179.5     60.3     -132.5      -0.69
  6  182   1979.0   1831.9     82.9      147.1       0.81
  7  156   1822.0   1598.0     61.9      224.0       1.17
  8  132   1253.0   1185.8     39.7       67.2       0.34
  9  137   1297.0   1178.9     39.0      118.1       0.60
 10  113    946.0    913.9     58.6       32.1       0.17
 11  137   1713.0   1561.0     78.4      152.0       0.82
 12  117   1024.0   1072.6     53.1      -48.6      -0.25
 13  137   1147.0   1115.2     44.3       31.8       0.16
 14  153   1092.0   1149.2     59.0      -57.2      -0.30
 15  117   1152.0   1187.2     69.7      -35.2      -0.19
 16  126   1336.0   1117.6     43.4      218.4       1.12
 17  170   1131.0   1914.4    116.7     -783.4      -4.80R
 18  182   1550.0   1597.7     62.8      -47.7      -0.25
 19  162   1884.0   1598.3     57.0      285.7       1.49
 20  184   2041.0   1776.6     70.7      264.4       1.41
 21  143    845.0   1048.4     58.9     -203.4      -1.06
 22  159   1483.0   1421.8     40.6       61.2       0.31
 23  108   1055.0   1130.7     97.9      -75.7      -0.43
 24  175   1545.0   1522.7     55.4       22.3       0.12
 25  108    729.0    695.5     99.6       33.5       0.19
 26  179   1792.0   1642.7     57.6      149.3       0.78
 27  111   1175.0   1224.0    107.2      -49.0      -0.29
 28  187   1593.0   1651.3     68.6      -58.3      -0.31
 29  111    785.0    781.1     80.9        3.9       0.02
 30  115    744.0    822.7     75.5      -78.7      -0.42
 31  194   1356.0   1480.7    133.6     -124.7      -0.83 X
 32  168   1262.0   1374.0     57.7     -112.0      -0.58
```

R denotes an observation with a large standardized residual.
X denotes an observation whose X value gives it large influence.

Figure 41

Minitab regression printout for altered grandfather clock data

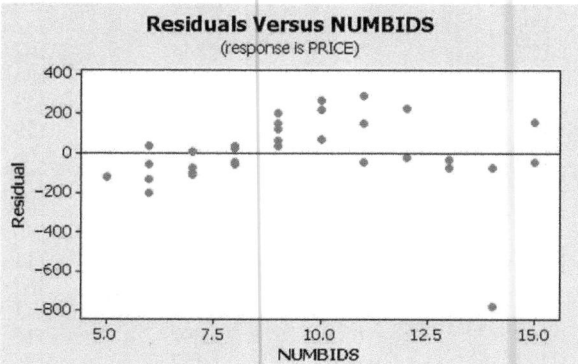

Figure 42

Minitab residual plot for altered grandfather clock data

Solution The residual plot dramatically reveals the one altered measurement. Note that one of the two residuals at $x_2 = 14$ bidders falls more than 3 standard deviations below 0. (This observation is highlighted on Figure 41.) Note that no other residual falls more than 2 standard deviations from 0.

What do we do with outliers once we identify them? First, we try to determine the cause. Were the data entered into the computer incorrectly? Was the observation recorded incorrectly when the data were collected? If so, we correct the observation and rerun the analysis. Another possibility is that the observation is not representative of the conditions we are trying to model. For example, in this case the low price may be attributable to extreme damage to the clock or to a clock of inferior quality compared to the others. In these cases, we probably would exclude the observation from the analysis. In many cases, you may not be able to determine the cause of the outlier. Even so, you may want to rerun the regression analysis excluding the outlier in order to assess the effect of that observation on the results of the analysis.

Figure 43 shows the printout when the outlier observation is excluded from the grandfather clock analysis, and Figure 44 shows the new plot of the residuals against the number of bidders. Now only one of the residuals lies beyond 2 standard deviations from 0, and none of them lies beyond 3 standard deviations. Also, the model statistics indicate a much better model without the outlier. Most notably, the s has decreased from 200.6 to 85.83, indicating a model that will provide more precise estimates and predictions (narrower confidence and prediction intervals) for clocks that are similar to those in the reduced sample.

```
The regression equation is
PRICE = 474 - 0.46 AGE - 114 NUMBIDS + 1.48 AGE_BIDS


Predictor      Coef    SE Coef      T      P
Constant      474.0      298.2    1.59  0.124
AGE          -0.465      2.107   -0.22  0.827
NUMBIDS     -114.12      31.23   -3.65  0.001
AGE_BIDS     1.4781     0.2295    6.44  0.000


S = 85.8286    R-Sq = 95.2%    R-Sq(adj) = 94.7%


Analysis of Variance

Source           DF        SS        MS       F      P
Regression        3   3933417   1311139  177.99  0.000
Residual Error   27    198897      7367
Total            30   4132314
```

Figure 43

Minitab regression printout when outlier is deleted

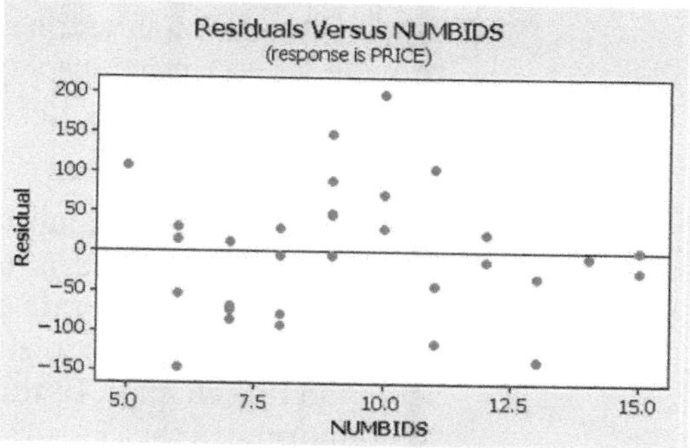

Figure 44

Minitab residual plot when outlier is deleted

ETHICS in STATISTICS

Removing observations from a sample data set for the sole purpose of improving the fit of a regression model without investigating whether the observations are outliers or legitimate data points is considered *unethical statististical practice*.

Look Back Remember that if the outlier is removed from the analysis when in fact it belongs to the same population as the rest of the sample, the resulting model may provide misleading estimates and predictions.

Now Work Exercise 120c

The next example checks the assumption of the normality of the random error component.

<table>
<tr><td>

Example 17

Using Residuals to Check for Normal Errors— Grandfather Clock Prices

</td><td>

Problem Refer to Example 16. Analyze the distribution of the residuals in the grandfather clock example, both before and after the outlier residual is removed. Determine whether the assumption of a normally distributed error term is reasonable.

Solution A histogram and normal probability plot for the two sets of residuals are constructed using Minitab and are shown in Figures 45 and 46. Note that the outlier appears to skew the histogram in Figure 45, whereas the histogram in Figure 46 appears to be more mound-shaped. Similarly, the pattern of residuals in the normal probability plot in Figure 46 (outlier deleted) is more nearly a straight line than the pattern in Figure 45 (outlier included). Thus, the normality assumption appears to be more plausible after the outlier is removed.

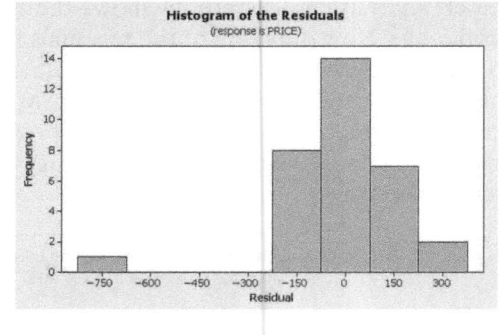

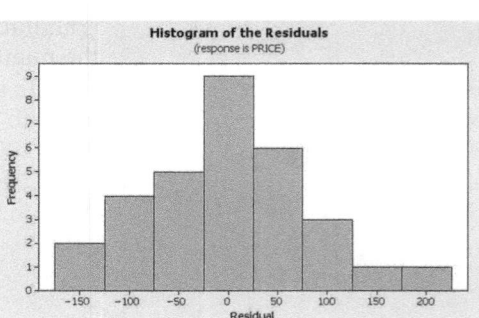

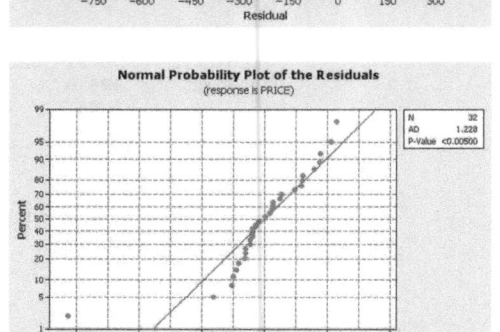

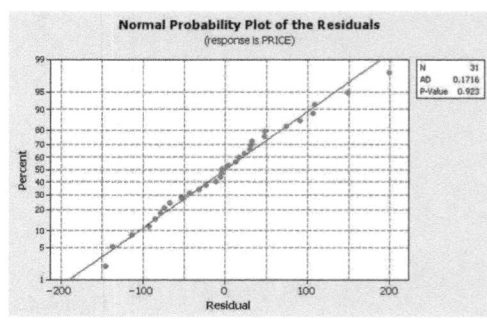

Figure 45
Minitab graphs of regression residuals for grandfather clock model (outlier included)

Figure 46
Minitab graphs of regression residuals for grandfather clock model (outlier deleted)

Look Back Although graphs do not provide formal statistical tests of normality, they do provide a descriptive display. Consult the references for methods to conduct statistical tests of normality using the residuals.

</td></tr>
</table>

Now Work Exercise 120d

Of the four assumptions in Section 1, the assumption that the random error is normally distributed is the least restrictive when we apply regression analysis in practice—that is, moderate departures from a normal distribution have very little effect on the validity of the statistical tests, confidence intervals, and prediction intervals presented in this chapter. In this case, we say that regression analysis is **robust** with respect to nonnormal errors. However, great departures from normality cast doubt on any inferences derived from the regression analysis.

Checking Assumption #4: Errors Independent

The assumption of independent errors is violated when successive errors are correlated. This typically occurs when the data for both the dependent and independent variables are observed sequentially over a period of time—called **time series data.** Time series data have a unique characteristic; the experimental unit represents a unit of time (e.g., a year, a month, a quarter). There are both graphical and formal statistical tests available for checking the assumption of independent regression errors. For example, a simple graph is to plot the residuals against time. If the residuals tend to group alternately into positive and negative clusters (as shown in Figure 47), then it is likely that the errors are correlated and the assumption is violated. If correlated errors are detected, one solution is to construct a **time series model** for $E(y)$.

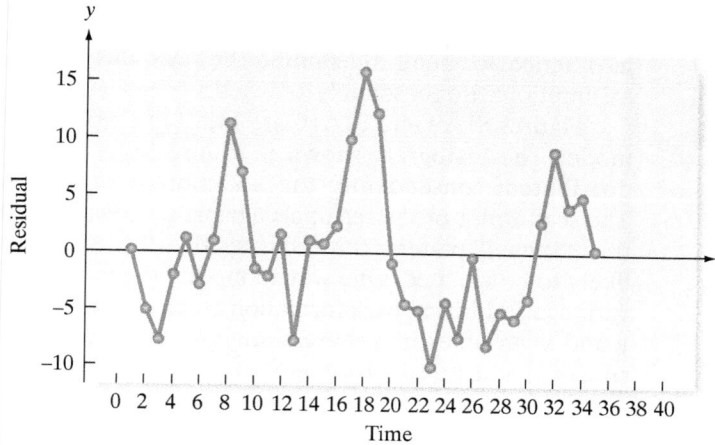

Figure 47

Hypothetical residual plot for time series data

Summary

Residual analysis is a useful tool for the regression analyst, not only to check the assumptions but also to provide information about how the model can be improved. A summary of the residual analyses presented in this section to check the assumption that the random error ε is normally distributed with mean 0 and constant variance is presented in the next box.

Steps in a Residual Analysis

1. Check for a misspecified model by plotting the residuals against each of the quantitative independent variables. Analyze each plot, looking for a curvilinear trend. This shape signals the need for a quadratic term in the model. Try a second-order term in the variable against which the residuals are plotted.

2. Examine the residual plots for outliers. Draw lines on the residual plots at 2- and 3-standard-deviation distances below and above the 0 line. Examine residuals outside the 3-standard-deviation lines as potential outliers and check to see that no more than 5% of the residuals exceed the 2-standard-deviation lines. Determine whether each outlier can be explained as an error in data collection or transcription, corresponds to a member of a population different from that of the remainder of the sample, or simply represents an unusual observation. If the observation is determined to be an error, fix it or remove it. Even if you cannot determine the cause, you may want to rerun the regression analysis without the observation to determine its effect on the analysis.

3. Check for nonnormal errors by plotting a frequency distribution of the residuals, using a stem-and-leaf display or a histogram. Check to see if obvious departures from normality exist. Extreme skewness of the frequency distribution may be due to outliers or could indicate the need for a transformation of the dependent variable. (Normalizing transformations are beyond the scope of this book, but you can find information in the references.)

4. Check for unequal error variances by plotting the residuals against the predicted values, $\hat{y}$. If you detect a cone-shaped pattern or some other pattern that indicates that the variance of ε is not constant, refit the model using an appropriate variance-stabilizing transformation on y, such as $\ln(y)$. (Consult the references for other useful variance-stabilizing transformations.)

A Residual Analysis

In the previous Statistics in Action Revisited section, we found the interaction model, $E(y) = \beta_0 + \beta_1 x_1 + \beta_3 x_2 + \beta_4 x_1 x_2$, to be both a statistically and practically useful model for predicting the cost (y) of a road construction contract. Recall that the two independent variables are the DOT engineer's estimate of cost (x_1) and bid status, where $x_2 = 1$ if a fixed bid and $x_2 = 0$ if a competitive bid. Before actually using the model in practice, we need to examine the residuals to be sure that the standard regression assumptions are reasonably satisfied.

Figures SIA9 and SIA10 are Minitab graphs of the residuals from the interaction model. The histogram shown in Figure SIA9 appears to be approximately normally distributed; consequently the assumption of normal errors is reasonably satisfied. The scatterplot of the residuals against $\hat{y}$ shown in Figure SIA10, however, shows a distinct "funnel" pattern; this indicates that the assumption of a constant error variance is likely to be violated. One way to modify the model to satisfy this assumption is to use a variance-stabilizing transformation (such as the natural log) on cost (y). When both the y and x variables in a regression equation are economic variables (prices, costs, salaries, etc.), it is often advantageous to transform the x variable also. Consequently, we'll modify the model by making a log transform on both cost (y) and DOTEST (x_1).

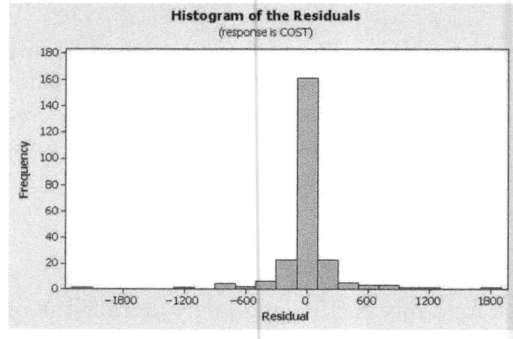

Figure SIA9

Minitab histogram of residuals from interaction model for road cost

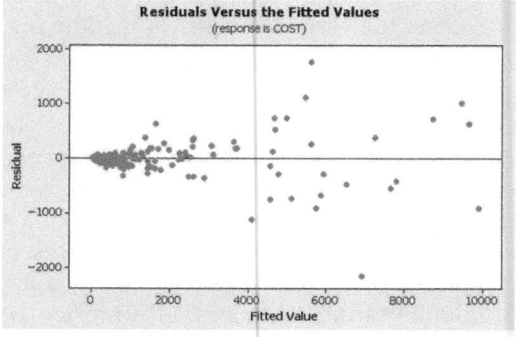

Figure SIA10

Minitab plot of residuals versus predicted values from interaction model for road cost

Our modified (log-log) interaction model takes the form

$$E(y^*) = \beta_0 + \beta_1 x_1^* + \beta_2 x_2 + \beta_3 (x_1^*) x_2$$

where $y^* = \ln(\text{COST})$ and $x_1^* = \ln(\text{DOTEST})$. The Minitab printout for this model is shown in Figure SIA11, followed by graphs of the residuals in Figures SIA12 and SIA13. The histogram shown in Figure SIA12 is approximately normal, and, more important, the scatterplot of the residuals shown in Figure SIA13 has no distinct trend. It appears that the log transformations successfully stabilized the error variance. Note, however, that the t-test for the interaction term in the model (highlighted in Figure SIA11) is no longer statistically significant (p-value = .420).

Consequently, we will drop the interaction term from the model and use the simpler modified model,

$$E(y^*) = \beta_0 + \beta_1 x_1^* + \beta_2 x_2$$

to predict road construction cost.

```
The regression equation is
LNCOST = - 0.162 + 1.01 LNDOTEST + 0.324 STATUS - 0.0176 STA_LNDOT


Predictor       Coef   SE Coef       T       P
Constant    -0.16188   0.05193   -3.12   0.002
LNDOTEST     1.00780   0.00798   126.23  0.000
STATUS        0.3243    0.1356    2.39   0.018
STA_LNDOT   -0.01762   0.02181   -0.81   0.420


S = 0.154922    R-Sq = 98.8%    R-Sq(adj) = 98.7%


Analysis of Variance

Source            DF       SS       MS       F       P
Regression         3   439.64   146.55  6105.87  0.000
Residual Error   231     5.54     0.02
Total            234   445.18
```

Figure SIA11

Minitab regression printout for modified (log-log) model of road construction cost

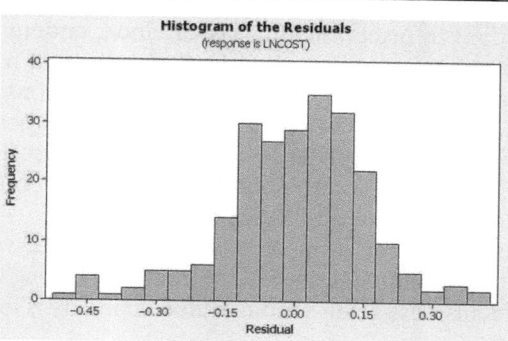

Figure SIA12

Minitab histogram of residuals from modified (log-log) model for road construction cost

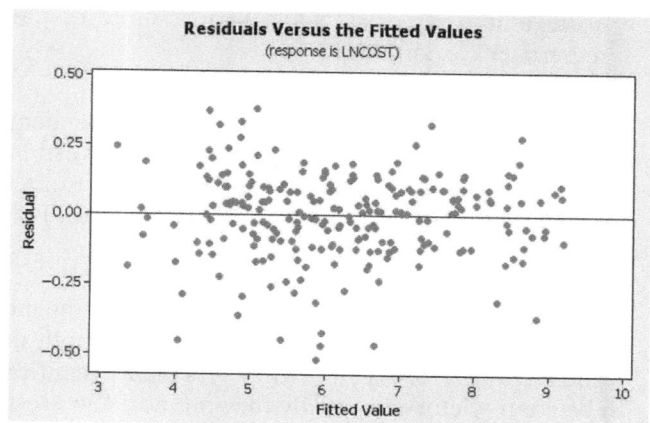

Figure SIA13

Minitab plot of residuals versus predicted values from modified (log-log) model for road construction cost

12 Some Pitfalls: Estimability, Multicollinearity, and Extrapolation

You should be aware of several potential problems when constructing a prediction model for some response y. A few of the most important are discussed in this final section.

Problem 1: Parameter Estimability

Suppose you want to fit a model relating annual crop yield y to the total expenditure for fertilizer x. We propose the first-order model

$$E(y) = \beta_0 + \beta_1 x$$

Now suppose we have 3 years of data and $1,000 is spent on fertilizer each year. The data are shown in Figure 48. You can see the problem: The parameters of the model cannot be estimated when all the data are concentrated at a single *x*-value. Recall that it takes two points (*x*-values) to fit a straight line. Thus, the parameters are not estimable when only one *x* is observed.

A similar problem would occur if we attempted to fit the quadratic model

$$E(y) = \beta_0 + \beta_1 x + \beta_2 x^2$$

to a set of data for which only one or two different *x*-values were observed (see Figure 49). At least three different *x*-values must be observed before a quadratic model can be fit to a set of data (that is, before all three parameters are estimable).

In general, the number of levels of observed x-*values must be one more than the order of the polynomial in* x *that you want to fit.*

For controlled experiments, the researcher can select an experimental design that will permit estimation of the model parameters. Even when the values of the independent variables cannot be controlled by the researcher, the independent variables are almost always observed at a sufficient number of levels to permit estimation of the model parameters. When the statistical software you use suddenly refuses to fit a model, however, the problem is probably inestimable parameters.

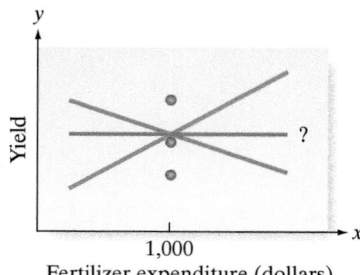

Figure 48

Yield and fertilizer expenditure data: Three years

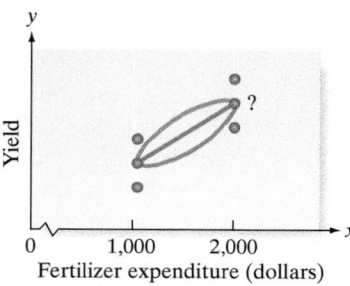

Figure 49

Only two *x* values observed: Quadratic model not estimable

Problem 2: Multicollinearity

Often, two or more of the independent variables used in a regression model contribute redundant information—that is, the independent variables are correlated with each other. For example, suppose we want to construct a model to predict the gas mileage rating of a truck as a function of its load, x_1 (in tons), and the horsepower, x_2 (in foot-pounds per second), of its engine. We would expect heavy loads to require greater horsepower and to result in lower mileage ratings. Thus, although both x_1 and x_2 contribute information for the prediction of mileage rating, *y*, some of the information is overlapping because x_1 and x_2 are correlated.

When the independent variables are correlated, we say *multicollinearity* exists. In practice, it is not uncommon to observe correlations among the independent variables. However, a few problems arise when serious multicollinearity is present in the regression variables.

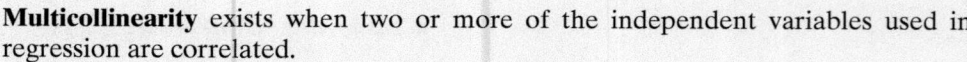

Multicollinearity exists when two or more of the independent variables used in regression are correlated.

First, high correlations among the independent variables increase the likelihood of rounding errors in the calculations of the β estimates, standard errors, and so forth. Second, and more important, the regression results may be confusing and misleading. Consider the model for gasoline mileage rating (*y*) of a truck:

$$E(y) = \beta_0 + \beta_1 x_1 + \beta_2 x_2$$

where $x_1 =$ load and $x_2 =$ horsepower. Fitting the model to a sample data set, we might find that the *t*-tests for testing β_1 and β_2 are both nonsignificant at the $\alpha = .05$ level, while the *F*-test for $H_0: \beta_1 = \beta_2 = 0$ is highly significant ($p = .001$). The tests may seem to be contradictory, but really they are not. The *t*-tests indicate that the contribution of one variable, say $x_1 =$ load, is not significant after the effect of $x_2 =$ horsepower has been accounted for (because x_2 is also in the model). The significant *F*-test, on the other hand, tells us that at least one of the two variables is making a contribution to the prediction of *y* (i.e., either β_1 or β_2 or both differ from 0). In fact, both are probably contributing, but the contribution of one overlaps with that of the other.

Multicollinearity can also have an effect on the signs of the parameter estimates. More specifically, a value of β_i may have the opposite sign from what is expected. In the truck gasoline mileage example, we expect heavy loads to result in lower mileage ratings, and we expect higher horsepowers to result in lower mileage ratings; consequently, we expect the signs of both the parameter estimates to be negative. Yet we may actually see a positive value of β_1 and be tempted to claim that heavy loads result in *higher* mileage ratings. This is the danger of interpreting a β coefficient when the independent variables are correlated. Because the variables contribute redundant information, the effect of $x_1 =$ load on $y =$ mileage rating is measured only partially by β_1.

How can you avoid the problems of multicollinearity in regression analysis? One way is to conduct a designed experiment so that the levels of the x variables are uncorrelated. Unfortunately, time and cost constraints may prevent you from collecting data in this manner. Consequently, most data are collected observationally. Because observational data frequently consist of correlated independent variables, you will need to recognize when multicollinearity is present and, if necessary, make modifications in the regression analysis.

Several methods are available for detecting multicollinearity in regression. A simple technique is to calculate the coefficient of correlation, r, between each pair of independent variables in the model to test for significantly correlated variables. If one or more of the r-values are statistically different from 0, the variables in question are correlated, and a multicollinearity problem may exist.* The degree of multicollinearity will depend on the magnitude of the value of r, as shown in the box.

Using the Correlation Coefficient r to Detect Multicollinearity

Extreme multicollinearity: $|r| \geq .8$

Moderate multicollinearity: $.2 \leq |r| < .8$

Low multicollinearity: $|r| < .2$

Other indications of the presence of multicollinearity include those mentioned above—namely, nonsignificant t-tests for the individual parameter estimates when the F-test for overall model adequacy is significant and estimates with opposite signs from what is expected.[†]

Detecting Multicollinearity in the Regression Model

1. Significant correlations between pairs of independent variables (see box above)
2. Nonsignificant t-tests for all (or nearly all) of the individual β parameters when the F-test for overall model adequacy is significant
3. Signs opposite from what is expected in the estimated β parameters

---

Example 18

Detecting Multicollinearity— Modeling Carbon Monoxide in Cigarette Smoke

Problem The Federal Trade Commission (FTC) annually ranks varieties of domestic cigarettes according to their tar, nicotine, and carbon monoxide contents. The U.S. Surgeon General considers each of these three substances hazardous to a smoker's health. Past studies have shown that increases in the tar and nicotine contents of a cigarette are accompanied by an increase in the carbon monoxide emitted from the cigarette smoke. Table 9 presents data on tar, nicotine, and carbon monoxide contents (in milligrams) and weight (in grams) for a sample of 25 (filter) brands tested in a recent

---

*Remember that r measures only the pairwise correlation between x-values. Three variables, x_1, x_2, and x_3, may be highly correlated as a group but may not exhibit large pairwise correlations. Thus, multicollinearity may be present even when all pairwise correlations are not significantly different from 0.

[†]More formal methods for detecting multicollinearity, such as variance-inflation factors (VIFs), are available. Independent variables with a VIF of 10 or above are usually considered to be highly correlated with one or more of the other independent variables in the model. Calculation of VIFs are beyond the scope of this introductory text. Consult the chapter references for a discussion of VIFs and other formal methods of detecting multicollinearity.

year. Suppose we want to model carbon monoxide content, y, as a function of tar content, x_1, nicotine content, x_2, and weight, x_3, using the model

$$E(y) = \beta_0 + \beta_1 x_1 + \beta_2 x_2 + \beta_3 x_3$$

The model is fit to the 25 data points in Table 9, and a portion of the Minitab printout is shown in Figure 50. Examine the printout. Do you detect any signs of multicollinearity?

Table 9	FTC Cigarette Data for Example 18		
Tar, x_1	Nicotine, x_2	Weight, x_3	Carbon Monoxide, y
14.1	.86	.9853	13.6
16.0	1.06	1.0938	16.6
29.8	2.03	1.1650	23.5
8.0	.67	.9280	10.2
4.1	.40	.9462	5.4
15.0	1.04	.8885	15.0
8.8	.76	1.0267	9.0
12.4	.95	.9225	12.3
16.6	1.12	.9372	16.3
14.9	1.02	.8858	15.4
13.7	1.01	.9643	13.0
15.1	.90	.9316	14.4
7.8	.57	.9705	10.0
11.4	.78	1.1240	10.2
9.0	.74	.8517	9.5
1.0	.13	.7851	1.5
17.0	1.26	.9186	18.5
12.8	1.08	1.0395	12.6
15.8	.96	.9573	17.5
4.5	.42	.9106	4.9
14.5	1.01	1.0070	15.9
7.3	.61	.9806	8.5
8.6	.69	.9693	10.6
15.2	1.02	.9496	13.9
12.0	.82	1.1184	14.9

Source: Federal Trade Commission

Data Set: FTC

Regression Analysis: CO versus TAR, NICOTINE, WEIGHT

```
The regression equation is
CO = 3.20 + 0.963 TAR - 2.63 NICOTINE - 0.13 WEIGHT


Predictor    Coef   SE Coef      T      P
Constant    3.202    3.462    0.93  0.365
TAR        0.9626   0.2422    3.97  0.001
NICOTINE   -2.632    3.901   -0.67  0.507
WEIGHT     -0.130    3.885   -0.03  0.974


S = 1.44573   R-Sq = 91.9%   R-Sq(adj) = 90.7%


Analysis of Variance

Source           DF      SS      MS      F      P
Regression        3  495.26  165.09  78.98  0.000
Residual Error   21   43.89    2.09
```

Correlations: TAR, NICOTINE, WEIGHT

```
             TAR  NICOTINE
NICOTINE   0.977
           0.000


WEIGHT     0.491     0.500
           0.013     0.011


Cell Contents: Pearson correlation
               P-Value
```

Figure 50

Minitab printout for model of carbon monoxide content, Example 18

Solution First, note that the F-test for overall model utility is highly significant. The test statistic ($F = 78.98$) and observed significance level (p-value $= .000$) are highlighted on the Minitab printout, Figure 50. Therefore, at, say $\alpha = .01$, we can conclude that at least one of the parameters—β_1, β_2, or β_3—in the model is nonzero. The t-tests for two of three individual β's, however, are nonsignificant. (The p-values for these tests are highlighted on the printout.) Unless tar (x_1) is the only one of the three variables useful for predicting carbon monoxide content, these results are the first indication of a potential multicollinearity problem.

The negative values for β_2 and β_3 (highlighted on the printout) are a second clue to the presence of multicollinearity. From past studies, the FTC expects carbon monoxide content (y) to increase when either nicotine content (x_2) or weight (x_3) increases—that is, the FTC expects *positive* relationships between y and x_2 and between y and x_3, not negative ones.

All signs indicate that a serious multicollinearity problem exists.

Look Back To confirm our suspicions, we had Minitab produce the coefficient of correlation, r, for each of the three pairs of independent variables in the model. The resulting output is shown (highlighted) at the bottom of Figure 50. You can see that tar (x_1) and nicotine (x_2) are highly correlated ($r = .977$), while weight (x_3) is moderately correlated with the other two x's ($r \approx .5$). All three correlations have p-values $\approx .01$ or less; consequently, all three are significantly different from 0 at, say, $\alpha = .05$.

Now Work Exercise 119

Once you have detected that multicollinearity exists, there are several alternative measures available for solving the problem. The appropriate measure to take depends on the severity of the multicollinearity and the ultimate goal of the regression analysis.

Some researchers, when confronted with highly correlated independent variables, choose to include only one of the correlated variables in the final model. If you are interested in using the model only for estimation and prediction (step 6), you may decide not to drop any of the independent variables from the model. In the presence of multicollinearity, we have seen that it is dangerous to interpret the individual β parameters. However, confidence intervals for $E(y)$ and prediction intervals for y generally remain unaffected *as long as the values of the x's used to predict* y *follow the same pattern of multicollinearity exhibited in the sample data*—that is, you must take strict care to ensure that the values of the x variables fall within the range of the sample data.

Solutions to Some Problems Created by Multicollinearity in Regression*

1. Drop one or more of the correlated independent variables from the model. One way to decide which variables to keep in the model is to employ stepwise regression (Section 10).

2. If you decide to keep all the independent variables in the model,

   a. Avoid making inferences about the individual β parameters based on the t-tests.

   b. Restrict inferences about $E(y)$ and future y values to values of the x's that fall within the range of the sample data.

Problem 3: Prediction Outside the Experimental Region

Many research economists had developed highly technical models to relate the state of the economy to various economic indices and other independent variables. Many of these models were multiple regression models, where, for example, the dependent

---

*Several other solutions are available. For example, in the case where higher-order regression models are fit, the analyst may want to code the independent variables so that higher-order terms (e.g., x^2) for a particular x variable are not highly correlated with x. One transformation that works is $z = (x - \bar{x})/s$. Other, more sophisticated procedures for addressing multicollinearity (such as *ridge regression*) are beyond the scope of the text. Consult the references at the end of this chapter.

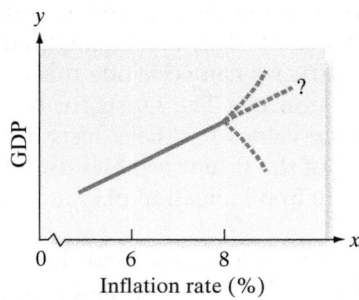

Figure 51
Using a regression model outside
the experimental region

variable y might be next year's gross domestic product (GDP) and the independent variables might include this year's rate of inflation, this year's consumer price index (CPI), and so on. In other words, the model might be constructed to predict next year's economy using this year's knowledge.

Unfortunately, these models were almost all unsuccessful in predicting the recession in the early 1970s and the late 1990s. What went wrong? One of the problems was that many of the regression models were used to **extrapolate** (i.e., predict y-values of the independent variables that were outside the region in which the model was developed). For example, the inflation rate in the late 1960s, when the models were developed, ranged from 6% to 8%. When the double-digit inflation of the early 1970s became a reality, some researchers attempted to use the same models to predict future growth in GDP. As you can see in Figure 51, the model may be very accurate for predicting y when x is in the range of experimentation, but using the model outside that range is a dangerous practice.

Exercises 119–131

Please be aware that some of the following problems may require knowledge of concepts that are not presented in this chapter.

Learning the Mechanics

119 Consider fitting the multiple regression model

NW

$$E(y) = \beta_0 + \beta_1 x_1 + \beta_2 x_2 + \beta_3 x_3 + \beta_4 x_4 + \beta_5 x_5$$

A matrix of correlations for all pairs of independent variables is given below. Do you detect a multicollinearity problem? Explain.

	x_1	x_2	x_3	x_4	x_5
x_1	—	.17	.02	−.23	.19
x_2		—	.45	.93	.02
x_3			—	.22	−.01
x_4				—	.86
x_5					—

120 Identify the problem(s) in each of the residual plots
NW shown below.

a.

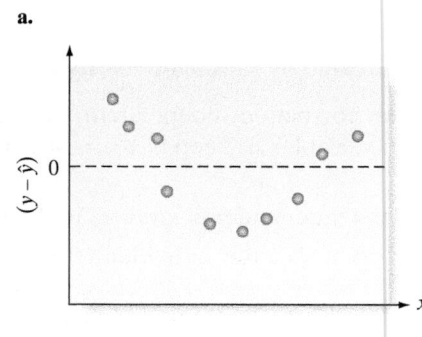

c.

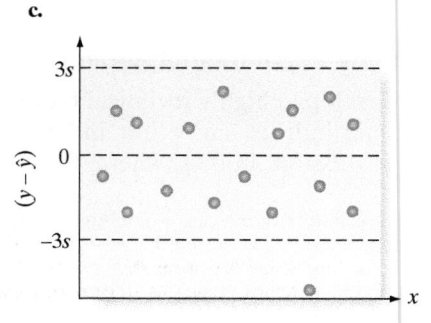

Applying the Concepts—Basic

121 State casket sales restrictions. Some states permit only licensed firms to sell funeral goods (e.g., caskets, urns) to the consumer, while other states have no restrictions. States with casket sales restrictions are being challenged in court to lift these monopolistic restrictions. A paper in the *Journal of Law and Economics* (Feb. 2008) used multiple regression to investigate the impact of lifting casket sales restrictions on the cost of a funeral. Data collected for a sample of 1,437 funerals were used to fit the model. A simpler version of the model estimated by the researchers is $E(y) = \beta_0 + \beta_1 x_1 + \beta_2 x_2 + \beta_3 x_1 x_2$, where y is the price (in dollars) of a direct burial, $x_1 = $ {1 if funeral home is in a restricted state, 0 if not}, and $x_2 = $ {1 if price includes a basic wooden casket, 0 if no casket}. The estimated equation (with standard errors in parentheses) is:

$$\hat{y} = 1{,}432 + 793x_1 - 252x_2 + 261x_1 x_2, \quad R^2 = .78$$
$$\quad\quad (70) \quad\quad (134) \quad\quad (109)$$

b.

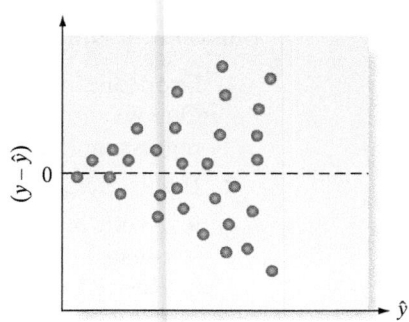

d.

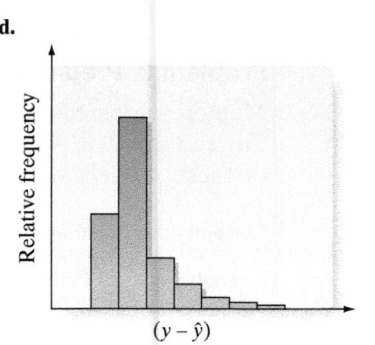

a. Calculate the predicted price of a direct burial with a basic wooden casket at a funeral home in a restricted state.

b. The data include a direct burial funeral with a basic wooden casket at a funeral home in a restricted state that costs $2,200. Assuming the standard deviation of the model is $50, is this data value an outlier?

c. The data also include a direct burial funeral with a basic wooden casket at a funeral home in a restricted state that costs $2,500. Again, assume that the standard deviation of the model is $50. Is this data value an outlier?

122 Personality traits and job performance. Refer to the *Journal of Applied Psychology* (Jan. 2011) study of the determinants of task performance, Exercise 94. In addition to x_1 = conscientiousness score and x_2 = {1 if highly complex job, 0 if not}, the researchers also used x_3 = emotional stability score, x_4 = organizational citizenship behavior score, and x_5 = counterproductive work behavior score to model y = task performance score. One of their concerns is the level of multicollinearity in the data. Below is a matrix of correlations for all possible pairs of independent variables. Based on this information, do you detect a moderate or high level of multicollinearity? If so, what are your recommendations?

	x_1	x_2	x_3	x_4
Conscientiousness (x_1)				
Job complexity (x_2)	.13			
Emotional stability (x_3)	.62	.14		
Organizational citizenship (x_4)	.24	.03	.24	
Counterproductive work (x_5)	−.23	−.02	−.25	−.62

123 Women in top management. The *Journal of Organizational Culture, Communications and Conflict* (July 2007) did a study on women in upper management positions at U.S. firms. Monthly data ($n = 252$ months) were collected for several variables in an attempt to model the number of females in managerial positions (y). The independent variables included the number of females with a college degree (x_1), the number of female high school graduates with no college degree (x_2), the number of males in managerial positions (x_3), the number of males with a college degree (x_4), and the number of male high school graduates with no college degree (x_5). The correlations are given in each part. Determine which of the correlations results in a potential multicollinearity problem for the regression analysis.

a. The correlation relating number of females in managerial positions and number of females with a college degree: $r = .983$.

b. The correlation relating number of females in managerial positions and number of female high school graduates with no college degree: $r = .074$.

c. The correlation relating number of males in managerial positions and number of males with a college degree: $r = .722$.

d. The correlation relating number of males in managerial positions and number of male high school graduates with no college degree: $r = .528$.

124 Factors identifying urban counties. The *Professional Geographer* (Feb. 2000) published a study of urban and rural counties in the western United States. Six independent variables—total county population (x_1), population density (x_2), population concentration (x_3), population growth (x_4), proportion of county land in farms (x_5), and 5-year change in agricultural land base (x_6)—were used to model the urban/rural rating (y) of a county, where rating was recorded on a scale of 1 (most rural) to 10 (most urban). Prior to running the multiple regression analysis, the researchers were concerned about possible multicollinearity in the data. Below is a correlation matrix for data collected on $n = 256$ counties.

Independent Variable	x_1	x_2	x_3	x_4	x_5
x_1: Total population					
x_2: Population density	.20				
x_3: Population concentration	.45	.43			
x_4: Population growth	−.05	−.14	−.01		
x_5: Farm land	−.16	−.15	−.07	−.20	
x_6: Agricultural change	−.12	−.12	−.22	−.06	−.06

Source: Based on Berry, K. A., et al. "Interpreting what is rural and urban for western U.S. counties," *Professional Geographer,* Vol. 52, No. 1, Feb. 2000, pp. 93–105 (Table 2).

a. Based on the correlation matrix, is there any evidence of extreme multicollinearity?

b. The first-order model with all six independent variables was fit, and the results are shown in the next table. Based on the reported tests, is there any evidence of extreme multicollinearity?

Independent Variable	β Estimate	p-value
x_1: Total population	0.110	0.045
x_2: Population density	0.065	0.230
x_3: Population concentration	0.540	0.000
x_4: Population growth	−0.009	0.860
x_5: Farm land	−0.150	0.003
x_6: Agricultural change	−0.027	0.580

Overall model:
$R^2 = .44$ $R_a^2 = .43$ $F = 32.47$ p-value $< .001$

Source: Berry, K. A., et al. "Interpreting what is rural and urban for western U.S. counties," *Professional Geographer,* Vol. 52, No. 1, Feb. 2000 (Table 2).

125 Accuracy of software effort estimates. Refer to the *Journal of Empirical Software Engineering* (Vol. 9, 2004) study of the accuracy of new software effort estimates, Exercise 114. Recall that stepwise regression was used to develop a model for the relative error in estimating effort (y) as a function of company role of estimator ($x_1 = 1$ if developer, 0 if project leader) and previous accuracy ($x_8 = 1$ if more than 20% accurate, 0 if less than 20% accurate). The stepwise regression yielded the prediction equation $\hat{y} = .12 - .28x_1 + .27x_8$. The researcher is concerned that the sign of the estimated β multiplied by x_1 is the opposite from what is expected. (The researcher expects a project leader to have a smaller relative error of estimation than a developer.) Give at least one reason why this phenomenon occurred.

Applying the Concepts—Basic

126 Reality TV and cosmetic surgery. Refer to the *Body Image: An International Journal of Research* (March 2010) study of the influence of reality TV shows on one's desire to undergo cosmetic surgery, Exercise 17 (p. 682). Simulated data for the study is saved in the file. In Exercise 17, you fit the first-order model, $E(y) = \beta_0 + \beta_1 x_1 + \beta_2 x_2 + \beta_3 x_3 + \beta_4 x_4$, where y = desire to have cosmetic surgery, x_1 is a dummy variable for gender, x_2 = level of self-esteem, x_3 = level of body satisfaction, and x_4 = impression of reality TV.

a. Check the data for multicollinearity. If you detect multicollinearity, what modifications to the model do you recommend?

b. Conduct a complete residual analysis for the model. Do you detect any violations of the assumptions? If so, what modifications to the model do you recommend?

127 Arsenic in groundwater. Refer to the *Environmental Science & Technology* (Jan. 2005) study of the reliability of a commercial kit to test for arsenic in groundwater, Exercise 16. Recall that you fit a first-order model for arsenic level (y) as a function of latitude (x_1), longitude (x_2), and depth (x_3) to data saved in the file. Conduct a residual analysis of the data. Based on the results, comment on each of the following:

a. assumption of mean error = 0

b. assumption of constant error variance

c. outliers

d. assumption of normally distributed errors

e. multicollinearity

128 Contamination from a plant's discharge. Refer to the U.S. Army Corps of Engineers data on fish contaminated from the toxic discharges of a chemical plant located on the banks of the Tennessee River in Alabama. In Exercise 18, you fit the first-order model, $E(y) = \beta_0 + \beta_1 x_1 + \beta_2 x_2 + \beta_3 x_3$, where y = DDT level in captured fish, x_1 = miles captured upstream, x_2 = fish length, and x_3 = fish weight. Conduct a complete residual analysis for the model. Do you recommend any model modifications be made? Explain.

129 Failure times of silicon wafer microchips. Refer to the National Semiconductor study of manufactured silicon wafer integrated circuit chips, Exercise 63. Recall that the failure times of the microchips (in hours) was determined at different solder temperatures (degrees Celsius). The data are repeated in the table in the next column.

a. Fit the straight-line model $E(y) = \beta_0 + \beta_1 x$ to the data, where y = failure time and x = solder temperature.

b. Compute the residual for a microchip manufactured at a temperature of 149°C.

c. Plot the residuals against solder temperature (x). Do you detect a trend?

Temperature (°C)	Time to Failure (hours)
165	200
162	200
164	1,200
158	500
158	600
159	750
156	1,200
157	1,500
152	500
147	500
149	1,100
149	1,150
142	3,500
142	3,600
143	3,650
133	4,200
132	4,800
132	5,000
134	5,200
134	5,400
125	8,300
123	9,700

Source: Gee, S., and Nguyen, L. "Mean time to failure in wafer level-CSP packages with SnPb and SnAgCu solder bmps," International Wafer Level Packaging Conference, San Jose, CA, Nov. 3–4, 2005 (adapted from Figure 7).

d. In Exercise 63c, you determined that failure time (y) and solder temperature (x) were curvilinearly related. Does the residual plot, part c, support this conclusion?

130 Cooling method for gas turbines. Refer to the *Journal of Engineering for Gas Turbines and Power* (Jan. 2005) study of a high-pressure inlet fogging method for a gas turbine engine, Exercise 103. Now consider the interaction model for heat rate (y) of a gas turbine as a function of cycle speed (x_1) and cycle pressure ratio (x_2), $E(y) = \beta_0 + \beta_1 x_1 + \beta_2 x_2 + \beta_3 x_1 x_2$. Use the data saved in the file to conduct a complete residual analysis for the model. Do you recommend making model modifications?

131 Agreeableness, gender, and wages. Refer to the *Journal of Personality and Social Psychology* (Feb. 2012) study of on-the-job agreeableness and wages, Exercise 107. Recall that the researchers modeled mean income, $E(y)$, as a function of both agreeableness score (x_1) and a dummy variable for gender ($x_2 = 1$ if male, 0 if female). Use the data saved in the file to analyze the residuals of the model,

$$E(y) = \beta_0 + \beta_1 x_1 + \beta_2 (x_1)^2 + \beta_3 x_2$$

What model modifications, if any, do you recommend?

◻ Chapter Notes

Key Terms

Adjusted multiple coefficient of determination
Base level
Categorical variable
Coded variable
Complete model
Complete second-order model
Dummy variable
Extrapolation
First-order model
Full model
General multiple regression model
Higher-order term
Indicator variable
Interaction
Interaction model
Interaction term
Least squares prediction equation
Level of a variable
Main effect terms
Mean square for error (MSE)
Method of least squares
Model building
Multicollinearity

Multiple coefficient of determination (R^2)
Multiple regression model
Nested model
Nested model F-test
Objective variable screening procedure
Paraboloid
Parameter estimability
Parsimonious model
Quadratic model
Quadratic term
Qualitative variable
Reduced model
Regression outlier
Regression residual
Residual analysis
Response surface
Robust method
Saddle-shaped surface
Second-order model
Second-order term
Stepwise regression
Time series data
Time series model
Variance-stabilizing transformation

Key Symbols

x_1^2	Quadratic form for a quantitative x
$x_1 x_2$	Interaction term
MSE	Mean square for error (estimates σ^2)
$\hat{\varepsilon}$	Estimated random error (residual)
SSE_R	Sum of squared errors, reduced model
SSE_C	Sum of squared errors, complete model
MSE_C	Mean squared error, complete model
$\ln(y)$	Natural logarithm of dependent variable

Key Ideas

Multiple regression variables
$y =$ **Dependent** variable (quantitative)
$x_1, x_2, \ldots, x_k$ are **independent** variables (quantitative or qualitative)

First-order model in k quantitative x's
$$E(y) = \beta_0 + \beta_1 x_1 + \beta_2 x_2 + \cdots + \beta_k x_k$$
Each β_i represents the change in $E(y)$ for every 1-unit increase in x_i, holding all other x's fixed.

Interaction model in 2 quantitative x's
$E(y) = \beta_0 + \beta_1 x_1 + \beta_2 x_2 + \beta_3 x_1 x_2$
$(\beta_1 + \beta_3 x_2)$ represents the change in $E(y)$ for every 1-unit increase in x_1, for fixed value of x_2
$(\beta_2 + \beta_3 x_1)$ represents the change in $E(y)$ for every 1-unit increase in x_2, for fixed value of x_1

Quadratic model in 1 quantitative x
$E(y) = \beta_0 + \beta_1 x + \beta_2 x^2$
β_2 represents the rate of curvature in $E(y)$ for x
($\beta_2 > 0$ implies *upward* curvature)
($\beta_2 < 0$ implies *downward* curvature)

Complete second-order model in 2 quantitative x's
$E(y) = \beta_0 + \beta_1 x_1 + \beta_2 x_2 + \beta_3 x_1 x_2 + \beta_4 x_1^2 + \beta_5 x_2^2$
β_4 represents the rate of curvature in $E(y)$ for x_1, holding x_2 fixed
β_5 represents the rate of curvature in $E(y)$ for x_2, holding x_1 fixed

Dummy variable model for 1 qualitative x
$E(y) = \beta_0 + \beta_1 x_1 + \beta_2 x_2 + \cdots + \beta_{k-1} x_{k-1}$
$x_1 = \{1$ if level 1, 0 if not$\}$
$x_2 = \{1$ if level 2, 0 if not$\}$
$x_{k-1} = \{1$ if level $k-1$, 0 if not$\}$
$\beta_0 = E(y)$ for level k (base level) $= \mu_k$
$\beta_1 = \mu_1 - \mu_k$
$\beta_2 = \mu_2 - \mu_k$

Complete second-order model in 1 quantitative x and 1 qualitative x (two levels, A and B)
$E(y) = \beta_0 + \beta_1 x_1 + \beta_2 x_1^2 + \beta_3 x_2 + \beta_4 x_1 x_2 + \beta_5 x_1^2 x_2$
$x_2 = \{1$ if level A, 0 if level B$\}$

Adjusted coefficient of determination, R_a^2
Cannot be "forced" to 1 by adding independent variables to the model.

Interaction between x_1 and x_2
Implies that the relationship between y and one x depends on the other x.

Key Formulas

$s^2 = MSE = \dfrac{SSE}{n - (k + 1)}$ — Estimator of σ^2 for a model with k independent variables

$t = \dfrac{\hat{\beta}_i}{s_{\hat{\beta}_i}}$ — Test statistic for testing $H_0: \beta_i$

$\hat{\beta}_i \pm (t_{\alpha/2}) s_{\hat{\beta}_i}$, where $t_{\alpha/2}$ depends on $n - (k + 1)$ df — $100(1 - \alpha)\%$ confidence interval for β_i

$R^2 = \dfrac{SS_{yy} - SSE}{SS_{yy}}$ — Multiple coefficient of determination

$R_a^2 = 1 - \left[\dfrac{(n - 1)}{n - (k + 1)} \right] (1 - R^2)$ — Adjusted multiple coefficient of determination

$F = \dfrac{MS\ (Model)}{MSE}$
$= \dfrac{R^2/k}{(1 - R^2)/[n - (k + 1)]}$ — Test statistic for testing $H_0: \beta_1 = \beta_2 = \cdots = \beta_k = 0$

$F = \dfrac{(SSE_R - SSE_C)/\text{number of } \beta\text{'s tested}}{MSE_C}$ — Test statistic for comparing reduced and complete models

$y - \hat{y}$ — Regression residual

Parsimonious model

A model with a small number of β parameters.

Recommendation for Assessing Model Adequacy

1. Conduct global F-test; if significant, then:
2. Conduct t-tests on only the most important β's (*interaction* or *squared terms*)
3. Interpret value of $2s$
4. Interpret value of R_a^2

Recommendation for Testing Individual β's

1. If *curvature* (x^2) deemed important, do not conduct test for first-order (x) term in the model.
2. If *interaction* ($x_1 x_2$) deemed important, do not conduct tests for first-order terms (x_1 and x_2) in the model.

Extrapolation

Occurs when you predict y for values of x's that are outside of range of sample data.

Nested models

Are models where one model (the *complete model*) contains all the terms of another model (the *reduced model*) plus at least one additional term.

Multicollinearity

Occurs when two or more x's are correlated.

Indicators of multicollinearity:

1. Highly correlated x's
2. Significant global F-test, but all t-tests nonsignificant
3. Signs on β's opposite from expected

Problems with Using Stepwise Regression Model as the "Final" Model

1. *Extremely large number of* t-*tests* inflate overall probability of at least one Type I error.
2. *No higher-order terms* (interactions or squared terms) are included in the model.

Analysis of Residuals

1. Detect **misspecified model:** *plot residuals vs. quantitative x* (look for trends, e.g., curvilinear trend)
2. Detect **nonconstant error variance:** *plot residuals vs. $\hat{y}$* (look for patterns, e.g., cone shape)
3. Detect **nonnormal errors:** *histogram, stem-leaf, or normal probability plot of residuals* (look for strong departures from normality)
4. Identify **outliers:** *residuals greater than $3s$ in absolute value* (investigate outliers before deleting)

Guide to Multiple Regression

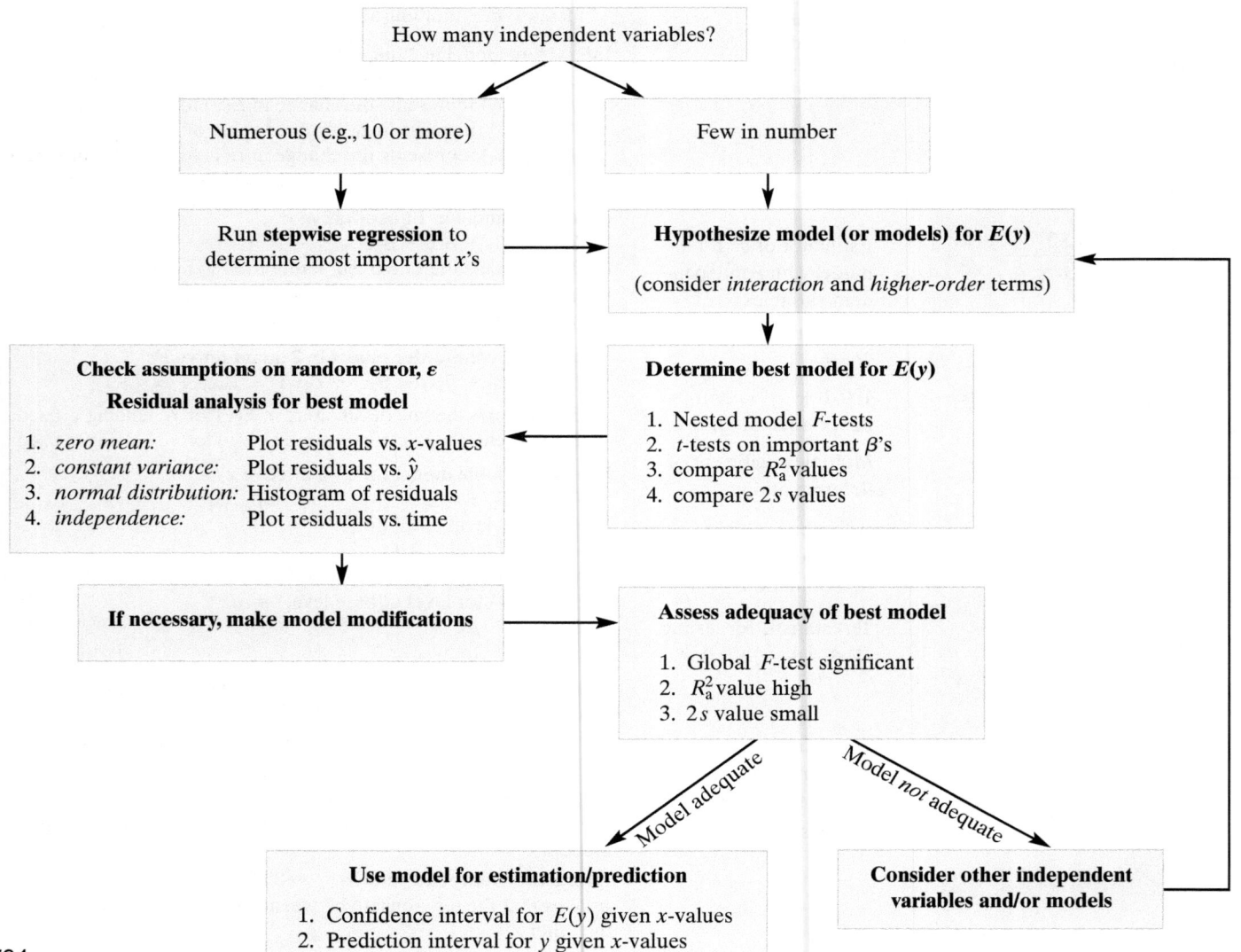

Supplementary Exercises 132–170

Please be aware that some of the following problems may require knowledge of concepts that are not presented in this chapter..

Learning the Mechanics

132 Suppose you have developed a regression model to explain the relationship between y and x_1, x_2, and x_3. The ranges of the variables you observed were as follows: $10 \leq y \leq 100$, $5 \leq x_1 \leq 55$, $.5 \leq x_2 \leq 1$, and $1,000 \leq x_3 \leq 2,000$. Will the error of prediction be smaller when you use the least squares equation to predict y when $x_1 = 30$, $x_2 = .6$, and $x_3 = 1,300$, or when $x_1 = 60$, $x_2 = .4$, and $x_3 = 900$? Why?

133 When a multiple regression model is used for estimating the mean of the dependent variable and for predicting a new value of y, which will be narrower—the confidence interval for the mean or the prediction interval for the new y value? Why?

134 Suppose you fit the model

$$y = \beta_0 + \beta_1 x_1 + \beta_2 x_1^2 + \beta_3 x_2 + \beta_4 x_1 x_2 + \varepsilon$$

to $n = 25$ data points with the following results:

$$\hat{\beta}_0 = 1.26 \quad \hat{\beta}_1 = -2.43 \quad \hat{\beta}_2 = .05 \quad \hat{\beta}_3 = .62 \quad \hat{\beta}_4 = 1.81$$
$$s_{\hat{\beta}_1} = 1.21 \quad s_{\hat{\beta}_2} = .16 \quad s_{\hat{\beta}_3} = .26 \quad s_{\hat{\beta}_4} = 1.49$$
$$\text{SSE} = .41 \quad R^2 = .83$$

a. Is there sufficient evidence to conclude that at least one of the parameters β_1, β_2, β_3, or β_4 is nonzero? Test using $\alpha = .05$.

b. Test $H_0: \beta_1 = 0$ against $H_a: \beta_1 < 0$. Use $\alpha = .05$.

c. Test $H_0: \beta_2 = 0$ against $H_a: \beta_2 > 0$. Use $\alpha = .05$.

d. Test $H_0: \beta_3 = 0$ against $H_a: \beta_3 \neq 0$. Use $\alpha = .05$.

135 Suppose you used Minitab to fit the model

$$y = \beta_0 + \beta_1 x_1 + \beta_2 x_2 + \varepsilon$$

to $n = 15$ data points and obtained the printout shown below.

```
The regression equation is
Y = 90.1 - 1.84 X1 + .285 X2


Predictor    Coef    SE Coef      T       P
Constant    90.10     23.10     3.90   0.002
X1          -1.836    0.367    -5.01   0.001
X2           0.285    0.231     1.24   0.465


S = 10.68    R-Sq = 91.6%    R-Sq(adj) = 90.2%

Analysis of Variance

Source           DF     SS      MS      F       P
Regression        2   14801   7400   64.91   0.001
Residual Error   12    1364    114
Total            14   16165
```

a. What is the least squares prediction equation?

b. Find R^2 and interpret its value.

c. Is there sufficient evidence to indicate that the model is useful for predicting y? Conduct an F-test using $\alpha = .05$.

d. Test the null hypothesis $H_0: \beta_1 = 0$ against the alternative hypothesis $H_a: \beta_1 \neq 0$. Test using $\alpha = .05$. Draw the appropriate conclusions.

e. Find the standard deviation of the regression model and interpret it.

136 The first-order model $E(y) = \beta_0 + \beta_1 x_1$ was fit to $n = 19$ data points. A residual plot for the model is provided below. Is the need for a quadratic term in the model evident from the residual plot? Explain.

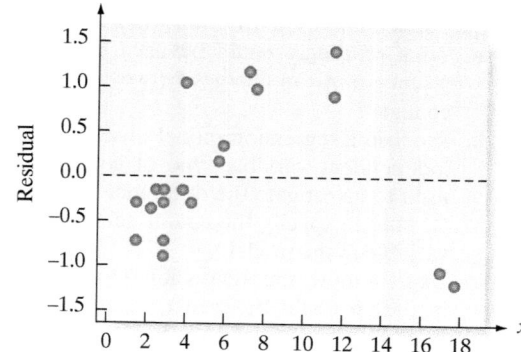

137 Write a model relating $E(y)$ to one qualitative independent variable that is at four levels. Define all the terms in your model.

138 It is desired to relate $E(y)$ to a quantitative variable x_1 and a qualitative variable at three levels.

a. Write a first-order model.

b. Write a model that will graph as three different second-order curves—one for each level of the qualitative variable.

139 Explain why stepwise regression is used. What is its value in the model-building process?

140 Consider relating $E(y)$ to two quantitative independent variables x_1 and x_2.

a. Write a first-order model for $E(y)$.

b. Write a complete second-order model for $E(y)$.

141 To model the relationship between y, a dependent variable, and x, an independent variable, a researcher has taken one measurement on y at each of three different x values. Drawing on his mathematical expertise, the researcher realizes that he can fit the second-order model

$$E(y) = \beta_0 + \beta_1 x + \beta_2 x^2$$

and it will pass exactly through all three points, yielding $\text{SSE} = 0$. The researcher, delighted with the excellent fit of the model, eagerly sets out to use it to make inferences. What problems will he encounter in attempting to make inferences?

142 Suppose you fit the regression model

$$E(y) = \beta_0 + \beta_1 x_1 + \beta_2 x_2 + \beta_3 x_2^2 + \beta_4 x_1 x_2 + \beta_5 x_1 x_2^2$$

to $n = 35$ data points and wish to test the null hypothesis $H_0: \beta_4 = \beta_5 = 0$.

a. State the alternative hypothesis.

b. Explain in detail how to compute the F-statistic needed to test the null hypothesis.

c. What are the numerator and denominator degrees of freedom associated with the F-statistic in part **b**?

d. Give the rejection region for the test if $\alpha = .05$.

Applying the Concepts—Basic

143 Comparing private and public college tuition. According to the *Chronicle of Higher Education Almanac*, 4-year private colleges charge, on average, five times as much for tuition and fees than 4-year public colleges. In order to estimate the true difference in the mean amounts charged for an academic year, random samples of 40 private colleges and 40 public colleges were contacted and questioned about their tuition structures.

a. What procedure could be used to estimate the difference in mean charges between private and public colleges?

b. Propose a regression model involving the qualitative independent variable type of college that could be used to investigate the difference between the means. Be sure to specify the coding scheme for the dummy variable in the model.

c. Explain how the regression model you developed in part **b** could be used to estimate the difference between the population means.

144 GPAs of business students. Research scientists at the Educational Testing Service (ETS) used multiple regression analysis to model y, the final grade point average (GPA) of business and management doctoral students. A list of the potential independent variables measured for each doctoral student in the study follows:

(1) Quantitative Graduate Management Aptitude Test (GMAT) score

(2) Verbal GMAT score

(3) Undergraduate GPA

(4) First-year graduate GPA

(5) Student cohort (i.e., year in which student entered doctoral program: year 1, year 3, or year 5)

a. Identify the variables as quantitative or qualitative.

b. For each quantitative variable, give your opinion on whether the variable is positively or negatively related to final GPA.

c. For each of the qualitative variables, set up the appropriate dummy variable.

d. Write a first-order, main effects model relating final GPA, y, to the five independent variables.

e. Interpret the β's in the model, part **d**.

f. Write a first-order model for final GPA, y, that allows for a different slope for each student cohort.

g. For each quantitative independent variable in the model, part **f**, give the slope of the line (in terms of the β's) for the year 1 cohort.

145 Comparing two orange juice extractors. The Florida Citrus Commission is interested in evaluating the performance of two orange juice extractors, brand A and brand B. It is believed that the size of the fruit used in the test may influence the juice yield (amount of juice per pound of oranges) obtained by the extractors. The commission wants to develop a regression model relating the mean juice yield $E(y)$ to the type of orange juice extractor (brand A or brand B) and the size of orange (diameter), x_1.

a. Identify the independent variables as qualitative or quantitative.

b. Write a model that describes the relationship between $E(y)$ and size of orange as two parallel lines, one for each brand of extractor.

c. Modify the model of part **b** to permit the slopes of the two lines to differ.

d. Sketch typical response lines for the model of part **b**. Do the same for the model of part **c**. Carefully label your graphs.

e. Specify the null and alternative hypotheses you would use to determine whether the model in part **c** provides more information for predicting yield than does the model in part **b**.

f. Explain how you would obtain the quantities necessary to compute the F-statistic that would be used in testing the hypotheses you described in part **e**.

146 Global warming and foreign investments. Scientists believe that a major cause of global warming is higher levels of carbon dioxide (CO_2) in the atmosphere. In the *Journal of World-Systems Research* (Summer 2003), sociologists examined the impact of foreign investment dependence on CO_2 emissions in $n = 66$ developing countries. In particular, the researchers modeled the level of CO_2 emissions in 1996 based on foreign investments made 16 years earlier and several other independent variables. The variables and the model results are listed in the table below.

a. Interpret the value of R^2.

b. Use the value of R^2 to test the null hypothesis, $H_0: \beta_1 = \beta_2 = \cdots = \beta_7 = 0$, at $\alpha = .01$.

Results for Exercise 146

$y = \ln(\text{level of } CO_2 \text{ emissions in 1996})$	β Estimate	t-value	p-value
$x_1 = \ln(\text{foreign investments in 1980})$	.79	2.52	$< .05$
$x_2 = \text{gross domestic investment in 1980}$	.01	.13	$> .10$
$x_3 = \text{trade exports in 1980}$	$-.02$	-1.66	$> .10$
$x_4 = \ln(\text{GNP in 1980})$	$-.44$	$-.97$	$> .10$
$x_5 = \text{agricultural production in 1980}$	$-.03$	$-.66$	$> .10$
$x_6 = 1 \text{ if African country, 0 if not}$	-1.19	-1.52	$> .10$
$x_7 = \ln(\text{level of } CO_2 \text{ emissions in 1980})$	.56	3.35	$< .001$

$R^2 = .31$

Source: Based on Grimes, P., & Kentor, J. "Exporting the greenhouse: Foreign capital penetration and CO_2 emissions 1980–1996," *Journal of World-Systems Research*, Vol. IX, No. 2, Summer 2003 (Table 1).

Correlation matrix for Exercise 147

Independent Variable	x_2	x_3	x_4	x_5	x_6	$x_7 = \ln(\text{level of } CO_2$ emissions in 1980)
$x_1 = \ln(\text{foreign investments in 1980})$	.13	.57	.30	−.38	.14	−.14
$x_2 = \text{gross domestic investment in 1980}$		.49	.36	−.47	−.14	.25
$x_3 = \text{trade exports in 1980}$			.43	−.47	−.06	−.07
$x_4 = \ln(\text{GNP in 1980})$				−.84	−.53	.42
$x_5 = \text{agricultural production in 1980}$					.45	−.50
$x_6 = 1 \text{ if African country, 0 if not}$						−.47

Source: Grimes, P., & Kentor, J. "Exporting the greenhouse: Foreign capital penetration and CO_2 emissions 1980–1996," *Journal of World-Systems Research,* Vol. IX, No. 2, Summer 2003 (Appendix B).

c. What null hypothesis would you test to determine if foreign investments in 1980 is a statistically useful predictor of CO_2 emissions in 1996?

d. Conduct the test, part **c**, at $\alpha = .05$.

147 Global warming and foreign investments (cont'd). Refer to Exercise 146. A matrix giving the correlation (r) for each pair of independent variables is shown above. Identify the independent variables that are highly correlated. What problems may result from including these highly correlated variables in the regression model?

148 Accuracy of software effort estimates. Refer to the *Journal of Empirical Software Engineering* (Vol. 9, 2004) study of the accuracy of software effort estimates, Exercise 73. Recall that the dependent variable (y) is measured as relative error of the effort estimate of a software development task. A total of eight independent variables were evaluated as potential predictors of relative error. Each of these was formulated as a dummy variable, as shown in the table below.

a. The eight independent variables were entered into a stepwise regression, and the following two variables were selected for entry into the model: x_1 and x_8. Write the main effects model for $E(y)$ as a function of these two variables.

b. The stepwise regression yielded the following prediction equation:

$$\hat{y} = .12 - .28x_1 + .27x_8$$

Give a practical interpretation of the β estimates multiplied by x_1 and x_8.

c. The researcher is concerned that the sign of $\hat{\beta}_1$ in the model is the opposite from what is expected. (The researcher expects a project leader to have a smaller relative error of estimation than a developer.) Give at least one reason why this phenomenon occurred.

Company role of estimator:	$x_1 = 1$ if developer, 0 if project leader
Task complexity:	$x_2 = 1$ if low, 0 if medium/high
Contract type:	$x_3 = 1$ if fixed price, 0 if hourly rate
Customer importance:	$x_4 = 1$ if high, 0 if low/medium
Customer priority:	$x_5 = 1$ if time of delivery, 0 if cost or quality
Level of knowledge:	$x_6 = 1$ if high, 0 if low/medium
Participation:	$x_7 = 1$ if estimator participates in work, 0 if not
Previous accuracy:	$x_8 = 1$ if more than 20% accurate, 0 if less than 20% accurate

149 Urban population estimation using satellite images. Can the population of an urban area be estimated without taking a census? In *Geographical Analysis* (January, 2007) geography professors at the University of Wisconsin–Milwaukee and Ohio State University demonstrated the use of satellite image maps for estimating urban population. A portion of Columbus, Ohio, was partitioned into $n = 125$ census block groups, and satellite imagery was obtained. For each census block, the following variables were measured: population density (y), proportion of block with low-density residential areas (x_1), and proportion of block with high-density residential areas (x_2). A first-order model for y was fit to the data with the following results:

$$\hat{y} = -.0304 + 2.006x_1 + 5.006x_2, \quad R^2 = .686$$

a. Give a practical interpretation of each β estimate in the model.

b. Give a practical interpretation of the coefficient of determination, R^2.

c. State H_0 and H_a for a test of overall model adequacy.

d. Refer to part **c**. Compute the value of the test statistic.

e. Refer to parts **c** and **d**. Make the appropriate conclusion at $\alpha = .01$.

150 Trust in e-retailers. Electronic commerce (or "e-commerce") describes the use of electronic networks to simplify a business operation. With e-commerce, retailers now can advertise and sell their products easily over the Web. In *Internet Research: Electronic Networking Applications and Policy* (Vol. 11, 2001), Canadian researchers investigated the factors that impact the level of trust in Web e-retailers. Five quantitative independent variables were used to model level of trust (y):

$x_1 = $ ease of navigation on the Web site

$x_2 = $ consistency of the Web site

$x_3 = $ ease of learning the Web interface

$x_4 = $ perception of the interface design

$x_5 = $ level of support available to the user

a. Write a first-order model for level of trust as a function of the five independent variables.

b. The model, part **a**, was fit to data collected for $n = 66$ visitors to e-retailers' Web sites and yielded a coefficient of determination of $R^2 = .58$. Interpret this result.

c. Compute the *F*-statistic used to test the global utility of the model.

d. Using $\alpha = .10$, give the appropriate conclusion for the test, part **c**.

151 Prototyping new software. To meet the increasing demand for new software products, many systems development experts have adopted a prototyping methodology. The effects of prototyping on the system development life cycle (SDLC) was investigated in the *Journal of Computer Information Systems* (Spring 1993). A survey of 500 randomly selected corporate-level MIS managers was conducted. Three potential independent variables were (1) *importance* of prototyping to each phase of the SDLC; (2) degree of *support* prototyping provides for the SDLC; and (3) degree to which prototyping *replaces* each phase of the SDLC. The table below gives the pairwise correlations of the three variables in the survey data for one particular phase of the SDLC. Use this information to assess the degree of multicollinearity in the survey data. Would you recommend using all three independent variables in a regression analysis? Explain.

Variable Pairs	Correlation Coefficient, *r*
Importance–Replace	.2682
Importance–Support	.6991
Replace–Support	−.0531

Source: Hardgrave, B. C., Doke, E. R., & Swanson, N. E. "Prototyping effects of the system development life cycle: An empirical study," *Journal of Computer Information Systems,* Vol. 33, No. 3, Spring 1993, p. 16 (Table 1). Copyright © 1993 by IACIS. Reprinted by permission of the author.

152 A CEO's impact on corporate profits. Can a corporation's annual profit be predicted from information about the company's CEO? Each year *Forbes* publishes data on company profit (in \$ millions), CEO's annual income (in \$ thousands), and percentage of the company's stock owned by the CEO. Consider a model relating company profit (y) to CEO income (x_1) and stock percentage (x_2). Explain what it means to say that "CEO income x_1 and stock percentage x_2 interact to affect company profit y."

153 "Sun safety" study. Numerous "sun safety" products exist on the market to prevent excessive exposure to solar radiation. But many people do not practice "sun safety" or recognize the effectiveness of these products. A group of University of Arizona researchers examined the feasibility of educating preschool (4- to 5-year-old) children about sun safety (*American Journal of Public Health*, July 1995). A sample of 122 preschool children was divided into two groups, the control group and the intervention group. Children in the intervention group received a *Be Sun Safe* curriculum in preschool, while the control group did not. All children were tested for their knowledge, comprehension, and application of sun safety at two points in time: prior to the sun safety curriculum (pretest, x_1) and 7 weeks following the curriculum (posttest, y).

a. Write a first-order model for mean posttest score, $E(y)$, as a function of pretest score, x_1, and group. Assume that no interaction exists between pretest score and group.

b. For the model, part **a**, show that the slope of the line relating posttest score to pretest score is the same for both groups of children.

c. Repeat part **a** but assume that pretest score and group interact.

d. For the model, part **c**, show that the slope of the line relating posttest score to pretest score differs for the two groups of children.

Applying the Concepts—Intermediate

154 Promotion of supermarket vegetables. A supermarket chain is interested in exploring the relationship between the sales of its store-brand canned vegetables (y), the amount spent on promotion of the vegetables in local newspapers (x_1), and the amount of shelf space allocated to the brand (x_2). One of the chain's supermarkets was randomly selected, and over a 20-week period x_1 and x_2 were varied, as reported in the table.

Week	Sales (\$)	Advertising Expenditures (\$)	Shelf Space (sq. ft.)
1	2,010	201	75
2	1,850	205	50
3	2,400	355	75
4	1,575	208	30
5	3,550	590	75
6	2,015	397	50
7	3,908	820	75
8	1,870	400	30
9	4,877	997	75
10	2,190	515	30
11	5,005	996	75
12	2,500	625	50
13	3,005	860	50
14	3,480	1,012	50
15	5,500	1,135	75
16	1,995	635	30
17	2,390	837	30
18	4,390	1,200	50
19	2,785	990	30
20	2,989	1,205	30

a. Fit the following model to the data:

$$y = \beta_0 + \beta_1 x_1 + \beta_2 x_2 + \beta_3 x_1 x_2 + \varepsilon$$

b. Conduct an *F*-test to investigate the overall usefulness of this model. Use $\alpha = .05$.

c. Test for the presence of interaction between advertising expenditures and shelf space. Use $\alpha = .05$.

d. Explain what it means to say that advertising expenditures and shelf space interact.

e. Explain how you could be misled by using a first-order model instead of an interaction model to explain how advertising expenditures and shelf space influence sales.

f. Based on the type of data collected, comment on the assumption of independent errors.

155 Yield strength of steel alloy. Industrial engineers at the University of Florida used regression modeling as a tool to reduce the time and cost associated with developing new metallic alloys (*Modelling and Simulation in Materials Science and Engineering*, Vol. 13, 2005). To illustrate, the engineers built a regression model for the tensile yield strength (y) of a new steel alloy.

The potentially important predictors of yield strength are listed in the accompanying table.

x_1 = Carbon amount (% weight)
x_2 = Manganese amount (% weight)
x_3 = Chromium amount (% weight)
x_4 = Nickel amount (% weight)
x_5 = Molybdenum amount (% weight)
x_6 = Copper amount (% weight)
x_7 = Nitrogen amount (% weight)
x_8 = Vanadium amount (% weight)
x_9 = Plate thickness (millimeters)
x_{10} = Solution treating (milliliters)
x_{11} = Aging temperature (degrees, Celsius)

a. The engineers discovered that the variable Nickel (x_4) was highly correlated with the other potential independent variables. Consequently, Nickel was dropped from the model. Do you agree with this decision? Explain.

b. The engineers used stepwise regression on the remaining 10 potential independent variables in order to search for a parsimonious set of predictor variables. Do you agree with this decision? Explain.

c. The stepwise regression selected the following independent variables: x_1 = Carbon, x_2 = Manganese, x_3 = Chromium, x_5 = Molybdenum, x_6 = Copper, x_8 = Vanadium, x_9 = Plate thickness, x_{10} = Solution treating, and x_{11} = Aging temperature. All these variables were statistically significant in the stepwise model, with R^2 = .94. Consequently, the engineers used the estimated stepwise model to predict yield strength. Do you agree with this decision? Explain.

156 Optimizing semiconductor material processing. Fluorocarbon plasmas are used in the production of semiconductor materials. In the *Journal of Applied Physics* (Dec. 1, 2000), electrical engineers at Nagoya University (Japan) studied the kinetics of fluorocarbon plasmas in order to optimize material processing. In one portion of the study, the surface production rate of fluorocarbon radicals emitted from the production process was measured at various points in time (in milliseconds) after the radio frequency power was turned off. The data are given in the next table. Consider a model relating surface production rate (y) to time (x).

Rate	Time	Rate	Time
1.00	0.1	0.00	1.7
0.80	0.3	−0.10	1.9
0.40	0.5	−0.15	2.1
0.20	0.7	−0.05	2.3
0.05	0.9	−0.13	2.5
0.00	1.1	−0.08	2.7
−0.05	1.3	0.00	2.9
−0.02	1.5		

Source: Takizawa, K., et al. "Characteristics of C_3 radicals in high-density C_4F_8 plasmas studied by laser-induced fluorescence spectroscopy," *Journal of Applied Physics,* Vol. 88, No. 11, Dec. 1, 2000 (Figure 7). Copyright © 2000 by American Institute of Physics. Reprinted with permission.

a. Graph the data in a scatterplot. What trend do you observe?

b. Fit a quadratic model to the data. Give the least squares prediction equation.

c. Is there sufficient evidence of upward curvature in the relationship between surface production rate and time after turnoff? Use α = .05.

157 Modeling peak-hour roadway traffic. Traffic forecasters at the Minnesota Department of Transportation (MDOT) use regression analysis to estimate weekday peak-hour traffic volumes on existing and proposed roadways. In particular, they model y, the peak-hour volume (typically, the volume between 7:00 and 8:00 A.M.), as a function of x_1, the road's total volume for the day. For one project involving the redesign of a section of Interstate 494, the forecasters collected n = 72 observations of peak-hour traffic volume and 24-hour weekday traffic volume using electronic sensors that count vehicles. The data are saved in the file. (The first and last five observations are listed in the table.)

Observation Number	Peak-Hour Volume	24-Hour Volume	I-35
1	1,990.94	20,070	0
2	1,989.63	21,234	0
3	1,986.96	20,633	0
4	1,986.96	20,676	0
5	1,983.78	19,818	0
⋮	⋮	⋮	
68	2,147.93	22,948	1
69	2,147.85	23,551	1
70	2,144.23	21,637	1
71	2,142.41	23,543	1
72	2,137.39	22,594	1

Source: Traffic and Commodities Studies Section, Minnesota Department of Transportation, St. Paul, Minnesota.

a. Construct a scatterplot for the data, plotting peak-hour volume y against 24-hour volume x_1. Note the isolated group of observations at the top of the scatterplot. Investigators discovered that all of these data points were collected at the intersection of Interstate 35W and 46th Street. (These are observations 55–72 in the table.) While all other locations in the sample were three-lane highways, this location was unique in that the highway widens to four lanes just north of the electronic sensor. Consequently, the forecasters decided to include a dummy variable to account for a difference between the I-35W location and all other locations.

b. Knowing that peak-hour traffic volumes have a theoretical upper bound, the forecasters hypothesized that a second-order model should be used to explain the variation in y. Propose a complete second-order model for $E(y)$ as a function of 24-hour volume x_1 and the dummy variable for location.

c. Using an available statistical software package, fit the model of part **b** to the data. Interpret the results. Specifically, is the curvilinear relationship between peak-hour volume and 24-hour volume different at the two locations?

d. Conduct a residual analysis of the model, part **b**. Evaluate the assumptions of normality and constant error variance and determine whether any outliers exist.

158 Improving Math SAT scores. *Chance* (Winter 2001) did a study of students who paid a private tutor (or coach) to help them improve their Scholastic Assessment Test (SAT) scores. Multiple regression was used to estimate the effect of coaching on SAT–Mathematics scores. Data on 3,492 students (573 of whom were coached) were used to fit the model, $E(y) = \beta_0 + \beta_1 x_1 + \beta_2 x_2$, where y = SAT–Math score, x_1 = score on PSAT, and $x_2 = \{1$ if student was coached, 0 if not$\}$.

a. The fitted model had an adjusted R^2 value of .76. Interpret this result.

b. The estimate of β_2 in the model was 19, with a standard error of 3. Use this information to form a 95% confidence interval for β_2. Interpret the interval.

c. Based on the interval, part **b,** what can you say about the effect of coaching on SAT–Math scores?

d. As an alternative model, the researcher added several "control" variables, including dummy variables for student ethnicity (x_3, x_4, and x_5), a socioeconomic status index variable (x_6), two variables that measured high school performance (x_7 and x_8), the number of math courses taken in high school (x_9), and the overall GPA for the math courses (x_{10}). Write the hypothesized equation for $E(y)$ for the alternative model.

e. Give the null hypothesis for a nested model F-test comparing the initial and alternative models.

f. The nested model F-test, part **e,** was statistically significant at $\alpha = .05$. Practically interpret this result.

g. The alternative model, part **d,** resulted in $R_a^2 = .79$, $\hat{\beta}_2 = 14$, and $s_{\hat{\beta}_2} = 3$. Interpret the value of R_a^2.

h. Refer to part **g.** Find and interpret a 95% confidence interval for β_2.

i. The researcher concluded that "the estimated effect of SAT coaching decreases from the baseline model when control variables are added to the model." Do you agree? Justify your answer.

j. As a modification to the model of part **d,** the researcher added all possible interactions between the coaching variable (x_2) and the other independent variables in the model. Write the equation for $E(y)$ for this modified model.

k. Give the null hypothesis for comparing the models, parts **d** and **j.** How would you perform this test?

159 Impact of advertising on market share. The audience for a product's advertising can be divided into four segments according to the degree of exposure received as a result of the advertising. These segments are groups of consumers who receive very high (VH), high (H), medium (M), or low (L) exposure to the advertising. A company is interested in exploring whether its advertising effort affects its product's market share. Accordingly, the company identifies 24 sample groups of consumers who have been exposed to its advertising, six groups at each exposure level. Then, the company determines its product's market share within each group.

MKTSHR

Market Share within Group	Exposure Level	Market Share within Group	Exposure Level
10.1	L	12.2	H
10.3	L	12.1	H
10.0	L	11.8	H
10.3	L	12.6	H
10.2	L	11.9	H
10.5	L	12.9	H
10.6	M	10.7	VH
11.0	M	10.8	VH
11.2	M	11.0	VH
10.9	M	10.5	VH
10.8	M	10.8	VH
11.0	M	10.6	VH

a. Write a regression model that expresses the company's market share as a function of advertising exposure level. Define all terms in your model and list any assumptions you make about them.

b. Did you include interaction terms in your model? Why or why not?

c. The data in the table above were obtained by the company. Fit the model in part **a** to the data.

d. Is there evidence to suggest that the firm's expected market share differs for different levels of advertising exposure? Test using $\alpha = .05$.

160 Downtime of a production process. An operations manager is interested in modeling $E(y)$, the expected length of time per month (in hours) that a machine will be shut down for repairs, as a function of the type of machine (001 or 002) and the age of the machine (in years). The manager has proposed the following model:

REPAIR

$$E(y) = \beta_0 + \beta_1 x_1 + \beta_2 x_1^2 + \beta_3 x_2$$

where

x_1 = Age of machine

$x_2 = 1$ if machine type 001, 0 if machine type 002

The following data were obtained for $n = 20$ machine breakdowns.

Downtime (hours per month)	Machine Age, x_1 (years)	Machine Type	x_2
10	1.0	001	1
20	2.0	001	1
30	2.7	001	1
40	4.1	001	1
9	1.2	001	1
25	2.5	001	1
19	1.9	001	1
41	5.0	001	1
22	2.1	001	1
12	1.1	001	1
10	2.0	002	0
20	4.0	002	0
30	5.0	002	0
44	8.0	002	0
9	2.4	002	0
25	5.1	002	0
20	3.5	002	0
42	7.0	002	0
20	4.0	002	0
13	2.1	002	0

a. Use the data (saved in the file) to estimate the parameters of this model.

b. Do these data provide sufficient evidence to conclude that the second-order term (x_1^2) in the model proposed by the operations manager is necessary? Test using $\alpha = .05$.

c. Test the null hypothesis that $\beta_1 = \beta_2 = 0$ using $\alpha = .10$. Interpret the results of the test in the context of the problem.

161 Forecasting daily admission of a water park. To determine whether extra personnel are needed for the day, the owners of a water adventure park would like to find a model that would allow them to predict the day's attendance each morning before opening based on the day of the week and weather conditions. The model is of the form

$$E(y) = \beta_0 + \beta_1 x_1 + \beta_2 x_2 + \beta_3 x_3$$

where

$y = $ Daily admission

$$x_1 = \begin{cases} 1 & \text{if weekend} \\ 0 & \text{otherwise} \end{cases} \quad \text{(dummy variable)}$$

$$x_2 = \begin{cases} 1 & \text{if sunny} \\ 0 & \text{if overcast} \end{cases} \quad \text{(dummy variable)}$$

$x_3 = $ predicted daily high temperature (°F)

These data were recorded for a random sample of 30 days, and a regression model was fitted to the data. The least squares analysis produced the following results:

$$\hat{y} = -105 + 25x_1 + 100x_2 + 10x_3$$

with

$$s_{\hat{\beta}_1} = 10 \quad s_{\hat{\beta}_2} = 30 \quad s_{\hat{\beta}_3} = 4 \quad R^2 = .65$$

a. Interpret the estimated model coefficients.

b. Is there sufficient evidence to conclude that this model is useful for the prediction of daily attendance? Use $\alpha = .05$.

c. Is there sufficient evidence to conclude that the mean attendance increases on weekends? Use $\alpha = .10$.

d. Use the model to predict the attendance on a sunny weekday with a predicted high temperature of 95°F.

e. Suppose the 90% prediction interval for part **d** is (645, 1,245). Interpret this interval.

162 Forecasting daily admission of a water park (cont'd). Refer to Exercise 161. The owners of the water adventure park are advised that the prediction model could probably be improved if interaction terms were added. In particular, it is thought that the *rate* at which mean attendance increases as predicted high temperature increases will be greater on weekends than on weekdays. The following model is therefore proposed:

$$E(y) = \beta_0 + \beta_1 x_1 + \beta_2 x_2 + \beta_3 x_3 + \beta_4 x_1 x_3$$

The same 30 days of data used in Exercise 161 are again used to obtain the least squares model

$$\hat{y} = 250 - 700x_1 + 100x_2 + 5x_3 + 15x_1 x_3$$

with

$$s_{\hat{\beta}_4} = 3.0 \quad R^2 = .96$$

a. Graph the predicted day's attendance, y, against the day's predicted high temperature, x_3, for a sunny weekday and for a sunny weekend day. Plot both on the same graph for x_3 between 70°F and 100°F. Note the increase in slope for the weekend day. Interpret this.

b. Do the data indicate that the interaction term is a useful addition to the model? Use $\alpha = .05$.

c. Use this model to predict the attendance for a sunny weekday with a predicted high temperature of 95°F.

d. Suppose the 90% prediction interval for part **c** is (800, 850). Compare this result with the prediction interval for the model without interaction in Exercise 161, part **e**. Do the relative widths of the confidence intervals support or refute your conclusion about the utility of the interaction term (part **b**)?

e. The owners, noting that the coefficient $\hat{\beta}_1 = -700$, conclude the model is ridiculous because it seems to imply that the mean attendance will be 700 less on weekends than on weekdays. Explain why this is *not* the case.

163 Sale prices of apartments. A Minneapolis, Minnesota, real estate appraiser used regression analysis to explore the relationship between the sale prices of apartment buildings and various characteristics of the buildings. The file contains data for a random sample of 25 apartment buildings. *Note:* Physical condition of each apartment building is coded E (excellent), G (good), or F (fair). Data for selected observations are shown in the table below.

APTS

Data for Exercise 163 (selected observations)

Code No.	Sale Price, y ($)	No. of Apartments, x_1	Age of Structure, x_2 (years)	Lot Size, x_3 (sq. ft.)	No. of On-Site Parking Spaces, x_4	Gross Building Area, x_5 (sq. ft.)	Condition of Apartment Building
0229	90,300	4	82	4,635	0	4,266	F
0094	384,000	20	13	17,798	0	14,391	G
0043	157,500	5	66	5,913	0	6,615	G
0079	676,200	26	64	7,750	6	34,144	E
0134	165,000	5	55	5,150	0	6,120	G
⋮	⋮	⋮	⋮	⋮	⋮	⋮	⋮
0019	93,600	4	82	6,864	0	3,840	F
0074	110,000	4	50	4,510	0	3,092	G
0057	573,200	14	10	11,192	0	23,704	E
0104	79,300	4	82	7,425	0	3,876	F
0024	272,000	5	82	7,500	0	9,542	E

Source: Robinson Appraisal Co., Inc., Mankato, Minnesota.

a. Write a model that describes the relationship between sale price and number of apartment units as three parallel lines, one for each level of physical condition. Besure to specify the dummy variable coding scheme you use.

b. Plot y against x_1 (number of apartment units) for all buildings in excellent condition. On the same graph, plot y against x_1 for all buildings in good condition. Do this again for all buildings in fair condition. Does it appear that the model you specified in part **a** is appropriate? Explain.

c. Fit the model from part **a** to the data. Report the least squares prediction equation for each of the three building condition levels.

d. Plot the three prediction equations of part **c** on a scatterplot of the data.

e. Do the data provide sufficient evidence to conclude that the relationship between sale price and number of units differs depending on the physical condition of the apartments? Test using $\alpha = .05$.

f. Check the data set for multicollinearity. How does this impact your choice of independent variables to use in a model for sale price?

g. Conduct a complete residual analysis for the model to check the assumptions on ε.

164 Light output of a bulb. A firm that has developed a new type of lightbulb is interested in evaluating its performance in order to decide whether to market it. It is known that the light output of the bulb depends on the cleanliness of its surface area and the length of time the bulb has been in operation. Use the data in the next table and the procedures you learned in this chapter to build a regression model that relates drop in light output to bulb surface cleanliness and length of operation. Be sure to conduct a residual analysis also.

LTBULB

Drop in Light Output (% original output)	Bulb Surface (C = clean) (D = dirty)	Length of Operation (hours)
0	C	0
16	C	400
22	C	800
27	C	1,200
32	C	1,600
36	C	2,000
38	C	2,400
0	D	0
4	D	400
6	D	800
8	D	1,200
9	D	1,600
11	D	2,000
12	D	2,400

165 Forecasting a job applicant's merit rating. A large research and development firm rates the performance of each member of its technical staff on a scale of 0 to 100, and this merit rating is used to determine the size of the person's pay raise for the coming year. The firm's personnel department is interested in developing a regression model to help them forecast the merit rating that an applicant for a technical position will receive after being employed 3 years. The firm proposes to use the following second-order model to forecast the merit ratings of applicants who have just completed their graduate studies and have no prior related job experience:

$$E(y) = \beta_0 + \beta_1 x_1 + \beta_2 x_2 + \beta_3 x_1 x_2 + \beta_4 x_1^2 + \beta_5 x_2^2$$

where

$y =$ Applicant's merit rating after 3 years
$x_1 =$ Applicant's GPA in graduate school
$x_2 =$ Applicant's total score (verbal plus quantitative) on the Graduate Record Examination (GRE)

The model, fit to data collected for a random sample of $n = 40$ employees, resulted in SSE $= 1,830.44$ and SS(model) $= 4,911.5$. The reduced model $E(y) = \beta_0 + \beta_1 x_1 + \beta_2 x_2$ is also fit to the same data, resulting in SSE $= 3,197.16$.

a. Identify the appropriate null and alternative hypotheses to test whether the complete (second-order) model contributes information for the prediction of y.

b. Conduct the test of hypothesis given in part **a**. Test using $\alpha = .05$. Interpret the results in the context of this problem.

c. Identify the appropriate null and alternative hypotheses to test whether the complete model contributes more information than the reduced (first-order) model for the prediction of y.

d. Conduct the test of hypothesis given in part **c**. Test using $\alpha = .05$. Interpret the results in the context of this problem.

e. Which model, if either, would you use to predict y? Explain.

166 Household food consumption. The data in the table on the next page were collected for a random sample of 26 households in Washington, D.C. An economist wants to relate household food consumption, y, to household income, x_1, and household size, x_2, with the first-order model

$$E(y) = \beta_0 + \beta_1 x_1 + \beta_2 x_2$$

DCFOOD

a. Fit the model to the data. Do you detect any signs of multicollinearity in the data? Explain.

b. Is there visual evidence (from a residual plot) that a second-order model may be more appropriate for predicting household food consumption? Explain.

c. Comment on the assumption of constant error variance, using a residual plot. Does it appear to be satisfied?

d. Are there any outliers in the data? If so, identify them.

e. Based on a graph of the residuals, does the assumption of normal errors appear to be reasonably satisfied? Explain.

167 State casket sales restrictions. Refer to the *Journal of Law and Economics* (Feb. 2008) study of the impact of lifting casket sales restrictions on the cost of a funeral, Exercise 121. Recall that data collected for a sample of 1,437 funerals were used to fit the model, $E(y) = \beta_0 + \beta_1 x_1 + \beta_2 x_2 + \beta_3 x_1 x_2$, where y is the price (in dollars) of a direct burial, $x_1 = \{1$ if funeral home is

Data for Exercise 166

Household	Food Consumption ($1,000s)	Income ($1,000s)	Household Size	Household	Food Consumption ($1,000s)	Income ($1,000s)	Household Size
1	4.2	41.1	4	14	4.1	95.2	2
2	3.4	30.5	2	15	5.5	45.6	9
3	4.8	52.3	4	16	4.5	78.5	3
4	2.9	28.9	1	17	5.0	20.5	5
5	3.5	36.5	2	18	4.5	31.6	4
6	4.0	29.8	4	19	2.8	39.9	1
7	3.6	44.3	3	20	3.9	38.6	3
8	4.2	38.1	4	21	3.6	30.2	2
9	5.1	92.0	5	22	4.6	48.7	5
10	2.7	36.0	1	23	3.8	21.2	3
11	4.0	76.9	3	24	4.5	24.3	7
12	2.7	69.9	1	25	4.0	26.9	5
13	5.5	43.1	7	26	7.5	7.3	5

in a restricted state, 0 if not}, and $x_2 = $ {1 if price includes a basic wooden casket, 0 if no casket}. The estimated equation (with standard errors in parentheses) is:

$$\hat{y} = 1,432 + 793x_1 - 252x_2 + 261x_1x_2, \quad R^2 = .78$$

$$\quad\quad (70) \quad\quad (134) \quad\quad (109)$$

a. Interpret the reported value of R^2.

b. Use the value of R^2 to compute the F-statistic for testing the overall adequacy of the model. Test at $\alpha = .05$.

c. Compute the predicted price of a direct burial with a basic wooden casket for a funeral home in a restrictive state.

d. Estimate the difference between the mean price of a direct burial with a basic wooden casket and the mean price of a burial with no casket for a funeral home in a restrictive state.

e. Estimate the difference between the mean price of a direct burial with a basic wooden casket and the mean price of a burial with no casket for a funeral home in a nonrestrictive state.

f. Is there sufficient evidence to indicate that the difference between the mean price of a direct burial with a basic wooden casket and the mean price of a burial with no casket depends on whether the funeral home is in a restrictive state? Test using $\alpha = .05$.

Applying the Concepts—Advanced

168 Modeling monthly collision claims. A medium-sized automobile insurance company is interested in developing a regression model to help predict the monthly collision claims of its policyholders. A company analyst has proposed modeling monthly collision claims (y) in the middle Atlantic states as a function of the percentage of claims by drivers under age 30 (x_1) and the average daily temperature during the month (x_2). She believes that as the percentage of claims by drivers under age 30 increases, claims will rise because younger drivers are usually involved in more serious accidents than older drivers. She also believes that claims will rise as the average daily temperature decreases because lower temperatures are associated with icy, hazardous driving conditions. In order to develop a preliminary model, data were collected for the state of New Jersey over a 3-year period. The data are saved in the file. (The first and last five observations are listed in the table below.)

a. Use a statistical software package to fit the complete second-order model

$$E(y) = \beta_0 + \beta_1x_1 + \beta_2x_2 + \beta_3x_1x_2 + \beta_4x_1^2 + \beta_5x_2^2$$

b. Test the hypothesis $H_0: \beta_4 = \beta_5 = 0$ using $\alpha = .05$. Interpret the results in practical terms.

c. Do the results support the analysts' beliefs? Explain. (You may need to conduct further tests of hypotheses to answer this question.)

Data for Exercise 168 (first and last 5 months)

Month	Monthly Collision Claims, y ($)	Percentage of Monthly Claimants under the Age of 30, x_1	Newark, N.J., Average Daily Temperature during the Month, x_2 (°F)
1	116,250	50.0	31.5
2	217,180	60.8	33.0
3	43,436	45.1	45.0
4	159,265	56.4	53.9
5	130,308	53.3	63.9
⋮	⋮	⋮	⋮
44	136,528	53.1	76.6
45	193,608	59.8	68.6
46	38,722	45.6	62.4
47	212,309	63.9	50.0
48	118,796	52.3	42.3

Sources: New Jersey Department of Insurance; *Weather of U.S. Cities*, 4th ed., Gale Research Inc., Detroit, 1992.

169 Developing a model for college GPA. Many colleges and universities develop regression models for predicting the GPA of incoming freshmen. This predicted GPA can then be used to make admission decisions. Although most models use many independent variables to predict GPA, we will illustrate by choosing two variables:

x_1 = Verbal score on college entrance examination (percentile)

x_2 = Mathematics score on college entrance examination (percentile)

The file contains data on these variables for a random sample of 40 freshmen at one college. (Selected observations are shown in the table.) Use the data to develop a useful prediction equation for college freshman GPA (y). Be sure to conduct a residual analysis for the model.

Verbal, x_1	Mathematics, x_2	GPA, y
81	87	3.49
68	99	2.89
57	86	2.73
100	49	1.54
54	83	2.56
⋮	⋮	⋮
74	67	2.83
87	93	3.84
90	65	3.01
81	76	3.33
84	69	3.06

Critical Thinking Challenge

170 IQs and *The Bell Curve*. *The Bell Curve* (Free Press, 1994), written by Richard Herrnstein and Charles Murray (H&M), is a controversial book about race, genes, IQ, and economic mobility. The book heavily employs statistics and statistical methodology in an attempt to support the authors' positions on the relationships among these variables and their social consequences. The main theme of *The Bell Curve* can be summarized as follows:

(1) Measured intelligence (IQ) is largely genetically inherited.

(2) IQ is correlated positively with a variety of socioeconomic status success measures, such as prestigious job, high annual income, and high educational attainment.

(3) From 1 and 2, it follows that socioeconomic successes are largely genetically caused and therefore resistant to educational and environmental interventions (such as affirmative action).

The statistical methodology (regression) employed by the authors and the inferences derived from the statistics were critiqued in *Chance* (Summer 1995) and *The Journal of the American Statistical Association* (Dec. 1995). The following are just a few of the problems with H&M's use of regression that are identified:

Problem 1 H&M consistently use a trio of independent variables—IQ, socioeconomic status, and age—in a series of first-order models designed to predict dependent social outcome variables such as income and unemployment. (Only on a single occasion are interaction terms incorporated.) Consider, for example, the model

$$E(y) = \beta_0 + \beta_1 x_1 + \beta_2 x_2 + \beta_3 x_3$$

where y = income, x_1 = IQ, x_2 = socioeconomic status, and x_3 = age. H&M employ t-tests on the individual β parameters to assess the importance of the independent variables. As with most of the models considered in *The Bell Curve*, the estimate of β_1 in the income model is positive and statistically significant at $\alpha = .05$, and the associated t-value is larger (in absolute value) than the t-values associated with the other independent variables. Consequently, *H&M claim that IQ is a better predictor of income than the other two independent variables*. No attempt was made to determine whether the model was properly specified or whether the model provides an adequate fit to the data.

Problem 2 In an appendix, the authors describe multiple regression as a "mathematical procedure that yields coefficients for each of [the independent variables], indicating how much of a change in [the dependent variable] can be anticipated for a given change in any particular [independent] variable, with all the others held constant." Armed with this information and the fact that the estimate of β_1 in the model above is positive, *H&M infer that a high IQ necessarily implies (or causes) a high income, and a low IQ inevitably leads to a low income*. (Cause-and-effect inferences like this are made repeatedly throughout the book.)

Problem 3 The title of the book refers to the normal distribution and its well-known "bell-shaped" curve. There is a misconception among the general public that scores on intelligence tests (IQ) are normally distributed. In fact, most IQ scores have distributions that are decidedly skewed. Traditionally, psychologists and psychometricians have transformed these scores so that the resulting numbers have a precise normal distribution. H&M make a special point to do this. Consequently, *the measure of IQ used in all the regression models is normalized (i.e., transformed so that the resulting distribution is normal), despite the fact that regression methodology does not require predictor (independent) variables to be normally distributed*.

Problem 4 A variable that is not used as a predictor of social outcome in any of the models in *The Bell Curve* is level of education. H&M purposely omit education from the models, arguing that IQ causes education, not the other way around. Other researchers who have examined H&M's data report that *when education is included as an independent variable in the model, the effect of IQ on the dependent variable (say, income) is diminished*.

a. Comment on each of the problems identified. Why do each of these problems cast a shadow on the inferences made by the authors?

b. Using the variables specified in the model above, describe how you would conduct the multiple regression analysis. (Propose a more complex model and describe the appropriate model tests, including a residual analysis.)

Activity 1 — *Insurance Premiums:* Collecting Data for Several Variables

Premiums for life insurance, health insurance, homeowners insurance, and car insurance are based on more than one factor. In this activity, you will consider factors that influence the price that an individual pays for insurance and how you might collect data that would be useful in studying insurance premiums. You may wish to look over statements from your own insurance policies to determine how much coverage you have and how much it costs you.

1. Suppose that you host an independent Web site that provides information about insurance coverage and costs. You would like to add a feature to your site where a person answers a few simple questions in order to receive an estimate of what that person should expect to pay for insurance with a major carrier. Pick one type of insurance and determine what five questions you would most like to ask the person in order to prepare an estimate.

2. Use your five questions from Exercise 1 to define five independent variables. What is the dependent variable in this situation? What would a first-order model for this situation look like?

3. The estimates provided on your Web site will be based on a random sample of policies recently purchased through major carriers. Because insurance rates change frequently, your Web site will need to be frequently updated through new samples. Design a sampling method that can easily be repeated as needed. Be specific as to how you will identify people who have recently purchased policies, how you will choose your sample, what data you will gather, and what method you will use to gather the data.

4. Once the data are collected, describe how you will organize them and use them to complete the model in Exercise 3.

References

Barnett, V., & Lewis, T. *Outliers in Statistical Data*. New York: Wiley, 1978.

Belsley, D. A., Kuh, E., & Welsch, R. E. *Regression Diagnostics: Identifying Influential Data and Sources of Collinearity*. New York: Wiley, 1980.

Chatterjee, S., & Price, B. *Regression Analysis by Example*, 2nd ed. New York: Wiley, 1991.

Draper, N., & Smith, H. *Applied Regression Analysis*, 2nd ed. New York: Wiley, 1981.

Graybill, F. *Theory and Application of the Linear Model*. North Scituate, Mass.: Duxbury, 1976.

Kutner, M., Nachtsheim, C., Neter, J., & Li, W. *Applied Linear Statistical Models*, 5th ed. New York: McGraw. Hill/Irwin, 2005.

Mendenhall, W. *Introduction to Linear Models and the Design and Analysis of Experiments*. Belmont, Calif.: Wadsworth, 1968.

Mendenhall, W., & Sincich, T. *A Second Course in Statistics: Regression Analysis*, 7th ed. Upper Saddle River, N.J.: Prentice Hall, 2011.

Mosteller, F., & Tukey, J. W. *Data Analysis and Regression: A Second Course in Statistics*. Reading, Mass.: Addison-Wesley, 1977.

Rousseeuw, P. J., & Leroy, A. M. *Robust Regression and Outlier Detection*. New York: Wiley, 1987.

Weisberg, S. *Applied Linear Regression*, 2nd ed. New York: Wiley, 1985.

Technology images shown here are taken from SPSS Statistics Professional 20.0, Minitab 16, XLSTAT for Pearson, and Excel 2010.

Note: Automated commands for generating combinations and permutations are not available in SPSS.

SPSS: Multiple Regression

Step 1 Access the SPSS spreadsheet file that contains the dependent and independent variables.

Step 2 Click on the "Analyze" button on the SPSS menu bar and then click on "Regression" and "Linear," as shown in Figure S.1. The resulting dialog box appears as shown in Figure S.2.

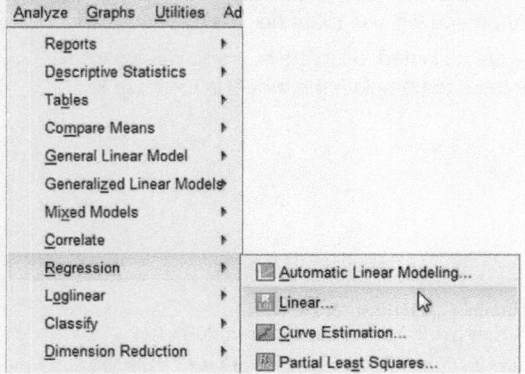

Figure S.1 SPSS menu options for regression

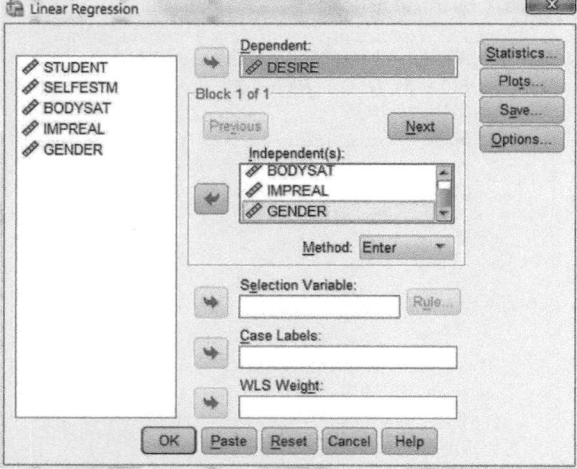

Figure S.2 SPSS linear regression dialog box

Step 3 Specify the dependent variable in the "Dependent" box and the independent variables in the "Independent(s)" box. [*Note:* If your model includes interaction and/or squared terms, you must create and add these higher-order variables to the SPSS spreadsheet file *prior* to running a regression analysis. You can do this by clicking the "Transform" button on the SPSS main menu and selecting the "Compute" option.]

Step 4 To perform a standard regression analysis, select "Enter" in the "Method" box. To perform a stepwise regression analysis, select "Stepwise" in the "Method" box.

Step 5 To perform a nested model *F*-test for additional model terms, click the "Next" button and enter the terms you want to test in the "Independent(s)" box. [*Note:* These terms, plus the terms you entered initially, form the complete model for the

nested *F*-test.] Next, click the "Statistics" button and select "R squared change." Click "Continue" to return to the main SPSS regression dialog box.

Step 6 To produce confidence intervals for the model parameters, click the "Statistics" button and check the appropriate menu items in the resulting menu list (see Figure S.3).

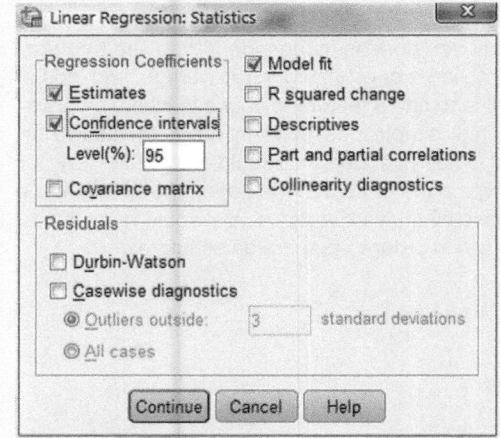

Figure S.3 SPSS linear regression save options

Step 7 To obtain prediction intervals for *y* and confidence intervals for *E(y)*, click the "Save" button and check the appropriate items in the resulting menu list. (The prediction intervals will be added as new columns to the SPSS data spreadsheet.)

Step 8 Residual plots are obtained by clicking the "Plots" button and making the appropriate selections on the resulting menu (see Figure S.4).

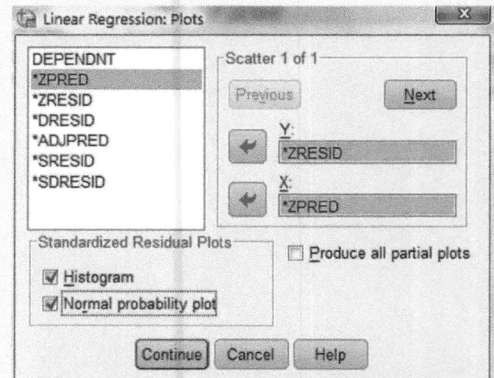

Figure S.4 SPSS linear regression plots options

Step 9 To return to the main Regression dialog box from any of these optional screens, click "Continue." Click "OK" on the Regression dialog box to view the multiple regression results.

Minitab: Multiple Regression

Multiple Regression

Step 1 Access the Minitab worksheet file that contains the dependent and independent variables.

Step 2 Click on the "Stat" button on the Minitab menu bar and then click on "Regression" and "Regression" again, as shown in Figure M.1.

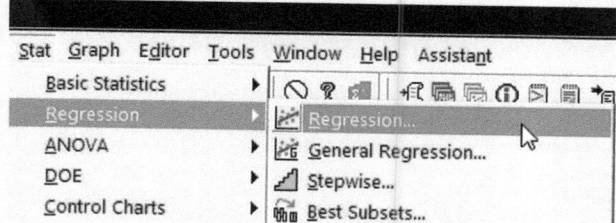

Figure M.1 Minitab menu options for regression

Step 3 The resulting dialog box appears as shown in Figure M.2. Specify the dependent variable in the "Response" box and the independent variables in the "Predictors" box. [*Note*: If your model includes interaction and/or squared terms, you must create and add these higher-order variables to the Minitab worksheet *prior* to running a regression analysis. You can do this by clicking the "Calc" button on the Minitab main menu and selecting the "Calculator" option.]

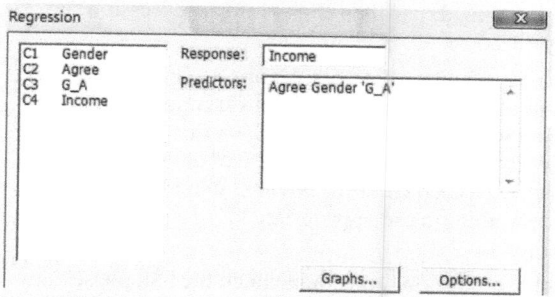

Figure M.2 Minitab regression dialog box

Step 4 To produce prediction intervals for y and confidence intervals for $E(y)$, click the "Options" button and then enter the values of the x's in the appropriate box on the resulting menu list (see Figure M.3).

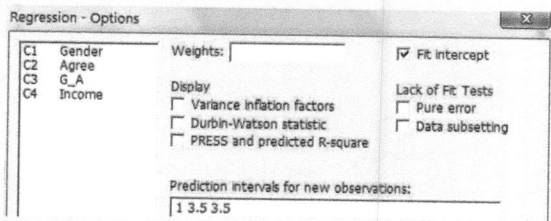

Figure M.3 Minitab regression options

Step 5 Residual plots are obtained by clicking the "Graphs" button and making the appropriate selections on the resulting menu (see Figure M.4).

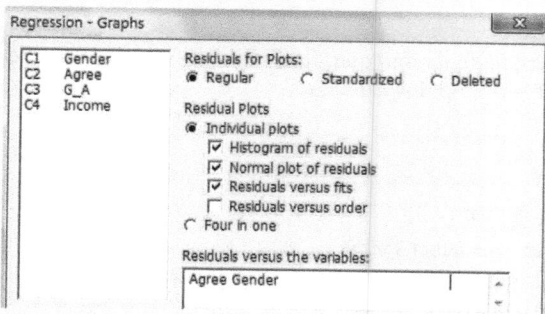

Figure M.4 Minitab regression graphs options

Step 6 To return to the main Regression dialog box from any of these optional screens, click "OK."

Step 7 When you have made all your selections, click "OK" on the main Regression dialog box to produce the Minitab multiple regression printout.

Stepwise Regression

Step 1 Click on the "Stat" button on the main menu bar; then click on "Regression" and click on "Stepwise" (see Figure M.1). The resulting dialog box appears like the one in Figure M.2.

Step 2 Specify the dependent variable in the "Response" box and the independent variables in the stepwise model in the "Predictors" box.

Step 3 As an option, you can select the value of α to use in the analysis by clicking on the "Methods" button and specifying the value. (The default is $\alpha = .15$.)

Step 4 Click "OK" to view the stepwise regression results.

Excel: Multiple Regression

Multiple Regression in Excel

Step 1 Access the Excel worksheet file that contains the dependent and independent variables. [*Note*: If your model includes interaction and/or squared terms, you must create and add these higher-order variables to the Excel worksheet *prior* to running a regression analysis.]

Step 2 Click "Data" from the Excel menu bar and then select "Data Analysis." The resulting menu is shown in Figure E.1.

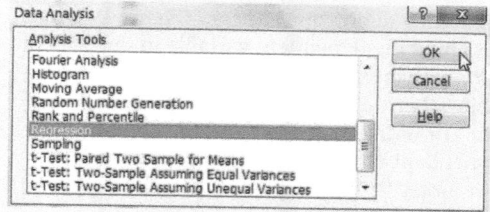

Figure E.1 Excel data analysis menu options for regression

Step 3 Select "Regression" from the drop-down menu and then click "OK." The resulting dialog box is shown in Figure E.2.

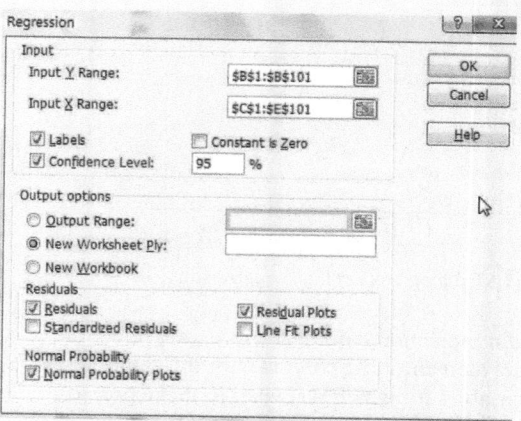

Figure E.2 Excel regression dialog box

Step 4 Specify the cell ranges for the y and x variables in the "Input" area of the Multiple Regression dialog box. [*Note*: The x variables must be in adjacent columns on the Excel worksheet.]

Step 5 Select the confidence level for confidence intervals for the model parameters.

Step 6 To produce graphs of the regression residual, select the "Residual Plots" and "Normal probability plots" options.

Step 7 After making all your selections, click "OK" to produce the multiple regression results.

Multiple Regression with Excel/XLSTAT

Step 1 Within XLSTAT, open the Excel spreadsheet with the data for the dependent and independent variables.

Step 2 Click the "XLSTAT" button on the Excel main menu bar, select "Modeling data," then click "Linear regression," as shown in Figure E.3.

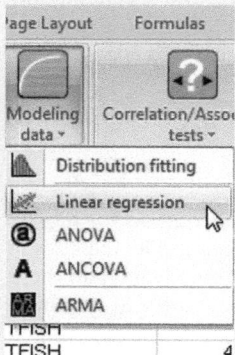

Figure E.3 XLSTAT menu options for multiple regression

Step 3 When the resulting dialog box appears (Figure E.4), enter the column containing the dependent variable in the "Y / Dependent variables" box. Depending on the type of independent variables, check either the "Quantitative" or "Qualitative" option (or both) and then enter the columns containing the independent variables in the appropriate "X / Explanatory variables" boxes.

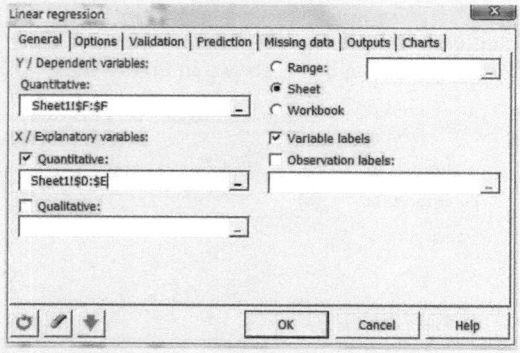

Figure E.4 XLSTAT dialog box for linear regression

Step 4 To obtain prediction/confidence intervals, select the "Prediction" tab, then enter the column with the values of the independent variables for which you want to make predictions in the "X / Explanatory variables" and "Quantitative" or "Qualitative" boxes, as shown in Figure E.5.

Step 5 Click "OK," then "Continue" to display the test results.

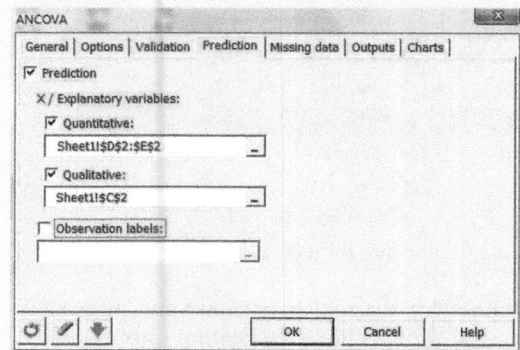

Figure E.5 XLSTAT dialog box for predictions

Stepwise Regression with Excel/XLSTAT

Step 1 Within XLSTAT, open the Excel spreadsheet with the data for the dependent and independent variables.

Step 2 Click the "XLSTAT" button on the Excel main menu bar, select "Modeling data," then click "Linear regression," as shown in Figure E.3.

Step 3 When the resulting dialog box appears (Figure E.4), enter the column containing the dependent variable in the "Y / Dependent variables" box. Depending on the type of independent variables, check either the "Quantitative" or "Qualitative" option (or both) and then enter the columns containing the independent variables in the appropriate "X / Explanatory variables" boxes.

Step 4 Select the "Options" tab, then check the "Stepwise" option under "Model selection," as shown in Figure E.6.

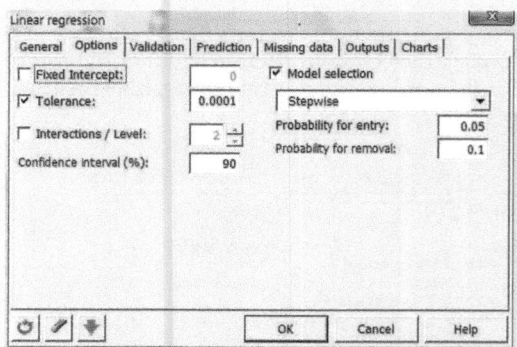

Figure E.6 XLSTAT regression options dialog box

Step 5 Click "OK," then "Continue" to display the stepwise results.

TI-84 Graphing Calculator: Multiple Regression

Note: Only simple linear and quadratic regression models can be fit using the TI-84 graphing calculator.

Quadratic Regression

I. Finding the Quadratic Regression Equation

Step 1 *Enter the data*

- Press **STAT** and select **1:Edit**

  Note: If the list already contains data, clear the old data. Use the up **ARROW** to highlight "**L1**" or "**L2**."

- Press **CLEAR ENTER**
- Use the **ARROW** and **ENTER** keys to enter the data set into **L1** and **L2**

Step 2 *Find the quadratic regression equation*

- Press **STAT** and highlight **CALC**
- Press **5** for **QuadReg**
- Press **ENTER**
- The screen will show the values for a, b, and c in the equation
- If the diagnostics are on, the screen will also give the value for r^2
- To turn the diagnostics feature on:
- Press **2nd 0** for **CATALOG**
- Press the **ALPHA** key and x^{-1} for **D**
- Press the down **ARROW** until **DiagnosticsOn** is highlighted
- Press **ENTER** twice

II. Graphing the Quadratic Curve with the Scatterplot

Step 1 *Enter the data as shown in part I above*

Step 2 *Set up the data plot*

- Press **Y =** and **CLEAR** all functions from the Y registers
- Press **2nd Y =** for **STAT PLOT**
- Press **1** for **Plot1**
- Set the cursor so that **ON** is flashing and press **ENTER**
- For **Type,** use the **ARROW** and **ENTER** keys to highlight and select the scatterplot (first icon in the first row)
- For **Xlist,** choose the column containing the *x*-data
- For **Freq,** choose the column containing the *y*-data

Step 3 *Find the regression equation and store the equation in Y1*

- Press **STAT** and highlight **CALC**
- Press **5** for **QuadReg** (*Note:* Don't press ENTER here because you want to store the regression equation in Y1)
- Press **VARS**
- Use the right **ARROW** to highlight **Y-VARS**
- Press **ENTER** to select **1:Function**
- Press **ENTER** to select **1:Y1**
- Press **ENTER**

Step 4 *View the scatterplot and regression line*

- Press **ZOOM** and then press **9** to select **9:ZoomStat**

Plotting Residuals

When computing a regression equation on the TI-84, the residuals are automatically computed and saved to a list called **RESID. RESID** can be found under the **LIST menu** (**2nd STAT**).

Step 1 *Enter the data*

- Press **STAT** and select **1:Edit**
- *Note:* If the list already contains data, clear the old data. Use the up **ARROW** to highlight "L1" or "L2."
- Press **CLEAR ENTER**
- Use the **ARROW** and **ENTER** keys to enter the data set into **L1** and **L2**

Step 2 *Compute the regression equation*

- Press **STAT** and highlight **CALC**
- Press **4** for **LinReg(ax + b)**
- Press **ENTER**

Step 3 *Set up the data plot*

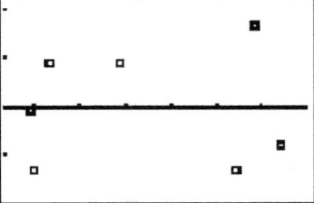

- Press **Y =** and **CLEAR** all functions from the Y registers
- Press **2nd Y =** for **STAT-PLOT**
- Press **1** for **Plot1**
- Set the cursor so that **ON** is flashing and press **ENTER**
- For **Type,** use the **ARROW** and **ENTER** keys to highlight and select the scatterplot (first icon in the first row).
- Move the cursor to **Xlist** and choose the column containing the *x*-data
- Move the cursor to **Ylist** and press **2nd STAT** for **LIST**
- Use the down **ARROW** to highlight the listname **RE-SID** and press **ENTER**

Step 4 *View the scatterplot of the residuals*

- Press **ZOOM 9** for **ZoomStat**

The Condo Sales Case

This case involves an investigation of the factors that affect the sale price of oceanside condominium units. It represents an extension of an analysis of the same data by Herman Kelting. Although condo sale prices have increased dramatically over the past 20 years, the relationship between these factors and sale price remains about the same. Consequently, the data provide valuable insight into today's condominium sales market.

The sales data were obtained for a new oceanside condominium complex consisting of two adjacent and connected eight-floor buildings. The complex contains 200 units of equal size (approximately 500 square feet each). The locations of the buildings relative to the ocean, the swimming pool, the parking lot, etc., are shown in the accompanying figure. There are several features of the complex that you should note:

1. The units facing south, called *ocean view*, face the beach and ocean. In addition, units in building 1 have a good view of the pool. Units to the rear of the building, called *bay-view*, face the parking lot and an area of land that ultimately borders a bay. The view from the upper floors of these units is primarily of wooded, sandy terrain. The bay is very distant and barely visible.

2. The only elevator in the complex is located at the east end of building 1, as are the office and the game room. People moving to or from the higher floor units in building 2 would likely use the elevator and move through the passages to their units. Thus, units on the higher floors and at a greater distance from the elevator would be less convenient; they would require greater effort in moving baggage, groceries, and so on and would be farther away from the game room, the office, and the swimming pool. These units also possess an advantage: there would be the least amount of traffic through the hallways in the area and hence they are the most private.

3. Lower-floor oceanside units are most suited to active people; they open onto the beach, ocean,

and pool. They are within easy reach of the game room, and they are easily reached from the parking area.

4. Checking the layout of the condominium complex, you discover that some of the units in the center of the complex, units ending in numbers 11 and 14, have part of their view blocked.

5. The condominium complex was completed at the time of the 1975 recession; sales were slow, and the developer was forced to sell most of the units at auction approximately 18 months after opening. Consequently, the auction data are completely buyer specified and hence consumer oriented in contrast to most other real estate sales data that are, to a high degree, seller and broker specified.

6. Many unsold units in the complex were furnished by the developer and rented prior to the auction. Consequently, some of the units bid on and sold at auction had furniture, others did not.

This condominium complex is obviously unique. For example, the single elevator located at one end of the complex produces a remarkably high level of both inconvenience and privacy for the people occupying units on the top floors in building 2. Consequently, the developer is unsure of how the height of the unit (floor number), distance of the unit from the elevator, presence or absence of an ocean view, etc., affect the prices of the units sold at auction. To investigate these relationships, the following data (saved in the data file) were recorded for each of the 106 units sold at the auction:

1. *Sale price.* Measured in hundreds of dollars (adjusted for inflation).

2. *Floor height.* The floor location of the unit; the variable levels are 1, 2, . . . , 8.

3. *Distance from elevator.* This distance, measured along the length of the complex, is expressed in number of condominium units. An additional two units of distance was added to the units in building 2 to account for the walking distance in the connecting area between the two buildings. Thus, the distance of unit 105 from the elevator would be 3, and the distance between unit 113 and the elevator would be 9. The variable levels are 1, 2, . . . , 15.

4. *View of ocean.* The presence or absence of an ocean view is recorded for each unit and specified

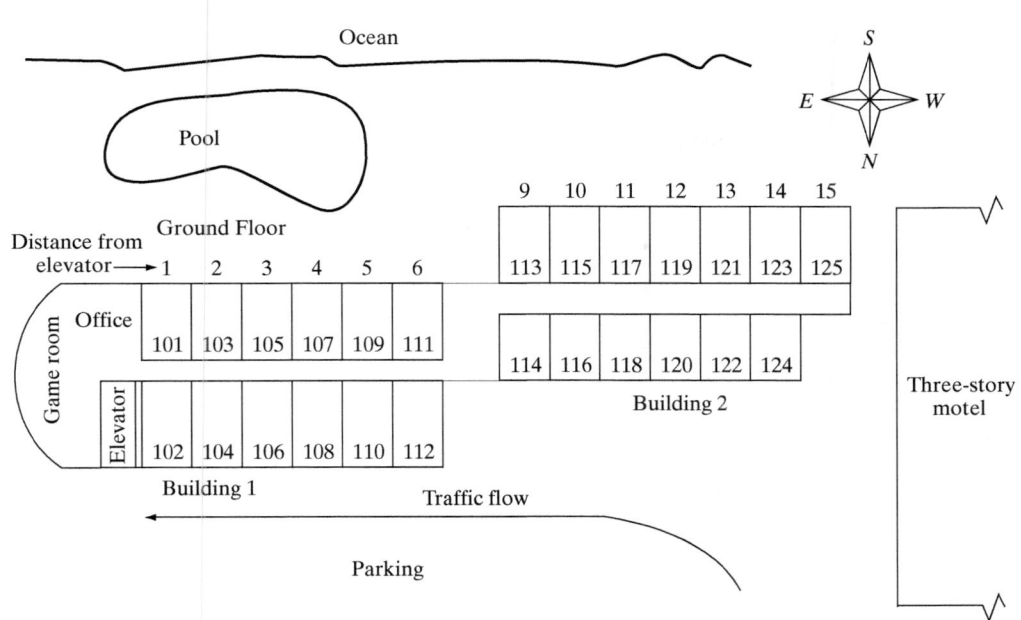

Figure C1 Layout of condominium complex

with a dummy variable (1 if the unit possesses an ocean view and 0 if not). Note that units not possessing an ocean view face the parking lot.

5. *End unit.* We expect the partial reduction of view of end units on the ocean side (numbers ending in 11) to reduce their sale price. The ocean view of these end units is partially blocked by building 2. This qualitative variable is also specified with a dummy variable (1 if the unit has a unit number ending in 11 and 0 if not).

6. *Furniture.* The presence or absence of furniture is recorded for each unit and is represented with a single dummy variable (1 if the unit was furnished and 0 if not).

Your objective for this case is to build a regression model that accurately predicts the sale price

of a condominium unit sold at auction. Prepare a professional document that presents the results of your analysis. Include graphs that demonstrate how each of the independent variables in your model affects auction price. A layout of the data file is described below.

Variable	Type
PRICE	QN
FLOOR	QN
DISTANCE	QN
VIEW	QL
ENDUNIT	QL
FURNISH	QL

(Number of Observations: 106) *Data Set:* CONDO

References Part I: First-Order Models with Quantitative Independent Variables

☐ Answers to Selected Exercises

1 a. $E(y) = \beta_0 + \beta_1 x_1 + \beta_2 x_2$ **b.** $E(y) = \beta_0 + \beta_1 x_1 + \beta_2 x_2 + \beta_3 x_3 + \beta_4 x_4$ **c.** $E(y) = \beta_0 + \beta_1 x_1 + \beta_2 x_2 + \beta_3 x_3 + \beta_4 x_4 + \beta_5 x_5$
3 a. $t = 1.45$, do not reject H_0 **b.** $t = 3.21$, reject H_0 **5** $n - (k + 1)$ **7 a.** Yes, $s = .117$ **b.** Yes, $F = 55.2$ **9 a.** \$93,002
b. \$98,774 **c.** 32% of sample variation in salary is explained by the model **d.** 95% confident that for each additional year of experience, mean salary will increase between \$2,700 to \$3,200, holding PhD status and manager status constant **e.** 95% confident that mean salary of PhDs will be \$11,500 to \$22,300 higher than salaries for non-PhDs, holding years of experience and manager status constant
f. 95% confident that mean salary of managers will be \$7,600 to \$14,600 higher than salaries for nonmanagers, holding years of experience and PhD status constant **11 a.** $F = 4.74$, p-value $< .01$, reject H_0 **b.** 13% of sample variation in Mach score can be explained by the model **c.** No **13 a.** $\hat{y} = 1.81231 + 0.10875 x_1 + 0.00017 x_2$ **c.** $(.027, .190)$ **d.** $(.00009, .00025)$
e. $\hat{y} = 1.20785 + 0.06343 x_1 + 0.00056 x_2$; $(.016, .111)$; $(.00024, .00088)$ **15 a.** $E(y) = \beta_0 + \beta_1 x_1 + \beta_2 x_2 + \beta_3 x_3 + \beta_4 x_4$
b. Reject H_0 **c.** Yes **d.** H_0: $\beta_1 = \beta_2 = \beta_3 = \beta_4 = 0$ **e.** $F > 3.37$ **f.** Thrill: reject H_0; Change: do not reject H_0; Surprise: do not reject H_0
17 a. $\hat{y} = 14.0107 - 2.1865 x_1 - .04794 x_2 - .3223 x_3 + .493 x_4$ **c.** Yes, $F = 40.85$ **d.** R_a^2 **e.** $t = -2.25$, reject H_0 **f.** $(.24, .74)$
19 a. $E(y) = \beta_0 + \beta_1 x_1 + \beta_2 x_2 + \beta_3 x_3 + \beta_4 x_4 + \beta_5 x_5$ **b.** $\hat{y} = 13,614.5 + 0.0888 x_1 - 9.201 x_2 + 14.394 x_3 + 0.35 x_4 - 0.848 x_5$
d. 458.83 **e.** $F = 147.3$, $p < .001$, reject H_0 **f.** .917 **g.** Yes, $t = -6.14$ **21 b.** $F = 5.11$, reject H_0 **23 a.** Model 1: $t = 2.58$,

reject H_0: $\beta_1 = 0$; Model 2: $t = 3.32$, reject H_0: $\beta_1 = 0$, $t = 6.47$, reject H_0: $\beta_2 = 0$, $t = -4.77$, reject H_0: $\beta_3 = 0$, $t = 0.24$, do not reject H_0: $\beta_4 = 0$; Model 3: $t = 3.21$, reject H_0: $\beta_1 = 0$, $t = 5.24$, reject H_0: $\beta_2 = 0$, $t = -4.00$, reject H_0: $\beta_3 = 0$, $t = 2.28$, reject H_0: $\beta_4 = 0$, $t = .014$, do not reject H_0: $\beta_5 = 0$ **c.** Model 2 **25 a.** 3.78 **b.** 4.68 **27 a.** 95% confident that mean desire is between 13.42 and 14.31 for all females with a self-esteem of 24, body satisfaction of 3, and impression of reality TV of 4 **b.** 95% confident that mean desire is between 8.79 and 10.89 for all males with a self-esteem of 22, body satisfaction of 9, and impression of reality TV of 4 **29 a.** (11,599.6, 13,665.5) **b.** (12,157.9, 13,107.1) **c.** Yes **31 a.** $\hat{y} = 130.22 + .169x_1 + .0259x_2 - 1.1115x_3$ **b.** $F = 100.06$, reject H_0 **c.** $(-5.76, 198.85)$ **33 a.** $\hat{y} = -3783 + .00875x_1 + 1.93x_2 + 3444x_3 + 2093x_4$ **b.** $F = 72.11$, reject H_0 **c.** (1,449, 2,424) **35 c.** Interaction is present **37 a.** $\hat{y} = -2.55 + 3.82x_1 + 2.63x_2 - 1.29x_1x_2$ **b.** Twisted plane **c.** $x_2 = 1$: $\hat{y} = .08 + 2.53x_1$; $x_2 = 3$: $\hat{y} = 5.34 - .05x_1$; $x_2 = 5$: $\hat{y} = 10.6 - 2.63x_1$ **e.** H_0: $\beta_3 = 0$ vs. H_a: $\beta_3 \neq 0$ **f.** $t = -8.06$, reject H_0 **39 a.** $E(y) = \beta_0 + \beta_1x_1 + \beta_2x_2 + \beta_3x_1x_2$ **b.** $(\beta_1 + 2.5\beta_3)$ **c.** $(\beta_1 + 5\beta_3)$ **d.** $(\beta_2 + 100\beta_3)$ **e.** H_0: $\beta_3 = 0$ **41 a.** $E(y) = \beta_0 + \beta_1x_1 + \beta_2x_2 + \beta_3x_1x_2$ **b.** $\beta_3 < 0$ **43 a.** $\hat{y} = 11.779 - 1.972x_1 + .585x_4 - .553x_1x_4$ **b.** 9.97 **c.** $F = 45.1$, reject H_0 **d.** .439 **e.** 2.35 **f.** $t = -2.00$, reject H_0 **45 a.** $E(y) = \beta_0 + \beta_1x_1 + \beta_2x_2 + \beta_3x_3 + \beta_4x_1x_3 + \beta_5x_2x_3$ **b.** $\hat{y} = 10,769 - 1,288x_1 + 218.8x_2 - 1,550.1x_3 - 10.99x_1x_3 + 19.99x_2x_3$ **c.** $t = -.93$, do not reject H_0 **d.** $t = 1.78$, do not reject H_0 **47 b.** $\hat{y} = .906 - .023x_1 + .305x_2 + .275x_5 - .003x_1x_2 + .002x_1x_5$; yes **49 a.** $E(y) = \beta_0 + \beta_1x + \beta_2x^2$ **b.** $E(y) = \beta_0 + \beta_1x_1 + \beta_2x_2 + \beta_3x_1x_2 + \beta_4x_1^2 + \beta_5x_2^2$ **c.** $E(y) = \beta_0 + \beta_1x_1 + \beta_2x_2 + \beta_3x_3 + \beta_4x_1x_2 + \beta_5x_1x_3 + \beta_6x_2x_3 + \beta_7x_1^2 + \beta_8x_2^2 + \beta_9x_3^2$ **51 a.** Yes, $F = 85.94$ **b.** H_0: $\beta_2 = 0$ vs. H_a: $\beta_2 > 0$ **c.** H_0: $\beta_2 = 0$ vs. H_a: $\beta_2 < 0$ **53 a.** Yes, $F = 25.93$ **b.** $t = -10.74$, reject H_0 **c.** $t = .60$, do not reject H_0 **55 b.** 22.6% of the sample variation in points scored is explained by the quadratic model **c.** No **d.** H_0: $\beta_2 = 0$ **57 b.** First-order model; first-order model; second-order model **59 a.** $E(y) = \beta_0 + \beta_1x_1 + \beta_2x_2 + \beta_3x_1x_2 + \beta_4x_1^2 + \beta_5x_2^2$ **b.** 14% of sample variation in attitude toward improving efficiency can be explained by the model **c.** Downward curvature in the relationship between attitude and congruence **d.** Evidence of interaction **61 a.** $E(y) = \beta_0 + \beta_1x$ **b.** $E(y) = \beta_0 + \beta_1x + \beta_2x^2$ **c.** Quadratic model **d.** $F = 57.75$, overall model is statistically useful; $t = 3.98$, sufficient evidence of curvature **e.** Quadratic model **63 a.** Curvilinear **b.** $\hat{y} = 154,243 - 1,908.9x + 5.93x^2$ **c.** $t = 5.66$, reject H_0 **65 b.** Possibly **c.** $\hat{y} = 2,802.4 + 122.95x$ **d.** $\hat{y} = 4,944.2 - 183.03x + 7.46x^2$ **e.** $t = 3.38$, reject H_0: $\beta_2 = 0$; 2nd-order **67** $E(y) = \beta_0 + \beta_1x_1 + \beta_2x_2$, where $x_1 = \{1$ level 1, 0 if not$\}$, $x_2 = \{1$ level 2, 0 if not$\}$; $\beta_0 = \mu_3, \beta_1 = \mu_1 - \mu_3, \beta_2 = \mu_2 - \mu_3$ **69 a.** Level 1: 10.2; Level 2: 6.2; Level 3: 22.2; Level 4: 12.2 **b.** H_0: $\beta_1 = \beta_2 = \beta_3 = 0$ **71 a.** Method: $x_1 = \{1$ manual, 0 if automated$\}$; Soil: $x_2 = \{1$ if clay, 0 if not$\}$, $x_3 = \{1$ if gravel, 0 if not$\}$; Slope: $x_4 = \{1$ if East, 0 if not$\}$, $x_5 = \{1$ if South, 0 if not$\}$, $x_6 = \{1$ if West, 0 if not$\}$, $x_7 = \{1$ if Southeast, 0 if not$\}$ **b.** $E(y) = \beta_0 + \beta_1x_1$ **c.** $E(y) = \beta_0 + \beta_1x_2 + \beta_2x_3$ **d.** $E(y) = \beta_0 + \beta_1x_4 + \beta_2x_5 + \beta_3x_6 + \beta_4x_7$ **73 a.** $E(y) = \beta_0 + \beta_1x$, $x = \{1$ if developer, 0 if not$\}$ **b.** $E(y) = \beta_0 + \beta_1x_1 + \beta_2x_2$, $x_1 = \{1$ if low, 0 if not$\}$, $x_2 = \{1$ if medium, 0 if not$\}$ **c.** $E(y) = \beta_0 + \beta_1x$, $x = \{1$ if fixed price, 0 if not$\}$ **d.** $E(y) = \beta_0 + \beta_1x_1 + \beta_2x_2$, $x_1 = \{1$ if time-of-delivery, 0 if not$\}$, $x_2 = \{1$ if cost, 0 if not$\}$ **75 a.** $x_1 = \{1$ if blond Caucasian, 0 if not$\}$, $x_2 = \{1$ if brunette Caucasian, 0 if not$\}$ **b.** $E(y) = \beta_0 + \beta_1x_1 + \beta_2x_2$ **c.** $\beta_0 + \beta_1$ **d.** β_1 **e.** $\beta_0 > 0$; $\beta_1 > 0$; $\beta_2 \approx 0$ **f.** Yes **77 a.** $x_1 = \{1$ if large/private, 0 if not$\}$, $x_2 = \{1$ if small/public, 0 if not$\}$, $x_3 = \{1$ if small/private, 0 if not$\}$ **b.** $E(y) = \beta_0 + \beta_1x_1 + \beta_2x_2 + \beta_3x_3$ **c.** Differences in mean likelihood of reporting sustainability policies among the four groups **d.** $x_1 = \{1$ if small, 0 if large$\}$, $x_2 = \{1$ if private, 0 if public$\}$ **e.** $E(y) = \beta_0 + \beta_1x_1 + \beta_2x_2$ **f.** Large/public: β_0; large/private: $\beta_0 + \beta_2$; small/public: $\beta_0 + \beta_1$; small/private: $\beta_0 + \beta_1 + \beta_2$ **g.** Public: $\mu_S - \mu_L = \beta_1$; private: $\mu_S - \mu_L = \beta_1$ **h.** $E(y) = \beta_0 + \beta_1x_1 + \beta_2x_2 + \beta_3x_1x_2$ **i.** Large/public: β_0; large/private: $\beta_0 + \beta_2$; small/public: $\beta_0 + \beta_1$; small/private: $\beta_0 + \beta_1 + \beta_2 + \beta_3$ **j.** Public: $\mu_S - \mu_L = \beta_1$; private: $\mu_S - \mu_L = \beta_1 + \beta_3$ **79 a.** $E(y) = \beta_0 + \beta_1x$, where $x = \{1$ if Lotion/Cream, 0 if not$\}$ **b.** $\hat{y} = .7775 + .1092x$ **c.** H_0: $\beta_1 = 0$ **d.** $t = .24$, do not reject H_0 **e.** $\hat{y} = 7.56 - 1.65x$; $t = -.46$, do not reject H_0 **81 a.** $E(y) = \beta_0 + \beta_1x_1 + \beta_2x_2$, $x_1 = \{1$ if group V, 0 if not$\}$, $x_2 = \{1$ if group S, 0 if not$\}$ **b.** $\hat{y} = 3.1667 - 1.0833x_1 - 1.4537x_2$ **c.** $F = 20.45$, reject H_0 **83 a.** $E(y) = \beta_0 + \beta_1x_1 + \beta_2x_1^2$ **b.** $E(y) = \beta_0 + \beta_1x_1 + \beta_2x_1^2 + \beta_3x_2 + \beta_4x_3$, where x_2 and x_3 are dummy variables **c.** add terms: $\beta_5x_1x_2 + \beta_6x_1x_3 + \beta_7x_1^2x_2 + \beta_8x_1^2x_3$ **d.** $\beta_5 = \beta_6 = \beta_7 = \beta_8 = 0$ **e.** $\beta_2 = \beta_5 = \beta_6 = \beta_7 = \beta_8 = 0$ **f.** $\beta_3 = \beta_4 = \beta_5 = \beta_6 = \beta_7 = \beta_8 = 0$ **85 a.** $\hat{y} = 48.8 - 3.4x_1 + .07x_1^2$; $\hat{y} = 46.44 + .3x_1 + .05x_1^2$; $\hat{y} = 41.3 - .7x_1 + .03x_1^2$ **87 a.** .58 **b.** .03 **89 a.** Model is statistically useful; reject H_0: $\beta_1 = \beta_2 = \cdots = \beta_{12} = 0$ **b.** No significant impact; do not reject H_0: $\beta_1 = 0$ **c.** Positive impact; reject H_0: $\beta_3 = 0$ **d.** $E(y) = \beta_0 + \beta_1x_3 + \beta_2x_5 + \beta_3x_6 + \cdots + \beta_9x_{12} + \beta_{10}x_3x_5 + \beta_{11}x_3x_6 + \cdots + \beta_{17}x_3x_{12}$ **91 a.** $x_2 = \{1$ if low, 0 if not$\}$, $x_3 = \{1$ if neutral, 0 if not$\}$ **b.** $E(y) = \beta_0 + \beta_1x_1 + \beta_2x_2 + \beta_3x_3$ **c.** $E(y) = \beta_0 + \beta_1x_1 + \beta_2x_2 + \beta_3x_3 + \beta_4x_1x_2 + \beta_5x_1x_3$ **d.** Part c **93 a.** $x_1 = \{1$ if channel catfish, 0 if not$\}$, $x_2 = \{1$ if largemouth bass, 0 if not$\}$ **b.** $E(y) = \beta_0 + \beta_1x_1 + \beta_2x_2 + \beta_3x_3$, where $x_3 = $ weight **c.** $E(y) = \beta_0 + \beta_1x_1 + \beta_2x_2 + \beta_3x_3 + \beta_4x_1x_3 + \beta_5x_2x_3$ **d.** $\hat{y} = 3.1 + 26.5x_1 - 4.1x_2 + 0.0037x_3$ **f.** $\hat{y} = 3.5 + 25.6x_1 - 3.47x_2 + 0.0034x_3 + 0.0008x_1x_3 - .0013x_2x_3$ **g.** .0042 **95 a.** $E(y) = \beta_0 + \beta_1x_1 + \beta_2x_1^2 + \beta_3x_2 + \beta_4x_3 + \beta_5x_4 + \beta_6x_1x_2 + \beta_7x_1x_3 + \beta_8x_1x_4 + \beta_9x_1^2x_2 + \beta_{10}x_1^2x_3 + \beta_{11}x_1^2x_4$, where $x_1 = $ sales volume and $x_2 - x_4$ are dummy variables for region **b.** $E(y) = (\beta_0 + \beta_5) + (\beta_1 + \beta_8)x_1 + (\beta_2 + \beta_{11})x_1^2$ **c.** $E(y) = (\beta_0 + \beta_3) + (\beta_1 + \beta_6)x_1 + (\beta_2 + \beta_9)x_1^2$ **d.** β_3 through β_{11} **e.** Yes, $F = 8.21$, $p = .000$ **97** a and b, a and d, a and e, b and c, b and d, b and e, c and e, d and e **99 a.** 5; 3 **b.** H_0: $\beta_3 = \beta_4 = 0$ **c.** $F = .38$, do not reject H_0 **101 a.** H_0: $\beta_4 = \beta_5 = 0$ **b.** Complete model: $E(y) = \beta_0 + \beta_1x_1 + \beta_2x_2 + \beta_3x_1x_2 + \beta_4x_2^2 + \beta_5x_1x_2^2$; reduced model: $E(y) = \beta_0 + \beta_1x_1 + \beta_2x_2 + \beta_3x_1x_2$ **c.** H_0: $\beta_3 = \beta_5 = 0$ **d.** Complete model: $E(y) = \beta_0 + \beta_1x_1 + \beta_2x_2 + \beta_3x_1x_2 + \beta_4x_2^2 + \beta_5x_1x_2^2$; reduced model: $E(y) = \beta_0 + \beta_1x_1 + \beta_2x_2 + \beta_4x_2^2$ **e.** H_0: $\beta_1 = \beta_3 = \beta_5 = 0$ **f.** Complete model: $E(y) = \beta_0 + \beta_1x_1 + \beta_2x_2 + \beta_3x_1x_2 + \beta_4x_2^2 + \beta_5x_1x_2^2$; reduced model: $E(y) = \beta_0 + \beta_2x_2 + \beta_4x_2^2$ **103 a.** $E(y) = \beta_0 + \beta_1x_1 + \beta_2x_2 + \beta_3x_1x_2 + \beta_4x_1^2 + \beta_5x_2^2$ **b.** H_0: $\beta_4 = \beta_5 = 0$ **c.** Complete model: $E(y) = \beta_0 + \beta_1x_1 + \beta_2x_2 + \beta_3x_1x_2 + \beta_4x_1^2 + \beta_5x_2^2$; reduced model: $E(y) = \beta_0 + \beta_1x_1 + \beta_2x_2 + \beta_3x_1x_2$ **d.** $SSE_R = 25,310,639$, $SSE_C = 19,370,350$, $MSE_C = 317,547$ **e.** $F = 9.35$ **f.** $F > 2.39$ **g.** reject H_0 **105 a.** $E(y) = \beta_0 + \beta_1x_1 + \beta_2x_2 + \beta_3x_3 + \beta_4x_4 + \beta_5x_1x_4 + \beta_6x_2x_4 + \beta_7x_3x_4$ **b.** $F = 24.40$, reject H_0 **c.** H_0: $\beta_5 = \beta_6 = \beta_7 = 0$ **d.** $F = 1.74$, do not reject H_0 **107 a.** Positive **c.** $E(y) = \beta_0 + \beta_1x_1 + \beta_2x_1^2 + \beta_3x_2 + \beta_4x_1x_2 + \beta_5x_1^2x_2$ **e.** H_0: $\beta_4 = \beta_5 = 0$ **f.** $F = .83$, do not reject H_0 **109 a.** $E(y) = \beta_0 + \beta_1x_1 + \beta_2x_2 + \beta_3x_3$ **b.** Add terms: $\beta_4x_1x_2 + \beta_5x_1x_3$ **c.** AL: β_1; TDS-3A: $\beta_1 + \beta_4$; FE: $\beta_1 + \beta_5$ **d.** Test H_0: $\beta_4 = \beta_5 = 0$ using a nested model F-test **111 a.** x_2 **b.** Yes **c.** Fit all models of the form $E(y) = \beta_0 + \beta_1x_2 + \beta_2x_i$ **113 a.** 7; $E(y) = \beta_0 + \beta_1x_i$ **b.** 6; $E(y) = \beta_0 + \beta_1x_1 + \beta_2x_i$ **c.** 5; $E(y) = \beta_0 + \beta_1x_1 + \beta_2x_2 + \beta_3x_i$ **115 a.** 11 **b.** 10 **d.** No interactions or squared terms; inflated Type I error rate **e.** $E(y) = \beta_0 + \beta_1(\text{AMAP}) + \beta_2(\text{NDF}) + \beta_3(\text{AMAP})(\text{NDF}) + \beta_4(\text{AMAP})^2 + \beta_5(\text{NDF})^2$ **f.** Test H_0: $\beta_3 = \beta_4 = \beta_5 = 0$ **117 a.** 11 **b.** 10 **c.** 1 **d.** $E(y) = \beta_0 + \beta_1x_{11} + \beta_2x_4 + \beta_3x_2 + \beta_4x_7 + \beta_5x_{10} + \beta_6x_1 + \beta_7x_9 + \beta_8x_3$ **e.** 67.7% of sample variation in overall satisfaction can be explained by the model

f. No interactions or squared terms in model; high probability of making at least one Type I error **119** Yes **121 a.** 2,234 **b.** No **c.** Yes, $z = 5.32$ **123 a.** No **b.** No **c.** Yes **d.** Possibly **125** Multicollinearity **127 a.** Satisfied **b.** Violated **c.** Some outliers **d.** Violated **e.** No **129 a.** $\hat{y} = 30,856 - 191.57x$ **b.** -1162.07 **c.** Yes, curvilinear trend **d.** Yes **131** Nonconstant error variance **133** Confidence interval **135 a.** $\hat{y} = 90.1 - 1.836x_1 + .285x_2$ **b.** .916 **c.** Yes, $F = 64.91$ **d.** $t = -5.01$, reject H_0 **e.** 10.68 **137** $E(y) = \beta_0 + \beta_1 x_1 + \beta_2 x_2 + \beta_3 x_3$, where $x_1 = \{1$ if level 2, 0 otherwise$\}$, $x_2 = \{1$ if level 3, 0 otherwise$\}$, $x_3 = \{1$ if level 4, 0 otherwise$\}$ **141** No degrees of freedom for error **143 a.** Confidence interval for $(\mu_1 - \mu_2)$ **b.** $E(y) = \beta_0 + \beta_1 x$, $x = \{1$ if public college, 0 if private college$\}$ **145 a.** Type of extractor is qualitative; size is quantitative **b.** $E(y) = \beta_0 + \beta_1 x_1 + \beta_2 x_2$, where $x_1 = $ diameter of orange, $x_2 = \{1$ if brand B, 0 if not$\}$ **c.** $E(y) = \beta_0 + \beta_1 x_1 + \beta_2 x_2 + \beta_3 x_1 x_2$ **e.** $H_0\colon \beta_3 = 0$ **147** x_4 and x_5 **149 a.** β_0: no practical interpretation; β_1: for every 1-unit increase in proportion of block with low-density areas, estimate density to increase 2.006 units; β_2: for every 1-unit increase in proportion of block with high-density areas, estimate density to increase 5.006 units **b.** 68.6% of sample variation in population density can be explained by the model **c.** $H_0\colon \beta_1 = \beta_2 = 0$ **d.** $F = 133.3$ **e.** reject H_0 **151** Importance and Support are correlated at .6991; no **153 a.** $E(y) = \beta_0 + \beta_1 x_1 + \beta_2 x_2$, where $x_2 = \{1$ if intervention group, 0 if control group$\}$ **b.** Slope $= \beta_1$ **c.** $E(y) = \beta_0 + \beta_1 x_1 + \beta_2 x_2 + \beta_3 x_1 x_2$ **d.** Intervention slope $= (\beta_1 + \beta_3)$; control slope $= \beta_1$ **155 a.** Possibly **b.** Yes **c.** No **157 b.** $E(y) = \beta_0 + \beta_1 x_1 + \beta_2 x_1^2 + \beta_3 x_2 + \beta_4 x_1 x_2 + \beta_5 x_1^2 x_2$, where $x_2 = \{1$ if 1-35W, 0 if not$\}$ **c.** Yes, $F = 457.73$ **d.** Assumptions satisfied **159 a.** $E(y) = \beta_0 + \beta_1 x_1 + \beta_2 x_2 + \beta_3 x_3$, where $x_1 = \{1$ if VH, 0 otherwise$\}$, $x_2 = \{1$ if H, 0 otherwise$\}$, $x_3 = \{1$ if M, 0 otherwise$\}$ **b.** No **c.** $\hat{y} = 10.2 + .5x_1 + 2.02x_2 + .683x_3$ **d.** Yes, $F = 63.09$ **161 b.** Yes, $F = 16.10$ **c.** Yes, $t = 2.5$ **d.** .945 **163 a.** $E(y) = \beta_0 + \beta_1 x_1 + \beta_2 x_6 + \beta_3 x_7$, where $x_6 = \{1$ if good, 0 otherwise$\}$, $x_7 = \{1$ if fair, 0 otherwise$\}$ **c.** Excellent: $\hat{y} = 188,875 + 15,617x_1$; good: $\hat{y} = 85,829 + 15,617x_1$; fair: $\hat{y} = 36,388 + 15,617x_1$ **e.** Yes, $F = 8.43$ **f.** $(x_1$ and $x_3)$, $(x_1$ and $x_5)$, $(x_3$ and $x_5)$ highly correlated **g.** Assumptions satisfied **165 a.** $H_0\colon \beta_1 = \beta_2 = \beta_3 = \beta_4 = \beta_5 = 0$ **b.** $F = 18.24$, reject H_0 **c.** $H_0\colon \beta_3 = \beta_4 = \beta_5 = 0$ **d.** $F = 8.46$, reject H_0 **e.** Second-order model **167 a.** 78% of sample variation in price is explained by the model **b.** $F = 1,693.55$, reject H_0 **c.** \$2,234 **d.** \$9 **e.** $-\$252$ **f.** yes, $t = 2.39$ **169** $\hat{y} = -11.5 + 0.189x_1 + 0.159x_2 - 0.00114x_1^2 - 0.000871x_2^2$

☐ Credits

☐ Technology Images

CONTENTS

Where We're Going

☐ Methods for Quality Improvement *Statistical Process Control*

STATISTICS in ACTION **Testing Jet Fuel Additive for Safety**

The American Society of Testing and Materials (ASTM) International provides standards and guidelines for materials, products, systems, and services. The Federal Aviation Administration (FAA) has a huge conglomerate of testing requirements for jet fuel safety that are spelled out in ASTM methods. This Statistics in Action involves an engineering firm that is developing a new method of surfactant detection in jet fuel.

Surfactants (surface active agents) are basically soaps that can form due to acids in the fuel but are more commonly caused by contamination from other products, such as engine cleaning additives. Although the surfactants do not directly cause problems, they reduce the ability of coalescing filters to remove water. Water in jet fuel carries bacteria that are deposited in tanks and engine components, causing major corrosion and engine damage.

The standard test for surfactants (described in ASTM Rule D-3948) is to use a miniature filter (Filter-A) with a pumping mechanism (Pump-A). A water/fuel mixture is pumped through the filter at a specific rate, and the amount of water that passes through the filter is detected with an optical transmittance test. Test measurements will typically yield a result between 80 and 85.

In an attempt to improve the precision of the surfactant test, the engineering firm compared the standard test (Pump-A with Filter-A) to three other pumping mechanism and filter option combinations—Pump-A with Filter-B, Pump-B with Filter-A, and Pump-B with Filter-B. Each day, a routine batch of jet fuel was created by adding 0.4 ppm of a surfactant solution. Twelve samples of the fuel were randomly selected and randomly divided into four groups of three samples each. The three samples in a group were tested for surfactants using one of the four pump/ filter combinations. Consequently, each day there were three test results for each

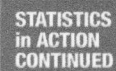

pump/filter method. This pattern of sampling continued for over 100 days. The test measurements are saved in four **JET** files. (Data for the first 5 days of the sampling experiment are listed in Table SIA1).

The firm wants to monitor the results of the surfactant tests and determine if one of the test methods yields the most stable process. In the Statistics in Action Revisited sections listed, we show how to analyze the data using methods for quality and process control.

Table SIA1	**Selected Data in the JET Files**						
Weekday	Month	Day	Sample	Pump-B Filter-A	Pump-A Filter-A	Pump-B Filter-B	Pump-A Filter-B
Tue	May	9	1	76	84	85	85
			2	81	91	84	84
			3	81	86	84	88
Wed	May	10	1	84	92	87	92
			2	81	93	82	95
			3	86	94	85	90
Thu	May	11	1	83	94	82	90
			2	82	96	85	87
			3	79	92	84	81
Fri	May	12	1	81	96	81	90
			2	84	91	82	91
			3	83	96	88	92
Mon	May	15	1	80	90	87	94
			2	88	92	85	94
			3	87	91	86	84

Data Sets: JETA-A, JETA-B, JETB-A, JETB-B

STATISTICS in ACTION REVISITED

▫ Monitoring the Process Mean

▫ Monitoring the Process Variation

Over the last several decades, U.S. firms have been seriously challenged by products (e.g., automobiles, electronics, cell phones) of superior quality from overseas, particularly from Japan. To meet this competitive challenge, more and more U.S. firms—both manufacturing and service firms—have quality-improvement initiatives of their own. Many of these firms stress **total quality management** (TQM) (i.e., the management of quality in all phases and aspects of their business, from the design of their products to production, distribution, sales, and service).

Broadly speaking, TQM is concerned with (1) finding out what it is that the customer wants, (2) translating those wants into a product or service design, and (3) producing a product or service that meets or exceeds the specifications of the design. In this chapter, we focus primarily on the third of these three areas and its major problem—product and service variation.

Variation is inherent in the output of all production and service processes. No two parts produced by a given machine are the same; no two transactions performed by a given bank teller are the same. Why is this a problem? With variation in output comes variation in the quality of the product or service. If this variation is unacceptable to customers, sales are lost, profits suffer, and the firm may not survive.

The existence of this ever-present variation has made statistical methods and statistical training vitally important to industry. In Sections 2–8 we present some of the tools and methods currently employed by firms worldwide to monitor and reduce product and service variation. But first, we provide a brief introduction to quality, processes, and systems—three key components of TQM.

1 Quality, Processes, and Systems

Quality

Before describing various tools and methods that can be used to monitor and improve the quality of products and services, we need to consider what is meant by the term *quality*. Quality can be defined from several different perspectives. To the engineers and scientists who design products, quality typically refers to the amount of some ingredient or attribute possessed by the product. For example, high-quality ice cream contains a large amount of butterfat. To managers, engineers, and workers involved in the production of a product (or the delivery of a service), quality usually means conformance to requirements, or the degree to which the product or service conforms to its design specifications. For example, in order to fit properly, the cap of a particular molded plastic bottle must be between 1.0000 inch and 1.0015 inches in diameter. Caps that do not conform to this requirement are considered to be of inferior quality.

Although quality can be defined from the perspective of either the designers or the producers of a product, in the final analysis both definitions should be derived from the needs and preferences of the *user* of the product or service. A firm that produces goods that no one wants to purchase cannot stay in business. We define *quality* accordingly.

> The **quality** of a good or service is indicated by the extent to which it satisfies the needs and preferences of its users.

To produce a high-quality product, it is necessary to study the needs and wants of consumers. What product characteristics are consumers looking for? What is it that influences users' perceptions of quality? This is the kind of knowledge that firms need in order to develop and deliver high-quality goods and services. The basic elements of quality are summarized in the eight dimensions shown in the box.

The Eight Dimensions of Quality*

1. **Performance:** The primary operating characteristics of the product. For an automobile, these would include acceleration, handling, smoothness of ride, gas mileage, and so forth.

2. **Features:** The "bells and whistles" that supplement the product's basic functions. Examples include CD players and digital clocks on cars and the frequent-flyer mileage and free drinks offered by airlines.

3. **Reliability:** Reflects the probability that the product will operate properly within a given period of time.

4. **Conformance:** The extent or degree to which a product meets preestablished standards. This is reflected in, for example, a pharmaceutical manufacturer's concern that the plastic bottles it orders for its drugs have caps that are between 1.0000 and 1.0015 inches in diameter, as specified in the order.

5. **Durability:** The life of the product. If repair is possible, durability relates to the length of time a product can be used before replacement is judged to be preferable to continued repair.

6. **Serviceability:** The ease of repair, speed of repair, and competence and courtesy of the repair staff.

7. **Aesthetics:** How a product looks, feels, sounds, smells, or tastes.

8. **Other perceptions that influence judgments of quality:** Such factors as a firm's reputation and the images of the firm and its products that are created through advertising.

Source: Based on "The Multiple Dimensions of Quality" from MANAGING QUALITY by David A. Garvin.

To design and produce products of high quality, it is necessary to translate the characteristics described in the box into product attributes that can be built into the product by the manufacturer—that is, user preferences must be interpreted in terms of product variables over which the manufacturer has control. For example, in considering the performance characteristics of a particular brand of wooden pencil, users may indicate a preference for being able to use the pencil for longer periods between sharpenings. The manufacturer may translate this performance characteristic into one or more measurable physical characteristics such as wood hardness, lead hardness, and lead composition. Besides being used to design high-quality products, such variables are used in the process of monitoring and improving quality during production.

Processes

In this chapter our attention is not on populations but on processes—such as manufacturing processes—and the output that they generate. In general, a process is defined as follows:

> A **process** is a series of actions or operations that transforms inputs to outputs. A process produces output over time.

In this chapter, we focus on organizational processes—those associated with organizations such as businesses and governments. Perhaps the best example is a manufacturing process, which consists of a series of operations, performed by people and machines, whereby inputs such as raw materials and parts are converted into finished products (the outputs). Examples include automobile assembly lines, oil refineries, and steel mills. Figure 1 presents a general description of a process and its inputs.

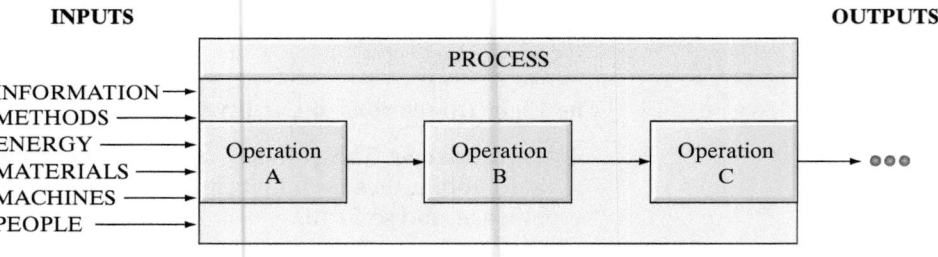

Figure 1

Graphical depiction of a process and its inputs

It is useful to think of processes as *adding value* to the inputs of the process. Manufacturing processes, for example, are designed so that the value of the outputs to potential customers exceeds the value of the inputs—otherwise the firm would have no demand for its products and would not survive.

Systems

To understand what causes variation in process output and how processes and their output can be improved, we must understand the role that processes play in *systems*.

> A **system** is a collection or arrangement of interacting processes that has an ongoing purpose or mission. A system receives inputs from its environment, transforms those inputs to outputs, and delivers them to its environment. In order to survive, a system uses feedback (i.e., information) from its environment to understand and adapt to changes in its environment.

Figure 2 presents a model of a basic system. As an example of a system, consider a manufacturing company. It has a collection of interacting processes—marketing research, engineering, purchasing, receiving, production, sales, distribution, billing, and so on.

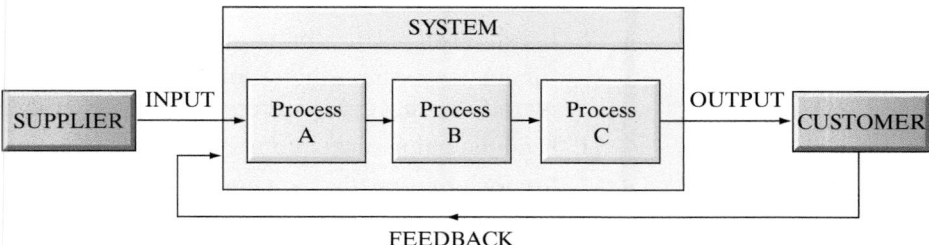

Figure 2
Model of a basic system

Its mission is to make money for its owners, to provide high-quality working conditions for its employees, and to stay in business. The firm receives raw materials and parts (inputs) from outside vendors that, through its production processes, it transforms to finished goods (outputs). The finished goods are distributed to its customers. Through its marketing research, the firm "listens" to (receives feedback from) its customers and potential customers in order to change or adapt its processes and products to meet (or exceed) the needs, preferences, and expectations of the marketplace.

Because systems are collections of processes, the various types of system inputs are the same as those listed in Figure 1 for processes. System outputs are products or services. These outputs may be physical objects made, assembled, repaired, or moved by the system; or they may be symbolical, such as information, ideas, or knowledge. For example, a brokerage house supplies customers with information about stocks and bonds and the markets where they are traded.

Two important points about systems and the output of their processes are as follows: (1) No two items produced by a process are the same; (2) variability is an inherent characteristic of the output of all processes. This is illustrated in Figure 3. No two cars produced by the same assembly line are the same: No two windshields are the same; no two wheels are the same; no two tires are the same; no two hubcaps are the same. The same thing can be said for processes that deliver services. Consider the services offered at the teller windows of a bank to two customers waiting in two lines. Will they wait in line the same amount of time? Will they be serviced by tellers with the same degree of expertise and with the same personalities? Assuming the customers' transactions are the same, will they take the same amount of time to execute? The answer to all these questions is no.

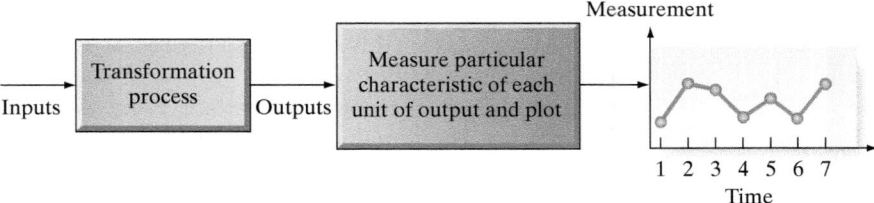

Figure 3
Output variation

Deming's 14 Points: Guidelines for Quality Improvement

1. Create constancy of purpose toward improvement of product and service, with the aim to become competitive, to stay in business, and to provide jobs.
2. Adopt the new philosophy.
3. Cease dependence on inspection to achieve quality.
4. End the practice of awarding business on the basis of price tag.
5. Improve constantly and forever the system of production and service, to improve quality and productivity, and thus constantly decrease costs.
6. Institute training.
7. Institute leadership.
8. Drive out fear, so that everyone may work effectively for the company.

9. Break down barriers between departments.

10. Eliminate slogans, exhortations, and arbitrary numerical goals and targets for the workforce that urge workers to achieve new levels of productivity and quality.

11. Eliminate numerical quotas.

12. Remove barriers that rob employees of their pride of workmanship.

13. Institute a vigorous program of education and self-improvement.

14. Take action to accomplish the transformation.

BIOGRAPHY

W. EDWARDS DEMING (1900–1993)
Deming's 14 Points

Born in Sioux City, Iowa, Ed Deming was raised on an Iowa farm until age 7, when his family moved to Wyoming. Because his parents emphasized the importance of education, Deming enrolled at the University of Wyoming in 1917, graduating 4 years later with a degree in electrical engineering. He eventually earned his PhD in mathematical physics from Yale University in 1928. Deming worked for both the U.S. Department of Agriculture and the Census Bureau before becoming a statistics professor at New York University and Columbia University. While studying under W. A. Shewhart in the 1930s, Deming become interested in the application of statistics to quality and process improvement for industry. He is probably most famous for his "14 Points for Management" (see preceding box)—guidelines that transform the organizational climate to one in which process-management efforts can flourish. In 1950, the Japanese Union of Scientists and Engineers invited Deming to present a series of lectures on these ideas. His expertise and advice on quality-control methods helped to revolutionize Japan's industry, leading to the Japanese economic boom in the twentieth century. (The *Deming Prize* is awarded every year to the corporation with the greatest accomplishment in quality improvement in the world.)

In general, variation in output is caused by the six factors listed below.

The Six Major Sources of Process Variation

1. People
2. Machines
3. Materials
4. Methods
5. Measurement
6. Environment

Awareness of this ever-present process variation has made training in statistical thinking and statistical methods highly valued by industry. By **statistical thinking** we mean the knack of recognizing variation and exploiting it in problem solving and decision making. The remainder of this chapter is devoted to statistical tools for monitoring process variation.

2 Statistical Control

For the rest of this chapter, we turn our attention to **control charts**—graphical devices used for monitoring process variation, identifying when to take action to improve the process, and assisting in diagnosing the causes of process variation. Control charts, developed by Walter Shewhart of Bell Laboratories in the mid-1920s, are the tool of choice for continuously monitoring processes. Before we go into the details of control chart construction and use, however, it is important that you have a fuller understanding of **process variation**. To this end, we discuss patterns of variation in this section.

The proper graphical method for describing the variation of process output is a *time series plot*, sometimes called a **run chart.** In a time series plot, the measurements of interest are plotted against time or are plotted in the order in which the measurements were made, as in Figure 4. Whenever you face the task of analyzing data that were generated over time, your first reaction should be

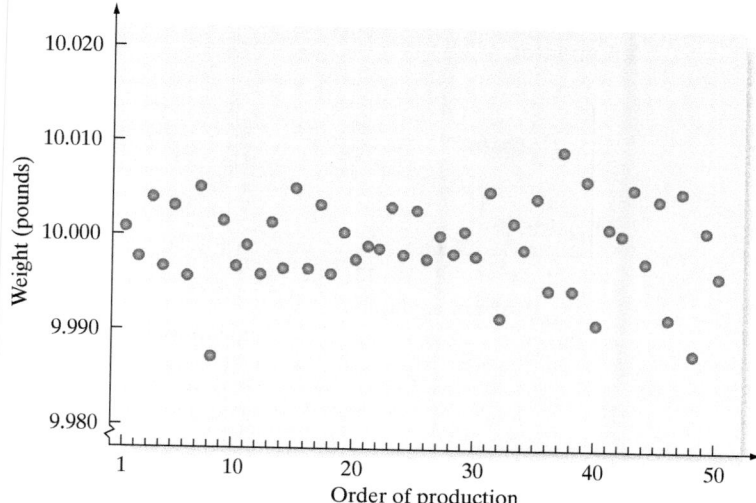

Figure 4

Time series plot of fill weights
for 50 consecutively produced
gallon cans of paint

to plot them. The human eye is one of our most sensitive statistical instruments. Take advantage of that sensitivity by plotting the data and allowing your eyes to seek out patterns in the data.

Let's begin thinking about process variation by examining the plot in Figure 4 more closely. The measurements, taken from a paint manufacturing process, are the weights of 50 one-gallon cans of paint that were consecutively filled by the same filling head (nozzle). The weights were plotted in the order of production. Do you detect any systematic, persistent patterns in the sequence of weights? For example, do the weights tend to drift steadily upward or downward over time? Do they oscillate—high, then low, then high, then low, and so on?

To assist your visual examination of this or any other time series plot, Roberts (1991) recommends enhancing the basic plot in two ways. First, compute (or simply estimate) the mean of the set of 50 weights and draw a horizontal line on the graph at the level of the mean. This **centerline** gives you a point of reference in searching for patterns in the data. Second, using straight lines, connect each of the plotted weights in the order in which they were produced. This helps display the sequence of the measurements. Both enhancements are shown in Figure 5.

Now do you see a pattern in the data? Successive points alternate up and down, high then low, in an **oscillating sequence.** In this case, the points alternate above and below the centerline. This pattern was caused by a valve in the paint-filling machine that tended to stick in a partially closed position every other time it operated.

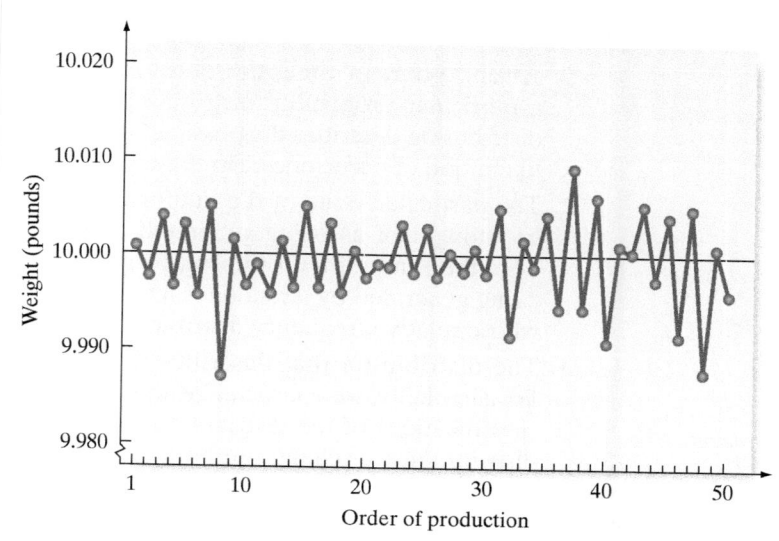

Figure 5

An enhanced version of the paint
fill time series

Other patterns of process variation are shown in Figure 6. We discuss several of them later.

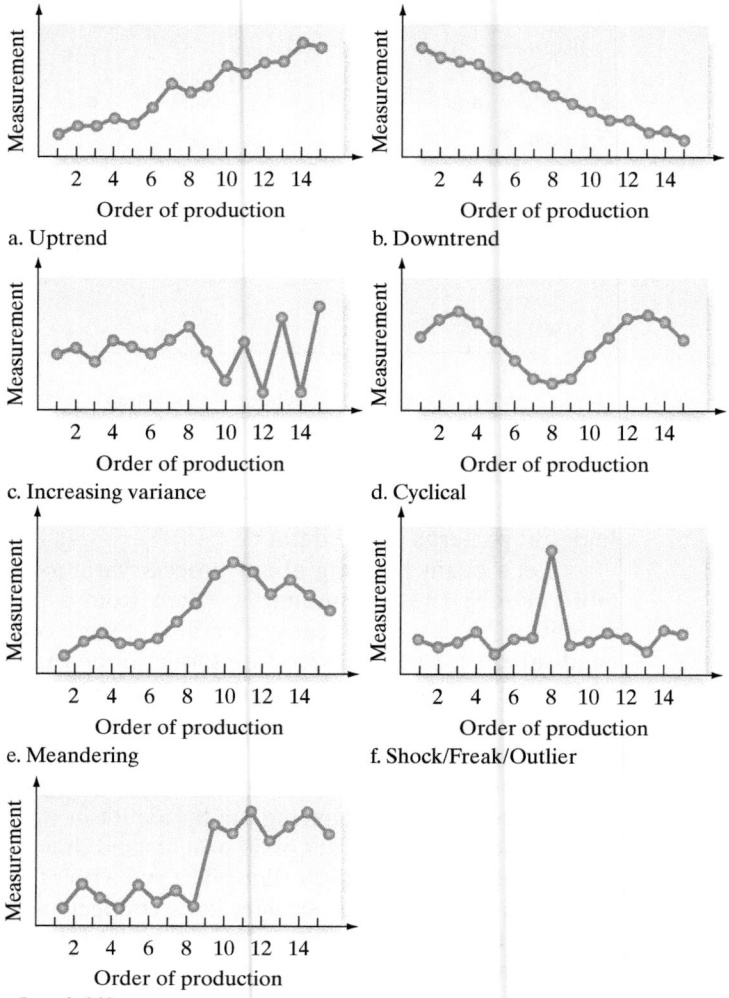

Figure 6

Patterns of process variation:
Some examples

In trying to describe process variation and diagnose its causes, it helps to think of the sequence of measurements of the output variable (e.g., weight, length, number of defects) as having been generated in the following way:

1. At any point in time, the output variable of interest can be described by a particular probability distribution (or relative frequency distribution). This distribution describes the possible values that the variable can assume and their likelihood of occurrence. Three such distributions are shown in Figure 7.

2. The particular value of the output variable that is realized at a given time can be thought of as being generated or produced according to the distribution described in point 1. (Alternatively, the realized value can be thought of as being generated by a random sample of size $n = 1$ from a population of values whose relative frequency distribution is that of point 1.)

3. The distribution that describes the output variable may change over time. For simplicity, we characterize the changes as being of three types: the mean (i.e., location) of the distribution may change; the variance (i.e., shape) of the distribution may change; or both. This is illustrated in Figure 8.

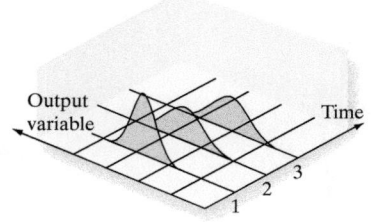

Figure 7

Distributions describing one output
variable at three points in time

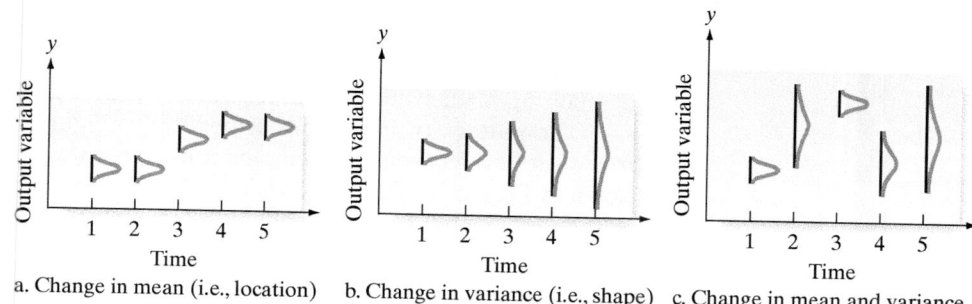

Figure 8

Types of changes in output variables

a. Change in mean (i.e., location) b. Change in variance (i.e., shape) c. Change in mean and variance

In general, when the output variable's distribution changes over time, we refer to this as a change in the *process*. Thus, if the mean shifts to a higher level, we say that the process mean has shifted. Accordingly, we sometimes refer to the distribution of the output variable as simply the **distribution of the process,** or the **output distribution of the process.**

Example 1

Models of Process Variation Patterns

Problem Reconsider the patterns of variation in Figure 6. These patterns are modeled in Figure 9. Interpret each graph.

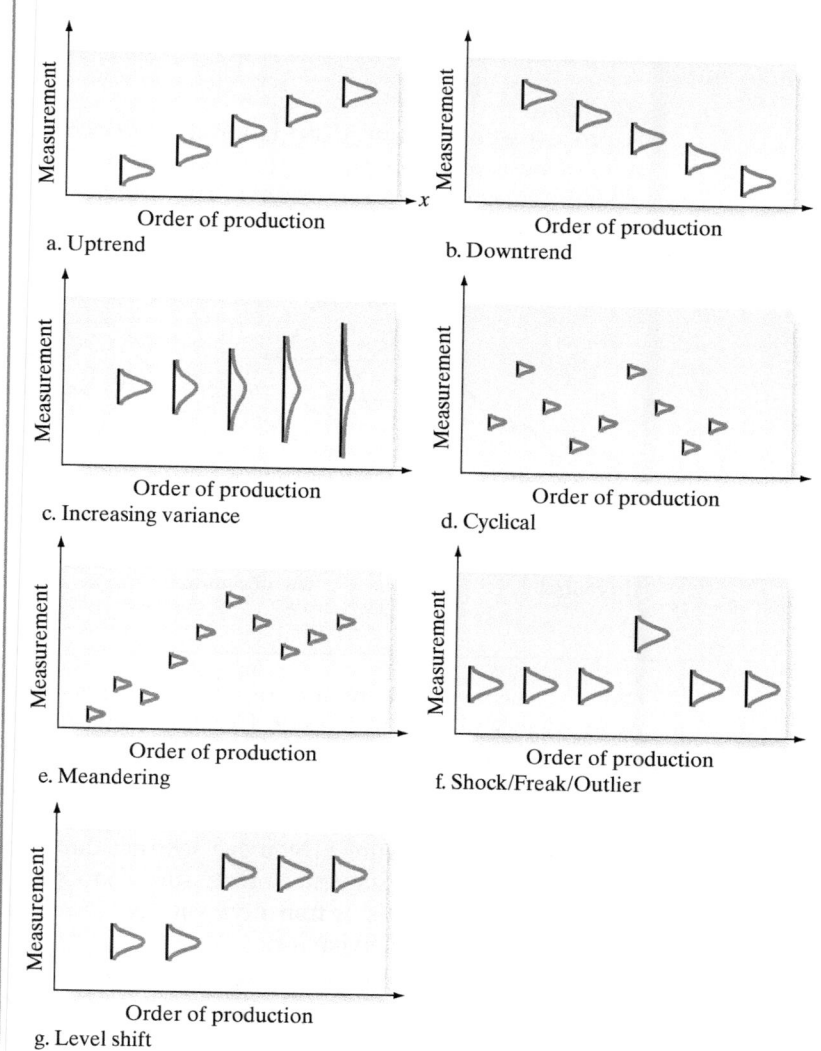

Figure 9

Patterns of process variation described by changing distributions

a. Uptrend
b. Downtrend
c. Increasing variance
d. Cyclical
e. Meandering
f. Shock/Freak/Outlier
g. Level shift

Solution The uptrend of Figure 6a can be characterized as resulting from a process whose mean is gradually shifting upward over time, as in Figure 9a. Gradual shifts like this are a common phenomenon in manufacturing processes. For example, as a machine wears out (e.g., cutting blades dull), certain characteristics of its output gradually change.

The pattern of increasing dispersion in Figure 6c can be thought of as resulting from a process whose mean remains constant but whose variance increases over time, as shown in Figure 9c. This type of deterioration in a process may be the result of worker fatigue. At the beginning of a shift, workers—whether they be typists, machine operators, waiters, or managers—are fresh and pay close attention to every item that they process. But as the day wears on, concentration may wane and the workers may become more and more careless or more easily distracted. As a result, some items receive more attention than other items, causing the variance of the workers' output to increase.

The sudden shift in the level of the measurements in Figure 6g can be thought of as resulting from a process whose mean suddenly increases but whose variance remains constant, as shown in Figure 9g. This type of pattern may be caused by such things as a change in the quality of raw materials used in the process or bringing a new machine or new operator into the process.

Look Back All the relative frequency distributions shown in Figure 9 appear to be mound-shaped and symmetric (i.e., normally distributed). In reality, one or more of the distributions are likely to be nonnormal.

One thing that the patterns in Example 1 have in common is that the distribution of the output variable *changes over time*. In such cases, we say the process lacks **stability.** We formalize the notion of stability in the following definition.

A process whose output distribution does *not* change over time is said to be in a state of **statistical control,** or simply **in control.** If it does change, it is said to be **out of statistical control,** or simply **out of control.** Figure 10 illustrates a sequence of output distributions for both an in-control and an out-of-control process.

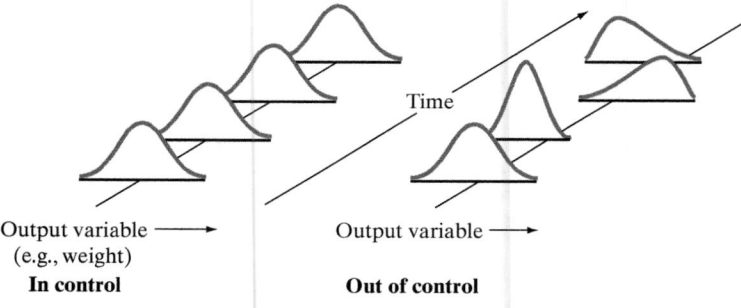

Figure 10

Comparison of in-control and out-of-control processes

Output variable ⟶
(e.g., weight)
In control

Output variable ⟶
Out of control

Time

Example 2

A Process "In Statistical Control"—Filling Paint Cans

Problem To see what the pattern of measurements looks like on a time series plot for a process that is in statistical control, consider Figure 11 (on the next page). These data are from the same paint-filling process we described earlier, but the sequence of measurements was made *after* the faulty valve was replaced. Interpret the graph.

Solution Examining Figure 11 you can see that there are no discernible persistent, systematic patterns in the sequence of measurements such as those in Figures 5 and 6a–6e. Nor are there level shifts or transitory shocks as in Figures 6f–6g. This "patternless" behavior is called **random behavior.**

Look Back The output of processes that are in statistical control exhibits random behavior. Thus, even the output of stable processes exhibits variation.

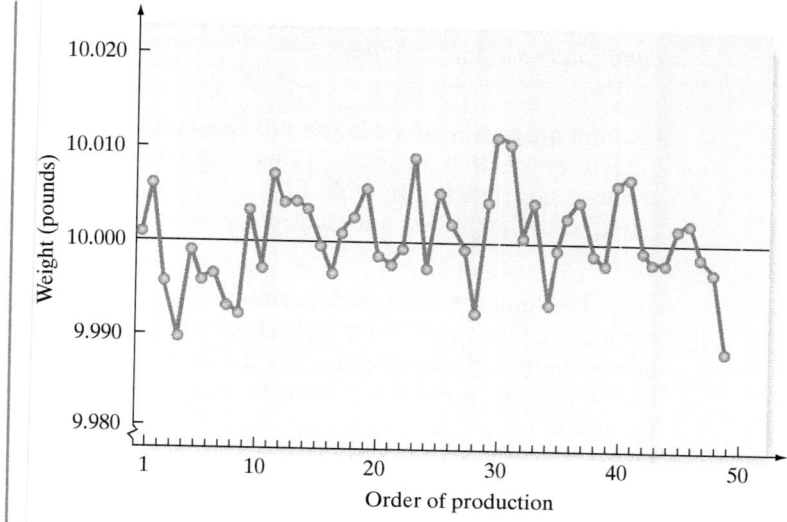

Figure 11

Time series plot of 50 consecutive paint can fills collected after replacing faulty valve

If a process is in control and remains in control, its future will be like its past. Accordingly, the process is predictable, in the sense that its output will stay within certain limits. This cannot be said about an out-of-control process. As illustrated in Figure 12, with most out-of-control processes, you have no idea what the future pattern of output from the process may look like.* You simply do not know what to expect from the process. Consequently, a business that operates out-of-control processes runs the risk of (1) providing inferior-quality products and services to its internal customers (people within the organization who use the outputs of the processes) and (2) selling inferior products and services to its external customers. In short, it risks losing its customers and threatens its own survival.

One of the fundamental goals of process management is to identify out-of-control processes, to take actions to bring them into statistical control, and to keep them in a state of statistical control. The series of activities used to attain this goal is referred to as *statistical process control.*

> The process of monitoring and eliminating variation in order to *keep* a process in a state of statistical control or to *bring* a process into statistical control is called **statistical process control (SPC).**

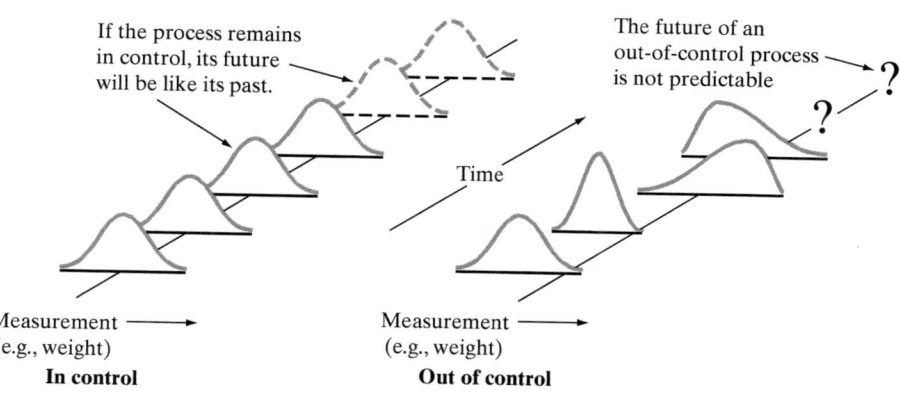

Figure 12

In-control processes are predictable; out-of-control processes are not

*The output variables of in-control processes may follow approximately normal distributions, as in Figures 10 and 12, or they may not. But any in-control process will follow the *same* distribution over time. Do not misinterpret the use of normal distributions in many figures in this chapter as indicating that all in-control processes follow normal distributions.

The variation that is exhibited by processes that are in control is said to be due to *common causes of variation*.

> **Common causes of variation** are the methods, materials, machines, personnel, and environment that make up a process and the inputs required by the process. Common causes are thus attributable to the design of the process. Common causes affect all output of the process and may affect everyone who participates in the process.

The total variation that is exhibited by an in-control process is due to many different common causes, most of which affect process output in very minor ways. In general, however, each common cause has the potential to affect every unit of output produced by the process. Examples of common causes include the lighting in a factory or office, the grade of raw materials required, and the extent of worker training. Each of these factors can influence the variability of the process output. Poor lighting can cause workers to overlook flaws and defects that they might otherwise catch. Inconsistencies in raw materials can cause inconsistencies in the quality of the finished product. The extent of the training provided to workers can affect their level of expertise and, as a result, the quality of the products and services for which they are responsible.

Because common causes are, in effect, designed into a process, the level of variation that results from common causes is viewed as being representative of the capability of the process. If that level is too great (i.e., if the quality of the output varies too much), the process must be redesigned (or modified) to eliminate one or more common causes of variation. Because process redesign is the responsibility of management, the *elimination of common causes of variation is typically the responsibility of management*, not the workers.

Processes that are out of control exhibit variation that is the result of both common causes and *special causes of variation*.

> **Special causes of variation** (sometimes called **assignable causes**) are events or actions that are not part of the process design. Typically, they are transient, fleeting events that affect only local areas or operations within the process (e.g., a single worker, machine, or batch of materials) for a brief period of time. Occasionally, however, such events may have a persistent or recurrent effect on the process.

Examples of special causes of variation include a worker accidentally setting the controls of a machine improperly, a worker becoming ill on the job and continuing to work, a particular machine slipping out of adjustment, and a negligent supplier shipping a batch of inferior raw materials to the process.

In the latter case, the pattern of output variation may look like Figure 6f. If instead of shipping just one bad batch the supplier continued to send inferior materials, the pattern of variation might look like Figure 6g. The output of a machine that is gradually slipping out of adjustment might yield a pattern like Figure 6a, 6b, or 6c. All these patterns owe part of their variation to common causes and part to the noted special causes. In general, we treat any pattern of variation other than a random pattern as due to both common and special causes.* Because the effects of special causes are frequently localized within a process, *special causes can often be diagnosed and eliminated by workers or their immediate supervisor*. Occasionally, however, they must be dealt with by management, as in the case of a negligent or deceitful supplier.

It is important to recognize that **most processes are not naturally in a state of statistical control.** As Deming (1986, p. 322) observed, *"Stability [i.e., statistical control] is seldom a natural state. It is an achievement, the result of eliminating special causes one by one…leaving only the random variation of a stable process"* (italics added).

---

*For certain processes (e.g., those affected by seasonal factors), a persistent systematic pattern—such as the cyclical pattern of Figure 6d—is an inherent characteristic. In these special cases, some analysts treat the cause of the systematic variation as a common cause. This type of analysis is beyond the scope of this text. We refer the interested reader to Alwan and Roberts (1988).

Process improvement first requires the identification, diagnosis, and removal of special causes of variation. Removing all special causes puts the process in a state of statistical control. Further improvement of the process then requires the identification, diagnosis, and removal of common causes of variation. The effects on the process of the removal of special and common causes of variation are illustrated in Figure 13.

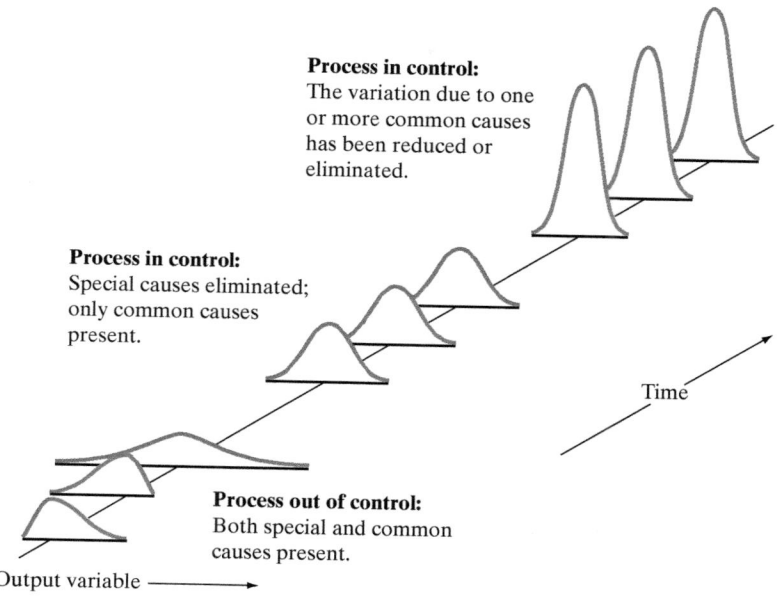

Process in control:
The variation due to one or more common causes has been reduced or eliminated.

Process in control:
Special causes eliminated; only common causes present.

Time

Process out of control:
Both special and common causes present.

Output variable ⟶

Figure 13
The effects of eliminating causes of variation

In the remainder of this chapter, we introduce you to some of the methods of statistical process control. In particular, we address how control charts help us determine whether a given process is in control.

3 The Logic of Control Charts

We use control charts to help us differentiate between process variation due to common causes and special causes—that is, we use them to determine whether a process is under statistical control (only common causes present) or not (both common and special causes present). Being able to differentiate means knowing when to take action to find and remove special causes and when to leave the process alone. If you take actions to remove special causes that do not exist—that is called *tampering with the process*—you may actually end up increasing the variation of the process and, thereby, hurting the quality of the output.

In general, control charts are useful for evaluating the past performance of a process and for monitoring its current performance. We can use them to determine whether a process was in control during, say, the past 2 weeks or to determine whether the process is remaining under control from hour to hour or minute to minute. In the latter case, our goal is the swiftest detection and removal of any special causes of variation that might arise. Keep in mind that **the primary goal of quality-improvement activities is variance reduction.**

In this chapter, we show you how to construct and use control charts for both quantitative and qualitative quality variables. Important quantitative variables include such things as weight, width, and time. An important qualitative variable is product status: defective or nondefective.

An example of a control chart is shown in Figure 14. A control chart is simply a time series plot of the individual measurements of a quality variable (i.e., an output variable), to which a centerline and two other horizontal lines called **control limits** have been added. The centerline represents the mean of the process (i.e., the mean of the quality variable) *when the process is in a state of statistical control.* The **upper control limit** and

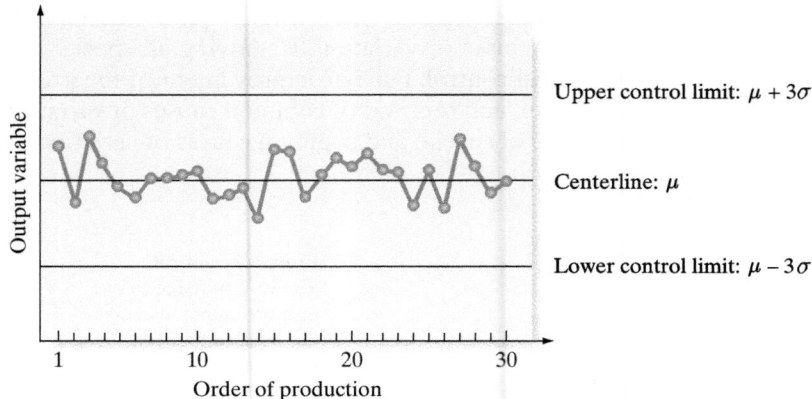

Figure 14
A control chart

the **lower control limit** are positioned so that *when the process is in control*, the probability of an individual value of the output variable falling outside the control limits is very small. Most practitioners position the control limits a distance of 3 standard deviations from the centerline (i.e., from the process mean) and refer to them as **3-sigma limits.** If the process is in control and following a normal distribution, the probability of an individual measurement falling outside the control limits is .0027 (less than 3 chances in 1,000). This is shown in Figure 15.

As long as the individual values stay between the control limits, the process is considered to be under control, meaning that no special causes of variation are influencing the output of the process. If one or more values fall outside the control limits, either a **rare event** has occurred or the process is out of control. Following the rare-event approach to inference described earlier in the text, such a result is interpreted as evidence that the process is out of control, and actions should be taken to eliminate the special causes of variation that exist.

Other evidence to indicate that the process is out of control may be present on the control chart. For example, if we observe any of the patterns of variation shown in Figure 6, we can conclude the process is out of control *even if all the points fall between the control limits*. In general, any persistent, systematic variation pattern (i.e., any nonrandom pattern) is interpreted as evidence that the process is out of control. We discuss this in detail in the next section.

You can make inferences about populations using hypothesis-testing techniques. In this case, we test

$$H_0: \text{Process is under control.}$$
$$H_a: \text{Process is out of control.}$$

Each time we plot a new point and see whether it falls inside or outside the control limits, we are running a two-sided hypothesis test. The control limits function as the critical values for the test.

Any time we reject the hypothesis that the process is under control and conclude that the process is out of control, we run the risk of making a Type I error (rejecting the null hypothesis when the null is true). Any time we conclude (or behave as if we conclude) that the process is in control, we run the risk of a Type II error (accepting the null hypothesis when the alternative is true). There is nothing magical or mystical

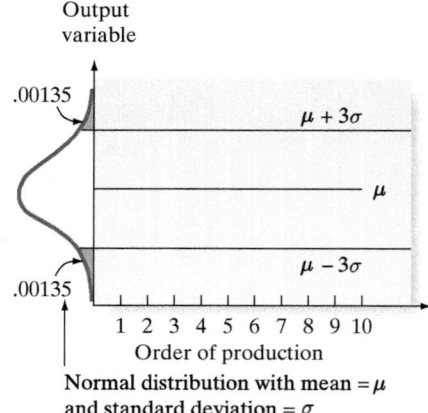

Figure 15

The probability of observing a measurement beyond the control limits when the process is in control

about control charts. Just as in any hypothesis test, the conclusion suggested by a control chart may be wrong.

One of the main reasons that 3-sigma control limits are used (rather than 2-sigma or 1-sigma limits, for example) is the small Type I error probability associated with their use. The probability we noted previously of an individual measurement falling outside the control limits—.0027—is a Type I error probability. Because we interpret a sample point that falls beyond the limits as a signal that the process is out of control, the use of 3-sigma limits yields very few signals that are "false alarms."

To make these ideas more concrete, we will construct and interpret a control chart for the paint-filling process discussed in Section 2. Our intention is simply to help you better understand the logic of control charts. Structured, step-by-step descriptions of how to construct control charts will be given in later sections.

Example 3

Control Chart for Individual Measurements—Filling Paint Cans

Problem The sample measurements from the paint-filling process, presented in Table 1, were previously plotted in Figure 11. Find the mean and standard deviation of the sample and use these values to construct a control chart for the individual measurements. What does the control chart imply about the behavior of the process?

Table 1		Fill Weights of 50 Consecutively Produced Cans of Paint							
Order	Weight	Order	Weight	Order	Weight	Order	Weight	Order	Weight
1	10.0008	11	9.9957	21	9.9977	31	10.0107	41	10.0054
2	10.0062	12	10.0076	22	9.9968	32	10.0102	42	10.0061
3	9.9948	13	10.0036	23	9.9982	33	9.9995	43	9.9978
4	9.9893	14	10.0037	24	10.0092	34	10.0038	44	9.9969
5	9.9994	15	10.0029	25	9.9964	35	9.9925	45	9.9969
6	9.9953	16	9.9995	26	10.0053	36	9.9983	46	10.0006
7	9.9963	17	9.9956	27	10.0012	37	10.0018	47	10.0011
8	9.9925	18	10.0005	28	9.9988	38	10.0038	48	9.9973
9	9.9914	19	10.0020	29	9.9914	39	9.9974	49	9.9958
10	10.0035	20	10.0053	30	10.0036	40	9.9966	50	9.9873

Data Set: CAN50

Solution An Excel/XLSTAT printout with descriptive statistics for the data is shown in Figure 16. The sample mean and standard deviation (highlighted on the printout) are $\bar{x} = 10$ and $s = .005$. Although these are estimates, in using and interpreting control charts, we treat them *as if* they were the actual mean μ and standard deviation σ of the in-control process. This is standard practice in control charting.

Descriptive statistics (Quantitative data):

Statistic	FillWt
No. of observations	50
Minimum	9.9873
Maximum	10.0107
Range	0.0234
1st Quartile	9.9965
Median	9.9995
3rd Quartile	10.0036
Mean	10.000
Variance (n-1)	0.000028
Standard deviation (n-1)	0.00527

Figure 16

Excel/XLSTAT summary statistics for 50 fill weights

The centerline of the control chart, representing the process mean, is drawn so that it intersects the vertical axis at $\bar{x} = 10$, as shown in Figure 17. The upper control limit (UCL) is drawn at a distance of $3s = 3(.005) = .015$ above the centerline, i.e., at $\bar{x} + 3s = 10 + .015 = 10.015$. The lower control limit (LCL) is $3s = .015$ below the

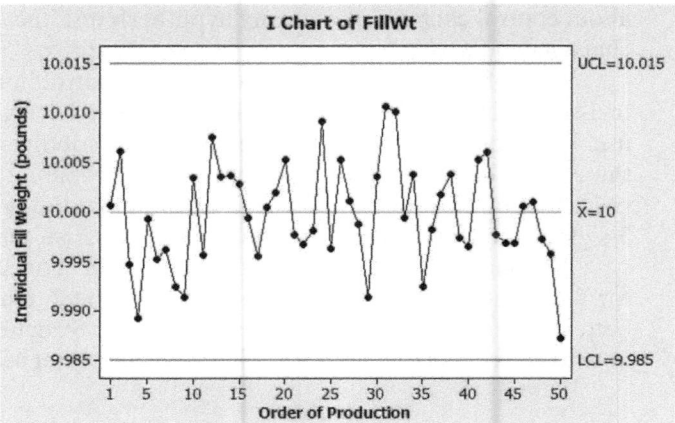

Figure 17

Minitab control chart of 50
consecutive fill weights

centerline, i.e., at $\bar{x} - 3s = 10 - .015 = 9.985$. Then the 50 sample weights are plotted on the chart in the order that they were generated by the paint-filling process.

As can be seen in Figure 17, all the weight measurements fall within the control limits. Further, there do not appear to be any systematic, nonrandom patterns in the data such as displayed in Figures 5 and 6. Accordingly, we are unable to conclude that the process is out of control—that is, we are unable to reject the null hypothesis that the process is in control. However, instead of using this formal hypothesis-testing language in interpreting control chart results, we prefer simply to say that the data suggest or indicate that the process is in control. We do this, however, with the full understanding that the probability of a Type II error is generally unknown in control chart applications and that we might be wrong in our conclusion.

Look Back What we are really saying when we conclude that the process is in control is that *the data indicate that it is better to behave as if the process were under control than to tamper with the process.*

We have portrayed the control chart hypothesis test as testing "in control" versus "out of control." Another way to look at it is this: When we compare the weight of an *individual* can of paint to the control limits in Example 3, we are conducting the following two-tailed hypothesis test:

$$H_0: \mu = 10$$
$$H_0: \mu \neq 10$$

where 10 is the centerline of the control chart. The control limits delineate the two rejection regions for this test. Accordingly, with each weight measurement that we plot and compare to the control limits, we are testing whether the process mean (the mean fill weight) has changed. Thus, what the control chart is monitoring is the mean of the process. **The control chart leads us to accept or reject statistical control on the basis of whether the mean of the process has changed or not.** This type of process instability is illustrated in the left graph in Figure 8. In the paint-filling process example, the process mean apparently has remained constant over the period in which the sample weights were collected.

Other types of control charts—one of which we will describe in Section 5—help us determine whether the *variance* of the process has changed, as in the center and right graphs of Figure 8.

The control chart we have just described is called an **individuals chart,** or an **x-chart.** The term *individuals* refers to the fact that the chart uses individual measurements to monitor the process—that is, measurements taken from individual units of process output. This is in contrast to plotting sample means on the control chart—for example, as we do in the next section.

Students sometimes confuse control limits with product *specification limits*. We have already explained control limits, which are a function of the natural variability of the process. Assuming we always use 3-sigma limits, the position of the control limits is a function of the size of σ, the process standard deviation.

> **Specification limits** are boundary points that define the acceptable values for an output variable (i.e., for a quality characteristic) of a particular product or service. They are determined by customers, management, and product designers. Specification limits may be two-sided, with upper and lower limits, or one-sided, with either an upper or a lower limit.

Process output that falls inside the specification limits is said to **conform to specifications.** Otherwise it is said to be **nonconforming.**

Unlike control limits, specification limits are not often dependent on the process in any way. A customer of the paint-filling process may specify that all cans contain no more than 10.005 pounds of paint and no less than 9.995 pounds. These are specification limits. The customer has reasons for these specifications but may have no idea whether the supplier's process can meet them. Both the customer's specification limits and the control limits of the supplier's paint-filling process are shown in Figure 18. Do you think the customer will be satisfied with the quality of the product received? We don't. Although some cans are within the specification limits, most are not, as indicated by the shaded region on the figure.

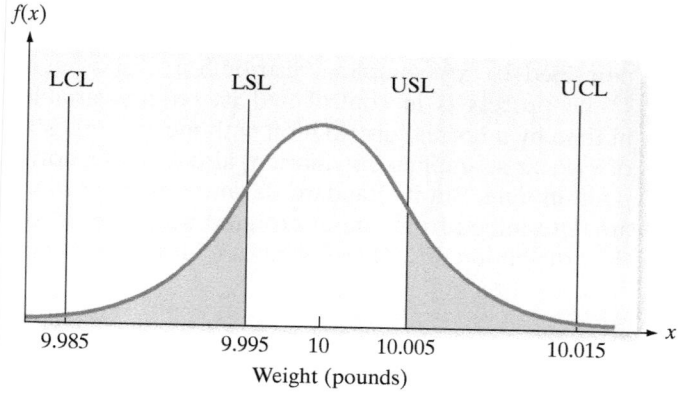

Figure 18

Comparison of control limits and specification limits

LCL = Lower control limit
UCL = Upper control limit
LSL = Lower specification limit
USL = Upper specification limit

4   A Control Chart for Monitoring the Mean of a Process: The $\bar{x}$-Chart

In the previous section, we introduced you to the logic of control charts by focusing on a chart that reflected the variation in individual measurements of process output. We used the chart to determine whether the process mean had shifted. The control chart we present in this section—the $\bar{x}$-**chart**—is also used to detect changes in the process mean, but it does so by monitoring the variation in the mean of samples that have been drawn from the process— that is, instead of plotting individual measurements on the control chart, in this case we plot sample means. Because of the additional information reflected in sample means (because each sample mean is calculated from n individual measurements), the $\bar{x}$-chart is more sensitive than the individuals chart for detecting changes in the process mean.

In practice, the $\bar{x}$-chart is rarely used alone. It is typically used in conjunction with a chart that monitors the variation of the process, usually a chart called an R-chart. The $\bar{x}$- and R-charts are the most widely used control charts in industry. Used in concert, these charts make it possible to determine whether a process has gone out of control because the variation has changed or because the mean has changed. We present the R-chart in the next section, at the end of which we discuss their simultaneous use.

For now, we focus only on the $\bar{x}$-chart. **Consequently, we assume throughout this section that the process variation is stable.**

Figure 19 is an example of an $\bar{x}$-chart. As with the individuals chart, the centerline represents the mean of the process, and the upper and lower control limits are positioned a distance of 3 standard deviations from the mean. However, because the chart is tracking sample means rather than individual measurements, the relevant standard deviation is the standard deviation of $\bar{x}$ not σ, the standard deviation of the output variable.

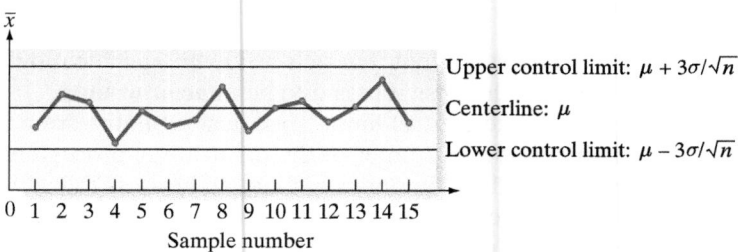

Figure 19

$\bar{x}$-chart

If the process were in statistical control, the sequence of $\bar{x}$'s plotted on the chart would exhibit random behavior between the control limits. Only if a rare event occurred or if the process went out of control would a sample mean fall beyond the control limits.

To better understand the justification for having control limits that involve $\sigma_{\bar{x}}$, consider the following. The $\bar{x}$-chart is concerned with the variation in $\bar{x}$, which is described by $\bar{x}$'s sampling distribution. But what is the sampling distribution of $\bar{x}$? If the process is in control and its output variable x is characterized at each point in time by a normal distribution with mean μ and standard deviation σ, the distribution of $\bar{x}$ (i.e., $\bar{x}$'s sampling distribution) also follows a normal distribution with mean μ at each point in time. But its standard deviation is $\sigma_{\bar{x}} = \sigma/\sqrt{n}$. The control limits of the $\bar{x}$-chart are determined from and interpreted with respect to the sampling distribution of $\bar{x}$, not the distribution of x. These points are illustrated in Figure 20.*

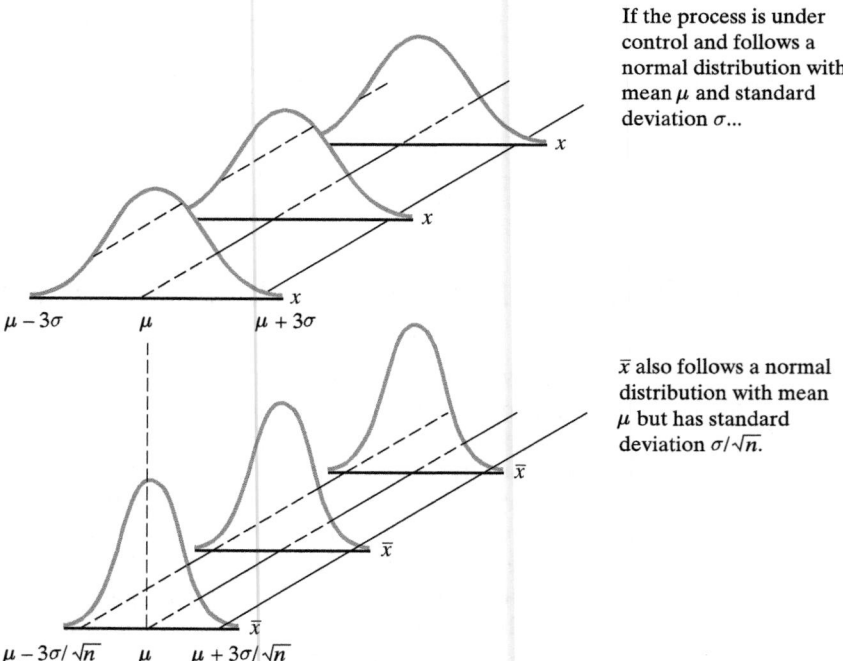

Figure 20

The sampling distribution of $\bar{x}$

*The sampling distribution of $\bar{x}$ can also be approximated using the Central Limit Theorem—that is, when the process is under control and $\bar{x}$ is to be computed from a large sample from the process ($n \geq 30$), the sampling distribution will be approximately normally distributed with the mean μ and standard deviation $\sigma/\sqrt{n}$. Even for samples as small as 4 or 5, the sampling distribution of $\bar{x}$ will be approximately normal as long as the distribution of x is reasonably symmetric and roughly bell shaped.

In order to construct an $\bar{x}$-chart, you should have at least 20 samples of n items each, where $n \geq 2$. This will provide sufficient data to obtain reasonably good estimates of the mean and variance of the process. The centerline, which represents the mean of the process, is determined as follows:

$$Centerline: \bar{\bar{x}} = \frac{\bar{x}_1 + \bar{x}_2 + \cdots + \bar{x}_k}{k}$$

where k is the number of samples of size n from which the chart is to be constructed and $\bar{x}_i$ is the sample mean of the ith sample. Thus $\bar{\bar{x}}$ is an estimator of μ.

The control limits are positioned as follows:

$$Upper\ control\ limit: \bar{\bar{x}} + \frac{3\sigma}{\sqrt{n}}$$

$$Lower\ control\ limit: \bar{\bar{x}} - \frac{3\sigma}{\sqrt{n}}$$

Because σ, the process standard deviation, is virtually always unknown, it must be estimated. This can be done in several ways. One approach involves calculating the standard deviations for each of the k samples and averaging them. Another involves using the sample standard deviation s from a large sample that was generated while the process was believed to be in control. We employ a third approach, however—the one favored by industry. It has been shown to be as effective as the other approaches for sample sizes of $n = 10$ or less, the sizes most often used in industry.

This approach uses the ranges of the k samples to estimate the process standard deviation, σ. The range, R, of a sample is the difference between the maximum and minimum measurements in the sample. It can be shown that dividing the mean of the k ranges, $\bar{R}$, by the constant d_2 obtains an unbiased estimator for σ. [For details, see Ryan (2011).] The estimator, denoted by $\hat{\sigma}$, is calculated as follows:

$$\hat{\sigma} = \frac{\bar{R}}{d_2} = \frac{R_1 + R_2 + \cdots + R_k}{k}\left(\frac{1}{d_2}\right)$$

where R_i is the range of the ith sample and d_2 is a constant that depends on the sample size. Values of d_2 for samples of size $n = 2$ to $n = 25$ can be found in Table IX in Appendix: Tables.

Substituting $\hat{\sigma}$ for σ in the formulas for the upper control limit (UCL) and the lower control limit (LCL), we get

$$UCL: \bar{\bar{x}} + \frac{3\left(\dfrac{\bar{R}}{d_2}\right)}{\sqrt{n}} \qquad LCL: \bar{\bar{x}} - \frac{3\left(\dfrac{\bar{R}}{d_2}\right)}{\sqrt{n}}$$

Notice that $(\bar{R}/d_2)/\sqrt{n}$ is an estimator of $\sigma_{\bar{x}}$. The calculation of these limits can be simplified by creating the constant

$$A_2 = \frac{3}{d_2\sqrt{n}}$$

Then the control limits can be expressed as

$$UCL: \bar{\bar{x}} + A_2\bar{R}$$
$$LCL: \bar{\bar{x}} - A_2\bar{R}$$

where the values for A_2 for samples of size $n = 2$ to $n = 25$ can be found in Table IX in Appendix: Tables.

The degree of sensitivity of the $\bar{x}$-chart to changes in the process mean depends on two decisions that must be made in constructing the chart.

The Two Most Important Decisions in Constructing an $\bar{x}$-Chart

1. The sample size, *n,* must be determined.
2. The frequency with which samples are to be drawn from the process must be determined (e.g., once an hour, once each shift, or once a day).

In order to quickly detect process change, we try to choose samples in such a way that the change in the process mean occurs *between* samples, not *within* samples (i.e., not during the period when a sample is being drawn). In this way, every measurement in the sample before the change will be unaffected by the change, and every measurement in the sample following the change will be affected. The result is that the $\bar{x}$ computed from the latter sample should be substantially different from that of the former sample—a signal that something has happened to the process mean.

Samples whose size and frequency have been designed to make it likely that process changes will occur between, rather than within, the samples are referred to as **rational subgroups.**

Rational Subgrouping Strategy

The samples (rational subgroups) should be chosen in a manner that

1. Gives the maximum chance for the *measurements* in each sample to be similar (i.e., to be affected by the same sources of variation)
2. Gives the maximum chance for the *samples* to differ (i.e., to be affected by at least one different source of variation)

The following example illustrates the concept of *rational subgrouping.*

Example 4

Selecting Rational Subgroups

Problem An operations manager suspects that the quality of the output in a manufacturing process may differ from shift to shift because of the preponderance of newly hired workers on the night shift. The manager wants to be able to detect such differences quickly, using an $\bar{x}$-chart. Develop a rational subgrouping strategy for the manager.

Solution Because the process may differ from shift to shift, it is logical to construct the control chart with samples that are drawn *within* each shift. None of the samples should span shifts—that is, no sample should contain, say, the last three items produced by shift 1 and the first two items produced by shift 2. In this way, the measurements in each sample would be similar, but the $\bar{x}$'s would reflect differences between shifts.

The secret to designing an effective $\bar{x}$-chart is to anticipate the *types of special causes of variation* that might affect the process mean. Then purposeful rational subgrouping can be employed to construct a chart that is sensitive to the anticipated cause or causes of variation.

The preceding discussion and example focused primarily on the timing or frequency of samples. Concerning the size of the samples, practitioners typically work with samples of size $n = 4$ to $n = 10$ consecutively produced items. Using small samples of consecutively produced items helps to ensure that the measurements in each sample will be similar (i.e., affected by the same causes of variation).

Constructing an $\bar{x}$-Chart: A Summary

1. Using a rational subgrouping strategy, collect at least 20 samples (subgroups), each of size $n \geq 2$.
2. Calculate the mean and range for each sample.

3. Calculate the mean of the sample means, $\bar{\bar{x}}$, and the mean of the sample ranges, $\bar{R}$:

$$\bar{\bar{x}} = \frac{\bar{x}_1 + \bar{x}_2 + \cdots + \bar{x}_k}{k} \qquad \bar{R} = \frac{R_1 + R_2 + \cdots + R_k}{k}$$

where

$$k = \text{number of samples (i.e., subgroups)}$$
$$\bar{x}_i = \text{sample mean for the } i\text{th sample}$$
$$R_i = \text{range of the } i\text{th sample}$$

4. Plot the centerline and control limits:

$$\text{Centerline: } \bar{\bar{x}}$$
$$\text{Upper control limit: } \bar{\bar{x}} + A_2\bar{R}$$
$$\text{Lower control limit: } \bar{\bar{x}} - A_2\bar{R}$$

where A_2 is a constant that depends on n. Its values are given in Table IX in Appendix: Tables, for samples of size $n = 2$ to $n = 25$.

5. Plot the k sample means on the control chart in the order that the samples were produced by the process.

Note: Most quality-control analysts use available statistical software to perform the calculations and generate the $\bar{x}$-chart.

When interpreting a control chart, it is convenient to think of the chart as consisting of six zones, as shown in Figure 21. Each zone is 1 standard deviation wide. The two zones within 1 standard deviation of the centerline are called **C zones;** the regions between 1 and 2 standard deviations from the centerline are called **B zones;** and the regions between 2 and 3 standard deviations from the centerline are called **A zones.** The box describes how to construct the *zone boundaries* for an $\bar{x}$-chart.

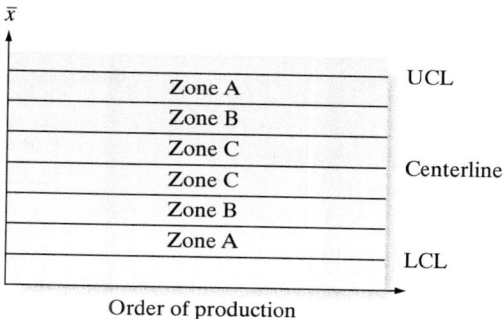

Figure 21

The zones of a control chart

Constructing Zone Boundaries for an $\bar{x}$-Chart

The zone boundaries can be constructed in either of the following ways:

1. Using the 3-sigma control limits:

$$\text{Lower and Upper } A–B \text{ boundaries: } \bar{\bar{x}} \pm \tfrac{2}{3}(A_2\bar{R})$$
$$\text{Lower and Upper } B–C \text{ boundaries: } \bar{\bar{x}} \pm \tfrac{1}{3}(A_2\bar{R})$$

2. Using the estimated standard deviation of $\bar{x}$, $(\bar{R}/d_2)/\sqrt{n}$:

$$\text{Lower and Upper } A–B \text{ boundaries: } \bar{\bar{x}} \pm 2\left[\frac{\left(\dfrac{\bar{R}}{d_2}\right)}{\sqrt{n}}\right]$$

$$\text{Lower and Upper } B–C \text{ boundaries: } \bar{\bar{x}} \pm \left[\frac{\left(\dfrac{\bar{R}}{d_2}\right)}{\sqrt{n}}\right]$$

Note: Again, statistical software programs that automatically find the zone boundaries for the control chart are available.

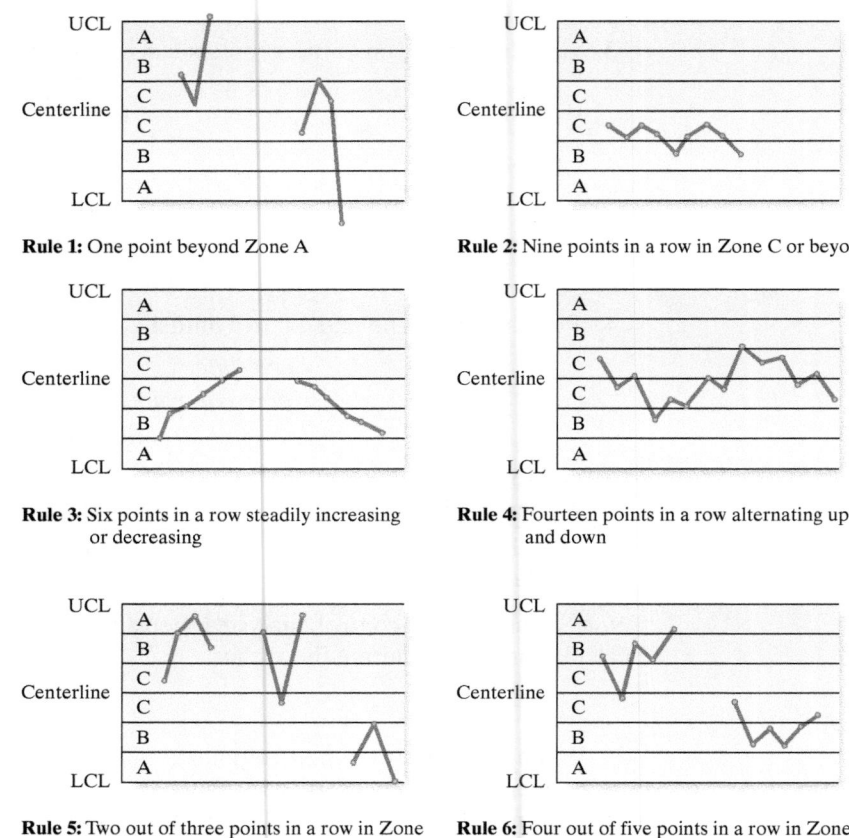

Figure 22

Pattern-analysis rules for detecting the presence of special causes of variation

Rule 1: One point beyond Zone A

Rule 2: Nine points in a row in Zone C or beyond

Rule 3: Six points in a row steadily increasing or decreasing

Rule 4: Fourteen points in a row alternating up and down

Rule 5: Two out of three points in a row in Zone A or beyond

Rule 6: Four out of five points in a row in Zone B or beyond

> Rules 1, 2, 5, and 6 should be applied separately to the upper and lower halves of the control chart. Rules 3 and 4 should be applied to the whole chart.

Practitioners use six simple rules that are based on these zones to help determine when a process is out of control. The six rules are summarized in Figure 22. They are referred to as **pattern-analysis rules.**

Rule 1 is the familiar point-beyond-the-control-limit rule that we have mentioned several times. The other rules all help to determine when the process is out of control *even though all the plotted points fall within the control limits*—that is, the other rules help to identify nonrandom patterns of variation that have not yet broken through the control limits (or may never break through).

All the patterns shown in Figure 22 are *rare events* under the assumption that the process is under control. We demonstrate this notion in the next example.

Example   5

Probabilities for Pattern-Analysis Rules

Problem Assume a process is under control and the data follow a normal distribution with mean μ and standard deviation σ.

a. What is the probability that an individual data point (x) will fall above upper Zone A? In upper Zone A? In upper Zone B? In upper Zone C?

b. Use these probabilities to evaluate the chance of an individual data point violating Rule 1.

c. Use these probabilities to evaluate the chance of an individual data point violating Rule 5.

Solution

a. Zone A is defined as the region that is between 2 and 3 standard deviations above (or below) the mean. (See Figure 21.) Because the data are normally distributed, we use the standard normal table (Table II in Appendix: Tables) to find

$P(x \text{ falls above upper Zone A}) = P(x > \mu + 3\sigma) = P(z > 3) = .5 - .4987 = .0013$

$P(x \text{ falls in upper Zone A}) = P(\mu + 2\sigma < x < \mu + 3\sigma) = P(2 < z < 3)$

$$= .4987 - .4772 = .0125$$

Now, Zone B is defined as the region that is between 1 and 2 standard deviations above (or below) the mean and Zone C as the region that is between 0 and 1 standard deviation above (or below) the mean. Thus, we have

$P(x \text{ falls in upper Zone B}) = P(\mu + \sigma < x < \mu + 2\sigma) = P(1 < z < 2)$

$$= .4772 - .3413 = .1359$$

$P(x \text{ falls in upper Zone C}) = P(\mu < x < \mu + \sigma) = P(0 < z < 1) = .3413$

b. An individual data point violates Rule 1 if it falls beyond Zone A. Thus, we desire the probability

$$P(x \text{ falls beyond Zone A}) = P(x \text{ falls above upper Zone A})$$
$$+ P(x \text{ falls below lower Zone A})$$

Because the normal distribution is symmetric, the two probabilities in the expression above are the same. Consequently, we have

$$P(x \text{ falls beyond Zone A}) = .0013 + .0013 = .0026$$

Thus, the probability of observing a point beyond the control limits (Rule 1) is only .0026. This is clearly a rare event.

c. Rule 5 is violated if two out of three points in succession fall in (say, upper) Zone A or beyond. For one point, the probability of this event is

$$P(x \text{ falls in or above upper Zone A}) = P(x \text{ falls in upper Zone A}) +$$
$$P(x \text{ falls above Zone } A) = .0215 + .0013 = .0228$$

Now we use the binomial distribution to find the probability of observing 2 out of 3 points in or beyond Zone A. The binomial probability of 2 successes in 3 trials when the probability of success is .0228 is

$$\binom{3}{2}(.0228)^2(.9972) = .0016$$

Again, if this occurs, it is clearly a rare event.

Now Work Exercise 18a

In general, when the process is in control and normally distributed, the probability of any one of these rules *incorrectly* signaling the presence of special causes of variation is less than .005, or 5 chances in 1,000. If all of the first four rules are applied, the overall probability of a false signal is about .01. If all six of the rules are applied, the overall probability of a false signal rises to .02, or 2 chances in 100. These three probabilities can be thought of as Type I error probabilities. Each indicates the probability of incorrectly rejecting the null hypothesis that the process is in a state of statistical control.

Explanation of the possible causes of these nonrandom patterns is beyond the scope of this text. We refer the interested reader to AT&T's *Statistical Quality Control Handbook* (1956).

We use these rules again in the next section when we interpret the *R*-chart.

Interpreting an $\bar{x}$-*Chart*

1. The **process is out of control** if one or more sample means fall beyond the control limits or if any of the other five patterns of variation of Figure 22 are observed. Such signals are an indication that one or more special causes of variation are affecting the process mean. We must identify and eliminate them to bring the process into control.

> **2.** The **process is treated as being in control** if none of the previously noted out-of-control signals are observed. Processes that are in control should not be tampered with. However, if the level of variation is unacceptably high, common causes of variation should be identified and eliminated.
>
> *Assumption:* The variation of the process is stable. (If it were not, the control limits of the $\bar{x}$-chart would be meaningless because they are a function of the process variation. The R-chart, presented in the next section, is used to investigate this assumption.)

In theory, the centerline and control limits should be developed using samples that were collected during a period in which the process was in control. Otherwise, they will not be representative of the variation of the process (or, in the present case, the variation of $\bar{x}$) when the process is in control. However, we will not know whether the process is in control until after we have constructed a control chart. Consequently, when a control chart is first constructed, the centerline and control limits are treated as **trial values.** If the chart indicates that the process was in control during the period when the sample data were collected, then the centerline and control limits become "official" (i.e., no longer treated as trial values). It is then appropriate to extend the control limits and the centerline to the right and to use the chart to monitor future process output.

However, if in applying the pattern-analysis rules of Figure 22 it is determined that the process was out of control while the sample data were being collected, the trial values (i.e., the trial chart) should, in general, not be used to monitor the process. The points on the control chart that indicate that the process is out of control should be investigated to see if any special causes of variation can be identified. A graphical method that can be used to facilitate this investigation—a *cause-and-effect diagram*—is described in Section 7. If special causes of variation are found, (1) they should be eliminated; (2) any points on the chart determined to have been influenced by the special causes—whether inside or outside the control limits—should be discarded; and (3) *new* trial centerline and control limits should be calculated from the remaining data. However, the new trial limits may still indicate that the process is out of control. If so, repeat these three steps until all points fall within the control limits.

If special causes cannot be found and eliminated, the severity of the out-of-control indications should be evaluated and a judgment made as to whether (1) the out-of-control points should be discarded anyway and new trial limits constructed, (2) the original trial limits are good enough to be made official, or (3) new sample data should be collected to construct new trial limits.

Example 6

Creating and Interpreting an $\bar{x}$-Chart—Paint-Filling Process

Problem Let's return to the paint-filling process described in Sections 2 and 3. Suppose instead of sampling 50 consecutive gallons of paint from the filling process to develop a control chart, it was decided to sample five consecutive cans once each hour for the next 25 hours. The sample data are presented in an Excel worksheet, Figure 23. This sampling strategy (rational subgrouping) was selected because several times a month the filling head in question becomes clogged. When that happens, the head dispenses less and less paint over the course of the day. However, the pattern of decrease is so irregular that minute-to-minute or even half-hour-to-half-hour changes are difficult to detect.

a. Explain the logic behind the rational subgrouping strategy that was used.

b. Construct an $\bar{x}$-chart for the process using the data in Figure 23.

c. What does the chart suggest about the stability of the filling process (whether the process is in or out of statistical control)?

d. Should the control limits be used to monitor future process output?

Solution

a. The samples are far enough apart in time to detect hour-to-hour shifts or changes in the mean amount of paint dispensed, but the individual measurements that make up each sample are close enough together in time to ensure that the process has

	A	B	C	D	E	F	G	H	I
1	Sample	Weight1	Weight2	Weight3	Weight4	Weight5		Mean	Range
2	1	10.0042	9.9981	10.001	9.9964	10.0001		9.99996	0.0078
3	2	9.995	9.9986	9.9948	10.003	9.9938		9.99704	0.0092
4	3	10.0028	9.9998	10.0086	9.9949	9.998		10.00082	0.0137
5	4	9.9952	9.9923	10.0034	9.9965	10.0026		9.998	0.0111
6	5	9.9997	9.9883	9.9975	10.0078	9.9891		9.99648	0.0195
7	6	9.9987	10.0027	10.0001	10.0027	10.0029		10.00142	0.0042
8	7	10.0004	10.0023	10.0024	9.9992	10.0135		10.00356	0.0143
9	8	10.0013	9.9938	10.0017	10.0089	10.0001		10.00116	0.0151
10	9	10.0103	10.0009	9.9969	10.0103	9.9986		10.0034	0.0134
11	10	9.998	9.9954	9.9941	9.9958	9.9963		9.99592	0.0039
12	11	10.0013	10.0033	9.9943	9.9949	9.9999		9.99874	0.009
13	12	9.9986	9.999	10.0009	9.9947	10.0008		9.9988	0.0062
14	13	10.0089	10.0056	9.9976	9.9997	9.9922		10.0008	0.0167
15	14	9.9971	10.0015	9.9962	10.0038	10.0022		10.00016	0.0076
16	15	9.9949	10.0011	10.0043	9.9988	9.9919		9.9982	0.0124
17	16	9.9951	9.9957	10.0094	10.004	9.9974		10.00032	0.0143
18	17	10.0015	10.0026	10.0032	9.9971	10.0019		10.00126	0.0061
19	18	9.9983	10.0019	9.9978	9.9997	10.0029		10.00012	0.0051
20	19	9.9977	9.9963	9.9981	9.9968	10.0009		9.99796	0.0046
21	20	10.0078	10.0004	9.9966	10.0051	10.0007		10.00212	0.0112
22	21	9.9963	9.999	10.0037	9.9936	9.9962		9.99776	0.0101
23	22	9.9999	10.0022	10.0057	10.0026	10.0032		10.00272	0.0058
24	23	9.9998	10.0002	9.9978	9.9966	10.006		10.00008	0.0094
25	24	10.0031	10.0078	9.9988	10.0032	9.9944		10.00146	0.0134
26	25	9.9993	9.9978	9.9964	10.0032	10.0041		10.00016	0.0077
27									
28							Averages	9.999937	0.010072
29									

Figure 23

Excel worksheet with 25 samples of $n = 5$ from paint-filling process

Data Set: CAN125

changed little, if at all, during the time the individual measurements were made. Overall, the rational subgrouping employed affords the opportunity for process changes to occur between samples and therefore show up on the control chart as differences between the sample means.

b. Twenty-five samples ($k = 25$ subgroups), each containing $n = 5$ cans of paint, were collected from the process. The first step after collecting the data is to calculate the 25 sample means and sample ranges needed to construct the $\bar{x}$-chart. The mean and range of the first sample are

$$\bar{x} = \frac{10.0042 + 9.9981 + 10.0010 + 9.9964 + 10.0001}{5} = 9.99996$$

$$R = 10.0042 - 9.9964 = .0078$$

All 25 means and ranges were computed using Excel and are displayed in Figure 23. Next, we use Excel to calculate the mean of the sample means and the mean of the sample ranges:

$$\bar{\bar{x}} = \frac{9.99996 + 9.99704 + \cdots + 10.00016}{25} = 9.99994$$

$$\bar{R} = \frac{.0078 + .0092 + \cdots + .0077}{25} = .010072$$

These values are highlighted on Figure 23. Now, the centerline of the chart is positioned at $\bar{\bar{x}} = 9.9999$. To determine the control limits, we need the constant A_2, which can be found in Table IX in Appendix: Tables. For $n = 5$, $A_2 = .577$. Then,

$$\text{UCL:} \; \bar{\bar{x}} + A_2\bar{R} = 9.99994 + .577(.010072) = 10.00575$$

$$\text{LCL:} \; \bar{\bar{x}} - A_2\bar{R} = 9.99994 - .577(.010072) = 9.99413$$

After positioning the control limits on the chart, we plot the 25 sample means in the order of sampling and connect the points with straight lines. The resulting trial $\bar{x}$-chart, shown in Figure 24, is produced using Minitab.

839

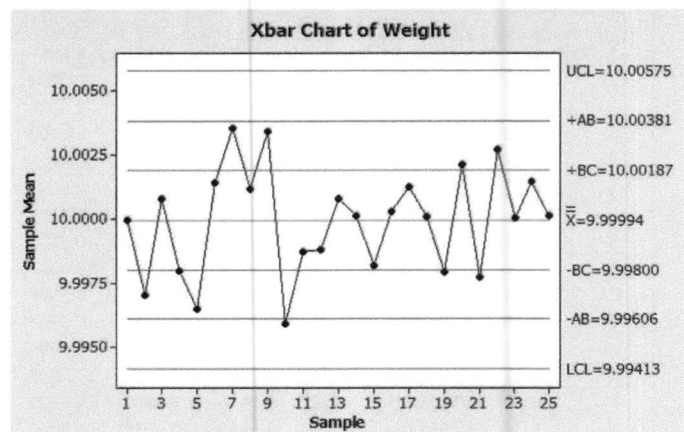

Figure 24

Minitab $\bar{x}$-chart for paint-filling process

c. To check the stability of the process, we use the six pattern-analysis rules for detecting special causes of variation, which were presented in Figure 22. To apply most of these rules requires identifying the A, B, and C zones of the control chart. These are indicated (with annotations) in Figure 24. We describe how they were constructed below.

The boundary between the A and B zones is 2 standard deviations from the centerline, and the boundary between the B and C zones is 1 standard deviation from the centerline. Thus, using $A_2\bar{R}$ and the 3-sigma limits previously calculated, we locate the A, B, and C zones above the centerline:

$$\text{A–B boundary} = \bar{\bar{x}} + \tfrac{2}{3}(A_2\bar{R}) = 9.99994 + \tfrac{2}{3}(.577)(.010072) = 10.00381$$

$$\text{B–C boundary} = \bar{\bar{x}} + \tfrac{1}{3}(A_2\bar{R}) = 9.99994 + \tfrac{1}{3}(.577)(.010072) = 10.00187$$

Similarly, the zones below the centerline are located:

$$\text{A–B boundary} = \bar{\bar{x}} - \tfrac{2}{3}(A_2\bar{R}) = 9.99606$$

$$\text{B–C boundary} = \bar{\bar{x}} - \tfrac{1}{3}(A_2\bar{R}) = 9.99800$$

A careful comparison of the six pattern-analysis rules with the sequence of sample means yields no out-of-control signals. All points are inside the control limits, and there appear to be no nonrandom patterns within the control limits—that is, we can find no evidence of a shift in the process mean. Accordingly, we conclude that the process is in control.

d. Because the process was found to be in control during the period in which the samples were drawn, the trial control limits constructed in part **b** can be considered official. They should be extended to the right and used to monitor future process output.

Look Back Most statistical software (like Minitab) will automatically calculate and plot the sample means and control limits. No hand calculations are needed to create an $\bar{x}$-chart.

■ **Now Work Exercise 7**

Example 7

Monitoring Future Output with an $\bar{x}$-Chart—Paint-Filling Process

Problem Ten new samples of size $n = 5$ were drawn from the paint-filling process of the previous example. The sample data, including sample means and ranges, are shown in the Excel worksheet, Figure 25. Investigate whether the process remained in control during the period in which the new sample data were collected.

Solution We begin by simply extending the control limits, centerline, and zone boundaries of the control chart in Figure 24 to the right. Next, beginning with sample number 26, we plot the 10 new sample means on the control chart and connect them with straight lines. This extended version of the control chart, produced using Minitab, is shown in Figure 26.

	A	B	C	D	E	F	G	H	I
1	Sample	Weight1	Weight2	Weight3	Weight4	Weight5		Mean	Range
2	26	10.0019	9.9981	9.9952	9.9976	9.9999		9.99854	0.0067
3	27	10.0041	9.9982	10.0028	10.004	9.9971		10.00124	0.007
4	28	9.9999	9.9974	10.0078	9.9971	9.9923		9.9989	0.0155
5	29	9.9982	10.0002	9.9916	10.004	9.9916		9.99712	0.0124
6	30	9.9933	9.9963	9.9955	9.9993	9.9905		9.99498	0.0088
7	31	9.9915	9.9984	10.0053	9.9888	9.9876		9.99432	0.0177
8	32	9.9912	9.997	9.9961	9.9879	9.997		9.99384	0.0091
9	33	9.9942	9.996	9.9975	10.0019	9.9912		9.99616	0.0107
10	34	9.9949	9.9967	9.9936	9.9941	10.0071		9.99728	0.0135
11	35	9.9943	9.9969	9.9937	9.9912	10.0053		9.99628	0.0141

Figure 25

Excel worksheet with 10 additional samples of $n = 5$ from paint-filling process

Data Set: CANNEW

Figure 26

Minitab extended $\bar{x}$-chart for paint-filling process

Now that the control chart has been prepared, we apply the six pattern-analysis rules for detecting special causes of variation (Figure 22) to the new sequence of sample means. First, notice that the mean for sample 32 falls below the lower control limit (Rule 1). Also, notice that six points in a row steadily decrease (samples 27–32). Rule 3 says that if we observe six points in a row steadily increasing or decreasing, that is an indication of the presence of special causes of variation. Notice that if you apply the rules from left to right along the sequence of sample means, the decreasing pattern also triggers signals from Rules 5 (samples 29–31) and 6 (samples 28–32). These signals lead us to conclude that the process has gone out of control.

Look Back Apparently, the filling head began to clog about the time that either sample 26 or 27 was drawn from the process. As a result, the mean of the process (the mean fill weight dispensed by the process) began to decline.

Now Work Exercise 8

Monitoring the Process Mean

The engineering firm that tests for surfactants in jet fuel additive is experimenting with different pump and filter combinations—Pump-A with Filter-A (the standard test), Pump-A with Filter-B, Pump-B with Filter-A, and Pump-B with Filter-B. To monitor the test results, three fuel samples were tested each day by each of the four methods, for a period of over 100 consecutive days. A "safe" surfactant additive measurement should range between 80 and 90, and this range represents the specification limits of the process.

We analyzed the data in the **JET** files using Minitab. Treating the three samples collected on the same day as a rational subgroup, four Minitab $\bar{x}$-charts are produced (one for each pump/filter method) in Figures SIA1a–d. As an option, Minitab will highlight (in red) any sample means that match any of the six pattern-analysis rules for

STATISTICS in ACTION REVISITED CONTINUED

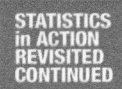

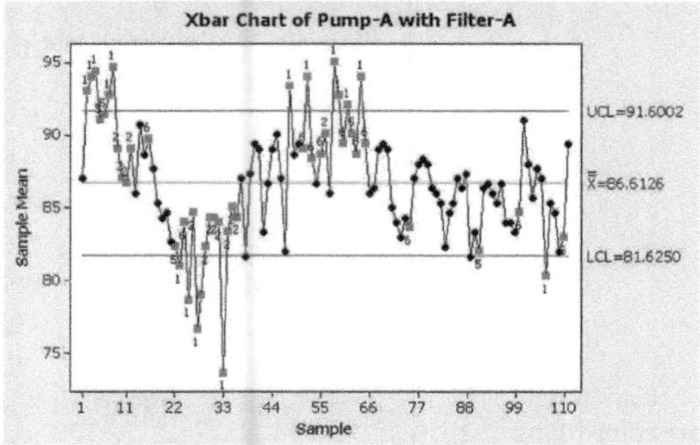

Figure SIA1a
$\bar{x}$-chart for Pump-A with Filter-A (standard) method

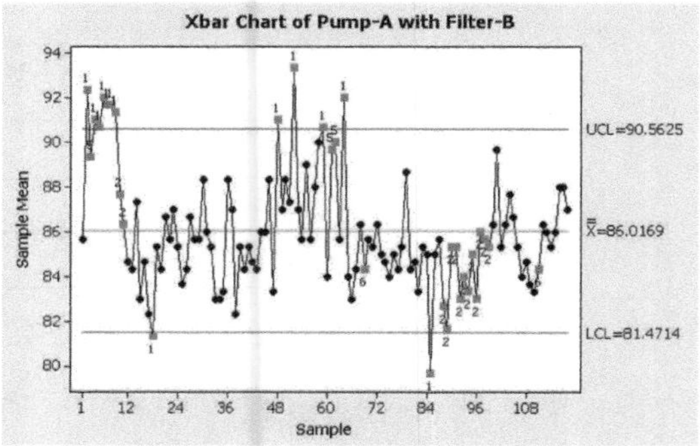

Figure SIA1b
$\bar{x}$-chart for Pump-A with Filter-B method

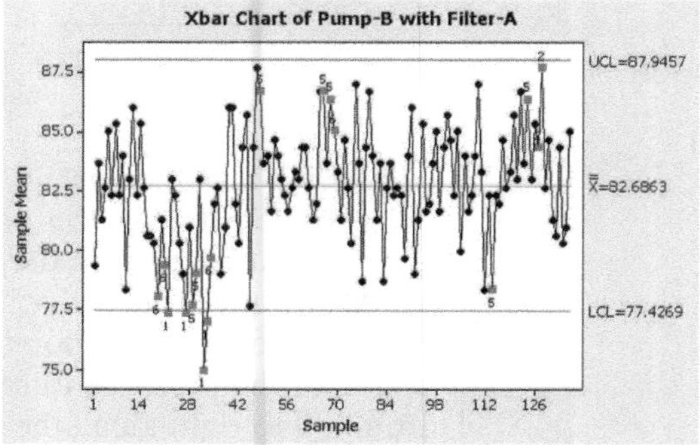

Figure SIA1c
$\bar{x}$-chart for Pump-B with Filter-A method

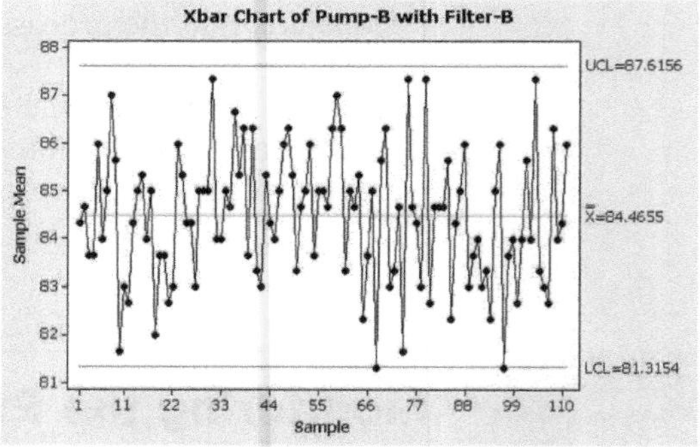

Figure SIA1d
$\bar{x}$-chart for Pump-B with Filter-B method

detecting special causes of variation. The number of the rule that is violated is shown above (or below) the sample mean on the chart.

You can see that only one of the process means is "in control"—the mean for the Pump-B with Filter-B test method—as shown in Figure SIA1d There is at least one pattern-analysis rule violated in each of the other three $\bar{x}$-charts. Also, each sample mean for Pump-B/Filter-B falls within the specification limits (80%–90%). In contrast, the other injection methods have several means that fall outside the specification limits of the process. Of the three nonstandard surfactant test methods, the Pump-B/Filter-B method appears to have the most promise. This analysis helped the company to focus on perfecting this method of surfactant testing in jet fuel.

Exercises 1–21

Learning the Mechanics

1 What is a control chart? Describe its use.

2 Explain why rational subgrouping should be used in constructing control charts.

3 When a control chart is first constructed, why are the centerline and control limits treated as trial values?

4 Which process parameter is an $\bar{x}$-chart used to monitor?

5 Even if all the points on an $\bar{x}$-chart fall between the control limits, the process may be out of control. Explain.

6 What must be true about the variation of a process before an $\bar{x}$-chart is used to monitor the mean of the process? Why?

7 Use the six pattern-analysis rules described in Figure 22 to
[NW] determine whether the process being monitored with the $\bar{x}$-chart shown below is out of statistical control.

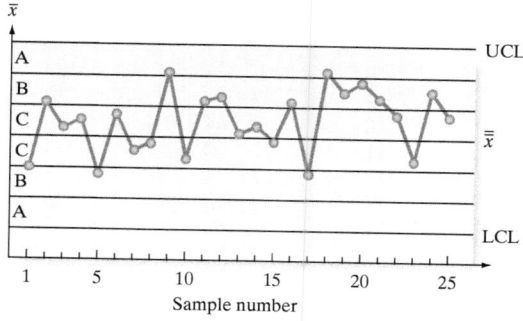

8 Consider the next $\bar{x}$-chart shown.
[NW]

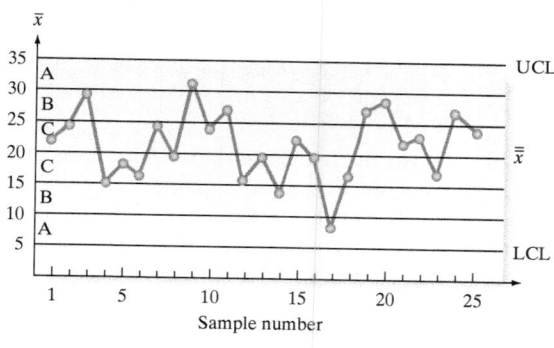

a. Is the process affected by special causes of variation only, common causes of variation only, or both? Explain.

b. The means for the next five samples in the process are 27, 29, 32, 36, and 34. Plot these points on an extended $\bar{x}$-chart. What does the pattern suggest about the process?

9 Use Table IX in Appendix: Tables to find the value of A_2 for each of the following sample sizes.

   a. $n = 3$

   b. $n = 10$

   c. $n = 22$

10 Twenty-five consecutive samples of size $n = 5$ were collected to construct an $\bar{x}$-chart. The sample means and
L13010 ranges for the data are shown in the next table.

   a. Calculate the mean of the sample means, $\bar{\bar{x}}$, and the mean of the sample ranges, $\bar{R}$.

   b. Calculate and plot the centerline and the upper and lower control limits for the $\bar{x}$-chart.

Sample	$\bar{x}$	R	Sample	$\bar{x}$	R
1	80.2	7.2	14	83.1	10.2
2	79.1	9.0	15	79.6	7.8
3	83.2	4.7	16	80.0	6.1
4	81.0	5.6	17	83.2	8.4
5	77.6	10.1	18	75.9	9.9
6	81.7	8.6	19	78.1	6.0
7	80.4	4.4	20	81.4	7.4
8	77.5	6.2	21	81.7	10.4
9	79.8	7.9	22	80.9	9.1
10	85.3	7.1	23	78.4	7.3
11	77.7	9.8	24	79.6	8.0
12	82.3	10.7	25	81.6	7.6
13	79.5	9.2			

   c. Calculate and plot the A, B, and C zone boundaries of the $\bar{x}$-chart.

   d. Plot the 25 sample means on the $\bar{x}$-chart and use the six pattern-analysis rules to determine whether the process is under statistical control.

11 The data in the following table were collected for the purpose of constructing an $\bar{x}$-chart.

L13011 **a.** Calculate $\bar{x}$ and R for each sample.

   b. Calculate $\bar{\bar{x}}$ and $\bar{R}$.

   c. Calculate and plot the centerline and the upper and lower control limits for the $\bar{x}$-chart.

   d. Calculate and plot the A, B, and C zone boundaries of the $\bar{x}$-chart.

   e. Plot the 20 sample means on the $\bar{x}$-chart. Is the process in control? Justify your answer.

Sample	Measurements			
1	19.4	19.7	20.6	21.2
2	18.7	18.4	21.2	20.7
3	20.2	18.8	22.6	20.1
4	19.6	21.2	18.7	19.4
5	20.4	20.9	22.3	18.6
6	17.3	22.3	20.3	19.7
7	21.8	17.6	22.8	23.1
8	20.9	17.4	19.5	20.7
9	18.1	18.3	20.6	20.4
10	22.6	21.4	18.5	19.7
11	22.7	21.2	21.5	19.5
12	20.1	20.6	21.0	20.2
13	19.7	18.6	21.2	19.1
14	18.6	21.7	17.7	18.3
15	18.2	20.4	19.8	19.2
16	18.9	20.7	23.2	20.0
17	20.5	19.7	21.4	17.8
18	21.0	18.7	19.9	21.2
19	20.5	19.6	19.8	21.8
20	20.6	16.9	22.4	19.7

Applying the Concepts—Basic

12 Detecting gender-related employment disparities. In the *Federal Reserve Bank of Atlanta, Working Paper Series* (Oct. 2008), researchers presented a novel approach to identifying firms that discriminate against women. The researchers used the Equal Employment Opportunity

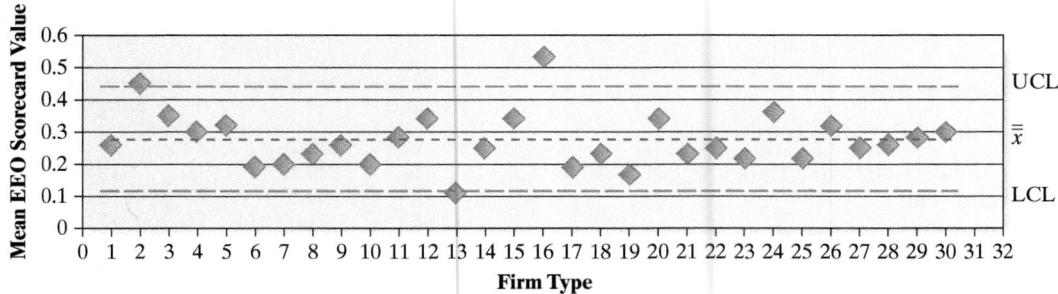

(EEOC) Systematic Gender Disparity Scorecard as a measure of the degree to which a firm complies with EEOC guidelines for eliminating gender bias. (EEOC Scorecard values range from 0 to 1, with larger values indicating a greater gender disparity.) In a hypothetical example, a sample of firms was selected for each of 30 different types of firms in the service industry (e.g., food service, financial services, oil and gas service, etc.). The mean scorecard values for the 30 firm types are plotted in the $\bar{x}$-chart shown above. The centerline and upper and lower control limits are shown on the chart.

a. Identify the rational subgroups used to construct the chart.

b. Identify the key variable plotted on the chart.

c. What are the approximate values of $\bar{\bar{x}}$, UCL, and LCL?

d. What conclusions can you draw from the chart? Are there any firm types that should concern the EEOC? Why?

13 **Pain levels of ICU patients.** Various interventions are available for nurses to help relieve patients' pain (e.g., heat/cold applications, breathing exercises, massage). The journal *Research in Nursing & Health* (Vol. 35, 2012) demonstrated the utility of statistical process control in determining the effectiveness of a pain intervention. The researchers presented the following illustration. Pain levels (measured on a 100-point scale) were recorded for a sample of 10 intensive care unit (ICU) patients 24 hours postsurgery each week for 20 consecutive weeks. The next table provides the means and ranges for each of the 20 weeks. To establish that the pain management process is "in control," an $\bar{x}$-chart is constructed.

a. Compute the value of the centerline for the $\bar{x}$-chart.

b. Compute the value of $\bar{R}$.

c. Compute the UCL and LCL for the $\bar{x}$-chart.

d. Plot the means for the 20 weeks on the $\bar{x}$-chart. Is the pain management process "in control"?

e. After the 20th week, a pain intervention occurred in the ICU. The goal of the intervention was to reduce the average pain level of ICU patients. To determine if the intervention was effective, the sampling of ICU patients was continued for 8 more consecutive weeks. The mean pain levels of these patients were (in order): 71, 72, 69, 67, 66, 65, 64, and 62. Plot these means on the $\bar{x}$-chart.

f. Apply pattern-analysis rules to the extended $\bar{x}$-chart, part **e**. Do you detect a shift in the mean pain level of the patients following the intervention? Explain.

Data for Exercise 13

Week	$\bar{x}$	Range
1	65	28
2	75	41
3	72	31
4	69	35
5	73	35
6	63	33
7	77	34
8	75	29
9	69	30
10	64	39
11	70	34
12	74	37
13	73	25
14	62	33
15	68	28
16	75	35
17	72	29
18	70	32
19	62	33
20	72	29

Source: Based on "Statistical Process Control in Nursing Research" by Denise F. Polit and Wendy Chaboyer from RESEARCH IN NURSING AND HEALTH, February 2012, Volume 35(1).

14 **Quality control for irrigation data.** Most farmers budget water by using an irrigation schedule. The success of the schedule hinges on collecting accurate data on *evapotranspiration* (ETo), a term that describes the sum of evaporation and plant transpiration. The California Irrigation Management Information System (CIMIS) collects daily weather data (e.g., air temperature, wind speed, and vapor pressure) used to estimate ETo and supplies this information to farmers. Researchers at CIMIS demonstrated the use of quality-control charts to monitor daily ETo measurements (*IV International Symposium on Irrigation of Horticultural Crops*, Dec. 31, 2004). Daily minimum air temperatures (°C) collected hourly during the month of May at the Davis CIMIS station yielded the following summary statistics (where five measurements are collected each hour): $\bar{\bar{x}} = 10.16°$ and $R = 14.87°$.

a. Use the information provided to find the lower and upper control limits for an $\bar{x}$-chart.

b. Suppose that one day in May the mean air temperature at the Davis CIMIS station was recorded as $\bar{x} = 20.3°$. How should the manager of the station respond to this observation?

15 **CPU of a computer chip.** The central processing unit (CPU) of a microcomputer is a computer chip containing millions of transistors. Connecting the transistors are slender circuit paths only .5 to .85 micrometer wide. A manufacturer of CPU chips knows that if the circuit paths are not .5–.85 micrometer wide, a variety of problems will arise in the chips' performance. The manufacturer sampled four CPU chips six times a day (every 90 minutes from 8:00 A.M. until 4:30 P.M.) for 5 consecutive days and measured the circuit path widths. These data and Minitab were used to construct the $\bar{x}$-chart shown below.

a. Assuming that $\bar{R} = .335$, calculate the chart's upper and lower control limits, the upper and lower A–B boundaries, and the upper and lower B–C boundaries.

b. What does the chart suggest about the stability of the process used to put circuit paths on the CPU chip? Justify your answer.

c. Should the control limits be used to monitor future process output? Explain.

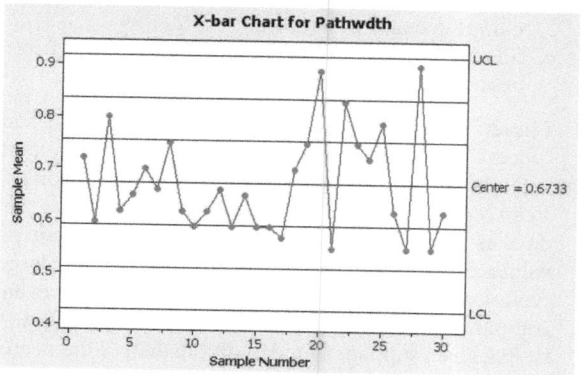

16 Cereal box manufacturing. A machine at K-Company fills boxes with bran flakes cereal. The target weight for the filled boxes is 24 ounces. The company would like to use an $\bar{x}$-chart to monitor the performance of the machine. To develop the control chart, the company decides to sample and weigh five boxes of cereal each day (at 8:00 and 11:00 A.M. and 2:00, 5:00, and 8:00 P.M.) for 20 consecutive days. The data are summarized in the SPSS printout below.

a. Construct an $\bar{x}$-chart from the summary statistics.

b. What does the chart suggest about the stability of the filling process (whether the process is in or out of statistical control)? Justify your answer.

Case Summaries[a]

DAY	MEANWT	RANGEWT
1	24.05	.22
2	23.96	.12
3	23.99	.32
4	24.02	.16
5	23.95	.26
6	24.01	.25
7	23.97	.17
8	23.98	.12
9	23.95	.28
10	24.00	.07
11	24.01	.21
12	24.02	.16
13	24.06	.16
14	23.96	.15
15	24.03	.12
16	24.03	.18
17	23.97	.19
18	24.00	.21
19	24.02	.13
20	23.97	.15

a. Limited to first 100 cases.

c. Should the control limits be used to monitor future process output? Explain.

d. Two shifts of workers run the filling operation. Each day the second shift takes over at 3:00 P.M. Will the rational subgrouping strategy used by K-Company facilitate or hinder the identification of process variation caused by differences in the two shifts? Explain.

Applying the Concepts—Intermediate

17 Improving public health waiting times. Statistical process control was utilized in an effort to improve the service delivery at a Women, Infants, and Children (WIC) health clinic in Minnesota (*American Journal of Public Health,* Sep. 2009). The health department sampled patients for 10 consecutive days and recorded each patient's lobby waiting time (in minutes). The mean lobby waiting times were (in order): 25.5, 16.5, 22.5, 18, 13, 10.5, 14, 4.5, 12.5, and 14 minutes. These means were plotted in an $\bar{x}$-chart to monitor the waiting time process.

a. Compute the value of the centerline for the $\bar{x}$-chart.

b. Critical boundaries for the $\bar{x}$-chart are listed as follows: UCL = 31.5, Upper A-B = 26, Upper B-C = 20.5, Lower B-C = 9.5, Lower A-B = 4, LCL = 0. Plot the 10 means in an $\bar{x}$-chart; include the critical boundaries on the chart.

c. Refer to part **b**. Apply pattern-analysis rules to the chart. Do you detect the presence of any special causes of variation?

d. After a 3-month time period, during which the clinic implemented new procedures, the health department conducted a second sampling of patients over 14 consecutive days. The mean lobby waiting times for these 14 days were (in order): 11.5, 12.5, 14.5, 11, 12.5, 11.5, 13.5, 11.5, 7.5, 13.5, 7, 10.5, 13.5, and 2 minutes. Critical $\bar{x}$-chart boundaries for the new data are listed as follows: UCL = 21.5, Upper A-B = 18, Upper B-C = 14.5, Lower B-C = 7.5, Lower A-B = 4, LCL = .5. Construct an $\bar{x}$-chart for the new data. Do you detect the presence of any special causes of variation?

e. Place the two $\bar{x}$-charts side by side. The health department concluded that a process shift occurred after the clinic implemented its new procedures. Do you agree?

18 Selecting the best wafer-slicing machine. Silicon wafer slicing is a critical step in the production of semiconductor devices (e.g., diodes, solar cells, transistors). Yuanpei (China) University researchers used control charts to aid in selecting the best silicon wafer-slicing machine (*Computers & Industrial Engineering,* Vol. 52, 2007). Samples of $n = 2$ wafers were sliced each hour for 67 consecutive hours and bow measurements (a measure of precision) were recorded. The resulting $\bar{x}$-chart for one of the machines tested revealed that the cutting process was out of control on the 19th, 40th, and 59th hours. For each of these 3 hours, the mean bow measurement fell above the upper control limit. Assume the mean bow measurements are normally distributed.

a. If the process is in control, what is the probability that a mean bow measurement for a randomly selected hour will fall above the upper control limit?

b. If the process is in control, what is the probability that 3 of 67 mean bow measurements fall above the upper control limit?

19 Detecting under-reported emissions. The Environmental Protection Agency (EPA) regulates the level of carbon dioxide (CO_2) emissions. Periodically these emissions

Data for Exercise 19

							Daily Average CO_2 Measurements for 30 Consecutive Days							
1	*2*	*3*	*4*	*5*	*6*	*7*	*8*	*9*	*10*	*11*	*12*	*13*	*14*	*15*
12.9	13.2	13.4	13.3	13.1	13.2	13.1	13.0	12.5	12.5	12.7	12.8	12.7	12.9	12.0
16	*17*	*18*	*19*	*20*	*21*	*22*	*23*	*24*	*25*	*26*	*27*	*28*	*29*	*30*
12.9	12.8	12.7	13.2	13.2	13.3	13.0	13.0	13.2	13.2	13.4	13.1	13.3	13.4	13.4

measurements are under-reported due to leakage or faulty equipment. Such problems are often detected only by an expensive test (RATA) that is typically conducted only once per year. Just recently, the EPA began applying an automated control chart methodology to detect under-measurement of emissions data (*EPRI CEM Users Group Conference*, Nashville, TN, May 13, 2008). Each day, the EPA collects emissions data by measuring CO_2 concentration for each of 6 randomly selected hours. The daily average CO_2 levels for each of 30 days are shown in the table above. The EPA considers these values to truly represent emissions levels because the RATA test was recently performed and showed no problems with under-reporting. The lower and upper control limits for the averages were established as LCL = 12.26 and UCL = 13.76.

a. Construct a control chart for the daily average CO_2 levels.

b. Based on the control chart, describe the behavior of the measurement process.

c. The following average CO_2 levels were determined for a later 10-day period: 12.7, 12.1, 12.0, 12.0, 11.8, 11.7, 11.6, 11.7, 11.8, 11.7. Make an inference about the potential under-reporting of the emissions data for this 10-day period.

20 Military aircraft bolts. A precision parts manufacturer produces bolts for use in military aircraft. Ideally, the bolts should be 37 centimeters in length. The company sampled four consecutively produced bolts each hour on the hour for 25 consecutive hours and measured them using a computerized precision instrument. The data are presented in the table below.

Hour	Bolt Lengths (centimeters)			
1	37.03	37.08	36.90	36.88
2	36.96	37.04	36.85	36.98
3	37.16	37.11	36.99	37.01
4	37.20	37.06	37.02	36.98
5	36.81	36.97	36.91	37.10
6	37.13	36.96	37.01	36.89
7	37.07	36.94	36.99	37.00
8	37.01	36.91	36.98	37.12
9	37.17	37.03	36.90	37.01
10	36.91	36.99	36.87	37.11
11	36.88	37.10	37.07	37.03
12	37.06	36.98	36.90	36.99
13	36.91	37.22	37.12	37.03
14	37.08	37.07	37.10	37.04
15	37.03	37.04	36.89	37.01
16	36.95	36.98	36.90	36.99
17	36.97	36.94	37.14	37.10
18	37.11	37.04	36.98	36.91
19	36.88	36.99	37.01	36.94
20	36.90	37.15	37.09	37.00
21	37.01	36.96	37.05	36.96
22	37.09	36.95	36.93	37.12
23	37.00	37.02	36.95	37.04
24	36.99	37.07	36.90	37.02
25	37.10	37.03	37.01	36.90

a. What process is the manufacturer interested in monitoring?

b. Construct an $\bar{x}$-chart from the data.

c. Does the chart suggest that special causes of variation are present? Justify your answer.

d. Provide an example of a special cause of variation that could potentially affect this process. Do the same for a common cause of variation.

e. Should the control limits be used to monitor future process output? Explain.

21 Chunky data. BPI Consulting, a leading provider of statistical process control software and training in the United States, recently alerted its clients to problems with "chunky" data. In an April 2007 report, BPI Consulting identified "chunky" data as data that result when the range between possible values of the variable of interest becomes too large. This typically occurs when the data are rounded. For example, a company monitoring the time it takes shipments to arrive from a given supplier rounded off the data to the nearest day. To show the effect of chunky data on a control chart, BPI Consulting considered a process with a quality characteristic that averages about 100. Data on the quality characteristic for a random sample of three observations collected each hour for 40 consecutive hours are given in the table below. (*Note:* BPI Consulting cautions its clients that out-of-control data points in this example were actually due to the measurement process and not to an "out-of-control" process.)

a. Show that the process is "in control," according to Rule 1, by constructing an $\bar{x}$-chart for the data.

b. Round each measurement in the data set to a whole number and then form an $\bar{x}$-chart for the rounded data. What do you observe?

Sample	Quality Levels			Sample	Quality Levels		
1	99.69	99.73	99.81	21	99.43	99.63	100.08
2	98.67	99.47	100.20	22	100.04	99.71	100.40
3	99.93	99.97	100.22	23	101.08	99.84	99.93
4	100.58	99.40	101.08	24	99.98	99.50	100.25
5	99.28	99.48	99.10	25	101.18	100.79	99.56
6	99.06	99.61	99.85	26	99.24	99.90	100.03
7	99.81	99.78	99.53	27	99.41	99.18	99.39
8	99.78	100.10	99.27	28	100.84	100.47	100.48
9	99.76	100.83	101.02	29	99.31	100.15	101.08
10	100.20	100.24	99.85	30	99.65	100.05	100.12
11	99.12	99.74	100.04	31	100.24	101.01	100.71
12	101.58	100.54	100.53	32	99.08	99.73	99.61
13	101.51	100.52	100.50	33	100.30	100.02	99.31
14	100.27	100.77	100.48	34	100.38	100.76	100.37
15	100.43	100.67	100.53	35	100.48	99.96	99.72
16	101.08	100.54	99.89	36	99.98	100.30	99.07
17	99.63	100.77	99.86	37	100.25	99.58	101.27
18	99.29	99.49	99.37	38	100.49	100.16	100.86
19	99.89	100.75	100.73	39	100.44	100.53	99.84
20	100.54	101.51	100.54	40	99.45	99.41	99.27

5 A Control Chart for Monitoring the Variation of a Process: The R-Chart

Recall from Section 2 that a process may be out of statistical control because its mean or variance or both are changing over time (see Figure 8). The $\bar{x}$-chart of the previous section is used to detect changes in the process mean. The control chart we present in this section—the **R-chart**—is used to detect changes in process variation.

The primary difference between the $\bar{x}$-chart and the R-chart is that instead of plotting *sample means* and monitoring their variation, we plot and monitor the variation of *sample ranges*. Changes in the behavior of the sample range signal changes in the variation of the process.

We could also monitor process variation by plotting *sample standard deviations*— that is, we could calculate s for each sample (i.e., each subgroup) and plot them on a control chart known as an **s-chart**. In this chapter, however, we focus on just the R-chart because (1) when using samples of size 9 or less, the s-chart and the R-chart reflect about the same information, and (2) the R-chart is used much more widely by practitioners than is the s-chart (primarily because the sample range is easier to calculate and interpret than the sample standard deviation). For more information about s-charts, see the references at the end of the chapter.

The underlying logic and basic form of the R-chart are similar to those of the $\bar{x}$-chart. In monitoring $\bar{x}$, we use the standard deviation of $\bar{x}$ to develop 3-sigma control limits. Now, because we want to be able to determine when R takes on unusually large or small values, we use the standard deviation of R, or σ_R, to construct 3-sigma control limits. The centerline of the $\bar{x}$-chart represents the process mean μ or, equivalently, the mean of the sampling distribution of $\bar{x}$, $\mu_{\bar{x}}$. Similarly, the centerline of the R-chart represents μ_R, the mean of the sampling distribution of R. These points are illustrated in the R-chart of Figure 27.

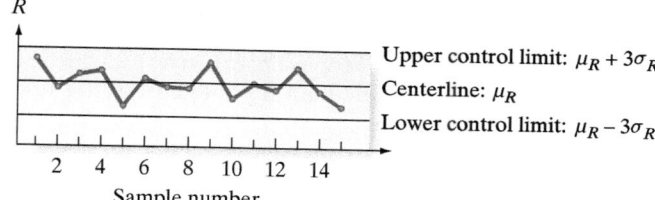

Figure 27
R-chart

As with the $\bar{x}$-chart, you should have at least 20 samples of n items each ($n \geq 2$) to construct an R-chart. This will provide sufficient data to obtain reasonably good estimates of μ_R and σ_R. Rational subgrouping is again used for determining sample size and frequency of sampling.

The centerline of the R-chart is positioned as follows:

$$\text{Centerline: } \overline{R} = \frac{R_1 + R_2 + \cdots + R_k}{k}$$

where k is the number of samples of size n and R_i is the range of the ith sample. $\overline{R}$ is an estimate of μ_R.

In order to construct the control limits, we need an estimator of σ_R. The estimator recommended by Montgomery (2009) and Ryan (2011) is

$$\hat{\sigma}_R = d_3\left(\frac{\overline{R}}{d_2}\right)$$

where d_2 and d_3 are constants whose values depend on the sample size, n. Values for d_2 and d_3 for samples of size $n = 2$ to $n = 25$ are given in Table IX in Appendix: Tables.

The control limits are positioned as follows:

$$Upper\ control\ limit: \overline{R} + 3\hat{\sigma}_R = \overline{R} + 3d_3\left(\frac{\overline{R}}{d_2}\right)$$

$$Lower\ control\ limit: \overline{R} - 3\hat{\sigma}_R = \overline{R} - 3d_3\left(\frac{\overline{R}}{d_2}\right)$$

Notice that $\overline{R}$ appears twice in each control limit. Accordingly, we can simplify the calculation of these limits by factoring out $\overline{R}$:

$$\text{UCL:}\ \overline{R}\left(1 + \frac{3d_3}{d_2}\right) = \overline{R}D_4 \qquad \text{LCL:}\ \overline{R}\left(1 - \frac{3d_3}{d_2}\right) = \overline{R}D_3$$

where

$$D_4 = \left(1 + \frac{3d_3}{d_2}\right) \qquad D_3 = \left(1 - \frac{3d_3}{d_2}\right)$$

The values for D_3 and D_4 have been tabulated for samples of size $n = 2$ to $n = 25$ and can be found in Table IX in Appendix: Tables.

For samples of size $n = 2$ through $n = 6$, D_3 is negative, and the lower control limit falls below zero. Because the sample range cannot take on negative values, such a control limit is meaningless. Thus, when $n \leq 6$, the R-chart contains only one control limit, the upper control limit.

Although D_3 is actually negative for $n \leq 6$, the values reported in Table IX in Appendix: Tables are all zeros. This has been done to discourage the inappropriate construction of negative lower control limits. If the lower control limit is calculated using $D_3 = 0$, you obtain $D_3\overline{R} = 0$. This should be interpreted as indicating that the R-chart has no lower 3-sigma control limit.

Constructing an R-Chart: A Summary

1. Using a rational subgrouping strategy, collect at least 20 samples (i.e., subgroups), each of size $n \geq 2$.

2. Calculate the range of each sample.

3. Calculate the mean of the sample ranges, $\overline{R}$:

$$\overline{R} = \frac{R_1 + R_2 + \cdots + R_k}{k}$$

where

k = The number of samples (i.e., subgroups)

R_i = The range of the ith sample

4. Plot the centerline and control limits:

$$Centerline: \overline{R}$$

$$Upper\ control\ limit: \overline{R}D_4$$

$$Lower\ control\ limit: \overline{R}D_3$$

where D_3 and D_4 are constants that depend on n. Their values can be found in Table IX in Appendix: Tables. When $n \leq 6$, $D_3 = 0$, indicating that the control chart does not have a lower control limit.

5. Plot the k sample ranges on the control chart in the order that the samples were produced by the process.

We interpret the completed R-chart in basically the same way as we did the $\bar{x}$-chart. We look for indications that the process is out of control. Those indications include points that fall outside the control limits as well as any nonrandom patterns of variation that appear between the control limits. To help spot nonrandom behavior, we include the A, B, and C zones (described in the previous section) on the R-chart. The next box describes how to construct the zone boundaries for the R-chart. It requires only Rules 1 through 4 of Figure 22; Rules 5 and 6 are based on the assumption that the statistic plotted on the control chart follows a normal (or nearly normal) distribution, whereas R's distribution is skewed to the right.*

Constructing Zone Boundaries for an R-Chart

The simplest method of construction uses the estimator of the standard deviation of R, which is $\hat{\sigma}_R = d_3(\overline{R}/d_2)$:

$$\text{Upper } A-B \text{ boundary: } \overline{R} + 2d_3\left(\frac{\overline{R}}{d_2}\right)$$

$$\text{Lower } A-B \text{ boundary: } \overline{R} - 2d_3\left(\frac{\overline{R}}{d_2}\right)$$

$$\text{Upper } B-C \text{ boundary: } \overline{R} + d_3\left(\frac{\overline{R}}{d_2}\right)$$

$$\text{Lower } B-C \text{ boundary: } \overline{R} - d_3\left(\frac{\overline{R}}{d_2}\right)$$

Note: Whenever $n \le 6$, the R-chart has no lower 3-sigma control limit. However, the lower A–B and B–C boundaries can still be plotted if they are nonnegative.

Interpreting an R-Chart

1. The **process is out of control** if one or more sample ranges fall beyond the control limits (Rule 1) or if any of the three patterns of variation described by Rules 2, 3, and 4 (Figure 22) are observed. Such signals indicate that one or more special causes of variation are influencing the *variation* of the process. These causes should be identified and eliminated to bring the process into control.

2. The **process is treated as being in control** if none of the noted out-of-control signals are observed. Processes that are in control should not be tampered with. However, if the level of variation is unacceptably high, common causes of variation should be identified and eliminated.

As with the $\bar{x}$-chart, the centerline and control limits should be developed using samples that were collected during a period in which the process was in control. Accordingly, when an R-chart is first constructed, the centerline and the control limits are treated as *trial values* (see Section 4) and are modified, if necessary, before being extended to the right and used to monitor future process output.

Example	8

Creating and Interpreting an R-Chart—Paint-Filling Process

Problem Refer to Example 6 and the paint-filling process. Recall that five paint cans were sampled each hour for 25 consecutive hours, and the can weights (oz.) were measured.

a. Construct an R-chart for the paint-filling process.

b. What does the chart indicate about the stability of the filling process during the time when the data were collected?

c. Is it appropriate to use the control limits constructed in part **a** to monitor future process output?

---

*Some authors (e.g., Kane, 1989) apply all six pattern-analysis rules as long as $n \ge 4$.

Solution

a. The first step after collecting the data is to calculate the range of each sample. These ranges were computed using Excel in Example 6 and are shown on the Excel spreadsheet, Figure 23. Next, calculate the mean of the ranges, $\overline{R}$. From Example 6, we have $\overline{R} = .010072$.

The centerline of the chart is positioned at $\overline{R} = .010072$. To determine the control limits, we need the constants D_3 and D_4, which can be found in Table IX in Appendix: Tables. For $n = 5$, $D_3 = 0$ and $D_4 = 2.114$. Because $D_3 = 0$, the lower 3-sigma control limit is negative and is not included on the chart. The upper control limit is calculated as follows:

$$\text{UCL: } \overline{R}D_4 = (.010072)(2.114) = .02130$$

After positioning the upper control limit on the chart, we plot the 25 sample ranges in the order of sampling and connect the points with straight lines. The resulting trial R-chart, produced using Minitab, is shown in Figure 28.

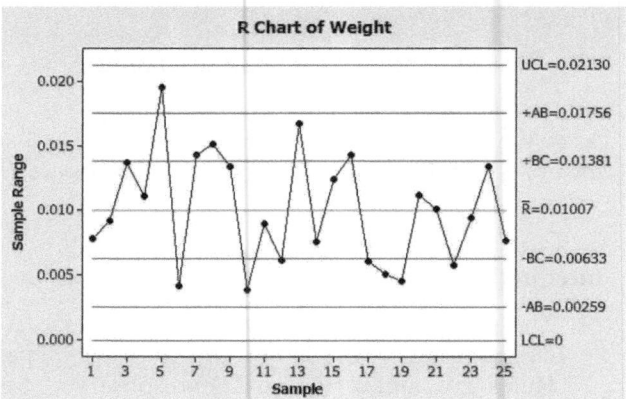

Figure 28

Minitab R-chart for paint-filling process

b. To facilitate our examination of the R-chart, we plot the four zone boundaries. Recall that, in general, the A–B boundaries are positioned 2 standard deviations from the centerline and the B–C boundaries are 1 standard deviation from the centerline. In the case of the R-chart, we use the estimated standard deviation of R, $\hat{\sigma}_R = d_3(\overline{R}/d_2)$, and calculate the boundaries:

$$\text{Upper A–B boundary: } \overline{R} + 2d_3\left(\frac{\overline{R}}{d_2}\right) = .01755$$

$$\text{Lower A–B boundary: } \overline{R} - 2d_3\left(\frac{\overline{R}}{d_2}\right) = .00259$$

$$\text{Upper B–C boundary: } \overline{R} + d_3\left(\frac{\overline{R}}{d_2}\right) = .01381$$

$$\text{Lower B–C boundary: } \overline{R} - d_3\left(\frac{\overline{R}}{d_2}\right) = .00633$$

where (from Table IX in Appendix: Tables) for $n = 5$, $d_2 = 2.326$ and $d_3 = .864$. Notice in Figure 28 that the lower A zone is slightly narrower than the upper A zone. This occurs because the lower 3-sigma control limit (the usual lower boundary of the lower A zone) is negative.

All the plotted R values fall below the upper control limit. This is one indication that the process is under control (i.e., is stable). However, we must also look for patterns of points that would be unlikely to occur if the process were in control. To assist us with this process, we use pattern-analysis Rules 1–4 (Figure 22). None of the rules signal the presence of special causes of variation. Accordingly, we conclude that it is reasonable to treat the process—in particular, the variation of the process—as being under control during the period in question. Apparently, no significant special causes of variation are influencing the variation of the process.

c. Yes. Because the variation of the process appears to be in control during the period when the sample data were collected, the control limits appropriately characterize the variation in R that would be expected when the process is in a state of statistical control.

■ **Now Work Exercise 25**

In practice, the $\bar{x}$-chart and the R-chart are not used in isolation, as our presentation so far might suggest. Rather, they are used together to monitor the mean (i.e., the location) of the process and the variation of the process simultaneously. In fact, many practitioners plot them on the same piece of paper.

One important reason for dealing with them as a unit is that the control limits of the $\bar{x}$-chart are a function of R—that is, the control limits depend on the variation of the process. (Recall that the control limits are $\bar{x} \pm A_2\bar{R}$.) Thus, if the process variation is out of control, the control limits of the $\bar{x}$-chart have little meaning. This is because when the process variation is changing (as in the rightmost graphs of Figure 8), any single estimate of the variation (such as $\bar{R}$ or s) is not representative of the process. Accordingly, **the appropriate procedure is to first construct and then interpret the R-chart. If it indicates that the process variation is in control, then it makes sense to construct and interpret the $\bar{x}$-chart.**

Figure 29 is reprinted from Kaoru Ishikawa's classic text on quality-improvement methods, *Guide to Quality Control* (1986). It illustrates how particular changes in a process over time may be reflected in $\bar{x}$- and R-charts. At the top of the figure, running across the page, is a series of probability distributions A, B, and C that describe the process (i.e., the output variable) at different points in time. In practice, we never have this information. For this example, however, Ishikawa worked with a known process (i.e., with its given probabilistic characterization) to illustrate how sample data from a known process might behave.

The control limits for both charts were constructed from $k = 25$ samples of size $n = 5$. These data were generated by Distribution A. The 25 sample means and ranges were plotted on the $\bar{x}$- and R-charts, respectively. Because the distribution did not change over this period of time, it follows from the definition of statistical control that the process was under control. If you did not know this—as would be the case in practice—what would you conclude from looking at the control charts? (Remember, always interpret the R-chart before the $\bar{x}$-chart.) Both charts indicate that the process is under control. Accordingly, the control limits are made official and can be used to monitor future output, as is done next.

Figure 29

Combined $\bar{x}$- and R-chart
Source: Based on GUIDE TO QUALITY CONTROL by Kaoru Ishikawa.

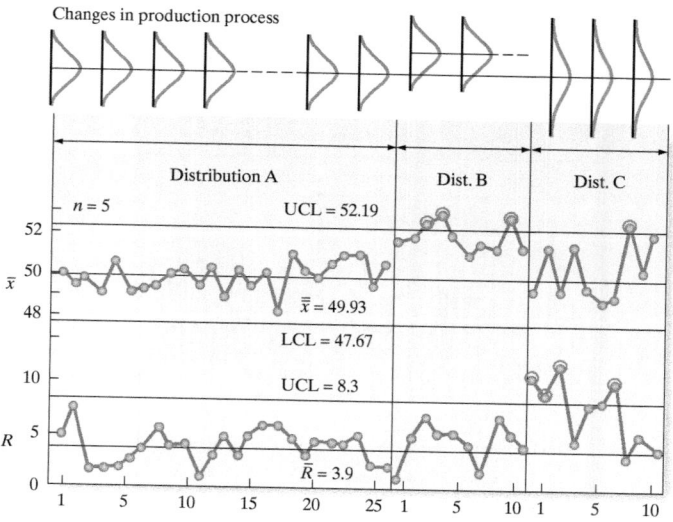

Toward the middle of the figure, the process changes. The mean shifts to a higher level. Now the output variable is described by Distribution B. The process is out of control. Ten new samples of size 5 are sampled from the process. Because the variation of the process has not changed, the R-chart should indicate that the variation remains stable. This is, in fact, the case. All points fall below the upper control limit. As we would hope, it is the $\bar{x}$-chart that reacts to the change in the mean of the process.

Then the process changes again (Distribution C). This time the mean shifts back to its original position, but the variation of the process increases. The process is still out of control but this time for a different reason. Checking the R-chart first, we see that it has reacted as we would hope. It has detected the increase in the variation. Given this R-chart finding, the control limits of the $\bar{x}$-chart become inappropriate (as described before), and we would not use them. Notice, however, how the sample means react to the increased variation in the process. This increased variation in $\bar{x}$ is consistent with what we know about the variance of $\bar{x}$. It is directly proportional to the variance of the process, $\sigma_{\bar{x}}^2 = \sigma^2/n$.

Keep in mind that what Ishikawa did in this example is exactly the opposite of what we do in practice. In practice, we use sample data and control charts to make inferences about changes in unknown process distributions. Here, for the purpose of helping you to understand and interpret control charts, known process distributions were changed to see what would happen to the control charts.

STATISTICS
in ACTION
REVISITED

Monitoring the Process Variation

Recall that the engineering firm discovered that tests for surfactants in jet fuel additive using Pump-B with Filter-B yielded an "in-control" process mean. However, as discussed in this section, the variation of the process should be checked first, before interpreting the $\bar{x}$-chart. Figure SIA2 is a Minitab R-chart for the test results using Pump-B with Filter-B. As an option, we again instructed Minitab to highlight (in red) any sample ranges that match any of the four pattern-analysis rules for detecting special causes of variation given in this section. (If a rule is violated, the rule number will be shown next to the sample range on the chart.)

Figure SIA2 shows that the process variation is "in control"—none of the pattern-analysis rules for ranges are matched. Now that we've established the stability of the process variance, the $\bar{x}$-chart of Figure SIA1d can be meaningfully interpreted. Together, the $\bar{x}$-chart and R-chart helped the engineering firm establish the Pump-B with Filter-B surfactant test method as a viable alternative to the standard test, one that appears to have no special causes of variation present and with more precision than the standard.

[*Note:* Extensive testing done with the Navy concluded that the improved precision of the "new" surfactant test was valid. However, the new test was unable to detect several light surfactants that can still cause problems in jet engines. The original test for surfactants in jet fuel additive remains the industry standard.]

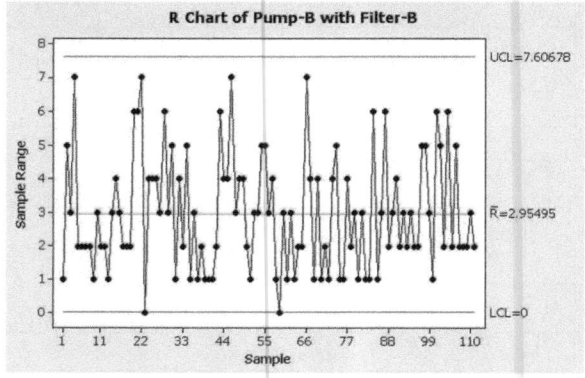

Figure SIA2

R-chart for Pump-B with Filter-B method

Exercises 22–36

Learning the Mechanics

22 What characteristic of a process is an R-chart designed to monitor?

23 In practice, $\bar{x}$- and R-charts are used together to monitor a process. However, the R-chart should be interpreted before the $\bar{x}$-chart. Why?

24 Use Table IX in Appendix: Tables to find the values of D_3 and D_4 for each of the following sample sizes.
  a. $n = 4$
  b. $n = 12$
  c. $n = 24$

25 Construct and interpret an R-chart for the data in Exercise 10.
NW
  a. Calculate and plot the upper control limit and, if appropriate, the lower control limit.
  b. Calculate and plot the A, B, and C zone boundaries on the R-chart.
  c. Plot the sample ranges on the R-chart and use pattern-analysis Rules 1–4 of Figure 22 to determine whether the process is under statistical control.

26 Construct and interpret an R-chart for the data in Exercise 11.
  a. Calculate and plot the upper control limit and, if appropriate, the lower control limit.

b. Calculate and plot the A, B, and C zone boundaries on the R-chart.

c. Plot the sample ranges on the R-chart and determine whether the process is in control.

27 Construct and interpret an R-chart and an $\bar{x}$-chart from the sample data shown below. Remember to interpret the
L13027 R-chart *before* the $\bar{x}$-chart.

Applying the Concepts—Basic

28 **Detecting gender-related employment disparities.** Refer to the *Federal Reserve Bank of Atlanta, Working Paper Series* (Oct. 2008) study of gender-related employment disparities, Exercise 12. Recall that the researchers used the Equal Employment Opportunity (EEOC) Systematic Gender Disparity Scorecard as a measure of the degree to which a firm complies with EEOC guidelines for eliminating gender bias. An R-chart for the data obtained by sampling firms for each of 30 different service industry firm types is shown below. The centerline and upper and lower control limits are shown on the chart.
  a. What are the approximate values of $\bar{R}$, UCL, and LCL?
  b. What conclusions can you draw from the chart? Are there any firm types that should concern the EEOC? Why?

Data for Exercise 27

Sample	Measurements							$\bar{x}$	R
	1	2	3	4	5	6	7		
1	20.1	19.0	20.9	22.2	18.9	18.1	21.3	20.07	4.1
2	19.0	17.9	21.2	20.4	20.0	22.3	21.5	20.33	4.4
3	22.6	21.4	21.4	22.1	19.2	20.6	18.7	20.86	3.9
4	18.1	20.8	17.8	19.6	19.8	21.7	20.0	19.69	3.9
5	22.6	19.1	21.4	21.8	18.4	18.0	19.5	20.11	4.6
6	19.1	19.0	22.3	21.5	17.8	19.2	19.4	19.76	4.5
7	17.1	19.4	18.6	20.9	21.8	21.0	19.8	19.80	4.7
8	20.2	22.4	22.0	19.6	19.6	20.0	18.5	20.33	3.9
9	21.9	24.1	23.1	22.8	25.6	24.2	25.2	23.84	3.7
10	25.1	24.3	26.0	23.1	25.8	27.0	26.5	25.40	3.9
11	25.8	29.2	28.5	29.1	27.8	29.0	28.0	28.20	3.4
12	28.2	27.5	29.3	30.7	27.6	28.0	27.0	28.33	3.7
13	28.2	28.6	28.1	26.0	30.0	28.5	28.3	28.24	4.0
14	22.1	21.4	23.3	20.5	19.8	20.5	19.0	20.94	4.3
15	18.5	19.2	18.0	20.1	22.0	20.2	19.5	19.64	4.0
16	21.4	20.3	22.0	19.2	18.0	17.9	19.5	19.76	4.1
17	18.4	16.5	18.1	19.2	17.5	20.9	19.6	18.60	4.4
18	20.1	19.8	22.3	22.5	21.8	22.7	23.0	21.74	3.2
19	20.0	17.5	21.0	18.2	19.5	17.2	18.1	18.79	3.8
20	22.3	18.2	21.5	19.0	19.4	20.5	20.0	20.13	4.1

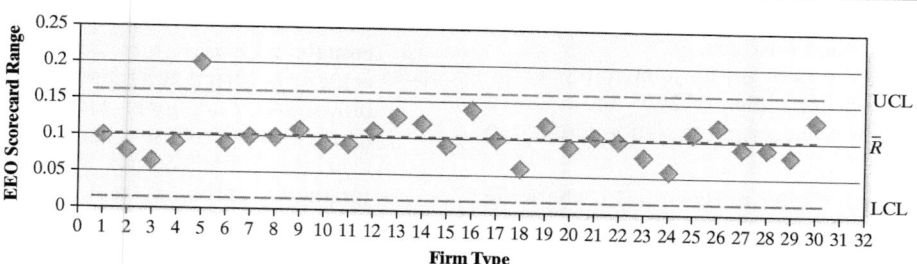

Control chart for Exercise 28

29 Pain levels of ICU patients. Refer to the *Research in Nursing & Health* (Vol. 35, 2012) study of the effectiveness of a pain intervention, Exercise 13. Recall that pain levels (measured on a 100-point scale) were recorded for a sample of 10 ICU patients 24 hours post surgery each week for 20 consecutive weeks. The data are repeated in the accompanying table. Now, you want to check process variation using an *R*-chart.

ICU

a. Compute the centerline for the chart.

b. Compute the UCL and LCL for the *R*-chart.

c. Plot the ranges for the 20 weeks on the *R*-chart. Does the variation of the pain management process appear to be "in control"?

d. Recall that after the 20th week, a pain intervention occurred in the ICU. The ranges of the pain levels for the samples of patients over the next 8 consecutive weeks were (in order): 22, 29, 16, 15, 23, 19, 30, and 32. Plot these ranges on the *R*-chart.

e. Apply pattern-analysis rules to the extended *R*-chart, part **d.** What do you observe?

Week	$\bar{x}$	Range
1	65	28
2	75	41
3	72	31
4	69	35
5	73	35
6	63	33
7	77	34
8	75	29
9	69	30
10	64	39
11	70	34
12	74	37
13	73	25
14	62	33
15	68	28
16	75	35
17	72	29
18	70	32
19	62	33
20	72	29

Source: Based on "Statistical Process Control in Nursing Research" by Denise F. Polit and Wendy Chaboyer from RESEARCH IN NURSING AND HEALTH, February 2012, Volume 35(1).

30 Quality control for irrigation data. Refer to Exercise 14 and the monitoring of irrigation data by the CIMIS. Recall that daily minimum air temperatures (°C) collected hourly during the month of May at the Davis CIMIS station yielded the following summary statistics (where five measurements are collected each hour): $\bar{\bar{x}} = 10.16°$ and $\bar{R} = 14.87°$.

a. Use the information provided to find the lower and upper control limits for an *R*-chart.

b. Suppose that one day in May the air temperature at the Davis CIMIS station had a high of 24.7° and a low of 2.2°. How should the manager of the station respond to this observation?

31 CPU of a computer chip. Refer to Exercise 15, where the desired circuit path widths were .5 to .85 micro-meter. The manufacturer sampled four CPU chips six times a day (every 90 minutes from 8:00 a.m. until 4:30 p.m.) for

5 consecutive days. The path widths were measured and used to construct the accompanying Minitab *R*-chart.

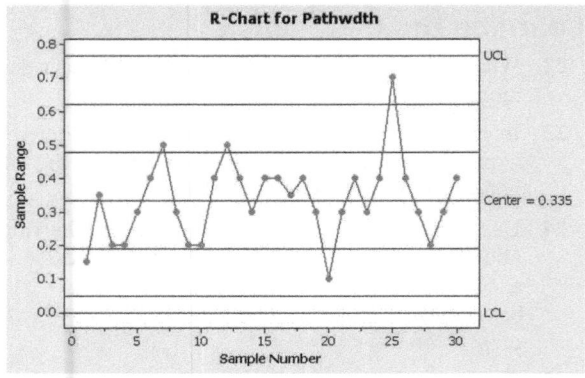

a. Calculate the chart's upper and lower control limits.

b. What does the *R*-chart suggest about the presence of special causes of variation during the time when the data were collected?

c. Should the control limit(s) be used to monitor future process output? Explain.

d. How many different *R* values are plotted on the control chart? Notice how most of the *R* values fall along three horizontal lines. What could cause such a pattern?

Applying the Concepts—Intermediate

32 Cola bottle filling process. A soft-drink bottling company is interested in monitoring the amount of cola injected into 16-ounce bottles by a particular filling head. The process is entirely automated and operates 24 hours a day. At 6:00 a.m. and 6:00 p.m. each day, a new dispenser of carbon dioxide capable of producing 20,000 gallons of cola is hooked up to the filling machine. To monitor the process using control charts, the company decided to sample five consecutive bottles of cola each hour beginning at 6:15 A.M. (i.e., 6:15 A.M., 7:15 A.M., 8:15 A.M., etc.). The data for the first day are saved in the file. An SPSS descriptive statistics printout for the data is shown on the next page.

COLA

a. Will the rational subgrouping strategy that was used enable the company to detect variation in fill caused by differences in the carbon dioxide dispensers? Explain.

b. Construct an *R*-chart from the data.

c. What does the *R*-chart indicate about the stability of the filling process during the time when the data were collected? Justify your answer.

d. Should the control limit(s) be used to monitor future process output? Explain.

e. Given your answer to part **c,** should an $\bar{x}$-chart be constructed from the given data? Explain.

33 Lowering the thickness of an expensive blow-molded container. *Quality* (Mar. 2009) presented a problem that actually occurred at a plant that produces a high-volume, blow-molded container with multiple layers. One of the layers is very expensive to manufacture. The quality manager at the plant desires to lower the average thickness for the expensive layer of material and still meet specifications. To estimate the actual thickness for this layer, the manager measured the thickness for one container

BLWMLD

SPSS output for Exercise 32

Descriptive Statistics for 25 Cola Samples

	Count	Mean	Minimum	Maximum	Range
1	5	16.01	15.98	16.03	.05
2	5	16.00	15.97	16.03	.06
3	5	16.01	15.98	16.04	.06
4	5	16.00	15.98	16.03	.05
5	5	16.01	15.97	16.04	.07
6	5	16.01	15.97	16.04	.07
7	5	16.00	15.96	16.05	.09
8	5	16.01	15.97	16.05	.08
9	5	15.99	15.95	16.03	.08
10	5	16.01	15.95	16.06	.11
11	5	16.00	15.93	16.07	.14
12	5	16.02	15.94	16.08	.14
13	5	15.99	15.96	16.01	.05
14	5	16.00	15.98	16.02	.04
15	5	16.00	15.98	16.03	.05
16	5	16.00	15.97	16.02	.05
17	5	16.01	15.99	16.05	.06
18	5	16.01	15.98	16.04	.06
19	5	15.98	15.96	16.01	.05
20	5	16.01	15.96	16.04	.08
21	5	16.01	15.97	16.05	.08
22	5	16.01	15.95	16.07	.12
23	5	16.02	15.95	16.07	.12
24	5	15.99	15.93	16.08	.15

from each of two cavities every 2 hours for 2 consecutive days. The data (in millimeters) are shown in the following tables.

a. Construct an R-chart for the data.

b. Construct an $\bar{x}$-chart for the data.

c. Based on the control charts in parts **a** and **b**, comment on the current behavior of the manufacturing process. As part of your answer, give an estimate of the true average thickness of the expensive layer.

Day 1

Time	7A.M.	9A.M.	11A.M.	1P.M.	3P.M.	5P.M.	7P.M.	9P.M.
Thickness	.167	.241	.204	.221	.255	.224	.216	.235
(mm)	.232	.203	.214	.190	.207	.238	.210	.210
Average	.1995	.2220	.2090	.2055	.2310	.2310	.2310	.2225
Range	.065	.038	.010	.031	.048	.014	.006	.025

Day 2

Time	7A.M.	9A.M.	11A.M.	1P.M.	3P.M.	5P.M.	7P.M.	9P.M.
Thickness	.223	.202	.258	.243	.248	.192	.208	.223
(mm)	.216	.215	.228	.221	.252	.221	.245	.224
Average	.2195	.2085	.2430	.2320	.2500	.2065	.2265	.2235
Range	.007	.013	.030	.022	.004	.029	.037	.001

34 Replacement times for lost ATM cards. In an effort to reduce customer dissatisfaction with delays in replacing lost automated teller machine (ATM) cards, some retail banks monitor the time required to replace a lost ATM card. Called *replacement cycle time,* it is the elapsed time from when the customer contacts the bank about the loss until the customer receives a new card (*Management Science,* Sept. 1999). A particular retail bank monitors replacement cycle time for the first five requests each week for

replacement cards. Variation in cycle times is monitored using an R-chart. Data for 20 weeks are presented below.

Week		Replacement Cycle Time (in days)			
1	7	10	6	6	10
2	7	12	8	8	6
3	7	8	7	11	6
4	8	8	12	11	12
5	3	8	4	7	7
6	6	10	11	5	7
7	5	12	11	8	7
8	7	12	8	7	6
9	8	10	12	10	5
10	12	8	6	6	8
11	10	9	9	5	4
12	3	10	7	6	8
13	9	9	8	7	2
14	7	10	18	20	8
15	8	18	15	18	21
16	10	22	16	8	7
17	3	18	4	8	12
18	11	7	8	17	19
19	10	8	19	20	25
20	6	3	18	18	7

a. Construct an R-chart for these data.

b. What does the R-chart suggest about the presence of special causes of variation in the process?

c. Should the control limits of your R-chart be used to monitor future replacement cycle times? Explain.

d. Given your conclusion in part **b** and the pattern displayed on the R-chart, discuss the possible future impact on the performance of the bank.

35 Chunky data. Refer to Exercise 21 and the hourly data collected by BPI consulting. Recall that the data are saved in the file.

CHUNKY

855

a. Construct an R-chart for the data. Is the process variation in control?

b. Round each measurement in the data set to a whole number, like in Exercise 21b. Form an R-chart for the rounded data. What do you observe?

Applying the Concepts—Advanced

36 Precision of scale weight measurements. The *Journal of Quality Technology* (July 1998) published an article examining the effects of the precision of measurement on the R-chart. The authors presented data from a British nutrition company that fills containers labeled "500 grams" with a powdered dietary supplement. Once every 15 minutes, five containers are sampled from the filling process, and the fill weight is measured. The table to the right lists the measurements for 25 consecutive samples made with a scale that is accurate to .5 gram, followed by the table below, which gives measurements for the same samples made with a scale that is accurate to only 2.5 grams. Throughout the time period over which the samples were drawn, it is known that the filling process was in statistical control with mean 500 grams and standard deviation 1 gram.

a. Construct an R-chart for the data that is accurate to .5 gram. Is the process under statistical control? Explain.

b. Given your answer to part **a**, is it appropriate to construct an $\bar{x}$-chart for the data? Explain.

c. Construct an R-chart for the data that is accurate to only 2.5 grams. What does it suggest about the stability of the filling process?

d. Based on your answers to parts **a** and **c**, discuss the importance of the accuracy of measurement instruments in evaluating the stability of production processes.

First table for Exercise 36

Sample	Fill Weights Accurate to .5 Gram					Range
1	500.5	499.5	502.0	501.0	500.5	2.5
2	500.5	499.5	500.0	499.0	500.0	1.5
3	498.5	499.0	500.0	499.5	500.0	1.5
4	500.5	499.5	499.0	499.0	500.5	1.5
5	500.0	501.0	500.5	500.5	500.0	1.0
6	501.0	498.5	500.0	501.5	500.5	3.0
7	499.5	500.0	499.0	501.0	499.5	2.0
8	498.5	498.0	500.0	500.5	500.5	2.5
9	498.0	499.0	502.0	501.0	501.5	4.0
10	499.0	499.5	499.5	500.0	499.5	1.0
11	502.5	499.5	501.0	501.5	502.0	3.0
12	501.5	501.5	500.0	500.0	501.0	1.5
13	498.5	499.5	501.0	500.5	498.5	2.5
14	499.5	498.0	500.0	499.5	498.5	2.0
15	501.0	500.0	498.0	500.5	500.0	3.0
16	502.5	501.5	502.0	500.5	500.5	2.0
17	499.5	500.5	500.0	499.5	499.5	1.0
18	499.0	498.5	498.0	500.0	498.0	2.0
19	499.0	498.0	500.5	501.0	501.0	3.0
20	501.5	499.5	500.0	500.5	502.0	2.5
21	501.0	500.5	502.0	502.5	502.5	2.0
22	501.5	502.5	502.5	501.5	502.0	1.0
23	499.5	502.0	500.0	500.5	502.0	2.5
24	498.5	499.0	499.0	500.5	500.0	2.0
25	500.0	499.5	498.5	500.0	500.5	2.0

Second table for Exercise 36

Sample	Fill Weights Accurate to 2.5 Grams					Range	Sample	Fill Weights Accurate to 2.5 Grams					Range
1	500.0	500.0	502.5	500.0	500.0	2.5	14	500.0	500.0	500.0	500.0	500.0	0.0
2	500.0	500.0	500.0	500.0	500.0	0.0	15	502.5	502.5	502.5	500.0	502.5	2.5
3	500.0	500.0	500.0	500.0	500.0	0.0	16	500.0	500.0	500.0	500.0	500.0	0.0
4	497.5	500.0	497.5	497.5	500.0	2.5	17	497.5	497.5	497.5	497.5	497.5	0.0
5	500.0	500.0	500.0	500.0	500.0	0.0	18	500.0	500.0	500.0	500.0	500.0	0.0
6	502.5	500.0	497.5	500.0	500.0	5.0	19	495.0	497.5	500.0	500.0	500.0	5.0
7	500.0	500.0	502.5	502.5	500.0	2.5	20	500.0	502.5	500.0	500.0	502.5	2.5
8	497.5	500.0	500.0	497.5	500.0	2.5	21	500.0	500.0	500.0	500.0	500.0	0.0
9	500.0	500.0	497.5	500.0	502.5	5.0	22	500.0	500.0	500.0	500.0	500.0	0.0
10	500.0	500.0	500.0	500.0	500.0	0.0	23	500.0	500.0	500.0	500.0	500.0	0.0
11	500.0	505.0	502.5	500.0	500.0	5.0	24	497.5	497.5	500.0	497.5	497.5	2.5
12	500.0	500.0	500.0	500.0	500.0	0.0	25	500.0	500.0	497.5	500.0	500.0	2.5
13	500.0	500.0	497.5	500.0	500.0	2.5							

Source: "The effects on the R-chart of precision of measurement" by A. Tricker, E. Coates, and E. Okell, in JOURNAL OF QUALITY TECHNOLOGY, July 1998, Volume 30(3). Copyright © 1998 by the American Society for Quality. Reprinted with permission.

6 A Control Chart for Monitoring the Proportion of Defectives Generated by a Process: The *p*-Chart

Among the dozens of different control charts that have been proposed by researchers and practitioners, the $\bar{x}$- and R-charts are, by far, the most popular for use in monitoring *quantitative* output variables, such as time, length, and weight. Among the charts developed for use with *qualitative* output variables, the chart we introduce in this section is the most popular. Called the **p-chart,** it is used when the output variable is categorical (i.e., measured on a nominal scale). With the p-chart, the proportion, p, of units produced by the process that belong to a particular category (e.g., defective or nondefective; successful or unsuccessful; early, on-time, or late) can be monitored.

The p-chart is typically used to monitor the proportion of defective units produced by a process (i.e., the proportion of units that do not conform to specification). This proportion is used to characterize a process in the same sense that the mean and variance are used to characterize a process when the output variable is quantitative. Examples of process proportions that are monitored in industry include the proportion of billing errors made by credit card companies, the proportion of nonfunctional semiconductor chips produced, and the proportion of checks that a bank's magnetic ink character-recognition system is unable to read.

As is the case for the mean and variance, the process proportion can change over time. For example, it can drift upward or downward or jump to a new level. In such cases, the process is out of control. **As long as the process proportion remains constant, the process is in a state of statistical control.**

As with the other control charts presented in this chapter, the p-chart has a centerline and control limits that are determined from sample data. After k samples of size n are drawn from the process, each unit is classified (e.g., defective or nondefective), the proportion of defective units in each sample—$\hat{p}$—is calculated, the centerline and control limits are determined using this information, and the sample proportions are plotted on the p-chart. It is the variation in the $\hat{p}$'s over time that we monitor and interpret. Changes in the behavior of the $\hat{p}$'s signal changes in the process proportion, p.

The p-chart is based on the assumption that the number of defectives observed in each sample is a binomial random variable. What we have called the process proportion is really the binomial probability, p. When the process is in a state of statistical control, p remains constant over time. Variation in $\hat{p}$—as displayed on a p-chart—is used to judge whether p is stable.

To determine the centerline and control limits for the p-chart, we need to know $\hat{p}$'s sampling distribution. Note that

$$\hat{p} = \frac{\text{Number of defective items in the sample}}{\text{Number of items in the sample}} = \frac{x}{n}$$

$$\mu_{\hat{p}} = p$$

$$\sigma_{\hat{p}} = \sqrt{\frac{p(1-p)}{n}}$$

and that for large samples, $\hat{p}$ is approximately normally distributed. Thus, if p were known, the centerline would be p and the 3-sigma control limits would be $p \pm 3\sqrt{p(1-p)/n}$. However, because p is unknown, it must be estimated from the sample data. The appropriate estimator is $\bar{p}$, the overall proportion of defective units in the nk units sampled:

$$\bar{p} = \frac{\text{Total number of defective units in all } k \text{ samples}}{\text{Total number of units sampled}}$$

To calculate the control limits of the p-chart, substitute $\bar{p}$ for p in the preceding expression for the control limits, as illustrated in Figure 30.

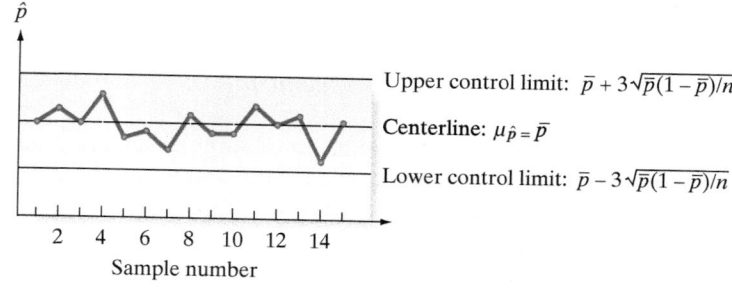

Figure 30

p-Chart

In constructing a p-chart, it is advisable to use a much larger sample size than is typically used for $\bar{x}$- and R-charts. Most processes that are monitored in industry have relatively small process proportions, often less than .05 (i.e., less than 5% of output is nonconforming). In those cases, if a small sample size is used, say $n = 5$, samples drawn from the process would likely not contain any nonconforming output. As a result, most, if not all, $\hat{p}$'s would equal zero.

We present a rule of thumb that can be used to determine a sample size large enough to avoid this problem. This rule will also help protect against ending up with a negative lower control limit, a situation that frequently occurs when both p and n are small. See Montgomery (2009) or Duncan (1986) for further details.

Sample-Size Determination for Monitoring a Process Proportion

Choose n such that $n > \dfrac{9(1 - p_0)}{p_0}$

where

n = Sample size

p_0 = An estimate (perhaps judgmental) of the process proportion p

---

For example, if p is thought to be about .05, the rule indicates that samples of at least size 171 should be used in constructing the p-chart:

$$n > \frac{9(1 - .05)}{.05} = 171$$

In the next three boxes, we summarize how to construct a p-chart and its zone boundaries and how to interpret a p-chart.

Constructing a p-Chart: A Summary

1. Using a rational subgrouping strategy, collect at least 20 samples, each of size

$$n > \frac{9(1 - p_0)}{p_0}$$

where p_0 is an estimate of p, the proportion defective (i.e., nonconforming) produced by the process. p_0 can be determined from sample data (i.e., $\hat{p}$) or may be based on expert opinion.

2. For each sample, calculate $\hat{p}$, the proportion of defective units in the sample:

$$\hat{p} = \frac{\text{Number of defective items in the sample}}{\text{Number of items in the sample}}$$

3. Plot the centerline and control limits:

$$\textit{Centerline: } \bar{p} = \frac{\text{Total number of defective units in all } k \text{ samples}}{\text{Total number of units in all } k \text{ samples}}$$

$$\textit{Upper control limit: } \bar{p} + 3\sqrt{\frac{\bar{p}(1 - \bar{p})}{n}}$$

$$\textit{Lower control limit: } \bar{p} - 3\sqrt{\frac{\bar{p}(1 - \bar{p})}{n}}$$

where k is the number of samples of size n and $\bar{p}$ is the overall proportion of defective units in the nk units sampled. $\bar{p}$ is an estimate of the unknown process proportion p.

4. Plot the k sample proportions on the control chart in the order that the samples were produced by the process.

As with the $\bar{x}$- and R-charts, the centerline and control limits should be developed using samples that were collected during a period in which the process was in control. Accordingly, when a p-chart is first constructed, the centerline and the control limits should be treated as *trial values* (see Section 4) and, if necessary, modified before being extended to the right on the control chart and used to monitor future process output.

Constructing Zone Boundaries for a p-Chart

$$\text{Upper } A\text{–}B \text{ boundary: } \bar{p} + 2\sqrt{\frac{\bar{p}(1 - \bar{p})}{n}}$$

$$\text{Lower } A\text{–}B \text{ boundary: } \bar{p} - 2\sqrt{\frac{\bar{p}(1 - \bar{p})}{n}}$$

$$\text{Upper } B\text{–}C \text{ boundary: } \bar{p} + \sqrt{\frac{\bar{p}(1 - \bar{p})}{n}}$$

$$\text{Lower } B\text{–}C \text{ boundary: } \bar{p} - \sqrt{\frac{\bar{p}(1 - \bar{p})}{n}}$$

Note: When the lower control limit is negative, it should not be plotted on the control chart. However, the lower zone boundaries can still be plotted if they are nonnegative.

Interpreting a p-Chart

1. The **process is out of control** if one or more sample proportions fall beyond the control limits (Rule 1) or if any of the three patterns of variation described by Rules 2, 3, and 4 (Figure 22) are observed. Such signals indicate that one or more special causes of variation are influencing the process proportion, p. These causes should be identified and eliminated in order to bring the process into control.

2. The **process is treated as being in control** if none of the above noted out-of-control signals are observed. Processes that are in control should not be tampered with. However, if the level of variation is unacceptably high, common causes of variation should be identified and eliminated.

Example 9

Creating and Interpreting a p-Chart—Order Assembly Process

Problem A manufacturer of auto parts is interested in implementing statistical process control in several areas within its warehouse operation. The manufacturer wants to begin with the order assembly process. Too frequently, orders received by customers contain the wrong items or too few items.

For each order received, parts are picked from storage bins in the warehouse, labeled, and placed on a conveyor belt system. Because the bins are spread over a 3-acre area, items that are part of the same order may be placed on different spurs of the conveyor belt system. Near the end of the belt system, all spurs converge and a worker sorts the items according to the order they belong to. That information is contained on the labels that were placed on the items by the pickers.

The workers have identified three errors that cause shipments to be improperly assembled: (1) pickers pick from the wrong bin, (2) pickers mislabel items, and (3) the sorter makes an error.

The firm's quality manager has implemented a sampling program in which 90 assembled orders are sampled each day and checked for accuracy. An assembled order is considered nonconforming (defective) if it differs in any way from the order placed by the customer. To date, 25 samples have been evaluated. The resulting data are shown in the Excel spreadsheet, Figure 31.

a. Construct a p-chart for the order assembly operation.

b. What does the chart indicate about the stability of the process?

c. Is it appropriate to use the control limits and centerline constructed in part **a** to monitor future process output?

	A	B	C	D
1	Sample	Size (n)	Defective Orders	Sample Proportion
2	1	90	12	0.133333333
3	2	90	6	0.066666667
4	3	90	11	0.122222222
5	4	90	8	0.088888889
6	5	90	13	0.144444444
7	6	90	14	0.155555556
8	7	90	12	0.133333333
9	8	90	6	0.066666667
10	9	90	10	0.111111111
11	10	90	13	0.144444444
12	11	90	12	0.133333333
13	12	90	24	0.266666667
14	13	90	23	0.255555556
15	14	90	22	0.244444444
16	15	90	8	0.088888889
17	16	90	3	0.033333333
18	17	90	11	0.122222222
19	18	90	14	0.155555556
20	19	90	5	0.055555556
21	20	90	12	0.133333333
22	21	90	18	0.2
23	22	90	12	0.133333333
24	23	90	13	0.144444444
25	24	90	4	0.044444444
26	25	90	6	0.066666667
27				
28	**Totals**	2250	292	0.129777778

Data Set: WAREHS

Figure 31

Excel worksheet with 25 samples of size $n = 90$ from warehouse order assembly process

Solution

a. The first step in constructing the p-chart after collecting the sample data is to calculate the sample proportion for each sample. For the first sample,

$$\hat{p} = \frac{\text{Number of defective items in the sample}}{\text{Number of items in the sample}} = \frac{12}{90} = .13333$$

All the sample proportions are computed using Excel and are displayed in Figure 31. Next, calculate the proportion of defective items in the total number of items sampled:

$$\bar{p} = \frac{\text{Total number of defective items}}{\text{Total number of items sampled}} = \frac{292}{2,250} = .12978$$

This value is also computed using Excel (and highlighted on Figure 31.) The centerline is positioned at $\bar{p}$, and $\bar{p}$ is used to calculate the control limits:

$$\bar{p} \pm 3\sqrt{\frac{\bar{p}(1 - \bar{p})}{n}} = .12978 \pm 3\sqrt{\frac{.12978(1 - .12978)}{90}}$$

$$= .12978 \pm .10627$$

$$\text{UCL: } .23605$$

$$\text{LCL: } .02351$$

After plotting the centerline and the control limits, plot the 25 sample proportions in the order of sampling and connect the points with straight lines. The completed control chart, obtained using Minitab, is shown in Figure 32.

b. To assist our examination of the control chart, we add the 1-and 2-standard-deviation zone boundaries. The boundaries are located by substituting $\bar{p} = .12978$ into the following formulas:

$$\textit{Upper A–B boundary: } \bar{p} + 2\sqrt{\frac{\bar{p}(1 - \bar{p})}{n}} = .20063$$

$$\textit{Lower A–B boundary: } \bar{p} - 2\sqrt{\frac{\bar{p}(1 - \bar{p})}{n}} = .05893$$

$$\text{Upper B–C boundary: } \bar{p} + \sqrt{\frac{\bar{p}(1-\bar{p})}{n}} = .16521$$

$$\text{Lower B–C boundary: } \bar{p} - \sqrt{\frac{\bar{p}(1-\bar{p})}{n}} = .09435$$

Note that three of the sample proportions fall above the upper control limit (Rule 1); thus, there is strong evidence that the process is out of control. None of the non-random patterns of Rules 2, 3, and 4 (Figure 22) are evident. The process proportion appears to have increased dramatically somewhere around sample 12.

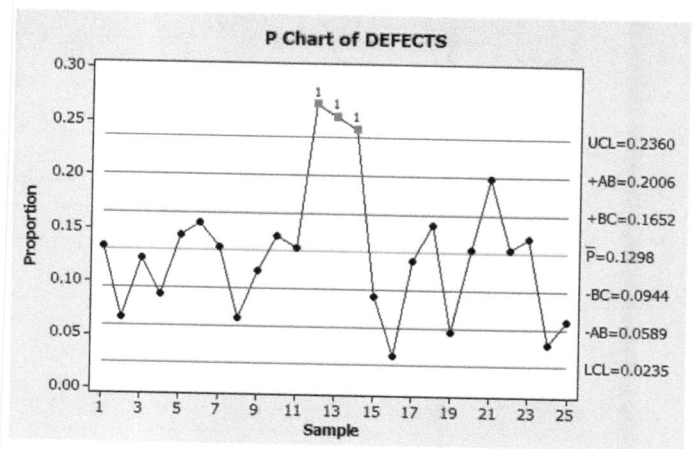

Figure 32

Minitab *p*-chart for warehouse order assembly process

c. Because the process was apparently out of control during the period in which sample data were collected to build the control chart, it is not appropriate to continue using the chart. The control limits and centerline are not representative of the process when it is in control. The chart must be revised before it is used to monitor future output.

In this case, the three out-of-control points were investigated, and it was discovered that they occurred on days when a temporary sorter was working in place of the regular sorter. Actions were taken to ensure that in the future, better-trained temporary sorters would be available.

Because the special cause of the observed variation was identified and eliminated, all sample data from the 3 days the temporary sorter was working were dropped from the data set, and the centerline and control limits were recalculated:

$$\text{Centerline: } \bar{p} = \frac{223}{1,980} = .11263$$

$$\text{Control limits: } \bar{p} \pm 3\sqrt{\frac{\bar{p}(1-\bar{p})}{n}} = .11263 \pm 3\sqrt{\frac{.11263(.88737)}{90}}$$

$$= .11263 \pm .09997$$

$$\text{UCL: } .21259 \quad \text{LCL: } .01266$$

The revised zones are calculated by substituting $\bar{p} = .11263$ in the following formulas:

$$\text{Upper A–B boundary: } \bar{p} + 2\sqrt{\frac{\bar{p}(1-\bar{p})}{n}} = .17927$$

$$\text{Upper B–C boundary: } \bar{p} + \sqrt{\frac{\bar{p}(1-\bar{p})}{n}} = .14595$$

$$\text{Lower A–B boundary: } \bar{p} - 2\sqrt{\frac{\bar{p}(1-\bar{p})}{n}} = .04598$$

$$\text{Lower B–C boundary: } \bar{p} - \sqrt{\frac{\bar{p}(1-\bar{p})}{n}} = .07931$$

The revised control chart appears in Figure 33. Notice that now all sample proportions fall within the control limits. These limits can now be treated as official, extended to the right on the chart, and used to monitor future orders.

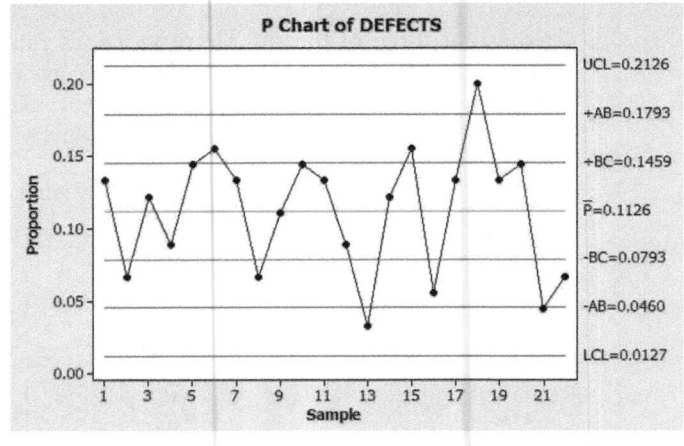

Figure 33

Revised Minitab *p*-chart for warehouse order assembly process

■ **Now Work Exercise 41**

Exercises 37–48

Learning the Mechanics

37 What characteristic of a process is a *p*-chart designed to monitor?

38 In each of the following cases, use the sample size formula to determine a sample size large enough to avoid constructing a *p*-chart with a negative lower control limit.
  a. $p_0 = .01$ **b.** $p_0 = .05$ **c.** $p_0 = .10$ **d.** $p_0 = .20$

39 The proportion of defective items generated by a manufacturing process is believed to be 8%. In constructing a *p*-chart for the process, determine how large the sample size should be to avoid ending up with a negative lower control limit.

40 To construct a *p*-chart for a manufacturing process, 25 samples of size 200 were drawn from the process. The number of defectives in each sample is listed in time order in the table that follows.

L13040

Defectives
16 14 9 11 15 8 12 16 17 13 15 10 9
12 14 11 8 7 12 15 9 16 13 11 10

a. Calculate the proportion defective in each sample.
b. Calculate and plot $\bar{p}$ and the upper and lower control limits for the *p*-chart.
c. Calculate and plot the A, B, and C zone boundaries on the *p*-chart.
d. Plot the sample proportions on the *p*-chart and connect them with straight lines.
e. Use pattern-analysis Rules 1–4 for detecting the presence of special causes of variation (Figure 22) to determine whether the process is out of control.

41 To construct a *p*-chart, 20 samples of size 150 were drawn from a process. The proportion of defective items found in each of the samples is listed in the next table.

NW

L13041

Sample	Proportion Defective	Sample	Proportion Defective
1	.03	11	.07
2	.05	12	.04
3	.10	13	.06
4	.02	14	.05
5	.08	15	.07
6	.09	16	.06
7	.08	17	.07
8	.05	18	.02
9	.07	19	.05
10	.06	20	.03

a. Calculate and plot the centerline and the upper and lower control limits for the *p*-chart.
b. Calculate and plot the A, B, and C zone boundaries on the *p*-chart.
c. Plot the sample proportions on the *p*-chart.
d. Is the process under control? Explain.
e. Should the control limits and centerline of part **a** be used to monitor future process output? Explain.

Applying the Concepts—Basic

42 **Rental car call center study.** A worldwide rental car company receives about 10,000 calls per month at its European call center. These calls typically involve customer issues with the level of service or the billing/invoice process. In an effort to reduce the proportion of issues that are not resolved on the customer's first call, management conducted a thorough study of the call center's procedures. The results were published in the *International Journal of Productivity and Performance Management* (Vol. 59, 2010). After making major changes at the call center, management constructed a *p*-chart to monitor the process improvements. Assume that 18 calls to the center were sampled each day for 60 consecutive days. The article reported that the proportion of all calls in the sample that had unresolved issues at the end of the call was .107. (This was a major improvement over the previous unresolved-first-call rate of .845.)

a. What is the centerline for the *p*-chart?

b. Compute the lower and upper control limits for the *p*-chart.

c. When the proportions of daily calls that resulted in unresolved issues are plotted on the *p*-chart, all fall within the LCL and UCL boundaries. What does this imply about the process?

43 Monitoring surgery complications. An article on the use of control charts for monitoring the proportion of post operative complications at a large hospital was published in the *International Journal for Quality in Health Care* (Oct. 2010). A random sample of surgical procedures was selected each month for 30 consecutive months, and the number of procedures with postoperative complications was recorded. The data are listed in the accompanying table.

POSTOP

a. Identify the attribute of interest to the hospital.

b. What are the rational subgroups for this study?

c. Find the value of $\bar{p}$ for use in a *p*-chart.

d. Compute the proportion of post-op complications in each month.

e. Compute the critical boundaries for the *p*-chart (i.e., UCL, LCL, Upper A–B boundary, etc.).

f. Construct a *p*-chart for the data.

g. Interpret the chart. Does the process appear to be in control? Explain.

Month	Complications	Procedures Sampled
1	14	105
2	12	97
3	10	115
4	12	100
5	9	95
6	7	111
7	9	68
8	11	47
9	9	83
10	12	108
11	10	115
12	7	94
13	12	107
14	9	99
15	15	105
16	13	110
17	7	97
18	10	105
19	8	71
20	5	48
21	12	95
22	9	110
23	7	103
24	9	95
25	15	105
26	12	100
27	8	116
28	2	110
29	9	105
30	10	120
Totals	294	2,939

Source: "The P-Control Chart: A tool for Care Improvement" by A. Duclos and N. Voirin, in INTERNATIONAL JOURNAL FOR QUALITY IN HEALTH CARE, Volume 22(5). Copyright © 2010 by Oxford University Press. Reprinted with permission.

44 Defective micron chips. A manufacturer produces micron chips for personal computers. From past experience, the production manager believes that 1% of the chips are defective. The company collected a sample of the first 1,000 chips manufactured after 4:00 P.M. every other day for a month. The chips were analyzed for defects; then these data and Minitab were used to construct the *p*-chart shown here.

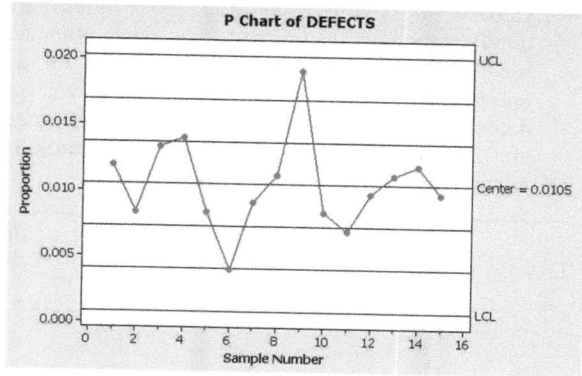

a. From a statistical perspective, is a sample size of 1,000 adequate for constructing the *p*-chart? Explain.

b. Calculate the chart's upper and lower control limits.

c. What does the *p*-chart suggest about the presence of special causes during the time when the data were collected?

d. Critique the rational subgrouping strategy used by the disk manufacturer.

Applying the Concepts—Intermediate

45 Monitoring newspaper typesetters. Accurate typesetting is crucial to the production of high-quality newspapers. The editor of the Morristown *Daily Tribune*, a weekly publication with a circulation of 27,000, has instituted a process for monitoring the performance of typesetters. Each week 100 paragraphs of the paper are randomly sampled and read for accuracy. The number of paragraphs with errors is recorded in the following table for each of the last 30 weeks.

TYPSET

Week	Paragraphs with Errors	Week	Paragraphs with Errors
1	2	16	2
2	4	17	3
3	10	18	7
4	4	19	3
5	1	20	2
6	1	21	3
7	13	22	7
8	9	23	4
9	11	24	3
10	0	25	2
11	3	26	2
12	4	27	0
13	2	28	1
14	2	29	3
15	8	30	4

Source: QUANTITATIVE ANALYSIS FOR MANAGEMENT, 6th ed., by Jerry Kinard and Brian Kinard. Copyright © 1997 by Prentice Hall, Upper Saddle Creek, NJ. Reprinted with permission of the author.

a. Construct a *p*-chart for the process.

b. Is the process under statistical control? Explain.

c. Should the control limits of part **a** be used to monitor future process output? Explain.

d. Suggest two methods that could be used to facilitate the diagnosis of causes of process variation.

46 Quality of rewritable CDs. A Japanese compact disc (CD) manufacturer has a daily production rate of about 20,000 CD-RW (rewritable disks). Quality is monitored by randomly sampling 200 finished CDs every other hour from the production process and testing them for defects. If one or more defects are discovered, the CD is considered defective and is destroyed. The production process operates 20 hours per day, 7 days a week. The table below reports data for the last 3 days of production.

Day	Hour	Number of Defectives	Day	Hour	Number of Defectives
1	1	13		6	3
	2	5		7	1
	3	2		8	2
	4	3		9	3
	5	2		10	1
	6	3	3	1	9
	7	1		2	5
	8	2		3	2
	9	1		4	1
	10	1		5	3
2	1	11		6	2
	2	6		7	4
	3	2		8	2
	4	3		9	1
	5	1		10	1

a. Construct a *p*-chart for the CD-RW production process.

b. What does it indicate about the stability of the process? Explain.

c. What advice can you give the manufacturer to assist them in their search for the special cause(s) of variation that is plaguing the process?

47 Leaky process pumps. *Quality* (Feb. 2008) presented a problem that actually occurred at a company that produces process pumps for a variety of industries. The company recently introduced a new pump model and immediately

Week	Number Tested	Number with Leaks
1	500	36
2	500	28
3	500	24
4	500	26
5	500	20
6	500	56
7	500	26
8	500	28
9	500	31
10	500	26
11	500	34
12	500	26
13	500	32

began receiving customer complaints about "leaky pumps." There were no complaints about the old pump model. For each of the first 13 weeks of production of the new pump, quality-control inspectors tested 500 randomly selected pumps for leaks. The results of the leak tests are summarized by week in the accompanying table. Construct an appropriate control chart for the data. What does the chart indicate about the stability of the process?

48 Rubber company tire tests. Goodstone Tire & Rubber Company is interested in monitoring the proportion of defective tires generated by the production process at its Akron, Ohio, production plant. The company's chief engineer believes that the proportion is about 7%. Because the tires are destroyed during the testing process, the company would like to keep the number of tires tested to a minimum. However, the engineer would also like to use a *p*-chart with a positive lower control limit. A positive lower control limit makes it possible to determine when the process has generated an unusually small proportion of defectives. Such an occurrence is good news and would signal the engineer to look for causes of the superior performance. That information can be used to improve the production process. Using the sample size formula, the chief engineer recommended that the company randomly sample and test 120 tires from each day's production. To date, 20 samples have been taken. The data are presented below.

Sample	Sample Size	Defectives
1	120	11
2	120	5
3	120	4
4	120	8
5	120	10
6	120	13
7	120	9
8	120	8
9	120	10
10	120	11
11	120	10
12	120	12
13	120	8
14	120	6
15	120	10
16	120	5
17	120	10
18	120	10
19	120	3
20	120	8

a. Use the sample size formula to show how the chief engineer arrived at the recommended sample size of 120.

b. Construct a *p*-chart for the tire production process.

c. What does the chart indicate about the stability of the process? Explain.

d. Is it appropriate to use the control limits to monitor future process output? Explain.

e. Is the *p*-chart you constructed in part **b** capable of signaling hour-to-hour changes in *p*? Explain.

7 Diagnosing the Causes of Variation

SPC consists of three major activities or phases: (1) monitoring process variation, (2) diagnosing causes of variation, and (3) eliminating those causes. A more detailed description of SPC is shown in Figure 34, which depicts SPC as a quality- improvement cycle. In the monitoring phase, statistical signals from the process are evaluated in order to uncover opportunities to improve the process. This is the phase we have dealt with in Sections 3–6. We turn our attention now to the diagnosis phase.

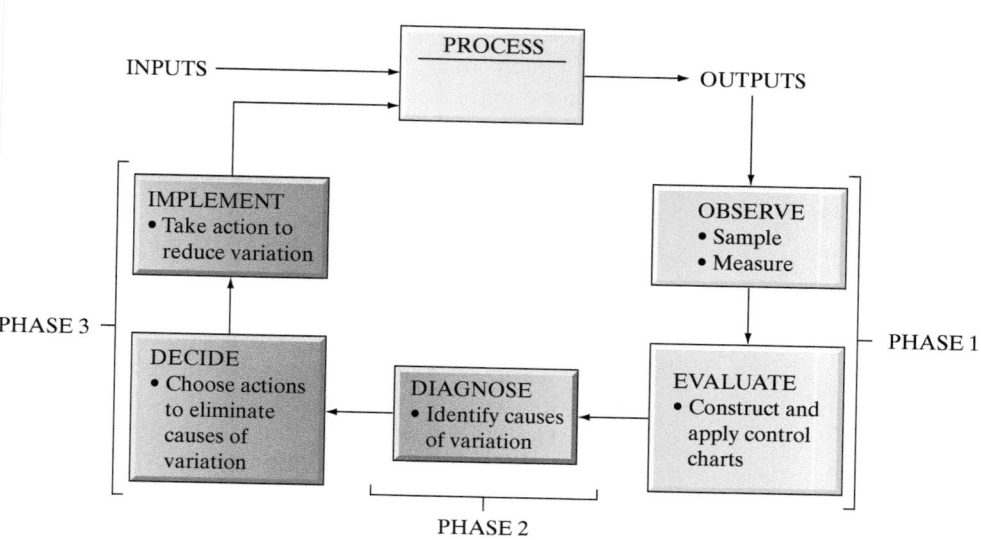

Figure 34

SPC viewed as a quality-improvement cycle

The diagnosis phase is the critical link in the SPC improvement cycle. The monitoring phase simply identifies *whether* problems exist; the diagnosis phase identifies *what* the problems are. If the monitoring phase detected the presence of special causes of variation (i.e., an out-of-control signal was observed on a control chart), the diagnosis phase is concerned with tracking down the underlying cause or causes. If no special causes were detected in the monitoring phase (i.e., the process is under statistical control) and further improvement in the process is desired, the diagnosis phase concentrates on uncovering common causes of variation.

It is important to recognize that the achievement of process improvement requires more than the application of statistical tools such as control charts. This is particularly evident in the diagnosis phase. The diagnosis of causes of variation requires expert knowledge about the process in question. Just as you would go to a physician to diagnose a pain in your back, you would turn to people who work in the process or to engineers or analysts with process expertise to help you diagnose the causes of process variation.

Several methods have been developed for assisting process experts with process diagnosis, including *flowcharting* and the simple but powerful graphical tool called *Pareto analysis.* Another graphical method, the **cause-and-effect diagram,** is described in this section.

The cause-and-effect diagram was developed by Kaoru Ishikawa of the University of Tokyo in 1943. As a result, it is also known as an *Ishikawa diagram.* The cause-and- effect diagram facilitates the construction of causal chains that explain the occurrence of events, problems, or conditions. It is often constructed through brainstorming sessions involving a small group of process experts. It has been employed for decades by Japanese firms but was not widely applied in the United States until the mid-1980s.

The basic framework of the cause-and-effect diagram is shown in Figure 35. In the right-hand box in the figure, we record the effect whose cause(s) we want to diagnose.

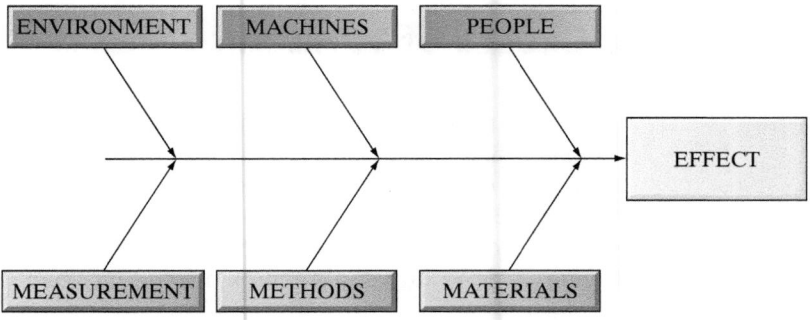

Figure 35

The basic framework for a cause-and-effect diagram

For instance, GOAL/QPC (a Massachusetts-based TQM consulting group) used the cause-and-effect diagram in Figure 36 to demonstrate why pizzas are delivered late on Fridays and Saturdays. As a second example, Figure 37 displays the reasons for high variation in the fill weights of 20-pound bags of dry dog food.

Examining Figure 35, we see the branches of the cause-and-effect diagram, which represent the major factors that influence the process and that could be responsible for the effect. These are often taken to be the six universal sources of process variation that we described in Section 1: people, machines, materials, methods, measurement, and environment. Notice that in the examples of Figures 36 and 37, these categories were tailored to fit the process in question. The set of categories must be broad enough to include virtually all possible factors that could influence the process. It is less important how many categories are used or how you label the categories.

The cause-and-effect diagram is constructed using effect-to-cause reasoning—that is, you begin by specifying the effect of interest and then move backward to identify *potential* causes of the effect. After a potential cause has been identified, you treat it as an effect and try to find its cause, and so forth. The result is a **causal chain.** A completed cause-and-effect diagram typically contains many causal chains. These chains help us to track down causes whose eradication will reduce, improve, or eliminate the effect in question.

After setting up the basic framework for the cause-and-effect diagram and recording the effect of interest in the box on the right, you construct the causal chains, proceeding backward from general potential causes to increasingly specific causes. Begin by choosing one of the universal cause categories—say, people—and asking, "What factors related to people could cause the effect in question?" In the pizza delivery example of Figure 36, two factors were identified: (1) drivers not showing up for work and (2) drivers getting lost. Each of these causes is written on a twig of the People branch. Next, each cause is treated as an effect and an attempt is made to identify its cause—that is,

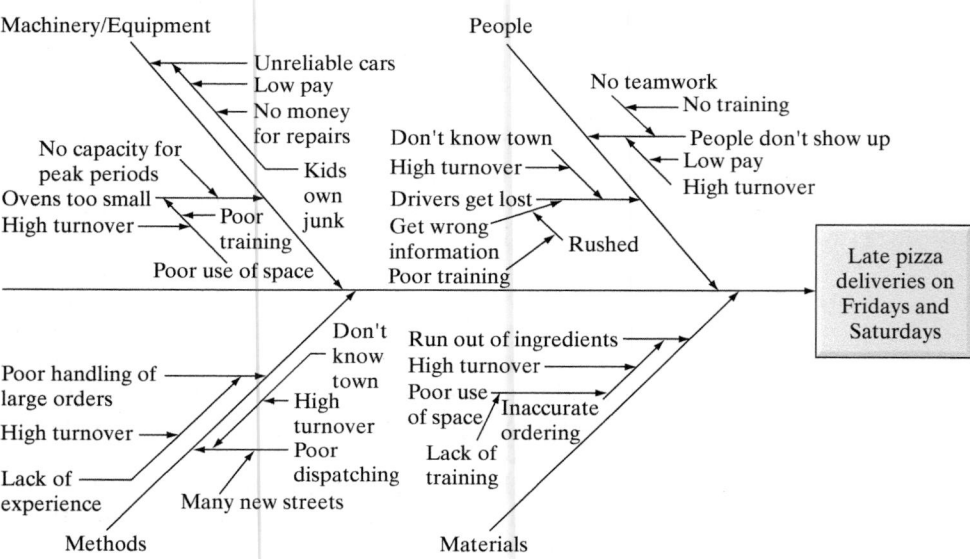

Figure 36

Cause-and-effect diagram for late pizza deliveries

Source: "Cause-and-effect diagram for late pizza deliveries," from THE MEMORY JOGGER II, pg 38. Copyright © 2010 by Goal/QPC. Reprinted with permission.

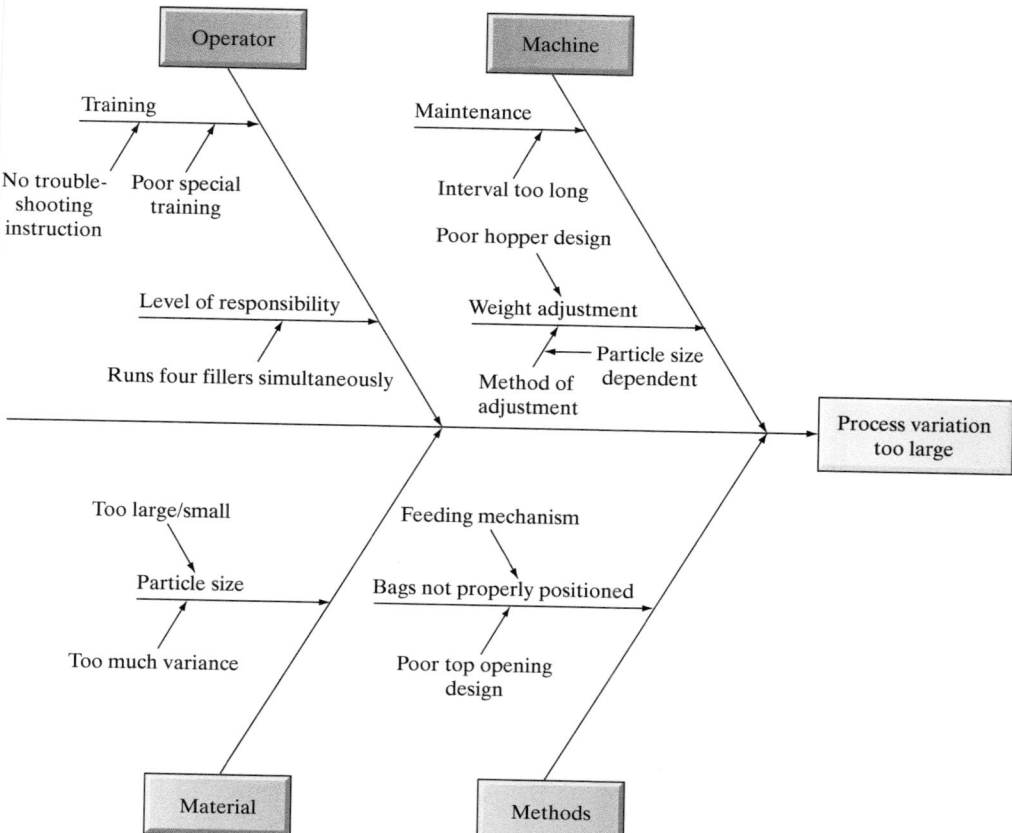

Figure 37

Cause-and-effect diagram for the
filling process for 20-pound bags of
dog food

Source: CONTEMPORARY
CONCEPTS AND METHODS, 1st Ed.,
by Richard E. Devor, Change Tsong-
How. Copyright © 1992 by Pearson
Education, Inc., Upper Saddle River, NJ.
Reprinted with permission.

we look for subcauses. For example, driver absenteeism was blamed on (1) high turnover and (2) no teamwork. The high turnover, in turn, was blamed on low pay, while lack
of teamwork was blamed on insufficient training. Thus, the "No show" twig has both a
"High turnover" twig and a "No teamwork" twig attached to it; and each of these twigs
has a cause twig attached. Multiple causal chains like this should be constructed for each
branch of the cause-and-effect diagram.

Once completed, the various causal chains of the cause-and-effect diagram must
be evaluated (often subjectively) to identify one or more factors thought most likely to
be causes of the effect in question. Then actions can be chosen and implemented (see
Figure 34) to eliminate the causes and improve the process.

Besides facilitating process diagnosis, cause-and-effect diagrams serve to document the causal factors that may potentially affect a process and to communicate that
information to others in the organization. The cause-and-effect diagram is a very flexible
tool that can be applied in a variety of situations. It can be used as a formal part of
the SPC improvement cycle, as suggested above, or simply as a means of investigating
the causes of organizational problems, events, or conditions. It can also help select the
appropriate process variables to monitor with control charts.

8 Capability Analysis

In the previous four sections, we pointed out that if a process were in statistical control,
but the level of variation was unacceptably high, common causes of variation should be
identified and eliminated. This was illustrated in Figure 13. Here, we describe a methodology that can be used to help determine when such variation is unacceptably high. The
methodology is called **capability analysis.** As we have seen, the achievement of process
stability is vitally important to process improvement efforts. But it is not an end in itself.
A process may be in control but still not be capable of producing output that is acceptable to customers.

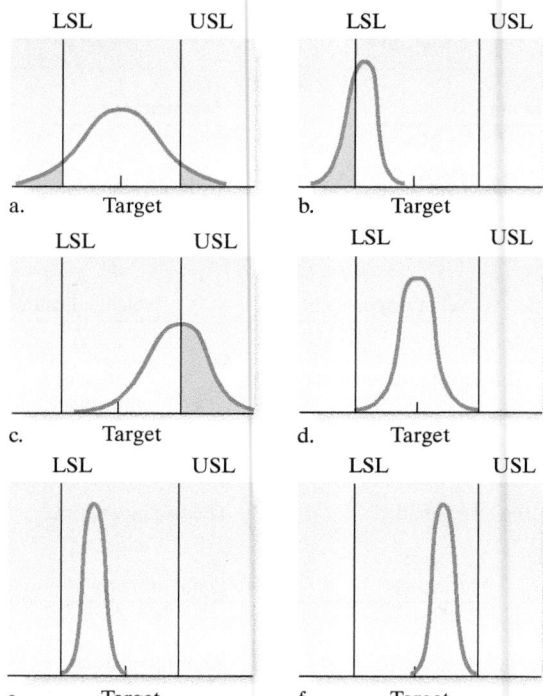

Figure 38

Output distributions of six different in-control processes, where LSL = lower specification limit and USL = upper specification limit

To see this, consider Figure 38. The figure displays six different in-control processes. Recall that if a process is under statistical control, its output distribution does not change over time, and the process can be characterized by a single probability distribution, as in each of the panels of the figure. The upper and lower specification limits (USL and LSL) for the output of each of the six processes are also indicated on each panel, as is the target value for the output variable. Recall that the specification limits are boundary points that define the acceptable values for an output variable.

The processes of panels a, b, and c produce a high percentage of items that are outside the specification limits. None of these processes is *capable* of satisfying its customers. In panel a, the process is centered on the target value, but the variation due to common causes is too high. In panel b, the variation is low relative to the width of the specification limits, but the process is off-center. In panel **c,** both problems exist: the variation is too high and the process is off-center. Thus, bringing a process into statistical control is not sufficient to guarantee the capability of the process.

All three processes in panels d, e, and f are capable. In each case, the process distribution fits comfortably between the specification limits. Virtually all of the individual items produced by these processes would be acceptable. However, any significant tightening of the specification limits—whether by customers or internal managers or engineers—would result in the production of unacceptable output and necessitate the initiation of process improvement activities to restore the processes' capability. Further, even though a process is capable, continuous improvement of a process requires constant improvement of its capability.

When a process is known to be in control, the most direct way to assess its capability is to construct a frequency distribution (e.g., dot plot, histogram, or stem-and-leaf display) for a large sample of individual measurements (usually 50 or more) from the process. Then, add the specification limits and the target value for the output variable on the graph. This is called a **capability analysis diagram.** It is a simple visual tool for assessing process capability.

The Minitab printout shown in Figure 39 is a capability analysis diagram for the paint-filling process found to be under statistical control in Examples 1 and 2. You can see that the process is roughly centered on the target of 10 pounds of paint, but a large number of paint cans fall outside the specification limits. This tells us that the process is not capable of satisfying customer requirements.

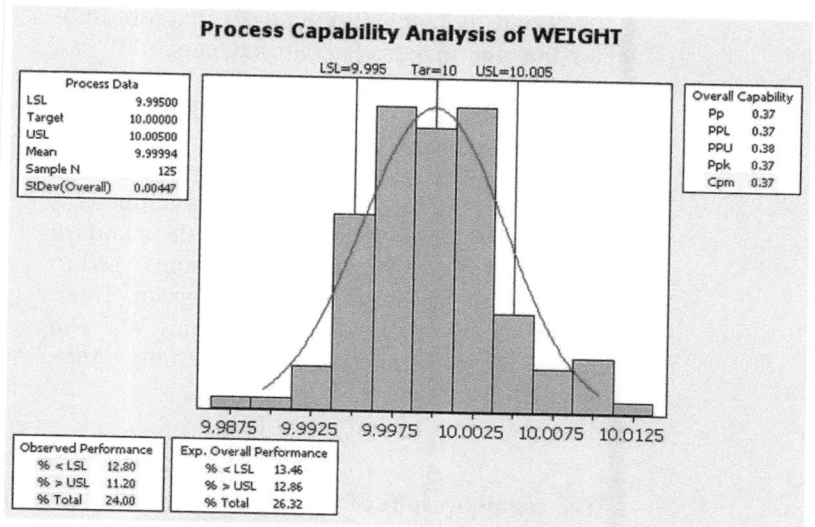

Figure 39

Minitab capability analysis diagram for the paint-filling process

Most quality-management professionals and statisticians agree that the capability analysis diagram is the best way to describe the performance of an in-control process. However, many companies have found it useful to have a numerical measure of capability. The ability to summarize capability in a single number has the advantages of convenience, simplicity, and ease of communication. However, it also has the major disadvantage of potentially misleading those who use it. Just as when you characterize a data set by its mean and ignore its variation, the information you provide to your audience is incomplete and may adversely affect their actions and decisions. (A more thorough discussion about the dangers of numerical measures of capability is presented later in this section.)

There are several different approaches to quantifying capability. We will briefly describe two of them. The first (and most direct) consists of counting the number of items that fall outside the specification limits in the capability analysis diagram and reporting the percentage of such items in the sample. The original data set or a graphical technique that displays the individual measurements—such as a stem-and-leaf display or a dot plot—can be used to obtain the needed count. Or, you can use the capability analysis option of a statistical software package.

The desired information for the paint data is provided in the lower-left corner of the Minitab printout, Figure 39. You can see that 24% of the 125 paint cans fall outside the specification limits (12.8% below 9.995 and 11.2% above 10.005). Thus, 24% of the 125 cans in the sample (i.e., 30 cans) are unacceptable.

When this percentage is used to characterize the capability of the process, the implication is that over time, if this process remains in control, roughly 24% of the paint cans will be unacceptable. Remember, however, that this percentage is an estimate—a sample statistic, not a known parameter. It is based on a sample of size 125 and is subject to both sampling error and measurement error.

If it is known that the process follows approximately a normal distribution, as is often the case, a similar approach to quantifying process capability can be used. In this case, the mean and standard deviation of the sample of measurements used to construct the capability analysis diagram can be taken as estimates of the mean and standard deviation of the process. Then, the fraction of items that would fall outside the specification limits can be found by solving for the associated area under the normal curve. As we said above, if you use this percentage to characterize process capability, remember that it is an estimate only and is subject to sampling error.

The second approach to measuring capability is to construct a **capability index.** Several such indexes have been developed. We will describe one used for stable processes that are centered on the target value—the C_p **index.***

---

*For off-center processes, its sister index, C_{pk}, is used. Consult the chapter references for a description of C_{pk}.

When the capability analysis diagram indicates that the process is centered, capability can be measured through a comparison of the distance between the USL and the LSL, called the **specification spread,** and the spread of the output distribution. The spread of the output distribution—called the **process spread**—is defined as 6σ and is estimated by $6s$, where s is the standard deviation of the sample of measurements used to construct the capability analysis diagram. These two distances are illustrated in Figure 40. The ratio of these distances is the capability index known as C_p.

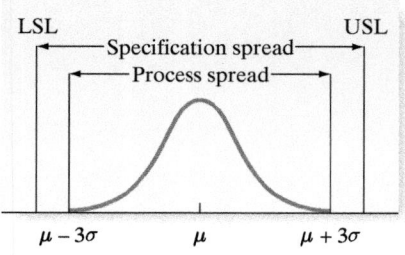

Figure 40
Process spread versus specification spread

The **capability index** for a process *centered on the desired mean* is

$$C_p = \frac{(\text{Specification spread})}{(\text{Process spread})} = \frac{(\text{USL} - \text{LSL})}{6\sigma}$$

where σ is estimated by s, the standard deviation of the sample of measurements used to construct the capability analysis diagram.

Interpretation of Capability Index, C_p

C_p summarizes the performance of a stable, centered process relative to the specification limits. It indicates the extent to which the output of the process falls within the specification limits.

1. If $C_p = 1$ (specification spread = process spread), process is capable.
2. If $C_p > 1$ (specification spread > process spread), process is capable.
3. If $C_p < 1$ (specification spread < process spread), process is not capable.

If the process follows a normal distribution,

$C_p = 1.00$ means about 2.7 units per 1,000 will be unacceptable.
$C_p = 1.33$ means about 63 units per million will be unacceptable.
$C_p = 1.67$ means about .6 units per million will be unacceptable.
$C_p = 2.00$ means about 2 units per billion will be unacceptable.

In manufacturing applications where the process follows a normal distribution (approximately), managers typically require a C_p of at least 1.33. With a C_p of 1.33, the process spread takes up only 75% of the specification spread, leaving a little wiggle room in case the process moves off-center.

Example 10

Finding and Interpreting C_p—Paint-Filling Process

Problem Let's return to the paint-filling process analyzed in Examples 6 and 8. Using 25 samples of size 5 (125 measurements), we constructed $\bar{x}$- and R-charts and concluded that the process was in a state of statistical control. The specification limits for the acceptable amount of paint fill per can are shown in the capability analysis diagram of Figure 39.

a. Is it appropriate to construct a capability index for this process?
b. Find C_p for this process and interpret its value.

Solution

a. Because the process is stable (under control), its output distribution can be characterized by the same probability distribution at any point in time (see Figure 12). Accordingly, it is appropriate to assess the performance of the process using that distribution and related performance measures such as C_p.

b. From the definition of capability index,

$$C_p = \frac{(\text{USL} - \text{LSL})}{6\sigma}$$

From the capability analysis diagram of Figure 39, we can see that the upper and lower specification limits are 10.005 pounds and 9.995 pounds, respectively. But what is σ? Because the output distribution will never be known exactly, neither will σ, the standard deviation of the output distribution. It must be estimated with s, the standard deviation of a large sample drawn from the process. In this case, we use the standard deviation of the 125 measurements used to construct the capability analysis diagram. This value, $s = .00447$, is highlighted in the upper left of the Minitab printout, Figure 39. Then

$$C_p = \frac{(10.005 - 9.995)}{6(.00447)} = \frac{.01}{.02682} = .373$$

(This value of C_p is highlighted in the upper right corner of Figure 39.) Because C_p is less than 1.0, the process is not capable. The process spread is wider than the specification spread.

Look Back The C_p statistic confirms the results shown on the capability analysis diagram (Figure 39), where 24% of the sampled cans were found to be unacceptable.

➡ **Now Work Exercise 58**

For two reasons, great care should be exercised in using and interpreting C_p. First, like the sample standard deviation, s, used in its computation, C_p is a statistic and is subject to sampling error—that is, the value of C_p will change from sample to sample. Thus, unless you understand the magnitude of the sampling error, you should be cautious in comparing the C_p's of different processes. Second, C_p does not reflect the shape of the output distribution. Distributions with different shapes can have the same C_p value. Accordingly, C_p should not be used in isolation, but in conjunction with the capability analysis diagram.

If a capability analysis study indicates that an in-control process is not capable, as in the paint-filling example, it is usually variation, rather than off-centeredness, that is the culprit. Thus, capability is typically achieved or restored by seeking out and eliminating common causes of variation.

Exercises 49–64

Learning the Mechanics

49 Explain why it is inappropriate to conduct a capability analysis study for a process that is not in statistical control.

50 Explain the difference between *process spread* and *specification spread*.

51 Describe two different ways to assess the capability of a process.

52 Why is it recommended to use and interpret C_p in conjunction with a capability analysis diagram rather than in isolation?

53 For a process that is in control and follows a normal distribution, interpret each of the following C_p values:
a. 1.00 **b.** 1.33 **c.** .50 **d.** 2.00

54 Find the specification spread for each of the following:
a. USL = 19.65, LSL = 12.45
b. USL = .0010, LSL = .0008
c. USL = 1.43, LSL = 1.27
d. USL = 490, LSL = 486

55 Find (or estimate) the process spread for each of the following.
a. $\sigma = 21$ **b.** $\sigma = 5.2$
c. $s = 110.06$ **d.** $s = .0024$

56 Find the value of C_p for each of the following situations:
   a. USL = 1.0065, LSL = 1.0035, s = .0005
   b. USL = 22, LSL = 21, s = .2
   c. USL = 875, LSL = 870, s = .75

Applying the Concepts—Basic

57 **Upper specification limit of a process.** An in-control, centered process that follows a normal distribution has a C_p = 2.0. How many standard deviations away from the process mean is the upper specification limit?

58 **Capability of an in-control process.** A process is in control
   `NW` with a normally distributed output distribution with mean 1,000 and standard deviation 100. The USL and LSL for the process are 1,020 and 980, respectively.
   a. Assuming no changes in the behavior of the process, what percentage of the output will be unacceptable?
   b. Find and interpret the C_p value of the process.

59 **Water use at a thermal power plant.** Thermal power plants use demineralized (DM) water for steam generation. Since it is costly to replace, power plants must conserve the use of DM water. DM water consumption was monitored at a thermal power plant in India and the results published in *Total Quality Management* (Feb. 2009). Plant management set the target for DM water consumption at .5%, the upper specification limit at .7%, and the lower specification limit at .1%. Based on data collected for a sample of 182 flow meter measurements, the overall standard deviation of the process was .265%. Use this information to find the capability index for this process. Interpret the result.

Applying the Concepts—Intermediate

60 **Cereal box filling process.** Refer to the data on weights
   of cereal boxes, Exercise 16. Assume the specifica-
   `CEREAL` tion limits for the weights are USL = 24.2 ounces and LSL = 23.8 ounces.
   a. Assuming the process is under control, construct a capability analysis diagram for the process.
   b. Is the process capable? Support your answer with a numerical measure of capability.

61 **Military aircraft bolts.** Refer to Exercise 20 and the data
   on lengths of bolts used in military aircraft. Management
   `BOLTS` has specified the USL and LSL as 37 cm and 35 cm, respectively.
   a. Assuming the process is in control, construct a capability analysis diagram for the process.
   b. Find the percentage of bolts that fall outside the specification limits.
   c. Find the capability index, C_p.
   d. Is the process capable? Explain.

62 **Bioreactor production of antibodies.** Benchtop bioreactors are used to produce antibodies for anti-cancer drugs.
   `BIOREC` Engineers calibrate bioreactors in order to maximize production. The *African Journal of Biotechnology* (Dec. 2011) published a study designed to achieve a high percentage of antibody production from a bioreactor. The variable of interest was the natural logarithm of the number of viable cells produced in a bioreactor run. Data were collected for a sample of four bioreactor runs every 6 hours for 20 consecutive time periods. These data (simulated from

information provided in the article) are listed in the accompanying table. Engineers have specified the following for the bioreactor runs: target mean = 6.3, LSL = 5.9, and USL = 6.5. Run a complete capability analysis on the data. How would you categorize the performance of the process?

Time Period	Hour	Run1	Run2	Run3	Run4
1	0	5.83	5.90	5.91	5.93
2	6	5.98	5.94	5.97	5.84
3	12	5.99	5.98	5.99	5.98
4	18	6.09	6.04	5.93	6.02
5	24	6.20	6.30	6.30	6.20
6	30	6.04	6.08	6.23	6.15
7	36	6.19	6.13	6.13	6.29
8	42	6.37	6.27	6.27	6.27
9	48	6.56	6.46	6.36	6.26
10	54	6.36	6.36	6.16	6.16
11	60	6.36	6.37	6.37	6.27
12	66	6.27	6.27	6.27	6.17
13	72	6.26	6.26	6.26	6.16
14	78	6.29	6.46	6.16	6.26
15	84	6.26	6.16	6.25	6.15
16	90	6.35	6.45	6.25	6.53
17	96	6.16	6.16	6.55	6.56
18	102	6.24	6.23	6.24	6.24
19	108	6.15	6.16	6.15	6.15
20	114	6.30	6.52	6.13	6.48

63 **New iron-making process.** *Mining Engineering* (Oct. 2004)
   published a study of a new technology for producing high-
   `CARBON` quality iron nuggets directly from raw iron ore and coal. For one phase of the study, the percentage change in the carbon content of the produced nuggets was measured at 4-hour intervals for 33 consecutive intervals. The data for the 33 time intervals are listed in the table below. Specifications state that the carbon content should be within 3.42 ± 0.3 percent.

Interval	Carbon Change (%)	Interval	Carbon Change (%)
1	3.25	18	3.55
2	3.30	19	3.48
3	3.23	20	3.42
4	3.00	21	3.40
5	3.51	22	3.50
6	3.60	23	3.45
7	3.65	24	3.75
8	3.50	25	3.52
9	3.40	26	3.10
10	3.35	27	3.25
11	3.48	28	3.78
12	3.50	29	3.70
13	3.25	30	3.50
14	3.60	31	3.40
15	3.55	32	3.45
16	3.60	33	3.30
17	2.90		

Source: "Tmk3-Application of a new ironmaking technology for the iron ore mining industry," by G. Hoffman and O. Tsuge, from MINING ENGINEERING, Volume 56(9). Copyright © 2004 by the Society for Mining, Metallurg, & Exploration. Reprinted with permission.

   a. Construct a capability analysis diagram for the iron-making process.

b. Determine the proportion of carbon measurements that fall outside specifications.

c. Find the capability index for the process and interpret its value.

64 Lowering the thickness of an expensive blow-molded container. Refer to the *Quality* (Mar. 2009) study of a plant that produces a high-volume, blow-molded container, Exercise 33. Recall that the quality manager at the plant wants to lower the average thickness for the expensive layer of material and still meet specifications.

Specification limits for individual thickness values are .10 to .30 millimeter.

a. Find the standard deviation of the process data.

b. Calculate the capability index, C_p, for the process and interpret the result.

c. Compare the LCL of the process (from Exercise 33) to the LSL. Does this imply that the average thickness of the material can be lowered and still meet specifications?

◻ Chapter Notes

Key Terms

A zone
B zone
capability analysis
capability analysis diagram
capability index
causal chain
cause-and-effect diagram
centerline
common causes of variation
conform to specifications
control chart
control limits
C_p index

C zone
distribution of the process
in control
individuals chart
lower control limit
nonconforming
oscillating sequence
out of (statistical) control
output distribution of the
  process
pattern-analysis rules
p-chart
process

process spread
process variation
quality
random behavior
rare event
rational subgroups
R-chart
run chart
s-chart
special (assignable) causes of
  variation
specification limits
specification spread

stability
statistical control
statistical process control
  (SPC)
statistical thinking
system
3-sigma limits
total quality management
trial values
upper control limit
x-chart
$\bar{x}$-chart

Key Formulas

Control Chart	Centerline	Control Limits	A–B Boundary	B–C Boundary
$\bar{x}$-chart	$\bar{\bar{x}} = \dfrac{\sum\limits_{i=1}^{k} \bar{x}_i}{k}$	$\bar{\bar{x}} \pm A_2\overline{R}$	$\bar{\bar{x}} \pm \frac{2}{3}(A_2\overline{R})$ or $\bar{\bar{x}} \pm 2\dfrac{(\overline{R}/d_2)}{\sqrt{n}}$	$\bar{\bar{x}} \pm \frac{1}{3}(A_2\overline{R})$ or $\bar{\bar{x}} \pm \dfrac{(\overline{R}/d_2)}{\sqrt{n}}$
R-chart	$\overline{R} = \dfrac{\sum\limits_{i=1}^{k} R_i}{k}$	$(\overline{R}D_3, \overline{R}D_4)$	$\overline{R} \pm 2d_3\left(\dfrac{\overline{R}}{d_2}\right)$	$\overline{R} \pm d_3\left(\dfrac{\overline{R}}{d_2}\right)$
p-chart	$\bar{p} = \dfrac{\text{Total number defectives}}{\text{Total number units sampled}}$	$\bar{p} \pm 3\sqrt{\dfrac{\bar{p}(1-\bar{p})}{n}}$	$\bar{p} \pm 2\sqrt{\dfrac{\bar{p}(1-\bar{p})}{n}}$	$\bar{p} \pm \sqrt{\dfrac{\bar{p}(1-\bar{p})}{n}}$

Key Symbols

LCL	Lower control limit
UCL	Upper control limit
$\bar{\bar{x}}$	Average of the sample means
$\overline{R}$	Average of the sample ranges
A_2	Constant obtained from Table IX in Appendix: Tables
D_3	Constant obtained from Table IX in Appendix: Tables
D_4	Constant obtained from Table IX in Appendix: Tables
d_2	Constant obtained from Table IX in Appendix: Tables
d_3	Constant obtained from Table IX in Appendix: Tables
$\hat{p}$	Estimated number of defectives in sample
$\bar{p}$	Overall proportion of defective units in all nk samples
p_0	Estimated overall proportion of defectives for entire process

SPC	Statistical process control
USL	Upper specification limit
LSL	Lower specification limit
C_p	Capability index

Key Ideas

Total quality management (TQM)

Involves the management of quality in all phases of a business

Statistical process control (SPC)

The process of monitoring and eliminating variation to keep a process in control

In-control process
Has an output distribution that *does not change over time*

Out-of-control process
Has an output distribution that *changes over time*

Dimensions of Quality
1. Performance
2. Features
3. Reliability
4. Conformance
5. Durability
6. Serviceability
7. Aesthetics
8. Reputation and Image

Major Sources of Process Variation
1. People
2. Machines
3. Materials
4. Methods
5. Measurement
6. Environment

Causes of Variation
1. Common causes
2. Special (assignable) causes

Types of Control Charts
1. $\bar{x}$-chart: monitors the process mean
2. *R*-chart: monitors the process variation
3. *p*-chart: monitors the proportion of nonconforming items

Specification limits
Define acceptable values for an output variable
LSL = lower specification limit

USL = upper specification limit
(USL − LSL) = specification spread

Capability analysis
Determines if process is capable of satisfying its customers

Capability index (C_p)
Summarizes performance of a process relative to the specification limits

$$C_p = (USL - LSL)/6\sigma$$

Pattern-analysis rules
Determine whether a process is in or out of control

Rational subgroups
Samples designed to make it more likely that process changes will occur between (rather than within) subgroups

Sample size for *p*-chart:

$$n > 9(1 - p_0)/p_0,$$

where p_0 estimates true proportion defective

Cause-and-effect diagram
Facilitates process diagnosis and documents causal factors in a process

Guide to Control Charts

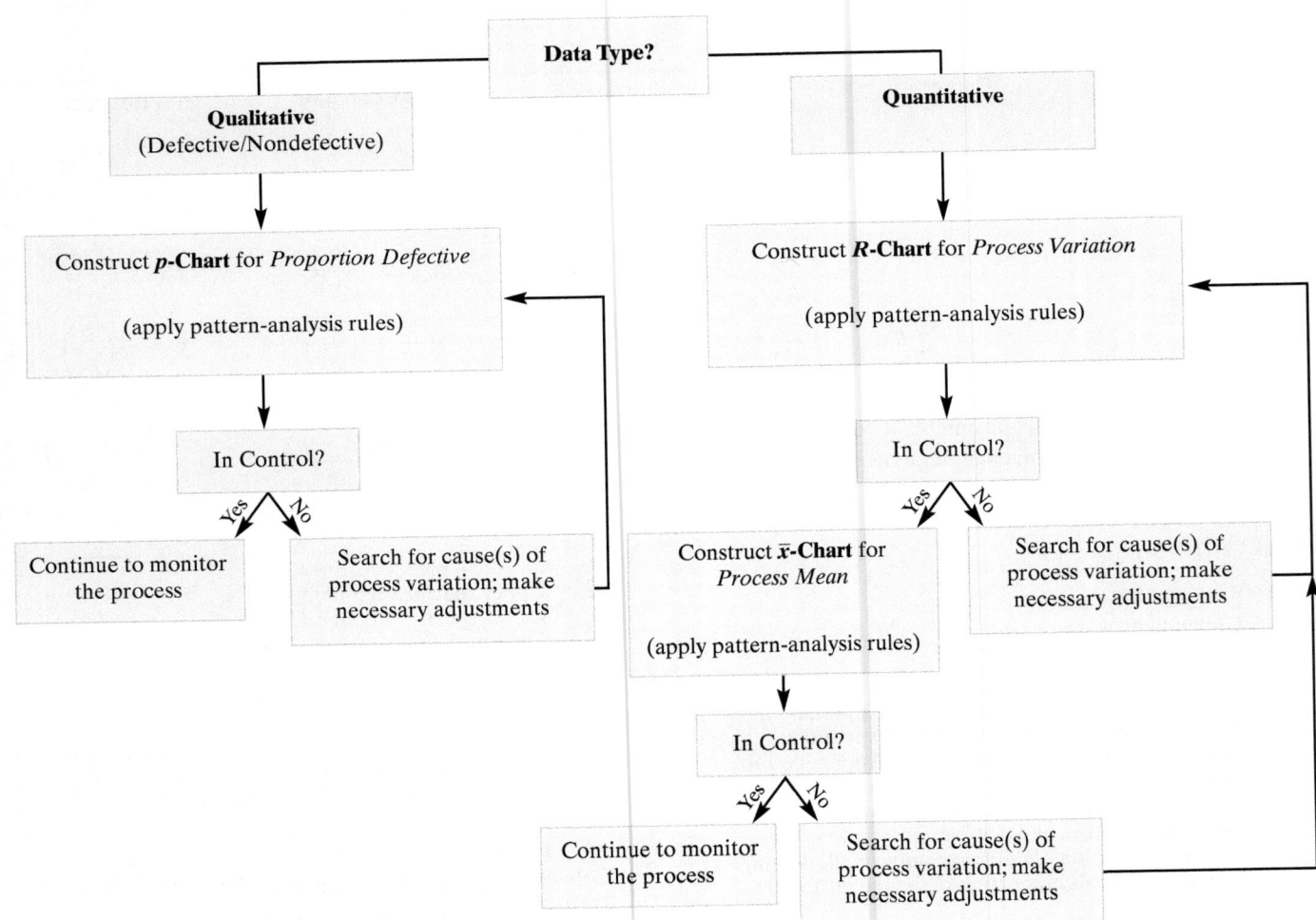

Supplementary Exercises 65–89

Learning the Mechanics

65 Define *quality* and list its important dimensions.

66 What is a process? Give an example of an organizational process.

67 What is a system? Give an example of a system with which you are familiar and describe its inputs, outputs, and transformation process.

68 Describe the six major sources of process variation.

69 Suppose all the output of a process over the last year was measured and found to be within the specification limits required by customers of the process. Should you worry about whether the process is in statistical control? Explain.

70 Select a problem, event, or condition whose cause or causes you would like to diagnose. Construct a cause-and-effect diagram that would facilitate your diagnosis.

71 In estimating a population mean μ using a sample mean $\bar{x}$, why is it likely that $\bar{x} \neq \mu$? Construct a cause-and-effect diagram for the effect $\bar{x} \neq \mu$.

72 Construct a cause-and-effect diagram to help explain why customer waiting time at the drive-in window of a fast-food restaurant is variable.

73 Processes that are in control are predictable; out-of-control processes are not. Explain.

74 Compare and contrast special and common causes of variation.

75 Explain the difference between control limits and specification limits.

76 Should control charts be used to monitor a process that is both in control and capable? Why or why not?

77 Under what circumstances is it appropriate to use C_p to assess capability?

78 A process is under control and follows a normal distribution with mean 100 and standard deviation 10. In constructing a standard $\bar{x}$-chart for this process, the control limits are set 3 standard deviations from the mean—that is, $100 \pm 3(10/\sqrt{n})$. The probability of observing an $\bar{x}$ outside the control limits is $(.00135 + .00135) = .0027$. Suppose it is desired to construct a control chart that signals the presence of a potential special cause of variation for less extreme values of $\bar{x}$. How many standard deviations from the mean should the control limits be set such that the probability of the chart falsely indicating the presence of a special cause of variation is .10 rather than .0027?

Applying the Concepts—Basic

79 **Weight of a product.** Consider the time series data for the weight of a manufactured product shown in the next column.

TIMEWT

   a. Construct a time series plot. Be sure to connect the points and add a centerline.

   b. Which type of variation pattern in Figure 6 best describes the pattern revealed by your plot?

Order of Production	Weight (grams)	Order of Production	Weight (grams)
1	6.0	9	6.5
2	5.0	10	9.0
3	7.0	11	3.0
4	5.5	12	11.0
5	7.0	13	3.0
6	6.0	14	12.0
7	8.0	15	2.0
8	5.0		

80 **Lengths of pencils.** The length measurements of 20 consecutively produced pencils are recorded in the table below.

PENCIL

   a. Construct a time series plot. Be sure to connect the plotted points and add a centerline.

   b. Which type of variation pattern in Figure 6 best describes the pattern shown in your plot?

Order of Production	Length (inches)	Order of Production	Length (inches)
1	7.47	11	7.57
2	7.48	12	7.56
3	7.51	13	7.55
4	7.49	14	7.58
5	7.50	15	7.56
6	7.51	16	7.59
7	7.48	17	7.57
8	7.49	18	7.55
9	7.48	19	7.56
10	7.50	20	7.58

81 **Applying pattern-analysis rules.** Use the appropriate pattern-analysis rules to determine whether the process being monitored by the following control chart is under the influence of special causes of variation.

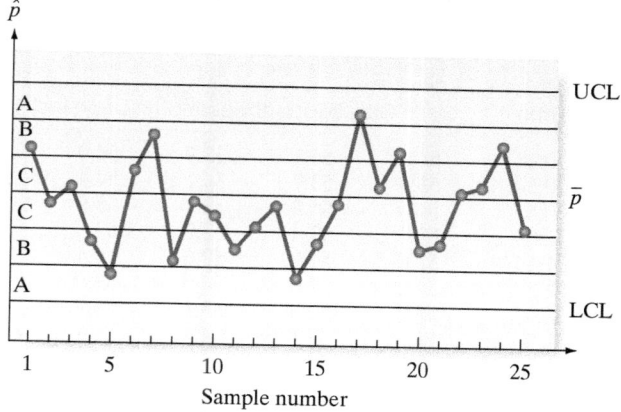

Applying the Concepts—Intermediate

82 **Defective plastic mold.** A company that manufactures plastic molded parts believes it is producing an unusually large number of defects. To investigate this suspicion, each shift drew seven random samples of 200 parts, visually inspected each part to determine whether it was defective, and tallied the primary type of defect present (Hart, 1992). These data are presented in the table at the top of the next page.

MOLD

Data for Exercise 82

Sample	Shift	# of Defects	Type of Defect				
			Crack	Burn	Dirt	Blister	Trim
1	1	4	1	1	1	0	1
2	1	6	2	1	0	2	1
3	1	11	1	2	3	3	2
4	1	12	2	2	2	3	3
5	1	5	0	1	0	2	2
6	1	10	1	3	2	2	2
7	1	8	0	3	1	1	3
8	2	16	2	0	8	2	4
9	2	17	3	2	8	2	2
10	2	20	0	3	11	3	3
11	2	28	3	2	17	2	4
12	2	20	0	0	16	4	0
13	2	20	1	1	18	0	0
14	2	17	2	2	13	0	0
15	3	13	3	2	5	1	2
16	3	10	0	3	4	2	1
17	3	11	2	2	3	2	2
18	3	7	0	3	2	2	0
19	3	6	1	2	0	1	2
20	3	8	1	1	2	3	1
21	3	9	1	2	2	2	2

a. From a statistical perspective, are the number of samples and the sample size of 200 adequate for constructing a p-chart for these data? Explain.

b. Construct a p-chart for this manufacturing process.

c. Should the control limits be used to monitor future process output? Explain.

d. Suggest a strategy for identifying the special causes of variation that may be present.

83 Robotics clamp gap width. University of Waterloo (Canada) statistician S. H. Steiner applied control chart methodology to the manufacturing of a horseshoe-shaped metal fastener called a *robotics clamp* (*Applied Statistics*, Vol. 47, 1998). Users of the clamp were concerned with the width of the gap between the two ends of the fastener.

CLAMP

Time	Gap Width (thousandths of an inch)				
00:15	54.2	54.1	53.9	54.0	53.8
00:30	53.9	53.7	54.1	54.4	55.1
00:45	54.0	55.2	53.1	55.9	54.5
01:00	52.1	53.4	52.9	53.0	52.7
01:15	53.0	51.9	52.6	53.4	51.7
01:30	54.2	55.0	54.0	53.8	53.6
01:45	55.2	56.6	53.1	52.9	54.0
02:00	53.3	57.2	54.5	51.6	54.3
02:15	54.9	56.3	55.2	56.1	54.0
02:30	55.7	53.1	52.9	56.3	55.4
02:45	55.2	51.0	56.3	55.6	54.2
03:00	54.2	54.2	55.8	53.8	52.1
03:15	55.7	57.5	55.4	54.0	53.1
03:30	53.7	56.9	54.0	55.1	54.2
03:45	54.1	53.9	54.0	54.6	54.8
04:00	53.5	56.1	55.1	55.0	54.0

Source: Based on "Grouped Data Exponentially Weighted Moving Average Control Charts" by Stefan H. Steiner from APPLIED STATISTICS-JOURNAL OF THE ROYAL STATISTICAL SOCIETY: SERIES C (APPLIED STATISTICS), Volume 47(2).

Their preferred target width was .054 inch. An optical measuring device was used to measure the gap width of the fastener during the manufacturing process. The manufacturer sampled five finished clamps every 15 minutes throughout its 16-hour daily production schedule and optically measured the gap. Data for 4 consecutive hours of production are presented in the accompanying table.

a. Construct an R-chart from these data.

b. Construct an $\bar{x}$-chart from these data.

c. Apply the pattern-analysis rules to the control charts. Does your analysis suggest that special causes of variation are present in the clamp manufacturing process? Which of the six rules led you to your conclusion?

d. Should the control limits be used to monitor future process output? Explain.

84 Package sorting time. AirExpress, an overnight mail service, is concerned about the operating efficiency of the package-sorting departments at its Toledo, Ohio, terminal. The company would like to monitor the time it takes for packages to be put in outgoing delivery bins from the time they are received. The sorting department operates 6 hours per day, from 6:00 P.M. to midnight. The company randomly sampled four packages during each hour of operation during 4 consecutive days. The time for each package to move through the system, in minutes, is given in the table on the next page.

TRNSIT

a. Construct an $\bar{x}$-chart from these data. For this chart to be meaningful, what assumption must be made about the variation of the process? Why?

b. What does the chart suggest about the stability of the package-sorting process? Explain.

c. Should the control limits be used to monitor future process output? Explain.

Data for Exercise 84

Sample	Transit Time (min.)			
1	31.9	33.4	37.8	26.2
2	29.1	24.3	33.2	36.7
3	30.3	31.1	26.3	34.1
4	39.6	29.4	31.4	37.7
5	27.4	29.7	36.5	33.3
6	32.7	32.9	40.1	29.7
7	30.7	36.9	26.8	34.0
8	28.4	24.1	29.6	30.9
9	30.5	35.5	36.1	27.4
10	27.8	29.6	29.0	34.1
11	34.0	30.1	35.9	28.8
12	25.5	26.3	34.8	30.0
13	24.6	29.9	31.8	37.9
14	30.6	36.0	40.2	30.8
15	29.7	33.2	34.9	27.6
16	24.1	26.8	32.7	29.0
17	29.4	31.6	35.2	27.6
18	31.1	33.0	29.6	35.2
19	27.0	29.0	35.1	25.1
20	36.6	32.4	28.7	27.9
21	33.0	27.1	26.2	35.1
22	33.2	41.2	30.7	31.6
23	26.7	35.2	39.7	31.5
24	30.5	36.8	27.9	28.6

85 Waiting times of airline passengers. Officials at Mountain Airlines are interested in monitoring the length of time customers must wait in line to check in at their airport counter in Reno, Nevada. To develop a control chart, five customers were sampled each day for 20 days. The data, in minutes, are presented in the table below.

CHECKN

Sample	Waiting Time (min.)				
1	3.2	6.7	1.3	8.4	2.2
2	5.0	4.1	7.9	8.1	.4
3	7.1	3.2	2.1	6.5	3.7
4	4.2	1.6	2.7	7.2	1.4
5	1.7	7.1	1.6	.9	1.8
6	4.7	5.5	1.6	3.9	4.0
7	6.2	2.0	1.2	.9	1.4
8	1.4	2.7	3.8	4.6	3.8
9	1.1	4.3	9.1	3.1	2.7
10	5.3	4.1	9.8	2.9	2.7
11	3.2	2.9	4.1	5.6	.8
12	2.4	4.3	6.7	1.9	4.8
13	8.8	5.3	6.6	1.0	4.5
14	3.7	3.6	2.0	2.7	5.9
15	1.0	1.9	6.5	3.3	4.7
16	7.0	4.0	4.9	4.4	4.7
17	5.5	7.1	2.1	.9	2.8
18	1.8	5.6	2.2	1.7	2.1
19	2.6	3.7	4.8	1.4	5.8
20	3.6	.8	5.1	4.7	6.3

a. Construct an *R*-chart from these data.
b. What does the *R*-chart suggest about the stability of the process? Explain.
c. Explain why the *R*-chart should be interpreted prior to the $\bar{x}$-chart.
d. Construct an $\bar{x}$-chart from these data.
e. What does the $\bar{x}$-chart suggest about the stability of the process? Explain.
f. Should the control limits for the *R*-chart and $\bar{x}$-chart be used to monitor future process output? Explain.

86 Waiting times of airline passengers (cont'd). Consider the airline check-in process described in Exercise 85.
a. Assume the process is under control and construct a capability analysis diagram for the process. Management has specified a USL of 5 minutes.
b. Is the process capable? Justify your answer.
c. If it is appropriate to estimate and interpret C_p for this process, do so. If it is not, explain why.
d. Why didn't management provide a LSL?

87 Credit histories with data-entry errors. A company called CRW runs credit checks for a large number of banks and insurance companies. Credit history information is typed into computer files by trained administrative assistants. The company is interested in monitoring the proportion of credit histories that contain one or more data-entry errors. Based on her experience with the data-entry operation, the director of the data processing unit believes that the proportion of histories with data-entry errors is about 6%. CRW audited 150 randomly selected credit histories each day for 20 days. The sample data are presented below.

CRW150

a. Use the sample size formula to show that a sample size of 150 is large enough to prevent the lower control limit of the *p*-chart they plan to construct from being negative.
b. Construct a *p*-chart for the data-entry process.
c. What does the chart indicate about the presence of special causes of variation? Explain.
d. Provide an example of a special cause of variation that could potentially affect this process. Do the same for a common cause of variation.
e. Should the control limits be used to monitor future credit histories produced by the data-entry operation? Explain.

Sample	Sample Size	Histories with Errors
1	150	9
2	150	11
3	150	12
4	150	8
5	150	10
6	150	6
7	150	13
8	150	9
9	150	11
10	150	5
11	150	7
12	150	6
13	150	12
14	150	10
15	150	11
16	150	7
17	150	6
18	150	12
19	150	14
20	150	10

88 Defects in graphite shafts. Over the last year, a company that manufactures golf clubs has received numerous complaints about the performance of its graphite shafts and has lost several market share percentage points. In response, the company decided to monitor its shaft production process to identify new opportunities to improve its product. The process involves pultrusion. A fabric is pulled through a thermosetting polymer bath and then through a long heated steel die. As it moves through the die, the shaft is

SHAFT1
SHAFT2

Shift Number	Number of Defective Shafts	Proportion of Defective Shafts
1	9	.05625
2	6	.03750
3	8	.05000
4	14	.08750
5	7	.04375
6	5	.03125
7	7	.04375
8	9	.05625
9	5	.03125
10	9	.05625
11	1	.00625
12	7	.04375
13	9	.05625
14	14	.08750
15	7	.04375
16	8	.05000
17	4	.02500
18	10	.06250
19	6	.03750
20	12	.07500
21	8	.05000
22	5	.03125
23	9	.05625
24	15	.09375
25	6	.03750
26	8	.05000
27	4	.02500
28	7	.04375
29	2	.01250
30	6	.03750
31	9	.05625
32	11	.06875
33	8	.05000
34	9	.05625
35	7	.04375
36	8	.05000

Source: CREATING QUALITY: CONCEPTS, SYSTEMS, STRATEGIES, AND TOOLS, by W. Kolarik. Copyright © 1995 by McGraw-Hill. Reprinted with permission.

cured. Finally, it is cut to the desired length. Defects that can occur during the process are internal voids, broken strands, gaps between successive layers, and microcracks caused by improper curing. The company's newly formed quality department sampled 10 consecutive shafts every 30 minutes, and nondestructive testing was used to seek out flaws in the shafts. The data from each 8-hour work shift were combined to form a shift sample of 160 shafts. Data on the proportion of defective shafts for 36 shift samples are presented in the table above.

a. Use the appropriate control chart to determine whether the process proportion remains stable over time.

b. Does your control chart indicate that both common and special causes of variation are present? Explain.

c. Data on the types of flaws identified are given in the table below. [*Note:* Each defective shaft may have more than one flaw.] To help diagnose the causes of variation in process output, construct a Pareto diagram for the types of shaft defects observed. Which are the "vital few"? The "trivial many"?

Type of Defect	Number of Defects
Internal voids	11
Broken strands	96
Gaps between layer	72
Microcracks	150

Critical Thinking—Challenge

89 Bayfield Mud Company case. In their text *Quantitative Analysis of Management* (2005), B. Render (Rollins College) and R. M. Stair (Florida State University) present the case of the Bayfield Mud Company. Bayfield supplies boxcars of 50-pound bags of mud treating agents to the Wet-Land Drilling Company. Mud treating agents are used to control the pH and other chemical properties of the cone during oil drilling operations. Wet-Land has complained to Bayfield that its most recent shipment of bags were underweight by about 5%. (The use of underweight bags may result in poor chemical control during drilling, which may hurt drilling efficiency, resulting in serious economic consequences.) Afraid of losing a long-time customer, Bayfield immediately began investigating their production process. Management suspected that the causes of the problem were the recently added third shift and the fact that all three shifts were under pressure to increase output to meet increasing demand for the product. Their quality-control staff began randomly sampling and weighing six bags of output each hour. The average weight of each sample over the last 3 days is recorded in the table below along with the weight of the heaviest and lightest bags in each sample. Does it appear that management's suspicion about the third shift is correct? Explain?

Data for Exercise 89

Time	Average Weight (pounds)	Lightest	Heaviest	Time	Average Weight (pounds)	Lightest	Heaviest
6:00 A.M.	49.6	48.7	50.7	1:00	49.0	46.4	50.0
7:00	50.2	49.1	51.2	2:00	49.0	46.0	50.6
8:00	50.6	49.6	51.4	3:00	49.8	48.2	50.8
9:00	50.8	50.2	51.8	4:00	50.3	49.2	52.7
10:00	49.9	49.2	52.3	5:00	51.4	50.0	55.3
11:00	50.3	48.6	51.7	6:00	51.6	49.2	54.7
12:00 P.M.	48.6	46.2	50.4	7:00	51.8	50.0	55.6

(Continued)

Data for Exercise 89 (continued)

Time	Average Weight (pounds)	Lightest	Heaviest	Time	Average Weight (pounds)	Lightest	Heaviest
8:00	51.0	48.6	53.2	8:00	49.8	49.0	52.4
9:00	50.5	49.4	52.4	9:00	50.3	49.4	51.7
10:00	49.2	46.1	50.7	10:00	50.2	49.6	51.8
11:00	49.0	46.3	50.8	11:00	50.0	49.0	52.3
12:00 A.M.	48.4	45.4	50.2	12:00 P.M.	50.0	48.8	52.4
1:00 A.M.	47.6	44.3	49.7	1:00	50.1	49.4	53.6
2:00	47.4	44.1	49.6	2:00	49.7	48.6	51.0
3:00	48.2	45.2	49.0	3:00	48.4	47.2	51.7
4:00	48.0	45.5	49.1	4:00	47.2	45.3	50.9
5:00	48.4	47.1	49.6	5:00	46.8	44.1	49.0
6:00	48.6	47.4	52.0	6:00	46.8	41.0	51.2
7:00	50.0	49.2	52.2	7:00	50.0	46.2	51.7
8:00	47.4	44.0	48.7	1:00 P.M.	48.9	47.6	51.2
9:00	47.0	44.2	48.9	2:00	49.8	48.4	51.0
10:00	47.2	46.6	50.2	3:00	49.8	48.8	50.8
11:00	48.6	47.0	50.0	4:00	50.0	49.1	50.6
12:00 A.M.	49.8	48.2	50.4	5:00	47.8	45.2	51.2
1:00	49.6	48.4	51.7	6:00	46.4	44.0	49.7
2:00	50.0	49.0	52.2	7:00	46.4	44.4	50.0
3:00	50.0	49.2	50.0	8:00	47.2	46.6	48.9
4:00	47.2	46.3	50.5	9:00	48.4	47.2	49.5
5:00	47.0	44.1	49.7	10:00	49.2	48.1	50.7
6:00	48.4	45.0	49.0	11:00	48.4	47.0	50.8
7:00	48.8	44.8	49.7	12:00 A.M.	47.2	46.4	49.2
8:00	49.6	48.0	51.8	1:00	47.4	46.8	49.0
9:00	50.0	48.1	52.7	2:00	48.8	47.2	51.4
10:00	51.0	48.1	55.2	3:00	49.6	49.0	50.6
11:00	50.4	49.5	54.1	4:00	51.0	50.5	51.5
12:00 P.M.	50.0	48.7	50.9	5:00	50.5	50.0	51.9

Source: QUANTITATIVE ANALYSIS FOR MANAGEMENT, 6th ed., by Jerry Kinard and Brian Kinard. Copyright © 1997 by Prentice Hall, Upper Saddle River, NJ. Reprinted with permission of the author.

Activity 1 *Quality Control*: Consistency

In some businesses, such as the food service industry, the consistency of a product contributes greatly to customer satisfaction. When a customer orders a particular menu item on a regular basis, he or she expects to receive a product that has approximately the same taste and appearance each time. The challenge for a national chain is not only to have a single worker be consistent but also to have thousands of workers nationwide produce the same menu item with little variation in taste and appearance.

1. The quality of some products, such as coffee and french fries, deteriorates quickly as the finished product is waiting to be purchased. Visit a coffee house or fast-food restaurant and ask specific questions about steps taken to guarantee a fresh product. If a customer complains that a product has been sitting too long, how have the employees been instructed to respond? Is there a policy regarding how many complaints must be received before a product is thrown out and a new batch made?

2. Visit a popular national chain restaurant and ask about measures taken to ensure consistency of portion size, flavor, and attractiveness of menu items among restaurants in the chain. Be sure to ask about vendors who supply the components of a dish. Does the chain allow for regional variations in the menu? If so, to what degree? Does the national chain have a system in place to check for consistency? If so, how does it work?

3. Did either of the establishments you visited indicate the use of statistical methods in checking for quality? If so, what were the methods? Identify at least one way each of the two places you visited could use control charts to track the quality of a product.

References

Alwan, L. C., & Roberts, H. V. "Time-series modeling for statistical process control," *Journal of Business and Economic Statistics,* 1988, Vol. 6, pp. 87–95.

Banks, J. *Principles of quality Control.* New York: Wiley, 1989.

Checkland, P. *Systems Thinking, Systems Practice.* New York: Wiley, 1999.

Deming, W. E. *Out of the Crisis.* Cambridge, Mass.: MIT Center for Advanced Engineering Study, 1986.

DeVor, R. E., Chang, T., & Southerland, J. W. *Statistical Quality Design and Control,* 2nd ed. Upper Saddle River, N.J.: Prentice Hall, 2007.

Duncan, A. J. *Quality Control and Industrial Statistics,* 5th ed. Homewood, Ill.: Irwin, 1986.

Feigenbaum, A. V. *Total Quality Control,* 4th ed. New York: McGraw-Hill, 2004.

Garvin, D. A. *Managing Quality.* New York: Free Press/Macmillan, 1988.

Gitlow, H., Gitlow, S., Oppenheim, A., & Oppenheim, R. *Quality Management: Tools and Methods for Improvement,* 3rd ed. Homewood, Ill.: Irwin, 2004.

Grant, E. L., & Leavenworth, R. S. *Statistical Quality Control,* 7th ed. New York: McGraw-Hill, 2000.

Gryna, F. M., Jr., Chua, R., & Defeo, J. *Juran's Quality Planning and Analysis for Enterprise Quality,* 5th ed. New York: McGraw-Hill, 2005.

Hart, M. K. "Quality tools for improvement," *Production and Inventory Management Journal,* First Quarter 1992, Vol. 33, No. 1, p. 59.

Ishikawa, K. *Guide to Quality Control,* 2nd ed. White Plains, N.Y.: Kraus International Publications, 1986.

Joiner, B. L., & Goudard, M. A. "Variation, management, and W. Edwards Deming," *Quality Process,* Dec. 1990, pp. 29–37.

Kane, V. E. *Defect Prevention.* New York: Marcel Dekker, 1989.

Latzko, W. J. *Quality and Productivity for Bankers and Financial Managers.* New York: Marcel Dekker, 1986.

Moen, R. D., Nolan, T. W., & Provost, L. P. *Improving Quality through Planned Experimentation.* New York: McGraw-Hill, 1991.

Montgomery, D. C. *Introduction to Statistical Quality Control,* 6th ed. New York: Wiley, 2009.

Nelson, L. "The Shewhart control chart—Tests for special causes," *Journal of Quality Technology,* Oct. 1984, Vol. 16, No. 4, pp. 237–239.

Roberts, H. V. *Data Analysis for Managers,* 2nd ed. Redwood City, Calif.: Scientific Press, 1991.

Rosander, A. C. *Applications of Quality Control in the Service Industries.* New York: Marcel Dekker, 1985.

Rummler, G. A., & Brache, A. P. *Improving Performance: How to Manage the White Space on the Organization Chart,* 2nd ed. San Francisco: Jossey-Bass, 1995.

Ryan, T. P. *Statistical Methods for Quality Improvement,* 3rd ed. New York: Wiley, 2011.

Statistical Quality Control Handbook. Indianapolis, Ind.: AT&T Technologies, Select Code 700-444 (inquiries: 800-432-6600); originally published by Western Electric Company, 1956.

Wadsworth, H. M., Stephens, K. S., & Godfrey, A. B. *Modern Methods for Quality Control and Improvement,* 2nd ed. New York: Wiley, 2001.

Walton, M. *The Deming Management Method.* New York: Dodd, Mead, & Company, 1986.

Wheeler, D. J., & Chambers, D. S. *Understanding Statistical Process Control,* 2nd ed. Knoxville, Tenn.: Statistical Process Controls, Inc., 1992.

USING TECHNOLOGY   Technology images shown here are taken from SPSS Statistics Professional 20.0, Minitab 16, XLSTAT for Pearson, and Excel 2010.

SPSS: Control Charts

Step 1 Access the SPSS spreadsheet file that contains the quality data.

Step 2 Click on the "Analyze" button on the SPSS menu bar and then click on "Quality Control" and "Control Charts," as shown in Figure S.1.

Figure S.1 SPSS menu options for control charts

Step 3 On the resulting dialog box (shown in Figure S.2), select the type of control chart you want to produce (*x*-bar, *R*- or *p*-chart) and whether the cases (rows) on the spreadsheet represent individual quality measurements ("Cases are units") or the subgroups ("Cases are subgroups") and then click the "Define" button.

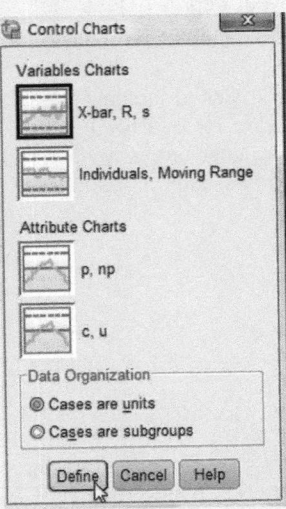

Figure S.2 SPSS control charts selection box

Step 4a If you selected an *x*-bar or *R*-chart where cases are units, the dialog box shown in Figure S.3 will appear. Make the appropriate selections (process variables and subgroup variable). (As an option, you can conduct a capability analysis by clicking the "Statistics" button and making the appropriate menu selections [specification limits, target value, and C_p statistic].)

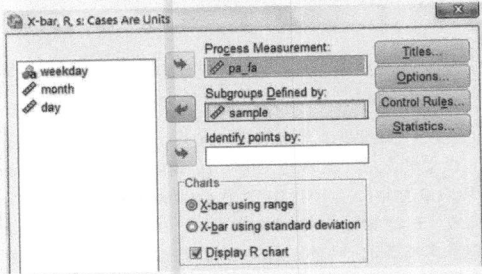

Figure S.3 SPSS dialog box for *x*-bar and *R*-charts

Step 4b If you selected a *p*-chart on the Control Charts dialog box (Figure S.2), the dialog box shown in Figure S.4 will appear. Specify the variables that represent the number nonconforming and the subgroups and specify the sample size.

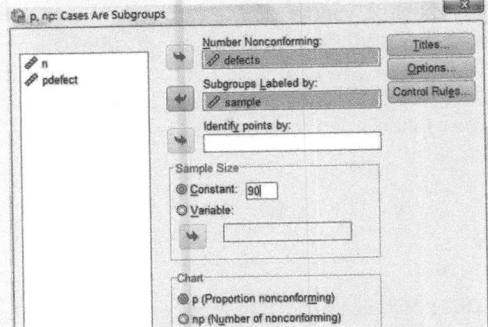

Figure S.4 SPSS dialog box for *p*-charts

Step 5 Click "OK" to view the SPSS control chart.

Minitab: Control Charts

x̄- or R-Chart

Step 1 Access the Minitab worksheet file that contains the quality data.

Step 2 Click on the "Stat" button on the Minitab menu bar and then click on "Control Charts," "Variables Charts for Subgroups," and either "Xbar" or "R," as shown in Figure M.1. The resulting dialog box is shown in Figure M.2.

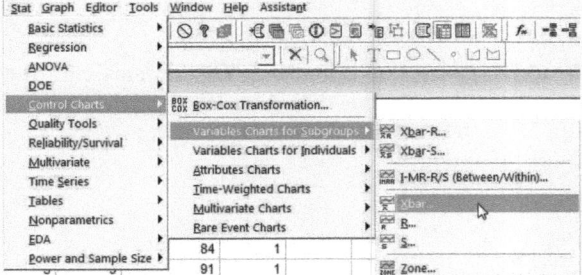

Figure M.1 Minitab menu options for control charts

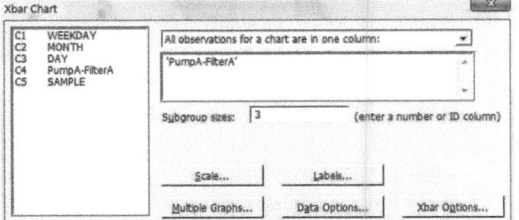

Figure M.2 Minitab dialog box for x-bar chart

Step 3 If each row on the worksheet represents an individual quality measurement, then specify "All observations for a chart are in one column:" (as shown in Figure M.2.) Enter the quality variable in the next box and specify the subgroup size.

If each row on the worksheet represents a subgroup, with columns representing the sample measurements, then specify "Observations for a subgroup are in one row of columns:" Enter the columns with the sample measurements in the next box.

Step 4 If you want Minitab to apply the pattern-analysis rules to the plotted points on the graph, click the "Xbar (or R) Options" button, click "Tests," and check the rules you want apply. Click "OK" to return to the Control Charts dialog box.

Step 5 Click "OK" to produce the Minitab control chart.

p-Chart

Step 1 Click on the "Stat" button on the Minitab menu bar and then click on "Control Charts" and "Attributes Charts" (see Figure M.1).

Step 2 On the resulting menu, select "P." The resulting dialog box appears similar to the one shown in Figure M.3.

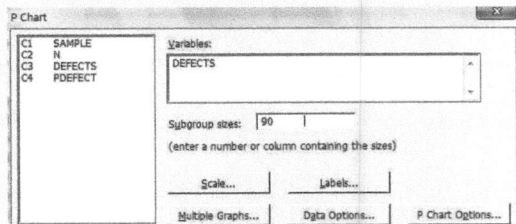

Figure M.3 Minitab dialog box for p-chart

Step 3 Specify the variable that represents the number of non-conforming items and specify the subgroup (sample) size.

Step 4 If you want Minitab to apply the pattern-analysis rules to the plotted points on the graph, click the "P Chart Options" button, click "Tests," and check the rules you want to apply. Click "OK" to return to the Control Charts dialog box.

Step 5 Click "OK" to produce the Minitab control chart.

Capability Analysis Diagram

Step 1 Click on the "Stat" button on the Minitab menu bar and then click on "Quality Tools," "Capability Analysis," and "Normal," as shown in Figure M.4. The resulting dialog box appears similar to the one shown in Figure M.5.

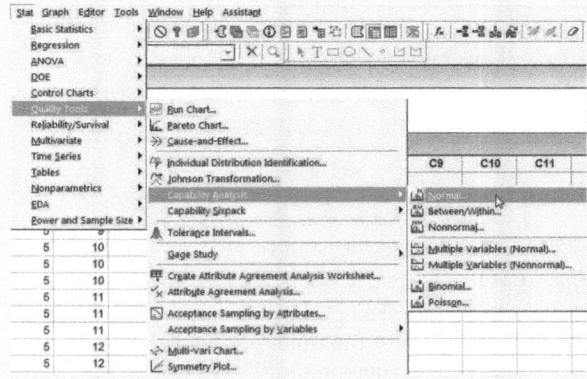

Figure M.4 Minitab menu options for capability analysis

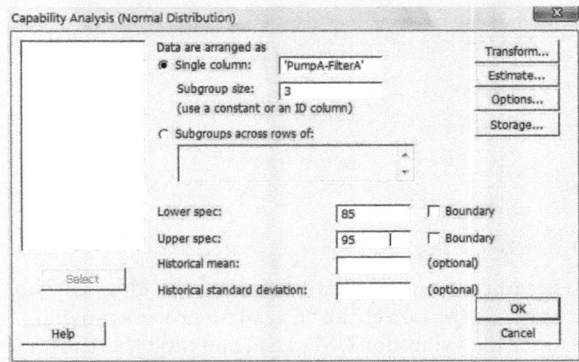

Figure M.5 Minitab dialog box for capability analysis

Step 2 Specify the quality variable of interest, subgroup size, and lower and upper specification limits on the menu screen.

Step 3 Click the "Options" button to specify the type of statistics (e.g., Cp and percents outside specification limits) to be displayed on the graph.

Step 4 Click "OK" to produce the Minitab capability analysis diagram.

Excel/XLSTAT: Control Charts

Step 1 Within XLSTAT, open the Excel spreadsheet containing the control chart data.

Step 2 Click the "XLSTAT" button on the Excel main menu bar, select "SPC," then click either "Subgroup charts" (for an x̄-chart or R-chart) or "Attribute charts" (for a p-chart), as shown in Figure E.1.

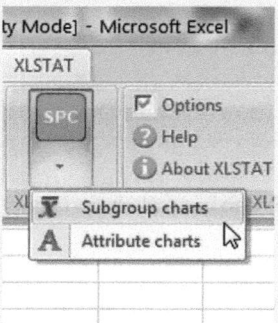

Figure E.1 XLSTAT menu options for control charts

Step 3 On the resulting dialog box, select the chart type (e.g., "X-bar chart"), as shown in Figure E.2.

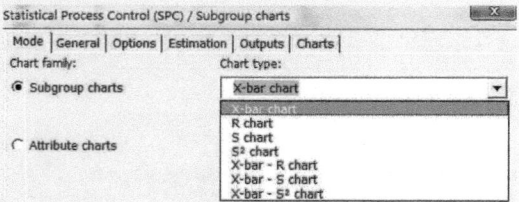

Figure E.2 XLSTAT dialog box for statistical process control

Step 4 Click the "General" tab. When the resulting dialog box appears (Figure E.3), click the appropriate "Data format" option (either data in one column or multiple columns), then specify the columns containing the data in the "Data" box and the column containing the subgroups in the "Groups" box.

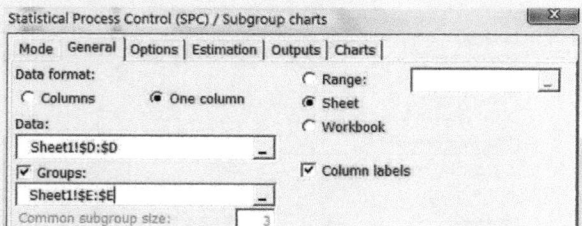

Figure E.3 XLSTAT dialog box for control charts data

Step 5 To determine process capability, click the "Options" tab. On the resulting dialog box check "Calculate process capabilities," then enter the values for USL, LSL, and target, as shown in Figure E.4.

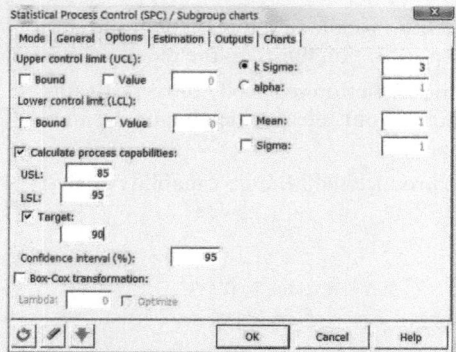

Figure E.4 XLSTAT dialog box for process capability

Step 6 To choose how the upper and lower control limits will be calculated, click the "Estimation" tab. On the resulting dialog box check the method for estimating the process standard deviation (e.g., using R bar), as shown in Figure E.5.

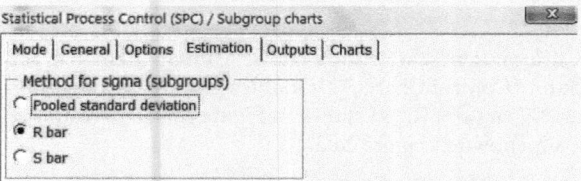

Figure E.5 XLSTAT dialog box for process capability

Step 7 To add A–B and B–C boundaries for the chart, click the "Outputs" tab. On the resulting dialog box check "Display zones (A, B, and C)," as shown in Figure E.6.

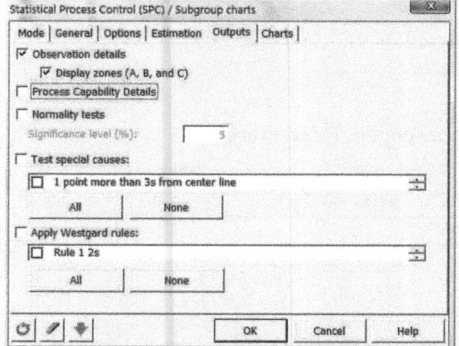

Figure E.6 XLSTAT dialog box for process capability

Step 8 Click "OK," then "Continue" to display the control chart and additional results.

TI-84 Graphing Calculator: Control Charts

Control charts are not available with the TI-84 graphing calculator.

MAKING BUSINESS DECISIONS

The Gasket Manufacturing Case

The Problem

A Midwestern manufacturer of gaskets for automotive and off-road vehicle applications was suddenly and unexpectedly notified by a major customer—a U.S. auto manufacturer—that they had significantly tightened the specification limits on the overall thickness of a hard gasket used in their automotive engines. Although the current specification limits were by and large being met by the gasket manufacturer, their product did not come close to meeting the new specification.

The gasket manufacturer's first reaction was to negotiate with the customer to obtain a relaxation of the new specification. When these efforts failed, the customer-supplier relationship became somewhat strained. The gasket manufacturer's next thought was that if they waited long enough, the automotive company would eventually be forced to loosen the requirements and purchase the existing product. However, as time went on, it became clear that this was not going to happen and that some positive steps would have to be taken to improve the quality of their gaskets. But what should be done? And by whom?

The Product

Figure C1 shows the product in question, a hard gasket. A hard gasket is composed of two outer layers of soft gasket material and an inner layer consisting of a perforated piece of sheet metal. These three pieces are assembled, and some blanking and punching operations follow, after which metal rings are installed around the inside of the cylinder bore clearance holes and the entire outside periphery of the gasket. The quality characteristic of interest in this case is the assembly thickness.

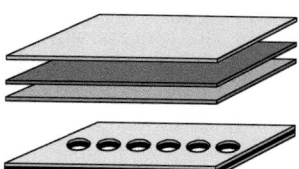

Figure C1

A hard gasket for automotive applications

The Process

An initial study by the staff engineers revealed that the variation in the thickness of soft gasket material—the two outer layers of the hard gasket—was large and undoubtedly responsible for much of the total variability in the final product. Figure C2 shows the roll mill process that fabricates the sheets of soft gasket material from which the two outer layers of the hard gasket are made. To manufacture a sheet of soft gasket material, an operator adds raw

material, in a soft pelletlike form, to the gap—called the *knip*—between the two rolls. The larger roll rotates about its axis with no lateral movement; the smaller roll rotates and moves back and forth laterally to change the size of the knip. As the operator adds more and more material to the knip, the sheet is formed around the larger roll. When the smaller roll reaches a preset destination (i.e., final gap/sheet thickness), a bell rings and a red light goes on, telling the operator to stop adding raw material. The operator stops the rolls and cuts the sheet horizontally along the larger roll so that it may be pulled off the roll. The finished sheet, called a *pull*, is pulled onto a table where the operator checks its thickness with a micrometer. The operator can adjust the final gap if he or she believes that the sheets are coming out too

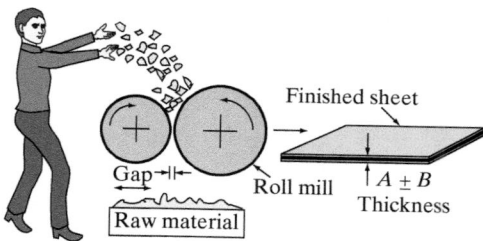

Figure C2

Roll mill for the manufacture of soft gasket material

thick or too thin relative to the prescribed nominal value (i.e., the target thickness).

Process Operation

Investigation revealed that the operator runs the process in the following way. After each sheet is made, the operator measures the thickness with a micrometer. The thickness values for three consecutive sheets are averaged, and the average is plotted on a piece of graph paper that, at the start of the shift, has only a solid horizontal line drawn on it to indicate the target thickness value for the particular soft gasket sheet the operator is making. Periodically, the operator reviews these evolving data and makes a decision as to whether or not the process mean—the sheet thickness—needs to be adjusted. This can be accomplished by stopping the machine, loosening some clamps on the small roll, and jogging the small roll laterally in or out by a few thousandths of an inch—whatever the operator feels is needed. The clamps are tightened, the gap is checked with a taper gauge, and if adjusted properly, the operator begins to make sheets again. Typically, this adjustment process takes 10 to 15 minutes. The questions of when to make such adjustments and how much to change the roll gap for each adjustment are completely at the operator's discretion, based on the evolving plot of thickness averages.

Figure C3 shows a series of plots that detail the history of one particular work shift over which

the operator made several process adjustments. (These data come from the same shift that the staff engineers used to collect data for a process capability study that is described later.) Figure C3a shows the process data after the first 12 sheets have been made—four averages of three successive sheet thicknesses. At this point, the operator judged that the data were telling her that the process was running below the target, so she stopped the process and made an adjustment to slightly increase the final roll gap. She then proceeded to make more sheets. Figure C3b shows the state of the process somewhat later. Now it appeared to the operator that the sheets were coming out too thick, so she stopped and made another adjustment. As shown in Figure Figure C3c, the process seemed to run well for a while, but then an average somewhat below the target led the operator to believe that another adjustment was necessary. Figures C3d and C3e show points in time where other adjustments were made.

Figure C3f shows the complete history of the shift. A total of 24 × 3, or 72, sheets were made during this shift. When asked, the operator indicated that the history of this shift was quite typical of what happens on a day-to-day basis.

The Company's Stop-Gap Solution

While the staff engineers were studying the problem to formulate an appropriate action plan, something had to be done to make it possible to deliver hard gaskets within the new specification limits. Management decided to increase product inspection and, in particular, to grade each piece of material according to thickness so that the wide variation in thickness could be balanced out at the assembly process. Extra inspectors were used to grade each piece of soft gasket material. Sheets of the same thickness were shipped in separate bundles on pallets to a sister plant for assembly. Thick and thin sheets were selected as needed to make a hard gasket that met the specification. The process worked pretty well, and there was some discussion about making it permanent. However, some felt it was too costly and did not get at the root cause of the problem.

The Engineering Department's Analysis

Meanwhile, the staff engineers in the company were continuing to study the problem and came to the conclusion that the existing roll mill process equipment for making the soft gasket sheets simply was not capable of meeting the new specifications. This conclusion was reached as a result of an examination of production data and scrap logs over the past several months. They had researched some new equipment that had a track record for very good sheet-to-sheet consistency and had decided to write a proposal to replace the existing roll mills with this new equipment.

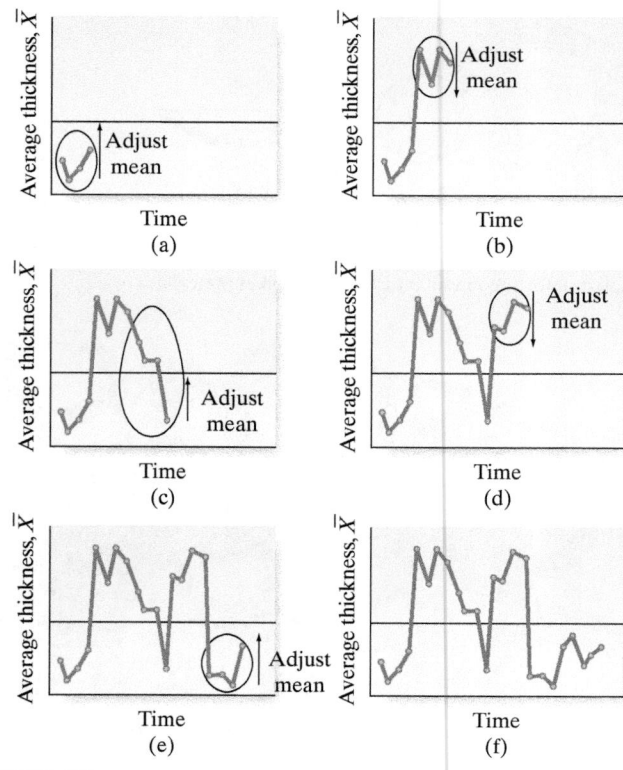

Figure C3

Process adjustment history over one shift

Table C1	**Measurements of Sheet Thickness**				
Sheet	w (in.)	Sheet	w (in.)	Sheet	w (in.)
1	0.0440	25	0.0464	49	0.0427
2	0.0446	26	0.0457	50	0.0437
3	0.0437	27	0.0447	51	0.0445
4	0.0438	28	0.0451	52	0.0431
5	0.0425	29	0.0447	53	0.0448
6	0.0443	30	0.0457	54	0.0429
7	0.0453	31	0.0456	55	0.0425
8	0.0428	32	0.0455	56	0.0442
9	0.0433	33	0.0445	57	0.0432
10	0.0451	34	0.0448	58	0.0429
11	0.0441	35	0.0423	59	0.0447
12	0.0434	36	0.0442	60	0.0450
13	0.0459	37	0.0459	61	0.0443
14	0.0466	38	0.0468	62	0.0441
15	0.0476	39	0.0452	63	0.0450
16	0.0449	40	0.0456	64	0.0443
17	0.0471	41	0.0471	65	0.0423
18	0.0451	42	0.0450	66	0.0447
19	0.0472	43	0.0472	67	0.0429
20	0.0477	44	0.0465	68	0.0427
21	0.0452	45	0.0461	69	0.0464
22	0.0457	46	0.0462	70	0.0448
23	0.0459	47	0.0463	71	0.0451
24	0.0472	48	0.0471	72	0.0428

Data Set: GASKET

To strengthen the proposal, their boss asked them to include data that demonstrated the poor capability of the existing equipment. The engineers, confident that the equipment was not capable, selected what they thought was the best operator and the best roll mill (the plant has several roll mill lines) and took careful measurements of the thickness of each sheet made on an 8-hour shift. During that shift, a total of 72 sheets/pulls were made. This was considered quite acceptable because the work standard for the process is 70 sheets per shift. The measurements of the sheet thickness (in the order of manufacture) for the 72 sheets are given in Table C1. The engineers set out to use these data to conduct a process capability study.

Relying on a statistical methods course that one of the engineers had in college 10 years ago, the group decided to construct a frequency distribution from the data and use it to estimate the percentage of the measurements that fell within the specification limits. Their histogram is shown in Figure C4. Also shown in the figure are the upper and lower specification values. The purple and red shaded parts of the histogram represent the amount of the product that lies outside of the specification limits. It is immediately apparent from the histogram that a large proportion of the output does not meet the customer's needs. Eight of the 72 sheets fall outside the specification

limits. Therefore, in terms of percent conforming to specifications, the engineers estimated the process capability to be 88.8%. This was clearly unacceptable. This analysis confirmed the engineers' low opinion of the roll mill process equipment. They included it in their proposal and sent their recommendation to replace the equipment to the president's office.

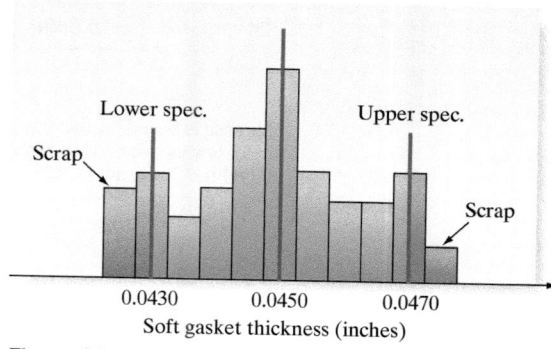

Figure C4

Histogram of data from process capability study

Your Assignment

You have been hired as an external consultant by the company's president, Marilyn Carlson. She would like you to critique the engineers' analysis, conclusion, and recommendations.

Suspecting that the engineers' work may be flawed, President Carlson would also like you to conduct your own study and make your own recommendations concerning how to resolve the company's problem. She would like you to use the data reported in Table C1 along with the data in Table C2, which she ordered be collected for you. These data were collected in the same manner as the data in Table C5.1. However, they were collected during a period of time when the roll mill operator was instructed *not* to adjust the sheet thickness. In your analysis, if you choose to construct control charts, use the same three-measurement subgrouping that the operators use.

Prepare an in-depth written report for the president that responds to her requests. It should begin with an executive summary and include whatever tables and figures are needed to support your analysis and recommendations. [The data file for this case is named **GASKET.** The file contains three variables: sheet number, sheet thickness, and a code for operator adjustments (A) or no adjustments (N).]

Table C2	Measurements of Sheet Thickness for a Shift Run with No Operator Adjustment				
Sheet	Thickness (in.)	Sheet	Thickness (in.)	Sheet	Thickness (in.)
1	0.0445	25	0.0443	49	0.0445
2	0.0455	26	0.0450	50	0.0471
3	0.0457	27	0.0441	51	0.0465
4	0.0435	28	0.0449	52	0.0438
5	0.0453	29	0.0448	53	0.0445
6	0.0450	30	0.0467	54	0.0472
7	0.0438	31	0.0465	55	0.0453
8	0.0459	32	0.0449	56	0.0444
9	0.0428	33	0.0448	57	0.0451
10	0.0449	34	0.0461	58	0.0455
11	0.0449	35	0.0439	59	0.0435
12	0.0467	36	0.0452	60	0.0443
13	0.0433	37	0.0443	61	0.0440
14	0.0461	38	0.0434	62	0.0438
15	0.0451	39	0.0454	63	0.0444
16	0.0455	40	0.0456	64	0.0444
17	0.0454	41	0.0459	65	0.0450
18	0.0461	42	0.0452	66	0.0467
19	0.0455	43	0.0447	67	0.0445
20	0.0458	44	0.0442	68	0.0447
21	0.0445	45	0.0457	69	0.0461
22	0.0445	46	0.0454	70	0.0450
23	0.0451	47	0.0445	71	0.0463
24	0.0436	48	0.0451	72	0.0456

Data Set: GASKET

This case is based on the experiences of an actual company whose identity is disguised for confidentiality reasons. The case was originally written by DeVor, Chang, and Southerland (*Statistical Quality Design and Control* [New York: Macmillan Publishing Co., 1992], pp. 298–329) and has been adapted to focus on the material presented in this chapter.

Answers to Selected Exercises

7 Out of control **9 a.** 1.023 **b.** 0.308 **c.** 0.167 **11 b.** $\bar{\bar{x}} = 20.11625$, $\bar{R} = 3.31$ **c.** UCL $= 22.529$, LCL $= 17.703$ **d.** Upper A–B: 21.725, Lower A–B: 18.507, Upper B–C: 20.920, Lower B–C: 19.312 **e.** Yes **13 a.** 70 **b.** 32.5 **c.** UCL $= 80.01$, LCL $= 59.99$ **d.** Yes **f.** Yes **15 a.** UCL $= .9175$, LCL $= .4291$, Upper A–B: .8361, Lower A–B: .5105, Upper B–C: .7547, Lower B–C: .5919 **b.** Out of control **c.** No **17 c.** 15.1 **c.** No **d.** No **e.** Yes **19 a.** $\bar{x} = 13.05$, Upper A–B: 13.55, Lower A–B: 12.55, Upper B–C: 13.3, Lower B–C: 12.8 **b.** Out of control **c.** Under-reporting likely **21 a.** $\bar{x} = 100.08$, $\bar{R} = .8065$, UCL $= 100.91$, LCL $= 99.26$, Upper A–B: 100.63, Lower A–B: 99.53, Upper B–C: 100.36, Lower B–C: 99.81; in control **b.** $\bar{\bar{x}} = 100.09$, $\bar{R} = .75$, UCL $= 100.86$, LCL $= 99.33$, Upper A–B: 100.61, Lower A–B: 99.58, Upper B–C: 100.35, Lower B–C: 99.84; out of control **25 a.** UCL $= 16.802$ **b.** Upper A–B: 13.853, Lower A–B: 2.043, Upper B–C: 10.900, Lower B–C: 4.996 **c.** In control **27** *R*-chart: $\bar{R} = 4.03$, UCL $= 7.754$, LCL $= 0.306$, Upper A–B: 6.513, Lower A–B: 1.547, Upper B–C: 5.271, Lower B–C: 2.789, in control; $\bar{x}$-chart: $\bar{\bar{x}} = 21.728$, UCL $= 23.417$, LCL $= 20.039$, Upper A–B: 22.854, Lower A–B: 20.602, Upper B–C: 22.291, Lower B–C: 21.165, out of control **29 a.** 32.5 **b.** UCL $= 57.75$, LCL $= 7.259$ **c.** Yes **e.** Out of control **31 a.** UCL $= .7645$ **b.** Process in control **c.** Yes **d.** 6 **33 a.** $\bar{R} = .0238$, UCL $= .0778$, LCL $= 0$, Upper A–B: .0598, Lower A–B: .0122, Upper B–C: .0418, Lower B–C: .0058; in control **b.** $\bar{\bar{x}} = .2214$, UCL $= .2661$, LCL $= .1767$, Upper A–B: .2512, Lower A–B: .1916, Upper B–C: .2363, Lower B–C: .2065; in control **c.** In control; .2214 **35 a.** $\bar{R} = .8065$, UCL $= 2.076$; yes **b.** $\bar{R} = .75$, UCL $= 1.931$; out of control **37** Proportion **39** 104 **41 a.** $\bar{p} = .0575$, UCL $= .1145$, LCL $= .0005$, Upper A–B: .0955, Lower A–B: .0195, Upper B–C: .0765, Lower B–C: .0385 **d.** No **e.** No **43 a.** Postoperative complication **b.** Months **c.** .10 **e.** UCL $= .191$, LCL $= .009$, Upper A–B: .161, Lower A–B: .039, Upper B–C: .130, Lower B–C: .070 **g.** Out of control **45 a.** $\bar{p} = .04$, UCL $= .099$, LCL $= 0$, Upper A–B: .079, A–B: .039, Upper B–C: .071, Lower B–C: .049; out of control **55 a.** 126 **b.** 31.2 **c.** 660.36 **d.** .0144 **57** 6σ **59** .377 **61 b.** .51 **c.** 3.9967 **d.** Yes **63 a.** LSL $= 3.12$, USL $= 3.72$ **b.** .152 **c.** $C_p = .505$ **69** Yes **79 a.** $\bar{x} = 6.4$ **b.** increasing variance **81** Out of control (Rule 2) **83 a.** $\bar{R} = 2.76$, UCL $= 5.83$ **b.** $\bar{\bar{x}} = 54.26$, UCL $= 55.85$, LCL $= 52.67$ **c.** Mean chart out of control **d.** No **85 a.** $\bar{R} = 5.455$, UCL $= 11.532$, Upper A–B: 9.508, Lower A–B: 1.402, Upper B–C: 7.481, Lower B–C: 3.429 **b.** In control **d.** $\bar{\bar{x}} = 3.867$, UCL $= 7.013$, LCL $= .721$, Upper A–B: 5.965, Lower A–B: 1.769, Upper B–C: 4.916, Lower B–C: 2.818 **e.** In control **f.** Yes **87 a.** $n > 141$ **b.** $\bar{p} = .063$, UCL $= .123$, LCL $= .003$, Upper A–B: .103, Lower A–B: .023, Upper B–C: .083, Lower B–C: .043 **c.** Out of control **e.** No **89** No

Credits

Technology Images

CONTENTS

Where We're Going

- Focus on methods for analyzing data generated by a process over time (i.e., *time series data*).

- Present descriptive methods for characterizing time series data (1–2)

- Present inferential methods for forecasting future values of time series data (3–9)

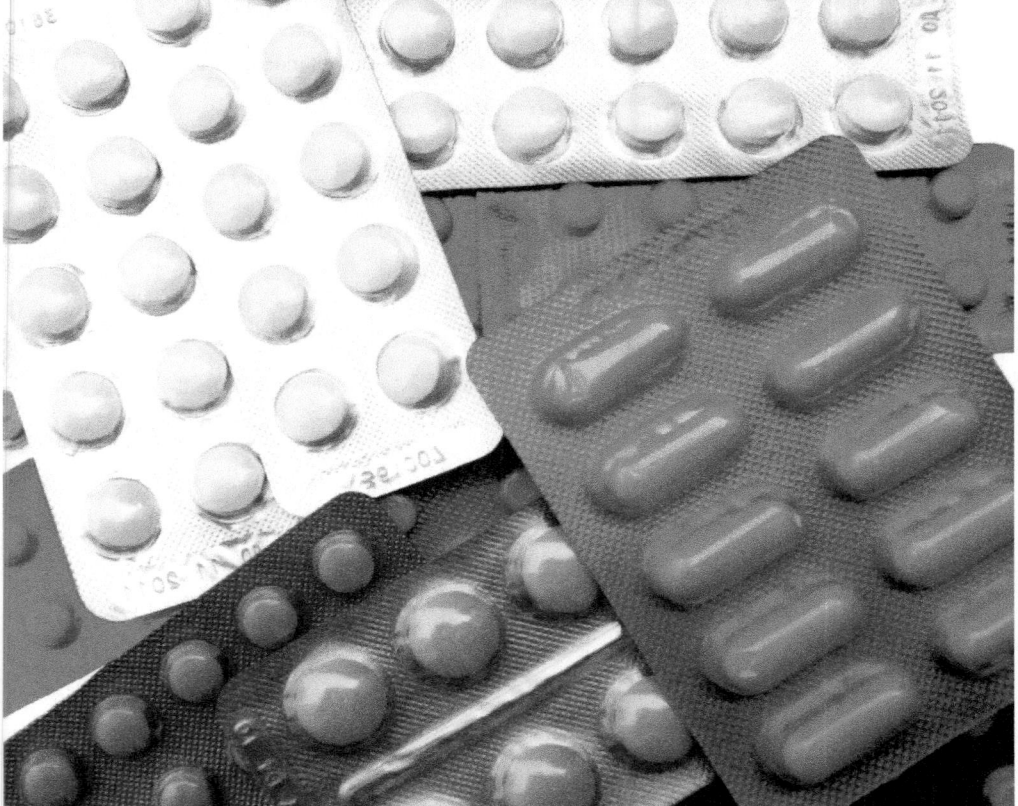

☐ Time Series *Descriptive Analyses,*

Models, and Forecasting

STATISTICS in ACTION
Forecasting the Monthly Sales of a New Cold Medicine

In the pharmaceutical industry, sales forecasting is critical to the success of a company. Accurate forecasts aid sales managers in improving decision making, the finance department in controlling and scheduling its operating costs and capital budget, the human resources department in projecting staffing, and the purchasing department in controlling inventories and production schedules. Due to the critical, life-and-death nature of the industry, pharmaceutical manufacturers rely on sophisticated analytical techniques to build their forecasts.

Several years ago, a major pharmaceutical company based in New Jersey introduced a new cold medicine called Coldex. (For proprietary reasons, the actual name of the product is withheld.) Coldex is now sold regularly in drugstores and supermarkets across the United States. Prior to launching the product nationally, the company hired consultants from the Graduate School of Management at Rutgers University (The State University of New Jersey) to help the company build a monthly forecast model for Coldex. This Statistics in Action involves a portion of the analysis conducted by the consultants.

Consider the task of forecasting the sales of Coldex for the first 3 months of the third year of the product's existence. The company provided data on the monthly sales (in thousands of dollars) for the first 2 years of the product's life. The data, saved in the **COLDEX** file, are listed in Table SIA1. In the Statistics in Action Revisited sections in this chapter, we demonstrate several forecasting methods used by the consultants.

Table SIA1			Coldex Monthly Sales Data				
Year	Month	Time	Sales	Year	Month	Time	Sales
1	Jan	1	3,394	2	Jan	13	4,568
	Feb	2	4,010		Feb	14	3,710
	Mar	3	924		Mar	15	1,675
	Apr	4	205		Apr	16	999
	May	5	293		May	17	986
	Jun	6	1,130		Jun	18	1,786
	Jul	7	1,116		Jul	19	2,253
	Aug	8	4,009		Aug	20	5,237
	Sep	9	5,692		Sep	21	6,679
	Oct	10	3,458		Oct	22	4,116
	Nov	11	2,849		Nov	23	4,109
	Dec	12	3,470		Dec	24	5,124

Source: Based on personal communication from Carol Cowley, Carla Marchesini, and Ginny Wilson. Rutgers University Graduate School of Management. *Data Set:* COLDEX

STATISTICS in ACTION REVISITED

▫ Forecasting with Exponential Smoothing

▫ Forecasting with Simple Linear Regression

▫ Forecasting with a Seasonal Regression Model

In this chapter, our concern is not with the improvement of the internal workings of processes but with describing and predicting the output of processes. The process outputs on which we focus are the streams of data generated by processes over time. Such data streams are called **time series** or **time series data.** For example, businesses generate time series data such as weekly sales, quarterly earnings, and yearly profits that can be used to describe and evaluate the performance of the business. The U.S. economy can be thought of as a system that generates streams of data that include the gross domestic product, the Consumer Price Index, and the unemployment rate.

The methods of this chapter focus exclusively on the time series data generated by a process. Properly analyzed, these data reveal much about the past and future behavior of the process. Time series data are subjected to two kinds of analyses: **descriptive** and **inferential.** Descriptive analyses use graphical and numerical techniques to provide a clear understanding of any patterns that are present in the time series. After graphing the data, you will often want to use them to make inferences about the future values of the time series (i.e., you will want to **forecast** future values). For example, once you understand the past and present trends of the Dow Jones Industrial Average, you would probably want to forecast its future trend before making decisions about buying and selling stocks. Because significant amounts of money may be riding on the accuracy of your forecasts, you would be interested in measures of their reliability. Forecasts and their measures of reliability are examples of **inferential techniques** in time series analysis.

1   Descriptive Analysis: Index Numbers

A common technique for characterizing a business or economic time series is to compute *index numbers.* Index numbers measure how time series values change relative to a preselected time period, called the *base period.*

> An **index number** measures the change in a variable over time relative to the value of the variable during a specific **base period.**

Two types of indexes dominate business and economic applications: **price** and **quantity indexes.** Price indexes measure changes in the price of a commodity or group of commodities over time. The Consumer Price Index (CPI) is a price index because it measures price changes of a group of commodities that are intended to reflect typical purchases of American consumers. On the other hand, an index constructed to measure the change in the total number of automobiles produced annually by American manufacturers would be an example of a quantity index.

Methods of calculating index numbers range from very simple to extremely complex, depending on the numbers and types of commodities represented by the index. Several important types of index numbers are described in this section.

Simple Index Numbers

When an index number is based on the price or quantity of a single commodity, it is called a *simple index number.*

A **simple index number** is based on the relative changes (over time) in the price or quantity of a single commodity.

For example, consider the price of silver (in dollars per fine ounce) between 1975 and 2011, shown in Table 1. To construct a simple index to describe the relative changes in silver prices, we must first choose a *base period.* The choice is important because the price for all other periods will be compared with the price during the base period. We select 1975 as the base period, a time just preceding the period of rapid economic inflation associated with dramatic oil price increases.

Table 1	Silver Prices, 1975–2011				
Year	Price ($/oz.)	Year	Price ($/oz.)	Year	Price ($/oz.)
1975	4.43	1988	6.53	2001	4.37
1976	4.35	1989	5.50	2002	4.60
1977	4.63	1990	4.83	2003	4.85
1978	5.42	1991	4.06	2004	6.65
1979	11.08	1992	3.95	2005	7.22
1980	20.98	1993	4.31	2006	11.57
1981	10.49	1994	5.29	2007	13.39
1982	7.92	1995	5.20	2008	15.02
1983	11.43	1996	5.20	2009	66
1984	8.14	1997	4.90	2010	20.16
1985	6.13	1998	5.54	2011	35.11
1986	5.46	1999	5.22		
1987	7.02	2000	4.95		

Source: Reprinted with permission of The Silver Institute.

Data Set: SILVER

To calculate the simple index number for a particular year, we divide that year's price by the price during the base year and multiply the result by 100. Thus, for the 1992 silver price index number, we calculate

$$1992 \text{ index number} = \left(\frac{1992 \text{ silver price}}{1975 \text{ silver price}}\right)100 = \left(\frac{3.95}{4.43}\right)100 = 89.2$$

Similarly, the index number for 2011 is

$$2011 \text{ index number} = \left(\frac{2011 \text{ silver price}}{1975 \text{ silver price}}\right)100 = \left(\frac{35.11}{4.43}\right)100 = 792.6$$

The index number for the base period is always 100. In our example, we have

$$1975 \text{ index number} = \left(\frac{1975 \text{ silver price}}{1975 \text{ silver price}}\right)100 = 100$$

	A	B	C
1	YEAR	PRICE	INDEX
2	1975	4.43	100.00
3	1976	4.35	98.19
4	1977	4.63	104.51
5	1978	5.42	122.35
6	1979	11.08	250.11
7	1980	20.98	473.59
8	1981	10.49	236.79
9	1982	7.92	178.78
10	1983	11.43	258.01
11	1984	8.14	183.75
12	1985	6.13	138.37
13	1986	5.46	123.25
14	1987	7.02	158.47
15	1988	6.53	147.40
16	1989	5.50	124.15
17	1990	4.83	109.03
18	1991	4.06	91.65
19	1992	3.95	89.16
20	1993	4.31	97.29
21	1994	5.29	119.41
22	1995	5.20	117.38
23	1996	5.20	117.38
24	1997	4.90	110.61
25	1998	5.54	125.06
26	1999	5.22	117.83
27	2000	4.95	111.74
28	2001	4.37	98.65
29	2002	4.60	103.84
30	2003	4.85	109.48
31	2004	6.65	150.11
32	2005	7.22	162.98
33	2006	11.57	261.17
34	2007	13.39	302.26
35	2008	15.02	339.05
36	2009	14.66	330.93
37	2010	20.16	455.08
38	2011	35.11	792.55

Figure 1

Excel workbook with simple index numbers for silver prices (base = 1975)

Source: The Silver Institute.

Index numbers below 100 indicate a decrease in the time series value; in contrast, index numbers above 100 indicate an increase. Thus, the silver price decreased by 11% (the difference between the 1992 and 1975 index numbers) between 1975 and 1992 and increased by 693% between 1975 and 2011. The simple index numbers for all silver prices between 1975 and 2011 were computed using Excel and are shown in the Excel spreadsheet, Figure 1. The index is also portrayed graphically in Figure 2. The steps for calculating simple index numbers are summarized in the next box.

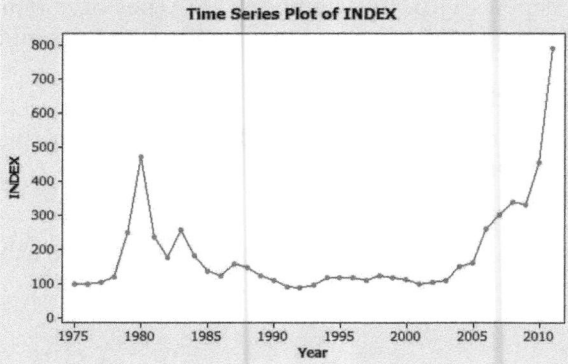

Figure 2

Minitab time series graph of simple silver price index

Source: The Silver Institute.

Steps for Calculating a Simple Index Number

1. Obtain the prices or quantities for the commodity over the time period of interest.

2. Select a base period.

3. Calculate the index number for each period according to the formula

$$\text{Index number at time } t = \left(\frac{\text{Time series value at time } t}{\text{Time series value at base period}} \right) 100$$

Symbolically,

$$I_t = \left(\frac{Y_t}{Y_0} \right) 100$$

where I_t is the index number at time t, Y_t is the time series value at time t, and Y_0 is the time series value at the base period.

Composite Index Numbers

A **composite index number** represents combinations of the prices or quantities of several commodities. For example, suppose you want to construct an index for the total number of sales of the two major automobile manufacturers in the United States: General Motors and Ford. The first step is to collect data on the sales of each manufacturer during the period in which you are interested, say 2000–2012. To summarize the information from both time series in a single index, we add the sales of each manufacturer for each year—that is, we form a new time series consisting of the total number of automobiles sold by the two manufacturers. Then we construct a simple index for the *total* of the two series. The resulting index is called a *simple composite index*. We illustrate the construction of a simple composite index in Example 1.

A **simple composite index** is a simple index for a time series consisting of the total price or total quantity of two or more commodities.

Example 1

Constructing a Simple Composite Index—High-Tech Stocks

Problem One of the primary uses of index numbers is to characterize changes in stock prices over time. Stock market indexes have been constructed for many different types of companies and industries, and several composite indexes have been developed to characterize all stocks. These indexes are reported on a daily basis in the news media (e.g., Standard and Poor's 500 Stocks Index and Dow Jones 65 Stocks Index).

Consider the 2011 monthly closing prices (i.e., closing prices on the last day of each month) given in Table 2 for three high-technology company stocks listed on the New York Stock Exchange. To see how this type of stock fared over the year, construct a simple composite index using January 2011 as the base period. Graph the index and comment on its implications.

Table 2	Monthly Closing Prices of Three High-Technology Company Stocks				
Year	Month	Time	IBM	Intel	Microsoft
2011	Jan	1	162.00	21.46	27.73
	Feb	2	161.88	21.47	26.58
	Mar	3	164.27	19.72	25.48
	Apr	4	165.05	23.15	25.92
	May	5	167.50	21.73	23.91
	Jun	6	181.85	22.53	26.02
	Jul	7	127.98	22.33	27.40
	Aug	8	166.98	19.64	25.80
	Sep	9	174.87	21.34	24.89
	Oct	10	186.38	23.74	26.25
	Nov	11	189.66	24.64	25.22
	Dec	12	183.88	24.25	26.96

Source: www.msn.com.

Data Set: HITECH

Solution First, we calculate the total for the three stock prices each month. These totals are shown in the "TOTAL" column in the Excel workbook displayed in Figure 3. Then the simple composite index is calculated by dividing each monthly total by the January 2011 total. The index values are given in the last column of Figure 3, and a graph of the simple composite index is shown in Figure 4.

	A	B	C	D	E	F	G	H
1	YEAR	MONTH	TIME	IBM	INTEL	MICROSOFT	TOTAL	INDEX
2	2011	JAN	1	162.00	21.46	27.73	211.19	100.00
3	2011	FEB	2	161.88	21.47	26.58	209.93	99.40
4	2011	MAR	3	164.27	19.72	25.48	209.47	99.19
5	2011	APR	4	165.05	23.15	25.92	214.12	101.39
6	2011	MAY	5	167.50	21.73	23.91	213.14	100.92
7	2011	JUN	6	181.85	22.53	26.02	230.40	109.10
8	2011	JUL	7	127.98	22.33	27.40	177.71	84.15
9	2011	AUG	8	166.98	19.64	25.80	212.42	100.58
10	2011	SEP	9	174.87	21.34	24.89	221.10	104.69
11	2011	OCT	10	186.38	23.74	26.25	236.37	111.92
12	2011	NOV	11	189.66	24.64	25.22	239.52	113.41
13	2011	DEC	12	183.88	24.25	26.96	235.09	111.32

Figure 3

Excel workbook with simple composite index for high-tech stock prices

Source: www.msn.com.

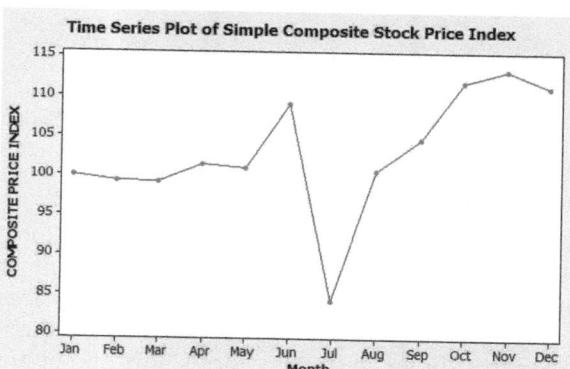

Figure 4

Minitab time series graph of simple composite index for high-tech stock prices

Source: www.msn.com.

The plot of the 2011 simple composite index for these high-technology stocks shows a dramatic drop in the stock market in July 2011, followed by an increasing trend. Overall, the composite price of these high-technology stocks increased about 11% from January (Index $= 100$) to December (Index $= 111.32$).

Look Back The difference between two index numbers gives the percentage change in the value of the time series variable between the two time periods.

Now Work Exercise 10c, d

A simple composite price index has a major drawback: The quantity of the commodity that is purchased during each period is not taken into account. Only the price totals are used to calculate the index. We can remedy this situation by constructing a *weighted composite price index*.

> A **weighted composite price index** weights the prices by quantities purchased prior to calculating totals for each time period. The weighted totals are then used to compute the index in the same way that the unweighted totals are used for simple composite indexes.

Because the quantities purchased change from time period to time period, the choice of which time period's quantities to use as the basis for the weighted composite index is an important one. A **Laspeyres index** uses the *base period quantities as weights*. The rationale is that the prices at each time period should be compared as if the same quantities were purchased each period as were purchased during the base period. This method measures price inflation (or deflation) by fixing the purchase quantities at their base period values. The method for calculating a Laspeyres index is given in the box below.

Steps for Calculating a Laspeyres Index

1. Collect price information for each of the k price series to be used in the composite index. Denote these series by $P_{1t}, P_{2t}, \ldots, P_{kt}$.

2. Select a base period. Call this time period t_0.

3. Collect purchase quantity information for the base period. Denote the k quantities by $Q_{1t_0}, Q_{2t_0}, \ldots, Q_{kt_0}$.

4. Calculate the weighted totals for each time period according to the formula

$$\sum_{i=1}^{k} Q_{it_0} P_{it}$$

5. Calculate the Laspeyres index, I_t, at time t by taking the ratio of the weighted total at time t to the base period weighted total and multiplying by 100—that is,

$$I_t = \frac{\sum_{i=1}^{k} Q_{it_0} P_{it}}{\sum_{i=1}^{k} Q_{it_0} P_{it_0}} \times 100$$

Example	2

Constructing a Laspeyres Index—High-Tech Stocks

Problem The 2011 January and December prices for the three high-technology company stocks are given in Table 3. Suppose that, in January 2011, an investor purchased the quantities shown in the table. [*Note:* Only two prices are used to simplify the example. The same methods can be applied to calculate the index for other months.] Calculate the Laspeyres index for the investor's portfolio of high-technology stocks using January 2011 as the base period.

Table 3	Prices of High-Technology Stocks with Quantities Purchased		
	IBM	Intel	Microsoft
Shares purchased	500	100	1,000
January price	162.00	21.46	27.73
December price	183.88	24.25	26.96

Source: www.msn.com.

Solution First, we calculate the weighted price totals for each time period, using the January quantities as weights. Thus,

$$\text{January weighted total} = \sum_{i=1}^{3} Q_{i,\text{ Jan.}} P_{i,\text{ Jan.}}$$

$$= 500(162.00) + 100(21.46) + 1,000(27.73)$$

$$= 110,876$$

$$\text{December weighted total} = \sum_{i=1}^{3} Q_{i,\text{ Jan.}} P_{i,\text{ Dec.}}$$

$$= 500(183.88) + 100(24.25) + 1,000(26.96)$$

$$= 121,325$$

Then the Laspeyres index is calculated by multiplying the ratio of each weighted total to the base period weighted total by 100. Thus,

$$I_{\text{Jan.}} = \frac{\sum_{i=1}^{3} Q_{i,\text{ Jan.}} P_{i,\text{ Jan.}}}{\sum_{i=1}^{3} Q_{i,\text{ Jan.}} P_{i,\text{ Jan.}}} \times 100 = \frac{110,876}{110,876} \times 100 = 100$$

$$I_{\text{Dec.}} = \frac{\sum_{i=1}^{3} Q_{i,\text{ Jan.}} P_{i,\text{ Dec.}}}{\sum_{i=1}^{3} Q_{i,\text{ Jan.}} P_{i,\text{ Jan.}}} \times 100 = \frac{121,325}{110,876} \times 100 = 109.42$$

Look Back The implication is that when weighted by quantities purchased, the total value of these stocks increased by about $(109 - 100)\% = 9\%$ from January to December in 2011.

Now Work Exercise 14b

The Laspeyres index is appropriate when the base period quantities are reasonable weights to apply to all time periods. This is the case in applications such as that described in Example 2, where the base period quantities represent actual quantities of stock purchased and held for some period of time. Laspeyres indexes are also appropriate when the base period quantities remain reasonable approximations of purchase quantities in subsequent periods. However, it can be misleading when the relative purchase quantities change significantly from those in the base period.

Probably the best-known Laspeyres index is the all-items Consumer Price Index (CPI). This monthly composite index is made up of hundreds of item prices, and the U.S. Bureau of Labor Statistics (BLS) sampled over 30,000 families' purchases in 1982–1984 to determine the base period quantities. Thus, beginning in 1988, the all-items CPI published each month reflects quantities purchased in 1982–1984 by a sample of families across the United States. However, as prices increase for some commodities more quickly than for others, consumers tend to substitute less expensive commodities where possible. For example, as gasoline prices rapidly inflated in the mid-2000s, consumers began to purchase more fuel efficient cars. The net effect of using the base period quantities for the CPI is to overestimate the effect of inflation on consumers because the quantities are fixed at levels that will actually change in response to price changes.

There are several solutions to the problem of purchase quantities that change relative to those of the base period. One is to change the base period regularly, so that the quantities are regularly updated. A second solution is to compute the index at each time period by using the purchase quantities of that period, rather than those of the base period. A **Paasche index** is calculated by using price totals *weighted by the purchase quantities of the period the index value represents*. The steps for calculating a Paasche index are given in the box.

Steps for Calculating a Paasche Index

1. Collect price information for each of the k price series to be used in the composite index. Denote these series by $P_{1t}, P_{2t}, \ldots, P_{kt}$.
2. Select a base period. Call this time period t_0.
3. Collect purchase quantity information for every period. Denote the k quantities for period t by $Q_{1t}, Q_{2t}, \ldots, Q_{kt}$.
4. Calculate the Paasche index for time t by multiplying the ratio of the weighted total at time t to the weighted total at time t_0 (base period) by 100, where the weights used are the purchase quantities for time period t. Thus,

$$I_t = \frac{\sum_{i=1}^{k} Q_{it} P_{it}}{\sum_{i=1}^{k} Q_{it} P_{it_0}} \times 100$$

<table>
<tr><td>**Example 3**

Constructing a Paasche Index—High-Tech Stocks</td></tr>
</table>

Problem The 2011 January and December prices and volumes (actual quantities purchased) in millions of shares for three high-technology company stocks are shown in Table 4. Calculate and interpret the Paasche index, using January 2011 as the base period.

Table 4	Prices and Volumes of High-Technology Stocks					
	IBM		Intel		Microsoft	
	Price	Volume	Price	Volume	Price	Volume
January	162.00	7	21.46	91	27.73	65
December	183.88	12	24.25	92	26.96	101

Source: S&P Daily Stock Price Record, moneycentral.msn.com.

Solution The key to calculating a Paasche index is to remember that the weights (purchase quantities) change for each time period. Thus,

$$I_{\text{Jan.}} = \frac{\sum_{i=1}^{3} Q_{i,\text{ Jan.}} P_{i,\text{ Jan.}}}{\sum_{i=1}^{3} Q_{i,\text{ Jan.}} P_{i,\text{ Jan.}}} \times 100 = 100$$

$$I_{\text{Dec.}} = \frac{\sum_{i=1}^{3} Q_{i,\text{ Dec.}} P_{i,\text{ Dec.}}}{\sum_{i=1}^{3} Q_{i,\text{ Dec.}} P_{i,\text{ Jan.}}} \times 100$$

$$= \frac{(12)(183.88) + (92)(24.25) + (101)(26.96)}{(12)(162.00) + (92)(21.46) + (101)(27.73)} \times 100 = \frac{7,160.52}{6,719.05} \times 100$$

$$= 106.6$$

The implication is that in 2011, December prices represent a $(106.6 - 100)\% = 6.6\%$ increase from January prices, assuming the purchase quantities were at December levels for *both* periods.

■ Now Work Exercise 14d

The Paasche index is most appropriate when you want to compare current prices to base period prices at *current* purchase levels. However, there are several major problems associated with the Paasche index. First, it requires that purchase quantities be known for every time period. This rules out a Paasche index for applications such as the CPI because the time and monetary resource expenditures required to collect quantity information are considerable. (Recall that more than 30,000 families were sampled to estimate purchase quantities in 1982–1984.) A second problem is that although each period is compared to the base period, it is difficult to compare the index at two other periods because the quantities used are different for each period. Consequently, the change in the index is affected by changes in both prices *and* quantities. This fact makes it difficult to interpret the change in a Paasche index between periods when neither is the base period.

Although there are other types of indexes that use different weighting factors, the Laspeyres and Paasche indexes are the most popular composite indexes. Depending on the primary objective in constructing an index, one of them will probably be suitable for most purposes.

ETHICS in STATISTICS

Intentionally selecting a base period in order to inflate or deflate an index number, without reporting the base period, is considered *unethical statistical practice*.

Exercises 1–14

Learning the Mechanics

1 Explain in words how to construct a simple index.

2 Explain in words how to calculate the following types of indexes:
  a. Simple composite index
  b. Weighted composite index
  c. Laspeyres index
  d. Paasche index

3 Explain in words the difference between Laspeyres and Paasche indexes.

4 The table below gives the prices for three products (A, B, and C) for the four quarters of last year.

Quarter	A	B	C
1	3.25	1.75	8.00
2	3.50	1.25	9.35
3	3.90	1.20	9.70
4	4.25	1.00	10.50

  a. Compute a simple index for the Quarter 4 price of product A, using Quarter 1 as the base period.
  b. Compute a simple index for the Quarter 2 price of product B, using Quarter 1 as the base period.
  c. Compute a simple composite index for the Quarter 4 price of all three products, using Quarter 1 as the base period.
  d. Compute a simple composite index for the Quarter 4 price of all three products, using Quarter 2 as the base period.

5 Refer to Exercise 4. The next table gives the quantities purchased for three products (A, B, and C) for the four quarters of last year.

Quarter	A	B	C
1	100	20	50
2	200	25	35
3	250	50	25
4	300	100	20

  a. Compute a Laspeyres index for the Quarter 4 price of all three products, using Quarter 1 as the base period.
  b. Compute a Paasche index for the Quarter 4 price of all three products, using Quarter 2 as the base period.

Applying the Concepts—Basic

6 **Annual median family income.** The table below lists the U.S. median annual family income every 5 years during the period 1975–2010. It also contains several values for each MEDINC of two simple indexes for median family income.
  a. Calculate the missing values of each simple index.
  b. Interpret the index for 1990.

Year	Income ($)	Base 1975 Index	Base 1980 Index
1975	13,719	–	65.26
1980	21,023	153.24	–
1985	27,735	202.16	–
1990	35,353	257.69	–
1995	40,611	–	–
2000	50,732	–	–
2005	56,194	–	–
2010	60,363	–	–

Source: U.S. Census Bureau, 2012.

7 Annual U.S. beer production. The table below describes U.S. beer production (in millions of barrels) for the period 1980–2010.

USBEER

  a. Use 1980 as the base period to compute the simple index for this time series. Interpret the value for 2010.

  b. Refer to part **a.** Is this an example of a quantity index or a price index?

  c. Recompute the simple index using 1990 as the base period. Plot the two indexes on the same graph. What pattern do you observe?

Year	Beer	Year	Beer	Year	Beer
1980	188	1991	203	2002	200
1981	194	1992	202	2003	195
1982	194	1993	203	2004	198
1983	195	1994	202	2005	197
1984	193	1995	199	2006	198
1985	193	1996	201	2007	199
1986	195	1997	199	2008	200
1987	195	1998	198	2009	196
1988	198	1999	198	2010	194
1989	200	2000	199		
1990	204	2001	199		

Source: 2011 BREWER'S ALMANAC. Copyright © 2011 by The Beer Institute. Reprinted with permission.

8 Quarterly single-family housing starts. The quarterly numbers of single-family housing starts (in thousands of dwellings) in the United States from 2007 through 2011 are recorded below.

HSTART

  a. Using Quarter 1, 2007, as a base period, calculate the simple index for this quarterly time series.

  b. Interpret the simple index for Quarter 2, 2010.

  c. By what percentage did the number of housing starts change between Quarter 1, 2007, and Quarter 4, 2011?

  d. By what percentage did the number of housing starts increase between Quarter 1, 2009, and Quarter 4, 2011?

Year	Quarter	Housing Starts
2007	1	260
	2	333
	3	265
	4	188
2008	1	162
	2	194
	3	163
	4	103
2009	1	78
	2	124
	3	138
	4	105
2010	1	114
	2	142
	3	119
	4	96
2011	1	90
	2	123
	3	118
	4	100

Source: United States Census Bureau.

9 Price of natural gas. The table below lists the price of natural gas (in dollars per 1,000 cubic feet) between 1980 and 2010.

NATGAS

Year	Price	Year	Price	Year	Price
1980	3.68	1997	6.94	2005	12.70
1990	5.80	1998	6.82	2006	13.73
1991	5.82	1999	6.69	2007	13.08
1992	5.89	2000	7.76	2008	13.89
1993	6.16	2001	9.63	2009	12.14
1994	6.41	2002	7.89	2010	11.20
1995	6.06	2003	9.63		
1996	6.34	2004	10.75		

Source: United States Census Bureau.

  a. Using 1980 as the base period, calculate and plot the simple index for the price of natural gas from 1990 through 2010.

  b. Use the simple index to interpret the trend in the price of natural gas.

  c. Is the index you constructed in part **a** a price or quantity index? Explain.

Applying the Concepts—Intermediate

10 Employment in farm and nonfarm categories. Civilian employment is broadly classified by the federal government into two categories—agricultural and nonagricultural. Employment figures (in thousands of workers) for farm and nonfarm categories for selected years from 1980 to 2010 are given in the table below.

CVEMP

Year	Farm	Nonfarm	Year	Farm	Nonfarm
1980	3,364	95,938	2000	2,464	134,427
1985	3,179	103,971	2005	2,197	139,532
1990	3,223	115,570	2010	2,206	136,858
1995	3,440	121,460			

Source: United States Census Bureau.

  a. Compute simple indexes for each of the two time series using 1980 as the base period.

  b. Which segment has shown the greater percentage change in employment over the period shown?

  NW **c.** Compute a simple composite index for total employment for the years 1980–2010. Use 1980 as a base period.

  NW **d.** Refer to part **c.** Interpret the composite index value for 2010.

11 GDP personal consumption expenditures. The gross domestic product (GDP) is the total national output of goods and services valued at market prices. As such, the GDP is a commonly used barometer of the U.S. economy. One component of the GDP is personal consumption expenditures, which is itself the sum of expenditures for durable goods, nondurable goods, and services. The GDP for these components (in billions of dollars) is shown in the next table, in 5-year increments from 1970 to 2010.

GDP

  a. Using these three component values, construct a simple composite index for the personal consumption component of GDP. Use 1970 as the base year.

  b. Suppose we want to update the index by using 1980 as the base year. Update the index using only the index values you calculated in part **a,** without referring to the original data.

c. Graph the personal consumption expenditure index for the years 1960–2010, first using 1970 as the base year and then using 1980 as the base year. What effect does changing the base year have on the graph of this index?

Year	Durables	Nondurables	Services
1970	90	229	330
1975	134	416	475
1980	226	573	956
1985	353	919	1,395
1990	497	994	2,344
1995	636	1,180	3,172
2000	916	1,543	4,371
2005	1,106	1,968	5,745
2010	1,089	2,336	6,923

Source: United States Census Bureau.

12 GDP personal consumption expenditures (cont'd). Refer to Exercise 11. Suppose the output quantities in 1970, measured in billions of units purchased, are as follows:

Durable goods: 10.9

Nondurable goods: 14.02

Services: 42.6

a. Use the outputs to calculate the Laspeyres index from 1960 to 2010 (same increments as in Exercise 11) with 1970 as the base period.

b. Plot the simple composite index of Exercise 11 and the Laspeyres index of part **a** on the same graph. Comment on the differences between the two indexes.

13 Hourly earnings for workers. The table below lists the average hourly earnings (in dollars) and the average number

HOURS

of hours worked per week for selected years from 1990 to 2010 for workers in three different industries.

a. Compute a simple index for average hourly earnings for manufacturing workers over the period 1990 to 2010. Use 1990 as the base year. Do the same for information and food services workers.

b. Plot the three simple indexes on the same graph and interpret the results.

c. Compute simple composite indexes for hourly earnings and weekly hours over the 40-year period. Use 1990 as the base year.

d. Plot the two composite indexes, part **c**, on the same graph and interpret the results.

14 Production and price of metals. The level of price and production of metals in the United States is one measure of the METALS strength of an industrial economy. The table at the bottom of the page lists the annual prices (in dollars per ton) and production (in millions of tons) for three metals—copper, aluminum, and iron scrap—from 2006 to 2010.

a. Compute the simple composite price and quantity indexes for the 5-year period, using 2006 as the base period.

NW **b.** Compute the Laspeyres price index for the 5-year period, using 2006 as the base period.

c. Plot the simple composite and Laspeyres indexes on the same graph. Comment on the differences.

NW **d.** Compute the Paasche price index for the 5-year period, using 2006 as the base period.

e. Plot the Paasche and Laspeyres indexes on the same graph. Comment on the differences.

f. Compare the Paasche and Laspeyres index values for 2008 and 2010. Which index is more appropriate for describing the change in this 2-year period? Explain.

Data for Exercise 13

Year	Manufacturing		Information		Food Services	
	Earnings	Hours	Earnings	Hours	Earnings	Hours
1990	10.78	40.5	13.40	35.8	5.70	25.9
2000	14.32	41.3	19.07	36.8	7.92	26.2
2005	16.56	40.7	22.06	36.5	8.80	25.7
2007	17.26	41.2	23.96	36.5	9.82	25.6
2008	17.75	40.8	24.78	36.7	10.23	25.4
2009	18.24	39.8	25.45	36.6	10.49	25.0
2010	18.61	41.1	25.86	36.3	10.68	25.0

Source: United States Census Bureau.

Data for Exercise 14

Year	Copper		Iron Scrap		Aluminum	
	Price	Production	Price	Production	Price	Production
2006	6,940	1.21	214	71	2,680	2.28
2007	7,230	1.27	249	77	2,690	2.55
2008	7,040	1.22	349	74	2,660	2.66
2009	5,320	1.11	208	80	1,750	1.73
2010	7,680	1.06	319	76	2,300	1.73

Source: US Geological Survey.

2 | Descriptive Analysis: Exponential Smoothing

As you have seen in the previous section, index numbers are useful for describing trends and changes in time series. However, time series often have such irregular fluctuations that trends are difficult to describe. Index numbers can be misleading in such cases because the series is changing so rapidly. Methods for removing the rapid fluctuations in a time series so the general trend can be seen are called *smoothing* techniques.

Exponential smoothing is one type of weighted average that assigns positive weights to past and current values of the time series. A single weight, w, called the **exponential smoothing constant,** is selected so that w is between 0 and 1. Then the exponentially smoothed series, E_t, is calculated as follows:

$$E_1 = Y_1$$
$$E_2 = wY_2 + (1 - w)E_1$$
$$E_3 = wY_3 + (1 - w)E_2$$
$$\vdots$$
$$E_t = wY_t + (1 - w)E_{t-1}$$

Thus, the exponentially smoothed value at time t assigns the weight w to the current series value and the weight $(1 - w)$ to the previous smoothed value.

For example, consider the silver price time series in Table 1. Suppose we want to calculate the exponentially smoothed series for the years 1982 through 2011 using a smoothing constant of $w = .3$. The calculations proceed as follows:

$$E_{1982} = Y_{1982} = 7.92$$
$$E_{1983} = .3Y_{1983} + (1 - .3)E_{1982} = .3(11.43) + .7(7.92) = 8.97$$
$$E_{1984} = .3Y_{1984} + (1 - .3)E_{1983} = .3(8.14) + .7(8.97) = 8.72$$
$$\vdots$$
$$E_{2011} = .3Y_{2011} + (1 - .3)E_{2010} = .3(35.11) + .7(14.54) = 20.71$$

All the exponentially smoothed values corresponding to $w = .3$ are given in the Minitab worksheet, Figure 5. (*Note:* Minitab gives the value of E_t in row $t + 1$.)

The actual silver prices and exponentially smoothed prices are graphed in Figure 6. Like many averages, the exponentially smoothed series changes less rapidly than the time series itself. The choice of w affects the smoothness of E_t. The smaller (closer to 0) is the value of w, the smoother is E_t. Because small values of w give more weight to the past values of the time series, the smoothed series is not affected by rapid changes in the current values and, therefore, appears smoother than the original series. Conversely, choosing w near 1 yields an exponentially smoothed series that is much like the original series—that is, large values of w give more weight to the current value of the time series, so the smoothed series looks like the original series. This concept is illustrated in Figure 7. The steps for calculating an exponentially smoothed series are given in the box on the next page.

SILVER2.MTP ***		
	C1	C2	C3
↓	YEAR	PRICE	SMOOTH3
1	1982	7.92	7.9200
2	1983	11.43	8.9730
3	1984	8.14	8.7231
4	1985	6.13	7.9452
5	1986	5.46	7.1996
6	1987	7.02	7.1457
7	1988	6.53	6.9610
8	1989	5.50	6.5227
9	1990	4.83	6.0149
10	1991	4.06	5.4284
11	1992	3.95	4.9849
12	1993	4.31	4.7824
13	1994	5.29	4.9347
14	1995	5.20	5.0143
15	1996	5.20	5.0700
16	1997	4.90	5.0190
17	1998	5.54	5.1753
18	1999	5.22	5.1887
19	2000	4.95	5.1171
20	2001	4.37	4.8930
21	2002	4.60	4.8051
22	2003	4.85	4.8186
23	2004	6.65	5.3680
24	2005	7.22	5.9236
25	2006	11.57	7.6175
26	2007	13.39	9.3493
27	2008	15.02	11.0505
28	2009	14.66	12.1333
29	2010	20.16	14.5413
30	2011	35.11	20.7119

Figure 5

Minitab worksheet with exponentially smoothed ($w = .3$) silver prices

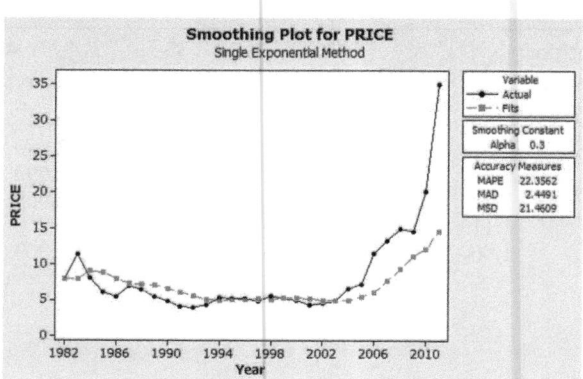

Figure 6

Minitab graph of exponentially smoothed ($w = .3$) silver prices

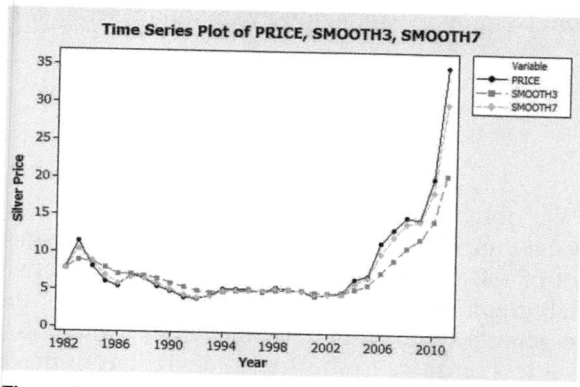

Figure 7

Minitab graph of exponentially smoothed ($w = .3$ and $w = .7$) silver prices

---

Steps for Calculating an Exponentially Smoothed Series

1. Select an exponential smoothing constant, w, between 0 and 1. Remember that small values of w give less weight to the current value of the series and yield a smoother series. Larger choices of w assign more weight to the current value of the series and yield a more variable series.

2. Calculate the exponentially smoothed series E_t from the original time series Y_t as follows:

$$E_1 = Y_1$$
$$E_2 = wY_2 + (1 - w)E_1$$
$$E_3 = wY_3 + (1 - w)E_2$$
$$\vdots$$
$$E_t = wY_t + (1 - w)E_{t-1}$$

Example	4

Exponential Smoothing— Annual Sales Revenue

Problem Annual sales data (recorded in thousands of dollars) for a firm's first 35 years of operation are provided in Table 5. Create an exponentially smoothed series for the sales time series using $w = .7$ and plot both series.

Table 5	A Firm's Annual Sales Revenues ($ thousands)		
Year	Sales Revenue	Year	Sales Revenue
1	5.8	19	103.2
2	4.0	20	85.4
3	5.5	21	86.2
4	15.6	22	89.9
5	25.1	23	89.2
6	20.3	24	99.1
7	31.4	25	100.3
8	48.0	26	111.7
9	46.1	27	102.2
10	35.9	28	115.5
11	35.5	29	119.2
12	53.5	30	125.2
13	48.4	31	136.3
14	61.6	32	146.8
15	65.6	33	150.1
16	71.4	34	151.4
17	83.4	35	150.9
18	93.6		

Data Set: SALE35

SALES35.MTW ***

↓	C1	C2	C3
	T	SALES	EXP7
1	1	5.8	5.800
2	2	4.0	4.540
3	3	5.5	5.212
4	4	15.6	12.484
5	5	25.1	21.315
6	6	20.3	20.605
7	7	31.4	28.161
8	8	48.0	42.048
9	9	46.1	44.885
10	10	35.9	38.595
11	11	35.5	36.429
12	12	53.5	48.379
13	13	48.4	48.394
14	14	61.6	57.638
15	15	65.6	63.211
16	16	71.4	68.943
17	17	83.4	79.063
18	18	93.6	89.239
19	19	103.2	99.012
20	20	85.4	89.484
21	21	86.2	87.185
22	22	89.9	89.086
23	23	89.2	89.166
24	24	99.1	96.120
25	25	100.3	99.046
26	26	111.7	107.904
27	27	102.2	103.911
28	28	115.5	112.023
29	29	119.2	117.047
30	30	125.2	122.754
31	31	136.3	132.236
32	32	146.8	142.431
33	33	150.1	147.799
34	34	151.4	150.320
35	35	150.9	150.726

Figure 8

Minitab worksheet with exponentially smoothed ($w = .7$) sales revenues

Solution To find the exponentially smoothed series with $w = .7$, we calculate

$$E_1 = Y_1 = 5.8$$
$$E_2 = wY_2 + (1 - w)E_1 = .7(4.0) + .3(5.8) = 4.54$$
$$E_3 = wY_3 + (1 - w)E_2 = .7(5.5) + .3(4.54) = 5.21$$

etc.

We obtained the exponentially smoothed values for all 35 years using Minitab. The values are shown on the Minitab worksheet, Figure 8, in the column labeled *EXP7*. A plot of the original time series and exponentially smoothed series is shown in the Minitab graph, Figure 9. You can see that the smoothed series provides a good picture of the general trend of the original series. Note, too, that the exponentially smoothed series is less sensitive to short-term deviations of the sales revenues from the trend that occurred in years 10, 11, and 19.

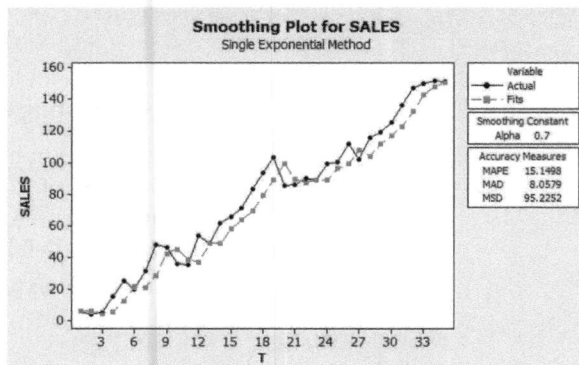

Figure 9

Minitab graph of exponentially smoothed ($w = .7$) sales revenues

Look Back If you desire a less variable exponentially smoothed series, then select a smoothing constant closer to 0 (e.g., $w = .5$ or $w = .2$).

Now Work Exercise 16

One of the primary uses of exponential smoothing is to forecast future values of a time series. Because only current and past values of the time series are used in exponential smoothing, it is easily adapted to forecasting. We demonstrate this application of exponentially smoothed series in Section 4.

Exercises 15–22

Learning the Mechanics

15 Describe the effect of selecting an exponential constant of $w = .2$. Of $w = .8$. Which will produce a smoother trend?

16 A monthly time series is shown in the table to the right.
L14016
NW
  a. Calculate the missing values in the exponentially smoothed series using $w = .5$.
  b. Graph the time series and the exponentially smoothed series on the same graph.

Applying the Concepts—Basic

17 Annual U.S. beer production. Refer to the annual U.S. beer production time series, Exercise 7.
USBEER a. Calculate the exponentially smoothed series for U.S. beer production for the period 1980–2010 using $w = .2$.
  b. Calculate the exponentially smoothed series using $w = .8$.

Month	t	Y_t	Exponentially Smoothed Series ($w = .5$)
Jan	1	280	—
Feb	2	281	—
Mar	3	250	265.3
Apr	4	246	255.6
May	5	239	—
Jun	6	218	—
Jul	7	218	—
Aug	8	210	—
Sep	9	205	—
Oct	10	206	—
Nov	11	200	—
Dec	12	200	—

  c. Plot the two exponentially smoothed series ($w = .2$ and $w = .8$) on the same graph. Which smoothed series best portrays the long-term trend?

18 Foreign fish production. Overfishing and pollution of U.S. coastal waters have resulted in an increased dependence by the United States on the fishing grounds of other countries. The table below describes the annual fish catch (in thousands of metric tons) in all fishing areas of Peru and Chile for the years 2000 to 2008.

FFTONS

Year	Chile	Peru
2000	4,692	10,665
2001	4,363	7,990
2002	4,817	8,775
2003	4,176	6,100
2004	5,584	9,627
2005	5,029	9,416
2006	4,971	7,046
2007	4,636	7,250
2008	4,398	7,406

Source: United States Census Bureau.

a. Compute an exponentially smoothed series for both Chile and Peru, using a smoothing coefficient of $w = .5$.

b. Plot both actual series and both smoothed series on the same graph. Describe the differences in variation of catches over time between the two countries. For example, do they move up and down together over time?

Applying the Concepts—Intermediate

19 Yearly price of gold. The price of gold is used by some financial analysts as a barometer of investors' expectations of inflation, with the price of gold tending to increase as concerns about inflation increase. The table below shows the average annual price of gold (in dollars per ounce) from 1990 through 2011.

GOLDYR

Year	Price	Year	Price
1990	384	2001	271
1991	362	2002	310
1992	344	2003	363
1993	360	2004	410
1994	384	2005	445
1995	384	2006	603
1996	388	2007	695
1997	331	2008	872
1998	294	2009	972
1999	279	2010	1,225
2000	279	2011	1,572

Source: Data from the London Bullion Market Association (LMBA). Copyright © 2012 by the World Gold Council. Reprinted with permission. www.kitco.com.

a. Compute an exponentially smoothed series for the gold price time series for the period from 1990 to 2011, using a smoothing coefficient of $w = .8$.

b. Plot the original series and the exponentially smoothed series on the same graph. Comment on the trend observed.

20 Personal consumption in transportation. There has been phenomenal growth in the transportation sector of the economy since 1990. The personal consumption expenditure figures (in billions of dollars) are given in the table in the next column.

TRNEXP

a. Compute exponentially smoothed values of this personal consumption time series, using the smoothing constants $w = .2$ and $w = .8$.

b. Plot the actual series and the two smoothed series on the same graph. Comment on the trend in personal consumption expenditure on transportation in the 2000s as compared to the 1990s.

Year	Expenditure on Transportation
1990	593.6
1991	553.2
1992	585.1
1993	611.4
1994	646.3
1995	658.6
1996	690.8
1997	730.7
1998	781.3
1999	832.1
2000	853.5
2001	872.1
2002	891.1
2003	913.0
2004	926.3
2005	905.9
2006	922.1
2007	925.2
2008	1,033.5
2009	890.7

Source: U.S. Census Bureau. *Statistical Abstract of the United States,* 2012.

21 OPEC crude oil imports. The data in the table below are the amounts of crude oil (millions of barrels) imported into the United States from the Organization of Petroleum Exporting Countries (OPEC) for the years 1990–2010.

OPEC

Year	t	Imports, Y_t
1990	1	1,283
1991	2	1,233
1992	3	1,247
1993	4	1,339
1994	5	1,307
1995	6	1,219
1996	7	1,258
1997	8	1,378
1998	9	1,522
1999	10	1,543
2000	11	1,659
2001	12	1,770
2002	13	1,490
2003	14	1,671
2004	15	1,948
2005	16	1,738
2006	17	1,745
2007	18	1,969
2008	19	1,984
2009	20	1,594
2010	21	1,654

Source: United States Census Bureau.

a. Construct two exponentially smoothed series for this time series, using $w = .1$ and $w = .9$.

b. Plot the original series and the two smoothed series on the same graph. Which smoothed series looks more like the original series? Why?

22 S&P 500 Stock Index. Standard & Poor's 500 Composite Stock Index (S&P 500) is a stock market index. Like the Dow Jones Industrial Average, it is an indicator of stock market activity. The data in the table are end-of-quarter values of the S&P 500 for the years 2004–2011.

a. Calculate and plot the exponentially smoothed series for the quarterly S&P 500 using a smoothing constant of $w = .3$.

b. Repeat part a but use $w = .7$.

c. Which exponentially smoothed series do you prefer for describing trends in the series? Explain.

Year	Quarter	S&P 500	Year	Quarter	S&P 500
2004	1	1,126.2	2008	1	1,322.7
	2	1,140.8		2	1,280.0
	3	1,114.6		3	1,164.7
	4	1,211.9		4	903.3
2005	1	1,180.6	2009	1	797.9
	2	1,191.3		2	919.3
	3	1,228.8		3	1,057.1
	4	1,248.3		4	1,115.1
2006	1	1,294.9	2010	1	1,169.4
	2	1,270.2		2	1,030.7
	3	1,335.8		3	1,141.2
	4	1,418.3		4	1,257.6
2007	1	1,420.9	2011	1	1,325.8
	2	1,503.3		2	1,320.6
	3	1,526.7		3	1,131.4
	4	1,468.4		4	1,257.6

Source: Standard & Poor's.

3   Time Series Components

In the previous two sections, we showed how to use various *descriptive* techniques to obtain a picture of the behavior of a time series. Now we want to expand our coverage to include techniques that will let us make statistical inferences about the time series. These *inferential techniques* are generally focused on the problem of *forecasting* future values of the time series.

Before forecasts of future values of a time series can be made, some type of model that can be projected into the future must be used to describe the series. Time series models range in complexity from **descriptive models,** such as the exponential smoothing models discussed in the previous section, to **inferential models,** such as the combinations of regression and specialized time series models to be discussed later in this chapter. Whether the model is simple or complex, the objective is the same: to produce accurate forecasts of future values of the time series.

Many different algebraic representations of time series models have been proposed. One of the most widely used is an **additive model*** of the form

$$Y_t = T_t + C_t + S_t + R_t$$

The **secular trend,** T_t, also known as the **long-term trend,** is a time series component that describes the long-term movements of Y_t. For example, if you want to characterize the secular trend of the production of automobiles since 1930, you would show T_t as an upward-moving time series over the period from 1930 to the present. This does not imply that the automobile production series has always moved upward from month to month and from year to year, but it does mean the long-term trend has been an increase over that period of time.

The **cyclical effect,** C_t, generally describes fluctuations of the time series about the secular trend that are attributable to business and economic conditions. For example, refer back to the monthly closing prices of three high-technology stocks for 2011, Table 2. Recall that a plot of the simple composite index (Figure 4) showed a generally decreasing secular trend. However, during periods of recession, the index tends to lie below the secular trend, while in times of general economic expansion, it lies above the long-term trend line.

---

*Another useful form is the *multiplicative model:* $Y_t = T_t C_t S_t R_t$. This can be changed to an additive form by taking natural logarithms (i.e., $\ln Y_t = \ln T_t + \ln C_t + \ln S_t + \ln R_t$). See Section 8.

The **seasonal effect,** S_t, describes the fluctuations in the time series that recur during specific time periods. For example, quarterly power loads for a Florida utility company tend to be highest in the summer months (Quarter III), with another, smaller peak in the winter months (Quarter I). The spring and fall (Quarters II and IV) seasonal effects are negative, meaning that the series tends to lie below the long-term trend line during those quarters.

The **residual effect,** R_t, is what remains of Y_t after the secular, cyclical, and seasonal components have been removed. Part of the residual effect may be attributable to unpredictable rare events (earthquake, presidential assassination, etc.) and part to the randomness of human actions. In any case, the presence of the residual component makes it impossible to forecast the future values of a time series without error. Thus, the presence of the residual effect emphasizes: No business phenomena should be described by deterministic models. All realistic business models, time series or otherwise, should include a residual component.

Each of the four components contributes to the determination of the value of Y_t at each time period. Although it will not always be possible to characterize each component separately, the component model provides a useful theoretical formulation that helps the time series analyst achieve a better understanding of the phenomena affecting the path followed by the time series.

4   Forecasting: Exponential Smoothing

In Section 2, we discussed exponential smoothing as a method for describing a time series that involves removing the irregular fluctuations. In terms of the time series components discussed in the previous section, exponential smoothing tends to de-emphasize (or "smooth") most of the residual effects. This, coupled with the fact that exponential smoothing uses only past and current values of the series, makes it a useful tool for forecasting time series.

Recall that the formula for exponential smoothing is

$$E_t = wY_t + (1 - w)E_{t-1}$$

where w, the *exponential smoothing constant*, is a number between 0 and 1. We learned that the selection of w controls the smoothness of E_t. A choice near 0 places more emphasis (weight) on *past* values of the time series and therefore yields a smoother series; a choice near 1 gives more weight to *current* values of the series.

Suppose the objective is to forecast the next value of the time series, Y_{t+1}. The **exponentially smoothed forecast** for Y_{t+1} is simply the smoothed value at time t:

$$F_{t+1} = E_t$$

where F_{t+1} is the **forecast** of Y_{t+1}. To help interpret this forecast formula, substitute the smoothing formula for E_t:

$$\begin{aligned}
F_{t+1} = E_t &= wY_t + (1 - w)E_{t-1} \\
&= wY_t + (1 - w)F_t \\
&= F_t + w(Y_t - F_t)
\end{aligned}$$

Note that we have substituted F_t for E_{t-1} because the forecast for time t is the smoothed value for time $(t - 1)$. The final equation provides insight into the exponential smoothing forecast: The forecast for time $(t + 1)$ is equal to the forecast for time t, F_t, plus a correction for the error in the forecast for time t, $(Y_t - F_t)$. This is why the exponentially smoothed forecast is called an **adaptive forecast**—the forecast for time $(t + 1)$ is explicitly adapted for the error in the forecast for time t.

Because exponential smoothing consists of averaging past and present values, the smoothed values will tend to lag behind the series when a long-term trend exists. In addition, the averaging tends to smooth any seasonal component. Therefore, exponentially smoothed forecasts are appropriate only when the trend and seasonal components are relatively insignificant. Because the exponential smoothing model assumes that the time series has little or no trend or seasonal component, the forecast F_{t+1} is used to forecast not only Y_{t+1}, but also all future values of Y_{t+1}, that is, the forecast for two time periods ahead is

$$F_{t+2} = F_{t+1}$$

and for three time periods ahead is

$$F_{t+3} = F_{t+2} = F_{t+1}$$

The exponential smoothing forecasting technique is summarized in the next box.

Calculation of Exponentially Smoothed Forecasts

1. Given the observed time series $Y_1, Y_2, \ldots, Y_t$, first calculate the exponentially smoothed values $E_1, E_2, \ldots, E_t$, using

$$E_1 = Y_1$$
$$E_2 = wY_2 + (1 - w)E_1$$
$$\vdots$$
$$E_t = wY_t + (1 - w)E_{t-1}$$

2. Use the last smoothed value to forecast the next time series value:

$$F_{t+1} = E_t$$

3. Assuming that Y_t is relatively free of trend and seasonal components, use the same forecast for all future values of Y_t:

$$F_{t+2} = F_{t+1}$$
$$F_{t+3} = F_{t+1}$$
$$\vdots$$

Two important points must be made about exponentially smoothed forecasts:

1. The choice of w is crucial. If you decide that w will be small (near 0), you will obtain a smooth, slowly changing series of forecasts. On the other hand, the selection of a large value of w (near 1) will yield more rapidly changing forecasts that depend mostly on the current values of the series. In general, several values of w should be tried to determine how sensitive the forecast series is to the choice of w. Forecasting experience will provide the best basis for the choice of w for a particular application.

2. The farther into the future you forecast, the less certain you can be of accuracy. Because the exponentially smoothed forecast is constant for all future values, any changes in trend or seasonality are not taken into account. However, the uncertainty associated with future forecasts applies not only to exponentially smoothed forecasts but also to all methods of forecasting. In general, time series forecasting should be confined to the short term.

Example 5

Forecasting with Exponential Smoothing— Sales Revenue

Problem Refer to Example 4. The annual sales data (recorded in thousands of dollars) for a firm's first 35 years of operation are reproduced in the Minitab worksheet, Figure 10. Apply the exponential smoothing technique to the data for years 1 to 32 in order to forecast sales revenue in years 33, 34, and 35. Make forecasts using both $w = .3$ and $w = .7$ and compare the results.

↓	C1 T	C2 SALES	C3 EXP3	C4 EXP7
1	1	5.8	5.800	5.800
2	2	4.0	5.260	4.540
3	3	5.5	5.332	5.212
4	4	15.6	8.412	12.484
5	5	25.1	13.419	21.315
6	6	20.3	15.483	20.605
7	7	31.4	20.258	28.161
8	8	48.0	28.581	42.048
9	9	46.1	33.836	44.885
10	10	35.9	34.456	38.595
11	11	35.5	34.769	36.429
12	12	53.5	40.388	48.379
13	13	48.4	42.792	48.394
14	14	61.6	48.434	57.638
15	15	65.6	53.584	63.211
16	16	71.4	58.929	68.943
17	17	83.4	66.270	79.063
18	18	93.6	74.469	89.239
19	19	103.2	83.088	99.012
20	20	85.4	83.782	89.484
21	21	86.2	84.507	87.185
22	22	89.9	86.125	89.086
23	23	89.2	87.048	89.166
24	24	99.1	90.663	96.120
25	25	100.3	93.554	99.046
26	26	111.7	98.998	107.904
27	27	102.2	99.959	103.911
28	28	115.5	104.621	112.023
29	29	119.2	108.995	117.047
30	30	125.2	113.856	122.754
31	31	136.3	120.589	132.236
32	32	146.8	128.453	142.431

Figure 10

Minitab worksheet with actual and exponentially smoothed ($w = .3$ and $w = .7$) sales revenues, years 1–32

Solution First, we used Minitab to calculate the exponentially smoothed series for years 1–32 using both $w = .3$ and $w = .7$. These smoothed values are shown in Figure 10 in the columns labeled *EXP3* and *EXP7*, respectively.

Now, the forecast for year 33 is simply the smoothed sales revenue value in the last year of the smoothed series, year 32. Consequently, we have

$$F_{33} = E_{32} = 128.45 \text{ for } w = .3 \quad \text{(values highlighted on Figure 10)}$$
$$142.43 \text{ for } w = .7$$

With exponential smoothing, the same forecasts are made for any future year. Thus, we have

$$F_{34} = E_{32} = 128.45 \text{ for } w = .3$$
$$142.43 \text{ for } w = .7$$

and

$$F_{35} = E_{32} = 128.45 \text{ for } w = .3$$
$$142.43 \text{ for } w = .7$$

Both sets of forecasts are shown in Table 6. Also shown are the actual sales revenue values and corresponding forecast errors for years 33–35. The **forecast error** is defined as the actual value minus the forecast value, i.e.,

$$\text{Forecast error} = (\text{Actual} - \text{Forecast})$$

Table 6	Sales Revenues (Years 33–35): Actual vs. Forecast Values				
Year	Actual	Forecast ($w = .3$)	Forecast Error	Forecast ($w = .7$)	Forecast Error
33	150.1	128.45	21.65	142.43	7.67
34	151.4	128.45	22.95	142.43	8.97
35	150.9	128.45	22.45	142.43	8.47

You can see that the forecast errors using $w = .7$ are considerably smaller than the forecast errors for $w = .3$. Consequently, future forecasts of the sales revenue time series will likely have a smaller forecast error when a smoothing constant of .7 is employed.

Look Back Note that both the $w = .3$ and $w = .7$ forecasts underestimate the sales revenues for years 33–35. This is because exponentially smoothed forecasts implicitly assume no trend exists in the time series. This example illustrates the risk associated with anything other than very short-term forecasting.

Now Work Exercise 25a

Many time series have long-term, or secular, trends. For such series, the exponentially smoothed forecast is inappropriate for all but the very short term. In the next section, we present an extension of the exponentially smoothed forecast—*Holt's method*—that allows for secular trend in the forecasts.

5 Forecasting Trends: Holt's Method

The exponentially smoothed forecasts for the sales revenue values in the previous section have large forecast errors, in part because they do not recognize the trend in the time series. In this section, we present an extension of the exponential smoothing method of forecasting that explicitly recognizes the trend in a time series. The **Holt forecasting model** consists of both an exponentially smoothed component (E_t) and a trend component (T_t).* The trend component is used in the calculation of the exponentially smoothed value. The following equations show that both E_t and T_t are weighted averages:

$$E_t = wY_t + (1 - w)(E_{t-1} + T_{t-1})$$
$$T_t = v(E_t - E_{t-1}) + (1 - v)T_{t-1}$$

Note that the equations require *two* smoothing constants, w and v, each of which is between 0 and 1. As before, w controls the smoothness of E_t; a choice near 0 places more emphasis on past values of the time series, while a value of w near 1 gives more weight to current values of the series and de-emphasizes the past.

The trend component of the series is estimated *adaptively,* using a weighted average of the most recent change in the level, represented by ($E_t - E_{t-1}$), and the trend estimate, represented by T_{t-1}, from the previous period. A choice of the weight v near 0 places more emphasis on the past estimates of trend, while a choice of v near 1 gives more weight to the current change in level.

The calculation of the components for Holt's model, which proceeds much like the exponential smoothing calculations, is summarized in the box.

> **Steps for Calculating Components of the Holt Forecasting Model**
>
> **1.** Select an exponential smoothing constant w between 0 and 1. Small values of w give less weight to the current values of the time series and more weight to the past. Larger choices assign more weight to the current value of the series.

*In some statistical sofware packages (e.g., Minitab), Holt's method is called *double exponential smoothing*.

2. Select a trend smoothing constant v between 0 and 1. Small values of v give less weight to the current changes in the level of the series and more weight to the past trend. Larger values assign more weight to the most recent trend of the series and less to past trends.

3. Calculate the two components, E_t and T_t, from the time series Y_t beginning at time $t = 2$ as follows:*

$$E_2 = Y_2$$
$$T_2 = Y_2 - Y_1$$
$$E_3 = wY_3 + (1 - w)(E_2 + T_2)$$
$$T_3 = v(E_3 - E_2) + (1 - v)T_2$$
$$\vdots$$
$$E_t = wY_t + (1 - w)(E_{t-1} + T_{t-1})$$
$$T_t = v(E_t - E_{t-1}) + (1 - v)T_{t-1}$$

[*Note:* E_1 and T_1 are not defined.]

Example 6

Applying Holt's Smoothing Method—Annual Sales Data

Problem Refer to the yearly sales data, Example 4 and 5. Using $w = .7$ and $v = .5$, apply Holt's smoothing method to the data for years 1 through 30. Give the values of the smoothed and trend components each year, then plot the data and the smoothing component, E_t, on the same graph.

Solution We used Minitab to perform Holt's calculations and generate the values of E_t and T_t for the annual series. The E_t and T_t values for each year are listed under the SMOOTH and TREND columns, respectively, on the Minitab worksheet, Figure 11. A

↓	C1	C2	C3	C4
	T	SALES	SMOOTH	TREND
1	1	5.8	5.800	4.14658
2	2	4.0	5.784	2.06525
3	3	5.5	6.205	1.24302
4	4	15.6	13.154	4.09629
5	5	25.1	22.745	6.84357
6	6	20.3	23.087	3.59251
7	7	31.4	29.984	5.24481
8	8	48.0	44.169	9.71482
9	9	46.1	48.435	6.99063
10	10	35.9	41.758	0.15666
11	11	35.5	37.424	-2.08837
12	12	53.5	48.051	4.26906
13	13	48.4	49.576	2.89711
14	14	61.6	58.862	6.09154
15	15	65.6	65.406	6.31783
16	16	71.4	71.497	6.20448
17	17	83.4	81.690	8.19890
18	18	93.6	92.487	9.49762
19	19	103.2	102.835	9.92306
20	20	85.4	93.608	0.34763
21	21	86.2	88.527	-2.36667
22	22	89.9	88.778	-1.05763
23	23	89.2	88.756	-0.53974
24	24	99.1	95.835	3.26953
25	25	100.3	99.941	3.68798
26	26	111.7	109.279	6.51272
27	27	102.2	106.277	1.75569
28	28	115.5	113.260	4.36909
29	29	119.2	118.729	4.91893
30	30	125.2	124.734	5.46225

Figure 11

Minitab worksheet with actual and Holt's smoothed ($w = .7$ and $v = .5$) sales revenues, years 1–30

*The calculation begins at time $t = 2$ rather than at $t = 1$ because the first two observations are needed to obtain the first estimate of trend, T_2. As an option, some statistical software packages use simple linear regression to estimate E_1 and T_1; for the model $E(Y_t) = \beta_0 + \beta_1 t$, $E_1 = \hat{\beta}_0$ and $T_1 = \hat{\beta}_1$.

graph of Y_t and E_t is shown in Figure 12. Note that the trend component T_t measures the general upward trend in Y_t.*

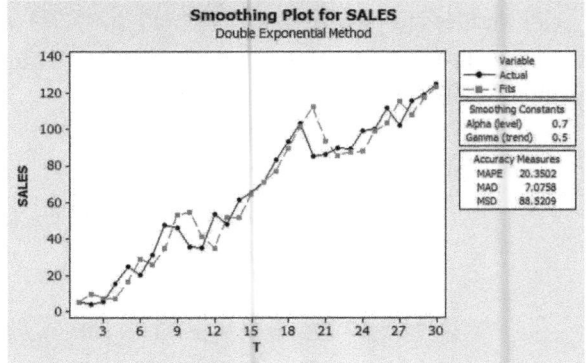

Figure 12

Minitab graph of Holt's smoothed ($w = .7$ and $v = .5$) sales data

Look Back The choice of $v = .5$ gives equal weight to the most recent trend and to past trends in the sales of the firm. The result is that the exponential smoothing component, E_t, provides a smooth, upward-trending description of the firm's sales.

Our objective is to use Holt's exponentially smoothed series to forecast the future values of the time series. For the one-step-ahead forecast, this is accomplished by adding the most recent exponentially smoothed component to the most recent trend component—that is, the forecast at time $(t + 1)$, given observed values up to time t, is

$$F_{t+1} = E_t + T_t$$

The idea is that we are constructing the forecast by combining the most recent smoothed estimate, E_t, with the estimate of the expected increase (or decrease) attributable to trend, T_t.

The forecast for two steps ahead is similar, except that we add estimated trend for *two* periods:

$$F_{t+2} = E_t + 2T_t$$

Similarly, for the k-step-ahead forecast, we add the estimated increase (or decrease) in trend over k periods:

$$F_{t+k} = E_t + kT_t$$

Holt's forecasting methodology is summarized in the box.

Holt's Forecasting Methodology

1. Calculate the exponentially smoothed and trend components, E_t and T_t, for each observed value of $Y_t (t \geq 2)$ using the formulas given in the previous box.

2. Calculate the one-step-ahead forecast using

$$F_{t+1} = E_t + T_t$$

3. Calculate the k-step-ahead forecast using

$$F_{t+k} = E_t + kT_t$$

*Minitab uses simple linear regression to calculate the initial smoothed and trend values.

Example	7

Forecasting with Holt's Method—Annual Sales

Problem Refer to Example 6 and Figure 11, which lists the sales revenue for years 1–30 along with Holt's smoothing components using $w = .7$ and $v = .5$. Apply Holt's forecasting methodology to forecast the firm's annual sales in years 31–35. Compute the forecast errors for each of these five years.

Solution From Figure 11 the smoothed and trend values (highlighted) for the last year (year 30) are $E_{30} = 124.73$ and $T_{30} = 5.46$. Consequently, the forecast for year 31 (the 1-year-ahead forecast) is

$$F_{31} = E_{30} + T_{30} = 124.73 + 5.46 = 130.19$$

The forecast 2 years ahead is

$$F_{32} = E_{30} + 2T_{30} = 124.73 + 2(5.46) = 135.65$$

For years 33–35 we find

$$F_{33} = E_{30} + 3T_{30} = 124.73 + 3(5.46) = 141.11$$
$$F_{34} = E_{30} + 4T_{30} = 124.73 + 4(5.46) = 146.57$$
$$F_{35} = E_{30} + 5T_{30} = 124.73 + 5(5.46) = 152.03$$

The forecasts and forecast errors for these five years are shown in Table 7. Note that unlike the constant exponential smoothing forecasts, Holt's forecast values increase from year 31 to year 35. This upward trend in the forecast is a result of Holt's estimated trend component. Note, also, that the forecast errors fluctuate in magnitude and in sign. This is due to the fact that the actual time series value (sales revenue) does not necessarily increase at the same rate as Holt's forecasted values.

Table 7	Sales Revenues (Years 31–35): Actual vs. Forecast Values		
Year	Actual	Forecast ($w = .7$, $v = .5$)	Forecast Error
31	136.3	130.19	6.11
32	146.8	135.65	11.15
33	150.1	141.11	8.99
34	151.4	146.57	4.83
35	150.9	152.03	−1.13

Look Back The selection of $w = .7$ and $v = .5$ as the smoothing and trend weights for the sales forecasts was based on the objectives of assigning more weight to recent series values in the exponentially smoothed component and of assigning equal weights to the recent and past trend estimates. Most forecasters will try several different combinations of weights when using Holt's forecasting model in order to assess the sensitivity of the forecasts to the choice of weights. The values of w and v that lead to the smallest forecast errors are typically used to make future forecasts.

Now Work Exercise 25b

In the following section, we demonstrate how to use the forecast errors to develop a single measure of forecast accuracy. These measures can then be used to compare and contrast different forecasting methodologies.

Exercises 23–31

Learning the Mechanics

23 How does the choice of the smoothing constant w impact an exponentially smoothed forecast?

24 Refer to Exercise 4. The table with the prices for product
NW A for the four quarters of last year is reproduced at right. Holt's smoothing method with $w = .2$ and $v = .6$ was applied to the data.

a. Find the missing trend value for Quarter 3.

Quarter	A	Smoothed Value	Trend
1	3.25	—	—
2	3.50	3.50	0.25
3	3.90	3.78	?
4	4.25	?	0.29

b. Find the missing smoothed value for Quarter 4.
c. Give the Holt's forecast for the price in Quarter 5.

Applying the Concepts—Basic

25 Annual U.S. beer production. Refer to Exercise 7 and the data on U.S. beer production (in millions of barrels) for the years 1980–2010.

a. Use the 1980–2007 values to forecast the 2008–2010 production, using simple exponential smoothing with $w = .3$. Repeat with $w = .7$.

b. Use Holt's model with $w = .7$ and $v = .3$ to forecast the 2008–2010 production. Repeat with $w = .3$ and $v = .7$.

26 Quarterly single-family housing starts. Refer to the quarterly housing start series, Exercise 8. Suppose you want to forecast the number of new housing starts in 2012 using data for 2010 and 2011.

a. Calculate the exponentially smoothed values for 2010 and 2011 using $w = .6$.

b. Plot the housing starts series and the exponentially smoothed series on the same graph.

c. Use the exponentially smoothed data from 2010–2011 to forecast the quarterly number of housing starts in 2012.

27 Consumer Price Index. The CPI measures the increase (or decrease) in the prices of goods and services relative to a base year. The CPI for the years 1990–2010 (using 1984 as a base period) is shown in the table below.

a. Graph the time series. Do you detect a long-term trend?

b. Calculate and plot the exponentially smoothed series for the CPI using a smoothing constant of $w = .4$. Use

the exponentially smoothed values to forecast the CPI in 2011.

c. Use Holt's forecasting model with trend to forecast the CPI in 2011. Use smoothing constants $w = .4$ and $v = .5$.

28 OPEC crude oil imports. Refer to the annual OPEC oil import data, Exercise 21.

a. Use the exponentially smoothed ($w = .9$) series you constructed in Exercise 21a to forecast OPEC oil imports in 2010.

b. Forecast OPEC oil imports in 2010 using the Holt's forecasting model with smoothing constants $w = .3$ and $v = .8$.

c. Calculate the errors of the forecasts, parts **a** and **b**. Which method yields the smallest forecast error?

Applying the Concepts—Intermediate

29 S&P 500 Stock Index. Refer to the quarterly Standard & Poor's 500 stock market index, Exercise 22.

a. Use exponential smoothing with $w = .7$ to smooth the series from 2004 through 2010. Then forecast the quarterly values in 2011 using *only* the information through the fourth quarter of 2010.

b. Repeat part **a** using $w = .3$.

30 S&P 500 Stock Index (cont'd). Refer to Exercise 29. Suppose you want to use only the 2009–2010 S&P values to forecast the quarterly 2011 values. Calculate the forecasts using Holt's model with $w = .3$ and $v = .5$. Repeat with $w = .7$ and $v = .5$.

31 Monthly gold prices. The fluctuation of gold prices is a reflection of the strength or weakness of the U.S. dollar. The table below shows monthly gold prices from January 2005 to December 2011.

a. Use exponential smoothing with $w = .5$ to calculate monthly smoothed values from 2005 to 2010. Then forecast the monthly gold prices for 2011.

b. Calculate 12 one-step-ahead forecasts for 2011 by updating the exponentially smoothed values with each month's actual value and then forecasting the next month's value.

c. Repeat parts **a–b** using Holt's method with $w = .5$ and $v = .5$.

Year	CPI	Year	CPI
1990	125.8	2001	177.1
1991	129.1	2002	179.9
1992	132.8	2003	184.0
1993	136.8	2004	188.9
1994	147.8	2005	195.3
1995	152.4	2006	201.6
1996	156.9	2007	207.3
1997	160.5	2008	215.3
1998	163.0	2009	214.5
1999	166.6	2010	218.1
2000	171.5		

Source: US Department of Commerce.

Data for Exercise 31

Month	2005	2006	2007	2008	2009	2010	2011
Jan	424.2	549.9	631.2	889.6	858.7	1,118.0	1,356.4
Feb	423.4	555.0	664.7	922.3	943.2	1,095.4	1,372.7
Mar	434.2	557.1	654.9	968.4	924.3	1,113.3	1,424.0
Apr	428.9	610.6	679.4	909.7	890.2	1,148.7	1,473.8
May	421.9	676.5	666.9	888.7	928.6	1,205.4	1,510.4
Jun	430.7	596.2	655.5	889.5	945.7	1,232.9	1,528.7
Jul	424.5	633.8	665.3	939.8	934.2	1,193.0	1,572.8
Aug	437.9	632.6	665.4	839.0	949.4	1,215.8	1,755.8
Sep	456.0	598.2	712.7	829.9	996.6	1,271.1	1,771.9
Oct	469.9	585.8	754.6	806.6	1,043.2	1,342.0	1,665.2
Nov	476.7	627.8	806.3	760.9	1,127.0	1,369.9	1,739.0
Dec	509.8	629.8	803.2	816.1	1,134.7	1,390.6	1,652.3

Sources: Standard & Poor's.

6 Measuring Forecast Accuracy: MAD and RMSE

As demonstrated in Example 5, forecast error (i.e., the difference between the actual time series value and its forecast) can be used to evaluate the accuracy of the forecast. Knowledge of a forecast's accuracy aids in the selection of both the forecasting methodology to be utilized and the parameters of the forecast formula (e.g., the weights in the exponentially smoothed or Holt forecasts). Three popular measures of forecast accuracy, all based on forecast errors, are the *mean absolute deviation (MAD)*, the *mean absolute percentage error (MAPE)*, and the *root mean squared error (RMSE)* of the forecasts. Their formulas are given in the box.

Measures of Forecast Accuracy for *m* Forecasts

Assume time series data for $t = 1, 2, 3, \ldots, n$ are used to make forecasts for the periods $t = n + 1, n + 2, \ldots, n + m$.

1. **Mean absolute deviation (MAD)**

$$\text{MAD} = \frac{\sum\limits_{t=n+1}^{n+m} |Y_t - F_t|}{m}$$

2. **Mean absolute percentage error (MAPE)**

$$\text{MAPE} = \frac{\sum\limits_{t=n+1}^{n+m} \left| \frac{(Y_t - F_t)}{Y_t} \right|}{m} \times 100$$

3. **Root mean squared error (RMSE)**

$$\text{RMSE} = \sqrt{\frac{\sum\limits_{t=n+1}^{n+m} (Y_t - F_t)^2}{m}}$$

Note that all three measures require one or more actual values of the time series against which to compare the forecasts. Thus, we can either wait several time periods until the observed values are available, or we can hold out several of the values at the end of the time series, not using them to model the time series, but saving them for evaluating the forecasts obtained from the model.

Example 8

Comparing Measures of Forecast Accuracy— Annual Sales

Problem Refer to the annual sales data of Examples 6 and 7. We want to use the data for all 35 years to forecast annual sales for years 36–40. Consider three alternative forecasting models: exponential smoothing with $w = .3$, exponential smoothing with $w = .7$, and Holt's method with $w = .7$ and $v = .5$. Minitab was used to obtain the forecasts for these alternative models. The Minitab printouts shown in Figures 13a–c give the forecasts (highlighted) for all three models. Suppose the actual sales values (in thousands of dollars) for years 36–40 are 150.2, 161.7, 159.3, 168.5, and 170.4, respectively. Find measures of forecast accuracy (MAD, MAPE, and RMSE) for each of the three forecasting models and use this information to evaluate the models.

Solution For ease of notation, we will number the forecasting models as follows.

Model 1: Exponential smoothing ($w = .3$)
Model 2: Exponential smoothing ($w = .7$)
Model 3: Holt's method ($w = .7, v = .5$)

Single Exponential Smoothing for SALES

```
Data     SALES
Length   35

Smoothing Constant
Alpha  0.3

Accuracy Measures
MAPE    21.485
MAD     13.187
MSD    249.068

Forecasts
Period  Forecast    Lower    Upper
36       143.188  110.879  175.497
37       143.188  110.879  175.497
38       143.188  110.879  175.497
39       143.188  110.879  175.497
40       143.188  110.879  175.497
```

Figure 13a

Minitab forecasts of annual sales—exponential smoothing $(w = .3)$

Single Exponential Smoothing for SALES

```
Data     SALES
Length   35

Smoothing Constant
Alpha  0.7

Accuracy Measures
MAPE    15.1498
MAD      8.0579
MSD     95.2252

Forecasts
Period  Forecast    Lower    Upper
36       150.726  130.985  170.467
37       150.726  130.985  170.467
38       150.726  130.985  170.467
39       150.726  130.985  170.467
40       150.726  130.985  170.467
```

Figure 13b

Minitab forecasts of annual sales—exponential smoothing $(w = .7)$

Double Exponential Smoothing for SALES

```
Data     SALES
Length   35

Smoothing Constants
Alpha (level)  0.7
Gamma (trend)  0.5

Accuracy Measures
MAPE    19.3874
MAD      7.0010
MSD     81.4953

Forecasts
Period  Forecast    Lower    Upper
36       155.474  138.322  172.626
37       157.713  136.058  179.368
38       159.952  133.404  186.501
39       162.192  130.539  193.844
40       164.431  127.552  201.310
```

Figure 13c

Minitab forecasts of annual sales—Holt's method $(w = .7$ and $v = .5)$

The forecasts for the three models as well as forecast errors are listed in the Excel workbook, Figure 14. These forecast errors are used to find the MAD, MAPE, and RMSE measures of forecast accuracy for each of the three models.

For example, for Model 1:

$$\text{MAD}_1 = \frac{|7.01| + |18.51| + |16.11| + |25.31| + |27.21|}{5} = 18.83$$

$$\text{MAPE}_1 = \left\{ \frac{\left|\frac{7.01}{150.2}\right| + \left|\frac{18.51}{161.7}\right| + \left|\frac{16.11}{159.3}\right| + \left|\frac{25.31}{168.5}\right| + \left|\frac{27.21}{170.4}\right|}{5} \right\} \times 100 = 11.44$$

$$\text{RMSE}_1 = \sqrt{\frac{(7.01)^2 + (18.51)^2 + (16.11)^2 + (25.31)^2 + (27.21)^2}{5}} = 20.16$$

	A	B	C	D	E	F	G	H	I	J	K
1	T	SALES	MODEL 1	ERROR 1		MODEL 2	ERROR 2		MODEL 3	ERROR 3	
2	36	150.2	143.19	7.01		150.73	-0.53		155.47	-5.27	
3	37	161.7	143.19	18.51		150.73	10.97		157.71	3.99	
4	38	159.3	143.19	16.11		150.73	8.57		159.95	-0.65	
5	39	168.5	143.19	25.31		150.73	17.77		162.19	6.31	
6	40	170.4	143.19	27.21		150.73	19.67		164.43	5.97	
7											
8		MAD	18.83			11.50			4.44		
9		MAPE	11.44			6.92			2.73		
10		RMSE	20.16			13.39			4.89		
11											
12											

Figure 14

Excel workbook with measures of annual sales forecast accuracy

The formulas for MAD, MAPE, and RMSE were programmed into Excel. The results are shown (highlighted) in Figure 14. For Model 2, $MAD_2 = 11.50$, $MAPE_2 = 6.92$, and $RMSE_2 = 13.39$. For Model 3, $MAD_3 = 4.44$, $MAPE_3 = 2.73$, and $RMSE_3 = 4.89$.

You can see that Model 3 has the smallest MAD as well as the smallest MAPE and the smallest RMSE. Of the three forecasting models, then, Model 3 (Holt's method with $w = .7$ and $v = .5$) yields the most accurate predictions of future annual sales.

Look Back We expect Holt's method to yield more accurate forecasts for annual sales because it explicitly accounts for trends in the sales data. The exponential smoothing forecasts do not account for any increasing or decreasing trends in the data; hence, they are the same for all five forecasted years. The accuracy of all three forecasting methods, however, will decrease the further we forecast into the future.

Now Work Exercise 32

[*Note*: Most statistical software packages will automatically compute the values of MAPE, MAD, and RMSE (equivalent to the square root of the *mean squared deviation, MSD*) for all *n* observations in the data set. For example, these statistics are shown in the middle of the Minitab printouts, Figures 13a–c.]

Criteria such as MAPE, MAD, and RMSE for assessing forecast accuracy require special care in interpretation. The number of time periods included in the evaluation is critical to the decision about which forecasting model is preferred. The choice depends on how many time periods ahead the analyst plans to forecast. With *N* time periods in your data, a good rule of thumb is to forecast ahead no more than *N*/2 time periods. Remember, however, that long-term forecasts are generally less accurate than short-term forecasts.

We conclude this section with a comment. A major disadvantage of forecasting with smoothing techniques (exponential smoothing or Holt's model) is that no measure of the forecast error (or reliability) is known *prior* to observing the future value. Although forecast errors can be calculated *after* the future values of the time series have been observed (as in Example 8), we prefer to have some measure of the accuracy of the forecast *before* the actual values are observed. One option is to compute forecasts and forecast errors for all *n* observations in the data set and use these "past" forecast errors to estimate the standard deviation of all forecast errors (i.e., the *standard error of the forecast*). A rough estimate of this standard error is the value of RMSE, and an approximate 95% prediction interval for any future forecast is

$$F_t \pm 2(\text{RMSE})$$

[An interval like this is shown at the bottom of the Minitab printouts, Figures 13a–c.] However, because the theoretical distributional properties of the forecast errors with smoothing methods (exponential smoothing or Holt's method) are unknown, many analysts regard smoothing methods as descriptive procedures rather than as inferential ones.

Predictions with inferential regression models are accompanied by well-known measures of reliability. The standard errors of the predicted values allow us to construct 95% prediction intervals. We discuss an inferential time series forecasting model in the next section.

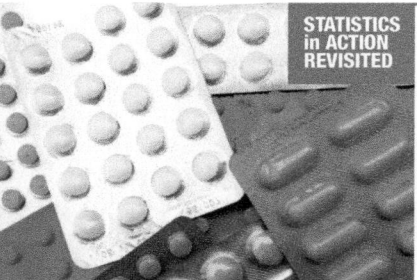

Forecasting with Exponential Smoothing

Recall that a pharmaceutical company hired consultants at Rutgers University to forecast monthly sales of a new brand of cold medicine called Coldex. The company provided monthly data on Coldex sales for the first 2 years of the product's life and desires forecasts of sales for the first 3 months of the third year. (The data are saved in the **COLDEX** file.) One forecasting model considered by the consultants was an exponential smoothing model with a smoothing constant of $w = .7$. Minitab was used to find the smoothed values of the monthly series. The Minitab plot of both the actual monthly sales and smoothed sales values is shown in Figure SIA1, followed by the exponentially smoothed forecasts in Figure SIA2.

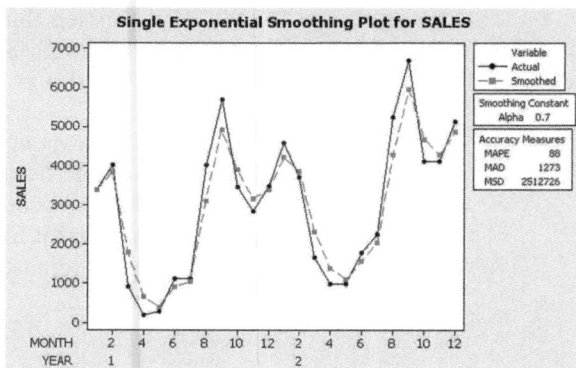

Figure SIA1

Minitab plot of monthly Coldex sales with exponentially smoothed values ($w = .7$)

The exponentially smoothed sales forecast for each of the first 3 months of year 3 is the smoothed value for the last month of the series (month 24). This value, highlighted on Figure SIA2, is 4,870 thousand dollars. Minitab also gives approximate 95% confidence bounds around the forecast. The interval (highlighted on the printout) is (1,750, 7,989). Thus, we are (approximately) 95% confident that the actual sales for the month will be between 1,750 and 7,989 thousand dollars. This wide interval was deemed unusable by the pharmaceutical company; consequently, the consultants searched for a better forecasting model. One of these models is presented in the next Statistics in Action Revisited.

Single Exponential Smoothing for SALES

```
Data     SALES
Length   24


Smoothing Constant

Alpha  0.7


Accuracy Measures

MAPE        88
MAD       1273
MSD    2512726


Forecasts
```

Period	Forecast	Lower	Upper
25	4869.91	1750.49	7989.34
26	4869.91	1750.49	7989.34
27	4869.91	1750.49	7989.34

Figure SIA2

Minitab forecasts of monthly Coldex sales using exponential smoothing ($w = .7$)

Data Set: COLDEX

Exercises 32–37

Applying the Concepts—Basic

32 Annual U.S. beer production. Refer to the beer production forecasts, Exercise 25. In part **a** you obtained forecasts of 2008–2010 beer production using exponential smoothing with $w = .3$ and $w = .7$.

USBEER

   a. Calculate the forecast errors for the $w = .3$ exponentially smoothed forecasts.

   b. Calculate the forecast errors for the $w = .7$ exponentially smoothed forecasts.

   c. Calculate MAD, MAPE, and RMSE for the exponential smoothing forecasts using $w = .3$.

   d. Calculate MAD, MAPE, and RMSE for the exponential smoothing forecasts using $w = .7$.

   e. Refer to parts **c** and **d.** Which forecast method do you recommend?

33 Annual U.S. beer production (cont'd). Refer to the beer production forecasts, Exercise 25. In part **b** you obtained forecasts of 2008–2010 beer production using Holt's method with $(w = .3, v = .7)$ and $(w = .7, v = .3)$.

USBEER

   a. Calculate the forecast errors for the $w = .3, v = .7$ Holt forecasts.

   b. Calculate the forecast errors for the $w = .7, v = .3$ Holt forecasts.

   c. Calculate MAD, MAPE, and RMSE for the $w = .3, v = .7$ Holt forecasts.

   d. Calculate MAD, MAPE, and RMSE for the $w = .7, v = .3$ Holt forecasts.

   e. Refer to parts **c** and **d.** Which forecast method do you recommend?

34 S&P 500 Stock Index. Refer to your exponential smoothing forecasts of the quarterly S&P 500 for 2011, Exercise 29.

SP500

   a. Calculate MAD, MAPE, and RMSE for the forecasts with $w = .7$.

   b. Calculate MAD, MAPE, and RMSE for the forecasts with $w = .3$.

   c. Compare MAD, MAPE, and RMSE for the two simple exponential smoothing forecast models. Which model leads to more accurate forecasts?

35 S&P 500 Stock Index (cont'd). Refer to your Holt forecasts of the quarterly S&P 500 for 2011, Exercise 30.

SP500

   a. Calculate MAD, MAPE, and RMSE for the forecasts with $w = .3$ and $v = .5$.

   b. Calculate MAD, MAPE, and RMSE for the forecasts with $w = .7$ and $v = .5$.

   c. Compare MAD, MAPE, and RMSE for the two Holt forecasts models. Which model leads to more accurate forecasts?

Applying the Concepts—Intermediate

36 Monthly gold prices. Refer to the monthly gold prices, Exercise 31. Two models were used to forecast the monthly 2011 gold prices: an exponential smoothing model with $w = .5$ and a Holt model with $w = .5$ and $v = .5$.

GOLDMN

   a. Use MAD, MAPE, and RMSE criteria to evaluate the two models' accuracy for forecasting the monthly 2011 values using the 2005–2010 data.

   b. Use the MAD, MAPE, and RMSE criteria to evaluate the two models' accuracy when making the 12 one-step-ahead forcasts, updating the models with each month's actual value before forecasting the next month's value.

37 U.S. school enrollments. The next table reports annual U.S. school enrollment (in thousands) for the period 1990–2010.

ENROLL

Year	Enrollment	Year	Enrollment
1990	60,267	2001	69,936
1991	61,605	2002	71,215
1992	62,686	2003	71,442
1993	63,241	2004	71,688
1994	63,986	2005	72,075
1995	64,764	2006	73,318
1996	65,743	2007	73,685
1997	66,470	2008	74,079
1998	66,983	2009	77,288
1999	67,667	2010	78,519
2000	68,146		

Source: United States Census Bureau.

   a. Use the 1990 to 2007 enrollments and simple exponential smoothing to forecast the 2008–2010 school enrollments. Use $w = .8$.

   b. Use Holt's method with $w = .8$ and $v = .7$ to forecast the 2008–2010 enrollments.

   c. Apply the MAD, MAPE, and RMSE criteria to evaluate the two forecasting models of parts **a** and **b.** Which model is better? Why?

7   Forecasting Trends: Simple Linear Regression

Perhaps the simplest **inferential forecasting model** is one with which you are familiar: the simple linear regression model. A straight-line model is used to relate the time series, Y_t, to time, t, and the least squares line is used to forecast future values of Y_t.

Suppose a firm is interested in forecasting its sales revenues for each of the next 5 years. To make such forecasts and assess their reliability, a time series model must be constructed. Refer again to the yearly sales data for a firm's 35 years of operation

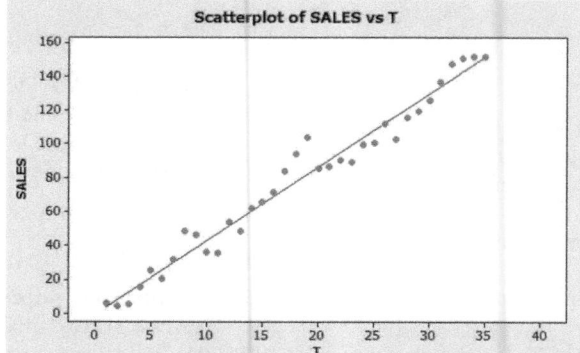

Figure 15

Minitab scatterplot of annual sales with least squares line

given in Table 5. A Minitab plot of the data (Figure 15) reveals a linearly increasing trend, so the model

$$E(Y_t) = \beta_0 + \beta_1 t$$

seems plausible for the secular trend. We fit the model to the data using SPSS; the resulting printout is shown in Figure 16. The least squares model (highlighted on the printout) is

$$\hat{Y}_t = \hat{\beta}_0 + \hat{\beta}_1 t = -.333 + 4.325t \quad \text{with} \quad R^2 = .969$$

(This least squares line is shown on Figure 15.)

We can now forecast sales for years 36–40. The forecasts of sales and the corresponding 95% prediction intervals are shown on the SPSS spreadsheet, Figure 17. For example, for $t = 36$, we have

$$\hat{Y}_{36} = 155.38$$

Model Summary

Mode l	R	R Square	Adjusted R Square	Std. Error of the Estimate
1	.985[a]	.969	.969	7.9863

a. Predictors: (Constant), T

ANOVA[b]

Model		Sum of Squares	df	Mean Square	F	Sig.
1	Regression	66789.029	1	66789.029	1047.172	.000[a]
	Residual	2104.753	33	63.780		
	Total	68893.782	34			

a. Predictors: (Constant), T

b. Dependent Variable: SALES

Figure 16

SPSS least squares regression of annual sales

Coefficients[a]

Model		Unstandardized Coefficients		Standardized Coefficients		
		B	Std. Error	Beta	t	Sig.
1	(Constant)	-.333	2.759		-.121	.905
	T	4.325	.134	.985	32.360	.000

a. Dependent Variable: SALES

Figure 17

SPSS spreadsheet with 95% prediction intervals for annual sales

	T	PRED_SALES	LOWER95CLI	UPPER95CLI
1	36	155.38	138.19	172.57
2	37	159.70	142.43	176.97
3	38	164.03	146.68	181.38
4	39	168.35	150.91	185.79
5	40	172.68	155.15	190.21

with the 95% prediction interval (138.2, 172.6). Similarly, we can obtain the forecasts and prediction intervals for years 37–40. Although it is not easily perceptible in the printout, the prediction intervals widen as we attempt to forecast further into the future. This agrees with the intuitive notion that short-term forecasts should be more reliable than long-term forecasts.

There are two problems associated with forecasting time series using a least squares model.

Problem 1

We are using the least squares model to forecast values outside the region of observation of the independent variable, t — that is, we are forecasting for values of t between 36 and 40, but the observed sales are for t-values between 1 and 35. It is risky to use a least squares regression model for prediction outside the experimental region.

Problem 1 obviously cannot be avoided. Because forecasting always involves predictions about the future values of a time series, some or all of the independent variables will probably be outside the region of observation on which the model was developed. It is important that the forecaster recognize the dangers of this type of prediction. If underlying conditions change drastically after the model is estimated (e.g., if federal price controls are imposed on the firm's products during the 36th year of operation), then for any forecasting model the forecasts and their confidence intervals are probably useless.

Problem 2

Although the straight-line model may adequately describe the secular trend of the sales, we have not attempted to build any cyclical effects into the model. Thus, the effect of inflationary and recessionary periods will be to increase the error of the forecasts because the model does not anticipate such periods.

Fortunately, the forecaster often has some degree of control over problem 2, as we demonstrate in the remainder of the chapter.

In forming the prediction intervals for the forecasts, we made the standard regression assumptions about the random error component of the model. We assumed the errors have mean 0, constant variance, and normal probability distributions, and are *independent*. The latter assumption is dubious in time series models, especially in the presence of short-term trends. Often, if a year's value lies above the secular trend line, the next year's value has a tendency to be above the line also — that is, the errors tend to be correlated (see Figure 15).

We discuss how to deal with correlated errors in Section 9. For now, we can characterize the simple linear regression forecasting method as useful for discerning secular trends, but it is probably too simplistic for most time series. And, as with all forecasting methods, the simple linear regression forecasts should be applied only over the short term.

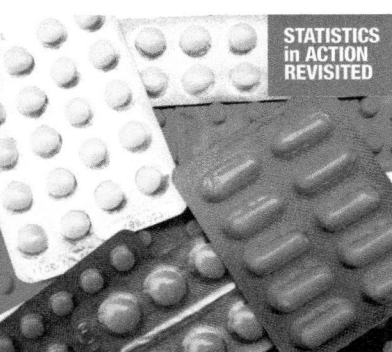

Forecasting with Simple Linear Regression

A second model considered by consultants to forecast monthly sales of a new cold medicine (Coldex) was a simple linear regression model with time (t) as the independent variable, where $t = 1, 2, 3, \ldots, 24$. The Minitab graph of the least squares line is shown in Figure SIA3, followed by the simple linear regression printout in Figure SIA4.

Note that the p-value for testing the slope coefficient is .047. Thus, at $\alpha = .05$, the model is statistically useful for predicting monthly sales. However, the coefficient of determination is low ($R^2 = .168$); only about 17% of the sample variation in monthly sales can be explained by the linear time trend.

The simple linear forecasts for each of the first 3 months of year 3 are shown on the Minitab worksheet, Figure SIA5. Minitab also gives a 95% prediction interval for

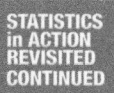

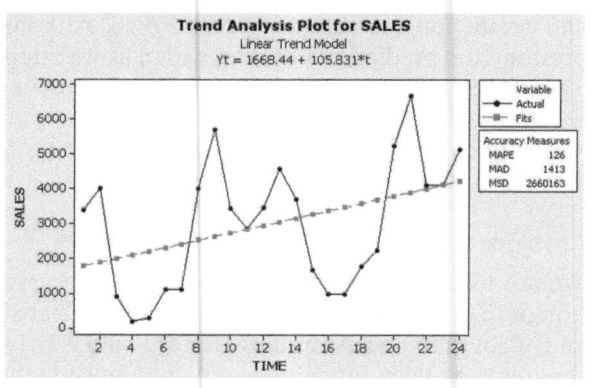

Figure SIA3

Minitab plot of least squares line for forecasting monthly Coldex sales

---

Regression Analysis: SALES versus TIME

```
The regression equation is
SALES = 1668 + 106 TIME


Predictor    Coef   SE Coef     T      P
Constant   1668.4    717.8    2.32   0.030
TIME       105.83    50.23    2.11   0.047


S = 1703.52   R-Sq = 16.8%   R-Sq(adj) = 13.0%


Analysis of Variance

Source           DF        SS        MS      F      P
Regression        1  12880305  12880305   4.44  0.047
Residual Error   22  63843919   2901996
Total            23  76724223
```

Figure SIA4

Minitab simple linear regression printout for the linear trend forecasting model

↓	C1	C2	C3	C4	C5	C6
	YEAR	MONTH	TIME	FORECAST	PL95LOW	PL95UPP
1	3	1	25	4314.22	480.528	8147.92
2	3	2	26	4420.06	549.731	8290.38
3	3	3	27	4525.89	616.500	8435.27

Figure SIA5

Minitab worksheet with simple linear regression forecasts of monthly sales

each forecast. The intervals for months 25, 26, and 27 are (480.5, 8,147.9), (549.7, 8,290.4), and (616.5, 8,435.3), respectively. For the first month of year 3 (i.e., month 25), we are 95% confident that the actual sales will fall between 480.5 and 8,147.9 thousand dollars. Similar interpretations are made for the other two forecasts.

As with the exponential smoothing model, these intervals were too wide to be of practical use by the pharmaceutical company. How can the forecasting model be improved? Examine Figure SIA3 and note the cyclical trends in the monthly sales data. Neither the exponential smoothing model nor the linear regression model account for this cyclical variation. A forecasting model is needed that explicitly accounts for such trends. Such a model is presented in the next Statistics in Action Revisited.

Data Set: COLDEX

8 Seasonal Regression Models

Many time series have distinct seasonal patterns. Retail sales are usually highest around Christmas, spring, and fall, with lulls in the winter and summer periods. Energy usage is highest in summer and winter, and lowest in spring and fall. Teenage unemployment rises in summer months when schools are not in session and falls near Christmas when many businesses hire part-time help.

Multiple regression models can be used to forecast future values of a time series with strong seasonal components. To accomplish this, the mean value of the time series,

$E(Y_t)$, is given a mathematical form that describes both the secular trend and seasonal components of the time series. Although the **seasonal model** can assume a wide variety of mathematical forms, the use of dummy variables to describe seasonal differences is common.

For example, consider the power load data for a Southern utility company shown in Table 8. Data were obtained for each quarter from 2001 through 2012. A model that combines the expected growth in usage and the seasonal component is

$$E(Y_t) = \beta_0 + \beta_1 t + \beta_2 Q_1 + \beta_3 Q_2 + \beta_4 Q_3$$

where

$t = $ Time period, ranging from $t = 1$ for Quarter 1 of 2001 to

$t = 48$ for Quarter 4 of 2012

$$Q_1 = \begin{cases} 1 & \text{if Quarter 1} \\ 0 & \text{if Quarter 2, 3, or 4} \end{cases}$$

$$Q_2 = \begin{cases} 1 & \text{if Quarter 2} \\ 0 & \text{if Quarter 1, 3, or 4} \end{cases}$$

$$Q_3 = \begin{cases} 1 & \text{if Quarter 3} \\ 0 & \text{if Quarter 1, 2, or 4} \end{cases}$$

The Minitab printout in Figure 18 shows the least squares fit of this model to the data in Table 8.

Note that the model appears to fit well, with $R^2 = .914$, indicating that the model accounts for about 91% of the sample variability in power loads over the 12-year period. The global $F = 114.88$ (p-value $= .000$) strongly supports the hypothesis that the model has predictive utility. The model standard deviation of 7.86 indicates that the

Table 8	Quarterly Power Loads (megawatts) for a Southern Utility Company, 2001–2012				
Year	Quarter	Power Load	Year	Quarter	Power Load
2001	1	68.8	2007	1	130.6
	2	65.0		2	116.8
	3	88.4		3	144.2
	4	69.0		4	123.3
2002	1	83.6	2008	1	142.3
	2	69.7		2	124.0
	3	90.2		3	146.1
	4	72.5		4	135.5
2003	1	106.8	2009	1	147.1
	2	89.2		2	119.3
	3	110.7		3	138.2
	4	91.7		4	127.6
2004	1	108.6	2010	1	143.4
	2	98.9		2	134.0
	3	120.1		3	159.6
	4	102.1		4	135.1
2005	1	113.1	2011	1	149.5
	2	94.2		2	123.3
	3	120.5		3	154.4
	4	107.4		4	139.4
2006	1	116.2	2012	1	151.6
	2	104.4		2	133.7
	3	131.7		3	154.5
	4	117.9		4	135.1

Data Set: POWER

Regression Analysis: LOAD versus T, Q1, Q2, Q3

```
The regression equation is
LOAD = 70.5 + 1.64 T + 13.7 Q1 - 3.74 Q2 + 18.5 Q3

Predictor      Coef   SE Coef      T       P
Constant     70.509     3.116   22.63   0.000
T           1.63621   0.08214   19.92   0.000
Q1           13.659     3.217    4.25   0.000
Q2           -3.736     3.212   -1.16   0.251
Q3           18.470     3.209    5.76   0.000


S = 7.85795   R-Sq = 91.4%   R-Sq(adj) = 90.6%

Analysis of Variance

Source          DF        SS       MS        F       P
Regression       4   28375.0   7093.7   114.88   0.000
Residual Error  43    2655.1     61.7
Total           47   31030.1
```

Figure 18

Minitab least squares fit to quarterly power load model

model predictions will usually be accurate to within approximately $\pm 2(7.86)$, or about ± 16 megawatts. Furthermore, $\hat{\beta}_1 = 1.64$ indicates an estimated average growth in load of 1.64 megawatts per quarter. Finally, the seasonal dummy variables have the following interpretations:*

$\hat{\beta}_2 = 13.66$ Quarter 1 loads average 13.66 megawatts more than Quarter 4 loads.

$\hat{\beta}_3 = -3.74$ Quarter 2 loads average 3.74 megawatts less than Quarter 4 loads.

$\hat{\beta}_4 = 18.47$ Quarter 3 loads average 18.47 megawatts more than Quarter 4 loads.

Thus, as expected, winter and summer loads exceed spring and fall loads, with the peak occurring during the summer months.

In order to forecast the 2013 power loads, we calculate the predicted value $\hat{Y}_k$ for $k = 49, 50, 51$, and 52, at the same time substituting the dummy variable appropriate for each quarter. Thus, for 2013,

$$\hat{Y}_{\text{Quarter 1}} = \hat{\beta}_0 + \hat{\beta}_1(49) + \hat{\beta}_2 = 70.51 + 1.636(49) + 13.66 = 164.3$$

$$\hat{Y}_{\text{Quarter 2}} = \hat{\beta}_0 + \hat{\beta}_1(50) + \hat{\beta}_3 = 148.6$$

$$\hat{Y}_{\text{Quarter 3}} = \hat{\beta}_0 + \hat{\beta}_1(51) + \hat{\beta}_4 = 172.4$$

$$\hat{Y}_{\text{Quarter 4}} = \hat{\beta}_0 + \hat{\beta}_1(52) = 155.6$$

The predicted values and 95% prediction intervals (highlighted) are given on the Minitab worksheet, Figure 19a, and graphed in Figure 19b. Also shown in Figure 19a are the actual 2013 quarterly power loads. Notice that all 2013 power loads fall inside the forecast intervals.

The seasonal model used to forecast the power loads is an **additive model** because the secular trend component $(\beta_1 t)$ is added to the seasonal component $(\beta_2 Q_1 + \beta_3 Q_2 + \beta_4 Q_3)$ to form the model. A **multiplicative model** would have the same form, except that the dependent variable would be the natural logarithm of power load; that is,

$$\ln Y_t = \beta_0 + \beta_1 t + \beta_2 Q_1 + \beta_3 Q_2 + \beta_4 Q_3 + \varepsilon$$

Figure 19a

Minitab worksheet with quarterly power load forecasts

QTRPOWERFORECASTS.MTP ***

↓	C1	C2	C3	C4	C5	C6	C7	C8	C9	C10
	T	YEAR	QTR	LOAD	Q1	Q2	Q3	PRED	LOWER95CLI	UPPER95CLI
1	49	2013	1	151.3	1	0	0	164.341	147.294	181.389
2	50	2013	2	132.9	0	1	0	148.583	131.536	165.630
3	51	2013	3	160.5	0	0	1	172.425	155.378	189.472
4	52	2013	4	161.0	0	0	0	155.591	138.544	172.639

*These interpretations assume a fixed value of t. In practical terms this is unrealistic, because each quarter is associated with a different value of t. Nevertheless, the coefficients of the seasonal dummy variables provide insight into the seasonality of these time series data.

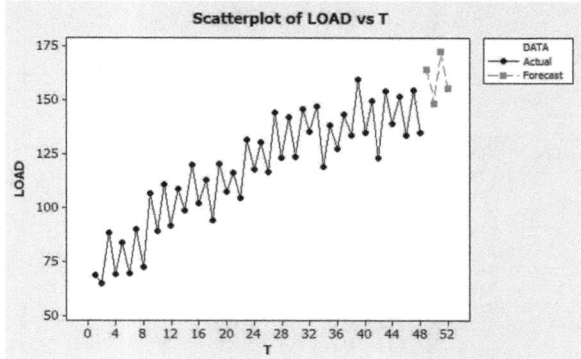

Figure 19b

Minitab graph of quarterly power loads with forecasts

To see the multiplicative nature of this model, we take the antilogarithm of both sides of the equation to get

$$Y_t = \exp\{\beta_0 + \beta_1 t + \beta_2 Q_1 + \beta_3 Q_2 + \beta_4 Q_3 + \varepsilon\}$$
$$= \underbrace{\exp\{\beta_0\}}_{\textbf{Constant}} \underbrace{\exp\{\beta_1 t\}}_{\substack{\textbf{Secular}\\\textbf{trend}}} \underbrace{\exp\{\beta_2 Q_1 + \beta_3 Q_2 + \beta_4 Q_3\}}_{\substack{\textbf{Seasonal}\\\textbf{component}}} \underbrace{\exp\{\varepsilon\}}_{\substack{\textbf{Residual}\\\textbf{component}}}$$

The multiplicative model often provides a better forecasting model when the time series is changing at an increasing rate over time.

When time series data are observed monthly, a regression forecasting model needs 11 dummy variables to describe monthly seasonality; three dummy variables can be used (as in the previous models) if the seasonal changes are hypothesized to occur quarterly. In general, this approach to seasonal modeling requires one dummy variable fewer than the number of seasonal changes expected to occur.

There are approaches besides the regression dummy variable method for forecasting seasonal time series. Trigonometric (sine and cosine) terms can be used in regression models to model periodicity. Other time series models, such as Holt's exponential smoothing model, do not use the regression approach at all, and there are various methods for adding seasonal components to these models. For example, the **Holt-Winters forecasting model** is a modification of Holt's model that includes a seasonality component.

We have chosen to discuss the regression approach because it makes use of the important modeling concepts and because the regression forecasts are accompanied by prediction intervals that provide some measure of the forecast reliability. While most other methods do not have explicit measures of reliability, many have proved their merit by providing good forecasts for particular applications. Consult the references at the end of the chapter for details of other seasonal models.

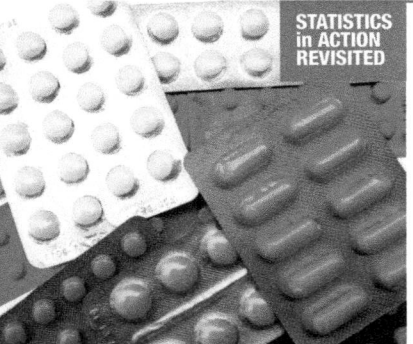

STATISTICS in ACTION REVISITED

Forecasting with a Seasonal Regression Model

The consultants hired by the pharmaceutical company detected a cyclical trend in the monthly sales data. They noted that sales of the cold medicine were higher during the winter and summer months as compared to the other months over the 2-year period. To account for this seasonal trend, they created 11 dummy variables ($x_1, x_2, \ldots, x_{11}$) for the 12 months of the year. The seasonal forecasting model takes the form

$$E(Y_t) = \beta_0 + \beta_1 t + \beta_2 x_1 + \beta_3 x_2 + \beta_4 x_3 + \beta_5 x_4 + \beta_6 x_5 + \beta_7 x_6 + \beta_8 x_7 + \beta_9 x_8$$
$$+ \beta_{10} x_9 + \beta_{11} x_{10} + \beta_{12} x_{11}$$

The Minitab regression printout for the model is shown in Figure SIA6, followed by the model forecasts in Figure SIA7. The global F-test (p-value $= .000$) indicates that the model is statistically useful for predicting monthly sales, and the model coefficient of

The regression equation is
SALES = 2961 + 74.2 TIME + 501 JAN + 306 FEB - 2329 MAR - 3101 APR - 3138 MAY
        - 2393 JUN - 2241 JUL + 623 AUG + 2111 SEP - 361 OCT - 744 NOV

Predictor	Coef	SE Coef	T	P
Constant	2960.5	320.2	9.25	0.000
TIME	74.25	11.65	6.38	0.000
JAN	500.8	365.5	1.37	0.198
FEB	305.5	361.6	0.84	0.416
MAR	-2329.2	358.0	-6.51	0.000
APR	-3101.0	354.8	-8.74	0.000
MAY	-3137.7	351.9	-8.92	0.000
JUN	-2393.5	349.4	-6.85	0.000
JUL	-2241.2	347.2	-6.45	0.000
AUG	623.0	345.5	1.80	0.099
SEP	2111.3	344.1	6.14	0.000
OCT	-361.5	343.1	-1.05	0.315
NOV	-743.7	342.5	-2.17	0.053

S = 342.314   R-Sq = 98.3%   R-Sq(adj) = 96.5%

Analysis of Variance

Source	DF	SS	MS	F	P
Regression	12	75435259	6286272	53.65	0.000
Residual Error	11	1288964	117179		
Total	23	76724223			

Figure SIA6

Minitab printout for seasonal regression model of monthly Coldex sales

Figure SIA7

Minitab worksheet with seasonal regression forecasts of monthly sales

↓	C1	C2	C3	C4	C5	C6
	YEAR	MONTH	TIME	FORECAST	PL95LOW	PL95UPP
1	3	1	25	5317.5	4285.83	6349.17
2	3	2	26	5196.5	4164.83	6228.17
3	3	3	27	2636.0	1604.33	3667.67

determination (R^2 = .983) indicates that over 98% of the sample variation in monthly sales can be explained by the seasonal model. Statistically, this model is a tremendous improvement over the linear trend model.

The 95% prediction intervals for sales in months 25, 26, and 27 (highlighted on Figure SIA7) are (4,285.8, 6,349.2), (4,164.8, 6,228.2), and (1,604.3, 3,667.7), respectively. Thus, for the first month of year 3 (month 25), we are 95% confident that the actual sales will fall between 4,285.8 and 6,349.2 thousand dollars. (Similar interpretations are made for the other two forecasts.) These intervals are much narrower than those for the previous two forecasting models, and they also reflect the expected drop in sales in March (month 3) from the winter months. This seasonal model was used successfully by the pharmaceutical firm to forecast monthly sales.

Data Set: COLDEX

Exercises 38–46

Learning the Mechanics

38 The annual price of a finished product (in cents per pound) from 1997 to 2012 is given in the table below. The time variable t begins with $t = 1$ in 1997 and is incremented by 1 for each additional year.

L14038

Year	t	Price, Y_t	Year	t	Price, Y_t
1997	1	21.73	2005	9	24.42
1998	2	24.32	2006	10	25.49
1999	3	25.31	2007	11	26.19
2000	4	26.36	2008	12	27.31
2001	5	27.31	2009	13	24.40
2002	6	27.58	2010	14	24.24
2003	7	24.79	2011	15	25.87
2004	8	25.36	2012	16	26.86

a. Fit the straight-line model, $E(Y_t) = \beta_0 + \beta_1 t$, to the data.

b. Give the least squares estimates of the β's.

c. Use the least squares prediction equation to obtain the forecasts for 2013 and 2014.

d. Find 95% forecast intervals for 2013 and 2014.

39 Retail sales in Quarters 1–4 over a 10-year period for a department store are shown (in hundreds of thousands of dollars) in the table below.

NW

L14039

	Quarter			
Year	1	2	3	4
1	8.3	10.3	8.7	13.5
2	9.8	12.1	10.1	15.4
3	12.1	14.5	12.7	17.1
4	13.7	16.0	14.2	19.2
5	17.4	19.7	18.0	23.1
6	18.2	20.5	18.6	24.0
7	20.0	22.2	20.5	25.1
8	22.3	25.1	22.9	27.7
9	24.7	26.9	25.1	29.8
10	25.8	28.7	26.0	32.2

a. Write a regression model that contains trend and seasonal components to describe the sales data.

b. Use least squares regression to fit the model. Evaluate the fit of the model.

c. Use the regression model to forecast the quarterly sales during year 11. Give 95% prediction intervals for the forecasts.

40 What advantage do regression forecasts have over exponentially smoothed forecasts? Does this advantage ensure that regression forecasts will prove to be more accurate? Explain.

Applying the Concepts — Basic

41 Mortgage interest rates. The level at which commercial lending institutions set mortgage interest rates has a significant effect on the volume of buying, selling, and construction of residential and commercial real estate. The data in the table are the annual average mortgage interest rates for conventional, fixed-rate, 30-year loans for the period 1987–2010.

Year	Interest Rate (%)	Year	Interest Rate (%)
1987	10.46	1999	7.46
1988	10.86	2000	8.08
1989	12.07	2001	7.01
1990	9.97	2002	6.56
1991	11.14	2003	5.89
1992	8.27	2004	5.86
1993	7.17	2005	5.93
1994	8.28	2006	6.47
1995	7.86	2007	6.40
1996	7.76	2008	6.23
1997	7.57	2009	5.38
1998	6.92	2010	4.86

Source: United States Census Bureau.

a. Fit the simple regression model

$$E(Y_t) = \beta_0 + \beta_1 t$$

where t is the number of years since 1987 (i.e., $t = 0, 1, \ldots, 23$).

b. Forecast the average mortgage interest rate in 2013. Find a 95% prediction interval for this forecast.

42 Price of natural gas. Refer to Exercise 9 and the annual prices of natural gas from 1990 to 2010. A simple linear regression model, $E(Y_t) = \beta_0 + \beta_1 t$, where t is the number of years since 1990, is proposed to forecast the annual price of natural gas.

a. Give the least squares estimates of the β's and interpret their values.

b. Evaluate the model's fit.

c. Find and interpret 95% prediction intervals for the years 2011 and 2012.

d. Describe the problems associated with using a simple linear regression model to predict time series data.

43 A gasoline tax on carbon emissions. In an effort to reduce gasoline consumption and curb carbon emissions, policymakers have proposed raising gasoline taxes. In the *Journal of Applied Econometrics* (Vol. 26, 2011), a group of economists investigated the effect of a gasoline tax

on gas consumption. The researchers used least squares regression to model gasoline consumption in month t (Y_t) as a function of the average inflation-adjusted after-tax price of gasoline in month t (X_t) and dummy variables for months.

a. Write a model for Y_t as a function of X_t that proposes a linear relationship between gasoline consumption and after-tax gasoline price.

b. Add dummy variables for months to the model, part **a.** Use December as the base level.

c. What statistical test would you conduct to determine whether mean gasoline consumption varies from month to month? Give the null hypothesis for the test.

d. Monthly data from January 1998 to March 2008 ($n = 123$ months) were used to fit the model, part **b.** In terms of the β's of the model, what is the forecast of gasoline consumption in January 2013?

Applying the Concepts — Intermediate

44 Predicting presidential elections. Researchers at the University of West Florida used regression analysis to build a model for predicting the outcome of presidential elections (*Political Analysis*, Vol. 17, 2009). The dependent variable of interest was Y_t = percentage of the two-party vote won by the incumbent party's candidate in election year t. Independent variables included in the model are similar to those listed below.

Fiscal policy of incumbent party in election year t: $X_{1t} = \{1 \text{ if expansion}, 0 \text{ if not}\}$

Duration of incumbent party: X_{2t} = number of consecutive terms served prior to election year t

Party of incumbent in election year t: $X_{3t} = \{1 \text{ if Democrat}, 0 \text{ if Republican}\}$

GDP trend in election year t: X_{4t} = number of quarters of the previous administration where the GDP $> 3.2\%$

GDP growth rate: X_{5t} = growth rate of the GDP in the first three quarters of election year t

---

a. Write a first-order regression model for $E(Y_t)$ as a function of the five independent variables.

b. The model, part **a,** was fit to data collected for $n = 24$ election years (from 1916 to 2008). The coefficient of determination was reported as $R^2 = .91$. Interpret this result, practically.

c. Use the value of R^2 to compute the F-statistic for testing the global adequacy of the model. Carry out the test using $\alpha = .05$.

d. The estimated β for X_{1t} was reported as -4.08 (p-value $< .05$). Interpret this result, practically.

e. The estimated β for X_{2t} was reported as -3.41 (p-value $< .05$). Interpret this result, practically.

f. The estimated β for X_{3t} was reported as -4.84 (p-value $< .05$). Interpret this result, practically.

g. The estimated β for X_{4t} was reported as .92 (p-value $< .05$). Interpret this result, practically.

h. The estimated β for X_{5t} was reported as .66. Interpret this result, practically.

i. The standard deviation of the model was reported as $s = 2.36$. Interpret this result, practically.

j. Do you recommend that the researchers use the model to predict the outcome of a future presidential election? Explain.

45 Life insurance policies in force. The table below represents all life insurance policies (in millions) in force on the lives of U.S. residents for the years 1980 through 2009.

LIFE

Year	No. of Policies (in millions)	Year	No. of Policies (in millions)
1980	402	1995	370
1981	400	1996	355
1982	390	1997	351
1983	387	1998	358
1984	385	1999	367
1985	386	2000	369
1986	391	2001	377
1987	395	2002	375
1988	391	2003	379
1989	394	2004	373
1990	389	2005	373
1991	375	2006	375
1992	366	2007	374
1993	363	2008	335
1994	366	2009	291

Source: U.S. Census Bureau. *Statistical Abstract of the United States,* 2012.

a. Use the method of least squares to fit a simple regression model to the data.

b. Forecast the number of life insurance policies in force for 2010 and 2011.

c. Construct 95% prediction intervals for the forecasts of part **b.**

d. Check the accuracy of your forecasts by looking up the actual number of life insurance policies in force for 2010 and 2011 in the *Statistical Abstract of the United States.*

46 Graphing calculator sales. The next table presents the quarterly sales index for one brand of graphing calculator

GCALC

Year	First Quarter	Second Quarter	Third Quarter	Fourth Quarter
2008	438	398	252	160
2009	464	429	376	216
2010	523	496	425	318
2011	593	576	456	398
2012	636	640	526	498

at a campus bookstore. The quarters are based on an academic year, so the first quarter represents fall; the second, winter; the third, spring; and the fourth, summer.

Define the time variable as $t = 1$ for the first quarter of 2008, $t = 2$ for the second quarter of 2008, etc. Consider the following seasonal dummy variables:

$$Q_1 = \begin{cases} 1 & \text{if Quarter 1} \\ 0 & \text{otherwise} \end{cases}$$

$$Q_2 = \begin{cases} 1 & \text{if Quarter 2} \\ 0 & \text{otherwise} \end{cases}$$

$$Q_3 = \begin{cases} 1 & \text{if Quarter 3} \\ 0 & \text{otherwise} \end{cases}$$

a. Write a regression model for $E(Y_t)$ as a function of t, Q_1, Q_2, and Q_3.

b. Find and interpret the least squares estimates and evaluate the usefulness of the model.

c. Which of the assumptions about the random error component is in doubt when a regression model is fit to time series data?

d. Find the forecasts and the 95% prediction intervals for the 2013 quarterly sales. Interpret the result.

9 Autocorrelation and the Durbin-Watson Test

Recall that one of the assumptions we make when using a regression model for predictions is that the errors are independent. However, with time series data, this assumption is questionable. The cyclical component of a time series may result in deviations from the secular trend that tend to cluster alternately on the positive and negative sides of the trend, as shown in Figure 20.

The observed errors between the time series and the regression model for the secular trend (and seasonal component, if present) are called **time series residuals.** Thus, if the time series Y_t has an estimated trend of $\hat{Y}_t$, then the time series residual* is

$$\hat{R}_t = Y_t - \hat{Y}_t$$

Note that time series residuals are defined just as the residuals for any regression model. However, we will usually plot time series residuals versus time to determine whether a cyclical component is apparent.

For example, consider the sales forecasting data in Table 5, to which we fit a simple straight-line regression model. The Minitab plot of the data and model is repeated in Figure 21, and a plot of the time series residuals is shown in Figure 22.

Notice the tendency of the residuals to group alternately into positive and negative clusters—that is, if the residual for year t is positive, there is a tendency for the residual

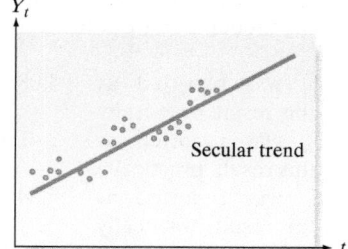

Y_t

Secular trend

t

Figure 20

Illustration of cyclical errors

---

*We use $\hat{R}_t$ rather than $\hat{\varepsilon}$ to denote a time series residual because, as we shall see, time series residuals often do not satisfy the regression assumptions associated with the random component ε.

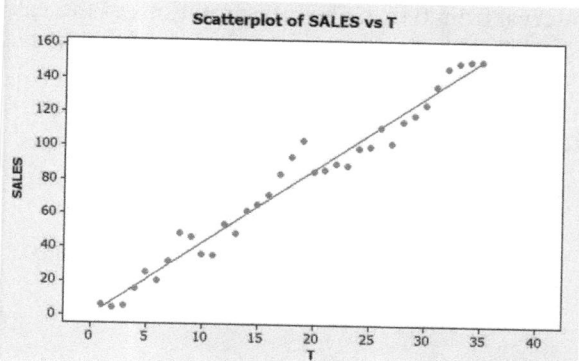

Figure 21

Minitab scatterplot of annual sales with least squares line

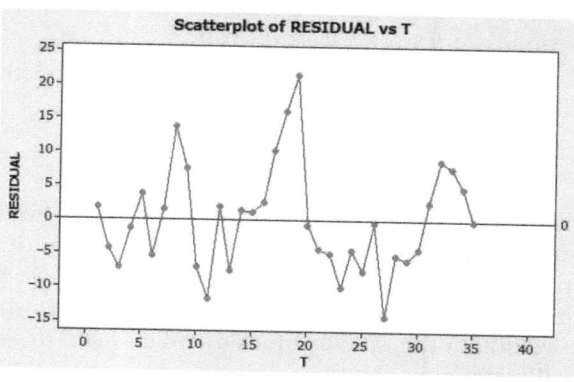

Figure 22

Minitab plot of residuals versus time

for year $(t + 1)$ to be positive. These cycles are indicative of possible positive correlation between neighboring residuals. The correlation between time series residuals at different points in time is called *autocorrelation,* and the autocorrelation of neighboring residuals (time periods t and $t + 1$) is called *first-order autocorrelation.*

> The correlation between time series residuals at different points in time is called **autocorrelation.** Correlation between neighboring residuals (at times t and $t + 1$) is called **first-order autocorrelation.** In general, correlation between residuals at times t and $t + d$ is called dth-order autocorrelation.

Rather than speculate about the presence of autocorrelation among time series residuals, we prefer to test for it. For most business and economic time series, the relevant test is for first-order autocorrelation. Other higher-order autocorrelations may indicate seasonality (e.g., fourth-order autocorrelation in a quarterly time series). However, when we use the term *autocorrelation* in this text, we are referring to first-order autocorrelation unless otherwise specified. So, we test

H_0: No first-order autocorrelation of residuals

H_a: Positive first-order autocorrelation of residuals

The **Durbin-Watson d-statistic** is used to test for the presence of first-order autocorrelation. The statistic is given by the formula

$$d = \frac{\sum_{t=2}^{n} (\hat{R}_t - \hat{R}_{t-1})^2}{\sum_{t=1}^{n} \hat{R}_t^2}$$

where n is the number of observations (time periods) and $(\hat{R}_t - \hat{R}_{t-1})$ represents the difference between a pair of successive time series residuals. The value of d always falls in the interval from 0 to 4. The interpretations of the values of d are given in the box. Most statistical software packages include a routine that calculates d for time series residuals.

Interpretation of Durbin-Watson d-Statistic

$$d = \frac{\sum_{t=2}^{n}(\hat{R}_t - \hat{R}_{t-1})^2}{\sum_{t=1}^{n}\hat{R}_t^2} \qquad \text{Range of } d: 0 \leq d \leq 4$$

1. If the residuals are uncorrelated, then $d \approx 2$.
2. If the residuals are positively autocorrelated, then $d < 2$, and if the autocorrelation is very strong, $d \approx 0$.
3. If the residuals are negatively autocorrelated, then $d > 2$, and if the autocorrelation is very strong, $d \approx 4$.

Durbin and Watson (1951) give tables for the lower-tail values of the d-statistic, which are shown in Tables X ($\alpha = .05$) and XI ($\alpha = .01$) of Appendix: Tables. Part of Table X is reproduced in Table 9. For the sales example, we have $k = 1$ independent variable and $n = 35$ observations. Using $\alpha = .05$ for the one-tailed test for positive autocorrelation, we obtain the tabled values $d_L = 1.40$ and $d_U = 1.52$. The meaning of these values is illustrated in Figure 23. Because of the complexity of the sampling distribution of d, it is not possible to specify a single point that acts as a boundary between the rejection and nonrejection regions, as we did for the z, t, F, and other test statistics. Instead, an upper (d_U) and lower (d_L) bound are specified. Thus a d-value less than d_L *does* provide strong evidence of positive autocorrelation at $\alpha = .05$ (recall that small d values indicate positive autocorrelation); a d value greater than d_U does *not* provide evidence of positive autocorrelation at $\alpha = .05$; and a value of d between d_L and d_U might or might not be significant at the $\alpha = .05$ level. If $d_L < d < d_U$, more information is needed before we can reach any conclusion about the presence of autocorrelation.

Table 9	Reproduction of Part of Table X of Appendix: Tables: Critical Values for the Durbin-Watson d-Statistic, $\alpha = .05$								
	$k = 1$		$k = 2$		$k = 3$		$k = 4$		$k = 5$	
n	d_L	d_U	d_L	d_U	d_L	d_U	d_L	d_U	d_L	d_U
31	1.36	1.50	1.30	1.57	1.23	1.65	1.16	1.74	1.09	1.83
32	1.37	1.50	1.31	1.57	1.24	1.65	1.18	1.73	1.11	1.82
33	1.38	1.51	1.32	1.58	1.26	1.65	1.19	1.73	1.13	1.81
34	1.39	1.51	1.33	1.58	1.27	1.65	1.21	1.73	1.15	1.81
35	1.40	1.52	1.34	1.58	1.28	1.65	1.22	1.73	1.16	1.80
36	1.41	1.52	1.35	1.59	1.29	1.65	1.24	1.73	1.18	1.80
37	1.42	1.53	1.36	1.59	1.31	1.66	1.25	1.72	1.19	1.80
38	1.43	1.54	1.37	1.59	1.32	1.66	1.26	1.72	1.21	1.79
39	1.43	1.54	1.38	1.60	1.33	1.66	1.27	1.72	1.22	1.79
40	1.44	1.54	1.39	1.60	1.34	1.66	1.29	1.72	1.23	1.79

Tests for negative autocorrelation and two-tailed tests can be conducted by making use of the symmetry of the sampling distribution of the d-statistic about its mean. The test procedure is summarized in the next box.

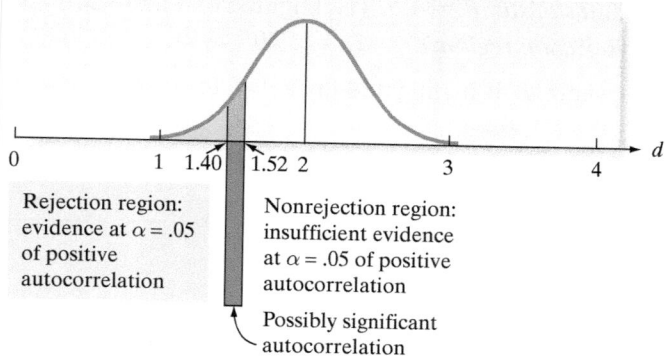

Figure 23
Rejection region for the Durbin-Watson d test: Sales example

GEOFFREY S. WATSON
(1921–1998)
The Durbin-Watson Test

Australian Geoff Watson was educated at the University of Melbourne, where he earned a mathematics degree in 1942. Following World War II, Watson moved to North Carolina State University to begin work on a graduate degree in statistics. He eventually earned his PhD in 1951. During his illustrious career as a statistics professor and researcher, Watson had appointments at Cambridge University, Australian National University, the University of Toronto, Johns Hopkins University, and Princeton University (where he was chairman of the statistics department). While visiting Cambridge in the late 1940s, Watson collaborated with James Durbin of the London School of Economics to develop their well-known Durbin-Watson test for serial correlation. His research interests covered a wide spectrum of statistical applications all across the world, including estimating the size of the penguin population (Antarctica), paleontology problems (Sweden), probability in quantum mechanics (Rome), molecular biology (Italy), and ozone depletion (U.S. Energy Information Administration). Outside his professional life, Watson was a serious painter (landscapes and hills) and an accomplished tennis player (effective lob).

Durbin-Watson d-Test for Autocorrelation

One-Tailed Test	Two-Tailed Test
H_0: No first-order autocorrelation	H_0: No first-order autocorrelation
H_a: Positive first-order autocorrelation (or H_a: Negative first-order autocorrelation)	H_a: Positive or negative first-order autocorrelation

Test statistic:

$$d = \frac{\sum_{t=2}^{n}(\hat{R}_t - \hat{R}_{t-1})^2}{\sum_{t=1}^{n}\hat{R}_t^2}$$

Rejection region:

$d < d_{L,\alpha}$
[or $(4 - d) < d_{L,\alpha}$
if H_a: Negative first-order autocorrelation]

where $d_{L,\alpha}$ is the lower tabled value corresponding to k independent variables and n observations. The corresponding upper value $d_{U,\alpha}$ defines a "possibly significant" region between $d_{L,\alpha}$ and $d_{U,\alpha}$ (see Figure 23).

Rejection region:

$d < d_{L,\alpha/2}$ or $(4 - d) < d_{L,\alpha/2}$

where $d_{L,\alpha/2}$ is the lower tabled value corresponding to k independent variables and n observations. The corresponding upper value $d_{U,\alpha/2}$ defines a "possibly significant" region between $d_{L,\alpha/2}$ and $d_{U,\alpha/2}$ (see Figure 23).

Requirements for the Validity of the d-Test

The residuals are normally distributed.

Example 9

Conducting the Durbin–Watson Test—Sales Revenue Model

Problem Refer to the straight-line regression model relating annual sales revenue, Y_t, to year t. Figures 21 and 22 provide graphical evidence of a potential residual correlation problem. Conduct a formal test for positive first-order autocorrelation by applying the Durbin-Watson test. Use $\alpha = .05$.

Solution We used SPSS to conduct the Durbin-Watson test. A portion of the SPSS printout for the least squares regression of annual sales is shown in Figure 24. The elements of the test follow:

H_0: No first-order autocorrelation

H_a: Positive first-order autocorrelation

Test statistic: $d = 1.02$ (highlighted on Figure 24)

Rejection region: $d < d_L = 1.40$

(where d_L is highlighted in Table 9 for $n = 35, \alpha = .05,$ and $k = 1$).

Figure 24

SPSS regression printout with Durbin-Watson statistic for annual sales model

Model Summary[b]

Model	R	R Square	Adjusted R Square	Std. Error of the Estimate	Durbin-Watson
1	.985[a]	.969	.969	7.9863	1.020

a. Predictors: (Constant), T

b. Dependent Variable: SALES

Conclusion: Because $d = 1.02$ is below the critical d_L value of 1.40, we reject H_0. Thus, there is sufficient evidence (at $\alpha = .05$) to conclude that the residuals of the straight-line model for sales are positively autocorrelated.

Look Back In the presence of autocorrelated residuals, the regression analysis tends to produce inflated t-statistics. Consequently, an analyst has a greater than α probability of committing a Type I error when testing a model parameter. For example, if a t-test is conducted on a β-parameter using $\alpha = .05$, the analyst will falsely reject H_0 more than 5% of the time when the regression errors are autocorrelated.

Now Work Exercise 49

Once strong evidence of autocorrelation has been established, as in the case of the sales example, doubt is cast on the least squares results and any inferences drawn from them. Under these conditions, a time series model that accounts for the autocorrelation of the random errors is required. Such time series models take the form

$$Y_t = E(Y_t) + R_t$$

where $E(Y_t)$ is the usual deterministic portion of the model and R_t is a term that represents autocorrelated error at time t. Consequently, the analyst must not only model the deterministic component but also the error component. For example, a model that is useful when the errors have first-order autocorrelation (called a *first-order autoregressive model*) is

$$R_t = \phi R_{t-1} + \varepsilon_t$$

where ε_t represents the usual independent error term. If the deterministic component can be modeled as a straight-line function of t, then the full model is

$$Y_t = \underbrace{\beta_0 + \beta_1 t}_{E(Y_t)} + \underbrace{\phi R_{t-1} + \varepsilon_t}_{R_t}$$

Consult the references at the end of this chapter for how to analyze these sophisticated time series models.

Exercises 47–56

Learning the Mechanics

47 Define autocorrelation. Explain why it is important in time series modeling and forecasting.

48 What do the following Durbin-Watson statistics suggest about the autocorrelation of the time series residuals from which each was calculated?

a. $d = 3.9$

b. $d = .2$

c. $d = 1.99$

49 For each case, indicate the decision regarding the test of the null hypothesis of no first-order autocorrelation against the alternative hypothesis of positive first-order autocorrelation.

a. $k = 2, n = 20, \alpha = .05, d = 1.1$

b. $k = 2, n = 20, \alpha = .01, d = 1.1$

c. $k = 5, n = 65, \alpha = .05, d = .95$

d. $k = 1, n = 31, \alpha = .01, d = 1.35$

Applying the Concepts—Basic

50 Forecasting monthly car and truck sales. Forecasts of automotive vehicle sales in the United States provide the basis for financial and strategic planning at large automotive corporations. The following forecasting model was developed for Y_t, total monthly passenger car and light truck sales (in thousands):

$$E(Y_t) = \beta_0 + \beta_1 x_1 + \beta_2 x_2 + \beta_3 x_3 + \beta_4 x_4 + \beta_5 x_5$$

where x_1 = average monthly retail price of regular gasoline, x_2 = annual percentage change in GDP per quarter, x_3 = monthly consumer confidence index, x_4 = total number of vehicles scrapped (millions) per month, and x_5 = vehicle seasonality. The model was fit to monthly data collected over a 12-year period (i.e., $n = 144$ months), with the following results: $R^2 = .856$, Durbin-Watson $d = 1.01$.

a. Is there sufficient evidence to indicate that the overall model contributes information for the prediction of monthly passenger car and light truck sales? Test using $\alpha = .05$.

b. Is there sufficient evidence to indicate that the regression errors are positively correlated? Test using $\alpha = .05$.

c. Comment on the validity of the inference concerning model adequacy in light of the result of part **b**.

51 Predicting presidential elections. Refer to the *Political Analysis* (Vol. 17, 2009) study on predicting presidential elections, Exercise 44. Recall that a regression model with five independent variables was fit to data collected for $n = 24$ election years in order to predict Y_t = percentage of the two-party vote won by the incumbent party's candidate in election year t. The Durbin-Watson d-statistic for the model was reported as $d = 1.77$. Is there evidence (at $\alpha = .05$) of positively correlated errors in the model? Explain.

52 The consumer purchasing value of the dollar, Y_t, from 1970
DOLLAR to 2010 is illustrated by the data in the table in the next column. The buying power of the dollar (compared with 1982) is listed for each year. The first-order model

$$Y_t = \beta_0 + \beta_1 t + \varepsilon$$

was fit to the data using the method of least squares. The Minitab printout and a plot of the regression residuals follow.

a. Examine the plot of the regression residuals against t. Is there a tendency for the residuals to have long positive and negative runs? To what do you attribute this phenomenon?

Regression Analysis: VALUE versus T

```
The regression equation is
VALUE = 1.90 - 0.0393 T

Predictor        Coef    SE Coef        T       P
Constant      1.89596    0.08948    21.19   0.000
T           -0.039274   0.003712   -10.58   0.000

S = 0.281263   R-Sq = 74.2%   R-Sq(adj) = 73.5%

Analysis of Variance

Source         DF        SS       MS        F       P
Regression      1    8.8534   8.8534   111.91   0.000
Residual Error 39    3.0852   0.0791
Total          40   11.9387

Durbin-Watson statistic = 0.0555155
```

b. Locate the Durbin-Watson d-statistic on the printout and test the null hypothesis that the time series residuals are uncorrelated. Use $\alpha = .10$.

c. What assumption(s) must be satisfied in order for the test of part **b** to be valid?

Year	t	Value, Y_t	Year	t	Value, Y_t
1970	1	2.545	1991	22	0.822
1971	2	2.469	1992	23	0.812
1972	3	2.392	1993	24	0.802
1973	4	2.193	1994	25	0.797
1974	5	1.901	1995	26	0.782
1975	6	1.718	1996	27	0.762
1976	7	1.645	1997	28	0.759
1977	8	1.546	1998	29	0.765
1978	9	1.433	1999	30	0.752
1979	10	1.289	2000	31	0.725
1980	11	1.136	2001	32	0.711
1981	12	1.041	2002	33	0.720
1982	13	1.000	2003	34	0.698
1983	14	0.984	2004	35	0.673
1984	15	0.964	2005	36	0.642
1985	16	0.955	2006	37	0.623
1986	17	0.969	2007	38	0.600
1987	18	0.949	2008	39	0.565
1988	19	0.926	2009	40	0.580
1989	20	0.880	2010	41	0.556
1990	21	0.839			

Source: United States Census Bureau.

Applying the Concepts—Intermediate

53 Mortgage interest rates. Refer to the data on annual mort-
MJR30 gage interest rate (Y_t), Exercise 41. You fit the simple linear regression model, $E(Y_t) = \beta_0 + \beta_1 t$, to the data for the years 1987 to 2010 ($t = 0, 1, 2, \ldots, 23$).

a. Find and plot the regression residuals against t. Does the plot suggest the presence of autocorrelation? Explain.

b. Conduct the Durbin-Watson test (at $\alpha = .05$) to test formally for the presence of positively autocorrelated regression errors.

c. Comment on the validity of the inference concerning model adequacy in light of the result of part **b**.

54 Price of natural gas. Refer to the annual data on natural
NATGAS gas price (Y_t), Exercise 42. You fit the simple linear regression model, $E(Y_t) = \beta_0 + \beta_1 t$, to the data for the years 1990 to 2010 ($t = 1, 2, \ldots, 21$).

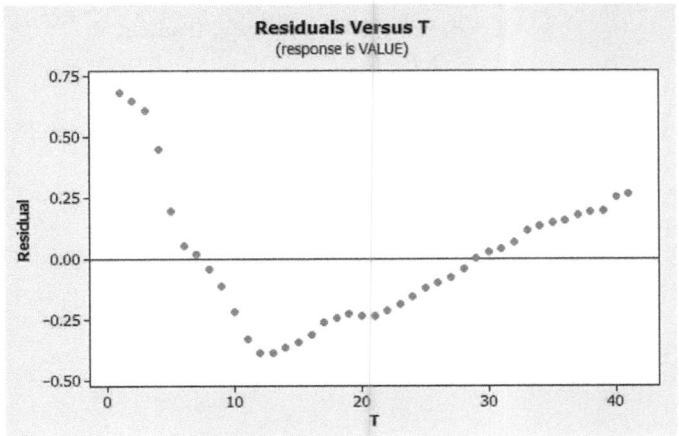

Residuals Versus T
(response is VALUE)

a. Find and plot the regression residuals against t. Does the plot suggest the presence of autocorrelation? Explain.

b. Conduct the Durbin-Watson test (at $\alpha = .05$) to test formally for the presence of positively autocorrelated regression errors.

c. Comment on the validity of the inference concerning model adequacy in light of the result of part **b.**

55 Modeling the deposit share of a retail bank. Exploratory research published in the *Journal of Professional Services Marketing* (Vol. 5, 1990) examined the relationship between deposit share of a retail bank and several marketing variables. Quarterly deposit share data were collected for 5 consecutive years for each of nine retail banking institutions. The model analyzed took the following form:

$$E(Y_t) = \beta_0 + \beta_1 P_{t-1} + \beta_2 S_{t-1} + \beta_3 D_{t-1}$$

where Y_t = deposit share of a bank in quarter t ($t = 1$, $2, \ldots, 20$), P_{t-1} = expenditures on promotion-related activities in quarter $t - 1$, S_{t-1} = expenditures on service-related activities in quarter $t - 1$, and D_{t-1} = expenditures on distribution-related activities in quarter $t - 1$. A separate model was fit for each bank with the results shown in the table.

a. Interpret the values of R^2 for each bank.

b. Test the overall adequacy of the model for each bank using $\alpha = .01$.

c. Conduct the Durbin-Watson d-test for positive residual correlation for each bank at $\alpha = .01$. What conclusions do you draw about autocorrelation?

Bank	R^2	p-Value for Global F-Test	Durbin-Watson d
1	.914	.000	1.3
2	.721	.004	3.4
3	.926	.000	2.7
4	.827	.000	1.9
5	.270	.155	.85
6	.616	.012	1.8
7	.962	.000	2.5
8	.495	.014	2.3
9	.500	.011	1.1

56 Life insurance policies in force. Refer to the annual data on number of life insurance policies in force (Y_t), **LIFE** Exercise 45. You fit the simple linear regression model, $E(Y_t) = \beta_0 + \beta_1 t$, to the data for the years 1980 to 2009 ($t = 1, 2, \ldots, 30$).

a. Find and plot the regression residuals against t. Does the plot suggest the presence of autocorrelation? Explain.

b. Conduct the Durbin-Watson test (at $\alpha = .05$) to test formally for the presence of positively autocorrelated regression errors.

c. Comment on the validity of the inference concerning model adequacy in light of the result of part **b.**

◻ Chapter Notes

Key Terms

Adaptive forecast
Additive model
Autocorrelation
Base period
Composite index number
Cyclical effect
Descriptive
Descriptive models
Durbin-Watson d-statistic
Durbin-Watson test
Exponentially smoothed forecast
Exponential smoothing
Exponential smoothing constant
First-order autocorrelation
Forecast
Forecast error
Holt forecasting model
Holt-Winters forecasting model
Index number
Inferential
Inferential forecasting model

Inferential models
Inferential techniques
Laspeyres index
Long-term trend
Mean absolute deviation
Mean absolute percentage error
Multiplicative model
Paasche index
Price
Quantity indexes
Residual effect
Root mean squared error
Seasonal effect
Seasonal model
Secular trend
Simple composite index
Simple index number
Time series or time series data
Time series residuals
Weighted composite price index

Key Formulas

$$I_t = \left(\frac{Y_t}{Y_0}\right)100 \qquad \text{Simple index}$$

$$I_t = \left(\frac{\text{Total of all } Y\text{-values at time } t}{\text{Total of all } Y\text{-values at time } t_0}\right)100 \qquad \begin{array}{l}\text{Simple composite} \\ \text{index}\end{array}$$

Weighted composite price indexes:

$$I_t = \left(\frac{\sum_{i=1}^{k} Q_{it_0} P_{it}}{\sum_{i=1}^{k} Q_{it_0} P_{it_0}}\right)100 \qquad \text{Laspeyres}$$

$$I_t = \left(\frac{\sum_{i=1}^{k} Q_{it} P_{it}}{\sum_{i=1}^{k} Q_{it} P_{it_0}}\right)100 \qquad \text{Paasche}$$

Exponential smoothing:

$$E_t = wY_t + (1 - w)E_{t-1}, \text{where } E_1 = Y_1$$

Forecast: $F_{t+k} = E_t$

Holt's method:

$$E_t = wY_t + (1 - w)(E_{t-1} + T_{t-1}),$$
$$\text{where } E_2 = Y_2, T_2 = Y_2 - Y_1$$

$$T_t = v(E_t - E_{t-1}) + (1 - v)T_{t-1}$$

Forecast: $F_{t+k} = E_t + kT_t$

$$\text{MAD} = \frac{\sum_{t=n+1}^{n+m} |Y_t - F_t|}{m}$$

Mean absolute deviation

$$\text{MAPE} = \frac{\sum_{t=n+1}^{n+m} \left| \dfrac{Y_t - F_t}{Y_t} \right|}{m} \times 100$$

Mean absolute percentage error

$$\text{RMSE} = \sqrt{\frac{\sum_{t=n+1}^{n+m} (Y_t - F_t)^2}{m}}$$

Root mean squared error

$$d = \frac{\sum_{t=2}^{n} \left(\hat{R}_t - \hat{R}_{t-1} \right)^2}{\sum_{t=1}^{n} \hat{R}_t^2}$$

Durbin-Watson test statistic

Key Symbols

Y_t	... Time series value at time t
I_t	... Index at time t
P_t	... Price series at time t
Q_t	... Quantity series at time t
E_t	... Exponentially smoothed value at time t
T_t	... Smoothed trend at time t
F_{t+k}	... k-step-ahead forecast value
MAD	... Mean absolute deviation
MAPE	... Mean absolute percentage error
RMSE	... Root mean squared error
$\hat{R}_t$	... Residual at time t
d	... Value of Durbin-Watson test statistic
d_L	... Lower critical value of d
d_U	... Upper critical value of d

Key Ideas

Time Series Data

Data generated by processes over time.

Index Number

Measures the change in a variable over time relative to a base period.

Types of index numbers:
1. **simple index number**
2. **simple composite index number** and
3. **weighted composite number (Laspeyres index or Paasche index)**

Time Series Components

1. **secular (long-term) trend**
2. **cyclical effect**
3. **seasonal effect** and
4. **residual effect**

Time Series Forecasting

Descriptive methods of forecasting with smoothing:
1. **exponential smoothing** and
2. **Holt's method**

An *inferential* forecasting method: **least squares regression**

Measures of forecast accuracy:
1. **mean absolute deviation (MAD)**
2. **mean absolute percentage error (MAPE)** and
3. **root mean squared error (RMSE)**

Problems with least squares regression forecasting:
1. *prediction outside the experimental region* and
2. *regression errors are autocorrelated*

Autocorrelation

Correlation between time series residuals at different points in time. A test for first-order autocorrelation: **Durbin-Watson test**

Guide to Time Series Analysis

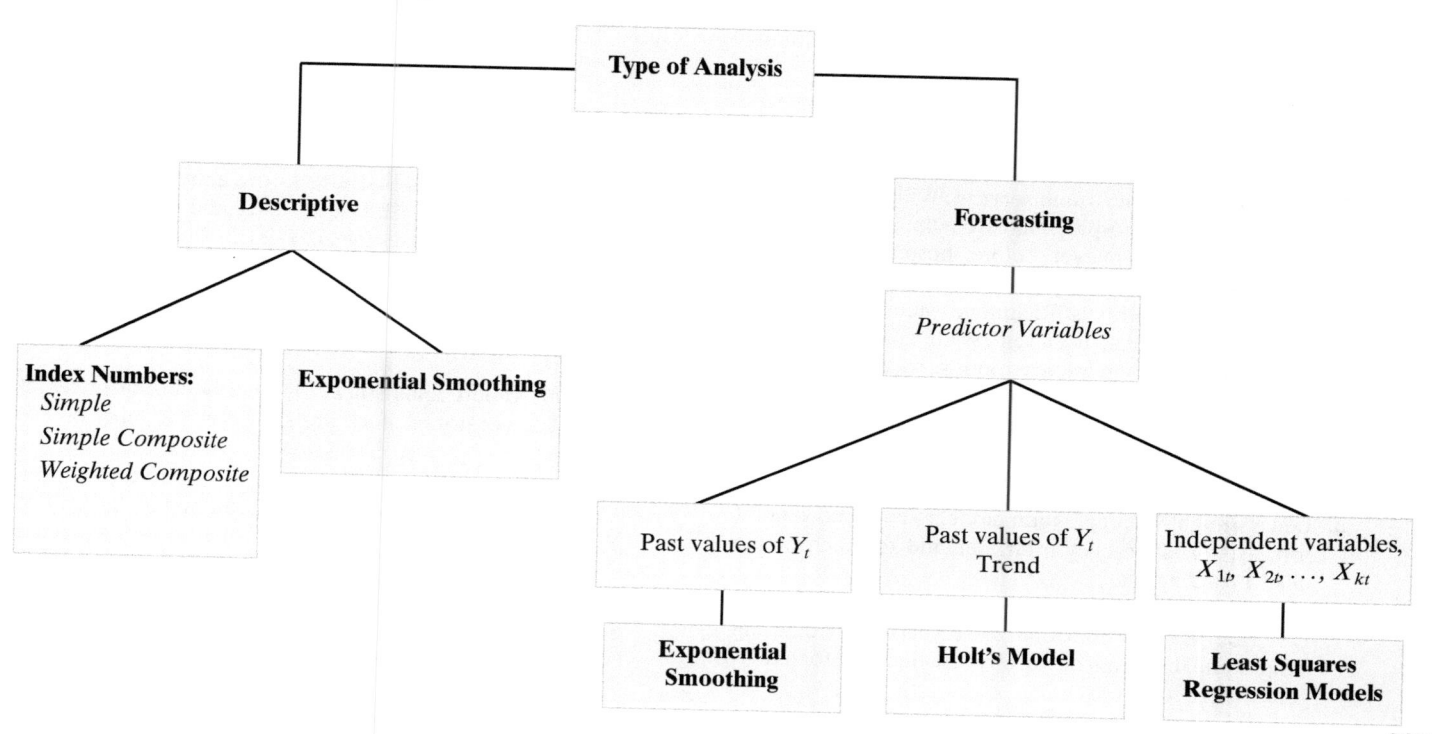

Supplementary Exercises 57–71

Applying the Concepts—Basic

57 Insured Social Security workers. Workers insured under the Social Security program are categorized as fully and permanently insured, fully but not permanently insured, or insured in the event of disability. The number of workers (in millions) in each insured category from 2000 to 2011 are provided in the accompanying table.

INSURE

Year	Fully, Permanent	Fully, not Permanent	Event of Disability
2000	140.9	44.9	139.5
2001	142.9	45.2	141.7
2002	144.9	45.3	143.5
2003	147.0	45.0	144.9
2004	149.0	44.8	146.2
2005	151.1	44.7	147.7
2006	153.3	45.1	150.1
2007	155.4	45.6	152.3
2008	157.4	46.0	154.5
2009	159.2	44.8	150.6
2010	161.1	44.6	151.7
2011	163.1	44.3	152.6

Source: The Social Security Administration.

a. Compute a simple composite index for the number of workers in the three insured categories using 2000 as the base period.

b. Is the index, part **a**, a price index or a quantity index?

c. Refer to part **a**. Interpret the index value for 2011.

58 Insured Social Security workers (cont'd). Refer to Exercise 57.

INSURE

a. Compute the exponentially smoothed series for the annual number of workers who are fully and permanently insured for Social Security. Use the smoothing constant $w = .5$.

b. Plot the number of workers and the exponentially smoothed values on the same graph.

c. Use exponential smoothing to forecast the number of fully and permanently insured workers in 2012 and 2013. What is the drawback to these forecasts?

59 Demand for emergency room services. With the advent of managed care, U.S. hospitals have begun to operate like businesses. More than ever before, hospital administrators need to know and apply the theories and methods taught in business schools. Richmond Memorial Hospital in Richmond, Virginia, uses regression analysis to forecast the demand for emergency room services. Specifically, Richmond Memorial uses data on patient visits to the emergency room during each of the past 10 Augusts to forecast next August's demand. Data for the month of August in a recent 10-year period are shown in the next table.

ER

a. Use a straight-line regression model to construct a point forecast for emergency room demand for each of the next three Augusts.

b. Provide 95% prediction intervals around the forecasts.

c. Describe the potential dangers associated with using simple linear regression to forecast demand for emergency room services.

Year t	Visits	Daily Average Y_t	Year t	Visits	Daily Average Y_t
1	1,367	44.09	6	3,019	97.38
2	1,642	52.96	7	2,794	90.12
3	1,780	57.41	8	2,846	91.80
4	2,060	66.45	9	3,001	96.80
5	2,257	72.80	10	3,548	114.45

d. Which other method described in this chapter would be appropriate for forecasting patient visits to the emergency room?

60 Retail prices of food items. In 1990, the average weekly food cost for a suburban family of four was estimated to be $154.40. The table below presents the retail prices of four food items for selected years from 1990 to 2010. Assume a typical suburban family of four purchased the following quantities of food, on average, each week during 1990:

FOOD4

Spaghetti	Ground Beef	Eggs	Potatoes
2 lb.	5 lb.	1 doz.	10 lb.

Year	Spaghetti ($/lb.)	Ground Beef ($/lb.)	Eggs ($/doz.)	Potatoes ($/lb.)
1990	.85	1.63	1.00	.32
1995	.88	1.40	1.16	.38
2000	.88	1.63	.96	.35
2005	.87	2.30	1.35	.50
2010	1.19	2.38	1.79	.58

Source: United States Census Bureau.

a. Calculate a Laspeyres price index for 1990 to 2010, using 1990 as the base year.

b. According to your index, how much did the above "basket" of foods increase or decrease in price from 1990 to 2010?

Applying the Concepts—Intermediate

61 Mortgage interest rates. Refer to the annual interest rate time series, Exercise 41. Use $w = .3$ and $v = .7$ to compute the Holt forecasts for 2011–2013. Compare these to the linear regression forecasts obtained in Exercise 41 using MAD, MAPE, and RMSE. [*Note:* You will need to obtain the actual values of the time series for 2011–2013 to complete this exercise.]

MJR30

62 Price of Abbott Labs stock. The yearly closing prices of Abbott Laboratories stock are shown in the table on the next page.

ABBLAB

a. Use exponential smoothing with $w = .8$ to forecast the 2012 and 2013 closing prices. If you buy at the end of 2011 and sell at the end of 2013, what is your expected gain (loss)?

b. Repeat part **a** using Holt's method with $w = .8$ and $v = .5$.

c. In which forecast do you have more confidence? Explain.

Data for Exercise 62

Year	Closing Price	Year	Closing Price
1990	45.00	2001	55.75
1991	68.07	2002	40.00
1992	30.03	2003	46.60
1993	29.05	2004	46.65
1994	32.05	2005	39.43
1995	41.05	2006	48.71
1996	50.75	2007	56.15
1997	65.50	2008	53.37
1998	49.00	2009	53.99
1999	36.31	2010	47.91
2000	48.44	2011	56.23

Source: Yahoo.com.

63 Price of Abbott Labs stock (cont'd). Refer to Exercise 62.

ABBLAB
  a. Fit a simple linear regression model to the stock price data.
  b. Plot the fitted regression line on a scatterplot of the data.
  c. Forecast the 2012 and 2013 closing prices using the regression model.
  d. Construct 95% prediction intervals for the forecasts of part **c.** Interpret the intervals in the context of the problem.
  e. Obtain the time series residuals for the simple linear model and use the Durbin-Watson d-statistic to test for the presence of autocorrelation.

64 Retirement assets. Annual retirement assets (in billions of dollars) for two fund types are given in the table below.

RETIRE
  a. Compute simple indexes for each of the two time series using 2000 as the base period.
  b. Construct a time series plot that displays both indexes.
  c. Using the results of parts **a** and **b,** compare and contrast the two types of funds.

Year	IRA	401(k)
2000	2,629	1,725
2004	3,299	2,189
2005	3,652	2,396
2006	4,207	2,768
2007	4,784	2,982
2008	3,759	2,275
2009	4,230	2,754

Source: United States Census Bureau.

65 Quarterly GDP values. The gross domestic product (GDP) is the total U.S. output of goods and services valued at market prices. The quarterly GDP values (in billions of dollars)

QTRGDP

Year	Quarter	GDP	Year	Quarter	GDP
2007	1	13,511		3	13,921
	2	13,738		4	14,087
	3	13,951	2010	1	14,278
	4	14,031		2	14,468
2008	1	14,151		3	14,606
	2	14,295		4	14,755
	3	14,413	2011	1	14,868
	4	14,200		2	15,013
2009	1	13,894		3	15,176
	2	13,854		4	15,319

Source: US Department of Commerce.

for the period 2007–2011 are given in the accompanying table. Using weights $w = .5$ and $\nu = .5$, calculate Holt forecasts for the four quarters of 2012.

66 Quarterly GDP values (cont'd). Refer to Exercise 65.

QTRGDP
  a. Use the simple linear regression model fit to the 2007–2011 data to forecast the 2012 quarterly GDP. Place 95% prediction limits on the forecasts.
  b. The GDP values given are *seasonally adjusted,* which means that an attempt to remove seasonality has been made prior to reporting the figures. Add quarterly dummy variables to the model. Use the partial F-test to determine whether the data indicate the significance of the seasonal component. Does the test support the assertion that the GDP figures are seasonally adjusted?
  c. Use the seasonal model to forecast the 2012 quarterly GDP values.
  d. Calculate the time series residuals for the seasonal model and use the Durbin-Watson test to determine whether the residuals are autocorrelated. Use $\alpha = .10$.

67 Quarterly GDP values (cont'd). Refer to Exercises 65 and 66. For each of the forecasting models, apply the MAD, MAPE, and RMSE criteria to evaluate the forecasts for the four quarters of 2012. Which of the forecasting models performs best according to each criterion? (You will need to obtain the actual 2012 GDP values to complete this exercise.)

QTRGDP

68 Revolving credit loans. A major portion of total consumer credit extended is in the category of revolving credit loans. Amounts outstanding (in billions of dollars) for the period 1990–2010 are given in the table.

LOANS

Year	Revolving	Year	Revolving
1990	239	2001	716
1991	264	2002	749
1992	278	2003	771
1993	310	2004	800
1994	366	2005	825
1995	444	2006	875
1996	508	2007	942
1997	538	2008	958
1998	579	2009	866
1999	609	2010	801
2000	683		

Source: United States Census Bureau.

  a. Use a simple linear regression model to forecast the 2011 and 2012 values. Place 95% prediction limits on each forecast.
  b. Calculate the Holt forecasts for 2011 and 2011 using $w = .7$ and $\nu = .7$. Compare the results with the simple linear regression forecasts of part **a.**

69 Using the CPI to compute real income. The number of dollars a person receives in a year is referred to as his or her *monetary* (or *money*) *income.* This figure can be adjusted to reflect the purchasing power of the dollars received relative to the purchasing power of dollars in some base period. The result is called a person's *real income.* The CPI can be used to adjust monetary income to obtain real income (in terms of 1984 dollars). To compute your real income for a specific year, simply divide your monetary

CPI

income for that year by that year's CPI and multiply by 100. In Exercise 27, we listed the CPI for 1990 and 2010 as 125.8 and 218.1, respectively.

a. Suppose your monetary income increased from $50,000 in 1990 to $95,000 in 2010. What were your real incomes in 1990 and 2010? Were you able to buy more goods and services in 1990 or 2010? Explain.

b. What monetary income would have been required in 2010 to provide equivalent purchasing power to a 1990 monetary income of $20,000?

70 IBM stock prices. Refer to Example 1 and the 2011 monthly IBM stock prices.

HITECH **a.** Use the exponentially smoothed series (with $w = .5$) from January to September 2011 to forecast the monthly values of the IBM stock price from October to December 2011. Calculate the forecast errors.

b. Use a simple linear regression model fit to the IBM stock prices from January to September 2011. Let time t range from 1 to 9, representing the 9 months in the sample. Interpret the least squares estimates.

c. With what approximate precision do you expect to be able to predict the IBM stock price using the regression model?

d. Give the simple linear regression forecasts and the 95% forecast intervals for the October–December 2011 prices. How does the precision of these forecasts agree with the approximation obtained in part **c**?

e. Compare the exponential smoothing forecasts, part **a**, to the regression forecasts, part **d**, using MAD, MAPE, and RMSE.

f. What assumptions does the random error component of the regression model have to satisfy in order to make

the model inferences (such as the forecast intervals in part **c**) valid?

g. Test to determine whether there is evidence of first-order positive autocorrelation in the random error component of the regression model. Use $\alpha = .05$. What can you infer about the validity of the model inferences?

71 Forecasting foreign exchange rates. T. C. Chiang considered several time series forecasting models of future foreign exchange rates for U.S. currency (*The Journal of Financial Research*, Summer 1986). One popular theory among financial analysts is that the forward (90-day) exchange rate is a useful predictor of the future spot exchange rate. Using monthly data on exchange rates for the British pound for $n = 81$ months, Chiang fit the model $E(Y_t) = \beta_0 + \beta_1 x_{t-1}$, where $Y_t = \ln(\text{spot rate})$ in month t, and $x_{i=1} = \ln(\text{forward rate})$ in month $t - 1$. The analysis yielded the following results:

$$t\text{-value} = 47.9, \quad s = .025, \quad R^2 = .957,$$
$$\text{Durbin-Watson } d = .962$$

a. Is the model statistically useful for forecasting future spot exchange rates for the British pound? Test using $\alpha = .05$.

b. Interpret the values of s and R^2.

c. Is there evidence of positive autocorrelation among the residuals? Test using $\alpha = .05$.

d. Based on the results of parts **a–c**, would you recommend using the model to forecast spot exchange rates?

Activity 1   Time Series

For this activity, select a recurring quantity from your own life for which you have monthly records for at least 2 years. This might be the cost of a utility bill, the number of cell phone minutes used, or even your income. If you do not have access to such records, use the Internet to find similar data, such as median monthly home prices in your area for at least 2 years.

1. Which methods from this chapter might apply to your data? Does there appear to be a seasonal component affecting the data? If so, can you explain the seasonal effect in simple terms?

2. Use methods from this chapter to predict the value of your quantity for the next year. Be prepared to defend your choice of methods.

References

Abraham, B., & Ledholter, J. *Statistical Methods for Forecasting.* New York: Wiley, 1983 (paperback, 2005; online, 2008).

Anderson, T. W. *The Statistical Analysis of Time Series.* New York: Wiley, 1971 (paperback, 1994).

Box, G. E. P., Jenkins, G. M., & Reinsel, G. C. *Time Series Analysis: Forecasting and Control,* 4th ed. New York: Wiley, 2008.

Chipman, J. S. "Efficiency of Least Squares Estimation of Linear Trend When Residuals Are Autocorrelated." *Econometrica,* Vol. 47, 1979.

Durbin, J., & Watson, G. S. "Testing for Serial Correlation in Least Squares Regression, I." *Biometrika,* Vol. 37, 1950, pp. 409–428.

Durbin, J., & Watson, G. S. "Testing for Serial Correlation in Least Squares Regression, II." *Biometrika,* Vol. 38, 1951, pp. 159–178.

Durbin, J., & Watson, G. S. "Testing for Serial Correlation in Least Squares Regression, III." *Biometrika,* Vol. 58, 1971, pp. 1–19.

Evans, M. *Practical Business Forecasting.* New York: Wiley-Blackwell, 2002.

Fuller, W. A. *Introduction to Statistical Time Series,* 2nd ed. New York: Wiley, 1996 (online, 2008).

Granger, C. W. J., & Newbold, P. *Forecasting Economic Time Series,* 2nd ed. New York: Academic Press, 1986.

Greene, W. H. *Econometric Analysis,* 7th ed. Upper Saddle River, N.J.: Prentice Hall, 2008.

Hamilton, J. D. *Time Series Analysis.* Princeton: Princeton University Press, 1994.

Harvey, A. *Time Series Models*, 2nd ed. Cambridge: MIT Press, 1993.

Maddala, G. S., & Lahiri, K. *Introduction to Econometrics*, 4th ed. New York: Wiley, 2010.

Makridakis, S., et al. *The Forecasting Accuracy of Major Time Series Methods*. New York: Wiley, 1984.

Nelson, C. R. *Applied Time Series Analysis for Managerial Forecasting*. San Francisco: Holden-Day, 1990.

Shively, T. S. "Fast Evaluation of the Distribution of the Durbin-Watson and Other Invariant Test Statistics in Time Series Regression." *Journal of the American Statistical Association*, Vol. 85, 1990.

Theil, H. *Principles of Econometrics*. New York: Wiley, 1971.

White, K. J. "The Durbin-Watson Test for Autocorrelation in Nonlinear Models." *Review of Economics and Statistics*, Vol. 74, 1992.

Willis, R. E. *A Guide to Forecasting for Planners*. Englewood Cliffs, N.J.: Prentice Hall, 1987.

USING TECHNOLOGY Technology images shown here are taken from SPSS Statistics Professional 20.0, Minitab 16, XLSTAT for Pearson, and Excel 2010.

SPSS: Forecasting

Exponential Smoothing or Holt's Method

Step 1 Within SPSS, open the data file containing the time series data.

Step 2 There are no point-and-click options for exponential smoothing in SPSS. Rather, you must enter the appropriate program commands (called syntax) to generate the results. Click the "File" button on the Excel main menu bar, then "New," and click "Syntax," as shown in Figure S.1.

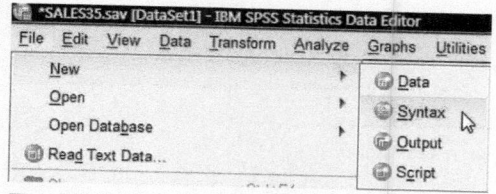

Figure S.1 SPSS menu options for creating program commands

Step 3 On the resulting dialog box, enter the commands for exponential smoothing (see Figure S.2) or Holt's method (see Figure S.3). In both programs, the time series variable to be forecasted (e.g., SALES) follows the "EXSMOOTH" command. Use "MODEL=SINGLE" for exponential smoothing and "MODEL=HOLT" for Holt's method. "ALPHA" represents the smoothing constant, and "GAMMA" represents the trend smoothing constant. Use the "INITIAL" command to specify the initial value in the forecast (this is usually the value of the time series variable at time 1).

Figure S.2 SPSS program commands for forecasting with exponential smoothing

Step 4 Click "Run," then "All" to generate the forecasts. (These forecasts will be added to the SPSS data file.)

Figure S.3 SPSS program commands for Holt's forecasting method

Regression

Step 1 Click the "Analyze" button on the SPSS main menu bar, then click on "Regression" and "Linear."

Step 2 Specify the dependent time series variable in the "Dependent" box and the independent variables in the model in the "Independent(s)" box. Click "Save" and make the appropriate menu selections to save the forecasted values as well as 95% prediction intervals.

Step 3 To conduct the Durbin-Watson test for autocorrelated errors, click on the "Statistics" button to obtain the menu shown in Figure S.4. Check the "Durbin-Watson" box and then click "Continue" to return to the "Linear Regression" dialog box. Click "OK" to view the results.

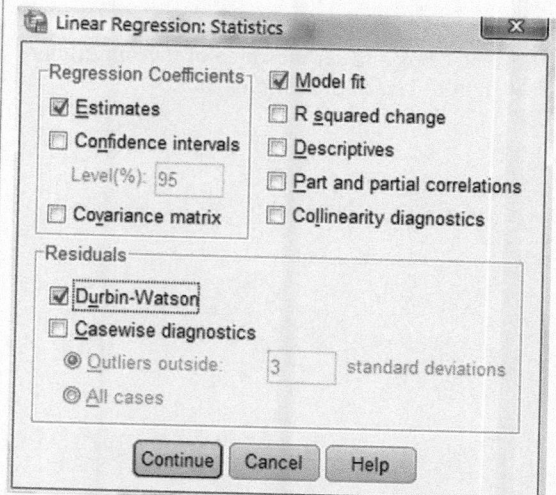

Figure S.4 SPSS linear regression statistics menu

Minitab: Forecasting

Exponential Smoothing or Holt's method

Step 1 Click the "Stat" button on the Minitab main menu bar and then click on "Time Series." This will produce the menu list shown in Figure M.1.

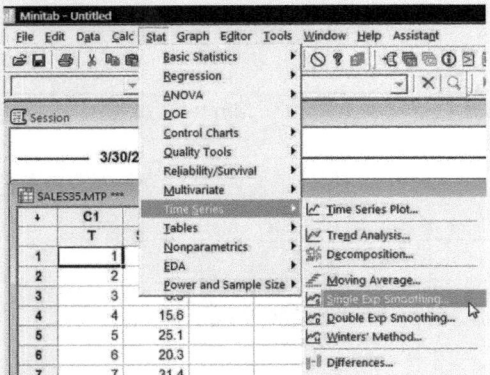

Figure M.1 Minitab options for time series analysis

Step 2 Click on "Single Exp Smoothing" for the exponential smoothing method or "Double Exp Smoothing" for Holt's method with trend. For example, clicking "Single Exp Smoothing" will result in the dialog box shown in Figure M.2.

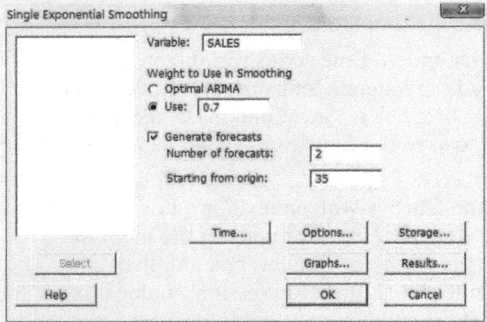

Figure M.2 Minitab exponential smoothing dialog box

Step 3 Select the quantitative variable to be smoothed and place it in the "Variable" box and set the value of the smoothing constant in the "Weight to Use in Smoothing" box.

Step 4 Select the "Options" box and specify "1" where Minitab asks for the number of observations to use for the initial smoothed value. As an option, you can store the forecast values by selecting "Storage" and making the appropriate selections.

Step 5 Click "OK" to view the results.

Regression

Step 1 Click the "Stat" button on the Minitab main menu bar and then click on "Regression" and "Regression" again.

Step 2 Specify the dependent time series variable in the "Response" box and the independent variables in the model in the "Predictors" box.

Step 3 Click "Options" to display the Regression Options dialog box. As shown in Figure M.3, you may select "Durbin-Watson statistic" to conduct a test for autocorrelated errors and/or make selections for producing a prediction interval for a future value of the time series variable.

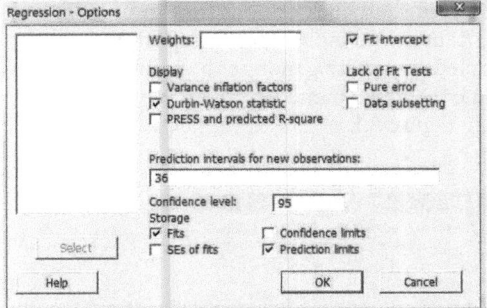

Figure M.3 Minitab regression options

Step 4 Click "Storage" and make the appropriate menu selections to save the forecasted values as well as 95% prediction intervals. (These values will appear on the Minitab worksheet.)

Step 5 Click "OK" on the Linear Regression dialog box to produce the forecasts.

Note: Time series forecasting methods are not yet available in the student version of Excel/XLSTAT.

Answers to Selected Exercises

5 a. 127.63 **b.** 116.37 **7 a.** $I_{2010} = 103.19$; beer production in 2010 increased by 3.19% over the beer production in 1980
b. Quantity **c.** $I_{2010} = 95.10$ **9 a.** $I_{1980} = 100.00, I_{1981} = 157.61, \ldots, I_{2010} = 304.35$ **c.** Price **11 a.** $I_{1970} = 100.00$,
$I_{1975} = 157.94, \ldots, I_{2010} = 1,594.45$ **b.** $I_{1970} = 36.98, I_{1975} = 58.40, \ldots, I_{2010} = 589.62$ **c.** Flattens the graph
13 a. Manufacturing: $I_{1990} = 100.00, I_{2000} = 132.84, \ldots, I_{2010} = 172.63$; Information: $I_{1990} = 100.00$,
$I_{2000} = 142.31, \ldots, I_{2010} = 192.99$; Food: $I_{1990} = 100.00, I_{2000} = 138.95, \ldots, I_{2010} = 187.37$ **c.** Earnings: $I_{1990} = 100.00$,
$I_{2000} = 138.25, \ldots, I_{2010} = 184.57$; Hours: $I_{1990} = 100.00, I_{2000} = 102.1, \ldots, I_{2010} = 100.2$ **15** $w = .2$ **17 a.** $E_{1980} = 188.0$,
$E_{1981} = 189.2, \ldots, E_{2009} = 198.1, E_{2010} = 197.3$ **b.** $E_{1980} = 188.0, E_{1981} = 192.8, \ldots, E_{2009} = 196.8, E_{2010} = 194.6$ **c.** $w = .2$ series
19 a. $E_{1990} = 384.00, E_{1991} = 366.40, \ldots, E_{2010} = 1168.78, E_{2011} = 1491.36$ **21 a.** $w = .1$: $E_{1990} = 1,283.0$,
$E_{1991} = 1,278.0, \ldots, E_{2009} = 1,618.9, E_{2010} = 1,622.4$; $w = .9$: $E_{1990} = 1,283.0, E_{1991} = 1,238.0, \ldots, E_{2009} = 1,632.6$,
$E_{2010} = 1,651.9$ **b.** $w = .9$ series **25 a.** $w = .3$: $F_{2008} = F_{2009} = F_{2010} = 198.16$; $w = .7$: $F_{2008} = F_{2009} = F_{2010} = 198.62$
b. $w = .7$ and $v = .3$: $F_{2008} = 198.84, F_{2009} = 199.11, F_{2010} = 199.38$; $w = .3$ and $v = .7$: $F_{2008} = 198.46, F_{2009} = 198.88, F_{2010} = 199.30$
27 a. Yes **b.** $F_{2011} = 212.67$ **c.** $F_{2011} = 225.62$ **29 a.** Forecast for all four quarters $= 1,215.8$ **b.** Forecast for all
four quarters $= 1,413.0$ **31 a.** Forecast for all 12 months $= 1,360.35$ **b.** $F_{\text{Jan}} = 1,360.35, F_{\text{Feb}} = 1,358.38$,
$F_{\text{Mar}} = 1,365.54, \ldots, F_{\text{Dec}} = 1,713.46$ **c.** Forecasts: $F_{\text{Jan}} = 1,436.48, F_{\text{Feb}} = 1,477.19, F_{\text{Mar}} = 1,517.88, \ldots, F_{\text{Dec}} = 1,884.14$;
one-step-ahead forecasts: $F_{\text{Jan}} = 1,436.49, F_{\text{Feb}} = 1,477.12, F_{\text{Mar}} = 1,404.48, \ldots, F_{\text{Dec}} = 1,781.32$ **33 a.** $1.54, -2.88, -5.30$
b. $1.16, -3.11, -5.38$ **c.** MAD $= 3.24$, MAPE $= 1.66$, RMSE $= 3.59$ **d.** MAD $= 3.22$, MAPE $= 1.65$, RMSE $= 3.65$
35 a. MAD $= 94.9$, MAPE $= 8.0$, RMSE $= 128.6$ **b.** MAD $= 119.9$, MAPE $= 10.0$, RMSE $= 153.7$ **c.** Holt's model with $w = .3$
and $v = .5$ **37 a.** Forecasts for all 3 years $= 73,558.2$ **b.** $F_{2008} = 74,402.6, F_{2009} = 75,068.8, F_{2011} = 75,735.0$ **c.** Exponential smoothing: MAD $= 3,070.5$, MAPE $= 3.9$, RMSE $= 3,595.9$; Holt's: MAD $= 1,775.6$, MAPE $= 2.29$, RMSE $= 2,064.0$;
Holt's model **39 a.** $E(Y_t) = \beta_0 + \beta_1 t + \beta_2 x_1 + \beta_3 x_2 + \beta_4 x_3$, where $x_1 = \{1 \text{ if Qtr. 1, 0 if not}\}$, $x_2 = \{1 \text{ if Qtr. 2, 0 if not}\}$,
$x_3 = \{1 \text{ if Qtr. 3, 0 if not}\}$ **b.** $\hat{Y}_t = 11.49 + .51t - 3.95x_1 - 2.09x_2 - 4.52x_3$; $F = 1,275.44$, reject H_0 **c.** Qtr. 1: $(27.22, 29.67)$; Qtr. 2:
$(29.59, 32.04)$; Qtr. 3: $(27.67, 30.12)$; Qtr. 4: $(32.70, 35.15)$ **41 a.** $\hat{Y}_t = 10.50 - .245t$ **b.** 4.14; $(2.12, 6.16)$ **43 a.** $E(Y_t) = \beta_0 + \beta_1 X_t$
b. $E(Y_t) = \beta_0 + \beta_1 X_t + \beta_2 x_1 + \beta_3 x_2 + \cdots + \beta_{12} x_{11}$, where $x_1 = \{1 \text{ if Jan., 0 if not}\}$, $x_2 = \{1 \text{ if Feb., 0 if not}\}, \ldots, x_{11} =$
$\{1 \text{ if Nov., 0 if not}\}$ **c.** subset F-test; $H_0: \beta_2 = \beta_3 = \cdots = \beta_{12} = 0$ **d.** $\hat{\beta}_0 + \hat{\beta}_1(180) + \hat{\beta}_2$ **45 a.** $\hat{Y}_t = 399.34 - 1.67t$
b. $F_{2010} = 347.46, F_{2011} = 345.79$ **c.** F_{2010}: $(311.85, 383.08)$; F_{2011}: $(309.95, 381.63)$ **47** Regression errors are correlated
49 a. Inconclusive **b.** Inconclusive **c.** Reject H_0 **d.** Fail to reject H_0 **51** No; do not reject H_0 **53 a.** Yes **b.** $d = 1.24$, reject H_0
c. Not valid **55 b.** Models statistically useful for Banks 1, 2, 3, 4, and 7 **c.** No evidence of positive autocorrelation for all nine
banks **57 a.** $I_{2000} = 100, I_{2001} = 101.4, \ldots, I_{2010} = 109.9, I_{2011} = 110.7$ **b.** Quantity **c.** Number of insured workers increased by
10.7% between 2000 and 2011 **59 a.** $\hat{Y}_t = 38.17 + 7.32t$; forecasts: 118.68, 126.00, 133.32 **b.** Year 11: $(100.61, 136.75)$; Year 12: $(107.06, 144.94)$; Year 13: $(113.40, 153.24)$ **61** $F_{2011} = 5.19, F_{2012} = 4.94, F_{2013} = 4.69$; Holt's forecast errors are larger
63 a. $\hat{Y}_t = 42.56 + .449t$ **c.** $F_{2012} = 52.44, F_{2013} = 52.89$ **d.** F_{2012}: $(29.30, 75.57)$; F_{2013}: $(24.49, 76.28)$ **e.** $d = 1.75$, do not reject H_0
65 $F_{2012,1} = 15,481.1$; $F_{2012,2} = 15,629.0$; $F_{2012,3} = 15,776.9$; $F_{2012,4} = 15,924.8$ **69 a.** \$39,746; \$43,558; 2010 **b.** \$34,674
71 a. Yes **c.** Yes **d.** No

Credits

The photo credits below are listed in order of appearance.

Varuka/Shutterstock
Bettmann/Corbis

☐ Technology Images

CONTENTS

Where We're Going

- Develop the need for inferential techniques that require fewer, or less stringent, assumptions (1)

- Introduce *nonparametric* tests that are based on ranks (i.e., on an ordering of the sample measurements according to their relative magnitudes) (2–7)

- Present a nonparametric test about the central tendency of a population (2)

- Present a nonparametric test for comparing two populations with independent samples (3)

☐ Nonparametric Statistics

STATISTICS in ACTION

How Vulnerable Are New Hampshire Wells to Groundwater Contamination?

Methyl tert-*butyl ether (commonly known as MTBE) is a volatile, flammable, colorless liquid manufactured by the chemical reaction of methanol and isobutylene. MTBE was first produced in the United States as a lead fuel additive (octane booster) in 1979 and then as an oxygenate in reformulated fuel in the 1990s. Unfortunately, MTBE was introduced into water-supply aquifers by leaking underground storage tanks (called USTs) at gasoline stations, thus contaminating the drinking water. Consequently, by late 2006 most (but not all) American gasoline retailers had ceased using MTBE as an oxygenate, and, accordingly, U.S. production has declined. Despite the reduction in production, there is no federal standard for MTBE in public water supplies; therefore, the chemical remains a dangerous pollutant, especially in states like New Hampshire that mandate the use of reformulated gasoline.*

A study published in *Environmental Science & Technology* (Jan. 2005) investigated the risk of exposure to MTBE through drinking water in New Hampshire. In particular, the study reported on the factors related to MTBE contamination in public and private New Hampshire wells. Data were collected for a sample of 223 wells. These data are saved in the **MTBE** file. One of the variables measured was MTBE level (micrograms per liter) in the well water. A detectible level of MTBE occurs if the value exceeds .2 micrograms per liter on the measuring instrument. Of the 223 wells, 70 have detectible levels of MTBE. (Although the other wells are below the detection limit of the measuring device, the MTBE values for these wells are recorded as .2 rather than 0.) The other variables on the data set are described in Table SIA1.

How contaminated are these New Hampshire wells? Is the level of MTBE contamination different for the two different well classes? For the two different

STATISTICS
in ACTION
CONTINUED

□ Present a nonparametric test for comparing two populations with paired samples (4)

□ Present nonparametric tests for comparing three or more populations using a designed experiment (5)

□ Present a nonparametric test for rank correlation (7)

aquifer types? What environmental factors are related to the MTBE level of a ground-water well? These are just a few of the research questions addressed in the study.

The researchers applied several nonparametric methods to the data in order to answer the research questions. We demonstrate the use of this methodology in four *Statistics in Action Revisited* examples.

Table SIA1	Variables Measured in the MTBE Contamination Study		
Variable Name	Type	Description	Units of Measurement, or Levels
CLASS	QL	Well class	Public or Private
AQUIFER	QL	Type of aquifer	Bedrock or Unconsolidated
DETECTION	QL	MTBE detection status	Below limit or Detect
MTBE	QN	MTBE level	micrograms per liter
PH	QN	pH level	standard pH unit
DISSOXY	QN	Dissolved oxygen	milligrams per liter
DEPTH	QN	Well depth	meters
DISTANCE	QN	Distance to UST	meters
INDUSTRY	QN	Industries in proximity	Percent of industrial land within 500 meters of well

 *Data Set:* MTBE

STATISTICS in ACTION REVISITED

□ Testing the Median MTBE Level

□ Comparing MTBE Levels of Wells

□ Comparing the MTBE Levels of Wells (continued)

□ Testing the Correlation of MTBE Level with Other Environmental Factors

1   Introduction: Distribution-Free Tests

The confidence interval and testing procedures all involve making inferences about population parameters. Consequently, they are often referred to as **parametric statistical tests.** Many of these parametric methods (e.g., the small-sample t-test or the ANOVA F-test) rely on the assumption that the data are sampled from a normally distributed population. When the data are normal, these tests are *most powerful*—that is, the use of these parametric tests maximizes power—the probability of the researcher correctly rejecting the null hypothesis.

Consider a population of data that are decidedly nonnormal. For example, the distribution might be very flat, peaked, or strongly skewed to the right or left (see Figure 1). Applying the small-sample t-test to such a data set may result in serious consequences. Because the normality assumption is clearly violated, the results of the t-test are unreliable: (1) The probability of a Type I error (i.e., rejecting H_0 when it is true) may be larger than the value of α selected; and (2) the power of the test, $1 - \beta$, is not maximized.

Figure 1

Some nonnormal distributions for which the t-statistic is invalid

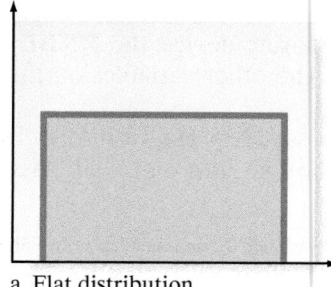

a. Flat distribution   b. Peaked distribution   c. Skewed distribution

A number of *nonparametric* techniques are available for analyzing data that do not follow a normal distribution. Nonparametric tests do not depend on the distribution of the sampled population; thus, they are called *distribution-free tests*. Also, nonparametric methods focus on the location of the probability distribution of the population, rather than on specific parameters of the population, such as the mean (hence, the name *nonparametrics*).

> **Distribution-free tests** are statistical tests that do not rely on any underlying assumptions about the probability distribution of the sampled population.

> The branch of inferential statistics devoted to distribution-free tests is called **nonparametrics.**

Nonparametric tests are also appropriate when the data are nonnumerical in nature but can be ranked.* For example, when taste-testing foods or in other types of consumer product evaluations, we can say we like product A better than product B, and B better than C, but we cannot obtain exact quantitative values for the respective measurements. Nonparametric tests based on the ranks of measurements are called *rank tests*.

> Nonparametric statistics (or tests) based on the ranks of measurements are called **rank statistics** (or **rank tests**).

In this chapter, we present several useful nonparametric methods. Keep in mind that these nonparametric tests are likely to be more powerful than their corresponding parametric counterparts in those situations where either the data are nonnormal or the data can be ranked.

In Section 2, we develop a test to make inferences about the central tendency of a single population. In Sections 3 and 5, we present rank statistics for comparing two or more probability distributions using independent samples. In Sections 4 and 6, the matched pairs and randomized block designs are used to make nonparametric comparisons of populations. Finally, in Section 7, we present a nonparametric measure of correlation between two variables.

2   Single Population Inferences

The z- and t-statistics can be used for testing hypotheses about a population mean. The z-statistic is appropriate for large random samples selected from "general" populations—that is, with few limitations on the probability distribution of the underlying population. The t-statistic was developed for small-sample tests in which the sample is selected at random from a *normal* distribution. The question is, how can we conduct a test of hypothesis when we have a small sample from a *nonnormal* distribution?

The **sign test** is a relatively simple, nonparametric procedure for testing hypotheses about the central tendency of a nonnormal probability distribution. Note that we used the phrase *central tendency* rather than *population mean*. This is because the sign test, like many nonparametric procedures, provides inferences about the population *median* rather than the population mean μ. Denoting the population median by the Greek letter η, we know that η is the 50th percentile of the distribution (Figure 2) and as such is less affected by the skewness of the distribution and the presence of outliers (extreme observations). Because the nonparametric test must be suitable for all distributions, not just the normal, it is reasonable for nonparametric tests to focus on the more robust (less sensitive to extreme values) measure of central tendency, the median.

*Qualitative data that can be ranked in order of magnitude are called *ordinal data*.

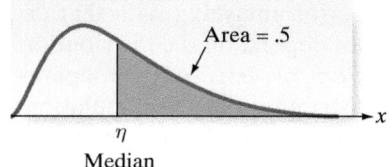

Figure 2

Location of the population median, η

Table 1	Substance Abuse Test Results						
.78	.51	3.79	.23	.77	.98	.96	.89

Data Set: ABUSE

For example, increasing numbers of both private and public agencies are requiring their employees to submit to tests for substance abuse. One laboratory that conducts such testing has developed a system with a normalized measurement scale, in which values less than 1.00 indicate "normal" ranges and values equal to or greater than 1.00 are indicative of potential substance abuse. The lab reports a normal result as long as the median level for an individual is less than 1.00. Eight independent measurements of each individual's sample are made. One individual's results are shown in Table 1.

If the objective is to determine whether the *population* median (that is, the true median level if an indefinitely large number of measurements were made on the same individual sample) is less than 1.00, we establish that as our alternative hypothesis and test

$$H_0: \eta = 1.00$$
$$H_a: \eta < 1.00$$

The one-tailed sign test is conducted by counting the number of sample measurements that "favor" the alternative hypothesis—in this case, the numbers that are less than 1.00. If the null hypothesis is true, we expect approximately half of the measurements to fall on each side of the hypothesized median, and if the alternative is true, we expect significantly more than half to favor the alternative—that is, to be less than 1.00. Thus,

Test statistics: $S =$ Number of measurements less than 1.00,
the null hypothesized median

If we wish to conduct the test at the $\alpha = .05$ level of significance, the rejection region can be expressed in terms of the observed significance level, or *p*-value of the test:

Rejection region: p-value $\leq .05$

In this example, $S = 7$ of the 8 measurements are less than 1.00. To determine the observed significance level associated with this outcome, we note that the number of measurements less than 1.00 is a binomial random variable and *if H_0 is true,* the binomial probability p that a measurement lies below (or above) the median 1.00 is equal to .5 (Figure 2). What is the probability that a result is *as contrary to or more contrary to H_0* than the one observed if H_0 is true? That is, what is the probability that 7 *or more* of 8 binomial measurements will result in Success (be less than 1.00) if the probability of Success is .5? Binomial Table I in Appendix: Tables (using $n = 8$ and $p = .5$) indicates that

$$P(x \geq 7) = 1 - P(x \leq 6) = 1 - .965 = .035$$

Thus, the probability that at least 7 of 8 measurements would be less than 1.00 *if the true median were* 1.00 is only .035. The *p*-value of the test is therefore .035.

This *p*-value can also be obtained using a statistical software package. The Minitab printout of the analysis is shown in Figure 3, with the *p*-value highlighted on the printout. Because $p = .035$ is less than $\alpha = .05$, we conclude that this sample provides sufficient evidence to reject the null hypothesis. The implication of this rejection is that the laboratory can conclude at the $\alpha = .05$ level of significance that the true median level for the tested individual is less than 1.00. However, we note that one of the measurements greatly exceeds the others, with a value of 3.79, and deserves special attention. Note that this large measurement is an outlier that would make the use of a *t*-test and its concomitant assumption of normality dubious. The only assumption necessary to ensure the validity of the sign test is that the probability distribution of measurements is continuous.

The use of the sign test for testing hypotheses about population medians is summarized in the box.

Sign Test for Median: Reading

Sign test of median = 1.000 versus < 1.000

Figure 3

Minitab sign test output

	N	Below	Equal	Above	P	Median
Reading	8	7	0	1	0.0352	0.8350

Sign Test for a Population Median η

One-Tailed Test	Two-Tailed Test
$H_0: \eta = \eta_0$	$H_0: \eta = \eta_0$
$H_a: \eta > \eta_0$ [or $H_a: \eta < \eta_0$]	$H_a: \eta \neq \eta_0$

Test statistic:

S = Number of sample measurements greater than η_0 [or S = number of measurements less then η_0]

S = Larger of S_1 and S_2, where S_1 is the number of measurements less than η_0 and S_2 is the number of measurements greater than η_0

Observed significance level:

p-value = $P(x \geq S)$

p-value = $2P(x \geq S)$

where x has a binomial distribution with parameters n and $p = .5$. (Use Table I, Appendix: Tables)

Rejection region: Reject H_0 if p-value $\leq .05$.

Conditions Required for Valid Application of the Sign Test

The sample is selected randomly from a continuous probability distribution. [*Note:* No assumptions need to be made about the shape of the probability distribution.]

Recall that the normal probability distribution provides a good approximation for the binomial distribution when the sample size is large (i.e., when both $np \geq 15$ and $nq \geq 15$). For tests about the median of a distribution, the null hypothesis implies that $p = .5$, and the normal distribution provides a good approximation if $n \geq 30$. (Note that for $n = 30$ and $p = .5$, $np = nq = 15$.) Thus, we can use the standard normal z-distribution to conduct the sign test for large samples. The large-sample sign test is summarized in the next box.

Large-Sample Sign Test for a Population Median η

One-Tailed Test	Two-Tailed Test
$H_0: \eta = \eta_0$	$H_0: \eta = \eta_0$
$H_a: \eta > \eta_0$ [or $H_a: \eta < \eta_0$]	$H_a: \eta \neq \eta_0$

Test statistic: $z = \dfrac{(S - .5) - .5n}{.5\sqrt{n}}$

[*Note:* S is calculated as shown in the previous box. We subtract .5 from S as the "correction for continuity." The null hypothesized mean value is $np = .5n$, and the standard deviation is

$$\sqrt{npq} = \sqrt{n(.5)(.5)} = .5\sqrt{n}$$

Rejection region: $z > z_\alpha$ — — — *Rejection region:* $z > z_{\alpha/2}$

where tabulated z-values can be found in Table II of Appendix: Tables.

Example 1

Sign Test Application— Failure Times of MP3 Players

Problem A manufacturer of MP3 players has established that the median time to failure for its players is 5,250 hours of utilization. A sample of 40 MP3 players from a competitor is obtained, and they are continuously tested until each fails. The 40 failure times range from 5 hours (a "defective" player) to 6,575 hours, and 24 of the 40 exceed 5,250 hours. Is there evidence that the median failure time of the competitor differs from 5,250 hours? Use $\alpha = .10$.

Solution The null and alternative hypotheses of interest are

$$H_0: \eta = 5,250 \text{ hours}$$
$$H_a: \eta \neq 5,250 \text{ hours}$$

Test statistic: Since $n \geq 30$, we use the standard normal z-statistic:

$$z = \frac{(S - .5) - .5n}{.5\sqrt{n}}$$

where S is the maximum of S_1, the number of measurements greater than 5,250, and S_2, the number of measurements less than 5,250.

Rejection region: $z > 1.645$ where $z_{\alpha/2} = z_{.05} = 1.645$

Assumptions: The distribution of the failure times is continuous (time is a continuous variable), but nothing is assumed about the shape of its probability distribution.

Because the number of measurements exceeding 5,250 is $S_2 = 24$ and thus the number of measurements less than 5,250 is $S_1 = 16$, then $S = 24$, the greater of S_1 and S_2. The calculated z-statistic is therefore

$$z = \frac{(S - .5) - .5n}{.5\sqrt{n}} = \frac{23.5 - 20}{.5\sqrt{40}} = \frac{3.5}{3.162} = 1.11$$

The value of z is not in the rejection region, so we cannot reject the null hypothesis at the $\alpha = .10$ level of significance.

Look Back The manufacturer should not conclude, on the basis of this sample, that its competitor's MP3 players have a median failure time that differs from 5,250 hours. The manufacturer will not "Accept H_0," however, because the probability of a Type II error is unknown.

Now Work Exercise 5

The one-sample nonparametric sign test for a median provides an alternative to the t-test for small samples from nonnormal distributions. However, if the distribution is approximately normal, the t-test provides a more powerful test about the central tendency of the distribution.

STATISTICS in ACTION REVISITED

Testing the Median MTBE Level

We return to the study of MTBE contamination of New Hampshire groundwater wells. The Environmental Protection Agency (EPA) has not set a federal standard for MTBE in public water supplies; however, several states have developed their own standards. New Hampshire has a standard of 13 micrograms per liter—that is, no groundwater well should have an MTBE level that exceeds 13 micrograms per liter. Also, only half the wells in the state should have MTBE levels that exceed .5 micrograms per liter. This implies that the median MTBE level should be less than .5. Do the data collected by the researchers provide evidence to indicate that the median level of MTBE in New Hampshire groundwater wells is less than .5 micrograms per liter? To answer this question, we applied the sign test to the data saved in the **MTBE** file. The Minitab printout is shown in Figure SIA1.

Sign Test for Median: MTBE

```
Sign test of median =  0.5000 versus < 0.5000

        N  Below  Equal  Above       P  Median
MTBE  223    180      0     43  0.0000  0.2000
```

Figure SIA1

Minitab sign test for MTBE data

We want to test $H_0: \eta = .5$ versus $H_a: \eta < .5$. According to the printout, 180 of the 223 sampled groundwater wells had MTBE levels below .5 micrograms per liter. Consequently, the test statistic value is $S = 180$. The one-tailed p-value for the test (highlighted on the printout) is .0000. Thus, the sign test is significant at $\alpha = .01$. Therefore, the data do provide sufficient evidence to indicate that the median MTBE level of New Hampshire groundwater wells is less than .5 micrograms per liter.

🔵 *Data Set:* MTBE

Exercises 1–13

Please be aware that some of the following problems may require knowledge of concepts that are not presented in this chapter.

Learning the Mechanics

1 Under what circumstances is the sign test preferred to the t-test for making inferences about the central tendency of a population?

2 What is the probability that a randomly selected observation exceeds the
   a. Mean of a normal distribution?
   b. Median of a normal distribution?
   c. Mean of a nonnormal distribution?
   d. Median of a nonnormal distribution?

3 Use Table I of Appendix: Tables to calculate the following binomial probabilities:
   a. $P(x \geq 7)$ when $n = 8$ and $p = .5$
   b. $P(x \geq 5)$ when $n = 8$ and $p = .5$
   c. $P(x \geq 8)$ when $n = 8$ and $p = .5$
   d. $P(x \geq 10)$ when $n = 15$ and $p = .5$. Also use the normal approximation to calculate this probability and then compare the approximation with the exact value.
   e. $P(x \geq 15)$ when $n = 25$ and $p = .5$. Also use the normal approximation to calculate this probability and then compare the approximation with the exact value.

4 Consider the following sample of 10 measurements.

L15004
| 8.4 | 16.9 | 15.8 | 12.5 | 10.3 | 4.9 | 12.9 | 9.8 | 23.7 | 7.3 |

Use these data to conduct each of the following sign tests using the binomial tables (Table I, Appendix: Tables) and $\alpha = .05$:
   a. $H_0: \eta = 9$ versus $H_a: \eta > 9$
   b. $H_0: \eta = 9$ versus $H_a: \eta \neq 9$
   c. $H_0: \eta = 20$ versus $H_a: \eta < 20$
   d. $H_0: \eta = 20$ versus $H_a: \eta \neq 20$
   e. Repeat each of the preceding tests using the normal approximation to the binomial probabilities. Compare the results.
   f. What assumptions are necessary to ensure the validity of each of the preceding tests?

5 Suppose you wish to conduct a test of the research hypothesis that the median of a population is greater than 75. You randomly sample 25 measurements from the population and determine that 17 of them exceed 75. Set up and conduct the appropriate test of hypothesis at the .10 level of significance. Be sure to specify all necessary assumptions.

Applying the Concepts—Basic

6 Caffeine in Starbucks coffee. Researchers at the University of Florida College of Medicine investigated the level of caffeine in 16-ounce cups of Starbucks coffee (*Journal of Analytical Toxicology*, Oct. 2003). In one phase of the experiment, cups of Starbucks Breakfast Blend (a mix of Latin American coffees) were purchased on 6 consecutive days from a single specialty coffee shop. The amount of caffeine in each of the six cups (measured in milligrams) is provided in the table.

CUPS6

564	498	259	303	300	307

   a. Suppose the scientists are interested in determining whether the median amount of caffeine in Breakfast Blend coffee exceeds 300 milligrams. Set up the null and alternative hypotheses of interest.
   b. How many of the cups in the sample have a caffeine content that exceeds 300 milligrams?
   c. Assuming $p = .5$, use the binomial table in Appendix: Tables to find the probability that at least four of the six cups have caffeine amounts that exceed 300 milligrams.
   d. Based on the probability, part **c**, what do you conclude about H_0 and H_a? (Use $\alpha = .05$.)

7 Salaries of experienced MBA graduates. According to *U.S. News & World Report's* Business School Rankings, the median earnings for graduates of full-time, highly ranked MBA programs 4 years after graduating is $125,000. A random sample of 50 recent graduates from a particular highly ranked MBA program was mailed a questionnaire and asked to report their annual earnings. Fifteen usable responses were received; nine indicated earnings greater than $125,000 and six indicated earnings below $125,000.
   a. Specify the null and alternative hypotheses that should be used in testing whether the median income of graduates of the MBA program is more than $125,000.
   b. Conduct the test of part **a** using $\alpha = .05$ and draw your conclusion in the context of the problem.
   c. What assumptions must hold to ensure the validity of your hypothesis test?

8 Lobster trap placement. The *Bulletin of Marine Science* (April 2010) did an observational study of lobster trap placement by teams fishing for the red spiny lobster in Baja California Sur, Mexico. Trap-spacing measurements (in meters) for a sample of seven teams of red spiny lobster fishermen are reproduced in the accompanying table. Test whether the average of the trap-spacing measurements for the population of red spiny lobster fishermen fishing in Baja California Sur, Mexico, differs from 95 meters.

93	99	105	94	82	70	86

Source: "Explaining catch variation among Baja California lobster fishers through spatial analysis of trap placement decisions," by G. G. Shester, in BULLETIN OF MARINE SCIENCE, 86.2.

a. There is concern that the trap-spacing data do not follow a normal distribution. If so, how will this impact the test you conducted above?

b. Propose an alternative nonparametric test to analyze the data.

c. Compute the value of the test statistic for the nonparametric test.

d. Find the *p*-value of the test.

e. Use the value of α you selected in the above test and give the appropriate conclusion.

9 Short-sale stock returns. On July 15, 2008, the Securities and Exchange Commission (SEC) temporarily suspended short sales of stocks of several financial firms in order to protect the firms from sudden stock price declines. The impact the temporary restriction had on the New York Stock Exchange was the subject of an article published in the *Journal of Financial Markets* (Vol. 13, 2010). For one portion of the study, the researchers examined the daily abnormal stock returns for a sample of 17 stocks subject to the short-sale restrictions 1 month after the SEC announcement. Of these 17 stocks, 6 had a positive abnormal return rate. In theory, if the SEC restriction was effective, half of all stocks with suspended short sales would have positive return rates and half would have negative return rates. Is there evidence to dispute this theory? Test using $\alpha = .05$.

Applying the Concepts—Intermediate

10 Performance of stock screeners. Stock screeners are automated tools used by investment companies to help clients select a portfolio of stocks to invest in. The annualized percentage returns on investment (as compared to the Standard & Poor's 500 Index) for 13 randomly selected stock screeners provided by the American Association of Individual Investors (AAII) are repeated below.

9.0	−.1	−1.6	14.6	16.0	7.7	19.9	9.8	3.2	24.8	17.6	10.7	9.1

Source: American Association of Individual Investors.

a. The *t*-distribution was used to find a 90% confidence interval for the average annualized percentage return on investment of all stock screeners provided by AAII. Explain why the resulting inference may be invalid.

b. A positive annualized return reflects a stock portfolio that performed better than the S&P 500. State the null and alternative hypotheses for a nonparametric test designed

to determine if more than half of all AAII stock screeners perform better than the S&P 500.

c. Conduct the test, part **b**, using $\alpha = .05$. Interpret your result in the context of the problem.

11 Radon exposure in Egyptian tombs. *Radiation Protection Dosimetry* (December 2010) did a study of radon exposure in Egyptian tombs. The radon levels—measured in becquerels per cubic meter (Bq/m^3)—in the inner chambers of a sample of 12 tombs are reproduced in the table below. Recall that for safety purposes, the Egypt Tourism Authority (ETA) temporarily closes the tombs if the level of radon exposure in the tombs rises too high, say 6,000 Bq/m^3. Conduct a nonparametric test to determine if the true median level of radon exposure in the tombs is less than 6,000 Bq/m^3. Use $\alpha = .10$. Should the tombs be closed?

50	910	180	580	7,800	4,000
390	12,100	3,400	1,300	11,900	1,100

Source: RADIATION PROTECTION DOSIMETRY, 2010.

12 Surface roughness of pipe. *Anti-Corrosion Methods and Materials* (Vol. 50, 2003) did a study of the surface roughness of coated interior pipe used in oil fields. The data (in micrometers) for 20 sampled pipe sections are reproduced in the table. Conduct a nonparametric test to determine whether the median surface roughness of coated interior pipe, η, differs from 2 micrometers. Test using $\alpha = .05$.

1.72	2.50	2.16	2.13	1.06	2.24	2.31	2.03	1.09	1.40
2.57	2.64	1.26	2.05	1.19	2.13	1.27	1.51	2.41	1.95

Source: "Coated pipe interior surface roughness as measured by three scanning probe instruments," by T. Pesacreta and F. Farshad, in ANTI-CORROSION METHODS AND MATERIALS, 2003.

13 Ranking PhD programs in economics. The *Southern Economic Journal* (Apr. 2008) published rankings of 129 PhD programs in economics. The number of publications published by faculty teaching in the PhD program and the quality of the publications were used to develop an overall productivity score for each PhD program. The following table gives the z-scores for the 10 PhD programs that specialize in agricultural and natural resource economics. Assume these 10 programs represent a random sample of all PhD programs that specialize in agricultural and natural resource economics. Give your opinion on whether the median productivity z-score of all such PhD programs differs from 0. Test using $\alpha = .05$.

School	z-Score
1 North Carolina State	0.37
2 Iowa State	0.35
3 Wyoming	−0.30
4 SUNY Binghamton	−0.48
5 Tulane	−0.65
6 Hawaii, Manoa	−0.69
7 New Mexico	−0.71
8 Rhode Island	−0.72
9 Utah State	−0.73
10 Colorado School of Mines	−0.76

Source: THE SOUTHERN ECONOMIC JOURNAL, April 2009.

3 Comparing Two Populations: Independent Samples

Suppose two independent random samples are to be used to compare two populations and the *t*-test is inappropriate for making the comparison. We may be unwilling to make assumptions about the form of the underlying population probability distributions or we may be unable to obtain exact values of the sample measurements. If the data can be ranked in order of magnitude for either of these situations, the **Wilcoxon rank sum test** (developed by Frank Wilcoxon) can be used to test the hypothesis that the probability distributions associated with the two populations are equivalent.

For example, suppose six economists who work for the federal government and seven university economists are randomly selected, and each is asked to predict next year's percentage change in cost of living as compared with this year's figure. The objective of the study is to compare the government economists' predictions to those of the university economists. The data are shown in Table 2.

Table 2	Percentage Cost-of-Living Change, as Predicted by Government and University Economists		
Government Economist (1)		University Economist (2)	
Prediction	Rank	Prediction	Rank
3.1	4	4.4	6
4.8	7	5.8	9
2.3	2	3.9	5
5.6	8	8.7	11
0.0	1	6.3	10
2.9	3	10.5	12
		10.8	13

Data Set: COL

Experience has shown that the populations of predicted percentage changes often possess probability distributions that are skewed, as shown in Figure 4. Consequently, a *t*-test should not be used to compare the mean predictions of the two groups of economists because the normality assumption that is required for the *t*-test may not be valid.

The two populations of predictions are those that would be obtained from *all* government and *all* university economists if they could all be questioned. To compare their probability distributions using a nonparametric test, we first *rank the sample observations as though they were all drawn from the same population*—that is, we pool the measurements from both samples and then rank the measurements from the smallest (a rank of 1) to the largest (a rank of 13). The ranks of the 13 economists' predictions are indicated in Table 2.

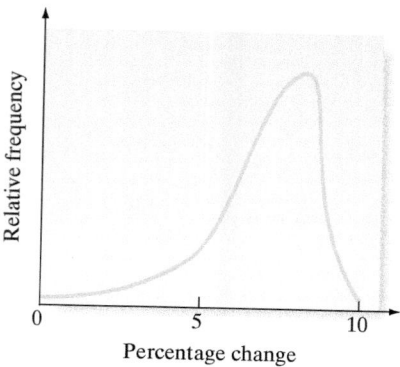

Figure 4

Typical probability distribution of predicted cost-of-living changes

If the two populations were identical, we would expect the ranks to be *randomly mixed* between the two samples. If, on the other hand, one population tends to have larger percentage changes than the other, we would expect the larger ranks to be mostly in one sample and the smaller ranks mostly in the other. Thus, the test statistic for the Wilcoxon test is based on the totals of the ranks for each of the two samples—that is, on the **rank sums.** The greater the difference in rank sums, the greater the evidence to indicate a difference between the populations.

For the economists' predictions, we arbitrarily denote the rank sum for government economists by T_1 and that for university economists by T_2. Then

$$T_1 = 4 + 7 + 2 + 8 + 1 + 3 = 25$$
$$T_2 = 6 + 9 + 5 + 11 + 10 + 12 + 13 = 66$$

The sum of T_1 and T_2 will always equal $n(n + 1)/2$, where $n = n_1 + n_2$. So, for this example, $n_1 = 6, n_2 = 7$, and

$$T_1 + T_2 = \frac{13(13 + 1)}{2} = 91$$

Because $T_1 + T_2$ is fixed, a small value for T_1 implies a large value for T_2 (and vice versa) and a large difference between T_1 and T_2. Therefore, the smaller the value of one of the rank sums, the greater the evidence to indicate that the samples were selected from different populations.

The test statistic for this test is the rank sum for the smaller sample; or, in the case where $n_1 = n_2$, either rank sum can be used. Values that locate the rejection region for this rank sum are given in Table XII of Appendix: Tables. A partial reproduction of this table is shown in Table 3. The columns of the table represent n_1, the first sample size, and the rows represent n_2, the second sample size. *The T_L and T_U entries in the table are the boundaries of the lower and upper regions, respectively, for the rank sum associated with the sample that has fewer measurements.* If the sample sizes n_1 and n_2 are the same, either rank sum may be used as the test statistic. To illustrate, suppose $n_1 = 6$ and $n_2 = 7$. For a two-tailed test with $\alpha = .05$, we consult part **a** of the table and find that the null hypothesis will be rejected if the rank sum of sample 1 (the sample with fewer measurements), T_1, is less than or equal to $T_L = 28$ or greater than or equal to $T_U = 56$. (These values are highlighted in Table 3.) The Wilcoxon rank sum test is summarized in the next box.

Wilcoxon Rank Sum Test: Independent Samples*

Let D_1 and D_2 represent the probability distributions for populations 1 and 2, respectively.

One-Tailed Test	Two-Tailed Test
H_0: D_1 and D_2 are identical	H_0: D_1 and D_2 are identical
H_a: D_1 is shifted to the right of D_2 [or H_a: D_1 is shifted to the left of D_2]	H_a: D_1 is shifted either to the left or to the right of D_2
Test statistic: T_1, if $n_1 < n_2$; T_2, if $n_2 < n_1$ (Either rank sum can be used if $n_1 = n_2$.)	*Test statistic:* T_1, if $n_1 < n_2$; T_2, if $n_2 < n_1$ (Either rank sum can be used if $n_1 = n_2$.) We will denote this rank sum as T.
Rejection region: T_1: $T_1 \geq T_U$ [or $T_1 \leq T_L$] T_2: $T_2 \leq T_L$ [or $T_2 \geq T_U$]	*Rejection region:* $T \leq T_L$ or $T \geq T_U$

where T_L and T_U are obtained from Table XII of Appendix: Tables.

Ties: Assign tied measurements the average of the ranks they would receive if they were unequal but occurred in successive order. For example, if the third-ranked and fourth-ranked measurements are tied, assign each a rank of $(3 + 4)/2 = 3.5$.

---

*Another statistic used for comparing two populations based on independent random samples is the *Mann-Whitney U-statistic*. The U-statistic is a simple function of the rank sums. It can be shown that the Wilcoxon rank sum test and the Mann-Whitney U-test are equivalent.

Conditions Required for a Valid Wilcoxon Rank Sum Test

1. The two samples are random and independent.
2. The two probability distributions from which the samples are drawn are continuous.

Table 3	Reproduction of Part of Table XII of Appendix: Tables: Critical Values for the Wilcoxon Rank Sum Test

$\alpha = .025$ one-tailed; $\alpha = .05$ two-tailed

n_2 \ n_1	3		4		5		6		7		8		9		10	
	T_L	T_U	T_L	T_U	T_L	T_U	T_L	T_U	T_L	T_U	T_L	T_U	T_L	T_U	T_L	T_U
3	5	16	6	18	6	21	7	23	7	26	8	28	8	31	9	33
4	6	18	11	25	12	28	12	32	13	35	14	38	15	41	16	44
5	6	21	12	28	18	37	19	41	20	45	21	49	22	53	24	56
6	7	23	12	32	19	41	26	52	28	56	29	61	31	65	32	70
7	7	26	13	35	20	45	28	56	37	68	39	73	41	78	43	83
8	8	28	14	38	21	49	29	61	39	73	49	87	51	93	54	98
9	8	31	15	41	22	53	31	65	41	78	51	93	63	108	66	114
10	9	33	16	44	24	56	32	70	43	83	54	98	66	114	79	131

Note that the assumptions necessary for the validity of the Wilcoxon rank sum test do not specify the shape or type of probability distribution. However, the distributions are assumed to be continuous so that the probability of tied measurements is 0, and each measurement can be assigned a unique rank. In practice, however, rounding of continuous measurements will sometimes produce ties. As long as the number of ties is small relative to the sample sizes, the Wilcoxon test procedure will still have an approximate significance level of α. The test is not recommended to compare discrete distributions for which many ties are expected.*

Example	2

Applying the Rank Sum Test—Comparing Economists' Predictions

Problem Test the hypothesis that the government economists' predictions of next year's percentage change in cost of living tend to be lower than the university economists'—that is, test to determine if the probability distribution of the government economists' predictions is *shifted to the left* of the probability distribution of the university economists' predictions. Conduct the test using the data in Table 2 and $\alpha = .05$.

Solution H_0: The probability distributions corresponding to the government and university economists' predictions of inflation rate are identical.

H_a: The probability distribution for the government economists' predictions lies below (to the left of) the probability distribution for the university economists' predictions.[†]

Test statistic: Because fewer government economists ($n_1 = 6$) than university economists ($n_2 = 7$) were sampled, the test statistic is T_1, the rank sum of the government economists' predictions.

Rejection region: Because the test is one-sided, we consult part **b** of Table XII for the rejection region corresponding to $\alpha = .05$. We reject H_0 only for $T_1 \leq T_L$, the lower value from Table XII, because we are specifically testing that the distribution of the government economists' predictions lies *below* the distribution of the university economists' predictions, as shown in Figure 5. Thus, we reject H_0 if $T_1 \leq 30$.

*Adjustments for ties are available with the Wilcoxon rank sum test. Consult the references at the end of this chapter.

[†]The alternative hypotheses in this chapter will be stated in terms of a difference in the *location* of the distributions. However, because the shapes of the distributions may also differ under H_a, some of the figures (e.g., Figure 5) depicting the alternative hypothesis will show probability distributions with different shapes.

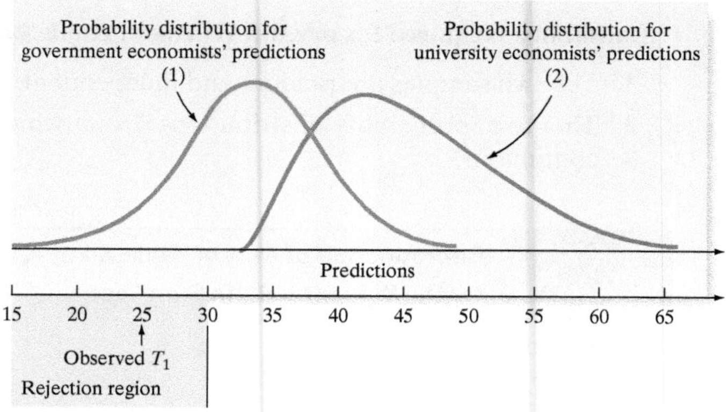

Figure 5

Alternative hypothesis
and rejection region for
Example 2

Because T_1, the rank sum of the government economists' predictions in Table 2, is 25, it is in the rejection region (see Figure 5). Therefore, we can conclude that the university economists' predictions tend, in general, to exceed the government economists' predictions. This same conclusion can be reached using a statistical software package. The SPSS printout of the analysis is shown in Figure 6. Both the test statistic ($T_1 = 25$) and two-tailed p-value ($p = .014$) are highlighted on the printout. The one-tailed p-value, $p = .014/2 = .007$, is less than $\alpha = .05$, leading us to reject H_0.

Mann-Whitney Test

Ranks

	ECONOMST	N	Mean Rank	Sum of Ranks
PCTCHNG	1	6	4.17	25.00
	2	7	9.43	66.00
	Total	13		

Test Statistics[b]

	PCTCHNG
Mann-Whitney U	4.000
Wilcoxon W	25.000
Z	−2.429
Asymp. Sig. (2-tailed)	.015
Exact Sig. [2*(1-tailed Sig.)]	.014[a]

a. Not corrected for ties.

b. Grouping Variable: ECONOMST

Figure 6

SPSS printout of rank
sum test

Look Back We remind you that the Wilcoxon rank sum test is equivalent to the Mann-Whitney test. The p-values for the tests are identical.

Now Work Exercise 15

Table XII of Appendix: Tables gives values of T_L and T_U for values of n_1 and n_2 less than or equal to 10. When both sample sizes n_1 and n_2 are 10 or larger, the sampling distribution of T_1 can be approximated by a normal distribution with mean and variance

$$E(T_1) = \frac{n_1(n_1 + n_2 + 1)}{2} \quad \text{and} \quad \sigma_{T_1}^2 = \frac{n_1 n_2(n_1 + n_2 + 1)}{12}$$

Therefore, for $n_1 \geq 10$ and $n_2 \geq 10$ we can conduct the Wilcoxon rank sum test using the familiar z-test. The test is summarized in the next box.

The Wilcoxon Rank Sum Test for Large Samples ($n_1 \geq 10$ and $n_2 \geq 10$)

Let D_1 and D_2 represent the probability distributions for populations 1 and 2, respectively.

One-Tailed Test	Two-Tailed Test
H_0: D_1 and D_2 are identical	H_0: D_1 and D_2 are identical
H_a: D_1 is shifted to the right of D_2	H_a: D_1 is shifted either to the
(or H_a: D_1 is shifted to the left of D_2)	right or to the left of D_2

$$\text{Test statistic: } z = \frac{T_1 - \dfrac{n_1(n_1 + n_2 + 1)}{2}}{\sqrt{\dfrac{n_1 n_2(n_1 + n_2 + 1)}{12}}}$$

Rejection region:
$z > z_\alpha$ (or $z < -z_\alpha$)

Rejection region:
$|z| > z_{\alpha/2}$

STATISTICS in ACTION REVISITED

Comparing the MTBE Levels of Wells

Refer to the study of MTBE contamination of New Hampshire groundwater wells. One of the objectives of the study was to determine if the level of MTBE contamination is different for private and public wells and for bedrock and unconsolidated aquifers. For this objective, the researchers focused on only the 70 sampled wells that had detectable levels of MTBE. Specifically, they wanted to determine if the distribution of MTBE levels in public wells is shifted above or below the distribution of MTBE levels in private wells, and, if the distribution of MTBE levels in bedrock aquifers is shifted above or below the distribution of MTBE levels in unconsolidated aquifers.

To answer these questions, the researchers applied the Wilcoxon rank sum test for two independent samples. In the first analysis, public and private wells were compared; in the second analysis, bedrock and unconsolidated aquifers were compared. The Minitab printouts for these analyses are shown in Figures SIA2 and SIA3, respectively. Both the test statistics and the two-tailed *p*-values are highlighted on the printouts.

```
Mann-Whitney Test and CI: PRIVATE, PUBLIC

            N   Median
PRIVATE    22   0.520
PUBLIC     48   1.035              I


Point estimate for ETA1-ETA2 is -0.390
95 Percent CI for ETA1-ETA2 is (-1.279,0.041)
W = 654.5
Test of ETA1 = ETA2 vs ETA1 not = ETA2 is significant at 0.1109
The test is significant at 0.1108 (adjusted for ties)
```

Figure SIA2

Minitab rank sum test for comparing public and private wells

```
Mann-Whitney Test and CI: UNCONSOL, BEDROCK

             N   Median
UNCONSOL     7   0.340
BEDROCK     63   0.970


Point estimate for ETA1-ETA2 is -0.590
95 Percent CI for ETA1-ETA2 is (-1.990,-0.010)
W = 139.5
Test of ETA1 = ETA2 vs ETA1 not = ETA2 is significant at 0.0337
The test is significant at 0.0336 (adjusted for ties)
```

Figure SIA3

Minitab rank sum test for comparing bedrock and unconsolidated aquifers

For the comparison of public and private wells in Figure SIA2, *p*-value = .1109. Thus, at $\alpha = .05$ there is insufficient evidence to conclude that the distribution of

MTBE levels differs for public and private New Hampshire groundwater wells. Although public wells tend to have higher MTBE values than private wells (note the sample medians in Figure SIA2), the difference is not statistically significant.

For the comparison of bedrock and unconsolidated aquifers in Figure SIA3, p-value $= .0337$. At $\alpha = .05$, there is sufficient evidence to conclude that the distribution of MTBE levels differs for bedrock and unconsolidated aquifers. Furthermore, the sample medians shown in Figure SIA3 indicate that bedrock aquifers tend to have the higher MTBE levels.

[*Note*: Histograms of the MTBE levels for public wells, private wells, bedrock aquifers, and unconsolidated aquifers (not shown) reveal distributions that are highly skewed. Thus, application of the nonparametric rank sum test is appropriate.]

Data Set: MTBE

Exercises 14–28

Please be aware that some of the following problems may require knowledge of concepts that are not presented in this chapter.

Learning the Mechanics

14 Specify the test statistic and the rejection region for the Wilcoxon rank sum test for independent samples in each of the following situations:
a. $n_1 = 10, n_2 = 6, \alpha = .10$
H_0: Two probability distributions, 1 and 2, are identical
H_a: Probability distribution for population 1 is shifted to the right or left of the probability distribution for population 2
b. $n_1 = 5, n_2 = 7, \alpha = .05$
H_0: Two probability distributions, 1 and 2, are identical
H_a: Probability distribution for population 1 is shifted to the right of the probability distribution for population 2
c. $n_1 = 9, n_2 = 8, \alpha = .025$
H_0: Two probability distributions, 1 and 2, are identical
H_a: Probability distribution for population 1 is shifted to the left of the probability distribution for population 2
d. $n_1 = 15, n_2 = 15, \alpha = .05$
H_0: Two probability distributions, 1 and 2, are identical
H_a: Probability distribution for population 1 is shifted to the right or left of the probability distribution for population 2

15 Suppose you wish to compare two treatments, A and B, based on independent random samples of 15 observations selected from each of the two populations. If $T_1 = 173$, do the data indicate that distribution A is shifted to the left of distribution B? Test using $\alpha = .05$.

16 Suppose you want to compare two treatments, A and B. In particular, you wish to determine whether the distribution for population B is shifted to the right of the distribution for population A. You plan to use the Wilcoxon rank sum test.
a. Specify the null and alternative hypotheses you would test.
b. Suppose you obtained the following independent random samples of observations on experimental units subjected to the two treatments. Conduct a test of the hypotheses described in part **a.** Test using $\alpha = .05$.

Sample A	37	40	33	29	42	33	35	28	34
Sample B	65	35	47	52					

17 Independent random samples are selected from two populations. The data shown in the table.

L15017

Sample 1		Sample 2		
15	16	5	9	5
10	13	12	8	10
12	8	9	4	

a. Use the Wilcoxon rank sum test to determine whether the data provide sufficient evidence to indicate a shift in the locations of the probability distributions of the sampled populations. Test using $\alpha = .05$.
b. Do the data provide sufficient evidence to indicate that the probability distribution for population 1 is shifted to the right of the probability distribution for population 2? Use the Wilcoxon rank sum test with $\alpha = .05$.

Applying the Concepts—Basic

18 Short Message Service for cell phones. Short Message Service (SMS) is the formal name for the communication service that allows the interchange of short text messages between mobile telephone devices. About 75% of mobile phone subscribers worldwide send or receive SMS text messages. Consequently, SMS provides an opportunity for direct marketing. In *Management Dynamics* (2007), marketing researchers investigated the perceptions of college students toward SMS marketing. For one portion of the study, the researchers applied the Wilcoxon rank sum test to compare the distributions of the number of text messages sent and received during peak time for two groups of cell phone users: those on an annual contract and those with a pay-as-you-go option.
a. Specify the null hypothesis tested in the words of the problem.
b. Give the formula for the large-sample test statistic if there were 25 contract users and 40 pay-as-you-go users in the sample.
c. The Wilcoxon test results led the researchers to conclude "that contract users sent and received significantly more SMS messages during peak time than

pay-as-you-go users." Based on this information, draw a graph that is representative of the two SMS usage rate populations.

19 Bursting strength of bottles. Polyethylene terephthalate (PET) bottles are used for carbonated beverages. A critical property of PET bottles is their bursting strength (i.e., the pressure at which bottles filled with water burst when pressurized). In the *Journal of Data Science* (May 2003), researchers measured the bursting strength of PET bottles made from two different designs—an old design and a new design. The data (pounds per square inch) for 10 bottles of each design are shown in the table. Suppose you want to compare the distributions of bursting strengths for the two designs.

| Old Design | 210 | 212 | 211 | 211 | 190 | 213 | 212 | 211 | 164 | 209 |
| New Design | 216 | 217 | 162 | 137 | 219 | 216 | 179 | 153 | 152 | 217 |

a. Rank all 20 observed pressures from smallest to largest and assign ranks from 1 to 20.

b. Sum the ranks of the observations from the old design.

c. Sum the ranks of the observations from the new design.

d. Compute the Wilcoxon rank sum statistic.

e. Carry out a nonparametric test (at $\alpha = .05$) to compare the distribution of bursting strengths for the two designs.

20 Gender attitudes toward corruption and tax evasion. Do men and women differ in their attitudes toward public corruption and tax evasion? This was the question of interest in a study published in *Contemporary Economic Policy* (Oct. 2010). The data for the analysis were obtained from a representative sample of over 30,000 Europeans. Each person was asked how justifiable it is for someone to (1) accept a bribe in the course of his or her duties and (2) cheat on his or her taxes. Responses were measured as 0, 1, 2, or 3, where 0 = "always justified" and 3 = "never justified." The large-sample Wilcoxon rank sum test was applied in order to compare the response distributions of men and women.

a. Give the null hypothesis for the test in the words of the problem.

b. An analysis of the "justifiability of corruption" responses yielded a large-sample test statistic of $z = -14.10$ with a corresponding *p*-value of approximately 0. Interpret this result.

c. Refer to part **b.** Women had a larger rank sum statistic than men. What does this imply about gender attitudes toward corruption?

d. An analysis of the "justifiability of tax evasion" responses yielded a large-sample test statistic of $z = -18.12$ with a corresponding *p*-value of approximately 0. Interpret this result.

e. Refer to part **d.** Again, women had a larger rank sum statistic than men. What does this imply about gender attitudes toward tax evasion?

21 The X-Factor in golf performance. Many golf teaching professionals believe that a greater hip-to-shoulder differential angle during the early downswing—dubbed the "X-Factor"—leads to improved golf performance. The *Journal of Quantitative Analysis in Sports* (Vol. 5, 2009) published an article on the X-Factor and its relationship to golfing performance. The study involved 15 male golfers with a player handicap of 20 strokes or fewer. The golfers

were divided into two groups: 8 golfers with a handicap of 10 strokes or fewer (low-handicapped group) and 7 golfers with a handicap between 12 and 20 strokes (high-handicapped group). The X-Factor, i.e., the hip-to-shoulder differential angle (in degrees), was measured for each golfer at the top of the backswing during his tee-shot. The researchers hypothesized that low-handicapped golfers will tend to have higher X-Factors than high-handicapped golfers. The researchers also discovered that the sample data were not normally distributed. Consequently, they applied a nonparametric test.

a. What nonparametric test is appropriate for analyzing these data?

b. Specify the null and alternative hypotheses of interest in the words of the problem.

c. Give the rejection region for this test, using $\alpha = .05$.

d. The researchers reported a *p*-value of .487. Use this result to draw a conclusion.

22 Homework assistance for accounting students. The *Journal of Accounting Education* (Vol. 25, 2007) did a study on homework assistance for accounting students. Students were randomly assigned different levels of assistance on the homework. Some (20 students) were given the completed solution, some (25 students) were given check figures at various steps of the solution, and the rest (30 students) were given no help. After finishing the homework, the students were all given a test on the subject and the knowledge gains (improvement in test scores) determined. The accompanying table gives the sample median knowledge gains for the three groups of students.

	No Solutions	Check Figures	Completed Solutions
Sample Size	30	25	20
Sample Median	3	2	2

Source: "How much help is too much help? An experimental investigation of the use of check figures and completed solutions in teaching and intermediate accounting," by L. M. Olsen and T. M. Lindquist, in JOURNAL OF ACCOUNTING EDUCATION, 25.3, pp. 103–117, 2007.

a. The researchers theorized that as the level of homework assistance increases, the test score improvement will decrease. Do the sample medians reported in the table support this theory?

b. What is the problem with using only the sample medians to make inferences about the population median knowledge gains for the three groups of students?

c. The researchers conducted the Wilcoxon rank sum test to compare the median knowledge gain of students in the "no solutions" group to the median knowledge gain of students in the "check figures" group. Based on the theory, part **a,** set up the null and alternative hypotheses for the test.

d. The observed significance level of the nonparametric test of part **c** was reported as .456. Using $\alpha = .05$, interpret this result.

Applying the Concepts—Intermediate

23 Children's recall of TV ads. The *Journal of Advertising* (Spring 2006) did a study of children's recall of television advertisements. Two groups of children were shown a 60-second commercial for Sunkist FunFruit Rock-n-Roll Shapes. One group (the A/V group) was shown the ad with both audio and video; the second group (the video only group) was shown only the video portion of the commercial. The number of 10 specific items from the ad recalled correctly by each child is shown in the table. The researchers theorized that children who receive an audiovisual presentation will have the same level of recall as those who receive only the visual aspects of the ad. Consider testing the researchers' theory using the Wilcoxon rank sum test.

A/V:	0 4 6 6 1 2 2 6 6 4 1 2 6 1 3 0 2 5 4 5
Video Only:	6 3 6 2 2 4 7 6 1 3 6 2 3 1 3 2 5 2 4 6

Source: "Children's Recall of Television Ad Elements," by R. H. Kolbe, M. Y. Hu and J. K. Maher, in JOURNAL OF ADVERTISING, 35.1, 2006.

a. Set up the appropriate null and alternative hypotheses for the test.
b. Find the value of the test statistic.
c. Give the rejection region for $\alpha = .10$.
d. Make the appropriate inference. What can you say about the researchers' theory?

24 Teamwork between nurses and doctors. In the treatment of critically ill patients, teamwork among health care professionals is essential. What is the level of collaboration between nurses and resident doctors working in the intensive care unit (ICU)? This was the question of interest in an article published in the *Journal of Advanced Nursing* (Vol. 67, 2011). Independent samples of 31 nurses and 46 resident doctors, all working in the ICU, completed the Baggs Collaboration and Satisfaction about Care Decisions survey. Responses to all questions were measured on a 7-point scale, where 1 = never and 7 = always. The data for the following two questions (simulated from information provided in the article) are listed at the bottom of the page.

a. Conduct a nonparametric test (at $\alpha = .05$) to compare the response distributions for nurses and doctors on Question 4. Practically interpret the result.
b. Conduct a nonparametric test (at $\alpha = .05$) to compare the response distributions for nurses and doctors on Question 5. Practically interpret the result.

25 Does rudeness really matter in the workplace? The *Academy of Management Journal* (Oct. 2007) did a study on rudeness in the workplace. 98 college students

enrolled in a management course were randomly assigned to one of two experimental conditions: rudeness condition (where students were berated by a facilitator for being irresponsible and unprofessional) and control group (no facilitator comments). Each student was asked to write down as many uses for a brick as possible in 5 minutes. The data are reproduced in the next table.

a. Show that although the data for the rudeness condition are approximately normally distributed, the control group data are skewed.
b. Conduct the appropriate nonparametric test (at $\alpha = .01$) to determine if the true median performance level for students in the rudeness condition is lower than the true median performance level for students in the control group.
c. Explain why a parametric 2-sample test is appropriate even though the data for both groups are not normally distributed. (Note that the nonparametric and parametric tests yield the same conclusions.)

Control Group:
1	24	5	16	21	7	20	1	9	20	19	10	23	16	0	4	9	13
17	13	0	2	12	11	7	1	19	9	12	18	5	21	30	15	4	
2	12	11	10	13	11	3	6	10	13	16	12	28	19	12	20	3	11

Rudeness Condition:
4	11	18	11	9	6	5	11	9	12	7	5	7	3	11	1	9	11	10	7
8	9	10	7	11	4	13	5	4	7	8	3	8	15	9	16	10	0	7
15	13	9	2	13	10												

26 Patent infringement case. *Chance* (Fall 2002) did a study of a patent infringement case brought against Intel Corp. The case rested on whether a patent witness's signature was written on top of key text in a patent notebook or under the key text. Using an X-ray beam, zinc measurements were taken at several spots on the notebook page. The zinc measurements for three notebook locations—on a text line, on a witness line, and on the intersection of the witness and text lines—are reproduced in the table.

Text Line:	.335	.374	.440			
Witness Line:	.210	.262	.188	.329	.439	.397
Intersection:	.393	.353	.285	.295	.319	

a. Why might the Student's *t*-procedure you applied in Exercise 19 be inappropriate for analyzing this data?

Question 4: Physicians and nurses cooperate in making decisions

Nurses:	1	1	1	1	2	2	2	2	2	2	2	2	2	2	3	3	3	3	3	3	3	4
	5	5	5	5	5	5	5	7	7													
Doctors:	1	1	1	1	1	1	1	2	2	2	3	3	3	3	3	3	3	3	3	3	4	4
	5	5	5	5	5	5	5	5	5	5	5	5	5	6	6	6	6	6	6	7	7	7	7	7

Question 5: In making decisions, both nursing and medical concerns about patients' needs are considered

Nurses:	1	1	2	2	2	2	3	3	3	3	3	3	3	3	4	4	4	4	4	4
	5	5	5	5	5	5	5	5	6	6	7									
Doctors:	2	2	2	2	2	3	3	3	4	4	5	5	5	5	5	5	5	5	5	5	5	5	5	5	5	5	5
	6	6	6	6	6	6	6	6	6	6	7	7	7	7	7	7	7	7									

Data for Exercise 24

b. Use a nonparametric test (at $\alpha = .05$) to compare the distribution of zinc measurements for the text line with the distribution for the intersection.

c. Use a nonparametric test (at $\alpha = .05$) to compare the distribution of zinc measurements for the witness line with the distribution for the intersection.

d. From the results, parts **b** and **c,** what can you infer about the median zinc measurements at the three notebook locations?

27 Cooling method for gas turbines. The *Journal of Engineering for Gas Turbines and Power* (Jan. 2005) did a study of gas turbines augmented with high-pressure inlet fogging. The data on engine heat rate (kilojoules per kilowatt per hour) are saved in the accompanying file. The researchers classified gas turbines into three categories: traditional, advanced, and aeroderivative. Suppose you want to compare the heat rate distributions for traditional and aeroderivative turbine engines.

a. Demonstrate that the assumptions required to compare the mean heat rates using a *t*-test are likely to be violated.

b. A Minitab printout of the nonparametric test to compare the two heat rate distributions is shown below. Interpret the *p*-value of the test shown at the bottom of the printout.

28 Is honey a cough remedy? The *Archives of Pediatrics and Adolescent Medicine* (Dec. 2007) did a study of honey as a children's cough remedy. 70 children who were ill with an upper respiratory tract infection were given either a dosage of dextromethorphan (DM)—an over-the-counter cough medicine—or a similar dose of honey. Parents then rated their children's cough symptoms, and the improvement in total cough symptoms score was determined for each child. The data (improvement scores) are reproduced in the accompanying table. The researchers concluded that "honey may be a preferable treatment for the cough and sleep difficulty associated with childhood upper respiratory tract infection." Use the nonparametric method presented in this section to analyze the data (use $\alpha = .05$). Do you agree with the researchers?

Honey Dosage:	12 11 15 11 10 13 10 4 15 16 9 14
	10 6 10 8 11 12 12 8 12 9 11 15
	10 15 9 13 8 12 10 8 9 5 12
DM Dosage:	4 6 9 4 7 7 7 9 12 10 11 6 3 4
	9 12 7 6 8 12 12 4 12 13 7 10 13 9
	4 4 10 15 9

Source: Data from ARCHIVES OF PEDIATRICS AND ADOLESCENT MEDICINE, 161.12, 2007.

Minitab output for Exercise 27

Mann-Whitney Test and CI: TRAD-HR, AERO-HR

```
            N   Median
TRAD-HR    39    11183
AERO-HR     7    12414


Point estimate for ETA1-ETA2 is -1125
95.3 Percent CI for ETA1-ETA2 is (-2358,1448)
W = 885.0
Test of ETA1 = ETA2 vs ETA1 not = ETA2 is significant at 0.3431
The test is significant at 0.3431 (adjusted for ties)
```

4   # Comparing Two Populations: Paired Difference Experiment

Nonparametric techniques can also be employed to compare two probability distributions when a paired difference design is used. For example, consumer preferences for two competing products are often compared by having each of a sample of consumers rate both products. Thus, the ratings have been paired on each consumer. Here is an example of this type of experiment.

For some paper products, softness is an important consideration in determining consumer acceptance. One method of determining softness is to have judges give a sample of the products a softness rating. Suppose each of 10 judges is given a sample of two products that a company wants to compare. Each judge rates the softness of each product on a scale from 1 to 20, with higher ratings implying a softer product. The results of the experiment are shown in Table 4.

Because this is a paired difference experiment, we analyze the differences between the measurements. However, a nonparametric approach developed by Wilcoxon requires that we calculate the ranks of the absolute values of the differences between the measurements—that is, the ranks of the differences after removing any minus signs. The absolute values of the differences are calculated and ranked (with ranks for negative differences highlighted) in Table 4. *Note that tied absolute differences*

Table 4			Softness Ratings of Paper		
	Product		Difference		
Judge	A	B	(A − B)	Absolute Value of Difference	Rank of Absolute Value
1	12	8	4	4	4.5
2	16	10	6	6	7
3	8	9	−1	1	1
4	10	8	2	2	2
5	15	12	7	7	8
6	14	17	−3	3	3
7	12	4	8	8	9
8	10	6	4	4	4.5
9	12	17	−5	5	6
10	16	4	12	12	10

T_+ = Sum of positive ranks = 45
T_- = Sum of negative ranks = 10

(e.g., the two differences of 4) are assigned the average of the ranks they would receive if they were unequal but successive measurements (e.g., 4.5, the average of the ranks 4 and 5). After the absolute differences are ranked, the sum of the ranks of the positive differences of the original measurements, T_+, and the sum of the ranks of the negative differences of the original measurements, T_-, are computed.

We are now prepared to test the nonparametric hypotheses:

H_0: The probability distributions of the ratings for products A and B are identical.

H_a: The probability distributions of the ratings differ (in location) for the two products. (Note that this is a two-sided alternative and that it implies a two-tailed test.)

Test statistic: T = Smaller of the positive and negative rank sums T_+ and T_-.

The smaller the value of T, the greater the evidence to indicate that the two probability distributions differ in location. The rejection region for T can be determined by consulting Table XIII of Appendix: Tables (part of the table is shown in Table 5). This

Table 5		Reproduction of Part of Table XIII of Appendix: Tables: Critical Values for the Wilcoxon Paired Difference Signed Rank Test					
One-Tailed	Two-Tailed	$n = 5$	$n = 6$	$n = 7$	$n = 8$	$n = 9$	$n = 10$
$\alpha = .05$	$\alpha = .10$	1	2	4	6	8	11
$\alpha = .025$	$\alpha = .05$		1	2	4	6	8
$\alpha = .01$	$\alpha = .02$			0	2	3	5
$\alpha = .005$	$\alpha = .01$				0	2	3
		$n = 11$	$n = 12$	$n = 13$	$n = 14$	$n = 15$	$n = 16$
$\alpha = .05$	$\alpha = .10$	14	17	21	26	30	36
$\alpha = .025$	$\alpha = .05$	11	14	17	21	25	30
$\alpha = .01$	$\alpha = .02$	7	10	13	16	20	24
$\alpha = .005$	$\alpha = .01$	5	7	10	13	16	19
		$n = 17$	$n = 18$	$n = 19$	$n = 20$	$n = 21$	$n = 22$
$\alpha = .05$	$\alpha = .10$	41	47	54	60	68	75
$\alpha = .025$	$\alpha = .05$	35	40	46	52	59	66
$\alpha = .01$	$\alpha = .02$	28	33	38	43	49	56
$\alpha = .005$	$\alpha = .01$	23	28	32	37	43	49
		$n = 23$	$n = 24$	$n = 25$	$n = 26$	$n = 27$	$n = 28$
$\alpha = .05$	$\alpha = .10$	83	92	101	110	120	130
$\alpha = .025$	$\alpha = .05$	73	81	90	98	107	117
$\alpha = .01$	$\alpha = .02$	62	69	77	85	93	102
$\alpha = .005$	$\alpha = .01$	55	61	68	76	84	92

table gives a value T_0 for both one-tailed and two-tailed tests for each value of n, the number of matched pairs. For a two-tailed test with $\alpha = .05$, we will reject H_0 if $T \leq T_0$. You can see in Table 5 that the value of T_0 that locates the boundary of the rejection region for $\alpha = .05$ and $n = 10$ pairs of observations is 8. Thus, the rejection region for the test (see Figure 7) is

$$Rejection\ region:\ T \leq 8 \quad for \quad \alpha = .05$$

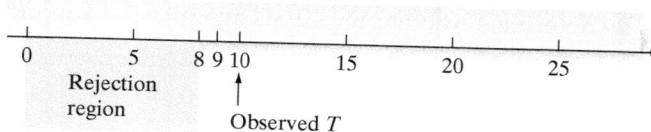

Because the smaller rank sum for the paper data, $T_- = 10$, does not fall within the rejection region, the experiment has not provided sufficient evidence to indicate that the two paper products differ with respect to their softness ratings at the $\alpha = .05$ level.

Note that if a significance level of $\alpha = .10$ had been used, the rejection region would have been $T \leq 11$, and we would have rejected H_0. In other words, the samples do provide evidence that the probability distributions of the softness ratings differ at the $\alpha = .10$ significance level.

The **Wilcoxon signed rank test** is summarized in the box below. Note that the difference measurements are assumed to have a continuous probability distribution so that the absolute differences will have unique ranks. Although tied (absolute) differences can be assigned ranks by averaging, the number of ties should be small relative to the number of observations to ensure the validity of the test.

Wilcoxon Signed Rank Test for a Paired Difference Experiment

Let D_1 and D_2 represent the probability distributions for populations 1 and 2, respectively.

One-Tailed Test	Two-Tailed Test
H_0: D_1 and D_2 are identical	H_0: D_1 and D_2 are identical
H_a: D_1 is shifted to the right of D_2 [or H_a: D_1 is shifted to the left of D_2]	H_a: D_1 is shifted either to the left or to the right of D_2

Calculate the difference within each of the n matched pairs of observations. Then rank the absolute value of the n differences from the smallest (rank 1) to the highest (rank n) and calculate the rank sum T_- of the negative differences and the rank sum T_+ of the positive differences. [*Note:* Differences equal to 0 are eliminated, and the number n of differences is reduced accordingly.]

Test statistic:	*Test statistic:*
T_-, the rank sum of the negative differences [or T_+, the rank sum of the positive differences]	T, the smaller of T_+ or T_-
Rejection region:	*Rejection region:*
$T_- \leq T_0$ [or $T_+ \leq T_0$]	$T \leq T_0$

where T_0 is given in Table XIII of Appendix: Tables.

Ties: Assign tied absolute differences the average of the ranks they would receive if they were unequal but occurred in successive order. For example, if the third-ranked and fourth-ranked differences are tied, assign both a rank of $(3 + 4)/2 = 3.5$.

Conditions Required for a Valid Signed Rank Test

1. The sample of differences is randomly selected from the population of differences.
2. The probability distribution from which the sample of paired differences is drawn is continuous.

Example 3

Applying the Signed Rank Test—Comparing Electrical Safety Ratings

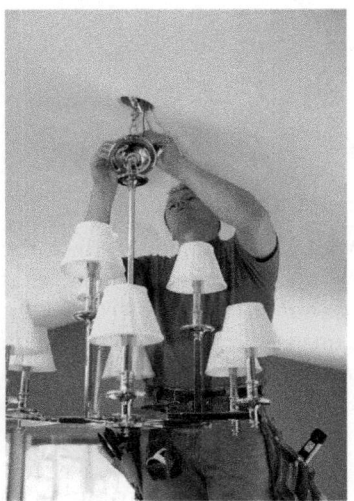

Problem Suppose the U.S. Consumer Product Safety Commission (CPSC) wants to test the hypothesis that New York City electrical contractors are more likely to install unsafe electrical outlets in urban homes than in suburban homes. A pair of homes, one urban and one suburban and both serviced by the same electrical contractor, is chosen for each of 10 randomly selected electrical contractors. A CPSC inspector assigns each of the 20 homes a safety rating between 1 and 10, with higher numbers implying safer electrical conditions. The results are shown in Table 6. Use the Wilcoxon signed rank test to determine whether the CPSC hypothesis is supported at the $\alpha = .05$ level.

Table 6	Electrical Safety Ratings for 10 Pairs of New York City Homes			
	Location		Difference	
Contractor	Urban A	Suburban B	(A − B)	Rank of Absolute Difference
1	7	9	−2	4.5
2	4	5	−1	2
3	8	8	0	(Eliminated)
4	9	8	1	2
5	3	6	−3	6
6	6	10	−4	7.5
7	8	9	−1	2
8	10	8	2	4.5
9	9	4	5	9
10	5	9	−4	7.5

Positive rank sum $= T_+ = 15.5$

Data Set: SAFETY

Solution The null and alternative hypotheses are

H_0: The probability distributions of home electrical ratings are identical for urban (A) and suburban (B) homes

H_a: The electrical ratings for suburban homes (B) tend to exceed the electrical ratings for urban homes (A)

Because a paired difference design was used (the homes were selected in urban-suburban pairs so that the electrical contractor was the same for both), we first calculate the difference between the ratings for each pair of homes and then rank the absolute values of the differences (see Table 6). Note that one pair of ratings was the same (both 8), and the resulting 0 difference contributes to neither the positive nor the negative rank sum. Thus, we eliminate this pair from the calculation of the test statistic.

Test statistic: T_+, the positive rank sum

In Table 6, we compute the urban minus suburban rating differences, and if the alternative hypothesis is true, we would expect most of these differences to be negative. Or, in other words, we would expect the *positive* rank sum T_+ to be small if the alternative hypothesis is true (see Figure 8).

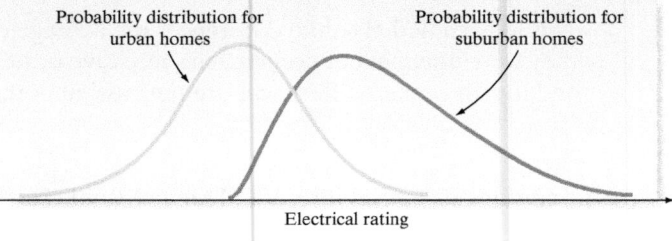

Figure 8

The alternative hypothesis for Example 3: We expect T_+ to be small

Rejection region: For $\alpha = .05$, from Table XIII of Appendix: Tables, we use $n = 9$ (remember, one pair of observations was eliminated) to find the rejection region for this one-tailed test: $T_+ \leq 8$.

Because the computed value $T_+ = 15.5$ exceeds the critical value of 8, we conclude that this sample provides insufficient evidence at $\alpha = .05$ to support the alternative hypothesis. We *cannot* conclude on the basis of this sample information that suburban homes have safer electrical outlets than urban homes.

Look Back An SPSS printout of the analysis, shown in Figure 9, confirms this conclusion. The two-tailed p-value of the test (highlighted) is .404. Because the one-tailed p-value, $.404/2 = .202$, exceeds $\alpha = .05$, we fail to reject H_0.

Wilcoxon Signed Ranks Test

Ranks

		N	Mean Rank	Sum of Ranks
SUBURB - URBAN	Negative Ranks	3[a]	5.17	15.50
	Positive Ranks	6[b]	4.92	29.50
	Ties	1[c]		
	Total	10		

a. SUBURB < URBAN

b. SUBURB > URBAN

c. SUBURB = URBAN

Test Statistics[b]

	SUBURB - URBAN
Z	−.834[a]
Asymp. Sig. (2-tailed)	.404

a. Based on negative ranks.

b. Wilcoxon Signed Ranks Test

Figure 9

SPSS printout of signed rank test

Now Work Exercise 30

As is the case for the rank sum test for independent samples, the sampling distribution of the signed rank statistic can be approximated by a normal distribution when the number n of paired observations is large (say, $n \geq 25$). The large-sample z-test is summarized in the next box.

Wilcoxon Signed Rank Test for Large Samples ($n \geq 25$)

Let D_1 and D_2 represent the probability distributions for populations 1 and 2, respectively.

One-Tailed Test	Two-Tailed Test
H_0: D_1 and D_2 are identical	H_0: D_1 and D_2 are identical
H_a: D_1 is shifted to the right of D_2 [or H_a: D_1 is shifted to the left of D_2]	H_a: D_1 is shifted either to the left or to the right of D_2

$$\text{Test statistic: } z = \frac{T_+ - [n(n+1)/4]}{\sqrt{n(n+1)(2n+1)]/24}}$$

Rejection region:
$z > z_\alpha$ [or $z < -z_\alpha$]

Rejection region:
$|z| > z_{\alpha/2}$

Assumptions: The sample size n is greater than or equal to 25. Differences equal to 0 are eliminated, and the number n of differences is reduced accordingly. Tied absolute differences receive ranks equal to the average of the ranks they would have received had they not been tied.

Exercises 29–42

Please be aware that some of the following problems may require knowledge of concepts that are not presented in this chapter.

Learning the Mechanics

29 Specify the test statistic and the rejection region for the Wilcoxon signed rank test for the paired difference design in each of the following situations:

a. $n = 30, \alpha = .10$

H_0: Two probability distributions, 1 and 2, are identical

H_a: Probability distribution for population 1 is shifted to the right or left of probability distribution for population 2

b. $n = 20, \alpha = .05$

H_0: Two probability distributions, 1 and 2, are identical

H_a: Probability distribution for population 1 is shifted to the right of the probability distribution for population 2

c. $n = 8, \alpha = .005$

H_0: Two probability distributions, 1 and 2, are identical

H_a: Probability distribution for population 1 is shifted to the left of the probability distribution for population 2

30 Suppose you wish to test a hypothesis that two treatments, A and B, are equivalent against the alternative that the responses for A tend to be larger than those for B.

a. If the number of pairs equals 25, give the rejection region for the large-sample Wilcoxon signed rank test for $\alpha = .05$.

b. Suppose that $T_+ = 273$. State your test conclusions.

c. Find the p-value for the test and interpret it.

31 Suppose you want to test a hypothesis that two treatments, A and B, are equivalent against the alternative hypothesis that the responses for A tend to be larger than those for B. You plan to use a paired difference experiment and to analyze the resulting data using the Wilcoxon signed rank test.

a. Specify the null and alternative hypotheses you would test.

b. Suppose the paired difference experiment yielded the data in the table. Conduct the test of part **a.** Test using $\alpha = .025$.

Pair	Treatment A	Treatment B	Pair	Treatment A	Treatment B
1	54	45	6	77	75
2	60	45	7	74	63
3	98	87	8	29	30
4	43	31	9	63	59
5	82	71	10	80	82

32 A paired difference experiment with $n = 30$ pairs yielded $T_+ = 354$.

a. Specify the null and alternative hypotheses that should be used in conducting a hypothesis test to determine whether the probability distribution for population 1 is located to the right of that for population 2.

b. Conduct the test of part **a** using $\alpha = .05$.

c. What is the approximate p-value of the test of part **b**?

d. What assumptions are necessary to ensure the validity of the test you performed in part **b**?

Applying the Concepts—Basic

33 Twinned drill holes. *Exploration and Mining Geology* (Vol. 18, 2009) did a study of drill twinned holes. The drilling of a new hole, or "twin," next to an earlier drill hole is a traditional method of verifying mineralization grades. The data in the table represent total amount of heavy minerals (THM) percentages for a sample of 15 twinned holes drilled at a diamond mine in Africa. Use a confidence interval based on Student's t-distribution to check for a difference in the true THM means of all original holes and their twin holes drilled at the mine.

a. Explain why the results of the confidence interval may be invalid.

b. What is the appropriate nonparametric test to apply? State H_0 and H_a for the test.

c. Compute the difference between the "1st hole" and "2nd hole" measurements for each drilling location.

d. Rank the differences, part **c.**

e. Compute the rank sums of the positive and negative differences.

f. Use the rank sums, part **e,** to conduct the nonparametric test at $\alpha = .05$. Can the geologists conclude that there is no evidence of a difference in the THM distributions of all original holes and their twin holes drilled at the mine?

Location	1st Hole	2nd Hole
1	5.5	5.7
2	11.0	11.2
3	5.9	6.0
4	8.2	5.6
5	10.0	9.3
6	7.9	7.0
7	10.1	8.4
8	7.4	9.0
9	7.0	6.0
10	9.2	8.1
11	8.3	10.0
12	8.6	8.1
13	10.5	10.4
14	5.5	7.0
15	10.0	11.2

Source: EXPLORATION AND MINING GEOLOGY, 18, 2009.

34 Performance ratings of government agencies. *The Public Manager* (Summer 2008) published performance ratings of government agencies. Evaluation scores for all agencies were obtained for two consecutive years and are saved in the file. Data for a random sample of five of these agencies are shown in the table on the next page. Suppose you want to determine whether the distribution of evaluation scores in year 2 is shifted above the distribution of evaluation scores in year 1.

a. Specify the null and alternative hypotheses for a Wilcoxon signed rank test of the data.

b. Compute the difference between the two scores for each sampled agency. Now rank the absolute values of these differences.

c. Sum the ranks of the positive differences, part **b.** Also, sum the ranks of the negative differences.

d. Use the results, part **c,** to find the test statistic.

e. Give the rejection region for the test using $\alpha = .05$.

f. Make the appropriate conclusion in the words of the problem.

Data for Exercise 34

Agency	Year 1 Score	Year 2 Score
GSA	34	40
Agriculture	33	35
HHS	37	35
USAID	32	42
Defense	17	32

Source: "Performance ratings of government agencies," by J. Ellig and H. Wray, from Measuring Performance Reporting Quality. THE PUBLIC MANAGER, Vol. 37.2, Summer 2008, p. 66. Copyright © 2008 by Jerry Ellig. Reprinted with permission.

35 **Healing potential of handling museum objects.** Does handling a museum object have a positive impact on a sick patient's well-being? To answer this question, researchers at the University College London collected data from 32 sessions with hospital patients (*Museum & Society*, Nov. 2009). Each patient's health status (measured on a 100-point scale) was recorded both before and after handling museum objects such as archaeological artifacts and brass etchings. The data (simulated) are listed in the accompanying table. The Wilcoxon signed rank test was applied to the data with the results shown in the accompanying SPSS printout.

MUSEUM

Session	Before	After	Session	Before	After
1	52	59	17	65	65
2	42	54	18	52	63
3	46	55	19	39	50
4	42	51	20	59	69
5	43	42	21	49	61
6	30	43	22	59	66
7	63	79	23	57	61
8	56	59	24	56	58
9	46	53	25	47	55
10	55	57	26	61	62
11	43	49	27	65	61
12	73	83	28	36	53
13	63	72	29	50	61
14	40	49	30	40	52
15	50	49	31	65	70
16	50	64	32	59	72

Source: MUSEUM AND SOCIETY, November 2009.

Wilcoxon Signed Ranks Test

Ranks

		N	Mean Rank	Sum of Ranks
AFTER - BEFORE	Negative Ranks	3[a]	3.83	11.50
	Positive Ranks	28[b]	17.30	484.50
	Ties	1[c]		
	Total	32		

a. AFTER < BEFORE
b. AFTER > BEFORE
c. AFTER = BEFORE

Test Statistics[b]

	AFTER - BEFORE
Z	−4.638[a]
Asymp. Sig. (2-tailed)	.000

a. Based on negative ranks.
b. Wilcoxon Signed Ranks Test

a. Use the information in the printout to find the large-sample Wilcoxon signed rank test statistic.

b. Does handling a museum object have a positive impact on a sick patient's well-being? Test using $\alpha = .01$.

36 **NHTSA new car crash tests.** The National Highway Traffic Safety Administration (NHTSA) compiled crash test data for new cars. Compare the chest injury ratings of drivers and front-seat passengers using the Student's t-procedure for matched pairs. Suppose you want to make the comparison for only those cars that have a driver's star rating of 5 stars (the highest rating). The data for these 18 cars are listed in the table below. Now consider analyzing these data using the Wilcoxon signed rank test.

CRASH5

Car	Chest Injury Rating	
	Driver	Passenger
1	42	35
2	42	35
3	34	45
4	34	45
5	45	45
6	40	42
7	42	46
8	43	58
9	45	43
10	36	37
11	36	37
12	43	58
13	40	42
14	43	58
15	37	41
16	37	41
17	44	57
18	42	42

a. State the null and alternative hypotheses.

b. Use a statistical software package to find the signed rank test statistic.

c. Give the rejection region for the test using $\alpha = .01$.

d. State the conclusion in practical terms. Report the p-value of the test.

37 **Impact of red-light cameras on car crashes.** The June 2007 Virginia Department of Transportation (VDOT) did a study of a newly adopted photo-red-light enforcement program. The VDOT provided crash data both before and after installation of red-light cameras at several intersections. The data (measured as the number of crashes caused by red light running per intersection per year) for 13 intersections in Fairfax County, VA, are reproduced in the table on the next page. The VDOT wants to determine if the photo-red enforcement program is effective in reducing red-light-running crash incidents at intersections. Use the nonparametric Wilcoxon signed rank test (and the accompanying Minitab printout) to analyze the data for the VDOT.

REDLIT

Wilcoxon Signed Rank Test: Difference

Test of median = 0.000000 versus median > 0.000000

	N	N for Test	Wilcoxon Statistic	P	Estimated Median
Difference	13	13	79.0	0.011	0.9650

Data for Exercise 37

Intersection	Before Camera	After Camera
1	3.60	1.36
2	0.27	0
3	0.29	0
4	4.55	1.79
5	2.60	2.04
6	2.29	3.14
7	2.40	2.72
8	0.73	0.24
9	3.15	1.57
10	3.21	0.43
11	0.88	0.28
12	1.35	1.09
13	7.35	4.92

Source: "The impact of red light cameras (photo-red enforcement on crashes in Virginia)" by Virginia Transportation Research Council, 2007.

Applying the Concepts—Intermediate

38 **Food availability at middle schools.** Most schools offer a la carte food items in the cafeteria for students at lunch. To **LUNCH** encourage students to eat healthy, the U.S. Department of Agriculture (USDA) requires schools to offer nutritional food items. Two methods for identifying and quantifying food items in the a la carte line—a detailed inventory approach and a checklist approach—were compared in the *Journal of School Health* (Dec. 2009). Data were collected for a sample of 37 middle schools. For each school, the accompanying table gives the percentage of a la carte food items deemed healthy as determined by both methods. The researchers used a nonparametric analysis to determine if the distribution of healthy food item percentages using the inventory method is shifted above or below the distribution of healthy food item percentages using the checklist method. If no significant difference is detected, the checklist method will be recommended since it is simpler and requires less resources. Conduct the appropriate analysis at $\alpha = .05$. Which method do you recommend?

School	Percentage Healthy Inventory	Percentage Healthy Checklist	School	Percentage Healthy Inventory	Percentage Healthy Checklist
A	100.0	100.0	T	46.3	60.0
B	95.5	66.7	U	44.2	70.0
C	90.6	62.5	V	43.8	50.0
D	77.8	71.4	W	43.5	60.0
E	66.7	66.7	X	42.2	40.0
F	64.5	50.0	Y	41.3	54.5
G	62.5	50.0	Z	40.7	55.6
H	55.1	63.6	AA	39.0	55.6
I	54.3	58.3	BB	38.5	42.9
J	54.3	55.6	CC	35.8	44.4
K	53.8	58.3	DD	32.4	50.0
L	53.7	58.3	EE	29.2	50.0
M	52.9	66.7	FF	28.9	45.5
N	52.0	54.5	GG	27.8	50.0
O	51.5	50.0	II	25.0	100.0
Q	50.0	100.0	HH	25.0	12.5
R	50.0	66.7	JJ	7.7	66.7
S	50.0	62.5	KK	6.3	66.7
P	50.0	50.0			

Source: "Inventory versus checklist approach to assess middle school a la carte food availability" by M. O. Hearst, et al., in JOURNAL OF SCHOOL HEALTH, 79.12 (table 3). Copyright © 2009 by John Wiley & Sons, Inc. Reprinted with permission.

39 **Taking "power naps" during work breaks.** According to the National Sleep Foundation, companies are encourag- **NAPS** ing their workers to take "power naps" (*Athens Daily News,* Jan. 9, 2000). Analyze the data collected by a major airline that had recently begun encouraging reservation agents to nap during their breaks. The number of complaints received about each of a sample of 10 reservation agents during the 6 months before naps were encouraged and during the 6 months after the policy change are reproduced in the table below. Compare the distributions of number of complaints for the two time periods using the Wilcoxon signed rank test. Use $\alpha = .05$ to make the appropriate inference.

Agent	Before Policy	After Policy
1	10	5
2	3	0
3	16	7
4	11	4
5	8	6
6	2	4
7	1	2
8	14	3
9	5	5
10	6	1

40 **Concrete pavement response to temperature.** Civil engineers at West Virginia University have developed a 3D **SLAB** model to predict the response of jointed concrete pavement to temperature variations (*The International Journal of Pavement Engineering,* Sep. 2004). To validate the model, model predictions were compared to field measurements on key concrete stress variables taken at a newly constructed highway. One variable measured was slab top transverse strain (i.e., change in length per unit length per unit time) at a distance of 1 meter from the longitudinal joint. The 5-hour changes (8:20 P.M. to 1:20 A.M.) in slab top transverse strain for 6 days are listed in the table below. Analyze the data using a nonparametric test. Is there a shift in the change in transverse strain distributions between field measurements and the 3D model? Test using $\alpha = .05$.

Day	Change in Temperature (°C)	Change in Transverse Strain Field Measurement	Change in Transverse Strain 3D Model
Oct. 24	−6.3	−58	−52
Dec. 3	13.2	69	59
Dec. 15	3.3	35	32
Feb. 2	−14.8	−32	−24
Mar. 25	1.7	−40	−39
May 24	−.2	−83	−71

Source: "Validation of 3DFE model of jointed concrete pavement response to temperature variations," by M. Riad, G. William and S. Shouky, in THE INTERNATIONAL JOURNAL OF PAVEMENT ENGINEERING, 5.3, 2004.

41 **Testing electronic circuits.** *IEICE Transactions on Information & Systems* (Jan. 2005) did a comparison of two **CIRCUIT** methods of testing electronic circuits. Each of the 11 circuits was tested using the standard compression/depression method and the new Huffman-based coding method and the compression ratio recorded. The data are reproduced in the table.

a. Use a parametric procedure to determine whether the Huffman-coding method will yield a smaller mean compression ratio than the standard method. Perform the alternative nonparametric test, using $\alpha = .05$.

b. Do the conclusions of the two procedures agree?

Circuit	Standard Method	Huffman-Coding Method
1	.80	.78
2	.80	.80
3	.83	.86
4	.53	.53
5	.50	.51
6	.96	.68
7	.99	.82
8	.98	.72
9	.81	.45
10	.95	.79
11	.99	.77

Source: "Huffman-Based Test Response Coding," by T. Inoue, M. Shintani and H. Ichihara, in IEICE Transactions on Information & Systems, Vol. E88-D (table 3), 2005.

42 Teachers who involve parents. Teachers Involve Parents in Schoolwork (TIPS) is an interactive homework process designed to improve the quality of homework assignments for elementary, middle, and high school students. TIPS homework assignments require students to conduct interactions with family partners (parents, guardians, etc.) while completing the homework. Frances Van Voorhis (Johns Hopkins University) conducted a study to investigate the effects of TIPS in science and mathematics homework assignments (April 2001). Each large group of middle school students was assigned to complete TIPS homework assignments. At the end of the study, all students reported on the level of family involvement in their homework on a 4-point scale (0 = Never, 1 = Rarely, 2 = Sometimes, 3 = Frequently, 4 = Always). The data for science and math for a random sample of 10 students selected from the large group are shown in the table. Conduct a nonparametric analysis to compare the level of family involvement in science and math homework assignments of TIPS students. Use $\alpha = 05$.

Student	Science	Math
1	0	2
2	4	3
3	3	0
4	1	1
5	3	1
6	2	3
7	4	0
8	2	1
9	3	1
10	4	1

Source: "The effects of teachers' use of interactive homework on middle grade student science learning," by Francis Van Voorhis. Presented at the annual meeting of the American Educational Research Association (AERA), April 2001. Copyright © 2001 by Francis Van Voorhis. Reprinted with permission.

5 Comparing Three or More Populations: Completely Randomized Design

We can use an analysis of variance and the F-test to compare the means of p populations (treatments) based on random sampling from populations that were normally distributed with a common variance σ^2. We now present a nonparametric technique — **Kruskal-Wallis H-test** — for comparing the populations that require no assumptions concerning the population probability distributions.

Suppose a health administrator wants to compare the unoccupied bed space for three hospitals in the same city. She randomly selects 10 different days from the records of each hospital and lists the number of unoccupied beds for each day (see Table 7). Because the number of unoccupied beds per day may occasionally be quite large, it is conceivable that the population distributions of data may be skewed to the right and that this type of data may not satisfy the assumptions necessary for a parametric comparison of the population means. We therefore use a nonparametric analysis and base our comparison on the rank sums for the three sets of sample data. Just as with two independent samples (Section 3), the ranks are computed for each observation according to the relative magnitude of the measurements *when the data for all the samples are combined* (see Table 7). Ties are treated as they were for the Wilcoxon rank sum and signed rank tests by assigning the average value of the ranks to each of the tied observations.

We test

H_0: The probability distributions of the number of unoccupied beds are the same for all three hospitals

H_a: At least two of the three hospitals have probability distributions of the number of unoccupied beds that differ in location

If we denote the rank sums for the k samples by $R_1, R_2, \ldots, R_k$, the test statistic is given by

$$H = \frac{12}{n(n+1)} \sum n_j (\bar{R}_j - \bar{R})^2$$

where n_j is the number of measurements in the jth sample, n is the total sample size, $\bar{R}_j$ is mean rank corresponding to sample j, and $\bar{R}$ is the mean of all the ranks [that is, $\bar{R} = (n+1)/2$]. The H-statistic measures the extent to which the k samples differ with respect to their relative ranks. Thus, $H = 0$ if all samples have the same mean rank, and H becomes increasingly large as the distance between the sample mean ranks grows.

If the null hypothesis is true, the distribution of H in repeated sampling is approximately a χ^2 (chi-square) distribution. This approximation for the sampling distribution of H is adequate as long as each of the k sample sizes exceeds 5. (See the references for more detail.) The degrees of freedom corresponding to the approximate sampling distribution of H will always be $(k-1)-1$ less than the number of probability distributions being compared. Because large values of H support the alternative hypothesis that the populations have different probability distributions, the rejection region for the test is located in the upper tail of the χ^2 distribution.

Example 4

Applying the Kruskal-Wallis Test—Comparing Available Hospital Beds

Problem Consider the data in Table 7. Recall that a health administrator wants to compare the unoccupied bed space of the three hospitals. Apply the Kruskal-Wallis H-test to the data. What conclusion can you draw? Test using $\alpha = .05$.

Solution As stated previously, the administrator wants to test

H_0: The distributions of the number of unoccupied beds are the same for the three hospitals

H_a: At least two of the three hospitals have unoccupied bed distributions that differ in location

For the data in Table 7, we have $k = 3$ samples with $n_1 = n_2 = n_3 = 10$ and $n = 30$. The rank sums are $R_1 = 120$, $R_2 = 210.5$, and $R_3 = 134.5$; consequently,

Table 7	Number of Available Beds				
Hospital 1		Hospital 2		Hospital 3	
Beds	Rank	Beds	Rank	Beds	Rank
6	5	34	25	13	9.5
38	27	28	19	35	26
3	2	42	30	19	15
17	13	13	9.5	4	3
11	8	40	29	29	20
30	21	31	22	0	1
15	11	9	7	7	6
16	12	32	23	33	24
25	17	39	28	18	14
5	4	27	18	24	16
$R_1 = 120$		$R_2 = 210.5$		$R_3 = 134.5$	

Data Set: BEDS

$\overline{R}_1 = 12.0, \overline{R}_2 = 21.05,$ and $\overline{R}_3 = 13.45.$ Also, the mean of all the ranks is $\overline{R} = (31)/2 = 15.5.$ Substituting these values in the test statistic formula, we have

$$\text{Test statistic: } H = \frac{12}{30(31)} [10(12.0 - 15.5)^2 + 10(21.05 - 15.5)^2 + 10(13.45 - 15.5)^2]$$

$$= \frac{12}{30(31)} [472.55] = 6.097$$

Now, when $k = 3$, the test statistic has a χ^2 distribution with $(k - 1) = 2\text{df}.$ For $\alpha = .05$, we consult Table IV of Appendix: Tables and find $\chi^2_{.05} = 5.99147.$ Therefore,

Rejection region: $H > 5.99147$ (see Figure 10)

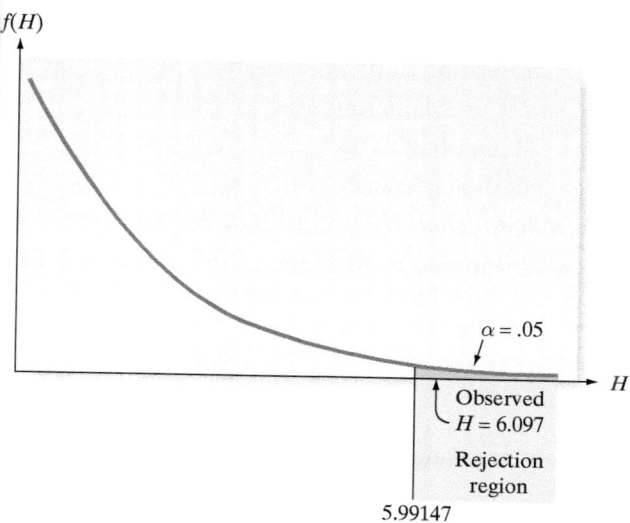

Figure 10

Rejection region for the comparison of three probability distributions

Conclusion: Because $H = 6.097$ exceeds the critical value of 5.99147, we reject the null hypothesis and conclude that at least one of the three hospitals has a distribution of unoccupied beds that is shifted above the distributions for the other hospitals. That is, at least one of the hospitals tends to have a larger number of unoccupied beds than the others.

Look Back The same conclusion can be reached from a computer printout of the analysis. The test statistic and *p*-value of the nonparametric test are highlighted on the Excel/XLSTAT printout shown in Figure 11. Because $\alpha = .05$ exceeds *p*-value $= .0474$, there is sufficient evidence to reject H_0.

Figure 11

Excel/XLSTAT Kruskal-Wallis test output

Kruskal-Wallis test:					
K (Observed value)	6.0988				
K (Critical value)	5.9915				
DF	2				
p-value (Two-tailed)	0.0474				
alpha	0.05				
An approximation has been used to compute the p-value.					

Now Work Exercise 45

The Kruskal-Wallis H-test for comparing more than two probability distributions is summarized in the box. Note that we can use the Wilcoxon rank sum test of Section 3 to compare the separate pairs of populations if the Kruskal-Wallis H-test supports the alternative hypothesis that at least two of the probability distributions differ.*

Kruskal-Wallis H-Test for Comparing k Probability Distributions

H_0: The k probability distributions are identical

H_a: At least two of the k probability distributions differ in location

$$\text{Test statistic:}^\dagger \quad H = \frac{12}{n(n+1)} \sum n_j (\overline{R}_j - \overline{R})^2$$

where

n_j = Number of measurements in sample j

R_j = Rank sum for sample j, where the rank of each measurement is computed according to its relative magnitude in the totality of data for the k samples

$\overline{R}_j = R_j/n_j$ = Mean rank sum for jth sample

$\overline{R}$ = Mean of all ranks = $(n+1)/2$

n = Total sample size = $n_1 + n_2 + \cdots + n_k$

Rejection region: $H > \chi_\alpha^2$ with $(k-1)$ degrees of freedom

Ties: Assign tied measurements the average of the ranks they would receive if they were unequal but occurred in successive order. For example, if the third-ranked and fourth-ranked measurements are tied, assign both a rank of $(3+4)/2 = 3.5$. The number of ties should be small relative to the total number of observations.

Conditions Required for the Validity of the Kruskal-Wallis H-Test

1. The k samples are random and independent.
2. There are five or more measurements in each sample.
3. The k probability distributions from which the samples are drawn are continuous.

STATISTICS in ACTION REVISITED

Comparing the MTBE Levels of Wells (continued)

In the previous *Statistics in Action Revisited*, we demonstrated the use of Wilcoxon rank sum tests to compare the MTBE distributions of public and private groundwater wells and of bedrock and unconsolidated aquifers. The environmental researchers also investigated how the combination of well class and aquifer affected the MTBE levels of the 70 wells in the **MTBE** file that had detectable levels. Although there are four possible combinations of well class and aquifer, there were data available for only three: Private/bedrock, Public/bedrock, and Public/unconsolidated.

The distribution of MTBE levels for these three groups of wells was compared using the Kruskal-Wallis nonparametric test for independent samples. The Minitab printout for the analysis is shown in Figure SIA4. The test statistic and p-value (highlighted) are $H = 9.12$ and p-value = .010. At $\alpha = .05$, there is sufficient evidence to indicate differences in the distributions of MTBE levels of the three class/aquifer types. Based on the medians shown on the printout, it appears that public wells with bedrock aquifers have the highest levels of MTBE contamination.

---

*A method similar to the multiple comparisons procedure can be used to rank the treatment medians. This nonparametric multiple comparisons of medians will control the experimentwise error rate selected by the analyst. Consult the references [Daniel (1990) and Dunn (1964)] for details.

†An alternative but equivalent formula for the test statistic is $H = \dfrac{12}{n(n+1)} \sum \dfrac{R_j^2}{n_j} - 3(n+1)$.

Kruskal-Wallis Test: MTBE versus WELL-ACQ

```
Kruskal-Wallis Test on MTBE

WELL-ACQ    N   Median   Ave Rank      Z
Priv/Bed   22   0.5200      29.8    -1.60
Pub/Bed    41   1.5000      41.2     2.81
Pub/Uncon   7   0.3400      19.9    -2.13
Overall    70               35.5

H = 9.12   DF = 2   P = 0.010
H = 9.12   DF = 2   P = 0.010   (adjusted for ties)
```

Figure SIA4

SAS Kruskal-Wallis test for comparing MTBE levels of wells

Data Set: MTBE

Exercises 43–53

Please be aware that some of the following problems may require knowledge of concepts that are not presented in this chapter.

Learning the Mechanics

43 Under what circumstances does the χ^2 distribution provide an appropriate characterization of the sampling distribution of the Kruskal-Wallis H-statistic?

44 Data were collected from three populations, A, B, and C, using a completely randomized design. The following describes the sample data:

$$n_A = n_B = n_C = 15$$
$$R_A = 230 \quad R_B = 440 \quad R_C = 365$$

a. Specify the null and alternative hypotheses that should be used in conducting a test of hypothesis to determine whether the probability distributions of populations A, B, and C differ in location.

b. Conduct the test of part **a.** Use $\alpha = .05$.

c. What is the approximate p-value of the test of part **b**?

d. Compute H using the alternative formula given in the footnote on the previous page. Verify that this formula yields the same value of H that you obtained in part **b**.

45 Suppose you want to use the Kruskal-Wallis H-test to compare the probability distributions of three populations. The following data represent independent random samples selected from the three populations:

L15045
NW

I	66, 23, 55, 88, 58, 62, 79, 49
II	19, 31, 16, 29, 30, 33, 40
III	75, 96, 102, 75, 98, 78

a. What type of experimental design was used?

b. Specify the null and alternative hypotheses you would test.

c. Specify the rejection region you would use for your hypothesis test, at $\alpha = .01$.

d. Conduct the test at $\alpha = .01$.

Applying the Concepts—Basic

46 **Containing wildfires.** The *International Journal of Wildland Fire* (Dec. 2011) published a study of the time it takes to contain wildfires, both with and without aerial support. Containment time (in hours) was estimated by fire management personnel for a particular wildfire scenario that had no aerial support. Fire management personnel were classified according to one of three primary roles—ground, office, or air support. Data for 21 fire managers (simulated, based on information provided in the article) are listed in the table. One objective is to compare the estimated containment times of the three groups of fire managers.

WILDFR

Ground	Office	Air
7.6	5.4	2.5
10.8	2.8	3.4
20.9	3.9	2.7
15.5	5.9	2.8
9.7	4.3	3.6
5.9	4.6	
	2.6	
	3.3	
	3.2	
	7.7	

a. Why is the ANOVA F-test inappropriate for analyzing these data? Use graphs to support your answer.

b. What is the appropriate nonparametric test to apply? State H_0 and H_a for the test.

c. Rank the 21 estimated containment times, and then find the rank sums for the three groups of fire managers.

d. Compute the nonparametric test statistic.

e. Find the rejection region for the test using $\alpha = .10$.

f. State the appropriate conclusion.

47 **Study of recall of TV commercials.** The *Journal of Applied Psychology* (June 2002) did a study of recall of television commercials. In a designed experiment, 324 adults were randomly assigned to one of three viewer groups: (1) watch a TV program with a violent content code (V) rating, (2) watch a show with a sex content code (S) rating, and (3) watch a neutral TV program. The number of brand names recalled in the commercial messages was recorded for each participant.

ADREC

a. Give the null and alternative hypotheses for a Kruskal-Wallis test applied to the data.

b. The results of the nonparametric test are shown in the Minitab printout on the next page. Locate the test statistic and p-value on the printout.

c. Interpret the results, part **b**, using $\alpha = .01$. What can the researchers conclude about the three groups of TV ad viewers?

Minitab output for Exercise 47

Kruskal-Wallis Test: RECALL versus GROUP

```
Kruskal-Wallis Test on RECALL

GROUP      N   Median  Ave Rank     Z
N        108    3.000     205.1   5.79
S        108    1.000     131.2  -4.26
V        108    2.000     151.2  -1.53
Overall  324              162.5

H = 36.04  DF = 2  P = 0.000
H = 37.15  DF = 2  P = 0.000  (adjusted for ties)
```

48 Commercial eggs produced from different housing systems.
Food Chemistry (Vol. 106, 2008) did a study of commercial
EGGS eggs produced from different housing systems for chickens.
The four housing systems investigated were (1) cage, (2)
barn, (3) free range, and (4) organic. Twenty-eight commercial grade-A eggs were randomly selected from supermarkets—10 of which were produced in cages, 6 in barns, 6 with
free range, and 6 organic. A number of quantitative characteristics were measured for each egg, including penetration
strength (newtons). The data (simulated from summary
statistics provided in the journal article) are given below.

Cage:	36.9 39.2 40.2 33.0 39.0 36.6 37.5 38.1 37.8 34.9
Free:	31.5 39.7 37.8 33.5 39.9 40.6
Barn:	40.0 37.6 39.6 40.3 38.3 40.2
Organic:	34.5 36.8 32.6 38.5 40.2 33.2

a. Rank the observations in the data set from 1 to 28.
b. Sum the ranks of the data for each housing system.
c. Use the rank sums to find the Kruskal-Wallis test
statistic.
d. Based on the result, part **c**, what do you infer about
the strength distributions of the four housing
systems?

49 Office rental growth rates. Real estate market cycles are
commonly divided into four phases that are based on
the rate of change of the demand for and supply of prop-
OFFICE erties: I—Recovery, II—Expansion, III—Hypersupply,
and IV—Recession. Glenn Mueller of Johns Hopkins
University studied the office market cycles of U.S. real
estate markets (*Journal of Real Estate Research*, July/Aug.
1999). For each of the four market cycles, office rental
growth rates (i.e., growth rates for asking rents) were
measured for a sample of six different real estate markets.
These data (in percentages) are presented in the table
below.

Phase I	Phase II	Phase III	Phase IV
2.7	10.5	6.1	−1.0
−1.0	11.5	1.2	6.2
1.1	9.4	11.4	−10.8
3.4	12.2	4.4	2.0
4.2	8.6	6.2	−1.1
3.5	10.9	7.6	−2.3

Source: "Real Estate Rental Growth Rates at Different Points in the
Physical Market Cycle," by G. R. Mueller, in JOURNAL OF REAL
ESTATE RESEARCH, 18.1, pp. 131-150, 1999.

a. Specify the null hypothesis for a Kruskal-Wallis test.
b. Rank the 24 measurements in the data set.
c. Find the rank sums and calculate the test
statistic.
d. Give the rejection region for the test at
$\alpha = .05$.
e. Is there sufficient evidence to conclude that the distributions of office rental growth rates differ among the
four market cycle phases?
f. What are the advantages and disadvantages of applying
the Kruskal-Wallis H-test in part **a** rather than the parametric F-test?

Applying the Concepts—Intermediate

50 Relieving pain with hypnosis. Rehabilitation medicine researchers at the University of Washington investigated
whether virtual-reality hypnosis can relieve pain in trauma
PAIN patients (*International Journal of Clinical and Experimental
Hypnosis*, Vol. 58, 2010). Study participants were 20 patients
treated at a major Level 1 trauma center. The patients
were randomly assigned to one of three treatment groups:
(1) VRH—virtual-reality hypnosis with posthypnotic
suggestions for pain reduction, (2) VRD—virtual-reality
distraction from pain without hypnotic suggestions for pain
reduction, and (3) Control—no virtual-reality hypnosis, but
standard care. Pain intensity was measured (on a 100-point
scale) prior to treatment and 1 hour after treatment. The
differences in pain-intensity levels (before minus after) are
listed in the accompanying table.

a. Conduct a nonparametric test to determine whether
the distribution of differences in pain-intensity levels
differs for the three treatments. Test using $\alpha = .05$.
What do you conclude?
b. Combine the patients in the VRD and Control groups
into a single treatment group (called non-posthypnotic
suggestion). Compare the VRH treatment patients to
the patients in this new group using the appropriate
nonparametric test (using $\alpha = .05$). What do you conclude?

VRH	VRD	Control
−20	−12	51
−56	63	21
−34	12	8
0	−7	0
16	29	4
0		
−14		
−7		
−44		
43		
−11		

51 Public defenders' salaries. Random samples of seven lawyers employed as public defenders were selected from
PUBDEF each of three major cities. Their salaries are recorded in the
table on the next page. You have been hired to determine
whether differences exist among the salary distributions
for public defenders in the three cities.

a. Under what circumstances would it be appropriate to
use the F-test for a completely randomized design to
perform the required analysis?

Data for Exercise 51

Atlanta	Los Angeles	Washington, D.C.
$39,600	$47,400	$43,000
89,900	140,000	81,900
66,700	68,000	53,000
43,900	48,700	77,600
82,200	74,400	78,200
88,600	102,000	56,800
64,800	54,500	60,000

Source: THE AMERICAN ALMANAC OF JOBS AND SALARIES, 2000-2001 EDITION. New York: Avon Books.

b. Which assumptions required by the *F*-test are likely to be violated in this problem? Explain.

c. Use the Kruskal-Wallis *H*-test to determine whether the salary distributions differ among the three cities. Specify your null and alternative hypotheses and state your conclusions in the context of the problem. Use $\alpha = .05$.

d. What assumptions are necessary to ensure the validity of the nonparametric test in part **c**?

52 Homework assistance for accounting students. Refer to the *Journal of Accounting Education* (Vol. 25, 2007) study of assisting accounting students with their homework, Exercise 22. A completely randomized design was employed, with students randomly assigned to receive one of three different levels of assistance on the homework: (1) the completed solution, (2) check figures at various steps of the solution, and (3) no help at all. The

ACCHW

response variable of interest to the researchers was the knowledge gain (or, test score improvement). The data (simulated from descriptive statistics published in the article) are saved in the file. Analyze the data with the appropriate nonparametric method. Interpret the results, practically.

53 Is honey a cough remedy? Refer to the *Archives of Pediatrics and Adolescent Medicine* (Dec. 2007) study of honey as a children's cough remedy, Exercise 28. In addition to the two experimental groups of children with an upper respiratory tract infection—one that was given a dosage of dextromethorphan (DM) and the other a similar dose of honey—a third group of children received no dosage (control group). The cough symptoms improvement scores for the children are reproduced in the accompanying table. Conduct a nonparametric test to compare the distributions of cough improvement scores for the three dosage groups. Use $\alpha = .01$.

HCOUGH

Honey Dosage:	12 11 15 11 10 13 10 4 15 16 9 14 10 6 10 8 11 12 12 8 12 9 11 15 10 15 9 13 8 12 10 8 9 5 12
DM Dosage:	4 6 9 4 7 7 7 9 12 10 11 6 3 4 9 12 7 6 8 12 12 4 12 13 7 10 13 9 4 4 10 15 9
No Dosage (Control):	5 8 6 10 8 12 8 7 7 1 6 7 7 12 7 9 7 9 5 11 9 5 6 8 8 6 7 10 9 4 8 7 3 1 4 3

Source: "Effect of honey, dextromethorphan, and no treatment on nocturnal cough and sleep quality for coughing children and their parents," from ARCHIVES OF PEDIATRICS AND ADOLESCENT MEDICINE, 161.12, 2007.

6 Comparing Three or More Populations: Randomized Block Design

We can employ an analysis of variance to compare k population (treatment) means when the data were collected using a randomized block design. The *Friedman F_r-test* provides another method for testing to detect a shift in location of a set of k populations that have the same spread (or scale).* Like other nonparametric tests, it requires no assumptions concerning the nature of the populations other than the capacity of individual observations to be ranked.

Consider the problem of comparing the reaction times of subjects under the influence of different drugs produced by a pharmaceutical firm. When the effect of a drug is short-lived (there is no carryover effect) and when the drug effect varies greatly from person to person, it may be useful to employ a *randomized block design*. Using the subjects as blocks, we would hope to eliminate the variability among subjects and thereby increase the amount of information in the experiment. Suppose that three drugs, A, B, and C, are to be compared using a randomized block design. Each of the three drugs is administered to the *same subject,* with suitable time lags between the three doses. The order in which the drugs are administered is randomly determined for each subject. Thus, one drug would be administered to a subject and its reaction time would be noted; then after a sufficient length of time, the second drug administered; etc.

Suppose six subjects are chosen and that the reaction times for each drug are as shown in Table 8. To compare the three drugs, we rank the observations within each subject (block) and then compute the rank sums for each of the drugs (treatments). Tied observations within blocks are handled in the usual manner by assigning the average value of the ranks to each of the tied observations.

*The Friedman F_r-test was developed by the Nobel Prize–winning economist Milton Friedman.

Table 8	Reaction Time for Three Drugs					
Subject	Drug A	Rank	Drug B	Rank	Drug C	Rank
1	1.21	1	1.48	2	1.56	3
2	1.63	1	1.85	2	2.01	3
3	1.42	1	2.06	3	1.70	2
4	2.43	2	1.98	1	2.64	3
5	1.16	1	1.27	2	1.48	3
6	1.94	1	2.44	2	2.81	3
		$R_1 = 7$		$R_2 = 12$		$R_3 = 17$

Data Set: REACT

The null and alternative hypotheses are

H_0: The populations of reaction times are identically distributed for all three drugs

H_a: At least two of the drugs have probability distributions of reaction times that differ in location

The **Friedman F_r-statistic,** which is based on the rank sums of the treatments, measures the extent to which the k samples differ with respect to their relative ranks within the blocks. The formula for F_r is

$$F_r = \frac{12b}{k(k + 1)} \sum (\overline{R}_j - \overline{R})^2$$

where b is the number of blocks, k is the number of treatments, $\overline{R}_j$ is the mean rank corresponding to treatment j, and $\overline{R}$ is the mean of all the ranks [(i.e., $\overline{R} = \frac{1}{2}(k + 1)$]. You can see that the F_r-statistic is 0 if all treatments have the same mean rank and becomes increasingly large as the distance between the sample mean ranks grows.

As for the Kruskal-Wallis H-statistic, the Friedman F_r-statistic has approximately a χ^2 sampling distribution with $(k - 1)$ degrees of freedom. Empirical results show the approximation to be adequate if either b or k exceeds 5. The Friedman F_r-test for a randomized block design is summarized in the next box.

Friedman F_r-Test for a Randomized Block Design

H_0: The probability distributions for the k treatments are identical
H_a: At least two of the probability distributions differ in location

Test statistic:* $\quad F_r = \dfrac{12b}{k(k + 1)} \sum (\overline{R}_j - \overline{R})^2$

where

b = Number of blocks

k = Number of treatments

R_j = Rank sum of the jth treatment, where the rank of each measurement is computed relative to its position *within its own block*

Rejection region: $F_r > \chi^2_\alpha$ with $(k - 1)$ degrees of freedom

Ties: Assign tied measurements within a block the average of the ranks they would receive if they were unequal but occurred in successive order. For example, if the third-ranked and fourth-ranked measurements are tied, assign each a rank of $(3 + 4)/2 = 3.5$. The number of ties should be small relative to the total number of observations.

---

*An alternative but equivalent formula for the test statistic is $F_r = \dfrac{12}{bk(k + 1)} \sum R_j^2 - 3b(k + 1)$.

> ## Conditions Required for a Valid Friedman F_r-Test
>
> 1. The treatments are randomly assigned to experimental units within the blocks.
> 2. The measurements can be ranked within blocks.
> 3. The k probability distributions from which the samples within each block are drawn are continuous.

Example	5

Applying the Friedman Test—Comparing Drug Reaction Times

Problem Consider the data in Table 8. Recall that a pharmaceutical firm wants to compare the reaction times of subjects under the influence of three different drugs that it produces. Apply the Friedman F_r-test to the data. What conclusion can you draw? Test using $\alpha = .05$.

Solution As stated previously, the firm wants to test

H_0: The population distributions of reaction times are identical for the three drugs

H_a: At least two of the three drugs have reaction time distributions that differ in location

For the data in Table 8, we have $k = 3$ treatments (drugs) and $b = 6$ blocks (subjects). The treatment rank sums are $R_1 = 7$, $R_2 = 12$, and $R_3 = 17$; consequently, $\overline{R}_1 = 7/6 = 1.167$, $\overline{R}_2 = 12/6 = 2.0$, and $\overline{R}_3 = 17/6 = 2.833$. Also, the mean of all the ranks is, $\overline{R} = (3 + 1)/2 = 2.0$. Substituting these values in the test statistic formula, we have

$$\textit{Test statistic:} \quad H = \frac{12(6)}{(3)(4)}[(1.167 - 2.0)^2 + (2.0 - 2.0)^2 + (2.833 - 2.0)^2]$$

$$= 6(1.388) = 8.33$$

Now, when $k = 3$, the test statistic has a χ^2 distribution with $(k - 1) = 2\,df$. For $\alpha = .05$, we consult Table IV of Appendix: Tables and find a $\chi^2_{.05} = 5.99147$. Therefore,

Rejection region: $H > 5.99147$ (see Figure 12)

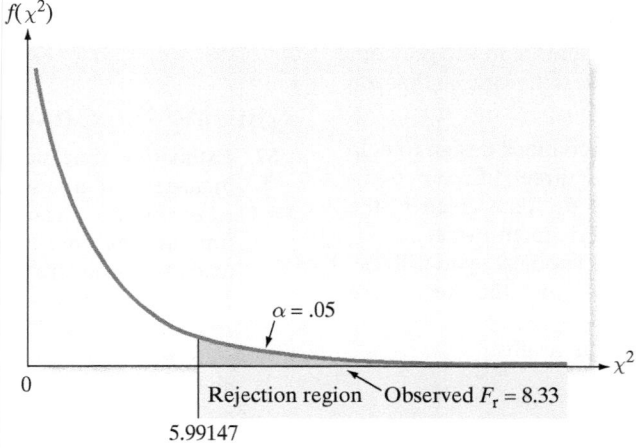

Figure 12

Rejection region for reaction time example

Conclusion: Because $H = 8.33$ exceeds the critical value of 5.99, we reject the null hypothesis and conclude that at least two of the three drugs have distributions of reaction times that differ in location. That is, at least one of the drugs tends to yield reaction times that are faster than the others.

A Minitab printout of the nonparametric analysis, shown in Figure 13, confirms our inference. Both the test statistic and p-value are highlighted on the printout. Because p-value $= .016$ is less than our selected $\alpha = .05$, there is evidence to reject H_0.

Friedman Test: REACTIME versus DRUG blocked by SUBJECT

```
S = 8.33   DF = 2   P = 0.016

                          Sum
                           of
DRUG   N   Est Median   Ranks
A      6      1.5283      7.0
B      6      1.7417     12.0
C      6      1.8950     17.0

Grand median = 1.7217
```

Figure 13

Minitab printout of Friedman test

Look Back Clearly, the assumptions for this test—that the measurements are ranked within blocks and that the number of blocks (subjects) is greater than 5—are satisfied. However, we must be sure that the treatments are randomly assigned to blocks. For the procedure to be valid, we assume that the three drugs are administered in a random order to each subject. If this were not true, the difference in the reaction times for the three drugs might be due to the order in which the drugs are given.

Now Work Exercise 55

Exercises 54–65

Please be aware that some of the following problems may require knowledge of concepts that are not presented in this chapter.

Learning the Mechanics

54 Data were collected using a randomized block design with four treatments (A, B, C, and D) and $b = 6$. The following rank sums were obtained:

$$R_A = 11 \quad R_B = 21 \quad R_C = 21 \quad R_D = 7$$

a. How many blocks were used in the experimental design?

b. Specify the null and alternative hypotheses that should be used in conducting a hypothesis test to determine whether the probability distributions for at least two of the treatments differ in location.

c. Conduct the test of part **b.** Use $\alpha = .10$.

d. What is the approximate p-value of the test of part **c**?

e. Compute the value of the F_r-test statistic using the alternative formula given in the footnote in the previous section. Verify that the test statistic is the same as that you obtained in part **c.**

55 Suppose you have used a randomized block design to help you compare the effectiveness of three different treatments, A, B, and C. You obtained the data given in the table below and plan to conduct a Friedman F_r-test.

a. Specify the null and alternative hypotheses you will test.

b. Specify the rejection region for the test. Use $\alpha = .10$.

c. Conduct the test and interpret the results.

Block	Treatment A	B	C
1	9	11	18
2	13	13	13
3	11	12	12
4	10	15	16
5	9	8	10
6	14	12	16
7	10	12	15

56 An experiment was conducted using a randomized block design with four treatments and six blocks. The ranks of the measurements within each block are shown in the table below. Use the Friedman F_r-test for a randomized block design to determine whether the data provide sufficient evidence to indicate that at least two of the treatment probability distributions differ in location. Test using $\alpha = .05$.

			Block			
Treatment	1	2	3	4	5	6
1	3	3	2	3	2	3
2	1	1	1	2	1	1
3	4	4	3	4	4	4
4	2	2	4	1	3	2

Applying the Concepts—Basic

57 **Estimating time needed to complete a task.** In project management, a key concern is the length of time it takes to perform a certain task. Managers have found that estimating the time in a series of short segments generally leads to an underestimation of the total time. This theory was tested in a study published in *Applied Cognitive Psychology* (Vol. 25, 2011). Each in a sample of 10 subjects was asked to visualize walking a familiar route for about 20 minutes. Subjects were then asked to provide an estimate of the distance walked in several shorter time segments (e.g., in 45-second intervals) until the destination was reached. The total walking time was then determined by adding up the time segments required to reach the destination. All subjects estimated total walking time (in minutes) under each of four time-segment conditions: 45-second intervals, 2-minute intervals, 3-minute intervals, and 5-minute intervals. The data (simulated from information provided in the article) are listed in the table on the next page. The researchers want to know if the distribution of walking times differs for the four time segments.

Data for Exercise 57

Subject	45 Sec.	2 Min.	3 Min.	5 Min.
1	13.0	10.5	17.2	16.0
2	10.6	14.0	18.0	16.5
3	7.5	6.0	17.0	15.0
4	10.0	12.7	10.2	12.0
5	10.5	7.5	13.5	14.5
6	7.4	15.0	10.0	15.0
7	11.0	10.6	17.5	16.0
8	7.0	15.1	13.0	12.8
9	11.0	14.7	17.5	19.0
10	12.0	16.4	21.5	20.0

Source: APPLIED COGNITIVE PSYCHOLOGY, 25, 2011.

a. Explain why the data should be analyzed using Friedman's test.
b. A Minitab printout of the analysis is shown below. Locate the test statistic and *p*-value on the printout.
c. Using $\alpha = .01$, what conclusion can you draw from the test?

Friedman Test: TIME versus INTERVAL blocked by SUBJECT

```
S = 14.37   DF = 3   P = 0.002
S = 14.52   DF = 3   P = 0.002 (adjusted for ties)

                            Sum of
INTERVAL   N   Est Median   Ranks
2min       10   11.653      21.5
3min       10   15.891      33.0
45sec      10    9.228      14.0
5min       10   15.291      31.5

Grand median = 13.016
```

---

58 Conditions impeding farm production. A review of farmer involvement in agricultural research was presented in the *Journal of Agricultural, Biological, and Environmental Statistics* (Mar. 2001). In one study, each of six farmers ranked the level of farm production constraint imposed by five conditions: drought, pest damage, weed interference, farming costs, and labor shortage. The rankings, ranging from 1 (least severe) to 5 (most severe), and rank sums for the five conditions are listed in the table below.

a. Use the rank sums shown in the table to compute the Friedman F_r statistic.

b. At $\alpha = .05$, find the rejection region for a test to compare the farmer opinion distributions for the five conditions.
c. Make the proper conclusion, in the words of the problem.

59 Peer mentor training at a firm. The *Journal of Managerial Issues* (Spring 2008) did a study of the impact of peer mentor training at a large software company. Participants volunteered to attend a 1-day peer mentor training session. The trainee's level of competence in peer mentoring (measured on a 7-point scale) was measured at three different times in the study: 1 week before training, 2 days after training, and 2 months after training. Data (simulated) for 15 trainees are displayed in the accompanying table. A Minitab nonparametric randomized block analysis is also provided below to compare the competence level distributions of the three time periods.

Trainee	Before	After 2 Days	After 2 Months
1	6	7	7
2	4	4	4
3	2	5	3
4	6	4	5
5	3	5	5
6	4	3	4
7	5	7	6
8	1	3	2
9	2	3	3
10	3	2	2
11	7	7	7
12	3	4	4
13	5	6	5
14	2	4	3
15	2	3	3

Friedman Test: LEVEL versus PERIOD blocked by TRAINEE

```
S = 5.20   DF = 2   P = 0.074
S = 7.09   DF = 2   P = 0.029 (adjusted for ties)

                             Sum of
PERIOD      N   Est Median   Ranks
After2Days  15   4.0000      35.0
After2Mons  15   4.0000      32.0
Before      15   3.0000      23.0

Grand median = 3.6667
```

		Condition				
		Drought	Pest Damage	Weed Interference	Farming Costs	Labor Shortage
	1	5	4	3	2	1
	2	5	3	4	1	2
Farmer	3	3	5	4	2	1
	4	5	4	1	2	3
	5	4	5	3	2	1
	6	5	4	3	2	1
	Rank sum	27	25	18	11	9

Source: Table from "An Illustrated Review of Some Farmer Participatory Research Techniques" by J. Riley and W. J. Fielding in JOURNAL OF AGRICULTURAL, BIOLOGICAL, AND ENVIRONMENTAL STATISTICS, 6.1 (table 1), pp. 5-14. Copyright © 2001 by International Biometric Society. Reprinted with permission.

a. Locate the rank sums on the printout.

b. Use the rank sums to find the Friedman F_r statistic.

c. Locate the test statistic and associated p-value on the printout.

d. Conduct the test and give the appropriate conclusion in the words of the problem.

60 **Rotary oil rigs.** *World Oil* (Jan. 2002) did a study of rotary oil rigs. Three months were randomly selected, and the number of oil rigs running in each of three states—California, Utah, and Alaska—was recorded. The data for the randomized block design are reproduced below. Consider a nonparametric test to compare the distributions of rotary oil rigs running in the three states.

a. State the null and alternative hypotheses for the test.

b. Rank the data within each month, then sum the ranks for each state.

c. Use the rank sums from part **b** to find the value of the test statistic.

d. Give the rejection region of the test at $\alpha = .05$.

e. State the conclusion in the words of the problem. Does the conclusion agree with that for the ANOVA *F*-test?

Month	California	Utah	Alaska
1	27	17	11
2	34	20	14
3	36	15	14

Applying the Concepts—Intermediate

61 **A new method of evaluating health care research reports.** *The Open Dentistry Journal* (Vol. 4, 2010) did a study of a new method of evaluating health care research reports. The assessment tool was validated on five systematic reviews (named R1, R2, R3, R4, and R5) on rheumatoid arthritis. For each review, scores on the 11 R-AMSTAR items (all measured on a 4-point scale) were obtained. The data are reproduced in the table below. One goal of the study was to compare the distribution of item scores for the five reviews. Conduct the analysis using the appropriate nonparametric test.

62 **Quality of research methodology in medical journals.** The journal *eCAM* (November 2006) published a study of the quality of the research methodology (e.g., statistical analysis) used in medical papers. For each in a sample of 13 research papers, the quality of the methodology on several dimensions was measured, with scores ranging from 1 (low quality) to 3 (high quality). The data in the table (next column) give the scores on three dimensions (labeled What, Who, and How) for each in a sample of 13 papers.

Paper	What	Who	How
1	3	2	2
2	3	1	3
3	2	1	1
4	2	2	2
5	2	2	1
6	2	1	2
7	2	2	2
8	2	1	3
9	1	2	1
10	2	1	2
11	2	1	3
12	2	2	1
13	3	2	2

Source: Table from "Evidence-based research in complementary in alternative medicine III: Treatment of patients with Alzheimer's disease" by Francesco Chiapelli et al., in EVIDENCE-BASED COMPLEMENTARY AND ALTERNATIVE MEDICINE (Table 1) eCAM, 3.4, pp. 411-424. Copyright © 2006 by Francesco Chiapelli under a Creative Commons Attribution license.

a. One goal of the study is to compare the mean scores of the three research methodology dimensions. Set up the null and alternative hypotheses for this test.

b. Explain why the data should be analyzed using a nonparametric randomized block ANOVA.

c. Conduct the analysis for the researchers. What do you conclude? (Use $\alpha = .10$.)

63 **Reducing on-the-job stress.** Kansas State did a study designed to investigate the effects of plants on human stress levels. The data (below) are given as finger temperatures for each of 10 students in a dimly lit room under three experimental conditions: presence of a live plant, presence of a plant photo, and absence of a plant (either live or photo). Analyze the data using a nonparametric procedure. Do students' finger temperatures depend on the experimental condition?

Student	Live Plant	Plant Photo	No Plant (control)
1	91.4	93.5	96.6
2	94.9	96.6	90.5
3	97.0	95.8	95.4
4	93.7	96.2	96.7
5	96.0	96.6	93.5
6	96.7	95.5	94.8
7	95.2	94.6	95.7
8	96.0	97.2	96.2
9	95.6	94.8	96.0
10	95.6	92.6	96.6

Source: "Reducing on-the-job stress," Copyright © 2012 by Elizabeth Schreiber, formerly of Department of Statistics, Kansas State University. Reprinted with permission.

Data for Exercise 61

Review	Item 1	Item 2	Item 3	Item 4	Item 5	Item 6	Item 7	Item 8	Item 9	Item 10	Item 11
R1	4.0	1.0	4.0	2.0	3.5	3.5	3.5	3.5	1.0	1.0	1.0
R2	3.5	2.5	4.0	4.0	3.5	4.0	3.5	2.5	3.5	1.5	1.0
R3	4.0	4.0	3.5	4.0	1.5	2.5	3.5	3.5	2.5	1.5	1.0
R4	3.5	2.0	4.0	4.0	2.0	4.0	3.5	3.0	3.5	1.0	1.0
R5	3.5	4.0	4.0	3.0	2.5	4.0	4.0	4.0	2.5	1.0	2.5

Source: "From systematic reviews to clinical recommendations to clinical-based health care: Validation of revised assessment of multiple systematic reviews (R-AMSTAR) for grading of clinical relevance," by J. Kung et al., in THE OPEN DENTISTRY JOURNAL, Vol. 4, 2010.

64   Absentee rates at a jeans plant. *New Technology, Work, and Employment* (July 2001) did a study of daily worker absentee rates at a jeans plant. Nine weeks were randomly selected and the absentee rate (percentage of workers absent) determined for each day (Monday through Friday) of the workweek. The data are reproduced in the table. Conduct a nonparametric analysis of the data to compare the distributions of absentee rates for the five days of the workweek.

Week	Monday	Tuesday	Wednesday	Thursday	Friday
1	5.3	0.6	1.9	1.3	1.6
2	12.9	9.4	2.6	0.4	0.5
3	0.8	0.8	5.7	0.4	1.4
4	2.6	0.0	4.5	10.2	4.5
5	23.5	9.6	11.3	13.6	14.1
6	9.1	4.5	7.5	2.1	9.3
7	11.1	4.2	4.1	4.2	4.1
8	9.5	7.1	4.5	9.1	12.9
9	4.8	5.2	10.0	6.9	9.0

Source: "The eradication of leisure," by J. J. Boggis, in NEW TECHNOLOGY, WORK, AND EMPLOYMENT, 16.2, pp. 118-129, July 2011.

65   Sealers used to retard metal corrosion. Corrosion of different metals is a problem in many mechanical devices. Three sealers used to help retard the corrosion of metals were tested to see whether there were any differences among them. Samples of 10 different metal compositions were treated with each of the three sealers, and the amount of corrosion was measured after exposure to the same environmental conditions for 1 month. The data are given in the table below. Is there any evidence of a difference in the probability distributions of the amounts of corrosion among the three types of sealer? Use $\alpha = .05$.

Metal	Sealer 1	Sealer 2	Sealer 3
1	4.6	4.2	4.9
2	7.2	6.4	7.0
3	3.4	3.5	3.4
4	6.2	5.3	5.9
5	8.4	6.8	7.8
6	5.6	4.8	5.7
7	3.7	3.7	4.1
8	6.1	6.2	6.4
9	4.9	4.1	4.2
10	5.2	5.0	5.1

7   Rank Correlation

Suppose 10 new car models are evaluated by two consumer magazines and each magazine ranks the braking systems of the cars from 1 (best) to 10 (worst). We want to determine whether the magazines' ranks are related. Does a correspondence exist between their ratings? If a car is ranked high by magazine 1, is it likely to be ranked high by magazine 2? Or do high rankings by one magazine correspond to low rankings by the other? That is, are the rankings of the magazines *correlated*?

If the rankings are as shown in the "Perfect Agreement" columns of Table 9, we immediately notice that the magazines agree on the rank of every car. High ranks correspond to high ranks and low ranks to low ranks. This is an example of *perfect positive correlation* between the ranks. In contrast, if the rankings appear as shown in the "Perfect Disagreement" columns of Table 9, high ranks for one magazine correspond to low ranks for the other. This is an example of *perfect negative correlation*.

Table 9	Brake Rankings of 10 New Car Models by Two Consumer Magazines			
	Perfect Agreement		Perfect Disagreement	
Car Model	Magazine 1	Magazine 2	Magazine 1	Magazine 2
1	4	4	9	2
2	1	1	3	8
3	7	7	5	6
4	5	5	1	10
5	2	2	2	9
6	6	6	10	1
7	8	8	6	5
8	3	3	4	7
9	10	10	8	3
10	9	9	7	4

In practice, you will rarely see perfect positive or negative correlation between the ranks. In fact, it is quite possible for the magazines' ranks to appear as shown in Table 10. You will note that these rankings indicate some agreement between the consumer magazines, but not perfect agreement, thus indicating a need for a measure of rank correlation.

Table 10	Brake Rankings of New Car Models: Less-than-Perfect Agreement			
	Magazine		Difference between Rank 1 and Rank 2	
Car Model	1	2	d	d^2
1	4	5	-1	1
2	1	2	-1	1
3	9	10	-1	1
4	5	6	-1	1
5	2	1	1	1
6	10	9	1	1
7	7	7	0	0
8	3	3	0	0
9	6	4	2	4
10	8	8	0	0
				$\sum d^2 = 10$

Spearman's rank correlation coefficient, r_s, provides a measure of correlation between ranks. The formula for this measure of correlation is given in the box on the next page. We also give a formula that is identical to r_s when there are no ties in rankings; this provides a good approximation to r_s when the number of ties is small relative to the number of pairs.

Note that if the ranks for the two magazines are identical, as in the second and third columns of Table 9, the differences between the ranks, d, will all be 0. Thus,

$$r_s = 1 - \frac{6\sum d^2}{n(n^2-1)} = 1 - \frac{6(0)}{10(99)} = 1$$

That is, *perfect positive correlation* between the pairs of ranks is characterized by a Spearman correlation coefficient of $r_s = 1$. When the ranks indicate perfect disagreement, as in the fourth and fifth columns of Table 9, $\sum d_i^2 = 330$ and

$$r_s = 1 - \frac{6(330)}{10(99)} = -1$$

Thus, *perfect negative correlation* is indicated by $r_s = -1$.

For the data of Table 10,

$$r_s = 1 - \frac{6\sum d^2}{n(n^2-1)} = 1 - \frac{6(10)}{10(99)} = 1 - \frac{6}{99} = .94$$

Spearman's Rank Correlation Coefficient

$$r_s = \frac{SS_{uv}}{\sqrt{SS_{uu}SS_{vv}}}$$

where

$$SS_{uv} = \sum(u_i - \bar{u})(v_i - \bar{v})$$

$$SS_{uu} = \sum(u_i - \bar{u})^2$$

$$SS_{vv} = \sum(v_i - \bar{v})^2$$

u_i = Rank of the ith observation in sample 1

v_i = Rank of the ith observation in sample 2

Shortcut Formula for r_s*

$$r_s = 1 - \frac{6\sum d_i^2}{n(n^2 - 1)}$$

where

$d_i = u_i - v_i$ (difference in ranks of ith observation for samples 1 and 2)

n = Number of pairs of observations (number of observations in each sample)

The fact that r_s is close to 1 indicates that the magazines tend to agree, but the agreement is not perfect.

The value of r_s always falls between -1 and $+1$, with $+1$ indicating perfect positive correlation and -1 indicating perfect negative correlation. The closer r_s falls to $+1$ or -1, the greater the correlation between the ranks. Conversely, the nearer r_s is to 0, the less the correlation.

Note that the concept of correlation implies that two responses are obtained for each experimental unit. In the consumer magazine example, each new car model received two ranks (one for each magazine), and the objective of the study was to determine the degree of positive correlation between the two rankings. Rank correlation methods can be used to measure the correlation between any pair of variables. If two variables are measured on each of n experimental units, we rank the measurements associated with each variable separately. Ties receive the average of the ranks of the tied observations. Then we calculate the value of r_s for the two rankings. This value measures the rank correlation between the two variables. We illustrate the procedure in Example 6.

Example 6

Spearman's Rank Correlation—Food Preservation Study

Problem Manufacturers of perishable foods often use preservatives to retard spoilage. One concern is that too much preservative will change the flavor of the food. Suppose an experiment is conducted using samples of a food product with varying amounts of preservative added. Both length of time until the food shows signs of spoiling and a taste rating are recorded for each sample. The taste rating is the average rating for three tasters, each of whom rates each sample on a scale from 1 (good) to 5 (bad). Twelve sample measurements are shown in Table 11.

Table 11	Data and Correlations for Example 6					
Sample	Days Until Spoilage	Rank	Taste Rating	Rank	d	d^2
1	30	2	4.3	11	−9	81
2	47	5	3.6	7.5	−2.5	6.25
3	26	1	4.5	12	−11	121
4	94	11	2.8	3	8	64
5	67	7	3.3	6	1	1
6	83	10	2.7	2	8	64
7	36	3	4.2	10	−7	49
8	77	9	3.9	9	0	0
9	43	4	3.6	7.5	−3.5	12.25
10	109	12	2.2	1	11	121
11	56	6	3.1	5	1	1
12	70	8	2.9	4	4	16
					Total =	536.5

Note: Tied measurements are assigned the average of the ranks they would be given if they were different but consecutive.

 *Data Set:* SPOIL

---

*The shortcut formula is not exact when there are tied measurements, but it is a good approximation when the total number of ties is not large relative to n.

a. Calculate Spearman's rank correlation coefficient between spoiling time and taste rating.

b. Use a nonparametric test to find out whether the spoilage times and taste ratings are negatively correlated. Use $\alpha = .05$.

Solution

a. We first rank the days until spoilage, assigning a 1 to the smallest number (26) and a 12 to the largest (109). Similarly, we assign ranks to the 12 taste ratings. [*Note:* The tied taste ratings receive the average of their respective ranks.] Because the number of ties is relatively small, we will use the shortcut formula to calculate r_s. The differences d between the ranks of days until spoilage and the ranks of taste rating are shown in Table 11. The squares of the differences, d^2, are also given. Thus,

$$r_s = 1 - \frac{6 \sum d_i^2}{n(n^2 - 1)} = 1 - \frac{6(536.5)}{12(12^2 - 1)} = 1 - 1.88 = -.88$$

The value of r_s can also be obtained using a computer. An SPSS printout of the analysis is shown in Figure 14. The value of r_s, highlighted on the printout, is $-.879$ and agrees (except for rounding) with our hand-calculated value. This negative correlation coefficient indicates that in this sample, an increase in the number of days until spoilage is *associated with* (but is not necessarily the *cause of*) a decrease in the taste rating.

Correlations

			DAYS	TASTE
Spearman's rho	DAYS	Correlation Coefficient	1.000	-.879**
		Sig. (2-tailed)	.	.000
		N	12	12
	TASTE	Correlation Coefficient	-.879**	1.000
		Sig. (2-tailed)	.000	.
		N	12	12

**. Correlation is significant at the 0.01 level (2-tailed).

Figure 14

SPSS printout of Spearman's rank correlation test

b. If we define ρ as the **population rank correlation coefficient** [i.e., the rank correlation coefficient that could be calculated from all (x, y) values in the population], this question can be answered by conducting the test

$H_0: p = 0$ (no population correlation between ranks)

$H_a: p < 0$ (negative population correlation between ranks)

Test statistic: r_s (the *sample* Spearman rank correlation coefficient)

To determine a rejection region, we consult Table XIV of Appendix: Tables, which is partially reproduced in Table 12. Note that the left-hand column gives values of n, the number of pairs of observations. The entries in the table are values for an upper-tail rejection region because only positive values are given. Thus, for $n = 12$ and $\alpha = .05$, the value .497 is the boundary of the upper-tailed rejection region, so that $P(r_s > .497) = .05$ if $H_0: \rho = 0$ is true. Similarly, for negative values of r_s, we have $P(r_s < -.497) = .05$ if $\rho = 0$—that is, we expect to see $r_s < -.497$ only 5% of the time if there is really no relationship between the ranks of the variables. The lower-tailed rejection region is therefore

Rejection region $(\alpha = .05)$: $r_s < -.497$

Because the calculated $r_s = -.876$ is less than $-.497$, we reject H_0 at the $\alpha = .05$ level of significance—that is, this sample provides sufficient evidence to conclude that a negative correlation exists between number of days until spoilage and the taste

Table 12	Reproduction of Part of Table XIV of Appendix: Tables: Critical Values of Spearman's Rank Correlation Coefficient			
n	$\alpha = .05$	$\alpha = .025$	$\alpha = .01$	$\alpha = .005$
5	.900	—	—	—
6	.829	.886	.943	—
7	.714	.786	.893	—
8	.643	.738	.833	.881
9	.600	.683	.783	.833
10	.564	.648	.745	.794
11	.523	.623	.736	.818
12	.497	.591	.703	.780
13	.475	.566	.673	.745
14	.457	.545	.646	.716
15	.441	.525	.623	.689
16	.425	.507	.601	.666
17	.412	.490	.582	.645
18	.399	.476	.564	.625
19	.388	.462	.549	.608
20	.377	.450	.534	.591

rating of the food product. It appears that the preservative does affect the taste of this food adversely.

Look Back The two-tailed p-value of the test is given on the SPSS printout, Figure 14, below the value of r_s. Because the lower-tailed p-value, $p = .000/2 = .000$, is less than $\alpha = .05$, our conclusion is the same: reject H_0.

Now Work Exercise 68

A summary of Spearman's nonparametric test for correlation is given in the box.

Spearman's Nonparametric Test for Rank Correlation

One-Tailed Test	Two-Tailed Test
$H_0: \rho = 0$	$H_0: \rho = 0$
$H_a: \rho > 0$ (or $H_a: \rho < 0$)	$H_a: \rho \neq 0$

Test statistic: r_s, the sample rank correlation (see the formulas for calculating r_s)

Rejection region: $r_s > r_{s,\alpha}$ (or $r_s < -r_{s,\alpha}$ when $H_a: \rho_s < 0$) where $r_{s,\alpha}$ is the value from Table XIV corresponding to the upper-tail area α and n pairs of observations	*Rejection region:* $\lvert r_s \rvert > r_{s,\alpha/2}$ where $r_{s,\alpha/2}$ is the value from Table XIV corresponding to the upper-tail area $\alpha/2$ and n pairs of observations

Ties: Assign tied measurements the average of the ranks they would receive if they were unequal but occurred in successive order. For example, if the third-ranked and fourth-ranked measurements are tied, assign each a rank of $(3 + 4)/2 = 3.5$. The number of ties should be small relative to the total number of observations.

Conditions Required for a Valid Spearman's Test

1. The sample of experimental units on which the two variables are measured is randomly selected.
2. The probability distributions of the two variables are continuous.

Testing the Correlation of MTBE Level with Other Environmental Factors

Refer, again, to the *Environmental Science & Technology* (Jan. 2005) investigation of the MTBE contamination of drinking water in New Hampshire. The environmental researchers also wanted an estimate of the correlation between the MTBE level of a groundwater well and each of the other environmental variables listed in Table SIA1. Because MTBE level is not normally distributed, they employed Spearman's rank correlation method. Also, because earlier analyses indicated that public and private wells have different MTBE distributions, the rank correlations were computed separately for each well class. The SPSS printouts for this analysis are shown in Figures SIA5a–e. The values of r_s (and associated *p*-values) are highlighted on the printouts. Our interpretations follow.

MTBE vs. pH level (Figure SIA5a): For private wells, $r_s = -.026$ (*p*-value = .908). Thus, there is a low negative association between MTBE level and pH level for private wells, one that is not significantly different from 0 (at $\alpha = .10$). For public wells, $r_s = .258$ (*p*-value = .076). Consequently, there is a low positive association (significantly different from 0 at $\alpha = .10$) for public wells between MTBE level and pH level.

Correlations

CLASS				MTBE	PH
Private	Spearman's rho	MTBE	Correlation Coefficient	1.000	−.026
			Sig. (2-tailed)	.	.908
			N	22	22
		PH	Correlation Coefficient	−.026	1.000
			Sig. (2-tailed)	.908	.
			N	22	22
Public	Spearman's rho	MTBE	Correlation Coefficient	1.000	.258
			Sig. (2-tailed)	.	.076
			N	48	48
		PH	Correlation Coefficient	.258	1.000
			Sig. (2-tailed)	.076	.
			N	48	48

Figure SIA5a

SPSS Spearman rank correlation test—MTBE and pH level

MTBE vs. Dissolved oxygen (Figure SIA5b): For private wells, $r_s = .086$ (*p*-value = .702). For public wells, $r_s = -.119$ (*p*-value = .422). Thus, there is a low positive association between MTBE level and dissolved oxygen for private wells, but a low negative association between MTBE level and dissolved oxygen for public wells. However, neither rank correlation is significantly different from 0 (at $\alpha = .10$).

Correlations

CLASS				MTBE	DISSOXY
Private	Spearman's rho	MTBE	Correlation Coefficient	1.000	.086
			Sig. (2-tailed)	.	.702
			N	22	22
		DISSOXY	Correlation Coefficient	.086	1.000
			Sig. (2-tailed)	.702	.
			N	22	22
Public	Spearman's rho	MTBE	Correlation Coefficient	1.000	−.119
			Sig. (2-tailed)	.	.422
			N	48	48
		DISSOXY	Correlation Coefficient	−.119	1.000
			Sig. (2-tailed)	.422	.
			N	48	48

Figure SIA5b

SPSS Spearman rank correlation test—MTBE and dissolved oxygen

MTBE vs. Industry percentage (Figure SIA5c): For private wells, $r_s = -.123$ (*p*-value = .586). This low negative association between MTBE level and industry percentage for private wells is not significantly different from 0 (at $\alpha = .10$). For public wells, $r_s = .330$ (*p*-value = .022). Consequently, there is a low positive association (significantly different from 0 at $\alpha = .10$) for public wells between MTBE level and industry percentage.

Correlations

CLASS				MTBE	INDUSTRY
Private	Spearman's rho	MTBE	Correlation Coefficient	1.000	−.123
			Sig. (2-tailed)	.	.586
			N	22	22
		INDUSTRY	Correlation Coefficient	−.123	1.000
			Sig. (2-tailed)	.586	.
			N	22	22
Public	Spearman's rho	MTBE	Correlation Coefficient	1.000	.330*
			Sig. (2-tailed)	.	.022
			N	48	48
		INDUSTRY	Correlation Coefficient	.330*	1.000
			Sig. (2-tailed)	.022	.
			N	48	48

* Correlation is significant at the 0.05 level (2-tailed).

Figure SIA5c

SPSS Spearman rank correlation test—MTBE and industry percentage

MTBE vs. Depth of well (Figure SIA5d): For private wells, $r_s = -.410$ (p-value = .103). This negative association between MTBE level and depth for private wells is not significantly different from 0 (at $\alpha = .10$). For public wells, $r_s = .444$ (p-value = .002). Consequently, there is a moderate positive association (significantly different from 0 at $\alpha = .10$) for public wells between MTBE level and depth.

Correlations

CLASS				MTBE	DEPTH
Private	Spearman's rho	MTBE	Correlation Coefficient	1.000	−.410
			Sig. (2-tailed)	.	.103
			N	22	17
		DEPTH	Correlation Coefficient	−.410	1.000
			Sig. (2-tailed)	.103	.
			N	17	17
Public	Spearman's rho	MTBE	Correlation Coefficient	1.000	.444**
			Sig. (2-tailed)	.	.002
			N	48	46
		DEPTH	Correlation Coefficient	.444**	1.000
			Sig. (2-tailed)	.002	.
			N	46	46

** Correlation is significant at the 0.01 level (2-tailed).

Figure SIA5d

SPSS Spearman rank correlation test—MTBE and depth

MTBE vs. Distance from underground tank (Figure SIA5e): For private wells, $r_s = .136$ (p-value = .547). For public wells, $r_s = -.093$ (p-value = .527). Thus, there is a low positive association between MTBE level and distance for private wells, but a low negative association between MTBE level and distance for public wells. However, neither rank correlation is significantly different from 0 (at $\alpha = .10$).

In summary, the only significant rank correlations were for public wells, where the researchers discovered low-to-moderate positive associations of MTBE level with pH level, industry percentage, and depth of the well.

Correlations

CLASS				MTBE	DISTANCE
Private	Spearman's rho	MTBE	Correlation Coefficient	1.000	.136
			Sig. (2-tailed)	.	.547
			N	22	22
		DISTANCE	Correlation Coefficient	.136	1.000
			Sig. (2-tailed)	.547	.
			N	22	22
Public	Spearman's rho	MTBE	Correlation Coefficient	1.000	−.093
			Sig. (2-tailed)	.	.527
			N	48	48
		DISTANCE	Correlation Coefficient	−.093	1.000
			Sig. (2-tailed)	.527	.
			N	48	48

Figure SIA5e

SPSS Spearman rank correlation test—MTBE and distance

Data Set: MTBE

Exercises 66–79

Please be aware that some of the following problems may require knowledge of concepts that are not presented in this chapter.

Learning the Mechanics

66 Use Table XIV of Appendix: Tables to find each of the following probabilities:
  a. $P(r_s > .508)$ when $n = 22$
  b. $P(r_s > .448)$ when $n = 28$
  c. $P(r_s \leq .648)$ when $n = 10$
  d. $P(r_s < -.738$ or $r_s > .738)$ when $n = 8$

67 Specify the rejection region for Spearman's nonparametric test for rank correlation in each of the following situations:
  a. $H_0: \rho = 0$; $H_a: \rho \neq 0$, $n = 10$, $\alpha = .05$
  b. $H_0: \rho = 0$; $H_a: \rho > 0$, $n = 20$, $\alpha = .025$
  c. $H_0: \rho = 0$; $H_a: \rho < 0$, $n = 30$, $\alpha = .01$

68 The following sample data were collected on variables x and y:

x	0	3	0	−4	3	0	4
y	0	2	2	0	3	1	2

  a. Specify the null and alternative hypotheses that should be used in conducting a hypothesis test to determine whether the variables x and y are correlated.
  b. Conduct the test of part **a** using $\alpha = .05$.
  c. What is the approximate p-value of the test of part **b**?
  d. What assumptions are necessary to ensure the validity of the test of part **b**?

69 Compute Spearman's rank correlation coefficient for each of the following pairs of sample observations:

  a.

x	33	61	20	19	40
y	26	36	65	25	35

  b.

x	89	102	120	137	41
y	81	94	75	52	136

  c.

x	2	15	4	10
y	11	2	15	21

  d.

x	5	20	15	10	3
y	80	83	91	82	87

Applying the Concepts—Basic

70 **Extending the life of an aluminum smelter pot.** The *American Ceramic Society Bulletin* (Feb. 2005) did a study of the life length of an aluminum smelter pot. Because the life of a smelter pot depends on the porosity of the brick lining, the researchers measured the apparent porosity and the mean pore diameter of each of six bricks. The data are reproduced in the table in the next column.
  a. Rank the apparent porosity values for the six bricks. Then rank the six pore diameter values.
  b. Use the ranks, part **a**, to find the rank correlation between apparent porosity (y) and mean pore diameter (x). Interpret the result.
  c. Conduct a test for positive rank correlation. Use $\alpha = .01$.

Brick	Apparent Porosity (%)	Mean Pore Diameter (micrometers)
A	18.8	12.0
B	18.3	9.7
C	16.3	7.3
D	6.9	5.3
E	17.1	10.9
F	20.4	16.8

Source: "Aluminosilicate refractories for aluminum cell linings," by P. Bonadia, in THE AMERICAN CERAMIC SOCIETY BULLETIN, 84.2, pp. 26-31 (table II), February 2005.

71 **Software millionaires and birthdays.** This exercise refers to the analysis of the disproportionate number of software millionaires who were born around the year 1955. On his Web blog (www.measuringusability.com), statistical consultant Jeff Sauro investigated this question by analyzing the data shown in the accompanying table.

Decade	Total U.S. Births (millions)	Number of Software Millionaire Birthdays	Number of CEO Birthdays (in a random sample of 70 companies from the *Fortune* 500 list)
1920	28.582	3	2
1930	24.374	1	2
1940	31.666	10	23
1950	40.530	14	38
1960	38.808	7	9
1970	33.309	4	0

Source: "Were most software millionaires born around 1955?" by Jeff Sauro, created from data by the National Center for Health Statistics. Copyright © 2010 by Jeff Sauro, www.measuringusability.com. Reprinted with permission.

  a. Compute Spearman's rank correlation coefficient, r_s, relating number (y) of software millionaire birthdays in a decade to total number (x) of U.S. births.
  b. Refer to part **a**. Is there evidence of positive rank correlation between y and x? Test using $\alpha = .05$.
  c. Compute Spearman's rank correlation coefficient, r_s, relating number (y) of software millionaire birthdays in a decade to number (x) of CEO birthdays.
  d. Refer to part **c**. Is there evidence of positive rank correlation between y and x? Test using $\alpha = .05$.

72 **Rankings of marketing journals.** College professors earn tenure by publishing in peer-reviewed academic journals. The rankings of these journals (often subjective) play a key role in the tenure process. A paper in the *Journal of Informetrics* (Vol. 4, 2010) investigated the merits of a new index designed for ranking journals and applied the index to recently published marketing journal articles. The new *hg*-index, based on Google Scholar searches, combines an assessment of both the quantity and quality of the papers published in the journal—the higher the *hg*-index score, the better the journal. This new index was compared to a count of the number of citations articles in the journal generated. Data on the *hg*-index score and number of citations for 20 (fictitious) marketing journals are provided in the table on the next page. The researchers used Spearman's rank correlation to measure the association between the two methods of ranking marketing journals.

a. Give one reason why the researchers' used Spearman's rank correlation rather than the usual (Pearson) correlation coefficient, r.

b. Rank the 20 hg-index scores.

c. Rank the 20 values of number of citations.

d. Compute Spearman's rank correlation coefficient, r_s. Practically interpret this value.

e. Conduct a test of hypothesis to determine if the true rank correlation in the population of all marketing journals is greater than 0. Test using $\alpha = .01$.

Journal	Score	Citations	Journal	Score	Citations
1	81.47	12583	11	23.52	1520
2	62.10	9420	12	22.55	1497
3	48.64	7139	13	22.30	951
4	36.96	2900	14	19.42	891
5	34.63	2866	15	7.58	101
6	29.65	2213	16	17.82	642
7	29.23	2051	17	14.75	459
8	28.02	2092	18	12.92	283
9	26.76	1276	19	11.90	255
10	25.76	1327	20	19.85	1439

Source: "Ranking marketing journals using the Google scholar-based hg-index" by M. Touzani and S. Moussa, in JOURNAL OF INFORMETRICS, 4 (table 1), 2010.

73 **Organizational use of the Internet.** Researchers from the United Kingdom and Germany attempted to develop a theoretically grounded measure of organizational Internet use (OIU) and published their results in *Internet Research* (Vol. 15, 2005). Using data collected from a sample of 77 Web sites, they investigated the link between OIU level (measured on a 7-point scale) and several observation-based indicators. Spearman's rank correlation coefficient (and associated p-values) for several indicators are shown in the table.

Indicator	Correlation with OIU Level	
	r_s	p-value
Navigability	.179	.148
Transactions	.334	.023
Locatability	.590	.000
Information richness	−.115	.252
Number of files	.114	.255

Source: "Organizational use of the internet: Scale and development and validation," by Y. Zhou and J. K. Brock in INTERNET RESEARCH, 1, pp. 67-87 (Table IV), 2005.

a. Interpret each of the values of r_s given in the table.

b. Interpret each of the p-values given in the table. (Use $\alpha = .10$ to conduct each test.)

Applying the Concepts—Intermediate

74 **Food availability at middle schools.** Refer to the *Journal of School Health* (Dec. 2009) study of identifying and quantifying food items in the a la carte line at a middle school, Exercise 38. Recall that two methods were compared—a detailed inventory approach and a checklist approach—for a sample of 36 middle schools. The data on percent of food items deemed healthy for each school are saved in the file. Use Spearman's rank correlation coefficient to measure the strength of the association between the percentage determined using the inventory

method and the percentage found using the checklist method. Conduct a test (at $\alpha = .05$) for positive rank correlation.

75 **In business, do nice guys finish first or last?** *Nature* (March 20, 2008) did a study of whether the saying "nice guys finish last" applies to business. College students repeatedly played a version of the game "prisoner's dilemma," where competitors choose cooperation, defection, or costly punishment. At the conclusion of the games, the researchers recorded the average payoff and the number of times punishment was used by each player. The data in the table are representative of the data obtained in the study. The researchers concluded that "punishers tend to have lower payoffs." Do you agree? Use Spearman's rank correlation statistic to support your conclusion.

Punish	Payoff	Punish	Payoff
0	0.50	8	−0.20
1	0.20	10	0.15
2	0.30	12	−0.30
3	0.25	14	−0.10
4	0.00	16	−0.20
5	0.30	17	−0.25
6	0.10		

76 **Media coverage of the 9/11 attacks and public opinion.** The terrorist attacks of September 11, 2001, and related events (e.g., the War in Iraq) have and continue to receive tremendous media coverage. How has this media coverage influenced the American public's concern for terrorism? This was the topic of research conducted by journalism professors at the University of Missouri (*International Journal of Public Opinion,* Winter 2004). Using random-digit dialing, a telephone survey of Americans was conducted. Each person was asked to rate, on a scale of 1 to 5, his or her level of concern for each of eight topics: long war, future terrorist attacks, effect on economy, Israel-Palestine conflict, biological threats, air travel safety, war protests, and Afghan civilian deaths. The eight scores were summed to obtain a "public agenda" score. The respondents were also asked how many days per week they read the newspaper, watch the local television news, and watch national television news. The responses to these three questions were also summed to obtain a "media agenda" score. The researchers hypothesized that the public agenda score would be positively related to the media agenda score. Consider a small survey of $n = 14$ Americans.

a. Spearman's rank correlation between the two scores was computed to be $r_s = .643$. Give a practical interpretation of this value.

b. Refer to part **a.** Conduct Spearman's rank correlation test of positive association at $\alpha = .01$.

c. The researchers removed the "long war" question from the data and recomputed the "public agenda" score. Spearman's rank correlation between the public agenda and the media agenda was then calculated as $r_s = .714$. Conduct Spearman's test for positive rank correlation using this value at $\alpha = .01$. Does the inference change?

77 **Assessmemt of biometric recognition methods.** Biometric technologies have been developed to detect or verify an individual's identity. These methods are based on physiological characteristics (called *biometric signatures*) such as facial features, eye irises, fingerprints, voice, hand shape, and gait. In *Chance* (Winter 2004), four biometric recognition algorithms were compared. All four methods were applied to 1,196 biometric signatures, and "match" scores were obtained. The Spearman correlation between match scores for each possible algorithm pair was determined. The rank correlation matrix is shown below. Interpret the results.

Method	I	II	III	IV
I	1	.189	.592	.340
II		1	.205	.324
III			1	.314
IV				1

78 Sweetness of orange juice. This exercise refers to the orange juice quality study. A manufacturer that has OJUICE developed a quantitative index of the "sweetness" of

Run	Sweetness Index	Pectin (ppm)
1	5.2	220
2	5.5	227
3	6.0	259
4	5.9	210
5	5.8	224
6	6.0	215
7	5.8	231
8	5.6	268
9	5.6	239
10	5.9	212
11	5.4	410
12	5.6	256
13	5.8	306
14	5.5	259
15	5.3	284
16	5.3	383
17	5.7	271
18	5.5	264
19	5.7	227
20	5.3	263
21	5.9	232
22	5.8	220
23	5.8	246
24	5.9	241

Note: The data in the table are authentic. For confidentiality reasons, the manufacturer cannot be disclosed.

orange juice is investigating the relationship between the sweetness index and the amount of water-soluble pectin in the orange juice it produces. The data for 24 production runs at a juice manufacturing plant are reproduced in the preceding table.

a. Calculate Spearman's rank correlation coefficient between the sweetness index and the amount of pectin. Interpret the result.

b. Conduct a nonparametric test to determine whether there is a negative association between the sweetness index and the amount of pectin. Use $\alpha = .01$.

79 America's most reputable companies. *Forbes* magazine publishes a list of America's most reputable companies COREP based on an annual survey conducted by the Reputation Institute. The rankings are based on a "global pulse" score (the higher the score, the more reputable the company). Global pulse scores for the top 20 companies in 2011 and 2010 are listed in the table. Is there evidence of a positive rank correlation between global pulse scores of firms in 2011 and 2010? Use $\alpha = .01$.

Company	2011	2010
Amazon.com	82.70	76.94
Kraft Foods	81.40	84.84
Johnson & Johnson	81.32	85.82
3M	81.00	77.15
Kellogg's	80.87	82.78
UPS	80.46	78.93
FedEx	79.63	77.59
Sara Lee	79.53	80.04
Google	79.25	79.31
Walt Disney Company	79.02	82.11
Texas Instruments	78.46	75.79
Caterpillar	77.95	78.07
Kohl's	77.91	71.43
Whirlpool	77.51	76.81
General Mills	77.44	78.46
HJ Heinz	77.29	77.46
Berkshire Hathaway	77.24	73.92
Eastman Kodak	76.85	77.73
Staples	76.50	77.70
Procter & Gamble	76.45	74.26

Source: Reputation Institute, FORBES, 2011.

◻ Chapter Notes

Key Terms

Distribution-free tests
Friedman F_r-statistic
Kruskal-Wallis H-test
Nonparametrics
Parametric statistical test
Population rank correlation
   coefficient

Rank statistics or rank tests
Rank sum
Sign test
Spearman's rank correlation
   coefficient
Wilcoxon rank sum test
Wilcoxon signed rank test

Key Formulas

Sign test, large-sample test statistic: $z = \dfrac{(S - .5) - .5n}{.5\sqrt{n}}$

Wilcoxon rank sum test, large-sample test statistic: $z = \dfrac{T_1 - \dfrac{n_1(n_1 + n_2 + 1)}{2}}{\sqrt{\dfrac{n_1 n_2(n_1 + n_2 + 1)}{12}}}$

Wilcoxon signed rank test, large-sample test statistic:

$$z = \frac{T_+ - \dfrac{n(n+1)}{4}}{\sqrt{\dfrac{n(n+1)(2n+1)}{24}}}$$

r_s ... Spearman's rank correlation coefficient
ρ ... Population correlation coefficient

Key Symbols

η ... Population median
S ... Test statistic for sign test
T_1 ... Sum of ranks of observations in sample 1
T_2 ... Sum of ranks of observations in sample 2
T_L ... Critical lower Wilcoxon rank sum value
T_U ... Critical upper Wilcoxon rank sum value
T_+ ... Sum of ranks of positive differences of paired observations
T_- ... Sum of ranks of negative differences of paired observations
T_0 ... Critical value of Wilcoxon signed rank test
R_j ... Rank sum of observations in sample j
H ... Test statistic for Kruskal-Wallis test
F_r ... Test statistic for Friedman test

Key Ideas

Distribution-Free Tests

Do not rely on assumptions about the probability distribution of the sampled population

Nonparametrics

Distribution-free tests that are based on **rank statistics**

One-sample nonparametric test for the population median — **sign test**

Nonparametric test for *two independent samples* — **Wilcoxon rank sum test**

Nonparametric test for *matched pairs* — **Wilcoxon signed rank test**

Nonparametric test for a *completely randomized design* — **Kruskal-Wallis test**

Nonparametric test for a *randomized block design* — **Friedman test**

Nonparametric test for *rank correlation* — **Spearman's test**

Guide to Selecting a Nonparametric Method

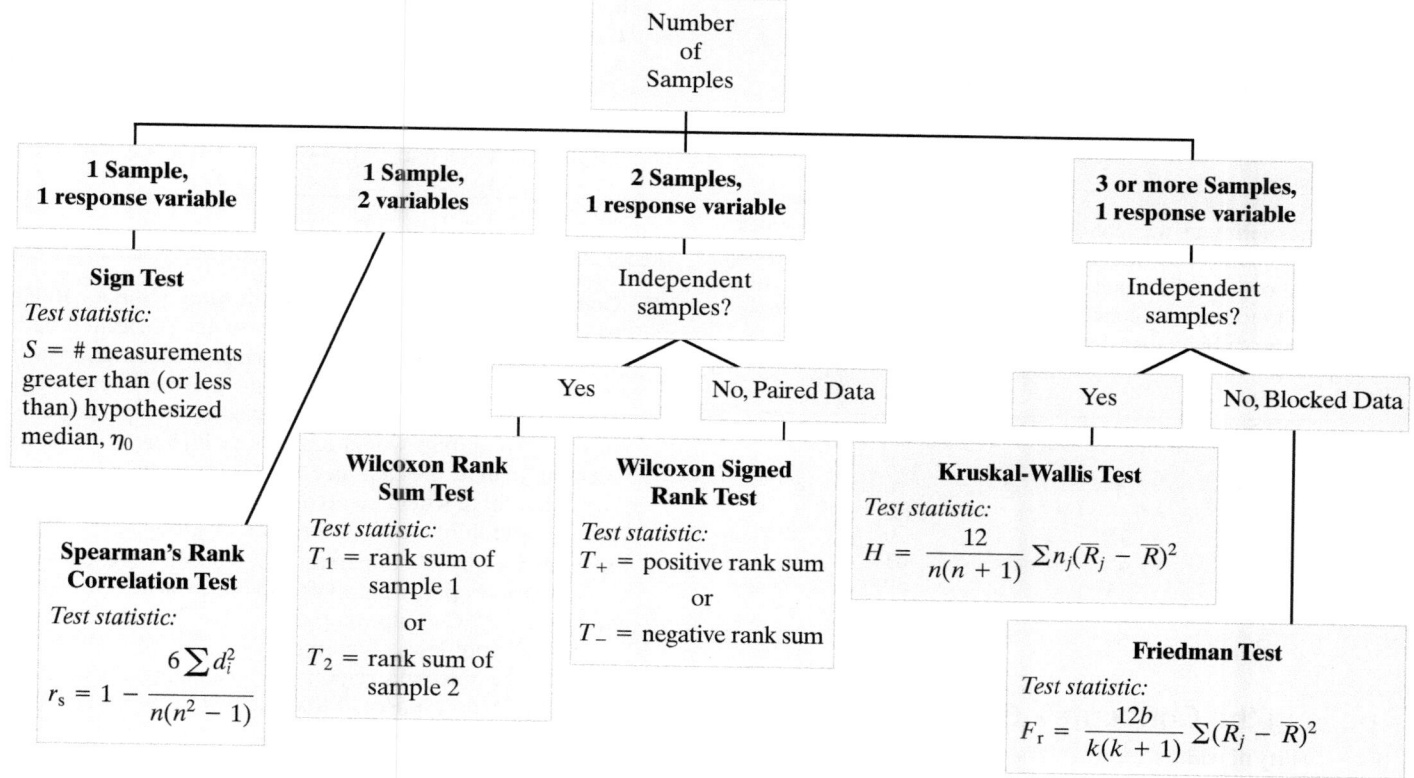

Supplementary Exercises 80–103

Please be aware that some of the following problems may require knowledge of concepts that are not presented in this chapter.

Learning the Mechanics

80

LI5080

The data for three independent random samples are shown in the table to the right. It is known that the sampled populations are not normally distributed. Use an appropriate test to determine whether the data provide sufficient evidence to indicate that at least two of the populations differ in location. Test using $\alpha = .05$.

Sample from Population 1		Sample from Population 2		Sample from Population 3	
18	15	12	34	87	50
32	63	33	18	53	64
43		10		65	77

81 A random sample of nine pairs of observations are recorded on two variables, x and y. The data are shown in the table below.

L15081

   a. Do the data provide sufficient evidence to indicate that ρ, the rank correlation between x and y, differs from 0? Test using $\alpha = .05$.

   b. Do the data provide sufficient evidence to indicate that the probability distribution for x is shifted to the right of that for y? Test using $\alpha = .05$.

Pair	x	y
1	19	12
2	27	19
3	15	7
4	35	25
5	13	11
6	29	10
7	16	16
8	22	10
9	16	18

82 Two independent random samples produced the measurements listed in the table below. Do the data provide sufficient evidence to conclude that there is a difference between the locations of the probability distributions for the sampled populations? Test using $\alpha = .05$.

L15082

Sample from Population 1		Sample from Population 2	
1.2	1.0	1.5	1.9
1.9	1.8	1.3	2.7
.7	1.1	2.9	3.5
2.5			

83 An experiment was conducted using a randomized block design with five treatments and four blocks. The data are shown in the table below. Do the data provide sufficient evidence to conclude that at least two of the treatment probability distributions differ in location? Test using $\alpha = .05$.

L15083

	Block			
Treatment	1	2	3	4
1	75	77	70	80
2	65	69	63	69
3	74	78	69	80
4	80	80	75	86
5	69	72	63	77

Applying the Concepts — Basic

84 **Quality of white shrimp.** In *The American Statistician* (May 2001), the nonparametric sign test was used to analyze data on the quality of white shrimp. One measure of shrimp quality is cohesiveness. Because freshly caught shrimp are usually stored on ice, there is concern that cohesiveness will deteriorate after storage. For a sample of 20 newly caught white shrimp, cohesiveness was measured both before storage and after storage on ice for 2 weeks. The difference in the cohesiveness measurements (before minus after) was obtained for each shrimp. If storage has no effect on cohesiveness, the population median of the differences will be 0.

If cohesiveness deteriorates after storage, the population median of the differences will be positive.

   a. Set up the null and alternative hypotheses to test whether cohesiveness deteriorates after storage.

   b. In the sample of 20 shrimp, there were 13 positive differences. Use this value to find the p-value of the test.

   c. Make the appropriate conclusion (in the words of the problem) if $\alpha = .05$.

85 **Computer-mediated communication study.** The *Journal of Computer-Mediated Communication* (Apr. 2004) did a study to compare those who interact via computer-mediated communication (CMC) to those who meet face-to-face (FTF). 48 undergraduate students were randomly divided into the two groups. Those in the CMC group communicated using the "chat" mode of instant-messaging software; those in the FTF group met in a conference room. The relational intimacy scores (measured on a 7-point scale) of the participants are reproduced in the accompanying table. The researchers hypothesized that the relational intimacy scores for participants in the CMC group would tend to be lower than the relational intimacy scores for participants in the FTF group.

   a. Which nonparametric procedure should be used to analyze the data?

   b. Specify the null and alternative hypotheses of the test.

   c. Give the rejection region for the test using $\alpha = .10$.

   d. Conduct the test and give the appropriate conclusion in the context of the problem.

CMC	4	3	3	4	3	3	3	3	4	4	3	4
	3	3	2	4	2	4	5	4	4	4	5	3
FTF	5	4	4	4	3	3	3	4	3	3	3	3
	4	4	4	4	4	3	3	3	4	4	2	4

86 **Computer-mediated communication study (cont'd).** Refer to Exercise 85. Relational intimacy scores (measured on a 7-point scale) were obtained for each participant after each of three different meeting sessions. The researchers hypothesized that relational intimacy scores for participants in the CMC group would tend to be higher at the third meeting than at the first meeting; however, they hypothesized that there would be no differences in scores between the first and third meetings for the FTF group.

   a. Explain why a nonparametric Wilcoxon signed rank test is appropriate for analyzing the data.

   b. For the CMC group comparison, give the null and alternative hypotheses of interest.

   c. Give the rejection region for conducting the test (at $\alpha = .05$), part **b.** Recall that there were 24 participants assigned to the CMC group.

   d. For the FTF group comparison, give the null and alternative hypotheses of interest.

   e. Give the rejection region for conducting the test (at $\alpha = .05$), part **d.** Recall that there were 24 participants assigned to the FTF group.

87 **RIF plan to fire older employees.** Reducing the size of a company's workforce in order to reduce costs is referred to as *corporate downsizing* or *reductions in force* (RIF) by the business community and media. Following RIFs, companies are often sued by former employees who allege that the RIFs were discriminatory with regard to age. Federal law protects employees over 40 years of age against such discrimination. Suppose one large company's employees have a median age of 37. Its RIF plan is to fire 15 employees with ages listed in the table below.

43	32	39	28	54	41	50	62
22	45	47	54	43	33	59	

a. Calculate the median age of the employees who are being terminated.

b. What are the appropriate null and alternative hypotheses to test whether the population from which the terminated employees were selected has a median age that exceeds the entire company's median age?

c. Conduct the test of part **b.** Find the significance level of the test and interpret its value.

d. Assuming that courts generally require statistical evidence at the .10 level of significance before ruling that age discrimination laws were violated, what do you advise the company about its planned RIF? Explain.

88 Forums for tax litigation. In litigating tax disputes with the IRS, taxpayers are permitted to choose the court forum. Three trial courts are available: (1) U.S. Tax Court, (2) Federal District Court, and (3) U.S. Claims Court. Accounting professors B. A. Billings (Wayne State University) and B. P. Green (University of Michigan-Dearborn) and business law professor W. H. Volz (Wayne State University) conducted a study of taxpayers' choice of forum in litigating tax issues (*Journal of Applied Business Research,* Fall 1996). A random sample of 161 court decisions was obtained for analysis. Two of the many variables measured for each case were taxpayer's choice of forum (Tax, District, or Claims Court) and tax deficiency DEF (i.e., the disputed amount, in dollars).

a. The researchers applied a nonparametric test rather than a parametric test to compare the DEF distributions of the three tax litigation forums. Give a plausible reason for their choice.

b. What nonparametric test is appropriate for this analysis? Explain.

c. The table below summarizes the data analyzed by the researchers. Use the information in the table to compute the appropriate test statistic.

d. The observed significance level (*p*-value) of the test was reported as $p = .0037$. Fully interpret this result.

Court Selected by Taxpayer	Sample Size	Sample Mean DEF	Rank Sum of DEF Values
Tax	67	$ 80,357	5,335
District	57	74,213	3,937
Claims	37	185,648	3,769

Source: "Selection of Forum for Litigated Tax Issues" by B. A. Billings, B. P. Green and W. H. Volz, in JOURNAL OF APPLIED BUSINESS RESEARCH, Vol. 12 (table 2). Copyright © 1996 by the Clute Institute for Academic Research. Reprinted with permission.

89 Wine-tasting experiment. Two expert wine tasters were asked to rank six brands of wine. Their rankings are shown in the table in the next column.

a. Use the rankings to compute r_s.

b. Do the data present sufficient evidence to indicate a positive correlation in the rankings of the two experts? Test using $\alpha = .05$.

Brand	Expert 1	Expert 2
A	6	5
B	5	6
C	1	2
D	3	1
E	2	4
F	4	3

Applying the Concepts—Intermediate

90 Employee suggestion system. An *employee suggestion system* is a formal process for capturing, analyzing, implementing, and recognizing employee-proposed organizational improvements. (The first known system was implemented by the Yale and Towne Manufacturing Company of Stamford, Connecticut, in 1880.) Using data from the National Association of Suggestion Systems, D. Carnevale and B. Sharp examined the strengths of the relationships between the extent of employee participation in suggestion plans and cost savings realized by employers (*Review of Public Personnel Administration,* Spring 1993). The data in the table are representative of the data they analyzed for a sample of federal, state, and local government agencies. Savings are calculated from the first year measurable benefits were observed.

a. Explain why the savings data used in this study may understate the total benefits derived from the implemented suggestions.

b. Carnevale and Sharp concluded that a significant moderate positive relationship exists between participation rates and cost savings rates in public sector suggestion systems. Do you agree? Test using $\alpha = .01$

c. Justify the statistical methodology you used in part **b.**

Employee Involvement (% of all employees submitting suggestions)	Savings Rate (% of total budget)
10.1%	8.5%
6.2	6.0
16.3	9.0
1.2	0.0
4.8	5.1
11.5	6.1
.6	1.2
2.8	4.5
8.9	5.4
20.2	15.3
2.7	3.8

Source: "The old employee suggestion box," by B. S. Sharp and D. G. Carnavale, in REVIEW OF PUBLIC PERSONNEL ADMINISTRATION, 13.2, pp. 82-92, 1993.

91 Number-one-selling fast-food item. According to the National Restaurant Association, hamburgers are the number-one-selling fast-food item in the United States. An economist studying the fast-food-buying habits of Americans paid graduate students to stand outside two suburban McDonald's restaurants near Boston and ask departing customers whether they spent more or less than $2.25 on hamburger products for their lunch. Twenty answered "less than"; 50 said "more than"; and 10 refused to answer the question.

a. Is there sufficient evidence to conclude that the median amount spent for hamburgers at lunch at McDonald's is less than $2.25?

b. Does your conclusion apply to all Americans who eat lunch at McDonald's? Justify your answer.

c. What assumptions must hold to ensure the validity of your test in part **a**?

92 Designing an atlas. An atlas is a compendium of geographic, economic, and social information that describes one or more geographic regions. Atlases are used by the sales and marketing functions of businesses, local chambers of commerce, and educators. One of the most critical aspects of a new atlas design is its thematic content. In a survey of atlas users (*Journal of Geography,* May/June 1995), a large sample of high school teachers in British Columbia ranked 12 thematic atlas topics for usefulness. The consensus rankings of the teachers (based on the percentage of teachers who responded they "would definitely use" the topic) are given in the table. These teacher rankings were compared to the rankings of a group of university geography alumni made 3 years earlier. Compare the distributions of theme rankings for the two groups with an appropriate nonparametric test. Use $\alpha = .05$. Interpret the results practically.

	Rankings	
Theme	High School Teachers	Geography Alumni
Tourism	10	2
Physical	2	1
Transportation	7	3
People	1	6
History	2	5
Climate	6	4
Forestry	5	8
Agriculture	7	10
Fishing	9	7
Energy	2	8
Mining	10	11
Manufacturing	12	12

Source: "Planning the next generation of regional atlases: Input from educators," by C. P. Keller, in JOURNAL OF GEOGRAPHY, 94.3, 1995.

93 Designing an atlas (cont'd). Refer to Exercise 92. In addition to high school teachers and university geography alumni, university geography students and representatives of the general public also ranked the 12 thematic topics. The rankings of all four groups are shown in the table in the next column. Compare the atlas theme ranking distributions of the four groups using a nonparametric test. Use $\alpha = .10$.

94 School property tax rates. An economist is interested in knowing whether property tax rates differ among three types of school districts—urban, suburban, and rural. A random sample of several districts of each type produced the data in the table in the next column (rate is in mills, where 1 mill = $1/1,000). Do the data indicate a difference in the level of property taxes among the three types of school districts? Use $\alpha = .05$.

Data for Exercise 93

	Rankings			
Theme	High School Teachers	Geography Alumni	Geography Students	General Public
Tourism	10	2	5	1
Physical	2	1	1	5
Transportation	7	3	7	2
People	1	6	2	3
History	2	5	9	4
Climate	6	4	4	8
Forestry	5	8	2	7
Agriculture	7	10	6	9
Fishing	9	7	10	6
Energy	2	8	7	10
Mining	10	11	11	11
Manufacturing	12	12	12	12

Source: Keller, C. P., et al. "Planning the next generation of regional atlases: Input from educators," *Journal of Geography,* Vol. 94, No. 3, May/June 1995, p. 413 (Table 1). Copyright 1995 by Taylor & Francis Informa UK Ltd.—Journals. Reproduced with permission of Taylor & Francis Informa UK Ltd.—Journals in the format Textbook and electronic usage via Copyright Clearance Center.

Data for Exercise 94

Urban	Suburban	Rural
4.3	5.9	5.1
5.2	6.7	4.8
6.2	7.6	3.9
5.6	4.9	6.2
3.8	5.2	4.2
5.8	6.8	4.3
4.7		

95 Satisfaction with MIS implementation. A *management information system* (MIS) is a computer-based information-processing system designed to support the operations, management, and decision functions of an organization. The development of an MIS involves three stages: definition, physical design, and implementation of the system. Thirty firms that recently implemented an MIS were surveyed: 16 were satisfied with the implementation results; 14 were not. Each firm was asked to rate the quality of the planning and negotiation stages of the development process, using a scale of 0 to 100, with higher numbers indicating better quality. (A score of 100 indicates that all the problems that occurred in the planning and negotiation stages were successfully resolved, while 0 indicates that none were resolved.) The results are shown in the table.

Firms with a Good MIS			Firms with a Poor MIS		
52	59	95	60	40	90
70	60	90	50	55	85
40	90	86	55	65	80
80	75	95	70	55	90
82	80	93	41	70	
65					

a. Use the Wilcoxon rank sum test to compare the quality of the development processes of successfully and unsuccessfully implemented MISs. Test using $\alpha = .05$.

b. Under what circumstances could you use the two-sample *t*-test to conduct the same test?

96 Flexible working hours program. A job-scheduling innovation that has helped managers overcome motivation and absenteeism problems associated with a fixed 8-hour workday is a concept called *flextime*. This flexible working hours program permits employees to design their own 40-hour workweek to meet their personal needs. The management of a large manufacturing firm may adopt a flextime program depending on the success or failure of a pilot program. Ten employees were randomly selected and given a questionnaire designed to measure their attitude toward their job. Each was then permitted to design and follow a flextime workday. After 6 months, attitudes toward their jobs were again measured. The resulting attitude scores are displayed in the table. The higher the score, the more favorable the employee's attitude toward his or her work. Use a nonparametric test procedure to evaluate the success of the pilot flextime program. Test using $\alpha = .05$.

Employee	Before	After
1	54	68
2	25	42
3	80	80
4	76	91
5	63	70
6	82	88
7	94	90
8	72	81
9	33	39
10	90	93

97 Fluoride in drinking water. Many water treatment facilities supplement the natural fluoride concentration with hydrofluosilicic acid in order to reach a target concentration of fluoride in drinking water. Certain levels are thought to enhance dental health, but very high concentrations can be dangerous. Suppose that one such treatment plant targets .75 milligrams per liter (mg/L) for their water. The plant tests 25 samples each day to determine whether the median level differs from the target.
   a. Set up the null and alternative hypotheses.
   b. Set up the test statistic and rejection region using $\alpha = .10$.
   c. Explain the implication of a Type I error and a Type II error in the context of this application.
   d. Suppose that one day's samples result in 18 values that exceed .75 mg/L. Conduct the test and state the appropriate conclusion in the context of this application.
   e. When it was suggested to the plant's supervisor that a *t*-test should be used to conduct the daily test, she replied that the probability distribution of the fluoride concentrations was "heavily skewed to the right." Show graphically what she meant by this and explain why this is a reason to prefer the sign test to the *t*-test.

98 Does fatigue lead to more defectives? A manufacturer wants to determine whether the number of defectives produced by its employees tends to increase as the day progresses. Unknown to the employees, a complete inspection is made of every item that was produced on one day, and the hourly fraction defective is recorded. The resulting data are given in the next table. Do they provide evidence that the fraction defective increases as the day progresses? Test at the $\alpha = .05$ level.

Hour	Fraction Defective
1	.02
2	.05
3	.03
4	.08
5	.06
6	.09
7	.11
8	.10

99 Union negotiation preferences. A union wants to determine the preferences of its members before negotiating with management. Ten union members are randomly selected, and an extensive questionnaire is completed by each member. The responses to the various aspects of the questionnaire will enable the union to rank in order of importance the items to be negotiated. The rankings are shown in the next table. Conduct a nonparametric test to determine whether evidence exists that the probability distributions of ratings differ for at least two of the four negotiable items. Use $\alpha = .05$.

Person	More Pay	Job Stability	Fringe Benefits	Shorter Hours
1	2	1	3	4
2	1	2	3	4
3	4	3	2	1
4	1	4	2	3
5	1	2	3	4
6	1	3	4	2
7	2.5	1	2.5	4
8	3	1	4	2
9	1.5	1.5	3	4
10	2	3	1	4

100 Hazardous organic solvents. The *Journal of Hazardous Materials* (July 1995) published a study of the chemical properties of three different types of hazardous organic solvents used to clean metal parts. Independent samples of solvents from each of the three types—aromatics, chloralkanes, and esters—were collected. The data on sorption rates for the three solvents are listed in the table. Use a nonparametric test to compare the sorption rate distributions at $\alpha = .01$.

Aromatics		Chloralkanes		Esters		
1.06	.95	1.58	1.12	.29	.43	.06
.79	.65	1.45	.91	.06	.51	.09
.82	1.15	.57	.83	.44	.10	.17
.89	1.12	1.16	.43	.61	.34	.60
1.05				.55	.53	.17

Source: "A review of polymeric geosynthetics used in hazardous waste facilities," by J. D. Ortego, in JOURNAL OF HAZARDOUS MATERIALS, 42.2, 1995.

101 Agent Orange and Vietnam vets. Agent Orange—the code name for an herbicide developed for the U.S. armed forces in the 1960s—was found to be extremely contaminated with TCDD, or dioxin. During the Vietnam War, an estimated 19 million gallons of Agent Orange was used to destroy the dense plant and tree cover of the Asian jungle. As a result of this exposure, many Vietnam veterans have dangerously high levels of TCDD in their blood and adipose (fatty) tissue. A study published in *Chemosphere* (Vol. 20, 1990) reported on the TCDD levels of 20 Massachusetts Vietnam vets who were possibly exposed to Agent Orange. The TCDD amounts (measured in parts per trillion) in both plasma and fat tissue of the 20 vets are listed in the accompanying table.

Vet	Fat	Plasma
1	4.9	2.5
2	6.9	3.5
3	10.0	6.8
4	4.4	4.7
5	4.6	4.6
6	1.1	1.8
7	2.3	2.5
8	5.9	3.1
9	7.0	3.1
10	5.5	3.0
11	7.0	6.9
12	1.4	1.6
13	11.0	20.0
14	2.5	4.1
15	4.4	2.1
16	4.2	1.8
17	41.0	36.0
18	2.9	3.3
19	7.7	7.2
20	2.5	2.0

Source: "Partitioning of 2, 3, 7, 8-chlorinated dibenzo-p-dioxins and dibenzofurans between adipose tissue and plasma lipid of 20 Massachusetts Vietnam veterans," by A. Schecter, in CHEMOSPHERE, Vol. 20, Nos. 7-9, pp. 954-55 (Tables I and II), 1990.

a. Medical researchers consider a TCDD level of 3 parts per trillion (ppt) to be dangerously high. Do the data provide evidence (at $\alpha = .05$) to indicate that the median level of TCDD in the fat tissue of these Vietnam vets exceeds 3 ppt?

b. Repeat part a for plasma.

c. Medical researchers also are interested in comparing the TCDD levels in fat tissue and plasma for Vietnam veterans. Specifically, they want to determine if the distribution of TCDD levels in fat is shifted above or below the distribution of TCDD levels in plasma. Conduct this analysis (at $\alpha = .05$) and make the appropriate inference.

d. Find the rank correlation between the TCDD level in fat tissue and the TCDD level in plasma. Is there sufficient evidence (at $\alpha = .05$) of a positive association between the two TCDD measures?

Applying the Concepts—Advanced

102 Comparing ethics of American and Mexican purchasing managers. In Mexico, the United States' third largest trading partner, purchasing has not fully evolved into a profession with its own standards of ethical behavior. Researchers at Xavier University investigated the question: Do American and Mexican purchasing managers perceive ethical situations differently (*Industrial Marketing Management*, July 1999)? As part of their

study, 15 Mexican purchasing managers and 15 American purchasing managers were asked to consider different ethical situations and respond on a 100-point scale with endpoints "strongly disagree" (1) and "strongly agree" (100). For the situation "accepting free trips from salespeople is okay," the responses shown in the table were obtained. Do American and Mexican purchasing managers perceive the given ethical situation differently? Explain.

American Purchasing Managers			Mexican Purchasing Managers		
50	15	19	10	15	5
10	8	11	90	60	55
35	40	5	65	80	40
30	80	25	50	85	45
20	75	30	20	35	95

Source: "Do American and Mexican Purchasing Managers Perceive Ethical Situations Differently? An Empirical Investigation," by S. Trevino, R. Moreno and R. Tadepalli, in INDUSTRIAL MARKETING MANAGEMENT, 28.1, pp. 369-380, 1999.

Critical Thinking Challenge

103 Self-managed work teams and family life. *Quality Management Journal* (Summer 1995) did a study of self-managed work teams (SMWTs). The researchers investigated the connection between SMWT work characteristics and workers' perceptions of positive spillover into family life (one group of workers reported positive spillover of work skills to family life while another group did not report positive work spillover). The data collected on 114 AT&T employees are described below. Compare the two groups of workers on each characteristic using parametric methods. Reanalyze the data using nonparametrics. Are the job-related characteristics most highly associated with positive work spillover the same as those identified in your previous comparison? Comment on the validity of the parametric and nonparametric results.

Variables Measured in the SMWT Survey	
Characteristic	Variable
Information flow	Use of creative ideas (7-point scale)
Information flow	Utilization of information (7-point scale)
Decision making	Participation in decisions regarding personnel matters (7-point scale)
Job	Good use of skills (7-point scale)
Job	Task identity (7-point scale)
Demographic	Age (years)
Demographic	Education (years)
Demographic	Gender (male or female)
Comparison	Group (positive spillover or no spillover)

References

Conover, W. J. *Practical Nonparametric Statistics,* 3rd ed. New York: Wiley, 1998.

Daniel, W. W. *Applied Nonparametric Statistics,* 2nd ed. Boston: PWS-Kent, 1990.

Dunn, O. J. "Multiple comparisons using rank sums," *Technometrics,* Vol. 6, 1964.

Friedman, M. "The use of ranks to avoid the assumption of normality implicit in the analysis of variance," *Journal of the American Statistical Association,* Vol. 32, 1937.

Gibbons, J. D. *Nonparametric Statistical Inference,* 4th ed. Boca Raton, FL: CRC Press, 2003.

Hollander, M., & Wolfe, D. A. *Nonparametric Statistical Methods,* 2nd ed. New York: Wiley, 1999.

Kruskal, W. H., & Wallis, W. A. "Use of ranks in one-criterion variance analysis," *Journal of the American Statistical Association,* Vol. 47, 1952.

Lehmann, E. L. *Nonparametrics: Statistical Methods Based on Ranks* (revised). New York: Springer, 2006.

Marascuilo, L. A., & McSweeney, M. *Nonparametric and Distribution-Free Methods for the Social Sciences.* Monterey, CA: Brooks/Cole, 1977.

Wilcoxon, F., & Wilcox, R. A. "Some rapid approximate statistical procedures," The American Cyanamid Co., 1964.

USING TECHNOLOGY Technology images shown here are taken from SPSS Statistics Professional 20.0, Minitab 16, XLSTAT for Pearson, and Excel 2010.

Note: Automated commands for generating combinations and permutations are not available in SPSS.

SPSS: Nonparametric Tests

Sign Test or Signed Rank Test

Step 1 Access the SPSS spreadsheet file that contains the sample data. It should contain two quantitative variables. (*Note:* For the sign test, one variable is the variable to be analyzed and the other variable will have the value of the hypothesized median for all cases. For the signed rank test, the two variables represent the two variables in the paired difference.)

Step 2 Click on the "Analyze" button on the SPSS menu bar, then click on "Nonparametric Tests," "Legacy Dialogs," and "2 Related Samples," as shown in Figure S.1.

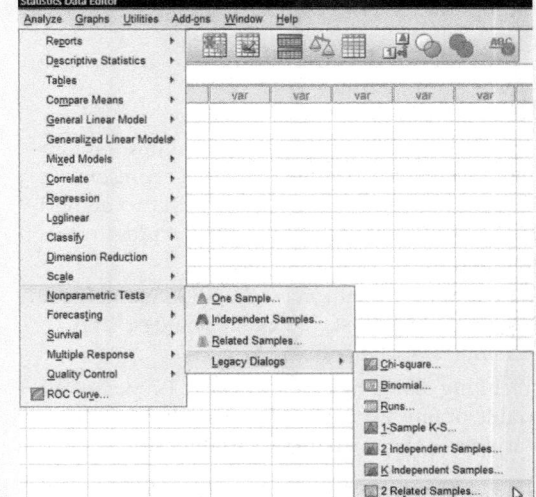

Figure S.1 SPSS menu options for sign test or signed rank test

Step 3 On the resulting dialog box (see Figure S.2), select the two quantitative variables of interest for "Variable 1" and "Variable 2" in the "Test Pairs" box.

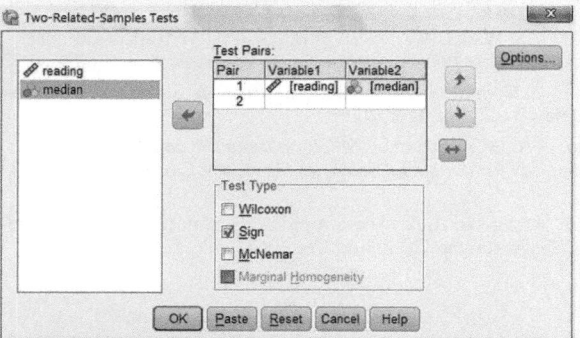

Figure S.2 SPSS Two-Related-Samples dialog box

Step 4 Under "Test Type," select the "Sign" option for a sign test or the "Wilcoxon" option for a signed rank test.

Step 5 Click "OK" to generate the SPSS printout.

Rank Sum Test

Step 1 Access the SPSS spreadsheet file that contains the sample data. It should contain two variables, one that represents the quantitative variable of interest and the other with two numerical coded values (e.g., 1 and 2). These two values represent the two groups or populations to be compared.

Step 2 Click on the "Analyze" button on the SPSS menu bar, then click on "Nonparametric Tests," "Legacy Dialogs," and "2 Independent Samples" (see Figure S.1).

Step 3 On the resulting dialog box (see Figure S.3), specify the quantitative variable of interest in the "Test Variable List" box and the coded variable in the "Grouping Variable" box.

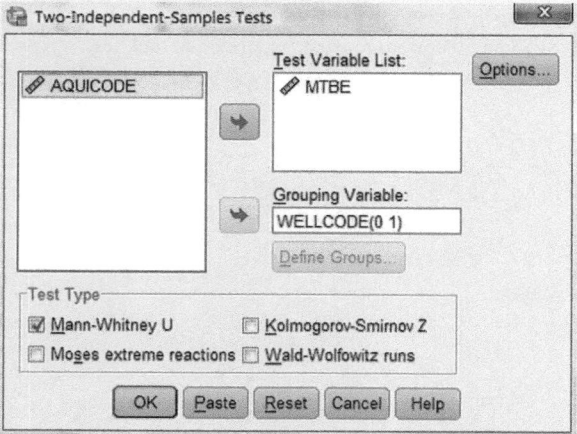

Figure S.3 SPSS Two-Independent-Samples dialog box

Step 4 Click the "Define Groups" button and specify the values of the two groups in the resulting dialog box. Then click "Continue" to return to the "Two-Independent-Samples" dialog screen.

Step 5 Select the "Mann-Whitney U" option under "Test Type."

Step 6 Click "OK" to generate the SPSS printout.

Kruskal-Wallis Test

Step 1 Access the SPSS spreadsheet file that contains the completely randomized design data. It should contain one

quantitative variable (the response, or dependent, variable) and one factor variable with at least two levels. (These values must be numbers, e.g., 1, 2, 3, etc.)

Step 2 Click on the "Analyze" button on the SPSS menu bar, then click on "Nonparametric Tests," "Legacy Dialogs," and "K Independent Samples" (see Figure S.1).

Step 3 On the resulting dialog box (see Figure S.4), specify the response variable in the "Test Variable List" box and the factor variable in the "Grouping Variable" box.

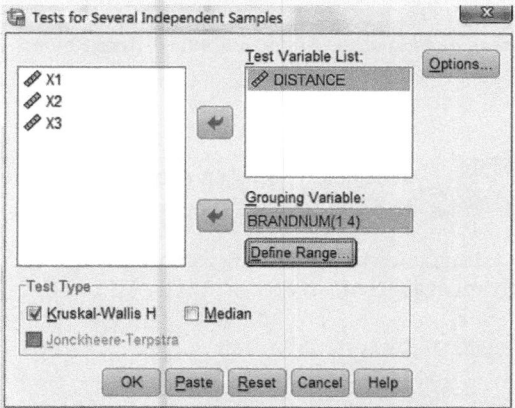

Figure S.4 SPSS K Independent Samples dialog box

Step 4 Click the "Define Range" button and specify the values of the grouping factor in the resulting dialog box. Then click "Continue" to return to the "K Independent Samples" dialog screen.

Step 5 Select the "Kruskal-Wallis" option under "Test Type."

Step 6 Click "OK" to generate the SPSS printout.

Friedman Test

Step 1 Access the SPSS spreadsheet file that contains the randomized block design data. It should contain k quantitative variables, representing the k treatments to be compared. (*Note:* The cases in the rows represent the blocks.)

Step 2 Click on the "Analyze" button on the SPSS menu bar, then click on "Nonparametric Tests," "Legacy Dialogs," and "K Related Samples" (see Figure S.1).

Step 3 On the resulting dialog box (see Figure S.5), specify the treatment variables in the "Test Variables" box.

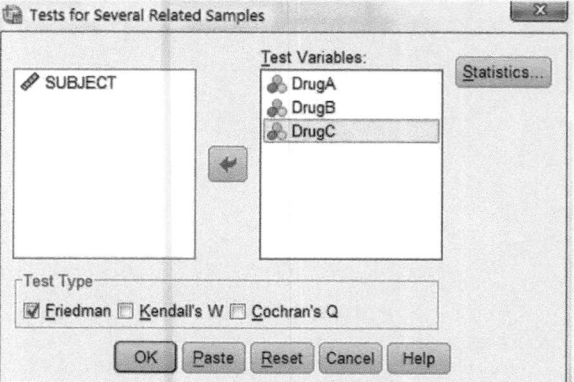

Figure S.5 SPSS K Related Samples dialog box

Step 4 Select the "Friedman" option under "Test Type."

Step 5 Click "OK" to generate the SPSS printout.

Rank Correlation

Step 1 To obtain Spearman's rank correlation coefficient for the two quantitative variables of interest, click on the "Analyze" button on the main menu bar, then click on "Correlate" and "Bivariate." The resulting dialog box appears in Figure S.6.

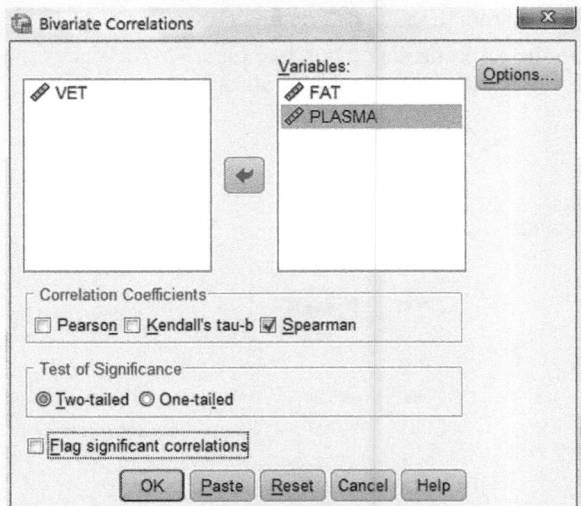

Figure S.6 SPSS Bivariate Correlations dialog box

Step 2 Enter the variables of interest in the "Variables" box.

Step 3 Check the "Spearman" option under "Correlation Coefficients."

Step 4 Click "OK" to obtain the SPSS printout.

Minitab: Nonparametric Tests

Sign Test

Step 1 Access the Minitab worksheet file with the sample data. It should contain a single quantitative variable.

Step 2 Click on the "Stat" button on the Minitab menu bar, then click on "Nonparametrics" and "1-Sample Sign," as shown in Figure M.1.

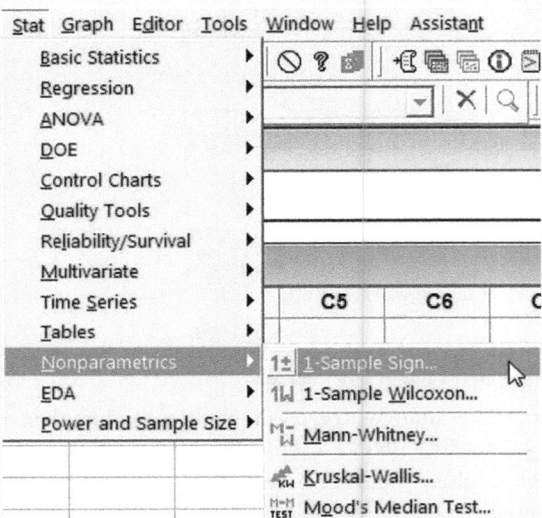

Figure M.1 Minitab nonparametric menu options

Step 3 On the resulting dialog box (see Figure M.2), enter the quantitative variable to be analyzed in the "Variables" box.

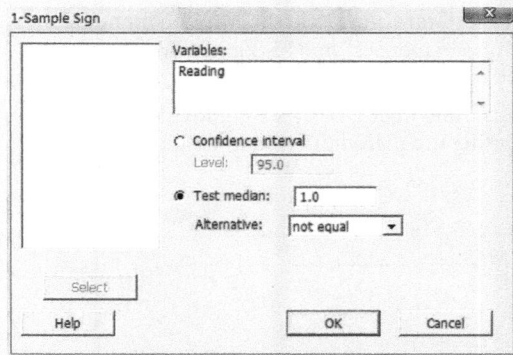

Figure M.2 Minitab 1-Sample Sign test dialog box

Step 4 Select the "Test median" option and specify the hypothesized value of the median and the form of the alternative hypothesis ("not equal," "less than," or "greater than").

Step 5 Click "OK" to generate the Minitab printout.

Rank Sum Test

Step 1 Access the Minitab worksheet file with the sample data. It should contain two quantitative variables, one for each of the two samples being compared.

Step 2 Click on the "Stat" button on the Minitab menu bar, then click on "Nonparametrics" and "Mann-Whitney" (see Figure M.1).

Step 3 On the resulting dialog box (see Figure M.3), specify the variable for the first sample in the "First Sample" box and the variable for the second sample in the "Second Sample" box.

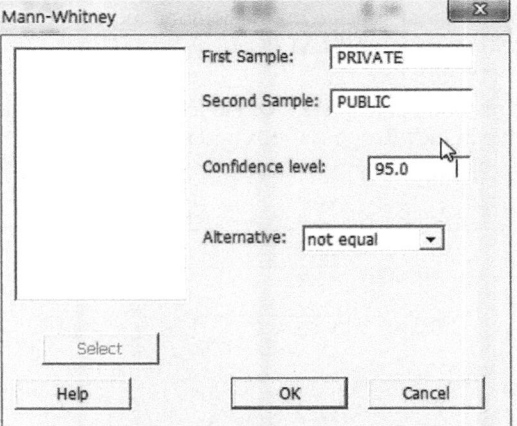

Figure M.3 Minitab Mann-Whitney (rank sum) test dialog box

Step 4 Specify the form of the alternative hypothesis ("not equal," "less than," or "greater than").

Step 5 Click "OK" to generate the Minitab printout.

Signed Rank Test

Step 1 Access the Minitab worksheet file with the matched pairs data. It should contain two quantitative variables, one for each of the two groups being compared.

Step 2 Compute the difference between these two variables and save it in a column on the worksheet. (Use the "Calc" button on the Minitab menu bar.)

Step 3 Click on the "Stat" button on the Minitab menu bar, then click on "Nonparametrics" and "1-Sample Wilcoxon" (see Figure M.1).

Step 4 On the resulting dialog box (see Figure M.4), enter the variable representing the paired differences in the "Variables" box.

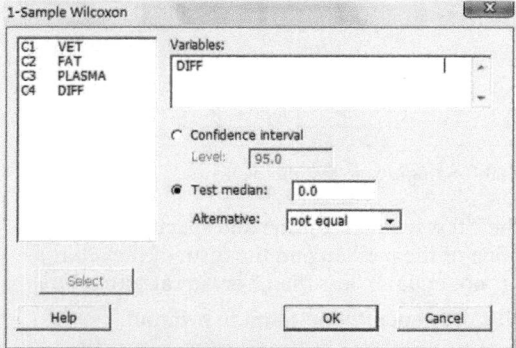

Figure M.4 Minitab 1-Sample Wilcoxon (signed rank) test dialog box

Step 5 Select the "Test median" option and specify the hypothesized value of the median as "0." Select the form of the alternative hypothesis ("not equal," "less than," or "greater than").

Step 6 Click "OK" to generate the Minitab printout.

Kruskal-Wallis Test

Step 1 Access the Minitab worksheet file that contains the completely randomized design data. It should contain one quantitative variable (the response, or dependent, variable) and one factor variable with at least two levels.

Step 2 Click on the "Stat" button on the Minitab menu bar, then click on "Nonparametrics" and "Kruskal-Wallis" (see Figure M.1).

Step 3 On the resulting dialog box (see Figure M.5), specify the response variable in the "Response" box and the factor variable in the "Factor" box.

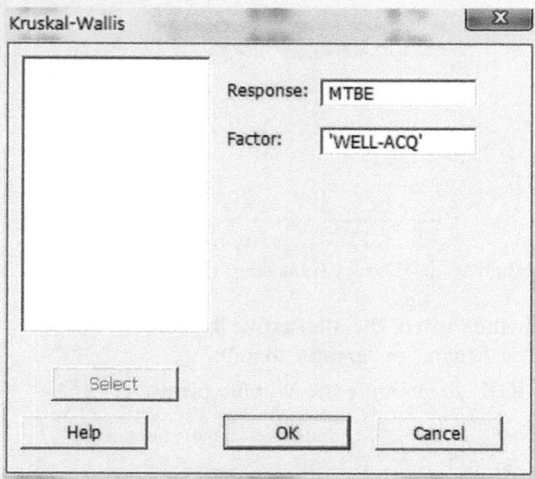

Figure M.5 Minitab Kruskal-Wallis test dialog box

Step 4 Click "OK" to generate the Minitab printout.

Friedman Test

Step 1 Access the Minitab spreadsheet file that contains the randomized block design data. It should contain one quantitative variable (the response, or dependent, variable), one factor variable, and one blocking variable.

Step 2 Click on the "Stat" button on the Minitab menu bar, then click on "Nonparametrics" and "Friedman" (see Figure M.1).

Step 3 On the resulting dialog box (see Figure M.6), specify the response, treatment, and blocking variables in the appropriate boxes.

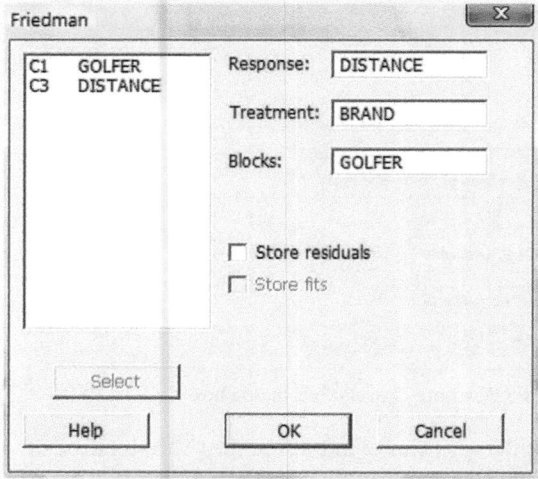

Figure M.6 Minitab Friedman test dialog box

Step 4 Click "OK" to generate the Minitab printout.

Rank Correlation

Step 1 To obtain Spearman's rank correlation coefficient in Minitab, you must first rank the values of the two quantitative variables of interest. Click the "Calc" button on the Minitab menu bar and create two additional columns, one for the ranks of the x-variable and one for the ranks of the y-variable. (Use the "Rank" function on the Minitab calculator as shown in Figure M.7).

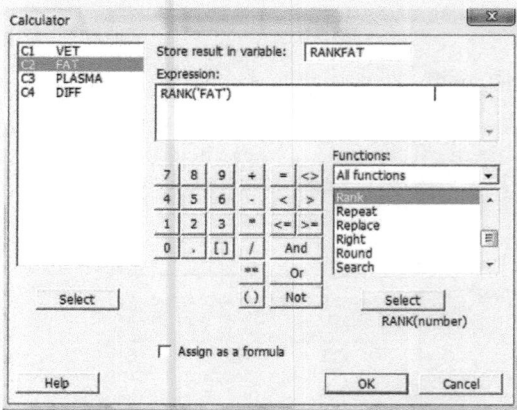

Figure M.7 Minitab calculator menu screen

Step 2 Click on the "Stat" button on the main menu bar, then click on "Basic Statistics" and "Correlation."

Step 3 On the resulting dialog box (see Figure M.8), enter the ranked variables in the "Variables" box and unselect the "Display p-values" option.

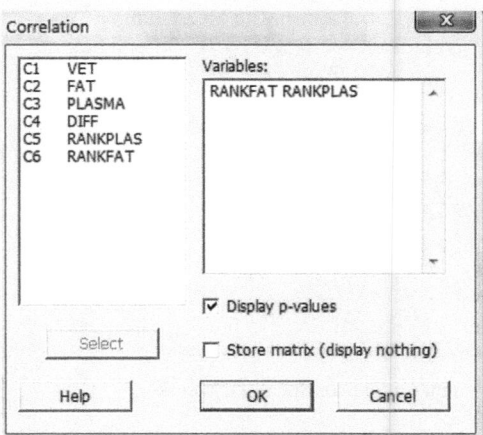

Figure M.8 Minitab correlation dialog box

Step 4 Click "OK" to obtain the Minitab printout. (You will need to look up the critical value of Spearman's rank correlation to conduct the test.)

Excel/XLSTAT: Nonparametric Tests

Sign Test or Signed Rank Test

Step 1 Within XLSTAT, open the Excel spreadsheet with the data. The file should contain two paired quantitative variables. (For the sign test, the second variable should contain the value of the hypothesized median for all cases.)

Step 2 Click the "XLSTAT" button on the Excel main menu bar, select "Nonparametric tests," then click "Comparison of two samples," as shown in Figure E.1.

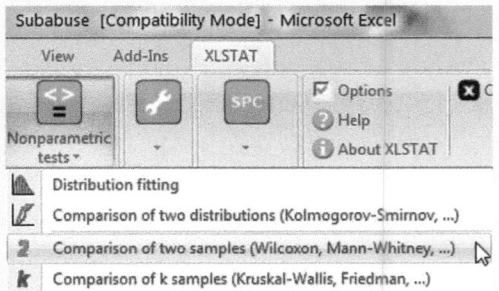

Figure E.1 XLSTAT menu options for sign test or signed rank test

Step 3 When the resulting dialog box appears (Figure E.2), click "Paired samples" in the "Data format" area, then specify the columns containing the variables in the "Sample 1" and "Sample 2" boxes.

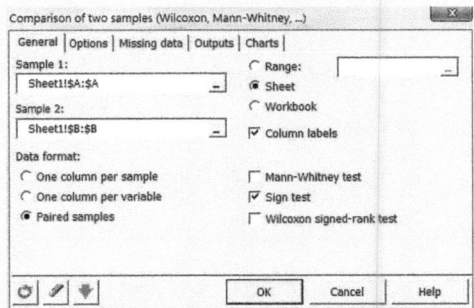

Figure E.2 XLSTAT nonparametric dialog box options for paired data

Step 4 Select ether "Sign test" or "Wilcoxon signed-rank test."

Step 5 Click "OK," then "Continue" to display the test results.

Rank Sum Test

Step 1 Within XLSTAT, open the Excel spreadsheet with the data. The file should contain two columns, one for each sample.

Step 2 Click the "XLSTAT" button on the Excel main menu bar, select "Nonparametric tests," then click "Comparison of two samples," as shown in Figure E.1.

Step 3 When the resulting dialog box appears (Figure E.3), click "One column per sample" in the "Data format" area, then specify the columns containing the variables in the "Sample 1" and "Sample 2" boxes.

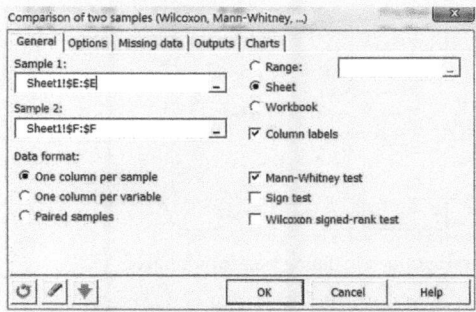

Figure E.3 XLSTAT nonparametric dialog box for two independent samples

Step 4 Select "Mann-Whitney test."

Step 5 Click "OK," then "Continue" to display the test results.

Kruskal-Wallis Test

Step 1 Within XLSTAT, open the Excel spreadsheet with the data. The file should contain two columns, one for the variable to be analyzed and one identifying the samples (treatments).

Step 2 Click the "XLSTAT" button on the Excel main menu bar, select "Nonparametric tests," then click "Comparison of k samples" (see Figure E.1).

Step 3 When the resulting dialog box appears (Figure E.4), click "One column per variable" in the "Data format" area, then specify the column containing the variable to be analyzed in the "Data" box and the column containing the samples in the "Sample identifiers" box.

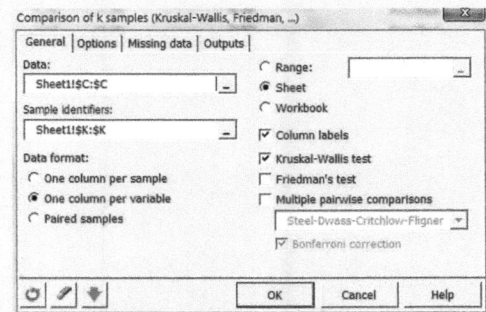

Figure E.4 XLSTAT nonparametric dialog box for k independent samples

Step 4 Select "Kruskal-Wallis test."

Step 5 Click "OK," then "Continue" to display the test results.

Friedman Test

Step 1 Within XLSTAT, open the Excel spreadsheet with the data. The file should contain multiple matched columns, one for each treatment (the rows represent the blocks).

Step 2 Click the "XLSTAT" button on the Excel main menu bar, select "Nonparametric tests," then click "Comparison of *k* samples" (see Figure E.1).

Step 3 When the resulting dialog box appears (Figure E.5), click "Paired samples" in the "Data format" area, then specify the columns containing data in the "Samples" box.

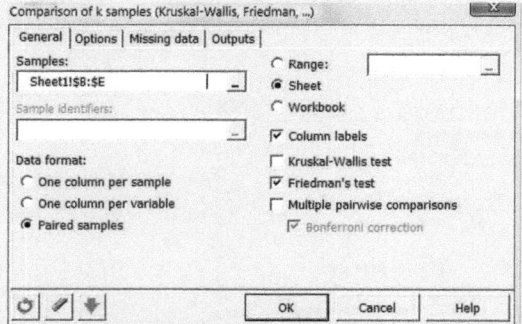

Figure E.5 XLSTAT nonparametric dialog box for *k* related samples

Step 4 Select "Friedman's test."

Step 5 Click "OK," then "Continue" to display the test results.

Rank Correlation

Step 1 Within XLSTAT, open the Excel spreadsheet with the data. The file should contain two quantitative variables.

Step 2 Click the "XLSTAT" button on the Excel main menu bar, select "Correlation/Association tests," then click "Correlation tests," as shown in Figure E.6.

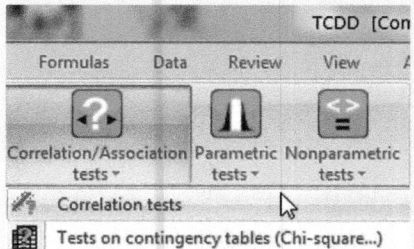

Figure E.6 XLSTAT menu options for Spearman's rank correlation

Step 3 When the resulting dialog box appears (Figure E.7), specify the columns containing the data in the "Observations/variables table" box, then specify "Spearman" for "Type of correlation."

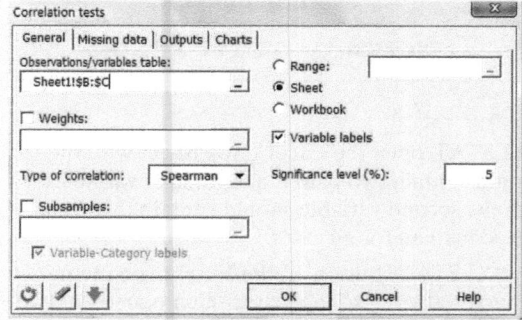

Figure E.7 XLSTAT dialog box options for correlation tests

Step 4 Click "OK," then "Continue" to display the test results.

MAKING BUSINESS DECISIONS

Detecting "Sales Chasing"

Many State Departments of Revenue (DOR) are tasked with reviewing each county's tax rolls to determine whether the appraised values of properties used to assess property taxes are being fairly determined. One common type of review performed by DORs is a sales ratio study, in which ratios of sales prices to appraised values are analyzed. Sales ratio studies aid in the detection of *sales chasing*. Sales chasing occurs when county property appraisers increase the appraised values of properties that sold within the last year by more than they increase the appraised values of properties that did not sell. One motivation for sales chasing is that the county property appraiser knows that the DOR will scrutinize the sold properties to determine how closely the appraised values and sales prices agree but will not be able to make that comparison for unsold properties.

Although the DOR obviously cannot know what sales prices would be for properties that did not sell, it can compare the changes in the appraised values of unsold properties from one year to the next to the changes in the appraised values of sold properties over the same time period. For example, suppose that a county's appraised values of sold properties increase by an average of 10% from one year to the next, but the appraised value of unsold properties increase by only 2%. This might lead the DOR to investigate whether this difference is attributable to real differences between the two sets of properties or is likely due to sales chasing on the part of the county appraiser.

The Problem and the Data

The Georgia DOR recently investigated potential sales chasing in a particular county. Data on all 82 sold properties and a random sample of 86 unsold properties in the county were used in the analysis. All sold properties were "qualified" (meaning no structural changes in the property from the previous year and that the sales are arms-length transactions). The randomly selected unsold properties were "qualified" as well. For each property, the percentage change in appraised value from last year to this year was determined as follows:

$$\text{Percentage change} = 100(AV_2 - AV_1)/AV_1$$

Table C6	Percentage Changes in Appraised Values of County's Sold and Unsold Properties							
Sold								
−4.95	−4.87	−2.99	−2.88	−2.70	−2.63	−2.42	−2.31	−1.93
−1.78	−1.66	−1.50	−1.48	−1.44	−1.40	−1.01	−0.93	−0.49
−0.37	0.00	0.00	0.00	0.00	0.00	0.00	0.00	0.00
0.00	0.00	0.31	0.58	0.71	0.76	0.89	1.00	1.27
1.29	1.45	1.47	2.16	2.36	2.60	2.64	3.08	3.12
3.25	3.43	3.60	3.61	3.61	3.71	4.10	4.17	4.22
4.70	4.91	4.92	5.54	5.56	5.69	5.83	6.11	6.49
6.68	6.86	7.08	7.21	7.50	7.83	8.14	8.84	9.08
9.12	9.32	10.04	10.36	11.29	11.50	11.66	11.82	14.12
14.80								
Unsold								
−1.43	−0.47	0.00	0.00	0.00	0.00	0.00	0.00	0.00
0.00	0.00	0.00	0.00	0.00	0.00	0.00	0.00	0.00
0.00	0.00	0.00	0.00	0.00	0.00	0.00	0.00	0.00
0.00	0.00	0.00	0.00	0.00	0.00	0.00	0.00	0.00
0.00	0.00	0.00	0.00	0.00	0.00	0.00	0.00	0.00
0.00	0.00	0.00	0.00	0.00	0.00	0.00	0.00	0.00
0.00	0.00	0.00	0.00	0.00	0.00	0.63	1.26	1.27
1.59	2.11	2.97	3.16	3.35	3.45	3.55	3.55	3.68
3.81	3.85	3.94	3.97	3.97	4.93	5.19	5.25	6.12
6.48	6.75	6.86	7.35	7.62				

Source: "Percentage changes in appraised values of County's Sold and Unsold Properties." Copyright © 2012 by Info Tech, Inc. Reprinted with permission.

(Making Business
Decisions Continued)

where AV_1 = last year's appraised value and AV_2 = this year's appraised value. The data, saved in the **GDOR** file, are shown in Table C6.

Variable	Type	Description
PROPERTY	QL	SOLD or UNSOLD
CHANGE	QN	Percentage change
APPRAISAL	QL	INCREASE, DECREASE, or SAME

(Number of observations: 168)　　🖸 *Data Set:* GDOR

Applying Statistical Methodology

Although statistical methods cannot reveal the cause of differences in sales ratios, they can be used to test the null hypothesis that there is no real difference between the year-to-year changes in appraised values of sold and unsold properties. Because both the distributions of property values and of the ratios of appraised values are often highly skewed and contain numerous outliers, nonparametric tests are often used to make the comparison. For example, a nonparametric test can be used to test the difference in the location of the two distributions, using the ranks of the appraisal changes. A chi-square test can also be conducted, classifying sales of sold and unsold properties' ratios into one of three categories: appraisal decreased, appraisal remained the same, or appraisal increased from one year to the next. This 2×3 table can then be tested to determine whether the distributions of the sold and unsold properties differ across the three categories. In either case, if the null hypothesis is rejected, the analysis provides some statistical evidence that the county property appraiser *may* be sales chasing. However, further investigation is typically required. Because the sales do not represent a random sample of properties in the county, there may be other explanations related to the differences in the characteristics (e.g., location, size, age, etc.) of the sold and unsold properties that would explain some or all of the difference.

Conduct the appropriate statistical analysis for the Georgia DOR. Is there evidence of potential sales chasing by the county appraisers? Prepare a document (include supporting materials) with your recommendations.

◻ Answers to Selected Exercises

1 Nonnormal data **3 a.** .035 **b.** .363 **c.** .004 **d.** .151; .151 **e.** .2122; .2119 **5** p-value = .054; reject H_0 **7 a.** H_0: $\eta = 125{,}000$, H_a: $\eta > 125{,}000$ **b.** $S = 9$, p-value = .304, do not reject H_0 **c.** Random sample **9** No; $S = 11$, p-value = .322 **11** $S = 9$, p-value = .073, reject H_0 **13** $S = 8$, p-value = .109, do not reject H_0 **15** Yes, $z = -2.47$ **17 a.** $T_1 = 62.5$, reject H_0 **b.** $T_1 = 62.5$, reject H_0 **19 b.** $T_1 = 104$ **c.** $T_2 = 106$ **d.** $T_1 = 104$ **e.** Do not reject H_0 **21 a.** Wilcoxon rank sum test **b.** H_a: Distribution of X-Factors for low-handicapped golfers is shifted to the right of distribution for high-handicapped golfers **c.** $T_2 \leq 41$ **d.** Do not reject H_0 **23 a.** H_0: Two sampled populations have identical probability distributions **b.** $z = -.66$ **c.** $|z| > 1.645$ **d.** Do not reject H_0 **25 b.** $z = 2.43$, reject H_0 **c.** Sample sizes large, Central Limit Theorem applies **27 b.** p-value = .3431, do not reject H_0 **29 a.** Smaller of T_+ or T_-; $T \leq 152$ **b.** T_-; $T_- \leq 60$ **c.** T_+; $T_+ \leq 0$ **31 a.** H_0: Two sampled populations have identical probability distributions **b.** $T_- = 3.5$, reject H_0 **33 a.** Nonnormal differences **b.** Signed rank test **e.** $T_+ = 65$; $T_- = 55$ **f.** Yes **35 a.** $z = -4.64$ **b.** Yes, p-value ≈ 0 **37** p-value = .011, reject H_0 at $\alpha = .05$; enforcement program is effective **39** $T_- = 3.5$, reject H_0 **41 a.** $T_- = 4$, reject H_0 **b.** Yes **43** $n \geq 5$ for each sample **45 a.** Completely randomized **b.** H_0: 3 probability distributions are identical **c.** $H > 9.21034$ **d.** $H = 13.85$, reject H_0 **47 a.** H_0: 3 probability distributions are identical **b.** $H = 36.04$, p-value = .000 **c.** Reject H_0 **49 a.** H_0: 4 probability distributions are identical **c.** $R_1 = 52.5$, $R_2 = 125.0$, $R_3 = 88.5$, $R_4 = 34.0$; $H = 16.23$ **d.** $H > 7.81473$ **e.** Reject H_0 **51 b.** Normal data and equal variances **c.** $H = .29$, do not reject H_0 **53** $H = 26.82$, reject H_0 **55 a.** H_0: Distributions for three treatments are identical **b.** $F_r > 4.60517$ **c.** $F_r = 6.93$, reject H_0 **57 a.** Data are not independent (blocked on subject) **b.** $F_r = 14.37$, p-value = .002 **c.** Reject H_0 **59 a.** $R_1 = 35$, $R_2 = 32$, $R_3 = 23$ **b.** $F_r = 5.20$ **c.** p-value = .074 **d.** Reject H_0 at $\alpha = .10$ **61** $F_r = 29.11$, p-value = .001, reject H_0 **63** No, $F_r = .20$ **65** Yes, $F_r = 6.35$ **67 a.** $|r_s| > .648$ **b.** $r_s > .45$ **c.** $r_s < -.432$ **69 a.** .4 **b.** $-.9$ **c.** $-.2$ **d.** .2 **71 a.** .8286 **b.** No **c.** .8117 **d.** No **73 b.** Navigability: do not reject H_0; transactions: reject H_0; locatability: reject H_0; information: do not reject H_0; files: do not reject H_0 **75** Yes; $r_s = -.829$, reject H_0 **77** Moderate positive rank correlation between Methods I and III; all other pairs have weak positive rank correlation **79** No, $r_s = .492$ **81 a.** No, $r_s = .40$ **b.** Yes, $T_- = 1.5$ **83** Yes, $F_r = 14.9$ **85 a.** Wilcoxon rank sum test **b.** H_0: CMC and FTF groups have identical probability distributions **c.** $z < -1.28$ **d.** $z = -.21$, do not reject H_0 **87 a.** 43 **b.** H_0: $\eta = 37$, H_a: $\eta > 37$ **c.** $S = 11$, p-value = .059, reject H_0 at $\alpha = .10$ **89 a.** .657 **b.** No **91 a.** No, at $\alpha = 0.5$; $S = 20$, $z = -3.71$ **b.** No; sample collected in Boston only **93** $F_r = .93$, p-value = .819, do not reject H_0 **95 a.** $z = 1.77$, do not reject H_0 **97 a.** H_0: $\eta = .75$, H_a: $\eta \neq .75$ **d.** p-value = .044, reject H_0 **99** $F_r = 6.21$, do not reject H_0 **101 a.** $S = 14$, p-value = .058, do not reject H_0 **b.** $S = 12$, p-value = .1796, do not reject H_0 **c.** $T = 50$, do not reject H_0 **d.** $r_s = .774$; yes **103** Evidence of difference in distributions (at $\alpha = .05$) for creative ideas and good use of skills

☐ Credits

The photo credits below are listed in order of appearance.

Liz Van Steenburgh/Shutterstock
Pizuttipics/Fotolia
Courtesy of the Department of Statistics, Florida State University
George Peters/iStockphoto
University College London Dept of Psychology

☐ Technology Images

Index

GREG DYKE

INSIDE STORY

GREG DYKE

INSIDE STORY

HarperCollins*Publishers*

First published in Great Britain by
HarperCollins*Publishers*
77–85 Fulham Palace Road,
Hammersmith, London W6 8JB

www.harpercollins.co.uk

Published by HarperCollins*Publishers* 2004
3

Copyright © Greg Dyke 2004

The Author asserts the moral right to
be identified as the author of this work

Extracts from *Point of Departure* by Robin Cook,
copyright © Robin Cook, 2003, 2004,
reprinted by permission of Simon & Schuster UK Ltd.

A catalogue record for this book
is available from the British Library

ISBN 0-00-719233-9

Typeset in Sabon by
Rowland Phototypesetting Ltd,
Bury St Edmunds, Suffolk

Printed and bound in Great Britain by
Clays Ltd, St Ives plc

To Sue

And to Matthew, Christine, Alice, and Joe

Contents

Illustrations

My mum and dad on their wedding day in 1939.
In the back garden of our hourse in Cerne Close, Hayes.
Aged seven, a pupil at Yeading Primary School in Hayes.
Form 1b at Hayes Grammar School in 1958.
The Hayes Grammar 'upper sixth' in 1965.
In my last year at school.
My leaving party at the *Hillingdon Mirror*, 1969.
Outside 1, Briggs Street, York. © *Jeffrey Wright*
With my dog Jake on the North Yorkshire moors, 1972. © *Jeffrey Wright*
The Six O'Clock Show team at LWT, 1982.
My leaving card from LWT: illustration by Carlo Roberto.
My family in 1989.
My message to LWT staff.
With Christopher Bland. © *Topfoto/UPPA*
The great match at Wembley in 1987.
Steve Cram chops me from behind.
The LWT joke poster.
LWT's top management and stars on the day we retained the franchise.
Celebrating Labour's victory, 1997. © *Justin Williams/The Sunday Times*
Sue and me on election night, May 1997. © *Andrew Shaw/The Daily Telegraph*
Outside Old Trafford, 1997. © *Tom Jenkins*.
With Alex Ferguson and other directors of Manchester United.

Directors and officials of Manchester United before the match in
   Barcelona.
Dr Dyke. © *Guzelian*
At Thora Hird's memorial service. © *Tim Rooke/Rex Features*
The BBC Board of Governors, July 2003. © *BBC Photo Library*
Outside Television Centre on the day I left the BBC. © *Fiona Hanson/
   PA Photos*
Taking out tea to the television crews. © *Stephen Lock/The Daily
   Telegraph*

Cartoons: Newman/NI Syndication; Franklin/NI Syndication; Richard
   Willson/NI Syndication; Heath/NI Syndication.

Acknowledgements

I've always believed that autobiographies are ridiculously self-serving and, as such, shouldn't be taken too seriously. That was before I had written one. I suspect in writing this book I've fallen into all the traps of self-justification that have made me laugh when I have read others' accounts of their lives. If I have, please forgive me. My dad always taught me that being pompous and self-important was just about the greatest sin of all; at least I hope I've avoided that in this book.

I started this book the weekend after I was fired from the BBC when my friend Melvyn Bragg rang me and told me that I had better write a book because if I didn't do something I'd drive my friends and my family mad. Melvyn is normally right about most things but on this occasion he got it wrong: I've driven my family mad anyway while writing this account of my life. They are almost as bored with Lord Hutton as I am.

But I sincerely believe we are living through something profound; that we are in the midst of a great political scandal; and if this book helps in a small way to expose that scandal, then I'll be happy.

There are people to thank. At HarperCollins there are Caroline Michel and Richard Johnson, whose enthusiasm has kept me going; there's my agent, Vivien Green (I've never had an agent before and she seems terribly nice); there's James Hogan, who suggested the title of the book; there are Jeff Wright, John Morrison, Alice Pearman, Trevor East, David Fairbairn, Clive Jones, Tony Cohen, Susan Spindler, Carolyn Fairbairn, Gavyn Davies and others who have helped me with different parts of the book. Then there's Christopher Bland, who read it all, corrected some facts, and tried to make some sense of my grammar; and finally there was

Melvyn Bragg, who gave me the confidence to start and has given invaluable advice chapter by chapter (not that he's agreed with all the sentiments in them).

I'll end by thanking my mum for just about everything but in particular for the wonderful words of advice she gave me when I rang and told her I was writing a book. She thought for a moment and said, 'I hope you're not going to cause trouble, dear.' I sincerely hope I am.

CHAPTER ONE

Three Days in January

As I left home on the morning of Tuesday 27 January 2004, I had no idea that within thirty-six hours my career as Director-General of the BBC would be over. I didn't even see it as a remote possibility that I would be fired by a board of BBC Governors behaving like frightened rabbits caught in the headlights – a board unnerved by a combination of the resignation of their Chairman, Lord Hutton's infamous report, and the prospect of the revenge the Government might seek to take against the BBC.

Of course very few people knew then that Lord Hutton's report, due to be published the following day, would so damn the BBC and would so totally exonerate the Government of any mistakes or wrongdoing. It was our view that the BBC had made some mistakes and was likely to be criticized but that the Government would deservedly suffer at least as much. Nor could anyone have known that within forty-eight hours the acting Chairman of the BBC would do lasting damage to the BBC's reputation at home and abroad by issuing the most grovelling of apologies to a vitriolic Government.

And who could possibly have foreseen that thousands of BBC employees, in all parts of the United Kingdom, would have taken to the streets to support me, or that they would have clubbed together to pay for a full-page advertisement in the *Daily Telegraph* backing me and challenging the Governors to defend the independence of the BBC? And how could anyone have known on that Tuesday morning that by the end of the week Lord Hutton's report would have been so comprehensively ridiculed by media and public alike, its findings dismissed as a crude

1

whitewash of the Government and yet another example of Number Ten spin?

Nevertheless, as I left home that morning I certainly knew that it was going to be a lively week.

With the publication of the Hutton Report imminent, the photographers and reporters were already camped outside my house in Twickenham, so even the most innocent of passers-by would have known that something was up. My partner Sue was away in Suffolk for the week, real evidence that we didn't expect a major crisis: if we had, then there was no way she would have gone. Only Joe and I were there that morning. Joe was sixteen at the time, the youngest of our four children and the only one at home. He was used to journalists and camera crews turning up outside our house and we both smiled when we saw them there that morning.

Our house backs onto nine acres of parkland that we share with forty or so other houses. This gives us numerous choices for getting in and out, making it virtually impossible for any reporter, photographer, or camera crew to catch me. We saw avoiding them as a game that we had been playing, on and off, for the four years I'd been Director-General. On some occasions Joe or my daughter Alice, who in January was away building a school in Africa, used to take pity on them and would tell them that I'd already left, but the journalists never believed them. Joe, Alice, and I quite enjoyed the game. Sue, on the other hand, hated these people intruding into our privacy in this way.

Because I had expected the press to arrive, I had already arranged for Joe to spend the next couple of days at a friend's house, so on that Tuesday morning we left together through the back door, with Joe pushing his bike and carrying a bagful of clothes. We got onto the road through the garden of Number 10a and when we got there I rang Bill, my driver, and he drove around the corner and picked me up. Meanwhile, Joe cycled off to college. An easy win that morning. The next time Joe and I were to meet was on Thursday evening, when I was no longer the Director-General and he had already started making jokes about leaving home if I was going to be there full time.

That Tuesday was Hutton publication day minus one, the day when all of those involved in the inquiry were to get an advanced copy of the report. We were to receive it exactly twenty-four hours before Hutton

pronounced, which meant we would get it around lunchtime. A total of twenty-two of us at the BBC had signed confidentiality agreements and we had agreed a timetable for the day. I was going to read the report alone in my office. Richard Sambrook, the Director of BBC News, and his deputy Mark Damazer would read it in the meeting room next door, along with Magnus Brooke, my acting business manager. Magnus was a lawyer whom I had picked from relative obscurity within the BBC for this job, and he was brilliant. During the summer he had gone back to the legal division for a period to help out on Hutton. The rest of the people entitled to read the report that day would be in rooms nearby. Andrew Gilligan, the journalist at the centre of the row, and his legal team also had a room allocated in the building.

We had all set aside four hours to read the report knowing that it was likely to be nearly 700 pages long; but as it turned out, we didn't need anything like as long as that. Halfway down page three I knew we were in trouble. It was on that page that Lord Hutton explained that he had decided to limit the scope of his inquiry and completely ignore the crucial question of what sort of weapons of mass destruction the Government was warning us about in the dossier they had published in September 2002. With this one inexplicable decision Lord Hutton had wiped out key parts of the BBC's evidence and a critical foundation of our case. The following week we were to discover perhaps the most damning fact of all: that the Prime Minister himself had no idea what sort of weapons of mass destruction he had referred to, even though he'd used the so-called evidence of their existence as the central theme of his own introduction to the dossier and a reason for going to war.

There was a crumb of comfort for everyone at the BBC at the bottom of page three when Hutton said he was satisfied that no one involved in the row, including the BBC, could possibly have realized that Dr David Kelly, the Government expert on weapons of mass destruction who had been the BBC's source for its original story, might take his own life. But these were virtually the only kind words about the BBC in the whole report, and even that reference was far kinder to those in 10 Downing Street and the Ministry of Defence than it was to the BBC. It was Number Ten and the MOD who had hounded Dr Kelly, not the BBC: we had gone to great lengths to keep his identity secret.

I tried to plough on through the report but rapidly discovered it was

a cut and paste job. It felt like Hutton, late in life, had learnt how to use Microsoft Word: the report was largely made up of tracts of evidence given to the inquiry with Hutton's opinion simply tacked on at the end, often without any explanation as to how or why he had reached his conclusions. When writing about the report later, the former editor of *The Times*, Lord Rees-Mogg, agreed. He called it a defective document in which the conclusions did not follow from the evidence.

I began to skim the document at about the same time as Mark Damazer stuck his head round the door to tell me that I only had to read the seven pages that made up Chapter 12 because the guts of the report was all there. This was the summary of Hutton's conclusions and I read them in total disbelief. This man wasn't on the same planet as the rest of us. Hadn't he listened to the evidence? Hadn't he listened to his own QC during the inquiry? How could he possibly have reached these conclusions?

Forty minutes after I started reading the report I walked into the adjoining meeting room where Sambrook, Damazer, and young Magnus Brooke were all sitting looking shell shocked. They tell me I said something like, 'Well, boys, we've been fucked, so what are we going to do about it?'

In the week or two before publication we had worked on a whole range of scenarios for what Hutton might say and how we should respond. The problem was that none of our scenarios was as bad as the reality. In our scenario planning it had only crossed our minds once, and then only fleetingly, that Hutton might find that the dossier had not been 'sexed up' at all. We all laughed and dismissed it, as the evidence was so clear cut. But that was exactly what Hutton had decided. There had been no sexing up; even worse, he had found against the BBC and for the Government on virtually every single count.

The four of us rapidly and prophetically agreed that this report was so one-sided we didn't believe it would turn out to be such good news for the Government as initially appeared to be the case. It was so much in their favour people would find it hard to believe. After all, dozens of journalists had sat through the inquiry and listened to the evidence. Surely they would see Hutton's findings as completely inconsistent with the evidence? And what about the wider public? They had followed the inquiry in large numbers and would surely see the same inconsistencies. Interestingly, over at *The Sun* newspaper, which, unbeknown to any of

us, had illicitly obtained a copy of the report, the reaction was very similar. There the paper's editor, Rebekah Wade, and her team immediately saw that the report might be seen as a complete whitewash.

The problem we faced on that Tuesday was: how long would it take before this happened, and what would our defence be in the meantime? We discussed a strategy and decided to stick to the plan we had developed in advance. We would say that most of the criticisms of the BBC had been acknowledged during the inquiry; that, as a result, we had taken steps to improve our procedures; and that we would soon announce changes to the BBC's editorial guidelines. However, I did add a new line. We would also say, on the crucial issue of reporting a confidential source, that we had real doubts whether Lord Hutton had got it right, that he had misunderstood the law, and that his conclusions were a threat to free journalism in the UK.

Around 2.30 p.m. we went down one flight of stairs to see the BBC Chairman Gavyn Davies. He was with the two other BBC Governors who had been allowed to read the report in advance – Pauline Neville-Jones and the Vice-Chairman, Lord Ryder. Both were very Establishment figures. Richard Ryder had been Chief Whip in the last Conservative Government and Neville-Jones had been a career civil servant at the Foreign Office and was a former Chair of the Joint Intelligence Committee (JIC). She had left the Foreign Office when she was not appointed Britain's Ambassador in Paris.

I can't say I liked Pauline Neville-Jones, but I did have some respect for her. She was one of a number of Governors who had fought against my appointment as Director-General four years earlier and was still a powerful voice on the current Board, which was a bit short of people with authority. She certainly worked harder than any other Governor in my time at the BBC, was obviously very clever in a manipulative Foreign Office sort of way, and had successfully sustained the BBC's close relation-ship with the Foreign Office. This mattered because it was the Foreign Office who funded the BBC World Service.

But neither I nor the two BBC chairmen I worked with, Christopher Bland and Gavyn Davies, ever totally trusted Pauline. She applied to be Deputy Chairman of the BBC when Lord Ryder was recruited and was turned down. She was incredibly ambitious but I always suspected she had not been as successful in life as she had wished or expected.

On the other hand, I did like Richard Ryder. I first met him at the Conservative Party Conference a decade or so earlier when I was Chief Executive of London Weekend Television and found him quiet and thoughtful, unlike most politicians. He had been one of the people who had worked with the public relations guru Gordon Rees back in the late 1970s transforming Margaret Thatcher's image, so he'd been around the fringes of politics for a long time. When he became Deputy Chairman of the BBC he was still on the Board of Ipswich Town Football Club, and as a former Director of Manchester United I had plenty to chat with him about. The problem with Richard was that he had been recruited as Deputy Chairman to help build a relationship with the Conservative Party but quite clearly disliked many of the people now leading it. He had failed to make a single speech since he was elevated to the House of Lords in 1997 and seemed reluctant even to attend, let alone host, lunches and dinners in the Lords in support of the BBC. People in both Public Affairs and the Secretary's office at the BBC complained all the time that he didn't work hard enough to be the Deputy Chairman.

When we met up with Gavyn, Pauline, and Richard they, too, seemed shocked. Pauline said she was horrified by the report; Richard said very little. Gavyn told us that he had been told by a close friend that we had made a mistake co-operating with Hutton in the first place and that from the moment this particular judge had been appointed the result was a foregone conclusion. Our only hope, according to Gavyn's friend, had been to attack the way Hutton ran the whole inquiry at every available opportunity: that way we would have been able to demonstrate that he had been appointed by the Government to deliver a verdict that would favour them. It was an interesting perspective but hardly relevant to the position we were now in. In the middle of this discussion Tara Conlan, a journalist on the *Daily Mail*, rang Gavyn on his mobile phone and asked him openly what was in the report. We all laughed as he gave her a very polite brush-off.

By late afternoon we moved to a bigger room, where we were joined by our legal and press teams. Our QC, Andrew Caldecott, turned up with a comprehensive argument detailing how Hutton had completely misunderstood the law on 'qualified privilege', which covered the rights journalistic organizations now possessed. In the end we split into two groups, one to plan strategy and the other practicalities.

I worked on a comparatively aggressive statement, which we would put out the following day and which we'd all agreed Gavyn was to deliver. Together we watched the result of the parliamentary vote on tuition fees, which took place around 7.00 p.m. We got even more depressed when the Government narrowly won, thanks to Gordon Brown delivering his supporters at the last minute. Our reaction was nothing to do with the pros and cons of the issue; we simply thought we'd get an easier time the following day if the Government had another crisis on its hands.

The whole team then had dinner together. I remember being pleased that someone had ordered something other than sandwiches. At the time I was on the Atkins diet, and January is also one of the two months in the year when I don't drink alcohol, so as I munched through two or three pieces of chicken, and drank my bottled water, I was feeling very virtuous.

By now Gavyn had begun to talk privately about resigning. I was strongly against it, but I thought it had to be his decision. As the hours went by he became more and more convinced it was the right and honourable thing for him to do. I certainly had no intention of resigning. We discussed the position briefly with Richard Ryder before he disappeared for the evening and we talked over the whole strategy with Pauline Neville-Jones later in the evening after she had returned from a drinks party.

The three of us – Gavyn, Pauline, and I – sat privately in a room together and weighed up the options, a conversation that was to take on greater importance later given what happened the following day. Gavyn said he believed it was right for him to resign because the Governors had been criticized for the actions they had taken. I disagreed and said that if someone had to go, then we should discuss whether it should be him or me, given that Lord Hutton had also criticized the management. I didn't believe it was necessary for either of us to go. I didn't believe then, and still don't believe today, that the BBC had done enough wrong to merit such a drastic response.

My view was that if Lord Hutton's criticisms required resignations, then the Chairman, all the Governors, the Director-General, and several senior people in BBC News should all go at once. Since I also knew that Tony Blair had told Gavyn in a private telephone conversation that, whatever happened, Number Ten would not be calling on either Gavyn or me to go, I was of the view we should all sit out the coming storm.

While Gavyn hadn't finally made up his mind he was of the view that at least one resignation was essential. As he says now: 'I was willing to resign in preference to apologizing for doing nothing wrong, indeed for telling the British people the truth about the September dossier. I was never going to grovel but I am not sure that a strategy of "no apology and no resignation" was ever viable after Hutton.'

Once Pauline realized that Gavyn was likely to go she turned to me and said it would be impossible for both of us to go at the same time. I agreed. Given what she did the following day, this was an interesting position, one that both Gavyn and I clearly remember her taking. I said that, in those circumstances, I would need the Governors to make it clear they supported me, and she agreed with that.

During the evening, Richard Sambrook took a call from the BBC's political editor, Andy Marr, who told us that *The Sun* had got a comprehensive leak of the report that made it very clear that Downing Street had been cleared and that the BBC had got the blame. It was a good scoop and the BBC's Ten O'Clock News reported the story in full. Tuition fees were now yesterday's news and, a day earlier than expected, Hutton was now the big story.

But where had the leak come from? I and a million others immediately assumed it was Alastair Campbell, that it was payback time for *The Sun* in recognition of the support they had given Tony Blair and the Government during the Iraq war. During his time in Downing Street Campbell had regularly given exclusives to *The Sun*, sometimes when they were other people's stories. As Alastair was no longer on the staff at Number Ten, my view at the time was that he had little to lose by leaking the document even if he was caught, and there wasn't much chance of that. Despite having spun his exit brilliantly we knew that Campbell had been pushed out. I had absolutely no evidence to support the view that Campbell leaked the story, and I now believe my immediate response was wrong. What I do know is that Downing Street was very scared that it would be blamed for the leak and that evening demanded that Rebekah Wade, *The Sun*'s editor, put out a statement making it clear that it wasn't Downing Street or Campbell who had leaked it.

Since then, it has been suggested to me that the leak might have come from someone on our side who was playing a very Machiavellian game to make it look like it originated with Campbell. I don't buy that because

it would have taken such a peculiar sort of mind to think that way, and what would have been the point? Another theory is that *The Sun* got the report from the printers. Lord Hutton set up an inquiry to try to discover who leaked his report, but I suspect we'll never know who actually did it.

At around 11 p.m. we all decided it was time to pack up and go home. I took the back way out of Broadcasting House to avoid any journalists but I did notice that Tara Conlan was still in reception. She rang me in the car about twenty minutes later, still digging.

I've always had a love–hate relationship with Tara, the *Daily Mail*'s TV editor. She was my bête noire when the *Daily Mail* was attacking me and the BBC virtually every day. She used to ask ridiculous questions at press conferences. I once replied to her by saying that her paper had already run the story in question on at least three separate occasions and yet she was now asking about it for the fourth time. Her answer was wonderful. 'Yes, I know,' she said, 'but my editor likes the story.' Later, when our relationship with the *Mail* improved, I grew to respect her. She worked incredibly hard, and when other journalists gave up she was always there.

On that Tuesday night I told her very politely that I was still bound by the confidentiality agreement we'd all signed and that I wouldn't break it (even though by then someone had broken it quite spectacularly). The only unauthorized person I had told about the contents of the report was Sue when I rang her in Suffolk. She asked what it was like. I answered in one word, 'Grim', and that was all I told her.

The next morning saw the same pattern as the day before. I left home early, escaping from my house via the back door and walking down to 10a, where Bill picked me up. There were even more journalists and crews outside my house than the previous day. I was glad that Sue was away and that I'd arranged for Joe to stay with a friend. Why should they have to put up with all this hassle simply because I was a public figure? I'd chosen that life, they hadn't.

It was an odd morning in the office. My PA for the past sixteen years, Fiona Hillary, arrived back from a holiday in Cuba not knowing that both our days at the BBC were numbered. By that evening she was in tears – not something I've seen from Fiona during the years we've worked together. She was also in a particularly difficult position: she is a close

friend of Tony and Cherie Blair (her husband, Barry Cox, the Deputy Chairman of Channel Four, had previously been their next-door neighbour).

I didn't really have enough to do on that Wednesday morning and yet I couldn't concentrate on anything else. So I hung around chatting to various people. Sally Osman, our ever smiling Head of Communications, wandered through. For me, one of the joys of working at the BBC was working with Sally: we managed to laugh our way through almost every crisis – and you get a lot at the BBC. Mark Damazer also joined us and, at one point during that morning, all three of us were in with Gavyn Davies trying to persuade him not to resign or, at the very least, to wait until later in the day. I did get him to agree that he wouldn't announce anything until after Hutton had made his public statement at lunchtime. Gavyn also made it clear that, as he was likely to resign, he would not now be able to be the person who responded to Hutton on behalf of the BBC. I would have to do that instead.

I had arranged for most of the members of my seventeen-strong executive team, which was known around the BBC as Exco, to watch Lord Hutton deliver his findings in a room in Broadcasting House where my office was based. We had arranged for lunch to be delivered and once again the Atkins dieters, of whom there were at least two others on Exco, were well provided for. So far Atkins had survived the crisis, and so had my abstinence from alcohol.

I warned my team it was bad news and on a confidential basis told them that Gavyn was seriously considering resignation. We all watched Hutton and then the statements in the House of Commons from the party leaders. I marvelled at how good Blair was. It is a great shame that his skills at people management and strategic leadership have never matched his skills as an orator or in public relations. If they had, he would have been a great Prime Minister.

The new Conservative leader, Michael Howard, had an impossible task, having only had the report for four hours; but I believe he made a crucial mistake in accepting Hutton's findings immediately. If he had delayed and given himself another forty-eight hours I believe he would have taken a different approach. In particular, he accepted Hutton's view that Blair had said nothing inappropriate to journalists about the naming of David Kelly when he was on the plane from Shanghai to Hong Kong.

Anyone who had followed the inquiry would have known that Hutton never questioned a single witness on that issue.

My own team were pretty badly shaken. I remember John Smith, the Director of Finance, saying something about resignations being needed (though I don't think he was referring to me) and Jenny Abramsky, the Director of Radio, sitting looking terribly serious in the corner, in the way that Jenny did. We all discussed the proposed statement I and the team had written. Virtually everyone wanted me to take out the more aggressive paragraphs, one of which said: 'We do have serious reservations about one aspect of the report which we believe could have significant implications for British journalism.' In effect I let them water down the proposed response. In retrospect I wish I hadn't because I believed then, as I do today, that the BBC had got the story largely right and that Downing Street's behaviour had been unacceptable. I was also convinced, as were our legal team, that Hutton had got the law wrong.

At 3.30 p.m. I recorded the statement and made it available to all news outlets. On BBC News 24 it was immediately interpreted as 'a robust response' from the BBC. Personally I thought it was conciliatory, but then being conciliatory is not necessarily one of my stronger points so perhaps I wasn't the best person to judge. I certainly wasn't going to roll over in the way Lord Ryder did the following day. Like Gavyn, I'd rather have resigned. I remember thinking at the time that it was a good job News 24 hadn't seen my original draft.

What did make me and the BBC look foolish later in the afternoon was the final paragraph of my statement, which said: 'The BBC Governors will be meeting formally tomorrow and will consider Lord Hutton's report. No further comment will be made until after that meeting.' Everyone had agreed that paragraph, but within half an hour of the statement being broadcast Andy Marr was back on the screens saying that he had it on very good authority that Gavyn Davies had resigned. Of course he only had a single unattributable source for his story, so under Lord Hutton's rules of journalism one wonders whether he should have broadcast it without corroboration. His source was a pretty good one though. It was Gavyn himself.

Gavyn was taking advice from his wife Sue, one of Gordon Brown's inner circle. Sue was very much of the view that it is better to resign on principle after being criticized than to be forced out later. As a strategy

it only made sense if you believed you would be forced out in the end, which Gavyn now did.

Gavyn believed that by resigning quickly it would be contrasted with the Government's 'awful' behaviour and help turn the tables on Hutton, which in many ways it did. And as he had made clear the night before, he was not going to apologize because he still believed the BBC had largely been right. Some people believe Gavyn's early resignation cost me my job and that he should have done a deal with the Governors that I should stay before making his resignation public. That may or may not be true, but he took his decision for the best and most honourable of reasons.

It was by complete chance that the Governors were due to meet that evening in a private session starting at 5 p.m. The meeting had been set up some time in 2003 when the annual BBC calendar was drawn up; when I discovered, a week or two earlier, that the meeting coincided with the publication of the Hutton report I urged Gavyn to cancel it. I told him I feared the Governors would rush around and make rash decisions, which is exactly what they did. Gavyn was against moving it and so was Simon Milner, the BBC Secretary who organized the Governors' meetings. Simon should have had the political nous to understand the dangers but unfortunately, while Simon had many talents, he lacked political judgement. Despite my efforts, the meeting stayed in the diary and I continued to tell them both it was a mistake.

The Governors started their meeting at 5 p.m. and virtually never left the room until the early hours of the following day. They didn't see Jon Snow on Channel Four News at 7 p.m. raising the question of whether Hutton was a whitewash. This was significant because throughout the inquiry we thought that Channel Four's news coverage of Hutton was the most authoritative, better than the BBC's Six O'Clock News. The Governors didn't see the same theme continued on *Newsnight*; they didn't see the BBC's former chairman Christopher Bland saying that one resignation was enough; and they didn't see the early edition of *The Independent* with its blank front page simply saying 'Whitewash'.

The Governors didn't want to see anyone. They wouldn't even meet Andrew Caldecott, the BBC's own QC, who sat outside all evening waiting to be called in to give his detailed and informed legal opinion on Hutton, which was very critical of the report. Andrew knew more about Hutton than all the Governors put together, but they never saw him. After waiting

for five hours he went home. At Andrew's hourly rate, keeping him waiting outside the meeting was criminal.

Later in the evening the Governors did agree to see the BBC's Director of Policy, Caroline Thomson, so she could give them a briefing: she had spent all evening gathering intelligence at Westminster. The BBC's Director of Human Resources, Stephen Dando, demanded to be seen and was allowed in. He told the Governors that getting rid of me would be a terrible blow to the staff and the BBC. But by then it was too late. The Governors had already made up their minds before speaking to either of them. They did what people under pressure often do: they turned inwards, talked to each other, and panicked.

I was there for the first forty minutes of the meeting. When they arrived, the Governors knew that Gavyn was going and some turned up with the view that they too should resign. In retrospect I should have let them. Instead I argued what I believed to be right: that the BBC couldn't be left without a Chairman and Governors because, in those circumstances, it would have no effective constitution. They agreed to stay.

When it came to discussing what should happen to members of the management team who had been criticized I offered to leave the meeting. I leant across to Simon Milner, who was sitting next to me, and reminded him what Gavyn and I had told him of our conversation the night before. It was his job to tell the Governors that if I was to continue I needed them to support me publicly. Gavyn and I then left the meeting for what I expected to be a half-hour discussion. As it turned out, I never went back that evening, and I will never have to go to another meeting of the BBC Governors again. There are some upsides in the whole affair.

As I walked down the corridor with Gavyn I saw Sarah Hogg scampering down the corridor the other way. She was late for the Governors' meeting. Sarah was never my favourite Governor. She had been Head of the Downing Street Policy Unit in John Major's Conservative Government and was the person who had invented 'Back to Basics' – one of the most disastrous policy initiatives introduced by any prime minister in the post-war years. She was recruited as a BBC Governor as a Tory, the view being that we were short of Conservative supporters on the Board. The irony was that by the end of my time at the BBC the Governors were dominated by people from the political Right. Virtually all the powerful players were Conservatives, with the exception of Gavyn, who in his

capacity as Chairman bent over backwards to hold the ring by being politically neutral. It was so typical of Blair's New Labour. They were so worried about newspaper charges of 'Tony's cronies' that they allowed the BBC's Board of Governors to be dominated by the Right. Could anyone have imagined Margaret Thatcher allowing the Board to be dominated by Labour supporters?

While being a strong supporter of the BBC, Sarah Hogg never left her politics or prejudices at the door of Governors' meetings, not that there was anything wrong with that. She was married to a patrician, land-owning Tory MP, Douglas Hogg, and lived in a political world. When we tried to change our political coverage to make it more appropriate for the twenty-first century it was Sarah who led the opposition on the grounds that we shouldn't upset the politicians. She was also upset by the lack of coverage of the Countryside March in September 2002 (probably the only march she'd ever been on). She insisted that the BBC was not covering rural affairs properly and demanded a full Governors' investigation, which she got – at the cost of many thousands of pounds. It always struck me as a classic case of special pleading from a Governor who lived on the family estate in rural Lincolnshire.

Sarah always gave the appearance that she was superior to most other people at Governors' meetings, sitting nodding in obvious support when she agreed with another Governor and shaking her head when she didn't, as if her opinion was the one that mattered most. Given that some of the other Governors were not as confident as Sarah, and didn't give the impression that they were born to rule, her opinions probably did matter a lot. Sarah and Pauline Neville-Jones were by far the most vocal Governors and I nicknamed them 'the posh ladies'. It was always clear to me that neither liked me much and Sarah, I now know, actively disliked me. The feeling was mutual.

Sarah's term as a Governor was due to finish at the end of January and she didn't want it renewed, which was just as well because neither did Gavyn or I. We both believed the right-wing bias of the Governors was unhealthy and that we needed more Governors without strong political views. So as Sarah ran past us in the corridor that night she only had a couple of days left as a Governor. It was her last chance to settle old scores. I now know that she came to the meeting determined to get rid of me.

I had been sitting in my office for maybe an hour and a half when

Simon Milner came in and said that Pauline and the Deputy Chairman wanted to see me downstairs. I'd thought their meeting was taking a long time, but it never crossed my mind that they would want me out. When I met them, Richard Ryder was pretty blunt. He said that the Governors had discussed the position and that they had decided I should go: if I stayed I'd be a lame-duck Director-General. It was a ridiculous argument: anyone who knew me well would know that there was never a chance of me being a lame-duck anything. I asked if this was the view of all the Governors. Typically, Richard told me he hadn't expressed a view but was reporting the views of the rest. Pauline said nothing.

Of course I should have seen it coming, but I hadn't. I was completely shocked. I had absolutely no idea what to say. I pointed out that I had a contract that they would have to honour, but I made it clear that if they didn't want me I wouldn't stay. It all took about five minutes and I said I needed to talk to Stephen Dando, the Head of Human Resources.

I went back to my office and sat there stunned. I had worked flat out for four years to try and turn round a deeply unhappy and troubled organization and was now being thrown out by the people I respected least in the whole place, the BBC Governors. I sat there in disbelief. Fancy being fired by a bunch of the great and the good, people whose contribution to the BBC was minimal to say the least, and who, in recent months, had become more and more obsessed about the survival of the Governors as an institution.

I asked Fiona to come into my room. We'd been together a long time at LWT, Pearson, and now the BBC. She'd arrived later than me at the BBC because Christopher Bland believed that her friendship with the Blairs would be a political liability for me and the BBC. That night I got up and gave her a hug and told her it was over, that the Governors wanted me out, and that I was going to resign.

Over the next hour or so I talked to Stephen Dando at some length. When he learnt what was happening he told the Governors that they were making a disastrous decision and warned them how the staff would react. Pat Loughrey, the Director of Nations and Regions, came in and told me not to go. He too went downstairs to demand to see the Governors, but they wouldn't let him in. Several members of my immediate team also came in and urged me not to resign.

Around 9 p.m. I changed my mind. I decided I wouldn't give the

Governors the satisfaction of getting rid of me without a fight. I asked Simon Milner to come and see me. He looked horrified when I told him that I didn't intend to resign and that they would have to sack me.

Ten minutes later I was back in a meeting with Ryder and Neville-Jones. I told them I wasn't going willingly and that I had never intended to resign, a veiled reference to the discussion Gavyn, Pauline, and I had had the night before. Richard Ryder got angry and slightly threatening, the sort of approach he must have adopted almost daily as a Chief Whip. I stayed firm and told them they must inform the other Governors that I wasn't resigning. I then went back to my office.

During that evening I talked on the phone with the three people who probably have more influence over me than anyone else. Firstly I reached Sue and told her what was happening. Her response was predictable: 'Fight the bastards, and if it means you get sacked, get sacked. Who cares?' That's my girl. She summed up the very reason why we've been together for twenty years. Sue was never very fond of my being at the BBC anyway. She thought the job was too time consuming, and she didn't like some of the senior people she met there. She thought they were lacking in fun, highly political, and falsely sycophantic.

I also phoned Christopher Bland, my former Chairman at LWT who'd gone on to become Chairman of the BBC and who, in turn, had persuaded me to join the organization in the first place. He had given up being Chairman two years earlier after he became the Chairman of BT, but before he did so he put his future in my hands. He told me: 'I brought you here so if you want me to stay I'll turn down BT and stay.' I thought he was right to take the BT job: he was in his sixties and he obviously fancied one last big challenge, so I advised him to go.

Christopher and I had been in battles together before. Some we'd won and some we'd lost, but he was great to have on your side. He never lost his nerve and I've known times when he supported me even though it was not in his personal interests to do so. I'd like to think I'd do the same for him. I loved working for him over the years, and he was always one of my two mentors. When I rang him and told him what was happening he couldn't believe that the Governors were trying to get me out and promised to do all he could. He appeared on *Newsnight* later in the evening. He also agreed with Sue and told me that I should tell them to 'fuck off'.

The third person I rang that evening was Melvyn Bragg, a close friend and my other mentor. Melvyn is probably the cleverest person I know; he knows so much about so many subjects. I first met him many years earlier when I was a young researcher at LWT and he was the famous Melvyn Bragg, editor and presenter of the *South Bank Show*. I remember being very flattered when he even remembered my name, but as a boy from a working-class background Melvyn had never lost the ability to relate to all around him, no matter what job they did. Much later, when I was Director of Programmes at LWT, I elevated the Arts Department into full departmental status just so that I could have Melvyn on my immediate team.

Melvyn was also one of the people who had encouraged me to join the BBC and had supported what I was trying to do there, although not uncritically. During those last three days at the BBC, he gave me all the support you could ask for from a friend, including writing a wonderful appraisal of what I had achieved in four years in that weekend's *Observer*. I got hold of him late on the Wednesday night, by which time I had had a further meeting with Ryder and Neville-Jones. They told me that the Board was adamant: I either resigned or was fired that night. Melvyn recognized that I was terribly upset and asked me how would I want it to be seen in six months' time: would I rather be seen to have resigned or to have been sacked? I answered 'Resigned'.

Normally when top executives leave or lose their posts these sorts of decisions are about pay-offs. But money was largely irrelevant in this case. The BBC would have had to pay up on my contract either way.

While all this was happening, Emma Scott – a feisty project manager who had worked with me from the first day I joined the BBC – decided she was going to rally my supporters by ringing around members of the executive team to get them to come in and support me. She persuaded Caroline Thomson to come back and talk to the Governors, Pat Loughrey stayed around for the whole evening, Andy Duncan, the BBC's outstanding Director of Marketing and now Chief Executive of Channel Four, turned up to support me, and Peter Salmon, the Director of Sport, phoned in to tell me to hang on in there.

Meanwhile Mark Byford, my recently appointed deputy, had been sitting outside the Governors' meeting for several hours, like the schoolboy summoned to the headmaster's study. Mark and I have always got on

well and I've always liked and respected him as a professional broadcaster, but I still wonder why he didn't just wander up one flight of stairs for a chat that evening. Instead, he just sat there on his own for hour after hour. I suspect he was under instructions from the Governors not to talk to me, which would explain it.

I always saw Mark as a possible successor to me within the BBC, but that evening, and in the days that followed, his chances of becoming Director-General were wiped out. It was clear to me that, with Gavyn and me both gone, any new Chairman would want his or her own Director-General, not someone tainted by the events of that night and the weeks that followed. To be fair to Mark, he was put in a terrible position by the Governors, a position that wasn't of his own making. I have no doubt he did what he thought was his duty: he is that sort of man.

The pressures of that day finally told and I succumbed. I abandoned both the Atkins diet and abstinence from alcohol and ate a whole pizza and drank at least half a bottle of wine while all sorts of people were coming in and out of my office. I'm not sure I can ever forgive a combination of Lord Hutton and the Governors for forcing me to break my diet.

Gavyn Davies, who had been out of the loop since we left the Governors' meeting together earlier that evening, decided at about 11 p.m. to go home. I had already told him that the Governors wanted me out, but we'd agreed there was little he could do about it. Before he left, he decided to say a final goodbye to his former colleagues, but when he walked into the room he found the atmosphere had changed completely in five hours. It was a very hostile environment, with the aggression mainly coming from Sarah Hogg, who, according to him, was 'seething'.

I've since discovered that Sarah had told Gavyn the day before that he shouldn't resign but that I should go. Gavyn had told her then that there were no circumstances in which he'd let me go while he stayed, and I genuinely think that that was one of the reasons Gavyn resigned. Gavyn and I had worked very closely together, particularly on Hutton, and we both believed we were right. I think his view was that if one of us should go it should be him and that way he would protect me. According to others at that meeting, when Gavyn walked in Sarah launched a ferocious attack on him, accusing him of 'cowardice under fire' .

In the end I announced at about one in the morning that I wasn't negotiating or discussing any more. I was going home. The Governors were still downstairs, but by then I'd had enough. I would decide whether to resign or be fired in the morning. Either way I knew I'd be leaving the BBC.

Outside there was thick snow everywhere and I remember thinking how sad that I'd hardly noticed it falling. I got into the car and told my driver Bill that I was leaving. He, too, got upset. He told me later that neither he nor his wife Ann slept a wink all night.

The following morning I took the usual precautions to avoid the journalists and the camera crews outside my house. In the car I got a call from John Smith, the BBC's Finance Director, wanting to know what was happening. I told him and he decided to set about working on some of the Governors. He was confident he could get them to change their minds. But I knew it was too late. Overnight I hadn't slept a lot, but I had taken a decision. I would resign, but over the next few days I would make it very clear I had been given little option by a bunch of intransigent Governors.

So why did I choose that path? Looking back now I am not sure I know. With the benefit of hindsight, I think I should have stayed and dared them to fire me. But at the time I felt isolated. I also felt hurt and had a deep sense of injustice. I didn't believe that I had done anything to justify resignation, nor did I believe the BBC had done anything seriously wrong. I wasn't to know then that the staff would react in the way they did and that Hutton would be dismissed so quickly and comprehensively. What I do remember thinking was that if I was to go, I wanted to do so with some dignity.

If the Governors had only waited another day or two there would have been no need for me to leave: by then, it was Blair's people who were on the run. By the weekend Number Ten couldn't understand what had happened. The report had exonerated them and yet the public hadn't. They had no concept then, and still don't have, of how fast Blair had lost the trust of the people in Britain, of how quickly he'd gone from being seen as an honest and open man to being regarded as a public relations manipulator, a man without real principles. Iraq and spin had destroyed his reputation.

I got into the office about ten past eight on that Thursday morning and immediately started rewriting a couple of draft statements I'd prepared the night before. The first was the public announcement I would make. The second, much more important to me, was the e-mail I would send to all the staff telling them I was going. I was determined that the staff would learn the news from me and that the e-mail would go out before any press or public announcement.

That morning all feels a blur now. I remember lots of people coming in and out, and lots of people crying. Most of my immediate support staff were either crying or trying to stop. I remember Carolyn Fairbairn, the BBC's Head of Strategy with whom I'd worked so closely over four years, turning up looking as if she'd been crying all the way from Winchester, where she lived. Melvyn Bragg had been presenting his Radio Four programme *In Our Time* that morning and he too came up to my office and was there for at least an hour, talking to me, advising me, and reassuring my staff. They loved him for showing so much care. In the end even he got upset.

All morning the e-mails had been pouring in from staff urging me not to resign, but at around 1.30 p.m. I sent out my e-mail statement to the staff. It was typical of my all-staff e-mails. I had started sending them almost as soon as I joined the BBC and found it an incredibly effective way for a Chief Executive to communicate with every member of staff. During my four years I refused to send out long, boring e-mails; I wanted people to read them, so they had to be short, to the point, and interesting. This one would certainly have an impact. It was only a few paragraphs long, free of jargon, and in a language everyone could understand. It said:

> This is the hardest e mail I've ever written. In a few moments I'll be announcing to the outside world that I'm leaving after four years as Director General. I don't want to go and I'll miss everyone here hugely. However the management of the BBC was heavily criticised in the Hutton Report and as the Director General I am responsible for the management.
>
> I accept that the BBC made errors of judgement and I've sadly come to the conclusion that it will be hard to draw a line under this whole affair while I am still here. We need closure. We need closure

to protect the future of the BBC, not for you or me but for the benefit of everyone out there. It might sound pompous but I believe the BBC really matters. Throughout this affair my sole aim as Director General of the BBC has been to defend our editorial independence and to act in the public interest.

In four years we've achieved a lot between us. I believe we've changed the place fundamentally and I hope those changes will last beyond me. The BBC has always been a great organization but I hope that, over the last four years, I've helped to make it a more human place where everyone who works here feels appreciated. If that's anywhere near true I leave contented if sad.

Thank you all for the help and support you've given me. This might sound schmaltzy but I really will miss you all.

Greg

As soon as the e-mail had gone I went downstairs to the entrance of Broadcasting House in Langham Place, where there was a massive, totally disorganized media scrum right on the BBC's own doorstep. I walked out through the revolving door, realized I was in danger of being crushed, stepped back into the drum, and revolved back into the building. After a couple of minutes there was enough room for me to move outside and, live on BBC News 24, Sky News, and the ITV News Channel, I announced I was leaving. The irony was that BBC News 24 almost missed the whole event because their crew was stuck at the back of the scrum and couldn't get a decent shot of me making the statement.

Then it was back upstairs and lots of drink and food with friends and colleagues. By then all thoughts of Atkins and abstinence had totally disappeared. Mark Damazer, whom I first worked with at TV-am twenty years earlier, made a short but funny speech talking about my strengths and weaknesses. I replied by telling everyone that this was not a day for bandstanding. I was going and they should protect their careers. I also told them to support Mark Byford, who was to be acting Director-General; he was a good bloke and had played no part in my demise.

Oddly, it was about that time that Mark was making a terrible mistake. He had agreed to stand with Lord Ryder while the acting Chairman recorded a statement. When asked to do this, Mark should have declined.

Instead, he stood by while Ryder made the most grovelling of apologies in which he said sorry for any mistake the BBC might have made, without actually defining what the mistakes were. He apologized 'unreservedly'. It was as if he had apologized for anything anyone in Government could accuse the BBC of. It was the style of delivery that made the apology seem so grovelling. The two of them looked like the leaders of an old Eastern European government: grey, boring, and frightened.

The statement was on the news bulletins all day and was seen throughout the world. Without realizing it, Lord Ryder had done enormous damage to the reputation of the BBC, and to himself.

When, that afternoon, Lord Ryder was asked at a special meeting of the BBC's executive committee whether his statement would be enough to satisfy the Government, he replied that he had been assured it would, leaving a number of members of the committee with the clear impression that he had discussed and cleared the statement with Downing Street before delivering it.

I have since had it confirmed by the BBC that, before he made his statement, Lord Ryder had been in contact with Number Ten telling them both of the content of the statement he planned to make and that I was going. The BBC now say this was only a matter of 'courtesy', but it has serious implications. The whole independence of the BBC is based on its separation from Government, and yet here was its acting Chairman effectively clearing a statement before he made it. We don't know if they asked for changes. What would he have done if they had?

It also brings into question whether or not Downing Street wanted my head. Gavyn had reached an agreement with Blair, in one of the many phone calls they had between June and December, that no matter what Hutton said the Government would not call for either of us to go. When he watched Blair in the House of Commons immediately after Hutton's press conference Gavyn realized the Prime Minister had gone back on his word. He told me: 'Blair skilfully piled the pressure on, and did nothing to discharge his promise that there should be no resignations at the BBC. I assumed he had reneged. Then I saw Campbell calling us liars, and demanding that heads should roll. I assumed that Blair had deliberately unleashed the dogs against us, and that there would be no peace with the Government until we either resigned or apologized.'

I, too, had been assured in advance, in discussions between myself and

Campbell's successor, Dave Hill – a more rational and reasonable man than Campbell – that when the Hutton report was published Number Ten would not criticize the BBC if we agreed not to criticize them. Hill had also assured me that they would be able to control Campbell, that he would be back inside Number Ten for the publication of the Hutton Report and would take orders. So on that Wednesday Blair could have stopped Campbell from calling for heads. He chose not to. And on the Thursday morning Downing Street was told what was happening at the BBC but Blair did nothing to prevent my 'resignation'. Since then, he has let it be known through friends that he didn't want either Gavyn or me to go and has even invited me to meet with him informally. I refused. I no longer regard Tony Blair as someone to be trusted.

Ryder's 'unreserved' apology had other repercussions. From that moment onwards the BBC stopped publicly arguing the case it had argued throughout the Hutton inquiry: that while it had made some mistakes, it had been right to broadcast Dr Kelly's claims that Downing Street had 'sexed up' the dossier to make a more convincing case for war. From that moment onwards no one from within the BBC was allowed to make that argument, and yet it is what I still believe happened and I will argue the case passionately in this book.

The real irony came several weeks later when *The Guardian* ran a story that said that Lord Hutton was 'shocked' by the reaction to his report and hadn't expected any heads to roll at the BBC. If this is true, he is a remarkably naive man.

My day and my time at the BBC were rapidly coming to an end. I was preparing to leave my office for the last time when I got a phone call from Peter Salmon at Television Centre. He told me that there were remarkable scenes happening and that I ought to come over. He said that hundreds of members of staff had taken to the streets with 'Bring Back Greg' posters and that the demonstration was getting bigger by the minute. I turned to Magnus and Emma and said we ought to go. Andrew Harvey, a friend and talented journalist whom I had brought in to edit *Ariel*, the BBC's in-house magazine, was with me at the time, so he came along too.

In all there were five of us in the car. It was a fifteen-minute drive and no one said anything. When we got to White City and drove down towards Television Centre we found the roads outside the BBC buildings thronged with chanting staff holding up placards. The scenes were amazing. As I

got out of the car people were applauding and trying to shake my hand. There were news crews everywhere trying to interview me. For a brief period of my life I suddenly found out what it was like to be an American presidential candidate or Madonna. It was frightening.

Someone thrust a megaphone into my hand and I made an impromptu speech. We were all a bit scared for our safety and Magnus and Emma tried to guide me through the crowd. We lost Andrew Harvey somewhere and didn't see him again that day. At one stage Emma even thumped a news cameraman who was getting a bit rough; but, inch by inch, we gradually moved towards the entrance to Stage Six, the home of BBC News.

Inside the building there were people everywhere shouting and applauding. I stopped for a quick but hassled interview with Kirsty Wark, the *Newsnight* presenter, whom I admired a lot. I then decided to go up to the BBC News room. As I walked in people started applauding and eventually I climbed onto a desk and spoke to them all. I told them that our journalism had to be fair but not to lose their nerve, unaware that it was being broadcast live to the nation on BBC News 24. I told the staff in the newsroom, and the rest of the world live on television, that all we had been trying to do was to defend the 'integrity and independence of the BBC'. I later discovered that this really upset Downing Street, but in truth it was exactly what the whole thing had been about. We were defending the BBC from a wholesale attack on its journalism by Alastair Campbell, a man whom some in the Labour Government are only now beginning to understand was a complete maverick and who had been given unprecedented power by Tony Blair.

I also went to visit the staff of the *Today* programme, on which Andrew Gilligan had worked. There was a more sombre mood amongst the *Today* staff.

We went quickly to others parts of the building and the response was overwhelming. I then decided it was time to go. We went outside and were surrounded yet again. Someone had written 'We love you Greg' on my car windscreen in lipstick, and if my driver Bill and a policeman hadn't stopped them they would have written all over the car. We drove out with hundreds of people still cheering and waving their placards.

Eventually I got back to my office at Broadcasting House to discover that what had happened at Television Centre was not a one-off. All over the country the staff had taken to the streets to protest that their boss

was leaving. In Cardiff, Glasgow, Belfast, Manchester, Newcastle, and Birmingham hundreds had walked out to protest. But it wasn't only in the big centres. The staff of local radio stations had also left their offices. At BBC Radio Shropshire in Shrewsbury all the staff had walked out, including the presenter who was on air. He had gone outside to express solidarity, whilst rightly continuing to broadcast live to the people of Shropshire.

In the next few days more than six thousand staff replied to my e-mail wishing me luck, thanking me for what I had done during my time at the BBC, and telling me how much they would miss me. I have chosen two examples – one from a producer in the World Service, and one from News; but there were thousands like them. The first said:

> Your greatest achievement was giving the kiss of life to a body of people who'd been systematically throttled, castrated and lobotomised. To leave us all very much alive and kicking, loving the BBC and respecting the role of Director General again, is a fantastic legacy.

And the second:

> The only way I can come to terms with the extraordinary events of the last 48 hours is to pay testimony to the vision and energy you have brought to the BBC. Men and women, even journalists, cried today. People came together and talked about their emotions, their fears, their frustrations all because the man who had embodied the hope, the vision, the pride they had begun to feel about the future of the organization had gone.

They came from all parts of the BBC and at all levels, all thanking me for changing the BBC. Well, all bar one. Amongst this great pile of e-mails my staff sifted out the only negative communication. It simply said:

> Fuck off Dyke, I'm glad you are going, I never liked you anyway.

That same night some of the staff in Factual Programmes and Current Affairs began collecting money to pay for an advertisement in the *Daily*

Telegraph to express their support. In twenty-four hours they collected twice as much as they needed, with all sorts of people contributing right across the BBC, from the lowest paid to the highest. Even people in the canteen who didn't work for the BBC, and who earned very little money, contributed. The spare money, nearly £10,000, was given to a charity of my choice. The *Telegraph* carried a full-page advertisement with a heading 'The Independence of the BBC' followed by a paragraph explaining that it had been paid for by BBC staff. It then said:

> Greg Dyke stood for brave, independent and rigorous BBC journalism that was fearless in its search for the truth. We are resolute that the BBC should not step back from its determination to investigate the facts in pursuit of the truth.
>
> Through his passion and integrity Greg inspired us to make programmes of the highest quality and creativity.
>
> We are dismayed by Greg's departure, but we are determined to maintain his achievements and his vision for an independent organization that serves the public above all else.

The page included just some of the thousands of names of BBC staff who had paid for the advertisement. They couldn't get all the names on the page. When I read it, I think it was the only time during the whole saga that I broke down and cried.

As I left Broadcasting House for the final time it seemed like everyone working there had come down to cheer me off. My own office staff all came out to the car: Fiona, Emma, Magnus, Orla, and Cheryl were all there to wave me goodbye, plus virtually the whole of the marketing department. I did a couple more quick interviews and in the middle of being interviewed live on Sky News my mobile phone rang. I answered it to find David Frost on the other end, so I offered him the opportunity to speak live to the world on Sky News. I don't think he quite understood what was happening.

And then I was gone. Four years to the very day that I had become Director-General I was driven away for the last time.

That evening Sue (who had driven back from Suffolk just for the night), Joe, and I went out for dinner. I think we were all on a strange high,

laughing and joking. We ended up round the corner with our good friends John Stapleton and Lynn Faulds Wood, where I promised to do a live phone interview for John's early morning programme on GMTV the following day. I decided then that I would only do three interviews: with John, because he's a good friend; with the *Today* programme the following morning, when I could put on record what I was feeling; and with David Frost on Sunday, again repaying the support and friendship that he and his wife Carina had shown Sue and me over the years.

For the *Today* interview, which I fixed up at about four in the morning, I suggested they send the radio car round to my house. When they turned up a BBC News television crew was already there so I thought I'd make everyone a cup of tea. It is ironic that, after three days of avoiding journalists and news crews outside the house, the pictures of me carrying out the tea for the crews is one of the memorable shots of the whole affair. Virtually everyone I know saw it and mentions it when we meet. I also know that the pictures caused great consternation inside 10 Downing Street. Who says there's no such thing as news management?

It was three days before I began to realize that perhaps all was not as it had seemed to be. The idea came to me when I was talking to someone from within the BBC who told me that she believed some of the Governors had been out to get me regardless of Hutton. It got me thinking: did some of the Governors have another agenda?

By then I knew that three of the eleven Governors had supported me in the crunch vote: the ballet dancer Deborah Bull, the Oxford academic Ruth Deech and voluntary sector consultant Angela Sarkis were all against my leaving. They were the three Governors who had most recently joined the Board. The 'posh ladies' had both been against me and Sarah Hogg, in particular, had led the charge. She had told the Board that she had never liked me.

I was surprised when I discovered that I had not received any support from the Governors representing Scotland, Wales, Northern Ireland, and the English regions. If I had achieved one thing in my time at the BBC it was to increase investment and improve morale outside of London, and yet when the crunch came the Governors with particular responsibility for the Nations and Regions had all voted against me.

Not that they were ever the strongest of Governors. Three of them –

27

Ranjit Sondhi, Fabian Monds, and Merfyn Jones – had said very little over the years. It always seemed to me that they were intimidated by the posh ladies. In the case of Ranjit, I understand he was in real trouble when he got home. His wife, Anita Bhalla, who works for the BBC as Head of Political and Community Affairs for the English Regions, was a big Dyke supporter and, reportedly, tore him to shreds for going along with the decision. Ranjit was a really likeable, incredibly hard-working Governor, but he was never likely to rock the boat about anything.

Only Robert Smith, an accountant and business leader from Scotland, had played a significant role at Governors' meetings in my time, and it was always difficult to judge where he was coming from. At that time we all knew he was after a big new job as chairman of a major public company, and like so many accountants he loved to look tough if the opportunity presented itself.

I began to think about the conversation Gavyn, Pauline Neville-Jones, and I had had the night before Hutton was published. Surely if Pauline had said that she thought it was impossible for Gavyn and me to leave at the same time, shouldn't she have been arguing on my behalf, given that Gavyn had already gone? And yet she hadn't stood up for me and had in fact voted the other way. I began to think some more.

Pauline Neville-Jones had always been a big supporter of Mark Byford. As the Governor with special responsibility for the World Service she had worked closely with him and clearly rated him highly. I suspect she also liked him because, like most of the BBC lifers, he was better at the politics of dealing with the Governors, better at playing the game of being respectful. It was a game that I refused to play. I saw no reason why I should treat the Governors any differently from the way I treated everyone else. I certainly wasn't going to regard the earth they walked on as if it was somehow holy ground. This wasn't a wilful decision. It was just the way I am.

After I had left the BBC one senior executive said to me that if I had been a bit more servile in my attitude to the Governors I would still be there today. I have no doubt that's true. Certainly both chairmen in my time at the BBC, Christopher Bland and Gavyn Davies, suggested on occasions that I ought to be more respectful and make fewer jokes at Governors' meetings, but in truth I was never going to do that. I have never been one to respect position for its own sake and I was hardly likely to start in my fifties, particularly when dealing with a group of people

most of whom knew absolutely nothing about the media, and who would have struggled to get a senior job at the BBC. In my time there were some excellent Governors, people like Richard Eyre and Barbara Young who had been on the Board when I joined, but I was not a fan of the system and made that obvious at times.

Whether this attitude to life is a weakness or a strength (and I suspect it is a bit of both) is largely irrelevant. That's the way my DNA is. I'm not particularly good at watching my back, and never have been. If you employ me you have to take me for what I am. In the commercial world that's not a problem because you are largely judged on the numbers. In the public sector, where accountability has become an obsession, you are judged on the strangest things, including how well you get on with the great and the good.

So why hadn't Pauline Neville-Jones supported me as I thought she would? Again I thought back a few months. One day in early December 2003, at our regular weekly meeting, Gavyn Davies told me that Pauline and Sarah Hogg had been to see him and were demanding that he call a meeting of the Governors without me being present so that they could appoint Mark Byford as my deputy and put him in charge of all the BBC's news output. I would then be told it was a *fait accompli*.

I laughed and told him that if they did that, then I would resign immediately. Gavyn told me that they were serious and were demanding he call the meeting. He asked me what he should do about it. I started by telling him that it was his problem but later said I'd think about it.

I'm certain Mark Byford didn't know anything about this move; in his time working for me Mark was always loyal and supportive. In many ways the proposal for Mark to become my deputy was a good idea. I had never had an official number two but Mark acted as my deputy, if he was around, when I was away and in fact I had suggested the move to Gavyn myself earlier that year. Mark had real strengths, many of which complemented mine. I tended to be broad brush, he was into detail. I was into big decisions and taking risks, whilst Mark, like many of the senior people who had worked their whole life at the BBC, tended to be cautious and process driven. We would have been a good fit. Gavyn was against it at that stage because it would have indicated that Mark was the Board's chosen successor to me when the time came for me to leave in three years' time when I reached the age of sixty.

My objection to the proposal from the posh ladies was, firstly, the way they were going about it by going behind my back; secondly, that it was nothing to do with them, that I was the DG and would suggest who my deputy should be, not them; and, thirdly, that they wanted to put Mark in charge of all the BBC's news output, thus effectively demoting the Director of News, Richard Sambrook. I was having none of that. However, with the Hutton report pending, even someone as naturally combative as me recognized that this was not a time for a big bust-up with the Governors and I had reached the conclusion we needed a change to the organization.

As Hutton had progressed, I had come to the view that our systems of compliance prior to and post broadcast needed to be brought together under one person, so I suggested to Gavyn that, as a way of appeasing the posh ladies, we should appoint Mark as my deputy and allow him to remain in charge of Global News but also take over all our compliance systems.

Gavyn took this proposal to the Governors and they agreed. The posh ladies seemed satisfied. On 1 January 2003, Mark Byford officially became my deputy. A month later I was gone and he was acting Director-General.

In the week after leaving I also discovered more about what had happened at that private Governors' meeting on the previous Wednesday. When I had left the meeting with Gavyn I had asked the Secretary, Simon Milner, to tell the Governors that I wanted their support if I was to stay. I later discovered he told them that I had resigned, a subtle but crucial difference. Of course Pauline Neville-Jones knew that wasn't what we had discussed the night before, so why didn't she question it? I also discovered that, later in the meeting, when they were discussing whether or not they should change their position on my going, Simon had intervened to say that it was a bad idea because they'd never be able to control me if that happened.

The week after my departure I discovered the Governors were having a secret meeting to review what had happened the week before. Sitting at home unemployed, I decided that there were things I wanted them to know. I phoned Simon Milner and told him I wanted to e-mail the Governors to tell them about the conversation Pauline Neville-Jones, Gavyn, and I had had the night before the crucial meeting. I suggested they might consider it odd that Pauline had neither mentioned the conversation to

them nor carried out what was agreed. I told them they should consult Gavyn for corroboration. It seemed to me important that they should understand the background to Gavyn's rapid departure and my surprise at the Governors' lack of support. Simon asked me what I wanted. Tongue in cheek, I told him I wanted my job back. What I really wanted was to make sure they all knew exactly how Pauline Neville-Jones had behaved.

The nature of my departure hit a nerve with the public. For a few weeks I became something of a hero in many people's eyes. They thought I had been badly treated and yet I must be a good bloke because why else would so many of the BBC's employees come out on my side? Of course I was helped by Alastair Campbell's performance on the day the Hutton report was published.

Standing on the stairs at the Foreign Press Association, Campbell gave about as pompous a performance as it's possible to imagine. For a man who was known to be economical with the truth, and who had certainly deliberately misled the House of Commons Foreign Affairs Select Committee during their Iraq hearings, he said that the Government had told the truth and that the BBC, from the Chairman and Director-General down, had not. He then called for heads to roll at the BBC.

Campbell is a man who has the ability to delude himself. He didn't realize how much he was disliked and distrusted by the British public, who saw him as Blair's Svengali. He believed throughout that he was right, and he now believed Hutton was right. The British public didn't. In attacking Gavyn and me he helped to put the public even further on our side. When asked about his response on the *Today* programme I said I thought that Campbell was 'remarkably graceless'. What I really felt was that he was a deranged, vindictive bastard, but I couldn't possibly say that on the radio.

The emotional response to my dismissal was not only from the staff. I received letters from all over Britain and all over the world – from people I'd never met, from people I'd met only occasionally, and from good friends. Everywhere I went people wanted to shake my hand: in the pub, in the supermarket, walking down the street, even at football matches. Sue and I went for dinner with Melvyn and his wife Cate in the House of Lords the following week and all sorts of people wanted to say hello and that they were sorry about what had happened. One Liberal

Democrat peer, an eminent lawyer, offered to take up my case against Hutton, whilst a prominent Tory peer offered to help pay for me to go to law. So many peers from all parties came up that Melvyn described it as 'a royal procession'.

I even got a message from my architect friend Chris Henderson, with whom I go riding every weekend, to say that the Hursley and Hambledon Hunt was 100 per cent behind me. I was eternally grateful – not that it will change my views about fox hunting. Even Ian, who cuts my hair, told me all his clients were on my side, with the exception of one. He also cuts the hair of the former Director-General of the BBC, John Birt.

Two weeks after I left the BBC we went with the Stapleton family to South Africa for a holiday and I met the same reaction there. Dozens of British tourists recognized me and wanted to shake my hand and say they thought I'd been treated badly and 'well done' for standing up to the Government. The funniest moment came when I was standing in the sea and a large tattooed man came up to me. 'Well done, mate,' he said. 'They're all fucking bastards.' And off he wandered into the deep.

Inside the television industry the reaction was the same. At the Royal Television Society's annual awards ceremony I was given a long standing ovation when I was presented with the annual judges' award for my contribution to television. The same happened a month later at the annual BAFTA awards, which were televised on ITV. First Paul Abbott, the brilliant writer of *Clocking Off* and *State of Play*, attacked the BBC Governors for getting rid of me, then I was given a standing ovation when I went up to present the award for best current affairs programme. I used the opportunity to have my first public dig at the BBC Governors.

Months after I had left the BBC all sorts of people I didn't know were still coming up to me saying they were sorry that 'they' had got me. So what was all this about, and who did they mean by 'they'? I can only presume they were talking about Blair, Campbell, and those around them, combined in their minds with Lord Hutton and the BBC Governors. To all these well-wishers, I was someone prepared to stand up against 'them'.

I even became a phenomenon amongst the business community. People from business schools all over the world were in contact. Every leader of an organization would like to think that if they were fired their people would take to the streets to support them, but most knew they wouldn't, so they were intrigued to know what had happened and why. It was best

32

summed up for me by a wonderful old man called Herb Schlosser, who was once President and CEO of NBC in the United States. He wrote, 'I saw on the internet BBC employees marching in support of a CEO. This is a first in the history of the Western World.'

And that was about the end of it. From the most powerful media job in the UK to unemployed in just three days. It was a remarkable period, but what were those crazy three days all about? Why did the Governors do what they did?

When you combine the unpredicted savagery of the Hutton Report towards the BBC, the whitewashing of Number Ten, Gavyn's early resignation, Pauline Neville-Jones's astonishing behaviour, the posh ladies' hostility towards me, their influence on a relatively weak Board, Richard Ryder's ineffectiveness as a leader, and my natural assumption that the majority of the Governors would want me to stay, you can understand what happened and why. Of course I was not without blame. I had made mistakes in how we dealt with the whole affair, and in those dying days I shouldn't have said I needed the Governors' support to stay. I certainly shouldn't have believed I would get it. I trusted certain people who were not to be trusted. In many ways it was a very British coup in which the Establishment figures got their opportunity to get rid of the upstart.

There are still questions to be answered. Why did Hutton write the report he wrote? Why did the British people reject Hutton out of hand, and so quickly? Why did it damage the Government instead of helping it? And why did people in the wider world sympathize so strongly with my position?

Why did my leaving create such a response inside the BBC? Why wasn't I perceived as just another suit, as most managers are? What had we done to the culture of the BBC in such a short period of time that provoked such emotion and such loyalty?

As one letter I received from within the BBC said so profoundly, 'How did a short, bald man with a speech impediment have such an impact?' I hope this book will go some way towards answering that question.

The First Thirty Years

Every so often I try to explain to my own kids what life was like growing up in a small West London suburban street in the 1950s, but I only get mocked for my efforts. I think they laugh because I make it sound too much like the Hovis advertisement where everyone was poor but happy, and the luxuries we aspired to were very simple.

We lived, for the first nine years of my life, in a very ordinary cul-de-sac on the borders between Hayes and Southall in Middlesex. My parents Joseph and Denise bought the house, a new, small suburban semi in a street called Cerne Close, in 1946 for £650. Today it would sell for close to £250,000. They moved there with my brothers Ian, then aged five, and Howard, who was only a few months old. I was born the following year in 1947, a year when there were more births in Britain than in any other year in history. It was the peak of the post-war baby boom with a million children born compared with an average of 600,000 a year today.

The reality was that most people did live very simple lives, compared with today. It's when I tell my kids that the milk was still delivered by horse and cart that they laugh. We walked to school in a big crowd – just kids, without any parents to escort us – and we all played football in the street with a tennis ball. No one in the street was divorced, and virtually all the children lived with two parents in a classic nuclear family, often with a grandparent in tow. Dad went out to work and Mum stayed behind to look after the children and the home. It was as simple as that.

My dad's job was selling insurance; as a result we were one of only two families in the street with a car, owned by his company, so we were seen as quite affluent. We also had a telephone for the same reason and

neighbours used regularly to knock on the door to ask if they could come in and use the phone.

We were luckier than most of the people in our street as we had at least three holidays each year. Every summer we stayed in a bungalow on the beach at Pevensey Bay in East Sussex, where the big treat of the week was a trip on a boat called the *William Olchorn*, which took holidaymakers out on trips around Beachy Head lighthouse. On the way back to the bungalow we would all have fish and chips, which we saw as something special. Every Easter we stayed for a week with my parents' best friends, Uncle Frank and Auntie Vi, in Bridgend in South Wales, and at Whitsun we stayed with 'Auntie' Edna and 'Uncle' Bill in Emneth near Wisbech in Cambridgeshire, where my Auntie Doreen was evacuated during the war; she was joined by my mum and my brother Ian towards the end of the war after their house in Bromley, Kent, had been bombed.

The years we lived in that little street in Hayes were happy times. No one was well off, but neither were they poor. We all had food and clothes, and life was uncomplicated by the choices that greater affluence has brought. I suspect it was also pretty dull, but as a child you didn't know that.

The Middlesex suburbs have never had a very good press and were widely looked down upon, particularly by the English upper-middle classes, but the criticism was, and is, unfair. These areas were largely populated by the aspiring English working class; most of the people who lived in this area of West London had moved there from pretty awful conditions in inner London. They wanted something better for themselves and, in particular, they wanted something better for their children. In most cases they achieved it.

My parents were typical. They had both been brought up in Hackney in East London. On my mother's side her father had been a soldier who had fought in the Boer War. He fell in love with South Africa and wanted to stay but his fiancée, my grandmother, refused to leave London and join him. Instead he came back to England, got married, and went to live on the Isle of Dogs, where he became a docker like the rest of his family. He was later injured in an accident at the docks and, after a long battle, won some compensation from the dock owners. With it he bought a small newsagent's and tobacconist's shop in Morning Lane, Hackney. My grandmother ran the shop while my grandfather spent the takings at the

local dog track. Whenever he had a big win he would come home in a taxi with his bike on the top.

My mum's mother, my gran, was one of six children who had been brought up by their grandparents in Farnham, Surrey, after both their parents had died when they were young. She always told how the local villagers were supposed to doff their caps to the gentry as they went by, but her grandfather wouldn't let them. He used to tell them 'You're as good as they are.' My grandmother went into 'service' at a young age and worked her way up from the scullery to become a ladies' maid at a big house in Sloane Square in London. Her life was tinged with tragedy. She never really got over the loss of all three of her brothers in the First World War. All were much younger than her, and she had helped to bring them up. During the war they lived with her in the shop in Hackney when they were home on leave. One by one they all died. Their loss was enormous. Right up until she died, in 1973, you could call in to see her and find her in tears thinking of her brothers and the waste of their lives.

My paternal grandfather came from a family of publicans in North London. They owned a series of pubs in Islington and Dalston and my father was born in one of these, the Trafalgar. They were a fairly affluent North London family and there is a Dyke family vault in the Abney Park Cemetery in Stoke Newington, near where Christine, my eldest daughter, now lives with her partner Martin. My grandfather died in his early thirties in the 1919 flu epidemic, which worldwide claimed more victims than the First World War. My dad was seven at the time.

His mother, my paternal grandmother, left home at the age of fourteen when her widowed mother took up with another man – known only in the family as Mr Sadgrove – and had an illegitimate child, Horace James. Years later, at her ninetieth birthday party, everyone kept pointing out Horace and saying, in very loud whispers, 'He's the illegitimate one, but don't mention it.' When she left home my grandmother got a job as a barmaid at one of the Dyke pubs and married out of her class when she became the wife of the publican's son, Leonard Dyke. He left my grandmother penniless when he died; any money he had he left in trust for my dad and his brother Leonard. My grandmother wasn't even allowed to continue running their pub because, as a woman, she couldn't hold a licence. Instead, the brewery offered her an off-licence and general grocer's

shop in Tresham Avenue, Hackney, where my father and his brother Len were brought up.

My grandmother Lil came from a big Walthamstow family that was dominated for more than half a century by four powerful sisters: Lil, Beat, Flo, and Ruby. They were known in the family as the big four, and all dominated their husbands. They all lived long lives; two of them received telegrams from the Queen on their hundredth birthdays. My grandmother died at the age of 101. She and I never really got on: according to the rest of the family we were too alike. We were both very competitive and hated losing (as a young boy I regularly beat her at cards). One of her brothers, Albert Silverton, worked as a commissionaire at Broadcasting House in Portland Place in the 1930s. When I joined the BBC it became a family joke – commissionaire to Director-General in only two generations.

My parents met at St John's Church in Hackney and got married in 1939, living first in Birmingham and later in Bromley. They moved to Hayes soon after the end of the war. As a family we weren't poor but we never had any money. Like most of those around us, we never went abroad for a family holiday – my first visit overseas came when I was sixteen on a school trip to Paris. And we certainly never ate in restaurants. The first time we ever ate out together as a family was at the Swan and Bottle, a Berni Inn steak bar in Uxbridge: I was 14 or 15 at the time.

Some things are memorable from that time. I vividly remember being told by my mother that King George VI had died: it was the same day in February 1952 that my brother Ian took the 11-plus exam. For my parents, the King represented something special because of the symbolic role he had played in the East End of London during the Second World War. People in the East End respected the King and Queen because they had stayed in London during the Blitz and had regularly visited the parts of East London that were badly bombed.

On the day of the King's funeral they both went to stand by the railway bridge in nearby Southall as the train carrying the King's body passed by on its way to Windsor. They thought it important that they pay their respects and I can remember to this day my dad leaving in his best suit and trilby hat and my mother in her best dress. They were dressed to the nines just to stand by a railway bridge. This was still the age of respect.

None of my memories of living in Cerne Close is as exciting as those

of the street party my mother helped organize to celebrate the coronation of Queen Elizabeth the following year. My brother Ian took part in a sketch put on by the older kids and I sang a song, pretending that the tennis racket I was holding was a guitar. We all had jellies and sandwiches in the street – it was a magical day for a six-year-old. Nearly fifty years later I sat in the royal box in the grounds of Buckingham Palace as the BBC put on two spectacular concerts to celebrate the fiftieth anniversary of the Queen's accession, and afterwards I wandered around the Palace meeting members of the Royal Family. It was a lifetime away from Cerne Close.

I remember the coming of television vividly. My early childhood was spent with *Listen with Mother* on the Home Service. Then television arrived. Initially, only two people in our street had television sets, the Riches at Number 21 and Mrs Unstead, who lived in the corner house, and all the kids in the street used to pile into one or other house to watch children's television. And then, in 1953, came the great day when Howard and I, walking home from school, were, by complete coincidence, counting the number of houses that had television aerials. Life in Hayes wasn't exactly exciting in those days and this was the sort of thing you did as a kid. We turned the corner and, lo and behold, there was an aerial on the roof of our house. We rushed in to find a television set, which my dad had bought so my mother could watch the Coronation and he could watch the Cup Final. We were really excited until about a week later when it stopped working. My dad called out the TV repair man, who came and plugged it back in. Dad was never a practical man, and I've followed in his footsteps.

Our set only received BBC and when ITV started in 1955 my dad refused to change the set, which meant that my brothers and I missed all those early ITV programmes like *The Invisible Man*, *Robin Hood*, *Take Your Pick*, and *Double Your Money*. I remember we felt very deprived that we couldn't join in the conversations at school about these pro-grammes. My dad was always of the view that the BBC was 'proper' television and that advertiser-funded television was inevitably inferior. He believed this until the day he died in 1990.

In our last years in Hayes, in the late Fifties, the area began to change rapidly. Southall became a massive centre for Indian immigrants and changed beyond recognition in just a few years. For those original resi-

dents who remained in the area the speed of change must have been traumatic. One moment you knew all your neighbours; the next, most of them were strangers from an entirely different culture who didn't speak your language.

After we had moved from our street some residents clubbed together to try to prevent Asian families from buying houses in the road. Of course they were branded as racist by some, but that was unfair. They weren't being unkind or reactionary – quite the opposite. They were simply scared by the pace and scale of change all around them and didn't understand its causes. They had seen the centre of Southall change beyond recognition and they didn't want to see the same happen to their street.

A couple of years ago I went back to the area when, as Director-General, I was invited to open the new hall at Yeading Junior school, where I was a pupil between 1954 and 1958. In 1958 the school was entirely populated by white working-class and lower-middle-class kids. Forty years later it was 80 per cent non-white, with children from dozens of different ethnic backgrounds. If a sociologist had moved into our house when we moved out in 1956, and had stayed to study Cerne Close and the surrounding area over the next forty years, he or she would have had a brilliant case study of the impact of immigration on a small community.

These were the days when the 11-plus dominated life for parents in streets like ours. If you were one of the 20 per cent who passed the exam you went to the local grammar school; if you didn't, you went to the secondary modern and, educationally, were effectively written off. No one we knew went to private school. I don't think anyone considered it an option: it wasn't on their radar screen even if they could have afforded it, which they couldn't.

One of the most traumatic memories I have of my childhood was when my eldest brother Ian failed the 11-plus. It was a family tragedy, and my parents were distraught. I took the exam six years later when there were four or five boys from our street taking it. Only one failed but his parents were broken hearted. My hatred of the 11-plus, and the whole concept of selection at the age of eleven, is rooted in those experiences. This was one of the main reasons why, later in life, I joined the Labour Party and Sue and I sent all our kids to comprehensive schools.

We left Hayes in 1957 to move to a bigger house three miles away in Hillingdon. My parents paid £4,500 for it: today it would be worth

somewhere between £350,000 and £400,000. We moved there when I was nine and it was certainly a move up market. We had a detached three-bedroomed house with a large garden where my father spent most Saturdays and Sundays tending his vegetables, when he wasn't fishing at a gravel pit in nearby Harefield.

Unlike Ian, both Howard and I passed the 11-plus and consequently went to Hayes Grammar School; neither of us was notably academic and one year I came bottom of the whole year – 132nd out of 132 pupils. Another year I remember Howard getting 7 per cent in his maths exam and his teacher saying in his school report that 'He thoroughly deserves this mark.' I also remember walking into a chemistry exam and the teacher saying to me 'Not a lot of point you coming in, Dyke.'

Our school was dominated by the headmaster, Ralph Scurfield. When I look back I think he was a really good headmaster, a great character, and a real leader, but we all lived in fear of him. After I left school I had no contact with him for nearly twenty years until I first hit the headlines at TV-am. One day Jane Tatnall, my secretary at the time, told me there was a Mr Scurfield on the phone. I picked it up and he said 'Is that you, Dyke?' My answer was entirely predictable. I said 'Yes, sir', as if nothing had changed over the intervening years. I was even tempted to stand up when I said it. Mr Scurfield had retired by then but was phoning on behalf of the new head teacher to ask me to give the prizes at speech day.

I went, and so did Mr Scurfield, who confided in me that day that he wished he had never used the cane while a headmaster. As I had been beaten by him on a couple of occasions, his conversion to non-violence didn't impress me. I wasn't ready for truth and reconciliation yet. Mr Scurfield is still alive and living in Sheffield and we write to each other once or twice a year.

Soon after I became Director-General I invited a few of my old teachers to dinner at the BBC, along with my brother Howard. I suppose I invited them so I could say to them 'OK, I didn't do so badly after all, did I?' All the teachers were retired and seemed to enjoy their evening, especially the red wine. After a few bottles one of them said to me that on the way there they had discussed my progress in life. 'We would like to say we spotted your potential,' he said, 'but in truth we all agreed you were one of the least likely pupils to succeed.' It's amazing how teachers can still wound, even after nearly forty years.

In Hillingdon we lived in a road called Cedars Drive, where I really enjoyed my teenage years. The street was full of boys (there were very few girls, except for my friend Val Clifton), and we did all the things boys did. Some of us became paper boys at the local newsagent's, which was run by a retired army officer, John Kane, known to us as Major John. We all liked working there, but he drove us all mad. He smoked like a chimney and would regularly leave his cigarette on the pile of newspapers he was marking up, which would then catch fire. But what really annoyed us about Major John was his habit of sleeping in so that when we turned up to collect our papers for delivery they were never ready for us. My first experience of being an 'activist' came at the age of fourteen or fifteen when I organized industrial action amongst the paper boys. We weren't bold enough to strike, but we decided that it was time we frightened Major John, so none of us turned up for our rounds until an hour after the normal time. I think he was a bit shocked but he quickly found out I was the ringleader and took me to task. He told me that if I didn't want to work on his terms and conditions I should leave. Forty years later I can understand what he was getting at, but at the time I thought he was being extremely unreasonable. My greatest success as a paper boy came when my friend Mick Higgins and I decided to go round to all our customers at Christmas, knock on their door, and wish them the compliments of the season. I think we got twice as many Christmas tips as anyone else.

Until girls came along, sport dominated the lives of all the boys on our estate and over the years we set up two football teams. The first, called Cedarwood Rangers, played in Newcastle United's black and white shirts; then, when we were older, we started Vine Athletic, who played in blue. The team was named after the local pub, the Vine, where we did most of our training. It was one of those pubs where you could be a regular at sixteen.

I've often wanted to make a documentary about kids from a typical street and tell the story of what happened to them in later life. In our street, the boys went on to do a whole range of things. Roger Weller became a teacher while his brother Keith was a senior civil servant in the Department of Education and ended up with an OBE. Mick Higgins went to work as a sales rep in the food industry, and Peter Hinley became a hairdresser but sadly died young. John Hayes did well in finance, while

Martin Webb worked for British Airways before joining his dad's business. Peter Bowden became an estate agent and Robin Cameron went into interior design. My brother Howard is currently a professor at the top university in South Korea while my brother Ian, after a life in the insurance industry, was the first to retire and was very proud of it.

I suppose I became the most famous by becoming Director-General of the BBC, but Christopher Barrett-Jolly came a close second. He came from the poshest family on our estate – at least we all thought they were posh because they had a double-barrelled name – and went off to be an airline pilot. At one time he ran a company flying live animals in and out of Birmingham Airport, which brought him a lot of flak from the animal rights lobby. Later, Chris hit bad times and received a good deal of publicity when he was sentenced to twenty years in jail for trying to smuggle £22 million worth of cocaine into the country. He had been caught flying a plane full of the drugs into Southend Airport. When he realized the police were waiting for him at the airport, he and his colleagues decided to try throwing the drugs out of the back of the plane, littering the runway with cocaine.

My best friend, then and now, is Richard Webb, who also lived on our estate. He had TB as a kid and as a result has a shortened left leg, which means he has had to wear a raised boot for most of his life – although you'd never have known it as you watched him playing football, cricket, or, in later life, in business. When people accuse me of being a competitive human being I always tell them they ought to meet my friend Richard. This was a man who impounded an easyJet plane, when it was full of passengers and just about to leave Stansted Airport for Nice, because he was owed £520 by the company. They refused to pay, so he went to the local County Court, representing himself, and got a court order. EasyJet still refused to pay so he got the bailiffs out and seized the plane. When an anxious easyJet executive rang and agreed to pay up, Richard made him send the money in cash by bike before he would release the plane.

Richard left school at sixteen and trained to become a chartered accountant. He's been my financial adviser for most of my life and in recent years has been involved in virtually all the business ventures I've undertaken. The only reason I've got lots of money today is because Richard has looked after it for me. I've only ever paid him for his advice

once. When we all made a lot of money out of London Weekend Television in the early Nineties I gave him a pile of my shares, explaining that it was his payment for life: twenty years in arrears and twenty years in advance. I'm a bit worried that the second twenty years ends in 2012.

I trust Richard more than anyone else I've ever met in my life. We've always argued and disagreed about all sorts of things, but we go back so far that it would never occur to either of us not to act in the other's best interests. Richard has access to every bank account I possess and he could completely clean me out if he wanted to, but of course it would never happen. That's what friendship is. When I was running the BBC and was criticized for retaining certain private business interests – on the grounds that I couldn't do more than one job at once – I tried to explain that they took up very little of my time because my friend Richard looked after my business interests for me. Of course for the journalists that spoiled a good story, so they ignored it.

I had a very happy childhood; as the third son in the family I had few of the battles with my parents that my elder brothers had had. In those days the vast majority of school leavers didn't go on to higher education; sadly, many of the brightest kids at my school left at sixteen because their families either couldn't afford, or didn't have the aspiration, for them to stay on. Although I had not done well at school my results picked up a bit in the last year or two and I passed six GCE O-levels. It was just about enough for me to stay on for the sixth form, but going on to university or college was never a realistic prospect.

I had a great time in my last two years at school. I played rugby for the First XV, was the school 440 yards running champion, was in all the school plays, and even sang in the choir. That's a slight exaggeration. I used to stand next to my good friend Dave Hornby, who had a great bass voice. He sang and I mimed. In fact we were together in the choir at the Royal Albert Hall on the night President Kennedy was assassinated. When people ask me where I was when JFK died, I always tell them I was miming at the Albert Hall.

I was enthusiastic about everything in those last two years, except academic work. I took A-levels in economics, and pure and applied maths, but didn't understand any of it. When I achieved a grade E in my combined maths A-level, which meant I had just passed, I was amazed – as was my maths teacher. When I met him in a pub about ten years after I left school

he told me he still used me as an example of why pupils shouldn't give up at the mocks 'because miracles could happen'.

On Saturdays I used to work in a shoe shop, first in Ealing and later in Acton. My greatest claim to fame at that time was that I sold Roger Daltrey a pair of plimsolls. We sold cheap shoes but it didn't stop people complaining. I'll always remember someone coming back unhappy, not unreasonably, because on getting home and opening the bag they'd found I'd sold them odd shoes – one was a size six, the other a size ten. What was strange was that we never found the matching pair.

While selling shoes, I learnt a lot about how salesmen con the public. If the shoes we were trying to sell were too big we'd explain that it was cool in our basement and that the customer's feet would expand when they got outside. If they were too small we'd say that they had been walking a lot and that their feet had expanded but that the shoes would be fine once they got home. The biggest scam was selling the shoes for which we got extra commission – the shoes people didn't want to buy. The trick was to bring the customer the wrong-sized shoes, and then miraculously pull out a pair that fitted perfectly, which just happened to be the pair on which we earned the largest commission.

When it came to leaving school and getting a proper job my mother had always warned me that I would have to 'buckle down' and that life wouldn't be as much fun any more. She was so right; in my first venture into the world of full-time work I became a trainee manager at Marks & Spencer, at the Watford branch in Hertfordshire. I got the job largely because my dad's brother, my Uncle Len, was a manager at M&S for more than thirty years and he put a word in for me. I started in September 1965, and hated every minute of it; it was purgatory.

In those days, M&S stores were largely managed by cautious public-school boys. Most of the bright people worked in head office, where they controlled almost everything. It was obvious to me that people in the stores were not encouraged to use their own initiative. When, many years later, M&S was in financial difficulties and the company decided to change the way they ran things, they announced that they wanted their managers to act as if they were franchisees. When I read this I nearly wrote to them to tell them that they had no chance of making this work. The people they now wanted to run their stores had either been sacked or had left in desperation over the years. The people they'd retained were those who

did what they were told and kept their noses clean. They didn't seem to understand that you can't change the fundamental culture of a company merely by announcing that you've done so. It's rather more complicated than that.

I remember being constantly in trouble, almost from the day I arrived at M&S. I set up the all-time broken biscuit record when I worked in the stockroom, got told off for not having my hair cut short enough, was told to stop chatting up the attractive shop girls, and was asked by the manager if I'd had any elocution lessons when I was at school. As a joke, I told him I'd gone to school in Hayes, where no one could even spell elocution, let alone take lessons in it. He didn't think it was at all funny.

After four months I got the sack. Because I was a management trainee they sent down some bigwig from head office to give me the news. With him came the latest of the Sieff family, who ran M&S. He was learning about human resources as he was fast tracked through the organization. I was shocked to be fired, but also absolutely delighted. They even gave me three months' money to leave. Years later, when I got a lot of publicity at TV-am, I was interviewed by one journalist and asked if I regretted not going into television earlier in life. My answer was that everyone should start their working life at Marks & Spencer, because it could only get better after that. Soon after the interview, David Frost bumped into Marcus Sieff, the then boss of M&S. Sieff said to him, 'I see you are employing one of our boys now,' so clearly someone had noticed.

The four months I spent at M&S had a profound influence on my future direction in life. It certainly prejudiced my views against public-school boys for many years, which, in turn, pushed my political views further in the direction of Labour. It also convinced me that my mother had been wrong. I decided there and then that I would never do a job and be miserable again; if I didn't like a job in the future I would leave. My dad, horrified that I was out of work, then tried to persuade me to follow him and my eldest brother into the insurance industry, or else try for a job in the local solicitor's office. I was having none of it. I'd tried work their way. Now it was my turn.

I was determined to find something exciting through which I could express myself. One day, when I was still unemployed, I wandered into the office of a fairly new local newspaper based in Uxbridge called the *Hillingdon Mirror* and met the editor, Brian Cummins. The paper was a

tabloid with a colour picture on the front page; the office was a complete tip. I had a long chat with Brian and told him why I wanted to be a journalist; as I left I remember thinking that I could enjoy life there. A few months later, while I was working in a temporary job, he rang me and offered me a job as a reporter.

Brian was 27 at the time but he seemed old to us youngsters in the office. Not only was he the boss, he had also spent two years in the RAF doing national service. We always used to joke that he'd spent his time learning to fly Sopwith Camels. He was a great man to work for and let us all get on with it. The paper was manned by indentured junior reporters, young kids who had signed up for three years at very little money to learn the business. It was Brian's job, along with his deputy, Peter Hurst, to teach us.

The newspaper group we all worked for, King & Hutchings of Uxbridge, was so mean they didn't even supply typewriters; you had to buy your own. I've still got mine. Expenses were virtually unheard of, although at a stretch they would pay bus fares, and the entertaining policy was straightforward: don't, and if you do you won't be reimbursed. I was always someone who challenged everything and after a couple of years I decided this was exploitation, particularly when we found out that the tele-ad girls earned more money than the indentured journalists. I organized a demonstration of junior reporters. Ray Snoddy, later to be an eminent media journalist on the *Financial Times* and *The Times*, was one of those who joined the protest. We demanded to see the top man.

We clearly got the company worried because in the end Mr Larriman agreed to meet us. Now everyone at King & Hutchings believed Mr Larriman was a mythical figure. No one knew him but when middle management talked about him it was in hushed tones. He was only ever known as Mr Larriman: no one knew his first name, let alone used it. He ran the whole newspaper group, ten or twelve prosperous papers stretching right across West London. When we met him we tried to explain that all the indentured juniors, and there must have been forty of us in all, were short of money and needed more. I can remember his reply to this day. He told us there was no point in increasing our wages because we were young and would only spend the money on things like records and portable radios. I think the Sixties youth revolution must have passed Mr Larriman by.

We all pretended we were proper big shot journalists and joined the National Union of Journalists so that we could flash the big NUJ membership card around. Having failed to impress Mr Larriman by organizing the junior journalists, I decided on a different approach and got myself elected as Father of the Chapel – the shop steward for all the journalists working in Uxbridge. I spent the next year or so trying to be a pain to the management.

On the *Hillingdon Mirror* we were trying to break the mould of local journalism. We didn't report the local court proceedings much, and we certainly didn't cover weddings and funerals. As a result we struggled to find enough to fill the paper, and consequently didn't sell that many copies. We'd spend our days on the road making 'contact calls', as Brian Cummins used to call them – trying to find stories. My best friend as a reporter was a tall, good-looking boy called Roy Eldridge, who ended up in the pop music industry. His version of contact calls was different from the rest of us – he ended up having a torrid affair with the woman who ran one of the local residents' associations. My girlfriend at the time was another reporter on the paper, Christine Webb. One day I was called in by Brian Cummins and told that his boss, the editor-in-chief, had seen us 'making contact' in the office one evening and that this wasn't appreciated.

I've always enjoyed working hard, so in my days on the *Hillingdon Mirror* I had a second job at the weekends to earn a bit more money. I worked for a news agency in Guildford called Cassidy and Leigh. If you talk to anyone who has run the newsdesk of a popular national paper they'll know about Cassidy and Leigh. Our job was to sell stories to them. Cassidy and Leigh were good, hard newsmen, but they also provided frothy stories for the tabloids. Not all these stories had to be 100 per cent true, just as long as the people you were writing about agreed they were. I remember, in particular, that we sold a whole string of stories about a Roman Catholic convent in Godalming whose nuns were terribly publicity conscious and getting headlines like 'Officiating at the Morning Service' – with a picture of a nun lying under a car wielding an enormous spanner.

My interest in politics really dates back to that time working on the *Hillingdon Mirror*. I became the paper's part-time political reporter and spent a lot of time with local councillors, MPs, and the like. I left the paper in 1969, initially to run the Staines regional office of the *Evening*

Mail, a brand-new evening paper that was being started in Slough, but within a few months I had become its full-time political reporter. I was now a specialist. At that time I shared a flat in Windsor with a photographer called Jeff Wright, whom I had first met at King & Hutchings and who had made the move to the *Evening Mail* a few months before me. Jeff and I are still close friends.

In my second year at the *Evening Mail* I began to think about going to university. Although I was told I didn't need a degree to have a good future as a journalist, I began to become conscious that I hadn't had much of an education. Someone I knew had got a place at university without the normal qualifications and I began to think about applying myself. I suppose I felt intellectually inferior to those who had been to university and needed to prove to myself, and to others, that I wasn't. I was also getting more and more interested in politics and wanted to study the subject.

I persuaded the editor of the Slough *Evening Mail*, John Rees, to give me a reference and set about filling in the appropriate university entrance forms. Much to my surprise I was offered interviews at Lancaster, East Anglia, and York, and then was offered places at all three. Although I only had my one maths A-level, all three were willing to take a chance on me. I chose to go to York because it was a beautiful campus and the people I met at the interview were both challenging and friendly. Twenty years later, after I had made a great deal of money, I decided that the risk the university had taken by offering me a place deserved to be rewarded. As a way of saying thank you, I gave them a quarter of a million pounds, which they used to build an all-weather sports pitch.

Changing from being a reporter on popular newspapers to studying politics required an enormous adjustment that took me at least a year to achieve. For the first time in my life I had to understand what academic study was all about. I remember vividly the first essay I wrote at York. I was asked to 'Discuss the causes of the English industrial revolution'. I remember reading one chapter of one book, thinking 'That's it, cracked that', and then just repeating what I'd read. It was pointed out to me by my tutor that academia was about collecting a range of opinion and assessing the strengths of different ideas, not just taking the first available option. I was no longer a pop journalist.

Gradually I grew to understand what it was all about and, as an older student who had made a positive decision to go to university, I worked pretty hard compared to most of those around me. In my politics course I tended to specialize in three areas. I wrote my dissertation on the origins of the Cuban revolution, and grew fascinated by the history of the Soviet Union; but the most exciting period came in my final year, 1974, when I was studying American politics. It coincided with the unfolding of the Watergate scandal – Richard Nixon resigned as President just after I had finished the course. The American Politics lecturers decided to abandon their usual course and rearrange the whole year around Watergate, which was a brilliant move as it meant you could study the theoretical base of US politics through what was actually happening during that year. The separation of powers between President, the Senate, and the Congress really meant something when the President was in the process of being impeached. I have been a Watergate groupie ever since, although even now I still don't fully understand why Nixon's people decided to burgle the Watergate building in the first place, and I'm not sure anyone else does.

I had long been interested in US politics and at the end of my first year at York spent the entire summer wandering around the United States. I went to the Democratic Party convention in Miami, where I worked briefly on the campaign for George McGovern, the US senator who was to stand for the Democrats in the 1972 presidential election. I then wandered off to find out about the USA. I hitched my way around the country, covering some eight thousand miles. I was on my own, which enabled me to discover America in a way I couldn't have done by any other means. From Europe we tend to see the USA as California and the Eastern seaboard. By hitching through the Midwest you discover another America.

The Vietnam War was still raging and in town after town in the Midwest there were very few young men in evidence – they were all away at the war. I also travelled down to El Paso in Texas to meet members of our extended family. Both my US cousins had fought in Vietnam, and both had been screwed up by the experience.

Being at York University in the early Seventies was an interesting experience. These were the days of sit-ins and radical action. Having gone to university from a job in which I'd been seen as a bit of a leftie, at York I was seen as a revisionist because I was a Labour Party supporter. The Socialist Workers Party and their like saw me as dangerous because,

although I was of the Left, I didn't agree with them that the true path to change was through revolution. I distinctly remember the leader of the hard Left at York walking into a meeting and apologizing for being late by explaining that he had 'been out working for the revolution'. All his fans applauded. His name was Peter Hitchens, now a right-wing columnist on the *Mail on Sunday*. I'm amazed when I discover that there are still Trotskyist organizations active in British universities, egged on by the last of the Trotskyist academics.

Unlike most students I did pretty well financially while at university. As I was 24 I got a full local authority grant and when I arrived at York decided I didn't want to live on campus but would rent my own house instead. I then rapidly came to the conclusion that it would be cheaper to buy than rent. My dad had just retired and one of his insurance policies had paid out, so I borrowed the lot, paying him a decent rate of interest, and bought a small terraced house in Briggs Street, near the Rowntree factory. I paid the princely sum of £1,200 for the house, got a local authority grant to add on a bathroom, and sold it for £5,000 when I left. When I was in York recently I was fascinated to see similar houses are now selling for £120,000. I wonder where the poor of York can now afford to live.

But my most memorable financial experience at university was my libel action against the local evening paper, the *York Evening Press*. They had run an article saying that a local printer wouldn't print a student newspaper because of an article written by me that was claimed to be obscene. While it was true that the printer wouldn't print the paper it had nothing to do with my article, which was about the California marijuana initiative (an attempt to make the drug legal on the West Coast of the United States). I asked for an apology but the editor of the *Evening Press*, unaware that he was dealing with a student who had trained as a journalist, refused. So I decided to sue. In the end I got a full apology, all my legal costs, and £250 as an out of court settlement. Given that a full grant in 1974 was just £420, this was a good day: my girlfriend at the time, later my wife, Christine Taylor and I had a good summer in France on the *York Evening Press*.

There is a postscript to the story. In 2003 I was invited as Director-General of the BBC to be the guest speaker and present the awards at the *York Evening Press* Annual Business Awards. As DG you get hundreds

of similar invites, but this was one I couldn't resist. Clearly no one at the paper was aware of the history; in my speech I told the whole story. I ended by thanking the *Evening Press* for making my life at York more comfortable.

Going to York as a mature student completely changed my life; it's why I've always been keen to encourage as many people as possible to go to university, particularly those who are older and who may have missed out on formal education the first time round. After I had left York I convinced Jeff Wright, my flatmate in Windsor, that although he didn't have a single O-level he was certainly clever enough to go to university. He ended up with a very good degree from Swansea University and went on to get a Masters. He was just another kid whose education was screwed up by the 11-plus.

In late 2003 I was appointed Chancellor elect of York University, which the *Sunday Times* recently named as University of the Year. For someone who went as a student with one A-level and caused a fair amount of trouble when I was there, I was both amazed and flattered to be asked to take on the role.

Unlike most students I haven't remained in close contact with many of my friends at York, with the exception of Marianne Geary, a girl from Northern Ireland. We've always enjoyed each other's company and she's very perceptive about me and what drives me. Just a few days after I left the BBC, I received an e-mail from Marianne telling me that Keith, her husband, had cancer and was about to have a kidney removed. At a time when I was feeling pretty sorry for myself it was a real awakening. By comparison, what was I making such a fuss about? Thankfully, it looks like Keith will make a full recovery.

When I left York after three incredibly stimulating years I wasn't sure what to do, so I went back to work in regional newspapers. My girlfriend Christine, who became my wife in 1975, was going to Newcastle University to do a one-year course to train as a probation officer, and it so happened that John Rees, my former editor on the Slough *Evening Mail*, was now the editor of the *Journal* in Newcastle. I wrote to him and he immediately offered me a job.

Going back to local journalism was a terrible mistake. Just as I had had to unlearn being a pop journalist when I went to university, so I was expected to forget all I had learnt while there and be a pop journalist

51

once again. I hated the experience. I wasn't the slightest bit interested in what some jumped-up councillor thought, nor was I prepared to create stories simply because someone said they were true when it was quite clear they were bullshit. The only good thing about the six months I spent on the *Journal* was that I met some people there who were to play a significant part in my future life. One was Peter McHugh, the industrial correspondent on the paper at the time, who later worked with me at TV-am and is now in charge of GMTV. The second was Nick Evans, who was doing a similar job to me on the regional evening paper, the *Evening Chronicle*.

Nick is a very close friend who always claims that he was the better reporter of the two of us, and it is certainly true that his shorthand was better than mine. Much later in life, Nick became famous when he wrote his first book, *The Horse Whisperer*, which became an international best-seller and was turned into a film starring Robert Redford. Nick played a big part in getting me my first job in television and later we worked together running a programme at London Weekend Television.

While in Newcastle I decided I didn't want to be a journalist any more – I wanted to do something more useful in society; so I got a job as a campaign organizer for Wandsworth Council for Community Relations. This meant Christine and me leaving Newcastle, which we both liked (even though I disliked my job), and moving to London, where she became a probation officer, also in Wandsworth. One day I was at home decorating our flat when she brought home a fellow probation officer, a very attractive girl called Sue Howes. Seven years later, after both our marriages had failed, Sue and I became an item, and still are.

My job involved organizing campaigns in the field of race relations. The Borough of Wandsworth had been a centre for both Asian and West Indian immigration in the 1960s and 1970s and the Community Relations Council was an organization that sought to bring representatives of the different ethnic minority communities together. I'm not sure anyone was really quite sure what a Community Relations Council was supposed to do, but my boss there, a man called Charles Boxer, believed that we should be a campaigning organization influencing local and national policy in the field of race. He employed me to set up campaigns and to get him, the organization, and the campaigns plenty of press publicity, which is exactly what I did.

I worked at WCCR for close on two years and discovered something profound: that no one, at any level, had solutions to some of the problems we identified. Worse still, neither did we – although of course we pretended we did by blaming the Government or the local council or claiming that more money would sort out all the problems. I had given up regional journalism because I thought it was superficial. Now I had found exactly the same thing in another area.

From this I began to recognize what I still believe today to be a fundamental difficulty in the relationship between pressure groups, media, and politics. Politicians are incapable of saying 'We don't know the solution to this', or even 'We don't think there is a solution'. If they did, they would be portrayed as weak or incompetent by the media. Pressure groups and opposition politicians play the same game by demanding that 'Something *must* be done', while politicians in power resort to saying 'Something *is* being done'. The whole process is damaging to media, politics, and the public understanding of the issues of the day.

Not that this growing understanding of the limitations of politics deterred me from following an ambition of mine that had developed in the years in Slough and afterwards: to be a politician. While I was at WCCR the opportunity arose for me to become the Labour Party's candidate for the Greater London Council election in Putney, one of four constituencies in the Borough of Wandsworth. The GLC was elected through the same constituencies as local MPs, so being the GLC candidate for Putney was quite a big deal.

I was nominated by one of the Labour branches in Battersea, where I was a member of the Party and where my friend Mark Mildred was also a member. I knew Mark, a successful lawyer who had worked on personal injury cases like Thalidomide, because his wife Sarah Rackham worked with me at WCCR. He put my name forward. Quite why Putney Labour Party wanted me I was never sure, but I was selected as their candidate for the 1977 GLC election. At that time Putney was a Labour seat both in Parliament and the GLC, but it was always going to be difficult to hang on to it.

The problem was that the Labour Government at the time, led by Jim Callaghan, was incredibly unpopular, so my chances of holding the seat seemed slim. And so it proved. I turned a Labour majority of 4,000 into a Conservative majority of 7,000, a massive 17 per cent swing to the

Conservatives. At the General Election two years later David Mellor, whom I had met and liked while I was active in Putney, also won the parliamentary seat for the Conservatives. During the GLC election I had met Ken Livingstone, who was organizing a left-wing grouping of potential GLC councillors. I joined his group, as he never ceases to remind me, but it was all in vain as very few of us won. Four years later he did the same thing again and became the Labour leader of the GLC, but by then my political ambitions had disappeared.

I often think how different my life might have been if I had won in April 1977. I would have become a full-time GLC councillor, and probably gone on to be a Labour MP, and would never have gone into the television industry. I have to say I am eternally grateful that I lost that election. I've seen too many people I really like go into politics only to find it frustrating and unrewarding.

A couple of months before the election I had resigned from WCCR, frustrated by all I had found in the race relations industry, which in those days was racked by the politics of race. On 20 May 1977 I celebrated my thirtieth birthday unemployed, having just turned a reasonably good Labour seat into a safe Conservative one. I was depressed and unsure of the future. I had always been ambitious and believed I would be a success in life, yet here I was with very little to show. I spent my birthday sitting on a log on Wandsworth Common asking myself 'Whatever happened to me?'

And then, just four months later, my life changed for ever.

CHAPTER THREE

Into Television

It was my friend from Newcastle, Nick Evans, who told me that there was a researcher's job going at London Weekend Television on *Weekend World*, ITV's prestigious but little watched current affairs show that was broadcast on Sunday lunchtimes. Nick had left Newcastle soon after me to become a researcher on *Weekend World* and had rapidly been promoted to become a producer. He told me if I applied for the job he would make sure the least I got was an interview; as I was unemployed at the time I didn't take much persuading.

I was interviewed by a whole range of people on the programme, including one who was very much against me. At that time Jane Hewland was a senior producer who was later to become Head of Features and Current Affairs at LWT. Today she runs a successful independent production company, Hewland International, which makes a lot of programmes for BSkyB. After meeting me, Jane decided I wasn't the right sort for LWT, although I only discovered this years later when, as Director of Programmes at LWT, I got access to my old file, and was able to read what Jane initially thought about me. By then Jane was working for me, so I included her comments about me in the speech I made at her leaving party. She's never forgiven me. I have her original report framed and hanging in my office. She said of me:

He was so glib, fast talking and sure of himself and so contemptuous of all the TV people he has met so far I fear we would never be able to break his spirit and bring him to see the light as we see it. I think he would just turn out to be a pain in the arse, get disgruntled with us and leave.

At the final interview for the *Weekend World* job I had been told by Nick Evans that the most important person on the Board was John Birt, who was then head of Features and Current Affairs and was all powerful. At the interview I thought I did pretty well, answering most of the questions intelligently, and getting a few laughs at the same time. In particular John Birt laughed quite a lot – or so I thought.

I discovered afterwards that I had muddled up the people on the Board and that the man who was laughing was actually Barry Cox, the head of Current Affairs. The only person on the Board I didn't take to was the person to my left, who kept asking me really awkward questions and didn't laugh once. When Nick Evans called to ask me how I had got on I described this man to him and discovered it had been John Birt.

I didn't get the job on *Weekend World,* but I must have done all right because I was asked to apply for another LWT job as a reporter on their regional current affairs programme, called *The London Programme*. I went in to meet the editor, Julian Norridge, and we ended up talking about the Cuban revolution, the subject of my thesis at university three years earlier. Quite what Cuba had to do with London I had no idea, but I got the job.

Suddenly one of the blackest periods in my life was over: I had got the job in television I'd always dreamed of having. There are three periods of my life that had a profound influence on me, on my career, and on the way I think. The first was the three years I spent at York University. The second was about to begin – the six years from 1977 to 1983 that I spent in the current affairs department at LWT. The third wouldn't come until 1989, when I went to the Harvard Business School.

When I joined LWT in the autumn of 1977 it was a really exciting place. The company had won its ITV franchise in 1968. After a disastrous start, when it nearly went broke, it had recovered and was looking for ways to ensure it got its franchise renewed by the Independent Broadcasting Authority in 1980. The Current Affairs and Features Department under John Birt was expanding fast. *Weekend World* had introduced a new, more intellectual form of current affairs on British television, and two well-funded local programmes had changed regional programming. The first was the *London Weekend Show*, a programme for teenagers presented by Janet Street-Porter. The second was the programme I was joining, *The London Programme*.

The LWT style of journalism had been pioneered by John Birt, who had developed the whole approach when editing *Weekend World*. Many in television, then and now, have mocked his philosophy, but I would defend it to this day. What John argued was that understanding the issue or story was more important than necessarily getting the right pictures, and that if you couldn't get the pictures it didn't mean you had to abandon the whole programme. But the approach went further. Birt argued that demonstrating there was a problem wasn't enough: you also had to explain what could be done about it. His thesis, known as 'The Bias Against Understanding', was first outlined in an article written by Birt and Peter Jay in *The Times* in 1975. What this analytical approach to television current affairs meant was that, first, you were able to tackle difficult subjects that weren't necessarily televisual, and, second, you couldn't get away with just saying that something was an outrage: you had to show that there was something the policy makers could do about it.

The programme I joined, *The London Programme*, had been the idea of Barry Cox when he was a producer at Granada. He'd had the idea of producing a weekly, well-resourced current affairs programme, in the style of *World in Action* but only about London stories and London issues, and taken it to John Birt. I joined for the third series.

It is difficult to explain how exciting working on a programme like that was for me at that time. It was intellectually satisfying compared to the other jobs I had had since leaving York. You had six weeks to make a single half-hour film about a particular issue, which meant you had four weeks to research it. In that time you could get to know a subject well. You were helped because you were from 'television', so you could get access to the experts in the field you were examining: television opens doors. But the real challenge was to understand the subject. In many ways it was more like being at university than being in the media. In those days people joked about the LWT current affairs department being 'Balliol on Thames', a place where programme makers spent weeks constructing theses and made programmes that no one except other programme makers, MPs, and Whitehall mandarins watched. It also kept up the tradition of the long summer vacation when the current affairs department would empty for weeks on end.

My first ever television programme was a story I had discovered while

working in community relations and was about landlords harassing tenants. This was followed by one about the chances of London flooding, and here I had an amazing piece of luck. The programme was made to commemorate the twenty-fifth anniversary of the great London flood of 1952. The Thames barrier was then being built and the programme asked what the chance was of London being flooded again before it was finished.

Three days after the programme was broadcast in the autumn of 1977 there was a surge tide, with the wind in the right direction, and London was inches from being under water. The Labour Government of the day was terrified and asked LWT to repeat the programme so that people would understand the danger and what they should do if the worst happened. Michael Grade, then the Director of Programmes at LWT, repeated it at 10.30 p.m. on the Friday night and we got an enormous rating, the largest for any *London Programme* that series.

I read recently that, according to some academic study or other, people born in May, like me, are the luckiest, and it's certainly been true in my case. My old managing director at LWT, Brian Tesler, once told me he would invest in any company I ran – not because I was brilliant, but because I had 'the luck' on my side. Most things I touched worked. When I was at TV-am in 1984 the astrologer Marjorie Orr did my chart and told me I could expect twenty wonderful years when all would go right. The trouble was, the twenty years ended in 2004. I must ask her some time if it was just coincidence that I was fired from the BBC the very moment the twenty years was up.

I had a pretty good first year at LWT and, at the end of it, was asked to join *Weekend World* as junior producer, progressing during the year to become a full producer. The programme I was most proud of while at *Weekend World* was one I made on the European Common Agricultural Policy, a system that only about six people in the world seemed to understand. I became the seventh and tried to explain it to the nation on this intellectual programme by telling a joke.

I told the story of a German cow. We saw it milked and then followed the cow's milk to the dairy, where it was made into powdered milk. The powdered milk was then bought by the EEC intervention board, who stored it in enormous sheds as part of the EEC milk mountain. Eventually it was sold back to the same farmer to be fed to the same cow who had produced the milk in the first place. When I finished the programme I

was convinced that the Common Agricultural Policy was doomed. It was so inefficient and made so little economic sense. How wrong I was. It's still going strong today, costing the average family of four in Britain something like £1,000 a year.

My year on *Weekend World* was not a happy time – not because of the work, but because of what happened in my private life. On getting a job in television I had thrown myself into it full time and in the process my marriage fell apart. Christine felt neglected and found another life without me. It was without doubt the worst time of my life, culminating in my sitting in the office one day trying to work with tears rolling down my face. I am forever grateful to a lovely PA called Julie Shaw, who, seeing how distressed I was, came up to me and said 'Why don't we go for a walk?' I also went in to see the editor of *Weekend World*, the brilliant but mad David Cox, and told him I needed a few days off because my marriage was collapsing. He just looked up and said, 'So is mine.'

Ever since then I've always tried either to talk or write to the people working for me when their life is in crisis because of a marriage break-down, a family tragedy, or some other major problem. A small gesture from the boss at a time of crisis can really mean something. I also learnt from that time onwards how important it was to keep a decent balance between work and the rest of your life, although I haven't always managed to achieve it. These were the days in television when you weren't seen as a 'proper' producer if you didn't sleep on the cutting room floor and ignore the rest of your life. It was complete nonsense.

In later years, when people came to see me and said their marriage was breaking down, I always told them to try again. Marriages and relationships inevitably go through difficult times, but sometimes they recover. And I've always insisted people take their holidays despite whatever crisis might be happening at work, because holidays matter in family life. I've only ever had to cancel two, the first when Granada launched a takeover bid for LWT in late 1993 and the other in the summer of 2003 after Dr Kelly committed suicide.

Thankfully, Christine and I had not had children so our break-up was relatively uncomplicated. We simply split what we owned and went our own ways. Some years later, when we were both with other people and Christine wanted to get married again, we discovered that, due to a mistake of our own making, we weren't actually divorced. We both had

to turn up in court to affirm that we no longer wanted to be married to each other – a very odd experience. We hadn't seen each other for some years and it was like meeting someone you were at university with, rather than meeting your ex-wife.

Much later, more than twenty years after we had split up and when I was Director-General of the BBC, the *Mail on Sunday* went in search of Christine with the obvious intent of getting her to dish the dirt on me. They found her at her home in Yorkshire, but when she said there was no animosity between us and that, although we no longer saw each other, we were still fond of one another, the reporter gave up and went back to London. No story there.

At the end of my year on *Weekend World* Nick Evans and I were asked to become a team to run *The London Programme*. He would be the editor and, after just two years in television, I would be his deputy. We had two small adjoining offices, the states of which reflected our differing personalities. His was always neat and tidy, with a completely clear desk at the end of the day. Mine was always a tip, with piles of paper every-where. My problem was that I really wanted a desk like his but could never quite achieve it; so on the nights when I was working late and he'd gone home, I used to sneak into his office and work at his desk. It was bliss.

Nick and his wife Jenny were great friends to me during this time. As anyone knows who has got divorced, or has seen a long-term relationship split up, these are times when the emotional swings are enormous. The highs are higher but the lows are much lower. Nick and Jenny helped me through so many of the low times. Sadly, much later, their own marriage split up as well and Nick has recently remarried.

Running a weekly current affairs show with one of your best friends was a lot of fun. What I discovered was the importance, in a creative business, of people with good ideas. In my relatively brief time in television I had always worked on stories that I had found myself, or on issue-based programmes I had suggested, so I had always assumed most producers worked on their own ideas. When I became an editor I discovered it wasn't true. There are brilliant producers who have few ideas themselves, but they can take an idea and make it into an outstanding programme.

What I discovered in the two years I was doing that job was that people with good ideas are worth their weight in gold. I discovered later that

the same applies in business. When I was at the Harvard Business School some years later, one of the professors came up with a great description of this when he said 'Man can live for three weeks without food, four days without water and five minutes without oxygen; but some men can live a lifetime without a good idea.'

The point is that in programme making you can screw up a good idea and make a bad programme, but you can never make a good programme out of a lousy idea. Whenever I've talked to people coming new into television I've always told them that you can learn the process of making programmes relatively easily; what really matters is the originality and quality of your ideas.

Nick and I ran *The London Programme* for two years. We had a good team with us and tried to make it a fun and exciting place to work. As always, we made some good programmes and some bad ones. The hardest job of being a programme editor is having to 'save' a programme – to try to turn a potentially disastrous programme into one that is at least average. I always remember Nick trying to do this with a programme on local government finance. The end product was totally incomprehensible, but at least Nick had made it look stylish: a week earlier it had both been incomprehensible and looked terrible. It is exactly the same in news. Producing a programme on a good news day is ten times easier than when there is nothing happening. The latter is the test of a good editor, as I was to discover later at TV-am.

In January 1982 LWT began another ten years as the weekend ITV broadcaster in London, which was good news for the company, although the renewal of the franchise wasn't unexpected. LWT's only challenger was from a consortium led by quizmaster Hughie Green. Even better news was that, instead of taking over – as usual – from Thames Television at 7 p.m. on Friday nights, LWT would in future start at 5.30. LWT had another hour and a half to fill each weekend, and another hour and a half's worth of advertising to sell.

I was given the job of filling some of that extra time – the hour between six and seven every Friday night. After just four years in television I was given my own programme. I was to be the editor of what became a mould-breaking programme called *The Six O'Clock Show*, which was due to launch in January 1982. It was only called that because we didn't have a name to put on the door of the office when we first brought the

team together in September 1981. In the next three months we came up with about twenty different names and put them all forward to Michael Grade, LWT's Director of Programmes at the time, for him to choose. In the end he chose the name on the door. The name of programmes doesn't really matter; it's the content that is important. Who in their right mind would call a situation comedy about a couple of wide boys from East London *Only Fools and Horses*, and yet it is one of the great television comedies of all time.

LWT in 1982 was a company with enormous confidence. It had won back its franchise and had a series of big hits on its hands. Cilla Black's *Surprise! Surprise!* was hugely popular and that year it launched another entertainment show called *Game for a Laugh*, which became Britain's Number One show in a matter of weeks. A new LWT drama called *Dempsey and Makepeace* became another big hit while *Weekend World* and *The South Bank Show* were there to prove that the company had an intellectual heart. Into this mix came *The Six O'Clock Show*.

The Six O'Clock Show broke the mould for a number of reasons. We were the first programme to use single-camera tape: up until then it had only been used for news. LWT had just got a union agreement allowing the company to use electronic news gathering (ENG) and we decided to see if we could use this new technology in an original and more creative way. We pre-planned every three- or four-minute item we were to shoot as if it were a thirty-minute documentary. We had a budget that people in television would dream about today, which meant we had a producer, a director, and a researcher on every short item. Because tape was so much cheaper than film, we shot masses of it on every item and only used a tiny proportion of it. As a result, we got some gems at times.

The aim of *The Six O'Clock Show* was to create a different feeling: that this was Friday night and Friday night was the beginning of the weekend. In fact, I wanted to call the show *Thank God it's Friday* and commissioned research to demonstrate that the public wouldn't be offended by the use of the word 'God' in this way. Unfortunately, the research showed exactly the opposite: it turned out that large numbers of people *would* be offended, so I had to drop the idea.

One of my complaints about most news and current affairs programmes is that they never deal with the good things in life, only problems and issues. If you had watched LWT's regional output at that time you

wouldn't have known that anyone in London ever actually enjoyed living there. I decided *The Six O'Clock Show* would counter that. Its aim would be to tell the funnier side of life in London, to put on the eccentrics, and to tell the sort of stories people told each other in the pub, in the shop, or at work – the stories that would never have found their way onto a news programme. My hunch was that these were the stories that people really wanted to hear.

For instance, we once found a small cutting in a local paper about an eccentric man who had spent ten years building a model of the *Titanic* out of matchsticks. When it was finally completed he had launched it on the pond on Wimbledon Common and, true to form, it had sunk on its maiden voyage. We decided that *The Six O'Clock Show* would raise the *Titanic*. We hired a frogman, put Janet Street-Porter into a rubber dinghy, and sent them, plus a camera crew, out to find the sunken model. Unfortunately, the pond was too shallow for our frogman to dive under the water so he could only walk up and down in his diving gear, with the boat's proud owner telling him roughly where his pride and joy had sunk. Sadly, our diver found the boat by treading on it and the *Titanic* ended up being raised in two pieces.

We made three pilots for *The Six O'Clock Show*. All three were bad, but the final one was spectacularly awful. The problem was we had a monkey on the show that escaped in the studio and ended up swinging around on the lighting rig. The poor director, Danny Wiles, had no idea whether to use his cameras to follow the monkey or concentrate on what was left of the show. I was very keen to shoot the monkey, but not with the cameras. At the drinks party afterwards I was downcast. I could see my career as an editor disappearing even before it had started. I cheered up when one of the team, Tony Cohen, who was then a researcher but who became my alter ego for many years and now runs one of the world's largest independent production companies, Fremantle Media, turned up with his wife Alison and their new-born baby.

After the drinks I was sitting with the show's executive producer, Barry Cox, discussing what we could do to save it when I got an agitated phone call from Tony. He explained that he was at the hospital because the monkey, which he claimed had got drunk in hospitality, had scratched his baby and the doctors were demanding to see it. I told the story to Barry who then uttered the immortal words, 'Did this happen on London

Weekend property?' All turned out OK in the end. We never found the monkey, but Tony's son Ben suffered no unpleasant after-effects and is now a strapping, six-foot-tall 22-year-old.

Despite the pilots, and to everyone's surprise, including mine, *The Six O'Clock Show* was a smash hit and became the most watched regional programme in Britain. One week we even got into the top ten programmes in London and were sent a case of champagne by the management. Looking back now I think its success was rooted in our ability to reflect the social, economic, and political changes that were happening in London at the time and talk about them in an entertaining way. It was a time when London was experiencing a massive change in social habits, when yuppies, cocktail bars, and crêperies were replacing traditional life in the working-class areas of the capital.

Every week we did three or four stories like the *Titanic* item, stories about another side of London. Michael Aspel presented the show. He was not Michael Grade's first choice – he wanted Terry Wogan to leave the BBC to do the show – but Michael turned out to be a great success. He was very witty and managed to stand above the chaos that was sometimes around him in the studio. The show sounded very London, with a cast of character reporters on the road and in the studio that included Janet Street-Porter, the former *Mastermind* winner and London cabbie Fred Housego, and the brilliant Danny Baker, all of whom had strong London accents. The team was completed by a small, wonderfully mad, rather posh man called Andy Price, who was an on-the-road reporter.

I decided that we should capitalize on Janet's accent and turn her into a working-class heroine. The problem was that Janet wanted to be seen as being cultured. It was fine to begin with, but one evening, after she had spent all day shooting an item about pigeon fancying, she burst into my office to tell me she'd had enough of being covered in pigeon shit and didn't want to be seen that way any more. She told me she wanted the audience to know she liked 'fucking opera', as she put it. I explained that that wasn't her role, that Michael was the cultured one in the team. As a result, Janet decided to leave and we replaced her with Paula Yates.

In many ways it was the juxtaposition between Michael Aspel and Danny Baker that made the show work. One represented suave London of the Sixties and Seventies, the other uppity London of the Eighties. Remember, this was the London of Ken Livingstone 'mark one', when

he was both dangerous and very funny and was hated by the Thatcher Government of the day. *The Six O'Clock Show* was also dangerous – and live. That's why it worked. Things went wrong. One week Tony Cohen fixed up for part of the show to come live from the beach at Southend but he mixed up the tide tables and halfway through the show the tide came in and wrecked the whole thing. On another occasion a live outside link went completely wrong when it was invaded by a bunch of kids. It was only saved as a piece of television when Andy Price, who was presenting, lost his temper and picked up one of the kids and threw him across the street. This was live on television.

For me, *The Six O'Clock Show* was the first programme that was completely mine, and totally under my control. From running it I learnt much about teamwork and leadership. I learnt about encouraging everyone, from the most junior to the most senior, to be part of the team and come up with ideas, and about the importance of celebrating success – and mourning failure – together as a team. And I learnt how important the leader was to the team. These were all themes that I developed further over the next twenty years as I went on to run larger and larger groups of people. I also learnt how important it was constantly to push the system and to defy the rules, because that way you got a better end result. But taking on the rules at LWT meant fighting both the management and the unions.

These were the days when the unions ran television. Earlier in my time at LWT I had been the trade union representative for the producers and directors; in fact when I became Managing Director of the company in 1990 I had to renegotiate some of the ridiculous deals that I had won from the management when I was a union negotiator. I learned just how ridiculous the whole thing was when, on my first ever shoot at LWT, a man turned up driving a car with no one and nothing in it. I asked who he was and was told he was the electrician's driver. So where was the electrician? I asked. I was told he liked to bring his own car as well so he could claim the mileage allowance on top of having a driver. In those days all the crews demanded expensive lunches every day in fairly upmarket restaurants. If they didn't get them they made your life a misery as a researcher or a producer.

The LWT management were feeble when it came to standing up to the unions. When another friend, Andy Forrester, and I were the union

negotiators for the producers and directors we demanded a 20 per cent wage increase. We nearly fell off our chairs when the management's second offer was 18 per cent – we couldn't get out of the room fast enough. We always called it the 'pop-up toaster deal' because on top of the 18 per cent we got everything else we had asked for, including company televisions and video recorders for all our members. We reckoned if we'd asked for a pop-up toaster we would have got that as well.

It is difficult to believe now, when there are so many outstanding women working in television, but in those days there was not a single woman director working in the Current Affairs and Features Department at LWT, and very few female producers. I was determined to break this and be the first to employ a female director. I had always been a strong supporter of the women's movement and wanted to put my beliefs into practice.

I found a great director for *The Six O'Clock Show* called Vikki Barras, who went on to invent *What Not to Wear* for the BBC. She applied for the job of director and got it, but the union objected as she hadn't got the right sort of union card. The LWT management immediately folded and agreed with the union that we couldn't employ her. I thought they were gutless bastards and decided to fight.

I was on holiday in Aberdovey in West Wales at the time and was fully dressed in a wet suit and about to go windsurfing when the phone rang. It was Roy Van Gelder, LWT's Director of Human Resources, who had called to tell me that the union had said 'No' to Vikki. Luckily Gavyn Waddell, the chairman of the shop stewards' committee, was with Roy. Gavyn was the cleverest, most articulate trade unionist I have ever met. He was a natural leader of men and would have made a great senior manager. Like many of the union people at LWT he was also a hardline Tory and he eventually resigned from the union, the ACTT, when they gave money to support the 1984 miners' strike.

Fully dressed in my wet suit I demanded to talk to Gavyn. Everyone at LWT knew that, where the union was concerned, Gavyn was the person you had to get on side. After ten minutes' discussion he agreed it was time we had a woman director and that he would withdraw the objection to my employing Vikki – which meant he would tell the activists in the union to back off. So when Vikki became our first woman director it was no thanks to the management.

In general the LWT management gave in to almost every demand from the unions. This was the company that, in the mid Seventies, paid a videotape engineer £150,000 a year, resulting in the joke 'What's the difference between an Arab oil sheikh and an LWT video engineer?' Answer: 'The engineer gets London weighting.' And it was the same management who, in the ITV national strike in 1979, allowed us to picket inside the building in case it rained – no cold nights and braziers for us. As usual we won the strike when the ITV managements around Britain folded and we all went back to work with another large increase in our wages.

The television unions of those days stifled creativity and good programme making by their obsession with restrictive practices. I decided to take them on whenever I could. Sometimes I did it as an editor, and thus as part of the management; but on other occasions a few of us did it as members of the union. When the management decided that crews would have first-class travel on flights to the USA the programme makers reversed the policy at the union meeting. We argued that the effect would be no more foreign shoots, and that the losers would be the viewers.

On *The Six O'Clock Show* we were 'advised' by management not to do single-camera live links into the programme because, although the unions had agreed we could do them, the management feared they wouldn't like it. Today these happen in almost every live programme, but in 1982 they were virtually unheard of. I did them from day one. Eventually the union demanded we had a floor manager on these shoots. I simply refused.

We were also told by the management that we had to have props people on location if we wanted to use any props at all. Again, we just ignored it. When we wanted a rubber boat for Janet to use on Wimbledon Common I sent a researcher out to buy one; and when we needed some golf balls sewn into the back of a pyjama jacket for an item on snoring, Tony Cohen persuaded his reluctant wife to do the job. We ignored the union's rules whenever and wherever we could, and more often than not we got away with it. It was a lesson I have applied in every job I have had since. As I learnt later at Harvard Business School, 'No one ever succeeded in an organization by following the rules.'

In the years since Christine and I had broken up I had, as a single man in his thirties in the television business, played the field quite a lot. But

in my last year on *The Six O'Clock Show* I had struck up a new relationship with the woman who had admired my decorating all those years earlier when Christine had brought her round to our flat in Wandsworth. The relationship was based on false pretences; because she'd seen me decorating she thought I was a handyman, whereas the truth was that this was the only time in my whole life I'd ever decorated a room. By then Sue had split from her husband and had taken her two children to live in Bradford upon Avon in Somerset. I began to go down for weekends after the show ended, and Sue and I quickly decided to set up home together.

I wanted Sue to come and live in Clapham, where I was then living, but an afternoon she spent wandering across Clapham Common soon put paid to that idea. The wonderful thing about the Common was that all of life was there – including people playing chess with enormous pieces, people with model boats, and lots of sportsmen. Unfortunately there were also a lot of drug dealers, pimps, and police and Sue absolutely refused to bring her children to live there. I think she was influenced by the fact that too many of her old clients as a probation officer lived nearby.

Instead we bought a house together further west in London, in Barnes. Matthew was five and Christine four when Sue and I set up home together, and overnight I became a family man – although like most people who haven't had kids of their own I had no idea what it meant. I think Sue's sister Anne summed it up best when she described visiting us as visiting Sue, her family, and her rather strange live-in lover. And then there was Jeff.

Jeff Wright, my old friend from my early newspaper days, had been living with me in Clapham when I sold up. He had nowhere else to go, and didn't have a job at the time, so he came too. Our neighbours in Barnes must have wondered what sort of people had moved in next door. Sue always joked that between Jeff and me she had just about got one decent partner, although he wasn't much good at decorating either.

Sue went back to work as a probation officer at Wandsworth Prison. She drove there early every morning, and I agreed to drop the kids at school before going into LWT on the train. My life as a family man was beginning to take shape. And then one day I got a phone call from a Conservative MP called Jonathan Aitken, and the world changed again.

CHAPTER FOUR

A Year at TV-am

TV-am was Britain's first ever venture into commercial breakfast television. Launched in February 1983, it was an instant failure with the audience, which in turn resulted in a bloodbath on the Board and the organization plunging into a deep financial crisis. All this happened in just a matter of weeks during which 'ailing' TV-am dominated the headlines. And then I was appointed to the job of Editor-in-Chief and was told I had one task and one task only: to save the station. An interesting challenge for a 35-year-old who had been unemployed just five years earlier.

I was originally asked to join TV-am six or seven months before it was due to be launched when Michael Deakin, TV-am's Director of Programmes, rang me and asked me to go along for a chat. At the time I was still running *The Six O'Clock Show* and had no intention of giving that up. I went along out of curiosity.

Michael was a flamboyant programme maker who had had a brilliant career in documentary making at Yorkshire Television. He had made some wonderful programmes and was a great raconteur, but he knew very little about news and magazine programming, the staple diet of breakfast television. In fact, he was never intended for the role of Director of Programmes at TV-am at all and had got the job by default.

When David Frost created his consortium to bid for Britain's first ever breakfast television franchise he brought together an odd bunch of high-profile people, most of whom were either too grand, or unsuitable, to do the jobs they were allocated. David mainly concentrated on building a team of five of the most famous presenters of the day. He recruited the

69

king of the chat show, Michael Parkinson; the two most famous female newsreaders of their day, Angela Rippon from the BBC and Anna Ford from ITN; and, as a real political heavyweight, Robert Kee from BBC Current Affairs. David believed that this combination would wow the viewers with their talent and sexual chemistry. The problem with this strategy was that the people who make or break television programmes are not the on-screen talent but the production teams. A great presenter has never saved a lousy show, while there have been many successful programmes with very average presenters.

Frost's group of presenters became known as the 'Famous Five', and although they never convinced the viewers of their combined talents they certainly convinced the members of the Independent Broadcasting Authority, who, to everyone's surprise, gave the franchise to their consortium. Frost persuaded Peter Jay, the former British Ambassador to Washington, to run the whole company as Chairman and Chief Executive, completely ignoring the fact that, although he was both a former *Times* economics editor and the former presenter of the prestigious LWT current affairs programme *Weekend World*, he had no experience of being in charge of a business. Like many economists, Jay was good at writing and talking about business but was not impressive when it came to running one. In putting his production team together, Frost tended to opt for programme executives whose track records in television would impress the 'great and the good' of the IBA, rather than people who had the proven skills to deliver three and a half hours of good television every morning, week in and week out.

When the Frost group won the breakfast franchise the Director of Programmes designate was another LWT man, Nick Elliot, a former Editor of *Weekend World*. But Nick, who has spent the past ten years as a highly successful head of drama for ITV, changed his mind after the franchise was won and decided that instead of 5 a.m. starts he would stick with LWT, where he had been offered a new job as Controller of Drama and Arts. History was to show that he made a very wise decision. Michael Deakin, who was in the original Frost consortium in charge of features, was instead promoted to the top programming job, despite his total lack of experience in this area of television.

My own meeting with Deakin convinced me that my instinct to stay with LWT was the right one. Michael said he wanted me to be number

three or four in the programme hierarchy but didn't seem to be able to describe what that hierarchy was, or who was doing what. Even more worrying was that he didn't seem to know what was going to be in the programme; he appeared to believe that filling three and a half hours of television a morning was going to happen by some sort of process of osmosis. Michael only became really animated when he talked about the building in Camden in North London that TV-am was planning to occupy, a building used today by MTV but known for years as Eggcup Towers. Designed by a young Terry Farrell, who went on to become one of Britain's top post-war architects, it was clear to me that Michael loved the building a lot more than he loved the prospect of breakfast television.

With Jay as Chairman and Chief Executive and Deakin as Director of Programmes TV-am had people in the two most important jobs in the company who were peculiarly unqualified for their particular roles. But it got worse. They had also promised the Independent Broadcasting Authority that they would produce a new and intellectual approach to news and current affairs because they had a 'mission to inform'. This completely ignored the fact that the most likely viewers to be attracted to breakfast television would be heavy television watchers, disproportionately women with children. Neither group was likely to be interested in the bill of goods the Frost consortium had sold to the IBA.

With the wrong Chief Executive, the wrong Director of Programmes, and a completely unrealistic remit, you could argue that TV-am's fate was sealed long before it went on air. Turning down Michael Deakin's offer of a job was one of the best decisions I ever made.

TV-am finally went live on Tuesday 1 February 1983 and was an instant disaster. Two weeks earlier, on Monday 17 January, the BBC had launched *Breakfast Time*, their first foray into early-morning television. It was unashamedly populist and was clearly a spoiler. TV-am had won their franchise promising to bring serious news and analysis to the early morning. The BBC had arrived with keep fit, horoscopes, and cookery. But it also had a very competent production team led by Ron Neill, an inspirational editor, and two very good presenters in Frank Bough and Selina Scott. Selina certainly brought sexual chemistry to breakfast television.

Within weeks TV-am turned from a disaster into a bloodbath. Peter Jay was ousted in a boardroom coup led by the Aitken cousins, Jonathan

and Tim. Michael Deakin only survived because he supported the Aitkens, but by then he was largely discredited. The programme had gone from bad to worse and David Frost had been replaced as the main presenter by a young sports presenter called Nick Owen. Ratings barely registered and there was virtually no advertising, partly due to the lack of ratings and partly to industrial action from the actors' union Equity, who wanted a new deal for their members for breakfast television. Most serious of all – although not publicly known at the time – was that TV-am Ltd was running out of money. The company had been under-capitalized from the beginning so that all the founders could have significant shareholdings without putting up a lot of cash. The problem was that the business plan required it to be a financial success from day one or it would have to raise more cash from the shareholders. In normal circumstances that would not have been an insurmountable problem, but the particular circumstances of TV-am made it very difficult. City institutions didn't like to be publicly associated with mayhem and failure, particularly when it was all over the front pages of the newspapers day after day. And the press, smelling blood, began to stalk the wounded station.

To raise more money TV-am had to convince institutional investors that they could get the programme right, and do it quickly. They needed a new programme head, and that was where I came in. It was around this time that I got my second approach to join TV-am; this time the phone call came from Jonathan Aitken, who, although he was still the Conservative MP for Thanet, had taken over from Jay as acting Chief Executive of TV-am, while former British Railways boss Dick Marsh, an ex-Labour MP, had become Chairman.

Aitken invited me to lunch at his grand house in Lord North Street in Westminster – the very same house his bankruptcy trustees sold eighteen years later to help pay off his debts after he lost his libel case against *The Guardian* and Granada Television (he was later sentenced to eighteen months in jail after pleading guilty to perjury and perverting the course of justice during the case). I remember the lunch very well. Most of all I remember the incredibly camp butler who served the lunch Kenneth Williams style. Julian and Sandy, the outrageously camp characters from *Round the Horne*, the popular radio programme of the 1960s, had nothing on Jonathan's butler.

While I sat intrigued by the butler, Jonathan set about trying to per-

suade me to join TV-am as Editor-in-Chief. He had approached me at just the right time. Despite the success of *The Six O'Clock Show* I was looking for a change after running the programme for eighteen months. And I was particularly incensed that LWT had refused to give me a company car whilst giving one to the Editor of *Weekend World*, a programme I had previously worked on as a producer. After all, *The Six O'Clock Show* added ratings while *Weekend World* lost them. My programme made money for the company, his lost it. Wasn't this supposed to be commercial television? Looking back now it is ridiculous that I decided my whole future on something as trivial as a company car; but I've never been a believer in grand career plans. My view has always been that you take the opportunities as they come and they either work for you or they don't.

I was intrigued by the challenge that the chaos at TV-am offered. It never crossed my mind that I wouldn't succeed in turning it around. As the novelist Maeve Haran, a former colleague on *The Six O'Clock Show*, always said about me, the only reason I had turned out to be successful in life was that I didn't have enough imagination to contemplate failure. I suspect there's some truth in that.

With all the confidence of a brash 35-year-old, and despite the fact that I was a relative newcomer to the television industry, I had no doubt I could make TV-am into a success. My view was that what was needed was, firstly, a programme vision that appealed to the sort of audience likely to watch breakfast television and, secondly, a programme team who could deliver it. In turn that meant I would need to bring in new people while also trying to convince a disillusioned staff that, together, we could succeed. As it turned out, the job was harder than that – but not a lot harder.

What I thought was a lunchtime chat with Jonathan Aitken was actually an interview, job offer, and negotiation all in one. He offered to double my current salary, buy out my pension, put me on a ratings-based bonus scheme, and, importantly in the circumstances, give me a smart company car. If everything worked out I would, by my standards in 1983, be comparatively well off for the first time in my life. Of course what I didn't know that day was that TV-am was rapidly running out of cash and that for me to get everything Jonathan was offering would be a long and hard fight.

Towards the end of the lunch Michael Deakin turned up and pretended that I would be working for him. I made it very clear that if I was to take the job I would have to have complete charge of all the programming. He was effectively redundant. I found out later that Jonathan was determined he wouldn't let me leave his house that day without my signing some sort of letter committing myself to TV-am. I think he was pretty desperate to get someone who knew about magazine programming, and the BBC's Ron Neill had already turned him down. Jonathan succeeded and I signed a letter, although I suspect what I actually signed had no legal value whatsoever. Jonathan was nervous that I would go home and change my mind so as I left the lunch he invited Sue and me for dinner on the following Sunday evening so we could cement the deal. This was clearly his attempt to persuade Sue that I should join TV-am. I persuaded her to come to the dinner, if only to meet the butler.

We duly turned up and were introduced to Jonathan's now famous wife Lolicia, the blonde who didn't pay the Paris hotel bill in his notorious libel case against Granada Television and *The Guardian*. She clearly had no interest in us and obviously didn't want to be there. It was a dull evening but two things happened that have had a profound effect on my life since then.

Firstly I met Clive Jones at the dinner. Today Clive is Chief Executive of ITV News; back then he had just been appointed Editor of TV-am by Jonathan and would work directly to me as Editor-in-Chief. It was the combination of Clive and myself that was to turn the whole place around, a combination of my ideas and leadership and his capabilities as a producer. Clive had an amazing capacity for work. A few weeks after I joined TV-am I reckoned the programme was still pretty awful. I said to him that it was only going to get better if one of us got in there at five every morning and drove the show from the gallery five days a week. I added that I thought it should be him, and that's what he did – week in and week out until it had improved. Over the years Clive and I have worked together on many occasions and he has turned out to be a good and trusted friend. In life there are some people whom you can be certain will always be there for you. Clive is one of those people.

But the more important event that night came when Sue and I left the house in Lord North Street. We'd only been living together for a few months and we were still learning about each other. As the butler shut

the front door she turned to me and said that if I wanted the job I should take it but that whatever I did I should never trust those people, referring to Jonathan and Lolicia.

In the years since I've learnt on many occasions that Sue's judgement of people is better than mine. I regularly, and naively, take people at face value. She doesn't. She knew instinctively that night that these were not our sort of people, that they came from different backgrounds, had different values, and played in a different world, one in which friendship and trust were commodities that were bought and sold. According to Sue, what Jonathan said and promised were not to be believed – a fact well and truly established at the Old Bailey sixteen years later.

I went back to LWT and told everyone I was leaving. As a result I was summoned to a meeting with LWT's then Director of Programmes John Birt, who had been promoted into the job when Michael Grade left to go to America in 1981. John told me that if I left there would be no way back into the company, ironic given that seven years later I became its Chief Executive. However, I stuck to my guns and told him I was definitely going, and after that we had a pleasant chat.

John asked me who was going to be the Chief Executive of TV-am. I told him exactly what Jonathan had told me: that he, Jonathan, was going to give up his parliamentary seat and become the full-time CEO. A few days later the story appeared in *The Guardian*; Jonathan immediately announced that it wasn't true and that if the paper didn't withdraw the article he would sue. Months later a sheepish John Birt rang me at TV-am to tell me he was helping *The Guardian* in their battle with Jonathan over the story and asked if I recollected what I had told him. I suddenly realized that he had been *The Guardian*'s source.

I had the usual LWT send-off with speeches and videos that were characteristically rude – no prisoners were ever taken at LWT leaving events. Danny Baker, one of the presenters on *The Six O'Clock Show*, ended the video sitting in a trap in a public toilet reading a limerick that went: 'There was a young fellow called Dyke/Largely did what he liked/Went to TV-am/Never heard of again/Fucking well served him right'. When I read my leaving card I also discovered that my immediate boss, David Cox, LWT's head of Current Affairs, had written in it 'Fuck off Dyke and good riddance'. When I returned to LWT just four years later as his boss I didn't need to remind him of this friendly message. He remembered it.

By the time I turned up for work at TV-am in May 1983 Jonathan Aitken had stepped down as Chief Executive and his cousin Timothy had taken on the job part time while continuing to run the family's merchant bank, Aitken Hume. Ratings and advertising were still non-existent and if anything the programme had got worse. I'll never forget watching it at home the week before I joined when Yehudi Menuhin was brought on to play the violin live. I sat there amazed. What producer in their right mind could possibly have believed that people rushing to work or struggling to get the kids to school had the time or the inclination to watch a classical violinist for five minutes in the morning?

When I was appointed Editor-in-Chief, TV-am had announced that I was to be its saviour and, for the first time in my life, I was all over the newspapers. My appointment even made the television news, much to my mother's excitement. TV-am had also announced that I would re-launch the whole weekday programme three weeks after joining. So what the previous management had got wrong in eighteen months of planning I was expected to fix in just three weeks!

On my first day at TV-am I had arranged to take Michael Parkinson out to lunch. Michael was one of the few successes at the station, largely because he had himself taken charge of the programming at the weekends as well as presenting the shows with his wife Mary. Michael is a rare breed in television: a great interviewer and presenter who is also a very good producer and motivator of the team around him. Melvyn Bragg is another. We had a pleasant lunch discussing the shambles that was TV-am and what could be done about it.

I went back to the office only to discover later in the afternoon that Tim Aitken had sacked two of the Famous Five without telling me. Both Angela Rippon and Anna Ford had been summarily dismissed for something they had done on the programme on the day Peter Jay left. They had said that 'treachery' was happening at TV-am and this had understandably upset the Aitkens because it implied that they were the perpetrators. Tim decided to get his revenge on the two women on my very first day by firing both of them. His nickname of Pol Pot was born that day. But both women got their revenge. First Anna very publicly threw a glass of red wine over Jonathan at a smart cocktail party and made sure it was in all the papers; and later both of them threatened to sue the company for breach of contract and were paid off.

My eventful first day ended when I went into the TV-am car park to collect my first company car only to find a battered BMW that had quite clearly been in a recent pile-up. I drove it home but got stopped by the police on the way on suspicion of driving an unroadworthy vehicle. So much for company cars! Luckily I didn't keep that car for long as one of the games we played at TV-am was executive car swap. Every time Tim fired another executive I would pinch his car and pass mine on to Clive Jones. We both ended up with very smart cars.

After the turmoil of my first day I already knew that the car wasn't the only thing that wasn't living up to Jonathan Aitken's promises. On the second day things only got worse. Overnight Michael Parkinson had decided he would go into battle to defend Anna Ford and Angela Rippon and had announced to the world that if they went he would go too.

Given that Michael produced and presented the only vaguely successful part of TV-am, it would not have been good news if he had left. My job was to persuade him not to go. But like so much at TV-am, even this descended into black comedy. I sat in my office with Michael, his wife Mary, and their agent John Webber trying to persuade him to stay. We were joined by the new Chairman, Dick Marsh, who had come in to help out. The trouble was that Dick had had a vasectomy that morning and every time he leaned forward to emphasize to Michael how important he was to TV-am he would end up clutching his crotch in agony.

Distracted by Dick Marsh's discomfort I didn't make much progress with Michael; in the end it was Tim Aitken who persuaded him to stay by the classic combination of flattery and bribery. He offered Michael a seat on the TV-am Board. It had clearly annoyed the other four members of the Famous Five that David Frost was the only one of their number who had a board seat. Now Michael was to join him. So Anna and Angela were forgotten and Michael announced to the scrum of reporters and photographers outside Eggcup Towers that he was to stay after all.

After the chaotic events of my first two days I had to get down to the programme relaunch itself. The problem I faced was that not only was it the wrong programme, as the appetite for a serious news and current affairs programme at that time in the morning was very limited, it was also badly produced. The news didn't start on time, the items were too long, and frankly it was boring. It had no character, no humour, and there was no team feeling amongst the presenters.

By then Clive Jones was in charge and was desperate to make changes to improve things. I told him his job was not to make the programme better but, if possible, to make it even worse, so that when we did unveil the much promised relaunch the contrast would be that much greater. I think those were the worst three weeks of his life in television.

The problem we both faced was the staff. There were some very talented young researchers and producers being led by much less talented people who were being paid far more money; but the one thing that virtually all of them shared was that they were shattered. They had joined with such high hopes: TV-am had advertised for staff with a picture of the Famous Five saying 'Join us and make history'. They had worked ridiculously hard only to find themselves and their programme publicly ridiculed. Four months into 'making history', most of them were desperate. They were trying to leave in their droves; many were very emotional. It was certainly different from LWT, which was full of smart, funny, and flamboyant people. In the end, Clive and I sat down together and worked out which members of staff we thought we could save and which were either so hopeless or so damaged by the experience of TV-am that they ought to leave. We settled on a list of sixty-odd people who had to go, and by one means or another we managed to lose all but two over the next six months.

The great thing about crisis – and TV-am was a very public crisis – is that while most people collapse, a few blossom. Lynn Faulds Wood, the consumer editor, turned up smiling in my office very proud of what she'd achieved. I agreed with her and doubled the number of slots she had in the schedule. Mark Damazer, then a young producer and now Deputy Head of News at the BBC, and Adam Boulton, now a great success at Sky News, had managed to produce some decent political coverage so I invented a morning political slot for them called 'Spotlight', edited by a talented producer called Andy Webb. I also brought in some people from outside. We desperately needed people who understood popular journalism and what the audience actually cared about, as opposed to what Peter Jay and Michael Deakin thought they ought to care about. I had known Peter McHugh since we worked together on the Newcastle *Journal* in the mid Seventies. He was, and still is, one of the best judges of a popular story I've ever met. He was working on the *Daily Mail* and hating it, so it wasn't difficult to persuade him to come. He's been a very successful

Director of Programmes at GMTV for the past decade. I also persuaded Eve Pollard – another journalist who understood the target audience – to leave her job as Assistant Editor of the *Sunday People* and join the features department at TV-am, promising her two on-screen gossip slots a week and that we'd teach her about television. She ended up as Features Editor before going back to Fleet Street, where she was editor of the *Sunday Mirror* between 1987 and 1991 and of the *Sunday Express* from 1991 to 1995.

Clive and I also put together a completely new team of on-screen presenters in a remarkably short period of time. Nick Owen had already become the male anchor, and we poached Anne Diamond from BBC's *Nationwide* to be the female lead. Clive had spotted a female weather presenter on Tyne Tees Television called Wincy Willis, so I phoned her and she joined us within a week. We brought former ITN newsreader Gordon Honeycombe out of semi-retirement to read the news and later we were joined by Lynn Faulds Wood's husband John Stapleton, who left *Newsnight* to do our serious political interviewing and a few bits beside. He's never forgiven me for asking him to read out the newspaper bingo numbers every morning.

I remember taking the new team of presenters out to lunch one day. I explained the scale of the problem we faced but how exciting it would be if we succeeded. I also warned them that if it worked they would become famous and at least one of them would become a monster. Of course it's not for me to say if that is what happened to any of them.

The relaunch went fairly well and we managed to increase our peak quarter-hour ratings in the first week from the pathetically small 0.2 (i.e. 0.2 per cent of the whole potential TV audience) to a not quite so pathetically small 0.3. We claimed a 50 per cent increase in ratings in the press and, for just about the first time, 'ailing' TV-am got some positive responses. We never mentioned that these figures were so small that, taking into account the margin for error in the research process, it was still quite possible we had no viewers at all.

It was around this time that we introduced Diana Dors and her diet on TV-am. Every Friday she would turn up and weigh in; over sixteen weeks she managed to lose 5 stone. One of my better ideas was that one Friday we should pull onto the set the amount of weight she had lost in lard. Seeing a pallet full of animal fat next to Diana had a dramatic effect.

Whether Diana actually lost all that weight I was never too sure. Clive and I always suspected she'd started her first weigh-in with a lead belt around her stomach and had then taken off one of the weights week by week. Either way, it was our most successful item and Fridays became our best day in terms of ratings, thanks to Diana.

When the diet was coming to an end Diana kept promising to tell the viewers the secret of how she had lost so much weight. We were all worried that she was intending to plug a commercial product, which would get us into real trouble with the Independent Broadcasting Authority; given that we already had enough problems with the IBA I was determined to stop her. So on the day of her final slot I told Clive that under no circumstances was she to take anything onto the set that could resemble a commercial product. Clive duly did the check, but I'm afraid Diana was far too smart for all of us.

As she sat down with John Stapleton for her usual Friday diet chat on the sofa she suddenly reached into her bra, which in Diana's case was pretty large, as her bosom had always been her trademark, and pulled out a cheap-looking calculator. She then announced that this Diana Dors Calorie Counter was the secret of her diet and that it was available for only £5.99 if people wrote directly to her at TV-am. Over the next week we received at least ten thousand letters from people wanting to buy the calculator, but I was so angry I refused to give them to Diana, arguing that they belonged to TV-am, not to her. She even took us to court to try to get them. She didn't win, she never got the letters, and the viewers didn't get their personally signed Diana Dors Calorie Counter.

Of course Diana had been a big star in the 1950s and 1960s, Britain's answer to Marilyn Monroe according to the tabloids. Although her best days were long gone she was still a massive personality and the public were still very much interested in her. I asked her agent once if she would be willing to present a show for TV-am on Sunday mornings. He came back and said that, being a Roman Catholic, her Sunday morning mass was very important to her, to which I said I assumed that meant she wouldn't do it. He replied, 'No, what it means is that it is going to cost you a lot of money.' Instead I asked David Frost to do the programme, thus bringing about the birth of *Frost on Sunday*, a programme that was still running (though on the BBC) twenty years later.

Diana died of cancer within a few months and because she was a

TV-am star we decided to do a special programme about her on the Saturday morning, the day after she had died. We invited on her friend, the singer Jess Conrad, who decided to use the opportunity to plug his latest record, and Barbara Windsor, who, like Diana, had also been a busty blonde film star. She was delightful about Diana on the set but when she came off she turned to me and said: 'You know I hated her, don't you?'

But while Diana made a difference to TV-am it was children's program-ming that proved to be the turning point for the station. In the June half-term week we ran half an hour of children's programming every day at 9 a.m. It was made by a very talented producer, Anne Wood, who later went on to fame and fortune by creating the Teletubbies. At this time Anne had discovered a talented puppeteer called David Claridge, who played a series of characters, the most important of whom was called Roland Rat. Little did I know then that the rat would haunt me for the next twenty years, with *The Sun* describing me as 'Roland Rat's dad' on more than one occasion. In this one half-term week our peak quarter-hour ratings increased by two points, and it happened when Roland was on. I decided there and then that our big chance for turning everything around would come in the school holidays in the summer.

It is important to understand the difference between David Claridge and Roland. David was a miserable, rather dull man who only came alive when he put his hand up this puppet's rear end. He then suddenly became clever and witty. As with so many puppeteers, I am not at all sure which was the real David, himself or the character he played. I certainly preferred the latter.

As David, he came to me one day to complain that Roland and his mate Kevin the Gerbil hadn't got an office. I looked at him as if he was mad and tried to explain that they weren't real and that, being puppets, they didn't need an office. David was having none of it: to him, they were real. In the end I relented, had the broom cupboard cleared out, and handed it over to Roland and Kevin.

On another occasion, when we were making Roland Rat in Switzer-land, David fell on the ski slopes and as a result took to his hotel room. Later that day the floor manager looked in to see if he was OK only to find David, Roland, and Kevin snuggled up in bed together. David was fast asleep, with Roland on one side of him and Kevin on the other.

But the funniest experience dealing with David Claridge came after the rat had saved TV-am – an event that led to the famous joke that it was the first time a rat had saved a sinking ship. By then Roland was our biggest star, so it clearly mattered when we got a call to the press office one Friday telling us that the *Daily Star* planned to run a story on their front page the following day in which they would claim that Claridge had hosted a Soho club called 'Skin Two' for rubber and latex fetishists. Almost anywhere else I've worked this would have led to a great crisis; but TV-am was in permanent crisis, and when Tim Aitken, Clive Jones, and I met to discuss this prospective story we couldn't stop laughing. Imagine it: the saviour of the station, the man behind the most popular children's characters of the day, involved in a sexual fetishists' club.

In the end we got lucky. I was deputed to phone the programme department of the Independent Broadcasting Authority to give them the news, but it was the day their Director was leaving and everyone had been out for a rather long leaving lunch at which the alcohol had clearly flowed generously. When I got through and explained the problem all I got from the other end was someone shouting rather loudly at me saying that he wasn't bothered about that sort of thing, and then the phone went dead.

Our luck held. The *Daily Star* didn't run the story on their front page after all; it was replaced by a story about Billy Connolly's divorce instead, and Claridge, Roland, and the rubber story were relegated to page seven or nine, where they duly disappeared.

In planning the TV-am schedule for the summer of 1983 Clive Jones and I decided to send the Rat out on the road. Anne Wood bought a 1957 Ford Anglia, which we painted bright pink, and off they went to produce a half-hour show every morning for six weeks. The difficult question was what to do with the other three hours in a period notoriously short of news.

Here we had the idea of doing the programme live from the seaside beaches of Britain. In fact it was the idea of a woman called Juliet Blake, who came looking for a job. We took her idea and gave her a job as compensation. Juliet now lives in Los Angeles but is still a good friend. We were lucky that it turned out to be a scorching summer, but that also had its downside as Eggcup Towers had no air conditioning and we were all dying from the heat. The story going the rounds at TV-am that boiling

summer was that the Board had had to choose between air conditioning and an executive flat when planning the building and they'd chosen the latter.

To produce *By the Seaside*, as I imaginatively called the idea, we needed an outside broadcast (OB) unit, a star, a producer, a director, and a union agreement in a matter of just a few weeks. In most organizations that would have been difficult to deliver, but at TV-am anything was always possible. In a matter of weeks we had them all.

We found an old OB unit sitting unused outside Ewart's studio complex in Wandsworth. The trouble was that Keith Ewart, who owned the studios, wanted £12,000 for it and TV-am was out of cash. I went to the finance director, who refused to sanction it; so instead I rang Tim Aitken, who was on holiday in the South of France. He was wonderfully pragmatic when I told him the finance director's view. 'Silly bastard. We're going bust anyway.' So I agreed to buy the OB unit and sent someone over to collect it. Luckily we managed to get it out of the yard, towing it because the engine didn't work, without actually handing over any cash. I think it was some years before Mr Ewart's cheque actually cleared.

Now a £12,000 OB unit isn't exactly television professionalism at its best. As John Stapleton always reminds me, it looked more like a Mr Whippy van than a traditional OB vehicle; in winter months you could only get the antenna up to broadcast the signal if you thawed it out with an electric fire first. But for *By the Seaside* it was fine.

For a presenter I turned to Chris Tarrant, whom I'd seen on *Tiswas*, the outrageous and brilliant ITV children's show, on Saturday mornings. I loved Tarrant's anarchic style. I met him and his agent Paul Vaughan one night for dinner and as I sat down at the table Chris just looked at me and said, 'Oh, so you're Mr TV fucking wonderman.' He was great to work with and became a good friend; I even appeared on his *This is Your Life*.

Chris's great advantage as a presenter is that he actually likes and admires ordinary people, the people so many television presenters dismiss. My friends John Stapleton and Lynn Faulds Wood are the same. Go on holiday with them and they never tire of signing autographs or chatting to the people who come up to them. They don't see it as a chore.

Tarrant was brilliant on *By the Seaside*, whether it was dancing with the local mayor and with someone dressed up as a gorilla on the beach

at Blackpool, or jokingly throwing fish back at the audience on the beach in Great Yarmouth after they'd started throwing them at him. In Brighton a rather strange man carrying a plastic bag wandered onto the set and stayed there. We later discovered he was a patient at a local institution, but Chris treated him as just another member of the team. This sort of television seemed a long way from Peter Jay's 'mission to inform', but it was original and funny and the audiences watched in large numbers.

When *By the Seaside* was over Chris came in to Eggcup Towers one day to fill in his expenses. I saw him from my office and told him to cancel everything he'd planned for the day because we needed him for our 'Stub it out with TV-am' anti-smoking campaign. We sent him straight out round the streets of London with a pair of scissors and a bucket of water: his job was to cut people's cigarettes in half and to threaten them with the bucket of water if they resisted. Not only did he agree, he actually soaked a couple of people, which they didn't regard as at all funny.

To produce *By the Seaside* we used one of our existing producers, Sally Bruce Lockhart, combined with Juliet Blake, whose idea it had been in the first place. For a director I got an Irishman called John McColgan, who has since become one of the richest men I know after he and his girlfriend, Moya Doherty, helped to create *Riverdance*. The trouble was that because McColgan was coming straight from Ireland he didn't have the relevant union ticket, and these were the days when the trade unions controlled commercial television. They blacked him for weeks.

I was so desperate to find a director that in the end I persuaded Noel Green, a friend from LWT, to moonlight for us. For one week he did *By the Seaside* in the mornings and worked for LWT Entertainment in the afternoons and evenings. Later Bob Merrilees, another person I brought from LWT, took over.

The combination of Roland Rat and Chris Tarrant live from the seaside turned the ratings around. After about three weeks of the summer holidays I was in Florida on vacation when I got a phone call from Clive Jones. He was so excited he just shouted down the phone: 'Our ratings have passed the BBC!' In three months we'd created a new show, done something totally different for the summer, reinvigorated the staff, and now we'd sailed past the BBC. I never doubted we could do it.

So we turned the ratings round, but soon we discovered that these weren't our only problem. We were always running out of money. On at

My mum and dad on their wedding day in 1939. They got married at their local church – St John's in Morning Lane, Hackney, which was opposite the newsagents run by my grandparents.

My mum with my two brothers (Ian and Howard) and me (bottom left) in the back garden of our house in Cerne Close, Hayes, in the summer of 1948. My parents bought the house for £650 in 1945; today it would sell for £250,000.

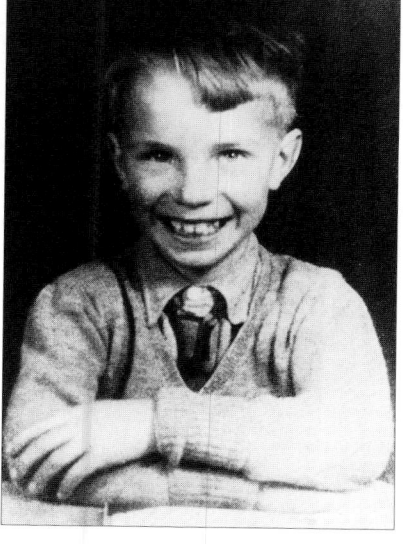

Aged seven, a pupil at Yeading Primary School in Hayes. Nearly fifty years later I was invited back to open the new school hall.

Top: Form 1b at Hayes Grammar School in 1958 (back row, fourth from right). I once came bottom of the whole year in the end-of-term exams.

Above: The Hayes Grammar 'upper sixth' in 1965 (sixth from right, second row from top). I left there to become a trainee manager at Marks & Spencer but was fired after three horrible months.

Left: In my last year at school.

Above: My leaving party when I left the *Hillingdon Mirror* in 1969. The paper itself was closed down in the 1970s.

Left: Outside 1, Briggs Street, York – the house I bought for £1,200 when I went to university. By then the beard and hair were getting longer.

Below: With my dog Jake on the North Yorkshire moors in 1972. By then I was a politics student at York University. In my time there I sued the local evening paper for libel.

Above: The Six O'Clock Show team at LWT in 1982: I'm standing behind Janet Street-Porter and Michael Aspel. This was my first job running my own show, and the programme was ground-breaking in many ways.

Left: The cartoon from my leaving card when I left LWT in 1983 to spend a bizarre year at TV-am. My team gave me the characteristic LWT send-off with very rude speeches.

least three occasions we sent out little notes to the staff saying 'Due to computer error your salary won't be in the bank this Friday'. Everyone knew that this meant that there was another financial crisis. In fact for a long period we paid no bills at all and ended up with a pile of writs in one corner of the finance department. We didn't mind writs because we could ignore them for twenty-eight days, and at a place like TV-am twenty-eight days was a long time.

The failure to pay bills did give us some problems. Our newsagent refused to deliver papers, something of a problem for a news organization, and the taxi firm refused to deliver guests for the morning show, which made producing three and a half hours of television difficult. However, we managed to find alternative suppliers for both. Worst of all was the day the London Electricity Board turned up while we were live on air one morning and said they would cut us off if we didn't pay their bill within half an hour. Breakfast television without newspapers and guests was one thing; breakfast television without electricity was impossible. We managed to persuade them to postpone the decision for twenty-four hours and someone managed to find some cash from somewhere.

Running a television station without cash sounds funny today, but at the time it made life very difficult for everyone at TV-am. Researchers who had signed for hotel bills found bailiffs coming round to their houses to claim their possessions; regional correspondents were forced to use public phone boxes because the office phone had been cut off; and crews would turn up at hotels to find TV-am had no credit because the last bill hadn't been paid. One day John Stapleton asked Jonathan Aitken if things were getting better. He replied 'Let's face it, we're still one step ahead of the sheriff.'

For those of us who lived through those days it was ridiculous but exciting, an experience we were unlikely to have again. My favourite moment came when our advertising agency said they would stop producing our promotions unless we paid up. I pointed out to them that would mean they would be moved out of one creditors' pile and into another. They asked what I meant. I explained that while one pile might, just might, get paid there was no chance of our paying the people who had withdrawn their services. They carried on making the promotions, and in the end everyone got paid.

It was around this time that we decided to open the mysterious filing

cabinet that Tim Aitken had found in his office. There were no keys so no one had bothered with it for months, but in the end curiosity got the better of us and we forced it open with a crowbar. Inside there were just bottles and bottles and bottles of pink champagne. We never found out who had bought them.

And then there were the mornings when the overnight editors used to come in to complain that Jonathan Aitken had been on the phone again in the middle of the night demanding that some unknown Arab should be interviewed on the show the following day. Once or twice they even got on. Much later we discovered why. The Arabs had put up all the money for the Aitken shares in TV-am and thus were, in effect, major shareholders, even though that was illegal at the time. Jonathan hadn't even told Timothy where the money had come from.

Summer moved into the autumn and on to the winter of 1984. The use of Roland Rat and Chris Tarrant had worked, the viewers who had found TV-am in the summer had stayed with us, and our ratings continued to rise. We consistently beat the BBC, which then did what the BBC always did. When they were winning they crowed about ratings, when they were losing they decided ratings didn't matter and we were too downmarket. It was a theme I was to come across on many occasions in my life in television.

But although the ratings were good the amount of advertising was still pitiful. I recollect that at one time we only had three regular advertisers, Ponds Cold Cream, Edam cheese, and Wall's pork sausages. In those circumstances I was concerned when Lynn Faulds Wood wanted to use her consumer slot to expose Wall's sausages for containing too much water. We both agreed that perhaps that was a story we should put into the drawer for a few months.

In early 1984 Tim Aitken asked me to become a member of the Board of TV-am Ltd. Today I would have declined and pointed out that, by my reckoning, we were close to trading insolvently. Back then I didn't know what trading insolvently meant, so I joined.

Unlike his cousin Jonathan, I grew to like and trust Tim Aitken. The grandson of Lord Beaverbrook, he was short, aggressive, and a lot of fun. He was also prepared to take risks. Anyone who knows me could see why I liked him. But there were problems – he spent most of his time at the

Aitken Hume Bank, knew absolutely nothing about running a television company, and had a pathological hatred of the trade unions. He relished being known as Pol Pot, and by and large he was unpopular with the staff, although those who got to know him grew to respect his qualities as a fighter. He had been brought up in North America and, despite his background, no more liked the British Establishment than I did.

The financial crisis at TV-am came to a head early in 1984 when we went back to our shareholders, including our two big new investors, Fleet Holdings, who owned the Express Group, and the Australian broadcasting magnate Kerry Packer, to ask for more investment because we'd run out of cash again. Tim decided we needed to demonstrate to the shareholders that we were a strong management team; we could do that by changing all the staff rosters, which would both save money and show we could stand up to the unions. That way, he believed, the shareholders would back us.

Clive and I agreed with the strategy and set about trying to deliver it. We cajoled and persuaded dozens of union members that it was necessary if we were to survive. In the end it all came down to one union meeting at which most of the staff would have a vote. The proposition was simple. If they voted in favour of the changes we would get the extra money and survive; if they voted against we would go into liquidation.

Tim Aitken decided he wanted to talk to the staff to warn them of the consequences of voting against. Given that he was so disliked by the union members, Clive and I reckoned this would probably lose us the vote. So as Tim's secretary, Jane Stanton, went round putting up the notices announcing Tim's address to the staff we had people going round taking them down. In the end Tim backed down but accused Clive and me of 'hooligan management'.

On the day of the vote all the management parked their cars outside the building in case the vote went against and the company went into liquidation. At least they could get home if that happened. Tim Aitken cleared his office, packed up all his pictures, and invited the union shop steward in to see what he was doing. I worked out that TV-am still owed me about £30,000 so I looked around for something I could take and then sell to get my money if all went wrong. I reckoned the only thing the company actually owned was the barge at the back of Eggcup Towers on the Grand Union Canal, so I pinched the keys. I somehow had this

mad idea that, as the company went into liquidation, I would chug away down the canal with its only saleable asset.

In the end the vote went our way and TV-am was saved yet again. This time, as it turned out, it was saved for the longer term. The shareholders put in the extra few million that was needed; I even put in the £10,000 that TV-am had finally paid me to buy out my LWT pension fund. I thought that as I'd never had that much money in my life I'd gamble it. I was the only person who had not taken part in the earlier financing exercises who was allowed to invest at this stage. Just a few years later that £10,000 was worth £360,000 when the company was floated on the stock exchange.

In early 1984, soon after the latest refinancing, Kerry Packer turned up to visit the station. Rumour had it that he was under investigation for something or other in Australia and had decided to spend some time in the UK. He brought with him the man who was his nominee on the TV-am Board, Bruce Gyngell. Packer was a legendary media figure in Australia and was known as one of the world's top gamblers. I once asked Packer why he'd invested in TV-am. He replied that for him it was just a punt and that he regularly won and lost more than the two million pounds he'd invested in TV-am at the race track or in the casino on a single day.

One day he came into my office, told me how impressed he was by what I had achieved, and asked me what was needed to really finish the job. He assured me that anything I said would be confidential; naively I believed him. I explained that, much as I liked and admired Tim, we needed a full-time Chief Executive, not one who spent half his time running a merchant bank. He thanked me and then, as I found out later, went straight in to see Tim Aitken to tell him that 'Dyke says I should sack you.' So much for a confidential conversation.

In the end it was agreed that Tim Aitken would go, but only if he was promoted to Chairman and if Bruce Gyngell stayed in the UK to run the business as Chief Executive. The trouble was that when the shareholder representatives came to carry out this plan at the board meeting no one had told the current Chairman, Dick Marsh, that he was on his way out. In a story I have heard David Frost tell on numerous occasions, the senior members of the Board whispered to each other at the meeting, asking each other very politely if they had had a word with Dick. When they

discovered no one had done so, Ian Irvine of Fleet had to tell him in front of the whole Board that his services were no longer required and that Tim, who was sitting opposite him, would be taking his job. David Frost, in a way that only David could, then proposed a vote of thanks to Dick for all he'd done for TV-am. An unusual way for a company to change its chairman.

The arrival of Bruce Gyngell was the beginning of the end for me. He was a delightful man but had odd hobbies like numerology, walking on hot coals, and encouraging everyone to wear pink. Bruce, although technically a married man when he arrived in Britain, was very much into women. I remember him distinctly clapping his arm around Adrian Moore, the Director of Production, and saying that he was relying on him to tell him which of the many attractive women at TV-am were an easy lay. Not that Adrian, a happily married man who didn't play around, would have known. This same man later became very friendly with Mrs Thatcher, married Kathy Rowan, one of the producers at TV-am who had earlier been at LWT, and within five years was lecturing Britain on its public morals.

Bruce and I went out to lunch on his first day and he insisted on applying numerology to our respective birth dates. He assured me that the result confirmed that we were going to get on wonderfully well together. I was gone within a month.

We fell out when he started telling me what should go in the programme. I pointed out to him that the programme was fine and doing well; when I had agreed to join TV-am Jonathan Aitken had assured me that I would have complete control over the station's output. I also pointed out that the problems of TV-am were no longer to do with ratings but were business difficulties and that it was his job to sort them out. What I didn't know was that Bruce wasn't a particularly smart businessman. His reputation in Australia was based on the fact that he had been the first ever presenter on Australian television.

To emphasize the point that I was in charge of the programme I called a meeting of my senior team, who told Bruce the same thing. We had turned TV-am's ratings around and we weren't having this upstart Australian telling us what to do. Within a year most of the people at that meeting had gone. People like John Stapleton, Lynn Faulds Wood, Clive Jones, Peter McHugh, Andy Webb and others were all out, and over the next

few years we were all systematically airbrushed out of the history of TV-am by Bruce. It was like being part of Stalin's Politburo when the political winds changed.

I left because Gyngell wanted me out and I couldn't be bothered to fight him. We'd achieved what I went to TV-am to achieve. Ratings and staff morale were unrecognizable compared with twelve months earlier, and I had been offered the role of Director of Programmes at TVS, another of the new ITV companies that had launched in 1982. Clive Jones joined me there within a couple of months as Controller of News, Current Affairs and Sport.

The twelve months I spent at TV-am were the most bizarre, the most stimulating, and the funniest of my life. I have never laughed so much. I made more good friends in that extraordinary period than at any other time. I learnt an enormous amount – not much about television but a lot about business for the first time, about leadership, and about life in a pressure cooker. I learnt that most people hated crisis but that I relished it. Most of all I learnt two things that were to influence what I did and how I did it for the next twenty years.

Firstly, I learnt that in crisis people would follow you if you led from the front and communicated openly and honestly with them. This I did instinctively, but up until TV-am I had only been able to see it work with small programme teams. Now I had tried it with a bigger organization and it had worked again.

Secondly, I learnt that if you demand, and are given, the whole train set to play with, it doesn't last for ever. In the end, someone will always want their train set back, or someone else will want to play with it.

Seven years later, in 1991, I organized the revenge of those who had turned TV-am around only to be thrown out of the company for their troubles. As Chief Executive of LWT, I put together the Sunrise consortium made up of LWT, Disney, the Guardian Group, and Scottish Television to bid for, and win, the ITV breakfast franchise for GMTV.

On 31 December 1992, TV-am closed down. Game set and match to us.

A cartoon published in 1984 after I left TV-am.
The same cartoon with the words changed could have been used
in 1994 when I left LWT and in 2004 when I left the BBC.

TVS and Back to LWT

If you believed the tabloid press, TV-am was saved by a combination of Roland Rat and me, in that order, so my departure from TV-am got quite a lot of publicity, although not as much as Roland when he left a year later to join the BBC.

I was now unemployed, because my next job wasn't yet vacant. By this time Michael Grade, my old boss at LWT, had announced that he was coming back from the USA to become Controller of BBC One and he rang a few times asking me to join him to make some shows for the BBC. I had decided by then that I wanted to stay in management and didn't want to go back to being a producer. When I look back now I think that was a mistake and that I stopped producing too early in my career. Whenever I go back and get involved in a production, as I did when I presented *Have I Got News For You* three months after leaving the BBC, I realize how much I miss it.

I had been approached to join TVS, another new ITV company, this one based in the South of England. The man who had asked me to join was the Managing Director, James Gatward, who was planning to oust the incumbent Director of Programmes and replace him with me. He hadn't quite succeeded in this when he and I first met. Eventually the deed was done and my predecessor left.

In September 1974 I became Director of Programmes at TVS and the family moved out of London and down south. Sue was six months pregnant so it was not exactly an ideal moment to move, but we found a big Victorian house that we thought, with a bit of work, we could make into a home. I remember the move well because Sue booked the removal firm

from an advert she'd found in *Time Out*; while the removers were quite effective they were unlike any other removal people I'd met. They were true 'heads', with very long hair, and they kept adding the word 'man' to the end of every sentence. When we got to the house, in a village called Swanmore, about ten miles out of Southampton, I went off for a wander around the large garden while the removers unloaded the van. In the greenhouse I found nothing but cannabis plants, the smallest of which was about five foot tall. I went to find Sue to tell her the news. She was talking to the removal men and one of them turned to me and asked, 'Is that a problem, man?' I explained that it wasn't a career-enhancing move for the Director of Programmes of the regional ITV station to have enough cannabis in his greenhouse to get half of Southampton stoned.

'Don't worry, man, we'll take it,' replied the removal man, and they did. They cleared most of the plants out of the greenhouse, piled them in the cabin of their removal van, and drove back to London, up to their waists in cannabis plants. I've often wondered how they would have explained this if they'd been stopped by the police on the M3. The following weekend I made a bonfire of the remainder of the plants, which probably had unintended effects on the state of the elderly couple who lived next door.

My period at TVS was, by the standards of most of my time in television, fairly uneventful. In my early days there I fell out with James Gatward because I believed I had joined on the basis that my job carried a place on the Board of TVS Ltd, the holding company for TVS, and he disagreed. Eventually he gave in, but only after I had threatened to leave the company. After that, he and I got on well together. When, some years later, he was fired from the company he had founded, I sent him a big bunch of flowers with a note that said, 'Don't let the bastards get to you.' We still see each other occasionally.

The irony of the ITV system in those days was that the company with the smallest share of viewers in its region, TVS, could charge the most for its advertising. I've spent years trying to explain this to people but they don't easily understand. It's all about supply and demand.

TVS was an incredibly successful company because of the region it covered. The South of England is the richest part of Britain, outside of London, and the people who live there watch more BBC programmes and fewer ITV programmes than the country as a whole does. It is very much

the BBC's heartland. This means that in the south people watch less advertiser-funded programming than in areas like Yorkshire, where ITV is very popular. But advertisers need the people in the south to see their adverts for cars or financial services because that's where the money is; this in turn means that advertisers have to buy more advertising spots in the south to have the same impact as they would in, say, Yorkshire. With the number of adverts allowed on ITV limited by the regulators, you had a classic case of demand outstripping supply, which led to higher prices. So the less successful TVS was in attracting an audience, the more money it made. It defied all normal business logic but, financially, it made TVS a very successful company.

In those days ITV was divided into two sorts of companies: the major companies, Thames, Granada, Yorkshire, Central, and LWT, that made most of the programmes for the ITV network, and the regional companies that largely made programmes for their particular areas and bought their network programming from the big five. But there was a growing problem. In terms of advertising revenue, TVS was now considerably bigger than Yorkshire and was fast catching up with both Granada and LWT. The reality was that, in terms of revenue, there was no longer a big five but a big six.

James Gatward and I decided to launch a campaign to persuade the Independent Broadcasting Authority to turn TVS into the sixth major ITV company. I wanted it because it would mean TVS making more network programming; James was in favour because he wanted TVS to be seen as a 'big' player. By nature both of us were the sort of people who hated being seen as 'junior partners'. We were supported in our campaign to change the system by Gus – now Lord – Macdonald, who was doing the same job as me at Scottish Television, and he wanted the system changed to suit his company.

The five major companies all opposed the move. They believed they should make all the programmes that mattered for ITV. But we persisted and although we didn't win the battle we did win the war. The whole system of majors and regionals was dismantled the next time the ITV franchises were advertised, in 1991, largely as a result of our campaign. Instead an ITV Network Centre was established and it commissioned all network programmes for ITV from the best ideas, wherever they came from.

There were some very good programme makers at TVS. Some were there when I joined, others we attracted to the region. My deputy was Anna Home, who was in charge of children's output and eventually became Controller of Children's Programming at the BBC. When she left I appointed Nigel Pickard to take on her children's role at TVS. Today Nigel is in charge of the whole ITV network.

My close friend from TV-am, Clive Jones, joined to run news, current affairs, and sport. Working for him in the sports department at TVS were Vic Wakeling and Mark Sharman, who later became big players in television when they ran Sky Sports. In fact Vic is still probably the most powerful man in television sport as he controls the purse strings at Sky for sports contracts. Factual programmes were run by Peter Williams, who had a real eye for popular documentaries. It was Peter and his crew who were with Robert Ballard when he first found and explored the submerged wreck of the *Titanic*.

Graham Benson joined to run drama and hit on a rich stream when he produced *The Ruth Rendell Mysteries* with George Baker as Inspector Wexford. An ex-LWT man, John Kaye Cooper, came to run entertainment for a very successful three years. In that time John and I discovered that we had both been born within a few hours of each other on the same day in 1947, so we celebrated our fortieth birthdays together. John later joined me back at LWT as Controller of Entertainment.

Although it was a new ITV company, TVS was no different from LWT in terms of the trade unions and cautious management, so we continued my policy of trying to break the rules wherever possible. At one time John and I wanted to launch a new network game show called *Catchphrase* with Roy Walker as the host. To make the pilot for the show we needed to buy some very expensive computer-generated graphics equipment, but if the show failed we would not get our money back. Someone, somewhere in facilities management refused to sanction the cost. We bought it anyway without telling them.

We bonded pretty well together as a team and most of us still meet up for dinner once a year to discuss old times. But you had to be very careful in a place like the South of England when recruiting staff. Too many people wanted to move there to live in the country and do as little real work as possible. When interviewing people I always asked if they enjoyed riding or sailing. If the answer was yes, I invariably didn't give them

the job. I was determined TVS was not going to be a refuge for the semi-retired.

In my time at TVS we regularly covered opera at Glyndebourne, which was broadcast on Channel Four; so, as a company, we used Glyndebourne to entertain people we already either regarded as friends of the company or people we wanted to be our friends. The first time Sue and I went we took the Director of Television at the Independent Broadcasting Authority, David Glencross, and his wife Liz. Glyndebourne is where the South of England upper classes go to play, and some of the accents you hear as you wander around the beautiful grounds are remarkably cut-glass. In fact one right-wing merchant banker friend of mine, Anthony Fry, says Glyndebourne is the only place in Britain that could turn him into a Marxist. Not that it stops him going.

On our first visit, Sue and I had no idea what the protocol was, but our driver at the time – a wonderful man called Michael Davies, now sadly dead – showed us what we had to do. I was dressed up in a dinner suit, we took the champagne and the picnic, and we had a wonderful evening, although I've no idea what opera we actually saw. As we were being driven home, sitting in the back of the car finishing off the champagne, Sue turned to me and said, 'You do know we've become the sort of people we wanted to blow up twenty years ago.'

For me it was during the years spent at TVS that I first learnt about being a family man. Sue and I had no sooner got together in Barnes than I was off to TV-am, and was hardly seen for a year. It was only in Hampshire that we became a proper family, helped by the fact that three months after we moved Alice was born on 28 November 1984. Sue had had her two other children in hospital and had hated the experience. This time she was determined that her baby would be born at home. I was terrified; what happened if anything went wrong? But Sue was adamant, and my views were irrelevant. After all, I was only the father. So Alice was born in our bedroom in the house in Swanmore.

Sue was right, of course, and Alice's being born at home was a magical experience. Within an hour of the birth we were all sitting on the bed very excited, Sue, me, Matthew, Christine, the dog, and of course the new baby. One of the lasting memories of my life is sitting on the rocking chair in the bedroom that night, when everyone else had gone to sleep, holding my first-born and singing 'Summertime' to her. As I am completely

tone deaf, I don't suppose it helped her much. It's probably the reason she cried non-stop for the next three months.

Two and a half years later Joe, too, was born in that same room, much to the annoyance of his older sister, who kept asking questions like 'When is that baby going home?' and 'Where have its parents gone?' – referring to the midwife and the doctor. As one who comes from a family of three sons, who in their fifties still raced each other on the beach to see who was the fastest, and even today still kick hell out of each other in our annual family football match, I understand all about sibling rivalry.

One morning while I was still in bed, about three years after I had joined TVS, I got a call from Brian Tesler, the Managing Director of LWT. He wanted to know if I could go up to London that afternoon to meet him and LWT's Chairman, Christopher Bland. I didn't ask what it was about, I just said yes, which I later discovered had puzzled Brian. He wanted to know why I hadn't asked him about the purpose of the meeting. I explained that if the Managing Director of LWT rings you at 7.30 a.m. and asks you to meet him, it's got to be worth saying yes.

Brian had been running LWT for thirteen years. He was not a great businessman, and would never have claimed to be; but he was as good a judge of programmes as I've ever met. His analysis of what was right and what was wrong about a programme was brilliant. He was also a pretty good judge of people: in his time as MD he appointed to the role of Director of Programmes at LWT three of the people who were to dominate British television management for the next twenty years, Michael Grade, John Birt, and then me.

When I got to the LWT offices on the South Bank I was shown into Brian's room, where Brian and Christopher were waiting. John Birt was with them. Of course I knew John well, and I knew Brian Tesler a bit at that time, but I had only met Christopher on a couple of occasions. They explained that Birt, who had been lined up to replace Brian Tesler as MD, was instead leaving to become Deputy Director-General of the BBC in charge of all news and current affairs programming. John looked a bit awkward and obviously wanted to know what I thought. I remember congratulating him but I was puzzled as to why he wanted to do the job. I thought he would have a lot more fun running LWT, and would certainly make more money.

John had been asked to look after the BBC's journalism by Michael

Checkland, an accountant who was formerly in charge of finance at BBC Television and who had recently been made Director-General. Checkland was the compromise candidate chosen by the BBC's Board of Governors after his predecessor, Alasdair Milne, had been fired by the BBC's new chairman, Duke Hussey. Hussey went on to fire Checkland six years later, replacing him with John Birt. When his autobiography was published, Hussey said he regretted not firing Birt as well. I often wondered whether Hussey ever thought that he himself might be the problem.

Brian Tesler and Christopher Bland told me that they wanted me to replace John as Director of Programmes. I had recently made the short list for the same job at Thames Television, which went to David Elstein instead, and John Birt had already hinted to me that when he became Managing Director of LWT he wanted me to be his Director of Programmes; so the offer wasn't completely out of the blue, although the timing was sooner than I had expected.

I knew immediately that I would take the job, but said I had to go back and discuss it with Sue. I realized it would mean dragging the whole family back up to London and I knew that wouldn't be popular, for by this time Sue had started lecturing in sociology at the local college and the older kids were settled in school. When we discussed it Sue agreed to the move, but with conditions. The first was that wherever we moved next we had to stay for at least ten years: she made the point that Matthew was only nine but had already been to three different schools. Now I'd be moving him to a fourth. I agreed.

The second condition was harder to deliver. She said she'd only move back to London if we could buy one of just six houses in a particular road in Barnes. Given that all six were occupied I wasn't sure I could meet this demand, but disingenuously I assured her I'd do my best. Amazingly, I discovered one of the six was for sale and we went to see it, taking our architect Chris Henderson, who is today also my horse-riding partner. It was the perfect house, but there were two problems. First, we'd have to spend another year with builders, having only just got rid of them from our existing house; second, Chris reckoned the whole back wall was about to fall off.

In the end, Sue relented and I was allowed to look further afield. We eventually found our present house, between Richmond and Twickenham, which had the great advantage of being in wonderful condition – not that

it stopped us knocking a few walls down here and there. I always remember the builder whom we'd asked to demolish a wall in the kitchen saying to me, 'Funny old world, isn't it, mate? I only built this wall last year.' I thought then that it was an unknowingly profound statement that could have been applied to the whole process of Western capitalism.

My appointment at LWT took some time to finalize as Brian and Christopher felt obliged to interview some internal candidates who also wanted the job. The internal runners were the Head of Entertainment, Alan Boyd, who went on to replace me at TVS, the Head of Drama and Arts, Nick Elliot, and my former boss at LWT, Barry Cox, who was Head of Current Affairs and Features. In the end, Brian and Christopher stuck with their original choice and gave the job to me. To take it I gave up some quite valuable stock options at TVS, which in the end didn't matter because their value evaporated a year or two later when TVS decided to expand in America and buy a large US production company called MTM, named after its founder, the actress Mary Tyler Moore. It was a disastrous buy and virtually bankrupted the company.

Instead I was awarded stock options in LWT and the traditional Dyke luck came into play yet again. The price of the options was to be based on the average price of the shares over a short period of time in October 1987. The lower the price the better it was for me, so I was one of the few big gainers on Black Monday, 19 October 1987, when the world's stock exchanges crashed. LWT's share price fell by a third in a week and my options were set at the new, lower price. As the share price recovered over the next year the value of my options went up with it.

In May 1987, soon after I had agreed to return to LWT, I took a call from David Frost, who offered me the most frightening experience of my life. Would I play in his football team against Jimmy Tarbuck's XI in a charity match? No problem with that. The scary bit was that the match was to be played at Wembley, in front of 80,000 people, just before the 1987 FA Cup Final between Coventry and Tottenham. I was to be in a Tottenham shirt and John Birt, who was also playing, would be in Coventry colours.

The rest of the teams were genuine celebrities, with people like Daley Thompson, Dennis Waterman, Steve Cram, Nick Berry, and Steve Davis all playing. I don't think the football fans in the stadium had any idea

who John and I were when we ran out onto the pitch. I always reckoned that David had invited us so he could maintain a good relationship with both ITV and the BBC, and make sure he had plenty of work over the next decade. Either way, I was scared to death. I was a park footballer, terrified of making a complete fool of myself in front of all these people. Late in the game I did one good sliding tackle and 40,000 Spurs fans cheered. At that moment I knew what it was like to be David Beckham.

The match was televised live on ITV and Jimmy Greaves, the former Tottenham and England forward, picked me out as the man of the match, which was flattering until he admitted he had done so because I was his new boss at LWT: it had nothing to do with my footballing abilities. I have always kept a picture of me being tackled by the World Championship winning runner Steve Cram on the wall in my study, and when he was little my son Joe always referred to it as 'when you were a footballer, Dad'. If only. Every couple of years I watch the video of the match to remind me of what might have been.

Returning to LWT was like going back to my spiritual home. I probably spent the happiest days of my working life there and made many good friends. To this day I still love that area along the South Bank of the Thames where the LWT building is based. I had left as a programme editor being told by my boss that if I went I would never be allowed back. Four years later I was back in the elevated position of Director of Programmes, a job that had two distinct roles at LWT. Firstly, I decided which programmes LWT made, both for the network and for the London region; secondly, I was responsible for scheduling the weekend for the whole of the ITV network, which meant deciding which network programmes went where.

I inherited a good team, the most important of whom was Nick Elliot, LWT's Head of Drama, a truly wonderful man who tended even then towards the eccentric. Every so often Nick would get so annoyed that a 'Nick Elliot memo' would turn up on my desk attacking everyone and everything. The trick with Nick was to wait forty-eight hours and then ask him to come up. By then he was usually deeply ashamed of the memo he'd sent and would crawl into the office like Uriah Heep. The letter Nick sent me when I left the BBC sums up his writing style:

I just wanted to say how sad and angry I am about what has happened – an appalling combination of all the people I hate in life – politicians, regulators, journalists, wankers. Our TV world is united behind you. Whenever you want me to join in a revenge attack just say.

As a head of drama Nick was, and still is, second to none in Britain. This really mattered because when I got to LWT I decided that we had to take the weekend schedule upmarket, particularly on Sunday nights, and the way to do that was to play more drama.

In those days, deciding to take ITV upmarket was a pretty radical decision. It meant getting rid of a lot of the cheap game shows that were in the schedule and using the money elsewhere. We did it because it was clear that the very nature of advertising was changing. The big growth area of the decade was financial services advertising – banks, building societies, and the like – aimed at more affluent and aspirational viewers.

An hour of drama is probably the most expensive hour you get on television, so if we were to run more drama I had to save money elsewhere. I scrapped *Weekend World* and replaced it with *Walden*, a show in which the former Labour MP interviewed major politicians of the day, as it seemed to me that the Brian Walden interview had become the most important part of the programme and the new format was significantly cheaper. I also scrapped the big Sunday night variety show *Live from the Palladium* starring Jimmy Tarbuck. I even scrapped my beloved *Six O'Clock Show*, which I thought looked tired and was too expensive. I used all the money I saved from such cuts to introduce double drama on a Sunday night, with an hour of family drama at eight and an hour of more adult drama at nine. It's a pattern that ITV still follows to this day and, more than fifteen years later, it continues to win Sunday nights for ITV.

We produced some of this drama ourselves at LWT – shows like *Poirot* and *London's Burning* – but were helped enormously by Yorkshire Television and their Director of Programmes, John Fairley. John is one of the most talented people I've met in the television business, but he's never been keen to work a full week. At Yorkshire he was known as 'rarely, therely, Fairley'. A few years later, when I was Chairman of ITV, I offered him the job of running the whole ITV network. He told me he would

take it if I could make it a Tuesdays-, Wednesdays- and Thursdays-only job. I didn't have the nerve to do that, but John could probably have managed it in just three days of the week. He was a brilliant creative executive.

I was once invited by the Royal Television Society to make a speech to their branch in Leeds and I decided to use it to pay tribute to what John had achieved. I praised the programme making department John had built and ended by saying, 'For John to have done all this is a great achievement in any circumstances, but to have done it all from a box at York races is quite remarkable.' John has now got his ideal job, running all the racing coverage for Channel Four as an independent producer.

John and Yorkshire Television decided to support my vision for a more upmarket Sunday night and they delivered all the David Jason programmes for Sundays, including *Frost*, plus a remarkable success story called *Heartbeat*. Initially we played *Heartbeat* on Fridays in the summer because we had been told by Yorkshire that they thought it was a 'dog' and they asked us to bury it somewhere. The ratings were low, but they grew over the series and, more importantly, the appreciation figures were enormous.

My Head of Planning, Warren Breach, and I realized that *Heartbeat* had real potential, so we moved it to Sunday nights; the rest is television history. Within a year it was pulling in over seventeen million viewers every week. *Heartbeat* was a classic example of what any commissioner or scheduler knows: that on many crucial calls you don't know anything. You can think something is going to be a big hit and then be proved spectacularly wrong. And exactly the same can happen the other way, as it did with *Heartbeat*.

My upmarket Sunday night was a big success with the sales team. The Director of Sales at LWT was one of the great figures of the whole industry, Ron Miller. A Barnado's boy, brought up in the East End of London with only a rudimentary education, Ron was a genius as a salesman. He understood that selling was about relationships, and Ron knew everyone and everyone knew Ron. He somehow managed to persuade the advertisers that an AB male watching television on a Sunday night was much more valuable than the same AB male watching television on a Monday night, when it just happened that Thames, and not LWT, were selling the advertising in London. It was complete bullshit, but all the

buyers went along with it because they liked Ron and they didn't much like his opposite number at Thames Television, a man called Jonathan Shier. He later went on to run, and create chaos at, ABC in Australia. Ron Miller believes to this day that ITV never had a better or classier Sunday night than my upmarket Sunday, with a line-up of *Heartbeat*, *Poirot*, *Hale and Pace*, the News, and the *South Bank Show*.

The combination of the new drama programming, our scheduling, and Ron's selling gave LWT a few really profitable years. We competed with our big rival, Thames Television, quite aggressively and we markedly increased our share of the London market in both ratings and advertising revenue.

In the area of entertainment – LWT had traditionally been an entertainment company – I was lucky; I had inherited *Blind Date*, which had been running for a couple of seasons when I became Director of Programmes. *Blind Date* was a clever format but it was made into a great show by Cilla Black – a considerable star whom I predict will return to her former glory. When I arrived back at LWT the actual dates, when the couple went out together, were covered by stills photographers but I soon decided to spend more money on the show and we sent a video crew on every date – a definite improvement.

The hardest thing for LWT to control was the after-show *Blind Date* party, where all the contestants met together and all sorts of people got off with each other. Quite often a contestant would decide that he or she had picked the wrong person and would make a play for one of the others. In the end, the producers used separate hotels for the boys and girls in a bid to keep them apart, largely to no avail.

Marcus Plantin was Head of Entertainment, a strange person to be in that role. While he picked good shows and was a very good producer, he didn't have much of a sense of humour. It was Marcus who spotted *Gladiators* on American television and introduced it into the UK, where it was a much bigger hit than it had been in the USA.

In those days Michael Barrymore was an exclusive artist at LWT. I'll always remember meeting Michael when Sue and I went to see Billy Connolly's one-man show. We chatted for a while and then Sue turned to him and asked him what he did. I didn't know whether to laugh or look embarrassed. Sue didn't bat an eyelid when I explained he was one of Britain's top comedians.

103

Michael was brilliant, but like a number of great comedians he was incredibly difficult to manage, and he surrounded himself with people who constantly pandered to him. These were the days when he was still married to Cheryl, although we all knew he was gay. There were times when he disappeared for days on end when he should have been making a show. His behaviour drove John K. Cooper, Marcus Plantin's successor as Head of Entertainment at LWT, completely mad. And yet he was the best popular comedian of his generation by a long way. Though he has recently been through some difficult times I hope he recovers because anyone with his talent should be working on British television.

Not everything I did as Director of Programmes at LWT was successful. One area where Marcus and I failed was situation comedy. We scrapped one comedy, called *Me and My Girl*, that was getting good ratings on a Friday night because neither of us liked the show and found the production company difficult. It was run by a man we used to call 'fucking Al Mitchell', whom I had never met. The following year I went over to introduce myself to a new neighbour in Twickenham and the man explained he too was in the television business and that his name was Al Mitchell. I looked at him and said, 'You're not "fucking Al Mitchell", are you?' It was the very same. We ended up good friends and he still sends me e-mails signed 'fucking Al Mitchell'.

We cancelled *Me and My Girl* because, despite its popularity with viewers, we were sure we could do better. But over the next seven years we didn't produce one new comedy that got the sort of ratings it used to attract.

Situation comedy is an incredibly valuable genre if you can get it right. It's cheaper than most drama to produce and it repeats well. Look how often *Dad's Army*, *Only Fools and Horses*, and *Fawlty Towers*, to name but three, have been successfully repeated. But situation comedy is probably the hardest thing to produce on television. Everyone struggles with it, but over the years the BBC has been the master and ITV an also-ran. That is still the case.

Another area where I tried to make changes and failed was religion. These were the days when ITV and BBC One were required to play religious programming at the same time on a Sunday evening. The God slot ran for thirty-five minutes between six and seven every Sunday evening. I regarded this requirement as deeply illiberal as it effectively

forced viewers to watch religious programmes regardless of whether they were believers or not. I proposed that the God slot should be scrapped, but naturally the idea did not go down well in religious circles. I even spoke at a religious conference at which I was heckled by members of the clergy. In the end a body called CRAC, the Central Religious Advisory Council, which was chaired by a bishop, not surprisingly voted against the proposal and the Independent Broadcasting Authority, as well as the BBC Governors, supported them.

This was less than twenty years ago but it demonstrates how much the world has changed since then. The idea of an enforced God slot on ITV and BBC One at the same time would now be seen as ridiculous. As it turned out, I was only slightly ahead of my time: the 1990 Broadcast Act effectively ended the enforced God slot. By the time the Act came into force in 1992 I was Chief Executive of LWT and scrapped the God slot on the first day it was legally possible to do so.

I've no doubt the religious lobby would describe it as dumbing down. I disagree. Religious programming is still there for those who want it, but is not being forced on those who don't. The recent Ofcom report, which asked people what sort of public service programming they valued most, had religious programming very near the bottom of the list.

As Director of Programmes at LWT I had a good team. My business manager was Sydney Perry, whom I inherited from John Birt, who, in turn, had inherited him from Michael Grade. Sydney was quite a lot older than the rest of us and over the years we changed his name from Sydney, to Syd, to old Syd, and finally to poor old Syd. Luckily he had a good sense of humour and gave us as good as he got. We eventually promoted him to run LWT International, which he did very successfully.

I replaced him with Mike Southgate, who had worked with me in several different organizations. Then there was Tony Cohen, who, since first working for me as a researcher on *The Six O'Clock Show*, had spent a year at the London Business School. He became my strategist. A few years later, when I joined Pearson Television, I explained that I didn't come alone: Tony Cohen came with me. I remember Frank Barlow, Managing Director of Pearson, asking what Tony did that I didn't do. I explained that Tony was the brains and that I did the PR. 'So why don't we just employ Tony?' he asked. 'Brains don't work without the PR,' I replied.

In 1989 Brian Tesler decided he would relinquish the role of Managing Director of LWT. Head hunters were brought in and eventually recommended that a man who sold bikes in the Midlands should get the job. Brian was unhappy, as he wanted the job to go to me, but Christopher Bland took some convincing: he didn't believe I had enough business experience. But in the end they offered me the job. So thirteen years after I had first joined LWT as a reporter I was to be its Managing Director.

To satisfy Christopher's concerns about my business skills we agreed that I would spend the autumn of 1989 on the Advanced Management Programme at the Harvard Business School and would take over as Managing Director of LWT early the following year. I was probably the first leader of an ITV company to go to business school. Many people in British television ridiculed me for it, but it was the first sign that British television was turning into a real business run by people who took business seriously. I later sent the top echelon of LWT to business school and introduced serious management training for many in senior and middle management.

Those twelve weeks I spent at Harvard were as exciting a period as I've spent anywhere. Sue advised me not to go. Knowing that I'm not a natural academic she said that I was an instinctive leader and that if I tried to intellectualize the process I could well screw it up. With that ringing endorsement in my ears I went anyway.

I was very nervous. I knew that I was a jumped-up television producer who worked in a monopoly industry. What the hell did I know about real business? There were 160 of us on the course, including half a dozen from Britain. Unlike the rest of the students we were required to wear business attire as we were on the most senior programme there. On occasions I insisted on wearing a white suit just to show that I wasn't from a 'normal' business. One day I remember a bunch of us walking along in our suits when we passed a group of MBA students coming the other way. They were half our age and as we walked by I heard one turn to another and say 'Jesus, is that what we're aspiring to be?'

Half way through the course, when all the natural competitiveness had died away and we had become mates, I discovered that I wasn't the only one who had been anxious about the programme. One of the great advantages age and experience give you is a better understanding of the human psyche. When I was first in the television business I used to respect

those in high places in television because I thought 'they must know'. Having now done those jobs myself I realize my confidence in them was misplaced. No one knows: you just pretend to know. The great myth of management is that somehow you know more than those you are leading, whereas the only real advantage you've got is the position and the power.

What that period at Harvard gave me was an intellectual rationale for running businesses and organizations the way I ran them instinctively. I came across a brilliant American professor called John Kotter, who was the first person I'd met who talked about the difference between being a manager and being a leader. This was 1989, the height of Thatcherism, when everyone in Britain still believed that successful management was all about being tough with your staff, the unions, your competitors, and virtually everyone else. I had never believed that, and Kotter reinforced my view of the world. When I turned up at the BBC a decade later I was amazed to find that the old view of management still persisted.

The biggest revelation through being at Harvard and listening to John Kotter was, for me, the discovery that the most successful organizations in the world were those that treated their staff properly. I believed in that concept but was surprised to discover it also led to competitive advantage and business success. The days when capital treated labour as if it was a commodity to be bought and sold increasingly didn't work. If you wanted a successful company you had to treat your people well.

When I came back from Harvard I rang up Peter Mandelson, whom I knew from when he was a producer at LWT and who was at that time in charge of communications for the Labour Party, to ask him to lunch. I explained that my experience at Harvard had given me a new vision for the Labour Party. The most successful companies in the world were treating their staff in the way that we, on the Left, had always argued people should be treated. The mistake we'd made was believing that state-owned organizations would be better at doing that than the private sector. Modern capitalism required an enthusiastic and fulfilled workforce if a company was to be successful; we could thus achieve what we had always aimed for within a mixed economy. Peter listened, and I think he took it in.

As a result of going to Harvard I decided to rejoin the Labour Party, which I don't think was the intention of Christopher Bland when he laid out $30,000 for me to go there. Christopher was a Tory and had been

chairman of the liberal Tory pressure group, the Bow Group. I became an early supporter of what New Labour was to stand for.

Later, in 1994, when Gail Rebuck, the head of the publishers Random House in the UK, asked me to write a book on management and leadership I told her that I didn't know enough to fill a pamphlet, let alone a book. I didn't feel I could do it, but I knew what the title should be: *Management Without Fear*.

I ended my time at Harvard by taking part in the sketch show that is put on at the end of every course. This was entertainment so I knew more about it than the bankers and industrial managers who made up most of the people on the course. I had great fun playing a thick, uneducated Texan who mocked the whole Harvard Business School experience by saying that it was impossible to fail so long as you had paid your $30,000 fee: after all, even he'd got a certificate saying he'd passed.

I came back to Britain with the task of running LWT and trying to put some of these ideas into practice.

Running and Losing LWT

On my first day in charge at LWT I put up an enormous picture of me in reception at our building on the South Bank with a notice saying that I was taking over the organization that day, that I would be spending the day wandering around trying to meet as many people as possible, and that everyone was invited to have a drink on me in the LWT bar at lunchtime. My aim was obvious: as a Managing Director I wanted to be seen as accessible, open, and friendly.

In that first year, 1990, I introduced a couple of policies that I hoped would demonstrate we were a 'caring' management. I started sending a bunch of flowers from the company to everyone who had a new baby. I had learnt from my own recent experience how important a day this was in your life and wanted people on the staff to know we recognized that. And at Christmas each year I put on an enormous party for the children and grandchildren of the people who worked for LWT. People in television worked very long hours, and this was a small way of thanking their families. That first year I played Father Christmas and gave out the presents to all the children, including my own. The cost of doing all this was pathetically small compared with the goodwill it fostered.

I discovered that it didn't take more than a small gesture to get people on-side. When we completely redesigned the monthly presentation of the accounts, which took an enormous effort from the finance department, I turned up with a few bottles of champagne to thank the people who had done the work. They never forgot it.

I also started a weekly breakfast meeting for the top forty people in the company at which, as well as discussing what was happening inside

LWT and in the industry generally, we'd have a lot of laughs. The meetings were key to the management spirit I was trying to engender. With humour, wit, speed, confidence, and fun we tried to give the place a sense of purpose.

Within days of my taking over at LWT my father died. He had had an operation for cancer of the colon three years earlier but the disease had reappeared in his lungs and we'd watched him getting worse month by month for the past year. I had been with him when he was told by the specialist, a wonderful man at Hammersmith Hospital called Karol Sikora, that he had a maximum of two years to live. My dad was not one who showed emotion, but that week he was devastated.

His own father had died when he was young. He had no role model as a father; yet to my brothers and me he was very special. Both he and my mother were always supportive of us, no matter what we did. When I was seventeen I bought a bubble car against his wishes. In fact I didn't tell him and he thought the car parked outside our house had been dumped there until my mother told him it was mine. It turned out to be a disastrous buy and was a hopeless vehicle, but he never said 'I told you so'. He just helped me try to make it work. He was a very conservative man who did a job he hated in the insurance industry, but he had a serene quality about him. He hated pompous people and was the only person I knew who would regularly stop and talk to the road sweeper, to make him feel like a real human being rather than someone doing a lowly job in society. That was my dad, and that was the way he brought us up.

My mother was wonderful looking after him in those last months but eventually we decided it would be best if he went into the local hospice. I remember that last weekend as if it was yesterday. It was 1990 and Manchester United were playing Crystal Palace in the FA Cup Final. I had tickets to take my son Matthew but in the end I decided to stay with my dad, who by then was no longer conscious. My brothers and I watched the match in the hospice.

On the Monday morning he was still alive and I made one of those inexplicable decisions that you have to live with for the rest of your life. I had my first big network meeting as Managing Director of LWT on that Monday and instead of staying with my dad I went to the meeting, promising to come back that afternoon. He died around midday and I wasn't there. Even as I write this now there are tears streaming down my

cheeks. Why did I go? It was only a bloody meeting. I'll never be able to justify that decision to myself and I shall always feel I let him down at the end.

In some ways it was a relief when he died: he had been so ill and the withered old man in that hospice bed bore no relation to the man who had brought us up and been such a great father. It was some months before it really hit me that he had gone, that he wouldn't see my kids growing up, that he wouldn't be there with that quiet word of support. Now, fourteen years later, not a week goes by when I don't think about him or tell my kids stories about him. My brothers and I were so lucky to have had the parents we did.

The problem I faced taking over LWT in 1990 was that its future was far from certain. The Thatcher Government had decided that ITV needed to be reformed. It was partly the fault of LWT. When Brian Walden had gone along to interview Mrs Thatcher several years earlier we had sent some forty-odd people to do a two-camera interview. Someone in Downing Street had counted them all in and counted them all out and had decided, quite rightly, that this was a ridiculous number of people to do just one interview. In those days the unions still effectively ran the ITV companies and Mrs Thatcher hated the unions, so it followed she hated ITV.

In 1985 she had set up a committee to look into the funding of television chaired by Professor Alan Peacock, an economist who had been teaching at York University when I was there. In fact the students had occupied his department for a while demanding that he should teach Marxist as well as market economics. In 1985 he was the Director of Edinburgh's David Hume Institute and had been asked by Mrs Thatcher to look into the whole question of putting advertisements on the BBC. To Mrs Thatcher's disappointment his report came out against the idea: there simply wasn't enough advertising revenue around to finance the BBC as well as ITV. As an afterthought he suggested that next time the ITV franchises were to be awarded they should be auctioned to the highest bidder. Everyone laughed at the suggestion, with the exception of Mrs Thatcher, who decided to implement it. So my job in 1990 was to prepare LWT for the auction of the ITV franchises that was to take place in 1991, with the new franchises due to begin in January 1993.

What I knew was that LWT had no chance of winning a franchise in

111

its current state. We had to reduce the size of the company and get rid of the excesses that we all knew were deeply embedded in the organization. This was a company where, like the rest of the ITV companies, the unions had been allowed to run riot for at least three decades. This had happened partly because over many years there had been a special tax on the profits of the commercial television companies – at one time they were paying something in excess of 90 per cent tax on any profits they made. As a result, no one in management worried too much about how much was spent as the taxpayer picked up the tab for almost all of it so long as the ITV companies stayed profitable. There was no incentive to be efficient, which was why the trade unions effectively ran ITV, and it was never financially worthwhile for the managements of the ITV companies to take them on.

On a couple of occasions Christopher Bland had prevented the management from taking on a small group of workers who could then have shut down the whole of LWT, leaving the company to continue paying the wages of the vast majority of the workforce with no advertising income coming in. Christopher's view was that if we were to take on the unions we had to take everyone on at the same time. If there was to be a bust-up, it had to be a big one. He was quite right.

The threat of an auction and the likelihood of your franchise going to the highest bidder changed the world. It meant that you had to become efficient as a company and fast. We were all helped in achieving this by what had happened at TV-am in 1987 when Bruce Gyngell sacked all his technicians after their union had called them out on strike. Initially the management had taken over all their jobs, but in the end Bruce employed non-union labour. The strikers never returned to TV-am.

I knew for the first time that change was possible at LWT when I went to a meeting with the unions while I was Director of Programmes. For years they had threatened to go on strike if management didn't give in to their demands. This time they were the exact opposite and accused us of trying to create a situation in which, as at TV-am, they would be locked out. I knew then that their many years of power were coming to an end. We got rid of scams like paying ridiculous multiples for overtime, paying enormous expenses, and employing technicians who often didn't turn up but still got paid, and we did it without a single day being lost through strike action.

112

The threat of a franchise auction coincided with the coming of independent producers, another of Mrs Thatcher's changes, which meant that ITV and the BBC would have to give 25 per cent of their commissions each year to the independent sector. As far as negotiating with the unions was concerned, this strengthened our hand enormously.

In fact when I first returned to LWT I had had a major confrontation with the unions over a drama production called *Betty* that was to star Twiggy. The set had been built at Shepperton Studios and shooting was about to get under way when the unions demanded that, even though it was an independent production, it should be made under ITV union agreements. For us this would have been a disaster as our union agreements were terrible and far too expensive. I decided to take a stand, cancelled the whole production, wrote off more than a million pounds, and publicly announced that I wouldn't be blackmailed by the trade unions.

This had three consequences. Firstly, the unions got the blame for the cancellation of *Betty*, which was never made, much to Twiggy's annoyance. As a result, all future independent productions for ITV were made under a different agreement. Secondly, at LWT we used this opportunity to tell our own people that if we didn't change our agreements all our drama in the future would be made by independent producers. They changed. Thirdly, my stand was obviously noticed in Downing Street. That was the only year I received a Christmas card from Margaret and Denis Thatcher.

If your political sympathies were on the Left, it was always difficult to explain why it was necessary to take on the trade unions in the television industry. My view was that most of the leaders of these unions, just like Fleet Street, were not the slightest bit interested in anything that resembled socialism. They didn't want a more egalitarian society in which opportunities were open to all, and they certainly didn't believe in efficiency. Worst of all I never saw any sign in those days that they were interested in making the best possible programmes for the audiences. They were only interested in their own power and in enriching themselves and their members. To round it off many of the union leaders at LWT at the time were hardline Thatcherites.

All this happened before I became Managing Director, but when I took over I decided I had to explain to the staff why we needed more change. In those days we employed about fifteen hundred people; by the time I

left that had been nearly halved to some eight hundred. I decided to talk to everyone in the company in groups of about twenty to explain what we were trying to achieve, and why we had to make more cuts to the organization to survive.

At that time we had a senior non-executive director on the Board of LWT called Roger Harrison, who was Deputy Chairman of Capital Radio but had formerly been Managing Director of *The Observer*. He was a very wise old bird and I always listened carefully to his advice. He told me that what he had discovered from the restructuring of Fleet Street was that you could afford to be very generous to the people you were making redundant as the savings were potentially massive. I followed his advice and did everything I could to help people to leave the organization feeling they had been well treated.

One day I went to the leaving party of some videotape engineers who had earned fortunes in their time at LWT but who didn't want to stay on in the new world when their wages, and in particular their overtime, would be cut dramatically. They had decided to take redundancy instead. One of them summed up the past when he said quite openly to me, 'You can't blame us, Governor. If the management were fools enough to give it, we were going to take it.' Who can disagree?

We decided to convert our resources division into a proper profit-and-loss company and put Mike Southgate in charge of it. We called the new company the London Studios and it proved to be a great and continuing success. I was back at the London Studios, on the South Bank, only months after I left the BBC when I was the guest presenter on *Have I Got News for You*, which, although a BBC show, has been made at the London Studios for many years for the independent producer Hat Trick.

Turning an old facilities business into a profit-and-loss operation meant that – for the first time – LWT programme makers had to negotiate prices for the studios and crews they used. In doing so we discovered the London Studios was losing £16 million a year. Mike's task was to make it a break-even business by the time the new franchises started in 1993, which he pretty much achieved by a combination of bringing in outside clients, a lot of restructuring, and a great many redundancies.

While I was trying to get the operating business right Christopher Bland, as the Chairman of LWT, began to think about the financing of the organization. Christopher's view was that, as a television company,

we should 'stick to our knitting': he therefore sold the company's two subsidiary businesses, the travel company Page & Moy and the publishers Hutchinson. He got good prices for both, which meant that LWT was sitting on a pile of cash. Then one morning in early 1989 he suggested to Brian Tesler and me that we undertake a management buyout. By using the cash we had in the business, plus borrowing, he reckoned the management could buy the whole of LWT.

In the end we didn't go for the total buyout, but a variation of it. We gave all the shareholders back a good deal of money, much of which we had borrowed, reduced the market capitalization of the business, and gave massive incentives to the management. Christopher's view was that by doing this we improved our chances in the franchise auction. We would have tied in a talented management who might otherwise have been attracted to rival bids; we would all be massively incentivized to make the company as efficient as possible; and we would have replaced much of the equity base of the company with cheaper debt, which meant we could bid more in the franchise round.

I was given the job of deciding who should qualify to be in the management scheme and I was determined we would include a wide range of people. In the end we had forty-four people who stood to make real money if we could increase the share price significantly over the coming years. As management we all put in our own money. Some had to mortgage their houses; others, like me, had enough valuable existing share options or shares in LWT that they didn't need to find any more cash. But we all took a risk, so it wasn't like a normal share option scheme. The idea was that if the share price rose from 83p to 240p over the next three years the number of shares we owned in the company would quadruple and the forty-four of us would end up owning 15 per cent of LWT. The details of the scheme were drawn up by Neil Canetty-Clarke, a young merchant banker who happened to be on a placement with LWT. He later became Finance Director.

There was some opposition to the scheme in the City, particularly from the Pearl, Eagle Star, and Scottish Amicable, but we got the 75 per cent of the shareholders we needed to vote in favour. When we launched the scheme the share price actually went down. We had paid 83p a share and now they were trading at 76p. Later, when people criticized the scheme for being too generous to the management, I regularly asked them why,

*Christopher Bland dreamt up a scheme whereby the LWT
management ended up owning 15 per cent of the company.
Becoming rich didn't make us universally popular in ITV.*

if it was that easy to predict how successful we would be, they hadn't invested when the shares were at 76p. That normally shut them up.

For the management there was no doubt it was a massive success. Having invested at 83p a share in 1990 we got back the equivalent of £30 a share just four years later. I ended up making £7 million, as did Brian Tesler and Ron Miller. Christopher, I think, made more, but then it was his idea in the first place. I had ensured that the scheme went down quite a long way in the management so people who had never imagined making a lot of money became comparatively rich. For instance, Peter Coppock, who ran the press office, made £1 million, which really upset the Fleet Street journalists. Not that the ordinary shareholders had anything to complain about: if they had invested in 1990 at 76p, or even 83p, they would have been able to sell out at £7.50p four years later.

When we finally cashed out I decided we should all share some of our gains with the staff at LWT who had worked for the company since the scheme was set up in 1990. I suggested to the forty-four participants in the scheme that we should all contribute on a sliding scale, depending on how much we'd made. It was a voluntary scheme but forty-three of the forty-four who had made money contributed to the pot. I think my share was about £220,000. The one member of the scheme who didn't put any money in criticized me in the newspapers for suggesting we should share some of our gains with the rest of the staff. He said I was a 'funny bloke' with socialist inclinations. I suppose I'd suggested giving some money to the rest of the staff because I'd never envisaged that we would all make so much and felt a degree of guilt that we hadn't included more of the people at LWT.

One of the reasons we made so much money was that we won back our franchise at a much smaller figure than we had estimated. Mrs Thatcher's original plan was a straight auction in which the highest bidder automatically won. As the Bill went through Parliament it was amended to add a quality threshold to the scheme. This clause was slipped into the Act by David Mellor, then a junior minister in the Home Office. I always suspected that David disliked the whole idea of the auction and did all he could to ensure that the good ITV companies survived. Under his clause any bidder had to satisfy the Independent Television Commission that they could both sustain the ITV system financially and deliver programmes of sufficient quality.

It was a mad system and by the mid Nineties it was very hard to find a Conservative MP who admitted to having voted for it, let alone proposing it in the first place. By then Margaret Thatcher had gone and she was blamed for the whole debacle. Two companies who discovered they had no opposition, Central and Scottish, bid just £2,000 a year for their franchises and won them, while others like TVS and Television South West bid £59 million and £16 million respectively and were ruled out by the ITC for having bid too much.

At LWT we thought long and hard about how much to bid. We knew we had only one competitor, London Independent Broadcasting, a franchise fronted by the music company Polygram and put together by a friend of mine, Tom Gutteridge, who had run York University TV while I was a student, after which he founded and ran a successful independent production company in the UK called Mentorn; he now runs Fremantle Television's operation in the United States. Tom is still a friend and, having forgiven him for bidding against us at LWT, Sue and I went to his wedding in 2003 when he married the wonderful Rosetta. The wedding was a classic Gutteridge production – no expense spared. There was even a bishop at the service: Tom and Rosetta had persuaded their local vicar that, although both of them were divorced, he should marry them in the local church. Tom always had that ability to sell anything to anyone. I think the bishop came along out of curiosity.

We didn't think much of the Polygram consortium and I dedicated a fortnight of my life to finding out everything I could about them. In that time I spoke to people who had been offered the job of Managing Director, to people who had been approached about finance, and to programme makers. I came to the conclusion that, no matter how much they bid, they couldn't win because they weren't properly financed. Unlike for his wedding, Tom hadn't raised enough money to pay for the project. He told me years later that if we'd offered him a couple of million pounds' worth of programming every year for Mentorn he would have pulled out. We'd guessed that might be the case at the time but we didn't dare risk it. If we'd been caught doing it there was a risk that we'd be ruled unfit to hold an ITV franchise. It didn't stop Gus Macdonald up in Scotland who gave programme deals to virtually every independent possible. Looking back now he was probably right to do so.

Having established Polygram's cash situation I was in favour of a

lowish bid, but it was Christopher's idea that we should bid a really low figure, one that was just enough to be respectable. We hit on the figure of £7.58 million and won. The Polygram consortium bid £35 million and lost. It was a truly ridiculous system.

The whole process leading up to the bids and afterwards was a cloak and dagger affair. One Friday I got a letter from someone saying he knew how much Polygram were going to bid and that if I paid him £5,000 he would tell me. He said that if I wanted to contact him I had to put an advert in the *Evening Standard* headed 'Something for the Weekend'. We didn't bother because we knew by then that our bid was going to be much lower than Polygram's. The funniest story I heard was about Yorkshire Television and Mersey Television getting together secretly to bid for the Granada franchise. They were due to have a confidential meeting at a hotel in Leeds but arrived to find that the hotel manager, in his enthusiasm, had put up a sign in the lobby saying that the hotel welcomed 'Yorkshire Television and Mersey Television'.

Ray Snoddy, the *Financial Times* media editor at the time and my former colleague in Uxbridge, managed to discover most of the bids for the different franchises around the UK, but not LWT's. He even tried exploiting our old friendship to try and persuade me to give him a hint, but I refused. When everyone discovered that we'd only bid £7 million, even though we had a serious competitor, they were all shocked, and that included members of the LWT Board. When I told our Director of Broadcasting, Robin Paxton, on the morning the results were expected, that we'd bid that low he went a deathly white. We'd taken a calculated gamble and it had come off; if it hadn't, I shudder to think what the staff's reaction would have been.

We also put together a bid for the ITV breakfast television franchise held by my old company TV-am. The rules only allowed us to own 20 per cent of the station, but because we'd put the bid together we managed to sell to the consortium an unused studio in our building, LWT crews, and the LWT transmission facilities. We bid too much for the franchise, £34.61 million a year, and it was a decade before GMTV started making a decent profit. But LWT made money from day one. It was a good deal for us.

Many conspiracy stories surround the size of our bid for the breakfast franchise. It has been suggested that we knew what our biggest rival, an

ITN-backed consortium, was likely to bid. This was perfectly true. I had found out the size of their bid and had told the members of our consortium how much extra we had to bid to win. We agreed to do it, upped our bid, and won. I've never revealed who told me the size of the ITN bid, and I never will, but I have said on many occasions that it wasn't Michael Green, whose company, Carlton, was part of the ITN consortium. After we had won he took up the last 20 per cent in our group and that started all the rumours that he'd doubled-crossed his group. But it wasn't true.

So on the day the results of the franchise auction were announced we had two things to celebrate at LWT: we'd won back our franchise and our consortium had also won the breakfast franchise. At lunchtime Christopher Bland, Brian Tesler, and I got a standing ovation from our staff in the LWT bar and that evening we had a great staff party that went on most of the night. I had prepared a speech I would make to the staff if we won the franchise battle and I duly delivered it that night; but I had never prepared for losing. I had asked Tony Cohen to draft me a losing speech because I couldn't face doing it, but he only admitted to me years later that he couldn't do it either. Thankfully, it wasn't needed.

There were still bodies lying around the building the morning after the party, people who were just too drunk or too tired to go home. I had been pretty confident of winning and had arranged for a lot of posters to go up all over London with the LWT comedians Hale and Pace saying 'LWT done the business'. My only fear was that I wouldn't be able to stop them going up if we'd lost. This nearly happened to Granada, who had arranged for a small bottle of champagne to be delivered to the home of everyone who worked for the company if they won. The trouble was the company commissioned to deliver the bottles started delivering them before the result was known. Luckily for them Granada had won.

It was a sad day at some ITV companies and I rang the managing directors of Thames, TVS, and TSW to say how sorry I was. I didn't ring Bruce Gyngell at TV-am – it was hardly appropriate, given that we had outbid him for his franchise. In truth, TV-am had never had much chance of winning. We'd calculated it was always going to be cheaper to run a breakfast service off the back of another broadcasting organization than run it as a stand-alone business, which meant we, or the ITN consortium that was also bidding, could always bid more than TV-am.

Losing still came as a shock to Bruce Gyngell. In his years in Britain, he had become a favourite of Margaret Thatcher, particularly after he'd taken on the television unions and beaten them, and she was distraught when his company lost its franchise as a result of legislation pushed through by her own Government. She wrote to Bruce to tell him how much she regretted it. Bruce clearly didn't feel the same way about her and he read her private letter out at a press conference at Eggcup Towers. Part of her letter ran:

> When I see how some of the other licences have been awarded I am mystified that you did not receive yours, and heartbroken. You of all people have done so much for the whole of television – there seems to have been no attention to that. I am only too painfully aware that I was responsible for the legislation.

It was typical of Margaret Thatcher that she automatically thought her friends would be immune to the impact of a really terrible piece of legislation, which her Government had pushed through. At that same press conference Bruce also said that GMTV would be dead inside two years. Twelve years later it is a profitable, thriving business.

I felt particularly sad for my friend Richard Dunn, who was in charge of Thames, the biggest of the ITV companies. He'd had a really strong bidder against him in Michael Green's Carlton and I'd always feared he might lose because he hadn't done enough cost cutting at Thames to allow him to make a knockout bid. I think he believed the Independent Television Commission would invoke the special circumstances clause, a discretionary power the legislation had given them, to save Thames. But Thames was very unpopular with the Government because of a programme called *Death on the Rock* about the killing by British soldiers of IRA terrorists in Gibraltar. Mrs Thatcher had attacked the programme and it would have taken a brave ITC to have treated Thames as a special case and not Mrs Thatcher's friend Bruce Gyngell. In the end they didn't use the special circumstances clause at all.

Richard Dunn and I had agreed some months earlier that we wouldn't bid for each other's franchise as second choice. It was a deal that suited LWT as we had decided to bid low, but I was never quite sure why it suited Richard. Losing Thames was a terrible blow to him, but he recovered and

121

was successfully rebuilding his career when, tragically, he was found dead at the bottom of his swimming pool in August 1998 having suffered a heart attack.

The results of the auction were announced in October 1991 but didn't take effect until fifteen months later, in January 1993. Guiding ITV through the interregnum was going to be difficult but interesting, and I decided I would try to do it by becoming the Chairman of ITV for a two-year period. At times we had representatives of twenty companies sitting around the table, twelve of whom had retained their franchises, four who had lost, and the four new franchise holders. The losers hated the winners and the winners didn't want to have anything to do with the losers. We even had to persuade Carlton that it was in their interests, and in the interests of ITV, to buy some of the Thames programmes like *The Bill*; but we made a mistake in not buying *Men Behaving Badly*, which later became a big hit on the BBC.

Overall, we managed the process and towards the end of 1992 the old ITV companies held a dinner for the losers. I made a speech praising Bruce Gyngell, eight years after he had fired me from TV-am. I no longer felt animosity towards him and told him how much a colourful character like him would be missed in ITV. Just over a year later I would join him on the outside.

It was June 1993 and, along with Mike Southgate and John K. Cooper, I had gone to Hilversum in Holland on business. We were sitting by a canal having lunch when the owner of the restaurant asked if there was a Mr Dyke in our party. He told me there was a phone call for me. It was Christopher Bland, who told me that it wasn't a good day to be out of the country as that morning Granada had gone into the market and bought 14.99 per cent of LWT at £5 a share. This cost Granada a total of £67.9 million and they had paid 30 per cent more per share than the closing price on the London Stock Exchange the day before. A week later they bought another 5 per cent, taking them up to 19.9 per cent, the maximum they were allowed to own.

On the plane home that day I was very down. I had made several million pounds that morning and yet I realized what it could mean. We were in danger of losing the company we loved.

There was much speculation at the time that the Government was going to change the ownership rules on ITV to allow any one company

to own two large franchises. Gerry Robinson and Charles Allen, two people from the catering industry who were now running Granada, had clearly decided that they wanted to own LWT if the opportunity arose and had made a pre-emptive strike.

A month earlier, in May 1993, LWT had bought a 14 per cent stake in Yorkshire/Tyne Tees Television in a friendly deal I did with the company's Chairman and Managing Director Clive Leach. As part of the deal we had taken over responsibility for selling Yorkshire's advertising time. In September of that year we found out that Yorkshire had been overstating its total advertising revenue. The company was about to declare a decent profit when in fact it had made a significant loss.

Ron Miller, LWT's Sales Director, had discovered this and as LWT's director on the Board of Yorkshire/Tyne Tees I had been the whistle blower. I had to go direct to the Chairman of the Audit Committee and tell him what we had found. As a result, Clive Leach resigned from the company and a Tyne Tees man, Ward Thomas, took over as Chairman. A couple of years later Bruce Gyngell became Managing Director of the company and stayed until it was sold to Granada in 1997.

Granada finally made their bid for LWT in December 1993. We knew it was coming and were ready. We had an alternative proposal to put to the shareholders. Instead of Granada buying LWT we, along with Anglia Television, would buy the whole of Yorkshire/Tyne Tees. We would own 80 per cent of the Yorkshire licence and 20 per cent of the Tyne Tees, while Anglia would own 80 per cent of Tyne Tees and 20 per cent of Yorkshire. Eventually, when the rules allowed it, we would merge all four companies to create a single ITV company to cover London and the East of England.

It was a brilliant plan and I believe to this day that it would have worked and that we could have seen off the Granada bid. We had an agreement to buy Yorkshire/Tyne Tees at £4 a share, which turned out to be a great price (it was eventually bought by Granada in June 1997 at £7 a share). But the directors of Anglia lost their nerve. Their merchant bank told them that the Granada takeover of LWT would happen and that Anglia would be left stranded. Gutlessly, they pulled out.

It was then a straight battle between Granada and LWT. We put up a spirited fight and forced Granada to increase their bid for the company on two occasions before 57 per cent of our shareholders finally accepted

the bid. We were a very successful management team with a brilliant track record – I believe we had been the fourth most successful company in Britain over the previous four years in terms of the increase in our stock price – and yet our shareholders sold us out. The real villain was a woman called Carol Galley who worked for Mercury Asset Management. When you met her she was charming but her nickname in the City was 'the ice maiden'. Mercury owned about 14 per cent of Granada and 14 per cent of LWT, and she decided to go against us even though we believed we had the better management. From that moment on I always described her as 'the witch'. She did exactly the same thing a couple of years later when Granada bought Forte: she sold out Forte. She was wrong both times. Carol Galley's reputation was bruised some years later when Unilever took Mercury to court claiming that they had mismanaged the Unilever pension fund. In the end Mercury had to pay £130 million into the fund. I opened a bottle of champagne that night and toasted a great result.

On the last day of the battle for LWT Christopher Bland and I considered doing something rather brave, if not reckless, to try to save the company. Christopher had been phoned that morning by an arbitrager (someone who buys in one market for immediate resale in another) who had built up a 3 per cent stake in the company. He was just about to sell out to Granada but told Christopher that if he offered a higher bid he could have the shares.

We knew the result of the takeover bid was going to be close, with shareholders like Warburg Pincus (an American venture capital business) and Fidelity supporting us, and when I got into the office Christopher suggested that he and I between us bought the shares we were being offered by the arbitrager. It would have cost us some £23 million. As neither of us had that sort of money we set about trying to raise it by borrowing it. After about an hour we both realized this could be madness: we could both lose an awful lot of money – as much as we'd made from the whole LWT scheme. I looked up at Christopher and said, 'If I go home tonight and we've lost I won't have a job. If we do this I might be penniless as well.' In the end the arbitrager's shares had gone before we could do it, which was just as well as we would still have lost the bid and we would have overpaid for the shares. But it certainly kept us busy for a couple of hours in a day that turned out to be our last in control of LWT.

Late in the afternoon of Friday 25 February 1994 Gerry Robinson rang Christopher and told him that Granada now had 57 per cent acceptances and owned LWT. That night we had another big party in the LWT bar, although it was more like a wake.

LWT and Granada had never been on friendly terms so it was ironic that we had been bought by the ITV company we disliked the most. In a speech to the Royal Television Society biennial symposium in Cambridge in September 1993, Christopher had explained how great the animosity was between the two companies when he said of John Birt: 'While at LWT he tried desperately to persuade Granada to act in the interests of the ITV system as a whole. In the end he left LWT and took on the much easier task of trying to modernize the BBC.'

The following week I met Gerry Robinson, who tried to persuade me to stay as Chief Executive of LWT. During the bid Granada had tried to split Christopher and me by making it clear that there was a good job for me in Granada if they won. I was having none of it during the bid and I was having none of it now. As far as I was concerned, Christopher was my friend and Granada was the enemy. There were no circumstances in which I would work for them, so I turned down the offer to stay, took the two years' pay my contract stipulated, and left LWT.

There was something about LWT at that time that was lost with the Granada takeover. It was a cocky, confident place where programme makers liked to work. As a result they made some extraordinary programmes. It was one big family, but with the takeover that came to an end. Over the next few years most of my team left, and when they did many of them rang me to tell me they were going, as if they wanted my approval.

It is difficult to explain today how devastated I felt then. Only a couple of things in my life – the failure of my marriage and the death of my father – had been as bad. I was 47 and my world had disappeared. I no longer knew what I was or who I was. I remember going to pick the kids up from school thinking everyone was watching me, seeing me as a has-been. Without the power, the title, the staff, the driver, the personal assistant, what was left? What was I?

That I was now rich didn't make any difference to how I felt. I remember going for lunch with a mate, the pop music promoter Harvey Goldsmith, and I started by telling him what we had done wrong. He looked

up and said, 'Greg, you've just walked away with £7 million. You didn't do anything wrong.' That wasn't how I saw it. I'd lost my job, my company, and my colleagues. Living through that period made what happened ten years later at the BBC so much easier to bear.

It was a truly miserable time and I made life at home truly miserable. When Clive Jones, by then an executive with Carlton, rang one day Alice answered the phone. Aged nine, she asked him if he could get me a job because I was driving everyone mad. That old line that politicians use so often when they are fired, that they wanted to 'spend more time with their family', didn't apply to me. I discovered that my family didn't want to spend that much more time with me.

I learnt a lot from the LWT experience, but it took me some time to understand it. I learned about money and City institutions and how it didn't matter how well you had done – they would still sell you out if it suited them. I learnt that, emotionally, you shouldn't get too tied into an organization because, just as had happened at TV-am ten years earlier, someone could take it away and there would be nothing you could do about it. And finally I had learnt that as the boss you could make a difference, that you could take a company through difficult times and still treat people properly and with respect.

I also learnt to live with suddenly being rich. Both Sue and I worried about the effect it would have on our life, our kids, and our attitude to

I left LWT when it was taken over by Granada. I was asked to stay on to carry on running the company but I didn't want to work for people I saw as 'the enemy'.

the world. We set up a charitable trust fund and gave quite a lot of money away: in particular we looked for opportunities to help individuals change their lives by helping with their education.

But we also enjoyed the money. We renovated a beautiful set of derelict barns near Stockbridge in Hampshire, which we turned into a place to relax and play. In one barn we built an indoor swimming pool and I insisted on having a chute from the floor above so you could get out of bed, wander along to the chute and go straight into the pool. We built our own football pitch, a tennis court, and some stables. At the age of 50, I took up horse riding, which I discovered could be quite dangerous. One day, when I'd come off yet again and my horse (appropriately named Big Horse) had arrived home without me, I asked Sue if she'd been worried when the horse had returned riderless. She replied that her only thought was, 'I'm rich.'

I found out later that becoming rich also turned you into a different sort of employee. Once you've got what is known as 'fuck-off money' you take more risks and become more cavalier in your attitude: if money is plentiful you don't have to take crap from your employer. In many ways you become more creative and more likely to succeed, but also more dangerous.

During this period I also began to make other investments with the money I'd made. It was in the middle of the recession and a lot of businesses were in trouble; there were bargains to be picked up. I bought a golf club and a number of cottages in Dartmouth in Devon from the receiver. After a few difficult years at the beginning it is now a very successful business. I also bought a restaurant, which taught me never to buy another one; and I began developing properties in the West Country. (When I joined the BBC I was allowed to keep these businesses, which meant that the newspapers were to crawl all over these activities a few years later.)

I was out of full-time work for most of the year. I was offered a few jobs I didn't fancy as I wanted to stay in the television business. Early on I was asked by the US media company Time Warner to get involved in a bid for Channel Five and I became a consultant for them, working a couple of days a week. Their partners were the media groups Pearson, who had recently bought the remnants of Thames Television, and United News and Media, who owned most of Meridian Television, which had

won the old TVS franchise. The idea was that I would become the Chief Executive if we won the Channel Five franchise.

After a few months Frank Barlow, the Managing Director of Pearson, decided that he would rather I was running his fledgling television business than be Chief Executive of a Channel Five bid that might, or might not, succeed. He offered me the job of Chairman and Chief Executive of Pearson Television and I decided to accept. I joined Pearson in January 1995.

I immediately asked Tony Cohen to leave the Granada-owned LWT and come and join me to help plan a strategy to build a significant television business. Pearson had already bought Thames Television from Thorn EMI at what turned out to be a ridiculously low price of £99 million. In the years to come we sold the Thames shares in SAS, the European satellite business, for £130 million and made a lot of money out of continuing to sell *The Bill* to ITV. On top of that there was a £30 million surplus in the Thames pension fund that was merged into the Pearson fund. By any standards Frank Barlow had done a great deal and Colin Southgate, Chairman of Thorn EMI, a terrible one.

Tony Cohen and I decided that the only way to expand was to go international. At the time Reg Grundy's business was for sale and we decided to try to buy it. Grundy Worldwide had started as an Australian business making game shows and soaps. Its greatest success was *Neighbours*, a big hit for the BBC that was making Grundy a lot of money. As a result he'd moved the business out of Australia to Bermuda. He had one of the most complicated tax structures I'd ever seen. Reg had made tax avoidance an art form.

A few years earlier he had decided to expand in Europe and by the time we were interested in buying the company he had three successful daily soaps running in Germany – *Gute Zeiten, Schlechte Zeiten* (Good Times Bad Times), *Unter Uns* (Among Us), and *Verbotene Liebe* (Forbidden Love). Reg, who owned the vast bulk of the business, was in the process of floating the company on the New York Stock Exchange when we intervened. He was interested in selling to us but needed to be assured that we would care for his company.

We arranged to meet at JFK Airport in New York in March 1995 and I flew out on Concorde for a four-hour meeting before flying back the same night. I met Reg and his wife Joy in a room at the airport and took a tough American merchant banker with me, Nancy Peretsman. Reg and

Joy were very emotional. Joy explained that the company was their baby: they had never had children, and losing it was terribly sad for them. At one time they were both crying.

Nancy looked at me as if to ask, 'What the hell is this?' But I understood how they both felt and tried to look and sound sympathetic. In the end they agreed to sell the company for $386 million and I then had the job of convincing Frank Barlow and the Board of Pearson that it was a good deal. Eventually they too agreed and we announced the deal, much to the surprise of the people working for Grundy and of their merchant bankers, who were in the middle of the US flotation.

It turned out to be a brilliant deal. Thanks to Mike Murphy, Grundy's head of drama in Europe, within two years we had two extra soaps running in Germany, a soap and a weekly serial in Italy, and a soap in Hungary. We doubled Grundy's profits and also opened up production companies right across Europe.

With the success of Grundy I had got the acquisition bug and with the help of Tony Cohen and a brilliant young French strategist called Cecile Frot Coutaz we set about buying some more companies. We next acquired SelecTV, the makers of *Birds of a Feather*, who also owned 15 per cent of the Meridian franchise. Buying it was difficult because it was a publicly quoted company, although the Managing Director, Alan McKeon, who was married to the comedienne Tracey Ullman, ran it more like a private business.

Eventually the deal went through, in February 1996, for £46 million and we immediately sold the shares in Meridian to Clive Hollick, the Chief Executive of Meridian's parent company United News and Media, for £27 million. He bought the broadcasting assets and we bought the production company and the programme library, which included a deal with the situation comedy writers Laurence Marks and Maurice Gran. In retrospect Clive got the better deal; sadly, in the time Marks and Gran were writing for Pearson they never produced the equivalent of *Birds of a Feather*.

After SelecTV we acquired a US movie distribution company called ACI, which we bought from a range of producers who made television movies for the US networks. Initially it was a good buy but in recent years the US networks have put more and more of their work in-house, squeezing out the independent producers.

Finally we bought All American, a big US production company that made *Baywatch* and, for the CBS network, *The Price is Right*. It also had a big library of game show formats, which was one of the businesses we were in across Europe. We bought it from an American of Italian descent called Tony Scotti and after acquiring it we heard some odd stories about the company. It seemed that a prostitute used to turn up in the Los Angeles offices every afternoon to satisfy one of the staff (not, I might add, Tony Scotti).

In four years we built Pearson Television into one of the biggest independent production companies in the world, with operations in twenty-five countries. We had also expanded our broadcasting business by being part of the consortium that won the Channel Five franchise in the UK. Our partners in Channel Five were Clive Hollick's United News and Media, RTL (the Luxembourg-based broadcasting company), and Warburg Pincus, who had been a shareholder in LWT and whose director, Dominic Shorthouse, I much admired. I also admired the way they had supported management all the way through the LWT takeover when it would have been much easier not to do so. When we needed a fourth shareholder I phoned Dominic.

The bidding process for Channel Five was comparatively simple. It was what happened soon after the bids were submitted that made it interesting. The Independent Television Commission had decided that they weren't going to let Ray Snoddy reveal the sizes of all the bids this time. Instead they were going to announce how much people had bid on the day they received them.

There were four bids. The highest was from UKTV, a consortium led by a Canadian Company called Can West, who owned broadcasters in Canada and Australia. While legally they met the ownership requirements, it was quite clear it was a foreign bid. They also bid a figure of £36 million, to be paid annually to the Treasury, which we all believed the ITC would decide was too high.

Amazingly the next two bidders, our group and a Virgin consortium, had both bid the identical sum, exactly £22 million and two thousand pounds a year. No one believed this was a coincidence and the press naturally portrayed it as a conspiracy. The only problem was that no one could explain why we would have chosen to have bid the same amount. If we had known the exact size of the Virgin bid we would have gone

higher; if Virgin had known ours, they would surely have bid higher too.

The strange thing was that on the morning the bids were submitted Clive Hollick and I had changed our bid. The bid had to be multiples of a thousand pounds and we had a long discussion about whether or not one thousand was a multiple of a thousand or not. In the end we decided to increase our bid by one thousand pounds without consulting our partners in the consortium. That one decision made the two bids identical. To this day I still don't know whether it was a bizarre coincidence or whether there was indeed some sort of conspiracy. While writing this book I've had a 'Come on, now, tell me the truth' conversation with Clive, but he denies that there was a plot, and I certainly wasn't involved in one, so maybe it was just a coincidence.

In the end it didn't matter because neither the Can West Consortium nor Virgin passed the quality threshold and, rather surprisingly, we were left the winner. The only other bidder to get through the quality threshold was a consortium involving BSkyB headed up by David Elstein. They were planning to bid £25 million and would have won, but at the last minute Rupert Murdoch dramatically reduced the bid to just £2 million. His partners in the consortium were furious with him because they knew that, at that level, it effectively meant they were dropping out. So why did he do this?

There had certainly been a campaign run in the non-Murdoch press against the BSkyB bid and Michael Grade, then Chief Executive at Channel Four, had written a very strong article arguing against his gaining control of Channel Five; but none of this would have been enough to stop the Murdoch bid. I've always suspected that he was told by the Prime Minister, John Major, or by one of his senior people, that for him to be in effective control of Channel Five, as well as BSkyB and all his national newspapers, was a step too far. Why else would he pull out when all the work had been done?

At Channel Five we set about doing the preparatory work for launching the channel. We changed our Chief Executive after a few months because we couldn't get it through to the management that, as the shareholders, we wanted preferential treatment in things like programme supply. We brought in David Elstein, who had been working for BSkyB since leaving Thames some years earlier. Soon afterwards I replaced Frank Barlow as Chairman of the company, a position I held until I joined the BBC in 1999.

The biggest task Channel Five faced was the retuning of about two-thirds of the nation's video recorders, which was no small challenge. We recruited an army of retuners and set about the task. We met a million problems, including the eccentricities of some of the residents of Britain. In one house the retuner found a sausage stuck in the back of the video. When asked why it was there the householder explained that he could only get his video to work when he had his finger in the same place. This had naturally proved tiring, so he had used a sausage instead.

The cost of retuning ended up being £165 million – about three times what we had set aside in our business plan. I am still not convinced it was necessary. In the few areas where we should have retuned, but didn't, it didn't seem to make any difference.

Our second major problem was that when we launched the channel the signal in London wasn't strong enough and the picture in many homes in the London area was awful. We only solved this problem when the ITC agreed that we could change our position on the mast at Crystal Palace, which broadcasts to the whole of the London area. By moving to a higher position on the transmitter the picture quality improved markedly.

In Dawn Airey, Channel Five had a charismatic Director of Programmes who was an outstanding leader of her team. Some time after I had left, the Board decided to replace David Elstein as Chief Executive with Dawn. She has since joined BSkyB and is now one of James Murdoch's main lieutenants, but I know she desperately misses running her own show.

Today, Channel Five gets between a 6 and 7 per cent share of all viewing in the UK and is now profitable. I doubt it has a long-term future as a stand-alone channel and believe it needs to be part of a bigger family of channels. Clive Hollick and I always envisaged the time when Channel Five and ITV would merge and Five would become an effective ITV2. Whether it ever happens time will tell, but it would be to the benefit of both organizations if it did.

Soon after Labour came to power I received a very curious call from Peter Mandelson asking if I had half an hour to spare for a chat. I duly went to meet him and he offered me the job of finishing and running the Millennium Dome at Greenwich. I couldn't think of anything I wanted to do less, but I was polite and told him I was happy at Pearson and didn't want to move. He looked up at me and said, in that sort of threatening way

that Mandelson has adopted, that if I didn't take the job the Prime Minister would be 'very disappointed'. Given what happened later to the Dome it was a pretty good decision on my part.

Later, when the Dome was opened, just a month before I became Director-General of the BBC, I was one of many people who were invited to the opening on Millennium night. Sue and I, plus Joe and one of his friends, went to Stratford Railway Station as instructed where we waited for close on three hours to get on a train to the Dome. I, to say the least, got very annoyed at the wait. At one time a policeman told me to calm down because I might start a riot. I said that was exactly what I was trying to do. I've always hated the way the British are happy to stand in a queue for hours on end.

When we finally got to the Dome I confronted Peter Mandelson and told him there were thousands of people stuck at Stratford. Many of them were not VIPs but ordinary people who had won competitions and the like and for them it was supposed to be the best night of their lives. Mandelson was dismissive. He said, 'It won't happen again.' That night killed the Dome because most of the editors of the national newspapers were standing in that queue and they never forgot.

In many ways the Dome saga tells you a great deal about New Labour. Tony Blair decided to go ahead with the project despite the opposition of the relevant Minister, Chris Smith, and most of the Cabinet. They discussed it and voted against, but Blair did it anyway. And of course although it was quite a good idea, it cost more than planned and didn't work very well. It was an early sign that New Labour wasn't great on delivery.

In my last year at Pearson it was clear to me that it didn't make sense for the television business to stay part of the wider Pearson Group. There were no synergies to be gained by Pearson owning a television business alongside an educational publisher, Penguin Books, and the *Financial Times*. I believed the television business needed to be in a group with European-wide broadcasting interests. The problem was that Marjorie Scardino, the colourful American Chief Executive of Pearson, liked the television business and wanted to keep it in her group. A few months after I left she merged Pearson's TV business with RTL, which was part of the deal I had been urging for months. It was a true case of Sod's Law.

It was Marjorie who really got me interested in joining the BBC. One

day she said she had read an article in which my name had been mentioned as a possible candidate to run the BBC. She looked up and in her delightful Texan drawl said, 'You know, if you get offered it you've got to do it. It really matters.'

So I did it.

CHAPTER SEVEN

Joining the BBC

It was about ten past six on the morning of 2 June 1999 when the phone rang. We are not early risers in our house and we regard ten past six as the middle of the night, so we were all fast asleep. I struggled to find the phone and when I eventually picked it up John Fallon, the head of public relations for the Pearson Group, was on the other end.

'Greg, did you hear the six o'clock news on Radio Four?' he asked. I remember thinking, 'This guy doesn't have to get into work until nine. What was he doing getting up at this unearthly hour, let alone listening to the radio?' There is some irony here as it was a broadcast at seven minutes past six on Radio Four that eventually led to my demise at the BBC.

I told John that I hadn't heard the six o'clock news and was only just awake. He told me I'd better wake up pretty fast and listen to the six-thirty bulletin.

What I learnt was that William Hague, the leader of the Conservative Opposition, had issued a statement overnight announcing that he had written to the Chairman of the BBC saying that I was an unsuitable person to become Director-General. He argued that I should be ruled out of the reckoning because I was a supporter of the Labour Party, to which I had given money over a number of years. BBC News had decided that this was the number one story of the day and were headlining it.

The argument William Hague was putting forward wasn't new. Peter Ainsworth, the Opposition spokesman on Culture, Media and Sport, had said similar things already, as had *The Times* and other newspapers. In particular they had pointed out that I had helped to fund Tony Blair's challenge for the Labour leadership back in 1994. But with this move the Conserva-

tives were really upping the ante. William Hague was the leader of Her Majesty's official Opposition. A real political heavyweight weighing in.

By the time Hague joined the game I was quite close to getting the job of Director-General and I've always suspected that this was a last-ditch attempt by the Conservative Party to stop me. As it turned out it had the opposite effect. I've also always believed that by coming out against me William Hague actually secured the job for me. That's not to say that Hague was my only opponent. The six months leading up to my appointment had been a lively time, but he put the BBC Governors in a difficult position. His intervention galvanized the Labour supporters on the BBC Board behind me and meant that if the BBC Governors rejected me they would be accused of bowing to political pressure. This, in turn, would have called into question the political independence of the whole of the BBC.

Once I had got the job I had to try to make my peace with William Hague, so along with the BBC Chairman Christopher Bland and the outgoing Director-General John Birt, I went to meet him to discuss the situation. I assured him I would be politically neutral and said that all I could ask was that he judged me on my performance. He was firm but likeable and accepted the position, not that he had much option.

In the years since then I've become a bit of a William Hague fan. After he had given up the leadership of the Conservative Party I persuaded him to come and speak to my monthly management meeting, a group of about a hundred people from all parts of the BBC. He wowed them all. He was clever, funny, and profound about British and world politics. Timing is all: I suspect William Hague got the job as leader of the Conservative Party too early in his career and at the wrong time. I would not be at all surprised to see him leading the party again in the years ahead.

My journey into the BBC had actually started more than a year earlier, in July 1998, when I went for breakfast at the Ritz with Christopher Bland, my former chairman at LWT who had become Chairman of the BBC. At the time I was Chief Executive of Pearson Television, a company we had built by acquisition in a short time into one of the largest independent production companies in the world. I had recently failed in my efforts to expand it further by putting together a very large merger that would have combined the television assets of four large groups, United

News and Media, the Luxembourg group RTL, the German company Bertelsmann, and Pearson. If the merger had worked my idea was that I would have been Chief Executive of the new company.

The trouble was that getting four companies to agree on a merger at the same time was too difficult. There's simply too much plate-spinning involved. Just as three of the companies agree on the way forward the fourth plate begins to wobble. In the end the deal fell apart, although at a later stage three of the companies, RTL, Bertelsmann, and Pearson, did merge their TV businesses to create a large pan-European broadcasting and production company that in Britain owns 66 per cent of Channel Five and produces programmes like *The Bill*. It is now totally owned by Bertelsmann.

Christopher and I had stayed close after we left LWT in 1994. He'd been offered, and accepted, the job as Chairman of the National Freight Corporation and had asked me to join him as Chief Executive. I hadn't taken the job as I couldn't see myself getting excited about the trucking business. Over our breakfast at the Ritz, I told Christopher that now my major deal had fallen through I'd decided I wouldn't stay at Pearson for much longer, I'd certainly leave in the next year, and that I was trying to work out what to do next.

He said why didn't I consider coming to the BBC as Director-General to succeed John Birt, who was due to leave in 2000, having been in the job for seven years?

I'd never really seen myself as a BBC man. I had always made jokes about the sort of people who made it to the top of the BBC, suggesting that they were disproportionately made up of the public school, Oxbridge brigade. My own background was very different from that and I'd never seen the BBC as a likely home. In fact when I left LWT I was interviewed by Alan Titchmarsh on a BBC daytime chat show and asked whether I would like to run the BBC. I replied that I thought Saddam Hussein had a better chance of getting the job than I had. Of course when I was eventually appointed Director-General the clip was replayed endlessly on BBC news bulletins. When I did finally join the BBC I discovered that my views about BBC people were outdated and that the top of the organization was no longer dominated by public-school boys in the way it had been a decade or so earlier. By then the grammar-school pupils were largely in control.

Although I had never worked for the BBC I had flirted with the idea of joining the Corporation on a few occasions, although I only ever officially applied for two jobs with them. The first was as a reporter on BBC Radio Teesside when it was set up in 1970. I went to two interviews but did not get the job. At the second interview I was asked if I thought the people of Middlesbrough would understand my London accent. I pointed out that the taxi driver must have understood me as how else could I have got there from the station? I don't think the joke went down well. My second application for a job at the BBC, nearly thirty years later, was to be Director-General. In the intervening years I had been offered an executive role at the BBC by Michael Grade back in the mid Eighties when Michael was Controller of BBC One. He wanted me to join to sort out *Wogan*, BBC One's failing, five-nights-a-week chat show, by becoming its executive producer. It didn't excite me a lot, but to try to persuade me Michael offered a big carrot. He told me I would replace him as Controller of BBC One as soon as he succeeded the legendary Bill Cotton, who would soon retire as Managing Director of BBC Television.

Bill Cotton, or Sir William as he is now known, was an outstanding head of entertainment for the BBC for many years. He was also the son of the famous bandleader and looks remarkably like him. He tells a wonderful story of the day his dad became ill and couldn't lead the band on tour. The band's manager asked Bill to do it instead. Bill pointed out that he had limited musical ability and couldn't conduct. The manager looked at him, sighed, and told him that was totally irrelevant. All he had to do was get on the stage and wave his arms around, the band would do the rest. And that's what he did every night for a month.

It was Bill who had brought Michael Grade back from the USA to run BBC One. I had known Michael from my LWT days and loved his sense of fun, as well as admiring his flair and his knowledge about talent. Working with him again was a very attractive proposition. The problem was that, in typical BBC fashion, no one would put the offer to run BBC One on paper and, despite getting assurances from both Michael and Bill that they wanted me for the job, I refused to join without a letter. The BBC had a famous reputation at that time for offering the same job to a number of people. It was just as well I turned the job down because it wasn't long before Michael was poached to take over at Channel Four and wasn't in a position to deliver. But I did work with him there when

I became a director of the channel in 1988, having been appointed as an ITV representative on the Board by the Independent Television Commission.

In 1998, with the Chairman of the BBC saying that if I applied for the post of Director-General I would have a very good chance of getting the job, I began to think seriously about the prospect of running the BBC for the first time. The downside of the job was that I knew there was an enormous amount to be done. While John Birt had achieved a lot in modernizing the BBC since becoming Director-General in 1993 it was a deeply unhappy organization and Birt's BBC was also under attack from many on the outside.

In his 1992 McTaggart lecture in Edinburgh, the most important lecture in the UK television calendar, Michael Grade, by then the Chief Executive of Channel Four, had described Birt's BBC as 'a secret and forbidding place to work ... an airtight fortress from which no stray opinion is permitted to escape'. When he spoke of Birt's approach to running the organization he described it as a 'pseudo-Leninist style of management'. The following year, in 1993, the playwright Dennis Potter had gone even further in his McTaggart lecture when he said 'there are legions of troubled and embittered employees at the BBC who can scarcely understand any of the concepts of the new management culture'.

Even though the BBC had lost some of its cachet in the outside world, and was seen as a boring, process-driven organization, I was fascinated by the idea of trying to change it. This was a real leadership challenge that I knew I would find both difficult and stimulating. How easy was it to motivate and inspire an organization that had 27,000 full-time employees and countless other freelance workers?

After my first year at the BBC I was asked to record a long private interview with Ron Neill, who had retired from the BBC the year before I joined. The interview was for BBC archive purposes only. I recently re-read it and discovered that I had explained to him why I decided to go for the BBC job in the first place.

> It was a job I wanted but it was also a job I could have lived without. I like doing jobs where I'm not sure I can do them and you could see it was a job which was going to be difficult, and I found that attractive.

Ron then asked about the doubts I'd had concerning my ability to do the job.

> Firstly I'd never worked for the BBC which was a very large organiz-ation and secondly in recent years I'd been running profit and loss companies which meant the culture and ethos was going to be very different.

Ron also asked me what Sue's view had been.

> Sue didn't care a lot either way until the campaign against me started. Sue is like me in many ways and when you tell her she can't have something she'll resist. Once the campaign against me started, which I didn't expect, we just said well bugger them we'll fight this.

At a later breakfast in September 1998, again at the Ritz, I asked Chris-topher Bland if he thought my politics would be a problem given that I was an advocate of Tony Blair and New Labour and that I had given money to the Labour Party. Christopher, who knew me well and knew I had always separated my politics from my work, dismissed it as 'irrel-evant', which I honestly believed it was. I had always been much more committed to the idea of independent broadcasting than I had been to Labour. When I had given the McTaggart lecture in August 1994 it had been on precisely that subject.

The donations I'd made to Labour totalled £55,000 over the previous five years, a significant sum but nothing compared to the £1 million I'd given to charity in the same period. That's not to say there haven't been times recently when I haven't been tempted to write to the Labour Party and ask for my money back.

Looking back now, I think Christopher and I convinced each other that my politics wouldn't be a major factor if I applied for the job. How wrong we were.

It was around this time that I shaved off the beard I'd had for thirty-three years. It is now part of Dyke mythology that I did it to make myself more presentable as a candidate for the post of Director-General, but the truth is less exciting. I grew it in the first place at the age of 19, when I was a

young reporter on a local paper, to make myself look older. I shaved it off at the age of 52 to make myself look younger. Sadly, as I had grown older my beard had grown whiter and my kids, in the way that only one's own kids can, kept telling me that I looked like an old man. I think it was my daughter Alice who told me I hadn't got the nerve to shave it off. I told them I'd do it the night before we were due to go for a week's skiing, which is exactly what I did.

After a couple of days on holiday we had a family and friends vote on whether it should stay off or not. I voted to grow it again but I was outvoted 6–3, with only our eldest son Matthew and our daughter Christine supporting me. For some weeks I kept seeing this image in the mirror that bore no relation to the me I knew, but in the end I got used to my new look. My mum certainly liked it; she thought she'd got her boy back.

The possibility of my becoming Director-General was first raised publicly in a feature article in *The Guardian* in January 1999. A *Guardian* reporter, Kamal Ahmed, later political editor of *The Observer*, rang and said his editor, Alan Rusbridger, wanted him to do a profile of me. I always suspected that my old friend Melvyn Bragg had told Alan that he believed I was going to be the next Director-General and that he should keep an eye on me. The feature was very flattering with the headline 'Greg Dyke: TV's Man of the People'. In it, Kamal wrote that I was a strong candidate to become Director-General. I think it was the first time anyone inside the BBC realized that the job might go to an outsider.

In the same month Ladbrokes started taking bets on who would be the next Director-General and I was made the 3–1 joint favourite with Michael Jackson, who was by then running Channel Four, having replaced Michael Grade in June 1997. Michael later dropped out of the running and I stayed the bookies' favourite throughout the whole process.

The BBC formally advertised the job in the *Sunday Times* in March 1999. It so happened that it was a weekend when Sue, Joe, and I were in Northern Ireland staying, along with a number of other guests, at Hillsborough Castle. We had all been invited by Mo Mowlam, then Secretary of State for Northern Ireland, who liked inviting her friends over for the weekend to share the castle with her.

I remember being struck by the affection there was for Mo amongst ordinary people in Northern Ireland. We had Saturday lunch in the pub up the road from the castle and as we sat eating two elderly women came

up to her and said, 'We just wanted you to know how much we love you, Mo.' It was very moving. Of course in the end Mo became too popular in the Labour Party for the Blairites. She always believed her downfall started when she got a standing ovation at the Labour Party conference during Tony Blair's speech.

On the Sunday morning someone in the party spotted the advert for Director-General in the *Sunday Times* and there was much discussion about whether or not I should apply. There were some BBC people amongst the guests that weekend, including Martha Kearney, the *Newsnight* and *Woman's Hour* presenter, and Jon Plowman, the BBC's Head of Comedy and the man who deserves enormous credit for spotting *The Office*, the best comedy, and probably the best programme, to come out of British television in the past decade. Months later, after starting at the BBC, I was at a meeting with staff at Television Centre when Jon walked up to me and gave me a rolled-up photograph that he knew would embarrass me: it was a picture he had taken in Hillsborough Castle of Sue and me sitting side by side on the thrones normally occupied by the Queen and Prince Philip.

Soon after the job of Director-General was advertised Matthew Horsman, the media analyst and former journalist, rang my office and said he wanted to join my campaign. I explained I didn't intend to run a campaign, that if I was asked to go for the job I would, but that was all I would do. Looking back now I realize how incredibly naive this position was. Given the campaigning that was to go on by those inside the BBC, by the candidates and other executives, I needed all the friends I could find if I was to succeed in getting the job, and Matthew would have been a valuable asset to any team.

To understand what happened in the coming months one has to understand John Birt. I had known him for many years and whilst we were not best friends we were mates. We originally got to know each other well at LWT playing football together every Friday lunchtime, when I was a reporter and he was my boss as Head of Current Affairs and Features. I played in the Friday game, on and off, for twenty years.

I owe John a lot. He played a big part in my getting a series of jobs, including succeeding him as Director of Programmes at LWT. In fact when he was due to become Director-General of the BBC he asked me to join as his deputy. I turned it down because by then I was Chief

Executive of LWT and had decided that, much as I liked him, I didn't want to work for him again. He was too much of a control freak. When I refused the job he lured Bob Phillis away from his job as Chief Executive at ITN to become Deputy Director-General. A few years later he effectively demoted him and tried to get him fired.

John Birt's autobiography, *The Harder Path*, might lead you to believe that he helped me become Director-General. When John's book was published in 2002 the press picked up on the story that he had 'rehearsed' me before my final interview with the Governors. They wrote that he had coached me. Journalists even found a few rent-a-gob politicians to denounce the appointment, saying that it had been a fix and unfair to the other candidates. The story simply wasn't true.

Whilst it was true I had spent an evening with John at the Governors' request I was certainly not coached by him, and in any case I knew by then the job was virtually mine. I only went for the dinner with John because I had been asked to go. I also knew by then how hard John had worked to stop me getting the job.

My memory of the evening was that John was much more concerned about how the press had discovered – and had published the previous weekend – the fact that he had been an active member of the Labour Party when he became Director-General. I now realize this had undermined one of the central arguments he had been using with the Governors to stop me being Director-General.

Nowhere in John's long and detailed book did he mention what he had done to stop me getting the job. All we were told was that he had helped me. We had to wait for the book (*The Fun Factory: A Life in the BBC*, published in 2003) written by Will Wyatt, Managing Director of BBC Broadcasting in John's time, to get the true story. It was typical of John to leave this out of his book. I can only presume it was because it was a battle lost, and according to John's account of his life he was always right and always won.

There is a story about the title of John's book that may or may not be true. Allegedly, his mother asked him what the title *The Harder Path* meant. John explained that you had a choice in life: you could take the easy route or the hard one. His mother looked at him and asked the obvious question, 'Why would anyone take the harder path if there was an easier one available?'

So why was John so hostile to my becoming Director-General when he had supported me in getting other jobs and, seven years earlier, had asked me to be his deputy when he took over the top job?

My own view is that John was desperate to go down in history as a great Director-General of the BBC. No story better illustrates this than the one about his portrait. As they retire, each Director-General has his portrait painted, which is then hung in the council chamber at Broadcasting House in central London. Before John, all the portraits were about the same size and depicted the subject from the waist up. And then came John's. He had a full facial portrait painted by Tai-Shan Schierenberg, which was done while he was still in the job, and thus ready to be unveiled as soon as he left, or soon after. It was a distinctive and brilliant portrait, but when it was hung it completely dominated the room, dwarfing everyone else's portrait. Wherever you sat, John's eyes followed you around the room. It was so typical of John. When the time came for John's picture to be hung Christopher made him dramatically prune the numbers he wanted to invite to the party for the official unveiling of his portrait.

I was never a great fan of the portraits. While I was a strong supporter of the BBC's heritage department I believed we should respect the past but not be dominated by it. With Broadcasting House currently being rebuilt, all the portraits are now in store or out on loan. I was asked what we should do with John's. Tongue in cheek, I suggested we should lend it to BBC Scotland, the part of the BBC where John was disliked the most. (I still have to have my portrait painted following my departure.)

When John left the BBC he went off to write his autobiography, which he wanted the BBC to make into a documentary. When Jane Root, the Controller of BBC Two, turned the idea down John wrote to her and complained, sending a copy of the letter to the Chairman, Christopher Bland. Typical John.

When I worked with him at LWT John Birt was great company, and widely respected. But the longer John was at the BBC, and he was there in all for thirteen years, the more he changed. He was constantly under attack and, as a result, became obsessed with himself and his image. He believed he had saved the BBC from Mrs Thatcher by making it more efficient, which is probably true. He also believed he had made a great financial sacrifice to join the BBC: again this was true. If he had stayed at LWT he could have made a fortune along with the rest of us. This was

illustrated at one session at the annual Edinburgh Television Festival when he was on the platform and he turned to me in the audience and asked what would I have preferred, 'public vilification or £7 million'? That summed up John's views. He had saved the BBC, he had made financial sacrifices to do it, and yet he wasn't given public credit for having done so. The fact that he was widely disliked, both inside and outside the BBC, only strengthened his view that he had been unfairly treated.

My view of John was that he was always a man who worked upwards, someone who desperately wanted to be part of the power elite, part of the new establishment. Peter Mandelson, an average producer when we were all at LWT together, later became one of John's best friends when he became powerful. When he left the BBC, John not only received a peerage, he also got a job even closer to the centre of power, working on long-term strategy inside Number Ten.

In his last years as Director-General John Birt had the whole organization working on his twenty-year master plan for the BBC. In my experience the only thing you can be certain about when dealing with long-term strategic plans is that they will turn out to be wrong: there are too many variables for them ever to be right. For instance, when the BBC outlined its future for the next ten years in a document called *Extending Choice*, published in 1992, it made no mention at all of the Internet. Over the next five years the BBC's online services turned out to be its most exciting initiatives.

The failure of strategic plans is nobody's fault; it's just that the world changes faster, or in different directions, than predicted by the strategic planners. I always liked Christopher Bland's definition of strategy. He told me that any commercial decision made for 'strategic reasons' actually meant 'loss making'.

John Birt wanted as his successor someone who would not disrupt what he had done so far and would carry out the first part of his twenty-year plan. He wanted someone from inside the BBC who would carry the Birtist flame, who believed in the Birt way of doing things. He certainly didn't want someone like me coming in from outside who would probably never even read his plan.

Succession planning for the job of Director-General is close to impossible. Appointing and getting rid of the Director-General is the best sport the Governors have. BBC Governors don't actually have a lot

to do and are removed from what is happening inside the BBC. But when it comes to hiring and firing the D-G they come into their own. In recent years the majority of D-Gs have left against their will. Hugh Carleton Greene was kicked upstairs to be a Governor in 1969, Alasdair Milne was fired in 1987, Michael Checkland was pushed out early against his wishes in 1992, and John only narrowly avoided an early departure in 1993 in a controversy over his tax arrangements. And then there was me.

After John Birt, the Chairman, Christopher Bland, and the majority of the Governors were of the view that they wanted to see a culture change at the BBC. They were tired of the staff loathing the management. So when it came to John's successor the Governors were not keen to appoint a Birtist from inside the organization, which meant they were interested in appointing an outsider.

Initially, John Birt encouraged all sorts of people inside the BBC to apply for the job. To his credit, he believed that everyone who wanted should be able to have the chance to go for it, even if they didn't have a realistic chance of getting the job. It was an egalitarian policy but in practice created real problems. People who had no chance of getting the job, people like the Head of Production Matthew Bannister, began to believe they might get it.

Contenders inside the organization began to work against anyone who might be a candidate, anyone who might stop them getting the job. They tried to kill off each other's chances. It was vicious, ruthless stuff, with BBC press officers being used full time to campaign for one candidate and against others inside the BBC.

The only candidate who seemed to steer well clear of the turmoil inside the organization was Mark Byford, who was Head of the World Service and had previously been the Director of Nations and Regions, responsible for the BBC's out of London activities. Mark was only forty at the time and, according to Will Wyatt in *The Fun Factory*, he was John Birt's chosen successor. When I first met Mark, having been appointed Director-General, I told him that I knew who had done what during the campaign and that by my reckoning he was completely clean. I thanked him for playing it straight.

A number of newspapers had taken against me, led by *The Times*, whose editor Peter Stothard had decided that, for political reasons, I

shouldn't be the next Director-General. He launched a ferocious attack against me. In the spring of 1999 he published article after article and leader after leader criticizing me. The fight to stop me becoming Director-General became his campaign, supported by some senior managers inside the BBC.

When I look back now at the articles and leaders in *The Times*, they appear to me to be both pompous and ridiculous. In one leader the paper conceded that I was no 'full pedigree poodle' but pointed out that I had given money to Tony Blair's leadership campaign and that 'for anyone ambitious to climb the greasy poles of new Labour Britain, this was doubtless money well and sincerely spent'.

Four years later, of course, things were rather different when the BBC and the Blair Government were at war with each other over the events surrounding the reporting of the Iraq war. Like all Rupert Murdoch's papers, *The Times* had followed their master's voice and supported Britain's involvement in Iraq. As a result, *The Times* were squarely on Tony Blair's side in the battle with the BBC. Who was the Labour poodle now?

The strange thing about the *Times* campaign against me was that the paper's media editor Ray Snoddy, the doyen of media reporters for more than twenty years, first on the *Financial Times* and then on *The Times* itself, was of the opposite view. The more *The Times* rampaged against me, the more Snoddy, to his great credit, supported me in his column. He refused point blank to play Stothard's's game. When I eventually got the job it was Snoddy who gave Stothard the news.

My friends in television rallied round. Clive Jones organized a letter to *The Times* signed by all sorts of people who had worked with me in the past, people like John Stapleton, Peter McHugh, Mark Damazer, Adam Boulton, Trevor Phillips, and David Cox, who all knew I had no history of trying to distort the editorial process to match my own political views. Barry Cox, the former Head of Current Affairs at LWT, also defended my journalistic experience, which *The Times* had described as 'limited', and the actor Nigel Havers wrote to the paper to tell them that I was 'a fine man [whose] programme-making, from grass roots to the chairman's office, has been of a very high calibre indeed'.

And throughout it all, Melvyn Bragg advised and supported me, lobbying from the sidelines wherever he could. The help I got from him and his wife Cate Haste was invaluable. They helped to keep me enthusiastic

despite the drivel that was being written in the papers, and they made sure I never got depressed.

The row went on in the columns of *The Times* for weeks but sitting in the Pearson building about half a mile away from Broadcasting House I wasn't that involved in it. I was still doing my day job at Pearson despite the furore going on around me.

Alan Yentob, the BBC's Director of Television at the time, then turned up in my office to say he wanted to join me and run as my deputy. I like Alan and think he is a talented man, and I could have done far worse than have him as my number two; but the last thing I was going to do was get involved in the inner politics of the BBC. Instead Alan announced his own candidacy, only to be publicly ridiculed as 'completely disorganized' by the other candidates and their press officers inside the BBC. It was nasty stuff.

Each candidate was asked to prepare a manifesto that was to be not more than three pages long. I had a lot to say, so the typeface I used got gradually smaller and smaller to ensure I could get it all on three pages. When I re-read my manifesto whilst writing this book I was pleasantly surprised by how much of it we had achieved in the four years I was at the BBC. In May 1999 I saw the BBC's single biggest problem as one of culture. I wrote then:

> Most of all I believe I could bring to the BBC a style of leadership which enables creative talent to flourish at the same time as being financially and managerially accountable. Internally, I believe the BBC has a cultural problem. It has moved to a culture which is very top-down in style, internally competitive, too centralized, and one in which people are reluctant to question. It is very clear to me that many of the people who work for the BBC today don't like the new culture.
>
> The interesting question this raises is: can the modernization process be continued and be successful with a different and more inclusive style of management? I believe it can. The most exciting organizations around the world are those with open and inclusive cultures. Interestingly, in terms of management style the BBC has moved in exactly the opposite direction to that chosen by the most successful companies of the 90's.

I believe the most important leadership challenge facing the next Director-General is to build an inclusive culture without losing the momentum for change.

I then listed what I believed needed changing in a number of areas. These included responding to devolution by expanding the BBC's production bases outside London, expanding the BBC's role as an international broadcaster, making the BBC's services more relevant to the young, and dramatically changing some of John Birt's internal organizational changes.

When I re-read it I also realized just how much of my manifesto was anti-Birtist. If he had read it, and I've little doubt one of the Governors would have shown it to him, I can understand why he didn't want me as his successor.

I had a series of interviews with different groups of Governors. The most bizarre was in a flat in Shepherd Market, Mayfair, which the BBC had hired for the day. It was later discovered it was normally used by prostitutes. I remember another where I told the Governors that I only had a certain amount of time as I was due to see Bruce Springsteen in concert at Earls Court. And I remember a final meeting with the whole Board, the day before I was appointed, at which Christopher had told me in advance that I was likely to get the job.

By the end there were four candidates left, two internal and two others who coincidentally both worked for the Pearson group. The internal candidates still in play were Mark Byford and the Head of News, Tony Hall. The two candidates from Pearson were Michael Lynton, an Americanized Briton who headed up Pearson-owned Penguin Books, and myself from Pearson Television. Michael didn't get offered the BBC job but was later offered the role of Chief Executive at Channel Four. He turned it down so it went to the BBC's Director of Television, Mark Thompson, instead. Michael went on to a major job in Hollywood as Chairman and Chief Executive of Sony Entertainment. Howard Davies, currently the Director of the London School of Economics, was also on the final list but he pulled out at the last moment.

To hear about both Pearson candidates Dennis Stevenson, the Chairman of Pearson, was invited along to see Christopher. To Dennis's surprise he found himself meeting the full Board of BBC Governors. I understand

he was full of praise for me and that swung some doubting Governors my way.

Towards the end of a lengthy and very public process John Birt, Will Wyatt and friends decided that they should try harder to stop me getting the job and tried to directly influence the Governors against me. I know for certain that John told Heather Rabbatts, at that time Chief Executive of Lambeth Council and a relatively new Governor, that she mustn't vote for me as an outsider. Ron Neill, who by this time had left, was sent to see the Governor for Wales, Roger Jones, to try to turn him against me, but Roger, an entrepreneur in the pharmaceutical industry, was having none of it. Mark Byford was Ron Neill's protégé so naturally he wanted him to become Director-General.

There was also a good deal of leaking going on. In his book Will Wyatt owns up to placing a story in *The Times* about my giving money to both Chris Smith and Mo Mowlam to help fund their offices when they were shadow secretaries of state for culture. The story was true, but it was hardly a scoop, as the piece implied, as it came from a letter I had written to *The Independent* some years earlier. To be fair to Will Wyatt, he was the only person who later admitted straight out to me that he had opposed my appointment because he didn't think someone with such strong links to a political party should be Director-General. Later he wrote publicly that he had been wrong to oppose me and thought I had done the job well.

The only time I was seriously unnerved was late in the process when the remaining candidates were asked to write a confidential letter to the Governors outlining their political and business interests, including any political donations they had made. I outlined mine in full only to find the letter printed verbatim in *The Times* two days later. I suddenly realized that at least one Governor was leaking against me. Today I could make a good guess as to who it was.

But it was all to no avail, I had enough supporters with Christopher Bland and his Deputy Barbara Young (then Chairman of English Nature), Richard Eyre (the former Director of the National Theatre who had encouraged me to apply in the first place), Heather Rabbatts, Roger Jones, plus the support of at least two others.

I think it was on Wednesday 23 June, just before midnight, that Christopher rang me in the car. Sue and I had been to dinner with Jeremy and

Sue Beadle and it was memorable because Jeremy was on an odd diet and had walked into the restaurant with a bag of ingredients that he'd asked the chef to cook. When I picked up the phone Christopher said 'I'm afraid it's bad news. You got the job.' By then I was pretty sure it was mine, but I was still excited. It had been a long, tortuous, and unpleasant process, but I had made it. The boy from Hayes was going to run one of Britain's great institutions.

According to Will Wyatt, 'John was low. His plans and his strenuous efforts to influence events had failed.'

The following day I went to Broadcasting House to arrange the details of my contract. As my appointment had not yet been announced, and because the BBC wanted to keep it secret for as long as they could, I was taken into the building through a tunnel that ran from another BBC building on the other side of the road. It was a bizarre experience, as though I was going for a job in the secret service rather than the media. Inside I met Margaret Salmon, the rather cold Director of Human Resources, who outlined what I was being offered. I didn't question a single thing. I took what was on offer – including, I discovered later, a pension deal that was far inferior to the one enjoyed by other people in the BBC, including Margaret Salmon.

My view was simple. I had made a lot of money over the previous ten years, and this job wasn't about money. I had earned just under a million pounds in my last year with Pearson and was coming to the BBC to earn about a third of that. But I didn't care. I accepted the package they offered me, which included stipulations as to which shares I could keep, which ones I had to sell, and by when. Some months later that became important. The worst was that I had to give up being a director of Manchester United and give up my four seats in the directors' box at Old Trafford as both the BBC and Manchester United rightly saw it was a conflict of interest. You couldn't be on both sides of the negotiating table. My kids have never forgiven me for that.

I was joining as Deputy Director-General and Director-General Designate, which meant my initials inside the BBC now read as GD, DDG, DGD. With initials like that it was quite clear that I had joined the public sector. It was agreed I would join in November but would not become Director-General until 1 April 2000 to allow a five-month handover

period – about four months longer than I reckoned was needed. In the end it was cut to three months because John Birt received his peerage and had to leave at the end of January 2000.

On Friday 25 June I turned up officially for the first time at Broadcasting House, where my appointment was to be announced, although it had been leaked and confirmed by the BBC the day before. I got there early and the only television crew outside was Sky News. The trouble was the cameraman had nipped off for a cup of tea and so missed my arrival. I felt sorry for him and restaged it.

We had a press conference with Christopher Bland, John Birt, and me on the podium. In discussions with James Hogan of the City public relations company Brunswick, who was advising me personally, I had decided that in the press conference or in any interviews I gave I would only talk about programmes because that was what I believed the BBC was all about. I also knew it was what the staff would want to hear and I had to start rebuilding morale immediately.

At the press conference virtually all the attention was on me, which was not surprising given that I was the new boy, but this immediately upset John Birt. I can only assume his ego was bruised. That weekend I took a call from Christopher saying that we had a problem with John, who was complaining that I hadn't been warm enough about him or praised his achievements enough at the press conference. In fact I don't think I'd mentioned John at all. I pointed out to Christopher that I was John's successor, not his mother; but as I certainly owed the job to Christopher's unswerving support, I did agree that from then on I would tell the staff at any meeting I attended what a great job John had done in modernizing the organization. But this would mean ignoring his biggest weakness: the fact that most of his staff hated him and everything he stood for.

I realized then what a long and miserable five months I faced before I finally took over and could truly speak my mind.

There were two further stories in the Murdoch newspapers that related directly to my joining the BBC. Both involved my private business dealings. When I'd first met up with Margaret Salmon, the BBC's Director of Human Resources, I'd offered to put all my business interests into a private trust, in the same way that politicians do when taking government office. She said that wouldn't be enough and that instead the BBC would

want me to sell a whole range of shares by 6 April 2000, six days after I became Director-General.

The shares I was being asked to sell, which had all been outlined in the BBC's offer letter, included my shares in Granada, which I owned as a result of the Granada takeover of LWT, Pearson, and Manchester United. I agreed without question and started to sell all my shares in media companies.

On 16 January the *Sunday Times* published a story saying that I still owned £6 million worth of shares in Granada, the largest of the ITV companies. The story was true but irrelevant because I had been given until 6 April to sell them. The *Sunday Times* ran it as if it was a great exclusive and a scandal. It was a typically exaggerated Sunday newspaper story and quoted one BBC Governor as saying, 'Of course it's a conflict of interests, he must sell now', as if it was news to the Governor in question that I owned the shares. Richard Brooks, the journalist who wrote the article, even quoted Lord Rees-Mogg, a former Deputy Chairman of the BBC, saying, 'If he did not reveal to the BBC Governors that he had the shares when he was appointed, he should resign now', even though all my holdings had been revealed at the time of my appointment. I had told Brooks this myself.

It was the usual way in which certain journalists turn a small story into a large one. They phone people up who know nothing about the story and get them to say things on the basis that the story is true. There are always people, particularly opposition politicians of all parties, who are willing to do this simply to get their names in the papers. It is why, after four years at the BBC, I had little regard for those politicians who never let the facts stand in the way of publicity.

Where both the BBC and I had made a mistake was in not considering whether the date by which I had to sell the shares – 6 April – should have been brought forward when John Birt was appointed to the House of Lords and my starting date as Director-General was consequently brought forward to 1 February. Changing the sell-by date hadn't crossed my mind, or the Chairman's. In the end I decided that I could kill the story simply by selling all the shares, which I did the following week.

In late January *The Times* ran a story saying that I was involved in a property business in Devon at the same time as being Deputy Director-General – again implying that this was scandalous. They quoted John

Tusa, a former Head of the BBC World Service, as saying 'Call me old-fashioned but I think if you are running the BBC it ought to be a full-time job.' This time I heard that some of the Governors were concerned about this story, particularly Pauline Neville-Jones, the former Foreign Office official who had opposed my becoming Director-General. Soon after I joined the BBC John Birt told me that I should never assume the BBC Governors remembered what they'd decided at an earlier meeting: you always had to remind them. He was to be proved right on countless occasions.

When the Governors were discussing my property interests at their next meeting I took in the letter I had sent them during the application process outlining all my business dealings, the very letter that one of them had leaked to *The Times*. This included details of my political payments and my business interests, including property development. I also pointed out that I had offered to put these interests into a blind trust but that the BBC had decided this would not be necessary and that they had not asked me to sell the property interests.

That was the end of that particular story, but what both stories showed me was that my battle with certain sections of the press, particularly the Murdoch press, was only just beginning. During the appointment process *The Times* and its editor Peter Stothard had been humiliated. They were unlikely to leave it at that.

On 29 January 2000 I became the BBC's thirteenth Director-General, and the first who had not been either to a public school or to Oxbridge. I was also the first Director-General in peace time who had never previously worked for the organization.

CHAPTER EIGHT

The BBC Years (1)

At the end of my first week at the BBC I woke up very early thinking about what I had discovered. I was deeply depressed, so I got up and decided to write down what I was feeling. I thought it was important that I captured these feelings, if only for myself. I couldn't believe how bureaucratic and paper-driven the whole place was.

The worst point had been getting into my car on the Tuesday or Wednesday evening of that first week and finding an enormous pile of papers more than a foot high on the back seat. This was my reading for tomorrow. I pointed out to Emma Scott – who had been assigned to look after me as my business manager in the early weeks but who remained on my staff for the whole four years – that I hadn't read that much in my life and certainly wasn't going to start now.

What I learned in my first few weeks was that the main activity at the executive level of the BBC seemed to be writing and reading documents, reports, and policy papers. The aim seemed to be to produce the perfect policy paper; when it was completed and approved, that in itself would be enough. Of course that wasn't the case. I remember a senior figure at the BBC telling me in those early days that I needed to understand that if everyone at a BBC meeting appeared to agree on something you couldn't assume that they did agree, and you certainly couldn't assume that they would then do what had been 'agreed'.

After a while the message began to get around that I was refusing to read these ridiculously long reports. Instead of making them shorter some people started doing two – what they called the 'proper' one and a condensed version for me. In the end I managed to get all papers shorter,

but the only way I could keep them that way was by complaining every few months when I spotted them getting longer again.

I'll always remember my first strategy conference. John Birt was still Director-General and he opened the session by saying that we weren't moving fast enough as an organization and that we had to get things done more quickly. He then proceeded to reject most of the detailed proposals on the agenda on the grounds that the papers that had been written for the conference weren't good enough. John was obsessed with getting everything dead right. Once a year he used to present his view of the BBC to the Governors' annual conference, usually held at a hotel somewhere in the South of England. His staff told me he would prepare as many as seventeen different versions of his presentation and rehearse it for days on end.

What I eventually worked out was that this was an organization that, at the top level, was risk averse. It commissioned more and more analysis and produced more and more papers to avoid taking risky decisions. The approach assumed, firstly, that the more analysis you undertook the more likely you were to take the right decision, not something that I have ever seen proven. Much more importantly, and the reason why the reports were so lengthy, was that if the policy went wrong you could point to an exhaustive paper trail to protect you. It was classic civil service mentality.

My own approach to organizations, business, and life is that you have to 'try things'. Some will work, others won't. If you try too many that don't work then you don't survive. It's as simple as that. On the other hand, if most of your initiatives work, then you end up being successful. What you can't do is analyse every good idea to death without taking a decision. If you do that everyone will lose enthusiasm for the project. At some time you have to decide to proceed, even if you are not 100 per cent certain, or else abandon the project – if only because everyone involved has had enough and is getting bored.

A good example of my approach came in my first year at the BBC when we decided to make a radical move, and make it quickly. The *Daily Telegraph* described it as follows:

This is a bad decision; for the BBC, for television in general, for the licence paying public, and for British political culture . . . In yielding

to the forces of Philistinism at the corporation Mr Dyke is clearly signalling his priorities. They are evidently very different from those of the BBC's core viewers . . . A philistine BBC is a supine BBC; a nation kept in ignorance is a nation easily led.

That was the *Daily Telegraph* leader on 15 August 2000. And the *Telegraph* wasn't alone. The media spokesmen for all three of the main political parties joined in the criticism of the BBC, as did some, though not all, of the other national newspapers.

According to the detractors, we were 'dumbing down' the BBC and the nation yet again. So what had we done? What momentous decision had we taken to bring such a tirade down on the heads of the BBC? The answer is that we had announced that we planned to move our nightly television news on BBC One from 9 p.m. to 10 p.m. Hardly the end of the civilized world as we knew it, but you wouldn't have known that from the reaction of politicians and the press.

ITV had occupied the ten o'clock slot with *News at Ten* for more than thirty-five years but had recently vacated it and were playing their news later. Their move had really upset the politicians and, under orders from Downing Street, Chris Smith, then Secretary of State for Culture, Media and Sport, had been trying desperately to 'persuade' ITV to move back. I had a lot of time for Chris and thought he was an excellent Secretary of State, and we were all surprised and disappointed when he was sacked after the 2001 election. But on this issue we disagreed.

Even before I joined the Corporation it was obvious to me that the BBC should move its news from nine o'clock into the 10 o'clock slot vacated by ITV. This would give the BBC two advantages. Firstly, it would increase the news ratings because the competition wasn't so strong at ten o'clock; secondly, it would allow the BBC to schedule more competitively at the crucial nine o'clock junction and enable us to start our drama, most of which couldn't be played before the nine o'clock watershed, at the same time as ITV rather than thirty minutes later.

We decided to make the move, got it unanimously approved by the BBC Governors, and agreed that I would announce it as part of the McTaggart lecture I was due to give at the Edinburgh Television Festival in August 2000, just six months after becoming Director-General. The story broke a day early, and I received an urgent phone-call from Chris

Smith asking me not to make the announcement. I told him I couldn't do that and phoned the BBC Chairman, Christopher Bland, to tell him what had happened. Christopher was indignant. His view was that the Governors had approved the change and that Chris Smith's view was therefore irrelevant. It was the Governors who were in control of the BBC, not the politicians.

So I went ahead and made the announcement and confirmed that we would be implementing the change some time during the following year, 2001. Then ITV announced on 21 September that they were going back to the ten o'clock slot that they had recently vacated. In a bizarre agreement between Charles Allen, the Chief Executive of Granada, and Patricia Hodgson, Chief Executive of the Independent Television Commission (who had clearly been heavily pressurized by the politicians), ITV had agreed to move their news back to ten o'clock but only on three days a week. Even more bizarrely, it wouldn't be the same three days every week. In return, the ITC was allowing ITV to run more advertisements in peak time. In scheduling terms the agreement was ridiculous. ITV's news eventually became known as *News at When* and its high reputation for news programming was seriously damaged.

When we heard about this our new Director of Television Mark Thompson and I decided we had two choices: scrap our plans or move quickly to implement them. We were helped by the weird proposal ITV had come up with. If their plan had been to move back into the slot five nights a week it would have made life difficult for us. As it was, Mark and I decided to press ahead quickly.

The Chairman, Christopher Bland, was all in favour and the Governors supported him. They all knew by then that the Government would take a dim view of it, but it was not, and must never be, the job of the BBC Governors to please the Government of the day – not that Governments and Secretaries of State ever fully understand that.

One journalist asked Christopher Bland if he would take the views of the Secretary of State into account when considering the matter of rescheduling the nine o'clock news. He famously replied: 'Yes, just like I would any other licence fee payer.' Downing Street was outraged; as I pointed out to Christopher, I thought he was there to stop me making injudicious remarks like that, not the other way round.

In my time at the BBC both Chris Smith and his successor, Tessa Jowell,

couldn't resist lecturing us on what should and should not be shown on television. Politicians watch less television than any other group in the country but, sadly, this has never stopped them thinking they know more about it than the professionals. One of the problems we face in a representative democracy today is that politicians increasingly believe that they should be involved in all aspects of our lives and want us to accept that they know something about pretty much everything. And yet the people who go into politics are increasingly drawn from a narrow group who, having decided (probably at university) that they wanted to become politicians, have done little else with their lives. I know: I was nearly one of them. What most of them know about, and are obsessed with, is politics full stop.

Just two months after I had announced our plan to move the news to ten o'clock we did it, giving everyone in the BBC just two weeks' notice of the precise date of the change. Again we came under attack for making the change quickly, something publicly funded organizations are not supposed to do; doing it early, in response to ITV's announcement that it was moving its news; and doing it competitively, because we wanted to occupy the slot before they did.

The move excited the people inside BBC News because it meant doing something different and new. When the unions began to make noises about the move it was the staff who told them to back off. When we finally made the move we also doubled the length of the late-night regional news from three and a half minutes to seven and made it an integral part of the ten o'clock bulletin. This proved very popular across the BBC newsrooms in the Regions and Nations. I only heard of one person directly related to the BBC who was against the move: Michael Buerk's wife. Michael was one of two main presenters of the nine o'clock news and his wife realized it would mean that he'd get home an hour later. Quite understandably she didn't fancy that.

Moving the news was the single best thing we did in my first couple of years at the BBC. We stopped the decline in the ratings for the BBC's flagship news bulletin, they even went up a little, and the freeing-up of the schedule at nine o'clock was a major factor in BBC One overtaking ITV as Britain's most watched channel a year or so later.

But the biggest impact of moving the news at two weeks' notice was the message it sent to the whole of the BBC. It told everyone that we didn't

have to be a large and unwieldy organization that analysed everything to death and couldn't take a decision quickly. We could move fast when we wanted to.

What the whole saga illustrated was the sort of intense public and political pressure an organization like the BBC comes under when it proposes even relatively minor changes. Opposition to change is not a new phenomenon at the BBC. As the Corporation's chief archivist said to me when I first joined: 'You do understand, don't you, the BBC has been accused of dumbing down from the day Reith invented it.'

In my McTaggart lecture I had foreseen the anguished cries we would get when I announced we were moving the news:

> Outrage from journalists, politicians, the great and the good and even some of the BBC's own staff at any change in BBC radio or television is a pattern you can find throughout the history of the BBC . . . The point is that the real genius of the BBC is that it *has* adapted and changed over the years . . . at crucial times in the BBC's history its leaders have recognized that change was essential and have taken the bold decision to introduce it despite loud protests from all around them.

I went on to say that change was essential at this particular time in the BBC's history:

> I believe the stark choice facing the BBC today is that we either change or we simply manage decline gracefully . . . The changes happening in technology, in the wider society, and in our competitive environment make this one of those times in history when change at the BBC is essential.

We were only able to change the timing of the main evening news because the BBC was not controlled by the politicians, unlike most of the rest of the public sector. We, management and Governors, made our own decisions and took our own risks without reference to political masters.

In theory, taking risks ought to be easier in the public sector than in profit-and-loss companies: in the former, you don't go bust if the risk

you take goes seriously wrong. But the reality is the opposite: publicly funded organizations are much more likely to avoid risk. The problem is that they are under much greater public scrutiny for the simple reason that they are spending public money. A single failure can be blown up by newspapers and politicians to such an extent that it does lasting damage to the organization, or to its leader.

As a result, there is a real danger that public-sector organizations err on the side of caution and do not take the calculated risks they ought to take if they want to improve the services they deliver to the public. For the downside of a risk going wrong in a publicly funded organization is public criticism, even public humiliation. Being wrong about the benefits of moving the news would have had serious consequences. On the other hand, the upside of taking the risk and being proved right was – what? I'm still waiting for the politicians and the newspaper editors who criticized our decision to concede it had, with hindsight, been the correct one.

The BBC I inherited would never have moved the news, and certainly not at the speed we did. There would have been at least a dozen policy papers on the issue, every possible ramification would have been considered at length – including the political opposition – and most likely nothing would have happened. Instead we just did it.

Moving the news was not the first major change I made at the BBC. Back in April 2000 a small group of us had produced a document entitled *One BBC*, which, amongst other things, proposed a new organizational structure for the Corporation. Soon after I'd arrived, John Birt and I had clashed over the appointment of a new Director of Broadcasting to replace Will Wyatt, who was due to retire in December 1999. John, who was still Director-General, wanted to make an immediate appointment. I didn't want to appoint a Director of Broadcasting at all. I couldn't see the point of the role and saw scrapping the Broadcasting Division in its totality as a good way of saving money.

The division had only been formed in 1995 as part of a McKinsey/Birt inspired reorganization known as the production/broadcasting split. In this everyone who produced programmes was put in one enormous division and had to sell their ideas to a much smaller but incredibly powerful Broadcasting Division. The important thing was that Broadcasting had all the money, and that gave it all the power. John had planned the

production/broadcasting split in secret with McKinsey and hadn't even told his deputy Bob Phillis about it. He had 'just jumped it' on the organization, to use his words, because he believed that was the only way he could get it implemented.

In John's reorganized BBC, the Director of Broadcasting was responsible for virtually all the services – television, radio, and online. The role puzzled me: surely that was what the Director-General was meant to do? Why did the people in charge of television or radio have to report to the Director-General through another layer of management? In effect this meant the Controller of BBC One had to report to the Director of Television, who in turn had to report to the Director of Broadcasting, who then reported to the Director-General. It was nuts.

Having just been appointed to run the BBC, I knew that if I made a stand against the appointment of a new Director of Broadcasting the Governors would have little choice but to back me against John. Instead I suggested that the whole issue be referred to a small group I had set up to look at the changes I wanted to make inside the BBC, a committee that later became known as the 'One BBC' group, after the title of their report.

The Governors agreed with this suggestion but John was mightily upset because he knew what it meant: that this was only the beginning of the dismantling of some of what he had done. John was very wary of my small group and on at least one occasion he took one of the people on the 'One BBC' group away to a quiet room and 'suggested' to them, in a threatening way, that their role was to defend the status quo. It made no difference and only convinced me that, whatever happened, the group would not report until after John had left the BBC.

I don't know why he was so surprised that I wanted to restructure the organization. That's what all new chief executives do. There is no perfect organizational structure and constant rethinking is healthy for any organization. Mark Thompson, my successor as Director-General, has done precisely that.

I announced the 'One BBC' changes at a studio session on 1 April 2000, which was to have been my first day in charge had John not been elevated to the House of Lords in February. We also sent every member of staff a booklet entitled *Building One BBC*, which outlined the whole range of changes we planned to put into effect as quickly as possible.

In my introduction to the booklet I outlined the problems we needed to overcome:

We have talked and listened to many people at all levels and in all parts of the BBC. We heard the same message again and again. People are proud to work for the BBC, but want to see changes . . . They think we have too many managerial layers and costly processes and that too much time is spent negotiating within the BBC. As a result, as an organization we simply move too slowly.

We disbanded the Broadcasting Division, saving about £5 million a year in the process, and in some areas like sport, children's programming, and radio we removed the artificial split between broadcasting and production altogether. Looking back now I wish we had been more radical and removed the split right across the BBC. I was too conservative and should have been bolder.

We divided the BBC's all-powerful Policy and Planning Department into two. I felt that the BBC's strategy was being too influenced by the policy people, who cared a great deal about what the politicians and Whitehall wanted and too little about the audience, the people who actually paid for the BBC. As a result of this decision Patricia Hodgson, who ran Policy and Planning, decided to leave the organization to become Chief Executive of the Independent Television Commission.

We centralized functions such as marketing so that there was only one Director of Marketing for the whole of the BBC rather than having a number of separate, competing marketing departments. This was an important change as marketing would clearly be taking on a bigger role in the BBC. In the multi-channel world more money has to be spent on marketing since there is no point spending millions on programmes if no one knows they are there or where to find them. We also set up a New Media department for the first time, bringing together all the online and interactive television departments across the BBC under a single director.

Probably the most controversial move came when we merged the old executive committee with the BBC's Board of Management; in future there would be only one management group running the BBC, the BBC Executive. In all there were to be seventeen in that group, all of whom would report directly to me. Some Governors asked, quite fairly, how

could that many people all report directly to one boss? I believed it was possible and looked around for examples from around the world. I found what I thought was a good one – Enron, then one of the fastest growing, most successful companies in the world. When the Enron scandal broke a year later I prayed no one on the Board of Governors would remember that I'd held them up as an example.

The organizational structure was drawn up on paper as a series of colourful petals, with me at the centre. Christopher Bland always said I had only done it that way because I couldn't get all the people reporting directly to me on a normal organizational chart. Harsh, but probably true. The petal diagram was actually the work of our new Director of Strategy, Carolyn Fairbairn, who had a great artistic touch. The idea of the layout was to demonstrate a less hierarchical organization.

In my years at the BBC Carolyn was probably my closest confidante, along with the Finance Director John Smith. A former journalist on *The Economist* and a consultant with McKinsey's (I forgave her that), Carolyn had worked in John Major's policy unit in Downing Street and had the advantage of being a fairly recent recruit to the BBC. She is incredibly clever and good fun to work with. Most of all she shared my view of the world – let's just work it out and then get on with it, risks and all.

Over four years together, Carolyn and I dreamt up all sorts of initiatives for the BBC: just before I left we were writing the BBC's plans for a new charter together. In many ways she took on the role my old friend and colleague Tony Cohen used to play in my life: she'd do the detailed analysis and find an intellectual rationale for the things I instinctively believed were a good idea. But she would also tell me, in no uncertain terms, if she thought it *wasn't* a good idea, and at the beginning of my time at the BBC there weren't many people who felt able to do that.

The most important thing about the 'One BBC' reorganization was that it resulted in more programme people at the very top of the Corporation – after all, outstanding programmes were what the BBC was all about and why the public paid their licence fees. So of the seventeen jobs on the Executive, nine went to programme makers. But structure was only one part of 'One BBC'. It was also about money and my avowed aim to spend more of the BBC's income on programming and less on running the BBC.

I have always understood finance and on arrival was surprised to find how complex the finances of the BBC appeared; after all, it was only a

spending organization. Everyone at the BBC used to say to me what a complicated organization it was. I used to reply that it didn't seem that way to me. We were given two and a half billion pounds a year and our job was to spend it. In the world I had come from, the hard bit was getting the two and a half billion.

The other thing I noticed at the senior levels of the BBC was that no one seemed to think anyone actually paid the licence fee. Even before I joined, I sat in a meeting discussing the likely licence fee settlement and was struck by how everyone just wanted as big an increase as possible. I suspect that most of the public sector is like this, but I kept thinking about the people 'out there', those for whom the licence fee is a lot of money. Shouldn't we have been talking about giving them value, not just seeing how big an increase we could get? This meeting simply assumed we gave them good value.

Within a couple of weeks of my becoming Director-General we got a comparatively generous licence fee settlement. Gavyn Davies, a distinguished economist who was later to become Chairman of the BBC, had written a brilliant paper on the funding of the BBC saying we needed more money and had recommended a two-tier licence fee in which people who had digital television and could receive the BBC's digital services would pay a larger fee. While it was a clever idea it was a non-starter. It met massive hostility from Rupert Murdoch's BSkyB, who believed it would be a deterrent to people going digital and as a result limit the potential of BSkyB's business. And, as I shall explain later, the New Labour Government was never likely to take on Rupert Murdoch.

However, the Prime Minister has always been a BBC supporter and he wanted a strong and vibrant BBC. In the end the licence fee agreement was an old-fashioned political carve-up. As so often happens in politics, Gavyn Davies's sophisticated analysis was largely irrelevant once the horse-trading started. There was initially a disagreement between Tony Blair and Chris Smith on one side and the Chancellor, Gordon Brown, on the other. Brown understandably didn't want to set a licence fee with an above-inflation increase for the next six years as he feared it would set a trend for the rest of the public sector.

But Blair and Smith were adamant. The BBC needed more money and some certainty about its funding, and in the end they got their deal – the BBC licence fee would increase by one and a half per cent a year above

inflation every year until 2007. As it turned out, virtually all of the rest of the public sector got bigger average increases over the next four years.

While the discussions about the licence fee agreement were going on, Patricia Hodgson, who was then still at the BBC, organized a private meeting between Chris Smith and myself to discuss the future. My job was to convince Chris that any extra money would be well spent. It was private because John Birt was still Director-General and neither Chris nor I wanted to offend him and he was still running the licence fee negotiations for the BBC. John did a brilliant job in achieving such a good settlement.

At the meeting I told Chris I thought BBC One was underfunded, that we needed to spend more money outside London, that we had exciting plans in education, and that it was important that the BBC compete in the digital world. If we were to do all of this we would need some extra funding. When Chris Smith announced the licence fee settlement in February 2000 he fed my four priorities straight back to the BBC as part of the agreement and said that these were what he wanted us to spend the extra money on.

Chris also urged us to raise any further money we needed by making savings within the BBC – by selling assets and by expanding our commercial activities. Interestingly, four years earlier Virginia Bottomley, the last Conservative Secretary of State, had also urged the BBC to become more commercial. As a result, we did increase our commercial activities quite significantly over the next four years, as we'd been asked to do, and brought more money into the BBC as a result, only to find ourselves under attack from all sides for becoming 'too commercial'. In all, Chris Smith challenged us to raise an additional £1.1 billion over seven years. When I left the BBC we were on target to do better than that, though we had probably spent more than expected as well.

Led by the BBC's talented Director of Finance, John Smith, who had sat on my 'One BBC' group, we worked out a plan that would allow us to spend more money in my early years at the BBC, and claw it back in the later years. The logic was straightforward. The digital revolution was under way and we needed to play a big part in it immediately, not four years later when we would have the cash. By then it would be much harder to compete and make an impact.

At that time, the BBC had quite a large cash surplus and our plan was to spend it all, and more, and go into debt for the next three or four

years. The increase in spending would then flatten off. The idea was to end the charter period in 2007 with little or no debt and with our annual income exceeding expenditure. To achieve this we knew that some time during that period we would have to sell one of the BBC's large assets. In my last year at the BBC we began the process of selling BBC Technology, the proceeds of which would repay the overdraft and reduce our expenditure on technology going forward.

I explained this financial strategy to the audience at Edinburgh in my McTaggart lecture in August 2000. Of course no one took much notice. They were far more interested in the sexier announcements. But what I said was this:

> By 2007 this [the licence fee settlement] will produce a real increase of £250 million in that year compared with our income in 1999. But 2007 is too late. If we want to shine in the new competitive digital age, and we must, we need to spend more money now, which is why I've spent so much time in my first six months as Director-General looking for ways to save money right across the BBC.

By the year 2000, when I gave the McTaggart lecture, the BBC was already a very different place from what it had been a decade earlier.

At the start of the Nineties, most television companies in Britain, including the BBC, had absolutely no idea about the true cost of anything. Large standing armies of cameramen, sound men, editors, make-up people, and the rest were employed and apportioned out to programme teams. The teams didn't pay for them and had little choice whom they got. The cost was carried in a massive central overhead and the people who ran these facilities budgets were kings. They handed out the resources and in many ways they controlled television.

Programme makers in areas like sport always did pretty well because they controlled tickets to sporting events: whenever you went to any of these the managers of the facilities divisions were always there, being well looked after. It was a corrupt, inefficient, appallingly organized system and needed to be changed. We changed it at LWT when I became Managing Director in 1990 and the BBC followed suit in the early Nineties.

When John Birt began to introduce change at the BBC it was on a massive scale. It was called 'producer choice' and I remember when I was

still at LWT being asked to go to meet two or three different groups who were being asked to come up with ways to modernize the BBC. On the first occasion I went to a breakfast meeting with one working party at Bush House, home of the World Service. I turned up to find we were all having a full silver-service breakfast with three people waiting on us.

As we started the discussion I asked who was paying for the waiters. I was the only non-BBC person there and everyone else looked at each other. One person finally said, 'Well, the BBC are paying,' to which I replied, 'Yes, but who? Whose budget is paying for them? Whose cash is it?' Silence again. So I said, 'Can I suggest that until you know who is paying for them the rest of this meeting is a waste of time.' Thankfully, John Birt's reforms meant that by the time I arrived at the BBC these sorts of excesses had disappeared. By then everyone knew what everything cost.

On another occasion I was taken by a group through their plans for 'producer choice'. What it meant was that every producer in the BBC would have the choice of either buying their resources, such as studios, film crews, and outside broadcast units, from inside the BBC or from outside providers. I applauded the idea of knowing what everything cost and having internal trading at proper market prices but I cautioned against going full scale down that route. I pointed out that if you had the people and resources you needed sitting idle while producers were spending real cash outside the building you were in danger of paying for everything twice. I was told, by a group of people who had only ever worked in the public sector, that I was not being ambitious enough, that this sort of change would only work at the BBC if it went all the way. No half-way solutions would work there. It was like meeting a group of zealots.

This was madness and the system was still in operation when I got to the BBC. One of the first things I did was to stop the Children's Department from moving *Blue Peter* to Granada's studios in Manchester. It was explained to me that this would be cheaper for the programme as Granada were offering a good deal, even though it meant laying out real cash both for the cost of the studios and travel and hotel accommodation every week to get the team to Manchester. I pointed out that while it might be cheaper for a particular programme, it would cost the BBC overall a lot more because it was already paying for the studio in London that *Blue Peter* was vacating.

No commercial organization would or did operate like this, and in my

first year I had to persuade all sorts of people that we needed a more pragmatic approach: producer choice was a good idea in principle, but not if you took it to extremes.

One of the first questions I asked when I joined the BBC was, what proportion of our expenditure was being spent on running the institution of the BBC itself? I was shocked to find that the figure was 24 per cent. It meant that almost a quarter of everyone's licence fee was being spent on the organization's overheads – going on things that had little to do with programmes or services. All organizations have overheads, but 24 per cent was a ridiculous figure and I set a target to reduce that to 15 per cent by 2004. In fact we did better than that: the figure for the financial year ending April 2004 was down to 12 per cent.

We achieved this partly by making some easy moves, such as not spending £20 million a year on outside consultants, most of which was going to McKinsey, and massively reducing the amount of internal charging between departments, which meant we could cut the spending on bureaucracy. We reduced the number of business units that could send invoices to each other from three hundred down to sixty. With the processing cost of each invoice at around £100 a transaction, this alone saved serious money.

We also made big savings in areas like personnel, where the BBC had one personnel employee for every forty members of staff whilst the average across British companies was closer to one for eighty. Too many managers at the BBC simply handed over people management to the Human Resources Department.

One particular cost-saving move got a good deal of publicity by accident. One day, early on, I said to my PA that I didn't want croissants at any of my meetings because I was putting on weight. I'm one of those people who will eat a croissant if it is there, even if I'm not hungry. She sent out an e-mail saying that I didn't want croissants at my meetings in future. Within days it was all over the newspapers that I had banned croissants from the BBC.

I didn't object to the publicity as I wanted everyone in the BBC to know that I intended to cut back on anything that diverted money away from programmes; but the story wasn't true. What I did ban was people taking cabs between the BBC's various sites in London. Instead I laid on a free bus service between the centres and saved hundreds of thousands

of pounds in the process. In his autobiography, *Chance Governs All* (2001), the former Chairman of the BBC, Duke Hussey, relates the tale of a taxi driver moaning bitterly to him about me for undermining the livelihood of London cabbies. The three C's – croissants, cabs, and consultants – thus became part of the legend of the spending cuts I was making all around the BBC.

But the biggest savings of all came as a result of changes in the finance area where we went through the agony of changing all our software systems across the organization to enable us to know far more about what we were spending and where. This meant we could have a more effective central purchasing system so that we could negotiate much better pan-BBC deals. We reduced the number of companies supplying services to the BBC from 150,000 to 9,000.

In doing all this we also found out some amazing things. For instance we discovered we were paying 120 different stationery suppliers, despite the fact that the BBC was supposed to use only one. We also discovered that 90 per cent of the bills we were paying did not have a proper purchase order. All this changed and we saved a fortune. We had far fewer bills to pay and overall we needed far fewer people working in finance. John Smith halved the size of the finance department from 1,000 staff to 500 over four years while also making the systems much more efficient.

As part of 'One BBC' every division inside the BBC was asked to produce its own plan to cut the overhead. By this initiative alone we cut 1,100 jobs. The total savings from 'One BBC' came to £166 million a year, significantly more than we received from the increase in the licence fee in my time at the BBC.

I explained all this in my McTaggart lecture in August 2000. Having announced to everyone that we were moving the news I went on to talk about money. I told the audience of broadcasters and programme makers that we were increasing the spend on programmes and services by £100 million that year, by £250 million the next year, and by a further £130 million the year after. I said:

That means in the year 2002/3 we will be spending £480 million a year more on our programmes and services than we spent last year, a 30 per cent real increase in programme spend over just three years. This amounts to the biggest increase in programme expenditure in

BBC history . . . More than half of that money will have been saved inside the BBC and this will not be achieved without real pain and a lot of people will have lost their jobs through no fault of their own . . . however, the obligation must be on us to spend as much as possible on programmes.

The next section of the lecture was the bit that really interested the audience. If we were increasing our spend by £480 million a year, where were we going to spend it? Most of the audience were interested because they wanted to know if they were going to get any of it. I explained briefly that some of the extra money had already been allocated to BBC One, which had been doing particularly badly in the ratings. It had been short of cash for some years, and was being widely criticized for being old-fashioned and out of touch. There were politicians who were saying we couldn't justify the licence fee if the figures for BBC One didn't improve. Four years later some of the same people were complaining it was too successful. This is the great dilemma all Director-Generals of the BBC face. When you do well in the ratings you are accused of 'dumbing down' and not taking minority programming seriously enough. When you are doing badly you are accused of failing the popular audience. As I've said many times, it is the only job in the world where you get crap for losing and crap for winning.

To try to revive the failing BBC One I had decided to increase the annual spending on it by £115 million a year, a 15 per cent increase. The Director of Television, Mark Thompson, and his new Controller of BBC One, Lorraine Heggessey, spent most of the additional money on drama. Some went on increasing *EastEnders* to four slots a week, *Holby City* to 52 weeks a year, and increasing the run of *Casualty*. But the vast bulk of the money went on drama series for the new 9 p.m. drama slot: *Waking the Dead*, *Judge John Deed*, *Merseybeat*, and *Red Cap* were all products of this new money. When Mark Thompson left the BBC for Channel Four his replacement, Jana Bennett, carried on very much the same strategy of investing heavily in drama.

What none of us knew at that time, in 2000, was that advertising revenue worldwide was about to drop dramatically. ITV's revenue was at an all-time high, but over the next two years it fell by 15 per cent, and in real terms it is unlikely to get back up to the 2000 figure until the

latter part of this decade. So at the very moment I had boosted spending on BBC One, ITV had to cut spending as its advertising fell. Within two years BBC One had overtaken ITV as Britain's most popular channel for the first time, not because BBC One's ratings share was growing dramatically but because ITV's was falling fast.

We also allocated a great deal of the extra money to developing a series of new digital channels. Anyone who had followed broadcasting developments in the United States over the previous twenty years understood what had happened to the big three broadcasters, CBS, NBC, and ABC. In his book *Three Blind Mice* Ken Auletta, the distinguished media columnist for the *New Yorker* magazine, had described how the three network companies had gone into decline because they failed to expand as the multi-channel world hit the USA. As a result, all three were bought by enormous conglomerates and have become small, if important, parts of the wider broadcasting landscape.

With the coming of BSkyB and cable television to Britain there was a danger of the same thing happening here. The advent of the digital revolution meant that there was more broadcasting capacity and many more channels would be made available. The BBC and ITV, who had both seen significant falls in their share of viewing since BSkyB was launched, were in danger of being marginalized over the coming years.

My predecessor, John Birt, had recognized this and had opened up new channels with BBC Choice, BBC Knowledge, and News 24 – but only News 24 had been properly funded. That day in Edinburgh, just six months after taking over at the BBC, I announced the biggest expansion in television services in the BBC's history. I said:

> We believe that in the age of digital television it will not be sufficient for the BBC to offer only two mixed genre channels which are somehow supposed to meet the needs of everyone. This is not how audiences will want to receive television in the future. We need a more coherent portfolio of channels.

I announced that we planned to scrap BBC Choice and BBC Knowledge and launch two children's channels (CBeebies and CBBC), a new network for younger people (BBC Three), and a cultural network (BBC Four) to add to BBC News 24 and BBC Parliament. I explained that this would

be our channel portfolio for the digital world and that there were a number of guiding principles involved.

One was that all the channels would eventually be available free to everyone whether on cable, satellite, or digital terrestrial. When the whole of Britain was digital, everyone would have access to all our channels. I explained that as the number of channels on digital terrestrial was limited, we therefore had to limit our expansion. I also explained that these initiatives represented the most we could afford.

By far the most important principle I outlined was that these would be overwhelmingly *British* channels, commissioning and broadcasting original *British* programmes. The greatest danger of multi-channel television is that it will lead to television around the world being dominated by American programming. As the richest market in the world, the USA can afford to make more programmes than any other country. The result could well see the world becoming dominated by US culture.

So far in Britain we have avoided that, largely because of the BBC and the way it is funded. We spend more money per head on original television programmes than any country in the world, including the USA, because of the way we fund the BBC. To compete with the BBC, both ITV and Channel Four have to spend a lot of money on original UK production. Take away the BBC and ITV would certainly spend less. In announcing a new tranche of channels for the BBC our aim was both to keep pace in the expanding multi-channel world and also to ensure that some of the new digital channels were overwhelmingly British, reflecting our society and our culture.

Having announced the channels we wanted to broadcast we still had to persuade the Secretary of State to give them the go-ahead. There was a lot of opposition to the children's channels from the large US media companies such as Disney, Viacom, and Rupert Murdoch's Fox, which had already started children's channels on satellite television in Britain. This was an easy battle to win.

These channels were overwhelmingly cartoon-based, broadcasting American programming on services littered with adverts. Our case was that British parents had the right to choose whether or not their children watched American channels or two BBC children's channels that were wholly British, reflected our culture, and carried educational material, all without ads. I met all sorts of US executives at that time bleating that it

173

wasn't fair that the BBC was using public money to compete with them. My reply was that it wasn't fair that they were building new businesses in Britain by 'dumping' US programming in the British market. I love winding up American media executives because so many of them suffer from the disease of not understanding that American hegemony might not be in the best interests of the world.

We secured permission for the children's channels and they were launched in February 2002. CBeebies was an instant hit amongst the under-fives but CBBC took longer to connect with the older audience at which it was aimed. Both are now very successful. There was little opposition to BBC Four, which was launched the following month in March 2002. The big battle was over BBC Three and it was a battle with Channel Four.

It was about this time that Mark Thompson left the BBC to take over as Chief Executive of Channel Four. I encouraged him to go, even though I didn't want to lose him. He had only ever worked at the BBC and needed wider experience if he was to succeed me as Director-General. At that time there were only two potential candidates as my successor inside the BBC – the two Marks, Thompson and Byford. While both had real talents, Mark Thompson was always the more likely to get the job.

Mark Thompson had moved around the BBC a lot: as he openly jokes, he never stayed anywhere long enough to be found out (an experience I fully understand). One of his great claims to fame was when, as editor of *Panorama*, he broadcast the programme revealing that Robert Maxwell was fiddling the 'Spot the Ball' competition in the *Daily Mirror*, which of course he owned. When I gave Mark's farewell speech at the BBC in 2002 I mentioned this, but also pointed out that the programme hadn't spotted that Maxwell had also stolen the whole of the Mirror Group's pension fund.

Mark had been an outstanding Controller of BBC Two and was a natural for the Channel Four job when Michael Jackson gave it up to go to the States. I always remember Mark's words to me when he told me he had got the job: he said that whatever happened at Channel Four, he would continue to support our application to launch BBC Three. Someone from Channel Four must have heard this because within days, before Mark had actually joined them, Channel Four came out against BBC Three on the grounds that it could damage their advertising revenue. Given that Channel Four's income had grown by 13 per cent per annum

for the past decade this was pathetic. The problem was that 2001 was the beginning of the slump in advertising revenue in the UK and people at Channel Four were panicking. For the first time their total revenue was falling.

In the middle of this process we had the 2001 General Election and Chris Smith was replaced by Tessa Jowell as Secretary of State at the Department of Culture, Media and Sport. Tessa had a terrible first couple of years and was regarded as a lightweight in the media industry. We all thought she was there because she was a Blairite who would do what Downing Street told her to do. That was certainly the case during the passing of the 2003 Communications Act: measures her department didn't agree with were put into the bill, and thus became law, at the initiative of Downing Street. There is no doubt that the change in the rules that allowed US media companies to own ITV, even though European companies are prevented from owning networks in the USA, was a Downing Street initiative and had nothing to do with Tessa Jowell and DCMS. In time, after the departure of Alastair Campbell (to whom Tessa was very close) and after Blair had been weakened by public reaction to the Iraq war, the general view across the industry has been that she became far more effective as a Minister. It was left to Tessa Jowell to make the decisions about our new channels, particularly BBC Three. In the end it got the go-ahead, and I have to admit that the channel was better for the process Tessa put it through. BBC Three was finally launched in February 2003.

The coming of the digital age did not only affect television. We recognized that we had to expand across the whole digital world, which meant moving into digital radio as well as digital television, developing interactive television, and expanding our online activities. Digital radio eventually took off in 2003 when the radio manufacturers finally decided to produce digital radio sets and, surprise, surprise, found there was a great demand for them. The consumer response was immediate; people were keen to get more radio stations and the better quality signal that came with digital radio.

Up until then the history of digital radio was a classic chicken and egg situation. The manufacturers wouldn't produce digital radios until there were more digital services available, and the BBC and commercial radio

stations wouldn't fund new digital services until the manufacturers produced and sold enough radios. It was Jenny Abramsky, the BBC's Director of Radio, who broke that deadlock. When the history of radio in this period is written, Jenny should get most of the credit for turning British radio digital.

Jenny is an infuriating person. Some days she is charming and reasonable; on others her paranoia that radio is a second-class citizen to television within the BBC makes her difficult to deal with. She believes passionately that inside the BBC radio is unloved and as a result is underfunded. Her argument is simply wrong: BBC radio stations are probably the best funded in the world, and are certainly significantly better funded than any competitors in Britain. The same, however, is not true of BBC One or BBC Two: ITV and Channel Four are at least as well funded. For instance, there is not a radio station anywhere in the world that receives the £70 million a year it costs to run Radio Four. As a lifelong Radio Four listener I am a true supporter of the channel; but sometimes it has to be acknowledged that it is well funded – just as it has to be recognized that Radio Four is a service that disproportionately appeals to, and serves, the South of England.

In the end it was the BBC who broke the stalemate with the radio manufacturers, and this was completely down to Jenny Abramsky. Without her commitment to, and promotion of, digital radio it simply wouldn't have happened. She persuaded, cajoled, and threatened everyone inside the BBC to support the plan to develop a series of new BBC digital radio services. And it was the arrival of those services that finally persuaded the radio manufacturers to start producing digital radios.

The BBC took the decision to spend £18 million a year on a range of new digital radio services at the same time as we committed to expanding our television portfolio. It was the right decision, even though it also meant our spending many more million actually paying for the transmission system that would enable 85 per cent of the population to receive digital radio. The truth is that none of us would have dared to suggest that we shouldn't set aside the money to fund our new digital radio stations when we were expanding in television. We would have all been too scared of incurring Jenny's wrath.

There was no problem persuading the Secretary of State to approve the new radio stations because the commercial radio companies were

actually in favour of the BBC expansion. They wanted digital radio to work and knew that only the BBC was big enough to drive it. So over the next eighteen months the BBC launched four new radio stations: Five Live Sports Extra, 1Xtra, 6 Music, and BBC 7. We also turned the Asian Network into a national network.

BBC Radio's share of the total market went up almost every year during my time at the BBC, driven mainly by the incredible success of Radio Two nationally but also by the performance of Radio Four in the London area, where it is the most listened-to radio station, ahead of all the commercial stations. When I joined the BBC, I hadn't listened to Radio Two for years. I still thought it was the service for my Auntie Muriel and thought of it as *Sing Something Simple* and *Friday Night is Music Night*. It was only when I started listening that I, like millions of others of my age, found it was now playing 'our' music. All my favourite artists – Bob Dylan, Bruce Springsteen, Crosby Stills & Nash, and others – were now all to be found on Radio Two.

But I suppose it was discovering Jonathan Ross's show on a Saturday morning that finally changed my attitude to Radio Two. In some ways I was responsible for the Ross family being on television and radio in the first place – I had given Paul, Jonathan's elder brother, his first job in television when I was running *The Six O'Clock Show* at LWT, and Jonathan followed Paul into the business. I was really touched when Jonathan gave £500 towards the fund to buy the advert in the *Telegraph* the weekend after I left the BBC. Jonathan's radio show is essential listening for me. I listen not for the music but to hear his banter, wit, and personal anecdotes. He has the same skill Victoria Wood possesses: that amazing ability to talk about the everyday things of life and make you laugh about them.

The third major growth area in my time at the BBC was online services. The BBC's online activity had started, like so many good ideas in many organizations, without anyone on top knowing much about it, but it was eventually championed by John Birt. The BBC spent a considerable amount of time, both before my arrival and after, deciding how much of the BBC's online services should be commercial and how much should be public service, funded by the licence fee. This was an occasion where moving comparatively slowly saved us from disaster.

When I arrived it was at the height of the dot-com boom, and with

the BBC owning the most visited websites in Europe there was a potential fortune there for the taking. But by the time we had worked out where the boundary between public service and commercial activity should lie, it didn't matter any more. The dot-com bubble had burst and it was clear that, other than in exceptional circumstances, people were not going to pay for information on the web. It became obvious that brilliant online services like BBC News, BBC Sport, and many of our educational sites could only exist if they were publicly funded.

Ashley Highfield joined us to run the newly created New Media division. Ashley is one of the most inventive people I know and our one-to-one monthly meetings were amongst the most creative and stimulating I had in my time as Director-General. He always had a new or different idea that he wanted to bounce around. With my limited knowledge of new media I enjoyed testing his ideas and acting as his technically illiterate sounding-board.

Ashley didn't have an easy task bringing all the BBC's online activity under one division, but he did it with great success. By early 2004, when I left, the BBC's website, bbc.co.uk, was reaching ten million adults every month, making it the BBC's fourth biggest service after BBC One, BBC Two, and Radio Two. More than 50 per cent of the people of Britain are now online, and nearly 50 per cent of them regularly use the BBC's sites.

The BBC is criticized by other British content providers on the web, particularly the national newspapers, for spending too much public money on its services and squeezing its competitors out of the available space. This is largely irrelevant. What is certain is that the BBC's websites are outstanding and that UK-originated sites of this quality would simply not have happened without the BBC and without public funding. Again the choice was straightforward: either the BBC developed and competed in this area or the Americans would have free rein to dominate the web in the UK. I'd challenge anyone to go onto, say, the CBeebies website and fail to recognize its value to the young children of Britain today.

The facts simply don't support the argument that if the BBC had not moved into providing online broadcasting services other British companies would have done so instead. It was *because* the BBC was publicly funded that it could be original, take risks, and develop sites in great depth. The commercial sector would never have done this: as the dot-com collapse demonstrated, there was no revenue base for these sorts of sites. Increas-

ingly, in the broadband era, the web will be used for delivering moving pictures as well as text, and then newspapers will be left far behind. What the BBC has achieved on the web is remarkable.

Ashley Highfield was also put in charge of developing interactive television on the BBC. Here he was starting with a clean sheet. His first big venture turned into an amazing success when BSkyB viewers were able to receive interactive Wimbledon coverage for the first time in 2001, enabling them to choose any one of four matches being played at the same time. In all, 63 per cent of the audience watching on the BSkyB platform pushed the red interactive button and watched the service at some time during the championships. BBCi, as the interactive service is called, now offers viewers the chance to vote, watch additional footage, and find out more information about a whole range of programmes from *Test the Nation* to *Restoration*, and from *Question Time* to coverage of the Chelsea Flower Show.

Looking back now I find it remarkable how fast we moved in that first year at the BBC. We reorganized the whole place, found ways of saving enormous amounts of money, and outlined what we planned to do over the next two years. We then simply did it.

CHAPTER NINE

The BBC Years (2)

For many years I have objected to, and feared, the stranglehold Rupert Murdoch has been securing on the British media. I could never understand why so few people seemed to understand or care about it. When it was recently suggested that Murdoch might move his papers in Britain en masse away from supporting Labour, virtually no one seemed alarmed that we had ended up in this country with such a significant concentration of power in the hands of one person. One person who is not even British: an Australian who is now a US citizen and who lives in New York. Similarly, when it was reported that Tony Blair had decided to hold a referendum on the issue of a European constitution as a way of trying to keep the Murdoch papers on side, it was remarkable how little reaction it caused.

It could be that Britain has grown to accept the power that Rupert Murdoch wields, but I still find it deeply offensive and worrying.

It is extraordinary that, after having had cross-media laws in this country since 1963, we have ended up in exactly the position those laws were intended to prevent. The legislation was aimed at stopping anyone getting too much power over the media, and as a result having too much power over the politicians. Yet in Rupert Murdoch that is precisely what we now have. Controlling 35 per cent of the national daily circulation of newspapers in this country, and 41 per cent of the Sunday market, makes him very powerful indeed. By chairing and effectively controlling BSkyB he also runs Britain's most financially successful broadcasting operation, which, if unchecked, could in the years to come dominate broadcasting in the way Murdoch's News International dominates the print media.

My family in 1989. We had this picture taken to give to my mum and dad, who were celebrating their golden wedding. Sadly my dad died the following year. The children are (from left to right) Christine, Alice, Joe and Matthew.

TO ALL
LWT STAFF

As you may know I am Managing Director of LWT
as from today (Thursday, March 1).

I will be spending the day going round the building
in the hope of meeting as many people as I can personally.

My apologies if I miss anybody today. Over the next few months
I'll be meeting with all staff again, section by section,
to listen to what you think about our company
and to answer any questions.

If you've any questions about the company
that you'd like to ask today,
please drop them into my office by lunchtime.

Michael Aspel will put them to me on your behalf
at 3.45 this afternoon on the set of Aspel & Company.
You can watch us on Channel 6 on the internal monitors.

Lastly, if you are around at lunchtime,
do drop by the bar to say hallo.

Greg Dyke

Above: The message I sent to LWT staff on my first day as managing director. I wanted them all to know that my approach was different.

Left: Christopher Bland and I were a good team both at LWT and the BBC, and I learned a lot from him and liked him enormously.

Above: The great match at Wembley when I played in David Frost's team against Jimmy Tarbuck's side immediately before the 1987 Cup Final. I was scared to death playing in front of all those people. John Birt (fifth from left, back row) played in the same match and even scored a goal. I'm standing next to Daley Thompson.

Right: Steve Cram chopping me from behind in the same match, which ended in a 1–1 draw with Daley Thompson scoring a great goal for our side.

Left: A joke poster we drew up at LWT as we bid to retain the London weekend franchise. We managed to keep the size of our bid confidential to the very end.

CARELESS TALK COSTS FRANCHISES

Below: LWT's top management with our stars on the day we retained the franchise. We partied all night. Front row (left to right): Michael Aspel, Denis Norden, Michael Barrymore, Cilla Black, myself, Jeremy Beadle, Brian Walden. Back row (left to right): Brian Tesler, Brian Moore, Marcus Plantin, Matthew Kelly, Melvyn Bragg, Trevor Phillips, Christopher Bland.

British broadcasting is in danger of sleepwalking into Murdoch's control.

Of course the editors of Murdoch's newspapers all pretend they don't jump to his tune, but no one doubts that on the really big issues he calls the shots. Murdoch was an avid supporter of the war against Iraq and all his 175 newspapers around the world supported the policy. The story that there was one exception, a small paper in Papua New Guinea, turns out not to be true. It simply gave prominence to a reader's letter that was against the war. All 175 newspapers just happened, by chance, to follow the Murdoch line.

So far Sky News, Murdoch's excellent television news operation in Britain, has followed the British broadcasting tradition of aspiring to political impartiality, but there is no guarantee that this will continue into the future. Fox News, Murdoch's 24-hour news channel in the USA, has been incredibly successful by adopting a blatantly right-wing agenda. During the Iraq war its ratings went up by 300 per cent and it overtook the market leader, CNN. Andrew Heywood, President of CBS News, was deeply concerned about the success of Fox News. He said that the long tradition of objective and fair journalism in the USA was threatened by the Fox effect. A University of Maryland study found that Fox News viewers in the USA were the most likely to believe three major misperceptions of 'facts' about the war: that US troops had found evidence of close pre-war links between the Saddam regime and al-Qaeda; that the US had found weapons of mass destruction in Iraq; and that world opinion was in favour of the US going to war.

When the Hutton report was published in January 2004, Fox News said on air that 'the BBC was forced to pay up for its . . . frothing at the mouth anti-Americanism that was obsessive, irrational and dishonest . . . it felt entitled to not only pillory Americans and George W. Bush but it felt entitled to lie'. There are some who believe that Murdoch wants Sky News to follow the same commercially successful route as Fox News. He reputedly calls Sky News 'BBC Light'.

The British Labour and Liberal parties should be very nervous of this happening: it would mark the beginning of the end of impartial broadcast news as we know it today in Britain. On both radio and television people in the UK have access to a range of political views in a way they don't in the newspapers they read. One of the reasons you buy the *Daily Mail* or *The Guardian* is that it tends to reflect your own political views. So

far that hasn't been true of broadcasting. One thing we can now be certain of in the UK is that the politicians are not strong enough successfully to resist Murdoch.

Back in the early Nineties, when I was Chief Executive of LWT, I persuaded Barry Cox, then Director of Corporate Affairs at LWT, to have a chat with his friend and former neighbour Tony Blair, at that time a rising star in the Labour Party. I wanted Barry to warn Blair about the scale of the operation Murdoch was building up with his expansion into television in Britain. Barry told me at the time that the warning had completely backfired. Tony Blair had recognized the danger but his reaction to the warning was not the one either of us expected. Blair had said, in effect, that he believed Labour might have to do a deal with this man.

Although unable to stand up to the Murdoch empire – for Blair and Alastair Campbell, having *The Sun* supporting Labour was much more important – when he became Prime Minister Tony Blair recognized that a strong BBC was essential as a counterweight to Murdoch, which is why he supported an increase in the licence fee. The great tragedy is that New Labour would have won the 1997 General Election with or without the support of Murdoch's newspapers and so could have campaigned on a policy to reduce the size and power of his empire. Sadly, after eighteen years out of power, they didn't have enough confidence to do it. Instead, New Labour has allowed Murdoch's power to grow and has done very little, if anything, in seven years that is likely to offend him.

In fact this Government would have allowed Murdoch's empire in Britain to grow even larger. Had the original Government bill outlining the 2003 Communications Act gone through, BSkyB would have been allowed to buy one of the traditional terrestrial broadcasters, Channel Five. Thankfully, the parliamentary joint committee chaired by Labour peer Lord Puttnam insisted that the Act should include a media plurality test, which makes it extremely unlikely that Murdoch will now be allowed to own a terrestrial television station. According to David Puttnam, he was not thanked by Downing Street for his efforts.

All of this might suggest I'm not a fan of Rupert Murdoch, which is not true. I admire the way he has built up his enormous media empire; I admire the loyalty he gets from his staff, and the speed at which he moves; and I admire his drive and imagination. He is without doubt the most successful media operator of the last twenty years. Whenever I've met

him I, like many others, have fallen under the Murdoch spell. But I find the way he uses politicians, as well as his attitude to democracy, worrying. He has found a way of subverting the democratic process to extend his own power and his own business interests. For electoral reasons politicians around the world, including both main political parties in Britain, have gone along with it.

Murdoch has never been a fan of the BBC. I suspect the idea that a publicly funded broadcaster should be so successful offends his very view of the world. It certainly limits his business potential in Britain. So whenever the opportunity arises, Murdoch or his people will always criticize the BBC, as they did on several occasions during my period as Director-General.

Now I'm no longer at the BBC I will happily admit that many of the moves I made in my years there, particularly in my last two years, were designed to ensure that the organization was big enough and strong enough to stand up to Murdoch. It was my view that Murdoch and his people would do all they could to damage the BBC, not because they believed it was in the public interest to do so, but because it was in their commercial interests to have a smaller and less influential BBC. To counter this, I believed anything I could do to limit the power and influence of BSkyB would, in turn, be very much in the public interest. In my last two years as Director-General we made two moves that I believed were to the long-term advantage of the BBC and broadcasting generally in Britain, moves which would prevent BSkyB from dominating broadcasting in this country. The first was perhaps the most important decision I took in my four years at the BBC: the launch of Freeview.

The story of Freeview goes back to 1998 when two ITV companies, Carlton and Granada, joined up with BSkyB to bid for the new digital terrestrial television (DTT) licences. At that time DTT was seen as an exciting new way of delivering digital television to the home through traditional television aerials. The On Digital consortium, as the three bidders called their new venture, were awarded the licences but existing broadcasters such as the BBC and Channel Four were also given additional spectrum on the new system.

Michael Green, Chairman of Carlton, was a DTT enthusiast from the beginning and his company did all the research and analysis for the bid. He believed it was an important strategic move for his company. Sadly,

it went seriously wrong for him. The Granada involvement was very different. Up to a couple of weeks before the consortium won the licences Granada had had no intention of bidding: they'd undertaken no research, and were only involved because they didn't want to be left out when they discovered that Carlton and BSkyB had joined together to bid. Granada bid blind.

The consortium's original business plan estimated that their maximum investment would be £350 million. After they'd lost £1.2 billion of their shareholders' money, Granada and Carlton finally pulled the plug and ITV Digital went bust in early 2002. Oddly, the company changed its name from On Digital to ITV Digital when it was in dire economic trouble, perhaps one of the worst branding decisions of all time.

Things began to go wrong for the company even before the services were launched. From the moment the European Commission ruled that it was anti-competitive for BSkyB to be part of the consortium, as they already dominated the satellite pay-television sector in the UK, the business was in trouble. That was the moment when Granada and Carlton made their crucial mistake. Instead of pulling out they decided to compete head to head with BSkyB in the pay-television market. They were murdered. BSkyB simply had too much money and muscle for the fledgling On Digital to compete.

When BSkyB started giving away digital boxes, On Digital had no option but to do the same, even though they couldn't afford to. And in June 2000, when football rights were being sold for enormous figures, On Digital was in there paying a fortune for the rights to broadcast Football League matches. They paid three times what they were worth.

But what really killed On Digital was that the technology didn't work. Only about 50 per cent of the population could get any sort of DTT picture, and less than a third of homes in the UK could get a clean, clear signal. In some homes the picture was interrupted by simple things like opening the fridge door or by a passing bus. As a result, the number of people giving up ITV Digital each month because of the quality of the picture meant the company was struggling to stand still.

In the autumn of 2001 it became clear that ITV Digital was in serious trouble. When we discovered this, Carolyn Fairbairn and I got talking and we dreamt up an idea. We went to Carlton and Granada and offered to help turn ITV Digital into a platform for free-to-air broadcasters like

the BBC, ITV, Channel Four, and Channel Five on which they could all develop new channels. We and others would help by marketing our digital channels, as Freeview was later marketed, to attract people who didn't want pay television. But every set-top box would also be capable of being used for pay television, allowing ITV Digital to try and persuade people to switch to pay once they had a box. That way Carlton and Granada could continue to bring in some income for the pay channels.

ITV Digital liked the idea but negotiating with Granada and Carlton was difficult because of a lack of mutual trust. Then one day, just before Christmas 2001, the Managing Director of Carlton, Gerry Murphy, whom I did trust, came to see me and told me to be careful. He honourably advised me to stop talking about this possible solution to their problems in public: even if we all reached a deal, he doubted whether there was enough money to keep ITV Digital going. From that moment on we began to develop version two. We called it Freeview.

Our research had shown that there were a lot of people who wanted a wider choice of television channels but didn't want to pay for it. They were the pay television rejecters, who tended to be older and more middle class; in effect, they were traditional BBC viewers and listeners. They wanted to have twenty or thirty channels but didn't want pay television. On the basis of this research we came up with Freeview. We first had to win the DTT licences that ITV Digital had handed back to the Independent Television Commission when the company went bust. I told my team, led by Carolyn Fairbairn, the BBC's Director of Marketing Andy Duncan (whom I had persuaded to join us from Unilever and who is now Chief Executive of Channel Four), and Emma Scott, that we had to win. So far I had won every bid for a licence I had been involved in – LWT, GMTV, and Channel Five. I didn't want to lose this 100 per cent record.

At a day's notice, I decided to turn up at a seminar being held at Number 11 Downing Street and outline the idea for Freeview. It was probably the concept's turning point.

The pitch was pretty simple. Part of the reason ITV Digital had failed was the failure of the technology: we knew how to fix that. They had also failed because they'd gone head to head with BSkyB: we had no intention of doing that because this would not be a pay service. Finally, ITV Digital became involved in buying expensive rights: we'd avoid this because we were only proposing a distribution system in which the risk

belonged to the channel providers. The great trick of Freeview would be to persuade consumers to buy the box and to see it in the way they saw their television set. If it didn't work it was their problem, not ours.

We got a break when Tony Ball of BSkyB phoned me to ask if we'd consider letting them in. It so happened that we needed someone to take up some of the spare channel capacity we would have if we won the bid as both Mark Thompson at Channel Four and ITV had turned us down, a decision history will show was a bad one for both of them, particularly for ITV. At the BBC we didn't want, and certainly couldn't afford, to take all the extra channels, so I welcomed Tony's approach. I was also keen on BSkyB's joining us because it meant they would be inside the proverbial tent rather than criticizing us from the outside. I've never really worked out quite why BSkyB wanted to help us build Freeview. To me, it was always obvious that if it worked it would undermine their own basic-tier pay business. This is now happening, and again, I think history will show that it was a business mistake for BSkyB to help us grow Freeview.

In a two-man consortium with Crown Castle, who owned the whole distribution system, including the masts, and with BSkyB as a partner in supplying channels, we bid for the licences and won. My 100 per cent track record was safe.

In less than two years Freeview has become a massive success. This doesn't surprise me. It was Andy Duncan's marketing department who came up with the basic selling idea – more 'normal' television but no contract. We started with Freeview boxes on the market for £99, although the price has now dropped dramatically. It is an easy sell. For a relatively small one-off payment you can get thirty television channels, including all the new BBC television and radio channels, and make no further payments. In twenty months four million homes had boxes able to receive Freeview, making it the fastest take-up ever for a new consumer electronic product in the UK. The four million are all in the 75 per cent of the country that can currently receive Freeview.

So what had all this to do with the BBC? Why should we have been interested in the first place? I can partially answer that with one simple statistic.

In traditional five-channel analogue homes, the BBC's share of viewing in 2003 was 49 per cent, nearly half of all viewing. In Freeview homes

the figure was just over 45 per cent, while in BSkyB homes it was 26 per cent. Given that the Government plans to turn off the analogue signal in the early part of the next decade, it is obviously very much in the BBC's interest for people to go digital via Freeview rather than through BSkyB. In Freeview homes, they watch 8 per cent less BBC programming than in traditional five-channel homes; but in Sky homes the loss is a massive 50 per cent.

There were two other reasons for the BBC's involvement. It was, and still is, important for the BBC that the UK goes fully digital because that is the only way to ensure that all the BBC services – on radio and television – are available to everyone. Given that everyone pays the licence fee, it is only right that, within a reasonable time, all its services are universally available. If we hadn't developed Freeeview the chances of the UK being able to turn off the analogue signal were virtually nil. In those circumstances it would have been hard to defend continuing with our range of digital services.

Freeview was also important to the BBC defensively. Opponents of the licence fee always argue that once everyone can get pay television the licence fee as a means of funding the BBC will be unnecessary. If people want the BBC they will choose to pay for it; and if they don't want it, then why should they pay for it? This is a superficially attractive argument that eventually some political party will fall for and adopt. But there is a good argument against and it is this: it is imperative that everyone can receive the BBC, even if they don't pay their licence fee. It is part of the glue that binds the UK together and must be available to everyone.

Freeview makes it very hard for any Government to try to make the BBC a pay-television service. The more Freeview boxes out there, the harder it will be to switch the BBC to a subscription service since most of the boxes can't be adapted for pay TV. I suspect Freeview will ensure the future of the licence fee for another decade at least, and probably longer.

The second move we made against BSkyB was a more obvious victory. When the BBC first put its television services onto BSkyB's digital platform it took the rather odd decision to pay BSkyB £5 million for the privilege of doing so. It was a decision taken back in 1998 and it was odd because BSkyB were desperate to get the BBC on board and would happily have paid them to get them. In Italy the state broadcaster RAI later looked at

what had happened in the UK and made sure that Sky paid them a lot of money to carry their services. The BBC were total mugs.

ITV stayed off the BSkyB platform for several years and only went on, reluctantly, in 2001. By then the platform was a roaring success and ITV needed to get on it, so they agreed to pay BSkyB's price of £17 million a year for the privilege – a decision that ITV appealed against to Oftel, the appropriate regulator. When Oftel decided it was a perfectly fair price, we at the BBC knew we were in trouble when our current contract with BSkyB ended in late 2003.

By then, however, two further things had happened. First, a new satellite had been launched with a smaller footprint that only covered the UK and part of Northern Europe. This meant that if we switched all our services to the new satellite we could beam our channels largely at our own home market. Second, I had discovered from my colleagues in the German equivalent of the BBC that they happily put their signals out unencrypted, even if it meant they were accessible all across Europe – this was allowed under European legislation on overspill.

With BSkyB telling us that eventually they would expect us to pay at least the price ITV was paying them we saw this as our opportunity to strike. If we decided to beam all the BBC services from the new satellite we could broadcast them unencrypted: we no longer had to pay BSkyB to scramble the signal and then unscramble it again.

This would bring real advantages for the BBC. In one move we'd be free of the BSkyB satellite monopoly; we would save a lot of money; and, finally, all our regional services would be available throughout the country. This would mean, for instance, that a Scot living in London would be able to watch BBC Scotland. I have to admit we also saw it as one in the eye for BSkyB, an organization that only respected you if you played it tough.

We did know, however, that BSkyB would hate it and would play tough themselves: if we got away with it the other terrestrial broadcasters were bound to follow suit over time, and this would cost BSkyB millions of pounds in lost revenue. We worked through all the things they could do to us and decided the risk was worth taking. For instance, we knew that the first thing they would do would be to try to demote the BBC from the good positions we had on the BSkyB electronic programme guide, but we also guessed that the Independent Television Commission wouldn't allow them to do this.

When Carolyn Fairbairn and I first came up with the idea of going unencrypted, everyone else in the BBC told us why it couldn't be done. No one was on our side. Jana Bennett's Television division said we wouldn't be able to buy films or US series because the Hollywood studios wouldn't sell to an unencrypted service. Peter Salmon's people in Sport said roughly the same thing, that it would prevent us acquiring sports rights; and the people in Pat Loughrey's Nations and Regions division objected because it could mean that the only way you could find their services on the electronic programme guide was down amongst the porn channels. My joke that it might increase the audiences was not well received.

I thought they were all behaving like wimps, but then I sometimes forget that not everyone else sees life like me. They don't relish battles the way I do. My reckoning was that we represented half the free television market: who in their right mind was going to try to sell sports rights or movies without half the market? Only we could do this, because only the BBC was big enough to take on BSkyB, the sports organizations, and the Hollywood studios in one go. I knew the Hollywood studios of old. The chances of their deciding together on a policy and sticking to it were nil. They would certainly get together and swear allegiance to each other in the battle with the BBC, but then one of them would break ranks if they could get a decent deal.

So despite everyone's fears we went ahead. We didn't give BSkyB any warning of the announcement and we planned our PR strategy very carefully. When we announced the move we blamed it on BSkyB for trying to charge us too much money. We argued that this was public money and that there were better things to do with it than hand it over to Rupert Murdoch. It worked brilliantly. It was a complicated move that journalists found difficult to explain; but they recognized that it was game, set, and match to us as there was little BSkyB could do about it.

At the BSkyB headquarters at Osterley there was a deafening silence. No one there had believed we would do it – after all this was the BBC. But the BBC had changed.

Predictably, the US studios all got together to protest, but Disney came round the back and did a deal, so that was the end of that. Once one studio had broken ranks, the rest of them folded one by one. As I told John Dolgen, the boss of Paramount, when he took Jana Bennett and me

out to lunch to tell us we were following the wrong strategy, I wasn't pleading with him to take the BBC's money and we were happy to spend it elsewhere.

In the sports area we were in the middle of negotiating a £280 million-plus deal with the Football Association. When they said that it was only a deal if our signal was encrypted our negotiators simply got up, said that there was no point continuing the discussion, and left. They were all soon back at the table. We got the deal and our signal remained unencrypted.

Then there was BSkyB's electronic programme guide. As we'd predicted, BSkyB immediately said that they could no longer keep BBC One at 101 and BBC Two at 102, the two best slots on the guide. In turn we appealed to the Independent Television Commission, arguing that BSkyB didn't have the right to do this. The ITC set up an investigation and the weeks passed. Then one day I got a call from a mutual friend who said that Tony Ball at BSkyB, whom I hadn't spoken to since we announced we were going unencrypted, would like a chat.

Although we were on opposite sides on this issue, I liked Tony and had always found him friendly and straight to deal with. I rang him and we had an affable conversation about sports rights and the coming FA contract. Over the next couple of weeks our conversations got friendlier still and we began to talk about a deal involving the FA contract, the electronic programme guide, and the possibility of what we called a regionalization service. We wanted to make sure that the right signals for BBC One and BBC Two went to the right regions in satellite homes and we were prepared to pay for that. We had to ensure that if you were in Wales and went to 101, not only would you get BBC One but you also got the service that included all the Welsh regional programmes.

I became suspicious: we were getting too good a deal. BSkyB even agreed to move BBC Three to slot 115 and BBC Four to 116 on their programme guide, slots we'd been trying to get for two years. And then it dawned upon me. BSkyB were keen to get an agreement with us *before* the ITC adjudication on our dispute was published and were prepared to be very generous to stop it being published. For a negotiator it was a wonderful position to be in; but in these circumstances it is important not to screw the opposition into the ground. I had discovered over the years that what goes around comes around.

Then I got the call from the ITC Chief Executive, Patricia Hodgson, who asked me, seemingly in all innocence, if we and BSkyB were likely to reach agreement before their publication date in a week's time. I said it looked like it and, as a result, we would withdraw our complaint, which meant the ITC's ruling would never be published. She laughed and said something like 'You appear to have got all you wanted.' It was very clear that the ITC had discovered something that would have been deeply embarrassing to BSkyB if it became public. That was why we had achieved such a good deal. Patricia has always refused to discuss it with me so, to this day, I don't know what the ITC found. But I do know they found something.

During my time at the BBC I had a high public profile – not always of my own choosing. According to sections of the press, I took every decision at the BBC and was personally responsible for making every programme on television and radio. The reality was exactly the opposite. I only ever commissioned one television programme the whole time I was at the BBC, a two-part biography of Nelson Mandela that played on BBC One in 2003.

I happened to be having breakfast with the South African High Commissioner, Lindiwe Mabuza, and told her that someone should make the definitive Mandela documentary and that we would love to do it. I heard no more until I was on holiday in Australia in the summer of 2002 and got an urgent message from my PA, Fiona Hillary, saying an outline of the project was needed within three days. There was no way I could do that; instead I wrote a couple of pages about why such a documentary needed to be made.

I quoted my daughter Alice, who was 15 at the time. I explained that, like most 15-year-olds, she had no interest in politics, no understanding of international affairs, and was obsessed by popular culture. (This was the same daughter who, when I told her I was going to run the BBC, told me I shouldn't do it because I'd only screw up Radio One.) And yet when I'd asked her whom she would like to meet most in the world it wasn't someone from film or pop music: it was Nelson Mandela. In my note I said that this was the reason we should make the documentary. Mandela had transcended politics and was an icon to young and old. It worked and we made two one-hour films.

The press also believed I was obsessed by ratings, which again wasn't true. When I first arrived at the BBC we certainly had to do something about the declining numbers on BBC One, and we did that by increasing our spend on the channel, largely in the areas of drama and sport. But if you look carefully at the numbers in my time at the BBC, BBC Television still lost share overall. The problem was that ITV was in free fall for a couple of years. We didn't overtake ITV by increasing our ratings; theirs simply fell faster than ours did. In fact, looking at a graph of what has happened to ITV's figures over thirty years, you find a pretty dismal picture, although there are some signs now that, under their new Director of Programmes, Nigel Pickard, ITV's decline has slowed down.

My real concern was that the whole television industry had now adopted the Channel Four model of commissioning, whereby a relatively small number of people decide which programmes should be made. They have all the money and, as a result, they take virtually every decision, even though they don't actually produce any programmes themselves. The danger of this system is that a channel only reflects the personalities and tastes of a very small number of people. The BBC adopted this system when John Birt introduced the producer/broadcaster split in June 1996, and although I changed some of it with my 'One BBC' changes when I first arrived, I didn't change it enough.

It meant that the production community in the BBC cared too much about what the channel Controllers wanted. I used to try to tell current affairs or documentary producers I came across that we wanted their ideas, not those of the channel Controllers; but at the end of the day the producers knew who had the money. I should have been more radical and done more to change this.

There were two other areas where I believe, over four years, we made a big difference to the BBC. The first was in the area of equal opportunities.

If anyone had walked round the BBC in the late Eighties they would have found it was still very white and very male. When I arrived a decade later it was no longer very male: women had broken through as a result of a series of positive initiatives introduced by John Birt, who felt passionately about the issue. This made it possible in my time for us to promote a lot of women, on merit, to the most senior positions in the BBC. By the time I left the Directors of Television, Radio, Strategy, and Policy and Legal were all women. Equally importantly so were the Controllers

of BBC One, BBC Two, Radio Two, Radio Four, BBC Northern Ireland, and BBC Wales.

Women were in charge of numerous parts of the organization, particularly in the regions, which until recent years had been very much a male preserve. Mark Byford tells the story of when, as Director of Nations and Regions in the mid Nineties, he organized a meeting of all his senior staff from around Britain to meet John Birt. They were virtually all men. John took Mark aside and told him this simply wasn't acceptable and *had* to change. Today it has changed and the glass ceiling for women, which existed for decades at the BBC, has been well and truly broken. However, in 1999, when I arrived, the same was not true for ethnic minorities.

As Director-General I was invited to speak at the annual Campaign for Racial Equality in the Media awards presentation in April 2000; in my speech I made it very clear that improving the ethnic mix of the staff at the BBC would be one of my priorities. I announced that we were to have targets so that, by the end of 2003, people from ethnic minorities would make up 10 per cent of the staff, as opposed to the 8 per cent figure in 1999, and that in management the figure would increase from the pathetically small 2 per cent to at least 4 per cent. I also said we wanted radically to change on-screen representation of ethnic minorities.

Soon afterward I was interviewed by Anvar Khan, the presenter of a Radio Scotland programme called *The Mix*. She asked me about ethnic representation in the media and didn't I think it was hideously white? I replied that I certainly thought the BBC was hideously white and thought no more about it until the comment appeared as the front-page lead story in the following week's *Mail on Sunday*, predictably followed by papers like the *Daily Telegraph*. The letters column of the *Telegraph* had to be seen to be believed. It seemed like every retired colonel in the Home Counties had written in to complain about me. Their argument was that the BBC was white because this was a white country.

Everyone assumed I would be embarrassed and realize I'd made a mistake in the interview. On the contrary, I was rather pleased with the publicity because it told people inside and outside the BBC that I was serious about change in this area. It also told the members of BBC staff from ethnic minorities that I was serious. This wasn't about being politically correct; it was about making sure the BBC properly reflected a significant change that was happening in our society.

After four years we hit our employment targets, just. It had been very hard work to get there and we only achieved them by introducing a 'name and shame' policy. Every three months the Executive would receive a report outlining which divisions were doing well and which were doing badly in our efforts to change. For instance, when the Asian Network was switched out of Nations and Regions and into the Radio Division it was suddenly apparent that we had a major problem in cities like Leeds, Manchester, and Birmingham where a high proportion of the population were from ethnic minorities. Andy Griffee, who was in charge of the English regions, told us that in two years he would change that and that if he didn't we should fire him. True to his word, he introduced a whole range of equal opportunity initiatives and delivered what he had promised. In January 2004, only a couple of weeks before I left the BBC, I announced another four-year target: by 2008, 12.5 per cent of staff were to be from ethnic minorities, whilst the figure for management would be increased to 7 per cent.

As for on-screen representation, there has been a big change in the number of Afro-Caribbeans appearing on the BBC, but we didn't do as well increasing the number of people of Asian descent, particularly Muslims. A great deal was achieved in drama, largely thanks to Mal Young, a Liverpudlian who was in charge of drama serials at the BBC. He changed the racial mix of programmes like *Holby City* and *Casualty* by making the producers go into hospitals and see what they were actually like. He pointed out that the existing racial mix in BBC hospitals was very different from the average UK hospital.

I was once on a train on my way back from watching a football match in Manchester when I found myself sitting opposite a black guy who had been in Manchester to see a play he had written. I didn't recognize him as Kwame Kwei-Armah, an actor from *Casualty*, and he didn't recognize me as the Director-General of the BBC. When we both found out who we were he told me the story of the day he saw another black actor being auditioned for *Casualty*. He'd said to himself, 'That's it, then. I'm out' – on the assumption that they only ever had one black actor in *Casualty*. Thanks to Mal Young those days are long past in BBC drama.

I think in this area I did make a difference. I suspect my determination over four years to change the mix of people working at the BBC means the process is now unstoppable, and I know that Mark Thompson regards

the issue as being as important as I did. I regularly got accused of promoting positive discrimination in favour of ethnic minorities, which wasn't true. What I wanted was a workforce that more properly represented twenty-first-century Britain. I believe multi-cultural Britain is an exciting place and I wanted more of that excitement to rub off on the BBC.

The other area in which I tried to make real change was in making the BBC less focused on London and the South of England. Historically, ITV had been the regional television system in Britain and the BBC more a national service. But as the ITV companies merged, and with greater commercial competition undermining their profitability, it was clear to me that ITV would have no option but to reduce its commitment to the regions. I thought this meant that, over time, our respective roles might be reversed and that the BBC would have to make more programming away from the South. Personally I saw it as an opportunity, not an obligation.

From the moment I joined the BBC I realized just how much a problem the bias towards the South of England was. In my early months, when I spent a lot of time out of London, I discovered a disillusioned workforce, people who believed that London stopped them doing this or that, who felt that London was biased against them and that you could only get on by working in London.

By making Mark Thompson the new Director of Television soon after I arrived at the BBC I created a vacancy for Director of Nations and Regions. In recent years the post had been given to high fliers on the way up – Byford followed by Thompson – but by promoting Pat Loughrey to the job we were promoting someone who had spent his whole career in Northern Ireland and had never worked in London. It was intended to give a signal to staff outside the capital.

Oddly, a lot of extra money had already been spent in Scotland, Wales, and Northern Ireland as a result of devolution, but it hadn't changed the relationship with 'head office'. In Scotland, in particular, the hostility towards London was very evident. For some reason the Scots and John Birt hadn't got on at all well.

My view was that devolution was very important and that it wasn't just about politics. It was about devolving real decision-making out of London. So we set aside an extra £50 million a year to be spent in all three countries, money without strings attached. I told the Controllers that my advice would be not to spend it just covering politics but to use

it to try to build the production industry in the three countries. But in the end I told them it was their decision. That was what devolution was about.

Over the four years I was Director-General we increased production in the nations for local consumption quite markedly, but we also succeeded in building up production for the network, particularly in Scotland, where network output doubled over four years. Interestingly, it transformed the relationship between London and Scotland. Suddenly BBC Scotland became a serious and well-respected player within the BBC.

Then it became very obvious that we had a problem in England, particularly in the North of England. The BBC regularly asks people what they think of the Corporation. What we found was that the further north you went in England the lower the BBC's approval figures were. It wasn't hard to see why. The vast majority of our programmes were made in the south. So early on we set aside some money and created the Northern initiative. As a result we got new northern dramas like *Cutting It* and *Merseybeat*; we developed an important writers' initiative across the North of England; Radio Four became active in Manchester again; and we introduced a completely new regional service for East Yorkshire based in Hull. We also decided to do a major research project on the impact of broadband in the city of Hull itself, and set up a new journalists' video training centre in Newcastle upon Tyne. The decision was taken that this should be out of London and the first suggestion was Oxford. I exploded and pointed out that Oxford was London in the country and could we please go further north. So it went to Newcastle.

We increased our spending on regional news with great effect. In terms of the numbers viewing, we overtook ITV's regional news in virtually every region in England; by the time I left we were only losing in the north-east, and BBC Scotland's news had even overtaken Scottish Television north of the border. That the BBC's regional news should become so successful had been unthinkable only five years earlier.

By spending a lot of time myself in the north, and encouraging other members of the BBC Executive to do the same, we improved morale in places like Manchester, Leeds, and Newcastle, but I still thought more needed to be done. Everyone in the UK pays a licence fee and it was wrong that so much of that money was being spent in the south. The BBC needed to reflect the whole of life in the UK, not just one part of it.

I therefore planned a major change. I wanted to move some of our services out of London to an expanded BBC operation in Manchester. My plan was to move Radio Five Live, both our children's channels, half our new media operation, and BBC Three to Manchester in the second half of this decade.

At the same time I planned to move other parts of the BBC out of London for more practical reasons. Our outside broadcast headquarters needed to be on a motorway somewhere, not in Acton in West London, whilst our back office operations did not have to be in Central London. We weren't big payers and many of our back office staff increasingly couldn't afford to live in London. I also planned that at least two members of the Executive would in future be based in Manchester.

When I told my Executive colleagues what I was proposing most, though not all, were against the idea. Jenny Abramsky threatened to resign if Radio Five Live were moved, although she never actually said so to me. Jana Bennett felt that BBC Three had to stay in London, while the Children's department were adamant they weren't going anywhere. They all said this had been tried before when 'Youth' and 'Religion' had been moved north a decade earlier and it hadn't been deemed a success. My point was that this plan moved the money to Manchester, not just a production department. The real reason most people objected was that it would disrupt their lives. My answer to that was, 'Bad luck'.

Sadly, this was unfinished business when I left the BBC. I took my plan to the Governors at the end of 2003 and they agreed with the proposal to move services to Manchester. The idea was that it would be announced as part of our commitment for the next charter period. And then I left. The plan still exists and the BBC say they are going to implement some of it, but I have no doubt that the forces against it are regrouping even as I write.

The opposition I hit was exactly the same as the opposition Gavyn Davies met when he made his speech suggesting that too much of the BBC's money was being spent on the southern middle class. He was savaged for daring to say such a thing. But then of course that is how a comparatively small South of England elite has managed to keep such a strong grip on the BBC and on this country for so long.

Why Did They Cry?
(Culture Change at the BBC)

In my manifesto for the post of Director-General of the BBC, written in the summer of 1999, I had said that the biggest challenge facing a new Director-General was to build an 'inclusive culture'. This was not based on any detailed analysis; it was simply something I sensed was a problem at the BBC from what I had heard. But I was shocked by what I found when I got there. It was worse than anything I had expected. Much worse.

When I joined the BBC I faced the prospect of spending five months shadowing John Birt and learning by his example, which is what I suspect he had in mind for his successor when he planned the ridiculous concept of a five-month handover. Five weeks would have been more than adequate. Instead I decided to find out about the BBC for myself, and so I took to the road. I spent a great deal of time outside London and talked to thousands of people who worked for the BBC in different parts of the UK.

The first thing I had to do was to put a stop to the whole pomp and paraphernalia that had traditionally surrounded visits from the Director-General over many years. This meant getting rid of the inevitable entourage and dissuading people from seeing me as a visiting dignitary. I didn't want the red carpet treatment that most Director-Generals had received in the past. On most of my visits I went alone or with one other person, Emma Scott, my business manager.

If this approach was to work it meant persuading the managers of the places I was visiting that I wanted to see business as usual, not a spruced-up version; more importantly, that I wanted to talk directly to the people who worked for the BBC, not just the local bosses. I therefore insisted on eating in the canteen with the staff instead of attending formal

lunches or dinners, and I wanted to have time to talk to people on a one-to-one basis.

The message began to get around. Early on I went to visit BBC Radio Lancashire in Blackburn to find I was being served tea in a cup and saucer, not the sort of thing you normally found in local radio. The boss, a great bloke called Steve Taylor, told me that he'd sent someone down to Blackburn Market to buy it especially but that I needn't worry about the expense as he was taking it back after my visit.

I went to BBC offices that no Director-General had visited in decades. I found that some of our staff were working in buildings that should have been condemned years earlier. I remember visiting our building in Leicester, the home of BBC Radio Leicester and the Asian Network, and saying to people afterwards how awful it was. I was told that if I thought it was bad I should wait until I went to Stoke. When I finally visited Stoke I was pleasantly surprised; it wasn't *that* terrible. But over the next four years BBC Radio Stoke moved to a better building. We also moved to a new building in Sheffield and started work on replacement premises in Birmingham, Leeds, Hull, Liverpool, Glasgow, and finally Leicester. We also renovated buildings right across the country.

On my visits I found staff doing what had been required of me in local newspapers thirty-five years earlier, when I had to buy my own typewriter. Some were buying their own recording equipment because the gear the BBC was supplying was so out of date. In particular the younger staff coming straight from media courses found they had to use equipment that was significantly inferior to what they'd been used to at college. Over the next four years we digitalized every local radio station in the BBC. I also found that many of the staff I met felt unloved, unwanted, and unnoticed.

Everywhere I asked the same two questions of the management and the staff. What do we need to change in order to improve our service? And what can I do to make your life better? Some of the suggestions were ridiculous, such as wanting their total budget doubled; but most of them were small and practical and would cost peanuts to implement. In most cases we did this in my first few months in charge. A few of the suggestions were more difficult because, in some areas, the Birt–McKinsey-inspired reorganizations of the BBC had resulted in institutional madness.

A classic example was the library service, a fundamental resource in

any broadcasting organization. Access to books, cuttings, and CDs had been priced at such a high level in the internal pricing system that many programme makers couldn't afford to use them, given the size of their budgets. In the case of CDs, for example, it was cheaper to go to the local High Street and buy them than borrow them from the BBC library. This was simply crazy and we put a stop to it as part of the 'One BBC' changes.

Worst of all was the climate of fear I found everywhere inside the BBC. I knew John Birt and his senior team weren't popular, but once I was on the inside I discovered that they were disliked, even loathed, by large numbers of people working for the BBC. Around the organization people didn't talk of the Director-General as 'John' or even 'Mr Birt': he was described only as 'Birt' in a disparaging tone. There was little affection for him or the wider leadership anywhere, and the further down I went into the organization the greater the feelings of hostility and distrust I found.

For instance, in local radio every station had to cut 2 per cent from its budget every year, year after year, because that was the saving that head office theoretically believed was achievable. Yet anyone who actually visited a local radio station could see they were being run on a shoestring and that more and more cuts would only damage the service. It may not have been fair but the staff in local radio blamed John Birt personally for this, and virtually every other problem they had.

I realized I would have to try to change the relationship between the Director-General and the staff at every level of the organization. It never occurred to me, for example, not to be friendly to the people on security or at the reception desk and I always chatted to the staff doing these jobs wherever I went. At Broadcasting House in Central London, where I was based, people on reception told me later that they had found my style very different from that of my predecessor, who had tended not to acknowledge them. He certainly never stopped and chatted. In contrast to this approach, I always wanted to get to know as many members of staff as possible.

I suspect John was intrinsically shy and found it difficult to be informal and friendly with people he didn't know. I don't do this naturally either, but over the years I've worked on it and learnt how to do it. Gareth Jones, whom I brought in to be Director of Human Resources, saw this in me and said one day, 'You're not really an extrovert at all, are you?'

He was right. Sadly, Gareth didn't like the BBC much and in particular he didn't take to the BBC Governors. He left after a year.

I also found that there was little trust between members of top management. Obviously there were friendships between people, but I detected no feeling of common purpose. They had learnt how to operate as competing individuals within a climate of fear, but I didn't feel they were a united team. When Jana Bennett returned to the BBC in 2002 to become Director of Television, after spending two years in the United States, she told the story of turning up late for her first Executive meeting. As she reached the room she heard laughter so she assumed she was in the wrong place. According to her, no one laughed at Executive meetings when she had last been at the BBC.

A year later, when things had begun to improve, I remember discussing what it had been like with a board-level colleague who had been a senior member of the previous regime. He told me that at the time he had genuinely believed in what they were doing and the way they were doing it and that their critics were totally wrong. He said he had since discovered a different world and what he had discovered in the process was that behaviour he had believed to be acceptable had actually been completely inappropriate and ineffective. Lorraine Heggessey, now the Controller of BBC One but then Joint Director of Factual Programming, demanded at an early meeting of the Executive, which she had just joined, that all those who had supported the Birt regime should explain and account for their actions. An uncomfortable silence followed, broken by a long-serving member saying, 'I vas only following orders.'

The reason I was so shocked by what I found at the BBC was that I couldn't conceive that anyone could have believed that this was the way to run a creative organization. What I knew for certain was that the traditional leadership model based on exaggerated status, self-importance, and ordering people around was over. It was obsolete. Expecting people to deliver because you, as their boss, told them to do so didn't work any more, and was certainly not the way to get the best out of staff.

I had discovered this for myself many years earlier when I first ran programme teams, but my views of management and leadership had developed over the years and had been reinforced by the period I had spent at the Harvard Business School back in 1989. The twelve weeks I spent there showed me that my gut feelings on how to run organizations

201

and motivate people had an intellectual rationale. That gave me the confidence to continue putting my ideas into practice as I found myself running larger and larger organizations.

In many ways my approach to leading groups of people is rooted in what my father taught my brothers and me all those years ago when he used regularly to talk to the local road sweeper. When he died, all three of us were asked to write a piece about him to be read out at his funeral. I wrote that, more than anything else, he had hated pompous people who thought that they were somehow better than those around them. He believed *everyone* was worthy of respect. It was always obvious to me that people would do a better job if their boss respected them and what they were doing. Once you grasp this simple human truth there are a set of ideas that logically follow, which I've used as a basis for running organizations over the years.

As a leader you need to be yourself. It is lethal to try to ape the behaviour of the stereotypical manager just because you've got a job in management. You were appointed because of who you are and you need to keep faith with that: if you are naturally rather eccentric, as I am, then *be* eccentric. Your staff will like you for it. On the other hand, if you try to be something you are not, you'll pay a high price, waste a lot of personal energy, and your staff will see straight through you. It takes courage to simply be yourself; it means you have to be confident, understand your strengths and weaknesses, and be willing to admit the latter. But the results are worth it.

As a leader, communication *really* matters. People working in the organization are more likely to support you and what you are trying to achieve if they feel they are involved in a two-way conversation with you. We used a variety of means at the BBC to try to do this. I sent regular e-mails always signed Greg, did frequent internal broadcasts, used our in-house magazine, and made a series of videos – all with the aim of creating a one-to-one relationship with nearly thirty thousand people. It is important to be direct and to the point; most important of all, never lapse into the language of management, the gobbledegook of consultants and business schools. Avoiding jargon is essential if you want to be a good leader.

For instance, when I publicly apologized for the *Question Time* programme that was broadcast the week of the September 11 disasters I

immediately sent an e-mail to all the staff saying very clearly why I thought it had been a mistake, that the programme hadn't matched the mood of the moment. I went on to say that we all made mistakes and that was the end of it. There would be no recriminations. This up-front approach worked. Many of the thousands of people who took to the streets, or who wrote to me following my departure from the BBC, had never met me, but they told me they felt we had a relationship.

As a leader you also have to be honest with your staff. It shouldn't be a problem to say, 'I'm sorry. I got that wrong.' The problem is pretending you are right when you know you are wrong. At the BBC we once tried to reform the expenses policy right across the organization. It was a good idea but I soon discovered by talking to the staff that we were being too mean and that some of the new allowances were too low. I listened, changed the policy, and personally took the blame, admitting the error on the front page of *Ariel*, the BBC's in-house magazine. Making the apology actually won me new friends.

As a leader you set the example. Don't tell your staff to do one thing and then do another yourself. They'll spot it immediately and your credibility will be undermined. It's about practising what you preach. If, for instance, you urge your managers to be less hierarchical and mix more with the staff then you, as the leader, need to be seen to be doing it yourself. Every day I got my sandwiches or salad from the canteen and talked to the people I met in the queue. It would have been easier and quicker to have sent someone from my office to get my lunch, but my going to the canteen sent an important and symbolic message to everyone: I was both accessible and one of them; that's what I wanted my managers to be.

As a leader you have to recognize that leadership is often about the stories told about you – either positive or negative – by others in the organization. You'll be judged more by those stories than by anything you say or write. As an example, in October 2002 there was a serious fire at my house that kept me up all night. The next day I was exhausted and up to my eyes dealing with the aftermath of the fire, but I had a long-standing commitment to speak to 350 BBC staff from the Nations and Regions at an event in East London. The organizers assumed I would cancel and made contingency plans. But I turned up, if only to tell those 350 people that they mattered. The downside of this approach is that, as

a leader, you are always under the spotlight. That's why big leadership jobs are so exhausting, if you do them properly.

As a leader in an organization you have to be able to convince those working for you that they are capable of achieving great things, more than they ever imagined. In turn, this means giving people responsibility and letting them get on with the job. I'm always amazed by how many so-called leaders manage to achieve the opposite. People perform better when they are trusted and encouraged rather than when they operate in a climate of fear or intimidation in which everything they do is double checked. When I arrived at the BBC such checking was institutionalized: in some areas nothing of real importance happened without being scrutinized by McKinsey, the management consultants. As a result, many senior managers in the BBC felt powerless and deeply frustrated.

As a leader you have to understand the finances. Numbers are far too important to be left to the accountants, who, in my experience, will only succeed in confusing you. You have to insist that the accountants give you the numbers in a form you can understand, not in a way that only they understand. This is a constant battle, for often finance people will not do this willingly. Managers who don't understand the finances are vulnerable: they are not really in charge. I found this all the time at the BBC, and I suspect this is a particular problem in the public sector. However, the problem doesn't only apply to finance. There's always a danger that other support services such as human resources, strategy, and facilities management end up running the operation. The leader's job is to understand enough to be able to remind them every so often that they are only the support machine.

Finally, if you are the leader of an organization you must care about the people who work for you, all of them, and show them you care. Only then can you succeed.

By the year 2000, when I took over at the BBC, this kind of thinking wasn't exactly rocket science. Business schools had been teaching the importance of leadership, as opposed to management, for more than a decade. But many organizations in Britain had continued to pursue the management philosophies of the 1970s and 1980s – years after most reputable academics had stopped teaching them. This was, and is, particularly true of the public sector.

Two years before I joined the BBC I had first-hand experience of this problem when I spent nearly a year looking around the National Health Service. In the summer of 1997, soon after Labour had been elected, I bumped into Margaret Jay, then Minister of State for Health, at David Frost's garden party, where the great and the good converge in large numbers every summer. It was at that same event six years later, when the Gilligan affair had just broken, that all the press photographers tried to get a picture of Alastair Campbell and me together. Instead we studiously avoided each other.

I told Margaret that as a committed Labour supporter and a believer in what the NHS stood for I would be happy to help if I could and that if there was anything I could do she should give me a ring. A few weeks later Margaret and the then Secretary of State for Health, Frank Dobson, asked me to come up with some new ideas for the Patients' Charter. With the help of Alison Nield, a former nurse and now a manager within the NHS, I spent nearly a year simply wandering around the organization. I quickly found the idea of the charter uninteresting but became fascinated by how you run and motivate an organization that employs a million people, the biggest employer in Europe.

What we found was an NHS whose frontline staff, particularly in the hospitals, overwhelmingly believed that what they achieved, they achieved *despite* their management, not thanks to it. I found small oases where the frontline staff and the leadership worked together in pursuit of common goals, but they were the exception. In my report I tried to tell the politicians that they didn't have a hope in hell of changing the NHS fundamentally unless they first addressed this problem, which was a problem of leadership.

In terms of culture I'm not sure much has changed since then, although the coming of foundation hospitals – in which the local management have real power – could make a big difference. I recently heard of an NHS Trust where one hospital had lost all its stars. The frontline staff had celebrated this because it was one in the eye for 'the management', who would now lose their bonuses. Until this ugly divide between 'us' and 'them' is tackled I do not think the NHS can move forward properly.

Changing the culture of the NHS will require real commitment over a number of years, but it also requires spending real money on change programmes. This is a difficult sell in the NHS. People both inside and

outside the service seem to believe that any NHS money not spent directly on health care is somehow wasted. And the likes of the *Daily Mail* would have great fun dismissing expenditure on culture change as wasted money when it could go on hip replacements. Yet every commercial organization in the world knows that you *have* to spend money on these things if you are to succeed.

In the introduction to my NHS report I wrote:

My approach to this task reflects my own approach to management. I believe that most people are capable of achieving outstanding performance – well beyond what many have been led to believe they can achieve – but that can only be brought out by an inclusive management style. I do not believe people are best motivated by fear but by being involved in the decision-making process, by taking part in the setting of goals for an organization and by being able to celebrate achieving them.

What the report recommended was that the top-down approach of running the NHS, which the Government was pursuing at the time, was largely doomed. I argued that, while the NHS needed a few central principles, power needed to be shifted quite radically from the centre towards the coalface. This was hardly revolutionary stuff, but it proved far too radical for the politicians and the Department of Health back then. By the time the report was published, in November 1998, Margaret Jay had moved on to become the Labour Leader in the House of Lords, and no one else was really interested in it or was in a position to deliver on its recommendations.

In my experience, politicians understand very little about how to manage and motivate a workforce. Few of them have held senior jobs in large organizations and they still tend to believe that the critical component in making change is deciding on the policy. It's not. The hardest thing is getting the support of the staff who have the job of implementing policy: they are the people who will determine whether it succeeds or fails. Most civil servants have the same problem: too much of their energy is focused on managing upwards.

As far as the NHS is concerned, I believe that it is only when the politicians stand well back and let the senior managers really become the

leaders that there is any chance of positive change. And the majority of those managers should come from the medical professions themselves rather than being 'professional' managers. This happens in almost every other organization, yet giving a doctor a management role in the NHS is somehow seen as a misuse of his or her training and talents. Only when this happens will the leadership have a chance of getting the staff on their side.

In one sense I wasted a year of my life on the NHS report, but in another it was invaluable experience, because when I joined the BBC I found myself facing many of the same challenges.

On my first day as Director-General I was determined to do something similar to what I had done a decade earlier on my first day as Managing Director of LWT. I wanted everyone to know that things were going to be different. But doing it in a relatively small organization where everybody worked in the same building was easy; it was going to be much harder getting that message across to the nearly thirty thousand BBC people working in more than six hundred offices in the UK and around the world. I could hardly buy them all a drink.

I decided to make a speech and hold a question and answer session in a studio at Television Centre in London that would be broadcast live across the BBC on the internal ring main. I insisted that we have a cross-section of staff in the studio audience, not just senior managers as had happened in the past. Compared with the kind of events we were running a couple of years later it was a rather conservative affair; but I did manage to make some jokes and to send some signals about the vision I had for the organization.

I said that my aim for the future was simple:

I joined the BBC because I wanted it to make wonderful programmes . . . So how do we do that? I think we need two things. We should spend more of our money on programme making and we must ensure we have a culture within the BBC where we believe everything and anything is possible.

In answer to one of the subsequent questions, I suggested that if people were so unhappy with the BBC that they felt the need to moan all the time, then they should consider leaving. There were thousands of people

outside who would be grateful for their jobs. To my amazement this drew a sustained round of applause.

Sue Lawley, who was MC of the event, asked me whether my management style was closer to Michael Grade's or John Birt's. I explained that I hoped to bring the flair of Grade and the analytical ability of Birt. I added that if I got it the other way round the organization could find itself in real trouble. When Michael Grade was appointed BBC Chairman in April 2004 he was asked a similar question about me and John Birt. He told Jon Snow on Channel Four News that he was a 'Dykeist' rather than a 'Birtist'.

So I made it clear to the staff that changing the culture of the BBC was on my agenda from day one. But it was two more years before I had the confidence really to do something about it, two years before I felt I'd earned sufficient credibility and support within the organization to launch a fully fledged culture-change initiative.

By then we'd restructured the organization, taken out several layers of management, put more programme people onto the BBC Executive, cultivated more collaboration, and encouraged the organization to move faster. We were also ahead of target in reducing the amount of money the BBC spent on overhead departments, which meant much more money was going into programmes.

I can't say I enjoyed my first year at the BBC and eighteen months after I joined the organization I was beginning to wonder whether I would ever be able to make real progress in the area that I knew mattered most: doing something about the entrenched BBC culture that had developed over decades. Like all big organizations the BBC was inbred, which made changing its culture even more difficult. BBC people tended to live their lives with other BBC people. They were their friends, their lovers, their husbands and wives. Even when they got divorced it was often to go off with or marry someone else from the BBC.

Parts of the BBC culture were very positive: a commitment to strong editorial values, a willingness to go the extra mile to achieve excellence, and a strong team spirit within certain units. But other aspects were negative. Many staff felt badly treated by their bosses and many more felt they weren't valued by the organization. Internal rivalry was rampant, and many people saw the competition as being someone else inside the BBC. There was little trust or collaboration; middle management

tended to be risk averse; and there was still contempt for many in senior management.

Our staff also told us that, despite producing some great programmes, it was a difficult place in which to be creative or innovative. The annual staff survey in 2001 showed that some things had improved since I arrived – staff believed the senior team had a much clearer vision of the future and they also felt communications were getting better; but, overall, the results of the survey painted a bleak picture of our internal culture. I hadn't made much of an impact.

The condition I'd identified in the NHS in 1998 was prevalent when I joined the BBC, and was still there. People still believed that what they achieved, they achieved *despite* the management.

In the end, a number of factors encouraged me to make the move to try and tackle the cultural problems in late 2001. The most significant was the arrival of three new people onto the BBC Executive team: Stephen Dando, who joined as Director of Human Resources; Andy Duncan as Director of Marketing and Communications; and Roger Flynn as Managing Director of BBC Ventures. They changed the balance on the Executive.

All three came from the private sector and all three had the same initial impressions of the BBC that I had had eighteen months earlier. They reminded me of my feelings that change to the ingrained culture was essential. Urged on by the three of them, I decided that this was a good time to make the move. In performance terms the BBC was in good health. Our revenue was secured, our output was strong, and our main commercial competitors were in trouble due to an advertising recession. I also believed, having channelled millions of pounds of extra money into programmes, that the production community was more on my side. Without the support of the programme makers there was little hope of effecting any real change in the culture since more than nineteen thousand of the staff worked directly in programme making or content creation.

My overall calculation was that the staff would now give me the benefit of the doubt if we went for wholesale culture change. In the end we finally decided to do it after three BBC executives – Andy Duncan, Alan Yentob, and BBC Two Controller Jane Root – went on a fact-finding trip around a number of successful companies and organizations in the USA. They came back like converts, preaching the gospel of culture change, corporate

values, and the importance of nurturing your staff. I was particularly taken by the slogans they brought back. My favourite was 'We employ people for attitude and train for skills', which came from Southwest Airlines in Dallas; but I also liked the Stanford Research Institute's advice to 'Kill the cynics'. I later went with another group of BBC executives on a similar trip and we saw what could be achieved for ourselves.

Having decided to back a culture change programme, the question was how to go about it. Over the years the BBC had been littered with the corpses of failed change programmes, which meant that BBC staff were likely to be cynical and resistant to yet another initiative. So the Director of Television, Mark Thompson, and his Radio counterpart, Jenny Abramsky, both veterans of previous ventures, offered to look back and see what lessons could be learnt.

They found that too often the programmes had been run by external consultants, had been owned only by management and imposed on the organization from the top, and that they'd been shot through with management jargon. As a result they'd tended to be short lived and had been resisted very effectively by an intelligent, articulate, and sceptical workforce. So we now knew what not to do. In particular, we knew that if we were to launch a change programme we had to see it through over a number of years. There's a lot of evidence to suggest that at about the time a change programme is having an impact on the staff the senior management have got bored and moved on to the next initiative.

On 7 February 2002, almost two years to the day since I'd become Director-General, we launched our culture change programme, which we called 'Making it Happen'. When I look back now, I'm not sure we knew what we were doing; we simply knew we had to do something. Luckily Susan Spindler, an experienced programme maker who, as a senior manager, had worked in a whole range of areas across the BBC, agreed to be director of the project for six months. In the end she did twenty. She was then replaced by another senior manager, Katharine Everett, who carried on the good work Susan and her team had started.

Susan took the job against the strong advice of her family and most of her senior BBC colleagues. They told her she was mad and that by getting involved in something that sounded like pure 'management bollocks' she was certain to blight her career. Having agreed to do the job, her biggest asset was her determination that this change programme would

not degenerate into meaningless management jargon like so many others before it.

The day before the launch of 'Making it Happen', we explained what we were planning to my 100-strong Director-General's briefing group. I had set up the group early on and used it as a way of communicating to the most senior managers in the BBC. Like most big organizations, the BBC tends to be too introverted, so I always invited a guest speaker to our monthly meetings to broaden everyone's horizons. These ranged from politicians to academics, from business leaders to senior clerics. In fact at one meeting Jonathan Sacks, the Chief Rabbi, made one of the most persuasive arguments in favour of public service broadcasting that I've ever heard – far more persuasive than most of the arguments the BBC has ever come up with.

I can't say that the briefing group was initially wild about 'Making it Happen'. I suspect they thought I had bounced the idea on them and that we were all being dangerously evangelical. But they gave me the benefit of the doubt and over the next two years fully supported the idea.

Next came the whole staff. In an ambitious studio session that was transmitted across the BBC I announced a new vision for the Corporation. I told them that John Birt's vision 'to be the best managed public sector organization in the world' was laudable and worthy but not designed to get creative people out of bed in the mornings. We were replacing it with an aim 'to become the most creative organization in the world'. I believed this best summed up what the BBC should be about.

In my off-the-cuff speech I urged everyone in the BBC to 'imagine, just imagine what a great place the BBC could be if we all worked together to change it'. But what the press picked up on, and which was by far the most publicized aspect of the event, was a yellow card emblazoned with the words 'CUT THE CRAP'. It was like a football referee's yellow card and I promised the staff that everyone who asked for one could have one, to use in meetings when they couldn't get something to happen. It was a good gimmick, if a little corny, and we sent out thousands of cards to staff right across the BBC. We even had it translated into Chinese and Arabic.

But the key message we were trying to get across was that the BBC did not have a 'God-given right to exist' and that we needed to pay more attention to our audiences. After all, they were our paymasters. In order

to do this we needed to address aspects of our own culture in the BBC.

At the same event we screened a video showing some of the good things already happening at the BBC that we wanted to see more of. One of them was the story of the atrium at our White City building. It demonstrated very clearly a lot of the things that were wrong at the BBC.

The White City building in West London was only built in the late 1980s, but it was a disgrace. It was a terrible off-the-shelf design and looked like it had been built by an old Eastern European communist state. Around the place it was called Ceausescu Towers, after the former communist leader of Romania. When I arrived at the BBC I noticed that the only nice part of the building, the open atrium in the middle, was actually closed to the staff. It had been closed since the building was first opened and to go into the atrium you had to wear a hard hat.

I asked why the staff weren't allowed to use it and was told the magic words: 'Health and Safety'. But because I was the Director-General I could push a bit more. I asked for an explanation of the Health and Safety problems. Some months later I was told staff couldn't use the atrium because there was no wheelchair ramp and it needed another exit to meet fire safety regulations. No one could explain why people had been wearing hard hats for the last decade!

I raised the matter at the BBC Executive. I asked everyone around the table if they'd known about all this and why they hadn't done something about it. I remember Mark Thompson, then Director of Television, saying 'We tried but it was too difficult, so we just gave up.' We all sympathized with this. We all knew changing things was hard.

So John Smith, who by now was in charge of property as well as finance, and I arranged for the fire exit and wheelchair ramp to be installed and opened up the atrium. On the opening day I wrote a piece in *Ariel* in which I asked, 'How many equivalents are there around the BBC, things which we can't do because someone, at some time, has told us it can't be done?'

I also held a party in the atrium that night for all the staff who worked in the building. As I wandered around many of them were excited and asked 'Does this mean we can go on the balconies now?' or 'Does it mean my office doesn't have to be painted grey?' I found the man from property and told him about this. His answer was a classic: 'Look what you've started now.'

The opening-up of the White City atrium became an incredibly important story around the BBC. It symbolized what 'Making it Happen' was trying to do and helped convince people that things could be changed. It showed the staff that the Director-General was on their side in attacking the mind-numbing negativity of much of the BBC bureaucracy. It also told the jobsworth bureaucrats that we were after them.

As part of 'Making it Happen' we set up seven working groups, each with a high-profile and powerful leader at the helm. Importantly, none of these came from the BBC Executive. They covered the areas we thought needed addressing: creativity, audiences, valuing people, improving leadership, transforming our work spaces, and attacking bureaucracy. The seventh group was asked to develop a set of written values for the BBC. These groups were charged with coming up with a five-year change plan to transform the BBC; at the same time we asked every division to form its own 'Making it Happen' team to suggest and implement more immediate change at a local level.

The launch event seemed to go down well and there were positive reactions reported in the BBC's in-house magazine, *Ariel*. One person said:

> It was the clearest sign yet that we've changed course and it's all hands on deck. It reminded me how much had been squashed out of the organization by the old regime. At last we've moved on to discussing the BBC's soul instead of being distracted by crazy charges for borrowing a CD.

Another commented:

> Some fantastic, inspirational stuff. This is something that everyone should own. Greg is backing us to question things and change them if we need to.

Perhaps less positively:

> Shame that after leaving the session I shared a lift with two 'BBC types' who said how funny it was hearing a cockney DG. Maybe we've got further to go than even Greg realizes.

'Making it Happen' was now up and running, with a decent budget, a good team, and an inspirational leader in Susan Spindler. What Susan and her team always believed was that it was very important that they reported directly to me as Director-General and weren't sidelined as a Human Resources initiative. They needed it to be seen that they were supported from the very top. The basic idea of 'Making it Happen' was that by getting rid of the crap, by freeing people to make their own decisions and to take their own risks, our programmes and services would improve.

Over the next two years we took communication within the BBC to a higher level. The BBC was full of great programme makers and writers and we started using them properly for the first time to tell stories about BBC people to people *inside* the organization. One example. We made a film to tell the story of two BBC engineers who were the real heroes on the day John Simpson 'liberated' Kabul. These two engineers had transported a satellite dish and other equipment through Russia and into Afghanistan. When their Russian lorry driver refused to go any further into the mountains they refused to give up. They hired thirty mules, divided up the equipment, and strapped it on the mules. They then walked for days with the mules through snow-covered passes and down into Kabul to be ready and waiting when John arrived. They were the true heroes of Kabul.

This sort of thing happened all the time at the BBC, but no one ever got to hear about it. We decided to change that and over the next two years made many similar films and showed them all around the organization. Many revealed for the first time the great work that was being done by staff outside London, which helped to offset the BBC's ingrained pro-London bias. One film featured the work of BBC Radio Leeds in a city-centre primary school in one of the most deprived areas of Britain. It showed how a comparatively small project had transformed the lives of the children, their families, and their community. It was impossible to watch it without getting a lump in your throat, tears in your eyes, or both. When I was next in Leeds I visited the school and the headmistress told me that, as a result of the project, the children's confidence had soared and their results had improved.

These films, and dozens of others like them, opened the eyes of BBC people to the scale and range of the organization and made them proud

of what was being achieved and of those involved. The real point about 'Making it Happen' was that it engaged people's emotions, not just their brains. Culture change is above all an emotional experience, not an intellectual one.

On launch day I'd promised staff that *everyone* would have a chance to be involved if they wanted. At the time I had no idea how we would do it, but Susan Spindler and her team found a way. They created something we called 'Just Imagine', borrowing the title from my launch speech. In the first six months more than ten thousand staff voluntarily took part at more than two hundred meetings all over the UK and across the world.

It is difficult now to remember how risky it felt to embark on something quite as radical as 'Just Imagine'. It was very non-BBC, an organization in which people tended to leave their emotions behind them when they came into work. In sessions ranging in size from fifty to four hundred, people paired up and took turns to interview each other about their positive experiences at the BBC. Instead of moaning, people talked about their proudest and most successful moments. They then discussed these in groups of ten, and finally the most powerful stories were shared with the whole group. Everyone was asked: If those great experiences were to become the norm, how would the organization have to change?

For thousands of people it was the first time anyone had ever listened to what they thought and felt about the BBC. These were often very moving occasions, and it wasn't unusual for people to shed a tear as their feelings of pride, loyalty, and deep affection for the BBC were reawakened. Often those feelings had been buried years earlier, to be replaced by disappointment and cynicism.

Many sceptics came to the meetings thinking this was 'happy-clappy management' but left excited after an incredibly rewarding experience. I was surprised by the success of these sessions and certainly found them an emotional experience myself, largely because some people I had secretly written off as 'change refuseniks' were transformed.

The data that came from the sessions – in all there were 25,000 separate ideas and suggestions – was analysed and then fed back to the divisional and pan-BBC change teams. Often good ideas that were popular at the sessions and easy to do were implemented almost immediately: simple things like putting a cash machine in the reception at BBC Cardiff or allowing staff to busk in the foyer of Bush House in London at lunchtime.

As a result of one suggestion at a 'Just Imagine' session we introduced job shadowing so everyone could learn about other parts of the BBC; and as a result of another we introduced news hotlines so that if a member of staff came across a story they knew who to ring. When this happened we told the world so that people could see change was happening and that their ideas were not being ignored.

Another vital aspect of 'Making it Happen' was the creation of a large group of senior leaders known as the 'Leading the Way' team. They came together for the first time in May 2002 at a two-day event in London's Docklands. This was the first time the top four hundred at the BBC had ever come together at one time. Some didn't want to come and protested vehemently that they didn't have time for this sort of nonsense. In my speech on the first day I said that in many ways the BBC was an immature organization, that I didn't know of any other company or institution of comparative size that did not bring its senior leaders together at least once a year to discuss strategy and performance and to build relationships.

I invited my old mentor from the Harvard Business School, John Kotter, to talk about leadership, and people were spellbound. The event was extremely effective in building a bigger group – a 400-strong team. People wanted us to hold more events of a similar nature.

Dave Gordon, a thirty-year veteran of BBC Sport, talked about the first meeting in a film made for his own area. He said:

> I've been in the BBC for thirty years and I've seen initiatives come and go. I went along to the event in Docklands thinking 'Oh my God, another one of those sessions', but within minutes I found the whole climate was so positive. I met people I'd never met before and we exchanged ideas. I came out feeling the BBC really did have a future.

All the 'Making it Happen' divisional groups produced action plans and new ideas and initiatives sprang up everywhere. Within a year staff opinion started to change. All those earlier responses from the staff survey that had convinced us we had to do something about the prevailing culture began to shift.

The amount of raw data that came from staff who had participated in the 'Just Imagine' sessions was worth its weight in gold. Most of all, it

gave me a powerful mandate for change. I no longer had to say, 'This is what I believe should happen' or 'This is what the Executive believes should happen'. I could look staff in the eyes and say, 'This is what you told us you wanted.'

A year after we launched 'Making it Happen' the cross-BBC groups came up with their proposals in the form of a single five-year change plan. Central to the plan was a new set of values that would guide everything that happened in the organization from now on. This was the first attempt in the BBC's eighty-year history to articulate the things the organization stood for. They were drawn up by a group from within the BBC that looked both at the way other successful organizations expressed their values and, crucially, boiled down the four thousand suggestions about values that had come in from the 'Just Imagine' sessions. These values hadn't originated with me or the Executive; they'd come from the staff, which made them easier to sell across the organization.

The six values were as follows:

- Trust is the foundation of the BBC: we are independent, impartial and honest.
- Audiences are at the heart of everything we do.
- We take pride in delivering quality and value for money.
- Creativity is the lifeblood of our organization.
- We respect each other and celebrate our diversity so that everyone can give their best.
- We are one BBC: great things happen when we work together.

These values were not necessarily what characterized the BBC at that time, but they were what the people at the BBC aspired to achieve.

Every value carried with it examples of what we, as individuals, needed to do if we were to achieve it. For instance: 'I support the best idea, not just my own' (creativity); 'We have internal debates and external unity: we are ambassadors for the BBC' ('One BBC'); 'We resist pressures on the output from political parties and lobby groups' (trust).

The largest and most expensive single element in the change plan was that the BBC would start one of the biggest ever leadership training programmes in the UK. With the help of Ashridge Business School we planned to give six thousand BBC leaders proper training over the next

five years. It was one of those initiatives that, historically, the staff would have said was a waste of money. Instead I told them all that the 'Just Imagine' data had overwhelmingly shown that the staff wanted better leaders; it had emerged as their highest priority. And for managers who didn't want to go on the programme I was able to tell them that their staff wanted them to go and that it wasn't voluntary. If you wanted to be a leader at the BBC you had to have leadership training. I spoke about my views of leadership on every course.

We also started an induction programme that was one of our quick wins. Everyone joining the BBC now had to spend three days getting to know the organization, learning some basic programme-making skills – even if they were working in accounts – and meeting other new recruits from other divisions. The idea was simple: we wanted to make them feel they were part of 'One BBC' from the outset. And we wanted to excite them about the organization.

The overall change plan consisted of more than forty separate initiatives, many of them involving quite radical changes to the status quo. We introduced coaching and mentoring for managers to give them support, and a new recruitment programme based on the BBC's newly stated values; we gave programme makers more and better information about audiences, and we gave people more control over the areas they worked in. In the area of creativity, there was a recognition that single acts of creative genius were the exception rather than the norm and that BBC people needed to learn how to work together, in creative teams, to come up with and improve on good ideas. Many in the independent production sector were already doing this.

The next challenge was how to launch the change plan so that as many people as possible would be aware of it and have a chance of being part of implementing it. We came up with the idea for something we called 'The Big Conversation' – a title that was later used by Downing Street. Our 'Big Conversation' involved seventeen thousand members of staff in a huge live discussion. We agreed to spend £250,000 permanently to extend the BBC ring main so that an additional eight thousand staff could watch and take part in this event. We tried to create a party atmosphere with four hundred large events. We had events in Delhi, Moscow, Cairo, and Nairobi, as well as right across the UK. At Television Centre in White City we followed the event with Cerys Matthews singing live in

the courtyard outside the studio. There was food and drink available to everyone and we all felt something special was happening.

The event began with a half-hour film in which I was the presenter. I explained the headlines of the change plan and linked all the initiatives back to what the staff had told us. This was not top down, it was bottom up. Everyone – all seventeen thousand of them – then discussed what they had seen in their separate meetings before joining together in a BBC-wide debate. For the first time, people could see the size, scale, and sheer variety of the organization. I believe this was the biggest and most ambitious staff communication event ever to take place in the UK.

It lasted two and a half hours and at the end of it I felt exhilarated. I thought we had achieved the impossible. Everyone seemed excited and there was an incredible sense that we all belonged to this huge, amazing, and wonderful organization. If we could only harness this spirit, everything would be achievable. As I left Television Centre that day I was accosted by a man who said to me, 'Greg, you've got to understand I'm about as cynical as you can get about the BBC, and even I thought that was pretty good.' Praise indeed.

Once the plans were announced we began to act on them very quickly. People began to see the difference and this was reflected in the results of the annual staff survey at the end of 2003. In 2001 the survey had revealed that just 28 per cent of people at the BBC felt valued by the organization. It was one of the main reasons we launched 'Making it Happen'. Two years later the figure stood at 58 per cent.

'Making it Happen' – and in particular the 'Just Imagine' sessions – changed the BBC profoundly. They helped the organization to grow up and to reduce the 'them and us' divide. People discovered that they didn't need permission to do things; they could do them for themselves. They also discovered management couldn't wave a wand and solve all their problems. They told us that, at last, they felt they were being treated as human beings, not just cogs in a machine.

It was a cathartic experience for many at the BBC, but not for all. Most of the BBC Governors were simply not part of it, which, given that their role only requires spending a day or two a month in the building, is not surprising. The main exception was the Chairman, Gavyn Davies, who understood about culture change programmes, having been through one at Goldman Sachs. Gavyn made the effort to attend the 'Just Imagine'

sessions himself. He had warned us at the beginning that we shouldn't start the process if we weren't intending to see it through. Richard Eyre, who had himself changed the culture of the National Theatre when he ran it, also understood what we were trying to achieve.

Sadly, when the BBC Governors decided my future that evening in January 2004 they didn't take into account what we had achieved with our staff – an achievement that is now a Harvard Business School case study and widely recognized as a highly effective change programme. The reason was most of the Governors didn't even begin to understand what had been achieved.

When I am asked, as I am all the time, why thousands of staff took to the streets in support of me, why they bought the ad in the *Telegraph*, and why my going was so emotional for so many of them, when I was forced to leave the BBC, my answer is: 'Making it Happen'.

In two short years we convinced most of our staff that we really wanted change, that we wanted to empower them, that we wanted to be better leaders ourselves, and that we wanted everyone working for the BBC to have more rewarding and more fulfilling working lives. They knew we weren't doing this just to be nice. It was the means of achieving the ambition we all shared for the BBC: to become 'the most creative organiz-ation in the world' and as a result make the best programmes and provide the best possible services to our audiences. But, most of all, I hope we persuaded them that we cared.

The street protests weren't really about me. In the eyes of the staff, I represented the changes that 'Making it Happen' had already brought about in the organization and their hopes for the future. They understood instinctively that the whole initiative itself would now be vulnerable. They had lived through the Prague Spring and feared they could hear the distant rumble of the tanks.

CHAPTER ELEVEN

Television and Sport

Sport has always played a big, even a dominant, part in my life. I was brought up in a household where winning at football was always more important than exam results, which was just as well given that the Dyke boys weren't exactly from the top drawer academically.

My eldest brother Ian was an outstanding sportsman and a particularly good footballer. He was a left winger, back in the days when there were still left wingers, and one of my earliest recollections as a child is that of Bill Dodgin senior, the manager of Brentford, turning up at our house to try to sign him up. These were the days of the £20 a week maximum wage for footballers and my dad made it very clear that Ian was not going to be a professional footballer but instead was going to get a 'proper' job. He ended up spending his life in the insurance industry just like my father. Both hated it.

Ian did join Brentford as a junior and we've all had an affection for the club ever since, although they were never first choice for any of us. My father had been a big Arsenal fan since he was a boy, and he talked endlessly about their great side of the 1930s. He was a particular fan of their winger Cliff (Boy) Bastin and their centre forward David Jack. According to him, there were no players in modern-day football who could match Bastin and Jack.

A couple of years before he died I took both my dad and my mum to the 1988 FA Cup Final and we watched one of the biggest upsets in modern footballing history when Wimbledon beat Liverpool. It was only the second Cup Final he'd ever been to – the first was when Arsenal beat Huddersfield in 1930 and he reckoned he'd watched the match from the

221

roof of the stand at Wembley. We worked out that there were fifty-eight years between his first final and his second.

When we were young my grandmother had a pub called the Seven Sisters in Markfield Road off Broad Lane in Tottenham, within walking distance of the Spurs ground. All the customers were Tottenham fans through and through so both my brothers followed suit, much to my father's dismay. If you are an Arsenal fan, there is nothing worse than your sons supporting Tottenham.

To be different from my brothers I perversely decided to support Manchester United, largely because John Rixon, a neighbour in our street in Hayes, was a United supporter. He was a friend of my eldest brother and was nearly ten years older than me, so I was always a bit in awe of him. Forty years later, in May 1999, I searched John out and took him with me in the private plane I had hired to fly to Barcelona to watch Manchester United in that amazing European Champions League Final. By then I was a Director of Manchester United and felt I owed John; if it hadn't been for him I might have had to support Tottenham for all those years, or – even worse – Arsenal.

As a sports freak it was natural that when I became Director of Programmes at LWT I also became Chairman of ITV Sport and took over responsibility for sport across the network. The full-time head of ITV Sport at that time was John Bromley, or Brommers as he was known, a legendary figure and one of the most loved men I have ever met. He never remembered anyone's name but overcame the problem by calling all women 'darling' and all men 'captain'.

Soon after I became Chairman we ran into problems concerning our contract with the American heavyweight boxer Mike Tyson. ITV had the exclusive rights for five Tyson world championship fights. As it turned out, the fifth was the big one: the fight between Tyson and the British boxer Frank Bruno. Suddenly Tyson's people, led by his manager Bill Cayton and Don King, the legendary US promoter, got a much bigger offer for the fight from the fledgling Sky and decided ITV didn't have a contract after all – even though we'd broadcast, and paid for, the first four fights.

We went to court to argue that we had the right to show the fight, although this was not without some risk. As always in such circumstances, our barrister told us we might win or we might not (I've often wondered

why we all pay barristers so much money to tell us the obvious). The problem was that the only written contract we had was an agreement signed in the Rififi Club, a private members' club and restaurant just off Berkeley Square in London's West End, and written on a Rififi club napkin. When John Bromley went into the witness box the barrister for Sky decided to try to embarrass him about this. 'Do you normally write contracts on napkins in clubs?' Brommers was asked. 'Absolutely,' he replied, and everyone in court fell about laughing. Bromley's wit didn't make any difference, however. We lost the case, very unfairly we all believed, and Sky showed the fight.

Brommers was a decade older than me and came from a different period in ITV's history, a time before ITV was in any sense a proper business. Bromley's expenses were legendary and as Chairman of ITV Sport I had to sign them off. I left them on the kitchen table once and Sue picked them up. She couldn't believe that anyone could possibly claim for so much food and drink, and it was certainly true that Brommers had great difficulty meeting anyone without both of them having a drink in their hand. Oddly, he didn't eat a lot himself; he merely paid for everyone else to eat.

My favourite Bromley story was when LWT's Managing Director had to try to defend Bromley's expenses before the Board of LWT. The Finance Director was in full flow about how much Bromley had charged the company while in Seoul covering the Olympics in 1988. 'And then we come to the boat,' he said. 'Ah,' replied the MD, 'I can explain that. The guys out in Seoul were working so hard that John decided to take them for a party on the boat. What's wrong with that?' The Finance Director looked up. This was the moment all finance directors dream of. 'That would be fine except this boat wasn't in Seoul, it was on the Thames,' he said. Like all good stories it's probably been exaggerated over the years, but it tells you all you need to know about ITV sport in those days.

When Brommers was dying of cancer a couple of years ago I went to visit him at the Cromwell Hospital in London. When I told the desk whom I was visiting the receptionist looked dismayed and said, 'Oh no, not another one.' I think the rules said that there were only supposed to be three visitors at a time around his bed but Brommers had never taken any notice of the rules at any stage in his life, and he certainly wasn't going to start in his dying days. In his room there were at least thirty

people. He'd had a bar set up in the corner and every night there was a party, while he lay in bed welcoming visitors.

I had been warned what to expect so I'd taken along a bottle of gin as a present. Brommers' voice was the same as it had always been, but the man in the hospital bed was a shrunken version of the wonderful character we'd all known. When he died there was standing room only at his memorial service held in St Martin-in-the-Fields in Trafalgar Square. It was a true celebration of the way he'd lived: LWT even picked up the bill for the celebrations afterwards. If you have to die, that's the way to go.

In those days boxing was big on ITV and one of my early sports decisions was that we should try to secure the rights for the fight between Frank Bruno and Joe Bugner for ITV. Bugner was coming out of retirement in Australia especially for the fight, and although it always had the look of a mismatch about it I believed it would be great box office. It was Barry Hearn's first ever fixture as a boxing promoter; up until then he was Mr Snooker in the UK, and this was the first time I'd ever met him.

Barry always tells the story that he asked me for a certain figure for the television rights to the fight; rather than arguing, I'd replied that if he could deliver the fight I'd pay him more. I don't remember this, but it didn't matter: the fight turned out to be a win for both of us. It was staged at White Hart Lane, the home of Tottenham Hotspur, and I even persuaded Sue to come and watch it. She hated the boxing but as a trained sociologist was fascinated by the mix of people who got all dressed up to watch it.

We got sixteen million viewers for the fight, the highest-rated sports programme on television in 1987, and it lasted eight rounds. Now how long a fight lasted was very important to ITV as you had to include as many advertisements as possible between rounds. A first- or second-round knockout might have been great for the crowds, but it was a disaster for a commercial broadcaster.

Barry is another of those big characters you find in sport. He walks around with a wad of notes in his wallet and has a new idea every day that he is prepared to back with his own money. Barry is the man who turned fishing into a spectator sport by building grandstands around a lake near Coventry where every year he stages *Fishomania* live on Sky

Sports. People sit all day, either in the grandstand or by the television set, watching motionless fishermen waiting to catch fish. It is a bit like watching paint dry, but Barry still manages to make money out of it. Amazingly, it has become an annual event.

My favourite Barry Hearn story was when Chris Eubank fought Dan Schummer of the USA in South Africa for the World Boxing Organization super middleweight world championship in October 1994. Eubank lost virtually every round. When it came to the end of the fight he sat down and asked Barry, who was his manager, 'What do you think?' At that very moment the WBO judge looked across at Barry and gave him a big wink, implying Eubank had retained his title. 'What do I think, Chris?' he said. 'What do I think? I think this is another country we can't come back to.' The crowd and the press went mad.

Barry once even asked me to be part of the English fishing team in the World Marlin Championships in the West Indies. I told him I'd never fished for big game and had certainly never caught a marlin. 'Don't be ridiculous. Neither has anyone else in the team,' he replied. He later sent me a tape: it was hilarious. I think there was only one marlin caught all week.

I also used to do business with another boxing promoter, Frank Warren, who was shot and wounded one night in Barking in London's East End. One of his boxers, Terry Marsh, was charged with the shooting but found not guilty. Soon afterwards Frank came for a lunch at LWT and I asked him if his business was going well. He replied that he was having a rough time and the banks weren't supporting him. Why not? I asked. 'Because banks don't like you if you get shot,' he explained.

During my years at ITV Sport I tried to refocus the network away from traditional magazine programming onto big sporting events. Early on I scrapped television wrestling and was threatened with Big Daddy and Giant Haystacks coming round to my house to sort me out. I believed the money spent on wrestling would be much better spent on boxing. But my five years as Chairman of ITV Sport were dominated by one sport above any other: football. It is difficult to believe today but until the mid Eighties there was virtually no live football on British television. Apart from the odd English international, the only live game was the FA Cup Final, and virtually everyone stayed indoors to watch it. In those days, towns were empty on FA Cup Final day.

225

But by the late Eighties pay television was emerging on the scene and out of the blue the fledgling British Satellite Broadcasting (BSB), the competitor to Sky before the two companies merged, bid for and was on the verge of winning the rights to broadcast live First Division matches on their pay channel, due to be launched in April 1990. It was around the same time that I came onto the sports scene and I decided my job was to try to derail the process and pinch these live football rights from BSB.

For advice on how I could go about this I turned to Trevor East, Deputy Head of Sport at Thames Television and a football specialist. I asked him whom we could talk to 'off the record' and he suggested we should meet David Dein, the Deputy Chairman of Arsenal and a member of the Football League management committee. The three of us met at

YES FOLKS, GREG DYKE IS BEING ASKED TO RECONSIDER HIS DECISION!

One of my first decisions when I was in charge of ITV Sport was to scrap Saturday afternoon wrestling. Many people hated me for taking that decision, including Big Daddy and Giant Haystacks. I did it because I wanted to change the image of ITV.

Suntory, a Japanese restaurant in London's West End, and David and I struck up a close friendship that lasts to this day.

We realized at once that we both had something to gain from each other. I wanted to pinch the football rights from BSB's grasp and he might be able to deliver them. He in turn wanted more money for his club and the other big clubs and I could afford to pay it. His view was very clear. The viewing public wanted to watch the big clubs on television so those clubs should get the bulk of the television money, which at that time was still spread around ninety-two clubs. In a series of meetings over a couple of weeks David, Trevor, and I worked out a plan. We would go direct to the big five clubs of the day – Arsenal, Liverpool, Manchester United, Tottenham, and Everton – and offer them a minimum of a million pounds a year each for the exclusive right to broadcast their home matches. This was massively more than any of them had received in the past. The Football League could sell the rest of the old First Division matches to whomever they wanted, but of course without the big clubs' home games they were worth much less.

I met the men who controlled the big five clubs in a bar one evening. Phil Carter of Everton, who was Chairman of the Football League at the time, came along with Martin Edwards from Manchester United, Irving Scholar, the Chairman of Tottenham, John Smith, Chairman of Liverpool, and of course David Dein from Arsenal. I took John Bromley with me for that first meeting but he was uneasy about doing a side deal with the big clubs so I didn't take him to the next one. That's a tactic I discovered was widely used at the BBC when I joined them a decade or so later. If someone doesn't agree, hold the next meeting without them.

In his book about his life in football – *Behind Closed Doors*, published in 1992 – Irving Scholar describes the turning point at this first meeting as the moment I admitted that I thought there had been a cartel between ITV and BBC to keep the price paid for televised football artificially low. The club chairmen had always believed it and I semi-confirmed it. From that moment on all five were on my side.

At our second meeting, held on a Sunday night, the five chairmen asked which club I supported. I told them I supported Manchester United, at which Martin Edwards beamed. A few years later this statement was to have real significance. At that second meeting we decided to extend the initial group of five to include five more clubs who would receive a lesser

227

figure: West Ham, Newcastle, Aston Villa, Nottingham Forest, and Sheffield Wednesday.

The problem for me during this period was that every time I went to lunch with David Dein the price tab for the contract went up. I even recollect having to pay for the lunches as well. But the strategy we had devised worked. Threatened with a rebellion by the top ten clubs in the First Division, the Football League folded and opened negotiations with ITV. We eventually reached agreement with the League to pay £11 million a year for twenty-one live matches, to be played mostly on Sunday afternoons. We also bought the recorded rights for ITV but chose not to use them. For the next four years there would be no *Match of the Day* on Saturday evenings on BBC One.

Early in the negotiations I'd invited Paul Fox, then Managing Director of BBC Television, to join us in trying to defeat the fledgling BSB but he told me that he didn't think it would help make the BBC popular with the Government at a time when the Corporation's charter was up for renewal. It's interesting that they didn't take the same view a few years earlier when they very nearly killed off TV-am by launching a competitive breakfast television service.

Within ITV, and particularly within LWT, there were those who believed I had overpaid by paying £11 million a year. Only two years earlier the Football League had received only £1.6 million in total from the BBC and ITV. Because virtually all the games would be played at the weekend, LWT would pay more than a quarter of the total £11 million bill, so I understood the concern within my own company. But I believed the doubters were wrong. Anyway the deal was done and there was little that could be done about it. Eight years later the same rights were sold for the unbelievable figure of £167 million a year, so perhaps it wasn't such a bad deal.

The ramifications of the way we had done the deal were enormous within the Football League. The old Second Division clubs were angry that they had been outmanoeuvred by the big clubs and took action that later would cost them dear. Phil Carter, the League's Chairman, was fired and David Dein was made to step down from the management committee as the Second Division clubs took total control of the Football League. In taking their revenge against the representatives of the big clubs they sowed the seeds of what was to come four years later.

ITV honoured the deal we'd made with the bigger clubs. They were all guaranteed a certain number of games a season on television, which we delivered, and all received the heady sums we'd promised them. But this strategy also made ITV vulnerable four years later. Where the old Second Division clubs had upset the big five, we'd upset the smaller clubs in the First Division, who became resentful about the deal we'd done with their stronger brethren. They, too, would have the opportunity to take their revenge.

Although, like so many sports contracts in those days, the deal was never actually signed by either party, it turned out to be a good one for both. ITV, in particular, got a real bonus at the end of the first season. The First Division title went right to the wire with Liverpool and Arsenal very close in first and second places respectively. Amazingly, the last game of the season was between the same two clubs and was to be played on a Friday night, live on ITV. Liverpool had won the FA Cup the previous Saturday and were three points clear of Arsenal, so the famous double was there for the taking. They only had to draw to become champions, while for Arsenal to take the title they had to win the match at Anfield by two clear goals. It was probably the most exciting end to a season ever.

Arsenal scored their second goal in the last minute to win 2–0 and to take the title. I had flown up to the game with members of the Arsenal Board and ended up celebrating with David Dein and the Arsenal team in the winners' dressing room. I found it revealing that only two of the Liverpool team, Bruce Grobbelaar and Peter Beardsley, came in to congratulate the Arsenal players that night. But the Liverpool fans were magnificent; they were obviously desperately disappointed but applauded the Arsenal team off the pitch. ITV got an audience of nearly eleven million, making the £11 million a season look cheap.

By the autumn of 1991 it was time to talk about the next football deal. Trevor East, David Dein, and I decided another dinner between ITV and the big five clubs was called for. We fixed the dinner and I offered to host it in London, in the hospitality suite on the eighteenth floor of the LWT building on the South Bank. Many have claimed they were the architects of the Premier League; but when the official history of the Premier League is written, this dinner meeting will surely be seen as the time and the place at which it became a reality.

By and large the same people turned up from the clubs as four years earlier, although by this time John Smith had retired as Chairman of Liverpool and had been replaced by Noel White. Just as we had four years ago, David Dein and I discussed tactics in advance. We agreed I would open up by saying I thought it unlikely we could do another deal with the Football League negotiators that would be as favourable to the big clubs as the last one, which was certainly true. So the big clubs had a choice: either take less money, as the total was likely to be spread around more clubs, or take radical action.

They were unanimous. They all resented the way Carter and Dein had been treated by the Football League and they opted for the radical approach. They very quickly decided that they wanted the First Division clubs to break away from the Football League and set up the Premier League, which would be run by the twenty member clubs in the interests of those clubs. They would sell their own television rights and the proceeds would go to them.

No one had predicted things would move so fast, but everyone remembered a few years back when a similar move had failed. This time they all agreed that if they were to succeed they needed to get the Football Association onside. Everyone knew that there had never been much love lost between the FA and the Football League. I once met Alan Hardaker's daughter at a football match and asked her why her father, the legendary Secretary of the Football League, had moved the organization's head-quarters to Lytham St Annes. Her reply was that he wanted to get it as far away from the FA as he could.

In 1992 the relationship between the two bodies was particularly bad and this made it more likely that the FA would support the clubs if they decided to break away; but it had to be handled properly, so another significant decision made that night was the choice of who would lead the delegation to meet Bert Millichip, the ageing Chairman of the FA. These were the days when Liverpool had dominated English football for at least a decade and they had to be seen to be onside; so the five clubs decided that the Chairman of Liverpool, Noel White, who was then and still is a member of the FA's international committee, would lead the delegation, supported by David Dein.

The rest is history. Within months the top clubs had resigned from the Football League and by the start of the following season the FA Premier

League was up and running. The only problem was that ITV didn't get the television rights. By then BSB had merged with Sky to form BSkyB and Rupert Murdoch was in control and very keen to win the rights.

It was probably my fault that we lost them. I'd been too complacent, believing that with the big five clubs supporting us we were bound to win. Trevor East tried to warn me that we ought to be spending more time with the smaller Premier League clubs, but I didn't take any notice. I've always hated making polite small talk in a bid to get people onside, a character trait that was later to cost me dear with the BBC Governors.

My view back in 1992 was that my strategy of working with the big clubs had been successful last time, so why wouldn't it be the same this time? Trevor himself had actually shaken hands on a deal with Rick Parry, the newly appointed Chief Executive of the Premier League, at a boxing match in Manchester, so we thought we were in pole position.

In fact I did have lunch with the Chief Executive of BSkyB, Sam Chisholm, during the bidding process. Chisholm was an overweight, mouthy Australian who had been brought up as one of Kerry Packer's henchmen and styled himself on Packer. He had been brought in by Murdoch to save the company. Over lunch he was pretty blunt. He told me that Rupert Murdoch had approved what he was about to say. 'Mr Dyke,' he said, 'why don't we get together to fuck these football clubs?' My view was that if he wanted a deal with us it meant we were in prime position and didn't need him. How wrong I was.

I also misjudged the situation because in the time between the Premier League actually being set up and the television contract being settled Irving Scholar had sold Spurs to Alan Sugar. Sugar owned the electronics company Amstrad, which at the time was the main supplier of satellite dishes to BSkyB, and he was very close to the Murdoch operation. As a result, Spurs switched sides and supported BSkyB.

In fact when it came to the crucial vote, Sugar played an important part. We had received intelligence from within the Premier League during the weekend before the meeting on Monday 18 May that we were in danger of losing. We worked all through Sunday night and on the day of the meeting we hit the clubs with a new offer, which Trevor East delivered personally to each club representative. He had also delivered the new bid to Rick Parry earlier that morning. It was high enough to be the winning bid.

A few minutes after the meeting at the Royal Lancaster Hotel started Trevor was standing outside the meeting room when Sugar came rushing out of the meeting and got on the phone. Trevor heard him say, 'You've got to blow them out of the water.' He was clearly talking to someone at BSkyB and – lo and behold – a new BSkyB bid arrived.

I also misjudged how much the Premier League contract mattered to BSkyB. Rupert Murdoch himself flew over to Britain to get involved and did his usual job of flattering the people who would be influential in the decision. In fact when ITV put in its final bid Alan Sugar wasn't the only person to ring BSkyB: Rick Parry had already done so. Between shaking hands with Trevor East on the deal and the meeting of the clubs actually taking place, Parry had been heavily courted by both Chisholm and Murdoch. They'd even flown him to Scotland in their private jet to show him the BSkyB call centre. Rick Parry told me later that 'Mr Murdoch was the most impressive man I ever met'.

In spite of all this, Trevor and I believed we had enough votes to win. When it came to the vote, six of the twenty Premier League clubs supported the ITV bid – four of the big five plus Leeds and Aston Villa. Two other clubs abstained. We lost by a single vote as seven clubs would have been enough to stop BSkyB. We discovered later that Nottingham Forest, whose Chairman had promised to vote for us, had actually sent along an office secretary because no one else was available. That vote in favour of BSkyB turned out to be crucial.

Actually, we would still have won had it not been for the personal intervention of the Chairman of the BBC, Duke Hussey. Again Rupert Murdoch was involved. When Murdoch took over the Times Group he kept Hussey, who had been a pretty disastrous Chairman of Times Newspapers, as a board member. They became friends, and there are even suggestions that it was Murdoch who suggested to Margaret Thatcher that she should appoint Hussey as Chairman of the BBC, a remarkable decision in itself given that Hussey didn't actually own a television set at the time. Personally I've always liked Hussey: he's loud, eccentric and a wonderful character, exactly the sort of person whose company I enjoy, although I'm not at all sure I would have enjoyed working for him. When he and John Birt were Chairman and Director-General respectively of the BBC they didn't talk to each other for months on end, though that was not necessarily all Hussey's fault.

In the run-up to the Premier League bid, as Hussey later admitted, he had discussed the issue with Rupert Murdoch. As a result, the BBC put in a bid of around £20 million a year for the *Match of the Day* rights but only on the condition that ITV didn't get the live rights. What it meant was that we at ITV had to bid £20 million more than BSkyB to win. As it turned out, that £20 million would have been enough to have swung the contract our way.

Knowing the BBC so much better now than I did then, I find Hussey's actions even more extraordinary today than I did at the time. What on earth was the Chairman of the BBC doing getting himself involved in football negotiations in the first place? That is not his role. The BBC had effectively used public money to favour the Murdoch bid following a conversation between Rupert Murdoch and the Chairman of the BBC. What was Hussey doing using money raised by the licence fee to favour Murdoch? It was, to say the least, questionable. But Rupert Murdoch's activities in Britain – first in the Thatcher/Major years and, since 1997, during the Blair era – have consistently escaped real political scrutiny. In other countries politicians intervened when it looked like their major football league was likely to end up on pay television; in Britain they didn't. Winning elections is too important to British politicians and the Murdoch press can influence who wins and who loses. As a result, most of them don't have the nerve to take on Murdoch.

So my days involved in sport at ITV ended on a disappointing note. By this time I had become Chief Executive of LWT and had moved away from any close involvement in programming. Once the Premier League negotiations were over I gave up being Chairman of ITV Sport and for a while wasn't involved in sport at all. It was only after LWT had been taken over by Granada and I was sitting at home unemployed that I got the chance to become involved again.

I received a call in the autumn of 1994 from Robert Charles, Head of Sport at Yorkshire Television, who told me that Channel Four wanted a new current affairs programme about sport and that Yorkshire were planning to bid for it. He wanted to know if they could use my name as the prospective presenter in their bid document. I agreed and we got the commission for a series of programmes called *Fair Game*. Now television broadcasters traditionally avoid making controversial programmes about sport for obvious reasons. If you expose wrongdoing or inefficiency in a

sporting organization they are unlikely to sell you their rights again; but this would not have been a problem for Channel Four because the channel wasn't reliant on sport.

By the time of *Fair Game* I had been around the boardroom of television companies for close on a decade, so going back on the road making programmes was a novel experience. If you run television companies you believe television production is an efficient, well-organised, well-oiled process. When you go back on the road you discover it is just as chaotic as it ever was. You spend hours hanging around, you shoot masses of material you never use, and there are always people who simply don't show up. One day we spent hours in a field waiting to meet a bent jockey. He never came. Why? Because he was a bent jockey and wasn't reliable.

We did programmes about a range of sports but the one that really hit the headlines was on rugby union and it led to Will Carling's being fired as captain of the England rugby team for something like thirty-six hours after he had described the Rugby Football Union's management committee as 'fifty-seven old farts'.

The aim of this particular programme was to demonstrate that the people running English rugby were from a different age. These were the days before the game went professional and the RFU's management committee really did believe the game was for them and that the players were largely irrelevant. When we interviewed Dudley Wood, the Secretary of the Rugby Football Union, for the programme we kept asking him about the players and in the end he got a bit agitated. 'You keep asking me about the players but I want to tell you what a wonderful job the committee does.' One has to wonder what planet he was living on.

Never in any sport have I met a bunch of players who so hated the people who ran the game as I found in rugby. It was a straight divide between a bunch of old blokes who loved the 'amateur' nature of rugby and players who trained and played like professional athletes but didn't get paid. It was a divide both of generations and of class.

When the producer of this particular programme first arranged to meet Carling and Rob Andrew in a pub, Andrew was late turning up; so the producer explained to Carling what the programme was likely to be about. When Andrew finally arrived Carling turned to him and said 'They're out to get the RFU. Are you up for that?' Both of them agreed they were 'up' for it.

234

I interviewed Carling at the Richmond Hill Hotel, the traditional meeting place for England players before an international. He said a lot of controversial things, including describing the committee as 'old farts'. Later there was some dispute about this particular statement with Carling saying it was said off the record when the camera wasn't running. The programme team denied it, although it was true they only had it on the audio tape not the video. My own recollection at the time was that Carling knew what he was saying and had been waiting a long time to say it. Although Carling initially complained to Channel Four, his agent later withdrew the complaint.

The programme, called 'State of the Union', was broadcast on Thursday 4 May 1995 at 8 p.m. On the following Saturday morning I got a phone call from John Bromley, by then a sports consultant, who had in turn taken a call from Carling's agent, Jon Holmes. 'They're going to fire Carling this morning,' Bromley told me, 'for disrespect to the committee. Jon Holmes is desperate to talk to you.' It was true, and Carling was fired.

Unfortunately for Dudley Wood and Dennis Easby, that year's President of the RFU, there was a game at Twickenham that afternoon with Wasps playing Bath in the final of the 1995 Pilkington Cup. The ground was full to capacity with 73,000 spectators. Word got around that the committee had fired the England captain for disrespect and as Dennis Easby walked onto the pitch the whole crowd started booing, and carried on booing. In one afternoon the RFU Committee had to face up to something they had spent years trying to avoid: they finally had to admit that the spectators, the people who paid to watch rugby and who indirectly paid for the committee's expenses and their grand dinners, regarded the players as infinitely more important than committee members.

The following day Jon Holmes persuaded me to go on a live radio discussion programme with Dennis Easby of the RFU. It was on Talksport and the presenter was another ITV man, Gary Newbon. Somehow, live on air, we managed to patch things up and Carling was reinstated.

In many ways the 'old farts' saga marked the death of one era of rugby in England and the birth of another. Not long afterwards the game went professional. The RFU was reformed, a more professional management team came in, and nine years later a professional England side won the Rugby World Cup. For my birthday that year my friend Jeff Wright gave me a car number plate as a present: GD 57 RFU 0.

What I'd discovered in making *Fair Game* was that the people who were organizing and running sport in the UK were largely hard-working, well-meaning, enthusiastic amateurs. Sadly, in many sports they still are. I remember Graham Taylor telling me that when he became manager of the England football team he expected to be quite an important figure at the Football Association. According to him, he quickly discovered he was less important than the FA council member for Norfolk.

Stories of committee members flying 'club class' while the competitors are back in goat class are still to be found in British sport. On one of the *Fair Game* programmes David Mellor captured all that was suspect in British sports administration when he said: 'Sport in Britain will only improve when a lot of old men in blazers fall on their swords.' Unfortunately, what we have discovered since is that there are always a lot of young men in blazers prepared to replace them. Without structural change in sport not much will improve.

I made two series of *Fair Game* whilst I was also holding down my new day job of running and building Pearson Television. In fact I was negotiating the deal to buy Grundy, the Australian production company, for $386 million while I was standing, freezing cold, on the Yorkshire moors filming a programme on horse racing. At the end of the second series I decided I couldn't be both a presenter and an executive so I wanted out of *Fair Game*. Channel Four and Yorkshire Television agreed there weren't that many more sports stories to cover so we all happily called it a day and my involvement in sport ended again, but only for a while.

The following year I took a call from Mike Southgate, who at that time was, amongst other things, responsible for sport at the ITV network. Mike is a great guy to have working for you. He works hard, is a good leader, but most of all he's a problem solver. Talk to Mike about a difficult issue and he'll be back the next day with a solution, and then he'll go away and actually get on with it. Any successful Chief Executive needs the Mike Southgates of this world. Mike is always complaining that I take him with me to new jobs and then leave him behind when I go, which is unfortunately true. When I first left LWT he stayed behind. I then lured him to TVS, back to LWT, to Pearson Television, and then to the BBC.

Mike had phoned to tell me that Martin Edwards of Manchester United

had been asking him where he could find me. So I rang Martin and fixed up to meet him for a drink at the Lancaster Hotel. When I turned up he was there with Sir Roland Smith, Chairman of Manchester United plc. They sat me down and told me they wanted someone with television experience to join the Board of Manchester United and that, after a long discussion, they had decided I was the person they wanted.

Of all the things that have happened to me in my life, this was the most humbling. I was a kid from Hayes who had supported United since the early Fifties. I'd cried myself to sleep on the night of the Munich air crash in February 1958; I'd celebrated the night we beat Benfica to win the European Cup in 1968; I'd despaired as Liverpool came to dominate English football and United didn't win the title for sixteen years. Suddenly I was to be elevated to the Board of Manchester United. Martin told me that with the place on the Board came four seats in the directors' box. I played it very cool and told Martin and Roland I would think about it and discuss it with Sue.

I rushed home and found Joe, my youngest son and a fellow United supporter. He was nine at the time. I told him that I was going to be a director of Manchester United. 'What does that mean, Dad?' he asked. I replied: 'It means tickets, Joe, tickets.'

Telling my partner Sue was a different proposition. She has always hated football with a passion and believes to this day that her greatest failure as a parent was in not preventing me from indoctrinating three of our four children with my love of football. Now I was going to tell her I'd be away at football matches most Saturdays, as well as midweek evenings, following United. It was not without some trepidation that I raised it. Amazingly, she was relaxed. 'I've been thinking you ought to be doing something just for you,' she said. I couldn't believe it. Was this the woman that I knew and loved? I thought about it and then said, 'Could you write that down and sign it, please?' Now all I had to do was to get the agreement of my employers, Pearson plc. I went to see the Chairman, Dennis, now Lord, Stevenson. I explained what I'd been offered and then said that if it came to a choice between United and Pearson, I'd opt for the former. He laughed and agreed.

The Chairman of Manchester United plc, Professor Sir Roland Smith, was another great character. He was a fount of fascinating and funny stories. He had been in and around big business for many years and at

one time he held more directorships in companies listed on the Stock Exchange than anyone else in Britain. He was Chancellor of UMIST, the second university in Manchester, had been on the Board of the Bank of England, and had also been Chairman of British Aerospace. As Chairman of House of Fraser he was the man who had sold Harrods to Mohamed Al Fayed and was threatened by Tiny Rowland in the process. In the battle for Harrods Roland had famously told Tiny Rowland to get his tanks off his lawn. In turn, Rowland said that after shaking hands with Roland Smith you had to count your fingers. It was Roland who had first suggested floating Manchester United on the stock market in 1991. I remember buying some shares back then out of loyalty. Richard Webb, my best friend, business partner and accountant, told me he didn't think they were a good buy but that I shouldn't worry about losing money because we needed some capital gains tax losses to offset against the profits we were making elsewhere. In fact it was a brilliant investment. I bought at 28p a share and sold at 214p.

The United Board had clearly been under pressure to recruit some proper independent non-executive directors. There was inevitably tension between the main plc Board, on which I sat, and the football club Board, which was supposed to run the actual footballing side of the business. As Mike Eddelson, still a member of the football club Board, once said to me: 'I don't care about the money or making profits. I want us to buy the best players so we can win.' Mike summed up the challenge facing any football club when you try to run it as a business. Virtually no one – not the manager, the players, the staff of the club, and certainly not the fans – cares whether you make any money. They'd rather you spent more money on players, and in football most of the income does go to the players. It is not unlike the movie business where most of the money goes to the on-screen talent. That old joke 'How do you make a small fortune in movies? Start with a large one' applies equally to football. The exception in Britain has been Manchester United and it was the duty of the main Board to make sure we made profits, paid dividends to the shareholders, and grew the overall value of the business. The two different concepts inevitably led to clashes.

When Manchester United bought Dwight Yorke for £12.6 million from Aston Villa in 1998 it was on the strict understanding that Ole Gunnar Solskjaer was to be sold to Tottenham for £5 million. I have my doubts

whether Alex Ferguson and the football club Board ever had any intention of selling him, and once Yorke had arrived, at a bigger price than we'd been told, suddenly Solskjaer didn't want to go. As it turned out, he won the European Champions League for United so the football club Board were probably right.

Martin Edwards was the Chief Executive of Manchester United and Chairman of the football club Board so he was on both boards. He was very interested in the share price because at that time he was the club's biggest shareholder. Of course running a football club is a thankless task because in the end the fans always turn on you, but this usually only happens when you are losing. With Martin it was different. In the time Martin was running United they won the Premier League seven times in nine years and yet every time he walked onto the pitch the fans booed him. They didn't believe he really loved the club in the same way as they did because, on at least three separate occasions, he'd tried to sell it and cash out. I was on the Board for the last of these, when Rupert Murdoch and BSkyB tried to buy the club. I ended up being the only director opposed to the sale for quite a long time, but being on my own in such circumstances has never worried me, and it didn't on this occasion. I think it was Enoch Powell who said, 'I've never felt being in a minority of one was in any way an indication that I might be in error.' On that I agree with him.

The first I knew that BSkyB wanted to buy Manchester United was at the beginning of July 1998 when I turned up at the monthly United board meeting to find that both Roland Smith and Martin Edwards wanted us to scrap the normal agenda to discuss something else – selling the business. It was to be another two months before the *Sunday Telegraph* broke the story, two months in which I did my best to kill the deal.

I should have known something was up at the earlier June board meeting. It was intended that we would discuss long-term strategy, not something the Board of Manchester United was used to doing. When we got there, however, Roland Smith announced that he had urgent business in London and was planning a truncated meeting. We were out of the room in a couple of hours. At the next meeting we were given the news of the BSkyB bid.

The plan to sell had been Martin's. We were told he'd had a series of meetings with Mark Booth, the Chief Executive of BSkyB, and that they

had agreed a deal. BSkyB would buy the whole of Manchester United at 212p a share, valuing the business at nearly £600 million. This compared with a share price at the time of 159p. Martin explained that Mark Booth had run the numbers and that 212p a share was the most BSkyB could afford to pay. I laughed and said, 'He would say that, wouldn't he?'

As the club's biggest shareholder, Martin was not only willing to sell; he was also willing to pledge his shares to support the bid, even at this early stage. He clearly wanted the cash. He had also got Roland on his side for more altruistic reasons. Roland truly believed United would benefit from being part of a large, high quality business with a strong balance sheet. I disagreed with Roland and for a whole range of reasons was against the deal.

I thought the price was too low. I didn't see any advantage to the club in being part of a large media empire; in particular I thought United had a strong enough balance sheet to survive on its own as, unlike many other football clubs, it had no debt. I also argued against the idea that BSkyB would put money into Manchester United. When companies pay a premium over the share price to buy another company they reckon on saving money, not putting more money into the new business.

I also said I had real doubts whether the deal would get through the competition authorities, since here was a single television company effectively buying Manchester United's television rights for ever. I had one final reason for being against the deal, though I didn't tell the Board. I didn't want my beloved Manchester United to be controlled by Rupert Murdoch, but I could hardly put that forward as a business reason for opposing the deal.

At that July meeting we decided, as a board, that we needed to do more work, to bring in our merchant bankers and make our own assessment as to whether or not it was a good deal. That work went on during July and August. I brought in Janice Hughes from Spectrum, a media consultancy, to give us a long-term view as to what television rights would be worth. She was pretty optimistic and I thought I might persuade the Board to drop the deal.

When Martin Edwards told Mark Booth that he was meeting opposition on the United Board, Booth increased BSkyB's offer to 220p a share. So much for 212p being the most he could afford to pay. Our bankers were HSBC, led by the remarkably named Rupert Faure-Walker.

At 220p a share they told us we had a fiduciary duty to put the offer to our shareholders to let them decide, as they thought it a good deal. I disagreed and pointed out to them that I didn't think this was an entirely unbiased view given that HSBC would make millions if the deal went through and a few hundred thousand if it didn't.

One by one the members of the Board began siding with Martin and Roland. By the end of August the only people against the deal were myself and the Finance Director David Gill, now the Chief Executive of Manchester United. Then the story broke. I was at my house in Hampshire on the afternoon of Saturday 5 September when I got a call from the Pearson press office saying that Neil Collins of the *Sunday Telegraph* had a story about BSkyB buying Manchester United. They'd laughed at the story but Collins had assured them it was true and said that he wanted to speak to me as I was known to be the director most opposed to the deal.

I didn't return the call but managed to get hold of David Gill and asked him to alert the rest of the Board. I also rang BSkyB and managed to speak to Mark Booth, whom I knew quite well, though we'd never discussed the takeover. I told him about the *Sunday Telegraph* story and we got on to talking about the deal. He asked me why I was against it. I gave him my reasons and also explained why I believed the deal would be thrown out by the Monopolies and Mergers Commission. We ended up making a £50 bet on whether it would go through or not. He duly paid up when it didn't.

It had been a good old-fashioned Sunday paper scoop and Neil Collins rightly won a number of awards for it. Everyone believed I had given him the story, but it wasn't in my interests for it to become public. I had more chance of stopping it if it remained confidential. To this day I have no idea who Collins' source was, but it was a good piece of journalism.

What happened next was politically interesting. On the Sunday morning the Sports Minister Tony Banks appeared on *Frost on Sunday* making it pretty clear that he was against the deal. He said that he was sure the Department of Trade and Industry would want to take a very close look at it. He and every other Government minister then disappeared and never said another word about the proposed takeover from beginning to end. The Labour Party had spent a long time wooing Murdoch and were not going to blow it over this. Banks had clearly been told to keep quiet.

The Manchester United Board met virtually non-stop for two days on

the Monday and Tuesday following the *Sunday Telegraph* article. It got pretty unpleasant at times. Late on the Monday night Martin Edwards threatened to sue me personally if my opposition stopped the deal, to which I pointed out that I was the only truly independent director on the Board and said I wouldn't be threatened by him. He later said it had been a joke, but it hadn't felt like it at the time.

Our stockbrokers, Merrill Lynch, supported me – they, too, thought the offer was too low – though they came under enormous pressure for doing so. Their top man in London told me that he'd been ordered by his bosses in New York to stop supporting me otherwise they wouldn't get their share of the impending US flotation of Fox – owned, of course, by Rupert Murdoch's News International. To their credit, Merrill Lynch remained steadfast. The pressure got worse. Early on the Tuesday morning Rupert Murdoch himself rang Roland Smith and warned him against me. He told him I shouldn't be allowed to vote as I was a known enemy of BSkyB.

I took my own legal advice from Stephen Cooke, at the City firm of Slaughter and May. Stephen had represented LWT in the takeover bid by Granada and I'd been impressed with his work. We had also become friends. His advice on this was clear: I had to recommend acceptance of an offer if I thought it was a good financial deal for the shareholders. According to him, the law was unambiguous: only the shareholders mattered. The fans, the players, the staff were all secondary to the shareholders in law.

By this time the bid was up to 230p and even David Gill had decided it was time to accept. I was now completely on my own. I came up with a proposal on the Tuesday morning that I would accept a price of 240p but I would simultaneously announce that any profit I made on the shares I owned as a result of the deal would be given to an appropriate charity in Manchester. I certainly didn't want to profit personally from this deal. I said that if the deal stayed at 230p I wouldn't oppose it but nor would I recommend it; I'd also put out a statement giving my view that there was no reason for Manchester United not to remain an independent company. Roland Smith, wise old bird that he was, knew that he had to have all his board onside and he instructed Martin Edwards to tell Mark Booth that the price was 240p or no deal. Booth went mad, saying that there was no way he would pay 240p and that the offer would come off the table at 5 p.m. that afternoon.

The BSkyB Board were meeting all afternoon in Isleworth, with Rupert Murdoch in attendance; we were at the HSBC offices in Lower Thames Street. It was now a game of chicken. Coincidentally, my chairman at Pearson, Dennis Stevenson, was also on the BSkyB Board at the time and he later told me that a number of profanities were used as adjectives in front of my name every time it was mentioned at the BSkyB meeting. Dennis stood up for me and said I was only doing what any non-executive board member should be doing – trying to maximize the return for the shareholders. I don't think he mentioned that I was also having great fun screwing Rupert Murdoch.

The question was, who would crack first? I was praying that the Board of BSkyB would stay firm because that way Manchester United would remain independent; but it wasn't to be. At about 4 p.m. they folded and agreed to pay 240p per share. I had won, but I had also lost.

The following day there was a press conference at Old Trafford at which a reporter from the *Daily Mirror* asked Mark Booth one of the great questions of sports journalism. 'Who plays left back for Manchester United?' Booth, an American who knew nothing about soccer, was completely lost and couldn't answer the question. In some ways I think the credibility of the deal collapsed with that question. At the same time, I made my announcement about giving the profit from my shares to a local charity. Our bankers had tried to persuade me, in the strongest fashion, not to make the announcement. I ignored them.

The takeover deal was duly referred to the Monopolies and Mergers Commission and hundreds of individuals and organizations submitted evidence arguing against the deal. Virtually no one outside of BSkyB and Manchester United plc argued in favour. In the end, the Commission took the view that a takeover of Manchester United by BSkyB would be anti-competitive. Their report was so conclusive that even a Government that had tried so hard not to offend Rupert Murdoch had to accept it. The BSkyB takeover of Manchester United was dead.

Being on the Manchester United Board meant that all sorts of people would ring you up to try to get that most precious of commodities – tickets. However, the oddest request I received during my time on the Board came from Downing Street, and it was not for tickets. Cherie Blair, whom I knew quite well, rang one Christmas to ask if I could get a

discount on a Manchester United shirt. I said I could and asked what name and number she wanted on the back. The reply came: Blair, number 7. Her son, Euan, wanted David Beckham's number. I offered to give her the shirt for free, but she insisted on paying. For a while I was tempted to keep the cheque Cherie sent me for the shirt and frame it; in the end I decided the money was more important than the memento, so I cashed it.

My last year on the United Board coincided with one of the most successful seasons in the club's history, by the end of which we'd won the treble. I took most of my family and a few friends, including John Rixon from Hayes, out to Barcelona to watch the third leg of the treble, the match with Bayern Munich. I very nearly didn't get in. I had enough tickets for my party but my personal ticket was being held by the United staff. I was due to meet them at the hotel in Barcelona to collect it but unfortunately the private plane I'd hired was late and the mini-bus driver who collected us from the airport didn't come from Barcelona and couldn't find the hotel. By the time I did get to the hotel everyone had left and I still didn't have a ticket. The only way to see the match was to bluff my way in. We got through the first police cordon by pretending we had more tickets than we had; after that at every barrier I insisted I was a director of Manchester United and asked to be escorted in. In the end I got onto the pitch itself before finding Ken Merrick, the secretary of Manchester United, who had my ticket and accreditation. It's amazing how far bullshit can get you.

In my time on the United Board two matches stand out above all others. I was at Villa Park in April 1999 on the night we knocked Arsenal out of the FA Cup with one of the greatest goals I've ever seen. Peter Schmeichel had already saved a penalty in the last minute of normal time and Roy Keane had been sent off when Ryan Giggs ran from the halfway line to score, having only touched the ball three or four times during a wonderful run. We went on to win the FA Cup, the second leg of the treble. The second game was that match in Barcelona just a couple of months later, where for eighty-eight minutes we were terrible and then scored twice to win the match. The following day I threw a party for all my staff at Pearson Television to celebrate.

My time on the United Board came to a natural end when I was appointed Director-General designate at the BBC. Everyone agreed that

Another celebration: Claire Rayner and I celebrating Labour's great victory in 1997.

Sue and I on election night in May 1997. We had waited a very long time for Labour to win again. I enjoyed the night, but Sue thought it was too triumphalist. She turned out to be right.

Outside Old Trafford soon after I became a director of Manchester United in 1997.

Left: With Alex Ferguson and other directors of Manchester United in 1999, the year we won the treble, which is probably the greatest achievement in the history of football in this country.

Below: Directors and officials of Manchester United before the match on that magic night in Barcelona when we scored twice in the last minute to win the European Champions League. I managed to blag my way onto the pitch without a ticket.

Left: The day I became Dr Dyke! In 1999 York University gave me an honorary doctorate. I received it twenty-five years to the day after I got my first degree. In 2004 I became Chancellor of the University.

Right: On the same day that I appeared before the Hutton Inquiry, I gave a reading at Thora Hird's memorial service. Victoria Wood and Alan Bennett paid moving tributes to a wonderful actress and a great character.

Below: The BBC's Board of Governors led by the chairman Gavyn Davies, in July 2003. The current system of governance is antiquated and needs to be changed. Back row, left to right: Lord Ryder, vice-chairman; Baroness Hogg; Professor Fabian Monds; Dermot Gleeson; Angela Sarkis; Sir Robert Smith; bottom row, left to right: Dame Ruth Deech; Ranjit Sondhi; Gavyn Davies, chairman; Professor Merfyn Jones; and Dame Pauline Neville-Jones. Seven of these voted to get rid of me.

Above: Outside Television Centre on the day I left the BBC. Thousands of staff in all parts of Britain took to the streets to protest about my departure. Many were in tears. I am forever grateful to them for their support.

Left: Taking out tea to the television crews outside my house the day after I left the BBC. The pictures were shown on the national news. I am not at all sure anyone drank the tea!

you couldn't be both the buyer and the seller of the same sports rights, and so I resigned. I also had to sell all my Manchester United shares. But it had been an interesting experience.

When I joined the BBC, sport was one of the biggest problems I faced. Until the late Eighties and the arrival of BSkyB, the BBC had been preeminent in sport and had most of the big sports contracts. But by 2000 many of these had been lost. The FA Cup and Formula One motor-racing had gone to ITV, cricket had gone to Channel Four, as had racing at Cheltenham and the Derby, we had no contract for the next football World Cup, and BSkyB had most of the domestic football.

The BBC had taken the decision not to compete for many of these sports. John Birt's view was quite logical: that the BBC had limited funds that could be better used in areas like drama and news where the BBC added more value. It was a perfectly rational strategy but, like so many of John's strategies, it ignored one factor: what the audience wanted. Our research showed the British public liked sport on the BBC, without advertisements, and were very resentful that it was no longer available. For many of them, that was why they paid their licence fee.

The second problem with BBC sport was easily fixed. For ideological reasons – driven by the consulting firm McKinsey – sport at the BBC had been split into two. There was Sports Broadcasting, the people who bought rights and were responsible for exploiting those rights on television and radio, and Sports Production, who produced the programmes that owning the rights entitled you to make. It was madness, and everyone involved knew it was madness – except of course for McKinsey and the people around John Birt. When I produced my first reorganization plan for the BBC, 'One BBC', I scrapped the system and recreated a BBC sports department that handled everything.

I then persuaded Peter Salmon, who at that time was Controller of BBC One, to take over BBC Sport. He was not only a natural leader prepared to take bold decisions but also a naturally caring person who, unlike some others at the BBC, saw it as his job both to inspire and look after the people who worked for him. When I started my culture change programme at the BBC he was an important part of it.

Sadly, before Peter took over the job in the autumn of 2000, things got worse: the BBC lost the rights to *Match of the Day* once again. In June 2000 the television rights to the FA Cup, the Premiership, and the

Football League were all sold in a single week – a week of madness when ridiculous prices were paid that I doubt will ever be paid for football rights again. At the BBC we wanted to retain *Match of the Day* and regain the FA Cup and the English internationals. ITV was not interested in recorded highlights but was desperate to retain the FA Cup.

The then Chief Executive of the FA, Adam Crozier, clearly wanted the FA Cup back on the BBC so he encouraged us and BSkyB to get together to bid. We ended up with a great deal for the BBC that rankled with Sky Chief Executive Tony Ball for some years. We paid only a third of the money and got all England's competitive home internationals live, as well as two matches from every round of the FA Cup, including the pick of the best game.

We were delighted when we were told unofficially that we'd got the deal. The trouble was that Adam Crozier also told ITV that they'd lost the FA Cup – something he denied later but which I know to be true. He didn't do it to be malicious; he was simply trying to be fair. Of course what happened was that the following morning, when all the final bids for Premier League rights had to be submitted, our £40 million bid for the *Match of the Day* rights, which was very expensive in any case, was dwarfed by ITV's bid of £60 million plus. If Crozier hadn't rung ITV we would have won both. Either way, it was the economics of the madhouse and was to cost ITV dear: they estimate they lost between £20 and £30 million a season on the contract. In fact things were worse than that for ITV because that was the same day that ITV Digital, the struggling digital service, bid £315 million to acquire the television rights to the Football League for the following three years. It was the size of this bid that eventually brought down the whole company and left the Football League short of £80 million a year.

The BBC and I were both savaged in the press for losing *Match of the Day*. No one was interested in our rather good FA deal, and the fact that ITV had massively overbid was ignored: most journalists know little about money but sports journalists know the least. This all happened while the European Nations Cup was happening in Belgium and Holland and the ITV sports boys out there gave our people a hard time.

In fact that 'mad' week, during which record prices were paid for the FA Cup, England internationals, Premier League and Football League rights, was the beginning of the end of the period of massive inflation in

sports rights. It had been fuelled by two things: the arrival of competing pay television platforms in the shape of BSkyB, ITV Digital, and the cable companies, and a massive boom in advertising revenue. In two years both these factors had disappeared, as I explained in a speech at the Manchester Evening News Business Awards in November 2001. By then ITV Digital and the cable companies were heading for bankruptcy and administration respectively, and ITV's advertising revenue was 15 per cent down year on year. The bubble had burst. 'So what does all this mean?' I asked in my speech. 'Well, if I was still on the Board of Manchester United I would be warning my fellow directors to be very careful. The boom in television revenues has funded an amazing escalation in players' wages in recent years but that boom is now coming to an end.' I was right, but I'd reckoned without Roman Abramovich and his Russian millions.

Despite losing the rights to *Match of the Day*, BBC Sport, under the leadership of Peter Salmon, gradually recovered. We had a great 2000 Olympics in Sydney, where the BBC was named by the International Olympics Committee as the number one broadcaster, and we wiped the floor with ITV when it came to the 2002 World Cup. First we had the exclusive rights to that wonderful night in Munich when England beat Germany 5–1, thus virtually qualifying for the finals. I was there that night and bumped into John Motson the following morning at the airport. He said it was such a great victory, wouldn't it be a good idea to repeat the match again that night? I grabbed Mark Thompson, the Director of Television, who was also at the airport and we both decided we should show it, if only so we could both see it again ourselves. We phoned Lorraine Heggessey, the controller of BBC One, from the airport and bullied her into changing that night's schedules.

When it came to the World Cup finals we completely outmanoeuvred ITV by playing hardball on the allocation of matches for the finals themselves. When negotiating the deal for the World Cup – which we got at a decent price because Kirsch, the organization selling the rights, was going bust – we told ITV that we wanted to change the way we split the matches. Once we'd both signed the contract we told them we were planning to show all the England matches live and didn't mind if they showed them live as well. The ITV people went berserk because they knew we'd attract twice or three times as many viewers as they would if we both broadcast the same match. In the end we took two England

matches and ITV took one. When we went head to head on the final we beat ITV by nearly four to one in ratings – 12.4 million viewers against their 3.6 million.

We retained the rights to both the Premier League and cricket for Radio Five Live; we won back the Derby and the whole of Five Nations rugby for BBC One, and we won athletics for BBC Two. But the comeback of BBC Sport was sealed in 2003 with the next round of football negotiations for the 2004/5 season. Not only did we agree a good deal with the FA by which we acquired all England's home internationals and three matches from each round of the FA Cup, we also won back the *Match of the Day* rights with a bid of £35 million – nearly half the figure ITV had been paying. In fact by the time I left the BBC we had more live and recorded football planned for the 2004/5 season than the BBC had ever had before.

The great advantage of being Director-General if you are a sports fan is you get access to tickets for virtually anything you want to watch. Every year I tried to arrange a couple of visits to Wimbledon as both Sue and I enjoyed watching tennis. At least one of them was usually in the Royal Box as a guest of the All England Lawn Tennis Club itself. One year we were in the front row of the box watching a match when someone announced that tea was served. The box emptied and Sue and I were on our own in the front row when the game finally ended. The players came up, looked up and bowed to us. It was hysterical. A couple of years later the Club ended the tradition of players bowing to the Royal Box.

Sport in Britain has changed beyond all recognition in the fifteen years I've been involved with sports broadcasting. The coming of pay television has brought billions of pounds into certain sports – the ones the public want to watch on television week in and week out – to the disadvantage of others. It has also changed when and where live sports events are played: the traditional Saturday afternoon football match, to take one example, is now close to disappearing as broadcasters want matches spread right across the weekend.

The traditionalists, including many sports journalists on newspapers, who hate the control broadcasters now have, constantly tell us what a terrible thing this is. But in today's sports world money is all. The broadcasters supply the cash, so they call the tune.

All sports organizations today face a dilemma: how much of their sport to put on pay television and how much on traditional terrestrial television.

The former pays more, the latter gets much bigger audiences and helps build the sport. The best example is rugby union. When England versus Wales at Twickenham was broadcast on Sky in 2002 it got an audience of only a few hundred thousand; Wales versus England at Cardiff the following season, on the other hand, was broadcast on BBC One and attracted seven million.

When I look back now, losing the rights to the Premier League back in 1992 was a blow for ITV but was probably inevitable. If it hadn't happened then it would have happened next time around. The value of Premier League football to a pay television operator is so much greater than it is for a traditional commercial broadcaster funded by advertising. Millions of people in Britain pay BSkyB £40 a month just to get their football; the advertising revenue involved is worth nothing like that.

Sport is a world in which money talks. All sorts of people and sports bodies promise you undying loyalty as a broadcaster because you cover their sport so well, only to sell the rights to someone else because they're prepared to pay more. But it goes both ways. Broadcasters often offer sports organizations the world to get their rights only to treat them in a cavalier fashion once they've won them.

In many ways sports organizations and broadcasters deserve each other.

Gilligan, Kelly, and Hutton

One of the standing jokes amongst my team at the BBC was that I always seemed to be away when the really big stories about the BBC hit the papers.

I had been on a beach in Barbados when the Secretary of State announced what the BBC's funding would be for the next six years. I had been sailing in Turkey when Rod Liddle had been forced to resign from the editorship of the *Today* programme after he wrote an article attacking the Conservatives and the Countryside Alliance. I had been in Australia when a potential bust-up about what a BBC website had said in a fictitious story about the death of the Queen Mother had surfaced. I remember it well because the then Chairman, Christopher Bland, had insisted on ringing me at 4 a.m. to 'discuss' it. And I was away skiing in France when the Queen Mother actually died and the colour of Peter Sissons' tie became a big issue.

Now, true to form, I was on holiday in the west of Ireland on the day – 29 May 2003 – when Andrew Gilligan's story on weapons of mass destruction in Iraq was broadcast on the *Today* programme on Radio Four. Once again my holiday was interrupted. But it wasn't the Gilligan story that was the controversial issue that particular week. That was to come later.

What dominated that week in Ireland was whether or not we should include pictures of dead British soldiers in Iraq in a documentary made for BBC Two's *Correspondent* series the following Sunday. Jana Bennett, the Director of Television, was in charge while I was away and her view, supported by Mark Damazer, the Deputy Head of News, was that we should.

I tended to agree, but it wasn't an easy call. The BBC had not done it before, *The Sun* had gone to town on the story, the relatives of the soldiers were understandably upset, and the Chairman of the BBC, Gavyn Davies, was worried. The argument in favour of showing the pictures was that we were planning to show pictures of dead US and Iraqi soldiers, so why not play a two-second shot of the unidentifiable British soldiers? Surely this was the reality of war?

In the end I backed Jana and Mark but made sure I got to see a tape when I arrived home on the Friday evening before *Correspondent* was broadcast on the Sunday, just in case I wanted to change my mind. I watched it and I didn't. When the BBC Governors' complaints committee considered the issue a couple of months later they took the view that we'd made the wrong decision and should not have broadcast the pictures. However, they recognized it had been a close call.

What this all meant was that another holiday had been disrupted. I'd sat out at sea in an open boat discussing the issue for hours on end with all sorts of people. At one time, distracted, with mobile phone in hand, I'd even untied the wrong boat on the quayside and was left with the task of stopping someone else's boat drifting out of the harbour.

In these circumstances none of us had taken much notice of the Gilligan story on the *Today* programme on 29 May. Although you can get a perfectly good Radio Four signal in that part of Ireland, I was on holiday and wasn't up in time to listen to the broadcast at seven minutes past six. Eight months later that broadcast would lead to my exit from the BBC.

My private view of the Iraq war, like that of the BBC's Chairman Gavyn Davies, was that I was marginally in favour of trying to get rid of Saddam Hussein. I regarded him as a nasty bastard whom the world could well do without. Mistakenly, as it has turned out, I had also been convinced that Tony Blair and the Government knew more about Iraq's weapons of mass destruction than they were able to tell us and that there was a real and serious threat. My support for the war made me very unpopular with some of my friends, one of whom described me publicly in her speech at her fiftieth birthday party as a neo-conservative.

In terms of my role as Director-General of the BBC my own feelings about the war were irrelevant. Our job was to report the events leading up to the war, and the war itself, as fairly as we could. It was certainly not the job of the BBC to be the Government's propaganda machine, but

nor was it our job disproportionately to represent the views of those protesting against the war. Our job was to be impartial, to tell the story as fairly as we could. At times we would get it wrong – journalism is not an exact science; but the duty we owed to the public was to do our best to tell the story as our journalists saw it. As our value statement made clear, 'Trust is the foundation of the BBC' and we should do nothing to endanger that trust, which was why we needed to avoid being seen as either side's mouthpiece.

It was Huw Wheldon, the former Managing Director of BBC Television, who had said that when Britain as a nation is divided the BBC is on the rack. It was clear from well before the war started that we were going to be on the rack this time: not since Suez had Britain been so divided over taking military action. History shows very clearly that it is at times of war that the relationship between the BBC and the government of the day is at its most tense. During Suez the Prime Minister, Anthony Eden, even considered taking over the BBC when it agreed to give the Leader of the Opposition, Hugh Gaitskell, airtime to explain why Labour was against the war, following Eden's broadcast explaining why he had gone to war.

Today such an even-handed approach is seen as the norm, but back then it brought accusations from Eden that the BBC was betraying the nation at a time of crisis. He wrote privately to Winston Churchill saying, 'The BBC is exasperating me by leaning over backwards to be what they call neutral and to present both sides of the case.' He asked William Clark, his press secretary, 'Are they enemies or just socialists?' Clark noted in his diary that Eden had a growing 'passion and determination to teach the BBC a lesson'. It is remarkable how history repeats itself. The same hostility from the Government was seen at the time of the Falklands war in 1982. When Dick Francis, a senior BBC executive, expressed the view that the grief of a widow in Buenos Aires was no less than that of a British widow, he was roundly condemned by a Government that told the nation it should 'rejoice' at military victories.

John Simpson, the BBC's brilliant World Affairs Editor, summed up the position in an article published just weeks before the Iraq war:

At the times of Suez, Biafra, Vietnam, the Falklands, the American bombing of Libya and the NATO attacks on Kosovo and Serbia,

the BBC reported the opposition to these wars fully. On every occasion the Government – Labour or Conservative – tried to bully the BBC into supporting the official line. On every occasion the BBC resisted; sometimes energetically, sometimes not as energetically as it ought to have done ... Governments have as much right as anyone to put pressure on the BBC; it's only a problem if the BBC caves in.

For Alastair Campbell and his team in the Downing Street press office our refusal to report what they wanted us to, in the way they wanted us to, made us a target even before the war itself began. It was easy to see why he was so anxious. With a million people on the streets of London protesting about the war, and a Labour rebellion on an unprecedented scale happening in the House of Commons, Tony Blair's whole future as Prime Minister was in the balance. In one letter Campbell even complained that we hadn't properly reported the views of the Labour MPs who had supported the Government – this on the day after 139 Labour MPs voted against their own leadership, the biggest backbench rebellion ever against a sitting Government.

The criticisms from Downing Street of the BBC's reporting in the run-up to the war were largely confined to complaints to Richard Sambrook and his people in BBC News. I heard nothing directly from Downing Street until the week the war started, when both Gavyn Davies and I received private letters from the Prime Minister. The Prime Minister's letter to me, sent on 19 March 2003, said that while he accepted that in a democracy it was right that 'voices of dissent' were heard, the BBC had gone too far and that he had been shocked by some of the editorializing of our interviewers and reporters. He said:

It seems to me there has been a real breakdown of the separation of news and comment ... I know too that Alastair has been pressing you to ensure more reference is made to reports from inside Iraq about the restrictions under which the media operate ...

Tony Blair went on to complain that our reports were full of complaints from 'ordinary' Iraqis but that there was no such thing in modern-day Baghdad, as anyone who criticized the regime risked execution or torture.

He ended by saying that he had never written to me or my predecessor in this way before and added:

I believe, and I am not alone in believing, that you have not got the balance right between support and dissent; between news and comment; between the voices of the Iraqi regime and the voices of Iraqi dissidents; or between the diplomatic support we have, and diplomatic opposition.

Gavyn was later told by an official at Number Ten that the Prime Minister hadn't wanted to send the letters in the first place. He'd been persuaded to send them by Alastair Campbell, and later regretted it. Gavyn and I discussed how we should respond. We agreed that he should send a conciliatory reply whilst mine should be more robust, since I deeply resented this obvious attempt by Campbell to try to bully us. The first three paragraphs of my letter to Tony Blair, sent on 21 March, said:

Firstly, and I do not mean to be rude, but having faced the biggest ever public demonstration in this country and the biggest ever back-bench rebellion against a sitting government by its own supporters, would you not agree that your communications advisors are not best placed to advise whether or not the BBC has got the balance right between support and dissent? Given these circumstances they are hardly in a position to make a reasoned judgement about the BBC's impartiality.

You have been engaged in a difficult battle fighting for your particular view of the world to be accepted and, quite understandably, you want that to be reported. We however have a different role in society. Our role in these circumstances is to try to give a balanced picture.

It is perfectly legitimate for you or your advisors to complain about particular stories – journalism is an imperfect profession – and if we make mistakes, as we inevitably do, under my leadership we will always say we were wrong and apologise. However for you to question the whole of the BBC's journalistic output across a wide range of radio, television and online services because you are

concerned about particular stories which don't favour your view is unfair.

My view was straightforward: if the Government was going to try to bully the BBC then I was going to fight back. Looking back now there is an argument that I should have been more circumspect, but I don't agree. I believed passionately in the argument I made in my reply to Blair: that the media and the Government had crucially different roles in a democracy and that one of the central roles of the broadcast media was to question the government of the day and to stand up to any bullying from them. That the BBC's charter was soon up for renewal was irrelevant to me.

I had first outlined my views on the relationship between broadcasters and government in my first McTaggart lecture back in 1994 and my opinions hadn't changed since then. Back then I had quoted Grace Wyndham Goldie, the former BBC News executive who had dealt with Eden during the Suez crisis in 1956. In her book, *Facing the Nation: Television and Politics, 1936–1976*, published in 1977, she expressed what I believed:

> Nowhere more than in broadcasting is the price of freedom eternal vigilance; resistance to political pressures has to be constant and continuous. But it must be realised that such pressures are inevitable, for the aims of political parties and those of broadcasting organizations are not the same.

The war in Iraq was not a moment of national unity. There were more than a million people marching through the streets of London opposed to it, and it was important that their voice, and what they represented, was properly and fairly reported. Writing this book more than a year after the war ended, it is quite clear now that Blair's Iraq policy has been disastrous for Blair, for the Labour Party, and for Britain's reputation virtually everywhere in the world other than in the United States. It would have been outrageous if the BBC hadn't tried properly to report the opposition to the war, which is in effect what Campbell wanted.

I think that from the moment my reply reached Number Ten all the gloves were off; that Campbell saw it as a personal rebuff, that I had humiliated him. I am told by people who know him well that he now

regarded it as personal. In a later letter, sent to me the day after he went ballistic in front of the Foreign Affairs Committee, he complained that my reply to the Prime Minister had been 'dismissive'.

Everything that happened later in the year has to be put into the context of the person with whom we were dealing. Alastair Campbell, while a brilliant operator, has a classic obsessive personality and he had decided that the BBC was the enemy. From then on, if not before, I suspect he was looking for revenge.

As the Director-General I believed I had already gone to great lengths to make sure we would report the run-up to the war, and the war itself, fairly and properly. I had set up and chaired an ad hoc group that met every morning to discuss our coverage of the Iraq issue. All the most senior editorial figures at the BBC were on that group. In particular I'd made strenuous efforts to ensure that the Government position was fairly reported.

It was this group that had decided to prevent any senior BBC editorial figures from going on the anti-war march if they wanted to be involved in the coverage of Iraq. It was this group that had decided there was a danger of our phone-in programmes being dominated by the anti-war lobby and had ordered more phone lines to be opened to ensure we got a proper balance. And it was this group that insisted we find a balanced audience for *Question Time* when it was hard to find many supporters of the war willing to come on the programme, even though the polls showed that the country was evenly split.

That same group had also discussed, on several occasions, the point the Prime Minister had made in his letter about whether or not our correspondents inside Baghdad were restricted in what they could and couldn't say. Our view was that this hadn't been the case and that, although all our reporters had Iraqi minders, they were not unduly hampered in their reporting. In fact, during the war itself, Rageh Omaar's minder even asked if he could have a day off because it was his child's birthday. Of course the American broadcasters pulled all their people out of Baghdad as soon as the war started, but then the US broadcasters were hardly a model of good and fair reporting during the war. In fact they were the opposite and most of them simply became cheerleaders for Bush, which is why viewing and listening figures for the BBC's services in the USA increased so markedly during the conflict.

I pointed out what we had done in terms of ensuring fairness to the Prime Minister in my reply to his letter. I said:

> My point is that we have discussed these sorts of issues at length and made the best judgements we could. That our conclusions didn't always please Alastair is unfortunate but not our primary concern.

I received no more complaints from Tony Blair during or after the war. But the complaints from Campbell never stopped. They arrived on Richard Sambrook's desk with regular monotony and Richard and I discussed them on several occasions. We both came to the conclusion that Campbell had become obsessed by the BBC. Peter Stothard, the former editor of *The Times* who spent thirty days following Blair during the war, said on the *Today* programme, when interviewed during the Hutton crisis, that he believed antagonism towards the BBC was 'hard wired into Downing Street'.

Andrew Gilligan was reporting from Iraq for the whole of the war and his reports were not always popular with Campbell. On one occasion we actually agreed with Campbell when Gilligan talked about a particular claim he said 'could be true rather than more rubbish from Central Command'. Campbell complained and we wrote back saying that we agreed the use of the word 'rubbish' was a mistake. On another occasion we received identical letters complaining about Andrew Gilligan from Campbell and the Chairman of the Culture, Media and Sport select committee, Gerald Kaufman. It was clear that Campbell's department had written this letter for him.

But the biggest argument came on the Monday after the war ended when Gilligan, who had been in Iraq for the whole of the war, filed a report for the *Today* programme in which he said that for many people in Baghdad conditions were more dangerous that morning than they had been before the war. He said:

> Baghdad may in theory be free but its people are passing their first days of liberty in a greater fear than they've ever known. The old fear of the regime was habitual, low level. This fear is sharp and immediate – the fear that your house will be invaded, your property will be taken away and your daughters will be raped.

Campbell and his team in Downing Street complained again. We discussed the complaint at some length but decided that what Gilligan had said was also being said by other journalists. We felt that his comments were reasonable: for some in Iraq, life was clearly now more dangerous. Of course within weeks many military people were saying very similar things, and no one could doubt that is the position in Iraq today. When Gilligan returned to the UK Richard Sambrook thanked him for staying on in Baghdad and putting his life at risk. He told him that some of his reporting had been very good, but he also told him that he needed to be more careful and that too often he went 10 per cent too far.

The war was over and we had a period of relative quiet in terms of our relationship with Downing Street. Then came Gilligan's broadcast of 29 May when I was away in Ireland.

One of the major criticisms of the BBC made by Lord Hutton when he published his report in January 2004 was that the BBC's editorial system that day was 'defective', implying that if the proper procedures had been followed Gilligan's broadcasts would never have got to air. This wasn't true. The BBC's own internal inquiry has recently reported that in fact the proper procedures *were* followed. Quite how Hutton reached this conclusion is beyond me: he never asked for evidence from the one person most responsible for implementing the editorial procedures on the *Today* programme, its editor, Kevin Marsh.

The BBC didn't put Marsh forward as a witness because our legal advice was that you didn't nominate witnesses; you waited for the inquiry team to call them. This was based on our QC's firm belief that all your bad days would come when your witnesses were in the witness box and all your best days would come when it was the turn of the Government witnesses. He was absolutely right; that is exactly what happened. But it did mean that Kevin Marsh was never given the opportunity to explain the editorial process the *Today* programme applied to the Gilligan report. As a result, Hutton has been allowed to create the myth that Gilligan's report went to air without any proper editorial control being exercised beforehand. It was one of the many myths Hutton has been allowed to foster. I shall discuss the others in the next chapter.

Gilligan's story began when he met Dr David Kelly – a former senior UN weapons inspector, a government adviser, and an international expert

in biological warfare – on 22 May 2003 over Appletize and Coca Cola at the Charing Cross Hotel in London.

Gilligan didn't expect to get a story at all; he was meeting Dr Kelly for a chat. When he realized that what Dr Kelly was telling him was indeed an important story he discovered he had no notebook with him. He therefore asked Dr Kelly if it was OK for him to take notes on his personal organizer. The story Gilligan was told is now well known. In essence, Dr Kelly told him of deep concern within intelligence that the Government's September 2002 dossier had been made 'sexier' by Alastair Campbell and others in Downing Street.

With a good, exclusive story on his hands, Gilligan began the process of checking and cross checking. He ran the story by a couple of senior government contacts. They were unable to confirm it, although one did encourage him to keep digging. He discovered that similar stories were circulating in the USA.

He also did extensive analysis of the 2002 dossier that suggested to him that the language had been hardened up in some areas. The dossier was supposed to be an assessment from the Joint Intelligence Committee (JIC). But Gilligan had seen earlier JIC assessments and the September dossier did not feel to him like the usual JIC product. The language was much more assertive than a conventional intelligence assessment, as the House of Commons Foreign Affairs Committee later pointed out.

Gilligan did a search of the cuttings, which threw up the remarkable fact that, although the claim that Iraq could deploy nuclear and biological weapons within 45 minutes had been made so much of when the dossier had been launched in September 2002, it had almost completely dropped out of government speeches over the following six months. This suggested that the Government did not place all that much faith in the claim.

Then there was the context. Firstly there was the second dossier, which the Government had published in February 2003 – just a few months before Gilligan spoke to Dr Kelly. This had been shown to have been based on a student thesis on Iraq, which had then been embellished in Downing Street to exaggerate the threat. The Government had form in this area.

Gilligan's suspicions were increased when he looked at the claim in the September dossier that Iraq had been trying to import uranium from Africa – one of the things Dr Kelly had raised questions about when they

met. The International Atomic Energy Authority had been very critical of this claim and said it was based on forged documents. Once again the claim had been dropped from ministerial speeches on the Iraqi threat.

There were other factors too. Gilligan's cuttings search revealed a number of press stories published shortly before the September dossier appeared saying that there was little new in the dossier, which was then circulating in draft form in Whitehall. This seemed to support Dr Kelly's claim that it had been 'transformed in the week before publication'. Later stories reported rows between Alastair Campbell and the intelligence services over the dossier, again supporting one of Dr Kelly's claims.

Then there was Robin Cook, who, in his speech given in the House of Commons after resigning from the Government in March 2003, said that he did not believe Iraq possessed weapons of mass destruction in the commonly understood sense of the term. And of course no weapons of mass destruction of any size had yet been found by the allies in Iraq.

None of this directly corroborated what Dr Kelly had said, but it did suggest he was not a lone voice with an axe to grind. He seemed to be well informed about the dossier. His claims were consistent with other information – and the extensive checks Gilligan had made had turned up nothing to suggest they were wrong. Gilligan also knew that Dr Kelly was a highly credible and authoritative source who had given him information before that had proved reliable. Finally, Gilligan knew that Dr Kelly was not a novice when it came to dealing with the media: he was perfectly aware of what journalists were likely to do with the information he gave them.

Gilligan spent six days checking out the story before he was sufficiently confident to take it to his editors on the *Today* programme. On Wednesday 28 May 2003 he rang the day editor, Miranda Holt, an experienced senior assistant editor. She was interested in the story but she thought she should run it by her editor, Kevin Marsh.

Marsh was still new to the job of editing *Today*, although he was not new to BBC radio news. Now approaching fifty, he'd joined the Corporation straight from Oxford in 1978 and, apart from a brief stint at ITN, he was a BBC lifer. In 1989 he became editor of Radio Four's *PM* programme, and four years later editor of *The World at One*. By 1998 he was editor of a group of Radio Four programmes that included both *PM* and *The World at One*, along with the newly launched Sunday morning

show *Broadcasting House*. In January 2003 he became the editor of *Today*.

Marsh is one of the BBC's most experienced editors and was long used to dealing with politicians upset by what he had broadcast. He also had extremely good contacts throughout Whitehall but was disliked by Campbell and New Labour because in his time editing *The World at One* he was a constant thorn in their side. When the BBC broadcast a drama called *The Project*, a film based on the early years of New Labour, the character of the BBC editor in the programme was widely thought to have been based on Marsh.

Marsh was interested in Gilligan's story. But, as any sceptical editor should, he raised a series of questions about it. In particular he wanted to know if the source was as senior as was being claimed; whether or not he was really in a position to make an informed judgement about the preparation of the dossier; whether or not he was credible and reliable and had a decent track record; what exactly the source had said to Gilligan; and how accurately Gilligan had recorded what he said. Marsh also wanted to know if the claims fitted into a broader picture.

Marsh was told that the anonymous source was a former Porton Down scientist; that he had been a lead United Nations weapons inspector in the 1990s; that Gilligan had known him for two years; that he was planning to return to Iraq as a senior member of the Iraq survey group; and that he would have seen much of the intelligence on chemical and biological weapons referred to in the September dossier. Miranda Holt also showed Marsh a note Gilligan had written for her. Among other things it recorded the source as saying there was a 30 per cent chance that Iraq had had a chemical weapons programme six months before the war started. Marsh took comfort from this because it indicated that the source did believe Iraq constituted some sort of threat – this was no pro-Iraqi peacenik trying to spin facts for a particular cause.

Marsh was now reassured on many of his concerns, but still not completely convinced. He decided to consider a number of other factors.

There had been a general feeling, since the revelation of the 'dodgy dossier' in February 2003, that government dossiers on Iraq were not to be wholly trusted – a feeling heightened by the doubts cast on the uranium claims in the earlier dossier.

There were the recent comments from Hans Blix, the UN Chief

Weapons Inspector, that intelligence offered to his inspectors by the UK and USA had turned out to be unhelpful, faulty, or misleading.

There was also the fact that stories in the press from reputable journalists alleging unhappiness in the intelligence services over information being 'spiced up' in the dossier had not been denied by the Government.

And there was more.

Marsh himself had two separate sources of unimpeachable authority who had given him information that lent credence to the source's claim about the inclusion of unreliable intelligence in the dossier. One was Clare Short, the former Cabinet Minister, who was still in her job at the time the dossier was produced. Marsh happened to have had lunch with her that very day. Short had insisted that she had seen no intelligence that conclusively demonstrated that Iraq was an imminent threat. She believed, she told Marsh, that policy had driven the interpretation and presentation of intelligence rather than – as is supposed to happen – intelligence driving policy. She had also told Marsh that she was convinced that Alastair Campbell had played a central role in the way intelligence had been presented to the wider public.

Marsh's second source was a very senior serving member of the intelligence services. Marsh and John Humphrys had recently had lunch with him, and Marsh had left the meeting with the clear impression that the intelligence available did not suggest that Iraq was the most immediate threat to the region and that Iran and Syria were a greater threat to British interests. Given this, it was difficult to justify attacking Iraq at that time.

On reflection, it seemed to Marsh that the story passed all the tests he had set. The source was senior, credible and reliable; was in a position to know what he was talking about; and it was obvious why he couldn't go on the record. Much of what the source was saying was validated by what he, Marsh, knew from other sources and he believed Gilligan's notes were full enough to justify the story. Finally, Marsh believed there was obvious public interest in broadcasting the story.

He decided to go ahead, but he made two further stipulations. One was that Gilligan should script his main report and that Marsh should see it before it was broadcast. The second was that, in the interests of balance, the bid that *Today* had already made for a Ministry of Defence minister (to respond to a different report about the coalition's use of

cluster bombs in Iraq) should be widened to include a response to Gilligan's story.

Marsh was now satisfied. He did not – nor was there any reason for him to do so – formally refer the story up to his own boss. However, I suspect that if Marsh had known the story would turn into the most celebrated BBC report of the century he would at least have discussed it with those above him. But then, at that point, who was to know?

There was one other decision to be made by the *Today* team – where the story should go in the running order. The cluster bomb story had more immediate appeal, so that was planned as the lead item, which now seems an odd decision. Gilligan's story would run some time later. It was decided that the minister who was due on the programme would first take questions on cluster bombs, and then on Gilligan's story.

The decision was taken to run Gilligan's scripted story some time between 7 and 8 a.m. but that, in accordance with usual practice, there would also be an unscripted 'two-way' between the presenter and reporter between 6 and 7 a.m.

Within the programme the early two-ways were seen as curtain-raisers, trails for the main event later in the programme. They were never scripted – although since they were based on the scripted item to be broadcast later in the programme, it was assumed that they would faithfully reflect the scripted content.

During that evening before the broadcast there were a number of phone calls to the Ministry of Defence both from the *Today* office and from Gilligan (who had been away from the office for the whole of the day). There is a dispute about what was said during these calls. Gilligan is sure that he outlined his story – that the dossier had been exaggerated at Downing Street's behest – to an MoD press officer, Kate Wilson. She is equally sure he did not and that they spoke mainly about cluster bombs. Since neither took notes the dispute is impossible to settle. Various members of the *Today* production team also put in calls to the MoD – and here too there is a dispute over what calls were made when, and who said what to whom. Neither side kept a good enough log of these calls.

Wherever the truth lies in these disputes, the Armed Forces Minister, Adam Ingram, did appear on *Today* the next morning, 29 May, and was sufficiently well briefed on the background to confirm one key piece of

information immediately: that the 45-minute intelligence came from a single source. And Mr Ingram, who has a reputation as a robust and direct minister who makes his complaints to *Today* personally, made no complaint about his treatment or suggested he had been 'ambushed'.

When Marsh arrived at the *Today* office early on that Thursday morning, he read Gilligan's proposed script for the planned 7.30 a.m. broadcast and passed it for transmission. The stage was now set. As it turned out, it was the early unscripted two-way conversation between Humphrys and Gilligan that was to cause all the trouble. I shall examine this in detail in the next chapter.

So Gilligan's story did not just fall onto the air. There was an extensive and well-tried editorial process in place which was followed, although it was not faultless. The record keeping of interview bids by the *Today* team was not what it should have been; it was unwise to break a story such as this in an unscripted two-way; and Downing Street should have been asked to comment on the story as well as the Ministry of Defence. But the process was fully in place, Kevin Marsh followed it, and the BBC's subsequent internal inquiry confirmed this.

Lord Hutton got this wrong. But then Lord Hutton got a lot wrong.

I returned from Ireland on the Friday night, 30 May, the day after Andrew Gilligan's reports on the *Today* programme, and went into the office on the Monday.

There was a bit of noise around about the *Today* programme story from the previous week but nothing particularly unusual. I later discovered that there had been a complaint on the day of the broadcast from Anne Shevas, a Downing Street press officer, that the Government's denial of the Gilligan allegations had not been properly reported. Reading the statement today is instructive as it included a paragraph saying: 'Any suggestion that there was any pressure or intervention from Downing Street is entirely false.' The evidence given to the Hutton inquiry some months later shows that statement to be wrong. There *was* pressure and it is obvious to me that John Scarlett, Head of the Joint Intelligence Committee in Downing Street, changed the dossier as a result of that pressure. But I am running ahead of events.

It so happened that I had one of my regular meetings with Stephen Whittle, the BBC's Head of Editorial Policy, on the following Wednesday

and we discussed the story. By then I had read an article by Andrew Gilligan that had appeared in the *Mail on Sunday* in which he had outlined the same story but, crucially, added that his source had told him the September dossier had been 'sexed up' by Alastair Campbell himself. Campbell was never named in any BBC programme.

That morning, Wednesday 4 June, the Chairman of the Labour Party, John Reid, had appeared on the *Today* programme and had attacked the story; in particular he'd attacked 'rogue elements in the security services' whom he believed had given the story to Andrew Gilligan.

I asked Stephen Whittle to take a look at Gilligan's original story and make sure we were happy with it and the process by which it went to air. He sent me back a two-page e-mail outlining the process and finished it with one line: 'As you can see, a strong and well sourced story.' When I was later criticized for not having involved myself early enough in the process I pointed to this action I had taken even before we had received our first complaint from Campbell. My mind was put at rest by Stephen's reply, although over the next week or so I did discuss the issue with Richard Sambrook. When we received Campbell's letters of complaint they were addressed to Richard so he dealt with them, which was the normal BBC process.

It was two days later that Alastair Campbell sent his first complaint. Campbell's complaint letters were often very long. He clearly suffered from verbal diarrhoea, which I always thought strange given his background as a tabloid journalist. In some of his letters it was also quite difficult to work out what he was actually complaining about.

In a four-page letter, dated 6 June, Campbell complained that Gilligan had failed to understand the role of the Joint Intelligence Committee and that we had broken our own BBC guidelines by the use of a single unattributable source. He ended the letter by saying he wondered why we had guidelines at all, given that they were so persistently breached. Richard Sambrook replied on 11 June and told Campbell quite clearly that there had been no breach of the guidelines and that the BBC had several sources who were expressing concern about the way intelligence was used and presented in the September dossier.

A day later came another letter from Campbell, again sent to Richard, again complaining that Gilligan had misunderstood the role of the Joint Intelligence Committee; and again he was complaining that Gilligan's

story had broken the BBC's reporting guidelines. Richard replied in detail on 16 June. This time he quoted the BBC guidelines, which made it clear they had not been broken. I had received copies of both Campbell's previous letters and at my suggestion Richard offered Campbell the opportunity to take his complaint through the BBC's official complaints process. If he had taken this route it could have eventually gone to the relevant Governors' committee for a final ruling. Campbell never replied to that invitation.

Campbell's letter of 12 June is very interesting and tells us a lot about him. In the final paragraph he complained that BBC news bulletins on Sunday 8 June had reported a *Sunday Telegraph* story saying that Campbell had written a letter of apology to Sir Richard Dearlove, Head of the Secret Intelligence Service (MI6), over the failings in the second, February, dossier. Campbell said this was untrue and he was demanding an apology. We later discovered that the story was essentially true: he had apologized to Sir Richard Dearlove. The only thing wrong in the article was that Campbell hadn't apologized by letter, but verbally.

This was a typical Campbell tactic. He would try to discredit an entire story by denying a tiny detail. Everyone was aware of this and it undermined the credibility of his complaints.

After this spurt of letters over ten days, complete silence. No more complaints from Campbell and we all assumed that the complaints and the story had gone the way of so many others. Richard Sambrook and I were later criticized for not taking the complaints seriously enough, which was unfair. Richard received letters like these from Campbell on such a regular basis that when he received the second letter he described it to me as 'just another Alastair rant'.

Around this time the House of Commons Foreign Affairs Select Committee was holding a series of hearings on the decision to go to war in Iraq and wanted Alastair Campbell to appear before it. In particular, they wanted to know about the 'dodgy' dossier, which Campbell's staff had taken from the Internet, changed to improve the case for going to war, and then published in February 2003 as their own work.

To get the full picture you have to go back a few weeks. The Foreign Affairs Select Committee announced their inquiry on 3 June 2003. One of their first actions was to ask Campbell to appear. He refused point blank.

But then things started to go wrong. Campbell began to attract a lot of criticism – particularly over the February dossier. Downing Street was forced to confirm that, in the wake of the 'dodgy' dossier, it had written to the heads of the intelligence agencies promising greater care would be taken in future.

On the same day Iain Duncan Smith, then leader of the Conservative Party, made his first intervention in the affair, calling for an independent inquiry into the way intelligence was used to make the case for war and pointing the finger at Campbell: 'My concern is the way that this was twisted and fiddled and spun by people like Alastair Campbell.'

Meanwhile, the flow of stories continued in the press, raising questions about misuse of intelligence. *The Observer* ran a story on 8 June saying that 'two vehicles that he [Blair] had repeatedly claimed to be Iraqi mobile biological warfare production units are nothing of the sort'. The *Mail on Sunday* ran a second piece by Gilligan. It didn't have much new to say but it kept the story on the boil – and Campbell's paranoia about the BBC at full pitch.

Then, on 9 June, Clare Short, who had resigned from the Cabinet over the war in May, before the broadcast, went on the attack. In the *New Statesman* she wrote: 'My conclusion is that our Prime Minister deceived us . . . He exaggerated the imminent threat from WMDs.'

The next day the Intelligence and Security Select Committee (ISC) published its annual report in which it criticized the way intelligence had been used in the 'dodgy dossier'. The report also contained a few lines of qualified support for the September dossier, but press comment, not surprisingly, focused on the 'dodgy' document. This upset Campbell. He later told Hutton: 'The BBC and other parts of the media chose to focus not on that part of their [the ISC's] report [concerning the September dossier] but on the part which criticised the Government over the February briefing paper.'

A week later, more bad news. Clare Short and Robin Cook gave evidence to the Foreign Affairs Select Committee in which they said that they had received intelligence briefings before the war that did not justify the claim of an imminent WMD threat from Iraq.

The next day it was the turn of Pauline Neville-Jones, a former JIC Chairman (and, incidentally, a serving BBC Governor), who, as usual, did not mince her words. The February dossier, she said, was 'a serious

mistake . . . it discredits the earlier material [the September dossier], it is a mistake. I think you should not do cut and paste jobs.'

By now the pressure was mounting for Campbell to appear before the Foreign Affairs Committee. But Downing Street was still holding firm. At Prime Minister's Questions on 18 June, Tony Blair, pressed on the issue, refused to give ground, citing an apparently unshakeable constitutional precedent: 'It has never been the case that officials have given evidence to Select Committees.'

The day after that another Foreign Affairs Committee witness, Ibrahim al-Marishi, whose doctoral thesis was the unacknowledged source for the 'dodgy dossier', said that the 'reckless' use of his work had endangered the lives of his family in Iraq.

The Foreign Affairs Committee now wrote to Campbell again asking him to appear. Campbell took a few days to reply.

It was now clear that the sheer weight of evidence against Campbell was likely to result in a report that was severely critical of him. The Sunday papers on 22 June were full of stories on this theme. The *Mail on Sunday* claimed that Campbell was 'on the brink of resignation' and that 'the powerful FAC has stepped up the fight to force him to answer for his actions'. The *Independent on Sunday* even managed to get a Labour member of the Committee, Eric Illsley, to go on the record: 'Given the evidence so far that Campbell's staff put this document [the 'dodgy dossier'] together, made a complete botch of it, and then put it out as serious research, I think the report is going to point the finger at him.' Campbell was later to tell Hutton: 'I sensed over that weekend, through reading some of the comments of the Labour MPs in the Sunday press, that the FAC was moving in a very, very bad direction for the Government.' What he meant, of course, was a very, very bad direction for Alastair Campbell.

By now Campbell's position was weakened. Even the usually loyal Foreign Secretary, Jack Straw, had told the Committee on 23 June that the February dossier was 'a complete Horlicks'.

Campbell decided the time had come to act. He consulted Tony Blair, who said the constitutional precedent was not so unshakeable after all and that Campbell could go before the FAC. On 25 June Campbell gave evidence.

*   *   *

The proceedings opened with the chairman making a feeble joke about 'Campbell in the soup' – an indication of the weakness of Campbell's position. But Campbell was not fazed for a moment. Instead he used his appearance to launch a full frontal verbal assault on the BBC. He accused it of lying and of running an anti-war agenda. It was an unprecedented attack on the BBC's journalism from the man in charge of all the Government's information services, a civil servant with unprecedented powers.

So why did Campbell do it? Why make such a public attack on the BBC, an attack that was eventually to lead to Campbell losing his job and which did lasting damage to the Labour Government he was supposed to be representing?

An article in *The Scotsman* the following morning captured what happened:

Mr Campbell did exactly what he wanted to do. He blunted the attack immediately by putting his hands up for the dodgy dossier and then used the remaining three hours to perform the oldest trick in the spin doctor's manual: distract attention from the government's shortcomings by feeding the media with an alternative story.

And the media – in particular the Murdoch press – lapped it up. *The Sun*'s headline the next morning was 'Campbell: BBC Liars'. *The Times* took the same tack: 'Campbell accuses BBC of lying'. No wonder Campbell was pleased. As he later told Hutton: 'I felt a lot better ... I had opened a flank on the BBC.'

It is clear that the whole attack on the BBC from Campbell was a means of diverting attention away from the 'dodgy dossier' and the disgraceful way he and his team had produced it. He decided that attack was the best means of defence. It was as cynical as that. And for Campbell, in the short term, it worked. Every time he was asked a difficult question by the Foreign Affairs Select Committee he attacked the BBC.

I suspect that Campbell had been wanting to 'get' the BBC for a long time as a way of exacting revenge for our refusal to follow his agenda during the Iraq war. In particular he had wanted to 'get' Gilligan and the *Today* programme. Campbell had told me personally how much he disliked the programme and we knew, in particular, he disliked its main

presenter, John Humphrys. We had also received complaints about Gilligan, who, in his time on the programme, had embarrassed both the Ministry of Defence and the Government with good stories. It was Gilligan who had shown up the tactical ineffectiveness of the bombing in Kosovo and the lack of any link between Saddam Hussein and al-Qaeda. He had also revealed that British troops had not been properly equipped on a number of occasions; and of course Campbell had hated Gilligan's reports from Baghdad during the war. But his dislike of Gilligan went back to 2000 when Gilligan had warned that a proposed European Union 'Code of Law' could be an EU Constitution that would form the basis of an EU super state. After that, Campbell called him 'gullible Gilligan'.

At the Select Committee Campbell personalized his attack by saying we had accused the Prime Minister of lying, which was completely untrue. Again this was a typical Campbell ploy. No one had ever mentioned the Prime Minister, but it suited Campbell to claim that criticism of Number Ten or the Government meant directly accusing the Prime Minister of lying. By the same logic the Prime Minister would have had to have taken personal responsibility for the 'dodgy dossier', even though no one had suggested that Blair himself knew it was nonsense. Campbell turned what Dr Kelly had told Gilligan into a personal attack by the BBC on the Prime Minister. To his discredit, Tony Blair later went along with this.

The ferocity and wide-ranging nature of the attack meant that the BBC had little choice but to go into battle. Campbell had attacked much of the BBC's output and in particular its coverage of the war. A comprehensive Cardiff University study later showed that, if anything, the BBC had slightly favoured the official Government position rather than an anti-war one.

On the day of Campbell's attack on the BBC at the Select Committee, 25 June, the BBC Executive was away at one of the strategy conferences we held three times a year. This time we were at Witley Park in Surrey, where we went every June. As usual we had some bonding activity, in which members of the Executive did silly things to make them feel more of a team. On paper these sorts of events seem ridiculous but they are very effective at bringing a team of people together as a group of friends.

At the 2003 BBC Executive conference we had an 'It's a Knockout' competition. We were halfway through when Richard Sambrook took a

call on his mobile phone. He walked over and told me that Alastair Campbell had gone ballistic at the Foreign Affairs Committee attacking the BBC; but as we only had the headlines we decided to carry on with the game, probably because my team was winning. We were still ahead until the last round when we all had to do country dancing. At that moment Alan Yentob came into his own and his team won on 'artistic merit'. What a joke!

An hour or so later we had the full report of what Campbell had said to the Committee and I agreed that we had to respond. Richard set off back to London to prepare himself for being interviewed on the *Today* programme about the attack the following morning; the rest of us stayed at the conference. We all agreed the next morning that Richard had done a pretty good job defending the BBC and making the point that it was not the BBC who had made the allegations against the Government but a high-level source who had been involved in preparing the September dossier.

I got home from the conference to find a fax Alastair Campbell had sent to the office. It was clearly an attempt to be friendly saying that he had always admired both my career and my commitment and that he was 'sorry' he had had to attack the BBC in the way he had. I didn't believe a word of it. Campbell had refused to take advantage of any of the official complaints channels open to him – going through our complaints process or taking his complaint to the Broadcasting Standards Commission, or even coming unofficially to Gavyn or myself. If he had wanted to be friendly he could have phoned to say that Number Ten regarded the Gilligan report extremely seriously and asked us to take a look at it.

It was very clear to me that Campbell's attack was a mixture of diversionary tactic and revenge against the BBC. He was not interested in a proper investigation: he wanted a public bust-up for political reasons. His letter to me was part of his game and I didn't want to play along with it. I decided not to respond.

Richard Sambrook, too, had received another three-page letter from Campbell in which, in typical Campbell style, he had demanded the answers to a series of questions, and wanted a reply that same day. He had also released his letter to the press.

On the Friday I was supposed to be one of a panel judging a competition to decide on the architect for the new BBC music centre planned for

White City. Ever since joining the BBC I'd taken a keen interest in the architecture of any new BBC buildings. At one time the BBC had wonderful buildings everyone could be proud of, but in recent years we had built inappropriate extensions and some really ugly new structures. I was determined that this wouldn't happen in my time as Director-General. John Smith, who was in charge of property, agreed with this approach, and Alan Yentob, a trained architect, played a major part in implementation.

After talking to Gavyn Davies first thing on the Friday morning I decided to pull out of the panel and spend the day with Richard Sambrook and Mark Damazer helping to draft the BBC's official reply to Campbell.

Replying quickly was a mistake, my mistake. We allowed ourselves to be driven by Campbell's timetable and, as I later explained to Lord Hutton, what I should have done that day was to stop the process, refer the whole complaint to the BBC's Programme Complaint Unit, and ask for a speedy judgement. We should then have told Downing Street what we had done and that they would have to wait for their reply.

Instead we sent a detailed response to Campbell that only upset him even more. He received it while he was watching the tennis at Wimbledon, got into his car, and drove to the studios of ITN. He demanded to be interviewed live on Channel Four News and laid into the BBC once more in a quite extraordinary fashion. He told Tony Blair what he was doing and Blair reluctantly agreed. Even Campbell later accepted that his behaviour had been over the top; Blair clearly had little control over him. We all thought that by then Campbell was completely out of control. Evidence is now emerging that suggests we were right.

According to *Alastair Campbell* by Peter Oborne (political editor of *The Spectator*) and Simon Walters (political editor of the *Mail on Sunday*), published in June 2004, Campbell rang Jon Smith, the Press Association's political editor, a few days later and started to shout at him when he wouldn't file a story about an issue that Campbell wanted reported. Smith told him to stop shouting and Campbell reportedly replied, 'I can't, I can't, they're after me, everybody's after me.' Smith told Campbell that he was 'going round the twist again'.

Campbell's diaries – parts of which were published on the Hutton Inquiry's website – show that his intention had been to 'fuck Gilligan'. According to Oborne and Walters, at a later event held by the Blairs to say

goodbye to Sir David Manning, who was leaving Number Ten to become Britain's Ambassador to Washington, Campbell is reported to have embarrassed people by saying openly that he wanted to wreak vengeance on 'that fucking little shit Gilligan'.

In one of a number of conversations Gavyn Davies had with Tony Blair over this period, all initiated by Blair, Gavyn said that he thought Campbell's behaviour was over the top. Blair replied, 'Don't we all'. Incidentally, Gavyn is convinced to this day that Blair had surmised what would be in the Hutton Report a couple of months before it was published because, suddenly, the calls from Blair dried up.

It was around this time that Mark Damazer remembered that *Newsnight* had run a story on weapons of mass destruction at about the same time as the *Today* programme report. When he pulled out the tape he found incredible similarities between the story on *Newsnight* by their science editor Susan Watts and Gilligan's reports on the *Today* programme. This was important because either Watts had a different source, in which case there were now two anonymous sources for the same story, or it was the same source and supported Gilligan. Either way, it was good news for the BBC because it corroborated the story.

Richard Sambrook saw Susan Watts and asked her who her source was. She refused to tell him. She also failed to tell him that she had recorded the conversation with her source, a fact that was not to come out for several weeks. She later complained to Lord Hutton that Richard had bullied her. She must be very sensitive, since Richard is about the least bullying person I know. Of course what we all found out later, when we heard the tapes, was that David Kelly was her source, that he'd given her the whole story before giving it to Gilligan, and that she'd missed it.

Watts herself seems to have realized this. The tape of her interview with Dr Kelly records her telling him: 'I've looked back at my notes [of her interview with him on 7 May] and you were actually quite specific at that time – I may have missed a trick on that one.' Later the editor of *Newsnight*, George Entwistle, asked Mark Damazer if he thought *Newsnight* had missed a great story.

Gilligan had given evidence to the Foreign Affairs Committee before Campbell's attack on the BBC. His appearance was barely reported – real evidence that the story was dying until it was reignited by Campbell. We

now thought the Committee should see the item on *Newsnight*, which was broadcast in two parts on 2 June and 4 June, before they published their report. We therefore sent them the tapes as a matter of urgency and pointed out their importance.

The *Newsnight* report only convinced us further that Campbell was running a vendetta against Gilligan and the *Today* programme. Why hadn't he complained about *Newsnight* since it had reported virtually the same story as the *Today* programme?

It is true that Susan Watts did not say the Government probably knew the 45-minute claim was wrong and had ordered it to be put into the dossier. But she did report her source saying that the 45-minute figure 'was seized on and it's unfortunate that it was. That's why there is the argument between the intelligence services and Cabinet Office/Number Ten, because they picked up on it and once they'd picked up on it you can't pull it back from them.'

Watts had also said that she had been told by 'a senior official involved with the process of pulling together the dossier' that 'in the run-up to publishing the dossier the Government was obsessed with finding intelligence on immediate Iraqi threats. The Government's insistence the Iraqi threat was imminent was a Downing Street interpretation of an intelligence conclusion.' She quoted her unnamed source (Dr Kelly) at length. For example, on the imminence of the Iraqi threat, Kelly had made it clear that while there might be a future threat, the current threat was less serious. 'But that unfortunately was not expressed strongly in the dossier because that takes away the case for war.' In other words, her reports made clear that the intelligence services were unhappy because Downing Street had exaggerated the scale of the threat from Iraq. In essence, this is exactly the claim made in Gilligan's report. The Prime Minister later said he would have had to resign if the Gilligan story was true, but he has never mentioned the Watts story. Surely if this had been true the same would have applied? And yet no one from Downing Street has ever denied the Watts story.

We had already told the Foreign Affairs Committee that if they unanimously told us that our report was wrong on the basis of concrete evidence that they had seen, then we would accept that the Gilligan report was wrong and that we would withdraw it and apologize. There was not much chance of that happening because Number Ten was, not surpris-

ingly, refusing to let the Committee see the various drafts of the September dossier.

We now know that if the Committee had seen the drafts its conclusions would have been embarrassing for Number Ten. When they were all revealed to the Hutton Inquiry, the drafts showed that not only had people in Number Ten suggested significant changes to the relevant parts of the dossier but that Campbell himself had deliberately misled the Foreign Affairs Committee. Campbell had told the Committee of the changes to the dossier that he himself had suggested but, crucially, he omitted any reference to the point he made about the 45-minute claim – the very detail they were interested in. He didn't tell the Committee that he had had an exchange with John Scarlett, the Chairman of the Joint Intelligence Committee, on this very point. If he had told the full story it would have supported what Kelly had alleged.

That neither Hutton nor the Committee has ever taken Campbell to task for misleading them is, at the very least, a failure of our democratic system. Hutton left it to the Committee and the Committee has since ducked it. It seems that if you are the Government's head of information you can mislead Parliament with impunity.

The story was not going away and during that week Gavyn was anxious that the Governors be given the opportunity to discuss the matter. He, personally, had investigated the whole thing in great detail since Campbell's public outburst and discussed it privately with a number of Governors who were concerned at the ferocity of the attack on the BBC's independence. With the Foreign Affairs Committee report due to be published the following week, he wanted to call an emergency Governors' meeting, but I cautioned against. I thought it wasn't necessary to bring the full force of the Governors into the battle at this stage and could see that it might leave the Governors in a difficult position if Gilligan's story was eventually shown to be wrong.

On the Friday, 4 July, I was in Northern Ireland for one of my regular out of London visits. In particular I was there to open the BBC's new roof gardens where the staff could relax at lunchtimes or in the evenings. It was a classic 'Making it Happen' initiative.

While in Belfast I got a phone call from Simon Milner, the BBC Secretary, to tell me that Gavyn had called a meeting of the Governors for that Sunday evening and that we would all be receiving a pack of

information over the weekend. I told Simon that I thought it was a mistake but that obviously I would be there.

The following morning *The Guardian* ran the story as their front-page lead story with the headline 'Dyke Summoned to BBC Crisis Meeting'. Later, when the Governors were accused of being management patsies, I regularly pointed to that headline to show that this wasn't how it was seen at the time.

On the Sunday Sue and I were due to go to Wimbledon for the men's tennis finals. As luck would have it, Cherie Blair was sitting in front of us, so the photographers had a field day. I've known Cherie for twenty years but that day she said hello to Sue and then looked straight through me as if I didn't exist. I remember thinking then how sad it was that she didn't recognize that old friendships are far more important than temporary battles. But then perhaps that can't apply to people who spend their lives in politics. As Enoch Powell once said, 'There are no friendships in politics, only alliances.'

I went straight from Wimbledon to the Governors' meeting, still in my cream suit. I remember being asked on the way into Broadcasting House one of those banal questions that journalists shout at you when it's clear you won't be interviewed. The question was, 'Is this the end of the BBC?' I replied with one word: 'Hardly'.

I agreed with Gavyn that I wouldn't go to the first part of the meeting. When I did go into the meeting, along with other members of the management team, Richard Sambrook and I were closely questioned about the story and the processes we'd followed. We'd been through all this with Gavyn over recent weeks and he understood all the detail. He hoped the Governors would support the position we had all taken. Interestingly, perhaps the most supportive Governor that day was Sarah Hogg, who was not physically at the meeting but was on the line from her home in Lincolnshire. She was adamant that we shouldn't show any weakness. The only waverer that day was the Deputy Chairman, Richard Ryder.

Of course at that time none of the Governors knew who Gilligan's source had been. At that meeting only Richard Sambrook knew Kelly's name, although I knew his position. At the meeting Richard described Andrew Gilligan as a reporter who tended to 'paint in primary colours', meaning that subtlety was not his strong point and that, as a result, he occasionally went too strongly on a story.

In the end the Board put out a statement that said that it 'emphatically rejects Mr Campbell's claim that large parts of the BBC had an agenda against the war' and it called on Campbell to withdraw the allegations. They also said that the *Today* programme had properly followed the BBC's producers' guidelines in broadcasting the Gilligan story and that it had been in the public interest to do so.

However, the Board did say that the *Today* programme could have put the allegation in the story to Number Ten as well as to the Ministry of Defence before it was broadcast – something we all agreed with – and that it intended to look again at rules under which BBC reporters and presenters were permitted to write for newspapers. I think the Governors felt that if Gilligan had not named Campbell in his newspaper article Campbell would not have reacted the way he did.

Finally, the Governors said the following:

> The Board wishes to place on record that the BBC has never accused the Prime Minister of lying, or of seeking to take Britain to war under misleading or false pretences. The BBC did not have an agenda in its war coverage, nor does it have any agenda which questions the integrity of the Prime Minister.

Later, Michael Grade (soon to be the next Chairman of the BBC) happened to be on *Question Time* and discussed the Governors' actions that night. His comments are very instructive. He said:

> I applaud the governors of the BBC. I wish I'd had them when I was at the BBC when we were going through *Real Lives* and everything else, because the first time there was ever a sabre rattled by Downing Street in our direction the governors shopped the management straight away ... I applaud Gavyn Davies and the governors for standing up to Downing Street and making sure that everyone understood that the independence of the BBC was not going to be compromised.

The day after the Governors' meeting, 7 July, the Foreign Affairs Committee report was published. It was a bit of a damp squib with both sides claiming victory. Jack Straw, the Foreign Secretary, came out and said

that the Committee had cleared Campbell and that the BBC should withdraw its allegations. He didn't point out that the report had divided on party lines and that it had cleared Campbell by one vote only.

We in turn pointed out that the Committee had said unanimously that the 45-minute claim did not warrant the prominence given to it in the September dossier and that the Committee had asked the Government to explain why it had done so. The Foreign Affairs Committee report also criticized the September dossier for using language that was too assertive in relation to the underlying intelligence – or, as some might say, 'sexed up'. The Committee also said the Government should set out whether or not it believed that what it had said in the dossier was still true.

Around that time there were two attempts to broker a peace between Downing Street and the BBC. First Peter Mandelson rang Caroline Thomson, the BBC's Director of Policy and an old friend of both of us. He suggested a way out; it required the BBC's accepting that Gilligan's story wasn't true whilst maintaining that we were right to broadcast it when we did. Caroline, Richard Sambrook, and I discussed this suggestion and agreed that we needed to try and find a compromise but that this wasn't it. We couldn't say the story wasn't true. When we discussed it with Gavyn he was against dealing with Mandelson at all because, he said, we couldn't be sure that our discussions would stay private and, more importantly, he didn't think there should be a backstairs deal on a matter of such public interest.

When Caroline took the message back to Mandelson, a former Labour spin doctor himself, he told her that the BBC would now have the full force of the Government's PR machine thrown at it. Nice people.

The second approach came on the morning of 7 July, the same day the Select Committee published its report, when the Prime Minister rang Gavyn Davies in what Blair said was an attempt to calm the whole thing down. He offered the same deal as Mandelson, but Gavyn told him that he couldn't agree to it because we were not prepared to withdraw the story. Blair also said he had told Campbell to back off and needed us to make a similar gesture. As a result, in a speech I was making at the Radio Academy Festival in Birmingham the following day, I added a phrase thanking Alastair Campbell for withdrawing his more outrageous remarks about the BBC. I suggested that we should all agree to disagree and that we should all move on. Some hope.

Whether Blair genuinely wanted to calm everything down is highly questionable. On the very day he spoke to Gavyn we now know he spent the rest of the morning in a series of meetings in Downing Street, none of them minuted, with political staff and civil servants deciding what should be done to exploit the fact that an official called David Kelly had now come forward to say he could have been Gilligan's source. Kelly had told the Ministry of Defence that, while he had talked to Gilligan, he hadn't said what Gilligan claimed he'd said. The strategy of how the Government should put Kelly's name into the public agenda was devised that day at a meeting attended by the Prime Minister.

For some reason Campbell, the Defence Secretary Geoff Hoon, and others had convinced themselves that once it was known that Gilligan's source was not an intelligence officer – which, to be fair, was how Gilligan had once mistakenly described him – the whole story would fall apart. Campbell's diary entry for that day notes that he and Hoon had agreed that it would 'fuck Gilligan' if Kelly turned out to be his source. Of course that didn't happen as the BBC refused to name its source even after Kelly had been named.

Over the next couple of days the Ministry of Defence and the Downing Street press office jumped through all sorts of hoops to make sure Kelly's name became known, including the farcical stunt of allowing journalists to suggest name after name until finally they hit on the right one, which the Ministry of Defence then confirmed.

On Monday 7 July Gavyn got a call from a Labour MP telling him that he'd had dinner the night before with a senior member of SIS (MI6) who happened to be an old friend. He had told the MP that Gilligan's story was absolutely right and that the original intelligence on the 45-minute claim had come through a reliable Iraqi contact who had been given the information by a brigadier in the Iraqi army. SIS had forwarded the information with provisos, only for these to be taken out, and what was left was then used as definite intelligence. Interestingly, when the Butler Inquiry, which reviewed the use of intelligence on weapons of mass destruction, reported in July 2004 it told virtually the identical story.

I got in touch with the MP and asked him if he could fix up a meeting between me and his friend. That was in the process of being arranged when David Kelly committed suicide. Gavyn also got a call from a Liberal Democrat peer who told him that a friend had been told by the Attorney

279

General himself that his original opinion on the legality of the war had been judged not sufficiently strong and needed to be strengthened. These were just two of many calls we were getting at that time from people in high places telling us to keep chasing and that the story was right. Some of them were from people close to the security services themselves. I myself was told by a very senior military official over dinner that it was very unlikely that they would find any weapons of mass destruction in the conventional sense and he personally doubted if there had ever been any.

At this time there were few moments of light relief but one came when I was phoned and offered a special number plate. I was asked if I'd like to buy it for £250. The number was MI6 WMD. I bought it with the intention of giving it to Richard Sambrook as a Christmas present when the whole story had died away. I still have it hidden away in a cupboard at home.

Once Dr Kelly had been named, the Foreign Affairs Select Committee wanted to interview him. I have no doubt that the Ministry of Defence and Number Ten believed Kelly would go before the Committee, say he was Gilligan's source, and then dump all over Gilligan. Instead when he appeared before the Committee on 15 July he convinced them that he was not Gilligan's source at all. He also told at least one deliberate lie when talking about dealing with Susan Watts. When the Conservative MP Richard Ottaway read from the transcript of the *Newsnight* programme Dr Kelly looked particularly uneasy.

I watched his appearance and was surprised that Kelly didn't play the game Campbell and others expected. By then I knew he was Gilligan's source and suspected he was also Susan Watts'; and yet the inept performance of members of the Committee in interviewing him had left them and the public totally confused. I felt terribly sorry for Dr Kelly: he looked like a man whom the politicians wanted to hang out to dry and who had been abandoned by everyone he'd worked with. He looked uncomfortable and his evidence was vague.

Two days later Andrew Gilligan gave evidence to the Committee for a second time, this time in private. It was a very hostile affair and some of the Labour members of the Committee had files in front of them that we suspected had been prepared for them by the Downing Street Information Department. So much for the independence of the legislature.

The Labour chairman of the Committee, the deeply unimpressive Donald Anderson, whom the Government had tried to dump from the chair after the last election, said after the session he thought Gilligan an 'unsatisfactory witness'.

Much later I had a long discussion with a senior member of the FAC who has asked for his name to be withheld. He told me that he now recognized that the Committee had made a great error. He said that they had disliked Gilligan and hadn't believed him, but that they had liked and respected Kelly and had believed what he'd told them. Now, he said, they recognized they had got it the wrong way round: Gilligan was telling the truth and Kelly wasn't.

We now know that at exactly the same time as Gilligan was being attacked by the Committee and Tony Blair was being given a standing ovation in Congress on his trip to Washington, having said that history would prove him and President Bush right with regard to their Iraq policy, Dr Kelly was lying dead in a field in Oxfordshire.

Until that happened I believed the story was running out of steam. Neither the BBC nor the Government were going to back down, nor were we going to say whether or not Dr Kelly was our source. All stories die in the end because the journalists covering them – and, more to the point, their editors and news desks – get bored with them. I thought that was happening to this story when the following morning, Friday 18 July, I took a call in the car on my way to work from Richard Sambrook, who told me the dramatic news that Dr Kelly was missing from home. He had left the day before to go for a walk and hadn't returned. We later heard that a body had been found. The story was back on all the front pages.

For the BBC this changed the world. We no longer had a source to protect. When she heard the news, Susan Watts told Richard Sambrook that Dr Kelly *had* been her source and that she had tape recorded her last conversation with him. Richard, Mark Damazer, and I all agreed that, with no source to protect, we should now tell the world that Dr Kelly had been our source, but that we couldn't do this until the body had been identified and we had informed Dr Kelly's family.

On the Saturday afternoon, after Dr Kelly's body had been identified, we told the family that we were going to make a statement and discussed

with them what it would say. They asked us to hold off until the Sunday, which we willingly did. The last thing we wanted to do in these terrible circumstances was to cause the family even more distress.

On the Sunday Sue and I were at the eighteenth birthday party of Michael Pallett, the son of my friend from university, Marianne Geary, and her husband Keith. To be truthful Sue was at the lunch party being held in the garden, I was in the house talking to all and sundry at the BBC. Midway through the afternoon I got a call from Mark Damazer asking me to ring Andrew Gilligan.

There were real worries inside the BBC about Gilligan's state of mind, and even fears that he might commit suicide. He was a relatively young man who lived on his own and was not known as someone with lots of friends. He was also under enormous pressure. Campbell had thrown the whole PR operation of the state against him, just as Peter Mandelson had promised, and he was being attacked by anyone and everyone. He was being blamed for Dr Kelly's death by politicians and journalists alike. I couldn't understand why he was being blamed as he'd done everything he could to keep the identity of his source confidential.

I rang him, left a message, and a few minutes later he rang back. We talked at some length and it was clear he was very agitated that he wasn't being allowed by the BBC to make a press statement. I judged that a controlled statement would do no harm and would certainly calm Andrew down, so I agreed. It did the trick and by the evening he seemed much more relaxed.

We got back home to find a *Sun* journalist outside the door of our house, so I parked the car further up the road and went in through one of the numerous other ways into the house. Later, when I thought the journalist had gone, I walked up the road to get the car only to find the journalist shouting at me, saying things like, 'Mr Dyke, haven't you got blood on your hands?' Who would willingly do a job like that?

In the week after Dr Kelly died we all gathered in the BBC lawyers' office – Gavyn, Richard, Mark Damazer, the lawyers, and me – to listen to Susan Watts' tape of her interview with Dr Kelly for the first time. The outside world still didn't know a tape existed but it proved to be remarkable in that it supported much of what Andrew Gilligan had reported back in May.

Here was Dr Kelly naming Alastair Campbell, talking about Number

Ten being 'desperate for information' to put into the dossier and about the 45-minute claim being a statement 'that just got out of all proportion' and about which he was 'uneasy'; he also said that it was difficult to get certain views into the dossier 'because people at the top of the ladder didn't want to hear some of the things'. Talking of Iraq, Kelly said that the concern wasn't the weapons that Saddam had but what he might have in the future, 'but that wasn't expressed strongly enough in the dossier because that takes away the case for war to a certain extent'.

It was remarkable stuff and showed very clearly that Dr Kelly hadn't told the truth either to the Ministry of Defence or to the Select Committee. Everyone in the room that day thought it massively strengthened the BBC's position, and Gilligan's. And yet Lord Hutton never seemed to take the Watts tape on board. It should have been dynamite at the inquiry but wasn't. It showed that Gilligan's story had been overwhelmingly true. Those who still believe that Gilligan exaggerated what Dr Kelly had told him should re-read the transcript of the tape. When Hutton replayed the tape in court it had been remastered and much of the really incriminating evidence was inaudible, so it didn't have the public impact it deserved. As William Rees-Mogg said later: 'I found Lord Hutton's report a defective document . . . he gave too little weight to crucial parts of the evidence, including David Kelly's interview with Susan Watts and the colourful extracts from Alastair Campbell's diary.'

There were two more events of note in the weeks that followed. First, I had another exchange of letters with the Prime Minister with me writing to complain that one Cabinet Minister had briefed journalists in the days after Dr Kelly died saying that 'the problem with the BBC was that it had too much money and Greg Dyke' and that after Hutton the Government would 'sort these things out'. The Minister had used the word 'revenge' on several occasions. The journalist who had been briefed said it sounded like the Minister had been reading from a script prepared by someone else.

In my letter to Tony Blair I said that both Gavyn Davies and I regarded this as 'a blatant threat to the funding and editorial independence of the BBC from a member of your Cabinet' and that while I was sure that the Prime Minister hadn't sanctioned the briefing I was also sure he would recognize 'the political and constitutional implications' of what was said. He sent back a letter in which he said he totally supported the

independence of the BBC and that there was no question of the licence fee decision being affected by any of this. He also said that he was fed up with stories driven by 'anonymous sources'. But mine wasn't an anonymous source – I knew for a fact which Cabinet Minister had done the briefing.

The second event was of course the resignation of Alastair Campbell. The BBC's Political Editor, Andy Marr, had got a very strong hint some weeks earlier that Campbell was going to go, but it wasn't until 29 August that he finally announced his departure. He spun himself out brilliantly, making it look like it was his decision, but it wasn't. Blair later told Gavyn Davies in one of their conversations that Campbell had to go.

From the moment Dr Kelly killed himself it was obvious that Campbell's decision to go to war with the BBC had backfired spectacularly on the Government, on Blair, and on Campbell himself. An eminent and loyal public servant had died. Campbell had wanted Kelly named. Now Kelly was dead and Blair was insisting that Campbell was out of Downing Street. Amongst other things, there was a real fear that his diaries would prove embarrassing and that the untruths he had told to the Foreign Affairs Committee about his involvement in the September dossier would rebound on the whole of Number Ten. By Campbell leaving, the Prime Minister would be able to say that Downing Street had cleaned up its act.

In many ways the death of Dr Kelly was the end of the whole saga for a while and things calmed down. The Government announced that Lord Hutton would conduct an inquiry and everything went quiet while we waited for the process to start. I'd persuaded my family that we should spend our summer holiday walking the Inca trail, cycling and white water rafting in Peru. Sadly, they all had to go without me. As they left, Sue said: 'I was only doing this because you wanted to go. Do you really think this is how I wanted to spend my summer holiday?' I did manage to get out for the second week, though I missed the difficult bit of walking the trail.

I arrived back from Peru for the first day of the Hutton Inquiry on 1 August. We were all impressed by the way the inquiry was run. I was particularly impressed by the barrister for the inquiry, James Dingemans, who seemed to be seriously interested in getting at the truth. The only time when I thought he and Hutton let themselves down was when they

were too reverential to Tony Blair when he gave evidence. He should have been recalled for cross-examination as there were questions that should have been put to him. In particular, he should have been asked about his role in the 'outing' of Dr Kelly as he clearly played a part. Hutton has since said he didn't recall Blair for cross-examination because he didn't want the Prime Minister to receive a public mauling. Surely Hutton's job was to get at the truth and not to be over-concerned about the sensitivities of the Prime Minister? This is an illustration of Hutton's whole attitude when it came to writing his report.

We judged that there were three particularly bad moments for the BBC during the inquiry. The first was when an e-mail from Kevin Marsh to his boss was revealed saying that Gilligan's report was 'marred by loose language'. I had never seen this before, or heard the sentiment expressed.

The second was when Gilligan was answering questions and said that when he reported Dr Kelly as saying that the Government 'probably knew it was wrong' it was not a direct quote but his interpretation of what Dr Kelly had told him. Again this was not what we believed he had told us.

The third was the e-mail that Gilligan had sent to the Liberal Democrat member of the Select Committee David Chidgey saying that Dr Kelly had been Susan Watts' source. At that time none of us – including Gilligan – knew this for a fact, and it was a totally unacceptable thing for Gilligan to have done.

Although these were all serious concerns, the Government and the Ministry of Defence faced even more embarrassing moments during the inquiry, particularly over the way in which they had conspired to 'out' Dr Kelly.

The day before I was due to appear before Hutton I rang my mother to warn her that there would be some more publicity. To cheer her up I told her that on the same morning I was doing a reading at Thora Hird's memorial service at Westminster Abbey. My mum thought for a moment and came back with two lines only an 88-year-old could come up with. On Hutton she just said, 'Yes, dear. I read in the paper you were going to a meeting'; and on Thora Hird she went quiet, thought for a moment, and then said: 'She's dead, you know.'

My own appearance before Hutton was rather a non-event. I wasn't called in the first round of witnesses, was called almost as an afterthought, and was not recalled for cross-examination. I was rather nervous and

GREG DYKE: INSIDE STORY

stuck very much to the witness statement I'd submitted in advance, as advised by our QC. When I wandered off it to try to point out something I thought was really important, Mr Dingemans rapidly chopped me to pieces. I realized then that this was the barristers' pitch and the barristers' game and that I had to play by their rules.

The inquiry closed on 25 September and Lord Hutton said he hoped to report before Christmas. In the end it was 28 January before he published his report. And when he did, it took virtually everyone by surprise.

Why Hutton Was Wrong

In the months after Gavyn Davies and I left the BBC, which in my case was the same day that Lord Ryder made his abject apology, the BBC stopped trying to defend the position it had taken throughout the Hutton Inquiry that it had been right to broadcast Andrew Gilligan reporting Dr Kelly's concerns.

What this has meant is that in the months since Lord Hutton's report was published a myth has been fostered. The myth is that Gilligan and the BBC made a series of very serious mistakes. This is simply not the case. Gilligan did make errors, a couple of which were serious; but it was Lord Hutton, not the BBC, who got it fundamentally wrong.

Over the months, the BBC could have countered this myth. Instead, led by the acting Chairman, the BBC ran for cover. From the moment Lord Ryder made his apology, with a worried acting Director-General by his side, no one from within the BBC has been allowed to argue the opposite case. This has done great damage to the BBC's integrity and to the reputation of its journalism both in Britain and, more importantly, around the world.

The Governors of the BBC have allowed the myth to become accepted wisdom for fear of reopening the whole issue and reigniting the battle with the Government, while some in management, who know the real story, were so badly bruised during the Hutton process that they have chosen to say very little in public. As a result, the fallacy that was at the heart of the Hutton Report has been left to fester undisturbed. It is time that was corrected.

We now know for certain that Andrew Gilligan's story was nothing

like the 'mountain of untruth' that Tony Blair described it as in the House of Commons on 4 February 2004. Nor was it '100 per cent wrong', as Alastair Campbell claimed in a letter to me of 26 June 2003. We know this because Lord Butler's Review of the intelligence on weapons of mass destruction told us so. It also meant that when Campbell said that the BBC – from Chairman and Director-General down – had lied, it was an inaccurate and disingenuous statement from a man who had himself deliberately misled the House of Commons Foreign Affairs Select Committee when giving evidence on the Kelly affair and who is not unknown for being economical with the truth.

There was a clear public interest in the BBC broadcasting what Dr Kelly had told Andrew Gilligan because of what it told us about the Government's case for going to war in Iraq, about how some in the security services disagreed with the way intelligence was used to justify that decision, and about the Blair Government's obsession with public relations and spin.

Lord Hutton got it wrong on many points, as I shall demonstrate later, but in particular he made a mistake on one crucial issue: his ruling that it was not part of his remit to consider what sort of weapons of mass destruction the Government's dossier on Iraq actually referred to. It is not going too far to say that the entire structure of Lord Hutton's report, and its recommendations, were deeply flawed because of that ruling.

This is not to say that Gilligan didn't make mistakes; he did, and he should not have made them. But his mistakes did not mean the story he was reporting wasn't valid, and not all the mistakes were of his making. Sometimes he reported accurately and in good faith something Dr Kelly had told him that later turned out to be an exaggeration by Dr Kelly himself.

The best way to understand what Hutton got wrong is to analyse what Gilligan actually said in that early-morning broadcast at seven minutes past six on 29 May 2003 and ask how it stacks up against what we know today. It was this early, unscripted, broadcast that caused all the problems.

First, there was an introduction from *Today*'s main presenter John Humphrys:

[JH]: The Government is facing more questions this morning over its claims about weapons of mass destruction in Iraq. Our defence

correspondent is Andrew Gilligan. This in particular, Andy, is Tony Blair saying they'd be ready within 45 minutes.

[AG]: That's right, that was the central claim in his dossier which he published in September, the main case if you like against Iraq and the main statement of the British Government's belief of what it thought Iraq was up to. And what we've been told by one of the senior officials in charge of drawing up that dossier was that actually the Government probably knew that that 45-minute figure was wrong even before it decided to put it in. What this person says is that a week before the publication date of the dossier it was actually rather a bland production. It didn't, the draft prepared for Mr Blair by the intelligence agencies, actually didn't say very much more than was public knowledge already and Downing Street, our source says, ordered it to be sexed up, to be made more exciting and ordered more facts to be discovered.

[JH]: When you say 'more facts to be discovered' does that suggest that they may not have been facts?

[AG]: Well, our source says that the dossier as it was finally published made the intelligence services unhappy because, to quote the source, he said there was basically – that there was, there was – unhappiness because it didn't reflect the considered view they were putting forward: that's a quote from our source. And essentially the 45-minute point was probably the most important thing that was added and the reason it hadn't been in the original draft was that it was – it was only, it came from – one source and most of the other claims were from two, and the intelligence agencies say they don't really believe it was necessarily true because they thought the person making the claim had actually made a mistake, it got – had got – mixed up.

[JH]: Does any of this matter now, all this – all these – months later? The war's been fought and won.

[AG]: Well, the 45 minutes isn't just a detail. It did go to the heart of the Government's case that Saddam was an imminent threat and

it was repeated four times in the dossier including by the Prime Minister himself in the foreword. So I think it probably does matter. Clearly, you know, if – if it was, if it was wrong in good faith, things do – things are – got wrong in good faith. But if they knew if it was wrong before they actually made the claim, that's perhaps a bit more serious.

In the course of his report Gilligan covered about a dozen points but serious questions were only ever raised about five of them. By far the most important, and the one that caused most of the fuss, was when Gilligan said he had been told by his source that 'the Government probably knew that the 45-minute figure was wrong even before it decided to put it in'. I shall return to that later but first I shall analyse the other four points.

First was Gilligan's description of Dr Kelly as 'one of the senior officials in charge of drawing up that dossier'. The mistake here was Dr Kelly's, not Gilligan's. Dr Kelly appears to have overstated his own role in the dossier. Gilligan told the Hutton Inquiry what had happened:

At the end of our May 22nd meeting I asked him how he wanted to be described in the reporting and offered him two alternatives, a senior official involved with the dossier or one of the senior officials in charge of drawing up the dossier. He was happy with both alternatives, he said: fine.

There is no reason to disbelieve Gilligan's account of what Dr Kelly told him, but from what we now know the first of these two descriptions ('a senior official involved with the dossier') is clearly the more accurate. Dr Kelly did draw up one part of the dossier, and he was consulted about the accuracy of the whole document. But he was not in charge of drawing up the dossier. Dr Kelly seems to have been quite keen to underline his role in the dossier. In the interview with him that Susan Watts of *Newsnight* taped he is heard saying: 'I reviewed the whole thing, I was involved with the whole process.'

In these circumstances Gilligan would have been covered by the law of qualified privilege, as defined under the Reynolds defence ruling of October 1999. (Reynolds provides a complete defence to media organiza-

tions, even where false allegations of fact have been reported, so long as publication was the result of 'responsible reporting' on a matter of 'legitimate public interest'.) Lord Hutton got the law wrong on this point when he said 'the right to communicate such information is subject to the qualification . . . that false accusations of fact impugning the integrity of others, including politicians, should not be made by the media'.

What this exposes is that Lord Hutton, who trained as a criminal lawyer, knew little about media law and yet this is what the whole inquiry was about. If Hutton's findings in this area had been a legal judgment they would, arguably, have completely rewritten the rules of journalism in the UK. Had the BBC been able to appeal, we could have shown that Hutton had misunderstood the law and that the whole inquiry was not a 'fair' legal process: the Government chose the judge and then he failed to permit full examination of the witnesses.

In any case, whether Gilligan properly described Dr Kelly is a relatively trivial matter as no one now questions the fact that Kelly had played an important role in drawing up the dossier. As the story unfolded the Government's public relations people did try to underplay Kelly's role. They initially dismissed him as 'a middle ranking official' and Tom Kelly, one of Campbell's lieutenants, famously called him a 'Walter Mitty character'. (Tom Kelly has since been promoted inside Downing Street.) But at the Hutton Inquiry there was no questioning of Dr Kelly's credibility as someone in a position to know about the dossier and weapons of mass destruction in Iraq.

The second point in Gilligan's broadcast that has been questioned was the use of the word 'ordered' in 'ordered more facts to be discovered'.

Gilligan accepted during the inquiry that he had no record of Dr Kelly's using this precise word. Again, on the face of it, this was a serious journalistic error. But in the light of the evidence revealed during the inquiry we can see that although 'ordered' was the wrong word to use, it was not all that far from the right one.

Gilligan's own notes record Dr Kelly as saying 'transformed week before publication to make it sexier'. Later there is a reference to 'Campbell', and then, two lines later, 'not in original draft – dull, he asked if anything else could go in'.

In his evidence to Hutton, Gilligan partially justified his use of the word 'ordered' by explaining that:

He [Kelly] clearly stated that the transformation of the dossier was the responsibility of Campbell, who had asked if anything else could be put in. So again, it was a reasonable conclusion to draw from what he had said.

Gilligan's logic here is not perfect. But we do know that Dr Kelly also told *Newsnight*'s Susan Watts: 'They were desperate for information. They were pushing hard for information that could be released.' What is clear is that the Government was not pushing for evidence that didn't support the case for war. Quite the opposite. It is also clear that pressure for that evidence was coming from the very top. On 3 September 2002 Tony Blair had said at a press conference held in his constituency of Sedgefield:

There is a real and existing threat we have to deal with . . . What is that threat? The threat is an Iraq that carries on building up chemical, biological, nuclear weapons capacity.

And yet on 3 September there was virtually no hard evidence to support that position. By 24 September, when the dossier was published, it had miraculously appeared.

What Dr Kelly told both Gilligan and Watts was strongly supported by the revelation during the Hutton Inquiry of a memo headed 'Questions from No 10'. This was written by someone in the Cabinet Office drafting team only a few days before the dossier went to the printers. It was addressed to the intelligence agencies and set out a number of areas where Downing Street was pressing hard for more information. It ends with the faintly despairing plea:

I appreciate everyone, including us, has been around at least some of these buoys before . . . But No 10 through the Chairman [of the JIC] want the document to be as strong as possible . . . This is therefore a last (!) call for any items of intelligence that agencies think can and should be included.

This doesn't amount to an 'order' in the strict technical sense of the word, but it's not far off it. Imagine yourself as a member of one of the intelligence agencies when this appeared in your e-mail box with all the majesty

of the Number Ten address at the top. Would it not feel like an order? Would you not respond as if it were an order? What would be the consequences of not reacting to such a high level 'request'?

There was another consequence of this relentless pressure to find new intelligence from the very top. As the Butler Report says, it resulted in dubious information being passed up the chain to satisfy the demands of the politicians:

Because of the scarcity of sources and the urgent requirement for intelligence, more credence was given to untried agents than would normally be the case.

This was to have serious consequences as we shall see later.

The third point is Gilligan's claim that Dr Kelly had told him the dossier was 'sexed up'. Hutton decided that this allegation was 'unfounded' and dismissed it out of hand. Yet the evidence on this point is unarguable.

Kelly certainly made the claim, although the actual word 'sexier' was not the sort of word he normally used. Gilligan probably introduced it into the conversation and Dr Kelly picked it up, as so often happens in interviews. Without doubt Gilligan's notes record Kelly as saying that the dossier 'was transformed in the week before it was published, to make it sexier', so Kelly clearly said it.

Another BBC reporter, Gavin Hewitt, having spoken to Kelly, said that it was Kelly's judgement that 'some Number Ten spin did come into play'. And Susan Watts of *Newsnight* taped Kelly saying, 'The word-smithing is actually quite important, and the intelligence community are a pretty cautious lot on the whole, but once you get people presenting it for public consumption then of course they use different words.'

It is clear that Kelly's allegation was of spin, that the dossier had been exaggerated to increase its impact. It was certainly the charge made by one of Kelly's colleagues, 'Mr A', a chemical weapons expert consulted in the preparation of the dossier. He e-mailed Kelly when the dossier was published and described it as 'another example supporting our view that you and I should have been more involved in this than the spin merchants of this administration'. When asked to explain this by the Hutton Inquiry, Mr A said: 'The perception was that the dossier had been round the

houses several times in order to try to find a form of words which would strengthen certain political objectives.'

The phrase to 'sex something up' has now gone into the language – as witnessed by the latest edition of the *Concise Oxford Dictionary* where it is defined as to 'present something in a more interesting or lively way'. But Hutton chose to interpret 'sexing up' in a totally different way, which just happened to support the Government's position. In his report he spells out the meaning he chose to put on it: '[that] the dossier had been embellished with intelligence known or believed to be false or unreliable'. This is a much more serious charge than Gilligan believed Kelly was making when using the term 'sexier'.

Yet even on Hutton's interpretation, the evidence that the wording of the dossier was tampered with in a way that fundamentally altered its meaning is overwhelming. Key passages were hardened up. Caveats were removed or softened, and conditional language was replaced with absolute language.

For example, the draft of 16 September says, in the section called Main Conclusions: 'The Iraqi military **may be able** to deploy these within forty-five minutes.' Three days later, in the draft of 19 September, the same section reads: 'The Iraqi military **are able** to deploy these within forty-five minutes.' A possibility had become a certainty.

Similarly, the first draft of the Executive Summary, written by Alastair Campbell and Tony Blair, says that: 'Intelligence **indicates** that Iraq **could deploy** [chemical and biological weapons] within 45 minutes.' But by the final draft the sentence has been hardened up to: 'We **judge** that Iraq has military plans for the use of chemical and biological weapons, some of which **are deployable** within 45 minutes.'

Now these two significant changes might have been justifiable if new intelligence had become available. But we know that there was no new evidence on the 45-minutes claim after 9 September; yet these redrafts took place after that date.

Throughout the dossier caveats were removed or softened, and conditional language was replaced with absolute language. When the Butler committee, which reviewed all the intelligence, reported in July 2004 it made this point in spades. It said:

The language in the dossier may have left readers the impression that there was fuller and firmer intelligence behind the judgements

than was the case; our view . . . is that judgements in the dossier went to (although not beyond) the outer limits of intelligence available.

A simpler way of putting it would have been to say that the dossier had been 'sexed up'. What Lord Butler conspicuously failed to tell us was who took out the caveats, who replaced the conditional language; in other words, who 'sexed up' the dossier.

These changes were what so upset Dr Brian Jones, Britain's most experienced intelligence official working on weapons of mass destruction, who had seen the original intelligence and knew that it did not reflect what was being said in the final draft of the dossier. For him, this change of language was not just a matter of spin, of putting the best gloss on available facts, of pushing intelligence to its outer limits. For Dr Jones, changing the language of an assessment was tantamount to changing the facts on which it was based.

When Dr Jones described to the inquiry the serious concerns his team had expressed on seeing the final draft of the dossier, Hutton interjected to ask if these concerns were just 'matters of language'. Dr Jones, a man of some dignity, gave a memorably withering reply: 'My Lord, they were about language, but language is the means by which we communicate an assessment so they were also about the assessment.'

This was not the view of those at the top, such as the Defence Secretary Geoff Hoon, who gave the impression that he simply couldn't understand what all the fuss was about over a few words here and there. 'I was aware,' Hoon told Hutton dismissively, 'that two officials had expressed some concern about certain language used in the dossier . . . I emphasize that this was of a *linguistic* kind.'

Hutton, as ever, came down against the views of the lower ranks in favour of those in higher places. But the evidence that the dossier was definitely 'sexed up' is there on the website for everyone to read. Hutton's verdict cannot change the truth revealed by the unexplained alterations to the drafts of the September dossier. And remember these were the very drafts that Downing Street refused to allow the Foreign Affairs Select Committee to see. We now know why.

The fourth point at issue is the assertion that the 45-minutes claim was not included in the early drafts of the dossier because it was single, not double, sourced. This was a straightforward mistake by Andrew Gilligan.

The reason the intelligence was included late in the drafting process was because it arrived late. Whether it should have been included because it was single sourced is itself a serious matter, particularly given the unreliability of the primary source, but it was not the reason for the lateness of its inclusion.

Gilligan's mistake was to link two of Kelly's concerns – that the information came late and that it was single sourced. He was wrong to have made such a connection, but was right to highlight both points.

It was the fifth point in the original broadcast that caused the most fuss, when Gilligan used the phrase: 'the Government probably knew that that 45-minute figure was wrong even before it decided to put it in'. This statement did more damage to the BBC case than any other during the inquiry when Gilligan told Lord Hutton that he now accepted that Dr Kelly did not use these precise words and that instead the phrase was his interpretation of what Dr Kelly had told him.

On the face of it, this was a serious mistake. But deeper analysis shows what Gilligan actually said is by no means indefensible. Gilligan himself defended his reporting by telling Lord Hutton:

He [Dr Kelly] did say that the statement that WMD were ready for use in 45 minutes was unreliable, that it was wrong and that it was included 'against our wishes'; and it was a logical conclusion to draw from this that those wishes had been made known.

Whether or not what Gilligan said is justifiable is entirely dependent on who knew what about the 45-minute claim and what they thought it meant.

To understand what happened here you have to retrace some steps. It was in January 2002 that President George W. Bush made his 'Axis of Evil' speech, naming Iraq, Iran, and North Korea as sponsors of terrorism. Of these, Iraq was quickly singled out as the next target. Bush was quite open about his objective: 'We support regime change.'

In London, Tony Blair rapidly adopted the new Washington line. John Scarlett, Chairman of the Joint Intelligence Committee (JIC), was instructed to start trawling the intelligence data so that the British Government could publish a dossier showing the dangers posed by the 'Axis of Evil' states, particularly Iraq. Other officials were instructed to start examining the legal basis for military action against Iraq.

The work rapidly ran into problems. There was *no* new intelligence to suggest Iraq was doing anything it hadn't been doing for years.

The Butler Report sets this out with remarkable clarity in a passage discussing Blair's change of policy in early 2002:

> There was a clear view [by the Government] that, to be successful, any new action to enforce Iraqi compliance . . . would need to be backed with the credible threat of force. But there was no recent intelligence that itself would have given rise to a conclusion that Iraq was of more immediate concern than the activities of some other countries.

And this was not the only problem. The officials charged with assessing the legal basis for action were being sticky too. President Bush might be gung-ho for regime change, but, as Lord Butler puts it:

> [British] officials noted that regime change of itself had no basis in international law.

The only way military action could be legally justified, said the officials, was if it could be proved that Iraq was in breach of its obligations under UN resolutions – but even then the proof would have to be 'incontrovertible and of large-scale activity'. Butler notes drily:

> The intelligence then available was insufficiently robust to meet that criterion.

But by now the die was cast. While this work was going on in the early part of 2002, Bush invited Blair to his ranch at Crawford in Texas. They met in early April and the two men had long discussions on Iraq, often with no officials present and no notes taken. Immediately afterwards Blair made a speech to an American audience and gave public endorsement to the Bush policy of removing Saddam by force. Blair said:

> We must be prepared to act . . . If necessary the action should be military and again, if necessary and justified, it should involve regime change.

It seems that Blair had committed himself to removing Saddam from power. But his officials were advising that this was illegal under international law unless 'incontrovertible' evidence of 'large-scale activity' by Iraq could be found. And Blair was being advised at this time that this evidence did not exist. Blair obviously wanted and expected to get United Nations support for his position, but was prepared to take military action alongside the USA if it wasn't forthcoming.

As it happened, military action was postponed and the dossier to demonstrate Iraqi guilt was put on ice. But in the summer, as war came closer, the dossier idea was revived. Only now there was a new element in the mix: Alastair Campbell.

Campbell had had nothing to do with the first draft of the dossier in early 2002. But now he was given an important role in the preparation of the document. He was to be in charge of presentation. At the end of August, on a flight back from a visit to Mozambique, Campbell and Blair agreed that a new dossier should be published. On 3 September Blair made a public announcement that the dossier was on its way. Campbell wrote in his diary: 'Why . . . now? Why Iraq? Why only Iraq . . .'. And he identified the 'toughest question' the dossier had to answer: 'What new evidence was there?'

The awkward truth was that at this stage there *was* no new evidence of the sort Blair needed, as Campbell discovered when he took his first look at the latest version of the March dossier. He immediately ordered a substantial rewrite. 'It had to be revelatory,' he wrote in his diary. But at this stage there was nothing new to reveal. And it was less than three weeks before the dossier was to be published.

But then Blair and Campbell had a remarkable stroke of luck. SIS helpfully came up with two brand new pieces of intelligence. The first had arrived on 29 August and was already wending its way through the JIC assessment process. It seemed to suggest that the Iraqis had chemical and biological weapons that could be ready for use within 45 minutes. Blair and Campbell had the revelation they needed.

Or did they?

According to Butler, this new evidence was based on an intelligence report that was 'vague and ambiguous'. A proper assessment of its significance, says Butler, would be something like:

A source has claimed some weapons may be deployed within 45 minutes of an order to use them, but the exact nature of the weapons, the agents involved and the context of their use is unclear.

According to Butler, that is the phrase that should have gone into the dossier, but it didn't because it wouldn't have convinced anyone that it was the basis for going to war. So a much stronger version was included. What the dossier said was: 'The Iraqi military are able to deploy these within 45 minutes.' And what Blair said in his introduction to the dossier was: 'We judge that Iraq has military plans for the use of chemical and biological weapons, some of which are deployable within 45 minutes.'

There was one thing all the officials handling the 45-minute intelligence agreed on: that the weapons were short-range battlefield munitions, not rocket warheads that could threaten other states. Again this was not how it appeared in the dossier. There the clear impression was given that these were weapons that could inflict mass destruction on British subjects.

How could this have happened?

We know from evidence revealed during the Hutton Inquiry and since that there were a significant number of people in Whitehall who had real concerns about the way the 45-minute claim was presented in the September dossier and that these included intelligence analysts in the Defence Intelligence Staff. One of these, Dr Brian Jones, took the almost unprecedented step of formally minuting his concerns to his boss. He told the *Independent* newspaper in February 2004:

My belief is that right up to publication of the dossier there was a unified view not only amongst my own staff but all the DIS experts that on the basis of the intelligence available to them the assessment that Iraq possessed a CW or BW capability should be carefully caveated.

On the 45-minute claim he said:

There was no indication the original or primary source had established a track record of reliability. Furthermore, the information reported by the source was vague in all aspects except, possibly, for the range of times quoted.

The Butler Report backs Dr Jones, concluding that the 45-minute claim should not have been included in the dossier

> without stating what it was believed to refer to. The fact that the reference . . . was repeated in the dossier later led to suspicions that it had been included because of its eye-catching character.

This was not the only time that intelligence on this issue would be massaged to make it more 'eye-catching'.

SIS, having produced the 45-minute evidence, then came up with their second revelation. The second piece of intelligence arrived on 10 September and caused great excitement. A brand-new source was reporting that 'the production of biological and chemical agents had been accelerated by the Iraqi Government, including through the building of further facilities throughout Iraq'.

At last, here was incontrovertible proof of large-scale activity by the Iraqis in breach of UN resolutions. Here was the evidence Blair needed. Except that it was not incontrovertible. It came from an entirely new and untested source with no track record. According to Butler, when the head of SIS, Sir Richard Dearlove, personally briefed Tony Blair on the news, he said that the case was 'developmental and that the source remained unproven'. What the Butler Report didn't tell us was that Alastair Campbell was also at that briefing meeting.

SIS were adamant that, to protect the source, this material should not be used in the dossier, although they agreed it could be used 'through assertion'. That was enough for Campbell and Blair. Four days later, Campbell, who had been at the SIS briefing with Blair, produced a draft of what Blair wanted to say in his foreword. It said that Blair had been briefed in detail about the intelligence concerning Iraq and that he now believed it established 'beyond doubt' that Iraq had continued to produce chemical and biological weapons. Yet both Blair and Campbell must have known this wasn't established 'beyond doubt' as Britain's top spy, the head of the SIS Sir Richard Dearlove, had told them personally that the case was 'developmental' and the source 'unproven'. Dearlove later made a specific point of explaining to Lord Butler that he had told them this.

Both Blair and Campbell chose to ignore these caveats; they were not included in Campbell's first draft of the foreword or in the later versions

which were approved by John Scarlett. It is clear to me that the Prime Minister's conviction was stronger than the evidence justified. In his foreword to the dossier Blair also hinted that he had information too secret to reveal, a claim which we now know was also partly based on evidence from this 'unproven' source. It, too, was used to convince us all of the threat from Iraq. Maybe there was a bit of 'sexing up' going on here.

We later discovered from the Butler report that this new source provided by SIS, a source so secret that his information didn't go through the proper assessment process, turned out to be unreliable. The evidence he supplied was withdrawn by SIS in July 2003, the month before the Hutton Inquiry started. Neither Sir Richard Dearlove nor John Scarlett, two eminent public servants, told Lord Hutton that the evidence was no longer regarded as reliable when they appeared before his inquiry.

This second new piece of intelligence was also used to support the first – the 45-minute claim. When Dr Jones complained about the over-strong use of language in the dossier on chemical and biological weapons, he was told that there was new intelligence, so secret that he was not allowed even to see it, that justified the language of the dossier.

And so the 45-minute claim, shorn of the caveats about its reliability, and presented in such a way as to make the implied threat much more serious, made its way into the dossier.

Jonathan Powell, the Chief of Staff inside Number Ten, drew attention to a serious problem in the dossier. Just before it went to the printers he sent an e-mail to Campbell and Scarlett. In it he pointed out that the paragraph in the latest draft of the dossier saying that

> Saddam is prepared to use chemical and biological weapons if he believes his regime is under threat

was actually an argument against going to war with Iraq, not one in favour of it. He described that phrase as

> a bit of a problem ... it backs up the argument that there is no chemical and biological weapons threat and we will only create one if we attack him.

Powell suggested that the relevant paragraph be redrafted. What John Scarlett then did is another example of how the dossier was 'sexed up' – changed not because there was new intelligence, but simply to make a better case for going to war. He took out the crucial qualification 'if he believes his regime is under threat' and in so doing changed the meaning of the dossier.

What is important here is not only *what* was changed but the timing of the changes. Powell's e-mail was sent, and Scarlett's redraft written, after the final deadline for changes to the dossier had passed. The redraft was never discussed by the rest of the Joint Intelligence Committee and yet any substantial changes to the dossier were supposed to go back to the full JIC for approval. Clearly Scarlett decided that the changes he was making were not substantial.

So it was Scarlett who took out the crucial line saying Saddam would only use his weapons if he was under threat. In doing so he changed a key emphasis of the dossier as a result of an e-mail from the Prime Minister's Chief of Staff, a political appointee. Scarlett's unilateral redraft meant that nowhere did the dossier say that attacking Saddam brought its own dangers. Nor did it say that the weapons of mass destruction it referred to were short-range munitions. As a result, the world was given the wrong impression.

In the same e-mail Powell also asked Alastair Campbell what the headline in the *Evening Standard* would be when the dossier was published, demonstrating that headlines about the dossier mattered to Downing Street. The answer was that the newspapers reporting the publication of the dossier put terrifying headlines on their stories such as:

45 MINS FROM ATTACK
(*Evening Standard*)

BRITS 45 MINS FROM DOOM
(*The Sun*)

Both papers talked of the threat to British troops in Cyprus and *The Sun* even suggested that tourists in Cyprus could be 'annihilated by germ warfare missiles launched by Iraq'. Other regional papers picked up on the same line.

Many in Whitehall – politicians, spooks, and civil servants alike – knew these newspaper stories were wrong and yet they made no attempt to correct this scaremongering. One can only assume they failed to do this because they got the headlines that Downing Street wanted. In fact Tony Blair built his case for war on the supposed imminence of the Iraqi threat to Britain and British interests. He did it in the dossier:

> I am in no doubt that the threat is serious and current, that he has made progress on WMD, and that he has to be stopped ... the document discloses that his military planning allows for some of the WMD to be ready within 45 minutes of an order to use them.

He did it again in the Commons on 24 September 2002:

> His [Saddam's] weapons of mass destruction programme is active, detailed and growing. The policy of containment is not working. The weapons of mass destruction programme is not shut down; it is up and running now ... he has existing and active military plans for the use of chemical and biological weapons, which could be activated within 45 minutes.

And just before the war began, in reference to the threat of weapons of mass destruction, he again raised the spectre of

> a real and present danger to Britain and its national security

when addressing the House of Commons in March 2003. We now know that the basis of all three of Blair's statements was wrong.

It is interesting to compare the Prime Minister's statements with an earlier e-mail of 17 September 2002 from Jonathan Powell. Writing to John Scarlett, with a copy to Campbell, he said, having read the latest draft of the dossier, that

> We will need to make it clear in launching the document that we do not claim we have evidence that he [Saddam] is an imminent threat.

And yet Tony Blair claimed exactly that.

303

What is certain is that the Head of the Secret Intelligence Service, Sir Richard Dearlove, knew that the intelligence concerning the threat of WMDs that could be fired in 45 minutes did not constitute a threat to Britain or British interests. During the Hutton Inquiry Sir Richard was asked by the inquiry counsel if he accepted that the 45-minutes claim had been given 'undue prominence'. His answer was astonishingly frank:

> Well, I think given the misinterpretation that was placed on the 45-minutes intelligence, with the benefit of hindsight you can say that is a valid criticism.

At this point Lord Hutton himself interjected to ask what Sir Richard meant by 'misinterpretation'. There was a significant pause before Sir Richard replied:

> Well, I think the original report referred to chemical and biological munitions and that was taken to refer to battlefield weapons. I think what subsequently happened in the reporting was that it was taken that the 45 minutes applied, let us say, to weapons of a longer range.

Sir Richard was not alone in knowing the truth. The then Leader of the House of Commons, Robin Cook, also knew it before the war was started. In his published diaries, entitled *Point of Departure* (2003), he records an intelligence briefing from John Scarlett, Chairman of the Joint Intelligence Committee, in February 2003 – just a month before the war began:

> My conclusion at the end of an hour is that Saddam probably does not have weapons of mass destruction in the sense of weapons that could be used against a large-scale civilian target.

According to Cook, he shared these concerns with Tony Blair shortly before the war began. His diary records what happened at the meeting:

> The most revealing exchange came when we talked about Saddam's arsenal. I told him, 'It's clear from the private briefing I have had that Saddam has no weapons of mass destruction in a sense of weapons that could strike at strategic cities. But he probably does

have several thousand battlefield chemical munitions. Do you never worry that he might use them against British troops?' [Blair replied:] 'Yes, but all the effort he has had to put into concealment makes it difficult for him to assemble them quickly for use.'

Cook says he was 'deeply troubled' by his conversation with the Prime Minister:

> Tony did not try to argue me out of the view that Saddam did not have real weapons of mass destruction that were designed for strategic use against city populations and capable of being delivered with reliability over long distances. I had now expressed that view to both the chairman of the JIC and to the prime minister and both had assented in it. At the time I did believe it likely that Saddam had retained a quantity of chemical munitions for tactical use on the battlefield. These did not pose 'a real and present danger to Britain' as they were not designed for use against city populations and by definition could threaten British personnel only if we were to deploy them on the battlefield within range of Iraqi artillery.

If Robin Cook's diary is an accurate record of his conversation with the Prime Minister it is inconsistent with Tony Blair's account of events in two important areas.

Firstly, it would mean that the Prime Minister knew that, even if these weapons of mass destruction did exist, they couldn't be used in 45 minutes because they had to be assembled first. Yet in his foreword to the September dossier the Prime Minister had talked about the 45-minute threat as if it was real and immediate and had done the same in his statement to Parliament the day the dossier was published. He has made no attempt to put the record straight on this.

Secondly, and more significantly, Blair's answer to Cook also suggests that by then he must have known that these were short-range weapons and that they couldn't threaten British interests, yet he has denied that he knew the truth about this until after the war was over. This means that either Cook's recollection of the conversation is suspect, or that Blair's subsequent denial of this knowledge has to be questioned. They cannot both be right.

Recent evidence published in Bob Woodward's book *Plan of Attack*, which was based on interviews with all the main US players, including President Bush, shows quite clearly that the CIA didn't believe the 45-minute claim. George Tenet, the Director of the CIA at the time, referred to the claim as 'they-can-attack-in-45-minutes shit'. Even more importantly, Woodward says that Tenet and the CIA had warned the British not to make the allegation, presumably before the dossier was published, as they believed the source was questionable and that the claim only referred to battlefield weapons.

The charge against Blair is damning. He was either incompetent and took Britain to war on a misunderstanding or he lied when he told the House of Commons that he didn't know what the 45-minute claim meant. Either way it can be argued that the Prime Minister should have known what sort of weapons he was talking about: after all, it was his foreword, his dossier, and subsequently his war. And in his foreword he did say: 'I and other ministers have been briefed in detail on the intelligence.'

The Defence Secretary, Geoff Hoon, accepts that he knew the truth although, he says, not until 'shortly after' the dossier was published, which was still six months before the war began. He told the Defence Select Committee on 5 February 2004:

I asked within the Ministry of Defence what kinds of weapons were in effect being referred to as part of the so-called 45 minutes claim, and the answer was . . . that they were of a battlefield kind.

It is interesting that Hoon didn't ask the question until *after* the dossier was published. As the member of the Government responsible for defence one would have thought he might have asked *before* it became a public document. What we learnt during the Hutton Inquiry was that Hoon was only a bit-part player, like many in Tony Blair's Cabinet, and was often excluded from the crucial discussions about Iraq. We do know that Hoon made no attempt to correct the public record when he discovered that the dossier was not clear on this point and that the public had been given totally the wrong impression.

John Scarlett certainly knew the truth before the dossier was published since he had seen all the original intelligence. At the BBC we also knew

he was 'uncomfortable' with the public case being made for the war because that is what he had told one journalist on a bench in the grounds of Ditchley Park, the exclusive Oxfordshire house used as a centre for high-level discussions on international affairs. Scarlett told the journalist he was particularly worried about the way the dossier had been interpreted in the press. He may have been worried, but Scarlett – like Hoon – didn't do anything about it.

I also find it difficult to believe that the group responsible for producing the dossier, which included Alastair Campbell and three other press officers from Number Ten, didn't know all the facts about the 45-minute claim before publication. Surely Campbell, a man who prides himself about knowing the detail on such matters, would have asked what actual weapons the dossier was referring to?

And yet the full picture on these points never made its way into the dossier. Why? One can only assume it was because it would have weakened the case for going to war.

Lord Hutton should have realized that Dr Kelly and his friends in the Defence Intelligence Services knew a whole range of things about this issue:

- They had serious doubts about the validity of the 45-minute claim and where it came from.
- They believed that the dossier presented the 45-minute claim to the press and public in a way that was misleading about Iraq's WMD capabilities.
- They knew that the 45-minute claim didn't refer to long-range weapons of mass destruction that could threaten Britain and British interests.
- They had been excluded from seeing the new evidence that SIS had presented directly to the Prime Minister, evidence that was formally withdrawn in July 2003.
- They knew that the September dossier had been changed at the very last moment. They suspected it had been done at the suggestion of people in 10 Downing Street.
- They knew that the very clear statement that Saddam would only be able to use his weapons of mass destruction against British interests if Britain attacked Saddam had been taken out of the dossier. Again, they suspected that this had been done at Number Ten's suggestion.

When Dr Kelly told Andrew Gilligan that the dossier had been sexed up by Downing Street we can see why he said it. From his perspective something very serious and unusual had happened. A deeply flawed dossier had been produced and he had grounds to believe, from what he knew, that this was as a direct result of interference from Downing Street. It is hardly surprising, then, that he told Andrew Gilligan, in so many words, that Downing Street probably knew it was wrong. That's what he clearly believed. Gilligan and the BBC only reported what Dr Kelly had told them, as they were perfectly entitled to do under the Reynolds legal ruling.

If Lord Hutton's remit was to find out the truth concerning the circumstances surrounding the death of Dr Kelly, then it was essential for him to understand and take on board what the 45-minute point meant. That was one of the key points of Dr Kelly's conversation with Gilligan. That Hutton failed to do this is a remarkable omission. Lord Butler understood this only too well. In his report he said the 45-minute report should not have been included without stating what sort of weapons it referred to.

One therefore has to ask, on what basis did Lord Hutton make the crucial decision that it was not relevant to his inquiry what sort of weapons of mass destruction the dossier referred to? How could he possibly have decided this?

It has been suggested that the Government constrained Lord Hutton's inquiry by the narrowness of the terms of reference. This is unfair to the Government and untrue. It was Lord Hutton himself who defined his terms of reference on this crucial point. It was Lord Hutton who chose not to consider the difference between a 45-minute claim based on battlefield deployment and one based on long-range use. In fact Lord Hutton included sixteen references to the '45-minute claim' in his report without once saying which of the two radically different meanings he was referring to.

His stated reason for making this decision was that the distinction between the two sorts of weapons was not made in the reports that Gilligan broadcast so it wasn't relevant. Lord Hutton said:

A consideration of this issue does not fall within my terms of reference relating to the circumstances surrounding the death of Dr Kelly.

When he appeared before the Public Administration Select Committee in May 2004 Hutton was asked why he hadn't gone into the nature of the intelligence or the 45-minute claim in his report. He replied that he didn't think he would have been able to resolve the issue and that it would require a different kind of inquiry. The question Lord Hutton didn't and doesn't answer is, why not? Surely his job was to find out what Dr Kelly was talking about?

The BBC's QC, Andrew Caldecott, made this one of his main points in the BBC's final submission to Lord Hutton:

> It seems to have been common knowledge within Government that the intelligence referred to battlefield munitions only, though this was never made clear in the dossier . . . the Government's failure to correct is wholly indefensible. The best governing minds of the country closely considered the outing of Dr Kelly, but on this fundamental misrepresentation to the public . . . there was nothing.

So it was pointed out to Lord Hutton how crucial the 45-minute point was. He chose to ignore it. Was there another reason for Lord Hutton's deciding that this issue was not relevant? Was it a genuine mistake or a deliberate decision not to probe into an area in which his findings would inevitably have been very embarrassing for Number Ten, for others in Government, and for some in the intelligence services? Did Lord Hutton just get it wrong, or was there a more sinister reason?

Lord Hutton's failure to take on board what sort of weapons Kelly was talking about when he met Gilligan was not his only mistake in this area of the inquiry. There were many others, as there were throughout the report.

Lord Hutton made no real attempt to explain why he accepted John Scarlett's evidence that he alone had made the change to the dossier that turned the threat from Saddam Hussein from a defensive threat to an offensive one. Lord Hutton seems totally to have disregarded Powell's e-mail and believed that Scarlett was acting unprompted. This was despite the fact that the rest of the JIC had signed off on the earlier interpretation.

Lord Hutton also refused to take on board the clear evidence that

Campbell had deliberately misled the Foreign Affairs Committee when he told them that the drafts of the dossier concerning the 45-minute issue had not changed, and had failed to tell them that he had suggested changes himself to this part of the dossier. Campbell also misled them about the number of changes he had suggested.

Lord Hutton gives no explanation for why Scarlett changed the title of the dossier from *Iraq's Programme for Weapons of Mass Destruction* to *Iraq's Weapons of Mass Destruction*. He did so late on without discussing it with the rest of the Joint Intelligence Committee, and of course in doing so radically changed the meaning of the title. Yet another example of 'sexing up'.

In his report Lord Hutton also refused to see any mitigation for the BBC's actions in view of the public nature of the attack from Campbell; he also made no reference to Campbell's failure to use the official complaints process and his decision instead to go public with his wide-ranging attack on much of the BBC's journalism. Lord Hutton also failed to allow Blair to be cross-examined while allowing Hoon to be cross-examined before Campbell's diary was made public, thus saving him from having to answer some very embarrassing questions. The mistakes are numerous.

There are countless stories in circulation about why Lord Hutton behaved in the way he did, virtually all of them unprintable because of Britain's libel laws. Personally I have never been a conspiracy theorist and have difficulty believing that there was some sort of sinister motive.

Lord Hutton clearly knew little about journalism, had spent many years living closely with the security services, and was naive about the way Blair's Downing Street operated – all of which could explain why he made the mistakes he did. He certainly had no experience of running a major public inquiry – the nearest he'd come to it before was an inquiry in Northern Ireland in relation to drainage works in a river. But does this explain why he did what he did?

What I do know is that Philip Gould, one of the architects of New Labour and very much part of Tony Blair's inner circle, was asked by one Labour member of the House of Lords before Hutton was published if he thought the Government faced a problem over the Kelly affair. Gould replied: 'Don't worry, we appointed the right judge.' So in appointing Lord Hutton the Government was pretty confident this was not a man to rock the boat. He was appointed because the Government believed he would deliver for

Blair, the security services, and the Establishment. He did precisely that.

Lord Hutton didn't intend to be biased, but those who selected him knew the man and his views on the world. His mistake was that he over-delivered; as a result the public, quite rightly, didn't believe him or accept his judgment.

Many people, including myself, have suffered as a result of Lord Hutton's report. But so has Lord Hutton's reputation, particularly since the publication of Lord Butler's report, which made him look foolish in a number of areas. There are some in the legal world who believe he has done lawyers in general, and judges in particular, a great disservice by producing such a lightweight, one-sided document.

What an analysis of the five controversial points tells us is that Gilligan's original story, although flawed in places, was nowhere near Tony Blair's 'mountain of untruth' or Campbell's '100 per cent wrong'. The 45-minute intelligence *was* misused. There *was* unhappiness in the intelligence community as a result. The government *did* want the dossier sexed up. They *did* demand that the intelligence agencies discover more facts to strengthen their case for going to war. And people inside Downing Street *did* know the impression given by the dossier, as reported in the press, was the wrong one.

In his role as Chairman of the Joint Intelligence Committee John Scarlett has a lot to answer for. It is very clear that the dossier was written in a way that included any information that supported the case for war and excluded any arguments against. If Scarlett's job was to insist that the document presented a fair and balanced picture based on the information available to the intelligence services at the time, he failed. Instead, Scarlett allowed what was supposed to be an intelligence dossier to be turned into a public relations document.

It was very clear to most people who listened to the evidence given to the Hutton Inquiry that while working in Downing Street John Scarlett crossed the line and became part of Blair's team. He went native. But then the story of a courtier trying to please the king is as old as time. Interestingly, the only time I ever met John Scarlett he sat next to my partner Sue at a dinner. I asked her what he was like. She thought him both interesting and charming but said, 'He likes Tony Blair a lot.' Even Lord Hutton suggested that Scarlett might have been influenced by his

closeness to Number Ten when, in one of the very few criticisms of anyone from the Government side, he said:

> I consider that the possibility cannot be completely ruled out that the desire of the Prime Minister to have a dossier which . . . was as strong as possible . . . may have subconsciously influenced Mr Scarlett . . . to make the wording of the dossier stronger than it would have been.

Logically, this statement from Lord Hutton must have meant that he believed the document was strengthened – even 'sexed up' – because of political pressure, whether it was done subconsciously or not. But Lord Hutton does not go on to say that. It's another fundamental contradiction in the Hutton Report.

Lord Butler is rather blunter; he believed that the pressure from above for a strong dossier that supported Tony Blair's position 'will have put a strain on them [SIS] in seeking to maintain their normal standards of neutral and objective assessment'.

It is little wonder that some in the intelligence services were upset by the dossier. They are reported to have told the Butler Inquiry that they were 'embarrassed' by what happened and that they never want to see their intelligence used in this way again. Given that much of their intelligence was misused this is hardly surprising.

In fact John Scarlett and the leaders of the intelligence services should be more than embarrassed by their role in the production of the September dossier. They should be ashamed. Virtually all the new intelligence they supplied was inadequate; much of it has turned out to be totally discredited. The intelligence from the 'unproven' source that Blair and Campbell used as the basis for hardening up the introduction to the dossier has now been withdrawn by SIS. It has also cast real doubts on the reliability of the 45-minutes report. The CIA tells us that Saddam's agents didn't try to buy 'significant amounts' of uranium from Niger as the dossier claimed; no mobile biological agent production facilities have been found in Iraq, which according to the dossier 'recent intelligence' said were there; the 'specialised aluminium tubes' that the dossier said were needed for Iraq's nuclear weapons programme we now know were actually for con-

ventional weapons only; above all, the dossier was called *Iraq's Weapons of Mass Destruction*, and we now know there weren't any.

Scarlett and the intelligence services should also be ashamed that they allowed themselves to be manipulated by the Downing Street machine to produce a political document, not an intelligence dossier, a piece of advocacy, not a dispassionate assessment. That John Scarlett should later be appointed to run SIS, having been responsible for the publication of such a document, does not bode well for the future of the intelligence services in this country.

Putting out documents of selective information to improve the Government's case was food and drink to Campbell and his team in Number Ten; it's what they had been doing for seven years. They simply did to weapons of mass destruction in Iraq what they had done to so many other issues in the years since New Labour came to power. Take the evidence, sift out the stuff that doesn't support your position and publish the rest, exaggerating it a bit if needs be. That was their trade.

Whether you should be doing that as a Government information organization is debatable; whether you should be doing it when the stakes are as high as people being killed in a war is not. The people of this country were entitled to know the full picture about Iraq and they were not given it by Campbell and Co.

Nothing illustrates the way the Downing Street information machine worked more clearly than the second dossier, which has become known as the 'dodgy dossier' and which was published in February 2003. It was Campbell's idea to produce it because he didn't think the September dossier was powerful enough. His department then simply found a twelve-year-old thesis on the Internet written by a PhD student, plagiarized it, and, most of important of all, changed it – or in Kelly and Gilligan's terms 'sexed it up' – to improve the case for going to war with Iraq. They then published it as if it was an original piece of work. The US Secretary of State Colin Powell described the document as 'a fine paper that the UK distributed'. In fact it was a travesty of the truth.

The best example of what Campbell's team did in the 'dodgy' dossier was when they changed the phrase 'aiding opposition groups in hostile regimes' to 'supporting terrorist organizations in hostile regimes', which has a completely different meaning. They changed and hardened the

313

language throughout the paper, and if a Cambridge academic hadn't spotted striking similarities between the dossier and a paper he had read on the Internet the 'dodgy' dossier would still have stood today, and no doubt Campbell would still be saying it was all true.

In a parliamentary statement on 3 February Tony Blair described the dossier as an 'intelligence report', and yet it was nothing of the sort. When Blair discovered the truth about how the dossier had been produced he should have been outraged and fired Campbell. That he didn't tells us a lot about Blair.

Doing this sort of thing was what Campbell's Number Ten information department saw as their job and they saw nothing wrong with it, until they were found out. But if anyone tried to point out what they were doing, as Dr Kelly did when he met Andrew Gilligan, they in turn became the enemy and had the whole apparatus of the state's PR machine turned on them.

To understand how this all came about one has to understand the whole psyche of Blair's Number Ten and the enormous power wielded by Alastair Campbell. In many ways Campbell is a political genius and there is enormous respect amongst the Conservative opposition for the way he operates. But over seven years he turned Downing Street into a place similar to Nixon's White House. You were either for them or against them. And if you opposed them on anything you became the enemy. As a Watergate groupie I was quite shocked when writing this book by these similarities between the Nixon White House and Blair's Downing Street.

Now all governments, of whatever political colour, get upset with the media. They all claim that what they are doing is what they promised when elected and that their policy is the right one. If the public disagree, governments always blame the media, saying that the public doesn't understand this or that because the media isn't reporting it properly. As a result, they all try to manipulate the media. It was just that Campbell took this to new extremes. Quite how such an obsessive man had become so powerful is interesting. This was a man whom a judge had described in a court action in May 1996 as 'less than completely open and frank'. The judge further said that 'I did not find Mr Campbell by any means a wholly satisfactory or convincing witness'. And yet, until he resigned a year later, he was in charge of all the government's information services,

and many regarded him as the most powerful man in the Government after Tony Blair and Gordon Brown.

When Labour was elected the law was changed to allow Campbell to become a civil servant and to control all the Government's information services whilst being a political appointee. As a result, he had unprecedented power and was able to order Cabinet Ministers around to do his bidding. Quite why they put up with it is, in itself, a sign of how our democratic system has been undermined.

As Director-General I always remember the hostility from Blair's Government to the BBC over the *Panorama* programme called 'Spin Doctors' back in 2000, the first programme to show that Labour were announcing the same spend on things time and time again – classic spin. The same happened in May 2001 when *Panorama* produced a not dissimilar programme called 'The Labour Years' the week before the general election. The team producing it were treated as enemies by the Labour Party press office led by Campbell.

There are legions of stories of Campbell helping friendly journalists, people like Tom Baldwin on *The Times*, while attacking journalists he saw as his enemies because they wouldn't run stories the way he wanted them run. I asked the editor of *The Times* if he wasn't embarrassed by Baldwin's closeness to Campbell. The reply was that 'he got very good stories'. The question is, at what cost?

When the BBC gave a confidential briefing to a team at *The Times* it was Baldwin who reported it word for word to Campbell. And guess which journalist first revealed that a Ministry of Defence employee had come forward and said he might be Gilligan's source? Baldwin again. But it was worse than that. Campbell's department regularly misled journalists in an attempt to try to kill stories they didn't want published. We had experience of this at the BBC.

In recent years Campbell's department had issued denials and then later changed their position when new 'facts' emerged on a whole range of stories, including the Martin Sixsmith 'resignation', the advice given by Peter Foster to Cherie Blair, the Britishness or otherwise of LNM (the steel company owned by billionaire Lakshmi Mittal, who was a big Labour Party donor), and the nature of a phone call between the then Italian Prime Minister (Romano Prodi) and Tony Blair involving discussions about Rupert Murdoch's business interests. The problem was

that the tactics Campbell employed in everyday life – spin, manipulation, and at times threats – were bound to catch up with the Government in the end, and they have with a vengeance over Iraq.

The Hutton Report was quickly dismissed by the British public. A poll in the *Daily Telegraph* two days after the report was published found that 56 per cent of the people interviewed agreed with the statement that 'Lord Hutton, as a member of the establishment, was too ready to sympathise with the Government and in the end produced something like a whitewash'. Another poll in *The Guardian*, published the same day, said that three times as many people trusted the BBC to tell the truth as trusted the Government.

Government ministers were genuinely shocked when the people of Britain treated Hutton with such contempt. As one minister said the weekend after, 'It cleared us and no one believed it, what are we supposed to do?'

So why did the public dismiss Hutton as a 'whitewash'? The answer to the question is that in many ways Lord Hutton was hoist by his own petard. He had held a ground-breaking inquiry. It was open to the public; all the evidence was available on the Internet, and Hutton ran it in a fair and open manner in an unprecedented way. The problem was that Lord Hutton's findings didn't line up with the evidence that the British public had seen and heard for themselves.

But the hostile reaction was based on more than that. By the time Hutton reported, the public increasingly didn't trust the Prime Minister. Blair's trust ratings, in fact, had collapsed. In 1997, according to the research organization Gallup, Tony Blair's trust rating was plus 37; by February 2004 a YouGov survey put the figure at minus 39. And the public certainly didn't trust a Downing Street information machine that had spun just once too often. Campbell's pompous and vitriolic performance on the steps of the Foreign Press Association certainly didn't help Blair's cause.

What all this tells us is that it was Government and the people in Number Ten who misled the British people, not Dr Kelly, Andrew Gilligan, or the BBC. The September dossier was only a public relations exercise designed to persuade sceptical Labour MPs and a sceptical public to support a policy of going to war in Iraq.

In fact most of the story broadcast on the *Today* programme on that May morning was right, and while Gilligan made mistakes they were nowhere near as serious as those made by Downing Street when producing their two dossiers warning about the threats from Iraq: the BBC was not sending British soldiers to war. In producing and promoting the September dossier Tony Blair and those involved, including John Scarlett, Alastair Campbell, and Geoff Hoon, sold the British people a false bill of goods.

Only Campbell has, so far, paid a price for this by being forced out of Downing Street, although he was planning to go at some stage anyway. But Blair and Hoon struggle on damaged, while Scarlett has got the job he always wanted as Head of SIS. Tony Blair could have stopped that appointment but didn't.

The king repaid the courtier.

CHAPTER FOURTEEN

Some Final Thoughts

This book has had three themes: broadcasting, politics, and me. I'll end by saying something about all three, beginning with broadcasting.

As I finish this book I am, oddly, more optimistic about the future of the BBC than I was before the whole Gilligan saga started. I'm of the view that the pressures the BBC will face in the renewal of its charter in 2007 will be significantly less as a result of the torrid events of 2003 and 2004.

The BBC has a good man as its new Chairman in Michael Grade, so long as someone can stop him trying to be the Director-General at the same time, which is bound to be a risk when you have a hands-on man like Michael in the Chairman's role. Michael was a good and brave Chief Executive of Channel Four, willing to stand up for his programme makers and willing to stand up against the bullying from politicians that all broadcasting organizations face – not that Channel Four ever faced the intensity of political pressure the BBC faced. I suspect that if Gilligan's report had been on Channel Four News it would have gone unnoticed.

To do his job well Grade needs better and more knowledgeable Governors than he currently has to support him. I hope that the six current Governors who voted to get rid of me – Dermot Gleeson, Merfyn Jones, Fabian Monds, Pauline Neville-Jones, Robert Smith, and Ranjit Sondhi – will realize, having read the Butler Report and my chapter on Hutton, that what they did on that January night was bow to pressure from a political thug called Alastair Campbell. What happened to me is irrelevant – Director-Generals come and go; but there is no greater betrayal of the principles on which the BBC is based than to fold under political pressure, particularly when it comes from the Government of the day. These Gov-

ernors got it seriously wrong and they should accept that. They should now resign. The BBC deserves better.

The BBC has a second good man in Mark Thompson, the new Director-General. He is both clever and potentially an outstanding leader. He sorted out the finances at Channel Four but wasn't there long enough to have an enormous impact on its programmes. He was a good Controller of BBC Two and made a big impact in his short period as Director of Television at the BBC. Both Michael and Mark are people who will not fear making changes and taking calculated risks, even when their decisions are unlikely to be popular with politicians, the press, or the BBC's commercial opponents. But the reason why I'm now optimistic about the BBC going forward is not because of its leadership but because Michael and Mark find themselves in a unique position with a unique opportunity.

Rather than being damaged by the Hutton affair the BBC has been strengthened by it. The battle over Hutton was so fierce that the public had to choose between the politicians and the BBC. The polls make it very clear that, overwhelmingly, they chose the BBC. What that means, I suspect, is that it will be a very long time before any Government tries to bully the BBC in the hysterical way that Campbell did and Tony Blair allowed him to do. And it will be a very long time before any Government will want to have another row on that scale with the BBC. There were no winners but the polls show quite clearly that public trust in the BBC wasn't damaged. The main casualty was the public's trust in Tony Blair and the Government.

In fact I don't believe Michael Grade would have become Chairman of the BBC had it not been for the Gilligan affair: he certainly believes that. When the staff took to the streets to support me, Downing Street was deeply unnerved. They had seriously misjudged the position. The advertisement in the *Daily Telegraph* and the demonstration organized by the trade unions protesting against Government interference in the BBC the week after my departure shocked them further. They thought they'd got the right result from Hutton. They hadn't. As a consequence Tessa Jowell, who had always favoured Grade becoming Chairman, was able to get her way despite the machinations of some inside Downing Street, particularly John Birt.

Birt and Grade, friends when they were both at LWT in the Seventies, had hated each other for nearly two decades. They fell out when John joined the BBC as Deputy Director-General and started trying to tell

319

Michael how to run the television service. Rather than be bossed around by John, Michael left the BBC and joined Channel Four. He later used the McTaggart lecture to launch a massive attack on Birt's BBC.

Inside Downing Street, Birt fought against Grade's appointment as Chairman of the BBC, tried to influence Tessa Jowell, and, when he lost, sent a letter to Tony Blair telling him that Grade's was the worst public appointment he had made since becoming Prime Minister.

But the whole affair had another beneficial impact on the BBC. It has led to a significant improvement in the relationship between the BBC and the Conservative Party: a party that was in danger of writing off the BBC as a bunch of pinkos and liberals has had to rethink. And of course they too must have recognized the strength of public opinion on the BBC's side.

Some things are bound to change with the BBC's next charter. In fact some things should change. The current system of governance should certainly be scrapped. You cannot carry on running one of the biggest media organizations in the world with a governance system more suited to a small charity: a system in which the great and the good are appointed for no obvious reason other than they are Welsh, Scottish, black, Asian, a businessman, a card-carrying former politician, a mate of the Minister's, or a trade unionist. This is particularly so when most of them bring with them little knowledge or understanding of broadcasting or the media.

And the logic of the current system whereby the Governors are both regulators and also responsible for management no longer holds water either. While it may have worked over the years it no longer stands up to intellectual analysis in a world more and more obsessed by accountability.

There needs to be a separation of powers with a BBC Board, made up of executives and knowledgeable non-executives, responsible for the running of the BBC, and an outside regulator with the job of checking on it. By the time I left the BBC most of the BBC Executive had come round to this way of thinking. We believed the BBC had spent too much time trying to defend the current system of governance: we had used up too much political capital trying to defend the indefensible. This wasn't true of the Board of Governors, who still hadn't changed their views and when I left were still fighting desperately to retain their current status. Michael Grade certainly knows and believes change is necessary.

This is not to argue that regulating the BBC should be the responsibility of the new communications super regulator Ofcom. It should not. It

would be too dangerous to have only one content regulator across the whole of British broadcasting. As a society we need a plurality of regulators, just as we need a plurality of broadcasters. There is too great a threat of a single regulator being 'captured' by the government of the day, in much the same way as John Scarlett was 'captured' when he was Chairman of the Joint Intelligence Committee.

But that isn't the only reason. Once the commercial sector and the BBC are regulated by the same body I fear that economic interests will predominate and the public interest will be left very much in second place. That will prevent the BBC from continuing to innovate and expand in the public interest as technology changes. My solution would be for the Government to establish a small and separate regulator for the BBC and the BBC alone, but place it outside the BBC and not make it responsible for the running of the organization. When I first joined the BBC Carolyn Fairbairn and the former BBC Secretary Michael Stevenson made a cogent argument on the BBC Executive for such a system. At the time it was rejected. They were right and the rest of us were wrong.

In a changing media world in which BSkyB will grow ever stronger it is essential there is a strong BBC to counterbalance the Murdoch interests; a BBC that is not overly constrained by the commercial sector; a BBC that is driven by the public interest in delivering the best possible services to as wide a group of the UK population as possible. The BBC is not and should not be there principally to please an intellectual, South of England elite.

A strong and well-funded BBC is particularly important given what has happened to ITV. In many ways it is sad that Granada bought LWT. It should have been the other way round since our management was far superior to theirs: we were committed broadcasters, they were cost-cutting caterers who knew little about television. They had no vision for ITV other than consolidation. That simply wasn't enough in a fast-changing media world. They screwed up over ITV Digital and made a serious mistake when not backing Freeview. As an ex-ITV man I feel terribly sad about the decline of ITV as a serious force in British broadcasting, and I am not confident it can recover without radical change.

I also worry that what we have seen in the USA is happening here to ITV. During the Iraq war the US broadcasters abandoned their role as

impartial observers to become cheerleaders for American involvement in the war. They did it for many reasons. The fear of the religious right, the after-effects of 11 September, and the fear of being accused of being anti-patriotic were just three of them. But I suspect there was a business agenda too. The big American media companies wanted a change in the ownership rules on US television to allow them to own more stations. If they had upset the Bush administration during the war this would not have happened.

This was exactly what I warned could happen in Britain in my first McTaggart lecture delivered in 1994. Now there are real signs that what has happened in the USA is beginning to happen to ITV in this country. In the last couple of years there have been at least three occasions when there has been attempted interference in programming from 'on top' because what was planned didn't suit the ITV companies' commercial interests. The first was with the drama *The Deal*, written by Peter Morgan and directed by Stephen Frears, which won the best single drama at the BAFTA awards in 2004. It told the story of the Brown/Blair pact. When it was broadcast, the piece was very sympathetic to Gordon Brown but far less so to Tony Blair. Nick Elliot, ITV's head of drama, commissioned the project for ITV and planned to play it on ITV. The powers that be inside Granada found out about it. With the company trying to persuade the Government to agree to the merger of Carlton and Granada they put enormous pressure on the ITV Network Centre for it not to go out on ITV. The drama eventually ended up on Channel Four.

The second came with a three-part factual series about Rupert Murdoch that the ITV Network Centre had actually commissioned. All was agreed and the programmes were about to be made when a senior executive stepped in and said that even if the series was made he would not broadcast the programmes, which were likely to be critical of Murdoch.

Thirdly, on the day the story came out that Michael Green was receiving a £15 million payout for leaving ITV, ITV's news provider ITN was asked by a senior executive of ITV not to run the story. To their credit the news people told him it was none of his business and ran the story anyway.

Successful commercial broadcasters only succeed if they care about more than just business. You can't have portion control television, nor can you only be obsessed about finance and management. Television is most of all a creative business and success comes if you recognize that.

If broadcasters end up as *just* commercial entities, as ITV is in danger of becoming, they will fail, both as broadcasters and as businesses. As I ended my McTaggart lecture back in 2000, 'It's the programmes, stupid.'

This book has also been about politics.

I first met him when he was sitting next but one to me at a dinner at Barry Cox's place. It was around 1980 and at the time I was a producer at London Weekend Television. I remember the evening well, and in particular I remember this fresh-faced young man with a very upmarket accent, which was unusual in the circles I moved in. In those days in the media, even people brought up with plums in their mouths spent most of the time pretending they didn't have them. This guy had no such inhibitions.

As part of polite conversation I asked him what he did. He told me he was a barrister but what he really wanted to do was to 'serve' his country. I remember thinking, what does he mean, 'serve'? I genuinely thought he meant that he wanted to join the priesthood. He later explained that by 'serve' he had meant that he wanted to serve his country by becoming a Labour MP.

I didn't say much but as the evening went on I returned to the subject. In those days I regarded myself as being from the Labour left and I thought one of the great problems of the Labour Party was that it was full of lawyers, barristers, journalists, and academics – people who had never actually run anything. Twenty-five years later my politics have moderated, but I still have the same view about many of the people who go into politics.

As the wine flowed I began to explain to my next but one neighbour that I didn't think his idea of becoming a Labour MP was a particularly good one and that I wasn't sure that the Labour Party needed another posh-sounding barrister as an MP. I think my exact words were, 'I think the Labour Party needs another barrister like it needs a hole in the head.'

Roll forward to May 1997. It had been a beautiful day and was a beautiful night. Sue and I were at the Festival Hall with the great and the good of the Labour Party to celebrate Labour's election victory. The man who had led the party to victory that night arrived amid huge jubilation in the early hours of the morning. I was one of many who had turned out to greet him.

It was the same man who had been my table companion at that house

in North London nearly twenty years earlier. I had told Tony Blair that the Labour Party needed him like a hole in the head.

My feelings the night New Labour won were mixed. It really hit me that I had been young when Labour had lost in 1979 – just thirty-two. I was about to be fifty and Labour had only just got back into power. But I enjoyed the night. Sue, on the other hand, hated all the triumphalism and she rightly had forebodings about the future.

We got home from the celebrations at the Festival Hall at about 5 a.m. The sun was just coming up. I remember the excitement of the following day as if it were yesterday. I had a couple of hours' sleep and then had to go to a meeting of the Pearson plc Board – not the natural home of the Labour Party. It was beautiful weather and on my way there everyone on the streets seemed to be smiling and waving. We all felt it was a new beginning, that New Labour would not only be in control but would bring new politics to Britain.

When I look back now maybe we were all ridiculously optimistic. I even remember one friend saying to me that Tony Blair was the first prime minister who looked like he might have been round Tesco's. I checked that out with Cherie at a later stage and she laughed at the idea. Seven years later all that optimism has gone. All that initial hope has gone. Tony Blair has turned out to be just another politician and in some ways worse than those before him. They never promised us a new sort of politics. He did.

For me, the disillusionment came late. In my time at the BBC I took no part in any political activity and studiously kept my feelings about politics to myself. And then came Iraq, Gilligan, and Hutton and suddenly it struck me how naive I had been.

It is now obvious; the decision to go to war was made first and the intelligence to support that move was discovered afterwards. The trouble was, the evidence wasn't right.

There was no current threat to British interests or to anyone else from Iraq's weapons of mass destruction. There were no weapons of mass destruction. There was no uranium being imported from Niger. Iraq played no part in the 11 September attacks. There were no international terrorists then operating out of Iraq, although there are today. In particular, Iraq was not supporting al-Qaeda. We now know that George W. Bush was obsessed with attacking Iraq *before* 11 September. Even the

moral arguments for getting rid of Saddam were damaged when we saw the way the Americans troops were then encouraged to behave in Iraq by people at the top.

One by one the reasons the Prime Minister gave us for going to war have been proved to be wrong. But it's even worse than that. He took us to war on the basis of intelligence about weapons of mass destruction and the 45-minute threat which, at the very least, he didn't understand and didn't question.

It was Mr Blair who said that Gilligan's reports were 'a mountain of untruth'. That wasn't the case. But there *were* 'mountains of untruth' – they were the dossiers he and his colleagues in Downing Street produced to justify going to war in Iraq. And yet the Prime Minister has never stood up and said to the British people, 'I am sorry.' There was a moment when he could have done so, and we might have forgiven him. That moment is past.

So why did we go to war? In researching this book I have become convinced that there is a relatively simple explanation. In April 2002 Tony Blair told George W. Bush that he would support him in a war against Iraq. He did so because he believed, as have all prime ministers since the Suez fiasco nearly fifty years ago, that Britain has to stay close to the USA, and in particular support their foreign policy. But unlike Harold Wilson, who supported the US involvement in Vietnam without committing British troops, Blair decided we should go to war alongside the USA; in April 2002 Blair committed us to support George W. Bush if he launched offensive action.

This left Blair with some problems. He had to persuade his Cabinet, Parliament, the Parliamentary Labour Party, the general public, and the Government's law officers to support him and follow his lead. He couldn't tell them his real reason for going to war. There was no legal basis for it, and he was clearly concerned that, across Britain and much of the world, if he did he would be seen as Bush's poodle. Instead he told us that Iraq had weapons of mass destruction; that work on them was increasing; and that they were a current threat to British interests. I've no doubt he believed this. He recruited the intelligence services to try to help him prove it and, to their eternal shame, they went along with it. As a result, intelligence turned into advocacy and public relations. In a series of speeches, press conferences, and two separate dossiers he outlined

the case for war. Unfortunately for Blair none of it turned out to be true. No matter. We are told by Mr Blair that a tyrant has gone, that history will show he was right, and that we should all rejoice.

It's not a complicated story, but what it means is that we were all duped. History will not be on Mr Blair's side. It will not absolve him but will show that the whole saga is a great political scandal. What is really frightening is that Tony Blair still doesn't believe or understand that what he did was fundamentally wrong.

If you look deeper you see our democracy is in trouble as a result of Blair's style of leadership. In the thirty years since I studied political theory Britain has moved, first with Thatcher and even more so with Blair, from cabinet government to a prime ministerial, even a presidential, system of government. But we have no separation of powers, and none of the checks and balances that such a system needs. As a result, the Prime Minister is now all powerful.

Parliament is supposed to hold the executive in check and yet with a Labour majority of 161 it has little chance of doing so, particularly when the Labour benches are disproportionately made up of people who, understandably, want to further their careers. In a system dominated by patronage they can only do that by currying favour with the very executive they are supposed to be holding in check.

As both the Hutton Inquiry and the Butler Report showed so clearly, most of the major decisions in Government are now made in Downing Street, with few elected politicians other than the Prime Minister being involved. The evidence presented to Hutton didn't give the impression that Geoff Hoon was in charge of Defence.

But, as we saw with the Foreign Affairs Select Committee during the Gilligan affair, we have too many MPs who are willing to do what the whips or the Prime Minister tell them to do; or, even worse, did what his unelected Director of Communications told them to do.

I don't subscribe to the theory that all politicians are liars and only out for themselves. I believe there are some very good people in all parties who are trying hard to do their best for their constituents, their country, and what they believe in. It is not the individuals who are flawed but our system of democracy in which the executive arm of government has been allowed to become all powerful.

A decade ago, in a very small way, I helped Tony Blair to become leader of the Labour Party by giving £5,000 towards a fund to help him run his leadership campaign. Of course he would have become the leader of the Labour Party without my money, but today I regret giving it. Not because he's not a decent man but because I don't like what he has allowed to happen to our political system. I don't like Number Ten's obsession with spin, and I believe he misled the nation on Iraq.

Tony Blair is, in electoral terms, the most successful Labour leader ever and New Labour can claim some real achievements. And yet I suspect Blair's legacy will be summed up in two words: 'Iraq' and 'spin'. The Gilligan affair was about both.

And then we come to me.

I have a cartoon on the wall of my study of me sitting in my office with a bullet hitting my back and a caption saying, 'Who shot Greg Dyke?' It was published when I left TV-am in May 1984, which was around the same time that the big story on *Dallas* was 'Who shot JR?' The irony is that that same cartoon could have been used again in 1994, when I left LWT, or in 2004, when I left the BBC.

Writing this book I have discovered the uncanny pattern that I was unemployed in the summer of 1974 when I left university and again in parts of 1984, 1994, and now 2004. I hope that by 2014 I'll be too old to be fired. At one point I was jokingly advised by my accountant and best friend Richard Webb that I had received so many tax-free payments as compensation for loss of office that there was a danger that the Inland Revenue might take a different view this time. He felt that the Revenue might say, 'No, Mr Dyke. This is not an exceptional tax-free compensatory payment for loss of office. This is how you earn your living.'

Soon after I'd left the BBC Sue, always one to get straight to the point, asked me a profound question. 'Why,' she said, 'don't you ever leave an organization like anyone else? Why is it always a drama?' I tried to point out that this wasn't entirely accurate, but when I looked back at my time in television I could only genuinely claim my departure from TVS as being without incident.

In the last few months, as I've been writing this book and thinking about my life, I've got to thinking more about what she said. Were the events of the last year somehow my fault? Was I simply too combative?

Do I look for confrontation when others don't? As I look back now on the whole Gilligan affair, as I call it, could I, or should I, have played it differently?

Having again reviewed all the evidence in the process of writing this book I am still of the view that the September dossier was sexed up and that there were people in Downing Street who knew that.

I believe that in Alastair Campbell the Government had a time bomb waiting to go off. He just happened to go off in the direction of the BBC.

Of course I could have backed down. Of course we could have done a deal. Of course I could have abandoned our people and settled. But to what purpose? If the BBC means anything it has to stand by what it believes to be fair and right.

For me to have been cowed by an out of control bully in the shape of Alastair Campbell, whom the Prime Minister himself was clearly unable to control, would have betrayed everything I believed in. So the answer is, no; I wouldn't have acted differently. I just wish the BBC had had a Board of Governors who understood that what they were doing in getting rid of me was giving in to political bullying. But it didn't.

So what of those three days in January 2004 now?

I have always believed that there are days of your life, some good, some bad, some truly exciting, but all of them days that stand out from the ordinary when you look back.

Some such days are intensely personal and mean much to you as an individual. For me, the days my children were born were like that, days that can never be replaced. Then there are days when everything goes right, like the day at LWT when we won two ITV franchises on the same day and ended up having the most amazing party. And days that are just memorable for you, like the one on which I played football at Wembley in front of 80,000 fans, or when I finally got to meet Bob Dylan, or the night I watched Manchester United win the European Champions League in Barcelona, or sat watching the Queen's Jubilee concert at Buckingham Palace.

But not all such days are happy. For me the day I knew my marriage was over and the day my father died are memorable for the wrong reasons. Luckily, in my life the good days have far outweighed the bad.

And then there are the days when memorable events happen to all of

328

us, like the first man walking on the moon, or when England won the football World Cup, or more recently when the English rugby team won the rugby World Cup. Again these days are not all good news days. For anyone of my age the assassination of John F. Kennedy was traumatic, and of course no one alive on 11 September 2001 will ever forget the events of that day.

So where does Thursday 29 January 2004 sit for me in those memories of special days? It was certainly special. It was a day when the swings in my emotions were enormous, ranging from the shock of being sacked from a job I loved through to the elation of finding just how many of the staff had been touched by what I had been trying to achieve over the previous four years.

It was both a good and a bad day, but I suspect over the years the reaction of the staff will play a bigger part in my memories. I suspect for some people working at the BBC that day will matter to them too; it will be one of those days that matters in their lives, a day when logic and rational behaviour were rejected and instead were overruled by emotion.

I found it exciting that thousands of people from different parts of the BBC and different parts of the UK believed enough in what we were trying to achieve together to go out onto the streets to express their emotions and their support for me. The fact that more than 20 per cent of the staff e-mailed me and thousands paid for the ad in the *Daily Telegraph* will always live in my memory. Jobs have come and gone in my life but the reaction of those people on that day will be with me forever. I thank them from the bottom of my heart for turning a terrible day into an uplifting one.

For me it was also special because of the reaction to the events of that day from people outside the media, ordinary people who saw what had happened and sensed that an injustice had been done to someone they didn't know but who was clearly liked and respected by the people who worked for him.

But everything needs to be put into context. Three weeks to the day after I had been fired I visited Robben Island off Cape Town, the prison where Nelson Mandela spent many of his twenty-seven years in captivity. Today it is a museum.

I found the visit an incredibly emotional experience. The man who showed us round was a former prisoner and I felt humbled just to be in

his company and to listen to the stories of people who had shown such dignity in such adversity; people who had been imprisoned for so many years by a barbarous regime that treated them appallingly. And yet these prisoners understood humility and forgiveness.

When I went to Robben Island, everything about me was still raw. I was still angry and upset about being fired from the BBC. As I wandered around the prison on that day my tears flowed quietly: tears for what had happened on this horrible island, but also tears for what had happened to me in those three days in January. But as I walked around, it put much into perspective. I began to ask myself, how dare I feel angry? Nobody had taken away my freedom, my possessions, my family, my friends. What I saw on Robben Island was real injustice, and what had happened to me was insignificant in comparison.

As I finish this book, what I still feel today is sadness. I am still sad that something so exciting was taken away from me and that my relationship with so many people at the BBC is no more. But perhaps if the events of 29 January 2004 had not happened I would never have known what I know now. I would have retired from the BBC, probably within a couple of years, and there would have been the boring statutory speeches at the statutory retirement parties and I would never have known what all those people felt about me. And I wouldn't have known what I felt about them.

From the day I left the BBC I've been determined that I wouldn't become obsessed by what happened. While writing this book has been cathartic, it hasn't helped me to put the whole business behind me. That time is now; it is time for me to move on, to do something else with my life.

Gavyn Davies and I left the BBC because we were criticized by Lord Hutton, we think wrongly and unfairly, for failing to ensure the BBC's editorial controls were sound on a particular story broadcast on one BBC radio station at seven minutes past six one May morning. Tony Blair took Britain into a war in which thousands were killed, including many British troops, on the basis of shoddy intelligence. Some of that intelligence he knew was unproven; and some of it he should have questioned and didn't. He is still the Prime Minister.

Index

331

TRAPPED

Also by Anna Smith

TRAPPED
ANNA SMITH

Quercus

First published in Great Britain in 2021 by

Quercus Editions Ltd
Carmelite House
50 Victoria Embankment
London EC4Y 0DZ

An Hachette UK company

A CIP catalogue record for this book is available
from the British Library

HB ISBN 978 1 52940 710 5

This book is a work of fiction. Names, characters,
businesses, organizations, places and events are
either the product of the author's imagination
or used fictitiously. Any resemblance to
actual persons, living or dead, events or
locales is entirely coincidental.

Printed ar ... af S.p.A.

Papers used by Quercus are from well-managed forests and
other responsible sources.

For Eilidh, our beautiful little angel,
whose light shines forever in our hearts.

We hope when we have nowhere else to go.
Hope gives us real power – the power never to give up.

PROLOGUE

Billy Dobson would do anything if the price was right. He didn't ask questions, he didn't need to know the background or why he was being asked to do a particular job. It was purely business. He had murdered and robbed; he had planted bombs almost as often as he'd planted drugs to smear whoever he was ordered to smear. In the Ulster Volunteer Force you did what you were told and you kept your trap shut. That was the reason he'd been chosen for this one. He would pick up fifteen grand when it was done, and a flight out of the country to wherever he wanted. Because once the shit hit the fan, it was crucial that neither he nor the UVF were on anyone's radar during the investigation. All he had to do once it was over, was to put the call in to his commander and say 'job done'. Then he had to get off his mark.

The first part of the task was easy. Executions were part of his life, and he'd carried out at least a dozen of them during the Troubles – usually a traitor who'd turned grass to the cops, or some guy who'd been blagging UVF money.

This one was no different, in terms of what he had to do. Earlier in the evening, as planned, he had executed the two men. He didn't know their story, only that they'd got greedy. It was swift and clinical, a bullet in the back of each head. Then he'd driven their car, the bodies slumped in the back seat, to the country road on the outskirts of Milngavie. He parked it well out of the way in a lay-by close to a dirt track road, and waited. The next part was going to be trickier, he'd been told. It involved some bird who'd be driving down the same road within twenty minutes. He'd assumed he had to put a bullet in her too, but that wasn't the deal here. This was different.

He waited at the roadside. He'd been told she'd left the place and was on her way down. But that she wasn't alone. His mobile pinged. They were only three minutes away. He got ready. He got out of the car and onto the roadside, when he saw the lights from the approaching car at the turn of the bend. He staggered and waved his hands urgently, as though he was injured and in need of help. The car slowed down and pulled in to the side of the road, hazards flashing. In seconds, as planned, his men came from the bushes, three of them, guns blazing. Then the car doors opened. An older guy climbed out, hands raised.

From where he stood, the full moon lighting up the dark, he could see the shock and rage on the old guy's face. Then he saw the woman get out of the back seat, hands in the air. She was tall, slim, youngish. And pregnant, by the looks of it.

'Don't move!' he shouted. 'Stay where you are or you'll all die right fucking here.'

He wondered if the old guy, standing silently fuming, was her father. He looked like he knew they were well and truly fucked.

Dobson watched, appreciating how swiftly his men worked. Rab Downey and Davey McKay had been hand-picked for this. The pair of them pulled the bodies out of the black BMW and dragged them over to the woman's car, wedging them into the back seat. Then they went back to the BMW and lugged over two holdalls – which he knew contained cocaine and sub-machine guns. Then as the woman stood horrified, they planted them in the boot of her car. Billy prowled around her, keeping his gun on her. She looked as though she was about to buckle. Maybe she was thinking about the baby she was carrying.

Dobson made his phone call.

'Job done,' he said.

He climbed into the BMW, and from his rear-view mirror, as he roared off, he could see the old guy peering into the back of their car where the dead men lay. Dobson put his boot down, almost going into a ditch on the bend. By the time the lights of the motorway came into view, he could hear the wail of the police siren. He smiled to himself. He was good at this shit.

CHAPTER ONE

Kerry Casey felt sick, a mixture of nerves, exhaustion and dread, as she was escorted in handcuffs by two female guards to the reception area of the prison entrance. From the corner of her eye, she could see the male officers looking at her from behind the glass reception. She tried to keep her eyes straight ahead, the tangle in her gut tightening, as she stood waiting for a few seconds. Then she heard a loud clunk and a low buzz as the door of the prison opened and she saw daylight, the rain coming down in sheets, bouncing off the steps and the ground beyond. She shivered, the icy blast slicing through the polo-neck sweater and jacket she was wearing. She felt grubby and unwashed, in the same clothes she'd slept in, her skin dry and irritated after splashing some water on it from the sink in the cell where she'd spent a sleepless night at Cornton Vale Women's Prison.

When they'd brought her here last night in the dark she

had almost been on the point of collapse, still in shock from what had happened just a couple of hours earlier. It was like being in the grip of some terrifying nightmare where you kept flailing around in the bed, trying to wake yourself to consciousness, but the hellish dream kept pulling you back in. At one point, as she was being registered at the reception area, Kerry's legs had buckled, and the two female police officers, who'd accompanied her from Stewart Street police station in Glasgow, helped her to a chair. A doctor was summoned, and she was taken to a side room. The middle-aged Asian woman GP sat next to her in the chair and spoke softly, asking her how far along she was in her pregnancy, and whether she had any history of fainting episodes or blood pressure issues. Kerry had struggled to speak. She was on the verge of tears and her throat was so tight with emotion that she kept halting and tightening her lips to stop herself from breaking down. She was aware of the two police officers glancing at each other and then at her. They'd have seen this before. She wouldn't be the first pregnant woman they'd brought in to face a night in the cells before appearing in court the following morning. Kerry might have looked and dressed better than some of the suspects brought in here, but right now she was no different, just another custody case awaiting her first appearance in court. The doctor had told her to lie on the narrow iron bed. And as she gently pressed the stethoscope onto her swelling stomach, again, Kerry filled up, her chest aching, thinking of the heartbeat inside her, ashamed and terrified that she had brought her unborn baby to this. Even though she was completely innocent of what she was being accused, she wouldn't have been targeted if she wasn't who she was. The doctor had smiled at her and told her the baby's heartbeat was strong and that she had to try as far as she could to relax and get some sleep overnight. Once the doctor had left, the officers helped her to her feet, then the door opened and a female prison guard came in and relieved the cops of their charge.

Kerry was told to follow her, and she walked behind her, handcuffs off as they went through the automatic door and through to an open area, with a staircase going up to a long row of cells above. The place was dimly lit and she assumed all the prisoners were sleeping as there wasn't a single sound.

'You're on the ground floor,' the officer said to her, pointing vaguely to a row of blue-painted cell doors. 'You'll be sharing with Natalie tonight, but you might be moved tomorrow.'

'Sharing?' The word was out before Kerry could stop it.

The officer glared at her and simpered a little.

'Did you think you were getting the presidential suite?'

Kerry cursed herself for being so naive, and despite her rage that she shouldn't be here, she knew it wouldn't be smart to argue. Self-preservation, she told herself.

'Of course not. I . . . I just wasn't sure if it was single cells.' She looked at the officer, then at the floor.

The officer walked on towards the last door on the corridor.

'As you're pregnant, you'll probably get moved to a different cell tomorrow, though you'll still be sharing. But tonight this is the only one free.' She was about to put the key in the door when she glanced over her shoulder at Kerry. 'Natalie is a bit of a handful, but just ignore her. Try to get some sleep.'

Kerry stood behind the officer, filled with dread as she eased open the door. Then, as soon as the light from the hall shone into the darkened room, there was an almighty roar from inside.

'Fuck is this! I haven't done anything. Fuck off!'

The officer opened the door wide and walked in, turning to beckon Kerry. She followed, her eyes adjusting to the dark. Jesus! There was a ghostly, skinny figure upright on the top bunk bed, clutching a bed sheet to her as though her life depended on it.

'It's okay, Natalie. Just calm down, now,' the officer said, firm but reassuring. 'This is Kerry. She'll be your cellmate for tonight. Just arrived. So just relax and go back to sleep.'

Natalie sat wide-eyed and scowling.

'She'd better no' touch my fucking stuff! Fucking tea leaves everywhere in here!'

'She's not interested in your stuff, Nat, now play nice and

get back to sleep while I get Kerry settled.' She turned to Kerry. 'Right. You're in the bottom bunk. There's a nightdress on the chair and some juice and a snack if you want.'

'That's my fucking snack! My nightdress!' Nat snapped.

'No, it's not, Natalie. You know that. You were told earlier you'd have a guest tonight. So button your lip and go to sleep. Be nice to Kerry. She's pregnant.'

Nat's eyes flicked Kerry up and down and rested briefly on her bump. She said nothing, then lay back down and turned to face the wall.

'Doors will click open at seven,' the officer said. 'If you need the toilet during the night just bang on the door and someone will come and take you.'

Then the officer turned and left, closing the door softly behind her, plunging Kerry into darkness, and leaving her standing in the middle of the stuffy, dingy room that smelled of sweat and something like very stale, cheap perfume. Kerry glanced around her, and from the window she could see nothing but the blackness outside. Her eyes tuned to the dark and now she could make out a chest of drawers across the room and on it were a couple of photos – one a framed picture of a little baby. Kerry softly picked her way across to the bottom bunk and sat down. She didn't even want to take her clothes off, to strip in this grim hole of a place and lie down. But she couldn't sleep in the clothes she had on as she'd been told she was going to have to appear in the custody court in the morning. Silently, she took off her sweater and folded it on the chair, then her bra, and her trousers. In the dark she could make out the silhouette of her swelling tummy and she touched it gently. She pulled on the nightdress which smelled clean and fresh, and then lay down on the bed, staring at the mattress on the bunk above. She was frozen with fear, barely breathing, listening to her heartbeat in her chest. Then the silence was broken by an anguished voice from the top bunk.

'I've got a wean, you know. They took him off me. The social work. Cunts!'

Kerry lay still, not sure whether to engage or stay quiet. She said nothing and the silence seemed to go on for ever, until from above she heard sniffing and heaving.

'Cunts took my wee laddie!' Nat sobbed.

Kerry held her breath, then she spoke. 'I'm so sorry,' she said softly.

For a long moment there was nothing, no sound from above, then soon there was the sound of her cellmate breathing deeply in slumber. Kerry turned on her side, curled up into a ball and wept.

Now, she was being nudged forward by the guards and they stepped outside into the rain. There was a large, dark blue van, like the ones Kerry had seen countless times on TV or when she had been a young lawyer, arriving or pulling away from court, transporting prisoners to and from jail. The windows were high and tiny with bars on them; a man in the passenger seat jumped out and dragged open the heavy door.

'On you go, Kerry.' The prison guard gave her a look and jerked her head towards the van.

The prison officer walked ahead and Kerry followed alongside the officer she was handcuffed to.

'You all right?' The guard turned to look at her, from dark brown, tired eyes.

Kerry nodded, swallowing hard again at the briefest touch of kindness. She took a breath as she stepped forward and into the van. *You can do this*, she told herself. *You have to*. Inside, she was plonked onto the thin plastic seats and the guard put her seatbelt on. Kerry expected the door to be slammed shut by the man who stood outside, the rain soaking his face, but it wasn't. She sat for a couple of minutes, shivering, then the prison doors opened again, and another two officers came out with a woman, handcuffed just as she had been. Kerry watched the scrawny dishevelled woman. She looked to be in her early thirties, and her dyed hair was matted and hanging like rats' tails. Her short denim skirt barely covered the tops of her thighs, and her black tights were laddered right down to her red sling-back shoes. She trembled in her tiny bomber jacket and plunging black T-shirt. She looked like a prostitute and teetered as she walked, jerking her arm away from the guard who was holding her. She stopped in her tracks as though she was refusing to go any further.

'Just fucking get your hands off,' the woman spat.

'Come on, Ash,' the guard said. 'Don't start with your crap now. You know how it ended the last time.'

The woman turned to her, defiant.

'Aye. But I shouldn't even be here,' she protested. 'This is all a fucking fit-up. That cunt of a cop.'

'Come on,' the guard said as she nudged her forward. 'Save it for your lawyer.'

The woman said nothing and walked on, climbing into the van. She stood for a moment as the door slammed shut, and gave Kerry a long hard look.

'Did they give you your glass of prosecco, hen?'

She might have been trying to smile but it was more of a snarl. Despite herself, in spite of the terror and anguish tearing at her insides, Kerry made eye contact with the woman and gave her a sympathetic smile, which she seemed to acknowledge, blinking smudged mascara eye-lashes to reveal bright blue eyes full of rage and hurt.

They drove from Cornton Vale to the motorway in silence. From where she was sitting, Kerry could see through a small space to the windscreen. They went past fields and cows and farmhouses, then onto the M8 motorway, rain lashing all the way towards the city centre. She thought of last night and of Natalie, and how this morning when the doors buzzed open, she had climbed down the ladder quietly, then had turned to her and said nothing, just stared blankly from eyes that seemed dead. Nat had been dressed in a T-shirt and jeans, and Kerry had glimpsed the slash marks on both wrists and forearms – some old, some recent – that made her look as though she was a self-harmer. When she'd left, Kerry had got dressed quickly but sat on her bunk as the corridor filled with the noisy chatter of women. From the vague smell of food coming from somewhere downstairs she'd assumed they were going to break-fast. Kerry hadn't followed Nat out of the cell, and when a prison guard stuck her head around a few minutes later, ask-ing if she wanted breakfast, she'd declined, saying she would just wait and eat the snack. The guard had shrugged and left her, the cell door open, so she could later peek outside and see prisoners moving around the communal area. In the weirdest way, it looked like business as usual.

The van weaved its way down to Clyde Street then across the Jamaica Bridge and on towards Glasgow Sheriff Court. She'd been told that her lawyer would meet her inside the court and she'd be taken downstairs. The officer who had been slightly pleasant turned to her.

'I don't know if you'll have been here before, Kerry, but you'll be taken to a holding cell, and your lawyer will come and talk to you. Then you'll go up for your appearance in front of the sheriff. Your brief will give you all the details.'

Kerry nodded as the van turned off the road and into what appeared to be the back of the Sheriff Court. It crossed her mind that there might be photographers out-side, if the news of the arrest of the head of a notorious

Glasgow crime family had leaked out through the police. It didn't take her long to find out. The van pulled up, and they sat for a few moments. Then she heard the sound of locks sliding and door opening.

'Okay, ladies,' the other guard said. 'Showtime!' She ushered Ash to her feet and marched her out of the van.

Kerry stood up, the nausea rising in her. She tried to breathe slowly as she was helped down the stairs out of the van. Then, in the drizzle, she heard the whirr of cameras and blinked as the flashes went off. Instinctively, she put her head down, as she'd seen prisoners do on news footage of them arriving in court. She was one of them now, whether she was guilty or not. The papers would be full of it in the morning. Christ! This was really happening.

'Fuck me, man!' Ash turned to her. 'Are you some kind of fucking celeb?'

'No,' Kerry said. 'I shouldn't even be here. I've done nothing.'

'Aye. Join the fucking club, mate. We all say that.'

'No. But really. I'm innocent.'

'Sure. But why are all these cameras here? Taking pictures of you? You famous or what?'

'No,' Kerry said. 'I'm a businesswoman.'

'Oh, right,' Ash said. 'A gangster?'

Kerry glanced at her but didn't answer. She went past the throng quickly and in through the back entrance, onto the charcoal-grey tiled floors and downstairs into the cells. Her senses were shocked and prickled by the noise, the smells of unwashed bodies and dirty clothes, the stench of fear and anger and shouts. Cloaked lawyers in smart suits walked briskly, clutching folders, rushing between clients who waited in cells. Kerry looked along the row of cells, some with two or three prisoners inside them, each cell guarded by a prison officer. Then she saw Marty Kane striding towards her like a vision of hope in all the gloom. It was all she could do to keep herself from bursting into tears.

'Kerry!' Marty said, as he reached her.

She wanted him to embrace her, this stalwart family friend, this uncle figure who had been her rock and her shoulder, especially in recent months. But he didn't. Here, Marty was her brief – no more. He shook her hand and held it for a long moment, but his eyes looked anguished behind his rimless glasses.

'Don't worry,' he whispered. 'Come on. Let's have a chat before you go upstairs.'

He led her and the officers to a cell and Kerry was ushered in and sat on a tubular plastic chair, the officer behind her.

'Do you mind taking the cuffs off?' Marty asked.

The guard stood for a moment, glanced around.

'I'm not supposed to.'

'Look. She's not going anywhere. You can see that.' He gave her a pleading look.

The guard said nothing, came across and unlocked the

cuffs. Kerry rubbed her wrists and put her hands on the table. Marty put his briefcase to one side and reached across and held her hand.

'Are you bearing up, Kerry?'

She swallowed.

'I'm trying to, Marty.' She felt her lip trembling. 'But Christ! What the hell happened? Where's Danny?'

Marty jerked his head.

'He's down the line a bit. I've already seen him. A good friend of mine will appear for Danny, as I'll be representing you. But we are working together. Danny is fine, but he's worried sick about you. Did the doctor come last night? I told them they had to get someone to see you.'

Kerry nodded. 'Yes. She examined me. Everything's fine.' She bit her lip. 'Well, I mean, as fine as it can be. I shared a cell last night with some girl who scared the living shit out of me. You've got to get me out of here, Marty.'

'Okay. I'll do everything in my power. Right. You'll know the sketch here, from your early days as a lawyer. You'll be taken up for a first appearance, they'll read the charges. We'll move for bail, obviously.'

Kerry watched as he looked away from her to his briefcase.

'Will you get bail, Marty?'

She'd been read the charges last night: murder, cocaine and possession of arms. Bail was at best a remote possibility.

'I hope so. It'll be difficult, given the charges, but it depends on who the custody sheriff is. The procurator fiscal who's taking custodies this morning is a bit of tough nut, making a name for himself. So it'll be a struggle.'

'Christ!' Kerry said. 'What if I don't get bail? I can't do a long wait in jail for a trial. I . . . I can't.'

Marty said nothing for a few beats. She knew he wouldn't lie to her, that he would have to lay it on the line.

'As I said, I'm hopeful. But if you don't get bail today, then we'll keep at it over the next few days. I'll move for it on health grounds, you being pregnant. You'll be back in Cornton Vale while I fight it, and while I move for an early pleading diet. But the most important thing is that I want to get these charges dropped. They're utterly ridiculous.'

Kerry was hearing it, but as if it was coming from a distance. A pleading diet. She knew what it was all right. She'd have to make a plea at some stage and then await trial. It could be anything up to one hundred and ten days that they could hold her. More than three months. Her mind raced and she felt nausea again. Her baby might even be born in jail.

'Jesus, Marty!'

'Let's keep it in perspective at the moment, Kerry,' Marty said. 'I'm not expecting this case even to go to trial. It will get ditched once they take a long hard look at the evidence and forensics. Even if you do get sent back to Cornton Vale, I don't expect you to be there long, before the charges are dropped.'

Kerry nodded. She had to stop herself being frustrated at Marty's calmness. This was his job. He was practical and pragmatic, while she was on the verge of hysteria.

'I have to believe that, Marty. But you make it sound as though it's easy.'

'I know it's not, sweetheart,' he said softly. 'Right.' He stood up. 'I'm going upstairs now to the court to see how far away your place is. When you go up, I'll be there. Just take it easy, try and stay calm. I know it's difficult.'

'Will Danny be there?'

'Yes,' Marty said. 'You'll be in the dock together.'

'Jesus.' Kerry shook her head. 'It's unreal.'

Marty pulled his lips to a sympathetic smile. Then he left.

CHAPTER TWO

The shriek of the flutes and thunder of the Lambeg drum at band practice upstairs was loud enough to hear at the far end of the White Horse pub. They were playing 'Derry's Walls', the anthem that celebrates the siege of Derry when the Irish rebels were defeated. The customers tapping their feet to the sounds of sectarian hate were happy enough though, and that's all that mattered. This pub was their spiritual home as much as Ibrox Stadium was on a Saturday afternoon. And it wasn't as if many tourists ventured down to Bridgeton looking for a bit of real Glasgow. If they did happen to wander in here, the death stares of the customers hugging the bar would make them swiftly turn on their heels.

Gimpy McGarvie was polishing tumblers behind the bar. He watched the swing doors as Gordy Thomson and a couple of his sidekicks walked in. One of the doors was held open and Dick Lambie entered, standing for a moment to soak up the atmosphere, like a general surveying his troops. Gimpy stared at this so-called band of brothers, a ruthless bunch of thugs who would pull out the lungs of anyone who dared cross them. Not that many did. It was unspoken in the White Horse that the UVF Glasgow section met here as they'd done all through the years of the Troubles. It was here in the back room that the flute bands practised, and later trained in weapons, assembling guns and taking instructions from uniformed UVF officers who led silent, double lives. The customers who were simply Rangers fans with no Loyalist connections may have known all of this, but if they did, they never spoke of it, because walls have ears, and if they were heard whispering in corners about the UVF or criticising them, then they would be history. Gimpy McGarvie hated the whole fucking lot of them. He hated football and everything that it meant in Glasgow, where you were on one side or the other. But he was trapped. He had nowhere to go, and he was paying off a hefty debt that right now felt like it would never come to an end.

'Awright, Gimpy?' Thomson said as he got to the bar. 'Cheer up, for fuck's sake. It might never happen.'

Gimpy snorted and managed as close to a smile as he could get with this wanker. His name was Steven, but they called him Gimpy on account of his right leg being shorter than his left, after having polio as a child.

'An' then again it might.' Gimpy shrugged.

He wasn't afraid of Thomson or the two pricks at his side now leaning on the bar hoping for a floor show. Lambie scared him though.

'You know what you need, Gimpy,' Thomson said, stabbing a finger at him. 'A right good ride. That would sort you out, big time.'

'Aye,' Billy Black chimed in, his skinny face and tongue darting out like a reptile. 'You'd need to get somebody to help you get your dodgy leg over though.'

'Fuck off!' Gimpy spat at Black. 'Enough of your shite. Drinks. What you want?' He glared at each of them, his expression flat, hoping the flush of rage he felt rising in his chest wouldn't reach his face.

Dick Lambie was already sitting in the corner where he could see who was coming through the doors and who was leaving. That kind of thing was important in any bar if you were Dick Lambie, drug dealer, loan shark, UVF Loyalist commander and feared killer.

Thomson sneered. He'd had his fun for the moment.

'Two vodkas with soda and lime for this pair of pussies, and Jack Daniel's and a dash of Coke for me and Dick.'

Gimpy didn't answer and was glad to turn away from them and face the gantry. As he picked up glasses and pushed them under the optics, he caught a glimpse of himself in the mirror and was raging that his face was red. He stood for a moment, chipping lumps out of the ice in the bucket, imagining it was the face of Gordy Thomson or any of these useless fuckers. But he knew he had to compose himself, and he did. He turned, added the mixers to the drinks and placed them on the bar. Thomson handed him a twenty pound note. He turned to the till and keyed in the order and took out six pounds change. He went to hand it to Thomson who had a Jack Daniel's in each hand.

'Keep it, son. You'll be able to get a hand job down at Glasgow Green for a fiver.' Thomson grinned.

The two picked up their drinks and sniggered as they turned their backs and headed across to where Lambie was sitting with his arms folded, his face serious, as though he hadn't heard any of the bullying.

Gimpy wiped the top of the bar and served another couple of customers, then sat down on a bar stool and looked up at the big-screen television mounted on the wall. He turned up the volume a little as the nine o'clock news came on, recognising the lead item showing images of Glasgow Sheriff Court. The strap headline at the bottom of the screen read, 'TWO IN COURT ON MURDER AND DRUGS CHARGES'.

Gimpy watched as the report followed.

A Glasgow businesswoman and her uncle appeared in court today charged with the murders of two men who died yesterday. Thomas Lumsden and Peter Hawkins were found last night near the switchback road on the outskirts of the city. Both had sustained gunshot wounds to the head and were pronounced dead at the scene. Kerry Casey and Daniel McGowan were arrested later by police and have been accused of the murders. They face additional charges relating to the possession of drugs and firearms. Both appeared in Glasgow Sheriff Court today and made no plea or declaration. They were remanded in custody.'

Gimpy turned down the volume as the news moved on to another story. He glanced down the length of the bar to where a group of customers had been watching the news in silence. The flutes upstairs struck up 'The Billy Boys', breaking the eerie quietness that had suddenly filled the bar. He knew that nobody would be talking about these murders – at least not in here. Most people in the bar would know the dead men, both customers, who worked for Dick Lambie. Gimpy knew them by name and reputation. They had shifted Lambie's drugs on the Manchester run and worked together on drops and picking up money. If they'd been murdered, no doubt it would have been a hit. The pair of them had been in here two days ago. If they'd stiffed Lambie for money he wasn't surprised that they'd ended up with bullets in their heads. But what he couldn't work out was why this Kerry Casey bird and her uncle were in the frame for it. The Casey family were big-time gangsters. Everybody knew that. They didn't get involved in small-time drug deals, so why would they be bumping off two of Lambie's thugs? He rinsed the cloth under the tap, wrung it out and wiped the length of the bar, making a furtive glance in the direction of Lambie and the boys who sat in silence, their faces like flint.

*

It was after midnight by the time Steven got back to the council flat on High Street in Glasgow's East End, where he lived with his mother. By the time he had climbed the tenement stairs to the second floor, his leg was aching from being mostly on his feet since his shift started at five. He pushed his key into the lock and went inside, careful to walk softly down the hall, as his mother would be asleep by this time. Or so he hoped. Then as he got to the kitchen, he heard her coughing. Her twenty fags a day lifetime habit was now taking its toll and rendered her more or less bed-ridden. It broke his heart. He knew she wouldn't be long for this world the way she coughed and was so breathless. But even though he knew her quality of life was getting worse every month, he couldn't bear the thought of her not being there. She'd been the rock of his life, her and only her. His father had pissed off when he was a toddler and it was his mum who'd taken on two jobs to keep the house and put food on the table. He'd watched her grow weaker over the years, the emphysema taking its toll, and the feisty bright woman, who in another life might have actually been some-body, was now breaking away in front of him. He stopped for a moment in the hallway and held his breath. He looked up at the fading pattern on the old wallpaper that had been there since he was a kid, and the damp patch spreading like varicose veins towards the ceiling. Like everything else in the flat, from the old fridge to the cooker, it needed fixing, but there was never enough money.

'That you, Steven?'

She was the only one who called him by his name.

'Aye, Ma. It's just me. You all right?'

He went to the slightly ajar bedroom door and stuck his head in. In the darkness he could see her head on the pillow, the duvet cover pulled up high under her chin. Her wispy grey hair was thinning and in the light from the street her cheekbones were emphasised and her face looked hollow. She had the grey, papery complexion of a lifelong smoker. She coughed again and he went forward, sat on the edge of the bed.

'Christ!' she managed to utter between coughs. 'This is a bastard, this cough.'

'You want me to get you something, Ma? I'm going to make a cup of tea. Did you eat your dinner?' Steven watched as she eased herself up a little on the pillow, wheezing.

'Aye, son,' she replied. 'A wee cup of tea would be lovely.'

'You want a bit of toast an' all?' Steven stood up.

'Only if you're making it,' she wheezed and lay back.

Steven smiled to himself as he left the room. Nearly every night it was the same routine. He tiptoed down the hall when he got in, hoping he wouldn't wake his ma. But nine times out of ten she'd call out for him, and nearly every night he made toast and they sat in her bedroom, him on the chair, her propped up on pillows, enjoying the toast and talking until he could see her eyes get heavy and she slipped off to sleep. She just wanted the company. He went into the kitchen and pushed two slices of bread into the toaster. Then he looked at the worktop and could see her dinner plate was already washed and on the rack. He went across to the bin and lifted the lid. Inside was half of his mum's mince and potatoes he'd left for her. That happened a lot these days; she seemed to be losing her appetite. He'd taken her down to the doctor and the GP told them it was part of her weakness, that she would eat smaller meals, but to do his best and make them nutritious. Steven often cooked ham soup, which at least got some vegetables inside her. But he knew this couldn't go on for ever.

'This is lovely, Steven,' his ma said, munching on the toast and sipping her tea. 'I was a wee bit peckish, and maybe that's why I couldn't get over to sleep.'

Steven sat on the old wicker chair by the window a few feet from her bed. He wanted to say to her that she was peckish because she hadn't eaten much of her dinner, but he knew it was pointless. There was nothing to be gained from giving her a row. He'd come to that way of thinking in the last year, when he'd seen how rapidly she was declining. At first he was angry, even with her, for her inability to do things for herself – like cooking sometimes, going outside, meeting people at the café nearby, all the things she used to love but had given up on. Then he realised that he was angry because the child in him knew he was losing her and raged against it, not wanting to consider a life without her. She was all he had, and he was annoyed with himself for that too. At thirty-seven he should have settled down by now, but it hadn't happened. Probably because the limp made him self-conscious and people had made fun of him since he was a little boy, so he lacked confidence. He didn't think anyone would be interested in a half-crippled man, and that was just how it had been. It was safer to be with his mum in the house away from all the crap that went on outside. Here he was loved and cared for, and there was always a warm smile for him any time he came in. Working in the pub, he'd listened to all sorts of stories from guys talking about their shitty marriages, their wives cheating, or themselves playing away, their kids driving them crazy. It struck him that there was a lot to be said for being on your own. He'd only had one girlfriend, when he'd been around seventeen, and it had lasted a while, but she'd got offered a job with her sister in Jersey and she'd taken the opportunity to get out of Glasgow. He couldn't blame her. But she'd broken his heart.

'So was it busy down in the pub tonight?'

'Not bad. Usual crowd,' he said. 'There was band practice so the racket from upstairs would burst your head.'

His mum shook her head. 'See all that stuff, Steven, all that hate? It makes me pig sick. I don't know how you can stand working in the place.'

He shrugged, ate his toast and took a swig of his tea.

'It's a job, Ma.'

Steven turned his head away and looked down at the

steady drizzle falling on the pavements and the roads shiny black from car head lights and the hazy glare of street lamps. He couldn't tell her it was more than a job. It would kill her if she knew that he was trapped in that bar because Dick Lambie and his mob had told him this was a job he would want. He had borrowed money from Lambie two years ago after his car had packed in and he wanted to take his mum on a holiday to the seaside. It had only been fifteen hundred pounds, and he took his mum to Ayr for a week and they'd had a fantastic time, but by the time he'd started paying the debt it'd quickly become two grand, because even the £50 a week he was paying barely touched the extortionate interest rates they were charging. Basically, all Lambie had wanted was someone he could manipulate. Steven had then been used to drive his men on a robbery. They'd broken into the home of an antique dealer and battered him almost to death and stolen some jewellery. He had only been the driver, but once he'd done that, there had been no way back. He'd told Lambie he wanted out and that he'd find a way to pay back his debt, which was now sitting at three and a half grand, but Lambie had said to do what he was told and get on with his job and then implied that worse would happen if he did not. So he had to listen, and hope to Christ he didn't get asked to do another job for them. But he knew it was only a matter of time. He looked across at his ma and could see her eyes heavy as she lay on the pillow. She'd eaten her toast but her half-empty mug was tilting from her hand.

'You looked tired, Ma. Why don't you try and get over to sleep?' He went across to her. 'Let me take this cup away.'

She didn't protest and he eased her back on the pillow, not too far as her chest got worse if she lay flat. He glanced at the oxygen canister in the corner.

'You want the oxygen on to help your breathing?'

'Aye, okay, son.'

Steven took the mask off the top of the canister and eased it onto his mother's head, making sure it was comfortable and covered her nose and mouth. Then he switched it on.

'How does that feel?'

'That's nice, son.' Her thin lips pulled back into a smile. 'You go and get to your bed now.'

Steven nodded. 'I will,' he said, as he turned towards the door. 'You want the light on or off?'

'Switch it off. There's enough light from the street lamps. That'll do me.'

He watched as she closed her eyes.

'Goodnight, Ma. See you in the morning.'

But she was already asleep.

Steven went into the living room and clicked the laptop on, going onto the news to see if there was any more information about the murders. He remembered Lumsden and Hawkins being in the pub and that Thomson had been talking to them. The boys had looked worried. There had to be something to that, but what puzzled him was why the Caseys were involved in it.

CHAPTER THREE

Kerry was being led up the stone stairs by a policeman. Her stomach was in knots, but she was glad to be out of the cell and the pit below, because a few minutes earlier all hell had broken loose. Police officers had been attempting to take a prisoner from his cell when he'd started lashing out, kicking and screaming abuse at them. Two more officers had waded in as they'd bundled the man out of the cell and into the main foyer. One of them had had him in a head-lock, but then from nowhere, the man had stabbed a policeman in the stomach. Kerry had heard the shouted 'He's stabbed me!' and she'd strained her neck to see the policeman, blood seeping out of his shirt. By this time, the man had been disarmed and pushed face down on the floor, his face bloodied from the force with which he'd hit the deck. There had been angry shouts from officers of 'Where did he get the fucking knife?' Then he'd been cuffed and dragged to his feet. Kerry had heard the officers being told to relay back upstairs to the court that there would be a delay in getting this prisoner up to the dock. Other prisoners in cells had egged him on, screaming of police brutality. The cop with the bloodied shirt had been ushered away along the hall to be treated.

Now at the top of the stairs, the door was opened and Kerry got her first glimpse of a courtroom in years.

It was the silence that hit her first, as she took in her surroundings. The sheriff up on the high bench, dressed in wig and gown, looked over the top of his half moon glasses then back to the papers in front of him. Marty Kane, in his black cloak, was seated at the huge square table below the sheriff's bench. He turned fully around to see her and gave her a sympathetic nod. The officer behind her nudged her forward. Then as she took a step, she saw Danny in the dock. He looked up at her, his face pale and tired, and for the first time since her mother had been killed she saw him look vulnerable. He tightened his lips as though to say to her it was okay. The policeman ushered her forward and as she stepped into the dock, she saw a flurry of activity in what was probably the packed press benches. This was a big story for the papers today – *Gangland crime boss in the dock for double murder.* She swallowed hard and shuffled into the dock, taking her seat next to Danny. Their knees touched and she turned her head to look at him as he whispered, 'You all right, sweetheart?' Kerry nodded but said nothing. She was far from all right. She was sitting in the dock next to her uncle, accused of crimes she had nothing to do with, surrounded by the public and a press bench who would be all over the story. The baby inside her was making a visit to the court, and it wasn't even born. There had to be some horrible irony in that. She thought of Vinny, of how mortified he would be if he had to see this, but how he would instinctively know she was innocent. For a fleeting moment she wondered if she would ever see him again, and with that thought she had to bite back tears.

A clerk from the front of the bench below the sheriff got to his feet and read out the charges. How do you plead? The cops urged both her and Danny to her feet.

'M'lud, I appear for Miss Casey on these charges. She pleads not guilty.' Marty sat down and Danny's solicitor stated that his client would also be pleading not guilty.

Opposite Marty, the depute fiscal got to his feet.

'M'lud, in view of the severity of the charges I move for no bail for either of the accused.'

'Objection, your honour!' Marty was on his feet.

The sheriff peered down at him.

'Go ahead, Mr Kane.'

'M'lud, my client, Miss Kerry Casey, is four months pregnant – and although in good health, the events of the last twenty-four hours have taken their toll on her. I move for the sake of her health that she be allowed bail, and if need be tagged. But I don't see that incarcerating her while we await proceedings would do any good; in fact it would be detrimental to her health and the health of her unborn child. She is of no absconding risk and could be monitored by daily visits to the police station and is willing to surrender her passport. I move that bail be granted.'

The sheriff said nothing.

'Mr Prentice?'

The depute fiscal was already standing up, hands in one pocket, a sheaf of papers in the other outstretched hand.

'M'lud, I have moved no bail for a reason. Miss Casey and her business empire have connections and residential property and businesses across Spain, and even if her passport has been surrendered I think there is still a risk of absconding. These are grave charges, the gravest of charges. Two men have been murdered, and a large quantity of cocaine and arms have been found in the boot of a car belonging to the Casey organisation. I believe there is a serious risk by allowing bail and I would move against it.'

The same for Danny.

The court was silent as the sheriff sat back. In the stillness he could be heard taking a long breath through his nose and letting it out slowly as he studied the charges, glancing up from time to time to look at Kerry and at Danny. Eventually he spoke.

'Bail refused.'

No explanation. Not that it was required, given what the fiscal had just said. And no words indicating that he had given much consideration to Marty's plea for bail. It was over. Kerry could feel a choking in her throat as Marty turned to face her then got up and came across. He put an arm out to touch her shoulder.

'Kerry, don't worry. We're working on this really hard, around the clock. These charges won't stick. I'm sure of that. Just try your hardest to bear up. I'll come down and see you before you go.'

He nodded to Danny.

'You bearing up, Danny?'

'I'm all right, Marty. This isn't my first rodeo.'

His voice was flat, with a hint of black humour. Danny obviously had learned how to remove himself from this by keeping focused. Kerry stood up but her legs felt shaky. The officer held her arm and guided her out of the box and down the stairs again to the cells.

'You all right?' the officer said to her once they were in the cell.

'Not really,' Kerry said, feeling tears in her eyes at the kindness. 'But I'm trying.'

The officer nodded. 'I'll get you a cup of tea for the journey.' She looked at her watch. 'They'll be leaving in about fifteen minutes. Just waiting for Ash.'

Kerry looked at her, wondering who Ash was, then the officer said, 'Ash, the woman who was with us on the journey in. She's up for shoplifting and police assault. She's broken her bail terms, so she'll be getting locked up until her trial.'

Kerry said nothing, remembering now, and the officer

went out of the cell and along the corridor and disappeared. For a few minutes Kerry sat alone, listening to the
shouts and arguments along the row of cells. It seemed
they were all fighting with police, blaming them for everything that had led to them being here, protesting every
time they were being moved. Only a couple of prisoners
went silently, and Kerry sat watching them being led along
towards the stairs, wondering what their stories were, how
different they would be from hers, and yet how close they
were at this moment.

'Fuck this shit! This is fucking pish, man!'

Even before the doors to the prison van opened, Kerry
just knew it was Ash. She watched as the door slid open,
and Ash stood, refusing to go any further, her hands in
cuffs, an officer on either side.

'Just get in the bus, Ash.' One of the officers forced her
forward. 'You're not going anywhere standing here.'

Ash stood for another moment, and Kerry watched as
her legs seemed to lose their stiffness and a defeated look
spread across her face. Ash glanced inside and her eyes met
Kerry's, and for a moment they locked, both in recognition
that whoever they were, whatever they'd done, they were
in the same boat – at least for the journey.

'Come on!' The officer pushed her again.

'Aye right, ya bitch. I'm going.' Ash gave up the protest
and climbed inside.

The officer gently eased her around so she was two seats behind Kerry on the opposite side. Kerry glanced back and their eyes met again, and she thought that somewhere in Ash's hooded, bloodshot, hopeless eyes, there was a glint of defiance. The engine revved as the minibus moved off. Kerry fixed her eyes on the gap she could see through the screen. They travelled through the town, towards High Street and then onto the motorway. She could see the turn-off that would have taken her up to her own house, her own bed, to the comforts of the life she had been living and taking for granted for the past few months. God knows when she'd ever see that again, the voice inside her nagged. But she ignored it. She couldn't think that way. She was a lawyer. She had studied criminal law as part of her degree, even though she hadn't practised it any more than was necessary to get her final qualification. But she knew enough to know that these charges surely wouldn't stick. Marty had assured her, and yet here she was, heading back to Cornton Vale to await her next court appearance and trial. As the minibus turned onto the M8, Kerry's mind drifted to the previous night, and she tried to go over every moment of it, before her life went into freefall.

Nothing had been any different from normal. She had been in Milngavie with Danny to see an old family connection, to look at buying some prime property that had suddenly come up and had to be acted upon swiftly.

Then they had been heading back towards her home, driving along a country road, when suddenly this guy had staggered around the road, waving them down. Danny had been immediately suspicious, even if she hadn't. He hadn't liked the look of it. But the man had been staggering, and Kerry had said we can't just drive past. What if it's a trap, Danny had said, and Kerry had argued that the guy was in trouble, blood on his face. They had to stop. Looking back now, at how quickly it happened, she knew she should have listened to Danny. But there was no point in thinking like that now. The question that was nagging her was *why*? Who would frame them like this in a clearly planned, professional operation? There was nobody in the city of Glasgow who would even think about doing that. Even the one or two shady characters who fancied their chances would be incapable of pulling this off. Sure, she'd made enemies of the Colombians, but as far as she knew that was over. Her mind was full of several scenarios, none of them making any sense. It occurred to her that Quentin Fairhurst could be behind it. Was that even possible? It had to be someone with a deep-seated grudge, so maybe even the Colombians were still in the frame after what she did to them.

In a way she was grateful to have these thoughts flooding through her mind, because it was keeping her from thinking about her situation right at this moment, as they turned off the main road and into the Cornton Vale entrance where she had no idea what lay in wait for her.

CHAPTER FOUR

Dick Lambie never shirked from a job, no matter what it was. He was a proud Loyalist, the son of a proud Loyalist, a soldier who would defend Queen and country no matter what it took. His UVF commanders had been able to see that he would take orders and ask no questions by the time he was a teenager. And by the time he was in his twenties, he had carried out a number of robberies, hits and beatings at the behest of the UVF. They had given him stripes for that and he was now Commander of the UVF Glasgow platoon. That was only part of his life though. On top of that he was allowed a free hand in drug dealing, and as long as he kept within his own turf and gave the UVF a slice of his profit, he could pretty much run his own show. He'd built up a reputation for getting things done swiftly and clinically. If Belfast accepted a job and it needed a foot soldier to make it happen, often the job would go to Lambie. He would be handsomely paid for his efforts, and over the years his business had built up. He had two bookies, a taxi firm which was handy in shifting drugs, and a haulage firm which was even better when transferring money and weapons back and forth to Belfast. He also had a substantial book in moneylending across the east side of the city where his henchmen ran a tight ship, with massive interest rates that doubled and tripled, trapping people for ever in their debt. He'd made a small fortune because people who couldn't pay would end up signing cars, houses and sometimes even businesses over to them. And lately, people-trafficking had become his new enterprise, where he was making a good skin out of supplying foreign women to brothels and escort agencies. Lambie knew nobody would think about taking him on or they'd face the UVF thugs.

When the job came up to frame the Caseys it had been something he'd had to take a second look at. He knew he couldn't, and wouldn't, refuse. But this was dangerous shit. This needed thinking through. If he fucked this up, the Caseys would be all over him like a raging inferno. The top UVF man, Wattie Townsley, had travelled from Belfast to meet him and give him the details of the job. They'd met in the White Horse and what was required had been laid out for him. Frame Kerry Casey had been the main goal. He'd known who she was – the bird that had taken over from Mickey Casey, that cocky Taig, who'd swaggered across the city with his sidekick Frankie Martin, taking scalps on every turf. They hadn't come for him though, and he'd been well puffed up with that, because it had made him feel too big for them.

But framing Kerry Casey in such a way that she wouldn't see the outside of a prison cell for a long time had been a big ask. Over two hours and several drinks, he and the Mid Ulster Brigade commander had gone over the possibilities and between them they had come up with murder, drugs and firearms. A triple whammy that would ruin the Caseys, and who knew, might just open the door for him to take over. But that was for another day. By the end of the night, he'd been told he had to make it happen, and if it involved sacrificing two of his bodies, then so be it. But you couldn't just wade in and take two random people off the street. They had to be dealers to make it look right. And the Caseys had to be seen to have been attacking them because of who they were and who they worked for. That was when Lambie had suggested going for the two pricks Lumsden and Hawkins, who he'd known were skimming off a bit too much of their share. On top of that, Lumsden had been riding his young cousin and had got her pregnant, and that was just not on. He was too thick to be bringing up a wean, and the wee cunt denying it made matters worse. So his days had been numbered anyway. It was all about planning the operation carefully and making sure they got Kerry Casey bang to rights. It had been a bonus to get her uncle Danny too, an old-fashioned hoodlum who'd lived to tell many tales. Lambie's gut had done a little anxious twist when he'd realised that there was no going back, after he'd seen her on the television going into court, the look on her face ... Tough shit. He'd done his job. And if you're caught with two stiffs in your car, a haul of coke in the boot and a couple of machine guns, you're going to need a very good lawyer to get you out of the hole.

Lambie could see that Billy Dobson was edgy and keen to get paid and out of Glasgow. They were sitting at a table in the White Horse in the early afternoon, a few feet away from where Thomson and his two sidekicks sat. There was no need to involve them in this part. Thomson's job had been to be on hand along with his boys to make sure Dobson got away from the murder scene before the cops arrived to catch Kerry Casey red-handed. It was them who had moved the stiffs into the back of her car and planted the guns and coke. They'd been well paid, and they were well paid anyway for the steady work they did for Lambie, enforcing, collecting and dealing out any slaps that had to be dealt. But Dobson was about to get handed a good wedge here, and it had to be just between the two of them. Lambie was glad the pub was quiet, but even if it had been busy, punters knew better than to barge into his company if he looked like he was having a meeting. He looked up at the bar, where Gimpy McGarvie was working away, stocking shelves. He'd clocked Gimpy stealing a couple of furtive glances across at them, and he made a mental note to get Thomson to keep an eye on the wee shite to make sure he wasn't getting curious or anything stupid. Lambie had had Gimpy on a tight rein anyway, ever since he'd driven the getaway van on a robbery, and even though Gimpy'd told him afterwards that he wanted out, Lambie had persuaded him otherwise; once you were in with Lambie's mob, you didn't get out. Well, not alive, anyway.

Lambie put his hand in the inside pocket of his jacket and brought out a brown padded envelope. He put it on the table and slid it across to Dobson.

'Your wages, mate. It's all there. As agreed.'

'Cheers, mate.' Dobson picked it up and stuffed it into his jacket and zipped the pocket. He gave Lambie a look. 'I know I don't need to count it.'

'Aye, not in here anyway,' Lambie said. He lifted his mug to his lips. 'Anyway. Good job, Billy. Not that I expected anything less. The boys across the water are well pleased.' He paused, looked up at the television. 'Did you see it in the news? The Caseys will be going fucking apeshit trying to figure this out.'

'I know,' Dobson said. 'That's why I'm fucking off to Barbados tonight.'

'You got a place there?'

'No. But I have friends.'

'Well, keep your head down.'

'No problems, Dick. I've been here before. Though this was a bit different.'

'Aye,' Lambie said. 'For me too. But I don't ask questions.'

'Yep.' Dobson stood up and zipped up his jacket. 'Right. I'm off. Good to see you, Dick. We'll talk again, I'm sure.'

'We will, brother. You look after yourself now.'

'I will.'

Dobson turned and walked towards the swing doors, and Lambie watched him as he left. He got up from the table and went across and sat beside Thomson and the boys.

'Listen, I know I don't need to tell you this, but you can guarantee the shit will be flying over this Casey bird and her uncle being in jail. They'll have top lawyers and investigators trying to prove they're innocent. So now, more than ever, it's important to keep your traps firmly shut. Understand?'

'Of course, boss,' Thomson said, and the other two nodded their heads vigorously.

'Now, are there any loose ends you've not told me about?' He looked from one to the other. 'Anything at all we need to mop up?'

There was an awkward silence which made Lambie suspicious. Thomson shifted in his seat.

'What?' Lambie leaned on the table, glaring at all three of them. 'Tell me.'

'Well.' Thomson picked at his fingernails, trying to avoid eye contact with his boss. 'There was a bit of a problem with the car – the one we used for getting us all away from the scene.'

'Aye. You were supposed to burn it.'

'I know. But it's not burned yet. It was all a bit mental, all happening that fast and the cops were all over the shop by the time we were two hundred yards down the road. We had to get off the road as quick as possible, and the last thing we wanted to do was torch a motor anywhere near it in case it attracted attention. In fact, torching any motor that night or the day after just seemed too risky.'

Lambie listened to Thomson and processed what he was saying. He had a point, even if he hadn't done what he was told.

'So where's the motor now?'

'We took it to the scrapyard, but even that's risky.'

Lambie thought for a moment before he answered.

'Well it needs to be dealt with quickly. You need to get the car torched, or drive it somewhere into a quarry or something. But it needs to be done.'

'I know.' Thomson jerked his head towards the bar. 'I was thinking about getting Bo and Gimpy to go today and take it out to the quarry. Just drive the fucking thing in and it will disappear.'

Lambie waited for a long moment. Gimpy wasn't a hard man, by any stretch of the imagination. But he would be handy enough to do something like this, and he knew he'd be too shit scared to open his mouth or ask questions.

'Aye, that's fine. Give him a couple of hundred quid.' He eyed Bo. 'And make sure you don't go opening your mouth about anything on the journey.'

He glanced at Thomson. They both knew that Bo had a coke problem, which he claimed he was keeping in check, but it was dodgy and Lambie didn't like it. Once this had all settled down, he might tell Thomson to take Bo for a long walk somewhere and make him disappear.

CHAPTER FIVE

Kerry hadn't slept much in her cell and had lain tossing and turning. She had heard the shouting and laughing, and sometimes crying, from other cells after lights out; and in some perverse way it had been like a sleepover on steroids. As she lay in bed waiting for the doors to buzz open, dreading what fresh hell she faced, she reflected on last night.

When she'd got back to jail after the court appearance, a senior guard had taken her to one side and told her she would still be sharing with Natalie until another cell became available, possibly the following day. The guard by now was well versed on who Kerry Casey was, and she'd fixed her eyes on her with a stern warning.

'You'll be a bit of a celebrity in here, Kerry, as your court appearance has already been on the lunchtime news. So be careful. I'd love to tell you there is a great bunch of girls in here but that's not the situation. There are one or two hard cases who will want to take you on.'

Kerry had put her hand up to stop her.

'Look,' she said. 'None of this is the way it's being presented. I've done nothing. I've been framed. I'm not some gangster looking to swagger around jail. Please believe me. That's not who I am. Christ, I'm pregnant and I'm sitting here, stuck in jail for something I absolutely didn't do.'

The guard hadn't looked convinced. She'd probably heard it all before.

'Fair enough. I hear you. But the best thing for you to do is just keep a low profile and get on with things until your lawyer can get you out – if that happens.'

Kerry nodded but didn't say anything.

'Now,' the guard said, 'here's the drill. As a remand prisoner, you don't have to work, because you've not been convicted of anything. So you're free to hang around your cell all day, but I wouldn't advise it. You'll go native. The best thing for you to do is be like the others, have a job and get on with it.'

A job, Kerry had thought. *In here*. She said nothing and waited.

'There are three areas you can work in to fill your time. There's the hairdressing salon, where you could help and learn a few things; there's the bicycle repair shop – that's one of the main jobs we do here, repair bikes for charity for them to sell on – or you can make greetings cards for charity. So that's something you might want to consider. We also grow our own vegetables and flowers so we have a good garden out there if you're into that. Up to you.'

Kerry had sat for a moment, trying to let this sink in. It was surreal. The guard had described it as though it was her first day at a holiday camp and these were the various activities that were available. But there was no mention of lights out, lock-up, the fact that there was no toilet in the cell, or that she was surrounded by broken women, some angry, some pathetically sad, some of them killers. There was nothing to do here but buckle down and hope Marty could get her out soon. Eventually, she spoke.

'I understand. And thanks. I suppose working with the greetings cards might be interesting.' Kerry could scarcely believe what she was saying, wondering who she was right now. 'But can I ask you a question? What about the girl Natalie I'm sharing with? Is she dangerous? She told me she has a baby the social work took off her, and she is very angry.'

The prison officer had sighed and sat back, stretching out her legs and studying her polished sensible shoes.

'Natalie,' she said. 'She's a bit of a poor soul, and like a lot of the people in here should probably be under psychiatric care. But she committed a crime and they sent her here. It's not the first time. She's in and out like a yo-yo. Drugs, mostly, shoplifting. But she stabbed someone in the street two months ago, and that's why she's here. She suffers paranoid episodes. She self-harms. It's a sad case, but we have to just do what we can for her.'

Kerry was worried that she might be angry with her for being pregnant, but didn't want to appear stupid by asking, so she just nodded.

'She was crying in the night.'

The guard shrugged. 'That happens. A lot of them do that. For most of them, there's been a shitload of misery before they ever got in here.' She looked beyond Kerry. 'But hey. It is what it is. And you're here now. So if you're wise, you'll just keep on people's good side and won't get involved in any of the shit that goes on – drugs, pills, the kind of stuff that seems to get smuggled in here no matter what we do.'

After what Kerry had felt was akin to a pep talk, she'd been given some clothes and showered and dressed before the evening meal.

When she'd walked into the big dining hall she had felt all eyes on her and the chatter had fallen silent.

'There's the Godmother in now!'

Kerry had heard the sarcastic cat-call and a few giggles and cackles, and glanced around to see where it was coming from, but blank faces had stared back at her. She'd picked up a tray and gone up to the canteen hatch where they'd been serving hot food. She'd filled her plate with stew and mashed potato and vegetables, and found that she was hungry despite the nausea she'd been feeling most of the day. She'd told herself that no matter what they served she'd have to eat because of the baby, even if she had to force herself, but this stuff hadn't looked too bad. She walked away from the counter with her tray, not quite sure where to sit as some of the girls were in groups and almost everyone was looking in her direction. She hadn't wanted to barge in to anyone's company so she'd sat at an empty table, and the murmuring had continued. She'd wondered if someone would approach her and had been trying to work out what to say. She hadn't had to wait long, because into the place walked Ash, who'd spotted her immediately and waved. Then she'd collected her food on a tray and came over and sat down, as though they were two old friends in a café who hadn't seen each other in a while.

The weirdness of it all had taken Kerry's mind off the hellishness of her plight. Because here in front of her were women with *real* problems, women whose lives had been very different from hers, and many of whom had ended up here because of drugs or mental health issues. They hadn't looked too dangerous, but this was prison so she'd had to assume that some of them at least were in for serious offences. She knew she was privileged compared to them, but she was in prison and pregnant, and somewhere she felt hurt and angry that it was all a bit of a lark to them to make fun of her. She hadn't been sure what to expect from other prisoners but she hadn't expected that.

'You all right, Kerry?' Ash had said as she plonked herself down.

'Yeah,' Kerry said. 'Kind of shellshocked, I suppose. Looks like people are enjoying me being in here – pregnant and all as I am.'

'I don't suppose you've been inside before?' Ash said, devouring a mouthful of mash which she'd smothered in gravy.

'No.' Kerry glanced at her, then back at her plate.

'I heard who you are, by the way,' Ash whispered. 'You're famous! Notorious!' Her eyes had widened as though she was in the company of a celebrity.

Kerry hadn't answered, and sipped from a glass of milk.

'They're all talking about the gangster boss.'

Kerry had given her a look and sighed. She hadn't wanted to have this conversation. But Ash had persisted.

'I knew as soon as I looked at you that you were different. Know what I mean?' she went on. 'You look well-heeled. That's why the other women will see you as different. Some of them will be fascinated by you, but I'm not going to lie to you, Kerry. There's one or two hard-faced bastards in here who might take a pop at you.'

'Christ! I don't want to fight or argue with anyone,' she said, putting down her knife and fork. 'Look, Ash, I run a business organisation.' As she'd said it she'd known it sounded ridiculous, even to her. She'd dabbed the corner of her mouth with a paper napkin. 'We have business interests in Glasgow and also abroad.' She'd paused, looking into Ash's eyes. 'But I have nothing to do with these charges against me. I have no clue why this happened. I swear to God.' She'd put her hand on her stomach. 'I swear on my baby's life. I have no idea. I'm completely innocent, and so is my uncle Danny. We were just driving home when we got flagged down by this guy who looked as though he was in trouble.'

Ash had nodded sagely. 'Fitted up then,' she said. 'Cops, probably. They fit people up as a matter of routine. Drugs mostly. If they want to do you, then they'll do you. If you're a gangster and they can't get you the right way, they'll set you up. That's the polis for you.'

Kerry had looked at her, perplexed. She hadn't suspected it was police, as she was sure there would have been some indication that they were looking at her beforehand, maybe some kind of gypsy warning. Danny still had some good friends in the police who had remained loyal to the Caseys.

'I don't know,' she'd said. 'But somebody fitted me and Danny up. Now I'm stuck in here, and anyone with any sense would know that I wouldn't get involved in the kind of crap that I'm charged with. It's ridiculous.'

She hadn't wanted to give the girl her life story, because Ash was too eager to talk and ask questions, and she would probably broadcast their conversation around the jail. 'Somebody did this to me. But I don't know who or why. My lawyers have a team working on it. And one way or another I will find out who is behind it.'

Ash had been silent for a moment, eating a few mouthfuls of food, then she'd sniffed and looked at her.

'Lucky you,' she said. 'A team working for you. People like me, we just get fucked in here and the duty lawyer gets handed a case that he'll have seen a million of, then he does his best to get you out. But this time I'm not so sure.'

'So what happened?' Kerry wanted to divert the attention from herself. 'I heard that you broke bail conditions.'

Ash had looked at her, a little surprised.

'Oh, I suppose the screw told you that,' she said. 'Yeah. That's right. I was picking up a bit of stuff from the shops' – she winked – 'you know, as you do, for the resetters, and I got caught. The store detective was a rough bastard and manhandled me so I knocked him on his arse. Then they held me till the cops came. It all ended up a bit messy.' She paused and held out her hands, shaking and bruised. 'I'm on methadone, trying to get off heroin, and doing not bad. But in here, they won't give me it as I'm on remand. So they gave me diazepam just to take the edge off it. But bottom line is by the time the cops came I was a bit wired, so I stuck the head in the officer. Blood everywhere. I think I broke his nose.'

'Oh,' Kerry said. 'You charged with police assault?'

Ash had shrugged. 'Aye. Not for the first time. But I was provoked.'

Kerry hadn't wanted to argue. She wondered where Ash came from, what her story was, how she ended up routinely being in and out of jail. No doubt it would be the same story she'd heard as a young lawyer, or reading the newspapers or watching the news. A different world.

'Where are you from?' Kerry ventured. 'If you don't mind me asking.'

Ash looked at her flatly. 'Ask away.' She shrugged. 'I'm from the East End – down by Glasgow Green. I grew up there – well if that's what you can call it. Dragged up, more like.'

'You got family?'

'Not any more.' Ash looked dark. 'My ma was dead by the time I was sixteen. It was her who put me on the game. So it's not as though I have a lot to thank her for.'

Kerry had sat in stunned silence. There was no answer to this.

'Your mum?' She couldn't help herself.

'Aye. She was a heroin addict. I grew up watching her inject. By the time I was thirteen I was smoking hash with my mates, dodging school and stuff. Then my ma decides that I'm old enough to earn my keep. She took me down to the Green and pimped me out. Well, not actually her, her pimp did that – cunt that he was. But she went along with it. Punters like the young ones, so I made good money. And now there were two of us earning, and she could afford more heroin.'

This was too much to take in and Kerry was chilled to the bone by her revelations, but suddenly felt as though she was intruding in Ash's life by letting her pour all this shocking information out. She found herself looking at Ash, almost in disbelief. How do you come back from your mum pimping you out to paedophiles at the age of thirteen? She didn't know what to do or ask or say, but she knew she was expected to say something.

'Christ, Ash,' she said. 'I'm shocked. How did you cope?' She'd shaken her head. 'So young.'

'Heroin,' she said. 'It takes all the pain away. Nothing can touch you when you get a wee smoke of that stuff. See the moment that shit kicks in, it's like being under a warm blanket and everything looks easy and all the things you've been crying about and were scared of just melt away.' She sniffed. 'And once you find that place, you're in. Your life has already gone.' She looked away, and for a long moment, Kerry could see that the memory was hurting.

'I can imagine,' Kerry said. Wanting to feel empathy she added, 'I have a good friend whose daughter was a drug addict. It was a terrible time for the family, but she's out of it now. She got into rehab.'

'Lucky her. There's no rehab for most of us though. Just a methadone script, and that keeps you going, unless you find money and can get smack to top it up. But I'm trying not to do that.'

They'd sat finishing their food, both of them silent, Kerry stealing glances at Ash, wondering at how a spirited girl like this, in other circumstances, could probably have been anything she chose to be. People would say that if you make the wrong choices you can end up hitting rock bottom. From where Kerry was sitting right now, she was as close to rock bottom as anyone else in here.

After dinner, there had been a couple of hours of free time for the prisoners, where some made phone calls to family and friends, lay around in their cells, or watched television in the communal area. Most of them had sat around on sofas or chairs that reminded Kerry of the big common room for sixth formers at school, though it was a world away. She had been on a couch with Ash, both of them drinking tea, a little further away from a group of women who sat together around a table.

'Don't look now,' Ash said, 'but see that big table, that's where two of the hardest cases in the jail sit. One of them, Big Aggie – the heavy one with the cropped hair – she's a lifer. In here for battering an old man to death when she was off her tits on drugs one night. Mind you, I don't know if it was just the drugs. She's out of her fucking tree any-way. Flies into fits of rage sometimes, and once she punched a prison warden so hard she nearly lost her eye. She got an extra four years for that. But I don't think she'll see day-light on the outside for the rest of her puff.'

Kerry risked a glimpse up from the magazine she was thumbing through. Big Aggie seemed to be holding court with the other girls, telling some story that had them in fits of laughter.

'That's her girlfriend,' Ash said. 'The wee fat one next to her with the black curly hair. Nicola. They're together.'

'I see,' Kerry said, not really knowing what to say.

'You get a lot of that in here,' Ash went on. 'You know, lassies being together. Sometimes they're not really lesbi-ans, but just gay in the jail, if you get my drift. Gets a bit lonely in here, and some of the girls just hook up with each other while they're inside.'

Kerry hadn't been sure what was coming next so she'd said nothing, then Ash had said, 'It's no' really my bag though. I like men. I had a boyfriend for a while, but we split up about six months ago. Drugs. He's just wasted. What about you?' She glanced at Kerry's bump. 'Is the da in the picture?'

Kerry had let out a sigh. She really hadn't wanted to go into it.

'Yes,' she said. 'But it's a long story, and he's away working at the moment.'

Ash nodded, as though she'd made her own mind up that the father had done a runner.

It had been getting close to lock-up and some of the girls had already drifted back to their cells. Kerry had been dreading going back into the cell with Natalie, wondering what was in store for her. She hadn't seen her around since the dinner hall, but now she spotted her coming along the corridor from their cell, striding towards where Kerry and Ash sat.

'Oh fuck!' Ash said. 'Here comes trouble.'

Kerry looked up to see Natalie standing over her, glowering, her face flushed and angry.

'You stole my fucking stuff,' she said, jabbing a finger.

Kerry, bewildered, looked up at her.

'I . . . I didn't take anything, Natalie. I don't know what you mean.'

'You took my perfume,' she spat. 'And my jumper. And that wee toy I keep for my boy. Where the fuck is the toy?'

The room had fallen silent, and all eyes had turned on Kerry. She'd glanced from Ash to her accuser.

'Nat. I didn't take anything,' she said. 'I didn't even see anything. I don't know what you're talking about.'

She could see Nat was shifting from one foot to the other, agitated. Kerry hadn't known what to do, and glanced around hoping to see a prison guard or anyone who could step in to help before this got out of hand.

'My toy!' she'd shrieked. 'You took my toy! Probably for that wean you've got in there. Well give it fucking back! It's for my wean not yours!'

'Nat—'

But before she could say anything else, Nat, as quick as lightning, had grabbed her by the hair, almost yanking her off the couch. Kerry yelped with the pain, feeling her hair being torn out by the roots. And in a few seconds all hell had broken loose. Ash had jumped to her feet and was all over Nat, trying to prise her hands off Kerry's hair, then two girls had jumped up from their chairs and seized Nat around the waist, one of them trying to gently coax her to let go. As she finally did, with a handful of hair, Nat had burst into tears and fled off down the corridor towards her cell. Kerry sat clutching her head, a searing pain at the temple where the hair had been wrenched.

'You all right?' Ash said, sitting down close to her. 'Let

me see.' She examined her head. 'Aye, she got a clump of your hair, all right.'

Kerry had swallowed her tears, sensing everyone's eyes on her. And then Big Aggie and a couple of the other women had come towards her. She had been terrified, but she'd got to her feet on shaky legs.

'Not a big hard woman then, eh? Not a gangster then?' Big Aggie said, smirking.

Kerry didn't answer.

'You better no' have taken her stuff.'

'I didn't take anything,' Kerry said. Her head had been pounding but she'd stood her ground. 'I would never do that.'

Aggie had stood legs apart and glared at her. 'Well, just so you know. Big-time gangster or no, Kerry Casey – we're watching you. You're nothing in here. You might be all rich and fancy outside, but in here you're just a fucking number like the rest of us.'

Kerry didn't reply, but she stood and stared Aggie down long enough for her to turn and walk away. When she did, Kerry sat back down, biting her lip.

'Well done, Kerry. That fat cunt knows you stood up to her there. But you need to watch your back now.'

She'd looked at Ash but said nothing, wondering what the hell was going to happen when she went to her cell later.

CHAPTER SIX

It had led to another night with not much sleep, Kerry lying terrified in case Nat was going to attack her again, her scalp aching from the hair having been torn out. When she'd come into the cell about an hour after the incident, Nat had lain in bed, silent, her face turned to the wall. Kerry had got dressed quietly and slipped into bed, barely breathing. Then the lights had gone out and the doors had clicked shut for the night, and Kerry had lain there, dreading what might happen. But then, out of the blue, Nat's voice had come from above.

'I'm sorry,' she said. 'I didn't mean to hurt you. I . . . I just can't cope sometimes.' Then the sobs.

'It's okay, Nat,' Kerry said. 'I understand. It's okay.'

It wasn't okay though, not by any stretch of Kerry's fevered imagination was anything okay, and she wondered if anything was ever going to get any better. She had lain thinking about Vinny. Remembering their last days together, his smile, their shared laughter and experiences, filling her head with any thoughts that would take her out of the hell she was in at the moment.

After breakfast, where Ash and Kerry sat together, Kerry was aware everyone was still looking at her, nobody speaking to her or nodding in her direction.

'That was some stooshie last night,' Ash said. 'Are you all right? Did you sleep?'

'Not much. But I'm fine. Nat said she was sorry. And she was crying. She's a poor soul, Ash.'

'Aye. But a dangerous one too. She shouldn't be in here.'

A prison guard approached their table, and looked towards Kerry.

'You'll be moving cells later,' she said, then turning to Ash. 'You too. The pair of you will be in together. On the first floor.'

They looked at each other, and Kerry could see Ash's eyes light up, and she wondered if hers had too. She didn't care how much Ash talked her head off, at least she wasn't going to turn on her.

The guard looked at her. 'And when you're finished here, I'll take you across to the mother and baby unit.'

Kerry smiled. 'Thanks.'

Later, as they left the main building and walked across the grounds to the mother and baby unit, the guard turned to her.

'They have everything there – cots, all sorts of baby clothes, bottles and breast pumps. It's lovely. We make sure a young mum and her baby are well looked after. It's not the baby's fault it's in here.'

Kerry looked at her, stung by the words. The mother and baby unit in prison? Had it really come to this? Not in any of her nightmares, in everything that had happened over the past few months and years, could she have ever imagined that she would be pregnant and in jail and being shown around the mother and baby unit in case she gave birth inside. The thought terrified her. She walked around the unit, which was bright and colourful, and in truth as welcoming as any baby nursery most young mums might create themselves. There were cupboards full of utensils, baby food, sterilisers, and packs full of nappies from newborn to a year old. And piles of baby clothes, pink and blue and white. Kerry gazed at them, thinking that if she'd been at home she would have been out shopping for all of these things, building her little nest for her baby. If the worst came to the worst and she had to give birth and come back here while awaiting trial, it wouldn't be the end of the world, even if it might seem that way at the time. At least it was safe and clean, and her baby wouldn't know, maybe would never know, the start it had in life. In a room off the main area, there was a young woman sitting on a chair bottle-feeding a baby that looked no more than a few weeks old. The girl looked up with tired eyes and a grey complexion, and she smiled at them.

As they left the building, Kerry looked at her watch again, as she had done from the moment she had woken up that morning. As she'd left her cell on the way to breakfast, she'd been met by a guard who'd told her she would have a visitor today, by the name of Sullivan. She had been thrilled. John Sullivan, the undercover detective she had arranged to meet at Bridgeton Cross yesterday, was coming to see her to talk about Vinny. Marty had called late last night to inform the reception. When Kerry had called Marty back this morning, he'd reported that Jack had gone to meet Sullivan, and told him what had happened: that Kerry had been set up and was in jail. Sullivan had been reluctant to identify himself even to Jack, so he had said very little. Jack had asked him to relay the information to him, but he'd refused, saying he would only speak to Kerry. He'd agreed to see her in jail, which he'd told Jack was a risk, but it was one, it seemed, he was prepared to take. Kerry wasn't even sure what the set-up was in terms of visiting, whether it would be in an open room with lots of other prisoners, or whether there would there be an opportunity for a private chat. She hoped so.

When they got back to the main building, Kerry joined the line of prisoners gathered in the communal area where she'd been told to wait to be taken to the prison visitors' café. She listened to the excited chatter of prisoners looking forward to seeing relatives and loved ones, still in a bit of shock that she was part of this. She'd barely had time to get her head around it. As she stood on her own, the other prisoners in groups, she was taken to the side by an officer and told she would be seeing her visitor in the family centre. Other prisoners looked at her and some glared, as she appeared to be getting preferential treatment. She didn't know if this was for remand prisoners, but hadn't presumed that anyone would be able to give her preferential treatment. But she followed the woman and the three other prisoners anyway. They were taken outside and across a courtyard, to the family unit. Inside, there were tables and chairs and pictures on the wall, giving it a pleasant bright look, like a café or a small community centre. She could see four people sitting at tables, two men and two women, one with a child. The women in front of her joined the men at the tables. Then at another table a man sat alone. She had no idea who she was looking for, but assumed it must be Sullivan. He had close-cropped hair, was unshaven and tired-looking. She saw him look at her as though he recognised her, and he half stood up. She walked towards where he sat.

'John?' she said softly as she got to the table.

He nodded, gesturing for her to sit opposite him. She slipped into plastic chair and they both looked at each other. His face was tanned and lean, with several days' stubble, and his eyes were bloodshot with dark shadows under them. She wondered what kind of role he had in the undercover operation. If he was undercover, moving among junkies, he looked like he would fit in no problem.

'Thanks for coming, John.'

'Christ, Kerry. I'm so sorry for what's happened here – I mean this.' He gestured the surroundings. 'It must be a nightmare for you.'

She nodded. 'I've done nothing. Nothing. I hope you know that. We were framed by someone and I have no idea who or why.' She shook her head. 'I was even more distraught that it happened because I couldn't come and see you as planned. Thanks for talking to Jack and coming here.'

He sat forward. 'I didn't want to say anything to him, I mean, no details. Obviously I don't know him from Adam and the only person I wanted to talk to is you. It's a huge risk for me coming here. If my bosses knew I'd be in serious trouble.'

'Thanks. I appreciate that.'

He sighed, frustrated, shook his head and rubbed his chin.

'It's a mess, Kerry. I'm not going to lie to you.'

Kerry blinked her acknowledgement. She wanted information, as fast as possible. She was so grateful to be next to someone who had actually been close to Vinny that it was all she could do to stop herself reaching out and touching him.

'I understand,' she said. 'We only have an hour, so if you can just tell me everything. I need to know what we can do about this.'

He swallowed. 'I just want to say I'm so sorry about

everything. I'm shattered and worried sick, and I'll be honest, I agonised about coming to you with this, but I didn't know what else to do.'

Sullivan looked edgy and watchful.

'So, tell me.' Kerry leaned across the table. 'I'm glad you got in touch. I've talked to my people. Anything we can do to find Vinny we will. He ... I ...'

He reached across but stopped short of touching her hand.

'I know,' he whispered. 'I know about the baby. Vinny told me. It was the first thing he said when he got back to Spain after he'd seen you in the hospital that time.' John smiled. 'He was so made up.' Then he shook his head.

They sat for a moment in silence, then Kerry spoke. 'So, what can you tell me? I mean, about the operation? I'm going to need places, locations and stuff like that, maybe some names, so I can get my people on the ground in Spain to make discreet enquiries.'

Kerry listened, making sure she took it all in, remembering all the details. He told it as though he was reliving it.

The two of them, he said, had been on their second stint working undercover together. He and Vinny had first worked together in Colombia three years ago – in Medellín and in Bogotá – infiltrating the cartels, and over time helping to snare a couple of mid-range hoodlums involved in transporting cocaine to Europe and Miami. The American Drugs Enforcement Agency officers had also worked with them over the years, but that had been three years ago, and in recent times they had been back in the UK, with Vinny working out of the Met in London most of the time. The operation they'd been sent on in the south of Spain was to infiltrate and gather intelligence on a Colombian gang that was looking to grow their set-up and take over a smaller gang of Albanian operators that had gained a foothold in Spain and was growing in Europe. Both he and Vinny lived in separate apartments and it was John's job to get himself in with the Albanian gang, while Vinny was winning over the Colombians and the Spanish hard men. It had been beginning to come together, he said.

'We both felt we were getting closer to being able to organise a move on these gangs. My cover with the Albanians was that I had connections in the UK and across Europe, so I was able to come up with some people who could help their smuggling operation. The Colombians always want to be top dog in any drug-smuggling operations, but they can't really ignore the Albanians, because they are a growing force, and just as brutal and ruthless as the Colombians when it comes to protecting what they have. So, it was working, and the people I was in with were meeting the guys Vinny had got himself in with.' He paused. 'You with me, Kerry?'

'Sure,' she said. Kerry knew he had to paint the picture, but she was anxious to hear what happened to Vinny. 'So, did it all fall apart? Is that what happened?'

John nodded, leaned in a little.

'I'm coming to that,' he said, taking a sip of tea. 'When Vinny and me would meet on our own, we were always totally meticulous in terms of where we went, and obviously made sure nobody knew we were working together. We know how to do this stuff.'

Kerry looked at him and thought he sounded as though he was trying to convince himself, and could see from the drawn look on his face that he must have asked himself a dozen times whether there was anything he had done wrong that could have led to Vinny being snatched. She didn't say anything. She just gave a slight nod in support.

'Mostly we talked on the phone, but every couple of days we would meet – always in a different café or restaurant, and always far enough away,' he said. 'We were both relaying our intelligence back to the bosses in the UK, and we knew that when the time was right we would be able to deliver the main players. We were working on intelligence about a shipment of cocaine coming in on a yacht to Cadiz in the coming weeks.'

He sat back, took a long breath and pushed out a sigh, eyes cast down at the table as though reliving the moment.

'Then, two months ago, I got a call from Vinny to say he was about to leave his apartment and would meet me in our usual place up in the hills behind Marbella. He said he had some hot stuff that was going to mean things would start to move quickly, and we'd have to talk about getting the bosses involved and how we were going to manage our own escape from this.' He stopped, swallowed. 'And then. Nothing. Fucking nothing.'

He fell silent, staring down at his hands as though looking for answers, and picking at his chewed fingernails. Kerry watched him, and for a while they sat there, as she tried to visualise Vinny leaving his apartment on the morning he disappeared, and how the scene might have unfolded. She blinked away images that were flooding her mind of him being grabbed, bundled into a car, hooded, and probably beaten. *Two months ago*, she thought. And who knew, maybe all this time he was being held somewhere on the Costa del Sol, perhaps even close to where her base was with Sharon and Vic and all her business interests. She tortured herself with the thought that he could have been so close. It was a long time to have been snatched with no move made by the kidnappers, not even to make any ransom demands. But maybe they didn't even want a ransom, she thought. Perhaps all they were required to do was find the mole in their outfit and eliminate him. These Colombian bastards were smart enough to know that if they'd discovered that Vinny was an undercover cop, then making him disappear would completely destabilise the authorities. They would enjoy that before they started posting parts of his body to his bosses. Kerry rubbed her face to try and blot out the terrifying thoughts in her head.

She took a deep breath, and stretched her hand across so that her fingers touched John's.

'John,' she said. 'We have to believe that Vinny is still alive.' She could see by his expression that he wasn't anywhere near convinced that Vinny was alive, but she had to make him believe it. 'I know, given your work and the stuff you get involved in, it's all pointing to the Colombians disposing of him. But maybe that's not happened. Maybe they're holding him, biding their time. What do you think?'

He sat back and for a moment said nothing, then he spoke.

'It's possible, Kerry,' he said. 'I want to believe that, and that's why I came to you.' He paused. 'Our bosses aren't doing much. I don't think there's a lot they can do. Once I found out from my own sources that Vinny was seen leaving the apartment and being bundled into the back of a car, I knew the game was up.'

'When did you pull out?' Kerry asked. 'How did that come about?'

'I just carried on as normal in my own undercover, meeting with my usual people, and keeping my ear to the ground. Then I was beginning to get some vibes that the Albanians and the Colombians were suspicious that there was more than one spy in the camp. The Colombians, I heard, were suspicious that it was the Albanians who were not being careful enough, and the Albanians were coming back to them saying that they were watertight. I was beginning to feel that the next person they looked at would be me. So the decision was made for me to pull out.' He paused. 'I didn't want to, but I knew I had to.'

Kerry kept her eyes on him and she could see from his expression that John was feeling guilty, he felt he'd abandoned his friend and colleague to save his own arse. Much as she didn't want to blame him, she couldn't help being angry that he was here and Vinny wasn't. She didn't know what to say, so she said nothing.

'I feel like shit, Kerry, and that's the truth,' he said, shaking his head. 'Why Vinny and not me? You know what I mean? That will haunt me every day until I know what happened to him. And if Vinny is out there, I need to find him. I need to bring him home. I'll do anything it takes.' He looked into Kerry's eyes. 'I'll take leave of absence from my job and pitch in with your guys. Anything.'

He looked as though he was struggling with emotion, and she could see how difficult this was for him. She nodded slowly.

'You might have to do that, John,' she said. 'If we're going to work on this together, you can't be a cop.'

He gave her a long hard look. 'I'm in,' he said. 'Whatever it takes.'

The guards checked their watches and glanced at each other, a sign that visiting was over. Couples hugged each other and the mother kissed her daughter. Kerry stood up and wasn't sure whether to shake John's hand in case it looked too formal. She leaned across and hugged him a little awkwardly. Then they stood apart.

'From now on, Jack will be in touch with you, once he knows what we're doing. I know he has plans in mind.' She leaned a little closer. 'It might involve you going there.'

'Whatever it involves,' he said. 'I'm ready.'

The doors were open and the visitors made their way out. As they left, the people stood there, some sniffing back tears, others with faces set in empty, determined silence. By the time Kerry got back to her cell, her mind was racing. She had to find out what had happened to Vinny. She had to find him and bring him home.

CHAPTER SEVEN

As soon as Steven arrived at the scrapyard to meet Bo Black, he could see from his eyes that he was coked up.

'Gimpy, ma man!' Bo greeted him like a long-lost friend, even though he'd only seen him yesterday when they'd been making arrangements.

Steven looked back at him, deadpan. He hadn't even been told what exactly he was going to be doing, only that he'd to come down to the scrapyard to go on a special job. He'd been suspicious as soon as the job had been given to him yesterday by Gordy Thomson. Lambie had plenty of foot soldiers. If they were having to ask him to be involved, it had to be something extra dodgy, something they didn't want to get their hands dirty with. Steven had reluctantly agreed, because he knew he had to, but also because he was told he would get three hundred quid upfront, even before the job was done. The money would come in handy to get the fridge-freezer fixed at his ma's house, and there would be some left over, so he could take her out shopping and maybe buy her a new coat. That would cheer her up. But right now, he didn't like what he was seeing. He stood in the yard, strewn with car wrecks, rusty engines, old wheels and burnt-out motors. Thomson's mate owned it and Steven knew it was the place where ringed cars were taken and rebuilt then sold on to one of his second-hand car dealers.

'So what's the job, Bo?' Steven asked, digging his hands into his trouser pockets, trying to look as though he wasn't worried.

Bo swaggered towards him and stood so close to him that Steven could smell his rancid breath. He could see his eyes were wild and bright from a recent line.

'You're not supposed to ask questions, Gimpy. You're job is to do what you're told, ya prick.'

Steven said nothing, but he could feel his face burning. He was sick of the ritual humiliation of this wanker and his mate who treated him like an imbecile. Steven stepped away from him and turned his back.

'Hey! Where you going, Gimpy? I'm talking to you, ya cunt.'

For a moment, Steven thought about turning around and decking him, but he knew the consequences would not be good. He was saved by a voice coming from the Portakabin behind him.

'Hey, Bo! What the fuck you doing, man? Behave your fucking self!'

Steven turned to see big Gordy coming down the steps

and striding towards them. He caught hold of Bo and turned him around.

'Look at you! Fucking idiot!' he spat, grabbing a handful of Bo's polo-neck jumper. 'What were you fucking told? Lay off that fucking charlie till we get the job done. Honest to Christ, man, you're a fucking liability, you are.' He let go.

Steven watched, uneasy, as Bo's eyes blazed. The cocaine had made him think he was a hard man.

'A fucking liability?' he snapped back. 'You weren't saying that the other night when I was dragging Lumsden and wee Hawkins into that bird's motor. I wasn't a liability when I put a bullet into Tam Gillespie's head because Dick wanted him out. Liability?'

The silence was deafening, the air crackling with rage and tension as it seemed to dawn on Gordy just what Bo had said out loud. Steven looked at the ground, trying his best to pretend he somehow hadn't heard Bo's mouthing off. But his head was buzzing with what he'd just witnessed. Did Bo really say it was him who dragged Lumsden and Hawkins out of that bird's car? That bird? What bird? It had to be Kerry Casey. Jesus Christ almighty! It must have been a set-up. They must have framed Kerry Casey and her uncle, so that they were now in jail charged with murder and possession of drugs and guns. Fucking hell! That was off the scale. And he also remembered Tam Gillespie's murder – he'd worked for Lambie but had been found in a shallow grave six months ago. Bo did that too? Steven wished the ground would open up and swallow him. Then the silence was broken by another voice on the steps of the hut.

'Gordy!'

Steven looked up. It was Lambie, standing with his arms folded. He had heard everything.

'Gordy!' he barked again. 'In here! Now!'

Gordy turned and walked towards the cabin, and Bo followed. Then Lambie called out again.

'You stay where you are, Bo.'

Bo stopped in his tracks. He sniffed, wiping his nose with the back of his hands. Steven heard him mumble.

'Ungrateful bastards.'

Steven wished he hadn't heard Bo's outburst, because he'd clocked Lambie glancing at him as Gordy walked towards the Portakabin. He stood around for a few minutes, nervous, wondering if Bo's rantings were that of a man coked out of his nut, or, even more worryingly, if he was actually telling the truth. After what seemed like an age, Gordy came back out of the hut and strode towards them.

'You've to go inside, Gimpy,' he said. 'Boss wants a word.'

Steven's gut dropped. He said nothing and limped across the yard and up the stairs.

Inside, Lambie was sitting behind a desk, and he got up and came around so that they were facing each other, a couple of feet apart. Lambie's six foot frame towered above him, and his jowly face had a pinkish, piggy complexion. Steven stood, barely breathing.

'See that shite out there, Gimpy?' he said. 'That pish that Bo was shouting?'

Steven blinked but kept quiet.

'Well, that's all it is. Pure pish. Bo's out of his tits on coke, and raving like a fucking lunatic as if he doesn't know the difference between something that he saw on the TV news and something that actually happened. You understand me, Gimpy?'

Steven nodded. 'Aye.'

'So,' Lambie went on, 'as far as you're concerned you never heard any of that shite. You pay no attention to it. Okay? I've told Gordy he'll need to deal with Bo. He's been at this coke too much now, and it's clouding his judgement, his ability to do the job. Can't tell reality from fantasy. Daft cunt. Know what I mean?'

'Aye.'

'So. You just ignore it. You've a job to go on with the pair of them. You'll be told what you've to do when you get there. You can drive one of the motors and Gordy will take the other – with Bo in it, so you don't need to listen to any more of his shite. Just follow Gordy's car. All right?'

'Aye.'

Lambie went into his pocket and took out a wedge of notes. He peeled off several fifty pound notes and handed them to Steven.

'Your wages,' he said. 'And remember.' He put his finger to his lips and looked at Steven, his eyes narrowed.

'Thanks,' Steven said, because he didn't know what else he could say. He just wanted to get out of here and far away. He felt he was suffocating.

During the drive out towards Stirling, Steven thought about nothing else but what he'd heard Bo shouting back at the scrapyard. What if it hadn't just been the rantings of a coked-out nutjob? What if Lambie, or whoever, had really set the Caseys up for murder? He couldn't understand why anyone would do that. All he knew about the Caseys was that they ran most of the show in Glasgow, and apparently a lot more on the Costa del Sol. They were gangsters, all right, but not in the way Lambie and his mob were, robbing and moneylending and running their protection racket on the east side of the city. Lambie was grubby. What he did was grubby, especially the loan-sharking. Over the past couple of years working in the pub, Steven had heard of some of the lowlife shit Lambie's boys had pulled to get money out of people whose debts had spiralled because of their extortionate interest rates. He was one of them, and he knew how trapped they felt, but Steven had to convince himself that he was working his way through it, that better days were coming. Otherwise he'd have given up and plunged into a depression. But the Caseys were different. He remembered the funeral of Mickey Casey and the carnage when some mobsters from Manchester came up and riddled the whole pub with bullets, like something out of a

Hollywood gangster movie. And he'd seen the funeral of Kerry Casey's mother on the television, and remembered feeling a bit sorry for what the woman was having to go through. If someone had done that to his mother, they'd be paying for it for the rest of their lives. But none of this led him to thinking why Lambie's boys would set them up. There had to be a reason for that. Whatever it was, he wasn't about to go and investigate. This was his day off from the pub, and he just wanted to get this job done and get back home in time to make his ma's dinner. He followed Gordy's car as it turned off the main road and onto a farm track that took them a couple of miles into the country. He saw a sign for Bannockburn, and they drove on, then Gordy took the cut-off to Cowiehill quarry.

The rain was coming down in sheets by the time the two cars trundled along the track that led to the quarry. It looked eerie under the leaden sky, the choppy water stretching for ever over a ridge that led up to the edge. Gordy's car stopped and Steven drew up alongside him. He pulled on his jacket and climbed out of the car, the rain lashing his face, the wind cutting through him. He watched as Gordy and Bo got out of their car. Gordy looked pale and edgy. He lit up a cigarette and handed one to Bo, who pushed it between his lips.

'Fucking freezing, man, isn't it!' Bo said, gazing out across the water.

'Aye,' Gordy said. 'Let's get this done and get the fuck out of here.'

Steven shuffled around from one foot to the other, not sure what he was supposed to do next. He didn't want to ask. Eventually, Gordy drew deep on his cigarette and tossed the rest of it away.

'Right, Gimpy,' he said. 'That motor you're driving. It's to go in the quarry.'

Steven glanced at him. He had gathered something like this was going to happen. They were getting rid of a car that they'd probably used in a robbery. Might even have been the car from the other night. He wasn't about to ask any questions. He said nothing.

'You're going to drive it to the edge, and then jump out, then we'll get behind it and shove it over. It's about fifty feet down from here so the impact as it hits the water and the weight of it will make sure it goes under quick and stays there.'

Steven nodded but said nothing. Bo stood looking at him, his face pale and his eyes a little heavy. Gordy must have told him again to lay off the coke till the job was done, because he'd lost the crazed look he'd had earlier.

'Right,' Gordy said. 'On you go, Gimpy. And go slow, for fuck's sake.'

Steven shivered with nerves and the cold. Right now, with these two thugs, he wasn't sure if he was actually going to be made to go into the quarry as well. Whatever they'd done with this car, they had to get rid of it, and he was a witness. He calmed himself down. They knew he wouldn't breathe a word of this. He took the steps to the car and got in, switching on the engine. It was only about fifteen feet from the front of the car to the edge of the quarry, so he had to concentrate as he edged slowly ahead, conscious that he was riding the clutch to make sure the car inched at a snail's pace. He kept it going until he could see the lip of the cliff, then he stopped, and switched the engine off. He got out and looked at Gordy and Bo, but they said nothing.

'That's fine, Gimpy,' Gordy said. 'Right. Get to the back of the car and get ready to push.'

Steven went to the back of the car, and for a second wondered why Gordy and Bo weren't following him. He stood behind the car, waiting for them, then, as he looked across the roof of the car, he froze.

'Right, Bo,' he heard Gordy say. 'In the motor. This is the end of the road for you.'

He saw the startled look on Bo's face. 'Wh ... What the fuck, Gordy! Don't even joke, man.'

He watched as Gordy put his hand inside his jacket and pulled out a handgun. He pointed it at Bo.

'In the fucking motor, Bo.'

Steven felt his mouth drop open. His legs suddenly started shaking and he had to steady himself against the car.

'Gordy!' he heard himself shout, his voice shaky. 'What the fuck, man?'

Gordy turned quickly and pointed the gun at him.

'Shut your fucking mouth, Gimpy. Just do as you're told.'

Bo burst into tears. 'Aw, come on, man!' he pleaded. 'Fucking stop it, Gordy. We're mates. Like brothers, man.'

'In. The. Fucking. Car.'

'But what for? I've no' done anything,' Bo whimpered.

'You've become a fucking liability. You can't be trusted. Shovin' that shit up your nose all the time.'

'I'll stop. I promise. I'll never take it again.'

'Shut it, Bo. I've got my orders. Now get in the car. It's nothing personal.'

Bo glanced around and for a moment Steven thought he was going to make a run for it, but he knew he had nowhere to go.

'Don't even think about it,' Gordy said. 'Get in.'

He moved closer to him, keeping the gun pointed, and with his free hand opened the door. He grabbed Bo by the back of the neck and pushed him, then put the gun to the back of his head. Bo put his hands up and got into the passenger seat. Steven could hear him screaming and crying and pleading. But it was only for a couple of seconds, because the next sound was the bang of a gunshot that echoed in the air and across the grey murky black water. Steven flinched, his legs like jelly. Gordy slammed the door shut, then turned to Steven. He waited for him to point the gun. He thought of his ma. How would she find out? He saw her sobbing, bewildered, going to pieces. He swallowed the lump in his throat.

'Right. Start pushing.' Gordy shoved his gun back in his jacket and walked to the back of the car.

Steven felt relieved that he'd been spared and terrified by what he'd just witnessed.

'Come on,' Gordy said. 'Don't just stand there like a pussy. Get your back into this.'

He bent down, put his shoulder to the metal and started to push, aware that his legs were weak and shaking.

'Come on to fuck, Gimpy!' Gordy strained. 'Push harder.'

Steven forced his legs to stop shaking and pushed with everything he had. He felt the car move forward a little. They kept pushing. He turned his face away from Gordy and gave it a huge heave until the car teetered on the edge of the quarry. Then they both gave one final push and over it went. Steven straightened up and tried to compose himself, his whole body trembling as though he was in shock.

'Right,' Gordy said. 'Let's go. You're driving.' He strode to the other car, got into the passenger seat.

For a couple of beats, Steven stood there, frozen, as his eyes scanned the landscape, the rain soaking his face and sweeping across the quarry. Nothing would ever be the same again. He went across to the car, got into the driver's seat, and with trembling hands turned on the ignition. He reversed away from the quarry and, in stunned silence, turned and headed back down the road they'd come.

CHAPTER EIGHT

In the weeks after Kerry and Danny's arrest, Jake Cahill worked quietly in the background, trying to dig up any intelligence on Vinny's disappearance. As a rule, he preferred to work alone, so whatever he did he was answerable only to himself. But he'd agreed to pitch in with this John Sullivan undercover cop, who had come to Spain to find out what had happened to his mate Vinny who'd gone missing.

It wouldn't be the first time. Jake had worked covertly with the police in several countries across the world. But you would never have seen it recorded in any documents, and nobody in any official capacity would ever admit that they had hired a hitman to do their dirty work. You would never hear it from Jake either. Nobody really knew for sure what he did or where he was, and that's how he preferred it. He lived in the shadows. It had to be that way if he wanted to stay alive. But he had always been particular about working with cops. He wouldn't simply just take on a hit for money if his conscience told him not to. He had never bumped anyone off who didn't tick the right boxes for him – a genuine threat to national security, a twisted psycho who had murdered innocent people, or a terrorist. He had never killed for cops so they could cover up their own shitty mess. He'd been asked to do that more than once, but he always refused. Not that he saw himself as any kind of crusader, for he had also taken people out of the game for gangsters like the Caseys, for the IRA, and one time for a politician whose child had been murdered and the killer had got off on a technicality. He'd done that one for free. Jake worked alone almost all the time. And he'd told big Jack when he called him that he wasn't keen to work with someone he didn't even know. But he'd agreed, because Jack had filled him in on what had happened to Kerry and that her and Danny were banged up on charges that they'd clearly been framed for. On top of that, Vinny was the father of Kerry's child, and he knew she'd be torn apart, so there was no question of him refusing. Like everyone else, Jake thought Vinny was probably dead by now. But he'd agreed. And now, as he sat and listened to this Sullivan cop giving him all the low-down of their operation, his mind had not changed.

They were having dinner in a restaurant in the Marbella hills that Jake knew was quiet and far enough away from the tourist haunts along the coast. There was a half-empty bottle of red wine on the table which they had drunk over the steak dinner while Sullivan updated him. None of the Albanian mobsters who Sullivan had infiltrated, he told him, knew that he was back in Spain, so he'd been keeping a low profile, talking only to the one trusted contact that he had. From what he'd told him it was not looking good. He talked, Jake listened.

'My man told me that he'd heard from a reliable inside source that it was the Colombians who took Vinny. He said his contact is Albanian and that they know nothing about the kidnapping, but they were well pissed off that the Colombians were accusing them. It caused a rift, but it's all died down a bit now and they're working as normal. He's going to be working with the Colombians in the next few days as they are cutting up and moving a batch of cocaine. The Albanians are transporting it to northern Spain and then to UK. So I'm told.'

Jake was glad to see that the couple of drinks before dinner, and the wine, had made Sullivan less agitated. He'd been edgy, obviously not happy to be back in Spain as he was probably a target by now. But he'd been impressed by his determination to come back and try to find his mate. That took balls. But Jake didn't want to tell him everything he'd been doing from his end, because the fewer people who knew, the better, so he simply listened and nodded in all the right places. He would tell him when the time was right.

It hadn't taken Jake long to discover for sure that it was the Colombians who took Vinny, so Sullivan's contact was spot on about that. Over the years in Spain, Jake had known a lot of people who moved in all sorts of high and low places. Some of them were lowlifes who got used by gangsters to put their names to bogus property deals for laundered money, or to open false bank accounts with fake ID to move dirty cash. Others were players. Some of them Colombians. Not all of them he would trust with this kind of enquiry. But yesterday one of his contacts had come back with what might turn out to be be solid information. A Brit, he said, was being held in a house down the coast in Tarifa while the Colombian cartel decided what to do with him. He'd been there for nearly two months, apparently, so the time frame would be right for the date Vinny disappeared. Of course, this could be any Brit the Colombians had picked up for various reasons. But if it was someone who had betrayed them he would be dead by now, unless they were planning to use him for some other purpose – ransom demands or whatever. If it was Vinny who was being held, and the Colombians knew he was an undercover cop, they might make a ransom demand. But in the unlikely event of the British authorities agreeing to meet it, Vinny would still get the chop. That much Jake was sure of. The Colombian kidnapping recently of Marty Kane's little grandson in Glasgow was different. He'd been an innocent child, and even though the Colombians were vicious, ruthless bastards, most of them would think twice about murdering a child. Plus, they'd thought they'd be getting a whole lot out of the Caseys by keeping him alive. But an undercover cop? No matter what the ransom, he would be murdered. Definitely. So, whatever was going on, Jake had to get closer to it. He had to find out where in Tarifa this Brit was being held. That was the first step, and he wasn't ready to tell Sullivan about it yet.

'So what do you think went wrong that blew Vinny's cover?' Jake looked at Sullivan. 'Or, both your covers? Because from what I hear, it makes me think that both your covers have been blown. How do you think that happened?'

Sullivan shook his head and pushed out a sigh.

'I don't know, Jake,' he replied. He lifted his glass to his lips and sipped. 'I mean, I have my thoughts, but I don't even know if I can go there.'

Jake gave him a long look.

'Well, you're going to have to if we're ever going to find out what's happening here. No point in holding out on me.'

Sullivan looked surprised, and a little hurt, a bit like a teenager who'd done something stupid and dangerous. He put a hand up.

'I'm not holding out on you, I promise you that.' He bit his lip. 'But I don't want to give you information that might not be accurate.'

'Listen.' Jake sat forward. He didn't want to say, listen,

mate, because he hated the way everyone was everyone else's mate these days – even strangers. 'Only when I have all the information in front of me – in front of us – can we decide what direction we're going in. So get it out there, for fuck's sake.' Jake waved the waiter across,.

Brandy?' Jake asked, and Sullivan nodded. He spoke to the waiter. '*Dos, por favor.*'

Jake watched the waiter go back to the bar, then turned to Sullivan and waited for him to talk. Finally, he did. The chatter in the restaurant had died down as a few of the other diners started to leave, so Sullivan pulled his chair a little closer and sat with his elbows on the table.

'Okay,' he said. 'I've got this niggle that someone we were dealing with from time to time has stuck us in it. Problem is, it's another cop.'

Jake raised his eyebrows. 'Seriously?'

'Not sure, but I've got my suspicions.'

'What kind of cop? Brit?'

'No. Spanish. Part of the DEA over here. We didn't deal with them every day or anything like that, but now and again we would give them some information, and the same with them – if they had any intel to give us, they'd pass it on.' He paused. 'It was a woman officer.'

Jake's face was impassive as he watched Sullivan stare into his brandy glass. A woman. That might explain a lot. It might explain his edginess and need to come back and see if he could dig Vinny out. Sullivan looked guilty as he made eye contact. Now they were beginning to get to the heart of the matter.

'A woman,' Jake said flatly, holding his gaze. 'Go on.' He had a feeling he knew what was coming next.

Sullivan took a gulp of the brandy, and Jake could see that he needed it.

'She was with the DEA – has been for about five years, and has been on the ground here most of that time. When Vinny and me first arrived, she was one of about three officers we met, and we agreed we would keep in contact, but Vinny and me were very much left to our own devices. We didn't get in touch with them much, until one time she called me and passed on some good inside stuff on the Albanians. I met with her, and after that we had dinner a couple of times.' He paused then corrected himself. 'More than a couple of times. And, well ... we kind of got involved.'

'You mean you had sex with her,' Jake said, matter-of-fact. 'Look, Sullivan, I'm not here to listen to your confession. You getting shacked up with some cop bird is down to you. I'm sure you've told yourself a million times that you should have known better. But hey, these things happen. Don't beat yourself up about it. Is that what you're doing? Is that why you're here? Do you think she double-crossed you?'

Sullivan looked defeated. He'd told none of this to Kerry, or she would have relayed it to Jake, but he was clearly depressed about it and feeling guilty. Jake didn't need someone working with him who was not a hundred per cent focused on the job at hand. So he had to hear the rest of the story, then put it to bed.

'I don't know for sure,' Sullivan said. 'We hadn't seen each other for about ten days, when she suddenly called me and we met up. In all the times me and Vinny met with DEA contacts we played it close to our chests, because we know how stuff gets out, and it was the same with Luisa – I never divulged anything to her that we were currently doing. But she knew the basics – that Vinny and me had infiltrated the Albanian and Colombian gangs and were working on the plans for a bust. That was all, though.' He paused for a long moment. 'That night, we slept together, but during the night I was a bit restless, and was aware that she had left the bed. I don't know why I was suspicious; I mean, she could have been in the bathroom for all I knew. But something told me to get up, and so I did. I quietly went into the hallway, and from where I stood, I could see that she had my phone in her hand, and although I couldn't be completely sure, it looked like she was reading my text messages.' He sighed, put his head back and looked forlorn. 'That's all I saw. I can't say if she was reading the texts, and anyway, Vinny and me were always careful what we texted to each other, so there would be nothing that crucial on it. But the fact that she was reading my texts . . . I mean, what the fuck! Why would she do that?' He shook his head. 'It was a couple of days later that Vinny disappeared. She hasn't been in touch since, and I haven't called her. Not even to tell her about Vinny.'

Jake had had a feeling from the moment he'd met Sullivan that he was deeply troubled, and not just about his missing cop mate. He could see now why finding Vinny was more important to him than any undercover job. They sat in heavy silence for a while, then Jake spoke.

'So, if this woman did betray you, who do you think she was working for? The Albanians? The Colombians?'

Sullivan shrugged. 'The Colombians would possibly make more sense – she spoke the language and has been here for a few years, so she would have seen how they've grown, known the main players.'

Again, they said nothing for a few moments.

'So how do you feel about getting in touch with her now?' Jake asked, then seeing the surprised look on his face he added, 'Maybe you could get some information out of her – see what she knows. If she's involved with these people, she might even know where Vinny is, if he's still alive. Or what has happened to him.'

Sullivan looked at him and blew out his cheeks.

'If I thought it would help, I've no problem with seeing her. But if she's set Vinny up, she's hardly going to tell me anything.'

Jake nodded slowly. 'Yeah,' he said. 'Might not be wise if she set him up. But if we could find a way to keep an eye on her, see who she's involved with. You never know where it might lead us.'

Sullivan said nothing, but from the look on his face, he was beginning to wonder what he'd got himself into by asking the Caseys for help.

CHAPTER NINE

Steven had slept very badly as he'd constantly replayed the scenes from the quarry. Every time he closed his eyes, he could see himself at the back of the car, heaving it to the edge and into the inky blackness. There was no way back from this. Whatever he felt, however repulsed he was about what had happened, the fact was that he was an accessory to murder. Actual murder. Christ! This was what people like Thomson and Lambie and scum like them did – and he'd heard tales of punishment beatings and whisperings about hits on individuals – but this wasn't who *he* was. Cold sweat prickled his body. What if the cops came calling? Even if he wanted to, he could hardly come clean and tell them what had happened. Because it was *his* shoulder pushing and shoving behind the car until it went over the edge. He was trapped. His chest felt like there was a belt tightening across it as he tried to breathe. He sat up, calming himself down until he managed a deep, slow breath. In the quietness, he could hear his mother, her phlegmy, rasping cough, and he sat until he could hear the coughing ease and the stillness return. From the crack in the curtains, he could see the rain heavy on the windows. He lay back down on the bed, praying for the morning to come. At least, then, he would be busy. He'd be making his mother breakfast, preparing a snack for her lunch, then heading to work in the pub. Much as he was dreading going to work, he knew he had to do it, get it over with. When they'd come back to Glasgow yesterday and Thomson had dropped him off outside his flat, he hadn't spoken. He'd simply said to him, 'See you tomorrow, Gimpy,' and turned away.

Steven was almost finished his shift at the bar, and he was counting down the minutes. All day, he'd been shattered, edgy, his head feeling like it was about to explode under the pressure. He wasn't even thinking straight, giving people the wrong change, the wrong drinks, or smashing a glass. He was like a zombie, barely getting through the day, all the time watching the door, expecting Lambie or Thomson to walk in. But they didn't, until fifteen minutes before he was due to clock off. When the door opened, it was Lambie he saw first and his stomach dropped as their eyes met. Lambie stood for a few beats staring straight at him, unblinking, until it was Steven who turned away. Thomson strolled up to the bar as Lambie took a seat in the corner.

'All right, Gimpy?' he said as he leaned on the bar.

Steven nodded.

'What can I get you, Gordy?'

Thomson leaned in a little, fixed him with a look, his mouth tight. 'I said you all right, Gimpy?'

Steven swallowed. 'Aye.' His mouth felt dry. He had no idea how to respond.

'Fine. Then keep it that way,' Thomson said. 'Two pints. Bring them over. Boss wants a word.'

Steven didn't answer. He was glad Thomson had turned to cross the bar, as his hands trembled a little when he lifted the pint tumblers and placed one under the font. *You have to calm down,* he told himself. *If these cunts get wind that you're shitting yourself, you'll be next.* Slowly, he pulled the pints, watched as his hands stopped shaking. He glanced around the bar; only four or five regulars were in, two of them playing pool and the others sitting with newspapers open in front of them, studying the horse racing. He picked up the pints of lager and came out from behind the bar, then crossed the room towards Lambie and Thomson. He placed the pints on the table, and stood awkwardly.

'Sit down, Gimpy,' Lambie said, his eyes flicking to the chair opposite him.

Steven sat down. He looked from Lambie to Thomson. He could hear his heart beat. He clasped his hands in front of his stomach in case they started shaking again.

Eventually, Lambie spoke. 'You all right, Gimpy?'

Steven managed a shallow breath and nodded.

'Aye.' Then he felt his face redden, and he couldn't stop himself. He leaned across the table. 'Well, er, I mean, fuck's sake, boss. I don't know what to say.'

Lambie lifted the pint to his lips and took a long drink. Thomson did the same. Steven felt light-headed. What the fuck was he supposed to say here?

'You don't know what to say?' Lambie said, his brows knitting as though he was confused or about to get angry. 'What do you mean?'

Steven looked from one to the other, frustration and fear and anger almost spilling over. But he knew he had to keep it in check.

'I mean, about yesterday, Dick.' He glanced at Thomson who was staring straight ahead. 'About Bo. About what happened.' He shook his head. 'Fuck me, man! I had no idea I was getting dragged into that.' He shifted uncomfortably in his seat. 'Fuck me!'

Again the silence. Then Lambie sighed and looked a little perplexed.

'Listen, son,' he said, in an almost fatherly tone. 'It was a bit of business that had to be dealt with. Bo was a fucking liability. You could see that yourself. Too much charlie and too big in the fucking mouth. There's no room for that in this business.'

A liability. He remembered Thomson saying that to him before he shot him.

'I mean, what if the cops find out?' As soon as he said it, Steven knew it was the wrong thing.

Thomson rolled his eyes in a Jesus-Fucking-Christ look. Lambie's face grew dark. He leaned across the table.

'Fuck the cops!' He lowered his voice. 'Get that out of your fucking head. Nobody is going to find out anything if you keep your mouth fucking zipped. Got that?'

'Of course. Christ! What the fuck would I want to tell anybody for? I was fucking there, for fuck's sake.'

'Aye. You were. And just remember that,' Lambie said, something close to a smirk on his lips. Then he said, 'Look, you did well enough yesterday, and you'll get a few extra quid on top of what I gave you. Okay?'

Steven said nothing. There was no point. Anything else he said here would be digging a hole for himself. The bar door opened and Geordie came in ready to start his shift.

'Time you were out of here,' Lambie said. 'On you go now.'

Steven stood up. Lambie gripped his wrist. 'And remember what I said. Keep it fucking shut.'

Steven looked down at him, then turned away towards the bar. He went into the back room, collected his jacket and went straight out of the door, without a glance in their direction.

On the way home, Steven took a detour and walked down to the Clydeside and along the Broomielaw, just to try and take his mind off where he was at this point. Once or twice he stopped, stood by the railing and looked down as the river flowed past, and he remembered one day years ago when he'd seen the cops and the riverboat picking up a bloated corpse from the river. Probably a suicide. Again, Steven was plunged into the image of the darkness of the quarry as the car went over. If he threw himself in here now, it would be over in a few minutes. All the fear, the hurt, the pain would be gone. But what about his ma? It would kill her. He walked on for another twenty minutes, the soft rain on his face and the physical exercise making him feel a little better. But he would never really feel better ever again, because everything had changed now. Everything. The lights on the hotels and bars along the Clyde and the traffic were all familiar, as if nothing had changed, but it had. And there was nothing he could do. He was a prisoner now. He looked at his watch. His mum would be expecting him home soon. He stopped at the supermarket on the way back and picked up some groceries that would do him and his mum for a couple of days. He had to put this shit out of his mind completely. He didn't know if he could do it, but he had no alternative but to try. Once into his street he turned into the tenement flat and went up to the second floor, pushing his key into the lock, surprised to find it open. Then as he went down the hallway, he stopped in his tracks. He could hear a man's voice. He froze. Then he heard his mother's voice. What the fuck! He took a couple of steps down the hall, his heart pounding.

'That you, son?'

'Aye, ma,' Steven said through a tight throat.

He walked towards the bedroom door and pushed it open, terrified of what would be on the other side. To his horror, it was big Gordy. Sitting there on the bedside chair next to his ma lying propped up on her pillows.

'I've got a visitor, Steven.' His mother smiled, but he could see it was more of a grimace. 'Your mate Gordy, from the pub.'

A cold calm came over Steven. Whatever he did here, he had to show nothing to his mother. This fucker was in his house for one reason only, to monster him. To let him know that he could get to him, to torment him with the thought that if he didn't keep his mouth shut, then Lambie and his mobsters could get to his mother. He suppressed the urge to scream, to cross the room and fucking throttle this cunt and throw him out of the window.

'Gordy!' he said. 'This is a surprise.' He glared at him. 'How did you get in?' He glanced at his mum. 'Ma, I told you not to open the door to anyone.'

'I didn't,' she said. 'Gordy said you must have left the lock off.'

Gordy smirked. Steven said nothing. No, he fucking didn't leave the lock off. He never did that. Even in the stupor he had been in that morning he would never leave without locking the front door. Gordy stood up.

'Anyway,' he said. 'I best be going now, Steven. I just popped round as I was in the area. But I'll away now and let you make your ma's dinner. She says you're a great cook, by the way.' He gave Steven a hefty squeeze that hurt his arm as he passed. 'You're full of surprises, you are.'

Steven said nothing. Rage and fear burning a hole in his gut.

'I'll let myself out,' Thomson said.

Then he left. Steven stood there, afraid to look at his ma for a moment, then he turned and rushed to the bathroom and promptly threw up. When he'd composed himself and came back into the bedroom, his ma was sitting on the side of the bed, trying to get up.

'Right, Steven,' she said, in a voice that used to reprimand him when he was young. 'You're in trouble, son, aren't you.'

Steven shook his head. 'No, Ma.' He knew she would see through him.

'Listen, son. I'm not going to hear any of your shit. Do you think I'm buttoned up the back? That bastard who came in here, was here for one reason. I know he broke in. But I'm a better liar than you and I played along with it. But I know why he was here. It was to threaten you. I'm right, am I not?'

Steven stood, tears in his eyes. He shook his head.

'Ma,' he said. 'I don't know what to do.'

'Tell me,' she said, motioning to the chair, wheezing, stretching her arms out for him to help her to her feet. 'Get me into the living room, and sit your arse down there and tell your ma what's going on. Because nothing and no bastard alive is going to threaten me or my boy.'

CHAPTER TEN

As the weeks went on, Kerry had buckled into prison life because there was nothing else for it. She'd taken a job in the workshop where the prisoners made greetings cards. The job was menial but hours went faster and the routine stopped her obsessing about her plight. She knew Marty would be working on all the legal aspects of the case to get her released, but it wasn't coming fast enough for her, and always there was the niggle that it might not even happen. The prospect of being stuck in here long term didn't even bear thinking about. She also knew that Jack and the troops would be all over Glasgow trying to find out who was behind the set-up, and retribution would be swift and deadly when they did. Kerry was even sleeping a little better since moving into a cell with Ash on the first floor. Despite Ash talking non-stop when they went to bed, at least she didn't feel under threat. She listened as Ash described her upbringing in the East End of Glasgow and how she had become resigned from an early age that there was no way out. In the darkness after lights out, Kerry had also found herself telling Ash some of her own story, about her father and of growing up in Maryhill, then being sent to Spain as a young teenager, away from any trouble in Glasgow. Ash was fascinated, and a good listener, and Kerry even told her about her brother Mickey's murder and her mum's shooting at the funeral, and that was how she reluctantly became head of the Casey empire, and how she was going to take them on to better things. Somehow, offloading all of this to a complete stranger had been liberating, and as the days went on, Kerry wondered if she was naive to hope that in Ash she might have forged a loyal friendship that could continue after they were both out of this place.

In the communal area after dinner, Kerry watched as the bickering between two women became more heated. The pair of them – girls in their early twenties – were already celebrities in the jail since their recent arrival. Their stories had been plastered all over the media after they had been caught red-handed with suitcases of cocaine smuggled from Spain. It was clear from early on that despite the prospect of lengthy jail sentences, the women were enjoying the notoriety that the high profile case had brought them. Kerry had kept well away from them – as she had with almost everyone else in the prison apart from Ash and one or two other women – as well as making sure she gave Big Aggie and her cronies a wide berth. The arrival of the two drug-smuggler girls – Tracy and Libby – had shifted the emphasis away from Kerry, and she was glad they were now getting all the attention. Every time an update of their case appeared on the news, a good-natured roar went up in the community room, and Kerry couldn't quite understand why they were celebrating when their lives were being squandered. But it wasn't lost on her that when everything was stripped back, she was no better than them. The Caseys had made a pile of cash from the huge haul of cocaine they'd stolen from the Colombians. While the Caseys had cleaned the drugs money and invested it in their hotel and property business on the Costa del Sol, drugs mules like these two girls were lower down the food chain and used as fodder. Kerry had plenty of time to reflect on this in the long hours in jail, and sometimes she felt ashamed at who the Caseys were, who she was. But there was nothing she could do to change that except stiffen her resolve to make things different for her and her organisation.

She sat, flicking through a magazine, as the women tried to keep their voices down while they quarrelled.

'It was your fucking fault anyway,' Tracy, the tall, skinny girl with the long dark hair spat at her friend. 'You were the one who said it was all going to be so fucking easy.'

Libby, petite, blonde, with angry narrow eyes, turned to her. 'My fault? My fucking fault?' She leaned across to her mate. 'If you hadn't got into so much fucking debt and done your job right, they wouldn't have forced you into it.' She shook her head. 'You were told to just sell the fucking pills in the clubs, but that wasn't enough for you. You had to get fucking hooked on it yourself. Like a fucking zombie you were.'

Her friend sat in silent, simmering rage. She glanced around, where everyone who had been listening and watching quickly turned away and pretended to be uninterested. The prison officer at the tea area flicked a glance to her mate on the other side of the hall. Kerry felt uncomfortable. Ash pulled her chair a little closer to her and whispered, 'I think this is about to kick off.'

Kerry didn't answer. She checked the clock on the wall and wished the twenty minutes to lock-up would move faster so she could get away from this. Suddenly it was mayhem. The tall, skinny girl picked up her cup of hot tea and threw it over her pal. The scalded girl shrieked.

'You've fucking roasted me, you skinny cunt!'

Tracy's hands went over her face but she lashed out with her feet, and then everyone was on the pair of them, the wardens dragged them away from each other kicking and screaming. An alarm wailed and two other wardens came rushing in to break it up. Big Aggie and her crew waded into the mayhem, booting a couple of the wardens and punching and kicking anyone who came near them. Then from the corridor Natalie came shrieking towards them and started banging her head against the wall until two wardens grabbed her and held her down to save her from herself. More wardens arrived to break up the mêlée and shout to everyone to calm down or nobody was getting out of their cells at all tomorrow. Kerry sat, horrified. She could see that Tracy's face was scalded but it didn't look blistered yet. The tea they served was never boiling hot the way you would make it yourself – probably in case this kind of thing happened – but it was hot enough to hurt and burn. When things calmed a little, Tracy was taken away, presumably to the hospital wing. Her co-drug mule was escorted out without protest, no doubt headed for the governor's office. Free time was over, one of the senior wardens shouted, and everyone was ordered to their cells. Kerry lay on the bottom bunk, wishing she'd wake up from this nightmare, terrified that this might be the life her child would be born into, guilty that she was only in here because of who she was. She wouldn't have been framed if she wasn't Kerry Casey. She lay on her side, touching her stomach. She suddenly felt a little flutter of life, and she promised that no matter what happened, her baby would never have a life like the people around her. She would make sure of that.

In the morning, Kerry awoke with the same sinking feeling she did every day. She thought of Vinny, wondered where he was and if she would ever see him again. But right now this was where she was, and that little life pushing against her was all she needed to get through these days. Ash was already up and dressed, sitting on the top bunk, her legs dangling. When the doors clicked open, they went down to the breakfast room, ready for the morning ritual. The room was buzzing with the chatter about scenes from last night. Tracy and Libby were nowhere to be seen.

'Awright, Kerry?' Ash said, spooning cereal into her mouth.

'Yeah,' Kerry said, sitting down. 'That was some carry-on last night.'

'Aye,' Ash said. 'As I was telling you last night, it's not the first time I've seen it all kicking off in here. One of the lassies got stabbed by another prisoner the last time I was in. It was all over the papers.'

Kerry sighed and went and got herself some breakfast at the hatch where the women were dishing up eggs, bacon and sausages or yoghurt. When she came back, Ash was buttering toast and sipping from a mug of tea.

'It's all quietened down now. I think that Tracy is in the hospital. She's not bad though.'

'What will happen now?' Kerry asked. 'Will her mate get charged with assault?'

Ash shrugged. 'Dunno. The guv might see if she can sort it out. I mean these lassies were best mates, and what happened last night was all the frustration – blaming each other and stuff.'

'Do you know much about the girls?' Kerry asked.

'Only what I hear from the other lassies. They were mates out in Ibiza and working the clubs. Selling drugs is normal out there. I think one of them got into it and was taking more than she was giving back to the dealers, so they put her under pressure to bring stuff in.'

'Christ!'

'Probably what's happened is the dealers offered to clear Tracy's debt and give them four grand each.' She paused, looked at Kerry. 'It's not as if they could refuse, know what I mean?'

'Yeah.' Kerry nodded.

She saw one of the wardens coming towards their table and looking at her.

'Kerry,' the warden said, 'you've got a visitor later today. Only got word last night, but we were in the middle of all the scene here, or you would have been told.'

Kerry looked up, surprised. 'Who is it? My lawyer?'

The warden looked at the clipboard and checked.

'Someone called Sharon.'

Kerry waited in the visiting room, a routine that she'd become used to now with visits from Marty, or Jack or Maria in the past days. Much as she longed for and was delighted to see people, when the actual visiting moment came, she was always anxious over what news they might bring. Every time Marty visited, and that was at least twice in the past week, she prayed that it would be news that things were moving forward. Poor Marty. He always tried to stay positive, urging Kerry to be the same, that soon this would all be over. But each time he came, not much had changed. They were working on it day and night, his team scanning every scrap of evidence the police had. And Jack too told her that they would get to the bottom of this. He was his usual determined self, confident that the Caseys would find out who framed them and make them pay. He already had top hands out there, picking up any word on the street. Someone had to be behind this, but so far nothing was coming up. Maria had mostly just cried when she came, and that had set Kerry off as well. Both of them sitting there in tears, holding hands across the table, both of them wondering where those carefree girls they'd been as children in the streets of Maryhill had gone. Kerry was looking forward to seeing Sharon, and was glad Jack had suggested bringing her over from Spain to pitch in while Kerry was inside. He'd brought Vic over too. Not that the Caseys were short on numbers or muscle, but Jack felt that Vic had proven to be a class act, between his role in the smuggling of the Colombian cocaine, and then escaping jail in Spain. He told Kerry it would be good to have a man like that at his side while Danny was being held in remand in Barlinnie prison.

As she waited, Kerry noticed Tracy was being brought in by one of the wardens. Her face was scarlet and angry from the scalding on one side, but not blistered, and she looked as though she'd been crying. Kerry sat a few places away from her, and made a sympathetic face when the girl sat down.

'Fuck are you looking at?' Tracy spat.

Kerry didn't answer, but looked away. There was no point in trying to make any conversation with Tracy, and the last thing she needed was to make any more enemies. Then the doors opened and the visitors filed in. When Sharon appeared, Kerry saw her stop in her tracks for a moment and look across at her. She flashed her perfect five grand smile and sashayed towards her. Then when she got within hugging distance, Sharon held out her hands in a gesture of how-the-hell-did-it come-to-this. Strangely, just seeing her, and the brassy confident way she strode into a place like this, gave Kerry a boost. If the tables were turned, Sharon would no doubt be running the show in here in a week. Kerry stood up and Sharon took her in her arms and hugged her hard. Kerry bit her lip to hold back the tears that were never far away these days. When they parted, Sharon gave the place a cursory glance around.

'Not the worst gaff I've been in.' She shrugged, planking herself on a chair.

'You've been in jail?'

'No. Not as a guest. But visited plenty,' she said. 'Obviously when Knuckles was inside. But also a couple of women I've known over the years ended up inside. Long time ago, but I can tell you it was nothing like this.'

'It's not exactly cushy,' Kerry said. 'I'm sharing a cell and there's not even a toilet or shower. Once you're locked up that's you in for the night!' She shook her head and smiled. 'I'm so glad to see you, Sharon.'

'How are you, girl?' Sharon searched her face. 'Are they looking after you all right? How you bearing up? I would have come sooner but I've been up to my eyes.'

In this kind of backs-to-the-wall mood, Kerry could see that the last thing Sharon would expect from Kerry was tears. She'd have to man up, and Sharon was just the woman to tell her that, if she started blubbing. She swallowed the lump in her throat and pulled herself up straight. She told her about the first couple of nights, sharing with Natalie, and then of the unprovoked verbal attack by Big Aggie which terrified her. But she didn't want to make a big deal of it in front of Sharon, who'd seen much more hardship in life than she had.

'It's not bad, actually. I mean, for a prison, it's not bad. You get fed all right, and your time is taken up. And to be honest, most of the girls are all right.' She shook her head. 'Some of them are poor souls. Girls who didn't even get a chance in life.'

Sharon nodded. 'Yeah. I'd say half of them are like that. Poor bastards.'

'I'm so glad you came, Sharon. Thanks. What about your Tommy? Did you bring him with you from Spain?'

'No. Little bugger wanted to come with me – bunk off

school for a bit and come here – but I wouldn't let him. He's staying with a good friend of the Caseys. Irish family, and he's mates with their son, so it's all good. And he's well protected with them.'

'So how are things over on the Costa? I feel as though I've been here for ages, not being on the phone every day being briefed by you and everyone else.'

Sharon sat forward, clasped her hands.

'Well, it's all going just about as well as it can over there. Fingers crossed, we're only a few months away from the grand opening of the best hotel complex on the Costa del Sol. So far there's been no trouble, security is tight as a duck's arse, and the place is looking fantastic.' She smiled. 'But don't worry, pet, you'll be out of here in no time and over there putting your own mark on it. I promise you that.'

For a long moment they sat there, Kerry appreciating her enthusiasm, but still her heart sinking a little.

'I hope so,' she said. 'But every time I see Marty or Jack – I know they are working their butts off – nothing's happening yet.'

'It will, pet. It will,' Sharon said. 'Sometimes, if you shake the trees at the right moment, something good falls out, and that's what will happen here. Trust me.'

Kerry nodded, more to please Sharon than to convince herself.

'So how are things since you came back? Is Jack doing all right?'

'Yes,' she replied. 'Vic and Jack are working away behind the scenes. Someone obviously set you and Danny up, so it's just a question of finding out who. Once that happens, the rest will be easy. Whoever did this will fall apart. So just give it a bit of time.'

Kerry managed a smile.. 'I felt the baby move a little last night. It happens mostly when I'm in bed.' As soon as she said it, Kerry regretted it, because she could feel her eyes filling up. She touched her mouth and tightened her lips. 'Sorry. I'm not going to cry, but it's always a great moment, and sometimes it gets to me that I'm feeling my baby move in a place like this.'

Sharon reached across and touched her hand. 'Never mind that, girl. Your little baby will know nothing of this, and by the time it's born, you'll be relaxing at home.'

Kerry smiled in appreciation. Then changed the subject.

'Still no news of Vinny,' she sighed. 'It's so hard to come to terms with it on top of everything else that's going on. Was there just nothing on the grapevine in Spain over the recent weeks?'

Sharon gave a perplexed sigh, shaking her head.

'No, love. Nothing at all. I'm not sure I would have heard anything anyway, given how these guys work undercover. But I know plenty of villains over there who hear things, and nobody's cracked a light, not even anything about a cop going missing.' She paused. 'But you've got Jake Cahill on the case, I hear, and that copper guy who was working with Vinny. So something will happen. I'd trust Jake with my life – more than that, he saved my life. If anyone can track down Vinny, then it's Jake. You just have to keep yourself up, make sure you eat properly and keep your spirits up. This will be over soon, Kerry. It will.'

Kerry nodded. Then she listened as Sharon told her about Vic and how it had been lovely to have him back in her life. She noted that Sharon was careful not to paint too rosy a picture because of Kerry's own situation, but she could see from her demeanour that she wasn't just being tough and determined, but that she was the happiest she'd ever seen her. And Kerry was happy for her. If anyone deserved a break it was her. Eventually the bell went, signalling visiting over, and Sharon stood up. She opened her arms.

'Come on then. Big hugs. Not tears, pet. That's not how big girls are.'

Kerry couldn't help but smile at the grittiness of her friend, and she resolved there and then to be brave and more like her.

CHAPTER ELEVEN

Once Steven had settled his ma in bed and put a movie on for her to watch, he sat in the living room staring blankly at the screen on his laptop. He felt ashamed and guilty that he'd buckled under the shock of Thomson's menacing visit, and had spilled everything out to her earlier. He'd had no option really, because she'd insisted he tell her what the hell was going on, and promised that no matter what he told her it wouldn't shock her. Steven had sat there, fighting back tears, and told her what had happened at the quarry, and that he was now a part of a murder. His ma had sat quietly listening, her mouth set in anger that he had been compromised by the hoodlums he worked for, but she'd said he should have told her before it got this far. He'd told her about what he'd overheard in the scrapyard from spaced-out Bo, that Kerry Casey and her uncle had been framed by Lambie and his mob for murder. He said he didn't know why they'd done it, but it was clear that they had. It was as though some steely rage had taken over his ma, as she'd listened, shaking her head occasionally in disbelief. They'd sat in silence for a while once he'd finished the story.

'So what do you know about this Kerry Casey and her mob then?' his ma had asked, finally breaking the silence.

Steven shrugged. 'Only what I've read in the papers, and stuff a while ago when her ma got killed at her brother's funeral. I'd heard of that Mickey – the brother who got killed by some mobsters from Manchester. But I don't know too much about them.' He paused. 'They're big stuff though. Bigger than Lambie and his crowd. But at the end of the day, they're all the same. Gangsters.'

His ma nodded. 'I suppose so. But that girl is in jail for something she didn't do, so right now she needs all the help she can get.'

Steven had looked at her, but said nothing. It had crossed his mind at one point that he should get in touch with them. But that would be like signing his own death warrant. Wouldn't it? His ma had said nothing more, just looked at him with a determination that he hadn't seen in her face for a very long time.

'Take me into my bed, son,' she'd said. 'Tomorrow's another day.'

Now alone, Steven typed in 'Kerry Casey murder charges' on his laptop on Google search, and several newspaper headlines with the story appeared. He called up the latest one, her court appearance, and saw that her lawyer was Marty Kane. He knew, from trials over the years, that Kane was the famous defence lawyer who always seemed to get criminals off serious charges. Then he searched for his legal firm in Glasgow and found the phone number. But at eight thirty in the evening, there would be nobody there. He looked and found an out-of-hours phone number, and before he could stop himself he pushed the call key on his mobile. A woman's voice answered.

'Kane Associates, can I help you?'

Steven found himself suddenly struck dumb. He hadn't even thought through his opening line. He wanted to hang up, call back when he'd worked out what he was going to say, then the voice again.

'Hello? Kane Associates? How may I help you?'

He swallowed and eventually spoke. 'Hello. Sorry. I was looking to speak to Mr Kane. Marty Kane? Is he there?' Steven cursed himself. As if a top lawyer would be sitting by the phone at this time of night.

'No. Mr Kane is not here, I'm afraid. This is the out-of-hours number for Kane Associates, but perhaps I can help? Are you a client of Mr Kane's? Have you been arrested by police?'

'No, no,' Steven blurted. 'Not a client. I . . . I've not been arrested. But I wanted to speak to Mr Kane. It's a . . . It's ab . . . about Kerry Casey.'

Silence from the other side for what seemed like a long time.

'Kerry Casey,' the woman finally said. 'Do you want to give me an idea what you want to talk about regarding Miss Casey?'

Steven was flustered. He did not want to go blurting anything out over the phone. He should hang up before it was too late. But he couldn't. He had to make some kind of move here.

'Actually I'd rather not say at the moment. But I'd like to speak to Mr Kane if that was possible?' He paused. 'I . . . I have some information that may help Kerry Casey.'

Another brief silence, then the woman spoke. 'Okay, do you want to give me a name, a number, and I can let Mr Kane know?'

Steven hesitated a few seconds. 'Yes.' He reeled off his name and mobile.

'Thank you,' the woman said. 'I'll get Mr Kane to call you. It may not be tonight though, possibly in the morning. But I'll pass your number on to him.'

'Thanks.' Steven hung up, and sat back on the chair. What the Christ was he doing? he asked himself.

He went into the kitchen and shoved the kettle under the tap and put it on to boil. He stood, looking out of the kitchen window at the drizzle. When his mobile rang at the same time as the kettle pinged, Steven jumped. He dashed into the living room and picked up his phone. It was a mobile, no name on the screen. He didn't say anything when he slid the accept key.

'Steven? Marty Kane here.' The voice was sharp, clear. 'You called my office? The out-of-hours lawyer passed your number.'

'Y-Yes. I called you, Mr Kane.'

'Good. I'm glad you did. You have some information regarding Kerry Casey, my assistant tells me?'

Steven took a breath and swallowed the dry ball in his mouth. The man sounded firm but friendly.

'Yes. I have,' Steven said. 'I know something. I . . . I know she didn't do that murder . . . I mean, kill them guys.'

A brief silence, then Kane spoke. 'Okay. And can I ask you, Steven, how you know this?'

'I . . . I don't know if I want to say anything over the phone. To be honest . . .' He paused, could feel the tension building up. 'I'm scared, Mr Kane. Because of what I know.'

Two beats, then Kane again. 'Okay, Steven. I understand that you may not want to speak on the phone, but if you have information, then as Kerry Casey's lawyer, I'd love to hear it. So how about we have a meeting? We could talk face to face?'

The lawyer seemed friendly, understanding. Steven stood for a moment, the phone pressed so hard to his ear it was beginning to hurt.

'Yes,' he finally said. 'We could meet. I'm okay with that.

But I don't want to go to any office. I . . . I can't be seen. You know what I mean?'

'I do, Steven. And don't worry. We will meet away from the office.' The lawyer paused. 'How about tonight? Can we meet tonight?'

'Tonight?' Surprised, Steven heard his voice go up an octave. 'You mean like now?'

'Sure. As soon as you can.'

'Oh. Well. Yes. Okay, I suppose.'

'Good stuff. Tell you what, Steven. Let me give one of my people a ring, and I'll call you back in five minutes. You okay with that?'

'Yes,' Steven said, not really knowing if he was okay or not, his mind almost paralysed with panic.

'Let me call you right back,' Kane said, and the phone went dead.

Steven stood for a moment, staring at the phone, catching his breath. He'd done it now. He'd made the call. He wasn't even sure he was doing the right thing, but right now he didn't have a lot of options. He went back into the kitchen and finished making his tea as though he was on automatic pilot, and somehow making a cup of tea normalised everything he was engulfed in. By the time he poured it into a mug, his mobile rang in his pocket.

'Steven.' The voice of Marty Kane.

'Hello, Mr Kane.'

'Are you in Glasgow?'

'Yes. I am.'

'Great. How about we meet in twenty minutes at Waxy O'Connor's? You know it? It's just off Queen Street Station. It's a quiet enough place.'

'Aye. Yes. I can go there. It's not that far from me.'

'Perfect. I'll see you there in twenty minutes and we can have a chat then. You okay with that?'

'Yes. I'll be there, Mr Kane.'

'Good. How will I recognise you?'

'I have a limp.'

'Okay. Twenty minutes then.'

The line went dead.

CHAPTER TWELVE

Jake had been tailing the Spanish undercover cop, Luisa, and it was looking more and more like she was a dirty cop. He'd enlisted the help of Sergio, one of his oldest contacts on the Costa del Sol, an ex-Guardia Civil cop, who'd been bumped out of the force for shooting a people-trafficker he was supposed to be arresting. Sergio knew who every player was among the various cartels who ran the show – from English to Dutch to Colombians, as well as the Spanish hard men who ran their own gangs and worked with all of them. As soon as Jake had mentioned Luisa's name to him, he'd known who she was. Sergio knew she was undercover, so it was no surprise when she'd been seen in the company of major drug dealers. But the people they'd observed her with over the last few days were not the kind of criminals she would be getting that close to if she was a cop. It was good to have Sergio's insight, but for now Jake was on his own.

He had watched from a safe distance as Luisa left her apartment in Mijas Costa, then followed her car all the way along the coast to Tarifa. The small town was as far south as you could go in Spain, and the next stop was the ferry to Tangier. Jake had trusted Sergio enough to tell him that he was trying to find a missing British undercover cop. But the Spanish ex-cop had been surprised that Jake's information indicated that Vinny may be being held in Tarifa. As far as Sergio knew, and he knew a lot, the cartels had no base of any note in Tarifa. The town was too small, and there were too many authorities swarming around because of the ferry traffic to Tangier to make it a viable base. But he supposed it just might be the kind of place they would keep someone they'd kidnapped holed up in an apartment. And now, Jake followed Luisa's car, keeping three vehicles behind as she drove into the warren of tight streets that made up the old town. She parked her car, and he ditched his close by, then he watched from a doorway as she disappeared into a building at the corner of a side street that led into the heart of the town. There were a few tourists wandering around some of the little gift shops, so he didn't look out of place as went into a small bar close by and sat at the counter so that he could still see onto the street. He ordered a coffee and some tapas as he scanned the building opposite. It looked more like local residential accommodation than the holiday rental apartments you saw dotted along the seafront. There were four floors, with one main security entrance, steel bars on all of the windows. Only the top floor had the steel shutters pulled down, which usually meant the residents were out for the day, or it was unoccupied. Jake sipped his coffee, nibbled at the tapas and waited. So much of what he did involved waiting and watching, and he was a patient man. Nearly an hour later, Jake was still waiting, on his second coffee and reading the newspaper for a third time. Then he noticed the main door of the apartment open and two men come out. They stood for a moment, glancing around them as one of them lit a cigarette and offered one to the other. They looked in their thirties or early forties, dark stubble and grubbily dressed. Jake kept his head in the newspaper but from behind his dark glasses, his eagle eyes homed in on the unmistakable bulge in the waistband of both the men. They were armed. For a few moments they stood there, not even talking or looking at each other. Then the door opened again, and Luisa came out. Jake kept his eyes on them as all three walked towards the bar where he was sitting.

They stood in the doorway, glancing around the empty place, one of them looking straight at him. Jake ordered another coffee from the barman and turned away from them to face the gantry. He was glad when two couples who looked like British tourists walked into the bar from the street. In the mirrored gantry, Jake watched as the Spaniards sat at a table in the corner, before one of them came up to the bar and ordered three beers, then ambled back, pulled out a chair and plonked himself down with the others. The Brits at the bar were ordering tapas and beers. They were just off the ferry from a trip to Tangier and were raving about the atmosphere and the industrial-scale hard selling of the Moroccans from the moment they'd stepped off the boat. As they opened their plastic bags and compared trinkets they'd bought, they were laughing. Jake was glad they were a distraction from his lone figure at the bar. He sipped his coffee, and in the pauses of the Brits' chatter, he listened hard, trying to pick up any thread of the Spaniards' conversation. It was difficult as they spoke quickly and in lowered voices, but his Spanish was good enough to make out some of what they said. One of the men seemed to be frustrated, looking at Luisa as he spoke. Jake was sure he said something about being pig sick of staying in the apartment, and it was only supposed to be for a few days. Luisa seemed to be trying to placate him, and he heard her whisper the words 'Soon it will be over'. *What will be over?* Jake wondered. Of course, they could be talking about a drug deal or anything in their personal lives, if it hadn't been for the fact that Luisa might be a bent cop, and her two amigos were armed. They might even have been undercover cops, but Jake suspected not. If they were talking about someone they were holding in the apartment, then the words, 'soon it will be over', were not good. If it *was* Vinny, and they had kidnapped him, then those sorts of people didn't just let their captives go free. Jake decided to sit tight. He read the newspaper again for a few minutes then watched as they drank up and left. When they did, they stood outside for a moment as Luisa spoke to them. Then one of the men went along the street towards a small supermarket, and the other went back into the house. Luisa went back to where she'd parked her car, and Jake wandered around the street behind the building to see if there was a fire escape outside. There wasn't. Only one way in. He allowed enough time for Luisa to be back in her car and on her way out of the village before he went back to his car, and followed.

Jake watched the look on Sullivan's face as he walked through the doors into Party Pam's lap-dancing bar tucked away in the backstreets of Fuengirola. The cop stood for a moment, scanning the dimly lit room. A stag party was in full, tacky swing, as a topless girl gyrated her hips over one of the lads who sat grinning, his hands firmly by his sides. The big black bouncer stood nearby, leaning on a fake stone pillar, poised in case any of the stags reached out to the girl. Sullivan eventually found Jake sitting at the circular bar, close to the edge of the stage where a half-naked waif wrapped herself around a metal pole. Jake, his arms leaning on the bar, swirled his glass of whisky and turned his head as Sullivan came up beside him.

'Party Pam's?' Sullivan rolled his eyes.

Jake shrugged. 'It's far enough away, and I'm friends with the owner.'

He jerked his head towards the bar where a brassy blonde in a leather miniskirt and thigh-high leather boots stood watching the pair of them.

'Is that Party Pam?' Sullivan asked, his face breaking into a smile.

'It is,' Jake said. 'But I've known her since she was just Pam.'

Sullivan snorted, bewildered, as the barmaid came over and leaned towards them, all cleavage and whiffs of perfume.

'What can I get you, sir?' She looked at him, then at Jake.

Sullivan pointed to Jake's glass. 'One of them, please,' he said.

'Jack Daniel's,' Pam said. 'You want another, Jake?'

Jake nodded, threw back the last of his drink and pushed the glass towards her. Pam poured two hefty measures of Jack Daniel's over ice and placed them on the bar. She caught Jake's eye and smiled, then retreated to the other side of the bar where two punters sat taking in the floor show.

'Surprised I didn't know about this place all the time I've been out here with Vinny,' Sullivan said, sitting up on a stool beside Jake. 'I mean, lap-dancing bars are not really my thing, but it might be the kind of place some of the low-ranking dealers would come to.'

'It's only been a lap-dancing bar for a year,' Jake said. 'It used to be just called Pam's. She ran it with her husband for years, but he died. Unknown to her, all the time she'd been running the place, her man was up to his arse in debt with the thugs who run the protection rackets along here. So suddenly, she's told that she either changes the bar to suit what they think will make money, or she fucks off with nothing. She's a good woman and a good friend. And one of these days those bastards will get their comeuppance.' He turned away from Sullivan, and flicked a glance at Pam. 'She knows a lot of people. Not much moves along the coast here that Pam doesn't hear about.'

Sullivan nodded but said nothing.

For a moment they didn't speak, then Jake asked, 'So, you heard anything on the ground since the other night?'

Sullivan sighed. 'A bit,' he said. 'I spoke to one of my Spanish contacts yesterday and he told me that he heard the Colombians did take an undercover cop. That was all he knew. But he said they killed him.' Sullivan shook his head, depressed. 'Shit. I hope he's got that wrong.'

After a long moment, Jake leaned a little closer.

'Listen, Sullivan. The word I'm getting is that an under-cover cop who got snatched might be in Tarifa. The guy told me he didn't know his name, but I don't suppose they're kidnapping undercover cops every day. So if it's true, it has to be Vinny.'

'Any more details? We should go there, should we not?' Sullivan suddenly brightened.

Jake looked at him for a few beats.

'I already did,' he said. 'I was there today.'

Sullivan's face fell. 'Oh.'

Jake could see the frustration and disappointment.

'Look, Sullivan,' Jake said, 'it wasn't the time to be going together. Trust me on that. And anyway, I was following your bird Luisa.'

'She's not my bird, Jake. Come on.'

'Fair enough. I'm not trying to put you down, but some things I am better doing alone. That's how I do business. You need to understand that. You're not in the cops now, with a team briefing every day. I do things my own way. Okay?' He paused, looking at Sullivan who swallowed the put-down. 'Anyway. I was tailing Luisa, and she went right into Tarifa.'

'Really?'

'More than that,' Jake said. 'I'd got a tip about Tarifa a couple of days ago, but was waiting for the right time. I wanted to do a recce first, to see if anything stood out. It's a funny little place – a lot of Moroccans live there, but lots of Spanish too, and there are also tourists around. And plenty of security around the harbour where the ferry goes to Tangier. It wouldn't be an ideal place to hide someone – plus it's well down the road from here. But if they had an apartment or something, they could blend in like locals.'

'So what happened?' Sullivan asked.

Jake told him about the bar and the building with the

shutters, and how two guys had come out of the building followed by Luisa. He told him about the snatches of conversation he'd overheard, and how the guys had stayed on but Luisa had gone back to her car.

'I followed her all the way back and she went into Marbella to a bar on the seafront. The place was busy, but she must have been meeting somebody. I managed to get a good vantage point and I watched as she met with these two guys.'

Jake picked up his phone from the bar and showed Sullivan a picture of Luisa sitting in the bar with a well-dressed middle-aged man and a younger, burly-looking guy who could be the older man's minder. He watched the shocked look on Sullivan's face as he took the phone from his hands and looked closely at the pictures.

'Christ, Jake.' He shook his head. 'That's Diego Lopez. The older guy. He's the top man, for fuck's sake! The Colombians sent him over here after Pepe Rodriguez got shot during the shitstorm with Kerry Casey's gang.'

He looked at Jake, who kept his face impassive. An image flashed into his mind of him firing his sniper rifle from high up in the hills right into Rodriguez's chest. One of his best hits.

'I heard on the grapevine,' Jake said, 'that the Colombians had sent someone to take over. But I've never seen him. From what I hear, he keeps in the background. Not flashy and strutting around the way Rodriguez did. And he doesn't do business with anyone from the UK or Dublin any more. Only deals with the Spanish and other crews . . . And, of course, perhaps the Albanians these days, as you discovered.'

'Do you think they took Vinny as some kind of revenge because of the Casey war? To get back at Kerry?'

Jake shrugged. 'I don't know. How would they even know who Vinny was? He was just an undercover cop, and even if they'd worked out that he was actually a cop, they wouldn't know there was any connection to Kerry Casey. How would they know that?'

Jake watched as Sullivan suddenly looked like he was going to fall off his stool. His head sank to his chest and he stayed that way for a few beats. Then he looked up at Jake, fear in his eyes. Jake knew the answer before Sullivan even spoke. He closed his eyes and let out a long sigh.

'Fuck me, Sullivan!' He glared at him and lowered his voice. 'You fucking told Luisa? What kind of fucking pillow talk was that, for Christ's sake?'

Jake controlled his rising anger. Rage never got people anywhere. But he couldn't believe how naive this guy was.

Sullivan put his head in his hands.

'What the fuck did you tell her? Did she ever meet Vinny?'

Sullivan nodded. 'Only once. We were all undercover cops. All in this together. Or so we believed.'

Jake shook his head in disbelief. 'Yeah. Until you're not

fucking in it together,' he said. 'What did you tell her? *When* did you tell her?'

Sullivan sat saying nothing as the music thumped out and the dancers swirled and twirled their routine. Pam was at the edge of the bar, watchful. Then he spoke.

'It was one night after a long dinner. When I was getting to know Luisa a bit more and finding out about her life, her family and background. We both talked about life and stuff. There was a lot of wine drunk, and we were talking about the Colombians and the way they operate. I mean, we were on the same side, Jake. We were working for the same thing. Then I told her about Vinny and the Caseys and that he was involved with Kerry Casey.'

'Did you tell her that she was pregnant with Vinny's baby?'

Sullivan dropped his head to his chest.

'Fuck's sake!' Jake muttered.

CHAPTER THIRTEEN

Waxy O'Connor's pub was big, shadowy and spread out, with dark corners and secret nooks that you could hide in if you wanted to keep your company private. Steven was glad of that, and also that the Irish bar was the kind of place customers of the White Horse would not be seen dead in. In the White Horse, anything Irish or Catholic was considered a no-go area, so at least he wouldn't bump into any punters who might mention that they'd seen him here. He was soaked through by the time he got to the pub, having been caught in a downpour as he left his flat and headed up to the place. Once inside, he shook the rain off his hair and stood just at the doorway, his eyes flicking around the main bar area. The place was quiet – only a handful of people were at a couple of tables. None of them looked in his direction as he came in, and from the images of Marty Kane he'd seen on his laptop, he definitely wasn't there. He looked at his watch, and he was bang on time.

The barman eyed him as he walked across the room and nodded to him, but he didn't order a drink. He went around a corner and into a dark wood-panelled area where there was another, smaller, bar. Two men were at a table and they both looked up. One of them was definitely Marty Kane. Steven acknowledged them and walked across. He was conscious of the other guy glancing at him as he limped towards them.

'Steven.' Marty Kane stood up, stretching his hand out. 'Thanks for coming.'

'Mr Kane,' he said, quietly. The lawyer's handshake was firm and warm.

Steven raised his eyebrows at the other man next to him who stood up.

'This is Jack,' Kane said. 'He's one of the main men in the Casey organisation, and a close friend of Kerry and Danny.'

Steven shook the outstretched hand of the big man, but his expression had none of the softness of Kane's. It made him feel a little uneasy, and the lawyer seemed to notice it.

'I asked Jack to accompany me, Steven,' he said, motioning them to sit down. 'He's helping run things for the organisation at the moment while Kerry and her uncle are being held.' He paused, lowered his voice. 'Jack is also very interested to hear any information or help you might be able to give us.' He put his hands out in a placating gesture. 'Now, just relax. You're not in any danger here, so don't worry. And listen: if you're concerned that you have something to tell us that might put you in danger, then don't worry. We will look after you.'

Steven didn't answer, because he didn't know what to say. But he guessed that Jack was one of the main hench-men in the Casey gang, and if Steven was going to throw any light on who might have framed Kerry, then this guy would be desperate to get his hands on them.

'What you drinking, Steven?' Jack asked, standing up.

'Just a pint of lager, please.'

Jack said nothing and went to the bar. Steven could see both their glasses were full. Kane's looked like a whisky and ice, and Jack's was a pint of Guinness.

They sat for a moment not speaking while Jack went to the bar. Steven wiped away a drip of rain that was trickling down his face, conscious that Kane was watching him.

'You all right?'

'Aye.' Steven nodded. 'Bit nervous though. I thought you'd be on your own.'

Kane glanced up at the bar.

'Don't concern yourself about Jack,' he said. 'He's one of the most decent men I know. Like family to the Caseys. As I said, we'll look after you. Okay?'

Steven nodded again. He got the message. Jack came back from the bar and placed the pint in front of Steven.

'There you go, mate,' he said, sitting down.

'Cheers.'

Steven didn't think he wanted to call this big guy 'mate',

not yet, anyway. He lifted his glass and took a long drink, then placed it back down. After a long moment, Kane leaned a little closer.

'So, Steven. You said on the phone that you knew that Kerry Casey was innocent.' He raised his eyebrows. 'How do you know that?'

Steven swallowed and nervously ran a hand across his face.

'Well . . . Because I know, or I think I know . . . actually I'm sure I know, who did it,' he said. 'It was a set-up.'

He saw Jack, his arms folded as he sat back, glance at Kane, but nobody spoke. He knew they were waiting for him to elaborate. He took a swig of his drink and sniffed.

'Look,' he said. 'It's best if I start at the beginning, fill you in on where I work and who I work for. And how I know who did it. Is that okay?'

'Of course,' Kane said. 'Take your time. Nobody is in a hurry here. Just tell whatever you want, however you want.'

Steven took a breath and puffed out as he tried to relax. The only thing to do now was to let it all go.

'I'm a barman in the White Horse,' he said. 'You know it?'

Jack nodded slowly but said nothing.

'I know it,' Kane said. 'Big Rangers pub down the road.'

'More than just Rangers, Mr Kane. It's a UVF shop. You know, Ulster Loyalists?' He leaned in and spoke in a whisper. 'Ulster Volunteer Force.' He glanced at Jack who was nodding silently and fixing him with dark eyes.

'I'm aware of that too,' Kane said. 'Oh, and please, not Mr Kane. Call me Marty, Steven.'

'Okay, er . . . Marty,' Steven said, a little awkwardly. 'You might know that the pub is owned by Dick Lambie?' He turned to Jack, whose eyes blinked a yes and looked at Kane.

Then Jack spoke. 'Yep. I know that too. I don't know Lambie, but I know of him. He's a bitter Orange bastard; more than that, a big UVF man. He does what he's told. Takes his orders from Belfast.'

Steven nodded. 'That's seems right. The bands practise in the back room of the pub on a Monday night, but it's all a front for UVF training. I've seen them in there – weapons and stuff.'

'Aye. Not at all surprised.'

Steven took a drink, and sat for a long moment. Whatever he said now, there was no going back. He would be a marked man for the rest of his life. He could feel the nerves in his stomach travel up to his chest and neck and his mouth was dry. He could see Jack and Marty looking at him, waiting. He had to say something.

'Look, guys,' he said. 'I'm honestly shitting myself here. If it ever gets back that I'm doing this there will be a bullet in my head. No doubt about it. I . . . I . . .' He covered his face with his hands for a second. Then he felt a hand on his. It was Jack, pulling his hands away and looking straight at him.

'Listen, son,' he said, his hand holding his wrist tight. 'You have nothing to fear, because once you tell us what you know, we will take over. You will be safe. You understand that?'

Steven almost buckled at the sincerity in the big man's face. He meant it. But could he really trust him? What if they just used him and disposed of him the way Lambie did with Bo? But he'd come this far, so it was too late to cut and run. If he didn't tell them now, they'd come looking for him and make him talk. Yet his gut told him there was something decent about this big guy, and he glanced at Marty who was waiting patiently for his next move.

'I . . . I've got my ma though,' Steven said. 'I live with my ma, and she's old and stuff and she's got emphysema. She's not well. So it's not just me I have to worry about, it's her an' all. I mean, for fuck's sake, I came into the house the other day and this fucker was sitting at her bedside. He'd just done that to frighten the shit out of me – broke in, to let me know that he could get to my ma if I opened my mouth.'

Steven stopped and bit his lip as tears sprang to his eyes. His head dropped to his chest. *These guys must think I'm a right tit*, he thought, trying to compose himself.

'I'm sorry,' he sniffed. 'It's just that she's the most important thing to me. And I've put her in danger.'

Marty reached across. 'Okay, listen, Steven. Just take your time. I know you're scared, but just take it easy.'

'Aye,' Jack said. 'Don't you worry about your ma. We'll look after her too.' He grabbed his arm again. 'Listen to me, son. We can get you and your ma away from here. If that's what you want.'

Steven looked at him, surprised. He hadn't expected this. Christ, he didn't know what he was expecting. He hadn't even thought this through. He just knew that he had nowhere to turn, and going to the Caseys had seemed his only option.

'You can? You'll make sure she's all right?'

'Of course.' Jack nodded slowly. 'Now, go on. Tell us from the start. Everything you know. In your own time.'

'Okay,' Steven said.

Then he began his story. He told them everything. He started with how long he'd worked at the bar, the insults and bullying of the hard men who drank in the place, who had slagged him about his limp. How they called him Gimpy – the name that had stuck with him all through childhood after he'd had polio. He could see they were hanging on his every word, glancing at each other from time to time, as he told them about how he'd been roped into the loan-sharking, had borrowed a small amount of money, and had had to work for Lambie as a result and would never be able to pay his debt because of the extortionate interest. And then he told them about Gordy Thomson, of Bo and the quarry, and how he'd been a part of it, forced to help in the execution, because that was what it had been. He said how he'd been shocked when Bo had said earlier that day that he was part of the set-up of Kerry Casey. And that he'd also executed another guy months earlier for Lambie's mob. And he told them how Lambie had told him to keep his mouth shut. He'd thought about going to the police there and then, because he knew that Kerry Casey was innocent, but it was too dangerous. Eventually, when he finished, he sat forward with his head in his hands. He had no idea what was going to happen from here, but the life that he'd been living was about to change and he would have no control over it. They sat for a long time in silence. Finally, Jack spoke.

'So it was Lambie and his men who did the hit. They executed these two guys and made it look like it was Kerry and Danny.' He spoke as though he was narrating the story, his eyes burning with rage. He shook his head, then whispered, 'Cunts. They won't know what hit them.'

Steven glanced at Marty whose face showed nothing. He wondered how much this guy was really involved in all the things they said the Caseys had done over the years. But right now it didn't matter. He was in their hands.

'So,' Steven eventually said. 'What now? I mean, what do I do now?'

Silence. Jack looked at Marty then to Steven.

'Here's what you do, Steven,' Jack said. 'You go to your work tomorrow as normal. Can you handle that?'

Steven puffed. 'I think so. I'll have to.'

'Right. You have to be able to pull that off. You go as if everything is normal, and you finish your shift, then you go home. And that's it. You'll be out of it for ever.'

'What? What do you mean?'

'You've told your ma everything, right?'

'Yeah, I have.'

'Okay. So how ill is she? I mean, can she move? Can she be moved out of the house to another place?'

Steven ran a hand through his hair.

'Aye. She can walk. But not far. She gets oxygen and medication. But she could be moved.'

'Okay. Then you go home from here. Get some stuff together you need – clothes or things you need to pack. Not everything you own. Just enough to keep you going. Get everything together, and we will take care of the rest.'

'What do you mean?'

'We'll find a place for you and your ma – away from here. A safe place. A safe flat somewhere on the outskirts of the city and you can stay there till we get this mess cleaned up.'

'You mean live somewhere else?'

'Yeah.' Jack looked at Steven. 'You can't stay in Glasgow once we start looking at this. You know that, don't you?'

'Aye. Yeah. I know. But my ma's lived there all her life, in that flat.'

'In High Street?' he said, something like a half smile breaking in his face. 'Well it's maybe time she went somewhere else. You said she doesn't even go out, didn't you?'

'Aye.'

'Well, we'll take her somewhere far enough away. Some place these fuckers won't get close to you.'

'Christ, man! I don't know how far I'd have to go once they start looking for me.'

Jack nodded slowly. 'You can let me worry about that. I won't let anything happen to you. I promise you that. And I know one thing, son. Kerry Casey won't let anything happen to you.'

Steven looked at Marty for confirmation. He nodded but said nothing. He was a lawyer, for fuck's sake. He wasn't about to say anything sitting here that would incriminate him, place him on the same page as serious criminals. But it was clear that he was leaving the heavy stuff to Jack. Kane would not be going to the police with this information, that's for sure. But one way or another, the guilty men would get their day.

When Steven pushed the door open to his flat, the blaring of the television from his ma's bedroom told him she'd probably fallen asleep while watching. But there was a sudden grip in his stomach that maybe someone had followed him and who knew, maybe they were already in here. He stood for a moment, feeling the nerves go straight to his legs. Then he heard the shout.

'That you, Steven? You all right, son?'

The sigh of relief he let out almost brought him to tears, and he quickly composed himself.

'Aye, Ma. I'm fine. Pissing down out there.'

He took off his jacket, shook the rain off it and hung it on a hook in a recess in the hall. Then he walked down to the bedroom. His ma was propped up watching some US crime show she followed about gangsters and hitmen and gangland executions. Something inside him almost smiled, and he wasn't sure if it was the irony of the moment or just the fact that he'd unburdened himself to some guys who had made him feel that they wouldn't abandon him. He went across to the bedside chair and sat down, leaning closer to the bed, and his ma pushed the remote to pause her television.

'Ma,' Steven said, 'how do you feel about going away from here for a while? Out of this flat. Maybe even out of Glasgow.'

His ma said nothing for a long moment, her eyes searching his face.

'You went to the Caseys, son?'

'I did.'

She was silent as she looked at him, then beyond him towards the open door into the hall. Then she took his hand.

'You did the right thing. Let the Caseys sort this out their way. I'm ready to go when you are.' Then she pushed the play button on the remote and started her show again, her eyes going from Steven to the television. 'Now go and get the kettle on and we'll have a cup of tea. Then we can pack.'

Steven stood up, the scene on the television a dark wood with some guy on his knees blindfolded and a gunman behind him aiming at his head. He left the room and went to the kitchen.

CHAPTER FOURTEEN

Jake was at the quiet end of the bar in Party Pam's, far enough away from the pole dancer and the blaring music. Pam had called his mobile to tell him she thought there was someone in the bar he might want to check out. Jake hadn't told her any details of what he was doing – only that he was looking for someone who may be being held in Tarifa. Even though he trusted her implicitly – and shared her bed on occasion – Jake always kept his own strict lines of secrecy when he was working. Pam knew what he was, though, how he made a living, and she never questioned, never judged. That was what made her so special to him, and why she was one of the few people in his life who ever got as close as she did. He was at the bar within ten minutes from his frontline beach apartment in Los Boliches, where he lived a completely anonymous life. Now he sipped the JD over ice and listened to Pam as she leaned across and spoke softly to him.

'Third guy down the bar,' she said. 'Just beyond the group of blokes with the champagne. Colombian, I'd say, given his accent. He's on his own now, but he was with two others, also Colombians I think – they left just before you came in.'

Jake took his time to sneak a discreet glance along the bar and into the mirrored gantry so he could see the guy sitting on the bar stool. From what he could make out, he was around forty, his lean face was unshaven and he wore a black shirt with sleeves turned up to his elbows. He was sipping whisky over ice and had a bottle of Sol beer on the side which he swigged from alternately.

'I see him,' Jake said. 'How many of them has he had?' He lifted his glass indicating to Pam.

'Four shorts,' Pam said. 'And as you know, my shorts are not short. And that's his second beer. The others who were with him were buying him drinks, and they'd had a fair skinful before they left him.'

'I wonder why he didn't go with them,' Jake said.

'Maybe he wants a dance.' Pam rolled her eyes. 'Who knows. The others left anyway, the usual back-slapping and man-hugging before they went. But the reason I called you is because of some stuff I overheard them saying. Might be nothing, but you never know.'

'Sure,' Jake said. 'I'm glad you did.'

He waited for her to speak. But before she did, she had to walk down the bar to serve a customer, and Jake watched as the Colombian eyed her as she bent down in her tight jeans to get some beers from the fridge. She came back to Jake and stood polishing glasses, leaning closer to talk.

'So. It was hard to make out exactly what they were saying – you know what it's like with the music and how fast they speak. But I distinctly heard one of the guys mentioning Tarifa, and that's when my ears pricked up. I had to busy myself behind the bar so they wouldn't think I was clocking their conversation. But I heard your man down there saying he didn't want to go back there, that he was bored shitless looking after the *coño*.'

'He actually said that?'

Pam nodded. 'Yes. Well, in Colombian. But that's what I heard. I'm sure.'

Jake took a second glance at the figure down the bar, but he didn't think he was any of the two men he'd seen when he'd been down in Tarifa for the recce. Maybe they rotated them, and he'd been there a couple of days before he arrived. Or it might even be nothing. But he had to find out.

'Anything else you could make out from their conversation?' Jake asked.

'Yes. Something about a boat. And a long swim. There was more than that, but I couldn't hear exactly what they were saying, and I didn't want to hang around too close.'

'Sure,' Jake said. He was already working out his next move. He looked her in the eye. 'I need to get him in a situation where I can ask him some questions, Pam. You get my drift?'

'Leave it to me,' she said softly as she turned away from him.

For the next twenty minutes, Jake watched as Pam paid more attention to the Colombian who had been sitting gazing at the pole dancer. Pam had slid a drink across to him and leaned on the bar so she was almost whispering in the guy's ear that this was on the house. The Colombian was swallowing the bait, suddenly sitting himself upright and leaning in on Pam, brushing his fingers on her arm as she got close to him. He couldn't take his eyes off her, and whenever she moved away to serve a customer, the Colombian eyed her and smiled at her each time she passed. Pam was good at this, and it wasn't the first time Jake had asked her to help him out like this, luring some lowlife into a trap.

Almost half an hour later, the shift change came into the bar, and that was Pam's cue to give the Colombian the nod. She owned an apartment upstairs from the bar, which she occasionally used if she didn't feel like driving to her villa down the coast in Elviria. She'd invited the Colombian upstairs for a drink, and the guy knocked back the dregs of his drink, his eager eyes waiting for the signal from Pam that it was time. Jake slipped off the bar stool and left through what looked like a cupboard door. From the other side, he went along the corridor behind the bar and pushed open the fire exit door that opened into the deserted backstreet. To the left was the tight steel staircase fire escape that led to the terrace of Pam's apartment. Jake stood in the shadows, waiting. The exit door was pushed open, and Pam came outside into the street, the Colombian close behind her, his hands reaching out to touch her as she turned towards the entrance of her apartment. He pushed himself close up behind her as she put her key into the lock. His arms went around her waist and he nuzzled her hair. Then just as Pam slowly unlocked the door, Jake was there. Before the Colombian had the chance to even turn around, Jake was on him, hustling him through, hurling him against the wall, then punching his face so hard he buckled. Jake knew he would be easy to overpower as the Colombian was half drunk. But whether he would talk, if he even knew anything, was another matter. He squeezed the Colombian's throat and held it as he gasped for breath. He saw his bulging eyes glance at Pam as she slipped past Jake and disappeared, the Colombian realising the set-up too late. He pulled the door closed behind him, and pushed the Colombian until he was lying on the stairs. Then Jake pulled out his gun and shoved it between his eyes, using his other hand to reach below the man's shirt and yank the pistol from the waistband of his jeans.

'Please, *señor*,' the Colombian pleaded. 'I sorry. She is your woman. I not know.'

Jake said nothing and cocked his gun. The Colombian looked like he was about to cry.

'Talk to me,' Jake said, bearing down on him, 'about Tarifa.'

The Colombian tried to feign confusion.

'Tarifa? *Que?* Please, *señor*. What you mean?'

Jake removed the gun from his forehead and quickly fired a shot that grazed the side of the Colombian's knee. He screamed in agony and blood pumped out.

'Next shot goes in your head. Talk,' Jake spat. 'You have the cop in Tarifa. You have five seconds to live or die. Five . . . four . . . three . . .' He cocked the gun again, pushed it into his head.

'Please. I am a dead man. They will kill me.'

'Fuck them! You have two seconds . . . Two . . .'

'Stop! Please! I not know. They tell me to sit. Guard the English boy. That's all.'

'His name?'

The Colombian shook his head. 'Vinn . . . I not know. We don't talk to him.'

'Is he hurt?'

The Colombian closed his eyes, bit his lip, shook his head vigorously.

'Not me! I not hurt him!'

'What happened?'

'I don't know. I promise you. They cut the finger off. Much blood. He is sick with infection. I not know. Please. I only there one day and one night.'

'Those men you were with at the bar. They your bosses?'

'*Si, mis jefes.* They tell me to go back tomorrow to Tarifa. They take the boy away the next day.'

'Where? Where are they taking him?'

The Colombian shook his head, snivelling as Jake forced the gun into his temple.

'I don't know. The boat, they said.'

Jake took the gun away from his forehead and stood over him.

'Okay. You have two choices here, *entiendes? Dos opciones.* You die now, or you do as I say and live.'

The Colombian was silent for a moment, swallowed, his Adam's apple moving in the redness of his neck.

'You police?'

'No.'

'My bosses. They will kill me.'

'Your choice. You help me, and you live. I'll make sure of it.'

'No. Please, *señor.* You cannot kill all these people. They will find me. They will find you.'

'They won't. Trust me. You work with me, or I kill you now.'

After a long moment the Colombian sat up and nodded his head. Jake grabbed him by the shirt and pulled him to his feet, holding the gun at his back as he walked on shaky legs out of the door. Jake pushed him towards his car and opened the boot.

'Get in.'

'Please no, *señor!* You are going to kill me.'

'No. I'm not. Get in.'

The Colombian climbed into the boot and curled up. He looked up at Jake, his face contorted as though waiting for the shot to be fired. Jake slammed the boot closed. Then, as he went around the car and opened the driver's door, he took his phone out and pressed the key for Sullivan's number.

'It's me. I've got someone we need to look after tonight. Meet me in Los Boliches – in Bar Sol. It's two streets back from the beach.' He hung up.

CHAPTER FIFTEEN

In her dream, Kerry was laughing and walking in the city centre with Vinny, his arm around her shoulder as they talked. The street lights lit up the pavements that were shiny from the rain, and they walked slowly, not clear where they were going. They were suddenly struck by how silent the town was: not a sound, no traffic, no people, just the two of them. Then in the dream she looked at Vinny as his face became concerned and he started to take a step backwards, touching her hand as he went. He wasn't speaking, just moving backwards, and all the time she was reaching out to him, but gradually he vanished into the darkness, and she tried to run after him, to catch him, but her legs were heavy and she couldn't move from the spot where she stood as she watched him disappear. When she woke up her face was wet from crying. It was then that she heard the commotion, an alarm sounding, urgent shouting, doors banging. Prison wardens were yelling at everyone to stay in their cells.

'What the fuck!' Ash said, as Kerry heard her stirring in the top bunk.

Kerry sat upright, the ceiling light blaring. She swung her legs out and stood closer to the door, her ear pressed against it, but all she could hear was the shouting, and wardens telling prisoners to calm down, that there had been an incident.

'Something's kicked off,' Ash said, getting out of bed.

'I heard the guards say there's been an incident.'

'Shit. That's bad,' Ash replied.

An incident. Kerry stood, trying to think what it could be. Perhaps another fight with the two girls from the other night. But it couldn't be because it was only seven and the doors were just about due to be opened and she was sure Tracy and Libby wouldn't be sharing a cell after what happened. She sat down, anxious, the noise outside getting quieter, but the low murmured voices of what she assumed were wardens could be heard around the area. It was only about fifteen minutes, but it seemed longer, as Kerry and Ash stood, clutching towels, ready for the communal shower area. Suddenly the doors clicked open, and the prisoners emerged from their cells. The wardens were walking up and down, ushering them to go for showers and then for breakfast, turning away whenever someone asked what was going on. As they made their way along the corridor, everyone was talking in hushed tones. Someone's topped themselves, one of the girls said – what else can it be? Kerry glanced around the line of people going downstairs, some of them filing off to the shower area, and others to breakfast. She and Kerry went straight in for breakfast and sat down.

'What's going on?' Kerry asked.

'Dunno for sure,' Ash replied. 'But I heard someone saying a lassie hanged herself during the night.'

'Christ! No way.'

'Dunno. That's what Miranda who works in the hairdresser's said, and the others are saying too. But the wardens are saying nothing.'

'That's awful,' Kerry said.

'Aye. I knew there was something up when they kept our cells locked. It's either some lassie has attacked a warden or someone's done themselves in. Fucking terrible, if that's what's happened.'

Kerry and Ash joined the queue at the breakfast hatch, but she had no appetite after all this. The very idea that a girl would hang herself and die alone. How desperate did you have to be to do that? She hoped it wasn't true. But she had to eat, for the sake of the baby, so she took some toast and cereal along with a tangerine and went across to the table. The room was filled with the low murmur between the women, as opposed to the usual chatter and arguing or banter that usually went on around the tables. It grew quiet when the doors opened and the governor walked in. Kerry looked up, and from the greyness of her face she could see that she was shocked. The governor, a big strapping woman in her forties, looked pale and drawn, and Kerry noted that the doctor who had examined her when she'd arrived stood beside her. Again, low whispers could be heard across the room. One of the wardens banged a table for quiet, and the place fell silent.

'Ladies,' the governor began. 'I know you're anxious to know what kept you in your cells this morning. I'm afraid I have some very bad news to impart to you.'

Kerry watched as the governor wrung her hands, glancing at the doctor as though looking for support. She paused to clear her throat, then went on.

'I'm afraid I have to report that there has been a death in the cells overnight. Linda Martin has died. Her death is under investigation, therefore there will be no further discussion about it. I ask you to remain calm and please have your thoughts and respect for Linda and for her family at this time.'

'Did she top herself, ma'am?' The brash voice came from Jenna, a thickset girl at the back who was in for stabbing a Glasgow Pakistani newsagent in the eye during an attempted robbery at his shop. 'Where were all you cunts when it happened?'

The atmosphere shifted from shock to anger.

'Aye. What happened? Wee Linda was just left on her own, was she? Left to fucking die?' Brenda, a lifer, shouted.

The words hung in the air, and the governor and the

prison wardens glared at her. Nobody spoke. The rest of the girls glanced at Jenna and then the chatter grew louder. A warden shushed at the girls to be quiet.

'Now everyone needs to calm down, please. The incident is under investigation. Just go back to your breakfast and if there is any more information available as the day goes on, then we will let you know.' The governor looked around the room, perhaps hoping to see a friendly face, but there were none. 'But please, ladies, think of Linda and her family at this time. And if anyone has any concerns then speak to a member of staff.'

With that, she turned and left. The low chatter became louder and the atmosphere heavy and edgy.

'Must be true,' Ash whispered to Kerry.

'Christ! That's just terrible.' She shook her head. 'What was Linda in for? I only saw her around, but she seemed to be all right, well as all right as you can be in here. Did you know her?'

'Aye. A bit,' Ash said. 'I met her the last time I was in, and she was okay. Just a bit mental and doing stupid things. She self-harmed. She had a lot of marks on her arms and neck from suicide attempts. But to be honest, she wouldn't be the only lassie in here with that.'

'Do you know what she was in for?'

'I know she was out, but then ended up back in just last week. So she must have done something to break her parole, as she got out early the last time.'

'Did you speak much to her in the last week since she came in?'

She shook her head. 'Only once. She remembered me from before, but she knew a few people here too. She told me she was raging that she was back in and this was all wrong. But she said nobody was listening to her.' She stopped, bit her lip. 'Fuck. I wish I'd listened more to her, or tried to get to the bottom of what she was feeling. Fucking place, this. I mean, some people are in here and they just shouldn't be here. They've got mental health issues and it's a psychiatric unit they should be in, not a jail. Wee Linda. She'd been through the children's home system stuff, so Christ knows what happened to her. She told me that ages ago, but she didn't know why she behaved that way. Sometimes she was up and high as a kite, then she could be in the depths of depression. I mean, you'd think someone might look at that before they pap her in here.'

'Do you think it's true? That she killed herself last night?'

'Oh aye. Bang on true, all right. Did you see the look on the governor's face, and the rest of them? They're shocked. A lassie has killed herself on their watch, and that's going to fuck them up big time. Know what I mean? You heard the reaction of the other girls here, because the fact is that it could be any one of us, and they managed to miss that something bad was happening. This could end up in a riot.'

'I hope not,' Kerry said, dreading scenes of fighting and wrecking. 'I don't know what good it would do, Ash. But there will be an investigation into it, and once the press get a hold of it and things like that, it will mean trouble. But what a tragedy for Linda. So young.'

'Aye. She was nineteen. Fucking ridiculous!'

For the rest of the morning, on the surface, it was business as usual, with prisoners going to their jobs and workshops. But Linda's death was everywhere. Prisoners spoke in whispered tones, angry, sad and anxious, many of them already mentally fragile. Kerry noticed that the wardens seemed more attentive, talking to girls and trying to allay their fears. During the lunchtime break in the canteen, the television news had Linda's death as the number one story, and everyone sat in silence as the newsreader said an investigation was under way into how the prisoner had been able to commit suicide. The blame game had already started and the media would whip it up, once any of Linda's relatives were tracked down and talking to the press. The atmosphere in the canteen was uneasy and heavy, and when the bell went for lock-up, nobody moved. It was as though everyone felt safer, less vulnerable, united if they had each other around them. Eventually, the wardens rounded people up firmly and ushered them to their cells. Before they went, they announced that there would be a service later in the prison chapel for anyone who wanted to attend and reflect on what had happened today. Nobody spoke and they shuffled in silence to their cells.

In the late afternoon, before dinner, the women who were around went to the chapel. Kerry made her way down the corridor and others also came from wherever they were. The chapel was non-denominational, just a wooden cross, and a solitary candle burning at the front. It smelled of polished wood. There was no music, nothing, just the gloominess of the place and all the girls sitting on pews in some kind of stunned silence. Then, from the back of the room, the minister came in alongside the Catholic priest. They stood at either side of the cross, and the girls looked at them expectantly.

The minister spoke first.

'I'm so glad so many of you have come along this afternoon to reflect on the tragic death of Linda, who was taken from us too soon.'

Everyone sat listening as he talked of the difficulties of life away from family and how hard it was to adjust to being in prison, and he appealed to anyone who had any worries or problems to share them with staff, or with himself or the Catholic priest. The women sat with glazed expressions on their faces.

Then the priest spoke. 'It's in moments like this that we feel bereft,' he said, looking around the chapel at the women. 'We feel abandoned and desperately sad that one of our own was so overwhelmed with the difficulties bearing down on her that she felt her life was worth nothing. That is what it must seem like to some of you, perhaps a lot of you here, not just today but in some of your darker moments. But you must understand that *your* life *is* important. From the day you are born, your life is important. Now I know that it may not seem that way in a place like this, and what brought you to this. But you must never feel that this is all there is, because there are people on your side. You are important, and one day, perhaps when you are out of here and you look back on the difficulties that this period of your life brought, you will understand that.

'So I appeal to you, please do not give up. Think of what your life can mean to so many people, even if you feel family and friends are not always on your side. You can make it different with the help available here, and with the help of God. He is always listening and watching, and he loves you no matter what you have done. His love is unconditional.

'Linda's childhood was tragic and she faced issues that overwhelmed her. That is the great sadness we feel today for her and for what has been lost. But for all of your sakes, don't let Linda's death be something that sets you back. Of course we feel sad. But we must try to live the life that Linda could not, wasn't able to, because of her state of mind. Is that not something worth thinking about? Perhaps as we sit here in the quietness of this chapel where all of us are equal, we could think of our own lives, what we can bring to them, and how we can turn around our futures. For ourselves and for Linda, who wasn't able to do that.'

As he stopped and stood back, Kerry glanced along the pews and could see some women in tears. Big Aggie and her partner sat holding hands, their faces tight more with anger than sorrow. Then the warden came forward and spoke.

'Most of you here only knew Linda from the time you met her inside, and it's the same for us staff. So we wanted to ask Linda's friend Josie, who probably knew her best, to come up and say a few words so that we can think of her today.'

The skinny girl in her early twenties, dyed blonde hair, the skin on her hollow cheeks dry and grey, came forward. Her eyes were red from crying and she was sniffing as she stood in front of the chapel clutching a piece of paper. She looked awkward, shifting from foot to foot. Then she took a breath, put her hand to her mouth to compose herself, and finally spoke. From where Kerry was sitting, some of the girls were already in tears and Josie hadn't even started.

'I knew Linda when we were both fifteen and cutting about Easterhouse together,' she began. 'I just wanted to say that she was more than what people thought about her – I mean by being in here. She was more than just ... this.' She spread her hands. 'Aye, we did some stupid things, got into trouble, and Linda got into some big trouble. It was all the drugs, I think – for me, anyway. But with Linda it was more than that, and she was up and down all the time, and it was like nobody really knew what to do with her.

She lost a lot of mates with her mood swings and some of the violent things she did. But her heart was big, man.' She broke down. 'Her heart was as big as the moon, man. And people just couldn't see that.' She stopped for a moment, swallowed, and around the chapel sniffs could be heard. Kerry could feel her throat tighten, stung by the courage and hurt in her voice. Then Josie unfolded the piece of paper she'd been holding, and wiped her nose with the back of her hand. She held up the paper.

'Linda wrote this for me when she first came in here last year. I wasn't in jail yet, but I'd been charged. I hadn't been to see her, well, because, well, I was just up to my neck in my own shit, drugs and stuff. But I kept it. And here it is. It's, well, it's not a poem, but it felt like a poem, or as close to a poem as I ever saw.' She wiped her nose again and read from the page. 'This is what she wrote.

' "One time on a bus trip to the beach with my ma – I was seven, I think – I saw a sunset, of orange and red and gold. It was awesome. It's where the miracles happen, my ma told me. I asked her do people live there, and she said she didn't know, and that was the secret of the sunset. But she said every day the sun comes up it's a miracle. I asked her can I go there, and stay in a place that's bright and gold and makes everything look beautiful, because it's dark here and grey all the time. And she said to me, one day, you'll be part of the sunrise and the sunset, and nobody will be able to touch you or hurt you and you will never

ever feel sad. When we went home that night, she put me
to bed and I fell asleep thinking of the place where the
miracles happen. In the morning when I woke up, my ma
was gone. I never saw her again." '

Josie looked at everyone, sniffing back her tears.

'I don't really know why she sent me it when she was in
jail, but maybe she was trying to encourage me or something. Who knows. But I used to read it sometimes, and
every time I saw the sunset or the sunrise I thought of
Linda. Maybe that's where she is now, in this place where
the miracles happen. Maybe we can think of her that way,
that she's not hurting or sad and the place she's in is beautiful, like the sunset, just the way she wanted it.'

Music floated out of the wall-mounted speakers, and
Kerry recognised it from the film, *The Mission*. Soulful,
moving. Kerry sat, tears streaming down her cheeks, the
grief and the pain of the girls palpable. In the time she'd
been in here, she'd spoken to only a few of them but knew
very little of their lives, what brought them to this, what
pain, suffering. Most of them she just saw in the corridor
or in the workshop and the canteen. You never knew what
shit they carried around on their shoulders. She wondered
what their lives were, vastly different from hers, one of
privilege and travel and opportunity. These girls, most of
them never had any of that. The strains of the music faded
and the women sat for a couple of minutes, then slowly
they filed out and into the corridor in silence.

CHAPTER SIXTEEN

Dick Lambie sipped his coffee and gazed out of the small, grimy window from his office in the back of the body repair shop. He'd be glad to get out of this fucking place for a couple of weeks. Even though the office was along a corridor and at the very back of the building, the stink of the fumes from the paint shop caught the back of his throat. It was one of the reasons he didn't like coming into his office, and did most of his business on the phone or in a quiet area of the White Horse. But the moneylending had to be done somewhere quiet and well out of the way. The body shop he owned was a perfect front for most of the business Lambie did, from shifting drugs to loan sharking. And every Friday morning he had to be here to make sure the punters he'd loaned money to were up to date and paying back on his lucrative terms. He left a lot of the basic stuff, like roughing up anyone who needed it, to Thomson and a couple of the lads, but on a Friday he liked to be there in person to collect the money and make sure other things were running smoothly. He looked at his watch. In a couple of days' time, he'd be sipping cocktails on the deck of a cruise ship around the Canary Islands with his wife Nora. It would be the first proper holiday they'd had in four years, as mostly it had been a week here and there in Alicante or Torrevieja, where he had money in a bar with two of his UVF mates. But it was his silver wedding anniversary next month, and Nora had insisted they go on a cruise. Truth was, he was actually looking forward to it, even if he was wary of the kind of pricks you met on a cruise ship and being stuck with them for ten days. He'd resolved to keep to himself. But all that aside, he would be out of here and away from the fumes and the shitty weather, and relaxing. He could hear footsteps in the corridor, and then a knock on the door.

'It's me, boss.'

'Come in.'

It was Thomson. He walked in and pulled a chair over to sit opposite his boss.

'There's a few punters out there already, boss,' he said. 'It's pissin' down. So they must be desperate.'

'Good,' Lambie said. 'That way I don't have to listen to their moaning about my terms. Are they new punters?'

'Two of them I haven't seen before, but one is wee Davey Johnson – he'll just be making his payment.'

'Fine. We'll bring them in shortly,' Lambie said. 'But

first, I want to go over a few things I need you to look at while I'm away.'

'Sure. No problem.'

Lambie was about to speak, when Thomson's mobile rang. He gave his boss a perplexed look as he took it from his pocket and pressed it to his ear.

'Jean, I'm in a meeting. What is it?'

Lambie assumed from the way he spoke to her that it was Jean, their cleaner at the White Horse. He watched the puzzled look on Thomson's face as he listened to what she was saying.

'Did you phone his mobile? Right. Okay. Give me a minute to sort it.'

Thomson hung up and Lambie could tell from the look on his face that something was wrong.

'Gimpy's not turned up for work. Jean's been in cleaning the bar.' He looked at his watch. 'It's twenty past eleven and the wee cunt's not there yet. He's not answering his phone. Seems to be switched off.'

Lambie did not like the sound of this at all. He knew Gimpy had been reluctant and scared of what they'd forced him to do over the last few days. But he knew he had no way out. He was into them for a lot of money and he had nowhere to go. Thomson had paid his sick ma a visit, just to let him know that they had him well stitched up.

'Try his number again,' Lambie said.

He watched as Thomson scrolled through his phone and

then pushed a key. After a few seconds he held the phone away from him on loudspeaker. An automated voice told them, 'This person's phone is switched off.'

'Fucking switched off,' Thomson said. 'I'll switch the wee cunt right off.'

'What do you think?' Lambie said. 'I mean Gimpy's not daft enough to do a runner. Maybe he's sick or something. Or his ma's taken a turn for the worse – especially after seeing your ugly mug at her bedside.'

Thomson didn't flinch at the sarcasm.

'Don't think so, boss. Something stinks. I feel it.'

'Send someone round to his flat. See if he's there.'

Thomson scrolled on his phone again and spoke to someone.

'Bobby. I need you go round to Gimpy's flat. You know where it is? High Street, above that newsagent shop. Go round there and see if he's in, or if anyone's in. Wee bastard hasn't turned up at the bar this morning. I need to know where he is so I can punch the fuck out of him.'

He hung up. Then keyed in another number.

'Terry. It's me. Listen, mate. Wee problem at the bar this morning. That fucker Gimpy's not turned up and the punters will be outside waiting for it to open. I know you're not due on until five, but can you go in and open up? Extra shift. Double time?' He glanced at Lambie and shrugged at his raised eyebrows. 'Fine. Thanks, mate.'

'Double fucking time? It's not a bastard charity I'm running.'

'I know, I know. But we just need the bar covered and smartish, until I find out where Gimpy is. I just don't like this.'

Lambie sat back and clasped his fingers across his stomach as he processed the possibilities. There was no way in the world Gimpy would just disappear. Even though he might be scared and worried about his part in Bo's death, it's not as if he could go to the cops. And he wouldn't run out on his ma. *He'll turn up*, he assured himself. *Just get on with the next couple of days, then it'll be sunshine and relaxation all the way.*

'We'll worry about Gimpy when we need to,' he said. 'Go and bring the punters in. Make sure you know who the new ones are first though, before I see them.'

Twenty minutes later, after tying up three new punters in loans with exorbitant interest rates they would never be able to repay, Lambie watched as Thomson wrote all the transactions down in the black book. Then he looked at his boss as his mobile rang. He pushed it onto loudspeaker.

'It's me, Gordy. He's not at his house. Door was locked, so I let myself in. But no sign of Gimpy. And guess what. His ma's not there either.'

'Fuck me, fucking gently,' Lambie muttered as Thomson finished the call.

*

Cal Ahern walked briskly, but made sure he didn't break into a run as he went towards Jack's car.

'How much did you get?' Jack asked when Cal climbed into the back seat.

Cal leaned through the space between the driver's and passenger seat and held out the wedge of cash.

'Three hundred quid,' he said. 'I asked for four, but they said they would up it in a couple of weeks, that they wanted to make sure I made my first payments on time.'

Cal glanced at Steven in the back seat. He'd only met him yesterday in Jack's office where they'd told him what the set-up was and what the job entailed. He didn't know much about the guy, but he seemed sound enough, and the fact that he'd been bullied by loan sharks meant that Cal took to him straight away. He still had nightmares about his mum and the scumbag sharks who'd had her in their grip. If there was a chance to do any moneylender over, he was up for it. Jack had told him the Caseys were going to be looking after Steven and his mum for the foreseeable future, because he had given them crucial information that could prove Kerry and Danny's innocence.

'Well done, son,' Jack said. 'So who did you deal with?'

'Thomson did the deal, setting up the terms and stuff. Lambie just sat there, didn't say too much until the end, till they gave me the money.'

'What did he say?'

'He asked why I didn't have a job. And I told him, I did

have a job at the supermarket but I got sacked four weeks ago for punching the duty night manager. He seemed to like that.' Cal smiled, hoping he'd said the right thing. 'Then he said to me that he would see how I got on with the repayments and that he might have some work for me.'

'Good,' Jack said. 'Let's hope it doesn't come to that.'

'Aye,' Cal said. 'You bet. Lambie said he was going on holiday in two days, and that when he comes back in a couple of weeks I should come and see him at the White Horse.'

'What? Lambie says he's going on holiday in two days?' Jack looked from Cal to big Gary, the driver.

'So he says.'

They were silent for a long moment, then Jack turned to Steven in the back seat.

'We'll need to move quick on this.'

In the White Horse, Lambie sat listening as Bobby told him how he'd been all over Gimpy's house looking for clues that he'd done a runner. He said there was nothing to suggest that he'd packed up and gone, because a lot of his clothes and his ma's clothes were still there. Bobby had searched through drawers and piles of papers and couldn't find any passports, but he suggested that maybe someone like Gimpy didn't even have a passport, as nobody could remember him ever going abroad. He hadn't found any stash of money, but that wasn't surprising, as Gimpy had none. Lambie nodded as Bobby spoke. It did occur to him that perhaps his ma was in hospital, or maybe they'd gone away for a couple of days, but he wouldn't have done that without letting them know, especially after what had happened with Bo. But the big problem was that Gimpy's phone was switched off. That meant he didn't want anyone to get in touch with him, and that could only be a bad sign. Lambie checked his mobile again. He still hadn't heard from Thomson, who'd gone out with Billy over an hour ago to move a package from a dealer and make sure it was put to the right guy to take it to Belfast. It was two kilos of cocaine that had been paid for, so it needed to be done. He rang his number again, but it went to messages, and the same for Billy. Where the fuck were they? He finished off his whisky and stood up. There was no point in sitting here getting paranoid. Thomson would probably phone him by the time he got to his house. He pulled on his coat and nodded to the barman.

'If Gordy comes in get him to phone me pronto.' He turned and left the bar.

Outside, the wind was whipping up and he buttoned his coat, even though his silver Mercedes was parked close to the door. The street was deserted and for a fleeting moment Lambie considered going back into the bar and getting one of the boys to drive him home. Christ. What the hell was happening to him? He was never usually spooked by anything, but something about Gimpy's disappearance made him deeply uneasy. He took a breath, cleared his throat and hawked onto the pavement, then unlocked his car.

It pinged and lit up as he went towards it. He got inside, sinking into the comfort of the leather seats like a cocoon, protected from everything. He pushed the button to start the engine and it purred to life, then he drove off. He headed out of the East End and towards the south side of Glasgow over the Jamaica Bridge. He turned on the radio as he got up past Shawlands Cross, and out towards Kilmarnock Road. Then suddenly he froze. The cold metal of a gun was pushed into the soft flesh just below his right ear.

'Take the next on the right, cunt. One word and your brains will be all over the windscreen.'

Lambie felt his bowels churn and for an awful moment he really thought he was going to shit his trousers. He said nothing. The gun pushed further. He turned right at the junction, his heart pounding, as he knew he was going down a darker, more deserted street that led to units and Portakabins. He slowed down.

'Did I tell you to slow down?'

The gun was pushed harder into his neck. He glanced quickly in the rear-view mirror and could see a figure in a black ski mask. He picked up speed again. 'Turn down here,' the voice said. 'Keep going till I tell you to stop.'

Lambie said nothing. Sweat trickled down his back and his face was flushed. He felt physically sick. He drove his car over potholes and puddles and kept going, past Portakabins, until he saw a light on in the very last one at the end of the deserted pitch-black road.

'Pull up right there,' the voice said.

He eased his car over the last few potholes and pulled over. He knew there was a gun in his glove compartment, but it was useless because he couldn't move a muscle. When the car stopped, a big shaven-headed guy built like a wrestler came out of the Portakabin and towards the car. He opened the door and shot him a maniacal grin. Then he popped open the glove compartment and took out his gun, grinning again as he stuck it in the waistband of his jeans.

'Listen,' Lambie said, aware that his voice was shaking. 'What is this, guys? Am I getting fucking robbed here? If it's money you're after, just say and I'll give you whatever you want.'

'Shut the fuck up!' The voice from behind him opened the back door, as the big guy kept a gun on him.

'Right! Out!' The masked man opened the driver's door and pushed the gun to the side of his head.

Lambie instinctively raised his hands as though he was being arrested and kept his head down as he got out of the car. His legs nearly gave way as he stood up.

'Move!'

The masked man got behind him and pushed him towards the Portakabin. The bald knuckle-trailer went ahead and opened the door. He walked up the wooden steps on shaky legs and was pushed inside, the harsh strip light making him strain his eyes, and the smell . . . the smell of fear and sweat. Then he saw Gordy. But he had to blink to make sure it was him, because his face was a mass of blood and his left eye was swollen up like a balloon. Standing at the desk with his arms folded was a big guy he knew only by sight. Jack Reilly. He'd never met him, but knew who he was. He worked for Kerry Casey. At that moment, Lambie knew he was well and truly fucked.

CHAPTER SEVENTEEN

The bar was three streets back from the front line beach cafés and restaurants in Los Boliches, and was mostly used by the Spanish locals. Jake Cahill liked it because when he was in there, he was never likely to encounter any nosy tourists and have to engage in conversation with them. He rarely spoke to the locals either, and that's what appealed to him about the Spanish. They were private people, didn't ask questions, didn't talk much about themselves – probably something that hung over from the Spanish Civil War, and the secrets and betrayal of each other that still lingered. That suited Jake perfectly. Especially tonight, with a terrified Colombian in the boot of his car. He looked up from his drink to see Sullivan coming through the doorway towards where he sat at a table close to the window.

'What's up?' Sullivan said as he drew back a metal chair and sat down. He looked around him. 'Thought you said you had someone.'

'I do,' Jake said.

'Who is it?' Sullivan said, then nodded to the hovering waiter to have the same as Jake.

'He's Colombian. He was in Party Pam's with a couple of his buddies earlier, and she overheard a conversation about Tarifa. She phoned me to come down.'

'Yeah?' Sullivan pulled his chair closer.

Jake nodded. 'She didn't pick up much of what they said, but enough to know that it was about watching someone in Tarifa. When I got to the bar he was on his own, and pretty pissed. He had the hots for Pam, so she lured him outside where I could have a chat with him.'

Sullivan's mouth curled to a wry smile.

'A chat?' He spread his hands. 'So where is he now?'

Jake jerked his head in the direction of the street, and watched as Sullivan looked out of the window. 'In the boot of my car.'

'Oh fuck! Did he say much?'

'After a bit of coaxing, he admitted he'd been in Tarifa looking after some English boy. Vinn.'

'Fuck me! He said that? He actually said Vinn?'

'He did. He's scared shitless, so I think he might work with us.'

'Christ, Jake. The Colombians will hunt him down.'

'That's *his* problem.'

'So what do we do now?' Sullivan took a swig of his Jack Daniel's, wincing at the strength of it.

'We have to take him somewhere we can talk to him properly. Your place, I think. My apartment is too exposed on the seafront. Someone might see us.'

Sullivan shrugged.

'Is he walking? I mean, can he walk?'

Jake's face was deadpan as he shrugged.

'He's got a bit of a knee situation, but he'll live.' He knocked back his drink and pushed his chair back. 'Let's go.'

Sullivan swirled the ice in his drink and took another gulp, wincing, then got up and followed him outside.

Jake was glad there was no sound coming from the boot as they got into his car and drove down towards the back roads into the outskirts of La Cala de Mijas a couple of miles away. He pulled the car into the spot Sullivan directed him to, just outside the back entrance to the chalet he was renting. The place was deathly quiet and a couple of hundred yards from other apartments, down a dirt track road. It had been more of an outhouse attached to villa than a house, but the owner must have fallen on hard times and was now renting it. It was ideal for what they needed right now. Once they were outside the back door, they got out and went around to the back of the car. Jake put his fingers under the lid and popped open the boot. Immediately the hands came up pleading, the eyes of the Colombian wide and terrified.

'Please, please, *señor*. No kill me.'

Jake put a forefinger to his lips and made no reply. He and Sullivan leaned in and yanked the Colombian out and he stood on shaky legs, blood on his knee and a hole in his jeans. He groaned in pain. Sullivan glanced at Jake.

'Christ! Did you kneecap him?'

'Not quite. Just grazed him. He'll be fine when he gets cleaned up.'

They both looked around and then helped the Colombian to the back door and into the house. Jake pushed him onto a chair in the kitchen, as Sullivan went to the fridge and brought out a bottle of water. He unscrewed the top and handed it to the Colombian, who nodded in thanks. They watched as he glugged the water down, dribbling it out of his mouth and down his chin. Sullivan switched on the kettle and took out three mugs and placed them on the worktop. He put spoons of black coffee in the mugs and took the milk out of the fridge. They stood in silence with only the sound of the kettle hissing away.

'We have to get him to talk more,' Jake said. 'And if he's going there, to Tarifa, then he needs to work with us.'

Sullivan nodded. 'Okay. Let's get some coffee into him and fix up his knee first.'

Sullivan went into a cupboard and took out some first aid bandages and iodine, then signalled to the Colombian to drop his jeans. He revealed caked blood and a wet wound on his knee, not quite a hole but damn near it. Hard blood had formed a trail down his legs. Sullivan poured iodine onto a rag and washed down the wound. The Colombian was shaking, his face contorted in pain. Sullivan finished cleaning it out and wrapped a bandage tightly around it. The Colombian looked up at him, the fear gone from his eyes. Then he looked at Jake, and his expression changed. Sullivan handed him the coffee and he sipped it.

Jake pulled up a chair opposite him.

'Now, you talk,' he said. 'Tell us about the English boy. Vinn . . .?'

The Colombian took a drink of his coffee and wiped his nose with the back of his hand. He pulled up his jeans.

'They will kill me,' he whimpered.

'Tell me,' Sullivan said. 'The English boy. He is my friend.'

'He is police. *Mi jefe* say he is police.'

'Who took him? Why did they take him?'

The Colombian shrugged. 'I not know. I only go there with two other people to guard him.'

'In Tarifa?' Jake said.

The Colombian nodded.

Jake pulled out his mobile and brought up a photo of the building where he had seen the men.

'In this place? He is in this place?'

The Colombian studied the picture. Then he pointed at the top floor. Jake glanced at Sullivan. They were in business.

'How long has he been there?'

The Colombian shrugged again. 'Maybe more than one,

two weeks. I go there two times to guard him. Two days I stay, each time.'

Jake looked at Sullivan who looked relieved that they were making a breakthrough.

'What happened to the English boy?' Jake said. 'You told me they cut off his finger. You see this? What happened?'

He shook his head. 'No. I not see. I come later – maybe two days after. By then is infected and English boy is maybe have fever. I was with one other guard, and I go to *farmacia* and get antibiotics and bandage.' He shook his head. 'But he is still sick. They cut his finger off because he won't tell them the information.'

'What information?'

The Colombian puffed. 'I not know for sure everything. But they said he is police and knows about the shipment. They are trying to find this from him, if the police know, in case they are waiting for them, but he won't talk.'

'What shipment?' Sullivan asked.

'The cocaine.' The Colombian looked surprised at Sullivan. 'Is the shipment coming in to Cadiz. Is from Colombia.'

For a long moment nobody spoke, and Jake could see the wheels in Sullivan's brain turning, processing what he could now do with this information. Jake touched his arm and gestured to the lounge.

'We're not here to get information for a drugs bust, Sullivan. I'm here to get Vinny out. That's all.'

Sullivan spread his hands. 'Of course, Jake. I know that. Christ! That's why I'm here; my bosses don't even know or they'd crucify me. All I want is to get Vinny out of there.'

Jake gave him a stern look, but wasn't all that convinced.

'Good. Well let's concentrate on that. This prick is either lying to keep me from shooting him, or he's so seriously scared that he knows he's fucked if the Colombians find him so he's spilling his guts to us. What do you think?'

Sullivan folded his arms. 'I think he's telling us what he knows. I believe him. He's only a foot soldier – fodder for the cartel. And he knows he's not getting out of here alive unless he cooperates.'

Jake nodded. 'Okay. Let's see if we can take him further.'

They went back into the room and the Colombian, who was sipping coffee, looked up at them.

'Okay. You said you have to go back to Tarifa. When is that?'

'Tomorrow afternoon.' He pointed at his knee. 'This is a problem. If they know I have been shot they will ask questions for sure.' He shook his head. 'Is not good that you did this.'

Jake glared at him but didn't answer. He wasn't about to apologise to the little prick. The Colombian looked down at his knee and said nothing. Jake turned to Sullivan and they both walked away from him.

'We need to keep him here tonight,' Jake said, his voice

low. 'Get him some sleep. Then we need to be telling him what's going to happen in Tarifa.'

Sullivan looked at him, a little confused.

'What's going to happen in Tarifa?'

Jake sighed. 'I don't know yet. But this will be our best chance, maybe our only chance, to get Vinny out of there.' He jerked his head towards the kitchen. 'So this little fucker is going to have to play along with whatever we want to do.'

'Christ, Jake! He's seriously shitting himself. I'm not sure he could carry something like that off. He might just buckle and blow the whistle as soon as he gets there, and then everyone will get done – Vinny first.'

Jake looked at him, eyebrows raised.

'You got a better plan?'

Sullivan shook his head. 'No.'

'Okay. Get him a place to sleep, and I'll organise some backup for tomorrow down in Tarifa.'

Sullivan said nothing and turned back into the kitchen.

CHAPTER EIGHTEEN

Lambie was roughly pushed onto a plastic chair alongside Thomson. Their eyes met and he saw a look of terror in his face that he had never seen before. Thomson was as hard and ruthless a bastard as you could get, and Lambie had witnessed him kicking the shit out of people until they were lying unconscious in a pool of blood. He'd seen him stab a guy in the chest and casually sip his drink while he bled out on the floor of the backroom in the White Horse. But now, as he caught a whiff of the fresh blood dripping from the gash on Thomson's eyebrow, he knew that things in this room were about to get a whole lot worse. He waited for someone to speak as he stared straight ahead. A suffocating silence filled the room. Lambie shifted in his seat, looking up to where Jack was still standing, his backside leaning on the table. Behind him was this big baldy fucker who was permanently wearing a weird smile like all his birthdays had come on one day.

Finally, Jack spoke.

'You know who I am, Lambie, don't you?'

'Aye.' Lambie looked at him, then glanced away.

'You know who I work for.'

It was a statement, not a question. Lambie nodded, but said nothing. He didn't want to say the name Casey. By saying it out loud, he was confirming that he knew why he was here.

'Who?' Jack persisted.

Lambie gave him a confused look.

'Who do I work for?'

Lambie knew he had to say it.

'Caseys.'

'That's right. Kerry Casey. You know her?'

Lambie shrugged. He had managed to calm himself a little so that his heart wasn't pounding in his chest the way it had been in the car. He had to find a level of self-control if there was any chance that he could talk, or buy, or deal his way out of this.

He heard Jack tut impatiently, and he looked up and saw him let out a bored sigh.

'Listen, Lambie. You're well fucked. So there's no point in trying to act the fucking wide boy. You'd better start talking if you want to have any chance of getting out of here alive.' Jack jerked his head in the direction of the henchman behind him. 'Right now, the big man here is choking to have a bit of fun with you. So, let's hear it.'

Lambie tried to moisten his lips, but his tongue was bone dry. He ran a trembling hand over his face.

'Jack. Look. I don't know why I'm here, and that's the truth.'

Nobody spoke for a few seconds and the sound of the big man cracking his knuckles echoed through the Porta-kabin.

'Kerry Casey is in jail,' Jack said. 'Along with Danny. You want to talk to me about that?'

'I . . . I don't know what to say, Jack,' he muttered. 'I saw it on the news.' He looked up and saw the irascible look on Jack's face. He was running out of patience.

Jack took a step towards him, and before he could brace himself, Lambie felt the shock and pain sear through him as Jack backhanded him so hard it nearly knocked him off the chair. He felt light-headed. He tasted blood.

'Listen, you fucking dirty UVF bastard. We know you put her there. We know it was you who set Kerry and Danny up, so don't even think about trying to fucking lie your way out of it. Don't waste any more of my time here. We know it was you and your mob. So the only reason you're still breathing is because I need names. I need the name of who gave you the job and why they gave you the job. You tell me that, and we can talk about the possibility of you having a future beyond the next fifteen minutes.'

Lambie swallowed the sick that had come into his mouth. Sweat broke out all over his body and he felt his arms grow heavy like lead. He glanced from the side of his eye to see Thomson doubled over, almost on the point of collapse. They knew. How the fuck did they know? It could only have been Gimpy. He knew that once Bo was out of the picture, there was not a single other person who would talk. Except Gimpy. Because Bo opened his trap, Gimpy knew. And now that he was missing, it had to be him. He would kill the fucker with his own hands if he could. Or maybe Thomson had broken and talked? Fuck knows. Right now none of that mattered. If Lambie spoke to this mob, and they acted on his information, the Belfast command would be on him like a ton of bricks. He'd be face down somewhere by the weekend. But if he didn't talk, these cunts would do him in the next ten minutes. He had to at least try to deny it.

'It wasn't me, Jack. You've got it wrong.' He managed to lift his head and look Jack in the eye. 'You've got this wrong. I don't know who's telling you this, but it's ... it's just wrong.'

Jack said nothing. The chat was over. He stood, arms folded, then turned to the big man behind him and nodded. Lambie and Thomson watched frozen as the knuckle-trailer clicked open a metal toolbox. The guy was built like a fridge and he had his back to them so they couldn't see what he was doing. But they could hear the sound of some-thing clicking onto something else, and then the sudden terrifying whirr of a drill. Fuck! Lambie could feel his breathing quicken as the big man turned to face them, clicking and revving the drill like a demented lunatic, the noise deafening. Lambie thought he was going to pass out as he came towards them. But it was Thomson he approached. Thomson flinched and pushed back on the chair as though if he pushed hard enough he could break out of the building. But the two minders behind him held him by the shoulders and grabbed his arm. He whimpered. Oh, fuck no. They planted his hand on the wooden desk and held it tight. Thomson was struggling and crying.

'Please, no. Aw, man. Please no!'

Then he let out a blood-curdling scream as the drill bit was placed on the back of his hand and the gorilla pressed the trigger. Lambie nearly passed out. He had never heard anything as sickening as the whirr of the drill, and the screams of Thomson. He heard the sound of bone and gristle being bored into, then just before Thomson passed out, he screamed, 'Fuck, boss! Just tell him! We're going to die here anyway!'

Thomson slumped forward, his hand drilled to the desk, blood, skin and bone splattered over the place. The big men behind him held him so he didn't fall to the floor. There was silence and then the sound of dribbling water hitting the lino floor as Thomson wet himself.

Lambie looked up at Jack, who shrugged.

'So,' he said. 'Let's hear it. I won't ask again.'

Lambie nodded. For a fleeting, surreal moment, he saw a

picture of himself on the cruise ship, the sun on his face, a colourful cocktail in his hand. It didn't get more ridiculous than that. He opened his mouth and began talking.

'I wasn't there,' he began. 'I was just given the job by Belfast.' He looked at Jack. 'You know what it's like. You don't say no. You can't say no. They gave me the job and told me to get it done. So I did.' He paused. 'It's not as though I had a fucking option.'

Jack said nothing and kept staring him down. Lambie knew he would want names, and he knew the moment he gave them it was like committing suicide. But what the fuck was he supposed to do now? Thomson was out for the count, the blood seeping out of his hand and the colour gone from his face. Nobody was even making a move to help him, or take the drill out now that he was talking. He knew he would have to keep going, because if he didn't, the next person to have the drill treatment would be him.

'The job was given to Billy Dobson. I gave it to him. He's a UVF man from Belfast. It was the commander there who suggested him. I've worked with him before. He's done stuff for me. So I got him to do it.'

Jack nodded. 'Who in Belfast gave you the job?'

Lambie looked at him and puffed out a breath.

'Fuck's sake, Jack. I can't do that. I can't give you his name. You might as well shoot me now.'

'Don't tempt me, cunt,' Jack spat. He looked past him at the big man with the drill and the other two behind him.

Lambie sat for a long moment, recollecting the scene in Belfast when he'd been given the job, around a month ago. It had been the usual few drinks in the pub on the Shankill, the meets and greets with the boys, all of them UVF, most of them killers and torturers and robbers. Lambie was comfortable in their company. He'd carried out their orders many times, but these days he didn't get his own hands dirty. He was rich enough and powerful enough to give orders back across the water to his Glasgow mob. He remembered the big boss, Wattie Townsley, sitting in the bar in Shankill, his power base, surrounded by his closest associates. It was always good to swap stories and talk about the good days. Also, for Lambie, being there and being seen among these men gave him a status and kudos that a lot of others didn't have. Wattie trusted him. They worked well together. Even in times when he was pulled in by cops as he arrived back in Glasgow airport or off the ferry at Cairnryan and he'd been quizzed as a person of interest, Lambie knew they'd had nothing on him. In fact he quite enjoyed the big-shot untouchable feeling when they glared at him as he walked away after questioning. Being a person of interest to the cops was like a badge of honour. He'd talk to Wattie in their own code about it after- wards, knowing their phones were being tapped, and they'd laugh it out. When a big job was going down, he always went across and saw the troops in person, as it was safer. That way nothing could get out. But now here he was, spilling his guts to a big-time organisation run by fucking Catholics. What the actual fuck was happening here?

'Wattie Townsley.' When he said it, the name echoed in his head. 'He's the head of the UVF. He gave me the job. I mean, it's not as if I could have refused.' He looked at Jack as though he was expecting a bit of sympathy, even though he knew it wouldn't be forthcoming. It wasn't. Jack glared at him.

'You mean he ordered you to hit Kerry Casey. Frame her?'

Lambie nodded sheepishly, seeing the disgust on Jack's face.

'Why? Did Townsley say why? Or do you just do what you're told, no questions asked, no matter what you're told to do?'

Lambie took a moment. Truth was he didn't know why, and he knew better than to ask Townsley why he wanted to frame Kerry Casey. But he recalled a moment during their conversation in Belfast, when Townsley had told him not to fuck this job up, because it came from somebody well up the line. He didn't quite know what that meant. The UVF did hits, robberies and punishment beatings on request and for a fee. That was standard. If the money was good enough, the Belfast command would take on any job. That's how they worked.

'I don't make the decisions,' Lambie ventured. 'Townsley would never tell me who ordered a job or why it was being done. But I do remember him saying that this had to be done right, because the order came from up the line.'

'Up the line? What the fuck does that mean?'

'I don't know. Could be anyone. Any of the Caseys' enemies.'

Jack didn't answer and Lambie could see his brain ticking over. He would know that the Caseys had a few enemies, but going to the trouble of framing Kerry Casey was something bigger than an ordinary hit. There had to be more to this. He could see that if Jack had any answers, then he wasn't going to share them with him.

'Okay. Go on. Walk me through the night it happened. Every detail. Everyone who was there and took part. Where they are now. Every fucking detail.'

Lambie swallowed, his mouth dry.

'Can I get a drink or something? A glass of water?'

Jack went across to the sink and filled a chipped mug with water and handed it to him. Lambie put it to his lips, hands shaking, and drank from it. He felt faint and tired and defeated. He went on talking.

'I had to make a plan. I knew it wouldn't be easy to lure Kerry Casey into a meet or a trap or anything like that. So the plan was fucking basic.' He turned his head to Thomson who was still out, his body twitching from the shock of the drill still attaching his hand to the desk. 'Thomson gave me the bodies – the boys who would be involved – and I okayed them. I brought Billy Dobson in from Belfast to do it. We decided to have someone stop in the middle of the road as if they were in trouble. We had been following her car for a couple of days. We knew she was coming back to the house but on the backroads. So we were waiting for her.'

'Give me all the names,' Jack said.

Lambie swallowed. 'The main man was Billy Dobson. He was organising it for Thomson. They were both there. And Bo – Billy Bo Black. But Bo's dead now. He had to be dealt with because he was coked out afterwards and shooting his mouth off about what'd happened. We couldn't have that, so we got rid of him.'

'At the quarry?' Jack glared at him.

'Aye. The bodies we put in Casey's car were Thomas Lumsden and Peter Hawkins. The pair of them were stealing from me, so they had to be got rid of anyway, and we used their bodies that night. Dobson had shot them both, earlier, before the Casey car arrived. Then the boys were lying in wait in the bushes when they stopped.'

Lambie wasn't surprised, but it confirmed everything he suspected. The little prick Gimpy had run to the Caseys and spilled his guts. Fucker.

'Gimpy came to you,' he said, deadpan.

'Shut the fuck up and keep telling the story. Give me names,' Jack hit back.

'Thomson, Rab Downey, Davey McKay. They're all my boys. They were the guys who ambushed her. The boys dragged the bodies over and put them in the Casey car.'

'So you just executed two of your own boys for convenience?' Jack said. 'What kind of fucking snake in the grass are you, Lambie?'

'It's not as if they were just innocent bystanders. They were two pricks who'd been stealing from me. They'd stiffed me on collections from a batch of heroin recently. They were on the road out anyway. I just brought it forward because it suited me.'

Jack didn't answer but the contempt was all over his face.

'Give me addresses and phone numbers. Tell me where these guys are.'

Lambie sat for a long moment. He had just ratted on everyone who was close to him, from Wattie Townsley to the guys he kicked around with every day. How the fuck was he going to get out of this? He went into his mobile and reeled off the names and numbers and rough addresses of where they lived and where to find them. One of Jack's men wrote them down. Then Lambie sat, waiting.

'Right,' Jack finally said. 'Here's what you're going to do. You're going to set up a meeting in Belfast with Townsley. You're going to wear a wire and talk to him about what happened. Get him to talk about the hit, that it came from him, that it was an ordered job. Then you give that to me.'

Lambie looked at him in disbelief.

'How the fuck am I going to suddenly set up a meet with Townsley and get him talking about the job? He'll be suspicious.'

'Well if he is, he'll shoot you. It'll save me doing it.'

'Fuck's sake. You'd be as well shooting me now.'

'Don't tempt me, arsehole.'

This was do-or-die stuff. If Lambie could pull this off, he might be able to do a runner and disappear for the rest of his life. He would have to. He had enough money. But he would have to go to the other side of the world.

'And what happens if I can make this work? What happens to me then?'

'We'll see,' Jack said, stone-faced.

'What about him?' Lambie jerked his head towards Thomson who was beginning to come to, groaning and crying.

'We'll see.'

'So what happens now?' Lambie said.

He knew one thing for sure – he wasn't going home to pack for the cruise. But what the Christ was he going to say to his wife?

'The boys will take you somewhere. For the night. Then tomorrow morning, you'll make the call to Townsley.'

'And tell him what?'

'You're the fucking mastermind,' Jack said. 'You can work that out.'

Jack looked at the two big men standing behind him, and nodded. They pulled Lambie to his feet, and walked him to the door. As he looked back, he saw Thomson half conscious, reaching out with his free hand.

'Dick. Wait. Don't leave me,' Thomson groaned.

Those were the last words he spoke. Lambie watched as one of the men stepped towards Thomson. He took a gun out of the waistband of his trousers, shoved it into the nape of Thomson's neck, and fired.

CHAPTER NINETEEN

A pall of grief hung over the prison in the days that followed the Linda's suicide. The usual banter and joshing
among the younger women had all but stopped, and it was
as though their spirit had gone. Even though most of the
girls hadn't known much about Linda, and in fact didn't
even know each other that well, Kerry had noticed that
there was a certain camaraderie that existed between the
women. Being locked up in jail, losing your freedom, and
for most of them, having not much of a future to look at
when they got out, somehow made their time inside feel
they were part of something. There was a level of protection in here, because many of the girls were from broken
homes, already scarred by the system, most of them on the
fringes of society. But in here, they found others in the
same boat. Someone Kerry used to know said that everyone
finds their own level in life. It had been a glib, snobbish,
remark, she thought, made to her at the start of her law

career, about some persistent reoffender in court again. Kerry always felt it was unfair to judge people immediately because you never knew what brought them to where they were. She was a bit of a bleeding heart that way. But in jail, she could see a completely different world rolled out in front of her. She was lucky because at least no matter what happened here, she'd already had something of a life; she'd travelled, seen places, had a successful career. But many of these girls had nothing. They'd come in here with nothing and they'd leave with nothing, and didn't have much to look forward to.

But Kerry noticed that after Linda's death, there was also anger brewing, and prisoners were unsettled and often aggressive, more often than not towards the prison officers. Some of the long-term offenders seemed to be high on drugs and there had been fury when the officers initiated cell searches after they'd discovered pills had been circulating. Free time in the evenings was beginning to take on an edginess that Kerry found disquieting, and more and more she wished she could be out of there. It came to a head one night over the drugs. Janice, a girl in her late twenties who had been in and out of jail for years, had arrived back two weeks ago, and rumour was that she was the one who had grassed about some diazepam that had been found. The night it happened, Kerry had been sitting in the communal area after dinner reading a book while others watched the TV.

'Don't look now,' Ash said to Kerry and the other two

girls who were on the sofa, 'but Aggie's spoiling for a fight. She's been bitching all day how she's going to batter Janice for grassing.'

'But does she know it was her?' Kerry felt naive as soon as she'd said it.

'No, but there's no courtroom in here, Kerry. It's the law of the jungle.'

The place went quiet as Aggie got to her feet and the others around her table glanced at each other as though they knew what was about to happen.

Janice sat by herself, reading a magazine. She looked up to see Aggie standing over her.

'Fuck!' Ash said. 'Look! Aggie's got a spanner! She must have stolen it from the bike shop.'

No sooner were the words out than Aggie lashed out with the spanner and hit Janice smack on the shoulder then the side of her head. The girl looked dazed, as she turned around.

'What the fuck are you doing, you fat bastard!'

'You're a skinny bastard grass!' Aggie said. 'And you're getting it.' She struck out again, this time hitting her above the eye where blood spurted out.

'Hey!' Kerry suddenly heard herself saying. 'Stop it. You're going to kill her.'

Everyone turned to Kerry, and Aggie swivelled around to face her as Janice slumped to the floor. Then Aggie ran the few steps across and lunged at Kerry, screaming, 'You and all the fucking Caseys are grasses! Your brother Mickey was a grass!'

For a second, despite her terror, the words stung Kerry. Mickey a grass? That was something she'd never heard before. But even as the thought streaked across her consciousness, Aggie had lifted the spanner and was about to strike her, when suddenly Ash jumped up and tackled Aggie from the waist, bringing her to the floor and knocking the spanner out of her hand. Two wardens came racing from the canteen area and one of them grabbed Aggie, sitting astride her. But she wriggled and elbowed the warden, trying to get to the spanner that was a couple of feet away from where they were struggling. Most of the girls were now in a circle surrounding the action, and Kerry then saw one of Aggie's lifer mates kick the spanner across to her so she was able to grasp it. And before the other warden could wade in, Aggie brought the spanner down heavily onto the officer's head. Then again.

Blood pumped out from the side of her head. As the siren wailed, the other officers came rushing as the prison officer lay in a pool of blood. None of the inmates came to help. Two officers forced Aggie onto her stomach, handcuffed her behind her back, then dragged her to her feet. Everyone watched as she was led away.

'Right! Show's over! Everyone into their cells!' one of the officers shouted.

Ash leaned in to Kerry. 'Aggie'll get another four years

for that. Look. The warden is unconscious. She's no' even moving. Maybe she's dead.'

Kerry stood looking around as the prisoners filed away, and the officer lay motionless on the floor, the trickle of blood oozing from her temple now flowing onto the tiled floor.

Back in the cells there was a deathly quiet outside in the communal area. Earlier, there had been some activity that Kerry assumed was paramedics arriving and stretchering the prison officer away. She could hear the crackling of police radios, so this was obviously going to be a major incident. Ash and she hadn't said much as they got undressed and into their beds. It was only in the silence and the blackness after lights out that Kerry finally broke down. She'd been holding back the tears and the tension of earlier, and everything over the last few days, and suddenly the floodgates opened.

'You all right, Kerry?'

'Yes,' she sniffed. 'I . . . I'm just a bit overwhelmed by all that stuff going on out there. It was terrible. I feel I'm trapped and I can't escape. I don't know if I can take much more of this, Ash. I really don't.'

Kerry heard Ash sit up on the bed and then climb down the ladder. She sat on the edge of her bed and took Kerry's hand.

'Listen, mate. We all get like that sometimes, when we can't see the end of the road. Especially when it's your first time locked up. But you'll be fine in time. You're a good woman, Kerry. And you're strong.'

'But I can't stand it. I can't bear the thought that if I don't get out of here and it goes to trial, I might have my baby in here.' Kerry sobbed.

'Sssh.' Ash wiped Kerry's tears with the sleeve of her pyjamas. 'Listen. You've got top people trying to get you out of here. Just hang on. It's just that shit tonight that pushed you over the edge. But hey. You stood up to Aggie. You told her to stop when she was beating the crap out of Janice. That was well brave.' Ash grinned. 'Good job she's away in handcuffs.'

Kerry stopped crying, and could see that Ash was trying to lighten the mood. She forced a smile.

'Jesus. I can't believe I did that. I hope to hell she doesn't appear back here in the morning.'

'Nah,' Ash said. 'She'll be locked up in isolation for a bit. They might even move her to another jail. She's a trouble-maker.'

'I hope I don't see her again. But what about her mates?'

'Don't worry. We'll keep out of their way. I've got your back anyway.'

'Thanks, Ash. You were brilliant, jumping in like that.'

'Aye. I'm a good fighter. Wiry.' She beamed.

With each passing week, the way things were going for Kerry, she didn't know if she would get out of there, but she had to keep hoping and believing. Marty kept telling her to keep her spirits up and that something would give. He said that they'd realise it was all too easy for the cops to find someone caught red-handed like this, with bodies in their car. That it was a process she had to go through, bear with, and that once they started looking hard, they would find – through forensics or DNA, that she and Danny had nothing to do with this. It was only a matter of time. Kerry hoped so. Because she was now almost six months pregnant, her bump showing, the life inside her kicking away. The idea that she might give birth behind bars was unthinkable. In her darker moments, and there had been many in recent days, she thought of Vinny. Not a trace or a sign that he was anywhere. She knew he would never do that. If he wanted to take himself out of the picture with Kerry, she knew him well enough to know that he would sit her down and tell her. He was too much of a man to do a runner. And even if he didn't want to be with her – and she understood that, given who she was – he would have told her. *One day at a time*, she told herself. And today, she had a visitor in the afternoon – Jack. She'd only seen him a few times since she was in, so she was looking forward to hearing what was going on outside.

Kerry was glad to see big Jack as she arrived along with other women into the prison visiting area. He'd got her a coffee and sat at the table waiting for her. He stood up when she approached.

'Hey, Kerry. Good to see you.' He opened his arms.

Kerry walked into his embrace and it was good to feel his strong arms around her. They stayed that way for a few seconds, and for a moment Kerry felt a little choked. When they parted, Jack searched her face, and she knew he could see it.

'You all right?'

'Yeah,' Kerry lied. 'I'm fine. It's just good to see you, Jack. Makes me homesick for everything when I see you.'

'I know.'

They sat down and Jack slid the coffee over to her.

'They don't do lattes in here apparently.' He smiled, lightening the moment.

'I know. But it's not that bad. I've got used to it.'

'So how are you coping?' Jack said. 'I saw on the news about the suicide of that young girl. That must have been awful.'

'It was,' Kerry said. She lifted the cup to her lips and sipped. 'She was only nineteen. All the women were really shattered by it. There's a few tough cookies in here, but something like that – the mood seemed to go from sorrow to anger. It's been a hard few days. There's been a bit of trouble among the prisoners and a warden got attacked by a lifer. She's a real hard case, and she's been having a go at me. She tried to hit me as well, and shouted at me that our Mickey was a grass – that all the Caseys were grasses. I mean, where the hell did that come from, Jack? I've never even heard anything about grassing, or our Mickey.'

Jack shrugged.

'I wouldn't worry about it, Kerry. Accusing someone of being a grass is just about the worst thing you can say to anyone. So she must have been mad or maybe just threatened because the head of the Caseys is in jail. I was worried that something like this would happen. But listen. Just keep your chin up. We'll get you out of here soon. I promise.'

They sat for a moment in silence. Kerry didn't really want to pour her heart out to Jack about everything she'd been feeling in recent days.

'So how are things going?' Kerry asked.

Jack nodded slowly and leaned forward a little.

'Good,' he said softly. 'There's been a bit of a development. A breakthrough.'

'Seriously?' Kerry wondered why it was Jack who was telling her this and not Marty.

'Yeah. We know who framed you. Who set it up. Who carried out the hit and planted the drugs, the guns. We have names.'

Kerry's stomach did a little jolt of delight. But if this was Jack giving her this information, then she knew it had to have been acquired by force. From where she was sitting, right now that didn't matter a damn. She was innocent, and she didn't care how her people went about proving it.

'Really? Tell me.'

Jack's voice dropped to a whisper. 'Wee guy came to us. His name is Steven. He worked in the White Horse for Dick Lambie's mob.' He paused. 'You'll not know them, Kerry, as you've been away. But they're UVF, violent loyalists. They carry out hits, robberies and stuff for big money. It all comes from Belfast. It was Lambie and his mob who set you up.'

'So this guy broke away from them and came to us? Why?'

'He's not one of them. Just worked for them in the bar. They've been bullying and using him for years. He's just a wee guy with a limp and not a lot going for him. But he's up to his eyes in debt with them – they're loan sharks as well – and they were extorting fortunes from him. He'd never have paid them off. It was all about bullying and abuse. They got him involved in a murder, and made a veiled threat that if he opened his trap then they'd kill his sick old mother. That was the last straw. But before he ran out on them, he overheard information that it was their mob who did the set-up on you and Danny.'

'Jesus! Is it definitely true?'

'Oh, it's true all right. We've already established that a hundred per cent.'

Kerry didn't reply. She was processing all this in her head.

'So where is the guy, this Steven and his mother? We've got them somewhere safe?'

Jack nodded and blinked in agreement.

'Of course. We've got them in one of our flats out of the way. The mother's a right old character – coughing her lungs up with emphysema. Steven is a good man, and he's been invaluable to us.' He paused. 'The information we've got will get you out of here, Kerry. I haven't spoken to Marty or Danny yet. But I'm sure this will make the cops and the prosecution think again.'

Kerry reached across and touched his hand. This was a game changer. It was all about how they approached the information now.

'So what about Lambie? What'll happen with him now?'

Jack sat back and folded his arms. He tried not to give anything away, but Kerry could see a glint in his eye that meant he knew he was winning.

'We've got him with us. He's helping the Caseys with their enquiries, so to speak.'

For the first time in a few days Kerry smiled. She didn't need to ask – at least not right now. She knew that no matter how much information they got from Lambie and his mob, that even if it did get her out of jail, the retribution for putting her there in the first place would be swift and deadly. Of course it was wrong. Of course it was something she would have run a mile from a year ago, even eight months ago. But right now, it all sat fine with her.

*

Steven watched his ma dunking her digestive biscuit into the mug of tea he'd put down on the table next to the armchair. She sat toasting her feet in front of the flame effect gas fire. Outside, the early evening gloom of a winter's night had settled over the street, and Steven gazed out, watching the well-heeled people getting out of their upmarket cars and heading to the front doors of their homes. The view was a world away from High Street. He'd lived three floors up from the day he was born and when you looked outside all human life was there, from the homeless guys sleeping in doorways to the sharp-suited lawyers heading down to the High Court on the Glasgow Green. Or just the typical Glasgow punters, heading to and from the station or into the city centre in search of shops, pubs or a day out. It was always interesting, an evolving picture every day. This place was different. Jack and Cal had taken him and his ma to some place on the edge of the West End of Glasgow, out towards the outskirts of the city. He knew the road well enough. He remembered going on it for bus runs with his ma as a kid, and eventually they'd get to the seaside town of Helensburgh. He remembered getting his picture taken with a wee monkey dressed in dungarees and a yellow polo-neck sweater. Looking back, the poor monkey was probably tranquillised, but back then as a wee guy, having a monkey on your shoulder for a photo, you were well made up.

In this street of large, smart, detached and semi-detached houses, people came and went to work early in the morning and returned at night. There were no shops nearby, no buses coming through, and it felt a bit isolated. But that was the only downside of it. The upside was how lovely it was. How Jack had looked after them, and how much his ma was loving every minute of their new surroundings, their new life. Everything had happened so fast, he'd scarcely had time to consider if this would indeed be a new life. He wondered what would happen once this all died down, but he was afraid to ask. He'd been assured at their first meeting with Jack and Marty that he would be looked after, and that they'd keep looking after him. He hoped so, because he knew if he put his head above the parapet anywhere in Glasgow city, someone would find him. He thought for a moment of how he'd gone to the addresses of Rab Downey and Davey McKay, and pointed them out as he sat in the back of the blacked-out car. That was all he'd had to do. Just show them the right guys and the Caseys' boys would do the rest. He could only imagine what would be happening to them right now. And he knew that Thomson would have been picked up by now and so would Lambie. He didn't care what happened to them. All of them deserved what they got. He was just grateful for the break, and he'd never slept so well as he had in the last few nights in the comfort of a warm cosy house after a meal with his ma. It gladdened his heart to see how happy she was. She even seemed to be breathing and moving around a little easier. Deep down he chastised himself for not making a bigger effort to make her life better. But he didn't have the means to do that – he'd had no real education, no trade and no finances. So he was never going to get out of the mire. Still he blamed himself. If he could have got his ma to a place like this years ago, she might not have got so ill. And maybe if he'd been living in a place like this, with a good job, he might even have found a girl to settle down with. All now water under the bridge, he told himself, but the thoughts were still there.

'You look miles away, Steven.' His ma sipped her tea. 'You all right?'

'Aye, Ma,' Steven replied. 'I'm fine. Just kind of trying to take things in. It's all happened that fast.'

'I know, son,' she said, her voice consoling. 'You're not regretting what you did though, are you?'

He looked at her, shook his head. 'No. There was no way out for me, Ma – for us. When I walked in to our house and saw that scumbag Thomson in your bedroom, my blood ran cold. If I'd have stayed, Christ knows what they would have lined up for me next. They thought they had me right where they wanted me.'

'But you showed them, son, did you not?'

Steven wished he shared his ma's triumphalism. He still felt that Lambie and his mob would hunt him down. But as long as the Caseys protected him he'd be safe.

'Aye,' he said. 'More like you showed them, Ma. The way you just made your mind up that night was enough. I don't know if I'd have had the courage to do what I did without you, and that's the truth.'

'Ach, nonsense. You're a good man, Steven. And you're a better man to come. When this settles down a bit and if that Kerry Casey gets out of jail, maybe you should see about working for them.'

Steven gave her a surprised look.

'The Caseys? But they're gangsters too. That might be like going out of the frying pan into the fire. I'm not even thinking that far ahead, Ma. We'll just wait and see what happens.'

'Aye,' she said. 'I suppose the Caseys are gangsters like all the rest of them. But I remember back in the old days, that Tim Casey fella – he'd be Kerry's old man, I suppose.'

'You knew them? You knew the father? You never mentioned it before.' Steven said, surprised.

'I knew of them,' she said, wistfully. 'Everyone did. I remember him, and he was a robber all right. But I remember he and his boys got involved in a big rumpus one time when a teenage girl was battered and they sorted it all out, and the boys who did it were beaten within an inch of their lives. The Caseys didn't need to get into that – it wasn't their affair, and not even in their area. Police were involved but they didn't even charge them. You got your own justice back then, and sometimes it was better than it is now. So maybe there's a bit of good in them somewhere, that's what I'm saying. I mean, they could have just given you a few quid after you helped them and sent us on our way without any protection.' She gestured with her hand. 'But look what they've done for us. They've got us well set up here and they're making sure we're fed and stuff. I don't know that they had to do that. But they have, and I've a bit of respect for them.'

Steven found himself smiling at his ma's logic.

'Jeez, Ma, you're beginning to sound like a gangster yourself.'

'Aye, well, if it comes to that . . .' She gave a hearty laugh that turned into a bout of coughing, but she was still smiling at the end of it.

CHAPTER TWENTY

Sharon sat on the chair next to where Kerry normally would have sat during meetings with her closest aides. In Kerry's absence, and with Danny gone too, she was overseeing everything that was going on in the organisation, but she didn't want to sit in Kerry's seat. She had too much respect for her to do that. Jack had already been to see Kerry in Cornton Vale, and Danny in Barlinnie, to let them know of the latest developments. Vic had been working closely with Jack and the boys to prepare the next step.

'So how are they bearing up, Jack?' Sharon asked.

In her own visit to Kerry, Sharon had sensed that she was feeling emotional but putting on a brave face for her.

'Danny is okay,' he said, nodding. 'It's a long time since he's seen the inside of a jail, but he's dealing with it fine. We've got a couple of people on the inside looking out for him. Danny's not as young as he was – or as he thinks he is – if any of the young blades try to take him on. So I talked to some people to make sure he's looked after.' Jack paused, sat back. 'But he's well buoyed up with the developments. And he's angry all right. Raging that he's not out here dealing with these bastards who brought all this on us. He said whatever it takes, just do it. Kerry is fuming too that they've been totally framed and she's banged up in jail, pregnant, and not knowing when the hell she'll get out.'

Sharon wasn't surprised to hear Danny's reaction, and she knew how upset Kerry was. The out-of-the-blue news that this little Glasgow guy Steven had come to them with information had changed everything. She knew that the retribution had already begun, but she hadn't asked Jack or Vic what they'd done with Thomson's body. As far as she was concerned, it wasn't relevant. He got what he deserved. Sharon didn't suffer from the crisis of conscience that she knew Kerry did when it came to the heavy-duty retribution, especially when it was carried out in cold blood. If someone had crossed the Caseys and placed them in a situation where they could lose everything and the head of their organisation was facing life in jail – there was only one way to deal with them. But she knew the show wasn't over yet. They had Lambie, and they were working on a plan.

'So, Jack,' Sharon said. 'Let's see how we can work this, so that when it comes down to the big questions, we actually have evidence that Marty can take to the prosecution.'

Jack glanced at Vic. 'We're on it, Sharon. I think we should hit this Wattie Townsley in Belfast. Go right to the heart of it. Apart from sending a message to these bastards, if it works out, we can get him talking about ordering the set-up.'

Sharon liked the idea, but how could they make that work?

'Townsley's UVF. Is there a snowball in hell's chance of him grassing anyone up?'

'Depends on how it's put to him,' Jack said, seriously. 'If he's no option but to squeal, then he will.'

Sharon clasped her hands on the table in front of her. She had to admit that stuff like this, organising how to extract information from thugs like Townsley, wasn't really her forte. Back in Spain, she'd been running the Casey businesses, getting the hotel ready for opening in a few months' time. Sure, she hadn't been shy when it came to putting a bullet in the Colombian after his thugs had kidnapped her and were going to murder her. Nor had she flinched when she'd shot the two bastards her late husband Knuckles Boyle had sent to execute her. But that was about survival, a spur-of-the-moment, white-heat reaction. Planning it in cold blood was a different matter.

'But going into Belfast, Jack,' she said. 'Townsley will be surrounded by guys who would take a bullet for him.'

Jack nodded, glanced at Vic. 'True. But we've thought of an alternative to that. Vic and me have talked a lot about this in the last couple of days, and we've come up with something. You need to hear it first, see what you think.'

Sharon waited, wondering what Vic had talked secretly with Jack about and not told her. They'd been living in Kerry's guest house together, since they'd both came back from Spain to help run things while Kerry and Danny were gone. Vic had always played his cards close to his chest in all the time she'd known him, but when they'd got together after he'd come out of jail, and now that they were both entrenched with the Caseys, Vic was more open. He knew she was running the show in Spain. But here in Glasgow, though she was overseeing things, Vic was more in his comfort zone with Jack. He'd been there when they picked up Thomson and Lambie, and he'd told her about Thomson's fate. And he'd been on the crew who rounded up the rest of Lambie's guys who'd set up Kerry. This kind of hardman stuff was meat and drink to him. And Sharon knew Vic felt he owed Kerry a huge debt. If it hadn't been for her blackmailing the Attorney General with compromising pictures and videos, he'd probably still be languishing in Belmarsh prison awaiting trial. He would do whatever was required to get her and Danny out of jail.

'I'm all ears,' Sharon said.

'Well, as you know, we have Lambie holed up, and he's being very cooperative.'

Sharon nodded. 'What kind of nick is he in? Did you not tell me he was supposed to be going on a cruise or something when you picked him up? Has he talked to his wife?'

'He has,' Jack said. 'He phoned her that night to say that something had come up, that they had to cancel, and that he'd been summoned to Belfast for a special job. He said his wife knew better than to ask questions. But he'll do whatever we tell him, because he thinks if he does, then he's going to get away with it if we get Kerry out.' Jack paused. 'Of course he's wrong about that, but we'll let Danny take care of that when, all going well, he gets out of jail.'

'And is he up for going to Belfast? I'd be worried about that.'

Jack nodded. 'He doesn't think it's a good idea. He said it would be too dangerous and that him suddenly pitching up in Belfast might get Townsley's hackles up and could get us all killed if it went tits up. So he says it's better if we can get Townsley over here.'

'How are we going to do that? Would Townsley not be more suspicious if an invite to Glasgow suddenly comes across his table?'

'Aye,' Jack said. 'He would. But he comes over quite a lot for the Old Firm matches. Next week is a quarter final of the Scottish Cup. It's midweek, so he might fly in and back the following day. Lambie can find out. If he does, then Lambie can talk to him about an offer on the table that looks like it will make him a huge amount of money. He says he might buy it, that he's greedy. He says Townsley is stashing away a lot of money for his future, and when the time comes, he wants to leave Belfast and go and live abroad. He said he has plans to buy a couple of bars in Spain. Set himself up there. Apparently he's well connected.'

Sharon puffed, a little indignant.

'Yeah. Well the bastard might find out when he gets there that other people are much better connected. So what kind of money-making deal are we talking about?'

'Lambie said he might be lured over by the promise of a big coke deal. One that would make him more money than ever.'

Sharon thought about it for a long moment. The Caseys didn't have a lot of cocaine around their organisation these days. Kerry had seen to that in recent months. Sure, they'd stolen the shipment of coke from the Colombians, but it was long gone, sold and profited from, and the money invested in legit businesses, helping them to grow both in Spain and the UK.

'Can we get our hands on a load of cocaine like that? I mean, would he not want to see it?' As she said it, Sharon felt she sounded a little naive.

Jack shrugged. 'He wouldn't need to see it if the offer is coming from Lambie. He trusts him completely. It was Townsley who pushed Lambie all the way to where he is now. They were a couple of scallies when they were younger and did work for Loyalists in the early days, earned their spurs. They trust each other. Totally.'

'So Lambie sets him up? Brings him over here? Then what?'

'Well, some of it will have to be played by ear. But if he comes here, ideally we'd get him to talk to Lambie about the hit. And after we've got that, we take it from there. Take him on a night out.'

Sharon glanced at Vic who raised his eyebrows.

'Fair enough. Sounds good. I'll leave you guys to it.'

Lambie hadn't slept much in the flat the Caseys had dumped him in yesterday. It was like being in jail. He'd been told he wouldn't be going anywhere until this was finished. They'd locked the bedroom door last night, and he knew that one of their henchmen was in the bedroom next to him or in the living room watching television late into the night. There was no chance he could get out, or alert anyone that he was here. They'd taken his mobile off him, and later in the evening someone came in and dropped off a couple of shopping bags with clothes for the next few days. They didn't speak to him or discuss anything, other than to tell him the takeaway food had arrived. He'd sat at the dining table in the living room while the Casey man ate on an armchair, one eye on the television, one eye on him. It occurred to him that he could grab a knife and have a go, but looking at the big burly bastard with the scar down one side of his face, it wouldn't be a good idea. There was nothing he could do but wait it out until they told him what was next. Lying in bed the previous night, he'd felt a twinge of guilt for Nora, who had built up to go on the cruise. But that was the least of his worries right now. She really didn't have a clue about anything, and never had. As long as he threw enough money at her all his life she pretty much let him do what he wanted. There was no point in dwelling on it, he decided. The next few days would be difficult and crucial. When he'd spoken to Jack last night, he'd convinced him that going to Belfast was not a good idea. He knew that even if he could find a way to warn Townsley once he got there, he would still get bumped off in due course for even bringing the Caseys to his turf. So it had to be Glasgow. Townsley had said a few weeks ago that he was coming over for the match on Wednesday and they'd planned to meet up for a drink and a bite to eat, as they usually did. This would be the trap he would lay for Townsley, the man he'd been loyal to most of his life. He knew the Caseys would execute Townsley as easily and coldly as they'd done with Thomson. But if that meant *he* could get out of this shitstorm alive, then so be it. It was all about *his* survival now. As soon as this was over, he would disappear, he told himself. Of course there was always the chance, the distinct possibility, that the Caseys would put a bullet in him too, but he didn't want to think about that. He heard the buzzer on the door and the voice of guy in the living room buzzing someone in. Then he heard Jack's voice. There was a knock on the door and the minder shouted, 'Lambie! Out here!'

'Right,' Lambie said, suppressing the rage that he was kowtowing to this fucker.

He took a deep breath, stood up and caught a glimpse of his ashen face in the mirror, sniffed and braced himself as he opened the door.

In the living room Jack stood with his hands in his jacket pockets, glaring at him. Beside him was another Casey man, a big stern-looking bastard called Vic, who'd driven them to this flat on the waterfront across from Kinning Park.

'You ready to make the call?' Jack said, his face like flint.

'Aye. I've no phone though. His number is on my mobile.'

Jack reached into the inside pocket of his jacket and took out Lambie's phone and switched it on. He stood for a moment as the phone pinged to life and registered messages and missed calls. He held the phone out to Lambie.

'Don't be doing anything stupid now, like making a panic call to someone. Because if you do, it'll be the last word you speak. Got that?'

Lambie nodded and said nothing. Before Jack handed it to him he took it back again.

'Have you got an app on there that lets people know where you are?'

'No,' Lambie said, wishing to fuck he had.

'Okay. Make the call. The usual kind of call you'd make

when Townsley's coming over for the match. And suggest a curry or something – whatever you normally do. But tell him you might have a wee business proposition to put to him.'

'You think I should say that now? This early?'

Jack seemed to think for a moment.

'Aye. Just tell him there's a chance to make a whole lot of money but that you can't talk on the phone.'

Lambie shrugged. He knew money and the possibility of making loads of it would give Townsley a hard-on.

'Okay.'

He knew Jack and the others were watching him as he scrolled down the phone for Townsley's mobile. Jack nodded to the minder who took out his gun, cocked it, and kept it on him. Lambie's mind was racing with thoughts of just blurting out to Townsley quickly what was going on, but he knew if he did, he'd be dead on the floor by the time he finished the first sentence, if he got that far. He held up the phone to show Townsley's number to Jack, who nodded but said nothing. Then he pushed the call key, and put the mobile on loudspeaker. A voice answered after four rings. Jack took a breath and composed himself.

'Wattie. How's it going?'

'Not too bad. What about you, brother?' The chirpy, sturdy Belfast accent filled the room.

'Aye, good. Just working away and stuff. Been a busy week.'

'You on loudspeaker, mate? You sound a bit distant.'

'Aye. Sorry. I'm getting ready to go out, running around like a blue-arsed fly.' He glanced at Jack with an expression that asked is it okay. 'Hold on till I switch the speaker off.' He switched the speaker off. 'That better?'

'Aye. Don't like them fucking speakers. Every fucker can listen in.'

'Aye. I won't keep you, man. But you still coming for the match?'

'Planning to. Got the flight booked and a hotel. Staying at the Radisson again.'

'Great stuff. You fancy going for a curry after? I've a couple of things I wanted to chat to you about.'

Silence. Then Wattie spoke. 'What like? Problems? With the recent job?'

'No, no, man. Far from it. Listen. I don't want to talk on the phone. You know what it's like. But something I think you might fancy. A wee proposition.'

'Aye? Throw in a couple of birds then as well, man. That'll get my interest up.'

Lambie heard Townsley's chuckling and was relieved that he wasn't at all suspicious.

'I'm sure that can be arranged, mate. What time you over?'

'I'm on the three o'clock flight. So I'll be in my hotel getting organised by back of four. Give me a shout and we'll meet for a pint before the match.'

'Perfect. See you Wednesday, mate.'

The line went dead, and Lambie stood for a long moment with the phone still at his ear. He was already in deep shit even before he made that phone call. Now there was no going back. He glanced at Jack who had his hand outstretched for the phone. He handed it to him, but Jack didn't speak. He just blinked in a kind of acknowledgement that he'd done what he'd been asked to do. Then he nodded to the guy next to him, and turned towards the door. As he opened it, he looked over his shoulder to where Lambie was standing.

'Talk later. I'll be back.'

He left and Lambie stood for a moment feeling isolated, lonely and fucking terrified.

CHAPTER TWENTY-ONE

Jake knew that Tarifa could turn into a battle if Mateo was right. So he was preparing for every eventuality, packing several guns and weapons into the hard-shell case he took with him on jobs. He always looked as though he travelled light, but inside the case was enough lethal weaponry to wipe out any mob. He packed a lightweight Kevlar bulletproof jacket and a spare one for Sullivan. It was important to be prepared. He sipped from a mug of coffee on his balcony, and gazed out over the sun twinkling on the sea. The village was beginning to get busy with people going about their business. He looked at his watch. If he picked up Sullivan and Mateo shortly, they could be in Tarifa by lunchtime. Then his mobile shuddered on the table and he could see Pam's name on the screen. He picked up the phone, curious as to why she was phoning him this early.

'Pam.'

The silence was brief, but Jake got a sense that something was wrong.

'Pam. You all right, sweetheart?'

Then he heard the sniffing.

'Oh, Jake. I'm sorry. I . . . I didn't have anyone else to phone.'

'What's up?'

Again the sniffing. Then she spoke. 'They came here. To the bar. Just now. They . . . they hit me, Jake.'

Cold rage flooded through him.

'Wait there. I'll be right over.'

He ended the call, shoved his phone into his pocket and went back into the apartment. From his case, he took a Glock pistol and pulled on a shoulder holster. Then he put his jacket on and went out the door, downstairs and into his car. As he drove the two miles through traffic to Fuengirola, Jake cursed out loud, blaming himself for bringing this shit to Pam's door. She didn't deserve this. In all the time he'd known her, Pam was a decent, hard-working, sometimes hard case of a woman. But she had the biggest heart, and would always go out of her way to do someone a good turn, give them a lift if they were down. Over the years, they'd become more than friends, and even when her husband had been alive, she'd shared Jake's bed from time to time. But it was more than that. Jake had never quite figured out what it was, because the way he lived his life meant he always ran a mile from any commitment, but Pam had filled the emptiness in his life – not just because of the sex, but because of her attitude, her charm, and her determination to see the good in a pile of crap. That's why she'd gone on for so long with the bar after the gangsters had steamed in and more or less taken it from her. The last thing she needed was to be dragged into his fight with the Colombians. He pulled his car off the main street and parked at the rear of the bar. The shutters were down and she wasn't quite open yet. So he punched in her number.

'I'm outside, Pam.'

'Okay.'

The shutters slowly went up, the noise filling the back alley, and then he saw her. Fuck! Her face was puffed up, one eye was red and swollen and her lip had been cut. He ducked under the shutter before it was fully up and dived inside. She buckled into his arms.

'Christ, Pam. I'm so sorry. They'll pay for this.'

He hugged her close and felt her sniffing on his shoulder. He held her tight, comforting her and stroking her hair as she sobbed.

'It's okay, sweetheart, you're safe now. Don't worry. I'll get these fucking Colombian bastards.'

She pulled away and looked up at him, her face tear-stained and puffy. It tore at his heart.

'It wasn't the Colombians, Jake.'

'What?'

'It wasn't them. It was the Spanish, the thugs who more or less took over the place, extorting money; the arseholes who made me change my bar into what it is. They came last night and said they needed me to move out of my apartment, that they were bringing girls in over the next few weeks, and that the place would also be a brothel upstairs. I told them to fuck off.'

'Why didn't you call me last night?'

'I . . . I didn't think they'd react like this. I thought maybe they'd send the boss and we'd come to an agreement. They've never been like this before, this heavy-handed. Something has changed now. It's all about money and women and all that shit.'

'So they told you the place was going to be a brothel.'

She bit her lip. 'I can't have that, Jake. I won't work here. My name is still on the deeds so I own the place on paper and they can't legally make me do it. But they can beat me into it.' She shook her head. 'I don't know what I can do now.'

Jake sat her down on a bar stool and sat opposite her, holding both her hands. In the darkness of the bar, her face was lit only by the neon of the bar taps and the gantry lights. She looked broken and bruised. Jake felt a dig of guilt that he was glad it hadn't been him who'd done this to her by dragging her into the Colombian shit. He hated himself for feeling that way, but he could never have forgiven himself if this had happened because she'd helped him last night.

'I'm going to fix this for you. I promise you that. I'll get these people, and I'll make sure they don't come near you again.'

She looked at him, her eyes pleading but hopeless.

'But, Jake, I don't know how you can. They run everything along this strip – all the protection for the shops and bars and restaurants.'

'I'll get them,' Jake said. 'But I need to go to Tarifa now. After last night. With the guy. Me and Sullivan are going down there now. But I'll be back in the next day or so. I promise you. Just lie low. Tell them you'll do what they ask, but that you need a bit of time to get organised and pack up your things. You got that?'

She nodded. Jake got off the stool and glanced at his watch.

'I have to move now. But I'll deal with this when I get back. Maybe you should take the day off and stay in the flat. Call them and tell them you'll agree to everything they ask. But say that you need time to get the legal stuff done. Can you do that?'

'Yes. I think so.'

He stepped towards her and pulled her close to him, kissing her cheek, and she buried her face in his neck. They stayed that way for a long moment, then he pulled away.

'I have to go, sweetheart. I'll call you. Don't worry.'

He turned and left, guilty at leaving her like this. But he

couldn't do much more right now. He considered taking her with him, but he didn't know what kind of shit was going to blow up in Tarifa, so she was probably safer here.

The Colombian had been silent for the entire journey down to Tarifa, and it crossed Jake's mind that he was either beginning to fall apart, or he was planning to double-cross them. Sullivan had said he wasn't sure they could trust him, but they both knew that right now they didn't have a lot of options. The Colombian had confirmed that Vinny was being held there, and he'd promised he would help them. But that would come at a cost.

As he drove, Jake reflected on the previous night when Mateo had opened up to them. Either he was a great bullshitter, or just a desperate man. Jake had decided he was desperate. Mateo had told them he'd been living on the Costa del Sol for three years with his wife and two-year-old son. He worked as a barman for the Colombian owner of the café in La Cala de Mijas, and though he knew it was a front for the cartel to wash their money, he didn't ask questions. When he'd got the job, he was told that if he kept his mouth shut he could have a good life here. But that if he talked to anyone about what he saw, he'd be a dead man. Mateo had said he'd tried to leave the job once to go and work on a building site, but he'd been told that leaving wasn't an option. You don't leave the cartel. They'd threatened to kill his wife and child. That was the moment Mateo had burst into tears, taking

Jake and Sullivan by surprise. They'd exchanged perplexed looks. They were stuck with this guy who was out of his depth with a bunch of hoodlums and he had nowhere to go. And now they were relying on him to help them. Anything could happen. Once Mateo had calmed down, Jake had told him that they would look after him. He'd said he would send someone to get his wife and child, and put them somewhere safe, and when this was all over, he would get them back together. To Sullivan's wide-eyed surprise, Jake had even promised they would be given a wedge of money to go and settle somewhere else, probably in the north of Spain. Mateo had agreed, and once he'd collapsed into a deep sleep, Jake had told Sullivan that he would keep his word. If they got Vinny out of this alive, with the help of this guy, then he would make sure he was looked after. By the time they were leaving Sullivan's apartment, Jake had got Mateo to ring his wife and tell her someone was going to come and pick them up, not to worry, just to go along with them, and that they would be safe. Jake had arranged for someone to do that. He didn't call Sharon or Jack to sanction any arrangement. He knew that if he'd phoned them they would tell him to do whatever it took to get Vinny. But he didn't want to tell them any of this anyway, or even that he knew where Vinny was, because it would only get their hopes up, and right now, he didn't know if he was going to be able to get Vinny out of this alive, or dead.

*

Jake pulled into the car park in the main area of the town so that they could let Mateo out. The arrangement was that once he was settled into the apartment and taking over his guard duty, he would come back out at some stage to go to the shop or bar, and he would phone Jake with whatever information he had picked up. As he was about to open the back door, Jake and Sullivan turned around to face him. He was pale and nervous, and hung-over, with dark bags under frightened eyes.

'Okay, Mateo,' Jake said. 'You are clear with everything we talked about, yes?'

Mateo nodded and looked at both of them, expression pleading.

'Please. You will make my wife and my son safe like you promised?'

'Like I promised,' Jake said. 'And when this is over, we will take you to them.'

'You are sure?'

'Mateo,' Jake said. 'I'm sure. Now it is up to you. You must be strong. You understand? You can do this. Just tell me once you know any information, and we will do the rest.' He paused. 'I told you. We will look after you. Today, this is over for you. Understand? For you, and your family.'

Mateo nodded again, opened the door and eased himself out of the car. They watched as he limped across the car park.

'Christ!' Sullivan said. 'He looks pathetic. I hope to fuck he doesn't go in there and completely burst.'

Jake kept his eye on Mateo until he disappeared out of sight in the direction of the apartment.

'I don't think he will,' he said. 'He's desperate. You know what the cartel is like. Once they have no further use for him, either in the bar or whatever drug-running shit they've involved him in, they'll just put a gun to his head. He knows that.'

Sullivan sighed, nodding.

'Yeah. That's about the size of it. Poor bastard.' He turned to Jake. 'What are you going to do with his wife and family?'

'One of my friends will pick them up this morning and take them to their home. It's up in the hills near Marbella. They'll be safe there. With Irish friends of mine.'

'Good. So is anyone else around here at the moment? I mean, your friends who you called last night?'

Jake nodded. He didn't want to go into a lot of detail about who was doing what. That's not how he worked. Sullivan would be told on a need-to-know basis, and he didn't need to know every move.

'Yes. Two of them are. They know where the apartment is, so they'll be on hand. These guys know what they're doing.' He narrowed his eyes, looking out towards the harbour. 'And I've got someone coming down on his boat this afternoon. I get the feeling that if anything is going to happen with Vinny – I mean if the Colombians are planning to get him out of there – then they'll do it under cover of darkness. Mateo said they told him they were taking Vinny for a swim. So we'll be here for a while.'

Jake and Sullivan sat in the café on a side street off the harbour in Tarifa. It had been two hours since Mateo had left them at the harbour, and it crossed Jake's mind that the Colombian had done a runner. The quayside was heaving with tourists coming off the boat from Tangier, laden with trinkets and heading for their tour buses. Other buses were arriving to catch the next ferry, and it would be easy for anyone just to disappear in the crowd. But his instinct told him that Mateo would stick with the plan, especially now that he'd told his wife to go with Jake's men. He was sure he wouldn't squeal to the Colombians, but his worry was if he got rumbled in any way and was asked awkward questions, he wouldn't be able to handle the pressure. Jake had already had a call from one of his own men saying he had a surprising development. They were waiting for him to come to the bar. Jake looked up as he could see him walking towards where they sat outside at one of the little wrought-iron tables.

'Here he comes,' Jake said to Sullivan.

A big man with dark cropped hair walked over to them with a swagger. As he approached, he pushed his aviator sunglasses onto his head, his piercing blue eyes scanning the harbour.

'Howsit going, Tommy boy?' Jake shook the big man's outstretched hand.

'All good so far, Jake.' A smile spread across his face. 'Even better than I hoped.' He shot a glance at Sullivan as he pulled a chair out and sat down.

'This is Sullivan, Tommy. He was undercover with Vinny,' Jake said.

Sullivan reached across the table and Tommy shook his hand, and gave him a kind of cold stare that Jake knew was about Tommy's basic distrust of cops. His brother had been shot dead by a British undercover cop in Belfast during the Troubles, and it was Jake who had talked Tommy into getting out of Northern Ireland rather than staying and seeking vengeance. He knew he would have ended up in jail. Jake could see that Sullivan wasn't fazed by Tommy as they shook hands.

'So what's the craic?' Jake said. 'Where's Bonzo?'

Bonzo was Tommy's best mate and the two of them worked together if they were ever required on anything Jake wanted them to do. Tommy pulled his chair close to the table and leaned in.

'We had a bit of a result this morning,' he said. 'We got on the road and came down here early, to have a decent recce and see if there was any movement in any of the other apartments. Believe it or not there was a time when the front door was left wide open by someone who was coming out, so the pair of us just went right in there.' He glanced from Jake to Sullivan, as though he was relishing telling his story.

'You walked right in?' Jake said. 'Is it not all locals in that place? Would you not be out of place?'

Tommy put his hand up. 'I don't think there is anyone in most of the flats. There are only about eight in total, and we'd watched for a while as people left looking like they were going to work. It was a chance we took. We'd seen some woman opening the shutters of her apartment and shaking out a rug, you know, like doing her housework. So we thought we would give her a knock.'

Jake put his hand to his eyes and massaged his brows. He really wasn't sure any of this was good news. But Tommy was no idiot, even if he did take flyers sometimes. He'd told him how crucial this operation was and how carefully they had to tread. So he had to trust the big man's judgement.

'You knocked on her door?'

'Yep,' Tommy said. 'She came out. Spanish woman. So I talked to her in Spanish and told her we were part of a film crew working on a documentary about Tarifa and the harbour and the tourist trade and stuff. And I asked her if it was possible to film and watch from her apartment over a day. That her window and balcony was a good vantage point.'

Jake was aware that Sullivan's mouth had dropped open. They exchanged glances and said nothing, but inside Jake was saying, 'Oh fuck!'

'So,' Tommy went on, 'she was a bit iffy in the beginning,

asking how long for, and for ID, and I gave her this old pass I had from a TV production company in London. Seemed to work. Then she said that she was going to work and wouldn't be back until later in the night and didn't know if she could trust us. All that shit.' Tommy looked from Jake to Sullivan. 'Then I offered her three hundred euros cash if we could work out of the apartment all day and into the evening.' He paused for effect. 'And she took it.'

'Fucking hell!' Jake said. He sucked in a breath through his teeth. 'Jesus, Tommy! Are you sure we can trust this woman? That she's not already in the police station telling them about the dodgy men in her apartment?'

Tommy spread his hands in a pleading gesture and shrugged, as though he did this sort of thing every day. 'Well,' he said. 'Truth is, you never really know. But she seemed sound enough. My instinct tells me she's hard-up and was glad of a wedge of money. Her eyes lit up when she saw the cash.'

'What about a man? Has she no husband or kids or any-one who's likely to wander in later?' Sullivan asked.

'No,' Tommy said curtly. 'She has one kid. There was a picture on the wall. Little boy about four, I'd say. She said he was with his gran up the coast a bit for the holiday weekend. That's where she was going to spend the day.' He paused. 'So she took the money, and off she went. Said she won't be back until around eleven this evening.'

Jake sat back and folded his arms. It was a good ploy – he

had to give Tommy ten out of ten for improvisation. He remembered the big Belfast man had been used by a TV investigation show years ago, to do undercover jobs when the programme was trying to expose villains. Who better to use for the job than a villain himself. Tommy used to regale them with stories of working with the production team, so his idea here might just work. In any case, it was already too late.

'So where's Bonzo?' Jake asked.

'He's already in the apartment, keeping a watchful eye on any comings and goings. The flat where you think Vinny is being held is the floor above, to the right. We've been in there two hours, and only heard the door being opened once. Two guys came out and down the stairs – we saw them in the street. They looked Colombian. And Bonzo saw one guy coming in. He looked Colombian too. He had a limp. But that's all the activity so far.'

Jake looked at Sullivan, then at Tommy, and half smiled.

'Okay. We'll see what the day brings.'

CHAPTER TWENTY-TWO

'The Billy Boys' anthem was being belted out in the packed White Horse pub as the Rangers fans crowded four deep at the bar. A quarter-final cup match between Celtic and Rangers was not just a big crowd puller, it was a chance for Lambie's boys to bang the drums around London Road that they were the team to beat. The song, as well as all of the vile chants from both Celtic and Rangers fans, had been banned from the football grounds a long time ago, so the only place the fans could vent their bigotry was in the bars around the football stadiums. The White Horse was on the London Road, where Celtic fans would be flocking to the stadium nearby for the match. It was always the dream of Rangers fans to beat them on their own turf. On any other Old Firm night, Lambie would have been counting the takings in his head as the tills rattled behind the bar and reckoning how many goals his team could put away to beat this Fenian scum. But not tonight. Because tonight, he felt like a condemned man. He tried to put that thought out of his mind, tried to convince himself that if he played the game the way the Caseys asked him, then they'd cut him loose as they'd promised. Of course, he couldn't come back here, or anywhere else in the UK, so he would be far away in the next few days. So he hoped. Jack had set him up with this tiny USB recording device which was inside his jacket pocket. It was completely undetectable, but every now and again, Lambie would put his hand in his pocket and just touch it. He wished he could just take it out of his pocket, bin it and keep on running. But he knew that was unlikely. Every now and then he glanced over his shoulder, and saw the two big brick shithouses – the Casey minders who were keeping an eye on him. One of them had been the guy who'd put a bullet in the back of Thomson's head in the Portakabin the other day, so he wasn't going to take any chances of upsetting him. He sipped from his pint and tried to look interested in the conversation between two of his old cohorts as they discussed the match and their team's chances. He looked at his watch. Townsley was due in any minute and they'd have a drink together before going to their season ticket holder seats for the match. There wouldn't be much chance to talk about this bogus coke deal in here, as it was noisy and he knew he wouldn't get much on the tape, but if it all went well, they'd meet up later for food and a night on the town. The swing door opened as far as it could in the throng, and in walked

Townsley, followed by two of his sidekicks. Lambie felt his gut flip a little as he strained his neck to look through the crowd. His eyes met Townsley's, and his friend's face cracked a smile; well, as much of a smile as Townsley was capable of. He had a jowly piggish face, ginger hair and thin lips. His cheeks were mottled from years of alcohol abuse. His minders pushed their way through the crowd, and anyone who was nudged out of the way looked around furiously, then their expressions changed when they saw the size of them. Many of the men in here would recognise the Belfast boys from Orange marches over there on the twelfth of July, or from Loyalist jobs over the years. But to anyone who was a visiting Gers fans, everyone was just a fan on their way to the match.

'Howsit going, mate?' Lambie managed a blustery smile and he stretched a hand out to Townsley who pumped it hard then held it a few seconds longer in a Masonic handshake.

'Good enough, mate. Good enough.' Townsley's beady eyes took in the packed room. 'You must be fucking coining it in here, you cunt,' he grinned. 'Fucking jam-packed.'

'Aye,' Lambie said, trying to give the smug look that was expected of him. 'These are the good days, mate. Makes up for all the fucking empty Tuesday nights in the winter, when it's pissing down and nobody's leaving the house.' He laughed. 'I'll take this any day of the week. What can I get you boys?' Lambie gestured to his minder at his side who seemed to know he was there to get the drinks in as well as take care of any trouble from hyped-up fans.

'Lager for me. Dying of fucking thirst.' Townsley turned to the others who mumbled lager too. 'Four pints of your finest, mate,' Townsley said to the squat skinhead with a sleeve tattoo of King Billy on his white horse in 1690.

'So how are things, Dick?' Townsley stood, legs apart, with his hands in his pockets. 'That was a right good job you and the boys did, by the way. Right good job.' He sniffed and drew the back of his hand across his nose. 'I've been watching the news and reading the papers. Looks like that bird and her uncle will be away for a long time. Fuck them! Taig cunts!'

'Aye,' Lambie said. 'It worked well. My boys did good.'

'Any repercussions? I mean from that Irish mob, the Caseys?'

Lambie shook his head. 'Nothing. Not a peep. They seem to have gone to ground, mate. Normally I hear on the grapevine a wee bit, but there's been nothing. I think this has hit them hard.'

Townsley nodded slowly. 'Aye. Good enough for them. But it might just look like they're lying low. Just be careful. I'd be surprised if they take this lying down.'

'They haven't a clue how it happened. I made sure of that. Left no edges anywhere, nothing for them to look at. It was a good job.'

The two minders came across with drinks and handed

them out. Townsley took a long thirsty drink and licked his lips.

'Fucking needed that.' He flicked a glance around the room. 'Where's your sidekick? Thomson? We usually have a bit of a side bet on who scores first in the matches. I'm fed up of taking fortunes off the cunt. Was going to dig him up.'

Lambie managed not to blink at the words 'dig him up', because right now if he wanted to speak to Thomson he would probably *have* to dig him up.

'Fucker's away on holiday. I gave him a good wedge for doing the job, so him and a couple of the boys are over in Benidorm. Getting pissed and laid, no doubt.'

Townsley sniggered. 'Quite right too.'

There was a moment of quiet, just the din of the crowd in the pub, then the banging of a Lambeg drum and the sound of flutes. In a few seconds the entire pub was singing 'The Sash'. Townsley and Lambie in full tilt, joining in.

'I fucking love this place,' Townsley said, taking a swig of his pint. 'Salt of the earth, these boys.'

'Aye,' Lambie said as enthusiastically as he could. 'We'll hump the Celts tonight, big time.'

'Hope so,' Townsley said. 'I've got a grand on at the bookies in the Shankill that Rangers will win two nil. They fucking better!'

'That's ambitious at Celtic Park, but I'd fucking love to see that. Wipe the floor with them.'

They made small talk for a couple of minutes about life

in Belfast, and holidays for the summer, as the crowd began to slowly trickle out of the bar singing and chanting. Once they'd finished their pints, they all buttoned up and did the same. On the way out, Townsley turned to Lambie.

'You fancy a curry after the match? Then we can go somewhere. I really need a ride.'

Lambie chuckled. 'Don't worry about that, mate. That's all sorted.'

CHAPTER TWENTY-THREE

Lambie had bought into the lap-dancing club three years ago. At the time it had been the haunt of stag-night lads on the lash as well saddos looking for a bit of no-strings titillation where nobody could see them. But as soon as he'd invested in it, along with an old mate who lived in Spain most of the time, they both saw the potential for it to make more money. Above the dancing bar there was enough floor space to make private rooms where clients who paid good money were able to have sex with any of the scantily clad women who paraded their wares around the bar. The girls were mostly East European and a few Vietnamese – women who had been bought by Lambie from the traffickers who'd imported them. Prostitution hadn't been something Lambie had really aspired to as a business venture, but the kind of money they were making was too easy to knock back. The girls were clean and drug free, and punters had to pay a hundred and fifty quid for a shag, which kept the lowlife riff-raff out. The clientele in the upstairs area were mostly business and wealthier men with money to burn. They bought the best champagne in the cocktail bar and used the rooms, and nobody got hurt. As far as Lambie was concerned, it was a licence to print money. The girls weren't housed in some shithole with no food. He made sure they were looked after. In fact, he was quite proud of what he'd achieved here. It wasn't the first time he'd entertained Townsley at his place, and he knew he'd be gagging to come back.

They were sitting in a shadowy corner of the cocktail bar with a couple of tumblers of large whiskies on ice in front of them. Townsley's minders were downstairs with Lambie's boys enjoying a few drinks to celebrate the Rangers humping Celtic two–nil. Townsley was six grand up, and already well-oiled from the beers before and after the match. Lambie had to make sure he was keeping up with Townsley in the drink stakes in case he aroused suspicion. He was somewhere between sober and getting drunk, but the nerves and the not knowing how the night would pan out somehow kept him from letting the alcohol take over his faculties. Jack hadn't told him what would happen tonight, or even if anything would happen. He'd just been told to get to a point where he could ask some questions and get Townsley talking about the set-up of Kerry and Danny. But he had no idea if Jack was going to phone him and tell him when it was over. He just had to wait and see.

'So what's with the deal you were talking about, man?'
Townsley stretched back, scratching his belly hanging over
his jeans. 'What are we looking at? Coke? Where did it
come from?'

Lambie looked at him. He'd been expecting this, and had
a vague script in his head.

'Stolen.'

'You stole some cunt's fucking coke?'

Lambie drew his lips back in a smug expression.

'You might say stolen,' he said. 'But it had been stolen in
the first place, so I figured that if we stole it, then it
wouldn't really be stealing.'

Townsley sniggered. 'Fuck me, you chancing Arab!'

'It's all about timing, mate,' Lambie elaborated.

'So who did you steal it off? I hope to fuck they're dead,
that's all I can say.'

'As good as dead,' Lambie said, picking up his glass and
swirling the whisky. The alcohol was making him more
confident, but he had to be careful not to make an arse of
this.

'What do you mean?'

'It was the Caseys' coke.'

'Kerry Casey? The Casey mob?'

'Yep,' Lambie said. 'I got word that they stole a right load
of coke from the Colombians a few months ago. The story
was doing the rounds, and the Caseys got away with millions of pounds' worth of the shit. And it's true. They did.

Then they moved it on.' He paused, seeing Townsley engrossed. 'But not all of it. Before they got a chance to move it, our boys got in and took a few kilos. The fuckers probably didn't even miss it.'

Townsley shook his head in admiration.

'Belter. So where is it? How good is it?'

'I can get you some tomorrow morning, before you go. But it's pure class. High end. Four kilos will get you enough to run the show for a while once you cut it.'

'So what do I need to pay?'

'We'll talk about that tomorrow, once you see it.'

'How do I know the Caseys aren't going to come after it?'

'They're fucked after what we did.'

'Aye,' Townsley said, elbows on the table. 'It was some fucking job. They'll get twelve years for that.'

There was a pause, then Lambie leaned forward.

'Where did this come from, Towns? I mean the hit. The order. It seemed to come from nowhere.' He hoped he hadn't gone too far. Townsley gave him a look, narrowing his eyes.

'You know the score, mate. We don't ask questions. We just do the job if the money is right. And it was.'

'But it was strange to want to hit Kerry Casey like that. I mean, she's kind of getting their mob out of the game and going legit, at least that's what they're saying, even if it is with coke they stole. I was just wondering why her, why hit her?'

They were quiet for a long moment. Then Townsley leaned across the table.

'Look,' he said. 'The job came from London. I was told that someone at the top of the tree wanted Kerry Casey and her mob destroyed.'

'What, another mob down there?'

'No. Not a mob.'

Lambie looked at him, bewildered.

'Not a mob? Not one of the London gangs?'

'No.' He sniffed and swallowed a drink of his whisky. 'Not a mob. I mean from high up,' he whispered. 'The government.'

Lambie looked at him, incredulous.

'The fucking government? You mean the fucking actual government?'

Townsley shrugged. 'Well, not officially. But then it never is when they want someone to do their dirty work. But it was someone high up on the government who wanted her hit. That's how it came to me.'

They sat for a long moment as Lambie tried to process the information. Someone high up in the government wanted to ruin Kerry Casey and her family? That was beyond him. The people Lambie and his mobsters moved among were the thugs and killers and hitmen, a world away from Whitehall and the corridors of power. He wondered if Townsley was drunk or if he was just dining out, trying to convince him that he was someone respected at every level.

'So you didn't ask any more questions.'

'Nope,' Townsley said. 'I was told what I would be paid, and told to organise the hit on Kerry Casey. The rest was down to you. It was your organisation of it that was fucking class, man. You did brilliant.' Townsley raised his glass and clinked it against Lambie's.

He half smiled but didn't answer. He didn't know what to say, but he hoped the tape he had under his shirt was working. Because this information might just save his neck.

Both of them looked up as the heavy dark-blue velvet curtain that separated the bar from the short corridor leading to the private rooms parted a little – enough for a tall, slim, semi-naked girl to slip out and into the bar. She stood for a moment and looked across at Lambie and Townsley. They both watched as her eyes settled on Townsley, giving him a sultry look. She raised a hand to her mouth and ran the tip of her forefinger across her lip, her tongue slowly pushing out a little to lick it. Townsley looked at Lambie and they both grinned.

'I think she likes you, mate,' Lambie said to Townsley.

Townsley didn't take his eyes off her. 'Where the fuck did you get this beauty?'

'She's new,' Lambie said, glad he approved. 'Ukrainian. Them birds know their way around.'

'I'll bet they do.'

Lambie raised a hand and beckoned her over to their

table. Townsley licked his lips as she stood close, her thigh touching his shoulder as she looked down at him, her lips parting, eyes full of longing.

'This is Ursula. Isn't she lovely?' Lambie enthused.

Townsley was entranced, shifting in his seat as the girl reached out and touched the back of his neck, his head. He closed his eyes for a second in ecstasy. He reached up and quickly pulled her onto his knee, glancing across to Lambie as he grinned.

'Fuck me, man,' he said, a hand running up the girl's thigh. 'You've excelled yourself this time, coming up with a stunner like this.'

Lambie watched as Ursula wriggled her backside so that she was over Townsley's crotch, and his eyes opened wide with delight.

'Fuck!' he croaked, his expression contorting a little in ecstasy. 'I think we should take this to a room, darlin'.'

Lambie feigned a smile and nodded.

'You know the way, Towns.' He jerked his head towards the curtain as Ursula looked at him. 'On you go, sweetheart.'

As he stood up, Lambie could see that Townsley was already aroused and he didn't even glance in his direction as Ursula led him by the hand through the velvet curtain.

Lambie sighed. He didn't know if he felt relief or fear because he didn't know what was going to happen next.

All he'd been told by Jack was that he had to bring him to the club and set him up with a girl. He swallowed a gulp of whisky and looked at his watch. He didn't have long to wait. Within a minute, he heard footsteps on the stairs leading to the bar, and muffled voices. As the door opened, one of Townsley's sidekicks was shoved in, his arms in the air, a gun in his back. Behind him was one of the minders he'd seen earlier in the pub, one of the guys who'd been watching him in the apartment. Then another of his henchmen was pushed in the same way, another Casey man had a gun in his back. Behind them, Jack came in, along with that Vic guy. Both were packing guns. Townsley's men were chalk white. Jack came forward.

'Where is he?'

Lambie stood up, a little light-headed. He pointed to the curtain. Last room on the left.

'Show me,' Jack said.

'B-But . . .' Lambie hadn't expected this.

He thought once he'd set Townsley up, they would do the rest. The last thing he wanted to do was look Townsley in the eye when he was ambushed.

'Move.' Jack pointed the gun at him.

Lambie moved towards the curtain, pulled it back and stepped into the dimly lit corridor. He looked over his shoulder and could see that Jack and Vic were behind him. He walked softly down the corridor and stopped at the door. He could hear the panting and groaning of Townsley inside. They all waited and for a few seconds the only sounds were of Townsley's ecstatic moans. Jack motioned at him to stand back from the door, then he reached down and turned the handle softly. Jack stepped quietly into the room, lit by an orange lamp on a bedside table. He was followed by Lambie who was pushed in with Vic's gun in his back. In the dimness they saw the naked backside of Townsley, trousers at his ankles, at the edge of the bed, lost in the throes of orgasm, as he thrust himself into Ursula on all fours on the bed. By the time he glanced over his shoulder Jack had already fired a bullet into his back. His face twisted in disbelief as he gasped, pulling himself back from Ursula. He turned, naked, his limp manhood hanging dead. As his eyes met Lambie's, he mouthed, 'What the fu—' Before he could finish, he was on the floor still conscious but gasping, as Jack stood over him.

'This is a wee message from Kerry Casey, you cunt.' Jack fired into his chest.

Lambie's legs buckled as Jack turned to him. He gripped the wall to steady himself. He knew there was no point in pleading for his life. His bottom lip trembled and he bit it to fight back tears. He closed his eyes tight and waited for the shot. But there was none. Only the dead silence in the room and the faint smell of the gunshot that had been pumped into Townsley, who was now lying in a pool of blood. Ursula was next to the bed, hurriedly pulling on her panties like some bizarre scene from a low-grade porn flick. Then she too stood silently, waiting. Eventually, Jack turned to Lambie.

'Open your eyes, you prick,' he commanded.

Lambie opened his eyes as Jack came towards him.

'You're not getting shot. Not today.'

Jack reached out and ripped open his shirt and yanked the device from him. Then he jerked his head towards the curtain.

'Move.'

Lambie's legs faltered as he walked along the corridor. Then, pulling back the curtain, he saw his two minders standing with guns at their backs, a look of sheer terror on their faces. As he stepped into the cocktail bar, Jack came in behind him. From the corner of his eye, he saw Jack nod to the men. And in perfect timing, both of them raised their guns to the back of the men's heads. Before they could protest, they'd hit the floor.

CHAPTER TWENTY-FOUR

Sharon watched out of the upstairs window as the steel automatic gates opened and Jack's car came in. She saw Jack climb out of the passenger seat and approach Vic who was standing in the yard, talking to one of the guards. Whatever was being said, Jack was nodding as though he was being briefed on something. He was carrying a small zipped bag and he and Vic disappeared into the back door of the house that led to the kitchen. Sharon guessed that inside the bag was the tape that he'd ripped off Lambie last night. She reflected on the moment Vic had come home after midnight. As he'd slipped into bed beside her, she'd woken up. She'd known where they'd been, she'd been told of the plan. Part of her had been afraid to ask. Vic had said nothing as he'd lain on his back in bed, and she'd kept quiet for a moment, wondering if he was actually going to say anything. It was only when she slid herself across to him, that he responded.

'How did it go?'

'Well. We got the tape from Lambie,' he said softly, then he turned to her, stroking her hair. 'But it didn't go well for Townsley.'

She hadn't answered, and for a moment they'd said nothing, and she'd turned to watch Vic's eyes wide open in the dark. His face showed nothing. Whatever had happened, whatever bloodbath he had just left, he didn't look fazed or disturbed, and there was something a little chilling about that. She'd decided not to ask any more for the moment.

She was sitting at the long table when Jack and Vic came into the room, both of them quiet, just nodding in greeting. She motioned at them to sit. She'd called the meeting early so that they could listen to the tape before calling Marty Kane.

'Have you listened to the recording yet, Jack?' Sharon asked.

He shook his head as he placed the bag on the table and unzipped it.

'No. I thought it best to hear it together. Not my place.' He unzipped the bag brought out his laptop and inserted the USB device.

Sharon said nothing. She was surprised that Jack would feel he had a 'place' where he didn't want to overstep his mark. But that was Jack. Respectful. Decent. But deadly when required. She couldn't think of a better right-hand man to be at Kerry's side.

'Okay. Let's have a listen then.'

Jack switched on the laptop and turned up the volume. At first it was just noise and the sound of singing and flutes and drums. Sharon screwed up her eyes and looked to Jack.

'What's this? In a pub or something?'

'Yep.' Jack nodded. 'It was in his pocket while he was in the White Horse – maybe when Townsley arrived. Our boys were there all the time in the background. They saw him come in.'

After a few seconds the singing and chants lessened and it was the din of chatter in the pub. Everyone strained their ears and leaned closer to the tape as though it would help. Eventually, they could hear a voice – Lambie talking, and someone, presumably Townsley, answering. From what they could hear it was football banter, nothing more. Then the recording stopped abruptly. Everyone looked at each other.

'Give it a minute or two. The way that sounded, they might have been leaving the pub for the match. Hopefully once it goes on a bit later in the night, it will get more interesting.'

They all sat waiting, listening, and the tape started again. This time the background noises were of crockery and glasses, and by the sound of it they were in a restaurant. They listened closely. They could hear Lambie asking how things were over there, which they took to mean in Belfast. Then Townsley was talking about a couple of problems with lads in east Belfast who'd got a bit out of hand and had had to be dealt with. Then they were discussing plans for the cup final, and families and holidays and all sorts of mundane nonsense. Sharon looked around the table and she could see they were all thinking the same thing.

'Christ, I hope it doesn't run out before they say anything interesting,' she said.

'It won't,' Jack said. 'The tape can last up to three hours. So far there's hardly any used up, though it seems a lot because we're sitting here waiting for something good.'

Vic nodded, and they kept listening. The next part was music and the sounds of a busy bar.

'I'm guessing that's them in the lap-dancing bar. We were already in there by that point. The boys were there waiting for them to come in.'

The recording went on, and the music and noise seemed to fade away.

'That'll be them up in the private area,' Jack said. 'There's no music there. It's a kind of VIP bar, and it's where they get the women.'

Sharon noticed that he shot her a glance in case he'd offended her. Then they could hear clear conversation. Lambie candidly talked about the Caseys' cocaine that his boys had stolen, and was offering it for sale to Townsley, who was chatting back. Everyone waited. And then, bingo! They started talking about the hit, about the Caseys, about

Kerry Casey, and even where the order had come from. Everyone's eyes widened when they heard that the job had come all the way from Whitehall.

'Fucking dancer!' Jack said. 'Smoking gun.'

'That's brilliant, Jack,' Sharon said. 'Wind it back so we can hear that again.'

Again, they heard the conversation. It was unequivocal. They'd done it, they'd set up Kerry Casey and it was a hit that had been ordered from someone high up. Eventually the tape moved on and the conversation turned to a girl, introduced by Lambie as Ursula. Then it went dead.

'I suppose that's when Townsley took the girl to the room. Lambie remained in the bar when he went into the room with the girl, so you won't hear any more.'

Sharon nodded.

'This is explosive stuff, guys. Great work. So what about Townsley?'

Stony silence then Jack looked at her.

'The tape is his evidence, Sharon,' Jack said. 'He's gone.'

Sharon took a breath. She was a little out of her depth here, especially in the legalities. But she had had to ask the question.

'I'm not up on all the legal stuff, but would he have been any good as a witness? I mean, to actually admit to the cops that he set Kerry up?'

Jack glanced at Vic and they both shook their heads.

'Not a chance,' Vic said. 'Firstly, as soon as you brought

cops in he would say he'd been kidnapped. Forced into saying things. And even if he did sign a confession, which he wouldn't, you can guarantee that he would never make it to any court, or trial. The lads he'd betrayed in the UVF would have him done in while he was in custody. That's how these things work. He would be a grass, and he'd be dead.'

'That's exactly it,' Jack said.

'What about Lambie?' Sharon asked.

'We've still got him,' Jack said. 'It might be a bit different if we can go to the cops with Lambie. He might be more cooperative if there is a chance he can get a deal from the cops and disappear. We're not sure. But we thought we'd keep him for the moment, and let you talk to Marty first, see what he thinks. But if it's decided that Lambie is of no further use, and this tape itself actually gets Kerry and Danny out, then we would leave Danny to deal with him. I think it's only fair.'

Sharon glanced from Jack to Vic, whose face showed nothing. They sounded like they were divvying up the spoils, and while part of her might be a little squeamish about that, she believed that Lambie should get his day after what he'd put Kerry through.

'Okay,' she said. 'I think I'll give Marty a ring and get him over for a listen to this tape. Why don't you guys go downstairs and have some breakfast and I'll see if Marty can come over this morning.'

They got up and left the room. Sharon sat back and took a long deep sigh.

An hour later, Marty Kane sat listening to the tape, then he went back to the beginning and listened again, taking notes, stopping at different parts, rewinding and listening again. When it came to an end he sat back and stretched out his legs, tapping the pen on the table.

'What do you think, Marty?' Sharon asked.

He put down the pen and folded his arms, adjusting his rimless glasses even though they didn't need adjusting. Then he took a breath and pushed it out slowly through his pursed lips.

'Well,' he said. 'On the face of it, when you hear Lambie and Townsley talking casually about what they did, then it does seem explosive. But the problem is – and it's a big problem – that this audio evidence alone is not proof of any-thing.' He paused, looked at each one of them. 'Because a defence lawyer could argue that this is just a couple of hoods making up a story. It could be anyone really, and it proves nothing as it is.' He glanced at Jack. 'Where is Townsley?'

In the long silence, Marty raised his eyebrows a little and glanced at Sharon. He knew the answer before Jack said it.

'He's dead.'

Marty put his hand up to stop him before he elaborated.

'What about Lambie?' he asked.

'He's still here,' Jack said. 'He's in a flat in the town.'

Marty nodded slowly. 'Okay. We're going to need him to talk. He'll have to go on the record to the police, make a full confession to his part in the job, hit, or whatever he wants to call it.'

Nobody answered for a long moment. Then Jack spoke.

'That might be signing his own death warrant – you know, with the UVF boys.'

Marty looked at him, then at Sharon.

'Well,' he said. 'I don't imagine he's got a great future anyway.'

Sharon watched as Marty took off his glasses and polished the lenses with his tie, as though he was looking for something to break the moment, something to do, as though he was uncomfortable with the truth that he knew was in front of him.

'Would he talk? To the police? The only way to make this evidence valid is if he can confirm being there, confirm that it is his voice, and that the other person is Townsley. In effect, he would be turning Queen's evidence. If he does that, and I can find a way to present it to the police and the Crown, then they will know that the case against Kerry and Danny is at the very least tainted. He would have to completely confess, though. If he does, then they may consider putting him on witness protection, getting him a new life and a new ID somewhere. But to do that, and to get that, he would have to confess to a lot more than this.'

'You mean like other things in his life as a crook? As a UVF man? As a drug dealer?'

'Yes,' Marty said. 'He would have to be able to drop some big names to the police that would help them pick up people for other crimes and put them away. That's how these things work. He should be behind bars anyway, it's not as though he's an innocent man. He took on this job to frame Kerry Casey. He has to admit that and provide information and evidence, but I know they'll want him to provide other scalps.' He paused, glanced at Jack and Vic. 'Do you think he will do it?'

Jack sat for a long moment, then he spoke.

'I don't think he has a lot of choices left, Marty.'

Marty closed his notebook and put the pen back in his pocket.

'Can I have the device? I'll put it in my safe in the office.' He stood up. 'Okay, you need to act swiftly though. You need to talk to Lambie and lay it on the line for him. Then if you get him to agree, let me know and I'll take it from there.'

Sharon stood up.

'Do you think it will work, Marty, if Lambie talks?'

Marty pursed his lips. 'I'd be hopeful,' he said. 'But let's see what you can get from him first.' He put the device inside his briefcase and snapped it shut.'Keep in touch, and the quicker we can do this, the better, as the Crown Office will be considering the evidence against Kerry and Danny by now to prepare a case.'

'What do you think of the line where Townsley says the job was ordered by figures in Whitehall?'

Marty almost smiled as he snorted.

'Well, I do think it's entirely possible, but we'll never prove that. Let's stick to what we can achieve and take it from there.' He walked towards the door. 'Keep me posted.'

CHAPTER TWENTY-FIVE

Deep down, Steven knew he was never really going to get off scot-free. He'd known that from the moment he'd spoken to the Caseys and told them everything. They had promised they would look after him and his mother, and they had. Still were. They couldn't have done enough for them. The flat they'd set them up in was perfect, from the decor to the internet and satellite television which his ma was loving. He couldn't remember when he'd last seen her this content. Steven hid his fears well from her and on the face of it he seemed to be enjoying the way they were living; he wasn't even that bothered that he couldn't go for a walk in the city or anywhere else in case he was spotted. But there was another added attraction to his new life – a woman called Maria, who worked for the Caseys, had been assigned to bring them food, and cook them the odd meal. Steven enjoyed her company, and visits from Maria and spending time in the house with her were the highlight of his day. She was really kind to his ma, and told them that she'd lost her mum when she was in her twenties, and how tough it had been. There was no hardness about her, and even though she worked for the Caseys, she never spoke of anything, other than to say she worked sometimes in the bookies, and that she had a son, Cal, and a daughter Jennifer. Cal, he knew, as he had been with them that day on the moneylending when he'd fingered Lambie for Jack. Jennifer, she said, was working in a hotel in the Highlands. Steven admired the way she'd dealt with being on her own and how she coped with family problems. And apart from that, she was attractive – though he didn't think for a moment the feeling was mutual. He'd gotten used to women not being attracted to him, or if they were, it was the half-drunk loonies in the bar who made a fuss of him when they were three sheets to the wind. He'd never really had a proper girlfriend, not since since he was seventeen, and he wasn't going to entertain the idea that that would change now. But it was good to have someone around who could be a friend. She didn't ask him why they had been moved there or anything about his life, though Steven got the impression she knew that if the Caseys were looking after him like this he must have done something for them.

Maria had just delivered some home-cooked lasagne to him and his ma, and was sitting at the kitchen table with Steven, drinking coffee before heading home. His ma was in the living room watching afternoon television.

'Your mum is a real character,' Maria said, smiling. 'Her patter is brilliant.'

Steven smiled back. 'Aye, she's funny. She's old-school. Born and bred in the Gallowgate, so she came up the hard way. Some of the stories she told me about growing up there – unbelievable how people lived. You couldn't make them up.'

'Does she miss not being there, Steven?' Maria said, then quickly added, 'Not that I'm prying or anything.'

Steven put a hand up to dismiss her worry.

'No problem. I know you don't ask questions. But I think she might miss some of her old pals. They used to meet up at the café and stuff, but it's been a while since she's been able to get out with her chest being bad. I think just being holed up in the flat was not good for her, but I couldn't do anything about it. Here, she's really happy. The best I've seen her in a while.' He shrugged. 'But I don't know how long we'll be here.'

He felt his face burn, suddenly aware that he'd said too much. He shouldn't have mentioned not knowing how long he'd be here. That could raise suspicions in Maria's mind. But if it did, she didn't show it, and just moved on.

'I didn't always live in a nice area either,' she said. 'I was up in the high flats, miserable as sin, skint and up to my neck in debt.'

Steven raised his eyebrows in surprise. He had just assumed she was part of the Casey clan and had never even questioned that she'd known anything else.

'Really?'

'Yeah. It was a real hard time. But it was Kerry who rescued me. No doubt about that. If it hadn't been for her ... To be honest, I was struggling to know how I could go on.' She sipped her coffee, holding the mug with both hands. 'She got me out of it. Helped my daughter, who was hopeless and on heroin. Kerry paid for her to go into rehab. And she gave my son a job – and me. Kerry and me go back a lifetime when we were kids playing in the streets of Maryhill. She did all that for me, but she didn't have to. She's a great friend and I'll never forget her.'

Steven wondered what she'd done for Kerry for her to save her like that, and it crossed his mind that she may have been involved in something as illegal as he was. He knew Cal wasn't doing a simple job for the Caseys and he knew that he was some kind of foot soldier, along with the Iraqi boy, Tahir. He'd seen the two of them working for Jack, and they always seemed to be busy, whatever they were doing. He wondered if she knew what her son did, and thought she probably didn't. He decided to change the subject.

'Did you ever get many holidays abroad, Maria? Like when you were younger?'

'As a teenager I did. Benidorm. Majorca. Places like that. But once I got married and had the kids, that was all gone.'

Steven looked at her and he thought he could see the hurt in her eyes.

'What about your husband? If you don't mind me asking.'

She sighed. 'Long gone. He was a soldier. Served in Iraq. Not sure what he did, but he had a lot of mental problems when he came back. Would never talk about it. The mood swings just got worse and worse, and he was in a deep depression. I felt for him, but I just couldn't reach him. None of us could.'

Steven watched as she swallowed hard, the memory obviously painful.

'That's a shame. A lot of guys who came back from those places suffered and it wasn't really recognised. Not fair.'

Maria nodded. 'I felt it most for our Cal. He adored his dad, and the fact that he was a soldier really appealed to a wee six-year-old boy in need of a hero. Cal was totally obsessed by him, and when he used to come home on leave, Cal dressed up as a soldier marching up and down the living room.' She shook her head at the memory. 'Then one day, amid all the depression, he just got up and went out. He never came back.' Her voice tailed off.

They sat for a long moment, and Steven didn't know what to say. He waited for her to go on.

'I don't know where he is, or even if he's still alive. The last communication I had from him was a letter from France saying that he was trying to sort himself out, but that he couldn't come back because he'd ruin our lives. That was five years ago. So I don't know if he's dead or alive.

To be honest, I'm angry at him for that. He just left us. I can live with it for me, and to a certain extent for Jen. But it really did Cal in. I'll always be angry at him for leaving his boy like that.'

'Cal is a good lad,' Steven said, because he couldn't think of anything else to say.

'Aye, he is,' Maria said. 'Despite his father, he's a good boy. He turned out good.'

Steven nodded in agreement, even though he knew Cal was a boy loyal to the Caseys and both his feet were firmly planted be in the criminal world. Steven and Maria's eyes met for a fleeting second, and there and then he was about to summon the courage to ask her if she would consider going for a coffee or a walk to the park with him some time, once things died down a little. From the look in her face Steven thought she might know what he was thinking.

But then the doorbell rang, crashing in on the moment's silence. Steven wasn't expecting anyone.

'I'll get it,' he said.

He got up and left the kitchen and went down the hall-way. He looked through the spyhole and could see Jack and Vic on the doorstep. He slid the chain across and opened the door. They stepped inside.

'All right, Steven?' Jack said. 'I meant to phone you first, but I need a wee word with you.'

Steven's stomach dropped. This was it. They were going to tell him the game was up. He was on his own now.

'Everything's all right.' Jack seemed to sense his unease. 'You're all right here. Don't worry. Just need to run some things past you.'

'Aye,' Steven said as he led them down the hall. 'That's fine. Maria's in the kitchen. She dropped off some lasagne for us, and we were just having a coffee. She's going now anyway.'

Maria was on her feet by the time they came into the kitchen.

'How's it going, Maria?' Jack said. 'All right?'

'Yeah. Fine, Jack. I'm just heading,' she said. 'Are you needing me to close up at the bookies later?'

'No, you're all right. I'll be going back in myself and I'll sort it out. I know you're back in the morning, so I'll leave some of the paperwork for you.'

She nodded, pulled on her coat, and said her goodbyes, smiling briefly at Steven, and left the room.

'Can I get you a coffee, guys? Tea?' Steven asked.

'Aye,' Jack said. 'Tea for me.'

'That'll do me too,' Vic said.

Steven shoved the kettle under the tap and filled it, then put it back and switched it on. He could hear the telly blaring in the living room and he closed the door. Despite what Jack had said, he could feel his hands were sweaty, and he rubbed them on his jeans and sat down.

Jack sat opposite him and took a breath.

'Okay, Steven,' he began. 'You know where we were the other day, and that we got Lambie and stuff.'

Steven nodded but said nothing, waiting.

'Well,' Jack went on, 'we're on our way to getting evidence to prove that Kerry and Danny were framed by Lambie and by his UVF boss Townsley. You were bang on with your information from the very start.'

Steven clasped his hands on the table then unclasped them, not knowing what to do with them.

'It all went very well,' Jack said. 'We've got Townsley actually admitting the set-up. Admitting everything on tape. And Lambie backing it up.'

Steven was wondering if they were both dead by now, and assumed they were.

'But here's the difficult bit, Steven, and this involves you.'

Christ, Steven thought. He knew a bombshell was coming. He listened, trying to keep his face straight.

'Townsley,' Jack said, pausing. 'Well, Townsley is no longer with us.' He glanced at Vic, whose face was like granite. 'But he left a full confession on tape – to everything.'

Steven's eyes darted from one to the other, but he didn't speak. He was trying to process it. 'Townsley is no longer with us' meant he was dead, bumped off. He was glad when the kettle pinged and he jumped to his feet like a boxer when the bell for the next round rang.

'I'll make the tea,' he said, realising how stupid that sounded. He went into the cupboard and brought out mugs, poured tea into a teapot and brought it to the table.

'So,' Jack said. 'Lambie is backing this up. He is going to talk to the police and confess everything.'

The word 'grass' was on the tip of Steven's tongue, but he knew he couldn't say if it out loud. At the end of the day he was a grass himself, even it was only to the Caseys. What he'd told them had certainly signed Townsley's death warrant – maybe even Lambie's. He nodded and said nothing.

'Lambie will be dealt with by the police. You know, like a protected witness. You'll never see him again. But his evidence will be used to back up our case. Our lawyer Marty Kane is already on it. Lambie has agreed to talk to the cops in return for a new life.'

Steven was imagining Lambie on the run, hiding in shadows, always looking over his shoulder.

'Will he have to go to court? Testify in the witness box?' Steven couldn't help asking.

Jack shrugged. 'Hopefully it won't come to that. But if it does he will. Marty is hoping that he'll present enough to the cops and the prosecutors and they'll see that they've got the wrong people in jail.'

Steven could see the logic in all of that, and he began to see where he would fit in. He dreaded it, but he knew it was coming.

'So what we want to do, you know, to build up the case, make it more solid, is to back up what Lambie has already told police, about the quarry, about the fact that you were forced into doing what you did. He's already admitted to us that he involved you in it without your knowledge, and he will admit it to the police.'

Steven felt a tension headache begin to throb around his temples. He was going to have to go and sit with police and tell them he was an accomplice to murder. What if this didn't work out? What if he ended up being thrown in jail?

'You mean you want me to tell the police I was a part of this? Of the murder of Bo?' he asked. 'But what if all they do is charge me as well?'

Jack glanced at Vic.

'We don't think that's going to happen. This will be done at a different level, Steven. It's not like you're going to the police station or anything. At this stage, you'll give a statement to Marty, and he will be the guy who will press on with this.'

'And then, will I have to go to cops, and go to court?'

Jack shook his head. 'No. As with Lambie, we don't think it will come to that. Lambie is going to throw some big fish to the cops involving other matters, other criminals, guys they've been trying to nail for years. And we are going to try to negotiate some kind of deal for him. At the end of the day, the police will know that Kerry and Danny are innocent, and that will be important to them. But it will be important to them to get some big names in pokey – drug dealers, Loyalist big shots. That kind of stuff.'

Steven nodded. He could see how that might work. But

he could also envisage how it might not. As he looked from Jack to Vic, he saw how easy they were in this life, sipping their tea, sitting back relaxed as they delivered the next chapter of his life. And his ma's. But he knew as he looked at them that they were waiting for answers and that he didn't have a lot of choice. They sat that way in the quietness, with the muffled blare of afternoon television coming from the living room. Then Steven looked at both of them and shrugged.

'Okay,' he said. 'Whatever it takes. But I worry about my ma. I mean, if something happens to me . . . you know?'

'Nothing's going to happen to you, Steven,' Jack reassured him. 'Don't worry.'

CHAPTER TWENTY-SIX

At breakfast, Kerry sat listening to Ash tell her about her news. She'd been called to the governor's office that morning to be told she was getting out. Her lawyer had managed to talk to social work and with the procurator fiscal's office, and they'd made the decision that the charges would be dropped. She was not deemed to be a danger to the public or herself – though they apparently had conceded that she might reoffend. That was a stick-on, Kerry thought, as Ash relayed all the information to her. But she was surprised to see that Ash was far from excited about the prospect of getting out of jail. She looked more depressed than elated, and Kerry watched her fidget as she listened.

'You don't seem all that happy about it though, Ash,' Kerry ventured.

Ash shoved her hands into her jeans pocket and leaned back. Kerry could see her hip bones sticking out of her skinny frame in her low-waist jeans.

'You know what, Kerry? The honest truth is I'm not looking forward to it. I mean, don't get me wrong, I shouldn't have been locked up here in the first place for that trumped up charge. But this time in here, I've felt something like family and I've never felt like that before in here, or on the outside.' She stopped and swallowed as she caught Kerry's eyes. 'I feel like you've been like a sister or a cousin or something to me, and you haven't judged me or anything and have just taken me as I am, warts and all.'

Kerry half smiled. If her time in this place had shown her anything it was that she was in no position to judge anyone. Many of the girls were here because of their circumstances, products of a broken family and a fractured system. Though from what she'd seen and experienced in the last couple of weeks there were some bad ones too. The drug addicts who had robbed and beaten an old woman or battered a man at the cashline, you could hardly call them victims, and Kerry could never reconcile herself to what they had done when she heard their crimes. Perhaps some of them had become addicts on the heroin that her brother Mickey had pushed in Glasgow before he'd got shot, before Kerry had come on the scene and started to change things. But his legacy was still there, and some of the people in here might be part of that legacy. And if she was the head of the family then it was her legacy. She'd tormented herself with thoughts like that through long sleepless nights in her cell. With too much time on her hands and riddled with guilt she'd promised herself she would make amends when and if she ever got out of here.

'I know what you mean, Ash.' Kerry eventually spoke. 'And I've felt the same kind of spirit in here because of people like you. To be honest, I don't know what I'd have done without you. You've been a real friend. And maybe everything that has happened – especially the death of Linda – made me feel it even deeper. I'll never forget that as long as I live, and the grief and sadness that hung over here.'

'Aye,' Ash said. 'I think that's why I'm not happy to be leaving. I've got support here, people to talk to who understand me, but outside I'm on my own. Just the usual pimps, dealers and robbers.'

'But did you not say you've got an auntie or something?'

'Yeah,' she said. 'But she's quite old now, and it's not as if I can go there, not to stay, anyway. I'm going to be getting methadone. But that's just to keep me going, stop me from stealing to get heroin. It'll never be enough. I need to get off the shit altogether.'

They sat for a long moment listening to the bustle of girls coming in and out and the cleaners with mops and buckets. Another day in jail was about to begin, Kerry thought. Not for Ash though. Her probation officer would come this morning to have a meeting with her and then she'd be gone. Dropped off in the city with a few pounds to get somewhere to stay for the night and some food. Tomorrow, she would meet the probation officer again. But she would feel abandoned. In another life, raised in different circumstances, it could have been her.

'Listen, Ash,' Kerry said. 'If you are serious about wanting to get off drugs and make your life different, I can help you.'

'Aye,' she said. 'I'm serious. I am.'

Kerry leaned across the table.

'Okay. I want to help you.' She looked around. 'God knows when I'll get out of here – hopefully soon. But I can give you a name and a phone number to talk to someone and they will sort you out.'

'What do you mean – sort me out how?'

'Well the first thing you need is rehab. I know there are no beds in the system, but if you are really serious, and I mean really serious, then I can get you in somewhere. Private.'

Ash's eyes lit up. 'Private? Christ! Like them celebrities? Like the Priory or something?'

Kerry nodded. 'Yes. Exactly.'

Suddenly Ash's eyes filled with tears and she tightened her lips.

'You'd do that for me? A wee bird from Easterhouse.'

'It's a chance. You deserve a chance,' Kerry said. 'I can give you that. The rest is up to you.'

Ash covered her face with her hands and started to cry.

'Sorry,' she sniffed. 'I'm a real shitebag, but I ... I'm just ... I mean, I can't believe you would do that. I'll never be able to pay you back.'

'You will,' Kerry said, feeling a lump to her throat. 'In fact you already did, being my friend in here, helping me when big Aggie was going to slap me around.' She manged a smile. 'And, if you get clean, I'll give you a job. You can come and work for me, for the Caseys. A job where you get paid and do ordinary things like get up, get showered and go to work, and bring home food and stuff. Like everyone else.'

Ash was sobbing now, and people were beginning to look at her.

Kerry leaned across and squeezed her wrist.

'Come on now,' she said. 'Dry your eyes and make your mind up. This is up to you now. I can make this happen for you – even from in here. But I need a complete, solid commitment from you.'

'I'll not let you down. I promise.'

Kerry looked her in the eye.

'If you do, that's up to you. I'm giving you one chance and one chance only. Things will change for you.'

Kerry went to the breakfast hatch and picked up a pen and piece of paper. She wrote down Jack's mobile phone number.

'Listen. My lawyer is coming in here this afternoon, so I'll get him to tell Jack to expect a call tonight from you. Jack will organise a place for you in rehab straight away, or as soon as it's possible.'

'Right away? Really? You can do that?'

'It's an unfortunate truth, Ash, but if you've got money you can do it.'

'But what will I tell my probation officer?'

'Tell her that you've got a relative who has just come on the scene and is going to help you get better. She'll understand. She'll be glad to get you off her hands, one less file in her workload.'

Ash shook her head. 'I can't believe this. I don't know what to say. I'm so grateful, Kerry.'

Kerry smiled; she could see one of the officers coming towards the table. It was time for Ash to go.

'Here's the woman with the keys to freedom coming,' Kerry joked. 'You're out of here, you lucky bugger.'

They both stood up, Ash blinded by tears, Kerry trying very hard to hold hers back. Ash stepped forward and put her arms around her, and they hugged each other tight. They stayed that way for a long moment, and Kerry could feel Ash sobbing onto her shoulder. She looked at the prison officer standing with her arms folded at a respectful distance. She'd probably seen so many girls go through the system, in and out like yo-yos every month.

'Come on, Ash,' the officer finally said. 'Before we change our minds.'

Kerry pulled away and Ash stood before her, flushed and tear-stained.

'On you go, girl,' Kerry said, biting her lip. 'It's all up to you now. Keep that number handy and call him as soon as you're out. Okay?'

'I will. I promise.' Then she whispered, 'And I'll never let you down. Ever, Kerry.'

Kerry smiled. She watched as Ash turned away and followed the prison officer towards the big door as it clicked open. Kerry stood there, suddenly feeling alone and isolated, and she swallowed hard. She had to pull herself together. Marty was coming to see her after lunch to give her an update. All she could do was hope it was something uplifting.

Kerry was glad to see Marty coming into the visiting room, and she stood up as he approached the table. A smile spread across his face and he opened his arms and they hugged.

'How are we doing, Kerry?'

He hugged her tight and she relished the warmth of his embrace. Then he eased himself away and flicked a glance up and down her body, resting for a second on the growing bump on her tummy. He smiled.

'Looking good, Kerry.'

She returned his smile as they sat down, knowing he was trying to keep her upbeat, but also knowing that it would be killing him to see her like this, pregnant and far from her family and friends.

'I feel okay, Marty,' she said, and she meant it. 'Just struggling some days to keep my spirits up.' She paused. 'Oh, before I forget, you know that girl Ash who has been in here with me from the start? Remember, the drug addict who was with me on the first morning I appeared in court?'

Marty nodded.

'Well she got out today. Charges dropped. But here's the thing, Marty. I got quite close to her while she was here, and my heart goes out to her. I know she's a bit of a hard case, and drugs and stuff, but I want to do something to help her.'

Marty smiled. 'You'll never change, Kerry. Ever since you were a little kid – I remember the day you brought all the stray dogs home and fed them everything that was in the house.'

Kerry smiled at the memory.

'I remember that too, Marty. My mum went nuts.' She stopped and sipped from her mug. 'But you know something, a lot of these people in here, they're a bit like strays themselves, and people like me and you, we never really see them, get to know them. Ash is one of them, and she deserves a chance. She helped me a lot in here, and to be honest I don't know what I'd have done without her. Do you know what I mean?'

He nodded gently. 'Of course I do. '

'Great. So I've given Ash Jack's phone number. I want you to tell him when you get back that he'll be getting a call from her. I want him to sort a place for her in the Priory – same as we did for Maria's daughter. As soon as possible.

Sooner if we can. Because give her a day or two or more, and she'll be back on the same road she was on before. I spoke to her this morning, and told her, and the poor girl was in tears. She's promised me if she's given the chance she'll be different. Can you tell Jack to expect a call from her tonight, please, Marty?'

'Of course. I'll call him as soon as I leave.' He reached across and touched Kerry's hand. 'You're a good person, Kerry. You probably don't realise that enough.'

She didn't answer, then he leaned across.

'Okay,' he said. 'I've got some good news.'

'You have? Jesus, Marty, I wish.'

'Well. I think it's good, and we're a bit away from it, but we are definitely on the road to getting you out of here.'

'But how? With all the evidence stacked against us.'

'The evidence was a lie, as you and Danny know. And if things go the way I'm hoping they do, then we can get these charges dropped. It's all behind the scenes stuff at the moment though.'

'What do you mean?'

He sat back and glanced over his shoulder in case anyone was listening, even though the other girls with visitors were several yards away at tables, and the officers were at the back wall, just watching.

'Well. I'll keep it simple rather than talk too much about the details in here. But let me put it this way: we have recorded evidence from the men behind the set-up, that it

was them who did it – them who framed you. We have
names, everything about the organisation, how it happened and why it happened.'

Kerry's eyes widened as she listened. A surge of excitement rushed through her and she felt a little light-headed.

'Jesus, Marty! You serious? You actually have that? Evidence recorded? Names? Who the hell was it? I mean,
why?' She paused. 'How did you get that?'

Marty was silent for a moment, and Kerry guessed he
wouldn't answer the last part of her question.

'I'm deadly serious, Kerry.' He leaned across, lowered his
voice to barely a whisper. 'It was a UVF hit. By a Glasgow
mob – you won't know him, but he's called Lambie. Owns
the White Horse in the East End. He's admitted everything.
It was a hit organised by the UVF by his boss in Belfast –
Wattie Townsley.'

Kerry couldn't speak as she tried to process all of this. A
UVF hit? But why? She knew the Caseys had always been
Irish by descent and loyalty, and that there had been whispers of involvement with the IRA over the years – especially
around Jake Cahill – though she didn't know for sure. But
why hit them now? They weren't trampling on each other's
turf.

'But why?' she asked again. 'Why would the UVF hit us?
I just don't get it.'

Marty nodded slowly and looked at her.

'I don't have any real facts on that and maybe never will,

Kerry. But from what Lambie could tell us, and from what Townsley has said on tape, he got the order from London.'

'London?'

'Yes. From Whitehall. All he said was that it was high up.'

Kerry actually felt her blood run cold. It could only be one man. But she didn't even want to utter his name, not even to Marty, because she knew he wouldn't be able to confirm it. But she vowed to herself that if she got out of this place then she would destroy Quentin Fairhurst once and for all.

CHAPTER TWENTY-SEVEN

In a shadowy alcove at the far end of La Lanterna restaurant, Marty Kane sat back, swirling the remains of his full-bodied red. He looked across at his old friend who had knocked back the dregs of his glass, then he summoned a waiter with a wave of his hand.

'You fancy a brandy, Joe?' Marty said. 'For the road?'

Joe made a could-do-worse face.

'Sure, you're a long while dead, Marty. Might as well.'

Marty ordered two cognacs and sat back, his hands clasped across his stomach. So far so good. This was the first step in the push to see if he could get the police to be amenable to listening to new evidence on Kerry's case. His dinner partner and long-time friend since secondary school was Joe Cassidy, the head of the Serious Crime Squad in Glasgow, and due for retirement in the next two years. Cassidy may have been old school, in a world where police officers now came with university degrees instead of size ten boots, but he could play the game better than any of them. He was respected by everyone from uniformed cops to the top of the tree. He'd risen through the ranks by putting away serial killers, terrorists on both side of the divide, and drugs barons. Much of his success was down to the way he managed things and people, and as Marty Kane knew, the fact that he didn't always play by the rules. That was why Marty had asked him here tonight. Because if he was going to get Kerry Casey out of jail then it wouldn't be by playing by the rules. In his leather-bound case, Marty had the recorded evidence and a full statement from Lambie that told the real story behind the frame-up. And on top of that, he had told Joe that Lambie was also prepared to spill the beans on a host of unsolved murders, robberies and terrorist attacks. He would give them the locations of various UVF arms dumps. He knew Joe would be keen, and if anyone could make this work then it would be him. But Marty knew there would be a stumbling block.

'So,' Joe said. 'To cut to the chase, Marty, we both know that this is big information your man has imparted. But what happens when it gets to the part where Townsley has disappeared off the face of the earth? How is that going to be answered?'

Joe gave Marty a long look. They both knew that Townsley hadn't just 'disappeared', well he had, but he wasn't coming back. Joe knew the Caseys and everything about them, and he knew that Marty was their closest associate and defence lawyer. Marty knew that Townsley had been bumped off, but he'd never discussed it openly with Jack who'd been about as vague as he'd have expected him to be. He knew that it was morally wrong, but that was not what Marty was here to discuss, and at the end of the day he knew that Joe wouldn't give a damn if Townsley had been swinging from a bridge – as far as he was concerned it was one more piece of scum off the face of the earth. But there was a little matter of getting it past the Crown Office and the prosecutors. Either they accepted what they had and went for everyone named in the dossier, or they nit-picked piddling little things like the fact that Townsley had been got rid of. Marty was counting on them taking the dossier and running with it.

'I can't answer that for you, Joe. You know that,' Marty said. 'I didn't ask, and if I had asked I know I would have been told some unbelievable story, so that's where we are. But I'm hoping the Crown will be glad to get what we have.' He sipped his brandy. 'It wouldn't be the first time they turned a blind eye to something that was staring them in the face, so that they could justify the ends they wanted to achieve. Don't you agree?'

Joe looked at his friend and his face softened to a smile.

'I do, Marty. I very much agree. If it was down to me, I wouldn't give a stuff about the big hole that Townsley may have fallen into. There's a lot more to be achieved by going with this dossier. That's my view.'

'And of course,' Marty said, 'there is some justice in the fact that an innocent woman, Kerry Casey, and her uncle Danny, are not going to be jailed for something they had no part in. That is something that shouldn't be lost here in all of this. They are innocent, and this evidence on the tape completely proves that.'

Joe nodded. 'You're right. I'm with you on that.' He sighed. 'Getting these guys at the Crown Office to agree with that and take what they've got is another matter. But I think I know who I can approach.' He paused. 'And by the way, Marty, is there any indication or hint as to why anyone would frame Kerry Casey? Why would anyone want to do that in such an elaborate way?'

Marty thought he knew the answer to that, from what Lambie had said. But he would leave it to Lambie to repeat it to the police when and if the time was right. And even then, the police would probably not be able to make the connections as to why someone high up in Whitehall would want to frame a Glasgow crime boss. He would leave it to them to puzzle out.

In the back of the big Land Rover Discovery, Lambie gazed out of the window, the outskirts of the city a blur as the car sped down the M8 motorway. It was as though he was in some kind of parallel world where he'd been watching himself unravel over the last few days. Now he was being driven down south and it had been made clear to him that the life he'd had before this no longer existed. Dick Lambie was dead. Officially he would only have been recorded as disappeared, perhaps a missing person. But he would not, could not, ever turn up again. He knew that, and he didn't need the Special Branch to tell him that he couldn't pitch up to his old life again. There would be a contract out on him in every corner of the world where there were Loyalist connections, and that pretty much meant every corner. He was told that once his new identity had been sorted, he would probably be sent to live somewhere in Europe – possibly Germany, Belgium or France. He would be anonymous, low-key, and that was how he would have to live out his life. There was no alternative. His wife would not be contacted by police to tell her of the arrangement. And he was forbidden to ever contact her. That hurt more than anything because Nora was an innocent woman in all of this and always had been. She knew what he was, or some of it, but she'd never questioned him. She liked the money, all right, and the lifestyle, but she loved and cared for him and if she'd known what was happening to him now, she would drop everything and join him. But he knew it didn't work that way. The fewer people who knew about this, the better.

Yesterday, in a basement office in Stewart Street police station, Lambie had sat across a table from two Special Branch officers. He had been told that Townsley's body had turned up. He had then reeled off the names of the men at the top of the UVF and all through the ranks, and he'd told them about weapons' stashes, where they were held and the types of ammo and stuff they routinely stored. He passed on the names of haulage companies who had complied with bringing money, drugs and weapons over, to and from Belfast, and gave them the names of the drivers he knew had done it. He'd admitted to being part of robberies, beatings and killings over the years and named the men who'd been there with him, or who'd carried them out on his behalf at the behest of the UVF. By the time he'd finished talking, he'd felt exhausted by the knowledge that there would be a whirlwind across Belfast and Glasgow as the police moved in, rounding people up. As the car raced down the motorway and they headed past Carlisle, he imagined the doors that would be kicked in over the coming days and weeks, and once it had all settled down and they were licking their wounds, the boys would notice that one man was missing in all of this – him. Then they would know. They would know he had grassed them all up, and his name would be spat on for generations as the traitor who brought the house down. But right now, even as the full force of his treachery and the consequences of that were beginning to sink in, none of that mattered to Lambie. He was alive, and he would survive.

CHAPTER TWENTY-EIGHT

Kerry stood in her cell taking one last look around it as she waited for the prison officer to arrive. She looked at the bunk beds, the blue duvet, the thin pillow, then at the table and chair where books and magazines sat. The towel she'd used that morning hung on the hook behind the cell door. It would be collected and replaced for the next occupant. It was grim and spartan, but it had been her home, and she had buckled down and accepted it, once she'd got over the initial shock of being banged up. But she was counting down the minutes until she could walk out of the door and reclaim her life, and she sure as hell would never set foot in a place like this again. It had been a strange feeling since Ash had left, and Kerry was surprised at how lonely she'd felt since her cellmate had gone. She'd been worried that the hard cases who she'd been giving a wide berth would gang up on her. But none of that had happened. Kerry had gone to work in the gift card workshop every day, and found that a few other girls were now talking to her and sitting with her at meal times. She had no idea why, but was just glad things hadn't turned hostile after the unrest of a few weeks ago. But now she was going home. So why was she feeling so nervous inside? She knew it was silly, but in here she was limited to very few activities, she never had to make any decisions. Everything, from meals to work, was ordered and organised and she barely had to think for herself except to keep her mood up. Going home, she had to take charge again, run the show, smile and be happy, look forward to the birth of her baby, feel protected and glad. She wondered how she would cope when they handed her a little baby that she had to make the world safe for. It was a daunting thought, especially without Vinny. She knew her apprehension would pass, and once she got home she would adapt, just as she had in here. She thought of Vinny, how constant he had been in her mind each night and first thing every morning. No news had come of him, and it seemed that Jake Cahill hadn't been in touch with Jack other than to say that he was working on it and would let them know if he had something to say. It was Jake's way of saying don't call me, I'll call you, and it was accepted. Kerry heard the footsteps in the hallway and the prison officer appeared in the open doorway.

'You all right, Kerry? It's time.'

Kerry turned to her. 'I'm ready.'

'Follow me,' the guard said. 'You can pick up your belong-
ings on the way to the exit. Someone collecting you?'

Kerry nodded.

She was looking forward to seeing Jack, and just the luxury of stepping into the car and being driven out of this
area, and towards the outskirts of Glasgow where she
could see the comforting church steeples and tower blocks
of her city begin to emerge on the skyline on the rise of the
M8 that took her home.

As she went out of the room, she saw a few of the girls
hanging around. She remembered them by name and by
offence – one of them was Tanya, one of the girls who
smuggled drugs in from abroad, the mule whose life would
now be in ruins for the foreseeable future. Everyone milled
around, Aggie arms folded, and her girlfriend by her side,
and Kerry wondered if there was some kind of protocol
among prisoners that they should shake hands or something. She saw Natalie milling around, her mouth tight
and downturned, a haunted look in her eyes. Kerry raised
her hand a little to acknowledge her, to try to convey that
she understood her pain, but in truth she would never
understand it.

'Take care, Kerry,' one of the girls said.

'Aye, go for it, Kerry. And you mind that wee baby when
it comes.'

Kerry walked past them, their faces displaying the pale
look of people who spend most of their lives indoors, the

sadness, and the hardness in their eyes. She felt choked as she nodded to them.

'Thanks, girls,' she said, stopping in her tracks. 'And you take care of yourselves.' There was nothing else to say that wouldn't sound trite. So she walked on without looking back.

She collected her handbag and jacket from the counter at the storage area before being led down a corridor towards the main exit. It felt strange to have her bag slung over her shoulder. A loud buzz signalled as the door slid across, and she stepped out. She stood for a moment, the damp drizzle on her face, and then she saw the car flash its lights from the car park. It eased its way out, drove along and then parked close to her. Jack got out and a smile spread across his face. Then Sharon got out of the back seat, a vision in her leather jacket and high boots.

'Well come on then, girl,' Sharon called out. 'Don't hang about! They might shout you back in.'

Kerry grinned and walked briskly towards them and into Jack's arms, feeling the warmth of his embrace. Her throat tightened with emotion.

'C'mere, you,' Sharon said, opening her arms to her.

'Oh, Sharon,' Kerry said as they hugged. 'Thanks for being here. I was beginning to think this day would never come.'

On the way back to Glasgow as the chatter slowed down, Kerry reflected on the last couple of days and how Marty had told her the good news about her release. Charges had been dropped. Marty hadn't told her any details of how it had come about as the news had only arrived via a phone call late yesterday afternoon, and there was no time to lose. He'd said Jack would fill her in.

'So tell me about it, Jack,' Kerry said. 'Marty just said the charges were dropped, but he did say when he visited a couple of days ago that there were things going on in the background.'

'Well that's one way of putting it.' Sharon gave Kerry a look of mischief as they sat in the rear seat.

From the front passenger seat, Jack turned around to face her.

'You want the full story, or the shortened version?' he asked.

'Well, as we've got half an hour's journey, let's have the full version. I know you told me while I was inside, but I want to hear it all again.'

'Okay,' Jack said. 'It all started with a phone call from some guy called Steven, who worked for Lambie – Marty will have told you who he is, yes?'

'Yeah,' she said. 'He mentioned. The White Horse, UVF.'

'Yep,' Jack said. 'The wee guy tipped us off that Lambie and his cohorts had been involved in a set-up to frame you.'

'He came to you with that? Out of the blue?'

'Pretty much, yes,' Jack said. 'To be honest, at that point we really didn't have a lot of intelligence on how the fuck it had come about. Nobody seemed to know anything, so before this guy got in touch, we were just clutching at straws, and that's the truth.'

'So did you meet him?'

'Yes,' Jack said. 'I went with Marty and we talked to him in a pub, and he spilled everything out. And a whole lot more.'

'Jesus. Does he have a death wish or something?'

'Well, you would think that, I suppose. But the fact is the wee guy had an axe to grind and Lambie and his mob had been bullying and extorting money from him for years. Anyway, he's safe now. We've got him in one of the flats. He's with his old mammy.'

'His mammy?' Kerry turned to Sharon, incredulous.

'Yes.' Sharon smiled. 'She's a real character. She's not well with some chest complaint. But Steven is devoted to her, so they came as a package.'

Kerry couldn't help but smile.

'Not that I'm complaining,' she said. 'I'll be glad to shake Steven's hand. So what then, Jack? What happened next?'

During the rest of the journey, Jack filled Kerry in on the turn of events, from the moment they'd identified and picked up Lambie and his sidekick Thomson, to the night at the lap-dancing brothel where Townsley had met his demise. Kerry listened intently, fascinated, finding herself excited at the power and decisiveness of Jack once he saw the end game. He hadn't hesitated, not once, in disposing of people like Thomson and Townsley once they'd no longer had use for them. She didn't like herself for feeling euphoric that people lost their lives the way they did, but told herself they were scum anyway. The truth was that if this hadn't been orchestrated by Jack the way it had been, then she'd still be in jail. And in any case, she was only in jail because the UVF took on the job, so they'd got what was coming to them. But her legal brain was trying to figure out why the police and the Crown Office had dropped the charges, but hadn't pursued the Caseys on whatever had happened to Townsley.

'So did the powers that be just take the evidence about Townsley not being around, and not ask what had happened to him?' Kerry asked.

Jack shrugged.

'Well, according to Marty they didn't make a big deal of asking about Townsley. Fact is, they'll be glad he's gone, because it's one less vicious bastard they have to worry about, track, follow, all that shit. They'll be shedding no tears. They were more interested in Lambie who spilled his guts on a raft of robberies and murders and drug deals. He threw in some big names and also pinpointed arms dumps in Scotland and in Belfast. All that shit is great publicity for them, and you'll probably see it in a few weeks' time when they decide to release pictures of the cops raiding some places and coming across a pile of sub-machine guns and ammo. Lambie dropped in a few big drug names too.'

'Jesus,' Kerry said. 'Talk about singing like the proverbial canary. So where is he now? I take it the cops are hiding him somewhere.'

'Yep. That was the deal. He would get his freedom for turning supergrass, but he would have to disappear. I don't know where they took him.' He paused. 'I'm guessing when Danny comes out, he'll be wanting to find out where he is. You know what he's like. Unfinished business.'

Kerry nodded and glanced at Sharon.

'Yeah. I suppose so, but I'm not interested so much in Lambie. He was just a vicious pawn in all of this. The guy who ordered the frame-up has to be Quentin Fairhurst. From what Lambie says it was someone high up in Whitehall. Who else could it be but Fairhurst?'

Nobody answered for a long moment. Then Sharon spoke. 'I'm sure it was him, Kerry. But proving it is another matter.'

'We don't need to prove it. It had to be him. There is nobody else in Whitehall who would go to that length to discredit me. He actually had me framed for murder. And Danny. I could have spent the next fifteen years in jail, my life and my baby's life ruined. That's the kind of guy Fairhurst is. So he'll get his comeuppance.'

Nobody answered, and Sharon and Jack glanced at each other. Kerry knew they would have expected nothing less from her. And they weren't offering any argument. For the remainder of the journey, Kerry listened as Sharon and Jack told her about the day-to-day stuff in the business.

Despite Sharon being in Glasgow, she'd still kept a tight rein on Spain and the Spanish hotel complex which was now almost finished. She filled Kerry in on what had to be done there, and how close they were to planning the big opening. Kerry listened, nodding in all the right places, but the elephant in the room that had not been mentioned was Vinny. Eventually she had to ask.

'Nothing from Jake yet?'

Sharon shook her head. 'No, pet. Nothing,' she said. 'Actually I haven't spoken to him in the last week or so, as I thought it was best to leave it to him.'

'It's taking such a long time,' Kerry said, gazing out of the window, thinking the worst. 'I thought something would have turned up by now, some information or some kind of trail.'

'Maybe it has, Kerry. But Jake isn't the kind of guy who has daily briefings, so to me no news is good news.'

Kerry automatically touched her swelling tummy.

'We have to believe that,' she said softly.

Kerry felt a wave of emotion as the gates of the Casey complex slid across and the Mercedes eased its way into the courtyard. The guards' familiar faces were all there, some working in the grounds, others by the gate, all vigilant. They smiled as the car pulled up. Then the kitchen door opened and Elsa came out, her apron on, beaming as Kerry got out of the car. For a moment she thought of her mother and father and how much this place had meant to them, how they had felt they had really arrived in life when they were able to afford to live here, away from the hardship of the council house scheme where she was brought up. She wondered what they would have made of all this. She wished they could be here. But what she saw around her now *was* her family. She was home.

CHAPTER TWENTY-NINE

Jake waited in the bar for Mateo to come out of the apartment. The Colombian had sent him a brief text – 'bar en cinco'. So he'd taken it that he would meet him in the bar with information. Ten minutes he'd been here, in a seat at the window, his eyes trained on the apartment, but no show. Jake had left Sullivan to cruise around the town in his car. So he was on foot like a tourist, but watching closely for any sign of anything resembling a Colombian mob arriving. But so far, nothing. Jake's mobile rang and he could see it was Tommy.

'Someone just came out of the apartment,' he said.

'Good,' Jake replied. Then he saw the apartment main door open and Mateo leave. 'I see him now.' He hung up.

Jake watched as Mateo limped across the street. The Colombian stood at the bar, then turned around and raised his chin in greeting to him. Jake nodded back as the old barman came shuffling out from somewhere behind glass string curtains. Once he'd filled the beer from the tap and pushed it across to Mateo, the old guy shuffled back and disappeared behind the curtains. After a moment, Mateo turned around to face Jake. There was nobody there to witness anything that the pair of them would say to each other, or even to see them talking, but Jake was very cautious. He folded the newspaper he was reading and went up to the bar, barely looking at Mateo. He went into his pocket and took out a five euro bill and left it on the counter, then he quietly turned to Mateo.

'*Que pasa?*'

Mateo glanced over his shoulder, put the glass of beer to his lips and took a long drink.

'They called my friend.' He jerked his head in the direction of the apartment. 'They are on their way. In next hour they say they will be there.'

Jake nodded. 'How is Vinny?'

Mateo puffed and shook his head.

'He is not good. He has fever, I think. Very hot, and he has been sick. Vomiting. The hand is swollen, red. Much more now.' Mateo indicated a swelling from the wrist towards the elbow. 'Is not good.'

'Is he conscious? Awake?'

Mateo made a face.

'Sometimes, but he is sleeping much. His body shaking.'

Jake shook his head slowly. This was not good at all. The infection from his severed finger was obviously spreading. If they didn't get him out of there and to a doctor soon, sepsis would set in, if it hadn't already. Time was running out. He looked at his watch, then out of the window where darkness was beginning to fall.

'What are they going to do with Vinny? Any more on that?'

Mateo nodded. 'There is a boat. Is coming soon to harbour. They are taking him to the boat. And then.' He drew a hand across his throat.

Jake spread his hands. 'Why are they doing this?'

Mateo shrugged. 'Because he won't tell them if police are watching the shipment coming to Cadiz. Is coming in a few days, but the cartel, they still not know if the police will be waiting.'

'Maybe Vinny doesn't know either?' Jake said.

Mateo shrugged. 'I not know. I only the guard.'

They stood in silence for a few moments. Jake took a long breath and let it out slowly.

'Okay,' he said. 'Then we will move soon.'

He handed him a twenty euro note. 'Go to the *farmacia* and get some more bandages and stuff to clean Vinny's wound, then give him some painkillers. Bandage it up as best you can.' He leaned closer to Mateo and lowered his voice to a whisper. 'Now I want you to do this: when you are fixing Vinny up, whisper this message to him. Tell him: "Jake is coming!" Okay? He will know what this means. Just say to him to hold on. Jake is coming.' He paused. 'Does the other guard speak English?'

Mateo shook his head. 'No. No English.'

'Good. Then you must make sure you pass the message to Vinny. Then just stay put, and we'll do the rest.'

Mateo's eyes dropped to the bar, then he looked at Jake.

'But what about me? You promised you get me out. My wife. My son?'

'Don't worry. You just keep your mouth shut and your head down whatever happens. Understand?'

The Colombian blinked in acknowledgment, finished his beer and wiped his mouth with the back of his hand. Then he turned and limped out of the bar towards the *farmacia*. Jake took out his mobile and punched in Sullivan's number.

'Head back to the bar. Bring the car. We need to move soon.'

Darkness had fallen in Tarifa and the stragglers from the last ferry from Tangier were leaving the town and heading for the motorway. The town itself would soon be busy with early evening tourists and locals going out for pre-dinner drinks or strolling in the harbour. But in half an hour, the harbour itself would be quiet, especially where Jake's mate had berthed the boat that would hopefully get them and Vinny away. It was risky going by sea, and Jake knew it, but making a fast getaway by road might be even riskier. At sea there was at best only one other boat to contend with if the Colombians had, as Mateo had told them, brought a boat to take Vinny out to sea and dump him. Jake decided that they could take the Colombians on if there was a battle at sea, and make their getaway fast up towards Malaga. By road, they'd run the risk of the Colombians ambushing them on the motorway, because they had no idea if they were coming down here mob-handed. Jake didn't think so, but didn't want to risk it.

The car was parked on a side street next to the apartment. Inside it Jake and Sullivan tooled up with Glocks and holsters, and Jake pulled his safari waistcoat over his eyes Kevlar vest, filling the pockets with ammunition. He shoved another pistol in the waistband of his trousers, just in case. When they were ready, he turned to Sullivan, also pulling on his Kevlar jacket.

'You all right? You ready?' he said. 'This could be a shit show.'

Sullivan nodded, mouth tight.

'I know. I'm good.' He glanced up at the apartment. 'I just want to get Vinny out.'

Jake pulled out his mobile and pushed the speed dial for Tommy.

'We're outside. Will be at the door in ten seconds.'

'Good.'

Jake put the phone back in his jacket pocket and opened the car door.

'Let's go.'

They walked briskly to the front door of the apartment,

and on their approach, they heard the security latch buzz, and they pushed open the door. Then they crept upstairs to the apartment as Tommy quietly opened the door. Inside the small apartment, Bonzo was standing with a sawn-off shotgun in his hand. Jake glanced at Tommy.

'Only one thing we can do, Jake. Blast our way in and keep firing. We don't have a lot of time.'

'I know,' Jake said. 'Let's go.'

They stepped downstairs to the landing outside the apartment where Vinny was being held. Everyone automatically stood back as Bonzo put the shotgun to the door. The blast echoed in the hallway and shattered the door into splinters as Bonzo kicked down what was left of it and climbed in. The others followed. Bonzo led, creeping along the hallway and past the kitchen which was filled with piled up dishes and rotting food. They went towards the closed door that presumably led to the lounge.

Jake stepped forward.

'*Guardia Civil!*' he shouted. '*Abierto! Ahora!*'

Silence. Everyone looked at each other but the door stayed shut.

'*Abierto!*' Jake shouted once more.

When there was no response he turned to the others. Then Bonzo stepped forward and booted the door in. It almost came off its hinges. It was wide open and as they stepped forward a shot rang out and everyone pushed themselves against the hallway wall. Another shot. Tommy dived to the floor and crawled his way in, and behind him Bonzo, who was firing shots, dived to the floor. The Colombians, at least one of them, was shooting back. Jake crept forward and saw Mateo. He indicated to him to dive down, which he did, and Bonzo fired again as the other Colombian stuck his head up from behind a chair. His head exploded across the wall. They were in. They glanced around quickly. Then they saw Vinny. He was barely recognisable. His bearded, bloodied face was bruised and thinner. He lay chained to the radiator. Vinny seemed to shake himself to consciousness and looked up at them. But his eyes were glazed. Sullivan stepped forward and knelt down.

'Vinny! Vinny! It's me! Sullivan!' he said. 'We're getting you out of here, mate.'

But Vinny stared at him and then collapsed.

'Stay with us, Vinny! We're getting you back home, mate.'

Jake looked around and went behind the chair where the dead Colombian was slumped, and pulled the keys to the padlock off him, then tossed it to Sullivan. Mateo lay down, hands covering his head.

'Get up, Mateo! Come on! Let's get out of here.'

He went across to Vinny and knelt beside him as Sullivan freed him from the chain.

'Vinny! It's me, Jake! Listen! You need to stand up, son. We need you walking so we can get you into the car and out of here.'

Vinny looked at him and tears came to his eyes.

'Jake.' Then at Sullivan. 'Sullivan. You came!' He shook his head and tried to lean on his arm, but his legs buckled.

Tommy and Bonzo came across the room and pulled him to his feet, arms over their shoulders.

'We've got you, mate. Come on. Let's go.'

A mobile rang on the dead Colombian, and everyone froze. Jake turned to Mateo.

'Answer it.'

Mateo pulled the phone from the dead Colombian's pocket and pushed it to his ear. He looked at Jake, his eyes filled with panic. They could hear him in Spanish telling them that the Colombian had gone to the supermarket but would be back in five minutes. Then he hung up.

'They be here in ten minutes. They are coming into Tarifa now.'

'Right,' Jake said. 'Let's get the fuck out of here.'

Tommy and Bonzo more or less carried Vinny out of the apartment and down the stairs to the main entrance. Outside, the street was quiet. They helped Vinny into the back seat of the car and Mateo got in beside them, Sullivan in the front. Behind them, Bonzo piled into Tommy's car.

'The harbour,' Jake said. 'Follow me.'

In the car, Jake keyed a number into his phone.

'Jimsy. On our way. Be there in three. There might be people after us, so be ready.' He hung up, and sped through the town and down towards the harbour and the quayside.

Once they were as close as possible to where the boat was moored, they screeched to a halt. They jumped out and as gently as they could, pulled Vinny from the back seat. Jimsy was on the quayside and helped them across to the boat and onto the narrow gangplank. Suddenly there was the squeal of car tyres. Everyone stopped in their tracks and looked around to see a car racing towards them.

'Get him in, Jimsy. Hurry.'

Vinny was being dragged, his legs trailing behind him, onto the gangplank onto the deck of the boat, where someone was waiting. They lifted him by his shoulders and lay him down on the deck. A shot was fired from the car that had just pulled up.

'You go, Jake,' Tommy said from the open driver's window. 'We'll take care of this.'

As Tommy and Bonzo got out of the car, Jake urged Mateo and Sullivan to get on the boat. Bonzo fired back towards the other car. Three Colombians were coming towards them, ducking and diving as bullets plinked off the headlights and body of the car. Then one of the Colombians fell down. More shots. There was the wail of sirens in the distance. Then the sound of the boat engine roaring. Jake jumped on just before they pulled up the gangplank. As shots were fired in the background, the boat sped out of the harbour and into the night, a frothy white trail in its wake. Jake went across and knelt down beside Vinny, whose whole body was twitching and drenched in sweat. Jake touched his forehead and pushed his hair back. He looked as though he was dying.

'You're going home, son. You'll be all right. Just hang in there.'

Vinny shook his head, his eyes rolling.

'I'm not.' Tears came to his eyes. He grabbed hold of Jake's wrist, and pulled him close. 'Tell Kerry. I . . . I love . . .' Then his eyes rolled back and his head dropped to the side.

Jake turned to the doctor who was crouched beside him.

'Is he . . .?' Jake asked.

The doc didn't answer. He knelt over Vinny and put his fingers to his neck and held it there for a moment. Then he looked at Jake.

'Pulse is there. But it's very weak.'

'Will he make it to the hospital in Marbella?'

The doc sighed and grimaced.

'I don't know. He is very bad.'

CHAPTER THIRTY

It had been so long since Kerry had enjoyed the simple things she'd taken for granted, that she wanted to take her time and enjoy every glorious moment. She'd decided to have a quiet dinner alone in her living room so that she could simply gaze around her and feel that her life was going back to some kind of normality – or whatever had passed for normality since the day she had come back to Glasgow to take over the family business all those months ago. That seemed like a lifetime ago. She could barely remember who she'd been before then, how she'd spent her days, what thoughts she would have had of an evening in her London apartment. Her life then had been full of work, and in her downtime she'd usually been exhausted and glad to have a night in. She sometimes felt that the past few months had been like watching someone else's life spiral out of control, the way events had unfolded. It had seemed as though just as they'd put out a fire in one place, another one would burst into life and that they were fighting a losing battle. She knew deep down that the time would come when this wouldn't be her life, but with every new step, her dream was being put on hold until they extinguished the latest fire. Even in jail, she'd had to step up to the plate and live the life that was in front of her, just do it day by day, one foot in front of the other. But now she was home, where she was protected and safe, she could start to sit back and enjoy what she had. She glanced down at the bulge in her white towelling bath robe as she lay back on the bed, fresh from the long, luxurious shower. She had already made an appointment tomorrow to see her obstetrician for another scan. The last one she'd had a couple of days before she'd been arrested, and although the doctors on the hospital wing of the prison had monitored her, there hadn't been a scan. She'd felt plenty of movement and that was what had kept her going, but she'd longed to see a screen image of her baby. Now that she was nearly seven months pregnant, tomorrow was the three-dimensional scan. She would be able to find out the sex of the baby, but she'd already decided she would wait. It was a decision she would have made with Vinny, but he wasn't here, so if he couldn't know the sex of their baby, then she didn't want to know either. She had to believe that she would hear some good news from Jake Cahill soon. She'd tried ringing his mobile when she'd got back to the house in the afternoon, and had left messages, but nothing.

She lay idly watching the television news, and knew that by tomorrow or the day after, the news would break that Kerry Casey had been released from jail and that all charges had been dropped. The newspapers would attempt to pull that apart and find out why. But nobody would get to the bottom of it. The only person who could give them answers was her, and she wasn't going to be giving any interviews. But what she could do was cause an explosion.

Over coffee when she'd come home late in the afternoon, she and Jack and Sharon had discussed doing something with the information she had about Fairhurst – the CDs and the tapes and photos they'd used to blackmail him. They both knew how much it meant to her, and that it was ninety-nine per cent certain he was behind it. She had later listened to copies of the tape from Lambie and Townsley and was even more convinced. There was no way it could have been anyone other than Fairhurst. He had been made to look a fool after Vic's release. And she thought it was plausible that people high up the chain of government used IRA and UVF people to do their dirty work. She'd heard stories about it before in the legal profession, but nothing provable and only anecdotal. Now she had a gut feeling, and she was going with it. She'd told Marty that she was going to drop the information to a journalist. She didn't know anyone by name, but she picked up the *Post* and saw the name Harry Foster on the front page. He'd written a story about allegations of corruption in the

Scottish government. She sat up and took a sip from a glass of iced water. Then she keyed in the newspaper number and asked for him. It was seven in the evening, so he probably wouldn't still be at work. She was surprised when he answered.

'Harry Foster.' His voice had a crisp urgency.

'Harry. My name is Kerry Casey.'

By the silence on the end of the phone, she knew that he recognised her name, and he would be as stunned as he would be excited to hear from her. An interview with Kerry Casey in the middle of her release from jail would be a scoop.

'Oh, Kerry Casey? The Kerry Casey who was just released from prison today?'

'You knew about this already?'

'We did. Within a couple of hours.'

'I'm surprised you didn't have a posse on my doorstep.'

'That wouldn't be the kind of thing we would do at this moment.'

Kerry almost smiled at the thought of it. Damn right you wouldn't send a bunch of hacks to her doorstep and expect to go back with anything other than a threatening look or worse.

Silence on the phone.

'I'm not phoning for a chat, Harry. I don't know you, but I saw your name on the front page of today's paper, and I decided to call you.'

'I'm glad you did, Kerry. Is it okay if I call you Kerry, by the way?'

'Yes.' She paused, knowing he was waiting for her next sentence. 'Look, Harry. I know there will be a lot of speculation in the papers as to why the charges against me were dropped. I won't be giving any interviews, but in essence, the charges have been dropped because they were never valid. I was innocent of those charges, as was my uncle Danny. We were framed. Simple as that. It was a set-up. And this is not an interview. Do you understand?'

'Yes, I do. But I could attribute your comments to an insider in your family or organisation if you would be prepared to do that?'

'We'll see. But the reason I'm phoning is that I have information that your paper might want to pursue. It's about the background of my arrest. Well, some of the background. And the reason I was framed.'

There was a moment's pause, then the reporter asked, 'Would you be in a position to say who framed you, Kerry? I mean off the record, if you want?'

'I can say that,' she said. 'But not on the phone.'

'And do you have any proof of this claim?' Then he added quickly, 'Not that I'm doubting you, but I know that when I go to my editor with this information the first thing he'll ask is whether I have proof.'

'I have. But I can only give you some parts of the proof. I don't want it all to come out because this information has already been passed to the police. Hence the reason I am out of jail.'

'So your information was believed. By police?'

'It was believed because it's true.'

'I'm not doubting your word.' Pause. 'Could we meet face to face if you are prepared to do that? I know you're just home and might be getting used to being free, but if you felt you were able to, I could meet you anywhere, anytime.'

'Okay. We can arrange that. I have information, documentation and photographs that will expose a top-level government official.'

Silence.

'What – in this framing allegation?'

'No. Not directly. But once you see what I have, and have the background – which you must keep to yourself, by the way – then you will see why I believe I was framed.'

There was a brief silence, and Kerry wondered if she was coming across as a nutcase, and whether she'd said too much.

'Okay. I understand. I'd be delighted to talk to you, as I said, anytime, whenever you can make it.'

Kerry thought for a moment. Was she being too hasty? She'd never dealt with the press before, and didn't want to suddenly find herself splashed all over the newspapers. This wasn't about her. She could be in the background. This was about Fairhurst. About exposing him. About ruining him. The first thing Danny had suggested when they'd got out of jail was that they should just get someone to bump Fairhurst off. It could be done, he said, and no comebacks. But that wasn't enough for Kerry. She wanted him alive, publicly shamed, his career ruined.

'Okay,' she said. 'I will meet you tomorrow. But remember. This story is not about me. I will give you information that you can look at and decide what to do with. But I don't want to find myself photographed or suddenly being all over your paper talking, because that is not what this is about. This is about exposing someone at top level who deserves to be exposed.'

Silence. Then:

'That's one of the reasons I get out of bed and go to work every day, Kerry. Where do you want to meet?'

'Name a place.' Then she paused. 'No. I'll tell you where. The Blythswood Hotel. You'll know where it is. It's quiet. Two o'clock tomorrow okay for you?'

'Absolutely. I'll be there.'

'Don't even think about bringing a photographer or taking my picture from behind some tree.'

She could hear him almost chuckle.

'Absolutely not, Kerry. You have my word. Just you and me.'

She hung up. Then she pushed the key for Jake Cahill again. Still nothing.

CHAPTER THIRTY-ONE

Kerry was wakened by the sounds that she'd almost forgotten about when she was in jail. She could hear the gate to the courtyard opening and closing and the quiet buzz of activity outside. That and the smell of food being cooked. At first when she'd come out of the deep sleep she was in, there was a second or two where she wondered where she was. In prison, there would have been the hum of conversation, the opening and clicking of doors and the sense that prisoners were making their way down to the dining room to start their day. She lay back and relished the feeling of being free and safe in her own home. But the relaxed feeling didn't last long as reality began to dawn on her. She picked up her mobile and checked it in case there had been anything from Jake, but nothing. She knew that to start her day by brooding over Vinny would plunge her into depression, because whatever was going on, whatever had happened to him was out of her control.

She had to find a way to push it to a manageable place in her mind and concentrate on the things around that she could manage. Her priority was to be healthy and to focus on her baby. In a couple of months' time she would give birth and she didn't even want to consider the prospect of doing that without Vinny. But right now, there was nothing she could do about that, so she had to put thoughts of Vinny to the side. She pushed back the duvet and got out of bed, padding across to the full-length mirror where she checked out her bulging tummy. She could feel the hardness of it. Just doing that, the simple touch, gave her a feeling as close to joy as she could achieve, and she tried to imagine what it would be like to have her own baby in her arms, to feed and clothe and care for another human being. She'd read that some mothers-to-be were filled with dread at the thought of their baby's arrival, but for Kerry this would be the best and most important thing she would ever do in her life. Nothing was going to get in the way of that, and worrying herself sick about Vinny was not going to stop the joy she felt. She knew that wherever he was, he would be telling her to do exactly that, to enjoy these moments, and that he would be with her some time. If only she could talk to him. If only she could hear a single word from him to say he was okay. She pushed the thought away.

Today was an important day in so many ways. She was going to the hospital for a scan, and afterwards she was meeting this reporter from the *Post* to drop the bomb on Fairhurst. This was payback time. What he had done had endangered her life and the life of her baby. She could leave it, and learn to live with it. But she didn't want him to get away with it, to live the way he did, high up in government, untouchable. He deserved everything that was coming to him. She went to the bathroom and turned on the shower, standing for a few seconds to relish the luxury she lived in. She would never again take anything in her life for granted.

Kerry was glad Maria had accompanied her to the hospital as she'd been with her at the first scan, and having her old friend with her was now part of the journey. Maria had become a feature of the Casey family, and if she was wary or didn't like what they did for a living, she never mentioned it. She'd been taken in by Kerry who'd looked after her when she'd most needed it. She was as loyal as any member of the organisation. Maria had been working mostly at the bookies and organising accounts, but had also been helping with this guy Steven and his mother, who Kerry was looking forward to meeting some time in the next couple of days. They sat in the ante-natal suite, Kerry on the bed as the sonographer put the gel on her stomach and placed the cold probe on her skin. She lay back, recalling the first time she'd been there and the nerve-racking wait to hear the heartbeat. Once again, there was an anxious moment, until the sonographer exchanged glances with her, then Maria.

'And here we are,' the sonographer said. 'If you don't want to know the sex of the baby, then look away while I do this bit.'

'I want it to be a surprise.' Kerry smiled. She closed her eyes.

'Okay. You can look now. Everything is looking great. We can see the baby moving and everything is ticking along nicely. Good size too. Looks like you're on course to have a big baby.'

Kerry glanced at her, a little worried.

'But not too big for this stage though?'

'No.' The sonographer smiled. 'Some babies thrive quicker than others, and yours is one. But everything is looking great.'

'Thanks. Are you sure?'

'Yes. Don't worry, Kerry. It's fine. A big healthy baby is not a problem. You might just give birth a little bit earlier than you were planning.'

'You mean like premature?'

'No, not necessarily.'

'Okay. As long as everything is fine.'

'It is.'

She pushed a button and printed out an image of the baby. She handed it to Kerry, who held it up to Maria.

'What do you think, Maria? Boy or girl?' Kerry asked.

'Just a beautiful wee baby, Kerry. Whatever it is, this baby will be lucky to have you as a mum.'

Kerry felt choked. 'I'm so excited.'

'I know. It's such a magical time. I can't wait either.'

An hour later, after Maria had gone back to work in the bookies, Kerry arrived at the Blythswood Hotel for her meeting with Harry Foster. She stood at the doorway wondering if she should wait outside or go in and wait for him. She turned when she heard the entrance door of the hotel open and saw a young man come from inside. He walked towards where she stood.

'Kerry?' he asked.

'Yes. Harry?'

He reached out a hand. 'Good to meet you. Thanks for seeing me.'

He was tall and handsome, but looked very young. Kerry wondered if she'd done the right thing by agreeing to meet the first name she could find. He held the door open and glanced inside.

'Looks nice and quiet here.'

'Yes,' Kerry said. 'It's one of my favourite hotels. Discreet.'

'Of course,' he said.

They sat down and both ordered tea. Kerry wondered if he would start the conversation or whether he was expecting her to do it. She watched and waited, then he spoke.

'Kerry, I want you to be absolutely clear that anything we talk about here is completely off the record. Unless you say otherwise, anything you give me or talk about is not attributable to you. Okay?'

Despite his boyish looks, he seemed mature and in command of his role here, and Kerry warmed to him. He couldn't have been any older than twenty-five, and she wondered what kind of frontline experience he would have had. But there was a look about him, something a little dark around his eyes, which she couldn't quite get.

'Yes. Absolutely. I don't want to be directly involved in anything I give you today. But you won't need anyone's involvement. Once you see the photos and hear what I have on tape, that will be enough.' She paused, knowing he was scanning her face. 'You look young, Harry, if you don't mind me saying. You been at the *Post* long?'

He smiled. 'Yeah. I've been there four years now, moving up the ranks. It's a great job. You get right in at the deep end of life.' He paused. 'Mind you, I grew up in Easterhouse, so I was born at the deep end of life.'

Kerry smiled back at him, and warmed to him even more. She wondered what life would have been like in Easterhouse when he was being raised, probably a good ten years after she grew up in Maryhill.

'Not the easiest place to grow up in,' she said. 'And I should know. I grew up in Maryhill.'

'Yeah. Well you'll know what I mean.'

'So, what made you go into newspapers?'

She saw his face darken a little and he glanced away from her.

'Well, I always wanted to write. That and a natural curiosity. But to be honest, I lost my sister to drugs when I was only about ten years old and she was seventeen. Heroin. It shaped everything about me. Still does. Made me want to go out there, get big stories, expose the bad guys.' He looked her straight in the eye, then turned away.

There was a long pause, and Kerry felt a flush of shame. This was a young man who'd lost his sister to drugs, and here he was talking to the head of a criminal gang who had made a fortune from dealing. She knew that the Caseys had only shifted heroin for a short time when her brother Mickey was in charge, and that he'd quickly switched their market to cocaine. But at the end of the day, a drug dealer was a drug dealer. It struck her that perhaps this guy was here to get inside information. Perhaps his goal was to expose her and her organisation. She waited for him to say something and when he didn't she knew she would have to address the issue.

'Harry,' she said. 'I don't know if you're aware of this, or you've read anything about it, but from the moment I took over the Casey organisation my goal has been to change things. I'm in the process of doing that. I . . . I—'

He put his hand up to stop her.

'Kerry, look. Please don't take this the wrong way,' he said. 'But what your organisation does to make money is something I can put to one side. Honestly. I'm not here to talk about that. In my line of business I work with all sorts of people and I get stories and lines to pursue from everyone from police, to drug dealers, to some homeless guy in the street who talks to me. I'm not here to expose you or look into your life. I just want to make that clear. Okay?' He paused. 'I might despise how some organisations make their money, but hey, I'm not here to judge. I'm here to listen to a story you have to tell.'

He was matter-of-fact and emphatic for one so young, and Kerry liked his honesty. But if he had an ulterior motive, then there was no point in being here. She would have to trust her gut. She was here now.

'Thanks for your honesty, Harry.' She spread her hands in a kind of surrender gesture. 'Okay. We're clear about that. So let me tell you, or show you, what I have here that you may be interested in.'

'Okay,' he said. His dark eyes shot a glance at the leather briefcase she had by her side. He watched in silence as she opened it and took out the buff envelope.

She took the photographs out and slid them across the table.

'I'm sure you'll know who these people are.'

He picked up each picture and studied them without

speaking, his expression flat. He looked at them again, then lay them on the table. To her surprise, his face almost broke into something between a smile and shock.

'Christ almighty, Kerry!' he whispered. 'Quentin Fairhurst? Henry Callaghan? Jesus! What the hell is this?'

'Photos that were brought to me some time ago. In case I ever wanted to use them.' She pulled out the DVD. There's film too!' She felt her face smile even though she tried not to. She could see how hooked he was.

'Christ!' he said. 'Who would bring this stuff to you?' He put a hand up. 'Obviously I don't expect you to tell me. But . . .' He shook his head. 'Why? I mean . . . how did they come to you?'

Kerry folded her arms. 'Would you believe it was more or less by accident?'

'Right now I don't know what to believe.'

'Well they came to me, kind of by accident, and it was only when I studied the photos that it meant something to me. I acted for a family years ago, when I was a rookie lawyer, who were suing a pharmaceutical company that had left their daughter paralysed. Fairhurst, long before he was who he is now, was a hotshot lawyer and he acted for the pharmaceutical company. To cut a long story short, we lost. But I always believed it had been fixed, you know. Witnesses had suddenly not been available or had changed their stories. It stank.'

He looked a little confused.

'So you thought this was a way to get back at him?'

Kerry blinked but didn't reply.

'But why now? I mean, how long have you had this for?'

'A few months. That's all.'

'Does he know you have it? Have you contacted him?'

She shrugged. 'He knows.'

Harry paused as though trying to process and work out his next question.

'Well,' he sighed. 'I'm totally stunned here, Kerry, and flying by the arse of my pants, so I'm just going to ask this. You don't have to tell me. But have you used it against him before – I mean recently?'

Kerry didn't answer, but she looked him in the eye and for a long moment she held his gaze. She could almost see him begin to figure it out in his head, until the penny dropped.

'So,' he said, puffing out his cheeks. 'So this frame-up of you and your uncle. You're saying Fairhurst did this?'

Kerry nodded slowly, but said nothing.

'But why? I mean why now? If he knew that this material was in existence, why didn't he do some deal with you so that you wouldn't use it?'

Kerry said nothing. She knew he would figure it out. Eventually he shook his head.

'Ah,' he said, 'and, completely off the record of course. But you *did* a deal with him before, using this as a threat to expose him, and now, months on, he decided to come after you. Am I on the right track?'

Kerry kept silent. Harry took a breath.

'You must have really fucked him over big time in whatever deal you did for him to get involved in a frame-up.' He shook his head. 'But how? I mean, he's the Attorney General. He's not a gangster. Are you saying he actually got someone to do this? Like a hit style job?'

'He did,' Kerry said.

'He did? Who did he get?'

'The UVF. A crew from Glasgow and Belfast. They did the frame-up.'

His eyes widened.

'You have evidence of this?'

'I do. Recorded evidence. Not of the Attorney General's involvement, but of UVF involvement.'

'Fuck! On tape? Of the actual story of what happened?'

'On a USB stick.. With the men behind it talking about doing it.'

'Jesus Christ! My editor will blow a gasket. Did these guys mention Fairhurst?'

'Sadly not by name. But they said it was someone high up in Whitehall who ordered the set-up. You can hear it yourself.'

He sat back, lifted the cup to his lips and took a gulp. Then he rubbed a hand across his forehead and through his mop of black hair.

'He's not named though. And even if he was, proving it is another matter. He's the Attorney General. You don't just go accusing him of hiring a team to carry out a hit on a Glasgow crime boss.' He didn't look embarrassed at using the words 'crime boss' to her face.

Kerry liked that. She gave him an understanding nod.

'You don't have to choose your words, Harry. I know what the organisation has been. But as I said, it is different now. I have moved us on.'

For a while they sat in silence, and Kerry wondered when the question was coming. It didn't take too long.

'So,' he said. 'These guys on the tape, talking about you being framed. Are they around? I mean now?'

Kerry looked at him, her face straight.

'One of them is,' she said. 'The other is not.'

He said nothing and just watched for a moment. He knew what she meant.

'So the one that is around. Is he anywhere I could get in touch with him?'

'No.' She took a breath. 'He's with the police. He turned Queen's evidence, informer. Told them everything, so as you can imagine, he's now well out of the way.'

'Witness protection?'

'Yeah.'

'Was he UVF?'

'Yes.'

'Anything you can tell me about him? Name? Anything. You say you have these guys on tape talking about the set-up. Could I listen to it?'

Kerry was learning that you just didn't throw information like this to a newspaper and expect them just to publish it. This guy wanted more, he would dig and dig, but there was only so much she wanted to give. But she could see that even though he wanted to believe her, he would need more evidence than just her word.

'Yes,' she said, going into her bag. 'I have a copy of the recording here, which you can listen to.'

'You do?' His eyes widened. 'That would be brilliant.'

Kerry took out the USB stick and her laptop and pushed the stick into the port. She didn't want to explain too much about the location of the conversation, because to say it was the White Horse pub and later the lap-dancing bar would identify the places, and might open up all sorts of questions as to what had happened that night.

'Okay,' she said. 'All I am prepared to tell you is that the two men in this recording are the people who framed me. One is from Glasgow and the other, as you'll hear, is from Belfast.'

'Can you name them?'

'I can. But I won't. You're the reporter. You can do some digging yourself.'

He nodded. 'Fair enough.'

She waited until the couple who were in the bar put on their jackets and walked out. Then she played the recording with the volume low and watched as Harry listened, engrossed. When it was finished he sat back and let out a sigh.

'I suppose my editor could say that might be anyone talking there. Could be somebody at the wind-up.'

'But it's not.'

His eyes narrowed as he leaned across, his elbows on the table.

'Is there anything more you can give me? A name? Anywhere I can dig and find out who these guys are?'

Kerry was itching to tell him. She had to convince him.

'Okay,' she said eventually. 'All I'm going to say to you is go to the White Horse bar, and see if the owner is around.'

Harry waited a moment for her to reveal more. When she didn't, he spoke.

'The owner. You mean the owner isn't around?'

Kerry shook her head but didn't answer, and they sat that way for a moment.

'That's all I can tell you,' she said. 'It's really up to you now. But look, Harry. For the moment, all you have to do is go away and look at the photos and the DVD of Fairhurst. That is a major story in itself. Just having material like this, so that your newspaper can ask what these photographs mean, is a story. In the pictures he's with Russian oligarchs. You'll see, if you dig deep enough, one of them in the picture died in some mysterious house fire in millionaires' row in Kensington a few months ago. You could just look at that story. That might be enough. At the very least you can link him to the photograph and ask what the Attorney General is doing in his company.'

He bit the inside of his cheek.

'Yes. Of course. There's enough here to cause a major storm. Definitely the resignation of Fairhurst and Callaghan.' He paused. 'But I also want to get the story that he framed you. That's mega.'

'But you can't actually prove it. He's never going to admit it. Nobody will.'

He sat back.

'I have to speak to my editor. And our lawyers. There are ways to write stories like this. I need some time to look and think.' He glanced at the material. 'Are you okay with me taking this? I suppose they're not the originals.'

She nodded. 'You can take them. I have copies of everything.' She paused. 'But remember. I am nowhere in this story talking to you. Are we absolutely clear about that?'

He gave her a long look as though he could sense the veiled threat in her words.

'Absolutely clear. Nothing here came from you. Nothing. As I say, there are ways to write a story like this.' He collected the material and slipped it onto his bag. He stood up. 'I'm desperate to get back, go into a quiet office and listen to the recording again and watch the DVDs.'

'Of course.' Kerry stood up. She put her hand out, and

gave him a firm handshake. 'Good. It's over to you now, Harry. Here's my mobile number.'

She relayed it and watched as he keyed it into his phone. She could see that he was bursting to get away.

'Thanks, Kerry. I'll be in touch.'

He turned and walked briskly to the door. She hoped she had done the right thing. But it was too late now if she hadn't.

CHAPTER THIRTY-TWO

Kerry was having a breakfast of toast and poached eggs in the kitchen, when the back door opened and one of her guards came in with a copy of the *Post*. He held it up then went across and put it on the table.

'Thought you might want a look at this, Kerry.' Then he left.

She knew something was coming, because so far there had been nothing reported in any of the papers about her being released from jail. So she was sure someone would be first to reveal the news. The front page jumped out at her. In huge letters the headline screamed: 'FRAMED'. There was a picture of Kerry that must have been taken at her mother's funeral. This wasn't what she had expected. At least not so soon. The headline on the story read: 'GANG-LAND BOSS FREED AS MURDER CHARGES DROPPED'. And the article went on to tell the story of how Kerry Casey, head of the notorious Casey empire, walked free from jail after a string of charges against herself and Danny were dropped by the Crown Office. It also had a few talking heads – a lawyer and a former prosecutor – asking how this could happen. Police were making no comment, and the Crown Office remained tight-lipped. But it was only when Kerry got towards the end of the story that she saw the lines: *The Post has begun a major investigation into the case. We have an exclusive story on the circumstances that led to Casey's arrest. Read tomorrow's* Post *for the truth behind the frame-up.* Kerry was surprised that they looked to be going with that story and not with the Fairhurst pictures she'd given them. The framed story was hard to prove without using names, so she wondered how they would do it. Her mobile rang and she could see Marty Kane's name on the screen.

'Marty,' Kerry said. 'How you doing?'

'How are *you* doing, Kerry?' he replied. 'Have you seen the *Post*?'

'Just reading it now,' she said. 'I didn't quite know what to expect, if I'm honest.'

There was a pause, and Kerry's gut told her Marty wasn't happy. He'd advised her not to go to the press with any story, but just to be glad she was free. But she hadn't listened.

'That's the problem, Kerry. When you go to the newspaper with a story, you really have no guarantees how it will turn out. They don't give you any editorial approval, so once you hand it over, it's out of your control. That's why I wasn't keen on it.'

Kerry let his words hang there for a moment. She knew Marty was too much of a decent guy to give her anything resembling a row, and he cared for her too much to say anything that might upset her. But the point was taken. He didn't think she should have done it.

'I know, Marty. I hear what you're saying,' she said. 'I'm a bit surprised the paper is going straight in tomorrow with the frame-up story. I did tell the reporter what happened and gave him the tapes of Lambie and Townsley, but he said he didn't think that was provable, because the newspaper can't actually speak to either of them. I was more interested in just dropping the bombshell of the Fairhurst tapes. I mean, that's just sitting there, easy to do. All they have to do is use the pictures and the film and ask themselves what is going on.'

After a long silence, Marty spoke.

'Yes. I agree with that. But I just think it was a bad idea to get involved with the newspapers.'

'I know you do, Marty. But Fairhurst tried to ruin my life. I can't forgive that, and he should pay for what he did.'

She heard Marty sigh, then he said, 'I know how you feel. But I worry that it might put you in danger. That's all.'

'I'm fine, Marty. I'm safe here at home. Whenever I go out, I'm with someone. I'm okay.' She changed the subject as she knew she would never get Marty's blessing for what she'd done. 'I went for a scan yesterday, and everything is looking great. The baby is going to be big.'

'That's good news then. And really that's why you should just take it easy in the next few weeks and enjoy this time. Just be glad you're where you are, Kerry.'

'I am, Marty. I will,' she said, thinking of Vinny.

'Okay. I've had a few calls from reporters from other newspapers this morning asking about this story, and what is coming tomorrow. So I've just said I have no idea, and that my client hasn't spoken to any newspaper. So let's keep it that way. I take it this reporter has agreed that nothing will be attributed to you?'

'Of course. I told him I don't want to be anywhere near it.'

'Let's hope he keeps his word. We'll talk tomorrow once the paper drops and we'll see what we are dealing with.' He paused. 'And please, slow down, relax and take care of yourself.'

'I will,' she said, as the line went dead.

It was late afternoon and Kerry was in the kitchen watching as Elsa cooked the meal for tonight's dinner. Sharon and Vic, as well as Jack and Danny were joining her for a celebratory dinner at the house. She'd invited Steven and his mother to join them as well. It was the first time she'd been around the table with everyone since she and Danny had been arrested. She'd spent last night at Danny's house having a quiet dinner, and it was the first time she'd really had a chance to talk to him about his experience inside. Apart from losing a little weight, he hadn't seemed fazed at all by it, and was quite buoyed up that he'd met up with people who were friends and family of old connections he'd had years ago. Kerry had joked to him that his stint on remand was a bit like summer camp. She had told Danny and Pat of her experience inside, and the sadness when Linda died, and of the girl Ash, who was now in rehab courtesy of the Caseys. Now she was looking forward to meeting Steven, the guy who had started the ball rolling to get her out of jail. She owed him a huge debt. The food was cooking away nicely and Kerry was about to go and get dressed when her mobile rang. Harry Foster's name came up.

'Kerry, sorry to trouble you. It's Harry,' he said.

'Yes. I see your name, Harry.' She was a little short as she'd had no conversation with him since the first time they met. She wanted to distance herself from him.

'I'm really sorry, Kerry, but would you have a few minutes to meet me? There's something really important I don't want to talk about over the phone.' He sounded a little edgy.

Kerry said nothing. She wasn't sure what to say here. What the hell was so important that he had to see her in person urgently?

'Well, it's a bit difficult at the moment. I'm busy tonight.' Silence.

'I understand. But it would only be a quick chat.'

She wanted to ask precisely what this was about, but she didn't want to say it on the phone, just in case she was being recorded. But she was curious. She wondered if he'd already started looking at the Fairhurst story and was ready to roll with it and needed her to answer a couple of questions. Perhaps they had already approached Fairhurst for comment. She didn't know, but she was curious enough to want to find out more.

'I don't know,' she said, checking her watch.

'It wouldn't be long.'

'Where are you?'

'I'm up in Garnet Street, off Sauchiehall Street. On the side street at the top of the steep hill. I could wait there for you.'

Kerry thought about it and if there was anything she was sure of it was that she shouldn't be doing this at short notice. But something about Harry didn't sound right. What if he was in some kind of trouble? If he was, it would have been her fault, even though she knew that wouldn't be the way he would look at it. He had been desperate to do this story, and his name would be on every reporter's lips for a long time to come.

'Okay. I'll see you. But ten minutes. That's all I can spare,' Kerry heard herself saying. She hung up.

Kerry picked up her phone and keyed in Jack's number. He answered in two rings, and when she told him about the call, he wasn't keen.

'I don't think you should go, Kerry. What if it's some kind of trap? It's a strange thing to do, isn't it? To just get in touch like this. I don't like the sound of it.'

Neither did she. But something compelled her to go.

'He's a newspaper reporter, Jack. He's not going to shoot me. I thought as long as we went with you and the driver it would be okay. It's the city centre and I wouldn't be out of anyone's sight.'

'Okay. I'll be there in five minutes.'

On the way up Charing Cross it was growing dark and the area was busy with traffic. They inched along then turned up to the street that ran parallel to Sauchiehall Street. At the top of the hill, just at the edge of Garnet Street, she saw Harry standing on the street, next to a car as though he had just climbed out and was waiting for her.

'That's him,' Kerry said. 'The reporter guy.'

Jack nodded to the driver to pull over. He pulled the car into the kerb and Kerry opened the door slowly. Harry looked pale and as she walked towards him she thought he was shaking a little. He looked jittery.

'Kerry, I'm sorry,' he said, by way of apology for pulling her out of her home.

Then it happened so quickly. Before she could answer, a shot was fired from somewhere. All she could see was the blood on the side of Harry's head and the stunned look as he fell to the ground. In a flash, Jack and the driver were out of the car and Jack rushed up and dived on Kerry, pinning her to the ground against the kerb. He looked around, the driver crouching at the side of his car, looking for a shooter. It seemed to have come from somewhere in the flats overlooking the street. Then another shot. It sounded like an engine backfiring, and then a figure came out from behind a hedgerow in the ground-floor garden. He fired a shot, and Kerry's driver fell over. Jack eased off Kerry and fired back. She lay, her face grazing the ground, her hands over her head, praying and terrified. From the corner of her eye she could see Harry lying there, a pool of blood trickling down the hill towards her. He was still moving though, his eyes wide open, and his lips seemed to be moving. He must have been forced to lure her up here where the gunmen were waiting. But how in the hell had they got to him so quickly? There was another shot, and as Jack keeled over beside her, she suddenly felt someone drag her by the ankles. Then a huge figure pulled her to her knees as a car screeched to a halt beside them. Before she could see who it was, she was punched hard on the side of the head and was losing consciousness as she was bundled into the back seat. The last thing she saw before she was slapped into oblivion, was someone going into her pocket and grabbing her mobile, smashing it against the window and throwing it out as the car sped away.

When she came to, the car was still moving, but this time slower, as though it was weaving its way through country lanes. Her head was thumping and she could taste blood in her mouth. Her first thought was of her baby and she reached down to feel the swell of her tummy. She opened one eye. It was pitch black outside, and somewhere a dog was barking. Then the car stopped. She could hear voices. Someone else was out there. Then she heard the Belfast accent.

'Bring her out.'

Her blood ran cold. The rear door of the car was pulled open and big hands reached in and roughly dragged her out.

'Please, I'm pregnant,' she pleaded.

They stood her up, propped her at the car as her legs buckled. In the darkness she saw someone in a black bala-clava step forward. He was so close she could smell his rancid sweat, and the alcohol on his breath. He put a gun to the side of her head. This was it. There was no way out of it. She was miles away from anywhere. Jack and the driver, even if they were alive, wouldn't have had a chance to phone anyone. She was going to die here, with her unborn baby in her stomach who never even had a chance to know how much she loved it. She thought of Vinny.

'This is what happens when you fuck with the big boys.'

The Belfast voice came from behind her, but she didn't dare move her head.

Then she heard the sudden blast of gunshot. But Kerry hadn't fallen down. Or had she? Was she already dead and in a place where a gun battle was raging? But there were lights somewhere in the distance. And again a sudden blast – more like a shotgun.

'Fuck!' The Belfast voice behind her. 'Let's get the fuck out of here. Shoot her.'

She closed her eyes tight, waiting. But another blast and the masked man fell at her knees. With every fibre of her strength she threw herself onto the ground and into a ditch, face down in the mud. She heard muffled voices and a car roar off. Then suddenly more lights in the distance and what sounded like a tractor. She was dizzy, but she felt herself being picked up and placed on something. She was on a bumpy road in the back of a tractor in a daze. Strong arms carried her into a house, and she saw a woman rushing towards her. Before she passed out, Kerry was conscious that water was running down her legs.

'Oh Jesus, Peter. The girl's in labour. Phone an ambulance.'

When Kerry awoke she felt sweat running down her back and the bed was soaked. For a moment she had no idea where she was. She could see daylight through vertical blinds. What had happened? Then it came to her. The baby. She suddenly realised she was in a hospital. Her head and neck ached as she turned to the side and saw she was hooked up to a machine making beeping noises. Her hand automatically went to her stomach, but it felt different, fleshy and no hardness. Empty. She turned her head to the other side. But there was no baby. *Where's my baby?* The sob came from somewhere deep in her soul, up through her gut and into her throat, but when she opened her mouth nothing came out. She couldn't catch her breath. Then she wailed, a primal scream, like a wild animal, lost and separated from its young.

CHAPTER THIRTY-THREE

Jake Cahill sat in the hospital café alone. He'd been there through the night and much of the morning, him and Sullivan taking turns to sit by Vinny's bedside. Jake had switched off his mobile after they'd been picked up from Malaga harbour by armed guards in a private ambulance, and once he'd made sure Mateo had been taken safely to his family, the concern that someone had caught up with them and was waiting to take potshots had faded the closer they got to Malaga, when he knew his boys would be lined up ready to take anyone on. His big worry had been that Vinny didn't look as though he was going to make it. He'd agonised as Vinny had drifted in and out of consciousness, his body going into spasms, the medic telling him that if they didn't get him into hospital soon he would be dead in a couple of hours. Jake had prayed for the first time in a very long time, because he didn't know how he was going to tell Kerry. He knew he had done everything he could, but Vinny had been weak and fading fast. As they'd got to the harbour and into the ambulance his heart had failed and they'd put the defibrillator paddles on him to bring him back. Sullivan had almost been in tears, holding his mate's hand, the expression in his eyes showing that he was thinking about his own stupid indiscretion with the bent Spanish female cop, and how that might have cost Vinny his life. By the time they got into hospital, Vinny had come back from the dead and was rushed to the operating theatre, but sepsis had set in and his system was beginning to shut down. It was now a case of waiting and hoping.

Sitting in the hospital café, Jake switched on his mobile and listened to a message from Kerry asking him to please call her. Then a message from Danny. He couldn't keep this up. Sooner or later he was going to have to tell them. He sipped his black coffee, wincing at the taste but at least it was keeping him up. Then he looked across the room as Sullivan came rushing in. Christ! He looked ashen. Jake stood up.

'He's come round,' Sullivan said, almost in tears. 'He's conscious.'

'Fuck!' Jake said. 'I thought the way you came running in that it was all over.' He shook head. 'Jesus! Let's go.'

As they walked briskly along the hospital corridor, Sullivan turned to him.

'He's going to be okay, Jake. He's asking for Kerry. That was the first thing he said after he recognised me. He's all right!' His eyes were filling with tears.

'What a fucking relief,' Jake said, surprised at how emotional he felt. 'I didn't know how I was going to tell her. It would have broken my heart. I've known Kerry since she was a kid.'

They walked along and into the room as a nurse was fussing round, checking his monitor and paraphernalia. Jake went across to the bed.

'Hey, hard man! You made it! You are one sight for sore eyes.' He squeezed Vinny's shoulder as he looked up, his eyes drowsy.

There was a bandage like a boxing glove on his hand.

'I need to talk to Kerry.' Vinny's voice was thick from drugs, barely audible.

Jake looked at him and nodded. He turned to Sullivan.

'I'll go outside and make a call. See if I can get hold of her.'

Jake knew that Kerry had been arrested and was in jail on remand along with Danny. But he purposely hadn't called anyone in the past couple of weeks. Christ! Vinny wouldn't know about Kerry's arrest, and this certainly was not the time to tell him. He walked out of the automatic doors exiting the hospital and took his phone out of his jacket pocket. He scrolled down until he saw Danny's name, then pushed the key. Danny answered after three rings.

'Jake! Christ, man! Been trying to get you for a few days.'

'I had to be off the grid,' he said. 'But mission accomplished, I've got Vinny.'

'Fuck! Jesus, man! Thank fuck for that. Is he okay?'

'He's alive. But not in great shape. Cunts cut his finger off and left it to fester. He's got sepsis. Just got to him in time.'

'Bastards. Is he going to be all right?'

'I think so. He's just regained consciousness. Wants to talk to Kerry. But I haven't even told him about her being in jail. Thought it might not be the best time.'

Jake listened, waiting for Danny to speak, and his hackles were up when the silence went on more than a few seconds.

'Jack! What's up?'

Again the silence.

'Christ, Jake. It's Kerry. She got out of jail a few days ago. All charges dropped. Will explain later. But there was a fucking ambush in the city centre. Jack got shot in the shoulder, but he's all right. Driver took a bullet too, but they're both all right. It was a set-up. But some fuckers kidnapped Kerry. She's in hospital.'

'Oh fuck! Is she okay? The baby?'

Silence.

'Oh no, Danny. Don't tell us that. Please tell me her baby is okay.'

Jake listened as Danny spoke, the croak in his voice.

'The baby might not make it. It's not looking good. She went into labour a bit early – in some fucking farmland outside Glasgow where these cunts took her to execute her. Belfast mob.'

Jake felt a surge of emotion that almost brought tears to his eyes. 'Bastards! I'll cut their fucking throats. Every one of them.'

'We're looking for them. But the baby – it's a wee boy – is in an incubator, all hooked up to a breathing machine and stuff. They're fighting to save him. I'm outside the hospital now. Pat's inside with Kerry. You can imagine the fucking state of the girl.'

'Jesus! But they can do all sorts of things these days with wee babies that are born too soon.'

After a long moment, Danny said, 'Aye. I know. We're all praying, mate. But I don't know if any fucker's listening.'

'What am I going to tell Vinny? He just woke up from being out since we got here last night, and the first thing he said is he needs to speak to Kerry. What the fuck am I going to tell him, Danny?'

He heard Danny push out a sigh.

'Christ knows. But we'll have to tell him something. He won't even know she was in the jail, so maybe you can tell him that part, and that she's in jail on remand, but that we're trying to get her out.' He paused. 'Is Vinny able to travel? I mean, when will he be able to get out of there and get home?'

'I don't know. He just came around. They'll be blasting him with intravenous antibiotics to kill the infection, but if that's the extent of it, then he might be able to leave in a day or so. I don't know. I'll have to ask the docs.'

'We need to get him home as soon as possible. We can't risk telling Kerry he's been found and he's alive. She'll want to talk to him, and she'll have to tell him about the baby. I don't think it's a good idea at the moment for him to be told. I mean the wee thing might not even make it through the day. The surgeon says if he gets through the next forty-eight hours there's a good chance he might make it.'

'So I'll just tell him that she's in jail, but hopefully she might get released in a few days?'

'Yeah. You're going to have to do that.'

Jake sighed, his heart sinking, as he thought of Kerry, of the little girl he had known since she was a kid, how she adored her father and was smart as a whip.

'He'll make it, Jack. He's a Casey.'

'I hope so. Let me know how you get on with Vinny and when you talk to the docs. But tell them he needs to get home.'

Jake stood gazing at the people coming in and leaving the hospital. He had to bring Vinny home safely to Kerry. Then there would be a reckoning for the fuckers who did this.

Jake went back into the hospital and along the corridor to where Vinny was being held in a private room. As he approached, the door opened and a tall middle-aged doctor in a white coat came out. He'd seen him when they'd arrived at the accident and emergency area, and he'd told Jake and

Sullivan that Vinny would be taken straight to surgery. The doctor pulled back his lips in a sympathetic smile to Jake.

'How is Vinny?' Jake asked. 'Is he going to be okay?'

For a moment the doctor didn't speak, but put his hand behind his back and pulled the door closed. He ushered Jake a few feet along the corridor.

'He was very sick when he came here, Mr er . . .'

'Jake,' he said. 'Jake Cahill.'

'Jake,' the doctor said. 'We almost lost him by the time we got him into theatre. The sepsis, you know? The poison of the blood?' Jake was glad the doctor's English was good. 'He went into cardiac arrest and we had to bring him back with the paddles, even before we operated.'

Jake nodded, grim faced, but said nothing. The doctor demonstrated with his hand.

'The operation on the hand. It was tricky. Because although only half the index finger was cut off, the poison had set in, and we had to remove all of the finger almost to the knuckle. We saved the knuckle as that is an important part, even without the finger.'

Jake didn't really know what to say.

'He had lost a lot of blood and was in septic shock, as I'm sure you saw.' The doctor paused. 'But the operation went well and the good news is that he is come back now and is conscious. He is talking and he is good, but obviously he is under a lot of heavy morphine painkilling drugs. He will be in pain for a long time.'

Jake shuffled his feet.

'When do you think I will be able to take him home, doctor? To Scotland? His family need to see him.'

The doctor took a deep breath and puffed his cheeks.

'If he is a quick healer, if he improves a lot, then he can go home. Right now he is sedated and just been operated on, so it is very early.'

Jake was already thinking ahead.

'But if the infection is going, then perhaps we can get him home and he can be in a hospital in the UK?'

The doctor gave him a long look.

'Can his family not come here to see him in Spain?'

Jake shook his head. 'No. I'm afraid his girlfriend has been in an accident, and is also in hospital. So she can't travel. I can't tell Vinny that. But I want to get him home.'

The doctor stood for a moment and Jake could see him studying his face.

'Who does such a thing to a man like this? I mean, who cuts a finger off?' The doc raised his hands a little in gesture of frustration. 'Is like a Mafia or something.'

Jake grimaced. 'Vinny is an undercover policeman. Bad people are after him.'

'I know he is a British policeman. I saw in his records.' He shook his head. 'Very dangerous people out there.'

'Yes. That's why I want him out of Spain and home to his family as soon as we can.'

The doctor nodded slowly.

'I understand. I will do my best for him. But you have to give him at least twenty-four hours to see if there is any reaction or lapse in his condition. These are crucial hours after surgery. If things are starting to get back to a little normal, then we will see.'

'Thank you, doctor.'

As he turned to walk away, the doctor said, 'You must be careful out there. Many bad people.'

'Of course,' Jake said, then he muttered under his breath, 'They'll get their day.'

He watched as the doctor walked briskly down the corridor then turned left out of sight.

CHAPTER THIRTY-FOUR

The nurse gently eased Kerry forward on the bed and put the pillow behind her to keep her upright. Just the smallest physical movement like that made her feel as though she'd walked a mile. She had never known exhaustion like she had felt over the last twenty-four hours. In fact she wasn't sure how many hours it had been, twenty-four, thirty-six . . . All she knew was that her baby was not by her side in a little perspex cot the way all the other babies were in the neonatal ward at the Glasgow maternity hospital. When she'd come to, whenever it was, she had gone into some kind of meltdown and passed out as she heard herself scream. She had vague recollections of the nurses around her, calming her and stroking her head, and a young doctor looking at her as they checked her vitals. Then she must have slept again for she dreamed she was in a park somewhere on a summer's day on a bench with her mother by her side. In front of her was a pram where her little baby lay snuggled and fast asleep. There was a stiff breeze sending petals from the cherry blossom trees behind them cascading down and making a soft pink path at their feet. She had never felt warmth like this in all her life as she sat with her mother holding her hand and telling her not to worry, that everything would be fine. But in her dream Kerry wondered why her mother was saying not to worry, because she had nothing to worry about. She was here with her mother, and her sleeping baby, safe in her pram. Then she sat forward and looked in the pram, but there was nothing there. No baby. Just an empty pram with blue fluffy covers and a small teddy bear with ink-black eyes staring up at her. She must have writhed and screamed in her sleep, because when she woke up, the nurses were round her bed again, soothing her, telling her everything would be fine. But once she was fully awake, she looked at their soft expressions and she knew everything would not be fine. The middle-aged paediatrician who had come in to see her yesterday gently took her hand and told her what had happened. Her little baby was struggling to survive, but they were doing everything they could. He had just come too early, she told her, with the trauma she understood that Kerry had suffered. In the end, the baby had had to be born by caesarean section, as it had got into difficulty and they couldn't detect a heartbeat during the panic rush of labour. She had been unconscious when her baby was born. When the paediatrician had come in to tell her that she had a little boy, who was fighting like a champ, Kerry had listened to the soft tones of her voice, tears streaming down her face, dripping off her chin. All this time she had waited. All these years of hoping and thinking she would never have a child, and now this. And no Vinny. She felt lost and helpless and completely abandoned. For hours afterwards she lay in the room, unable to make sense of it all, but slowly she began to gain strength and she had no idea where it came from. The midwives had told her she could visit her baby just to see how he was doing, but it was very early and too soon to say how things would progress. But so far, he was still fighting.

Now, as she sat up on the bed, the nurses eased her onto her feet, then they helped her into the wheelchair. She felt like an old, frail woman as they wheeled her out of her single room and past the other rooms where she couldn't help but notice that the new mums had their babies by their side and that some were breastfeeding. Kerry bit her lip and swallowed hard. She was going to see her baby boy. All was not lost, and it would not be lost until his last breath had been taken. She sniffed back tears as they entered the closed doors of the neonatal intensive care unit. It was warm and stuffy and the silence was broken only by the buzz and ping of alarms going off on the six or seven cots dotted around the room. It looked like some kind of weird scientific experiment, and she had to peer into the cots to see if there were any babies in them at all, because all she could see was equipment and oxygen masks and tubes and wires. She was wheeled along past two cots until she got to the one at the window.

'There's your little guy,' the midwife said, pushing her up close to the cot. 'There's the wee man.'

Kerry's eyes homed in on the tiny pink figure in the cot, his little tummy puffing in and out in time to the beeps of the machine, and in that single moment she was overwhelmed by a love she could never have believed would have been possible for another person. She sniffed back tears.

'He's tiny,' she croaked. 'Look at him. He's just a wee soul. Look at his fingers! And his feet! Oh God, please don't take him from me! Please, God!'

'Here.' The nurse pointed to two holes in the cot. 'You can put your hand into the gloves and touch him. Just for a moment.'

Kerry slipped her hand inside the socket and touched the warm little body of her baby boy. Her son. She could barely see his face for the tubes and the tapes and the wires and the helmet that was breathing for him. But this was her son. Again, the tears came as she thought of her mother, of her father, and how they would have loved this moment. And Vinny. Where was Vinny? He had to come back to her to see what he had here. She swallowed her tears and eased her hand back out. Then she sat for a few moments just gazing at him, engrossed in his skin and the silky, downy hair covering his body. She looked up at the nurses.

'Is he doing okay?'

The nurse smiled down.

'He's doing the best he can. Every hour of every day is crucial. And this wee fella looks like he's up for the fight.' She pointed to the monitors. 'His blood oxygen is getting better and the tests we've done are still being looked at. He was very early, as you know, but you got to the hospital in the nick of time.'

'Will he make it?' Kerry knew they wouldn't answer, but she wanted someone to give her more hope. 'I mean, other babies born early survive, don't they?'

'Of course. And younger too.' She paused. 'As I said, every hour is a bonus. He's got a bit to go before he's out of the woods. Next two days are crucial. So we'll just wait and watch.' She took hold of the back of the wheelchair. 'Let's get you back to your room. You need to rest, Kerry. You've been through a lot.'

'Thank you,' Kerry said, sniffing. 'Thank you for bringing me here. And for everything.'

They wheeled her back along the corridor towards her room as she wiped tears from her cheeks with the back of her hands. Then they helped her get back into bed and puffed up her pillows. She was exhausted. She closed her eyes, and the image she could see behind them was her little son, all pink and soft and breathing in and out. It was a picture she would carry in her head for ever. She drifted off to sleep.

CHAPTER THIRTY-FIVE

Jake knew Vinny would be anxiously waiting for his return to ask him about Kerry. He braced himself as he walked back towards his room, and hoped to Christ his face didn't give the truth away. He had to make sure it didn't. When he opened the door he was glad to see Vinny propped up and sipping some kind of juice through a straw in a plastic tumbler. Sullivan sat by his bedside.

'You're looking well, Vinny,' Jake said, as chipper as he could. 'Great to see you sitting up like that. Honest to God, man, it was hard going yesterday, so you're a hundred per cent better from then.'

'I'm feeling okay. Just desperate to get out of here.' He glanced at his bandaged hand. 'Did you manage to get hold of Kerry?'

Vinny took a slow breath and pulled up a plastic chair on the other side of the bed from where Sullivan sat.

'Well. No. Not exactly.'

Vinny's eyes screwed up, confused.

'What does that mean?' Then he looked worried. 'Is something wrong?'

'Look, Vinny. While me and Sullivan were looking all over for you, we . . . well I . . . have been out of contact with anyone back in Glasgow. That's how I work, and my only priority was to find you and bring you home. That was my instruction from Kerry.' He paused to see how Vinny was taking this.

'Yeah. I see that. And I'll never be able to thank you – and Sully – enough for saving my life. But have you been able to tell Kerry I'm okay?'

'That's what I was coming to,' Jake said. 'You see, while I've been out of touch, there's been a big development over there. Kerry and Danny are in jail.'

'What?' Vinny interrupted. 'Jail? What for? Is she all right? The baby?'

'Kerry's on remand,' Jake said. 'They were set up by someone – framed – for a murder and drugs and weapons haul. Total set-up. But the way it was done it looked open and shut. But Marty Kane is working on it, and we're hoping she will be out very soon.'

'Fuck me! Who the hell set them up? What are the cops saying?' He turned to Sullivan. 'You can make a few calls, mate – see what's going on.'

Sullivan nodded. 'I will.' He stood up and took his phone out of his pocket.

At that moment a nurse came into the room and glanced at the monitor Vinny was hooked up to. She peered at the readings, then at Jake and Sullivan.

'You can leave please for a moment. I need to check the patient.'

'Is he all right?' Sullivan asked.

'*Si*. But the blood pressure and heartbeat is up.' She pointed to the door. 'Please. Let me check things.'

Her timing was perfect as far as Jake was concerned, and he ushered Sullivan out of the door. As they walked down the corridor he turned to him.

'That nurse couldn't have timed that any better. Fuck!'

'What? What do you mean? Were you lying your arse off in there?'

'I was. Did it show?'

'I was suspicious, but Vinny doesn't know you so he probably wasn't. So what's up?'

Jake stopped and shook his head.

'It's all pretty much fucked up back in Glasgow. The bit about Kerry and Danny being banged up is true – well it was until three days ago. They were framed, as you know. But they've been out for a few days – all charges dropped – and then Kerry goes to meet someone and gets fucking kidnapped. Beaten up. Dumped in the countryside. Remember, she's well on in her pregnancy. So she goes into labour and the fucking baby is born and is now fighting for its wee life.'

'Oh, fuck!'

'Exactly. So I was just talking to Danny when I was outside and he told me not to tell Vinny what had happened – just to say that she was in jail. That would be easier for him to take rather than being told his baby might not make it.'

'Christ, man, this is terrible. You were right though. It's not a good time to tell Vinny that kind of news. Did you see his blood pressure and heart rate shot up just telling him that Kerry was in jail? We've got to keep that news from him.'

'We need to get him home, pronto.'

'I know. But we need to make sure for the moment he doesn't see any British newspapers. I imagine there will have been something in them about Kerry getting out of jail and charged dropped. If he sees that he'll know we've been lying.'

'I know. That's why we need to move fast. I spoke to the surgeon a little while ago and he said he was doing well but it might be a couple of days before he can look at getting out. But it needs to be sooner than that. I want us out of here tomorrow.' He paused, looked around. 'Even if we have to fucking smuggle him out.'

'Christ, Jake. That could be well dodgy, and dangerous.'

Jake looked at him. 'Like nothing we've done in the last twenty-four hours has been dodgy or dangerous?'

'Yeah. But we need to make sure he's strong enough to be out and to travel.'

'We'll see by the end of the day,' Jake said. 'But I'm booking flights for tomorrow afternoon. We have to get him home. Kerry needs him.'

The door opened and the nurse came back out.

'You can go in now. He is okay.'

They both nodded in thanks and went back into the room.

'Did you talk to anybody, Sully?' Vinny asked as soon as they came in.

'Can't get a hold of anyone at the moment, mate. But I'll keep trying. Anyway. Thing is to get you better and get out of here. You'll see Kerry soon enough.'

'I want out of here tomorrow or the next day at the latest,' Vinny said, shifting in the bed. 'I'm fine now. The painkillers will keep me going till I get home.' He turned to Jake. 'What do you think, Jake? Did you talk to the doctor or anything?'

'I bumped into him a little while ago and we talked. He said you were doing well, and that the antibiotics were killing the infection. But he said you've been very ill. Nearly lost you.'

'Yeah yeah,' Vinny said, impatient. 'I know it was bad. But I'm getting better. And I don't want to be stuck in here. Did he say when I can get out?'

'He said maybe a couple of days.'

'No.' Vinny shook his head. 'That's too long. Listen, guys. Check out what medication I'm on here and go to the *farmacia.* You can buy just about anything over the counter in Spain. Get me enough painkillers and antibiotics to do me till I get to Glasgow. I want out of here tomorrow.' He turned to Jake. 'Can you organise that, Jake? Please? I need to see Kerry.'

Jake nodded slowly. 'Don't worry, son. We'll get you home.'

Jake was glad when his mobile shuddered in his jeans pocket and he was able to get away from this. He pulled it out and could see Tommy's name on the screen. He glanced at Sullivan.

'I need to go and take this call,' he said, as he turned and left the room.

Outside in the foreground of the hospital, Jake listened as Tommy spoke.

'Howsit goin', Jake? How's the boy Vinny? Did he make it? He looked well fucked.'

'He did. It was touch and go. And by all accounts they nearly lost him in the emergency room at the hospital. But he's pulled through. Lost a finger and had sepsis, but he's alive. I'm at the hospital now, and was just with him.' He paused, looked out across the pale grey sky. 'To be honest I've never been as glad to see someone wake up as I was when he came to.'

'Great stuff, Jake. Thank fuck for that.' There was a moment's pause, then Tommy went on. 'Anyway, reason

I'm phoning you. You know these fuckers who were shooting at us back at the harbour?'

'Yeah?' Jake said hoping to Christ he wasn't about to say they were coming after them.

'Well, we downed two of them on the spot, and took another two with us. We slapped them around a bit and we've still got them. What do you want me to do with them?'

Jake was delighted to hear that.

'Did you get anything out of it? Any reason why they would kidnap Vinny? Or who was behind it?'

'A bit,' Tommy said. 'It was the Colombians for sure. And one of the fuckers said something about a Spanish cop. Not sure what that means, but sounds like someone was working for them – like a cop or something. Fuck me!'

'Yeah. That sounds about right,' Jake said. 'You got any name or anything like that? I mean of the Colombian they're working for?'

'Yep. They told us a name, Diego Lopez – whether it's true or not I don't know – but they said where we could find him. It's out past Estepona. Near Puerta de la Duquessa – down that way.'

'What – a house or what?'

'Aye. A villa. But there's a party tonight. In San Pedro, nearby. It's an anniversary party for him and his wife or something. That's as much as they said. But they told us where.'

'Christ! Some fucking foot soldiers they are. So much for any *omertà*!' he joked. 'He actually told you where the party is?'

'Yeah. Couldn't believe it myself. Unless he's bullshitting.'

Jake looked at his watch.

'Only one way to find out.'

CHAPTER THIRTY-SIX

Jake sat in the pavement café in San Pedro, sipping a glass of cold beer and watching the people arrive at La Bodega restaurant across the street. From what he could see, it looked like the information given to Tommy was bang on the money, because the people going into the restaurant looked as though they were there for a celebration. Some carried gift bags and floral arrangements. The women were dressed up and the men in suits or smart casual. Jake clocked that some of the men just had a look about them. You could dress them up in the best of clothes, but underneath they were thugs. He noted that some of the arrivals had a bulge in the back of their jackets, which meant they must be carrying.

'So what are you thinking, Jake? How we going to do this?'

Tommy sat opposite him next to Bonzo. The guys they'd ambushed at the harbour had given Tommy a picture of the Colombian he'd named, so they knew who they were looking for.

'We'll wait to see if our man comes and how many are covering him,' Jake said. 'But you'll have noticed that plenty of these bastards are carrying.'

Tommy nodded. He'd nipped into the restaurant a couple of hours ago on a recce, so they both knew where the top table was situated, where the band was, and he'd sneaked a photo on his mobile he could show to Jake. He'd also noted there was a back door entrance next to the gents' toilet, so they could make some kind of plan to get all of them inside.

'Look.' Jake pointed to the big black Merc with the blacked-out windows gliding along the street. 'This could be them.'

The three of them watched as the car pulled into the kerb outside the restaurant, and the driver, a huge mountain of a guy, got out and opened the door. They saw a man get out of the back seat and stand for a moment while a woman followed him. As the man stood, he glanced around as another car pulled up and the doors opened simultaneously and four thickset men got out. Jake thought they looked like Colombians. He watched the way the main man preened himself, his slicked back hair, his blue shiny suit and white open-neck shirt. He was short and swarthy-looking.

'That's our man. That'll be Diego,' Jake said.

The others nodded but said nothing.

By the time darkness was falling, the music from La Bodega was getting louder, and there was the sound of clapping and cheering. Perhaps the Colombian was making his anniversary speech. They could see two men posted outside. Earlier they had been standing either side of the door, but now that everyone was inside, they seemed more relaxed, and were sitting at a table sipping beer. The music came to a stop, and then struck up again and everyone was cheering and clapping. *The anniversary waltz,* Jake was thinking. *Little prick.*

'Okay, lads,' he said, finishing his beer. 'Let's move. Just the way we discussed it earlier. You all right?'

'Sound,' Tommy said, and Bonzo nodded.

Jake waited until Tommy and Bonzo crossed the street and went in the opposite direction of the bar for a couple of hundred yards, then saw them coming back into sight. But from where the minders were sat, his boys were shaded by the trees on the pavement, so he hoped they might not be able to see them. Then they disappeared. Jake got to his feet, and squared his shoulders. He put his hand inside his jacket and could feel the Glock in his holster. He walked across the street towards the restaurant, just as a couple of guests had come out to smoke a cigarette in the covered patio area. One of the minders started chatting to an attractive dark-haired woman in a figure-hugging dress split to her thigh. Jake took the opportunity of the distraction to slip past them and inside the restaurant. He knew he wouldn't have long so he had to quickly make sure that he'd clocked the boss as his eyes roved the busy room. He found him, going from table to table, chatting and glad-handing guests who exchanged hugs and handshakes.

Moments later it happened. Boom! The explosion had been timed to go off right at that moment in the old Ford Fiesta that Tommy had parked twenty yards away on a patch of waste ground. It was far enough away from the restaurant and bars not to kill anyone but close enough to make a big enough noise and create panic that would bring everyone running. And it did. Inside, guests dived under tables and ran for cover to the back of the room. The minders came in, guns raised, and scanned the place. But Diego Lopez was nowhere to be seen. Then Jake spotted him below a table near where the band was. He dived to the floor himself and crawled close to him. He knew he wouldn't know who he was and would presume he was the husband of a friend. As Jake crawled close, they came face to face, and he met the Colombian's eyes.

'My friend Vinny,' he said.

The Colombian's eyes widened in terror as he recognised that this man wasn't a guest. Jake pushed the Glock to the side of his neck and fired. In the noise and confusion nobody even noticed him as he got to his feet, went out of the back door and walked briskly up the street. Two minders were on the ground outside the back door, blood pumping out where Tommy and Bonzo had shot them. Job done.

On the way back to the meeting point, he took out his phone and pushed the key for Party Pam.

'Jake. You okay? I've been worried about you.'

Jake was cool and calm as only he could be after killing someone.

'I'm good, Pam,' he said. 'Listen. I'm probably going to the UK tomorrow, so how about you call up these bastards who are extorting you and get them to come to your bar and tell them you're signing over the whole shooting match to them?'

'Jesus, Jake,' she said. 'You mean . . . Sign it over? My bar?'

'No, Pam. I mean just *tell* them you're going to sign it over. Leave the rest to me.'

Silence. And Jake knew she was processing the info and hoped she could go through with it.

'Can you do that, Pam?'

'Yes. I'll do it.'

'Okay. Make the meet in the morning – about eleven. I've got things to do after that.'

He hung up. Then he called Tommy.

'Tommy. You free tomorrow morning?'

'Sure, Jake. What's the craic?'

'Bit of business.'

He told them where and when to meet him.

'What about these two fuckers from the harbour shoot-out though?'

'Dump them somewhere tonight.'

'Will do.'

Before he'd gone to bed last night, Jake had booked flights for himself, Vinny and Sullivan from Malaga airport for the following afternoon. He'd phoned Sullivan and told him, and asked him to speak to the consultant and plead with him to let Vinny out. He knew Vinny would be echoing that when he spoke to his doctor himself, so given that he seemed to be improving as the day went on, Jake was hoping he wouldn't have to smuggle him out of hospital. Because right now, he had enough stress on his plate, as he sat in Pam's apartment above the bar. He'd got there early in the morning, so he could lay out the plan with Pam before she went downstairs to open up and met the Spanish thugs who were thinking they were coming to push her out of the place she'd built up for fifteen years. Pam had been understandably nervous, but over breakfast and coffee, Jake had explained to her that all she had to do was stick to the script. She already had the official papers they'd hand delivered to her weeks ago telling her that she had to sign. All you have to do, Jake had told her, is look worried and heartbroken, and tell them you'll sign on the dotted line, that you just want to start a new life. We will do the rest when the time is right. He told her to ring his mobile twice, for the signal that it was about to happen. Then he and the boys and would pounce. He watched from the kitchen window that backed onto the alley behind the bar, and he could see Tommy and Bonzo arrive, as arranged. They entered through the door Pam had left ajar, and came upstairs. Jake was waiting for them at the top of the landing.

'All right, lads?'

'Aye,' Tommy said. 'All good here.'

'Did you get rid of these fuckers from the harbour last night?'

Tommy glanced at Bonzo who nodded.

'Yep. Fish food by now. Down off the coast a bit. I know the spot. It'll be months before what's left of them ever washes up.'

'Perfect,' Jake said. 'In you come, guys. Coffee's ready.'

They sat in the kitchen drinking coffee and keeping a watchful eye on any unusual cars or arrivals outside the bar.

'So these fuckwits, Jake,' Tommy said. 'Are they no marks? Spanish thugs? Not connected?'

'As far as I can gather they are local gangsters who own this area and operate a protection racket. A couple of the bar owners and the shops nearby told me they have to pay a few hundred to them every week if they want to stay in business. Fucking hooligans.'

Tommy nodded and they sat listening to the noise from the open windows of the cafés and traffic below. Then from the edge of the window looking onto the main street, Jake could see the big four-by-four pull into the kerb. A squat driver got out and another tall, skinny guy got out from the passenger seat. The driver opened the rear door, and the man in the back stepped out. He wore khaki trousers, moccasin leather shoes and a pale blue open-neck shirt. He stood for a moment, hands in the pocket of his suede bomber jacket as he glanced around the area. Then they made their way to the door of the bar.

'That's our men gone in,' Jake said. 'Three of them. They'll all be carrying. So be careful.'

'Will there be anyone else in the bar?' Tommy asked.

'No,' Jake said. 'Not at this time. Pam just left the shutters half open so they could come in, but it doesn't open to customers for another hour. So we've got time.'

The minutes ticked past and Jake checked his watch again. They'd been inside now for nearly five minutes. He hoped Pam was okay and was beginning to feel a bit edgy. Then his phone rang on the table. Two rings. Both Tommy and Bonzo looked at Jake. He picked up his phone as it rang off.

'Right, lads. Game on.'

Carefully, silently, the three of them crept down the stairs that led from the flat to the back alley. At the foot of the stairs, Jake jerked his head towards the gap in the fire exit door. He was glad it was still open, as that meant that the thick bastards inside were so cocky that they didn't even think they had to check the place out. Perfect. That gave him the element of surprise. Jake pointed his finger to his chest, indicating he would go first, then made a gesture with both hands, which he knew they would understand, meaning they should immediately follow him. Tommy and Bonzo stood, guns in their hands. Jake took out his weapon and held it casually in his hand, dropped behind his back. He peered through the gap in the door and could see the two minders sitting on bar stools a few feet away from where Pam was behind the bar, leaning and pointing to the document that was placed on the bar. The main man appeared to be reading it. He could see Pam was sniffing back tears. So far so good. Then Jake slipped inside the bar, and the minders turned around.

'Oh, sorry. Bar not open yet?' he asked, feigning surprise.

Before Pam had a chance to answer, Jake raised his gun and strode across the room.

'The first fucker to move gets this.'

The minders were so startled they didn't even have time to get off their bar stools before Tommy and Bonzo piled in and the three of them spread out, making a semicircle that nobody was going to escape from. The main man glared at Pam. He shook his head and waved a finger.

'This not clever, Pam.' He tutted.

In a few strides, Jake was on him, the gun pushed into the side of his head.

'No,' Jake said. 'You not clever, you fucking prick.'

The man put his hands up in submission.

'Please. I promise. We only want to do business here with Miss Pam.'

That brought a swift pistol whip on the side of his cheek from Jake and he tottered on his stool as though he was dizzy. Blood oozed from the cut above his eyebrow.

'The kind of business that involves beating Pam up?' Jake grabbed his chin and turned his face towards Pam.

Again the man put his hands up.

'Please. Is no my fault. I tell them no hurt anyone. My boys. They made a mistake.'

He shot a pleading glance at Pam, as if he was hoping she would help him. She glared right through him.

'Get down!' Jake said, gesturing for him to get off the stool. Then he turned to the others. 'All of you.'

Tommy and Bonzo kept their guns on the other two as they went into their jackets, pulled out their weapons and slid them along the bar, far enough away. Jake did the same with the main man.

'Please, don't kill me, man,' the main guy pleaded. 'I have children. Please. I do anything. I pay you.'

'Nobody wants your fucking money,' Jake said. 'Your money is no good here, and you were told that months ago. But you kept coming back. You do it all along the streets here.' He leant closer to his face. 'You are filth. A parasite on these people who only want to earn a living. Who do you work for?' he rasped.

'Nobody,' he said. 'I the boss. We only work together. But please. I sorry. No more. Not here. Not anywhere.'

There was silence, the air crackling with tension.

'Aye. You'll move somewhere else. Make other people's lives a misery.'

'No, no. Please. Is finish, I promise.'

Jake glanced at Tommy and Bonzo and could see the colour had drained from the faces of both minders. They knew how these things worked. When the talking stopped they knew they were waiting for a bullet. Jake looked at Tommy. Then he turned to the main man. He lowered his gun, held it at close range to his knee and fired. The man let out a high-pitched squeal as he buckled to the ground. He lay bleeding in agony. Then Tommy and Bonzo kneecapped the minders, and they buckled, their agonising screams filling the stillness of the empty bar. Then Jake went forward and aimed the gun at the main man's chest. He writhed on the ground, his hands up for protection as though that would save him.

'Please. Please. My children.'

Jake looked at Pam, whose hand was at her mouth, shocked by what she was seeing. Then he saw her slowly shake her head. Enough. Jake turned to the main man.

'You listen to me, you *coño*,' he spat. 'Today you live. But you come back here one time, or any of your fucking thugs, and you are dead. From now on. Every time you take a step, you will limp and you will remember this moment. You understand?'

'Yes, yes . . . please. I understand.' He was sobbing now, blood from his knee on his hands where he was pressing on the injury as though trying to hold it together. 'I remember. I'm sorry. *Los siento*, Pam. *Los siento*.'

Jake moved away from them and beckoned Pam to the other end of the bar. She had tears in her eyes and her hands were shaking uncontrollably.

'Christ, Jake!' she said. 'I don't know what to say.'

Jake took a breath and reached across and touched her hand.

'Don't say anything. The boys will clean this up. They'll dump them somewhere, and drive their car out of the way.' He paused, half smiled. 'You did good, Pam.'

She stood, biting her lip. 'I was so scared.'

'Not any more,' he said.

They stood that way for a long moment, and Jake felt anger that she'd been made to feel vulnerable and that she'd had to put up with so much. A decent good woman.

'Listen, Pam, I've got to go back to the UK tonight. But I'll be back soon. This is all behind you now.' He looked around him. 'Maybe best to close the bar for another day and take a breather.'

He could see the look in her eye, the sarcastic twinkle that always attracted him to the tough-talking sassy woman. That was more like it.

'A breather?' She shook her head.

Jake turned to his men.

'Guys. Can you sort this pronto and give me a shout when it's done? I'm on a flight out later, so I need to square up with you before I go.'

'No worries, Jake.'

He went over to them, shook their hands and walked out of the bar into the bright sunlight.

CHAPTER THIRTY-SEVEN

Kerry listened and tried to concentrate on the words the paediatric consultant was telling her. But she only wanted to hear hope, not the string of complications and difficulties that her baby son might suffer. Just tell me if he's still alive, she wanted to ask. Will he still be alive tomorrow? Can I hold him? But in the pit of her stomach was the agonising feeling that he was preparing the ground to tell her that her baby might not make it. Of course she'd known that the moment she went into labour far too early, and she'd known it before she was put to sleep for the emergency section to deliver her baby. But she'd seen him now with her own eyes. She'd seen his little tummy swell in and out and out, felt his tiny fingers move in hers and grasp her pinky tight. Nothing this doctor was saying to her now would make her give up hope. He looked at her with tired eyes that said no matter how many times he broke this news to parents, it never got any easier. But Kerry was refusing to believe any bad news. She lay back on the pillow after he left, and the tears came again. Her eyes were tight from crying, her throat continually tight with emotion. Even when she'd been visited by Danny and Pat, and later by Sharon and Maria, she went through the motions, but she could see on their faces that they felt this was not going to end well. She didn't want to hear that. She didn't want to talk about it. Her son was along the corridor in a little glass cot, and as long as there was a beat in his heart she would never give up hope. Additionally, she'd sensed Danny had been a little vague when she'd asked if there was any news from Jake Cahill about Vinny. He'd simply said he couldn't get hold of him but was hoping to talk to him before the day was out. She'd studied Danny's face when he said that and was wondering if he was telling the truth, that perhaps he was hiding some terrible news from her so as not to make things worse. But she didn't have the energy to quiz him, and part of her was afraid if she probed too much she might hear something she couldn't handle right now. For the moment it was just her and her baby son. She had this time with him, and no matter what happened, nobody could take this away from her. She eased herself off the bed and pulled on her robe and pushed her feet into her slippers. She was able to visit the neonatal unit several times a day and just sit with her baby. The midwives encouraged it, as it helped with bonding for new mums who weren't able to hold their babies in the normal way. In the past couple of days, Kerry had watched the other mums in the critical care unit as they sat watching and hoping. They would look up when she went into the room, a nod or as close to a smile as they could muster, an acknowledgement that they were all the same, just waiting and hoping. She left her hospital room and walked along the corridor; the silence, the heat, the beeping of monitors in what had now become her world. Inside the room, she could see two nurses at either side of her baby's cot and her heart sank.

'He's okay, Kerry.' One of them gave her an understanding look. 'We're just checking his cannula.'

As she approached she could see his tummy rising and falling. He was still here. She swallowed hard and sat down close to the cot. She studied every inch of him from the fuzzy blond hair on his head and the nape of his neck, to his eyebrows, the shape of his ears, his wrists, his legs and his little toes. He was just perfect.

Jake was glad when the plane touched down at Glasgow airport, and he breathed a sigh of relief that he didn't have to keep up the pretence any more. Danny would be waiting for them at arrivals, and he was the one who was going to break the news to Vinny about Kerry and the baby. Jake hoped Vinny would understand why he'd had to lie to him. At least he had managed to get him out of hospital without having to smuggle him out. Sullivan had met with the doctor and pleaded with him to let Vinny go home, and he had confided in him that there was an urgency about his newborn baby, but made him promise not to tell Vinny about it. That appeared to be the clincher, and the doctor had allowed him to travel, loading them up with enough medication for the next couple of days. Jake had watched Vinny drift in and out of restless sleep as he'd sat next to him on the plane, and he guessed he'd have that twitching, stressful sleep for some time to come.

At arrivals, close to the automatic door, Jake spotted Danny, and waved to him as all three of them walked towards him.

'Jake!' Danny said, giving him a handshake and a short but hard bear hug. 'Good to see you, big yin.'

Without asking Jake any more, Danny turned to Vinny.

'Vinny! Jesus, man! Are you a sight or what!' He stepped forward and gave Vinny a hug. Vinny returned it, his heavily bandaged hand over Danny's shoulder in the embrace.

'Thanks, Danny,' Vinny said. 'For everything. For my life.'

'No sweat, son. I'm just glad you're okay. It was Jake here who did all the work.'

Danny glanced at Jake, then at Sullivan, unsure of who he was, until Vinny spoke.

'Danny, this is John Sullivan. We were working together undercover when I got snatched. As you know it was him who went to Kerry for help.' He paused. 'How is she, Danny? What about the baby? She's nearly due. Have you told her

I'm home? Did you talk to her? I heard about the jail, the frame-up! Christ!'

Danny glanced at Jake, and then took Vinny by the arm. Jake and Sullivan waited as they moved a few feet away.

'Vinny,' Danny said, 'come with me a minute, son. I want to talk to you.'

Jake could see Vinny hesitate for a moment. He glanced back at him, then walked with Danny. He couldn't hear what Danny was saying, but he could see by the way Vinny's head went into his hands that he'd told him about the baby. Vinny was looking around him frantically for a way to get out of this situation and to hospital. They came back as the car pulled up beside them.

In the back of the car, Vinny turned to Jake.

'I can see why you didn't level with me.'

'I couldn't,' Jake said. 'It would have been too much for you, being so far away and all.'

Vinny nodded. 'Can you take me straight there, Danny?'

'That's the plan. Don't worry.'

'Have you spoken to Kerry today? Does she know I'm coming?'

'No.'

Kerry was watching again as the nurses and the paediatric consultant came in and were hovering over the baby's cot, glancing at the monitors. She could feel her heart pounding in her chest, terrified they were going to tell her something awful. The monitors were going up and down but she had no idea what that meant, but at least there was no alarm going off. Then the consultant turned to her, his pale tired expression suddenly changing to a bright smile.

'Well, Kerry,' he said. 'Your wee boy is looking good. He's passing all the tests here, and now that we're two days down the line, his oxygen levels are going up and we're going to be able to take this helmet off him and just put the oxy tube in his nose.'

'Really?' Kerry felt a sob somewhere in her chest. 'Is he going to be all right?'

'Early doors. He's not out of the wood yet, and a bit to go, but this is the first step.' He gestured to the nurses and they began to gingerly loosen the helmet, then their expert fingers very gently eased a tube up into his nostril. The consultant studied the monitor, his eyebrows knitted in concentration as they did it. Then the helmet was removed, and no alarms had gone off. He nodded slowly.

'You can have a hold of him now.'

'I can?' Tears spilled out of Kerry's eyes. 'Oh God!'

Very slowly and carefully, the nurses lifted the baby out, so tiny and pink with his little blue wool hat on. They placed him in her arms on her bare chest. She felt the warmth of his soft body on hers. As long as she lived nothing would ever come close to this moment. She touched his back, skin so soft, so fragile, his calves, his legs, and the tears spilled out of her eyes so much that the nurse leaned over and dabbed her cheeks with a tissue. Then the door opened, and she looked up, blinking.

It was Vinny. It was. It really was.

'Oh, Vinny! Oh, Vinny! Look at our baby!'

Vinny stood, rooted for a moment, his face a mask of disbelief and joy at the same time. Then he was across in two strides and dropped to his knees beside her, his arm around her as he broke down.

'Oh, Kerry! It's our baby. Is . . . Is he all right? Jake told me what happened to you. I'm so sorry I wasn't here.'

Kerry sniffed. 'You're here now.'

'Did you . . . Has he got a name?'

She shook her head. 'I was waiting for you.'

'You choose, Kerry. Whatever you want.'

'I-I thought we could call him Tim, after my father.'

Kerry looked down at the little pink face and vowed that this Tim Casey's life was going to be so very different.

Four months later . . .

Kerry walked at the water's edge, watching her footprints with every step. The baby was in a harness around her. Little Tim was sound asleep, his face beneath his sunhat and snuggled into her chest. The warmth of his skin on hers gave her a surge of joy she never would have believed possible. She stood for a moment, gazing out at the sun twinkling on the ocean, and closed her eyes, grateful for everything she had. But even now, as the days and weeks had flown past, there was still the niggle of worry at how quickly this could all be taken away. She folded her arms across the harness, subconsciously trying to protect her baby, even though she knew that this sun-kissed lagoon was the safest place she could be.

Kerry had moved to Spain as soon as it was deemed safe for Tim to travel abroad. She had left Glasgow and set up home in Nerja on the Costa del Sol, with Vinny and their son. It had been a huge step and commitment for both of them, and they were still finding their way together, determined to make it work. Vinny was exploring the possibility of working as a private eye for Brits abroad who ended up in trouble or in jail, and his job would be to hook them up with lawyers and the help that they needed. It was a world away from being an undercover cop rattling the cages of drugs barons from Glasgow to Colombia. But so far he was happy. The Casey empire was flourishing across the south of Spain, and the flagship hotel would be open by the autumn in a blaze of publicity. The Caseys were legit, and they could sit at the top table with any company bosses in UK and abroad. She had done everything she had dreamed of, and she'd walked away, leaving it to Sharon and her growing staff to run the show. This afternoon, their baby would be christened in the little chapel in the town, and Kerry couldn't wait to see Danny and Pat, Jack, and Maria, who'd made the trip across. Cal and Tahir were coming too – they were now based on the Costa del Sol learning the Caseys' real-estate business, and by all accounts doing well, and it made Kerry happy that she'd given them a new start. It was up to them now. Even Steven and his mother would be there. They'd relocated to Spain, where Steven worked as a bar manager for the Caseys three bars along the coast, and his mother was thriving in the warm climate. Ash, who was now working for the Caseys in the kitchen of a restaurant they'd bought over in Glasgow's West End, had been thrilled to be flown to Spain for the baptism. She was drug free and relishing her new job, and was planning to go to college to train as a chef. Kerry stood with her back to the sea, as she saw Vinny coming down to the beachside café and waving to her as he sat down and opened the newspaper he was carrying. She walked back to the café, picking her feet through the warm sand. As she was about to sit down she was struck by the front page of the newspaper Vinny was holding up for her.

'ATTORNEY GENERAL RESIGNS'. Beneath the headline was a picture of Quentin Fairhurst skulking out of Whitehall, ashen faced. Below it a picture of him with a Russian, and another with money changing hands and two women. She sat down and picked up the newspaper. There was now a police probe into allegations of corruption and backhanded payments. The article said he could face years in jail if found guilty. Staring at the lurid headlines was the sweetest revenge for Kerry. Had he not cheated and humiliated her as a young lawyer, her entire life may have been a different story. She may still have been a lawyer, a champion of people who had been abandoned, let down. By framing her, he was determined to completely destroy her, but it was Fairhurst who now stood to lose everything. She saw the byline that read Harry Foster and smiled. She hadn't heard from Harry since the day she'd seen him shot and bleeding in the street as she was being kidnapped. But she'd never ever believed he'd betrayed her. Perhaps one day he would tell her exactly what happened, but right now that didn't matter. As she scanned the story, her eye caught a paragraph at the foot of the page, urging the reader to turn to page five:

The body fished out of the river in Utrecht in Holland has been confirmed as missing Glasgow bar owner Dick Lambie. He was identified by dental records, as the name on the driving licence found in his possession was a pseudonym.

Job done, Kerry thought. She was looking forward hearing all about it later from Uncle Danny.

ACKNOWLEDGEMENTS

Where to start, in a year like this, a year overshadowed by grief and a global pandemic.

But we are still here, still working, still hoping. I have so many people to thank for their love and support.

But first of all my nephew Christopher Costello and his wife Laura, who have shown such courage after the recent loss of their newborn baby girl. They put one foot in front of the other every day, and keep going for their wee boy Ruairi. And they still find time to support me.

To my sister Sadie, who has had to live through the tragedy of that day, and remains my rock and greatest supporter, as well as her husband Matt.

For her family, Katrina and Iain, Matthew and Katie, who have all pulled together in these hard times. And the kids Jude, Max and Cillian who make us laugh even in the dark days. Also brother Des who has always been one of my biggest supporters.

Life is going on, though not as we knew it. During lock-down the only upside was I finished *Trapped* ahead of schedule.

I also want to thank the friends I seldom see these days but hope we will soon be able to share a drink and a laugh.

To Mags, Annie, Eileen, Mary, Phil, Liz, Helen, Donna, Louise, Barbara, Jan and cousins Annmarie, Anne, and Alice and Debbie in London.

My old journalist pals – I hope we get together soon – Simon and Lynn, Mark, Annie, Keith and Maureen. And the cherished veteran hacks, Brian, Gordon, Ian, David, Jimmy and Brian. And to Tom Brown and Marie let's hope next year is better.

Special thanks to Bruce McKain for his legal expertise, and Tom Fox for his insight into life in HM Prison Cornton Vale.

Thanks also to my cousins the Motherwell Smiths who missed their trip to Dingle for the first time in nearly twenty years.

And my good friends back west, Mary and Paud, Sioban and Martin, Sean Brendain.

I'm grateful and blessed to have such good people around me. My lovely friends in La Cala de Mijas – Lisa, Yvonne, Mara, Wendy, Jean, Maggie, Fran, Sally, Sarah, Donna, Lillias and Natalie.

My agent Euan Thorneycroft for his help driving my ideas and ambitions forward.

At Quercus, my editor Jane Wood, for her encouragement and great advice over the years, and Florence Hare for her great edit on *Trapped*. And all the team at Quercus who push and promote my books.

And last, but not least, the growing gang of readers I have out there who have followed my novels and enjoyed them. Thank you. Without you, I wouldn't be writing this.